International
Encyclopedia
of
Women Composers

AARON I. COHEN

Second Edition
Revised and Enlarged

Volume 2

SAI — ZYB
APPENDICES

Books & Music (USA) Inc.

NEW YORK   LONDON

Published by BOOKS & MUSIC (U.S.A.) Inc.
P.O. Box 1301, Cathedral Station, New York, NY 10025

UK and European Distributors
Books and Music UK, 25/26 Poland Street, London WI

Printed and bound by National Book Printers, 1987.

ISBN 0-9617485-0-8 (Vol. 1)
ISBN 0-9617485-1-6 (Vol. 2)
ISBN 0-9617485-2-4 (Set.)

Library of Congress Cataloging in Publication Data
Library of Congress Catalog Card Number: 86-72857
COHEN, Aaron I.
International Encyclopedia of Women Composers
(Second Edition)

1. Women Composers - Biography
2. Music - Bibliography 1. Title

British Library Cataloguing in Publication Data
COHEN, Aaron I.
International Encyclopedia of Women Composers
2nd ed.

1. Women Composers - Biography
I. Title
780'.92'2   ML390

PRINTING HISTORY

First Edition
International Encyclopedia of Women Composers
Copyright © 1981 by Aaron I Cohen
Pp. XVIII + 597. New York NY. R. R. Bowker Co.
ISBN 0-8352-1288-2

First Edition
International Discography of Women Composers
Copyright © 1984 by Aaron I. Cohen
Pp. XXII + 254. Westport CT. Greenwood Press.
ISBN 0-313-24272-0

Contents

VOLUME 2

Guide to Use

ACCENTS. Owing to serious computer problems, the *umlauts* had to be eliminated and after consultation with the language authorities in the various countries, the letter *e* was added to all the characters concerned. The French, Spanish and Portuguese accents had to be added by hand and dealt with by the Optical Character Reader. This illustrates the difficulties facing the International Performing Rights Societies in their endeavour to set up a standard computerised program to cover the composers' names throughout the world.

BIOGRAPHIES of women composers are arranged alphabetically by name, with cross-references from variant names, pseudonyms and maiden names to the main entry. As the information applies, entries have been divided into five main parts: (a) biographical information; (b) compositions; (c) publications; (d) bibliography; (e) references.

a. *BIOGRAPHICAL INFORMATION* includes the composer's name, variant names, current nationality, instrument specialization, occupational activities, place and date of birth and death, a description of her musical career with emphasis on her music education, commissions, awards and distinctions. The word DISCOGRAPHY indicates that some of her works have been recorded and that the listing appears in the *Discography* at the end of this book. The word PHOTOGRAPH indicates the inclusion of her picture in the *Photographs* section immediately following the biographies.

b. *COMPOSITIONS* is a listing of the composer's works, grouped under the categories: orchestra; chamber; solo instrument; vocal; sacred; ballet; opera; theatre; electronic etc. The instruments for which a particular work was composed are listed in parenthesis after the title; names of instruments etc. are given in abbreviated form which are explained in the list of *Abbreviations*. Other information provided for individual compositions includes where available, the date of composition, the publisher and date of publication, dedicatory and commissioning information.

c. *PUBLICATIONS* is a listing of books and articles written *by the composer*.

d. *BIBLIOGRAPHY* is a listing of books and articles written *about the composer*.

e. *REFERENCE* concludes each entry, with a list of reference numbers which are keyed to consecutively numbered sources in the *Bibliography* section of the book. In instances where the composer herself supplied the information for the entry, the word 'composer' precedes the list of reference numbers. The names of individuals who supplied information also precede the reference numbers.

BIBLIOGRAPHY is divided into three sections viz (a) numerical, which relates to the reference numbers at the foot of each biography; (b) the alphabetical listing of these books by author; and (c) the alphabetical listing of the books by title.

PHOTOGRAPHS of women composers appear alphabetically by name following the bibliographical section.

Appendix 1. Information Wanted. This is a list of women composers about whom little or nothing is known. It would be appreciated if readers having knowledge of any item would communicate with the

Director, International Institute for the Study of Women in Music, California State University, Northridge, Los Angeles, CA 91330, USA.

Appendix 2. Music Key Signatures in 25 Languages. This has been provided as an aid towards the identification of the works of the women composers when performed, published or recorded in different countries.

Appendix 3. Comparative Distribution of Composers by Century. This tabulation illustrates the century-wise growth in the number of the women composers in each of the countries. Unfortunately there are quite a number of composers whose nationality and period of activity were not available at the time of going to press.

Appendix 4. Composers by Country and Century. This is a list of composers arranged alphabetically by country and, within each country, chronologically by century. Composers' names appear under their country of birth or subsequent nationality and within the century in which their creative musical abilities were most manifest. Changes in the names and boundaries of countries were taken into consideration in the classification of composers by country. The retention of a country's earlier name was usually influenced by the number of composers, as in the case of Bohemia under which 18 composers are listed. Croatian and Serbian composers are assigned to Yugoslavia; composers from England, Scotland, Northern Ireland and Wales to the United Kingdom and biblical composers to Israel, etc.

Appendix 5. Pseudonyms of the Women Composers. This is a list of pseudonyms used by the women composers in order to get their works published.

Appendix 6. Operas and Operettas by Women Composers. This is a list of the operas and the operettas which were composed by the women.

Appendix 7. Composers influenced by Shakespeare. This is a list of the women composers who were influenced by Shakespeare and lists the resultant works and their music form.

Appendix 8. Composers by Instrument and Music Form. This is a list of composers arranged alphabetically and chronologically by century under the instrument and form or type of music for which they composed.

Appendix 9. Composers by Calling, Occupation and Profession. This is a list of composers arranged alphabetically by occupation, profession or calling and within each category, chronologically by century.

Appendix 10. Composers by the Instruments they Play. This is a list of composers arranged alphabetically and chronologically by century under the musical instrument on which they were proficient.

Appendix 11. International Council of Women and Affiliates. This gives details about this important world wide organization and the addresses of the constituent affiliations in each country throughout the world.

Appendix 12. International Music Societies (selection) and other music organizations pertinent to women composers, and includes national information centers.

Appendix 13. International Performing Rights Societies. This is the most recent listing of all the performing rights societies and their addresses throughout the world.

Appendix 14. National Federation of Music Clubs. This is a listing of the affiliated bodies and senior music clubs of the National Federation of Music Clubs in the United States.

DISCOGRAPHY. This is a fairly complete listing as at the time of going to press, of the albums and recordings of the women composers (classical and serious music only). Where available the performers are listed, otherwise they are substituted by a series of asterisks (* * *). Record labels are indicated by five letter codes which are listed against the actual label names and their relative recording companies or distributors and their addresses where available.

Abbreviations

MUSICAL

A alto voice
a-cap a cappella
a-cl alto clarinet
a-fl alto flute
a-rec alto recorder
a-sax alto saxophone
acc accompaniment
acdn accordion
amp amplified
arr arranged for or by

B bass voice
B-Bar bass baritone voice
b-cl bass clarinet
b-dr bass drum
b-rec bass recorder
b-trb bass trombome
Bar baritone voice
bar-sax baritone saxophone
bsn bassoon

c-bsn contra bassoon
c-fl contra flute
ca circa
cel celeste
ch chorus
cham chamber
chil children
cl clarinet
clav clavichord
comm commissioned by or for
cond conductor
cong congregation
Cont contralto voice
cor cornet
cym cymbals

d-b double bass
ded dedicated to
dir director
diss dissertation
dr drum

elec electronic
ens ensemble
euph euphonium

fl flute

glock glockenspiel
gtr guitar

har harmonica
hn horn
hon honorary
hons honours
hp harp
hpcd harpsichord

inaug inauguration of
inst instrument

lib libretto by

m men's
m-Cont mezzo contralto voice
m-S mezzo soprano voice
man mandolin
mar marimba
med medium
mix mixed
mvt movement

n/a not available
narr narrator
no number

ob oboe
obb obbligato
op opus
opt optional
orch orchestra
org organ

perc percussion
perf performer/performed
pf piano

picc piccolo
prep prepared

qnt quintet
qrt quartet

rec recorder
rev revised

S soprano voice
sax saxophone
s-rec soprano recorder
str string
sym symphony
syn synthesizer

T tenor voice
t-rec tenor recorder
t-sax tenor saxophone
t-trb tenor trombone
tam tamborine
tba tuba
timp timpani
trad traditional
trans translated by
trb trombone
tri triangle
trp trumpet

unacc unaccompanied

var various
vce voice
vib vibraphone
vir virginal
vl viol
vla viola
vlc violoncello
vln violin

w women
ww woodwind

xy xylophone

About the Editor

AARON I. COHEN was born in Cape Town on 1st Feb. 1906, and spent most of his life in Johannesburg. He is a town-planner and an authority on shopping centers and land development. He is also an inventor and one of his inventions is the Colorscope, an instrument that expresses music in a series of variable patterns and colors. His vast collection of classical records of some 70 years' standing is based on the representative works of about 5 000 composers. This included about 350 women, and out ot this came the decision to embark upon the search for the women composers, which he commenced in 1974.

Eight years later, after working in 90 odd major music libraries and innumerable university and minor libraries as well as delving through the shelves of music antiquarians in 18 countries, this research led to the publication of the first International Encyclopedia of Women Composers in December 1982. This 600 page book (now out of print), listing some 4900 women over a time-scale of 44 centuries, had a remarkable impact on the hitherto highly prejudiced masculine world of music. It filled a great gap in music history.

The present 1240 page edition in two volumes listing nearly 6200 women composers completes almost 13 years of intensive research. Despite the outright restriction of his entry into any of the "iron curtain" countries, his listing of the women composers in these countries is unique and unsurpassed.

His entire collection of phonograph records, his extensive library of music reference books and all the working papers and data relating to the Encyclopedia have been donated to the new annexe to the music library of the California State University at Northridge, Los Angles.

His other hobbies are woodworking and gardening. He and his wife have been married over 50 years and have a son and a daughter and six grandchildren.

Biographies of
Women Composers

SAI — ZYB

SAINT GEORGE TUCKER, Ida. See TUCKER, Tui St. George

SAINT-GEORGES, Didia (Alexandra)
Rumanian pianist, accompanist and composer. b. Botosani, September 24, 1888. She studied at the Iasi Conservatory from 1905 to 1907 and then attended the Leipzig Conservatory, where for three years she studied theory, solfege, harmony and counterpoint under Emil Paul; composition and musical form under Stephan Krehl and the piano under Robert Teichmuller. She worked in Botosani, Bucharest, and Iasi as a piano accompanist. In 1943 one of her compositions won an honorable mention in the Georges Enesco competition.
Compositions
PIANO
De la musique avant tout chose, Rumanian suite, op. 4 (1930)
Illustratii muzicale pe un cintec vechi francez
Sonatina, op. 6 (1943)
Three ballet waltzes, op. 7 (1958)
Twelve variations on a Jewish song, op. 3 (1929)
VOCAL
Amurg (V. Tulbure) (1960)
Four songs, op. 1 (St. O. Iosif, M. Eminescu, O. Goya) (Leipzig, 1913)
Seven Rumanian folk songs, op. 5 (1933)
Two songs (Ricardo Huch) (1914)
Vier Lieder (Eichendorff, Biernbaum, Moericke) (Leipzig, 1913)
Ziorel de ziua (M. Dumitrescu) (1960)
Ref. 94, 196

SAINT GILLES, La Chatelaine de
12th-13th-century French minstrel and composer.
Composition
VOCAL
Un seigneur pauvre avoir pour fille
Ref. British Library

SAINT HELIER, Ivy
British composer.
Composition
PIANO
Ring up

SAINT JEAN-DU-SACRE COEUR, Soeur. See CADORET, Charlotte

SAINT JOHN, Georgie Boyden
American composer. She died in the Windsor Hotel fire in New York City in 1899.
Compositions
VOCAL
Songs incl.:
Bonny Prince Charlie
Cupid at the bar
In dreamland
Toujours amour
Ref. 276, 347, 433

SAINT JOHN, Kathleen Louise
American pianist, lecturer and composer. b. Long Beach, CA, May 28, 1942. She completed her early piano studies with Angelon Hoffmeister in Los Angeles. From 1962 to 1966 she attended San Diego State College where she majored in music studying under Dr. John Blyth (piano), Dr. David Ward-Steinman (orchestration) and Gilbert Back (piano and strings). From 1966 to 1971 she attended the Juilliard School of Music where she majored in the piano in 1968, having studied composition under Ania Dorfmann. In 1971 she studied under Luciano Berio, Hugo Weisgall, Vincent Persichetti, Hal Overton, Stanley Wolfe and Norman Grossman. She studied orchestration with Jacob Druckman and the piano and strings with George Macanovitsky graduating with a B.M. Between 1968 and 1979 she attended the Columbia-Princeton Electronic Music Center where she studied under Vladimir Ussachevsky, Bulent Arel, Mario Davidovsky and Alice Shields (q.v.) and classes at Darmstadt Ferienkurse fuer neue Musik, at Tanglewood in the Berkshires, at Johnson State College Composers Conference, at the Instituut voor Sonologie and the California Institute of the Arts. She worked as a music transcriber for Dr. Laura Boulton at Columbia University from 1968 to 1970. She has worked as a tape technician and guest lecturer. She is the recipient of numerous awards including the Juilliard award in composition and outstanding work for music theater in 1970, the Irvine foundation scholarship in composition from 1977 to 1978 and the Marie A. Lovelace scholarship in classical music, from the California Institute of the Arts, 1978 to 1979. She received five residency fellowships from the MacDowell Colony and the Virginia Center for Creative Arts. In 1976 she was designated a Norlin foundation fellow by the MacDowell Colony in special tribute to Aaron Copland. She has given extensive performances as a pianist and has had a number of works commissioned. PHOTOGRAPH.
Compositions
ORCHESTRA
And many of the eternal ones laughed (vln and orch)
Garden of the ever-present (mar and orch)
Amongst those of the Elysian Fields (string orch)
Canto I (vln and string orch)
Destruction of a monolith
Disguised (cham orch)
Odë to the death of Socrates (cham orch) (1980)
The sacred mountain (string orch)
Sarabande
Serenade
The soloist (1968)
Valse triste (string orch and cl)
BAND
Caboclinha (1965)
Serenade
CHAMBER
Silent fugue (infinite strs) (1969)
Meditations and madrigals, solo songs (12 insts) (1977)
The cage (cl and cham ens) (1969)
A shiny shilling-worth (brass ens) (1979)
Song of a weeping heron, on the death of a nightingale (ob and 8 insts) (1979) (comm Music Project Contemporary Ensemble)
Such a bunch (octet) (1967)
The gathering (septet) (1967)
A conversation (pf qnt) (1968)
Harvest (qnt) (1980)
Heliotrope (ww qnt) (1979)
Melancholia (str qnt) (1968)
Project I (qnt)
Quintet (1967)
The winds of Aeolus (ww qnt) (1980)
Divertimento (qrt) (1979)
Harlequin (cl, vla, hp and perc) (comm William Powell, California Inst. of the Arts) (1978)
Ideas on a 28-note ditty (qrt) (1967)

Innermission (perc and trio) (comm John Fitzgerald) (1978)
Meditation, hymne and dance of repose (qrt) (1980)
Quartet of a prophecy (str qrt) (1980)
A string quartet to a swan (1967)
Andante (str trio) (1981)
Clotho, Lachesis and Atropos (3 solo insts) (1976)
Cocquette: To the feelings of an aging clown (trio) (1981)
The mount of Luna (trio) (1980)
Rondeau à La Toulouse-Lautrec (trio) (1981)
The tender graces took thee up in their bosom, O Lily! (wind trio) (1978)
Trio (picc, cl and ob) (1983)
Trio sonata plus (str trio) (1967)
Frail life! (perc trio) (1981)
Canto (vln and keyboard) (1981)
Duo (ob and cl) (1977)
Interlude (cl and pf) (1981)
Maze (ob and hpcd) (1979)
Nova (hn and pf) (comm Rachel Dalevoryas) (1978)
Postlude (post time!) (cl and pf) (1981)
Prelude (cl and pf) (1978)
Rhapsody (vln and gtr) (1977)
The sacrifice of Iphigenia (cl and pf) (1979)
Stereo (cl and trp) (1977)
Waltz (fl and pf) (1978)
Lied (bsn) (1981)
Miniatures (bsn) (1980)
PIANO
An afternoon at the zoo (1978)
Calliope's song to Apollo (1980)
Night music, 6 nocturnes (1979)
VOCAL
A cantilena on the fable of Aornos (S and str orch) (1976)
Celestia (B-reader, perc qrt and string orch) (1976)
Centipede (ch a-cap, perc and str orch) (1978)
Mosquito (ch a-cap, perc and orch) (1972)
Praying mantis (ch a-cap and orch) (1980)
Sakura no hana (S and orch) (1981)
Socrates on the divination of swans (vce and orch) (1968)
Sonnet of the confined (m-S and orch) (1975)
Dear one (2-ch, vla and cel) (1978)
The Devil-bird: A South American myth (boys ch or w-ch, cl, mar and perc) (comm William Powell) (1974)
Cantus (Cont and ch a-cap) (1980)
Mendelssohn's muse (ch a-cap) (1981)
O mistress mine! (S and w-ch) (1977)
Sonnet 29 (Bar reader and cham ens) (1969)
An inscription on Smenkhare's coffin? (S, sextet, str trio and perc) (comm Kaaren Herr, California Inst of the Arts) (1978)
Ach Schatz (Bar, vce and pf) (comm Robert S. Gray, Juilliard) (1970)
Go find a new lover (vce and gtr) (1980)
His angel (vce and keyboard) (1980)
O thrive, faire five, madrigal (w-ch) (1978)
O thy sweet blood divine (S and pf) (1978)
Quartet of a prophecy I (S and str qrt) (1980)
Song of Anna Blue (vce and pf) (1970)
Songs from the Land of Dawn (Cont and pf) (1979)
Sweetsongs to the lament of the Sibyl (vce and keyboard) (1980)
Trois poèmes (S and gtr) (1980)
The unicorn and the white doe (Cont and pf) (1978)
Vestigia (m-S and inst trio) (1970)
SACRED
A prayer (ch a-cap and str orch) (1979)
BALLET
Adam and Eve, Oh! (pf) (1980)
Arcana (The reincarnation of Osiris) (comm Patricia Gage, California Institute of Arts) (1978)
The gold-bug (concert band) (1968) (comm James A. Hansen, Astoria High School)
Highnoon at Peace Rock (qrt) (1980)
OPERA
The Clouds (Aristophanes) (1971)
ELECTRONIC
Kaleidoscope (tape and inst ens) (1969)
MULTIMEDIA
The lips of a strange woman drop honey, oratorio (solo, ch, insts, visuals and lights) (1975)
Ayre and dialogue: On an houre-glasse (S, mar, vlc, perc and lights) (1980)
The crying of water (3 S, Bar-reader, vln and lights) (1976)
The delirious Caitanya (orch and lights) (1977)
Her drifting from me these days (Bar, perc, vla and lights) (1976)
Fleur de lys (S, w-ch, org, insts and lights) (1977) (comm Sweet Briar College
Fragrances (pf, orch and lights) (1976)
Isadora: Daughter of the sun (S, 9 insts, m-ch, dancers, sculpture and lights) (1977) (comm The Music Project Repertory Cham Ens)

Mimosa pudica (dancer, qrt and lights) (1976)
Ophelia (tape, readers and lights) (1970) (comm J. Krusberg, Journey of Dreams and Company)
The Revelation of St. John the Divine (tape, dancers, actors, musicians and lights) (1970) (comm William Powell, Juilliard)
The Sibyl, in contemplation (S or m-S, octet and lights) (1976) (comm The Music Project Repertory Chamber Ens)
A vision of the ethereal cosmos (tape, dancers and lights) (1970)
Where young Adonis oft reposes (T, S, cham ens and lights) (1979)
Ref. composer, 494, 622, 625

SAINT MARIE, Sister Cecile du Sacre-Coeur. See BEAUCHEMIN, Marie

SAINT-SIMON, Comtesse de. See BAWR, Alexandrine Sophie

SAINT OF PANDHARPUR. See JANABAI

SAINTON-DOLBY, Charlotte Helen

English pianist, singer, teacher and composer. b. London, May 17, 1821; d. London, February 18, 1885. Her earliest piano teacher was Mrs. Montague. From 1832 she studied at the Royal Academy of Music, under J. Bennett, Elliot and then Crivelli. Elected King's scholar in 1837, she remained at the academy for five years and was elected honorary member on leaving. She made her first appearance in a quartet at the Philharmonic in 1841 and in 1842 as a solo singer. In the winters of 1846 and 1847, Mendelssohn, who had been delighted by her singing in oratorios at St. Paul's, obtained an engagement for her at the Gewandhaus Concerts at Leipzig where she appeared with Jenny Lind (q.v.) with great success. He dedicated his *Six songs, op. 57* to her and wrote the contralto arias in *Elijah* for her. Her success in Leipzig was followed by several concert tours in Holland and France where she established a reputation as a singer. In 1860 she married violinist M. Prosper Sainton and retired from public life ten years later. In 1872 Charlotte opened her singing school where she trained artists such as Fanny Moody. Upon her death the Royal Academy of Music founded a scholarship in her memory.

Compositions
VOCAL
Florimel, cantata (w-vces)
The legend of St. Dorothea, cantata (solos, ch and orch)
The story of the faithful soul, cantata
Thalassa, cantata
Songs incl.:
A-sailing we will Go
Coming home
In August
Is it forever?
A stream of golden sunshine
Watching and waiting
Ballads

Publications
Tutor for English Singers: A Complete Course of Practical Instruction in Singing. London.
Ref. 2, 6, 8, 9, 26, 74, 102, 129, 226, 276, 361, 433, 572

SAITO-NOTA, Eva

American pianist, teacher and composer of Japanese origin. b. Edmonton, Canada, June 25, 1921. She has a B.S. in music education from Columbia University and is an A.R.C.M. and L.R.S.M. for performance and teaching. She also has a Master of Sacred Music degree from Union Theological Seminary and the Dalcroze Certificate from the Dalcroze School, both in New York. She taught the piano and the fundamentals of music in Canada, the United States and in Japan. In 1976 she was chosen composer of the year at the Ohio Music Teachers' Association State Convention.

Compositions
CHAMBER
Sonatine (fl, vlc and pf) (1976)
Concerto gioco (pf and perc) (1976)
Tankas (Impressions for the children of war) (fl and hpcd) (1968)
Black and White (pf, 4 hands) (1976)
Ref. 185

SAIZ-SALAZAR, Marina

Panamanian composer. b. 1930.
Composition
PIANO
Sonata, in 3 mvts (1955)
Ref. 52

SAKALLI-LECCA, Alexandra

Greek pianist, singer and composer. b. Corfu, 1927. She studied lieder singing at the Athens Odeum, graduating in 1929 with a diploma in the piano and music theory. Later she studied classical and 12-tone composition in Munich under the composer George Tsouipoulos and in Greece under Papaioanou. PHOTOGRAPH.

Compositions
CHAMBER
    Lento (fl and pf) (1967)
    Rondo (vln and pf) (1974)
VOCAL
    At Leukatas (to Sapphos) (1966)
    Apoichos (Tsatsos-Sefere) (vce and pf) (1981)
    Apparition (1965)
    Barkarola (1966)
    The grave (ded composer's deceased son) (1963)
    He (1972)
    Hero (1967)
    It's getting late my love
    The journey (1968)
    My two hands in your hands (1966)
    Perles (1972)
    Return (1968)
    When I miss you (1966)
    Wind upon the flowers (1967)
    With Chopin (1967)
    With Mozart (1967)
SACRED
    Maria Magdalena No. 1 (ch a-cap) (1964)
    Maria Magdalena No. 2 (S and insts)
    Sacraments (1965)
    Two psalms
ARRANGEMENTS
    The birds, based on a 12-tone row of Arnold Schoenberg
    Yellow roses
Ref. composer, 94

SALAMAN, Ivy Frances. See KLEIN, Ivy Frances

SALE, Sophia

English organist, teacher and composer. d. Westminster, May 3, 1869. She composed hymns and songs.
Ref. 6, 226, 276, 433

SALICCO, Betty Lou. See EVERETT-SALICCO, Betty Lou

SALIGNY, Clara

19th-century German composer. She composed pieces for the piano.
Ref. 226, 276

SALIUTRINSKAYA, Tatiana

20th-century Russian composer.
Composition
ORCHESTRA
    Concerto (1958, rev 1963)
Ref. R. Dearling (Spaulding U.K.)

SALLAMA AL-QASS (Selema al Cas, Selamet ol-Kass)

Arabian songstress and composer. b. ca. 722. She was a freed slave educated in Medina. She took the name Qass from a pious Koran reader in Medina who loved her, but controlled his passion for her out of holy fear of the sensual pleasures she offered him. She belonged first to a Quraish noble named Suhail. When he died his son Musab sold her to Yazid II, before he became caliph, for 3 000 pieces of gold and even after his death she continued to wield political and musical influence at court. Her teachers included Jamila (q.v.), Ma'bad, Ibn Aisha and Malik. She specialized in funeral songs and was able to move her hearers to tears.
Ref. 171, 234

SALLAMA AL-ZARQA

Arabian songstress of the Umayyad period. b. ca. 665. One of the four outstanding singers of the Umayyad period, the blue-eyed Sallama was taught her art by Jamila (q.v.). At the court of Yazid I (680 to 683) she was presented to the poet Al-Ahwas, who fell in love with her. She was later bought by Jafer, the son of Suleiman, for 80 000 dirhem. Suleiman reprimanded his son for this extravagance, but after hearing her sing, said no more. She is also known to have sung at the court of Yazid II (720 to 724). She was famous for her beauty and passed into the ownership of several masters, all of whom seem to have fallen in love with her. Her sister Rayya (q.v.) also achieved some fame as a songstress.
Ref. 171, 234

SALM-DYCK, Constance-Marie de Theis, Princess

French writer and composer. b. Nantes, November 7, 1767; d. Paris, April 13, 1845. She wrote the libretto for the opera *Sappho*.
Compositions
VOCAL
    Several romances incl.:
    Conseil aux femmes
    La fievre
    L'inconstant
    Le méchant
Publications
    L'Eloge de Pierre Gavinies. Paris, 1802.
Ref. 26, 128, 129, 312, 347

SALMANOVA, R.

20th-century Bashkir Soviet composer.
Compositions
VOCAL
    Songs (Bashkir composers)
    Songs in Liubliu tebia, zemlia ottsov (Moscow: Sovietski Kompozitor, 1980)

SALOMONI, Mlle.

Early 19th-century Russian violinist and composer. She was the daughter of the choreographer Giuseppe Salomoni. She often appeared in concert. She composed a violin concerto and music for several of her father's ballets.
Ref. 156

SALQUIN, Hedy

Swiss concert pianist, critic, orchestral conductor, writer and composer. b. Lucerne, October 13, 1928. She studied the piano at the Conservatory of Geneva under Dinu Lipatti, composition under Charles Chaix, solfege under Lydie Malan and conducting under Samuel Baud-Bovy. She studied accompaniment at the Paris Conservatoire under Nadia Boulanger (q.v.) and was the first woman to be admitted to the conservatoire's orchestral conductors' class, under Professor Louis Fourerstier. Her international career as a pianist and orchestral conductor led her throughout Europe. From 1966 she was the artistic director for the chamber music festival Schlosskonzerte Schauensee Kriens. She received prizes as a performer, conductor and composer in 1982 and was the first woman to receive first prize for conducting from the Paris Conservatoire, where she also won first prize for accompaniment. DISCOGRAPHY.
Compositions
ORCHESTRA
    Suite for string orchestra and piano (1947) (prize, Geneva Conservatory)
    Concerto for flute, string orchestra and timpani
CHAMBER
    Trio (vln, vla and pf)
    Duo (fl and ob)
    Solitotales (perc and pf) (1985)
    Thuner suite (fl and pf) (1984) (Sorriso)
PIANO
    Christmas perpetuum (1983)
    Incontro (1985)
    Noël, Christmas piece (1982) (Sorriso)
    November am Thunersee (1982)
    Seventeen, 3 pieces (1945) (Sorriso)
    Sonatine in G (1947)
    Sorriso (1984)
    Theme and variations (1945) (Sorriso)
    Toccata in Es (1984)
VOCAL
    Tantum ergo (4 vce ch) (1945)
    Three Venetian island-songs (Anna Coriolani) (vce and pf) (1982) (Sorriso)
Bibliography
    Musik. Kurt Pahlen. Walter-Edition.
    Les Pionnieres de l'Histoire. Claude Pasteur. Paris: Albin Michel, Paris.
    Schweizer Komponistinen der Gegenwart. Zurich: Editions Hug.
    Tendenzen und Verwirklichungen. Atlantis Edition.
Ref. composer, 651

SALSBURY, Janet Mary

English organist, professor and composer. b. Pershore, Worcester, May 13, 1881. She received a doctorate in music from Dunelm in 1910. She was professor of music and honorary organist at Ladies' College, Cheltenham and professor of music-by-correspondence and theoretical examiner for Trinity College of Music, London.

Compositions

VOCAL

    A ballad of Eversham (ch) (Weekes)

    From Shakespeare's garden, song cycle (J. Williams)

SACRED

    Christmas carols (Stainer and Bell)

Publications

    Analysis of Mozart's Piano Sonatas. Weekes.

    Staff-Sight-Singing Tests. Books I and II. J. Williams.

Ref. 23, 105, 226

SALTER, Mary Elizabeth (nee Turner) (Mrs. Sumner)

American singer, lecturer and composer. b. Peoria, IL, March 15, 1856; d. Orangeburg, NY, September 13, 1938. She was educated at Burlington, IA, where she studied singing with Alfred Arthur and Max Schilling and later continued her studies in Boston with O'Neill and Rudersdorff. After 1875 she was soprano soloist for about 20 years in churches in Boston, New York, New Haven, Syracuse, Buffalo, and Atlanta. She gave concerts with many noted artists and choral societies. From 1879 to 1881 she taught at Wellesley College, when she married Sumner Salter, organist and composer.

Compositions

VOCAL

    Songs incl.:

    Come to the garden, love

    The cry of Rachel

    Eight songs, op. 24 (1912) (New York: Schirmer)

    A fair white flower (Church)

    Five songs, op. 6 (1905)

    Five songs, op. 34 (1916) (Schirmer)

    Four songs, op. 26 (1913) (Schirmer)

    Four songs, op. 33 (1916) (Ditson)

    From old Japan, op. 23, cycle of 6 songs (1911) (Summy)

    In some sad hour

    The lamp of love

    Little boy, good night (Ditson)

    Love's epitome, cycle of 5 songs (1905) (Schirmer, 1905)

    Lyrics from Sappho, op. 18 (Schirmer, 1909)

    A night in Naishapur, cycle of 6 songs (Schirmer, 1906)

    Outdoor sketches, set of 6 songs (1908) (Schirmer)

    The pine tree

    Remembrance

    Serenity

    Set of seven songs (1909) (Schirmer)

    Songs of the 4 winds, op. 12 (1907) (Schirmer, 1904)

    Three spring songs, op. 4 (1904) (Schirmer, 1904)

    Unseen

    The veery

    A water lily (Ditson; Pond)

    The willow

    Duets

    Part songs

SACRED

    Christmas song (1936)

    Church music

Ref. 22, 39, 40, 70, 74, 85, 89, 226, 228, 260, 276, 292, 297, 347, 610

SALVADOR, Matilde

Spanish pianist, lecturer and composer. b. Castellon de la Plana, March 23, 1918. She studied the piano and composition under Vicente Asencio at the Conservatorio Superior de Musica in Valencia and taught there.

Compositions

ORCHESTRA

    Pieces

CHAMBER

    Piano pieces

VOCAL

    Llanto por la muerte de Falla, cantata (vce, ch and orch) (1946)

    Tres canciones valencianas (S and orch) (prize) (1937)

    Com es la lluna (mix-ch) (1933)

    Songs incl.:

    Canciones antiguas

    Canciones de nana y desvelo

    Canciones españolas

    Lieder

BALLET

    Judas, choreographic poem (1955)

    Missa de Lledo, choreographic poem (1964)

    Romance de la luna (Garcia Lorca) (1937)

    El Segoviano esquivo (Granada, 1953)

OPERA

    La filla del rei Barbut, prologue and 3 act puppet opera

    Mujeres de Jerusalem (1972)

    Vinatea (1966)

THEATRE

    Retablo de Navidad (1953)

Bibliography

    Temprano, A. *Tesoro sacro mus.* LVI, 1973.

Ref. 17, 107, 361

SAMAMA AZUMA. See SERVOZ, Harriet

SAMIOU, Domna

20th-century Greek composer.

Composition

FILM MUSIC

    For an Unimportant Reason (1974)

Ref. 497

SAMPSON, Peggy

20th-century American composer. DISCOGRAPHY.

Compositions

CHAMBER

    Theme for viola da gamba

MISCELLANEOUS

    Improvisation

Ref. 563

SAMSON, Valerie Brooks

American violinist, lecturer and composer. b. St. Louis, MO, October 16, 1948. She studied under Hugo Norden at Boston University graduating with a B.A. in 1970. Later she studied under Andrew Imbrie and Ollie Wilson at the University of California, Berkeley, where she obtained her M.A. in 1973. She was radio programmer-announcer for WTBS from 1960 to 1970 and Music Director of the Picchi Youth Orchestra in Oakland, from 1971 to 1972. She currently lives in San Francisco where she plays the Chinese violin and concentrates on Chinese music.

Compositions

ORCHESTRA

    Encounter (cham orch) (1973)

    Night visits (cham orch) (1976)

CHAMBER

    Quartet (fl, cl, vla and vlc) (1973)

    Mousterian meander (rec, vlc and pf) (1976)

    Blue territory I (vln and pf) (1975)

    Experimental shorts (vln and pf) (1969)

    Oboe duet (1972)

PIANO

    Winter dances (prepared pf)

    Pieces

MULTIMEDIA

    Montage: A journey through youth (3 S, pf, dancer and lights) (1975)

Ref. composer, 142, 625

SAMSUTDINOVA, Magira

Soviet singer and composer. b. 1896; d. 1929. She broke with old customs by appearing and performing Kazakh songs with the domra and Russian and Tatar songs to the accordion at fairs and bazaars. In an autobiographical song she explains how she appeared in defense of the rights of Kazakh women for equality in artistic activity.

Ref. 453

SAMTER, Alice

West German pianist, teacher and composer. b. Berlin, June 11, 1908. She began composing in childhood and later studied the piano under Else Blatt, Amalie Iwan and Dr. Starck; composition and improvisation under Gerhard Wehle and choral work under Karl Ristenpart. At the Music Academy, Berlin, she studied school music under Professor Heinrich Martens. Her career was interrupted by the war and she only appeared in concert after 1945, when she began teaching in Berlin high schools. She gave numerous performances in Germany and abroad as well as on radio. She was co-founder of the Berlin Chamber Music Circle and a foundation member of the Verband Deutscher Musikerzieher und Konzertierender Kuenstler. DISCOGRAPHY. PHOTOGRAPH.

Compositions

ORCHESTRA
　Konzertstueck (pf and orch)

CHAMBER
　Quintetto giocoso (fl, ob, vln, vlc and pf)
　Rivalites (fl, cl, vlc and pf)
　Dedikation (cl, hn and pf)
　Les extremes se touchent (cl, vlc and pf)
　Sketch (ob, cl and bsn)
　Zuneigung (fl, trp and pf)
　Kontrapost (fl, a-rec and pf) (1974)
　Nelly-Sachs-Trio (vln, vlc and pf)
　Piano trio
　Aspects (fl and hpcd) (1972)
　Dialogue (vln and pf)
　Episodes (vln and pf)
　Essay (vln and cim) (1977)
　Facets (fl and pf)
　Fraternité (vlc and pf)
　Hundert Takte (pf and gtr)
　Kaleidoskop (fl and vln) (1973)
　Metamorphosis (pf and hpcd)
　Mobile (ob and bsn)
　Mosaic (d-b and pf)
　Permutation (vlc and pf)
　Rotation (fl and cim)
　Three Dance Miniatures (cl and pf) (1955)
　Trilogy (vln and pf)
　Floetenmonolog (fl)
　Monolog (vlc) (1975)
　Monolog einer Geige (vln) (1974)

PIANO
　Duo ritmico (4 hands)
　Gemini (4 hands)
　Drei Aphorismen
　Drei Phasen (1969)
　Eskapaden
　Match
　Varianten (1976)
　Prisma (also org) (1973)

VOCAL
　Ringelnatz (4 solos and ch)
　Berlin-Zyklus (A. Gustas) (vce and pf)
　Choere nach der Mitternacht, 3 choruses (N. Sachs) (S, m-S, Bar and pf)
　Erfindungen, 5 tercets (C. Morgenstern) (S, T, Bar, rec and fl) (1967)
　Getretner Quark (J.W. von Goethe) (vocal qrt and 4 hand pf)
　Drei Lieder (Rainer Maria Rilke) (med-vce and pf)
　Drei Lieder (Stefan George) (S and pf) (1968)
　Drei Lieder (Sachs) (S, org and pf)
　Fuenf Oboenlieder (vce and ob)
　Gott schuf die Sonne (S, cim and pf)
　Grimace d'Artiste (Edith Soedergrau) (med-vce and pf)
　Hellbrun-Zyklus, 6 songs (med-vce, fl, ob and bsn)
　Herbst (Guillaume Apollinaire) (med-vce and pf)
　Im Atemholen (Goethe) (m-S and pf)
　Katzenverfassung (Christa Reinig) (S and pf)
　Mein Besitz (Reinig) (vce, speaker and pf) (1970)
　Mit Katzenaugen (Angelike Wiebach) (S and pf)
　Morgenmahlzeit (J. Prevert) (w-speaker and pf)
　Ode an Singer (P. van Ostaijen) (m-S, speaker and pf)
　Reklame (Ingeborg Bachmann) (S, speaker and pf) (1969)
　'S gibt hungrige Leute (Solano Trindade) (speaker or female speaker and pf)
　Der Schaffner (Jacques Prevert) (Bar, speaker and pf)
　Sechs Lieder, texts and pictures by Rosita Magnus (med w-vce and pf)
　Sechs Wechselgesaenge nach chinesischen Gedichten (Klabund) (m-S, Bar and small perc)
　Die Selbstkritik (3 vces and pf)
　Song of yourself (Hans-Juergen Heise) (middle vce and pf)
　Songs (vce and ww) (1976)
　Taenzerinnen, 3 songs (N. Sachs, E. Lasker-Schueler, G. von der Vring) (1975)
　Three duets (Wilhelm Busch) (S, Bar, cl, small perc and pf)
　Ulkiade, der Kartoffelpuffer (E. Lasker-Schueler) (S, T, pf and speaker)
　Vier Lieder (C. Morgenstern) (med-vce and pf)
　Winter, 2 songs (Arno Holz and Wolfgang Borchert) (med-vce and pf)

OPERETTA
　Der falsche Graf, for children (freely adapted from Gottfried Keller) (1957)

THEATRE
　Die Kartenhexe, melodrama (Walter Mehring) (speaker and pf) (1967)

INCIDENTAL MUSIC
　Die drei Spinnerinnen, masked play (Grimm) (1967)
　Music for Proteus (Paul Claudel)
　Music for Die Schule der Witwen (Jean Cocteau)
　Das Zauberhorn, masked play, after a Hungarian folk tale (1958)

MULTIMEDIA
　Drei Klavierstuecke zu Plastiken von Josef Magnus (slides)

ARRANGEMENTS
　Die Battleroper (Gay-Pepusch) (small orch)
　Die Nachtwache, play (N. Sachs)

Ref. composer, 474, 563, 622

SAMUEL, Caroline

Belgian pianist and composer. b. Liège, November 1, 1822; d. Liège, March 15, 1851. She was the sister of composer Adolphe Samuel. She studied at the Liège Conservatory where her teacher for the piano, harmony and composition was Daussoigne-Mehul, director of the Conservatory. At the age of 11 she won second prize for the piano. She received first prize for the piano in 1935 and in 1936, first prize for harmony. She gave several performances and used her earnings to support her mother and sisters. She died of a chest illness at the age of 29.

Compositions

PIANO
　Two fantasies (Brussels: Lahou)

VOCAL
　Melodies (vce and pf) (Lahou)

Ref. 14, 26, 129

SAMUEL, Marguerite

20th-century American pianist, teacher and composer. b. Paris. She composed for the piano.

Ref. 347, 448

SAMUEL, Rhian

British lecturer and composer. b. Aberdare, Wales, February 3, 1944. In 1967 she moved to the United States where she graduated from Washington University with a Ph.D. and was then appointed to the faculty of the St. Louis Conservatory. She returned to the United Kingdom to teach composition at the University of Reading. In 1979 she was awarded first prize at the Greenwich Festival, London and in 1983 was joint winner of the ASCAP Rudolph Nissim award. DISCOGRAPHY.

Compositions

ORCHESTRA
　Elegy symphony (comm St. Louis Symphony, 1981)

CHAMBER
　Encounter (bsn and str trio) (1983)
　Rondo pizzicato (str qrt) (1982) (Richard Schamer)
　Midwinter spring (ob, cl, bsn and hn) (1984)
　Shadow dance (fl, ob and pf) (1984)
　Caprice (fl and pf) (1985)

VOCAL
　La belle dame sans merci (ch and cham orch) (1982)
　Intimations of immortality (T and cham orch) (1978)
　Changes (mix-ch and vib) (1978)
　Jacobean lyrics (school mix-ch) (1978)
　Opposites (mix-ch) (1979)
　So long ago (mix-ch) (1979)
　The hair in the moon (S, vib, mar and d-b; also S and pf) (1978)
　In the hall of mirrors (med-vce and pf) (1984)
　April rise (m-S and pf)
　Songs of earth and air: April rise; The kingfisher (med-vce and pf) (1983)
　Songs with guitar (med-vce and gtr) (1985)

INCIDENTAL MUSIC
　For Pasquinade (12 insts) (1984)

Ref. composer, AMS 1985

SAMUELSON, Laura Byers

20th-century American composer. DISCOGRAPHY.

Composition

THEATRE
　Shades: A new musical for the bi-centennial (composer)

Ref. 563

SAMVELIAN, Sofia Vardanovna

Soviet lecturer and composer. b. Erivan, June 1, 1927. In 1951 she graduated from the Erivan Conservatory where she studied composition under E. Mirzoyan. She then lectured in solfege at the A. Spendiarov Music School.

Compositions
ORCHESTRA
Scene (orch of folk insts) (1949)
Mir pobedit voinu, symphonic portrait
Piece (orch of folk insts) (1954)
CHAMBER
Suite (str qrt) (1951)
Piece (vln and cl) (1949)
PIANO
Children's pieces (1954)
Sonata (1951)
Two preludes (1952, 1953)
Variations (1948)
VOCAL
Sovietskaya Armenia (ch) (1951)
Romances (Armenian poets)
ARRANGEMENTS
Armenian folk songs (vce and folk insts or pf)
Ref. 87

SANCHEZ, Manuela Cornejo de
Argentine teacher and composer. b. Salta, 1854; d. 1902. She taught at the Escuela Normal.
Compositions
VOCAL
Songs incl.:
A mi patria
Canto a Guemes
Canto patriotico
La escuela
Himno a Colon
Himno a Rivadavia
Larmes du coeur
El sol de julio
El sol de majo
SACRED
Songs
Ref. 297, 390

SANCHEZ DE LA MADRID, Ventura
19th-century Spanish composer.
Compositions
OPERA
Iginia d'Asti (1842)
La Maga (1854)
Malek-adel (1850)
Ruggero (1841)
Ref. 431

SANCIN, Mirca
Slovene-Yugoslav pianist, professor and composer. b. Ljubljana, March 3, 1901. She studied composition under A. Michl at the Graz Conservatory and then under L.M. Skerjanc in Ljubljana. She was professor of the piano in Celje and Ljubljana and at the State Higher Teachers' College, Trieste.
Compositions
PIANO
Fantasticno kolo
Improvizacija Nos. 1 and 2
Iz mladih dni
Kmecki ples
Komar i muha
Koracnica
Mali plesni impromptu
Mladinska igra
Na igriscu
Pomladni valcek
Preludij
Retovje
Romansa
Scherzoso
Silhuette
Spanski ples
Uspavanka
Valce campestre
Vesela mladina
VOCAL
Songs incl.:
Begunka
Ljubavna pesma
Med nama je vse polno zlatnih nit
Mene ni pozela kosa

Nesreca
Pomlad je prisla
Rosica
Tih vecer
Trenutak
Ref. 145

SANDELS, Ellen
20th-century editor and composer. She was editor of *Damernas Musik-blad* from 1901 to 1913. This newspaper published salon and dance music, songs and arrangements from operas and included some of her works.
Compositions
PIANO
Bla prinsen, march
Folj mej! Damernas egen pas de quatre (1901)
Gif akt i bataljon, march (1899)
Glittrande bolja, waltz (1902)
Arrangements for piano of popular melodies from operettas
Ref. 642

SANDERS, Alma
Late 19th-century English concert pianist, professor and composer. She studied at Trinity College, London and was professor of the piano there. She performed at concerts in London from 1880 and in 1883 won the Sir Michael Costa prize from Trinity College.
Compositions
CHAMBER
Piano quartet (1883)
Piano trio (Sir Michael Costa prize, 1883)
Four pieces (vln and pf)
Sonata (vln and pf)
Piano pieces
Ref. 6, 260

SANDERS, Alma M.
American pianist, singer, teacher and composer. b. Chicago, March 13, 1882; d. New York, December 15, 1956. She attended the Chicago Musical College on a scholarship and studied singing under William Castle.
Compositions
CHAMBER
Pieces
VOCAL
Songs incl.:
Dreaming of Louise
The hill of Connemara
Hong Kong
Little town in the ould county down
My home in the County Mayo
No one to care
That tumble-down shack in Athlone
Two blue eyes
THEATRE
Musicals incl.:
The Chiffon Girl
Elsie
The Houseboat on the Styx
Tangerine
Ref. 39, 40, 142, 347

SANDFORD, Lucy A.
19th-century composer.
Composition
VOCAL
Stars of the summer night (S, A and pf) (New York: W. Hall, 1849)
Ref. 228

SANDIFUR, Ann Elizabeth
American editor, poetess, teacher and composer. b. Spokane, WA, May 14, 1949. She studied under Robert Asheley at Mills College in California where she received a B.A. (composition) and an M.F.A. (electronic music and recording media). She also studied under Charles Bestor at Willamette University, Paul Creston at Central Washington State College, Stanley Linetta in Sacramento, CA, and Alden Jenks at the San Francisco Conservatory. She is a teacher of music and broadcast engineering in California and an instructor in television and radio communications. She is founder and president of Rosonant Communications Network and editor of a publishing company. From 1980 to 1982 she held the position of vice-president of the Metropolitan Mortgage and Securities Company where she was in charge of data processing and in 1983 completed a five year commisssion for 'Cosmography' monumental multimedia sculpture. She received a prize and grant for her works. PHOTOGRAPH.

Compositions
CHAMBER
>Prenatal (cham ens) (1968)
>Shared improvisations (pf, 4 hands) (1976) (Berkeley: Arsciene, 1977)
>Double chamber music (1976) (Arsciene, 1977)

ELECTRONIC
>Big belly
>Biorhythms of performance (1976) (Arsciene, 1978)
>Bridging space (1970)
>Columbia river (syn, elec and acoustic pfs) (1981)
>Five-part Fugue for the collective consciousness (1976) (Arsciene, 1978)
>Fugue for touch (1976) (Arsciene, 1978)
>In celebration of movement (pf and tape) (1974) (Arsciene, 1978)
>Jona one (1973)
>Learning to talk (vce and digital syn) (1984)
>Poetry is sleeping (vce and tape) (1980)
>P.P.G.
>Rite of birth (1969)
>Scored improvisation (acoustic or electric keyboard) (1977) (Arsciene)
>Still still (mix-ch, fl, ob, elec pf and d-b) (1971) (Arsciene, 1977)
>TVCOMOO1.TEL (digital syn) (1984)

THEATRE
>I Extol the nestle and cuddle, play (1972)
>Sequence II

MULTIMEDIA
>Letting go of home, musical sculpture (1984)
>Word Park, musical sculpture (1984)

Ref. composer, 142, 228, 625

SANDRESKY, Margaret Vardell
American organist, associate professor and composer. b. Macon, GA, April 28, 1921. She studied the organ under her father, Charles Vardell, graduating with a B.M. from Salem College, NC, in 1942 and continued her study of the organ under Harold Gleason and Helmut Walcha. She studied composition under Charles Vardell and at the Eastman School under Howard Hanson and Bernard Rogers, graduating with an M.M. in 1944. From 1955 to 1956 she studied composition under Kurt Hessenberg in Frankfurt. She held a Fulbright scholarship for study in Germany and received several commissions for her works. She was lecturer in theory and composition at Oberlin Conservatory from 1944 to 1946, then at the University of Texas, North Carolina School of the Arts, and Salem College. She was head of the organ department at Salem College from 1950 to 1955 and at North Carolina School of the Arts from 1965 to 1967. Since 1968 she has been an associate professor at Salem College. PHOTOGRAPH.

Compositions
ORCHESTRA
>Brief assemblage (cham orch) (1969)
>Nicole and Roland (1946)
>Sinfonietta (1943)
>The three Marys, tone poem (1945)

CHAMBER
>Seven Japanese drawings (ww qnt) (1970)
>Piano trio (pf, vln and vlc) (1958)
>Two pieces (rec and 2 vla)
>Toccata 11-16 (hpcd) (1972)

ORGAN
>Die Koenige aus Saba kamen da, chorale prelude (1970)
>Du Friedefurst, Herr Jesu Christ, chorale prelude (1970)

PIANO
>Nocturne (1938)
>Quiet Shining (1984)
>Ricercare (1970)
>To be played in the mountains (1974)

VOCAL
>Jericho, cantata (mix-ch and pf) (1970)
>Windows, cantata (w-vces, org and hp) (1972)
>Two Italian songs (mix-ch and handbells) (1971)
>Marie Brunette, song (1945)
>My heart's in the Highlands (S and pf) (1970)
>To the chief musician: A new song (S, fl, pf and perc) (1984)

SACRED
>Come Gracious Spirit, anthem (mix-ch and org) (1966)
>King of glory, King of peace, unison anthem (1961)
>Psalm 92, anthem (mix-ch and org) (1966)
>Jubilate Deo omnis terra (1974) (homage to Guillaume Dutay, 1474)
>My soul doth magnify the Lord (S and org) (1958)
>Overture to the common glory (1949)

Publications
Researches in the analysis of 15th-century music.
Ref. composer, 40, 137, 142, 347, 622, 625

SANDRINI, Marie. See BOERNER-SANDRINI, Marie

SANDSTROEM, Alice Charlotte. See TEGNER, Alice Charlotte

SANDY, Grace Linn
20th-century American organist, teacher and composer. b. Greencastle, IN. She composed piano pieces and songs.
Ref. 347

SANFILIPPO, Margherita Marie
American cellist, clarinetist, double-bassist, flautist, horn player, percussionist, pianist, saxophonist, tuba player, violinist, violist, conductor, teacher, writer and composer. b. San Jose, CA, June 4, 1927. She graduated from San Jose State University with an A.B. in 1950. Her teachers included Herold Johnson, Frank Erickson, Robert Aichele, Leonard Klein, Joseph Hoffman, Gibson Walters, Alma Lowery Williams, Allan Wendt, William Erlendson, Valbort Leland, Rodger Nixon, Charlene Archibeque and Anthony Circne. She studied lyric writing and all the instruments she plays privately. She taught in Californian schools for 29 years and conducted the All-City Orchestra.

Compositions
CHAMBER
>Camel caravan
>Moreland overture
>A rickshaw ride
>United Nations processional march

VOCAL
>Carlo
>El burrito
>The spotted duckling

Publications
Position Studies for Strings.
The Young Orchestra/String Orchestra Concert Book.
Ref. 494

SANFORD, Grace Krick
American accompanist, teacher and composer. b. Indianapolis, September 10, 1904. She studied conducting, singing and sacred music accompaniment. She obtained her B.M. and M.M. from the Oberlin Conservatory, Ohio, and then completed a five year fellowship in composition at the Juilliard School of Music where she studied under Rubin Goldmark. She later obtained her M.Sac.M. oratorio solo at the Union Theological Seminary. She then taught and became a concert accompanist. PHOTOGRAPH.

Compositions
CHAMBER
>Quintet for piano and strings
>String quartet in B-Minor
>String quartet in C-Minor
>Sonata in D (vln and pf) (1931-1932)
>Romanza (vlc and pf) (1945)
>Theme and variations in F-Minor

PIANO
>Canzonetta
>Fugue in A-Minor
>Fugue in 3 voices
>Improvisation (1940)
>Legend
>Scherzo in A-Minor
>Serenade
>Valse noble

VOCAL
>The presentation (w-ch, vln and org) (H.W. Gray Co., New York, 1939)
>October noon (1937)
>Peace
>Song of childhood
>To Ruth
>Values, song

SACRED
>Bethlehem (mix-ch; also w-ch a-cap)
>The spread table, communion prayer (mix-ch a-cap) (1948)
>Settings for many texts

Ref. composer

SANGIACOMO, Olivieri. See RESPIGHI, Elsa

SANGUESA, Iris
20th-century Chilean percussionist, pianist, conductor and composer. She studied at the National Conservatory of Music under Herminia Raccagni, Flora Guerra and German Berner and graduated in the piano in 1959. She studied percussion under Jorge Canelo, conducting under Augustin Cullel and composition under Gustavo Becerra. She received a fellowship from the Instituto De Tella in Buenos Aires where she studied in 1967 and 1968. She later studied composition under Alberto Ginastera.

Compositions
ORCHESTRA
Sincresis (perc and orch) (1963)
Abastractas (1965)
Aforismos del Bhagavad-Gita (1965)
Estudios orquestrales (1966)
Transiciones (1967)
CHAMBER
Quartet (perc) (1968)
Quartet (wind insts) (1967)
Sonata (d-b and pf) (1968)
Sonata (fl and pf) (1965)
Sonata (hp)
PIANO
El pianista chileno, for children (1963)
Pieces for children (1969)
Variations (1962)
SACRED
Hymn for Liceo Gabriela Mistral
Hymn for Liceo Manuel de Salas (1963)
Hymn for the Swiss College
BALLET
Copahue, on an Auracanian legend (1963)
Los trabajos del bailarin (1967)
INCIDENTAL MUSIC
Music for the 1970 Exhibition in Arica (Chile)
MULTIMEDIA
Integracion (tape, dance, slides and engravings) (1968)
Ref. University of Chile

SANI, Maria Teresa

Italian composer.
Compositions
VOCAL
Songs incl.:
A mosca cieca, op. 58, no. 1 (Milan: Ricordi)
A un arpa estia, op. 19, no. 5 (Ricordi)
Canto di giovinezza, op. 63, no. 5 (Ricordi)
Canto di nostalgia, op. 63, no. 8 (Ricordi)
Canto notturno, op. 32, no. 1 (Ricordi)
Canzone, op. 3, no. 4 (Ricordi)
La canzone di Sir di Falkenstein, op. 43, no. 4 (Ricordi)
Il crepusculo si stende, op. 58, no. 1 (Ricordi)
O guancie vezzose, op. 47, no 4 (Ricordi)
Il lieto aracano, op. 71, no. 3 (Ricordi)
Ricordo, op. 63, no. 2 (Ricordi)
Tu dici ch'io m'inganno, op. 32, no. 6 (Ricordi)
ARRANGEMENTS
Works by Brahms, incl.:
Two songs, op. 91: Desio sopito; Ninna nanna mistica (Cont, vla and pf)
Ref. Ricordi

SANNA CAMPAGNA, Myriam

20th-century Italian poetess, writer and composer. Her pieces were greatly praised by critics.
Ref. 56

SANTA-COLONA-SOURGET, Eugenie de (Helene de) (Colomma, Colona, Colonna)

French pianist, singer and composer. b. Bordeaux, February 8, 1827; d. Bordeaux, 1895. She received her first piano lessons from Dufresne at the age of five. She studied in Paris under Zimmermann and Bertini and appeared in public as a singer in Bordeaux when she was 14. She then studied harmony under Colin and voice under Arregui.
Compositions
CHAMBER
String Trio
VOCAL
C'est ton nom (Gerard)
Le chant du crepuscule (1847) (Meissonnier)
Chant Madeleine (1847) (Meissonnier)
Une étoile (1842) (Escudier)
Une jeune fille (1847) (Meissonnier)
OPERA
L'image (1864) (Gerard)
Ref. 26, 105, 129, 225, 269, 433

SANTA-COLONA-SOURGET, Helene de. See SANTA-COLONA-SOURGET, Eugenie

SANTIAGO-FELIPE, Vilma R.

Philippine pianist, critic, playwrite, assistant professor and composer. b. Manila, January 11, 1932. She received her B.Mus. from the Philippine Women's University and studied at the Juilliard School of Music and privately. She premiered Bartok's *Third Piano Concerto* with the Manila Concert Orchestra in 1952 and 1953. As a scriptwriter she wrote music appreciation broadcasts from 1953 to 1956 and was music critic and columnist for the *Times Journal* and *Manila Journal* in 1973. She was associate and assistant professor in music at the Philippine Women's University in 1975 and a recipient of various awards.
Composition
PIANO
Dedication
Ref. 206

SANTINI, Maria

Early 18th-century Italian composer.
Compositions
CHAMBER
Sonatas and vespers (org)
SACRED
Libro di sonate d'organo d'intavolatura fatto per commodo da sonare alle messe, vespri completi ed altro
Ref. 128

SANTOJA, Mari Carmen

20th-century composer.
Composition
FILM MUSIC
At the Service of Spanish Womanhood (1978)
Ref. 497

SANTOS BARRETO, Adelina

Brazilian composer.
Composition
BAND
Percussion music (chil band) (São Paulo: Irmãos Vitale)

SANTOS-OCAMPO DE FRANCESCO, Amada Amy

American pianist, lecturer and composer. b. Manila, Philippines, June 23, 1927. She studied the piano under her aunt, Mercedes M. Santos-Campo and won a first prize for her performance. She then studied under Rizalina Bartolome and the next year enrolled as a special student at the Conservatory, University of the Philippines, where she studied under Rosario Lopes Garcia (piano), Antonino Buenaventura and Felipe P. DeLeon (theory) and the piano privately under Mrs. Garcia. She received her piano music teacher's diploma from St. Paul College Manila in 1943; a B.Mus. (composition and conducting) from the Centro Escolar University Conservatory, Manila, in 1948; an M.Mus. (composition) from DePauw University, Greencastle, Indiana in 1960. She did postgraduate studies at Indiana University in Bloomington, from 1960 to 1964. She held scholarships from the Music Promotion Foundation of the Philippines; DePauw University; Indiana University; and Altrusa International. She was a faculty member of Centro Escolar University from 1955 to 1958 and 1964 to 1967; and Stella Maris College from 1965 to 1967. From 1967 she was a music consultant and pianist in residence and accompanist at Pennsylvania State University. She married Rio Tamayo de Francesco, artist, publisher and composer. PHOTOGRAPH.
Compositions
ORCHESTRA
Two symphonies
Piano concerto in A-Minor (1957)
Prelude and fugue (str orch) (1955)
Sunset by the beach, tone poem (orch) (1955)
Variations for orchestra (1960)
CHAMBER
Woodwind quintet (1961)
String quartet No. 2 (1963 to 1973)
Romance in G (vln and pf) (1960)
Sonata (cl and pf) (1960) (Videorama Music Co.)
Sonata (vln and pf) (1965)
Orchesis (vln and pf) (1978)
PIANO
Concert piece (2 pf) (1962)
If after every tempest come such calm (1959)
Impromptu, op. 2 (1942)
Romance in G (1943)
Rustic suite (1954)
Sonata in D (1942)
Twinkling stars (1956)
Variations on Leron Leron Sinta (Musical Journal of the Philippines)
VOCAL
A song (high vce and orch)
A song cycle (m-S and orch)
Where mountains meet the sea (S and orch) (1963)

Cupid and death (3 part ch) (1960)
A song of ascents (mix-ch) (1959)
To the sea the river flows (mix-ch and pf)
Piece for recorder, percussion ensemble, chant and piano (1968)
The beggar (Bar and pf) (1967)
Chrysalis (S and pf) (1959)
Fifty-five years (Bar and pf) (1966)
Gloom casts the candle (Bar and pf) (1966)
I want you (S and pf) (1955)
In an orchard (vce and pf) (1964)
Love song (m-S and pf) (1962)
Morning on the San Francisco peaks, song cycle
Universal peace (m-S and pf) (1974)
DANCE SCORES
Modern Dance pieces (1959-1960 and 1967-1975)
ELECTRONIC
Alon (1956)
Ref. composer

SANZ, Rocio (Carmen Rocio Sanz Quiros)

Costa Rican poetess, teacher, writer and composer. b. San Jose, January 28, 1934. She had some musical training with her mother, Rosita Quiros, then attended the Conservatorio de Costa Rica in 1950 and 1951 and the Los Angeles City College from 1952 to 1953, majoring in music. She studied under Carlos Jimenez Mabarak, Blas Galindo and Rodolfo Halffter among others at the Conservatorio Nacional de Mexico from 1954 to 1958 and took a course on electronic music from 1969 to 1970. She was awarded a scholarship to study composition under Vladimir Giorgyevich Fere at the Moscow Tchaikovsky Conservatory in 1965 and 1966. She has been active as a teacher since 1956 and composed since 1958. She taught for 14 years at the Fine Arts Institute's School of Dance and Dramatic Art and at the University's Theater Centre in 1977. She worked as stage manager and music consultant for several dance and theatre companies between 1959 and 1964. In 1963 she was resident composer for the Theatre of the Universidad Veracruzana in Jalapa, Mexico and is a member of the Liga de Compositores. She was in charge of special projects for the Folk-lore Ballet of Mexico in 1970 and 1971. Since 1966 she has been an active member of Radio Universidad de Mexico; being involved in the daily organization of broadcasting programs of serious music since 1972; been writer and producer of a weekly program for children and since 1973, has been head of the record library department of Radio Universidad. She is a recipient of numerous prizes and awards, including first prize in the Independence Musical Competition in 1971. She lives in Mexico City. PHOTOGRAPH.
Compositions
ORCHESTRA
Ballet suite (1959)
Suite hilos (str orch)
CHAMBER
Four brief pieces (wind qnt) (1962)
Two brief dances (str qrt) (1972)
Piece (vlc and pf)
Rondo (pf) (4 hands) (1981)
Sonata (fl and pf) (1966)
Suite for recorders (themes of children's games from Costa Rica)
VOCAL
Independence cantata (B, ch and symphonic band) (1971) (1st prize music competition, San Jose)
Canciones de la muerte (composer) (S and str orch)
Four brief songs of death (S and str orch)
Five villancicos (Juana Ines de la Cruz) (mix-ch) (1976) (Christmas choral music prize)
Six villancicos (mix-ch)
Two songs (Pablo Neruda) (mix-ch) (1958)
Canciones de la noche, five songs of the night (composer) (S and pf) (1975)
El sabanero (1980)
Five songs for children (Carlos Luis Saenz) (1979)
Five songs for children (m-S and pf) (1962)
Five songs of summer (composer) (m-S and pf) (1972)
Nine songs for children (vce, gtr and perc) (1975)
Three songs (Carlos Luiz Sanz) (S and pf) (1959)
BALLET
El forastero, sound collage (Mexico, 1973)
Letania erotica para la paz (elec insts) (1973)
THEATRE
Los Argonautas (Sergio Magana) (1967)
La Culpa busca la pena (Juan Ruiz de Alarcon) (1962)
The exception and the rule (Bertolt Brech) (1961)
The good soul of Sezuan (B. Brecht) (1964)
Lances de amor y fortuna (1981)
Macbeth (Shakespeare) (1963)
The mandrake-root (Niccolo Maquivelo) (1963)
Pastores de la ciudad (Emilio Carballido) (1959) (Universidad Veracruzana, 1962)

La ronda de la hechizada (Hugo Arguelles) (1967)
The Tempest (Shakespeare) (1964)
Two classical Spanish plays (1962)
Two plays for children (E. Carballido and Sergio Magana)
Two short plays (Friedrich Duerrenmatt) (1962)
FILM MUSIC
Figurillas de Jaina (tape) (1969)
Imagen 68, documentary (1968) (comm committee for Olympic Games)
Juegos de Arcilla, documentary (1971)
Manicomio (musique Concrete) (1969)
Palenque, documentary (1971) (award, best documentary film of the year)
La Sunamita (1965) (award, 1st competition of experimental films)
Ref. composer

SANZ QUIROS, Carmen Rocio. See SANZ, Rocio

SAPAROFF, Andrea

20th-century American guitarist, conductor and composer. She studied the guitar, conducting and composition at California State University, Northridge and did post-graduate study in conducting, electronic music and composition.
Compositions
CHAMBER
Spectrums five for six (comm Sylmar Chamber Ensemble)
FILM MUSIC
I don't Know who I am
A rainy Day
The Tie that Binds
Women and Alcohol: Through the Drinking Glass
Ref. International Women's Year Conference

SAPPHO

Greek flautist, kithara player, poetess and songstress. b. Eresos, Lesbos, ca. 630 B.C.; d. ca. 570 B.C. (In Aeolian dialect Psappha or Psappho). She lived in the town of Mytilene. In common with the other women of the Aegean world, the women of Lesbos had high social, political, literary and religious status. They owned their own property, were well educated, especially in poetry and music and enjoyed the company of both sexes, taking part in literary and political discussions and religious functions. Sappho's father was probably Scamadronymus, a rich noble said to be a wine merchant. Her mother was Cleis. Sappho was a woman of independent wealth and married Cercola (or Cercylos) a young man of the island of Andros. They had a daughter, also Cleis, but Cercola died young and Sappho was determined never to love again. According to a widely spread legend, she soon fell in love with Phaon and followed him to Sicily. He was untouched by her love, poetry and music and in sheer disappointment, Sappho committed suicide by throwing herself into the sea near Cape Ceucata on the island of Leucatia. But Phaon is not mentioned in any of the fragments of her poetry. References to Phaon date to the 5th-century and the story of Sappho's leap appears over a century later. Sappho formed an academy of music and poetry for girls, who came to the academy from all over Greece. Sappho and her pupils officiated at religious festivals and her epithalamia (wedding songs) were so famous that she and her girls were frequently employed at weddings. The poetic form of her epithalamia was the model used by other writers for nearly a thousand years in Greece, Rome and Europe. Her favorite instruments to accompany her songs were the golden lyre (kithara) and sweet-toned flute. She was reputed to have developed a stringed instrument called the pectis and to have introduced the plectrum for the lyre. Sappho frequently engaged in social and poetical sparring with Alcaeus, the other famous poet of Lesbos. They appear to have sung a tenso between them – a sort of poetical dialogue between kindred spirits. Plato called Sappho the tenth muse. She was also called the mortal muse, the feminine Homer and the muses' sister. Sappho was credited by Aristoxenos with having evolved the mixolydian mode and a new style of music by breaking up the meter: she also wrote elegies, epigrams, hymns, and nine books of lyric poetry. Only a few fragments of her poetry and none of her music survive, but her verses and melodies were regarded by contemporaries and critics of the golden age as being perfect.
Bibliography
Bascoul, J. M. F. La Chaste Sappho de Lesbos et Stecichore Paris, 1913.
Carman, Bliss. Sappho, One Hundred Lyrics. Boston, 1904.
Sitzler, J. Bibliography on Sappho. Jahresbericht ueber die Fortschritte der klassischen Altertumswissenschaft. 1907 and 1919.
Ref. 24, 116, 209, 264, 281, 310, 382

SAPTEFRATI, Liana Alexandra. See ALEXANDRA, Liana

SARASIN de GEYMULLER, Marguerite. See GEYMULLER, Marguerite Camilli Louise

SARASWATIBAI
20th-century Indian composer of film music.
Ref. National Council of Women in India

SARGENT, Cora Decker
19th-century American composer.
Compositions
VOCAL
    Songs incl.:
    Spanish
    A summer girl
Ref. 226, 276, 433

SARNECKA, Jadwiga
Polish concert pianist, teacher and composer. b. Slawuta, Wolynia, 1877; d. Cracow, December 29, 1913. She studied the piano under Szopski in Cracow, Melcer and A. Michalowkski in Warsaw and then under I. Leschetizky in Vienna. She toured Austria, Germany and Poland. Her piano pieces and songs with her own words reflected the grief and suffering that characterized her life.
Compositions
PIANO
    Four ballads (1 won an honor, in the Competition, Lvov, 1910)
    Sonata
    Variations in E-Minor
    Other salon pieces
VOCAL
    Songs (vce and pf) (some publ Cracow: A. Piwarski)
Ref. 8, 105, 118, 226

SAROVA, Dagmar. See ADDENDUM

SARRET DE COUSSERGUES, Mlne.
18th-century French composer. She composed a collection of harpsichord pieces.
    Ref. Otto Harrassowits (Wiesbaden)

SARTORIS, Mrs. See KEMBLE, ADELAIDE

SARTORIUS, Lili. See REIFF, Lili

SASSOLI, Ada
Italian harpist, pianist, lecturer and composer. b. Bologna, 1886; d. Rome, 1946. She studied the harp at the Bologna Conservatory and the Paris Conservatoire. She worked as a soloist and accompanied singers, including such names as Dame Nellie Melba. In 1916 she joined the staff at the Conservatory of Santa Cecilia in Siena. She composed works for both the harp and the piano.
Ref. 502

SATO, Masashiko
20th-century Japanese composer.
Composition
FILM MUSIC
    Belladonna (1973)
Ref. 497

SATOH, Kimi
Japanese composer. b. Senai, March 5, 1949. She graduated from the Toho School of Music where she studied composition under Yoshiro Irino. In 1972 she attended the International Summer School in Darmstadt and went on to study composition under Olivier Messiaen at the Paris Conservatoire. In 1977 she received a French government scholarship and first prize on graduation from the Paris Conservatoire. DISCOGRAPHY.
Compositions
ORCHESTRA
    Espace (1974)
CHAMBER
    Le bleu de ciel (12 strs) (comm French government, 1977)
    Beyond space, sound (pf) (1976)
    Le cadre blanc (fl) (1972)

MISCELLANEOUS
    Ailleurs
    Journal d'été
    Sol diese
Ref. Yamaha Foundation, Japan

SAUGEON, Zelie (nee Faget)
French teacher and composer. d. Tresne, Gironde, 1878. She was a pupil of Pierre Galin and Aime Paris and married Saugeon, the author on music. She taught the Meloplaste system for 30 years at Bordeaux. She composed piano pieces and songs.
Ref. 26

SAUNDERS, Carrie Lou
American singer and composer. b. Mexia, TX, August, 1893. She studied at the Texas Technological College. She sang in choirs and became a member of ASCAP in 1961.
Compositions
VOCAL
    Green grass and still waters
SACRED
    My Saviour came
    Stay Close to God
Ref. 39

SAUTER, Maya
Swiss pianist and composer. b. Bienne, 1910. She completed her piano studies in Neuchatel in 1933 and received a prize for her virtuosity. She composed pieces for the piano and the flute.
Ref. composer

SAUVAL, Marc. See SOULAGE, Marcelle Fanny Henriette

SAUVREZIS, Alice
French composer. b. Nantes, April, 1885; d. Paris, April, 1946. She lived in Paris and studied under Cesar Franck and P. Vidal. She was president of the Société Artistique et Litteraire de l'Ouest.
Compositions
ORCHESTRA
    Francen-ar-Mor, lyric legend
    Symphonic poem
    Two symphonic suites
CHAMBER
    Sonata (vln and pf)
    Sonata (2 pf)
VOCAL
    Veillée (vce and orch)
    About 50 songs
Ref. 23, 70, 81, 105, 226, 465, 622

SAVAGE, Jane
Late 18th-century English harpsichordist and composer.
Compositions
CHAMBER
    A favourite duet for two performers, op. 6 (pf or hpcd) (Longman & Broderip, ca. 1790)
    Six easy lessons, op. 2 (hpcd or pf)
    Six rondos, op. 3 (hpcd or pf) (Longman, ca. 1790)
VOCAL
    Stephan and Flavia, op. 4, cantata (Longman, ca. 1790)
    God save the King, op. 8, adapted as a double lesson
    Hall the woodman, op. 5, a favourite song (Longman, 1790)
Ref. 6, 65, 85, 347, 405

SAWATH, Caroline
19th-century German composer. She composed pieces for the piano.
Ref. 226, 276

SAWYER, Elizabeth
b. 1931.
Composition
CHAMBER
    The seasons, suite. (Charm Orch) (1955)
Ref. 594

SAWYER, Harriet P. (Hattie)
19th-century American composer.
Compositions
VOCAL
Songs incl.:
Across the dreary sea
Who'll tell
Willie darling
SACRED
Pieces
Ref. 276, 292, 347, 433

SAWYER, Hattie. See SAWYER, Harriet P.

SAXTORPH, Gudrun
Danish pianist, singer, lecturer and composer. b. Copenhagen, November 19, 1885. She studied at the Royal Conservatory of Copenhagen and in Chicago in 1908. She taught at the Central Conservatory of Chicago. She toured the United States and Europe and was a singing teacher in Copenhagen. She published her own works in 1933.
Compositions
ORCHESTRA
Sommernat i Danmark
Valse sentimente
CHAMBER
Romance (vln) (1941)
VOCAL
Frihed og fred (1940)
Six Icelandic songs (1939)
Ref. 96

SAZ, Leyla. See HANIM, Leyla

SCALETTI, Carla
American harpist and composer. b. Ithaca, NY, April 28, 1956. DISCOGRAPHY.
Composition
VOCAL
Motet (narr, m-S, b-cl and hp) (Hoffman)
Ref. AMC, 622

SCAPINELLI, Countess Isabella D. See PIO DI SAVOJA, Isabella D.

SCAPUS, Mit. See SCHEEPERS-VAN DOMMELEN, Maria

SCEK, Breda Friderika
Slovenian (Yugoslav) conductor, lecturer, singer and composer. b. Trieste, August 20, 1895; d. Ljubljana, March 11, 1968. She studied at the Tartini Conservatory in Trieste and at the Music Liceo Martini in Bologna. She worked for a time in Trieste as a singer and conducted choirs there and in Ljubljana, where she became a lecturer in music.
Compositions
ORCHESTRA
Mala suita (cham orch) (1926)
PIANO
Preludiji (1926)
Zvonovi v praznik, 8 pieces (1928)
VOCAL
Hasanaginica, cantata (solo, ch and pf) (1955)
Soci, cantata (m-ch and orch) (1945)
Jugoslavija, 8 pieces (youth ch) (1939)
Kadar jaz, dekle, umrla bom, 33 folk songs (ch) (1933)
Pojmo spat, 11 pieces (youth ch) (1936)
Cez pohorje sinje, 8 songs (vce and pf) (1935)
Dekle na vrtu zelenem (vce and pf) (1945)
Juhej, jaz pa v gorco grem (vce and pf) (1945)
Med rozami, 4 solo songs (1955)
Oj vrba, 5 songs (vce and pf) (1954)
Raste mi raste, 7 songs (vce and pf) (1934)
Starka zima, book for youth (1967)

SACRED
Sveti Andrej, 23 pieces (m-ch) (1938)
V Nazaretu roza raste, 12 pieces (m-ch) (1934)
Other pieces
Ref. 109, 145, 193

SCHADEN, Nanette von
Late 19th-century Austrian pianist and composer. She lived in Salzburg.
Compositions
ORCHESTRA
Two piano concertos
PIANO
Pieces incl.:
Rondos
Sonatas
Ref. 226, 276

SCHAEFFER, Theresa
19th-century German composer.
Compositions
ORCHESTRA
Festival overture
PIANO
Capriccio, op. 16
Etincelles (Schlesinger)
Lamentations erotique, op. 1
Mazurka, op. 5
Nocturne, op. 15
Rondo brilliant, op. 14
Scherzo, op. 17
Serenade, op. 27
VOCAL
Cradle song, op. 22 (Schroeder)
Two songs, op. 6 (Siegel)
Two songs, op. 7 (Siegel)
Ref. 226, 276, 297, 433

SCHAFF, Merle S. See POLIN, Claire

SCHAFMEISTER, Helen
American concert pianist, teacher and composer. b. Ossining, NY, October 5, 1900. She attended Ossining School and studied under Frank La Forge, Ernesto Berumen, Egon Petri, Charles Haubiel and Emerson Whithorne. She performed as a soloist, appearing in concert at such places as Carnegie and Steinway Halls.
Compositions
ORCHESTRA
Festival overture
BRASS BAND
Barnegat bay
The dawn and you
Psalm 46, duet
Entreat me not
Forever
Gypsies
Illusion
The jaunting car
The music of your love
A night myth
Prairie
Reasons
Sea swept fantasy
Spring song
Then and now
To and from town
We are to-gether
Ref. 190, 494, 622

SCHALE, Mademoiselle
Composition
PIANO
Menuet
Ref. Frau und Musik

SCHAPIRA, Ilana. See MARINESCU-SCHAPIRA, Ilana

SCHARLI, Ruth
Swiss flautist, pianist, music therapist, teacher and composer. b. 1929. She taught the piano and the flute and was a music therapist. DISCOGRAPHY.
Compositions
CHAMBER
Ein Portraet (b-cl and pf)
Parthenon (b-cl and pf)
Ref. Carus-Verlag (Stuttgart), 563

SCHARWENKA-STRESOW, Marianne
German pianist, violinist and composer. b. February 25, 1856; d. Berlin, October 23, 1918. She studied the violin under Marsick and Sarasate. She also studied the piano and composition.
Composition
CHAMBER
Concertino, op. 5 (vln and pf) (Schuberth & Co., 1911)
Ref. 7

SCHATZELL, Pauline von (Mrs. von Decker) (pseud. P.F. Marxhausen)
German singer and composer. b. Berlin, 1812. She was the granddaughter of the singer Margarethe Schick. She took singing lessons with the court singer, H. Stuemer and made her debut in 1828 as Agathe in *Der Freischuetz* at the Court theatre. She became famous and her operatic roles covered a wide range. After retiring from the operatic stage she sang in concerts and oratorios.
Compositions
VOCAL
Duet, op. 5 (2 S)
Two duets, op. 17 (S and A)
Ten songs incl.:
So weit, op. 15, no. 3
Ref. 129, 276, 347

SCHAUFF, Marie
18th-century German composer.
Compositions
CHAMBER
Variazioni per il clavicembalo (hpcd) (1799)
VOCAL
Das Geheimnis und das Bestaendige, op. 3 (Lenau) (Vienna: Diabelli & Co.)
Ref. 128

SCHAUROTH, Delphine (Adolphine) von
German concert pianist and composer. b. Magdeburg, 1814; d. after 1881. She was a pupil of Kalkbrenner and became a concert pianist. Mendelssohn became infatuated with her during his visit to Munich in 1830 and dedicated his *Concerto in G* and his *Venetian Gondellied, No. 6* to her. Schumann also admired her playing.
Compositions
PIANO
Sonatas incl.:
Capriccio
Sonata brilliant in C-Minor
Other pieces
Ref. 85, 226, 276, 347

SCHAUSS-FLAKE, Magdalene
German composer. b. 1921. DISCOGRAPHY.
Compositions
CHAMBER
Suite in G (brass and ww)
VOCAL
Der Morgenstern ist aufgedrungen (Daniel Rumpius) (S, ch and 4- 6 wind insts)
Variationen ueber das Lied 'es ist ein Schnitter, heisst der tod' (narr and trb)
SACRED
Ohren gabst du mir (Ruppel) (ch)
Befiehl dem Herrn deine Wege
Befiehl du deine Wege
Du meine Seele singe
Jauchzet dem Herrn, alle Welt
Jauchzet, ihr Himmel
Nun lasst uns Gott, dem Herrn

MISCELLANEOUS
Serenade
ARRANGEMENTS
Variationen ueber ein Thema von Anton Dvorak (trp and trb)
Ref. 266, 563

SCHEEPERS-VAN DOMMELEN, Maria (pseud. Mit Scapus)
Dutch singer and composer. b. Antwerp, November 17, 1892. She was a member of the Belgian Vocal Trio with Tolkowsky and Roitel. She composed more than 60 songs.
Ref. 1

SCHEICHER, Caroline. See KRAEHMER, Caroline

SCHEIDL-HUTTERSTRASSER, Lili. See HANS, Lio

SCHEIN, Suzanna Fedorovna
Soviet lecturer and composer. b. Baku, March 9, 1921. She studied composition under L. Rudolf from 1936 to 1938 and under B. Zaidman in 1944, and then graduated from the Baku Conservatory. From 1946 to 1948 she lectured in composition, instrumentation and harmony and was head of the department of theoretical subjects at the Music School of Baku. From 1948 to 1950 she lectured in the history of music department at the Music School in Moscow, and after 1953 returned to Baku to teach composition and polyphony at the music school there.
Compositions
ORCHESTRA
Symphony (1945)
Violin concerto (1946)
Poem on a Moldavian theme (vln and orch) (1947)
Poem (1944)
CHAMBER
Quartet (1949)
Trio (1948)
Six preludes (pf) (1950)
VOCAL
Arrangements of Russian folk songs (mix-ch) (1954)
Mingechaur, poem (M. Plyama) (1945)
Three romances (S. Burgin) (1944)
Ref. 87

SCHEINZER, Hilda. See KUCZOR, Hilda

SCHELLER ZEMBRANO, Maria
Argentine composer. b. Buenos Aires, 1917; d. 1944. She graduated from the Conservatorio Nacional de Musica y Arte in 1937 and studied under Rafael Gonzalez, Ricardo Rodrigues and Jose Andre.
Compositions
ORCHESTRA
Concerto in A-Minor (pf and orch) (1939)
CHAMBER
Quartet in F-Major (str qrt) (1936)
Sonata (vln and pf) (1939)
PIANO
Four sonatas
Sonata in E-Flat (1938)
Suite (1937)
Ref. 390

SCHENK, Annette. See THOMA, Annette

SCHERCHEN, Mme. See HSIAO, Shu-Sien

SCHERCHEN (Scherchen-Hsiao), Tona
Swiss conductor, lecturer and composer. b. Neuchatel, March 12, 1938. The daughter of conductor Herman Scherchen and Hsiao Shu-sien (q.v.), she lived in China from the age of 11 and studied Chinese classical music at the Peking Conservatory and the Shanghai Music Academy from 1958 to 1960. She then went to Switzerland and spent two months at her father's Gravesano studio. From 1961 to 1963 she studied under Henze at the Mozarteum in Salzburg. She studied at the Paris Conservatoire under Messiaen from 1963 to 1966 and privately in Vienna under Ligeti from 1966 to 1967. In 1972 she lectured in Denmark and in 1976 in the United States where she also conducted the Saint Paul Chamber Orchestra. Since 1972

she has lived in France. In 1964 she won first prize at the Paris Conservatoire and in 1967 first prize of the Gaudeamus Foundation Composers' competition. In 1972 she received the Prix Stephane-Chapelier-Clergue-Gabriel-Marie from the French Society of Authors, Composers and Publishers of Music. She received a grant from the Concert Artists' Guild, New York in 1973 and in the same year won the Grand Prix Herve Dugardin in Paris. DISCOGRAPHY.

Compositions

ORCHESTRA

Khouang (hpcd and orch) (1968) (Universal Edition)
Tao (vla and orch with 3 Jew's harps) (from Histoire de Ziguidor)
L'invitation au voyage (cham orch) (1977) (Boosey and Hawkes)
Oeil de chat (1977)
'S....' (1975) (Universal)
Shen (6 perc or perc orch) (1968) (Universal)
Tjao-houen (cham orch) (1973) (Universal)
Tzang (cham orch) (1966)
Vague-t'Ao (1975) (Universal)

CHAMBER

Lo (trb and 12 strs) (Boosey)
Bien (Mutations) (12 insts) (1973) (Universal)
Hsun (ob, trp, trb, perc and 2 vlc) (1968) (Universal)
Tzing (brass qnt) (1979)
Ziguidor (wind qnt) (1977) (Boosey)
Tzoue (fl or cl and vlc or c-bsn and hpcd) (1970) (Universal)
Escargot volants (cl) (1979)
In (fl) (1965) (Peschek)
Lien (vla) (1973) (Universal)
Once upon a time (hp) (1979) (Musicales)
Radar (pf) (1984)
Sin (fl) (1965)

VOCAL

Tzi (ch a-cap) (1970) (Universal)
Wai (m-S, perc and str qrt) (1966) (Universal)

BALLET

Tzan-shen (1971) (Universal)

THEATRE

Labyrinteromysfloraquatarabiscocotiques, musical
Nouvelles legendes ..., musical
La tarme du crocodile (vce) (Musicales)

ELECTRONIC

Yun-yu (vln or vla and vib) (1972) (Universal)
Yi (2 players on one marimbaphone or 2 other insts) (1973) (Universal)

Bibliography

Shiffer, Brigitte. *Tona Scherchen. Tempo* No. 117. Boosey and Hawkes, June 1976.

Ref. 17, 70, 189, 403, 563, 594, 622, 637

SCHERCHEN-HSIAO, Tona. See SCHERCHEN, Tona

SCHEYWYCK, Marie. See MATTHYSSENS, Marie

SCHIATTI, Catherine. See MAIER, Catherine

SCHIAVO DE GREGORIO, Maria. See ADDENDUM

SCHICK, Philippine

German pianist, lecturer, writer and composer. b. Bonn, February 9, 1893; d. Munich, January 13, 1970. She studied at the State Academy of Music, Munich under Friedrich Klose from 1914 to 1918 (theory and composition) and under Waltershausen (composition). Later she studied composition privately under Waltershausen and the piano under Ruoff, Schmid-Linder and Herman Zilcher from 1921 to 1925. From 1946 to 1956 she was a lecturer in music, theory, English language and literature at the University of Munich. She founded the music section of GEDOK and in 1943 was awarded the Advancement prize of Munich.

Compositions

ORCHESTRA

Piano concerto, op. 10 (1923)
Ueber das Magnificat, passacaglia and choral fugue, op. 37 (2 pf and orch) (1939)
Schottische Tanzsuite, op. 36 (1938)

CHAMBER

String quartet, op. 3 (1920)
Trio, op. 21 (vln, vlc and pf) (1930)
Norwegische Suite, op. 33 (vln and pf) (1936) (Verlag Elisabeth Thomi-Berg)
Sonata, op. 43 (vlc and pf) (1941) (Thomi-Berg)
Sonata in F-Sharp, op. 14 (vln and pf) (1926)
Passacaglia and fugue, op. 11 (org) (1924)

PIANO

Eleven old German folk songs, op. 57 (4 hands) (1953)
Four intermezzos, op. 31 (1936)
Metamorphosen, op. 52 (1951)
Six miniatures, op. 13 (1924)
Sonata, op. 1 (1918)
Variationen und Fantasie ueber ein Theme von Waltershausen, op. 7 (1923)

VOCAL

Von unvergaenglicher Liebe, op. 47, cantata (after M. Claudius) (S and ch)
Alte deutsche Liebeslieder, op. 16 (mix-ch and orch) (1928) (E. Schneider)
Der Geiger von Gmund, op. 26, ballad (I. Kerner) (A and orch) (1934)
Komm, suesser Schlaf, op. 55 (S, m-S and strs) (1953)
Five Shakespeare songs, op. 56 (vce and str trio)
Fuenf Kinderlieder, op. 4 (Ruekert) (S) (1921)
Liebesfruehling, 7 Lieder, op. 18 (S) (1928)
Lieder der Sehnsucht, op. 12 (B) (1924)
Lieder des Todes, op. 8 (A) (1922)
Maedchen Lieder, op. 2 (Ritter) (S) (1923)
Neue Kinderlieder, op. 9 (S) (1922)
Der Pilger, cycle (Eichendorff), op. 24
Pyrrhussieg, op. 6, cycle (S) (1922)
Sententia latinae, op. 54 (6 to 8 vces)
Sieben Lieder, op. 5 (1923)
Sieben Lieder, op. 15 (Morgenstern) (B) (Berlin: Verlag Deutscher Tonkuenstler)
Vom Frieden der Liebe, op. 29 (S and pf) (Thomi-Berg)

SACRED

Welt der Liebe, op. 23, oratorio (Tagore) (1931)
Der Einsame an Gott, op. 17, cantata (Hesse) (S, B, w-ch, pf, strs and orch) (Deutscher Tonkuenstler)
Gespraeche mit Gott, 3 psalms (B and orch) (1929)

BALLET

Three ballet pantomimes, ops. 42, 47 and 48 (1939-1943) (H. Pawlinin) incl.:
Vergessene Gaeste

OPERA

Severina, op. 35 (1939)

OPERETTA

Der Blumenzwist (1906)

Publications

Deutsch-englisches Musikwoerterbuch. With H. Leuchtmann. Berlin, 1964.
Harmonielehre. 1950.
Kontrapunkt und Fuge. 1950.

Bibliography

Wuerz, A. *Philippine Schick. Zeitschrift fuer Musik.*

Ref. 14, 15, 17, 86, 109, 111, 200, 622

SCHIEVE, Catherine

American accordionist, flautist, arranger, painter and composer. b. Fountain Hill, PA, March 6, 1956. She obtained her B.Mus. and M.Mus from the University of Texas in 1978 and 1980 and Ph.D. from the University of California, San Diego. She studied composition under Kenneth Gaburo, Barton McLean, Joseph Schwantner, Bernard Rands, Eugene Kurtz and Pauline Oliveros (q.v.). She has performed widely in several experimental, early music, ethnic and chamber ensembles. In 1981 she was awarded the first prize at the International League of Women Composers and she has held fellowships at the Universities of Texas and San Diego. DISCOGRAPHY.

Compositions

CHAMBER

Mablick (12 fl)
String figures (pf, hpcd, hp, 2 gtr, 2 vln, 2 vlc and d-b)
Serpentine (fl, b-fl, cl, b-cl and pf)
Tiger's eye (b-Flat cl and op cl ch) (1980)
Labyrinth (1977)

VOCAL

Drone (4 vces, 4 trb, 4 fl, 2 pf, 2 vlc)
The flying sea sings (vce, 2 trp and trb) (1976)
I offer songs, intoxicating flowers (vce, fl, vla, vlc and gtr)
Pajaro (vce, cl, b-cl and perc)
Weaving (vce, fl, perc and strs) (1981)

DANCE SCORES

Duet (fl and dancer) (1975)

INCIDENTAL MUSIC

Music for theatre, film, dance and television

ELECTRONIC

Piece for percussion and synthesizer (1977)
Catalysts in a sonic soup (audience and syn) (1977)

Ref. 563

SCHIMON, Anna (nee Regan)
Bohemian singer, teacher and composer. b. Carlsbad, September 18,
1836. She studied under Halevy.
Compositions
VOCAL
Pieces
OPERA
List un list
Stradella
Ref. 276, 307

SCHINDLER, Alma Maria. See MAHLER, Alma Maria

SCHINDLER, Livia
19th-century composer.
Compositions
PIANO
Valsas brilhantes
Ref. 399

SCHIRMACHER, Dora
English concert pianist and composer. b. Liverpool, September 1, 1857.
She was a pupil of Wenzel and Reinecke at the Leipzig Conservatory for
three years, was awarded first prize and made her debut at the Gewand-
haus, Leipzig at the age of 20. She played with great success in England
and on the continent.
Compositions
PIANO
Romanze, op. 4
Sonata
Suite
Tonbilder, op. 5
Valse de concert, op. 6
Other pieces
VOCAL
Songs
Ref. 6, 226, 276, 433

SCHJELDERUP, Mon Marie Gustava
Norwegian pianist and composer. b. June 16, 1870. She studied the piano
under Agathe Backer-Groendahl (q.v.) and theory under Raif, Succo and
Bargiel in Berlin and Massenet in Paris. She made her debut in Christi-
ania, in 1894.
Compositions
CHAMBER
Violin sonata (1895)
VOCAL
Four-part male choruses
Songs
THEATRE
Prelude to The Wild Duck (Ibsen) (1891)
Ref. 23, 105, 113

SCHLECHTRIEM, Theresia
German composer.
Compositions
VOCAL
Drei Chorlieder nach Gedichten (ch a-cap)
Fink und Frosch (ch a-cap)
Ref. Frau und Musik

SCHLEDER, Griselda Lazzaro
Brazilian pianist, choral conductor, teacher, writer and composer. b. São
Paulo, 1889. She graduated at the National School of Music at Rio de
Janeiro, majoring in the piano and harmony. She directed the First Brazil-
ian choir which played during the opera seasons at the Rio de Janeiro
Municipal Theatre. She performed at various concerts and directed sev-
eral orchestras. She was awarded the National School of Music gold
medal.
Compositions
OPERETTA
E o teu amor
THEATRE
A Cigarra e a Formiga, musical fantasy
A Folha do Pica-Pau
Publications
Noções Sucintas de Teoria Musical.
Ref. 268

SCHLEICHER, Caroline. See KRAEHMER, Caroline

SCHLICK, Elise, Countess of
19th-century German composer.
Compositions
VOCAL
Songs incl.:
Geisternacht (Cranz)
Gute Nacht (Cranz)
Lieder der Nacht (Cranz)
Ref. 226, 276, 433

SCHLOSS, Myrna Frances (nee Margulius)
Canadian pianist, lecturer and composer. b. New Westminster, January
30, 1941. She received her B.A., M.A. and B.Mus from the University of
British Columbia; M.Mus from Lewis and Clark College, Portland, OR, in
1980 and a Ph.D. (ethnomusicology) from the Wesleyan University. She
studied composition under Alvin Lucier, Vincent McDermott and Harry
Freedman and the piano under Audrey Mallinson and Robert Rogers at
the University of British Columbia. She taught the piano and music in
schools from 1965 to 1982 and at the Wesleyan and British Columbian
Universities.
Compositions
CHAMBER
Thirteenth summer (fl, vlc and gtr) (1979)
Intertwine II (fl, ob and a-sax)
Intertwine I (cl and a-sax)
Eruption (pf) (1980)
Golden streams (vln) (1980)
VOCAL
Oregon landscape (mix-ch)
Dome (Bar, vlc and hn) (1981)
Gender (S) (1980)
The glass castle (S, cl and org) (1979)
Image, No. 1, 2, 2, (vce, pf, har and tape)
ELECTRONIC
Erotium's song (S and tape) (1978)
Guitar varia (gtr, hpcd and syn) (1980)
Intertwine III (ob, a-sax and syn) (1980)
Music for King Lear (vce, tape and perc)
Overture, interlude and coda (tape) (1979)
MULTIMEDIA
Green hollows (S, Bar, vlc, vib, xyl, dr, pf, chimes and projections)
(1981)
Triptych plus (tape and projections)
Ref. composer

SCHMELING, Elisabeth Gertrud. See MARA, La

SCHMEZER, Elise
19th-century German composer.
Compositions
VOCAL
Berg und See aus Amaranth, op. 11, duet (Bachmann)
Jung Walther aus Amaranth, op. 14 (Bachmann)
Romances and Ballads, op. 4 (Heinrichshofen)
Die Verwandlung, op. 13 (Bachmann)
Zwei Lieder, op. 19 (Raabe)
OPERA
Otto der Schuetz (1823)
Ref. 226, 276, 297, 347, 433

SCHMIDHUBER, Caecilie
Composition
SACRED
Deutsche Messe
Ref. 465

SCHMIDT, Carola
German composer. b. 1905.
Compositions
SACRED
Freuet euch in dem Herrn allezeit
Steh auf, Herr Gott
Ref. Hanssler verlag

SCHMIDT, Diane Louise

American accordionist and composer. b. Seattle, November 23, 1948. She obtained her B.Mus. from the University of Puget Sound and in 1973 studied composition with William O. Smith and Robert Suderburg at the University of Washington as a doctoral candidate. She was the winner of the World Accordion Competition, Mozarteum, Salzburg.

Compositions
ACCORDION
　Theme and variations
　Two contemporary fugues
Ref. 142

SCHMIDT, Margot Alice

German composer. b. Schoenlanke, January 18, 1897. She lived in Landsberg, Prussia. She composed choruses and songs with songs with original texts.
Ref. 105, 226

SCHMIDT, Mia

Compositions
CHAMBER
　Friedensappelle (hpcd)
　Sonata (pf)
Ref. Frau und Musik

SCHMIDT-DUISBURG, Margarete Dina Alwina

German pianist, teacher and composer. b. Dusseldorf, August 1. She studied at the Hochschule fuer Musik, Cologne Music School under Uzielli (piano) and H. Unger and Professor Jarnach (composition). She performed extensively on the radio and in concert and in 1950 won the composition prize at the 700th Anniversary of Goethe in Weimar. She taught in Frankfurt. PHOTOGRAPH.

Compositions
ORCHESTRA
　Prelude in A
　Zwei Tango espagnole (Aufnahmen)
CHAMBER
　Elegie and Humoreske (balalaika and pf) (Urauffuehrugen, 1970, 1977)
PIANO
　English waltz (2 pf)
　Jazz-etude (2 pf)
　Rhythmus aus dem Sueden (4 hands)
　Streitende Haende (4 hands)
　Aeolische Suite
　Capriccio Etude
　Drei Klang-Stucke
　Rhythmus aus dem Sueden
VOCAL
　Cantatas
　Jaegerlieder (Bar and orch)
　Marienlegende (S and w-ch)
　Zwei Floetenlieder (S, fl and pf)
　Lieder (vce and pf)
　Songs incl.:
　Indischer Liederzyklus
Ref. composer

SCHMIDTOVA, Lydie. See BOESGAARDOVA-SCHMIDTOVA, Lydie

SCHMIT-FONTYN, Jacqueline. See FONTYN, Jacqueline

SCHMITT, Alois (pseud. Czanyi)

German composer. b. 1851; d. 1906. Her husband was a celebrated musician.

Compositions
VOCAL
　Songs incl.:
　Deep in my heart
　Stars are brightly beaming
Ref. 276, 347, 433

SCHMITT-LERMANN, Frieda

German pianist and composer. b. Wuerzburg, May 24, 1885. She studied the piano privately in Augsburg in 1904 and studied counterpoint and composition under Josef Schmid in Munich.

Compositions
ORCHESTRA
　Allerseelen, symphonic poem (1928)
　Indische Maerchen, symphonic poem (1928)
　Serenade
VOCAL
　Liebeslied (1925)
　Lied vor de Trauung (Boehm und Sohn, 1923)
　Songs (Halbreiter, 1925)
SACRED
　Offertorium fuer Christi Himmelfahrt (mix-ch and orch) (1927)
　Graduale fuer Mariae Empfangnis (ch and org) (1926)
　Mass in F (1921)
　Deutsche Schulmesse (2 vces and org) (1926)
THEATRE
　Das Lied von der Glocke, melodrama (Schiller) (ch and pf) (1923)
INCIDENTAL MUSIC
　Music for television
Ref. 70, 111, 226

SCHMITZ-GOHR, Else

German pianist, professor and composer. b. Cologne, August 12, 1901. She studied the piano and composition at the Cologne Conservatory under Dr. Otto Klauwell, Fritz Hans Rehbold and Professor Franz Bolsche. She made her debut at the age of 17 under the baton of Herman Abendroth. She continued her piano studies in Berlin at the Stern Conservatory under Professor James Kwast and composition under Professor Wilhelm Klatte. In 1922 she was awarded the Gustav-Hollander medal. She toured in Germany and abroad. In 1927 she lectured on the piano at the Stern Conservatory. In 1944 she taught at the Rheinische Musikschule in Cologne and from 1958 to 1966 was a lecturer at the State Academy of Music in Cologne. In 1960 she became a professor. Her pupils included the Kontarsky brothers, Joachim Volkmann, Bernhard Klee, and Dietmar von Capitaine. DISCOGRAPHY.

Compositions
ORCHESTRA
　Overture in G-Minor (1917)
CHAMBER
　Allegro moderato in E-Minor (pf trio) (1919)
　Andante in G-Minor (pf trio) (1919)
　Allegro in G-Minor (vln and pf) (1916)
　Capriccio in E-Major (vln and pf) (1914)
　Kleine Floeten Duette in Kirchentonarten (1957)
PIANO
　Fantasie in F-Major (1918)
　Suite (1945)
　Elegie for the left hand only in A-Major (1926)
Publications
　Festchrift zur Feier der Gruendung des Koelner Konservatoriums im Jahre 1850 und der Staatlichen Hochschule fuer Musik Koeln im Jahre, 1925. Cologne: 1950.
Ref. 192

SCHNEIDER, Caroline. See WISENEDER, Caroline

SCHNEIDER, June (nee Benjamin)

South African pianist, lecturer, music psychotherapist and composer. b. Johannesburg, June 15, 1939. The daughter of the pianist Rose Benjamin, She studied the piano under Isador Epstein and became an A.T.C.L. and L.T.C.L. in 1959 and 1960. She gained her B.Mus. and B.Mus. hons. (first class) in the same years at the University of the Witwatersrand. She was granted a master's exemption and in 1962 obtained her Ph.D. in music, being the youngest person to whom it had been awarded at that university. Her studies were supervised by Professor F.H. Hartmann of the Vienna State Academy. She was awarded a Julius Robinson grant and a British Council grant and was invited by the Menuhin family to conduct research. She was invited to the International Festival of Contemporary Music in Athens; Domaines Musicales in Paris and 'New Music in Action 1974' at the University of York, England. She was senior lecturer in the department of music and education at the University of the Witwatersrand; lecturer at the Teachers' Training College for Nursery School Teachers, Johannesburg and received various guest lectureships; was music psychotherapist at Tara Hospital, Johannesburg; correspondent for *Dance News* of New York, wrote articles and gave broadcasts. She lives in the United States.

Compositions
ELECTRONIC
　Encounter 2
　Music for ballet
　Nongause music for Euripides' Electra

MULTIMEDIA
Encounter time and space
Bibliography
Eyton, Audrey. *'Don't Laugh at Dr. Schneider.* Johannesburg *Sunday Times*, September 26, 1976.
Ref. composer, 377, 625

SCHNEIDER-STEINEE, Lina. See STEIN-SCHNEIDER, Lena

SCHNORR VON CAROLSFELD, Malvina (nee Garrigues)
Danish singer, lecturer and composer. b. Copenhagen, December 7, 1825; d. Karlsruhe, February 8, 1904. She studied singing for three years under Manuel Garcia in Paris and made her debut in 1846 at the Breslau Opera. From 1849 to 1853 she sang at the court of Duke Ernst II of Saxe-Coburg-Gotha. She sang for a short while in Hamburg and in 1854 received a ten year contract to sing in Karlsruhe, where she taught singing from 1865. She then taught at the Frankfurt Conservatory from 1881 to 1884. She married the singer Ludwig Schnorr von Carolsfeld.
Compositions
VOCAL
Ich hoert ein Baechlein rauschen (vce and pf)
Mignon's Four Lieder, op. 3
Nine Lieder (with Ludwig Schnorr von Carolsfeld) (Aibl, 1867)
Six Lieder (1853) (vce and pf) (ded Jenny Lind q.v.)
Ref. 276, 297, 433, 622

SCHOLL, Amalie
German composer. b. Dresden, September 28, 1823; d. Dresden, September 18, 1879.
Compositions
PIANO
Pieces
VOCAL
Fuenf Lieder, op. 2
Die Sprachschuelerin, op. 3
Zwei Lieder, op. 4
Zwei Lieder, op. 5
Ref. 226, 276, 297, 433

SCHONE, Elna
20th-century Swedish composer.
Compositions
SACRED
Andeliga sanga (composer) (1926)
Nya borrinjholmska visor (composer) (1926)
Ref. 331

SCHONTHAL, Ruth E.
American pianist, lecturer and composer. b. Hamburg, June 27, 1924. She studied at the Stern Conservatory in Berlin from 1929 to 1936 and then at the Royal Academy in Stockholm from 1942 to 1945. She studied at Yale University on a full scholarship from 1946 to 1948 graduating with her B.M. She studied composition under Etthoven in Berlin and Manuel M. Ponce and Paul Hindemith at Yale University. Among her piano teachers were Simon Barere and Sasha Gorodnitzky. She gave concerts of her own compositions in Europe and Mexico and performed her *Piano concerto* in Mexico City in 1944. She gave concerts and performances in New York and other centers in the United States. In 1979 she gave a concert of her own works at Wigmore Hall, London and in 1982 and 1983 in Germany. She was awarded the Delto Omicron 3rd International award for her *String quartet*. She taught at New York University and Westchester Conservatory. DISCOGRAPHY. PHOTOGRAPH.
Compositions
ORCHESTRA
Symphony (1957)
Concerto No. 2 (pf and orch)
Concerto romantico (pf and orch) (1942)
The beautiful days of Aranjuez (hp and str orch) (1981)
Music for horn and chamber orchestra (1979)
Serenade for strings (1962)
CHAMBER
String quartet No. 1 (1964) (Leonarda)
String quartet No. 2 (1983)
Fantasy, op. 47 (vln and pf) (1949)
Loveletters (cl and vlc) (1979)
Sonata (vln and pf; also cl and pf) (1964)
Sonata concertante (vlc and pf; also vla and pf; also cl and pf) (1975)
Fantasy in a nostalgic mood (gtr) (1978)

Four epiphanies (vla) (1975) (OUP)
Interlude (hp) (1980)
Rhapsodie (vla)
Sonata (vlc)
Twelve inventions a due voici (hpcd; also pf) (1984)
PIANO
Capriccio español (1945)
Eleven pieces (Gestures) (1978)
Fiestas y danzas (1961)
Five sonatas
Fragments from a woman's diary (1982)
Gestures (1978)
In homage of ... 24 preludes (1978)
Miniatures, vols. 1-3 (Galaxy Music)
Minuscule (Carl Fischer)
Near and far (Fischer)
Potpourrie (Fischer)
Reverberations (prep pf)
Sonata breve (1976) (OUP)
Sonatensatz (1975)
Sonatina (1939) (Stockholm: Lundgren)
Three elegies for a murder victim (1981)
Variations in search of a theme (1975)
Teaching pieces
VOCAL
Nine lyric dramatic songs (Yeats) (m-S and cham orch) (1960)
By the roadside (Walt Whitman) (S and pf) (OUP)
Seven songs of love and sorrow (S and pf) (1977)
The solitary reaper (T, vln, pf, vlc and pf) (1978)
Songs (R.M. Rilke) (S and pf) (1939-1942)
Three canciones (Lorca) (S, fl, vla, vlc and hp) (1956)
Three songs (Li Po) (S and pf) (1942)
Totengesaenge (S and pf) (1963)
Totenglocken, song cycle (1963)
Two canciones (Lorca) (m-S and pf) (1943)
BALLET
Candide, after Voltaire (orch) (1955)
The Transposed Heads (orch)
OPERA
The Courtship of Camilla, in 1 act (1980)
FILM MUSIC
Lantern Love
Ref. composer, 40, 142, 190, 347, 563, 622, 625

SCHORLEMMER, Erna von (pseud. Erny Chaloix)
German composer. b. Dessau, June 30, 1875. She lived in Berlin-Charlottenburg and was a pupil of O. Lessman, E. Behm, Luria and von Dulong. She composed songs, marches and ballet music for the theater.
Ref. 70, 226

SCHORR-WEILER, Eva
West German organist, pianist and composer. b. Crailsheim, Wuerttemburg, September 28, 1927. Her father, an organist and music teacher was her first teacher. She performed her own compositions when she was eight years old and in 1942 won first prizes for the organ and composition in a youth competition in Wuerttemberg. She concluded her studies at the State Music Academy, Stuttgart, where her teachers included J.N. David (composition) and Hermann Keller and Anton Nowakowski (organ and piano). She attended lectures given by O. Messiaen at the Darmstadt Holiday School and won gold medals at four international competitions for women composers in Buenos Aires. Her compositions were performed in concert on the radio in Germany and abroad. She married Dieter Schorr, a music editor. PHOTOGRAPH.
Compositions
ORCHESTRA
Chamber symphony
Septuarchie, violin concerto (1974)
Sinfomobil (1978)
Suite for string orchestra (1963)
CHAMBER
Wind quintet (1971)
Initialen FGHS quartet (S-rec, ob, viola da gamba and hpcd)
Rondo and ten variations (str qrt)
Pas de trois (vla, vln and vlc) (1981)
Trio (fl, vla and bsn) (1981)
Dialog (hp and org) (1981)
Erscheinungen (org and perc) (1982)
Ludus mobilis (fl and pf) (1969)
Mixed suite (fl and gtr) (1983)
Ritornell (vln and org) (1983)
Moving play (fl and hpcd) (1971)
Sonata (fl and pf)
Sonata in D-Major (vln and pf) (1973)

ORGAN
Ceremonial music and fugue
Partita on Wie soll ich dich empfangen
Toccata and fugue in E-Minor
Two chorale preludes (1951)
PIANO
Concert piece (2 pf)
Eight preludes and fugues (1949)
Four rhythmic etudes (1961)
Six pictures (1967)
Sonata in F-Major
Toccata
Twelve pieces for piano, Der Tierkreis (1958)
Variations (1957)
VOCAL
Die vier Elemente (soloists, mix-ch and orch)
Zeit zu (soloist and str qrt) (1974)
Drei Lieder fuer mittlere Stimme und Klavier (1982)
Drei Lieder (W.G. Benn) (S and pf) (1959)
Drei Lieder nach Texten von Gabriele Wohmann (1982)
Fuenf Lieder (Nelly Sachs) (S and pf) (1962)
Fuenf Lieder (J. Poethen) (S and pf) (1968)
Fuenf Lieder (Chr. Morgenstern) (middle vce and hpcd) (1972)
Der Tanz um den weissen Gott (J. Poethen) (speaker and fl) (1973)
SACRED
German Mass (1952)
Psalm 97 (soli, ch and org)
Six motets (mix-ch)
Ref. composer, 70

SCHOTTENSACK, Margarete. See MATZEN, Margarete

SCHREINZER, F.M.
German pianist, singer and composer. b. Danzig, ca. 1812; d. 1873.
Compositions
PIANO
Six eclogues, op. 7, 2 suites (Leipzig: Kistner)
Three characteristic pieces, op. 11 (Kistner)
VOCAL
Three poems, op. 19 (vce and pf) (Kistner)
Three poems, op. 39 (vce and pf) (Berlin: Guttentag)
Ref. 26, 276

SCHROEDER, Beatrice
20th-century American harpist and composer.
Composition
CHAMBER
The enchanted harp (pedal or Irish hp)
Ref. 344

SCHROEDER, Inge Maria
20th-century German composer.
Composition
ORCHESTRA
Concerto, op. 34 (ob and str orch)
Ref. Barenreiter (Kassel)

SCHROETER, Corona Elisabeth Wilhelmine
German actress, artist, teacher, singer and composer. b. Guben, January 14, 1751; d. Ilmenau, August 23, 1802. She was the daughter of Johann Friedrich Schroeter, oboist in the court orchestra. Her family moved from Guben to Warsaw when she was very young and then finally settled in Leipzig. She began her musical studies under her father's guidance and continued under the composer Johann Adam Hiller. She made her first appearance at a Leipzig Grosses Konzert at the age of 14 and continued to sing in Leipzig for the next six years. She lived in London with her family between 1772 and 1774. She made Goethe's acquaintance in 1766 and through his influence, became Kammersaengerin to the Dowager Duchess Anna Amalia. She worked closely with Goethe, being one of the first to set his poems to music and appeared in the first performance of *Iphigenia* in 1779 in which Goethe himself played the part of Orestes. She composed all the music for and appeared in his play *Die Fischerin*. From 1782 to 1784 she sang at the Leipzig Gewandhaus but thereafter appeared seldom in public, devoting herself to composition, a few pupils, drama and painting. Her musical settings of some of Schiller's poems were highly praised by him. In 1778 Goethe mentioned in his diary that he had received the manuscript of her autobiography, but it has never been found. He praised her in 'Dichtung und Wahrheit'.

Compositions
VOCAL
Book I: 25 Lieder (Weimar, 1786)
Book II: 16 Gesaenge mit Begleitung des Fortepiano ... (Weimar, 1794)
THEATRE
Die Fischerin, a play (Goethe)
Bibliography
Duentzer. *Charlotte von Stein and Corona Schroeter.* 1876.
Keil. *Corona Schroeter.* 1875.
Pasig, P. *Goethe und Corona Schroeter.* 1902.
Stuemcke, H. *Corona Schroeter.* 1904.
Ref. 2, 8, 15, 20, 26, 44, 65, 74, 105, 116, 119, 128, 177, 226, 276

SCHROTER, Corona Elisabeth. SCHROETER, Corona Elisabeth Wilhelmine

SCHUBARTH, Dorothe
Swiss choir conductor, teacher and composer. b. Basle, September 11, 1944. She studied theory under Klaus Huber and Robert Suter in Basle and under Harald Genzmer in Munich, choral conducting under Fritz Schieri in Munich and Paul Schaller in Basle, and composition under Cesar Breesge and Juerg Baur in Salzburg and Cologne. She taught music and conducted a choir in Lucerne till 1978, when she went to Galicia, Spain, to do field research in folk music for the Instituto de Lingua Galega with Professor Dr. Anton Santamarina.
Compositions
ORCHESTRA
Two pieces
CHAMBER
Wind quintet
String quartet
Trio (fl, trb and vib)
Meditation (org)
Viola sonata
VOCAL
La puerta, cantata (Jorge Guillen) (speaking ch and orch)
Cantata (vce, fl and pf)
A choral song (old anonymous Spanish text)
La penitencia del Rey Rodrigo, ballad (A, 2 Bar and Bass)
Six songs (Bernd Hohnoff) (m-S, fl and gtr)
Three choral songs (Alvaro Cungueiro and Martin Codax)
Three songs (Lorca) (A, cl and pf)
SACRED
Choral motets (2-5 part ch)
Five liturgical songs (A and org)
Geistliche Musik (ch and wind insts)
Passionsmusik (A, small ch and org)
Ref. 651

SCHUBERT, Georgine
German concert singer and composer. b. Dresden, October 28, 1840; d. Potsdam, December 26, 1878. She was the daughter of Franz Schubert (1808 to 1878) and Maschinka Schubert, who was her first singing teacher. She was also a pupil of Jenny Lind (q.v.) and Manuel Garcia in London between 1857 and 1859. She sang in various European cities and composed songs.
Ref. 226, 276

SCHUBERT, Myra Jean
American concert pianist, adjudicator, teacher and composer. b. Borger, TX, June 9, 1938. She graduated with both her B.Mus. and M.Mus. (piano performance) from Oklahoma University in 1964 and 1967 respectively having studied under Lytle Powell and Dr. Clarence Burg. She has given piano performances in 20 countries around the world and taught the piano privately for the past 33 years. Since 1975 she has been a faculty member of the American College of Musicians and in 1978 was voted Outstanding Alumnus of Bethany Nazarene College. She was selected to the Hall of Fame through the Guild of Piano Teachers. PHOTOGRAPH.
Compositions
PIANO
Give Him glory (1981)
Give Him praise (1983)
VOCAL
Lush stereo-phonic choir (Lillenas Publishing Company, 1972)
TEACHING PIECES
Hymns we play and sing (Bk 1 to 6) (piano)
O coro canta (Bk 1 and 2) (vocal) (Lillenas Pub. Co., 1976 and 1984)
Teen sound (Bk 1 to 3) (vocal) (Lillenas Pub. Co., 1966-1969)
The quick choir (Bk 1 and 2) (Lillenas Pub. Co., 1968 and 1973)
Ref. composer, 643

SCHULTE, Eleonore

German composer. b. Gelsenkirchen, January 16, 1876. She lived in Kreuzlingen, Switzerland.
Compositions
ORCHESTRA
Tone poem
VOCAL
Songs (some with orch)
Ref. 70, 226

SCHULTZ-ADAJEWSKY, Ella. See ADAJEWSKY, Ella

SCHULTZOWA, Barbara. See ADDENDUM

SCHULZ, Madeleine (nee von Braun)

German composer. b. Lyon, France, January 18, 1866. She grew up in Michelstadt, Odenwald and Waldheim am Main and attended the Hochschen Conservatory in Frankfurt am Main. She composed piano pieces, a vocal quartet and songs.
Ref. 70, 226

SCHULZE-BERGHOF, Luise Doris Albertine

German pianist, teacher and composer. b. Potsdam, June 14, 1889. She studied the piano privately in Potsdam until 1906. For the next five years she studied at the Berlin Academy and under Johannes Schulze (piano). She was a pupil of Gustav Kulenkampff, studying counterpoint and composition until 1916. She was a concert pianist and teacher in Berlin and also played on Berlin Television.
Compositions
PIANO
Pieces
VOCAL
Lieder and ballads (Schueler, Liliencron, Dehmel, Knodt, Busse, Salus and composer)
THEATRE
Frau Einsamkeit
Ref. 105, 111

SCHULZOVA, Anezka

19th-century Bohemian composer.
Compositions
VOCAL
Songs
OPERA
Hedy, Fibich, Zdenek, op. 43 (1896)
Ref. 465

SCHUMAKER, Grace L.

20th-century American teacher and composer. b. Lafayette, IN. She composed chamber music, violin pieces and songs.
Ref. 347

SCHUMANN, Clara Josephine (nee Wieck)

German pianist, violinist, teacher and composer. b. Leipzig, September 13, 1819; d. Frankfurt am Main, May 20, 1896. She was the daughter of piano teacher Friedrich Wieck and his first wife, the pianist Marianne Tromlitz and she began to study the piano under her father when she was five years old. He also introduced her to music theory and laid the basis for her ability to transpose and improvise. Clara received her first tuition in composition from T. Weinlig and Heinrich Dorn and wrote her first compositions when she was ten years old. After 1834 she studied composition and instrumentation under C.G. Reissiger in Dresden and the violin and singing under Miecksch. In 1827 she played Mozart's *E-Flat Minor piano concerto* before an invited audience and a year later played in the Leipzig Gewandhaus. During the following three years she visited Weimar, where she played for the 82-year-old Goethe. Later she went to Kassel where she impressed Spohr; Frankfurt am Main, Mainz, and to Paris, where she met Berlioz, Kalkbrenner and Chopin. Clara was one of the first pianists to perform and make known Chopin's work; her concert repertoire expanded to include works by Beethoven, Bach, Mendelssohn and Scarlatti and in 1832 she gave the first of many performances of her own *Piano concerto*. In 1833 she appeared in Leipzig with Beriot and Pauline Garcia and in the same period visited Berlin, Paris, Prague and Vienna, being acclaimed everywhere. In Vienna in 1837 and 1838 she was honored by the Empress with the title 'Kammermusikerin', the first foreigner to be so honored. She inspired Grillparzer to write his poem 'Clara Wieck und

Beethoven'. In Vienna she performed a number of Schumann's works for the first time, including his *Carnaval, op. 9*. She was nine years old when Robert Schumann became a pupil of her father's and a frequent visitor in the Wieck household. Her father, fearful that marriage would put an end to his daughter's career, did all he could to prevent it and only in 1840, with the consensus of the court, were they able to marry. In the first few years after marriage she performed less and concentrated on literature and studying Bach, Mozart and Beethoven, although in 1841 she played a composition of Liszt's for two pianos, with the composer. In the next few years she toured, sometimes with her husband, to Hamburg, Copenhagen and St. Petersburg, and in 1844 because of Robert's health they moved from Leipzig to Dresden, where they lived till 1850. She devoted these years to performing and making known her husband's compositions. His *Piano concerto* quintet, quartet and trios, among other pieces, were first played by her. They moved again, to Duesseldorf, but Robert's health was declining. He attempted to commit suicide in 1854 and died in 1856. To support her seven children she was obliged to resume her concert career. She moved to Berlin where her mother, who had divorced Wieck and married Bargiel, was living, and then in 1863 she bought a house in Lichtental, near Baden-Baden. She toured, particularly in England, often with Joseph Joachim or the singer Julius Stockhausen, playing mainly her late husband's compositions and those of Brahms, who was an intimate friend of the Schumanns. In 1878 she accepted the position of principal piano teacher at Hochschen Conservatory in Frankfurt, establishing herself as a teacher of such ability that merely to be a pupil of hers was considered an honor. Hearing difficulties compelled her to give up this post in 1892, but she continued to teach privately till her death. Clara Schumann was considered the most important pianist of her time and her compositions were praised by Chopin as early as 1835. Several of her themes were used by Robert Schumann in his *Impromptus, op. 5* in the Andantino of his *Sonata in F-minor, op. 14*, and in *Davidsbuendlertaenze, op. 6*. DISCOGRAPHY. PHOTOGRAPH.
Compositions
ORCHESTRA
Piano concerto in A-Minor, op. 7 (ded Louis Spohr) (Leipzig: Hofmeister, 1832)
CHAMBER
Trio in G-Minor, op. 17 (vln, vlc and pf) (Breitkopf & Hartel)
Three romances, op. 22 (vln and pf) (ded Johann Joachim) (Breitkopf)
PIANO
Andante and allegro (Leipzig: J. Schuberth & Co.)
Caprices en forme de valse, op. 2 (Leipzig: Hofmeister)
Deuxieme scherzo, op. 14 (Breitkopf)
Drei Praeludien und Fugen, op. 16 (Breitkopf)
Drei Romanzen, op. 21 (Breitkopf)
Marsch (1879)
Quatre pieces caracteristiques, op. 5 (Leipzig: F. Whistling)
Quatre polonaises, op. 1 (Hofmeister)
Quatre pièces fugitives, op. 15 (Breitkopf)
Romance variée, op. 3 (ded Robert Schumann) (Hofmeister)
Rondo (1833)
Scherzo, op. 10 (Breitkopf)
Soirées musicales, op. 6 (Hofmeister)
Sonatine: Allegro und Scherzo (1841)
Souvenir de Vienne, impromptu, op. 1 (Vienna: A. Diabelli)
Trois romances, op. 11 (ded Robert Schumann) (Vienna: P. Plechetti)
Valse romantique, op. 4 (Hofmeister)
Variations de concert, sur la Cavatine du Pirate de Bellini, op. 8 (Vienna: Haslinger)
Variationen ueber ein Tyroler Lied (1830)
Variationen ueber ein Originalthema (1830)
VOCAL
Am Strande (vce and pf) (J. Schuberth & Co.)
Liebeszauber (Geibel)
Six songs, op. 13 (Breitkopf)
Six songs (from Rollet's Jucunde)
Three songs (Rueckert) (in R. Schumann's op. 37, nos. 2, 4, 11, op. 12) (Breitkopf)
Three mixed choruses (Geibel)
Der Traum (Tedge)
ARRANGEMENTS
Cadenza to Mozart's piano concerto in C-Minor (K466) (Leipzig: Winterthur)
Cadenzas to Beethoven's piano concertos in C-Minor and G-Major, ops. 37 and 38 (Winterthur)
Arrangement of Robert Schumann's quintet, op. 44 (4 hands pf) (Breitkopf)
Arrangements of other works by Robert Schumann
Publications
Fingeruebungen und Studien aus Carl Czernys grosse Pianoschule.
Jugendbriefe von Robert Schumann, nach den originalen mitgeteilt. Leipzig: Breitkopf and Hartel, 1885; 4th printing, 1910.
Robert Schumann's Liederalbum fuer die Jugend. Arr. for voice and piano by Clara Schumann. Leipzig: Breitkopf and Hartel.
Robert Schumann's Works. Series I-XIII, XIV ed. by Clara Schumann and Johannes Brahms. Leipzig: Breitkopf and Hartel, 1879-1893.

Bibliography

Alley, Marguerite and Alley, Jean. *Une amitie passionee: Clara Schumann, Johannes Brahms.* Paris: Laffont, 1955.

Burk, John Naglee. *Clara Schumann: A Romantic Biography.* New York: Random House, 1940.

Chissell Joan - *Clara Schumann, A dedicated Spirit.* London. H. Hamilton, 1983.

Fang, Siu-Wan Chair. *Clara Schumann as Teacher.* (D.M.A., Performance, University of Illinois, 1978)

Ginder, C. Richard. *Great Musical Women of Yesterday.* Etude, September 1941.

Hanslick, E. *Clara Schumann und Amalie Joachim, Concerte, Componisten und Virtuosen der letzten fuenfzehn Jahre 1870-1885.* Berlin, 1896.

Henning, L. *Die Freundschaft Clara Schumann mit Johannes Brahms.* Zurich, 1952.

Hoecker, Karla. *Clara Schumann.* Regensburg: Bosse Verlag, 1838. p. 93.

Holman, Grethe. *Clara Schumann.* Gyldendal, Copenhagen, 1970.

Kleefeld, W. *Clara Schumann.* Bielefeld, 1920.

De Lara, Adelina. *Finale.* London, Burke, 1953.

Litzmann, B. *Clara Schumann.* 3 vols. Leipzig, 1902, 1906, 1908. (English trans. G.E. Hadow - abridged; 2 vols. London, 1913.)

Manfred, Willfort. *Clara Schumann.* Neue Zeitschrift fuer Musik 132 (May 1971): 239-243.

May, F. *The Girlhood of Clara Schumann.* London, 1912.

Meichsner, A. von. *Friedrich Wieck und seine Tochter.* Leipzig. 1875.

Munte, Frank. *Verzeichnis des deutschsprachigen Schrifttums ueber Robert Schumann 1856-1870; Anhang; Schrifttum ueber Clara Schumann.* Hamburg: Karl Dieter Wagner, 1972.

Quednau, Werner. *Clara Schumann.* Berlin: Altberliner Verlag Grosser, 1955, p. 318.

Reich, Nancy B. *Clara Schumann. The Artist and the Woman.* Cornell University Press, 1985.

Schumann, Robert. *Music and Musicians: Essays and Criticisms.* Trans. by Fanny Raymond Ritter. London: William Reeves, n.d., p. 418.

Stephenson, Kurt. Clara Schumann. Bonn: Inter Nationes, 1969.

Susskind, Pamela Gertrude. *Clara Wieck Schumann as Pianist and Composer: A Study of Her Life and Works.*

Tracey, James. *Some of the World's Greatest Women Pianists: Short, Interesting Biographies of Great Performers from Clara Schumann to the Present Day.* Etude, 1907, pp. 773-774.

Walch-Schumann, Kathe, ed. *Friederich Wieck, Briefe: Aus den Jahren 1830-1838.* Cologne: Arno Volk-Verlag, 1968.

Ref. 2, 8, 9, 13, 14, 15, 20, 22, 26, 41, 44, 52, 70, 72, 74, 86, 88, 100, 102, 103, 105, 113, 121, 129, 132, 177, 192, 193, 201, 210, 211, 226, 231, 264, 276, 297, 332, 347, 361, 391, 394, 404, 455, 518, 563, 570, 572, 622, 637, 653.

SCHUMANN, Meta

American soprano and composer. b. St. Paul, MN, 1887. Her father, a well-known singer and choral conductor was her first teacher. At 16 she began vocal study under Dr. C.C. Carman and later continued her studies under Carina Mastinelli and John Acton. Returning from her studies under Acton in London, she appeared in concerts, recitals and oratorios and with a number of symphony orchestras. Meta was well known as an artist accompanist but later devoted her time exclusively to vocal instruction and composition.

Compositions
VOCAL
Songs incl.:
Recompense
Thee
Thou, immortal night
Ref. 292, 347

SCHUPPE, Anna. See BENFEY-SCHUPPE, Anna

SCHUPPE-BENFEY, Anna. See BENFEY-SCHUPPE, Anna

SCHURZMANN, Katharina

German teacher, writer and composer. b. Liegnitz, September 24, 1890. She was a pupil of Gernsheim in Berlin.
Compositions
ORCHESTRA
Serenade (str orch)
PIANO
Pieces
VOCAL
Songs

Publications
Von Tonart zu Tonart.
Wie erkenne ich die musikalische Begabung meines Kindes.
Ref. 70, 226

SCHUSSLER-BREWAEYS, Marie Antoinette

Belgian pianist, authoress, editor, poetess, singer and composer. b. Anderlecht, June 15, 1912. The daughter of composer and organist Charles Brewaeys, she studied under her father as a young child and at the Brussels Royal Conservatory from 1924 to 1931. She obtained first prize with distinction for solfege, history of music, chamber music and the piano. She was the editor of *Pax Hominibus.* In 1967 she received the Silver Medal of the Arts, Sciences and Letters from the City of Paris and in 1967 the Prix Thorlet from the French Academy. She received a bronze medal from the European Council of Arts and Aesthetics for her composition and writing. PHOTOGRAPH.
Compositions
VOCAL
Je chante, op. 2 (S, mix-ch and pf) (1949) (Pax Hominibus)
Hommage à centenaire, op. 6 (m-S and pf, or 4 vces a-cap) (1969) (Hominibus)
A mon pauvre ami, op. 15 (m-S and pf) (1977) (Hominibus)
Ces doux noms, op. 14 (m-S and pf) (1977) (Hominibus)
Dialogue d'immortelle et de rose, op. 8 (S and pf) (1974) (Hominibus)
Hirondelle, op. 16 (m-S and pf) (1977) (Hominibus)
In den Storm, op. 1 (m-S and pf) (1947) (Hominibus)
La mort du vieux chêne, op. 7 (m-S and pf) (1970) (Hominibus)
Parenthèse à la tentation de St. Antoine, op. 10 (m-S and pf) (1974) (Hominibus)
Poésies d'autrefois ... de A a Z, plaquette of 26 poems, op. 5 (1965) (Hominibus)
Portraits d'aujourd'hui, 26 cliches en rimes de A a Z, op. 12 (1974-1977) (Hominibus)
Requiem pour un amour, op. 9 (m-S and pf; also 3 vces and perc) (1974) (Hominibus)
Roses de Toussaint, op. 4 (m-S and pf) (1965) (Hominibus)
Vieux jardin de mes jeunes ans, op. 3 (m-S and pf; also 2 vces) (1950) (Hominibus)
SACRED
Controverse à la grande gloire de Dieu, op. 11 (m-S and pf) (1974)
THEATRE
Polichinellespel, pour theatre de toone, op. 13 (1974)
Ref. composer, 188

SCHUSTER, Doris Dodd

American organist, pianist, assistant professor, choir director and composer. b. Belmont, MA, May 10, 1924. She graduated with a Mus.B. from Yale University in 1946 and a Mus.M. in 1951. She was a faculty member at Oklahoma State University during 1946 and 1947 and held the post of assistant professor in the department of music at Madison College, Harrisonburg from 1947 to 1950. She lectured at the Plymouth State College. She taught the piano privately from 1955 and from 1944 to 1961 was the organist and choir director at Laconia, New Hampshire.
Compositions
PIANO
Six pieces (1976)
Three preludes on Gospel hymns for organ (1972)
Ref. 475

SCHUSTER, Elfriede

German pianist, teacher and composer. b. Berlin, November 26, 1894. She studied composition under Wilhelm Klatte and taught the piano at the Stern Conservatory. She composed a piano concerto, a piano trio, piano pieces and songs.
Ref. 70

SCHUYLER, Georgina

19th-century American composer.
Compositions
VOCAL
Songs incl.:
Across the world I speak to thee
Album of songs (m-S or Cont) (Schirmer)
The apology
Autumn song
Cupidon-marche (vce and pf) (Societe Libre)
Go lovely rose
Grow old along with me
In a gondola
The page sings to the queen

Song from the last tournament
Song from the new day
Sunflower song
This is the spray the bird clung to
To Ellen at the south
To Lucasta
When the tide comes in
When we two parted
Ref. 226, 276, 297, 433

SCHUYLER, Philippa Duke

Black American concert pianist, poetess, writer and composer. b. New York, August 22, 1932; d. Da Nang, Vietnam, May 9, 1967. She was the daughter of George Schuyler, editor of the *Pittsburgh Courier*. She began composing at the age of three and at four had composed 10 original works with national recognition. At 12 an award-winning symphonic work was played by the Detroit Symphony Orchestra. She studied the piano privately and at the age of 14 made her debut with the New York Philharmonic. Under the auspices of the U.S. State Department she made three world tours and she was guest artist at independence celebrations. In Leopoldville, Ghana and Madagascar she played command performances for Emperor Haile Selassie, the King and Queen of Malaya and Queen Elizabeth of Belgium. She also appeared as guest soloist of her own works with major symphony orchestras in the United States. She was killed in a plane crash in Vietnam. DISCOGRAPHY.

Compositions
ORCHESTRA
    Manhattan nocturne, symphonic poem (1943) (first prize Grinnell Foundation Contest, Detroit)
    Rhapsody of youth (1948) (medal of merit and honor from President Paul E. Magloire)
    Rumpelstilskin, fairy-tale symphony (1943) (also pf)
    The Nile fantasy
PIANO
    Eight little pieces
    Three little pieces (1938)
    White Nile suite (musical saga depicting Arab history in Egypt and the Sudan) (1965)
VOCAL
    Rococo (Swinburne) (1961)
    Three songs (1967)
ARRANGEMENTS
    African rhapsody (1965)
    Around the world suite (1960)
    Chisamharu the Nogomo (Mozambique)
    Country boy (1967)
    Cynthia (1957)
    Legend of the Mahdi (based on themes from Omdurman, Sudan) (1965)
    No bed of roses (1957)
    New moon (1960)
    Old Father William: Arabian love song; Hymn to Proserpina; Maelstrom (ca. 1948)
    Sleepy hollow sketches (1946)

Publications
Adventures in Black and White. New York: Robert Speller and Sons, 1960.
Good Men Die. Denver, Colorado: Twin Circle, 1969.
Jungle Saints. Herder and Herder, 1963.
Kingdom of Dreams (with Josephine Schuyler). New York: Speller, 1966.
Who Killed the Congo? New York, 1962.
A Baby on Death, poem. *Washington Post*, May 10, 1967.
Moroccan Andalusian Music. Schuyler, P.D.

Bibliography
Harlem Prodigy. Time, June 22, 1936.
Music by Philippa. Newsweek, August 14, 1944.
Music of Modern Africa. Musical Journal, October, 1960.
Philippa Duke Schuyler. The Crisis, May 1950; April 1954; June 1967.
Philippa Duke Schuyler. Revue Musica Chilena, January 1955.
Philippa Duke Schuyler. Musical America, November 15, 1956.
Philippa Duke Schuyler. Musical Courier, May 15, 1954; October 1954; 1959.
Philippa Duke Schuyler Back from Europe. Musical Courier, January 1, 1954.
Philippa Schuyler: American Pianist Played for Monarchs and Desert Saint. Musical Courier, May 1959.
Philippa Schuyler Makes Orchestral Debut in Buenos Aires. From Porteno Press on Philippa's Argentina debut. Reprinted in *The Crisis*, December 1954.
Schuyler, Josephine. *My Daughter Philippa*. Sepia, May 1959.
U.S. Pianist Killed in Vietnam Crash. New York Times, May 10, 1967.
Up and Down the Guild Keyboard. Musical Courier, January 1, 1956.
Ref. 39, 133, 136, 142, 347, 353, 549

SCHWARTZ, Julie

American pianist, teacher and composer. b. Washington, D.C., April 17, 1947. She studied under Ron Nelson, Hall Overton and Jacob Druckman; under Julius Eastman, Frederic Rzewski and Gordon Mumma at New Music Center in New Hampshire, 1973. She received a National Federation of Music Club's junior award for a piano composition in 1962. From 1973 she taught at the Arts Center, Albany, New York.

Compositions
CHAMBER
    Matrix I (winds and strs)
    Rounds (cham ens)
    In return (str qrt)
    And so do I like to bang and tootle? (fl and perc)
    Breathplace (ob)
VOCAL
    Homespun (vocal qrt, strs and perc)
Ref. 142

SCHWARTZ, Nan Louise

American pianist, arranger, singer and composer. b. Burbank, CA, February 25, 1953. She came from a musical family, her father was an active studio musician and lead clarinetist with the Glenn Miller Band. She studied the piano from an early age and began singing professionally at the age of 11. She received her B.A. (cum laude) (radio, television and film) from the California State University, Northridge in 1973. She began work as a television production assistant after graduating and in 1977 began her career of film scoring. After a skiing accident she began studying composition and orchestration under Dr. Albert Harris and music education under Billy Byers. She currently studies composition under George Tremblay. PHOTOGRAPH.

Compositions
CHAMBER
    Woodwind, op. 1 (Nantz Music, 1976)
    Horn quintet
    Two woodwind quintets
    Horn, op. 1 (Nantz Music, 1977)
VOCAL
    Collaboration
    Jim and Andy's
    Sambistro
ARRANGEMENTS
    For film and television
Ref. composer, 494

SCHWARZ, Friederike

Czech pianist, teacher and composer. b. Prague, January 15, 1910. She taught the piano in Prague.

Compositions
CHAMBER
    Pieces incl.:
    Clarinet quintet
PIANO
    Pieces incl.:
    Sonata
VOCAL
    Songs
Ref. 105, 347

SCHWARZ-SIGMAND, Hermina

Late 19th-century German pianist and composer. Her compositions included four piano pieces.
Ref. 226

SCHWARZKOPF-DRESSLER, Maria

Bohemian composer. b. Warnsdorf, November 28, 1889. After 1908 she lived in Dresden and was a pupil of Mraczek.

Compositions
PIANO
    Pieces
VOCAL
    Favola die Natale
    Songs (some with cham orch)
    Other pieces
Ref. 105, 226

SCHWEIZER, Gertrude

German teacher and composer. b. Mannheim, May 5, 1894. She studied under A. Schmid-Lindner, H.W. de Waltershausen and Ernest Toch.
Compositions
PIANO
Teaching and other pieces
VOCAL
Duets
Songs
SACRED
Our Father (w-ch)
Ref. 105, 225

SCHWERDTFEGER, E. Anne (Alt. name Sister M. Ernest O.P.)

American lecturer and composer. b. Galveston, TX, February 1, 1930. She studied at the Dominican College, Houston under Arthur Hall, the University of Texas under Clifton Williams (B.Mus., 1953), and at the University of Notre Dame under Carl Hager, (M.Mus., 1963). She was the recipient of a Fulbright Scholarship to France in 1963 and 1964. She was head of the music department of Dominican College from 1962 to 1972. She did further study at the Pontificio In tituto-orientale in Rome and received a B. oriental liturgy in 1975 and a Lic. oriental liturgy in 1977. She now lives in Rome. PHOTOGRAPH.
Compositions
ORCHESTRA
Symphony in one movement (1963)
Christus Rex (cham orch) (1960)
Exaudi Domine (str orch) (1959)
CHAMBER
Variations on an Irish air (6 hp) (1962)
Modal suite (hp and tba) (1960)
Fugue (org) (1957)
PIANO
Charivari (1966)
Modal suite (1965)
Three pieces (1965)
Toccatina (1962)
VOCAL
Two pieces (Tagore) (w-vces and single org line) (1969)
SACRED
Mass of St. Martin de Porres (unison vces and org) (1965)
Amo Christum (w-ch) (1957)
Ave Maris Stella (w-vces) (1958)
Hymn of St. Francis (w-vces) (1960)
O Sacrum convivium (w-vces) (1961)
Ref. composer, 142

SCHWERTZELL, Wilhelmine von

19th-century German composer.
Compositions
VOCAL
Part-songs
Songs (1, 2 and 3 vces)
Zwoelf Lieder (Kistner)
Ref. 226, 276, 297

SCHYTTE, Anna

Danish concert pianist and composer. b. Copenhagen, November 20, 1880. The daughter of composer Ludwig Schytte, she studied under Ove Christensen, F. Neruda and J. Rontgen in Amsterdam, A. Reisenauer in Leipzig and I. Friedmann in Berlin. She concert toured in Denmark, Germany (playing inter alia at the Leipzig Gewandhaus under Nikisch), Amsterdam, Stockholm, and other European cities. She was a member of the Bohemian String Quartet and the Brussels Quartet in Copenhagen. She taught in Copenhagen.
Compositions
PIANO
Pieces incl.:
Capriccietto, study in staccato
Ref. 96, 331

SCHYTTE-JENSEN, Caroline

Norwegian composer. b. 1848; d. 1935.
Compositions
VOCAL
For Norge (4 w-vces)
About 200 songs incl.:
Boerne sange, many vols. of children's songs
Blomster-eventyr (1904)

Du aer min ro
For de smaa (1907)
I slen
Karin Mansdottere vaggvisa
SACRED
Jesu haender og mine
Choral pieces
Ref. 20

SCIBOR, Maria

20th-century composer.
Composition
INCIDENTAL MUSIC
L'Annonce fait à Marie (Paul Claudel) (1943)
Ref. Philip Martin Catalogue (London)

SCLIAR, Esther (Ester)

Brazilian concert pianist, conductor, teacher and composer. b. Porto Alegre, September 28, 1926. She studied the piano under Judite Pacheco and at the Instituto de Belas Artes of Porto Alegre under Enio de Freitas e Castro (harmony) and Demofilo Xavier (piano) and graduated in 1945. She did postgraduate studies in composition in Rio de Janeiro under Joachim Koellreutter, Claudio Santoro (orchestration) and Edino Krueger. She taught in Porto Alegre and Rio from 1949; formed the choir Coro da Associação Juvenil Musical of Porto Alegre (1952) among others and was a performer with the Porto Alegre Symphonic Orchestra for several years. She was a recipient of many prizes and awards. DISCOGRAPHY.
Compositions
ORCHESTRA
O auto da barca do inferno, prelude (1962)
CHAMBER
String quartet (1963)
Imbricata (fl, ob and pf)
Sonata (fl and pf) (1962)
Etude No. 1 (gtr)
PIANO
Sonata (National Composition prize, 1961)
VOCAL
Beira mar, in 4 mvts (ch)
A busca da identidade entre o homem e o rio (ch) (1971)
Canto menor com final heroico (ch) (1964)
Desenho leve (ch) (1962)
Ofulu loreree, in 4 mvts (Oxala) (mix-ch) (1974)
Para peneirar, in 4 mvts (ch)
Entre o ser e as coisas (vce and pf) (1973)
Six choral songs
FILM MUSIC
Derrota (Mario Fiorani) (Festival Nacional de Cinema, Brasilia, 1966)
Ref. 333

SCOTT, Alicia Ann Spottiswoode. See SCOTT, Lady John Douglas

SCOTT, Clara H.

19th-century American composer. b. 1841; d. 1897.
Compositions
PIANO
Dearborn, waltz (Brainard)
Floating clouds (Brainard)
Grand Girard, mazurka (Brainard)
Lillie, schottische (Brainard)
Snowflakes (Brainard)
VOCAL
As the hart panteth (Curwen)
But one sweet face (w-vces) (Summy)
Carol, sweet Carol
Gently evening bendeth (3 w-vces) (Summy)
Guard the heart
Gushing rill
O when shall I be free (Ditson)
When winds are raging, duet
SACRED
I love the Lord (mix-ch) (Church)
Lead me to the rock (qrt; also ch with S obb) (Brainard; Church)
They that trust in the Lord (mix-ch) (Church)
Go bring the Gospel of His Son
Gospel temperance battle song
I will extol Thee
Make a joyful noise
Royal anthem book (Ditson)
Ref. 226, 276, 297, 433

SCOTT, Georgina Keir

20th-century Scottish cellist, organist, pianist, violinist, teacher and composer. She was a pupil of B. Mansell Ramsey and John Scott, whom she later married. She taught the piano, the organ, the violin and theory in Dunkeld, and played the piano, the violin and the cello in her husband's orchestra.

Compositions
PIANO
  Pieces
VOCAL
  Songs incl.:
  In exile
  The hoose on the brae
  The silver lining
  The way of nature
MISCELLANEOUS
  Highland music: Marches; Strathspeys; Reels
Ref. 467

SCOTT, Hazel

20th-century composer.
Compositions
PIANO
  Five solos from boogie woogie to the classics
Ref. Frau und Musik

SCOTT, Isabella Mary. See GIBSON, Isabella Mary

SCOTT, Lady John Douglas (Alicia Ann) (nee Spottiswoode)

Scottish composer. b. Spottiswoode, Berwickshire, 1810; d. Spottiswoode, March 12, 1900. DISCOGRAPHY.
Compositions
VOCAL
  Annie Laurie (vce and pf) (Paterson & Roy, 1838)
  Douglas tender and true
  Durisdeer
  Ettrick
  Farewell to thee
  Foul fords
  Katherine Logie
  Lammermoor
  Mother, oh sing me to rest
  Shame on ye, gallants
  Think on me (vce and pf)
  When we first rode down to Ettrick
Ref. 6, 63, 74, 76, 226, 276, 433, 563

SCOTT, M.B.

19th-century American composer.
Composition
VOCAL
  Bird of beauty (vce and pf) (Boston: O. Ditson, 1856)
Ref. 228

SCOTT, Molly. See ADDENDUM

SCOTT-HUNTER, Hortense

20th-century American composer. She studied at the Peabody Conservatory.
Compositions
VOCAL
  Love song (1961)
SACRED
  Ad Te Domine, levavi, cantata (1960)
BALLET
  Maid of the mist
OPERA
  Harlequin in Search of his Heart, chamber opera
  Pelleas and Melisande, chamber opera
INCIDENTAL MUSIC
  The Little World of Kim Hai (1959)
Ref. 142

SCOVILLE, Margaret Lee

American composer. b. Pasadena, CA, May 3, 1944. She studied at the State University of New York, Buffalo under William Kothe, Ramon Fuller, Lejaren Hiller and Morton Feldman. DISCOGRAPHY.

Compositions
CHAMBER
  Ephemerae (vln, 2 vla and vlc)
  Time out of mind (2 perc)
PIANO
  Ostinato, fantasy and fugue
  Pentacycle
VOCAL
  Four fragments from Empidocles (S, fl and pf)
ELECTRONIC
  Electric Sunday (magnetic tape)
  Number 9 (tape)
  Thirteen ways of looking at a blackbird (cham ens and tape)
Ref. 142, 563

SCRIABINE, Marina

Russian-French organist, musicologist and composer. b. Moscow, January 30, 1911. She is the daughter of Alexander Scriabin. After her father's death, she lived with her mother in Kiev and Moscow before going to Belgium. She studied at the Ecole Nationale des Arts Decoratifs, Paris and studied music theory under Rene Leibowitz. She worked on electronic techniques at Radiodiffusion Française. In 1967 she received a doctorate in aesthetics for her thesis.

Compositions
CHAMBER
  Pieces
BALLET
  Bayalett (1952)
ELECTRONIC
  Suite radiophonique (1951)
Publications
  Le langage musical. Paris, 1963.
  Le miroir du temps. Paris, 1973.
  Problemes de la musique moderne. With her uncle, Boris de Schloezer. Paris, 1959.
Ref. 22

SCRUGGS, Mary Elfrida. See WILLIAMS, Mary Lou

SEALE, Ruth

20th-century American composer. b. Alabama. She studied at the New Orleans Baptist Seminary, the Tulane Music School and the American Conservatory of Music, Chicago.
Compositions
CHAMBER
  Twelve ballet songs (pf)
  Solo (org)
VOCAL
  It's wonderful (soloist and 3 w-vces)
SACRED
  Alleluia
  Christ is risen
  Restore unto me (4 mix-vces)
  Unworthy as I am
Ref. 448

SEALY, Helen

20th-century composer
Compositions
CHAMBER
  Pekinese (vln and pf)
  Rosemary (vln and pf)
  Sybilla (vln and pf)
Ref. 63

SEARCH, Sara Opal

American composer. b. Fort Worth, TX, 1890.
Compositions
ORCHESTRA
  Symphony No. 1, in C-Minor (also str orch) (ca. 1941)
CHAMBER
  Allegro giocoso (fl; also pf or orch acc)
Ref. 190, 322, 594

SEARS, Helen
20th-century American composer. b. Massachusetts. She composed piano pieces and songs.
Ref. 40, 347, 433

SEARS, Ilene Hanson
American pianist, lecturer and composer. b. Crookston, MN, August 31, 1938. She studied under Bernard Heiden and Thomas Beversdorf at Indiana University. She was piano teacher at Salem College in Winston-Salem, North Carolina from 1967 to 1968 and lecturer in theory and piano at the Winston-Salem University.
Compositions
CHAMBER
    Cello sonata
    Sonatina (pf)
SACRED
    Three Christmas carols (ch)
Ref. 142, 347

SEAVER, Blanche Ebert
American authoress and composer. b. Chicago, IL, September 15, 1891. She studied under her father, Amalie Hanning and Brahm van der Berg. She was awarded the following honorary degrees; a L.H.D. from the University of Southern California in 1966; a D.F.A. from Seaver College, Malibu in 1968; an L.L.D. from Pomona College in 1970; a D.B.A. from Woodbury College in 1970; a D.H. from Oklahoma Christian College in 1972 and a D.P.S. from MacMurray College in 1973. She was the recipient of numerous awards including the Jane Addams Award from Rockford College, Illinois and was named Woman of the Year by the *Los Angeles Times* in 1964. DISCOGRAPHY.
Compositions
ORCHESTRA
    Pieces
VOCAL
    Songs incl.:
    Just for today (vce and orch)
    Calling me back to you
    The flowers
    Morrow rock
    No llores yo volvere
    Remember me
SACRED
    Alone with Thee
    Battle hymn of the Republic
    Close at Thy feet, my Lord
    If God send me you
    Mass
    Pontifical mass
    Stay with me, O Lord
Ref. 39, 40, 142, 347, 494, 563, 622

SEAY, Virginia
American musicologist and composer. b. Palo Alto, CA, August 8, 1922. She composed chamber and piano pieces, choral works and songs.
Ref. 347, 353

SEBASTIANI, Pia
Argentine pianist and composer. b. Buenos Aires, February 27, 1925. Her father was the Italian harpist Augusto Sebastiani and she was a pupil at the National Conservatory and the Beethoven Conservatory. She studied the piano under Lalewicz, composition under Gilard and Messiaen, Paris, under Copland at the Berkshire Music Center, Tanglewood, MA, and Milhaud in Boston. She performed internationally with symphonic orchestras and on TV in Europe and the United States. She was a recipient of honors and awards, including the title of Chevalier and Officer of the Belgian Crown in 1961 and Officer of the Arts of France in 1965. She retired from the concert platform in 1948.
Compositions
ORCHESTRA
    Piano concerto (1941) (1st prize, Palmes d'or, Belgium, 1948)
    Coral, fuga y final (1945)
    Estampas (1946)
CHAMBER
    Sonatina (2 vln) (1948)
PIANO
    Cuatro preludios (1944-1947)
    Cancion de cuna para Bibi, lullaby (1947)

VOCAL
    Songs incl.:
    Cancion popular (1945)
    Cuatro marinas (Leopoldo Lugones) (1943)
    Trois chansons françaises (Paul Verlaine) (1941)
Ref. 17, 77, 390

SEBAULT, Pauline. See THYS, Pauline

SEEGER, Ruth Crawford. See CRAWFORD SEEGER, Ruth

SEEMAN, Elsa Laura. See WOLZOGEN, Elsa Laura von

SEGHIZZI, Cecilia
Italian violinist, teacher, choral conductor and composer. b. Gorizia, September 5, 1908. She obtained diplomas in violin teaching and composition from the Conservatory at Milan and in choral song and choral conducting at Salzburg. She made her debut as a violinist in 1928 and as a conductor in 1940. She taught at the Conservatories of Trieste and Gorizia and gave concerts abroad as conductor of a polyphonic chorus. She was awarded first prize in a national competition of polyphonic song in Rome and first prize in several other choral competitions as well as a gold medal 'Premio Epifania.'
Compositions
CHAMBER
    Quartets
    Sonatas (vln and ob)
    Piano pieces
VOCAL
    Dieci canti popolari friulani e grandesi, choral and lyrical music (ch a-cap) (Padova: Zanibon, 1975)
Ref. 77

SEGOVIA, Paquita. See MADRIGUERA RODON, Paquita

SEHESTED, Hilda
Danish pianist and composer. b. Broholm, April 27, 1858; d. Copenhagen, April 15, 1936. She studied in Copenhagen and Paris. Her teachers included C.E.F. Horneman and Orla Rosenhoff and Mme. Massart in Paris.
Compositions
ORCHESTRA
    Miniaturer (1914)
    Nocturne
    Poème lyrique
    Rhapsody (1914)
    Suite (b-cor and orch) (1906)
CHAMBER
    Fyenske billeder (cl, vlc and pf) (1920)
    Intermezzi (vln, vlc and pf) (1903)
    Fantasy Pieces (vlc and pf) (1909)
    Morceau pathetique (bsn and pf) (1923)
    Suite (cor and pf) (1906)
PIANO
    Fantasy pieces
    Sonata (1904)
    Three pieces (1906)
VOCAL
    Cantata for Danish Women's Association (1916)
    Agnete og Haumanden
    Foraarsvers og sommersange (J. Jorgensen) (1908)
    Songs incl.:
    Acht Gedichte fuer Mezzo-Sopran mit Klavierbegleitung, op. 2 (Hermann von Gilm)
    Dagning
    Folkevise
    I natten
    Jeg ved en roee
    Kys
    Nadjesda
    Stjernen
Ref. 20, 96, 113, 226, 331

632

SEIBERT, Irma

American concert harpist, accompanist and composer. b. Bloomfield, NJ, October 27, 1888. She was a pupil of Gertrude Ina Robinson and Elizabeth Sloman. She appeared frequently as a soloist in recitals in New York after her debut in 1910 and was an accompanist for Alice Nielsen. Seibert composed chamber music for the harp.
Ref. 226

SEIDENWEBERIN, Metzi

12th-century Swiss nun. She composed songs of Jesus.
Ref. 476

SEIDERS, Mary Asenath

20th-century American pianist, teacher and composer. b. Walnut Hill. She taught the piano for 50 years.
Compositions
OPERETTA
Cinderella
The Little White Door
Ref. 374

SEILER, Amalie. See GROEBENSCHUETZ, Amalie

SEIPT, Sophie

19th-century German composer of Cologne.
Compositions
CHAMBER
Drei Romanzen (vlc and pf)
Fantasie (vlc and pf)
Other pieces for cello and piano
Ref. 266, 276, 347

SELAMET OL-KASS. See SALLAMA AL-QUASS

SELDEN, Gisela. See SELDEN-GOTH, Gizella

SELDEN, Margery Stomme

20th-century American composer.
Composition
CHAMBER
String quartet No. 1

SELDEN-GOTH, Gizella (Selden, Gisela)

Hungarian pianist, musicologist, writer and composer. b. Budapest, June 6, 1884. She studied the piano under Istvan Thoman and then composition under Bela Bartok from 1906 to 1908. She lived in Berlin from 1912 to 1924; in Florence and then New York from 1938 to 1950, before returning to Florence. She owned a large collection of manuscripts, from J.S. Bach to Bartok. Some of her compositions were performed by prominent musicians of her time. Her symphonic poem *The pilgrim* was performed in Budapest, Zurich and Berne. She wrote articles on music for newspapers in Berlin, Prague, Switzerland and Budapest.
Compositions
ORCHESTRA
Symphonic poem
Humoresque (1908)
CHAMBER
String quartet No. 1
String quartet No. 2
String quartet No. 3 (1958)
String quartet No. 4 (1960)
String trio (1959)
Suite (vln and pf) (1911)
PIANO
Prelude and fugue (2 pf) (Universal Edition) (1956)
Scherzo
VOCAL
Cantata (1941)
The pilgrim, poem (Bar, mix-ch and orch)
Songs

Publications
Ferruccio Busoni, Versuch eines Portraits. Vienna, 1922.
Fuenfundzwanzig Busoni Briefe. Vienna, 1937.
Felix Mendelssohn, Letters. New York, 1945; London, 1946.
Ref. 105, 226, 375

SELEMA AL CAS. See SALLAMA AL-QUASS

SELMER, Kathryn Lande

American singer and composer. b. Staten Island, NY, November 6, 1930. She studied at the Eastman and Juilliard Schools of Music. She is a member of ASCAP.
Compositions
VOCAL
Songs incl.:
Let's go to the toy shop
For sleepyheads only
Let's have a party
Song for little folk
OPERETTA
The Princess and the Pea
The Princess Who Couldn't Laugh
Shoemaker and the Elf
INCIDENTAL MUSIC
Birthday house
Captain Kangaroo
Ref. 39, 94, 142

SELTZNER, Jennie

American teacher and composer. b. Bristol Township, WI, January 19, 1895. She graduated from the American Conservatory in Chicago in 1929 where she studied under Aletta Tenold and Adolf Weidig, with whom she continued studying privately. She taught privately after 1913.
Compositions
CHAMBER
Forest in spring (vlc, vln and pf) (1932)
Shady terrace (vln and pf) (1932)
PIANO
Tone Pictures incl.:
Dolly's lesson
Fireflies
Goodnight
In merry mood
Petite Valse
The shepherd
Singing and swinging
Sleep song
Slumber song
Springtime
Through the forest
Twilight
The white bunny
TEACHING PIECES
Elves (1926)
Ref. 347, 496

SELVA, Blanche

French pianist, professor and composer. b. Brive, 1884; d. 1942. She studied at the Paris Conservatoire and with Vincent d'Indy at the Schola Cantorum, where she later taught. She was awarded a professorship at the Prague and the Strasbourg Conservatories. She composed sonatas and arrangements of classical pieces.
Publications
L'enseignement musical de la technique du piano.
Ref. 268

SEMAD. See THAMAD

SEMEGEN, Daria

American electronic instrumentalist, professor and composer. b. Bamberg, Germany, June 27, 1946. She became an American citizen in 1957. She began writing music concurrently with her piano studies at the age of seven. She studied composition under Gauldin, Burrill Phillips and Samuel Adler at the Eastman School of Music (B.Mus., composition, 1968). She studied composition in Warsaw as a Fulbright scholar under Witold Lutoslawski and electronic music under Wlodzimierz Kotonski at the Warsaw Conservatory from 1968 to 1969. She received a Yale University Fellowship and studied composition and electronic music under Bulent Arel and theory under Alexander Goehr, graduating with her M.Mus. (composition) in 1971. At Columbia University, where she was awarded scholarships for continuing studies in composition and electronic music, she studied under Vladimir Ussachevsky, completing her doctoral work at the School of Arts in 1973. From 1971 to 1973 she taught at Columbia-Princeton Electronic Music Center, where she was full-time technician and administrative manager from 1973 to 1974. After 1971 she was technical assistant to Otto Luening and V. Ussachevsky in the creation and modification of electronic music materials, and teacher at the Center. After 1974 she taught composition and electronic music at the State University of New York at Stony Brook where she is currently an associate professor. She was awarded BMI awards from 1967 to 1969; Chautauqua, Tanglewood, and MacDowell Colony fellowships in 1967 and 1968; the Woods Chandler and Bradford-Keeley prizes in composition from Yale University in 1970 and 1971; two prizes in the Mu Phi Epslon Composition Contest in 1968; a National Academy of Recording Arts and Sciences award in 1972; a National Endowment for the Arts Commission in 1973 for the completion of an electronic music work, grants in both 1980 and 1981 and a prize in the International Electronic Music Competition of the ISCM-League of Composers. She has been awarded numerous other awards and grants. She has served as judge in the BMI awards to student composers. Her works have been performed live and on radio broadcasts in the United States and abroad. DISCOGRAPHY. PHOTOGRAPH.

Compositions
ORCHESTRA
 Fantasia for orchestra (1963)
 Triptych for orchestra (1966)
CHAMBER
 Study for sixteen strings (1968)
 Composition for string quartet (1965)
 String quartet No. 1 (1963)
 String quartet No. 2 (1964)
 Jeux des quatres (cl, trb, vlc and pf) (1970)
 Quattro (fl and pf) (1967)
 Suite for flute and violin (1965)
 Three pieces for clarinet and piano (1968)
 Music for contrabass solo (1980)
 Music for clarinet solo (1981)
 Music (vln) (1973)
PIANO
 Five early pieces
 Three pieces (1966)
VOCAL
 Dans la nuit (Bar and cham orch) (1969)
 Poem (R. Sward) (ch) (1967)
 Lieder auf der Flucht (S and 8 players) (1967)
 Silent, silent night (T and pf) (1965)
SACRED
 Psalm 43 (ch) (1967)
 Prayer of Hannah (S and pf) (1968)
DANCE SCORES
 Epicycles: Electronic music for dancers (1982)
 Music for dancers (1977)
FILM MUSIC
 Out of Into
ELECTRONIC
 Electronic composition No. 1 (1972)
 Spectra: Electronic composition No. 2 (1979)
 Music for cello and tape (1980)
 Six plus (tape and live insts) (1965)
 Trill study (tape) (1971)

Bibliography
MOMA. *Women Composers: Summergarden Concert. High Fidelity/ Musical America* 25. December 1975.
National Music Council 35. Spring 1976: 18. Biographical sketch of Daria Semegen.
Ref. composer, 94, 142, 185, 206, 228, 347, 359, 415, 474, 563, 611, 622, 625

SENEKE, Teresa
Italian composer. b. Chieti, ca. 1848; d. Chieti or Rome, November 1875.
Compositions
PIANO
 Pieces
VOCAL
 Songs incl.:
 'Addio
 Ad una giovinetta
 Una corona di fiori
 Il disinganno
 Il lamento

 Il mio destino
 Oltre la tomba
 Il pensiero dominante
 La preghiera
 Rimembranze di Roma
OPERA
 Le due amiche (Rome, 1869)
Ref. 26, 50, 105, 225, 226, 276, 297, 307

SENFTER, Johanna
German pianist, violinist and composer. b. Oppenheim, November 27, 1879; d. Oppenheim, August 11, 1961. She studied at the Hoch'schen Conservatory in Frankfurt am Main, where she was a pupil of I. Knorr (composition), A. Rebner (violin) and Friedberg (piano). At the Leipzig Conservatory she studied under Max Reger.
Compositions
ORCHESTRA
 Nine symphonies
 Violin concerto
 Twenty-six orchestral works, some with voice or instrumental solo
CHAMBER
 Octet for strings and winds
 Four sonatas (vln and pf)
 Sonata (cl and pf)
 Sonata (vla and pf)
 Sonata, op. 10 (vlc and pf) (Andre, 1913)
 Sonata (vln)
 Organ pieces
VOCAL
 Maria vor dem Kreuz (4 vces and str qrt)
 Choral works with orchestra
 Songs, some with orchestra
Ref. 17, 41, 94, 111, 219, 226

SENIOR, Kay
20th-century British composer.
Composition
SACRED
 Mass of Benediction (1981)
Ref. *Composer* (London)

SEPULVEDA, Maria Luisa
Chilean pianist, violinist, violist, folklorist, professor, singer and composer. b. Chile, August 14, 1898; d. Santiago, 1959. She studied at the Conservatorio Nacional de Santiago under Bindo Paoli (piano), Jose Varalla (violin), Luis Esteban Giarda (viola and voice), and Domingo Santa Cruz and D. Brescia (composition). She graduated in 1905 (piano) and in 1918 (composition). She taught from 1912, was a professor at the National Conservatory from 1918 to 1931 and later taught at the Escuela Vocacional de Educacion Artistica, where she encouraged the study of Chilean folk music. She was a recipient of numerous prizes and awards.
Compositions
ORCHESTRA
 Symphonic studies
 Suite (pf and orch)
 Greco (also pf)
 Song of the Corhuillas y Trutruka (Indian insts of the Mapuches)
CHAMBER
 Pieces for guitar and harp
 Pieces for violin and piano
 Guitar solos
PIANO
 Studies and preludes (2 pf)
 Meditation
 Song of my land
 Studies
 Three miniatures
 Two descriptive pieces
 Solos
VOCAL
 Asi lo hace Juan (ch and orch)
 El aire (mix-ch)
 El imposible (mix-ch)
 Fourteen songs (mix-ch)
 Sinfonia de la trilla (mix-ch)
 Te quiero porque te quiero (mix-ch)
 Bouree (prize)
 Cancionero chileno (vce and gtr; also vce and pf)
 Canciones e tonadas del siglo XIX
 Cantos escolares (prize, Amigos del Arte)

Musica folclorica infantil (vce and pf)
Quodlibet on Chilean popular melodies
Ronda de paz (G. Mistral)
Ronda primaveral (G. Mistral)
Tres tonadas
Tonada (prize, Ateneo de Valparaiso)
Zamacueca estilizada (prize, Ateneo de Valparaiso)
Arrangements on folklore themes
SACRED
Album de Navidad (ch) (prize, Amigos del Arte)
Two religious songs
TEACHING PIECES
El amigo del nino
Piano manuals
Ref. 8, 70, 90, 100, 107, 226

SERA, Beatrice del
17th-century Italian nun and composer.
Ref. 264

SERANUS. See HARRISON, Susan Frances

SERENA, Amalie. See AMALIE, Marie Friederike Augusta, Princess

SEROVA, Valentina Semyonovna (nee Bergmann)
Soviet music critic and composer. b. Moscow, 1846; d. Moscow, 1924. She studied at the St. Petersburg Conservatory under her future husband, Alexander Nikolayevich Serov and under Anton Rubinstein.
Compositions
PIANO
Pieces
VOCAL
Songs
OPERA
Der Branntweinbrenner (1894)
Ilia Murometz (1899)
Khai Dievka
Maria d' Orval
Uriel Acosta (Gutzov) (1885)
Publications
Autobiography. 1916.
Reviews for 'Music and Theatre' and other magazines.
Ref. 2, 108, 135, 226, 297, 307, 330, 379, 431

SERRANO REDONNET, Ana
Argentine guitarist, conductor, music critic and composer. b. Buenos Aires, December 30, 1916. She studied the guitar under A. Sinopali and composition under G. Gilardi and J. Pahissa. She has conducted since 1942 and was director of folklore programs in Buenos Aires from 1941 to 1945 and of the program 'La Musica Nacional' on national radio in 1947. She was music critic for the daily newspaper 'Tribuna' for several years.
Compositions
CHAMBER
Guitar pieces
VOCAL
Songs inc.:
La soledad, poem (soloist, ch and str orch)
Quebradenas (vce, fl, ob, cl, bsn, gtr and caja (folk inst))
Arreos (vce and gtr)
Bagualas de chaya (vce and gtr)
Coplas tuyas (vce and gtr)
Danza (vce and gtr)
La generala (vce and gtr)
Indianas (S, fl and caja)
Lamento (vce and gtr)
El maule (vce and gtr)
Melisma de la soledad (vce and gtr)
Seis aires argentinos (vce and pf) (1939)
Vidala (vce and gtr)
Yo se lo que estoy cantando (vce and gtr)
THEATRE
La chaya, mimic-drama (1944)
El nino alcalde, legend (1943)
Tierra, choreographic poem (1945)
Publications
Panorama estetico de la musica argentina.
Ref. 100, 390

SERTORIUS, Lili. See REIFF, Lili

SERVIER, Mme. H.
19th-century French pianist, teacher and composer.
Compositions
PIANO
Simple melodie, op. 5 (4 hands)
Three airs variees, op. 3 (4 hands)
Variations, op. 5 (4 hands)
Exercise sur le trille, op. 10
Four bagatelles
Publications
Methode elementaire et progressive de chant à l'usage de toutes les voix. Paris: Schoenberger.
Ref. 26, 226, 276, 433

SERVOZ, Harriet (pseud. Azuma Samama)
French composer. b. Marseille, June, 1885; d. Paris, April, 1939. She studied music privately.
Composition
CHAMBER
Violin sonata (vln and pf) (1927)
Ref. 81

SESSA, Marianne. See SESSI, Marianne

SESSA, Claudia
16th-century Italian nun, musician, singer and composer. b. Milan. She was of aristocratic descent and a nun of the Annunciata in Milan. She was praised for her musical talent by P.A. Della Chiesa and Quadrio. She declined an offer by Queen Margaret of Austria to join the Spanish court, remaining at the convent where she died at a very young age.
Compositions
VOCAL
Songs incl.:
Occhi io vissi di voi
Vattene pur lasciva (in Patto's collection, 1613)
Bibliography
Borsieri. Supplemento alla Nobilta di Milano.
Ref. 118, 180, 653

SESSI (Sessa, Sessi-Natorp), Marianne (Marianna)
Italian opera singer and composer. b. Rome, 1771; d. Vienna, March 10, 1847. In 1792 she began singing at the Italian Opera in Vienna and soon became a celebrity. After her marriage to Baron van Natorp in 1795, she was known as Sessi-Natorp. She toured Europe in the early years of the 19th-century.
Compositions
VOCAL
Amare un infedele veder si abandonare
Canzonette italiane (vce and pf) (Breitkopf)
Di puri affeti miei
E dunque vero, torna il mio bene
Ecce quel fiero instante
Nasce nel vago aprile porporea rosa
Non t'accostar a l'urna
Placido zeffiretto
Sempre piu t'amo
Stanco di pascolar le pecorelle
Ref. 35, 103, 128, 297, 347

SESSI-NATORP, Marianne. See SESSI, Marianne

SETO, Robin
American pianist, teacher and composer. b. New York, November 25, 1957. At the age of 11 she entered the Junior Conservatory Camp in East Burke, VT, on a scholarship to study solfege, orchestration, harmony, counterpoint and analysis under Grace Newson Cushman. She continued to study there after it became the Walden School and later she became a teacher. At the Peabody Conservatory, Baltimore, she received degrees in the piano and musicianship. She studied composition under David Hogan, Stephen Albert, Donald Wheelock and later Ronald Perence. She

obtained her B.A. in music from Smith College, Northampton, in 1979. She received the Grace Newson Cushman Memorial award for composition and the Goldman award for outstanding performance. In 1970 she won the Delta Omicron award for musicianship, first place in the National Federation of Music Clubs Cavalcade for Creative Youth for composition from 1971 to 1974 and the Fred Waring award in 1975. She has twice been finalist in the composition contest sponsored by the Music Teachers' National Association. She was awarded the Fatman prize for composition, Smith College, 1976; the Devora Nadworney award and honorable mention in the Victor Herbert (ASCAP) composition contest sponsored by the National Federation of Music Clubs in 1977. PHOTOGRAPH.

Compositions
CHAMBER
Sonata (vln and pf) (1974)
PIANO
Pieces incl.:
If I ran the zoo (1973)
Octatonic suite for children, op. 1 (169)
VOCAL
Instruments I and II (S, fl, perc and pf) (Madeleine L'Engle) (1976)
Miracles, song cycle (S and pf) (children around the world) (1977)
ELECTRONIC
Fantasy (cl and elec tape) (1978)
Ref. composer

SETTI, Kilza (Kilza Setti de Castro Lima)

Brazilian teacher, folklorist and composer. b. São Paulo, January 26, 1932. She studied at Conservatorio Dramatico e Musical of São Paulo and obtained her teacher's diploma in 1953. She trained in Lisbon at the Arquivos Sonoros Portugueses under the direction of ethnologist Michel Giacometti and composer Fernando Lopes Graça and made her debut in 1959 with the Municipal Symphony Orchestra in São Paulo. She was active in stimulating interest in folklore and folklore music in educational institutions and is a founder member of the Brazilian Folklore Association. She is teacher of Brazilian folklore at the Escola Superior de Musica Santa Marcelina of São Paulo.

Compositions
ORCHESTRA
Baião (strs, picc, cl and fl) (1961)
Folganca, suie (cham)
Suite (Toada Caterete Interludio)
Toada
CHAMBER
Variations, on a popular theme for children (str qrt) (1957) (M. Andrade)
Cantilena (cl and pf) (1959)
Dois momentos (fl and pf) (1972)
PIANO
Ciranda
Duas peças: Canto de Yemanja; Canto de Ere (1969)
Interludio (in memory of J.C. Nobre) (1959)
A moda de Luiz Gonzaga, baiao
Oito variacões
Roda (1958)
Samba-lenco
Serie para piano: Peças sobre Mucama Bonita
Tanguinho (1958)
VOCAL
Balada do rei das sereias, cantata in 4 mvts (M. Bandeira) (mix-ch a-cap) (1959)
Quatro canções: As penas do meu martirio; Voce me faz esperar; Coração entristecido; A moda da chimarrita (Silvio Romero) (vce and str qrt) (1958)
Jogo da condessa (F. de C. Pires de Lima) (ch and perc) (1973)
Lenda do ceu, in 4 mvts (M. Andrade) (ch and perc) (1962)
Dois corais mistos a capela: Obiala koro; Yemanja oto, in 4 mvts (2 mix-ch a-capela)
Poesia II, in 4 mvts (ch)
Songs incl.:
Cantorias Paulistas
Dois poemas (G. Campos)
A estrela (M. Bandeira)
Olhos do meu benzinho, Os. (G. Barroso)
Poema da tua luza (C. Guarnieri) (1962)
Quadrinhas (S. Romero) (1956)
Raro dom (S. de Campos)(1958)
Serenata (V. Carvalho)
Tres lembrancas do folclore infantil: Jogo de tantague; Jogo da lua nova; Jogo do varisto (S. Romero) (1961)
Trova de muito amor para um amado senhor (H. Hilst)
Voce gosta de mim (Cantos Populares do Brazil, S. Romero) (1959)
Bibliography
Catalogo de partituras de autores brasileiros. Universita de San Paulo, 1977.
Ref. 333

SEUEL-HOLST, Marie (Holst, Marie Seuel)

American organist, pianist, teacher and composer. b. Parsonage on the Hill, Hochheim, WI, 1877. She played and sang melodies at the age of three and at the age of six began to study music. At 17 she was a pupil of Hans Bruenning at the Wisconsin Conservatory in Milwaukee. From 1900 to 1902 she studied under Ganz, Borowski and Falk at the Chicago Musical College. In 1902 Mrs. Holst joined the faculty of Bush Conservatory where she taught the piano, history and theory, studying under Fannie Bloomfield Ziegler. From 1912 to 1932 she was the dean of education and teacher of the piano and theoretical studies at the Wheeler Conservatory in Madison, WI. In 1912 she became the organist of the Emmanuel Lutheran Church at Madison. In 1929 she attended the British American Music conference at Lausanne, Switzerland, where she played her own compositions.

Compositions
ORCHESTRA
In Elfland, op. 26, miniature concerto (pf and str orch)
CHAMBER
In the foothills
In the northland
Sonata mignonne
Sonata mignonne No. 2
PIANO
Drowsy poppies
Forest idyls
Playing the drone bass
Three and twenty pirates
Twenty-nine tunes
Two slumber sketches
Work and pleasures
VOCAL
Songs
Part songs
Choruses
Ref. 40, 280, 292, 347

SEVERY, Violet Cavell

American professor and composer. b. Pasadena, CA, May 26, 1912. She studied under W.B. Olds and Wayne Bohrnstedt, receiving her B.Mus. and M.Mus. from the University of Redlands. She also studied under Juan Orrego Salas at Indiana University, John Barnes Chance at the University of Kentucky and privately under Frances Marion Ralston. From 1956 she was been assistant professor at Morehead State University.

Compositions
CHAMBER
Harpsichord sextet (ww-qnt and hpcd) (1970)
Toccata and fugue (hpcd) (1971)
Pieces for flute and oboe
VOCAL
Pieces
SACRED
Psalmotet (m-S, Bar, ch, org and plucked inst) (comm Music Teachers' National Association and Kentucky Music Teachers' Association, 1970)
Ref. 142

SEWALL, Maud Gilchrist

American organist, violinist and composer. b. Urbana, OH, February 18, 1872. She studied the violin under Stribelli in Glasgow, Faini in Florence, Walter in Munich and J. Kaspar in Washington, DC. Self-taught in the organ and theory, she was organist at the Church of the New Jerusalem, Washington. She composed a string quartet, organ pieces, vocal choruses and songs.
Ref. 226

SHADWELL, Nancy

20th-century American composer. DISCOGRAPHY.
Composition
CHAMBER
Theme and variations for trumpet
Ref. 562, 563

SHAFFER, Jeanne Ellison

American organist, professor and composer. b. Knoxville, TN, May 25, 1925. She received her A.A. in music from Stephens College, Columbia in 1944; a B.Mus from Samford University, Birmingham in 1954 (sacred music, voice and organ); an M.Mus. (voice and composition) from Birmingham Southern College, Birmingham, AL, in 1958; and a Ph.D. from the George Peabody College, Nashville, 1970. She studied composition under

Hugh Thomas, Gilbert Trythall, Newton Strandberg and Betty Louise Lumby (q.v.). Jeanne lectured in music at the University of Alabama, Tuscaloosa, 1961; at Birmingham Southern College from 1957 to 1962, at Southeastern Bible College, Birmingham from 1960 to 1962. She taught in community districts and metropolitan schools in Illinois and Tennessee from 1964 to 1967 and also worked as studio instructor for WDGN-TV. As co-ordinator of instruction she worked jointly for Peabody College and Blair Academy of Music from 1967 to 1970, was associate professor of music at Union University, Jackson from 1970 to 1971 and at Peabody College in 1971 and 1972. From 1972 to 1973 she served as associate professor and chairlady of fine arts in an inter-disciplinary program. From 1973 she was professor and chairlady of the division of fine arts at Judson College in Marion, GA. PHOTOGRAPH.

Compositions
CHAMBER
    Heart of Dixie (strs, fl, ob, cl, trp, trb, gtr and perc) (1980)
    Broadman duets, 10 duets (org and pf) (1964)
    Duet on Promised Land (pf and org) (1975) (Broadman Press)
ORGAN
    Hymn tune meditations (Broadman: Vol. I, 18 preludes, 1961; vol. II, 12 preludes, 1966)
    Prelude on Picardy (1974) (Broadman)
VOCAL
    Golgotha (mix-ch) (1977)
    Jingle bell (1965) (Summy-Birchard)
    On garden, minutes and butterflies (vce and ens) (1980)
    Balm in Gilead (arr) (1953) (Broadman)
SACRED
    Lenten cantata: The words from the Cross (1969) (Abingdon Press)
    Sing Noel, cantata (mix-ch) (1963) (Broadman)
    Ask, and I will be given to you (mix-ch) (1960) (Broadman)
    Be with me Lord (mix-ch) (1960) (Broadman)
    His star shineth clear (mix-ch) (1953) (Broadman)
    Hope (mix-ch) (1956) (Broadman)
    Laudate Dominum omnes gentes (mix-ch, continuo and strs) (1972) (Concordia)
    Lord of Hosts, be Thou my refuge (mix-ch) (1960) (Broadman)
    O Lord of heaven and earth and sea (mix-ch) (1960) (Broadman)
    O Thou whose gracious presence (mix-ch) (1957) (Broadman)
    Sing we alleluia (mix-ch) (1958) (Broadman)
    Within a lowly manger (mix-ch) (1953) (Broadman)
    Alleluia, clap your hands (1981)
    The carpenter shop (1957) (Choral Services)
    For children who have never heard (w-vces) (1953) (Broadman)
    An earthen vessel (1956) (Broadman)
    Four advent anthems (1977)
    From henceforth, O my soul (1967) (Canyon Press)
    Gentle Jesus (w-vces) (1956) (Broadman)
    God's word (1975)
    The hands of God (1966) (Broadman)
    He hath made them everyone (1956) (Broadman)
    I know a name (1953) (Lorenz Publishing)
    Light of this dark world (1967) (Broadman)
    A long, long time ago (unison vces) (1956) (Broadman)
    A man went forth to die (1967) (Broadman)
    My sheep hear my voice (S) (1974) (Broadman)
    Show me, O Lord (1966) (Canyon Press)
    Two hymn tune preludes (1977)
    When David was a young boy (1965)
BALLET
    Rainbows (1978)
OPERA
    The Ghost of Susan B. Anthony, chamber opera (1977)
Ref. composer, 185, 359, 468, 622

SHAGIAKHMETOVA, Svetlana Georgievna
Soviet composer. b. Bashkiria, 1939. She studied under Leman at the Kazan Conservatory and graduated in 1964. Her music makes use of Bashkir themes.
Compositions
ORCHESTRA
    Bashkir suite
CHAMBER
    Piano trio
    Sonatas for clarinet
    Other pieces
PIANO
    Twenty pieces
Ref. 420

SHAIMARDANOVA, Shakhida
Soviet composer. b. China, 1938. She attended the Tashkent Conservatory from 1957 to 1964. DISCOGRAPHY.

Compositions
ORCHESTRA
    Symphony in C-Major
    Violin concerto (1964)
    Sinfonietta
VOCAL
    Songs
Ref. 217, 420

SHARIYYA
After Oraib, she was the greatest Arabian songstress of the Abbasid period, ca. 815. Like the most famous songstresses of her time she came from Basra. Her father was alleged to be a man of the tribe of Banu Sama ibn Lu'ai who, however, did not recognize his daughter, whose mother was a slave. Consequently Shariyya was born a slave. In another version she was stolen from her parents, sold into slavery and came into the possession of a woman who brought her up, taught her singing and took her to Baghdad to sell her. In yet another version, this woman was her own mother, of the Banu Zuhra, a branch of the Quraish. She must have already shown exceptional talent, for she was only seven years old and the two most significant musicians of the time, Ishaq al-Mausili and Ibrahim Ibn al-Mahdi, both attended the auction. When Shariyya's venal mother realised how much money she could make with her daughter, she did not wish to be separated from her, and great bargaining and intrigue ensued. Finally she was purchased by Ibrahim Ibn al-Mahdi. Her mother tried to have the sale invalidated, saying that Shariyya was of the Quraish, who may never be sold as slaves, but omitted to say that she herself had sold her. To keep her, Ibrahim freed her and married her. Versions differ as to whether this was a marriage only in legal form. The Khalif Al-Mutasim himself offered Ibrahim 70,000 dinars for her, but he refused it. Shariyya grew up in Ibrahim's house together with other slave girls to whom she taught music. One of the slaves was Raiq, who taught Shariyya. After Ibrahim's death, it was revealed that he had not really married her and that she was still his slave. Shariyya herself did not know this. She belonged in succession to the Khalifs Al-Mutasim (833 to 842), Al-Watiq (842 to 847), Al-Mutawakkil (847 to 861), Al-Muntasir (861 to 862), Al-Mustain (862 to 866)j, Al-Mutazz (866 to 869) and Al-Mutamid (870 to 892). Her most productive period was during the Khalifate of Al-Watiq. During the Khalifate of Al-Mutawakkil there developed great rivalry between Shariyya, representing the Persian-Romantic school of music, and Oraib, representing the conservative classical tradition. At first the two women sang together for the Khalif but predictably fell out. Baghdad and Samarra were divided into supporters of the two prima-donnas and there were contests between the two and their respective slave-pupils. The songstress Farida was the most famous of Shariyya's pupils. However, when she threatened to steal some of Shariyya's limelight, they became bitter enemies and Shariyya determined never to teach anyone again, or at least no one who was likely to rival her. One of her last protectors was the Khalif Al-Mutamid (870 to 892). She set his poems to music and he rewarded her richly. He also bought several slaves from her singing-school. It is not known whether she lived to see the end of his Khalifate or the end of Samarra as capital city. With her death, there ended one of the most brilliant epochs of Arabian culture.
Ref. 224

SHARPE, Anna Wright
American composer. b. 1914.
Composition
CHAMBER
    One little hour (vln and pf) (Southgate)
Ref. 63

SHARPE, Emma
Hawaiian autoharp and ukulele player, pianist, teacher and composer. b. 1904. She was a member of Hawaii's musical Farden family and one of 11 brothers and sisters who played various instruments. Emma played the ukulele, the autoharp and the piano. She composed and taught the hula and chanting for many years.
Composition
VOCAL
    Ulupalakua
Ref. 438

SHASHINA, Elizaveta Sergeyevna
19th-century Russian composer. DISCOGRAPHY.

Compositions
VOCAL
Drei Worte
I go alone along the road
Sehnsucht nach Ruhe
Vykhozhu odin ya na dorogu
Ref. 493, 563

SHATAL, Miriam
Dutch/Israeli composer. b. Amsterdam, December 12, 1903. Having first taken a doctorate in biology, she studied composition under Paul Ben Chaim, Arthur Geldrun, and Chaim Alexander. PHOTOGRAPH.
Compositions
VOCAL
Songs incl.:
Four ballads (English text) (vce and gtr) (1970)
SACRED
Al har gawoah (adapted for mix-ch by M. Lushig) (1956)
Barchie nafshi, psalm 104, Verse 4 (mix-ch) (1960)
El artsie (w-ch) (1960)
Heed (w-ch) (1958)
Shalom aleichem, prayer (ch) (1965)
Hisybati etchem (1965)
Ketal chermon, psalm 133, verse 3 (1957)
Kina (wordless w-ch and vln) (1962)
Prayer (1967)
MISCELLANEOUS
Echo
Ref. composer, 206

SHATIN, Judith Allen. See ALLEN, Judith Shatin

SHATTUCK, Grace. See BAIL, Grace Shattuck

SHAVERZASHVILI, Tamara Antonovna
Soviet pianist, lecturer and composer. b. Kutais, Georgia, October 14, 1891; d. Tbilisi, September 18, 1955. From 1910 she studied the piano under I. Aisberg at the Tiflis Music School graduating in 1923. In 1935 she graduated with distinction in composition, which she studied under I. Tuskia and V. Shcherbachev. She continued postgraduate studies under P. Ryazanov, taught the piano from 1923 to 1925 and theory, solfege and music appreciation at the Z. Paliashvili Central Music School in Tbilisi from 1935 to 1938. From 1938 she lectured at the Conservatory, becoming senior lecturer in general and special polyphony in 1946. In that year she received the title 'Honored Worker in Art of the Georgian SSR' and was awarded a medal.
Compositions
ORCHESTRA
Suite (1935)
Twelve pieces from children's suite (1946)
Two marches (1940)
CHAMBER
String quartet (1938)
Suite (wind insts) (1938)
Suite (vlc and pf) (1949)
PIANO
Children's album, 40 pieces (1946)
Pastorale (1948)
Polyphonic suite (1940)
Twenty children's pieces (1952)
VOCAL
Pesni gor (vce and pf) (1981)
Collection of 12 children's songs (1925)
Fifty songs for school children (1923-1929)
Sozhalenie (I. Grishashvili) (vce and pf) (1920)
Two lullabies (I. Chavchavadze) (1925-1926)
THEATRE
Vesna
Vesna i leto
Ref. 87, 94

SHAW, Alice Marion
American accompanist, teacher and composer. b. Rockland, ME, August 22, 1890. She was accompanist to many noted artists such as George Barrere, Eddie Brown and Scipione Guidi.

Compositions
CHAMBER
Pieces for violin, flute and cello
Piano pieces
Organ pieces
VOCAL
Songs incl.:
The little man in grey
May noon
Once on a radiant morning
One April day
Pussy willows
There is a little lady
To go and forget
Waiting
SACRED
The first day of the week, anthem (mix-ch)
Ref. 40, 347, 374

SHAW, Carrie Burpee
American organist, pianist, teacher and composer. b. Rockland, ME, 1850; d. 1946. She studied the piano and the organ under Stephen Emery, E.E. Perfield, Kotschmann, Mrs. Virgil, B.J. Lang, Thomas Tapper, Frederick Lamond and Goetschius. She was a founder of the Rockland Rubinstein Club in 1873 and was an organist at various churches and teacher of music in various schools.
Compositions
CHAMBER
Instrumental works
Piano pieces
VOCAL
The field sparrow, part-song (w-ch)
Humpty Dumpty, part-song (m-ch)
Prairie Dog Town, part-song (m-ch)
There was a little man, part-song (m-ch)
All is o'er
Dandelions, part-song
My sunshine
SACRED
The Lord is great in Zion (mix-ch) (1914)
Ref. 40, 347, 374, 433

SHELDON, Lillian Tait
American organist and composer. b. Gouverneur, NY, September 10, 1865; d. Gouverneur, NY, January 10, 1925. Sheldon composed choral works and songs.
Ref. 347, 353

SHELLEY, Margaret Vance
20th-century American composer.
Compositions
VOCAL
Choral works (two-part and mix-ch) (Belwin-Mills)
Ref. 40, 347

SHELLEY, Mary Wollstonecraft
British composer. b. 1795; d. 1851. She married the poet Percy B. Shelley and composed songs.
Ref. 465

SHELTON, Margaret Meier
American pianist and composer. b. New York City, July 3, 1936. She received her B.Mus. (music education and piano) from the Eastman School of Music in 1958; her M.A. (composition) from the California State University, Los Angeles and in 1983 received a Ph.D. (composition) from the University of California, Los Angeles. She studied under Roy Travis, Paul Reale and Alden Ashforth. Her awards include the Axel Stordahl Scholarship and the Atwater Kent award in composition. PHOTOGRAPH.
Compositions
ORCHESTRA
Mythical muliebrity (1972)
CHAMBER
Stances (fl and str trio) (1980)
Petronella (fl, cl and pf) (1978)
Dialogues (fl and pf) (1977)

PIANO
Forward motion (1982)
Reflections of Robert (1974)
VOCAL
The Spanish gypsy, cantata (m-S and cham orch) (1982)
The Catherine wheel, song cycle (m-S, fl, cl, pf and str trio)
I will sing (mix-ch) (Lawson-Gould) (1982)
Smog (mix-ch, pf and perc) (Thomas Music) (1978)
Eschatos, 2 songs (m-S and a-fl) (1981)
Sense and nonsense (Thomas) (1977)
A woman's heart, 3 songs (m-S and pf) (1982)
SACRED
This child, cantata (ch and perc) (1977)
The three Mary's, cantata (w-ch) (1980)
Three prophets (mix-ch) (1979)
Creation (m-S and a-fl) (1981)
Kings from Persian lands (Gentry) (1976)
ELECTRONC
Isaiah sketches (tape) (1980)
Restless (tape) (1976)
Ref. composer, 625

SHELTON, Mrs. Henry. See SAFFERY, Eliza

SHEMER, Naomi
Israeli composer.
Compositions
VOCAL
Jerusalem of Gold
Children's songs
Lieder
Ref. 497

SHEPARD, Jean Ellen
American composer. b. Durham, NC, November 1, 1949. She studied at the Peabody Conservatory under Stefan Grove and Robert Hall Lewis (composition) and Elizabeth Katzenellenbogen (piano) receiving a B.Mus in 1973 and an M.Mus (composition) in 1974. Continuing her studies in composition she was a pupil of Milko Kelemen in Stuttgart, as a recipient of a graduate fellowship from the International Rotary foundation from 1975 to 1976. She received the Gustav Klemm composition award and won second prize in a Mu Phi Alpha Sinfonia contest. PHOTOGRAPH.
Compositions
ORCHESTRA
Movement (str orch) (1970)
The clock strikes three (1973)
CHAMBER
Serenade (perc, winds and strs) (1973)
String quartet movements (1974)
Fantasy (winds) (1971)
Trio (fl, vlc and pf) (1972)
Duo (fl and pf) (1975)
Four duos (cl and bsn) (1971)
Four pieces (hn) (1972)
Music (vlc) (1976)
Two pieces (org) (1971)
PIANO
Fantasie (1976)
Nocturne (1971)
Soliloquy (1973)
VOCAL
To a child dancing in the wind (speaker and 4 insts) (1972)
SACRED
Alleluia, God is ascended, anthem (4-part ch)
DANCE SCORES
Textures of morning, modern dance (1977)
MISCELLANEOUS
Ode to Swath (1971)
Ref. composer, 142

SHEPPARD, Suzanne
20th-century American composer.
Compositions
CHAMBER
Fleetings, (fl) (1983)
Suite for solo marimba (1985)
Fantasy (pf) (David Bates award, 1981)
Ref. AMC 1985, 25

SHER, Rebecca
Pianist, songwriter and composer. b. Munich, Germany, May 30, 1950, now resident in the United States. She was educated at the New York School of Music. She obtained her B.A. at CUNY and after furthering her studies at the Manhattan School of Music returned to CUNY to complete her Ph.D. (music). She has given numerous piano recitals in New York.
Ref. 457

SHERBOURNE, Janet
English composer. b. Southampton, September 28, 1952. She graduated with a B.A. (hons) from York University in 1975, and M.A. (ethnomusicology) from Queen's University, Belfast in 1978. She performs regularly with local ensembles, chamber groups and orchestras. PHOTOGRAPH.
Compositions
MISCELLANEOUS
Everyday (1978)
Slower than molasses (1981)
Slowly (1978)
Still (1980)
Streets ahead (1982)
FILM MUSIC
French film pieces (1979)
Ref. composer

SHERIDAN, Helen Selina. See DUFFERIN, Lady Helen Selina

SHERMAN, Elna
American composer. b. Massachusetts, 1889; d. 1964.
Compositions
CHAMBER
For an Oriental bazaar, suite (3 rec)
Sonata lyrica (CFE)
Other pieces
SACRED
St. Francis and the birds (vce, 3 rec, vlc and hpcd) (1951) (ACA)
Ref. 68, 142

SHERMAN, Ingrid
German lecturer, writer and composer. b. Cologne, June 25, 1919. She studied at the Piano Conservatory of Cologne and was awarded 15 honorary degrees from various countries. Her awards included the Golden Laurel Wreath and the United Poets Laureate.
Compositions
VOCAL
Color harmony
A million songs
Wake up
I walk the earth
You are an angel
SACRED
I worship Thee
O Lord, I'm asking you
Pathway to light
Ref. 457, 625

SHERMAN, Kim Daryl
American pianist and composer. b. Elgin, IL, August 6, 1954. She studied composition and theory under Homer Keller, the piano under Erno Danie and operetta under Clarence Stephenson. She obtained her B.Mus. (piano, 1976) from the Conservatory at Lawrence University, WI, studying the piano under Robert Belon, composition under James Ming and Kenneth Timme and music theory under Marjory Irvin and James Ming. From 1976 to 1977 she studied composition under Thea Musgrave (q.v.) in California.
Compositions
CHAMBER
Heavenly orbs of different colours (vlc, fl and pf)
Fog (vla) (1978)
Phasis (fl) (1978)
Song for Wednesday night (ob) (1977)
Spring night on a mountain (ob) (Mark Seerup) (1979)
VOCAL
Sea changes (ch, str, ob, fl and pf) (1979)
First vision (ch, vlc, fl, ob and pf) (1979)
OPERA
Claire (1979)

THEATRE
  Accidentally exalted (1978)
  Dinosaurs, passenger pigeons, clowns and other things obsolete (1980)
  Florida (1979)
  Goodbye suite (1979)
  The last clown (1978)
  Orlando Orlando (1977)
Ref. composer

SHERREY, Mae Ayres

Late 19th-century American pianist and composer. b. St. Louis. She studied at the Beethoven Conservatory and the Western Conservatory, St. Louis under Marcus Epstein, Roscoe Warren Lucy and Victor Ehling.
Composition
OPERETTA
  Dreamland Beauties (ca. 1898)
Ref. 460, 465

SHERRINGTON, Grace

English singing teacher and composer. b. Preston, 1842. She was the sister of the soprano and composer Helena Lemmens Sherrington (q.v.). She composed songs.
Ref. 276, 347, 433

SHERRINGTON, Helena Lemmens (Mrs. Nicholas Jacques Lemmens)

English professor, singer and composer. b. Preston, October 4, 1834; d. Brussels, May 9, 1906. Her sister Grace Sherrington (q.v.), born at Preston, 1842, was also a talented composer of songs and a well-known vocal teacher. Helena studied in Rotterdam in 1838 and later under Verhulst. In 1852 she entered the Brussels Conservatory. She made her first appearance in London in 1856. She was a professor of singing at the Brussels Conservatory from 1880 to 1891 and at the Royal Academy of Music in London from 1891. She composed songs.
Ref. 6, 85, 276, 347, 433

SHEVITZ, Mimi

American composer. b. Los Angeles, December 14, 1953. She obtained her B.A. (music, 1976) at the University of California, Santa Cruz, majoring in voice, electronic music and composition and her Master of Fine Arts in electronic music and recording media from Mills College. She has also studied computer animation graphics and is currently studying computer science so as to incorporate kinetic-acoustic sound sculptures into her work.
Compositions
VOCAL
  A composition (S, str qrt, perc, fl and picc)
  As I said (1977)
  Discus (1978)
  I beams (1977)
  Sojourn (wind, vce and perc) (1975)
  Swingset (1978)
ELECTRONIC
  Variance, in 3 parts (syn) (1975)
  Leviathans (syn) (1977)
  Piece for voice and feed back (vce and syn) (1975)
Ref. composer

SHIBATA, Haruna. See MIYAKE, Haruna

SHIDA, Shoko

20th-century Japanese composer, now resident in West Germany.
Compositions
VOCAL
  Cypress sun-up (vce and perc) (1983)
BALLET
  Orpheus (vce, pf and perc) (1984)
ELECTRONIC
  Chutney sweet
  Lazy garnet (vce, fl and tape) (1982)
  Vocalize (vce and tape) (1983)
  Summer talk (perc and tape) (1979)
Ref. composer

SHIELDS, Alice Ferree

American teacher, singer and composer. b. New York, 1943. She studied composition under Vladimir Ussachevsky and Otto Luening at Columbia-Princeton electronic music center, earning a B.S. (Music) and an M.A. (composition) from Columbia University. She followed a career as a singer with the Metropolitan Opera and Lake George Opera Festivals. She is teaching assistant in electronic music at Columbia University. Among honors awarded her were a Presser Foundation grant in 1970 and a Martha Baird Rockefeller fund for music grant for voice in 1973. DISCOGRAPHY.
Compositions
VOCAL
  The storyteller, cantata (b-Bar and orch)
  Neruda songs (vces and vlc)
  Spring music (S, trp and ob)
  Wildcat songs (S and picc) (ACA)
SACRED
  O sacred light (mix-ch) (ACA)
OPERA
  Odyssey, in 1 act (2 m-vces, ch of 6 men and cham orch) (ACA)
  Shaman
INCIDENTAL MUSIC
  Barabbas, theatre (1968)
  Domino, dance (1967)
  Witches' scenes from Macbeth (1967)
ELECTRONIC
  Coyote
  Domino (for dance)
  Egyptian Book of the Dead (1970)
  Electronic music for the ghost scenes in Hamlet (1967)
  Rhapsody (pf and tape)
  Study for voice and tape (1969)
  The transformation of Ani (tape piece for manipulated vce) (1970)
  Waking on the surface of the sun
  The winter king (resonator bells and pf)
MISCELLANEOUS
  Farewell to a hill
Ref. 77, 142, 282, 622, 624, 625

SHIMANOVSKAYA, Maria Agata. See SZYMANOWSKA, Maria Agata

SHIOMI, Mieko

Japanese composer. b. December 13, 1938. She graduated from Tokyo University of Arts in 1961 having studied under Minao Shibata. Between 1964 and 1965 she studied in New York. DISCOGRAPHY.
Compositions
VOCAL
  Bird dictionary (S and pf)
  If we were a pentagonal memory device (vocal ens)
  In the afternoon or structure of the dream (vce and pf)
  Spring
  The sun sets over the prairie
ELECTRONIC
  Amplified dream I and II
  As it were floating granules No. 1-6
  Collection of events
  Phantom
  Polarization
Ref. Japanese Federation of Composers, Otto Harrassowitz (Wiesbaden)

SHIRLEY, Constance Jeanette

American pianist, teacher and composer. b. Los Angeles. Her father was a baritone soloist and her mother a concert pianist and soprano soloist. She graduated with an A.A. from the Los Angeles Junior College and a B.Mus and an M.Mus from Chapman College, Los Angeles. She made her first public appearance as a pianist at the age of four, having studied under her mother. She studied composition with Dr. Mary Carr Moore (q.v.) and Arnold Schonberg, orchestration with Dr. Lucien Caillet, string quartet and fugue with Dr. Charles Pemberton, composition with Dr. Howard Hanson and the Schillinger System with David Holguin. She received many honors and awards and was the recipient of an honorary Mus.D. from Temple Hall College and Seminary, Illinois.
Compositions
PIANO
  Poem in retrospect (also orch)
MISCELLANEOUS
  Caprice brilliant
  Elephantasia (circus suite)
  Flight of wild geese
Ref. 496

640

SHLEG, Ludmila Karlovna
Composition
ORCHESTRA
Fair's sketches
Ref. Otto Harrassowitz (Wiesbaden)

SHLONSKY, Verdina (Vardina Chlonsky)
Israeli pianist, teacher and composer. b. Krementshug, Ukraine, January 22, 1905. The sister of the poet Abraham Shlonsky and singer Nina Valery, she was Israel's first woman composer. She studied the piano at the Dnepropetrovsk Conservatory and at the Hochschule fuer Musik in Berlin under Egon-Petri and Arthur Schnabel. In Paris she studied composition under Nadia Boulanger (q.v.), Edgard Varese, Max Deutsch, and Darius Milhaud. She received a prize for composition for her *Poem Hebraique*. She was also awarded the Bela Bartok prize, Budapest and the Akum Publication prize for her *String quartet*. She has lived in Israel since 1929. PHOTOGRAPH.
Compositions
ORCHESTRA
Symphony (1935)
Symphony
Piano concerto with orchestra (1944)
Violin concerto
Dapim Miyoman suite (small orch)
Euphony (cham orch)
Introduction and scherzo (1964)
Meditation (1971) (Tel Aviv: Israeli Music)
Movement at the air (1983)
Suite for string orchestra (compiled from music for the Hebrew Theatre)
Trilogie (orch, wind inst and perc) (1983)
CHAMBER
Divertimento (wind qnt) (1954)
Woodwind quintet
String quartet (1948) (Bela Bartok prize) (1949)
Dialogue (vlc and pf)
Hora (vln and pf) (Salabert)
Sonata No. 1 (vln and pf) (1948)
Sonata No. 2 (vln and pf) (1954)
Trio (cl and pf) (1984)
Two pieces (vlc and pf) (1967) (Israeli Music)
PIANO
Ballade No. 3
Eleven postcards for children, educational piece (1955) (Israeli Music)
Fantasy in twelve movements
Five sketches
Mosaic (1972) (Cologne: Gering)
Pages from the diary (Tel Aviv: Merkaz Letarbut Ulechinuch)
Youth suite (New York: Mills Music)
VOCAL
Hodaja, cantata (solo, ch and orch) (1948)
Shirai lechem va-mayim, cantata (A. Shlonsky)
Five songs (Nelly Sachs) (vce and cham orch) (1966) (Israeli Music)
Al milet, song cycle (A. Shlonsky)
Eight songs in popular style (Merkaz Letarbut Ulechinuch)
Gluehende Raetsel, 5 songs (N. Sachs)
Images (vce and pf)
Let's sing, children's songs (Tel Aviv: Massada)
Poeme Hebraique (vce and pf) (1st prize, Women Composers' Competition, 1931)
Silhouetto (vce and perc)
Space and esprit, trio (vce, bsn and pf) (1961) (Israeli Music)
Three songs (vce and pf) (Merkaz Letarbut Ulechinuch)
THEATRE
Incidental music for the Habima and Ohel theatres
MISCELLANEOUS
Movement of the air
Ref. composer, 18, 139, 205, 379, 622

SHORE, Clare
American teacher and composer. b. Winston, Salem, NC, December 18, 1954. She received her B.A. (cum laude) from Wake Forest University where she studied under Annette LeSiege and Donald Hoirup, a M.Mus (composition) from the University of Colorado studying under Charles Eain and Cecil Effinger. She received a scholarship to attend the Juillard School of Music, where she studied under David Diamond and obtained her D.Mus, and where she is currently a teaching fellow. In 1981 she received the Irving Berlin Fellowship. Her works have been performed extensively throughout the United States.

Compositions
ORCHESTRA
Passacaglia (1978)
CHAMBER
Rondo (handbell ens) (1977)
Woodwind quintet (1978)
String quartet (1978)
Four for three (perc) (1977)
Sonata (cl and bsn) (1980)
Weltanschauung (bsn) (1976)
PIANO
Passacaglia (1977)
Prelude and variations (1980)
VOCAL
Inum coeli (mix-ch and cham orch)
July remembrances (S and cham orch) (1981)
Fire (mix-ch and pf) (1975)
Five songs (S and pf) (1976)
Lucy's lament (S, pf and perc) (1977)
Rock me gently, friend (S and hpcd)
SACRED
Mass to St. Michael (mix-ch and orch) (1979)
ELECTRONIC
Constancy (rec and tape) (1977)
Ref. composer, 622, 625

SHOTWELL, Phyllis
20th-century composer.
Composition
FILM MUSIC
California Split (1974)
Ref. 497

SHREVE, Susan Ellen
American choral director and composer. b. Detroit, November 24, 1952. She studied at Wayne State University, Detroit, earning a B.S. (music, 1973) and an M.A. She also studied at the Bordeaux Conservatory of Music in France. She worked in the music listening lab at Wayne State University from 1971 to 1973 and since that time has worked as an instrumental and vocal music teacher in Michigan schools. She was placed second out of 5000 applicants to receive an award for an original composition from the National Board of Mu Phi Epsilon in 1972. She also received a first class award for her leadership of a marching band in 1968. She is the director of a children's choir and assistant director of the St. Anastasian adult choir in Troy, MI. She served as president and vice-president of the Phi Kappa chapter of Mu Phi Epsilon. PHOTOGRAPH.
Compositions
ORCHESTRA
Piano concerto in G-Minor (1972)
CHAMBER
Brass quintet (1977)
Duos (hn) (1975)
Music (fl and pf) (1977)
Sonata (fl)
Sonata (sax)
Three pieces (hn) (1974)
Ref. composer, 142

SHRUDE, Marilyn
American teacher and composer. b. Chicago, IL, July 6, 1946. She completed her B.Mus. at Alverno College in 1969 and her M.Mus. at Northwestern University in 1972. Her composition teachers included Alan Stout, M. William Karlins and W. Mays. Her works have been performed throughout the United States and Europe. She is a recipient of many grants and awards. She teaches at Bowling Green State University in Ohio.
Compositions
ORCHESTRA
Notes to the unborn (sym orch) (1975) (ACA)
Psalms for David (1983) (ACA)
CHAMBER
Infinity (wind ens) (1981) (ACA)
Quartet for saxophones (1972) (Southern)
Masks (sax qrt) (1982)
Evolution V (sax qrt) (1976)
B.E.R.G. (2 hn) (1980) (ACA)
Music for soprano saxophone and piano (1974) (ACA)
Shadows and dawning (S-sax and pf) (1982) (ACA)
Enuma elish (org) (1980) (ACA)
Invocation, antiphons and psalms (1977) (ACA)
Four meditations: To a mother and her firstborn (1975) (ACA)
Arctic desert (1979) (ACA)

PIANO
   Six pieces (1972) (ACA)
   Solidarnosc (1982) (ACA)
MULTIMEDIA
   Drifing over a red place (cl, slides, echo and dancer) (1982) (ACA)
Ref. composer, 622, 625

SHUKAILO, Ludmila Fedorovna
20th-century Soviet composer.
Compositions
ORCHESTRA
   Concertino (vln, pf and str orch) (Kiev: Muzychna Ukraina, 1977)
CHAMBER
   Rhapsodies (vla and pf)
Ref. Otto Harrassowitz (Wiesbaden)

SHUPPE, Anna. See BENFEY-SCHUPPE, Anna

SHURTLEFF, Lynn Richard
American conductor and composer. b. Vallejo, CA, November 3, 1939. She studied at the Vienna Academy (B.A.), the Brigham Young University (M.A.), Indiana University and privately under Merrill Bradshaw (composition). In 1970 she won the conductor's competition at the Vienna Symposium. She is currently at the University of Santa Clara and a member of BMI.
Composition
CHAMBER
   Dialogues (cham orch)
   Charlie Brown suite
VOCAL
   Echoes from Hungry Mountain (mix-ch and perc) (Mark Foster) (1979)
SACRED
   Sing a new song to the Lord (ch)
   O be joyful
   Spectrum
Ref. 137, 468, 625

SHUTENKO, Taisiya Ivanovna
Soviet composer. b. Kharkov, October 5, 1905.
Ref. 94, 420

SHUTTLEWORTH, Anne-Marie
South African composer. b. Bloemfontein, January 5, 1961. She graduated from the University of the Witwatersrand with a B.Mus. in 1982.
Compositions
ORCHESTRA
   Kontaka (1986)
CHAMBER
   Three mood pictures (cl, pf and vlc) (1982)
   Three jazzettes (cl and pf) (1981)
VOCAL
   Conversations (vce, elec gtr and perc) (1982)
   Myth for the end of time (vce, trb, trp and rock band) (1986)
   Song-cycle (S, fl, hp and cl) (1981)
   Song-cycle (S and pf) (1982)
ELECTRONIC
   Music with a painting
Ref. composer

SICK, Anna (Anne-Laurie) (nee Manir)
German pianist and composer. b. Munich, July 10, 1805. She first studied the piano under Mozart's sister and thereafter in Vienna under Charles Czerny and under Foerster (harmony). She was invited to Stuttgart in the capacity of court pianist and as *Mistress of Piano* to the princess in the royal family. In 1834 she married M. Sick, assessor of the royal court in Stuttgart after which time she performed in public.
Compositions
PIANO
   Pastoral
   Three variations
VOCAL
   Songs
Ref. 26, 226, 276, 433

SIDDALL, Louise
American teacher and composer. b. Winston-Salem, NC; d. Sumter, SC, December 8, 1935. She composed choral works and organ pieces.
Ref. 347, 353

SIDORENKO, Tamara Stepanovna (Maliukova)
Soviet pianist, professor and composer. b. Krasnoye, February 15, 1919. She studied the piano at the Nikolayev Music School and composition at the Odessa Conservatory where she studied under S.D. Orfeyev and graduated in 1946. She then taught theoretical subjects and composition at the conservatory and became a professor in 1966. She held the position of head of the department of theory and composition at the Odessa Music School until 1970.
Compositions
ORCHESTRA
   Symphony No. 1 (1946)
   Symphony No. 2 (1950)
   Suite of ancient dances (1947)
   Overture: Bogdan Khmelnitzky (1954)
CHAMBER
   String quartet No. 1 (1945)
   String quartet No. 2, on Ukrainian themes (1952)
   Kolkhoz, collective farm work (str qrt) (1952)
   Pieces for viola and for piano and cello (1952)
PIANO
   Cycle piece in old style (1969)
   Preludes (1950)
   Sonatas (1967)
VOCAL
   Do zirok, cantata (1963)
   K. zvzdam vvys, cantata (V. Bobrov) (ch and orch) (1963)
   Lenin vsegda s nami, cantata (L. Barabanov) (ch and orch) (1969)
   Oda korabelnoi stolitse, cantata (E. Yanvarov) (ch and orch) (1970)
   Pamyati Pablo Nerudy, cantata (A. Voznesensky) (ch and orch) (1974)
   Lesnoi yantar, suite (V. Karpeko) (ch a-cap) (1949)
   Song of Moscow (S. Vasiliev) (ch a-cap) (1949)
   Tsvetushchaya Odessa, suite (L. Barabanov) (ch and pf) (1959)
   Four ballads (F. Garcia Lorca) (vce and pf)
   Numerous choruses (Shevchenko, Lesa Ukrainka, Nekrasov and other poets)
   Numerous romances and songs (Yesenin, Shevchenko, A. Tolstoy and others)
   Seven romances (Lesa Ukrainka) (vce and pf)
   Arrangements of Russian, Ukrainian, Polish and Czech folk songs
THEATRE
   Music for theatre and film
Ref. 21, 87, 330

SIEBER, Susanne
Pianist, recorder player, violinist, teacher and composer. b. Schneidemuehl, Germany, 1929 and resident of Canada since 1952. She studied the piano under Dr. Friedrich Brand and the violin under Wilhelm Wulf. She taught the Orff method of music at the Volkskindergarten in Braunschweig. She currently teaches the recorder and performs in Canada.
Compositions
VOCAL
   Four sketches (mix-ch and mix-ch)
Ref. 94

SIEFERT, Justina
17th-century German composer.
Compositions
VOCAL
   Da antworteten Laban und Bethuel (5 vces) (1645)
   Ich hab gewagt und zugesagt ehelich mit ihm zu leben (1645)
Ref. 128

SIEGRIED, Lillie Mahon
20th-century American composer. b. Buffalo, NY.
Compositions
VOCAL
   Songs incl.:
   The beautiful Land of Nod
   Lullabies
OPERETTA
   One operetta
Ref. 260, 347

SIEGMANN, Margaret Krimsky. See KRIMSKY, Katrina

SIEGMUND, Hermine
19th-century German composer.
Compositions
PIANO
Blaetter und Blueten, op. 1 (Breslau: Schuetz)
Leuchtende Sterne, gavotte, op. 2 (Becher: Hoffmann) (also orch) (Carisch)
Maienmorgen, idyll, op. 22 (Gleis)
Toujours fidele, march, op. 5 (also orch) (Becher)
Zingaresca, op. 10 (Becher; Carisch)
ZITHER
Alpengruesse, idyll, op. 6 (4 zithers)
In dulci jubilo, march (4 zithers) (Schuetz)
Je t'aime, gavotte, op. 7 (4 zithers)
Elly-Walzer, op. 8 (1, 2, 3 and 4 zithers)
Alpenlieder-Potpourri, op. 16 (2 or 3 zithers) (Ragotsky)
Im Walde, charakteristisches Tongemaelde (Ragotzky)
Inspiration, fantasie, op. 11
Resignation, valse mignon (Domkowsky)
Taendelei (Domkowsky)
Ref. 297

SIEGRIST, Beatrice (nee Houllier)
French organist, lecturer and composer. b. Paris, December 21, 1934. She studied at the Paris Conservatoire and at the Ecole Normale de Musique where she obtained first prize for counterpoint and fugue. She has been an organist in Paris for 19 years. She taught in several schools in Paris and Toulouse as well as teaching solfege at the Toulouse Conservatory. She gained an honorable mention for composition in the Prix de Rome.
Compositions
CHAMBER
Suite (4 trb)
Tarantelle (3 wind insts) (1963)
Variations on a chorale by Luther (wind insts) (1962)
Essai (2 perc) (1976)
Five pieces (trb and pf) (1974)
Three pieces (trp and pf) (1974)
Trucs in B-Flat (cl and pf) (1966) (Paris: Editions Françaises de Musique)
Two pieces (fl and pf) (1974)
VOCAL
Chorus for three equal voices (1977)
Soleils couchants (Verlaine) (1963)
Melodies (Paul Fort) (1962)
Ref. composer

SIEROVA, Mme. See SEROVA, Valentina Semyonovna

SIESLEY, Mme de. See COURMONT, Countess von

SIGAL, Mme.
French composer.
Composition
OPERA
A propos (Paris, 1906)
Ref. 431

SIKORA, Elzbieta
Polish composer. b. Lwow, October 20, 1943. She attended the Warsaw Academy of Music from 1963 to 1968 where she studied under Professor A. Karuzas and graduated with her M.A. She returned to study theory, composition and conducting at the same academy from 1972 to 1977 where her teachers included Zbigniew Rudzinski and Tadeusz Baird. In 1981 she studied computer music in Paris and music analysis and composition with Betsy Jolas (q.v.). She also studied computer music at Stanford, USA in 1983. She is the recipient of a number of awards and scholarships including a scholarship from the Groupe de Recherches Musicales. She made her debut as a composer in Warsaw in 1971. DISCOGRAPHY. PHOTOGRAPH.

Compositions
ORCHESTRA
First Symphony (1983)
Cercles (1975)
CHAMBER
String quartet (1975)
String quartet No. 2 (1980) (Ariadne Verlag)
...According to Pascal (trp, vlc and hpcd) (1976)
Il viaggio I (tba and pf)
Interludes (fl and hp) (1980)
Sands (fl and perc) (1980) (Ariadne)
Journey No. 3 (fl) (1981)
Eine Kleine Tagmusik (1983)
Piano prelude (1979)
Solo (vln) (1983)
VOCAL
Guernica – Hommage à Pablo Picasso (ch a-cap) (1975)
The creation of the World (vocal ens and cham orch) (1976)
Salve Regina (ch and org) (1981)
Heart brightening songs (S, fl and hpcd) (1983)
BALLET
Blow-up (magnetic tape) (1979)
OPERA
Ariadna, chamber opera (1977) (Cracow: PWM)
1968 (1983)
ELECTRONIC
First name (tape) (1970)
The head of Orpheus (tape) (1981)
In the night, face to heaven (tape) (1978)
Janek Wisniewski-December-Poland (tape) (1981)
Journey No. 1 (d-b and 2 tape recorders) (1974)
Journey No. 2 (tape) (1976)
Letters to M. (tape) (1980)
Rapsodie for the death of republic (tape) (1979)
Stress (perc and tape) (with Marta Ptaszynska q.v.)
Uncertainty of summer (tape) (1973)
The view from the window (tape) (1971)
Waste land (magnetic tape) (1979)
MULTIMEDIA
Behind his double (vce, inst ens and electronic sounds) (1983)
Intervention, music parable (2 perc, b-tba and small orch on tape) (1971)
Ref. composer, 199, 563, 622

SILBERTA, Rhea
American pianist, singer, teacher and composer. b. Pocahontas, VA, April 19, 1900; d. New York, December 6, 1959. She studied at the Ethical Culture School, at the Juilliard School of Music, and studied voice privately. She made her debut as a pianist when she was seven and has toured the United States as a singer. From 1922 to 1959 she taught singing.
Compositions
ORCHESTRA
Pieces
CHAMBER
Fantaisie ballade (pf)
VOCAL
The nightingale and the rose (narr, soli, ch and orch)
Songs incl.:
Lullaby for Judith
The message
Samson said
Wild geese
Yahrzeit
You shall have your red rose
Ref. 39, 40, 142, 347, 353, 622

SILESIAN NIGHTINGALE. See BABNIGG, Emma

SILNI, Max. See PAIGNE, Mme.

SILSBEE, Ann Loomis
American lecturer and composer. b. Cambridge, MA, July 21, 1930. She studied under Irving Fine at Radcliffe College (A.B., 1951) and graduated from Syracuse University (M.Mus.) in 1969 where she studied under Earl George. In 1978 she graduated with a D.M.A. from Cornell University having studied under Karel Husa. In 1964 she was a participant in the Ferienkurs fuer neue Musik in Darmstadt where her work River was performed. From 1970 to 1971 she was a member of the music faculty at the

State University College at Cortland, NY, and lecturer in music theory at Cornell University from 1971 to 1973. She studied in Paris from 1973 to 1974. She attended the Composers' Conference in Vermont and is the recipient of a number of fellowship awards and grants. She was one of the winners of the Burge-Eastman Prize and her works have been widely performed. She is on the boards of the ACA and the ILWC. DISCOGRAPHY.

Compositions

ORCHESTRA

Spirals (also str qrt; also pf) (1975)
Seven rituals (1977)
Trois historiettes (1974)

CHAMBER

Another river (4 solo vlc and 3 perc) (1975)
Quartet (cl, vln, vlc and pf) (1980)
Quest (str qrt) (1977) (ACA)
Go gentle (3 ww; also 3 strings) (1980)
Pathway (timp, perc and strings) (1979)
Spirals (pf and str qrt) (1975)
Pharos (vlc, pf and perc) (1977)
Three chants (fls) (1975)
Trialogue (vln, cl and pf) (1976) (ACA)
Expressions (cl or pf) (1969)
Gylphs (gtr and hpcd) (1979)
Journey (fl and perc) (1982)
Phantasy (ob and hpcd) (1973)
Runemusic (vlc) (1979)
Spirals

PIANO

Bagatelle (1963)
Corrai (prepared pf) (1980)
Doors (1976) (Burge-Eastman prize)
In and out the window (1984)
Letter from a field biologist (1979)

VOCAL

Pictures from Brueghel (S and mix-ch) (1982)
Dona nobis pacem (mix-ch) (1981)
Icarus (8 vces, rec and bongo drs) (1972)
De amore et morte (S or Cont and cham ens) (1978)
Scroll (S and cham ens) (1977) (ACA)
An acre for a bird, motet (1983)
Bourn (A.R. Ammons) (S, T, vlc and hpcd) (1974)
Diffraction (e.e. cummings) (S, fl, pf and 2 perc) (1974)
Huit chants en brun (Federico Garcia Lorca, trans into French by Andre Belamich) (1975)
Leavings (S, perc and prep pf) (1976)
Mirages (e.e. cummings) (B, vlc and quarter-tone hpcd) (1969)
Now (e.e. cummings) (1969)
Only the cold bare moon, song cycle (8 Chinese prose poems) (S, fl and pf) (1971)
Raft (narr and 5 perc) (A.R. Ammons) (1976) (ACA)

SACRED

A canticle (S, ob and hpcd) (1974) (after the Song of Solomon)
Hymn (A.R. Ammons) (S, ob and pf) (1968)

OPERA

The Nightingale's Apprentice, story opera

INCIDENTAL MUSIC

River (2 groups of players and opt dancers) (1974)

ELECTRONIC

Prometheus, a dramatic cantata (B, mix-ch, cham ens and tape) (1973)

MISCELLANEOUS

... and who so witnessed (comm Boston Musica Viva) (1984)
Ref. composer, 474, 563, 594, 622, 625

SILVA, Eloisa d'Herbil de

Cuban pianist and composer. b. 1842; d. Buenos Aires, 1944. She was the daughter of the Baron of Saint Thomas, Joseph d'Herbil, who was exiled to America after the French Revolution. She was a child prodigy and studied under Gottschalk. In 1870 she settled in Argentina, and performed in charity concerts. She lived to the age of 102.

Compositions

PIANO

A orillas del mar, waltz
Minuet con variaciones
Saltarello
Scherzo
Other pieces

VOCAL

Songs incl.:
La caridad
Remember
Serenata

Ref. 390

SILVER, Sheila Jane

American composer. b. Seattle, WA, October 3, 1946. She studied under Erhard Karkoschka in Stuttgart, Germany from 1969 to 1971, under Arthur Berger, Gyorgy Ligeti, Seymour Shifrin, Harold Shapero and Martin Boykan at Brandeis University from 1971 to 1974, and under Jacob Druckman at Tanglewood in 1972. In 1969 she received the Prix de Paris from the University of California, Berkeley and from 1972 to 1974 an Irving Fine Memorial fellowship from Brandeis University. In 1975 she received a prize for chamber music from GEDOK and also a Rome Prize fellowship. In 1978 and 1979 she received an award in musical composition from the American Academy, Rome. DISCOGRAPHY.

Compositions

ORCHESTRA

Galixidi (comm Seattle Philharmonic Orchestra) (1976)

CHAMBER

Passtense (12 insts) (1973)
Two string quartets (1975, 1983)
Ode to Julius (2 pf and perc) (1972)
Quarthym (a-rec) (1971)

VOCAL

Fantasy quasi theme and variations (mix-ch) (G. Schirmer) (1980)
Two songs on Elizabethan poems (mix-ch) (G. Schirmer) (1982)
Chariessa, cycle of 6 songs (Sappho) (S and pf; also S and orch) (1978)
Canto (Bar and cham ens)
Canto XXXIX of Ezra Pound (comm Berkshire Music Center) (1979)
Ek ong kar (1983)

Publications

Analysis of Webern Op. 11. Neue Methoden der Analyse Doering Verlag. 1976.
Pitch and Registral Distribution in Arthur Berger's Music for Piano. Perspectives of New Music, 1978.

Ref. 142, 403, 622, 625

SILVERBURG, Rose

20th-century American organist and composer. She was organist of the Holy Trinity Court in Shreveport.

Compositions

VOCAL

Springtime is love time

SACRED

Ave Maria
Sacred Memory

Ref. 448

SILVERMAN, Faye-Ellen

American pianist, teacher and composer. b. New York, October 2, 1947. She received her early training at Dalcroze School of Music and at the Manhattan Preparatory School of Music. At Mannes College she was a pupil of William Sydeman; she also studied at Barnard College under Otto Luening (B.A., hons, 1968) and under Leon Kirchner and Lukas Foss at Harvard University (M.A., composition, 1971). She then studied under Jack Beeson and Vladimir Ussachevsky at Columbia University (B.A., composition, 1974). She taught the piano, the clarinet and theory in various schools and privately between 1968 and 1972. From 1971 she taught in schools and colleges and since 1972 has been a teaching assistant at Columbia University and associate editor of *Current Musicology*. Her works have been peformed on radio and television. She was the recipient of a Regents Scholarship and teaching fellowships and won the Stokowski composition contest in 1961. Since 1980 she has been the piano soloist with the Brooklyn Philharmonia and is currently teaching graduate courses at the Peabody Institute of John Hopkins University. She is the acting director of the Peabody Electronic and Computer Music Center. DISCOGRAPHY. PHOTOGRAPH.

Compositions

ORCHESTRA

Shadings (1978) (New York: Seesaw Music)
Stirrings (cham orch)
Winds and sines (1981)

CHAMBER

No strings (fl, picc, ob, B-cl, bsn, a-sax, hn, trb, trp and perc) (1983)
Quantum quintet (brass qnt) (1983)
Windscape (ww qnt) (1977)
String quartet (1976)
Three by three (perc trio)
Yet for him (fl, vib and vlc) (1975)
Conversations (a-fl and cl) (1975)
Dialogue (hn and tba) (1976)
Speaking together (vln and pf) (1981)
Trysts (2 trp) (1982)
Memories (vla) (1974)
Oboe-sthenics (ob) (1980)
Settings (pf)
Speaking alone (fl)
Three movements for saxophone alone (1971)

VOCAL
Madness (narr and orch) (1972)
For showing truth (w-vces) (1972)
Echoes of Emily (A and cor anglais)
In the shadow (S, gtr and cl) (1972)
To Love? (bar and pf) (1980)
Volcanic songs (1984) (comm Baltimore Chamber Music Society)
OPERA
The Miracle of Nemirov, in 1 act (1974)
ELECTRONIC
K 1971 (male and female narr, T, B, w-ch, fl, cl, vla, vlc, c-bsn and electronic tape)
Layered lament (tape) (1982)
On four (1983)
Publications
Articles in *Current Musicology*.
Beethoven today would be exploring new form. Evening Sun, 1983.
Gesualdo: Misguided or Inspired Fall. 1973.
Report from New York City on Computer Arts Day.
Twentieth Century Section of the Schirmer History of Music. Schirmer Books; MacMillan, 1982.
Ref. composer, 141, 142, 185, 228, 301, 494, 563, 622, 625

SIMIC, Darinka
Yugoslav pianist, professor and composer. b. Belgrade, February 19, 1937. She studied the piano under Professor Emil Hajek and composition under Predrag Milosevic at the Music Academy in Belgrade, graduating in 1962. From 1962 to 1966 she was professor of piano at the music school Josip Slavenski. Since then she has been music editor with Radio Belgrade. Her compositions have been performed in many Yugoslav and Soviet cities as well as in Rome, Lausanne, Prague, Sofia and Bucharest. In 1964 she received the April 4th award of Federation of Students. PHOTOGRAPH.
Compositions
CHAMBER
Sonata (vln and pf) (1963 (UKS)
Igre, dances (bsn and pf)
Pieces
VOCAL
Gradinar, song cycles (m-S and pf) (Tagore) (1962)
Vrati mi moje Krpice, song cycle (Vasko Popa) (S, m-S, vln, fl, hp and vlc) (1964)
Ref. composer, 70, 145

SIMMONS, Kate
19th-century American composer.
Compositions
PIANO
Dances incl.:
Racquet galop
Ref. 276, 347, 433

SIMON, Cecile Paul
20th-century French composer. b. Paris.
Compositions
ORCHESTRA
Etude symphonique
Poème, symphonic poem
CHAMBER
Trio (pf, vln and vlc) (Durdilly)
Fantaisie-sonata (pf and vln) (Rouart, 1905)
Sonata (pf and vln) (Rouart, 1910)
Pieces for wind instruments
Piano and other pieces
VOCAL
Selection of melodies
THEATRE
L'aumone de Don Juan
La belle au bois dormant
Casanova
Fleur de pêche (L. Payen)
Marchand de regrets (Fernand Creronelink)
Ref. 41, 107, 226, 361

SIMON, Louise Marie. See ARRIEU, Claude

SIMONCELLI-PRINCIPE, Giulia
20th-century Italian composer. She married the composer Remy Principe.

Compositions
HARP
I burattini di Mangiafuoco
Leggenda
Meditazione
Omaggio a Rossini
Trittico
Ref. 228

SIMONE, Nina. See ADDENDUM

SIMONIAN, Nadezhda Simonovna
Soviet composer. b. Rostov-on-the-Don, February 26, 1922. In 1945 she graduated from the Leningrad Conservatory, where she studied the piano under G. Muchar and in 1950 received her diploma in composition. Her teacher was O. Chishko. She continued postgraduate studies under V. Pushkov and was awarded a medal.
Compositions
ORCHESTRA
Piano concerto (1953)
Poem-concerto (pf and orch) (1976)
CHAMBER
Sonata (vln and pf) (1948)
Pieces (pf) (1945-1950)
VOCAL
Ozero Sevan, cantata (I. Alterman) (1949)
Romances
Songs
THEATRE
Akh serdtse
Strekoza
Yuzhneve 38 paralleli
FILM MUSIC
The duel (1974)
The flying carpet (1956)
Green dale
The lady with the dog (1960)
The only one (1976)
INCIDENTAL MUSIC
Golden Apples, radio play
On the Bank of Sevan, radio play
Story of Turkey, radio play
Three Bears, radio play
The Year of my Birth, radio play
Music for circus
Ref. 87, 497

SIMONS, Lorena Cotts
American conductor, poetess, teacher and composer. b. Sherman, TX, January 16, 1897. She attended Kidd Key College from 1913 to 1914 and St. Joseph Academy in 1915. She then continued her studies at the American Conservatory and the Juilliard School of Music. In 1969 she attended St. Olav's Academy, Sweden (Mus.D.) hons. She was the organizer and director of the Schubert Violin Choir in Port Arthur from 1919 to 1955. She was named Poet Laureate of various districts and in 1969 her name was added to the International Poets' Hall of Fame.
Compositions
ORGAN
Meditation (1967)
VOCAL
Songs incl.:
Freedom's light (1963)
In search for growth (1963)
I was a donkey
I was a lamb
I was a star
Live expectantly (1962)
SACRED
What can I do for Jesus (1963)
Ref. 433, 475

SIMONS, Netty
American pianist, teacher and composer. b. New York, October 26, 1913. She received her early musical training at the Third Street Music School, Manhattan where she taught from 1928 to 1933. She taught the piano, theory and composition privately from 1928 to 1956. She was producer and performer of a weekly radio program of the piano and chamber music from 1931 to 1932. She began studies at New York University's School of Fine Arts in 1931. A one-year scholarship in 1933 enabled her to study the piano under Alexander Siloti at the Juilliard School of Music. From 1934 to 1937 she resumed her studies at New York University's

School of Fine Arts where her composition teachers included Marion Bauer (q.v.) and Percy Grainger. From 1938 to 1941 she became a private student of Stefan Wolpe. She was producer and co-ordinator of composer's concerts at Carnegie Recital Hall from 1960 to 1961; she was one of ten contemporary women composers in an American exhibition of the music division of the New York Public Library Composers Alliance from 1966 to 1971; producer and scriptwriter of a contemporary music program at the University of Michigan in 1971 and recipient of a recording-publication award from the Ford Foundation in 1971. Her works have been performed in the United States, Europe, Japan and Australia and on such new music series as Monday Evening Concerts, Los Angeles; at the Museum of Contemporary Art, Chicago, at Town Hall and the Carnegie Recital Hall, New York; at the Centre Culturel Americain and the Theatre de la Cite Internationale, Paris; and at Osaka Geijutsu Centre, Japan. DISCOGRAPHY. PHOTOGRAPH.

Compositions
ORCHESTRA
Illuminations in space (vla and orch) (comm Karen Phillips) (1972) (Merion Music; Theodore Presser)
Big Sur (1984)
Lamentations No. 1 (1961) (Merion; Theodore Presser)
Lamentations No. 2 (1966) (Merion)
Piece for orchestra (1949) (Merion)
Scipio's dream (1968) (ACA)
Variables (1967) (ACA)
BAND
A journey sometimes delayed (1977) (Merion)
Summer's outing (1977) (Merion)
CHAMBER
Piece for percussion and ensemble (12 players) (1978) (comm Jan Williams)
Time groups No. 2 (cl, hn, bsn, 2 vln, vla, vlc, c-bsn) (1964) (Merion)
Quintet (winds and str bass) (New York: Pioneer Editions, 1953)
Variables (inst ens, any 5 insts or multiples of 5; also orch) (Merion)
Cityscape (sax, B-cl, mar and vib) (1984) (comm Duo Contemporain, Holland)
Facets 4 (str qrt) (Merion)
Quartet for flute and strings (1951) (ACA)
String quartet (1950) (ACA)
Design groups for percussion, graphic score (1-3 players, vib, xyl and perc) (Merion)
Facets 1 (hn, vln and pf) (1961) (ACA)
Facets 2 (fl or picc, cl and c-bsn) (1961) (Merion)
Facets 3 (ob or vla and pf) (1962) (ACA)
The great stream silent moves (pf, hp and prc) (1973)
Design groups No. 2 (duo for any combination of a high and a low-pitched inst) (1958) (Merion)
Duo (vln and vlc) (1939) (ACA)
Sonata (2 vln) (1954) (ACA)
Wild tales told on the river road (cl and perc) (1966) (Merion)
Design groups No. 1 (perc)
PIANO
Illuminations, aleatoric (2 pf) (1970) (ACA)
Two dot, graphic score (2 pf) (1970)
Four little pieces (1953) (ACA)
Night sounds (1953) (Merion)
Piano work (1952) (ACA)
Time groups No. 1 (1963) (ACA)
Windfall, aleatoric (1965) (ACA)
VOCAL
Pied Piper of Hamelin (Browning) (narr, fl, pf and str orch) (1955) (Merion Music)
Diverse settings (S and cham) (ACA)
She's down the road by Miss Winnie (narr, perc solo and perc ens)
Set of poems for children (J. Stephens, R.L. Stevenson, C. Sandburg, C. Rossetti) (narr, fl, ob, cl, bsn, vln, vla, vlc and c-bsn) (Merion)
Songs for Jenny (vce, pf and str bass) (1975) (Merion)
Songs for Wendy (Keats, Blake, Rosetti) (vce and vla) (1976) (Merion)
Three songs (H. Morley) (m-S and pf) (ACA)
Trialogues I (Dylan Thomas) (m-S or A, Bar and vla) (1963) (Merion)
Trialogues II (Dylan Thomas) (M-S or A, Bar and vla) (1968) (Merion)
Trialogues III (Dylan Thomas) (m-S or A, Bar and vla) (1973) (ACA)
SACRED
For all blasphemers (S.V. Benet) (m-ch a-cap) (1951) (ACA)
Sing, O Daughter of Zion (Bible, Zephaniah) (A, T, Bar and mix-ch a-cap) (ACA) (1960)
OPERA
Bell Witch of Tennessee, American folktale (J. Simon) (1956) (Merion)
MULTIMEDIA
Buckeye has wings, theatre piece, graphic score (any number of players, opt dancer and slides) (comm Ken Dorn) (1971) (Merion)
Circle of attitudes (vln and opt dancer) (1960) (ACA)
Design groups 1, graphic score (1-3 perc) (Ford Foundation award) (Merion)
Design groups 2, graphic score (duo for any combination of a high and a low-pitched inst) (Ford Foundation award) (Merion)

Gate of the hundred sorrows, dance suite (pf and opt dancer) (1963)
Puddintame (limericks), graphic score (narr and players) (color coded) (1972) (ACA)
The sea darkens, theatre piece, graphic score (any number of players) (color coded) (Merion)
Silver thaw, graphic score (1-8 players) (1969) (Ford Foundation award) (Merion)
This slowly drifting cloud, theatre piece, graphic score (1977) (Merion)
Too late - the bridge is closed, theatre piece, graphic score (also ballet) (one to any number of players) (color coded) (1972) (Merion)
Publications
Contributions to Cage, J. *Notations.*
Gallery of Living Composers: *Composers of the Americas.*
Landsman, J. *Anthology of American Violin Music.*
Bibliography
BMI. The Many Worlds of Music. Issue 4, 1977.
Ref. composer, 17, 40, 52, 77, 80, 84, 94, 142, 146, 185, 189, 190, 347, 371, 397, 415, 622, 625

SIMONS, Virginia Mary
20th-century American composer. She obtained her Ph.D. from the University of Utah in 1973.
Composition
MISCELLANEOUS
GheGhetto
Ref. University of Utah, Ph.D. dissertation

SIMONS-CANDEILLE, Amelie or Emilie. See CANDEILLE, Amelie

SIMPSON, Mary Jean
American concert flautist, assistant professor and composer. b. Bryan, TX, January 31, 1941. She gained her B.S. (music) from the Juilliard School of Music in 1965, M.Mus. from the University of Texas in 1968 and D.M.A. from the University of Maryland in 1982. She was flautist for several major orchestras; lectured in music at the Centenary College for two years; was assistant professor of music, University of Montana for nine years and a private teacher and freelance flautist.
Composition
VOCAL
Reflections (m-S and fl)
Publications
Musical Instruments in the Dayton C. Miller Flute Collection at the Library of Congress, 1984. Co-author vols 2 and 3.
Alfred G. Badger (1815-1892), Nineteenth-Century Flutemaker: His art, innovation and influence. Doctoral dissertation, 1982.
Ref. 643

SINDE RAMALLAL, Clara
Argentine teacher, guitarist and composer. b. Buenos Aires, December 28, 1935. She took advanced studies in composition, voice and the guitar which she studied under Consuelo Mallo Lopez. She made her guitar debut in 1945 and her voice debut in Salta-Argentine in 1952. She toured as a soloist in the major cities of Argentina, Chile, Equador, Peru, Colombia, Uruguay and Venezuela; she has given performances in concert halls and for musical societies and recordings and broadcasts in Caracas and major Argentinian cities. She has premiered works by composers A. Galluzzo, Bianchi Pinero and E. Calcagno; she toured South America as a member of the Sinde Ramallal Trio, with Silvia Molinari and Gloria Boschi, (both her students), and appeared on radio and TV in 1971. She teaches advanced guitar privately and in national music schools. She is a recipient of prizes and awards, including the honorary diploma of the Argentine Association for Chamber Music in 1953.
Compositions
GUITAR
Barmi aire de milonga (Argentina: Ricordi, 1975)
Prelude No. 1 (Ricordi, 1973)
ARRANGEMENTS
Allegro, op. 100, (M. Giuliani) (1977)
Concierto en Re (3 gtr) (Vivaldi) (1973)
Estudio en Mi menor by Sor (1975)
Prelude No. 1 (Bach) (1976)
Rondo No. 2 (M. Carcassi) (1977)
Sonata-gavota (D. Scarlatti) (Ricordi, 1972)
Ref. composer, 206

SINGER, Jeanne

American pianist, teacher and composer. b. New York, August 4, 1924. She received her B.A. (music) magna cum laude from Barnard College, Columbia University in 1944. She studied the piano for 15 years under Nadia Reisenberg. She is an active concert pianist, having performed as a soloist and with chamber music ensembles for over 30 years. She also made appearances on the radio and TV where she included many of her own works. In 1955 she was awarded an artist's diploma from the National Guild of Piano Teachers plus two first rating gold medals in their international piano recording festival. She formed the Long Island Trio in 1969 for which she composed seven trios. At present she is working with several contemporary poets on musical settings of their poetry. She received eight awards for composition, including prizes from Composers, Authors, Artists of America, from 1971 to 1975; from the National League of American Pen Women she received 12 first prizes and seven second prizes between 1974 and 1976. She was recently awarded an honorary doctorate in music from the World University. PHOTOGRAPH.

Compositions

CHAMBER

Grandmother's attic (fl, ob, vln and vlc) (1982) (L'Amore di Musica) (1982)

Dream stirrings, trio (vln, cl and pf) (1974)

From the green mountains, trio (vln, cl and pf) (1974) (Harold Branch)

Rhapsody: Trio (vln, cl and pf) (1970)

Sweet Stacy suite, trio (vln, cl and pf) (1970) (national award) (West Babylon, NY: H. Branch, 1977)

Then and now (theme and variations), trio (1971) (national award)

Dialogue for violin and piano (1972)

Legend No. 1 (fl or vln and pf) (1978)

Nocturne (cl and pf) (1972) (National League of American Pen Women, national award) (Massapequa, NY: Cor Pub.)

Romance (vln and pf)

Suite for horn and harp (1979) (Cor)

Arietta (gtr) (1973)

Suite for harpsichord (or Pianoforte) (also suite in harpsichord style for pianoforte or harpsichord) (national award) (Branch, 1976)

PIANO

American short subjects (2 pf) (1962)

Four pieces for piano: Baroque frolic; Etude; Remembrance; Toccatina (also as six pieces for piano) (National League of American Pen Women, national award)

Introduction and caprice (1972) (National League of American Pen Women, national award)

Ricky's rondo (1972) (national award)

VOCAL

Ballad of changing times (m-ch and pf) (1983)

Choral art (w-ch and pf) (1979)

Come greet the spring (w-ch and pf) (1979) (1st prize, Composer's Guild National Competition) (Plymouth Music)

Composer's prayer (O.P. Stewart) (w-ch and pf) (1977)

Madrigal (mix-ch a-cap) (1977)

The seaman's wife (m-ch and S) (1978)

All beauty brings you close (S and pf) (1972) (national award)

American Indian song suite, traditional (S or m-S and pf) (Branch, 1977)

Arno is deep (F. Blankner) (m-S or Bar and pf) (1st prize, Art Songs)

Banquet (S and hn) (1977)

The bargain (vce and pf) (1983)

Betrothal (vce and pf) (1983)

A cycle of love, 4 art songs (1975) (Branch, 1976)

Dirge (M. Mason) (Bar or m-S and pf) (1972)

Downing the bell tower (S. Dale) (m-S or Bar and pf) (1974)

Elegy (vce and pf) (1983)

Five galgenlieder (vce and pf) (1982)

Four songs of reverence (vce and pf) (1981) (1st prize, Composer's Guild)

From Petrarch (m-S, hn and pf; also m-S, cl and pf) (Cor)

Gift (P. Benton) (S and pf) (1977)

Hannah (L. Schwartz) (m-S or vce and pf)

Harvest (vce and pf) (1983)

I would sing now (vce and pf) (1983)

Intelligencia (vce and pf) (1979)

Lament (S and pf) (1971) (national award)

Memento (vce and pf) (1982)

Memoria (F. Blankner) (1st prize, Art Songs, New York Poetry Forum, 1977)

Of time lost (vce and pf) (1983)

The old wild woman (vce and pf) (1983)

Pantoum (vce and pf) (1981) (M. Buonecote)

Reverie (vce and pf) (1983)

The salt cathedral (T, vln and pf) (1979) (1st prize, Composers, Authors and Artists of America)

Sanguinaria (B. Grebanier) (m-S or Bar and pf) (National League of American Pen Women, national award)

Sonnet (Benton) (S or m-S, vln and B-flat cl or vla) (1972)

Summons (Benton) (Bar or m-S and pf) (Branch, 1975)

To stir a dream (S, cl obl and pf)

Where do the wild birds fly (S or m-S or Bar and pf)

Winter identity, duet (2 S and pf)

SACRED

Ave Maria (mix-ch)

Carol of the bells (w-ch and pf) (1974)

For the night of Christmas (B. Grebanier) (w-vces and opt pf) (1972)

Go in peace (m-ch and T) (prize, 1982 Composer's Guild contest)

Mary's Boy (mix-ch, pf or org) (1981)

MISCELLANEOUS

A decade

Suite

ARRANGEMENTS

Arrangements of Bach, Debussy, Gershwin and Stoessel

Bibliography

Jeanne Singer wins four awards at convention. The Manhasset Mail. Manhasset, NY, April 11, 1974.

LI Trio Presents Program. Long Island Press, October 29, 1972. *M'set Musician Wins Four Awards.* Manhasset Press. April 18, 1974. *Premiere to Open Music Season.* The Manhasset Mail. Manhasset, NY, October 26, 1972.

Ref. composer, 206, 228, 359, 457, 474, 475, 622, 625

SIRIN

Persian songstress at the court of Bahram III, Sassanid King, ca. 293. Ref. 305

SIRMEN (Syrmen), Maddalena Laura di (nee Lombardini)

Italian harpsichordist, violinist, singer and composer. b. Venice ca. 1735; d. Venice ca. 1800. She studied voice at the Conservatorio dell'Ospedaletto dei Mendicanti in Venice and the violin under G. Tartini in Venice and under Padua, becoming his favorite pupil. She concert-toured Italy from 1760 to 1768 and gained such popularity that she was considered a worthy rival of the famous violinist Nardini. In 1768 she performed her own works at the *Concerts Spirituels* in Paris and appeared in London in 1771 and 1772 as a harpsichordist and in 1774 as a singer. She sang at the Court of Saxony, Dresden in 1782 and reappeared as a violinist in Paris in 1785. She married the German violinist and composer Ludwig Sirmen.

Compositions

CHAMBER

Six concertos for violin and instruments (Amsterdam: Hummel)

Concerto a violino obbligato, in Si b con orchestra

Six concertos for the harpsichord or pianoforte, op. 3 (adapted for the hpcd by S. Giordani) with accompaniments (London: W. Napier, 1773; Longman & Broderip, ca. 1785)

Quartetto in Si b (2 vln, vla and vlc)

Six string quartets (Paris: Breault, 1769)

Six trios à deux violons et violoncello oblige, op. 1 (Hummel; London: Welcker & Genaud, 1770)

Terzetto in Re, trio

Terzetto in Sol, trio

Six concertanti for two violins, ops. 2 and 3 (Hummel)

Six sonatas, op. 4 (2 vln) (Hummel, 1770)

Six duos pour violon (W. Napier, 1773)

Bibliography

Bouvet, C. *Une Leçon de G. Tartini et une femme violiniste au XVIII siècle* Lombardini M. Paris: P. Senart, 1915.

Brenet, M. *Les concerts en France sous L'Ancien Régime.* Paris, 1900. Lombardini M. *Madame Syrmen.*

Ref. 2, 7, 12, 13, 26, 41, 65, 70, 74, 85, 102, 105, 119, 123, 128, 129, 155, 177, 216, 226, 260, 276, 347, 405, 653

SIROONI, Alice

20th-century American pianist, teacher and composer. She obtained a postgraduate diploma from the Juilliard School of Music. She made her debut at Town Hall in New York and toured in concert and gave radio performances in the United States.

Compositions

PIANO

Prelude in E-Minor

Rondo in E-Flat Major

Ref. 77

SISTEK-DJORDJEVIC, Mirjana

Yugoslav professor and composer. b. Belgrade, 1935. She completed her studies at the Music Academy under Professor Stanojlo Rajcic. She is professor of harmony and counterpoint at the Mokranjac Music School in Belgrade. PHOTOGRAPH.

Compositions
ORCHESTRA
Symphony in one movement (1972)
Piano concerto (1969)
CHAMBER
String quartet (1962)
Piano trio
Theme with six variations (2 cl) (1966)
Three sketches (vln and pf) (1971)
Study (fl) (1973)
PIANO
Klavirska suita (1957)
Sonata (1958)
Suites (1970)
Variations (1960)
VOCAL
Trazim Pomilovanje, poem (reciter, w-ch and orch)
Mrazova Sestrica (mix-ch) (1957)
Ref. composer

SISTER Johane d'Arcie. See DECARIE, Reine

SISTER Mary Ann Joyce. See BERNARDONE, Anka

SISTER Mary Gabriel. See O'SHEA, Mary Ellen

SIU JUNN. See WONG, Betty Ann

SIVRAI, Jules de. See ROECKEL, Jane

SKABO, Signe-Lund. See LUND, Signe

SKAGGS, Hazel Ghazarian
American pianist, authoress, music psychologist, teacher and composer. b. Boston, MA, August 26, 1924. She obtained a diploma in pedagogy from the New England Conservatory, Boston in 1942. She received a B.A. in 1969 and an M.A. from Fairleigh Dickinson University, New Jersey in 1971 and an artist diploma from the American College of Musicians. She also attended Northeastern College and the Universities of Colorado, Wisconsin and Minnesota. As a private piano student she studied under Ernst Levy, Goding, Madame Gladys Ondricek in Boston, and Dr. Clarence Adler in New York from 1942 to 1950. She taught in schools in Boston, the Catskills, and in New Jersey from 1950 to 1961 and held piano classes in adult education schools from 1960 to 1970. From 1961 she worked as a group piano specialist. From 1956 to 1969 she toured the United States as adjudicator for the National Guild of Piano Teachers. She appeared in concerts and on radio as composer-pianist. She is a member of ASCAP.
Compositions
CHAMBER
Basketball
Impressions of snow
Petite ballerina
Polka dot clown
Spring showers
PIANO
Humoresques
Prelude and fugue
Sonata
Many recital pieces
VOCAL
Songs for soprano
MISCELLANEOUS
Little girl from Mars
Publications
Thumbs Under. Technical work.
Contributions to several music journals incl.: *Ararat, Clavier, Etude, Keyboard,* and *Piano Quarterly.*
Ref. composer, 39, 40, 84, 206, 347

SKALSKA-SZEMIOTH, Hanna Wanda
Polish editor, teacher and composer. b. Warsaw, April 29, 1921; d. Warsaw, April 10, 1964. She studied composition under K. Sikorski at the State Music College in Lodz and received her diploma in 1953. She was a music editor with the Polish Radio from 1953 to 1955 and then taught at the Frederic Chopin Music School until 1958. She was chief editor of the journal *Praca Swietlicowa.* PHOTOGRAPH.
Compositions
ORCHESTRA
Czerwona rapsodia (small sym orch; also club-room band) (1950)
CHAMBER
String quartet (1948)
Variations on a folk theme (cl and pf) (1949)
PIANO
Epigrams, miniatures (1944)
Fraszki, miniatures (1944)
Inventions (1948)
Variations (1947)
VOCAL
Ballada o Krakowiance (mix-ch a-cap) (1945)
Songs (vce and pf) (1941-1944)
BALLET
Piosenka, ballet music (small sym orch) (1945)
INCIDENTAL MUSIC
Light music (1955-1958)
Ref. 118

SKARECKY, Jana Milena
Canadian horn player, organist, pianist, teacher and composer. b. Prague, Czechoslovakia, November 11, 1957. She moved to Canada in 1968 and became a citizen in 1973. She graduated from Wilfrid Laurier University, Ontario, with a B.Mus. in 1980, where her teachers included H. Barrie Cabena (composition), Erhard Schlenker (piano), Felix Acevedo (horn), and J. Nixon, McMillan and Jan Overduin (organ). She teaches composition and the piano and is assistant to the director of music at the First United Church in Waterloo.
Compositions
ORCHESTRA
Fanfare (12 trp, org and orch) (1982) (Ontario: Jana Skarecky)
BAND
Processional (1978) (Skarecky)
CHAMBER
Brass quintet (2 trp, hn and 2 tbn) (1983) (Skarecky)
Prelude and fugue (ww-qnt) (1980) (Skarecky)
Music for tower bells (bells) (1982) (Skarecky)
ORGAN
Fantasy on Aurelia (org) (1980) (Skarecky)
Wedding processional (org) (1980) (Skarecky)
VOCAL
Requiem (mix-ch) (1983) (Skarecky)
Arise my love (S, picc and org) (1980) (Skarecky)
Drink to me only with thine eyes (vce and pf) (1982) (Skarecky)
The lonely land (S, ob and pf) (1978) (Skarecky)
SACRED
Gloria, cantata (S, Bar, T, mix-ch, org and brass qrt) (1980) (Skarecky)
Arise, shine (mix-ch) (1977) (Skarecky)
Be to me now my life (mix-ch, brass qrt and org) (1979) (Skarecky)
Bethlehem lullaby (ch, pf and org) (1980) (Music Plus)
Communion motet (mix-ch) (1979) (Skarecky)
Easter (S, Bar, mix-ch and org) (1979) (Skarecky)
Four Czech Christmas carols (mix-ch) (1977) (Music Plus)
Golden mornings (mix-ch and org) (1979) (Skarecky)
In celebration (mix-ch) (1982) (Music Plus)
I sing as I arise today (mix-ch) (1980) (Skarecky)
Jacob's ladder (mix-ch and fl) (1979) (Skarecky)
Love is come again (mix-ch) (1979) (Ontaria)
Magnificat and Nunc dimittis (mix-ch) (1979) (Skarecky)
Mass in the Lydian mode (mix-ch) (1979) (Skarecky)
O come let us sing (ch and pf) (1980) (Skarecky)
Psalm 8 (mix-ch and org) (1981) (Music Plus)
The secret flower (S and mix-ch) (1981) (Music Plus)
Et incarnatus est (Bar, hn and pf) (1981) (Skarecky)
The prayer of St. Francis (Cont, pf and org) (1980) (Skarecky)
ELECTRONIC
City of a hundred towers (tape) (1979) (Skarecky)
The singer (fl, cl, vlc and tape) (Skarecky)
Ref. composer

SKEENS, Gwendolyn
20th-century American composer.
Composition
OPERA
The Prince and the Pauper (1974)
Ref. 519

SKELTON, Nellie Bangs

American pianist and composer. b. Lacon, IL, August 15, 1859. She was a pupil of Rice and Mme. de Roode. She composed songs, a gavotte and pieces for the piano.
Ref. 226, 276, 433

SKELTON, Violet. See DUNLOP, Isobel

SKINNER, Fannie Lovering

19th-century American singer, teacher and composer. She studied under Mme. Rudersdorf.
Compositions
VOCAL
Songs incl.:
Gypsy
Rapture
Rose
Spring
Ref. 226, 433

SKINNER, Florence Marian (Mrs. Stuart Stresa) (Mme. Stewart)

19th-century English composer who lived in Italy for many years. Her operas were performed in Naples, San Remo and Turin.
Compositions
OPERA
Maria Regina di Scozia (1883)
Suocera (1877)
Ref. 6, 26, 226, 276, 307, 433

SKOLFIELD, Alice Jones Tewksbury

American organist, pianist, choral conductor and composer. b. Paris, May 1, 1944; d. November 11, 1932. She studied the piano and the organ under W. Emminger and Herman Kotzschmar and voice under W. Dennett and W. Davis. She was the organist and choral conductor at various churches.
Compositions
SACRED
Requiem Mass, service music
Many hymn tunes
Ref. 374

SKORIK, Irene

20th-century French composer.
Composition
PIANO
Musiques pour la leçon de danse
Ref. MLA *Notes*

SKOUEN, Synne

Norwegian critic, editor and composer. b. 1950. She studied composition under Professor Alfred Uhl and Dieter Kaufmann, at the Music Academy in Vienna from 1969 to 1973. She continued her studies under Professor Finn Mortensen at the Norwegian State Academy of Music, receiving a diploma in composition in 1976. She is editor of *Ballade*, a periodical for contemporary music. DISCOGRAPHY. PHOTOGRAPH.
Compositions
ORCHESTRA
Tombeau to Minona
PIANO
Hail Domitila!
THEATRE
What did Schopenhauer say (actor and cham ens)
BALLET
Evergreen, for television
FILM MUSIC
The Guardian
Ref. NWI

SKOVGAARD, Irene

20th-century Danish composer.
Compositions
SACRED
Tolv Juleviser (with Werner W. Glaser) (1945)
Ref. 331

SKOWRONSKA, Janina

Polish composer. b. Germakowka, USSR, February 8, 1920. She studied in Wroclaw (Breslau) at the pedagogical and conducting faculties of the State Music College. She studied composition under T. Szeligowski at the State Music College and received her diploma in 1961.
Compositions
ORCHESTRA
Symphony (1961)
CHAMBER
Theme and variations (str qrt) (1956)
PIANO
Preludes (1965)
Rondo (1957)
Waltz (1958)
VOCAL
Od Krakowa do Wroclawia, suite of folk dances (ch and orch) (A. Waligorski) (1955)
Moda pani czepca nie ma, folk song (mix-ch a-cap) (1964)
O wy corne kawki, folk song (mix-ch a-cap) (1965)
Pokoju czas (R. Heniszowa) (mix-ch a-cap) (1969)
Samotne drzewa (L. Turkowski) (mix-ch a-cap) (1969)
Ziemio moja (mix-ch a-cap) (1959)
Parodie (W. Marianowicz) (spoken vces, Bar and S, bsn and str orch) (1962)
Drugi brzeg (S, ob, 2 cl and hn) (1964)
Tu bedziemy (A. Burcla) (vce and pf) (1970)
Two folk songs (S and pf) (1956)
Arrangements of folk songs
THEATRE
Pieces
Ref. V. Pigla (Warsaw)

SLAUGHTER, Marjorie

English composer. b. London 1888. Her operettas were performed in London.
Compositions
OPERETTA
Als es noch kuehne Ritter gab (1907)
Der hoelzerne Schuh (1906)
Ref. 431

SLAVKOVSKA, Johanna. See KRALIKOVA, Johana

SLAVYANSKAYA, Olga Khristoforovna Agreneva

19th-century Russian composer.
Composition
VOCAL
Songs (ch; also vce)
Ref. 123

SLEETH, Natalie

American organist and composer. b. Evanston, IL, October 29, 1930. She studied under Hubert Lamb at Wellesley College graduating with her B.A. in 1952. She studied the organ under Lloyd Pfautsch at the Southern Methodist University in 1969 and at the Northwestern University. She was church organist in Glencoe, IL, from 1952 to 1954 and church music secretary from 1968 at the Highland Park Methodist Church, Dallas.
Compositions
VOCAL
Christmas is a feeling (unison ch or duo, pf and opt fl; also S, pf and opt fl) (Chapel Hill: Hinshaw Music, 1975)
Down the road (mix-ch and pf; also duo and pf) (Hinshaw, 1975)
Fa la la fantaisie (mix-ch, opt pf and d-b) (New York: C. Fischer, 1972)
Halleluyah day (mix-ch and pf) (Fischer, 1971)
Joy in the morning (mix-ch, brass qrt and opt org or pf) (Carol Stream: Hope, 1976)
Little by little (m-ch, w-ch and pf) (Hinshaw, 1975)
This land of ours (mix-ch or choral duo, perc, 2 pfs and opt 2 trp; also mix-ch and symphonic band) (Fischer, 1975)
Weekday songbook (choral unison and duo and pf) (Hinshaw, 1977)
Spread joy (3 vces, pf and opt trp) (Fischer, 1972)
SACRED
Amen, so be it (duo, org or pf and opt d-b) (Fischer, 1973)
Blessing (unison vces, hp or org or pf and opt fl) (Dallas: Choristers Guild, 1974)
Christmas festival (ch)
Feed my lambs (choral unison, 2 fl, hp or org or pf) (Fischer, 1972)

Jazz gloria (mix-ch, 3 trps, d-b, bongo drums, pf and opt gtr) (Fischer, 1970)

Lord Jesus, be near me (solo S or choral unison, hp or org or pf and opt cl or vlc) (Fischer, 1975)

Noël, Noël, a boy is born (duo or unison vces, hp or org or pf and opt handbells) (Minneapolis: Art Masters Studio, 1973)

Thy church, O God (unison vces with descant, hps or org or pf) (Nashville: Broadman Press, 1970)

Were you there on that Christmas night? (duo and org or pf) (Hope, 1976)

Long time ago

Other pieces

Ref. 142, 147, 228

SLEIGH, Mrs.

19th-century English composer.

Composition

VOCAL

Come buy my sweet flowers, ballad (London: Broderip & Wilkinson, 1800)

Ref. 65

SLENCZYNSKA, Ruth

American pianist, professor, writer and composer. b. Sacramento, CA, January 15, 1925. She studied at the University of California, Berkeley and the piano under Egon Petri, Arthur Schnabel, Alfred Cortot, Sergei Rachmaninoff, Nadia Boulanger (q.v.) and composition under Dendelot. She made her first appearance at the age of four in Oakland and performed in Berlin and Paris when she was six and seven. She made her debut in New York in 1933 and then gave concerts in Europe and America. She was professor of music at the College of Our Lady of Mercy, Burlingame, CA, from 1948 to 1952 and professor of the piano at the Southern Illinois University in Edwardville.

Compositions

PIANO

Cadenzas for Beethoven's Piano concertos Nos. 1 and 3

Small piano works

Publications

Forbidden Childhood. With L. Biancolli. New York and London, 1961.

Music at your Fingertips: Aspects of Pianoforte Technique. With A.M. Lingg, New York and London, 1961.

Ref. 14, 17, 77, 84, 455

SLENDZINSKA, Julitta

Russian harpsichordist, pianist, teacher and composer. b. Wilna, July 31, 1927. She obtained her M.A. from the State Conservatory in Warsaw and her piano virtuoso diploma in 1958. She studied under Harry Neuhaus at the Moscow Conservatory and the harpsichord under M. Trombini-Kazuro. In 1974 she received a diploma of merit in the harpsichord master course at the Academy of Chigiana, Siena, Italy. She toured extensively throughout Europe, China, Cuba and Korea.

Compositions

PIANO

Etudes de concert

Ref. 457

SLIANOVA-MIZANDARI, Dagmara Levanovna

Soviet pianist, teacher and composer. b. Kutais, December 28, 1910. She began studying the piano at the age of 12 and in 1933 graduated from the Tiflis Conservatory where she studied the piano under A. Tulashvili. In 1935 after studying under M. Bagrinovsky and I. Tuskia, she received her diploma in composition. She continued with postgraduate studies under I. Tuskia, B. Arapov, and P. Ryazanov. From 1932 she taught theoretical subjects at the conservatory and after 1938 at the music school. She wrote articles on music teaching and was co-author with O.I. Baramishvili of a book of solfege using Georgian themes. She received two medals.

Compositions

ORCHESTRA

Piano concerto (1938)

Children's suite (1934)

Heroic poem (1935)

CHAMBER

Quintet (vln, cl, vlc, fl and bsn) (1936)

Quartet for string and wind instruments, in 3 mvts

Page of the album (cl and pf) (1931)

PIANO

Five children's pieces (1935)

Nocturne (1937)

Six preludes and fugues (1931)

Sonata (1944)

Sonatas, in 3 mvts

Three preludes (1937)

VOCAL

Domik v gori, ballad (vce and orch)

Vozhdiu, ballad (vce and orch)

Numerous revolutionary songs (vce and pf)

Romances and songs incl.:

Elegiya (A. Pushkin) (1936)

Poslaniye v Sibir (A. Pushkin) (1937)

Tucha (A. Pushkin) (1936)

Ref. 87, 458

SLOMAN, Jane

19th-century American composer.

Compositions

PIANO

The Ericsson Schottische (New York: W. Hall, 1853)

VOCAL

Roll on silver moon (S, mix-ch and pf) (New York: Firth, Pond, 1848)

Forget thee? (vce and pf) (Boston: W.H. Oakes, 1843)

Queen of the night (vce and pf) (Boston: White-Smith, 1873)

So far away (W. Hall, 1869)

Ref. 228

SMART, Harriet Anne (Mrs. Callow)

English composer. b. London, October 20, 1817; d. London, June 30, 1883. Her brother was Henry Thomas Smart, organist and composer. She composed songs, vocal pieces and sacred hymns.

Ref. 6, 226, 276, 433

SMEJKALOVA, Vlasta

Czech pianist, teacher and composer. b. Tabor, January 26, 1915. She studied the piano at music schools in Tabor and in Pribram, where she continued her piano studies under Frantisek Forst from 1934 to 1935 and after passing the state examinations, under E. Mikelka, K. Hoffmeister, and L. Escha. She studied choral singing under B.V. Aim and harmony, counterpoint, and composition under Frantisek Spilka in 1941. She taught music in middle schools and conducted children's choirs. She composed orchestral, horn and piano pieces as well as choruses and songs.

Ref. 197

SMELTZER, Mary Susan (Snyder)

American clarinetist, harpsichordist, organist, pianist, teacher, violinist, violist and composer. b. Sapulpa, OK, September 13, 1941. She composed her first original work at five and performed a composition of her own on television at ten. She received her early music training in Sapulpa where she studied the clarinet under George Brite from 1951 to 1959 and attended Sapulpa High School. Between 1954 and 1959 she also attended Tulsa University, as a special preparatory student, studying the clarinet under Dwight Daily, principal clarinetist of the Tulsa Philharmonic Orchestra from 1958 to 1959. During the summers of 1956 to 1958, she studied the clarinet under Dr. Revelli and Ferde Grofe, and the violin and the viola under Dr. Rush, at the Summer Music Festival at Western State College in Gunnison, CO, as a scholarship student. She won first prize at the festival for an original work for the piano, and was the principal violist in the Beginning Orchestra in 1958. She also studied the violin and the viola under Betty Roller in Sapulpa from 1957 to 1958. She won many honors for the clarinet throughout the Midwest between 1953 and 1959. In 1963 she graduated with a B.M. from Oklahoma City University having studied under Dr. Clarence Burg, Robert Laughlin and Ernestine Scott and been the recipient of many honors during her studies there. She studied chamber music at the University of Southern California, Los Angeles and at Mt. St. Mary's College, Los Angeles from 1964; As a teacher she taught the piano privately in Oklahoma and California, and in schools, churches, universities and conservatories in Oklahoma, California and Texas from 1956. She was the organist at churches in Oklahoma and California from 1957 to 1971 and as a professional accompanist she has performed in concerts since 1961 in cities throughout the Midwest, in Oklahoma, Los Angeles and in Houston, including Houston Grand Opera Concerts together with visiting artists. In 1962 she was a member of the Beginner's String Trio at Oklahoma City University, and Southern California (M.M., hons., 1967), having studied under Lillian Steuber. From 1964 to 1969 she performed in chamber groups in Los Angeles and as a harpsichordist she gave a concert with the American Youth Symphony under the direction of Mehli Mehta in 1969. She attended master classes at the University of Southern California in 1967 studying under Lillian Steuber and Gregor Piatigorsky in 1969. From 1969 to 1970 a Fulbright Grant enabled her to study in Vienna under Prof. Dr. Joseph Dichler at the Akademie fuer Musik where she worked towards an Artists' Diploma. In 1970 and 1971 she attended the Master Classes of Piatigorsky, Mme. Rosina Lhevinne and Daniel Polack at the University of Southern California. From 1970 to 1972 she again performed in chamber groups in the Los Angeles area, and from 1972 onwards continued to give harpsichord performances in the Houston area, and since 1972 she has been artist-in-residence at the College of Mainland, Texas City. She has given radio performances in the United States and abroad and toured Europe as a concert artist. She was the American representative to the Van Cliburn International Piano Competition. She has received numerous awards in California, Oklahoma, Colorado and Texas and in 1974 she was awarded a National Award 'Sword of Honor' at the Triennial National Convention, Kansas City; she was a finalist in the Oklahoma City composition competition and received a Distinguished Alumni Award from Oklahoma City University in 1976. She was the New York Judge for the National Piano Guild Audition in 1977. PHOTOGRAPH.

Compositions
BAND
   The Bald Eagle march (1976)
   The Mainlander's march (also as Brotherhood march) (also ch) (1976)
CHAMBER
   An American tribute for a Royal marriage (org, 2 hn and 8 trp) (1981)
   Christmas fantasy (brass ens) (1960)
   Bird calls (hpcd) (1982)
   German chorale for harpsichord (1961)
   Piece for organ (1961)
   Study for harpsichord (1961)
   Study for harpsichord with romantic touches (1961)
   Two studies for harpsichord (1964)
PIANO
   Piece in 12-tone style (2 pfs) (1960)
   Theme and variations (2 pfs) (1961)
   Bach's nightmare
   Dialogue
   Fanfare
   Folk dance
   Furious wind (1950)
   Kaleidoscope (1962)
   Lazy practice room at noon on the moon
   Little song
   El matador (1957)
   Rat-race toccata
   Reverie (1962)
   Train whistle
   Twelve mood pictures, variations on Yankee Doodle
VOCAL
   A doctor date with Dr. Brute, 1980 (S and pf)
   Jonathan Richard my bicentennial baby (S, pf, dr, 2 fl and 2 trp)
SACRED
   Psalm 121 (ch, pf and orch)
THEATRE
   A Midsummer Night's Dream, play
ARRANGEMENTS
   Battle Hymn of the Republic (cl qrt)
   Chamber, vocal and sacred
Publications
Selected Orchestrations of Poetic Expressions.
Bibliography
Houston Chronicle, April 1975. C. Ward.
Houston Post, April 1975. C. Cunningham.
Musical Journal, July 1975. Turner.
New York Times, April 1975.
Newhouse Newspapers, April 21, 1975. Critic at Large - Byron Belt.
Piano Guild Notes, March-April, 1976.
Ref. composer, 468, 474, 624, 625

SMILEY, Pril
American teacher and composer. b. Lake Mohonk, March 19, 1943. She studied under Henry Brant, Louis Calabro and Vivian Fine (q.v.) at Bennington College, Vermont. She received an award in the First International Electronic Music Competition, Dartmouth in 1968. Since 1963 she has been the composer and instructor at Columbia Princeton Electronic Music Center. From 1968 to 1974 she was the electronic music consultant at the Lincoln Center Repertory Theatre. DISCOGRAPHY.
Compositions
VOCAL
   Secret (chil-vces and str qrt) (ACA)
OPERA
   Elephant Steps, occult opera (1968)

THEATRE
   The Balcony (1967)
   Bananas (1969)
   The Increased Difficulty of Concentration (1970)
   Inner Journey (1969)
   King Lear (Shakespeare) (1968)
   Macbeth (Shakespeare) (1966)
   Operation Sidewinder (1970)
   Richard III (Shakespeare) (1968)
   Satyricon (1969)
   St. Joan (1968)
   Tiger at the Gates (1968)
   Music for 19 major theatre productions in New York, Tanglewood, Cleveland, Baltimore and Cincinnati
FILM MUSIC
   Incredible Voyage (1969)
   The Trip (1970)
ELECTRONIC
   Can you hear me? (1967)
   Eclipse (1967) (4 elec tapes)
   Kolyosa (1970)
INCIDENTAL MUSIC
   Music for 2 television documentaries and 4 films
Ref. 142, 415, 622, 625

SMIRNOVA, Galina Konstantinovna
Soviet composer. b. Moscow, January 20, 1910. She studied music history and theory at the Moscow Conservatory from 1932 to 1935 and composition under V. Shebalin from 1935 to 1940. DISCOGRAPHY.
Compositions
VOCAL
   A dedication to Leningrad, oratorio (chil-ch and orch) (Moscow: Sovetski Kompozitor, 1984)
   Northern wind (vocal qrt)
   Children's choral pieces (vocal qrt)
   Dobrove utro (M. Tanka) (1950)
   Pesni zapadnikh slavyan (Pushkin) (1937)
   Pesnya materei, Russian folk song (O. Kolchev)
   Svadevnaya, Russian folk song (A. Nedogonov)
FILM MUSIC
   Italianskaia suita, 10 songs (D. Rodari and S. Marshak)
Ref. 87, 223, 518, 563

SMIRNOVA SOLODCHENKOVA, Tatiana Georgievna
Soviet composer. b. 1940. DISCOGRAPHY.
Compositions
CHAMBER
   Sonata-Ballada (trp and pf)
VOCAL
   Six pictures from Russian folk poetry (vce and pf)
Ref. 267

SMITH, Alice Mary (Mrs. Meadows White)
British composer. b. London, May 19, 1839; d. London, December 4, 1884. She was a pupil of Sir W. Sterndale Bennett and Sir George Macfarren. She was elected associate of the Philharmonic Society in 1867 and was an honorary member of the Royal Academy of Music. She married Frederick Meadows White, director of the Royal Academy of Music in London. DISCOGRAPHY.
Compositions
ORCHESTRA
   Symphony in C-Minor (1863)
   Symphony in G
   Clarinet concerto (1872)
   Introduction and allegro (pf and orch) (1865)
   Overture to Endymion (Keats) (1864, rev 1871)
   Overture to Jason, or the Argonauts and Sirens (1979)
   Overture to Lalla Rookh (T. Moore) (1865)
   Overture and two intermezzi to the Masque of Pandora (Longfellow) (1878)
CHAMBER
   Piano quartet in B-Flat (pf, vln, vla and vlc) (1861)
   Piano quartet in D (1864)
   Piano quartet in E-Minor
   Piano quartet in G-Minor
   String quartet in A (1870)
   String quartet in B-Flat (1862)
   String quartet in D (1862)
   String quartet in G (Novello)
   Trio in G (pf, vln and vlc) (1862)
   Melody and scherzo (vlc and pf)

PIANO
  Impromptu
  Six short pieces
  Vale of Tempe, rondo
VOCAL
  Ode to the north east wind, cantata (Kingsley) (soli, ch and orch) (1878) (Novello)
  Ode to the passions, cantata (Collins) (soli, ch and orch) (1884) (Novello)
  Ruedesheim (or Gisela) cantata (solos, ch and orch) (1865)
  Song of the Little Baltung, cantata (Kingsley) (m-vce and orch) (1883) (Novello)
  The dream, part-song (1863)
  Oh that we two were maying, duet
  Part-songs, duets and solos
Ref. 2, 6, 14, 17, 22, 41, 70, 102, 105, 129, 226, 276, 361, 563

SMITH, Anita

American composer. b. New York, December 19, 1922. She studied under Karol Rathaus on a scholarship to Queens College.
Compositions
CHAMBER
  Violin suite
  Homage to Gershwin
  Perambular funiculi
VOCAL
  Three concert songs on Lindsay texts
  Three settings of Carl Sandburg texts
Ref. 94, 142

SMITH, Edith Gross

American assistant professor and composer. b. Boston, March 2, 1937. She was educated at Carleton College, MN, and graduated from Boston University with a B.A. in 1958. She also attended Norfolk College of William and Mary in Virginia, and graduated from Mills College as a scholarship student with a M.A. (composition) in 1965. She obtained her D.M.A. (composition) from Stanford University in 1971 and studied the piano under Denise Lassmonne and Joan Fay. She was a teacher at the Castilleja School from 1967 to 1970, a teaching fellow at Stanford University from 1970 to 1971 and since 1971 has held the position of assistant professor at Orange Coast College in California. She received a Young Composer's award in 1962; Copley award in 1963; Fromm prize, Aspen, in 1963; and the Elizabeth Crothers Mills prize in 1965.
Ref. 77

SMITH, Eleanor

American singer, lecturer and composer. b. Atlanta, June 15, 1858; d. Midland, MI, June 30, 1942. She studied singing under Fannie Root and Julius Hey and composition under Frederick G. Gleason and later under Moritz Moszkowski in Berlin for three years. She taught in schools; lectured at the University of Chicago from 1902 to 1904 and founded and headed the Hull House School of Music from 1893 to 1935.
Compositions
VOCAL
  The golden asp, cantata
  Songs incl.:
  Cradle song
  Eleanor Smith series (1911)
  Modern music series (1905)
  The quest (Cont)
  The shadow (Summy)
  She kissed with her eyes
  Song for the year
  Songs for little children (1887)
  Songs of life and nature (1899)
  The swing
  Where go the boats
  Windy nights (Summy)
SACRED
  Christmas carol (Rossetti)
  Wedding music (8 vces, pf and org)
  In another land and time, hymn (1931)
Ref. 226, 276, 292, 297, 347, 353, 433, 622, 646

SMITH, Eleanor Louise

American organist, pianist and composer. b. St. Louis, MO, 1873.
Ref. 347

SMITH, Ella May Dunning

American organist, pianist, authoress, music editor, teacher and composer. b. Uhrichsville, OH, February 20, 1860; d. Oak Park, IL, 1934. She was a pupil of Edgar Stillman Kelley. She composed piano pieces and songs.
Ref. 226, 347, 353

SMITH, E.M. Monica

British composer. b. 1896.
Compositions
CHAMBER
  Poems (fl and pf)
Ref. 41

SMITH, Ethel

20th-century British composer.
Composition
CHAMBER
  Sonata in C-Minor (vlc and pf) (1981)
Ref. *Composer* (London)

SMITH, Eva Munson. See SMITH, Mrs. Gerrit

SMITH, Florence Beatrice. See PRICE, Florence Beatrice

SMITH, Gertrude

19th-century American composer. b. New York. She was the daughter of Dr. Norman Smith.
Compositions
VOCAL
  Songs incl.:
  An die grosse Glocke
  Rose in Thal
  Waechterruf
Ref. 226, 276, 291, 433

SMITH, Hannah

19th-century American pianist, writer and composer.
Compositions
PIANO
  Twelve duets with a very easy bass staff (4 hands)
  Little tunes for little hands, op. 7 (Schirmer)
  One hundred two-part canons (J.H. Schroeder)
  Songs and dances for little hands, op. 2 (J.H. Schroeder)
  Three old-fashioned dances, op. 6
  Twelve little melodies, op. 8 (Schirmer)
Publications
Music, how it came to be.
Progressive exercise in sight reading for piano. Parts 1-12.
Ref. 226, 297

SMITH, Hilda Josephine

American organist, pianist, teacher and composer. b. Dell Rapids, SD, December 1, 1884. She was a pupil at the Wolcott School in Denver, and at the Chicago Musical College. She composed songs and anthems.
Ref. 226

SMITH, Ida Polk

20th-century American composer. She composed pieces and an arrangement of hymns.
Ref. 40, 347

SMITH, Joan Templar

American flautist, lecturer and composer. b. Topeka, KA, May 12, 1927. She graduated with a B.Mus. hons from the University of Kansas in 1951; M.Mus. in 1952 and Ph.D. in 1976 from the Eastman School of Music. She was flautist with the North Carolina Orchestra from 1952 to 1953 and lectured on theory and wind instruments at Mary Hardin Baylor College from 1953 to 1954; on theory and on the flute at the University of Texas from 1953 to 1954 and the flute at University of Colorado from 1965 to 1971. She is a member of Mu Phi Epsilon.

Composition

ORCHESTRA

Sonnet (fl and cham orch) (Kendor)

Ref. 643

SMITH, Julia Frances (Vielehr)

American pianist, authoress, lecturer and composer. b. Denton, TX, January 25, 1911. She studied with Harold von Mickwitz at the Institute of Musical Art, Dallas and obtained her B.A. from North Texas State University, Denton in 1930. She studied composition under Rubin Goldmark and Frederick Jacobi at the Juilliard School of Music, where she also studied the piano under Lonny Epstein and Carl Friedberg from 1930 to 1939. She studied orchestration under Bernard Wagenaar. She received her M.A. in 1933 and Ph.D. in 1952 from New York University where she studied composition under Marion Bauer (q.v.), Vincent Jones and Virgil Thomson. She was a member of the theory department at the Juilliard School of Music from 1940 to 1942 and founder and head of the Department of Music Education, Julius Hartt College of Music, University of Hartford, CT from 1940 to 1945. From 1944 to 1946 she was on the faculty of the New Britain State Teachers' College in Connecticut. In 1963 she was named one of ten leading women composers by the National Council of Women of the United States. She was the recipient of two Martha Baird Rockefeller grants and was chairlady of AWC (NFMC) until April 1979. DISCOGRAPHY. PHOTOGRAPH.

Compositions

ORCHESTRA

Folkways symphony (1948)

Concerto (pf and orch; also 2 pf) (1939)

American dance suite (also 2 pf) (1935) (Presser Rental, 1960)

Episodic suite (orch; also pf) (Presser)

Hellenic suite (Presser, 1942) (ded Frederique Petrides)

Liza Jane (1940)

BAND

Sails aloft, overture (with Cecile Vashaw) (1965) (Mowbray)

Fanfare for Alma Mater (Mowbray)

CHAMBER

Work and play (inst ens) (with Cecile Vashaw)

Octet for woodwinds (1980)

String quartet (Mowbray, 1966)

Trio-Cornwall (vln, vlc and pf) (Mowbray, 1956)

Nocturne and festival piece (vla and pf) (Mowbray, 1942)

Sonatine in G (fl and pf)

Five pieces for double-bass and piano (Mowbray, 1985)

Prelude in D-Flat (org) (Mowbray, 1967)

PIANO

Characteristic suite (Mowbray, 1951)

Prelude (Presser, 1952)

Sonatine in C (Mowbray, 1941)

Variations humoresque on a theme by Arturo Somohano (Mowbray, 1950)

VOCAL

Remember the Alamo (narr, ch and band; also orch) (Presser, 1965)

Enrich your life with music (ch and pf) (Mowbray, 1969)

Glory to the green and white (mix-ch or m-ch) (Mowbray, 1966)

Our heritage (ch and pf) (Mowbray, 1959)

Prairie kaleidoscope (vce and pf; also vce and str qrt) (1981)

To all who love a song (1949) (S, A and pf)

Three love songs (Karl Flaster) (1955)

SACRED

Invocation (w-ch or vce and pf) (Mowbray, 1967)

OPERA

Cockcrow (Presser, 1954)

Cynthia Parker (1939, rev 1977)

Daisy (Mowbray; Presser 1973)

The Gooseherd and the Goblin (Presser, 1949)

Shepherdess and the Chimney Sweep, Christmas opera (1966) (Presser)

The Stranger of Manzano (1945-1946) (Mowbray)

Publications

Aaron Copland, New York: Dutton, 1955.

A Directory of American Women Composers. Chicago, 1970.

Master Pianist: The Career and Teaching of C. Friedberg. New York, 1963.

String Method. Books I, II and II. With Cecile Vashaw.

Bibliography

Craig, M. *Composer and Ambassadress of U.S. Music. Musical Courier*, July 1959, p. 7.

Ref. composer, 17, 39, 40, 68, 85, 94, 141, 142, 146, 190, 195, 228, 280, 321, 322, 347, 353, 397, 415, 474, 463, 477, 494, 594, 610, 611, 622, 625

SMITH, La Donna Carol

American pianist, violinist, violist, lecturer and composer. b. Birmingham, AL, March 2, 1951. She began to study the piano at the age of seven at Birmingham Southern Conservatory, then she attended the University of Alabama where she continued to study for 15 years. She studied the viola and the violin under Henry Barrett at the University of Alabama in 1972, graduating with a B.Mus. (theory and composition) in 1976 and an M.Mus. She also studied electronic music at the Peabody College, Nashville and string technique and teaching methods at James Madison University, Harrisonburg, VA. She taught theory and electronic music at the University of Alabama from 1973 to 1976. In 1974 she was the co-founder and director of a spontaneous music ensemble, 'Transcend Provisation'. which received attention in the United States and abroad. She is currently music director of the fine arts program of Tuscaloosa city schools. DISCOGRAPHY. PHOTOGRAPH.

Compositions

ORCHESTRA

Orchestrophes (perc, pf, hp, strs and orch) (Tuscaloosa, AL: Transmuseq, 1975)

Six movements (youth orch) (1977)

Solo (amateur orch) (Transmuseq, 1976)

Three movements (1974)

VOCAL

Amplified Jude (16 vces and cham ens) (Transmuseq, 1976)

Vision (vce and pf) (1974)

ELECTRONIC

Electronic lullaby (tape and Arp 2600) (1976)

Polymusic (tape and Arp 2600) (1976)

Prelude, day music (tape and concrete music) (1976)

Sforces (tape and Moog III) (175)

MULTIMEDIA

Amerigreen (perc, strs and 4 amp lawn mowers) (Transmuseq, 1976)

Vairocana (dancers and improvised ens) (1976)

MISCELLANEOUS

Armed forces day

Montage (1977)

Raudelunas pataphysical revue

School

USA concerts

Ref. composer, 228, 563

SMITH, Laura Alexandrine

19th-century English authoress and composer.

Compositions

VOCAL

Music of the waters, collection of sea chanties (London: Kegan Paul, 1888)

Songs incl.:

My castle in Spain

Ref. 6, 85, 347, 433

SMITH, Lilian

Compositions

PIANO

Betty's diary

Three rhythmic studies

Ref. 473

SMITH, Linda Catlin

American composer. b. White Plains, NY, April 27, 1957. She studied composition under Allen Shawn and then attended at the State University of New York, Stony Brook. She received her B.A. and M.A. from the University of Victoria in Canada where she studied under Rudolf Komorovs and John Celona (composition) and under Erich Schwandt (harpsichord). Her work *Peripheri* was one of the winners of the 1979 ILWC competition. PHOTOGRAPH.

Compositions

ORCHESTRA

Link (cham orch) (1981)

CHAMBER

Peripheri (pf and unspecified ens) (1979) (prize)

Scroll (6 insts) (1981)

Clay (str qrt) (1980)

Silhouette (cor) (1981)

VOCAL

Grey broken (S, fl and hpcd) (1981)

Ref. composer

SMITH, Margit

20th-century American composer. b. Germany. She is a resident of the Ivory Coast and the United States and composes music incorporating the use of exotic wind, string and percussion instruments. She composes with Marrie Bremer (q.v.) using both old and modern instruments but their music is firmly rooted in tradition. DISCOGRAPHY.

Compositions

CHAMBER

Traject I (org, baroque and Peruvian fl)

Traject II (org, 2 African fl, gemshorn, shakuhachi, b-fl, Nepalese and Thai fl)

Chroai (chin, hpcd, pf and kayagum)

Elevensevenseven (kayagum and Renaissance b-fl)

ORGAN

Maqam

Mobile

Ombre

Ref. 563

SMITH, Mary Barber

Canadian composer of English origin. b. 1878. She lived in Edmonton and composed organ pieces and vocal works.

Ref. 133

SMITH, May Florence

19th-century American writer and composer. She composed songs and sacred music.

Publications

A key to perfect reading or Transposition studies at a glance.

Ref. 276, 347, 433

SMITH, Mrs. Gerrit (Eva Munson)

American lecturer, singer and composer. b. Monkton, VT, July 12, 1843. After school she became the head of the music department of Otoe University, Nebraska City.

Compositions

PIANO

Home sonata

VOCAL

Songs incl.:

Joy (1868)

Woodland warbling

Ref. 226, 276, 433

SMITH, Nellie von Gerichten

American composer. b. 1875.

Composition

OPERA

The Twins of Bistritz

Ref. 307

SMITH, Nettie Pierson

19th-century American composer.

Compositions

VOCAL

Songs incl.:

'Neath the lilies sleeping

We meet no more

Ref. 276, 292, 347, 433

SMITH, Rosalie Balmer

19th-century American musician and composer.

Compositions

VIOLIN

Romanza

Sonatas

Ref. 276, 347, 433

SMITH, Ruby Mae

American artist, authoress, publisher, teacher and composer. b. Joplin, MO, March 20, 1902. She teaches the piano, the guitar, the organ and singing and leads her vocal quartet 'Ruby Smith and The Rubytones.' She is owner and president of Rubytone Record and Publishing Co., Portland, OR.

Compositions

VOCAL

That beautiful city

The bells

Hard luck blues

Worth more than gold

Rise or fall

SACRED

The Lord will come

When Jesus shall come

Ref. 39, 646

SMITH, Selma Moidel

American violinist, lawyer and composer. b. Warren, OH, April 3, 1919. She studied the violin and theory at the Hollywood Conservatory from 1930 to 1935 and then studied at the University of California, Los Angeles, the University of Southern California and the Pacific Coast University where she obtained her LI.B. She studied the piano both privately and at UCLA. PHOTOGRAPH.

Compositions

PIANO

Pieces incl.:

Bagatelle, op. 111 (1967)

Barcarole (1956)

Beguine in A-Minor (1960)

Beguine in F-Minor (1953)

Bolero in A-Minor (1959)

Caravan (1955)

Dark waltz (1957)

El argentino (1966)

Espana antigua (1956)

The Great Wall of China (1955)

Melody in D-Minor (1954)

Mission of the Orient (1957)

Nocturne, op. 136 (1982)

Nocturne in A-Minor, op. 132 (1972)

Nocturne in C-Minor, op. 3 (1953)

Nocturne in G-Minor (1959)

Oracion de un torero (1959)

Prelude in C-Minor (1954)

Reflections, op. 26 (1955)

Reverie (1958)

Tango in A-Minor (1953)

Tango in B-Minor, op. 6 (1954)

Tango in C-Minor, op. 20 (1955)

Tango in D-Minor, op. 4 (1954)

Tango in F-Minor, op. 124 (1968)

Tango in G-Minor (1954)

Waltz in B-Minor (1977)

Waltz in C-Minor, op. 17 (1954)

Waltz in G (1958)

Waltz in G-Minor, op. 68 (1959)

Publications

The American Composer; Classics West. February, 1972.

Ref. composer, 475

SMITH, Sharon

20th-century Canadian composer.

Compositions

ORCHESTRA

Raining heart (1980)

CHAMBER

Buque (cl) (1981)

Kaya (fl) (1980)

Piano pieces (1975-1978)

Ref. Assoc. of Canadian Women Composers

SMITH, Zelma

20th-century American composer.

Composition

OPERA

The Gallant Tailor

Ref. 141

SMYSLOVA, Natalia Nikolayevna. See LEVI, Natalia Nikolayevna

SMYTH, Ethel Mary, Dame

English pianist, conductor, writer and composer. b. London or Kent, April 23, 1858; d. Woking, Surrey, May 8, 1944. She was a pupil of composer, Colonel Ewing and studied for a short while at the Leipzig Conservatory under Carl Reinecke and S. Jadassohn in 1877 where she took private lessons with Heinrich von Herzogenberg whom she followed to Berlin. She went to England in 1909 and received an honorary D.Mus. from Durham University in 1910, Oxford in 1926 and St. Andrews University in 1928. She was the first woman composer to have an opera performed at Covent Garden with her *The Wreckers* in 1910 and in 1922 she was made a Dame of the British Empire. She was a militant leader of the suffragette movement and imprisoned for two months as a result of this involvement. She composed *March of the women* which became the battle song of the Women's Social and Political Union of which she was an avid supporter and the story is that she conducted fellow suffragettes in this march with a toothbrush from her cell window. She later felt that any neglect of her work was due to prejudice against women. DISCOGRAPHY. PHOTOGRAPH.

Compositions

ORCHESTRA
Concerto for violin and horn (also as Horn concerto) (London: Curwen, 1927)
Anthony and Cleopatra, overture (1890)
March of the women (Curwen, 1911)
Serenade in D-Major (1890)
Suite for strings (1891) (Leonard)

CHAMBER
The dance and chrysilla (fl, hp, tri, tam and strs) (1909)
Quintet, op. 1 (2 vln, vla and 2 vlc) (Leipzig: Peters 1884)
Six quartets
String quartet in E-Minor (Vienna, 1914)
Piano trio (incomplete) (ca. 1880)
String trio (1880)
Trio (vln, hn and pf) (1927)
Two trios (vln, ob and pf) (Curwen, 1927)
Two interlinked French folk melodies (from Entente Cordiale) (fl, ob and cl) (OUP, 1929)
Sonata (vln and pf) (1887)
Sonata in A-Minor (vlc and pf) (1887)
Violin sonata in A-Minor (1887)

PIANO
Prelude and fugue (1887)
Sonata in D, in 2 mvts
Suite
Two sonatas (1887)
Variations (1887)
Incomplete pieces

ORGAN
Chorale prelude on an Irish air (1939)
Five short chorale preludes, Nos. 1, 3, 4 and 5 (also strs; also solo insts) (1913)

VOCAL
The song of Love, op. 8, cantata (solos, ch and orch) (1888)
Hey nonny no (ch and orch) (1910)
Sleepless dreams (ch and orch) (1926)
A spring canticle (ch and orch) (1926)
Three Anacreontic odes (vce and orch) (1909)
Three moods of the sea (m-S or bar and orch)
The prison (ch a-cap) (1930)
Soul's joy (ch a-cap) (1923)
Three songs of sunrise (ch a-cap) (1911)
Bonny sweet Robin, variations (fl, ob and pf) (1928)
Chrysilla (m-S or Bar)
Wood spirits' song
Songs

SACRED
Mass in D-Major (solos, ch and orch) (Novello, 1893)

OPERA
The Boatswain's Mate (1916)
Der Wald (1902)
Entente Cordiale (1923)
Fantasio (1898)
Fête galante, a dance-dream (1923)
The Forest (1901)
On the Cliffs of Cornwall
The Wreckers (Strandrecht, original title Les Naufrageurs) (1906, rev 1939)

Publications

As Time went-on. London and New York, 1935.
Beecham and Pharaoh. London, 1935.
Female Pipings in Eden. London, 1934.
A Final Burning of Boats. London and New York, 1928.
Impressions That Remained. 2 vols. London and New York, 1919; Da Capo, 1945.
Maurice Baring. 1937.
Streaks of Life. London and New York, 1921.
A Three-legged Tour in Greece. London, 1927.
What Happened Next. London and New York, 1940.

Bibliography

Beecham, T. *Dame Ethel Smyth (1858-1944).* In ML (1958).
Dale, K. *Dame Ethel Smyth.* In ML (1944).
Dale, K. *Ethel Smyth and Prentice Work.* In ML (1949).

Le donne compositrici. Musica d'oggi 4 (1922): 14.
Famous Women Composers. Etude April 1917: 237-238.
Hurd, M. *Dame Ethel M. Smyth.* In MGG 12 (1965).
St. John, Christopher. *Ethel Smyth: A Biography.* Additional chapters by V. Sackville West; K. Dale. London and New York, 1959.
Ref. 2, 6, 9, 14, 15, 17, 20, 22, 23, 41, 44, 70, 74, 85, 86, 89, 96, 100, 105, 108, 141, 149, 165, 177, 189, 226, 260, 276, 284, 295, 297, 307, 322, 335, 361, 398, 415, 433, 477, 488, 563, 572, 609, 612, 622, 637, 645, 646, 653

SNEED, Anna (Mrs. Cairn)

19th-century American composer.
Compositions
VOCAL
Songs incl.:
Break, break o sea
Ref. 226, 276, 433

SNELL, Lillian Lucinda

American pianist, saxophonist, trombonist and composer. b. Dexter, May 15, 1873. Her teachers include Professor Fowler, Carter, Greenley and Leonard. She was the assistant Director of the Dexter orchestra club and organized Snell's band and orchestra.
Compositions
VOCAL
Songs incl.:
Just for tonight
Ref. 374

SNELREWAARD-BOUDEWIJNS, Nelly. See LINDEN-VAN SNELREWAARD-BOUDEWIJNS, Nelly van der

SNIFFIN, Allison

20th-century American pianist and composer.
Compositions
VOCAL
Now I lay (with everywhere around) (S and pf) (1985)
Six significant landscapes (W. Stevens) (S and pf) (1985)
THEATRE
Lunar Baedeker (singing actor, cl and perc) (1985)
Ref. AMC newsletter 1985

SNIZKOVA-SKRHOVA, Jitka

Czech pianist, professor, writer and composer. b. Prague, September 14, 1924. She studied the piano under Jan Herman, S. Sima and O. Kredba at the Masters' School of the Prague Conservatory in 1948, composition under Alois Haba and privately under K. Hofmeister and F. Spilka. At the philosophical faculty of Charles University she studied musicology, aesthetics and Czechoslovak literature. She appears in concerts and recitals and is particularly interested in Czech music from the 15th to the 17th-centuries. She is a professor at Prague Conservatory. PHOTOGRAPH.
Compositions
ORCHESTRA
Small sinfonietta (cham orch) (1957)
Interludes (fl and str orch) (1958)
Two overtures (cham orch) (1959)
CHAMBER
Chora (str qrt) (1966)
String quartet No. 1 (1948)
String quartet No. 2 (1953)
String quartet No. 3 (1956)
Laconic concertino (pf, fl and perc) (1965)
Satiticon (fl, d-b and pf) (1967)
Tercet (fl, d-b and pf) (1967)
Trio (fl, ob and hp) (1955)
Trio inquietto (fl, ob and bsn) (1962)
Trio ritmico (vln, vlc and pf) (1961)
Inquiette (fl and pf) (1966)
Inventions (fl and ob) (1972)
Pascua (ob and pf) (1974)
Suite (fl and hpcd)
Sonata (vla and pf) (1947, rev 1963)
Sonata (vlc and pf) (1958)
Sonatina (fl and pf) (1957)
Dance compositions (pentatonic) (hp) (1944)
Epithalamia (fl) (1970)
Gothic dream, 20 etudes (hp) (1944)
The mosaics, cycle (hp)

PIANO
  Signal-duo (2 pf) (1962)
  Ritmicon (4 hands) (1970)
  Start (4 hands) (1961)
  Concertino (1962)
  Megi, piano fairy tale (1943)
  Sonata
  Several quarter-tone compositions
ORGAN
  Medieval reminiscences (1969)
  Other pieces
VOCAL
  Eternal woman, cantata (Z. Rotrekl) (B, w-ch and pf) (1970)
  The flame of Hus, cantata (J.B. Capek) (mix-ch, solos and pf) (1974)
  The home circle, cantata, dramatic recital (1972)
  On J.A. Comenius, cantata (J.B. Capek and J.G. Leibnitz) (mix-ch) (1969)
  The song of songs, musical poem (Solomon's song, trans J. Seifert) (A, recitative, hp and cham orch) (1960)
  The bell (Latin, Italian and Old Slavonic texts on peace) (m-ch) (1967)
  Canons (chil ch a-cap) (1954-1955)
  Cantica latina (ancient dance songs) incl. O. Venus regina (w-ch) (1956)
  Choruses (Tagore) (m-ch and w-ch) (1970-1973)
  The magic wand (V. Rostocilova) (chil-ch and vla) (1963)
  Mixed choruses (J. Patova-Vrchotova) (1958-1959)
  Panegyricus on Komensky (Comenius) (Leibnitz) (ch) (1956)
  The path (m-ch) (1968)
  Salve amice (Ovid) (mix-ch) (1973)
  Tale of Jizerka (mix-ch) (1960)
  To Albert Schweitzer (J.B. Capek) (mix-ch) (1966)
  Arabesques (Armenian folk poetry) (A and pf) (1950)
  Ariadne, dramatic mvt aria (S and speaker) (1971)
  Boats on the sea (Cont and gtr) (1960)
  Brac, cycle (Vl. Narer, in Czech and Croat) (high vce) (1963)
  Children's songs with flute (1955)
  Dante canzonas (A, fl and vlc) (1965)
  Gitanjali (Tagore) (1971-1972)
  Goetheanum (Aphorisms by J.W. Goethe) (1974)
  In Sheherazade's night (J. Hilcr) (speaker, S, vlc and pf) (1973)
  Lullabies (1964)
  Partisan songs (Bohac, 1946)
  The Portuguese sonnets (E. Browning) (S) (1953)
  Prague pictures for children (Jiri Hutina) (vce and pf) (1963)
  Premyslovna (M. Vlcek) (vce) (1973)
  Rubaiyat (Persian poetry) (A) (1953)
  Songs from the war (1946)
  Songs to the pictures of J. Capek (S and pf) (1950)
  Songs for a boy (J. Seifert) (S, vln and pf) (1954)
  Songs about B. Nemcova (S and fl) (1963)
  Songs of a woman (V. Rostocilova) (1967)
  Spring greeting, cycle of melodramas (J. Kutina) (w-vce, fl and pf) (1971)
  Spring song (T) (1970)
  Swan song (Petr Bezruc) (vce and pf) (1963)
  Three songs for Amadeus (J. Hilcr) (S and pf)
  Triptych on one string (J. Vrchotova) (1972)
  Wedding songs (m-S and hp) (1950)
  Musica polyfonica Bohemiae, arrangements of works of 16th and 17th-centuries (vces)
SACRED
  Oratorio on St. Vojtech, (Latin legends with interpretations by J.B. Capek and M. Vlcek) (solos, m-ch, chil-ch and org) (1971-1972)
  Fons bonitatis, mass (solo vces) (1970)
  Motets (A, fl and ob)
THEATRE
  The Miner, drama (Petr Bezruc) (1963)
TEACHING PIECES
  Pieces incl.:
  Works for violin and ensemble
Publications
  Numerous articles in Czech musical journals.
Ref. composer, 81, 193, 197, 206

SNODGRASS, Louise Harrison

American pianist, lecturer and composer. b. Cincinnati, OH, 1890. She graduated from the Cincinnati Conservatory in 1910 and then studied with Lhevinne in New York. She studied composition under Dr. Sidney Durst and Frank Van der Stueken and began composing in 1924. She was on the faculty of the Cincinnati Conservatory, the Minneapolis School of Music and the College of Music, Cincinnati. Louise also taught privately both in Cincinnati and New York and was an accompanist. She was a pianist with Leo Ditrichstein in the Belasco production *The concert*.

Compositions
CHAMBER
  String quartets
  Trios for piano, violin and viola
  Solo pieces for piano, violin and cello
VOCAL
  Cantata (w-vces)
  Choruses
  Songs incl.:
  Beside the door
  Enchantment claims its own
  London girl
  Mountain love song
  Star wishes
  With all of Dublin lookin' on
  You are the tide
Ref. 292

SNOW, Mary McCarty

American assistant professor and composer. b. Brownsville, TX, August 26, 1928. She studied under Anis Fuleihan at Indiana University where she obtained a B.Mus. and under Burrill Phillips at the University of Illinois where she graduated with a M.Mus. She was assistant professor at Texas Technological University from 1974 to 1978 and received a grant from the university to compose a work based on arid and semi-arid land cultures. In 1977 and 1980 she received the National Endowment of Arts grant.
Compositions
CHAMBER
  Toccata (cl and pf)
  Five monodies (cl)
ELECTRONIC
  The Bacchae (Euripides)
  Hieroglyphs (insts and tape)
  Indians
  Mandora (vln and tape)
  Marat-Sade
  Obsidion II (1979)
  Voyages: Columbus/Apollo II (tape) (1977)
MULTIMEDIA
  Ezekiel I (actor, dancer and tape) (1975)
Ref. 142, 185, 625

SNYDER, Amy

American conductor, singer and composer. b. Ft. Belvoir, VA, November 29, 1949. She graduated with a B.A. in the piano and composition from Bennington College and studied composing and conducting with Henry Brant. From 1971 she worked as a freelance conductor, orchestrator, singer and composer in America and Holland. She received the Sherrill C. Corwin award for excellence in music composition. DISCOGRAPHY.
Compositions
ORCHESTRA
  Buffalo grass (1982)
  Prairie schooner (1984)
CHAMBER
  Ozark brush – meeting II (vla, man, banjo, vlc, hp and mar) (1984)
  Road map (cl, ob, hn, bsn, vln and vlc) (1980)
  Ozark brush – meeting I (picc, fl, vlc, man and hp) (Amsterdam: Haast, 1983)
  Feast of the stones (perc and 30 trp) (1981)
VOCAL
  Cactus (S, ob, perc and vlc) (1976)
  The last words of Copernicus (vocal qrt, org, str qrt and trb) (1984)
  Okra (S, fl, hp, man, pf, a-sax, hn, cl, ob and bsn) (1984)
  Vitreous floaters (S, vlc and perc) (1971)
Ref. composer

SNYDER, Mary Susan Smeltzer. See SMELTZER, Mary Susan

SODRE (Nunes Sodre), Joanidia

Brazilian pianist, organist conductor, professor and composer. b. Porte Alegre, December 22, 1903; d. Rio de Janeiro, September 9, 1975. She studied the piano in Rio de Janeiro under Alberto Nepomuceno and harmony at the Institute Nacional de Musica under Agnelo Franca, the piano under Joao Nunes and Henrique Oswald and composition, counterpoint and fugue under Francisco Braga. She received her teacher's diploma in 1925. She won a scholarship prize to study composition at Berlin's Hochschule fuer Musik under Paul Juon and conducting under Ignatz Waghalter. Joanidia graduated in orchestral conducting at the Stadtische Oper at

Charlottenburg and became a professor of solfege, harmony and morphology at the National School of Music in 1925 and between 1946 and 1950 was director of that school. She was the first South American *Maestrina* to conduct the Bonn Philharmonic Orchestra in Germany. In 1939 she formed the Orquestra da Juventude in Brazil and conducted a number of orchestras. She was director of the Escola Nacional de Musica, in Rio from 1946 to 1967. She was appointed honorary professor at the Pernambucan Conservatory.

Compositions
CHAMBER
  Incendio de Roma, (str qrt)
  Trio (pf, vln and vlc)
  Casa forte
  Cheia do Paraiba
Ref. 268

SOEDERG, Gerda
Composition
PIANO
  Marsch und Vals (1949)
Ref. Frau und Musik

SOENSTEVOLD, Maj
Norwegian pianist, lecturer and composer. b. Soleftea, Sweden, September 9, 1917. She studied the piano in Stockholm under Sven Brandel and Gotfried Boon and in London under Billy Mayerl. At the Akademie fuer Musik und darstellende Kunst, Vienna, she studied composition under Hanns Gelinek and Karl Schiske from 1960 to 1967, graduating with distinction. From 1971 she lectured on composition, instrumentation, keyboard harmony and jazz at the University of Oslo and at the Oslo Broadcasting Corporation. She married composer Gunnar Soenstevold. DISCOGRAPHY. PHOTOGRAPH.

Compositions
ORCHESTRA
  Den gamle majors forunderlige droemme, suite (1970)
  Sorlandsommer, suite (1956)
CHAMBER
  Festival overture (timp, perc, hp, vlc and strs) (1983)
  Juleglede (cel, hp, hpce, bsn and vlc)
  But it was my melody, the double-bass said (d-b and pf)
  Theme with five variations (treble insts and perc) (Norsk Musikforlag, 1965)
  Three Spanish aquarelles (fl and hp)
  Veien min vise vil vandre (keyboard harmony and improvisation)
  Very little piece for harp (1964)
  Prelude and fugue (1963)
PIANO
  A-B-C jazz (Oslo: Edition Lyche, 1954)
  Eleven polytonal blues
  Sonata, op. 3 (1964)
  Suite, op. 1 (1962)
  Sweet and swing (1947)
  Theme with dour variations, op. 2 (1963)
  Thoughts of Latin America (1983)
  Var det en vals (1980)
VOCAL
  Sex par sko (narr and orch) (1962)
  Varvon, ballad (Per Sivle) (2 m-ch, T and orch) (1965)
  Stillhet (8 vces, fl, cl, vla, vlc, pf and perc)
  Nine haiku (A, fl and hp) (1965)
  The Selma Broeter, ballad
SACRED
  In Nasaret, oratorio for children (1980)
BALLET
  The cat with the seven mile boots (1959)
THEATRE
  Elias rekefisker (1958)
  Lan meg din kone (1958)
  Matchstick Girl (H.C. Andersen) (1959)
  Snow White and the Seven Dwarfs
  Thorn Rose
  Toya (1956)
  Trost i taklampa (A. Proeysen) (1955)
ELECTRONIC
  Insektlek (fl, hp, cel and insects on tape) (1979)
Ref. composer, NMI, 20, 94, 114, 206, 280, 563

SOERLIE, Caroline Volla
Norwegian choir conductor and composer. b. 1869; d. 1953.
Ref. NMI

SOEUR M. Louise-Andrée. See BARIL, Jeanne

SOEUR St. Marie Cecile du Sacre-Coeur. See BEAUCHEMIN, Marie

SOEUR St. Jean-du-Sacre Coeur. See CADORET, Charlotte

SOHNIUS, Elfriede
Composition
PIANO
  Sonata, 2 mvts
Ref. Frau und Musik

SOKOLL, Christa
Composition
CHAMBER
  Bees buzz around: a light journey through music history (1-5 rec) (Baerenreiter, 1982)
Ref. MLA *Notes*

SOLLIMA, Donatella
20th-century Italian composer.
Composition
CHAMBER
  Dieci pezzi facili (pf) (Bergen, 1977)
Ref. MLA *Notes*

SOLOMON, Elide M.
American pianist, authoress, publisher, teacher and composer. b. Switzerland, December 22, 1938. She studied the piano and composition at the Milan Conservatory and then studied at the American College of Musicians where she obtained a certificate in 1976. Her composition teacher was Ronald Herder and she studied musicianship under Anthony La Magra, Filippini, Brancaleoni and Robeda. She was a founding director of the Purchase music ensemble and school for composers. PHOTOGRAPH.

Compositions
ORCHESTRA
  Piano concerto for chamber orchestra (Rydet)
CHAMBER
  Self portrait (cl, fl, ob, picc, pf and vln) (1976)
  Scenes from childhood (hn, cl, vln, vlc) (1982)
  Song for winter (cl and pf)
  Stangetziana (T-sax and pf) (1980)
PIANO
  Hommage à Picasso (Rydet, 1980)
  Rhapsody (1976)
VOCAL
  Divertimenti pastorali (mix-ch) (1983)
Publications
  Composing with Visual Aids.
Ref. composer, 622, 624, 625

SOLOMON, Joyce Elaine
American assistant professor and composer. b. Tuskegee, AL, May 11, 1946. She gained a B.A. from Vassar College; her M.A.T. from Rutgers University; a M.F.A. from Sarah Lawrence College and in 1982 graduated with an Ed.D. from the Teachers College, Columbia University. She is the adjunct assistant professor at the Borough of Manhattan Community College and on the faculty of the Brooklyn Music School and Henry Street Music School. In 1976 she was awarded a NEA jazz study grant and in 1981 the AMC copying assistance grant. PHOTOGRAPH.

Compositions
ORCHESTRA
  Ethereal (str orch) (1976)
  The flood (pf and str orch) (1977)
  The soul of nature (1975)
CHAMBER
  Among the snow capped peaks (pf, perc and str qrt) (1976)
  Clarinet quintet (cl and str qrt) (1974)
  Oceana (fl, B-cl, d-b, perc and pf) (1978)
  Jazz quintet (2 trp, hn, trb and tba) (1978)

Trio (ob, tba and pf) (1978)
Sonatina (fl, vlc, pf) (1972)
Fantasy (vln and pf) (1979)
Elegy for solo cello (1970)
Solo for seated percussionist (1982)
Three pieces for flute (1970)
PIANO
Variations on a theme (1971)
Suite (1973)
A summer afternoon in South Carolina (1983)
A young black woman's impressions of New York City (1978)
VOCAL
Sing my people (mix-ch, picc, fl, cl, ob, B-cl, bsn, 2 trp, trb, pf and perc) (1980)
All music is (S and pf) (1973)
Dance of the streets (T, fl, vlc, perc and pf) (1978)
Drei besondere klangfarben (B, mar and bsn) (1971)
Repose (B, fl, cl and gtr) (1970)
A setting of five poems by Longton Hughes (T, hn, xyl and bsn) (1979)
A setting of a poem from Sirens, Knuckles, Boots by Dennis Brutus (B and pf) (1978)
South Africa (B and pf) (1978)
ELECTRONIC
Apocalypse (tape) (1980)
Trio (tape, pf and perc) (1980)
Ref. composer, 625

SOLOMON, Mirrie Irma (Hill, Mirrie Irma)

Australian pianist, professor and composer. b. Sydney, December 1, 1892. She studied at the New South Wales Conservatorium where she held a scholarship for composition and chamber music. She was professor of harmony and aural culture at the conservatory. She married the Australian composer Alfred Hill. DISCOGRAPHY.
Compositions
ORCHESTRA
Arnhem Land symphony (1954)
Symphony in A
Avinu malkenu (vln and orch) (1971)
Duo (vln and orch)
Rhapsody in A-Major (pf and orch) (1918)
Three Aboriginal dances (pf and orch) (1950)
Carnival night (1971)
Cinderella suite (1925)
The little dream, suite, 5 pieces based on John Galsworthy (1930)
Andante (1975)
CHAMBER
String quartet in D-Major
Eleven short pieces (str qrt)
Piano Trio in B-Minor
Come summer (cl and pf) (1969)
Dancing faun (fl and pf) (1969)
Improvisations (vln and pf)
PIANO
Numerous piano pieces incl.:
All in a day, 7 solos (1950)
Blue tongue lizard (1952)
Bonny Oh! (1973)
Willow wind
VOCAL
Numerous songs incl.:
Aboriginal themes (m-S, B and orch) (1971)
And everyone will love me
Caprice in C
Down in the sunlit glades, in A
I heard a sound of singing, in F
Let your song be delicate (S and pf)
My bird singing, in D
SACRED
God be in my head
OPERETTA
Old Mr. Sundown (1935)
Publications
Aural Culture.
Ref. 70, 77, 105, 280, 412, 440, 442, 446, 563

SOMELLERA, Josefa

Argentine pianist and composer. b. Buenos Aires, 1810; d. 1885. She was the niece of Candelaria Somellera de Espinosa (q.v.) and studied at the Escuela de Musica y Canto under Picasarri y Esnaola.
Composition
VOCAL
La Muerte de Corina, song (Juan Cruz Varela) (El Cancionero Argentino, 1837)
Ref. 390

SOMELLERA DE ESPINOSA, Candelaria

19th-century Argentine composer. She was the aunt of Josefa Somellera (q.v.).
Composition
CHAMBER
Minuet (pf)
Ref. 390

SOMMER, Silvia

Austrian pianist and composer. b. Vienna, April 9, 1944. She began studying the piano at the age of eight under Professor Landa at the Vienna Musikhochschule, then under J. Dichler. She studied composition under A. Uhl. She began composing when she was eleven and frequently performed her own piano compositions in Austria and abroad. She won the prize for progress from the City of Vienna in 1970.
Compositions
CHAMBER
Caprice (fl, vln, vlc and pf) (1971)
Fuenf Bilder (vln and pf) (1969)
Sonatine (fl and pf) (1969)
Fuenf israelische Taenze (pf) (1975)
Other pieces
VOCAL
Kiryat Shmona (vce and orch) (1974)
Drei Lieder von Hesse, Storm und R.M. Rilke (vce and pf) (1969)
INCIDENTAL
Music for play (Audiberti) (1967)
Music for play (Moliere) (1968)
Ref. Oesterreichische Komponisten der Gegenwart, 194

SOMMERS, Daria E.

American pianist and composer. b. Peoria, IL, October 21, 1956. She grew up in Thailand, the Philippines and the United States. While in Bangkok she studied under Piyabhand Snitwongse. Between 1974 and 1975 she had her first formal composition training when she studied under Christopher Yavelow in Boston and then continued her studies at Oberlin College for four years where she was a pupil of Richard Hoffman. During this period she spent time in the Philippines where she studied the ethnic music of that country.
Compositions
CHAMBER
Malacandra (unspecified ens)
Orion (str qrt) (1974)
PIANO
Prelude to Memnon (1975)
Delphius (1975)
ELECTRONIC
Untitled work for computer (1979)
MISCELLANEOUS
Cepheus (1976)
Disorientale (1979)
Four by two (1977)
Let's deal (1980)
Ref. composer

SONGSTRESS

Prior to the invention of written musical notation, ca. 11th-century, the song was the principal if not sometimes the only means of musical communication and entertainment. The songstress composed the music for her songs as distinct from the singer whose songs were not of her own composition. These songstresses have been traced back as far as the 25th-century B.C.; the earliest in recorded music history being the Egyptian Iti (q.v.) (see frontispiece). (See also AMBUBAJAE, AMON SONGSTRESSES)

SONNTAG, Brunhilde

German harpsichordist, organist, professor and composer. b. Kassel, September 27, 1936. She studied the organ, the harpsichord and composition under Professor Kurt Hessenberg and at the University of Music in Vienna under Professor Gottfried von Einem. She gained her M.Sc. in 1977 from the University of Marburg and in 1977 graduated with her D.Ph. (musical science). She was musical science assistant at the University of Giessen from 1968 to 1974 and from 1975 to 1978 the assistant at the University of Muenster. From 1982 she held the position of professor of composition at the University of Duisburg.
Compositions
CHAMBER
String quartet (1984)
Fuenf Miniaturen fuer Orgel (1984)
Klavierstueck Nr. 4 (1984)
VOCAL
Von guten Maechten (Bonhoeffer) (ch a-cap) (1982)
Floetenspiel, 3 Gedichte nach Hermann Hesse (S, rec and org) (1984)

SACRED
Aber ich sage Euch: liebet eure Feinde (speaker, ch and org) (1983)
Drei Lieder nach Gedichten von P. Celan (S and pf) (1983)
ELECTRONIC
EKG (str qrt, org and tape)
Ref. composer

SONNTAG, Henriette. See SONTAG, Henriette

SONSTEVOLD, Maj. See SOENSTEVOLD, Maj

SONTAG (Sonntag), Henriette (Gertrud Walburga) (later Countess Rossi)

German singer and composer. b. Koblenz, January 3, 1806; d. Mexico, June 17, 1854. Her parents were singers and soon after Henriette's birth, moved to Darmstadt. She appeared in Gotter's *Medea* at the age of four and when she was six sang in Kauer's *Donauweibchen* in Mannheim and Prague with great success. She sang by ear and with no formal training until she was ten years old although she received advice from Josephine Fodor-Mainvielle. Her mother was then persuaded to send her to the Prague Conservatory which accepted her although she was two years under the minimum age. Her teachers were Triebensee (theory), Pixis (piano), Bayer and Czegka (singing). She left the Conservatory early to pursue her operatic career which took her all over Europe and finally to America where her reception almost surpassed that in Europe. She died of cholera.
Composition
VOCAL
Il naufragio fortunato, cantata
Bibliography
Gautier, Theophile. *Portraits contemporains*. Paris, 1847.
Pirchan, E. *Henriette Sontag*. Vienna, 1946.
Ref. 8, 121, 347, 637

SOOK-JA, Oh. See OH, Sook-Ja

SOPHIA CHARLOTTE

German composer. b. ca. 1732. She was the mother of the sons of Frederick the Great, his queen Elizabeth being childless.
Compositions
VOCAL
Songs
OPERA
I Trionfi di Parnasso (ca. 1700)
Ref. 465

SOPHIE ELISABETH, von Braunschweig (Elisabeth Christine), Duchess

German viola da gamba player and composer. b. Guestrow, August 20, 1613; d. Luchow, July 12, 1676. She was the daughter of Johann Albrecht of Mecklenburg-Guestrow and the wife of Duke August of Braunschweig-Wolfenbuettel. She studied the viola da gamba under William Brade. Her court became a place of asylum for refugees and she did much to help the poor.
Compositions
VOCAL
Christfuerstliches Davids Harpfen-Spiel mit Arien: 63 Lieder with basso continuo (texts by her stepson Duke Anton Ulrich von Braunschweig) (Nuremberg, 1667)
Friedens Sieg (ch) (Wolfenbuttel, 1642)
Glueckwuenschende Freudendarstellung (ch) (Luneberg, 1652)
Vinetum evangelicum (Wolfenbuttel, 1647)
SACRED
Piece (pub anon)
OPERETTA
Ballet der Zeit (1655)
Minerva Banquett (1655)
Bibliography
Chrysander, F. *Geschichte der Braunschweig Wolfenbuettelschen Capelle*. Leipzig, 1863.
Daetrius, B. *Koeniges Davids Hertzens-Lust*. Wolfenbuettel, 1677.
Ref. 15, 85, 128, 129

SORALINA, Ana

20th-century composer.
Composition
FILM MUSIC
The Woman of Everyone (1969)
Ref. 497

SORLIE, Caroline Volla. See SOERLIE, Caroline Volla

SOUBLETTE, Sylvia (Sylvia Soublette de Valdes)

Chilean choral conductor, lecturer, singer and composer. b. Antofagasta, February 5, 1924. She studied privately and at the Conservatorio Nacional de Musica in Santiago de Chile under Clara Oyuella (voice), F. Heinlein (interpretation) and Santa Cruz (composition). From 1944 to 1950 she taught at the Catholic University of Valparaiso, formed the women's choir *Vina del Mar* and the choir of the Catholic University of Valparaiso which she directed in numerous concerts. In 1951 she received a scholarship from the French government to study composition and choir-conducting at the Paris Conservatoire under Darius Milhaud and O. Messiaen. Sylvia toured Brazil and Argentina as a soloist with the symphonic and chamber orchestras of Chile. She taught voice and was director of the Conjunto de Musica Antigua of the Catholic University of Santiago, Chile from 1960 and toured extensively with the group throughout Latin America, Eastern and Western Europe and the United States. She was awarded the Elizabeth Sprague Coolidge (q.v.) gold medal in 1964.
Compositions
ORCHESTRA
Preludio y fuga (1949)
CHAMBER
Suite in three movements (fl and pf) (1960)
Sonatina (pf) (1953)
VOCAL
Eva, cantata (1950)
Three choruses for children: Alleluya; Tambuen ganadico; Villancico (1955)
Cancion Madre de Copacabana (S and 3 rec) (1958)
Donde estoy? (S and cham) (1955)
Muy ma clara que la luna (S and 4 rec) (1955)
La pajita (vce and cham) (1946)
Suite pastoril (S, T, fl, vln and hp) (1948)
Three fables: La cigale et la fourmi; Le corbeau et le renard; Le Loup et l'agneau (La Fontaine) (mix-vces) (1954) (prize, Faculdad de Ciencias y Artes Musicales)
Songs incl.:
Balada (G. Mistral) (1956)
Del rosal vengo (Gil Vicente) (1956)
Isla (1955)
Lluvia (Juana Ibarbourou) (1950)
No es porque to quiero (1956)
Unos ojos bellos (Josef Valdivielso) (1956)
SACRED
Te Deum (soloists, ch and orch)
Aquel Pastorcito (Jose M. Peman) (4 mix-vces) (1957)
Cancion de Cuna (G. Mistral)
Hallazgo
THEATRE
Alicia in the Country of Mirrors, play (by G. Eliot from Lewis Carroll)
Le Sicilien, play (Moliere)
Ref. composer, 17, 70, 90

SOUERS, Mildred

American pianist, authoress, teacher and composer. b. Des Moines, IA, February 26, 1894. She studied under Francis J. Pyle at Drake University and Marion Bauer (q.v.) in New York. She won first prize for a choral work from the National Federation of Music Clubs. She was a member of ASCAP.
Compositions
CHAMBER
Pieces
PIANO
Impromptu
Passacaglia
VOCAL
April weather
The immortal
Winter nocturne
SACRED
What Christmas means to me
BALLET
Bar and technique melodies for dance studio
Ref. 39, 40, 142, 347

SOULAGE, Marcelle Fanny Henriette (pseud. Marc Sauval)
French pianist, critic, lecturer and composer. b. Lima, Peru, December 12, 1894. She studied at the Paris Conservatoire under Mme. Marcou, Nadia Boulanger (q.v.), Dallier, Vidal d'Indy, Philipp Caussade, Estyle and M. Emmanuel. She won first prizes for accompaniment in 1913, counterpoint in 1915 and composition. From 1921 to 1925 she taught the piano and harmony at the Orleans Conservatory and from 1949 to 1965 solfege at the Paris Conservatoire. She was a music critic.
Compositions
ORCHESTRA
Badinages (1931)
Danse orientale (1928)
Invocation à la nuit (1928)
CHAMBER
Quartet with piano (1925)
Three string quartets
Piano trio (1921)
Compositions for two harps
Duo (2 hp)
Sonata in D-Minor (vln and pf) (Evette & Schaeffer)
Sonata (vlc and pf) (Paris: Lemoine) (Prix de Amis de la Musique, 1920)
Sonata (vla and pf) (1921)
Sonata in G (fl and pf) (Evette)
Suite in C (Lepaulle, 1918)
Choral et danse (hp)
Variations (pf)
Other instrumental works
VOCAL
Proses d'amour et de mort, song cycle (vces and orch) (1945)
Le repos en Egypte (w-ch)
Ocean (1946)
Songs
SACRED
Hymn des creatures (St. Francis of Assisi) (3 vces a-cap) (Lemoine)
THEATRE
Vive la Chanson, musical comedy (with P. Guedy) (1929)
Publications
Le Solfege. Paris: PUF, 1962.
Ref. 13, 15, 17, 23, 41, 70, 86, 94, 96, 105, 172, 193, 226

SOURGET, Eugenie. See SANTA-COLOMA-SOURGET, Eugenie de

SOUTHAM, Ann
Canadian pianist, music director, lecturer and composer. b. Winnipeg, February 4, 1937. At the Royal Conservatory of Toronto she studied the piano under Pierre Souverain and composition under Samuel Dolinand under Gustav Ciamaga at the electronic music studio of the University of Toronto. She is an instructor in the electronic music studio of the Royal Conservatory in Toronto. She was musical director with the New Dance Group, called the Toronto Dance Theatre after 1969. She is affiliated with the BMI Canada and is the recipient of numerous grants and commissions. DISCOGRAPHY. PHOTOGRAPH.
Compositions
ORCHESTRA
Divertimento (str orch)
Waves (str orch) (1976)
CHAMBER
Momentum (2 perc, hpcd, pf, vla and vlc) (1967)
Towards green (fl, cl, vln and vlc) (1967)
Rhapsodic interlude (vln) (1963)
PIANO
Altitude lake (1963)
Counterparts (1966)
Five pieces in a jazz manner (1970)
Four bagatelles (1961)
Quodlibet (1967)
Rivers, 2nd set, No. 8
Sea flea (1963)
Sonata in one movement (1966)
Suite (1960)
Three in blue (1965)
Toccata (1966)
DANCE SCORES
Against sleep (1969) (comm Toronto Dance Theatre)
ELECTRONIC
Counterparts (full orch and tape)
Antic Eden (1974)
Arrival of all time (1975)
L'assassin menace (1974)
Bernarda Alba (1969)
Boat, river, moon (1972) (comm Toronto Dance Theatre)

Configurations (pf and tape) (1973)
Continuum (1969)
Counterplay (str qrt and tape) (1973)
Eight-way Jones (Sean O'Huigin) (1971)
Encounter (1969)
Figure in the pit (1972)
Fliques (1970)
Harold Morgan's delicate balance (Sean O'Huigin) (1973)
Integruities (narr, pf and tape) (1975) (comm CBC)
Mito (1968)
Mythic journey (1974)
Prospect Park (1971) (comm Ontario Arts Council)
The recitation (1968)
Sky sails (Sean O'Huigin) (1973)
A summer song (1974)
A thread of sand (1969)
Three plus three (1968)
Untitled solo (Sean O'Huigin) (1970)
Walls and passageways (1974)
MISCELLANEOUS
Emerging ground (1983)
Reprieve (1975)
Ref. 4, 81, 288, 329, 402, 563, 622

SOUTHGATE, Dorothy
English composer. b. 1889; d. 1946.
Compositions
CHAMBER
Dorothy's lullaby (vln and org)
Mispah (vln and org)
Serenade espagnole (vln and org)
Thanksgiving (vln and org)
Ref. 63

SOUTHGATE, Elsie
English composer.
Compositions
CHAMBER
Thanksgiving (vln and org)
Vale egyptienne (vln and org)
Ref. 63

SOUTZO, Rodica. See SUTZU, Rodica

SPAGNOLO, Aurelia
20th-century Italian composer.
Composition
PIANO
Dodici studietti
Ref. 228

SPAIN-DUNK, Susan (nee Folkestone), (Mrs Henry Gibson)
English violinist, violist, conductor, teacher and composer. b. London, February 22, 1880; d. January 1, 1962. She studied and taught at the Royal Academy of Music. Two of her compositions, *Trio for piano, violin and cello in A-Minor* and her *First sonata for violin and piano in B-Minor* won prizes in the Cobbett international competition. She played the viola in Mr. Cobbett's quartet.
Compositions
ORCHESTRA
Cantilena (cl and orch)
Spanish dances (pf and orch)
Elaine, symphonic poem
Stonehenge, symphonic poem
Andred's weald (military orch) (1927)
Suite in B-Minor (str orch)
Idyll for strings
Kentish downs, overture
The water-lily pool, overture
CHAMBER
Phantasy (str qrt)
Trio in A-Minor (pf, vln and vlc)
Sonatas (vln and pf)
Flute solos
Violin solos
Ref. 41, 70, 105, 322, 433, 467

SPALDING, Eva Ruth

English lecturer, pianist and composer. b. Blackheath; d. 1969. She studied with L. Auer and Carl Weber and is an L.R.A.M. She taught the piano and the violin privately and at Bradfield College.

Compositions
CHAMBER
String quartets, Nos. 1-5 (Senart)
Sonata No. 2 (pf and vln) (Senart)
VOCAL
Five sonnets from Spencer's Amoretti (vce, 2 vln, vla and vlc)
Songs
Ref. 41, 226, 490

SPALDING, G.F.

American composer. d. Newton Center, MA, December 12, 1933. She was the grandniece of composer William Billings.
Ref. 105

SPANHEIM, Jutta von. See SPONHEIM, Sister Jutta von

SPAULDING, Florence Atherton

19th-century composer.
Composition
THEATRE
Lady Nancy, musical (White)
Ref. 297

SPAULDING, Virginia

American pianist, lyricist, poetess and composer. b. Houlton, ME, July 6, 1906. She wrote music and lyrics for songs and other poetry.
Ref. 374

SPEACH, Sister Bernadette Marie (C.S.J.)

American organist, pianist, teacher and composer. b. Syracuse, NY, January 1, 1948. She obtained her B.S. (music education) from the College of Saint Rose, Albany, NY. She taught the piano, the guitar, the organ, choir and church liturgy.
Compositions
PIANO
Reaching for the sun
VOCAL
To share a dream (vce and pf)
SACRED
The new Jerusalem (ch and org)
Ref. 77

SPEARE, Sally. See LUTYENS, Sally

SPECHT, Anita Socola

American pianist, singer and composer. b. New Orleans, 1869; d. New Orleans, 1959. She studied in New Orleans under Professor Hubert Rolling, Marguerite Samuel, Professor Otto Weber and Professor Lenfant, in New York under Alexander Lambert and singing in Chicago under Professor Seeboeck and Signor Arcangelo. At the age of 18 she was acclaimed at the World Fair in Chicago. She was elected president of the State Federation of Music Clubs in 1921 and was active in the founding of the New Orleans Symphony Orchestra.
Compositions
PIANO
Nocturne (also orch)
Other pieces
Ref. 347, 448

SPECHT, Judy Larise

Canadian accordionist, flautist, organist, pianist, teacher and composer. b. Prince Rupert, British Columbia, 1943. She graduated from the University of British Columbia (B.Mus. theory and composition) in 1975, (M.Mus., composition) in 1980 having studied under Elliott Weisgarber. She is an A.R.C.T. and the recipient of several scholarships. She has taught music appreciation, the piano, theory and composition in Vancouver and Prince Rupert. PHOTOGRAPH.

Compositions
ORCHESTRA
Celebration (1982)
CHAMBER
String quartet
Duo (fl and pf) (1978)
Bachianas (pf) (1979)
VOCAL
Chamber operation (mix-ch and cham ens)
Three Canadian folk songs (chil-ch) (1981)
Mosaic (fl, S, hn, vla and vlc) (1984)
Song with words and Song without words (Cont, fl, cl, vib, d-b and timp) (1977)
Three songs (T and pf) (1978)
SACRED
Missa brevis (S, A and org) (1984)
INCIDENTAL MUSIC
Deus ex Machina, theatre piece (1978)
Easy Street, music for a silent movie (1978)
Ref. composer, Assoc. of Canadian Women Composers

SPEKTOR, Mira J. (Myra)

20th-century American poetess, singer and composer. She graduated from the Sarah Lawrence College and did post-graduate work at Mannes and the Juilliard School of Music. She founded and directed the Atlantic Opera Singers for six years and the Aviva Players. DISCOGRAPHY.
Compositions
VOCAL
Magen Yerushalaim (boys-ch)
Four songs on poems by Ruth Whitman (vce, vln, vlc)
Love is more thicker than forget (e.e. cummings) (w-vce, vln and pf)
SACRED
Sunday Psalm (Bar and pf) (1980)
OPERA
Lady of the Castle
THEATRE
The Housewives' Cantata, musical (Joan Siegel)
Publications
The Changeling – Poems from a Journal. 1980-1982.
Bibliography
AMC Newsletter. Vol. 20, no. 3.
Music Journal, January 1979, p. 42.
Ref. 563, 622, 625

SPENA, Lita

Argentine composer. b. Buenos Aires, 1904. She studied at the Conservatorio de Musica y Arte Escenico. She began her musical career in 1929 as member of the Chamber Music Trio Argentino. Her songs for children received several prizes.
Compositions
PIANO
Cuatro preludios impresionistas (1938)
Sonata (1937)
VOCAL
Coplas jujenas (vce and pf) (1939)
Treinta canciones infantiles
Ref. 390

SPENCER, Fannie Morris

19th-century American composer. b. Newburgh, NY.
Compositions
VOCAL
Songs incl.:
Awake my love
Homeward
Well-a-day
When I know
SACRED
Anthems
Thirty-two hymn tunes
Ref. 226, 276, 292, 433

SPENCER, Georgiana, Duchess of Devonshire. See CAVENDISH, Georgiana

SPENCER, Marguerita (nee McQuarrie)

Canadian cellist, organist, pianist, violinist, teacher and composer. b. Cape Briton, Glace Bay, Nova Scotia, December 28, 1892. She studied in Glace Bay under Hilda Irwin; at the Halifax Conservatory, Nova Scotia, under Harry Dean, Romeo Corteri and Mrs. Pianconka; in Saskatoon under E.V. Morton, Mary Mitchener, Lyell Gustin and Madame Sherry; in Montreal under Clara Liechtenstein and Walter Clapperton and in Madison under Conn. She is an A.T.C.M. and hold an L.Mus. from McGill University. She was church organist, teacher and piano recitalist in Sydney, Nova Scotia and Saskatoon. During World War II she played in cinemas for silent films and performed piano recitals and gave CBC broadcasts. All her published works have been performed in Canada, the United States and Europe. In 1975 she was one of fifty women honored for her position as woman of status by the civic committee. A television documentary on her life and music was shown on Canadian TV. PHOTOGRAPH.

Compositions
CHAMBER
String Quartet
Trio (vln, vlc and pf)
PIANO
Piano duo Corelli
Arabesque (1940)
Dolls' suite
Early morning impressions (1949)
Four waltzes
Pastorale (1940)
Prelude for Easter
Prairie suite I, II and II
Reverie (1940)
Song without words (1936)
Twenty-four preludes
Three intermezzi
ORGAN
Sunday morning
Sunday evening
VOCAL
A birthday (1969)
Five Shakespeare songs
Girl in a yellow sweater
Innocence (1974)
June magic
The little caterpillar
Meadow larks in April
A portrait of Irene (1952)
Tell my love (1952)
Time cannot take (1952)
Who seeketh beauty (Shakespeare)
Four commissioned songs:
Reality
Spring song
Wild horses
Ref. composer, 77, 85, 133, 347

SPENCER, Williametta

American organist, musicologist, professor and composer. b. Marion, IL, August 15, 1932. She studied at Whittier College under Ernst Kanitz and Tony Aubin (B.A.) and at the University of Southern California (M.Mus., Ph.D.). She studied in Paris from 1953 to 1954 on a Fulbright scholarship and is currently associate professor at Rio Hondo College in Whittier, CA. She won national competition awards and MOE first prizes for her *Sonata* in 1951 and *Madrigals* in 1958 and in 1968 the Southern California Vocal Association national award for composition. She contributes articles to a number of local publications. DISCOGRAPHY. PHOTOGRAPH.

Compositions
ORCHESTRA
Movements for symphony band
Passacaglia and double fugue for string orchestra
Overture (Amy Beach award)
CHAMBER
String quartet No. 1
Trio for brass instruments
Adagio and rondo (ob and pf) (1960) (Los Angeles: Western International Music Co., 1968)
Lyric piece (ob and pf)
Music for flute and clarinet
Sonata (trb and pf; also cl and pf)
Suite (fl and pf)
Improvisation and meditation on 'Gott sei gelobet' (org)
VOCAL
The fisherman and his wife (S, Bar and cham orch)
At the round earth's imagined corners (mix-ch) (1st prize, Southern California Vocal Assoc.) (Delaware Water Ga, PA: Shawnee Press, 1968)

Death be not proud (mix-ch) (Shawnee, 1971)
Four madrigals to poems of James Joyce (mix-ch) (1st prize MOE National competition) (Champaign, IL: Foster Music, 1970)
Give me the splendid sun (mix-ch) (Foster, 1976)
The mystic trumpeter (mix-ch) (Anaheim, National Music Co., 1969)
Adam lay ybounden (Assoc. Music)
As I rode out this enders night (Assoc. Music)
As I sat under a sycamore tree (Assoc. Music)
Bright cap and streamers (Foster, 1976)
Green grow the rashes, O (National Music)
In the dark pine wood (Foster, 1976)
O my luv's like a red, red rose (National Music)
Past 3 o'clock (National Music)
Songs from The Tempest (National Music)
These are the days when birds come back (Foster)
Three songs from William Shakespeare
Trylow, trylow (Foster)
Two glees (National Music)
Winter has lasted too long (vce, cl and pf)
SACRED
Cantate Domino, cantata (Shawnee)
Make we joy, cantata (Foster)
Missa brevis (mix-ch) (1972) (Foster, 1974)
Nova, nova, ave fit ex Eva (mix-ch) (National Music, 1969)
There is no rose of such virtue, carol (mix-ch) (Music Pub., 1969)
Angelus ad virinem (Foster)
A babe is born (Assoc. Music)
Gabriel's message (Foster)
Gloria in excelsis (Assoc. Music)
Nowell, out of your sleep, carol (Assoc. Music)
Two Christmas madrigals
Wassail, wassail all over town, carol (Assoc. Music)
Welcome Yule, carol (Assoc. Music)
Ref. composer, 77, 137, 142, 146, 206, 228, 563, 625

SPENCER PALMER, Florence Margaret (Peggy)

English pianist, teacher and composer. b. Thornbury, Gloucestershire, July 27, 1900. She was educated at the Tobias Matthay School in London where she was awarded a scholarship to London University (B.Mus.). She studied the piano under Vivian Longrish, composition under B.J. Dale and Sir Ivor Atkins. She was senior music mistress at Clarendon School Malvern for 18 years, visiting teacher in Bristol schools and taught privately. She was awarded the Chappell gold medal in 1923 and received the Horatio Lumb competition award for hymn tunes and anthems. PHOTOGRAPH.

Compositions
CHAMBER
Three pieces (vlc and pf) (1924)
Other pieces
PIANO
Burlesque (Ascherberg, 1925)
Three festive pieces (1922)
Variations on Barbara Allen (1923)
VOCAL
Solo and part-songs (J.B. Cramer & Co., 1934)
Songs incl.:
SACRED
Anthems (J.B. Cramer & Co., 1934)
The gate of the year
Publications
The Pianist's Book of Chime. 1953.
Simplified Sightreading. 1970.
Wings, Part I (set of religious poems, words by Amy Carmichael, music by various composers), 1960.
Ref. composer, 77, 206

SPENCER PALMER, Peggy. See SPENCER PALMER, Florence Margaret

SPENGER, M.T. See DICHLER-SEDLACEK, Erika

SPICER, Marjorie

Australian composer. b. 1921.
Compositions
VOCAL
Come to the river (mix-ch and cham orch) (1976)
OPERA
Paul, rock opera (1974)

662

THEATRE
The Blue Miracle, musical (1968)
Cyclone, musical
Folk Elijah, musical (1965)
The Paul Story, musical (1967)
The Rice Bowl Nativity, musical (1965)
Ref. 442

SPIEGEL, Laurie

American guitarist, lutenist, teacher and composer. b. Chicago, IL, September 20, 1945. She studied at Shimer College (A.B.) in 1967. From 1966 to 1968 she studied independently at Oxford University and privately (classical guitar, theory and composition) under J.W. Duarte in London from 1967 to 1968. From 1969 to 1972 she studied the guitar under Oscar Ghiglia at the Juilliard School of Music and Renaissance and Baroque lute under Suzanne Bloch and Fritz Rikko. During that time she also studied privately under Alexander Bellow and Michael Czajkowski. From 1972 to 1975 she studied composition privately under Jacob Druckman and computer composition under Emmanuel Ghent. At Brooklyn College she was a pupil of Jacob Druckman and obtained her M.A. in 1975. Since 1970 she has been the guitar teacher at Bucks County Community College and electronic music teacher since 1971. Since 1971 she has been assistant to the director of electronic music at the Aspen Music Festival and a teacher since 1972. She was resident visitor with Bell Telephone Research Laboratories for composing with the Groove System from 1973 to 1974 and was awarded a Rockefeller grant as junior research fellow at the Institute for Studies in American Music, 1973 to 1974. She was awarded *Meet the Composer* grants from the New York State Council on the Arts in 1975, 1976 and 1977, a CAPS grant in 1975 and 1976 and an ASCAP award in 1976. She received a WNET Experimental Television Laboratory production support grant and artist-in-residence status in 1976. From 1980 to 1981 she held the position of director of the electronic music studio and composition teacher at the Cooper Union for the Advancement of Science and Art, NY, and during 1982 she was the director of the computer music studio at New York University. She also works as a freelance consultant in computer music. She has performed at numerous museums, galleries, universities and festivals, including the Museum of Modern Art in New York and the Aspen Music Festival. She has also appeared on radio and television. DISCOGRAPHY.
Compositions
CHAMBER
Hearing things (1983) (comm Mostly Modern Cham Orch)
A stream (man)
BALLET
Waves (9 acoustic insts and pre-recorded tape) (1975) (comm American Dance Festival)
INCIDENTAL MUSIC
The Clinic (Robert Goldman)
The House of Bernarda Alba
The Library of Babel (Paul Ahrens) (1972)
White Devil (John Webster)
ELECTRONIC
Appalachian Grove No. 1 (1974)
Drums
Expanding universe (1975)
Harmonic spheres (1971)
Old wave
Orchestras (1971)
The Orient Express (1974)
Patchwork (1976)
Pentachrome
Purification (1973)
Raga (1972)
Return to zero (1971)
Sediment (1972)
Sunsets (1973)
The unquestioned answer
Voices within
DANCE SCORES
Music for dance
Ref. composer, 142, 206, 269, 494, 563, 622, 625

SPIEGEL VON UND ZU PECKELSHEIM, Charlotte. See SPORLEDER Charlotte

SPINAROVA, Vera
20th-century Czech composer. DISCOGRAPHY.
Composition
MISCELLANEOUS
Andromeda
Ref. 563

SPINDLE, Louise Cooper
20th-century American lecturer and composer. b. Muskegan, MI. She studied under her mother and at the Chicago Musical College. Her other teachers included Glen Dillard, Gunn, Hans von Schiller, Dr. Falk, Max Wald, Felix Borowski, Chas, Vogan and Lawrence Powell. She taught at Columbia University and is a member of ASCAP.
Compositions
ORCHESTRA
Southland suite
CHAMBER
Sonata in E
PIANO
Bouncy balls
Holiday in Naples
Parade of the bunnies
Ping-pong
Somersaults
Swaying pussywillows
Other pieces
VOCAL
Choral pieces
Songs incl.:
Moon magic
My dream ship
SACRED
The City Eternal, cantata
Christmas roundelay
God's gift supreme
TEACHING PIECES
Pieces
Ref. 39, 40, 94, 142, 347

SPIZIZEN, Louise Myers
American harpsichordist, critic, lecturer, singer-accompanist and composer. b. Lynn, MA, August 4, 1928. She studied at Vassar College (A.B.) in 1949 and the University of California, San Diego (M.A.) in 1972 and composition privately under Wallingford Riegger, Robert Erickson, Kenneth Galburo and Wilbur Ogdon. She was music director of Interplayers, Inc., New York from 1949 to 1952 and singer-accompanist with the Westchester County Civic Opera from 1954 to 1957. She was singer-accompanist-composer with the Madrigal Singers in Westport, CT from 1959 to 1965 and with the First Unitarian Church, Westport, from 1960 to 1963. From 1960 she taught privately, in adult schools and community colleges in Connecticut, Washington DC, and San Diego. From 1972 she taught at the University of California. She was co-founder of San Diego mini concerts, founder of Basically Baroque Symposium and served as music critic and columnist in La Jolla, CA, from 1975. She has contributed articles to journals and has performed as solo harpsichordist with chamber groups and orchestras throughout the western United States. She received a Vassar College prize in composition for a dance score and was awarded two commissions from the Westport Madrigal Singers. She published numerous teaching pieces. PHOTOGRAPH.
Compositions
VOCAL
Three games for ten players (mix-ch and str qnt) (1971)
Three rounds for mothers (mix-ch a-cap) (1962)
Weary with toil (mix-ch a-cap) (1966) (Theodore Presser)
SACRED
Sacred service, for Reformed Jewish congregation (2 part w-vces and org) (1963-1965)
DANCE SCORES
Sweep it clean, musical comedy (1948)
BALLET
Birthday of the Infanta (hpcd, cham orch and pf) (1949)
Publications
Numerous teaching pieces. Editions and realizations of 17th/18th century works by Fasch, Locatelli, Leclair and Biber.
Ref. composer, 142, 625

SPOENDLIN, Elisabeth
Swiss pianist, violinist, violist, psychologist and composer. b. Zurich, February 8, 1923. As a child she studied the violin and then the viola which she played for many years in the Solothurn Orchestra. After leaving school she studied social work and in 1969 opened her own practice as a child psychologist. She began piano studies and composing at the age of 40. Although lacking in formal composition education she felt she had learnt much from working together with Zurich composer and conductor Thuering Braem. PHOTOGRAPH.
Compositions
ORCHESTRA
In memoriam (1984)
Sine nomine, 4 movements (1984)
Spielen, concert piece (school orch) (1985)
Traeumen (1984)

CHAMBER
> Invention, concert piece (9 insts) (1983)
> Geigengesang (vln and 5 insts) (1983)
> Drei Miniaturen, concert piece (cor anglais, vla and hp) (1985)
> String trio (1981)
> Streiten? (keyboard insts and bongo) (1985)
> Trio (pf, vln and vlc) (1985)
> Oboe soll a geben (ob) (1983)
> Solo piece (vln) (1981)

PIANO
> Aufbaeumen
> Flucht in die Andacht
> Heftig
> Mobile mit Metallplaetchen
> Nach den Radioafnahmen
> Still
> Wo ist der Schlag
> Four pieces

VOCAL
> Songs
> Children's songs

INCIDENTAL MUSIC
> Six pieces for radio program, Musikmacher ohne Oeffentlichkeit (1981)

Ref. composer, 651

SPOERRI-RENFER, Anna-Margaretha

Swiss pianist composer. b. Biel-Bienne, Canton Bern, 1896. She began her piano studies at the age of 11. She studied theory at the Bern Conservatory from 1918 to 1920 and at the University of Bern in 1935. She continued her studies at the Conservatory of Bienne and studied theory, the piano and singing in Gstaad. Her piano teachers included E. Fisher, Cherbulier, E. Levi, A. Aeschbacher, R. Serkin, H. Pembauer and H. Scherchen. She is a member of the Swiss Tonkuenstler. PHOTOGRAPH.

Compositions
CHAMBER
> String quartet in G-Major
> Sonata in C-Minor (vlc and pf) (1968)

PIANO
> Sketches
> Small variations
> Studies for the left hand

VOCAL
> Eight songs (J. Reinhart) (S and pf) (1924)
> Forty-four songs (vce and pf)

SACRED
> Pax, Christmas cantata (solos, ch, org and small orch) (1971)
> Easter Cantata (solos and ch)
> Geistliche Gesaenge (ch a-cap)
> Magnificat (5-part ch a-cap)
> Psalm 23 (trans Martin Buber)

Ref. composer

SPONDLIN, Elisabeth. See SPOENDLIN, Elisabeth

SPONGBERG, Viola

20th-century American organist, pianist, violinist, singer and composer. b. New York, NY. She graduated from Hunter College (A.B.), Columbia University (M.A.), New York University (Ph.D.) and obtained a Teacher's Licence in Music from the New York College of Music. Her teachers include Henry Holden Huss and Pompilio Malatesta. She made her debut as a violinist at the age of ten; performed extensively in both the United States and abroad; and was the organist for several churches in New York. She wrote a string quartet, string trio, a concerto for the violin and the piano, a piano concerto, violin pieces and organ pieces.

Publications
> *The Philosophy of Erik Gustaf Geijer.* 1945.
> Articles for numerous publications.

Ref. 496

SPONHEIM, Sister Jutta von

Early 12th-century teacher and composer. She was the abbess of the Benedictine nunnery at Disibodenberg and sister of the Count of Sponheim. She was the teacher of Hildegard von Bingen (q.v.) and composed hymns.

Ref. Donne in Musica (Rome)

SPOONER, Dorothy Harley

West Indian pianist, accompanist, choral conductor, teacher and composer of Trinidad. b. March 23, 1921. She is an L.R.S.M. She was accompanist for music festivals and ballet exams and taught the piano at St. Peter's School in Trinidad. She was also choir mistress and piano teacher there. She was honored at the Trinity College of Music exhibitions in 1934 and 1935.

Compositions
SACRED
> Our Father

MISCELLANEOUS
> Airport
> Barbecue

Ref. 359

SPORLEDER, Charlotte (nee Baroness Spiegel von und zu Peckelsheim)

German composer. b. Kassel, November 8, 1836; d. Kassel, January 9, 1915.

Compositions
CHAMBER
> Concertante (vln and pf)

PIANO
> Grand sonata
> Die Kaskaden von Wilhelmshohe, op. 19, idyll for the left hand (Monopol-Verlag)
> Preussischer Siegesmarsch, op. 14 (Andre)
> Valse brillante, ballad

VOCAL
> Der Vater ist am Steuer: Die Nacht ist dunkel, op. 1, ballad
> Four songs, op. 15
> Two songs (Dufayel): Ich hab'im Traum geweinet; Ich will meine Seele tauchen, op. 11
> Weihnachtslied, op. 20
> Other choruses and songs

Ref. 70, 105, 226, 297, 433

SPORRI-RENFER, Anna-Margaretha. See SPOERRI-RENFER, Anna-Margaretha

SPOTTISWOODE, Alicia Ann. See SCOTT, Lady John Douglas

SPRAGG, Deborah J. See ADDENDUM

SPRAGINS, Florence

20th-century American composer of choral works.
Ref. 40, 347

SPROD, Anna. See SPROED, Anna

SPROED (Sprod), Anna

20th-century composer.
Composition
MISCELLANEOUS
> Unspunnen-Taenze, group and pair dances (with Klar Stern and Louise Witzig) (Schweizerische Trachtenvereinigung)

Ref. Verlag Hug

SQUIRE, Hope (Mrs. Frank Merrick)

English composer. b. 1878; d. 1936. DISCOGRAPHY.
Composition
PIANO
> Variations on Black-eyed Susan

Ref. 563

STAEHLI, Violette

Compositions
PIANO
> Auf einer Alp
> Vorfruehlingstag

VOCAL
> Kleines, schlichtes Lied (vce and pf)

Ref. Frau und Musik

STAINKAMPH, Eileen Freda (Mrs. Morris)

Australian teacher, writer and composer. b. Kensington, Victoria, June 25, 1904; d. November 14, 1981. Her teachers included Drs. J Steele and A.E. Nickson. She held her L.Mus.A. and was an L.R.S.M. and an A.T.C.L. She specialized in teaching music through correspondence and wrote numerous books on this subject. PHOTOGRAPH.

Publications

Essential Harmony for Students.
Essential Rudiments.
My First Theory Book.
Preliminary Theory Papers for Beginners.
Essential Questions and Exercises of School Leaving Standard.
Essential Theory Papers.
Essential Technic for Junior Pianists.
Form and Analysis of 27 Haydn Pianoforte Sonatas.
Form and Analysis of Mozart Pianoforte Sonatas.
Form and Analysis of Beethoven Pianoforte Sonatas.
Essential Tests (aural work).
Essential Scale and Arpeggios Manual.
Sight Reading Exercises for the Pianoforte.
Classical Analysis of Modern Chord Symbols.
Ref. Mr. J. Morris

STAIR, Patty (Martha Green)

American organist, pianist, choral conductor, lecturer and composer. b. Cleveland, OH, November 12, 1869; d. Cleveland, April 26, 1926. She studied at the Cleveland Conservatory from 1882 to 1893 and was a pupil of Franklin Bassett. From 1889 she taught at the Conservatory and from 1892 at the University School where she was also an organist. She frequently appeared in concerts in Cleveland. In 1914 she was the first woman in Ohio to become a fellow of the American Guild of Organists. For some years she was active as conductor of women's club choirs.

Compositions
ORCHESTRA
    Intermezzo
    Small pieces
CHAMBER
    Pieces (org, vln and pf)
    Sweet simplicity, berceuse (vln and pf)
VOCAL
    Minuet (4 part ch a-cap) (Schirmer)
    Part-songs incl.: Jenny kissed me (m-vces) (Schirmer)
OPERETTA
    The Fair Brigade, in 3 acts
    An Interrupted Serenade
Ref. 22, 40, 85, 89, 226, 276, 292, 297, 347, 353, 415, 433

STAIRS, Louise E. (pseud. Sidney Forrest)

American organist, pianist, conductor, teacher and composer. b. Troupberg, NY, 1892.

Compositions
PIANO
    Floating clouds
    Soldiers at play
    To whit, to whoo
    A woodland concert
VOCAL
    Choral cantata (Presser)
SACRED
    Lift up your heads, ye gates of brass
    Lord, speak to me
    So longeth my soul for thee
    There is an eye that never sleeps
Ref. 40, 142, 292, 347

STALEWSKA, Jadwiga

19th-century Polish composer.

Composition
PIANO
    Przelotne mysli, waltz (Warsaw: Gebethner, 1860)
Ref. 118

STANEKAITE-LAUMYANSKENE, Elena Ionovna

Soviet pianist, professor and composer. b. Radzivilishka, Lithuania, July 4, 1880. In 1907 she graduated from the Moscow Conservatory where she studied the piano under A. Scriabin and K. Igumnov. She studied composition under A. Ilinsky. From 1908 she taught the piano at schools in Moscow and Vilna and in 1930 founded the Lithuanian National Conservatory in Kaunas, of which she was the principal. From 1940 she taught the piano at the Vilna Conservatory and became a professor in 1946. She gave concerts in Vilna, Kaunas and Moscow. DISCOGRAPHY.

Compositions
CHAMBER
    Mazurka (vln and pf) (1923)
    Memories (vln and pf) (1923)
    Remembrance (vln and pf)
    Romance (vlc and pf) (1923)
    Tarantella (vln and pf) (1923)
PIANO
    More than 200 pieces incl.:
    Miniatures
    Preludes
    Children's pieces
VOCAL
    Choral works and songs of Lithuanian poets
    Approximately 100 romances in Lithuanian language
    Evening
    I was sad in the night
    It is good for your heart (1923)
    Understood
Ref. 87, 563

STANG, Erika

Norwegian pianist and composer. b. 1861; d. 1898. She was a pupil of Agathe Backer-Groendahl (q.v.) and H. Barth.

Compositions
PIANO
    Bryllupsmarsch
    Menuet
    Other pieces
VOCAL
    Songs incl.: Vaarvise
SACRED
    Songs
Ref. 20

STANLEY, Helen Camille (Mrs. Denby Gatlin)

American pianist, violinist, violist, lecturer and composer. b. Tampa, FL, April 6, 1930. She studied under Hans Barth and Ernst von Dohnanyi and at the Cincinnati Conservatory (B.Mus) in 1951. In 1954 she graduated from Florida State University (M.Mus.) and in 1961 from Muskingum College, OH, (B.S.). She is a piano judge and teacher and has been a violinist with the El Paso Symphony; music director at the Ballet Center, El Paso; lecturer at the School of Broadcasting, Jones College in 1965 and 1966; and at Jacksonville University from 1962 to 1967, then she became a free-lance lecturer and presented master classes to teachers. She has appeared on TV and her works have been performed on various radio stations throughout the United States. She became composer-in-residence of the Florida Contemporary Ensemble in 1986. Her awards include a graduate fellowship, Florida State University; the C. Hugo Grimm prize for ensemble composition; the Louis Pogner Chamber Music award and the Florida State Music Teachers Association award in 1972. She has received a number of commissions. PHOTOGRAPH.

Compositions
ORCHESTRA
    Symphony No. 1
    Passacaglia
CHAMBER
    Woodwind quintet
    Brass quartet
    String quartet (1980)
    String quartet No. 1 (1951)
    Piece (hn, perc and pf)
    Fantasy and fugue (brass)
    Overture for timpani and brass (1951)
    Two pieces (wind insts and pf)
    Sonata (trb and pf) (comm W. Cramer)
    Suite for tuba (1986)
PIANO
    Etudes
    Modal suite
    Sonatina
VOCAL
    Night piece (w-ch and orch) (W.C. Hugo Grimm prize)
    Battle hymn at St. Paul's by-the Sea (ch, org, perc, trp and fl) (1976)
    Songs incl.:
    Credo
    The isle
BALLET
    Birthday of the Infanta
ELECTRONIC
    Rhapsody (tape and orch)
    Duo-sonata (tape and pf)
    Electronic prelude
    Meditation (pf and tape)
    Study (elec tape)

OPERETTA
Lunar Encounter (tape)
MISCELLANEOUS
My sky-yearning soul (1976)
Ref. composer, 77, 142, 347, 475, 625

STANLEY, Marion Isabel

20th-century American singer, teacher and composer. b. Boston. She studied singing under Jessie Hubbard and I. Braggiotti and pantomime under Clayton Gilbert at the New England Conservatory. She taught opera at the Venello-Johnson School of Opera and in Europe.
Compositions
VOCAL
If I were a red rose
SACRED
A prayer for peace
Ref. 374

STANLEY, Mrs. P. See HENDERSON, Rosamon

STARBUCK, Anna Diller

American organist, pianist, teacher and composer. b. Lancaster, PA, August 29, 1868. She studied at the Leipzig Conservatory and at the Zurich Musikschule.
Compositions
CHAMBER
Fugue (org)
Pieces (pf)
VOCAL
Songs
THEATRE
Music for a Greek play
Ref. 226

STARCK, Ingeborg Lena von. See BRONSART VON SCHELLEN-DORF, Ingeborg Lena von

STARK, Lola Aloisia Maria. See BERAN-STARK, Lola Aloisia Maria

STECHER, Marianne

German organist and composer. b. Mannheim, ca. 1760. She lived in Mannheim until about 1811.
Compositions
CHAMBER
Three sonatas for piano and flute oblige, op. 8 (1803)
ORGAN
Eight fugues (also hpcd) (1802)
Fugue, op. 7 (Schott)
Fugue, op. 6 (also hpcd) (Leipzig: Breitkopf and Haertel)
Six fugues, op. 13 (Breitkopf)
HARPSICHORD
Nine pieces (1793)
Thirteen variations, op. 5 (Breitkopf and Hartel)
Twelve variations and a rondo, op. 6 (Munich, 1799)
PIANO
Grosse grand Sonate in B (4 hands) (Breitkopf)
Pieces (2 hands)
Ref. 26, 226, 260, 297, 347

STECKLER, Anne-Marie. See KRUMPHOLTZ, Anne-Marie

STEEL, Ann (pseud. Theodosia)

English composer. b. Broughton, Hampshire, May, 1716; d. Hampshire, November 11, 1778. She was the daughter of a Baptist minister. After her fiance drowned she devoted herself to good works and composing hymns.
Compositions
SACRED
Miscellaneous pieces (under pseud) (1760)
Hymns
Publications
Hymns, Psalms and Poems. London 1863.
Ref. 502, 646

STEELE, Helen (Mrs. Wager S. Harris)

American pianist, authoress, choral conductor, teacher and composer. b. Enfield, CT, June 21 1904. She attended Mount Holyoke and Wellesley Colleges, where she obtained her B.A. and studied music privately. She is a member of ASCAP.
Compositions
VOCAL
America, our heritage
Duerme
Lagrimas
The legend of Befana
Ref. 39, 94, 142, 646

STEELE, Lynn

American arranger, conductor, teacher and composer. b. Beaumont, TX, May 27, 1951. She graduated from Smith College, Northampton, MA, (A.B.) in 1973 where she studied composition with Alvin Etler and conducting with Iva Dee Hiatt. In 1982 she graduated from the American University, Washington, MA, having studied composition with Jerzy Sapieyevski and singing with Elizabeth Kirkpatrick Vrenios. She teaches singing, the piano and composition privately and has worked as an arranger. Since 1982 she has been a member of the Oratorio Society of Washington.
Compositions
ORCHESTRA
Pavane (cham orch) (1979)
Sartre's wall (cham orch) (1980)
CHAMBER
Balladette (ww qnt) (1967)
Aquarelles, 3 pieces (fl, vlc and pf)
Fugue for recorders (3 rec) (1979)
Suite for flute, bassoon and piano (1980)
Berceuse (fl and pf) (1980)
Minuetto (2 fl) (1967)
Tarentelle (fl and pf) (1983)
HANDBELLS
Carillon de nuit (Bell Tower Pub. Corp.) (1981)
Her garden (Bell Tower) (1981)
Little fugue (1981)
Petits fours (1982)
Wild geese (1981)
VOCAL
Requiem for women's voice and handbells (1982) (soli, ch and bells) (comm Reston Chorale, VA)
Seven poems (Edna St Vincent Millay) (S and pf) (1980)
OPERA
Dominique (1982)
OPERETTA
Flea circus (1969)
Ref. composer, 625

STEFANOVIC, Ivana

Yugoslav violinist, music director and composer. b. Belgrade, 1948. She studied the violin and composition at the Faculty of Music and Arts in Belgrade and advanced studies in composition under Enriko Josif. Since 1967 she has been a music director with Radio Belgrade. She won a prize for original music for drama and a prize for the best music program in the International Competition, Monte Carlo in 1974. PHOTOGRAPH.
Compositions
CHAMBER
String quartet (1970)
Trio sonata (1967)
Suite (pf) (1966)
Variations (vln) (1968)
VOCAL
Kabana, vocal poem (solo, mix-ch and orch)
Kasto su ti suze (mix-ch)
Dve pesme (H. Micheaux)
Glad mi je beskrajna (R. Drainac)
Moj svet (D. Maksimovic)
INCIDENTAL MUSIC
Music for radio and television dramas
Ref. Union of Yugoslav Composers

STEIGMAN, Mrs. B.M. See BARTHELSON, Joyce Holloway

STEIN, Gladys Marie

American authoress, teacher and composer. b. Meadville, PA, October 19, 1900. She graduated from the Pennsylvania College of Music in 1922 and from the New England Conservatory in 1924. She also attended the Thiel College, the Pittsburgh Musical Institute, the Erie Conservatory and the University of Pittsburgh. She founded and taught at the Stein School of Music in Erie, PA, from 1929. She contributed articles to numerous publications.

Compositions

BAND
 Dancing along
 Dancing Americans
 Happy little robin
 Hummer's waltz
 In tulip time
 Polish dance
 Redbird
 Scouts on parade
 Song of the young braves
 Spring time frolic
 Waltz of the toys
PIANO
 Melodies to play
 Red feather
 Soldiers on parade

Publications

Tuned Time Bell. 1936.
Rhythm Band Instruction. 1936.
Tuned Resonator Bell and Rhythm Instructor. (Ludwig and Ludwig) (1935).
Ref. 475, 496

STEIN, Nannette (Mrs. Streicher)

Austrian pianist and composer. b. Augsburg, January 2, 1760; d. Vienna, January 16, 1833. She was the daughter of Johann Andreas Stein the famous Viennese piano builder. Her father tried to turn her into a *Wunderkind*, taking her on concert tours and in 1777 she played at the Viennese court. Although her playing was praised by many, Mozart dismissed her as *not a genius*. Together with her husband and brother she took over her father's piano business after his death and then called themselves *Frère et soeur Stein*. She met Beethoven when he was 17 and supported him through the turbulent years between 1813 and 1818.

Compositions

CHAMBER
 March for wind instruments
 Variations (pf)
VOCAL
 Klage ueber den fruehen Tod der Junger Ursula Sabina Stage in Augsburg (1788)
Ref. 25, 26, 335

STEIN-SCHNEIDER, Lena

German writer and composer. b. Leipzig, January 3, 1874. She studied counterpoint under Hermann at the Berlin Academy of Arts. She worked as a writer and composer in Berlin and was a member of the Verband Deutscher Buehnenschriftsteller. In 1923, 1924, 1925 and 1928 she toured the United States.

Compositions

ORCHESTRA
 Valse d'amitie, op. 54
CHAMBER
 Nocturne in E, op. 53 (vlc and pf)
 Berceuse in C, op. 52 (pf)
VOCAL
 Das Veilchen (1914)
 Der neugierige Kater, song, op. 20
 Hinter dem Glanz deiner Augen, op. 99
 Kronprinzen' Marsch Song, op. 103
 Lied von verlorenen Glueck
 Sehnsucht, op. 100
 Other songs
 Children's songs
OPERETTA
 Auto und Schimmel
 Composer's Dream (New York, 1928)
 Ein Hundert Kuesse (1928)
 Koenig Drosselbart (1916)
 Prinz Heidenmut (1914)
 Der luftikus, op. 59
 Die lustige Liebe
Ref. 111, 226

STEINBOCK, Evalyn

20th-century American composer

Composition

OPERA
 The Proposal (Anton Chekov) (1983)
Ref. AMC newsletter

STEINER, Emma Roberto

American conductor and composer. b. Baltimore, 1852; d. February 27, 1929. She began composing at seven and produced a piano duet at the age of nine; at 11 she wrote one and a half acts of a grand opera *Aminaide*. In 1873 she became assistant music director to the Rice and Collier Iolanthe Company in Chicago. She conducted for a number of companies and produced Gilbert and Sullivan and other light operas and became known for her own operatic works. Her opera *Fleurette* was produced in San Francisco in 1889 and in New York in 1891. In 1894 she conducted the 80 member Anton Seidl Orchestra in New York in a program of her own works. In 1902 she spent a season working with Heinrich Conried in New York, who in 1903 became the manager of the Metropolitan Opera and who would reputedly have liked to appoint her as conductor at the Metropolitan Opera. In 1921 she presented *Harmony and Discord*, a program of her own works, at New York's Museum of Natural History. She composed over 400 works in her lifetime and conducted over 6 000 performances of more than 50 different operas and operettas.

Compositions

ORCHESTRA
 Gavotte Menzeli or Mengeli (pf and orch) (New York: MacDonald and Steiner, 1914)
PIANO
 Dream of the angels, theme with variations (Brainard)
VOCAL
 The flag, forever may it wave (vce and orch) (1918)
 Beautiful eyes (M.L. Glentworth) (vce and pf) (MacDonald, 1921)
 Florence Laurence, op. 417 (M.M. MacDonald) (vce and pf) (MacDonald)
 I envy the rose (M.G. Millais) (vce and pf) (MacDonald and Steiner) (1921)
 My love, so fair (S and T) (Brainard)
 Rapture (S and fl ad lib) (Brainard)
 Tecolate (St. Henri) (vce and orch; also vce and pf) (MacDonald, 1921)
OPERETTA
 The Alchemist
 La belle Marguerite
 Brigands (1894)
 Burra Pundit
 Day Dreams (1894)
 Fleurette, comic opera in two acts
 The Little Hussar
 The Man from Paris (1900)
MULTIMEDIA
 I'm a rattler, character song and dance (Brainard)
ARRANGEMENTS
 Orchestral arrangements
Ref. 226, 228, 264, 292, 297, 307, 415, 433

STEINER, Gitta Hana

American pianist, poetess, professor and composer. b. Prague, April 17, 1932. She received a diploma in composition in 1963 and graduated from the Juilliard School of Music (B.Mus.) in 1967 and (M.S.) in 1969 where her teachers included Elliott Carter and Vincent Persichetti. She was a pupil of Gunther Schuller at Tanglewood in 1966. As a pianist she has played orchestral and chamber music in the United States and abroad. Since 1960 she has taught the piano privately and from 1962 to 1966 she was a teacher of theory at the Brooklyn Conservatory and co-director of the Composer's Group for International Performance in 1968. She was professor of composition at the faculty of Brooklyn Conservatory from 1983 to 1984. She was awarded the Gretchaninoff memorial prize for her string orchestra work in 1966 and received the Marion Freschl award for vocal works with original texts in 1966 and 1967. She won the ASCAP standard annual award in 1972 and was honored at the Composer's Forum, Donell Library, 1966. In 1967 she became a fellow of the Berkshire Music Center, Tanglewood.

Compositions

ORCHESTRA
 Piano concerto (Seesaw, 1967)
 Violin concerto (1963)
 Music for string orchestra
 Tetrark (str orch) (1965)
 Three movements for orchestra (1981)
CHAMBER
 Movement for eleven (fl, 2 cl, 2 trp, hn, trb, tba, vln, vla and vlc)
 Brass quintet (Seesaw, 1964)
 Percussion quartet (1968)
 String quartet (1968, 1983)
 Piano trio (1968)
 String trio (Seesaw, 1964)
 Suite (fl, cl and bsn) (Seesaw, 1958)
 Trio (2 perc and pf) (Seesaw, 1969)
 Music for strings
 Duo (hn and pf) (1979)

Duo (vib and mar; also trb and perc) (1980, 1982)
Duo (vlc and perc) (1971)
Fantasy (cl and pf; also mar) (1964, 1980)
Five pieces (trb and pf)
Jouissance (fl and pf) (1965)
Percussion music for two (1971) (Seesaw, 1975)
Dialogue (perc) (1975)
Eight miniatures (vib)
Five pieces (trb)
Four bagatelles (vib) (Seesaw, 1975)
Night music (mar)
Refractions (vln) (1967)
Sonata (vib) (1982)
Three pieces (vib) (1968)
Violin sonata (1981)
Suite (1958)
PIANO
Fantasy piece (Seesaw, 1966)
Nine melodious pieces (1959)
Sonata (Seesaw, 1964)
Three pieces (Seesaw, 1961)
VOCAL
Concert piece for seven, nos. 1 and 2 (S and cham ens) (1968)
Five choruses (1965)
Five poems (mix-ch) (1970)
Four choruses (1972)
Four choruses of Emily Dickinson
Four settings (ch) (1970)
Music for 4 players (S, d-b and 2 perc)
Trio (vce, pf and perc) (1971)
Pages from a summer journal (vce and pf) (1963)
Cantos (vce and vib) (1975)
Dream dialogue (vce and perc) (1975)
Four Songs (med-vce and vib) (1970)
Interludes (vce and vib) (1968)
Three songs (med-vce) (1960)
Three songs by James Joyce
Three poems (1960)
Two songs (1966)
Ref. 40, 52, 80, 94, 142, 146, 185, 190, 206, 322, 347, 477, 494, 594, 611, 622, 625

STEINKRAUS-FISCHER, Edith. See FISCHER, Edith Steinkraus

STEMANN, Petronella
Danish composer. b. Soroe; d. Copenhagen, 1839.
Composition
PIANO
Smaacompositioner med portraet (1854)
Ref. 413

STENHAMMAR, Fredrika (nee Andree)
Swedish pianist, operatic singer and composer. b. Visby, September 19, 1836; d. October 7, 1880. She was the sister of the composer Elfrida Andree (q.v.). She studied under W. Soehrling in Visby before proceeding to the Leipzig Conservatory, where she studied the piano, theory and singing from 1851 to 1854. In Paris she studied under Duprez from 1857 till his death the following year. In the 1860s and 1870s she was considered one of the most outstanding singers in Stockholm, her roles ranging from Wagner (she was one of the first Swedish sopranos to sing in his operas) and Mozart to Rossini.
Compositions
VOCAL
Der Abschied Johannas (Schiller)
Aftonen, romans
Aftonstjernan
An der Quelle sass der Knabe (Schiller)
Droemmen (Heine)
Five songs with piano (Stockholm, 1869) (ded Laura Netzel)
Granen (Heine)
Hektors Abschied
Hjertesorg (Geibel)
Laengtan (Immermann)
Lullaby
Das Maedchen in der Fremde
Des Maedchens Klage
Under vindens sus och boeljors dans, marsch
Naer varens dagar nalkas
Oforstadd kaerlek (Heine)
Pa Nova Sembljas fjaell, i Ceylons branda dalar

Ritter Toggenborg Ballade (Schiller)
Til din vagga feer komma
Till Syster Frida
Vaarlaengtan
Wid Mormor Gerles graf
Ref. 20, 95, 167

STEPANIUGINA, E.
Soviet composer. b. ca. 1930.
Compositions
VOCAL
Songs incl.:
Druzhno khleb my ubirayem
Poliushko kolkhoznoye
Radostno na dushe
Vane nochenku ne spitsya
Ref. 441

STEPHEN, Roberta Mae
Canadian pianist, violinist, singer, teacher and composer. b. Calgary, April 17, 1931. She studied the piano under Dorothy Hare and the violin at the Mount Royal College Conservatory. She played first violin in a youth orchestra. She attended the University of Calgary where she majored in music and then taught at public schools in both Edmonton and Calgary. In 1960 she began writing music, mostly songs for children. She graduated from the University of British Columbia faculty of music in 1973 having majored in composition. She founded the R. Stephen Contempra Ensemble to perform vocal music of the 20th-century. Most of the songs performed at these concerts were composed by her.
Compositions
ORCHESTRA
The playground suite (fl and string orch) (1973)
Salt sea and prairie grass (string orch) (1978)
CHAMBER
Lines and spaces (pf, hn, fl and perc) (1970)
Prelude and canon (vln and pf) (1978)
VOCAL
Courtship (vce and pf) (1974)
Song to Naomi (vce and pf) (1967)
ARRANGEMENTS
Blood on the saddle, folk song (1980)
Canadian folk songs (1974-1975)
Hush you bye, folk song (1980)
Moon of wintertime, folk song (1979)
Ref. composer

STEPHENSON, Maria Theresa
19th-century English composer.
Composition
VOCAL
Victoria anthem (Celtic)
ARRANGEMENTS
An ancient Argyllshire melody (presented by the Marquis of Lorne as a Diamond Jubilee tribute from loyal Scots abroad to Queen Victoria)
Ref. 123

STERLING, Antoinette. See MacKINLEY, Mrs. J.

STERLING, Jean. See TAYLOR, Mary Virginia

STERNICKA-NIEKRASZOWA, Ilza
Polish pianist and composer. b. Petersburg, September 20, 1898; d. Warsaw, June 27, 1932. She studied the piano under W. Drozdow and then at the Petersburg Conservatory where she also studied theoretical subjects, instrumentation and composition under W. Kalafati, J. Witol and Glazunov. Later in Warsaw she studied under Statkowski, Melcer, Szymanowski and was awarded diplomas in the piano in 1927 and in composition in 1929.
Compositions
ORCHESTRA
Basn (pf and orch) (1927)
Szachy, symphonic grotesque (1931)
CHAMBER
Variations (str qrt)
Double fugue (str qrt)
Grotesque for children (fl, cl and bsn)

PIANO
  Colours, ballet suite
  Fragments
  Oberek
  Sonata in F-Minor
VOCAL
  Children's songs
SACRED
  Oratorio (K. Niekrasz) (soli, ch and orch)
  Ojcze nasz (vce and pf)
  Agnus Dei
Ref. 8, 118

STEVENS, Isadore Harmon
American organist and composer. b. Pomona, FL. She was educated at Bates College and Brown University.
Compositions
VOCAL
  Pines of Maine (w-ch)
SACRED
  Service music and songs
Ref. 374

STEVENS, Joan Frances (nee Wollerman)
New Zealand pianist, lecturer and composer. b. Palmerston North, NZ, January 14, 1921. She was educated at the Wellington Teachers' College and is an L.R.S.M., an L.T.C.L. and a licenciate of the Graduate School of Music, Trinity (music therapy). She taught music at schools and lectured at the Wellington Teachers' College.
Compositions
VOCAL
  A child's song of the New Zealand bush
  Koo the kiwi and Kip the kangaroo
  The penguin
  Song to A Tui
Ref. 457

STEVENS, Mrs Fred P. See STEVENS, Isadore Harmon

STEVENSON, Mrs. George. See BARNETT, Alice

STEWART, Annie M.
19th-century American composer.
Compositions
VOCAL
  Songs incl.:
  Summer's crowning day
Ref. 276, 347, 433

STEWART, Elizabeth Kirby
South African composer. b. London, 1832; d. Alice, South Africa, October 2, 1919.
Compositions
PIANO
  Flowers of melody waltz (London: Reid Bros.)
  Pretty Polly Hopkins mazurka (King Williamstown: Hay Brothers)
VOCAL
  The Victoria East march (vce and pf) (Hay)
SACRED
  The anchor within the veil (vce and pf) (Hay)
  The joy of angels (Lord Kinloch) (vce and pf) (Grahamstown: T. & G. Sheffield)
  I will give thee rest (vce and pf)
Ref. 184, 377

STEWART, F.M.
19th-century American composer. She composed piano pieces and songs.
Ref. 276, 347, 433

STEWART, Hascal Vaughan
American lecturer and composer. b. Darlington, SC, February 17, 1898. She studied at Winthrop College and did post-graduate work at Teachers' College in New York. She studied composition privately under Gustave Weigl and was on the music faculty of Winthrop College from 1921 to 1922.
Compositions
CHAMBER
  Pieces pieces
VOCAL
  Songs incl.:
  As a premiere
  Overtones
  Sleep to wake
SACRED
  Mary in Christendom
  Threshold of Christmas
Ref. 142

STEWART, Katherine (nee Brown)
English piano teacher and composer. b. Plymouth, 1891. She is an L.R.A.M. She taught the piano, elocution and singing in schools from 1914 to 1925, and composed works for the piano and songs.
Ref. 490

STEWART, Madame. See SKINNER, Florence Marian

STEWART, Mrs. See WAINRIGHT, Harriet

STEWART, Ora Pate
20th-century American composer. DISCOGRAPHY.
Compositions
PIANO
  March of the Gadiantons (pf) (Provo, Utah: Fernwood, 1975)
VOCAL
  The battle line of home (w-ch and pf) (Fernwood, 1966)
  Golden promise (w-ch and pf) (Fernwood, 1968)
  I cried when I sang of babes in the wood (w-ch and pf) (Fernwood, 1967)
  Jamie's Christmas (w-ch and pf) (Fernwood, 1977)
  Likewise (w-ch) (Fernwood, 1974)
  Mother-song (w-ch) (Fernwood, 1973)
  Our glorious land (w-ch and pf; also S and pf) (Fernwood, 1965)
  Pebble beach (w-ch and pf) (Fernwood, 1973)
  Song of love (w-ch and pf; also S and pf) (Fernwood, 1965)
  This is the land (mix-ch and pf; also brass and str) (Fernwood, 1974)
  To a child (A, pf or w-ch, vln and vla ad lib) (Fernwood, 1964)
  A tree stood tall (w-ch and pf) (Fernwood, 1967)
  What was that song (mix-ch) (Fernwood, 1969)
  Claim thou my heart (w-ch) (Fernwood, 1965)
  Crossing the bar (2 S, pf and/or org) (Fernwood, 1965)
Ref. 228, 563

STEWART, Rosina. See VRIONIDES, Rosina

STEWART-BAXTER, Maud
Scottish violinist and composer. b. Perthshire, 1892. She was a pupil of Emil Sauret at the Royal College of Music.
Compositions
CHAMBER
  Haymakers' dance (2 vln and pf)
  In Corbar Woods (2 vln and pf)
  Gigue (vln and pf)
  A lament (vln and pf)
  Melody in A (vln and pf)
  Pavanne (vln and pf)
  Ruritanian dance (vln and pf)
  Sarabande (vln and pf)
  Scotch air (vln and pf)
VOCAL
  Songs incl.:
  Across the valley
  A call from the deep
  Cruisers
  In August
  Loveliness more fair
  Lovers' sighs

O cold grey sea
One hour of love
Our lady's bedstraw
Primeval
A rainy day
The soul of the Moor
Ref. 467

STEWART-NORTH, Isabel
English composer.
Compositions
VOCAL
Book of lullabies (James Kenyon)
Songs
Bibliography
Musical Observer. Vol. 14, no. 5, May 1917.

STILLING, Kemp
American composer.
Compositions
MISCELLANEOUS
The giant talks
The great adventure
Ref. 92

STILMAN, Ada Julia. See STILMAN-LASANSKY, Julia

STILMAN-LASANSKY, Julia (Stilman, Ada Julia)
American pianist and composer. b. Buenos Aires, February 3, 1935. She studied in Buenos Aires where she pursued private piano studies under Roberto Castro from 1951 to 1956 and composition under Gilardo Gilardi from 1956 to 1958. She graduated from the University of Maryland (M.Mus.) in 1968 (D.M.A.) in 1973 and did post-doctoral studies at Yale University in 1974 under Krysztof Penderecki. Other composition teachers included Morton Subotnick and Lawrence Moss at the University of Maryland and Leon Kirchner at the University of Buffalo, 1959. She received a graduate school fellowship from 1970 to 1973, a Phi Kappa Phi award in 1972, and an N.E.A. fellowship-grant in 1974. She has lived in the United States since 1964. PHOTOGRAPH.
Compositions
CHAMBER
Cello quartet (cl, trp, xyl and vlc) (1959) (CFE; NY)
Etudes (ww qnt) (1968) (CFE)
Etudes (str qrt) (1967) (CFE)
Visiones primera, sonata (pf) (CFE)
VOCAL
Cantata No. 1, El oro intimo (Amado Nervo) (B and orch) (1961)
Cantata No. 2, Cantares de la madre joven, poem no. 61 from Gitanjali by R. Tagore) (7 women soloists and cham ens)
Cantata No. 3, Barcarola (Pablo Neruda) (S, m-S, A, triple mix-ch and cham orch)
Cantata No. 4, Magic Rituals of the Golden Dawn (Yeats) (soloist, ch and orch) (comm National Endowment for the Arts for the Bicentennial)
Cuadrados y Angulos (Alfonsina Storni) (A, trp, E-flat sax, pf and tim)
Ref. composer, 137, 206, 228, 280, 347, 622, 625

STINSON, Ethelyn Lenore. See ADDENDUM

STIRLING, Elizabeth (Mrs. Frederick A. Bridge)
British organist, pianist and composer. b. Greenwich, February 26, 1819; d. London, March 25, 1895. She studied the organ and the piano under W.B. Wilson and E. Holmes and harmony under Hamilton and Macfarren. She was appointed organist of All Saints' Poplar at the age of 20, a position that she retained for nearly 20 years and later at St. Andrews, Undershaft (after winning a competition) until 1880. In 1856 she submitted an exercise for a Mus.B. at Oxford. Though accepted it was not performed as there was no precedent at that time for conferring degrees on women. As an organist she was one of the first women to play Bach's fugues and give performances at the Apollonicon, in various London churches and at the International Exhibition of 1862.
Compositions
PIANO
God save the Queen (4 hands) (Augener)
All among the barley, galop and waltz (Augener)
ORGAN
Pedal fugues, six and eight slow movements (Novello)
Two grand voluntaries (Novello)
Arrangements of works by Bach, Handel and Mozart (various publishers, incl. Augener)

VOCAL
About 50 pieces incl.:
Dream (ch) (Curwen)
Faded flowers (mix-ch) (Ashdown)
Friendship, love and truth (m-ch) (Novello)
The hermit (mix-vces) (Novello)
Nine choral songs (ch and pf ad lib)
Now autumn strews on every plain (Harvest) (mix-ch) (Novello)
Portrait (mix-vces) (Ashdown)
Red leaves are falling (ch) (Curwen)
Sleeping, why, now sleeping, serenade (m-ch) (Novello)
Woodman's walk (mix-ch and pf or harm) (Pitman)
All among the barley, part-song
Leonora (vce and pf) (Ascherberg)
Parted friends (vce and pf) (Novello)
SACRED
Psalm 130 (5 vces and orch) (1856)
Ref. 2, 6, 8, 22, 70, 74, 85, 102, 123, 132, 226, 260, 264, 297, 347, 353, 400, 433, 622, 646

STIRLING, Jean. See TAYLOR, Mary Virginia

STIRLING, Magdalene
18th-century Scottish composer.
Compositions
MISCELLANEOUS
Twelve tunes (1796)
Ref. 65

STIRLING-MAXWELL, Lady W. See NORTON, Hon. Mrs.

STITH, Mrs Townsend
19th-century American composer.
Composition
VOCAL
Our friendship (vce and pf) (Philadelphia: G. Willig, 1830)
Ref. 228

STITT, Margaret McClure
20th-century American composer. She composed pieces for instrumental ensembles, choirs, songs and an opera and children's songs.
Ref. 40, 347

STOBAEUS, Kristina. See ADDENDUM

STOCKER, Clara
Compositions
PIANO
Two little pieces (1937)
Ref. 473

STOCKER, Stella (nee Prince)
American pianist, lecturer, singer and composer. b. Jacksonville, IL, April 3, 1858; d. 1925. She graduated from the University of Michigan, and studied at Wellesley College from 1876 to 1877 and later at the Sorbonne in Paris. Her early training was at Jacksonville Conservatory. She studied the piano under Frau Gliemann in Dresden and Xaver Scharwenka in Berlin. She sang with Sbriglia in Paris and studied counterpoint and composition under Klein in New York from 1910 to 1913. She was a specialist in the music of the American Indians and made use of their melodies in their original form in her compositions. These melodies appear frequently in the choruses of her plays. She lectured in the United States and abroad on Indian music and legends and was a member of the New York and Chicago Manuscript Societies.
Compositions
PIANO
Pieces
VOCAL
Songs incl.:
A sea song
While thou wert by
OPERA
Beulah
Ganymede
Queen of hearts
Raoul

THEATRE
 The Marvels of Manabush, 3 act Indian pantomime
 Sieur du Lhut, 4 act play
Ref. 74, 276, 292, 433

STOCKHAUSEN, Elizabeth von. See HERZOGENBERG, Elizabeth von

STOCKTON, Morris. See TERHUNE, Anice

STOEPPELMANN, Janet

American electronic instrumentalist, harpsichordist and composer. b. St. Louis, December 5, 1948. She obtained her B.A. (harpsichord and composition) from Barry College, Miami and an M.Mus. (composition and theory) from the University of South Florida. She did graduate work in composition and ethnomusicology under de Oliveira. She studied electronic music under Hilton Jones and Japanese Noh drama under Agnes Takako and Miyazaki Youngblood. She also studied multiphonic singing under D.J. Mizelle.
Compositions
CHAMBER
 Sindhura (hp) (1973)
VOCAL
 Seashore of endless worlds (w-ch) (1972)
 Parallax (1973)
 Piece (S and ens)
 Three Japanese haiku concerning butterflies (w-vce)
 Tollite jugum meum, motet (1971)
 Trisagion (1972)
THEATRE
 The Great Wall of China, after Kafka (theatre piece) (4 channel tape and narr) (1973)
ELECTRONIC
 Metallon (tape tamtams, perc and sculpture)
MULTIMEDIA
 Lila (1973)
 Raise high the roofbeam, carpenters (1974)
 The river merchant's wife: a letter (1974)
 Water music (1975)
 Piece for contemporary dance (comm)
Ref. composer, 77, 142, 625

STOLBERG, Louise von (Countess)

19th-century German composer.
Compositions
VOCAL
 Nicht im Leben, nicht im Lieben (m-ch)
 Umtoente mich der wilde Laerm der Schlacht (m-ch)
 Alles wo ich weil' und gehe
 Bluet' und Ranken
 Ich bin von aller Ruh' geschieden
 Ich wandre ueber Berg und Tal (1 or 3 vces)
 O Herz, sei endlich stille
 Poetisches Tagebuch (Klemm)
 Die Winde sausen am Tannenhang
 Du zarte Ros' im Morgentau (1, 2 or 3 vces)
Ref. 128, 297

STOLL, Helene Marianne

20th-century German composer.
Compositions
VOCAL
 Ich singe dir mit Herz und Mund, cantata (1960)
 Der Morgenstern ist aufgedrungen, cantata (S, T, org, ob or vln)
 Ein feste Burg ist unser Gott (w-ch, 2 trp or vln, drs, timp and org)
Ref. 465

STOLLEWERK, Nina von

Austrian composer. b. Vienna, ca. 1825. She was a pupil of Simon Sechter. She wrote her first lieder when she was 16 years old.
Compositions
ORCHESTRA
 Two symphonies
 Piano pieces
VOCAL
 Men's choruses
 Drei Lieder (Kistner): Der Einsame; Die Traene; Du bist ferne
 Eliza's erstes Begegnen (vce and pf) (Cranz)

Grubenfahrt, op. 2 (Cranz)
 Liebchen, wo bist du?, op. 3 (Cranz)
 Matrosenlied, op. 6, No. 2 (Cranz)
 Two poems, op. 5 (Witzendorf)
 Wunsch und Gruss, op. 6, No. 1 (Cranz)
 Songs
SACRED
 Mass (1846)
Ref. 26, 226, 276, 297

STOLTZ, Rosina (Rosina, Victorine Noeb, Rose Niva)

French mezzo-soprano and composer. b. Paris, February 13, 1815; d. Paris, June 30, 1903. She married a baron and then two princes. She composed six songs and an arrangement of quadrilles and contradances from Donizettis *Favorita*.
Ref. 332, 462

STORY, Pauline B.

20th-century American pianist and composer. b. Cincinnati. She composed piano pieces.
Ref. 347

STOWE, Charlotte Caroline. See BACHMANN, Charlotte Caroline

STOWE, Harriet Beecher

American authoress, teacher and composer. b. Litchfield, CT, June 14, 1811; d. Hartford, CT, July 1, 1896. She composed hymns but became famous as the authoress of *Uncle Tom's Cabin*.
Publications
The Mayflower, or Sketches of Scenes and Characters among the Descendants of the Pilgrims.
Uncle Tom's Cabin; or, Life Among the Lowly. 1852.
A Key to Uncle Tom's Cabin.
Dred: A Tale of the Dismal Swamp.
The Minister's Wooing. 1859.
Pearl of Orr's Island. 1862.
Ref. 208, 502, 646

STRANTZ, Louise von

German pianist, singer and composer. b. Tippelskirch, May 2, 1825. She studied the piano and theory under Pax and singing under Constanze Blank and Jaehn.
Compositions
ORCHESTRA
 Pieces
PIANO
 Berliner Einzugs-Marsch (Bote)
 Dell-Era Walzer (Bote)
 Fest-Walzer (S. Majestaet) (Bote)
 Flora-Polka (Bote)
 Hubertsburger Friedens-Marsch (Bote)
 Kaiser-Koenig-Marsch (Bote)
 Maiblueten, Walzer (Bote)
 Prinz Friedrich-Marsch (Bote)
 Santa-Lucia Marsch (Bote)
 Schneeflocken, Walzer (Bote)
 Victoria-Walzer (1858) (Bote)
 Wilhelm-Marsch (Bote)
 Reverie (Bote)
VOCAL
 Des Kaisers Ruh' schutz' Vater du, cantata (solos and ch) (Bote)
 Songs incl.:
 Anna-polka (Bote)
 Klage dem Liebchen (Bote)
 Zwei Lieder (Bote)
Ref. 121, 297

STRATTON, Anne (Mrs. Thomas S. Holden)

American composer. b. Cleburne, TX, 1887. After three years at the Universiy of Texas she turned to composition and for a brief period studied in New York.

Compositions
VOCAL
Songs incl.:
Ah, love, how soon? (New York: H. Flammer)
Boats of mine (Flammer)
Dusk come floating by (Flammer)
From out the long ago (Flammer)
Home time (Flammer)
May magic (Flammer)
My goal (Flammer)
November (Flammer)
Parting at morning (Flammer)
The sun at last (Flammer)
Sun of my soul (Flammer)
Wash day (Flammer)
Ref. 228, 292, 347

STRAUSS, Elizabeth
German music teacher and composer. b. December 27, 1881; d. Landsberg, June 25, 1934. She composed piano pieces and songs.
Ref. 226

STREATCH, Alice
20th-century American composer. She composed choral pieces and songs.
Ref. 40, 347

STREATFIELD, Mrs. R. See PATERSON, Wilma

STREATFIELD, Valma June
British pianist, recorder player, violinist, singer, teacher and composer. b. Lahore, Pakistan, October 13, 1932. In 1977 she graduated with a B.Mus. from Auckland University where she studied under John Rimmer and Douglas Noeurs. She holds a B.Mus, an L.T.C.L., an A.T.C.L., and an A.Mus.A. She is qualified as a teacher and a member of the British Guild of Composers. She studied the piano, the violin and the recorder. At Melbourne Conservatory she studied singing with Carrie Cairndoff and her piano teachers included Allan Jankins and Larry Litsky. She played in several major orchestras including the Sydney Symphony and the Canberra Symphony. In 1969 she studied composition under Dorothea Hranshi in Auckland, in 1970 with Len Hischer in Canberra and the piano with Allan Jenkins. In 1971 she studied the piano with May Clifford and composition with Eileen Stainkampf. She represented Australia at the Trinity College of Music centenary celebrations having moved to England in 1972. She continued her composition studies under Charles Lealey at Trinity College. She is currently director of music at a small private school in Reading, England. PHOTOGRAPH.
Compositions
ORCHESTRA
Campbell's Bay overture (1976)
Little orchestra waltz (1981)
Minuet and trio (1969)
Second time around (1969)
CHAMBER
Three blind mice (fl, hn, xyl, vib, vln and pf) (1975)
Opus 2 (2 cl, vln and pf) (1968)
Carawal (trp and 2 cl) (1980)
Minuet and trio (pf, vln and cl) (1965)
Pink rabbits (sax, cl and org) (1980)
Rondo (vln, vla and vlc) (1977)
Trio (fl, cl and vlc) (1977)
The wooden horse (2 vln and wood block) (1977)
Katrina's polka (2 cl) (1965)
Minuet (ob and bsn) (1976)
The jagged rock (vln) (1977)
Mountain songs (org) (1977)
Regal march (org) (1982)
Ten simple studies for violin, 1st position (1968)
Two waltzes, op. 1 and 2 (org) (1982)
PIANO
Ali Baba (1971)
Follow my lead (1977)
Finches in spring (1978)
Petit-point (1979)
Sea-horses (1979)
Serial composition (1979)

Snowflakes (1982)
The storm (1977)
Windmills (1978)
Elementary piano book (1982)
VOCAL
All but blind (m-S, pf, fl and vln) (1976)
Aotearoa (S, fl, ob, cl, trp, trb, vln, vlc and pf) (1977)
Eskimo Song; Ipes and kilts; Polish dance; German dance, Clog song; Mexico; Canada (1968)
The Highlands (1981)
Jean Pierre; Little maid from Austria; Danish dance; Little Hao from Old Macao (1967)
New Zealand (1969)
Sea-scape (1981)
Seventy-two songs incl. Nature songs; Rhythm songs; Weather songs, Health songs; Songs of the seasons (1953)
Silver (S and pf) (1981)
Sir Richard Granville (1977)
Who has seen the wind? (S and pf) (1981)
Windy nights (1983)
Yugoslavia; Tonga (1970)
SACRED
Blake's cradle song (1977)
Bright the vision that delighted (1982)
Cherry tree carol (1977)
Dark the night (mix-ch)
Eternal ruler of the ceaseless round (1982)
Fair waved the golden corn (1982)
Flemish carol (1977)
From out of a wood a cuckoo did fly (1982)
A gallery carol (1977)
Gloria in excelsis Deo (1982)
Go man go (1982)
God of mercy, God of grace (1982)
Green grow'th the holly (1977)
Hail to the Lord who comes (1982)
Hark the sound of holy voices (1982)
I look to thee in every need (1982)
Jesus, gentlest Saviour (1982)
Jesus, meek and gentle (1982)
Little Jesus sweetly lay (1954)
Lute book lullabye (1982)
Mighty God which angels bless thee (1982)
O happy band of pilgrims (1982)
O heavenly Jerusalem (1982)
O Trinity of blessed light (1982)
Puer nobis (1982)
See the conqueror mounts in truimph (1982)
Sing around on this day (1977)
Soldiers of Christ arise (1982)
Sussex carol (1977)
Take heart, the journey's ended (1982)
Take up Thy cross (1982)
There were ninety and nine (1982)
When spring unlocks the flowers to paint the laughing soil (1982)
The winter's sleep was long and deep (1982)
ELECTRONIC
Singapore melange (1977)
Ref. composer

STREET, Arlene Anderson
Composer b. 1933. DISCOGRAPHY.
Composition
PIANO
Drowsy Dilemma
Ref. 563

STREICHER, Lyubov Lvovna
Soviet violinist, lecturer and composer. b. Vladikavkas, Ordzhonikidze, March 3, 1888; d. Moscow, March 31, 1958. She studied the violin under L. Auer at the St. Petersburg Conservatory, graduating in composition, which she studied under Liadov and Steinberg at the same time as teaching solfege. From 1913 to 1915 she taught the violin and solfege at the Yekaterinodar Music School and conducted the symphony orchestra there. From 1915 to 1921 she taught theoretical subjects, first at the music school in Rostov-on-the-Don and then at the Rostov Conservatory. From 1922 to 1924 she taught at the Glinka Music School in Petrograd; from 1932 to 1937 at the Leningrad Conservatory; and from 1946 to 1952 at the Gnesin Institute in Moscow where she lectured on composition. After 1953 she taught at the Moscow School of Music.

Compositions
ORCHESTRA
    Jewish poem (1927)
CHAMBER
    Armenian quartet (1936)
    Quartet (1955)
    Suite (str qrt) (1930)
    Suite on folk themes of the peoples of the Soviet Union (str qrt) (1941)
    Improvisation (vlc and pf) (1933)
    Sonata (vlc and pf) (1944)
    Pieces for violin and piano
PIANO
    Six pieces
    Sonata
    Twelve children's pieces on folk themes of the USSR
VOCAL
    Zhenshchina vostoka (E. Polonskaya) (ch and sym orch) (1937)
    Klyatva (E. Polonskaya) ballad (vce and pf) (1931)
    Children's songs
    Romances (F. Tyuchev, P. Verlaine)
    Seven poems from Eugene Onegin (Pushkin) (vce and pf) (1954)
    Songs about Lenin, Kirov
    Ten Jewish work-songs (Jewish poets) (vce and pf) (1949)
    Ya lesom shla, musical story (vce and pf) (1949)
    1905 god, song cycle
BALLET
    Noch fialki (1914)
OPERETTA
    Chasi, for children (E. Polonskaya) (1932)
ARRANGEMENTS
    Folk songs of USSR, Czechoslovakia, Hungary and Rumania
Ref. 17, 87

STREICHER, Mrs. See STEIN, Nannette

STREIT, Else

German pianist, violinist, lecturer and composer. b. Lauenburg, Pomerania, July 27, 1869. She studied the violin under Heinrich Deeke and theory and composition under Stephan Krehl at the Karlsruhe Conservatory from 1893 to 1897 and continued her studies at the Stern Conservatory, Berlin from 1898 to 1902 where her teachers included Gustav Hollaender (violin) and Max Loewengar (instrumentation and composition). She taught the violin in Berlin at various music schools and the New Conservatory, Charlottenburg until 1916 and then at the Bromberg Conservatory she taught the violin, the piano, theory and composition until 1920 when she taught the violin privately and at the Klindworth-Scharwenka Conservatory, Berlin.

Compositions
ORCHESTRA
    Festmarsch for infantry (1896)
    Symphonietta (str orch) (1908)
    Theme and variations (1904)
CHAMBER
    Romance in B-Minor (vln and pf) (1897)
    Sonata (vln and pf) (1925)
    Violin pieces
VOCAL
    Songs with violin and cello, or piano, incl.:
    Drei Lieder: Still dahin; Colombine; Schelmenlied, op. 25 (Schlesinger)
    Es war einmal, op. 7 (Schlesinger)
    Vier Lieder: Trost; Stummer Abschied; Herbst; Zwei Glueckliche, op. 21 (Schlesinger)
    Vier Lieder: Aus meinem Grabe; Abendlied; Nachtgeschwaetz; Rauhfrostmorgen, op. 22 (Schlesinger)
SACRED
    Psalm (S, vln and org) (1926)
    Weihnacht (Bierbaum) (vce and pf or org) (1925)
OPERA
    Fairy tale opera
    St. Nikolaus und seine Gehilfen, Christmas opera (1928)
Ref. 111, 226, 297

STRELLA, Evgenia. See KUZNETSOVA, Zhanetta Aleksandrovna

STRICKLAND, Lily Teresa

American organist, authoress, teacher and composer. b. Anderson, SC, January 25, 1887; d. Hendersonville, NC, June 6, 1958. She studied at Converse College in Spartanburg, SC, under A. Mildenburg, in New York at the Institute of Musical Art under A.J. Goodrich, W.H. Humiston, W.J. Henderson and Thomas Tapper and on scholarship at the Juilliard School

of Music under Goetschius. In 1924 she was awarded an honorary Mus.D. from Converse College. From 1927 to 1928 she composed the Indian dance music for the Derishawn Dancers' production with the Ziegfeld Follies. From 1920 to 1930 she traveled in the Far East and India. She was a prolific songwriter and on her return to the United States a number of her songs were published. DISCOGRAPHY.

Compositions
ORCHESTRA
    Piano concerto
    Carolina suite
    Charleston sketches
    East Indian night
    Flight fantasy
    Moorish dance
    Oasis (1942)
    Prelude
    Symphonic suite on Negro themes
    Three Egyptian scenes (hp, pf and strs)
PIANO
    Bird fantasy
    Blue Ridge idyls, suite
    From a caravan, suite
    From the southwest, suite
    Impromptu
    Jungle nocturne
    Moroccan mosaics, suite
    Saharan silhouettes, suite
    Through an Indian gateway
    To the burning gnat
    Two East Indian nautches
VOCAL
    Fog in the harbor, tone poem (ch and orch)
    From a Sufti's tent (ch)
    Songs incl.:
    At dawn
    At eve I heard a flute
    Because of you
    Colleen o' mine
    Compensation
    Dreamin' time
    Four Aztec love songs
    Here in the high hills
    Little white bird
    Lonesome moonlight
    Mah Lindy Lou
    Moon of Iraq
    My love is a fisherman
    Oubangi, African song cycle
    Songs of India
SACRED
    St. John the Beloved, cantata (8 solos, ch and orch)
    Song of David
OPERA
    Jewels of the Desert
    Joseph
    Woods of Pan
BALLET
    Ballet Indienne, in 4 mvts)
    Other Ballet music
Publications
    Oriental and Character Dances. With Helen Frost. New York, 1930.
Bibliography
    Howe, Ann Whitworth. *Lily Strickland: Her Contribution to American Music in the Early Twentieth Century.* Ph.D. dissertation, Catholic University of America, 1969.
Ref. 22, 39, 70, 74, 85, 94, 142, 228, 280, 292, 347, 415, 477, 496, 563, 610

STROZZI, Barbara (Barbara Valle) (Barbara di Santa Sofia)

Italian aristocrat, singer and composer. b. Venice, August 6, 1620; d. ca. 1664. She was the adopted natural daughter of the librettist Giulio Strozzi and her mother was Isabella Garzoni. Barbara was referred to as Barbara Valle and later Barbara di Santa Sofia by her father. She first studied under Giulio Strozzi and then Francesco Cavalli, becoming famous as a singer and was called 'virtuosissima cantatrice' by Nicolo Fontein in his *Bizarrie Poetiche* in 1836. She sang at her father's Accademia degli Unisoni and appears to have been one of the first women composers to compose in the cantata form. She was the authoress of eight volumes of vocal works, published in Vienna between 1644 and 1664. DISCOGRAPHY.

Compositions
VOCAL
    Cantate, ariette a 1-3 voci, op. 3 incl.: Lamento: su'l rodano severo (S, clav, vlc and hp), S'io mi giuro mia vita (Gardano, 1654)
    Cantate, ariette e duetti, op 2 inc. Chiamata a nuovi amori; (Gardano, 1651)
    Un anante doglioso

Ariette a voce sola, op. 6 incl.: Risolveteri pensieri; Non pavento co di te sospira e respira (ded Francesco Carafa Principe di Belvedere e Marchese d'Anzi (Magni, 1657)
Arie, op. 8 (ded Sofia, Duchess of Brunswick and Luneburg) (Gardano, 1664) incl. Donne belle; Ferma il piede; Hor che Apollo, serenade with violins; Non c'e piu fede; Tu me ne puoi ben dire; Astrate; Lucibelle; Aure giacche non posso; Che si puo fare; Cieli stelle; E giungera pur mai
Arie e ariette, incl. Amore e badito; Amor dormiglione; Con le belle non ci vuol fretta; Consiglio amoroso (S, A and B); Lacrime mie; Presso un ruscello; Soccorrete, luci avare; Spesso per entro al petto; Tradimento
Avere torto
Moralita amorosa (S, clav, vlc and hp)
Non ti doler mio cor
Il Primo Libro de' Madrigali a 2-5 voci, 25 madrigals op. 1 inc. Dolcissimi respiri, madrigal; Pietosissimo amore, madrigal; Vel misero usignolo, madrigal (G. Strozzi) (ded Granduchessa di Toscana D. Vittoria della Rovere (Venice: Alessandro Vincenti, 1644)

SACRED
Sacri musicali affetti, Libro 1, op. 5 (vce and acc) (Magni, 1655) (ded Anna of Austria, Archduchess of Innsbruck)

OPERA
Diporti di Euterpe, overo Cantate et ariette a voce sola, op. 7 (Venice: Magni, 1659) (ded Nicolo Sagredo, Cavalier e Procuratore di S. Marco)

Bibliography
Rosand, Ellen. *Barbara Stozzi, virtuosissima cantatrice: the composer's voice.* Journal of the American Musicological Society XXXI/2. Summer 1978.
Ref. 8, 13, 17, 25, 65, 88, 105, 116, 129, 157, 160, 216, 226, 264, 297, 335, 361, 405, 433, 563, 653

STRUCK, Ilse

20th-century German organist and composer. b. Parchim, Mecklenburg. She was an organist in Flensburg and Leipzig. She composed pieces for chamber orchestra, the organ and the recorder and for sacred and secular choruses and songs.
Ref. 70

STRUTT, Dorothy

English cellist, pianist, violinist, singer and composer. b. Hornchurch, Essex, May 5, 1941. She studied the violin from the age of seven and later the piano, the cello and singing and taught herself composition. From 1970 to 1971 she was a pianist for Moreley College Music Theatre. She is a member of the Barnard-Strutt-Owen Trio, founded in 1972, and also a member of a jazz orientated music tape workshop at the Arts Center. She has performed in concerts and recitals and given lecture demonstrations in schools. She was recently commissioned to add a choral part to Beethoven's 5th symphony adapting words from the psalms.

Compositions
ORCHESTRA
Allegro maestoso (1961)
Wilderness orchestrated (1965)
CHAMBER
Music for wind ensemble, based on an oriental scale (1961)
Septet (fl, B-flat cl, B-cl, str qrt and perc) (1962)
Serenata breva (6 ob and cor anglais) (1964)
Study (vlc and rec qrt) (1962)
Wind quintet (ob, cl, bsn, hn and trp) (1962)
Adagio (str qrt) (1962)
Fanfare (4 trb) (1961)
Four string quartets (1962)
Pentatonic music (str qrt) (1961)
Quartet on haiku (Charles Ford) (fl, cl, gtr and vln) (1974)
String quartet (1961, 1969)
Allegro (str trio) (1961)
Andante (str trio) (1961)
Burton Woods, based on Over Burton Woods (Peter C. Owen) (pf, vlc and cl) (1973)
Cello ensemble (1964-1965)
Music (descant and t-recs) (1961)
Music (ob, bsn and hn)
Music (fl, ob and cl in A) (1961)
Sea dirge (rec, a-fl and vla) (1961)
Sonata in E-Flat (vln, vla and vlc) (1960)
Sonata in whole tones (vln, vla and vlc) (1960)
Study (treble rec, t-vla and vlc) (1963)
Suite on Greek modes (ob, cl and bsn) (1961)
Trio (cl, vlc and pf) (1973)
Allegro moderato (b-rec and pf) (1964)
Andante and adagio on anonymous 18th-century theme (b-rec and vlc) (1964)

The blue fawn (cl and pf) (1976)
Cello duets, Set 1, nos. 1-3 (1964)
Elegies for Alpha (cl and pf) (1978)
Fantasy (vln and pf) (1970)
Five haiku (cl and pf) (1975)
Four duets (school recs) (1961)
Lacrymae (vlc and pf) (1972)
Peace (vlc and pf) (1972)
Piece for Laura (t-rec and pf) (1971)
Piece on three (ob and gtr) (1971)
Poem (fl and vlc) (1973)
Exercise in twelve note row (rec consort) (1961)
Sonata (ob and cl) (1960)
Study (ob and vlc) (1963)
Two movements (cl and pf) (1973-1974)
Adagio (b-rec) (1964)
Andante and allegro (treble rec) (1962)
Eight pieces (ob) (1965)
Essay (vlc) (1961)
Fanfare for Dick (trp) (1971)
Five grotesque dances (cl in A) (1961)
Five pieces (ob) (1961)
Gamba music (1963)
Grey light (gtr) (1971)
Improvisation and andante (descant rec) (1969)
Piece on 4 (d-b) (1971)
Prelude, andante and allegro (vln) (1964)
Sonata (fl) (1974)
Sonatina (vlc) (1969)
Suite (ob) (1970)
Suite (vlc) (1963; 1971)
Three landscapes (ob) (1961)
Three pieces (cl)
Variations (B-flat cl) (1961)
Variations (fl) (1963)
Wilderness (org) (1964)
PIANO
Bi-tonal tune (1961)
Four sketches (1964)
Pieces on three (1971)
Sonata (1969)
Sonata on six (1973)
Sonorities (1972)
VOCAL
The folding of a paper, cantata (Mallarme, Valery and Baudelaire) (2 T and cham orch) (1962)
Three koans (mix-ch) (1974)
And I will rest (S, T and pf or Cont and cl) (1974)
Bamboo shadows (Japanese text) (Cont and pf) (1972)
Before dawn (Dorothy Strelt) (T) (1971)
Credo (Cont and pf) (1972)
The eagle and the panther (B-Bar and pf) (1972-1973)
Epigram on a sundial (T, cl and bsn) (1961)
A flower was offered me (Blake)
Hanny Ashingyo (Cont and perc) (1972)
Men who march away! song cycle (T and fl) (1969)
A plea for unicorns (A or T) (1971)
Sky fragments (Cont and cl) (1977)
Snow girl (1977)
Song of experience (S and 2 and 3 T) (1961)
Three German songs (B-Bar and vlc) (1974)
Three stanzas (Lord Byron) (T and pf) (1973)
To Belshazzar (Byron) (T and pf) (1973)
Two songs for Milarepa (vce and cl) (1977)
Voices (De La Mare) (T or A) (1968)
SACRED
John the Baptist, oratorio (ch and orch) (1968)
By the rivers of Babylon (mix-ch) (1969)
Carol tune (mix-ch) (1968)
Missa brevis (mix-ch a-cap) (1970)
Processional for Christmas (boys vce and ch) (1968)
When Jesus Christ was yet a child (mix-ch) (1967)
Agnus Dei (B-Bar and Cont) (1973)
Carol (boys and m-vces) (1960)
Judica me Deus (1971)
Kyrie (Cont) (1973)
Lumen de lumine (org) (1970)
Retiring voluntary for Lent (1968)
Rorate coeli desuper (1971)
Sanctus (vce and pf) (1974)
Three motets (4 vces) (1961)
Trinity (vce and org) (1969)
Verbum caro factum est (1971)
THEATRE
Eternal Mind (composer) (1972)

DANCE SCORES
Circle (3 dancers and pf) (1973)
Words at Castlerigg (vlc and dancers; also vlc and pf) (1976)
Ref. composer, 230, 322

STUART, Peggy. See COOLIDGE, Peggy Stuart

STUART-BERGSTROM, Elsa Marianne (pseud. Kaimen)
Swedish pianist, critic and composer. b. April 26, 1889; d. May 19, 1970.
She studied at Stockholm Conservatory under Lundberg, Kerstin Stroemberg (piano) and Saul (theory). She was a music critic for several Stockholm newspapers and composed orchestral pieces, choruses and songs.
Publications
Kurt Atterberg. 1925.
Johann Sebastian Bach. 1922.
Articles on music.
Ref. 20

STUART STRESA, Mrs. See SKINNER, Florence Marian

STUBENBERG, Countess Anna Zichy (Buttler-Stubenberg)
Austrian composer. b. Graz, August 9, 1821; d. Graz, December 1, 1912.
She showed great musical talent as a child and soon turned to composition. She spent her youth in Hungary and the influences of Hungarian folk music and gypsy music were apparent in many of her works.
Compositions
PIANO
An der Elbe, polka-mazurka, op. 49
An der Wolga, Tonbild, op. 134
Auf Wiedersehen! Trauermarsch, op. 42
Aus des Herzens Tiefe, Lied ohne Worte, op. 48
Aus schoener Zeit, polka-mazurka, op. 96
Buttler-Marsch, op. 45
Ein Traum, Tanzgemaelde, op. 97
Einst und Jetzt, Gavotte, op. 52
Emma, polka-mazurka, op. 41
Gavotte, op. 56
Im Zauberbaum, polka-mazurka, op. 95
Jubel-Marsch, op. 47
Jugendtraeume, waltz, op. 107 (Pechel)
Konzert-Laendler, op. 148 (Eberle)
Letzter Gruss! Trauermarsch, op. 94
Mein Stern, Lied ohne Worte, op. 39 (Bosworth)
Philomele, polka-mazurka, op. 46
Schockel-Hexe, Fant. polka, op. 51
Styrian dances, waltzes, op. 67 (Eberle; Presser)
Tarantelle, op. 43
ZITHER
Heimatsklange, Laendler, op. 44
VOCAL
Gruss aus den Bergen (m-ch) (Wiener Musikverlagshaus; Eberle)
Noet gift'n!, op. 109 (T, m-ch and humming ch) (F. Blumei) (Eberle)
's anzige Straeusserl, op. 106 (m-ch) (Eberle)
's Hoamatlied (m-ch) (F. Bluemel) (Pechel)
Ergebung, op. 104 (vce and pf) (Eberle)
Elegie auf den Tod der Kaiserin Elisabeth von Oesterreich, op. 112 (Eberle)
Es war einmal, op. 127 (Eberle)
Jugendtraum und Leben, op. 125 (Eberle)
Lieder-Album, 10 lieder (Eberle)
Meine Lieb' ist wie Lenzwind, op. 150 (Eberle)
Narzissen (vce and pf) (Eberle)
Stilles Heimatdorf, op. 143 (Eberle)
Todesmuede, op. 110 (Eberle)
Songs incl.:
Abschiedsgesang: Es geht ein lindes Wehen, op. 65
Aus! Ob jeder Freude sehe ich schweben, op. 77
Bluehen und Vergehen: Geniesse was der Tag dir bringt, op. 69
Blumen am Grabe, op. 58
Drei Zigeuner, op. 60
Mein Herz ist schwer, mein Auge wacht, op. 70
Die Perle: In meines Herzens tiefstem Grund, op. 68
Ref. 105, 226, 276, 297, 500

STUDENY, Herma
German violinist and composer. b. Munich, January 4, 1896. She studied under Sevcik and Marteau and made a career as a virtuoso violinist. She composed violin pieces and songs.

Publications
Buechlein vom Geigen.
Ref. 70

STULTS, Grace Hayhew. See MAHEW, Grace

STULTZ, Marie Irene
American choral conductor, teacher and composer. b. San Antonio, TX, April 13, 1945. She studied conducting under Carlton Young and Lloyd Pfautsch and singing under Catherine Akos at the Southern Methodist University. She graduated with a B.Mus.Ed. in 1967 and a M.Mus. (history) in 1973. She studied composition under Robert Sirota at Boston University in 1978 and under Anthony Milner and John Heiss. She taught singing in Texas, Kansas and Massachusetts. She founded the Treble Chorus of New England in 1975. DISCOGRAPHY.
Compositions
CHAMBER
Caprice au vent, op. 5, cycle in 4 movements using 12-tone technique (1983)
Serenade, The silver swan, op. 9 (cl and org) (1985)
Romanze, op. 8 (vln) (1982)
VOCAL
Horseshoe nail (w-ch)
Mirth and mischief (mix-ch a-cap) (1980)
Ode to Shelley, op. 11 (w-ch) (1985)
Fireside amusements, song cycle based on nursery rhymes (w-vces, pf and fl) (1980)
Maiden of Edo, op. 6 (S, hp, fl) (1983)
Winter on Avon, op. 4 (Shakespeare)
SACRED
Suite Nativitat, op. 3 (S, m-S, mix-ch and orch) (1980)
Missa illuminare, op. 10 (S, Bar and mix-ch) (1981)
Song of jubilation, op. 2 (S, mix-ch and org) (1981)
King Jesus is born (w-ch) (1979)
Psalm 30, op 7 (S, T, mix-ch, 2 hp, hn, trb, timp, gong, cymbal and org) (1983)
OPERETTA
Nursery rhymes for holiday times (1979)
The Worthy Gift, for children (1980)
THEATRE
The Tethered Colt, op. 1, musical drama (1980)
Arrangements for choruses
Ref. composer

STURE VASA, Mary O'Hara (pseud. Mary O'Hara)
American novelist, script writer and composer. b. Cape May Point, July 10, 1885; d. Chevy Chase, October 15, 1980. Although writing was her major love, Mary started composing while at school and later had several compositions published (Schirmer, New York, Presser, Philadelphia) and a Christmas carol performed by the Paulist Fathers' Choir in 1942.
Composition
SACRED
A christmas carol
Publications
Green Grass of Wyoming. 1946.
My Friend Flicka. 1941.
Son of Adam Wyngate.
Thunderhead. 1943.
Wyoming Summer.
Bibliography
Current Biography. 1944.
Obituary, *NY Times.*
Ref. 347

STURKOW-RYDER, Theodora (Theodora Sturkow Ryder)
American pianist, teacher and composer. b. Philadelphia, 1876. She was a pupil of Louis Staab, Regina Watson and Carl Wolfsohn. She toured in concerts and gave recitals. She composed a suite for the violin and the piano, cello pieces, piano pieces and songs.
Ref. 226, 347, 353

STUTSMAN, Grace May
American concert pianist, writer and composer. b. Melrose, MA, March 4, 1886; d. April 30, 1970. She attended Boston University and won a scholarship for private piano study at the New England Conservatory, 1920 to 1922 where her teachers included Bridge, Johns and Mason. She wrote articles for the *Christian Science Monitor* for 25 years. She won an Endicott prize for song composition. Some of her piano recitals included her own works.

Compositions
CHAMBER
  Piano pieces
SACRED
  In Bethlehem 'neath starlit skies, hymn (Methodist Hymnal, 1964)
  Wait's Carol, hymn (Methodist Hymnal, 1964)
Ref. 646

STYLES, Dorothy Geneva
American organist, pianist, choral conductor, librettist, poetess, teacher, writer and composer. b. Eldorado, AR, December 13, 1922. At the age of 10 she performed on WEXL-Radio and taught after the age of 12. She graduated from the Detroit Institute of Musical Arts in 1945. She obtained a B.Mus. from the University of Detroit in 1945, a B.S. from Columbia University in 1954 and an M.A. in 1970 from the University of Michigan, Ann Arbor. She was organist and pianist at Hazel Park Baptist Tabernacle and choral conductor at St. Timothy's Evangelical Lutheran Church in Wayne, MI from 1975 to 1976.
Compositions
VOCAL
  I sing a song (1975)
  Lullaby (1966)
  Mother, tell me (1977)
  Mrs Santa Claus loves Mr Santa Claus (1976)
  The pledge of allegiance to the flag (1976)
SACRED
  Hymn arrangements
Publications
  Young Verses for the Early Old.
  An Extension of the Idea of Countability as Applied to Real Numbers. 1966.
  A Prime Number Theorum. 1971.
  Projections of the Natural Harmonic Series: Some Implications. 1978.
Ref. 27, 475

SUARDA, Maria Virginia
Late 17th-century Italian composer. She was a nun of the monastery of Saint Maria del Paradiso in Bergamo. She was one of the few women composers of that era who turned from vocal to instrumental composition.
Compositions
ARRANGEMENTS
  A collection of Balletti, correnti, minuetti arranged into eleven suites (2 vlns, vlc or spinet) (Venice: Giuseppe Sala, 1692)
Ref. 335

SUBBALAKSHMI, M.S.
20th-century singer from South India. She sings her own devotional songs and those of other Indian composers in many Indian languages and gave a recital at the United Nations.
Ref. 414

SUBBALAXMI, M.S. See SUBBALAKSHMI, M.S.

SUBLIGNY, Mme.
18th-century composer.
Composition
VOCAL
  Come fill up ye bow, minuet (London, ca. 1700)
Ref. 65

SUBOTNIK, Joan. See LA BARBARA, Joan

SUCCARI, Dia
Composition
PIANO
  Nuit du destin (Jobert, ca. 1978)

SUCHY (Guchy), Gregoria Karides
20th-century American pianist, conductor, professor and composer. b. Milwaukee, WI. She obtained her B.S. from Milwaukee State Teacher's College in 1945 and her M.Mus. from Northwestern University in 1951. She studied composition under J. Thomas Oakes and Alexander Tcherepnin

at De Paul University, Rudolph Ganz at Chicago Musical College, Anthony Donata at Northwestern University and Ralph Shapey. She taught instrumental music in Milwaukee public schools from 1943 to 1944; the piano and instrumental music at the Northwestern Conservatory, 1944 to 1947; theory and instrumental music at Carroll Music Studios, Milwaukee, 1945 and from 1946 she was a faculty member of the Department of Music, School of Fine Arts at the University of Wisconsin, Milwaukee, becoming professor of theory and composition. Her music was performed in premieres by the late Rudolph Ganz and at the Wisconsin Contemporary Music Forum. She is the recipient of various Wisconsin Federation of Music Clubs awards; 1960, 1961, 1962, 1964, 1966 and 1967 and research grants for musical composition from the Graduate School of the University of Wisconsin, 1960, 1963, 1965 and 1968. She received a faculty fellowship to participate in a special computer applications workshop from the University of Wisconsin in 1967 and won competitions for musical composition, including a first prize from the Musician's Club of Women, Chicago, IL.
Compositions
ORCHESTRA
  Symphonic piece with trumpet and piano obbligato
  Three lovers (2 pf and sym orch)
  Argument
  Greek rhapsody (1962)
CHAMBER
  Triophony (fl, cl or vla and vlc or bsn)
  String quartet No. 1 (1st prize, 1966)
  Soliloquy sans C (vln)
PIANO
  A fantasy circle dance in 7/8 (1st prize, 1964)
  A fantasy (1st prize, 1966)
  Mo-goose revisited
  Mother goose rhyme in 12-Tone
  Saturn's ring
  Sousta (award winner, 1962)
  Suite on Greek themes (award winner, 1961)
  Two sketches
VOCAL
  The ass in the lion's skin
  Entries (narr, B, tim, perc and pf)
  Twelve Greek maxims, set of 12 songs (S)
  Other songs
SACRED
  A Christmas carol (mix-ch)
BALLET
  Skins and exposures (tape)
Ref. 40, 84, 137, 142, 228, 347

SUESSE, Dana (Nadine)
American organist, pianist, arranger, playwright and composer. b. Kansas City, MO, December 3, 1911. When she was nine she won the Tri-State American Federation of Music prize for composition. In Kansas City she studied the piano, harmony and the organ. When she was 16 she refused a full scholarship to a leading Chicago Conservatory but went instead to New York to work with Alexander Siloti, a pupil of Franz Liszt, and to study composition under Rubin Goldmark. From 1947 to 1950 she studied privately in Paris under Nadia Boulanger (q.v.). She gave her first concert in Kansas City and toured in concert in the southern and western United States, performing her own works. She was the only American composer other than George Gershwin to be invited as composer-pianist in the General Motors Symphony Concert Series of coast-to-coast broadcasts. DISCOGRAPHY. PHOTOGRAPH.
Compositions
ORCHESTRA
  Concerto in E-Minor (2 pf and orch) (D.S. Music Co., 1943)
  Concerto romantico (pf and orch) (D.S. Music, 1945)
  Concertino (pf and orch) (D.S. Music, 1945)
  Concertino in three rhythms (pf and orch) (D.S. Music, 1932)
  Coronach (in memory of Casper Reardon) (D.S. Music, 1941)
  Eight waltzes (pf and orch) (1933)
  Jazz concerto in D-Major (Concerto in rhythm) (3-piece combo and orch) (D.S. Music, 1955)
  Piano concerto in A
  Young man with a harp, suite (hp and orch) (D.S. Music, 1939)
  Two Irish fairy tales (1933)
PIANO
  Afternoon of black faun (Robbins Music Co., 1938)
  American nocturne (Robbins, 1939)
  At the fountain (D.S. Music, 1926)
  Balalaika waltz (D.S. Music, 1930)
  Berceuse (D.S. Music, 1932)
  Blue moonlight (Harms, 1935)
  The cocktail suite (D.S. Music, 1942)
  Jazz nocturne (Famous Music, 1930)
  Midnight in Gramercy square (D.S. Music, 1933)

Night sky (D.S. Music, 1947)
Rockette (Robbins, 1939)
Rondeau (D.S. Music, 1947)
Serenade to a skyscraper (D.S. Music, 1940)
Swamp bird (D.S. Music, 1926)
Syncopated love song (Harms, Inc., 1930)
Whirligig (D.S. Music, 1937)
110th St. Rumba (D.S. Music, 1941)
VOCAL
Ode to Aphrodite (Sappho) (Cont and orch) (1945)
More about the pear tree (Hugh A. Carter) (Bourne Music, 1972)
Songs incl.:
The girl without a name
Have you forgotten?
My silent love
The night is young and you're so beautiful
You oughta' be in pictures
THEATRE
The Man who sold the Eiffel Tower, play
Publications
It Takes Two. Comedy.
Mrs. Mooney. Play.
The Voice of the Hyena. Play.
Ref. composer, 39, 142, 280, 347, 353, 610, 563

SUGAI, Esther
20th-century composer.
Compositions
CHAMBER
Five poems (Andre Breton) (fl, cl, sax, tbn and perc) (1983)
Kokoro (3 fl) (1980)
Three movements (S-sax and a-fl) (1983)
Ref. AMC newsletter

SUH, Kyung-Sun
20th-century Korean lecturer and composer. b. Seoul. She began her music studies under her mother, attended the Seoul Arts High School and then entered the College of Music, Seoul National University graduating with honors in 1964 and obtaining her Master's degree in composition in 1968. In 1972 she won a scholarship to study at the Graduate School of Massachusetts where she obtained an M.A. (theory). On her return she taught theory in the faculty of music of the National University, Seoul. Since 1977 she has been president of the composition department of the University of Hanyang. She is a member of the Society for Contemporary Music and in 1971 represented Korea at the Festival of contemporary music in Taipei.
Compositions
CHAMBER
An illusion (fl, hp and perc)
Three movements (cl and vlc)
Pieces (small inst ens)
VOCAL
Two images (S, vln and pf)
Ref. Korean National Council of Women

SULLIVAN, Marion Dix
19th-century American composer.
Compositions
VOCAL
Songs:
The field of Monterey (Boston: O. Ditson, 1846)
Jessie Cook (Boston: Prentiss & Clark, 1844)
Juniata ballads (Boston: N. Richardson, 1855)
Marion Day (Ditson, 1844)
Mary Lindsey (Ditson, 1848)
O'er our way when first we parted (Ditson)
Oh! boatman row me o'er the stream (Ditson, 1844)
We cross the prairie as of old (Boston: E.H. Wade, 1854)
Ref. 228

SULPIZI, Mira (Pratesi)
Italian composer. b. Milan, December 28, 1923. She graduated from the Universita Cattolica del Sacro Cuore in Milan and studied composition under Soresina. DISCOGRAPHY.
Compositions
CHAMBER
Eight medieval songs (gtr) (1972)
Organ sonata (1968)
PIANO
Introduzione-aria-finale (1969)
Sonata breve (1963)

VOCAL
Filastrocche popolari italiane (boys-ch and perc ad lib; also fl, xyl and gtrs) (Ricordi)
Antichi canti spagnoli
Lyrics (Langston Hughes) (1968)
Three lyrics (G. Azzi) (1970)
Three lyric poems (Giovanni Serafini) (1958)
Two rispetti toscani (1959)
SACRED
Messa melodica
Vigilia di Pentecoste (1965)
Ref. composer, 563

SULTAN, Aishe
Turkish composer. b. 1887; d. 1960. She composed military marches, a waltz, a mazurka, a lullaby and songs.
Ref. National Council of Turkish Women

SULTAN, Fatma
Turkish composer. b. 1904. She composed instrumental music and songs.
Ref. National Council of Turkish Women

SULTAN, Hatidje
Turkish composer. b. 1870; d. 1938. She composed military marches and songs.
Ref. National Council of Turkish Women

SULTANOVA, Asya Bakhish kyzy
Soviet composer. b. Baku, October 16, 1925. In 1950 she graduated from the Moscow Conservatory where she studied composition under E. Golubiev and V. Shebalin.
Compositions
ORCHESTRA
Concert march (1955)
Waltz (1955)
CHAMBER
Variations (vln and pf) (1946-1947)
PIANO
Sonata (1946)
Sonatina (1954)
VOCAL
Oda (vce and sym orch) (Bolotin and T. Sikorska) (1952)
Ya ob otchizne poyu (soloists, ch and orch) (Registan) (1953)
Dyetski sad, cycle of 6 children's songs (Registan) (1954)
Lieder (vce and pf) (Bajan)
Rodina (Safarli) (1954)
Schastye (D. Zeinalli)
Ref. 87

SUMNER, Clare
Canadian organist, pianist, teacher and composer. b. Birmingham, UK, 1886. She studied at the Midland Institute in Birmingham under William Hartland. She studied the piano under Mme. Fromme and the organ under W. Hoyle and W. Newey. She holds an L.R.A.M. and Licentiate Tonic Sol Fa diploma. She moved to Canada in about 1914, where she taught music and for several years was supervisor of music in a public school in Point Grey, British Columbia.
Compositions
PIANO
April (2 pf)
Aspiration (2 pf)
Fantasia (2 pf)
Flight (2 pf)
Vaurka (2 pf)
Campanella che cantano
Study in F-Minor
VOCAL
Via Vancouver (vce and orch)
Apple blossom (ch)
Easter Eve (ch)
My lady sleeps (ch)
Birmingham over the sea
Heart's garden
The scented hour
Song of the ace

Sunset
There are fairies at the bottom of our garden
Wanderlust
When I am dead
SACRED
Nunc dimittis (ch)
Ref. 133

SUMNER, Mrs. See SALTER, Mary Elizabeth

SUMNER, Sarah
20th-century American violinist and composer. She studied the violin under Paul Stassevitch in New York, composition under Irvin Fine and Walter Piston at Harvard University and also under Nadia Boulanger (q.v.) in Paris on a Fulbright Scholarship. She composed songs.
Ref. 142

SUMOWSKA, Helena
19th-century Polish composer.
Compositions
PIANO
Ha laczee, waltz (Gebethner)
Marsz rycerzy, march (Gebethner)
Oryginal, galop (Gebethner)
Secesja, waltz (Gebethner)
Sfinks, waltz (Gebethner)
Zuch bartek, mazurka (Gebethner)
Ref. 297

SUMPF, Luisa. See GREGER, Luisa

SUNDBLAD-HALME, Heidi Gabriella Wilhelmina
Finnish pianist, conductor, lecturer and composer. b. Pietarsaari, September 29, 1903; d. Helsinki, April 30, 1973. She studied the piano and composition at the Helsinki Conservatory from 1927 to 1933 then privately under V. Raitio and L. Funtek and conducting in Berlin under C. Kraus in 1938 and under D. Dixon in Lund in 1954. In 1938 she founded the Helsinki Women's Orchestra and conducted it until 1968. She taught at the Helsinki Public Conservatory, at the Helsinki Swedish Workers' Institute and privately. In 1968 she received the honorary title of 'Director Musices'.
Compositions
ORCHESTRA
At a marionette theatre (1935) (FMIC)
At the dam (1932)
Ballad (1950)
Finnish folk songs (1940)
The gipsy (1938)
Hungarian fantasy (1938)
In the dark (1949)
Intrada (1945) (FMIC)
Jutta's arrival at the Folkungs (1938)
Karelian folk songs (1931) (FMIC)
Life is great (1956)
May night (1932)
Menuets precieux (1932)
Midsummer dance (1932)
The net (1949)
Non-existent country (1949)
Nocturno (1949)
Pan's flute (1945)
Prelude and fugue (1941) (FMIC)
Rondo capriccio (1940) (FMIC)
Song on the hill (1938)
South Ostrobothnian rhapsody, op. 5 (1932)
Suite, op. 11 (1930) (FMIC)
Starry sky (FMIC)
Suite of Finnish folk songs (1940)
Towards evening (1938)
Vihnu (1932)
Yellow nocturne (1949)
CHAMBER
Piano pieces
VOCAL
Songs for Tellervo, 4 songs (S and orch) (L. Onerva) (1955) (FMIC))
BALLET
The Enchanted Belt (1937)

TEACHING PIECES
Eight Christmas songs for the primary school (3 vces) (1932)
ARRANGEMENTS
For child violinists and pianists
Ref. 280, FMIC

SURIANI, Alberta
Italian harpist, arranger and composer. b. 1920. Some of her arrangements for the harp of 17th-century lute music were published by Bongiovanni, Bologna.
Ref. 344

SUSSMAN, Ettel
Israeli violinist, singer, teacher and composer. b. Poland, June 24, 1926. She learned to play the violin for several years before studying singing in Tel Aviv under Ely Kurz. In Lyons, France, she studied harmony and counterpoint under organist Marcel Pehu and orchestration under Jacques Boisgallais. In 1946 and 1947 she received first prizes for singing and lyric art at the Lyon Conservatory and two years later was Laureate d'Execution Musicale in Geneva, Switzerland. She toured five continents as a singer of opera and Lieder. After 1969 she taught singing at the Glate Seminary for Teachers of Music, Tel Aviv. PHOTOGRAPH.
Compositions
ORCHESTRA
Symphony Caesarea: Triptych (Israeli Music Pub., 1965)
PIANO
Impromptu les hirondelles (Israeli Music, 1966)
Three Israeli dances (1962)
VOCAL
Magic rituals of the golden dawn, cantata No. 4 (1935)
Song of songs (high vce, narr and small orch) (Israeli Music, 1962)
Cerises (vce and pf) (1960)
Chinese poets on animal life (vce and hpcd or pf) (Israeli Music, 1961)
Deux onomatopeides (S, m-S and Cont) (1962)
Insomnie (vce and pf) (1960)
Pour les petits brigards (high vce and pf) (Giboulees d'Avril) (1960)
Le reveil (vce and pf) (1960)
Ronde (vce and pf) (1960)
Six extraits du livre, Caractères de la bruyère (vce and hpcd or pf) (1962)
Three Israeli folk songs (vce and str qrt; also vce and pf) (1968)
Yefeh Nof (S and str qrt or pf) (1968)
Ref. composer, Israeli Music Publ., 594

SUSZCZYNSKA, Anna
Polish pianist, teacher and composer. b. Poznan; d. Poznan, August, 1931. She studied at the Scharwenka Conservatory in Berlin and then in New York. On her return she founded and directed her own music school, Lutnia, in Poznan, and appeared in concerts. She returned to New York to found a music school in Binghamton without interrupting her concert career. In 1918 she returned to Poland and devoted herself to teaching and composing.
Compositions
ORCHESTRA
War symphony (1914)
Piesn o pokoj, piano concert in E-Minor
Why is it so? fantasy
Ref. 118

SUTHERLAND, Margaret O.B.E.
Australian pianist, lecturer and composer. b. Adelaide, South Australia, November 20, 1897. In 1914 she was awarded a scholarship to study the piano under Edward Goll and composition under Fritz Hart at the Marshall Hall Conservatory and in 1915 moved to the University Conservatory. She continued her studies there under Goll on another scholarship. Later she taught the piano and theory and worked as an assistant to Goll. In 1923 she went to Europe, spending time in London and Vienna. In 1925 she returned to Australia where she taught privately and at the Melbourne Conservatory for nine years. In 1969 she was awarded an honorary doctorate of music from the University of Melbourne and in 1970 she was awarded the Order of the British Empire. DISCOGRAPHY.
Compositions
ORCHESTRA
Adagio (2 vln and orch) (1946)
Violin concerto (1954)
Concertino (pf and orch) (1940)
Fantasy (vln and orch) (1960)
Concertante (small orch)

Overture, movement and rondel (junior orch) (1945)
Prelude and jig (str orch) (1939)
Rondel (junior orch) (1945)
Suite in E-Minor (str orch)
Threesome (junior orch) (1947)
Ballad overture (timp, perc and strs) (1948)
Bush ballad (timp, perc and strs)
Concerto grosso (vln, vla, hpcd and strs)
Concerto for strings
Concertante (obs, perc and strs) (1962)
Concertante (vln, vla, hpcd and strs) (1960)
Four symphonic studies (1954)
Haunted hills, poem (1953)
Homage to J. Sebastian (1947)
Movement (1959)
Open air piece (1953)
Outdoor overture (1953)
Pavane (1938)
Simply string pieces
Suite on a theme of Purcell (1935)
Three temperaments (1958)
Triptych
Vistas
Walking tune (1947)
CHAMBER
Discussion (str qrt) (1958)
Fantasy quartet for Winds
House quartet (cl or vln, vln, hn or vlc and pf) (1936)
Quartet (cl and strs) (1967)
Quartet (cor anglais and strs) (L'Oiseau Lyre, 1955)
String quartet (comm Aus. Perf. Rights Assoc.) (1967)
Adagio and allegro giocoso (2 vln and pf) (1945)
Divertimento (vln, vla and vlc) (1958)
Little suite (wind trio) (1957)
Trio (ob, vln and vla)
Trio (ob and 2 vln) (Kurrajong Press, 1951)
Trio in C-Major (cl, vln and pf) (1934)
Ballad and nocturne (vln and pf) (1944)
Cavatina (vln and pf)
Concerto (fl and hp)
Contrasts (2 vln) (1953)
Fantasy (vln and pf) (1960)
Fantasy sonatina (sax and pf) (1935)
Nocturne (vln and pf) (1944)
Rhapsody (vln and pf) (1934)
Six bagatelles (vln and vla) (1956)
Sonata (cl or vla and pf) (1944)
Sonata in one movement (cl or vla and pf) (1947)
Sonata (vln and pf) (L'Oiseau Lyre, 1925)
Sonata in B-Flat (cl and pf)
Sonatina (ob or vla and pf) (Kurrajong, 1958)
Air (vln; also pf)
Sonatina (hpcd)
Three pieces (hpcd)
Simple string pieces for school class work (1967)
PIANO
Burlesque and movement (2 pf) (1958)
Pavan and canonical piece (2 pf) (1957)
Bagatelle
Chiaroscuro 1 and 2 (1968)
First suite (1938)
Holiday tunes (1936)
Miniature ballet suite (1936)
Miniature sonata (1939)
Mischief in the air (1936)
Nocturne in A-Flat
Nocturne in B-Flat
Extension (1967)
Second suite (1937)
Six profiles (1946)
Sonata (1966)
Sonatina (1958)
Two choral preludes on Bach's chorales (1935)
Valse descant (1968)
Variations on a clockwork instrument
Voices I and II (1968)
Waltz in C
VOCAL
The passing (mix-ch and orch) (1939)
Quietly as rosebuds (mix-ch a-cap) (1934)
The soldier (vce and orch) (1938)
Youth and age (mix-ch a-cap)
The zoo (mix-ch a-cap)
And now Mr. Ferritt
Blue of Australian skies (1953)
Break of day (1934)

Chez nous (1969)
Country places (1935)
The green singer (1934)
Heart of spring
Land of ours (1935)
Song of the south (vce and pf)
Two blue slippers
The pathfinders
Songs incl.
Arab love song (J. Albert & Son, 1973)
Cradle song (Albert, 1973)
Five songs (John Shaw Neilson) (1936)
O mistress mine (Albert, 1973)
Old Australian bush ballads (Allans Music, 1948)
The orange tree (J.S. Neilson) (vce, cl and pf) (1938)
September (Albert, 1973)
Sequence of verse into music (Maie Casey) (speaking vce, fl, vla and bsn) (1964)
Six Australian songs (Judith Wright) (1967)
Strange requiem (Albert, 1973)
Three songs (Francis Thompson) (1930)
The world and the child (vce and str trio) (1960)
SACRED
A company of carols, five carols (mix-ch a-cap) (1966)
BALLET
Dithyramb (1941)
The Selfish Giant
OPERA
The Young Kabberli, chamber opera (Maie Casey) (1965)
INCIDENTAL MUSIC
The Knight of the Burning Pestel
A Midsummer Night's Dream (Shakespeare) (1941)
Publications
Young Days in Music. Melbourne, 1968.
Bibliography
Brozel, Nada. *For Margaret Sutherland on her Seventy-fifth Birthday.*
Coles, Helen. *Margaret Sutherland: Australian Composer.* In *Lip 1978-1979.*
Covell, Roger. *Australia's Music: Themes of a New Society.* Melbourne: *Sun Books,* Melbourne, 1967.
Garretty, J.D. *Three Australian Composers. M.A. Thesis,* University of Melbourne, 1963.
Harris, Laughton. *Australian Composition in the Twentieth Century.* Melbourne: *OUP,* 1978.
McCredie, Andrew *Catalogue of 46 Australian Composers and Selected Works.*
Murdoch, James. *Australia's Contemporary Composers. Macmillan* Australia, 1972.
Sinclair, J. *Australian Journal of Music Education.*
Ref. AMC, 4, 5, 14, 17, 58, 70, 77, 94, 203, 280, 412, 440, 446, 563, 622

SUTRO, Florence Edith (nee Clinton)
American pianist, teacher, writer and composer. b. England, May, 1865; d. April 29, 1906. She was a pupil of Dudley Buck and Dr. William Mason. She was the first woman in the United States to receive a Mus.D. and the first woman to enroll in the women's law class of New York University, where she was a valedictorian. She was the founder of the National Federation of Music Clubs.
Compositions
PIANO
Pieces
VOCAL
Fugue (4 vces)
Songs incl.:
My first love
Publications
Women in Music and Law. New York, 1895.
Ref. 85, 191, 260, 269, 276, 292, 347, 433

SUTZU (Soutzo), Rodica
Rumanian pianist, professor and composer. b. Iasi, April 15, 1913. At the Iasi Conservatory she studied the piano under Aspasia Burada, theory and solfege under Sofia Teodoreanu and harmony under Gavriil Galinescu and Elinescu. She graduated in 1930 and proceeded to the Ecole Normale in Paris where she continued her piano studies under Blanche Basscouret de Geraldi, Lazare Levy, Alfred Cortot, accompaniment under Ginette Waldmeyer, chamber music under Diran Alexanian, harmony under George Dandelot and music history under Nadia Boulanger (q.v.). She received her diploma in 1935. From 1937 until 1955 she was piano soloist and master of sound with the Rumanian Radio. At the same time she performed under prominent conductors with orchestras and in chamber recitals, accompanying such performers as George Enesco, Mircea

Barsan and Theodor Lupu. In 1959 she became professor of piano at the George Enesco Music School and lectured at the Pedagogic Institute in Bucharest until 1968. In 1933 she won the George Enesco prize for composition and in 1953 was awarded the Workers's medal. PHOTOGRAPH.

Compositions
CHAMBER
    Prelude for oboe and piano, op. 28 (1961)
    Piece for cello and piano, op. 4 (1940)
PIANO
    Concert waltz (2 pf)
    Album of piano pieces
    Ballad in C-Minor, op. 4 (1957)
    Etude, op. 12 (1954)
    Five miniatures, op. 27 (1961)
    Five pieces
    Obsession, op. 1 (1933)
    Perpetuum mobile, op. 11 (1954)
    Rondo, op. 13 (1955)
    Sonata in C-Major, op. 7 (1950)
    Suite, op. 25 (1960)
    Suite for children
    Three nocturnes, op. 10 (1954)
    Toccata, op. 23 (1960)
    Two preludes, op. 5 (1940)
    Virtelnita, op. 21 (1958)
VOCAL
    Ballad (vocal sextet, 2 pf and orch)
    Divertisement, op. 22 (ch) (1959)
    Five love songs (Armenian troubadours) (1953)
    Gazel op. 15 (M. Eminescu) (1957)
    Imi sint ochii plini de soare, duet (1966)
    Songs to verses of Eminescu and Cazimir
    Three miniatures, op. 16 (Otilia Cazimir) (1957)
    Waltz for voice and piano, op. 24 (1961)
    Light songs
THEATRE
    Allonsy d'un pas flaneur, play (L. Delesco)
    Ghici-ghici, puppet theatre (N. Stroescu) (1968)
    Tu comprendras, play (E. Peretz)
Ref. 87

SUZUE, Mariko

20th-century Japanese composer.
Composition
CHAMBER
    String quartet No. 2
Ref. Jeannie Pool (Los Angeles)

SVANIDZE, Natela Damianovna

Soviet lecturer and composer. b. Akhalkhitse, Georgia, September 4, 1926. From 1944 to 1946 she studied at Tbilisi University and in 1950 graduated from the Conservatory of Tbilisi having studied composition under A. Balanchivadze. From 1952 to 1954 she lectured on theoretical subjects at the Kultprosvet School and after 1955 at the Music School.

Compositions
ORCHESTRA
    Samgori (on a poem by G. Leonidze) (1951)
    Symphonic dances, suite (1950)
CHAMBER
    Improvisation (vln and pf) (1955)
    Theme with variations (pf) (1948)
VOCAL
    Sad Kartli, poem (G. Leonidze) (ch and sym orch) (1949)
    Rassvet (G. Orbeliani) (w-ch a-cap) (1954)
    Gkazaniye ob odnoi dyevyshke (I. Noneshvili) (vce and pf) (1953)
Ref. 87

SVOBODOVA, Bozena. See JAHNOVA, Bozena

SWADOS, Elizabeth

American singer, writer and composer. b. Buffalo, NY, 1950. She studied creative writing and music at Bennington College, Vermont. Since 1977 she has held the position of composer-in-residence at the La Mama Experimental Theatre Club New York. PHOTOGRAPH.

Compositions
ORCHESTRA
    Symphonic overture
VOCAL
    Sylvia Plath song cycle (1973)

BALLET
    Truth and variations (1979)
THEATRE
    Nightclub cantata
    Dispatches (1979)
    Lullabye and Goodnight (1980)
    New York and Gypsy Suite (1980)
    Runaways (1978)
    Wonderland in Concert (1978)
INCIDENTAL MUSIC
    Agamemnon (1976)
    Barn Burning (1979)
    Cherry orchard (1976)
    Electra (with Andrei Serban)
    Ghost Sonata (with Andrei Serban)
    The Good Woman of Setzuan
    Medea (with Andrei Serban)
    Step by Step (1978)
    Sky Dance (1979)
    Too Far to Go (1978)
    The Trojan Woman (with Andrei Serban)
MISCELLANEOUS
    Conference of the birds (1973)
Publications
    For All Our Children. 1980.
    The Girl with the Incredible Feeling.
    Lullaby. 1980.
    Runaways. 1979.
Bibliography
    Many Worlds of Music. No. 4. Broadcast Music, 1977.
Ref. BMI, 610

SWAIN, Freda Mary

English flautist, pianist, violinist, professor and composer. b. Portsmouth or Southsea, Hants, October 31, 1902; d. January 29, 1985. She was educated at the Tobias Matthay Piano School and the Royal College of Music where she studied the piano under Arthur Alexander, whom she later married, and composition under Stanford and Achille Rivarde. She studied the violin under Maurice Sons and played the flute in the college orchestra. She was also associate board exhibitioner for the piano. In 1924 she was appointed professor of the piano at the Royal College of Music, a position she held until 1940. In 1936 she founded and later became director of the British Music Movement. In 1940 she went to Cape Town, South Africa, as a lecturer and gave recitals with her husband. She was founder and director of NEMO concerts and NEMO Music Centre. She became an F.R.C.M. in 1961; was awarded the Sullivan prize for composition in 1917; the Ellen Shaw Williams piano prize in 1917; the Ada Lewis scholarship for the piano in 1917 and the Portsmouth-Whitcombe scholarship for composition in 1917. PHOTOGRAPH.

Compositions
ORCHESTRA
    The air mail concerto (pf and orch) (1939)
    Piano concerto
    The harp of Aengus (after Yeats) (vln and orch) (1924)
    The Lion of England, march (orch and trp) (1953)
    Concertino (cl, hn and strs) (1948)
    Concerto (pf and str orch)
    Marshland, tone poem (cham orch)
    Miniature suite (str orch) (1952)
    A pastoral fantasy (1936-1937)
    Walking and dream tide (str orch)
CHAMBER
    Fanfare for a duchess (3 trp, 3 trb, drs or 6 trp) (1976)
    Suite (6 trp) (1952)
    Dance rhythms from an unknown country (vla, fl, ob, cl and pf) (1957)
    Piano quintet (1938)
    Solemn salutation (2 trp, 2 hn and trb) (1951)
    Piano quartet
    The sea (vln, vla, vlc and pf) (1938)
    String quartet in E-Minor, No. 1 (The Norfolk) (1924-1935)
    String quartet in G-Minor, No. 2 (1950)
    Lamentations (2 vlc and pf) (1960)
    Terzet for strings (vln, vla and vlc) (1966)
    Ballade (vln and pf)
    Bobolink (rec and pf)
    Berceuse (vln and pf)
    By the loch (vlc and pf) (1960)
    Danse barbare (vln and vlc)
    Derry down (cl and pf) (1953)
    Duets (2 vln)
    Eight pip tunes for Janet (cl and pf) (1965)
    Les elegants (cl and pf) (1963)
    Fanfare for a queen (brass) (1977)
    Festival suite (hn, drs and pf) (1967)

Fanfare (3 trp) (1952)
Fantasy, suite (ob and pf) (Bourne Music, 1957)
Fantasy, march (sax and pf) (1983)
Heather hill (cl and pf) (1953)
Highlands hill (vln and pf) (1952)
Laburnum tree (cl and pf) (British & Continental Music, 1959)
Lamenta (vln and pf)
Love song (vlc and pf) (1929)
Mauresque (vln and pf) (1919)
La pasadita (vln and pf) (Schott, 1930)
Paspy (ob or fl and pf) (Chappell & Co., 1963)
Piece for open strings (vln and pf) (Schott, 1965)
Pipe tunes (cl and pf) (1965)
Poem (vln and pf) (1959)
Rhapsody (cl and pf) (1950, 1960)
The river (vln and pf) (1925)
Rhapsody No. 2 (vla and pf) (1958)
Royal fanfare to precede a national anthem (brass) (1977)
Satyr's dance (cl and pf; also a-sax and pf) (Bourne, 1937)
Shushan waltz (cl and pf) (1965)
Sonata in C-Minor (vlc and pf) (1922)
Sonata in B-Minor (vln and pf) (1925)
Summer rhapsody No. 1 (cl or vln and pf) (1936)
Tambourin gai (ob or vln or fl and pf) (Chappell, 1964)
Three fantasies (vlc and pf) (1959)
Three movements (vln and pf) (1955)
Three pleasant pieces (vln and pf)
Two rhapsodies (vla and pf)
La vielle marquise (ob or vln and pf) (1963)
The waving grass (cl and pf) (British & Continental)
The willow tree (cl; also cl and pf) (1946)
Willow waltz (sax and pf) (1940)
Nature suite (sax) (1939)
Slow worm (rec)
Sonata (vln) (1933)
Suite (sax) (1937)
The tease (sax) (1965)
Three pieces (vlc) (1962)
Three whimsies (ob) (Bourne, 1965)
Teaching pieces
PIANO
Barbaric scherzo (3 pf) (1923)
Flourish (2 pf) (1968)
Perceptions (2 pf) (1968)
Whirling wheels (2 pf) (1965)
Autumn landscape (1953)
The blank wall (1928)
Bluebottle (1963)
The breezes (1945)
Camp fires
Caricatures (1928)
Chinese procession (1924)
A country outing, 4 pieces
Crossbow castle, 4 pieces
The croon of the sea (1924)
Cycle of life, 7 pieces (1928)
The deep ravine (1925)
The desolate lake (1941)
Dog daisy, caricature suite (1928)
An English idyll (1941)
Glory hallelujah (1967)
The greenawn (1934)
Grey landscape (1929)
Humoresque (1924)
Irish jig (1953)
Kalahari croon (1958)
Lazy waters (1941)
Marionette on holiday (1953)
Melodies (Burns)
Melancholy thistle (1928)
Merry thought (1917)
The mountain ash (1935)
The musical box (1924)
Name pieces (1963)
Prelude, jubilation (1973)
Prelude and toccata with interlude (1955)
The red flower (1929)
Reflections at night, sound setting on poem by W. Hart-Smith (1941)
The return (1934)
Romance (1941)
The sea, sonata-poem in F-Minor
Six name pieces (1965-1966)
Sonata (1 or 2 hands) (1956-1957)
Sonata No. 1, The Skerries (1956)
Sonata No. 2 in F-Sharp Minor (1950)
Sonata saga (1925-1929)

March with fanfare (The Lions of England) (1953)
Spring joy (1953)
Spring mood (1945)
Star pieces
Suite-quiddities (1977)
Tetrad, sonatina, in 4 mvts (1930)
Three descriptive pieces (1967)
Three movements (1963)
Toccata in D (1941)
Two South African impressions (1940)
Valse charming
The water mill (1937)
Wayward waltz (1953)
West wind
The windmill (1924)
The winds (1945)
ORGAN
English pastoral (1950)
Sonatina (Novello)
VOCAL
Perihelion (vce without words and str orch) (1963)
The indwelling, song cycle (L.A.G. Strong, Ruth Pitter, Edward Faw-cett) (Bar, T, 2 S, Cont, mix-ch, 2 vln, vla and vlc)
Country love (w-ch) (1960)
Sweet content (R. Greene) (w-ch)
The bird of the wilderness, song cycle (vce, pf and vln) (Rabindranath Tagore) (1961)
Enigma (from the Japanese of Yoni Noguchi) (1922)
Evening (Mark Tait) (1942)
Five settings of poems by Burns (1924-1925)
The harvesters' song (George Peel) (vce and gtr) (1946)
In exile (David Gamble) (1942)
The lovely lady (John Masefield) (1922)
Montanus, sonnet (Thomas Lodge) (1946)
November (Sir Donald Ross) (1942)
Seven settings from A Shropshire lad (A.E. Housman) (1927-1928)
She is my love (P.A. Graves) (1924)
Six settings of Chinese poems (trans Arthur Waley) (1921-1923)
Six sonnets (Shakespeare) (1934-1946)
Sympathy (Emily Bronte) (1934)
Thirteen settings of poems by A.E. Coppard (1928-1938)
The travelling companion (Lord Alfred Douglas) (1934)
The twilight shore (Robert Bridges) (1924)
Two settings of poems by L.A.G. Strong (1936)
Two settings of poems by Gwen Grant (1942)
Two songs (A.E. Coppard) (vce and strs) (1929-1934)
Two unaccompanied ballads (1946)
Numerous songs for schools
Many other songs
SACRED
A prayer (vce and pf; also S and orch) (1941, 1946)
In memoriam, cantata
Bells of heaven (ch and pf) (1964)
Carol of the seasons (ch and pf)
A Gaelic prayer (ch and org) (1965)
The holly and the ivy (mix-ch a-cap) (1964)
Jubilate (ch and org) (1966)
Psalm 121 (ch and org) (1976)
Te Deum (ch and org) (1965)
Unseen heralds (Swain) (ch and pf; also vce and 2 pf) (1964)
Breathe on me, breath of God (1960)
Psalm 150 (Bar and org) (1972)
A queen's prayer (Elizabeth I) (1977)
Anthems
Hymns
BALLET
Ship ahoy, unfinished
OPERA
The Shadowy Waters (Yeats)
Ref. composer, MLA Notes, 2, 8, 41, 68, 74, 76, 84, 86, 96, 172, 226, 280, 465, 622

SWART, Anna. See RUDOLPH, Anna

SWARTZ, Elsa Ellen
American teacher and composer. b. El Paso, IL, June 25, 1878. She was a pupil of A.K. Virgil, Frederick Grant Gleason and Gertrude H. Murdogh. She taught in Illinois.
Compositions
PIANO
Children's pieces
Studies
Ref. 226

SWEDISH NIGHTINGALE. See LIND, Jenny

SWEPSTONE, Edith

19th-century English lecturer and composer. She studied at the Guildhall School of Music. She lectured on music at the City of London School.

Compositions
ORCHESTRA
Unfinished symphony
Les ténèbres, elegiac overture
Minuet in C-Major (str orch) (Schott Soehne)
Tarantelle in A-Minor (str orch) (Schott Soehne)
CHAMBER
Quintet in F-Minor (pf and strs)
Quartet in G-Minor (strs)
Several works for cello and piano incl.:
Fantastic; plaintive
Cavatina violin pieces
Piano pieces
VOCAL
Ice king, cantata
Idylls of the morn, cantata
Songs
Ref. 6, 41, 226, 276, 322, 433

SWIFT, Gertrude H.

19th-century American composer.

Compositions
VOCAL
Songs incl.:
Art thou same
A fancy
Hark, hark the lark
Serenade
Ref. 226, 276, 292

SWIFT, Kay (Mrs. Paul Warburg)

American pianist and composer. b. New York, April 15, 1905. She studied composition at the Juilliard School of Music on a faculty scholarship, under Arthur E. Johnstone, at the Institute of Musical Art and under Charles Martin Loeffler at the New England Conservatory. Her other teachers included Heinrich Gebhard (piano) and Percy Goetschius (counterpoint and orchestration). She was accompanist to touring concert artists and staff composer at Radio City Music Hall for two years. She was also the first magazine radio columnist and music chairlady for the 1939 New York World Fair, as well as piano soloist with the New York Philharmonic at the Lewisohn Stadium.

Compositions
ORCHESTRA
Century 21, suite
CHAMBER
Theme and variations (vlc and pf)
Piano pieces
VOCAL
Man have pity on man (soloists, ch and orch) (1970)
Reaching for the brass ring (S and orch) (1950)
Calliope
Can this be love?
Can't we be friends?
Forever and a day
I gotta take my hat off to you
In between age
A moonlight memory
Once you find your guy
Up among the chimney pots
BALLET
Alma Mater
THEATRE
Century 21 (1962)
Fine and Dandy, musical comedy (Paul James)
Garrick Gaieties (1930)
Nine-fifteen Revue
One Little Girl (1960)
Paris '90, musical comedy
Songs for Little Show (1929)
FILM MUSIC
Never a Dull Moment, songs
The Shocking Miss Pilgrim, adaptation of Gershwins' music
Bibliography
Never a Dull Moment. Autobiography.
Ref. 39, 40, 142, 347, 392, 610

SWISHER, Gloria Agnes Wilson

American pianist, lecturer and composer. b. Seattle, WA, March 12, 1935. She studied under John Verrall at the University of Washington graduating summa cum laude (B.A.) in 1956 and under Darius Milhaud at Mills College (M.A.). She graduated from the Eastman School of Music (Ph.D.) in 1960, having studied under Howard Hanson and Bernard Rogers. She also studied under Egon Petri. From 1960 to 1961 she taught at Washington State University; from 1969 to 1970 at Pacific Lutheran University and since 1969 she has been an instructor at Shoreline Community College and is currently secretary of the board of directors of the Sigma Alpha Iota Philanthropies. She won the Tahalia Symphony Orchestra contest in 1981, received a Woodrow Wilson fellowship from 1956 to 1957 and received the Capital Choir Contest award in 1961. She is a member of Phi Beta Kappa. PHOTOGRAPH.

Compositions
ORCHESTRA
Cancion (fl and orch) (1966)
Concerto (cl and orch) (1960)
Yuki no niigata (koto and orch)
Lincoln memorial (1962)
Two pieces (1969)
BAND
The mountain and the island (sym band) (1971)
Processions (sym band) (1974)
Three pieces (pf and band) (1954)
CHAMBER
Suite (wind sinfonietta and pf)
Suite (3 A, sax and pf)
Theatre trio (trp, sax and pf)
Sonata (cl and pf) (1959)
Theme and variations (fl) (1963)
PIANO
Canon (4 hands) (1972)
J-O-E-L, variations (1984)
Variations on an original theme (1963)
VOCAL
Words to a grandchild (mix-ch and wind ens) (1983)
Death, be not proud (mix-ch a-cap)
Two faces of love (Shakespeare) (mix-ch and pf)
Love's shadow comes slow (S or m-S and pf)
Rest, love (m-S and pf)
Sisters (S or m-S and pf)
Sonnets (S and pf) (1983)
Vocalise (1969)
SACRED
God be merciful unto us (mix-ch) (1963)
God is gone up with a merry noise (mix-ch and org or pf) (1961)
Be Thou my judge, O Lord (1971)
Thanksgiving
Unto Thee, O Lord (1964)
OPERA
The Artist and the Other, chamber opera (Willy Clark) (1982)
The Happy Hypocrite, chamber opera (1965)
THEATRE
The Promise, musical (1953)
INCIDENTAL MUSIC
For Such a Time as This (1983)
MISCELLANEOUS
Dance for Tomorrow
One Nation Indivisible (1961)
Publications
Syllabus for Music Theory. 1st and 2nd Years. 1974.
Ref. composer, 77, 94, 142, 228, 474, 625

SYBIL OF THE RHINE. See HILDEGARDE, Saint

SYMIANE, Magdaleine

19th-century French composer.
Compositions
OPERA
Le proces verbal (1906)
Une simple formalité (1906)
Ref. 431

SYNER, Sonia

English pianist, teacher and composer. b. Worcester, 1892. She was an L.R.A.M. and taught the piano, singing and musical appreciation at schools between 1916 and 1936.

Compositions
PIANO
Eight miniature sketches
VOCAL
The dream ship
Quest of the lost song
School song
OPERETTA
The Birthday Cake
Ref. 467

SYNGE, Mary Helena

19th-century Irish pianist, singer and composer. b. Parsonstown. She studied the piano and singing at Brussels Conservatory.
Compositions
PIANO
Pieces
VOCAL
Songs incl.:
Fate
Spring (vocal trio)
Time and eternity
Ref. 85, 276, 347, 433

SYNOWIEC, Ewa

20th-century Polish composer.
Compositions
ORCHESTRA
String concerto (1978)
Synfonia for 58 string instruments (1976)
CHAMBER
Seasons of the year (fl, vln, vla and vlc) (1978)
Still life No. 4 (fl, trp and vib) (1976)
Alternations I (2 pf) (1978)
Postscript (pf and perc) (1977)
One-sided composition (vln) (1976)
Version No. 3 (vln) (1976)
SACRED
Psalmodia (A and ch) (1968)
Ref. Polish Music, 465

SYRMEN, Maddalena Laura di. See SIRMEN, Maddalena Laura di

SZAJNA-LEWANDOWSKA, Jadwiga Helena

Polish pianist, teacher and composer. b. Brody, Russia, February 22, 1912. She began her musical studies at the Lvov Conservatory, where she was a pupil of M. Soltysowa. At the State Music College in Wroclaw, she studied composition under T. Szeligowski, P. Perkowski and S.B. Poradowski, graduating in 1956. From 1943 she taught in schools and privately and played in theatres in Wroclaw..
Compositions
ORCHESTRA
Piano concerto
Funerailles (pf, perc and str orch; also 2 pf) (1971)
Concertino (fl and str orch) (1954)
Polish capriccio (pf and str orch) (1973)
Three fragments (pf and str orch) (1968)
Two etudes (pf and str orch) (1962)
CHAMBER
Capriccio (cl and str qrt) (1956)
Four dances in the old style (fl, ob, 2 cl, bsn and perc) (1979)
Five pieces for piano quintet (Agencja Autorska, 1980)
Mythological preludes (fl and pf) (1955)
Six pieces (pf and str qrt) (1978)
Six triolets (fl and pf)
Sonatina (ob and pf) (1954)
PIANO
Concertino (2 pf) (1965)
Sonatina giocosa (PWM, 1958)
Three legerezze (1965)
VOCAL
Rhymes of Mr. Lear, 2 songs (E. Lear) (spoken vce, B and orch) (1968)
Song cycle (T. Zasadny) (S and cham orch) (1964)
Three jocular songs (L.J. Kern) (2 vce w-ch, str qrt and perc) (1964)
Poetry (M. Jasnorzewska-Pawlikowska) (S and str qrt) (1972)
The fly is asleep (H. Januszewska, 1978)
The lion (H. Januszewska, 1978)
Six children's songs (W. Bronikowski)

BALLET
Abduction in Tiutiurlistan, for children (1966)
Pinocchio, for children (1956)
Tais, in 3 acts (1969)
OPERETTA
Blekitny Kot, for children
THEATRE
Little Donkey's Hide, musical comedy (Perrault) (1971)
Ref. composer, 70, 118

SZALIT, Paulina. See SZALITOWNA, Paulina

SZALITOWNA (Szalit), Paulina

Polish pianist and composer. b. Lvov, 1886; d. 1920. She studied at the Lvov Conservatory and then in Vienna where she was a pupil of E. d'Albert, J. Hofman and T. Leschetizky. She was acclaimed a child prodigy by Hanslick and made numerous appearances in Vienna, Germany and Poland.
Compositions
PIANO
Klavierstuecke: Impromptu in F, op. 3; Intermezzo in G Sharp; Praeludium, capriccio (F-Minor) (Ries & Erler)
Miniatures
Morceaux: Intermezzo, op. 2; Mazurka, valse; Reverie, impromptu; Tendresse, scène de ballet (Ries & Erler)
Traeumerei
Bibliography
Das Klavier und seine Meister. 1901.
Ref. 8, 70, 81, 118, 297

SZARVADY, Wilhelmine Clausz

Bohemian pianist and composer. b. Prague, December 13, 1834; d. Paris, November 1, 1907. She was a pupil of Joseph Proksch and at the age of 15 began a career as a pianist, touring widely and being acclaimed by Liszt, Spohr and Schumann. After 1857 she settled in Paris. She arranged works by C.P.E. Bach, Pergolesi, Scarlatti, Rameau, Couperin and others.
Ref. 50, 276, 297, 433

SZCZUKA-JEZIERSKA

Early 18th-century Polish composer. She lived in Warsaw and composed a mazurka and a waltz for the piano.
Ref. 118

SZEKELY, Katalin

Hungarian professor and composer. b. Budapest, June 12, 1953. She studied at the Ferenc Liszt Academy of Music in Budapest where she became professor of music theory. Her works have been performed in Hungary, Yugoslavia and Norway and recorded for Hungarian radio. In 1981 she won the Society of Hungarian Musicians' prize for young composers. PHOTOGRAPH.
Compositions
ORCHESTRA
Summernight music (orch) (1979)
Windows of the time (orch) (1982)
Concerto grosso, hommage à Corelli (str orch) (1983)
CHAMBER
Atem (8 fl) (1977)
Quintet (wind insts) (1973)
Nine short pieces (str qrt) (1975)
Aforismi (vlc and mar) (1984)
Sketches (vln and per) (1976)
Violin duos, twelve studies (1982)
Miniatures (gtr) (1981)
Pièce avec interludes (gtr) (1981)
VOCAL
Missa Esztergom (S and gtr orch) (1983)
Missa traditionalis (ch and orch) (1982)
Flashings (S, fl and cl) (1974)
SACRED
Madrigale, omaggio à Sancto Francesco d'Assisi (mix-ch)
Missa brevis, hommage à Palestrina (w-ch) (1981)
Ref. composer

SZOENYI, (SZONYI) Erzsebet

Hungarian pianist, choral conductor, lecturer and composer. b. Budapest, April 25, 1924. She studied composition under Janos Viski and the piano under Erno Szegedi at the Liszt Academy. She also attended teaching and choir conducting classes graduating in 1947. In the same year she won a French State scholarship to study at the Paris Conservatoire where her teachers included Nadia Boulanger (q.v.), Tony Aubin and Olivier Messiaen. In 1948 she received the Conservatoire's prix de composition. That year she began teaching solfege and theory at the Ferenc Liszt Academy in Budapest and in 1960 became director of the academy's school music faculty. She worked in close co-operation with Zoltan Kodaly and played an important part in realizing his ideas for music education in schools. In 1959 she won the Erkel prize for composition. Her compositions have been played both in Hungary and abroad. She has been the supervisor of music conservatories in Hungary since 1951 and is a member of the board of directors of the International Society for Music Education. She has lectured on Hungarian music education in many countries. DISCOGRAPHY. PHOTOGRAPH.

Compositions
ORCHESTRA
  Concerto for organ and orchestra (Budapest Editio Musica; Boosey & Hawkes)
  Trio concertino (vln, vlc, pf and str orch) (Boosey)
  Allegro (Boosey, 1969)
  First divertimento (Edito Musica) (1948)
  Musica festiva suite (1965)
  Parlando e giusto (Artisjus, 1947)
  Piccola introduzione (strs) (Boosey)
  Prelude and fugue (1969)
  Second divertimento (Editio Musica; Boosey)
  Three ideas, 4 mvts (1980)
  Two pieces for orchestra (Boosey)
CHAMBER
  Trio (ob, cl and bsn) (Editio Musica; Boosey)
  Trio for young people (vln, vlc and pf) (Editio Musica, 1952)
  Trio sonata (vln, vlc and pf) (Editio Musica; Boosey)
  Twenty Hungarian folksongs (2 rec and gtr) (1978)
  Air (vln and pf) (Editio Musica, 1946)
  Duo (vln and vla) (Editio Musica, 1955)
  Evocation (pf and org) (1985)
  French suite (vla and pf) (1983)
  Five folk songs (vln and pf) (1948)
  Melody (vlc and pf) (1958) (Editio Musica)
  Play (vlc and pf) (1954) (Editio Musica)
  Preludium (vln and pf) (1958) (Editio Musica)
  Serenade and dance (vln and pf) (1954)
  Sonata (d-b and pf) (1982)
  Sonatina (vln and pf) (Editio Musica, 1963)
  Sonatine for children (vln and pf) (1965) (Editio Musica)
  Fantasy (hp) (1983)
  Introduzione, passacaglia, e fuga (org)
ORGAN
  Introduction, passacaglia and fugue (Editio Musica, 1965)
  Six pieces (Editio Musica, 1955)
PIANO
  Play (2 pf) (1946)
  Small chamber music (duet) (1963)
  Colours, suite (1946)
  Fantasy and fugue (1948)
  Five preludes (Editio Musica, 1963)
  Sonata (1953)
  Two sonatinas (1944, 1946)
VOCAL
  A didergo kiraly, children's oratorio (1959) (Editio Musica)
  A gay lament, oratorio (1979)
  A hazug katona, oratorio (1960)
  Story of the Gyula-castle, oratorio (mix-ch, T, B, brass and orch) (1983) (Musica Budapest)
  Tinodi egri summaja, youth oratorio (1960) (Editio Musica)
  Attila Jozsef, cantata (1968)
  Radnoti cantata, (Miklos Radnoti) (1975)
  Anakreon (ch) (1969) (Editio Musica)
  A song (m-ch) (1983) (Editio Musica)
  Balatoni kepek (ch) (1953) (Editio Musica)
  Canticum sponsae (ch) (1953) (Editio Musica)
  Egy aldomast; Kelj fel Jancsi (L. Benjamin) (mix-ch) (1965) (Editio Musica)
  Elotted a kuzdes (Janos Arany) (mix-ch) (1974) (Editio Musica)
  Fifteen two-three part choruses on folk-songs from Asia (chil-ch) (1985)
  Fifty bicinia on Japanese, American and Canadian folk songs (ch) (1971) (Editio Musica)
  For St. Dominic's day, canon (I. Grany) (chil-ch) (1970) (Editio Musica)
  Four children's choruses (chil-ch) (1979) (Editio Musica)
  Huszonegy enekesjatek (vocal games) (2 S and cham ens) (1948) (Editio Musica)
  Japanese songs (D. Kosztolanvi) (chil-ch) (1970) (Editio Musica)
  Lament (w-ch, fl, vln and hpcd) (1967) (Editio Musica)
  Motets (m-ch and org) (1983)
  Nine two-three part choruses on Israeli folksongs (chil-ch) (1985)
  Orban, tintasuveg (Sandor Petofi) (chil-ch) (1973) (Editio Musica)
  Ode to the present (mix-ch) (1979) (Editio Musica)
  Paysage (mix-ch) (1983) (EMB)
  Running to the meadow (S. Devecseri) (mix-ch) (1970) (Editio Musica)
  Savaria (Maria Virag) (mix-ch) (1973) (Editio Musica)
  Sicut cervus (m-ch) (1976) (Editio Musica)
  Soldiers' song (Balint Balassa, 17th century) (m-ch) (1956)
  Something has spoken to me in the night (T. Wolfe) (mix-ch) (1972) (Editio Musica)
  Sonnet (Petrarch) (mix-ch) (1978)
  Thirty-three easy small choruses, based on Hungarian folk songs (chil-ch) (1967) (Editio Musica)
  Three madrigals (S. Petofi) (mix-ch) (1985)
  Two mixed choruses (L. Benjamin) (1970)
  Two sonnets by Petrarch (ch, hp and cl) (1960)
  Two songs on poems by Balint Balassa (mix-ch and cham ens) (1979) (Editio Musica)
  Uj varak epultek (ch) (1947) (Editio Musica)
  Vakacio elott (L. Szabbo) (chil-ch) (1973) (Editio Musica)
  Ad aristium fascum, Ode by Horace (S or T, 2 pf and perc) (1965)
  Melodies (Ady, Kosztolany, Babits) (S, m-S, T and Bar)
  Duet (S and m-S) (1958)
SACRED
  Stabat Mater (mix-ch and org) (1982) (Editio Musica)
BALLET
  The Cricket and the Ants, for children (1953)
  Garden Tale, for children (1949)
  Pantomime (1949)
OPERA
  Adashiba, in 1 act (Karoly Szakonyi) (1980)
  Break of Transmission (Karoly Szakonyi) (1980)
  Dalma, in 3 acts (Mor Jokai) (1952)
  Elfrida, in 1 act (Laszlo Arany) (1985)
  Firenzei tragedia, in 1 act (Oscar Wilde) (1957)
OPERETTA
  Az aranyszarnyu mehecske, in 1 act (1974)
  Az igazmondo juhasz, in 1 act (Magda Donaszy)(1979)
  Makrancos Kiralylany, in 2 acts (Edit Kovats) (1955)
THEATRE
  Kepzelt beteg, musical (1963)
  Kis rongyos, for children (1962)
  Szaz cifra Kodmon, musical (1965)
  Vidam sirato egy bolyongo porszemert, in 2 acts (Andras Suto) (1979)

Publications
La Formation musicale de l'oreille musicale. Montreal: Beauchemin, 1965.
Kodaly's Principles in Practice. Budapest: Corvina, 1973.
Kodaly Zoltan nevelesi eszmei. Tankonyvkiado, 1984.
The Method of Musical Reading and Writing. 3 vols. In Hungarian (Budapest Editio Musica, 1954), in English (Boosey & Hawkes, 1972), in Japanese (Zen-On, 1971). 4th vol.
Musical Education for Children from the Age of Three to Ten in Hungary. Panton Ed. Prague. 1968.
Sol-fa Teaching in Musical Education (English, German, Japanese). Budapest: Corvina.
20th-Century Music Methods, EMB.
Utazasok ot Kontinensen. Gondolat, 1978.
Ref. composer, 9, 17, 30, 70, 77, 94, 96, 280, 563, 622

SZPINTER-KINIECKA, Maria

Polish composer. b. 1942.
Compositions
VOCAL
  Small cantata (S and w-ch) (1968)
  Interventions (vce and orch) (1972)
  Characters (soli and inst ens)
  Composition (S, fl and hp) (1969)
  Songs
Ref. 465

SZTARAY, Margit (Countess)

19th-century Polish composer.
Composition
SACRED
  Ave Maria (4 w-vces and org)
Ref. 226, 276

SZUMINSKA, Flora
19th-20th-century Polish composer.
Compositions
VOCAL
Songs incl.:
To imie Helena, op. 4
Za czym gonisz, op. 3
Ref. 118

SZYMANOWSKA, Filipina. See BRZEZINSKA, Filipina

SZYMANOWSKA (Shimanovskaya), Maria Agata (nee Wolowska)
Polish pianist, teacher and composer. b. Warsaw, December 14, 1789; d. St. Petersburg, July 24, 1831. Her first music teachers were Antonie Lisowski and Tomay Gremm. In 1810 she went to Paris where she inspired Cherubini to dedicate a *Fantasia* to her. In the same year she married Jozef Szymanowski, a Polish landowner but the marriage ended in divorce ten years later. Her daughter Celina married the poet Adam Mickiewicz. Maria began a career as a touring concert pianist in 1815, traveling to London, Berlin and other German cities and in 1822 became pianist at the court of the Tsar in St. Petersburg. At this time Hummel and Field dedicated compositions to her. In 1821 she met Goethe and she is perhaps best known for the infatuation she inspired in him. Goethe praised her playing above Hummel's and was inspired to write his poem *Aussoehnung* in his *Trilogie der Leidenschaft*. Her 12 concert etudes were highly praised by Schumann. She was often described as *the feminine Field*, Field being the originator of the nocturne. In 1828 she settled in St. Petersburg and retired from performing to dedicate herself to teaching. She died three years later of cholera. DISCOGRAPHY.
Compositions
CHAMBER
Divertissement (vln and pf) (Leipzig: Breitkopf & Haertel)
Fanfare duet (2 hn or trp)
Serenade (pf and vlc) (ded Prince Antoine Radziwill) (Breitkopf)
Theme varié (fl and pf or vln) (ded Princess de Lowicz) (Breitkopf)
PIANO
Grand valse (4 hands) (Breitkopf)
Quatre valses (3 hands)
Caprice sur la romance de Jocande (ded John Field) (Breitkopf)
Cotillon du valse figurée (Paris: Henry)
Danse polonaise (Henry)
Dix-huit danses de different genre (Breitkopf)
Early Polish music
Fantaisie (Breitkopf)
Menuet in E-Major
Le murmure, nocturne (Henry)
Nocturne in A-Flat Major
Nocturne in B-Major
Nocturne in F-Minor (Breitkopf)
Polonaise sur l'air national favori du feu Prince Joseph Poniatowski (Breitkopf)
Polish pre-romantic music
Preludium in B-Major
Romance de Monsieur le Prince Alexandre Galitzin (Breitkopf)
Etude in C-Major
Etude in E-Major
Etude in E Flat Major
Etude in F Major
Etude in D-Minor
Serenada
Six marches (Breitkopf)
Six menuets (Breitkopf)
Temat wariacji in B-Minor
Twenty-four mazurkas (Breitkopf)
Valse in D-Minor
Vingt exercises et preludes (Breitkopf)
VOCAL
Songs incl.:
Alpuhara, Piesn z wiezy, Wilia, w Tych przedsionkach szczescie gosci (W. Skarbek)
Ballade (m-S and pf) (Saint-Onge)
Le depart (Cervantes)
Jadwiga, krolowa polska (Warsaw, 1816)
Jan Albrycht duma o kniaziu Michale Glinskim (Warsaw, 1816)
Kazimierz Wielki
Nie bede lez ronic (A. Gorecki) (1822)
Piec spiewow historychnych (J.U. Niemcewicz) (1816)
Peine et plaisir, romance du saule (Shakespeare)
Romance à Josephine, apres avoir fait la terre
Romance à la nuit, le connais tu (de Bernis)
Se spiegar potessi oh Dio
Six romances

Spiewka na powrot wojsk polskich (L.A. Dmuszewski) (Warsaw, 1822)
Stefan Czarniecki
Switezianka (A. Mickiewicz) (1828)
Trzy spiewy z poematu Adama Mickiewicza Konrad Wallenrod (1828)
Bibliography
Belza, I.M. *Szymanowska*. Moscow, 1956.
Iwanejko, M. *M. Szymanowska*. Cracow: PWM, 1960.
Mirski, J. *Zapomniana artystka polska*. Warsaw: Musyka, 1931.
Ref. 2, 8, 9, 15, 17, 20, 22, 26, 44, 52, 70, 118, 129, 226, 258, 276, 282, 297, 361, 400, 563, 622

SZYMANSKA, Iwonka Bogumila
Polish pianist and composer. b. Warsaw, July 11, 1943. She made her debut as a pianist in 1951 and her first composition appeared in 1965. She studied the piano at the State Music College in Gdansk and in 1965 went to the State Music College, Warsaw, where she studied composition and graduated in 1972. She created the 'Sonnet' a new musical form. She has also performed on the radio.
Compositions
ORCHESTRA
Three symphonies (1956, 1966, 1973)
Trylogia, 3 compositions (large orch) (1973-1974)
Third sonnet (2 pf and orch) (1972)
Mahoniowy koncert (orch and vln)
Wiosenny koncert (orch and pf)
First sonnet (1970)
Mobil
Play of colours (1969)
Second play of colours (1973)
BRASS BAND
Dyptyk (large band) (1970)
Tryptyk (large band) (1970)
CHAMBER
First string quartet (1968)
Second string quartet (with fl) (1969)
Third string quartet (1970)
Fourth string quartet (1973)
Freski kameralne (hn, cl and hp) (1971)
Dwoj eseje (hp) (1971)
Other instrumental pieces
PIANO
Arabeski (2 pf) (1971)
Esej (pf and perc) (1969)
Trzy sonety (1969-1972)
VOCAL
Sonnet II (2 S, ch and orch) (1971)
Promienie swiatla, suite (ch a-cap) (1968)
Ref. composer, 206

TABARY, M.A.C. de
18th-century composer.
Compositions
VOCAL
Numa Pompilio alla grotta d'Egeria (D. Gonnella) (vce and orch)
MISCELLANEOUS
Sesostri, op. 2
Ref. 161, 431

TACK, Annie (nee De Kluis)
South African organist, choral conductor, critic, lecturer, singer and composer. b. Utrecht, Holland, May 3, 1930. She studied the organ under Jacob Byster in Holland and received an L.R.S.M. an L.T.C.L. and an U.U.L.M. for singing and U.O.L.M. for the organ. At the University of South Africa she received a B.Mus. in 1974, D.Mus. hons. in 1975 and M.Mus. in 1981 for the organ. In 1961 she became organist at the Lindenpark Dutch Reformed Church, Johannesburg and in 1971, choral conductor of the choir Studia Musica, concentrating on Renaissance, baroque and modern works. She gave performances on radio, in cathedrals and for a music society in the Orange Free State. As a singer she appeared in concert in the main centers in South Africa. She lectured to trainee teachers on Orffschulwerk and from 1974 to 1976 was a music critic. PHOTOGRAPH.
Compositions
CHAMBER
Birds (fl, flageolet, cl and 2 pf) (1981)
De Kluizensuite (pf) (1982)
VOCAL
Die Andreas Cyclus (A. van de Coht) (solo, ch and insts) (1978)
Three compositions on three paintings of Dirk Meerkotter (ch and pf) (1977)
Three Dutch poems: Het enige houvast; Carpe Diem; 1, Cor. 13 (N. Beuschop) (vce, fl and pf) (1972)
Uiteindelik vir almal (C. Cilliers) (13 soloists, m-ch, w-ch, mix-ch, fl, cl, flageolet and hp) (1982)

SACRED
Christmas cantata (Cilliers) (soli, ch, org, fls, cls, hp and trp) (1973)
Weerloos vir die Seun van God, cantata (Cilliers) (solos, youth ch, ch, rec and org) (1979)
Die vier vroue by die Kruis, Easter cantata (Cilliers) (solos, ch and org) (1972)
Psalm 121 (ch a-cap) (1981)
ELECTRONIC
Gebrauchsmusik, Orffschulwerk (vce, elec gtr, gtr, vln, fl, cl and fagot) (1982)
Ref. composer, 77

TAILLEFERRE, Germaine

French professor and composer. b. Parc Saint-Maur, near Paris, April 19, 1892; d. Paris, November 7, 1983. Against parental opposition, she attended the Paris Conservatoire from 1904, where she was a pupil of Widor, Dallier and Causcade and won first prizes for solfege, harmony, counterpoint and accompaniment. She was a pupil of Milhaud, Koechlin and later Ravel. She made Satie's acquaintance and in 1918 became the only female member of the group known as 'Les Six', together with Honegger, Milhaud, Poulenc, Auric and Durey. These six composers were of widely diverse characters, having in common only hostility to French Wagnerianism and Impressionism. However, Tailleferre later showed great admiration for the French composers of the 18th-century. In 1936 she took over the sponsorship of the group 'Jeune France'. From 1942 to 1946 she lived in the United States. From 1970 to 1972 she was professor of accompaniment at the Schola Cantorum. Among other awards, she received the decoration of Officier de la Legion d'Honneur and the Grand Prix de Musique, Academy of Fine Arts, 1973. DISCOGRAPHY. PHOTOGRAPH.
Compositions
ORCHESTRA
Piano concerto (1924)
Violin concerto (1937)
Ballade (pf and orch) (1919)
Concertino (hp and orch; also pf and orch) (1927)
Concertino (fl, pf and cham orch) (1952)
Concertino in D-Minor (pf and orch)
Largo (vln and orch) (1934)
A l'exposition (1937)
Jeu de plein air (also 2 pf) (1918)
Pastorale (small orch) (1920)
La guirlande de Campra (1952)
Ouverture (1932)
Pavane, nocturne, finale (1929)
CHAMBER
Images (pf, fl, cl, cel, and str qrt) (1918)
String quartet (1919)
Partita, hommage à Rameau (2 pf and perc) (1964)
Piano trio
Arabesque (cl and pf)
Pastorale (fl and pf; also vln and pf) (1942, 1941)
Sonata (vln and pf) (Durand, 1921)
Clarinet sonata (1958)
Harp sonata (Paris: Meridian, 1957)
PIANO
Two waltzes (2 pf) (1951)
Partita (Rongwen, 1951)
Scènes de cirque (1951)
Sicilienne (Heugel, 1928)
Fleurs de France, 6 easy pieces (also orch as Suite a danser) (1930)
La forêt enchantée, 10 pieces (1951)
Three pastorales: D, 1918; A-Major, 1928; C, 1929
Tombeau de Couperin
VOCAL
Cantate du Narcisse (vce and orch) (1937)
Concerto grosso (mix-ch, 2 pf, sax qrt and orch) (Presser, 1934)
Concerto des vaines paroles (Bar and orch) (1956)
Six chansons françaises, 15th, 16th and 17th-century chants (vce and orch) (1929)
Two concertos for voice (S and orch) (1953)
C'est facile à dire (vce and pf) (1955)
Pancartes pour une porte d'entrée (R. Pinget) (1959)
Paris, sentimental (M. Lacloche) (1951)
BALLET
Le marchand d'oiseaux, in 1 act (1923)
Paris-magie, in 1 act (1949)
OPERA
La fou sense (1951)
Le maitre, chamber opera (Ionesco) (1951)
Le marin de Bolivar (1937)
Memoires d'une bergère, opera bouffe (1959)
Parisiana, comic opera (1955)
La petite sirène, in 3 acts (1958)
OPERETTA
Dolores (1950)
Il était un petit navire (1951)
THEATRE
Parfums, musical comedy (1951)
INCIDENTAL MUSIC
Les maries de la Tour Eiffel, 1 act farce (with Cocteau and members of Les Six, its failure causing the breakup of the group) (1951)
Music for stage, film, radio and TV, incl.:
Claudel's Sous le rempart d'Athènes (1925)
Bibliography
Chamfory, Claude. *Hommage à Germaine Tailleferre. Le Courier Musical de France 37. 1972: 119.*
Trickey, S.M. Les Six. Denton, TX, 1955.
Ref. 2, 8, 9, 13, 15, 17, 20, 22, 44, 52, 63, 64, 70, 73, 74, 75, 88, 94, 96, 100, 105, 107, 135, 138, 172, 177, 183, 206, 226, 280, 361, 563, 622, 637

TAITE (Tait), Annie

English pianist and composer. d. Eastbourne, February 24, 1886. She was a pupil of G.A. Macfarren at the Royal Academy of Music. She died at an young age.
Compositions
CHAMBER
Trio (pf and strs)
Sonata in F (pf)
VOCAL
Songs
Ref. 6, 226, 276, 347, 433

TAJANI MATTONE, Ida (pseud. Janita Dino)

Italian pianist, singer, teacher and composer. She studied voice and the piano under Enricho Ricci and composition under Cesare Dobici. She performed in concert and later taught singing.
Compositions
PIANO
Pieces
VOCAL
Romances
OPERETTA
Pantagruel (P. Reni) (under pseud)
Second operetta (with Giuseppe Guerra)
Ref. 86

TAKAMI (Braun-Takami), Toyoko

Japanese pianist, teacher and composer. b. Shimane, January 1, 1945. Her parents were a composer and a music teacher and she commenced her piano lessons at the age of six. She studied at Tokyo University, receiving a B.A., a music teaching diploma and then her M.A. in 1971. Since 1971 she has lived in Germany. She studied under Professor Genzmer at the University of Munich until 1973. She teaches music in schools. PHOTOGRAPH.
Compositions
ORCHESTRA
Symphonic movement (1970)
Two symphonic movements (1968)
CHAMBER
Sextet (4 sax, vib and mar) (1967)
Quintet (cl and str qrt) (1969)
Wind quintet (1973)
So-mon (org, fl and bsn) (1975) (hon mention, 6th-International Women Composers' competition, 1975)
VOCAL
So (vce, fl, vlc and perc) (1976)
Four Songs (Bar and pf) (1967)
Three Songs (Bar and pf) (1973)
Ref. composer

TAKASHIMA, Midori

Japanese composer. b. Tokyo, April 20, 1954. She graduated from the Graduate School of Tokyo University of Arts in 1982 having studied under Ishiketa Mareo, Mami-Ya Michio and Yamada Kazou. Her *Statue* was first performed at the Contemporary Music Exhibition, 1985. DISCOGRAPHY.
Compositions
ORCHESTRA
Piano concerto (1977)
Elegie (1982)
CHAMBER
Statue (vln and pf) (1985)

VOCAL
Blue message (ch) (1984)
Two sonatas sentimentales (m-ch and pf) (1985)
MISCELLANEOUS
Five movements in a pastel-coloured scene
Seishun no Jujika (1983)
Serenade, from the Greek myth
Ref. Japanese Federation of Composers

TAL, Marjo

Dutch concert pianist, teacher and composer. b. The Hague, January 15, 1915. At the Amsterdam Conservatory she studied the piano under Nelly Wagenaar. She won a Dutch government scholarship to study abroad and became a pupil of Franz Osborn in London for three years. She studied composition and counterpoint under Sam Dresden. As a concert pianist she toured Europe and Israel. She teaches theory and the piano in Amsterdam. Many of her compositions were lost during the war. DISCOGRAPHY.

Compositions
CHAMBER
String quartets
Two string trios
A version of old Irish country songs (rec, hp and vla da gamba or fl, pf and vlc) (1978)
Three encores, songs without words (descant rec and pf) (1979) (Amsterdam: Donemus)
Seven pieces for a gentleman and his recorder (treble rec) (1979) (Donemus)
Violin sonata
Violoncello sonata
VOCAL
Acht Engelsman liederen (1973) (Donemus)
After, 6 songs (Rupert Brooke) (high vce and pf) (1978) (Donemus)
Cent et cinquant chansons littéraires (Prevert, Queneau, Eluard, Desnos, Paul Fort Apollinaire, Geraldy, Aragon, Fombeure etc) (1967)
Dix chansons de Jacques Prevert (Paris: Ray Ventura)
En Sourdine, 5 songs (Prevert, Desnos, Apollinaire, Baudelaire) (fl and S) (1982)
Les sept poèmes d'amour en guerre (Paul Eluard) (1982)
Siete canciones española, 23 pieces (Lorca) (med-vce and pf; also pf; also other insts) (1973) (Donemus)
Six songs (Russian poets) (1975) (Donemus)
Tendre et dangereux, 6 songs (vce and pf) (1980) (Donemus)
SACRED
Mass (ch and org) (1976)
Publications
Solfeggio. 1978.
Ref. composer, 563

TAL, Ya'ara

Israeli concert pianist and composer. b. Israel, February 27, 1955. She started playing the piano at the age of six under Azriel Beresowski and later studied at the Rubin Music Academy in Tel Aviv under Ilona Vincze and Arie Vardi. She studied composition under Abel Ehrlich and Andre Hajdu and completed piano masters courses under Leon Fleischer, Magda Tagliaferro, Claude Granck, Gina Bachauer and Vladimir Horbowski. She also studied in Munich at the Hochschule fuer Musik under Hugo Steurer and Ludwig Hoffmann. She played in concerts and recorded for radio and television. PHOTOGRAPH.

Compositions
ORCHESTRA
Juni 1973, Abel Ehrlich gewidmet (1973)
CHAMBER
Berceuse for market dragonflies (2 pf, 2 vlc and 6 vln) (1973)
The owl, for children (pf) (1978)
VOCAL
Film and soundtrack (Shavit, Tagore, Virgil) (narr, soloists, ch and orch) (1973)
I've lost her (Jean Cocteau) (narr, pf, cl, 2 orff xyl, box, rec and chil-orch) (1972)
Achsiw songs (Yehuda Amichai) (A, pf, vln and vlc) (1974)
But she ....(composer) (singing and speaking pianist) (1977)
Song No. 1 (composer) (S, pf and snare drum) (1973)
Song No. 2 (composer) (A, vlc, fl, vib and cel) (1973)
BALLET
Hommage à un homo (fl and pf)
Ref. composer

TALMA, Louise

American organist, pianist, professor and composer. b. Arcachon, France, October 31, 1906. Her mother, an opera singer, gave Louise her first lessons in the piano and solfege. She attended the Institute of Musical Art, New York City, from 1922 to 1939, studying theory under George Wedge, ear training under Franklin Robinson, counterpoint under Percy Goetschius and composition under Howard Brockway. Every summer from 1926 to 1939 as well as in 1949, 1951 and 1961, she attended the Fontainebleau School of Music where she studied the piano under Isidore Philipp and harmony, counterpoint, fugue, composition and the organ under Nadia Boulanger (q.v.). She obtained her B.Mus. from New York University in 1931 and M.A. from Columbia University in 1933. Her numerous awards included two Guggenheim fellowships in 1946 and 1947 – she was the first woman to win the award twice – the Isaac Newton Seligman prize for composition at the Institute of Musical Art in 1927, 1928 and 1929; the Pleyel prize for the piano, Fontainebleau, 1927; the senior Fulbright research grant for ten months in Rome to compose her opera *The Alcestiad*, 1955 to 1956; the Stovall prize for composition, Fontainebleau, 1938 and 1939; the Juilliard publication award for her *Toccata for orchestra*; 1946 and the French Government Prix d'Excellence de Composition in 1951. She taught theory and ear training at the Manhattan School of Music, 1926 to 1928 and for a number of summers, taught solfege at Fontainebleau, being the only American teacher there. After 1928 she taught at Hunter College, New York, becoming professor of music in 1952. She received two honorary degrees: in 1983, doctor of humane letters from Hunter College, City University of New York and in 1984, doctor of arts from Bard College. DISCOGRAPHY. PHOTOGRAPH.

Compositions
ORCHESTRA
Dialogues for piano and orchestra (1964)
Introduction and rondo giocoso (1946)
Toccata (1944) (Carl Fischer, 1965)
CHAMBER
Summer sounds (qnt for cl, 2 vln, vla and vlc) (1973)
The ambient air (fl, vln, vlc and pf) (1983)
String quartet (1954)
Textures (str qrt) (1978)
Sonata (vln and pf) (1962)
Song and dance (vln and pf) (1951)
Studies in spacing (cl and pf) (1982)
Three duologues for clarinet and piano (1968)
Wedding piece: Where thou goest I go, canon (org) (1946)
PIANO
Four-handed fun (1939) (Fischer, 1943)
Alleluia in form of toccata (Fischer, 1945)
Italian suite (1949)
Passacaglia and fugue (1962)
Pastoral prelude (Fischer, 1950)
Six etudes (1954) (G. Schirmer, 1955)
Sonata No. 1 (1943) (Fischer, 1945)
Sonata No. 2 (1955) (Fischer, 1959)
Sound shorts, 20 short pieces (1974)
Textures (1977) (comm International Society for Contemporary Music)
Three bagatelles (1955)
Two dances (1934)
Up and down the day, 20 short pieces (1974)
VOCAL
Celebration cantata (w-ch and small orch)
A time to remember (speeches of John F. Kennedy) (mix-ch and orch) (1967)
The tolling bell, triptych (Shakespeare, Marlow, Donne) (Bar and orch) (comm MacDowell Club, Milwaukee, 1969) (nominated Pulitzer prize, 1970)
La belle dame sans merci (Bar, w-ch and org) (1929)
La corona, 7 sonnets (John Donne) (mix-ch a-cap) (1955)
The leaden echo and the golden echo (Gerard Manley Hopkins) (S, mix double ch and pf) (1951)
Let's touch the sky (e.e. cummings) (mix-ch, fl, ob and cl) (1952)
Birthday song (Edmund Spencer) (T, fl and vla) (1960)
Diadem (Confucius) (T, fl, cl, vln, vlc and pf) (1979) (comm Da Capo Chamber Players)
A child's fancy, cycle (Edith Gould) (1935)
Five sonnets from the Portuguese (E.B. Browning) (1934)
Have you heard? Do you know, divertimento in 7 scenes (composer) (S, m-S, T and inst ens) (1976)
I fear a man of scanty speech (Emily Dickinson) (1938)
Late leaves (Landor) (1934)
Leap before you look (W.H. Auden)
Letter to St. Peter (Elma Dean)
Never seek to tell thy love (Blake) (1934)
One need not be a chamber to be haunted (E. Dickinson) (S and pf) (1941)
Pied beauty; spring and fall (Hopkins) (1946)
Rain song (S and pf) (1973)
Song of the songless (Meredith) (1928)
Terre de France, song cycle (S and pf) (1945)
Thirteen ways of looking at a blackbird (w-vces and pf) (Stevens, 1938)
Three madrigals (w-vces and str qrt) (1929)
Two sonnets (Hopkins) (Bar and pf) (1950)

SACRED
The divine flame, oratorio (m-S, B, mix-ch and orch) (1948)
All the days of my life, cantata (Bible) (T, cl, vlc, pf and perc) (1965)
(comm Koussevitzky Music Foundation)
Celebrations (excerpts from Psalms, Desiderata, etc) (w-ch and small orch) (1977)
In principio erat verbum (St. John) (mix-ch and org) (1939)
Psalm 84, (mix-ch a-cap) (1978) (comm Corpus Christi Church of New York)
Voices of peace (The Missal, Bible, St. Francis of Assisi, Hopkins) (mix-ch and strs) (1973)
Carmina Mariana: Ave Maria; Regina Coeli; Salve Regina (2 S and pf) (1943)
OPERA
The Alcestiad, in 3 acts (Thornton Wilder; German trans H. Herlitschka) (1958) (Frankfurt Opera Co. 1962: 1st work of American woman produced by leading European opera house)
Publications
Harmony for the College Student. 1966.
Functional Harmony. With James S. Harrison and Robert Levin. 1970.
Ref. composer, 2, 4, 5, 17, 21, 22, 40, 52, 71, 77, 81, 86, 94, 137, 138, 141, 142, 146, 152, 191, 195, 226, 228, 280, 282, 397, 415, 468, 477, 560, 563, 611, 622, 625

TAMBLYN, Bertha Louise
20th-century Canadian pianist, singer and composer. b. Oshawa, Ontario. She attended the Whitby Ladies' College and Royal Conservatory in Toronto, studying the piano, voice and composition under Drs. Vogt and Anger, D.D. Slater, Leo Smith and T.J. Crawford.
Compositions
PIANO
In holiday mood (1945)
Light and shadow (Woodland dance) (1946)
One bright morning, march (1950)
Valse in G
VOCAL
Chloris in the snow (w-vces or chil-vces) (1943) (Canadian Music Sales)
Come in lady moon (w-vces or chil-vces) (1940) (Hall & McCreary Co.)
Evensong (1932) (Lorenz, Dayton)
Flower time and you (1943) (B.L. Tamblyn)
Good night, good morn (1943) (Tamblyn)
Grey rocks and greyer sea (1943) (Tamblyn)
Life's lovely things (1930) (Waterloo Music)
Life and love, wedding song (1943) (Tamblyn)
Mumps (1932) (Tamblyn)
A soldier's socks, patriotic song (1940) (Waterloo)
Such a little way together (1950) (Waterloo)
A toast to Canada, patriotic song (1933) (G.V. Thompson)
The Wasted Crust (Canadian Music)
We are seven, 7 songs (1928) (Thompson)
SACRED
Dear little Christ Child, duet (S and A) (1943) (Canadian Music)
Four anthems (1940) (Lorenz, Dayton)
Glad tidings, Christmas anthem (1942) (Canadian Music)
God is near (1950) (Waterloo)
Holly time songs, 15 Christmas songs (1938) (Thompson)
Lord give us peace, anthem (1949) (F. Harris)
Three anthems (1949) (Canadian Music)
Several other pieces
Ref. 133

TAMMELIN, Bertha
19th-century Swedish composer.
Composition
VOCAL
I Furuskog, jag gick mig ut att vandra (1865)
Ref. 167

TANN, Hilary (Presslaff)
Welsh editor, professor and composer. b. Llwynpia, November 2, 1947. She received a B.Mus. 1st class hons in 1968, from the University of Wales and from 1976 to 1970 did graduate research on Roberto Gerhard at the University of Southampton. She was a visiting fellow at Princeton University from 1972 to 1977 and then studied there until 1981 gaining her M.F.A in 1975 and Ph.D. in 1981. From 1965 to 1968 she was a teaching assistant and composer at Princeton; from 1977 to 1980, assistant professor of music at Bard College, Annandale and from 1980 assistant professor of music at Union College, Schenectady. She was editor of composer societies newsletters. She married the composer and jazz pianist, Jeffrey

Tann Presslaff and is a permanent resident in the United States. She was awarded a Princeton fellowship from 1973 to 1977 and a Pew Memorial Trust award, Union College, 1983. Her works have been performed in Wales and the United States. PHOTOGRAPH.
Compositions
ORCHESTRA
As ferns (str orch) (1977)
CHAMBER
Duo (ob and vla) (1981)
A sad pavan forbidding mourning (gtr) (1982)
PIANO
Aftermath (1973)
Doppelgaenger (1984)
VOCAL
Sound dawn (m-ch and pf) (1983)
ELECTRONIC
Templum (computer and syn tape) (1975)
Ref. composer, 624

TANNER, Hilda
20th-century American composer.
Compositions
CHAMBER
Modal suite (2 fl) (1977)
PIANO
Three plus three plus two (1 or 2 pf) (1977)
Suite (1977)
VOCAL
The singing bird (m-S, fl, cl and pf) (1969)
Ref. 228

TANTU, Cornelia
20th-century composer.
Composition
FILM MUSIC
The Wall (1978)
Ref. 497

TAPPER, Bertha (nee Feiring) (Mrs. Thomas)
Norwegian pianist, editor, lecturer and composer. b. Oslo, January 25, 1859; d. New York, September 2, 1915. She studied the piano under Agathe Backer-Groendahl (q.v.) in Norway and Leschetizky in Vienna and moved to America in 1881, teaching the piano at the New England Conservatory from 1889 to 1897. From 1905 to 1910 she taught at the Institute of Musical Art, New York. She composed piano pieces and songs and published some of the piano works of Edvard Grieg.
Ref. 85, 347, 353, 433

TARBE DES SABLONS, Mme.
French composer.
Composition
OPERA
I Batavi, lyric drama in 3 acts (on La Siege de Leyde) (1864)
Ref. 26

TARBOS (Tarbox), Frances
20th-century American pianist and composer. b. St. Paul, MN. She composed an opera and songs.
Ref. 347. 353

TARBOX, Frances. See TARBOS, Frances

TARDIEU DE MALLEVILLE, Charlotte
19th-century French pianist and composer.
Compositions
PIANO
Berceuse, op. 7
Carillon, op. 6
First and second preludes, ops. 4 and 5
Grande valse brillante, op. 2
Romances sans paroles, op. 3
Other pieces
Ref. 26, 276, 433

688

TARIHI, Kamu Yarari Karar
20th-century Turkish composer.
Compositions
CHAMBER
 Toccata (cl and insts)
 Danse rustique
 Danse melancolique
 Esquisse turque, tanzara
SACRED
 Epitaphio
Ref. National Council of Turkish Women

TARLOW, Karen Anne
American pianist, lecturer and composer. b. Boston, September 19, 1947. She studied at the University of Massachusetts, under Philip Bezanson, Charles Fussell, Robert Stern and Frederick Tillis, obtaining her B.Mus. (composition and theory) in 1970 and M.Mus. (composition and theory) in 1973 and her doctorate in composition from Boston University, in 1983. In 1970 she received an alumni grant for study in Germany for one year and there she studied musicology and German literature and language at the University of Freiburg; composition under Wolfgang Fortner and the piano under Seemann and Solter at the Freiburger Musikhochschule. Other teachers of composition were Malcolm Peyton and David del Tredici. She taught at the University of Massachusetts and later at Boston University. Since 1966 she has been a private music teacher and a performer. She was awarded a special honors in music from the University of Massachusetts in 1968 to 1970, a fellowship from the Boston University from 1975 to 1979 and a Howard Lebow memorial scholarship in 1972. She won first prizes in the 1978 Boston University annual composition competition and for music theory from 1975 to 1976. In 1982 she was voted one of the Outstanding Young Women of America.
Compositions
ORCHESTRA
 Bachanale (small orch) (1978)
CHAMBER
 Music for wind quintet (Seesaw Press, 1973)
 Games for three (ob, pf and vla) (1970)
 Three household miniatures (cl and bsn) (1978)
 Zenana (vln and pf) (1978)
 Uchronia (hp) (1982)
VOCAL
 Fields of sorrow (w-ch, fl, hp or pf) (1975) (Seesaw)
 Five Yiddish poems (ch a-cap) (1984)
 Salvacion de la primavera (w-vces) (1973)
 Lieblingstier (soli, 4 ww and vlc) (1969)
 The lowest trees have tops (2 soli and cham ens) (1972)
 Renascence (S, cl and pf) (1977) (New Valley Press, Smith College, 1981)
 Two songs (vce and pf) (1962)
ELECTRONIC
 Chansons innocents (w-ch, amp hpcd and vlc) (1974) (Seesaw)
MULTIMEDIA
 Concerto for orchestra (timbre-play, time-line, mathematical proportions and projected co-ordination with mvt and light) (1983)
 The Emperor and the Nightingale (chil-ballet, small ens, Chinese folksongs, light and mvt) (1980)
 Uncle Wiggily and the Duck Pond (spoken text, chil-ballet, and small) (1979)
Ref. 142, 185

TARNER, Evelyn Fern
American teacher and composer. b. September 2, 1912. She received her B.S. and elementary teacher's certificate from the Kutztown State Teachers' College.
Compositions
SACRED
 The risen Lord, cantata
 The Saviour has come, cantata
 Bless the Lord, O my soul
 Dear little Jesus
 The followers for Jesus
 God's little lamb
 I know God is love
 I know the Lord
 Psalm one hundred
 Show me a window
 The steps of a good man
 Walk with the years
 Wedding prayer
Ref. 494

TARNOCZY, Malvine. See O'DONNEL, Malvine, Countess

TARNOWSKA, Julia
Polish composer.
Composition
PIANO
 Polonaise

TARRONI, Antonia
17th-century Italian composer.
Compositions
VOCAL
 Libro de Madrigali a 5 v. con 2 a 8 nel fine, madrigals (5 vces) (Venice: Amadino, 1612)
Ref. 128

TARTAGLIA, Lidia (Lydia)
Italian pianist and composer. b. Rome, October 20, 1898. She graduated from the Conservatorio di Santa Cecilia and studied under Giovanni Sgambati, Alfredo Casella and M. Pelissier. She toured Italy, England and Germany as an pianist.
Compositions
CHAMBER
 Piano pieces
VOCAL
 Inno di guerra, anthem (1915)
Ref. 70, 86, 105

TARTAGLINI, Rosa. See TIBALDI, Rosa

TASCA (Tosca), Mme.
18th-century French violinist and composer.
Composition
ORCHESTRA
 Concerto (after Vivaldi) (ca. 1750)
Ref. 226

TASHJIAN, B. Charmian
American lecturer and composer. b. Detroit, February 4, 1950. She obtained her B.M. (theory and composition) in 1976 and A.B.D. (composition) in 1976 from Northwestern University where she studied composition under Alan Stout and Williams Karlins. She graduated with an M.A. from Stanford University in 1974, where she studied composition under Gyoergy Ligeti and computer generated composition under John Chowning. She then lectured at DePaul University, Chicago and became a private teacher of music theory, aural skills, counterpoint, composition, music history and appreciation. Her *Antiphonies* won the Padrone-Kantscheidt award for composition from Northwestern University. In 1982 she was awarded a summer study scholarship at the Massachusetts Institute of Technology. Her works have been performed in concert and on television. DISCOGRAPHY. PHOTOGRAPH.
Compositions
ORCHESTRA
 Work for full orchestra
CHAMBER
 Antiphonies I (1977)
 Armenechos (1966)
 Refractions (1967)
VOCAL
 Songs for chorus and brass sextet (mix-ch, 2 cor, 2 hn and 2 euph) (1978)
 Songs of the sea (m-S, pf and hn or vla) (1982)
ELECTRONIC
 Resan (hn, d-b, vla, amp hpcd and perc ens) (1978)
Ref. composer, 468, 563, 622, 625

TASSO, Joan Maria
20th-century English composer.
Compositions
CHAMBER
 Nine fantasies for two instruments (Italian instrumental music of the Renaissance) (with Bernardo Lupacchino) (London: Pro Musica, 1977)
Ref. MLA *Notes*

TATE, Phyllis (Margaret Duncan)

English pianist, tympanist and composer. b. Gerrards Cross, April 6, 1911. She studied composition under Harry Farjeon at the Royal Academy of Music, London, from 1928 to 1932 and worked as a free-lance composer. She studied the piano and the timpani and became a F.R.A.M. in 1964. Several of her compositions were commissioned by the BBC and for festivals. DISCOGRAPHY.

Compositions

ORCHESTRA
Symphony suite (1938)
Cello concerto (1933)
Occasional overture (1955)
Concerto for alto saxophone and strings (1944) (also reduction for pf) (1974) (OUP)
Duo concertante (trp, bsn and small orch) (1962)
New work (str orch) (1977)
Panorama (str orch) (1977) (OUP)
Prelude, interlude and postlude (cham orch) (OUP, 1942)
Song without words (trp, bsn and cham orch) (OUP)
Valse lointaine (small orch) (OUP, 1941)

BRASS BAND
Illustrations for brass band (1969)

CHAMBER
St. James' Park, a lakeside reverie (timp, perc, pf duet and/or cel and strs) (OUP)
Hampstead Heath rondo for roundabouts (timp, perc, pf duet and strs) (OUP)
Divertimento (str qrt)
The rainbow and the cuckoo (ob and str trio; also ob qrt) (1975) (OUP)
String quartet in F (1952) (OUP)
Air and variations (vln, cl and pf) (1958) (OUP)
Sonata (cl and vlc; also T, str qrt, har and pf) (1952) (1968) (OUP)
Prelude, aria, interlude and finale (cl and pf) (1981)
Triptych: prelude, scherzo and soliloquy (vln and pf) (OUP, 1957)
Sad humoresque (gtr) (OUP)
Seascape (gtr) (OUP)
Three pieces (cl) (1979) (OUP)
Variegations (vla) (1970) (OUP)

PIANO
London waifs (2 pf)
Sonatina (2 pf) (1957)
Let's play duets, 6 duets (OUP)
Exploration around a troubadour song (OUP, 1973)
Sonatina pastorale (1976)

VOCAL
All the world's a stage (ch and orch) (OUP)
Saint Martha and the dragon (Charles Causley) (narr, S and T, chil-ch, ch, perc and orch) (OUP)
Secular requiem, setting of The phoenix and the turtle (Shakespeare) (mix-vces, org and orch) (1961) (OUP)
Wassail all over the town (mix-ch, timp and perc or orch) (OUP)
Choral scene from the Bacchae of Euripides (trans Gilbert Murray) (double mix-ch and opt org) (OUP, 1953)
Cielito lindo (2 part ch) (OUP)
Close to your mother (2 part ch) (OUP)
Dry bones (mix-ch a-cap) (OUP)
Engraved on the collar of a dog (mix-ch a-cap) (OUP)
The foolish boy (2 part ch) (OUP)
Four Negro spirituals (2 part ch and strs) (OUP)
Go to the market, daughter fair (2 part ch) (OUP)
De Gospel train (mix-ch) (OUP)
Hurry, hurry, quickly, shepherd boy (2 part ch) (OUP)
I'se the b'y that builds the boat (2 part ch) (OUP)
Old MacDonald had a farm (2 part ch) (OUP)
Postman's song (unison ch) (OUP)
The sailor and young Nancy (2 part ch) (OUP)
Seven Lincolnshire folk songs (ch and insts) (1966) (OUP)
The shepherd boy's song (mix-ch) (OUP)
Street sounds, concertante suite (wordless ch, pf and perc) (1979)
To words by Joseph Beaumont (w-ch) (1970) (OUP)
When I am a-roaming (2 part unison ch) (OUP)
Witches and spells, choral suite (Herrick, Peele and anon) (1959)
Hearken brethren (unison vces) (OUP)
A pride of lions (Ian Serraillier) (narr, vces, gtr, recs, perc and opt insts) (OUP)
The story of Lieutenant Cockatoo (Ronald Eyre) (vces, tuned and untuned perc and opt insts) (OUP)
Nocturne for four voices (S. Keyes) (vocal qrt, b-cl, str qrt, d-b and cel) (OUP, 1946)
Apparitions (T, har, str qrt and pf) (OUP)
The Lady of Shalott (T and insts) (1956)
Ballad of reading Gaol (Bar, vlc and org) (1980)
Billy Boy (OUP)
Brother James Air (med vce) (OUP)
Coastal ballads (Bar and insts) (1969)
The frog in the well (2 S and A a-cap) (OUP)

Good-nature to animals (Christopher Smart) (2 S and 2 A) (OUP)
How deep the snow (w-vce) (OUP)
The lark in the clean air (OUP)
O bonny fisher lad (OUP)
Scenes from Tyneside (m-S, cl and pf) (1978)
Scenes from Kipling (Bar and pf) (1978)
Soldier, won't you marry me? (A and 2 S a-cap) (OUP)
Songs of sundrie kinds (T and lute) (OUP, 1977)
Songs of sundry natures (Elizabethan poets) (Bar, fl, cl, bsn, hn and hp) (1945)
Three Gaelic ballads (S and pf)
Trois chansons tristes (vce and gtr) (OUP)
Two ballads (OUP)
A Victorian garland, poems (Matthew Arnold) (S, Cont, hn and pf) (OUP, 1972)
Water of Tyne (OUP)

SACRED
Christmas ale (soloist, ch and orch) (1967)
Compassion (ch and orch) (1978) (OUP)
Serenade to Christmas (m-S, mix-ch and orch) (1972) (OUP)
Carol for Christmas Eve (John Pudney) (mix-ch, org or pf) (1980) (OUP)
Peace on earth to men (trans J.M. Neale) (mix-ch) (OUP)
The Virgin and the Child, carol (mix-ch) (OUP)
How deep the snow, Christmas lullaby (French and English texts) (2 S and 2 A a-cap) (OUP)
Long ago in Bethlehem, Moravian carol
Ring out, sing out, festival carol for spring or summer (vces, vlns, vlcs and pf) (OUP)

OPERA
Dark Pilgrimage, for television (1962)
The Lodger, in 2 acts (David Franklin) (1960) (OUP)
The What d'ye Call it (V.C. Clinton-Bradley) (1966)

OPERETTA
The Policeman's Serenade (A.P. Herbert) (1932)
A Pride of Lions (OUP, 1971)
Scarecrow, for children (1983)
Solar, for children (unison vces and orch) (1983)
Twice in a Blue Moon (Christopher Hassall) (speaking guide, 2 ch, opt 2 pf, perc and d-b) (OUP, 1971)

Bibliography

Carner, M. *The Music of Phyllis Tate*. Music and Letters. April 1954.
Searle, H. *Phyllis Tate*. The Musical Times. 1955.

Publications

New Viola Books. With Eleanor Murray. 3 vols.
Ref. 2, 8, 15, 17, 22, 27, 68, 74, 76, 77, 81, 84, 94, 96, 141, 177, 193, 347, 422, 518, 563, 622, 624, 637

TATTON, Madeleine

20th-century American composer.

Compositions

CHAMBER
Five for fun (fl, vln and vla)
Two duets (fl and vla)
Ref. 40, 347

TAUBER, Lotti

Swiss pianist, artist, teacher and composer. b. Winterthur, July 4, 1944. She studied the piano under Walter Frey and Christof Lieske at the Konservatorium Winterthur and the Music Academy, Zurich. Unable to pursue her career as a pianist for eight years as a result of an accident, she studied astrology, painting, psychology, meditation and the Tarot and worked as an existentialist psychotherapist. Her music is meditative and frequently improvised. She teaches the piano, drawing, painting, astrology and psychology in Zurich. DISCOGRAPHY. PHOTOGRAPH.

Compositions

PIANO
Aufgehoben (1981)
Bestimmung (1982)
Courage (1982)
I Ging (1984)
Planeten (1983)
Roundabout Ways (1981)
Von Zeit zu Zeit (1982)
Ref. composer

TAUHERT

Ancient Egyptian songstress of Isis. Mention of her was on the tomb of the priests of Amun, found near the Hatshepsut Temple at Deir el-Bahri and now at the Victoria Museum, Upsalla.
Ref. 428

TAUTU, Cornelia
Rumanian folklorist and composer. b. 1938. She studied at the Ciprian Porumbescu Conservatory, Bucharest and received her diploma in 1967. From 1965 she pursued research in musical folklore at the Institute of Ethnography and Folklore at Bucharest. From 1971 to 1972 she studied in New England at Long Island University. PHOTOGRAPH.
Compositions
ORCHESTRA
Symphonic movement (1967)
Concertino (str orch) (1967)
Counterpoint (str orch) (1968)
Des (1971)
Prometheus (1974)
Segments (str orch) (1969)
CHAMBER
Concerto for twelve instruments (1967)
String quartet No. 1 (1965)
String quartet No. 2 (1972)
Trio (pf, hp and fl) (1965)
Zig-zag (2 ob) (1971)
PIANO
Inventions (1971)
Sonata (1973)
VOCAL
Divertisment folcloric (mix-ch and perc) (Editions Muzicala, 1977)
La belle sans corps (V. Hilmu, after Eminescu) (1974)
Kaltes Herz (Covali) (1973)
La maîtresse d'auberge (Goldoni) (1973)
INCIDENTAL MUSIC
Medea (Seneca) (1974)
La Première (John Cromwell) (1971)
Prometheus (Aeschylus) (1972)
FILM MUSIC
Stejar (1974)
Ref. composer

TAVEIRA, Eva
Composition
INCIDENTAL MUSIC
No hay plata, tango (Ricordi)
Ref. Ricordi

TAYLOR, Eleanor
20th-century American composer. She composed orchestral and organ pieces and songs.
Ref. 40, 347

TAYLOR, Iris
Composition
CHAMBER
Dreamy afternoon (pf)
Ref. 473

TAYLOR, Mary Virginia (pseuds. Sue Wood, Jean Stirling)
American authoress, teacher and composer. b. August 7, 1912.
Compositions
VOCAL
Deck the hut with coconut
Fair weather love
SACRED
Sleep my little Lord Jesus, anthem
ARRANGEMENTS
John Henry
Hosanna, we build a house
Ref. 494, 646

TAYLOR, Maude Cummings
American organist, teacher and composer. b. Bermuda, February 19, 1897. She attended the Chicago Extension University, the Columbia University and Matlock College of Engineering, the Salzburg Mozarteum and the Fontainebleau Conservatory. She was music minister at the Cornerstone Baptist Church, Brooklyn for over 40 years.
Compositions
SACRED
They shall run and not be weary (mix-ch)
The day is nearly done
He hath put a new song in my mouth, anthem
Ref. 494

TAYLOR, Mrs. A.H.
19th-century American composer.
Compositions
SACRED
Songs incl.:
Oft when my soul
Rock of ages '
There is a land
Ref. 226, 276, 292, 347, 433

TE RANGI-PAI, Princess (Fanny Rose Howie)
Maori singer and composer. DISCOGRAPHY.
Composition
VOCAL
Hine e hine, lullaby
Bibliography
Andersen, Johannes C. *Maori Music*. Memoirs of the Polynesian Society. Vol. 10, 1934.
Ref. 563

TECK, Katherine (nee Weintz)
American horn player, journalist and composer. b. Mineola, NY, December 31, 1939. She obtained her B.A. from Vassar College in 1960, studied at Mannes College of Music from 1961 to 1962 and received her M.A. from Columbia University in 1964. She studied the horn under Harry Berv and George Squires. From 1964 to 1966 she worked in the concert music department of Broadcast Music. She was president of the Modern Listeners' Record Club from 1966 to 1967 and on the editorial staff of Dover Publications from 1967 to 1969. She was the horn player with the Westchester Philharmonic Symphony, Yonkers Civic Philharmonic Orchestra, Westchester County Band and the Performing Arts Opera Society. She composed several pieces for wind instruments.
Publications
Contributions to publications incl.:
Three Facets to French Horn. 1964.
Ref. 206

TEDESCHI, Angela
Italian composer.
Composition
VOCAL
Quando cadran le foglie, melody (L. Steccheti) (Ricordi)
Ref. Ricordi (Milan)

TEGNER, Alice Charlotte (nee Sandstroem)
Swedish pianist, teacher and composer. b. 1864; d. 1943. She studied the piano under S. Haegg, Norman and Lundberg and composition under Lindegren. She taught music in schools in Stockholm and Djursholm till 1906. She was particularly interested in music as the best means to form children's character and her children's songs of a Nordic romantic character, were composed with this in mind. DISCOGRAPHY.
Compositions
PIANO
Fraan mormors mormors tid (4 hands) (1925)
Hemma och borta, 2 vols (1929)
Music for physical exercises (1917)
VOCAL
Four cantatas, incl. one to commemorate the inauguration of a school in Djursholm (1911)
Betlehems Stjarna (ch)
Sjung svenska, folk song collection (1905, rev 1951)
Unga roester, song collection (1904, rev 1940)
Children's songs incl.:
Lillebrors segelfaard (1921)
Mors lille Olle
Naar lillan kom till jorden
Sjung med oss, Mamma, collection (1934)
Sockerbagaren
Ute blaaser sommarvind
Videvisan
Ref. 95, 113, 130, 563, 642

TEICHMUELLER, Anna
German teacher and composer. b. Goettingen, May 11, 1861. She studied in Tartu, Estonia, Jena and Berlin and after 1900 lived and taught in the Schreiberhau.

Compositions
CHAMBER
Suite (vln and pf)
PIANO
Die georgische Prinzessin, op. 43
Seven small pieces, op. 44
Other pieces
VOCAL
Abendlied, op. 21 (2 S and A)
Hymne an die Nacht, op. 23 (S, Bar, vlc and pf)
Lieder, ops. 3-5, 7-19, 24-25, 43
Tercet a capella
Waldnacht, op. 22 (vce, vln and pf)
O Welt du Wunder, op. 27, tercet (S, A, Bar, pf and vln)
Duets
SACRED
Ostergesang, op. 6, cantata (soli, mix-ch and pf)
Mass (Ilse von Stach) (soli, ch, org and orch)
Benedictus, op. 20 (S, A, Bar and pf or org)
OPERA
One opera
Ref. 70, 105, 11, 226, 297

TEICHMULLER, Anna. See TEICHMUELLER, Anna

TELESILLA OF ARGOS

Lyric poetess, musician, warrior and composer from Argos. ca. 546 B.C.
When the Spartans under Kleomenes threatened Argos, Telesilla is reputed to have composed rousing war marches and gathered weapons from
homes and temples to give to the women of Argos, whom she led against
the enemy and thus greatly contributed to the victory. In memory of this
exploit, her statue was erected in the temple of Aphrodite at Argos. She
was famous for her hymns and political and lyrical songs and partheneia
(songs sung by a chorus of maidens in ceremonies in honor of various
gods, particularly Apollo or Artemis). Of her compositions, only two
verses survive, part of a hymn and a call to maidens. These were bound
together by Neuc in his work *De Telessilae Argivae Reliquiis Comentation*
(Dorpat, 1843).
Ref. 264, 268, 281, 382

TELFER, Nancy Ellen

Canadian horn player, pianist, choral conductor, singer, teacher and composer. b. Brampton, Ontario, May 8, 1950. She received a B.A. (music
education and mathematics) in 1971 and a B.Mus. (theory and composition) in 1979, from the University of Western Ontario. She studied the piano
under Jean-Paul Bracey and voice under Constance Newland and compo-
sition and theory under Ken Bray, Jack Behrens, Gerhard Wuensch, Peter
Kaprowski and Alan Heard. She attended the London Teachers' College
from 1971 to 1972 and taught choral and instrumental music to elementary
classes in England until 1976, when she turned to composition. She was
commissioned by several associations and performers. DISCOGRAPHY.
PHOTOGRAPH.
Compositions
ORCHESTRA
Dance #1 (str orch) (1982) (comm)
Dance #2 (1982)
SYMPHONIC BAND
Release the captives (1984)
CHAMBER
Bird flight (fl ens)
Inner space (brass qnt) (1981)
String quartet (1983)
String trio (1983)
Trio for violin, clarinet and cello (1983)
Festive dance (trp and org) (1984)
High park suite (fl and vlc) (1981)
Offertory (fl and org) (1984)
ORGAN
Meditations for Lent (1982)
Processional for a princess (1981)
Toccata and fugue (1983)
PIANO
Pieces incl.:
Dreams (1983)
Fantasy (1983)
In the evening (1983)
Puzzle (1983)
Shades of colour (1983)
Two-part invention in D (1983)

VOCAL
A child's Christmas in Wales (narr and orch) (1984)
Winter flowers (A, mix-ch and orch) (1980)
Apple skin (easy mix-ch and pf) (Waterloo Music) (comm)
Child's play (2 mix-ch, unison ch, rec, pf and perc) (1982) (comm)
Dark little king of the north (mix-ch and pf) (1981)
Fourteen three-part Canadian folk songs (mix-ch) (1982) (Harris, 1985)
(comm)
Going to the movies (easy mix-ch and pf) (comm)
The golden cage (mix-ch and cham insts) (1979)
Grizzly (easy mix-ch and pf) (Waterloo) (comm)
Heritage (mix-ch) (1979)
Late march (mix-ch and pf) (1981)
The man under the bed (mix-ch) (1982)
Monday's child (easy mix-ch and pf) (comm) (1982)
The sailing day (mix-ch and ww qnt) (1979)
Songs of love and Loneliness: Grey-beast; In the rain; Again with mu-
sic (mix-ch) (1979) (Waterloo)
Spectrum (easy mix-ch and pf) (comm) (1982)
The spell of times long past: A love song; Solitude; A wind and the
flower; The sailor's sweetheart (mix-ch and pf) (1982) (Frederick Har-
ris, 1984) (comm)
Sixteen two-part Canadian folk songs (ch) (1981) (Harris, 1985) (comm)
Ten four-part Canadian folk songs (mix-ch) (1983) (Harris, 1985) (comm)
Visions: Elegy; I get high on butterflies; Bushed (mix-ch and pf) (1981)
(Waterloo, 1984)
Watching the veiled moon (mix-ch and strs) (1979)
The ballad of Princess Caraboo (m-S and pf) (1982) (Harris) (comm)
High flight (2 S and A) (1982) (Waterloo)
In the head's fierce caves (S and pf) (1984)
Lullaby of the Iroquois (2 S and A) (1984)
Portraits (S and pf) (comm Lynn Blaser) (1984)
Seven sound scores (chil-vces) (1981) (Holt Rinehart)
The yak (2 S and A) (1984)
SACRED
The journey, oratorio (m-S, mix-ch and strs) (comm) (1982) (Gordon V.
Thompson)
B'not tzeeyon, cantata (mix-ch and pf) (1981)
The wisdom of Solomon, cantata (soloists, mix-ch and org) (1979)
Break forth into singing, anthem (mix-ch) (1980)
Come, Holy Spirit (mix-ch and org) (1983) (Waterloo, 1984)
Doth not wisdom cry? anthem (mix-ch and org) (1980) (Son-Key, 1984)
From quiet winter skies (speaker, mix-ch, fl, ob and org) (1981)
Glory be to thee, anthem (mix-ch) (1981)
His father was a carpenter (mix-ch, fl and org) (1980)
Hodie (mix-ch) (1982) (Shawnee Press)
Hope's lantern (mix-ch, brass and org) (comm Bicentennial Com-
mittee of Stratford) (1984)
Prayer for Lent, anthem (mix-ch) (1981)
Psalm 116, anthem (mix-ch and org) (1979)
Silence, anthem (mix-ch) (1982) (Waterloo)
Sing praises to God (mix-ch) (1984)
This holy time (mix-ch, rec or ww ens and keyboard) (1983) (comm)
To everything there is a season (2 S, A, mix-ch, org and brass) (1983)
Carol (S, A and pf) (1983) (comm)
Christ is the saving grace, hymn (1984)
Jesus, my love, my Lord (S and pf) (1983) (Harris, 1984)
Missa brevis (2 S and A) (1983)
Now join we to praise the creator (m-S, speaker and org) (1982)
The spirit is among us, hymn (1982) (Thompson) (comm)
MULTIMEDIA
He hath made everything beautiful in his time (org and slides) (1982)
TEACHING PIECES
I love my dog (vln and pf) (1984)
I'm not scared (pf) (1984)
Put on your dancing shoes (pf) (1984)
The sun, the moon, the wind and the rain (vln and pf) (1984)
Treetoads and friends (pf) (1983)
Ref. composer

TEMPLAR, Joan

20th-century American composer.
Composition
CHAMBER
Sonata (fl)
Ref. 142

TEMPLE, Hope (Mrs. Messager) (real name Dotie Davies)

English pianist and composer. b. Dublin, 1859; d. Folkstone, May 10, 1938.
She studied the piano under J.F. Barnett, E. Silas and Andre Messager,
whom she married. She planned to become a concert pianist but after a
hand injury at the age of 17, abandoned this goal to become a composer.
Many of her songs gained popularity.

Compositions
CHAMBER
Instrumental pieces
Piano pieces incl.:
Summer's dream, waltz
VOCAL
Songs incl.:
A golden Argosy (Boosey)
In sweet September (various publ.)
Lights o'home (vce and vln ad lib) (Chappell)
Mary Grey
A mother's love (Boosey; Ditson)
My lady's bower
A nursery story
An old garden (various)
Scent of the mignonette
A soldier's song
'Tis all that I can say (vln and pf: also man and pf) (various)
Duets
BALLET
Une aventure de la Guimard
Le chevalier aux fleurs
Les deux pigeons
Scaramouche
OPERETTA
The Wooden Spoon
Ref. 6, 226, 276, 297, 433

TENGBERGEN, Maria Elizabeth van Ebbenhorst

Dutch organist, lyricist, teacher and composer. b. Hoorn, July 11, 1885.
She had her first music lessons from her aunt, Maria Elizabeth Gerlings,
an organist. Other teachers were Jean Baptiste de Pauw and Steven van
Groningen. In Amsterdam Maria studied harmony under Sem Dresden,
counterpoint under Wilhelmina ter Huppen and began composing. She
taught and composed many songs for youngsters, writing most of the
words herself. PHOTOGRAPH.
Compositions
CHAMBER
Kleine suite (vln and pf)
PIANO
Drie tertsencirkels (Alsbach)
Four sonatines (Broekmans en van Poppel)
Fifty polyphone stukjes (Broekmans)
Klimmen en dalen, early etudes (Broekmans)
Studies in wit en zwart (Alsbach)
Other teaching works
VOCAL
Zwenken en Keren I & II (2 part ch) (Alsbach)
Trekvogels, 14 canons (Alsbach)
Als duizend sterren schijnen (vce, pf and vln) (Broekmans)
Christmas songs
Children's songs
OPERETTA
Sneeuwit en Rozerood (Broekmans)
Ref. composer

TENNEY, Mrs. John F. See BRANSCOMBE, Gena

TENNYSON, Emily Sarah, Lady

English musician and composer. b. 1813; d. Aldworth, August 10, 1896.
She married Lord Alfred Tennyson. She was an accomplished musician
and composed settings for several of her husband's poems.
Compositions
VOCAL
Airy fairy Lilian, in E
Hands all around
Home they brought him, in D-Flat
In love, if love be love; in A-Flat
Lady let the rolling drums, in D
Look through mine eyes, in D
Rifleman, form, in E-Minor
To sleep, to sleep, in E (from The foresters)
Ref. 208, 226, 276, 433

TENTIOH

Egyptian songstress of Mut. ca. 950 B.C. Mention of her was on the tombs
of the priests of Amun found near the Hatshepsut temple at Deir el-Bahri.
Ref. 428

TENTNAU

Ancient Egyptian songstress of the 8th-century B.C.

TERESA

16th-century Spanish composer of songs.
Ref. 465

TERHUNE, Anice (nee Potter) (pseud. Morris Stockton)

American organist, pianist and composer. b. Hampden, MA, October 27,
1873; d. Pompton Lakes, NJ, November 9, 1964. She studied at the Cleve-
land Conservatory; the organ, the piano and harmony under Louis
Coenen in Rotterdam; under Bowman in New York and under Franklin
Bassett. She was organist at a Cleveland church and later moved to New
York.
Compositions
PIANO
Child's kaleidoscope (1913)
Country sketches (1914)
The hill (1917)
VOCAL
Songs incl.:
Song at dusk (m-ch) (1910)
Barnyard ballads (1911)
Syrian woman's lament (1911)
SACRED
Bridal song
Easter morn
Faith
OPERA
Hero Nero (1904)
OPERETTA
The woodland princess (1911)
MISCELLANEOUS
Exaltation
In an old garden
The little dream horse (1913)
Romance in G-Minor (1906)
Serenade (1907)
Publications
Music-Study for Children. 1922.
Across the Line. Autobiography. New York, 1945.
Home Musical Education for Children. 1903.
Several song books for children incl.:
Chinese Child's Day; Colonial Carols; Dutch Ditties; Our Very Own
Book.
Ref. 22, 70, 74, 94, 142, 226, 433

TERRIER-LAFFAILLE, Anne

French composer. b. Laval, July 22, 1906. She was a pupil of d'Indy at the
Schola Cantorum.
Compositions
ORCHESTRA
Prélude pour la mort de la terre (after J. Laferque)
Other pieces
CHAMBER
Quartets
Trios
PIANO
Derniers murmures du soir, impressions (Leduc)
Et comment, polka-marche (Bethune)
Italie en deuil (Meaux-Alger)
Marche des insouciants (Bethune)
Menuet bleu (Leduc)
Mogador, marche (Bethune)
Sonata (also vocal)
Pieces (A. Terrier et Valsien, possibly same as Terrier-Laffaille)
VOCAL
Songs incl.:
Amours et saison, chanson-marche (Marseille: Gauthier)
C'est la femme (Marseille: Cidale)
Ca r'vient cher (Gauthier)
Comprendre (Gauthier)
Convoi (Gauthier)
Filial amour (Paris: Journal Musical)
Je suis marcheuse (Bordeaux: New Edition)
Ou donc tu vas? (Mayol)
Très content! (Mayol)
Choruses and melodies
Ref. 297, 347

TERRY, Frances

American pianist, teacher and composer. b. East Windsor, CT, 1884; d. Northampton, MA, January 1965. She studied under Scharwenka, Saar and Mr. and Mrs. Edmund Severn. She taught the piano in New York and Passaic, NJ, later moving to Northampton.

Compositions

CHAMBER

    Theme and variations (str qrt)

    Sonata in F-Sharp, op. 15 (vln and pf) (prize, SPAM, 1931)

PIANO

    Pieces incl.:

    Ballade hongroise

    Dramatic and program studies

    Impromptu appassionato

    Improvisation

    Seven reveries

    Suite, idylls of an inland sea

    Ten silhouettes

    Three impromptus

    Volume of etudes

Ref. 40, 70, 94, 142, 168, 292, 347

TERZIAN, Alicia

Argentine pianist, conductor, lecturer, musicologist and composer. b. Cordoba, July 1, 1938. She graduated in the piano in 1954 and composition in 1958 from the National Conservatory in Buenos Aires, with a first prize and a gold medal. She studied under A. Ginastera, R. Gonzalez, R, Garcia Morillo, F. Ugarte and G. Gilardi. She studied religious and medieval Armenian music, specializing in that from the 4th to the 12th-century, under Padre Dr. Leoncio Dayan in Venice in 1961 and gained a B.A. from the National University. She lectured internationally and at the National Conservatory, Escuela Superior de Bellas Artes de la Universidad Nacional de la Plata, the Municipal Conservatory and the Colon Theatre. From 1969 she directed the festivals of contemporary Argentine music as the artistic director of the Encounters of Contemporary Music Foundation. She was a recipient of many prizes and awards from 1956 to 1958 and the Outstanding Young Musician of Argentina prize in 1970. DISCOGRAPHY.

Compositions

ORCHESTRA

    Visual symphony

    Concerto for violin and orchestra (1960) (national composition prize, 1970) (Ricordi)

    Recitativo dramatico del mensagero (d-b and orch) (1957)

    Atmosferas II, No. 3 of Imagenes cosmicas I (1970)

    Carmen criaturalis (hn, perc and str orch) (1970)

    Gris de la noche, No. 6 of Imagenes cosmicas I (kettle dr and str orch) (1969)

    Imagenes cosmicas II (1970)

    Movimiento sinfonico (1958)

    Movimientos constrastantes I (Buenos Aires Municipal, prize, 1964) (Ricordi)

    Primera sinfonia (prize, Direccion de Cultura, 1957)

    Proagon (vln and str orch) (1969)

SYMPHONIC BAND

    Movimeintos para banda sinfonica (1968) (Ricordi)

CHAMBER

    Cuadrados magicos, No. 4 of Imagenes cosmicas (sextet)

    Pastoral (str qrt) (1954)

    Primer cuarteto de cuerdas (str qrt) (1956) (prize Direccion de cultura, 1956)

    String quartet (1968)

    Tres piezes, op. 5 (str qrt) (1959)

    Libro de imagenes (org) (1975)

PIANO

    Atmosferas, No. 2 of Imagenes cosmicas (2 pf) (ded C. Gulbenkian, 1970)

    Danza criolla (1954) (Barry y Ca)

    Juegos para Diana (1956) (Ricordi)

    Suite (1954)

    Toccata (1954) (Ricordi)

VOCAL

    Cantata de la tarde (orator, mix-ch and orch) (prize Direccion de cultura, 1958)

    Introduction y cantico de primavera (ch and orch) (prize Direccion de cultura, 1958)

    Oracion de Jimena, aria (from El Cid) (S and orch) (1957)

    Ab ovo, No. 1 of Imagenes cosmicas I (vce, perc and strs) (1969) (International Festival of Contemporary Music, Buenos Aires)

    Embryo, No. 5 of Imagenes cosmicas I (1969) (vce and vla)

    Escena lirica (1957)

    Songs incl.:

    Canciones para niños (G. Lorca) (1960)

    Dos canciones (A. Machado) (1956)

    Libro de canciones de Lorca (1960)

    Tres canciones (Byron) (1954)

    Tres retratos (G. Lorca) (1954)

    Tristeza (Byron) (1956)

SACRED

    Padre Nuestro y Ave Maria (mix-ch a-cap) (1966)

    Tres madrigals (w-ch a-cap) (1960)

BALLET

    Genesis (1972)

    Hacia la luz (1968)

INCIDENTAL MUSIC

    Correspondencias (1969)

    Shantiniketan (vce, fl and dance) (1970)

ELECTRONIC

    Musidanza vision (1972)

    Sinfonia visual en dos movimientos (1972)

Publications

    La Notacion Musical Armenia. Rev. Musical Chilena, 1965.

    La Musica Argentina Contemporanea. Study of 66 composers in British Encyclopaedia in Portuguese.

Bibliography

    Arizaga, R. *Enciclopedia de la Musica Argentina.* Fondo Nacional de las Artes, Buenos Aires, 1971.

Ref. composer, 20, 70, 77, 79, 109, 390, 563, 622

TESCHKE, Herma

B. 1962.

Composition

CHAMBER

    Pentachromatika (fl, ob and cl) (1980) (prize Verbanc composition contest, 1981) (Otto Harrassowitz)

Ref. Otto Harrassowitz (Wiesbaden)

TESIER, Maria Reiset de. See GRANDVAL, Marie Felicie Clemence

TESTORE, Lidia

20th-century Italian composer. b. Milan.

Compositions

OPERETTA

    Baccante (Zimar Baldo) (Milan, 1917)

    Il Bagno di Venere, in 3 acts (A. Franci) (Milan, 1915)

    La Perla dell'atelier, in 3 acts (C. Bonapace) (Bergamo, 1920)

THEATRE

    L'azzurrina, play in 2 acts (A. Barilatti)

Ref. 86. 105

TEYBER, Hellene. See ASACHI, Elena

THAIN, Lillian

American composer.

Compositions

VOCAL

    Songs incl.:

    In the heart of you (vce and keyboard)

Ref. 190

THAMAD (Semad)

Arabian songstress. b. ca. 610. She and Qu'ad (q.v.) were the oldest known Arabian songstresses and called the jaradatan (the two grasshoppers) of the emir of the Banu Amaliq, Mu'aiwiya ibn Bakr. They appear in the story of the destruction of the people of 'Ad, reputedly in South Arabia. When the land was afflicted by a drought, a deputation was sent to Makuraba (Mecca) to seek divine aid. The emir entertained them with the music of his jaradatan and the suppliants neglected their mission. In anger the deity sent a storm to break over 'Ad, destroying the whole race. Qu'ad and Thamad are also referred to in the Kitab al'Agani as belonging to the Quraish chief Abdallah ibn Judan, in a period just prior to the dawn of Islam. He gave them to his friend Umayya ibn Abil-Salt (d. 630), a pagan poet of Mecca.

Ref. 171, 234

THAMM, Ida

German pianist and composer of Berlin. b. ca. 1828.

Compositions

PIANO
   Potpourri (Fra Diavolo) (Berlin: Wagenfuehr)
   Romanz in E-Flat (Wagenfuehr)
   Rondo in G (Berlin: Paez)
   Sechs Variationen (Wagenfuehr)
   Walzer (Wagenfuehr)
VOCAL
   Songs incl.:
   Hoeret meiner Sehnsucht Klage, op. 18 (Fremery) (Berlin: Kecht, 1830)
   Mit dem Fruehling kam sie her (Berlin: Trautwein)
   Schaefer und Reiter (La motte fouque) (Wagenfuehr, 1829)
Ref. 121

THEANO

Greek poetess, philosopher and composer of the 5th-century B.C. She was the wife of Pythagoras and with him, taught that the spheres and the stars of heaven moved to music in eternal song and dance. They organized rites for their followers so that each person might achieve inner harmony of spirit by taking part in the music and the dance.
Ref. 264, 382

THECLA. See THEKLA

THEGERSTROEM, Hilda Aurora

Swedish pianist, lecturer and composer. b. September 17, 1838; d. December 6, 1907. After studying at A.F. Lindblad's Music School in Stockholm she became a piano pupil of Franz Berwald and in 1857, after winning a state scholarship to study abroad, studied under A.F. Marmontel in Paris and then Liszt in Vienna. She returned to Sweden to give concerts, settled in Gothenburg and resumed piano studies in Berlin under C. Tausig, 1864 to 1869. She taught at the Stockholm Conservatory from 1872 to 1903 and privately.
Compositions
PIANO
   Nocturne och rondoletto, op. 2
   Souvenirs svedois, op. 1
   Other pieces
   Teaching pieces
VOCAL
   Songs
Ref. 20, 95, 98, 103, 113, 226, 276

THEGERSTROM, Hilda Aurora. See THEGERSTROEM, Hilda Aurora

THEKLA (Thecla)

Late 9th-century Byzantine nun.
Composition
SACRED
   Inno alla Vergine
Ref. 502

THEMAR, Rosalie

Composition
PIANO
   Les feux-follets, tarentella (L. Lonsdale, ca. 1851)
Ref. H. Baron catalogue, 125

THEMMEN, Ivana Marburger

American concert pianist, accompanist, lecturer, painter, poetess and composer. b. New York, April 7, 1935. She studied the piano from the age of seven. Her principal teacher in New York was Jean Rosenblum. At the New England Conservatory, she studied composition under Carl McKinley in 1954, and Francis Judd Cooke, 1953. She studied at the Eastman School, Rochester and the Berkshire Music Center, Tanglewood, under Lukas Foss in 1954. During the mid-1960s she lived in Europe and appeared in concert in Scandinavia and Britain and studied chamber music under Otto Schulhof. On her return to New York she studied orchestration under Nicholas Flagello. She received several commissions and awards, including funds provided by the New Jersey Arts Council in 1976 for completion of an opera. She taught at Hampton Conservatory and was accompanist for the American Ballet Theatre. She was the first woman to compose a guitar concerto, which made her the only woman finalist for the 5th annual Kennedy Center Friedheim composition competition in 1982. DISCOGRAPHY. PHOTOGRAPH.
Compositions
ORCHESTRA
   Guitar concerto (1981)
   Trombone concerto
   Fasching (also 2 pf) (1963)
   Triptych (1952)
   Cupid and Psyche (1982) (comm Queens Symphony and NY State Arts Council)
CHAMBER
   Sextet (1953)
   Music for friends perhaps (pf, cl, vln, vla and vlc) (1959)
   Quintet (fl, cl, hn, vln and vlc) (1952)
   Wind game (sax qrt) (1971)
   Circles (fl, hn and pf) (1971)
   Fanfares (3 trp) (1973)
   Little etudes (3 trp) (1959)
   Concepts (2 vla or cl and vla) (1972)
   Duets (fl and b-cl) (1953)
   For two trombones (1952)
   Piece (fl and pf) (1951)
   Sonata (vlc and pf) (1951)
   Ten cantos (2 hn) (1973)
   Tetrachiron (pf, 4 hands) (1952)
   Montages (hp) (1976)
VOCAL
   The mystic trumpeter (Walt Whitman) (vce and orch; also cham orch; also pf) (Lyra Music, 1975)
   Ode to Akhmatova (vce and orch or pf) (1977)
   Shelter this candle from the wind, 5 poems (Edna St. Vincent Millay) (S and orch) (Lyra Music, 1978)
SACRED
   Requiem (4 soli, ch and orch) (1973)
   Magnificat (large ch and insts) (1977)
BALLET
   One ballet
OPERA
   Lucien, in 2 acts (1977)
MULTIMEDIA
   Green willow, a Japanese fairy tale (narr, opt dancers and cham ens) (1954)
Ref. composer, Bridgeport Post October 5 1982, 185, 228, 563, 622, 625

THEODOSIA. See STEEL, Ann

THEODOSIA

Byzantine nun of the late 9th-century. She composed a song in honor of St. Johanna.
Ref. 502

THERESA (pseud. of Giovanna Emma Valadon)

French dancer, singer and composer. b. La Bazoche-Gouet, Eure-et-Loire, April 25, 1837; d. Paris, May 15, 1913. Her father was a musician and Theresa studied dancing from an early age, becoming a dancer at the Theatre Porte-Saint-Martin in Paris. She later studied singing, made her debut at the Caffe-Concert dell'Alcazar and became a favorite of the public in Paris between 1863 and 1888. DISCOGRAPHY.
Compositions
VOCAL
   Joy is like the rain (chil-ch)
   Songs incl.:
   Chanson de la Reine Carotte
   Lettre d'une grand'mère
   Voila se que je voudrais être
Bibliography
   Theresa et ses memoires. La chanteuse célèbre del'Alcazar d'été. Paris. 1865.
Ref. 105, 563

THERESE, Princess of Saxe-Altenburg and of Sweden

German born princess and composer. b. 1836; d. 1914. She married Prince August, brother of Princess Eugenie of Sweden (q.v.). DISCOGRAPHY. PHOTOGRAPH.

Compositions
PIANO
   Eugenie, waltz
   Funeral, march
   Lied ohne Worte
   Romance
   Parade, march
VOCAL
   Drinking song
   Gedanken an die liebe Mutter zum Geburtstage
   Gondoliera
Ref. Bernadotte Biblioteket, Royal Palace, Stockholm, 563

THICKNESSE, Miss
18th-century English viola da gamba player and composer. As players she and Abel were unrivalled in their time. She composed pieces for her instrument.
Ref. 119, 129

THIELE, Isabel Aretz. See ARETZ, Isabel

THIELE, Leonore. See PFUND, Leonore

THIEME, Kerstin Anja (pseud. Karl Thieme)
West German organist, pianist, lecturer, writer and composer. b. June 23, 1909. She studied philosophy, psychology, the science of history, music and pedagogics at the University of Leipzig from 1929 to 1935 and gained a Ph.D. She taught music in school and at the university and was a music critic and journalist. She was the recipient of many prizes in Germany and abroad, including the Premio Citta di Trieste in 1970, 1971 and 1974 for symphonic compositions and the Stamitz prize in Stuttgart, 1973. PHOTO-GRAPH.
Compositions
ORCHESTRA
   Omaggio a Tartini, concerto (vln and orch) (Astoria)
   Rapsodia festiva doppio, concerto (a-sax, pf and orch) (1960) (Berlin: Astoria Verlag)
   Capriccio (large orch) (1946) (Hamburg: Simrock)
   Divertimento II (large orch; also 2 pf) (1959)
   Erzgebirgische, suite (large orch) (1932) (Leipzig: Breitkopf & Haertel)
   Suite Burleske (1947)
   Laendliche Taenze (small orch) (1939) (Berlin: Kistner & Siegel)
   Mascherata piccola, concertino (pf and small orch; also 2 pf) (1958) (Heidelberg: Sueddeutscher MV)
   Variati 'Bach' (1970) (Astoria)
   Variations from a theme of Hindemith (1934) (Breitkopf & Haertel)
CHAMBER
   Der Vetter Muchel, Serenade (wind insts and strs) (1939) (Wolfenbuettel: GKV)
   Mosaici, concerto (strs) (1971) (Astoria)
   Serenade (strs) (1938) (GKV)
   String quartet (1958)
   Giorni del sole, divertimento (fl and pf) (1958)
ORGAN
   Tre invocazioni (1967) (Sueddeutscher MV)
   Toccata (1932)
   Vom Himmel hoch (1949) (Sueddeutscher MV)
   Verleih uns Frieden, Phantasie (1966) (Sueddeutscher MV)
PIANO
   Variations (2 pf) (1932)
   Tre capriccetti amorosi (1972) (Astoria)
VOCAL
   Stufen des Lebens, oratorio (2 soli, mix-ch, chil-ch, org and orch) (1963)
   Der Tagkreis, oratorio (2 soli, mix-ch, chil-ch, org and orch) (1952) (Sueddeutscher mv)
   Hoffnung, cantata (Nelly Sachs) (1973) (Astoria)
   Musica, du liebliche Kunst, cantata (2 soli, mix-ch, w-ch, audience-ch and small orch) (1954) (Sueddeutscher mv)
   So reimt sich das, cantata (solo, chil-ch, mix-ch and small orch) (1937) (Sueddeutscher mv)
   Was kost'die Welt, cantata (soloist, mix-ch and small orch) (1960) (Sueddeutscher mv)
   Fraenkischer Sommer, 3 songs (w-ch) (1956) (Sueddeutscher MV)
   Das kleine Lalula, 7 madrigals (Morgenstern (m-ch) (1950) (Sueddeutscher MV)
   Licht muss wieder werden, 3 motets (mix-ch) (1952) (Sueddeutscher MV)
   Ein Mensch geht, 4 madrigals (Eugen Roth) (mix-ch) (1954) (Sueddeutscher MV)
   Der Rutsch vorbei, 5 madrigals (J. Ringelnatz) (Bar, m-ch, pf and perc) (1937) (Sueddeutscher MV)
   Spieglein an der Wand, 4 chansons (S, w-ch, pf and perc) (1961) (Sueddeutscher MV)
   Troestliche Einkehr, 5 motets (Eichendorff) (mix-ch) (1949) (Sueddeutscher MV)
   Tu der Voelker Tuere auf, Motette (mix-ch) (1952) (Sueddeutscher MV)
   Waehlte das Leben, Motette (mix-ch) (1952) (Sueddeutscher MV)
   Wer zuletzt lacht, 5 madrigals (Wilhelm Busch) (mix-ch) (1947) (Sueddeutscher MV)
SACRED
   Hymnus des Glaubens (solo, mix-ch and orch) (1936)
   Psalm Triptychon (2 soli, ch and org) (1965) (Sueddeutschen mv)
Ref. composer

THISSE-DEROUETTE, Rose
20th-century Belgium composer. She was a winner of the Prix de Rome.
Compositions
VOCAL
   Wallonische Volkstaenze (mix-ch)
   Songs
OPERA
   Cour d'Amour, comic opera in 2 acts (1928)
THEATRE
   Les bucherons, lyric drama in 3 acts, on a legend from Brittany (1948)
   L'étoile qui danse, fairy scene in 4 acts, on a legend from Brittany (1948)
Publications
   Chansonniers maternels pour l'enseignement de la musique au jardin d'enfants. Liege: Desoer.
   Les dances anciennes de Wallonie.
Ref. Otto Harrassowitz (Wiesbaden)

THOMA, Annette (nee Schenk)
German folk song collector, linguist, writer and composer. b. Neu-Ulm, January 23, 1886; d. Ruhpolding, Upper Bavaria, November 26, 1974. After studying French and English abroad, she settled in Riedering in 1910. DISCOGRAPHY.
Compositions
SACRED
   Deutsche Bauernmesse (3 part w-ch) (1933)
   Die kleine Messe
Publications
   Das Volkskied in Altbayern und seine Saenger. Munich, 1952.
   Numerous articles in newspapers and journals.
Ref. 17, 563

THOMAS, Adelaide Louise
19th-century English pianist, administrator, authoress and composer. b. Clapham, London. In 1893, after passing all the examinations for her B.Mus. at Oxford, she was refused her degree because she was a woman. Her compositions included a festival setting of Magnificat and Nunc dimittis.
Publications
   The Royal Road to Pianoforte Playing.
Ref. 6, 226, 276, 347, 433

THOMAS, Connie
20th-century American composer.
Composition
INCIDENTAL MUSIC
   No Vacancy, music play (with Ann Barton q.v.) (3 soli and youth-ch) (Flammer, 1978)
Ref. MLA *Notes*

THOMAS, Elizabeth
British lecturer and composer. b. Towyn, Merion, Wales, March 22, 1935. She was head of the music department at Totnes High School from 1958 to 1961 and at Ingestre Hall, Stafford in 1962 and a lecturer at the College of Further Education, Salop from 1968. She was chairlady of the West Midlands Arts Council from 1980. She composed three chamber and three vocal pieces.
Ref. Rev. Harold Bacon (UK)

THOMAS, Florence. See MARSHALL, Florence

THOMAS, Georgina. See WELDON, Georgina

THOMAS, Gertrude Auld
20th-century American composer.
Composition
OPERA
Hazila
Ref. 321

THOMAS, Gertrude Evelyn
20th-century British organist and composer. She studied under Dr. Joseph Parry, Mendelssohn Parry, Mander Fox, Misses Clarke and Hazell, W.E. Edwards and E.G. Richards. She was the organist at Bedwas Parish church.
Compositions
SACRED
Arise, shine, for thy light is come, Christmas anthem
Father of mercies, harvest anthem
I am He that liveth, Easter anthem
Chants and kyries
Ref. 467

THOMAS, Helen (Helen Thompson Thomas)
20th-century American authoress, singer and composer. b. East Liverpool, OH. She studied under her mother and later at the New England Conservatory. Her private teachers included Sidney Dietch and Estelle Liebling. She sang in operas and operettas, with symphony orchestras and in concert.
Compositions
CHAMBER
Piano pieces
VOCAL
Songs incl.:
The Christmas tree
The circus
Circus fantasy, 8 songs
The hurdy gurdy
In London Town at night
The love song
Shelter lullaby
Tippie's tunes
When I go back to Paris
When you come home some day
SACRED
Christmas carol
OPERETTA
Song of Yesterday
Ref. 3, 40, 142, 347

THOMAS, Janet Owen
20th-century composer.
Composition
PIANO
Fantasy sonata
Ref. *Composer* (London)

THOMAS, Karen P.
American pianist, conductor and composer. b. Seattle, September 17, 1957. She received her B.A. (music) from the Cornish Institute, Seattle in 1979, after studying under Bern H. Herbolsheimer (composition), Joseph Levine (piano) and Melvin Strauss (conducting). She did graduate composition studies under William Bergsma and Diane Thome (q.v.) and conducting under Robert Feist (conducting) at the University of Washington, Seattle. Her works have been performed in festivals in America and Norway.
Compositions
ORCHESTRA
Echo: Metamorphoses on a theme of John Barth (large orch) (1981)
CHAMBER
Metamorphoses on a Machaut Kyrie (str qrt) (1983)
Contention (cl and pf) (1979)
Sonata for solo flute (1977)

PIANO
Soliloquy: Black with red (1978)
Sonata (1977)
VOCAL
Anactoria (m-S, vla and pf) (1978)
Acheron (2 S, m-S, cl, trp, pf and vlc) (1980)
Five songs on poems of Sappho (S, fl, ob, cl and bsn) (1978)
Folk songs (S, cl, vla and perc) (1979)
Lament on the death of Hec (counter-T, T and B) (1978, rev 1981)
SACRED
Mass (double-ch and wind ens) (1976)
Stabat Mater (m-S, speaker, double-ch, pf and perc) (1979)
ELECTRONIC
Aria with Montana Fix (typist and tape, improvising ens) (1979)
Ref. composer

THOMAS, Lydia Georgina Edith. See AYLOTT, Lydia Georgina Edith

THOMAS, Marilyn Taft
American organist, pianist, assistant professor and composer. b. McKeesport, PA, January 10, 1943. She received her B.F.A. (piano and composition) from the Carnegie-Mellon University in 1964 and her M.F.A. (composition) in 1965. From the University of Pittsburgh she gained her Ph.D. (theory and composition) in 1982. She was the director of music, the organist and the pianist at the First Unitarian Church, Pittsburgh from 1963 to 1981 and visiting composer and music consultant to the Quaker Valley School District from 1981 to 1982. She lectured in theory and the piano at universities, becoming assistant professor of theory, composition, harmony and computer music at Carnegie-Mellon University in 1981. She won first prize in the Young Composers' contest run by the National Federation of Music Clubs in 1964. She is a member of ASCAP.
Compositions
ORCHESTRA
Concert piece (pf and cham orch) (1980)
Soundscapes (comm McKeesport Symphony Orch)
CHAMBER
Elegy (ob, hp and str qrt) (1980)
Five pieces for five players (ww qnt)
VOCAL
Songs of family
SACRED
He was my son
ELECTRONIC
Eighty & disparities (elec tape and ens) (1982) (Fischer)
Publications
Using Eurhythmics in Private Teaching, Dalcroze Society 1978.
Ref. 625

THOMAS, Mary Virginia (nee Ice) (Mrs. Michael Daraban)
20th-century American organist, pianist, violist, teacher and composer. b. Elkins, NY. She composed her first piece at the age of nine. She later studied under Professors Franc Antonio Migliaccio, Gerald Gaddis, Dave Vining, Cora Marsh Atchison and Charles Wakefield Cadman. She taught the piano and the organ. She was a member of a chamber music trio with her brother and sister and played the organ in churches, funeral parlours and movie theatres from the age of 14 years. She appeared in concerts throughout the southern United States, many of which were recorded for radio. She taught the piano and the organ privately. All of her compositions were lost in floods in Elmira in 1972. PHOTOGRAPH.
Compositions
CHAMBER
Sketches (org)
Sketches (pf)
VOCAL
Songs incl.:
The answer
Can't keep from crying
Don't have the answer
Li geet
Na canzone d'amore
Pour me stardust
Wan chi
What do you do?
Why should I keep wishing?
Ref. composer, 40, 347

THOMAS, Mrs. See TAPPER, Bertha

THOMAS, Muriel Leonora Duncan (nee Budge)

British concert pianist, singer, teacher and composer. b. Calcutta, January 1, 1898. Halfway through school she moved to England and later became a teacher, when her interest in music was renewed. She studied singing under Edward Daires, becoming an L.R.A.M. in singing and appearing in local concerts and on the radio. She continued singing and composition studies, becoming a A.R.C.M. at the age of 40 years.

Compositions

VOCAL

Buds in spring (Boosey & Hawkes)
Faithless as the winds (Snell)
Four songs for children, settings, from R.L. Stevenson's Child's garden of verse (Leeds: Arnold & Son)
Let my voice ring out (Snell)
Music when soft voices die (pf) (prize Royal Welsh National Eisteddford, 1950) (Snell)
My true love hath my heart (pf) (Boosey & Hawkes)
Settings of classical poems by famous British poets incl.:
She walks in beauty (pf) (prize Royal Welsh National Eisteddford, 1956) (Snell)
A world of song (Byd o Ganu) (Snell)

Ref. composer

THOME, Diane

American pianist, professor and composer. b. Pearl River, NY, January 25, 1942. She studied composition under Robert Strassburg and Darius Milhaud at Aspen; under Roy Harris at the Inter-American University of Puerto Rico; under A.U. Boscovitch in Israel and under Milton Babbitt at Princeton University. She was a piano student of Dorothy Taubman. She obtained a performer's certificate in the piano and a B.Mus. from Eastman School of Music in 1963. She received her M.A. (theory and composition) from the University of Pennsylvania in 1965 and her M.F.A. from Princeton University in 1970. She is distinguished as the first woman to earn a Ph.D. from Princeton (1973) and the first woman to write computer synthesized music. She taught the piano at Princeton University from 1970 to 1974, theory and 20th-century music at SUNY, Binghamton from 1974. She is on the faculty of the University of Washington School of Music, Seattle. She received fellowships from the Woodrow Wilson Foundation, Columbia University (hon), University of Pennsylvania, Princeton, Tanglewood and Inter-American University in Puerto Rico. DISCOGRAPHY.

Compositions

ORCHESTRA

S'embarquement (cham orch) (1971) (ACA)
Three movements (pf, perc and str orch) (1962)

CHAMBER

Constellations (large chamber ens) (1966) (ACA)
Three movements (perc, pf and strs) (1962)
Quartet (fl, vln, vla and vlc) (1961)
String quartet
Silver deer (vln and pf) (1981) (ACA)
Sonatine (fl and pf) (1960)
Suite (vln and pf) (1961)
Three movements (vlc and pf) (1958)
Three pieces (fl and vla) (1958)

PIANO

Pianismus (1982) (ACA)
Sonatine (pf) (1959)

VOCAL

Cantata based on Bhagavad-Gita (1964) (ACA)
Ash on an old man's sleeve (T and cham orch) (1962)
Three sonnets by Sri Aurobindo (S and orch) (1984) (ACA)
The Yew tree (S and large cham ens) (1979) (ACA)
Songs on Chinese verses (S, fl, B-flat cl, vla and perc) (1964) (ACA)
Spring and fall: To a young child (G.M. Hopkins) (Bar and str trio) (1962)

SACRED

Three Psalms (Bar, mix-ch, fl, vln, vla, vlc and hp) (1979) (ACA)
Two Psalms (mix-ch and inst ens) (1980) (ACA)

ELECTRONIC

Alexander Boscovich remembered (vla, pf and tape) (1975) (ACA)
Anais (vlc, pf and tape) (1976) (ACA)
Le berceu de miel (S, a-fl, str qrt and tape) (1968) (ACA)
January variations (computer synthesized tape) (1973) (ACA)
Los nombres (pf, perc and computer synthesized tape) (1974) (ACA)
Polyvalence (computer, fl, cl, pf, vlc, vln, vla and perc) (1972) (ACA)
Spechtrophonie (fl, a-fl, electric hpcd, vla, man and amplified d-b) (1969) (ACA)
Sunfower space (fl, pf and tape) (1978) (ACA)
Winter infinities (7 players and stereo tape) (1980) (ACA)

MULTIMEDIA

Caprice, ballet and story for children (pf, fl and dancers) (1957)
In my garden (Bialik, trans Maurice Samuel) (S, Bar, dancers and small inst ens) (1956)
Night passage, environmental theatre piece (1973) (ACA)

FILM MUSIC

Music for films

MISCELLANEOUS

The golden messengers (comm Seattle Arts Commission)

Ref. composer, Composers' Forum Inc. Fall 1985, Working papers on women in music, 142, 206, 227, 563, 622, 625

THOMPSON, Alexandra

19th-century English composer. The daughter of the Archbishop of York, the Rev. W. Thompson, she studied under Dr. Naylor.

Compositions

VOCAL

The battle of the Baltic (ch and orch)
Shepherd's elegy: Holiday in Arcadie
Madrigals

Ref. 6, 226, 276, 433

THOMPSON, Caroline Lorraine

Australian pianist and composer. b. Albury, NSW, December 23, 1948. She came from a musical family and studied and performed ballet and music from an early age. She obtained her Dip.Mus. (education) from New South Wales Conservatory and a teacher's certificate from the department of Education. She studied music theatre at Morley College, London and acting and voice production in Sydney. She also studied the jazz piano under Chuck Yates and Serge Ermoll and composition under Dr. Michael Hannon. She performs in the production of many of her works and has composed many commercial songs.

Compositions

DANCE SCORES

Series F (1978)

THEATRE

Annonomations I, II, III (1977)
Antipodium Diem (1975)
Aspect, dance theatre (1981)
Basta! (D.H. Lawrence) (1978)
Between Silence and Light, dance theatre (1979)
The Capuccino Family- Not Everyone's Cup of Tea, music drama (1979)
Corpuscle Chaos, choreopoems (1981)
Days Untold, dance theatre (1981)
Doors, dance theatre (comm The One Extra Dance Theatre) (1980)
The Dunce (1978)
Fine Lines (1982)
Hans Anderson, for children (1978)
In Search of a Landscape, dance theatre (1977)
In Terms of Love (1977)
Noddy Comes to Town, for children (1978)
Noddy Comes to Stay, for children (1978)
New Adventures of Pinocchio, for children (1978)
A Remnant (1975)
Satura (1982)
To Paint a Portrait of a Bird (vce, fls and gtr) (1978)
Veloce (1978)
A Well Shaped Pair of Legs, for children (co-writer) (1981)
What's Mime is Yours, music mime (1979)

FILM MUSIC

Lost Moments (1978)

Ref. composer

THOMPSON, Ellen

20th-century American choral conductor, professor and composer. She received her B.Mus. from Houghton College, NY, her M.A. (music) from Teachers' College, Columbia University and her M.Mus. (piano) from the American Conservatory in Chicago, where she studied under Lillian Powers-Wadsworth and Stella Roberts. She became professor of theory and the piano and chairlady of the theory department at Wheaton College Conservatory, IL, after teaching there from 1951.

Publications

Teaching and Understanding Contemporary Piano Music. Text and reference. Kjos West.

Ref. Neil A. Kjos (CA)

THOMPSON, Lady Henry. See LODER, Kate Fanny

THOMPSON, Leland

20th-century American composer. She composed piano pieces and songs.
Ref. 42, 347

THOMPSON, Mary Frances (Mrs. W. Dewey)
American composer. b. Little Rock, AR, April 4, 1912. She studied at Little Rock Junior College and obtained a B.S. from George Peabody College for Teachers, Nashville, TN. She was awarded an M.Mus. (education) from Southern Methodist University in 1962.
Compositions
SACRED
Herald Angel, cantata, on the story Raphael, the Herald Angel (m-ch; also w-ch; also mix-ch)
Silver flute, cantata (bible) (4 solo, school-ch and insts)
Ref. composer, 146

THOMPSON THOMAS, Helen. See THOMAS, Helen

THOMSEN (Muchova-Thomsenova), Geraldine
Czech composer. b. London, July 5, 1917. She studied music at the London Royal Academy of Music under Benjamin Dale and Allan Busch. She completed her studies in 1942 and went to Czechoslovakia in 1945, where she married the writer Jiri Mucha. Her compositions were influenced by Scottish, English, Czech and Slovak folk music. Some of her works were performed on Czech radio.
Compositions
ORCHESTRA
Fantasy (vlc and orch) (1946)
Piano concerto (1960)
Overture (1951)
Picture of sumava (1952)
CHAMBER
Variations for nonet (1959)
Wind quintet, serenata (1964)
String quartet (1962, 1963)
First sonata in G-Minor (vln and pf) (1947)
Sea scenes (vln and pf) (1961)
Second sonata (vln and pf) (1961)
Sonatina (vla and pf) (1945)
PIANO
Children's pieces (1953)
Miniatures (1962)
Parting and teasing (1942)
Sixteen variations on a Scottish folk song (1957)
VOCAL
Two women's choruses (16th-cent English poet) (1956, 1958)
Collection of Czech and Slovak folk songs (B and pf) (1943)
Folk lullabies (vce and pf) (1952)
Song of songs (recitor, fl and hp) (1961)
Sonnets (Shakespeare) (recitor, fl and hp) (1961)
BALLET
Macbeth (1965)
Ref. 70, 94, 197

THOMSON, Geraldine
Composition
PIANO
Stately dance (OUP, 1941)
Ref. 473

THOREAU, Rachel
20th-century composer.
Composition
FILM MUSIC
Gigi (1949)
Ref. 326

THORESON, Janice Pearl (Milevic)
Canadian pianist, teacher and composer. b. Lethbridge, Alberta, December 17, 1926. She gained her L.R.S.N. (piano) from the associated board of the Royal Schools of Music, her Mus.G. (pedogogy) from the University of Western Ontario and her B.Mus. (composition) from the University of Calgary. She taught the piano privately for many years. PHOTOGRAPH.
Compositions
PIANO
Fog
Little donkey
Little waltz
Parallels
Running
Sunday afternoon suite: Waltzing; Quite time; Perpetual morning; Floating; Marching (Ontario: E.C. Kerby)
Ref. composer

THORKELSDOTTIR, Mist Barbara
American/Icelandic pianist, teacher and composer. b. Urbana, IL, August 2, 1960. She attended school in Iceland and obtained her B.A. (composition) from the Hamline University St. Paul, MN, in 1982, where her teacher was Dr. Russel Harris. In 1983 she studied for a short period at the State University of New York, Buffalo, under Morton Feldman and Lejaren Hiller. She lives in Iceland and teaches the piano and music history at Gardabaer Children's Music School. Several of her compositions have been performed in concert and on radio and television and a choral work was presented at the Aisa Cantat in Japan and a work performed at the Rostrum of Composers in Paris, 1984. PHOTOGRAPH.
Compositions
CHAMBER
A movement for strings (str qrt) (1982)
Notflot (fl, cl and bsn) (1983)
In aeternum (fl and pf) (1982)
Grand music for Asthildur (pf) (1983)
No skal eg lettur lida (vla) (1982)
VOCAL
Scissors (ch a-cap) (1984)
SACRED
David, 116 (Bar and cham orch) (1984)
Ref. composer

THORNE, Beatrice
English pianist and composer. b. London, May 9, 1834; d. December 26, 1916. She was the daughter of the pianist and composer Edward Henry Thorne. She made her debut as a pianist at Prince's Hall in 1888.
Compositions
PIANO
Gavotte
Other pieces
Ref. 6, 85, 347

THORNE, Edgar. See MERRICK, Marie E.

THREADGILL-MARTIN, Ravonna
American composer. b. October 18, 1954. She received her B.A. (music education) from the University of Alaska-Fairbanks in 1980 and her M.A. (music history) in 1983, after she studied vocal literature under Sister Suzanne Summerville. She also studied vocal literature under Herr Werner Wais in Berlin. Several of her works have been performed in and out of America. She received a commission from the University Community Chorus at the University of Alaska-Fairbanks, to write a cantata based on Alaskan Moravian traditions for choir and chamber group and she won an award from the University of Alaska Foundation to write a solo cantata on Anne Bradstreet poems for the United States Frontier, early American and present day Alaska conference, 1983.
Compositions
CHAMBER
Six studies for two clarinets (1982)
Alaskan animal miniatures (pf) (1983) (Galaxy)
VOCAL
Beauty art thou (ch and pf) (1983) (Lawson-Gould)
There is a season (ch and pf) (1982)
Meditations (m-S and pf) (1983)
T'is you that are the music (m-S and pf) (1982)
SACRED
Christmas Psalm (ch, org, perc and ww) (1982)
THEATRE
Swashbuckler I and II, musical drama (vces, perc, pf and lyrics) (1983)
ARRANGEMENTS
Were you there? (ch, pf and chimes) (1982)
Ref. composer

THURBER, Nettie C.
19th-century American composer of songs.
Ref. 276, 347, 433

THYMELE
Ancient Greek actress, musician and composer. She lived in the reign of Domitian. A dance Themelinos, was attributed to her as well as the use of an altar in the theatre. She frequently acted with Latinus.
Ref. 334, 382

THYS, Pauline (Sebault) (Thys-Sebault) (Labault, Pauline Thys)
French librettist, writer and composer. b. Paris, 1836. She was the daughter of Alphonse Thys, musician and composer. Her chansonettes enjoyed some popularity in her day. She devoted herself almost entirely to the compositions of operettas and comic operas, for most of which she wrote her own librettos. She also wrote novels.
Compositions
VOCAL
Chansonettes and romances (Heugel)
OPERA
La congiura di Chevreuse, opera seria, in 2 acts (composer) (1881)
OPERETTA
Le cabaret du pot-casse, in 3 acts (1878)
Dieu le garde (1860)
L'éducation d'Achille, in 1 act (with G. Durval) (1881)
Le fruit vert, in 3 acts
Giuditta, in 3 acts (1891)
L'heriter sans le savoir
Manette, in 2 acts
Le mariage de Tabarin (1876)
Nedgeya, in 2 acts (Nemo) (1880)
Le pays de Cocagne, in 2 acts (Deforges) (1862)
La perruque de Bailli (1860)
La pomme de Turquie, in 1 act (1857)
Quand Dieu est dans le ménage (1860)
Le roi jaune (1887)
Ref. 26, 105, 108, 129, 225, 276, 307, 347, 394

THYS-SEBAULT, Pauline. See THYS, Pauline

TIBALDI, Rosa (nee Tartaglini) (Mrs. Giuseppe Luigi)
Italian singer and composer. d. Bologna, November 17, 1775. She was a member of the Accademica della Filarmonica of Bologna, an honor awarded to only two other women composers of the 18th-century. She composed a duet in a volume printed by her husband, Giuseppe Luigi Tibaldi.
Ref. 85, 347, 502

TIBERGE, Mme. See NATIBORS

TIBORS
Provençal troubadour. b. ca. 1130; d. 1182. Probably the earliest of the women troubadours, she was the sister of the troubadour Raimbuat d'Orange. Her family held title to the castle of Sarenom, now Serignan, near Grasse, Alpes Maritimes. Her husband Bertrand de Baux, an important patron of the troubadours and allied with Barcelona, was assassinated in 1181, on the orders of his enemy Raimon V of Toulouse. Only one of Tibor's songs survives, beginning *Bels dous amics, ben vos posc en ver dir que anc non fo qu'lieu estes ses desir pos vos conven que us tenc per fin anam....*
Ref. 375

TICHARICH, Zdenka
Hungarian concert pianist, lecturer and composer. b. Budapest, 1900. She studied under Istvan Tomka and in Berlin under Schreker, Busoni and Sauer. She gave concerts in the capitals of Europe and the United States. After 1947 she taught at the Budapest Academy of Music. She composed orchestral and piano works and songs.
Ref. 375

TIDEMAN-WIJERS, Bertha (Albertha Wilhelmina) (nee Wijers)
Dutch pianist and composer. b. Zutphen, January 8, 1887. Her mother and sister were her first teachers. In 1900 she went to the Stern Conservatory in Berlin, where she was a pupil of Max Loewengaard and Wilhelm Klatte. At the Berlin Hochschule fuer Musik she studied the piano under Ernst von Dohnanyi and composition under Richard Roessler. After her graduation she went to the Dutch East Indies where she lived for 17 years, returning to Holland in 1929. PHOTOGRAPH.
Compositions
CHAMBER
Two concertinos (vln) (1927)
Violin pieces for children
Eight compositions (car) (1959-1973)

PIANO
Beo's lied (1921)
Berceuse (1950)
Karozang (1921)
Oosterse impressie (1925)
Pieces for children
Seven elegies (1935)
Tobafantasie (1921)
VOCAL
Two cantatas (w-ch) (1942)
Three songs (m-ch) (1937)
Four songs (1919)
Four songs and duets (1918)
Three poems (E. Eybers) (Amsterdam: Broekmans & van Poppel)
Three songs (1952)
Other songs
Publications
Articles in *Die Taalgenoot*, January 1959.
Ref. composer, 377

TILBURY, Adeline. See DE LARA, Adelina

TILICHEYEVA, Elena Nikolayevna
Soviet lecturer, writer and composer. b. Moscow, November 17, 1909. She studied composition under A. Aleksandrov at the Moscow Conservatory and graduated in 1937. From 1937 to 1941 and 1943 to 1947 she lectured at the Ippolotov-Ivanov music school, Moscow and from 1941 to 1943 at the music school in Tomsk. She wrote books on the teaching of music to children.
Compositions
ORCHESTRA
Symphony (1938)
CHAMBER
Sonata (inst ens) (1938)
String quartets (1945, 1955)
Children's pieces (vln and pf)
Poem (vln and pf) (1943)
Suite (vln and pf) (1944)
Piano pieces for children (1946)
VOCAL
Pamyati pogibshikh geroev, oratorio (S. Blizky) (1942)
Lenin, cantata (Ivensen) (chil-ch) (1960)
Spasibo, spasibo, rodnaya strana, cantata (Nekrasova) (chil-ch) (1959)
Novogodine pesni (E. Trutneva) (vce and orch) (1954)
Pechora (M. Golbukova) (vce and orch) (1954)
Three songs, folk words (vce and orch) (1954)
Kak u nashikh u vorot (ch a-cap) (Muzgiz, 1949)
Osenneye utro (ch and pf) (Muzgiz, 1954)
Prekrasni vy polya zemli rodnoi (Lermontov) (ch) (1979)
Rechushka bezymyannaya (V. Gurian) (ch and pf) (Muzgiz, 1954)
Rodina (ch a-cap) (1976)
Song about Lise Chaikina (ch and pf) (Muzgiz, 1954)
Three Pioneer songs (ch and pf) (Muzgiz, 1951)
Vechernyaya pesnya (ch) (1978)
Children's songs (ch and pf) (Muzgiz, 1955)
Romances (Gurkov) (vce and pf) (1942)
Romances (Lermontov) (vce and pf) (1937)
Romances (Soviet poets)
THEATRE
Sobaka na sene, play (1943)
Music for radio and theatre
Ref. 87, 94, 441

TILLETT, Jeanette
20th-century American composer of piano and choral works.
Ref. 40, 347

TIMMERMANN, Leni
West German pianist, poetess, teacher and composer. b. Witten, Ruhr, March 5, 1901. She studied at the conservatories of Recklinghausen and Essen and at the Westphalian Academy of Music, Muenster. She worked as a pianist and teacher in Marl-Huels, Westphalia for many years and organised and participated in many charity concerts. She composed mainly light and folk music. DISCOGRAPHY. PHOTOGRAPH.
Compositions
VOCAL
Songs incl.:
Denk daran
Der Sommer 'achtundsiebzig/ Wir gratulieren unserer Duesseldstadt
Erster Fruehling, children's song

Gehst du der Sonne entgegen
Herrlicher Rhein
Lieder aus dem Sauerland
Nun geht die Sonne sur Ruh', lullaby
Stolzer November
Wer die Heimat kennen und lieben will
Wir lieben die Sonne, rambling song
SACRED
Leise schwebend auf Engelshaenden
Three German carols (OUP, 1983)
Weihnachtserwartung
Wunder von Bethlehem
Ref. Dr. F.H. Timmermann (composer's son)

TIMOFEYEW, Mrs.

20th-century American director, opera producer and composer. Her opera won the National Women's Composers' award in 1978.
Composition
OPERA
Aza
Ref. Music Clubs magazine summer 1979

TINDAL, Adele. See MADDISON, Adele

TIRINANZI, Nannette

Early 18th-century composer.
Composition
HARPSICHORD
Huit variations sur l'air quand l'amour (Ratisbon: Keyser)
Ref. 128

TIRS, Katharina

German nun, choral conductor, soprano and composer of the Augustine convent Niesing, near Muenster. d. August, 1604. Almost nothing is known of her life. The nuns of the convent led a communal life and had much to do with life outside the convent. The influence of lively dance melodies and ring dances with hand clapping is apparent in Katharina's songs. The Reformation, which caused great upheaval and confusion and was reflected in the music of other contemporary convents, left no mark on Katherina's songs, so that they are considered the last source of spiritual song in the Middle Ages on German ground. Her *Liederbuch* consists of 80 songs of which 72 were composed by herself, the remainder either by contemporaries or later revisors. The first 16 are Latin Christmas songs, the others are a mixture of Latin and Low German. It is thought that many were accompanied by percussion instruments such as wooden blocks and handbells.
Compositions
SACRED
Das Liederbuch der Katherina Tirs, consisting of 80 songs incl.:
Four or 5 part choral songs (Latin and Low German) (S)
Sixteen Latin Christmas songs
Ref. 476

TISHMAN, Fay

20th-century American composer. She wrote musicals for community and non-profit institutions with Harriett Bailin (q.v.).
Ref. 39

TISSOT, Mireille

20th-century French organist and composer. DISCOGRAPHY.
Composition
ORGAN
Meditation
Ref. 563

TKACH, Zlata Moiseyevna

Soviet teacher and composer. b. Kishinev, Moldavia, May 16, 1928. She graduated from the Kishinev Conservatory after studying under L.S. Gurov. From 1963 she taught composition at G. Musichesky.
Compositions
ORCHESTRA
Violin concerto (Muzyka, 1977)
Dyetskaya, suite (1963)
Kontsert (vln, timp and str orch)
Surovii napev, triptych (1975)

CHAMBER
Funny stories: six pieces (cl and str qrt)
Pieces (vln and pf) (1976)
Sonata (vla and pf) (1976)
VOCAL
Gorod dyeti, solntse, cantata (Y. Telyeuk) (1962)
Lenin, cantata (V. Galaik) (1969)
Pesnya o dnestre, cantata (E. Lotyan) (1957)
Pionveri, cantata (V. Galaik) (1974)
Cycle of 6 children's songs (G. Viyer) (1964)
The new house, children's songs (vce and pf)
Poema pamyat (1977)
Romances
BALLET
Andriyesh (1980)
OPERA
Golubi i kosuyu linyeiku (1974)
OPERETTA
Koza s tremya kozlyatami, for children (1966)
Ref. 420

TOBIN, Candida

English pianist, lecturer, writer and composer. b. Chingford, Essex, January 5, 1926. She studied at the Royal Academy of Music and Trinity College, London. She received an honorary F.T.C.L. in recognition of her Tobin music system, which enables a non-music specialist to teach classroom music and assists in the teaching of the classical guitar and the recorder to large groups. She was the originator of the circular graph. She lectured in America, Canada, Australia, Japan and Europe. PHOTOGRAPH.
Publications
Audio Visual Kit on Composition. Helicon Press, 1977.
Classical Guitar Instruction Kit. Helicon Press, 1978.
Colour Piping Books I and II. Helicon Press, 1969
Manual. Helicon Press, 1977.
First and Second Steps to Music. Helicon Press, 1980.
First Steps to Music Literacy Manual. Guide to Tobin Music System. Helicon Press, 1979.
Guitar Music Packs I, II and III. Helicon Press, 1978.
Music Work Books. Helicon Press, 1969.
Wizard's Way Recorder Books I and II. Helicon Press, 1976, 1981.
Ref. composer

TOBIN, Sister Clare

Australian composer. b. 1931.
Compositions
PIANO
Chaque fleur s'évapore ainsi qu'un encensoir, op. 4 (1971)
Reflection, op. 6 (1972)
VOCAL
Autumn evening, op. 5 (Japanese Haiku verse) (S and pf) (1971)
SACRED
O filii et filiae, op. 7, Easter hymn (mix-ch and orch)
I see his blood upon the rose, op. 2 (mix-ch)
Light eternal, op. 9, mass for the dead (2 part-ch a-cap and org) (1973)
Good Shepherd mass, op. 11
Lochinvar mass. op. 10
Ref. 440, 446

TOBLER, Mina

20th-century Swiss teacher and composer, living in Germany. She studied at the Zurich Conservatory and later in Leipzig, Brussels and Berlin. She was a music teacher in Heidelberg.
Compositions
PIANO
Sechs kleine Klavierstuecke
Ref. 276

TODD, Alice Weston

American cellist, organist, pianist, singer and composer. b. Madison, February 23, 1884; d. January 31, 1957. She attended the New England Conservatory and received special voice training in New York. She was a church organist for several years.
Compositions
VOCAL
Fire Pictures
June Days
Song of the Kennebec (1913)
State of Maine (1931) (Boston: J. Worley)

Publications
Life on Grandpa's Farm. 1954.
Ref. 374

TODD, Esther Cox
20th-century American composer.
Compositions
CHAMBER
Swans (pf)
Other pieces for piano
Pieces for violin
VOCAL
Songs
Ref. 40, 347

TODD, M. Flora
20th-century American composer. She composed choral pieces.
Ref. 40, 347

TOLER, Anne
20th-century English composer.
Compositions
VOCAL
Four moon poems
Three magic songs
Ref. 422

TOLKOWSKY, Denise
Belgian pianist and composer. b. Brighton, England, August 11, 1918. Her father was a Russian and her mother Anna Kennes, the Belgian singer and actress of the Royal Flemish Opera of Antwerp. Denise studied at the Royal Flemish Conservatory in Antwerp; the piano under E. Durlet, harmony under E. Verheyden, counterpoint and fugue under K. Candael and composition under Flor Alpaerts. She won first prizes in the piano, chamber music, solfege, harmony, fugue, history of music, history of art and literature. With her husband she organized Recontres Musicales d'Anvers, for young musicians and after her husband's death she dedicated herself to founding and developing the Alex de Vries Foundation, which helps young musicians throughout the world and now has the support of numerous world-renowned performers. PHOTOGRAPH.
Compositions
ORCHESTRA
Piano concerto (1958)
Adagio on an old Flemish theme (str orch)
CHAMBER
Hommage à Bela Bartok (fl, vln, pf and perc) (1953)
Dance of the Sulamith (fl and pf)
Six Hebraic songs (vln and pf)
PIANO
Pieces incl.:
Suite for two pianos
Etudes
Metamorphoses
Preludes
Rhythmic
Sonatine
VOCAL
Het kamp (Marcel Coole) (vce and orch)
Songs (Flemish, French, English and German poets) (vce and pf)
BALLET
Le jeu du coeur
La Sulamite
La terre et les hommes (1946)
Van't kwezelke (1939)
Ref. composer, 44, 94

TOLLEFSEN, Augusta
American composer. b. January 5, 1885.
Compositions
VOCAL
The grave of love (high vce and pf) (Composers Press)
To a snowflake (high vce and pf) (Composers Press)
Winter (high vce and pf) (Composers Press)
Ref. 190

TONDEUR, Wilhelmine
German pianist and composer. b. Berlin, ca. 1797; d. Berlin, March 1, 1838. She studied the piano under Wilhelm Schneider and then the chamber musician Schwarz in Berlin, where she made her first public appearance in 1811. In 1818 she became a member of the Berlin String Academy.
Compositions
PIANO
Eight variations on an Austrian folk song (Berlin: Tondeur, 1822)
VOCAL
Wiedersehen (vce and pf) (Tondeur, 1822; Leipzig: Klemm)
Ref. 121

TONEL, Leonie
19th-century French composer.
Compositions
PIANO
Pieces incl.:
Perles et diamants
Ref. 226, 276, 433

TORRA, Celia
Argentine violinist, choral conductor and composer. b. Concepcion del Uruguay, Entrerrios, September 18, 1889; d. 1962. She studied the violin under Alberto Williams and Athos Palma. In 1909 she won the conservatory prize, Gran Premio Europe, enabling her to study in Europe. There she followed courses under Zoltan Kodaly in Budapest, Vincent d'Indy and Paul le Flem in Paris and improved her technique under C. Thompson and R. Hubay. In 1911 she won the Grand Prix for violin at the Brussels Conservatory and the Van Hall prize. Two years later she received the title of Violin Virtuoso in Budapest. In 1919 she was awarded a grant by the government of Entrerrios, Argentina to further her studies in Europe. In 1921 she returned to Argentina and taught, conducted and composed. In 1930 she was founder-director of the Asociacion Coral Femenina which later amalgamated with the Asociacion Sinfonica Femenina. She conducted its orchestra and choir in concerts of large-scale works.
Compositions
ORCHESTRA
Suite en 3 tiempos: En Piragua, Cortejo y Fiesta indigena (1937)
Suite incaica (1938)
Suite y rapsodia entrerriana (1931)
Tres piezas para arcos (str och)
CHAMBER
Pieces (vln and pf)
Sonata en la menor (pf)
VOCAL
El arroyo y luna y nieve en Huillapina (mix-ch and cham orch)
Himno a la raza (mix-ch and orch)
Coqueando (w-ch and pf)
El aguila (w-ch and pf)
Atardecer
El sauce
Himno de la paz
Oracion a la bandera
Pampeana (m-vces)
SACRED
O Maria Virgo pia (w-ch and org)
Tota pulchra (w-ch and org)
ARRANGEMENTS
Las Campanas, from 17th-cent melody by Juan Hidaldo (mix-ch)
Ref. 8, 54, 100, 276, 322, 361, 390

TORRANCE, Mrs. Joe Taylor
American authoress and composer. b. Manchester, TN, May 29, 1899. She was a member of ASCAP.
Compositions
VOCAL
Alone
Come greet the dawn
Down by the river
Dreaming
I'll be shoutin' again
Sweet peace
SACRED
I bring my love to Thee
Lord you know I've got a troubled soul
Ref. 39

TORRENS, Grace
19th-century English pianist and composer. She was accompanist to the singer Dame Clara Butt. DISCOGRAPHY.
Composition
VOCAL
How pansies grow
Ref. Ace of Diamonds Record Co.

TORRENS, Merce
Spanish composer. b. Barcelona, February 12, 1930. She studied at the Conservatorio del Liceo, Barcelona.
Compositions
ORCHESTRA
Squitxos, suite
CHAMBER
Triptic (vlc and pf)
PIANO
Impressions
Suite de danses
VOCAL
Songs, poems (J. Carner, S. Espriu)
Ref. International Council of Women

TORRY, Jane Sloman
19th-century American composer.
Compositions
PIANO
Pieces
VOCAL
Songs incl.:
Barbara Fritchie
Butterfly, waltz song (Ditson)
Carina, waltz song (White)
Come the bark is moving, waltz song
Constancy (White)
Don't be jealous darling
Drifting away (White)
Estella, waltz song (Ditson)
Love's whisper, waltz song (White)
Margery Daw
Milkmaid's song (Ditson)
Mon amie, waltz song (White)
Only flirting (White)
Poem of love, waltz song (White)
Queen of the night (White; Ashdown)
Return of spring (Ditson)
So far away (Ditson)
Springtime, waltz song (Ditson)
Star of the morn, waltz song
Star of my life, scherzo song (Schroeder)
Take back the ring (Ditson)
Titania
Under the maples (Ditson)
Waiting at the brookside (Ditson)
Waiting heart, or Glide, gondola (Ditson)
Weary heart (Ditson)
Zephyr, waltz song (Ditson)
Ref. 276, 292, 347, 433

TOSCA, Mme. See TASCA, Mme.

TOWER, Joan
American pianist, lecturer and composer. b. New Rochelle, NY, September 6, 1938. She obtained her B.A. from Bennington College, VT, her M.A. (theory and history of music), in 1967 and D.M.A. (composition) from Columbia University. From 1968 to 1971 she studied composition under Henry Brant, Louis Calabro, Wallingford Riegger and Darius Milhaud. Her composition teachers at Columbia included Otto Luening, Jack Beeson, Vladimir Ussachevsky, Chou Wen-Chung, Charles Wourinen, Ralph Shapey, Allen Sapp and Ben Boretz. She taught at Bard College after 1972. When at Columbia, she left the Greenwich House School of Music, New York, to organize the Da Capo Players, a chamber group that won the Naumberg award for chamber music, 1973. She received three grants from the National Endowment for the Arts, an award from the American Academy and the Institute of Arts and Letters and a fellowship from the MacDowell Colony. DISCOGRAPHY. PHOTOGRAPH.
Compositions
ORCHESTRA
Cello concerto
Amazon II (1979)

Composition (also ob) (1976)
Sequoia (1981)
CHAMBER
Breakfast rythms I and II (fl or picc, vln, vlc, mar, 3 tom-toms, vib, woodblock and pf) (1974)
Noon dance (fl, cl, vln, vlc, pf and perc) (1983)
Amazon (fl, cl, vla, vlc and pf) (1977)
Prelude (fl, ob or vln, cl, bsn or vlc and pf) (1970)
Percussion quartet (1963 rev 1969) (Music Percussion Inc.)
Pillars (2 pf and perc) (1961)
Trio (1960)
Brimset (fl and perc) (ACE)
Opa Eboni (ob and fl) (1967)
Movements (fl and pf) (ASUC)
Snowdrops (fl and gtr) (comm Schubert Club, St. Paul) (1983)
Hexachords (fl)
Petroushkates (1980)
Platinum spirals (vln) (1976)
Six variations (vlc) (1971)
Wings (cl) (1981) (Associated Press)
PIANO
Circles (1964)
Fantasia (1966)
Red garnet, waltz (1977)
Ref. composer, *Minnesota Monthly* April 1973, *Musical America* September 1982, 94, 137, 142, 146, 206, 228, 397, 415, 563, 622

TOWERSEY, Phyllis Mary
English teacher and composer. b. London, 1914. She is an L.R.A.M., A.R.C.M. and L.G.S.M.. She obtained her teacher's certificate from the Bognor Training College and taught music in schools from 1950 to after 1961.
Compositions
CHAMBER
Sonata (vln and pf)
VOCAL
Songs
Choral pieces
Ref. 490

TOWNSEND, Jill
20th-century American composer.
Compositions
ORCHESTRA
Carnival time: Music for a festive occasion (str orch) (Chester, 1985)
The circus comes to town (Chester, 1981)
Ref. MLA *Notes*, Otto Harrassowitz (Wiesbaden)

MANSFIELD. See TOWNSEND, Marie

TOWNSEND, Marie (Townsend Allen) (Mansfield Townsend)
19th-century American composer.
Compositions
VOCAL
Hammock song, quartet
Summer days, quartet
Duets
OPERA
Hawaii
Ref. 226, 276, 291, 347, 433

TOWNSEND, Natalie. See TOWNSEND, Pearl Dea Etta

TOWNSEND, Pearl Dea Etta (Natalie) (Mme. Lawrence)
English composer. b. 1886.
Compositions
CHAMBER
Berceuse (vln and pf; also vce and pf) (Ricordi)
Sérènade rustique (vln and pf) (Ricordi)
Sandringham, march
VOCAL
A Spanish girl's love song (H. Huntington) (vce and pf)
The thought of you (Huntington) (vce and pf)
Ref. 63

TOWNSEND-ALLEN, Marie. See TOWNSEND, Marie

TOYAMA, Michiko Françoise
Japanese pianist, conductor, professor and composer. b. 1913. She studied in Paris under Nadia Boulanger (q.v.) and returned to Japan in 1948 to teach counterpoint and the piano as assistant professor at the Osaka Academy of Music. In 1952 she returned to France to study under Milhaud, Messiaen and Noel Gallon at the Paris Conservatoire. Whilst there she met Pierre Shaeffer of Radiodiffusion Française, a lecturer on musique concrete. Impressed by his demonstration, she went to Columbia University to study electronic music under Dr. Otto Luening, laboratory experimentation under Dr. Ussachevsky and Nobuo Yoneda of Tokyo University, who helped her as technical assistant and flautist. She also received advice from Edgard Varese. In 1955 she went to Tanglewood as a scholarship student, studying under Roger Sessions. She studied conducting at Ecole Monteux and at Columbia University. At present she is research fellow in the department of electronics at Kyoto University. DISCOGRAPHY.
Compositions
ORCHESTRA
    Japanese suite
VOCAL
    Voice of Yamato (S and cham orch) (1937)
    Two old folk songs with koto: Torianse: Takai yama kara
ELECTRONIC
    Aoi no ue, music drama (tape and narr)
    Waka, inspired by 9th-century folk song adapted to the Gagali imperial court music; poetry taken from Hyaku-nin Shu; dated from Kamakura period, 12th-century (narr and tape) (1958)
Ref. 563, 622

TOYAMA, Mihoko
Japanese composer. b. Chiba, January 19, 1944. She graduated from the Graduate School of Tokyo University of Fine Arts in 1971 and in 1979 was awarded first prize in the composition section of the 39th-music concours.
Composition
CHAMBER
    Accumulation of three groups of instruments
Ref. Yamaha Music Foundation

TRAEGER, Elinor Meissner
American pianist, teacher, writer and composer. b. Chicago, July 10, 1906. She studied under Clara Meissner, Mrs. Cory, Bess Ressiguie, Antoinette Lauer, Edna Hansen and Len Cleary. She taught the piano privately from 1948. She was the recipient of various honors. She wrote musical and book reviews.
Compositions
VOCAL
    The carousel (Pro Art)
    Cradle song (Willis)
    Sleepytime (Pro Art)
Ref. 206

TRAIN, Adelaine
19th-century American composer.
Compositions
VOCAL
    Songs incl.:
    Persian serenade
    The rose
    Snowflakes
Ref. 226, 276, 292, 433

TRANETTINA
Italian composer of a cantata.
Ref. 128

TRAVANET, Mme. B. de. See TRAVENET, Mme. B. de

TRAVASSOS LOPES, Maria de Lourdes Alves
Portuguese poetess and composer. b. Santa Maria Maior, 1924.

Compositions
CHAMBER
    Marches, fados
VOCAL
    Songs (composer)
OPERETTA
    Olha par isto (co-composer)
Ref. 268

TRAVENET (Travanet), Mme. B. de
18th-century French poetess and composer.
Compositions
VOCAL
    Two collections of romances and chansons with piano or harp accompaniment (Paris: Gerber, 1798)
Ref. 128, 226, 433

TREADWAY, Maude Valerie
20th-century American singer and composer. DISCOGRAPHY.
Compositions
VOCAL
    Five poems (Judith Brown) (m-S)

TREBICKA, Maria
20th-century Polish composer.
Composition
PIANO
    Suity elegijnej, op. 9
Ref. W. Pigla (Warsaw)

TREHERNE, Georgina. See WELDON, Georgina

TREMBLAY, Gertrude. See BAKER, Gertrude Tremblay

TREMBLOT DE LA CROIX, Francine
20th-century French composer.
Compositions
ORCHESTRA
    Concerto (org and orch)
CHAMBER
    Le tombeau de Goya, sur des thèmes de Tony Aubin (tr and pf) (Leduc, 1982)
Ref. MLA *Notes*, Otto Harrassowitz (Wiesbaden)

TRENT, Anthony. See CLARKE, Rebecca

TRETBAR, Helen
19th-century American writer and composer. b. Buffalo. She became known for her translations of texts of musical works.
Compositions
VOCAL
    Songs incl.:
    From youth's happy day
Publications
    Analytical works.
Ref. 226, 292, 347

TREVALSA, Joan
DISCOGRAPHY.
Composition
VOCAL
    My treasure, Victorian ballad
Ref. Ace of Diamonds Record Co.

TREW, Mrs. Charles A. See TREW, Susan

TREW, Susan (Mrs. Charles A.)
19th-century English pianist and composer.
Composition
CHAMBER
Sonata (vln and pf) (1893)
Ref. 6, 85, 347

TRICHT, Nora von
20th-century West German composer.
Composition
CHAMBER
Deux pièces (vlc and pf)
Ref. Frau und Musik

TRIMBLE, Joan
Irish concert pianist, professor and composer. b. Enniskillen, June 18, 1915. She gained her B.A. in 1936 and Mus.B. in 1937 from the Dublin University. She also studied at the Royal Irish Academy of Music in Dublin under Claud Biggs, Annie Lord, F. Grossi and J.F. Larchet and at the Royal College of Music, London, under Arthur Benjamin (piano) and Herbert Howells (composition), gaining her L.R.A.M. (piano performance) and A.R.C.M. She formed a piano duo with her sister Valerie in 1938 and they performed in the Wigmore Hall, Albert Hall, on radio and with many of the major orchestras. Joan was a professor at the Royal College of Music. She received the Sullivan prize of the Royal College of Music in 1939 and 1940; Dublin Feis Coeil composer's prizes in 1938, 1939 and 1940; Wesley Exhibition for improvisation; the Cobbett prize; Thomas Moore centenary prize, Radio Eireann, in 1952. PHOTOGRAPH.
Compositions
ORCHESTRA
In Glenade (str orch) (1942)
Suite (str orch) (1953)
BRASS BAND
Erin go bragh (1943)
CHAMBER
Phantasy trio (pf, vln and vlc) (1939)
Air for two Irish harps (1969)
The pool among the rushes (cl and pf) (1940)
PIANO
The bard of Lisgoole (2 pf duet)
Buttermilk point (2 pf) (1939)
The green bough (2 pf) (1941)
The humours of Carrick (2 pf) (1938)
Pastorale (2 pf) (1943)
Puck Fair (2 pf) (1951)
Sonatina (2 pf) (1941)
The cows are a-milking (1945)
VOCAL
The county Mayo (Bar and 2 pf) (1949)
Green rain (vce and pf) (1938)
The lamb, duet (1953)
The milkmaid, duet (1953)
My grief on the sea (vce and pf) (1937)
OPERA
Blind Raftery (1957)
FILM MUSIC
The Voice of Ulster
ARRANGEMENTS
The Coolin (vlc and pf) (1939)
Polka (2 pf duet) (1939)
La calinda (2 pf duet) (1947)
Gartan mother's lullaby (2 pf duet) (1949)
The heather glen (2 pf duet) (1949)
Jamaican rum (pf duet) (1953)
Ref. composer, 74, 77, 177

TRINITAS, Sister M.
20th-century American teacher and composer. b. Union City, IN. She composed choral works and songs.
Ref. 347

TRIPP, Ruth
20th-century American composer. She composed pieces for the flute and orchestra, choral pieces, operas, operettas and songs.
Ref. 40, 347

TRISTAN, Joyeuse
Compositions
VOCAL
Alhambra (vce and pf) (Milan: Ricordi)
Au Tsar, chanson russe (Ricordi)
Buona notte! (Shelley) (Ricordi)
Chanson du XIII siècle (vce and pf) (Ricordi)
Chanson de Marsa (vce and pf) (Ricordi)
Saint Blaise (vce and pf) (Ricordi)
Souhaits (vce and pf) (Ricordi)
Ref. Ricordi (Milan)

TROENDLE, Theodora
20th-century American violinist and composer. b. Chicago. She composed piano pieces.
Ref. 347, 353

TROMBONE, Giuseppina
20th-century Italian composer.
Composition
CHAMBER
Sei piccoli pezzi facili e progressivi (vln and pf)
Ref. 228

TROOSTWYCK, Hendrika
20th-century Dutch composer.
Composition
CHAMBER
Springtime (vln and pf)
Ref. 63

TROSCHKE UND ROSENWEHRT, Wilhelmine von, Baroness
Early 19th-century German composer of Silesia.
Compositions
VOCAL
Two collections of variations (Glogau, 1801)
Variationen ueber Tyroler sind lustig
Ref. 128

TROTT, Josephine
20th-century violinist, teacher and composer. She studied and taught in Berlin and Paris. She published study material for the violin.
Ref. 226

TROUP, Emily Josephine
English composer. d. 1912.
Compositions
CHAMBER
Sketches (vln and pf)
Piano pieces
VOCAL
Songs incl.:
Hark! the lark! (w-trio)
On a faded violet
Portuguese love song
Song by the river (w-trio)
Spring flowers
Ref. 6, 226, 276, 433

TROWBRIDGE, Leslie Eliot
19th-century English soprano and composer. She studied at the Royal Academy of Music and gave her first concert in 1883.
Compositions
VOCAL
Songs incl.:
My rose
Our love
SACRED
Mass in D
Ref. 6

TRUETTE, Everette
19th-century composer.
Compositions
ORGAN
Canon, op. 15 (Ditson)
Evening star (Wagner; Thompson)
Finale, op. 17 (Ditson)
Five interludes, op. 16 (Ditson)
Melody (Ditson)
Organ voluntaries collection
SACRED
Blessed be the Lord God (vce and pf) (Schmidt)
Ref. 297

TRUMAN, Irene
20th-century British concert pianist and composer. b. Nottingham. She is
an L.R.A.M. and A.T.C.L. and composed a choral prelude and songs.
Ref. 490

TS'AI, Yen
Chinese poetess, singer and composer. ca. 162 to 239. She was the daughter of the scholar and poet Ts'ai I. After being widowed, she was captured and taken North by the Huns. She bore two sons to a Hun chief and after 12 years was ransomed back to China, but her joy was mixed with grief at having to leave her sons. Her *Eighteen verses* describe war, the barbaric ways of the Huns and her immeasurable grief. She was the first Chinese poetess of whom there is any information.
Compositions
VOCAL
Eighteen verses (in the song she describes herself as singing to acc of lute and Tatar horn)
Ref. 464

TSCHETSCHULIN, Agnes
19th-century German composer.
Compositions
CHAMBER
Alla zingaresca (vln and pf)
Berceuse (vln and pf)
Violin pieces
VOCAL
Songs
Ref. 226, 276

TSCHIERSCHKY, Wilhelmine von
19th-century German composer of songs.
Ref. 226, 276

TSCHITSCHERIN, Theodosia de
19th-century Russian composer. Her *Grand festival march* was played at the 25th-anniversary of the coronation of Tsar Alexander II.
Composition
ORCHESTRA
Grand festival march (large orch)
Ref. 226, 276

TUCKER, Irene
Australian composer. b. 1920.
Compositions
BRASS BAND
Celebrating (Manly-by-the-Sea) march (1975)
Grand occasion – ceremonial march (1974)
VOCAL
Baci Ami (vce and orch) (1975)
Mau Piu (vce and small ens or orch) (1974)
Australia – with fanfare (med to large ch) (1970)
Christmas in the sunshine (vce or chil-ch) (1971) (Castle Music)
The happiest Christmas Day (vce or chil-ch) (1969) (Castle Music)
Little town of Hay (vce or small ch) (1959)
Mother's day, waltz song (solo vce or 2 vces and small ens) (1963)
THEATRE
Blue Heaven, musical (1949)
Luck's a Fortune, musical (1974)
Paradise Island, musical (1976)
Ref. 442, 440

TUCKER, Mary Jo
20th-century American composer. She composed choral pieces.
Ref. 40, 347

TUCKER, Tui St. George (Tu St. George Tucker)
American recorder player, conductor and composer. b. California, 1924.
Compositions
CHAMBER
String quartet (1956-1957)
Lift up your heads (ob, bsn and cl)
Ye mighty gates (ob, bsn and cl)
The bullfinch sonata (rec) (1960)
Violin sonata
PIANO
Little pieces for quarter-tone piano
Two sonatas
VOCAL
Drum taps, cantata (Bar) (1975)
Music for bass recorder (narr) (1972)
Choral works and songs
Ref. 142, 415, 465

TUCZEK, Felicia
20th-century Bohemian composer.
Composition
CHAMBER
String quartet in F-Minor (Steingraeber)
Ref. 297

TUICHEVA, Zumrad
20th-century Soviet composer of Uzbekistan. She studied under Boris Zeidman at the Tashkent Conservatory and continued postgraduate studies under him.
Compositions
ORCHESTRA
Overture
CHAMBER
String quartet
Aria with variations (vln and pf)
VOCAL
The voice of the heart, cycle (E. Vachidov) (vce and orch)
Ref. 420

TUMANIAN, Elizaveta Artashesovna
Soviet composer. b. Moscow, June 16, 1928. In 1955 she graduated with distinction from the Moscow University, having studied composition under N. Peiko.
Compositions
ORCHESTRA
Double fugue (1954)
Scherzo (1954)
CHAMBER
Piece for string quartet (1951)
String quartet (1953-1954)
Piece (vla and pf) (1948)
Variations (vln and pf) (1952)
PIANO
Variations on Russian Themes (1949)
Pieces (1950)
VOCAL
Fugue (ch a-cap)
Five romances (Burns) (1951-1954)
Russian folk songs (1950)
Songs (S. Marshak)
Ref. 87

TUMANISHVILI, Ketevana Dmitirevna
Soviet pianist, lecturer and composer. b. Tbilisi, August 31, 1919. She studied the piano at the Tbilisi Music School under K. Dzhaparadze, graduating in 1938. In 1943 she graduated from Tbilisi Conservatory, having studied the piano under V. Kuftina and A. Balanchivadze and composition under P. Ryazanov. In 1949 she completed postgraduate studies in composition at the Moscow Conservatory, where she was a pupil of V. Shebalin, D.B. Kabaevsky and then of Y. A. Shaporin. From 1943 to 1945 she lectured on theoretical subjects at the No. 3 Music School in Tbilisi and after 1949 at the Central Music School, becoming headmistress in 1952.

Compositions

ORCHESTRA

Gamzrdeli, poem (A. Tsereteli) (1943)

Piano concerto (1943, rev 1952)

Violin concerto (1948)

CHAMBER

Trio (1946)

Sonata (vla and pf) (1952)

Sonata (vlc and pf) (1949)

Sonata (vln and pf) (1944)

Other pieces (vln and pf)

PIANO

Etude (1950)

Kartinki pionerskogo lagera, children's suite (1955)

Preludes: 6 (1942); 2 (1944); 4 (1951)

Sonata

Zimnie kartiny, 4 children's pieces (Tbilisi: Muzfond, 1952)

VOCAL

Amirani, cantata (I. Evdoshvili) (1955)

Rodina vozhdya, cantata (soli, ch and orch) (1948)

Cycle of romances (R. Tavadze, I. Mosashvili and other Soviet poets)

Kogda zashumit vesna (V. Reimeris, trans from Lithuanian)

Molchu, molchu (A. Faizi, trans from Tatarian)

Nichego chto v moikh volosakh sedna (vce and pf)

Six romances incl. O, mir! (R. Tagore)

Tishe, serdtse (vce and pf) (1941)

Utro v Kolhide (I. Mosashvili, trans from Georgian)

V mire dvukh devushek net u tebya liubumykj (V. Luks, trans from Latvian) (1948)

Other songs

Ref. 87, 458

TUNISON, Louise

20th-century American composer.

Compositions

VOCAL

Songs incl.:

Dying rose

Good night

Next summer

Song of a heart

Ref. 276, 347, 433

TUORNABUONI (Tornabuoni), Lucrezia

Italian musician and composer. d. 1482. She married Piero Medici and was the mother of Lorenzo the Magnificent. She composed Christmas carols.

Ref. 264

TURGEON, Frances (Mrs. Daniel W. Wiggin)

American composer. b. Lewiston, ME, October 4, 1891. She studied at Bates, William Smith, Seneca, Geneva and New York Colleges and gained her B.A. She studied under Helen Winslow, Lyon, Lanphere, Elizabeth Quaille (q.v.) and Anne Neily (q.v.).

Compositions

CHAMBER

Three dances: Minuet; Gigue; Gavotte (vln, vla and pf)

PIANO

Gigue in E (or any key)

Arrangements of Chopin etude, op. 25, no. 8

VOCAL

Bonum omen (solo and m-ch)

Little hand of pioneers (composer) (mix-ch)

Songs incl.:

Applecumjockaby

Children's songs (Rossetti)

Five encore songs (Rossetti)

The horseman

House of dreams

I've never been to winkle (Vilda Owens)

Love (Charlotte Michaud)

Pierrot at fifty (Garrison)

Queen Anne's lace (Mary Newton)

Red geraniums (Elizabeth Dillingham)

Someone

Tartary

Who loves the rain?

SACRED

Alma Mater (Elizabeth Hawthorne, 1914)

Publications

Biographical Dictionary of Maine Composers. 1958.

Directory of Maine Composers. 1946.

Maine Composers and Their Music.

Thumbnail Sketches of Maine Composers. With Helen J. Dubbs. 1958.

Ref. 40, 347, 374

TURMAND, Eta Moiseyevna. See TYRMAND, Eta Moiseyevna

TURNELL, Margaret Hoberg

20th-century American organist, pianist and composer. b. Terre Haute, IN. She composed pieces for the harp, two vocal suites and songs.

Ref. 75, 347

TURNER, Eliza

British composer. d. 1756.

Compositions

HARPSICHORD

Giga

Minuetto

Savoyard

Tambourine

Ref. 473

TURNER, Elizabeth

18th-century English composer.

Compositions

VOCAL

At even ere the sun was set (vce and pf) (Abbott)

A collection of songs with symphonies and a thorough bass, with 6 lessons for hpcd (London, 1756)

To Celia (Forgive, thou fairest of thy kind) (London Magazine, 1750)

Two songs (Vincent)

SACRED

Benedicite, omnia oera (Abbott)

Christ is risen (Abbott)

God from on high hath heard (Abbott)

Great and marvellous (Abbott; Schirmer, Jr.)

Lord gave the word (Abbott)

Magnificat and Nunc dimittis (also in E-Flat) (Abbott)

O clap your hands together (Abbott; Schirmer)

O death where is thy sting? (vce and pf) (Abbott)

Praise the Lord (ch and cong) (Abbott)

Sun of my soul (mix-ch) (Abbott; Ditson; Schirmer)

Te Deum (Abbott)

Ref. 65, 91, 150, 297, 405

TURNER, Harriet

19th-century composer of songs and one song cycle.

Ref. 465

TURNER, Mary Elizabeth. See SALTER, Mary Elizabeth

TURNER, Mildred Cozzens (Mrs. Huntington) (alt. name Mrs. Huntington-Turner)

American pianist, authoress, conductor, singer, teacher and composer. b. Pueblo, CO, February 23, 1897. She graduated from the University of Wisconsin School of Music. She studied the piano under Francis Schwinger and later C. Overstreet and Emil Leibling. She was a public school supervisor in Mineral Point, WI. She conducted a boys' orchestra and sang with the Minneapolis Symphony Orchestra. Her extensive travels gave her the inspiration for her songs. DISCOGRAPHY. PHOTOGRAPH.

Compositions

VOCAL

Answer (1950)

Dalmation lullaby (also Gregorian chant) (1940)

Galaxy (1940)

Geisha (1940)

Hawaii calls at twilight

I'm the spell of the moon (1950)

I wish they didn't mean goodbye

My charro (1950)

Songs for amateur plays

Ref. composer, 39, 40, 142, 347, 563

TURNER, Myra Brooks

American choral conductor, lecturer, playwright and composer. b. Knoxville, January 13, 1936. She studied at the Juilliard School of Music, from 1947 to 1951 and obtained a B.Mus. in 1955 and M.Mus. in 1956 from the Southern Methodist University, Dallas. She served as music specialist in schools in Dallas from 1956 to 1960 and was musical director of choral music at Knoxville, from 1960 to 1964. She was composer-in-residence at Birmingham Children's Theatre in Alabama from 1967 to 1969. As lecturer and performing artist she was active in community services, clubs and musical organizations in Atlanta from 1973 and choir director with the St. Cecilia Choir and St. Martin-in-the-Fields Episcopalian Church from 1973. She was awarded several prizes, including first prize, 19th-National Playwriting Contest, Seattle, 1968; special music therapy award, Mu Phi Epsilon, 1972; special merit awards, National Federated Music Clubs, 1971 to 1973.

Compositions
PIANO
    Fantasy in A-Minor (1968)
    The jazz man suite (1968)
    Man speaks through music (1965)
    Praise the Lord Jesus Christ (1966)
VOCAL
    Choral works and songs
THEATRE
    Cinderella, musical drama (1966)
    Flibberty-gibbet, musical drama (1966)
    The Green Dragon, musical drama (1965)
    Javoho Junction, musical drama (1959)
    Mid-Summer-Night's Dream, musical drama (1965)
    Pinocchio, musical drama (1965)

Publications
    Contributions to *The Metronome* and *The Triangle*.
Ref. 84, 142, 475

TURNER, Olive Mary

English operatic singer and composer. b. New Barnet, 1894. She studied at the Royal Academy of Music, where her teachers were Professors Agnes Larkcom, Cuthbert Whitemore and Frederick Corder. For two years she was prima donna of the D'Oyley Carte Opera Company. She was a medallist of the Worshipful Company of Musicians and received the Betzemann gold medal for opera.

Compositions
PIANO
    Cap and bells, humouresque (2 pf) (OUP, 1937)
    Cornish sketches: The pottery wheel: Sea shanty (2 pf) (OUP, 1937)
    Five preludes
    Teaching pieces
VOCAL
    Songs incl.:
    The Christmas minstrel
    Cradle song of the coast
    The dawn
    Life is like a song
    The visitor
    Ballads
INCIDENTAL MUSIC
    Cinema background music
Ref. 467

TURNER, Sara Scott

Canadian percussionist, lecturer and composer. b. 1926. She obtained her B.Mus. from the University of Louisville in 1948 and was named outstanding student of the year. The summer of 1945 she spent at the Juilliard School of Music, where she studied percussion under Saul Goodman. She did post graduate study at the Peabody College for Teachers, studied composition under Lennox Berkeley and at the Berkshire Music Center studied orchestral work under Leonard Bernstein and choral work under Robert Shaw. She lectured at various colleges and universities.

Compositions
CHAMBER
    Crab canon (fl, cl, vln, vlc and interposed pf fugue)
    String quartet (1980)
    Variations bn a canon (str qrt) (1946)
    Piece for brass (1948)
VOCAL
    Early Tudor lyrics (mix-ch) (1950)
    Rounds (mix-ch and rec) (1979)
    Canadian folk songs (vce and rec) (1980)
    Thy fingers make early flowers of all things (2 S and A) (1947)
    Two pieces (narr, pf, vla and perc) (1976)
Ref. composer

TURNER-MALEY, Florence

American music critic, singer, teacher and composer. b. Jersey City, NJ, August 23, 1871; d. Point Pleasant, NJ, January 3, 1962. She was a pupil of Jacques Bouhy, Oscar Saenger, Joseffy, G. Becker, Alberta Lawrence, Mme. Marchesia and Joseph Barnaby. She also studied at the University of Geneva and made her debut at Carnegie Hall in 1898. She appeared as guest soloist with the New York Symphony and the Cincinnati Orchestra and as soloist at the Church of the Pilgrims in Brooklyn and the Brick Presbyterian Church in New York. She also performed with oratorio societies. She taught privately.

Compositions
CHAMBER
    Piano pieces
VOCAL
    Songs incl.:
    The fields of Ballyclare
    I see him everywhere
    In a garden wild
    In a little town near by
    Lass o'mine
    Light at evening time
    Long and long ago
    Song of sunshine
    Songs for children incl.:
    Jingly ringly rhymes
    Just for children
    Some songs to play
    Some songs to sing
    Songs for kindergarten
    Ten tiny songs of fantasy
    Choral pieces
Ref. 39, 226, 292, 347

TURNEY, Ruthyn

American violinist, teacher and composer. b. Luray, MO, September 11, 1867. She was a pupil of August Aamold. She composed a violin concerto and pieces for the violin and other instruments.
Ref. 226

TURRIETTA, Cheryl Renee

American flautist, pianist, lecturer and composer. b. November 6, 1956. She gained her B.A. (composition and theory) and M.M. (composition and theory). From 1976 to 1982 she was a private piano teacher and then on the faculty of performing and fine arts at the University of Portland, teaching computer and electronic music, counterpoint and orchestration. She specializes in the composition of computer and electronic music.

Compositions
BAND
    Accents (concert band) (1980)
CHAMBER
    Notes (fl, cl, vln and vlc) (1977)
    String quartet (1979)
    String trio (1975)
    Duet on a row (vln and vlc) (1979)
VOCAL
    Four sonnets (E. Browning) (vces, pf, vla and perc) (1979-1980)
ELECTRONIC
    Allusion (ch, loudspeakers and tape delay) (1975)
    Building blocks and icicles (tape) (1983)
    Friendly fog monster (tape) (1982)
    Duet for piano and tape (1981)
    Electronic studies (untitled) (tape) (1975, 1976, 1978)
    To the nightingale (recitor and tape) (1982)
MULTIMEDIA
    Artists' musician (slides and tape) (1982)
Publications
    Articles in *Music Educators' Journal*; *T.M.E. Journal*; *Technological Horizons in Education*; *Apple Journal of Courseware Review*; *Association for Educational Data Systems Proceedings*. All 1983.
Ref. composer

TURTYGINA, Pava Grigorevna

Soviet pianist and composer. b. Gomel, Russia, December 26, 1902. From 1915 to 1919 she studied the piano at the Yekaterinoslav Music School and from 1921 to 1922 at the Gnesina Music School, where she was a pupil of the founder. From 1938 to 1940 she attended classes at the Moscow Conservatory. She worked as a pianist.

Compositions
VOCAL
Krasnoflotskaya (Y. Rodionov) (Muzgiz, 1941)
Pod znamenem slavy (A. Kovalenkov) (1937)
Pokhodnaya komsomolskaya (I. Molchanov) (Muzgiz, 1934)
Songs
Ref. 87

TUSSENBROEK, Hendrika van
Dutch pianist, teacher and composer. b. Utrecht, December 2, 1854; d. Utrecht, June 22, 1935. She was a pupil of Richard Hol and Johan Wagenaar. She taught singing and the piano in Amsterdam and was best known for her music for children.
Compositions
VOCAL
Choral works (Utrecht: Wagenaar) incl.:
Een oud sprookje, op. 20 (chil-ch and pf)
Twee fabels van De la Fontaine, op. 34, nos. 1 and 3 (w-ch and pf)
Duets
Children's songs
OPERA
Miniature operas
THEATRE
Music
Ref. 26, 44, 70, 105, 226, 276

TUTTLE, Thelma Kent
American pianist, lecturer and composer. b. Milwaukee, IA, September 30, 1902. She received her M.Mus. from the American Conservatory of Music, Chicago in 1928 and then commenced post-graduate work at the Juilliard School of Music. She taught the piano at Drake University, Des Moines from 1956 to 1966 and privately in the same city. She received an honorable mention for her *Moods* in the centennial competition.
Compositions
PIANO
Nocturne (duet or solo) (1962)
Umbrella in the wind (duet or solo) (1957, 1955)
Fog horn warning (1952)
Shadows in the lagoon (1951)
Sleepy bugler (1954)
Tower chimes (1957)
Moods (1964) (J. Fischer)
Teaching pieces
Ref. 206

TUXEN, Elisabeth
20th-century Danish composer.
Compositions
VOCAL
Frem paa marsch (vce and pf)
Maj-sangen (Mads Nielsen) (vce and pf)
Ref. 331

TUY
Egyptian songstress of the Min dynasty, 1320 to 1200 B.C. A wooden statue of her is in the Louvre, Paris.
Ref. 428

TWOMBLY, Mary Lynn
American pianist, conductor and composer. b. New York, January 8, 1935. She studied under Meyer Kupferman at Sarah Lawrence College from 1952 to 1954, under Vittorio Giannini at Manhattan School of Music from 1954 to 1958 and electronic music under Elias Tannenbaum from 1971 to 1972. She was composer and conductor for films and records at Weston Woods Children's Library from 1966 to 1967 and participated in workshops at Fairleigh Dickinson University in 1973. She received commissions from the Little Orchestra Society in 1960 and obtained the Harold Bauer piano award in 1957.
Compositions
ORCHESTRA
Symphonic statements (pf and str orch)
VOCAL
Songs of Christmas (1964)
SACRED
The Eternal Word (S, T, narr, mix-ch and orch)

OPERETTA
The Little Match Girl (chil-ch) (1964)
Who are the Blind (1969)
BALLET
Alice in Wonderland (opt narr) (1960)
Ref. 142, 280

TWOREK, Wandy
Danish concert violinist and composer. b. Copenhagen, June 25, 1913. She made her violin debut at the age of six and appeared in concert, on radio and television all around the world. She composed concert works, songs and modern music.
Publications
My Life.
Violin Method.
Ref. 643

TWYMAN, Grace
American composer.
Compositions
VOCAL
Little west wind (Boston Music, 1918)
SACRED
God save our men (w-vces and pf) (Boston Music)
Ref. 190

TYER, Norma Phyllis
Australian composer. b. Sydney, 1928. She studied at the Sydney Conservatory and graduated from the Sydney University in the history of art.
Compositions
ORCHESTRA
Fantasie on a theme of Bach
Franz Josef: Impressions of a glacier (1971)
CHAMBER
String quartet
VOCAL
The canticle of the rose (soli, ch and pf)
The new sunrise (soli, ch and pf)
Spring, the sunset spring (ch a-cap)
SACRED
Kyrie eleison (A, ch and orch)
Fragments: Corpus Christi pageants (15th-cent) (ch a-cap) (Chappell & Co., 1961)
Missa brevis: Kyrie; Sanctus; Hosanna; Benedictus; Agnes Dei (soli and ch a-cap) (1967)
Ref. 280, 440

TYRELL, Agnes
Austrian pianist and composer. b. Bruenn, September 20, 1846; d. Bruenn, April 18, 1883. She studied theory under Otto Kitzler. In Vienna she studied the piano under Professor Pacher. Poor health prevented her touring. Her piano compositions were highly praised by Liszt.
Compositions
ORCHESTRA
Symphony
Piano concerto
Three overtures
Smaller works
CHAMBER
Pieces
PIANO
Fantasias
Mazurka
Twelve etudes, op. 48 (ded Liszt)
Two nocturnes
Other pieces
VOCAL
Over 100 songs
SACRED
Die Koenige Israels, oratorio
OPERA
Bertram de Born
Ref. 74, 105, 129, 226, 276, 433

TYRMAND, Eta Moiseyevna
Soviet pianist, concert mistress, lecturer and composer. b. Warsaw, February 23, 1917. In 1938 she graduated from the choral faculty of the Warsaw Conservatory, where she studied under S. Kazuro. She then went to

the Minsk Conservatory, graduating in the piano in 1949, after studying under G. Shershevsky. She studied composition under A. Bogatyrev in 1952. After 1949 she lectured in the piano at the same Conservatory. During World War II she taught and was choreographer and concertmistress of the opera in Frunze, Kirghiz SSR. DISCOGRAPHY.
Compositions
ORCHESTRA
Piano concerto (1952)
CHAMBER
Poem (vln and pf)
Sonata (vln and pf) (1950)
Cycle of pieces (pf)
VOCAL
Partia vedet Kommunism, cantata (1951)
Words (M. Bogdanovich) (ch a-cap)
Cycle (G. Lorca) (vce and pf)
Ref. 87, 420, 563

TYSON, Mildred Lund (Mrs. Harold Canfield)
American organist, pianist, conductor, lecturer and composer. b. Moline, IL, October 3, 1900. She studied under Carl Beecher at Northwestern University, where she obtained a B.Mus. and at Columbia University. She taught the piano and voice at Pomona College and was an organist and choir conductor in Sidney, NY. DISCOGRAPHY.
Compositions
VOCAL
Songs incl.:
Lilacs are in bloom (w-ch and pf) (G. Schirmer, 1934)
May in Japan (w-ch and pf) (F. Fischer, 1934)
One little cloud (w-ch and pf) (Schirmer, 1936)
Sea moods (mix-ch and pf) (Schirmer, 1936)
The great divide (vce and pf) (Schirmer, 1938)
Like barley bending
Noon and night (vce and pf) (Schirmer, 1939)
Ref. 142, 228, 563, 622

UBAIDA (Ubayda, Obeidet)
Arabian tunbur player and songstress. ca. 830. Ubaida learned to play the tunbur with Al-Zubaidi al-Tunburi, who stayed at her father's house. The tunbur (pandora) was a skin-bellied stringed instrument and Ubaida was considered the best tunbur player of her time. Ishaq al-Mausuli, the greatest musician and theorist of Islam up to this time, said of her *In the art of tunbur playing, anyone who seeks to go beyond Ubaida makes mere noise.* She became a public singer after her parents' death, was bought by Ali ibn al-Faraj al-Zajhi and had a daughter by him. Her virtuosity as an instrumentalist was universally acknowledged and Masdud, the most celebrated tunbur player at the time, refused to play in competition with her. Her tunbur was given to her by the son of the Caliph Al-Mamun and was inscribed 'In love one can endure almost anything except faithlessness'. But Ubaida was true only to her art; she had many lovers, who spent vast sums on gifts for her.
Ref. 171, 234

UBAYADA. See UBAIDA

UCCELLI, Carolina (nee Pazzini)
Italian composer. b. Florence, 1810; d. Florence or Paris, 1855. She was an amateur musician from a noble family in Florence and in 1845 went to Paris with her young singer daughter Giulia and they both toured, giving concerts in Belgium, Holland and Switzerland.
Compositions
OPERA
Emma (Anna) Resburgo (G. Rossi) (1835)
Eufemio di Messina (1833)
Saul (1830)
Ref. 26, 105, 108, 129, 225, 226, 268, 276, 307, 431, 502

UCHENDU, Nellie Uchendu Edith
Nigerian singer and composer. b. Uwani-Enugu, July 3, 1953. She studied music in school, attended the School of Agriculture and became a principal cultural officer, Ministry of Information and Social Welfare, Unugu. She sang with several choirs including the Nigerian Festac Choir in 1977 and on television and radio. She obtained seven first class certificates from the 1966 Nigerian Festival of Arts, two first class certificates from the 1974 Enugu Festival of Arts, a national honours award of Member of the Order

of the Niger in 1979 and a Solidra Circle Oscar award of excellence in in 1983 and a diploma from IBC, England, 1984. She contributes articles to several magazines and newspapers. DISCOGRAPHY. PHOTOGRAPH.
Compositions
ORCHESTRA
Aka bu eze (1978)
Chukwu nyelu m onu (1978)
Ezigbo dim (folk music) (1982)
Green eagles (1981)
Hossanah (1980)
Love nwantinti (1977)
Mama-ausa (1978)
Nwa bialy ije (1978)
Ogadili gi nma (1982)
Okwu di nlo (1978)
Oma bu nwunye m (1978)
Yegheyeghe (1982)
Ref. composer, 643

UGALDE, Delphine Beauce (Mme. Valcollier)
French pianist, singer, teacher and composer. b. Paris, December 3, 1829; d. July, 1910. She was the granddaughter of the guitarist Porro and studied mainly under him and her mother, who was also an excellent musician. From the age of six Delphine played the piano and at the age of nine gave lessons. When she was 11 she performed in concert with distinguished artists at La Salle Herz. As a result of that performance she was engaged to sing solos at the meetings of the Society of Classical Singing. It was there that she received her practical instruction. She also studied under Damoreau Cinti (q.v.). Following her debut at the Opera-Comique in 1848 she enjoyed a brilliant career at the Theatre-Lyrique till 1858, when she supervised the Bouffes-Parisien and triumphed in the operettas of Offenbach and Serpette, including *Le songe d'une nuit d'été.* She taught pupils as eminent as Marie Sass and her own daughter Marguerite. She married the musician Ugalde.
Compositions
PIANO
Bebe, gavotte (Enoch)
Paillette d'or, polka (Enoch)
Two polkas brillantes (Heugel)
VOCAL
L'élève de saint (vce and pf) (Enoch)
Femme honnête (vce and pf) (Enoch)
On d'mande une institutrice (vce and pf) (Enoch)
Pauvre bergère (vce and pf) (Legouix)
Sabots (vce and pf) (Sulzbach)
Trottinette, valse chantee (vce and pf) (Enoch)
SACRED
Ave Maria in D (Lebeau)
OPERA
Halte au Moulin, comic opera (Bornemann)
OPERETTA
Le Page de Stella (Paris, 1895)
Seule, à un seul personnage (Noel)
Ref. 26, 85, 105, 225, 297, 394

UIES (Uies-Gruetzner), Margret
20th-century German composer.
Compositions
CHAMBER
Melodiespiel auf der Altblockfloete; 17 Uebungen in melodischer Folge (Wilhelmshaven; Noetzel, 1978)
Ref. Otto Harrassowitz (Wiesbaden)

UIES-GRUETZNER, Margret. See UIES, Margaret

UKELELE LADY. See BREEN, May Singhi

ULAYYA
8th-century Arabian songstress. She was the daughter of Maknuna (q.v.), a slave songstress whom al-Mahdi bought for 100,000 dirhem and Caliph al-Mahdi (775 to 785) and half-sister of the later Caliph Harun al-Rashid and Ibrahim ibn al-Mahdi. The latter was a talented musician who became leader of the Persian romantic music movement in opposition to the classical conservative school of Ibrahim and Ishaq al-Mausuli. Harun took great interest in the musical education of his younger half-brother and half-lsister and encouraged them to perform with the court musicians.

Ulayya inherited her mother's talent and beauty, but was religious and abstemious and passed her time praying, studying and writing. Many of her songs were sung by Oraib (q.v.) and other songstresses.
Ref. 171, 234

ULEHLA (Ulehlova), Ludmila

American professor and composer of Czech origin. b. New York, May 20, 1923. The daughter of the violinist Joza Ulehla, Ludmila received her B.Mus. in 1946 and M.Mus. in 1947 from the Manhattan School of Music, where Giannini was one of her teachers. She began composing when she was eight and at 15 composed a piano quintet. She received numerous ASCAP awards and several commissions. She taught composition, theory and analysis at the Manhattan School from 1947, becoming chairlady of composition in 1981. She was made a professor at the Hoff-Barthelson Music School, Scarsdale in 1968. DISCOGRAPHY.

Compositions
ORCHESTRA
    Five over twelve (also pf) (New York: General Music)
    Michelangelo, tone portrait (1971)
    Suite
CHAMBER
    Piano quintet (1938)
    Contrasts and interludes for string quartet (1979)
    La muse naisante, parody (hpcd) (1971)
    Pieces inspired by Slovak folk themes
PIANO
    Slovak phantasy
    Songs without words (General Music)
    Variations on a theme of bach (General Music)
VOCAL
    Sonnets from Shakespeare (vce and cham orch) (1951)
    Gargoyles (S, pf and bsn)
    Time is a cunning thief (vce and pf)
ELECTRONIC
    Elegy for a whale (fls and taped whale calls)
Publications
    Contemporary Harmony: Romanticism Through the Twelve-Tone Row. New York: Free Press, 1966.
Ref. 40, 142, 197, 563, 622, 625

ULEHLOVA, Ludmila. See ULEHLA, Ludmila

ULRICHSEN, Ingeborg

20th-century Danish composer.
Composition
CHAMBER
    Vaarblomster, mazurka (pf)
Ref. 331

UMM AL-HIRAM

11th-century Arabian poetess and composer of Spain. She composed women's verses and love songs.
Ref. 476

UNA DONNA DE GASCOINA. See ALAMANDA

UNDERWOOD, Frances Evangeline

South African pianist, teacher and composer. b. Natal, 1890. She studied under Adolphe Wouters at the Brussels Conservatory and taught music in schools in South Africa, 1910 to 1919, before opening her own music school, teaching the piano, singing, elocution and composition. She composed a string quartet, solos for the piano and the violin and songs.
Ref. 490

UNGHER-SABATIER, Caroline

Austrian contralto and composer. b. Stuhlweissenburg, October 28, 1803; d. Florence, March 23, 1871. She was a pupil of Aloysia Lange, sister of Mozart's wife and of Johann Michael Vogel, Schubert's favorite interpreter. She was chosen by Beethoven to sing in the premieres of his *Ninth symphony* and *Missa solemnis*. She sang in over a hundred operas: Belli-

ni, Donizetti, Mercadante and Pacini wrote operas for her and Rossini was one of her ardent admirers. She married Francois Sabatier, a French art historian who translated into French many of the German poets whose works she set to music.
Compositions
VOCAL
    Songs incl.:
    Ballade
    Canzonette
    Frauenliebe
    Ich danke dein
    Je suis a toi
    Klage nicht
    Lieder, melodies et stornelli, album of 46 songs
    Der Maedchen Friedenslieder
    Naehe des Geliebten
    Nocturno
    Sehnsucht
    Staendchen
    Stornello fiorentino
    Stornello toscano
    Wanderspruch
Ref. 246, 297, 433

UNSCHULD, Marie von

Austrian concert pianist, violinist and composer. b. Olmutz, May 17, 1881. She studied the piano under Leschetizky and Stavenhagen at the Vienna Conservatory, the violin under Dont and composition and counterpoint under Graedner. She toured Europe as a pianist and in 1904 established the von Unschuld University of Music, Washington, DC. She composed for the piano.
Publications
    Art of and Means for Pianoforte Instruction. 1915.
    The Graded Course. 1912.
    The Hand of the Pianist. 1901.
    The Handbook of General Musical Knowledge. 1915.
    The Scale Practice. 1910.
Ref. 433

UNTERSTEINER, Antonietta (nee Gambara)

Italian pianist and composer. b. Constantinople, Turkey, 1846; d. Milan, May 27, 1896. She studied at the Milan Conservatory from 1874 to 1876 and graduated with a prize.
Compositions
ORCHESTRA
    Dio e Satana, symphonic poem (also 2 pf) (Ricordi)
VOCAL
    Songs and romances (French and Italian)
THEATRE
    Sul Baltico, melodramatic fantasy
Ref. 105

UPTON, Anne

20th-century American authoress and composer. b. Marble City, AR. She was a student at the Fred Palmer Institute and a radio writer and producer. She is a member of ASCAP.
Compositions
ORCHESTRA
    Cattle at eventide, symphonic poem
VOCAL
    Remember the four (J.F. Kennedy memorial)
SACRED
    Children emancipate, oratorio
    Life of Jesus, cantata
OPERA
    Book of Ruth
Ref. 39

URAIB. See ORAIB

URBANYI-KRASNODEBSKA, Zofia Jadwiga

Polish pianist, conductor, lecturer and composer. b. Bydgoszcz, March 18, 1936. She studied the piano at school and then studied composition, theory, operatic and orchestral conducting at Warsaw High School of Music (B.A.) in 1961. She held choral and orchestral conducting posts and conducted at the Great Theatre, Warsaw and the State Opera House, Wroclaw and lectured at the Academy of Music, Wroclaw, from 1980.

Composition
SACRED
The pilgrim, chorale hymn (C.K. Norwid) (ch) (1983)
Ref. 643

URGEL, Louise. See ADDENDUM

URNER, Catherine Murphy
American lecturer, linguist, soprano and composer. b. Mitchell, IN, March 23, 1891; d. San Diego, April 30, 1942. She studied at the Peabody Institute of Music and then the University of California. She won the George Ladd Prix de Paris, which enabled her to study composition under Koechlin in Paris from 1920 to 1921; she later collaborated with him. She was director of vocal music at Mills College from 1921 to 1914 and then a singer in the United States, France and Italy. She researched into American Indian tribal melodies, using their characteristics in her compositions. She married the composer Charles Shatto.
Compositions
ORCHESTRA
Flute concerto (1940)
The bride of a god, symphonic poem
Elegy (1921)
Esquisses normandes (1929)
The partheneia (1916)
Prologue
Three movements for chamber orchestra (1940)
CHAMBER
Chant funèbre (str sextet) (1920)
Suite (str qrt and fl) (1929)
Quartet (strs)
Quartet in A-Minor (strs)
Quartet in C-Sharp Minor (strs)
Quartet in E-Minor (strs)
Quartet in G-Sharp Minor (strs) (1926)
Sonatine (fl, vla, vlc and hp or pf; also vlc and pf) (1932)
Sonata (2 vln and pf)
Trio in B-Flat or A (fl and 2 cl; also str trio; also fl, cl and vlc) (1932)
Trio in B-Minor (pf, vln and vlc)
Trio in D-Minor (strs) (1929, rev 1931)
Adagio in A (cl and pf)
Allegretto (fl and pf) (1929)
Chant (vlc and pf) (1926)
Choral and fugue (pf and org)
Etude chromatique in B-flat, or A (cl and pf)
Jubilee suite (fl and pf) (1931)
Lamento (vla and pf) (1930)
Petit suite (fl and vla; also fl, vln, vla and vlc; also hpcd or hp and fl) (1929, 1930, 1932)
Sonata in C (vln and pf) (1942)
Sonata in C-Major (vln and pf) (1942)
Sonata in C-Sharp Minor (vln and pf) (1939)
Sonata in E-Minor (vln and pf)
Valse sentimental (pf and fl obb) (1932)
Comme une berceuse
ORGAN
Adagio sostenuto (1929)
Allegretto scherzando (1938)
Andante moderato
Barcarolle (1932)
Chant pour la Toussaint (1929)
Choral-lento molto espressivo
Choral-molto lento
Choral in D-Minor
Deux fugues (1931)
Fourteen hymns
Fugue in D-Minor (1937)
Fugue in E-Flat minor
Fugue in G
Fugue in G-Minor (1937)
Grave
Impromptu in E-Flat (1941)
Litany (1939)
Madonna's lullaby
Nocturne
Pastorale
Prayer (with Charles Shatto)
Quasi adagio (1930)
Suite for children
Three holiday chorals
Two chorals in A-Minor (1933)
Two traditional Indian songs (1978)
Versets (1930)
PIANO
Sonata Noel (2 or 1 pf)
Adagio (1930)

Andante quasi adagio (1937)
L'attente
Carcassone
Choral pour Noël (1932) (also org)
Chorals for C.R.S. (1938)
Crossing Arizona Sands (1929)
Fantasie-etudes
Four sketches, La Jolla
Four songs (1930)
From a car window in France, 6 sketches
Fughetta
Hymn for Mother's birthday (1933)
Images, 6 sketches on Richard Aldington's poetry (1926)
Prelude (1932)
Preludes
Seven short preludes (1930)
Soir
Suite for children
Tendrement à un Ami (1930)
Three chorals
Three songs
Two nocturnes
Two short pieces
Western suite
Woodland reveries
Yaltah-danseuse orientale
VOCAL
The mystic trumpeter, cantata (mix-ch and trp)
Rhapsody of Airmairgin of the golden knee (B, mix-ch and orch) (1936)
Over 100 songs incl.:
After parting (Sarah Teasdale)
Come away death (Shakespeare)
Dusk at sea (Thomas Jones, Jr.)
Four melodies (S and pf) (Paris: M. Senart, 1928)
The lake isle of Innisfree (Yeats)
Music I heard with you (C. Aiken)
Nichts ist dauernd (Ludwig Boerne)
Song from April (I. Rutherford McLeod)
Song from fruit gathering (Rabindranath Tagore) (vce, fl and pf)
Sonnet (M. Meagher)
OPERETTA
Anoemone, in 2 acts (I.S. Churchman) (chil-soli, chil-ch and pf)
Pan (C. van Lerberghe) (incomplete)
The Sun Pilgrim (English trans of French novel) (incomplete)
ARRANGEMENTS
Numerous arrangements of works by J.S. Bach, Faure, Mendelssohn, Franck and others
Bibliography
Kirk, Elise Kuhl. *The Chamber Music of Charles Koechlin*. Ph.D. Dissertation. Catholic University of America. 1977. Block/Neuls-Bates.
Kirk, Elise Kuhl. *A Parisian in America: The Lectures and Legacies of Charles Koechlin*. Current Musicology, 25, 1978, 50-60.
Ref. University of California Music Library, 226, 228, 477

URRETA, Alicia
Mexican electronic instrumentalist, pianist, conductor, lecturer and composer. b. Veracruz, October 12, 1935; d. December 18/19, 1986. From 1948 to 1954 she studied the piano under Joaquin Amparan. At the National Conservatory of Music, Mexico, she studied harmony under R. Halffter and chamber music under Sandor Roth. She made her debut as a concert pianist in 1957. She studied electronic music under Jean-Etienne at the electronic studio of the RTF, Paris. She founded the Camerata de Mexico and taught chamber music at the music academy of the National Autonomous University of Mexico and electronic music at the Polytechnic Institute of that University.
Compositions
ORCHESTRA
Piano concerto
Rallenti
CHAMBER
Homage (str qrt)
Estudio I and II (gtr)
Salmodia I and II (pf)
BALLET
Cubos
Luiz negra
Mujer flor
OPERA
Romance de Dona Balada, chamber opera (1972)
ELECTRONIC
Un dia de Luis, ballet, collage
De natura mortis, i verdadera historia de Caperucita roja (vces, insts and tapes) (1972)
Music concrete for No-theatre and films
Tantra, ballet (music concrete)

FILM MUSIC
    Several films
Ref. MLA *Notes*, 17, 70, 94, 109

USHER, Ethel Watson

20th-century concert accompanist, organist and composer. b. Gorham. She studied under Mary G. Jordan in Portland, Leopold Godowsky in Berlin, Heinrich Gebhard in Boston, Frank La-Farge in New York and Leon Rothier. She accompanied and toured with many leading concert artists. She was organist and musical director of several American churches.
Compositions
VOCAL
    Group of three songs (Oliver Herford) (1915)
    The Panaesthesa or Birth of the senses, song cycle (Dr. Frank Miller) (7 solos) (1915)
SACRED
    Lullaby (1916)
Ref. 374

USHER, Julia

English flautist, pianist, lecturer and composer. b. Oxford, July 21, 1945. She studied composition under Richard Orton in her final year at Neunham College, Cambridge and then completed her postgraduate teaching certificate in 1968, studying composition under Robert Sherlaw-Johnson. She taught music in schools and lectured at the Philippa Fawcett College until 1971, when she gave her full time to composition. She received several commissions. In 1980, with Enid Luff (q.v.), she formed the music publishing company Primavera. PHOTOGRAPH.
Compositions
ORCHESTRA
    The bridge (1980)
    Gordale Scar (youth orch) (1974)
    De revolutionibus (cham orch) (1975)
    An ocean of light (str orch) (London: Primavera, 1980)
    Peace offering (str orch) (London: Primavera, 1980)
CHAMBER
    Burning bush (cham ens) (1976)
    RAI (10 wind insts)
    The waste remains (vln, vla, vlc, d-b, perc and wind qnt) (Primavera 1984)
    The angel standing in the sun (brass qnt) (Primavera, 1985)
    Encounter (cl qnt) (1973)
    Secret gatherings (fl and viols) (1979)
    L'isole dela laguna (rec and pf) (Primavera, 1984)
    Ode to the west wind (trp and pf) (1980)
    Subsequent darkness (cl and pf) (1981)
    Venezia, 6 sketches (tba and pf) (Primavera, 1984)
    Exits and entrances (d-b) (1977)
    Pentimento (pf) (1979)
    A reed in the wind (ob) (1980) (prize, Wangford Festival) (1980)
    Riddle music (cl) (1977)
FLUTE
    Asolando (1975)
    Byzantine mosaics (1968)
    Constellations
VOCAL
    Dust life (T and cham orch) (1974)
    Hey mister butterfly (chil-vces and orch)
    Phoenix (T and cham orch) (1967)
    Dance for the sun-rising (mix-ch, brass, ww and strs) (1976-1977)
    Ordnance survey: 7 poems (T, fl, cl, vla and vlc) (Primavera, 1980)
    Rites of transition (S, A, T and B) (comm David Johnson)
    Due canti (T and ens) (1970)
    Sacred physic (vce and ens) (Primavera, 1980)
    The causeway (S, trp and str trio) (Primavera, 1984)
    Aquarelles (A, fl and picc) (Primavera, 1980)
    A chess piece (S and 3 cl) (1980)
    Ruin (T and pf) (1977)
    Tell me where is fancy bred, jazz song (vce and pf)
INCIDENTAL MUSIC
    Tempest, for children
Ref. composer, *Composer* (London)

USTVOLSKAYA, Galina Ivanovna

Soviet lecturer and composer. b. Petrograd, June 17, 1919. She studied at the Leningrad Arts School from 1937 to 1939, before entering the conservatory, graduating in 1947 after studying composition under Dmitri Shostakovich and Maximilian Steinberg and in 1947, Rimsky-Korsakov. She continued postgraduate studies under Shostakovich until 1950. From 1948 she taught composition at the music school of the same university. DISCOGRAPHY.

Compositions
ORCHESTRA
    Concerto in G-Minor (pf and orch)
    Piano concerto (1947)
    Podvig geroya, symphonic poem (1957)
    Children's suite (1955)
    Ogni v stepi (1958)
    Pioneer suite (1951)
    Second symphony (cham orch)
    Simfonietta (1951)
    Sportivnaya suite (1958)
    Three suites (1948, 1950, 1952)
CHAMBER
    Composition (8 ob, perc and pf) (1973)
    Octet (4 vln, 2 ob, pf and tim) (1951)
    Composition (fl, 4 bsn and pf) (1975)
    Composition (fl, tba and pf) (1971)
    String quartet (1945)
    Trio (vln, cl and pf) (1949)
    Duet (vln and pf)
    Grand duo (vln and pf) (1959)
    Sonata (vln and pf) (1947)
    Sonatina (vln and pf) (1947)
PIANO
    Three sonatas (1948, 1950, 1952)
    Twenty preludes
VOCAL
    Dawn over the Fatherland (N. Gleisarov) (chil-ch and orch) (1952)
    The dream of Stenka Razin (B and orch) (1948)
    Hail, youth (V. Lebedev-Kumach) (ch and orch) (1950)
    The man from the high mountain (N. Gleisarov) (soloist, ch and orch) (1952)
    Symphony (2 boy S and orch; also vce, perc, pf and wind insts) (1955, rev 1964)
FILM MUSIC
    Boldinsky Autumn (orch) (1951)
    Gogol (1954)
    Mordvin Autonomous Soviet Socialist Republic (1952)
    Russian Museums (1954)
Bibliography
Gojowy, Detlef. *Symposion: Unbekannte neue musik bei der Zagreber Biennale '77*. Mf XXX/4. 1977. 515-16.
Ref. 4, 5, 17, 22, 81, 87, 94, 223, 330, 419, 420, 563, 622

UTTER, Betty

20th-century American composer.
Composition
THEATRE
    Heidi, musical (composer)
Ref. 518

UYEDA, Leslie (pseud. Charles Brown)

American flautist, pianist, singer and composer. b. Lancaster, PA, September, 1962. She attended the Conestoga Valley High School and studied the piano and composition privately under Dr. Mary Bainbridge Vyner (q.v.). She received many prizes from the state and National Federation of Music Clubs, for piano performance and composition.
Compositions
ORCHESTRA
    Quinderni, toccata
    Vitamente
CHAMBER
    String quartet
    Valley forge revolutionary suite (fl and vlc)
    Sonata for violin
PIANO
    Chasing my shadow
    The grasshopper
    March for Chesapeake (also orch) (1st prize, junior composers' contest)
    Piacere, sonata
    Remember 1776
    The Orc's caper
Ref. *Music Clubs Magazine* summer 1979

UYTTENHOVE, Yolande

Belgian concert pianist, lecturer and composer. b. Leuze, July 25, 1925. She received her early musical training from her mother and first played the piano in public at the age of four. She studied at the Royal Conservatory in Brussels, where she obtained first prizes in the piano, chamber music, solfege, harmony (Martin Lunssens prize), counterpoint, fugue and music history. She studied under Henry Sarly, Jean Absil, Marcel Poot and Eduardo del Pueyo. Her studies culminated in a higher diploma in chamber music and she is an L.R.A.M. for performance, awarded in 1953. She performed in concert throughout Europe, frequently appearing with her flautist husband René De Macq. She taught the piano at the Academy of Music, Brussels and then became headmistress of the Academy of Music, Braine-'Alleud. She holds an honorary diploma from the International Competition of Pianists in Barcelona. In 1950 she was honored with the bronze medal from the Acedemy of Arts, Sciences and Literature in Paris. Her compositions have been broadcast over the radio in Europe. DISCOGRAPHY.

Compositions
ORCHESTRA
Concertino (trb and orch) (1963)
Violin concerto, op. 102 (1982)
Symphoniette, op. 101 (chil-orch) (1982)
CHAMBER
Three pieces, op. 106 (cl ens) (1983)
Trio (trp, 4 kettledrums and pf) (1965)
Quatuor pour harpes chromatiques (1958)
Le cygne d'or, op. 107 (2 fl) (1984)
Duo for clarinet in B, op. 85 (1979)
Elègie for cello and piano, op. 86 (1979)
Meditation and fantasy for flute and piano, op. 88 (1979)
Le pâtre et son étoile (fl and pf) (1969)
Sonata, op. 94 (fl and hpcd) (1969)
Sonata, op. 95 (vln and pf; also fl and pf) (1980)
Suite pour deux harpes chromatiques (1959)
For two girls and two boys, op. 89 (rec) (1979)
Improvisation (cl) (1974)
Petit histoire (fl) (1971)
La petite fille d'autrefois (hp) (1974)
Pièce (hn)
Pièce triste (trp) (Maurer, 1962)
Prélude and allegro, op. 90 (bsn) (1979)
Romance à l'étoile (fl) (1968)
Sonatine, op. 105 (hpcd) (1982)
Triptyque (fl) (1969)
PIANO
La chanson d'autrefois (6 hands) (1971)
Rochemaure, teaching piece (6 hands) (1971)
Cendrillon, op. 93 (4 hands) (1980)
Berceuse (1958)
Chiffres et poèsie (1961)
Diner à Cajarc (Maurer, 1967)
Fables de la Fontaine (1970)
Interlude (1967)
Le jardin de Beau-Minet (Maurer, 1974)
Leçon de solfege (1973)
Methode de piano (Maurer, 1964)
Petite maman de bonheur (1959)
Petite toccata (1959)
Le sire du Lusigny (Maurer, 1967)
Sonatine (Maurer, 1962)
Toccata miniature (1967)
VOCAL
Levé-toi mon amie, op. 100 (S and 4 fl) (1981)
Seizoenkrans, op. 108 (4 vces) (1983)
Three incantations, op. 102 (S, fl, pf, cl and vlc) (1982)
A elle me suis donne (Jehan de la Fontaine) (vce and pf) (1970)
Campanule (1959)
Cancale (A. Lepage) (vce and pf) (Maurer, 1967)
Rejouis-toi, Marie, op. 98 (1981)
Retour (A. Lepage) (vce and pf) (Maurer, 1967)
SACRED
Psalm 120 (solo and ch) (1970)
Psalm 46 (solo and 2 fl) (1968)
Salve Regina, op. 99 (3 vces and org) (1981)
INCIDENTAL MUSIC
Receuils de dictées atonales (1966)
Ref. composer, 77, 188, 359, 643

UZEINZADZE, Adilea
20th-century Soviet composer of Azerbaijan. Her compositions were influenced by the folk music of that region.
Compositions
ORCHESTRA
Symphonic poem (ded heroes of labor)
VOCAL
Vetenin, cycle (Vurgun, Raghim and other Azerbaijanian poets) (vce and orch)
OPERA
One opera on Azerbaijanian folklore
Ref. 223

VACCARO, Judith Lynne
American operatic soprano, lecturer and composer. b. Downey, CA. She obtained a B.A. (music) from California State University in 1967; a certificate from the International Opera Studio, Zurich in 1969 and studied at the Academy of Performing Arts, Vienna, under Erik Werba, 1970 to 1971. She was a soloist at the Zurich Opera House in 1968; at the City of Angels Opera from 1973 to 1975 and Las Vegas Chamber Players, 1974 to 1976. Her operatic roles included that of Suzanne in *Secret of Suzanne* and Marcelena and Cherubino in *Marriage of Figaro*. She taught singing privately, at the University of Nevada and then became vocal coach for Disneyland and Disney World.
Compositions
VOCAL
Dr. Nuwine's travelling show (ch)
SACRED
Ceremony of the Advent wreath (ch)
MISCELLANEOUS
Jeremy's wizard tale
Sam's emporium (Willis Music, 1982)
Ref. 625

VAKHVAKHISHVILI, Tamara Nikolayevna
Soviet pianist, lecturer and composer. b. Warsaw, December 23. 1893. She studied at the music school in Tbilisi. From 1912 to 1916 she studied the piano under N. Nikolayev and from 1917 to 1921, composition under F. Hartmann. In 1927 she graduated from the Paris Conservatoire, having studied composition under P. Vidal. From 1921 to 1923 she was director of the Tbilisi music school and head of the music department of the S. Rustaveli Theatre from 1922 to 1926 and the K. Mardzhanishvili Theatre from 1928 to 1933, when she moved to Moscow. In 1940 she was awarded the title of Honored Artist of the Georgian Soviet Socialist Republic.
Compositions
ORCHESTRA
Concerto (vln and orch)
Dance suite
March of the heroes
Symphonic etude (1930)
VOCAL
Cantata (B. Bronevsky and N. Tikhonov) (soloist, ch and sym orch)
Citation from S. Rustaveli, cycle (Russian trans K. Balmont) (soloist and sym orch) (1938)
Georgian folk ballad (orator and sym orch) (1928)
BALLET
The festival of Bacchus (1919)
The herb of love (1920)
Spartacus (1937)
THEATRE
Don Khil, musical comedy (1924)
Iranian pantomime (1914)
Khandzari, pantomime (1949)
Mzeta-Mze, pantomime (1949)
Ref. 87

VALADON, Giovanna Emma. See THERESA

VALCOLLIER, Mme. See UGALDE, Delphine Beauce

VALDES, Marta
Cuban guitarist and composer. b. Havana, July 6, 1934. She studied philosophy and literature at the University of Havana. She studied harmony and composition under Harold Gramatges and was a pupil of Francisqueta Vallalta, Guyun and Leopoldina Nunez. She was the vice-president of the Cuban Society of Composers and performed on radio and television and in cabaret.
Compositions
VOCAL
Songs incl.:
Cancion de la plaza vieja
En la imaginacion
No es preciso
Si vuelves
Tu dominas
Tu no sospechas
INCIDENTAL MUSIC
Music for theatre incl.:
El becerro de oro
El perro del hortelano
Et alma buena de Se-Shuan

La casa de Bernarda Alba
Pasado a la criolla
Music for films incl.:
Desarraigo
Lucia
Ref. 604

VALDES, Sylvia Soublette de. See SOUBLETTE, Sylvia

VALGAY, Devisme de. See DEVISME, Jeanne-Hippolite Moyroud

VALENTINE, Ann
English organist and composer. b. Leicester, ca. 1762. d. Leicester, October 13, 1842. The daughter of John Valentine, a prominent musician in their home town, she became organist at St. Margaret's church.
Composition
CHAMBER
Ten sonatas, op. 1 (pf or hpcd with vln or German fl)
ARRANGEMENTS
Monny Musk (Scottish air) (rondo for pf) (London: Cahusac & Sons, ca. 1798)
Ref. Dr. Karl Kroeger (University of Colorado), 6, 65, 226, 276, 335, 433

VALERO, Matilde
19th-century Spanish pianist and composer.
Compositions
PIANO
Pieces incl.:
Las orillas del seña
Ref. 389

VALGRAND, Clemence. See GRANDVAL, Maire Felicie

VALKYRIE OF THE PIANO. See CARRENO, Teresa

VAMOS, Grace Becker
20th-century American composer.
Compositions
ORCHESTRA
Fantasy concerto (pf and str orch) (1951)
MISCELLANEOUS
Gypsy
Legend of the redwoods
Ref. 280

VAN AARDT, Madelene (nee Olivier)
South African teacher and composer. b. Graaff Reinet, Cape Province, August 14, 1896. She lived in Somerset-East.
Compositions
PIANO
Fusion (1935)
VOCAL
Heimwee (Justus Latsky) (Johannesburg: Voortrekkerpers, 1945)
I'll be waiting (Mary Astor) (Voortrekkerpers, 1944)
I wonder why (composer) (Cape Town: Felix de Cola)
Onthou jy nog? (J. Latsky) (Felix de Cola, 1935)
Ref. 184

VAN ALSTYNE, Mrs. Frances Jane. See CROSBY, Fannie

VAN APPLEDORN, Mary Jeanne
American pianist, professor and composer. b. Holland, MI, October 2, 1927. She obtained her B.Mus. (piano) in 1948. She studied composition under Bernard Rogers and Alan Hovhaness at the Eastman School of Music, where she received an M.Mus. (theory) in 1950 and a Ph.D., 1966.

She received the Delta Kappa Gamma international scholarship from 1958 to 1960 and was voted one of the three most outstanding Texan women composers in 1971. In 1973 she was designated a member of the Texas Composers' Hall of Fame, with manuscripts entered in the archives of the Dallas public library. She won awards in Mu Phi Epsilon composition contests and from 1967 was professor and chairlady of graduate studies in music and chairlady and founder of the annual symposium of contemporary music at Texas Technical University, 1950 to 1975. She studied computer-synthesized sound techniques at the Massachusetts Institute of Technology for a short period and in 1982 received a Texas Technical University development award. DISCOGRAPHY.
Compositions
ORCHESTRA
Piano concerto (1954)
Trumpet concerto (1961)
Passacaglia and chorale (1973)
SYMPHONIC BAND
Concerto for trumpet and band (Carl Fischer)
CHAMBER
Liquid gold (sax and pf) (1982) (Dorn Publ.)
Matrices (sax and pf) (1979) (Dorn)
A celestial clockwork (carillon)
Sonnet (org)
Passacaglia (1959)
PIANO
Contrasts (1948)
Eight pieces, for children (1972)
Fort Davis salute (1978)
Nine pieces (Charles Scribner & Sons, 1972)
Scenes from Pecos Country (C. Fischer, 1975)
Set of five (1953) (OUP, 1975)
Sun devils (1978)
Three pieces (1971)
VOCAL
West Texas suite (chil-ch and wind orch) (1975)
Peter Quince at the clavier (narr, w-ch, fl, ob, hn and pf) (1959)
Azaleas (Bar, fl, a-fl and pf)
Communique, song cycle (S and pf)
SACRED
Rising night after night, cantata (narr, mix-ch and orch) (1977)
Darest thou now, O soul (solo, w-ch and org) (1975)
MISCELLANEOUS
Cacophony
Lux: Legend of Sankta Lucia
Publications
Functional Piano for the College Student.
In Quest of the Roman Numeral.
Keyboard: Singing and Dictation Manual. 1968.
A Stylistic Study of Claude Debussy's Opera 'Pelleas and Melisande'. 1965.
Ref. composer, 137, 347, 563, 622, 625

VAN BARENTZEN, Aline Isabelle. See HOYLE, Aline Isabelle

VAN BUREN, Alicia Keisker
American composer. b. Louisville, March 5, 1860. d. April 11, 1922.
Compositions
CHAMBER
String quartet (Breitkopf & Haertel)
VOCAL
Songs incl.:
Afar (Breitkopf)
Book of songs (1896) (Breitkopf)
Constancy (Breitkopf)
Five songs (1900) (Breitkopf)
June song (Breitkopf)
Six songs (1909)
Ref. 276, 292, 433

VAN DE VATE, Nancy Hayes (pseuds. Helen and William Huntley)
American pianist, professor and composer. b. Plainfield, NJ, December 30, 1930. She studied the piano at the Eastman School of Music from 1948 to 1949 and received her A.B. from the Wellesley College, 1952. She also studied the piano under Bruce Simonds of Yale University in 1954, composition under Arthur Kreutz from 1956 to 1958 and John Boda, 1963 to 1964 and 1967 to 1968. At the University of Mississippi she received a M.Mus. in 1958, then a Mus.D. from Florida State University, 1968. During the summer of 1972 she pursued study at the Electronic Music Institute at Dartmouth College and the University of New Hampshire. She was a private

piano teacher from 1957 to 1963; lecturer at the University of Mississippi in 1960; assistant professor at Memphis State University from 1964 to 1966; lecturer at the University of Tennessee in 1967 and associate professor at Knoxville College, 1968 to 1969. She was a lecturer at Maryville College from 1973 to 1974. As visiting professor she taught in the music department of the University of Hawaii in 1975, from 1977 to 1978 she lectured in music at Hawaii Loa College and from 1978 to 1980 was associate professor of music. She founded the League of Women Composers in 1975. She was commissioned to compose a number of works. Honors awarded to her included: Rochester prize scholarship and George Eastman scholarship at Eastman School; election as Composer of the Year, Knoxville Music Teachers' Association; Presser scholarship from 1949 to 1952; grant from the French Government for special study in French from 1950 to 1952; Wellesley College scholar; ASCAP awards from 1973 to 1975; Delius award for brass quintet in 1975; residence awards at Yaddo and Ossabaw Island (GA) Project and 3rd prize, Stowe composition competition, 1975 and a National Endowment for the Arts composer fellowship to write orchestral works, 1987 to 1988. She affiliated with BMI in 1982. She received four awards from Meet the Composer. She spent several years in Jakarta, Indonesia and now lives in Vienna. DISCOGRAPHY. PHOTOGRAPH.

Compositions
ORCHESTRA
Piano concerto (1968)
Journeys (large orch) (1984)
Distant Worlds (1985)
Dark nebulae (large orch) (1981)
Adagio (1957)
Concert piece for cello and small orchestra (1978)
Gema jawa (str orch) (1984)
Variations for chamber orchestra (1959)
CHAMBER
Three sound pieces for brass and percussion (2 trp, 2 hn, 2 trb, tba and 6 perc) (1973)
Music for quintet (fl, vln, d-b, cl, vlc or pf) (1975) (1st prize, Los Alamos chamber music competition, 1979)
Quintet for brass (2 trp, hn, trb and tba) (1974, rev 1979)
Diversion for brass (hn, 2 trp and trb) (1964)
Short suite for brass quartet (2 trb and 2 trp) (1960)
String quartet No. 1 (1969)
Student string quartet (1977)
Woodwind quartet (1964)
Incidental piece for three saxes (1976)
Music for viola, percussion and piano (1976)
String trio (1974)
Trio for bassoon, percussion and piano (1980)
Trio for violin, cello and piano (1983)
Lento (ob and pf) (1969)
Sarabande (fl and pf) (1974)
Sonata (ob and pf) (1970)
Sonata (vla and pf) (1964)
Three sound pieces (brass and perc) (1973)
Variations (cl and pf)
Fantasy for harpsichord (1982)
Six etudes (vla) (1969)
Six etudes (vln) (1979)
Sonata for harpsichord (1982)
Suite for viola (1975)
Suite for violin (1975)
PIANO
Contrast (2 pf)
Encore (1981)
Bicycle ride (as Helen Huntley) (Buffalo: Montgomery Music)
Hoe-down (as Helen Huntley) (Willis Music)
Mississippi (as Helen Huntley) (Montgomery)
Nine preludes (1974-1978) (New York: North/South Consonance)
Second sonata
Sonata (1978) (Arsis Press)
Syncopated soldier (as Helen Huntley) (Montgomery)
Topsy turvy (as Helen Huntley) (Montgomery)
Twilight (1962)
VOCAL
Cantata for women's voices (w-ch and ens) (1979)
An American essay (mix-ch, pf and perc) (1972)
The pond (mix-ch) (1970)
Cradlesong (C. Brentano) (m-S and pf) (1962)
Death is the chilly night (m-S and pf) (1962)
Five somber songs (m-S and pf) (1970)
How fares the night (w-ch and pf) (Montgomery, 1977)
Letter to a friend's loneliness (S and str qrt) (1976)
Lo-yang
Songs for the four parts of the night (vce and pf) (1983)
To the east and to the west (high vce) (1972)
Youthful age (m-S and pf) (1960)
SACRED
Make a joyful noise unto the Lord (as William Huntley)
Psalm 121 (mix-ch) (1960)

OPERA
The Death of the Hired Man, chamber opera (R. Frost) (m-S, T and pf) (1960)
In the Shadow of the Glen, chamber opera (J.M. Synge) (S, 2 T, Bar and pf) (1960)
THEATRE
A Night in the Royal Ontario Museum (S and tape) (1983)
ELECTRONIC
Invention I (magnetic tape) (1973)
Invention II (magnetic tape) (1973)
MISCELLANEOUS
Sound Piece III
Publications
Women in Music: The Second Stage. Vol. 1, No. 1. Newsletter of the International Congress of Women in Music.
Articles to various music journals.
Ref. composer, 68, 77, 80, 94, 137, 142, 146, 185, 206, 347, 415, 454, 474, 563, 622, 624, 625

VAN DEN BEEMT, Hedda
American composer. b. Dordrecht, Netherlands, October 31, 1880; d. Philadelphia, February 15, 1925.
Composition
ORCHESTRA
Aucassin and Nicolette, introduction and shepherd scene, from an opera based on 13th-century French legend (1913)
Ref. 322

VAN DEN BOORN-COCLET, Henriette
Belgian professor and composer. b. Liège, January 15, 1866; d. Liège, March 6, 1945. She studied at the Liège Conservatory under J.T. Radoux and Sylvan Dupuis. In 1895 she won the Prix de Rome for her *Callirrhoe* and in 1907 her *Sonata for piano and violin* won a prize in Paris. Her compositions attracted considerable attention in Paris and Brussels. She became a professor of solfege and harmony at the Liège Conservatory.
Compositions
ORCHESTRA
Andante symphonique (1909)
Renouveau, symphonic poem (1913)
Symphonie Wallonne (1928)
CHAMBER
Serenade (vlc and pf)
Sonata for violin and piano in D-Minor (Brussels: Breitkopf & Haertel) (prize, Paris, 1907)
PIANO
Caprice
Mazurka
Twelve melodies (also vce)
Vers l'infini, tarantella
VOCAL
Callirrhoe, cantata (1895)
Ref. 22, 41, 100

VAN DEN BRANDELER, Henriette. See BRANDELER, Henriette van den

VAN DEN HEEVER, Catharina Maria. See KRUGER, Catherina Maria

VAN DER MARK, Maria (nee de Jong)
South African librettist and composer. b. Rotterdam, Netherlands, August 12, 1912. She commenced her musical studies at the age of six at the Toonkunst Muziekschool in Rotterdam. She emigrated to South Africa in 1935 and studied composition at the University of the Witwatersrand, Johannesburg, under Dr. K. van Oostveen, 1959 to 1968. She wrote words and music for many songs which were used for music therapy with epileptic patients. PHOTOGRAPH.
Compositions
CHAMBER
A suite (fl, cl and bsn) (1968)
Technique (fl, cl and bsn) (1967)
Seven inventions (2 vln) (1966)
Ten tone poems (fl and pf) (1969)
PIANO
Aangebed
Geertjie gans
Little suite, 7 pieces (1966)
Marionet

Meester mong
Die nuwe more
Op my fluitjie
Sonatine
Songolslos
VOCAL
Maryna (ch)
My bosveldduifie (ch)
Bosveld liedjies, 11 songs
Bruilofswals
Dender-liedeken (E. Hiel)
Ek hoor... (N.P. van Wyk Louw)
Engel aarselde (Albe)
Gees van die vuur (1966)
In die warm, beskutte koringvelde
In the park
In the Tsitsikama mountains (1980)
Journey (Carl Kirchner)
Klossie, jy bewe en bibber (1980)
Kriekie, jy wat op die solder sanik (1980)
Langs die stroompie in die berge (vce and gtr)
Nagliedjie (van Wyk Louw)
Nagrit (van Wyk Louw)
Ons is die geest wat dwaal (van Wyk Louw)
Die ossewaens ry deur die land
Reenvoel (vce and gtr)
Rooidag (van Wyk Louw)
Soos 'n borrelende vink sy hart verlos (1980)
Soos 'n kers se vlam brand daardie boom se top
Tussen al die klawers, 6 songs
Vogeltjie uit morgenrood (J.L. den Belcher)
Waarmee, lief (van Wyk Louw)
Wanneer ek eens groot Ben (P. van Duyse)
Wat kan ek vir jou gee (van Wyk Louw)
Wintersong
Yskoud is dit in die Lande
Zorgen en zegen (Rene de Clerq)
SACRED
O stralende lig, Christmas cantata
Paaskantate, cantata (soli, mix-ch and pf)
Star of heaven, Christmas cantata (vce and pf)
Die wonders, cantata (soli, mix-ch and pf)
Motet (New Testament) (4 vces and cor anglais) (1968)
OPERA
Volund, in 1 act (1968)
OPERETTA
Diepwater se hoek (1959)
Hanepoot en muskadel (1967)
Lente caprice, song and dance play (1956)
Publications
Fourteen little songs. Cape Town: Studio Holland.
With Open Eyes.
Ref. composer, SAMRO, 295, 377

VAN DIJCK, Beatrice Madeleine
Dutch teacher and composer. b. Soerabaja, Indonesia, August 9, 1930. She studied music and movement for five years at the Rotterdam Conservatory, gaining the first official certificate for teaching this subject in Holland. She taught music and movement in schools and institutes for 15 years, when an accident ended her teaching career. From 1982 to 1983 her composition teacher was Jan van Dijck. She then devoted her time to composing and studied at the Dalcroze School, Geneva. PHOTOGRAPH.
Compositions
ORCHESTRA
Petit poème symphonique (1983)
Petit sérénade pour cordes (str orch) (1983)
Symphonietta (1983)
CHAMBER
Little dance-music for 6 string instuments (1983)
First clarinet quartet (1982)
First saxophone quartet (1983)
First string quartet (1982)
Poème (pf, fl and vlc) (1983)
Duet for flutes (1983)
Duet for saxophones (1983)
Bagatelle *at fantasy* (pf and fl) (1982)
Adagio and allegretto (pf and sax) (1983)
PIANO
Adagio (1983)
Autumn-thoughts (1983)
Early birds (1983)
Little suite (1982)
Petit souvenir musicale (1983)

Romance (1982)
Three meditations, with poems (1983)
Twelve miniatures (1982)
VOCAL
An orchestra (vce and orch)
Ref. composer

VAN EPEN-DE GROOT, Else Antonia (pseud. Derek Laren)
Dutch pianist, conductor, teacher and composer. b. Amsterdam, December 19, 1919. The daughter of Hugo de Groot, conductor, composer and singer, she showed musical talent early in life but studied to be a medical analyst. In 1942 she turned again to music and studied composition at the Hilversum Music Lyceum under Hugo Godron and Jacques Beers. She studied instrumentation under her father and passed the state examination in the piano and theory. For a short time she taught and played the piano in ballet schools but soon found composition took up all her time. She conducted her own works on several occasions. DISCOGRAPHY.
Compositions
ORCHESTRA
Suite for mouth organ and orchestra (1970)
Episodes from the bible (vol 1 and 2)
Jacqueline waltz (1961) (Chappel)
De klop op de deur
CHAMBER
Music for a historical era (ens) (as Derek Laren)
Woodwind quintet (1945)
Trio for flute, viola and guitar (1956)
VOCAL
Een dag uit het leven van .... (2 soli, ch and orch) (1969)
In lichte laaie (soli, ch and orch) (1964)
Van vrijers and vrijsters (ch and orch) (1963)
BALLET
Music for ballets
THEATRE
Music for musicals and cabaret
Music for plays: Alkestis; Oedipus; Faust
INCIDENTAL MUSIC
Het huis, waltz theme for film
Other music for television and films (as Derek Laren) (London: de Wolfe Music Library)
Approx 150 radio plays
MISCELLANEOUS
Arrangements of folk music
Music for children
Ref. composer, 563

VAN ETTEN, Jane (Mrs. Alfred Andrews)
Early 20th-century American operatic singer and composer. b. St. Paul, MN. She studied under Signor Grecco in New York and Matilde Marschesi and Sbriglia in Paris. Later she continued her studies under Randegger in London and studied composition under Bernard Ziehn and Alexander von Fielitz. She toured Europe as an opera singer and her works were performed in the western United States. In 1926 she was awarded the David Bispham medal by the American Opera Society of Chicago for *Guido Ferranti*.
Compositions
VOCAL
Songs:
Come with me (Ricordi)
O thou fairest among women (Ricordi)
Rise up, my love (Ricordi)
Stir not up nor awake, my love (Ricordi)
SACRED
The Song of Solomon (Ricordi)
OPERA
Guido Ferranti (lib from the Duchess of Padua, Oscar Wilde; adapted Elsie Wilbor)
Ref. 141, 226, 292, 304, 347, 415

VAN EYE, Thelma. See BUTT, Thelma

VAN HAUTE, Anna-Maria (Mieke)
Belgian concert pianist, conductor, lecturer and composer. b. Kortrijk, June 28, 1948. She studied the piano and theory at the Royal Conservatory of Brussels and in Amiens. She was a composition pupil of Tony Aubin, Victor Legley and Roland Coryn. At the conservatory she won first prizes for the piano, counterpoint, fugue and harmony. She studied conducting under P. Dervaux in Paris and Quebec. She teaches the piano and har-

mony and is director of the Ecole Communale de Musique d'Heverlée and of the Academie de Musique d'Izegem. She performed as a concert pianist in Belgium, France, Spain, Hungary and Canada and as a conductor in France.

Compositions
ORCHESTRA
Sinfonietta for strings, op. 4
CHAMBER
Visions, op. 8 (sax sextet)
Preludes, op. 3 (wind qnt)
Lucioles, op. 8 (sax qrt)
Theme and variations, op. 3 (str qrt)
Pantomines, op. 9 (fl and pf) (Maurer)
Intermezzi voor winderkind, op. 10 (cl)
Prelude, op. 6 (gtr)
ORGAN
Espaces I, op. 7
Espaces II, op. 7
Sonata, op. 2
Thème avec variations, op. 7
Toccata, op. 2
PIANO
Empreintes, op. 9 (Andel)
Il mattachione, op. 1 (Maurer)
Menuet, op. 1 (Maurer)
Preludes op. 1 (Maurer)
Sonatine, op. 1 (Maurer)
VOCAL
Fantasie weg fantasie, op. 11 (chil-ch and orch)
Lieder: De gierzwaluwen; Antwoorde aan een vriend (Guido Gezelle) (3 part ch)
Lieder: Ma mère est tombée; J'ai mal (A. Werfel) (A)
Ref. Belgium Music Info. Center

VAN KATWIJK, Viola Edna Beck
American pianist, lecturer and composer. b. Denison, TX, February 26, 1894. She studied composition and the piano under Percy Grainger and the piano under Richard Burmeister in Berlin. She made her debut with the St. Louis Symphony in Dallas. She served on the piano faculty at the Southern Methodist University, 1922 to 1955. She won first prizes in Mu Phi Epsilon national contests in 1928 and 1930 and two first places in San Antonio Club piano composition contests.

Compositions
PIANO
Pieces incl.:
Dusk on a Texas prairie
Gamelan
The jester
VOCAL
Songs incl.:
My terrace (1930)
Winter valley (1930)
Ref. 142

VAN NESTE, Rosane Micheline Lucie Charlotte
Belgian concert pianist, teacher and composer. b. Kortrijk, August 21, 1911. She studied at the Royal Conservatory, Brussels, where her composition teacher was Joseph Jongen. She won first prizes for harmony and the piano in 1927, counterpoint and practical harmony in 1928 and fugue in 1930, the violin in 1935 and song, 1938. She also won first prize for the piano from the Royal Conservatory, Antwerp, 1938. PHOTOGRAPH.

Compositions
ORCHESTRA
Orchestration, op. 21: Introduction; Allegro; Carlo Van Neste (vln and orch)
Suite pour orchestra sur des thèmes gregoriens, op. 2:
Prèlude; Interlude; Scherzo (1930)
CHAMBER
L'art de l'archet (vln and pf) (Metropolis Antwerp)
Serenade (vln and pf) (1930)
Suite breve, op. 1: Nostalgie; Tendresse; Badinage (vln and pf) (1930)
Two pieces (vlc and pf) (1930)
Realisation basse chiffrée, op. 20
Tartini variations
ORGAN
Gregoriana I, op. 16, 12 preludes (1930)
Gregoriana II, op. 17, 12 preludes (1930)
PIANO
Arlequin, op. 6 (1930)
Concertstudie, op. 3 (1930)
Cortège chinois, op. 7 (1930)
Fox-trot, op. 4 (1930)

Pictures for Guino, op. 22, 14 easy pieces (1980) (Metropolis)
Preludes, op. 18
Preludes, op. 19
Sonatine, op. 23: Burleske; Wiegelied; Scherzo (1981)
Valse-caprice, op. 5 (1930)
VOCAL
Cantique, op. 11 (S and org) (1930)
Gy badt of Enen Berg, op. 14 (B and pf) (1930)
Lied, op. 12 (S and pf) (1930)
Lieder van Moeder, op. 15 (S and pf) (1930)
Menuet, op. 10 (S and pf) (1930)
Prière, op. 13 (S and pf) (1930)
Ref. composer

VAN OHLEN, Deborah
American composer. b. Seattle, September 19, 1955. She studied under David P. Robbins, James Eversole, Hale Smith and Jane Brockman. She received her B.Mus. from the Pacific Lutheran University in 1977 and M.Mus. from the University of Connecticut in 1980.

Compositions
ORCHESTRA
Of all things most yielding (1978)
CHAMBER
October country (6 perc and hpcd) (1976)
Brass septet (trps, trbs and hns) (1976)
Bestekar quartet (strs) (1976)
Littoral (fl, cl, ob and bsn) (1980)
Piece for string quartet in two sections (1980)
Soft rain (euph and 2 perc) (1978)
Facets and nuances (fl and cl) (1978)
Papillon (d-b and pf) (1978)
Nocturnes (vlc) (1980)
PIANO
Crystals (1979)
Mobius (1978)
VOCAL
Five songs (S and pf)
Variations on an ending (m-S, T, Bar, a-fl, cor anglais, hpcd and perc) (1978)
OPERA
A Prayer, chamber opera (1981)
ELECTRONIC
The sky was candy xuminous (cl, ob and tape) (1976)
Ref. composer, 625

VAN SOLDT, Suzanna
17th-century composer. DISCOGRAPHY.
Compositions
VIRGINAL
Almande
Almande brun smeedelin
Almande d'amour
Almande de la nonnette
Almande prynce
De France galliard
Ref. Arion Records

VAN TUYLL VAN SEROOSKEREN, Isabella. See CHARRIERE, Isabella Agneta Elisabeth de

VAN TWINKLE, Kate. See VANNAH, Kate

VAN VLIET, Pearl H.
20th-century American pianist and composer. b. Cedar Rapids, IA. She composed chamber music and songs.
Ref. 347

VAN ZUYLEN, Belle. See CHARRIERE, Isabella Agneta Elisabeth de

VANDEN HEUVEL, Countess Marie. See MELY, Marie

VANDENBURGH, Mildred
20th-century composer.
Composition
ORCHESTRA
Carlsbad caverns, suite (1966)
Ref. 280

VANDERPOEL, Kate
19th-century American composer.
Compositions
VOCAL
Songs incl.:
Cradle song
Please smile
Where love is
Ref. 276, 292, 347

VANDEVERE, J. Lilien
20th-century American teacher and composer of piano pieces.
Ref. 93, 94

VANE, Florence
19th-century American composer.
Composition
VOCAL
Are we almost there? (vce and pf) (Boston: O. Ditson, 1845)
Ref. 228

VANIER, Jeannine
Canadian organist, lecturer and composer. b. Laval, Quebec, August 1, 1929. She commenced her musical studies at the Nazareth Institute for the Blind and then gained her B.Mus. at the University of Montreal, studying composition under Jean Papineau-Couture and Clermont Pepin, history and orchestration under Jean Vallerand and the organ under Conrad Letendre, Françoise Aubut and Georges Lindsay. She was the organist at St. Paul-de-la-Croix Church from 1952 to 1974 and taught theory and the organ at the Nazareth Institute, 1955 to 1970. In 1967 she returned to Montreal University, teaching ear training and keyboard harmony. She won second prize in the Casavant Organ Society competition in 1948. DISCOGRAPHY.
Compositions
CHAMBER
Fantasia for recorder trio (1962) (CAMMAC prize)
Cinq pièces pour enfants (pf) (Sarah Fischer scholarship)
SACRED
Salve Regina (ch and orch)
Ref. CMC, Catalog of Chamber Music 1967, 93, 94, 485, 631

VANNAH, Kate (pseud. Kate van Twinkle)
American organist, pianist, poetess, writer and composer. b. Gardiner, ME, October 27, 1855; d. October 11, 1933. She played the organ and the piano, showing a creative ability from an early age. She was a pupil of Professor Eversmann, Ernest Perabo and George W. Marston. She obtained her doctorate from St. Joseph's College, Emmittsburg, M.D.
Compositions
ORCHESTRA
Small pieces
PIANO
Sunbeam polka
Sweetheart's march
VOCAL
Songs incl.:
At sea
Come back to me
Cradle song
Eily
Goodbye sweet day (L.H. Ross, 1891)
Gray rocks and grayer seas
Mary O
My bairnie
Oh night unforgotten
Sunset
SACRED
Ave Maria
Singing in God's acre
Tears of Christ

OPERETTA
Heligoland (Elinore Bartlett)
Publications
Hit or Miss Papers.
From Heart to Heart. Poetry. 1897
Verses. Poetry. 1833.
Newspaper articles.
Ref. 40, 276, 292, 347, 353, 374, 433, 622

VANTOURA, Suzanne Haik. See HAIK-VANTOURA, Suzanne

VANZO, Vittoria Maria
Italian conductor, teacher and composer. b. Padua, April 29, 1862. She studied at the Conservatory of Milan and was one of the leading conductors of Wagnerian music in Italy. She composed pieces for the violin and cello, the piano and songs.
Ref. 226

VARAPRADA. See LOPAMUDRA

VARGAS, Eva
20th-century German composer. DISCOGRAPHY.
Compositions
VOCAL
Von zeit zu zeit (vce and gtr)
Wenn Gott es will (vce and gtr)
Ref. 563

VARISI, Giulia
16th-century Italian composer. She composed madrigals and motets for salons in Milan.
Ref. 502

VASCONCELOS, Maria Regina Quintanilha de
Portuguese pianist, journalist and composer. b. Lisbon, 1930. She gave her first public recital at the age of four years. At the age of six she commenced studies under Elisa Sousa Pedrosa. A later concert tour of Brazil led the newspapers of that country to call her the 'Queen of the Keyboard' and the Brazilian government to offer to sponsor her musical studies; an offer which she declined, in order to return to Portugal to study with Viana da Mota. She studied under Tio Aprea, graduated from the Santa Cecilia Conservatory in Rome and continued her studies in Portuguese and Swiss schools and at the Lisbon Music School. She toured the world as a concert pianist and was a correspondent for several Mexican newspapers and journals.
Ref. 268

VASCONELLOS, Nana
20th-century composer.
Composition
FILM MUSIC
The Castaways of Turtle Island (1976)
Ref. 497

VASHAW, Cecile
20th-century American composer.
Compositions
BAND
Pieces
CHAMBER
Work and play (inst ens) (with Julia Smith q.v.) (1960)
VOCAL
Remember the Alamo (opt narr, mix-ch and orch) (Lt. Col. W.B. Travis and Gladys W. Wright) (Presser)
Publications
String Method. Books I, II and III. With Julia Smith. Presser.
Ref. 40, 280, 347, 448

VASILIEVA, Tatiana Ivanovna

Soviet lecturer and composer. b. Irkutsk, February 27, 1943. She studied theoretical subjects and composition at the Moscow Conservatory and graduated in 1968. She lectures on theory and history at the Krasnodarsk Institute of Culture.

Compositions
ORCHESTRA
Symphony (1968)
Piano concerto (1972)
Piece (1964)
Bela, suite based on Lermontov (1964)
CHAMBER
Quintet for woodwind, timpani and triangle (1967)
Piece for string quartet (1968)
Two pieces (str qrt) (1963)
Sonata (pf) (1963)
VOCAL
Lenin, cantata (solo, ch and orch) (1969)
Ten choruses (S. Yesenin) (ch a-cap) (1963)
Two choruses (V. Mayakovsky) (mix-ch) (1964)
Cycle (vce and pf)
Songs
OPERETTA
Aleshi i chernaya kuritsa, for children (1966)
Ref. 21

VAUBOURGOIN, Jeanine

20th-century French composer.
Composition
CHAMBER
Aria pour Jacqueline (pf)

VAUGHAN, Freda (nee Cameron)

Compositions
VOCAL
Gardens, song cycle (L. Ramsden) (Ricordi)
The herb garden
Interlude
The rose garden
The water garden
SACRED
God's garden
Ref. Ricordi (Milan)

VAURABOURG, Andrée. See HONEGGER-VAURABOURG, Andrée

VAZQUEZ, Alida

American guitarist, pianist, choral conductor, lecturer and composer. b. Mexico City, 1931. She studied the piano at the Conservatory of Queretaro and the National Conservatory of Mexico, where she obtained her teacher's diploma. She gained her B.A. from the University of Mexico. In 1948 she moved to New York and studied eurythmics and improvisation at the Dalcroze Music School, 1948 to 1951. She won a scholarship to study at the Diller-Quaille Music School from 1952 to 1954 and took courses in music therapy at the Turtle Bay Music School, 1954 to 1959. She gained her doctorate in composition from Columbia University. She studied the piano under Esperanze Cruz, Claudio Arrau, Grete Sultan; composition under B. Wagenaar, Chou Wen-Chung, J. Serebrier, J. Meeson; electronics under M. Davidovsky and Ussachevsky; choral direction under D. Randolph and Jose Serebrier; the classical guitar under L. Boletine and F. Had and music therapy under Marian Chance. From 1948 she taught, from 1960 to 1965 was therapy supervisor of dance and music at Hillside Hospital, conducted classes and lectured on music therapy in summer camps and schools in New York and Mexico. She was the recipient of honors, prizes and grants, including that of the National League of American Pen Women, for the best musical work by a woman composer.

Compositions
ORCHESTRA
Five pieces
Incidental music for strings (str orch) (1970)
CHAMBER
Music for seven instruments (2 fl, ob, bsn, hn, trp and vla) (New York: Seesaw Music, 1974)
Mexico (str qrt)
String quartet No. 2 (1975) (ded C. Arrau)
Piece for clarinet and piano (Seesaw, 1974)
Piece for violin and piano (1970)

PIANO
Crepusculo (1969)
Suite para Piano (1966)
VOCAL
Acuarelas de Mexico (vce and pf) (1968)
Song cycle
BALLET
Dances for Claudia (elecs and sym orch)
ELECTRONIC
Danzas de la vida y de la muerte (tape and dancers)
Electronic moods and piano sounds (1977)
Ref. *Heterofonia* No. 59, The Best in Contemporary Music catalog, 228, 594, 622

VAZQUEZ, Lilia

20th-century Mexican bassoonist, pianist and composer. She studied at the composition workshop of CENIDIM.
Composition
MISCELLANEOUS
Donde habita el Olvido
Ref. *Latin American Music Review* Vol. 4 No. 1 Spring/Summer 1983

VEDRUNA, Dolores

19th-century Spanish pianist and composer. She lived in Barcelona ca. 1830 and was highly thought of in musical circles. She composed piano pieces.
Ref. 389

VEGA, Paulina

Late 19th-century Portuguese composer of piano suites.
Ref. 398

VEHAR, Persis Anne

American harpsichordist, pianist, lecturer and composer. b. New Salem, NY, September 29, 1937. She gained her B.M. from Ithaca College and M.M. from the University of Michigan. She studied composition under Warren Benson, Rose Lee Finney, Roberto Gerhard and Ned Rorem. She did postgraduate piano study with Ada Kopetz-Korf at the Manhattan School of Music. Persis was a piano lecturer at the University of Bridgeport, 1961 to 1963 and on the faculty of the piano and accompaniment at the New England Music Camp, Oakland, 1962 to 1966. As a harpsichordist and pianist she performed and recorded widely. She won a Meet the Composer grant, was voted one of the Outstanding Young Women in America in 1967 and was John Dwyer, *Buffalo News* music critic's 'Critic's Choice' in 1980 for her song cycle *Emily D.*

Compositions
ORCHESTRA
Four attitudes (str orch) (1982)
CHAMBER
Quintus-concertino (a-sax and wind ens) (1980)
Promenade and cakewalk (sax qrt) (1981) (Studio P/R)
Aria and caprice (cl and pf) (1982)
Four pieces (a-sax and pf) (1980) (Tenuto)
Sounds of the outdoors (sax)
Suite (trp) (1984)
VOCAL
Faith, hope, LOVE (w-vces, str orch and 2 hn) (1982)
In praise of mercy (S and str orch) (1981)
The mourning bird (mix-ch and opt pf) (1982)
Beach at sundown (S, A and pf) (1980)
Emily D., song cycle (vce, fl, ob and pf) (1980)
Hearing music (vce, fl, ob and pf) (1982)
Ho-la-li-days (3 part vces and opt 2 rec, fl or vlc) (1983)
The laughing song (S and str qrt) (1981)
She never told her love (vce, fl and pf) (1980)
What the lark said (3 part vces, 2 fl and pf)
The yellow monster (2 S, A, 4 perc and pf) (1980)
SACRED
For God is love (mix-ch) (1981) (Palladium Press)
Gertrude Stein addressing the congregation of St. Patrick's Cathedral (mix-ch) (1982)
Ref. composer, 622, 625

VEIGA OLIVEIRA, Sofia Helena da

20th-century Brazilian composer. DISCOGRAPHY.
Composition
VOCAL
Murmurios de um regato (E.F. Guimaraes) (m-S and pf)
Ref. 563

VEILUVA, Giuseppina Cerruti
19th-century Italian composer.
Composition
PIANO
Maria, waltz (for the marriage of the Princess Maria Pia of Savoy)
Ref. 399

VELA DE ARNAO, Sofia
19th-century Spanish singer and composer. She was well known in Madrid in the 1840s. Her compositions, mainly sacred songs, were highly thought of and frequently played in the court churches.
Ref. 389

VELLERE, Lucie Weiler
Belgian pianist, violinist, pharmacist and composer. b. Brussels, December 23, 1896; d. October 12, 1966. She began to study solfege and the piano at the age of six under her father. Later she became a pupil of Emile Chaumont (violin), Paul Miry (harmony) and Joseph Jongen (composition). By profession she was an assistant pharmacist, composition being her hobby. In 1935 she was awarded first prize for her *O blanche fleur* by the National Committee for Promotion of Belgian Music; in 1958 a second prize for her *Petite symphonie* by the Province of Brabant and in 1957 the prize for her *Air de syrinx* in a competition funded by the American section of the International Council of Women. DISCOGRAPHY. PHOTOGRAPH.
Compositions
ORCHESTRA
Fantaisie, in 3 mvts (vln and orch) (1958)
Epitaphe pour un ami (vln and cham orch) (Brussels: CeBeDeM, 1964)
Nuits, suite for strings (1946)
Petite symphonie (str orch) (1956) (prize)
La route ascendante (cham orch) (1962)
CHAMBER
Prelude (fl, ob, cl and bsn) (1961) (Brussels: Maurer)
Quartet (4 cl) (Maurer, 1963)
Quartetto (fl, ob, cl and bsn) (1964)
String quartet in D-Minor (1937)
String quartet in E-Minor (1942)
String quartet No. III (1951)
String quartet No. IV (1962)
Bagatelles (3 cl) (1960)
Deux essais (trp, hn and trb) (1965)
Piano trio (1947)
Quatre bagatelles for wind trio (1960) (Maurer)
String trio, prelude and scherzo (1949)
Chanson nocturne (vln and pf) (1920)
Dialogue (ob and pf) (Maurer, 1960)
Divertissement (vln and pf) (1962)
Intermède (fl and pf)
Nocturne (pf and cl) (1954)
Pirouettes (2 vln) (CeBeDeM, 1964)
Sonata (vln and pf) (1952) (CeBeDeM, 1978)
Sonata for violin and cello (1961)
Arlequinade (trp) (Maurer, 1959)
Sérénité (cl) (Maurer, 1959)
Soliloque (vln) (1961)
Fantaisie, en trois mouvements (1958)
PIANO
Capriccio (1959)
Deux danses pour Akarova (1930)
Divertissement (1953)
Feuillets épars, 10 pieces
Figurines, 4 pieces (1920)
Préludes pour la jeunesse, 12 pieces (Maurer, 1950)
Promenade au bord du lac, 6 pieces (Maurer, 1950)
Sonatine (1960)
Sonatina No. 2 (1965) (Maurer)
Trois tanagras (L'Art Belge, 1918)
VOCAL
Ce fut un trouvère qui chanta et une âme qui en mourut (Gerardy) (mix-ch and orch or pf) (1949)
Ophélie (Marsalleau) (w-ch and cham orch) (1941)
Vieille chanson de Xe siècle (S or T and pf; also vce and str qrt or orch) (1919)
Vous m'avez dit tel soir (Verhaeren) (vce and pf or orch) (1940)
Air de syrinx (Paul Claudel) (w-ch a-cap) (Maurer, 1956)
La belle chanson que voila (P. Delaby) (w-ch a-cap) (1965)
Deux poèmes de C. van Lerberghe (mix-ch a-cap) (1957)
Mon âme elle est la-bas (Verhaeren) (mix-ch a-cap) (1959)
Procession nocturne (J. Aderca) (qrt or mix-ch a-cap) (1959)
Trois poèmes d'Apollinaire (ch a-cap, S, m-S and Bar) (1957)

Berceuse (Francis Carco) (vce and pf) (1930)
Chansonnettes, 6 pieces (Pierre Loran) (Maurer, 1964)
Chansons enfantines, 5 pieces (Maurice Careme) (chil-vces) (Maurer)
Les chants de l'ombre, 4 pieces (Marie Maurel) (vce and pf) (1964)
Les Cloches (Apollinaire) (vce and pf) (1964)
Croquis, 6 pieces (Careme) (Brogniaux, 1948)
Désespois (Marie Brunfaut) (S or T and pf; also vce and str qrt) (1937)
Entre les biches et les daims (C. van Lerberghe) (vce and pf) (1948)
Egarement (S or T and pf) (1952)
Faune (Georges Marlow) (S or T and pf) (1933)
Harmonie lunaire (Paul Fort) (vce and pf) (Bosworth, 1917)
La mort des voiles (Fort) (vce and pf) (1917)
O blanche fleur (van Lerberghe) (vce and pf) (1934)
Pastels, 4 melodies (m-S and B a-cap) (1959)
Petites histoires, 6 pieces for children (R. de Bourmant, J. Richepin, J. Moreas, Verlaine, Vicaire) (1948)
La ronde (Paul Fort) (vce and pf) (Bosworth, 1917)
Toi et moi, 5 pieces (Paul Gerady) (vce and pf) (1921)
Trois petites poèmes (Brunfaut) (vce and pf) (Cranz, 1963)
THEATRE
Puck, children's musical (Odette Robert)
Ref. composer's daughter, CeBeDeM, 474, 563, 622

VELLUCCI, Leonilde
Italian composer. She was a member of the Societa Autori.
Ref. 56

VELTHEIM, Charlotte
German pianist, singer and composer. b. Breslau, March 30, 1803; d. April 27, 1873. She composed piano variations and songs.
Ref. 226, 276, 433

VELTHUYSEN, Abesritz von
Composer of a piano trio.
Ref. Frau und Musik

VENDELHAVEN, Harriet
20th-century Danish composer.
Composition
VOCAL
Dansk jagdforenings jubilaeumskantate, cantata (Adam Jensen) (vce and pf) (1934)
Ref. 331

VENIER DE PETRIS, Teresa
18th-century Venetian aristocrat and composer.
Composition
VOCAL
Tiolemo su el fagoto, song (S and basso continuo)
Ref. 105, 160

VENTH, Lydia Kunz
19th-century American pianist and composer. She lived in Brooklyn.
Compositions
PIANO
Brooklet
Mazurka
Moments musicales
Sonatina
Ref. 226, 276, 292, 433

VENTURE, Anna
Compositions
PIANO
A vos pieces, march
Austricana, march
Cheer up!, march
Darling devils, polka-march (also orch and pf)

Dulce soberana, caprice
Fleur d'orient, valse (also orch and pf)
Frissons d'avril, reverie
Illusions fauchées, valse lente
Mia diletta, chanson napolitaine
Rose de Grenade
Vision du passe, waltz
Ref. 297

VERBRUGGHE, Marguerite. See LEFEBURE Marguerite

VERCOE, Elizabeth

American professor and composer. b. Washington, DC, April 23, 1941. She obtained her B.A. (music theory and history) from Wellesley College in 1962, her M.M. (composition) from the University of Michigan in 1963 after studying under Ross Lee Finney and Leslie Bassettand her D.M.A. (composition and music theory) from Boston University, where she studied under Gardner Read. She taught at Westminster Choir College from 1969 to 1971, lectured in music theory in Princeton, NJ, and was assistant professor of music at Framingham State College, 1973 to 1974. She was music scriptwriter and programmer for WUOM-FM in Ann Arbor, MI, from 1963 to 1965. DISCOGRAPHY. PHOTOGRAPH.

Compositions
ORCHESTRA
Concerto (vln and orch) (1976)
Children's caprice (timp, 2 per, hp and str orch) (1963)
CHAMBER
Balance: duo for violin and cello (1974) (Arsis Press, 1978)
Pasticcio: Pattern and imagery from Paul Klee (vlc and pf) (1965)
Sonaria (vlc) (1980) (award, Felipe Espinosa International Competition, 1980)
Fanfare (comm Wellesley College)
PIANO
Fantasy (ded Evelyn Zuckerman) (1975) (Arsis)
Persona (1980) (comm 1st National Congress of Women in Music, New York, 1981)
Six gratitudes (1978)
Three studies (1973) (Arsis)
VOCAL
Irreveries from Sappho (ch and pf) (1981)
Eight riddles from symphosius (m-S or Cont and pf) (1964)
Herstory I: Song cycle for soprano, vibraphone and piano (1975)
Herstory II: 13 Japanese lyrics (S, pf and perc) (1979) (award, GEDOK International Competition, 1981)
ELECTRONIC
Synapse for viola and computer
Synthesism (computer)
Ref. composer, AMC newsletters, 474, 563, 622, 625

VERGER, Virginie Morel du (alt. name Christiane)

French pianist, teacher and composer. b. Metz, 1779; d. Castle Verger, 1870. She studied at the Paris Conservatoire where she received first prize in the piano. She also studied harmony under Antonin Reicha and received advice and guidance from Clementi and occasional lessons from Hummel.

Compositions
CHAMBER
Tre duettini (vln and pf)
PIANO
Fantaisie on an English air
Huit études melodiques
Sonata
Valse brillante, la mascara
Variations brillantes on a German air
Virgiania valse
VOCAL
Poems (Queneau, Rimbaud, Prevert, Hugo, Fombeure and Soupault)
Ref. 26, 276, 433

VERHAALEN, Sister Marion

American pianist, editor, professor and composer. b. Milwaukee, WI, December 9, 1930. She took her B.M. in the piano at Alverno College in Milwaukee, 1954; her M.M. in the piano at Catholic University in Washington, DC, 1962 and Ed.D. in music education at Teachers' College, Columbia University, NY, 1971. She taught in schools and colleges from 1954. From 1967 to 1969 she was teaching assistant to Dr. Robert Pace at Teachers' College. She lectured and worked as a clinician in music edu-

cation workshops sponsored by the National Piano Foundation in Chicago from 1964, in the United States and Brazil. As staff editor of *Musart Magazine* from 1963 to 1969 she was responsible for an elementary classroom column. She received two Teachers' College scholarships in 1968 and one in 1969. The Organization of American States awarded her a research grant to study the music of Francisco Mignone and Camargo Guarnieri in Brazil from 1969 to 1970. In 1980 she was named the Outstanding Milwaukee Musician by the Wisconsin Federation of Music Clubs.

Compositions
CHAMBER
Outburst (trp and org) (1983)
Samba (gtr) (1983)
Three postludes (org) (SSSF Music Ministry, 1976)
PIANO
Canon in D (2 pf, 8 hands) (Hal Leonard, 1984)
Aura Lee, duet (Hal Leonard, 1983)
Duets on four Brazilian songs (Lee Roberts, 1973)
Every night, duet (Leonard, 1983)
Folk songs From America, set I and II, duet (Roberts, 1984)
Joshua fit the battle, duet (Leonard, 1984)
Old Joe Clark, duet (Leonard, 1983)
Sandy land, duet (Leonard, 1983)
The water is wide, duet (Leonard, 1984)
City set, 4 pieces (Roberts, 1968)
Fantasy suite, in 4 mvts (1979) (Leonard, 1983)
Johnny has gone for a soldier (Leonard, 1983)
Modes in miniature (1975)
Phrygian toccata (Summy-Birchard, 1966)
VOCAL
Patriotic medley (w-ch, pf, strs, fl and perc) (1959)
Song cycle for young singers (vce or w-ch and pf) (1964)
The kings of Tarsis (w-ch and pf)
The Prairie Woman, song cycle of poems (Tom Montag) (S and pf) (1979)
Six for three, poems (S. Kevin Robertson) (2 S and A a-cap) (1981)
SACRED
Judith, oratorio (4 soloist, mix-ch and cham orch) (comm for 6th-national Workshop on Christian-Jewish Relations, Milwaukee, 1981)
Alverno sacred music series (Gregorian Institute of America) incl.:
Lord God, let your spirit come, hymn (cong and org) (1981)
Our soul awaits Yahweh, anthem (solos, mix-ch, cong and org) (1968)
A text of St. Paul (mix-ch and elec tape) (1969)
Four offertory motets
Mass hymn suites (1969); Mass in the Dorian mode; Hymn of praise; Nunc transitus (2 S, 2 A and T a-cap) (1982)
Papal procession in holiday at the Vatican (Gregorian Institute, 1962)
Two offertory notets for the Sundays of Advent
Several songs in 'Praise and Song' for elementary school (McLaughlin & Reilly, 1962)
DANCE SCORES
Four dances of affliction (pf, vln and fl) (1966)
Haves and the have-nots (pf and perc) (1965)
THEATRE
Under the Greenwood Tree, musical (chil-ch, pf, cl, fl and strs) (1964)
INCIDENTAL MUSIC
Imaginary Invalid (Moliere) (mix-ch and pf) (1965)
ARRANGEMENTS
Six modal miniatures of Everett Stevens (str orch) (Presser, 1968)
Pieces incl. Memory; Parade of wooden soldier; Claire de Lune

Publications
Camargo Guarnieri-Brazilian Composer. 1973.
Guided Listening Units. Vols I and II. For junior high school. McLaughlin-Reilly. 1968.
Handbook of Delta Mu Theta. 1963.
Keyboard Dimensions I, II, III, IV. New piano course for Milwaukee public schools. M.P.S. 1983. 1984.
Music for Piano and Skills and Drills. Group instructional method of Robert Pace. Translation-adaptation to Portuguese with Vera Silvia Camargo Guarnieri. Sao Paulo, Brazil: Ricordi Brasileira. 1973.
Articles, mainly on teaching, in *Musart* and other journals.
Ref. composer, 77, 301

VERNAELDE, Henriette. See ADDENDUM

VERNE, Adela (born Wurm)

English pianist and composer. b. Southampton, February 27, 1877; d. London, February 5, 1952. With her sisters, Mary Wurm (q.v.), Alice Verne-Bredt (q.v.) and Matilde, she changed the family name to Verne. Adela took her earliest piano lessons from her sisters and later from Marie Schumann, daughter of Clara Schumann (q.v.). The composer Paderewski, who was impressed with her playing, invited Adela to stay with his family periodically at Morges in Switzerland and to study under him.

At the age of 14 she made her debut under Manns at the Crystal Palace Concerts and became one of London's foremost pianists, appearing frequently in chamber music concerts at St. James Hall, often with such eminent artists as Joachim and Piatti. Her considerable repertory included Brahm's *Second Concerto in B-Flat Major*. She traveled extensively, visiting the United States on more than one occasion, where she was regarded as one of the finest players of her day. Ill health forced her to withdraw from concert performances, but she later returned, impressing audiences with her virtuosity and musicality. Her son, John Vallier, was also a talented pianist and composer.

Compositions
VOCAL
Songs incl.:
For me (Enoch)
I wonder why (Enoch)
Ref. 8, 297

VERNE, Mary J.A. See WURM, Mary J.A.

VERNE-BREDT, Alice (born Wurm)

English pianist and composer. b. Southampton, August 9, 1868. Alice and her sisters Adela (q.v.) and Matilde changed the family name to Verne.

Composition
CHAMBER
Trio-phantasie (pf, vln and vlc) (prize in a Cobbett competition)
Ref. 8, 41

VERNON, Sylvia

20th-century English composer.
Composition
PIANO
Waltz in E-Flat
Ref. 230

VERRALL, Pamela Motley

British teacher and composer. b. Penrhiwseiber, South Wales, August 13, 1915. Her father was a musician. She gained her B.A. hons. from the University of Wales, Cardiff and a teacher's diploma from King's College, London. She is an L.R.A.M. in school music and was head of the music department in several schools. She presented her own works on radio and television. PHOTOGRAPH.

Compositions
CHAMBER
Woodwind ensemble (ob, cl and bsn) (1977)
Clarinets in chorus, in 3 parts (1975)
Clarinets in concert, in 3 parts (1972)
Seven romantics (cl and pf)
Six conversations (cl and pf) (1970)
Six dance duets (rec and pf) (1975)
Six miniatures for recorders (1977)
Old English music (1974)
VOCAL
Songs incl.:
Balloons for sale (Forsyth Brothers)
Cossack's riding song (Herald Music Services)
The dove (Bosworth)
Far from my home (Herald)
The frost fairy (Forsyth)
Get on board ev'rybody (Forsyth)
Get together, song book (Forsyth)
The gypsy dance (Forsyth)
Hopalong Fred (Forsyth)
If only (Forsyth)
An Irish lilt (Forsyth)
I love to walk (Forsyth)
Johnny will you dance with me? (Forsyth)
The king's carol (Forsyth)
The lollipop tree (Bosworth)
The music box (Forsyth)
My friend Joe (Forsyth)
Night magic (Forsyth)
O nightingale (Forsyth)
The pipers are coming (Forsyth)
Sammy the snail (Forsyth)
Shepherds on the mountain (Forsyth)
Singalong tunes with guitar (Feldman)
Song of the match-girl (Forsyth)
Song of the sea shell (Forsyth)

Swing song (Forsyth)
Wake up shepherds! (Forsyth)
Wiggly Willy (Forsyth)
SACRED
Cross over the road, hymn (Herald)
Hymn collections incl.:
Hymns for today (1969) (Herald)
It's all in the book (1973) (Vanguard)
Rejoice and sing (1971) (Chester Home)
So much to sing (1971) (five by composer)
Tell ev'rybody (Herald)
Christmas carol collections incl.:
Caribbean carol (1970)
A Christmas journey (1972)
King of love is on his way (1974)
The little King's carol (1972)
Long ago (Peter & Payne, 1978)
Mary's song (1975)
No room at the top (Peter & Payne, 1978)
The open door (Peter & Payne, 1978)
The organ-grinder's carol (1975) (Cramer)
Peace on earth (1970)
Peter Piper's carol (Cramer)
Play musicians! (Peter & Payne, 1978)
Ring-a-ding bells (1972)
Rose of Bethlehem (1972)
Sing a lullaby for Jesus (1971)
The song of the bells (1972)
Snow-flakes carol (Peter & Payne, 1978)
A stable bare (1971)
Star bright, starlight (1971)
Star carol (1972)
Star for Maria (1972)
Swinging angels (Peter & Payne, 1978)
Take my hand (Peter & Payne, 1978)
Thirty carols based on Chinese folk songs (1977)
THEATRE
Musicals for young people incl.:
Around the World (F. Drake) (1975) (British & Continental)
Babushka, Christmas play (1977)
The Gingerbread Man (comm BBC)
Grand Tour of Europe (comm BBC)
Johny Appleseed (1973) (Feldman)
The Legend of the Yellow River (1976) (Herald)
Miracle Man (1977)
Move Over, Mr. Noah (1967) (Herald)
A Sea Spell (1977) (Lengrich & Co.)
The Silver Arrow (Peter & Payne)
Son of Assisi (1972) (comm BBC) (Feldman)
Summer Water (1970) (Bosworth)
Ref. composer

VERRILL, Louise Shurtleff Brown

American pianist and composer. b. Portland, ME, March 23, 1870; d. February 17, 1948. She studied the piano and composition under distinguished masters in Berlin and Dresden for many years.

Compositions
PIANO
Alone
The birch tree
Chaconne
Du bist wie eine Blume
Exultation
Four moods of a gnome
Ghosts on parade
It happened in Spain
It is spring
Jennie kissed me
The lonely pine
March of the patriot
Reverie
Rumpelstiltskin
Tenderness
Tone pictures
Tone poem
Walhalla
Waltz
When shadows fall
Yellow moon
VOCAL
Songs incl.:
Winter joy (solo and ch)
Pleasant dreams
You came like the dawn
Ref. 30, 347, 374

VERTOA DA BERGAMO, Sister Agostina
16th-century nun and composer.
Composition
MISCELLANEOUS
Gagliarda
Ref. 164

VESPERMANN (Vespermann-Goerres), Marie (Maria) (Mrs. Arndt)
German pianist, poetess and composer. b. Munich, April 5, 1823; d. Munich, May 3, 1882. She played in public at a very young age. She married the Viennese pandectist, Ludwig Arndt.
Compositions
CHAMBER
Four-hand pieces, op. 5 (pf)
VOCAL
Aus den Bergen, op. 8
Choruses
Songs
SACRED
Sacred songs, op. 3 (org obb)
Ref. 70, 226, 276, 347

VESPERMANN-GOERRES, Maria or Marie. See VESPERMANN, Marie

VESVALI, Felicita
Polish composer. b. Stettin; d. Warsaw, April 3, 1880.
Composition
OPERA
Die Papstwahl (1875)
Ref. 431

VETLUGINA, Natalia Alekseyevna
20th-century Soviet composer.
Composition
ORCHESTRA
Children's orchestra for children and youth (various vocal and inst ens) (Moscow; Muzyka, 1976)
Ref. Otto Harrassowitz (Wiesbaden)

VETTER, Cato
20th-century Dutch composer. She participated in a Dutch music festival in 1912.
Ref. Wouter Paap (Ghent)

VEVERS, Doris. See CRAIB, Doris

VEZZANA, Lucretia Orsina. See VIZANA, Lucretia Orsina

VIALA, Georgette
20th-century Belgian composer. Her works include three operettas, film music and songs.

VIARDOT, Louise Pauline. See HERITTE-VIARDOT, Louise Pauline

VIARDOT-GARCIA, Pauline Michelle Ferdinande
French lecturer, pianist, singer and composer. b. Paris, July 18, 1821; d. Paris, May 18, 1910. She was the daughter of Manuel del Popolo Garcia, tenor and teacher and of Joaquina Sitcher Garcia, opera singer and younger sister of Maria Felicitas Malibran (q.v.). When she was three years old, Pauline went with her parents to London, where her father was engaged by the Italian Opera and then to New York and Mexico. She received piano lessons from Marcus Vega until 1826 when the family returned to Europe. On the voyage she received her first singing lessons from her father. In Europe she studied the piano under Meysenberg and when she was seven, accompanied her father's singing lessons. She later

said that she learned more from her father this way than as his pupil, her mother being her only effective teacher. After her father's death when Pauline was ten, her brother Manuel took over her tuition, although Rossini wished to have her as his pupil. She also studied harmony, counterpoint and composition with Antonin Reicha and in 1838 became a piano pupil of Franz Liszt. Pauline accompanied her sister Maria in concerts when she was 14 or 15 years old. Liszt later encouraged her to become a concert pianist. However, she had already made her debut as a singer in Brussels, in 1837. Thereafter she toured in Germany, returned to Paris and made her first appearance in London in the role of Desdemona in Rossini's Otello in 1839. She was engaged for the Paris Theatre-Italien in the same year by its director Louis Viardot, who married her in 1840 or 1841. He managed extensive tours for her throughout Europe in the following years. Every year from 1848 to 1858 she appeared in London for a season at the Italian Opera. In 1859 she sang, at Berlioz's invitation, his revival of Gluck's Orpheus which became one of her greatest roles and was performed 150 times. Then she retired from the opera and lived in Baden-Baden until 1871, when as the wife of a Frenchman she was obliged to leave Germany. She moved to Paris and Bougival, devoted herself to composition and developed a fine reputation as a singing teacher both at the Paris Conservatoire and privately. Schumann wrote his Cycle of songs, op. 24 for her; Brahms composed his Alto rhapsody for her and she was the model for the heroine of Consuelo written by her friend George Sand. Turgenev, who was in love with Pauline and lived with the family for many years, wrote A month in the country, a semi-autobiographical work that described the menage à trois between Pauline, her husband and himself. His works Smoke and Torrents of spring were also inspired by her. Her daughter Louise Pauline Marie Heritte-Viadot (q.v.) taught singing and composed. Two other daughters became concert singers and her son became a highly esteemed violinist and composer. DISCOGRAPHY. PHOTOGRAPH.
Compositions
CHAMBER
Six pièces pour piano et violon (Gerard)
PIANO
Defile bohemien (4 hands) (Miran)
Polonaise (4 hands) (Miran)
Suite armenienne (4 hands) (Miran)
Album russe de 12 romances (Troupenas)
Deux airs de ballet (Miran)
Gavotte
Mazourke (Miran)
Second album russe
VOCAL
Die Sterne: Ich starrte und stand unbewegliche (vce, pf and vlc) (Breitkopf)
Six chansons du XVe siècle (2-3 vces and fl) (Heugel)
Choeur bohemien (soli and 3 w-vces) (Enoch)
Choeur des elfes (soli and 3 w-vces) (Enoch)
Over 60 songs incl.:
A la fontaine (Heugel)
Abricotier, chansons serviene (Schott)
Attraits (Enoch)
Au jardin de mon père (Fromont)
Bonjour mon coeur (Enoch)
Canzonetta de concert: Gia la notte s'avvicina (Heugel: Bessel)
La chamelle à Marier (vce and wind qnt)
Chanson de la pluie (Enoch)
Chanson de mer (Enoch)
Chêne et la roseau (Schott)
Désepoir (Enoch)
Die Klagende (Schlesinger)
Dinderindine, vieille chanson (2 ces)
Dites, que fuat-il faire (vce and pf)
Elle passe! Paroles et musique (Miran)
Fluestern, Athemscheues, Lauschen (vce and pf)
Grands oiseaux blancs (Enoch)
Une heure d'étude (Bote; Gutheil; Schirmer)
In der Fruehe (Ries & Erler)
La jeune république, military song (Pierre Dupont) (1848-1849)
Lamento (Enoch)
Four Lieder (Bote)
Marquise (Durand)
Mignonne (Enoch)
Parmé (Enoch)
Poursuite (Se per fuggir) (Miran)
Pushkin songs: Des Nachts, Das Voeglein, Die Beschwoerung (vce and pf)
Raetsel (Heugel; Ries & Erler)
Réssemblance (Durand)
Rossignol et rossignolet (Miran)
Sara la baigneuse (Miran)
Savetier et le Financier (Miran)
Six airs italiens du XVIIIe siècle
Six melodies
Ta chevelure, chanson napolitaine (Miran)

Toreador (Miran)
Toskanische Gedichte (Breitkopf)
Trois jours de vendange (Enoch)
Zwoelf Gedichte (Breitkopf)
SACRED
Ave Maria (Enoch)
OPERA
Cendrillon
OPERETTA
Conte de fées (1879)
Le Dernier Sorcier (Der letzte Zauberer) (I. Turgenev) (1869)
L'Ogre (I. Turgenev) (1868)
Trop des Femmes (I. Turgenev) (1867)
ARRANGEMENTS
Air de Xerxes, Handel (vce, fl, vlc and vln)
Bohemiennes (d'après les danses hongroises de J. Brahms) (duet or
w-ch; also pf) (Hamelle)
Six mazurkas, Chopin (vce) (Gerard; Breitkopf & Hartel)
Waltzes, F. Schubert (2 vces) (Schirmer)
Zigeunerlied (gypsy song) J. Brahms (duet) (Simrock)
Publications
L'école classique du chant.
P. Viardot-Garcia to J. Rietz. *Letters of Friendship* in *Music Quarterly*,
July, 1915-1916.
Bibliography
Fitzlyon, A. *The Price of Genius: A Life of Pauline Viardot.* New York,
London, 1964.
Heritte-Viardot, L. *Une famille des grands musiciens.* 1923.
Kaminski, C.H. *Lettres à Mlle. Viardot d'Ivan Tourgenev.* Paris, 1907.
Mara, La. *P. Viardot-Garcia.* Leipzig, 1882.
Marix-Spire, T. *Gounod and his Interpreter, Pauline Viardot.* 1945.
Rachmanowa, A. (pseud.) *Die Liebe eines Lebens: I. Turgenev und
Pauline Viardot.* Frauenfeld, 1952.
Torrigi, L.H.P. *Viardot-Garcia, Sa biographie, ses compositions, son
enseignement.* Geneva, 1901.
Waddington, P. *P. Viardot-Garcia as Berlioz's Counsellor and Physi-
cian.* 1973.
Ref. H. Baron (London), 128, 2, 8, 17, 20, 22, 26, 70, 74, 88, 100, 102, 103, 105,
106, 107, 113, 129, 132, 135, 177, 193, 201, 226, 276, 282, 297, 307, 347,
387, 394, 563

VICOUNTESS OF CHARTRES. See CHARTRES, La Vidame de

VICTORIA MARIA LOUISA, Duchess of Kent
B. Germany, 1786; d. 1861. She was the mother of Queen Victoria and
spent most of her mature life at court. She was one of the most enthusias-
tic and prolific royal composers of the 19th-century, producing a new
piece for every occasion. PHOTOGRAPH.
Compositions
PIANO
Galoppade, for her daughter (1840)
Galops
Quicksteps
Waltzes
VOCAL
I am weary (1840)
Lieder
Ref. 262

VIDAMPIERRE, Comtesse de
18th-century French composer.
Compositions
VOCAL
Le baiser, ariette (Paris: Mercure de France, 1772)
L'heureuse securité (Mercure de France, 1772)
Le regret, ariette (Mercure de France, 1772)
Ref. 65

VIDAR, Jorunn
Icelandic pianist, teacher and composer. b. Rejkjavik, December 7, 1918.
She studied music first with her mother and Pall Isolfsson and later at the
Rejkjavik Conservatory under Arni Kristjansson. She graduated in 1936
and then attended the Hochschule fuer Musik, Berlin for two years. At the
Juilliard School of Music she studied under Giannini and then in Vienna
under Viola Tern, 1959 to 1969. She made her debut in Rejkjavik in 1947
and thereafter appeared in concerts and on radio and television. She also
taught.

Compositions
ORCHESTRA
Concerto (pf and orch)
CHAMBER
Suite (vln and pf) (for Icelandic radio on occasion of 1,100 years' settle-
ment in Iceland) (1973)
Variations on Icelandic song (vlc and pf)
Five meditations on Icelandic themes (pf)
VOCAL
Olafsrimur graenlendings (ch and str orch) (1950)
An old Christmas song (vce and pf) (ITM)
Fifteen songs (Halldor Laxness, Stein Steinarr, Tomas Gudmundsson,
Einar Bragi and Jakobina Johnson)
Icelandic folk songs (vce and pf) (ITM)
Love song (mix-ch and pf)
Six songs (vce and pf) (ITM)
BALLET
Fire (1951)
Olafur liljuros (1952)
INCIDENTAL MUSIC
Music for plays and films
Ref. composer, IMI

VIELANDA, Mengia (nee Bisozia)
18th-century Swiss composer. b. Ticino. Her works are in the library of the
University of Basle.
Composition
SACRED
Collection: Ovretta musicale chi consista in certas canzuns spirituales
da diversa materia et in diversas melodias (Scuol, 1769)
Ref. 101, 651

VIENNE, Marie-Louise de
French singer, teacher and composer. b. Paris, 1905. She attended the
University of Paris and was a laureate of the Paris Conservatoire. She was
a soprano at the National Opera from 1929 to 1930 and a concert soloist
from 1932. From 1945 she taught interpretation courses in French, Ger-
man, Italian and Russian.
Compositions
BAND
The Ordinance Corps march
SACRED
Ave verum (homage to Pope Jean XXIII)
Rotary Club La Defense hymn
INCIDENTAL MUSIC
Musical fancies for films and ballets incl.:
Waltz of my life
Ref. 490

VIERK, Lois
American pianist, choral conductor and composer. b. Hammond, IN, Au-
gust 4, 1951. She is a Phi Beta Kappa, summa cum laude graduate of the
University of California, Los Angeles, where she obtained her B.A. (1974).
In 1976 she entered the California Institute of the Arts, receiving an M.F.A.
in 1978 and winning the Bruno Maderna composition fellowship to study at
Tanglewood. During this period her composition teachers included Jacob
Druckman, Mel Powell, Leonard Stein and Morton Subotnick. From 1971
she studied gagaku (Japanese court music) under Suenobu Togi at the
University of California. Lois continued her Gagaku studies in Japan in
1982 and performed her own works there. At the California Institute of the
Arts she studied conducting under Paul Vorwerk. She conducted the Uni-
versity Lutheran Chapel Choir, Westwood, CA, and was pianist with the
Cal Arts Contemporary Players. PHOTOGRAPH.
Compositions
CHAMBER
Trombone (18 t-trb) (1980)
Photosphere (2 trp, 3 trb, vln, vla, vlc and bsn) (1976)
Ginko (fl, cl, ob, bsn, 2 vln, vla and vlc; also pf and vib) (1977, 1979)
Inverted fountain (6 t-trb) (1978)
Desert heat (3 cl in A) (1977)
Processional music (3 trp) (1976)
Song for three clarinets (1977)
Trio (fl, cl and bsn) (1974)
VOCAL
Kana for three tenors and three basses (1976)
Ni-Zwei (S, fl, cl, bsn and pf) (1975)
SACRED
Gradual for Easter Sunday (speakers, ch and 2 trp) (1976)
ELECTRONIC
Guitars (5 miked or elec gtr; also 4 pre-recorded gtr and 1 live gtr)
(1981)
Ref. composer

VIEU, Jane (Jeanne)

French composer. b. 1871.

Compositions

ORCHESTRA

Colombine, air de ballet (pf and orch) (Enoch)

Griserie de caresses, valse chantée (pf and orch; also vce; also pf) (Ricordi)

Ivresse et parfums, valse (pf and orch; also pf) (Enoch)

Marquise Bergers, chanson Louis XV (pf and orch; also pf) (Ricordi)

Morceaux detachées: Le tableau (pf and orch); contredanse (pf and orch)

Nymphes et papillons (pf and orch) (Enoch)

Tarantelle (pf and orch; also pf; also hp) (G. Verdalle) (Ricordi)

Valse des merveilleuses, extraite du divertissement les merveilleuses (also pf)

CHAMBER

Minuetto (str qrt and pf) (Ricordi)

Amoroso intermezzo (vln and pf; also man and pf) (Enoch)

Au coin de feu (vln and pf; also ch) (Hachette)

Castillante, valse de concert (man and pf; also pf) (Enoch)

Lever de l'aurore, air de ballet (vln and pf) (Vieu)

Marche des alguazils (man and pf) (Enoch)

Seduction, valse chantée (vln and pf; also pf) (Ricordi)

Sérénade d'aldin, valse lente (vln and pf; also pf) (Ricordi)

Vaines tendresses (vlc and pf) (Ricordi)

Valse des rousses (vln and pf; also pf) (Ricordi)

Morceaux detachées: Sortie (org)

Chanson du soir (Hachette)

Vers le rêve (Enoch)

PIANO

Images en musique, 10 easy pieces (4 hands) (Vieu)

Andalouse, habanera (Enoch)

Andalouse, melodie imitative (Enoch)

Arabesque

Caprice (Enoch)

Defile du cortège de la raison (Enoch)

Ensorceleuse, valse (Hachette)

Leçon de danse, minuet (Vieu)

Libellules, scherzo (Enoch)

Magicienne, air de ballet (Enoch)

Menuet du lys (Enoch)

Menuet de la princesse (Enoch)

Menuet royal (Vieu)

Minuetto (Ricordi)

Nocturne en La bemol (Ricordi)

Pompadour (Enoch)

Sieste (souvenir de Seville) (Enoch)

Suite espagnole (Enoch)

Tendrement, valse (Hachette)

VOCAL

Choeur du printemps (w-ch)

Ange de rêve, duo (Ricordi)

Au bord du grand chemin (S or T)

Songs (vce and pf) incl.:

Aprés le bal (Hachette)

Avril chante (Ricordi)

Les deux baises, rondenas espagnoles (Enoch)

Barcarolle (Ricordi)

Carillons blancs (Enoch)

Celle qui passe (Ricordi)

Celle qu'on rêve (Ricordi)

Chanson breve (Enoch)

Chanson d'automne (Ricordi)

Chanson de la bergère (Heugel)

Chanson douce (Gross)

Chanson du matin (Ricordi)

Chanson fleurie, chanson Louis XV (Ricordi)

Chant de berger (Hachette)

Chantons les roses, mélodie (Schott-Freres)

Charite (Enoch)

Chevalier printemps, valse chantée (Vieu)

SACRED

Ave Maria

Je vous salue (Salut à Vous Marie)

O salutaris

OPERA

Aladin, feërie chantée, 15 tableaux (Enoch)

La Belle au Bois dormant, feërie illustrée (vln and pf; also pf) (Enoch)

Madame Tallien, historic piece in 5 acts and 8 scenes (Theresia Cabarus)

OPERETTA

Arlette

Piège d'Amour

BALLET

Au Bal de Flore, pantomime (pf and orch; also other insts)

ARRANGEMENTS

Au pays parfume, valse (vln and pf) (Enoch)

Menuet de l'enfante, extrait de Piège d'amour, operetta (pf) (Hachette)

Sur le pont de bambou, promenade chinoise, from Aladin (vce and pf) (Enoch)

Ref. 226, 297, 322, 307

VIGGO, Eleanor Margaret Green, Princess

Danish composer. b. November 5, 1895; d. July 3, 1966.

Compositions

VOCAL

Fire sange (W. Hansen, 1949)

Ref. 331

VIGNERON-RAMAKERS, Christiane-Josée (pseud. Jo Delande)

Belgian organist, pianist, conductor, professor and composer. b. Leopoldsburg, January 25, 1914. She studied harmony and counterpoint in Hasselt at the Limburg Organ School under Professors Arthur and Herman Meulemans and received her diplomas in the organ and the piano and teaching in 1934. She studied orchestration and fugue by correspondence with Paul Gilson. Five of her compositions were awarded the Prix Koopal of the Ministry of Education and Culture in 1961. From 1934 to 1969 she taught music and singing at the Athenne Royal of Eisden. In 1945 she founded the Academy of Music in Eisden, which was later taken over by the community of Maasmechelen in September 1972 under the name Gemeentelijke Muziekakademie Maasmechelen. She was conductor of the Eisden orchestra and chamber orchestra from 1945 to 1970, director professor of harmony and history of music at the Academy in Eisden and in 1956 she founded Jeugd en Muziek, Eisden. She composed light music and literary works under the name Jo Delande. PHOTOGRAPH.

Compositions

ORCHESTRA

Concertino, op. 5 (ob, cor anglais and cham orch; also ob, cor anglais, hpcd and str orch) (1958, 1970)

Etudes, op. 4, in 4 mvts (1957)

CHAMBER

Mobiles, op. 14 (cl qrt, perc and strs) (1969)

Octet for clarinets, Hommage à Maurice van Guchte, op. 7 (1958)

Quartet for saxophones, op. 7 (1959)

Petit cortège presque chinois, op. 10 (pf and 2 tim) (1968)

Alternato, op. 17 (cor anglais and pf) (1971)

Duo rapsodique, op. 6 (cl and pf) (Brussels: Maurer, 1958)

Three etudes, op. 9 (sax or ob) (1968)

Hautes fagnes, op. 15 (org) (1968)

Variations sur un cramignon liegeois, op. 16 (gtr) (1969)

Ten vocalises, sonatina, teaching pieces (ob and org) (1984)

PIANO

Ballade, op. 13 (Oiseaux captifs) (1968)

Six mini-studi, op. 11 (1968)

Deux préludi, op. 12 (1968)

VOCAL

Three songs, op. 3 (A. Berbier) (m-S and cham orch) (1963)

Drie zangen van Liefde en Dod, op. 19 (Trudo Hoewaer) (mix-ch a-cap) (1972)

Eight melodies, poems (A. Berbier) (middle vce and pf) (1982)

Four songs, op. 2 (m-S and pf) (1943)

Rossignol-es-tu damne? op. 1 (A. Berbier) (A and pf) (1943)

Vocalise for middle voice. op. 18 (1972)

Vocalise II, op. 20 (stile espressivo) (S, A, B and pf) (1981) (Oostende: Andel)

THEATRE

Het daghet, based on Limburg folk elements (ch and orch) (Y.P. Stasse) (1938)

Publications

Door volkslied tot notenleer II.

Metode dictees.

La notenboekje.

Van kleuterdreun naar notenleer I.

Articles for various magazines.

Ref. composer, 84

VIGNERY, Jeanne Emilie Virginie

Belgian violinist, lecturer and composer. b. Ghent, April 11, 1913; d. Luttre, August 15, 1973. She studied at the Royal Conservatory of Ghent, winning prizes for harmony, counterpoint and fugue. Then she studied the violin at the Ecole Normale de Musique in Paris and became a pupil of Nadia Boulanger (q.v.) and J. de la Presle. In 1941 she won a mention at the Prix de Rome; in 1942 she won the Priz Emile Mathieu and in 1943 the Prix Irene Fuerison of the Royal Belgian Academy. After 1945 she taught harmony at the Royal Conservatory of Ghent.

Compositions
ORCHESTRA
Vision de guerre, symphonic poem
CHAMBER
Sonata (vln and pf; also hn and pf)
VOCAL
La fille de Jephte (soli and orch)
Songs
Bibliography
Le Vie Musicale Belge. July/August, 1974.
Ref. 96

VIGNY, Louise von
19th-century German composer.
Compositions
PIANO
Four mazurkas (Bote)
VOCAL
Drei Lieder (A and pf) incl.:
Ich war mit meiner Lieb; O weine ueber sie (Heinrichshofen)
Vier Lieder (B and pf) incl.:
Abends; was wollt ihr noch (Bote)
SACRED
Psalm 27, op. 2 (S and pf) (Heinrichshofen)
Ref. 226, 276, 297

VIKTOR, Denise
B. 1933.
Composition
PIANO
Burla (Paris: Combre, 1984)
Ref. Otto Harrassowitz (Wiesbaden)

VILLA-LOBOS, Arminda Neves de Almeida
20th-century Brazilian poetess, professor and composer. Of Portuguese parents, she graduated from the National Music Insitute of Rio de Janeiro and was choral professor at the Rio de Janeiro Music Conservatory. She married and worked with the composer Heitor Villa-Lobos and he dedicated some of his compositions to her, calling her Mindinha. After her husband's death, Arminda became curator of the Villa-Lobos museum in Rio.
Ref. 268

VILLAN, Marcelle Henriette Marie. See VILLIN, Marcelle Henriette

VILLARD, Nina de
19th-century French composer.
Compositions
PIANO
Nocturne
Paroles d'une rose à un rayon de soleil (Bosworth)
Valse brillante
Ref. 226, 276, 297, 347, 433

VILLARINI, Awilda
American concert pianist, lecturer and composer. b. Puerto Rico, February 6, 1940. She studied at the Peabody Conservatory of Music and obtained a B.Mus. in 1961, an M.Mus. in 1973 and a Ph.D. from New York University in 1979. She studied the piano under D. Weber from 1965 to 1968, W. Panhofer from 1968 to 1970 at the Vienna Academy of Music and the Juilliard School of Music from 1973 to 1975 and Alexander Gorodnitzky and chamber music under Claus Adam and William Kroll at the Peabody Conservatory. She received awards from the Institute of Culture in 1970 and the Peabody Conservatory and scholarships from the University of Puerto Rico in 1971 and the Ford Foundation, 1973. She taught privately and in schools and at the Santa Maria University of Puerto Rico. She performed as a soloist with the Puerto Rico Symphony from 1974 to 1976 and concertized widely in Europe, the United States and Latin America.
Compositions
ORCHESTRA
Suite portoricinses (also pf) (1979, 1977)
CHAMBER
Three fantastic pieces (cl and pf) (1977)
Ten preludes (pf) (1979)
VOCAL
Four songs (vce and pf)
Ref. composer

VILLENEUVE, Marie-Louise Diane (Rev. Soeur Maire-Helise S.S.A.)
Canadian organist, pianist, choral conductor, teacher and composer. b. St. Anne des Plaines, Quebec, August 15, 1889. She studied theory, composition, singing, the piano, the organ and choral conducting under R.O. Pelletier, Raoul Paquet, Rodolphe Matthieu, Auguste Descarries, Reverend Ethelbert Thibault, Fleurette Contant and Jean Charbonneau. She obtained a Mus.Bac. at the Quebec Conservatory. She was a music teacher at convents of the Soeurs de Sainte-Anne.
Compositions
PIANO
Prelude No. 1
Prelude No. 2
VOCAL
Chemin faisant
Le semeur
SACRED
Adorate
Cor Jesu
O salutaris
La Samaritaine
Ref. 133

VILLIN, Marcelle Henriette Marie
French organist, pianist and composer. b. Plomion, Aisne, May 8, 1927. She began to study the piano at an early age and entered the National Conservatory of Lille at the age of 11. There she studied the piano under Kara Chatteleyn and composition under Edmond Gaujac and at the age of 13 won the Conservatory's first prize. She performed in recitals in France and the United States. She attended the Collegium Musicum de France and was admitted to the Société des Auteurs, Compositeurs et Editeurs de Musique. She was organist of the Sacre-Coeur Church in Antibes.
Compositions
CHAMBER
Badinage (vln and pf) (1957)
Chant d'amour mystique (vln and org) (1974)
Extrait, Tuerkesse (vln and pf) (1950)
Lui et elle (vln and pf) (1955)
PIANO
Allors se dressant, il commanda au vent et à la mer (1961)
Attente (1950)
Elle court .... Elle court .... la micheline (1969)
L'espiegle jongleur
Esquisses de vacances
Evocations (1950)
Fantaisie (1950)
Gyoniam ipsi consolabuntur (1953)
Heures sylvestres (1954)
Loins dans la montagne
Marche funèbre (1961)
Marche romaine (1961)
Mon chien et moi (1950)
Prélude (1957)
Le quatuor s'amuse (1970)
Scherzo (1957)
Theatre d'enfants, theme and progressive variations (1961)
Trois pièces: Au bois joli; L'heure qui tir et qui chante (1972) (Lemoine)
En ce lieu savage, il y a bien longtemps, étude (left hand) (1962)
Teaching pieces
VOCAL
Dormeuse, lullaby (1953)
O navire immobile, melody
Près d'un étang (vce and pf) (1964)
Six melodies (1957)
SACRED
Au Christ-roi, cantata (B, T and mix-ch) (1960)
Jesus en sa crèche (ch, chil-vces and org) (1956)
Cantum ergo (mix-ch and org) (1959)
Annonce de Pacques (B and ch) (1968-1969)
Tendre invocations au Sacre-Coeur (B and ch) (1968)
Chant d'allegresse pour l'Ascension (mix-ch) (1961)
Deux mélodies (chil-ch) (1960)
Je crois en Dieu (mix-ch)
Je vous salue Marie (mix chil-ch) (1961)
Kyrie eleison (mix-ch) (1961)
Dans ta demeure, Seigneur (vln and org) (1956)
Adoration pour une nuit de Noël (org) (1959)
Ave Maria (1971)
Hymne à St. Jeanne d'Arc (1959)
Meditation devant un crucifix (org) (1971)
Nos âmes s'elancent vers toi, Seigneur Jesus (vln and pf or org) (1956)

Pater Noster (B, vln and org) (1969)
Sonate de Noël (pf) (1959)
Sunt unum, melodie pour un marriage (1970)
THEATRE
Les fourberies de Scapin (Moliere)
Ref. composer, Billaudot (Paris)

VILLINES, Virginia
20th-century American composer.
Compositions
VOCAL
Songs incl.:
Bird in the bamboo
Chopin at candlelighting
The color poet
I got a glory, Negro spiritual
The passionate shepherd
The rain
Sea call December song
Serenade to a child, lullaby
Thoughts
To a singer (ded Gerard Souzay)
The trinket
The vagabond songs, poems (Don Blanding)
SACRED
It must have been, Christmas song
Star faith, song
Ref. Composers Press Inc.

VINETTE, Alice (Rev. Soeur Marie-Jocelyn, S.S.A.)
Canadian organist, pianist, teacher and composer. b. Saint-Urbain, Quebec, April 24, 1894. She studied the piano under R.O. Pelletier, the organ and harmony under Raoul Paquet, composition under Rodolphe Matthieu and Auguste Descarries and singing under Fleurette Contant. She received a Mus.Bac. She taught harmony, counterpoint, voice, the piano and the organ at the Institute Pedagogique des Soeurs de Saint-Anne.
Compositions
CHAMBER
Prelude (pf)
SACRED
Messe breve (3 equal vces) (Editions de la Violette, 1950)
Si tu savais le don de Dieu, poème evangélique
Ref. 133

VINNING, Rosetta. See O'LEARY, Rosetta

VINOGRADOVA, Vera
20th-century Soviet concert pianist and composer. b. Leningrad. She studied under L. Nikolayev and M. Steinberg at the Leningrad Conservatory and traveled outside Russia as a concert pianist.
Compositions
ORCHESTRA
Piano concerto
Ballade (pf and cham orch)
CHAMBER
String quartet
Suite (vln and pf)
Other small compositions
Ref. 38

VINTULE, Ruta Evaldovna
Soviet concertmistress and composer. b. Riga, Latvia, January 6, 1944. She studied composition under Y. Ivanov at the Latvian Conservatory, graduating in 1967. After being concertmistress at the Conservatory she was concertmistress of the Latvian Philharmonic Orchestra till 1968.
Compositions
ORCHESTRA
Concertino for piano and string orchestra (1969)
Simfonietta (1971)
The year 1905, poem (1967)
CHAMBER
String quartet (1967)
PIANO
Sonata (1966)
Sonatina (1968)

VOCAL
Solitse mira, cantata (I. Mezhnor) (ch) (1967)
Vocalise (ch) (1969)
Winter impressions, cycle (vce and pf) (1971)
Choruses, romances and other songs
Songs (Latvian poets) (1972)
Ref. 21

VIOLIN VIRTUOSO. See TORRA, Celia

VIRGIL, Antha Minerva Patchen
American pianist, teacher, writer and composer. b. Elmira, NY, ca. 1855; d. New York, 1939. She wrote for musical journals and with her husband, who invented the Virgil silent-practice keyboard, she patented improvements for the pedal and keyboard.
Compositions
PIANO
Over 200 pieces incl.:
Etudes, studies and short pieces
Op. 21 in 4 numbers
Op. 22 in 3 numbers
Op. 23 in 3 numbers
Ref. 226, 347, 353, 433

VIRTUE, Constance Cochnower (Mrs. Clark W.)
American organist, pianist, editor, lecturer and composer. b. Cincinnati, OH, January 6, 1905. She received a B.Mus. from the College of Music at the University of Cincinnati in 1927. In 1933 she was the originator of the Virtue Notagraph, a seven-line semitone staff notation; this she later further simplified and made more widely serviceable. In 1980 came the inclusion and description of the Notagraph in the 6th edition of the Grove Dictionary. She received an MOE research award in 1938 and her master's degree in sacred music from the Union Theological Seminary in New York in 1945. As a private teacher she taught the piano, the organ and theory. She was organist-director at a number of churches, including Mt. Auburn Presbyterian; St. Luke's Evangelical Lutheran in New York in 1945 and Mission Hills Congregational in San Diego from 1955 to 1957 and the First Unitarian in San Diego, 1960 to 1965. She taught the organ at the Convent of the Sacred Heart from 1960 to 1968 and at Grossmont College, 1961 to 1963. She played the piano for local artist concerts and toured with the opera program for Alaska Music Trails in 1968. She gave lectures on 19th- and 20th-century music at the University of California and served as editor, partner and president of Virtue Notagraph Editions. She received numerous awards, including five first prizes in composition contests. PHOTOGRAPH.
Compositions
ORCHESTRA
Mystic sonnet: To a tree in bloom (also pf) (prize)
CHAMBER
String quartet in G (1923)
Romanza (vln, vlc and pf) (1925)
Fairy tale for a sleepy child (vlc) (1941)
For spring returning (vln) (1941)
VOCAL
Love is like a rose, song (New York: G. Schirmer)
Six songs from the chronology of love (1941)
SACRED
I will lift up mine eyes, anthem (1926) (New York: H.W. Gray)
THEATRE
What gift to the king? Christmas music drama (1924)
The Queen of Camelot, music drama (E. Kruckemeyer) (vces and orch) (1931)
ARRANGEMENTS
America, the beautiful (1938)
Publications
Design for a Modern Notation. 1945. Copies in the British Museum, Bibliotheque Nationale, Index of New Musical Notation, New York Library, Lincoln Center.
Music Without Accidents. In the Triangle of MOE. 1975-1976.
Ref. composer, 84, 359

VIRTUOSISSIMA CANTATRICE. See STROZZI, Barbara

VISCONTI, Caterina
Italian composer.
Composition
VOCAL
Aria (vce and basso continuo)
Ref. 160

VISCONTI, Leila

Italian harpsichordist, pianist, teacher and composer. b. Novara, June 20, 1954. She completed her musical studies at the Verdi Conservatory in Milan, under Bruno Canino (piano), E. Giordani Sartori (harpsichord) and A. Maggiori (composition). She was the recipient of several prizes and awards. PHOTOGRAPH.

Compositions
ORCHESTRA
   Ensembler (vln and orch) (1976) (Milan: Suvini E. Zerboni)
   Ruinhlach (fl and orch) (prize Citta di Belveglio) (1979) (Suvini E. Zerboni)
   Zadkiel (pf and orch) (prize G.F. Malipiero, Treviso, 1978) (Zerboni)
   Souce Saison claire (1979) (Zerboni)
CHAMBER
   Paperworld (vln and pf) (1st prize, Citta di Varese, 1978) (Zerboni)
   Ywis (fl and hpcd) (1978) (Zerboni)
   Ailes (pf) (1979) (hon mention, 1979) (Zerboni)
VOCAL
   Aux foules de comprende (cham ch and 5 insts) (1980) (Zerboni)
Ref. composer

VISVAVARA

Poetess-musician member of the priestly family of Atreya, India. ca. 1200 B.C. She was of the Atri race and reputed to have lived a spiritual, unworldy life. In the Rig-Veda, there are references to women and their authority in religion, music and social life, which show that women in early Aryan society were respected and protected without having their personal ability limited. A marriage-hymn to Agni, the fire god, invoking perfection of the bond between husband and wife, is ascribed in the Rig-Veda to Visvavara.
Ref. 264. 414

VITALI-AUGUSTI, Giuseppina

Italian poetess, singer and composer. b. Odessa, ca. 1855; d. Rome, February, 1915. She was the daughter of the singer Raffaele Vitali and married the tenor Paolo Augusti. She achieved success in Europe with her performances of Verdi's operas. Rossini wrote several variations for her on *Gazza Ladra*.

Compositions
VOCAL
   Songs on her own poems (Ricordi)
Publications
   Divagazioni notturne.
   Pensieri poetici.
Ref. 105

VITALIANI, Contessa Raffaela. See ROZWADOWSKI, Contessa Raffaela

VITALIS, Sister Mary

American choral conductor, lecturer singer, pianist and composer. b. Evansville, IN, December 11, 1898. She graduated from the Immaculate Conception College in Oldenburg, IA, in 1914, having studied under Sister M. Adele and was later a scholarship student of the piano and voice at the Cincinnati Conservatory of Music, studying under Leo Paalz and Mary Ann Kaufman and gaining her B.M. in 1925 and M.M. in 1932. She taught in elementary and high schools and then colleges, becoming head of the music department and director of choral ensembles at Marian College in 1940.

Compositions
SACRED
   Angelus Domini (J. Fischer)
   Dignare me laudare D (J. Fischer)
   Ite ad Joseph (J. Fischer)
   Pater Noster Franciscus (J. Fischer)
   Tu es sacerdos (J. Fischer)
Ref. 496

VITO-DELVAUX, Berthe di

Belgian pianist, lecturer and composer. b. Angleur, Liège, May 17, 1915. She came from a musical family and her father was an organist. She was a student at the Royal Music Conservatory of Liège where she studied solfege, the piano, harmony, counterpoint and fugue and was awarded first prize with honors. Afterwards she studied composition at the Royal Music Conservatory in Brussels under Leon Jongen. She was a teacher at the Royal Conservatory of Liège from 1938. She was the recipient of numerous honors and awards including: the prize Marie from the city of Liège; the Prix de Rome (1943); the Prix Modeste Gretry (1962); scholarships to work and travel from the Ministry of National Education and Culture (1963); two gold medals from the Association des Arts, Sciences et Lettres of France; first prize in the competition of Melodies Les Arts en Europe (1965); the Prix du Salon for her *Sonatines* and a Palmes d'or de la couronne civic medal for her 25 year career (1967). DISCOGRAPHY. PHOTOGRAPH.

Compositions
ORCHESTRA
   Concerto de Noël, op. 91 (vln and orch) (1963)
   Concerto No. 1, op. 93 (1963)
   Concerto No. 2 (hn and str orch) (1965)
   Concerto pour piano, op. 120 (1969)
   Five pieces, op. 27 (fl and orch) (1943)
   Improvisation et finale, op. 30 (pf and orch) (1946)
   Neilovim (insaisissable), op. 123 (trp and orch) (1970)
   Barcarolle, op. 97 (fl and str orch) (1965)
   Capriccio, op. 43A (vln and cham orch) (1949)
   Eclogue, op. 52 (fl and cham orch) (1952)
   Esquisse mythologique, op. 114 (ballet Pavlova) (small orch; also pf) (1966)
   Fantaisie sur un air populaire, op. 47 (1951)
   Folletti, op. 33 (1946)
   Images d'Espagne, op. 13 (1941)
   La Malibran, op. 56, suite (1952)
   Ouverture dramatique, op. 32 (1946)
   Polichinelle mélodie, op. 104 (Maurice Careme) (also pf) (1965)
   Scherzo, op. 8 (1939)
   Trois airs à danser, op. 48 (cham orch; also pf, op. 49) (1951)
   Variations sur la chanson flamande, op. 78 (Te Hasselt lang de baan) (str orch) (1957)
   Variations sur un vieux cramignon, op. 132 (prix de la Province de Liège)
   Xenia, overture, op. 9 (1939)
CHAMBER
   Sons de'Ovifat (4 trp, 4 trb, tba and vln) (1981)
   Quintette, op. 101 (ww) (1965)
   Suite pour quintette, op. 59 (str qrt and fl) (Hassels Meiliedeken) (1953)
   Suite. op. 62 (str qrt and fl) (1954)
   Woodwind quintet, op. 112 (1966)
   Jeux d'enfants, op. 19 (sax qrt) (1942)
   Suite, op. 23 (sax qrt) (1943)
   Suite, op. 35 (str qrt) (1947)
   Trio, op. 44 (ob, cl and bsn) (1949)
   Trio serenade, op. 43b (vln, vlc and pf) (1949)
   Adagio, op. 68 (vlc and pf) (1954)
   Concertino, op. 50 (trb and pf) (1952)
   Divertissement, op. 26 (cl and pf) (1943)
   Eclogue, op. 51 (fl and pf) (1952)
   Entrata e rondo, op. 90 (vln and pf) (1963)
   Les feux de la nuit (perc and pf) (1981)
   Prélude et finale (bsn and pf) (1941)
   Sonate, op. 81 (vln and pf) (1959)
   Sonatine, op. 61 (cl and pf) (1953)
   Sonatina, op. 76 (vln and pf) (1957)
   Suite, op. 14 (cl and pf) (1941)
   Suite, op. 15 (bsn and pf) (1941)
   Trevoga (angoisse) op. 128, concert piece (ob and pf) (1971)
   Histoires pour guitare, op. 139 (1979) (Schott)
   Suite, op. 16 (vln) (1941)
PIANO
   Trois mouvements, op. 99 (2 pf) (1964)
   Fantaisie sur un air populaire, op. 69, Zeg kwezelken wilde dij danson (pf reduction, 4 hands) (1954)
   Burlesque, op. 18 (1941)
   Danse du faune et bacchanale, op. 119 (1968)
   Entrata et rondo, op. 64 (1954)
   Festi dei bimbi, op. 119, pieces pour debutantes (1968)
   Mits mats variations sur le chanson populaire Le long de la route de Hasselt, op. 66 (1954)
   Solfege à deux clés, op. 118 (1968)
   Sonata, op. 7 (1939)
   Sonata, op. 60 (1953)
   Sonatine No. 1, op. 102 (1965)
   Sonatine No. 2 in F-Major, op. 108 (1966)
   Sonatine No. 3 in F-Major, op. 110 (1966)
   Suite, op. 63 (1954)
   Toccatina, op. 129, no. 1 (1971)
   Trois pièces, op. 17: En voyage; Pochade; Tambour (1941)
   Variations, op. 96 (1965)
VOCAL
   Hero et Leandre, op. 11, cantata (Felix Bodson) (1940)
   Le navigation d'Ulysse, op. 20, cantata (solos, ch and orch) (Prix de Rome, 1943)
   Le légend de la flute magique, op. 38 (narr, chil-ch, fl solo and cham orch) (1949)
   Pièce concertante. op. 105 (Cont and orch) (1965)

Les sapins, chantet, op. 36 (rec, ch and orch) (1948)
Le lanterne magique, op. 107 (mix-ch a-cap) (1965)
Petit chanson d'automne, op. 53 (mix-ch) (1952)
Pommier, op. 126 (m-ch) (1976)
Quatre choeurs (ch a-cap) (1979)
Sur la route de Cricqueboeuf, op. 126 (mix-ch) (1971)
Vieille chanson, op. 88 (m-ch a-cap) (1961)
Andante et scherzo, op. 28, no. 1 (A and pf) (1943)
La chamelle à marier, op. 103, melody (vce and qnt) (1965)
Chanson, op. 28, no. 2 (Bilitis de P. Louys) (2 w-vces) (1943)
Le critique, op. 116 (Paul Valery) (vce and ww qrt) (1968)
Demain, op. 75 (w-vces) (1956)
Elle gardait, op. 3 (2 w-vces) (G. Vicaire) (1938)
Il etait une fois, op. 4 (J. Adalbert) (2 w-vces) (1938)
Hymne au travail, op. 31 (m-vces a-cap) (prix de la deputation permanente du Limbourg) (1946)
Minon, op. 79 (narr and pf) (1959)
Sonate, op. 60, série noire (A and pf) (1953)
Tovle Mozan, op. 5 (ch; also vce and pf) (1939)
Trois satires, op. 65, série noire (F. Bodson) (vce and pf) (1954) (1st prize Arts en Europe, 1965)
Vocalise, op. 124 (Pro Civitate) (high vce and pf) (1971)
Songs:
Alleluia d'amour-te souviens tu, op. 22, 2 melodies (1943)
L'amour vainqueur, op. 46, cycle (1951)
La bien-aimée, no. 1, op. 106, cycle (Maurice Careme) (1965)
Chanson d'ami, op. 54 (1952)
Chanson medievale, op. 39, mélodie (1949)
Deux chansons tristes, op. 64 (1952)
Devinettes, op. 94, mélodie (1964)
Les etoiles, op. 21, mélodie (1943)
Extases, op. 25, 6 love songs (N. de Sart) (ded C. Panzera, 1943)
Instant, op. 58, mélodie (1952)
Mélodies, op. 131 (1972)
Nostalgia, op. 111 (M. Careme) (1966)
Nuage gris, nuage bleu, op. 80, mélodie (1959)
Nuit de Decembre (vce and pf) (1981)
Offrande, op. 125, mélodie De La Haye (1971)
Pelegrinage, op. 86, mélodie (1961)
Pluit dans le nuit, op. 40 (1949)
Quatre chansons à Tescaly, mélodie (1980)
Quinze chansons enfantines, op. 130 (1972)
Rupture, op. 89, mélodie (B. Bolsee) (1961)
Silence, op. 42 (1949)
Les sept peches capitaux, op. 117 (1968)
Six melodies, ops. 1 and 2 (1938)
Six papueretes, op. 67, children's songs (1954)
Solitude, op. 57, melodie (M. Voilier) (1952)
Solitude, op. 127, melodie (Riga Bonvosin) (1971)
Source enchantée, op. 41 (1949)
Souvenir, op. 53 (1952)
Voeux a l'aimée, op. 84, melodie (1959)
SACRED
Gethsemani, op. 133, oratorio (S. Berthe) (T, ch and orch) (1973)
L'enfant prodigue, op. 10, cantata (Liebrecht) (1940)
Psaume, op. 12 (solos, ch and lg orch) (1941)
Messe des Disciples (m-ch) (1979) (CeBeDeM)
Noël, op. 121 (w-ch) (1968-1969)
Concerto de Noël, op. 91 (vln) (1962-1963)
Salve Regina (4 chil-vces and org) (1981)
BALLET
L'Ambitieux puni, op. 72, in 1 act (1955)
Amours paiennes, op. 24, ballet (N. de Sart) (solos, ch and orch) (1943)
Et les cancans ...., op. 113 (ww qnt) (1966)
Un jour de vacances, op. 73, in 1 act (1957)
Pourquoi? op. 85, in 2 acts and 4 tableaux (A. Bordaloue)
Le prisonnier, op. 71, in one act (1955)
Le semeur du mal, op. 77, in 2 acts (ch) (1957)
Sous le chapiteau, op. 83, 12 circus scenes (1957)
OPERA
Abigail, op. 45, in 4 acts (Jean de Sart)
Les Amants de Sestos, op. 37, tragedy in 3 scenes (F. Bodson) (1949)
Magda, l'ange dans les tenebres, op. 87, opera-ballet in 4 acts (J. de Sart) (1961)
La Malibran, op. 29 (N. de Sart) (1946)
Maribel, op. 115, comic opera in 4 acts (Nestor Eermans) (1967)
Monsieur Gretry, with adaptation, in 4 acts (1979)
Nouvel acte Abigail, op. 74 (1956)
La Palette, tryptique, op. 95 (N. Eermans) (1964)
Spoutnik, op. 82 (C. Morraye) (1959)
OPERETTA
La Leçon, op. 55, comic opera in 1 act, for children (1952)
THEATRE
L'Amant Timide, op. 34, musique de scène (Tirso Demolina, adapted by F. Maret) (orch) (1949)
Ref. composer, 563

VIVADO ORSINI, Ida

Chilean pianist, lecturer and composer. b. Tacna, August, 1916. She studied at the National Conservatory of the University of Chile, under E. Castrillon and A. Spikin Howard and graduated in the piano in 1942. She studied composition under D. Santa Cruz and Free Focke and was awarded a grant by the Italian Government for the study of contemporary Italian music. She lectured at the National Conservatory and her teaching manuals are used in national conservatories. DISCOGRAPHY.

Compositions
PIANO
Ochos trozos, 4 hands (prize, Instituto del Chile, 1976)
Anoranza
Dos momentos: Con expresion doliente; Con gracia (1976)
Estudios, 15 pieces (11 in C. Botto's El pianista chileno) (1966)
Six studies (1967)
Six pieces for children (1964)
Suite (1955)
Tres preludios y tema con variaciones; originally Cuatro preludios (1952) (prize, 1952)
VOCAL
Ay Huasa, divertimento (vce and orch) (1972)
Picaresca (vce and orch) (1977) (Facultad de Artes Musicales)
Himno (ch and pf)
Tres poemas y una cancion (1949) (Spikin Howard) (Santiego: University of Chile, 1952)
Ref. 90, 563

VIZANA (Vizani, Viziani, Vezzana) Lucretia (Lucrezia) Orsina

Italian musician, singer and composer. b. Bologne, ca. 1593; d. March 7, 1662. She was a nun at the convent of Saint Christina in Bologna and wrote publications on counterpoint and harmony.

Compositions
SACRED
Componimenti musicali de motetti a une e piu voci di Donna Lucretia Orsini Vizana Monaca nel Sacro Coleggio di Santa Christini di Bologna Della Congregatione Camaldolense (ded. alla medesme Monache Anno 1623) (Venice: Gardano, appresso Bartholomeo Magni, 1623)
Concerto musicali, raccolta di madrigali a piu voci (Gardano, 1623)
Ref. 26. 105, 216, 226, 242, 260, 276, 335, 347, 653

VIZANI or VIZIANI, Lucretia Orsina. See VIZANA, Lucretia Orsina

VLAD, Marina

20th-century Rumanian composer. DISCOGRAPHY.
Compositions
CHAMBER
String quartet No. 2
Sonata (pf)

VLADERACKEN, Geertruida van

Dutch soprano, writer and composer. b. Haarlem, April 18, 1880; d. Naarden, January 2, 1947. She studied under Bernard Zweers and A. Tierie, but was mainly self-taught. She traveled in England, France, Germany, Austria and Scandinavia.

Compositions
VOCAL
Bloemencantate
Lenteliedjes (vce and pf) (Utrecht: De Haan)
Children's songs
SACRED
Ave Virgo (S, vln and pf)
Plange Sion (vce and org)
OPERETTA
Goudhaartje en de Troubadour, for children
De Koningskeuze, for children
De Sneeuwmannetjes, for children
De Tooverbal, for children
Publications
Beter zingen. 1946.
Het Klavier bij Bach. 1948.
Muziek. 1946.
Ref. 26, 44, 110

VOELLMY-LIECHTI, Grety

Swiss organist, pianist, teacher and composer. b. Fribourg, 1904. Her first piano teacher was her father, then at 16 she became a pupil of Abbé Joseph Bovet in Fribourg, who taught her the organ, the piano, theory and composition and encouraged her to publish her work. Later in Paris she continued her piano studies under Alfred Cortot and counterpoint and composition under Nadia Boulanger (q.v.). She then taught in Murten. The influence of Bach and Wagner can be discerned in her work.

Compositions
CHAMBER
Pieces
Piano pieces
VOCAL
Songs (Foerisch)
SACRED
Gott und die Menschen, cantata (Walter Dietiker) (ch and org) (1928)
Second cantata
Ref. 651

VOIGT, Henriette (Henny)
German choir conductor, singer, teacher and composer. b. Potsdam, October 12, 1872. She studied at the Berlin Academy and in Holland under Julia Culp. She traveled widely, singing in concerts and then conducted a women's choir and taught music in Potsdam. She composed piano pieces, an operetta and songs.
Ref. 70, 226

VOIGT, Henny. See VOIGT, Henriette

VOIGT-SCHWEIKERT, Margarete
German pianist, teacher, writer and composer. b. Karlsruhe, February 16, 1887. She studied composition under S. de Lange and Joseph Haas in Karlsruhe and Stuttgart and was a virtuoso pianist. She composed violin pieces, a children's operetta and songs.
Ref. 70, 105, 226

VOJACKOVA-WETCHE, Ludmila
Czech pianist, accompanist, teacher and composer. b. Northern Hungary, August 2, 1872. She studied in Prague, at the Royal Academy of Music, London and under Theodore Ysaye and Richter at the Geneva Conservatory. She made her debut in 1890 at the Prague Conservatory and as Sevcik's accompanist, toured Europe, England and the United States. She taught in the United States.
Ref. 226

VOLKART, Hazel
20th-century American organist, pianist, teacher and composer. She began playing the piano at the age of three, after listening to her elder sister's lessons. She studied at the Oklahoma College for Women under Bertha Hornaday (organ) and Drs. John Thompson, Wiktor Labunskid and DeRubertus at the Kansas City Conservatory; at the University of Missouri, Kansas City under Drs. Francis Buebendort, George Simpson and Wiktor Labunski and at the University of Kansas under Dr. Hanson. She also studied under Sir Carl Busch. She was a private piano teacher in Kansas and Missouri for 45 years. She won first place in Mu Phi Epsilon Convention in 1963 for her *Sonatina in C*.

Compositions
BAND
Victory entree march
TEACHING PIECES
Reverie (2 vln, pf and vlc)
Over 300 organ and piano pieces for children incl.:
Bob o-link
Coral sea
The frog
Gavotte in E-Flat
Gavotte in G
Japanese doll dance
Marionette
Mid-night
Nocturne in C
Nocturne in G
Pirate king
Sonatina in C (prize, Mu Phi Epsilon)
That certain thing
That crazy tune
MISCELLANEOUS
Memories of days gone by
Merry Christmas to you
Tear drops
Ref. Merriam Music Study Club, 40, 347

VOLKART-SCHLAGER, Kaethe
Austrian concert pianist, teacher and composer. b. Vienna, February 7, 1897. She entered the Stuttgart Music Academy in 1913 and studied the piano under Max Pauer and Wilhelm Kempff and composition under Joseph Hass, graduating in 1917. She continued her studies under Wilhelm Kempff and others until 1929. In Vienna, Hanover and other cities she gave advanced courses for teachers as well as concerts and traveled to Sweden, Turkey and Finland. From 1947 to 1969 she taught composition and improvisation in Stuttgart and became head of the music teaching department in a school there.

Compositions
CHAMBER
Cycle (ob and vla; also vla and vlc)
Moravian suite (ob and pf) (1936)
Singende Windrose (vln and pf) (1974)
Sonate in C-Minor (vln and pf)
Sonate in G-Minor (vln and pf)
Two sonatinas (ob and pf or vln and hpcd) (1937)
PIANO
Der Spielgarten (4 hands)
Mohrentanz und Mummenschanz (4 hands)
Wir musizieren an 2 Klavieren (1937)
Allerlei fuer drei, 2 vols (1937)
Der bunte Tonkreis, I and II (1939)
Fuer Klavierleute (1937)
Jahrmarkt, 12 pieces
Kleine Welt, 10 pieces
Rumelian suite (1945)
Zu zweit mit Freud, I and II (1937)
Teaching and other pieces
VOCAL
About 200 songs
Ref. composer, 81

VOLKMANN, Ida
German pianist, teacher and composer. b. Insterberg, East Prussia, August 28, 1838. She composed elementary teaching pieces for the piano, in collaboration with Lina Ramann (q.v.)
Ref. 226

VOLKONSKAYA, Zinanda Alexandrovna, Princess
Russian contralto, poetess, writer and composer. b. Turin, December 14, 1792; d. Rome, February 5, 1862. She was the daughter of a diplomat and in her youth wrote verses and songs for amateur concerts. After her marriage to Prince Volkonsky in 1810 she lived in Petersburg and then in Paris. Her salon was a meeting place of numerous poets and musicians. She published collections of poems and other works and composed secular cantatas and romances.
Ref. 330

VOLKSTEIN, Pauline
German composer. b. Quedlinburg, January 19, 1894; d. Weimar, May 6, 1925. She lived in Dresden, Merano and Naples before settling in Weimar in 1905. She then composed about 1200 songs, including 20 with guitar accompaniment, which were published in collections.
Ref. 105

VOLLENHOVEN, Hanna van
Dutch pianist and composer. b. The Hague, January 12, 1894. At the Amsterdam Conservatory she studied under Julius Roentgen, Louis Coenen, Hugo Riemann and Leopold Godowsky. She made her debut in 1909 and visited the United States in 1915.

Compositions
ORCHESTRA
Galathea, symphonic poem
CHAMBER
String quartet
VOCAL
Folk songs
Songs
Ref. 226

VON BINGEN, Hildegarde. See HILDEGARDE, Saint

VON BRAUN, Madeleine. See SCHULZ, Madeleine

VON DECKER, Pauline. See SCHATZELL, Pauline von

VON GUNDEN, Heidi

American lecturer and composer. b. San Diego, April 13, 1940. She studied under Matt Doran at Mount St. Mary's College, under Byong-Kon at California State University and composition and theory under Pauline Oliveros (q.v.), Robert Erickson and Kenneth Gaburo at the University of California, San Diego, receiving a Ph.D.. She was teaching assistant at the University of California from 1972 to 1974 and later on the theory-composition faculty of the University of Illinois.

Compositions
CHAMBER
  Diathrosis (org, hpcd, 2 trb, 2 acdn, cel and pf)
  Triptych (org, hpcd and perc)
VOCAL
  Zen gestures, series of short pieces (Paul Reps) (1980)
ELECTRONIC
  Fantasy (org, pipes, cl, perc and tape)
MULTIMEDIA
  Mass for Pentecost (ch, resonating tubes, org, tape and projected score)
Ref. 142

VON HAGEN, Elizabeth

Composition
CHAMBER
  The country maid, or L'amour est un enfant trompeur (pf or hpcd)
Ref. 228

VON HOFF, Elizabeth (nee Chamberlaine)

English organist, pianist, teacher and composer. d. before 1890. She studied under W.S. Bennett at the Royal Academy of Music and in 1843 was a King's Scholar. She married the tenor, composer and teacher Henry von Hoff. From 1857 she was the organist of the Rectory Church in Marylebone. She composed piano pieces.
Ref. 6, 85, 347

VON KOENNERITZ, Nina. See ESCHBORN, Georgine Christine Maria

VON KRALIK, Mathilde. See KRALIK VON MAYERSWALDEN

VON PECHY, Valerie

American harpist, teacher and composer. b. Cleveland, December 11, 1947. She gained degrees from Baldwin-Wallace College, OH, and the University of Miami. She was second harpist with the Miami Philharmonic Orchestra and principal harpist with the Miami Opera Orchestra and the Fort Lauderdale Symphony Orchestra.
Composition
CHAMBER
  Sweet is my layde love (hp)
Ref. 206

VON ROSSOW, Helene. See HROSWITHA

VON SCHORLEMMER, Erna. See SCHORLEMMER, Erna von

VON SCHULTZ, Ella. See ADAJEWSKY, Ella

VON ZEDLITZ, Baroness. See KINGSTON, Marie Antoinette

VON ZIERITZ, Grete

Austrian pianist, professor and composer. b. Vienna, March 10, 1899. From 1912 to 1917 she attended the Styrian Conservatory in Graz where she studied the piano under H. Kriemer and composition under R. van Mojsisovics-Mojsvar. She graduated with distinction in all subjects. She moved to Berlin in 1917 and furthered her piano studies under Martin Krause and R.M. Breithaupt and composition under Franz Schreker. She taught the piano at Stern Conservatory, Berlin and toured in Germany and abroad. She won the Mendelssohn state prize for composition in 1928 and a Schubert scholarship of the Columbia Phonograph Company, New York. In 1958 she was nominated Professor by the Austrian Federal President, Dr. Schaerf, being the first woman composer so honored. DISCOGRAPHY. PHOTOGRAPH.

Compositions
ORCHESTRA
  Bilder vom Jahrmarkt (fl and orch: also fl and pf) (Ries & Erler, 1936)
  Concerto for one player on four different flutes and orchestra (1970)
  Sizilianische Rhapsodie (vln and orch) (Astoria, 1956)
  Symphonic music (pf and orch) (1928)
  Triple concerto (fl, cl, bsn and orch) (Astoria, 1950)
  Zigeunerkonzert in 6 Bildern (vln and orch) (1982)
  Das Gifhorner Konzert (fl, hp and str orch) (1940)
  Divertimento (cham orch) (1962)
  Gebet (small orch) (1916)
  Intermezzo diabolico (1932)
  Kleine Abendmusik (str orch) (1916)
  Musik der Pferde, suite (1937)
  Serenata (small orch) (1949)
CHAMBER
  Concertino (cl, hn, bsn and str qnt) (1982) (Ries & Erler)
  Sextet (bsn and str qnt) (Astoria, 1965)
  Quintet (trp, trb, 2 pf and perc) (rev 1973) (Astoria, 1959)
  Serenade (fl, ob, cl, bsn and hn) (Astoria, 1965)
  Suite in four movements (fl, ob, cl, bsn and pf) (1937)
  String quartet (1916)
  Two pieces (str qrt) (1926)
  Tanzsuite (gtr or hp, bsn and perc) (1958)
  Die Jagd, concert piece (cl, hn and pf) (1957)
  Trio (cl, hn and pf; also ob, cl and bsn) (1955) (Ries & Erler, 1971)
  Bockelberger suite (fl and pf) (Ries & Erler, 1971)
  Danza (2 gtr) (1979)
  Fantasie in two movements (vln and pf) (1921)
  Folkloristische Fantasie (vln and pf) (1982)
  Fuenf Aphorismen (vln and vlc) (Ries & Erler, 1971)
  Ildiko und Attila, scene (vln and 5-str d-b)
  Kaleidoskop (vln and vla) (1969)
  Ligaea, die Sirene (vln and pf) (Astoria, 1964)
  Music (cl and pf) (Frankfurt am Main: Wilhelm Zimmermann, 1957)
  Sonata (vla and pf) (1940)
  Suite (a-cl and pf) (1952)
  Variationen ueber Signale u. Maersche der alten k.u.k. Oesterreichischen-ungarischen Monarchie (hn and pf) (1956)
  Verurteilter Zigeuner (vln and pf) (1956)
  Le violon de la mort (danses macabres) (vln and pf; also vln, pf and orch; also vla, hps and pf) (Ries & Erler, 1952)
  '1914' Fantasie-sonata (vln and pf) (1917)
  Autobiographie (vln) (Astoria, 1965)
  Une humoresque diabolique (d-b) (1980) (Ries & Erler)
  Le roi à fait battre tambour (oboe d'amour) (1973)
  Suite (vla) (1976)
  Triptychon (1 player on fl, a-fl and picc) (Astoria, 1968)
  Der Waldspaziergang (cl) (1983)
  Zigeunerromanze (vln) (1984)
PIANO
  Doppelfuge, cis-moll (1924)
  Fuenf kurze Skizzen (1919)
  Praeludium und Fuge (also org) (Ries & Erler, 1924)
  Sechs Daemonentaenze aus dem chinesischen Gespensterbuch (1948)
  Sonata (1928)
  Suite in six movements (1926)
  Zwei Fugen (Ries & Erler, 1921)
  Other pieces (1915, 1959, 1963)
VOCAL
  Bergthora, overture (w-ch, org and large orch) (1917)
  Die Zigeunerin Agrippina, 6 songs (S and orch) (1956)
  Hymne (Novalis) (B and orch) (1943)
  Hymnus der Erde, 6 songs (Ina Seidel) (S and orch) (1937)
  Passion im Urwald, 6 songs (S and orch) (1930)
  Vogellieder, 5 songs (Eleonora Kalkowska and composer) (S, fl and orch) (1933)
  Berglied (mix-ch a-cap) (Vienna: Ludwig Krenn, 1962)
  Dem Sonnengott (Hoelderlin) (4 part w-ch a-cap) (Astoria, 1940)
  Five Portuguese and Spanish songs (8 part mix-ch a-cap) (Astoria, 1966)
  Kosmische Wanderung, 7 choruses (mix-ch a-cap, timp and perc) (Astoria, 1969)
  Sieben Gesaenge, auf Dichtungen moderner Neger-Lyrik (8 part mix-ch a-cap) (Astoria, 1966)
  Three choruses (m-ch a-cap) (1973)

Three choruses (Fontane) (mix-ch a-cap) (1973)
Two choruses (mix-ch a-cap) (1948)
Vier alt-aztekische Gesaenge (8 part mix-ch a-cap) (Astoria, 1966)
Acht arabische Gesaenge (Bar and pf) (1941-1944)
Aus den Klageliedern Jeremiae (2 w-vces and pf) (1915)
Das ewige Du (von Below) (A and pf) (1938)
Das goldene Herz, 4 songs (Decarlie) (coloratura S and pf) (1947)
Der letzte Weg, 8 songs (Molse) (A and pf) (1950)
Drei Gesaenge (Bluecher von Wahlstatt) (Bar, vlc and pf) (1946)
Fiebergeschichte (Hamsun) (A and pf) (1933)
Five songs (Rilke & Herse) (T and pf) (1943)
Five sonnets (Louise Labe) (S and pf) (1942)
Four songs (Agnes Miegel) (S and pf) (1930)
Fuenf Gesaenge (Nietzsche) (4 vces and pf) (1935)
Kinderlied, from Des Knaben Wunderhorn (S and pf) (1927)
Lieder des Hafis (Bar and pf) (1924)
Muse von Kerkyra, 3 songs (dramatic S and pf) (1924)
Nachtwachen der Liebe, 3 songs (Schuetz) (Bar and pf) (1941)
Quartett (S, ob, cl and hp) (1972)
Sechs Gesaenge (George) (Bar and str qrt) (1935)
Sechs Balladen (Schuetz) (Bar and pf) (1946)
Sechs Kinderlieder (S and pf) (1938)
Stimmen im Walde (coloratura S and fl) (1954)
Three songs (T and pf) (1921)
Three songs in praise of Polish poets: In praise of health (Kolchan-owski); In praise of the Fatherland (Mickiewicz); In praise of peace (Iwaszkiewicz) (m-S and pf) (1979)
Two songs (J. Franz Schueta) (Bar and pf) (1924)
Wiegenlied (Ibsen) (S and pf) (1915)
Zigeunermusik (S, fl, vlc and pf) (1955)
Zlatarog, monodrama (Bar, cl, hn and pf) (1959)
SACRED
Psalm 60 (Bar, mix-ch and orch) (1929)
Vier geistliche Lieder (Bar, fl and orch) (1926)
Ref. composer, 17, 70, 77, 105, 109, 111, 189, 201, 206, 226, 280, 347, 359, 563

VONDRACKOVA, Helena
20th-century Czech composer. DISCOGRAPHY.
Compositions
ORCHESTRA
Isle of Helena
FILM MUSIC
Several films
Ref. 563

VORLOVA, Miroslava. See VORLOVA, Slavka

VORLOVA, Slavka (Miroslava) (nee Johnova) (pseud. Mira Kord)
Czech pianist, choir conductor, singer, teacher and composer. b. Nachod, March 15, 1894; d. Prague, August 24, 1973. She received her first instruction in the piano from her mother. She went to Vienna to study singing under Rose Papier at the Music Academy, but returned to Czechoslovakia after losing her voice. In Prague she became a pupil of Vitezslav Novak in composition and Vaclav Stepan in the piano in 1916. She passed state examinations in the piano, composition and choir conducting and taught for a while in Nachod. After her marriage in 1919 she returned to Prague. Her music evenings were attended by M. Sadlo, K. Hoffmann, Alois Haba and the Ondricek Quartet. She resumed her piano studies under Frantisek Maxian and took private lessons with Jaroslav Ridky, before joining his master class in composition at the Prague Conservatory in 1945. The first woman to receive a degree in composition in Czechoslovakia, she graduated in 1948 with her Symphony, op. 18 dedicated to Jan Masaryk. Before that, her wartime compositions were of a patriotic nature; at this time the folklore element in her work is evident. She later turned to the unusual use of instruments, particularly in concertos and after 1960 used aleatorics, dodecaphony and serial techniques. She wrote a large number of songs and jazz compositions under the pseudonym of Mira Kord. DISCOGRAPHY. PHOTOGRAPH.
Compositions
ORCHESTRA
Symphony, Jan Masaryk, op. 18 (1948)
Concerto in D-Minor, op. 41 (cl and orch) (1952)
Double concerto, op. 59 (ob, hp and orch) (1963)
Emergence, op. 93 (vln and orch) (1973)
Fantasie, op. 6 (vlc and orch) (1940)
Pastoral concerto in E-Flat Major, op. 28 (ob and orch) (1952)
Polarisation, op. 84 (hp, perc and wind orch) (1970)
Slovak concerto, op. 35 (vla and orch) (1954)
Spring concerto, op. 48 (fl and orch) (1959)
Chamber concerto for double bass and strings, op. 74 (1968)
Concerto for bass clarinet and strings, op. 50 (1961)

Correlations, op. 75 (b-cl, pf and str orch) (1969)
Bhukhar, birds of Horecky, op. 67 (1965) (Panton, 1970)
Bozena Nemcova, suite in 8 symphonic pictures, op. 24 (1951)
Charades for symphony orchestra, op. 32b (1956)
Cybernetic studies, op. 56 (1962)
Dedication, op. 64 (1956)
Doublebske dances, op. 36 (1954)
Memento, experimental symphonic, op. 43 (1957)
Model kinetic, op. 69 (1966)
Symphonic prelude, op. 25 (1951)
Three Czech dances, op. 29 (1953)
Thuringian dances, op. 44 (1957)
CHAMBER
Nonet F, op. 10 (1944)
Six for five, quintet, op. 71 (brass insts) (1967)
Wind quintet (1967)
The Beskyds, op. 1 (str qrt) (1933)
Colloqui, op. 82 (4 rec) (1969)
Dessins tetraharpes, op. 60, sketches (4 hp) (1963)
Immanence, op. 87 (fl, b-cl, pf and perc) (1971)
Melodic variations, op. 22, no. 3 (str qrt) (1939)
String quartet, op. 5, no. 2 (1939)
Tema con variazioni, op. 3 (str qrt) (1938)
Serenata desta, op. 58 (fl, b-cl and pf) (1962)
Spectra, op. 86 (cl, vlc and pf) (1970)
Christmas fantasy, op. 85 (b-cl and pf) (1970)
Sonata lirica da tre, op. 62 (vln, vla and gtr) (1964)
Esoterics, op. 87 (fl and gtr) (1971)
Five bagatelles, op. 15 (vlc and pf) (1947)
From home, suite on folk songs, op. 77 (b-cl and pf) (1969)
Melancholy lullaby and dance, op. 16 (vln and pf) (1947)
Miniature (bsn and pf) (1962)
Miniatures, op. 55 (b-cl and pf) (Panton, 1962)
Serenade, op. 57 (ob and hp) (1962)
Variations on a theme by Handel, op. 68 (b-cl and hpcd or pf) (1965)
Droleries basclarinettiques, op. 63 (1964)
Ephemeras, op. 83 (cymbalom) (1970)
Fantasy on a Czech folk song from the 14th-century, op. 33 (vla; also op. 33b, b-cl) (1953, 1969)
Il fauno danzante, op. 66 (b-cl) (1965)
Pantums, op. 46 (hp) (1959)
PIANO
Charade, op. 32 (2 pf) (1953)
Gay intervals, op. 54 (pf, 4 hands) (Panton, 1961)
Coloured notes, op. 9, 9 preludes (1944)
Paraphrases of Hussite songs, op. 34 (1953)
Two dance fantasies, op. 20 (1950)
Variations at the crossroads, op. 21 (1949)
Other pieces
VOCAL
A little country, op. 7, cantata (mix-ch and orch) (1949)
Magellan of the Universe, op. 49, cantata (new age oratorio) (V.H. Roklan) (soli, chil and mix-ch and orch) (1960)
Songs of Gondowana, op. 19, cantata, full-length epic (V.H. Roklan) (mix-ch and orch) (1949)
We, people of the 20th-Century, op. 46, cantata (symphoniade) (V.H. Roklan) (chil-ch, mix-ch and orch) (1959)
Prospects, with prologues to the verses of V.H. Roklan, op. 90 (orch) (1971)
Tango cantabile, op. 23 (V.H. Roklan) (vce and orch) (1944)
White clouds, op. 8, 10 songs (w-ch and orch) (1943)
Aesop, op. 12, 10 choruses (w-ch a-cap) (1945)
The dear little moon, op. 39 (K.H. Macha) (w-ch and pf) (1956)
Maliniarky, op. 51 9 songs (P.O. Hviezdoslav) (double ch) (1961)
Ten folk songs, op. 11 (chil-ch) (1944)
Three spells, op. 76 (F. Branislav) (chil-ch and pf) (1968)
White requiem, op. 80 (V. Nemec) (4 mix-ch) (1961)
The gift of song, op. 40 (V. Halek) (1956)
Gipsy songs, op. 53 (Bar and pf) (1961)
Longing, op. 13, song cycle (Olga Scheinpflugova) (middle vce and pf) (1946)
On love, op. 17 (middle vce and pf) (1947)
Trebon Madona's ring, op. 72 (Jaroslav Seifert) (T and pf) (1967)
Unkempt thoughts, op. 70 (Stanislaw Jerzy Lec) (Bar and pf)
Numerous other songs
OPERA
The Golden Bird, fairy tale opera in 6 scenes (V.H. Roklan) (1959)
Nachod Cassation, op. 37, historical opera in 6 scenes (V.H. Roklan) (1955)
Two Worlds, op. 45, in 1 act (V.H. Roklan) (1958)
OPERETTA
Rozmarynka, op. 30, in 4 acts (after V. Halek by V.H. Roklan) (1955)
INCIDENTAL MUSIC
The Gamekeeper's Wife, op. 38 (P.O. Hviezdoslav) (1956)
Caesar and Cleopatra, op. 42 (G.B. Shaw) (1957)
Ref. 8, 17, 96, 109, 197, 563

VORONINA, Tatiana Aleksandrovna
Soviet pianist, lecturer and composer. b. Leningrad, January 12, 1933. She graduated from the Leningrad Conservatory in 1957, having studied composition under O.A. Evlakhov and the piano under M. Y. Khalfin. She then taught chamber music at the same conservatory. Her compositions were influenced by Russian folk music.
Compositions
ORCHESTRA
Concert ballad (pf and orch) (1961)
Suite (1955)
CHAMBER
String quartet No. 1 (1959)
String quartet No. 2 (1969)
Suite (str qrt)
Poema (vln and pf)
Sonata (vln and pf) (Sovietski Kompozitor, 1978)
PIANO
Aria and humoresque (1965)
Concert fantasy on War and Peace (Prokofiev) (1962)
Concert scherzo (1962)
Preludii (1952)
Six pieces (Sovietski Kompozitor, 1976)
Skazki (1964)
Sonata
Vesennyaya muzyka (1968)
VOCAL
Pamyat lyndskaya, cantata (Chernushenko and Azarov) (soli, ch and orch) (1957)
Pamyatnik (Lunacharski) (ch, org and orch) (1967)
Choral cycle (Proletarian poets) (1961)
Dumy o mire (N. Khikmet, M. Aliger, Shilya, Darye and Chernushenko) (vce and pf) (1956)
Girl from Hiroshima (Khikmet) (vce and pf)
Pesni odinokogo strannika (Basyo) (vce and str trio) (1966)
Rich and poor (Emin) (vce and pf)
The sun of peace (vce and pf)
Veresk, cycle (R. Burns) (vce and pf) (1970)
Vocal, cycle (R. Tagore) (vce and pf) (1961)
The widow's ballad (Aliger) (vce and pf)
Ref. 74, 223, 277, 420

VORONTSOVA, M.
19th-century Russian composer.
Compositions
VOCAL
Songs incl.:
Esli zhizn tebya obmanet (Jurgenson)
Eshche tomlius (Jurgenson)
Mne tverdili mapevaya, polyubi plutovka (Jurgenson)
To byli vremena chudes (Jurgenson)
Ty vsegda khorosha nesravnenno (Jurgenson)
Ya ne mogu ne proiznest (Jurgenson)
Ref. 297

VORWERK, Henrietta
German composer. b. Erkelenz, August 13, 1843. She studied under Professor Sieber of Berlin.
Compositions
CHAMBER
Piano pieces
VOCAL
An den Abendstern (mix-ch) (Leuckart)
Es weht aus Sueden ein warmer Hauch (mix-ch) (Leuckart)
Flohen die Wolken (mix-ch) (Leuckart)
Songs
Ref. 226, 276, 297

VOSS, Marie Wilson
20th-century American composer.
Compositions
PIANO
Pleasure pier waltzes
VOCAL
We fight for right
SACRED
Judge me, O God, song
Ref. 448

VOYNICH, Ethel Lillian
Compositions
VOCAL
The golden net, cantata
The submerged city (B) (ca. 1895)
Ref. 465

VRABELY-WURMBACH-STUPPACHOVA (Wurmbrand) (Vrabely), Stefania (Stephanie) (pseud. Ernest Wurmbach-Stuppach)
Czech pianist and composer. b. Bratislava, October 26, 1849. She studied under L. Karl Tausig. She wrote music articles. Her compositions were published under her pseudonym.
Compositions
CHAMBER
Sonata, op. 24 (vln and pf) (Doblinger)
PIANO
Konzertstueck in ungarischem Stile (4 hands) (Doblinger)
Fuenf Klavierstuecke, op. 25 (Doblinger)
Fuenfzehn Fantasiestuecke (Doblinger)
Konzert-Paraphrase ueber Fruehlingsstimmen, Walzer von Joh. Strauss, op. 41 (Cranz)
Libelle, Charakterstueck (Bosworth)
Lied ohne Worte; Elfenreigen, Fruehlingslied (Heinrichshofen)
Mimosa; Andalusierin; Lied; Prelude; Orpheus, op. 38 (Eberle)
Novelletten, op. 31 (Doblinger)
Ozean, Konzert-Etude, op. 43 (Eberle)
Paraphrase ueber 2 ungarische Volkslieder, op. 40 (Eberle)
Tanzszenen, op. 27 (Doblinger)
Walzer, op. 42 (Eberle)
Other pieces
INCIDENTAL MUSIC
Music for Die schoene Melusine
Ref. 197, 216, 226, 276, 297, 347, 433

VREE-BROWN, Marion F.
20th-century American teacher and composer. She taught at Pierce College, Los Angeles.
Compositions
VOCAL
Fum, fum, fum (w-ch and pf) (Theo Presser)
SACRED
Consecration (2 part ch, pf and org) (Presser, 1978)
Ref. composer, 40, 142, 347

VRIONIDES, Rosina (Stewart)
American organist, violinist and composer. d. November, 1943. Her first husband was James Stewart, the raconteur of the 'Uncle Josh' records, popular in the 1930s. After she was widowed, she married the conductor and composer Christos Vrionides.
Compositions
VOCAL
Out of the rolling ocean the ground (w-ch) (M. Baron Co.)
Ref. Mrs. Helen Vrionides, 190

VUYET, Caroline. See WUIET, Caroline

VYNER, Mary Bainbridge
American concert pianist, lecturer and composer. b. Uniontown, September 4, 1933. She obtained her B.Mus. (1952), M.Mus. (1953) and D.Mus. (1954) from the Philadelphia Music Academy. She was a faculty member at Franklin and Marshall College and founder-director of the Lancaster Conservatory of Music (1953).
Compositions
ORCHESTRA
Twelve symphonies
Twenty-one piano concertos
Four symphonic poems
CHAMBER
Eighteen pieces
Three sonatas (fl and hp)
Eight violin sonatas
PIANO
Nine sonatas
Four preludes
VOCAL
Bicentennial symphony (narr and orch)
Ref. 359, 475

WAALER, Fredrikke Holtemann (nee Rynning)

Norwegian violinist, choir conductor, teacher and composer. b. May 7, 1865; d. February 2, 1952. She studied the violin under F. Ursin and G. Boehn and theory under L.M. Lindeman and J. Haarklou. She played first violin in the Oslo Musikforening orchestra in 1885. In 1893 she founded and led the first orchestra in Hamar. At the same time she conducted a choir, taught and was a strong influence on the musical life of that city.

Compositions

VOCAL

    Hamarsanger, op. 7 (mix-ch) (1915)

    Blomstersange (vce and pf) (1912)

    Spinnersken (B. Bjornson) (vce and pf) (1888)

    Other songs

Ref. 20

WADDINGTON, Miss. See LLANOVER, Lady

WADIA, Sabra

19th-century composer.

Composition

PIANO

    Valse de concert (Crevel)

ARRANGEMENT

    Recueils d'airs orientaux, of No. 6 Marche Orientale (Crevel)

Ref. 297

WAGENSONNER, Maria. See WAGENSONNER, Mimi

WAGENSONNER, Mimi (Maria)

Austrian lecturer, lyricist and composer. b. Aussig Elbe, March 13, 1897; d. Vienna, August 21, 1970. She studied under R. Stohr at the Music Academy in Vienna, where she also taught. She wrote lyrics and composed piano pieces and songs.

Ref. 70

WAGNER, Melinda

20th-century composer.

Composition

MISCELLANEOUS

    Circles, stone and passage (1981)

Ref. AMC

WAGNER, Virginia de Oliveira Bastos

Portuguese composer. b. Lisbon, 1959. She married Leopold Wagner, a great music lover and a relative of the famous composer.

Compositions

CHAMBER

    Cello pieces

    Organ pieces

    Piano pieces

SACRED

    Ave Maria

    Marcha religiosa

MISCELLANEOUS

    Canção da inocencia

    Fantasia capricho

    Impromptu

    Marcha triunfal

    Nocturno

    Pensamento melodico

    Reverie

    Romanza, Nos. 1 and 2

    Um grito de alma

Ref. 268

WAINWRIGHT, Harriet (Mrs. Stewart)

English writer and composer. b. ca. 1780; d. ca. 1840.

Compositions

VOCAL

    Comala, dramatic poem (Ossian)

    Merrily, merrily passes the day

    Collections of songs, duets, trios and choruses

Publications

    Critical Remarks on the Art of Singing. London: Brown & Stratton, 1836.

Ref. 6, 85, 226, 276, 347, 433

WAKEFIELD, Augusta Mary

English pianist, lecturer, singer and composer. b. Sedgwick, near Kendal, August 19, 1853; d. Grange-over-Sands, September 16, 1910. She studied singing under Randegger, Henschel and Blumenthal in London and Alari in Rome, where she also took piano lessons from Sgambati. As an amateur contralto singer she was a success, appearing at charity concerts in London. She also sang at the Gloucester Festival in 1880 and at other important concerts. In 1885 she started a competitive festival at her home in Sedgwick, which later transferred to Kendal, where it flourished as the Westmorland Music Festival. Later, in 1890 she lectured on music and illustrated her own lectures.

Compositions

VOCAL

    Queen of sixty years (ch) (1897)

    Songs incl.:

    Bunch of cowslips

    May time in mid-winter

    More and more

    No sir! Yes sir!

    Ballads

Publications

    Ruskin on Music. Editor. Anthology.

    Contributions to various periodicals.

Ref. 2, 6, 8, 276, 433

WALBERG, Emilie

19th-century composer.

Compositions

PIANO

    Alte Erinnerungen, fantasie (Hansen)

    En loenlig Stund (Hansen)

    Entschwundene Traeume, fantasie (Hansen)

    Freundicher Gruss, fantasie (Hansen)

    Fruehlingsfeier, fantasie (Hansen)

    In der Daemmerung, fantasie (Hansen)

    Morgendaemmerung, fantasie (Hansen)

    Sommerfrische, fantasie (Hansen)

    Stimmung, fantasie (Hansen)

    Was die Voeglein erzaehlen, fantasie

Ref. 297

WALBURGA, Gertrud. See SONTAG, Henriette

WALDBURG-WURZACH, Julie von, Princess

Austrian composer. b. Vienna, April 27, 1841. Over 60 of her compositions were published.

Compositions

PIANO

    Hochzeitsfanfare, march (Bosworth)

    Mitzi-polka (Bosworth)

    Ohne Ende, op. 15, polka-mazurka (Ruhle)

    Sonnenblumenwalzer (Ruhle)

    Tagesneuigkeiten, op. 12, polka (Ruhle)

VOCAL

    Es faellt ein Stern herunter, op. 26 (Bosworth)

    Frau Nachtigall, op. 25 (Bosworth)

    Lebe wohl, op. 15 (Ruhle)

    O du, vor dem die Stuerme schweigen, op. 24 (Bosworth)

    O Herz du musst dich fassen, op. 23 (Bosworth)

    Ungarisches Lied, Ueber mir zieht eine traenenschwere Wolke Hin, op. 13 (vce and pf) (Ruhle)

    Other songs

Ref. 226, 276, 297, 347

WALDENBURG, Eveline von

Early 19th-century German composer of Berlin. She may have been the wife of Prince August of Prussia.

Compositions

PIANO

    Ecossaise (Berlin: Schlesinger, 1813)

    Waltz

Ref. 121

WALDIN, Hugues. See BLANC DE FONTBELL, Cecile

WALDO, Elisabeth

American violinist, folklorist, lecturer and composer. b. Tacoma, WA, June 18, 1923. She studied the violin from the age of 5 and won a scholarship to study at the Cornish School of Music in Seattle and then as a scholarship student under Efrem Zimbalist at the Curtis Institute of Music, Philadelphia, where she went on Jascha Heifetz recommendation. She was first violinist of the All American Youth Symphony under the directorship of Leopold Stokowski for two years and first violinist with the Los Angeles Philharmonic Orchestra in California. She lectured at California State Universities in Los Angeles and Occidental College. As researcher she worked at the Inter-American University in Panama City, the Fine Arts Library at the University of New Mexico in Albuquerque and the Na-Balom Museum in Chiapas, Mexico. She taught at summer workshops (music and dance heritage of Latin America and the American Southwest) and went on solo tours of Central and South American capital cities. She was solo violinist with the Mexico City Radio Network (XEW) and other inter-American orchestras. She founded the Pan-American Ensemble (1970) and the Pan-Asian Ensemble, who perform on rare traditional instruments dating from the time of the Han Dynasty (ca. 202 B.C.) in combination with Western instruments of contemporary times. She was the recipient of a bronze finalist award, 1973, for TV score, from the Information Film Producers of America; and was a gold medal winner, April, 1977, Mexico City, Latin American Network of Announcers and Journalists for contributions to International Understanding of Pan American Music. She won an award of excellence, 1976, presented by the Hollywood Film Advisory Board for an original film score and ASCAP awards (1971 1973, 1974 and 1976): She also won the Third Annual Special Composers award for contributions to American Music; the 15th-annual radio-televison award for noteworthy achievement in field of serious music and an Emmy Award nomination, 1977, for Best Entertainment Special. DISCOGRAPHY. PHOTOGRAPH.

Compositions
ORCHESTRA
Concierto indo-americano (vln and sym orch) (1976)
The Barrio suite (sym orch) (1975)
Siembra (sym orch) (1958)
Bossa Pan-Americana (1972)
Entrance of the Conquistadores
Jarabes mestizos (str orch) (1974)
Mejorana y Socavon (Latin orch) (1946)
Rites of the Pagan
The Serpent and the Eagle
CHAMBER Con quistadores, suite (ens)
Feng-Huang (western and Chinese insts; also wind qnt) (1983)
Minority suite (ethnic and western insts)
Saga of Lady Tsai Wen Chi (western and Chinese insts; also sym orch)
El Gran Quivira (gtr, d-b and str qrt) (1977)
Alabado (trp and perc)
The De Anza march
VOCAL
Inca sun dance (Realm of the Incas suite) (vces and orch with modern and pre-Hispanic insts)
Viva California (ch and orch)
Winneduma, a Paiute legend (narr and mix-ch) (Mary Austin) (comm Sacramento Chorale)
SACRED
Misa de la Raza (mix-ch and cham ens) (1974)
People of the Book: Religious musical pageant (folk ens) (1968)
BALLET
Angels Theme from Entering the Stream
El Popol Vuh, modern score (pre-Columbian insts; also orch)
OPERA
Ballad of Lola Montez
Los pastores
INCIDENTAL MUSIC
Chac (Mayan rain god), film
History of Mexico, TV (pre-Columbian insts; also wind and perc ens)
Who will weep when all is gone, film (cham ens) (1975)
MISCELLANEOUS
Oil over the Andes (comm Occidental Petroleum Corp)
Publications
American Folklore.
Latin American Music.
Spanish American Folk Songs.
Ref. composer, 494

WALDROP, Uda

20th-century American composer.
Composition
VOCAL
Nec-natama (J. Wilson Shields) (1914)
Ref. 304

WALES, Evelyn

20th-century American composer.
Composition
OPERA
Little Gypsy Boy
Ref. 141

WALKER, Caroline Holme

American accompanist, teacher and composer. b. St. Louis, MO. June 14, 1863. She studied under Anna Strothotte, James North and Robert Goldbeck in St. Louis and Mme. Linda Ostrander (q.v.) and Professor Kuhn in Denver.
Compositions
MISCELLANEOUS
The lonely garden
When the dew is falling
Ref. 226, 460

WALKER, Ella May (Mrs. D.H.)

American organist, pianist and composer. b. Windom, MN, 1892. She attended the McGill Conservatory where she studied the organ and the piano and later studied at Northwestern University in Chicago. Among her teachers were Alfred White, Dean P.C. Sutkin, Arne Oldberg, Percy Grainger and Norman Wilks in Alberta. She was organist at Knox Church and at the Allan Theatre in Edmonton.
Compositions
CHAMBER
Piano pieces
VOCAL
The Eternal Guest (ch)
Ref. 2, 94, 622

WALKER, Gwyneth van Anden

American assistant professor and composer. b. New York, March 22, 1947. She gained a B.A. Mus. hons. from Brown University, Rhode Island, in 1968, an M.Mus. in 1970 and a D.M.A. in 1976, from Hartt College of Music, University of Hartford. She studied primarily under Arnold Franchetti. She spent several years on the faculty of the Oberlin College Conservatory as assistant professor and later the Hartford Conservatory. She left teaching to become a free-lance composer. She was the recipient of numerous awards and received several commissions. PHOTOGRAPH.
Compositions
ORCHESTRA
Fanfare for the Washington Festival Orchestra (1978) (Studio Pub. Inc.)
Match point
Orchestral study No. 1 (1965); No. 2 (1968)
CHAMBER
Coffa (vlc and wind ens) (1972)
The story of Jorket Hayforks, ballad (wind ens) (1974)
Four movements for dance (fl and pf) (Walker, 1981)
Etude for flute and piano (1979)
Inner dances (vlc and pf) (Walker, 1981)
Sonata (fl and pf) (1978)
Sonata (vla and pf) (Walker, 1982)
Three violin duets (1965)
Fantasy for Lute (1979)
Four pieces for contemporary lute (Walker, 1977)
Rhapsody for clarinet (1974)
Rondo, variations (gtr) (Walker, 1976)
Sonata (fl) (1978) (Arsis Press)
Sonata (vlc) (1981)
Two woodwind fugues (1968)
Interlude and finale (Walker, 1980)
ORGAN
Ayre and variations on a country dance (Walker, 1976)
Passacaglia and fugue (Walker, 1976)
Song for organ (1968)
PIANO
April rag and fantasy (Walker, 1977)
Cantos (Walker, 1980)
Complete piano works (Walker, 1976)
Five pieces (1972)
Preludes (1974)
Sonata No. 1 (Walker, 1980)
Sonata No. 2 (Walker, 1982)
Sonata No. 3 (Walker, 1983)
Suite (1969)
VOCAL
Cantata, on texts by British poets (1970)
Upon her leaving, cantata (B and cham ens)
Runes and poems (ch and orch) (1975)

Lift up your voice to the sun! (ch and brass qrt or pf) (Walker, 1983)
As a branch in May (ch and pf) (Walker, 1983)
As the stars had told (ch and org) (Walker, 1980)
The nocturnal nibbler (mix-ch and pf)
So far from here (w-ch) (1973)
Collected songs (1976)
Elizabethan songs (B, ob, pf and perc) (1975, rev. 1979)
In memoriam (also vlc) (1980)
Minnow Minnie songs (1981)
Songs of '66 (1966)
Songs of '77 (1977)
Songs of the night wind (S, vlc or pf) (Walker, 1981)
Songs for voice and guitar (Walker, 1976)
Three songs for soprano, violoncello and piano (1975)
Three songs for three voices (T, Bar, counter-T and gtr) (Walker, 1983)
Though love be a day (high vce and pf) (Walker, 1980)
Tulips (S, fl, pf and perc) (Walker, 1983)
Variations on Hebrides folk songs (vce and fl) (1983)
A wonder told shyly, madrigal (vib and d-b) (1978)
SACRED
Born this night, anthem (ch and org) (Walker, 1980)
The radiant dawn, anthem (ch, org and vlc) (1978)
Mass in E-Minor (1967)
DANCE SCORES
Inner dances (vlc, pf and dancer) (1981)
Four movements for dance (fl and pf) (1981)
OPERA
Mary, come running! chamber opera (30 vces, fl, ob, vlc, pf, perc, gtr and trp)
Opera buffet (S, vce and gtr) (1982)
MISCELLANEOUS
My love walks in velvet
The pasture (1967)
Upon her leaving (1977)
Ref. composer, 228, 468, 474, 622, 624, 625

WALKER, Ida
19th-century American composer.
Compositions
PIANO
Carnival, scherzo fantastique (Goggan)
Carnival of the butterflies (Goggan)
Chrysanthemum, mazurka (Goggan)
Francesca, Hungarian dance (Goggan)
Grand rush to victory, military march (Goggan)
Hunter's dash, grand march (Goggan)
Mathilde, polonaise militaire (Goggan)
Memory bells (Ditson)
On the Gulf of Mexico, waltzes (Goggan)
Student's bolero (Goggan)
Student's minuet (Goggan)
Student's waltz (Goggan)
Valse noble (Goggan)
Yule-tide, waltzes
VOCAL
Daughter of Mendoza (vce and pf)
I love the night (vce and pf)
Oh! come to me (vce and pf)
Sweetest lass in all thy land (vce and pf)
There is no song in my sad (vce and pf)
We two (vce and pf)
SACRED
Give me thine heart (vce and pf) (Goggan)
My soul is dark
We seek for a city (Goggan)
Ref. 226, 276, 297, 433

WALKER, Louise
20th-century Austrian guitarist, teacher and composer. She was a pupil of M. Llobet, J. Zuth, J. Ortner and H. Albert at the Academy of Music and Performing Arts in Vienna. She toured as a concert guitarist in Europe, America and Japan and taught the guitar at the Musikhochschule in Vienna. In 1968 she was awarded the Cross of Honor for the Arts and Sciences by the Austrian Federal President. DISCOGRAPHY.
Compositions
GUITAR
Concert pieces
Small variations on a Catalonian folk song
Studies
Technical exercises
Ref. 282

WALKER, Mrs. D.H. See WALKER, Ella May

WALKER, Nina
English composer. b. ca. 1927. She composed two chamber pieces.
Ref. composer, 94

WALKER, Sarah-Jane Layton. See CAHIER, Mrs. Charles

WALKER, Shirley. See ADDENDUM

WALLACE, Kathryn
American composer. b. Shawnee, OK, October 21, 1917. She studied at Oklahoma University where she received a B.F.A. in 1938. She also studied under Warren M. Angell at Oklahoma Baptist University from 1957 to 1958.
Compositions
PIANO
Moods
Tin soldier parade
SACRED
Be thou, O God, exalted
For the beauty of the earth
The Lord is my Shepherd
Ref. 142

WALLACE, Mildred White
American authoress, editor, singer and composer. b. Columbiana, OH, August 25, 1887. She obtained her B.A. from the Birmingham Conservatory. She studied under Ruth Chandler and Clara Harper Steele. On radio she was known as 'The Dixie Bluebird'.
Compositions
VOCAL
Alone with thee
Black belt lullaby
Close of day
Dream boat
I would be near you then
Since your path crossed mine
Sometime, somehow, somewhere
Trust only in His love
Ref. 347

WALLACE, Phyllis Joy
American singer and composer. b. Ottawa, KS, April 6, 1920.
Compositions
ORCHESTRA
Concertos incl.:
Father forgive them (vln and orch)
Moon concerto (1942)
THEATRE
Through difficulty, musical
MISCELLANEOUS
Marches
Waltzes
Rock songs
Ref. 475

WALLACH, Joelle
20th-century American pianist, lecturer and composer. b. New York. As a pupil of Meyer Kupferman at Sarah Lawrence College, she took her B.A. in 1967. After studying composition under Chou Wen-Chung and Jack Beeson at Columbia University, she obtained her M.A. in 1969. From 1955 to 1971 she studied the piano under Ruth Geiger, Jean Williams (q.v.), Edmund Haines, Joel Spiegelmain and William Beller. At the Juilliard School of Music she continued her composition studies under Stanley Wolff; her vocal teachers were Clara Burling Roesch, Joyce McLean, Oren Brown, Shirley Meier and Edith Bers. Her graduate study after 1967 included composition, electronic music and theory and analysis. She taught musical subjects at the City University of New York and was the recipient of a number of awards. The New Jersey State Council on the Arts awarded her one of their fellowships for 1984 and 1985 in recognition of outstanding artistic merit and achievement. PHOTOGRAPH.
Compositions
ORCHESTRA
Concerto for four winds and orchestra (1969)
Glimpses (1981)
Turbulence, stillness and saltation (cham orch) (1983)

CHAMBER
    The kiss of Anima Mundi, a samba of moans and whispers (perc sextet) (1983)
    Adagio for strings (str qrt)
    Coalescence (sax qrt) (1980)
    Movement for string quartet (1968)
    Quartet (winds and strs) (1966)
    Quartet for saxophones (1980)
    Quartet movement (fl, cl, vln and vlc) (1967)
    String quartet (1964) (New York: CFE, 1968)
    Trio (fl and 2 ob) (1965)
    Trio (3 reed insts) (1968)
    Duo (cl and vlc) (1964)
    Duo (vln and vlc) (1966)
    Forewords (trp and hn) (1983) (prize)
    Little duet (vln and pf) (1966)
    Organal voices (bsn and vib) (1983)
    Pas de deux (fl and hpcd) (1967)
    Contemplations (cl) (1978)
    Moment (ob) (1967)
PIANO
    Andante cantabile (1982)
    Piano study in open-ended form (1965)
    Three pieces (1967)
    Wisps (1978)
VOCAL
    The happy prince (narr, mix-ch and cham orch)
    Five American echoes (mix-ch a-cap) (prize)
    In the mist (ch)
    Look down fair moon (mix-ch a-cap)
    On the beach at night alone (mix-ch a-cap) (C.F. Peters) (prize)
    Plaint for a prince and king (m-ch and keyboard) (1982)
    Tears (mix-ch a-cap)
    Three Whitman visions (mix-ch a-cap)
    Two introits (cham ch) (1974)
    Cords (S and d-b) (1973)
    Deirdre (m-S and pf) (1963)
    Mourning madrigals (S, T, fl and hp) (1980)
    Of honey and of vinegar (m-S and 2 pf) (1983)
    Youth's serenade (m-S, fl, bsn, hp and harmonium) (1982)
    Force that through the green fuse (S and ob) (1965)
SACRED
    A prophesy and psalm (ch and orch) (1981)
    Prayers of steel (mix-ch and org) (1977)
    Three short sacred anthems (ch) (1980) (prize)
    Thirty ecumenical responses (mix-ch) (1977)
    Amen (vce and inst) (1975)
    Five-fold Amen (2 vces) (1974)
ELECTRONIC
    Prelude and toccata (pf and tape) (1967)
Ref. composer, 142, 228, 457, 468, 474, 569, 622, 625

WALLNEROVA, Bibiana
Czech editor, librettist, translator and composer. b. Bratislava, December 14, 1932. She studied philosophy, history and German at Bratislava University. She has translated musical texts, songs, arias and choral works and was an editor for Czech Broadcasting from 1964. She composed a symphony in 1974, songs for adults and children, dramatic works and a children's musical.
Ref. 77

WALPURGIS. See MARIA ANTONIA WALPURGIS, Princess of Bavaria

WALSH, Elizabeth Jameson
American pianist, singer, teacher and composer. b. Panhandle, TX, October 23, 1913. She received a B.Mus. from North Texas State University and a teaching diploma from the American Conservatory, Chicago. She studied under Paul van Katwijk at the Southern Methodist University and privately under Silvio Scionti, Alexander Uninsky and Larry Walz. She was a soloist with orchestras in Dallas and Denton and gave recitals throughout Texas. She appeared in leading roles with the Dallas and Amarillo Little Theatre. She received a prize in a national recording contest, sponsored by the National Piano Guild, 1973.
Compositions
VOCAL
    Songs
OPERETTA
    Day in Mexico (1971)
Publications
    A Stylistic Analysis of the Piano Works of Debussy and Ravel. 1942.
Ref. 77

WALSH, Helen Mary
20th-century composer.
Composition
OPERA
    Daniel in the Lion's Den
Ref. 141

WALTER, Ida
English composer. b. London, 1886. She studied at the Royal Academy of Music.
Compositions
CHAMBER
    Andante con variazioni (pf) (Ascherberg)
VOCAL
    O let the solid ground
    The sea hath its pearls (Ascherberg)
OPERA
    Florian, in 4 acts
Ref. 6, 225, 226, 276, 297, 307, 433

WALTERS, Teresa
20th-century American pianist and composer. b. Lincoln, NE. She gained her B.A. and M.A. (music) from the University of Nebraska and then studied for a certificate at the Ecole Normale de Musique, Paris in 1979. She gained her D.Mus. from the Peabody Conservatory in 1982. She won an Alpha Delta award; two Vreeland awards and a Boucher medal.
Compositions
CHAMBER
    Music for organ and two trumpets (1977) (Trinity Press)
    Sonata (prep pf) (1977)
SACRED
    The kingdom, cantata (1974) (Salter Publ.)
    One man, cantata (1976) (Trinity)
    Wedding service of scripture and song (1977) (St. John's Press)
Ref. 625

WALTON, Constance
20th-century American composer. She won the National Federation of Music Club's adult composer award in 1977.
Composition
PIANO
    Duo dimensions, in four parts: Mass on mass; Inteaction: Out of step; New relationships (2 pf)
Ref. National Music Clubs journal

WANDERMAN, Dorothy
American pianist and composer. b. New York, October 20, 1907. She studied under Philipp, Saperton and Scoville. She is a member of ASCAP.
Compositions
PIANO
    Four waltzes: In a French cafe; Swiss alpine waltz; In a Viennese garden; Valse tragic
    The playful mouse
Ref. 39

WANG, An-Ming
American pianist, authoress and composer. b. Shanghai, China, November 7, 1926. She studied the piano and music theory at the Central China University in Wuchang where she obtained her B.Ed. (1947). In the United States she studied at the Wesleyan Conservatory, Macon, Georgia, where she obtained her B.Mus. cum laude in 1950; the Juilliard School of Music and graduated with her M.A. from Columbia University, 1951. PHOTOGRAPH.
Compositions
ORCHESTRA
    Symphonic projections (1977)
    Introduction and allegro (1982)
    Overture to Lan Ying (1983)
CHAMBER
    Promenade (ww, brass and timp) (1980)
    Scenes from Pingchow (vla, vln, vlc and pf) (1981)
    Sonata for violin and piano (also cl) (1978)
    Dialogue (fl, cl and pf) (1983)
    Jestures (fl, cl and pf) (1983)
    East wind (vln and pf) (1982)

PIANO
Arabesque (1978)
Dance chinois (1978)
The Mahjong suite: The flowers, The words, The winds (1977)
Petite valse (1978)
Toccata (1979)
VOCAL
Autumn leaves (mix-ch) (1978)
A Chinese lullaby (chil-ch) (General Commodities Co., 1980)
In paradisum (ch) (1982)
Autumn winds (S) (1974)
The fairy hill upon the void obscure
A hundred loves
Life's dreary gloom
Little yellow bird (w-vce) (1980)
The nightingale (S) (General Commodities, 1978)
Nights of spring
Rain (m-vce) (1979)
The rain of night
Sky (w-vce) (1980)
The song of endless sorrow (S) (1976)
Songs for all seasons (vce and pf) (1982)
War's alarms
SACRED
Agnus Dei (m-ch) (1981)
Anna meets baby Jesus (chil-ch) (1977)
A Christmas gift (chil-ch) (1980)
God created people (chil-ch) (1979)
Introit, requiem (mix-vces) (1980)
Libera me (mix-ch) (1982)
Lux aeterna (mix-ch) (1981)
Mary's lullaby, anthem (mix-ch)
O praise the Lord (mix-vce) (1976)
Offertoire (B and mix-ch) (1981)
Sanctus (w-ch) (1981)
In eternal wedlock bliss (w-vce) (1977)
Kyrie (S and A) (1981)
Pie Jesu (T and B) (1981)
Ref. composer, 494, 622, 625

WANG, Jiu-Fang
Chinese composer. b. 1937. DISCOGRAPHY.
Compositions
ORCHESTRA
Red lady, symphonic poem (with Ju Wei) (1983)
Ref. China Records Co.

WANG, Qiang
Chinese violinist, teacher and composer. b. Yan Tai, Shan Dong, January 23, 1935. She began violin lessons at the age of 12 and in 1955 commenced composition lessons with Professor Ding Shan De, harmony with Professor Sang Tong and polyphony with Professor Chen Ming Zhi at the Shanghai Conservatory, from which she graduated in 1960 with distinction. She was awarded a gold medal at the Seventh International Youth Festival for her *Rivers of Happiness* and in 1960 received the title of Women's Red-Banner Pacesetter in Shanghai for distinction in learning. DISCOGRAPHY.
Compositions
ORCHESTRA
Ga da mei lin (vlc and orch) (The People's Music Publishing House, 1982)
CHAMBER
Hong Hu's songs (fl, vla and hp) (1981)
Trumpet and drum
Folk dance-jiu-jie-bian (Nine-Join-Whip)
VOCAL
Rivers of happiness, cantata (ch and orch) (1959, rev 1961) (Shanghai Literature and Art Publishing House, 1959) (prize)
FILM MUSIC
Aurora (orch) (Shanghai Film Studio, 1979)
The girls selling cakes (orch) (Shanghai Film Studio, 1981)
The magic gourd (orch) (Shanghai Lit., 1963)
Song of life (orch) (Liaoning Film Studio, 1983)
Wait till tomorrow (orch) (Shanghai Lit., 1962)
Xue Hua and Lizi Qiu (orch) (Shanghai Film Studio, 1980)
Ref. composer

WARBURG, Mrs. Paul. See SWIFT, Kay

WARD, Adelaide. See NEWTON, Adelaide

WARD, Amy. See WOODFORDE-FINDEN, Amy

WARD, Beverly A.
American composer.
Composition
SACRED
Benedictus es, Domine (ch and org)
Ref. 142

WARD, Clementine
19th-century English organist, singer and composer. She was the daughter of the organist and composer John Charles Ward.
Compositions
PIANO
Clementine gavotte (Weekes)
Dickens series (Weekes)
March
VOCAL
Doll's house party, cantata (Curwen)
Doll's wedding, cantata (Curwen)
Path of the pilgrims, cantata (Curwen)
Spirit of the wood, cantata (Curwen)
Away o'er the dashing spray (mix-ch; also duets) (Curwen)
Beautiful rainbow, school song (ch and pf) (Curwen)
Black and white (vce and pf) (Curwen)
Granny's patchwork quilt, school song (vce and pf) (Curwen)
Smiles and tears, 2-part song (vce and pf)
Winter (vce and pf) (Bayley)
Work's the thing, 2-part song (vce and pf) (Curwen)
OPERA
Princess Ju Ju (Curwen)
OPERETTA
Beauty and the Beast (Curwen)
H.M.S. Alphabet (Bayley)
Zurika, the Gypsy Maid (Curwen)
Ref. 6, 85, 297, 347

WARD, Corajane Diane Bunce. See WARD, Diane

WARD, Diane (Corajane Diane Bunce)
American actress, authoress, operatic singer, teacher and composer. b. Jackson, MI, January 10, 1919. She attended Cleary College and Jackson Junior College where she obtained an A.A. She also studied at Michigan State University where she obtained a B.A. and an M.A., at the University of Michigan, Interlochen and at the American Conservatory under Barre Hill. She also studied under Robert Long, Laura Koch and Robella Manong. She sang in operas, in concerts, musicals, theatre and on radio and TV. She produced scripts for radio and TV. She taught in schools and music and drama privately. She founded the Ward Institute of Arts in Michigan.
Compositions
VOCAL
Two poems (ch)
OPERA
Visiting the Bancrofts
OPERETTA
The Little Dipper
Ref. 39, 142

WARD, Emily. See NEWTON, Adelaide

WARD, Kate Lucy
English composer. b. Wiltshire, 1833. She studied at the Royal Academy of Music, London. Her compositions were highly praised by Felix Mendelssohn.
Compositions
VOCAL
Songs incl.:
Ah, my heart is weary
Mother, the winds are at play
True hearts
THEATRE
The Tempest
Small stage productions
Ref. 226, 276, 433

WARD, Louise Taylor

20th-century American composer of Texas. She holds an M.M.
Composition
ORCHESTRA
Piano concerto
Ref. 147

WARD, Nancy

20th-century American composer.
Compositions
ORCHESTRA
The fall (pf and orch) (Broadcast Music)
Cajun track (trp and str orch) (Broadcast Music)
Ref. 403

WARD, Sister Mary Louise

American organist, pianist, teacher and composer. b. Georgetown, MI, September 23, 1890. She obtained her B.M. from the Detroit Institute of Music in 1928 and her M.M. (organ) from the University of Michigan in 1932 and M.M. (music theory) in 1943. She studied the piano under Margaret Mannebach, John Kollen and Joseph Brinkman and the organ under Dr. Edward Manniles and Palmer Christian. In 1928 she became an associate of the American Guild of Organists. From 1913 to 1935 she was a music teacher at the St. James Academy in Adrian, MI, and then joined the Sienna Heights College where she was head of the music department. She was organist at the Holy Rosary Chapel, Detroit.
Composition
SACRED
Mass in honor of St. Joseph (1932)
Ref. 496

WARDE, Ann Maury

American gamelan and mrdungam player, oboist, pianist and composer. b. Stamford, CT, December 6, 1956. She studied the piano under Joan Balloo Mathes and Walid Raja Howrani at the Mozarteum, Salzburg, Austria. She studied composition under George Cacioppo and the oboe under John Hanulik and Thomas Stacy. She obtained her B.A. in anthropology and music from the University of Michigan and her M.A. from Wesleyan University, CT. She studied the Javanese gamelan and the South Indian mrdungam, (a type of barrel drum).
Compositions
CHAMBER
Close together, far apart (8 vlc) (1981)
Music for two horns (1979)
Piece for cello and flute (1981)
Two movements for solo oboe (1979)
PIANO
Inside lines (4 players) (1982)
Musical poem (1983)
VOCAL
Vereinsamt (S and pf)
DANCE SCORES
Outside lines (1982)
MISCELLANEOUS
Lines and shapes
Ref. composer

WARDER, Marie

19th-century composer.
Compositions
VOCAL
Ach du liebe gute Butterpflanze
Backfischfragen
Danen-Couplets (Dietrich)
Eine Hofmusikantin oder die Strassengeisha
Eine Maid fuer alles
Die Landstreicherin
Die Strohwitwe
Der Seusse Emil
Ref. 297

WARE, Harriet

American concert pianist and composer. b. Waupun, WI, August 26, 1877; d. New York, NY, February 9, 1962. She married Hugh M. Krumbhaar, architect, engineer and musician. She studied at the Pillsbury Academy in Owatonna, Minnesota and the piano under Dr. William Mason and George Sweet in New York. She then went to Paris where she studied composition and the piano under Sigismund Stojowski and voice under Mme. de la Grange and Juliani. Later in Berlin she studied composition under Mme. Grunewald and H. Kaun. She made her debut at the age of 15 when she played with an orchestra in St. Paul. She appeared at the Biennial Convention of Women's Clubs in St. Paul which devoted its program to five women composers, which included Amy Beach (q.v.), Clara Schumann (q.v.), Cecile Chaminade (q.v.) and Margaret Lang (q.v.). She was piano soloist with symphony orchestras and toured throughout the United States.
Compositions
ORCHESTRA
Piano concerto
The artisan, symphonic poem (1929)
PIANO
Midnight waltz
Mountain pictures, suite
Song of the sea
Victory prelude
VOCAL
Sir Oluf, cantata (C. Fanning) (S, B, w-ch and orch) (1929) (G. Schirmer)
Trees, choral cycle
Women's triumphal march (ch) (National Song, Federation of Women's Clubs of America)
Songs incl.:
Boat song
The call of Radha
A day in Arcady, duet
Fay song
In an old garden, song cycle
The forgotten land
Fresh lilacs
From India (composer)
Hindu slumber song
Joy of the morning
Last dance
The nightingale and the ant
Princess of the morning
Stars
Sunlight
This day is mine
'Tis spring
Waltz song
Wind and lyre
SACRED
The Cross, choral march (E. Markham) (vce, pf and orch)
Christmas Angels
OPERA
Priscilla
Sinner's Saint
Undine, lyric tone poem in 1 act (E. Markham) (w-ch, pf and orch) (Presser)
OPERETTA
The Love Wagon
Waltz for three
Ref. 53, 70, 94, 141, 142, 226, 292, 304, 347, 353, 610

WARE, Helen

American violinist and composer. b. Woodbury, NJ, September 9, 1887; d. 1962. She studied the violin under Frederic Hahn in Philadelphia and composition under Hugh Clarke at the University of Pennsylvania. She studied in Vienna under Sevcik and for two years in Budapest under Hubay. She made her debut at Budapest in 1912 and was the first American violinist to tour in Hungary. She also toured throughout the United States.
Compositions
CHAMBER
Caprice genett (vln and pf)
Gentle shadows (vln and pf) (Witmark)
Hungarian camp songs (vln and pf) (Presser)
Hungarian love-song (vln and pf) (Presser)
Hungarian phantasy, Cinka panna (vln and pf) (Fischer)
Transcriptions (Fischer; Schirmer)
VOCAL
Songs
Ref. 53, 85, 90, 347, 353

WARING, Kate

American flautist, teacher and composer. b. Alexandria, LA, April 22, 1953. She gained her B.Mus. (flute) and M. Mus. (composition) from the Louisana State University, Baton Rouge and her D.Mus. from the Sorbonne, Paris. She has appeared in concert and on television as a flautist. Her compositions have been performed in Europe and the United States. She has received numerous commissions and is the president of the European Chapter, College Music Society.

Compositions
ORCHESTRA
    Ulterior motives (8 sax and str orch) (1984)
    Collage cachique (wind qrt and str orch) (1985)
CHAMBER
    Trio (fl, vlc and pf) (1975)
    Variations (fl and hpcd) (1984)
VOCAL
    Thirteen ways of looking at a blackbird (S and ww qnt) (1977)
    Assemblages (S, fl, trb, pf and perc) (1977)
BALLET
    Acteon, in 3 acts (large orch) (1982)
Ref. composer, 643

WARNE, Katharine Mulky
American professor and composer. b. Oklahoma City, October 23, 1923. She studied under Darius Milhaud at Mills College, under Bernard Wagenaar at the Juilliard School of Music and under Donald Erb at the Cleveland Institute of Music. She was a lecturer at the University of Kansas from 1947 to 1950, an assistant professor from 1950 to 1953 and 1957 to 1960. She performed at the University of Kansas Symposium and Cleveland Contemporary Arts Festival. She received first prize in the Mills College composition contest (1944 and 1945), a full fellowship in composition at the Juilliard School of Music and first and second prizes at the Kansas Federation of Music Clubs Contest in 1959.
Compositions
ORCHESTRA
    Apollo-Orion (cham orch)
    Epigenesis (1974)
CHAMBER
    String quartet (1952)
    Fugal consequences (perc ens) (1979)
    Les deux (2 vln and 2 fl) (1983)
    Fête (2 vln and pf) (1959)
    Interplay (picc, trp and vlc)
    Airplane music (vln and pf) (1980)
    Colored reflections (rec and hp) (1982)
    Cryptic evocations (fl and pf) (1976)
    Fantasy (vln and pf) (1980)
    Friendly conversation (cl and pf) (1979)
    Now (2 fl) (1976)
    Uncamouflaged (fl and pf) (1978)
    Dispositions (hp) (1975)
    Easy head joint (1980)
    Meditation (org) (1982)
    Tedrad (perc)
PIANO
    Rondo (2 pf) (1967)
    Anaphora (1972)
    Claude et francois (1975)
    Passacaglia (1950)
    Serenata scherzando (1978)
    Suite No. 3 (1952)
    Theme and variations (1946)
    Toccata (1982)
VOCAL
    Andromache (vce and insts) (1984)
    Cradle song (S and hp) (1963)
    The joining cousins (S, bsn and hp) (1980)
    Songs (Bar and pf) (1951)
    Songs (S and pf) (1963)
SACRED
    O God our help in ages past (ch, org, bells and perc) (1981)
    Thy Church O God in ev'ry age (mix-ch, org, bells and perc)
    Psalm 36 (S, cl and org) (1974)
    Psalm 69 (3-part w-vces and hp) (1950)
MULTIMEDIA
    Ta matete (fl, vla, hp and dance) (1977)
Ref. composer, 142, 625, 643

WARNER, Sally Slade
American carillonist, organist, choral conductor, teacher and composer. b. Worcester, Mass, September 6, 1932. She studied at the New England Conservatory (1950 to 1952); gained her choir master and associate certificate from the Guild of Organists and studied under Piet van den Broek to gain a diploma from the Royal Carillon School, Mechelen, Belgium, 1979. She was organist and music director at Church St. John, Boston and taught the carillon at Phillips Academy, Andover.
Compositions
CARILLON
    Passacaglia on E-A-C (1981)
    Variations on Die alder soetse Jesus
Ref. 625

WARNER, Sylvia Townsend
English music historian and composer. b. Harrow on Hill, December 6, 1893; d. 1978. She studied composition under Percy C. Buck and specialized in notation.
Compositions
CHAMBER
    Memorial (str qrt)
VOCAL
    Children of the earth, song cycle
    Rhapsody
    Songs
Publications
    The Point of Perfection in XVI-Century Notation. Proc. Mus. Ass XLV. 1918-1919.
    Article on notation in the Oxford History of Music. Oxford, 1929.
    Editions of old Tudor music.
Ref. 17, 85, 201, 226, 347

WARREN, Betsy (Frost Warren-Davis)
20th-century American singer, teacher and composer. b. Boston. She gained her B.A. and M.A. from Radcliffe College. She performed as a singer and taught singing privately.
Compositions
CHAMBER
    Quartet (sax) (1981)
    Trio (fl, ob and pf) (1981)
    Sonata (fl and hp) (1982)
    Suite (vln and vlc) (1983)
    The blue goat (gtr) (1982)
    Night watch in city of Boston (1980)
SACRED
    Jonah, cantata (1983)
Ref. 625

WARREN, Elinor Remick
American concert pianist, accompanist and composer. b. Los Angeles, February 23, 1905. She began her musical studies at the age of five, composing short piano pieces at an early age. She began serious study of composition at the age of 14 and while she was still in high school her compositions were published by leading New York firms. She studied for one year at Mills College in Los Angeles and then in New York under various teachers: Kathryn Cocke, Olga Steeb, Paulo Gailico, Ernesto Berumen and Frank La Forge. She also studied under Dr. Clarence Dickinson (harmony, counterpoint and orchestration) and later under Nadia Boulanger (q.v.) in Paris; also under Gertrude Ross. She was pianist-accompanist for well-known singers such as Lawrence Tibbett, Richard Crooks and Lucrezia Bori. As an accomplished concert pianist she performed her own works with orchestras, including the Los Angeles Philharmonic and the Hollywood Bowl Orchestra and in tours and recitals throughout the United States. Her awards included election as Woman of the Year in Music by the Los Angeles Times in 1955; annual ASCAP awards from 1958 onward and an honorary music doctorate given by Occidental College, Los Angeles in 1960. She was chosen, together with Igor Stravinsky and Walter Piston, to participate as a composer in the first Los Angeles International Music Festival in 1961 and was the recipient of the first prize in the Gedok International Choral and Orchestral competition in Germany in 1962. She received numerous first prizes in contests organized by the American League of Pen Women. She also received many commissions and published well over 160 works. DISCOGRAPHY. PHOTOGRAPH.
Compositions
ORCHESTRA
    Symphony in one movement (1970) (New York: Carl Fischer) (comm Stanford University)
    Along the western shore, 3 sketches: The Dark Hills; Nocturne; Sea rhapsody (C. Fischer)
    The crystal lake (C. Fischer)
    The fountain (also pf)
    Intermezzo (from The Legend of King Arthur) (H.W. Gray: Belwin-Mills)
    Scherzo (also pf)
    Suite for orchestra (C. Fischer)
    Theme for the Hollywood Bowl (1959)
CHAMBER
    Pieces, incl:
    Quintet for woodwinds or French horn
    Processional march (org or pf) (New York: G. Schirmer, 1969)
PIANO
    The fountain
    Poem (1946) (C. Fischer)
    Processional march (G. Schirmer, 1969)
    Scherzo

VOCAL

The harp weaver, cantata (Edna St. Vincent Millay) (Bar, w-ch, hp and orch; also pf and vce) (H.W. Gray; Belwin-Mills)

The passing of King Arthur, cantata (Tennyson) (T, Bar, ch and orch or pf) (H.W. Gray)

Singing earth, cantata (C. Sandburg) (S or T and orch or pf) (Theodore Presser)

Four sonnets (Edna St. Vincent Millay) (S and str orch or str qrt; also pf and vce) (C. Fischer, 1965)

Good morning, America (C. Sandburg) (narr, mix-ch, orch or cham ens; also vce and pf) (1976) (C. Fischer) (comm Occidental College)

The little betrothed (w-ch and opt orch; also vce and pf) (C. Fischer)

To my native land (H.W. Longfellow) (mix-ch a-cap or mix-ch and orch; also vce and pf) (E.C. Schirmer)

Sleeping beauty (Tennyson) (S, Bar, mix-ch and cham ens or pf) (H.W. Gray)

Transcontinental (A.N. Sullivan) (Bar, mix-ch and cham ens or pf; also vce and pf) (Presser)

Our beloved land (S. Bonner) (mix-vces and opt orch or org or pf) (Presser)

At the crossroads (m-ch)

Autumn sunset (m-ch) (H.W. Gray)

Children of the moon (w-ch; also vce and pf) (H. Flammer)

From this summer garden (P. Romay) (w-ch) (C. Fischer, 1970)

The gate of the year (mix-ch a-cap) (H. Flammer)

The heart of the night (w-ch) (H. Flammer)

Little choral suite (w-ch and pf) (C. Fischer, 1975)

Night rider (R.L. Stevenson) (mix-ch and pf) (Gould, 1975)

The night will never stay (E. Farjeon) (w-ch and pf) (Gould)

Now welcome, summer (mix-ch and pf) (1984)

Rolling rivers, dreaming forests (mix-ch a-cap) (C. Fischer)

Songs of the seasons (ch a-cap)

White horses of the sea (m-ch; also vce and pf) (G. Schirmer)

White iris (w-ch) (Galaxy)

Windy nights (m-ch) (H. Flammer)

Windy weather (J. Stephens) (w-ch and pf) (E.C. Schirmer, 1942)

Awake! put on strength! (mix-vces and pf or org) (Concordia)

My heart is ready (mix-vces and pf or org) (Gould)

To the farmer (mix-vces and pf or org; also vce and pf) (C. Fischer)

Other choral pieces

Songs incl:

For you with love (L. Untermeyer) (vce and pf) (G. Schirmer)

Heather (T and pf)

I saw a little tailor (vce and pf) (Ditson)

Idyll (vce and pf) (H.W. Gray)

My lady Lo Fu

Now welcome summer!

O, sleep

Other (vce and pf) (H.W. Gray)

Poem (C. Fischer)

Snow towards evening (vce and pf) (G. Schirmer)

Songs for young voices (mix-ch and pf) (Gould, 1976)

Sweetgrass range

Tawny (T and pf)

Time you old gypsy man

To a blue-eyed baby (vce and pf) (Presser)

We two (S or Bar and pf) (G. Schirmer)

When you walk through the woods (vce and pf) (Ditson)

SACRED

Abram in Egypt (ch and orch) (1961)

Hymn of the city (W.C. Bryant) (mix-vces and opt orch or org or pf) (C. Fischer, 1970)

Requiem (Latin and English texts) (mix-ch, m-S, Bar and orch or pf or org) (Gould) (comm R. Wagner)

Sanctus (S, Bar, mix-ch and orch or pf or org) (Gould)

Hymn to the night sea (w-ch) (Oliver Ditson)

More things are wrought by prayer (Tennyson) (mix-ch a-cap; also vce and pf or org) (H.W. Gray; Belwin Mills)

Now thank we all our God (mix-ch and org) (Fred Bock Co., 1981)

Prayer of St. Francis (ch a-cap) (H.W. Gray)

Praises and prayers (mix-ch and org or ch a-cap and opt brass qrt) (Neil Kjos)

Arise, my heart and sing! for Easter (mix-vces and pf or org) (H.W. Gray)

Christmas candle (mix-vces and pf or org; also mix-vces a-cap, w-ch or m-ch or ch a-cap, or vce and pf) (G. Schirmer)

Christ went up into the hills (mix-vces and pf or org) (H.W. Gray)

Come to the stable (mix-vces and pf or org) (H.W. Gray)

God be in my heart (mix-vces a-cap; also vce and pf) (Ditson)

God is my song (mix-vces and pf or org) (Boosey & Hawkes)

A joyful song of praise (mix-vces and pf or org) (H. Flammer)

Let the heavens praise Thy wonders (mix-vces and pf or org) (H.W. Gray; Belwin-Mills)

Christms morn (S and A) (H. Flammer)

Glory of His presence (vce and pf) (H.W. Gray)

God, our refuge (vce and pf) (H.W. Gray)

Jesus from Thy throne on high

ARRANGEMENTS

Concert transcription of three Stephen Foster melodies (pf) (Ditson)

If Thou Art Near, from Bach Air (pf) (H. Flammer)

Ref. composer, 22, 40, 68, 74, 77, 94, 142, 146, 190, 226, 228, 292, 322, 415, 474, 477, 494, 563, 594, 611, 622, 625, 643, 653

WARREN, Mrs. H. Jnr. See DAVIS, Jean Reynolds

WARSHAW, Dalit Paz

American concert pianist and composer. b. Manhattan, August 6, 1974. Her only piano teacher is her mother, Ruti, a former concert pianist and graduate of the Rubin Academy, Tel Aviv. Dalit gave her first public performance at the age of four and started to compose at the age of seven. At eight she won the Aaron Copeland International Young Composers' Competition and at nine, a BMI award for student composers up to the age of 26 years, both times being the youngest composer ever to do so. Her *In the Beginning* was performed by several leading orchestras and at the New York Philharmonic's Young People's Concert, 1984, this being the first time that a person under the age of 16, except for Mozart, had a composition played by the Philharmonic. In 1983 she won the Rockland County Music Teachers' Guild piano concerto competition. In 1986 her *Ruth* was premiered at the Israel International Music Festival of Women Composers. Most of her compositions have been performed by leading orchestras in the United States. PHOTOGRAPH.

Compositions

ORCHESTRA

Conflicts in Genesis (1985)

In the beginning, suite (1983) (BMI award, 1984)

Ruth (1986) (comm)

CHAMBER

Horah and variations (vln and pf) (1985)

Short pieces (vln and pf)

Waltz (vln and pf) (1983)

PIANO

Pieces incl.:

Fun suite (Aaron Copland Award, 1983; IBM student composer award, 1984)

VOCAL

The War of Gettysburg (brother, Hilan) (vce and pf) (1985)

Ref. composer, *New York Magazine* December 17 1984

WARSKA, W.

Composition

FILM MUSIC

The Curio lake (1974)

Ref. 497

WARTEL, Atala Therese Annette (nee Adrien)

French pianist, accompanist, professor and composer. b. Paris, July 2, 1814; d. Paris, November 6, 1865. She was the daughter of a violinist at the Opera and leader of the Conservatoire Orchestra. She studied at the Paris Conservatoire, worked there as an accompanist and from 1931 to 1938, as a professor. She was the first woman instrumentalist engaged by the Société des Concerts and also appeared in London. She married Pierre Wartel, a pianist, composer and writer on music.

Compositions

PIANO

Leçons écrites sur les sonates de Beethoven (Girod)

Souvenirs des Huguenots, fantaisie (Kistner)

Ref. 8, 226, 276, 297, 433

WARWICK, Mary Carol

American pianist, arranger, librettist, assistant professor and composer. b. Lumberton, October 28, 1939. She gained her B.A. (1961) and B.M. (1962) from Meredith College, Raleigh in piano performance and M.M. (1964) and B.M. (1985) in composition and theory from Florida State University. She studied opera composition and libretto writing under Carlisle Floyd, University of Houston (1981 to 1985); contemporary piano techniques under Virginia Gaburo, University of California Extension Studies from 1971 to 1984; applied opera vocal training under Stella Roman, Los Angeles from 1972 to 1975 and orchestration, canon and fugue under Kent Kennan at the University of Texas from 1965 to 1968. She was head opera coach, Houston Baptist University from 1982 to 1985, graduate assistant and, opera coach at Florida State University from 1978 to 1981, assistant professor of the piano and theory at Pembroke State University from 1977

to 1978 and composer, arranger, rehearsal pianist for the Theater under the Stars, Houston from 1983 to 1985. She is a member of Phi Kappa Phi and Pi Kappa Lambda.
Compositions
ORCHESTRA
Suite
CHAMBER
Alto aspects (a-sax and pf) (1981) (comm Pat Meighan, Florida State University)
Five movements (b-sax and pf) (1979)
Metaphysical meditations
DANCE SCORES
Cabin in the sky (orch) (1985)
One man band (orch) (1985)
Sin city ballet (orch) (1985)
Teen Charlie burlesque (orch) (1985)
OPERA
Lealista, in 2 acts (1985)
Sisters of Faith, in 1 act (1985) (comm Southwest Texas State University)
Ref. composer, 643

WASIAKOWA, M.
20th-century Polish composer.
Composition
PIANO
Rythmique
Ref. Polonaises de Musique 1954

WASKO, Christine
American composer. b. Philadelphia, PA, October 18, 1953. She graduated from the Mozarteum, Salzburg, in 1976, majoring in composition and in 1980 graduated from the Temple University Music School, Philadelphia, majoring in composition magna cum laude.
Compositions
CHAMBER
Woodwind quartet (1979)
Iskra (fl and pf) (1980)
Piano pieces (1977-1982)
VOCAL
The mustard seed (mix-ch and pf) (1981)
Alias evidence (S and pf) (1978)
Haiku (S and pf) (1977)
ELECTRONIC
Metropolis (str qrt, pf and elec tape) (1981)
Music for harp and electronic tape (1979)
Ref. composer

WASSALS, Grace (Chadbourne)
20th-century American composer. Her compositions were sung by such artists as Gadski and Bispham.
Composition
VOCAL
Shakespearean song cycle (4 vces)
Ref. 226, 347

WATARI, Kyoto (pseud. of Kyoko Natsume)
Japanese composer. b. February 24, 1915.
Compositions
MISCELLANEOUS
Chatting on a side walk
On the beach one day
Outside the window
Ref. Japan Phonograph Record Assoc.

WATERHOUSE, Frances Emery
American pianist, writer and composer. b. Kennebunk, April 5, 1902. Her music was influenced by the eight years she spent in Central America. She was tourist attachée for Guatamala and was devoted to the cause of Inter-American solidarity and the interest of Mexican labourers resident in Kennebunk.
Compositions
PIANO
Waltz trio: Symphony of Guatamala, Symphony of Maine, Jungle Memories
VOCAL
Songs incl.:
Another christmas

Banana paradise
Certain music
Tipitapa
Tiquisate
Yo lo dudo
Publications
Banana Paradise. New York: Stephen-Paul. Travel book of the year, 1947.
Ref. 347, 374

WATERSTONE, Satella S.
American pianist, teacher and song composer. b. Greenwood Lake, NY; d. South Orange, NJ, June 1938. She studied at Columbia University and in Germany. She published works on musical education for young people including the training of rhythm bands and children's symphonies.
Ref. 226

WATKINS, Mary
20th-century American composer.
Composition
CHAMBER
String quartet
Ref. I.L.W.C.

WATSON, Gwendolyn
20th-century American cellist, improvisor, lecturer and composer. She is on the staff of the Stanford University. She travels extensively performing and giving workshops for modern dance musicians and dancers and has been commissioned by several leading modern dance companies.
Composition
DANCE SCORE
Improvisation (dancer, vlc and orch)
Ref. AMC

WATSON, Mabel Madison
American composer. She composed piano pieces.
Ref. 292

WATSON, Regina
English composer. b. Germany, 1854.
Compositions
PIANO
An Arabian night (Summy)
Bourrée la gigue (Summy)
Dansons la gigue (Summy)
Mazourka étude (Summy)
Mignon, a portrait (Summy)
Scherzino (Summy)
VOCAL
Aus Drang und Lieb fuer dich (vce and pf)
Cupid's blunder (vce and pf)
An explanation (vce and pf)
Lune blanche (vce and pf)
Ref. 297, 347

WATSON OR WATSON-HENDERSON, Ruth. See HENDERSON, Ruth Watson

WAUGH, Jane
20th-century English composer.
Composition
MISCELLANEOUS
Scissors, paper and stone
Ref. 230

WAYMON, Eunice. See SIMONE, Nina in ADDENDUM

WEATHERALL, Nellie G.
Australian composer. b. Geelong, Victoria, May 11, 1878.

Compositions
CHAMBER
    Piano pieces (Sydney: Paling & Co.)
    Teaching pieces (Melbourne: Allan & Co.)
VOCAL
    Songs (Paling & Co.)
FILM MUSIC
    Facade
Ref. 23, 105, 226, 442

WEAVER, Carol Ann

American pianist, lecturer and composer. b. Harrisonburg, VA, May 6, 1948. She obtained a B.M. (1970), M.M. (1972) and a D.M. (composition, 1982) from Indiana University, Bloomington. She studied theory and composition at the University of Michigan, Ann Arbor (summer 1974) and the piano and composition under various teachers including John Eaton, Bernard Heiden, Juan Orrego-Salas and Higo Hirado (composition) and Gyorgy Sebok, Robert Weisz and Enrica Cavallo Gulli (piano). She studied theory under Mary Wennerstrom (q.v.), Vernon Kliewer and Elaine Barkin (q.v.). She was teacher of music at the Eastern Mennonite College in Harrisonburg, where she taught the piano, theory and composition from 1972. She appeared as guest solo pianist at recitals at the Eastern Mennonite College, Ohio State University and Bridgewater College in Virginia. She was winner of a piano competition sponsored by the Virginia Music Teachers Society in Harrisonburg in 1966 and is the recipient of several grants. She was assistant lecturer at Indiana University, 1970 to 1972.
Compositions
ORCHESTRA
    Glimpses (str sextet and orch) (1976)
    Orogeny (1974)
CHAMBER
    Ranges (str sextet, 3 vln, vla and 2 vlc) (1976)
    Ad cappellam fortem (4 pf, perc, fl, ob, B-cl and vla) (1972)
    City primeval (2 vln, ob, cl, B-gtr, perc and pf) (1978)
    Algonquin night (cl, man, vla, vlc, perc and pf) (1982)
    Four statements of Meine Hoffnung (wind ens) (1982)
    Stephen's feast (wind ens) (1982)
    Dance of the earth creatures (ob, cl, 2 vln and vlc) (1978)
    Four psalm tones (fl, ob, B-cl, vla and perc) (1972)
    Procession (man, gtr and pf) (1982)
    Three fragiles (ob, cl and bsn) (1969)
    Duo for horn and piano (1970)
    Psalm (a-sax and pf) (1981)
    Streams (a-sax and pf) (1981)
    We wish you (vln and pf) (1974)
    Lyra (man) (1983)
    Moods of cello (vlc) (1970)
    Morning of the sixth day (perc) (1978)
PIANO
    Before Jehovah's aweful throne: A commentary (1972)
    Summer suite (1966)
    Three moments in time: Late of the day; Between a dream; Ice dawn (1971)
VOCAL
    Come (ch, fl, ob, trb, gtr, perc, pf and org) (1978)
    Two affirmations (ch a-cap) (1970)
    Four songs of Donna Carol Burkhart (S and cl) (1971)
    Four preludes of T.S. Eliot (S and pf) (1969)
    Lullaby (S, fl and vla) (1978)
    Must happen (1967)
    The two-born soul (S, 2 fl, 2 cl, 2 bsn and perc) (1977)
SACRED
    Mass (ch and orch) (1976)
    God can work miracles (chil-ch, pf and rec) (1967)
    Jericho (chil-ch and pf) (1979)
    Psalm 57 (ch and pf) (1981)
    Psalm 68 (ch, brass, perc and 2 pf) (1979)
    Psalm 96 (ch and pf) (1979)
    Worthy the lamb (ch and pf) (1980)
    Amazing grace (S and pf) (1981)
    Grant us thy peace (m-S, a-sax and pf) (1981)
    Jesus walked (S and pf) (1980)
    Magnificat (S and pf) (1979)
    Voices of Eve (m-S, fl, cl, vib and vlc) (1981)
ELECTRONIC
    Rejoice (ch, elec gtr and orch) (1980)
    Beyond soundless stars (pf and tape) (1973)
    Gathering (ch, elec gtr, perc and amp pf) (1975)
    Sing praises (speakers and tape) (1976)
    Tower of Babel (ch a-cap, elec gtr, perc and amp pf) (1972)
    Erscheinen (tape) (1972)
    Mini-Moog-scape (mini-Moog) (1970)
Ref. composer, 77

WEAVER, Harriet

American composer.
Composition
VOCAL
    O lovely world (vce and pf) (Presser)
Ref. 190

WEAVER, Marion

American organist, pianist, authoress and composer. b. Marietta, PA, December 18, 1902. She studied the organ and voice at Temple University Music School and the piano under S. Becker von Grabill. She played the piano for silent films from the age of 14 and was the organist and pianist in various Eastern Pennsylvanian cities.
Compositions
VOCAL
    Music in the night
    One star
SACRED
    I walked into the garden, hymn
INCIDENTAL MUSIC
    Plain Betsy
Ref. 494

WEAVER, Mary (alt. name Mary Watson Weaver)

American pianist, authoress, lecturer and composer. b. Kansas City, MO, January 16, 1903. She studied at Smith College and Ottawa University where she received a B.A. and B.M. She also studied with Rosario Scalero and Deems Taylor at the Curtis Institute of Music and privately in New York and France. She gave recitals and lecture recitals from 1927 to 1957. She taught the piano at the Kansas City Conservatory, the Curtis Institute and the University of Missouri, Kansas City (1946 to 1957) and at the Manhattan School of Music (1957 to 1970). She also taught at the Henry Street School of Music, New York.
Compositions
VOCAL
    Enchanted islands (w-ch, org or pf) (St. Louis: G. Scholin, 1952)
    Cradle song (S and pf) (New York: G. Schirmer, 1940)
    Heart of heaven (S or A and pf) (New York: Galaxy Music, 1952)
SACRED
    All weary men (mix-ch and org) (Galaxy Music, 1949)
    Confess Jehovah (mix-ch and org) (Galaxy Music, 1951)
    God's love enfold (mix-ch and org) (New York: Belwin-Mills, 1952)
    Hail, Jesu Bambino (mix-ch and org) (Delaware Water Gap, PA: Shawnee, 1967)
    Like doves descending (mix-ch and org) (Galaxy Music, 1952)
    Like the young sheep (mix-ch and org) (Galaxy Music, 1950)
    New Mexican lullaby (w-ch, org or pf) (Belwin-Mills, 1953)
    O Holy Child (w-ch, org or pf) (G. Scholin, 1952)
    On the eve of the First Christmas (mix-ch and org) (Galaxy Music, 1948)
    Rise up all men (mix-ch and org) (Galaxy Music, 1953)
    When Jesus lay by Mary's side (mix-ch and org) (G. Schirmer, 1951)
Ref. 39, 40, 142, 228, 347

WEBB, Allienne Brandon

American choir conductor and composer. b. Palestine, TX, January 2, 1910; d. Dallas, November 16, 1965. She graduated with a B.A. from Southern Methodist University in Dallas. She studied voice under Peter Tchach and was local soloist and church choir director for 12 years at Park Cities Baptist Church in Dallas.
Compositions
ORCHESTRA
    Sleepy head (Adolph Schmid) (also med-vce) (Theodore Presser)
VOCAL
    The endless song (mix-ch) (Mills Music)
    Last night I walked in the garden (med-vce) (Presser)
    The mule's tail (med-vce) (Carl Fischer)
SACRED
    Father teach me to pray (mix-ch) (Hansen Music)
    He's walking with me, hymn anthem (mix-ch) (Hansen)
    Hosanna to His name, Christmas anthem (mix-ch) (Mills)
    My father's prayer, Father's Day anthem (mix-ch; also w-ch) (Mills)
    Nine short choral responses for Protestant Churches (mix-ch) (Hansen)
    Are he gone, have he went (Mills)
    Our Wedding prayer (Hansen)
TEACHING PIECES
    Piano pieces:
    Balky donkey (Leeds)
    Ballerina of the ice (Leeds)

Indian feather (Leeds)
Gremlins (E.B. Marks)
Hopscotch (E.B. Marks)
Skates on the Zuider Zee (E.B. Marks)
Three solos (E.B. Marks)
Ref. composer, 142

WEBB, Fannie Edith Starke. See EAGAR, Fannie Edith Starke

WEBB, Mary
20th-century composer.
Composition
PIANO
Twilight tapestry (Cramer, 1950)
Ref. 473

WEBENAU, Julie
German composer. b. 1813; d. 1887.
Composition
VOCAL
Eigne Bahn (J.N. Vogl)
Ref. Openbare Musiekbibliotheek, Amsterdam

WEBER, Bertha
20th-century composer.
Composition
OPERA
The Mysterious Characters of Mr. Fu
Ref. 141

WEBER, Carole
20th-century American flautist, artist, dancer, director, teacher and composer. b. Rochester, NY. She studied music and art at the California State University and was a member of a folk ensemble which specialized in music of the Middle East. She taught in elementary schools for eight years and was the musical director for the Long Beach City College dance concerts.
Ref. 633

WECKWERTH, Nancy
American horn player, pianist, teacher and composer. b. Montevideo, MA, December 11, 1951. In 1975 she graduated with a B.Mus. from the University of Wisconsin and in 1979, with a M.Mus. from the University of Miami. Her teachers included Philp Farkas, Frank Brouk, Jerry Peel and Robert Elworthy. She was the principal horn player with the Fort Lauderdale Chamber Orchestra. She has been teaching the piano and French horn for a number of years and traveled extensively with various orchestras. A number of her works are written under a pseudonym.
Compositions
CHAMBER
Symphony for eight winds (Trombacor Music)
Brass quintet (Trombacor)
Ritual dance (ww qnt) (Trombacor)
Woodwind quintet (Trombacor)
Noodletown rag (brass qrt) (Trombacor)
Sonata for trumpet and piano (Trombacor)
Trombacor suite (hn and trp) (Trombacor)
Ceremonial suite (Trombacor)
Ref. composer

WEEL, Heleen van der
20th-century Dutch carillonneur and composer. She is city carillonneur of The Hague.
Compositions
CARILLON
Invencie
Fughetta
Ref. University of California, Riverside

WEGENER-FRENSEL, Emmy Heil
Dutch pianist, violinist and composer. b. Amsterdam, June 14, 1901; d. January 11, 1973. She was the daughter of Bertha Frensel Wegener-Koopman (q.v.) She studied under Sam Dresden.

Compositions
ORCHESTRA
Dance (cl and orch)
Rhapsody (pf and orch) (1930) (Henmar)
Suite (naar illustraties van Walter Crane bij fragmenten van Shakespeare) (Henmar, 1929)
CHAMBER
Sextet (fl, ob, cl, bsn, hn and pf) (1927)
String quartet (1929)
Suite (vln, vla and vlc) (1925)
Oboe suite (ob and pf) (1929)
Sonata (vln and pf) (1929)
Sonata in one movement (vlc and pf) (1927)
Toccata (pf) (Broekmans en van Poppel, 1929)
VOCAL
Gekwetst ben ik van binnen (mix-ch) (1928)
Ik zag Cecilia komen (1928)
Ref. 17, 44, 70, 226, 280, 461

WEGENER-KOOPMAN, Bertha Frensel
Dutch pianist and composer. b. Bloemendaal, September 27, 1874; d. Amsterdam, July 17, 1953. She was the mother of Emmy Heil Wegener-Frensel (q.v.).
Compositions
VOCAL
Cantata (w-vces)
Songs, incl.:
Droomevrouw
Love songs (Tagore)
SACRED
Stabat Mater
Ref. 44, 94, 169, 226

WEICHSEL, Elizabeth. See BILLINGTON, Elizabeth

WEIGL, Vally
American pianist, lecturer, music therapist and composer. b. Vienna, September 11, 1889; d. December 25, 1982. She studied the piano privately in Vienna under Richard Robert, musicology under Guido Adler and composition under Karl Weigl (whom she later married) at Vienna University. She taught as Professor Robert's assistant and at Vienna University's musicological Institute. In the summers she worked in music festivals with visiting students. In 1928 she went to the United States and taught at the institute for Avocational Music and the American Theatre Wing, becoming an American citizen in 1943. In 1955 she gained her M.A. from Columbia University and pursuing her lifelong interest in music therapy, worked as chief music therapist at the New York Medical College. She taught at the Roosevelt Cerebral Palsy School, Long Island, NY, and directed research projects at Mt. Sinai Hospital's psychiatric division and the Home for the Jewish Aged in New York. She lectured in the United States, Canada and Europe and was chairlady of the Friends' Arts for World Unity Committee. She was a fellow of the MacDowell Colony association where she was twice composer-in-residence and was a member of the ACA, AMC and other professional organizations. She was awarded several recording grants and was the recipient of prizes and honors. Her music was widely performed and published by E.C. Schirmer, Theodore Presser, Jelsor Music and Broadcast Music, Inc. DISCOGRAPHY. PHOTOGRAPH.
Compositions
CHAMBER
Five occurrences, op. 27 (ww qnt) (1977)
Mood sketches, suite in 4 movements (ww qnt) (1953-1954)
Adagio for strings (str qrt)
Andante for strings (str qrt)
Dear earth (hn, vln, vla and tim)
To Emily, adagietto (str qrt)
Brief encounters (ww trio)
The cherry tree (hn, ob or fl and pf)
Echoes from poems (P. Benton) (hn or cl, vln and pf)
New England suite (cl or f, vlc and pf)
Old time divertimento (3 hn)
Prelude for three (fl, vla and hp)
Trialogue (fl, vla and hp or pf)
Dialogue (fl and cl)
Old time burlesque (vlc or trb and pf) (1937)
Three discourses (fl or vln and vlc)
Oiseau de la vie (fl or cl)
PIANO
Bagatelles (4 hands) (1953)
Capriccio (4 hands)
Dance of the Grasshoppers and Kittens

Frolicking Kittens (1961)
Kitten Stories, educational (1953)
Lonesome Kitten (1961)
Toccatina
Two children's pieces (4 hands)
Who is afraid of 5 black keys
Other pieces
VOCAL
The people, yes, chamber cantata (C. Sandburg) (1977) (ded President Jimmy Carter)
Fins (m-ch and str qrt)
Ode to beauty (mix-ch, hn and pf or strs)
Three choral songs of the South West (mix-ch)
Along the moving darkness, song cycle
Beat, old heart (C. Sandburg)
Beyond time, song cycle (F. Blankner)
Birds in springtime (G.S. Bail)
The blackbird (H. Wolfe)
Bless the four corners of this house (A. Guiterman)
Bold heart (mix-ch a-cap)
Cardinal in March (E.R. Weigl)
Challenger (E. Segal)
City birds (M. Mason)
Day and night (H. Van Dyke)
Dearest, dearest sleepest thou?
Death snips proud men by the nose (Sandburg)
Der Tod (M. Claudius)
Do not awake me, song cycle (M. Edey)
Drums of war
Echoes from poems by Patricia Benton
The elf and the dormouse (O. Herford)
Evolution
The fairies have never a penny to spend (R. Fyleman)
Fairy song (Keats)
Fear no more (Shakespeare)
Fog (Sandburg)
Four choral songs on death and man (C. Sandburg)
Four songs (Swinburne, Rossetti, G. Cooper, D. Harris)
Five songs of remembrance (Dickinson)
Four songs of concern
From the far corners
From time and eternity (Dickinson)
Fruehling (Springtime) (E. Shyber)
Gifts (J. Thompson)
Glimpse of hope (R. List)
Hoarfrost and silence (C. Sandburg)
Heart's content
Hoffnungsschimmer (R. List)
The huntsmen (R.L. Stevenson)
I saw two birds (E. Segal)
In just spring (cummings)
In the meadow (C. Rosetti)
In springtime
Killers (C. Sandburg)
Let down the bars, O death (Dickinson)
Let my country awake
Listen (C. Fischer)
The little singers (E. Hammond)
Lullaby (from Native Island) (Kennedy)
Lyrical suite
Mich (R. Fyleman)
Mist marches across the valley (C. Sandburg)
Mother's day
Nature moods, from the green kingdom (H. Woodeburne)
The night will never stay (E. Farjean) (vce and pf)
Nightfall in the mountains
No boundary
No loveliness is ever lost (N. Bird Turner)
Not Avalon in April (N. Bird Turner)
Not Earth alone (J.J. Keith)
Ode: We are the music makers (A. Shoughnessy)
Oh! fair to see (Rossetti)
Other hearts (E. Segal)
Other summers (E. Segal)
People, yes, out of what is their change
The people know the salt of the sea
The people know what the land knows
Pippa's song (R. Browning)
Playthings of the wind (C. Sandburg)
Practical earth satellites
Rabbles of tattered leaves (C. Sandburg)
Rain at night (Regennacht) (H. Hesse)
Rain summer (Longfellow)
Regennacht (H. Hesse)
Revelation (S and str qrt) (1982)
The rock-a-bye lady (E. Field)

The salutation of the dawn (Sanskrit)
The sea moves always (C. Sandburg)
Seal lullaby (Kipling)
Sea sunsets (C. Sandburg)
Seven rounds in Various Moods
Seven songs (Vachel Lindsay, D. Aldis, N.B. Turner)
Shelter for all
Shepherdess moon
Silver (de la Mare)
Song of hope
Song of the shadows (de la Mare)
Songs beyond time (F. Blankner)
Songs for a child
Songs from native island (G. Kennedy)
Songs from no boundary (L. Marshall)
Songs newly seen in the dusk
Songs of love and leaving (C. Sandburg)
Soon (E. Segal)
Spring cries (C. Sandburg)
Spring grass (C. Sandburg)
Summer grass (C. Sandburg)
Summer stars (C. Sandburg)
Summer's end (O. Maar)
Swiftly along flows the river
Take my hand (E. Segal)
Thanks (C. Fischer)
Thistle, yarrow, clover (K. Porter)
Thoughts about grasshoppers (F.P. Jacques)
Upstream (C. Sandburg)
When the vision dies (Perhaps) (V. Brittain)
Where go the boats (R.L. Stevenson)
Who goes there through the night?
Who has seen the wind?
Winter night (M.F. Butts)
Wynken, blynken and nod (E. Field)
The year (C. Sandburg)
SACRED
All faith prayer for peace (mix-ch) (1950-1958)
Benediction (mix-ch)
Christmas in the Holy Land (M.H. Jones) (mix-ch) (1958)
Easter morning (mix-ch)
Hear ye, all ye people (mix-ch) (1958)
Hymn (mix-ch a-cap) (1941)
Hymnus (mix-ch)
Long, long ago (mix-ch, rec or fl and pf)
Madrigal (F. Blankner) (mix-ch)
Night of prayer (T.N. Hahn) (10 S soli ad lib and mix-ch)
O see of good (God) in Human Kind (E. Yarnell) (mix-ch) (1946)
On Christmas Eve (mix-ch)
Our world is one (F. Blankner) (mix-ch)
Peace hymn (Whittier) (w-ch)
Psalm 130 (mix-ch) (1945-1946)
Te Deum (soloists, mix-ch and pf)
This is the day of light (mix-ch)
Thou art the way (F. Blankner) (mix-ch)
To Zion (mix-ch a-cap)
When the song of the angels is stilled (H. Thurman) (mix-ch)
Who bids us sing (mix ch and fl or cl and pf)
A Christmas carol (S and w-vces)
Christmas folk song (w-vces and pf)
A Christmas lullaby (Mary Jones) (vce)
The firstborn (vce and pf) (1951-1952)
Pax hominibus (with Blake) (vce)
Prayer of St. Francis of Assisi (w-vces, fl and pf; also vce) (1945)
Requiem for Allison (P. Davies) (S and strs)
Road to peace (unison vces)
Ref. composer, 77, 142, 347, 468, 474, 563, 622, 624

WEIMAR, Auguste. See GOETZE, Aguste

WEINFIELD, Christine. See BERL WEINFIELD, Christine

WEINLICH, Josepha or Josephine. See AMANN, Josephine

WEINREICH, Waltraut. See ADDENDUM

WEINTZ, Katherine. See TECK, Katherine

WEIR, Judith
Scottish lecturer and composer. b. 1954. After studying composition under John Tavener she attended the Massachusetts Institute of Technology where she became interested in computer music. From 1973 to 1976 she studied under Robin Holloway at King's College, Cambridge. In 1975 she won the Koussevitsky Fellowship at Tanglewood and worked with Messiaen. From 1976 to 1979 she worked for the English organisation, The Southern Arts Association and after 1979 occupied the chair of composition at the University of Glascow. Her works for orchestra and chamber were commissioned and performed at festivals in England and America. Her *Out of the Air* won a competition for young composers in 1976 and was performed by the Vega Wind Quintet in the Purcell Room in the same year.
Compositions
ORCHESTRA
    Isti mirant stella (Novello, 1984)
    Where the shining trumpets blow (str orch)
CHAMBER
    Black birdsong (cham ens)
    Piano sextet
    Out of the air (wind qnt)
    Wind quintet
    A Serbian cabaret (pf qrt) (1984)
    Music for 247 strings (vln and pf)
    An mein klavier (pf)
    Harmony and invention (hp)
    Variations
VOCAL
    Ballad (vce and orch)
OPERA
    King Harald's Saga, in 3 acts (S a-cap) (Novello, 1982)
MISCELLANEOUS
    The art of touching the keyboard
    Ascending into heaven
    Between ourselves
    Campanile (Scottish composers' award, 1974)
    Hans the hedgehog
    Ohime
Ref. BMIC, *Tempo* No 148, 69, 422, 622

WEIR, Mary Brinckley
American composer. b. 1783; d. New York, November 12, 1840. She composed songs.
Ref. 347

WEISMANN, Julia. See KERWEY, Julia

WEISS, Amalie. See JOACHIM, Amalie

WEISS, Arleta
B. 1965.
Composition
CHAMBER
    Pan-Epikon (2 rec) (1984) (Celle: Moeck, 1985)
Ref. Otto Harrassowitz (Wiesbaden)

WEISS, Helen L.
American composer. b. 1920; d. 1948. DISCOGRAPHY.
Composition
SACRED
    I am the people, cantata (mix-ch)
Ref. 190, 563

WEISS-MANN, Edith
German pianist, teacher and composer of songs. b. Hamburg, May 11, 1885.
Ref. 226

WEISSBERG, Julia Lazarevna
Russian editor, teacher, translator and composer. b. Orenburg, now Chkalov, December 25, 1878, d. Leningrad, March 1, 1942. She graduated from the Women's University in St. Petersburg in 1903 and then studied at the St. Petersburg Conservatory under Kryshanovsky (harmony) and Rim-

sky-Korsakov, whose son Andrei she married. She studied orchestration under Glazunov. She intended to make a career as a singer, but her voice was badly affected by the climate of St. Petersburg and she turned to composition. She was expelled from the Conservatory in 1905 for her political activities. In 1907 she moved to Berlin to become a pupil of Max Reger and Humperdinck. She returned to St. Petersburg in 1912 and graduated with an honors degree in composition from the conservatory in the same year. She edited a journal *Musical Contemporary* from 1915 to 1917 and taught choral singing at the Music School for Working Youth, Leningrad, 1921 to 1923. She was interested in folklore, particularly of the East, but her main work was composing for children. She wrote several essays on music, translated books on musical history by Romain Rolland and directed research work on folklore.
Compositions
ORCHESTRA
    Symphony in G-Minor, op. 4
    Nochyu, symphonic poem based on F. Tiuchiev (1929)
    Ballad based on King Harald, op. 10 (Heine) (1930)
    Dramatic scherzo, op. 6
    Fairy tales, based on Meyer, op. 13 (1928)
    Fantasy, op. 5
    Sailors' dances (1936)
CHAMBER
    Four pieces (2 vln and pf) (1937)
VOCAL
    Cantata
    Dvenadtsat, op. 21, cantata (A. Blok) (mix-ch and orch) (1928)
    Five children's songs: Babochka, Zainka (V. Katayev), Myshi, Loshag and Korablik (Marshak) (vce and orch) (1929)
    Komsomol i dedy (Vs. Rozhdestvenski) (vce and orch) (1938)
    Poet-pechalniy golos (F. Solodub) (vce and orch) (1924)
    Rautendelein, cycle (Hauptmann) (S and orch) (1912)
    Merry march, Locomotive, Festival Song (chil-ch and pf)
    Pechka (S. Marshak) (chil-ch and pf)
    Veselii trud (composer) (chil-ch and pf) (1927)
    Children's songs: Song riddles; Pioneer suite; The platoon
    Eastern songs
    Foma i Yerema (S. Marshak) (2 vces and pf)
    Four Chinese songs, op. 7, after Shi-King and Li-Tai-Po (vce and pf)
    Garafitsa, Moldavian folk songs (vce and hp or pf) (1938)
    Gypsy songs, op. 27
    Lunnaya skazka (P. Dehmel) (vce, fl and str qrt) (1929)
    Negro lullaby, op. 33
    Pesnya vesni (Sarodzhini Nandu)
    Poyedinok s sudboi (R. Kuch) (1912)
    Svyrel zapela (A. Blok) (2 vces and pf) (1930)
    Tak eto pravda? (R. Tagore) (1924)
    Testament to the memory of Kirov, op. 36
    Three romances (M. Konopinskaya) (1911)
    Two songs after Verlaine, op. 2 (vce and pf) (1911)
    Zadrozhali zazvuchali (F. Solodub) (2 vces and pf)
    Numerous other songs
OPERA
    Gulnara, based on Thousand and One Nights (with S. Parnok) (1935)
    Gusi-levedi, op. 18, based on Russian folk tale, in 1 act (with S. Marshak) (1937) (ded Professor Yevgenia Gnessina)
    Myorvaya Tsarevna, radio opera (Pushkin) (1937)
    Rusalochka (H.C. Andersen) (S. Parnok) (1923)
    Zaikin dom (with V. Veltman) (1937)
Ref. 2, 8, 9, 14, 22, 61, 70, 74, 87, 105, 109, 193, 226, 322, 556, 622

WELANDER, Svea Goeta (nee Nordblad)
Swedish organist, pianist, lecturer and composer. b. Linhamm, Malmo, July 24, 1888. She took organ examinations before specializing in the piano in Malmo and later in Copenhagen under Henrik Knudsen. She studied composition under Lars-Erik Larsson. From 1928 to 1963 she was the organist at Bjurlov and later taught at the Music Institute in Malmo. She married the composer Waldemar Welander.
Compositions
ORCHESTRA
    En liten skanemusik (str orch)
    Liten svit (str orch)
    Scherzando (str orch)
    Serenade (str orch)
    Vals serenade
CHAMBER
    String quartet No. 1
    Divertimento (vln, cl and vlc)
    Mazurka No. 2 (vln, vlc and pf)
    Melody, burlesque (fl, cl and bsn)
    Monica's mazurka (vln, vlc and pf)
    Preludium (fl, cl and bsn) (1966)
    Preludium (3 cl or 3 a-sax) (1961)
    Preludium for three wind instruments on a synagogue theme (1955)

Sonatina in old style (vln, cl and vlc)
Trio (vln, vlc and pf)
Dialogue and fugue for two woodwind instruments
Humoresque (vlc and pf) (1942)
Sonatina (cl and bsn) (1966)
Sonatina (vla and pf) (1945)
Choral preludes (org)
Preludium (cl) (1962)
PIANO
Sonatina
Vals serenade
VOCAL
Arioso (Eric Rembert) (S and str orch) (1956)
Sista resan (Axel Ahlman) (solo, ch and orch)
Berceuse (Lopa de Vega) (w-ch and pf) (1956)
Brollopsang (E. Rembert) (vce and org) (1947)
Impromptu (Gabriel Jonsson) (vce and pf)
Med manga kulorta iyktor (Nils Ferlin) (vce and pf)
Varregn (Sten Gelander) (S and strs) (1945)
Numerous songs (vce and pf) incl.:
Armodets son (1954)
Bebadelse
De evige tre (1948)
For en underbar stjarnas skull (1956)
Jag har fragat en stjarna (1948)
Kvall (1935)
Tyck sa mycket om mig (1948)
SACRED
Cantata (solo and ch)
Cantata for the installation of the Dean (S, T, ch and strs)
A little cantata (H. Schiller) (solo, w-ch and org) (1943)
Hymn (H. Schiller) (solo, w-ch and org) (1943)
I Betlehems stall (N. Bolander) (vce and pf)
Loven herren (vce and org)
Two Indian hymns (mix-ch) (1953)
Ref. composer, 94

WELDON, Georgina (nee Thomas) (later Treherne)

English choir conductor, singer and composer. b. London, May 24, 1837; d. Brighton, January 11, 1914. She studied singing, making her first public appearance in 1870. She toured Wales with her pupil Gwendoline Jones and became a member of Leslie's choir. Later she sang in many popular concerts. Her romantic liaison with Gounod is well known. She helped train his choir in London and established an orphanage at her residence in order to give musical training to poor children. In 1879 she sang at Riviere's Promenade Concerts with a women's choir which she trained and directed herself. This gave rise to a protracted lawsuit which was a matter of considerable notoriety. Her last professional engagement was at a popular music hall in 1884. In addition to her own compositions she published songs by Gounod and other composers.
Compositions
VOCAL
Songs incl.:
The brook (Tennyson)
Chant du passereau
Le petit garçon et le nid du rouge-gorge
Publications
Autobiography of Charles Gounod.
Hints for Pronunciation in Singing. London, 1872.
Musical Reform. London, 1872.
Ref. 8, 85, 276, 347, 433

WELLNER, Elsa

Czech composer. b. Pilsen, 1892. She completed her studies under Mandyczewski in Vienna.
Compositions
ORCHESTRA
Eight minuetti con coda (str orch)
Serenade (str orch)
CHAMBER
Quartets
Variations (ob and pf)
PIANO
Passacaglia
Other pieces
VOCAL
Neugriechische Skolien, cantata (mix-qrt and pf)
Women's choral works
Duets in canon
Songs
Ref. 105

WELLS, Jane

20th-century British composer.
Compositions
CHAMBER
Duet (pf)
MISCELLANEOUS
Reflection
There is a light
Under the redwood tree
Ref. *Composer* (London)

WELLS, Karolyn. See BASSETT, Karolyn Wells

WELMAN, Sylvia

German composer. b. 1946.
Compositions
VOCAL
Melospectaculum (speakr, ob, trp, 4 perc and vln) (Donemus, 1975)
OPERA
Vision, fantasy freely adapted from Dostoyevsky's Idiot (Donemus, 1978)
Ref. Otto Harrassowitz (Wiesbaden)

WENDELBURG, Norma Ruth

American pianist and composer. b. Stafford, KS, March 26, 1918. She won a scholarship to Bethany College, Lindsborg and received a B.M., then attended the University of Michigan where she obtained an M.M., studying composition under Ross Lee Finney and the piano under John Kollen. In 1948 she received a fellowship from the Composers' Conference and Chamber Music Center and studied under Otto Luening. She continued her study under Bernard Rogers at the Eastman School of Music, receiving an M.M. and Ph.D. (composition, 1969). She studied composition under Carlos Chavez at the Berkshire Music Center, Tanglewood, in 1953. From 1953 to 1955 she studied composition and the piano as a Fulbright scholar in Austria under Cesar Bresgen at the Mozarteum in Salzburg and Karl Schiske at the Academy of Music in Vienna. Whilst studying for her Ph.D. she held a fellowship as research scholar at the Eastman School.
Compositions
ORCHESTRA
Symphony No. 1 (1967)
Andante and allegro (1951)
Concert piece (bsn and str orch) (1952)
Concertino (ob and str orch) (1956)
Poem (fl and str orch) (1947)
Triptych (1961)
CHAMBER
Festival piece (brass and tim) (1959)
String quartet No. 1 (1952)
String quartet No. 2 (1956)
Woodwind quartet (1951)
Four dances (3 ww) (1958)
Affirmation (trb and pf)
Concenter (cl and pf) (1971)
Five duos for flute and clarinet
Sonata (ob and pf) (1951)
Suite No. 1 (vln and pf) (1951)
Suite No. 2 (vln and pf) (1964)
To nature, suite (vln and pf) (1964-1972)
Variants (perc) (1972)
ORGAN
Chorale fantasy (1961)
Interlacings
Six choral preludes
PIANO
American fantasy (1976)
Eight sketches (1950)
Six preludes (1954)
Sophisticated daughter
Transformations
Teaching pieces
VOCAL
Chinese cycle from The book of songs (w-ch and orch) (1962)
Boating song (Li Po) (mix-ch and pf) (1960)
Eve (Ralph Hodgson) (w-ch and pf) (1956)
Song on May morning (Milton) (w-ch a-cap) (1956)
Three miniatures (Rachel Field) (w-ch and pf) (1973)
Velvet shoes (Elinor Wylie) (w-ch a-cap) (1956)
Great stars of our time, cycle (vce and pf)
Song of the white clouds, cycle (S, 2 fl or pitch pipes and pf) (from the Fountain of old poems, trans from Chinese) (1969)

The songs of William Blake (vce and pf) (1953)
The stone drums (trans from Chinese) (1965)
Three songs from kaleidoscope (Betty Bird) (1971)
Three songs from Emily Dickinson (1951)
SACRED
Alleluia (mix-ch a-cap) (1951)
Apostles' Creed (mix-ch and opt org) (1962)
Arise, O God, to judge the earth (Psalm 82) (mix-ch and opt org) (1972-I1973)
Blessed series (mix-ch, trp, fl and org) (1976)
Create in me a clean heart, O God (solos, ch, cong and insts) (1969)
Delight in the Lord, Psalm 37 (mix-ch and opt org) (1973)
Doors of heaven (Robert Nathan) (mix-ch a-cap) (1957)
Help, O Lord all godly men, Psalm 12 (mix-ch and opt org) (1973)
Hymn (Stephen Crane) (w-ch and pf) (1953)
If I take the wings of morning, Psalm 139 (mix-ch and fl) (1971) (Hopkins)
It is good, Psalm 92 (w-ch and org or pf) (1973)
The Lord reigns over us, Psalm 93 (w-ch and org) (1973)
Lord, your blessing please, Psalm 67 (mix-ch and org) (1973)
My Lord, chastise me not in anger, Psalm 6 (mix-ch and opt org) (1973)
My prayers like incense rising, Psalm 141 (mix-ch and opt org) (1973)
O God, we wait upon You now, Psalm 130 (mix-ch and opt org) (1973)
Oh, how I love Thy word, Psalm 119 (w-ch or m-ch or mix-ch and opt org) (1973)
Praise the Lord, Psalm 146 (mix-ch and opt org) (1973)
Praise the Lord of Creation, Psalm 148 (mix-ch and org) (1973)
The promised gifts, Psalm 85 (T, mix-ch, cong, trp and org)
Silent Night (Mohr) (mix-ch a-cap) (1968)
Psalm 13 (mix-ch and opt org) (1955)
Psalm 83 (mix-ch a-cap) (1961)
Psalm 100 (mix-ch and ww qnt) (1971)
Psalm 147 (mix-ch and org or pf)
We three Kings of Orient are (mix-ch and fl) (1972)
Ref. composer, 625, 643

WENNERBERG-REUTER, Sara Margareta Eugenia Euphrosyne
Swedish organist and composer. b. Ottestad, February 11, 1875; d. March 3, 1959. She was the niece of composer and organist Gunnar Wennerberg. She studied harmony and the organ under Elfrida Andree (q.v.) and passed the examinations of organist and church singer of the Stockholm Conservatory in 1895. From 1896 to 1898 she studied at the Leipzig Conservatory under Reinecke, Jadassohn and Ewald. At the Berlin Academy she was a pupil of Max Bruch from 1901 to 1902. She was the organist of the Sofia Church, Stockholm from 1906 to 1945. She won the Litteris et Artibus award, 1931.
Compositions
ORCHESTRA
Festival march, military march
CHAMBER
Im Traum, Andante (vln and pf)
Violin sonata in E-Minor (1904)
Organ pieces
Violin pieces
PIANO
Pas de quatre
Other pieces
VOCAL
Skogsraet, cantata (G. Trollrunor) (solos, ch and orch) (1915)
Necken (solos, ch and orch)
Der Harfner und sein Sohn (vce and pf)
Tvanne sanger (Lundquist)
Wo steckst du denn Marie?
Twenty men's quartets
SACRED
Cantata for Inauguration of Sofia Church (solo, ch and org) (1905)
Fran Oestersalt, national hymn
Motet (mix-ch)
Hymns, incl.:
Easter hymn
Ref. 20, 297, 642

WENNERSTROM, Mary Hannah
American pianist, critic, professor and composer. b. Grand Rapids, MI, December 12, 1939. She studied at the Indiana University to obtain her B.Mus. (piano, 1961); M.Mus. (theory, 1963) and Ph.D. (theory, 1967). She lectured at the Indiana University School of Music from 1964, becoming chairlady of the theory department in 1979. She was visiting professor at the University of Oklahoma. She composes church music.
Publications
Anthology of Musical Structure and Style. 1983.
Anthology of 20th-century music. 1969.
Aspects of 20th-century music. Co-author. 1975.
Ref. 643

WENSLEY, Frances Foster
19th-century English pianist and composer. She was a pupil of Kalkbrenner.
Compositions
VOCAL
Set of four songs (1823)
SACRED
Variations on God save the Queen
Ref. 6, 226, 276, 433

WENTZ-JANACEK, Elisabet (nee Wentz)
Swedish organist, choir conductor, teacher and composer. b. Stockholm, August 20, 1923. She studied the organ and choral singing at Lund University, obtaining her organist's and precentor's certificate in 1948. She taught choral singing to children in the parish of Lund Cathedral and wrote articles for music journals. She married Bedrich Janacek, cathedral organist in 1951.
Compositions
ORGAN
Then som frisker aer och sund, partita, Scandinavian melody (Hakan Ohlssohns, 1973)
Oss kristna boer tro och besinna, partita, Scandinavian variation (Hakan Ohlssohns, 1973)
Arrangements of Scandinavian themes (1973-1974)
VOCAL
Songs, incl.:
Ja, jag vill sjunga (Verbum, 1973)
Satt en ring paa hans hand (Hakan Ohlssohns, 1972)
Tystnad, ljus (Proprius, 1973)
SACRED
Chorale melodies for congregational singing
Chorale 106
Easter music
Tvaa skaanska koraler: I himmelen; Den signade dag (Ohlssohns, 1973)
ARRANGEMENTS
Folk songs (chil-ch and recs)
Nu vilar hela jorden (Enninger) (m-ch)
Ref. STIM

WENTZEL, Elisabet von (nee Wartenberg)
German pianist, teacher and composer. b. Rastatt, Baden, December 23, 1889. She was a virtuoso pianist and taught in Berlin. She composed piano pieces and songs.
Ref. 70, 226

WERBER, Elise
Compositions
VOCAL
Drei Lieder: Das verlassene Maegdelein; Hingebung: Nordisches Lied (Ruckmich)
Vier Lieder, op. 2: Am Flusse; Das Blumelein; Im Herbste; Steh'balde still und ruehr dich nicht (Ruckmich)
Ref. 297

WERFEL, Alma Mahler. See MAHLER, Alma

WERFEL-LACHIN, Assia
20th-century Belgian composer.
Compositions
VOCAL
Cinq melodies: Scherzo; Un oiseau chante; Touraine; Rome; Je gravis lentement (S and pf) (Brussels: J. Maurer, 1971)
Ref. 188

WERNER, Hildegard
Swedish pianist, teacher and composer. b. 1834; d. 1911. She studied the piano under Drake at the Stockholm Conservatory in 1856. She settled in Newcastle-on-Tyne in 1871 and founded a music school and women's choir in 1885. Her compositions included men's vocal quartets.
Ref. 642

WERNER, Tara Louise
New Zealand lecturer and composer. She obtained her B.A. hons. and
B.Mus. (composition) from Victoria University. In 1976 she taught music at
Victoria University. In 1977 she won the Wellington City Council music
prize for composition. PHOTOGRAPH.
Compositions
ORCHESTRA
    Variations (1980)
CHAMBER
    Pieces
BALLET
    Ballet music
Ref. composer

WERTHEIM, Rosy
Dutch choir conductor, lecturer and composer. b. Amsterdam, February
19, 1888; d. Lare, May 27, 1949. She was a pupil of B. Zweers, S. Dresden,
and L. Aubert. She taught at the Music Lyceum in Amsterdam and directed
choirs. She lived in Paris from 1929 to 1935.
Compositions
ORCHESTRA
    Piano concerto (Henmar)
    Divertimento (Henmar)
    Overture (Henmar)
CHAMBER
    Violin sonata
    String quartet
    Pieces
VOCAL
    Choral works
    Songs
Ref. 26, 44, 81, 280, 622

WESLEY, Alice. See PITTMAN, Alice Locke

WESSELS, Judith Brent
20th-century South African composer.
Compositions
PIANO
    Five etudes
    Study in G-Major
    Waltz in G-Major
VOCAL
    Die gebreklike (S.J. Pretorius) (vce and pf)
    Diep rivier (Eugene Marais) (vce and pf)
    Ek sing van die wind (C. Louis Leipoldt)
    In daardie laaste nag van trae wonder, sonnet (Elisabeth Eybers)
    Ken jy die land waar die boerevolk woon? (C.F. Visser)
    Krulkop klonkie (C. Louis Leipoldt)
    O, koele water van die spruit (C.M. van den Heever)
    Skoppensboer (E. Marais) (vce and pf)
    Winternag (E. Marais) (vce and pf)
Ref. 295

WESSELS, Marlene
South African composer. b. Ventersburg, July 31, 1939. She received her
music diploma from the University of the Orange Free State, where she
studied under Adolph Hallis, Isador Epstein, Isabella Stengel, Laura
Searle and Peggy Haddon. She started her own publishing company *Eu-
mar* to encourage the advancement of Afrikaans music. PHOTOGRAPH.
Compositions
VOCAL
    Ek en jy (1968)
    Ek hou van jou (1976)
    Ek leef van jou (1975)
    Geelvink (Schutte) (1972) (Eumar)
    Kosmos (1976)
    Mymering (1935)
    Nag (1982)
    Net om (1981)
    Op die rante van die wolke (1980)
    Rooivlerkspreeu (1970)
    Sawens as die windjie waai (1969)
    Seemeeu (Erasmus) (1980)
    Sonneblom (1979)
    Splinternuut (1979)
    'n Sprokie (1973)
Ref. composer

WEST, Lottie
English pianist, contralto and song composer. b. South Hackney, Novem-
ber 5, 1865.
Ref. 85, 347

WESTBROOK, Helen Searles
American organist and composer. b. Southbridge, MA, October 15, 1889;
d. Chicago, ca. 1965. She received a B.M. from the American Conservatory where she studied under Frank Van Dusen, Wilhelm Middles-
chulte and Adolf Weidig. She was theatre organist in Chicago and organ
soloist with the Chicago Symphony Orchestra and music director at the
Central Church in Chicago. She wrote material for radio. She won a
young American Artists award and a gold medal from the American
Conservatory.
Compositions
ORGAN
    Andante religioso
    Chanson triste
    Concert piece in D
    Dust at friendship lake
    Intermezzo
    Laughing sprites
    Melodie
    Menuett in olden style
    On the Ontonagon River
    Pastorale scherzo
    Poem for autumn
    Retrospection
    Waltz circle
VOCAL
    Songs incl.:
    Alabaster
    Hindu cradle song
    If you call me
    Invincible
    Six Indian songs
SACRED
    March beside him, Lord, song
Ref. 39, 142

WESTENHOLZ, Eleonore Sophie Marie (nee Fritscher)
German harpsichordist, pianist, singer and composer. b. ca. 1780; d. early
19th-century. She married Carl August Friedrich Westenholz, composer
and Kapellmeister to the Duke of Mecklenburg-Schwerin. She was a sing-
er at the same court as her husband and was also a virtuoso harpsichord-
ist, mainly playing music in Bach's style.
Compositions
CHAMBER
    Rondo alla polacca (pf) (Berlin: Schlesinger)
VOCAL
    Arien (vce and orch)
Ref. 26, 128, 129, 465

WESTGATE, Elizabeth
20th-century American organist, pianist, teacher and composer. b.
Nantucket, MA. She composed piano pieces, secular songs and sacred
music.
Ref. 226

WESTON, Mildred
20th-century American teacher and composer. b. Gallitzen, PA. She composed piano pieces.
Ref. 347, 353

WESTROP, Kate
19th-century English organist, pianist and composer. She was the daugh-
ter of Henry John Westrop, a composer, violinist and organist and suc-
ceeded him as organist at St. Edmund, until 1887.
Compositions
ORGAN
    Four short voluntaries (Novello, 1885)
VOCAL
    Songs
Ref. 6, 226, 297, 347, 433

WESTRUP-MILNER, Maria
20th-century Danish composer.
Compositions
PIANO
Un compromis melodramatique ou Les trois bons amis
The flying fleet
VOCAL
Den danske Haers Kongehymne (vce and pf)
Henblick, tyrolsk serenade (vce and pf)
Ref. 331

WETTE, Adelheid
19th-century German librettist and composer. She was the sister of Humperdinck and wrote the libretto to his *Hansel and Gretel*.
Composition
OPERETTA
The Frog King, 2 act fairy play
Ref. 226, 291

WEYBRIGHT, June
American pianist, choral conductor, teacher and composer. b. Jeffersonville, IN, June 15, 1903. She attended the Perfield Pedagogical School, NY, the Leo Miller Institute of Music, St. Louis, Washington University, St. Louis, and the Juilliard School of Music. From 1925 to 1959 she taught in various schools, directed choirs and organized lecture-workshops. She was the recipient of numerous awards and a member of the Mu Phi Epsilon International Music Fraternity.
Compositions
CHAMBER
Cello and violin pieces
PIANO
Ensemble
To the moon and beyond (1953)
We cowboys (1955) (Belwin-Mills)
Wings over the world (1944) (Willis Music)
Other pieces
VOCAL
Oh no, John! (1942)
Polly, put the kettle on (1942)
TEACHING PIECES
Numerous pieces incl.:
Belwin piano methods (1964) (Belwin-Mills)
Christmas music books (1950) (Belwin-Mills)
Courses for pianists (1949) (Belwin-Mills)
Double play, duet book (1951) (Belwin-Mills)
Mildly contemporary books (1964) (Belwin-Mills)
My first Christmas book, Best of June Weybright, vol I, II and III Early American Folk Collection (Clayton Summy Music Co.) (1948)
Piano music in the home (1952) (Belwin-Mills)
Piano solo album books (1955) (Belwin-Mills)
Techniques for pianists (1947) (Belwin-Mills)
Theory workbooks (1949) (Belwin-Mills)
Bibliography
Who's Who of American Women. Chicago: Marquis.
Ref. 40, 347

WEYRAUCH, Anna Julie von (Anne de Weyrauch)
Early 19th-century German composer. In 1794 one Madame von Weyrauch was the first singer at the ducal court in Weimar. It is not known whether this was Anna Julie or Sophie Auguste (q.v.).
Compositions
PIANO
Nouvelles danses (4 and 3 hands) (with Sophie Auguste von Weyrauch)
Six danses
Three etudes (Klemm)
Ref. 128, 297

WEYRAUCH, Augusta Henriette von
19th-century German composer.
Compositions
CHAMBER
Ouverture in D, op. 3 (pf, 4 hands) (Hofmeister)
VOCAL
Der liebste (Simrock)
Nach Osten (Challier)
Zwoelf ausgewaehlte Lieder (Blosfeld)
Ref. 297

WEYRAUCH, Sophie Auguste von
Early 19th-century German singer and composer. In 1794 one Madame von Weyrauch was first singer at the ducal court at Weimar. It is not known whether this was Sophie Auguste or Anna Julie (q.v.).
Compositions
PIANO
Nouvelles danses (4 and 3 hands) (with Anna Julie von Weyrauch)
Differentes danses dont le derniere tirée de l'opera Der Freischutz (after 1821)
Six danses
Ref. 128

WHEAT, Margaret Anne
Composition
THEATRE
The Eumenides, play
Ref. 147

WHEELER, Edwina Florence. See WILLS, Edwina Florence

WHITE, Claude Porter
20th-century American composer.
ORCHESTRA
Pieces
CHAMBER
Harp pieces
Piano pieces
VOCAL
Choral works
Songs
BALLET
One ballet
OPERA
Grass Roots
Ref. 40, 347

WHITE, Elizabeth Estelle
English composer. b. South Shields, Durham, 1925.
Compositions
VOCAL
Songs incl.:
Harvey, book of songs (McCrimmon)
January brings the snow, song
You can't climb a river, book of songs
SACRED
He is the light of the world
It is the living spirit
A mass for our time
Mass for young people
Mass of the spirit
Walk with me, Oh my Lord
Ref. composer

WHITE, Elsie Fellows (Mrs. Bruce M.)
American violinist, authoress and composer. b. Skowhegan, ME, November 14, 1873; d. March 22, 1953. She studied the violin at the New England Conservatory under Adamowski and Campanari, harmony under Emery and theory under L.C. Elson. She later studied under Kneisel for seven years. She continued her studies in Vienna under Jacob Grun and Max Lewinger and gave several recitals there. She attended special courses at Colby College in 1897 and 1898 in harmony and counterpoint with Eugene Gruenberg. She made her debut in Boston with the Cecilia Society under B.J. Lang and in New York with Nordica at a Bagby Concert at the Waldorf-Astoria. She also toured the United States and Canada. She was first violinist with the New York Women's Symphony Orchestra.
Compositions
CHAMBER
The Angelus (vln and pf or org) (1912)
Bluebird (vln and pf) (1914)
Etude caprice (vln and pf) (1922)
Fairy tale (vln and pf)
Prelude in G (vln and pf or org) (1923)
VOCAL
Madrigal (S, Cont, 30 w-vces, pf and vln) (1927)
For remembrance (vce and vln obb) (1910)
In the silence

My love is come
Song of the dawn (C. Rossetti)
Song to maine
Spring song (vce and vln obb) (E.F. White) (1916)
Twilight

Publications

History of Music in Old Bloomfield. Chapter on music in Louise Colburn's *Skowhegan on the Kennebec.*

Contributions of articles to various magazines and newspapers including: *Chicago Music News, Music Quarterly, Musical Observer, New Music Review* and *Violin World.*

Ref. 142, 226, 292, 433

WHITE, Emma C.

19th-century American composer of piano pieces and songs.
Ref. 226, 276, 433

WHITE, Grace

American pianist, violinist, lecturer and composer. b. Sioux City, IA, November 12, 1896. She began to study the piano and composition at the age of five under her mother. In Sioux City she studied under Cecil Burleigh from 1911 to 1914. She went to New York the following year where she studied under Schradieck, Percy Goetschius and W.J. Henderson until 1916. She also studied under Burleigh, Leopold Auer, Ernest Bloch and Daniel Gregory Mason. She taught at Syracuse University, New York. At one time she was the only woman representative in the United States among composers of violin concertos.

Compositions

ORCHESTRA

Violin concerto in B-Flat
Violin concerto in E-Flat Minor, op. 18 (rev 1916)
Ref. 7

WHITE, Mary Louisa

English teacher and composer. b. Sheffield, September 2, 1866; d. London, January, 1935. She studied under John Farmer in London in 1885 and gave frequent concerts of her own works in London and Paris.

Compositions

PIANO

Short lyrics
Sketch book: Gavotte; Hunting song; March; Minuet; Pastorale; Waltz
Spinning Wheel (Williams)
Two waltzes (Williams)

VOCAL

Hush-a-bye
Jubilate (treble vce trio)
Night's rhapsody, 2-part song (Novello)
Prelude of spring
School song for girls (Novello)
Sleep, sweetly sleep
To the river (Williams)

OPERETTA

The Babes in the Wood, op. 42
Beauty and the Beast, op. 41
Ref. 22, 23, 70, 105, 226, 297, 433

WHITE, Maude Valerie

English composer. b. Dieppe, France, June 23, 1855; d. London, November 2, 1937. She studied harmony and composition under W.S. Rockstro and Oliver May in London before entering the Royal Academy of Music in 1876, where she became a composition pupil under Sir G.A. Macfarren. She was the first woman to win the Mendelssohn Scholarship in 1879 and continued her studies under Macfarren and F. Davenport. In 1881 she went to South America for health reasons and in 1883 completed her studies in Vienna before returning to London. DISCOGRAPHY.

Compositions

CHAMBER

Naissance d'amour (vlc and pf)
Violin and cello pieces

PIANO

Pieces, incl.:
Scherzetto (4 hands)
Allegretto giocoso (Lucas)
Barcarolle (Lucas)
Four sketches
Pictures from abroad, 14 pieces (Ashdown)

VOCAL

Ich habe gelebt und geliebet (Schiller) (S and orch)
My soul is an enchanted boat (Shelley)
Settings of poems by Heine incl.: Du bist wie eine Blume; Im wunderschoenen Monat Mai; Wenn ich in deine Augen seh (vocal qnt)
Four albums of German songs; Es muss doch Fruehling werden; Isdotta Blanzesman
Settings of poems by Herrick incl.: To blossoms; To daffodils; To electra; To music to becalm his fever
Settings of poems by Victor Hugo incl.: Chantez, chantez, jeune inspirée; Heureux qui peut aimer
Other songs incl.:
Absent yet present
Among the roses
The bonny curl
Canzone di Taormina
Crabbed age and youth
The devout lover
A faithful heart (Boosey)
A farewell song (Ricordi)
Four volumes of German songs (Lucas, Leonard)
How do I love thee
In memoriam
It is na Jean
John Anderson, my Jo
King Charles
Ophelia's song
Prière
Risposta
Romanza
The spring has come
So we'll go no more a'roving
A Song of the Sahara (Ricordi)
The throstle
Three little songs
To Althea from prison
To Mary

SACRED

Agnus Dei (orch)
Ave Maria
Lead kindly light
Mass

BALLET

The captured butterfly

OPERA

Figlia della Dora (Lima, 1868)
Jocelyn
Smaranda

Publications

Friends and Memories. Autobiography. London: Edward Arnold, 1914.
My Indian Summer. London: Grayson & Grayson, 1932.
Ref. 2, 8, 15, 70, 100, 102, 105, 177, 297, 335, 361, 431, 433, 488, 572, 609, 622, 637, 653

WHITE, Mrs. Bruce M. See WHITE, Elsie Fellows

WHITE, Mrs. Meadows. See SMITH, Alice Mary

WHITE, Ruth Eden

American church organist and composer. b. Florence, SC, December 25, 1928. She studied at Coker College and was organist at Calvary Baptist Church, Florence after 1963. She composed sacred choral pieces.
Ref. 142, 347

WHITE, Ruth S.

American pianist, lecturer and composer. b. Pittsburgh, PA, September 1, 1925. She studied at the Carnegie-Mellon University under Nikolai Lopatnikoff, receiving a B.F.A. (piano and composition, 1948) and M.F.A. (composition, 1949). She also studied privately under George Antheil in Los Angeles from 1951 to 1953. She won the first prize for composition from the National Society of Arts and Letters and became a fellow of the Huntington Hartford Foundation in 1964. From 1951 to 1959 she was supervisor of the University of California Demonstration School, Los Angeles and in 1955 became president of Rhythms Production Records. In 1959 she was made vice-president of the Cheviot Corporation. DISCOGRAPHY.

Compositions

DANCE SCORES

Motifs for dance compositions
Motivations for modern dance
Music for contemporary dance

ELECTRONIC
Flowers of evil (tape) (1969)
Pinions (tape) (1968)
Seven trumps from the Tarot cards (tape) (1968)
Short Circuits (tape) (1970)
Variations on Couperin's Rondeau
THEATRE
Capture the Sun (1971)
Mr. Windbag Multi-Media Series, six programs (1972)
Ref. 84, 142, 228, 347, 563, 622, 625

WHITECOTTON, Shirley Ellen

American choral conductor, singer, teacher and composer. b. Aurora, IL, September 23, 1935. She studied under Jack Goode at Wheaton College, IL, and graduated with a B.Mus. (voice). She also studied at the Aspen Music School, CO, and Northwestern University. She taught singing privately from 1960 to 1973 and then at a high school. She directed a children's choir at a Presbyterian church.
Compositions
VOCAL
Light (ch) (Broadman Press, 1973)
Aftermath (Shawnee Press, 1981)
Don't wake the baby (Broadman, 1982)
Flow not so fast, ye fountains (Shawnee, 1981)
Four pastoral songs (Somerset Press, 1975)
Gratitude (Hope Pub. Co., 1980)
Like the thrush in winter (Roger Dean Co., 1980)
Little things (Broadman, 1987)
Michael (Somerset, 1973)
The omen (Neil A. Kjos, 1983)
A star (Heritage, 1975)
Three Scottish songs, Bks. I and II (Heritage, 1974)
To a caged bird
To live beautifully (Somerset, 1976)
Two idylls (Galaxy, 1974)
Unheard (Shawnee, 1982)
Wildflowers, cycle (Kjos, 1987)
SACRED
Christmas comes in the morning, cantata (1973)
We have a King, cantata (Choristers Guild, 1971)
Awake my soul (Hope, 1970)
Because He loves us all (Ward, 1973)
The Bethlehem innkeepers speak (Curtis Music, 1982)
The Call
Carol for all seasons (Ward, 1976)
Children of the Heavenly King (Ward, 1974)
A Christmas carol (1973)
A Christmas sonnet (Belwin-Mills, 1982)
Fanfare and alleluia for Easter (Hope, 1975)
The fourth shepherd (1974)
God of all power (Richmond Press, 1984)
God is watching (Hope, 1972)
Hymn to spring (1984)
Joyful music (Heritage, 1980)
The lamb (Broadman, 1975)
Let faith be my shield (Broadman, 1982)
Missa brevis (1974)
Noel dance (Shawnee, 1973)
None other lamb (Ward, 1973)
Two old spanish carols (Galaxy, 1981)
Welcome carol for the King (Shawnee, 1974)
Words of life (Hope, 1974)
Ref. composer, 142, 347, 625

WHITEHEAD, Alison

20th-century Australian composer.
Composition
INCIDENTAL MUSIC
The Good Doctor (Neil Simon)
Ref. 442

WHITEHEAD, Gillian

New Zealand lecturer and composer. b. Whangarei, April 23, 1941. She studied at the universities of Auckland and Victoria and received her B.Mus. in 1963. She obtained her M.Mus. from Sydney University in 1965, after studying under Peter Scutthorpe. The next year she attended a course given by Peter Maxwell Davies at Adelaide University and in 1967 became his student in London. From 1969 to 1970 she worked in Portugal and Italy on a New Zealand Arts Council grant. She taught composition at Auckland University in 1975 and became composer-in-residence at Northern Arts, England. In 1971 she won the New Zealand Broadcasting Corporation String Quartet prize. DISCOGRAPHY.

Compositions
ORCHESTRA
Punctus solis (1971)
Te tangi a apakura (str orch) (1975)
CHAMBER
Te-akua-te-atarangi (str qrt) (1970)
Piano trio (1972)
Trio (hpcd, vln and vlc) (1974)
Moonstone (vla and pf)
Aria (vlc) (1969)
Ricercare (vla) (1976)
PIANO
La cadenza sia corta (1974)
Fantasia on three notes: Wai-te-ata (1966)
Voices of Tane, 7 pieces for children (1975)
VOCAL
Babel, part I (solos, 3 eight-part choirs and orch) (1969-1970)
Riddles (w-ch and hp) (1973)
Pakurn (S, fl, cl, vla, vlc, hpcd and perc) (1967)
Riddles, 2nd version (m-S, fl, mar, gtr and hpcd) (1975)
Six songs of Umberto Saba (S and cl) (1968)
Three songs of Janet Frame (S, fl, ob, cl or b-cl, hn, trp, gtr and d-b) (1972)
Whaka-tau-ki (m-vce, fl, ob, cl, hn, trp, trb, vln, vln or vla, vlc, d-b and perc) (1970)
SACRED
Laude spirituale, 5 songs of Hildegard von Bingen (ch) (1976)
Missa brevis (mix-ch) (1963)
Qui natus est (mix-ch) (1966)
Christmas music (1972)
OPERA
Tristan and Iseult, chamber opera (singers, narrs, puppets and mime) (1975)
MULTIMEDIA
Marduk (m-S, mime dancers and inst ens) (1973)
MISCELLANEOUS
Tamatea tutahi
Bibliography
Tristan and Iseult. Bryony Phillips. CANZ Newsletter, 37-38. October, 1978.
Ref. New Zealand Composers' Assoc.

WHITELY, Bessie Marshall

American pianist, teacher and composer. b. St. Louis, 1871. She studied at the Oakland Conservatory of Music and under H.G. Pasmore, J.P. Morgan and Louis Lesser. She taught music in Kansas City until 1921.
Compositions
ORCHESTRA
Five symphonic sketches
VOCAL
Muramadzu (T and orch)
The four winds (m-qrt)
The garden of Buddha (w-vce and m-qrt)
The landing of the pilgrims
The shadders (vce and pf) (G. Schirmer) (prize)
Three madrigals: The nights s'spring; O lady leave thy silken thread: A spring ditty (mix-ch a-cap)
OPERA
Hiawatha's Childhood (composer)
Pandora
Sarita
Ref. 141, 190, 347, 460, 465

WHITLOCK, E. Florence (nee Williams)

New Zealand cellist, pianist, violinist, violist, conductor, teacher and composer. b. Redruth, Cornwall, November 10, 1889. She studied the violin for eight years under H.V. Pearce. From the age of 13 she played in the Camborne and Redruth Oratorio orchestra. In 1910 she became a pupil of Hans Wessely. From 1911 to 1912 she taught in Bury St. Edmunds and later in Taunton and Ashford, where she also led the local orchestra. From 1919 to 1923 she attended the teachers' training course run by the Music Teachers' Association. Her teachers were Frederick Moore (piano), Stewart MacPherson (musical appreciation) and again Hans Wessely. In 1925 she sailed for New Zealand and taught the violin, the cello and chamber music in Havelock Bay. She became conductor of the Hastings Orchestral Society. After her marriage in 1926 she continued conducting and performing in Hastings and Napier as well as teaching privately. Returning to England in 1952, she taught the violin and the viola and performed chamber music. At the same time she studied composition under Alan Bush. She returned to New Zealand and resumed teaching. PHOTOGRAPH.

Compositions
ORCHESTRA
Violin concerto No. 1 in B, op. 9 (vln and cham orch) (1963)
Violin concerto No. 2 in F, op. 14 (vln and cham orch) (1964)
CHAMBER
Concerto for seven solo instruments, op. 15 (2 vln, vla, vlc, d-b, cl and hn) (1965)
A sad story, op. 11 (str ens) (1971)
Quintet, op. 12 (fl and str qrt) (1964)
String quintet, op. 17 (2 vln, vla and 2 vlc) (1968)
String quartet No. 1 in A, op. 7 (1969)
String quartet No. 2 in B-Minor, op. 7 (1961)
String quartet No. 3 in F, op. 7 (1962)
Two trios, op. 19 (2 vln and pf) (1972)
Evening, op. 11 (vln and pf) (1961)
In the style of a scherzo, op. 11 (vln and pf) (1963)
Spring song, op. 1 (vln and pf) (1960)
Gavotte in D-Minor (vln) (1968)
A variation on a theme of Corelli (vln) (1968)
PIANO
The fairy garden, on the chromatic scale of D, op. 4 (1958)
Theme and variations on a folk tune, op. 2 (1955)
VOCAL
Chorus with string chamber orchestra (ded Redruth Choral Society) (org ad lib) (1970)
Ode to St. Cecilia, op. 5, dramatic song (John Dryden) (1958)
Spring prayer, op. 16 (Emerson) (2 S or S and m-S and pf) (1968)
Ref. composer

WHITNER, Mary Elizabeth
20th-century American composer.
Composition
VOCAL
Weep you no more, sad fountains (mix-ch) (Carl Fischer)
Ref. 190

WHITTAKER, Vivian
Australian composer. b. 1930.
Compositions
THEATRE
The Mermaid's Tail, pantomime (ch and pf) (1965)
Platypus in Boots, pantomime (ch and pf) (1964)
St. George and the Burley Griffin, children's fantasy (mix-ch and pf) (1963)
Trebizond, musical (ch and pf) (1966)
Ref. 442

WHITTINGTON, Joan
South African artist, poetess, writer and composer. b. Standerton, Transvaal, February 28, 1933. After graduating from the University of Potchefstroom with a B.A. she studied music for three years at the University of South Africa under Professors Woehler and Rhoode and Tessa Uys.
Compositions
CHAMBER
Siklus nagmusiek (vlc and pf)
Overture (pf)
Nagmusiek vir tjello en klavier
VOCAL
Hoe speel die lente (mix-ch and pf)
Die lewe is tog so lekker (2 part ch)
In die veld (A.J. Pretorius) (w-ch)
Gooi weg, jul griffels en leie (boy's-ch)
Die wals en die draai ons wakis (mix-ch and pf)
Songs (vce and pf) incl.:
Die velde roep
Hier waar ons
Jy is die lied (Alma Strydom) (1978)
Jy moet vir my 'n liedjie sing
'n Meisie in 'n woonhuisie
Nooientjie fyn
Ons is honger, Ma!
Soos kinderstemme
Temalied: Die wildernis is ongerep en skoon
Windswaal (C.L. Leipoldt) (1978)
Wys my die plek (Leipoldt) (1978)
School anthems and songs
SACRED
Die Here is my lig (mix-ch and pf)
Psalm 121 (mix-ch and pf) (1978)
Corinthians I (Bar) (1984)

'n Kersgebedjie
Maria I
Maria II
OPERETTA
By die water van Likwa
Pionierslied
ARRANGEMENTS
Jy daar Voëltjie, Grieg's notturno op. 54 no. 4
Ref. composer, 295

WHITTLE, Chris Mary-Francine
Belgian harpsichordist, concert pianist, teacher and composer. b. Antwerp, May 23, 1927. She was educated in France and at the Royal Conservatory in Antwerp where she studied the piano, harmony, chamber music, music history and won several prizes, including the Albert de Vleeschower prize for composition. At the Ecole Normale de Musique de Paris she attended Alfred Cortot's interpretation course and then began a career of almost 20 years of concert touring, playing the piano in France, Switzerland, Germany, Belgium, Poland and Great Britain. At the same time she taught and composed. She then took an interest in the harpsichord and studied in Amsterdam under Gustav Leonhardt. She taught at the Wynegem Music School and gave harpsichord concerts and recitals. She married Luc Jageneau, a harpsichord builder.
Compositions
ORCHESTRA
Variation on an old Scottish song (1952)
Concerto (pf) (1948)
CHAMBER
Quintet (fl, ob, cl, bsn and hn) (1951) (Albert de Vleeschower prize)
Trio, op. 11 (vln, vlc and pf) (1949)
Trio en forme de suite, op. 24 (tr, hn and bsn) (1955)
Capriccio, op. 7 (vln and pf) (1947)
Sonata (vln and pf) (1951)
Toccata per il cembalo (hpcd) (Schott-Freres, 1969)
Variations for carillon, op. 1 (1951)
PIANO
Two small pieces, op. 25 (4 hands) (1960)
Ballade, op. 15 (1949)
Berceuse, op. 4 (1947)
Diurne, op. 22 (1965)
Impromptu, op. 27 (Schott-Freres, 1966)
Ondine, op. 12 (1952)
Scottish dances, op. 16 (Schott-Freres, 1951)
Sonata, op. 4 (1947)
Sonata, op. 9 (1948)
Sonatine, op. 30 (Schott-Freres, 1967)
Twenty-four preludes, op. 14 (Schott-Freres, 1952)
Two nocturnes, op. 6 (1967-1968)
Two suites, op. 1 (1943)
VOCAL
Odelette, op. 20 (m-S, pf and orch) (1951)
Kerstliederens, op. 28 (ch)
Six lieder, op. 23 (1966)
SACRED
Regina coeli, op. 17 (ch) (1950)
Christmas songs, op. 28 (ch) (1966)
Missa brevis, op. 2 (1944)
Publications
Work on Anna Magdalena Bach. Editions Matropolis Antwerp.
Ref. composer

WICHERN, Caroline (Karoline)
German choral conductor, singer, teacher and composer. b. Horn, near Hamburg, September 13, 1836; d. Horn, March 19, 1906. She studied under Graedener, Hoffner and Weitzmann and for 20 years conducted a men's and boys' choir in Hamburg. From 1881 to 1896 she lived in Manchester and taught singing and then returned to Hamburg. In 1900 she conducted an orchestral concert in which only her compositions were performed.
Compositions
CHAMBER
Welsh harp songs (vln and pf; also vlc and pf; also pf) (Vieweg & Breitkopf)
PIANO
Moment musical, caprice
Poesies musicales, op. 40 (Cranz)
VOCAL
Six songs, op. 42 (m-ch and pf) (Cranz)
Totenfeier: Es sind die Leiden dieser Zeit (mix-ch; also vce and org) (Heinrichshofen)
Part-songs (w-qrt)
Twenty-five children's songs, op. 43 (1 or 2 vces) (Cranz)
Six songs, op. 41, incl. Die Heide Blume von Tiefensee; Du liebe Taube; Die Tuerteltaube; Am Abend (Cranz)

754

SACRED
    Le campane del Natale (1880)
    Collection of ancient and modern Christmas songs (1879)
Ref. 105, 226, 276, 297, 344

WICHERN, Karoline. See WICHERN, Caroline

WICHMANN, Fredrika. See WICKMAN, Fredrika

WICKER, Irene
    20th-century American composer.
    Compositions
    OPERA
        Abraham Lincoln the Boy (New York: ABC Music, 1941)
        George Washington the Boy (ABC Music, 1941)
        Hail New World or Tobacco Bride
        Look and Long
    Ref. 141

WICKERHAUSER, Nathalie
    19th-century German composer.
    Compositions
    PIANO
        Danse des fées, op. 3 (Cranz)
        Deux impromptus, op. 1 (Cranz)
        Erinnerung an Huetteldorf, Impromptus, op. 10 (Bosworth)
        Invocation, melodie (Bosworth)
        La perte, Le rêve, morceau caracteristique (Cranz)
        Scherzo, op. 2 (Cranz)
        Sechs Lieder ohne Worte, op. 6 (Kahnt)
        Toujours, jamais, morceau caracteristique, op. 8 (Bosworth)
        Traumbilder op. 11, 4 pieces
    VOCAL
        Six romances (Bosworth)
        Two songs, op. 7 (A and pf) (Bosworth)
    Ref. 226, 276, 297

WICKHAM, Florence Pauline
    American singer and composer. b. Beaver, PA, 1880; d. New York, October 20, 1962. She studied singing under Alice Groff in Philadelphia and Mme. Mallinger and Franz Emerich in Berlin. She made her debut in Wiesbaden and sang in Germany and London, before returning to the United States. She sang at the New York Metropolitan Opera, 1909 to 1912.
    Compositions
    VOCAL
        Choral pieces
        Songs
    OPERETTA
        Ancestor Maker
        Legend of Hex Mountain (1950)
        Rosalynd (based on As You Like It)
    Ref. 40, 74, 141, 142, 226, 347

WICKINS, Florence
    19th-century English composer.
    Compositions
    CHAMBER
        Better land (2 vln, fl, vla, vlc and cor ad lib; also vln and pf; also pf)
        Narcissus, danse (2 vln, fl, vla and vlc ad lib; also vln and pf; also pf)
        Minuetto (2 vln, fl and cor ad lib; also vln and pf)
        Recollections of Bonnie Scotland, Ould Ireland and Merrie England (2 vln, fl, vla, vlc and cor ad lib; also vln and pf; also pf)
        Reverie and two danses (2 vln, vla, vlc, fl, cor or cl; also pf)
        Arrangements of excerpts from Gounod's Faust (cham ens)
    PIANO
        Easy duets: Gavotte in F; March in E-Flat; Mazurka in C
        Autumn pieces
        Bolero
        Bourree Pompadour
        Golden harvest
        Impromptu
        Menuetto
        Old folks at home
        Numerous fantasias on operatic themes
        Pieces for children
        Teaching pieces

VOCAL
    Alas! 'twas but a dream, in D or F
    At love's sweet will
    Hush! 'tis the twilight (solo or duet)
    Pourquoi
    Song of harvest
    Tell me
    Three duets, old Scottish melodies
    Other songs
SACRED
    Pilgrim's progress (solos, ch and pf or org)
    O shepherd divine
    Of heaven's joys (Bar)
    Shadow of the Cross (vce and vlc obb)
Ref. 297

WICKMAN (Wichmann), Fredrika
    Swedish operatic singer and composer. b. 1852. She made her debut at the Royal Theatre in 1869, where she remained for a year, before changing to concert singing.
    Compositions
    PIANO
        Grande Valse: Di gioia insolita, op. 9 (Richordi)
        Trois morceaux de salon: Reverie, Impromptu, Berceuse, op. 12 (Hansen)
    VOCAL
        Fiskaren
        Floden
        Flyttfoglarne
        Kaerlekssaang
        Laangt fjaerran
        Mjoelnarflickan
        Over de hoeje fjelle!
        Rosen i oeknen
        Vaaren
        Vackra sky, som ensam taagar
        Wandrarens visa
        Other songs and romances
    SACRED
        Ave Maria (S, vln and pf) (Schott)
    Ref. 67, 297, 642

WICKS, Camilla
    American violinist, professor and composer of Norwegian origin. b. Long Beach, CA, 1928. She studied the violin under the guidance of her father, the violinist Ingwald Wicks. She then became a pupil of Persinger Temianka and made her debut in New York in 1942. She toured in the United States and Europe and in 1971 became professor of violin at the Music Academy, Oslo.
    Compositions
    CHAMBER
        Har du sett noko till kjerringa mi (vln and pf)
        Jeg lagde meg sa silde (vln and pf)
        Jeg rodde meg ut (vln and pf)
    Ref. 20, 63, 74, 130

WIECK, Clara Josephine. See SCHUMANN, Clara Wieck

WIECK, Marie
    German pianist, teacher and composer. b. Leipzig, January 17, 1832. She was the half-sister of Clara Schumann (q.v.) and like her sister, studied under their father Friedrich Wieck. She appeared in concerts in Germany, Sweden and England and had a good reputation in Dresden as a teacher. She was appointed court pianist to the Prince of Hohenzollern in 1858. She edited some of her father's compositions.
    Compositions
    PIANO
        Fantasie ueber skandinavische Volkslieder (also vlc and pf, vla and pf) (Wernthal)
        Scherzo
        Traugesang (also org) (Forberg)
        Studies and polonaises (published under her father's name)
        Three etudes for the left hand (Hoffarth)
    VOCAL
        Abendlieder, Nun ist der Tag geschieden (Hoffarth)
        Fruehlingsabend (Hoffarth)

SACRED
Ave Maria (4 vces) (Oppenheimer)
Christkindlein (Hoffmann)
Publications
Aus dem Kreise Wieck-Schumann. 1912.
Ref. 8, 85, 276, 297, 347, 653

WIEGAND, Elizabeth Grieger
Composition
SACRED
God the Blessed Trinity
Ref. *ASCAP in Action* Fall 1983

WIEL, Elise
19th-century Danish composer.
Compositions
PIANO
Foer vi kan noderne, ganske lette stykker (4 hands)
Fem smaastykker, op. 2: Mazurka, vals, romance, vaarstemning, menuet (Warmuth)
Fem smaastykker, op. 3: Praeludium, alumblad, capriccietto, arietta, vuggevise (Warmuth)
Til alle smaa elever, op. 4, 5 lette stykker (Warmuth)
VOCAL
Sex smaa sange, op. 1: I skoven; I en tung stund; Ungbirken; Det maate ingen vide; I maandeski; Her klokkerne ringe til ave (Warmuth)
Ref. 297

WIELE, Aimee van der
Belgian harpsichordist, pianist and composer. b. Brussels, March 8, 1907. She studied at the Brussels Conservatory. She won the Laure van Cutsem prize for the piano, which she studied under E. Bosquet. She also won first prizes for harmony, counterpoint, composition and music history. In Paris she studied the harpsichord under Wanda Landowska (q.v.) and musicology under A. Pirro. She gave harpsichord recitals in various cities in Belgium, Italy, France and England and played with various orchestras.
Compositions
ORCHESTRA
Poem
CHAMBER
Inventions (hpcd)
Other pieces
Piano pieces
VOCAL
Transcriptions of cantatas and sonatas
Ref. 8, 26, 44, 80, 94

WIENECKE, Henriette Stadfeldt
19th-century Danish composer.
Composition
SACRED
Psalmer, og aandelige sange af Kingo, Brorson, Grundtvig, Ingemann (4 vces; also vce and and pf) (Copenhagen: T. Michaelsen & Tillge, 1861)
Ref. 331

WIENECKE, Sigrid Henriette
Early 20th-century Danish composer.
Compositions
VOCAL
Songs (P.E. Benzon, H.C. Andersen, Klopstock, Nyegaard and others) incl.:
Aftensang (vce and pf)
Dannebrogslied (vce and pf)
De tvende draaker (vce and pf)
Hvidtfeld (vce and pf)
Koenig Christian (vce and pf)
Min lille fugl (vce and pf)
Se jeg vil sende min engel (vce and pf)
Vinterfuglen (vce and pf)
SACRED
Gud tilgive dig (vce and pf)
Maria Magdalene (H.H. Nyegaard)
To psalmer (4 vces; also vce and pf)
Tre psalmer: Jo stoerre Kors, des bedre Boenner; Ak, som en Droem er manges liv; Klokken slaaer

THEATRE
Fadervor, melodrama (Klopstock)
Ref. 331

WIENER, Elisabeth
Compositions
FILM MUSIC
The singing goodbye (1975)
The wise guys (1977)
Ref. 497

WIENER, Eva Hannah
American composer. b. New York, March 2, 1956. She attended Barnard College at Columbia University where she obtained her B.A. cum laude. From 1977 to 1980 she studied at the Juilliard School and in 1982 she obtained her M.A. from Brooklyn College. She studied under Charles Dodge.
Compositions
CHAMBER
Orbits (cl, sax, hn, trp and trb) (1981)
String quartet (1980)
Aurora (orch bells and perc) (1980)
Fantasy (vln) (1978)
PIANO
Prism (2 pf) (1980)
Dream (1982)
Etude (1978)
VOCAL
Moesta et Errabunda (T and pf) (1976)
Ref. composer

WIENIAWSKA, Irene Regine (Lady Dean Paul) (pseud. Poldowski)
English pianist and composer. b. Brussels, May 16, 1880; d. London, January 28, 1932. She was the daughter of the Polish violinist and composer Henryk Wieniawski. She entered the Brussels Conservatory at the age of 12 or 13 and studied under F.A. Gevaert (composition) and Stork (piano). She won first prizes for solfege and preparation. She went to London where she studied under Percy Pitt and Michael Hambourg and then to Paris to study under Gedalge. She married Sir Aubrey Dean Paul. After the death of her first child, she returned to London for a while before entering the Schola Cantorum, to study under Vincent d'Indy. DISCOGRAPHY.
Compositions
ORCHESTRA
Pat Malone's wake (pf and orch)
Nocturnes, symphonic sketch
Tenements, symphonic sketch
CHAMBER
Suite miniature de chansons à danser (wws, 2 fl, ob, ob d'amore, cor anglais, cl, hn and b-cl)
Berceuse de l'enfant mourant (vln and pf)
Sonata in D-Minor (vln and pf) (Cobbett)
Tango (vln and pf)
PIANO
Caledonian market, suite of 8 pieces
Dansons la gigue
The Hall of Machinery (Wembley)
L'heure exquise
Sonatina
Study
VOCAL
Denholm dream (Chappell)
Impression fausse (Verlaine) (m-S and pf)
Thirty songs (Verlaine, Anatole Le Braz, Jean Dominique, Jean Moreas, Albert Samain, Blake and Adolphe Ratte)
OPERETTA
Laughter
Bibliography
Miniature Essay. Biography. Anon. London: J.W. Chester, 1924.
Ref. 2, 8, 15, 22, 41, 63, 85, 163, 204, 226, 282, 297, 347, 361, 563, 653

WIERUSZOWSKI, Lili
German organist, choral conductor and composer. b. Cologne, December 10, 1899. She studied at the Cologne Conservatory and the Hochschule fuer Musik, Berlin.

Compositions
ORGAN
Cantus-Firmus-Praeludien, vol. II
Chorale preludes, vols I, II, III
Dreiundvierzig Choralvorspiele (1956)
Forty-two Choralintonationen zum deutsch-schweizerichen (1952)
Hugenottenpsalmen, chorale prelude
Orgelchoraele Schweizerischer Komponisten
Fuenfundzwanzig choralvorspiele (1948)
Verkuendigung 1 and 2, chorale prelude
Weichnachtschoralvorspiele
SACRED
Chorale prelude for wind instruments
Danket dem Herrn und ehret
Singt mit froher Stimm, Voelker, jauchzet ihm
Wir stehen vor dir, O Vater
Ref. 3, 85, 266, 347, 477

WIESENEDER, Caroline. See WISENEDER, Caroline

WIGGIN, Kate Douglas. See WIGGINS, Kate Douglas

WIGGIN, Mrs Daniel W. See TURGEON, Frances

WIGGINS (Wiggin), Kate Douglas (Mrs. George C. Riggs)
American pianist and composer. b. Philadelphia, September 28, 1856; d. August 24, 1923.
Compositions
VOCAL
Nine love songs and a carol (1924)
Collections for children incl. Kindergarten chimes
Ref. 226, 374

WIGGINS, Mary
American organist, pianist, teacher and composer. b. Indiana, PA, February 10, 1904; d. Pittsburgh, April 17, 1974. She studied composition privately under Gladys W. Fisher and Harvey B. Gaul. At Carnegie-Mellon University she was a pupil of Roland Leich. She taught the organ at Schenley High School from 1951 to 1957 and the piano privately and at the Pittsburgh Musical Institute from 1959 to 1962. She received an award from the National Federation of Music Clubs in 1973. She composed chamber pieces for the violin, the bassoon, the organ and the piano as well as teaching pieces. Her vocal pieces included choral and solo works.
Ref. Ruth E. Wiggins, 40, 142, 347

WIGHAM, Margaret
20th-century American composer. b. Minnesota.
Compositions
ORCHESTRA
Concerto (2 pf and orch)
CHAMBER
Piano pieces
Ref. 40, 142, 347

WIKSTROM, Inger
20th-century Swedish pianist and composer. DISCOGRAPHY.
Compositions
VOCAL
Songs incl.:
An die Musik, op. 12, no. 2 (vce and pf)
Du bist die Zukunft, grosses Morgenrot, op. 12, no. 3 (vce and pf)
Liebeslied, op. 12, no. 1 (vce and pf)
Orfeus Eurydike Hermes, op. 11 (vce and pf)
Sechs Lieder, op. 10 (vce and pf)

WILBER, Clare Marie O'Keefe
American lecturer and composer. b. Denver, March 21, 1928. In 1950 she graduated from Fordham University and in 1972 received her M.M. from Colorado State University. She taught at Webster College from 1951 to 1952 and at Colorado State University from 1972. She managed the Fort Collins Symphony Orchestra for a period of years and was the recipient of awards and grants.
Composition
CHAMBER
Fantasie romantique (pf) (1972)
Ref. 506

WILBRAHAM, Mrs.
18th-century English composer.
Composition
SACRED
A favourite anthem (Westminster: Rock, 1795)
Ref. 65

WILBRANDT, Susan
20th-century American composer.
Composition
CHAMBER
Creatures (2nd prize, Pittsburgh Flute Club's contest, 1981)
Ref. ILWC

WILCOCK, Anthea
20th-century composer. DISCOGRAPHY.
Composition
SACRED
Christus natus est
Ref. 563

WILDSCHUT, Clara
Dutch pianist, violinist and composer. b. Deventer, June 11, 1906; d. Amsterdam, August 27, 1950. At the Conservatory of 's-Gravenhage she studied composition under Dr. Johan Wagenaar, the piano under E. van Beinum and the violin under Andre Spoor, F. Broer van Dijk and Vegt. In 1930 she won a state scholarship for composition. She went to Vienna and became a pupil of Joseph Marx. She returned to Amsterdam in 1937.
Compositions
ORCHESTRA
Fuga en romance, fantasy (str orch)
Entrata capricciosa, small overture
CHAMBER
Serenade (fl, ob, cl, bsn and hn)
String quartet
Sonata (vln and pf)
Sonatina (vln and pf)
Two sonatines (ob and pf; one arr for ob and orch as concertino)
PIANO
Theme with twelve variations and fugue
Small pieces
VOCAL
Pieces (ch a-cap)
Over 70 songs (vce and pf)
Ref. 26, 44, 94, 110

WILENS, Greta
20th-century English composer of German origin. b. Bielefeld, Germany. She studied at the London School of Economics.
Compositions
CHAMBER
Blue brocade gavotte (pf and strs) (Keith Prowse Music)
PIANO
Bless you
Isola bella (Bosworth & Co.)
Waiting for the night
Ref. composer

WILES, Margaret Jones
American violinist, violist, conductor, lecturer and composer. b. Hamilton, OH, December 25, 1911. She received her B.Mus. from De Paul University and studied at the Royal Academy of Music in London under Arthur Catteral, 1933 to 1934. At New York College she was a pupil of Raphael Bronstein. She was a member of the Durban Symphony Orchestra, 1941 to 1945 and for 15 years a soloist in concert and on the South African radio. From 1945 to 1951 she was concertmistress of the Pietermaritzburg Symphony

Orchestra. On her return to the United States in 1957 she became assistant concertmistress of the Eastern Connecticut Symphony Orchestra. She taught the violin and viola at Connecticut College and conducted the college orchestra. She composed 50 string quartets.
Ref. 77, 206

WILEY, Dora
American singer and composer. b. Bangor, NY, 1853; d. Bangor, November 2, 1924. She sang in churches, concerts and at the Boston opera.
Composition
VOCAL
The ferryman, waltz song (1890)
Ref. 374

WILHELM, Grete
20th-century German composer.
Compositions
PIANO
Memento
Zweistimmiges Thema mit 7 Variationen
VOCAL
Besinnliches Singen (1959)
Sechs Choere nach Texten von H. Hesse (1960)
Ref. Frau und Musik

WILHELMINA, Caroline of Anspach (Caroline, Queen of England)
B. 1683; d. November 20, 1737. She was the wife of George II. Her composition is still played today before church parades in some army units.
Composition
SACRED
Church call
Ref. 177

WILHELMINA, Sophie Friederike, Princess of Prussia, Margravine of Bayreuth
B. Berlin, July 3, 1709; d. Bayreuth, October 14, 1758. She was the daughter of Frederick William I and the sister of Frederick the Great. She showed an early inclination towards literature and the arts. In 1731 she married Prince Frederick of Bayreuth and moved to Bayreuth. Under her influence the Bayreuth opera played almost exclusively the Italian operas by Graun, Hasse, Bernasconi and other composers. Many of her compositions were lost. DISCOGRAPHY.
Compositions
ORCHESTRA
Concerto for harpsichord, flute and string orchestra in G-Minor
OPERA
Argenore
Six arias for L'Huomo
Ref. 177, 200, 347

WILHELMJ, Maria
19th-century Dutch composer.
Composition
CHAMBER
Andante (vln and pf) (Heinrichshofen)
Ref. 297

WILKINS, Elizabeth
British composer of sacred songs. b. ca. 1750.
Ref. 465

WILKINS, Margaret Lucy
English harpist, conductor, lecturer and composer. b. Surrey, November 13, 1939. When she was 12 she won a junior exhibition to study at Trinity College of Music, London. Later she studied at the University of Nottingham and obtained a B.Mus. and became an L.R.A.M. She performed on the minstrel harp with the Scottish Early Music Consort, conducted her own works and broadcast on the BBC and CBC. Her compositions have been performed in Scotland, England, Canada and Switzerland. From 1976 she has been the senior lecturer at the School of Music, Huddersfield Polytechnic. PHOTOGRAPH.

Compositions
ORCHESTRA
Callanish (1972)
Concerto grosso (2 ob, bsn, hn and str orch) (1970) (prize, New cantata orchestra of London's competition for young British composers, 1970)
Dance Variations (cham orch) (1972)
CHAMBER
Circus (9 insts) (1974)
Postlude: Ave Maria Stella (early insts) (1971)
Double reed Nos. 1, 2 and 4 (ob, bsn and pf) (1981)
Etude (str trio) (1974)
Aspects of night (rec and gtr; also rec and hpcd) (1981)
Suite for two: Five dances (vln and vla) (1968)
Orpheus (vln and pf) (1973)
Allemande, courante, sarabande and gigue for harpsichord (1980)
A dance to the music of time, op. 33 (hpcd) (1980)
Deus ex Machina (org) (1982)
Study in black and white (pf) (1983)
VOCAL
Gitanjali (mix-ch) (1981)
L'allegro (counter-T, rec and hpcd) (1979)
The silver casket (S and ens) (1970) (Capianni Prize for Women Composers, 1971)
The tree of life (T, Bar, B, fl, cl, vln, vlc, pf and perc) (1979)
Witch music (m-S and ens) (1971)
SACRED
Three Skelmanthorpe carols (m-ch) (1980)
Ave Maria (m-S and ens) (1975)
Dieux est (S and ens) (1969)
Hymn to Creation (1973)
ELECTRONIC
Lest we forget (mix-ch and syn) (1982)
Music for an exhibition (music concrete) (1970)
Sci-fi (elec tape) (1972)
TEACHING PIECES
Instrumental interludes (1973) (prize, Halifax international competition for teaching music, Canada, 1973)
MISCELLANEOUS
Music for the spheres (1976)
Ref. composer, 77, 177, 206, 230, 622

WILKINSON, Constance Jane
British professor and composer. b. England, February 20, 1944. She obtained her B.A. and B.M. from Cambridge University, United States, and M.A. and Ph.D. from the University of California. She studied composition under Richard Orton, W. Kotonski and Richard Felciano. She then lectured at the same university for two years. She was assistant professor at the University of Virginia for three years before accepting a position at the University of Pennsylvania. DISCOGRAPHY
Compositions
CHAMBER
Phoenix 1 (hp)
VOCAL
Songs of a courtesan (12 w-vces, 2 pf, fl and vlc) (1976)
Comparatives (S and vla) (1978)
Crossworlds (1978)
Movements (S, fl, cl and perc) (1975)
Ref. AMC newsletter

WILL, Madeleine
French organist, lecturer and composer. b. Mulhouse, November 1, 1910. She studied in Mulhouse and Basle and taught the organ, harmony, counterpoint and composition at the Ecole Nationale de Musique, Mulhouse. PHOTOGRAPH.
Compositions
ORCHESTRA
Concerto (org and orch)
Concerto grosso
Divertissement (3 trp and orch)
Divertissement (pf and orch)
Partita (str orch)
Sinfonia (bsn and orch)
Sinfonia (hn and orch)
Sinfonia (ob and orch)
Sinfonia (trp and str orch)
Suite (str and 7 wind insts)
Concertino (vla and str orch)
Concertino (hpcd and str orch)
Divertissement (3 trp, 3 trb and str orch)
CHAMBER
Chamber pieces
Organ pieces
Piano pieces

SACRED
Mass
Motets
Ref. composer, 95

WILLAERT, Caterina
20th-century German composer. She was the neice of the composer Adrian Willaert. She composed operas.
Ref. 433

WILLIAMS, Alice Crane
Compositions
ORGAN
Grand choeur
Marche triomphale
Meditation
Voix celeste
Vox humana
Ref. Frau und Musik

WILLIAMS, Carol
American composer. b. 1939. She studied composition under Robert Kelly and Stella Roberts and graduated from the American Conservatory.
Compositions
PIANO
Bells (1969)
Sonata
Teaching pieces
Ref. 52

WILLIAMS, Frances
20th-century American conductor, editor and composer. b. Caernarvonshire, Wales. She studied on a scholarship at the Cornish School of Music, Seattle and under Rubin Goldmark and James Friskin at the Juilliard School of Music. Other teachers included Calvin Brainerd Cady and Anna Dall. She was on the staff of Harold Flammer, music publishers and later became editor-in-chief.
Compositions
VOCAL
More than 300 pieces, incl.:
Hear ye, O mountains (ch)
Let there be music (ch)
Night (w-ch and pf) (Harold Flammer)
Snowflakes (ch)
Song to April (w-ch) (Flammer)
Spring's awakening (ch)
Spring song (ch)
To the dawn (ch)
SACRED
Christ is the risen Lord, cantata (ch)
Give thanks (ch)
In Bethlehem's lowly manger (ch)
I shall not live in vain (high vce and pf) (Flammer)
Psalm 23
Ref. 39, 40, 142, 190, 347, 646

WILLIAMS, E. Florence. See WHITLOCK, E. Florence

WILLIAMS, Grace Mary
Welsh scriptwriter, teacher and composer. b. Barry, Glamorganshire, February 19, 1906; d. Barry, February 10, 1977. She studied at the University of Wales, Cardiff, receiving her B.Mus. in 1926 and at the Royal College of Music in London, 1926 to 1930, where she was a pupil of Vaughan Williams and Gordon Jacob. She won a traveling scholarship from the Royal College of Music, enabling her to study composition under Egon Wellesz in Vienna, 1930 to 1931. She taught at the Camden School for Girls in London until 1947, when she returned to Glamorganshire. She wrote mainly educational scripts for the BBC and contributed to children's programs. Most of her works have been performed by prominent orchestras and were broadcast on the BBC in Wales. She received the John Edwards Memorial Award for her services to Welsh music and was vice-president of the guild for the promotion of Welsh music. DISCOGRAPHY.
Compositions
ORCHESTRA
Symphony No. 1, symphonic impressions
Symphony No. 2 (1956)
Carillons (ob and orch) (1965)
Sinfonia concertante (pf and orch) (1941)
Trumpet concerto (1963)
Violin concerto (1950)
Ballads (1968)
Castell Caernarfon (for Investiture of Prince of Wales at Caernarfon Castle) (1962)
Concert overture Hen Walia (1930)
The Dark Island, suite (str orch) (1950)
Elegy (str orch) (1936, rev. 140)
Fantasie on Welsh nursery rhymes (1940)
Owen Glendower, symphonic impressions after Shakespeare's Henry IV, Part 1 (1943)
Penillion, suite (1955)
Processional (1962)
Rhiannon, symphonic legend (1939)
Sea sketches (str orch) (1944)
CHAMBER
Hiraeth (hp) (1961)
PIANO
Polish polkas (1945)
Three nocturnes: serenade; passacaglia; masque
VOCAL
All seasons shall be sweet, choral suite (S and orch) (1959)
Fairest of stars (S and orch) (1973)
Harp song of the Dane women (Kipling) (ch and orch) (1975)
Mariner's song (Beddoes) (ch and orch)
The merry minstrel (after Grimm) (narr and orch) (1949)
The dancers, choral suite (Hillaire Belloc and others) (S, w-ch and strs) (1951)
The billows of the sea, song cycle (1969)
The ballad of the trail of Sodom (V. Watkins) (S, T and trp) (1965)
Four medieval Welsh poems (Cont, hp and hpcd) (1962)
In convertando, song (S and cham ens)
Six poems of Gerard Manley Hopkins (Cont and str sextet)
Songs (Byron, Lawrence, Herrick)
Super plumina, song (S and cham ens)
Three songs of sleep (S, a-fl and hp) (1959)
Arrangements of folks songs, incl. Six Welsh oxen songs (1937)
SACRED
Ave Maris Stella (ch and orch)
Missa Cambrensis (solos, ch and orch) (1971)
Benedicite (youth ch and orch) (1964)
Hymn of praise (Gogonedawg Arglwydd) (trans composer from the Black Book of Carmarthen, 12th-century) (ch and orch) (1939)
The Song of Mary, based on the Magnificat (S and cham) (1939)
OPERA
The Parlour, based on Guy de Maupassant's En Famille (1961)
INCIDENTAL MUSIC
Blue Scar (1949)
David (1951)
Bibliography
Thomas, A.F.L. *Grace Williams: The Musical Times*. 1956.
Ref. composer, 8, 9, 15, 17, 77, 84, 94, 96, 150, 172, 177, 280, 477, 563, 622, 637, 645

WILLIAMS, Irma
20th-century Argentine pianist, lecturer and composer. b. Buenos Aires. She was the daughter of composer Charles Lee Williams and started her study of the piano, solfege, harmony, counterpoint and composition under her father. She attended the Conservatory of Buenos Aires from a very young age and received first prize in solfege in 1920, first prize and gold medal in the piano in 1921 and composition in 1926. She taught the piano at the Conservatory and in 1941 became deputy-director. She composed piano pieces and songs, the words being by La Quena.
Ref. 54, 100

WILLIAMS, Jean E.
Compositions
ORCHESTRA
Concerto in A-Minor (pf and orch)
Concerto in C (pf and orch)
Concerto in F (pf and orch)
Fourth concerto in C (pf and orch)
CHAMBER
Piano pieces
VOCAL
Choral pieces
Ref. 40, 142, 347

WILLIAMS, Joan
19th-20th-century English composer.

Compositions
SACRED
Blessed is He that cometh
Glorious land
Glory to our King
Hark! the cherubic host
I heard the voice
Let heaven
O lovely voices of the sky
Thanks be to God
Thou wilt keep him
While shepherds watched
Ref. 297

WILLIAMS, Joan Franks

Israeli-American composer. b. New York, April 1, 1930. She received a B.M. (musical education) from the Eastman School of Music in 1952 and B.M. and M.M. in composition from the Manhattan School of Music in 1959 and 1961. Her teachers included Wayne Barlow, Vittorio Giannini, Ralph Shapey, Vladimir Ussachevsky and Roman Haubenstock-Ramati. She lives in Israel.
Compositions
ORCHESTRA
Haiku (1972) (also fl, vlc and perc)
CHAMBER
String quartet (1964)
Await the wind (trio) (1966)
Composition in three movements (vln and pf) (1962)
Concert piece for solo violin (1965)
PIANO
Etude from Moscow, Idaho (ACA)
Three miniatures (1963)
VOCAL
Cassandra (S, vln, vlc, fl, trp and perc) (1969)
From Paterson (S, pf, vlc and trp) (1968)
In celebration
Listen! The wind! three songs (S, fl and pf)
ELECTRONIC
Frogs (vce, pf, tape and 12 strs) (1973)
MISCELLANEOUS
Humpty Dumpty sat on a waltz
Ref. composer, 40, 80, 94, 190, 347, 501

WILLIAMS, Kimberley

Australian composer. b. 1952.
Composition
PIANO
Piece for two players (1970)
Ref. 446

WILLIAMS, Linda

20th-century American pianist and composer.
Composition
CHAMBER
Edge of light (pf, perc and c-bsn) (1980)
Ref. AMC newsletter

WILLIAMS, Margaret

19th-century American composer. b. Tennessee. She studied at the Peabody Conservatory in Baltimore, where her *Overture* was performed by the Symphonic Orchestra.
Compositions
ORCHESTRA
Overture
OPERA
Columbus, in 5 acts (composer)
Ref. 226, 292, 347, 433

WILLIAMS, Mary. See BELCHER, Mary Williams

WILLIAMS, Mary Lou (Mary Elfrieda) (nee Scruggs)

Black American jazz pianist, arranger, conductor and composer. b. Pittsburgh, PA, May 8, 1910; d. May 28, 1981. She studied music with B. Sterzio, A. Alexander, Ray Lev and Don Redman. She received a grant from the Guggenheim Foundation for composition and was awarded an honorary doctorate of human letters, by Fordham University. From 1926 to 1928 she was the pianist in the jazz orchestra of John Williams, saxophonist, whom she later married. She was an arranger for Benny Goodman, Louis Armstrong, Duke Ellington, Cab Calloway and others. After 1942 she conducted her own jazz group and appeared with the New York Philharmonic Orchestra in 1946. She frequently appeared in concerts with her own trio and made radio and TV appearances. She toured Europe, 1952 to 1954. DISCOGRAPHY.
Compositions
ORCHESTRA
The zodiac suite (1946)
CHAMBER
Zoning fungus II (2 pf, d-b and drs)
PIANO
Camel hop
Cloudy
The devil (also ch)
Dirge blues
Easy blues
Froggy bottom
A fungus amungus
A keyboard history
In the land of OO-bla-dee
It ain't necessarily so
The juniper tree
Little Joe from Chicago
Miss D.D. (ded. Doris Duke)
Pretty-eyed baby
Walking and swinging
VOCAL
A grand nite for swinging (vce and pf)
Gloria (vce and pf)
My blue heaven (vce and pf)
My Mama pinned a rose on me
What's your story, morning glory, lyrical blues
Zoning fungus II (vce and insts)
SACRED
Black Christ of the Andes, cantata
Mass
Mass of the Lenten season
Mary Lou's Mass
Anima Christi
Elijah and the juniper tree (ch)
Gloria
Glory to God
Music for peace
Praise the Lord
St. Martin de Porres, liturgy
Bibliography
Pianist and Composer who Helped Improvise the History of Jazz: Mary Lou Williams. Life, 1976, p. 54.
Profiles. Mary Lou Williams as Pianist, Composer and Arranger up to the 1960s. New Yorker, May 2, 1964.
Ref. *Helicon Nine* Nos 12/13 1985, 1, 39, 70, 109, 136, 142, 282, 347, 549, 622,

WILLIAMS, Nora Osborne

19th-century English composer.
Compositions
PIANO
Air de ballet (Ashdown)
Chant de matelot (Chappell)
Grand valse de concert (Novello)
Valse joyeuse (Ashdown)
VOCAL
Ho! for the chase (Ascherberg)
Nell of Hewhaven (Duff)
Phoebe (Boosey)
Ref. 297

WILLIAMS, Sioned

British concert harpist, professor and composer. b. Mancot, Clwyd, Wales, July 1, 1953. She studied at the Welsh College of Music and Drama from 1971 to 1974 and at the Royal Academy of Music, gaining a recital diploma in 1976. She is an L.W.C.M.D. and L.R.A.M. She made her concert debut in 1977 and appears worldwide with leading orchestras and on radio and television. She was professor of the harp at the Royal College of Music junior department. She contributes articles to harp journals. She received several prizes, awards and bursaries.
Compositions
HARP
Cyfres i'r Delyn (1973) (prize, 17th International Harp Week)
Serenade e danza (1983)
Ref. 643

WILLIAMS, Stella
20th-century British pianist and composer. b. Southampton. She studied at the Mathilde Verne School of Music in London and won the Schumann scholarship. At the age of 14 she played the *D'Albert Concerto* under the conductorship of Nikisch.
Compositions
PIANO
Elegy
Fairy suite
My dolls suite
Prelude in E-Minor
Other pieces
INCIDENTAL MUSIC
Three plays with music (co-composer)
Ref. 467

WILLIAMSON, Esther. See BALLOU, Esther Williamson

WILLMAN, Regina Hansen
American composer. b. Burns, WY, October 5, 1914; d. Portland, OR, October 28, 1965. She studied at the University of Wyoming, and received a B.M. in 1945. She obtained an M.M. from the University of New Mexico in 1961. She studied privately under Darius Milhaud at Mills College and under Roy Harris at Colorado College. She also attended the University of California, Berkeley, the Juilliard School of Music, the Sorbonne and the Lausanne Conservatoire. She was resident composer of the Wurlitzer Foundation, Taos from 1956 to 1957 and 1960 and 1961.
Compositions
ORCHESTRA
Anchorage (Alaska), symphony
Design for orchestra I
Design for orchestra II
PIANO
Steel mill (2 pf)
The little tailor, suite
VOCAL
Vocalise (equal vces and low strs)
Choral pieces
SACRED
First holy sonnet (John Donne) (vce and str trio)
BALLET
Legend of the Willow Plate (cham orch)
THEATRE
Music for Medea (Euripides)
Ref. 142, 347

WILLS, Edwina Florence (nee Wheeler)
American cellist, choral director, lecturer and composer. b. Des Moines IA, December 5, 1915. She received a B.A. from Grinnell College and also studied at Drake College, the University of Washington, Washington State University and Chico University. She played the cello in the Des Moines Symphony Orchestra and the Salem and Eugene Symphony Orchestras, as well as in various chamber groups in the northwestern states. She became principal cellist of the Portland Chamber Orchestra in 1971. She taught chamber music at Lewis and Clark Colleges, Portland and held a teaching fellowship at Washington State University.
Compositions
CHAMBER
String quartet In G-Minor (1st award of Washington State Federation of Music Clubs Competition, 1941)
Theme and variations (vlc and pf) (1940)
Fugue in F-Major (pf)
ARRANGEMENTS
Adagio, from 4 part chorus, Radiance and Glory (Fra Giovanni, 1513) (pf, vln and vlc; also vce)
Ref. composer, 206

WILLS, Harriet Burdett
19th-century American composer.
Compositions
VOCAL
Songs incl.:
My lady's eyes
A night song
A Norse lullaby
Ref. 276, 347, 433

WILMORE, Mrs. Louisa Aubert. See PYNE, Louisa Aubert

WILSON, Addie Anderson
19th-century American carillonist, organist and composer. b. Lawrenceville, AL. She studied under Mary Carr Moore and M. Wilson.
Compositions
CHAMBER
Piano pieces
VOCAL
Songs incl.:
Apple blossoms
Evening song
Hi, Mr. sunshine
Lullaby
Under the rose
Whenever skies are gray
MISCELLANEOUS
Music dramas
Ref. 292, 347

WILSON, Carrie Bell. See ADAMS, Carrie Bell

WILSON, Elizabeth
American composer. B. Neenah, WI, August 19, 1867; d. Los Angeles, August 17, 1957. She studied at the Lawrence University, Appleton, 1882-1890 and at Oxford University, England. She worked for the Y.M.C.A. from 1891 until her retirement in 1928. She was ordained in the Methodist Church, Appleton.
Compositions
VOCAL
Songs incl.:
Love song
Robin m'aime (vce, fl and pf)
Summer song (high vce and pf)
When Ulysses waited (vce and pf)
Yout eyen two (vce and pf)
SACRED
Father of Lights, in whom there is no shadow
Ref. 190, 646

WILSON, Gertrude Hoag
American pianist and composer. b. Christiansburg, VA, March 1, 1888. She studied at Randolph-Macon Women's College and at the Institute of Applied Music, New York. She was also a pupil of Harry Rowe Shelley. She performed with orchestras and in recitals and composed songs and fugues for the piano.
Ref. 226

WILSON, Hilda (Matilda Ellen) (pseud. Douglas Hope)
English singer, teacher and composer. b. Monmouth, April 7, 1860; d. December 1, 1918. She made her debut in Handel's *Messiah* at the age of 15. She studied at the Royal Academy of Music in London in 1879 and from 1880 to 1881 she was a Westmoorland scholar. She was Parepa-Rosa prizewinner in 1882. She composed songs under her pseudonym.
Ref. 6, 226

WILSON, Joan Dolores
American harpist, teacher and composer. b. Santa Ana, CA, May 28, 1933. She studied at the University of California (Chico) and was a pupil of Janet Leigh-Taylor, Dorothy Ramsen, Robert Maxwell, Ann Stephens, Beverly Bellows and Julie Gustavson. She was the harpist in various orchestras and performed on radio and television.
Compositions
CHAMBER
Harper's tunes for troubadours (hp)
Paradise in blue (pf)
VOCAL
Le jardin de Versailles
Wind song
Ref. 77

WILSON, Karen

American lecturer and composer. b. Cincinnati, OH, January 9, 1942. She studied at Bob Jones University under Dwight Gustafson and Frank Garlock and was a pupil of Roger Hannay at the University of North Carolina, where she obtained an M.M. in 1972. From 1966 to 1969 and in 1972 she taught at Bob Jones University and from 1970 to 1972 was a graduate assistant at the University of North Carolina.

Compositions
PIANO
  Sonatina
  Other pieces
Ref. 142, 347

WILSON, Lynn

American pianist and composer. b. 1948. She studied composition under Ruth Still.

Compositions
CHAMBER
  Cello and piano (1978)
  Preludes (pf) (1980)
Ref. *Heresies* 10

WILSON, Marion

20th-century Australian composer.

Compositions
BRASS BAND
  Aurora australis
VOCAL
  Nine songs for special days in Australia (J. Albert & Son, 1969)
  Pantomime (Albert, 1974)
  The rolling sea (Albert, 1974)
  Songtime, nine children's songs (Albert, 1974)
Ref. 440

WILSON, Matilda Ellen. See WILSON, Hilda

WILSON, Mrs. Cornwall Baron

English poetess and composer. b. 1797; d. London, January 12, 1846. In 1837 she won the Melodist Club prize and also won medals at Bardic Festivals in Wales.

Compositions
VOCAL
  The lyrist's offering
  Water music, a collection of national melodies (vce and gtr)
  Song of the ship
  Songs (composer)
Publications
  Memoirs of the Duchess of St. Albans.
  Poetry for Parry's Welsh Melodies. Vol. 3.
Ref. 6, 226, 276, 347, 433

WIMMER, Marianne

19th-century German composer.

Compositions
ZITHER
  Aus der Rettenbachklamm, Laendler (Munich: Dondl)
  Couragiert, march
  Stilles Sehnen, song without words
  Traum-wellen, waltz
Ref. 297

WINDSOR, Helen J.

20th-century American composer.

Compositions
OPERA
  The Adventures of Thumbelina (H.C. Andersen)
  The Emperor's Nightingale (H.C. Andersen) (G. Schirmer, 1966)
Ref. 40, 141, 347

WING, Helen

20th-century American pianist, violinist and composer.
Ref. 347, 353

WINGATE, Maud. See DE LYLE, Carlyon

WINKEL, Therese Emilie Henriette aus dem (pseud. Comale)

German virtuoso harpist, teacher and composer. b. Weissenfels, December 20, 1784. Under her pseudonym she published articles on the construction of the harp. She taught the harp in Dresden till 1850.

Composition
CHAMBER
  Three sonatas (vln and hp) (Dresden: Arnold)
Ref. 26, 129, 226, 276

WINKLARDE FORAZET, Aloyse. See POTT, Aloyse

WINKLER, Blanka

Compositions
OPERA
  Humor auf Reisen
  Four other operas
Ref. 465

WINOKUR, Roselyn M.

American pianist, lecturer and composer. b. Trenton, NJ. She gained her B.A. (1956) and M.F.A. (1976) from Sarah Lawrence College. She was guest lecturer at the Amsterdam Sweelinck Conservatory in 1979. Her awards included an ASCAP prize, 1980 to 1984.

Compositions
THEATRE
  Byline Nellie Bly, musical (prize, Alliance Theatre Co. playwriting competition, 1982)
MISCELLANEOUS
  Mainly Mozart (1982)
  The nutcracker and the mouse king (1978)
  Once upon a woodwind (1978)
  The Princess who talked backwards (1980)
  Rip Van Winkle (1981)
  Silents, please! (1979)
Ref. *ASCAP* Fall 1983, 625

WINROW, Barbara

20th-century English composer.

Compositions
CHAMBER
  String quartet
  Soliloquy (cl)
VOCAL
  Vainly burning (S and 9 players)
Ref. 263

WINTER, Sister Miriam Therese (Gloria Frances)

American professor, singer, writer and composer. b. Passaic, NJ, June 14, 1938. She obtained her B.M. from the Catholic University in 1964 and her M.R.E in 1976 from the McMaster Divinity College. She obtained her PhD from Princeton Theological Seminary. She taught from 1955 and became associate professor of Hartford Seminary Foundation in 1980. DISCOGRAPHY.

Compositions
SACRED
  Gold, incense and myrrh (S, A, mix-ch and gtr) (New York: Vanguard Music, 1972)
  I know the secret (S, A, w-ch and gtr) (Vanguard, 1966)
  Joy is like the rain (S, A, w-ch and gtr) (Vanguard, 1966)
  Knock, knock (S, A, w-ch, perc and gtr) (Vanguard, 1968)
  Sanstone (ch and pf) (1980)
  Seasons (S, A, w-ch, gtr and perc) (Vanguard, 1970)
  God gives his people strength
  Spirit of God in the clear running water
  Over 100 songs and hymns
  Six mass service settings
Ref. 228, 624, 646

WINTLE, Virginia

Late 19th-century composer.

Composition
OPERETTA
  Vingt-et-un (London, 1893)
Ref. 431

WINTZER, Elisabeth
German composer. b. Suderode, Harz, June 16, 1863; d. Bremen, June 12, 1933. She studied under Reinecke and Jadassohn in Leipzig. She married the artist Otto Gerlach.
Compositions
CHAMBER
Flute pieces
Piano pieces
Violin pieces
VOCAL
Als Grossmama ein Maedchen war, op. 10, duet (Simrock)
Hinterm Gartenzaun, op. 11 (2 w-vces) (Simrock)
Klein Maryke, op. 12 (vce and pf) (Simrock)
Tanzlied der Dorfdirnen, op, 15, duet (Simrock)
Children's songs (some with gtr)
THEATRE
Johannisnacht, fairy tale
Maria in Tann, fairy tale
Ref. 70, 105, 226, 297

WIRE, Edith
20th-century American composer. She composed piano pieces.
Ref. 40, 347

WISENEDER (Wieseneder), Caroline (nee Schneider)
German teacher and composer. b. Brunswick, August 20, 1807; d. Brunswick, August 25, 1863 or 1868. After a good musical education she married the opera singer Wiseneder. She founded several singing societies and the Wiseneder Music School for the blind in 1860, which became the model for numerous similar institutions in Germany. She invented a movable chart for use by the blind.
Compositions
VOCAL
Abschied, op. 9 (Bauer)
Es sitzt eine Jungfrau gefangen, op. 16 (Ruehle)
Die Kraft der Erinnerungen, op. 8 (vce and pf) (Bauer)
Lebewohl an Maria, op. 10 (Bauer)
Songs
Children's songs
Teaching works for kindergarten and advanced pupils
OPERA
Das Jubelfest, oder Die drei Gefangenen (1849)
Die Palastdame (1848)
Melodramas
Ref. 26, 129, 225, 226, 276, 297, 307

WISHART, Betty Rose
American pianist, teacher and composer. b. Lumberton, NC, September 22, 1947. She studied composition under Richard Bunger at Queens College, Charlotte, NC, graduating with a B.Mus. in 1969. At the University of North Carolina, Chapel Hill, she was a composition pupil of Roger Hanny from 1970 to 1972. Other teachers were Evelyn Reynolds, Michael Zenge and Wolfgang Rose (piano) and Stanley Wolf (composition). She received her M.M. in 1973. She taught the piano, theory and composition at Kohinoor Music Company from 1972 to 1973 and was on the staff of Argo Classical Records in 1973. She started composing in 1974. PHOTOGRAPH.
Compositions
CHAMBER
Ch'ien (4 vln and Chinese temple blocks)
Experience (2 vln, 2 vla and vlc)
Memories of things unseen (vln, fl, cl and vlc) (1973)
Memories II (vln, fl, cl and vlc) (1983)
Dreams (cl and pf) (1983)
ORGAN
Meditations for Trinity (1976)
Prelude (1975)
Sounds (1972)
PIANO
Apprehensions (1971)
Illusion, suite (1968)
Kohinoor, sonata (1971)
Leukoplakia (1968)
Reflections (1983)
Reverie (1983)
Salute (1982)
VOCAL
Lullabies for peace (vce and pf)
Melancholy lullaby (vce and pf) (1968)
Shanti (vce and pf)

SACRED
Go now in peace (S and A) (1982)
Hymn for the children (vce and pf) (1979)
Ref. composer, 142, 185, 206, 347

WITBECK, Ariel Lea
20th-century American composer.
Composition
CHAMBER
Motet (str qrt)

WITKIN, Beatrice
American pianist and composer. b. New York, May 13, 1916. She studied the piano under Edward Steuerman and composition under Roger Sessions, Mark Brunswick and Stefan Wolpe. She received her B.A. from Hunter College and did graduate work at New York University School of the Arts Composers' Electronic Workshop. She received grants from the Rockefeller Foundation, the Ford Foundation, the National Endowment for the Arts, the Hebrew Arts Music School and a Creative Arts public service grant as well as several awards. DISCOGRAPHY.
Compositions
ORCHESTRA
Stephen Foster variations for orchestra
Twelve-tone variations derived from the Beatles
SYMPHONIC BAND
Stephen Foster revisited (1980)
CHAMBER
Combinations for thirteen instruments (1965)
Parameters for eight instruments (1964)
Triads and things (brass qnt)
Cantillations I (2 cl and pf) (1982) (Belwin Mills)
Cantillations II (2 cl) (1983) (Belwin)
Cantillations III (2 vln)
Chiaroscuro (vlc and pf) (1968)
Duo (vln and pf) (1960 to 1961)
Work for 2 B-Flat clarinets (comm, 1981)
Contour (pf) (1964)
Interludes for flute (1960)
VOCAL
Prose poem (J.F. Farrell) (S, narr, vlc, hn and perc) (1963-1964)
THEATRE
Does Poppy live here? children's musical comedy (1957)
ELECTRONIC
Reports from the Planet of Mars (orch and tape)
Breath and sounds (tba and tape) (1972)
Echologie (fl and quadrophonic tape) (1973)
The electronic Mother Goose (elec tape)
Glissines (tape) (1972)
Homage to Handel (elec tape)
Wild, wild world of animals, for televison (1973)
Ref. composer, 142, 190, 280, 347, 397, 494, 622, 625

WITKOWSKA-JABLONSKA, Maria
19th-century Polish composer.
Composition
CHAMBER
Berceuse, op. 10 (vln and pf; also vlc and pf) (Gebethner)
Ref. 297

WITNI, Monica
20th-century American double-bass player, organist, pianist, teacher and composer. b. Fairfax, MN, May 6, 1930. She began learning the piano at the age of six. She attended Southern Illinois University and James Millikin University Decatur. Her piano teacher was Jose Eschniz. She received scholarships in the double-bass from both universities which enabled her to pursue composing. She taught briefly and played bass in a jazz trio and with the Milwaukee Symphony Orchestra. DISCOGRAPHY.
Compositions
ORCHESTRA
First symphony (1947)
Second symphony (1956)
Concerto for organ and orchestra in C-Minor (1948)
Piano concerto in F-Minor (1949)
Viola concerto in C (1956)
Tambores subsurrantes, symphonic rumba
CHAMBER
String quartet in E-Minor (1969)
March, fantasia, fugue for organ (1966)
Pieces for viola

Dimensions in rhythm
Modal etude (1948)
Summer holiday
Sweet one
Twilight serenade
BALLET
Zarea and the purple rainbow (1968)
OPERA
Children of the Sun, in 3 acts (1975)
The Dark of Summer, in 1 act (1967)
El Pope, in 1 act (1950)
THEATRE
The Wizard, musical (1964)
ELECTRONIC
Tapestry (cor anglais, hp, cel, vib and d-b)
Ref. composer, 94, 190, 347, 563

WITTICH, Martha von
German song composer. b. November 9, 1858; d. Berlin, November 5, 1931.
Ref. 226

WITTMAN, Therese
French composer. b. 1869; d. 1942.
Compositions
PIANO
Dear Alice, danse anglaise (Ricordi)
Fleur d'hiver, valse berceuse (Ricordi)
Laments, valse hongroise (Ricordi)
Maman, souvenir, marche française (Ricordi)
Marche des jolies parisiennes (Ricordi)
VOCAL
Bateau des amours, song
Pauv' boscotte
Sorellina
Trois petites miss, air anglais
Ref. Ricordi (Milan)

WITZIG, Louise
Swiss teacher and composer. d. 1969. She gave courses in folk dancing. She was instrumental in the introduction of the Week of Swiss Folk Song.
Compositions
DANCE SCORES
Unspunnen-Taenze, group and pair dances (with Klar Stern and Anna Sproed q.v.) (Schweizerische Trachtenvereinigung)
ARRANGEMENTS
Swiss folk dances (Schweizerische Trachtenvereinigung)
Ref. Verlag Hug

WOHL, Maria Viktoria. See ADDENDUM

WOJCIECHOWSKA-MYSZINSKA, Leokadia. See MYSZINSKA-WOJ-CIECOWSKA, Leokadia

WOLCOTT, Ellen. See ADDENDUM

WOLDE, Elsa. See FLACH, Elsa

WOLDE-FLACH, Elsa Anna Clara. See FLACH, Elsa

WOLDERSLEBEN, Juliane Charlotte
18th-century German composer.
Composition
VOCAL
Die Umstimmung der Misstoene des widrigen Schicksals der leidenden ... In 16 Gesaengen am Pianoforte von ihr selbst in Musik gesetzt (1792)
Ref. 128

WOLF, Ilda von
German choral conductor, teacher and composer. b. Metz, October 10, 1883. She moved to Dresden in 1905 and founded a women's choir in 1913. She taught in schools and toured in concert till 1930. She composed chamber pieces, choruses - some with string quartet accompaniment - and songs.
Ref. 70, 105, 226

WOLF, Maria Carolina
Bohemian composer. b. ca. 1750. She was a member of the Benda family and married the German composer A.F. Wolf.
Composition
CHAMBER
Melodien zu dem Mildheimischen Liederbuch (pf) (Gotha, 1817)
Ref. Openbare Muziekbibliotheek, Amsterdam, 177

WOLF, Winifried
19th-century German composer.
Composition
PIANO
Klavier-Konzert, op. 13 (1952)
Ref. R. Dearling (Spaulding, UK)

WOLF-COHEN, Veronika
American lecturer and composer. b. Hungary, 1944. She settled in the United States in 1956. She received her B.M. from the Peabody Conservatory and her M.M. from Yale University. Her teachers included Grace Cushman, Robert Hall Lewis, Gunther Schuller and Bulent Arel. She obtained a doctorate in electro-acoustic music from the University of Illinois in 1980. She taught music theory and education at universities in the United States then settled in Israel, where she was employed by the Ministry of Education and by the faculty of the Rubin Academy of Music, Jerusalem, and Tel-Aviv University. DISCOGRAPHY.
Composition
ELECTRONIC
Bat David
Ref. Israeli Electro-Acoustic Music

WOLFF, Luise (Aloysia)
Austrian concert agent, music dealer, secretary, writer and composer. b. Bruenn, March 25, 1855; d. Berlin, June 25, 1935. She was the wife of Hermann Wolff and secretary to Anton Rubinstein. She composed piano pieces.
Ref. 226

WOLFF-FRITZ, Sophie
German singer, teacher, writer and composer. b. Kirchlotheim, July 15, 1858. She studied singing in Darmstadt under Luise Muller. She taught in a nursery school there and at the Kirschbaum Institute before going to Buenos Aires in 1891 where she was principal of a music school till 1904. After 1907 she taught singing in Berlin.
Compositions
VOCAL
Ein Bild (Johst) (vce and pf)
Friede (Kundt) (vce and pf)
Fuenf Lieder (1912-1922)
Kinderlieder (1912-1928)
Schicksal (Kroppin) (vce and pf)
Weddigen (Brennent) (vce and pf)
Ref. 219

WOLL, Erna
German professor and composer. b. Ingbert/Saar, March 23, 1917. She studied music and German at the Heidelberg University, 1936 to 1938 and in Munich. Her teachers of composition were Fortner, Geierhaas, Haas and Lemacher. She taught at the church music institute in Speyer and the music gymnasium Weissenhorn, in Munich and in Augsburg, where she was honorary professor. Her compositions won several prizes, including the Deutscher Allgemeiner Saengerbund prize, 1976. DISCOGRAPHY. PHOTOGRAPH.
Compositions
ORCHESTRA
Spielmusik in A (str orch) (Cologne: Verlag Gerig, 1958)
VOCAL
Canticum fuer Liebende, cantata (ch, ob and fl) (Moeseler, 1984)
Mohn, roter Mohn, cantata (Wolfenbuettel: Moeseler, 1957)
Siehe die Sonne, cantata (Verlag Gerig)
Zur Sonnenwende, cantata (Moeseler)
Der Fischzug des Simon Petrus, cantata (1978)
Clownballade, choral cycle (Moeseler)
Suesses Saitenspiel, choral cycle (Tonger)
Toene Lied meine Floete, choral cycle (Tonger, 1966)
Zeit, Verkuendigung, choral cycle (Tonger, 1963)
Apfelkantate (T. Hermann Claudius) (3 vces, 2 vln, vlc, 2 fl and glock) (Frankfurt: Peters, 1964)

Aus Ton gemacht: 20 songs for children and adults (Wilhelm Williams) (Moeseler, 1976)
Eine Grenze haben sie gezogen (Moeseler)
Le Fort-Motetten
Lieder der Liebe (Ruth Schaumann) (vce and pf) (Tonger, 1962)
Neue Lieder zur Feier
Neue Lieder zur Verlobung und Hochzeit: Dasein fuereinander Strassenkreuz (Moeseler)
Wir loben dich, O Musica (Fidula)
Wo die Seele
Zauber und Segen, Bergengruenmotetten (Moeseler, 1961)
SACRED
Augsburger Kyrie (ch a-cap) (1984)
Gelobt seist Du, Jesus Christ, cantata (Regensburg: Pustet, 1964)
Komm, Herr Jesu, cantata (Sikorski, 1965)
Stille Huegel, cantata (Sikorski, 1965)
Zur heiligen Nacht, cantata (S and T, mix-ch, rec, strs and org) (Haenssler, 1967)
Und alles preist Dich, Gott, den Herrn, cantata
Zwei Marienkantaten (Trier: Paulinus)
Drei lateinische Proprien (ch and orch) (1955-1967)
Alle Zeit ist Gottes Zeit (ch) (Fidula, 1968)
Three motets: O faltet die Fluegel; Wer die Unendlichkeit liebt; Ich bleibe der Verratene (mix-ch a-cap) (Sueddeutscher Musikverlag, 1976)
Dies soll euch zum Zeichen sein, neue Weihnachtslieder (ch and insts) (Moeseler, 1979)
Feier der Weihnacht (ch) (Fidula, 1970)
Feier des Advent (ch) (Fidula, 1969)
Ich singe da die Nact noch dunkel ist (ch) (Fidula, 1973)
Im Schatten deiner Fluegel (ch) (Fidula, 1968)
Requiem fuer Lebende (mix-ch, ob, picc, d-b and perc) (Moeseler, 1977)
Lieder von neuen leben
Martin Luther: Ich glaube, dass mich Gott geschaffen hat (mix-ch and inst ens) (1983)
Alleluja und Jubilusrufe (Coppennath-Altoetting)
An der Krippe zu singen (1981)
Anrufungen: Herr, wir leben in Suende und Schuld
Ave Maria, dich lobt die suesse Musik (Tonger)
Bausteine fuer den Gottesdienst (Haenssler)
Bibellieder fuer Kinder (Fidula, 1975)
Children's mass (vces, fl and Orff insts) (Fidula, 1960)
Der Herr wird kommen, mass for Advent (Laumann)
Deutsche Christnachtmesse (Munich: Uni-Druck)
Deutsche Mitternachtsmesse (Paulinus)
Deutsches Requiem (Munich: Uni-Druck)
Deutsches Weihnachtsevangelium (Laumann, 1970)
Du hast uns gerufen (Christophorus, 1969)
Eer aan God, Dutch Mass (Amsterdam: Annie Bank, 1967)
Es begab sich aber
Ewigkeit im Augenblick
German Psalms 26, 123, 62, 68, 177 (Christophorus, 1963)
Gott hat die Erde fuer uns gemacht (1977)
Gott ist dabei, for children (Fidula)
Gott wir freuen uns (1979)
Gott wir suchen dich, mass for young people (Laumann)
Herr, mache deine Kirche zum Werkzeug deines Friedens
Ihr seid mir Wasser (Taufe)
Liedersingen in dir, cycle of motets (Fidula, 1960)
Messe fuer Kinder und ihre Eltern
Messe in E (Moeseler, 1956)
Missa choralis (Schwann-Peters, 1961)
Mit Dank und Amen (Fidula, 1978)
Neue Weihnachtslieder fuer Kinder (Fidula, 1974)
Ordinarium in Rufen (Paulinus)
Osterevangelium (Laumann)
Pfingstevangelium (Laumann)
Proprium zu Allerheiligen (Paulinus)
Psalm Triptychon (vce and org) (Mueller, 1981)
Sieben Leben moecht' ich haben, choral cycle (1967)
Singen auf Hoffnung hin (1968)
Singmesse nach Gotteslobliedern (Christophorus)
Stern, goldner Stern (Fidula, 1975)
Versichert hat sich die Gemeinde
Wir glauben, mass (Fidula, 1965)
Wo die Seele fluegelbebend (vce and pf) (1971)
Zwischen Babel und Jerusalem
Publications
Articles on programmed learning. Munich: Ehrenwirth. Wolfenbuettel: Moeseler. Frankfurt: Diesterweg.
Ref. composer, 563

WOLLERMAN, Joan Frances. See STEVENS, Joan Frances

WOLLNER, Gertrude Price
American pianist, authoress, conductor, lecturer and composer. b. New York, May 15, 1900. She studied conducting, orchestration and composition under Albert Stossel of New York University; improvisation and composition under Joseph Schillinger, Dr. Ernest Ferand and Frederick Schlieder; counterpoint under Hugh Kander; the piano under Katherine Ruth Heyman and E. Robert Schmitz; chamber music under Melzar Chaffee; pedagogy under Harriet Seymour; rhythms under Alys Bentley and eurhythmics under Dalcroze. She taught in New York, Washington, Boston and Newton, MA, and lectured in music at New York University, Boston University and the New England Conservatory.
Compositions
ORCHESTRA
Exaggerated Impressions (perc and str orch)
Suite (str orch)
CHAMBER
Quartet (cor anglais, vln, vla and vlc) (1950)
Trio (vln, cl and vlc) (1950)
Allegro (ob and bsn) (1950)
Cello sonata (1946)
PIANO
A dance to my daughter
Impressions of tour of old marblehead
VOCAL
We catch a fish, from we do things (vce and orch)
Poem by Tagore (1937)
These August nights (Melville Cane) (1935)
THEATRE
After Paul Draper, for dance (1944)
Music for Caesar and Cleopatra
Music for Scarlet Letter
Music-Narration-Pantomime-Dance
Reed-drum, for dancers (1940
Publications
Improvisation in Music. Boston: Branden Press.
Articles in *Tomorrow, Etude* and other journals.
Ref. composer, 142, 347

WOLOWSKA, Maria Agata. See SZYMANOWSKA, Maria Agata

WOLZOGEN, Elsa Laura von (nee Seeman)
German lutanist and composer. b. Dresden, August 5, 1876. She was the wife of Ernst Wolzogen, with whom she toured the United States from 1910 to 1911.
Composition
VOCAL
Folk songs (vce and lute)
OPERA
Der Heiligenschein
Ref. 226, 500

WONDER CHILD. See LA GUERRE, Elisabeth-Claude

WONG, Betty Ann (Siu Junn)
American banjo and gong player, pianist, Chinese recorder player, zither player, lecturer and composer of Chinese descent. b. San Francisco, September 6, 1938. She was a pupil of Morton Subotnick, Nathan Rubin and Colin Hampton at Mills College and received her B.A. (music, 1960). She studied composition under Pauline Oliveros, Robert Erickson and Kenneth Gaburo at the University of California (San Diego), graduating with an M.M. in 1971. She also pursued Chinese studies under her parents' tuition, her mother being a schoolteacher and her father a scholar and poet. In addition to her university courses she studied Chinese music under David Liang, Lawrence Lui and Leo Lew. She worked as a piano teacher at the San Francisco Music Conservatory and at the University of California (San Diego) and as an arts and crafts instructor and co-ordinator for the Community Center Chinese Music Workshops, a joint project of the Community Center and the San Francisco Conservatory of Music through a Rockefeller grant. She is co-manager and a performer of the Flowing Stream Ensemble, a Chinese silk and bamboo orchestra whose repertoire covers 25 centuries. She also formed the Phoenix Spring Ensemble, a group that introduces new works for ancient indigenous instruments of different cultures.
Compositions
THEATRE
Music for The Good Citizen, an adaptation of The Good Woman Setzuan
Village, interracial, big wheels (tape)

ELECTRONIC
   Check one-people control the environment, people are controlled by the environment (tape) (1970)
   Submerged still capable (tape) (1969)
MULTIMEDIA
   All sound is music when you let it flow
   Dear friends of music, this is your piece as well as mine (with audience) (1971)
   Furniture music or two-way stretch on a swivel chair (tape and visuals) (1971)
   A mad tea party (film and tape)
   Private audience with Pope Pius XII (tape and slides) (1971)
   Quiet places in the environment (tape, 9 performers and audience) (1971)
   Riding on to glory (film and tape)
Publications
   Magic of Chinese Music. 1974.
   Ref. composer, 142, 347, 625

WONG, Hsiung-Zee

American artist, designer and composer. b. Hong Kong, October 24, 1947. She went to the United States in 1966 and until 1968, studied at the University of Hawaii and under Ernst Krenek and Chou Wen-Chung. She studied electronic music under Robert Sheff and Dane Rudhyar at Mills College in 1970 and received her F.F.A. in industrial design from the California College of Arts and Crafts in 1972 having worked as a free-lance graphic designer and illustrator since 1967. She was initiator of Hysteresis, a women's creative arts group at Mills College and performed with Flowing Stream Ensemble.
Compositions
VOCAL
   Piano ritual I (vce, pf, perc, Chinese woodblock and opera gong)
   Songs (vce and gtr) (1964-1972)
ELECTRONIC
   The cry of women in the wilderness (pf, Chinese gong and amplified Zen bell) (1972)
   Earth rituals (tape with chanting and sound improvisation) (1973)
   Maturity (taped pf improvisation) (1972)
   The sounding of the sane (tape with audience chanting)
MULTIMEDIA
   They move, don't they? (sound calligraphic score with visual slides) (1973)
   Ref. 142, 347

WONG, Zhao, Princess (Zhoo Jun Wong)

Chinese musician and composer. b. Zi Qui.
Composition
VOCAL
   Song of the Monarch who goes to Mongolia (vce and pipa – traditional Chinese str inst)
   Ref. Patricia Adkins Chiti (Rome)

WOOD (Wood-Hill), Mabel

American teacher and composer. b. Brooklyn, NY, March 12, 1870; d. Stamford, CT, March 1, 1954. In 1917 she became a pupil of Cornelius Rubner at Columbia University. She also studied under Henry Rothwell and attended Smith College. The first recital of her songs was in 1918 and her vocal compositions were well known before she began writing in larger forms. She was associated with the New York Music School Settlement and helped to found the Brooklyn Music School Settlement and the Hudson River Music School.
Compositions
ORCHESTRA
   Grania overture
   Fables of Aesop, suite (1926)
   The Wind in the Willows, suite (1936)
   Outdoor suite, incl.: Before night (str orch)
   From a far country
   Reactions to prose rhythms of Fiona McLeod (1856-1905)
   Tone poems after Yeats' The Land of Hearts' Desire
CHAMBER
   Two string quartets
   Trio (pf, hn and cl) (1937)
   Two preludes (org)
VOCAL
   Captain Bing (m-ch and pf) (Axelrod)
   Gaelic rune of hospitality (vocal octet) (Hall & McCreany)
   I am not so bad (w-ch and pf)
   I laid me down so softly (mix-ch and pf) (Riker, Brown & Wellington)
   O fetch the water (mix-ch and pf) (Riker)
   The riders (m-ch and pf) (G. Schirmer)
   Sheep and lambs (mix-ch and pf) (Riker)
   A song for courage (m-ch and pf ad lib) (Boston Music)
   Ebb tide (vce and pf)
   French-Canadian folk songs
   The gull (vce and pf) (Riker)
   Morgengebet (vce and pf)
   Roetnam's Knut in F
   Snow on the hills (8 vces and pf)
   Songs from Calliope or The vocal enchantress (vce and pf) (Axelrod)
   The tidy dawn (vce and pf)
   Where? (vce and pf) (Axelrod)
   Les yeux (vce and pf) (J. Hamelle)
OPERA
   The Jolly Beggars
BALLET
   Interpretive solo dance (pf and perc) (1937)
   Pinocchio, ballet pantomime (1936)
ARRANGEMENTS
   Ah, ola, ola in A-minor
   Ref. 39, 40, 44, 74, 110, 124, 141, 190, 226, 280, 322, 347, 433

WOOD, Marilyn

20th-century avant-garde composer.
Compositions
MISCELLANEOUS
   Citysenses (1971)
   Events in environments (with T. Burns)
   Ref. Source: *Music of the Avant Garde*

WOOD, Mary Knight

American pianist and composer. b. Easthampton, MA, April 7, 1857; d. Florence, Italy, December 20, 1944. She was a pupil of A. Foote and B. Lang in Boston, of H. Huss in New York and of A. Parsons and J. Cornell.
Compositions
CHAMBER
   Trio (vln, vlc and pf)
VOCAL
   Afterward (vce and pf) (Ditson; Pond)
   Ashes of roses (vce and pf) (Schirmer)
   At dawn (vce and vlc obb) (Ditson)
   Autumn (Ditson)
   Clover blossoms (vce and pf) (Schirmer)
   Dodelinette (vce and pf) (Schirmer)
   Don't cry (vce and pf) (Ditson; Pond)
   Love blows into the heart (Ditson; Pond)
   Love's missing bow (vce, vlc and pf) (Ditson)
   Meadow lark (Schroeder)
   On land or sea (Ditson; Pond)
   The name
   Pine and palm, duet (Ditson)
   A romance (Ditson)
   Queen whims
   Song of joy
   Songs of sleep
   Songs of Tangier
   Thy name (Ditson; Pond)
   To my lady (Ditson; Pond)
   Wailing (Pond)
   When (Schoeder)
   A wild rose
   Other songs
SACRED
   Christmas comes but once a year (mix-ch) (Novello)
   Thou (vce and vln or vlc obb) (Schirmer)
   A Song of Solomon (vce and pf) (Pond)
   Ref. 226, 276, 292, 297, 347, 653

WOOD, Mrs. George

19th-century American composer.
Compositions
VOCAL
   Songs incl.:
   Go, lovely rose
   Hope on
   The promised kiss
   The sword and the crimson bow
   Ref. 226, 276, 292, 347

WOOD, Ruzena Alenka Valda
British musicologist, poetess, writer and composer. b. Macclesfield, Cheshire, March 17, 1937. She obtained her M.A. in English literature from Edinburgh University in 1959 and studied musical composition with Ronald Stevenson. From 1959 she worked in the music department of the National Library of Scotland, Edinburgh, where she was involved in music research. From 1980 she was music advisor for Cantilena.
Compositions
CHAMBER
    Galway hornpipe (fl and pf)
SACRED
    Hear the tidings of joy (1978)
    Oh will you come with us to Bethlehem (1961)
    Rowan tree psalm (1979)
    Sleep Baby Jesus (1980)
Publications
    Edition of John Hebden's Six Concertos in 7 parts.
    The Palace of the Moon. London: Andre Deutsch, 1981.
Ref. composer, 457, 643

WOOD, Sister Mary Davida
20th-century American composer.
Compositions
VOCAL
    Songs
SACRED
    Mass in English (1967)
Ref. 465

WOOD, Sue. See TAYLOR, Mary Virginia

WOODBRIDGE, Charlotte Louise
20th-century American organist and composer of Pasadena, CA. She composed approximately 30 works for solo, chamber and vocal media.
Ref. UCLA Music Library

WOODFORDE-FINDEN, Amy (nee Ward)
English composer. b. Valparaiso, Chile; d. London, March 13, 1919. She was a pupil of Adolph Schoesser, Winter and Amy Horrocks (q.v.).
DISCOGRAPHY.
Compositions
VOCAL
    Songs incl.:
    Indian love lyrics (Hope) (Cochrane & Southgate)
    Allah be with us (Towne)
    A lover in Damascus, cycle
    A dream of Egypt, song cycle (Boosey)
    The eyes of Firozee (Boosey)
    A little fleet of cloud-boats, in D and F (Boosey)
    Little Japanese songs (Boosey)
    A night in June
    O flower of all the world (Boosey)
    On Jhelem River (Boosey)
    Pale hands I loved, Kashmiri song
    A request (Leonard)
    A sonnet
Ref. 23, 62, 105, 177, 226, 297, 370, 488

WOOD-HILL, Mabel. See WOOD, Mabel

WOODHULL, Mary G.A.
Late 19th-century American composer.
Compositions
VOCAL
    Songs incl.:
    Love is ever
Ref. 433, 276

WOODRUFF, Edith S.
American pianist, professor and composer. b. Andover, MA, April 14, 1887. She studied at Vassar College where she obtained her B.A. and her M.A. and then attended the Northwestern University where she graduated with a B.M. in 1924. Her teachers included Theordore A. Hoeck (piano), Jean Batalla, R. Wikarski, George C. Bow, Peter C. Lutkin and Arne Oldberg. She studied writing, analysis and composition under Nadia Boulanger (q.v.), R.O. Morris, Knut Jeppesen and Normand Lockwood. She was a member of the faculty of Vassar College from 1914 to 1915 and 1920 to 1921 and Smith College from 1918 to 1919. She rejoined the staff of Vassar College as an associate professor and taught courses in harmony and counterpoint.
Compositions
CHAMBER
    Diversion (fl and strs)
    Ballade (vln and pf)
VOCAL
    Part songs
    Songs
Publications
    Harmonic Writing.
Ref. 496

WOODS, Eliza
19th-century American composer. She graduated from the Peabody Conservatory. She composed an orchestral overture, piano pieces, a sonata, a double fugue and songs.
Ref. 292, 347

WOODS, Joan Shirley LeSueur
American pianist, conductor, lecturer, writer and composer. b. Phoenix, September 5, 1932. Her studies included periods at Brigham, Arizona, Columbia, the Mozarteum, Salzburg and York, England, Universities and masterclasses under Lili Kraus at Texas Christian University from 1975 to 1978. She taught the piano in school and the piano, piano teaching, theory and composition at the Northern Arizona University. She conducts ensembles. She composed numerous piano duos, trios and duets.
Ref. 643

WOODWARD, Martha Clive
American flautist, teacher and composer. b. Wilmington , DE, April 26, 1946. She studied the flute under Blaisdell, Rampal, Dwyer, Pappoutsakis, Nyfenger and Moyse. She gained her B.A. from Smith College (1968) after study under Alvin Etler and M.A. from Harvard University. She has performed as a soloist and with orchestras and taught the flute.
Compositions
VOCAL
    The far field (ch and orch) (1968)
    Sonnets pour Hélène (1972)
Ref. 625

WOOGE, Emma
German composer. b. Hamburg, April 2, 1857; d. Berlin, April 13, 1935. She was a pupil of Behm and Richard Eichberg.
Compositions
PIANO
    Lyrische Weisen, op. 11: Romanze; Mazurka; Laendliche Weise
    Three pieces, op. 6: Capriccio; Intermezzo; Scherzo
VOCAL
    Vier Lieder, op. 1: Ach, wie kuehle; Ich weiss nicht, was werden soll; Im Walde; Wuensche (Eisoldt)
    Vier Lieder, op. 2: Kindertraenen; Spaziergang; Suchen und finden; Unersaettlich (Eisoldt)
    Three duets: Abschied: Der Morgen: Elfenreigen (Sulzer)
    Other songs, ops. 5 and 7
SACRED
    Drei Taufsprueche, op. 10: Herr, hoer auf mein; Heiliges Sakrament; Lasset das Kindlein (2 vces and pf, org or har) (Jonasson)
    Zwei Weihnachtslieder, op. 12: Christnacht, Heil'ge Nacht mit Engelsschwingen; Froehlich geweihte Nacht (1 or 2 vces) (Eisoldt)
Ref. 226, 297

WOOLF, Sophia Julia
English pianist and composer. b. London, 1831; d. Hampstead, September 27, 1893. She began learning music when she was five years old and in 1846 entered the Royal Academy of Music, becoming a pupil of Cipriani Potter. She was elected King's scholar in 1846 and 1848. She became an A.R.A.M. and an F.R.A.M.
Compositions
CHAMBER
    Piano pieces
VOCAL
    Songs

OPERA
    Carina, comic opera
Ref. 6, 85, 225, 276, 307, 347, 433

WOOLSLEY, Mary Hale

American editor, writer and composer. b. Spanish Fork, UT, March 21, 1899; d. 1969. She studied at Brigham Young, Utah and Columbia Universities. She held several editorial positions.
Compositions
VOCAL
    Songs incl.:
    Colorado
    Lost melody
    O lovely night
    Shangri-la
    When it's springtime in the Rockies
OPERETTAS
    The Enchanted Attic
    The Giant Garden
    The Happy Hearts
    Neighbors in the House
    Starflower
Publications
    The Keys and the Candle.
Ref. 39, 40, 142, 347, 433

WORALECK, Josephine

German composer of songs. b. 1781; d. 1897.
Ref. 465

WORGAN, Mary

18th-century English organist and composer. She was probably the wife of the organist James Worgan and succeeded him at St. Dunstan's Church on his death.
Compositions
VOCAL
    Songs incl.:
    The constant lover (ca. 1745)
    The dying nightingale (ca. 1745)
    The power of gold (ca. 1750)
Ref. 6, 8, 15, 65, 226, 276, 347, 433

WORRELL, Lola Carrier

20th-century American composer. b. Michigan. She lived mostly in Denver and was prominent in musical life there, specializing in recital programs of compositions by American women.
Compositions
CHAMBER
    Violin pieces
    Piano pieces
VOCAL
    Songs incl.:
    Autumn bacchanal
    Hohe liebe
    In a garden
    It is June
    Mistress mine
    Song of the chimes
    Who knows?
Ref. 292, 347

WORTH, Adelaide

19th-century American song composer.
Compositions
VOCAL
    Songs incl.:
    Land that is kissed
    True hearts
Ref. 292, 433

WORTH, Amy

American organist, choir director, teacher and composer. b. St. Joseph, MO, January 18, 1888; d. April 29, 1967. She studied music under Jessie Gaynor, Frederick Beale, Mary Lyon and Arthur Garbett.

Compositions
PIANO
    Purple heather (2 pf)
    Gavotte Marianne
VOCAL
    Songs incl.:
    The evening is hushed
    Israel
    Madrigal
    Midsummer
    Pierrot
    Song of the angels
    The time of violets
SACRED
    Mary, the Mother, Christmas cantata (ch)
    Christ rises (ch)
    He came all so still (ch)
    The Little Lamb
    Sing of Christmas (w-vces)
Ref. 39, 40, 142, 347, 433, 646

WRANA, Emilie

20th-century composer.
Composition
OPERA
    Maerchen der Liebe (1924)

WRIGHT, Agnes

19th-century British composer.
Compositions
VOCAL
    Songs
OPERA
    The Lost Clown
Ref. 465

WRIGHT, Ellen (nee Ryley) (pseud. Mrs. Sydney Harper)

English composer. b. Elm Tree Lodge, Clapham; d. Long Ditton, Surrey, July 29, 1904. She was a pupil of Alma Saunders, Henry Gadsby, and F.W. Davenport and later studied harmony and singing under Frederick Walker at the Royal Academy of Music, London. Her songs enjoyed great popularity at the time; half a million copies of *Violets* were sold.
Compositions
VOCAL
    As a dove (Chappell)
    Cycle of love songs: Accept, my love, as true a heart; Didst thou but know; I arise from dreams of thee; O, my love's like a red, red rose; To Julia; When I awake (Chappell)
    Dawn of life
    Fidelity
    Had I but known
    In my garden
    Longing (Chappell)
    Love's entreaty
    Maid in the moon
    Queen of my days
    Set of six songs, poems (Burns, Prior and others)
    She walks in beauty (Leonard)
    Starlight (Boosey)
    Two lyrics: The parting hour; Spring again
    Violets (Leonard)
    With my guitar (Chappell)
Ref. 6, 105, 276, 297, 347, 433

WRIGHT, Nannie Louise

American pianist, teacher and composer. b. Fayette, MO, June 30, 1879. She graduated from Howard Payne College in Fayette and the Columbia School of Music, Chicago. She was a pupil of Josef Lhevinne in Berlin and Mary Wood Chase in Chicago. She returned to Fayette to become director of music and president of the Missouri State Music Teachers' Association.
Compositions
ORCHESTRA
    Piano concerto, op. 42
PIANO
    Autumn
    The circus parade
    Humoreske

The juggler
Twelve etudes
Twelve preludes
Winter and spring
Ref. 226, 292, 347, 460

WRIGHTEN, Mary Ann. See POWNALL, Mary Ann

WRONIKOWSKI, Florence F.
American composer. b. Milwaukee, WI, June 3, 1916. She composed piano pieces and songs.
Ref. 347

WUERTEMBERSKA-CZARTORYSKA, Maria, Duchess
Polish authoress and composer. d. Paris, 1854. Her brother was Prince Adam Czartoryski. She lived mainly in Paris.
Compositions
CHAMBER
Piano pieces (Kiev: A. Kocipinski, 1862)
VOCAL
Stefan Potocki (Warsaw: Ragoczy, 1817)
Publications
Malwina. Novel. Warsaw: Ragoczy, 1817. Also in French.
Ref. 35, 118

WUIET (Vuyet), Caroline (Aufdiener; Auffdiener) (pseud Donna Elidora)
French pianist, novelist, teacher and composer. b. Rambouillet, 1766; d. Paris, 1835. Her father was an organist and her first teacher. At the age of five she was considered a child prodigy. She aroused the attention of Queen Marie Antoinette, who gave her a stipend for her further studies. She studied literature under Beaumarchais and Demoustier, music under Gretry and art under Greuze. Because of her connections with the royal family she was deported from France during the revolution and went to England, finally settling in Holland where she earned a living by teaching. She returned to Paris under the directorate and became known as a novelist and composer. In 1807 she married Auffdiener and accompanied him to Portugal where she assumed the name Donna Elidora. She returned alone to Paris where she was elected as an honorary member of the French Academy. She taught and wrote novels.
Compositions
CHAMBER
Trois sonates pour clavecin avec violon et basse, op. 1 (Paris, 1785)
Pot-pourri pour clavecin (Paris: Boyer)
VOCAL
Songs incl.:
Comme, elle était jolie
Moi, j'aime la danse
Six romances avec accompagnement de piano (1798)
OPERA
L'heureuse erreur (composer) (Theatre Beaujolais, Paris, 1786)
Ref. 26, 119, 129, 225, 226, 276, 347, 433

WUNSCH, Ilse Gerda
American organist, pianist, choral conductor, professor and composer. b. Berlin, December 14, 1911. After beginning her piano studies in Berlin she received her M.M. from the Chicago Music College, after studying the piano under Rudolf Ganz and composition under Max Wald. She taught at the New York College of Music from 1948 to 1968; at the Stern College for Women, Yeshiva University from 1960 to 1964 and became an associate professor of music education at New York University in 1968. She was organist and choir director at the Temple Beth-El, Cedarhurst, from 1949 to 1968.
Compositions
PIANO
Twelve progressing tone plays (1972)
SACRED
Young Faith, a sabbath evening and morning service, 2 vols (1956)
Ref. 142

WURM, Mary (Marie) J.A. (pseud. Mary Verne)
British pianist, conductor and composer of German parentage. b. Southampton, May 18, 1860; d. Munich, January 21, 1938. She studied the piano and composition at the Stuttgart Conservatory under Dr Stark and Pruckner and later became a piano pupil of Clara Schumann (q.v.), Raff, Frank Taylor, Anna Mehlig, Marie Krebs and Joseph Wieniawski. She studied composition in London under Stanford, Arthur Sullivan and Bridge, winning the Mendelssohn Stipend (founded by Jenny Lind) three times in succession. In 1886 she continued composition studies in Leipzig under Dr. Reinecke. She had made her debut at London's Crystal Palace in 1882 and followed this appearace with numerous others in London, Leipzig, Meiningen and Berlin. Germany was her home for most of her life; she lived in Hanover, Berlin and Munich. In Berlin she established a women's orchestra, with which she conducted and toured until 1900. Her sisters, Adela (q.v.), Alice (q.v.) and Matilde changed the family name to Verne and pursued careers as pianists in England.
Compositions
ORCHESTRA
Piano concerto in B-Minor
Concert overture
Dalila's Traum (str orch)
Estera gavotte (str orch; also pf)
Meteor-walzer (str orch) (Kahnt)
CHAMBER
String quartet in B-Flat, op. 40 (London, 1894)
Lullaby, op. 7 (vln and pf; or vlc and pf; or pf)
Lullaby, op. 43 (vln and pf; or pf) (Heinrichshofen)
March, lullaby (vln and pf) (Augener)
Sonata (vlc and pf)
Sonata, op. 17 (vln and pf)
PIANO
Four duets, op. 24 (Augener)
Tanzweisen, op. 28 (4 hands) (Breitkopf)
Barcarolle (Ashdown)
Clotilde Kleeberg, gavotte (Leonard)
Fairy music (Ashdown)
Gavottes in D and G (Boosey)
Josef Hoffmann, gavotte (Leonard)
Kleine Stuecke im Jugendstil, op. 30 (Steingraeber)
Maien-Walzer (Nagel)
Mazurka (Boosey)
Muenchener Kindl-Polka (Nagel)
Quatre morceaux, op. 47: Scherzo; Menuet; Romanze; Gavotte Royale (Forberg)
Rosen-Walzer (Steingraeber)
Serenate, op. 50 (Steingraeber)
Suite: Prelude; Fugue; Minuet; Loure; Gavotte (Ashdown)
Sylph dance (Ashdown)
Valse de concert, op. 27 (Augener)
Zwei Klavierstuecke: Petite berceuse; Gavotte mignonne (Hoffheinz)
Zwei kleine Fantasien ueber Weihnachslieder (Steingraeber)
Zwei Sonatinen alten Stils in modernen Tonarten, ohne Oktavenspannung (Steingraeber)
VOCAL
Mag auch heiss das Scheiden brennen, op. 39 (solos, w-ch, str orch or pf) (Oertel)
About the sweet bag of a bee (w-ch) (Novello)
Albion (w or boys' ch) (Novello)
Einst taet ein Lied erklingen (w-ch) (Novello)
Good night (Gute Nacht) (w-ch) (Novello)
Hoffnung (w or boys' ch) (Novello)
O dass des Herzens (w- or boys' ch) (Novello)
Some strain that once thou heardest (w-ch) (Novello)
Sturm nur, O Wind (w or boys' ch) (Novello)
To the March winds (w or boys' ch) (Novello)
Under the greenwood tree (w-ch) (Novello)
Unter des Laubdaches Hut (w-ch) (Novello)
Whenever life some joy does bring (w-ch) (Novello)
Wo nur dem Leben Lust erblueht (w-ch) (Novello)
Abschied eines Slowaken: Gebt mir meine Wandertasche (Bote)
Drei Lieder, op. 55 (Heinrichshofen)
Ein Eiland kenn'ich (w or boys' vces) (Novello)
Fly not, summer hours (w or boys' vces) (Novello)
Four love songs (Landy)
Neun Lieder, op. 25 (Plothow)
Pfeil und das Lied (Bote)
Scots Guards' band is playing, vocal march (Ashdown)
Wiegenlied in Sommer (Bote)
Wiegenlied, schlaf lieb' Kindlein (Simrock)
OPERA
Die Mitschuldigen (Goethe) (Leipzig, 1921)
OPERETTA
Prinzessin Lisa's Fee, Japanese children's operetta (1896)
Publications
Das ABC der Musik. Leipzig.
Praktische Vorschule zur Caland Lehre. Hanover, 1914.
Ref. 2, 8, 17, 22, 70, 74, 105, 107, 108, 226, 276, 297, 322, 347

WURMBACH-STUPPACH, Ernest. See VRABELY-WURMBACH-STUPPACHOVA, Stefania

WURTEMBERSKA-CZARTORYSKA, Maria. See **WUERTEMBER-SKA-CZARTORYSKA, Maria**

WURZER, Gabriella
19th-century German composer.
Compositions
VOCAL
Am Abend (Schmid)
Denkst du daran
Der alte Garten
Der Freund
Die Nacht
Elfe
Fuenf Lieder: Liebesglueck; Nachts; Rueckkehr; Wiegenlied; Zur Hochzeit
Gedichte-Daemmerung senkte sich von oben: April; Wunderliches Buch der Buecher; St. Nepomuks Vorabend
Der Entherzte; Durcheinander; Lieber alles; Guter Rat; Tusch Ziguenerin
Ref. 297

WYER, Berenice Crumb. See **CRUMB, Berenice**

WYETH, Ann (Mrs. John W. McCoy II)
American pianist, artist and composer. b. Chaddes Ford, PA, March 15, 1915. Her brother is the artist Andrew Wyeth. She studied the piano under William Hatton Greene and composition under Harl McDonald.
Compositions
ORCHESTRA
Christmas fantasy
In memoriam (ded her father)
Maine summer
PIANO
Children's pieces: About a little boy; Music for Christopher; Portrait of Newell
Maine preludes: Cannibal shore; Fog; The green dory
VOCAL
Songs
Ref. 40, 142, 347, 374

WYLIE, Betty Jane.
American composer. DISCOGRAPHY.
Composition
VOCAL
Beowulf, based on Anglo-Saxon poem (with Victor Davies) (ch and orch)
Ref. 563

WYLIE, Ruth Shaw
American flautist, pianist, professor and composer. b. Cincinnati, OH, June 24, 1916. She received a B.A. in 1937 and an M.A. in 1939 from Wayne State University, Detroit. She earned a Ph.D. in 1943, from the Eastman School of Music, where she studied under Bernard Rogers and Howard Hanson. At the Berkshire Music Center she was a pupil of Arthur Honneger, Samuel Barber and Aaron Copland. She was lecturer of music theory and composition at the University of Missouri from 1943 to 1949. At Wayne State University she was assistant professor in 1960, chairlady of the music department from 1961 to 1962 and head of composition from 1958 to her retirement in 1969. As founder and director of the Wayne State University Improvisation Chamber Ensemble from 1965 to 1969 she gave concerts throughout the Midwest. She was awarded a fellowship at the Eastman School of Music in Orchestration from 1942 to 1943; was a resident fellow at the Huntington Hartford Foundation, Pacific Palisades, CA from 1952 to 1953 and resident fellow at the MacDowell Colony (Peterborough, NH) in 1954 and 1956. In 1984 she was the recipient of an Inter American music award and a Mu Phi Epsilon national composition contest. She won numerous ASCAP standard awards. DISCOGRAPHY. PHOTOGRAPH.
Compositions
ORCHESTRA
Symphony No. 1, op. 6 (1943)
Symphony No. 2, op. 11 (1948)
Clarinet concertino No. 1, op. 24 (1967)
Concerto grosso, op. 5 (7 ww and str orch) (1952)
Holiday overture, op. 14 (1951)
Involution, op. 24, no. 2 (1967)

The long look home, op. 30, no. 2 (1975)
Shades of Anasazi (1984)
Suite (str orch) (1941)
Suite, op. 2 (1942)
Suite, op. 3 (for a little nephew) (cham orch) (1942)
CHAMBER
Airs above the ground, op. 32, no. 2 (fl, cl, vln, 4 or 8 vlc)
Scenes from Arthur Rackham, op. 37, no. 1 (2 fl, ob, vln, vlc, pf and 2 perc) (1983)
Imagi, op. 29 (fl, cl, vln, ob, vlc and perc)
Incubus, op. 28 (fl, cl, perc and vlc ens) (1973)
Nova, op. 30 (fl, cl, vln, vlc, perc and mar) (1975)
Toward Sirius (fl, ob, pf, vln, vlc and hpcd) (1976)
Five occurrences, op. 27 (ww qnt) (1971)
Memories of birds, op. 32, no. 1 (2 picc, 2 hn and perc)
Nova, op. 30, no. 1 (fl, cl, vln, perc and mar)
Terrae incognitae, op. 34 (fl, vla, gtr, pf and perc)
Three inscapes, op. 26 (fl, vla, gtr, pf and perc) (1970)
String quartet No. 1, op. 1 (1941)
String quartet No. 2, op. 8 (1946)
String quartet No. 3, op. 17 (1956)
String quartet No. 4, op. 37, no. 3 (1983)
Wistful piece, op. 16, no. 2 (fl, vln or ob and pf) (1953)
Music for three sisters (fl, cl and pf) (1981)
November music (vlc and pf) (1982)
Sonata, op. 16, no. 3 (vla and pf) (1954)
Sonata, op. 20 (fl and pf) (1960)
Song and dance, op. 9 (cl and pf) (1947)
PIANO
Five preludes, op. 12 (1949) (Camara Music)
Psychogram, op. 25 (1968)
Sonata No. 1, op. 7 (1945)
Sonata No. 2, op. 16 (1953)
Sonatina, op. 7, no. 1 (1945)
The white raven (Henmar: Peters, 1983)
Soliloquy for left hand alone, op. 23 (1966)
Teaching pieces
VOCAL
Echo (Christina Rossetti) (w-ch and str orch)
Toward nowhere (mix-ch)
... In just spring, op. 19, no. 1 (w-ch, 2 fl, pf and perc) (1958)
Five madrigals to poems by William Blake, op. 13, no. 1 (1950)
Light (Elizabeth Scott), op. 16, no. 4 (vce and pf) (1954)
The wanderer (Jeanne Torosian) (vce and pf) (1950)
SACRED
God's grandeur. op. 13, no. 2 (G. Manley Hopkins) (1950)
BALLET
Facades, op. 18, no. 1 (Edith Sitwell) (fl, cl, perc and pf) (1956)
The ragged Heart, op. 21 (1961)
Spring Madness (pf) (1951)
Publications
Contributions to *Dance Magazine, Criticism* and *American Journal of Aesthetics.*
Ref. composer, 52, 137, 206, 228, 280, 282, 322, 347, 359, 474, 494, 594, 622, 625

XENOPOL, Margareta
Rumanian pianist, singer and composer. b. Iasi, January 28, 1892; d. Bucarest, July 8, 1979. Her first piano teacher was Margareta Sakellary (1902 to 1907) and she later studied under Aspasia Sion Burada and then Walter Bachmann in Dresden. She studied singing under Alexandru Zirra, harmony under Paul Constantinescu and composition and counterpoint under Martian Negrea in Bucharest. DISCOGRAPHY. PHOTOGRAPH.
Compositions
CHAMBER
Elegie (vlc and pf)
PIANO
Etude classique
Etude de concert (1947)
Idylle (Leipzig: C.G. Roder, 1912)
Prélude
Le rêve de colombine, valse choreographique
Sonatine
Suite russe (1950)
Thème avec variations
Valse mélancholique
VOCAL
Allons marin (m-ch)
Numerous songs (composer and Rumanian poets) incl.:
Chant d'automne
Four romances
Fumée bleue de cigarette
J'ai voulu te fuir
J'aime comme je n'ai jamais aime

Je rest à te regarder
Les jours passent, mais l'amour demeurre
Nocturne
Pourquoi je me lie d'in rêve
Que tu oublie la romance
Retour
La romance de l'automne
Romances sans musique
Three romances
Vocal waltzes, tangos (vce and pf) (1937-1952)
SACRED
Prière (Eminescu) (ch)
Psalm 19 (mix-ch)
OPERETTA
Incomplete operetta (1972)
Ref. composer, 563

YAGLING, Victoria
Russian cellist and composer. b. 1946. She graduated from the Moscow Conservatory in the cello in 1969 and with a master's degree in 1972. She studied composition under Professors D. Kabalyevska, I. Khrennikov and A. Pyriumov. She is a notable cellist and won first prize at an international competition in Florence in 1969 and second prize at the 4th-international Tshaikovsky competition in 1970. As a performer she has a large repertoire from Bach to contemporary Soviet composers and is well-known in the USSR and internationally. DISCOGRAPHY.
Compositions
ORCHESTRA
Concerto (vlc and str orch) (1968)
CHAMBER
Pieces (vlc and pf)
Three sonatas (vlc and pf)
Sonata (vlc)
VOCAL
Song cycle (Briusov, Kamoens, Frenkel, Tarkovsky) (vce and pf)
Ref. 330

YAKHNINA, Yevgenia Yosifovna
Soviet teacher and composer. b. Kharkov, December 30, 1918. She studied composition under V. Shebalin at the Moscow Conservatory and graduated in 1945. She taught theoretical subjects at the Moscow School of Music from 1944 to 1948 and after 1952 at an evening school.
Compositions
ORCHESTRA
Children's scenes, 6 pieces (symphonic orch) (1975)
Dramatic poem (1955)
CHAMBER
String quartet (1946)
Concerto for oboe and piano (1953)
Sonata (vln and pf)
Suite (cl and pf) (1952)
Akvareli, cycle (hp) (1976)
Prelude, cycle (pf) (1954)
VOCAL
Poem, cantata (N. Tikhonov) (1945)
Three choruses (Pushkin, Lermontov) (mix-ch a-cap) (1947)
Poemy serdtsa (vce and pf) (Sovietski Kompozitor, 1976)
Romances and songs (Pushkin, Lermontov, A. Blok, V. Shefner and other Soviet poets)
Ref. 87, 227

YAKUBOVITCH, Elizaveta
19th-century Russian composer.
Composition
VOCAL
Solovei, song cycle (vce and pf) (Idzikowski)
Ref. 297

YAMAGUCHI, Kazuko. See HARA, Kazuko

YAMASHITA, Mika
Japanese composer. b. 1968. DISCOGRAPHY.
Composition
PIANO
Dance of a comic doll
Ref. Yamaha Music Foundation

YAMASHITA, Toyoko
20th-century Japanese composer.
Composition
CHAMBER
Wa (vlc and pf) (1983)
Ref. Frau und Musik

YAMPOLSCHI, Roseane
Brazilian pianist, singer and composer. b. Rio de Janeiro, July 18, 1956. She began piano lessons at an early age and attended the graduated courses of stage direction and composition at the Federal University of Rio de Janeiro. She also completed a perception and ear training course at the University of Uni-Rio and studied singing privately under Ghyta Taghy. In 1978 she won first prize in a composition contest. PHOTOGRAPH.
Compositions
CHAMBER
Wind quintet (1984)
Two pieces for string quartet (1977)
Four pieces for wind trio (1982)
Duet for oboe and cello (1983)
Sonata for clarinet and piano (1978)
Piece for piano (1984)
Two micro-pieces for clarinet (1983)
VOCAL
Agridoce (ch a-cap) (1983)
Andante (Bar and pf) (1983)
Serenata prum gato (Bar and pf) (1983)
Ref. composer

YAROSHEVSKAYA, Ludmila Anatolievna
Soviet pianist, concertmistress and composer. b. Kiev, September 14, 1906; d. Lvov, March 27, 1975. She studied the piano under V. Pukhalsky at the I. Lysenko Music-Drama Institute in Kiev, graduating in 1930. From 1927 to 1930 she studied theoretical subjects at the same institute and from 1923 to 1926 was concertmistress at the Lvov Music School.
Compositions
ORCHESTRA
Cello concerto (1940)
Violin concerto (1954)
Heroic overture (1946)
Suite on Volga themes
Year 1654, overture (1954)
CHAMBER
Capriccio (vlc and pf) (1954)
Exprompt (vln and pf) (1946)
Scherzo (vln and pf) (1935)
Sonata (cl and pf) (1954)
PIANO
Fantasy on Gutsul themes
Nocturne (1951)
Preludes
Variations (1935)
VOCAL
Cycle (A. Prokofiev) (vce and pf) (1954)
Romances (P. Tychina, M. Rylsky and Y. Kupala) (1936)
Songs
Ref. 87

YAZBECK, Louise
20th-century American teacher and composer. b. Shreveport, LA.
Compositions
CHAMBER
Lebanon-Syrian marches in D and G-Major (pf)
VOCAL
Echoes
Good old Southern blues
Songs
Ref. 347, 448

YDETTE, Arline
20th-century composer.
Composition
THEATRE
Christopher Columbus, mini musical (vce, opt perc, pf, gtr and hp)
Ref. MLA *Notes*

YDSTIE, Arlene Buckneberg

American organist, choral conductor, teacher and composer. b. Larson, ND, April 28, 1928. At Concordia College, Moorhead, NM, she studied choir conducting under Paul J. Christiansen and received her B.A. in 1952. In Portland she studied composition at Central Washington State University. She taught singing in Benton City, WA, and was church organist and choir director at Richland Lutheran Church. PHOTO-GRAPH.

Compositions
VOCAL
   Songs incl.:
   Down the aisle country style (w-ch) (Edward B. Marks, 1977)
   Erie Canal boogie (w-ch) (Marks, 1977)
   How many ways? (mix-ch) (Schmitt Music, 1977)
   If there's a song (mix-ch or w-ch) (Schmitt; Hall; McLeary, 1975)
   Make your own world (w-ch) (Schmitt; Hall; McLeary, 1974)
   My valley (mix-ch) (Marks, 1977)
   Ready or not, here he comes (w-ch) (Neil Kjos, 1977)
   Somewhere there's a song (mix-ch) (1980)
   There is a treasure (mix-ch) (1982)
   As you come and go (S, A and B) (1979)
   I sing of a maiden (1982)
   If you need a friend (1981)
   Many generations ago (1981)
   Serendipity (S and A) (1979)
   Ten generations ago, bicentennial pageant (1976)
   To be or not to be (m-ch) (Neil Kjos, 1974)
SACRED
   Sermon on the Mount, cantata (1978)
   As heaven's rain (mix-ch) (Neil Kjos, 1977)
   The Family of God (ch) (1978)
   Hosanna today (w-ch) (Schmitt; Hall; McLeary, 1976)
   Little Samuel (w-ch) (Schmitt; Hall; McLeary, 1977)
   Song of the shepherds (ch) (Neil Kjos, 1974)
   Five loaves and two little fishes (Schmitt; Hall; McLeary, 1977)
   Moses smote the rock (1984)
   Walk to me, Jesus (Schmitt; Hall; McLeary, 1976)
THEATRE
   The Case of the Counterfeit Santa, musical (1984)
   Christopher Columbus, musical (1982)
   The Return of the Star, musical (1983)
   The Townhall Christmas Tree, musical
Ref. composer

YEARWOOD, Kathleen

20th-century composer of a piece for electric guitar and tape.
Ref. *Canadian Composer* April 1983

YEATMAN, Ethel

19th-century English composer.
Compositions
ORCHESTRA
   Olden times (also vln and pf; also pf) (Ascherberg)
CHAMBER
   Masks and faces (pf) (Jefferys)
Ref. 297

YELCHEVA, Irina Mikhailovna. See ELCHEVA, Irina Mikhailovna

YI, Heung-Yull

Korean professor and composer. b. July 17, 1909. She graduated from the Tokyo School of Music in 1931 and received a Ph.D. from Sukmyong Women's University in 1972. She taught at Kyongsong Poyuk School, 1933 to 1937, and Pungman Girls' Middle and High Schools, 1947 to 1957. She organized a piano trio in 1933, the Kyongsong Radio Orchestra in 1936 and the Apollo Chorus in 1938. She was a professor at Korea University from 1957 to 1964 and from 1963, at the College of Music, Sukmyong Women's University. She became vice-president of the Korean Composers' Association in 1955. She received the Seoul City cultural award in 1961, the Presidential cultural order in 1963 and the National Academy of Arts award in 1967.
Compositions
VOCAL
   Three collections of songs: Flower garden (1937); For you (1965); The place I want to live
MISCELLANEOUS
   Collection, 2 vols (1934, 1955)

Publications
   An Outline of New Music. 1962.
   Synthetic Study of Music. 1958.
Ref. 77

YOGUCHI, Rie

Japanese concert pianist and composer. b. 1971. She attended the Yamaha special advanced music course and has toured extensively. DISCOGRAPHY.
Compositions
PIANO
   Fantasy of chateau and silhouette
   Gypsy girl
   Kangaroo march
Ref. Yamaha Music Foundation

YOSHIDA, Kazuko

20th-century Japanese composer.
Composition
CHAMBER
   Esquisse No. 1, poem (Hurbert Juin) (ob and hp) (1980)
Ref. Otto Harrassowitz (Wiesbaden)

YOUNG, Corrine

19th-century composer of songs.
Ref. 433

YOUNG, Donel Marie

American pianist and composer. b. Wellsboro, PA, March 5, 1962. She graduated with a B.Mus. from the Moravian College where she studied composition under Larry Lipkis and the piano under Dimitri Toufexis.
Compositions
CHAMBER
   Theme and variations (pf and vln) (1981)
   Four piano pieces (1982)
VOCAL
   The way (ch and inst ens) (1982)
Ref. composer

YOUNG, Eliza (nee Mazzucato) (Mrs. Bicknell)

American composer. b. 1858. Her father was Chevalier Alberto Mazzucato, the director of the conservatory and the conductor at La Scala, Milan.
Compositions
CHAMBER
   Staccato etude (pf) (ded William H. Sherwood) (Summy)
VOCAL
   Le roi Don Juan, French romantic song (vce and orch)
   Songs (vce and pf)
SACRED
   How is come salvation and strength (Summy)
   Resurrection, chant (Summy)
OPERA
   The Maid and the Reaper, in 1 act (orch)
   Mr. Samson of Omaha (1880)
Ref. 226, 297, 307, 431

YOUNG, Fredricka Agnes Robinson

American concert pianist, arranger, choral conductor, professor and composer. b. Charleston, SC, October 18, 1928. She gained a B.A. in music from Fisk University, Nashville in 1950; M.Ed. from the University of Minnesota in 1960 and a D.M.A in music education from the Catholic University of America, Washington, DC, 1975. She gave piano-vocal recitals in the Southeastern states in New York in the 1950s and 1960s. She was music teacher supervisor for public schools in Columbia and Florence, SC, 1950 to 1960. She joined the music department of Claflin College, Orangeburg, SC, in 1960, was college accompanist until 1962; then choir director and teacher, 1962 to 1970 and from 1975, professor of music. She won Omega Psi Phi talent hunt scholarships in 1946 and 1947.
Compositions
VOCAL
   Nobody knows the trouble I see (ch) (1964)
   Plenty good room (ch) (1981)
SACRED
   Once to every good man and nation, choral anthem (m-ch, w-ch and pf or org)
Ref. 643

YOUNG, Gayle

Canadian pianist and composer. b. St. Catharines, Ontario, 1950. After studying the piano, choral and folk music she studied composition and contemporary music at York University from 1974 until 1977. Her teachers included Richard Teitelbaum, Louis Debra, David Rosenboom, James Tenney and Casey Sokol. She graduated with an F.F.A. hons. and was awarded the BMI prize in composition. She designed and built the columbine, a percussion instrument of forty steel bells with nineteen pitches to each octave, intended to explore the intonational resources of proportional frequency. In 1980 she built the amaranth, which is a twenty-four stringed instrument with a movable bridge system which reproduces any system of pitches. Since 1974 she has worked with and written for a wide variety of electronic and acoustic instruments and received several awards and commissions. PHOTOGRAPH.

Compositions
CHAMBER
In motion (3 columbine) (1979)
Lacustrine (fl, columbine and amaranth) (1980)
Through a haze (pf and cl) (1978)
Amiranda (amaranth) (1982)
Passagere (columbine) (1982)
Patterns for unwinding (1976)
VOCAL
According to the moon (S and A) (1978)
Capriccio (S, A, wood block, columbine, amaranth and vln) (1978)
Krohnohs (S, A, vln and columbine) (1980)
Suite of 3 songs: Sometimes in the evening; Out wandering around; Listen
Vio-voi (S and vln) (1978)
ELECTRONIC
Aquilegia (tape and syn) (1979)
Cuesta (computer and amaranth) (1981)
Lunatic phases (amaranth and computer generated tape)
Theorein (tape of vce and perc)
Usque ad mare (syn qrt) (1981)

Bibliography
New Instruments Come from Experimental Urge. Lorraine Le Page, St. Catharines Standard, Jan. 28, 1982.
Composer Creates New Instruments. Isobel Harry, *Canadian Composer,* No. 162, June, 1981.
Composer Devises Musical Instruments. Jean Southworth, *Ottawa Journal,* April 9, 1980.
New Instruments Unveiled. Lauretta Thistle, *Ottawa Citizen,* April 10, 1980.
According. Review. Barry Edwards, *Music Magazine,* Volume 4, Number 3, May, 1981.
According. Review. Raymond Gervais, *Parachute,* Winter, 1981.
Ref. composer

YOUNG, Harriet Maitland

English composer. b. 1838.
Compositions
VOCAL
Songs:
In sunny Spain (w-ch and pf) (Ashdown)
Ah! si vous saviez (Chappell)
Bella pescatorina (Weekes)
Golden days and silvery nights (Boosey)
Lullaby (vce and vlc) (Cramer)
La mia bella (Ashdown)
Out of reach (Weekes)
Secret is my own (Ashdown)
Where the roses are, duet (Boosey)
OPERETTA
An Artist's Proof (1882)
The Holy Branch
Queen of Hearts (1888)
When One Door Shuts
Ref. 226, 276, 297, 347

YOUNG, Jane Corner

American pianist, music therapist, lecturer and composer. b. Athens, OH, March 25, 1915. She graduated from Ohio University with a B.M. cum laude in 1936 and obtained an M.M. in the piano and composition at the Cleveland Institute of Music in 1953. She studied the piano under Beryl Rubinstein and Arthur Loesser, composition under Marcel Dick, theory under Ward Lewis and pedagogy under Ruth Edwards. She has a B.M. hons in Dalcroze eurhythmics, which she studied under Elsa Findlay and Ann Lombardo. She was awarded a music fellowship from Ohio University, 1942 to 1943 and the alumni award in composition (1961). She taught for over 27 years in public schools, privately, and was a faculty member at the Cleveland Institute and director of music therapy at Hawthornden State Hospital. DISCOGRAPHY.

Compositions
CHAMBER
Essences, concert piece in 4 mvts (2 vln) (Alumni Composers' prize, 1961)
PIANO
Andante espressivo
Caprice (1976)
Children's picture pieces
Dramatic soliloquy (1961)
First journey
Five duets for matched students
Five tone thoughts and summary (1971) (1st prize, Mu Phi Epsilon, Cleveland Heights alumni chapter composers' contest)
Four recital pieces: The chase; Patterns; Shadows; Waltz
I won't go
Piano gambol
Schumannianna: Tema, Elegia; Humoresque; Romanze; Toccatella, Intermedietto; Allegretto, Supplicando; Imbroglio, Sereno (1974)
Two humorous pieces: Going away; March for clowns
Two short studies: Counting; Two melodies
Two study pieces: Half-steps; Whole steps
Variations: American sea chantey
Yesterday/today
VOCAL
The story of Fay (vce, fl, vln, ob, bsn, trp, pf and zither)
We people, song cycle (high dramatic vce, vlc and pf) (1967)
Blues-art song: Who' there to know
Captive (L. Kenney)
Fantasy (L. Kenney)
Untidy sun (L. Kenney)
How I like a wild tame bird (vce and pf)
Such is her love (vce and pf)
Ref. composer, 142, 347, 562, 563, 622

YOUNG, Maria or Mary. See BARTHELEMON, Mary

YOUNG, Polly. See BARTHELEMON, Mary

YOUNG, Matilda

19th-century composer.
Compositions
CHAMBER
Il bacio d'amore, waltz (pf) (Ricordi)
VOCAL
L'addio supremo, romanza
Un fiore, stornello
Lasciatemi morir, romanza
La riccintella, barcarolle
Ref. Ricordi (Milan)

YOUNG, Rolande Maxwell

American pianist, actress, authoress and composer. b. Washington, DC, September 13, 1929. After studying at Catholic University, she became a pupil of Harold Bauer at the Manhattan School of Music and of Vittorio Giannini at the Juilliard School of Music. She made her debut as a pianist in New York in 1953. She is a member of ASCAP.

Compositions
PIANO
Pieces incl.:
Little acorns
VOCAL
Songs incl.:
How can I?
Somehow there's magic in you
There's a dream in my heart
When the trains came in
Ref. 39, 142, 347

YOUSE, Glad Robinson

American composer. b. Miami, October 22, 1898. She studied at Stephen's College and was a composition pupil of Tibor Serly in New York. In 1955 she was nominated by the National Federation of Music Clubs as one of the three top women composers. She was the composer and director of Jenkins' music conferences, Kansas City, 1948-1966. DISCOGRAPHY.

Compositions
VOCAL

A salute to America (ch and pf)
April is forever (w-ch and pf; also S and pf) (Bourne, 1953)
Winds of the prairie (w-ch and pf) (Bourne, 1958)
The little lost boy (S and pf) (C. Fischer, 1947)
My dream of springtime (S and pf)
Red bird (S and pf) (G. Schirmer, 1943)
Some lovely thing (S and pf) (C. Fischer, 1957)

SACRED

As long as children pray (w-ch and pf; also S and pf) (Bourne, 1941)
Behold, God is my salvation (mix-ch and pf) (C. Fischer, 1958)
Glorious Easter morning (mix-ch and pf) (St. Louis: C.A. Scholin, 1954)
Great is Thy mercy (mix-ch and pf) (C. Fischer, 1955)
He who believes in Me (mix-ch) (Remick Music, 1960)
Hear me Lord (mix-ch and pf; also solo S and pf) (Bourne, 1942)
Hungry pagan (mix-ch and pf) (C. Fischer, 1966)
O, it is lovely, Lord (w-ch and pf) (C. Fischer, 1961)
Ring out ye bells! Sing out ye voices! (mix-ch and pf) (Remick Music, 1956)
This nation under God (mix-ch and pf) (Bourne, 1958)
The Beatitudes (S and pf) (Bregman, Vocco & Conn, 1946)
I knelt at Thy altar (S and pf) (Chappell, 1953)
Thou wilt light my candle (S and pf)
Ref. 39, 40, 142, 347, 563

YSELDA. See ISELDA

YUKHNOVSKAYA, Ninel Grigorievna
Composition
OPERA

Pavel Korchagin (V. Sokol)
Ref. 465

ZACCAGNINI, Giuliana
Italian composer. b. 1933.
Composition
ELECTRONIC

Mobile 570 (4 speaking vces, vce, perc and 2 tapes) (1963)
Ref. 301

ZAFFAUK, Theresa
19th-century Austrian composer of songs.
Ref. 465

ZAIDEL-RUDOLPH, Jeanne
South African pianist, conductor, lecturer and composer. b. Pretoria, July 9, 1948. She began piano tuition at the age of five under her aunt Goldie Zaidel and composed from an early age. She obtained her B. Mus. cum laude from Pretoria University Conservatory in 1969, and an M.Mus. in 1971. She is an L.T.C.L., a F.T.C.L. and an L.R.S.M.. She obtained her certificate for advanced study in 1973. She was awarded a scholarship from the Ernest Oppenheimer Memorial Trust to do advanced post-graduate work at the Royal College of Music, London in 1973 which was renewed for study in 1974. She studied composition under John Lambert and the piano under John Lill and worked in the Royal College of Music electronic studio under Tristram Carey. She attended courses at the Tanglewood Summer School, Boston, MA, and worked on composition with Ligeti at the Hamburg Hochschule. She took part in composers' seminars at Darlington and at the Musica Nova Seminar in Glasgow and studied for her Ph.D. in composition at the University of Pretoria, becoming the first South African woman to be awarded a doctorate in composition, 1979. She conducted performances of her own symphonic works at the Royal College of Music where she was awarded the R.O. Morris prize and a Cobbett prize, both for composition. She lectured at the music department of the University of the Witwatersrand in Johannesburg. She was commissioned to write a work for competitors in the SABC music competition in 1974. She was invited to attend the festival *Donne in Musica 82* in Rome where she received a standing ovation for her *Five original works*. Amongst those who sponsored her attendance at the festival was Eva Harvey, a fellow South African composer. In 1986 Jeanne won the Total Oil Co. competition with *Tempus Fugit*. Her works have been performed in England, Germany, Rome and Tel Aviv. PHOTOGRAPH.

Compositions
ORCHESTRA

Construction symphony (youth orch) (1985)
At the end of the rainbow (comm National Youth Orchestra, 1987)
Concert overture (1979)
Fanfare festival overture (comm SABC, 1985)
Five chassidic melodies (small orch) (1981)

CHAMBER

Tempus fugit (brass ww, large perc and strs) (1986) (winner, Total Oil composition competition, 1986)
Chamber concertino, in 3 mvts (11 insts) (1979)
Kaleidoscope (wind insts and perc) (1971)
Brass quintet – and all that jazz (2 trp, hn, trb and tba) (comm SABC)
Margana (fl, vln, vlc and 2 perc) (1985)
Canonetta for four (trp, bsn, vla and vib) (1973)
Reaction (pf, vlc and perc) (1973)
Three Chassidic pieces (fl, vln and vlc) (1982)
Four minims (vlc and pf) (1982) (comm SABC) (Seesaw: NY)
The fugue that flew out of the window (fl and pf)
Tango for Tim (gtr) (1973)
Mereko (mar) (1986)

PIANO

Seven variations on an original theme (1971)
Sonata No. 1 (1969)
Three dimensions (1974) (comm SABC)
Virtuoso one (comm for International Piano Competition, 1988)

VOCAL

Dialogue of self and soul (W.B. Yeats) (8 soloists and speech ch a-cap) (1971)
Boy on a swing (w-ch, pf and perc) (1983) (ded. A.I. Cohen)
It's a women's world (ch and pf) (1984)
Five original works (S and ww qnt) (1976)
Back to basics (narr, prep pf and pf)
Setting of the Swaziland national anthem (vce and pf)
Song cycle on the occasion of the centenary of the poet Totius (Bar and ens) (1976)
Vaalvolk, etc (Afrikaans poems) (vce and pf) (1968)

BALLET

The River People (comm SAMRO, 1987)

OPERA

Animal Farm (1978)
A Rage in a Cage, rock opera (soloists, ch and cham group) (1983)

Bibliography

Springer, D. *Rainier, Gerstman, Zaidel-Rudolph. Their Lives, Times and Music.* B.Mus. thesis, Wits University, 1984.
Clough, Penelope J. *Jeanne Zaidel, a Contemporary Woman in Music.* B.Mus. thesis.
Lesicnik, Leah. *An Analytical Study of 'Four Minims for Cello and Piano' by Jeanne Zaidel-Rudolph.* B.Mus. hons. thesis, University of South Africa, 1985.
Nabarro, Dr. M. *Jeanne Zaidel-Rudolph. Scenario*, Nov. 1985.
Ref. composer, 377

ZAIMONT, Judith Lang
American pianist, musicologist, professor and composer. b. Memphis, November 8, 1945. She studied the piano and theory at the Juilliard School of Music from 1958 to 1964. In 1966 she obtained a diploma from the Long Island Institute of Music. She graduated with a B.A. magna cum laude in music from Queens College in 1966 and received an M.A. in music composition from Columbia University in 1968. Her composition teachers included Hugo Weisgall from 1965 to 1966, Jack Beason from 1966 to 1967, Otto Luening from 1967 to 1968 and Andre Jolivet in Paris from 1971 to 1972. From 1967 to 1971 and after 1972 she was accompanist and resident composer of the Great Neck Choral Society, New York. She was lecturer in musicology from 1970 to 1971 at the New York City Community College and also lectured at Adelphi University on contemporary music techniques. From 1972 to 1976 she was instructor in theory and assistant professor of music at Queens College. Since 1980 she has been professor of music in the theory division at the Peabody Conservatory of Music in Baltimore, Maryland. She performed as a duo-piano recitalist with her sister from 1960 to 1967, making her debut at Carnegie Hall in 1963. Among her honors were a Guggenheim Foundation fellowship in composition for 1983 and 1984, a National Endowment for the Arts consortium commission grant in 1982, MacDowell Colony fellowship in 1971 and 1976, a Debussy scholarship for study in France at the Alliance Française from 1971 to 1972, and a Woodrow Wilson National Foundation fellowship, 1966 to 1967. She received the Queens College award in 1965 and 1966, the Karol Rathaus Memorial Prize in 1966, the BMI award in 1966, 1st prize in the Gottschalk Competition in 1971, 2nd prize in the Delius composition contest in 1971, a performance prize in the same contest in 1975, the judges' award in the 1978 Los Alamos International chamber music contest award and ASCAP standard awards annually since 1977. Her works have been performed extensively and she has had numerous commissions. DISCOGRAPHY. PHOTOGRAPH.

Compositions

ORCHESTRA

Piano concerto (1972)

CHAMBER

Stone (pf and strs) (1981)
Sky curtains (fl, cl, bsn, vla and vlc) (1983)
Two movements (wind qrt) (1967)
De infinitate caeleste (str qrt) (1980)
Trio (fl, vla and pf) (1971)
Wind trio (ob, cl and bsn) (comm La Chambre d'Anches)
Experience (fl and pf) (1966)
Grand tarantella (vln and pf) (1970)
Music for two (any 2 treble winds) (1971)
Trumpet and piano sonata (1971)
Capriccio (fl) (1971)
Flute sonata (1962)
Valse romantique (fl) (1971)

PIANO

Duo in concert (4 hands)
Snazzy sonata (4 hands) (1972)
Calendar collection (1977) (Alfred Pub., 1980)
A calendar set, 12 preludes (1975)
Solitary pipes (1977) (Yorktown Music Press, 1978)
Judy's rag, reflective rag (1974) (Leonarda Productions, 1982)
La fin de siècle, nocturne (1978) (Galaxy Music, 1983)
Portrait of a city, suite (1961)
Black velvet waltz (1983)
Deceit (1979)
Scherzo (1969)
Solitary pipes (1977)
Sweet Daniel (1979)
Toccata (1968)
Variations (1965)
White-key waltz (1966)

VOCAL

Man's image and his cry (Bar, A, ch and orch) (1968)
Serenade: To music (cham ch and orch) (1981)
The chase (mix-ch and pf) (1972) (Galaxy 1984)
Lamentation (ch, pf and perc) (1982)
Moses supposes (w-ch and perc) (1975) (Alexander Broude, 1978)
Sunny airs and sober, 5 madrigals (ch a-cap) (Walton Music)
They flee from me ... (fl and mix-ch) (1966)
Three ayres (mix-ch a-cap) (Broude, 1976)
The tragical ballad of Sir Patrick Spens (mix-ch and pf) (1980)
The magic world (Ritual music for three) (Bar, pf and perc) (1979)
The ages of love (Bar and pf) (1971) (ACA, 1976)
Chansons nobles et sentimentals (high vce and pf) (1974) (ACA, 1976)
Coronach, 5 songs (S and pf) (1970)
Four songs (e.e. cummings) (m-S and pf) (1965)
From the great land: Woman's songs (m-S, cl, pf and Eskimo drum) (1982) comm University of Alaska)
Greyed sonnets, 5 songs (S and pf) (1975) (1st song: Galaxy Music, 1982)
High flight (vce and pf) (1980)
In the theatre of night: Six dream songs of poems of Karl Shapiro (vce and pf) (1983)
Song cycle (1984) (comm Dalton Baldwin and A. Auger)
Songs of innocence, 4 songs (Blake) (S, T, fl, vce and hp) (1974)
Two songs for soprano and harp (1978) (Lyra Music, 1983)
A woman of valor, tone poem (m-S and str qrt) (1977) (ACA, 1977)

SACRED

Psalm 23 (Bar, fl, vlc and pf) (1978)
Sacred service for the Sabbath evening (Bar, ch and orch) (1976) (Galaxy, 1979)
A solemn music cycle (Bar) (1967)

OPERA

The Thirteen Clocks, chamber opera (1983)

Publications

Twentieth Century Composition Techniques.
A Selective List of Twentieth Century Repertoire for Piano.
Contemporary Concert Music by Women. A Directory of the Composers and Their Works. With Karen Famera. Greenwood Press, 1981.
Piano Teachers' Guidebook. N.Y.: Yorktown Music Press, 1979.
The Musical Woman: An International Perspective. With Catherine Overhauser and Jane Gollhet. Greenwood Press. 1984.

Bibliography

Peter G. Davis. Pianos Still Stir Composers' Souls. New York Times, 1981.
Judith Lang Zaimont: Composer, Pianist. Judith Finell Music Services, Inc., NY.
Ref. composer, 142, 185, 206, 228, 347, 415, 454, 457, 474, 477, 494, 562, 563, 594, 611, 622, 625

ZAKRZEWSKA-NIKIPORCZYK, Barbara Maria

Polish composer. b. Poznan, January 1, 1946. She studied composition at the State College of Music under Florian Dabrowski. She obtained her doctorate at the Institute of History of Poznan University, 1976. She completed a course in sonology at the University of Utrecht in 1981. From 1981 she was head of the department of musical collections and from 1983, head of the department of special collections at the University Library in Poznan. Some of her works were performed at the Poznan Spring Music Festival and the Warsaw Autumn International Festival of Modern Music. She had articles published in several publications. PHOTOGRAPH.

Compositions

ORCHESTRA

Les carillons (pf and orch) (1980)
Star dust (vln and orch) (1978)
Arrampicata (1977)
Miazga (1983)
Orazione (1981)
Tetragonos tri fatos (1969)

CHAMBER

Spacery kosmiczne (inst ens) (1983) (prize)
Aenigma (fl, ob, cl, bsn, sax, vln and vlc) (1979) (prize)
Tempus (fl, 2 trp, 2 trb, hp and timp) (1976)
Platonic music II (perc and strs) (1974)
Erotic (3 fl, vib, cel and hp) (1982)
Medium (pf, vib, d-b, sax and cmb) (1974)
Muchy (5 d-b) (1977)
Platonic music (pf, org, vln, cel and perc) (1974)
Dream (str qrt) (1979)
Na mlecznej drodze (str qrt) (1980)
Do swiatla (hn, vln and hp) (1975)
S.O.S. (fl, sax and vln) (1978)
Solitude (fl, d-b and perc) (1980)
Rytm swiatel i cieni (org and timp) (1967)
Deus meus (org) (1980)
Lokomotywa (perc) (1976)
Repetition (clav) (1979)
Rifflettere (fl) (1967)
Tryptyk perkusyjny (perc) (1975)

PIANO

Sonatina (1965)
Swiat dziecka (1980-1983)
Variations (1964)

VOCAL

A ave, reciter (S, m-ch and cham orch) (1970) (prize, Young Polish Composers' competition)
Contrary music (m-ch and orch) (1977)
Genetrix (S and str orch) (1974)
Cisza i ciemnosc (mix-ch) (1984)
Witaj jasnosci (m-ch) (1978)
Fortepian (S, mar and bells) (1968)
Four songs for children (1980)
Pokolenie (S, trp, d-b and cmb) (1969)
Skrzypce (S, hpcd and tam) (1968)
Two songs for children (1981)
Wiecznosc (S and perc) (1966)

SACRED

Hail to the Light (m-ch a-cap) (1978)
Three songs (vce and pf) (1981)

BALLET

Krolewna Sniezka (1976)

Publications

The musical life in Pomerania in the years 1815-1820. Gdansk.
Ref. composer

ZALLMAN, Arlene

American professor and composer. b. Philadelphia, PA, September 9, 1934. She studied at the Philadelphia Conservatory of Music, the Juilliard School of Music, where she obtained a diploma, the Luigi Cherubini Conservatorio and the University of Pennsylvania where she graduated with her M.A. She studied composition under Vincent Persichetti and Luigi Dallapiccola. She is currently associate professor of theory and composition and chairlady of the music department at the Wellesley College.

Compositions

ORCHESTRA

Focus (cham orch) (1967)

CHAMBER

Le malade imaginaire (vlc, pf and fl; also vce and insts) (1974)
Variations (vln, cl and pf) (1977)
Analogy (fl) (1973)
Five pieces (cl) (1961)
Serenade (vlc) (1979)
Tramonto (fl) (1968)

PIANO

Preludes (1978)
Racconto (1965)
Temples at Paestum (1962)
Toccata (1978)

VOCAL
> The locust tree in flower (mix-ch) (1969)
> Kyrie (mix-ch) (1966)
> Ballata (T and pf) (1968)
> The Greek anthology (speaker and pf) (1965)
> Per organo di Barberia (S and vlc) (1976)
> Songs from Quasimodo (S, a-fl, vlc and pf) (1976) (1st prize, National Composers' competition, 1982)
> Sonnet (S and pf) (1958) (prize, Freschl award for vocal composition)
> Two sonnets (Shakespeare) (Bar, hn and pf) (1979)
> Willow poem (Bar, cl, hn, vla and gtr) (1978)
> Winter (S and pf) (1972)

Ref. composer, 622

ZAMOYSKA, Countess Gizycka. See GIZYCKA-ZAMOYSKA, Ludmilla

ZAMOYSKA, Maria

Polish singer and composer. b. Paris, May 15, 1860. She studied singing under Della Ledia and Pauline Viardot-Garcia (q.v.) in Paris.

Compositions
VOCAL
> Bory litewskie
> Sa chwile w zyciu
> Slonko

SACRED
> Agnus Dei
> Ave Maria
> Maria Mater

Bibliography
Loza, S. *Czy wiesz, kto to jest?* Warsaw, 1938.
Ref. 35, 118, 128

ZAMOYSKA (Zamoyska Czartoryska), Zofia, Princess

Polish singer and composer. b. 1779; d. Florence, Italy, 1837. She was president of the Musical Society of Amateur and Professional Musicians in Warsaw in 1815, which later became the Warsaw Conservatory.

Compositions
VOCAL
> Do zulemy (S. Okraszewski) (vce and pf) (Warsaw, 1817)
> Songs about her illustrious ancestor, Jan Zamoyski (in Niemczewicz's *Spiewy historyczne*, Warsaw, 1816)

Bibliography
Niemczewicz, J.U. *Zofia Zamoyska*. Paris, 1837.
Ref. 35, 118, 128, 276

ZAMOYSKA CZARTORYSKA, Zofia, Princess. See ZAMOYSKA, Zofia

ZAMPARELLI, Dionisia

18th-century Italian composer. b. Naples.

Compositions
OPERA
> Artaserse, tragedy in 3 acts (P. Metastasio) (Livorno, 1731)
> Roma liberata dalla Signoria dei Re, tragedy in 3 acts (G.B. Montecatini) (Lucca, 1760)
> Il Teuzzone, tragedy in 3 acts (A. Zeno) (Livorno, 1753)
> La Zoé, tragedy in 3 acts (F. Silvestri) (Livorno, 1746)

Ref. 108

ZAMPIERI, Elizabetta

18th-century Italian pianist, teacher and composer. b. Venice. She taught the piano at the Philharmonic Institute in 1815.

Compositions
PIANO
> Sonata (Ricordi)
> Tema variata (Ricordi)
> Variazioni (Ricordi)

Ref. 105, 297

ZANARDI, Patricia

20th-century composer.

Composition
ELECTRONIC
> Mandala (1981)

Ref. 62

ZANETTOVICH Daniele

20th-century Italian composer. b. 1950.

Composition
CHAMBER
> Invenzione sopra un tritono (strs) (1976)

Ref. R. Dearling (Spaulding, UK)

ZANTEN, Cornelia van

Dutch singer, lecturer and composer. b. Dordrecht, August 2, 1855. She studied singing in Holland before attending the Cologne Conservatory. She studied under Geul, Karl Schneider and Francesco Lamperti in Milan and made her debut in Turin as Leonora in *Favorita*. She performed in Germany, Russia, the United States and finally her own country. She was a member of the National Opera Company in America from 1886 to 1887 and began teaching at the Conservatory in Amsterdam in 1895. She retired from the stage in 1903 to teach singing in Berlin. She composed songs in Dutch and German and published *The Way to the Art of Singing* in 1903.
Ref. 105, 347, 433

ZAPATER, Rosaria

Spanish pianist, poetess, singer, teacher and composer. b. 1840. Her libretto for Aguirre's opera *Gli amanti di Tervele* was considered one of the best ever written. She composed songs and wrote books for the teaching of the piano and singing.
Ref. 226, 276

ZARANEK, Stefania Anatolyevna

Soviet pianist, artistic director, lecturer and composer. b. Kotelnich, near Kirov, September 23, 1904; d. Leningrad, January 17, 1972. She studied the piano under S. Savshinsky and composition under M. Steinberg at the Leningrad Conservatory, graduating in 1926. From 1926 to 1936 she taught the piano at the Conservatory and the Worker's High School. From 1942 to 1944 she was artistic director of the Philharmonia in Gorky.

Compositions
ORCHESTRA
> Piano concerto (1930)
> Ballad of the Ukraine, triptych of symphonic portraits to commemorate the 300th anniversary of the re-inclusion of the Ukraine in Russia (1954)
> Dance suite (1935)
> Kartini duma pro Ukrainu

CHAMBER
> Sonata (pf) (1926)

VOCAL
> Fizkulturnaya (L. Rakovsky) (1934)
> Four song-dances (M. Shiffman): Polonaise; Mazurka; Krakoviak; Gopak (1955)
> Iz dnevnika shkolnitsy, song cycle (E. Aplaksina and A. Churkin) (1948)
> Pesnya o narodnom Kitaye (I. Lukovski) (1950)
> Pesnya o Vietname (I. Lukovski) (1950)
> U Ryazanskikh prichalov (L. Khaustov) (1950)
> Za mir i svobody, song cycle (B. Rayevsky, B. Kezhun and B. Khanchev) (1950)

BALLET
> Chudesnaya fata (1947)
> Golub mira (1951)
> Mechta (1947)

OPERETTA
> Chest mundira (E. Pavlov) (1937)
> Schastlivui put (E. Pavlov) (1939)
> Taina morya (1954)
> Zolotoi fontan (K. Guzynin and A. Maslennikov) (1949)

THEATRE
> Music for over 20 plays

FILM MUSIC
> Kholmogorsk
> Mars
> Other documentary films

Ref. 87, 94, 330

ZARIPOVA, Naila Gatinovna

Soviet teacher and composer. b. Kapraly Armeisk, Tatar Autonomous Republic, October 15, 1932. She studied at the Kazan Music School until 1954 and then became a composition pupil of A.S. Leman at the Kazan Conservatory. She taught music in schools in Kazan after 1964.

Compositions
ORCHESTRA
Suite (1959)
CHAMBER
String quartet (1959)
Melody and dance (vln and pf) (1954)
Piece (fl and pf) (1970)
Quartetino (gtr) (1953)
PIANO
Children's suite (1951)
Little suite (1971)
Sonata (1952)
Sonatina (1952)
VOCAL
Children's songs
Romances (Tatar poets) (vce and pf)
INCIDENTAL MUSIC
Music for radio
Ref. 21

ZAUBITZER, Ida
19th-century German zither player and composer of numerous zither pieces.
Ref. 226, 276, 347

ZAULECK, Gertrud
German composer. b. 1921.
Compositions
CHAMBER
Musik zu Pole Poppenspaeler (fl, pf and Orff insts)
Stueck fuer Altblockfloete and Klavier (a-rec and pf)
PIANO
Theme mit vier Variationen
Zweistimmige Invention
VOCAL
Abraham baute
Ein Fischlein stand im Kuehlen Grund
Vier Kinderlieder
Choral works
Ref. Frau und Musik

ZAVALISHINA, Maria Semyonovna
Soviet lecturer and composer. b. St. Petersburg, December 26, 1903. She studied composition under M. Glinka at the Leningrad Musical College and graduated in 1929. In 1939 she studied composition at the Conservatory of Odessa under P. Molchanov. From 1929 to 1934 she was head of the music department of the Northern Siberian Dramatic Theatre and from 1938 to 1941, an inspector of the Odessa Art Department. From 1941 to 1944 she founded and was headmistress of the Music School in Sovetsk, Kirov region, lectured in theoretical subjects at the Music School in Kirov and composed for the theatre. From 1944 to 1955 she was on the Artistic Committee of the Moldavian SSR and from 1945 to 1951 lectured at the Odessa Conservatory. After 1951 she was a deputy of the artistic director of the Philharmonia. DISCOGRAPHY.
Compositions
ORCHESTRA
Igrushki, children's suite (1939)
CHAMBER
Elegy, romance (hn and pf) (1962)
Happy piece, song (ob and pf) (1964)
Melody (vln and pf) (1938)
Melody, nocturne, little waltz (vlc and pf) (1963)
Romance (vln and pf) (1938)
Three pieces (vln and pf) (1969)
PIANO
Children's album (1952)
Pro zaiku, 6 pieces (1964)
Suite (1937)
Ten children's pieces (1961)
VOCAL
Idut kommunisty (A. Chepurov) (ch a-cap) (1951)
Lipka (P. Voronko) (ch a-cap) (1950)
K portretu (Lermontov) (vce and pf) (1938)
Nad Dniepnom (I. Radchenko) (vce and pf) (1951)
Pyatnadtsat let (Pushkin) (vce and pf) (1937)
S toboiu mysl moya (V. Gete) (vce and pf) (1939)
Skazka (A. Grash) (vce and pf) (1947)
Trostnik (Lermontov) (vce and pf) (1938)
Songs (Soviet poets)
Children's songs
Arrangements of folk songs

OPERA
Esli druzya (1966)
OPERETTA
Kol i druzie, in 3 acts, for children (Muzichna Ukraina, 1978)
INCIDENTAL MUSIC
Music for more than 80 plays and films
MISCELLANEOUS
Toys (Children's suite)
Ref. 21, 87, 563

ZBYSZEWSKA-OLECHNOWSKA, Maria (pseud. P. Ratuld)
Polish authoress and composer. b. Lublin, 1865. She composed piano pieces.
Publications
Nauka i rozrywka. Warsaw.
Ref. 118

ZECHLIN, Ruth (nee Oschatz)
East German harpsichordist, organist, pianist, conductor, professor and composer. b. Grosshartmannsdorf, near Freiberg, June 22, 1926. She studied at the Hochschule fuer Musik in Leipzig, 1943 to 1949, the organ under Straube and Ramin, the piano under Rohden and Fischer and composition under J.N. David. She married the pianist Dieter Zechlin. She taught harmony, counterpoint, composition and the harpsichord at the same academy, 1949 to 1950, and lectured on composition at the Berlin Music Academy, becoming a professor in 1969. In 1962 she won the Goethe prize of the City of Berlin; in 1965 the arts prize of the German Democratic Republic and in 1968 the Hanns Eisler prize. She became a member of the Academy of Arts of the German Democratic Republic in 1970. She performs the music of J.S. Bach and his contemporaries on the harpsichord and the organ and conducts. DISCOGRAPHY.
Compositions
ORCHESTRA
Symphony No. 1 (1965)
Symphony No. 2 (1967)
Symphony No. 3 (1971)
Piano concerto
Organ concerto No. 1 (1974)
Organ concerto No. 2 (1975)
Piano concerto (1974)
Violin concerto (1963)
Theme with five variations (large orch) (1969)
Chamber symphony No. 1 (1967)
Chamber symphony No. 2 (1973)
Concertino (fl and cham orch)
Concertino (ob and cham orch) (1969)
Briefe Emotionen
Handel, variations (cham orch) (1958)
Kristalle, concerto (hpcd and str orch) (1975)
Linear meditations (str orch) (1968)
Metamorphosen (1982)
Musik (1980) (Berliner Festlage, 1981)
Music zu Bach: Epitaph und Polyphonie (1983) (Peters, 1985)
Polyphonic meditations (str orch) (1968)
Prager Orgelkonzert (1980) (Prager Fruehling, 1981)
Reflexionen (str orch) (Peters, 1983)
Sinfonietta fuer Kinder (1969)
Situationen (1980) (Komische Oper, Berlin, 1981)
Terzinen
CHAMBER
Thoughts on a piano piece of Prokofiev (pf and 10 insts) (1967)
Amor und Psyche (hpcd and cham ens) (1966)
Begegnungen (ob, trb, perc, pf, vla, vlc and d-b) (1977)
Stationen (wind qnt and keyboard insts) (1972)
Hommages à PHL (str qnt and perc) (1973)
Aktionen (str qnt) (1978)
String quartets (1959, 1965, 1970)
Two string quartets (1971)
Apollo und Daphne (fl, ob and hpcd) (1980)
Katharsis (ob, vlc and perc) (1981)
Trio (ob, vla and vlc) (1957)
Exercitien (fl and hpcd) (1974)
Sonata (fl and pf)
Sonatine (fl and hpcd) (1955)
Sonatine (vln and hpcd) (1956)
Beschwoerungen (perc) (1980)
Epitaph (hpcd) (1973)
Kontrapunkte (hpcd; also pf) (1970)
Pour la flute = Linien und Register (fl) (1973)
Toccata and Passacaglia (hpcd) (1962)

ORGAN
 Genesis und Evolution
 Orpheus (1975)
 Spektrum (Leipzig: Deutscher Verlag fuer Muzik, 1975)
 Wandlungen (Deutscher Verlag fuer Muzik, 1975)
 Work for the Martin Luther King Festival in East Germany (1983)
PIANO
 Sonatine (1955)
 Suite (1953)
 Variations on Eisler's Einheitsfrontlied (1960)
VOCAL
 Der Himmel senkt sich, oratorio (soli, ch and orch)
 Wenn der Wacholder blueht, oratorio (1960)
 Lidice, cantata (Berlin: Verlag Neue Musik, 1958)
 Canzoni alla notte, after Quasimodo (B and orch) (Leipzig: Peters, 1974)
 Das Hohelied (T and orch) (1979) (Leipzig: Gewandhaus, 1980)
 Ode an die Luft (Neruda) (m-S and orch) (1962)
 Die Wolken (S and orch)
 Aphorismen ueber die Liebe (ch a-cap) (1972)
 Apparition (Mallarme) (w-ch and fl) (1965)
 Five songs by Brecht (cham ch) (1960)
 Zauberlehrling (Goethe) (Bar, 4-part boy's ch and pf) (1981)
 An Aphrodite (3 vces)
 Keunergeschichten (Brecht) (speaker and cham ens) (1966)
 Lieder (Brecht) (1956)
 Sieben Borchert Lieder (vce and pf) (1964)
 Three Love Songs from Carmina Burana (vce and hpcd or pf) (1968)
OPERA
 Reineke Fuchs (1962)
THEATRE
 Egmont (Goethe) (1974)
Ref. composer, 70, 79, 94, 193, 206, 280, 465, 518, 563, 622

ZECKWER, Camille
20th-century American composer. She composed piano pieces.
Ref. 347

ZEGERS, Isidora (nee Zegers Y Montenegro)
Chilean guitarist, harpist, pianist, singer and composer of Flemish origin. b. Madrid, January 1, 1803; d. Chile, July 17, 1869. She studied voice under Massimino and composition under Paer. She also studied the piano, the guitar and the harp. Her home was the cultural gathering center of Chilean society and she had one of the best private music libraries in Latin America, later donated to the National Conservatory in Santiago. With C. Drewtcke she co-founded the Sociedade Filarmonica and brought about the foundation of the first conservatory in Chile from 1849 to 1850 and was later president of the Academia Superior de Musica, 1852. With J. Zapiola she formed the Semanario Musical in the same year and founded a Sociedad Filarmonica in Copiaco in 1862, singing at its inauguration. Many of her compositions were lost.
Compositions
PIANO
 La camille
 La flore
 Over a dozen pieces in the style of Mercedes 'Contradanzas'
VOCAL
 Pieces (French and one Spanish text) (vce and pf) (1822)
Ref. 90

ZEINER, Marliese
B. 1944.
Compositions
VOCAL
 Fuenf Stuecke (chil-ch) (1980)
Ref. Otto Harrassowitz (Weisbaden)

ZELIKOVSKAYA, Fania Mordukhovna
Soviet pianist and composer. b. Kiev, October 12, 1912. She studied composition under M.A. Gozenpud at the Kiev Conservatory, graduating in 1939. After 1942 she was a pianist at the V.I. Military Academy in the Bashkir Autonomous Republic. She moved to Moscow in 1944.
Compositions
CHAMBER
 Piano trio (1934)
 Barcarolle (vlc and pf) (1935)
 Mazurka (vlc and pf) (1935)

PIANO
 Sonata (1939)
 Theme and variations (1936)
VOCAL
 Romances (T. Shevchenko)
 Songs
 Arrangements of Ukrainian folk songs
Ref. 21

ZELINSKA, Lydia
20th-century composer. She won a prize in a competition for orchestral work in Paris in 1983.
Ref. Frau und Musik

ZENTA, Hermann. See HOLMES, Augusta Mary Anne

ZENTNER, Clary
19th-century Italian composer.
Compositions
PIANO
 Divertissement, op. 6
 Elegie harmonique, op. 7
 Fantaisie brillant, op. 9
 Fantaisie in C
 Fantaisie sur Semiramide, op. 5
 Recreation ou passe temps, op. 14
 Variations, op. 15
 Other pieces
Ref. 226, 260, 276, 347

ZERNICKOW, Elise
19th-century German composer.
Compositions
PIANO
 Pieces incl. (Portins):
 Als die Linden bluehten
 Dein eigen
 Froehliches Wiedersehen
 Im leichten Kahn
 Lenzesgruss
 Maedchentraeume
 Mein alles
 Neckteufelchen
 Pfingstgruss
 Seerosen
 So lieb
 Sommerabend
 Stille Traeume
 Waldieschen
 Wiesenbaechlein
Ref. 297

ZERR, Anna
German composer. b. 1822; d. 1881.
Composition
OPERA
 Astrifiammante
Ref. 307

ZEUTA, Hermann. See HOLMES, Augusta Mary Anne

ZHUBANOVA, Gaziza Akhmetovna
Soviet composer. Zhana-Turmys, Kazakhstan, December 2, 1928. She was the daughter of Akhmet Zhubanov, the first Kazakh composer to embrace Western music. She was a pupil at the Gnessin Music School in Moscow before studying composition under Y. Shaporin at the Moscow Conservatory. She graduated in 1954 and continued her studies under the same teacher. She was chairlady of the Kazakh Composers' Union, Alma-Ata. Her music made use of rhythmic and melodic features of Kazakh classical music. DISCOGRAPHY.

Compositions
ORCHESTRA
Zhiger, symphony (1971)
Violin concerto (1958)
Aksak-Kulan, symphonic poem (1954)
Utro Temirtau, symphonic poem (1964)
Festive overture
Heroic poem (1972)
CHAMBER
Lyrical poem (str qrt) (1952)
String Quartet
Elegy (vln and pf) (1950)
Melody (vln and pf) (1950)
Poem (vlc and pf) (1967)
Two pieces (trp and pf) (1968)
Variations (vln and pf) (1951)
Three preludes (pf) (1950)
VOCAL
Lenin, oratorio (soloists, ch and orch) (1969)
Zarya nad stepiyu, oratorio (1960)
Kantata o Partii (1970)
Nights beneath the Urals, cantata in 6 parts (K. Yergaliyev) (1957)
Pesnaya radosti, cantata (Dzhamvili) (1953)
Skaz o Mukhtari Avezov, cantata (1963)
Aria (S and orch) (1959)
Pesnaya o Partii (D. Abilev) (soloists, ch and orch) (1954)
Songs to the night (Bar and orch) (1976)
Kazakh song of Lenin (A. Tazhibayev) (soloists and ch) (1957)
Kazakh melodies (ch) (1953)
Solitary oak tree (ch a-cap)
Four Kazakh folk songs (vce and pf) (1952)
Korean, Mongolian and Chinese folk songs (vce and pf) (1955)
Pesnaya o Tselinye (K. Ailibyekov)
Twelve songs (Shakenov and Tazhibayev)
Two children's songs (Shakenov)
Young Pioneer song (Z. Sain) (1957)
BALLET
Hiroshima, Alma-Ata (1966)
Legenda O Beloi Ptitsa, on a Kazakh legend (1965)
Tragedy in Kara-kum (1972)
OPERA
Kurmangazy (1971)
Tungi-Saryn, in 1 act (M. Auezov) (1955)
Yenlik and Kebek, in 3 acts (S. Zhienbayev) (1972)
THEATRE
On the Banks of the Irtysh (S. Khusainov) (1957)
Bibliography
Muhambetova, Asija. *A Genuine Tradition Grows and Develops.*
Ref. Rilm Abstracts X11 1978, 17, 21, 70, 87, 94, 109, 223, 277, 280, 330, 420, 563, 571

ZHUBINSKAYA, Valentina Yanovna
Soviet pianist, concertmistress, lecturer and composer. b. Kharkov, May 17, 1926. She was concertmistress at the Kharkov State Theatre until 1948 while studying the piano under M. Pilstrom and composition under V. Barabashov at the Kharkov Conservatory. She graduated with distinction in 1949 and did postgraduate studies in Moscow. She became a lecturer on the piano at the Gnessin School in Moscow in 1961.
Compositions
ORCHESTRA
Piano concerto (1950)
CHAMBER
Romance and serenade (vln and pf) (1946)
PIANO
Children's album, 12 pieces (1946)
Collection of children's pieces (1960)
Eight pieces (1960)
Fifteen pieces (1969)
Four etudes (1946)
Lullaby and humoresque (1946)
Russian variations (1963)
Sonata (1948)
Song and waltz (1946)
Three improvisations (1963)
Waltz (1948)
VOCAL
Dobruy khleb, cycle (ch) (1972)
Children's songs (1971)
Cycle of works by Bulgarian poets (1962)
Molodezhnaya (Malykhin) (vce and pf) (1968)
Pesnya o Taimyre (M. Arons) (vce and pf) (1947)
Razvernis garmonika (A. Prokofiev) (vce and pf) (1947)
Rodina (D. Althausen) (vce and pf) (1948)
Two Ukrainian folk songs (ch a-cap) (1948)
Vremena goda, cycle for children (vce and pf) (1959)
Ref. 21, 87

ZHVANETSKAYA, Inna Abramovna
Soviet pianist, lecturer and composer. b. Vinnitsa, January 20, 1937. In 1964 she graduated from the Gnessin School in Moscow, where she studied composition under N.I. Peiko. She taught the piano until 1965 when she became a lecturer in score-reading and instrumentation at the Gnessin School.
Compositions
ORCHESTRA
Concerto (d-b and orch; also d-b and pf)
Overture (1963)
Suite (str orch) (1965)
CHAMBER
Six pieces (wind qnt) (1969)
String quartet (1962)
Burlesque (vln and pf) (1959)
Sonata (vln and pf) (Sovietski Kompozitor, 1976)
PIANO
Partita (1966)
Polyphonic fantasy (1962)
Toccata (1961)
Variations on a theme of Brahms (1958)
VOCAL
Zemlya! Tvoye tvorenye-cholovek (Soviet poets) (ch and orch) (1972)
Cycle (A. Izaakian) (vce and pf) (1960)
Romances (V. Bryusov and other poets)
Yanvarskie stroki (S. Smirnov) (vce and pf) (1968)
Songs
Ref. 21, 277

ZIBEROVA, Zinaida Petrovna
Soviet pianist, conductor and composer. b. Darmstadt, Germany, December 1, 1909. After 1925 she lived in Rostov-on-the-Don. In 1928 she graduated from the music school there, where she studied the piano under A. Alper. In 1931 she studied composition under N. Heifetz, I. Gottweiter and E. Broomberg. From 1925 to 1929 she worked as a pianist in clubs; from 1929 to 1941 she was conductor and artistic director of amateur activities in Rostov. She was active in local government.
Compositions
ORCHESTRA
Rodnoi gorod, march (wind orch) (1941)
Tam gole shli boi, symphonic poem (1950)
CHAMBER
Nocturne (vce and pf) (1946)
Plyasovaya (xy and pf) (1946)
PIANO
Prelude (2 pf) (1956)
Vdali ot rodiny
Vozvrashenie (1955)
VOCAL
Osvobozhdennomu gorodu (E. Shirman) (vce and orch) (1941)
Zhdi menya (K. Simonov) (vce and orch) (1941)
Don (A. Pushkin) (ch and pf) (1940)
Eleven songs (V. Shak) (1948-1953)
Lesnaya tropa, cycle of 12 songs (A. Olenicha-Gneneko) (1952)
Marsh studentov (E. Zinovev) (1949)
Pesnaya o Lenine (D. Althausen) (1952)
Over 120 other songs
Arrangements of folk songs
BALLET
Buratino (1959)
OPERETTA
Kot v sapogakh
THEATRE
Approx 150 pieces for theatre in Rostov, incl.:
Aul Gidzhe (Shestakov) (1930)
Ignoramus (D. Fonvizin) (1933)
The Misanthrope (Moliere) (1934)
William Tell (Schiller) (1935)
Ref. 14, 21, 87

ZIEGLER, Natalia Sophie von
German concert pianist, lecturer and composer. b. Dorpat (now Tartu), Estonia, December 7, 1865. She studied at the Rollfuss Music Academy in Dresden under Hermann Scholtz, Felix Draeseke and Bernhard Schneider. She studied theory under Alexander Wolf, the piano under Bertrand Roth and music history under Eugene Schmitz. She taught at the same academy after 1889 and toured in Germany on concert.
Compositions
CHAMBER
Sonata, op. 6 (vln and pf) (1927)
PIANO
Sonata, op. 7 (1929)
Three pieces, op. 3
Other pieces

VOCAL
Weihnachtslied
Other songs
Ref. 105, 111, 226

ZIELINSKA, Lidia
Polish violinist, lecturer and composer. b. Poznan, October 9, 1953. She studied at the State Higher School of Music in Poznan and in 1978 obtained her M.A. From 1972 to 1975 she played the violin in the State Philharmonia in Poznan and in the Jeunesses Musicales Chamber Orchestra. She lectured on electronic music at the State Higher School of Music, Poznan, from 1983.
Compositions
ORCHESTRA
Paradies artificiels (fl, bsn, vln, vlc and orch) (1980)
Violin concerto (1979) (prize, Jeunesses Musicales, Belgrade, 1979)
Adieu Mr. Toorop (1983)
Epitafium (1981)
Polyethylene diptych (1979)
CHAMBER
De quattris, church music (fl, cl, t-sax, b-sax, 2 vln, vla, vlc, perc and 4 xy) (1983)
Stabile, mobili e passacaglia (7 perf) (1979)
Two dances (strs) (1981)
Litany (str qrt)
Passacaglia (a-fl, vla and 2 insts)
Six pieces (str qrt) (1979)
Traite (ob, vlc, vln and vla) (1982)
Minuten-sonate (tba ad lib) (1981)
Sonatina (vln) (1979)
Violin solo (1977)
VOCAL
Cascando (after Beckett) (vce and 2 mix-ch) (1983)
Solfatara (mix-ch) (1981) (Polish choir music contest, Legnica, 1981)
THEATRE
Play, children's instrumental theatre (1977)
Lady Koch, tragic farce in one act (solo vces, vocal ens, inst ens and tapes) (1981)
ELECTRONIC
Prelude and fugue (solo, fl or a-sax and quad tape) (1981)
MULTIMEDIA
En, Joe (mime and tape of vce and orch) (1978)
Ref. composer, Polish Music 4/79

ZIERITZ, Grete von. See VON ZIERITZ, Grete

ZIFFER, Fran
20th-century American composer of incidental music.
Ref. 40, 347

ZIFFRIN, Marilyn Jane
American professor and composer. b. Moline, IL, August 7, 1926. She earned a B.M. from the University of Wisconsin (Madison), an M.A. from Columbia University Teacher's College and a Ph.D. from the University of Chicago. She studied composition privately under Karl Ahrendt and Alexander Tcherepnin. From 1961 to 1966 she was assistant professor at Northeastern Illinois State College. She was associate professor of music at New England College in Henniker, NH, until 1982 when she became a composition teacher at St. Paul's School, Concord. She was the recipient of many awards and prizes including two second prizes, International Society for Contemporary Music, Chicago Chapter contest, 1955 and 1964; special mention in the Delius Composition Competition, 1971; and a Delius award, 1972. She was awarded the Alfred Noyes scholarship, a Knapp scholarship at the University of Wisconsin and a grant-in-aid for a biography of Carl Ruggles from the American Council of Learned Societies, 1974. She received ASCAP grants in 1981, 1982 and 1983 and in 1961, 1963, 1971, 1977 and 1980 she was resident fellow at the MacDowell Colony in Peterborough, NH. DISCOGRAPHY.
Compositions
ORCHESTRA
Orchestra piece No. 1 (1977)
Prelude and fugue (sym orch) (1953)
A small suite (str orch) (1963)
Waltz (1955, rev 1957)
BAND
Overture for concert band (1958)

CHAMBER
Thirteen for chamber ensemble (1969)
Concerto for viola and woodwind quintet
Make a joyful noise (rec qnt) (1966)
Quintet for oboe and string quartet (1976)
String quartet (1970)
Trio (vln, vlc and pf) (1975)
For Angie and Jim, mvts (b-Flat cl and perc) (1972)
In the beginning (perc and pf) (1968)
The little Prince, suite (cl and bsn) (1953)
Sonata (org and vln)
Sono (vlc and pf)
Four pieces for tuba (1973)
Rhapsody (gtr) (1958)
Toccata and fugue (org) (1956)
PIANO
Suite, op. 4 (1955)
Theme and variations (1949)
VOCAL
Drinking song and dance from Captain Kidd (B, ch, 2 gtr, S-rec and perc ens) (1971)
Haiku, song cycle (S, vla and hpcd) (1971)
Three songs (w-vces) (1957)
Trio (S, xy and tba) (1973) (comm Barton Cummings)
SACRED
Death of Moses, cantata (narr, soloists, mix-ch and orch) (1954)
Prayer (mix-ch) (1966)
Jewish prayer (1950)
OPERA
Captain Kidd (1959)
Publications
Ruggles' Continuous Flight for Linear Compositions.
Interesting Lies and Curious Truths About Carl Ruggles. College Music Society Symposium.
Carl Ruggles: Music Critic, the American Music Teacher. Contributions to various magazines and music publications including Grove's *Dictionary of Music and Musicians.*
Ref. composer, 40, 77, 94, 137, 142, 228, 280, 347, 468, 474, 563, 569, 594, 622, 625

ZILIOTTO, Elisa
Italian musician and composer. b. 1825.
Compositions
OPERA
La Cena Magica (Venice, 1855)
MISCELLANEOUS
La gondola veneziana a Fontainebleau (Ricordi)
Ref. 26, 297, 307

ZIMMER, Nellie
20th-century American publisher and composer. She composed chamber music for the Irish harp.
Ref. 344

ZIMMERMAN, Phyllis
20th-century American composer.
Compositions
SACRED
Alleluia (ch)
An Easter carol (1967)
Hodie Christus natus est (1976)
Ref. 142, 147

ZIMMERMANN, Agnes Marie Jacobina
German pianist, teacher and composer. b. Cologne, July 5, 1847; d. London, November 14, 1925. She left Germany when young and at nine entered the London Royal Academy of Music to study the piano and composition under Cipriani Potter, Charles Steggal, Ernst Pauer and George Macfarren. She won the King's scholarship in 1860 and 1862 and received two silver medals. In the following years she appeared in concerts in Leipzig, Hanover and Cologne, often performing her own compositions. In the United Kingdom she was one of the most frequently engaged artists at the Halle concerts, in Edinburgh, Glasgow and London, where she also taught at the Royal Academy.
Compositions
CHAMBER
Suite in D-Minor, op. 19 (vln, vlc and pf) (Novello)
Sonata in G-Minor, op. 17 (vlc and pf) (Schott, 1872)
Three sonatas, ops. 16, 21 and 23 (vln and pf) (Novello, 1871)

PIANO
Barcarolle, op. 8 (Novello)
Bolero, op. 9 (Novello)
Bourree
Caprice, Auf dem Wasser, scherzo
Gavotte in D, op. 14 (Novello)
Gavotte in E-Minor, op. 20 (Novello)
Kanon, Sarabande und Gigue (Breitkopf)
March in D-Minor
Mazurka, op. 11 (Novello)
Presto alla tarantella, op. 15
Suite: Prelude; Mazurka; Scherzo; March, op. 22 (Novello)
Two pieces: Sunshine; Twilight (Novello)
VOCAL
Andromeda et Perseus (vce and orch)
Come, follow me (mix-ch) (Novello)
Flowers (mix-ch) (Novello)
Gone forever (mix-ch) (Novello)
Good morrow (mix-ch) (Novello)
Good night (mix-ch) (Novello)
Lordly gallants (mix-ch) (Novello)
To daffodils (mix-ch)
True love (w-ch) (Novello)
Songs incl.:
Adieu (vce and pf) (Chappell)
After war (Novello)
Blow, blow, thou winter wind (Novello)
Blow, breezes, blow (Chappell)
Der Verbannte (Novello)
Ephemeral (Only a year ago, love) (Novello)
Fairy song (Novello)
Far from home (Chappell)
Lebewohl (Novello)
Love, I may not tarry here (Novello)
My heart is sair for somebody (Novello)
O! That we two were maying (Novello)
Ringlet-your ringlets-O ringlet (Novello)
Stars are with the voyager (Novello)
Sweetly glows the early morn (Novello)
SACRED
Childrens' prayer (mix-ch) (Novello)
Hymn of trust (mix-ch) (Novello)
ARRANGEMENTS
Works by Bach (vlc)
Works by Schumann, Beethoven, Corelli, Handel (pf)
Ref. 8, 26, 70, 74, 100, 102, 132, 192, 226, 297, 347, 369, 465

ZIMMERMANN, Margrit
Swiss pianist, conductor, teacher and composer. b. Berne, August 7, 1927. She began her music studies under Jeanne Bovet and Walter Furrer in Berne and graduated with a diploma in the piano from the Ecole Normale de Musique in Paris where she also studied composition under Arthur Honegger. At the Lausanne Conservatory she studied under Denise Bidal and Alfred Cortot. She then concentrated on conducting and attended courses with I. Markevitch in Monte Carlo and Hans Swarowski and Aurelio Maggioni in Ossiach. She attended the Verdi Conservatory in Milan where she studied opera conducting under Umberto Cattini and graduated with a diploma in composition in 1978. She taught music in Berne and from 1973 conducted an orchestra.
Compositions
ORCHESTRA
Ghasel, symphony-ballet (1981)
Introduzione e allegro (large sym orch) (1979)
CHAMBER
Musica per nove archi (1977)
Per sei (fl, vln, vla, d-b, timp and pf) (1980)
Aus Black-Box (ob, cl, hn and bsn) (1982)
String quartet (comm Woman and Art, Lucerne)
String quartet, op. 7, no. 1 (1979)
String quartet, no. 2 (1980)
String quartet, op. 16, no. 3 (1981)
Duetto (fl and gtr)
Duetto (vlc and gtr) (1982)
Musica (vlc and pf) (1980)
Senza parole (pf and gtr)
Sonata (fl and pf)
Suite for cello and piano
Suoni (vln and pf) (1978)
Aus Pezzi brevi (gtr)
Suite for solo violin, op. 33
PIANO
Blanc et noir, 10 etudes
Six études de l'oeuvre, op. 36
Sonata, op. 27

VOCAL
Capriccio (vce and pf) (1982)
Drei Lieder (Heinz Peyer) (1978)
Drei Sonetten von Petrarca, op. 35 (vce, fl and gtr)
Plis, op. 37 (vce and insts)
Der Politiker (H. Peyer) (vce, d-b and pf) (1978)
Spiegelungen des Tages, concertino (T and ens)
BALLET
Ghasel (1981)
Jason und Medeia (lg orch) (1982)
Ref. composer, 651

ZINGLER-SCHREINER, Martha
American teacher and composer. b. February 11, 1869. From 1911 to 1916 she taught music in Frankfurt, Germany. She composed piano pieces.
Ref. 70

ZIPRICK, Marjorie Jean (nee Affeldt)
American organist, pianist, lecturer and composer. b. Lansing, MI, January 1, 1915. At 13 she won the Music Teachers' Association of Michigan piano competition. She gained a B.Mus. (1937) and an M.Mus. (1966) from the Michigan State University, Lansing and from 1966 to 1970 did further graduate studies at the University of California, Riverside. Her piano teachers included Mabel Whitney, Professor Osborne, Mrs. Moon Hallett, Amparo Iturbi and Bendetson Netzorg. She attended master piano classes. Her organ teachers included Professor Harold Hannum, Dr. Ernest Douglas and Raymond Boese and she attended master classes for the organ. She studied trio ensemble performance under the cellist Alexander Schuster. Her teaching career started in 1936 and included private teaching and lecturing at Wilde Conservatory, Lansing, San Diego Academy and Loma Linda University. From 1947 to 1949 she was the organist at White Memorial Church, Loma Linda University and 1957 to 1979 substituted as the organist in various churches. PHOTOGRAPH.
Compositions
ORGAN
Dorian
Thoughts
Three part canon
PIANO
Aeolian fugue
Chromatic fugue
Contemporary fugue
Fugue
Three voice fugue
VOCAL
Song of the Chaparral (comm as theme song by Chaparral poets)
SACRED
All sixty six
Benedictus
Chorale and fugue-Ach Gott and Herr, wie gross and schwer
Christus, der ist mein Leben
Evening hymn
He will always see you through
Lamentations
The Lord is my light
Merry Christmas
So little time
Thou wilt keep Him in perfect peace
Ref. composer, 643

ZITHER OF THE HOLY SPIRIT. See HILDEGARD, Saint

ZITTELMANN, Helene
Late 19th-century German composer. She composed piano pieces and songs.
Ref. 226, 276

ZIVKOVIC, Mirjana
Yugoslav (Serbian) pianist, professor and composer. b. Split, May 3, 1935. She attended the Josip Slavenski Secondary Music School in Belgrade, studying the piano under Alisa Besevic and proceeded to the Music Academy of Belgrade to study composition under Stanoljo Rajicic and to pursue postgraduate studies. Her graduation composition Sinfonia polifonica won the Stevan Hristic prize and the prize of the Belgrade Radio Television. From 1967 to 1968 she studied in France under Olivier Messiaen

and Nadia Boulanger (q.v.). Her composition *Basma* won the first prize of the Fontainebleau Conservatory. She is a professor of harmony, counterpoint and composition at the Josip Slavenski Music School. PHOTOGRAPH.

Compositions

ORCHESTRA
   Koncertante metamorfoze (pf and orch) (1974)
   Simfonijsi torzo (1967)
   Sinfonia polifonica (1964)
CHAMBER
   Paean (fl, vln, cl, bsn and pf) (1967)
   Prelude and passacaglia (wind qnt)
   Two brass quintets (1962)
   Two movements (wind qnt)
   Miniatures, for children (vln and pf) (1972)
   Studies I, II and III (vlc and pf) (1965, 1969, 1974)
   Variations (vln and pf) (1961)
   Zapis (vln and pf) (1975)
   Dodecaphonic passacaglia (vln) (1965)
PIANO
   Little suite (1959)
   Rondo (1960)
   Scherzo (1960)
   Two impressionistic pieces (1958)
   Two preludes (1968)
VOCAL
   O zivotu i smrti, cantata (solos, mix-ch and orch) (1971)
   Basma, incantation (m-S and 4 timp) (1968)
   The anticipation of autumn on the city pavement (vce and pf) (1960)
   Cetiri pohvale, song cycle (1975)
   Igracka vjetrova (vce and pf) (1959)
   Tuzaljka (vce, fl, vlc and pf) (1958)
   Two songs on the text of B. Brecht (vce and pf) (1973)
THEATRE
   Park (Margarette Dura) (1965)

Publications
   Analytical Study of Josip Slavenski's Musical Language.
   Ref. composer, 109, 145, 206, 280, 418

ZOECKLER, Dorothy Ackerman
   American organist, authoress, choral conductor and composer. b. Wheeling, WV, August 19, 1915. She was educated at Cincinnati Conservatory and studied under Marcian Thalberg, Robert Goldsand and Parvin Titus. She was the organist and choir director at St. Matthew's Episcopal Church.

Compositions

SACRED
   God speaks to me
   Too good not to be true
   When I kneel down to pray
MISCELLANEOUS
   The Cabanera
   Fiesta
   Latinera
TEACHING PIECES
   Works for the piano
   Ref. 39

ZORKA. See KOZINOVIC, Luiza

ZRELC, Celeste
   20th-century Yugoslav composer of Rijeka.
   Ref. 416

ZSCHOCK, Marie von
   German composer. b. Berlin, 1819. She entered the Berlin Sing-Akademie at the age of 12 to study singing under Stumer and composition under Grell. Her oratorio was performed at her parents' home.

Composition

SACRED
   Nebukadnezar, 2 part oratorio (1840)
   Ref. 121

ZUBANOVA, Gaziza. See ZHUBANOVA, Gaziza

ZUBELDIA, Emiliana de
   Spanish pianist, conductor, lecturer and composer. b. Vasconia, September 5, 1948. She studied music in Spain and later in Paris at the Schola Cantorum, the piano under Blanche Selva, composition under Vincent d'Indy, Gedalge and others and took courses in conducting. She was a pupil of and worked with Augusto Novaro, whose theories she has diffused by means of her own works. She concert-toured Europe and the United States and formed the choir of the University of Hermosillo, with which she toured Mexico and border U.S. towns. She lives in Mexico, has lectured in Mexican universities and is a teacher in the music department of the University of Hermosillo. DISCOGRAPHY.

Compositions

ORCHESTRA
   Four symphonies
   Concierto inolvidable
CHAMBER
   Two string quartets
   Sonata (vla and pf)
PIANO
   Bitonal danza de titeres
   Cinco estudios para piano (Sophie Cheiner)
   Once tientos (Ricordi)
   Sonata
VOCAL
   Cinco canciones (R. Schweinfurth)
   Songs, poems (Guillen, G. Lorca, Lopes Velarde and others)
   Choral Arrangements
SACRED
   Misa de la Asuncion, mass (mix-ch)
   Ref. Esperanza Pulido (Mexico City), 563, 622

ZUCKERMANN, Augusta. See MANA-ZUCCA

ZUMSTEEG, Emilie
   German pianist, choral conductor, singer, teacher and composer. b. Stuttgart, December 9, 1796; d. Stuttgart, August 1, 1857. She was the youngest daughter of Johann Rudolf Zumsteeg, composer and concertmaster of the Wurttemberg ducal court. She studied the piano and voice and appeared with considerable success at the Stuttgart Museum Concerts at a very young age. She later acquired a reputation as a distinguished teacher and choir director.

Compositions

ORCHESTRA
   Overture to Die Geister Insel
PIANO
   Three polonaises
VOCAL
   Three and four part choral works incl.: Grablied aus der Sonnenjungfrau (Schott); Lied an Emma von Rudersdorf (Schott); Sizilianisches Schiffergebet (Schott); Abschied von der Schweiz; Heimat; Weine nicht; Sangers Trost, op. 7
   Der Abend (vce and pf) (Simrock)
   Des Kaufmanns Liebeswerben (vce and pf) (Simrock)
   Gut' Nacht, fahr' wohl, op. 5 (vce and pf)
   Mitternacht-Scheide nur nicht, op. 6 (vce and pf)
   Ulrichs Lied aus Hauffs Liechtenstein (vce and pf) (Augener)
   Other songs
   Ref. 26, 103, 226, 335, 347, 433, 653

ZUZAK, Doris
   20th-century American composer who lived in Louisiana.

Compositions

PIANO
   Valse romantique
   Other pieces
VOCAL
   In all my dreams
   In memoriam
   Ref. 347, 448

ZWEIG, Esther
   American teacher, ensemble director and composer. b. New York, July 29, 1906. She studied at Hunter College, New York University, University of Vienna and the Jewish Theological Seminary. Her instructors included Walter Damrosch and Kurt Weill. She taught choral music in the Hebrew schools of New York from 1927 to 1937. From 1949 to 1950 she directed the Esther Zweig Ensemble, New York. She received an award from the Jewish Theological Seminary in 1927 and a merit certificate from the University of Vienna.

Compositions
VOCAL

The Conquerors of Canaan, cantata
Songs incl.:
I close my eyes and dream
I sing to you, America
Ref. 142, 347

ZWILICH, Ellen Taaffe

American violinist, lecturer and composer. b. Miami, April 30, 1939. She received her B.M. and M.M. from Florida State University, where she studied under John Boda and Carlisle Floyd. She was the first woman to receive a doctorate in composition from the Juilliard School of Music, 1975. Her major teachers were Elliott Carter and Roger Sessions. She married the violinist Joseph Zwilich. She taught at college for seven years and was a violinist for the American Symphony Orchestra under Leopold Stokowski for seven years. Her works have been performed in concerts in Italy, Switzerland, Holland, Scotland, Hungary and in the United States at various colleges and universities, including the Juilliard School of Music, University of Miami and Hunter College as well as in the Donnell Library, New York Historical Society, Carnegie Recital Hall and Alice Tully Hall. Her works have been performed on the radio in Budapest, New York and Boston. Ellen was chosen to be one of three composers featured on the broadcast entitled *The Young American Composer* in the series entitled *Speaking of American Music*. In 1983 she was awarded the Pulitzer prize for her *Symphony No. 1*. Among other honors awarded to her are the Elizabeth Sprague Coolidge chamber music prize (1974); a gold medal in the International Composition Competition J.B. Viotti (Vercelli, Italy) (1975); the Marion Freschl prize (1971, 1972, and 1975); a Guggenheim fellowship, a National Endowment for the Arts composer fellowship grant (1976); an ASCAP award (1977); a Creative Artists public service fellowship grant (1977); a Martha Baird Rockefeller fund for music grant (1974) and scholarships and fellowships for study at Florida State University, the Rogers and Hammerstein scholarship award from Juilliard School of Music, as well as three prizes from the Florida Composers' League. DISCOGRAPHY. PHOTOGRAPH.

Compositions
ORCHESTRA

Symphony No. 1, in 3 mvts (Pulitzer prize, 1983)
Symphony No. 2, in 3 mvts (1985)
Celebration (comm Indianapolis Symphony Orch)
Chamber symphony (1979)
Prologue and variations (str orch) (1983)
Symposium (1973)

CHAMBER

Double quartet for strings (1984)
Clarino quartet (picc, 2 b-flat trp and Cont-trp) (1976)
Intrada (fl, cl, vln, vlc and pf) (1983)
Divertimento (fl, cl, vln and vlc) (1983)
String quartet (vla, vln, vlc and d-b) (1974)
String trio (1981)
Sonata in three movements for violin and piano (1973, rev 1974)
Fantasy (hpcd) (Merion Music, 1985)
Impromptu (hp) (1974)

VOCAL

Einsame Nacht, song cycle of poems (Hermann Hesse) (B and pf) (1971)
Elisabeth (vce and pf)
Emlekezet (S and pf) (Sandor Petofi)
Erik a gabona (S. Petofi) (S and pf) (1976)
Im Nebel (H. Hesse) (Cont and pf) (1972)
Mueckenschwarm (vce and pf)
Passages (S and cham ens)
Schicksal (vce and pf)
Trompeten (S and pf) (1974)
Ueber die Felder (vce and pf)
Wie sind die Tage schwer (vce and pf)
Wohl lieb ich die finstre Nacht (vce and pf)
Ref. composer, *Time* November 25 1985, 142, 228, 347, 563, 569, 610, 622, 625

ZYBINE, Mme. S.

19th-century French composer.
Compositions
VOCAL

Glyba (vce and pf) (Wasiljew)
Hymne des fleurs (solo and ch) (Gutheil)
I fior di primavera, Italian barcarolle (vce and pf) (Gutheil)
J'aime le soir, waltz (2 vces) (Gutheil)
Jadis fidele: Ministrel (Gutheil)
Lilea (vce and pf) (Wasiljew)
Quand loin de toi, Oh! n'insultez jamais (vce and pf) (Bessel)
Quand tu chantes (Gutheil)
Rêve (Gutheil)
S'il est aupres de moi (Gutheil)
Secret (Gutheil)
Situ le vois (Gutheil)
Sous ton balcon j'attende le jour, aubade (Gutheil)
Sur le grand fleuve (Gutheil)
Ref. 297

Bibliography

NUMERICAL REFERENCES

1. Corbet, A. and Paap, W. *Algemene muziekencyclopedie.* Antwerp: Zuid-Nederlandse Uitgeverij, 1957-1963; supplement, ed. Jozef Robijns. Ghent-Louvain: Wetenschappelijke Uitgeverij E. Story-Scientia, 1972.

2. Blom, E., comp. *Everyman's Dictionary of Music.* London: Dent, 1971.

3. Sartori, C. *Dizionario Ricordi della musica e dei musicisti.* Milan: Ricordi, 1959.

4. Vinton, J., ed. *Dictionary of Twentieth-Century Music.* London: Thames & Hudson, 1974.

5. Vinton, J., ed. *Dictionary of Contemporary Music.* New York: Dutton, 1974.

6. Brown, J.D. and Stratton, S.S. *British Musical Biography: A Dictionary of Musical Artists, Authors and Composers Born in Britain and Its Colonies.* Birmingham: Stratton, 1897. Repr., New York: Da Capo Press, 1971.

7. Emery, F.B. *The Violin Concerto.* Chicago: Violin Literature Publ., 1928. Repr., New York: Da Capo Press, 1969.

8. Grove, G. *Dictionary of Music and Musicians.* 5th ed. Blom, Eric, ed. London: Macmillan, 1961. New York: St. Martin's Press. 6th ed., 1970.

9. Michel, F. et al., eds. *Encyclopedie de la musique.* Paris: Fasquelle, 1958-1961.

10. Corte, A. della and Gatti, G.M., eds. *Dizionario di musica.* Turin: Peravia, 1959.

11. Jacobs, A. ed. *Penguin Dictionary of Music.* Harmondsworth, Middlesex: Penguin, 1967.

12. Honegger, M. *Dictionnaire de la musique.* Paris: Bordas, 1970.

13. Dufourcq, N., ed. *Larousse de la musique.* Paris: Larousse, 1957.

14. Gatti, G.M. and Basso, A. *La musica: Enciclopedia Storica.* Turin: Unione Tipografica - Editrice Torinese. 1966.

15. Blume, F., ed. *Die Musik in Geschichte und Gegenwart.* Kassel: Baerenreiter Verlag, 1949-1967.

16. Castillo, J. *La musica maya quiche: Region de Guatemala.* Guatemala: Homenaje, 1977.

17. Riemann, H. *Musik Lexikon.* Wilibald Gurlitt, ed. Mainz: Schott's Soehne, 1972-1975.

18. Scholes, P.A. *Concise Oxford Dictionary of Music.* 2nd ed. Ward, John Owen, ed. London: Oxford University Press, 1964.

19. Scholes, P.A. *Oxford Companion to Music.* 2nd ed. London: Oxford University Press, 1943.

20. *Sohlman's Musiklexikon.* Stockholm: Sohlman Foerlag, 1975-1979.

21. Bernandt, G.B. and Yampolski, I.M. *Sovietske kompozitory i muzykoviedy.* Moscow: Sovietski Kompozitor, 1978.

22. Baker, T. *Baker's Biographical Dictionary of Musicians.* 5th & 6th ed. & suppl. rev. Nicolas Slonimsky. New York: Schirmer, 1971 and 1978.

23. Hull, A.E., ed. *Dictionary of Modern Music and Musicians.* London: Dent, 1924.

24. Sainsbury, J.S. *A Dictionary of Musicians from Earliest Ages to the Present Time...* London: Sainsbury, 1824. Repr., New York: Da Capo Press, 1966.

25. Linker, R.W. *Music of the Minnesinger and Early Meistersinger: A Bibliograhy.* Chapel Hill, NC.: University of North Carolina Press, 1962.

26. Fetis, F. *Biographie universelle des musiciens et bibliographie générale de la musique.* 2nd ed. Paris: Firmin Didot Frères, 1866-1870. Repr., Brussels: Culture et Civilisation, 1972.

27. Mize, Dr. J.T.H., ed. *International Who is Who in Music.* 5th ed. Chicago: Who Is Who in Music, 1951.

28. Fontanals, M. *De los trovadores en España: estudio lengua y poesia provenzal.* Barcelona: Libreria de Joaquin Verdaguer, 1861.

29. McCredie, A.M. *Catalogue of 46 Australian Composers and Selected Works.* Canberra: Advisory Board, Commonwealth Assistance to Australian Composers, 1969.

30. Vannes, R. *Dictionnaire des musiciens (compositeurs).* Brussels: Larcier, 1947.

31. Canadian Broadcasting Corporation. *Thirty-four Biographies of Canadian Composers.* Montreal: Canadian Broadcasting Corporation, 1964.

32. Gardavsky, C. *Contemporary Czechoslovak Composers.* Prague: Panton, 1965.

33. Baptie, D. *Musical Scotland: Past and Present.* Hildesheim: Georg Olms Verlag, 1972.

34. *Who's Who in Music and Musicians' International Directory.* St. Clair Shores, MI.: Scholarly, 1935.

35. Sowinski, W. *Dictionnaire Biographique: Les musiciens polonais et slaves, anciens et modernes.* Paris: A. Le Clerc, 1857. Repr., New York: Da Capo Press, 1971.

36. Swiss Composers' League. *Forty Contemporary Swiss Composers.* Amriswill: Bodensee Verlag, 1956.

37. Huskisson, Y. *Bantu Composers of South Africa*. Johannesburg: South African Broadcasting Corporation, 1969.

38. Vodarsky-Shiraeff, A., comp. *Russian Composers and Musicians: A Biographical Dictionary*. New York: Wilson, 1940. Repr., New York: Da Capo Press, 1969.

39. American Society of Composers, Authors and Publishers. *ASCAP Biographical Dictionary of Composers, Authors and Publishers*. 3rd ed. Lynn Farnol Group, ed. New York: ASCAP, 1966.

40. Smith, J. *Directory of American Women Composers*. Chicago: National Federation of Music Clubs, 1970.

41. Cobbett, W.W., comp. *Cyclopedic Survey of Chamber Music*. 2nd ed. London: Oxford University Press, 1963.

42. Thompson, K.A. *A Dictionary of Twentieth Century Composers, 1911-1971*. New York: St. Martin's Press, 1973.

43. Charles, Sidney R. *Handbook of Music and Music Literature in Sets and Series*. New York: Free Press, 1972.

44. *Encyclopedie van de muziek*. Amsterdam: Elsevier, 1956.

45. Aretz, I., comp. *America Latina en su musica*. Paris: Unesco, 1977.

46. Marrou, H.I. *Les troubadours*. Paris: Seuil, 1971.

47. Bouws, J. *Suid-Afrikaanse komponiste*. Stellenbosch: Albertyn, 1957.

48. Cooper, M., ed. *The Concise Encyclopedia of Music and Musicians*. London: Hutchinson, 1958.

49. Sandved, K.B. *World of Music: A Treasury for Listener and Viewer*. London: Waverley Books, 1957.

50. Fleischmann, A., ed. *Music in Ireland: A Symposium*. Dublin: Cork University Press, 1952.

51. *Dictionnaire des musiciens français*. Paris: Seghers, 1961.

52. Hinson, M. *Guide to the Pianist's Repertoire*. Freundlich, Irwin, ed. Bloomington, IN.: Indiana University Press, 1973.

53. Claghem, C.E. *Biographical Dictionary of American Music*. New York: Parker, 1973.

54. Slonimsky, Nicolas. *Music of Latin America*. New York: Crowell, 1945. Repr., New York: Da Capo Press, 1972.

55. Raynaud, G. *Bibliographie des chansonniers français des XIIIe et XIVe siècles*. Paris: Vieweg, 1884.

56. Recupito, M.V. *Artisti e musicisti moderni: Cenni storici, critici e bibliografici con speciale riguardo alla scuola ed all'esegesi*. Milan: La Fiamma, 1933.

57. Davies, H., comp. *International Electronic Music Catalogue*. Paris: Groupe de Recherches Musicales de L'ORTF. New York: Independent Electronic Music Center, 1968.

58. Covell, R. *Australia's Music*. Melbourne: Sun Books, 1967.

59. Schuh, W., et al. *Schweizer Musiker-lexikon: Dictionnaire des musiciens suisses*. Zurich: Atlantis, 1964.

60. *Catalogo de obras de compositores españoles: Sinfonicas de camara, corales, lieders, solistas y ballets; and Catalogo de obras que forman el archivo sinfonico de la Sociedad General de Autores de España*. Madrid: Archivo Sinfonico de la SGAE, 1972.

61. Moisenko, R. *Realist Music*. London: Meridian Books, 1949.

62. Richards, D. *The Music of Finland*. London: Evelyn, 1968.

63. Creighton, J. *Discopaedia of the Violin, 1889-1971*. Toronto: University of Toronto Press, 1974.

64. Kelen, P.P. *Manuel de la musique*. Paris: Centurion, 1961.

65. Schnapper, E., ed. *British Union Catalogue of Early Music Printed Before the Year 1801*. London: Butterworths, 1957.

66. Lichtenthal, P. *Dizionario e bibliografia della musica*. Milan: Fontana, 1826.

67. Yoell, J.H. *The Nordic Sound*. Boston: Crescendo Publishers, 1974.

68. Barrett, H. *The Viola: Complete Guide for Teachers and Students*. University, AL.: University of Alabama Press, 1972.

69. Foreman, L. *British Music Now*. London: Elek, 1975.

70. Frank, P. and Altmann, W. *Kurzgefasstes Tonkuenstlerlexikon*. 15th ed. Regensburg: Bosse, 1936; Wilhelmshaven: Heinrichshofen, 1974.

71. Goss, M. *Modern Music Makers*. New York: Dutton, 1952.

72. De Candé, R. *La musique: Histoire, dictionnaire, discographie*. Paris: Seuil, 1969.

73. Prieberg, F.K. *Lexikon der neuen Musik*. Munich: Alber, 1958.

74. Thompson, O. ed. *The International Cyclopedia of Music and Musicians*. 4th ed., Slonimsky, Nicolas, ed. London: Dent, 1942; 10th ed., Bohle, Bruce, ed. London: Dent, 1975.

75. Zingel, H.J. *Verzeichnis der Harfenmusik*. Hofheim am Taunus. Hofmeister.

76. Londeix, J.M. *125 ans de musique pour saxophone*. Paris: Leduc, 1971.

77. Kay, E. *International Who's Who in Music*. 7th ed. Cambridge, England: International Who's Who in Music, 1975.

78. *Phaidon Book of the Opera*. Oxford: Phaidon, 1979.

79. Raynaud, G. *Bibliographie des altfranzoesischen Liedes*. Spanke, Hans, ed. Leiden: Brill, 1955.

80. Grodner, M. *Comprehensive Catalog of Available Literature for the Double Bass*. 2nd ed. Bloomington, IN.: Lemur Musical Research, 1964.

81. Pedigo, A. *International Encyclopedia of Violin-Keyboard Sonatas and Composer Biographies*. Booneville, AR: Arriaga, 1979.

82. Garcia, F.M. *Pequeñas biografias de grandes musicos mexicanos*. Mexico: Ediciones Framong, 1966.

83. Ferrara (City of). *Catalogo delle opere musicali... citta di Ferrara*. Parma: Associazione dei Musicologi Italiani, 1917.

84. Kay, E. *The World's Who's Who of Women*. Cambridge, England: Melrose Press, 1975.

85. Hixon, D.L. and Hennessee, D. *Women in Music: A Bio-bibliography*. Metuchen, NJ.: Scarecrow Press, 1975.

86. De Angelis, A. *Dizionario dei musicisti*. Rome: Ansonia, 1922.

87. Bernandt, G.B. and Dolzhansky, A. comps. *Sovietske kompozitory: Kratkii biograficheskii spravochnik*. Moscow: Sovietski Kompozitor, 1955.

88. *Enciclopedia Garzanti della musica*. Rome: Garzanti, 1974.

89. Pratt, W.S. *The New Encyclopedia of Music and Musicians*. rev. ed. New York: Macmillan, 1929.

90. Claro, S.V. and Blondel, J.U. *Historia de la musica en Chile*. Santiago: Editorial Orbe, 1973.

91. Backus, E.N., comp. *Catalogue of Music in the Huntington Library Printed Before 1801*. San Marino, CA.: Huntington Library, 1949.

92. Pistoia (City of). *Catalogo delle opere musicali... citta di Pistoia*. Parma: Associazione dei Musicologi Italiani, 1936-1937.

93. Napier, R.A. *Guide to Canada's Composers*. Ontario: Avondale Press, 1976.

94. Bull, S. *Index to Biographies of Contemporary Composers*. Metuchen, NJ.: Scarecrow Press, 1974.

95. Norlind, T. *Allmaent musiklexikon*. Stockholm: Wahlstroem & Widstrand, 1916.

96. *Musikens hvem hvad hvor: politikens musikleksikon*. Copenhagen: Politikens Forlag, 1950.

97. Schacht, M.H. *Musicus Danicus eller Danske sangmester*. ed. & commentary, G. Skjerne. Original Latin manuscript, 1687; Danish, Copenhagen: Hagerups, 1928.

98. Hamburger, P. *Aschehougs musikleksikon*. Copenhagen: Aschehougs, 1957-1958.

99. Mazza, J. *Dicionario biografico de musicos portugueses*. Lisbon, 1770..Repr., Occidente, vol. 24, 1944.

100. Pena, J. *Diccionario de la musica Labor*. Barcelona: Labor, 1954.

101. Refardt, E. *Historisch-biographisches Musikerlexikon der Schweiz*. Leipzig: Gebrueder Hug & Co., 1928.

102. Champlin, J.D. *Cyclopedia of Music and Musicians*. New York: Scribner, 1888-1890.

103. Hoeijer, J.L. *Musik-Lexikon*. Stockholm: Lundquist, 1864.

104. Vieira, E. *Diccionario biographico de musicos portugueses: Historia e bibliographia da musica em Portugal.* Lisbon: Moreira & Pinheiro, 1900-1904.

105. Schmidl, C. *Dizionario universale dei musicisti.* Milan: Sonzogno, 1926-1937.

106. Mariz, V. *Dicionario bio-bibliografico musical: Brasileiro e internacional.* Rio de Janeiro: Livraria Kosmos, 1948.

107. Torrellas, A.A. *Diccionario enciclopedico de la musica.* Barcelona: Central Catalana de Publicaciones, 1947-1952.

108. Manferrari, U. *Dizionario universale delle opere melodrammatiche.* Florence: Sansoni, 1954.

109. Kovacevic, K., ed. *Muzicka enciklopedija.* Zagreb: Jugoslavenski Leksikografski Zavod, 1971.

110. Keller, G. and Kruseman, P., eds. *Geillustreerd Muzieklexicon.* 's-Gravenhage: Kruseman, 1932.

111. Mueller, E.H., ed. *Deutsches Musiker-Lexikon.* Dresden: Limpert, 1929.

112. Allorto, R. and Ferrari, A. *Dizionario di musica.* Milan: Ceschina, 1959.

113. Panum, H. and Behrend, W. *Illustreret musikleksikon.* Hamburger, Povl, ed. Copenhagen: Aschehoug, 1940.

114. Society of Norwegian Composers. *Contemporary Norwegian Orchestral and Chamber Music.* Oslo: Grundt Tanum Forlag, 1970.

115. Einstein, A. *Das neue Musiklexikon.* Berlin: Hesse, 1926.

116. Borde, J.B. de la. *Essai sur la musique ancienne et moderne.* Paris: Ph.D. Pierres, 1780.

117. Pillet, A. *Bibliographie der Troubadours.* Carstens, H., ed. Halle: Niemeyer, 1933.

118. Chominski, J., ed. *Slownik muzykow polskich.* Warsaw: Polskie Wydawnictwo Muzyczne, 1962.

119. Choron, A.E. and Fayolle, F.J.M. *Dictionnaire historique des musiciens, artistes et amateurs, morts ou vivants.* Paris: Valade, 1810-1811. Repr., Hildesheim: Olms Verlag, 1971.

120. Boutiere, J. and Schutz, A.H. *Biographies des troubadours: Textes provençaux des XIIIe et XIVe siècles.* Paris: Didier, 1950; Nizet, 1964.

121. Ledebur, C. von. *Tonkuenstler-Lexicon Berlins von den aeltesten Zeiten bis auf die Gegenwart.* Berlin: Rauh, 1861.

122. Sonneck, O.G.T. *Catalogue of Opera Librettos Printed Before 1800.* Washington, DC.: Library of Congress, 1914.

123. British Museum. *Catalogue of the King's Music Library.* Squire, Willian Barclay. London: The Museum, 1927-1929.

124. Reis, C. *Composers in America: Biographical Sketches of Living Composers with a Record of their Works, 1912-1937.* New York: Macmillan, 1938; rev. & enl. ed., New York: Macmillan, 1947.

125. Schlager, K. ed. *Internationales Quellenlexikon der Musik Einzeldruecke vor 1800.* London: Baerenreiter, 1971.

126. Gerber, E.L. *Historisch-biographisches Lexikon der Tonkuenstler, 1790-1792; und, Neues historisch-biographisches Lexikon der Tonkuenstler, 1812-1814.* Wessely, Otmar, ed. Graz: Akademische Druck - und Verlaganstalt, 1966.

127. Eitner, R., ed. *Bibliographie der Musik-Sammelwerke des XVI und XVII Jahrhunderts.* Berlin: Liepmannssohn, 1877.

128. Eitner, R., ed. *Biographisch-bibliographisches Quellen-Lexikon der Musiker und Musikgelehrten christlicher Zeitrechnung bis Mitte des neunzehnten Jahrhunderts.* Graz: Akademische Druck - und Verlaganstalt, 1960.

129. Mendel, H. *Musikalisches Conversations-Lexikon: Eine Encyclopaedie der gesammten musikalischen Wissenschaften.* Berlin: Heinemann, 1870-1879.

130. Sorenson, S. et al., eds. *Gads musikleksikon.* Copenhagen: Gad, 1976.

131. Carlson, E.B. *A Bio-bibliographical Dictionary of Twelve Tone and Serial Composers.* Metuchen, NJ.: Scarecrow Press, 1970.

132. Riemann, H. *Dictionary of Music.* New ed., trans. Shedlock, S.J. London: Augener, 1908.

133. Kallmann, H., ed. *Catalogue of Canadian Composers.* Rev. enl. ed., Ottawa: Canadian Broadcasting Corporation. Repr., St. Clair Shores, MI.: Scholarly Press, 1972.

134. Sabaneyeff, L. *Modern Russian Composers.* London: Lawrence, 1927.

135. Allorto, R., ed. *Nuovo dizionario Ricordi della musica e dei musicisti.* Milan: Ricordi, 1976.

136. Williams, O., ed. *American Black Women in the Arts and Social Sciences: A Bibliographic Survey.* Metuchen, NJ.: Scarecrow Press, 1973; rev. and enl. ed., 1978.

137. Jacobi, H.W., comp. *Contemporary American Composers.* California: Paradise Arts, 1975.

138. Friskin, J. and Freundlich, I. *Music for the Piano: A Handbook of Concert and Teaching Material from 1580-1952.* New York: Rinehart, 1954. Repr., New York: Dover, 1973.

139. Rothmueller, A.M. *The Music of the Jews: An Historical Appreciation.* London: Vallentine Mitchell, 1953.

140. Gillespie, J. *Five Centuries of Keyboard Music.* New York: Dover, 1965. Repr., 1972.

141. Northouse, C. *Twentieth Century Opera in England and the U.S.A.* Boston: Hall, 1976.

142. Anderson, E.R. *Contemporary American Composers.* Boston: Hall, 1976.

143. Selfridge-Field, E. *Venetian Instrumental Music from Gabrieli to Vivaldi.* Oxford: Blackwell, 1975.

144. Krueger, K. *The Musical Heritage of the United States.* New York: Society for the Preservation of the American Musical Heritage, 1974.

145. Savez Kompozitora Jugoslavije. *Kompozitori i muzicki pisci Jugoslavije: clanovi saveza kompozitora Jugoslavije, 1945-1967 katalog.* Miloslavjevic-Pesic, Melina, ed. Belgrade: Savez Kompozitora Jugoslavije, 1968.

146. Eagon, A. *Catalog of Published Concert Music by American Composers.* 2nd ed. Metuchen, NJ.: Scarecrow, 1969; supls., 1971 and 1974.

147. Texas Music Educators' Association. *A Bibliography of Master's Theses and Doctoral Dissertations in Music Completed at Texas Colleges and Universities, 1919-1972.* Houston: The Association, 1974.

148. Brancusi, P. and Calinoiu, N. *Muzica in Romania Socialista.* Bucharest: Editura Muzicala a Uniunii Compozitorilor, 1973.

149. Harris, C.A. and Hargrave, M. *The Story of British Music and Earlier French Musicians.* London: Waverley Books, 1919.

150. Young, P.M. *A History of British Music.* London: Benn, 1967.

151. Sendrey, A. *Music in the Social and Religious Life of Antiquity.* Madison, NJ.: Fairleigh Dickinson University Press, 1974.

152. Thomson, V. *American Music Since 1910.* Twentieth Century Composers, vol. 1. New York: Holt, Rinehart & Winston, 1971.

153. Searle, H. and Layton, R. *Britain, Scandinavia and the Netherlands: Twentieth Century Composers.* vol. 3. London: Weidenfeld & Nicolson, 1972.

154. Gaoldbeck, F. *France, Italy and Spain: Twentieth Century Composers.* vol. 4. London: Weidenfeld & Nicolson, 1974.

155. Naples (City of). *Catalogo generale... città di Napoli.* Parma: Associazione dei Musicologi Italiani, 1918.

156. Mooser, R. Aloys. *Annales de la musique et des musiciens en Russie au XVIIIe siècle.* Geneva: Editions du Mont-Blanc, 1948-1951.

157. Modena (City of). *Catalogo delle opere musicalici... città di Modena.* Parma: Associazione dei Musicologi Italiani, 1916.

158. Florence (City of). *Catalogo delle opere musicali... città di Firenze.* Parma: Associazione dei Musicologi Italiani, 1929.

159. Bologna (City of). *Catalogo delle opere musicali... città di Bologna.* Parma: Associazione dei Musicologi Italiani, 1910.

160. Venice (City of). *Catalogo generale delle opere musicali... città di Venezia.* Parma: Associazione dei Musicologi Italiani, 1913.

161. Parma (City of). *Catalogo generale delle opere musicali... città di Parma.* Parma: Associazione dei Musicologi Italiani, 1911.

786

162. Bertini, G. *Dizionario storico-critico degli scrittori di musica e de piu celebri artisti di tutti le nazioni si antiche che moderne.* Palermo: Tipografia Reale di Guerra, 1814.

163. La Mara (pseud. of Marie Lipsius). *Musikalische Studienkoepfe.* Leipzig: Breitkopf & Haertel 1883.

164. Brown, H.M. *Instrumental Music Printed before 1600: A Bibliography.* Cambridge, MA.: Harvard University Press, 1965.

165. Ballo F. et al., eds. *Il Libro della Musica.* Florence: Sansoni, 1940.

166. *Il mondo della musica: Enciclopedia alfabetica con ampie trattazioni monografiche.* Rome: Garzanti.

167. Helmer, A. *Svensk solosang, 1850-1890, pt. 1: En genrehistorisk studie.* Stockholm: Almqvist & Wiksell, 1972.

168. Howard, J.T. and Mendel, A. *Our Contemporary Composers: American Music in the Twentieth Century.* Philadelphia: Blakiston, 1943.

169. Reeser, E., ed. *Music in Holland: A Review of Contemporary Music in the Netherlands.* Amsterdam: Meulenhoff.

170. Ribera, J. *Music in Ancient Arabia and Spain: Being "La Musica de las Cantigas".* Stanford University Press, 1929. Rper., New York: Da Capo Press, 1970.

171. Farmer, H.G. *A History of Arabian Music to the XIIIth Century.* London: Luzac, 1973.

172. Coeuroy, A. *Dictionnaire critique de la musique ancienne et moderne.* Paris: Payot, 1956.

173. Detheridge, J., comp. *Chronology of Music Composers.* Birmingham: Detheridge, 1936.

174. Lombard, M. *The Golden Age of Islam.* Trans. Spencer, Joan. Amsterdam: North-Holland Publishing Co., 1975.

175. Bouws, J. *Komponiste van Suid-Afrika.* Stellenbosch: Albertyn, 1971.

176. Bingley, W. *Musical Biography.* 2nd ed. London: Colburn, 1834. Repr., New York: Da Capo Press, 1971.

177. Dearling, Robert. et al. *The Guinness Book of Music Facts and Feats, 1976.* Middlesex: Guinness, 1976.

178. Spiess, L. and Stanford, T. *An Introduction to Certain Mexican Musical Archives.* Detroit Studies in Music Bibliography, no. 15. Detroit: Information Co-ordinators, 1969.

179. Kemp-Welch, A. *Of Six Mediaeval Women.* Williamstown, MA.: Corner House Publishers, 1979.

180. Villani, C. *Stelle feminili: dizionario bio-bibliografico.* New ed. Rome: Albrighi, Segati & Co., 1915.

181. Levati, A. *Dizionario biografico cronologico.* Milan: Bettoni, 1822.

182. Orestano, F. *Eroine, ispiratrici e donne di eccezione.* Milan: Istituto Editoriale Italiano Bernard Carlo Tossi.

183. Willemze, T. *Spectrum muzieklexicon.* Utrecht: Spectrum, 1975.

184. Van der Merwe, F.Z. *Suid-Afrikaanse Musiekbibliografie.* Cape Town: Tafelberg, 1974.

185. *Composium: Directory of New Music.* Washington, DC.: Crystal Record Company, 1971-1979.

186. Farmer, H.G. *Music: The Priceless Jewel, from the Kitab al-iqd al-farid of ibn-Abd Rabbihi.* Bearsden: The Author, 1942.

187. Riemann, H. *Dictionnaire de musique.* Paris: Payot, 1931.

188. Huys, B. *Catalogue des partitions musicales édites en Belgique et acquises par la bibliothèque Royale Albert I, 1966-1975.* Brussels: Bibliothèque Royale Albert 1, 1976.

189. Internationales Musikinstitut Darmstadt. *Katalog der Abteilung Noten.* Darmstadt: The Institute, 1966.

190. American Music Center Library. *Catalogue of Choral and Vocal Works.* Finell, Judith Greenberg, comp. New York: American Music Center, 1975.

191. Skowronski, J. *Women in American Music: A Bibliography.* Metuchen, NJ.: Scarecrow Press, 1978.

192. Fellerer, K.G. ed. *Rheinische Musiker.* Cologne: Arno Volk-Verlag, 1962.

193. Andreis, J. ed. *Muzicka enciklopedija.* Zagreb: Izdanje i Naklada Leksikografskog Zavoda Fnrj, 1958.

194. Oesterreichischer Komponistenbund. *Orchesterkatalog zeitgenoessicher oesterreichischer Komponisten.* Lubej, Emil et al., eds. Vienna: Lafite, 1977

195. Pavlakis, C. *The American Music Handbook.* New York: Free Press, 1974.

196. Cosma, V. *Muzicieni Romani: Compozitori si muzicologi.* Bucharest: Uniunii Compozitorilor, 1965 and 1970.

197. *Cesko slovensky hudebni slovnik osob a instituci.* Prague: Statni Hudebni Vydavatelstvi, 1963-1965.

198. Vernillat, F. and Charpentreau, J. *Dictionnaire de la chanson française.* Paris: Larousse, 1968.

199. Boydell, B., ed. *Four Centuries of Music in Ireland.* London: British Broadcasting Corporation, 1979.

200. Gojowy, D. *Neue sowjetische Musik der 20er Jahre.* Regensburg: Laaber, 1980.

201. Goodman, A.A. *Musik von A-Z: vom Gregorianischen Choral zu Jazz und Beat.* Munich: Suedwest Verlag, 1971.

202. Koch, W.A. *Musisches Lexikon: Kuenstler, Kunstwerke und Motive aus Dichtung, Musik und bildender Kunst.* 3rd ed. Stuttgart: Kroener, 1976.

203. Murdoch, J. *Australia's Contemporary Composers.* Sydney: Macmillan, 1972.

204. Hamel, F. and Huerlimann, M. *Enciclopedia de la musica.* 7th ed. Barcelona: Grijalbo, 1979.

205. Gradenwitz, P. *Music and Musicians in Israel.* Tel Aviv: Israeli Music Publications, 1959.

206. Gaster, A., ed. *International Who's Who in Music and Musicians' Directory.* 8th ed. London: International Who's Who in Music, 1977.

207. Hickmann, H. *Musik des Altertums: Aegypten. Musikgeschichte in Bildern.* vol. 2, pt. 1, ed. Besseler, Heinrich Schneider, Max. Leipzig: VEB Deutscher Verlag fuer Musik, 1961.

208. *Encyclopaedia Britannica: A New Survey of Universal Knowledge.* Chicago: Encyclopaedia Britannica, 1946.

209. Elson, L.C. *Curiosities of Music: A Collection of Facts Not Generally Known, Regarding the Music of Ancient and Savage Nations.* Boston: Ditson.

210. *Manuel de bibliographie biographique et d'iconographie des femmes célèbres... par un vieux bibliophile.* Paris: Nilsson, 1892.

211. Paloschi, G. comp. *Annuario musicale storico, cronologico, universale.* 2nd ed. Milan: Stabilimento Musicale Ricordi, 1878.

212. Amari, R. *Calendario di donne illustri italiane.* Florence: Tipografia di Federigo Bencini, 1857.

213. Vincenti, E. *Bibliografia antica dei trovatori.* Milan: Ricciardi, 1963.

214. Sartori, C. *Bibliografia della musica strumentale italiana stampata in Italia fino al 1700.* Biblioteca di Bibliografia Italiana. Florence: Olschki, 1952.

215. Kornmueller, P.U. *Lexikon der kirchlichen Tonkunst.* Regensburg: Coppenrath, 1891.

216. Gaspari, G. *Catalogo della biblioteca del liceo musicale di Bologna.* Bologna: Libreria Romagnoli dall'Acqua, 1890.

217. Nikolov, N. *Bulgarski kompozitori i muzikovedi: Spravochnik.* 1971.

218. Briquet, F.B. *Dictionnaire historique, litteraire et bibliographique des françaises, et des étrangères naturalisées en France.* Paris: Treuttel & Wuertz, 1804.

219. Reich, T. *Susreti sa suvremenim kompozitorima jugoslavije.* Zagreb: Skolska Knjiga, 1972.

220. Chabaneau, C. *Les biographies des troubadours en langue provençale.* Toulouse: Privat, 1885.

221. *Histoire litteraire des troubadours.* Paris: Dur & Neveu, 1774.

222. Bergert, F. *Die von den Trobadors genannten oder gefeierten Damen.* Halle a.S.: Verlag Max Niemeyer, 1913.

223. Gibelli, V. *Storia della musica sovietica: compositori e composizioni della Russia europea e asiatica*. Pavia: Tipografia del Libro, 1964-1965.

224. Stigelbauer, M. *Die Saengerrinnen am Abbasidenhof um die Zeit des Kalifen al-Mutawakkil*. Vienna: Verband der wissenschaftlichen Gesellschaften Oesterreichs, 1975.

225. Dassori, C. *Opere e operisti: Dizionario lirico universale, 1541-1902*. Genoa: Sordomuti, 1903.

226. Wier A.E., comp. *The Macmillan Encyclopaedia of Music and Musicians*. London: Macmillan, 1938.

227. Melby, C., comp. *Computer Music Compositions of the United States, 1976*. Cambridge, MA.: Massachusetts Institute of Technology, 1976.

228. Block, A.F. and Neuls-Bates, C. comp. *Women in American Music: A Bibliography of Music and Literature*. Westport, CT.: Greenwood Press, 1979.

229. Kenneson, C. *Bibliography of Cello Ensemble Music*. Detroit Studies in Music Bibliography. Detroit: Information Co-ordinators, 1974.

230. Jacobs, A., ed. *British Music Yearbook: A Survey and Directory with Statistics and Reference Articles for 1976*. New York: Bowker, 1976.

231. Moser, Hans Joachim. *Musik Lexikon*. Berlin: Hesses Verlag, 1935.

232. Azevedo, D.M.A. de. *Portugal illustrado pelo sexo femino: Noticia historica*. Lisbon: Pedro Ferreira, 1734.

233. Wallaschek, R. *Primitive Music*. London: Longmans Green, 1893. Repr., New York: Da Capo Press, 1970.

234. Hammer-Purgstall. *Literaturgeschichte der Araber*. Vienna: Staatsdruckerei, 1850.

235. D'Erlanger, R. *La musique arabe*. Paris: Geuthner, 1949.

236. Arnold, C.R. *Organ Literature: A Comprehensive Survey*. Metuchen, NJ.: Scarecrow Press, 1973.

237. Vaschalde, H. *Histoire des troubadours*. Paris, 1889.

238. *Ceske hudebni skladatelky, k mezinarodnimu dni zen*. Brno, Czechoslovakia: Universitni Knihovna v Brne, 1957.

239. Petersen, K. and Wilson, J.J. *Women Artists: Recognition and Reappraisal from the Early Middle Ages to the Twentieth Century*. New York: Harper & Row, 1976.

240. Reck, D. *Music of the Whole Earth*. New York: Scribner, 1977.

241. Cerulli, E. *Nuove ricerche sul libro della scala e la conoscenza dell'Islam in occidente*. Vatican: Biblioteca Apostolica Vaticana, 1972.

242. Frati, L. *Studi e notizie riguardanti la storia della musica*. Bologna: Forni, 1976.

243. Lindsay, J. *The Troubadours and Their World of the Twelfth and Thirteenth Centuries*. London: Muller, 1976.

244. Livermore, A. *A Short History of Spanish Music*. London: Duckworth, 1972.

245. Shepherd, J. et al. *Whose Music: An Anthology of Musical Languages*. London: Latimer, 1977.

246. Williams, M.D. *Source: Music of the Avant Garde: Annotated List of Contents and Cumulative Indices*. MLA Index and Bibliography Series, no. 19. Ann Arbor, MI.: Music Library Association, 1978.

247. Barillon-Bauche, P. *Augusta Holmès et la femme compositeur*. Paris: Fischbacher, 1912.

248. Mill, J.S. *The Subjection of Women*. London: Longmans, Green, 1869.

249. De Li Arienti, J.S. *Gynevera de la clare donne*. Bologna: Presso Romagnoli dall'Acqua, 1888.

250. Cattan, B. *Nell'Arabia antica: La donna nella famiglia e nella societa*. Rome: Tipografia Ponteficia nell'Istituto Pio IX, 1915.

251. Bier, W.C., ed. *Woman in Modern Life*. New York: Fordham University Press.

252. Wahl, J.A. *The Exclusion of Woman from Holy Orders*. Washington, DC.: Catholic University of America Press, 1959.

253. Pescerelli, B. *Maddalena Casulana: Madrigalista del cinquecento*. Bologna: Universita degli Studi di Bologna, 1974.

254. Notor, G. *La femme dans l'antiquite grecque*. Paris: Renouard, 1901.

255. Sendrey, A. *Music in Ancient Israel*. London: Vision Press, 1969.

256. Harrison, F. *Time, Place and Music: An Anthology of Ethnomusicological Observation, c. 1550 to c. 1800*. Amsterdam: Knuf, 1973.

257. Levis, J.H. *Foundations of Chinese Musical Art*. 2nd ed. New York: Paragon, 1963.

258. Erhardt, L. *Music in Poland*. Warsaw: Interpress, 1975.

259. Malm, W.P. *Music Cultures of the Pacific, the Near East and Asia*. Englewood Cliffs, NJ.: Prentice-Hall, 1967.

260. Elson, A. *Woman's Work in Music*. Maine: Longwood Press, 1976.

261. Montagu-Nathan, M. *A History of Russian Music*. Maine: Longwood Press, 1977.

262. Fairbairn, N. and Unger-Hamilton, C., eds. *Royal Collection: A Historical Album of Music Composed Exclusively by Members of the Royal Family of Great Britain and Ireland*. Sevenoaks: Novello, 1977.

263. Gabet, C. *Dictionnaire des artistes de l'école française aux XIXe siècle*. Paris: Vergne, 1851.

264. Drinker, S. *Music and Women: The Story of Women in Their Relation to Music*. Washington, DC.: Zenger, 1948; repr., 1977.

265. Pfeiffer, W.R. *Filipino Music: Indigenous, Folk, Modern*. Dumaguete City: Silliman Music Foundation, 1976.

266. Chase, G. *America's Music: From the Pilgrims to the Present*. New York: McGraw-Hill, 1955.

267. Verona (City of). *Catalogo delle opere musicali... città di Verona*. Parma: Associazione dei Musicologi Italiani, 1936.

268. Oliveira, A.L. de and Viana, M.G. *Dicionario mundial de mulheres notaveis*. Porto: Lello & Irmao, 1967.

269. Pool, Jeannie Gayle. *Women in Music History: A Research Guide*. New York: The author, 1977.

270. Rexroth, K. and Chung, L., eds. *The Orchid Boat: Women Poets of China*. New York: McGraw-Hill, 1972.

271. Hughes, R. *Biographical Dictionary of Musicians*. New rev. ed., Taylor, Deems and Kerr, Russell. New York: Blue Ribbon Books, 1971.

272. Key, M.R. *Male/Female Language*. Metuchen, NJ.: Scarecrow Press, 1975.

273. Raming, I. *The Exclusion of Women from the Priesthood: Divine Law or Sex Discrimination*. Trans., Adams, Norman R. Metuchen, NJ.: Scarecrow Press, 1976.

274. Goodwater, L. *Women in Antiquity: An Annotated Bibliography*. Metuchen, NJ.: Scarecrow Press, 1975.

275. Swidler, L. *Women in Judaism: The Status of Women in Formative Judaism*. Metuchen, NJ.: Scarecrow Press, 1976.

276. *Women Composers. A biographical Handbook of Womens Work in Music*. New York: Chandler-Ebel, 1913.

277. *Muzykalnaya literatura iz SSSR*. Moscow: Vsesoyuznoye Obyedinenie, 1976.

278. Thompson, A.F. *An Annotated Bibliography of Writings About Music in Puerto Rico*. MLA Index and Bibliography Series, no. 12. Ann Arbor, MI.: Music Library Association, 1975.

279. Wilhelm, J.J., ed. *Medieval Song: An Anthology of Hymns and Lyrics*. London: Allen & Unwin, 1971.

280. American Society of Composers, Authors and Publishers. *ASCAP Symphonic Catalog*. 3rd ed. New York: Bowker, 1977.

281. Michaelides, S. *The Music of Ancient Greece*. London: Faber, 1978.

282. Maleady, A.O. *Index to Record and Tape Reviews 1976*. California: Chulainn Press, 1977.

283. *Donemus General Catalogue: Dutch Contemporary Music*. Amsterdam: Donemus, 1977.

284. Gilder, E. and Port, J.G. *Dictionary of Composers and Their Music*. London: Paddington Press, 1978.

285. Southern, E. *The Music of Black Americans: A History*. New York: Norton, 1971.

286. Roberts, J.S. *Black Music of Two Worlds*. New York: Praeger, 1972.

287. Abdul, R. *Blacks in Classical Music*. New York: Dodd, Mead & Co., 1977.

288. Jarman, L. ed. *Canadian Music: A Selected Checklist, 1950-1973*. Toronto: University of Toronto Press, 1976.

289. Caldwell, J. *Medieval Music*. Bloomington, IN.: Indiana University Press, 1978.

290. *Grande enciclopedia Portuguesa e Brasileira*. Lisbon: Editorial Enciclopedia Lda.

291. Bruechle, B. *Horn Bibliographie*. Wilhelmshaven: Heinrichshofen, 1970.

292. Barnes, E.N.C. *American Women in Creative Music*. Washington, DC.: Music Education Publications, 1936.

293. Dziebowska, E., ed. *Polska wspotczesna kultura muzyczna, 1944-1964*. Cracow: Polskie Wydawnickwo Muzyczne, 1964.

294. Dibelius, U. *Moderne Musik, 1945-1965*. Munich: Piper, 1966.

295. Drone, J.M. *Index to Opera, Operetta and Musical Comedy Synopses in Collections and Periodicals*. Metuchen, NJ.: Scarecrow Press, 1978.

296. Martin, J. *Nos auteurs et compositeurs dramatiques*. Paris: Flammarion, 1897.

297. Pazdirek, F. *Universal-Handbuch der Musik-literatur aller Zeiten und Voelker*. Vienna: Pazdirek, 1904-1910. Repr., Hilversum: Knuf, 1967.

298. Slonimsky, N. *A Thing or Two About Music*. Westport, CT.: Greenwood Press, 1948; repr., 1972.

299. Zimmermann, W. *Desert Plants: Conversations with 23 American Musicians*. Vancouver: ARC Publications, 1976.

300. De Vasconcellos, J. *Os musicos portuguezes*. Porto: Imprensa Portugueza, 1870.

301. Edwards, J.M. *Literature for Voices in Combination with Electronic and Tape Music: An Annotated Bibliography*. MLA Index and Bibliography Series, no. 17. Ann Arbor, MI.: Music Library Association, 1977.

302. Walther, J.G. *Musikalisches Lexicon oder musikalische Bibliothek*. Leipzig: Deer; facsimile reprint ed., Richard Schaal. Kassel: Baerenreiter, 1953.

303. Bogin, M. *The Women Troubadours*. London: Paddington Press, 1976.

304. Hipsher, E.E. *American Opera and Its Composers*. Philadelphia: Presser, 1927. Repr., New York: Da Capo Press, 1978.

305. Farmer, H.G. *Musik des Mittelalters und der Renaissance: Islam. Musikgeschichte in Bildern*. vol. 2, pt. 3, Besseler, Heinrich and Schneider, Max, eds. Leipzig: VEB Deutscher Verlag fuer Musik, 1976.

306. Carpentier, A. *La musica en Cuba*. Mexico: Fondo de Cultural Economica, 1946; repr., 1972.

307. Towers, J., comp. *Dictionary-Catalogue of Operas and Operettas*. Morgantown, WV.: Acme, 1910. Repr., New York: Da Capo Press, 1967.

308. Al-Hasan ibn-Ahmad ibn-Ali al-Katib. *La perfection des connaissances musicales: Kitab kamal Adab al-Gina*. Trans. Amnon Shiloah. Paris: Geuthner, 1972.

309. Donakowski, C.L. *A Muse for the Masses: Ritual and Music in the Age of Democratic Revolution, 1770-1870*. Chicago: University of Chicago Press, 1977.

310. Robinson, D.M. *Sappho and Her Influence: Our Debt to Greece and Rome*. New York: Cooper Square. 1963.

311. Nettl, B. *Music in Primitive Culture*. Cambridge, MA.: Harvard University Press, 1956; repr., 1977.

312. Gardeton, C. *Bibliographie musicale de la France et de l'étranger*. Paris: Niogret, 1822. Repr., Geneva: Minkoff, 1976.

313. Polin, C.C.J. *Music of the Ancient Near East*. New York: Vantage Press, 1954. Repr., Westport, CT.: Greenwood Press, 1976.

314. Gardeton, C. *Annales de la musique; ou, Almanach musical pour l'an 1819 et 1820*. Paris: Annales de la Musique, 1820., Repr., Geneva: Minkoff, 1978.

315. Cazeaux, I. *French Music in the Fifteenth and Sixteenth Centuries*. Oxford: Blackwell, 1975.

316. Ribera y Tarrago, J. *La musica andaluza medieval en las canciones de trovadores, troveros y minnesinger*. Madrid: Revista de Archivos, 1923. Repr., New York: AMS Press, 1974.

317. De Beauvoir, S. *The Second Sex*. Trans. and ed., Parshley, M.M. Harmondsworth, Middlesex: Penguin Books, 1972; repr., 1976.

318. Balsdon, J.P.V.D. *Roman Women: Their History and Habits*. London: Bodley Head, 1962; repr., 1977.

319. Allen, W.D. *Philosophies of Music History: A Study of General Histories of Music, 1600-1960*. New York: Dover, 1962.

320. *Contemporary Hungarian Composers*. 3rd rev. and enl. ed. Budapest: Editio Musica, 1967.

321. Mattfeld, J. *A Handbook of American Operatic Premieres, 1731-1962*. Detroit Studies in Music Bibliography, no. 5. Detroit: Information Co-ordinators, 1963; repr., 1973.

322. Philadelphia, Free Library. *The Edwin A. Fleisher Collection of Orchestral Music in the Free Library of Philadelphia: A Cumulative Catalog, 1929-1977*. Boston, MA.: Hall, 1979.

323. Pahlen, K. *Great Singers: From the Seventeenth Century to the Present Day*. New York: Stein & Day, 1974.

324. Russcol, H. *The Liberation of Sound: An Introduction to Electronic Music*. Englewood Cliffs, NJ.: Prentice-Hall, 1972.

325. Adler, I. et al., eds. *Yuval Studies of the Jewish Music Research Centre*. Jerusalem: Magnes Press, 1968.

326. Limbacher, James L., ed. *Film Music: From Violins to Video*. Metuchen, NJ.: Scarecrow Press, 1974.

327. Ferri, P.L. *Biblioteca femminile italiana*. Padua: Tipografia Crescini, 1842.

328. Cuney-Hare, M. *Negro Musicians and Their Music*. Washington, DC.: Associated Publishers, 1936.

329. Macmillan, K. and Beckwith, J., eds. *Contemporary Canadian Composers*. Toronto: Oxford University Press, 1975.

330. Keldysh, Y.V., ed. *Muzykalnaya entsiklopedia*. Moscow: Sovietski Kompozitor, 1973- .

331. Clausen, P.G., comp. *Dansk musik: katalog over statsbibliotekets samling af trykte musikalier*. Aarhus: Universiteitsforlaget, 1977.

332. Stevenson, R. *Renaissance and Baroque Musical Sources in the Americas*. Washington, DC.: Organization of American States, 1970.

333. *Enciclopedia da Musica Brasileira: Erudita, folclorica et popular*. Sao Paulo: Art Editora, 1977.

334. Betham, M. *Biographical Dictionary of Celebrated Women of Every Age and Country*. London: Crosby, 1804.

335. Green, M.D. *Study of the Lives and Works of Black Women Composers in America*. Ann Arbor, MI.: Xerox University Microfilms, 1975.

336. Plowden, A. *Tudor Women: Queens and Commoners*. London: Weidenfeld & Nicolson, 1979.

337. Bagnall, A.D. *Musical Practices in Medieval English Nunneries*. Ann Arbor, MI.: Xerox University Microfilms, 1975.

338. Putnam, E.J. *The Lady: Studies of Certain Significant Phases of Her History*. Chicago: University of Chicago Press, 1970.

339. Baudot, A. *Musiciens romains de l'antiquité*. Canada: Les Presses de l'Université de Montreal and Editions Klincksieck, 1973.

340. Dlabacz, G.J. *Allgemeines historisches Kuenstler Lexikon fuer Boehmen, etc.* Prague: Haase, 1915. Repr., Hildesheim: Georg Olms Verlag, 1973.

341. Reinhard, K. and Reinhard, U. *Turquie: Les traditions musicales*. Paris: Buchet, 1969.

342. Pan American Union. *Music of Latin America*. 3rd ed. Washington, DC.: The Union, 1953.

343. Vidal, A. *La Chapelle St. Julien-des-ménestriers et les ménestrels à Paris*. Paris: Quantin, 1878.

344. Zingel, H.J. *Lexikon der Harfe*. Regensburg: Laaber, 1977.

345. Moore, F.L. *Crowell's Handbook of World Opera*. New York: Crowell, 1961.

346. Bedford, F. and Conant, R. *Twentieth Century Harpsichord Music: A Classified Catalog*. Hackensack, NJ.: Boonin, 1974.

347. Stern, S. *Women Composers: A Handbook*. Metuchen, NJ.: Scarecrow Press, 1978.

348. Baker, D.N. et al., eds. *The Black Composer Speaks*. London: Scarecrow Press, 1978.

349. Vasconcelos, A. *Raizes da musica popular brasileira, 1500-1889*. Sao Paulo: Martins, 1977.

350. Levati, A. *Dizionario delle donne illustri*. Milan: 1821.

351. Clement, F. and Larousse, P. *Dictionnaire des operas*. Rev., Pougin, Arthur. Paris: Larousse, 1905. Repr., New York: Da Capo Press, 1969.

352. Elson, L.C. *The History of American Music*. New York: Macmillan, 1904.

353. Ireland, N.O. *Index to Women of the World from Ancient to Modern Times: Biographies and Portraits*. Westwood, MA.: Faxon, 1970.

354. Chase, G. *The Music of Spain*. New York: Dover, 1959.

355. Gingras, C. *Musiciennes de chez nous*. Montreal: Editions de l'Ecole Vincent d'Indy, 1955.

356. Fahmy, M. *La condition de la femme dans la tradition et l'évolution de l'Islamisme*. Paris: Alcan, 1913.

357. Boase, R. *The Troubadour Revival: A Study of Social Change and Traditionalism in Late Medieval Spain*. London: Routledge & Kegan Paul, 1978.

358. Chase, G. *A Guide to the Music of Latin America*. Washington, DC.: Pan American Union & Library of Congress, 1962.

359. Kay, Ernest., ed. *Dictionary of International Biography*. Cambridge, England: International Biographical Centre, 1979.

360. Honegger, M. and Massenkeil, G. *Das grosse Lexikon der Musik*. Freiburg; Herder, 1976.

361. Matas, J.R. *Diccionario biografico de la musica*. 2nd ed. Barcelona: Iberia, 1966.

362. Aubry, P. *Trouveres and Troubadours: A Popular Treatise*. New York: Cooper Square Publishers, 1969.

363. Kendall, A. *The Tender Tyrant, Nadia Boulanger*. London: MacDonald & Jane's, 1976.

364. Guelke, P. *Moenche/Buerger Minnesaenger: Musik in der Gesellschaft des europaeischen Mittalalters*. Vienna: Boehlaus, 1975.

365. Hughes, A. *Medieval Music: The Sixth Liberal Art*. Toronto: University of Toronto Press, 1974.

366. Audiau, J. *Les troubadours et l'Angleterre*. Paris: Libraire Philosophique J. Vrin, 1927.

367. Mottini, G.E. *La donna e la musica*. Milan: Vallardi, 1931.

368. *Tablettes de renommée des musiciens, auteurs, compositeurs, virtuoses, amateurs et maîtres de musique vocale et instrumentale, les plus connus en chaque genre*. Paris: Cailleau, 1785. Repr., Geneva: Minkoff, 1971.

369. Dunstan, R. *A Cyclopaedic Dictionary of Music*. London: Curwen, 1980.

370. Fuld, J.J. *The Book of World-Famous Music: Classical, Popular and Folk*. Rev. and enl. ed. New York: Crown Publishers, 1971; repr., 1975.

371. *Compositores de America/Composers of the Americas*. Washington, DC.: Secretaria General, 1955-1972.

372. Sonneck, O.G.T. *Early Concert-Life in America, 1731-1800*. Leipzig: Breitkopf & Haertel, 1907. Repr., New York: Da Capo Press, 1978.

373. Rezits, J. and Deatsman, G. *The Pianist's Resource Guide: Piano Music in Print and Literature on the Pianistic Art 1978-1979*. San Diego, CA.: Pallma Music Co., 1979.

374. Wiggin, F.T. *Maine Composers and Their Music: A Biographical Dictionary*. Portland, ME.: Maine Federation of Music Clubs, 1959; Maine Historical Society, 1976.

375. Szabolcsi, B. and Toth, A. *Zenei lexikon*. Budapest: Zenemukiado Vallalat, 1965.

376. Kelly, J.W. *The Faust Legend in Music*. Detroit: Information Co-I ordinators, 1976.

377. Malan, J.P., ed. *South African Music Encyclopedia, vol. 1-4*. Cape Town: Oxford University Press, 1979.

378. Morris, J. *The Lady Was a Bishop: The Hidden History of Women with Clerical Ordination and the Jurisdiction of Bishops*. New York: Macmillan, 1973.

379. Ravina, M. and Skolsky, S., comps. *Who Is Who in ACUM: Authors, Composers and Music Publishers- Biographical Notes and Principal Works*. Israel: ACUM, 1965.

380. Such, P. *Soundprints: Contemporary Composers*. Toronto: Clarke, Irwin, 1972.

381. Stevenson, R. *Music in Mexico: A Historical Survey*. New York: Crowell, 1952.

382. Smith, W. *A New Classical Dictionary of Biography, Mythology and Geography*. 2nd ed. London: Murray, 1853.

383. Raynor, H. *A Social History of Music from the Middle Ages to Beethoven*. London: Barrie & Jenkins, 1972.

384. Sachs, C. *The Wellsprings of Music*. The Hague: Nijhoff, 1962. Repr., New York: Da Capo Press, 1977.

385. Osborne, C., ed. *The Dictionary of Composers*. London: Bodley Head, 1977.

386. Harman, A. et al. *Man and His Music*. London: Barrie & Jenkins, 1962.

387. Chailley, J. *40,000 Years of Music, Man in Search of Music*. New York: Macdonald, 1964.

388. Oram, D. *An Individual Note of Music: Sound and Electronics*. London: Galliard, 1972.

389. Saldoni, B. *Diccionario biografico-bibliografico de efemerides de musicos espaõles*. Madrid: Dubrull, 1881.

390. Arizaga, R. *Enciclopedia de la musica argentina*. Buenos Aires: Fondo Nacional de las Artes, 1971.

391. Adkins, Cecil and Dickinson, Alis, eds. *International Index of Dissertations and Musicological Works in Progress*. New York: American Musicological Society and International Musicological Society, 1977.

392. Green, S. *Encyclopaedia of the Musical Theatre*. New York: Dodd, Mead, 1976.

393. Fey, H. *Schleswig-Holsteinische Musiker, von den aeltesten Zeiten bis zur Gegenwart: ein Heimatbuch*. Hamburg: Holler, 1922.

394. Bisson, A. and Lajarte, T. de. *Petite encyclopedie musicale*. Paris: Hennuyer, 1884.

395. Fink, R. et al., eds. *Directory of Michigan Composers*. Michigan: Western Michigan University, 1977.

396. Lavalliere, L. *Ballets, opera et autres ouvrages lyriques, par ordre chronologique depuis leur origine avec une table alphabetique des ouvrages et des auteurs*. Paris: Baudre, 1760. Repr., London: Baron, 1967.

397. Machlis, J. *Introduction to Contemporary Music*. 2nd ed. New York: Norton, 1979.

398. Bergmans, C. *La musique et les musiciens*. Ghent: Siffer, 1902.

399. Santos, M.A.M. *Catalogo de musica manuscritta*. Lisbon: Biblioteca da Ajuda, 1958.

400. Melchior, E.A. *Wetenschappelijk en biographisch woordenboek der Tonkunst*. 2nd ed. Schiedam: Roelants, 1889.

401. Famera, K.M. *Catalog of the American Music Center Library: Chamber Music*. New York American Music Center Library, 1978.

402. Laplante, L., ed. *Compositeurs canadiens contemporains*. Montreal: Les Presses de l'Université du Quebec, 1977.

403. Broadcast Music Inc. *Symphonic catalogue*. Rev. ed. New York: Broadcast Music Inc., 1971; supplement, 1978.

404. Macksey, J. and Macksey, K. *The Guinness Guide to Feminine Achievements*. London: Guinness Books.

405. British Museum. *Catalogue of Printed Music Published Between 1487 and 1800*. Squire, William Barclay ed. In British Museum. London: The Museum, 1927.

406. Kondracki, M. et al. *International Electronic Music Discography*. Mainz: Schott, 1979.

407. Composers' Guild of Great Britain. *British Orchestral Music*. London: British Music Information Centre, 1958.

408. Composers' Guild of Great Britain. *Chamber Music by Living British Composers*. London: British Music Information Centre, 1969.

409. Composers' Guild of Great Britain. *Instrumental Solos and Duos by Living British Composers*. London: British Music Information Centre, 1972.

410. Composers' Guild of Great Britain. *Keyboard Solos and Duos by Living British Composers*. London: British Music Information Centre, 1974.

411. Composers' Guild of Great Britain. *Orchestral Music by Living British Composers*. London: British Music Information Centre, 1970.

412. Callaway, F. and Tunley, D., eds. *Australian Composition in the Twentieth Century*. Melbourne: Oxford University Press, 1978.

413. Fog, D. *Dansk musikfortegnelse*. Copenhagen: Dan Fog Musikforlag, 1979.

414. Verma, H.N. and Verma, A. *Indian Women Through the Ages*. New Delhi: Great Indian Publishers, 1977.

415. Ammer, C. *Unsung: A History of Women in American Music*. Westport, CT.: Greenwood Press, 1980.

416. Kovacevic, K. *Muzicko stvaralastvo u Hrvatskoj, 1945-1965*. Zagreb: Udruzenje Kompozitora Hrvatske, 1966.

417. Mizgalski, G. *Podreczna encyklopedia muzyki Koscielnej*. Warsaw: Wojciecha, 1959.

418. Pericic, V. *Muzicki stvaraoci u Srbiji*. Belgrade: Prosveta, 1969.

419. Polyakova, L. *Soviet Music*. Moscow: Foreign Languages Publishing House.

420. Gibelli, V. *Musicisti di oggi nell' U.R.S.S.* Milan: Giuffre, 1972.

421. Pleasants, H. *The Great Singers*. New York: Simon & Schuster, 1970.

422. Jacobs, A., ed. *British Music Yearbook, 1980*. 6th ed. London: Black, 1980.

423. Scott, M. *The Record of Singing to 1914*. London: Duckworth, 1977.

424. De Mirimonde, A.P. *Sainte-Cécile: Metamorphoses d'un Thème Musical*. Geneva: Minkoff, 1974.

425. Scott, M. *The Record of Singing, 1914-1925*. London: Duckworth, 1979.

426. Martens, F.H. *A Thousand and One Nights of Opera*. New York: Appleton, 1926. Repr., New York: Da Capo, 1978.

427. Béhague, G. *Music in Latin America: An Introduction*. Englewood Cliffs, NJ.: Prentice-Hall, 1979.

428. Porter, B. and Moss, R.L.B. *Topographical Bibliography of Ancient Egyptian Hieroglyphic Texts, Reliefs and Paintings*. 2nd ed. Oxford: Clarendon Press, 1960.

429. Johnson, H.E. *First Performances in America to 1900*. Detroit: Information Co-ordinator for College Music Society, 1979.

430. Oztuna, Y. *Turk musikisi ansiklopedisi*. Istanbul: Milli Egitim Basimevi, 1974.

431. Stieger, F. *Opernlexikon*. Tutzing: Schneider, 1977.

432. Seland, M. *Kvinnelige Komponister: en bio-bibliografi*. Oslo: Statens bibliotekskole, 1976.

433. Laurence, A. *Women of Notes: 1,000 Women Composers Born Before 1900*. New York: Rosen Press, 1978.

434. Brook, D. *Violinists of Today*. London: Salisbury Square, 1948.

435. Andreis, J. *Music in Croatia*. Zagreb: Institute of Musicology, 1974.

436. Mooser, R. Aloys. *Operas, Intermezzos, Ballets Cantates, Oratorios*. Geneve, Imprimerie A. Kundig, 1945.

437. Glyn, Margaret H. *Elizabethan Virginal Music and Its Composers*. 2nd Ed. London, William Reeves, 1934.

438. Kanahele, George S., ed. *Hawaiian Music and Musicians. An Illustrated History*. Honolulu: The University Press of Hawaii. 1979.

439. Brenet, Michel. *Musique et Musiciens de la Vieille France*. Editions d'aujourd'hui, 1977.

440. Catalogues of Australian Compositions IV. *Vocal and Choral Music*. Sydney: Australia Music Centre, 1976.

441. Institute of History of the Arts. *History of Russian Soviet Music*. Moscow: 1956.

442. Catalogues of Australian Compositions V. *Dramatic Music*. Sydney: Australia Music Centre, 1977.

443. Catalogues of Australian Compositions VI. *Military and Brass Band Music*. Sydney: Australia Music Centre, 1977.

444. *Catalogue of Instrumental and Chamber Music*. Sydney: Australia Music Centre, 1976.

445. *Catalogue of Orchestral Music*. Sydney: Australia Music Centre, 1976.

446. *Catalogue of Keyboard Music*. Sydney: Australia Music Centre, 1976.

447. Pirie, Peter J. *The English Musical Renaissance*. London: Victor Gollancz Ltd., 1979.

448. Zelenka, Karl. *Komponierende Frauen*. Cologne: Ellenberg Verlag, 1980.

449. *Le Biografie Trovadoriche*. Edizione Integrale. Bologna: Libreria Antiquaria Palmaverde, 1961.

450. *American Music before 1865 in Print and on Records*. New York: Institute for Studies in American Music, 1976.

451. Jackson, Richard. *Sources of Bibliography and Collective Biography*. United States Music. New York: Department of Music, 1973.

452. Goertz, Harald. *Oesterreichische Komponisten der Gegenwart*. Munich: Doblinger, 1979.

453. Beliaev, Viktor M. *Central Asian Music*. Middletown, CT.: Wesleyan University Press, 1975.

454. Lepage, Jane Weiner. *Women Composers, Conductors and Musicians of the Twentieth Century*. London: Scarecrow Press, Inc., 1980.

455. Camner, James., ed. *The Great Instrumentalists in Historic Photographs*. New York: Dover Publications, 1980.

456. Engman Bo. *Svensk 1900-talsmusik fraan opera till pop 2000 biografier*. Stockholm: Bokfoerlaget Natur och Kultur, 1978.

457. Gaster, Adrian., ed. *International Who's Who in Music and Musicians' Directory*. Cambridge, England: Melrose Press, 1980.

458. Chkhikvadze, Grigori. *Composers of the Georgian Soviet Socialist Republic*. Musical Fund of the Georgian Soviet Socialist Republic, 1949.

459. Hadley, Benjamin., ed. *Britannica Book of Music*. New York: Doubleday & Company, Inc., 1980.

460. Krohn, Ernst C. *Missouri Music*. New York: Da Capo Press, 1971.

461. Robijns, Prof. Dr. J. and Zijlstra Miep. *Algemene Muziek Encyclopedie*. Bussum: Unieboek bv., 1980.

462. Parkhurst, Winthrop, and Bekker L.J. de. *The Encyclopedia of Music and Musicians*. New York: Crown Publishers, 1937.

463. Stoykova Kichka and Tsenkov Tsenko. *Bulgarian Orchestral Music*. Sofia Press.

464. Barnstone, Aliki and Barnstone, Willis, eds. *A Book of Women Poets from Antiquity to Now*. New York: Schocken Books, 1980.

465. Stewart-Green, Miriam. *Women Composers: A Checklist of Works for the Solo Voice*. Boston: G.K. Hall & Co., 1980.

466. Krustev, Venelin. *Bulgarian Music.* Sifoa Press, 1978.

467. Ronald, Sir Landon., ed. *Who's Who in Music.* London: Shaw Publishing Co. Ltd., 1937.

468. Christ, Peter, ed. *Composium., Annual Index of Contemporary Compositions.* Washington: Crystal Musicworks, 1981.

469. Dearling, Robert and Dearling, Celia. *The Guinness Book of Music.* 2nd ed. Enfield: Guinness Superlatives Ltd., 1981.

470. Regli, Francesco., comp. *Dizionario Biografico.* Turin: Coi Tipi Di Enrico Dalmazzo, 1860.

471. Weston, Pamela. *Clarinet Virtuosi of the Past.* Kent: Novello & Co. Ltd., 1976.

472. Weston, Pamela. *More Clarinet Virtuosi of the Past.* Kent: Novello & Co. Ltd., 1977.

473. British Broadcasting Corporation Music Library. *Piano and Organ Catalogue I and II.* London: J. Smethurst and Co. Ltd., 1973.

474. Zaimont, Judith Lang, and Famera, Karen. *Contemporary Concert Music by Women.* Westport, CT.: Greenwood Press, 1981.

475. *Who's Who of American Women.* 11th ed., 1979-1980. Chicago: Marquis Who's Who.

476. Weissweiler, Eva. *Komponistinnen aus 500 Jahren.* Frankfurt: Fischer Taschenbuch Verlag, 1981.

477. Meggett, Joan M. *Keyboard Music by Women Composers.* Westport, CT.: Greenwood Press, 1981.

478. Schreijer, Cobi. *Sara, Je Rok Zakt af.* Vrouwenliedboek. Amsterdam: Feministische Uitgeverij Sara, 1980.

479. Room, Adrian. *Naming Names.* London: Routledge & Kegan Paul, 1981.

480. Riemann, Dr. Hugo. *Opern-Handbuch.* Hildesheim: Georg Olms Verlag, 1979.

481. Rieger, Eva. *Frau, Musik und Maennerherrschaft.* Frankfurt: Verlag Ullstein GmbH, 1981.

482. Rogal, Samuel J. *Sisters of Sacred Song.* New York: Garland Publishing Inc., 1981.

483. Mayr, Giovanni Simone. *Biografie di Scrittori e Artisti Musicali.* Bologna: Forni Editore, 1875.

484. McHenry, Robert., ed. *Liberty's Women.* Springfield, MA.: G and C Merriam Co., 1980.

485. Kallmann, H., Potvin, G. and Winters, K. eds. *Encyclopedia of Music in Canada.* Toronto: University of Toronto Press, 1981.

486. Martini, Giovanni Battista. *Storia Della Musica, tomo 1, Bologna.* Graz: Akademischer Druck - und Verlaganstalt, 1967.

487. Prunières, Henry. *Nouvelle Histoire de la Musique.* Paris: Aux Editions Rieder, 1934.

488. Wyndham, H. Saxe, ed. *Who's Who in Music.* London: Sir Isaac Pitman and Son, 1915.

489. Hixon, Donald L. *Music in Early America.* Metuchen, NJ.: Scarecrow Press, Inc., 1970.

490. Townend, Peter and Simmons, David., eds. *Who's Who in Music.* London: Burke's Peerage, 1962.

491. Burton, Captain Sir Richard F. *Personal Narrative of a Pilgrimage to Al-l Madinah & Meccah.* New York: Dover Publications Inc., 1964.

492. Holmes, John L. *Conductors on Record.* Westport, CA.: Greenwood Press, 1982.

493. Bennett, John R., ed. *Melodiya; A Soviet Russian L.P. Discography.* Westport, CA: Greenwood Press, 1981.

494. *ASCAP Biographical Dictionary.* New York: Jaques Cattell Press; R.R. Bowker Co., 1980.

495. *German Music Archive of the German Library.* Bonner Katalog. Munich: K.G. Saur, 1982.

496. Mize, Dr. J.T.H., ed. *The International Who Is Who in Music.* 5th ed. Chicago: Who Is Who in Music, Inc. Ltd., 1951.

497. Limbacher, James L. *Keeping Score. Film Music 1972-1979.* Metuchen, NJ.: Scarecrow Press, 1981.

498. Koltypina and Pavlova, N.G. *Soviet Literature and Music.* Moscow: Sovietski Kompozitor, 1979.

499. Danish Composers' Society. *Danske komponister af i dag.* Copenhagen: Dansk Komponistforening, 1980.

500. Suppan Wolfgang., ed. *Steirisches Musiklexikon.* Graz: Akademische Druck - und Verlaganstalt, 1966.

501. Keren, Zvi. *Contemporary Israeli Music.* Israel: Bar Ilan University Press, 1980.

502. Chiti, Patricia Adkins. *Donne in Musica.* Rome: Bulzoni Editore, 1982.

503. Knape, Walter. *Karl Friedrich Abel.* Bremen: Schuenemann Universitaetsverlag, 1973.

504. *Mata encyklopedia muzyki.* Warsaw: Panstwowe Wydawnictwo Naukowe, 1981.

505. Parkhurst, Winthrop and Bekker L.J. de. *The Encyclopedia of Music and Musicians.* Cleveland, OH.: The World Publishing Co., 1943.

506. *Who's Who of American Women.* Chicago, IL.: Marquis Who's Who Inc., 1981.

507. Stahl, Dorothy. *A Selected Discography of Solo Song.* Detroit, MI.: Information Co-ordinators, Inc., 1972.

508. Stahl, Dorothy. *A Selected Discography of Solo Song.* Sup. Detroit, MI.: Information Co-ordinators, Inc., 1976.

509. Thiel, Joern. *International Anthology of Recorded Music.* Vienna and Munich: Jugend & Volk, 1971.

510. Coover, James and Colvig, Richard. *Medieval and Renaissance Music on Long-Playing Records.* Detroit, MI.: Detroit Studies in Music Bibliography, 1964.

511. Cooper, David Edwin. *International Bibliography of Discographies.* Littleton, CO.: Libraries Unlimited Inc., 1975.

512. Gray, Michael H. and Gibson, Gerald D. *Bibliography of Discographies.* Classical Music, 1925-1975. New York: R.R. Bowker Co., 1977.

513. Coover, James and Colvig, Richard. *Medieval and Renaissance Music on Long Playing Records.* Sup. Detroit, MI.: Information Co-ordinators Inc., 1973.

514. Celletti, Rodolfo. *Il Teatro D'Opera.* Milan: Rizzoli Editore, 1976.

515. Zelenina, M.E. *Zarubuzhnaya muzyka XX veka.* Moscow: Kniga, 1979.

516. Manson, Adele P. *Calendar of Music and Musicians.* Metuchen, NJ.: Scarecrow Press, 1981.

517. Sublette, Ned., ed. *A Discography of Hispanic Music in the Fine Arts Library of the University of New Mexico.* Westport, CT.: Greenwood Press, 1973.

518. Weiser, Marjorie P.K. and Arbeiter, Jean S. *Womanlist.* New York: Atheneum, 1981.

519. *Music: Books on Music and Sound Recordings.* Washington, DC.: Library of Congress, 1975-1980.

520. Levy, Michael S. *Catalogue of Serious Music, Original Works, Arrangements and Orchestrations by members of SAMRO.* Johannesburg: SAMRO, 1982.

521. Schulz, Ferdinand F. *Pianographie.* Recklinghausen: Piano Verlag, 1982.

522. Jacobs, Arthur and Barton, Marianne, eds. *British Music Yearbook 1982.* London: Adam & Charles Black, 1982.

523. Lerma, Dominique-René de. *Black Concert and Recital Music.* Bloomington, IN.: Afro-American Music Opportunities Assoc., 1975.

524. Dziebowska, Elzbieta, ed. *Encyklopedia Muzyczna.* Cracow: Polskie Wydawnictwo Muzyczne, ab and cd, 1979.

525. Hilton, Ruth B. *An Index to Early Music in Selected Anthologies.* Clifton, NJ.: European American Music Corporation, 1978.

526. Coover, James. *Music Lexicography.* Carlisle, PA.: Carlisle Books, 1971.

527. Duckles, Vincent. ed. *Music Reference and Research Materials.* New York: Free Press, 1974.

528. Marco, Guy A. *Information on Music: A Handbook of Reference Sources in European Languages.* Vol. 1. Basic and Universal Sources. Littleton, CO.: Libraries Unlimited Inc., 1975.

792

529. Marco, Guy A. *Information on Music: A Handbook of Reference Sources in European Languages.* Vol. 2. The Americas. Littleton, CO.: Libraries Unlimited Inc., 1977.

530. Mixter, Keith E. *General Bibliography for Music Research.* Detroit, MI.: Information Co-ordinators, 1975.

531. Dickinson, Edward. *Music in the History of the Western Church.* New York: Greenwood Press, 1969.

532. Studi e Ricerche, 1948-1960. *Rome, Accademia Nazionale di S. Cecilia.* RAI Radiotelevisione Italiana.

533. Martini, Giovanni Battista. *Storia della Musica.* Graz: Akademische Druck - und Verlagsanstalt, 1967.

534. Bickerman, E.J. *Chronology of the Ancient World.* London: Thames & Hudson, 1980.

535. Lipman, Samuel. *Music after Modernism.* New York: Basic Books Inc., 1979.

536. Spiess, Lincoln Bunce. *Historical Musicology.* Westport, CT: Greenwood Press, 1980.

537. Krummel, D.W., Geil, Jean., Dyen, Doris J., and Root, Deane L. *Resources of American Music History.* Chicago, IL.: University of Illinois Press, 1981.

538. Higgins, Ardis O. *Windows on Women.* Hollywood, CA.: Halls of Ivy Press, 1975.

539. Von Ende, Richard Chaffey. *Church Music: An International Bibliography.* Metuchen, NJ.: Scarecrow Press, 1980.

540. Eric Werner, ed. *Contributions to a Historical Study of Jewish Music.* New York: KTAV Publishing House Inc., 1976.

541. Croucher, Trevor, comp. *Early Music Discography.* London: Library Association, 1981.

542. Fellowes, Edmund Horace. *The English Madrigal Composers.* Oxford: Clarendon Press, 1921.

543. *New Larousse Encyclopedia of Mythology.* Hamlyn Publishing Group Ltd., 1981.

544. Bauer, Marion and Peyser, Ethel. *How Music Grew.* New York and London: G.P. Putnam's Sons, 1939.

545. Caroso, Marco Fabrizio. *Nobilta' Di Dame.* Arnaldo Forni Editore, 1980.

546. Lieberman, Fredric. *Chinese Music, An Annotated Bibliography.* New York and London: Garland Publishing Inc., 1979.

547. Baker, Derek., ed. *Medieval Women.* Oxford: Blackwell, 1978.

548. Baumgartner, Alfred. *Alte Musik.* Salzburg: Kiesel Verlag, 1981.

549. *Compositores Contemporaneos Puertorriquenos.* Puerto Rico: Centro de Investigaciones y Ediciones Musicales, 1981.

550. Roche, Jerome and Roche, Elizabeth. *A Dictionary of Early Music.* London: Faber Music Limited, 1981.

551. Moser, Hans Joachim. *Musik Lexikon.* Hamburg: Musikverlag Hans Sikorski, 1963.

552. *Der Schweizerische Tonkuenstlerverein Im zweiten Vierteljahrhundert seines Bestehens.* Zurich: Atlantis Verlag, 1950.

553. Golitsma, A.M. *Sovietski Operi.* Moscow: Sovietski Kompozitor, 1982.

554. Donington, Robert. *The Rise of Opera.* London: Faber & Faber, 1981.

555. Neuls-Bates, Carol., ed. *Women in Music.* New York: Harper & Row, 1982.

556. *Pierre Key's Music Year Book.* New York: Pierre Key, Inc., 1926.

557. Ayala, Dr. Cristobal Diaz. *Musica Cubana.* San Juan and Puerto Rico: Editorial Cubanatan, 1981.

558. Haefeli, Anton. *Die Internationale Gesellschaft fuer Neue Musik.* Zurich: Atlantis Musikbuch-Verlag, 1982.

559. *Ars Electronica, Linz, im Rahmen des Internationalen Brucknerfestes.* Linz: Bruckner Haus.

560. Ewen, David. *American Composers.* New York: G.P. Putnam's Sons, 1982.

561. Laade, Wolfgang. *Musik Der Goetter Geister und Menschen.* Baden-Baden: Verlag Valentin Koerner, 1975.

562. Oja, Carol J., ed. *American Music Recordings.* New York: Institute for Studies at American Music Conservatory of Music, 1982.

563. Cohen, Aaron I. *international Discography of the Women Composers.* Westport, CT.: Greenwood Press, 1983.

564. Borroff, Edith. *Music in Europe and the United States.* Englewood Cliffs, NJ.: Prentice-Hall, Inc., 1971.

565. Reese, Gustave. *Music in the Middle Ages.* London: J.M. Dent & Sons Ltd., 1941.

566. Rosenberg, Samuel N. and Tischler, Hans., eds. *Chanter M'Estuet, Songs of the Trouveres.* London: Faber Music Ltd., 1981.

567. Duncan, Edmiondstoune. *The Story of Minstrelsy.* London: Walter Scott Publishing Co. Ltd., 1907.

568. Hoppin, Richard H. *Medieval Music.* New York: W.W. Norton & Co., 1978.

569. *Musical America.* New York: ABC Leisure Magazines, 1983.

570. Adkins, Cecil and Dickinson, Alis. *International Index of Dissertations and Musicological Works In Progress.* American-Canadian Supplement. Philadelphia, PA.: American Musicological Society, 1979.

571. Brook, Barry S., editor in chief. *International Repertoire of Music Literature (RILM) New York, International RILM Center.* 1966.

572. Norris, Gerald. *A Musical Gazetteer of Great Britain and Ireland.* London: David & Charles, 1981.

573. Gustafson, Bruce. *French Harpsichord Music of the 17th-Century.* Ann Arbor, MI.: University Microfilms International, 1977.

574. Gifford, Virginia Snodgrass. *Music for Oboe, Oboe D'Amore and English Horn.* Westport, CT.: Greenwood Press, 1983.

575. Frey, Linda., Frey, Marsha and Schneider, Joanne., eds. *Women in Western European History.* Westport, CT.: Greenwood Press, 1982.

576. *The Holy Bible.*

577. Al Faruqi, Lois Ibsen, comp. *An Annotated Glossary of Arabic Musical Terms.* Westport, CT.: Greenwood Press, 1981.

578. Gimbutas, Marija. *The Goddesses and Gods of Old Europe.* London: Thames & Hudson, 1982.

579. Hamm, Charles. *Music in the New World.* New York: W.W. Norton, 1983.

580. Seeger, Horst. *Musiklexikon.* Leipzig: VEB Deutscher Verlag fuer Musik, 1981.

581. Partnow, Elaine., comp and ed. *The Quotable Woman.* Los Angeles, CA.: Pinnacle Books Inc., 1977.

582. Sayers, Janet. *Biological Politics.* London: Tavistock Publications, 1982.

583. Mackay, Andy. *Electronic Music.* Minneapolis, MN.: Control Data Publishing, 1981.

584. Navaretta, Cynthia. *Guide to Women's Art Organizations and Directory for the Arts.* New York: Midmarch Associates, 1982.

585. Barton, Marianne and Jacobs, Arthur., eds. *British Music Yearbook.* London: Classical Music, 1982.

586. Tjepkema, Sandra L. *A Bibliography of Computer Music.* Iowa: University of Iowa Press, 1981.

587. Valenzuela Tobar, Paulina. *Lista De Autores y Compositores Registrados en DAI-Chile a Septiembre de 1979.* Editorial Universitaria SA, 1979.

588. Maillard, Jean. *Anthologie de Chants de Trouveres.* Paris: Editions Aug. Zurfluh, 1967.

589. *Komponisten und Musikwissenschaftler der Deutschen Demokratischen Republik.* Berlin: Verlag Neue Musik, 1959.

590. Tick, Judith. *American Women Composers before 1870.* Ann Arbor, MI.: UMI Research Press, 1979.

591. Gevaert, Aug. *Histoire et Theorie de la Musique de L'Antiquite.* Hildesheim: Georg Olms Verlagsbuchhandlung, 1965.

592. Paratore, Ettore. *Musical Poesia Nell'Antica Roma.* Cremona: Fondazione Claudio Monteverdi, 1981.

593. Friedland, Bea. *Louise Farrenc, 1804-1875.* Ann Arbor, MI.: UMI Research Press, 1980.

594. *Music for Orchestra, Band and Large Ensemble*. New York: American Music Center, 1982.

595. Kinsky, George. *Album Musical*. Paris: Librairie Delagrave, 1930.

596. Raynor, Henry. *Music and Society Since 1815*.

597. Hinding, Andrea., Bower, Ames Sheldon and Chambers, Clarke A., eds. *Women's History Sources*. New York: R.R. Bowker Co., 1979.

598. Brun, Henry J. *Women of the Ancient World*. New York: Richards Rosen Press Inc., 1976.

599. *Finnish orchestra works, vocal works with orchestra, operas, ballets*. Foundation for promotion of Finnish Music. 1973.

600. Gradenwitz, Peter. *Musik zwischen Orient und Okzident*. Hamburg: Heinrichshofen's Verlag.

601. Shera, F.H. *The Amateur in Music*. London: Oxford University Press, 1939.

602. Lloyd, Norman. *Grosses Lexikon der Musik*. Bertelsmann Lexikon-Verlag, 1968.

603. Burns, Edward McNall. *Western Civilizations*. 8th ed. New York: W.W. Norton and Company Inc., 1973.

604. Orovio, Helio. *Diccionario de la musica cubana*. Cuba: Editorial Letras Cubanas, 1981.

605. Song, Bang-Song. *An Annotated Bibliography of Korean Music*. Providence, RI.: Asian Music Publications; Brown University, 1971.

606. Graves, Robert. *New Larousse Encyclopedia of Mythology*. London: Hamlyn, 1959.

607. Collaer, Paul and Linden, Albert Vander. *Historical Atlas of Music*, London: George G. Harrap & Co.

608. Brunschwig, Chantal., Calvet, Louis-Jean and Klein, Jean-Claude. *Cent ans de chanson française*. Editions du Seuil, 1981

609. Stevens, Denis., ed. *A History of Song*. New York: W.W. Norton & Co., 1970.

610. Jablonski, Edward. *The Encyclopedia of American Music*. Garden City, NY: Doubleday & Co. Inc., 1981.

611. Butterworth, Neil. *A Dictionary of American Composers*. New York: Garland Publishing, 1984.

612. Arnold, Denis., ed. *The New Oxford Companion to Music*. Oxford: Oxford University Press, 1983.

613. Utas, Bo., ed. *Women in Islamic Societies*. Curzon and Humanities Press, 1983.

614. Futrell, Jon., Gill, Chris., St. Pierre, Roger., Richardson, Clive., Trengove, Chris., Fisher, Bob., Sheehy, Bill and Wesker, Lindsay. *The Illustrated Encyclopedia of Black Music*. London: Salamander Books Ltd.

615. Charbon, Marie H. *Catalogue of the Music Library, The Hague Gemeentemuseum; Vocal Music 1500-c.1650*. New York: Da Capo Press, 1973.

616. Weisser, Albert. *The Modern Renaissance of Jewish Music*. New York: Da Capo Press, 1983.

617. McHenry, Robert, ed. *Famous American Women*. Springfield, MA.: Merriam-Webster Inc., 1980.

618. Seeger, Horst. *Opern Lexikon*. Hamburg: Heinrichshofen's Verlag, 1979.

619. Basart, Ann. *Perspectives of New Music; An Index, 1962-1982*. Berkeley, CA.: Fallen Leaf Press, 1984.

620. Short, Craig R., ed. *Directory of Music Faculties in Colleges and Universities, U.S. and Canada*. College Music Society, 1982-1984.

621. Barton, Marianne, ed. *British Music Yearbook 1984*. London: Classical Music, 1983.

622. Zaimont, Judith Lang., Overhauser, Catherine and Gottlieb, Jane., eds. *The Musical Woman*. Westport CT.: Greenwood Press, 1984.

623. Utas, Bo, ed. *Women in Islamic Societies*. London: Curzon Press Ltd.; Humanities Press, 1983.

624. *Directory of New Music, 1982/1983*. Composium.

625. Press, Jaques Cattell, ed. *Who's Who in American Music*. New York: R.R. Bowker Co., 1983.

626. Trollope, T. Adolphus. *A Decade of Italian Women*. London: Chapman & Hall, 1859.

627. Naumann, Emil. *The History of Music*. London: Cassell & Co., 1891.

628. Pomeroy, Sarah B. *Goddesses, Whores, Wives and Slaves*. New York: Schocken Books, 1975.

629. Stone, Merlin. *When God was a Woman*. San Diego: Harcourt Brace Jovanovich Publishers, 1978.

630. Weaver, Robert Lamar and Weaver, Wright Norma. *A Chronology of Music in the Florentine Theatre 1590-1750*. Detroit: Information Coordinators Inc., 1978.

631. Poirier, Lucien, ed. *Canadian musical works 1900-1980: A Bibliography of general and analytical sources*. Canadian Association of Music Libraries, 1983.

632. Stainer, John. *The Music of the Bible*. London: Novello & Co., 1914.

633. *Scores, An Anthology of New Music*. New York: Schirmer Books, 1981.

634. Evans, Mary J. *Woman in the Bible*. Exeter: Paternoster Press, 1983.

635. Williams, James G. *Women Recounted*. Sheffield: Almond Press, 1982.

636. Warnicke, Retha M. *Women of the English Renaissance and Reformation*. Westport, CT.: Greenwood Press, 1983.

637. Uglow, Jennifer S., comp and ed. *The Macmillan Dictionary of Women's Biography*. London: Macmillan Press.

638. *New English Bible*. Oxford University Press; Cambridge University Press, 1970.

639. Starkie, Walter. *Spain; A Musician's Journey through Time and Space*. Geneva: Edisli-At Editions Rene Kister, 1958.

640. Kaufmann, Walter. *Musical References in the Chinese Classics*. Detroit: Information Co-ordinators Inc., 1976.

641. Burbank, Richard. *Twentieth Century Music*. London: Thames and Hudson, 1984.

642. Oehrstroem, Eva. *Kvinnliga Komponister i Sverige under 1800 och 1900-Talen*. Stockholm: Haesselby Slott, 1981.

643. *International Who's Who in Music and Musicians' Directory*. 10th ed. Cambridge, England: International Who's Who in Music, 1985.

644. Verma, H.N., and Verma, Amrit. *100 Great Indians Through the Ages*. New Delhi: Great Indian Publishers, 1975.

645. Crawford, Anne., Hayter, Tony., Hughes, Ann., Prochaska, Frank., Stafford, Pauline and Vallance, Elizabeth, eds. *The Europa Biographical Dictionary of British Women*. Europa Publications, 1983.

646. Claghorn, Gene. *Women Composers and Hymnists; A Concise Biographical Dictionary*. Metuchen, NJ: Scarecrow Press, 1984.

647. Imamuddin, S.M. *Muslim Spain 711-1492 A.D.* Leiden: E.J. Brill, 1981.

648. Cattin, Giulio. *Music of the Middle Ages I*. Cambridge: Cambridge University Press, 1984.

649. Frasier, Jane. *Women Composers; A Discography*. Detroit: Information Co-ordinators, 1983.

650. *Who's Who of Indian Musicians*. New Delhi: Sangeet Natak Akademi, 1984.

651. Ehrismann, Sibylle and Meyer, Thomas, ed. *Schweizer Komponistinnen der Gegenwart*. Zurich: Musik Hug & Co., 1985.

652. Spiegl, Fritz. *Music Through The Looking Glass*. London: Routledge & Kegan Paul, 1984.

653. Bowers, Jane and Tick, Judith, eds. *Women making Music*. Chicago: University of Illinois Press, 1986.

ALPHABETICAL BY AUTHOR

Abdul, R. *Blacks in Classical Music*. New York: Dodd, Mead & Co., 1977. (Ref. 287)

Adkins, Cecil and Dickinson, Alis., eds. *International Index of Dissertations and Musicological Works in Progress*. New York: American Musicological Society & International Musicological Society, 1977. (Ref. 391)

Adkins, Cecil and Dickinson, Alis. *International Index of Dissertations and Musicological Works In Progress*. American-Canadian Supl., Philadelphia, PA.: American Musicological Society, 1979. (Ref. 570)

Adler, I., et al., eds. *Yuval Studies of the Jewish Music Research Centre*. Jerusalem: Magnes Press, 1968. (Ref. 325)

Al Faruqi, Lois Ibsen, comp. *An Annotated Glossary of Arabic Musical Terms*. Westport, CT.: Greenwood Press, 1981. (Ref. 577)

al-Hasan ibn-Ahmad ibn-Ali al-Katib. *La perfection des connaissances musicales: Kitab kamal Adab al-Gina*. Trans. Amnon Shiloah. Paris: Geuthner, 1972. (Ref. 308)

Allen, W.D. *Philosophies of Music History: A Study of General Histories of Music, 1600-1960*. New York: Dover, 1962. (Ref 319).

Allorto, R., ed. *Nuovo dizionario Ricordi della musica e dei musicisti*. Milan: Ricordi, 1976. (Ref. 135)

Allorto, R. and Ferrari, A. *Dizionario di musica*. Milan: Ceschina, 1959. (Ref. 112)

Amari, R. *Calendario di donne illustri italiane*. Florence: Tipografia di Federigo Bencini, 1857. (Ref 212).

American Music before 1865 in Print and on Records. New York: Institute for Studies in American Music, 1976. (Ref. 450)

American Music Center Library. *Catalogue of Choral and Vocal Works*. Finell, Judith Greenberg comp. New York: American Music Center, 1975. (Ref. 190)

American Society of Composers, Authors and Publishers. *ASCAP Biographical Dictionary of Composers, Authors and Publishers*. 3rd ed. New York: ASCAP, 3rd ed., 1966. (Ref. 39)

American Society of Composers, Authors and Publishers. *Symphonic Catalog*. 3rd ed. New York: R.R. Bowker Co., 1977. (Ref. 280)

Ammer, C. *Unsung: A History of Women in American Music*. Westport, CT.: Greenwood Press, 1980. (Ref. 415)

Anderson, E.R. *Contemporary American Composers*. Boston: Hall, 1976. (Ref. 142)

Andreis, J., ed. *Muzicka enciklopedija*. Zagreb: Izdanje i Naklada Leksikografskog Zavoda Fnrj, 1958. (Ref. 193)

Andreis, J. *Music in Croatia*. Zagreb: Institute of Musicology, 1974. (Ref. 435)

Aretz, I., comp. *America Latina en su musica*. Paris: Unesco, 1977. (Ref. 45)

Arizaga, R. *Enciclopedia de la musica argentina*. Buenos Aires: Fondo Nacional de las Artes, 1971. (Ref. 390)

Arnold, C.R. *Organ Literature: A Comprehensive Survey*. Metuchen, NJ.: Scarecrow Press, 1973. (Ref. 236)

Arnold, Denis., ed. *The New Oxford Companion to Music*. Oxford: Oxford University Press, 1983. (Ref. 612)

Ars Electronica, Linz, im Rahmen des Internationalen Brucknerfestes. Linz: Bruckner Haus. (Ref. 559)

ASCAP Biographical Dictionary. New York: Jaques Cattell Press; R.R. Bowker Co., 1980. (Ref. 494)

Aubry, P. *Trouveres and Troubadours: A Popular Treatise*. New York: Cooper Square Publishers, 1969. (Ref. 362)

Audiau, J. *Les troubadours et l'Angleterre*. Paris: Libraire Philosophique J. Vrin, 1927. (Ref. 366)

Ayala, Dr. Cristobal Diaz. *Musica Cubana*. San Juan, PR.: Editorial Cubanatan, 1981. (Ref. 557)

Azevedo, D.M.A. de. *Portugal illustrado pelo sexo femino: Noticia historica*. Lisbon: Pedro Ferreira, 1734. (Ref. 232)

Backus, E.N., comp. *Catalogue of Music in the Huntington Library Printed Before 1801*. San Marino, CA.: Huntington Library, 1949. (Ref. 91)

Bagnall, A.D. *Musical Practices in Medieval English Nunneries*. Ann Arbor, MI.: Xerox University Microfilms, 1975. (Ref. 337)

Baker, D.N., et al., eds. *The Black Composer Speaks*. London: Scarecrow Press, 1978. (Ref. 348)

Baker, Derek, ed. *Medieval Women*. Oxford: Basil Blackwell, 1978. (Ref. 547)

Baker, T. *Baker's Biographical Dictionary of Musicians*. 5th & 6th ed. & suppl. rev. Slonimsky, Nicolas. New York: Schirmer, 1971 and 1978. (Ref. 22)

Ballo, F., et al. *Il libro della musica*. Florence: Sansoni, 1940. (Ref. 165)

Balsdon, J.P.V.D. *Roman Women: Their History and Habits*. London: Bodley Head, 1962; Repr., 1977. (Ref. 318)

Baptie, D. *Musical Scotland: Past and Present*. Hildesheim: Georg Olms Verlag, 1972. (Ref. 33)

Barillon-Bauche, P. *Augusta Holmès et la femme compositeur*. Paris: Fischbacher, 1912. (Ref. 247)

Barnes, E.N.C. *American Women in Creative Music*. Washington, DC.: Music Education Publications, 1936. (Ref. 292)

Barnstone, Aliki and Barnstone, Willis., eds. *A Book of Women Poets from Antiquity to Now*. New York: Schocken Books, 1980. (Ref. 464)

Barrett, H. *The Viola: Complete Guide for Teachers and Students*. Alhambra: University of Alabama Press, 1972. (Ref. 68)

Barton, Marianne and Jacobs, Arthur., eds. *British Music Yearbook*. London: Classical Music, 1982. (Ref. 585)

Barton, Marianne, ed. *British Music Yearbook 1984*. London: Classical Music, 1983. (Ref. 621)

Basart, Ann. *Perspectives of New Music; An Index, 1962-1982*. Berkeley, CA.: Fallen Leaf Press, 1984. (Ref. 619)

Bauer, Marion and Peyser, Ethel. *How Music Grew*. New York; London: G.P. Putnam's Sons, 1939. (Ref. 544)

Baudot, A. *Musiciens romains de l'antiquite*. Canada: Les Presses de l'Université de Montreal and Editions Klincksieck, 1973. (Ref. 339)

Baumgartner, Alfred. *Alte Musik*. Salzburg: Kiesel Verlag, 1981. (Ref. 548)

British Broadcasting Corporation Music Library. *Piano and Organ Catalogue I and II*. Composers. London: J. Smethurst & Co., 1973. (Ref. 473)

Bedford, F. and Conant, R. *Twentieth Century Harpsichord Music: A Classified Catalog*. Hackensack, NJ.: Boonin, 1974. (Ref. 346)

Béhague, G. *Music in Latin America: An Introduction*. Englewood Cliffs, NJ.: Prentice-Hall, 1979. (Ref. 427)

Beliaev, Viktor M. *Central Asian Music*. Middletown, CT.: Wesleyan University Press. 1975. (Ref. 453)

Bennett, John R., ed. *Melodiya; A Soviet Russian L.P. Discography*. Westport, CT: Greenwood Press, 1981. (Ref. 493)

Bergert, F. *Die von den Trobadors Genannten oder Gefeierten Damen*. Halle a. S.: Verlag Max Niemeyer, 1913. (Ref. 222)

Bergmans, C. *La musique et les musiciens*. Ghent: Siffer, 1902. (Ref. 398)

Bernandt, G.B. and Dolzhansky, A., comps. *Sovietske kompozitory: Kratkii biograficheskii spravochnik*. Moscow: Sovietski Kompozitor, 1955. (Ref. 87)

Bernandt, G.B. and Yampolski, I.M. *Sovietski kompozitory i muzykoviedy*. Moscow: Sovietske Kompozitor, 1978. (Ref. 21)

Bertini, G. *Dizionario storico-critico degli scrittori di musica e de piu celebri artisti di tutti le nazione si antiche che moderne*. Palermo: Tipografia reale di Guerra, 1814. (Ref. 162)

Betham, M. *Biographical Dictionary of Celebrated Women of Every Age and Country*. London: Crosby, 1804. (Ref. 334)

Bickerman, E.J. *Chronology of the Ancient World*. London: Thames & Hudson, 1980. (Ref. 534)

Bier, W.C., ed. *Woman in Modern Life*. New York: Fordham University Press. (Ref. 251)

Bingley, W. *Musical Biography.* 2nd ed. London: Colburn, 1834. Repr., New York: Da Capo Press, 1971. (Ref. 176)

Biografie Trovadoriche. Edizone Intergale. Bologna: Libreria Antiquaria Palmaverde, 1961. (Ref. 449).

Bisson, A and Lajarte, T. de. *Petite encyclopedie musicale.* Paris: Hennuyer, 1884. (Ref. 394)

Block, A.F. and Neuls-Bates, C., comps. *Women in American Music: a Bibliography of Music and Literature.* Westport, CT.: Greenwood Press, 1979. (Ref. 228)

Blom, E., comp. *Everyman's Dictionary of Music.* London: Dent, 1971. (Ref. 2)

Blume, F., ed. *Die Musik in Geschichte und Gegenwart.* Kassel: Baerenreiter Verlag, 1949-1967. (Ref. 15)

Boase, R. *The Troubadours Revival: A Study of Social Change and Traditionalism in Late Medieval Spain.* London: Routledge & Kegan Paul, 1978. (Ref. 357)

Bogin, M. *The Women Troubadours.* London: Paddington Press, 1976. (Ref. 303)

Bologna (City of). *Catalogo delle opere musicali ... città d Bologna.* Parma: Associazione dei Musicologi Italiani, 1910. (Ref. 159)

Borde, J.B. de la. *Essai sur la musique ancienne et moderne.* Paris: Ph.D. V. Pierres, 1780. (Ref. 116)

Borroff, Edith. *Music in Europe and the United States.* Englewood Cliffs, NJ.: Prentice-Hall, Inc., 1971. (Ref. 564)

Boutiere, J. and Schutz, A.H. *Biographies des troubadours: Textes provençaux des XIIIe et XIVe siècles.* Paris: Didier, 1950; Nizet, 1964. (Ref. 120)

Bouws, J. *Komponiste van Suid-Afrika.* Stellenbosch: Albertyn, 1971. (Ref. 175)

Bouws, J. *Suid-Afrikaanse komponiste.* Stellenbosch: Albertyn, 1957. (Ref. 47)

Bowers, Jane and Tick, Judith, eds. *Women making Music.* Chicago: University of Illinois Press, 1986. (Ref. 653)

Boydell, B., ed. *Four Centuries of Music in Ireland.* London: British Broadcasting Corporation, 1979. (Ref. 199)

Brancusi, P. and Calinoiu, N. *Muzica in Romania Socialista.* Bucharest: Editura Muzicala a Uniunii Compozitorilor, 1973. (Ref. 148)

Brenet, Michel. *Musique et Musiciens de la Vieille France.* Editions d'aujourd'hui, 1977. (Ref. 439)

Briquet, F.B. *Dictionnaire historique litteraire et bibliographique des françaises, et des étrangéres naturalisées en France.* Paris: Treuttel & Wuertz, 1804. (Ref. 218)

British Museum. *Catalogue of Printed Music Published Between 1487 and 1800.* Squire, William Barclay. London: The Museum, 1927-1929. (Ref. 405)

British Museum. *Catalogue of the King's Music Library.* Squire, William Barclay. London: The Museum, 1927. (Ref. 123)

Broadcast Music Inc. *Symphonic Catalogue.* Rev. ed. New York: Broadcast Music Inc., 1971; supl. no. 1, 1978. (Ref. 403)

Brook, Barry S. Editor in chief. *International Repertoire of Music Literature (RILM).* New York: International RILM Center, 1966. (Ref. 571)

Brook, D. *Violinists of Today.* London: Salisbury Square, 1948. (Ref. 434)

Brown, H.M. *Instrumental Music Printed before 1600: A Bibliography.* Cambridge, MA.: Harvard University Press, 1965. (Ref. 164)

Brown, J.D. and Stratton, S.S. *British Musical Biography: A Dictionary of Musical Artists, Authors and Composers born in Britain and its Colonies.* Birmingham: Stratton, 1897. Repr., New York: Da Capo Press, 1971. (Ref 6)

Bruechle, B. *Horn Bibliographie.* Wilhelmshaven: Heinrichshofen, 1970. (Ref. 291)

Brun, Henry J. *Women of the Ancient World.* New York: Richards Rosen Press, Inc., 1976. (Ref. 598)

Brunschwig, Chantal., Calvet, Louis-Jean and Klein, Jean-Claude. *Cent ans de chanson française.* Editions du Seuil, 1981. (Ref.608)

Bull, S. Index to Biographies of Contemporary Composers. Metuchen, NJ.: Scarecrow Press, 1974. (Ref. 94)

Burbank, Richard. *Twentieth Century Music.* London: Thames & Hudson, 1984. (Ref. 641)

Burns, Edward McNall. *Western Civilizations.* 8th ed. New York: W.W. Norton & Company Inc., 1973. (Ref. 603)

Burton, Captain Sir Richard F. *Personal Narrative of a Pilgrimage to Al-Madinah & Meccah.* New York: Dover Publications Inc., 1964. (Ref. 491)

Butterworth, Neil. *A Dictionary of American Composers.* New York: Garland Publishing, 1984. (Ref. 611)

Caldwell, J. *Medieval Music.* Bloomington, IN: Indiana University Press, 1978. (Ref 289)

Callaway, F. and Tunley, D., eds. *Australian Composition in the Twentieth Century.* Melbourne: Oxford University Press, 1978. (Ref. 412)

Camner, James, ed. *The Great Instrumentalists in Historic Photographs.* New York: Dover Publications, 1980. (Ref. 455)

Canadian Broadcasting Corporation. *Thirty-four Biographies of Canadian Composers.* Montreal: Canadian Broadcasting Corporation, 1964. (Ref. 31)

Carlson, E.B. *A Bio-bibliographical Dictionary of Twelve Tone and Serial Composers.* Metuchen, NJ.: Scarecrow Press, 1970. (Ref. 131)

Caroso, Marco Fabrizio. *Nobilta' di Dame.* Arnaldo Forni Editore, 1980. (Ref. 545)

Carpentier, A. *La musica en Cuba.* Mexico: Fondo de Cultural Economica, 1946; Repr., 1972. (Rep. 306)

Castillo, J. *La musica maya quiche: Region de Guatemala.* Guatemala: Homenaje, 1977. (Ref. 16)

Catalogo de obras de compositores espanoles: Sinfonicas de camara, corales, lieders, solistas y ballets; and Catalogo de obras que forman el archivo sinfonico de la Sociedad General de Autores de España. Sinfonico de la SGAE, 1972. (Ref. 60)

Catalogue of Instrumental and Chamber Music: Sydney: Australia Music Centre, 1976. (Ref. 444)

Catalogues of Australian Compositions IV. *Vocal and Choral Music.* Sydney: Australia Music Centre, 1976. (Ref. 440)

Catalogues of Australian Compositions V. *Dramatic Music.* Sydney: Australia Music Centre, 1977. (Ref. 442)

Catalogues of Australian Compositions VI. *Military and Brass Band Music.* Sydney: Australia Music Centre, 1977. (Ref. 443)

Catalogue of Keyboard Music. Sydney: Australia Music Centre, 1976. (Ref. 446)

Catalogue of Orchestral Music. Sydney: Australia Music Centre, 1976. (Ref. 445)

Cattan, B. *Nell'Arabia antica: La donna nella famiglia e nella societa.* Rome: Tipografia Ponteficia nell'Istituto Pio IX, 1915. (Ref. 250)

Cattin, Giulio. *Music of the Middle Ages I.* Cambridge: Cambridge University Press, 1984. (Ref. 648)

Cazeaux, I. *French Music in the Fifteenth and Sixteenth Centuries.* Oxford: Blackwell, 1975. (Ref. 315)

Celletti, Rodolfo. *Il Teatro D'Opera.* Milan: Rizzoli Editore, 1976. (Ref. 514)

Cerulli, E. *Nuove ricerche sul libro della scala e la conoscenza dell'Islam in occidente.* Vatican: Biblioteca Apostolica Vaticana, 1972. (Ref. 241)

Ceske hudebni skladatelky, k mezinarodnimu dni zen. Brno: Universitni Knihovna v Brne, 1957. (Ref. 238)

Cesko slovensky hudebni slovnik osob a instituci. Prague: Statni Hudebni Vydavatelstvi, 1963-1965. (Ref. 197)

Chabaneau, C. *Les biographies des troubadours en langue provençale.* Toulouse: Private, 1885. (Ref. 220)

Chailley, J. *40,000 Years of Music: Man in Search of Music.* New York: Macdonald, 1964. (Ref. 387)

Champlin, J.D. *Cyclopedia of Music and Musicians.* New York: Scribner, 1888-1890. (Ref. 102)

Charbon, Marie H. *Catalogue of the Music Library, The Hague Gemeentemuseum; Vocal Music 1500-c.1650.* New York: Da Capo Press, 1973. (Ref. 615)

Charles, Sidney R. *Handbook of Music and Music Literature in Sets and Series.* New York: Free Press, 1972. (Ref. 43)

Chase, G. *A Guide to the Music of Latin America.* Washington, DC.: Pan American Union & Library of Congress, 1962. (Ref. 358)

Chase, G. *America's Music From the Pilgrims to the Present.* New York: McGraw-Hill, 1955. (Ref. 266)

Chase, G. *The Music of Spain.* New York: Dover, 1959. (Ref. 354)

Chiti, Patricia Adkins. *Donne in Musica.* Rome: Bulzoni Editore, 1982. (Ref. 502)

Chkhikvadze, Grigori. *Composers of the Georgian Soviet Socialist Republic.* Musical Fund of the Georgian Soviet Socialist Republic, 1949. (Ref. 458)

Chominski, J., ed. *Slownik muzykow polskich.* Warsaw: Polskie Wydawnictwo Muzyczne, 1962. (Ref. 118)

Choron, A.E. and Fayolle, F.J.M. *Dictionnaire historique des musiciens, artistes et amateurs, morts ou vivants.* Paris: Valade, 1810-1811. Repr., Hildesheim: Olms Verlag, 1971. (Ref. 119)

Christ, Peter, ed. *Composium., Annual Index of Contemporary Compositions.* Washington: Crystal Musicworks, 1981. (Ref. 468)

Claghem, C.E. *Biographical Dictionary of American Music.* New York: Parker, 1973. (Ref. 53)

Claghorn, Gene. *Women Composers and Hymnists; A Concise Biographical Dictionary.* Metuchen, NJ.: Scarecrow Press, 1984. (Ref. 646)

Claro, S.V. and Blondel, J.U. *Historia de la musica en Chile.* Santiago: Editorial Orbe, 1973. (Ref. 90)

Clausen, P.G., comp. *Dansk musik: Katalog over statsbibliotekets samling af rykte musikalier.* Aarhus: Universitetsforlaget, 1977. (Ref. 331)

Clement, F. and Larousse, P. *Dictionnaire des operas.* Rev. Pougin Arthur. Paris: Larousse, 1905. Repr., New York: Da Capo Press, 1969. (Ref. 351)

Cobbett, W.W., comp. *Cyclopedic Survey of Chamber Music.* 2nd ed. London: Oxford University Press, 1963. (Ref. 41)

Coeuroy, A. *Dictionnaire critique de la musique ancienne et moderne.* Paris: Payot, 1956. (Ref. 172)

Cohen, Aaron I. *International Discography of the Women Composers.* Westport, CT.: Greenwood Press, 1983. (Ref. 563)

Collaer, Paul and Linden, Albert Vander. *Historical Atlas of Music.* London: George G. Harrap & Co. (Ref. 607)

Composers' Guild of Great Britain. *British Orchestral Music.* London: British Music Information Centre, 1958. (Ref. 407)

Composers' Guild of Great Britain. *Chamber Music by Living British Composers.* London: British Music Information Centre, 1969. (Ref. 408)

Composers' Guild of Great Britain. *Instrumental Solos and Duos by Living British Composers.* London: British Music Information Centre, 1972. (Ref. 409)

Composers' Guild of Great Britain. *Keyboard Solos and Duos by Living British Composers.* London: British Music Information Centre, 1974. (Ref. 410)

Composers' Guild of Great Britain. *Orchestral Music by Living British Composers.* London: British Music Information Centre, 1970. (Ref. 411)

Compositores Contemporaneos Puertorriquenos. Puerto Rico: Centro de Investigaciones y Ediciones Musicales, 1981. (Ref. 549)

Compositores de America/Composers of the Americas. Washington, DC.: Secretaria General, 1955-1972. (Ref. 371)

Composium: Directory of New Music. Washington, DC.: Crystal Record Co. 1971-1979. (Ref. 185)

Contemporary Hungarian Composers. 3rd rev. & enl. ed. Budapest: Editio Musica, 1967. (Ref. 320)

Cooper. David Edwin. *International Bibliography of Discographies.* Littleton, CO.: Libraries Unlimited, Inc., 1975. (Ref. 511)

Cooper, M., ed. *The Concise Encyclopedia of Music and Musicians.* London: Hutchinson, 1958. (Ref. 48)

Coover, James and Colvig, Richard. *Medieval and Renaissance Music on Long-Playing Records.* Detroit, MI.: Detroit Studies in Music Bibliography, 1964. (Ref. 510)

Coover, James and Colvig, Richard. *Medieval and Renaissance Music on Long Playing Records.* Supl. Detroit, MI.: Information Coordinators, 1973. (Ref. 513)

Coover, James. *Music Lexicography.* Carlisle, PA.: Carlisle Books, 1971. (Ref. 526)

Corbet, A. and Paap. W. *Algemene muziekencyclopedie.* Antwerp: Zuid-Nederlanse Uigeverij, 1957-1963; supl. Robijns, Jozef ed. Ghent-Louvain: Wetenschappelijke Uitgeverij E. Story-Scientia, 1972. (Ref. 1)

Corte, A. della and Gatti, G.M., eds. *Dizionario di musica.* Turin: Peravia, 1959. (Ref. 10)

Cosma, V. *Muzicieni Romani: Compozitori si muzicologi.* Bucharest: Uniunii Compozitorilor, 1965 and 1970. (Ref. 196)

Covell, R. *Australia's Music.* Melbourne: Sun Books, 1967. (Ref. 58)

Crawford, Anne., Hayter, Tony., Hughes, Ann., Prochaska, Frank., Stafford, Pauline and Vallance, Elizabeth. *The Europa Biographical Dictionary of British Women.* Europa Publications, 1983. (Ref. 645)

Creighton, J. *Discopaedia of the Violin, 1889-1971.* Toronto: University of Toronto Press, 1974. (Ref. 63)

Croucher, Trevor, comp. *Early Music Discography.* London: Library Association, 1981. (Ref. 541)

Cuney-Hare, M. *Negro Musicians and Their Music.* Washington, DC.: Associated Publishers, 1936. (Ref. 328)

D'Erlanger, R. *La musique Arabe.* Paris: Geuthner, 1949. (Ref. 235)

Danish Composers' Society. *Danske Komponister af i dag.* Copenhagen: Dansk Komponistforening, 1980. (Ref. 499)

Dassori, C. *Opere e operisti: Dizionario lirico universale, 1541-1902.* Genoa: Sordomuti, 1903. (Ref. 225)

Davies, H., comp. *International Electronic Music Catalogue.* Paris: Groupe de Recherches Musicales de l'ORTF & New York Independent Electronic Music Center, 1968. (Ref. 57)

De Angelis, A. *Dizionario dei musicisti.* Rome: Ansonia, 1922. (Ref. 86)

De Beauvoir, S. *The Second Sex.* Trans. & ed. Parshley, H.M. Harmondsworth: Penguin Books, 1972; Repr., 1976. (Ref. 317)

De Cande, R. *La musique: Histoire, dictionnaire, discographie.* Paris: Seuil, 1969. (Ref. 72)

De Li Arienti, J.S. *Gynevera de la clare donne.* Bologna: Presso Romagnoli dell'Acqua, 1888. (Ref. 249)

De Mirimonde, A.P. *Sainte Cécile: Metamorphoses d'un Thème Musical.* Geneva: Minkoff, 1974. (Ref. 424)

De Vasconcellos, J. *Os Musicos portuguezes.* Porto: Imprensa Portugueza, 1870. (Ref. 300)

Dearling, Robert, et al. *The Guinness Book of Music Facts and Feats, 1976.* Middlesex: Guinness, 1976. (Ref. 177)

Dearling, Robert and Celia. *The Guinness Book of Music.* 2nd ed. Enfield: Guinness Superlatives Ltd., 1981. (Ref. 469)

Der Schweizerische Tonkuenstlerverein im zweiten Vierteljahrhundert seines Bestehens. Zurich: Atlantis Verlag, 1950. (Ref. 552)

Detheridge, J., comp. *Chronology of Music Composers.* Birmingham: Detheridge, 1936. (Ref. 173)

Dibelius, U. *Moderne Musik, 1945-1965.* Munich: Piper, 1966. (Ref. 294)

Dickinson, Edward. *Music in the History of the Western Church.* New York: Greenwood Press, 1969. (Ref. 531)

Dictionnaire des musiciens français. Paris: Seghers, 1961. (Ref. 51)

Directory of New Music, 1982/1983. Composium. (Ref. 624)

Dlabacz, G.J. *Allgemeines historisches Kuenstler Lexikon fuer Boehmen, etc.* Prague: Haase, 1915. Repr., Hildesheim: Georg Olms Verlag, 1973. (Ref. 340)

Donakowski, C.L. *A Muse for the Masses: Ritual and Music in the Age of Democratic Revolution, 1770-1870*. Chicago: University of Chicago Press, 1977. (Ref. 309)

Donemus General Catalogue: Dutch Contemporary Music. Amsterdam: Donemus, 1977. (Ref. 283)

Donington, Robert. *The Rise of Opera*. London: Faber & Faber, 1981. (Ref. 554)

Drinker, S. *Music and Women: The Story of Women in Their Relation to Music*. Washington, DC.: Zenger, 1948; Repr., 1977. (Ref. 264)

Drone, J.M. *Index to Opera, Operetta and Musical Comedy Synopses in Collections and Periodicals*. Metuchen, NJ.: Scarecrow Press, 1978. (Ref. 295)

Duckles, Vincent, ed. *Music Reference and Research Materials*. New York: Free Press, 1974. (Ref. 527)

Dufourcq, N., ed. *Larousse de la musique*. Paris: Larousse, 1957. (Ref. 13)

Duncan, Edmondstoune. *The Story of Minstrelsy*. London: Walter Scott Publishing Co., 1907. (Ref. 567)

Dunstan, R. *A Cyclopaedic Dictionary of Music*. London: Curwen, 1908. (Ref. 369)

Dziebowska, Elzbieta, ed. *Encyklopedia Muzyczna*. Vol 1 & 2. Cracow: Polskie Wydawnictwo Muzyczne, 1979. (Ref. 524)

Dziebowskia, E., ed. *Polska wspotczesna kultura muzyczna, 1944-1964*. Cracow: Polskie Wydawnickwo Muzyczne, 1964. (Ref. 293)

Eagon, A. *Catalog of Published Concert Music by American Composers*. 2nd ed. Metuchen, NJ.: Scarecrow Press, 1969; supl. 1971 and 1974. (Ref. 146)

Edwards, J.M. *Literature for Voices in Combination with Electronic and Tape Music: An Annotated Bibliography*. MLA Index and Bibliography Series, no. 17. Ann Arbor, MI.: Music Library Association, 1977. (Ref. 301)

Ehrismann, Sibylle and Meyer, Thomas, eds. *Schweizer Komponistinnen der Gegenwart*. Zurich: Musik Hug & Co., 1985. (Ref. 651)

Einstein, A. *Das neue Musiklexikon*. Berlin: Hesse, 1926. (Ref. 115)

Eitner, R., ed. *Bibliographie der Musik-Sammelwerke des XVI und XVII Jahrhunderts*. Berlin: Liepmannssohn, 1877. (Ref. 127)

Eitner, R., ed. *Biographisch-bibliographisches Quellen-Lexikon der Musiker und Musikgelehrten christlicher Zeitrechnung bis Mitte des neunzehnten Jahrhunderts*. Graz: Akademische Druck-und Verlaganstalt, 1960. (Ref. 128)

Elson, A. *Woman's Work in Music*. ME.: Longwood Press. 1976. (Ref. 260)

Elson, L.C. *Curiosities of Music: A Collection of Facts Not Generally Known, Regarding the Music of Ancient and Savage Nations*. Boston: Ditson. (Ref. 209)

Elson, L.C. *The History of American Music*. New York: Macmillan, 1904. (Ref. 352)

Emery, F.B. *The Violin Concerto*. Chicago: Violin Literature Publishing, 1928. Repr., New York: Da Capo Press, 1969. (Ref. 7)

Enciclopedia da Musica Brasileira: Erudita, folclorica et popular. San Paulo: Art Editora, 1977. (Ref. 333)

Enciclopedia Garzanti della musica. Rome: Garzanti, 1974. (Ref. 88)

Encyclopaedia Britannica: A New Survey of Universal Knowledge. Chicago: Encyclopaedia Britannica, 1946. (Ref. 208)

Encyclopedie van de muziek. Amsterdam: Elsevier, 1956-1957. (Ref. 44)

Engman, Bo. *Svensk 1900-talsmusik fraan opera till pop 2000 biografier*. Stockholm: Bokfoerlaget Natur och Kultur, 1978. (Ref. 456)

Erhardt, L. *Music in Poland*. Warsaw: Interpress, 1975. (Ref. 258)

Evans, Mary J. *Woman in the Bible*. Exeter: Paternoster Press, 1983. (Ref. 634)

Ewen, David. *American Composers*. New York: G.P. Putnam's Sons, 1982. (Ref. 560)

Fahmy, M. *La condition de la femme dans la tradition et l'évolution de l'islamisme*. Paris: Alcan, 1913. (Ref. 356)

Fairbairn, N. and Unger-Hamilton, C., eds. *Royal Collection: A Historical Album of Music Composed Exclusively by Members of the Royal Family of Great Britian and Ireland*. Sevenoaks: Novello, 1977. (Ref. 262)

Famera, K.M. *Catalog of the American Music Center Library: Chamber Music*. New York: American Music Center Library, 1978. (Ref. 401)

Farmer, H.G. *A History of Arabian Music to the XIIIth Century*. London: Luzac, 1973. (Ref. 171)

Farmer, H.G. *Music: The Priceless Jewel, from the Kitab al-iqd al-farid of ibn-Abd Rabbihi*. Bearsden: Author, 1942. (Ref. 186)

Farmer, H.G. *Musik des Mittelalters und der Renaissance: Islam. Musikgeschichte in Bildern*. Vol. 2, pt. 3, ed. Besseler, Heinrich and Schneider, Max. Leipzig: VEB Deutscher Verlag fuer Musik, 1976. (Ref. 305)

Fellerer, K.G., ed. *Rheinische Musiker*. Cologne: Arno Volk-Verlag, 1962. (Ref. 192)

Fellowes, Edmund Horace. *The English Madrigal Composers*. Oxford: Clarendon Press, 1921. (Ref. 542)

Ferrara (City of). *Catalogo delle opere musicali ... città di Ferrara*. Parma: Associazione dei Musicologi Italiani, 1917. (Ref. 83)

Ferri, P.L. *Biblioteca femminile italiana Padua*. Tipografia Crescini, 1842. (Ref. 327)

Fetis, F.J. *Biographie universelle des musiciens et bibliographie génèrale de la musique*. 2nd ed. Paris: Firmin Didot Freres, 1866-1879. Repr., Brussels: Culture et Civilisation, 1972. (Ref. 26)

Fey, H. *Schleswig-Holsteinische Musiker, von den aeltesten Zeiten bis zur Gegenwart: ein Heimatbuch*. Hamburg: Holler, 1922. (Ref. 393)

Fink, R., et al., eds. *Directory of Michigan Composers*. Michigan: Western Michigan University, 1977. (Ref. 395)

Finnish Orchestra Works, Vocal Works with Orchestra, Operas, Ballets. Foundation for the Promotion of Finnish Music, 1973. (Ref. 599)

Fleischmann, A., ed. *Music in Ireland: A Symposium*. Dublin: Cork University Press, 1952. (Ref. 50)

Florence (City of). *Catalogo delle opere musicali ... citta di Firenze*. Parma: Associazione dei Musicologi Italiani, 1929. (Ref. 158)

Fog, D. *Dansk musiskfortegnelse*. Copenhagen: Dan Fog Musikforlag, 1979. (Ref. 413)

Fontanals. M. *De los trovadores en España: Estudio lengua y poesia provenzal*. Barcelona: Libreria de Joaquin Verdaguer, 1861. (Ref. 28)

Foreman, L. *British Music Now*. London: Elek, 1975. (Ref. 69)

Frank, P., and Altmann, W. *Kurzgefasstes Tonkuenstlerlexikon*. Regensburg: Bosse, 1936; 15th ed. Wilhelmshaven: Heinrichshofen, 1974. (Ref. 70)

Frasier, Jane. *Women Composers; A Discography*. Detroit: Information Co-ordinators, 1983. (Ref. 649)

Frati, L. *Studi e notizie riguardanti la storia della musica*. Bologna: Forni, 1976. (Ref. 242)

Frey, Linda., Frey, Marsha and Schneider, Joanne., eds. *Women in Western European History*. Westport, CT.: Greenwood Press, 1982. (Ref. 575)

Friedland, Bea. *Louise Farrenc, 1804-1875*. Ann Arbor, MI.: UMI Research Press, 1980. (Ref. 593)

Friskin, J. and Freundlich, I. *Music for the Piano: A Handbook of Concert and Teaching Material from 1580-1952*. New York: Rinehart, 1954. Repr., New York: Dover, 1973. (Ref. 138)

Fuld, J.J. *The Book of World-Famous Music: Classical, Popular and Folk,* Rev. & enl. ed. New York: Crown Publishers, 1971; Repr., 1975. (Ref. 370)

Futrell, Jon., Gill, Chris., St. Pierre, Roger., Richardson, Clive., Trengove, Chris., Fisher, Bob., Sheehy, Bill and Wesker, Lindsay. *The Illustrated Encyclopedia of Black Music*. London: Salamander Books Ltd. (Ref. 614)

Gabet, C. *Dictionnaire des artistes de l'école française aux XIXe siècle*. Paris: Vergne, 1851. (Ref. 263)

Gaoldbeck, F. France, Italy and Spain. *Twentieth Century Composers*. Vol. 4. London: Weidenfeld & Nicolson, 1974. (Ref. 154)

Garcia, F.M. *Pequeñas biografias de grandes musicos mexicanos*. Mexico: Ediciones Framong, 1966. (Ref. 82)

Gardavsky, C. *Contemporary Czechoslovak composers*. Prague: Panton, 1965. (Ref. 32)

Gardeton, C. *Annales de la musique: ou, Almanach musical pour l'an 1819 et 1820*. Paris: Annales de la Musique, 1820. Repr., Geneva: Minkoff, 1978. (Ref. 314)

Gardeton, D. *Bibliographie musicale de la France et de l'étranger*. Paris: Niogret, 1822. Repr., Geneva: Minkoff, 1976. (Ref. 312)

Gaspari, G. *Catalogo della biblioteca del liceo musicale di Bologna*. Bologna: Libreria Romagnoli dall'Acqua, 1890. (Ref. 216)

Gaster, A., ed. *International Who's Who in Music and Musicians' Directory*. 8th ed. London: International Who's Who in Music, 1977. (Ref. 206)

Gaster, Adrian., ed. *International Who's Who in Music and Musicians' Directory*. Cambridge, England: Melrose Press, 1980. (Ref. 457)

Gatti, G.M. and Basso, A. *La musica: Enciclopedia storica*. Turin: Unione Tipografico-Editrice Torinese, 1966. (Ref. 14)

Gerber, E.L. *Historisch-biographisches Lexikon der Tonkuenstler, 1790-1792; und, Neues historisch-biographisches Lexikon der Tonkuenstler, 1812-1814*. Othmar, Wessely ed. Graz: Akademische Druck-und Verlaganstalt, 1966. (Ref. 126)

German Music Archive of the German Library. Bonner Katalog. Munich: K.G. Saur, 1982. (Ref. 495)

Gevaert, F. Aug. *Histoire et Theorie de la Musique de L'Antiquite*. Hildesheim: Georg Olms Verlagsbuchhandlung, 1965. (Ref. 591)

Gibelli, V. *Storia della musica sovietica: Compositori e composizioni della Russa europea e asiatica*. Pavia: Tipografia del Libro, 1964-1965. (Ref. 223)

Gibelli, V. *Musicisti di oggi nell' U.R.S.S.* Milan: Giuffre, 1972. (Ref. 420)

Gifford, Virginia Snodgrass. *Music for Oboe, Oboe D'Amore and English Horn*. Westport, CT.: Greenwood Press, 1983. (Ref. 574)

Gilder, E. and Port, J.G. *Dictionary of Composers and Their Music*. London: Paddington Press, 1978. (Ref. 284)

Gillespie, J. *Five Centuries of Keyboard Music*. New York: Dover, 1965; repr., 1972. (Ref. 140)

Gimbutas, Marija. *The Goddesses and Gods of Old Europe*. London: Thames & Hudson, 1982. (Ref. 578)

Gingras, C. *Musiciennes de chez nous*. Montreal: Editions de l'Ecole Vincent d'Indy, 1955. (Ref. 355)

Glyn, Margaret H. *Elizabethan Virginal Music and Its Composers*. 2nd ed. London: William Reeves, 1934. (Ref. 437)

Goertz, Harald. *Oesterreichische Komponisten der Gegenwart*. Munich: Doblinger, 1979. (Ref. 452)

Gojowy, D. *Neue sowjetische Musik der 20er Jahre*. Regensburg: Laaber, 1980. (Ref. 200)

Golitsma, A.M. *Sovietski Operi*. Moscow: Sovietski Kompozitor, 1982. (Ref. 553)

Goodman, A.A. *Musik von A-Z: vom Gregorianischen Choral zu Jazz und Beat*. Munich: Suedwest Verlag, 1971. (Ref. 201)

Goodwater, L. *Women in Antiquity: An Annotated Bibliography*. Metuchen, NJ.: Scarecrow Press, 1975. (Ref. 274)

Goss, M. *Modern Music Makers*. New York: Dutton, 1952. (Ref. 71)

Gradenwitz, Peter. *Music and Musicians in Israel*. Tel Aviv: Israeli Music Publications, 1959. (Ref. 205)

Gradenwitz, Peter. *Musik zwischen Orient und Okzident*. Hamburg: Heinrichshofen's Verlag. (Ref. 600)

Graves, Robert. *New Larousse Encyclopedia of Mythology*. London: Hamlyn, 1959. (Ref. 606)

Gray, Michael H. and Gibson, Gerald D. *Bibliography of Discographies. Classical Music 1925-1975*. New York: R.R. Bowker Co., 1977. (Ref. 512)

Green, M.D. *Study of the Lives and Works of Black Women Composers in America*. Ann Arbor, MI.: Xerox University Microfilms, 1975. (Ref. 335)

Green, S. *Encyclopaedia of the Musical Theatre*. New York: Dodd; Mead, 1976. (Ref. 392)

Grodner, M. *Comprehensive Catalog of Available Literature for the Double Bass*. 2nd ed. Bloomington, IN.: Lemur Musical Research, 1964. (Ref. 80)

Grove, G. *Dictionary of Music and Musicians*. London: Macmillan, 1890; 5th ed. Blom Eric, ed. New York: St. Martin's Press, 6th Ed., 1970. (Ref. 8)

Guelke, P. *Moenche/Buerger Minnesaenger: Musik in der Gesellenschaft des europaeischen Mittelalters*. Vienna: Boehlaus, 1975. (Ref. 364)

Gustafson, Bruce. *French Harpsichord Music of the 17th-Century*. Ann Arbor, MI.: University Microfilms International, 1977. (Ref. 573)

Grande enciclopedia portuguesa e brasileira. Lisbon: Editorial Enciclopedia Lda. (Ref. 290)

Hadley, Benjamin, ed. *Britannica Book of Music*. New York: Doubleday & Company, Inc. 1980. (Ref. 459)

Haefeli, Anton. *Die internationale Gesellschaft fuer neue Musik*. Zurich: Atlantis Musikbuch-Verlag, 1982. (Ref. 558)

Hamburger, P. *Aschehougs musikleksikon*. Copenhagen: Aschehougs, 1957-1958. (Ref. 98)

Hamel, F. and Huerlimann, M. *Enciclopedia de la musica*. 7th ed. Barcelona: Grijalbo, 1979. (Ref. 204)

Hamm, Charles. *Music in the New World*. New York: W.W. Norton, 1983. (Ref. 579)

Hammer-Purgstall. *Literaturgeschichte der Araber*. Vienna: Staatsdruckerei, 1850. (Ref. 234)

Harman, A., et al. *Man and His Music*. London: Barrie & Jenkins, 1962. (Ref. 386)

Harris, C.A. and Hargrave, M. *The Story of British Music and Earlier French Musicians*. London: Waverley Books, 1919. (Ref. 149)

Harrison, F. *Time, Place and Music: An Anthology of Ethnomusicological Observation, ca. 1800*. Amsterdam: Knuf, 1973. (Ref. 256)

Helmer, A. *Svensk solosang, 1850-1890, pt. 1: En genrehistorisk studie*. Stockholm: Almqvist & Wiksell, 1972. (Ref. 167)

Hickmann, H. *Musik des Altertums: Aegypten*. Musikgeschichte in Bildern. Vol. 2, pt. 1. Besseler, Heinrich and Schneider, Max, eds. Leipzig: VEB Deutscher Verlag fuer Musik, 1961- . (Ref. 207)

Higgins, Ardis O. *Windows on Women*. Hollywood, CA.: Halls of Ivy Press, 1975. (Ref. 538)

Hilton, Ruth B. *An Index to Early Music in Selected Anthologies*. Clifton, NJ.: European American Music Corporation, 1978. (Ref. 525)

Hinding, Andrea., Bower, Ames Sheldon and Chambers, Clarke A., eds. *Women's History Sources*. New York: R.R. Bowker Co., 1979. (Ref. 597)

Hinson, M. *Guide to the Pianist's Repertoire*. Freundlich, Irwin, ed. Bloomington, IN.: Indiana University Press, 1973. (Ref. 52)

Hipsher, E.E. *American Opera and Its Composers*. Philadelphia: Presser, 1927. Repr., New York: Da Capo Press, 1978. (Ref. 304)

Histoire litteraire des troubadours. Paris: Dur & Neveu, 1774. (Ref. 221)

Hixon, D.L. and Hennessee, D. *Women in Music: A Bio-bibliography*. Metuchen, NJ.: Scarecrow Press, 1975. (Ref. 85)

Hixon, Donald L. *Music in Early America*. Metuchen, NJ.: Scarecrow Press, Inc., 1970. (Ref. 489)

Hoeijer, J.L. *Musik-Lexikon*. Stockholm: Lundquist, 1864. (Ref. 103)

Holmes, John L. *Conductors on Record*. Westport, CA.: Greenwood Press, 1982. (Ref. 492)

Holy Bible. (Ref. 576)

Honegger, M. and Massenkeil, G. *Das grosse Lexikon der Musik*. Freiburg: Herder, 1976. (Ref. 360)

Honegger, M. *Dictionnaire de la musique*. Paris: Bordas, 1970. (Ref. 12)

Hoppin, Richard H. *Medieval Music*. New York: W.W. Norton & Co. 1978. (Ref. 568)

Howard, J.T. and Mendel, A. *Our Contemporary Composers: American Music in the Twentieth Century*. Philadelphia: Blackiston, 1943. (Ref. 168)

Hughes, A. *Medieval Music: The Sixth Liberal Art*. Toronto: University of Toronto Press, 1974. (Ref. 365)

Hughes, R. *Biographical Dictionary of Musicians*. Rev. ed., Deems, Taylor and Kerr, Russel. New York: Blue Ribbon Books, 1971. (Ref. 271)

Hull, A.E., ed. *Dictionary of Modern Music and Musicians*. London: Dent, 1924. (Ref. 23)

Huskisson, Y. *Bantu Composers of South Africa*. Johannesburg: South African Broadcasting Corporation, 1969. (Ref. 37)

Huys, B. *Catalogue des partitions musicales édites en Belgique et acquises par la bibliothèque Royale Albert 1, 1966-1975*. Brussels: Bibliothèque Royale Albert 1, 1976. (Ref. 188)

Imamuddin, S.M. *Muslim Spain 711-1492 A.D.* Leiden: E.J. Brill, 1981. (Ref. 647)

Institute of History of the Arts. *History of Russian Soviet Music*. Moscow, 1956. (Ref. 441)

International Who's Who in Music and Musicians's Directory. 10th ed. Cambridge, England: International Who's Who in Music, 1985. (Ref. 643)

Internationales Musikinstitut Darmstadt. *Katalog der Abteilung Noten*. Darmstadt: The Institute, 1966. (Ref. 189)

Ireland, N.O. *Index to Women of the World from Ancient to Modern Times: Biographes and Portraits*. Westwood, MA.: Faxon, 1970. (Ref. 353)

Jablonski, Edward. *The Encyclopedia of American Music*. Garden City, New York: Doubleday and Co., 1981. (Ref. 610)

Jackson, Richard. United States Music. *Sources of Bibliography and Collective Biography*. New York: Department of Music, 1973. (Ref. 451)

Jacobi, H.W., comp. *Contemporary American Composers*. California: Paradise Arts, 1975. (Ref. 137)

Jacobs, A., ed. *British Music Yearbook: A Survey and Directory with Statistics and Reference Articles for 1976*. New York: R.R. Bowker Co., 1976. (Ref. 230)

Jacobs, A., ed. *British Music Yearbook 1980*. 6th ed. London: Black, 1980. (Ref. 422)

Jacobs, A., ed. *Penguin Dictionary of Music*. Harmondsworth: Penguin, 1967. (Ref. 11)

Jacobs, Arthur and Barton, Marianne, eds. *British Music Yearbook 1982*. London: Adam & Charles Black, 1982. (Ref. 522)

Jarman, L., ed. *Canadian Music: A Selected Checklist, 1950-1973*. Toronto: University of Toronto Press, 1976. (Ref. 288)

Johnson, H.E. *First Performances in America to 1900*. Detroit: Information Co-ordinators for College Music Society, 1979. (Ref. 429)

Kallman, H., ed. *Catalogue of Canadian Composers*. Rev. & enl. ed. Ottawa: Canadian Broadcasting Corporation. Repr., St. Clair Shores, MI.: Scholarly Press, 1972. (Ref. 133)

Kallmann, H., Potvin, G. and Winters, K., eds. *Encyclopedia of Music in Canada*. Toronto: University of Toronto Press, 1981. (Ref. 485)

Kanahele, George S., ed. *Hawaiian Music and Musicians: An Illustrated History*. Honolulu: University Press of Hawaii, 1979. (Ref. 438)

Kaufmann, Walter. *Musical References in the Chinese Classics*. Detroit: Information Co-ordinators Inc., 1976. (Ref. 640)

Kay, E. *International Who's Who in Music*. 7th ed. Cambridge: International Who's Who in Music, 1975. (Ref. 77)

Kay, E. *The World's Who's Who of Women*. Cambridge, England: Melrose Press, 1975. (Ref. 84)

Kay, Ernest., ed. *Dictionary of International Biography*. Cambridge, England: International Biographical Centre, 1979. (Ref. 359)

Keldysh, Y.V., ed. *Muzykalnaya entsiklopedia*. Moscow: Sovietski Kompozitor, 1973- . (Ref. 330)

Kelen, P.P. *Manuel de la musique*. Paris: Centurion, 1961. (Ref. 64)

Keller, G. and Kruseman, P., eds. *Geillustreed Muzieklexikon*. 's Gravenhage: Kruseman, 1932. (Ref. 110)

Kelly, J.W. *The Faust Legend in Music*. Detroit: Information Co-ordinators, 1976. (Ref. 376)

Kemp-Welch, A. *Of Six Mediaeval Women*. Williamstown, MA.: Corner House Publishers, 1979. (Ref. 179)

Kendall, A. *The Tender Tyrant, Nadia Boulanger*. London: MacDonald & Jane's, 1976. (Ref. 363)

Kenneson, C. *Bibliography of Cello Ensemble Music*. Detroit Studies in Music Bibliography. Detroit: Information Co-ordinators, 1974. (Ref. 229)

Keren, Zvi. *Contemporary Israeli Music*. Israel: Bar Ilan University Press, 1980. (Ref. 501)

Key, M.R. *Male/Female Language*. Metuchen, NJ.: Scarecrow Press, 1975. (Ref. 272)

Kinsky, George. *Album Musical*. Paris: Librairie Delagrave, 1930. (Ref. 595)

Knape, Walter. *Karl Friedrich Abel*. Bremen: Schuenemann Universitaetsverlag, 1973. (Ref. 503)

Koch, W.A. *Musisches Lexikon: Kuenstler, Kunstwerke und Motive aus Dichtung, Musik und bildender Kunst*. 3rd ed. Stuttgart: Kroener, 1976. (Ref. 202)

Koltypina, and Pavlova, N.G. *Soviet Literature and Music*. Moscow: Sovietski Kompozitor, 1979. (Ref. 498)

Komponisten und Musikwissenschaftler der Deutschen Demokratischen Republik. Berlin: Verlag Neue Musik, 1959. (Ref. 589)

Kondracki, M., et al. *International Electronic Music Discography*. Mainz: Schott, 1979. (Ref. 406)

Kornmueller, P.U. *Lexikon der kirchlichen Tonkunst*. Regensburg: Coppenrath, 1891-1895. (Ref. 215)

Kovacevic, K., ed. *Muzicka enciklopedija*. Zagreb: Jugoslavenski Leksikografski Zavod, 1971. (Ref. 109)

Kovacevic, K. *Muzicko stvaralastvo u rvatskoj, 1945-1965*. Zagreb: Udruzenje Kompozitora Hrvatske, 1966. (Ref. 416)

Krohn, Ernst C. *Missouri Music*. New York: Da Capo Press, 1971. (Ref. 460)

Krueger, K. *The Musical Heritage of the United States*. New York: Society for the Preservation of the American Musical Heritage, 1974. (Ref. 144)

Krummel, D.W., Geil, Jean., Dyen, Doris J., and Root, Deane L. *Resources of American Music History*. Chicago, IL.: University of Illinois Press, 1981. (Ref. 537)

Krustev, Venelin. *Bulgarian Music. Sofia Press, 1978*. (Ref. 466)

La Mara (pseud. of Marie Lipsius). *Musikalische Studienkoepfe*. Leipzig: Breitkopf & Haertel, 1883. (Ref. 163)

Laade, Wolfgang. *Musik der Goetter, Geister und Menschen*. Baden-Baden: Verlag Valentin Koerner, 1975. (Ref. 561)

Laplante, L., ed. *Compositeurs Canadiens contemporains*. Montreal: Presses de l'Universite du Quebec, 1977. (Ref. 402)

Laurence, A. *Women of Note: 1,000 Women Composers Born Before 1900*. New York: Rosen Press, 1978. (Ref. 433)

Lavalliere, L. *Ballets, opera et autres ouvrages lyriques, par ordre chronologique depuis leur origine avec une table alphabetique des ouvrages et des auteurs*. Paris: Baudré, 1760. Repr., London: Baron, 1967. (Ref. 396)

Ledebur, C. von. *Tonkuenstler-Lexikon Berlins von den aeltesten Zeiten bis auf die Gegenwart*. Berlin: Rauh, 1861. (Ref. 121)

Lepage, Jane Weiner. *Women Composers, Conductors and Musicians of the Twentieth Century*. London: Scarecrow Press, Inc., 1980. (Ref. 454)

Lerma, Dominique-René de. *Black Concert and Recital Music*. Bloomington, IN.: Afro-American Music Opportunities Assoc., 1975. (Ref. 523)

Levati, A. *Dizionario biografico cronologico*. Milan: Bettoni, 1822. (Ref. 181)

Levati, A. *Dizionario delle donne illustri*. Milan, 1821. (Ref. 350)

Levis, J.H. *Foundations of Chinese Musical Art*. 2nd ed. New York: Paragon, 1963. (Ref. 257)

Levy, Michael S. *Catalogue of Serious Music, Original Works, Arrangements and Orchestrations by members of SAMRO*. Johannesburg: SAMRO, 1982. (Ref 520)

Lichtenthal, P. Dizionario e bibliografia della musica. Milan: Fontana, 1826. (Ref. 66)

Lieberman, Fredric. *Chinese Music, An Annotated Bibliography*. New York; London: Garland Publishing Inc., 1979. (Ref. 546)

Limbacher, James L., ed. *Keeping Score. Film Music 1972-1979*. Metuchen, NJ.: Scarecrow Press, 1981. (Ref. 497).

Limbacher, James L., ed. *Film Music: From Violins to Video*. Metuchen, NJ.: Scarecrow Press, 1974. (Ref. 326)

Lindsay, J. *The Troubadours and Their World of the Twelfth and Thirteenth Centuries*. London: Muller, 1976. (Ref. 243)

Linker, R.W. *Music of the Minnesinger and Early Meistersinger: A Bibliography*. Chapel Hill, NC.: University of North Carolina Press, 1962. (Ref. 25)

Lipman, Samuel. *Music after Modernism*. New York: Basic Books, Inc., 1979. (Ref. 535)

Livermore, A. *A Short History of Spanish Music*. London: Duckworth, 1972. (Ref. 244)

Lloyd, Norman. *Grosses Lexikon der Musik*. Bertelsmann Lexikon-Verlag, 1968. (Ref. 602)

Lombard, M. *The Golden Age of Islam*. Trans Spencer, Joan. Amsterdam: North-Holland Publishing Co., 1975. (Ref. 174)

Londeix, J.M. *125 ans de musique pour saxophone*. Paris: Leduc, 1971. (Ref. 76)

Machlis, J. *Introduction to Contemporary Music*. 2nd ed. New York: Norton, 1979. (Ref. 397)

Mackay, Andy. *Electronic Music*. Minneapolis, MN.: Control Data Publishing, 1981. (Ref. 583)

Macksey, J. and Macksey, K. *The Guinness Guide to Feminine Achievements*. London: Guinness Books. (Ref. 404)

Macmillan, K. and Beckwith, J., eds. *Contemporary Canadian Composers*. Toronto: Oxford University Press, 1975. (Ref. 329)

Maillard, Jean. *Anthologie de Chants de Trouveres*. Paris: Editions Aug. Zurfluh, 1967. (Ref. 588)

Malan, J.P., ed. *South African Music Encyclopedia*. Cape Town: Oxford University Press, 1979. (Ref. 377)

Maleady, A.O. *Index to Record and Tape Reviews 1976*. California: Chulainn Press, 1977. (Ref. 282)

Malm, W.P. *Music Cultures of the Pacific, the Near East and Asia*. Englewood Cliffs, NJ.: Prentice-Hall, 1967. (Ref. 259)

Manferrari, U. *Dizionario universale delle opere melodrammatiche*. Florence: Sansoni, 1954. (Ref. 108)

Manuel de bibliographie biographique et d'iconographie des femmes célébres ... par un vieux bibliophile. Paris: Nilsson, 1892. (Ref. 210)

Manson, Adele P. *Calendar of Music and Musicians*. Metuchen, NJ.: Scarecrow Press, 1981. (Ref. 516)

Marco, Guy A. *Information on Music: A Handbook of Reference Sources in European Languages*. Vol. 1. Basic and Universal Sources. Littleton, CO.: Libraries Unlimited, Inc., 1975. (Ref. 528)

Marco, Guy A. *Information on Music: A Handbook of Reference Sources in European Languages*. Vol. 2. The Americas. Littleton, CO.: Libraries Unlimited, Inc., 1977. (Ref. 529)

Mariz, V. *Dicionario bio-bibliografico musical.*, Brasileiro e internacional. Rio de Janeiro: Livraria Kosmos, 1948. (Ref. 106)

Marrou, H.I. *Les troubadours*. Paris: Seuil, 1971. (Ref. 46)

Martens, F.H. *A Thousand and One Nights of Opera*. New York: Appleton, 1926. Repr., New York: Da Capo, 1978. (Ref. 426)

Martin, J. *Nos auteurs et compositeurs dramatiques*. Paris: Flammarion, 1897. (Ref. 296)

Martini, Giovanni Battista. *Storia della Musica, tomo 1, Bologna*. Graz: Akademische Druck - und Verlagsanstalt, 1967. (Ref. 486)

Martini, Giovanni Battista. *Storia Della Musica*. Graz: Akademische Druck - und Verlagsanstalt, 1967. (Ref. 533)

Mata encyklopedia muzyki. Warsaw: Panstwowe Wydawnictwo Naukowe, 1981. (Ref. 504)

Matas, J.R. *Diccionario biografico de la musica*. 2nd ed. Barcelona: Iberia, 1966. (Ref. 361)

Mattfeld, J. *A Handbook of American Operatic Premieres, 1731-1962*. Detroit Studies in Music Bibliography, no. 5. Detroit: Information Co-ordinators, 1963; Repr., 1973. (Ref. 321)

Mayr, Giovanni Simone. *Biografie di Scrittori e Artisti Musicali*. Bologna: Forni Editore, 1875. (Ref. 483)

Mazza, J. *Dicionario biografico de musicos portugueses*. Lisbon, 1770. Repr., Occidente, vol. 24, 1944. (Ref. 99)

McCredie, A.M. *Catalogue of 46 Australian Composers and Selected Works*. Canberra: Advisory Board, Commonwealth Assistance to Australian Composers, 1969. (Ref. 29)

McHenry, Robert, ed. *Famous American Women*. Springfield, MA.: Merriam-Webster Inc., 1980. (Ref. 617)

McHenry, Robert, ed. *Liberty's Women*. Springfield, MA.: G and C Merriam Co. 1980. (Ref. 484)

Meggett, Joan M. *Keyboard Music by Women Composers*. Westport, CT.: Greenwood Press, 1981. (Ref. 477)

Melby, C., comp. *Computer Music Compositions of the United States, 1976*. Cambridge, MA.: Massachusetts Institute of Technology, 1976. (Ref. 227)

Melchior, E.A. *Wetenschappelijk en biographisch woordenboek der Tonkunst*. 2nd ed. Schiedam: Roelants, 1889. (Ref. 400)

Mendel, H. *Musikalisches Conversations-Lexikon: Eine Encyclopaedie der gesammten musikalischen Wissenschaften*. Berlin: Heinemann, 1870-1879. (Ref. 129)

Michaelides, S. *The Music of Ancient Greece*. London: Faber, 1978. (Ref. 281)

Michel, F., et al., eds. *Encyclopèdie de la musique*. Paris: Fasquelle, 1958-1961. (Ref. 9)

Mill, J.S. *The Subjection of Women*. London: Longmans; Green, 1869. (Ref. 248)

Mixter, Keith E. *General Bibliography for Music Research*. Detroit, MI.: Information Co-ordinators, 1975. (Ref. 530)

Mize, Dr. J.T.H., ed. *The International Who's Who in Music*. 5th ed. Chicago: Who Is Who in Music, Inc., 1951. (Ref. 27, 496)

Mizgalski, G. *Podreczna encyclopedia muzyki Koscielnej*. Warsaw: Wojciecha, 1959. (Ref. 417)

Modena (City of). *Catalogo delle opere musicalici ... città di Modena*. Parma: Associazione dei Musicologi Italiani, 1916. (Ref. 157)

Moisenko, R. *Realist Music*. London: Meridian Books, 1949. (Ref. 61)

Mondo della musica: Enciclopedia alfabetica con ampie trattazioni monografiche. Rome: Garzanti. (Ref. 166)

Montagu-Nathan, M. *A History of Russian Music*. ME.: Longwood Press, 1977. (Ref. 261)

Moore, F.L. *Crowell's Handbook of World Opera*. New York: Crowell, 1961. (Ref. 345)

Mooser, R. Aloys. *Annales de la musique et des musiciens en Russie au XVIIIe siècle*. Geneva: Editions du Mont-Blanc, 1948-1951. (Ref. 156)

Mooser, R. Aloys. *Operas, Intermezzos, Ballets Cantates, Oratorios*. Geneva: Imprimerie A. Kundig, 1945. (Ref. 436)

Morris, J. *The Lady Was a Bishop: The Hidden History of Women with Clerical Ordination and the Jurisdiction of Bishops*. New York: Macmillan, 1973. (Ref. 378)

Moser, Hans Joachim. *Musik Lexikon*. Berlin: Hesses Verlag, 1935. (Ref. 231)

Moser, Hans Joachim. *Musik Lexikon*. Hamburg: Musikverlag Hans Sikorski, 1963. (Ref. 551)

Mottini, G.E. *La donna e la musica*. Milan: Vallardi, 1931. (Ref. 367)

Mueller, E.H., ed. *Deutsches Musiker-Lexikon*. Dresden: Limpert, 1929. (Ref. 111)

Murdoch, J. *Australia's Contemporary Composers*. Sydney: Macmillan, 1972. (Ref. 203)

Music: Books on Music and Sound Recordings. Washington DC.: Library of Congress, 1975-1980. (Ref 519)

Music for Orchestra, Band and Large Ensemble. New York: American Music Center, 1982. (Ref. 594)

Musical America. New York: ABC Leisure Magazines, 1983. (Ref. 569)

Musikens hvem hvad hvor: Politikens musikleksikon. Copenhagen: Politikens Forlag, 1950. (Ref. 96)

Muzykalnaya Literatura iz SSSR. Moscow: Vsesoyuznoye Obyedinenie, 1976. (Ref. 277)

Napier, R.A. *Guide to Canada's Composers*. Ontario: Avondale Press, 1976. (Ref. 93)

Naples (City of). *Catalogo generale ... città di Napoli*. Parma: Associazione dei Musicologi Italiani, 1918. (Ref. 155)

Naumann, Emil. *The History of Music*. London: Cassell & Co., 1891. (Ref. 627)

Navaretta, Cynthia. *Guide to Women's Art Organizations and Directory for the Arts*. New York: Midmarch Assoc., 1982. (Ref. 584)

Nettl, B. *Music in Primitive Culture*. Cambridge, MA.: Harvard University Press, 1956; repr., 1977. (Ref. 311)

Neuls-Bates, Carol., ed. *Women in Music*. New York: Harper & Row, 1982. (Ref. 555)

New English Bible. Oxford University Press; Cambridge University Press, 1970. (Ref. 638)

New Larousse Encyclopedia of Mythology. Hamlyn Publishing Group, 1981. (Ref. 543)

Nikolov, N. *Bulgarski kompozitori i muzikovedi: Spravochnik*. 1971. (Ref. 217)

Norlind, T. *Allmaent musiklexikon*. Stockholm: Wahlstroem & Widstrand, 1916. (Ref. 95)

Norris, Gerald. *A Musical Gazetteer of Great Britain and Ireland*. London: David & Charles, 1981. (Ref. 572)

Northouse, C. *Twentieth Century Opera in England and the U.S.A.* Boston: Hall, 1976. (Ref. 141)

Notor, G. *La femme dans L'antiquité grecque*. Paris: Renouard, 1901. (Ref. 254)

Oehrstroem, Eva. *Kvinnliga Komponister i Sverige under 1800 och 1900 Talen*. Stockholm: Haesselby Slott, 1981. (Ref. 642)

Oesterreichischer Komponistenbund. *Orchesterkatalog zeitgenoessischer oesterreichischer Komponisten*. Lubej Emil et al., eds. Vienna: Lafite, 1977. (Ref. 194)

Oja, Carol J., ed. *American Music Recordings*. New York: Institute for Studies in American Music Conservatory of Music, 1982. (Ref. 562)

Oliveira, A.L. de and Viana, M.G. *Dicionario mundial de mulheres notaveis*. Porto: Lello & Irmao, 1967. (Ref. 268)

Oram, D. *An Individual Note of Music, Sound and Electronics*. London: Galliard, 1972. (Ref. 388)

Orestano, F. *Eroine, ispiratrici e donne di eccezione*. Milan: Istituto Editoriale Italiano Bernard Carlo Tossi. (Ref. 182)

Orovio, Helio. *Diccionario de la musica cubana*. Cuba: Editorial Letras Cubanas, 1981. (Ref. 604)

Osborne, C., ed. *The Dictionary of Composers*. London: Bodley Head, 1977. (Ref. 385)

Oztuna, Y. *Turk musikisi ansiklopedisi*. Istanbul: Milli Egitim Basimevi, 1974. (Ref. 430)

Pahlen, K. *Great Singers: From the Seventeenth Century to the Present Day*. New York: Stein & Day, 1974. (Ref. 323)

Paloschi, G., comp. *Annuario musicale storico, cronologico, universale*. 2nd ed. Milan: Stabilimento Musicale Ricordi, 1878. (Ref. 211)

Pan American Union. *Music of Latin America*. 3rd ed. Washington, DC.: Union, 1953. (Ref. 342)

Panum, H., and Behrend, W. *Illustreret musikleksikon*. ed. Hamburger Polv. Copenhagen: Aschehoug, 1940. (Ref. 113)

Paratore, Ettore. *Musica e Poesia Nell'Antica Roma*. Cremona: Fondazione Claudio Monteverdi, 1981. (Ref. 592)

Parkhurst, Winthrop and Bekker L.J. de. *The Encyclopedia of Music and Musicians*. Cleveland, OH.: World Publishing Co., 1943. (Ref. 505)

Parkhurst, Winthrop and Bekker L.J. de. *The Encyclopedia of Music and Musicians*. New York: Crown Publishers, 1937.

Parma (City of). *Catalogo generale delle opere musicali ... città di Parma*. Parma: Associazione dei Musicologi Italiani, 1911. (Ref. 161)

Partnow, Elaine, comp. and ed. *The Quotable Woman*. Los Angeles, CA.: Pinnacle Books Inc., 1977. (Ref. 581)

Pavlakis, C. *The American Music Handbook*. New York: Free Press, 1974. (Ref. 195)

Pazdirek, F. *Universal-Handbuch der Musik-literatur aller Zeiten und Voelker*. Vienna: Pazdirek, 1904-1910. Repr., Hilversum: Knuf, 1967. (Ref. 297)

Pedigo, A. *International Encyclopedia of Violin-Keyboard Sonatas and Composer Biographies*. Booneville, AR: Arriaga, 1979. (Ref. 81)

Pena, J. *Diccionario de la musica Labor*. Barcelona: Labor, 1954. (Ref. 100)

Pericic, V. *Muzicki stvaraoci u Srbiji*. Belgrade: Prosveta, 1969. (Ref. 418)

Pescerelli, B. *Maddalena Casulana: madrigalista del Cinquecento*. Bologna: Universita degli Studi di Bologna, 1974. (Ref. 253)

Petersen, K. and Wilson, J.J. *Women Artists: Recognition and Reappraisal from the Early Middle Ages to the Twentieth Century*. New York: Harper & Row, 1976. (Ref. 239)

Pfeiffer, W.R. *Filipino Music: Indigenous, Folk, Modern*. Dumaguete City, R.P.: Silliman Music Foundation, 1976. (Ref. 265)

Phaidon Book of the Opera. Oxford: Phaidon, 1979. (Ref. 78)

Philadelphia, Free Library. *The Edwin A. Fleisher Collection of Orchestral Music in the Free Library of Philadelphia: A Cumulative Catalog, 1929-1977*. Boston, MA.: Hall, 1979. (Ref. 322)

Pierre Key's Music Year Book. New York: Pierre Key Inc., 1926. (Ref. 556)

Pillet, A. *Bibliographie der Troubadours*. Carstens H., ed. Halle: Niemeyer, 1933. (Ref. 117)

Pirie, Peter J. *The English Musical Renaissance*. London: Victor Gollancz Ltd., 1979. (Ref. 447)

Pistoia (City of). *Catalogo delle opere musicali ... città di Pistoia*. Parma: Associazione dei Musicologi Italiani, 1936-1937. (Ref. 92)

Pleasants, H. *The Great Singers*. New York: Simon & Schuster, 1970. (Ref. 421)

Plowden, A. *Tudor Women: Queens and Commoners*. London: Weidenfeld & Nicolson, 1979. (Ref. 336)

Poirier, Lucien., ed. *Canadian musical works 1900-1980: A Bibliography of general and analytical sources*. Canadian Association of Music Libraries, 1983. (Ref. 631)

Polin, C.C.J. *Music of the Ancient Near East*. New York: Vantage Press, 1954. Repr., Westport, CT.: Greenwood Press, 1976. (Ref. 313)

Polyakova, L. *Soviet Music*. Moscow: Foreign Languages Publishing House. (Ref. 419)

Pomeroy, Sarah B. *Goddesses, Whores, Wives, and Slaves*. New York: Schocken Books, 1975. (Ref. 628)

Pool, J.G. *Women in Music History: A Research Guide*. New York: Author, 1977. (Ref. 269)

Porter, B. and Moss, R.L.B. *Topographical Bibliography of Ancient Egyptian Hieroglyphic Texts, Reliefs and Paintings*. 2nd ed. Oxford: Clarendon Press, 1960. (Ref. 428)

Pratt, W.S. *The New Encyclopedia of Music and Musicians*. Rev. ed. New York: Macmillan, 1929. (Ref. 89)

Press, Jaques Cattell., ed. *Who's Who in American Music*. New York: R.R. Bowker Co., 1983. (Ref. 625)

Prieberg, F.K. *Lexikon der neuen Musik.* Munich: Albert, 1958. (Ref. 73)

Prunieres, Henry. *Nouvelle Histoire de la Musique.* Paris: Aux Editions Rieder, 1934. (Ref. 487)

Putnam, E.J. *The Lady: Studies of Certain Significant Phases of Her History.* Chicago: University of Chicago Press, 1970. (Ref. 338)

Raming, I. *The Exclusion of Women from the Priesthood: Divine Law or Sex Discrimination.* Trans. Adams, Norman R. Metuchen, NJ.: Scarecrow Press, 1976. (Ref. 273)

Ravina, M. and Skolsky, S., comps. *Who Is Who in ACUM: Authors, Composers and Music Publishers Biographical Notes and Principal Works.* Israel: ACUM, 1965. (Ref. 379)

Raynaud, G. *Bibliographie des altfranzoesischen Liedes.* Spanke, Hans ed. Leiden: Brill, 1955. (Ref. 79)

Raynaud, G. *Bibliographie des chansonniers français des XIIIe et XIVe siècles.* Paris: Vieweg, 1884. (Ref. 55)

Raynor, H. *A Social History of Music from the Middle Ages to Beethoven.* London: Barrie & Jenkins, 1972. (Ref. 383)

Raynor, Henry. *Music and Society Since 1815.* (Ref. 596)

Reck, D. *Music of the Whole Earth.* New York: Scribner, 1977. (Ref. 240)

Recupito, M.V. *Artisti e musicisti moderni: Cenni storici, critici e bibliografici con speciale reguardo alla scuola ed all 'esegesi.* Milan: Fiamma, 1933. (Ref. 56)

Reese, Gustave. *Music in the Middle Ages.* London: J.M. Dent & Sons, 1941. (Ref. 565)

Reeser, E., ed. *Music in Holland: A Review of Contemporary Music in the Netherlands.* Amsterdam: Meulenhoff. (Ref. 169)

Refardt, E. *Historisch-biographisches Musikerlexikon der Schweiz.* Leipzig: Gebrueder Hug & Co., 1928. (Ref. 101)

Regli, Francesco., comp. *Dizionario Biografico.* Turin: Coi Tipi Di Enrico Dalmazzo, 1860. (Ref. 470)

Reich, T. *Susreti sa suvremenim kompozitorima jugoslavije.* Zagreb: Skolska Knjiga, 1972. (Ref. 219)

Reinhard, K. and Reinhard, U. *Turquie: Les traditions musicales.* Paris: Buchet, 1969. (Ref. 341)

Reis, C. *Composers in America: Biographical Sketches of Living Composers with a Record of Their Works, 1912-1937.* New York: Macmillan, 1938; rev. & enl. ed., New York: Macmillan, 1947. (Ref. 124)

Rexroth, K. and Chung, L., eds. *The Orchid Boat: Women Poets of China.* New York: McGraw-Hill, 1972. (Ref. 270)

Rezits, J. and Deatsman, G. *The Pianist's Resource Guide: Piano Music in Print and Literature on the Pianistic Art, 1978-1979.* San Diego, CA.: Pallma Music Co., 1979. (Ref. 373)

Ribera, J. *Music in Ancient Arabia and Spain: Being La Musica de las Cantigas.* Stanford, CA.: Stanford University Press, 1929. Repr., New York: Da Capo Press, 1970. (Ref. 170)

Ribera Y Tarrago, J. *La musica andaluza medieval en las canciones de trovadores, troveros y minnesinger.* Madrid: Revista de Archivos, 1923. Repr., New York: AMS Press, 1974. (Ref. 316)

Richards, D. *The Music of Finland.* London: Evelyn, 1968. (Ref. 62)

Rieger, Eva. *Frau, Musik und Maennerherrschaft.* Frankfurt: Verlag Ullstein GmbH, 1981. (Ref. 481)

Riemann, Dr. Hugo. *Opern-Handbuch.* Hildesheim: Georg Olms Verlag, 1979. (Ref. 480)

Riemann, H. *Dictionary of Music.* New ed. Trans. Shedlock, J.S. London: Augener, 1908. (Ref. 132)

Riemann, H. *Dictionnaire de musique.* Paris: Payot, 1931. (Ref. 187)

Riemann, H. *Musik Lexikon.* Gurlitt, Wilibald ed. Mainz: Schott's Soehne, 1972-1975. (Ref. 17)

Roberts, J.S. *Black Music of Two Worlds.* New York: Praeger, 1972. (Ref. 286)

Robijns, Prof. Dr. J. and Zijlstra Miep. *Algemene Muziek Encyclopedie.* Bussum: Unieboek bv., 1980. (Ref. 461)

Robinson, D.M. *Sappho and Her Influence: Our Debt to Greece and Rome.* New York: Cooper Square, 1963. (Ref. 310)

Roche, Jerome and Roche, Elizabeth. *A Dictionary of Early Music.* London: Faber Music, 1981. (Ref. 550)

Rogal, Samuel J. *Sisters of Sacred Song.* New York: Garland Publishing Inc., 1981. (Ref. 482)

Ronald, Sir Landon., ed. *Who's Who in Music.* London: Shaw Publishing Co., Ltd., 1937. (Ref. 467)

Room, Adrian. *Naming Names.* London: Routledge & Kegan Paul, 1981. (Ref. 479)

Rosenberg, Samuel N. and Tischler, Hans. eds. *Chanter M'Estuet, Songs of the Trouveres.* London: Faber Music Ltd., 1981. (Ref. 566)

Rothmueller, A.M. *The Music of the Jews: An Historical Appreciation.* London: Vallentine Mitchell, 1953. (Ref. 139)

Russcol, H. *The Liberation of Sound: An Introduction to Electronic Music.* Englewood Cliffs NJ.: Prentice-Hall, 1972. (Ref. 324)

Sabaneyeff, L. *Modern Russian Composers.* London: Lawrence, 1927. (Ref. 134)

Sachs, C. *The Wellsprings of Music.* The Hague: Nijhoff, 1962. Repr., New York: Da Capo Press, 1977. (Ref. 384)

Sainsbury, J.S. *A Dictionary of Musicians from Earliest Ages to the Present Time.* London: Sainsbury, 1824. Repr., New York: Da Capo Press, 1966. (Ref. 24)

Saldoni, B. *Diccionario biografico-bibliografico de efemerides de musicos españoles.* Madrid: Dubrull, 1881. (Ref. 389)

Sandved, K.B. *World of Music: A Treasury for Listener and Viewer.* London: Waverley Books, 1957. (Ref. 49)

Santos, M.A.M. *Catalogo de musica manuscritta.* Lisbon: Biblioteca da Ajuda, 1958. (Ref. 399)

Sartori, C. *Bibliografia della musica strumentale italiana stampata in Italia fino al 1700.* Biblioteca di Bibliografia Italiana. Florence: Olschki, 1952. (Ref. 214)

Sartori, C. *Dizionario Ricordi della musica e dei musicisti.* Milan: Ricordi, 1959. (Ref. 3)

Savez Kompozitora Jugoslavije. *Kompozitori i muzicki pisci Jugoslavije: Clanovi saveza kompozitora Jugoslavije, 1945-1967 katalog.* Miloslavjevic-Pesic Milan, ed. Belgrade: Savez Kompozitora Jugoslavije, 1968. (Ref. 145)

Sayers, Janet. *Biological Politics.* London: Tavistock Publications, 1982. (Ref. 582)

Schacht, M.H. *Musicus Danicus eller Danske sangmester.* Ed and commentary Skjerne, G. Original manuscript, 1687. Copenhagen: Hagerups, 1928. (Ref. 97)

Schlager, K., ed. *Internationales Quellenlexikon der Musik Einzeldruecke vor 1800.* London: Baerenreiter, 1971. (Ref. 125)

Schmidl, C. *Dizionario universale dei musicisti.* Milan: Sonzogno, 1926-1937. (Ref. 105)

Schnapper, E., ed. *British Union Catalogue of Early Music Printed Before the Year 1801.* London: Butterworths, 1957. (Ref. 65)

Scholes, P.A. *Concise Oxford Dictionary of Music.* 2nd ed. Ward, John Owen ed. London: Oxford University Press, 1964. (Ref. 18)

Scholes, P.A. *Oxford Companion to Music.* 2nd ed. London: Oxford University Press, 1943. (Ref. 19)

Schreijer, Cobi. *Sara, Je Rok Zakt af.* Vrouwenliedboek. Amsterdam: Feministische Uitgeverij Sara, 1980. (Ref. 478)

Schuh, W., et al. *Schweizer Musiker-lexikon: Dictionnaire des musiciens suisses.* Zurich: Atlantis, 1964. (Ref. 59)

Schulz, Ferdinand F. *Pianographie.* Recklinghausen: Piano-Verlag, 1982. (Ref. 521)

Schweizerische Tonkuenstlerverein im zweiten Vierteljahundert seines Bestehens. Zurich: Atlantis Verlag, 1950. (Ref 552.)

Scores, An Anthology of New Music. New York: Schirmer Books, 1981. (Ref. 633)

Scott, M. *The Record of Singing to 1914.* London: Duckworth, 1977. (Ref. 423)

Scott, M. *The Record of Singing, 1914-1925.* London: Duckworth 1979. (Ref. 425)

Searle, H. and Layton, R. *Britain, Scandinavia and the Netherlands. Twentieth-Century Composers.* Vol. 3. London: Weidenfeld & Nicolson, 1972. (Ref. 153)

Seeger, Horst. *Musiklexikon.* Leipzig: VEB Deutscher Verlag fuer Musik, 1981. (Ref. 580)

Seeger, Horst. *Opern Lexikon.* Hamburg: Heinrichshofen's Verlag, 1979. (Ref. 618)

Seland, M. *Kvinnelige komponister: En bio-bibliografi.* Oslo: Statens bibliotekskole, 1976. (Ref. 432)

Selfridge-Field, E. *Venetian Instrumental Music from Gabrieli to Vivaldi.* Oxford: Blackwell, 1975. (Ref. 143)

Sendrey, A. *Music in Ancient Israel.* London: Vision Press, 1969. (Ref. 255)

Sendrey, A. *Music in the Social and Religious Life of Antiquity.* Madison, NJ.: Fairleigh Dickinson University Press, 1974. (Ref. 151)

Shepherd, J., et al. *Whose Music: An Anthology of Musical Languages.* London: Latimer, 1977. (Ref. 245)

Shera, F.H. *The Amateur in Music.* London: Oxford University Press, 1939. (Ref. 601)

Short, Craig R., ed. *Directory of Music Faculties in Colleges and Universities, U.S. and Canada.* College Music Society, 1982-1984. (Ref. 620)

Skowronski, J. *Women in American Music: A Bibliography.* Metuchen, NJ.: Scarecrow Press, 1978. (Ref. 191)

Slonimsky, Nicolas. *A Thing or Two About Music.* Westport, CT.: Greenwood Press, 1948; Repr., 1972. (Ref. 298)

Slonimsky, Nicolas. *Music of Latin America.* New York: Crowell, 1945. Repr., New York: Da Capo Press, 1972. (Ref. 54)

Smith, J. *Directory of American Women Composers.* Chicago: National Federation of Music Clubs, 1970. (Ref. 40)

Smith, W. *A New Classical Dictionary of Biography, Mythology and Geography.* 2nd ed. London: Murray, 1853. (Ref. 382)

Society of Norwegian Composers. *Contemporary Norwegian Orchestral and Chamber Music.* Oslo: Grundt Tanum Forlag, 1970. (Ref. 114)

Sohlman's musiklexikon. Stockholm: Sohlman Foerlag, 1975-1979. (Ref. 20)

Song, Bang-Song. *An Annotated Bibliography of Korean Music.* Providence, RI.: Asian Music Publications, Brown University, 1971. (Ref. 605)

Sonneck, O.G.T. *Catalogue of Opera Librettos Printed Before 1800.* Washington, DC.: Library of Congress, 1914. (Ref. 122)

Sonneck, O.G.T. *Early Concert-Life in America, 1731-1800.* Leipzig: Breitkopf & Haertel, 1907. Repr., New York: Da Capo Press, 1978. (Ref. 372)

Sorenson, S. et al., eds. *Gads musikleksikon.* Copenhagen: Gad, 1976. (Ref. 130)

Southern, E. *The Music of Black Americans: A History.* New York: Norton, 1971. (Ref. 285)

Sowinski, W. *Dictionnaire Biographique: Les musiciens polonais et slaves, anciens et modernes.* Paris: A. le Clerc, 1857. Repr., New York: Da Capo Press, 1971. (Ref. 35)

Spiess, L. and Stanford, T. *An Introduction to Certain Mexican Musical Archives.* Detroit Studies in Music Bibliography, no. 15. Detroit: Information Co-ordinators, 1969. (Ref. 178)

Spiegl, Fritz. *Music Through The Looking Glass.* London: Routledge & Kegan Paul, 1984. (Ref. 652)

Spiess, Lincoln Bunce. *Historical Musicology.* Westport, CT.: Greenwood Press, 1980. (Ref. 536)

Stahl, Dorothy. *A Selected Discography of Solo Song.* Detroit, MI.: Information Co-ordinators, Inc., 1972. (Ref. 507)

Stahl, Dorothy. *A Selected Discography of Solo Song.* Supl., Detroit, MI.: Information Co-ordinators, Inc., 1976. (Ref. 508)

Stainer, John. *The Music of the Bible.* London: Novello & Co. 1914. (Ref. 632)

Starkie, Walter. *Spain; A Musician's Journey through Time and Space.* Geneva: Edisli-At Editions Rene Kister, 1958. (Ref. 639)

Stern, S. *Women Composers: A Handbook.* Metuchen, NJ.: Scarecrow Press, 1978. (Ref. 347)

Stevens, Denis., ed. *A History of Song.* New York: W.W. Norton & Co. 1970. (Ref. 609)

Stevenson, R. *Music in Mexico: A Historical Survey.* New York: Crowell, 1952.

(Ref. 381)

Stevenson, R. *Renaissance and Baroque Musical Sources in the Americas.* Washington, DC.: Organisation of the American States, 1970. (Ref. 332)

Stewart-Green, Miriam. *Women Composers: A Checklist of Works for the Solo Voice.* Boston: G.K. Hall & Co., 1980. (Ref. 465)

Stieger, F. *Opernlexikon.* Tutzing: Schneider, 1977. (Ref. 431)

Stigelbauer, M. *Die Saengerinnen am Abbasidenhof um die Zeit des Kalifen al- Mutawakkil.* Vienna: Verband der wissenschaftlichen Gesellschaften Oesterreichs, 1975. (Ref. 224)

Stone, Merlin. *When God was a Woman.* San Diego: Harcourt Brace Jovanovich Publishers, 1978. (Ref. 629)

Stoykova Kichka and Tsenkov, Tsenko. *Bulgarian Orchestral Music.* Sofia Press. (Ref. 463)

Studi Ricerche, 1948-1960. *Rome, Accademia Nazionale di S. Cecilia.* RAI Radiotelevisione Italiana. (Ref. 532)

Sublette, Ned., ed. *A Discography of Hispanic Music in the Fine Arts Library of the University of New Mexico.* Westport, CT.: Greenwood Press, 1973. (Ref. 517)

Such, P. *Soundprints: Contemporary Composers.* Toronto: Clarke, Irwin, 1972. (Ref. 380)

Suppan Wolfgang., ed. *Steirisches Musiklexikon.* Graz: Akademische Druck-und Verlaganstalt, 1966. (Ref. 500)

Swidler, L. *Women in Judaism: The Status of Women in Formative Judaism.* Metuchen, NJ.: Scarecrow Press, 1976. (Ref. 275)

Swiss Composers League. *Forty Contemporary Swiss Composers.* Amriswill: Bodensee Verlag, 1956. (Ref. 36)

Szabolcsi, B. and Toth, A. *Zenei lexikon.* Budapest: Zenemukiado Vallalat, 1965. (Ref. 375)

Tablettes de renommée des musiciens, auteurs, compositeurs, virtuoses, amateurs et maîtres de musique vocale et instrumentale, les plus connus en chaque genre. Paris: Cailleau, 1785. Repr., Geneva: Minkoff, 1971. (Ref. 368)

Texas Music Educators' Association. *A Bibliography of Master's Theses and Doctoral Dissertations in Music Completed at Texas Colleges and Universities, 1919-1972.* Houston: Association, 1974. (Ref. 147)

Thiel, Joern. *International Anthology of Recorded Music.* Vienna; Munich: Jugend & Volk, 1971. (Ref. 509)

Thompson, A.F. *An Annotated Bibliography of Writings About Music in Puerto Rico.* MLA Index and Bibliography Series, no. 12. Ann Arbor, MI.: Music Library Association, 1975. (Ref. 278)

Thompson, K.A. *A Dictionary of Twentieth Century Composers, 1911-1971.* New York: St. Martin's Press, 1973. (Ref. 42)

Thompson, O., ed. *The International Cyclopedia of Music and Musicians.* 4th Ed. Slonimsky, Nicolas ed. London: Dent, 1942; 10th ed., Bohle, Bruce ed. London: Dent, 1975. (Ref. 74)

Thomson, V. *American Music Since 1910.* Twentieth Century Composers, vol. 1. New York: Holt, Rinehart & Winston, 1971. (Ref. 152)

Tick, Judith. *American Women Composers before 1870.* Ann Arbor, MI.: UMI Research Press, 1979. (Ref. 590)

Tjepkema, Sandra L. *A Bibliography of Computer Music.* Iowa: University of Iowa Press, 1981. (Ref. 586)

Torrellas, A.A. *Diccionario enciclopedico de la musica.* Barcelona: Central Catalana de Publicaciones, 1947-1952. (Ref. 107)

Towers, J., comp. *Dictionary-Catalogue of Operas and Operettas.* Morgantown, WV: Acme, 1910. Repr., New York: Da Capo Press, 1967. (Ref. 307)

Townend, Peter and Simmons, David., eds. *Who's Who in Music.* London: Burke's Peerage, 1962. (Ref. 490)

Trollope, T. Adolphus. *A Decade of Italian Women.* London: Chapman & Hall, 1859. (Ref. 626)

Uglow, Jennifer S., comp. & ed. *The Macmillan Dictionary of Women's Biography.* London: Macmillan Press. (Ref. 637)

Utas, Bo., ed. *Women in Islamic Societies*. Curzon Press; Humanities Press, 1983. (Ref. 613, 623)

Valenzuela Tobar, Paulina. *Lista de Autores y Compositores Registrados en DAI-Chile a Septiembre de 1979*. Editorial Universitaria SA, 1979. (Ref. 587)

Van der Merwe, F. *Suid-Afrikaanse musiekbibliografie*. Cape Town: Tafelberg, 1974. (Ref. 184)

Vannes, R. *Dictionnaire des musiciens (compositeurs)*. Brussels: Larcier, 1947. (Ref. 30)

Vaschalde, H. *Histoire des troubadours*. Paris, 1889. (Ref. 237)

Vasconcelos, A. *Raizes da musica popular brasileira, 1500-1889*. San Paulo: Martins, 1977. (Ref. 349)

Venice (City of) Catalogo generale delle opere musicali ... città di Venezia. Parma: Associazione dei Musicologi Italiani, 1913. (Ref. 160)

Verma, H.N. and Verma, A. *Indian Women Through the Ages*. New Delhi: Great Indian Publishers, 1977. (Ref. 414)

Verma, H.N. and Verma, A. *100 Great Indians Through the Ages*. New Delhi: Great Indian Publishers, 1975. (Ref. 644)

Vernillat, F. and Charpentreau, J. *Dictionnaire de la chanson française*. Paris: Larousse, 1968. (Ref. 198)

Verona (City of). *Catalogo delle opere musicali ... città di Verona*. Parma: Associazione dei Musicologi Italiani, 1936. (Ref. 267)

Vidal A. *La Chapelle St.Julien-des-ménestriers et les ménestrels à Paris*. Paris: Quantin, 1878. (Ref. 343)

Vieira, E. *Diccionario biographico de musicos portugueses: Historia e bibliograpia da musica em Portugal*. Lisbon: Moreira & Pinheiro, 1900-1904. (Ref. 104)

Villani, C. *Stelle feminili: Dizionario bio-bibliografico*. New ed. Rome: Albrighi, Segati & Co., 1915. (Ref. 180)

Vincenti, E. *Bibliografia antica dei trovatori*. Milan: Ricciardi, 1963. (Ref. 213)

Vinton, J., ed. *Dictionary of Contemporary Music*. New York: Dutton, 1974. (Ref. 5)

Vinton, J., ed. *Dictionary of Twentieth-Century Music*. London: Thames & Hudson, 1974. (Ref. 4)

Vodarsky-Shiraeff, A., comp. *Russian Composers and Musicians: A Biographical Dictionary*. New York: Wilson, 1940. Repr., New York: Da Capo Press, 1969. (Ref. 38)

Von Ende, Richard Chaffey. *Church Music: An International Bibliography*. Metuchen, NJ.: Scarecrow Press, 1980. (Ref. 539)

Wahl, J.A. *The Exclusion of Woman from Holy Orders*. Washington, DC.: Catholic University of America Press, 1959. (Ref. 252)

Wallaschek, R. *Primitive Music*. London: Longmans Green, 1893. Repr., New York: Da Capo Press, 1970. (Ref. 233)

Walther, J.G. *Musikalisches Lexikon oder musikalische Bibliothek*. Leipzig: Deer. Facsimile reprint Schaal, Richard ed. Kassel: Baerenreiter, 1953. (Ref. 302)

Warnicke, Retha M. *Women of the English Renaissance and Reformation*. Westport, CT.: Greenwood Press, 1983. (Ref. 636)

Weaver, Robert Lamar and Weaver Wright, Norma. *A Chronology of Music in the Florentine Theater 1590-1750*. Detroit: Information Co-ordinators Inc., 1978. (Ref. 630)

Weiser, Marjorie P.K. and Arbeiter, Jean S. *Womanlist*. New York: Atheneum, 1981. (Ref. 518)

Weisser, Albert. *The Modern Renaissance of Jewish Music*. New York: Da Capo Press, 1983. (Ref. 616)

Weissweiler, Eva. *Komponistinnen aus 500 Jahren*. Frankfurt: Fischer Taschenbuch Verlag, 1981. (Ref. 476)

Werner, Eric., ed. *Contributions to a Historical Study of Jewish Music*. New York: KTAV Publishing House Inc., 1976. (Ref. 540)

Weston, Pamela. *Clarinet Virtuosi of the Past*. Kent: Novello & Co., 1976. (Ref. 471)

Weston, Pamela. *More Clarinet Virtuosi of the Past*. Kent: Novello & Co., 1977. (Ref. 472)

Who's Who in Music and Musicians' International Directory. St. Clair Shores, MI.: Scholarly, 1935. (Ref. 34)

Who's Who of American Women. 11th ed., 1979-1980. Chicago: Marquis Who's Who. (Ref. 475)

Who's Who of American Women. Chicago, IL.: Marquis Who's Who, 1981. (Ref. 506)

Who's Who of Indian Musicians. New Delhi: Sangeet Natak Akademi, 1984. (Ref. 650)

Wier, A.E., comp. *The Macmillan Encyclopaedia of Music and Musicians*. London: Macmillan, 1938. (Ref. 226)

Wiggin, F.T. *Maine Composers and Their Music: A Biographical Dictionary*. Portland, ME.: Maine Federation of Music Clubs, 1959; Maine Historical Society, 1976. (Ref. 374)

Wilhelm, J.J., ed. *Medieval Song: An Anthology of Hymns and Lyrics*. London: Allen Unwin, 1971. (Ref. 279)

Willemze, T. *Spectrum muzieklexicon*. Utrecht: Spectrum, 1975. (Ref. 183)

Williams, James G. *Women Recounted*. Sheffield: Almond Press, 1982. (Ref. 635)

Williams, M.D. *Source: Music of the Avant Garde: Annotated List of Contents and Cumulative Indices*. MLA Index and Bibliography Series, No. 19. Ann Arbor, MI.: Music Library Association, 1978. (Ref. 246)

Williams, O., ed. *American Black Women in the Arts and Social Sciences: A Bibliographic Survey*. Metuchen, NJ.: Scarecrow Press, 1973; rev. and enl. ed., 1978. (Ref. 136)

Women Composers. Brooklyn, NY.: Chandler-Ebel Music Co., 1913. (Ref. 276)

Wyndham, H. Saxe., ed. *Who's Who in Music*. London: Sir Isaac Pitman & Son, 1915. (Ref. 488)

Yoell, J.H. *The Nordic Sound*. Boston: Crescendo Publishers, 1974. (Ref. 67)

Young, P.M. *A History of British Music*. London: Benn, 1967. (Ref. 150)

Zaimont, Judith Lang and Famera, Karen. *Contemporary Concert Music by Women*. Westport, CT.: Greenwood Press, 1981. (Ref. 474)

Zaimont, Judith Lang., Overhauser, Catherine and Gottlieb, Jane., eds. *The Musical Woman*. Westport, CT.: Greenwood Press, 1984. (Ref. 622)

Zelenina, M.E. *Zarubuzhnaya muzyka XX veka*. Moscow: Kniga, 1979. (Ref. 515)

Zelenka, Karl. *Komponierende Frauen*. Cologne: Ellenberg Verlag, 1980. (Ref. 448)

Zimmermann, W. *Desert Plants: Conversations with 23 American Musicians*. Vancouver: ARC Publications, 1976. (Ref. 299)

Zingel, H.J. *Lexikon der Harfe*. Regensburg: Laaber, 1977. (Ref. 344)

Zingel, H.J. *Verzeichnis der Harfenmusik*. Hofheim am Taunus: Hofmeister. (Ref. 75)

ALPHABETICAL BY TITLE

Album Musical. Kinsky, George. Paris: Librairie Delagrave, 1930. (Ref. 595)

Algemene Muziek Encyclopedie. Robijns, Prof. Dr. J. and Zijlstra, Miep. Bussum: Unieboek bv., 1980. (Ref. 461)

Algemene muziekencyclopedie. Corbet, A., and Paap. W. Antwerp: Zuid- Nederlanse Uitgeverij, 1957-1963; supplement, ed., Jozef Robijns. Ghent-Louvain: Wetenschappelijke Uitgeverij E. Story-Scientia, 1972. (Ref. 1)

Allgemeines historisches Kuenstler Lexikon fuer Boehmen, etc. Dlabacz, G.J. Prague: Haase, 1915. Repr., Hildesheim: Georg Olms Verlag, 1973. (Ref. 340)

Allmaent musiklexikon. Norlind, T. Stockholm: Wahlstroem & Widstrand, 1916. (Ref. 95)

Alte Musik. Baumgartner, Alfred. Salzburg: Kiesel Verlag, 1981. (Ref. 548)

Amateur in Music. Shera, F.H. London: Oxford University Press, 1939. (Ref. 601)

America Latina en su musica. Aretz, I., comp. Paris: Unesco, 1977. (Ref. 45)

American Music Handbook. Pavlakis, C. New York: Free Press, 1974. (Ref. 195)

American Black Women in the Arts and Social Sciences: A Bibliographic Survey. Williams, O., ed. Metuchen, NJ.: Scarecrow Press, 1973; rev. & enl. ed., 1978. (Ref. 136)

American Composers. Ewen, David. New York: G.P. Putnam's Sons, 1982. (Ref. 560)

American Music before 1865 in Print and on Records. New York: Institute for Studies in American Music, 1976. (Ref. 450)

American Music Recordings. Oja, Carol J., ed. New York: Institute for Studies in American Music Conservatory of Music, 1982. (Ref. 562)

American Music Since 1910. Thomson, V. Twentieth Century Composers, vol. 1. New York: Holt, Rinehart & Winston, 1971. (Ref. 152)

American Opera and Its Composers. Hipsher, E.E. Philadelphia: Presser, 1927. Repr., New York: Da Capo Press, 1978. (Ref. 304)

American Women Composers before 1870. Tick, Judith. Ann Arbor, MI.: UMI Research Press, 1979. (Ref. 590)

American Women in Creative Music. Barnes, E.N.C. Washington, DC.: Music Education Publications, 1936. (Ref. 292)

America's Music From the Pilgrims to the Present. Chase, G. New York: McGraw-Hill, 1955. (Ref. 266)

Annales de la musique et des musiciens en Russie au XVIIIe siècle. Mooser, R. Aloys. Geneva: Editions du Mont-Blanc, 1948-1951. (Ref. 156)

Annales de la musique: ou, Almanach musical pour l'an 1819 et 1820. Gardeton, C. Paris: Annales de la Musique, 1820. Repr., Geneva: Minkoff, 1978. (Ref. 314)

Annotated Bibliography of Korean Music. Song, Bang-Song. Providence, RI.: Asian Music Publications, Brown University, 1971. (Ref. 605)

Annotated Bibliography of Writings About Music in Puerto Rico. Thompson, A.F. MLA Index and Bibliography Series, no. 12. Ann Arbor, MI.: Music Library Association, 1975. (Ref. 278)

Annotated Glossary of Arabic Musical Terms. Al Faruqi, Lois Ibsen., comp. Westport, CT.: Greenwood Press, 1981. (Ref. 577)

Annuario musicale storico, cronologico, universale. 2nd ed. Paloschi, G., comp. Milan: Stabilimento Musicale Ricordi, 1878. (Ref. 211)

Anthologie de Chants de Trouveres. Maillard, Jean. Paris: Editions Aug. Zurfluh, 1967. (Ref. 588)

Ars Electronica, Linz, im Rahmen des Internationalen Brucknerfestes. Linz: Bruckner Haus. (Ref. 559)

Artisti e musicisti moderni: Cenni storici, critici e bibliografici con speciale reguardo alla scuola ed all 'esegesi. Recupito, M.V. Milan: La Fiamma, 1933. (Ref. 56)

ASCAP Biographical Dictionary. New York: Jaques Cattell Press; R.R. Bowker Co., 1980. (Ref. 494)

ASCAP Biographical Dictionary of Composers, Authors and Publishers. 3rd ed. American Society of Composers, Authors and Publishers. New York: ASCAP, 1966. (Ref. 39)

ASCAP Symphonic Catalog. 3rd ed. American Society of Composers, Authors and Pubishers. New York: R.R. Bowker Co., 1977. (Ref. 280)

Aschehougs musikleksikon. Hamburger, P. Copenhagen: Aschehoug, 1957-1958. (Ref. 98)

Augusta Holmès et la femme compositeur. Barillon-Bauche, P. Paris: Fischbacher, 1912. (Ref. 247)

Australia's Contemporary Composers. Murdoch, J. Sydney: Macmillan, 1972. (Ref. 203)

Australia's Music. Covell, R. Melbourne: Sun Books, 1967. (Ref. 58)

Australian Composition in the Twentieth Century. Callaway, F., and Tunley, D., eds. Melbourne: Oxford University Press, 1978. (Ref. 412)

Baker's Biographical Dictionary of Musicians. 5th & 6th ed. & suppl. Slonimsky, Nicolas. Baker, T. New York: Schirmer, 1971 and 1978. (Ref. 22)

Ballets, opera et autres ouvrages lyriques, par ordre chronologique depuis leur origine avec une table alphabetique des ouvrages et des auteurs. Lavalliere, L. Paris: Baudre, 1760. Repr., London: Baron, 1967. (Ref. 396)

Bantu Composers of South Africa. Huskisson, Y. Johannesburg: South African Broadcasting Corporation, 1969. (Ref. 37)

Bibliografia antica dei trovatori. Vincenti, E. Milan: Ricciardi, 1963. (Ref. 213)

Bibliografia della musica strumentale italiana stampata in Italia fino al 1700. Sartori, C. Biblioteca di Bibliografia Italiana. Florence: Olschki, 1952. (Ref. 214)

Bibliographie der Musik-Sammelwerke des XVI und XVII Jahrhunderts. Eitner, R., ed. Berlin: Liepmannssohn, 1877. (Ref. 127)

Bibliographie der Troubadours. Pillet, A. Carstens, H., ed. Halle: Niemeyer, 1933. (Ref. 117)

Bibliographie des altfranzoesischen Liedes. Raynaud, G. Spanke, Hans, ed. Leiden: Brill, 1955. (Ref. 79)

Bibliographie des chansonniers français des XIIIe et XIVe siècles. Raynaud, G. Paris: Vieweg, 1884. (Ref. 55)

Bibliographie musicale de la France et de l'etranger. Gardeton, D. Paris: Niogret, 1822. Repr., Geneva: Minkoff, 1976. (Ref. 312)

Bibliography of Cello Ensemble Music. Kenneson, C. Detroit Studies in Music Bibliography. Detroit: Information Co-ordinators, 1974. (Ref. 229)

Bibliography of Computer Music. Tjepkema, Sandra L. Iowa: University of Iowa Press, 1981. (Ref. 586)

Bibliography of Discographies. Classical Music, 1925-1975. Gray, Michael H., and Gibson, Gerald D. New York: R.R. Bowker Co., 1977. (Ref. 512)

Bibliography of Master's Theses and Doctoral Dissertations in Music Completed at Texas Colleges and Universities, 1919-1972. Texas Music Educators' Association. Houston: The Association, 1974. (Ref. 147)

Biblioteca femminile italiana Padua. Ferri, P.L. Tipografia Crescini, 1842. (Ref. 327)

Bio-bibliographical Dictionary of Twelve Tone and Serial Composers. Carlson, E.B. Metuchen, NJ.: Scarecrow Press, 1970. (Ref. 131)

Biografie di Scrittori e Artisti Musicali. Mayr, Giovanni Simone. Bologna: Forni Editore, 1875. (Ref. 483)

Biografie Trovadoriche. Edizione Integrale. Bologna: Libreria Antiquaria Palmaverde, 1961. (Ref. 449)

Biographical Dictionary of American Music. Claghem, C.E. New York: Parker, 1973. (Ref. 53)

Biographical Dictionary of Celebrated Women of Every Age and Country. Betham, M. London: Crosby, 1804. (Ref. 334)

Biographical Dictionary of Musicians. New rev. ed., Taylor Deems and Kerr, Russel. Hughes, R. New York: Blue Ribbon Books, 1971. (Ref. 271)

Biographie universelle des musiciens et bibliographie générale de la musique. 2nd ed. Fetis, F.J. Paris: Firmin Didot Frères, 1866-1879. Repr., Brussels: Culture et Civilisation, 1972. (Ref. 26)

Biographies des troubadours: Textes provençaux des XIIIe et XIVe Siècles. Boutiere, J. and Schutz, A.H. Paris: Didier, 1950; Nizet, 1964. (Ref. 120)

Biographies des troubadours en langue provençale. Chabaneau, C. Toulouse: Privat, 1885. (Ref. 220)

Biographisch-bibliographisches Quellen-Lexikon der Musiker und Musikgelehrtennchristlicher Zeitrechnung bis Mitte des neunzehnten Jahrhunderts. Eitner, R., ed. Graz: Akademische Druck- und Verlaganstalt, 1960. (Ref. 128)

Biological Politics. Sayers, Janet. London: Tavistock Publications, 1982. (Ref. 582)

Black Concert and Recital Music. Lerma, Dominique-René de. Bloomington, IN: The Afro-American Music Opportunities Association, 1975. (Ref. 523)

Black Music of Two Worlds. Roberts, J.S. New York: Praeger, 1972. (Ref. 286)

Blacks in Classical Music. Abdul, R. New York: Dodd, Mead & Co., 1977. (Ref. 287)

Book of Women Poets from Antiquity to Now. Barnstone, Aliki and Barnstone, Willis, eds. New York: Schocken Books, 1980. (Ref. 464)

Black Composer Speaks. Baker, D.N., et al., eds. London: Scarecrow Press, 1978. (Ref. 348)

Book of World-Famous Music: Classical, Popular and Folk. rev. & enl. ed. Fuld, J.J. New York: Crown Publishers, 1971; repr., 1975. (Ref. 370)

Britain, Scandinavia and the Netherlands. Twentieth-Century Composers. vol. 3. Searle, H. and Layton, R. London: Weidenfeld & Nicolson, 1972. (Ref. 153)

Britannica Book of Music. Hadley, Benjamin., ed. New York: Doubleday & Company, Inc. 1980. (Ref. 459)

British Music Now. Foreman, L. London: Elek, 1975. (Ref. 69)

British Music Yearbook: A Survey and Directory with Statistics and Reference Articles for 1976. Jacobs, A., ed. New York: R.R. Bowker Co., 1976. (Ref. 230)

British Music Yearbook 1980. 6th ed. Jacobs, A., ed. London: Black, 1980. (Ref. 422)

British Music Yearbook 1982. Jacobs, Arthur and Barton, Marianne., eds. London: Adam and Charles Black, 1982. (Ref. 522)

British Music Yearbook 1984. Barton, Marianne., ed. London: Classical Music, 1983. (Ref. 621)

British Music Yearbook 1983. Barton, Marianne and Jacobs, Arthur., eds. London: Classical Music, 1982. (Ref. 585)

British Musical Biography: A Dictionary of Musical Artists, Authors and Composers Born in Britain and Its Colonies. Brown, J.D., and Stratton, S.S. Birmingham: Stratton, 1897. Repr., New York: Da Capo Press, 1971. (Ref 6)

British Orchestral Music. Composers' Guild of Great Britain. London: British Music Information Centre, 1958. (Ref. 407)

British Union Catalogue of Early Music Printed Before the Year 1801. Schnapper, E., ed. London: Butterworths, 1957. (Ref. 65)

Bulgarian Music. Krustev, Venelin: Sofia Press, 1978. (Ref. 466)

Bulgarian Orchestral Music. Stoykova Kichka and Tsenkov Tsenko. Sofia Press. (Ref. 463)

Bulgarski kompozitori i muzikovedi: Spravochnik. Nikolov, N. 1971. (Ref. 217)

Calendar of Music and Musicians. Manson, Adele P. Metuchen, NJ.: Scarecrow Press, 1981. (Ref. 516)

Calendario di donne illustri italiane. Amari, R. Florence: Tipografia di Federigo Bencini, 1857. (Ref. 212)

Canadian Music: A Selected Checklist, 1950-1973. Jarman, L., ed. Toronto: University of Toronto Press, 1976. (Ref. 288)

Canadian musical works 1900-1980: A Bibliography of general and analytical sources. Poirier, Lucien, ed. Canadian Association of Music Libraries. 1983. (Ref. 631)

Catalog of Published Concert Music by American Composers. 2nd ed. Eagon, A. Metuchen, NJ.: Scarecrow Press, 1969; supl. 1971 and 1974. (Ref. 146)

Catalog of the American Music Center Library: Chamber Music. Famera, K.M. New York: American Music Center Library, 1978. (Ref. 401)

Catalogo de musica manuscritta. Santos, M.A.M. Lisbon: Biblioteca da Ajuda, 1958. (Ref. 399)

Catalogo de obras de compositores españoles: Sinfonicas de camara, corales, lieders, solistas y ballets; and Catalogo de obras que forman el archivo sinfonico de la Sociedad General de Autores de España. Madrid: Archivo Sinfonico de la SGAE, 1972. (Ref. 60)

Catalogo della biblioteca del liceo musicale di Bologna. Gaspari, G. Bologna: Libreria Romagnoli dall'Acqua, 1890. (Ref. 216)

Catalogo delle opere musicali ... città di Bologna. Bologna (City of). Parma: Associazione dei Musicologi Italiani, 1910. (Ref. 159)

Catalogo delle opere musicali ... città di Ferrara. Ferrara (City of). Parma: Associazione dei Musicologi Italiani, 1917. (Ref. 83)

Catalogo delle opere musicali ... città di Firenze. Florence (City of). Parma: Associazione dei Musicologi Italiani, 1929. (Ref. 158)

Catalogo delle opere musicalici ... città di Modena. Modena (City of). Parma: Associazione dei Musicologi Italiani, 1916. (Ref. 157)

Catalogo delle opere musicali ... città di Pistoia. Pistoia (City of). Parma. Associazione dei Musicologi Italiani, 1936-1937. (Ref. 92)

Catalogo delle opere musicali ... città di Verona. Verona (City of). Parma: Associazione dei Musicologi Italiani, 1936. (Ref. 267)

Catalogo generale ... città di Napoli. Naples (City of). Parma: Associazione dei Musicologi Italiani, 1918. (Ref. 155)

Catalogo generale delle opere musicali ... città di Parma. Parma (City of). Parma: Associazione dei Musicologi Italiani, 1911. (Ref. 161)

Catalogo generale delle opere musicali ... città di Venezia. Venice (City of). Parma: Associazione dei Musicologi Italiani, 1913. (Ref. 160)

Catalogue des partitions musicales édites en Belgique et acquises par la bibliotheque Royale Albert 1, 1966-1975. Huys, B. Brussels: Bibliotheque Royale Albert 1, 1976. (Ref. 188)

Catalogue of Canadian Composers. Rev. & enl. ed. Kallman, H., ed. Ottawa: Canadian Broadcasting Corporation. Repr., St. Clair Shores, MI.: Scholarly Press, 1972. (Ref. 133)

Catalogue of Choral and Vocal Works. Finell, Judith Greenberg, comp. American Music Center Library. New York: American Music Center, 1975. (Ref. 190)

Catalogue of Instrumental and Chamber Music. Sydney: Australia Music Centre, 1976. (Ref. 444)

Catalogue of Keyboard Music. Sydney: Australia Music Centre, 1976. (Ref. 446)

Catalogue of Music in the Huntington Library Printed Before 1801. Backus, E.N., comp. San Marino, CA.: Huntington Library, 1949. (Ref. 91)

Catalogue of Opera Librettos Printed Before 1800. Sonneck, O.G.T. Washington, DC.: Library of Congress, 1914. (Ref. 122)

Catalogue of Orchestral Music. Sydney: Australia Music Centre, 1976. (Ref. 445)

Catalogue of Printed Music Published Between 1487 and 1800. British Museum. In British Museum. By William Barclay Squire. London: Museum, 1927. (Ref. 405)

Catalogue of Serious Music, Original Works, Arrangements and Orchestrations by members of SAMRO. Levy, Michael S. Johannesburg: SAMRO, 1982. (Ref. 520)

Catalogue of the King's Music Library. By William Barclay Squire. British Museum. London: Museum, 1927-1929. (Ref. 123)

Catalogue of the Music Library, The Hague Gemeentemuseum; Vocal Music 1500-c.1650. Charbon, Marie H. New York: Da Capo Press, 1973. (Ref. 615)

Catalogue of 46 Australian Composers and Selected Works. McCredie, A.M. Canberra: Advisory Board, Commonwealth Assistance to Australian Composers, 1969. (Ref. 29)

Cent ans de chanson française. Brunschwig, Chantal., Calvet, Louis-Jean., and Klein, Jean-Claude. Editions du Seuil, 1981. (Ref. 608)

Central Asian Music. Beliaev, Viktor M. Middletown, CT.: Wesleyan University Press, 1975. (Ref. 453)

Ceske hudebni skladatelky, k mezinarodnimu dni zen. Brno: Universitni Knihovna v Brne, 1957. (Ref. 238)

Cesko slovensky hudebni slovnik osob a instituci. Prague: Statni Hudebni Vydavatelstvi, 1963-1965. (Ref. 197)

Chamber Music by Living British Composers. Composers' Guild of Great Britain. London: British Music Information Centre, 1969. (Ref. 408)

Chanter M'Estuet, Songs of the Trouveres. Rosenberg, Samuel N., and Tischler, Hans. eds. London: Faber Music Ltd., 1981. (Ref. 566)

Chapelle St.Julien-des-ménestriers et les ménestrels à Paris. Vidal A. Paris: Quantin, 1878. (Ref. 343)

Chinese Music, An Annotated Bibliography. Lieberman, Fredric. New York, London: Garland Publishing Inc., 1979. (Ref. 546)

Chronology of Music in the Florentine Theater 1590-1790. Weaver, Robert Lamar and Weaver, Wright Norma. Detroit: Information Coordinators Inc., 1978. (Ref. 630)

Chronology of Music Composers. Detheridge, J., comp. Birmingham: Detheridge, 1936. (Ref. 173)

Chronology of the Ancient World. Bickerman, E.J. London: Thames & Hudson, 1980. (Ref. 534)

Church Music: An International Bibliography. Von Ende, Richard Chaffey. Metuchen, NJ.: Scarecrow Press, 1980. (Ref. 539)

Clarinet Virtuosi of the Past. Weston, Pamela. Kent: Novello & Co., 1976. (Ref. 471)

Composers in America: Biographical Sketches of Living Composers with a Record of Their Works, 1912-1937. Reis, C. New York: Macmillan, 1938; rev. & enl. ed., New York: Macmillan, 1947. (Ref. 124)

Composers of the Georgian Soviet Socialist Republic. Chkhikvadze, Grigori. Musical Fund of the Georgian Soviet Socialist Republic, 1949. (Ref. 458)

Compositeurs canadiens contemporains. Laplante, L., ed. Montreal: Les Presses de l'Université du Quebec, 1977. (Ref. 402)

Compositores Contemporaneos Puertorriquenos. Puerto Rico: Centro de Investigaciones y Ediciones Musicales, 1981. (Ref. 549)

Compositores de America/Composers of the Americas. Washington, DC.: Secretaria General, 1955-1972. (Ref. 371)

Composium: Annual Index of Contemporary Compositions. Christ, Peter., ed. Washington: Crystal Musicworks, 1981. (Ref. 468)

Composium: Directory of New Music. Washington, DC.: Crystal Record Company, 1971-1979. (Ref. 185)

Comprehensive Catalog of Available Literature for the Double Bass. 2nd ed. Grodner, M. Bloomington, IN.: Lemur Musical Research, 1964. (Ref. 80)

Computer Music Compositions of the United States, 1976. Melby, C., comp. Cambridge, MA.: Massachusetts Institute of Technology, 1976. (Ref. 227)

Concise Encyclopedia of Music and Musicians. Cooper, M., ed. London: Hutchinson, 1958. (Ref. 48)

Concise Oxford Dictionary of Music. 2nd ed. Scholes, P.A. Ward, John Owen, ed. London: Oxford University Press, 1964. (Ref. 18)

Condition de la femme dans la tradition et l'évolution de l'islamisme. Fahmy, M. Paris: Alcan, 1913. (Ref. 356)

Conductors on Record. Holmes, John L. Westport, CA.: Greenwood Press, 1982. (Ref. 492)

Contemporary American Composers. Anderson, E.R. Boston: Hall, 1976. (Ref. 142)

Contemporary American Composers. Jacobi, H.W., comp. California: Paradise Arts, 1975. (Ref. 137)

Contemporary Canadian Composers. Macmillan, K. and Beckwith, J., eds. Toronto: Oxford University Press, 1975. (Ref. 329)

Contemporary Concert Music by Women. Zaimont, Judith Lang and Famera, Karen. Westport, CT.: Greenwood Press, 1981. (Ref. 474)

Contemporary Czechoslovak composers. Gardavsky, C. Prague: Panton, 1965. (Ref. 32)

Contemporary Hungarian Composers. 3rd rev. & enl. ed. Budapest: Editio Musica, 1967. (Ref. 320)

Contemporary Israeli Music. Keren, Zvi. Israel: Bar Ilan University Press, 1980. (Ref. 501)

Contemporary Norwegian Orchestral and Chamber Music. Society of Norwegian Composers. Oslo: Grundt Tanum Forlag, 1970. (Ref. 114)

Contributions to a Historical Study of Jewish Music. Werner, Eric. ed. New York: KTAV Publishing House Inc., 1976. (Ref. 540)

Crowell's Handbook of World Opera. Moore, F.L. New York: Crowell, 1961. (Ref. 345)

Curiosities of Music: A Collection of Facts Not Generally Known, Regarding the Music of Ancient and Savage Nations. Elson, L.C. Boston: Ditson. (Ref. 209)

Cyclopaedic Dictionary of Music. Dunstan, R. London: Curwen, 1980. (Ref. 369)

Cyclopedia of Music and Musicians. Champlin, J.D. New York: Scribner, 1888-1890. (Ref. 102)

Cyclopedic Survey of Chamber Music. 2nd ed. Cobbett, W.W., comp. London: Oxford University Press, 1963. (Ref. 41)

Dansk musik: katalog over statsbibliotekets samling af trykte muskalier. Clausen, P.G., comp. Aarhus: Universitetsforlaget, 1977. (Ref. 331)

Dansk musikfortegnelse. Fog, D. Copehagen: Dan Fog Musikforlag, 1979. (Ref. 413)

Danske Komponister af i dag. Danish Composers' Society. Copenhagen: Dansk Komponistforening, 1098. (Ref. 499)

De los trovadores en España: estudio lengue y poesia provenzal. Fontanals, M. Barcelona: Libreria de Joaquin Verdaguer, 1861.

Decade of Italian Women. Trollope, T. Adolphus. London: Chapman & Hall, 1859. (Ref. 626)

Desert Plants: Conversations with 23 American Musicians. Zimmermann, W. Vancouver: ARC Publications, 1976. (Ref. 299)

Deutsches Musiker-Lexikon. Mueller, E.H., ed. Dresden: Limpert, 1929. (Ref. 111)

Diccionario biografico-bibliografico de efemerides de musicos espanoles. Saldoni, B. Madrid: Dubrull, 1881. (Ref. 389)

Diccionario biografico de la musica. 2nd ed. Matas, J.R. Barcelona: Iberia, 1966. (Ref. 361)

Diccionario biographico de musicos portuguezes: Historia e bibliografia da musica em Portugal. Vieira, E. Lisbon: Moreira & Pinheiro, 1900-1904. (Ref. 104)

Diccionario de la musica cubana. Orovio, Helio. Cuba: Editorial Letras Cubanas, 1981. (Ref. 604)

Diccionario de la musica Labor. Pena, J. Barcelona: Labor, 1954. (Ref. 100)

Diccionario enciclopedico de la musica. Torrellas, A.A. Barcelona: Central Catalana de Publicaciones, 1947-1952. (Ref. 107)

Dicionario bio-bibliografico musical. Mariz, V. Brasileiro e internacional. Rio de Janeiro: Livraria Kosmos, 1948. (Ref. 106)

Dicionario biografico de musicos portugueses. Mazza, J. Lisbon, 1770. Repr., Occidente, vol. 24, 1944. (Ref. 99)

Dicionario mundial de mulheres notaveis. Oliveira, A.L. de and Viana, M.G. Porto: Lello & Irmao, 1967. (Ref. 268)

Dictionary-Catalogue of Operas and Operettas. Towers, J., comp. Morgantown, WV: Acme, 1910. Repr., New York: Da Capo Press, 1967. (Ref. 307)

Dictionary of American Composers. Butterworth, Neil. New York: Garland Publishing, 1984. (Ref. 611)

Dictionary of Composers. Osborne, C., ed. London: Bodley Head, 1977. (Ref. 385)

Dictionary of Composers and Their Music. Gilder, E., and Port, J.G. London: Paddington Press, 1978. (Ref. 284)

Dictionary of Contemporary Music. Vinton, J., ed. New York: Dutton, 1974. (Ref. 5)

Dictionary of Early Music. Roche, Jerome and Roche, Elizabeth. London: Faber Music Limited, 1981. (Ref. 550)

Dictionary of International Biography. Kay, Ernest., ed. Cambridge, England: International Biographical Centre, 1979. (Ref. 359)

Dictionary of Modern Music and Musicians. Hull, A.E., ed. London: Dent, 1924. (Ref. 23)

Dictionary of Music. New ed. Riemann, H., ed. Trans. Shedlock, J.S. London: Augener, 1908. (Ref. 132)

Dictionary of Music and Musicians. Grove, G. London: Macmillan, 1890; 5th ed., ed. Blom, Eric. New York: St. Martin's Press; 6th ed., 1970. (Ref. 8)

Dictionary of Musicians from Earliest Ages to the Present Time... Sainsbury, J.S. London: Sainsbury, 1824. Repr., New York: Da Capo Press, 1966. (Ref. 24)

Dictionary of Twentieth Century Composers, 1911-1971. Thompson, K.A. New York: St. Martin's Press, 1973. (Ref. 42)

Dictionary of Twentieth-Century Music. Vinton, J., ed. London: Thames & Hudson, 1974. (Ref. 4)

Dictionnaire Biographique: Les musiciens polonais et slaves, anciens et modernes. Sowinski, W. Paris: A. le Clerc, 1857. Repr., New York: Da Capo Press, 1971. (Ref. 35)

Dictionnaire critique de la musique ancienne et moderne. Coeuroy, A. Paris: Payot, 1956. (Ref. 172)

Dictionnaire de la chanson française. Vernillat, F. and Charpentreau, J. Paris: Larousse, 1968. (Ref. 198)

Dictionnaire de la musique. Honegger, M. Paris: Bordas, 1970. (Ref. 12)

Dictionnaire de musique. Riemann, H. Paris: Payot, 1931. (Ref. 187)

Dictionnaire des artistes de l'école française aux XIXe siècle. Gabet, C. Paris: Vergne, 1851. (Ref. 263)

Dictionnaire des musiciens (compositeurs). Vannes, R. Brussels: Larcier, 1947. (Ref. 30)

Dictionnaire des musiciens français. Paris: Seghers, 1961. (Ref. 51)

Dictionnaire des operas. Rev. Arthur Pougin. Clement, F. and Larousse, P. Paris: Larousse, 1905. Repr., New York: Da Capo Press, 1969. (Ref. 351)

Dictionnaire historique des musiciens, artistes et amateurs, morts ou vivants. Choron, A.E., and Fayolle, F.J.M. Paris: Valade, 1810-1811. Repr., Hildesheim: Olms Verlag, 1971. (Ref. 119)

Dictionnaire historique litteraire et bibliographique des françaises, et des étrangères naturalisées en France. Briquet, F.B. Paris: Treuttel & Wuertz, 1804. (Ref. 218)

Directory of American Women Composers. Smith, J. Chicago: National Federation of Music Clubs, 1970. (Ref. 40)

Directory of Michigan Composers. Fink, R., et al., eds. Michigan: Western Michigan University, 1977. (Ref. 395)

Directory of Music Faculties in Colleges and Universities, U.S. and Canada. The College Music Society. 1982/1984. Short, Craig R., ed. (Ref. 620)

Directory of New Music, 1982/1983. Composium. (Ref. 624)

Discography of Hispanic Music in the Fine Arts Library of the University of New Mexico. Sublette, Ned., ed. Westport, CT.: Greenwood Press, 1973. (Ref. 517)

Discopaedia of the Violin, 1889-1971. Creighton, J. Toronto: University of Toronto Press, 1974. (Ref. 63)

Dizionario Biografico. Regli, Francesco, comp. Turin: Coi Tipi Di Enrico Dalmazzo, 1860. (Ref. 470)

Dizionario biografico cronologico. Levati, A. Milan: Bettoni, 1822. (Ref. 181)

Dizionario dei musicisti. De Angelis, A. Rome: Ansonia, 1922. (Ref. 86)

Dizionario delle donne illustri. Levati, A. Milan, 1821. (Ref. 350)

Dizionario di musica. Allorto, R. and Ferrari, A. Milan: Ceschina, 1959. (Ref. 112)

Dizionario di musica. Corte, A. della, and Gatti, G.M., eds. Turin: Peravia, 1959. (Ref. 10)

Dizionario e bibliografia della musica. Lichtenthal, P. Milan: Fontana, 1826. (Ref. 66)

Dizionario Ricordi della musica e dei musicisti. Sartori, C. Milan: Ricordi, 1959. (Ref. 3)

Dizionario storico-critico degli scrittori di musica e de piu celebri artisti di tutti le nazione si antiche che moderne. Bertini, G. Palermo: Tipografia reale di Guerra, 1814. (Ref. 162)

Dizionario universale dei musicisti. Schmidl, C. Milan: Sonzogno, 1926-1937. (Ref. 105)

Dizionario universale delle opere melodrammatiche. Manferrari, U. Florence: Sansoni, 1954. (Ref. 108)

Donemus General Catalogue: Dutch Contemporary Music. Amsterdam: Donemus, 1977. (Ref. 283)

Donna e la musica. Mottini, G.E. Milan: Vallardi, 1931. (Ref. 367)

Donne in Musica. Chiti, Patricia Adkins. Rome: Bulzoni Editore, 1982. (Ref. 502)

Dramatic Music. Catalogues of Australian Compositions V. Sydney: Australia Music Centre, 1977. (Ref. 442)

Early Concert-Life in America, 1731-1800. Sonneck, O.G.T. Leipzig: Breitkopf & Haertel, 1907. Repr., New York: Da Capo Press, 1978. (Ref. 372)

Early Music Discography. Croucher, Trevor, comp. London: Library Association, 1981. (Ref. 541)

Edwin A. Fleisher Collection of Orchestral Music in the Free Library of Philadelphia: A Cumulative Catalog, 1929-1977. Philadelphia: Free Library; Boston, MA.: Hall, 1979. (Ref. 322)

Electronic Music. Mackay, Andy. Minneapolis, MN.: Control Data Publishing, 1981. (Ref. 583)

Elizabethan Virginal Music and Its Composers. 2nd ed. Glyn, Margaret H. London: William Reeves, 1934. (Ref. 437)

Enciclopedia alfabetica con ampie trattazioni monografiche. Il mondo della musica. Rome: Garzanti. (Ref. 166)

Enciclopedia da Musica Brasileira: Erudita, folclorica et popular. Sao Paulo: Art Editora, 1977. (Ref. 333)

Enciclopedia de la musica. 7th ed. Hamel, F., and Huerlimann, M. Barcelona: Grijalbo, 1979. (Ref. 204)

Enciclopedia de la musica Argentina. Arizaga, R. Buenos Aires: Fondo Nacional de las Artes, 1971. (Ref. 390)

Enciclopedia Garzanti della musica. Rome: Garzanti, 1974. (Ref. 88)

Encyclopaedia of American Music. Jablonski, Edward. Garden City, NY: Doubleda & Co., 1981. (Ref. 610)

Encyclopaedia Britannica: A New Survey of Universal Knowledge. Chicago: Encyclopaedia Britannica, 1946. (Ref. 208)

Encyclopaedia of the Musical Theatre. Green, S. New York: Dodd Mead, 1976. (Ref. 392)

Encyclopaedia of Music and Musicians. Parkhurst, Winthrop and Bekker L.J. de. Cleveland, OH.: World Publishing Co., 1981. (Ref. 505)

Encyclopaedia of Music and Musicians. Parkhurst, Winthrop and Bekker L.J. de. New York: Crown Publishers, 1937. (Ref. 462)

Encyclopedia of Music in Canada. Kallmann, H., Potvin, G. and Winters, K. eds. Toronto: University of Toronto Press, 1981. (Ref. 485)

Encyclopedie de la musique. Michel, F., et al., eds. Paris: Fasquelle, 1958- 1961. (Ref. 9)

Encyclopedie van de muziek. Amsterdam: Elsevier, 1956-1957. (Ref. 44)

Encyklopedia Muzyczna. Vol. 1 & 2. Dziebowska, Elzbieta., ed. Kracow: Polskie Wydawnictwo Muzyczne, 1979. (Ref. 524)

English Madrigal Singers. Fellowes, Edmund Horace. Oxford: Clarendon Press, 1921. (Ref. 542)

English Musical Renaissance. Pirie, Peter J. London: Victor Gollancz Ltd., 1979. (Ref. 447)

Illustrated Encyclopedia of Black Music. Futrell, Jon., Gill, Chris., St. Pierre, Roger., Richardson, Clive., Trengove, Chris., Fisher, Bob., Sheehy, Bill and Wesker, Lindsay, eds. London: Salamander Books Limited. (Ref. 614)

Illustreret musikleksikon, Panum, H. and Behrend, W. Povl Hamburger, ed. Copenhagen: Aschehoug, 1940. (Ref. 113)

Index to Biographies of Contemporary Composers. Bull, S. Metuchen, NJ.: Scarecrow Press, 1974. (Ref. 94)

Index to Early Music in Selected Anthologies. Hilton, Ruth B. Clifton, NJ.: European American Music Corporation, 1978. (Ref. 525)

Index to Opera, Operetta and Musical Comedy Synopses in Collections and Periodicals. Drone, J.M. Metuchen, NJ.: Scarecrow Press, 1978. (Ref. 295)

Index to Record and Tape Reviews 1976. Maleady, A.O. California: Chulainn Press, 1977. (Ref. 282)

Index to Women of the World from Ancient to Modern Times: Biographies and Portraits. Ireland, N.O. Westwood, MA.: Faxon, 1970. (Ref. 353)

Indian Women Through the Ages. Verma, H.N. and Verma, A. New Delhi: Great Indian Publishers, 1977. (Ref. 414)

Individual Note of Music, Sound and Electronics. Oram, D. London: Galliard, 1972. (Ref. 388)

Information on Music: A Handbook of Reference Sources in European Languages. vol. 1. Marco, Guy A. Basic and Universal Sources. Littleton, CO.: Libraries Unlimited Inc., 1975. (Ref. 528)

Information on Music: A Handbook of Reference Sources in European Languages. vol. 2. Marco, Guy A. The Americas. Littleton, CO.: Libraries Unlimited, Inc., 1977. (Ref. 529)

Instrumental Music Printed Before 1600: A Bibliography. Brown, H.M. Cambridge, MA.: Harvard University Press, 1965. (Ref. 164)

Instrumental Solos and Duos by Living British Composers. Composers' Guild of Great Britain. London: British Music Information Centre, 1972. (Ref. 409)

International Anthology of Recorded Music. Thiel, Joern. Vienna; Munich: Jugend & Volk, 1971. (Ref. 509)

International Bibliography of Discographies. Cooper, David Edwin. Littleton, CO.: Libraries Unlimited Inc., 1975. (Ref. 511)

International Cyclopedia of Music and Musicians. Thompson, O. Slonimsky, Nicolas, ed., 4th ed. London: Dent, 1942; 10th ed., ed., Bohle, Bruce. London: Dent, 1975. (Ref. 74)

International Discography of the Women Composers. Cohen, Aaron I. Westport, CT.: Greenwood Press, 1983. (Ref. 563)

International Electronic Music Catalogue. Davies, H., comp. Paris: Groupe de Recherches Musicales de l'ORTF and New York Independent Electronic Music Center, 1968. (Ref. 57)

International Electronic Music Discography. Kondracki, M., et al. Mainz: Schott, 1979. (Ref. 406)

International Encyclopedia of Violin-Keyboard Sonatas and Composer Biographies. Pedigo, A. Booneville, AR.: Arriaga, 1979. (Ref. 81)

International Index of Dissertations and Musicological Works in Progress. Adkins, Cecil and Dickinson, Alis, eds. New York: American Musicological Society & International Musicological Society, 1977. (Ref. 391)

International Index of Dissertations and Musicological Works In Progress. Adkins, Cecil and Dickinson, Alis. American-Canadian Supplement. Philadelphia, PA.: American Musicological Society, 1979. (Ref. 50)

International Repertoire of Music Literature (RILM) New York, International RILM Center. Brook, Barry S., editor in chief. 1966. (Ref. 571)

International Who's Who in Music. 7th ed. Kay, E. Cambridge, England: International Who's Who in Music, 1975. (Ref. 77)

International Who's Who in Music and Musicians' Directory. 8th ed. Gaster, A., ed. London: International Who's Who in Music, 1977. (Ref. 206)

International Who's Who in Music and Musicians' Directory. Gaster, Adrian, ed. Cambridge, England: Melrose Press, 1980. (Ref. 457)

International Who's Who in Music and Musicians's Directory. 10th ed. Cambridge, England: International Who's Who in Music, 1985. (Ref. 643)

International Who Is Who in Music. 5th ed. Mize, Dr. J.T.H., ed. Chicago: Who is Who in Music, 1951. (Ref. 27, 496)

Internationale Gesellschaft fuer neue Musik. Haefeli, Anton. Zurich: Atlantis Musikbuch-Verlag, 1982. (Ref. 558)

Internationales Quellenlexikon der Musik Einzeldruecke vor 1800. Schlager, K., ed. London: Baerenreiter, 1971. (Ref. 125)

Introduction to Certain Mexican Musical Archives. Spiess, L. and Stanford, T. Detroit Studies in Music Bibliography, no. 15. Detroit: Information Co-ordinators, 1969. (Ref. 178)

Introduction to Contemporary Music. 2nd ed. Machlis, J. New York: Norton, 1979. (Ref. 397)

Karl Friedrich Abel. Knape, Walter. Bremen: Schuenemann Universitaetsverlag, 1973. (Ref. 503)

Katalog der Abteilung Noten. Internationales Musikinstitut Darmstadt. Darmstadt: Institute, 1966. (Ref. 189)

Keeping Score. Film Music 1972-1979. Limbacher, James L. Metuchen, NJ.: Scarecrow Press, 1981. (Ref. 497)

Keyboard Music by Women Composers. Meggett, Joan M. Westport, CT.: Greenwood Press, 1981. (Ref. 477)

Keyboard Solos and Duos by Living British Composers. Composers' Guild of Great Britain. London: British Music Information Centre, 1974. (Ref. 410)

Komponierende Frauen. Zelenka, Karl. Cologne: Ellenberg Verlag, 1980. (Ref. 448)

Komponiste van Suid-Afrika. Bouws, J. Stellenbosch: Albertyn, 1971. (Ref. 175)

Komponisten und Musikwissenschaftler der deutschen Demokratischen Republik. Berlin: Verlag Neue Musik, 1959. (Ref. 589)

Komponistinnen aus 500 Jahren. Weissweiler, Eva. Frankfurt: Fischer Taschenbuch Verlag, 1981. (Ref. 476)

Kompozitori i muzicki pisci Jugoslavije: Clanovi saveza kompozitora Jugoslavije, 1945-1967 katalog. Savez Kompozitora Jugoslavije. Miloslavjevic-Pesic, Milena, ed. Belgrade: Savez Kompozitora Jugoslavije, 1968. (Ref. 145)

Kurzgefasstes Tonkuenstlerlexikon. Frank, P., and Altmann, W. Regensburg: Bosse, 1936; 15th ed. Wilhelmshaven: Heinrichshofen, 1974. (Ref. 70)

Kvinnelige komponister: En bio-bibliografi. Seland, M. Oslo: Statens bibliotekskole, 1976. (Ref. 432)

Kvinnliga Komponister i sverige under 1800 och 1900- Talen. Oehrstroem, Eva. Stockholm: Haesselby Slott, 1981. (Ref. 642)

Lady: Studies of Certain Significant Phases of Her History. Putnam, E.J. Chicago: University of Chicago Press, 1970. (Ref. 338)

Lady was a Bishop: The Hidden History of Women with Clerical Ordination and the Jurisdiction of Bishops. Morris, J. New York: Macmillan, 1973. (Ref. 378)

Larousse de la musique. Dufourcq, N., ed. Paris: Larousse, 1957. (Ref. 13)

Lexikon der Harfe. Zingel, H.J. Regensburg: Laaber, 1977. (Ref. 344)

Lexikon der neuen Musik. Prieberg, F.K. Munich: Alber, 1958. (Ref. 73)

Lexikon der kirchlichen Tonkunst. Kornmueller, P.U. Regensburg: Coppenrath, 1891-1895. (Ref. 215)

Liberation of Sound: An Introduction to Electronic Music. Russcol, H. Englewood Cliffs NJ.: Prentice-Hall, 1972. (Ref. 324)

Liberty's Women. McHenry, Robert, ed. Springfield, MA.: G & C Merriam Co., 1980. (Ref. 484)

Libro della Musica. Ballo, F. et al., eds. Florence: Sansoni, 1940. (Ref. 165)

Lista de Autores y Compositores Registrados en DAI-Chile a Septiembre de 1979. Valenzuela Tobar, Paulina. Editorial Universitaria, SA, 1979. (Ref. 587)

Literature for Voices in Combination with Electronic and Tape Music: An Annotated Bibliography. Edwards, J.M. MLA Index and Bibliography Series, no. 17. Ann Arbor, MI.: Music Library Association, 1977. (Ref. 301)

Literaturgeschichte der Araber. Hammer-Purgstall. Vienna: Staatsdruckerei, 1850. (Ref. 234)

Louise Farrenc, 1804-1875. Friedland, Bea. Ann Arbor, MI.: UMI Research Press, 1980. (Ref. 593)

Libro della musica. Ballo, F., et al., eds. Florence: Sansoni, 1940. (Ref. 165)

Maddalena Casulana: madrigalista del Cinquecento. Pescerelli, B. Bologna: Universita degli Studi di Bologna, 1974. (Ref. 253)

Maine Composers and Their Music: A Biographical Dictionary. Wiggin, F.T. Portland, ME.: Maine Federation of Music Clubs, 1959; Maine Historical Society, 1976. (Ref. 374)

Male/Female Language. Key, M.R. Metuchen, NJ.: Scarecrow Press, 1975. (Ref. 272)

Man and His Music. Harman, A., et al. London: Barrie & Jenkins, 1962. (Ref. 386)

Manuel de bibliographie biographique et d'iconographie des femmes celebres... par un vieux bibliophile. Paris: Nilsson, 1892. (Ref. 210)

Manuel de la musique. Kelen, P.P. Paris: Centurion, 1961. (Ref. 64)

Mata encyklopedia muzyki. Warsaw: Panstwowe Wydawnictwo Naukowe, 1981. (Ref. 504)

Medieval and Renaissance Music on Long-Playing Records. Coover, James and Colvig, Richard. Detroit, MI.: Detroit Studies in Music Bibliography, 1964. (Ref. 510)

Medieval and Renaissance Music on Long Playing Records. Coover, James and Colvig, Richard. Supl. Detroit, MI.: Information Co-ordinators, Inc., 1973. (Ref. 513)

Medieval Music. Caldwell, J. Bloomington, IN: Indiana University Press, 1978. (Ref. 289)

Medieval Music. Hoppin, Richard H. New York: W.W. Norton & Co., 1978. (Ref. 568)

Medieval Music: The Sixth Liberal Art. Hughes, A. Toronto: University of Toronto Press, 1974. (Ref. 365)

Medieval Song: An Anthology of Hymns and Lyrics. Wilhelm, J.J., ed. London: Allen Unwin, 1971. (Ref. 279)

Medieval Women. Baker, Derek, ed. Oxford: Basil Blackwell, 1978. (Ref. 547)

Melodiya; A Soviet Russian L.P. Discography. Bennett, John R., ed. Westport, CT.: Greenwood Press, 1981. (Ref. 493)

Military and Brass Band Music. Catalogues of Australian Compositions VI. Sydney: Australia Music Centre, 1977. (Ref. 443)

Missouri Music. Krohn, Ernst C. New York: Da Capo Press, 1971. (Ref. 460)

Modern Music Makers. Goss, M. New York: Dutton, 1952. (Ref. 71)

Modern Renaissance of Jewish Music. Weisser, Albert. New York: Da Capo Press, 1983. (Ref. 616)

Modern Russian Composers. Sabaneyeff, L. London: Lawrence, 1927. (Ref. 134)

Moderne Musik, 1945-1965. Dibelius, U. Munich: Piper, 1966. (Ref. 294)

Moenche/Buerger Minnesaenger: Musik in der Gesellschaft des europaeischen Mittelalters. Guelke, P. Vienna: Boehlaus, 1975. (Ref. 364)

Mondo della musica: Enciclopedia alfabetica con ampie trattazioni monografiche. Rome: Garzanti. (Ref. 166)

More Clarinet Virtuosi of the Past. Weston, Pamela. Kent: Novello & Co. Ltd., 1977. (Ref. 472)

Muse for the Masses: Ritual and Music in the Age of Democratic Revolution, 1770-1870. Donakowski, C.L. Chicago: University of Chicago Press, 1977. (Ref. 309)

Music: Books on Music and Sound Recordings. Washington DC.: Library of Congress, 1975-1980. (Ref 519)

Music: The Priceless Jewel, from the Kitab al-iqd al-farid of ibn-Abd Rabbihi. Farmer, H.G. Bearsden: Author, 1942. (Ref. 186)

Music after Modernism. Lipman, Samuel. New York: Basic Books, Inc., 1979. (Ref. 535)

Music and Musicians in Israel. Gradenwitz, P. Tel Aviv: Israeli Music Publications, 1959. (Ref. 205)

Music and Society since 1815. Raynor, Henry. (Ref. 596)

Music and Women: The Story of Women in Their Relation to Music. Drinker, S. Washington, DC: Zenger, 1948; Repr., 1977. (Ref. 264)

Music Cultures of the Pacific, the Near East and Asia. Malm, W.P. Englewood Cliffs, NJ: Prentice-Hall, 1967. (Ref. 259)

Music for Oboe, Oboe D'Amore and English Horn. Gifford, Virginia Snodgrass. Westport, CT.: Greenwood Press, 1983. (Ref. 574)

Music for Orchestra, Band and Large Ensemble. New York: American Music Center, 1982. (Ref. 594)

Music for the Piano: A Handbook of Concert and Teaching Material from 1580-1952. Friskin, J. and Freundlich, I. New York: Rinehart, 1954. Repr., New York: Dover, 1973. (Ref. 138)

Music in Ancient Arabia and Spain: Being La Musica de las Cantigas. Ribera, J. Stanford, CA.: Stanford University Press, 1929. Repr., New York: Da Capo Press, 1970. (Ref. 170)

Music in Ancient Israel. Sendrey, A. London: Vision Press, 1969. (Ref. 255)

Music in Croatia. Andreis, J. Zagreb: Institute of Musicology, 1974. (Ref. 435)

Music in Early America. Hixon, Donald L. Metuchen, NJ.: Scarecrow Press, Inc., 1970. (Ref. 489)

Music in Europe and the United States. Borroff, Edith. Englewood Cliffs, NJ.: Prentice-Hall, Inc., 1971. (Ref. 564)

Music in Holland: A Review of Contemporary Music in the Netherlands. Reeser, E., ed. Amsterdam: Meulenhoff. (Ref. 169)

Music in Ireland: A Symposium. Fleischmann, A., ed. Dublin: Cork University Press, 1952. (Ref. 50)

Music in Latin America: An Introduction. Béhague, G. Englewood Cliffs, NJ.: Prentice-Hall, 1979. (Ref. 427)

Music in Mexico: A Historical Survey. Stevenson, R. New York: Crowell, 1952. (Ref. 381)

Music in Poland. Erhardt, L. Warsaw: Interpress, 1975. (Ref. 258)

Music in Primitive Culture. Nettl, B. Cambridge, MA.: Harvard University Press, 1956; repr., 1977. (Ref. 311)

Music in the History of the Western Church. Dickinson, Edward. New York: Greenwood Press, 1969. (Ref. 531)

Music in the Middle Ages. Reese, Gustave. London: J.M. Dent & Sons Ltd., 1941. (Ref. 565)

Music in the New World. Hamm, Charles. New York: W.W. Norton, 1983. (Ref. 579)

Music in the Social and Religious Life of Antiquity. Sendrey, A. Madison, NJ.: Fairleigh Dickinson University Press, 1974. (Ref. 151)

Music Lexicography. Coover, James. Carlisle, PA.: Carlisle Books, 1971. (Ref. 526)

Music of Ancient Greece. Michaelides, S. London: Faber, 1978. (Ref. 281.)

Music of Black Americans: A History. Southern, E. New York: Norton, 1971. (Ref. 285)

Music of Finland. Richards, D. London: Evelyn, 1968. (Ref. 62.)

Music of Latin America. 3rd ed. Pan American Union. Washington, DC: Union, 1953. (Ref. 342)

Music of Latin America. Slonimsky, Nicolas. New York: Crowell, 1945. Repr., New York: Da Capo Press, 1972. (Ref. 54)

Music of Spain. Chase, G. New York: Dover, 1959.

Music of the Ancient Near East. Polin, C.C.J. New York: Vantage Press, 1954. Repr. Westport, CT.: Greenwood Press, 1976. (Ref. 313)

Music of the Bible. Stainer, John. London: Novello, 1914. (Ref. 632)

Music of the Jews: An Historical Appreciation. Rothmueller, A.M. London: Vallentine Mitchell, 1953. (Ref. 139)

Music of the Middle Ages 1. Cattin, Giulio. Cambridge: Cambridge University Press, 1984. (Ref. 648)

Music of the Minnesinger and Early Meistersinger: A Bibliography. Linker, R.W. Chapel Hill, NC.: University of North Carolina Press, 1962. (Ref. 25)

Music of the Whole Earth. Reck, D. New York: Scribner, 1977. (Ref. 240)

Music Reference and Research Materials. Duckles, Vincent, ed. New York: Free Press, 1974. (Ref. 527)

Music Through The Looking Glass. Spiegl, Fritz. London: Routledge & Kegan Paul, 1984. (Ref. 652)

Musica: Enciclopedia Storica. Gatti, G.M. and Basso, A. Turin: Unione Tipografica - Editrice Torinese, 1966. (Ref. 14)

Musica andaluza medieval en las canciones de trovadores, troveros y minnesinger. Ribera y Tarrago, J. Madrid: Revista de Archivos, 1923. Repr., New York: AMS Press, 1974. (Ref. 316)

Musica Cubana. Ayala, Dr. Cristobal Diaz. San Juan, PR.: Editorial Cubanatan, 1981. (Ref. 557)

Musica e Poesia Nell'Antica Roma. Paratore, Ettore. Cremona: Fondazione Claudio Monteverdi, 1981. (Ref. 592)

Musica maya guiche: Region de Guatemala. Castillo, J. Guatemala: Homenaje, 1977. (Ref. 16)

Musical America. New York: ABC Leisure Magazines, 1983. (Ref. 569)

Musical Biography. 2nd ed. Bingley, W. London: Colburn, 1834. Repr. New York: Da Capo Press, 1971. (Ref. 176)

Musical Poesia Nell'Antica Roma. Paratore, Ettore. Cremona: Fondazione Claudio Monteverdi, 1981. (Ref. 592)

Musical Practices in Medieval English Nunneries. Bagnall, A.D. Ann Arbor, MI.: Xerox University Microfilms, 1975. (Ref. 337)

Musical References in the Chinese Classics. Kaufmann, Walter. Detroit: Information Co-ordinators Inc., 1976. (Ref. 640)

Musical Scotland: Past and Present. Baptie, D. Hildesheim: Georg Olms Verlag, 1972. (Ref. 33)

Musiciennes de chez nous. Gingras, C. Montreal: Editions de l'Ecole Vincent d'Indy 1955. (Ref. 355)

Musiciens romains de l'antiquité. Baudot, A. Canada: Presses de l'Université de Montreal and Editions Klincksieck, 1973. (Ref. 339)

Musicisti di oggi nell' U.R.S.S. Gibelli, V. Milan: Giuffre, 1972. (Ref. 420)

Musicus Danicus eller Danske sangmester, Schacht, M.H. ed. and commentary, Skjerne, G. Original manuscript, 1687. Copenhagen: Hagerups, 1928. (Ref. 97)

Musik der Goetter Geister und Menschen. Laade, Wolfgang: Baden-Baden, Verlag Valentin Koerner, 1975. (Ref. 561)

Musik des Altertums: Aegypten. Musikgeschichte in Bildern, vol. 2, pt. 1; Hickmann, H. Besseler, Heinrich and Schneider, Max, eds. Leipzig: VEB Deutscher Verlag fuer Musik, 1961. (Ref. 207)

Musik des Mittelalters und der Renaissance: Islam. Farmer, H.G. Musikgeschichte in Bildern, vol. 2, pt. 3. Besseler, Heinrich and Schneider, Max, eds. Leipzig: VEB Deutscher Verlag fuer Musik, 1976. (Ref. 305)

Musik Lexikon. Wilibald, Gurlitt and Riemann, H. Mainz: Schott's Soehne, 1972-1975. (Ref. 17).

Musik Lexikon. Moser, Hans Joachim. Berlin: Hesses Verlag, 1935. (Ref. 231)

Musik Lexikon. Moser, Hans Joachim. Hamburg: Musikverlag Hans Sikorski, 1963. (Ref. 551)

Musik-Lexikon. Hoeijer, J.L. Stockholm: Lundquist, 1864. (Ref. 103)

Musik von A-Z: vom Gregorianischen Choral zu Jazz und Beat. Goodman, A.A. Munich: Suedwest Verlag, 1971. (Ref. 201)

Musik zwischen Orient und Okzident. Gradenwitz, Peter. Hamburg: Heinrichshfen's Verlag. (Ref. 600)

Musikalische Studienkoepfe. La Mara (pseud. of Marie Lipsius). Leipzig: Breitkopf & Haertel, 1883. (Ref. 163)

Musikalisches Conversations-Lexikon: Eine Encyclopaedie der gesammten musikalischen Wissenschaften. Mendel, H. Berlin: Heinemann, 1870-1879. (Ref. 129)

Musikalisches Lexikon oder musikalische Bibliothek. Walther, J.G. Leipzig: Deer; facsimile reprint ed., Schaal, Richard Cassel: Baerenreiter, 1953. (Ref. 302)

Musikens hvem hvad hvor: Politikens musikleksikon. Copenhagen: Politikens Forlag, 1950. (Ref. 96)

Musiklexikon. Seeger, Horst. Leipzig: VEB Deutscher Verlag fuer Musik, 1981. (Ref. 580)

Musique et Musiciens de la Vieille France. Brenet, Michel. Editions d'aujourd'hui, 1977. (Ref. 439)

Musisches Lexikon: Kuenstler, Kunstwerke und Motive aus Dichtung, Musik und bildender Kunst. 3rd ed. Koch, W.A. Stuttgart: Kroener, 1976. (Ref. 202)

Muslim Spain, 711-1492 A.D. Imamuddin, S.M. Leiden: E.J. Brill, 1981. (Ref. 647)

Muzica in Romania Socialista. Brancusi, P. and Calinoiu, N. Bucharest: Editura Muzicala a Uniunii Compozitorilor, 1973. (Ref. 148)

Muzicieni Romani: Compozitori si muzicologi. Cosma, V. Bucharest: Uniunii Compozitorilor, 1965, 1970. (Ref. 196)

Muzicka enciklopedija. Andreis, J., ed. Zagreb: Izdanje i Naklada Leksikografskog Zavoda Fnrj, 1958. (Ref. 193)

Muzicka enciklopedija. Kovacevic, K., ed. Zagreb: Jugoslavenski Leksikografski Zavod, 1971. (Ref. 109)

Muzicki stvaraoci u Srbiji. Pericic, V. Belgrade: Prosveta, 1969. (Ref. 418)

Muzicko stvaralastvo u Hrvatskoj, 1945-1965. Kovacevic, K. Zagreb: Udruzenje Kompozitora Hrvatske, 1966. (Ref. 416)

Muzykalnaya entsiklopedia. Keldysh, Y.V., ed. Moscow: Sovietski Kompozitor, 1973. (Ref. 330)

Muzykainaya Literatura iz SSSR. Moscow: Vsesoyuznoye Objedinenie, 1976. (Ref. 277)

Naming Names. Room, Adrian. London: Routledge & Kegan Paul, 1981. (Ref. 479)

Negro Musicians and Their Music. Cuney-Hare, M. Washington, DC.: Associated Publishers, 1936. (Ref. 328)

Nell'Arabia antica: La donna nella famiglia e nella societa. Cattan, B. Rome: Tipografia Ponteficia nell'Istituto Pio IX, 1915. (Ref. 250)

Neue Musiklexikon. Einstein, A. Berlin: Hesse, 1926. (Ref. 115)

Neue sowjetische Musik der 20er Jahre. Gojowy, D. Regensburg: Laaber, 1980. (Ref. 200)

New Classical Dictionary of Biography, Mythology and Geography. 2nd ed. Smith, W. London: Murray, 1853. (Ref. 382)

New Encyclopedia of Music and Musicians. Rev. ed. Pratt, W.S. New York: Macmillan, 1929. (Ref. 89)

New English Bible. Oxford University Press; Cambridge University Press, 1970. (Ref. 638)

New Larousse Encyclopedia of Mythology. Graves, Robert. London: Hamlyn Publishing Group, 1959. (Ref. 606)

New Larousse Encyclopedia of Mythology. Hamlyn Publishing Group, 1981. (Ref. 543)

New Oxford Companion to Music. Arnold, Denis, ed. Oxford: Oxford University Press, 1983. (Ref. 612)

Nobilta' di Dame. Caroso, Marco Fabrizio. Arnaldo Forni Editore, 1980. (Ref. 545)

Nordic Sound. Yoell, J.H. Boston: Crescendo, 1974. (Ref. 67)

Nos auteurs et compositeurs dramatiques. Martin, J. Paris: Flammarion, 1897. (Ref. 296)

Nouvelle Histoire de la Musique. Prunieres, Henry. Paris: Aux Editions Rieder, 1934. (Ref. 487)

Nuove ricerche sul libro della scala e la conoscenza dell'Islam in occidente. Cerulli, E. Vatican: Biblioteca Apostolica Vaticana, 1972. (Ref. 241)

Nuovo dizionario Ricordi della musica e dei musicisti. Allorto, R., ed. Milan: Ricordi, 1976. (Ref. 135)

Oesterreichische Komponisten der Gegenwart. Goertz, Harald. Munich: Doblinger, 1979. (Ref. 452)

Of Six Mediaeval Women. Kemp-Welch, A. Williamstown, MA.: Corner House Publisers, 1979. (Ref. 179)

Operas, Intermezzos, Ballets Cantates, Oratorios. Mooser, R. Aloys. Geneva: Imprimerie A. Kundig, 1945. (Ref. 436)

Opere e operisti: Dizionario lirico universale, 1541-1902. Dassori, C. Genoa: Sordomuti, 1903. (Ref. 225)

Opern-Handbuch. Riemann, Dr. Hugo. Hildesheim: Georg Olms Verlag, 1979. (Ref. 480)

Opern Lexikon. Seeger, Horst. Hamburg: Heinrichshofen's Verlag, 1979. (Ref. 618)

Opernlexikon. Stieger, F. Tutzing: Schneider, 1977. (Ref. 431)

Orchesterkatalog zeitgenoessischer oesterreichischer Komponisten. Lubej, Emil et al., eds. Oesterreichischer Komponistenbund. Vienna: Lafite (1977?). (Ref. 194)

Orchestral Music by Living British Composers. Composers' Guild of Great Britain. London: British Music Information Centre, 1970. (Ref. 411)

Orchid Boat: Women Poets of China. Rexroth, K. and Chung, L., eds. New York: McGraw-Hill, 1972. (Ref. 270)

Organ Literature: A Comprehensive Survey. Arnold, C.R. Metuchen, NJ.: Scarecrow Press, 1973. (Ref. 236)

Os Musicos portuguezes. De Vasconcellos, J. Porto: Imprensa Portugueza, 1870. (Ref. 300)

Our Contemporary Composers: American Music in the Twentieth Century. Howard, J.T. and Mendel, A. Philadelphia: Blackiston, 1943. (Ref. 168)

Oxford Companion to Music. 2nd ed. Scholes, P.A. London: Oxford University Press, 1943. (Ref. 19)

Penguin Dictionary of Music. Jacobs, A., ed. Harmondsworth: Penguin, 1967. (Ref. 11)

Pequeñas biografias de grandes musicos mexicanos. Garcia, F.M. Mexico: Ediciones Framong, 1966. (Ref. 82)

Perfection des connaissances musicales: Kitab kamal Adab al-Gina. Trans. Amnon Shiloah. al-Hasan ibn-Ahmad ibn-Ali al-Katib. Paris: Geuthner, 1972. (Ref. 308)

Personal Narrative of a Pilgrimage to Al-Madinah & Meccah. Burton, Captain Sir Richard F. New York: 1964. Dover Publications, 1964. (Ref. 491)

Perspectives of New Music: An Index, 1962-1982. Basart, Ann. Berkeley CA: Fallen Leaf Press, 1984. (Ref. 619)

Petite encyclopedie musicale. Bisson, A., and Lajarte, T. de. Paris: Hennuyer, 184. (Ref. 394)

Phaidon Book of the Opera. Oxford: Phaidon, 1979. (Ref. 78)

Philosophies of Music History: A Study of General Histories of Music, 1600-1960. Allen, W.D. New York: Dover, 1962. (Ref. 319)

Pianist's Resource Guide: Piano Music in Print and Literature on the Pianistic Art, 1978-1979. Rezits, J. and Deatsman, G. San Diego, CA.: Pallma Music, 1979. (Ref. 373)

Piano and Organ Catalogue I and II. BBC Music Library. Composers. London: J. Smethurst & Co., 1973. (Ref. 473)

Pianographie. Schulz, Ferdinand F. Recklinghausen: Piano-Verlag, 1982. (Ref. 521)

Pierre Key's Music Year Book. New York: Pierre Key, Inc., 1926. (Ref. 556)

Podreczna encyclopedia muzyki Koscielnej. Mizgalski, G. Warsaw: Wojciecha, 1959. (Ref. 417)

Polska wspotczesna kultura muzyczna, 1944-1964. Dziebowska, E., ed. Cracow: Polskie Wydawnickwo Muzyczne, 1964. (Ref. 293)

Portugal illustrado pelo sexo femino: Noticia historica. Azevedo, D.M.A. de. Lisbon: Pedro Ferreira, 1734. (Ref. 232)

Primitive Music. Wallaschek, R. London: Longmans Green, 1893. Repr., New York: Da Capo Press, 1970. (Ref. 233)

Quotable Woman. Partnow, Elaine, comp and ed. Los Angeles, CA.: Pinnacle Books, Inc., 1977. (Ref. 581)

Raizes da musica popular brasileira, 1500-1889. Vasconcelos, A. San Paulo: Martins, 1977. (Ref. 349)

Realist Music. Moisenko, R. London: Meridian Books, 1949. (Ref. 61)

Record of Singing, 1914-1925. Scott, M. London: Duckworth, 1979. (Ref. 425)

Record of Singing to 1914. Scott, M. London: Duckworth, 1977. (Ref. 423)

Renaissance and Baroque Musical Sources in the Americas. Stevenson, R. Washington DC: Organisation of the American States, 1970. (Ref. 332)

Resources of American Music History. Krummel, D.W., Geil, Jean., Dyen, Doris J., and Root Deane L. Chicago, IL.: University of Illinois, 1981. (Ref. 537)

Rheinische Musiker. Fellerer, K.G., ed. Cologne: Arno Volk-Verlag, 1962. (Ref. 192)

Rise of Opera. Donington, Robert. London: Faber & Faber, 1981. (Ref. 554)

Roman Women: Their History and Habits. Balsdon, J.P.V.D. London: Bodley Head, 1962; Repr., 1977. (Ref. 318)

Roma, Accademia Nazionale di S. Cecilia. Studi Ricerche, 1948-1960. RAI Radiotelevisione Italiana. (Ref. 532)

Royal Collection: A Historical Album of Music Composed Exclusively by Members of the Royal Family of Great Britian and Ireland. Fairbairn, N. and Unger- Hamilton, C., eds. Sevenoaks: Novello, 1977. (Ref. 262)

Russian Composers and Musicians: A Biographical Dictionary. Vodarsky-Shiraeff, A., comp. New York: Wilson, 1940. Repr., New York: Da Capo Press, 1969. (Ref. 38)

Saengerinnen am Abbasidenhof um die Zeit des Kalifen al-Mutawakkil. Stigelbauer, M. Vienna: Verband der wissenschaftlichen Gesellschaften Oesterreichs, 1975. (Ref. 224)

Sainte Cécile: Metamorphoses d'un Thème Musical. De Mirimonde, A.P. Geneva: Minkoff, 1974. (Ref. 424)

Sappho and Her Influence: Our Debt to Greece and Rome. Robinson, D.M. New York: Cooper Square, 1963. (Ref. 310)

Sara, Je Rok Zakt af. Vrouwenliedboek. Schreijer, Cobi. Amsterdam: Feministische Uitgeverij Sara, 1980. (Ref. 478)

Schleswig-Holsteinische Musiker, von den aeltesten Zeiten bis zur Gegenwart: ein Heimatbuch. Fey, H. Hamburg: Holler, 1922. (Ref. 393)

Schweizer Komponistinnen der Gegenwart. Ehrismann, Sibylle and Meyer, Thomas, eds. Zurich: Musik Hug & Co., 1985. (Ref. 651)

Schweizer Musiker-lexikon: Dictionnaire des musiciens suisses. Schuh, W., et al. Zurich: Atlantis Verlag, 1964. (Ref. 59)

Schweizerische Tonkuenstlerverein im zweiten Vierteljahrhundert seines Bestehens. Zurich: Atlantis Verlag, 1950. (Ref. 552)

Scores, An Anthology of New Music. New York: Schirmer Books, 1981. (Ref. 633)

Second Sex. De Beauvoir, S. Trans. & ed., Parshley, H.M. Harmondsworth: Penguin Books, 1972; repr., 1976. (Ref. 317)

Selected Discography of Solo Song. Stahl, Dorothy. Detroit, MI.: Information Co-ordinators Inc., 1972. (Ref. 507)

Selected Discography of Solo Song. Supl. Stahl, Dorothy. Detroit, MI.: Information Co-ordinators Inc., 1976. (Ref. 508)

Short History of Spanish Music. Livermore, A. London: Duckworth, 1972. (Ref. 244)

Sisters of Sacred Song. Rogal, Samuel J. New York: Garland Publishing, Inc., 1981. (Ref. 482)

Slownik muzykow polskich. Chominski, J., ed. Warsaw: Polskie Wydawnictwo Muzyczne, 1962. (Ref. 118)

Social History of Music from the Middle Ages to Beethoven. Raynor, H. London: Barrie & Jenkins, 1972. (Ref. 383)

Sohlman's Musiklexikon. Stockholm: Sohlman Foerlag, 1975-1979. (Ref. 20)

Soundprints: Contemporary Composers. Such, P. Toronto: Clarke, Irwin, 1972. (Ref. 380)

Source: Music of the Avant Garde: Annotated List of Contents and Cumulative Indices. Williams, M.D. MLA Index and Bibliography Series, No. 19. Ann Arbor, MI.: Music Library Association, 1978. (Ref. 246)

Sources of Bibliography and Collective Biography. Jackson, Richard. United States Music. New York: Department of Music, 1973. (Ref. 451)

South African Music Encyclopedia. Vol. 1-4. Malan, J.P., ed. Cape Town: Oxford University Press, 1979. (Ref. 377)

Soviet Literature and Music. Koltypina, and Pavlova N.G. Moscow: Sovietski Kompozitor, 1979. (Ref. 498)

Soviet Music. Polyakova, L. Moscow: Foreign Languages Publishing House. (Ref. 419)

Sovietske kompozitory: Kratkii biograficheskii spravochnik. Bernandt, G.B., and Dolzhansky, A., comps. Moscow: Sovietske Kompozitor, 1955. (Ref. 87)

Sovietske kompozitory i muzykoviedy. Bernandt, G.B., and Yampolski, I.M. Moscow: Sovietske Kompozitor, 1978. (Ref. 21)

Sovietski Operi. Golitsma, A.M. Moscow: Sovietski Kompozitor, 1982. (Ref. 553)

Spain; A Musician's Journey through Time and Space. Starkie, Walter. Geneva: Edisli-At Editions Rene Kister, 1958. (Ref. 639)

Spectrum muzieklexicon. Willemze, T. Utrecht: Spectrum, 1975. (Ref. 183)

Steirisches Musiklexikon. Suppan, Wolfgang, ed. Graz: Akademische Druck-und Verlaganstalt, 1966. (Ref. 500)

Stelle feminili: Dizionario bio-bibliografico. New ed. Villani, C. Rome: Albrighi, Segati & Co., 1915. (Ref. 180)

Storia della Musica. Martini, Giovanni Battista. Graz: Akademische Druck-und Verlaganstalt, 1967. (Ref. 533)

Storia della musica, tomo 1, Bologna. Martini, Giovanni Battista. Graz: Akademische Druck-und Verlaganstalt, 1967. (Ref. 486)

Storia della musica sovietica: Compositori e composizioni della Russa europea e asiatica. Gibelli, V. Pavia: Tipografia del Libro, 1964-1965. (Ref. 223)

Story of British Music and Earlier French Musicians. Harris, C.A. and Hargrave, M. London: Waverley Books, 1919. (Ref. 149)

Story of Minstrelsy. Duncan, Edmiondstoune. London: Walter Scott Publishing Co., 1907. (Ref. 567)

Studi e notizie riguardanti la storia della musica. Frati, L. Bologna: Forni, 1976. (Ref. 242)

Study of the Lives and Works of Black Women Composers in America. Green, M.D. Ann Arbor, MI.: Xerox University Microfilms, 1975. (Ref. 335)

Subjection of Women. Mill, J.S. London: Longmans; Green, 1869. (Ref. 248)

Suid-Afrikaanse komponiste. Bouws, J. Stellenbosch: Albertyn, 1957. (Ref. 47)

Suid-Afrikaanse musiekbibliografie. Van der Merwe, F. Cape Town: Tafelberg, 1974. (Ref. 184)

Susreti sa suvremenim kompozitorima jugoslavije. Reich, T. Zagreb: Skolska Knjiga, 1972. (Ref. 219)

Svensk solosang, 1850-1890, pt. 1: En genrehistorisk studie. Helmer, A. Stockholm: Almqvist & Wiksell, 1972. (Ref. 167)

Svensk 1900-talsmusik fraan opera till pop 2000 biografier. Engman, Bo. Stockholm: Bokfoerlaget Natur och Kultur, 1978. (Ref. 456)

Symphonic Catalog. 3rd Ed. American Society of Composers, Authors and Publishers. New York: R.R. Bowker Co., 1977. (Ref. 280)

Symphonic Catalogue. Rev. ed. New York: Broadcast Music Inc., 1971; supplement no. 1, 1978. (Ref. 403)

Tablettes de renommée des musiciens, auteurs, compositeurs, virtuoses, amateurs et maîtres de musique vocale et instrumentale, les plus connus en chaque genre. Paris: Cailleau, 1785. Repr., Geneva: Minkoff, 1971. (Ref. 368)

Teatro D'Opera. Celletti, Rodolfo. Milan: Rizzoli Editore, 1976. (Ref. 514)

Tender Tyrant, Nadia Boulanger. Kendall, A. London: MacDonald & Jane's, 1976. (Ref. 363)

Thing or Two About Music. Slonimsky, Nicolas. Westport, CT.: Greenwood Press, 1948; Repr., 1972. (Ref. 298)

Thirty-four Biographies of Canadian Composers. Canadian Broadcasting Corporation. Montreal: Canadian Broadcasting Corp., 1964. (Ref. 31)

Thousand and One Nights of Opera. Martens, F.H. New York: Appleton, 1926. Repr., New York: Da Capo, 1978. (Ref. 426)

Time, Place and Music: An Anthology of Ethnomusicological Observation, ca. 1800. Harrison, F. Amsterdam: Knuf, 1973. (Ref. 256)

Tonkuenstler-Lexikon Berlins von den aeltesten Zeiten bis auf die Gegenwart. Ledebur, C. von. Berlin: Rauh, 1861. (Ref. 121)

Topographical Bibliography of Ancient Egyptian Hieroglyphic Texts, Reliefs and Paintings. 2nd ed. Porter, B. and Moss, R.L.B. Oxford: Clarendon Press, 1960. (Ref. 428)

Troubadours. Marrou, H.I. Paris: Seuil, 1971. (Ref. 46)

Troubadours and Their World of the Twelfth and Thirteenth Centuries. Lindsay, J. London: Muller, 1976. (Ref. 243)

Troubadours et l'Angleterre. Audiau, J. Paris: Libraire Philosophique J. Vrin, 1927. (Ref. 366)

Troubadours Revival: A Study of Social Change and Traditionalism in Late Medieval Spain. Boase, R. London: Routledge & Kegan Paul, 1978. (Ref. 357)

Trouveres and Troubadours: A Popular Treatise. Aubry, P. New York: Cooper Square Publishers, 1969. (Ref. 362)

Tudor Women: Queens and Commoners. Plowden, A. London: Weidenfeld & Nicolson, 1979. (Ref. 336)

Turk musikisi ansiklopedisi. Oztuna, Y. Istanbul: Milli Egitim Basimevi, 1974. (Ref. 430)

Turquie: Les traditions musicales. Reinhard, K. and Reinhard, U. Paris: Buchet, 1969. (Ref. 341)

Twentieth Century Composers. Vol. 4. Gaoldbeck, F. France, Italy and Spain. London: Weidenfeld & Nicolson, 1974. (Ref. 154)

Twentieth Century Harpsichord Music: A Classified Catalog. Bedford, F. and Conant, R. Hackensack, NJ.: Boonin, 1974. (Ref. 346)

Twentieth Century Music. Burbank, Richard. London: Thames & Hudson, 1984. (Ref. 641)

Twentieth Century Opera in England and the U.S.A. Northouse, C. Boston: Hall, 1976. (Ref. 141)

Universal-Handbuch der Musik-literatur aller Zeiten und Voelker. Pazdirek, F. Vienna: Pazdirek, 1904-1910. Repr., Hilversum: Knuf, 1967. (Ref. 297)

Unsung: A History of Women in American Music. Ammer, C. Westport, CT.: Greenwood Press, 1980. (Ref. 415)

Venetian Instrumental Music from Gabrieli to Vivaldi. Selfridge-Field, E. Oxford: Blackwell, 1975. (Ref. 143)

Venice (City of) Catalogo generale delle opere musicali ... città di Venezia. Parma: Associazione dei Musicologi Italiani, 1913. (Ref. 160)

Verzeichnis der Harfenmusik. Zingel, H.J. Hofheim am Taunus: Hofmeister. (Ref. 75)

Viola: Complete Guide for Teachers and Students University. Barrett, H. University of Alabama Press, 1972. (Ref. 68)

Violin Concerto. Emery, F.B. Chicago: Violin Literature Publishing, 1928. Repr., New York: Da Capo Press, 1969. (Ref. 7)

Violinists of Today. Brook, D. London: Salisbury Square, 1948. (Ref. 434)

Vocal and Choral Music. Catalogues of Australian Compositions IV. Sydney: Australia Music Centre, 1976. (Ref. 440)

Von den Trobadors Genannten oder Gefeierten Damen. Bergert, F. Halle a.S.: Verlag Max Niemeyer, 1913. (Ref. 222)

Wellsprings of Music. Sachs, C. The Hague: Nijhoff, 1962. Repr., New York: Da Capo Press, 1977. (Ref. 384)

Western Civilizations. 8th ed. Burns, Edward McNall. New York: W.W. Norton & Co., 1973. (Ref. 603)

Wetenschappelijk en biographisch woordenboek der Tonkunst. 2nd ed. Melchior, E.A. Schiedam: Roelants, 1889. (Ref. 400)

When God was a Woman. Stone, Merlin. San Diego: Harcourt Brace Jovanovich Publishers, 1978. (Ref. 629)

Who is Who in ACUM: Authors, Composers and Music Publishers –Biographical Notes and Principal Works. Ravina, M. and Skolsky, S., comps. Israel: ACUM, 1965. (Ref. 379)

Who is Who in Music. 5th ed. Mize, Dr. J.T.H., ed. Chicago, IL: Sterling Publishing Co., 1951. (Ref. 496)

Who's Who in American Music. Press, Jaques Cattell. ed. New York: R.R. Bowker Co., 1983. (Ref. 625)

Who's Who in Music. Ronald, Sir Landon, ed. London: Shaw Publishing Co., 1937. (Ref. 467)

Who's Who in Music. Townend, Peter and Simmons, David, eds. Burke's Peerage, London, 1962. (Ref. 490)

Who's Who in Music. Wyndham, H. Saxe, ed. London: Sir Isaac Pitman & Son, 1915. (Ref. 488)

Who's Who in Music and Musicians' International Directory. St. Clair Shores, MI.: Scholarly, 1935. (Ref. 34)

Who's Who of American Women. 11th ed., 1979-1980. Chicago, IL: Marquis Who's Who. (Ref. 475)

Who's Who of American Women. Chicago, IL.: Marquis Who's Who, Inc., 1981. (Ref. 506)

Who's Who of Indian Musicians. New Delhi: Sangeet Natak Akademi, 1984. (Ref. 650)

Whose Music: An Anthology of Musical Languages. Shepherd, J., et al. London: Latimer, 1977. (Ref. 245)

Windows on Women. Higgins, Ardis O. Hollywood, CA.: Halls of Ivy Press, 1975. (Ref. 538)

Women Artists: Recognition and Reappraisal from the Early Middle Ages to the Twentieth Century. Petersen, K. and Wilson, J.J. New York: Harper & Row, 1976. (Ref. 239)

Woman in Modern Life. Bier, W.C., ed. New York: Fordham University Press. (Ref. 251)

Women in Music. Neuls-Bates, Carol, ed. New York: Harper & Row, 1982. (Ref. 555)

Woman in the Bible. Evans, Mary J. Exeter: Paternoster Press, 1983. (Ref. 634)

Women in Western European History. Frey, Linda., Frey, Marsha and Schneider, Joanne, eds. Westport, CT: Greenwood Press, 1982. (Ref. 575)

Womanlist. Weiser, Marjorie P.K. and Arbeiter, Jean S. New York: Atheneum, 1981. (Ref. 518)

Woman's Work in Music. Elson, A. ME.: Longwood Press. 1976. (Ref. 260)

Women Composers: A Biographical Handbook of Womens Work in Music. Brooklyn, NY.: Chandler-Ebel Music Co., 1913. (Ref. 276)

Women Composers: A Checklist of Works for the Solo Voice. Stewart-Green, Miriam. Boston: G.K. Hall & Co., 1980. (Ref. 465)

Women Composers: A Handbook. Stern, S. Metuchen, NJ.: Scarecrow Press, 1978. (Ref. 347)

Women Composers: A Discography. Frasier, Jane. Detroit: Information Co-ordinators, 1983. (Ref. 649)

Women Composers, Conductors and Musicians of the Twentieth Century. Lepage, Jane Weiner. London: Scarecrow Press, 1980. (Ref. 454)

Women Composers and Hymnists; A Concise Biographical Dictionary. Claghorn, Gene. Metuchen, NJ.: Scarecrow Press, 1984. (Ref. 646)

Women in American Music: A Bibliography. Skowronski, J. Metuchen. NJ.: Scarecrow Press, 1978. (Ref. 191)

Women in American Music: a Bibliography of Music and Literature. Block, A.F. and Neuls-Bates, C., comps. Westport, CT.: Greenwood Press, 1979. (Ref. 228)

Women in Antiquity: An Annotated Bibliography. Goodwater, L. Metuchen, NJ.: Scarecrow Press, 1975. (Ref. 274)

Women in Islamic Societies. Utas, Bo, ed. Curzon Press; Humanities Press, 1983. (Ref. 613, 623)

Women in Judaism: The Status of Women in Formative Judaism. Swidler, L. Metuchen, NJ.: Scarecrow Press, 1976. (Ref. 275)

Women in Music. Neuls-Bates, Carol, ed. New York: Harper & Row, 1982. (Ref. 555)

Women in Music: A Bio-bibliography. Hixon, D.L. and Hennessee, D. Metuchen, NJ.: Scarecrow Press, 1975. (Ref. 85)

Women in Music History: A Research Guide. Pool, J.G. New York: Author, 1977. (Ref. 269)

Women in Western European History. Frey, Linda., Frey, Marsha and Schneider, Joanne, eds. Westport, CT.: Greenwood Press, 1982. (Ref. 575)

Women making Music. Bowers, Jane and Tick, Judith, eds. Chicago: University of Illinois Press, 1986. (Ref. 653)

Women of Note: 1000 women Composers Born Before 1900. Laurence, A. New York: Rosen Press, 1978. (Ref. 433)

Women of the Ancient World. Brun, Henry J. New York: Richards Rosen Press, 1976. (Ref. 598)

Women of the English Renaissance and Reformation. Warnicke, Retha M. Westport, CT.: Greenwood Press, 1983. (Ref. 636)

Women Recounted. Williams, James G. Sheffield: Almond Press, 1982. (Ref. 635)

Women Troubadours. Bogin, M. London: Paddington Press, 1976. (Ref. 303)

Women's History Sources. Hinding, Andrea., Bower, Ames Sheldon and Chambers, Clarke A., eds. New York: R.R. Bowker Co., 1979. (Ref. 597)

World of Music: A Treasury for Listener and Viewer. Sandved, K.B. London: Waverley Books, 1957. (Ref. 49)

World's Who's Who of Women. Kay, E. Cambridge, England: Melrose Press, 1975. (Ref. 84)

Yuval Studies of the Jewish Music Research Centre. Adler, I., et al., eds. Jerusalem: Magnes Press, 1968. (Ref. 325)

Zarubuzhnaya muzyka XX veka. Zelenina, M.E. Moscow: Kniga, 1979. (Ref. 515)

Zenei lexikon. Szabolcsi, B. and Toth, A. Budapest: Zenemukiado Vallalat, 1965. (Ref. 375)

100 Great Indians Through the Ages. New Delhi: Great Indian Publishers, 1975. (Ref. 644)

125 ans de musique pour saxophone. Londeix, J.M. Paris: Leduc, 1971. (Ref. 76)

40,000 Years of Music, Man in Search of Music. Chailley, J. New York: Macdonald, 1964. (Ref. 387)

FOR FURTHER READING

Armstrong, Toni L. *We Shall Go Forth, Directory Resources in Women's Music*. Chicago: The Author, 6208 Hermitage, 1982.

Barbacci, R. *La inferioridad mental de la mujer y su refleio en la actividad musical*. In Revista Musical Peruana 1, Sept. 1939, 1-5.

Barnes, E.N.C. *American Women in Creative Music*. Washington DC.: Music Education Publications, 1936.

Borroff, Edith. *Women Composers: Reminiscences and History*. College Music Symposium, 15.

Bowen, Jean. *Women in Music: Their fair share?* High Fidelity/Musical America 24, Aug. 1974.

Briffault, R. *The Mothers*. New York: Macmillan, 1927.

Britain, Radie. *Musical Composition: A New World for Women*. Instrumentalists 25, Nov. 1970.

Brower, Edith. *Is the Music Idea Masculine?* Atlantic Monthly (March 1894).

Burns, Don. *The Distaffed Composers*. Music Journal, March 1974.

Camner, James. *The Great Opera Stars in Historic Photographs*. New York: Dover, 1978.

Caplan, D.B. *In Township Tonight*. South Africa's black music. Johannesburg: Ravan Press, 1985.

Comay and Brownrigg. *Who's Who in the Bible*. New York: Bonanza Press, 1980.

De Braut, Guy. *Composers and their Mothers*. Etude 58, May 1940.

Denmark, Florence. *Who Discriminates against Women*. Beverly Hills, CA: Sage, 1974.

Drewes, H. *Maria Antonia Walpurgis als Komponistin*. Leipzig, 1934.

Drummond, Andrew. *American Opera Librettos*. Metuchen, NJ: Scarecrow Press, 1973.

Een, Jo-Ann D. and Rosenberg-Dishman, Marie B. *Women and Society - Citations 3601 to 6000; an annotated bibliography*. Beverley Hills, CA.: Sage Publications, 1978.

Freedman, Estelle B. *The New Woman: Changing views of Women in the 1920s*. Journal of American History 61, Sept. 1974.

Freer, E.E. *Woes of a Woman Composer*. Overland Monthly 82, Oct. 1924.

Gilman, Lawrence. *Women and Modern Music: Phases of Modern Music*. New York: Harper, 1904.

Greene, Richard L. *Male Oppression of Women Composers*. Saturday Review 55, Jan. 8, 1972.

Haddon, C. *Women and Music*. Musical Courier 47, 1903.

Hardester, Jane S. *Women in Choral Music*. Choral Journal 15, 1974.

Hentoff, Nat. *Cherchez la femme*. Downbeat 19, Dec. 3, 1952.

Hughes, Robert. *Women Composers*. Century Magazine 55, March 1898.

Jepson, Barbara. *American Women in Conducting*. Feminist Art Journal 4/4, Winter 1975/6.

Krehm, Ida. *Why not Women Conductors?* Music Journal 27, Feb. 1969.

Ladd, G. *Why Women cannot compose Music*. New Haven: Yale Publication Association, 1917.

Laufer, Beatrice. *A Woman Composer Speaks Out*. ASCAP Today 1, 1967.

Lebrecht, Norman. *The Book of Musical Anecdotes*. London: Andre Deutsch, 1985.

Lerner, Ellen. *Music of Selected Contemporary American Women Composers: A Stylistic Analysis*. Master's Thesis, University of Massachusetts, Amherst, 1976.

Lyle, Wilson. *Dictionary of Pianists*. London: Robert Hale, 1985.

Maier, Guy. *A great Woman Composer? When?* Etude 72, May 1954.

McCullough, Joan. *First of All*. New York: Holt Rinehart & Wilson, 1980.

McLeod, Enid. *The Order of the Rose: The Life and Ideas of Christine de Pizan*. Totowa, NJ: Rowman & Littlefield, 1976.

Moeller, Heinrich. *Can Women Compose?* Musical Observer 15, May 1917.

Montagu, Ashley, Why Wagner was no Lady. High Fidelity 8, March 1958.

Neely, M.D. and James C. *Gender, the Myth of Equality*. New York: Simon & Schuster, 1981.

Neuls-Bates, Carol. *Five Women Composers, 1587-1875*. Feminist Art Journal 5/2, Summer 1976.

Osborn, Judith E. *Women in Music*. Research paper, University of Colorado, 1974.

Petrides, Frederique Joanne. *Outline of a Prejudice*. Musical Review IV/6, Sept-Oct 1935.

Ritter, Fanny Raymond. *Woman as a Musician*. New York: Edward Schuberth, 1877.

Rorem, Ned. *Women: Artist or Artist-ess?* Vogue 155, April 1970.

Rosenberg Marie B. and Bergstrom Len V. *Women and Society: A critical review of the Literature with a selected Annotated Bibliography*. Beverly Hills, CA.: Sage Publications, 1975.

Rubin-Rabson, Grace, and Rosen, Judith. *Why Haven't Women Become Great Composers?* High Fidelity, Feb. 1973.

Russell, Letty M., ed. *Feminist Interpretation of the Bible*. London: Basil Blackwell, 1985.

Sanday, Peggy Reeves. *Female Power and Male Dominance*. Cambridge, England: Cambridge University Press, 1981.

Seager, Joni and Olsen, Ann. *Women in the World*. London: Pan Books, 1986.

Seashore, C.E. *Why no great Women Composers?* Musical Education Journal 24, March 1939.

Shapiro, Marianne. *The Provençal Trobaritz and the Limits of Courtly Love*. Signs 3/3, Spring 1978, pp. 560-571.

Smyth, Ethel Mary. *Streaks of Life*. New York: Knopf, 1922.

Stanton, Lady Elizabeth. *The Women's Bible*. Edinburgh: Polygon Press, 1985.

Starr, Susan. *The Prejudice against Women*. Music Journal 32, March 1974.

Stewart Green, Miriam. *Women: From Silence to Song*. American Music Teachers' Journal 24, Sept-Oct. 1974.

Swinyard L. *Female Quiristers (sic)*. Musical Opinion 98, April 1975.

Tick, Judith. *Towards a History of American Women Composers Before 1870*. Ph.D diss. City University of New York, 1979.

Tick, Judith. *Why Have There Been No Great Women Composers?* Instrumental Musician 74, July 1975.

Tjepkema, Sandra L. *A Bibliography of Computer Music*. Iowa, IA.: University of Iowa Press, 1953.

Towers, J. *Women in Music*. Musician, April-June 1897.

Upton, George R. *Woman in Music*. Chicago: A.C. McClurg, 1886.

Van de Vate, Nancy. *The American Women Composers: Some Sour Notes*. High Fidelity/Musical America 25, June 1975.

Van de Vate, Nancy. *Every Good Boy (Composer) Does Fine*. Symphony News 24, Dec. 1973.

Williams, James G. *Women Recounted*. Sheffield: Almond Press, 1982.

Women Composers En Route: Results of an Editorial Survey. High Fidelity/Musical America 25, June 1975.

Women in Music. Heresies 3/2, Summer 1980.

Women of Music. Music Journal-New York, 30/1, Jan. 1972.

Wood, Elizabeth. *Review Essay: Women in Music*. Signs 6/2, Winter 1980.

Working Papers on Music. Journal of the International Institute for the Study of Women in Music. California State University, Northridge, CA.

Wurm, Marie. *Woman's Struggle for Recognition in Music*. Etude 54, Nov. 1936.

Gastove, Amedée. *Les Primitifs de la Musique Française*. Paris: Henri Laurens, 1922; Duesseldorf: Frau und Musik.

AARON, Yvonne

ABEJO, Sister M. Rosalina

ABORN, Lora

AESCHLIMANN-ROTH, Esther

AGUDELO MURGUIA, Graciela

AINSCOUGH, Juliana Mary

ALCALAY, Luna

ALEXANDRA, Liana

ALLEN, Judith Shatin

ALLOUARD CARNY, Odette

ALOTIN, Yardena

ALT, Hansi

ALVES DE SOUSA,
Berta Candida

ANDERSON, Beth

ANDERSON, Jay

ANDERSON-WUENSCH,
Jean Mary

ARCHER, Violet Balestreri

ARIMA, Reiko

Photo: C.V.M. Germann, Utrecht

ARRIEU, Claude

AUSTER, Lydia Martinovna

AUSTIN, Dorothea

AYLOTT, Lydia Georgina Edith

Photo: B.J. Dorys. Warsaw

BACEWICZ, Grażyna

BACKER GRÖNDAHL,
Agathe Ursula

BADIAN, Maya

BAGANIER, Janine

BAHMANN, Marianne Eloise

BAIL, Grace Shattuck

BAILEY, Judith Margaret

BAILLY, Colette

Photo: Cairo Museum.

BAKIT

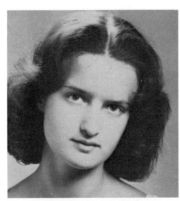

BANCER, Teresa Barbara

BANDT, Rosalie Edith

BARADAPRANA, Pravrajika

BARBERIS, Mansi

BARDEL, Germaine

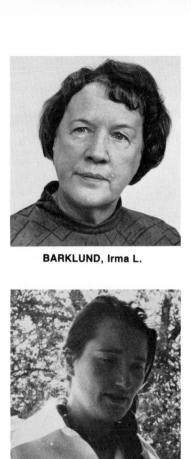

BARKLUND, Irma L.

BARNETT, Carol Edith

BARRAINE, Elsa

BARRIERE, Françoise

BARTHEL, Ursula

**BARTHELSON,
Joyce Holloway**

BASSOT, Anne-Marie

BEACH, Amy Marcy

BEAHM, Jaqueline Yvette

BEAT, Janet Eveline

BEATH, Betty

**BEATRICE MARY,
Princess of Battenberg**

BECKON, Lettie Marie

BEECROFT, Norma Marian

BEEKHUIS, Hanna

BEHREND, Jeanne

BELINFANTE-DEKKER,
Martha Suzanna Betje

BELL, Elizabeth

BENEDICENTI, Vera

BERK, Adele

BIANCHINI, Virginie

BIENVENU, Lily

BINGHAM, Judith

BIRCSAK, Thusnelda

BITGOOD, Roberta

BLACKWILL, Anna Gee

BLOOD, Esta Damesek

Photo: Peabody Institute, John Hopkins University

BLOOMFIELD-ZEISLER, Fannie

Photo: Inge Reunert, Bergen.

BODENSTEIN-HOYME, Ruth E

BÖHN, Liselotte

Photo: National Portrait Gallery, London

BOLEYN, Anne
Queen of England

BOND, Victoria Ellen

BORDERS, Barbara Ann

BORROFF, Edith

Photo: Roger Viollet, Paris.

BOULANGER, Lili Juliette
Marie Olga

Photo: Roger Viollet, Paris

BOULANGER, Nadia Juliette

BOUTRON, Madeleine

BRANDMAN, Margaret Susan

BRANSCOMBE, Gena

BRIGGS, Nancy Louise

BRINK-POTHUIS,
Annie van den

BRITAIN, Radie

BRODIN, Lena Birgitta Elise

BROOK, Gwendolyn Giffen

BRUSH, Ruth Damaris

BUCZEK, Barbara Kazimiera

BULTERIJS, Nina

BURSTON, Maggie

BUTLER, Anne Lois

CABRERA, Silvia Maria Pires

CALAME, Genevieve

CAMEU, Helza

CAMPOS, Joaquina
Araujo de

CANNING, Effie I.

CAPUIS, Matilda

CARL, Tommie Ewert

CARR-BOYD, Ann Kirsten

CECCONI-BOTELLA, Monic

CHAMINADE, Cécile
Louise Stephanie

CHARLES, S. Robin

CIANI, Suzanne Elizabeth

CIOBANU, Maia

CLARK, Florence Durrell

CLARK, June

CLARK, Mary Margaret

CLEMENS, Margaret

CLEVE, Cissi

CLINGAN, Judith Ann

COATES, Gloria Kannenberg

COCCIA, Maria Rosa

COCQ, Rosina Suzanna de

COLACO OSORIO-SWAAB, Reine

COLE, Ulric

COLERIDGE-TAYLOR,
Avril Gwendolen

COLONNA, Victoria
Duchess of Amalfi

CONSTANTINESCU, Domnica

COPLEY, Maria Kriel

COQUET, Odile Marie-Lucie

COTRON, Fanou

COULOMBE SAINT-MARCOUX,
Micheline

COULTHARD, Jean

CRAWFORD, Dorothy Lamb

CREES, Kathleen Elsie

CROKER, Catherine Munnell

CURRIE, Edna R.

DAMASHEK, Barbara

DASCALESCU, Camelia

DAVIES, Eiluned

DAVIS, Eleanor Maud

DE BIASE BIDART, Lycia

DE FREITAS, Elvira Manuela Fernandez

DE PURY, Marianne

DECARIE, Reine

DELMOULY, Marie Mathilda

DEMBO, Royce

DENBOW, Stephania Bjoerson

DESPORTES, Yvonne Bertha

DEYTON, Camilla Hill

DIANDA, Hilda

DIEMER, Emma Lou

DINESCU, Violeta

DLUGOSZEWSKI, Lucia

Photo: Broadcast Music Inc., New York.

DONCEANU, Felicia

DREYFUS, Kay Francis

DRYNAN, Margaret

DU PAGE, Florence Elizabeth

DUSHKIN, Dorothy Smith

EASTES, Helen Marie

ECKHARDT-GRAMATTE,
Sophie-Carmen

EGGLESTON, Anne E.

EIRIKSDOTTER, Karolina

ELEANOR OF AQUITAINE

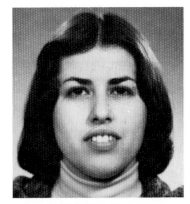

ELKOSHI, Rivka

ELLIOTT, Marjorie Reeve

ELWYN-EDWARDS, Dilys

ERNST, Siegrid

ETHRIDGE, Jean

EUGENIE, Princess of Sweden

EVEN-OR, Mary

EZELL, Helen Ingle

FALCINELLI, Rolande

FARRENC, Louise

FEIGIN, Sarah

FEININGER, Leonore Helene

FERREYRA, Beatriz

FINZI, Graciane

FIRKNEES, Gertrude

FISCHER, Edith Steinkraus

FISHER, Katherine Danforth

**FLEISCHER-DOLGOPOLSKY,
Tsipporah**

FONTYN, Jacqueline

FOWLER, Jennifer Joan

FRAJT, Ludmila

FRANGS, Irene

FRASIER, Jane

FREED, Dorothy Whitson

GABUS, Monique

GAMILLA, Alice Doria

GARDINER, Mary Elizabeth

GARSCIA-GRESSEL, Janina

GARTENLAUB, Odette

GENTILE, Ada

GEYMULLER, Marguerite
Camille-Louise de

GHANDAR, Ann

GIDEON, Miriam

GIFFORD, Helen Margaret

GILBERT, Janet Monteith

GILLES, Yvette Marie

GILLICK, Emelyn Mildred

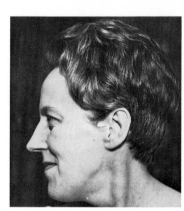

GIPPS, Ruth

GITECK, Janice

GLANVILLE-HICKS, Peggy

GLATZ, Helen Sinclair

GLAZIER, Beverly

GLEN, Irma

GOERSCH, Ursula Margitta

GOLDSTON, Margaret
Nell Stumpf

GOLSON-BATEMAN, Florence

GOMM, Elizabeth

GOOLKASIAN-RAHBEE,
Diane Zabelle

GOULD, Janetta

GRAD-BUCH, Hulda

GRAHAM, Janet Christine

GRAINGER, Ella Viola
Strom-Brandelius

GRAY, Victoria Winifred

GREENE, Margo Lynn

GRIEBLING, Karen Jean

GROSSMAN, Deena

Photo: Christian Steiner

GRUDEFF, Marian

GUBITOSI, Emilia

GWILY-BROIDO, Rivka

Photo: G. Mehwald, Steyr.

HAGER-ZIMMERMANN, Hilde

HAJDU, Julia

Photo: Norsk Komponisforening, Oslo.

HALL, Pauline

HALPERN, Stella

HALSTED, Margo

HARA, Kazuko

HARDY, Helen Irene

HARPER, Marjorie

HARRIS, Ruth Berman

HARVEY, Eva Noel

HAWLEY, Carolyn Jean

HEDOUX, Yvonne

HELLER-REICHENBACK,
Barbara

HELSINGIUS, Barbara

HEMON, Sedje

HENDERSON, Ruth Watson

HENSEL, Fanny Cäcilia

HICKS, Marjorie Kisbey

HILDERLEY, Jeriann G.

HILL, May

HINLOPEN, Francina

HOFFERT, Brenda

Photo: Eva Everything, Toronto.

HOLBERT, Diana Brown

HOLLAND, Dulcie Sybil

HOLMES, Augusta Mary Anne

Photo: Bibliothèque Nationale, Paris.

HOLST, Imogen Clare

HOOVER, Katherine

Photo: Canadian Music Centre, Toronto.

HOVDA, Eleanor

Photo: Gloria Defilips-Brush Duluth, MN.

HULFORD, Denise Lovona

HULL, Kathryn B.

Photo: Bronson Photography Glendale, CA.

HURLEY, Susan

HUTSON, Wihla L.

HUTTON, Florence Myra

HYDE, Miriam Beatrice

IRMAN-ALLEMANN, Regina

Photo: Barbara Davitz, Zurich.

JACKSON, Elizabeth Barnhart

JACOB, Elizabeth Marie

JENNY, Sister Leonore

Photo: Barbara Davitz, Zurich.

JEPPSSON, Kerstin Maria

JEREA, Hilda

JESI, Ada

JIRÁCKOVÁ, Marta

JOHN, Patricia Spaulding

JOHNSON, Eloise Lisle

JOLAS, Betsy

JOLLY, Margaret Anne

JOLY, Suzanne

JORDAN, Alice Yost

JOSEPHINE,
Queen of Sweden & Norway

JÜNGER, Patricia

KABAT, Julie Phyllis

KALOGRIDOU, Maria

KALTENECKER, Gertraud

Kamlen, Anna

KANACH, Sharon E.

KAPRÁLOVÁ, Vítězslava

KASILAG, Lucrecia R.

KATS-CHERNIN, Elena

KAVASCH, Deborah Helene

Photo: Fotokombinat No. 2 Yerevan.

KAZANDJIAN, Sirvart

Photo: Adonis Photos, Vancouver.

KEEFER, Euphrosyne

KELLER, Ginette

**KEMP, Dorothy Elizabeth
Walter**

KENDRICK, Virginia Catherine

KENT, Ada Twohy

KETTERING, Eunice Lea

KICKINGER, Paula

KIRKBY-MASON, Barbara

KIRKWOOD, Antoinetta

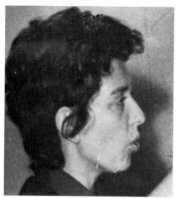

KJAER, Kirsten

KLEBE, Willemyntje

KOBLENZ, Babette

KONISHI, Nagako

KOPTAGEL, Yuksel

KORHOREN, Gloria

KRAUSZ, Susan

KRULL, Diana

KUKUCK, Felicitas

KUZMENKO, Larysa

KUZMYCH, Christina

LA GUERRE,
Elizabeth-Claude Jacquet de

LACHARTRE, Nicole Marie

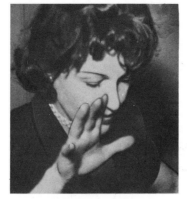

LALAUNI, Lila

LAMEGO, Carlinda J.

LANG-BECK, Ivana

LARSEN, Elizabeth Brown

LAST, Joan Mary

LATZ, Inge

LAUBER, Anne Marianne

Photo: Michel Blanc/SMB, Geneva.

LAUFER, Beatrice

LAZAR, Ella

LEAHY, Mary Weldon

LEE, Young Ja.

LEFANU, Nicola Frances

LEIVISKA, Helvi Lemmiki

Lejet, Edith

LEON, Tania Justina

LEONARD, Mamie Grace

LINDEMAN, Hjelle Signe

LINNEMANN, Maria Catharina

LLUNELL SANAHUJA, Pepita

LOCKSHIN, Florence Levin

LOH, Kathy Jean

LOMON, Ruth

LOOTS, Joyce Mary Ann

LOUDOVÁ, Ivana

LOWENSTEIN, Gunilla Marike

LUMBY, Betty Louise

LUND, Gudrun

MAGOGO KA DINIZULU,
Princess Constance

Photo: Ralf Ndawo.

MALMLÖF-FORSSLING, Carin

MAMLOK, Ursula

Photo: Broadcast Music Incorp.,
New York.

MANZIARLY, Marcelle de

Photo: Camilla Jessel, Twickenham.

MARAIS, Abelina Jacoba

MARBE, Myriam

MARCUS, Ada Belle Gross

MAREZ-OYENS, Tera de

MARI, Pierrette

MARIE ANTOINETTE
Queen of France

MARKIEWICZOWNA,
Wladyslawa

MARKOV, Katherine Lee

MARSHALL, Kye

MARTIN, Judith Reher

MATHIESON, Ann Emily

MATUSZCZAK, Bernadetta

MAZOUROVÁ, Jarmila

MEACHEM, Margaret McKeen
Ramsey

MEKEEL, Joyce

MELL, Gertrud Maria

MENEELY-KYDER,
Sarah Suderley

MERIT

MERRIMAN, Margarita Leonor

MILENKOVIĆ, Jelena

MILLER, Elma

MITCHELL, Janice Misurell

MOLAVA, Pamela May

MONTGOMERY, Merle

MOON, Chloe Elizabeth

MOORE, Dorothy Rudd

MOORE, Mary Carr

MORLEY, Angela

MORLEY, Nina Dianne

MOSSAFER RIND, Bernice

MOSUSOVA, Nadezda

MOSZUMANSKA-NAZAR,
Krystyna

MRACEK, Ann Michelle

MUNDINGER, Adele Franziska

Photo: Eric Thorburn, Glascow.

MUSGRAVE, Thea

McCOLLIN, Frances

McILWRAITH, Isa Roberta

McINTOSH, Diana

McLEAN, Priscilla Anne Taylor

Photo: Broadcast Music Inc., New York.

McMILLAN, Ann Endicott

NIEMACK, Ilza Louise

NIXON, June

NOBLITT, Katheryn Marie
McCall

NORDENSTROM,
Gladys Mercedes

NORRE, Dorcas

OBROVSKÁ, Jana

ODAGESCU, Irina

ØRBECK, Anne-Marie

OFFICER, Bronwyn Lee

OH, Sook Ja

OLIVEIRA, Jocy de

ORAM, Daphne Blake

ORE, Cecilie

OSAWA, Kazuko

OSTROFF, Esther

OWEN, Angela Maria

OWEN, Blythe

PALMER, Jane Hetherington

PALMER, Lynne Wainwright

Photo: Dana C. Lutes Eugene, OR.

PARKER, Alice

PAULL, Barberi

PAYNE, Maggi

PENGILLY, Sylvia

PENNER, Jean Priscilla

Photo: Canadian Music Centre, Toronto.

PENTLAND, Barbara Lally

PERETZ-LEVY, Liora

PERONI, Wally

PETROVÁ-KRUPKOVÁ, Elena

PFEIFFER, Irena

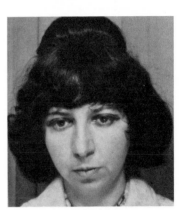

PHILIBA, Nicole

PHILIPPART, Renée

Credit: Capitol Studio, Auckland.

PHILLIPS, Bryony

PHILLIPS, Karen Ann

PHILLIPS, Linda

Photo: Tom Flora Photography, Shawnee

PHILLIPS, Vivian Daphne

PIERCE, Sarah Anderson

PILIS, Heda

PIRES DOS REIS, Hilda

PIZER, Elizabeth Faw Hayden

POLIN, Claire

POOL, Jeannie Gayle

POPOVICI, Elise

PRADELL, Leila

PREDIĆ-ŠAPER, Branislava

PROCACCINI, Teresa

PTASZYNSKA, Marta

RABER DE REINDERS, Esther

RACOVITZA-FLONDOR, Florica

RADERMACHER, Erika

RADIGUE, Eliane

RAYMOND, Madeleine

REED, Marlyce Rae Polk

REHNQVIST, Karen Birgitta

REID, Sarah Johnston

REISER, Violet

RESPIGHI, Elsa

REYNOLDS, Erma Grey Hogue

RHENE-Jaque

RHOADS, Mary R.

RICHTER, Marga

Photo: Univ of Colorado Inf. Service.

RICKARD, Sylvia

RILEY, Ann Marion

ROBERT, Lucie

ROBERTS, Gertrud Hermine

ROBERTS, Megan L.

ROCHAT, Andrée

ROCHEROLLE,
Eugenie Katherine

ROE, Eileen Betty

ROE, Helen Mary Gabrielle

ROE, Marion Adelle

ROGER, Denise

ROGERS, Ethel Tench

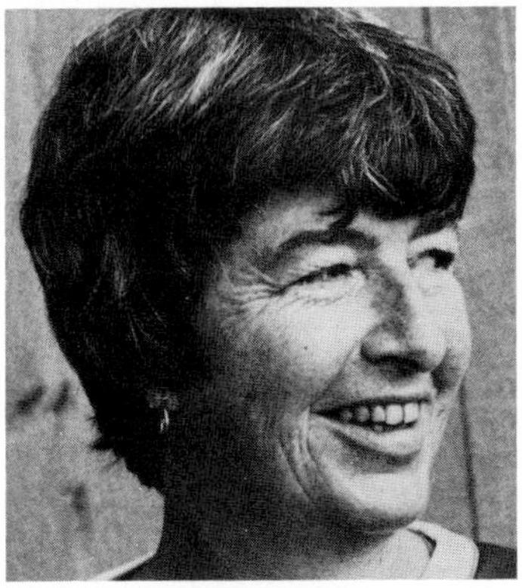

ROGERS, Patsy

ROHDE, Q'Adrianne

ROOTH, Anna-Greta

Photo: Per-Ola Holm, Västeras.

ROSAS FERNANDES,
Maria Helena

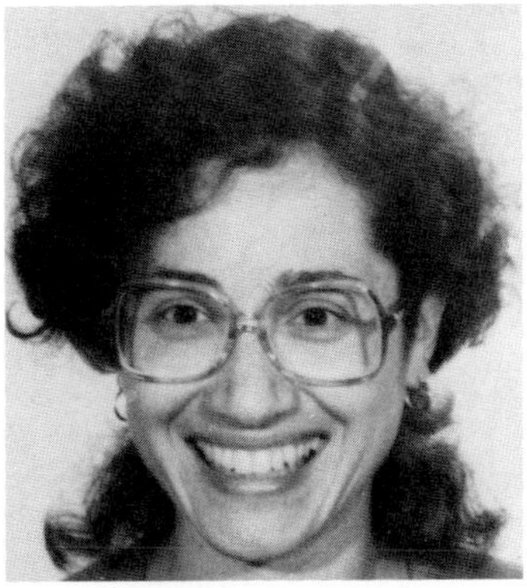

RUBIN, Anna Ita

RUFF-STÖHR
Herta Maria Klara

RUSCHE, Majorie Maxine

SAINT JOHN, Kathleen Louise

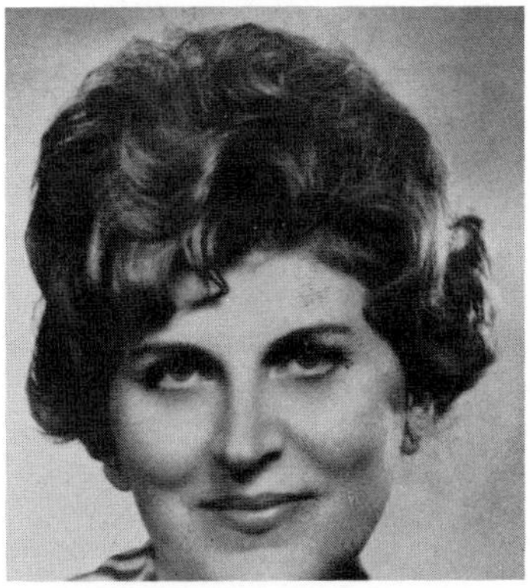

SAKALLI-LECCA, Alexandra

SAMTER Alice

SANDIFUR, Ann Elizabeth

SANDRESKY, Margaret Vardell

SANFORD, Grace Krick

SANTOS-OCAMPO DE
FRANCESCO, Amada Amy

SANZ, Rocio

SCHMIDT-DUISBERG,
Margaret Dina Alwina

SCHONTHAL, Ruth E.

SCHORR-WEILER, Eva

SCHUBERT, Myra Jean

SCHUMANN, Clara Josephine

SCHUSSLER-BREWAEYS,
Marie Antoinette

SCHWARTZ, Nan Louise

SCHWERDTFEGER, E. Anne

SEMEGEN, Daria

SETO, Robin

SHAFFER, Jeanne Ellison

SHATAL, Miriam

SHELTON, Margaret Meier

SHEPARD, Jean Ellen

SHERBOURNE, Janet

SHLONSKY, Verdina

SHREVE, Susan Ellen

SIKORA, Elzbieta

SILVERMAN, Faye-Ellen

SIMIĆ, Darinka

SIMONS, Netty

SINGER, Jeanne

SISTEK-DJORDJEVIĆ, Mirjana

SKARECKY, Jana Milena

SKOUEN, Synne

Photo: Jan Nordby, Oslo.

SMELTZER, Susan Mary

Photo: James Abresch, New York.

SMITH, Julia Frances

SMITH, Ladonna Carol

SMITH, Linda Catlin

SMITH, Selma Moidel

Photo: Stan Marsal, Prague.

SNÍZKOVÁ-SKRHOVA, Jitka

Photo: Jan Nordby, Oslo

SONSTEVOLD, Maj

SOLOMON, Elide M.

SOLOMON, Joyce Elaine

SOUTHAM, Ann

SPECHT, Judy Lavise

SPENCER PALMER,
Florence Margaret

SPENCER, Marguerita

SPENCER, Williametta

SPIZIZEN, Louise Myers

SPÖNDLIN, Elisabeth

SPOERRI-RENFER,
Anna-Margaretha

STAINKAMPH, Eileen Freda

STANLEY, Helen Camille

STEFANOVIC, Ivana

STILMAN-LASANSKY, Julia

STREATFIELD, Valma June

STULTZ, Marie Irene

SUESSE, Dana

SUSSMAN, Ettel

SUTZU, Rodica

Photo: Broadcast Music Inc.

SWADOS, Elizabeth

SWAIN, Freda Mary

**SWISHER,
Gloria Agnes Wilson**

SZÉKÉLY, Katalin

SZÖNYI, Erzsébet

TACK, Annie

TAILLEFERRE, Germaine

TAKAMI, Toyoko

TAL, Ya'ara

TALMA, Louise

TANN, Hilary

TASHJIAN, B. Charmian

TAUBER, Lotti

TAUTU, Cornelia

TELFER, Nancy Ellen

**TENGBERGEN, Maria
Elizabeth von Ebbenhorst**

THEMMEN, Ivana Marburger

**THERESE, Princess of Saxe-
Altenburg and of Sweden**

THIEME, Kerstin Anja

THOMAS, Mary Virginia

THORESON, Janice Pearl

THORKELSDOTTIR,
Mist Barbara

TIDEMAN-WIJERS, Bertha

TIMMERMAN, Leni

TOBIN, Candida

TOLKOWSKY, Denise

TOWER, Joan

TRIMBLE, Joan

TURNER, Mildred Cozzens

UCHENDU, Nellie Uzonna Edith

USHER, Julia

VAN DE VATE, Nancy Hayes

VAN DER MARK, Maria

VAN DIJCK, Beatrice Madeleine

VAN NESTE, Rosane Micheline Lucie Charlotte

VELLERE, Lucie Weiler

VERCOE, Elizabeth

VERRALL, Pamela Motley

Photo: Downing St. Studios, Farnham.

VIARDOT-GARCIA, Pauline Michelle Ferdinande

Photo: Bibliotéque Nationale, Paris.

VICTORIA, MARIA LOUISA, Duchess of Kent

Photo: National Portrait Gallery, London.

VIERK, Lois

VIGNERON-RAMAKERS, Christiane-Josée

VIRTUE, Constance
Cochnower

VISCONTI, Leila

VITO-DELVAUX, Berthe di

Photo: Nina von Jaanson, Berlin.

VON ZIERITZ, Greta

VORLOVA, Slavka

WALDO, Elisabeth

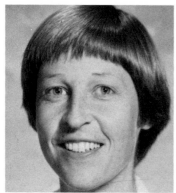

WALKER, Gwyneth van Anden

WALLACH, Joelle

WANG, An-Ming

WARREN, Elinor Remick

WARSHAW, Dalit Paz

WARWICK, Mary Carol

Photo: Broadcast Music Inc., New York.

WEIGL, Vally

WERNER, Tara Louise

WESSELS, Marlene

WHITLOCK, E. Florence

Photo: The Courier, Dundee.

WILKINS, Margaret Lucy

WILL, Madeleine

WISHART, Betty Rose

WOLL, Erna

WYLIE, Ruth Shaw

XENOPOL, Margareta

YAMPOLSCHI, Roseane

YDSTIE, Arlene Buckneberg

YOUNG, Donel Marie

YOUNG, Gayle

ZAIDEL-RUDOLPH, Jeanne

ZAIMONT, Judith Lang

**ZAKRZEWSKA-NIKIPORCZYK,
Barbara Maria**

ZIPRICK, Marjorie Jean

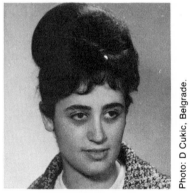

ZIVKOVIĆ, Mirjana

Photo: D Cukic, Belgrade.

ZWILICH, Ellen Taaffe

Photo: Whitestone Photo., New York.

**It is regretted that over 200 additional photographs could not be used
owing to the fact that the permission to reproduce them could not be
obtained, mainly because the photographers could not be traced.**

APPENDIX 1

Information Wanted

This appendix lists women composers about whom the editor has no information as at the date of this publication. Readers having information about any of the composers listed below are earnestly requested to communicate with the Director, International Institute for the Study of Women in Music, California State University, Northridge, CA 91330, United States of America.

12th Century A.D.
CLUZEL, Irene

13th Century A.D.
SCHOENAU, Elisabeth von

16th Century A.D.
SILVA, Helena Da
TOLETANA, Angela Sygaea

17th Century A.D.
CAZZOLANI

19th Century A.D.
BATHMANN, Charlotte
BAXTER, Lydia
BUSI, Leonida
CHALOTI, Helene
DLUZYNSKA, Zofia
FONTRY, Mme. de
GNATKOWSKA, Paulina
GWOZDECKA, Gabriela
HARRADEN, Beatrice
HEYERDAHL, Vally
KISZWALTER, Adamina
KONTSKI, Eugenie de
KOSSAKOWSKA, Antonina
KRAINDL, Sophie de
LEBER, Antonia
MANSILLA DE GARCIA, Eduarda
MARCINKIEWICZ, Kamilla
MORACZEWSKA, Ksawara
MOTTE, Nicola del
MRASECK, Fraulein
MUSSINI, Adele Branca
PHILIPPON, Aimee-Jeanne
PISARONI, Benedetta
POPLAWSKA, Maria Paulina
POSSANER, Emma Baronini
PROENCA-A-VELVHA, Countess
STANDT, Elsie
THIRKLEBY, Laura Taylor
ZAGRODZKA, Eugenia

20th Century A.D.
ACHMATOWICZ-KRYCZYNSKA, Maria
ADACHI, Motohiko

AGNES, Marie Jacobina
ALBRECHT, Wendy
ALCANTARA FERREIRA, Lucemar de
ALEGRO, Amelia Guilhermina
ANDERSON, Kristine
ANDERSON, Laurel Everette
ANDRE-FOUET, M.
APPLE, Lorraine
ARNDT, Nola
ATHANASIU-GARDEEV, Esmeralda
AUSTIN, Frances
BAKER, Deborah Jean
BALLAS, Barbara
BANG, Ragnhild
BARBE, Henriette
BARBIERI, Anna
BARELLA, Yvonne
BARNES, Anna
BARREAU, Gisele
BASSI, Giulia
BATEMAN, Florence G.
BAUD, Madeleine
BECKMAN, Debora
BEETH, Lola
BELL, Dorothy
BENNETT, Virginia H.
BENSON, May
BENTIA, Ana
BERNARD, Simone
BERT, Martha
BERTILLE, Janine
BIEDRZYCKA, Helena
BIERMANN, Petra
BLAZQUEZ, Eladia
BO, Sonia
BONNETTE, Jeanne
BOSTWICK, Sara
BOUCK, Marjorie
BOUSSARD, Marguerite
BOUVET, Denise
BOWMAN, Frances
BOXALL, Maria
BRAND, Margaret
BRANNON, Gertrude Legler
BREDOW, Maria de
BREGUET, May

BRENNEN, Sister Rose Immacula
BRIDGES, Myrtle M.
BRUNETEAU, Simone
BRUSH, Mrs. J.M.
BULL, Patricia
BURNETT, Mildred R.
BURSEY, Rosetta
CAHIER, Mme. Charles
CAMPODONICO, Beatrice
CAPDEVILLE, Constanca
CASKIE, Helen
CASTILLO, Graciela
CECCHI, Gabriella
CHAPMAN, Joyce
CHARLES, Anna Maria
CHEFALIADY-TEBAN, Maria
CHENIER, Monique
CHIAPPARIN, Solange
CHOJNOWSKA, Zofia
CIESLAKOWNA, Maria
CLARKE, Lucia
CLAYTON, Jay
COCHEREAU, Nicole
COOK, Rosalind
CORCORAN, Lillian Hague
COSSAR, Louanne
COSTANTINI, Andreina
CRUZ, Sor Juana Ines de la
CURPHY, Geraldine
CWIORI, Barbara
CZAPLICKA, J.
DACH, Charlotte von
DARGE, Moniek
DAVALOS, Julia Elena
DAVENPORT, Caroline
DAVIS-BERRYMAN, Alice
DE CASTRO, Blanca
DE COMPEIGNE, Laetitia
DE HERVE, Zelina
DEAN, Lynn C.
DEGRAFF, Grace Clark
DELFIN, Carmelina
DELLA, Hinerangi
DENNISON, Barbara
DESBOURDIEUX, Yvonne
DESCAVES, Lucette

DESCHAMPS, Anne-Marie
DESSOIR, Susanne
DIJK, Antoinette van
DIMARIAS, Esperanza
DODDSON, Ora
DOE, Elaine
DOLMETSCH, Cecile
DRAPPIER, Yvonne
DRIESSLER QUISTORP, Monica
DUBOIS, V.
DUNLAP, Judy
EGLI, Johanna
EMANUELSON, Elsa
EMERY, Emma Wilson
EPPERSON, Hilda
ERDELY, Isolda
ERMAN, Sarah
ESCHWEILER, Geneva
ESTELLE, Sister Rita
EWING, Nona
EYMAR, Jacqueline
EZZAR, Katherine
FAGANDINI, Maddalena
FALCONER, Bertha
FERRELL, Billie
FIJAL, Anne-Marie
FOISON, Michelle
FONTANA, Annie
FOWKE, Edith Fulton
FOX, Charlotte
FOX, Doris H.
FOX, Pauline S.
FRANKLIN-PYKE, Elinor
FREIBERGER, Katherine
GABRIELY, Irith
GADDY, Carol
GALANTI, Laura
GANEVAL, Emilienne
GARNIER, Ilse
GARRETT, Elizabeth
GAUTIER, Josie
GEISTLENER, Barbara
GERARD, S.
GERVAIS, Francoise Jeanne
GILIOLI, Fiorenza
GILLE, Paule
GILLILAND-HERNDON, Marianne
GISELA, Sister Mary
GNEDEL, Mimi
GODART, L.
GOLBIN, Elsa
GOLD, Diana
GOLDSTEIN, Anne
GORE, Virginia
GOW, Dorothy
GREENWOOD, Neva Garner
GREWE SOBOLEWSKA, Mme.
GRIFFITH, Corinne
GROBEL, Marily A.
GROBICKA, Eugenia
GROEGEROVA, Bohumila
GRUENBERG, Irma
GUSEINZADE, Sofia Asgatovna
GUTMAN, Natalia Grigorievna
HAENSCH, Delle
HAIRSTON, Jessie
HALL, Marian Wilson
HALL, Marleen van
HARKNESS, Joan
HARRAH, Madge
HAWARDEN, Caroline Anna May Oyle,
   Viscountess
HEARDING, Elizabeth
HECKSCHER-SCHNEEKLAUS, Marga
HECQ, Olia
HENDEL, Tikva
HESS, Alyssa Nan
HIRSCHLER, Ziga
HOBBS, Barbara
HOBSON, Nancy
HOFFMAN, Laura

HOLLINGSWORTH, Thekla
HORIOT, Evelyne
HOUSER, Kitty
HOWLETT, May
HUDGINS, Mary
HURLBUTT, Patricia
HURST, Olive
HUTCHINS, Helene Owen
HYDE, Georgina Colvin
HYNES, Eloise
IMPERIAL, Ruth
IRGENS, Sofie
ISLE, Harriet L.
IVANOWSKA-PLOSZKO-
   OSSEN-DOWSKA, Zofia
JEHAN, Noor
JOWETT, Diane
JOWETT, Jennifer
KADIZADE, Celal
KAMINSKA, Wiktoria
KANT-BENEKER, H.
KATENE-HORVATH, Dovey
KATONOVA, S.
KEARNY, Moira
KEISER, Lauren Keith
KELLNER, Sybil
KENNEDY, Gurney
KERR, Heather
KHAIRUTDINOVA, Luisa
KHERESKO, Lidia Petrovna
KHODZHAEVITCH, Asja
KHOLOPOVA, Valentina Nikolayevna
KILICHEVSKAYA, A.
KLINGENSMITH, Anne
KNERR, Katrina
KOH, Bunya
KOHN, Doris
KOOL, Rie
KOSSAKOWSKA, Wiktoryna
KRASINSKA, Karolina
KROKIEWICZOWA, Apolonia
KRUITHOF VAN DIGGELEN, M.
KRUSZEWSKA, Zofia
KULLIN, Marta
KUTTEN, Rachel
KWIATKOWSKA-MARCZYK, Krystina
KYRIAKOU, Rena
LA HALLE, Yvonne
LAMBA, Huguette
LAND, Mary
LASKINE, Lily
LE MENN, Michelle
LECOUNA, Ernestina
LEES, Christine Brown
LERCHE, Juliane
LESNIEWICZOWA, Iza
LEVINE, Amy Miller
LEVITAS-GOLDIS, Lea
LEWIS, Margery de
LINEBARGER, Iva B.
LINFORD, Shirley Ann
LIU, Shea-An
LOEVENSKJOLD, Hannah
LOWTHER, T.
LUBICZ-DZIERZBICKA, Zofia
LUCAS, Marie
LUNDBERG, Harriet
LUTHI-WEGMANN, Elvira
MacENULTY, Rosalind
McCAIN, Eula Louise
McCALLUM, Nance
McCARRY, Betty
McDONAL, Carey
McDONALD, Kirsten
McDONALD, Marna Service
McDOWELL, Jennifer
McGUIRE, Valerie
MAIZANI, Azucena
MANDANICI, Marcella
MARADEIX, Suzanne
MARANCA, Lucia

MARIS, Barbara
MARSTRANDER, Sigrid Borrensen
MARTIN, Genevieve
MARTIN, Mary
MAST-BOLDREY, Joyce
MATHIS, Kitty
MATURANO, Liliana Ester
MAY, Laure Castellanes
MAYER, Bernadette
MESHKO, Nina
MILEVIC, Janice
MISONNE, Claude
MOLINA, Olivia
MOORE, Margaret Crammond
MORRIS, Mary S.
MORVAI, Suzanne
MOUNTFORT, Helen
MUELLER, Ann
MUGNAINI ROBOTTI, Teresa
MUNTHE, Margarethe
MURAD, Elizabeth
MURAWSKA, Marietta
MYERS, Monda
NAIMSKA, Joanna
NASH, Wendy
NAZLI, Shamin
NEWBARR, Carol
NIEMANN, Charlotte
NIKOLAYEVA, Galina Alexandrovna
NUNES, Elizabeth Zamorano
OBTULOWICZ, Zofia
OCHOA, Elvira
OHLSSON, Grettel
OHLSSON, Sarah
OKADA, Kyoko
OKI, Hideko
OLIVERO, Betty
OLSON, Mrs. Herbert V.
O'NEILL, Denise
OSHCHERETOVSKAYA, N.
OSTERTAG, Gertrud
OWEN, Mollie O.
PADGETT, Betty
PANZANI, Iris Piera
PARRONDO, Maria
PARRY, Enid
PERDEW, Ruth
PERONNE, Pauline
PERRY, Kathryn
PIAZZA, Paola
PICKEN, Emele M.
PILATI, Maria
PILNY, Josepha
PINE-BLUSTEIN, Cathia
PISTON, Julia
PISTONO D'ANGELO, Piera
PLISZKA RAMSEWICZOWA, Katarzyna
PODGORSKA, Ewa
POLIAKOVA, Ludmila Viktorovna
POLLARD, Bessie
POND, Ida L.
POOLE, Anne
PORBERGS, Ingibjorg
POSSE, Monica
POWERS, Jennifer
PREYSS, Adelina
PRINCE, Mary Lou
PRUNEDER, Frau
PRUSIECKA, Jadwiga
QUITTNER, Katharine
RADOSZEWSKA, A.J.
RADULESCU-VLAD, Sofia
RAINER, Sara
RAMPAZZA, Teresa
RAWLS, Kathryn Hill
REYNOLDS, Barbara
REYNOLDS, Darcy
RICHARDS, Deborah
RIGAUX, Clotilde
RIVENBURG, Leah Patt
ROBERTS, Helen
ROBINSON, Jean

ROGERS, Cornelia P.
ROLLIN, Monique
RORICH, Mary
ROWE, Helen
RUBIN, Basia Izrailevna
RUPNIEWSKA, Janina
RZEPECKA, Maria
SABININA, Marina Dimitrevna
SAGI, Noa
SALTYKOVA, Tamara Sergeyevna
SAM, Carole Nelsom
SANDER, Jacqueline
SANDERFOSS, Mme.
SANDERS, Joan
SAZERAC, Genevieve
SCARPA, Eugenia
SCHAGER-LATACZOWA, Wanda
SCHARLOT, Debaro
SCHEFFEL, Conny
SCHERTZ, Helen Pitkin
SCHMOLKE, Anneliese
SCHNEIDER, Susan F.
SCHOPPIG-PIOTROWSKA, Claire
SCOTT, Dorothy
SCOTT, Ruth
SEIEROE MORTENSEN, Anne
SERTIMA, Theresia Elizabeth van
SHASUTDINOVA, Maria
SHEHAN, Helen Falvey
SHEPHERD, Doris
SHIMIZU, Chisako
SHIRAISHI, Iris
SHORE, Elaine
SIMONCINI, Simona
SIMONE, Mercedes
SINCLAIR, Margaret
SKIRBINSKA, Wladyslawa
SKORIK, Marcelle
SKREBKOVA, M.
SKUDRA, Ruta Evaldova
SLIWINSKA, Josefa
SLOCZYNSKA, Cecylia
SMITH, Doreen Wilhelmina
SMOLSKA, Jolanta
SOHET-BOULNOIS, Suzanne
SORIA, Isobel
SOUDERE, Valery
SPALETTI, Giuliana
SPECKNER, Anna Barbara
STANDRING, Helen
STAWOWY, Ludomira
STEEL, Jeanette
STEINBERG, Carolyn
STEPANOVA, V.
STOPHER, Vashti
STREEB, Barbara Ellen
STROMBERG, Ruth
SUAREZ, Erna
SUGAREVA, Parashkeva
SULKOVSKA, Eliza
SULZBOECK, Toni
SUPINSKA J.
SUSANA, Graciela
SZADURSKA, W.
TAMIA
TANAKA, Tomoko
TARGONSKA, Izabela
TAYAR-GUICHARD, Marguerite
TEAKLE, Robyn
TOKARSKA, Emilia
TOUREL, Alona
TRAUTH, Dorothy Kyle
TRUCHET, Pauline
TURNBULL, Sister Fedora
TURNER, Hilda
TUSOWSKA-SKRZETUSKA, M.
TYEPKEMA, Sandra
UHL, Danuta
UNO, Evelyn
VALEANU, Elisa
VALLADARES, Leda

VAN STEENBERG, Michelim
VANDERVELDE, Jan
VARLEY, Rene G.
VERHAAR, Jacqueline
VIGOT, Therese
VILLAMANJNA, Ada Comandoli
VIVIER, Odile
VIZCAINO, Gloria Tapia de
VORBOND, Wanda
WAAL, Lies de
WAHL, Miriam
WALDECKER, Matilde R.
WALSH, Maria Elena
WANSKA, Anna
WASOWSKA-BADOWSKA, Maria
WEBB, Helen
WEGMANN-BOLOZE, N.
WEINGARTNER-STUDER, Carmen
WELLS, Elsie
WILSON, Alice
WOLF, Gwendolyn
WOLSKA, Aleksandra Aniela
WOODLEY, Joyce
YEGEROVA, V.
ZDZIENNICKA, Zofia

Century unknown
AIR, Kathleen
ALLARD DEMERS, Cecile
ALLEN, Mary
AMARD, Anna
AMATO, Maria
AMONKAR, Kishri
ANDERSON, Edythe
ANDERSON, Joyce
ANDERSON, Lucy
ARGIL, Louise
ARMSTRONG, Susannah
ASHBY, Gertrude
AUGUSTI, Giuseppina Vitali
AUSTIN, Roberta Martin
BARTLETT, Gertrude
BASSI, Laura
BATTY, Florence
BISETTI-BALICE, Rina
BISHOP, Anna
BLOOMER, Nancy
BOGINSKI, Barbel
BONDURANT, Dorothy
BRELING, Jossie
BRENT, Miss
BRESSON, Marie
BRET, Mme. le
BRIL, France-Yvonne
BRUCK, Ester
BRUNET, Jacqueline
BRUNNER, Miriam
BUCKLEY, Caroline Kemper
BUMSTEAD, Gladys
BURNHAM, Mazel
CANTONI, Giulia
CARBALLO, Celeste
CARLEY, Isabel McNeill
CARLUCCI, Filippina
CASPARY, Marie
CASSINIS, Giovannina
CASTELBARCO, Albani Angeline
CATALANOTTO, Marisa
CAUMONT-DADE, Mme. la Comtesse de
CAWKER, Lenore H.
CHARPENTIER, Louise
CHARPENTREAU, Simone
CHAZOT-LAUCHER, Mme.
CHIARLANTINI, Paola
CHRISTENSEN, Betty
CLEAVER, Esther
CODET-BOISSE, Catherine
COLANGELO, Rita
COMFORT, Annabel
CORNEA, Nely
COUNTRYMAN, Alice

COWELL, Mrs. Sidney
CRAMM, Helen L.
CRANE, Charlotte M.
CREPTAX, Rosette Tribor
CROSBY, Marie
CROWLEY, Anne
CUNNINGHAME, Agnes Jane Winifred
DAHLSTROM, Greta
DARION, Mlle.
DARTY, Paulette
D'AUBISSON, Marguerite
DAUPHIN, Madeleine
DAUVERGNE DE BEAUVAIS, Mlle.
DAVID, Elizabeth H.
DE CASTRO, Jessie
DELARUE, Eugenie
DENNO, Antonietta
DEPEYSAC, Comtesse
DESANGLES, Anny
DINSART, Madeleine
DONATI, Albasini Giuseppina
DONETS-TESSEIR, Marija
DORFNER, Elisabet
DROLENVAUX, Mme.
DUPRE, Mme.
DUROT, Maria
DUSMESNIL, Louise
ECHOLS, Mrs. James
ECKERT, Antonie
EICHHORN, Marianne
ENOCH, Yvonne
ERB, Mae Aileen
ERVIN, Emily L.
ESCOMBE, Ester
FORE, Burdette
FORTIER, Julia
FOSSEY, Elizabeth Jarrell
FRANK-AUTHENRID, Hedwig
FULLAM, Victoria
FUNCKE, Kathleen Paula
GABORIT, Marie Josephe
GABRIEL, Alma
GALLOS, Mme.
GATEHOUSE, Lady
GAUTHIER, Simone
GINA, Valentina
GOW, Dorothy
GRACE, Norah
GRAHAM, Susan Christine
GRIEVE, Annette
GRINDELL, Clara Kyle
GUSTAFSON, Vera
HARRINGTON, Mrs. W.C.
HARTLEY, Evaline
HAUSENFLUCK, Frances W.
HEFNER, Leah
HOFFMANN, Mary
HOFFMEYER, Zantha
HOHENBURG, Abbess von
HOLDBERG, Margaret
HOLZWEISSIG, Erika
HOSCHEK-MUHLHEIM, Klare
HUNT, Wynn
IDZIK, Danuta
JACQUET, Marie-Louise
JENNINGS, Marjorie
JENSON, Carol
JOHANSEN, Irene
JOHNDREAU, Audrey
JOHNSON, Myrna
KALLENBACH, Dagmar
KAVELIN, Nellie
KHRISTOVA, Milina
KLEMM, Roberta
KORANDA, Lorraine
KROESEN, Jill
LAIRD, Nancy
LANGFORD, Olivia
LASON, Olga
LAVINE, Rhoda J.
LEA, Annie

LEBARRON, M.H.
LEMERT, Gladys Fulbright
LENKEI, Gabriella
LEQUIEN, Colette
LEVAILLANT, Irma
LEVAN, Mrs. D.B.
LIVELY, Katherine Allen
LIVINGSTONE, Dorothy
McCOY, Nadine
McIVER WOOD, Mrs. Jules
McLARRY, Beverley
MACIEJASZ-KAMINSKA, Anna
MADISON, Ada
MAGARIA, Elvira
MAHLE, Maria Aparecida
MALVEZZI, Peppina
MAN, Nanda
MANGIONE, Amelia
MANOUKIAS, Virginie
MANTIA, Simone
MARKS, Florence Mary
MARREGA, Serenella
MARSHALL, Elisabeth
MARTIN, Elizabeth B.
MARTIN, Gloria
MATTHISON, Adela
MENKE, Emma
MEZZACAPO, Elena
MIGLIARI FERNANDES, Marlene
MOMONT, Heidi
NICOLINI, Maria
O'BUCHALLA, Maire
OLMSTEAD, Bess Heath
ORMAND, Lilla
ORTWEIN, Gerhild
PADULA, Elvira
PARET, Betty

PEREYERA LIZASO, Nydia
PERRY, Nina
PERUGIA, Noemie
PERWICH, Susanna
PETER, Lily
PICCARDI, Silvia
PLEE, Jo
PRICE, Janet
PULER, Clara P.
QUAILLE, Elizabeth
QUENEDEY, Aglae
RAMOS, Natalia
RAPOPORT, Ruth
REED, Edith Lobdell
REYNOLDS, Florence
RILEY, Alice
RIND, Bernice M.
RISTAD, Eloise
RODGERS, Irene
ROMA, Elsie P.
ROSENKRANZ, Maria
ROSSI, Gabriella
ROSSMAN, Floy
RUSSELL, Velma Armistead
RUTTER, Ida
SACHSEN, Caroline von
SANKS, Mary C.
SANS-SOUCI, Gertrude
SAVOY, Anne
SCHAFER, Ruth
SCHIEMANN, Agnes
SCHMIDT, Susan
SCHMITT, Alma C.
SEITZ, Inez Rae
SHAFFER, Helen Louise
SHERWOOD, Josephine
SHINDLER, Mary Dana

SIEDOFF, Elizabeth
SMITH, Mildred Price
SMITH, Virginia B.
SOMOGI, Judith
SORELLI, Mariella
STANZELEIT, Barbara
STEEMSON, Miss
STERN, Klara
STRONG, May A.
SURACE, Sandra Caratelli
SUTTON, Theodora
TAIROVA, S.
THORBERGS, Ingeborg
TRAMMER, Gaynor
TRUSTEDT, Ulrike
VERESS, Jolan
VESELA, Alena
VESTERINE, Marja
WARD, Willa
WATERMAN, Constance Dorothy
WHITE, Evelyn Davidson
WICKDAHL, Lillian S.
WICKHAM, Carol S.
WICKOP, Eta
WIESENFELDT, Eva
WILLERT-ORFF, Gertrud
WILSON, Dorothy
WINTULE, Ruta
WOLLIN, Natalie
WOODSTOCK, Mattie
WOOLLATT, Ethel Elizabeth
WOOTTON, Meredith E.
WOZERCRAFT, Marion
ZANETTI, Emilia
ZEDDA, Anna Paolone
ZIEREN-FRANK, A.M.

Appendix 2.

Music Key Signatures in 25 languages

English	Hungarian	Hebrew	Greek	German	French	Finnish	Dutch	Danish	Czecho-Slovakian	Chinese	Bulgarian	Afrikaans	English
A flat	asz	la bemol	la ifesi	as	la bemol	as	as	as	As	chiang A	La bemol	A mol	A flat
A	a	la	la	A	la	A	A	A	a	A	La	A	A
A sharp	aisz	la diese	la thiesi	ais	la diese	ais	ais	ais	ais	sheng A	La diez	A kruis	A sharp
B flat	b	si bemol	si ifesi	B	si bemol	B	bes	B	bes	chiang B	si bemol	B mol	B flat
B	h	si	si	H	si	H	B	H	b	B	si	B	B
C flat	cesz	do bemol	do ifesi	ces	do bemol	ces	ces	ces	ces	chiang C	do bemol	C mol	C flat
C	C	do	do	C	ut/do	C	C	C	C	C	do	C	C
C sharp	cisz	do diese	di thiesi	cis	do diese	cis	cis	cis	cis	sheng C	do diez	C kruis	C sharp
D flat	desz	re bemol	re ifesi	des	re bemol	des	des	des	des	chiang D	re bemol	D mol	D flat
D	d	re	re	D	re	D	D	D	d	D	re	D	D
D sharp	disz	re diese	re thiesi	dis	re diese	dis	dis	dis	dis	sheng D	re diez	D kruis	D sharp
E flat	esz	mi bemol	mi ifesi	es	mi bemol	es	es	es	es	chiang E	mi bemol	E mol	E flat
E	e	mi	mi	E	mi	E	E	E	E	E	mi	E	E
F	f	fa	fa	F	fa	F	F	F	F	F	fa	F	F
F sharp	fisz	fa diese	fa thiesi	fis	fa diese	fis	fis	fis	fis	sheng F	fa diez	F kruis	F sharp
G flat	gesz	sol bemol	sol ifesi	ges	sol bemol	ges	ges	ges	ges	chiang G	sol bemol	G mol	G flat
G	g	sol	sol	G	sol	G	G	g	g	G	sol	G	G
G sharp	gisz	sol diese	sol thiesi	gis	sol diese	gis	gis	gis	gis	sheng G	sol diez	G kruis	G sharp
Major	dur	Major	megalos (maggiore)	dur	majeur	duuri	Majeur	dur	dur	Dah-Tyau	Major	Majeur	Major
Minor	moll	Minor	mikros (minore)	moll	mineur	molli	Mineur	moll	moll	Sheau-Tyau	Minor	Mineur	Minor

English	Yugoslavian	Turkish	Swedish	Spanish	Rumanian	Portuguese	Polish	Norwegian	Japanese	Italian	Indonesian	English
A flat	as	la bemol	ass	la bemol	la bemol	la bemol	as	ass	hen-i	la bemolle	as	A flat
A	a	la	A	la	la	la	a	a	i	la	A	A
A sharp	ais	la diyez	aiss	la sostenido	la diez	la sostenido	ais	aiss	ei-i	la diesis	ais	A sharp
B flat	b	si bemol	B	si bemol	si bemol	si bemol	b	b	hen-ro	si bemolle	bes	B flat
B	h	si	H	si	si	si	h	h	ro	si	B	B
C flat	ces	do bemol	cess	do bemol	do bemol	do bemol	ces	cess	hen-ha	do bemolle	ces	C flat
C	C	do	C	do	do	do	do	C	ha	do	C	C
C sharp	cis	do diyez	ciss	do sostenido	do diez	do sostenido	cis	ciss	ei-ha	do diesis	cis	C sharp
D flat	des	re bemol	dess	re-bemol	re bemol	re bemol	des	dess	hen-ni	re bemolle	des	D flat
D	do	re	D	re	re	re	d	d	ni	re	D	D
D sharp	dis	re diyez	diss	re sostenido	re diez	re-sostenido	dis	diss	ei-ni	re-diesis	dis	D sharp
E flat	es	mi bemol	ess	mi bemol	mi bemol	mi bemol	es	ess	hen-ho	mi bemolle	es	E flat
E	e	mi	E	mi	mi	mi	e	e	ho	mi	E	E
F	f	fa	F	fa	fa	fa	f	f	he	f	F	F
F sharp	fis	fa diyez	fiss	fa sostenido	fa diez	fa sostenido	fis	fies	ei-he	fa diesis	fis	F sharp
G flat	ges	sol bemol	gess	sol bemol	sol bemol	sol bemol	ges	gess	hen-to	sol bemolle	ges	G flat
G	g	sol	G	sol	sol	sol	g	g	to	sol	G	G
G sharp	gis	sol diyez	giss	sol sostenido	sol diez	sol sostenido	gis	giss	ei-to	sol-diesis	gis	G sharp
Major	dur	major	dur	mayor	major	mayor	dur	dur	Chocho	maggiore	majeur	Major
Minor	mol	minor	moll	menor	minor	menor	moll	moll	Tancho	minore	mineur	Minor

International Encyclopedia of Women Composers (© Aaron I. Cohen).

Appendix 3.

Women Composers
Comparative distribution by century

Century	Total	20th	19th	18th	17th	16th	15th	14th	13th	12th	11th	10th	9th	8th	7th	6th	5th	4th	1st-3rd	B.C.	Century not known
Arabia	39										1		16	11	5	3				2	1
Argentina	49	44	5																		
Australia	87	85	2																		
Austria	91	37	42	8	3	1															
Belgium	58	51	6						1												
Bohemia before 1918	18	4	13	1																	
Brazil	57	51	6																		
Britain before 1700	14				6	4				1	2					1					
Bulgaria	7	7																			
Byzantium	6						1						4					1			
Canada	136	136																			
Chile	10	8	2																		
China	12	7											1						1		3
Colombia	4	4																			
Costa Rica	2	2																			
Croatia before 1918	6	4	2																		
Cuba	21	20	1																		
Czechoslovakia	31	29	2																		
Denmark	78	59	18	1																	
Dominica	7	4	2			1															
Egypt	21																			17	4
Eire	7	1	1	1													1				3
El Salvador	1	1																			
Esthonia	1	1																			
Finland	10	9	1																		
France	447	203	130	48	5	1	2	11	13	14											
Germany before 1945	363	118	185	27	7	5	3		4	2	1						1				18
Germany East	6	6									1										11
Germany West	54	54																			
Greece	21	8														1	1		1	9	1
Hawaii	15	12	3																		

Women Composers
Comparative distribution by century

Century	Total	20th	19th	18th	17th	16th	15th	14th	13th	12th	11th	10th	9th	8th	7th	6th	5th	4th	1st-3rd	B.C.	Century not known
Hong Kong	1	1																			
Hungary	21	14	6	1																	
Iceland	4	4																			
India	20	7			1	2	1	2					1							2	4
Iran (Persia)	2																			2	
Israel	32	30																	2		
Italy	314	104	75	24	38	33	1			1									2		36
Jamaica	3	3																			
Japan	55	55																			
Java	1	1																			
Korea	10	10																			
Lithuania before 1945	2	2																			
Malta	1	1																			
Mexico	19	15	2	2																	
Monaco	1				1																
Netherlands	71	60	8		2																1
Neth. East Indies	1	1																			
New Zealand	40	40																			
Nigeria	1	1																			
Norway	43	32	10	1																	
Pakistan	2	2																			
Panama	1	1																			
Peru	9	3	6																		
Philippines	7	7																			
Poland	189	115	65	6	1				2												
Portugal	31	16	9	2	1	2						1									
Puerto Rico	5	5																			
Rumania	35	33	2																		
Russia before 1917	58	28	27	2	1																
Slovakia before 1918	8	7	1																		
South Africa	48	46	2																		

International Encyclopedia of Women Composers (© Aaron I. Cohen)

Women Composers
Comparative distribution by century

Century	Total	20th	19th	18th	17th	16th	15th	14th	13th	12th	11th	10th	9th	8th	7th	6th	5th	4th	1st-3rd	B.C.	Century not known
Spain	69	44	16	1	1	2	3		1		1										
Sri Lanka	2	2																			
Sumeria	2																			2	
Surinam	1	1																			
Sweden	66	40	25	1																	
Switzerland	64	54	7	2																	1
Trinidad & Tobago	1	1																			
Turkey	17	15	1	1																	
United Kingdom	587	318	206	50																	13
United States	2 009	1 746	162	1																	100
Uruguay	2	2																			
U.S.S.R. after 1918	175	175																			
Venezuela	9	8																			1
Vietnam	1	1																			
Yugoslavia after 1918	21	21																			
Nationality unknown	459	169	52	3	2	1				1											231
Total	6 196	4 200	1 103	184	69	52	11	12	22	20	6	1	22	11	5	5	3	1	6	33	430

Continental Distribution
Excluding Nationalities Unknown

	Total	20th	19th	18th	17th	16th	15th	14th	13th	12th	11th	10th	9th	8th	7th	6th	5th	4th	1st-3rd	B.C.	Century not known
Africa	71	49	2																	16	4
Asia	103	85			1	2	1	2				2							1	2	7
Asia Minor	75	30									1		16	11	5	3			2	6	1
Australasia & Pacific	150	145	5																		
Europe	2 997	1 673	861	177	66	48	10		21	19	5	1	4			2	3	1	2	9	83
North America	2 164	1 897	164	3																	100
South & Cent. America	181	157	22				1														1
Ancient Near East to 11 cent. A.D.	82										1		20	11	5	4	1	1	3	30	6

International Encyclopedia of Women Composers (© Aaron I. Cohen)

APPENDIX 4

WOMEN COMPOSERS BY COUNTRY

ARABIA
9th Century B.C.
  MILH AL-ATTARA
7th Century B.C.
  RAYYA AL-ZARQA
6th Century A.D.
  HIND BINT'UTBA
  HURAIRA
  KHULAIDA II
7th Century A.D.
  AZZA AL-MAILA
  MAYSUNAH
  QU'AD
  SALLAMA AL-ZARQA
  THAMAD
8th Century A.D.
  ALYA
  BASBAS
  HABBABA
  INAN
  JAMILA
  KHULAIDA I
  MAKNUNA
  MUTAYYAM AL-HASHIMIYYA
  SALLAMA AL-QASS
  SHARIYYA
  ULAYYA
9th Century A.D.
  BADHL
  BANAN
  BID'A
  DANANIR AL BARMAKIYYA
  FADL(1)
  FADL(2)
  FARIDA
  IRFAN
  MAHBUBA
  NASIB AL-MUTAWAKKILIYA
  ORAIB
  QALAM
  QALAM AL-SALAHIYYA
  QAMAR
  RAIQ
  UBAIDA
11th Century A.D.
  UMM AL-HIRAM
Century unknown
  DILAL

ARGENTINA
19th Century A.D.
  GARCIA, Eduarda Mansilla de
  MANSILLA DE GARCIA, Eduarda
  SANCHEZ, Manuela Cornejo de

SOMELLERA DE ESPINOSA,
  Candelaria
SOMELLERA, Josefa
20th Century A.D.
  ANIDO, Maria Luisa
  ARETZ, Isabel
  BARON SUPERVIELLE, Susana
  BENAVENTE, Regina
  BLAZQUEZ, Eladia
  CABRERA, Ana S. de
  CALCAGNO, Elsa
  CARRIQUE, Ana
  CASTILLO, Graciela
  CIMAGLIA DE ESPINOSA, Lia
  CURUBETO GODOY, Maria Isabel
  DAVALOS, Julia Elena
  DIANDA, Hilda
  EISENSTEIN DE VEGA, Silvia
  FERREYRA, Beatriz
  FREGA, Ana Lucia
  GARCIA MUNOZ, Carmen
  GARCIA ROBSON, Magdalena
  GOMEZ CARRILO, Maria Ines
  KERSENBAUM, Sylvia Haydee
  KOHAN, Celina
  MAIZANI, Azucena
  MARANCA, Lucia
  MORETTO, Nelly
  PARASKEVAIDIS, Graciela
  PARRONDO, Maria
  PATINO ANDRADE, Graziela
  POSSE, Monica
  RAINER, Sara
  RODRIGUEZ BELLA, Catalina
  SACCAGGIO, Adelina Luisa Nicasia
  SCHELLER ZEMBRANO, Maria
  SEBASTIANI, Pia
  SERRANO REDONNET, Ana
  SIMONE, Mercedes
  SINDE RAMALLAL, Clara
  SPENA, Lita
  SUAREZ, Erna
  SUSANA, Graciela
  TERZIAN, Alicia
  TORRA, Celia
  VALLADARES, Leda
  WALSH, Maria Elena
  WILLIAMS, Irma

AUSTRALIA
19th Century A.D.
  MENK-MAYER, Florence
  WEATHERALL, Nellie G.

20th Century A.D.
  ANDERSON, Julia McKinley
  ANDERSON, Olive Jennie Paxton
  BAINBRIDGE, Beryl
  BANDT, Rosalie Edith
  BARKER, Patricia
  BATCHELOR, Phyllis
  BAULD, Alison
  BEATH, Betty
  BLOM, Diane
  BOTTAGISIO, Jacqueline
  BOYD, Anne Elizabeth
  BRANDMAN, Margaret Susan
  BRIGHT, Ann
  CADDEN, Jill
  CALCRAFT, Sharon
  CALLINAN, Maureen
  CARR-BOYD, Ann Kirsten
  CHILD, Marjorie
  CLINGAN, Judith Ann
  COGAN, Morva
  COHEN, Dulcie M.
  DAVY, Ruby Claudia Emily
  DE JONG, Sarah
  DOBIE, Janet
  DOBSON, Elaine
  DODD, Dorothy
  DOE, Elaine
  DOYLE, Beth
  DREYFUS, Francis Kay
  EAGLES, Moneta M.
  EVANS, Winsome
  FOWLER, Jennifer Joan
  GHANDAR, Ann
  GIBBS, Prue
  GIFFORD, Helen Margaret
  GRAHAM, Sybil
  HARRHY, Edith
  HESSE, Marjorie Anne
  HILL, Sister M. Mildred
  HOLLAND, Dulcie Sybil
  HOWLETT, May
  HYDE, Miriam Beatrice
  JOWETT, Diane
  JOWETT, Jennifer
  KATS-CHERNIN, Elena
  KATTS, Letty
  KELLNER, Sybil
  LASDAUSKAS, Jacqueline
  LAVIN, Marie Duchesne
  McALISTER, Mabel
  McFARLANE, Jenny
  McKENZIE, Sandra
  MAGEAU, Mary Jane

MAHLER, Hellgart
MATHIESON, Ann Emily
MENDOSA, Dot
MILNE, Lorraine
MORGAN, Mary Hannah
MORONEY, Sister Mary Emmeline
MORRISSEY, Elizabeth
MURDOCH, Heather
MYERS, Monda
NASH, Wendy
NIXON, June
OKEY, Maggie
O'SHEA, Mary Ellen
PHILLIPS, Linda
RADIC, Maureen
ROFE, Esther
SOLOMON, Mirrie Irma
SPICER, Marjorie
STAINKAMPH, Eileen Freda
STANDRING, Helen
SUTHERLAND, Margaret
TEAKLE, Robyn
THOMPSON, Caroline Lorraine
TOBIN, Sister Clare
TUCKER, Irene
TYER, Norma Phyllis
VERHAAR, Jacqueline
WHITEHEAD, Alison
WHITTAKER, Vivian
WILLIAMS, Kimberley
WILSON, Marion
WOODLEY, Joyce

AUSTRIA
16th Century A.D.
MARGARET OF AUSTRIA
17th Century A.D.
BACHMANN, Judith
BIBER, Maria Anna Magdalena von
ENTHALLER, Sidonia
18th Century A.D.
AUENBRUGG, Marianna von
AURENHAMMER, Josefa Barbara
  von
BAYER, Karoline
EBERLIN, Maria Barbara Caecilia
FIELD, Miss A.
MARTINEZ, Marianne
MUELLNER, Johanna
WOHL, Maria Viktoria
19th Century A.D.
AMANN, Josephine
AUENHEIM, Marianna
BARONI-CAVALCABO, Guilia
BENFEY-SCHUPPE, Anna
BLAHETKA, Marie Leopoldina
BRINKMANN, Wilhelmine
BUERDE, Jeanette Antonie
CIBBINI, Katherina
ELSCHNIG, Marietta
ELSSLER, Fanny
GEIGER, Constanze
GOUBAU D' HAVORST, Leopoldine
GRUNBAUM, Theresa
HAENEL DE CRONENTHAL, Louise
  Augusta Marie Julia
HENDRICH-MERTA, Marie
JOACHIM, Amalie
KRALIK VON MAYERSWALDEN,
  Mathilde
KREBS, Mrs.
KUCZOR, Hilda
KURZBOECK, Magdalene von
LILIEN, Antoinette von, Baroness
LORINSER, Gisela von
MIER, Countess Anna von
MOSEL, Catherine de
MOZART, Maria Anna Walburga
  Ignatia

PACHLER-KOSCHAK, Marie
  Leopoldine
PAPPENHEIM, Marie, Countess
PARADIS, Maria Theresia von
PESCHKA, Minna
PESSIAK-SCHMERLING, Anna
POSSANER, Emma Baronini
POTT, Aloyse
SCHADEN, Nanette von
STANDT, Elsie
STEIN, Nannette
STOLLEWERK, Nina von
STUBENBERG, Anna Zichy,
  Countess
TYRELL, Agnes
UNGHER-SABATIER, Caroline
WALDBURG-WURZACH, Julie von,
  Princess
WOLFF, Luise
ZAFFAUK, Theresa
20th Century A.D.
ALCALAY, Luna
BACH, Maria
BALENOVIC, Draga
DANIELA, Carmen
DICHLER-SEDLACEK, Erika
ERDMANNSDOERFER, Pauline
ERDOEDY, Luisa, Countess
ESTERHAZY, Alexandrine, Countess
FAHRBACH, Henrietta
FISCHER, Emma Gabriele Marie von,
  Baroness
FRYDAN, Kamilla
GARY, Marianne
GEYER, Marianne
HAGER-ZIMMERMANN, Hilde
HALACSY, Irma von
HANS, Lio
HOFER, Maria
HUEBNER, Ilse
JUENGER, Patricia
KAHRER, Laura Rappoldy
KERN, Frida
KHOSS VON STERNEGG, Gisela
KICKINGER, Paula
KODOLITSCH, Michaela
MAHLER, Alma Maria
MAYER, Lise Maria
MIKUSCH, Margarethe von
MUELLER-HERMANN, Johanna
NEUWIRTH, Goesta
PETYREK, Felika
PRENTNER, Marie
SOMMER, Silvia
UNSCHULD, Marie von
VOLKART-SCHLAGER, Kaethe
VON ZIERITZ, Grete
WAGENSONNER, Mimi
WALKER, Louise

BELGIUM
13th Century A.D.
HADEWIJCH OF BRABANT
19th Century A.D.
LANNOY, Clementine-Josephine-
  Françoise-Thérèse, Countess
LEFEBURE, Marguerite
MATTHYSSENS, Marie
MICHEL, Josepha
MONGRUEL, Georgiana Catherine
  Eugénia Leonard
SAMUEL, Caroline
20th Century A.D.
BARELLA, Yvonne
BOUSSARD, Marguerite
BULTERIJS, Nina
COLIN, Jeanne
COME, Tilde
DAILLY, Claudine
DANEAU, Suzanne
DARGE, Moniek

DE HERVE, Zelina
DE MOL, Josephine
DEBRASSINE-PRIJAT, Laure
DELIRE, Alice
DENEUVILLE, Irene
DUVOSEL, Seraphien Lieven
ELLEN, Mary
EVERAERTS-ZLICA, Mme.
FOLVILLE, Eugenie-Emilie Juliette
FONTYN, Jacqueline
FRANCK, Philippine
FRESON, Armande
GERARD, S.
GODART, L.
GRANJE, Rosa
HECQ, Olia
HILLIER-JASPAR, Jeanne
LAOUREUX DE GUCHTENAERE,
  Marguerite
LEBIZAY, Marguerite
LEMAIRE-SINDORFF, Jeanne
LEPLAE, Claire
MESTDAGH, Hélène
MISONNE, Claude
NESTE, Rosane van
PILNY, Josepha
RAMAKERS, Christiane Josee
ROZET, Sonia
SANDERFOSS, Mme.
SCHUSSLER-BREWAEYS, Marie
  Antoinette
THISSE-DEROUETTE, Rose
TOLKOWSKY, Denise
UYTTENHOVE, Yolande
VAN DEN BOORN-COCLET,
  Henriette
VAN HAUTE, Anna-Maria
VAN NESTE, Rosane Micheline Lucie
  Charlotte
VELLERE, Lucie Weiler
VIALA, Georgette
VIGNERON-RAMAKERS, Christiane-
  Josee
VIGNERY, Jeanne Emilie Virginie
VITO-DELVAUX, Berthe di
WERFEL-LACHIN, Assia
WHITTLE, Chris Mary-Francine
WIELE, Aimée van der

BOHEMIA, BEFORE 1918
18th Century A.D.
WOLF, Maria Carolina
19th Century A.D.
AUSPITZ-KOLAR, Augusta
BARTH, Elise
BLEITNER, Rosa
BRDLIKOVA, Josefina
DUSCHEK, Josefina
DUSSEK, Olivia
DUSSEK, Veronica Rosalie
JAHNOVA, Bozena
KENDIKOVA, Zdenka
RINGELSBERG, Matilde
SCHIMON, Anna
SCHULZOVA, Anezka
SZARVADY, Wilhelmine Clausz
20th Century A.D.
BERAN-STARK, Lola Aloisia Maria
FALTIS, Evelyn
SCHWARZKOPF-DRESSLER, Maria
TUCZEK, Felicia

BRAZIL
19th Century A.D.
CASTRO GUIMARAES, Floripes de
CASTRO, Maria Guilhermina de
  Noronha E.
DE CASTRO, Alice
LEONARDO, Luisa
MATOS, A. de
OLIVEIRA, Alexandrina Maciel de

20th Century A.D.
ALCANTARA FERREIRA, Lucemar de
ANACLETO, Aurea
ARAUJO, Gina de
BARBOSA, Cacilda Campos Borges
BRAGA, Henriqueta Rosa Fernandes
CABRERA, Silvia Maria Pires
CAMEU, Helza
CAMINHA, Alda
CAMPOS ARAUJO DE, Joaquina
CARVALHO, Dinora de
CATUNDA, Eunice do Monte Lima
CHALITA, Laila Maria
COSTA, Maria Helena da
DE BIASE BIDART, Lycia
DINIZ, Thereza da Fonseca Borges
EMIDIO TAVORA, Florizinha
FERNANDES, Maria Helena Rosas
FERNANDEZ, Helen Lorenzo
FIUZA, Virginia Salgado
GONZAGA, Chiquinha
GREGORI, Nininha
JABOR, Najla
LAMEGO, Carlinda J.
LEITE, Clarisse
MACIEL, Argentina
MALHE, Maria Aparecida
MARQUES, Fernandina Lagos
MARQUES, Maria Adelaide
NUNES, Elizabeth Zamorano
OLIVEIRA, Alda de Jesus
OLIVEIRA, Babi de
OLIVEIRA, Jocy de
OLIVEIRA, Sophie Marcondes
de Mello
PEREIRA DA SILVA, Adelaide
PIRES DE CAMPOS, Lina
PIRES DE PIRES, D. Maria
Clementina
PIRES DOS REIS, Hilda
POLONIO, Cinira
PRIOLLI, Maria Luisa de Matos
ROSALINA, Ana
ROSAS FERNANDES, Maria Helena
ROSATO, Clorinda
SANTOS BARRETO, Adelina
SCHLEDER, Grizelda Lazzaro
SCLIAR, Esther
SETTI, Kilza
SODRE, Joanidia
VEIGA OLIVEIRA, Sofia Helena da
VILLA-LOBOS, Arminda Neves de
Almeida
YAMPOLSCHI, Roseane

BRITAIN, BEFORE 1700
6th Century A.D.
GUINEVERE, Queen
11th Century A.D.
ADELINE
MARGARET, Queen of Scotland
12th Century A.D.
MARIE DE FRANCE
16th Century A.D.
BOLEYN, Anne, Queen of England
ELIZABETH I, Queen of England
MARY STUART, Queen of Scots
MILDMAY, Lady
17th Century A.D.
BIRNIE, Patie
CLIFFORD, Anne
DERING, Lady Mary
DILCARO, Mrs.
HUME, Agnes
MacLEOD, Mary

BULGARIA
20th Century A.D.
BANKOVA-MARINOVA, Angelina
BAYEVA, Vera
KARASTOYANOVA, Elena

KLINKOVA, Zhivka
LESICHKOVA, Lili
LIDGI-HERMAN, Sofia
PETROVA, Mara

BYZANTIUM
4th Century A.D.
MACRINA, Saint
9th Century A.D.
KASIA
MARTHA
THEKLA
THEODOSIA
15th Century A.D.
PALAEOLOGINA

CANADA
20th Century A.D.
ACKLAND, Jeanne Isabel Dorothy
ACKLAND, Jessie Agnes
ALBRECHT, Wendy
ALLIK, Kristi
ANDERSON-WUENSCH, Jean Mary
ANTHONY, Gina
ARCHER, Violet Balestreri
AUBUT-PRATTE, Françoise
BARIL, Jeanne
BEAUCHEMIN, Marie
BECKMAN, Debora
BEECROFT, Norma Marian
BELLAVANCE, Ginette
BENSON, May
BERRY, Margaret Mary Robinson
BERTRAND, Ginette
BINET, Jocelyne
BLOMFIELD-HOLT, Patricia
BOESE, Helen
BOUCHARD, Linda L.
BOUCHER, Lydia
BOYD, Liona Maria
BRANSCOMBE, Gena
BROWNING, Bertha Hecker
BUCK, Era Marguerite
BUCKLEY, Beatrice Barron
BURCHELL, Henrietta Louise
BURROWES, Katherine
BURSTON, Maggie
BUTLER, Patricia Magahay
CADORET, Charlotte
CADZOW, Dorothy Forrest
CAMPBELL, Edith Mary
CARON-LEGRIS, Albertine
CHARLES, S. Robin
CHENIER, Monique
CHITTENDEN, Kate Sara
CLAMAN, Dolores Olga
CLARK, Florence Durrell
CLARKE, Phyllis Chapman
CLEMENS, Margaret
COONEY, Cheryl Lee
COTE, Helene
COULOMBE SAINT-MARCOUX,
Micheline
COULTHARD, Jean
CULLEN, Trish
DECARIE, Reine
DELORME, Isabelle
DRYNAN, Margaret
DUGAL, Madeleine
ECKHARDT-GRAMATTE, Sophie-
Carmen
EGGLESTON, Anne E.
ETHRIDGE, Jean
FOOT, Phyllis Margaret
FRANCHERE-DESROSIERS, Rose de
Lima
FRITZ, Sherilyn Gail
FULLER, Jeanne Weaver
GARDINER, Mary Elizabeth
GEDDES-HARVEY, Roberta
GRAY, Victoria Winifred

GRUDEFF, Marian
GUILBERT, Christiane
GUMMER, Phyllis Mary
HANSEN, Joan
HARDIMAN, Ellena G.
HARDY, Helen Irene
HARRISON, Susan Frances
HAZELRIG, Sylvia Jean Earnhart
HENDERSON, Ruth Watson
HICKS, Marjorie Kisby
HOBBS, Barbara
HOFFERT, Brenda
JACOB, Elizabeth Marie
KEEFER, Euphrosyne
KENT, Ada Twohy
KERR, Bessie Maude
KILBY, Muriel Laura
KUZMENKO, Larysa
KUZMICH, Natalie
LAFLEUR, Lucienne
LAJEUNESSE, Emma, Dame
LATIMER, Ella May Elizabeth
LAUBER, Anne Marianne
LEE, Hope Anne Keng-Wei
LEFEBVRE, Françoise
LEMON, Laura G.
LOUIE, Alexina Diane
McINTOSH, Diana
McINTYRE, Margaret
McKELLAN, Irene Mary
MARGLES, Pamela
MARSHALL, Kye
MILETTE, Juliette
MILEVIC, Janice
MILLER, Elma
MORGAN, Hilda
MORIN-LABRECQUE, Albertine
MORLEY, Nina Dianne
MORTIFEE, Ann
MOSHER, Frances Elizabeth
NORBURY, Ethel F.
PALMER, Catherine M.
PAQUIN, Anna
PAQUIN, Louisa
PARR, Patricia
PENNER, Jean Priscilla
PENTLAND, Barbara Lally
PICHE, Eudore
PIGGOTT, Audrey Margaret
RAYMOND, Madeleine
RENSHAW, Rosette
RHENE-JAQUE
RICHARDSON, Cornelia Heintzman
RICKARD, Sylvia
ROBINSON, Jean
RODRIGUE, Nicole
SCHLOSS, Myrna Frances
SIEBER, Susanne
SINCLAIR, Margaret
SKARECKY, Jana Milena
SMITH, Mary Barber
SMITH, Sharon
SOUTHAM, Ann
SPECHT, Judy Lavise
SPENCER, Marguerita
STEPHEN, Roberta Mae
STREET, Arlene Anderson
SUMNER, Clare
TAMBLYN, Bertha Louise
TELFER, Nancy Ellen
THORESON, Janice Pearl
TURNER, Sara Scott
VANIER, Jeannine
VILLENEUVE, Marie-Louise Diane
VINETTE, Alice
YOUNG, Gayle

CHILE
19th Century A.D.
HUNEEUS, Isidora Zegers de
ZEGERS, Isidora

20th Century A.D.
ALEXANDER, Leni
CANALES PIZARRO, Marta
MATES, Vega
MacKENNA, Carmela
SANGUESA, Iris
SEPULVEDA, Maria Luisa
SOUBLETTE, Sylvia
VIVADO ORSINI, Ida

CHINA
2nd Century A.D.
TS'AI, Yen
9th Century A.D.
HSUEH, T'ao
20th Century A.D.
HSIAO, Shu-Sien
LEE, Bo-Chas
LIU, Tyan-Khua
LU, Yen
LUO, Jing-Jing
WANG, Jiu-Fang
WANG, Qiang
Century unknown
CAI, Wen Ji, Princess
DE, Li, Princess
WONG, Zhao, Princess

COLOMBIA
20th Century A.D.
ACOSTA, Josefina, Baroness
BRIDGEWATER, Violet Irene
BUENAVENTURA, Isabel
NOVA SONDAG, Jacqueline

COSTA RICA
20th Century A.D.
CASTEGNARO, Lola
SANZ, Rocio

CROATIA, BEFORE 1918
19th Century A.D.
ATANASIJEVIC, Slavka
PUCIC-SORKOCEVIC, Yelena
20th Century A.D.
CHUDOBA, Blanka
FOSIC, Tarzicija
HIRSCHLER, Ziga
PEJACEVIC, Dora, Countess

CUBA
19th Century A.D.
POSADA Y TORRE, Ana
20th Century A.D.
ALVARES-RIOS, Maria
ARIZTI SOBRINO, Cecilia
BERROA, Catalina
BLANCK, Olga de
BOTET, Maria Emma
CARRILLO, Isolina
CASTELLANOS, Tania
CERVANTES, Maria
DE CASTRO, Blanca
DE LA MARTINEZ, Odaline
DELFIN, Carmelina
FERNANDEZ, Terresita
FLEITES, Virginia
HERNANDEZ-GONZALO, Gisela
LECOUNA, Ernestina
LOPEZ ROVIROSA, Maria Isabel
MARTINEZ DE LA TORRE Y
    SHELTON, Emma
RODRIGUEZ, Esther
SILVA, Eloisa d'Herbil de
VALDES, Marta

CZECHOSLOVAKIA, AFTER 1918
19th Century A.D.
KAVALIEROVA, Marie
VOJACKOVA-WETCHE, Ludmila

20th Century A.D.
BODOROVA, Sylvie
DONATOVA, Narcisa
GROGEROVA, Bohumila
JANACEKOVA, Viera
JIRACKOVA, Marta
JIRKOVA, Olga
KAPRALOVA, Vitězslava
KNOBLOCHOVA, Antonie
KOLARIKOVA-SEDLACHOVA, Marie
KOSTAKOVA-HERODKOVA, Marie
KOZANKOVA, Anna
KRALIKOVA, Johana
KUCEROVA-HERSTOVA, Marie
LACMANOVA, Anna
LEHOTSKA-KRIZKOVA, Ludmila
LOUDOVA, Ivana
MAZOUROVA, Jarmila
OBROVSKA, Jana
PETROVA-KRUPKOVA, Elena
SCHWARZ, Friederike
SMEJKALOVA, Vlasta
SNIZKOVA-SKRHOVA, Jitka
SPINAROVA, Vera
THOMSEN, Geraldine
VONDRACKOVA, Helena
VORLOVA, Slavka
VRABELY-WURMBACH-STUPPA
    CHOVA, Stefania
WALLNEROVA, Bibiana
WELLNER, Elsa

DENMARK
18th Century A.D.
AHLEFELDT, Marie Theresia,
    Countess
19th Century A.D.
AUGUSTENBURG, Caroline
    Amelia of
BRAASE, Albertine
CUMAN, Harriet Johanna Louise
EBERLIN, Anna Margrethe
FENGER, Johanne
FONSECA, Ida Henriette da
HEIBERG, Johanne Louise
HOEGSBRO-CHRISTENSEN, Inge
MATTHISON-HANSEN, Nanny
    Hedwig Christiane
MEYER, Elizabeth
MUNCH, Natalie
NIELSEN, Henriette
RECKE, Caroline
ROSENHOFF, Orla
SCHNORR VON CAROLSFELD,
    Malvina
STEMANN, Petronella
WIEL, Elise
WIENECKE, Henriette Stadfeldt
20th Century A.D.
ALSTED, Birgitte
ANDERSSON, Ellen
BANG, Sophy
BEHREND, Emilie
BENTZON, Karen Johanne
BENZON, Julie
BOISEN, Elisabeth
BRAASE, Sophie
CHRISTIANSEN, Cecilie
DAHL, Vivian
DALBERG, Nancy
FEDERHOF-MOLLER, Betty
GREVENKOP CASTENKIOLD, Olga
GRIEBEL WANDALL, Tekla
GYLDENKRONE, Clara
HANSEN, Thyra
HARMS, Signe
HEINE, Eleanor
HELLMERS, Ellen
HELSTED, Bodil
HERMANSEN, Gudrun
IRGENS-BERGH, Gisela, von

IRMINGER, Caroline
JENSEN, Helga
JOERGENSEN, Christine
JOEST, Emma
KJAER, Kirsten
LIEBMANN, Nanna Magdalene
LINNET, Anne
LUND, Gudrun
LUND, Hanna
MEYER, Ilse
MOE, Benna
MOELLER, Agnes
MOELLER, Paulette
MORITZEN, Gunda
MUNTHE-MORGENSTIERNE, Anna
NIELSEN, Olga
NORUP, Helle Merete
NOVI, Anna Beate
OGILVIE, Signe
OLSEN, Sophie
OSIANDER, Irene
PADE, Else Marie
RABEN-LEVETZAU, Nina
ROEMER, Hanne
RYGAARD, Christine
SAXTORPH, Gudrun
SCHYTTE, Anna
SEHESTED, Hilda
SEIEROE MORTENSEN, Anne
SKOVGAARD, Irene
TUXEN, Elisabeth
TWOREK, Wandy
ULRICHSEN, Ingeborg
VENDELHAVEN, Harriet
VIGGO, Eleanor Margaret Green,
    Princess
WESTRUP-MILNER, Maria
WIENECKE, Sigrid Henriette

DOMINICAN REPUBLIC
16th Century A.D.
GINES, Teodora
19th Century A.D.
ABREU, Lucila
HARTMANN, Emma Sophie
    Amalie
20th Century A.D.
ABREU, Julieta Licairac
KOH, Bunya
LAPEIRETTA, Ninon de
    Brouwer
LUNA DE ESPAILLAT, Margarita

EGYPT
27th Century B.C.
HEMRE
25th Century B.C.
HEKENU
ITI
16th Century B.C.
BAKIT
HATSHEPSUT, Queen
15th Century B.C.
AHMES-NEFRETERE, Queen
MERIT
13th Century B.C.
TUY
10th Century B.C.
HENUTTAUI
MUTYUNET
9th Century B.C.
TENTIOH
8th Century B.C.
MERESAMENT
TENTNAU
7th Century B.C.
'ANKH-AMENARDAIS
'ANKH-SHEPENWEPT
6th Century B.C.
DE-ESIHEBSED
NEIT

MERELLE, Mlle.
MOLINOS-LAFITTE, Mlle. A.
MONTGEROULT, Hélène de Nervode
MONTGOMERY, Mme. de
NEUVILLE, Mme. Alphonse de
OLAGNIER, Marguerite
PAIGNE, Mme.
PAPOT, Marie Anne
PEAN DE LA ROCHE-JAGU,
  E. Françoise
PERRIERE-PILTE, Anais, Countess of
PERRONNET, Amélie
PERRY-BIAGIOLI, Antoinette
PFEIFFER, Clara-Virginie
PHILIPPON, Aimée-Jeanne
PIERPONT, Marie de
PIERRET, Phedora
PLEYEL, Marie Felicity Denise
POLLET, Marie Nicole Simonin
PROHASKA, Bernhardine
PUGET, Loise
RENAUD-D'ALLEN, Mlle. de
REVIAL, Marie Pauline
REYNAC, Mme. de
RIVAY, Mlle.
ROBERT-MAZEL, Hélène
RONDONNEAU, Elise
RONSSECY, Mme. de
ROTHSCHILD, Matilde, Baroness
  Willy de
ROUSSEAU, Louise
SABATIER-BLOT, Mme.
SAINT-CROIX, Caroline de
SALM-DYCK, Constance-Marie de
  Theis, Princess
SANTA-COLONA-SOURGET,
  Eugenie
SAUGEON, Zélie
SCHALE, Mlle.
SERVIER, Mme. H.
SIGAL, Mme.
STOLTZ, Rosina
SYMIANE, Magdaleine
TARDIEU DE MALLEVILLE, Charlotte
THERESA
THYS, Pauline
TONEL, Leonie
UGALDE, Delphine Beaucé
URGEL, Louise
VERGER, Virginie Morel du
VIARDOT-GARCIA, Pauline Michelle
  Ferdinande
VILLARD, Nina de
WARTEL, Atala Thérèse Annette
WUIET, Caroline
ZYBINE, Mme. S.
20th Century A.D.
AARON, Marcelle
AARON, Yvonne
ACCART, Eveline
ALAIN, Marie Claire
ALLAIN, Edmée J.
ALLOUARD CARNY, Odette
ANCONA, Solange
ANDRE-FOUET, M.
ARRIEU, Claude
AUBERT, Pauline Louise Henriette
AUZEPY, Michele
BAGANIER, Janine
BAILLY, Colette
BALUTET, Marguerite
BARAT, Eliane
BARBILLON, Jeanne
BARDEL, Germaine
BARRAINE, Elsa
BARREAU, Gisele
BARRIERE, Françoise
BASSOT, Anne-Marie
BECLARD D'HARCOURT,
  Marguerite
BENSUADE, Jane

BERGE, Irènée
BERNARD, Jeanne
BERNARD, Simone
BERTILLE, Janine
BIANCHINI, Virginie
BIASINI, Marcelle
BIENVENU, Lily
BONHOMME, Marie Therese
BONINCONTRO, Gabrielle
BOULANGER, Lili Juliette Marie Olga
BOULANGER, Nadia Juliette
BOUQUET, Marie-Thérèse
BOUTRON, Madeleine
BOUVET, Denise
BRACQUEMOND, Marthe Henriod
BRENET, Thérèse
BREUIL, Hélène
BRUNETEAU, Simone
CANAL, Marguèrite
CECCONI-BOTELLA, Monic
CHALLAN, Annie
CHAMINADE, Cécile Louise
  Stephanie
CHARBONNIER, Janine Andrée
CHRETIEN-GENARO, Hedwige
CLAUDE, Marie
CLOSTRE, Adrienne
COQUET, Odile Marie-Lucie
COTRON, Fanou
DARGEL, Maude
DE CHAMY, Berthe
DE COMPEIGNE, Laetitia
DEDIEU-PETERS, Madeleine
DELAHAYE, Cécile
DELBOS, Claire
DEMARQUEZ, Suzanne
DEMESSIEUX, Jeanne
DERHEIMER, Cécile
DESBOURDIEUX, Yvonne
DESCAT, Henriette
DESCAVES, Lucette
DESCHAMPS, Anne-Marie
DESPORTES, Yvonne Berthe Melitta
DOLMETSCH, Hélène
DOMMEL-DIENY, Amy
DRAPPIER, Yvonne
DUCOUREAU, Mme. M.
EHRMANN, Rosette
FALCINELLI, Rolande
FEJARD, Simone
FERRAND-TEULET, Denise
FERRARI, Gabriella
FIJAL, Anne-Marie
FINZI, Graciane
FLEMMING, Martha
FLEURY, Hélène
FOISON, Michelle
FRANCE, Jeanne Lelen
GABUS, Monique
GANEVAL, Emilienne
GARTENLAUB, Odette
GAUTHIER, Brigitte
GAUTHIEZ, Cécile
GERVAIS, Françoise Jeanne
GILLE, Paule
GILLES, Yvette Marie
GIROD-PARROT, Marie-Louise
GOLDSTEIN, Anne
GOTKOVSKY, Ida-Rose Esther
GOURY, Suzanne
GRAUBNER, Hannelore
GRIMAUD, Yvette
HAIK-VANTOURA, Suzanne
HANSEN, Hanna Marie
HANSEN, Renée
HARDELOT, Guy d'
HEDOUX, Yvonne
HERICARD, Jeanne
HERSCHER-CLEMENT, Jeanne
HONEGGER-VAURABOURG, Andrée
HORIOT, Evelyne

HUBLER, Evelyne
INGEBOS, Louise-Marie
JAELL-TRAUTMANN, Marie
JAMET, Marie-Claire
JOLAS, Betsy
JOULAIN, Jeanne-Angèle-Desirée-
  Yvonne
KELLER, Ginette
KRONING, Mlle.
LA HALLE, Yvonne
LABEY, Charlotte Sohy
LACHARTRE, Nicole Marie
LALAUNI, Lila
LARA, Catherine
LARHANTEC, Marie Annick
LARUELLE, Jeanne-Marie
LASKINE, Lily
LASRY-HERRBACH, Yvonne
LE BORDAYS, Christiane
LE DENTU, Odette
LE MENN, Michelle
LEANDRE, Joelle
LECLERC, Michelle
LEFEVRE, Armande
LEFEVRE, Jeanne
LEJET, Edith
LEJEUNE-BONNIER, Eliane
LELEU, Jeanne
LEPEUT-LEVINE, Jeannine
LESUR, Mme. A.R.
LORIOD, Yvonne
LOUVIER, Nicole
LUCAS, Blanche
LUCAS, Marie
MAGUY LOVANO, Marguerite
  Schlegel
MAIXANDEAU, Marie-Vera
MANZIARLY, Marcelle de
MARADEIX, Suzanne
MARI, Pierrette
MARTENOT-LAZARD, Ginette-
  Geneviéve
MARTIN, Geneviéve
MAURICE, Paule
MAURICE-JACQUET, H.
MEGEVAND, Denise
MEL-BONIS
MIMET, Anne Marie
MIREILLE, Saint Planté
MONNOT, Marguerite Angéle
MORHANGE-MOTCHANE, Marthe
PANZERA, Magdeleine
PERISSAS, Madeleine
PHILIBA, Nicole
PHILIPPART, Renée
PIERROT, Noelie Marie Antoinette
PISTON, Julia
PLE-CAUSSADE, Simone
POLIGNAC, Armande de, Countess
  of Chabannes
POULET DEFONTAINE Madeleine
PRESTI, Ida
QUANTIN-SAULNIER, Denise
RADIGUE, Eliane
RAVIZE, Angele
RAYNAL, Germaine
RENIE, Henriette
RIBONI, Liliane
RICHEPIN, Eliane
RICHER, Jeannine
RIGAUX, Clotilde
ROBERT, Lucie
ROGER, Denise
ROGET, Henriette
ROKSETH, Yvonne
ROLLIN, Monique
RUEFF, Jeanine
SANTA CRUZ
SAUVREZIS, Alice
SAZERAC, Genevieve
SCRIABINE, Marina

SELVA, Blanche
SERVOZ, Harriet
SIEGRIST, Beatrice
SIMON, Cécile Paul
SKORIK, Irene
SKORIK, Marcelle
SOUDERE, Valery
SOULAGE, Marcelle Fanny Henriette
TAILLEFERRE, Germaine
TAMIA
TAYAR-GUICHARD, Marguerite
TERRIER-LAFFAILLE, Anne
TISSOT, Mireille
TREMBLOT DE LA CROIX, Francine
TRUCHET, Pauline
VAUBOURGOIN, Jeanine
VIENNE, Marie-Louise de
VIGOT, Thérèse
VILLIN, Marcelle Henriette Marie
VIVIER, Odile
VOIGT, Henriette
WAHL, Miriam
WILL, Madeleine
WITTMAN, Thérèse
Century unknown
ACHARD, Marguerite
ARGIL, Louise
BAZIN, Mlle.
CAUMONT-DADE, Mme. la
Comtesse de
CODET-BOISSE, Catherine
CREPTAX, Rosette Tribor
DAUPHIN, Madeleine
DELARUE, Eugenie
DEPEYSAC, Comtesse
DESCHAMPS, Jacqueline
DUSMESNIL, Louise
GAUTHIER, Simone
GRAZIANA
GUEDON DE PRESLES, Mlle.
JACQUE, Emilie
JOUVENEL, Germaine de
RIVET, Jeanne
TARBE DES SABLONES, Mme.

GERMANY, BEFORE 1945
11th Century A.D.
HROSTWITHA
12th Century A.D.
HILDEGARDE, Saint
SPONHEIM, Sister Jutta von
13th Century A.D.
GERTRUDE OF HELFTA, Saint
MECHTHILD
ROTTERIN ALHEIT
SCHOENAU, Elisabeth von
15th Century A.D.
BUNGE, Jungfer Gertrud
HATZLERIN, Sister Clara
HOYA, Katherina von
16th Century A.D.
BARIONA, Madelka Simone
BRAUNSCHWEIG, Anna Maria,
Duchess
CATERINA
ECHENFELD, Katharina
RUFFIN, Fraulein
17th Century A.D.
AMALIE JULIANE, Countess of
Schwarzenberg
ERPACH, Amalia Katharina, von,
Countess
FRANCK, Elsbeth
HOFF, Regina Clara
SIEFERT, Justina
SOPHIE ELISABETH von
Braunschweig, Duchess
TIRS, Katharina
18th Century A.D.
ANNA AMALIA, Duchess of Saxe-
Weimar

ANNA AMALIA, Princess of Prussia
AUBIGNY VON ENGELBRUNNER,
Nina d'
AURELIA, Sister
BACH, Maria Barbara
BACHMANN, Charlotte Caroline
Wilhelmine
BRANDENSTEIN, Charlotte von
BRANDES, Charlotte Wilhelmina
Franziska
BRUCKENTHAL, Bertha von,
Baroness
CONTAMINE, Mlle. de
DANZI, Maria Margarethe
EICHNER, Adelheid Marie
GRAEFIN, Sophia Regina
HUEBNER, Caroline
KANZLER, Josephine
KAUTH, Maria Magdalena
LEBRUN, Franziska Dorothea
MARIA ANTONIA WALPURGIS,
Princess of Bavaria
MARIA CHARLOTTE AMALIE,
Princess of Saxe-Meiningen
MUELLER, Elise
REICHARDT, Bernhardine Juliane
SCHAUFF, Marie
SCHROETER, Corona Elisabeth
Wilhelmine
SOPHIA CHARLOTTE
STECHER, Marianne
WILHELMINA, Sophie Friederike,
Princess of Prussia
WOLDERSLEBEN, Juliane Charlotte
19th Century A.D.
ABRECHT, Princess of Prussia
ADELUNG, Olga
AMALIE, Marie Friederike Augusta,
Princess of Saxony
ANNA, Duchess of Mecklenburg-
Schwerin
ARNIM, Bettina von
AUGUSTA MARIA LOUISE, Queen of
Prussia
BABNIGG, Emma
BACHMANN, Elise
BAER, Louisa
BATHMANN, Charlotte
BATTA, Clementine
BAU, Elise
BAUDISSIN, Sofie, Countess Wolf
BAUER, Charlotte
BAUER, Katharine
BAUM, Katherine
BAUR, Constance Maud de
BEHR, Louise
BELLANI, Caroline
BELLEVILLE-OURY, Emilie
BERNARD, Vincenzia
BERNOUILLY, Agnes
BIEHLER, Ludmilla
BOCHKOLTZ-FALCONI, Anna
BOCK, Anna
BOERNER-SANDRINI, Marie
BOPP VON OBERSTADT, Countess
BOVET, Hermine
BRANDHURST, Elise
BRINKMANN, Minna
BRONIKOWSKA, Charlotte von
BRONSART VON SCHELLENDORF,
Ingeborg Lena von
BRUCKEN-FOCK, Emilie von
BUCHLEITNER, Therese
BUELOW, Charlotte von
BUTTENSTEIN, Constanze von
CHARLOTTE, Friederike Wilhelmine
Louise, Princess
CHRIST, Fanny
DAHL, Emma
DAMCKE, Louise
DECKER, Pauline

DEICHMANN, Julie
DIETRICH, Amalia
DOCKHORN, Lotte
DREIFUSS, Henrietta
DRIEBURG, Louise von
DROSTE-HUELSHOFF, Annette Elise
von, Baroness
DULCKEN, Louisa
DULCKEN, Sophie
EDELSBERG, Philippine von
ESCHBORN, Georgine Christine
Maria Anna
FELSENTHAL, Amalie
FLOTOW, Marthe von
FRANCOIS, Emmy von
FRANKEL, Gisela
GASCHIN-ROSENBERG, Fanny,
Countess
GOETZE, Auguste
GORONCY, Emilie
GOSSLER, Clara von
GRAB, Isabella von
GROEBENSCHUETZ, Amalie
HAASS, Maria Catharina
HADELN, Nancy von
HAMBROCK, Mathilde
HEIDENREICH, Henrietta
HEINEMANN, Jenny
HEINKE, Ottilie
HEITMANN, Matilde
HELLER, Ottilie
HENN, Angelica
HENSEL, Fanny Caecilia
HERTZ, Hedwig
HERZOGENBERG, Elizabeth von
HEUBERGER, Jenny
HINRICHS, Marie
HUBER, Nanette
HUND, Alicia
HUNDT, Aline
JENTSCH, May
JONAS, Anna
KAINERSTORFER, Clotilde
KALKHOEF, Laura von
KERN, Louise
KINKEL, Johanna
KLAGE, Marie
KLENZE, Irene von
KOENIG, Marie
KRAEHMER, Caroline
KRAUSE, Anna
KRAUSE, Ida
KRUMPHOLTZ PITTAR, Fanny
KRUMPHOLTZ, Anne-Marie
LANG, Josephine
LANGHANS, Louise
LEAVITT, Josephina
LIEBMANN, Helene
LOEWE, Auguste
LUDWIG, Rosa
MAILLART, Aimee
MANNKOPF, Adolphine
MARCHESI, Mathilde de Castrone
MARIE ELIZABETH, Princess of
Saxe-Meiningen
MAYER, Emilie
MENTER, Sophie
MENTZEL-SCHIPPEL, Elisabeth
METZGER-VESPERMANN, Clara
MOLIQUE, Caroline
MOLITOR, Friederike
MOMY, Valerie
MRASECK, Fraulein
MUELLER-BENDER, Mme.
NATHUSIUS, Marie
NICOLAY, Maria Antonia
NIEDERSTETTER, Emilie
OLIVIER, Charlotte
PESADORI, Antoniette de
PFEIFFER, Charlotte Birsch
PFEILSCHIFTER, Julie von

PLITT, Agathe
POLKO, Elise Vogel
RAMANN, Lina
RAPP, Marguerite
REICHARDT, Louise
RICHTER, Pauline
ROSENTHAL, Pauline
RUTTENSTEIN, Baroness Constance
SABININ, Martha von
SAINT-DIDIER, Countess
SALIGNY, Clara
SAWATH, Caroline
SCHAEFFER, Theresa
SCHATZELL, Pauline von
SCHAUROTH, Delphine von
SCHLICK, Elise, Countess of
SCHMEZER, Elise
SCHMITT, Alois
SCHOLL, Amalie
SCHREINZER, F.M.
SCHUBERT, Georgine
SCHUMANN, Clara Josephine
SCHWARZ-SIGMAND, Hermina
SCHWERTZELL, Wilhelmine von
SEIPT, Sophie
SICK, Anna
SIEGMUND, Hermine
SONTAG, Henriette
SPORLEDER, Charlotte
STOLBERG, Louise von
STRANTZ, Louise von
THAMM, Ida
TONDEUR, Wilhelmine
TROSCHKE UND ROSENWEHRT,
　Wilhelmine von, Baroness
TSCHETSCHULIN, Agnes
TSCHIERSCHKY, Wilhelmine von
VELTHEIM, Charlotte
VESPERMANN, Marie
VICTORIA MARIA LOUISA, Duchess
　of Kent
VIGNY, Louise von
VOLKMANN, Ida
VORWERK, Henrietta
WALDENBURG, Eveline von
WEBENAU, Julie
WESTENHOLZ, Eleonore Sophie
　Marie
WETTE, Adelheid
WEYRAUCH, Anna Julie von
WEYRAUCH, Augusta Henrietta von
WEYRAUCH, Sophie Auguste von
WICHERN, Caroline
WICKERHAUSER, Nathalie
WIECK, Marie
WIMMER, Marianne
WINKEL, Therese Emilie Henriette
　aus dem
WINTZER, Elisabeth
WISENEDER, Caroline
WOLFF-FRITZ, Sophie
WOLZOGEN, Elsa Laura von
WORALECK, Josephine
WURZER, Gabriella
ZAUBITZER, Ida
ZERNICKOW, Elise
ZERR, Anna
ZIEGLER, Natalie Sophie von
ZIMMERMANN, Agnes Marie
　Jacobina
ZITTELMANN, Helene
ZSCHOCK, Marie von
ZUMSTEEG, Emilie

20th Century A.D.
AGNES, Marie Jacobina
AUTENRIETH, Helma
BALCKE, Frida Dorothea
BARTHEL, Ursula
BELOW-BUTTLAR, Gerda von
BEUSCHER, Elisabeth

BLAUHUTH, Jenny
BRAUER, Johanna Elisabeth
CHARLOTTE, Princess of Saxe-
　Meiningen
CLEMENT, Mary
DERLIEN, Margarete
DESSOIR, Susanne
DOMBROWSKY, Maria
ERNST, Siegrid
FAISST, Clara Mathilde
FEHRS, Anna Elisbeth
FEININGER, Leonore Helene
FEIST-STEINHAUSEN, Alwine
FLACH, Elsa
FROMM-MICHAELS, Ilse
FRONMUELLER, Frieda
GEIGER-KULLMANN, Rosy Auguste
GINDLER, Kathe-Lotte
GOEBELS, Gisela
GOLDSCHMIDT, Lore
GREGER, Luisa
GREGORY, Else
HAENSCH, Delle
HAMPE, Charlotte
HANEFELD, Gertrud
HECHLER, Ilse
HEGELER, Anna
HEIDRICH, Hermine Margaret
HEINRICHS, Agnes
HEINSIUS, Clara
HELLER-REICHENBACH, Barbara
HERZ, Maria
HEYNSSEN, Adda
HOEK, Agnes
HOPPE, Clara
HORST, Carita von
HUEGEL, Margrit
INJADO
JACOBINA, Agnes Marie
JAEGER, Hertha
JOLY, Suzanne
JOSEPH, Rosa
KALTENECKER, Gertraud
KARG, Marga
KAZORECK, Hildegard
KEETMAN, Gunild
KERWEY, Julia
KICKTON, Erika
KIRCHNER, Elisabeth
KLEES, Gabriele
KOEHLER, Estella
KOLLER-HOPP, Margarete
KOPPEL-HOLBE, Maria
KRUSE, Lotte
KUKUCK, Felicitas
KUNTZE, Olga
LANGE, Anny von
LANKMAR, Helen
LE BEAU, Louisa Adolpha
LEMCKE, Anna
LEWING, Adele
MAEDLER, Ruth
MATZEN, Margarete
MAUR, Sophie
MENDELSSOHN, Erna
MENDELSSOHN, Luise
MUELLER, Charlotte
NAESER-OTTO, Martha
NAUMANN, Ida
NIEMANN, Charlotte
NIKISCH, Amelie
NOETHLING, Elisabeth
OHE, Adele aus der
PERSCHMANN, Elfriede
PETERSEN, Else
PFERDEMENGES, Maria Pauline
　Augusta
QUIEL, Hildegard
QUITTNER, Katharine
REIFF, Lili

RITTMAN, Trude
RUFF-STOEHR, Herta Maria Klara
SCHARWENKA-STRESOW,
　Marianne
SCHAUSS-FLAKE, Magdalene
SCHICK, Philippine
SCHMIDT, Carola
SCHMIDT, Margot Alice
SCHMITT-LERMANN, Frieda
SCHMITZ-GOHR, Else
SCHORLEMMER, Erna von
SCHORR-WEILER, Eva
SCHROEDER, Inge Maria
SCHULTE, Eleonore
SCHULZ, Madeleine
SCHULZE-BERGHOF, Luise Doris
　Albertine
SCHURZMANN, Katharina
SCHUSTER, Elfriede
SCHWEIZER, Gertrude
SENFTER, Johanna
STEIN-SCHNEIDER, Lena
STRAUSS, Elizabeth
STREIT, Else
STUDENY, Herma
SULZBOECK, Toni
TEICHMUELLER, Anna
VIEU, Jane
VOIGT-SCHWEIKERT, Margarete
VOLKSTEIN, Pauline
WEISS-MANN, Edith
WENTZEL, Elisabet von
WIERUSZOWSKI, Lili
WITTICH, Martha von
WOLF, Ilda von
WOOGE, Emma

Century unknown
BOGINSKI, Barbel
BOTIANO, Helene von
DANZIGER, Rosa
ECKERT, Antonie
HOHENBURG, Abbess von
PFUND, Jeanne
PHILIPPINA, Charlotte, Duchess of
　Brunswick
ROSENKRANZ, Maria
ROST, Emilie
SCHMIDHUBER, Caecilie
WERBER, Elise

GERMAN DEMOCRATIC REPUBLIC
20th Century A.D.
BAUMGARTEN, Chris
BODENSTEIN-HOYME, Ruth E.
BOLL, Christine E.
MEISTER, Marianne
MUNDINGER, Adele Franziska
ZECHLIN, Ruth

GERMAN FEDERAL REPUBLIC
20th Century A.D.
AHRENS, Sieglinde
ALSCHANSKY, Serafine
BACKES, Lotte
BAMBERGER, Regina
BIRNSTEIN, Renate Maria
BIZONY, Celia
BOEHN, Liselotte
BOESSER, Dagma
BOHMANN, Hedwig
BRUECKNER, Monika
CHAMPION, Stephanie
DIECKMANN, Jenny
EHRHARDT, Else
ERDING, Susanne
EUTENEUER-ROHRER, Ursula
　Henrietta
FIRNKEES, Gertrud
FRITSCH, Magda von
GOERSCH, Ursula Margitta

HECKSCHER-SCHNEEKLAUS,
  Marga
HIRSCHFELDT, Ingrid
HOELSZKY, Adriana
ISSLE, Christa
KIRCHGASSNER, Elisabeth
KOBLENZ, Babette
KOCHER-KLEIN, Hilda
KUBISCH, Christina
LATZ, Inge
LINNEMANN, Maria Catharina
MATTHEISS-BOEGNER, Helga
MERTENS, Dolores
MOYSEOWICZ, Gabriela
NIVELLI SCHWARTZ, Gina
PFUND, Leonore
ROHNSTOCK, Sofie
ROSENBACH, Ulrike
SAMTER, Alice
SCHMIDT-DUISBURG, Margarete
  Dina Alwina
SCHMOLKE, Anneliese
SHERMAN, Ingrid
SONNTAG, Brunhilde
STOLL, Helene Marianne
STRUCK, Ilse
THIEME, Kerstin Anja
THOMA, Annette
TIMMERMANN, Leni
TRICHT, Nora von
UIES, Margret
VARGAS, Eva
WEINREICH, Waltraut
WELMAN, Sylvia
WILHELM, Grete
WILLAERT, Caterina
WOLF, Winifried
WOLL, Erna
ZAULECK, Gertrud

GREECE
  7th Century B.C.
    DAMOPHILA
    ERINNA
    MEGALOSTRATA OF SPARTA
  6th Century B.C.
    MYRTIS
    SAPPHO
    TELESILLA OF ARGOS
  5th Century B.C.
    PRAXILLA
    THEANO
  4th Century B.C.
    MOERO
  1st Century A.D.
    THYMELE
  5th Century A.D.
    AZADE
  6th Century A.D.
    CORINNA
  20th Century A.D.
    DELMOULY, Marie Mathilde
    KALOGRIDOU, Maria
    KYRIAKOU, Rena
    KYROU, Mireille
    MIHALITSI, Sophia
    OIKONOMOPOULOS, Eleni N.
    SAKALLI-LECCA, Alexandra
    SAMIOU, Domna
  Century unknown
    ELENA

HAWAII
  19th Century A.D.
    EVERETT, Alice
    LIKELIKE, Miriam Cleghorn,
      Princess
    LILIUOKALANI, Queen of Hawaii
  20th Century A.D.
    ALULI, Irmgard Keali'iwahinealo-
      hanohokahaopuamana

BEAMER, Helen Desha
BEKEART, Edna
KAHANANUI, Dorothy
KANAKA'OLE, Edith Ke-Kuhikuhi-I-
  Pu'u-one-o-Na-Ali'i-O-Kohala
MACHADO, Lena
MOSSMAN, Bina
NAMAKELUA, Alice K.
PARIS, Ella Hudson
PUKUI, Mary Abigail
ROES, Carol
SHARPE, Emma

HONG KONG
  20th Century A.D.
    LAM MAN YEE, Violet

HUNGARY
  18th Century A.D.
    KOHARY, Marie, Countess of
  19th Century A.D.
    BAKA-BAITZ, Irma
    GERZSO, Angela
    HOVORST, Mme. Gouban d'
    KELEMEN, Berta Zathureczky
    KELEMEN, Mrs. Lajos
    LASZLO, Anna von
  20th Century A.D.
    BERG, Lily
    GEYER, Stefi
    HAJDU, Julia
    KAUFMAN, Barbara
    KISTETENYI, Melinda
    KODALY, Emma
    LINZ VON KRIEGNER, Marta
    MAJLATH, Julia
    MERO, Jolanda
    MORVAI, Suzanne
    SELDEN-GOTH, Gizella
    SZEKELY, Katalin
    SZOENYI, Erzsebet
    TICHARICH, Zdenka

ICELAND
  20th Century A.D.
    EIRIKSDOTTIR, Karolina
    PORBERGS, Ingibjorg
    THORKELSDOTTIR, Mist Barbara
    VIDAR, Jorunn

INDIA
  25th Century B.C.
    APALA
  13th Century B.C.
    VISVAVARA
  9th Century A.D.
    KODHAI
  14th Century A.D.
    JANABAI
    RUPAMATI, Rani
  15th Century A.D.
    PEPARARA, Laura
  16th Century A.D.
    MIRA BAI
    MRIGANAYANA, Queen
  17th Century A.D.
    BAHINABAI
  20th Century A.D.
    ANNAPURNA, Devi
    ATRE, Prabha
    AVAZARALA
    DARUWALA, Zarine
    KHANNA, Usha
    SARASWATIBAI
    SUBBALAKSHMI, M.S.
  Century unknown
    AMONKAR, Kishri
    GHOSHA
    LOPAMUDRA
    MUDDUPALANI

IRAN (PERSIA)
  3rd Century A.D.
    AFARIN
    SIRIN

ISRAEL
  13th Century B.C.
    MIRIAM
  12th Century B.C.
    DEBORAH
  20th Century A.D.
    ALOTIN, Yardena
    ARBEL, Re Chaya
    CHEN, Nira
    ELKOSHI, Rivka
    EVEN-OR, Mary
    FEIGIN, Sarah
    FLEISCHER-DOLGOPOLSKY,
      Tsipporah
    GHERTOVICI, Aida
    GRAD-BUCH, Hulda
    GWILY-BROIDO, Rivka
    HENDEL, Tikva
    INGBER, Anita Rahel
    JACOB-LOEWENSOHN, Alice
    KADIMA, Hagar Yonith
    KLEPPER, Anna Benzia
    LAZAR, Ella
    LEVITAS-GOLDIS, Lea
    LEVITE, Miriam
    OLIVERO, Betty
    PERETZ-LEVY, Liora
    RAN, Shulamit
    ROZMAN, Sarah
    SAGI, Noa
    SCHARLOT, Debaro
    SHATAL, Miriam
    SHEMER, Naomi
    SHLONSKY, Verdina
    SUSSMAN, Ettel
    TAL, Ya'ara
    TOUREL, Alona

ITALY
  1st Century A.D.
    CALPURNIA
  2nd Century A.D.
    CECILIA, Saint
  12th Century A.D.
    ISABELLA
  15th Century A.D.
    TUORNABUONI, Lucrezia
  16th Century A.D.
    AGOSTINO, Corona
    ALEOTTI, Raffaela-Argenta
    ALEOTTI, Vittoria
    ANIMUCIA, Giovanna
    ARCHILEI, Vittoria
    ARCHINTA, Marguerite
    BAGLIONCELLA, Francesca
    BELLINA, Madonna
    BERNARDI-BELLATI, Eleonora
    BOLOGNESE, Isabella
    BORGHI, Faustina
    BOVIA, Laura
    CAMALDULI, Sorella
    CAPPELLO, Laura Beatrice
    CARAFA, Livia
    CASULANA, Maddalena
    CHIERICATI, Lucrezia
    CIERA, Hippolita
    COLONNA, Vittoria, Duchess of
      Amalfi and Marchioness of
      Pescara
    COTTA, Anastasia
    FERRA, Susana
    LA MAINA
    LA PEREGO
    MANCINI, Eleonora
    MASSARENGHI, Paola

MEDICI ORSINI, Isabella de, Duchess
of Bracciano
MOLZA, Tarquinia
ORSINI, Eleanora, Duchess of Segni
PIGNETELLI, Mariana
RICCI, Cesarina di Tingoli
SESSA, Claudia
VARISI, Giulia
VERTOA DA BERGAMO, Sister
Agostina

17th Century A.D.
ANGELINI, Maria Vittoria
ASSANDRA, Catterina
BADALLA, Rosa Giacinta
BAPTISTA, Gracia
BARONI BASILE, Adriana
BARONI, Eleanora
BASSANO, Mlle.
BEMBO, Antonia
BERTOLAJO-CAVALETTI, Orsola
CACCINI, Francesca
CACCINI-GHIVIZZANI, Settimia
CALEGARI, Cornelia
CALEGARI, Leonarda
CAMPANA, Francesca
CAZZOLANI
CEPPARELLI, Soura Costanza
CERVONI, Isabella di Colle
CLARISSE DE ROME, Sister
COZZOLANI, Chiara Margarita
DOROTHEA SOPHIA, Duchess
FEDELE, Diacinta
FRANCESCHINI, Petronia
GRECA, Antonia La
LEONARDA, Sister Isabella
MEDA, Sister Bianca Maria
MURATORI SCANNABECCHI,
Angiola Teresa
NASCIMBENI, Maria Francesca
PATTARINA, Maria
PERUCONA, Sister Maria Saveria
PRIOLI MORISINA, Marietta
QUINCIANI, Lucia
QUINZANA, Sister Rosalba
RUSCA, Claudia Francesca
SERA, Beatrice del
STROZZI, Barbara
SUARDA, Maria Virginia
TARRONI, Antonia
VIZANA, Lucretia Orsina

18th Century A.D.
AGNESI-PINOTTINI, Maria Teresa d'
ALESSANDRA, Caterina
BARTALOTTI, Signora
BON, Anna
BONITA, Domina S. Delia
CAMATI, Maria
CAMBIASI BRANCA, Cirilla
CAZATI, Maria
CERINI, Geronda
CUZZONI, Francesca
DONI, Antonia
GRAZIANINI, Caterina Benedicta
GRIMANI, Maria Margherita
GUIDICCIONI, Laura
LANTI, Teresa
MATTEI, Beatrice
PIO DI SAVOJA, Isabella D.
ROSSI, Camilla de
SANTINI, Maria
SIRMEN, Maddalena Laura di
TIBALDI, Rosa
VENIER DE PETRIS, Teresa
ZAMPARELLI, Dionisia
ZAMPIERI, Elizabetta

19th Century A.D.
ACQUAVIVA-D'ARAGONA, Sofia
ADDI, Renee d'
ALESSI, Antonietta
APPIANI, Eugenia
ASPRI, Orsola

BALLIO, Hilda
BARONI-PASOLINI, Silvia
BATTAGINI, Giuseppina
BEDINI, Guendalina
BELLINCIONI, Gemma
BERTELLI, Clotilde
BERTINOTTI, Teresa
BLAND, Maria Theresa
BLANGINI, Mlle.
BOTTINI, Marianna, Marchioness
BRAGGIOTTI, Augusta
BRAMBILLA, Marietta
BRANCA-MUSSINI, Adele
BRIZZI-GIORGI, Maria
BUSKY-BENEDETTI, Albina
CALOSSO, Eugenia
CAPUCCI, Lida
CASELLA, Felicita
CATALANI, Angelica
COCCIA, Maria Rosa
COEN, Anna
COLTELLANI, Celeste
CONFORTINI-ZAMBUSI, Lucietta
CONTIN, Mme.
CORRER, Ida, Countess
CRESCIMANO, Fiorita
CRETI, Marianna de Rocchis
CRUVELLI, Sofia
DE MICCO, Lora
DELLE GRAZIE, Gisella
DELL'ACQUA, Eva
FERRARI, Carlotta
FRUGONI, Bertha
GALLONI, Adolfa
GAMBARO, Alceste
GAMBOGI, Federica Elvira
GERMANO, Vittoria
GIULIANI-GIULELMI, Emilia
GUERINI, Rosa
GUIDI LIONETTI, Teresa
LANZARINI DE ISAJA, Antonietta
LUCILLA D.
MARCHISIO, Barbara
MARINELLI, Maria
MARRA, Adelina
MASINI, Giulia
MELIA, Gabrielle
MERSANNE, Maddalena
MILANOLLO, Teresa Domenica
Maria
MORPURGO, Irene
MURIO-CELLI, Adelina
MUSSINI, Adele Branca
NAVA D'ADDA, Francesca,
Countess
NEGRONE, Luisa
ORSINI, Teresa
PATTI, Adelina
PELLEGRINI CELONI, Anna
PERRELLI, Giuseppina
PISARONI, Benedetta
POZZONE Maria
PUZZI, Fanny
REBAUDI, Virginia
RICOTTI, Onestina
SENEKE, Teresa
SESSI, Marianne
UCCELLI, Carolina
UNTERSTEINER, Antonietta
VANZO, Vittoria Maria
VEILUVA, Giuseppina Cerruti
VOLKONSKAYA, Zinanda
Alexandrovna, Princess
ZENTNER, Clary
ZILIOTTO, Elisa

20th Century A.D.
ANGELI-CATTINI, A. de
BALDACCI, Giovanna Bruna
BARBI, Alice
BARBIERI, Anna
BASSI, Giulia

BELOCH, Dorotea
BENEDICENTI, Vera
BIANCHERA, Silvia
BIANCHINI, Emma
BLASIS, Teresa de
BO, Sonia
BORRONI, Virginia
BRESCHI, Laura
BRONDI, Rita Maria
BRUSA, Elizabetta
CAMPODONICO, Beatrice
CAPUIS, Matilde
CAPURSO, Elisabetta
CECCHI, Gabriella
CHARTRES, Vivien
CINTOLESI, Liliana
CITATI-BRACCI, Clelia
COEN, Augusta
COLBRAN, Isabella Angela
CONTINI ANSELMI, Lucia
COSTANTINI, Andreina
DE MONTEL, Adalgisa
DEL CARRETTO, Cristina
FILIPPONI, Dina
FONTANA, Annie
FURGERI, Bianca Maria
GALANTI, Laura
GAMBARINI, Costanza
GARELLI DELLA MOREA, Vincenza
GASPARINI, Jola
GENNAI, Emanuela
GENTILE, Ada
GHILARDI, Syra
GIACCHINO CUSENZA, Maria
GILIOLI, Fiorenza
GIURANNA, Elena Barbara
GOLIA, Maria
GRAMEGLIA-GROSSO, Emma
GRIECO, Ida
GRILLI GALEFFI, Elvira
GUBITOSI, Emilia
JESI, Ada
KAZURO-TROMBINI, Margerita
LISSONI, Giulia
LOTTI, Silvana di
MANDANICI, Marcella
MANZONI, Eugenia Tretti
MARCHI, Giuliana
MARIANI-CAMPOLIETI, Virginia
MARINI, Giovanna
MEINI-ZANOTTI, Maddalena
MICHELI AGOSTINI, Fausta
MOLA, Corradina
MORMONE, Tamara
MOTTA, Giovanna
MUGNAINI ROBOTTI, Teresa
MURRI, Alceste
NARRONE, Claudia
NOVELLI, Mimi
ODDONE SULLI-RAO, Elisabetta
OLIVIERI SAN GIACOMO, Elsa
PALLASTRELLI, Giannina, Countess
PANZANI, Iris Piera
PARPAGLIOLO, Iditta
PERONI, Wally
PIAZZA, Paola
PICCONI, Maria Antonietta
PILATI, Maria
PISTONO D'ANGELO, Piera
PROCACCINI, Teresa
RAMPAZZA, Teresa
RAVINALE, Irma
RECLI, Giulia
RESPIGHI, Elsa
RICCIOLI FRAZZI, Eva
ROGATIS, Teresa de
ROMITELLI, Sante Maria
ROSSELLI-NISSIM, Mary
RUTA, Gilda, Countess
SADERO GENI, Maria Scarpa
SANNA CAMPAGNA, Myriam

SEGHIZZI, Cecilia
SIMONCELLI-PRINCIPE, Giulia
SIMONCINI, Simona
SOLLIMA, Donatella
SORALINA, Ana
SPAGNOLO, Aurelia
SPALETTI, Giuliana
SULPIZI, Mira
SURIANI, Alberta
TARTAGLIA, Lidia
TESTORE, Lidia
TROMBONE, Giuseppina
VILLAMANJNA, Ada Comandoli
VISCONTI, Leila
VITALI-AUGUSTI, Giuseppina
ZACCAGNINI, Guiliana
ZANETTOVICH, Daniele
Century unknown
AMATO, Maria
AMENDOLA, Mariannina
AUGUSTI, Giuseppina Vitali
BASSI, Laura
BELLAMANO, Marietta
CANTONI, Giulia
CARAFA D'ANDRIA, Anna
CARLUCCI, Filippina
CATALANOTTO, Marisa
CERUTTI, Paolina
CESIS, Sister Sulpizia
CONSOLINI, Gabriella Elsa
CUBONI, Maria Teresa
CUSENZA, Maria Giacchino
DENNO, Antonietta
FORTI, Elsa
GALEOTTI, Margherita
GALLI, Signora
MAN, Nanda
MANGIONE, Amelia
MARREGA, Serenella
MINGHELLA, Aida
MONACHINA
PICCARDI, Silvia
PREZIOSI, Antonietta
PROSDOCIMI, Ada
ROSATI, Elvira
ROSSI, Gabriella
SANI, Maria Teresa
SCHIAVO DE GREGORIO, Maria
SURACE, Sandra Caratelli
TAJANI MATTONE, Ida
TEDESCHI, Angela
TRANETTINA
VISCONTI, Caterina
ZEDDA, Anna Paolone

JAMAICA
20th Century A.D.
LEWIN, Olive
LISTON, Melba
NARCISSE-MAIR, Denise Lorraine

JAPAN
20th Century A.D.
ABE, Kyoko
ADACHI, Motohiko
AKIYOSHI, Toshiko
AOKE, Haruna
ARIMA, Reiko
HARA, Kazuko (1)
HARA, Kazuko (2)
HASHIMOTO, Kunihiko
HAYAKAWA, Kazuko
HORI, Etsuko
IWAUCHI, Saori
KABE, Mariko
KANAI, Kikuko
KITAZUME, Yayoi
KONISHI, Nagako
KUBO, Mayako
KUBOTA, Minako
KURIMOTO, Yoko

KUROKAWA, Manae
MASSUMOTO, Kikuko
MIYAKE, Haruna
MIZUNO, Shuko
MORI, Junko
MURAKUMO, Ayako
MURAO, Sachie
NAGAYO, Sueko
NAITO, Akemi
NAKAMURA, Sawako
NARITA, Kasuko
NATSUDA, Shoko
NISHIKI, Kayoko
NISHIMURA, Yukie
NISHUDA, Yamiko
NOZAWA, Kazuyo
OBAYASHI, Nobichiko
OKADA, Kyoko
OKI, Hideko
OSAWA, Kazuko
RANTA-SHIDA, Shoko
SATO, Masashiko
SATOH, Kimi
SHIDA, Shoko
SHIMIZU, Chisako
SHIOMI, Mieko
SUZUE, Mariko
TAKAMI, Toyoko
TAKASHIMA, Midori
TANAKA, Tomoko
TOYAMA, Michiko Françoise
TOYAMA, Mihoko
WATARI, Kyoko
YAMASHITA, Mika
YAMASHITA, Toyoko
YOGUCHI, Rie
YOSHIDA, Kazuko

JAVA
20th Century A.D.
BANDARA, Linda

KOREA
20th Century A.D.
HONG, Sung-Hee
KIM, Kwang-Hee
LEE, Chan-Hae
LEE, Hwaeja Yoo
LEE, Young Ja
MATURANO, Liliana Ester
OH, Sook Ja
PAGH-PAAN, Younghi
SUH, Kyung-Sun
YI, Heung-Yull

LITHUANIA
20th Century A.D.
BIELEFELD, Ljuba
LAUMYANSKENE, Elena Iono

MALTA
20th Century A.D.
MALLIA-PULVIRENTI, Josie

MEXICO
18th Century A.D.
DOLORES, Maria Francisca de los
RODRIGUES, Maria Joachina
19th Century A.D.
MOTTE, Nicola del
PERALTA CASTERA, Angela
20th Century A.D.
AGUDELO MURGUIA, Graciela
ALONSO, Julia
CANCINO DE CUEVAS, Sofia
CHARLES, Anna Maria
CRUZ, Sor Juana Ines de la
DIMARIAS, Esperanza
ELIAS, Graciela Morales de
GREVER, Maria
GURAIEB KURI, Rosa
HERRERA Y OGAZON, Alba

RENART, Marta Garcia
SORIA, Isobel
URRETA, Alicia
VAZQUEZ, Lilia
VIZCAINO, Gloria Tapia de

MONACO
17th Century A.D.
MARGARITA da Monaco

NETHERLANDS
17th Century A.D.
GEERTSOM, Joanne van
HOIJER, Anna Ovena
19th Century A.D.
AMERSFOORDT-DYK, Hermina
   Maria
BROES, Mlle.
GRAEVER, Madeleine
HORTENSE, Queen of Holland
LUND, Baroness van der
REES, Cathrine Felicie van
WILHELMJ, Maria
ZANTEN, Cornelia van
20th Century A.D.
ANDRIESSEN, Caecilia
APPELDOORN, Dina van
BEEKHUIS, Hanna
BELINFANTE-DEKKER, Martha
   Suzanna Betje
BESSEM, Saar
BEYERMAN-WALRAVEN, Jeanne
BOETZELAER, Josina Anna
   Petronella
BORDEWIJK-ROEPMAN, Johanna
BOSMANS, Henriette Hilda
BRANDELER, Henriette van
   Heukelom van den
BREMER, Marrie Petronella
BRINK-POTHUIS, Annie van den
CAMPAGNE, Conny
CHAPIRO, Fania
COCQ, Rosina Susanna de
COLACO OSORIO-SWAAB, Reine
DAHMEN, Mona Scholte
DIJK, Antoinette van
ELST, Nancy van der
HALL, Marleen van
HARTZER-STIBBE, Marie
HEMON, Sedje
HINLOPEN, Francina
HOENDERDOS, Margriet
JAMA, Agnes
KANT-BENEKER, H.
KLEBE, Willemijntje
KOOL, Rie
KRUITHOF VAN DIGGELEN, M.
KUYPER, Elizabeth
LAMBRECHTS-VOS, Anna Catharina
LENNEP, Henrietta van
LINDEN VAN SNELREWAARD-
   BOUDEWIJNS, Nelly van der
MAREZ-OYENS, Tera de
MESRITZ-VAN VELTHUYSEN, Annie
MONTIJN, Aleida
MULDER, Johanna Harmina Gerdina
MULDER, Maria Antonia
MURDOCH, Marjolijn
OOSTERZEE, Cornelia van
OVERMAN, Meta
RABER DE REINDERS, Esther
RENNES, Catharina van
SCHEEPERS-VAN DOMMELEN,
   Maria
TAL, Marjo
TENGBERGEN, Maria Elizabeth van
   Ebbenhorst
TIDEMAN-WIJERS, Bertha
TROOSTWYCK, Hendrika
TUSSENBROEK, Hendrika van
VAN DIJCK, Beatrice Madeleine

VAN EPEN-DE GROOT, Else Antonia
VETTER, Cato
VLADERACKEN, Geertruida van
VOLLENHOVEN, Hanna van
WAAL, Lies de
WEEL, Heleen van der
WEGENER-FRENSEL, Emmy Heil
WEGENER-KOOPMAN, Bertha
  Frensel
WERTHEIM, Rosy
WILDSCHUT, Clara
Century unknown
ZIEREN-FRANK, A.M.

NETHERLANDS EAST INDIES
20th Century A.D.
GESELSCHAP, Maria

NEW ZEALAND
20th Century A.D.
BELL, Dorothy
BIBBY, Gillian Margaret
BUCHANAN, Dorothy Quita
CASKIE, Helen
DANIELSON, Janet Rosalie
DELLA, Hinerangi
FALCONER, Bertha
FRANCHI, Dorothea
FREED, Dorothy Whitson
HENDERSON, Moya
HOBSON, Nancy
HULFORD, Denise Lovona
HUTTON, Florence Myra
KATENE-HORVATH, Dovey
KERR, Heather
LOCKWOOD, Annea Ferguson
McCALLUM, Nance
McDONAL, Carey
McDONALD, Kirsten
McDONALD, Marna Service
McGUIRE, Valerie
McLEOD, Jennifer Helen
MARTIN, Mary
MOON, Chloe Elizabeth
MOUNTFORT, Helen
OFFICER, Bronwyn Lee
PATTERSON, Andra
POLLARD, Bessie
SAARINEN, Gloria Edith
SANDERS, Joan
SCOTT, Dorothy
SHEPHERD, Doris
SHORE, Elaine
STEEL, Jeanette
STEVENS, Joan Frances
TE RANGI-PAI, Princess
WERNER, Tara Louise
WHITEHEAD, Gillian
WHITLOCK, E. Florence
WILSON, Alice

NIGERIA
20th Century A.D.
UCHENDU, Nellie Uzonna Edith

NORWAY
18th Century A.D.
ENGELBRETSDATTER, Dorthe
19th Century A.D.
BACKER-GROENDAHL, Agathe
  Ursula
BUGGE, Magda
CORMONTAN, Theodora
DEDEKAM, Sophie
EGEBERG, Anna
EGEBERG, Fredrikke Sophie
ENGER, Nelly
HEYERDAHL, Vally
NATHAN, Matilde Berendsen
STANG, Erika

20th Century A.D.
AAS, Else Berntsen
BAKKE, Ruth
BANG, Ragnhild
BJELKE-ANDERSEN, Olga
BODOM, Erica
CLEVE, Cissi
HALL, Pauline
HEBER, Judith
HEDSTROEM, Ase
HOLCK, Sine
HOLMBERG, Betty
HOLMSEN, Borghild
IRGENS, Sofie
JASTRZEBSKA, Anna
LINDEMAN, Anna Severine
LINDEMAN, Hjelle Signe
LOEVENSKJOLD, Hannah
LUND, Inger Bang
LUND, Signe
MARSTRANDER, Sigrid Borrensen
MOESTUE, Marie
MUNTHE, Margarethe
NORDRAAK-FEYLING, Gudrun
OERBECK, Anne-Marie
ORE, Cecilie
SCHJELDERUP, Mon Marie Gustava
SCHYTTE-JENSEN, Caroline
SKOUEN, Synne
SOENSTEVOLD, Maj
SOERLIE, Caroline Volla
TAPPER, Bertha
WAALER, Fredrikke Holtemann

PAKISTAN
20th Century A.D.
JEHAN, Noor
NAZLI, Shamin

PANAMA
20th Century A.D.
SAIZ-SALAZAR, Marina

PERU
19th Century A.D.
ARANCIBIA, Francisca
BENAVIDES, Elena
PLASENCIA, Ubalda
RABORG, Rosa Ortiz de Zerallos de
RAMOS, Eudocia
RIVERA, Eusebia
20th Century A.D.
ALARCO, Rosa
AYARZA DE MORALES, Rosa
  Mercedes
JIJON, Ines

PHILIPPINES
20th Century A.D.
ABEJO, Sister M. Rosalina
GAMILLA, Alice Doria
IMPERIAL, Ruth
KASILAG, Lucrecia R.
MACEDA, Corazon S.
MAQUISO, Elena G.
SANTIAGO-FELIPE, Vilma R.

POLAND
13th Century A.D.
HEDWIG, Sister
KUNEGUNDE, Queen
17th Century A.D.
CONSTANCE OF AUSTRIA, Queen of
  Poland
18th Century A.D.
CZARTORYSKA, Izabela de,
  Princess
JACOBSON, Henrietta
KIERNICKA, Anna
LESZCZYNSKA, Marie, Queen
SZCZUKA-JEZIERSKA
ZAMOYSKA, Zofia, Princess

19th Century A.D.
ACHMATOWICZOWA, Helena
BADARZEWSKA-BARANOWSKA,
  Tekla
BAJEROWA, Konstancje
BEYDALE, Cecile
BRZEZINSKA, Filipina
BRZOWSKA-MEJEAN, Jadwiga
CAETANI-RZEWUSKA, Calista,
  Princess
CHODKIEWICZ, Comtesse
CHRZASTOWSKA, Pelagia
CZETWERTYNSKA, Marie, Princess
CZETWERTYNSKA-JELOWICKA,
  Janina, Princess
DABROWSKA, Konstancja
DABROWSKA, Waleria
DLUZYNSKA, Zofia
FECHNER, Paulina
FILIPOWICZ, Elize-Minelli
GIZYCKA-ZAMOYSKA, Ludmilla,
  Countess
GLOWACKA, Ludwika
GNATKOWSKA, Paulina
GRABOWSKA, Clementine,
  Countess
GRISI. Mme.
GRODZICKA-RZEWUSKA, Julia
GROTTGEROWA, Krystyna
GWOZDECKA, Gabriela
JESKE-CHOINSKA-MIKORSKA,
  Ludmila
KISZWALTER, Adamina
KLETZINSKY, Adele
KOCHANOWSKA, Franciszka
KOMOROWSKA, Stephanie,
  Countess
KOSSAKOWSKA, Antonina
KOSSAKOWSKA, Wanda
KOWALOWSKA, Wiktoria
KRAINSKA, Justyna
KRYSINSKA, Maria
LATY, Mme.
LESSEL, Helena
LIPINSKA-PARCZEWSKA, Natalia
MARCINKIEWICZ, Kamilla
MARKOWSKA-GARLOWSKA, Eliza
MILASZEWSKA
MORACZEWSKA, Ksawara
NARBUTOWNA, Constance
NIEMIERZYC, Antonia
NIEWIAROWSKA-BRZOZOWSKA,
  Julia
PAPARA, Teodozja
PARIS, Salomea
PLATEROWA-BROEL-ZYBERK,
  Maria
POLANOWSKA, Teofila
POPLAWSKA, Maria Paulina
POTOCKA-PILAVA, Laura
RADZIWILL, Princess
ROZWADOWSKI, Contessa Raffaela
RUCINSKA, Lucja
STALEWSKA, Jadwiga
SUMOWSKA, Helena
SZTARAY, Margit
SZUMINSKA, Flora
SZYMANOWSKA, Maria Agata
VESVALI, Felicita
WITKOWSKA-JABLONSKA, Maria
WUERTEMBERSKA-CZARTOR
  YSKA, Maria, Duchess
ZAGRODZKA, Eugenia
ZAMOYSKA, Maria
ZBYSZEWSKA-OLECHNOWSKA,
  Maria
20th Century A.D.
ACHMATOWICZ-KRYCZYNSKA,
  Maria
ALLINOWNA, Stefania
ANDRZEJOWSKA, Alina

BACEWICZ, Grazyna
BANCER, Teresa Barbara
BIALKIEWICZOWNA-ANDRAULT DE
  LANGERON, Irena
BIEDRZYCKA, Helena
BIELICKA, Eugenia
BORKOWICZ, Maria
BREDOW, Maria de
BRUZDOWICZ, Joanna
BRZOZOWSKA, U.
BUCZEK, Barbara Kazimiera
BURZYNSKA, Jadwiga
CHOJNOWSKA, Zofia
CIESLAKOWNA, Maria
CWIORI, Barbara
CZAPLICKA, J.
DORABIALSKA, Julia Helena
DREGE-SCHIELOWA, Lucja
DUBANOWICZ, Wanda
DUCZMAL-JAROSZEWSKA,
  Agnieszka
DZIELSKA, Jadwiga
DZIEWULSKA, Maria Amelia
GAERTNER, Katarzyna
GAJDECZKA, S.
GARR, Wieslawa
GARSCIA-GRESSEL, Janina
GARSTKA, Ewa
GARZTECKA-JARZEBSKA, Irena
GEISTLENER, Barbara
GNUS, Ryta
GREWE SOBOLEWSKA, Mme.
GROBICKA, Eugenia
GRZADZIELOWNA, Eleonora
HAENDEL, Ida
HUSSAR, Malgorzata
ISZKOWSKA, Zofia
IVANOWSKA-PLOSZKO-OSSEN-
DOWSKA, Zofia
JANOTHA, Natalia
KACZURBINA-ZDZIECHOWSKA,
  Maria
KAMINSKA, Wiktoria
KIELANOWSKI, Alina
KLECHNIOWSKA, Anna Maria
KOMIAZYK, Magdalena
KOSSAKOWSKA, Wiktoryna
KRASINSKA, Karolina
KROKIEWICZOWA, Apolonia
KRUSZEWSKA, Zofia
KRZANOWSKA, Grazyna
KRZYZANOWSKA, Halina
KWIATKOWSKA-MARCZYK,
  Krystina
LACHOWSKA, Stefania
LANDOWSKA, Wanda
LESNIEWICZOWA, Iza
LOPUSKA-WYLEZYNSKA, Helena
LUBICZ-DZIERZBICKA, Zofia
MARKIEWICZOWNA, Wladyslawa
MATUSZCZAK, Bernadetta
MODRAKOWSKA, M.
MOSZUMANSKA-NAZAR, Krystyna
MURAWSKA, Marietta
MYSZINSKA-WOJCIECHOWSKA,
  Leokadia
NAIMSKA, Joanna
NIEWIADOMSKA, Barbara
OBTULOWICZ, Zofia
OTTAWOWA, Helena
PFEIFFER, Irena
PIECHOWSKA, Alina
PLISZKA RAMSEWICZOWA,
  Katarzyna
PODGORSKA, Ewa
PREYSS, Adelina
PRUSIECKA, Jadwiga
PSTROKONSKA-NAVRATIL,
  Grazyna Hanna
PTASZYNSKA, Marta
RADOSZEWSKA, A.J.

RUPNIEWSKA, Janina
SARNECKA, Jadwiga
SCHAGER-LATACZOWA, Wanda
SCHOPPIG-PIOTROWSKA, Claire
SCHULTZOWA, Barbara
SIKORA, Elzbieta
SKALSKA-SZEMIOTH, Hanna Wanda
SKIRBINSKA, Wladyslawa
SKOWRONSKA, Janina
SLIWINSKA, Josefa
SLOCZYNSKA, Cecylia
SMOLSKA, Jolanta
STAWOWY, Ludomira
STERNICKA-NIEKRASZOWA, Ilza
SULKOVSKA, Eliza
SUPINSKA J.
SUSZCZYNSKA, Anna
SYNOWIEC, Ewa
SZADURSKA, W.
SZAJNA-LEWANDOWSKA, Jadwiga
  Helena
SZALITOWNA, Paulina
SZPINTER-KINIECKA, Maria
SZYMANSKA, Iwonka Bogumila
TARGONSKA, Izabela
TARNOWSKA, Julia
TOKARSKA, Emilia
TREBICKA, Maria
TUSOWSKA-SKRZETUSKA, M.
UHL, Danuta
URBAYI-KRASNODEBSKA, Zofia
  Jadwiga
VORBOND, Wanda
WANSKA, Anna
WASIAKOWA, M.
WASOWSKA-BADOWSKA, Maria
WOLSKA, Aleksandra Aniela
ZAKRZEWSKA-NIKIPORCZYK,
  Barbara Maria
ZDZIENNICKA, Zofia
ZIELINSKA, Lidia

PORTUGAL
  10th Century A.D.
    ASSUNCÃO, Sister Arcangela Maria
    de
  16th Century A.D.
    DE CASTRO, Maria
    SILVA, Helena Da
  17th Century A.D.
    LACERDA, Bernarda Ferreira de
  18th Century A.D.
    ARCANGELA-MARIA, Sister
    MARIA TERESA BARBARA DE
    BRAGANCA, Queen of Spain
  19th Century A.D.
    BORGES, Deolinda Eulalia Cordeiro
    COSSOUL, Genoveva Virginia
    DE SOUSA HOLSTEIN, Donna Teresa
    LARCHER, Maria Amalia
    PROENCA-A-VELVHA, Countess
    PUSICH, D. Antonia Gertrudes
    RIBAS, Medina N.
    VEGA, Paulina
    WAGNER, Virginia De Oliveira
    Bastos
  20th Century A.D.
    ALVES DE SOUSA, Berta Candida
    BENOIT, Francine Germaine Van
    Gool
    BORBOM, Maria de Melo Furtado
    Caldeira Giraldes
    CABREIRA, Estefania Loureiro de
    Vasconcelos Leao
    CAPDEVILLE, Constanca
    CHAVES, Laura da Fonseca
    COELHO, Ernestine Leite
    DE FREITAS, Elvira Manuela
    Fernandez
    FRONDONI LACOMBE, Madalena
    LIMA CRUZ, Maria Antonietta de

MARQUES, Laura Wake
MARTINS, Maria de Lourdes
PAVIA DE MAGALHAES, Isaura
POLICARPO TEIXEIRA, Maria
  Margarida Fernandes
TRAVASSOS LOPES, Maria de
  Lourdes Alves
VASCONCELOS, Maria Regina
  Quintanilha de

PUERTO RICO
  20th Century A.D.
    ALEJANDRO-DE LEON, Esther
    ARTEAGA, Genoveva de
    DELIZ, Monserrate
    FERRER OTERO, Monsita
    Monserrate
    RIVERA, Graciela

RUMANIA
  19th Century A.D.
    ASACHI, Elena
    BOCK, Bertha
  20th Century A.D.
    ALEXANDRA, Liana
    ATHANASIU-GARDEEV, Esmeralda
    BADIAN, Maya
    BARBERIS, Mansi
    BENTIA, Ana
    BRATU, Emma
    CASSIAN, Nina
    CHEFALIADY-TEBAN, Maria
    CIOBANU, Maia
    CONSTANTINESCU, Domnica
    CORNEA-IONESCU, Alma
    DASCALESCU, Camelia
    DIMITRIU, Florica
    DINESCU, Violeta
    DONCEANU, Felicia
    ERDELY, Isolda
    GHIKA-COMANESTI, Ioana
    GRUNBERG, Janeta
    JEREA, Hilda
    MARBE, Myriam
    MARINESCU-SCHAPIRA, Ilana
    NEMTEANU-ROTARU, Doina
    ODAGESCU, Irina
    PETRA-BASACOPOL, Carmen
    POPOVICI, Elise
    RACOVITZA-FLONDOR, Florica
    RADULESCU-VLAD, Sofia
    SAINT-GEORGES, Didia
    SUTZU, Rodica
    TAUTU, Cornelia
    VALEANU, Elisa
    VLAD, Marina
    XENOPOL, Margareta

RUSSIA, BEFORE 1917
  17th Century A.D.
    CHURAI, Marusya
  18th Century A.D.
    DASHKOVA, Ekaterina Romanovna,
    Princess
    MAIER, Catherine
  19th Century A.D.
    ADAJEWSKY, Ella
    ADAMOWITSCH, Elisabeth
    ALEXANDRA JOSEPHOWNA, Grand
    Duchess
    ALEXANDROVA, A.
    CHERTKOVA, A.
    DANILEVSKAYA, V.
    DUPORT, Marie
    GORYAINOVNA, A.
    JANINA, Olga
    KOCHETOVA, Aleksandra
    Dorimedontovna
    KONTSKI, Eugenie de
    KOTSBATREVSKAYA
    LINEVA, Yevgeniya Eduardovna

MARIA PAULOWNA, Grand Duchess
of Weimar
NIKOLSKY, Mlle.
OLGA, Grand Duchess
PURGOLD, Nadezhda Nikolayevna
RADECKI, Olga von
ROSE
RUDERSDORF, Erminie
SALOMONI, Mlle.
SEROVA, Valentina Semyonovna
SHASHINA, Elizaveta Sergeyevna
SLAVYANSKAYA, Olga
Khristoforovna Agreneva
TSCHITSCHERIN, Theodosia de
VORONTSOVA, M.
YAKUBOVITCH, Elizaveta
20th Century A.D.
CHICHERINA, Sofia Nikolayevna
DIMENTMAN, Esfir Moiseyevna
ERDELI, Xenia Alexandrovna
GAIGEROVA, Varvara Andrianovna
GALIKIAN, Susanna Avetisovna
GARUTA, Lucia Yanovna
GNESINA, Yelena Fabianovna
GOLUB, Martha Naumovna
GUSEINZADE, Adilia Gadzhi Aga
HOFFMANN-BEHRENDT, Lydia
IORDAN, Irina Nikolayevna
IVANOVA, Lidia
KASHPEROVA, Elizaveta Vadimovna
KASHPEROVA, Leokadia
Alexandrovna
KESAREVA, Margarita
Alexandrovna·
KOMPANUETS, Lidia
KOSHETZ, Nina
MESHKO, Nina
NAIKHOVICH-LOMAKINA, Fania
Filippovna
NAZAROVA, Tatiana Borisovna
NURPEISSOVA, Dina
RAMM, Valentina Iosifovna
ROMM, Rosalina Davidovna
RUBIN, Basia Izrailevna
SALIUTRINSKAYA, Tatiana
SHASUTDINOVA, Maira
SKUDRA, Ruta Evaldova
STEPANOVA, V.

SLOVAKIA, BEFORE 1918
19th Century A.D.
CZICZKA, Angela
20th Century A.D.
BOESGAARDOVA-SCHMIDTOVA,
Lydie
DRDOVA, Marie
DREVJANA, Anna
EMINGEROVA, Katerina
FALLADOVA-SKVOROVA, Anežka
REISSEROVA, Julie
RYLEK-STANKOVA, Blažena

SOUTH AFRICA
19th Century A.D.
NEUMANN, Elizabeth
STEWART, Elizabeth Kirby
20th Century A.D.
ALLEN, Denise
ARNOLD, Rosanna Luisa Swann
BARKER, Phyllis Elizabeth
BRICE, Jean Anne
BURGER, Hester Aletta Sophie
BURTON, Pixie
COPLEY, Maria Kriel
CRAIB, Doris
DE VILLIERS, Justina Wilhelmina
Nancy
EAGAR, Fannie Edith Starke
EGNOS, Bertha
FRANGS, Irene
GERSTMAN, Blanche Wilhelminia

HART, Alice Maud
HARVEY, Eva Noel
JOLLY, Margaret Anne
KEARNY, Moira
KING, Rebecca Clift
KRUGER, Catharina Maria
LAPIN, Lily
LAVOIPIERRE, Therese
LOOTS, Joyce Mary Ann
MAGENTA, Maria
MAGOGO KA DINIZULU, Constance,
Princess
MARAIS, Abelina Jacoba
MEARS, Caroline
MICHELOW, Sybil
MIEROWSKA, Jean
NEPGEN, Rosa Sophia Cornelia
NEWMAN, Adelaide
NIAY, Apolline
RAW, Vera Constance
RORICH, Mary
RUDOLPH, Anna
SCHNEIDER, June
SERTIMA, Theresia Elizabeth van
SHUTTLEWORTH, Anne-Marie
TACK, Annie
UNDERWOOD, Frances Evangeline
VAN AARDT, Madelene
VAN DER MARK, Maria
WEBB, Helen
WESSELS, Judith Brent
WESSELS, Marlene
WHITTINGTON, Joan
ZAIDEL-RUDOLPH, Jeanne

SPAIN
11th Century A.D.
QASMUNA
13th Century A.D.
PEREZ, Maria
15th Century A.D.
ALEGRE, Gracieuse
GONZAGA, Margherita
PINAR, Florencia del
16th Century A.D.
TERESA
TOLETANA, Angela Sygaea
17th Century A.D.
ESCAMILLA, Manuela de
18th Century A.D.
AGUDIEZ, Eliza
19th Century A.D.
BUIXO, Paulina
FERNANDEZ DE LA MORA, Pilar
GONZALEZ, Dona Paz
LANUZA Y VAZQUEZ, Agustina
LEONARD, Antonia Sitcher de Mendi
MENA, Carolina
MENTES, Maria
MUNGAY Y PIZARRO, Dona Carolina
PRECIADOS Y MANESCAU, Cecilia
RODRIGO, Maria
ROSALES, Cecilia
SANCHEZ DE LA MADRID,
Ventura
VALERO, Matilde
VEDRUNA, Dolores
VELA DE ARNÃO, Sofia
ZAPATER, Rosaria
20th Century A.D.
BARRIENTOS, Maria
BOFILL, Anna
BORRAS I FORNELL, Teresa
BROCA, Carmen L. de
CALVO-MANZANO, Maria Rosa
CAMPMANY, Montserrat
CAPDEVILA I GAYA, Merce
CAPSIR-TANZI, Mercedes
CARMEN MARINA
CASAGEMAS, Luisa
CHACON LASAUCA, Emma

CHEVALLIER SUPERVIELLE, Marie
Louise
DA SILVA, Adelaide
FARGA PELLICER, Onia
FREIXAS Y CRUELLS, Narcisa
GARCIA ASCOT, Rosa
GUELL, Elizabeth
GUELL, Maria Luisa
IBANEZ, Carmen
JAQUETTI ISANT, Palmira
KARR Y DE ALFONSETTI, Carmen
LLUNELL SANAHUJA, Pepita
LOPEZ Y PENA, Maria del Carmen
MADRIGUERA RODON, Paquita
MATEU, Maria Cateura
MILA, Leonora
MIRET, Emilia
MURILLO CABALLERO, Juliana
OLLER BENLLOCH, Maria Teresa
OZAITA, Maria Luisaria Luisa
PABLOS CEREZO, Maria de
PELEGRI, Maria Teresa
PEY CASADO, Diana
PONSA, Maria Luisa
PRIETO, Maria Teresa
PUCHE, Sofia
REBULL, Teresa
REIS, Manuela Cancio
ROLDES FREIXES, Mercedes
ROMERO BARBOSA, Elena
SALVADOR, Matilde
SANTOJA, Mari Carmen
TORRENS, Merce
ZUBELDIA, Emiliana de

SRI LANKA
20th Century A.D.
FERNANDO, Sarathchandra
Vichremadithya
PEREIRA, Diana Maria

SUMERIA
30th Century B.C.
INANNA
24th Century B.C.
ENHEDUANNA

SURINAM
20th Century A.D.
KENSWIL, Atma

SWEDEN
18th Century A.D.
OLIN, Elizabeth
19th Century A.D.
AARUP, Caia
BROOMAN, Hanna
EUGENIE, Charlotte Augusta Amalia
Albertina, Princess
GYLLENHAAL, Matilda Valeriana
Beatrix, Duchess of Orozco
HAXTHAUSEN, Aurore M.G.Ch. von
HJORT, Thecla
HOLMBERG, Emelie Augusta
Kristina
JOSEPHINE, Queen of Sweden and
Norway
KYNTZELL-HAGSTROMER, Louise
LIND, Jenny
LUNDBERG, Ada
MYRBERG, Anne Sophie
NYSTROEM, Elisabeth
PEYRON, Albertina Fredrika
RIDDERSTOLPE, Caroline Johanna
Lovisa
RON, Helene de
RONTGEN, Amanda
SAHLBERG, Alma
STENHAMMAR, Fredrika
TAMMELIN, Bertha
THEGERSTROEM, Hilda Aurora

THERESE, Princess of Saxe-
    Altenburg and of Sweden
WERNER, Hildegard
WICKMAN, Fredrika
20th Century A.D.
ALMEN, Ruth
ANDREE, Elfrida
AULIN, Laura Valborg
BARKLUND, Irma L.
BERGMAN, Ellen
BERGSTROM, Anna
BRODIN, Lena Birgitta Elise
DOMINIQUE, Monica
EMANUELSON, Elsa
HAMMARBERG-AKESSON, Sonja
HEIBERG, Ella
HYLIN, Birgitta Charlotta Kristina
JEPPSSON, Kerstin Maria
KRULL, Diana
KULLIN, Marta
LIEDBERGIUS, Camilla
MALMLOEF-FORSSLING, Carin
MELL, Gertrud Maria
MUENTZING, Paula
MUNKTELL, Helena Mathilda
NILSSON, Christine
NORDENFELT, Dagmar
NORDENSON, Ruth
NORLING, Signe
NORRE, Dorcas
OHLSSON, Grettel
OHLSSON, Sarah
PEGELOW, Hanna G.
RAHMN, Elza Loethner
REHNQVIST, Karin Birgitta
ROOTH, Anna-Greta
SANDELS, Ellen
SCHONE, Elna
STOBEAUS, Kristina
STROMBERG, Ruth
STUART-BERGSTROM, Elsa
    Marianne
TEGNER, Alice Charlotte
WELANDER, Svea Goeta
WENNERBERG-REUTER, Sara
    Margareta Eugenia Euphrosyne
WENTZ-JANACEK, Elisabet
WIKSTROM, Inger

SWITZERLAND
12th Century A.D.
SEIDENWEBERIN, Metzi
18th Century A.D.
CHARRIERE, Isabella Agneta
    Elisabeth de
VIELANDA, Mengia
19th Century A.D.
BECKER, Ida
CERRINI DE MONTE-VARCHI,
    Anna von
CONSTANT, Rosalie de
GERING, Karoline
HUENERWADEL, Fanny
KIRCHER, Maria Bertha
LAVATER, Magdalena Elisabeth
20th Century A.D.
AESCHLIMANN-ROTH, Esther
ALIOTH, Marguerite
BAADER-NOBS, Heidi
BARBE, Henriette
BARBLAN-OPIENSKA, Lydia
BAUD, Madeleine
BIRCHER-REY, Hedy
BOSCH Y PAGES, Luisa
BREGUET, May
BRUGGMANN, Heidi
BRUNNER, Maria
CALAME, Genevieve
DACH, Charlotte von
DALBERT, Anny
DE PURY, Marianne

DUBOIS, V.
EGLI, Johanna
EICHENWALD, Sylvia
GENTIL, Alice
GEYMULLER, Marguerite
    Camille-Louise de
HEGNER, Anna
HELBLING, Elsa
HOFER-SCHNEEBERGER, Emma
IRMAN-ALLEMANN, Regina
JENNY, Sister Leonore
KAESER-BECK, Aida
LAGO
LOHR, Ina
LUTHI-WEGMANN, Elvira
MERLI-ZWISCHENBRUGGER,
    Christina
MUELLER-WELTI, Hedwig
NIEDERBERGER, Maria A.
PERONNE, Pauline
PEYROT, Fernande
RADERMACHER, Erika
RICHNER-HEIM, Erika
ROCHAT, Andrée
ROESGEN-CHAMPION, Marguerite
    Sara
RUEGGER, Charlotte
RYBNER, Dagmar de Corval
SALQUIN, Hedy
SAUTER, Maya
SCHARLI, Ruth
SCHERCHEN, Tona
SCHUBARTH, Dorothé
SPOENDLIN, Elisabeth
SPOERRI-RENFER, Anna-Marga-
    retha
TAUBER, Lotti
TOBLER, Mina
VOELLMY-LIECHTI, Grety
WEGMANN-BOLOZE, N.
WEINGARTNER-STUDER, Carmen
WITZIG, Louise
ZIMMERMANN, Margrit

TRINIDAD & TOBAGO
20th Century A.D.
SPOONER, Dorothy Harley

TURKEY
18th Century A.D.
KALFA, Dilhayat
19th Century A.D.
HANIM, Durri Nigar
20th Century A.D.
GAZAROSSIAN, Koharik
HANIM, Leyla
HANIM, Tamburi Faize
KADIZADE, Celal
KAZANDJIAN, Sirvart
KIP, Yuksel
KOKDES, Veveser
KOPTAGEL, Yuksel
OSMANOGLU, Gevheri
OZDENSES, Semahat
PARS, Melahat
SCARPA, Eugenia
SULTAN, Aishe
SULTAN, Fatma
SULTAN, Hatidje
TARIHI, Kamu Yarari Karar

UNITED KINGDOM
18th Century A.D.
BARTHELEMON, Cecilia Maria
BARTHELEMON, Mary
BOYD, Elisabeth
CAMPBELL, Caroline
CANTELO, Anne
CARVER, Miss
CASSON, Margaret
CATLEY, Anne

CAVENDISH, Georgiana
CLARKE, Jane
CLARKSON, Jane
COSWAY, Maria Cecilia Louise
CROUCH, Anna Maria
CUMBERLAND, Mrs. William
DALL, Miss
DAWSON, Nancy
DE GAMBARINI, Elisabetta
ESSEX, Margaret
FLEMING, Lady
GUEST, Jeanne Marie
HARDING, Elizabeth
HARLOW, Clarissa
HODGES, Ann Mary
HOFFMANN, Miss J.
HUDSON, Mary
HUNTER, Henrietta Elizabeth
JORDAN, Mrs.
KNIGHT, Julia Baylis
MacINTOSH, Mary
MELLISH, Miss
MORE, Isabella Theaker
MURRAY, Lady Edith
PARKER, Mrs.
PHILHARMONICA, Mrs.
POOLE, Caroline
POOLE, Maria
POWNALL, Mary Ann
REYNOLDS, Marie Hester
RICHMOND, Heiress
SAVAGE, Jane
STEEL, Ann
STIRLING, Magdalene
THICKNESSE, Miss
TURNER, Eliza
TURNER, Elizabeth
VALENTINE, Ann
WILBRAHAM, Mrs.
WILHELMINA, Caroline of Anspach
WILKINS, Elizabeth
WORGAN, Mary
19th Century A.D.
ABBOTT, Jane
ABRAMS, Harriet
ADAMS, Sarah
ALEXANDER, Mrs. Cecil Frances
ALSOP, Frances
AMES, Mary Mildred
AMES, Mrs. Henry
ANDREWS, Jenny
ANSPACH, Elizabeth, Margravine of
ARKWRIGHT, Mrs. Robert
ARMSTRONG, Annie
ASTLE-ALLAM, Agnes Mary
AUSTEN, Augusta Amherst
AYLWARD, Florence
BACHE, Constance
BAILY, Mrs. James S.
BARKER, Laura Wilson
BARNARD, Charlotte
BARNETT, Emma
BARTHOLOMEW, Ann Sheppard
BARTHOLOMEW, Mrs. M.
BARTLETT, Agnes
BEARDSMORE, Mrs.
BENINGFIELD, Ethel
BINFIELD, Hanna R.
BISSET, Elizabeth Anne
BLEWIT, Gionata
BORTHWICK, Jane Laurie
BORTON, Alice
BOUNDY, Kate
BOYCE, Ethel Mary
BRAY, Anna Eliza
BRINE, Mary D.
BRONTE, Anne
BROWN, Caroline Curtis
BRYAN, Mrs. M.A.
BUTLER, Mary
CAMPBELL, Mary Maxwell

CANTELLO, Annie
CAREW, Lady Henry
CARTWRIGHT, Mrs. Robert
CASPERS, Agnes B.
CHAMBERLAYNE, Edith A.
CIANCHETTINI, Veronica Elisabeth
CLARKE, Jessie Murray
CLAY, Melesina
COLE, Charlotte
COLLETT, Sophia Dobson
COOK, Eliza
CORRI-DUSSEK, Sofia Giustina
CRAMENT, J. Maude
DAVIES, Llewela
DAVIS, Marianne
DAVIS, Miss
DE LACKNER, Mrs.
DIBDIN, Isabelle Perkins
DICK, Edith A.
DICKSON, Ellen
DUFFERIN, Lady Helen Selina
EATON, Frances
ELLIOTT, Charlotte
EUAN-SMITH, Lady
FARE, Florence
FARMER, Emily Bardsley
FARNINGHAM, Marianne
FINCH, Miss
FLOWER, Eliza
FORREST, Margret
FORTEY, Mary Comber
FOWLER, Eliza
FOWLES, Margaret F.
GABRIEL, Mary Ann Virginia
GADE, Margaret
GIBSON, Isabella Mary
GIBSON, Louisa
GILBERT, Florence
GOODEVE, Mrs. Arthur
GORE, Katharina
GRAY, Louisa
GREATOREX, Martha
GREENE, Edith
GROOM, Mrs.
GYDE, Margaret
HACKETT, Marie
HAGUE, Harriet
HAMPDEN, Elizabeth
HARRADEN, Beatrice
HARTLAND, Lizzie
HAVERGAL, Frances Ridley
HAWES, Maria
HAYES, Mrs.
HOLLAND, Caroline
HOLMES, Mary
HUNTER, Anne
INVERARITY, Eliza
IRVINE, Jessie Seymour
KALLEY, Sara Poulton
KEMBLE, Adelaide
KERR, Louisa
KINGSTON, Marie Antoinette
KNYVETT, Mrs. Edmund
LAMBERT, Agnes
LANGRISHE, May Katherine
LAWRENCE, Elizabeth S.
LEHMANN, Amelia
LIGHTFOOT, Mils
LINDSAY, Miss M.
LINWOOD, Mary
LLANOVER, Lady
LODER, Kate Fanny
LONSDALE, Eva
LOWTHIAN, Caroline
MACIRONI, Clara Angela
MADDISON, Adele
MALLARD, Clarisse
MARSHALL, Florence A.
MARSHALL, Mrs. William
MASSON, Elizabeth
MILLAR, Marian

MILLARD, Mrs. Philip
MITFORD, Eliza
MONCRIEFF, Lynedock
MOODY, Marie
MORGAN, Lady
MOUNSEY, Elizabeth
MULLEN, Adelaide
MUNDELLA, Emma
NAIRNE, Carolina, Baroness
NEWCOMBE, Georgeanne
NEWTON, Adelaide
NORTON, Caroline Elizabeth
   Sarah
NORTON, The Hon. Mrs.
NOVELLO, Mary Sabilla
NUNN, Elizabeth Annie
OCKLESTON-LIPPA, Katherine
OLDHAM, Emily
O'LEARY, Rosetta
OLIVER, Mary
ORGER, Caroline
OSTIERE, May
PARK, Jane
PARKE, Maria Hester
PARKYNS, Beatrice
PATON, Mary Anne
PENNA, Catherine
PHILP, Elizabeth
PRATTEN, Mrs. Robert Sidney
PRESCOTT, Oliveria Louisa
PYNE, Louisa Aubert
RADNOR, Helen, Countess of
RALPH, Kate
RAMSAY, Lady Katherine
RAWLINSON, Angela
RICHINGS, Caroline
RIGHTON, Mary
ROBERTSON, Mrs.
ROBINSON, Fanny
ROECKEL, Jane
SAFFERY, Eliza
SAINTON-DOLBY, Charlotte
   Helen
SALE, Sophia
SANDERS, Alma
SCOTT, Lady John Douglas
SHELLEY, Mary Wollstonecraft
SHERRINGTON, Grace
SHERRINGTON, Helena Lemmens
SKINNER, Florence Marian
SLEIGH, Mrs.
SMART, Harriet Anne
SMITH, Alice Mary
SMITH, Laura Alexandrine
SQUIRE, Hope
STEPHENSON, Maria Theresa
STIRLING, Elizabeth
SWEPSTONE, Edith
SYNGE, Mary Helena
TAITE, Annie
TENNYSON, Emily Sarah, Lady
THIRKLEBY, Laura Taylor
THOMAS, Adelaide Louise
THOMPSON, Alexandra
THORNE, Beatrice
TORRENS, Grace
TOWNSEND, Pearl Dea Etta
TREW, Susan
TROWBRIDGE, Leslie Eliot
VON HOFF, Elizabeth
WAKEFIELD, Augusta Mary
WARD, Clementine
WARD, Kate Lucy
WATSON, Regina
WENSLEY, Frances Foster
WEST, Lottie
WESTROP, Kate
WHITE, Maude Valerie
WICKINS, Florence
WILLIAMS, Nora Osborne
WILSON, Hilda

WILSON, Mrs. Cornwall Baron
WOODFORDE-FINDEN, Amy
WOOLF, Sophia Julia
WRIGHT, Agnes
WRIGHT, Ellen
WURM, Mary J.A.
YEATMAN, Ethel
YOUNG, Harriet Maitland

20th Century A.D.
ACOCK, Gwendolyn
ADAIR, Yvonne Madeleine
AINLEY, Julie
AINSCOUGH, Juliana Mary
ALDRIDGE, Amanda Ira
ALLITSEN, Frances
ANDERSON, Avril
ANTHONY, Evangeline
ARKWRIGHT, Marian Ursula
ATKINSON, Dorothy
AXTENS, Florence
AYLOTT, Lydia Georgina Edith
BAGA, Ena Rosina
BAILEY, Freda
BAILEY, Judith Margaret
BAILY, Margaret Naismith Osborne
BAIRD, Edith Anna
BAIRD, Irene
BARCROFT, E. Dorothea
BARNES, Anna
BARNS, Ethel
BARRATT, Carol Ann
BARRELL, Joyce Howard
BARTLETT, Ethel Agnes
BATE, Jennifer
BAYLIS, Lilian Mary
BEAT, Janet Eveline
BEATRICE, Mary Victoria Feodore,
   Princess of Battenberg
BERTRAM, Madge
BILLINGTON, Elizabeth
BILTCLIFFE, Florence
BINGHAM, Judith
BIRKETT, Gwenhilda Mary
BLEWITT, Lorna
BLOCKSIDGE, Kathleen Mary
BOOSEY, Beatrice Joyce
BRADSHAW, Susan
BRAGGINS, Daphne Elizabeth
BRAND, Margaret
BRIGHT, Dora Estella
BROADWOOD, Lucy E.
BROWN, Rosemary
BROWN, Veronica
BRUCKSHAW, Kathleen
BULL, Patricia
BURRELL, Dianne
BURSEY, Rosetta
CARMICHAEL, Mary Grant
CARRIVICK, Olive Amelia
CARROL, Ida Gertrude
CARSWELL, Francis
CARTER, Rosetta
CARWITHEN, Doreen
CHANDLER, Mary
CHAPMAN, Joyce
CLARK, June
CLARKE, Emily
CLARKE, Rebecca
CLAYTON, Susan
COCKING, Frances M. Hefford
COHEN, Harriet
COLEMAN, Ellen
COLERIDGE-TAYLOR, Avril
   Gwendolen
COOKE, Edith
COOPMAN, Rosalie
CORRI, Ghita
COWL, Doreen
COX, Alison Mary
COX, Sally
CREES, Kathleen Elsie

CRISWICK, Mary
DAIKEN, Melanie
DALE, Kathleen
DALE, Phyllis
DANIELS, Nellie
DARE, Margaret Marie
DAVENPORT GOERTZ, Gladys
DAVIES, Eiluned
DAVIES, Margaret
DE LARA, Adelina
DE LYLE, Carlyon
DEL RIEGO, Theresa
DERBYSHIRE, Delia
DICK, Ethel A.
DINN, Freda
DOLMETSCH, Cecile
DONIACH, Shula
DOROW, Dorothy
DRING, Madeleine
DUNLOP, Isobel
EARLEY, Judith
EGGAR, Katharine
ELLICOTT, Rosalind Frances
ELLIS, Vivian
ELWYN-EDWARDS, Dilys
ERHART, Dorothy
EVANS, Patricia Margaret
FAGANDINI, Maddalena
FAULKNER, Elizabeth
FELIX, Margery Edith
FISHER, Charlotte Eleanor
FLOWER, Amelia Matilda
FORSTER, Dorothy
FOSTER, Cecily
FOX, Charlotte
FOX, Erika
FOX, Kalitha Dorothy
FRASER, Shena Eleanor
FRAZER, Mrs. Allan H.
FRICKER, Anne
FRIEDBERG, Patricia Ann
FULCHER, Ellen Georgina
FURZE, Jessie
GIPPS, Ruth
GLATZ, Helen Sinclair
GLYN, Margaret Henriette
GODDARD, Arabella
GODWIN-FOSTER, Dorothy
GOMM, Elizabeth
GOODWIN, Amina Beatrice
GOOSSENS, Marie Henriette
GOULD, Doris
GOULD, Janetta
GRAHAM, Janet Christine
GREENE, Pauline
GREENFIELD, Marjorie
HALL, Beatrice Mary
HAMER, Janice
HARRADEN, R. Ethel
HARRIS, Dorothy
HARRISON, Annie Fortescue
HARRISON, Pamela
HAWARDEN, Caroline Anna May
    Oyle, Viscountess
HEALE, Helene
HELYER, Marjorie
HIND O'MALLEY, Pamela
HO, Wai On
HOLLAND, Ruby
HOLLINS, Dorothea
HOLLWAY, Elizabeth L.
HOLST, Imogen Clare
HORROCKS, Amy Elsie
HOWELL, Dorothy
HUBICKI, Margaret Olive
HUGH-JONES, Elaine
HUME, Phyllis
HUNTER, Hilda
HYDE, Cicely
JACKSON, Barbara May
JARRATT, Lita

JOHNSTON, Alison Aileen Annie
JONES-DAVIES, Maude
JUDD, Margaret Evelyn
KAHN, Esther
KEAL, Minna
KELLY, Denise Maria Anne
KEMP-POTTER, Joan
KENNEDY-FRASER, Marjory
KERCHER, Eleanor
KIRKBY-MASON, Barbara
KIRKWOOD, Antoinette
KISCH, Eve
KLEIN, Ivy Frances
KNIGHT, Judyth
LAMBELET, Vivienne Ada Maurice
LANE, Elizabeth
LARKIN, Deirdre
LAST, Joan Mary
LAWRENCE, Emily M.
LEE, Michelle
LEES, Christine Brown
LEFANU, Nicola Frances
LEGINSKA, Ethel
LEHMAN, R.
LEHMANN, Liza
LIDDELL, Claire
LINFORD, Shirley Ann
LITTLEJOHN, Joan Anne
LONGWORTH, Helen
LOWENSTEIN, Gunilla Marike
LOWTHER, T.
LUCAS, Mary Anderson
LUFF, Enid
LUTTRELL, Moira
LUTYENS, Elisabeth
LYELL, Margaret
MACONCHY, Elizabeth
MacFARREN, Emma Marie
McALLISTER, Rita
McGILL, Gwendolen Mary Finlayson
McQUATTIE, Sheila
MAIRE, Jacqueline
MARSHALL, M.E.
MASON, Gladys Amy
MAY, Florence
MENDOZA, Anne
MEREDITH, Margaret
MILDREN, Margaret Joyce
MILKINA, Nina
MILNE, Helen C.
MOODY, Pamela
MORE, Margaret Elizabeth
MORGAN, Maud
MORISON, Christina W.
MORLEY, Angela
MOSELEY, Caroline Carr
MOSS, Katie
MUKLE, May Henrietta
MURDOCH, Elaine
MURRAY, Margaret
MUSGRAVE, Thea
NASH, Phyllis V.
NEEDHAM, Alicia Adelaide
NEWPORT, Doreen
NIECKS, Christina
NOVELLO-DAVIES, Clara
OLIVE, Vivienne
ORAM, Daphne Blake
ORTMANS, Kay Muriel
OWEN, Morfydd Llwyn
PAIN, Eva
PALMER, Florence Margaret
    Spencer
PALMER, Jane Hetherington
PARKE, Dorothy
PARKER, Phyllis Norman
PARRY, Enid
PATERSON, Wilma
PATTERSON, Annie Wilson
PENGILLY, Sylvia
PERKIN, Helen

PHILLIPS, Bryony
PHILLIPS, Lois Elisabeth
PIKE, Eleanor B. Franklin
PLUMSTEAD, Mary
POINTON, Barbara
POSTON, Elizabeth
PRICE, Beryl
PRITCHARD, Gwyn
PYKE, Helen
QUINLAN, Agnes Clune
RADMALL, Peggy
RAINIER, Priaulx
REEKS, Kathleen Doris
REES, Winifred Emily
REYNOLDS, Barbara
RICHARDSON, Enid Dorothy
ROBLES, Marisa
ROE, Eileen Betty
ROE, Evelyn
ROE, Helen Mary Gabrielle
ROGERS, Clara Kathleen
ROGERS, Melicent Joan
ROWE, Helen
ROWE, Victoria
RUDALL, Eleonor C.
SAINT HELIER, Ivy
SALSBURY, Janet Mary
SAMUEL, Rhian
SANDER, Jacqueline
SCHIRMACHER, Dora
SCOTT, Georgina Keir
SENIOR, Kay
SHERBOURNE, Janet
SLAUGHTER, Marjorie
SMITH, E.M. Monica
SMITH, Ethel
SMYTH, Ethel Mary, Dame
SOUTHGATE, Dorothy
SOUTHGATE, Elsie
SPAIN-DUNK, Susan
SPALDING, Eva Ruth
SPENCER PALMER, Florence
    Margaret
STEWART, Katharine
STEWART-BAXTER, Maud
STEWART-NORTH, Isabel
STREATFIELD, Valma June
SWAIN, Freda Mary
SYNER, Sonia
TANN, Hilary
TASSO, Joan Maria
TATE, Phyllis
TEMPLE, Hope
THOMAS, Elizabeth
THOMAS, Gertrude Evelyn
THOMAS, Muriel Leonora
    Duncan
TOBIN, Candida
TOLER, Anne
TOWERSEY, Phyllis Mary
TRIMBLE, Joan
TROUP, Emily Josephine
TRUMAN, Irene
TURNBULL, Sister Fedora
TURNER, Olive Mary
USHER, Julia
VERNE, Adela
VERNE-BREDT, Alice
VERNON, Sylvia
VERRALL, Pamela Motley
WAINWRIGHT, Harriet
WALKER, Nina
WAUGH, Jane
WEBB, Mary
WEIR, Judith
WELDON, Georgina
WELLS, Jane
WHITE, Elizabeth Estelle
WHITE, Mary Louisa
WIENIAWSKA, Irene Regine
WILCOCK, Anthea

WILENS, Greta
WILKINS, Margaret Lucy
WILKINSON, Constance Jane
WILLIAMS, Grace Mary
WILLIAMS, Joan
WILLIAMS, Sioned
WILLIAMS, Stella
WINROW, Barbara
WOOD, Ruzena Alenka Valda
Century unknown
GOW, Dorothy
GRAHAM, Susan Christine
HARVEY, Ella Doreen
HOGBEN, Dorothy
HUNT, Wynn
LEVAN, Mrs. D.B.
MacDONNELL, Lilly
PARGETER, Maude
PRICE, Janet
SMITH, Lilian
STEEMSON, Miss
WALTER, Ida
WATERMAN, Constance Dorothy

UNITED STATES OF AMERICA
18th Century A.D.
DEMILLIERE, Marthesie
19th Century A.D.
ABLAMOWICZ, Anna
ALLEN, Mary Wood
ANDREWS, Mrs. George H.
ANLEY, Charlotte
ARENS-ROGER, Adelia
ATHERTON, Grace
BAKER, Maude
BAXTER, Lydia
BELLCHAMBERS, Julliet
BENNETT, Mimi
BISLAND, Margaret Cyrilla
BLACK, Jennie Price
BLAKE, Mary
BLOCK, Isabelle McKee
BRADSHAW, Nellie Shorthill
BRANDLING, Mary
BRANHAM, Norma Wood
BRIGHAM, Helena
BROWN, Clemmon May
BROWNE, Augusta
BUGBEE, L.A.
BURNHAM, Georgiana
BURTIS, Sarah R.
CAMMACK, Amelia
CAPPIANI, Luisa
CARMICHAEL, Anne Darling
CARTER, Christine Nordstrom
CASSEL, Flora Hamilton
CHICKERING, Mrs. Charles F.
CLARKE, Helen Archibald
COATES, Kathleen Kyle
COLE, Elizabeth Shirk
COLLINS, Laura Sedgwick
CROWNINGSHIELD, Mary Bradford
CRUMB, Berenice
DALY, Julia
DAMON, Frances Brackett
DANA, Mary S.B.
DANZINGER, Laura
DE LISLE, Estelle
DEMING, Mrs. L.L.
DOLE, Caroline
DONALDS, Belle
DRAPER, Mrs. J.T.
ESTABROOK, G.
EVERSOLE, Rose M.
FARLEY, Marion
FISCHEL, Marguerite
GARRETT, Mrs. William
GATES, Alice Avery
GERARD, Miss
GRO, Josephine
HABICHT, Mrs. C.E.

HAHR, Emma
HALE, Irene
HAMMER, Marie von
HARDY, Mrs. Charles S.
HART, Imogine
HASWIN, Frances R.
HAWES, Charlotte W.
HERRESHOFF, Constance
HEWITT, Estelle
HIBLER, Nellie
HODGES, Faustina Hasse
HOHNSTOCK, Adele
HUTET, Josephine
JENKS, Maude E.
JEWELL, Althea Grant
JOYCE, Florence Buckingham
KERBY, Caroline
KING, Frances Isabella
KNAPP, Phoebe Palmer
KNUDSEN, Lynne
LAIGHTON, Ruth
LAMSON, Georgie
LEMMEL, Helen Howarth
LOUD, Annie Frances
LOUD, Emily L.
MACKENZIE, Grace
MacKINLEY, Mrs. J.
McKINNEY, Ida Scott Taylor
MARCKWALD, Grace
MARTIN, Angelica
MEADER, Emily Peace
METZLER, Bertha
MORANDI, Jennie Jewett
MOULTON, Mrs. Charles
MYERS, Emma F.
OLCOTT, Grace
ORTH, Lizette Emma
OWEN, Anita
PALDI, Mari
PARCELLO, Marie
PARK, Edna Rosalind
PARKHURST, Susan
PEASE, Jessie L.
PITTMAN, Alice Locke
POWELL, Mrs. Watkins
PRICE, Sara A.
RAYMOND, Emma Marcy
READ, Sarah Ferriss
REES, Clara H.
RICHARDSON, Jennie V.
RING, Claire
RITTER, Fanny Malone Raymond
ROBERTS, Nellie Wilkinson
RONALDS, Belle
ROOT, Grace W.
RUNCIE, Constance Owen Faunt Le
  Roy
SAINT JOHN, Georgie Boyden
SANDFORD, Lucy A.
SARGENT, Cora Decker
SAWYER, Harriet P.
SCHUYLER, Georgina
SCOTT, Clara H.
SCOTT, M.B.
SIMMONS, Kate
SKELTON, Nellie Bangs
SKINNER, Fannie Lovering
SLOMAN, Jane
SMITH, Eleanor Louise
SMITH, Gertrude
SMITH, Hannah
SMITH, May Florence
SMITH, Mrs. Gerrit
SMITH, Nettie Pierson
SMITH, Rosalie Balmer
SNEED, Anna
SPENCER, Fannie Morris
STEWART, Annie M.
STEWART, F.M.
STITH, Mrs. Townsend
STOWE, Harriet Beecher

SULLIVAN, Marian Dix
SUTRO, Florence Edith Clinton
SWIFT, Gertrude H.
TAYLOR, Mrs. A.H.
THURBER, Nettie C.
TORRY, Jane Sloman
TOWNSEND, Marie
TRAIN, Adelaine
TRETBAR, Helen
TURNER, Harriet
TURNEY, Ruthyn
VANDERPOEL, Kate
VANE, Florence
VENTH, Lydia Kunz
WALKER, Caroline Holme
WALKER, Ida
WEIR, Mary Brinckley
WHITE, Emma C.
WHITELY, Bessie Marshall
WIGGINS, Kate Douglas
WILLIAMS, Margaret
WILLS, Harriet Burdett
WILSON, Addie Anderson
WOOD, Mrs. George
WOODHULL, Mary G.A.
WOODS, Eliza
WORTH, Adelaide
YOUNG, Eliza
ZINGLER-SCHREINER, Martha
20th Century A.D.
ABESON, Marion
ABORN, Lora
ACE, Joy Milane
ACKERMANN, Dorothy
ADAIR, Dorothy
A'DAIR, Jeanne
ADAIR, Mildred
ADAM, Margie
ADAMS, Carrie Bell
ADAMS, Elizabeth Kilmer
ADAMS, Julia Aurelia
ADERHOLDT, Sarah
AGUIRRE, Diana V.
AHRENS, Peg
AIN, Noa
AKERS, Doris Mae
ALBRIGHT, Janet Elaine
ALBRIGHT, Lois
ALDEN, Zilpha May
ALDERMAN, Pauline
ALLAN, Esther
ALLBRITTON, Florence Ziegler
ALLEMAND, Pauline L'
ALLEN, Judith Shatin
ALLEN, Mimi
ALMESAN, Irma
ALPERT, Pauline Edith
ALT, Hansi
ALTER, Martha
ALTMAN, Adella C.
AMACHER, Maryanne
AMATI, Orlanda
ANCELE, Sister Mary
ANDERSEN, Helen Somerville
ANDERSON, Beth
ANDERSON, Jay
ANDERSON, Kristine
ANDERSON, Laurel Everette
ANDERSON, Laurie
ANDERSON, Pauline Barbour
ANDERSON, Ruth
ANDREWS, Virginia
ANDRUS, Helen Josephine
APPLE, Lorraine
APPLETON, Adeline Carola
ARAUCO, Ingrid Colette
ARBUCKLE, Dorothy M.
ARENA, Iris Mae
ARLEN, Jeanne Burns
ARMER, Elinor Florence
ARNDT, Nola

ARQUIT, Nora Harris
ARVEY, Verna
ASHFORD, Emma Louise
ASHMORE, Grace Flournoy
AUFDERHEIDE, May
AUSTIN, Dorothea
AUSTIN, Frances
AUSTIN, Grace Leadenham
AYLWIN, Josephine Crew
BABITS, Linda
BACHELLER, Mildred R. Thomas
BACON, Viola Ruth Orcutt
BAHMANN, Marianne Eloise
BAIL, Grace Shattuck
BAILEY-APFELBECK, Marie Louise
BAILIN, Harriett
BAINBRIDGE, Katharine
BAIRD, Lorine Chamberlain
BAKER, Deborah Jean
BAKER, Gertrude Tremblay
BAKER, Mary Winder
BALDWIN, Esther Lillian
BALL, Frances de Villa
BALL, Ida W.
BALLANDS, Etta
BALLAS, Barbara
BALLASEYUS, Virginia
BALLOU, Esther Williamson
BAMPTON, Ruth
BANKS, Hilda
BANNISTER, Mary Jeanne Hoggard
BARADAPRANA, Pravrajika
BARBER, Gail Guseman
BARBOUR, Florence Newell
BARD, Vivien
BARKIN, Elaine
BARLOW, Betty
BARNES-WOOD, Zilpha
BARNETT, Alice
BARNETT, Carol Edith
BARRETT-THOMAS, N.
BARROWS, Margaret Bentley
  Hamilton
BARTHELSON, Joyce Holloway
BARTLETT, Floy Little
BARTON, Ann
BASSETT, Henrietta Elizabeth
BASSETT, Karolyn Wells
BATEMAN, Florence G.
BATES, Anna Craig
BATES, Katherine Lee
BAUER, Emilie Frances
BAUER, Marion Eugenie
BEACH, Amy Marcy
BEACH, Priscilla A.
BEAHM, Jacquelyn Yvette
BEAN, Mabel
BEARD, Katherine K.
BEARER, Elaine Louise
BEATON, Isabella
BEAUMONT, Vivian
BECK, Martha Dillard
BECKMAN, Ellen Josephine
BECKON, Lettie Marie
BEESON, Elizabeth Ruth
BEHREND, Jeanne
BELCHER, Mary Williams
BELL, Carla Huston
BELL, Elizabeth
BELL, Judith
BELL, Lucille Anderson
BELLAMY, Marian Meredith
BELLEROSE, Sister Cecilia
BELLMAN, Helene M.
BENARY, Barbara
BENNETT, Claudia
BENNETT, Elsie M.
BENNETT, Virginia H.
BENNETT, Wilhelmine
BENTLEY, Berenice Benson
BERBERIAN, Cathy

BERCKMAN, Evelyn
BERGEN, Sylvia
BERGER, Jean
BERGERSEN, Marie Christine
BERK, Adele
BERL WEINFIELD, Christine
BERLINER, Selma
BERNADONE, Anka
BERRYMAN, Alice Davis
BERT, Martha
BETHEA, Kay
BEYER, Johanna Magdalena
BEZDEK, Sister John Joseph
BILBRO, Anne Mathilde
BILLSON, Ada
BIRCSAK, Thusnelda
BIRD, Sister Mary Rafael
BISH, Diane
BISHOP, Dorothy
BITGOOD, Roberta
BLACKWELL, Anna Gee
BLAIR, Kathleen
BLAKE, Dorothy Gaynor
BLAUSTEIN, Susan Morton
BLAUVELT, Bula Caswell
BLEY, Carla
BLIESENER, Ada Elizabeth
  Michelman
BLISA, Alice
BLISS, Marilyn S.
BLISS, Pearl
BLISS, Tamara
BLOCH, Suzanne
BLOOD, Esta Damesek
BLOOM, Jane Ira
BLOOM, Shirley
BLOOMFIELD-ZEISLER, Fannie
BOBROW, Sanchie
BOCARD, Sister Cecilia Clair
BOESING, Martha
BOLZ, Harriet
BOND, Carrie Jacobs
BOND, Victoria Ellen
BONDS, Margaret
BONNETTE, Jeanne
BOONE, Clara Lyle
BOOZER, Patricia P.
BORDERS, Barbara Ann
BORGE, Michele
BORON, Marion
BORROFF, Edith
BOSTELMANN, Ida
BOSTWICK, Sara
BOTSFORD, Talitha
BOUCK, Marjorie
BOWMAN, Frances
BOYACK, Jeanette
BOYCE, Blanche Ula
BOYD, Jeanne Margaret
BOYKIN, A. Helen
BRADLEY, Ruth
BRANDT, Dorothea
BRANNING, Grace Bell
BRANNON, Gertrude Legler
BREASEALE, Jayne
BRECK, Carrie Ellis
BREEN, May Singhi
BREILH, Fernande
BRENNER, Rosamond Drooker
BRES, Dorothy
BRIDGES, Myrtle M.
BRIGGS, Cora Skilling
BRIGGS, Dorothy Bell
BRIGGS, Mary Elizabeth
BRIGGS, Nancy Louise
BRINGUER, Estela
BRINK, Emily R.
BRITAIN, Radie
BRITTON, Dorothy Guyver
BROCK, Blanche Kerr
BROCKMAN, Jane E.

BROGUE, Roslyn Clara
BROOK, Gwendolyn Giffen
BROOKS, Alice M.
BROOKS, Myra Lou
BROUK, Joanna
BROUWER, Margaret Lee
BROWN, Elizabeth Bouldin
BROWN, Elizabeth van Ness
BROWN, Gertrude M.
BROWN, Gladys Mungen
BROWN, Mary Helen
BROWN, Norma
BROWN, Zilda Jennings
BRUNDZAITE, Konstantsiya Kazyo
BRUNER, Cheryl
BRUSH, Mrs. J.M.
BRUSH, Ruth Damaris
BRUSSELS, Iris
BRYAN, Betty Sue
BRYANT, Verna Mae
BUCHANAN, Annabel Morris
BUCKLEY, Dorothy Pike
BUCKLEY, Helen Dallam
BUMP, Mary Crane
BURDICK, Elizabeth Tucker
BURKE, Loretto
BURNETT, Helen Roth
BURNETT, Mildred R.
BURROUGHS, Jane Johnson
BURT, Virginia M.
BUSH, Gladys B.
BUSH, Grace E.
BUTCHER, Jane Elizabeth
BUTLER, Anne Lois
BUTT, Thelma
BUTTERFIELD, Hattie May
BYERS, Roxana Weihe
BYLES, Blanche D.
CADY, Harriette
CAESAR, Shirley
CAHIER, Mme. Charles
CALBRAITH, Mary Evelene
CALDER, Hattie M.
CALDWELL, Mary Elizabeth Glockler
CALE, Rosalie Balmer Smith
CALL, Audrey
CALLAWAY, Ann
CALVIN, Susan Heath
CANNING, Effie I.
CAPERTON, Florence Tait
CAREY, Elena
CARL, Tommie Ewert
CARLOS, Wendy
CARMON, Helen Bidwell
CARNO, Zita
CARP, Susan
CARR, Bess Berry
CARR, Wynona
CARRINGTON-THOMAS, Virginia
CARROLL, Barbara
CARSON, Ruby B.
CARSON, Zeula Miller
CARTER PAULENA, Elizabeth
CARTER, Buenta MacDaniel
CASTAGNETTA, Grace Sharp
CATO, Jane Dickson
CAWTHORN, Janie M.
CECCONI-BATES, Augusta
CHAMBERS, Wendy
CHAMPION, Constance MacLean
CHANCE, Nancy Laird
CHASE, Mary Wood
CHAVES, Mary Elizabeth
CHEATHAM, Kitty
CHENOWETH, Vida
CHERTOK, Pearl
CHERUBIM, Sister Mary Schaefer
CHESTER, Isabel
CHESTNUT, Lora Perry
CHEVALIER, Charlotte Bergersen
CHILDS, Mary Ellen

CHLARSON, Linda
CHRISTENSEN, Anna Mae Parker
CHURCHILL, Beatrice
CIANI, Suzanne Elizabeth
CLARK, Jane Leland
CLARK, Mary Elizabeth
CLARK, Mary Margaret Walker
CLARK, Ruth Scott
CLARKE, Lucia
CLARKE, Mary Gail
CLARKE, Rosemary
CLARKE, Urana
CLAYTON, Jay
CLAYTON, Laura
CLEMENT, Sheree
COATES, Gloria Kannenberg
COBB, Hazel
CODY, Judith
COFFMAN, Lillian Craig
COHEN, Marcia
COLE, Ulric
COLGAN, Alma Cecilia
COLLARD, Marilyn
COLLINS, Janyce
COLLVER, Harriet Russell
COLTRANE, Alice McLeod
CONRAD, Laurie M.
CONWAY, Olive
COOK, Rosalind
COOKE, Marjorie Tibbets
COOLIDGE, Elizabeth Sprague
COOLIDGE, Peggy Stuart
COOPER, Esther Sayward
COOPER, Rose Marie
COPLAND, Berniece Rose
CORCORAN, Lillian Hague
CORDULA, Sister M.
CORNING, Karen Andree
CORY, Eleanor
COSSAR, Louanne
COUPER, Mildred
COUTURE, Priscilla
COVERT, Mary Ann Hunter
COWLES, Cecil Marion
COWLES, Darleen
CRANE, Helen
CRAWFORD SEEGER, Ruth
CRAWFORD, Dawn Constance
CRAWFORD, Dorothy Lamb
CRAWFORD, Louise
CREWS, Lucille
CRISP, Barbara
CROCHET, Sharon Brandstetter
CROFTS, Inez Altman
CROKER, Catherine Munnell
CROMIE, Marguerite Biggs
CROSBY, Fannie
CROWE, Bonita
CULP, Paula Newell
CUNIBERTI, Janet Teresa
CURPHY, Geraldine
CURRAN, Pearl Gildersleeve
CURRIE, Edna R.
CURRIER, Marilyn Kind
CURTIS, Elizabeth
CURTIS, Natalie
CURTWRIGHT, Carolee
CURZON, Clara-Jean
CUTLER, Mary J.
DAIGLE, Sister Anne Cecile
DAMASHEK, Barbara
DANA, Lynn Boardman
DANFORTH, Frances A.
DANIELS, Mabel Wheeler
DANOWSKI, Helen
DAVENPORT, Anne Bridges
DAVENPORT, Caroline
DAVIDSON, Tina
DAVIS, Eleanor Maud
DAVIS, Eva May
DAVIS, Fay Simmons

DAVIS, Genevieve
DAVIS, Hazel E.
DAVIS, Hilda Emery
DAVIS, Jean Reynolds
DAVIS, Katherine Kennicott
DAVIS, Margaret Munger
DAVIS, Mary
DAVIS, Sharon
DAVIS-BERRYMAN, Alice
DAVISON, Martha Taylor
DAVISSON, Genevieve
DAWSON, Alice
DE CEVEE, Alice
DE FAZIO, Lynette Stevens
DE LEATH, Vaughn
DEACON, Mary Connor
DEAN, Laura
DEAN, Lynn C.
DEGRAFF, Grace Clark
DEMAREST, Alison
DEMAREST, Anne Shannon
DEMBO, Royce
DENBOW, Stefania Bjoerson
DENNISON, Barbara
DEPPEN, Jessie L.
DEYO, Ruth Lynda
DEYTON, Camilla Hill
DIAMOND, Arline
DICKISON, Maria Bobrowska
DIEFENTHALER, Margaret Kissinger
DIEHL, Paula Jespersen
DIEMER, Emma Lou
DILLER, Angela
DILLER, Saralu C.
DILLON, Fannie Charles
DIRKS, Jewel Dawn
DITMARS, Elizabeth
DITTENHAVER, Sarah Louise
DIXON, Esther
DLUGOSZEWSKI, Lucia
DOANE, Dorothy
DOBBINS, Lori
DODDSON, Ora
DODGE, Cynthia
DODGE, May Hewes
DOLAN, Hazel
DOLLEY, Betty Grace
DONAHUE, Bertha Terry
DORTCH, Eileen Wier
DOUGAN, Vera Warnder
DOUROUX, Margaret Pleasant
DOWNEY, Mary
DRAKE, Elizabeth Bell
DRATTELL, Deborah
DRENNAN, Dorothy Carter
DRETKE, Leora N.
DROSTE, Doreen
DRYE, Sarah Lynn
DU PAGE, Florence Elizabeth
DUBOIS, Shirley Graham
DUDLEY, Marjorie Eastwood
DUFFENHORST, Irma Habeck
DUGGAN, Beatrice Abbott
DUNFORD, Nancy Ridenhour
DUNGAN, Olive
DUNLAP, Judy
DUNN, Rebecca Welty
DURAND, Nella Wells
DUSHKIN, Dorothy Smith
DUTTON, Theodora
DVORKIN, Judith
DYER, Susan
EAGER, Mary Ann
EAKIN, Vera O.
EAKLOR, Vicki
EASTES, Helen Marie
EDGERLY, Cora Emily
EDICK, Ethel Vera Ingraham
EDWARDS, Clara
EDWARDS, Jessie B.
EFREIN, Laurie

EGERT, Nina
EICHHORN, Hermene Warlick
EILERS, Joyce Elaine
EISENSTEIN, Judith Kaplan
EISENSTEIN, Stella Price
EKIZIAN, Michelle
ELKAN, Ida
ELKIND, Rachel
ELLERMAN, Helen
ELLIOTT, Janice Overmiller
ELLIOTT, Marjorie Reeve
ELLIOTT, Mary Sims
ELLIS, Cecil Osik
ELMORE, Cenieth Catherine
ELVYN, Myrtle
EMERY, Dorothy Radde
EMERY, Emma Wilson
EMIG, Lois Irene
ENDE, Amelia von
ENDRES, Olive Philomene
ENGBERG, M. Davenport
EPPERSON, Hilda
ERICKSON, Elaine M.
ERMAN, Sarah
ERNEST, Sister M.
ESCHWEILER, Geneva
ESCOT, Pozzi
ESTELLE, Sister Rita
EUBANKS, Rachel Amelia
EVANTI, Lillian
EVERETT-SALICCO, Betty Lou
EWING, Nona
EZELL, Helen Ingle
EZZAR, Katherine
FAHRER, Alison Clark
FAIRCHILD, Helen
FAIRLIE, Margaret C.
FARR, Hilda Butler
FAUTCH, Sister Magdalen
FAXON, Nancy Plummer
FAY, Amy
FELDMAN, Joann Esther
FELLOWS, Mrs. Wayne Stanley
FENASCI, Dorothy
FENNER, Beatrice
FENSTOCK, Belle
FERRE, Susan Ingrid
FERRELL, Billie
FERRIS, Isabel D.
FINE, Sylvia
FINE, Vivian
FINK, Emma C.
FINLEY, Lorraine Noel
FIRESTONE, Elizabeth
FIRESTONE, Idabelle
FISCHER, Edith Steinkraus
FISHER, Doris
FISHER, Gladys Washburn
FISHER, Jessie
FISHER, Katherine Danforth
FISHER, Linda
FISHER, Renee Breger
FISHER, Susan
FISHMAN, Marian
FITZGERALD, Sister Florence
  Therese
FLAGG, Mary Houts
FLEMING, Shari Beatrice
FLEMMING, Elsa
FLICK-FLOOD, Dora
FLORING, Grace Kenny
FODY, Ilona
FONDER, Sister Mary Teresine
FORD, Mrs. Raymond C.
FORD, Nancy
FORD, Olive Elizabeth
FORMAN, Addie Walling
FORMAN, Ellen
FORMAN, Jeanne
FORMAN, Joanne
FORSYTH, Josephine

FORTENBERRY, Myrtis
FOSTER, Dorothy Godwin
FOSTER, Fay
FOWLER, Marje
FOX, Doris H.
FOX, Pauline S.
FRANCO, Clare
FRANK, Jean Forward
FRASER-MILLER, Gloria Jill
FRASIER, Jane
FREEHOFF, Ruth Williams
FREER, Eleanor Warner Everest
FREIBERGER, Katherine
FREITAG, Dorothea Hackett
FRENCH, Tania
FRERICHS, Doris Coulston
FRITTER, Genevieve Davisson
FROHBEITER, Ann W.
FRUMKER, Linda
FRYZELL, Regina Holmen
FUCHS, Lillian
FULLER, Sarah
FULLER-HALL, Sarah Margaret
GABURO, Elizabeth
GADDY, Carol
GAINSBORG, Lolita Cabrera
GALAJIKIAN, Florence Grandland
GALBRAITH, Nancy Riddle
GALLI-CAMPI
GANNON, Helen Carroll
GANNON, Ruth Ellen
GARDNER, Kay
GARDNER, Mildred Alvine
GARLAND, Kathryn
GARNETT, Luisa Aires
GARRETT, Elizabeth
GARWOOD, Margaret
GASTON, Marjorie Dean
GAUTIER, Josie
GAYNOR, Jessie Love
GEBUHR, Ann K.
GENET, Marianne
GENTEMANN, Sister Mary Elaine
GEORGE, Lila-Gene
GERRISH-JONES, Abbie
GESSLER, Caroline
GEST, Elizabeth
GHIGLIERI, Sylvia
GIDEON, Miriam
GILBERT, Janet Monteith
GILBERT, Marie
GILBERT, Pia
GILENO, Jean Anthony
GILLICK, Emelyn Mildred Samuels
GILLILAND-HERNDON, Marianne
GILLUM, Ruth Helen
GISELA, Sister Mary
GITECK, Janice
GLANVILLE-HICKS, Peggy
GLASER, Victoria Merrylees
GLAZIER, Beverly
GLEN, Irma
GLICK, Henrietta
GLICK, Nancy Kay
GODLA, Mary Ann
GOETSCHIUS, Marjorie
GOLBIN, Elsa
GOLD, Diana
GOLDSTON, Margaret Nell
  Stumpf
GOLLAHON, Gladys
GOLSON-BATEMAN, Florence
GOODE, Blanche
GOODMAN, Lillian Rosedale
GOODSMITH, Ruth B.
GOOLKASIAN-RAHBEE, Dianne
  Zabelle
GORE, Virginia
GORELLI, Olga
GOULD, Elizabeth Davies
GOVEA, Wenonah Milton

GRAINGER, Ella Viola Strom-
  Brandelius
GRANT, Louise
GRAU, Irene Rosenberg
GRAY, Dorothy
GRAY, Judith
GREEN, Mary Thompson
GREENE, Genevieve
GREENE, Margo Lynn
GREENFIELD, Lucille
GREENWALD, Jan Carol
GREENWOOD, Neva Garner
GRESHAM, Ann
GREY, Edith
GRIEBLING, Karen Jean
GRIEBLING, Margaret Ann
GRIEF, Marjorie
GRIFFINS, Vashti Rogers
GRIFFITH, Corinne
GRIGSBY, Beverly
GRIMES, Doreen
GROBEL, Marylin A.
GRONOWETTER, Freda
GROOM, Joan Charlene
GROSSMAN, Deena
GRUENBERG, Irma
GUDAUSKAS, Giedra
GUERRANT, Mary Thorington
GULESIAN, Grace Warner
GUNDERSON, Helen Louise
GUSTAVSON, Nancy Nicholls
GYRING, Elizabeth
HABAN, Sister Teresine M.
HACKLEY, Emma Azalia Smith
HADDEN, Frances Roots
HAGAN, Helen Eugenia
HAGEMANN, Virginia
HAHN, Sandra Lea
HAIMSOHN, Naomi Carrol
HAINES, Julia Howell
HAIRSTON, Jacqueline Butler
HAIRSTON, Jessie
HALL, Frances
HALL, Marian Wilson
HALPERN, Stella
HALSTED, Margo
HAMBLEN, Suzy
HAMILL, Roseann
HAMILTON, Gertrude Bean
HAMILTON, Marcia
HAMMANN, Rebecca
HAMMOND, Fanny Reed
HANCHETT, Sybil Croly
HANKS, Sybil Ann
HANSON, Fay S.
HARDING, Mildred Thompson
HARKNESS, Joan
HARKNESS, Rebekah West
HARLEY, Frances Marjorie
HARLOW, Barbara
HARPER, Marjorie
HARRAH, Madge
HARRIS, Ethel Ramos
HARRIS, Letitia Radcliffe
HARRIS, Margaret R.
HARRIS, Ruth Berman
HARROD, Beth Miller
HARSHMAN, Margaret B.
HART, Elizabeth Jane Smith
HARTER, Louise C.
HARVEY, Vivien
HARWOOD, Sylvia Rowell
HASKELL, Doris Burd
HATCH, Edith
HATCH, Mabel Lee
HAUSMAN, Ruth Langley
HAVEY, Marguerite
HAWLEY, Carolyn Jean
HAYS, Doris Ernestine
HAYWARD, Mae Shepard
HAZEN, Sara

HEARDING, Elizabeth
HEATON, Eloise Klotz
HECKSCHER, Celeste de Longpre
HEGGE, Mrs. M.H.
HEILBRON, Valerie
HEIMERL, Elizabeth
HEIMLICH, Florentine
HEINRICH, Adel Verna
HEINY, Margaret Harris
HELLER, Ruth
HEMENWAY, Edith
HEMMENT, Marguerite E.
HENDERSON, Elizabeth
HENDERSON, Rosamon
HERBERT, Dorothy
HERBERT, Muriel
HERBISON, Jeraldine Saunders
HERTEL, Sister Romana
HESS, Alyssa Nan
HETRICK, Patricia Anne
HEYMAN, Katherine Ruth Willoughby
HIER, Ethel Glen
HIGGINBOTHAM, Irene
HIGGINS, Esther S.
HILDERLEY, Jeriann G.
HILDRETH, Daisy Wood
HILER, Charlotte Ailene
HILL, May
HILL, Mildred J.
HILSTON, Lucille
HINEBAUGH, Bessie
HINKLE, Daisy Estelle
HIRSCH, Barbara
HOFF, Vivian Beaumont
HOFFMAN, Laura
HOFFMAN, Phyllis Sampson
HOFFMANN, Peggy
HOFFRICHTER, Bertha Chaitkin
HOKANSON, Margrethe
HOLBERT, Diana Brown
HOLCOMB, Louanah Riggs
HOLDEN, Bernice
HOLLINGSWORTH, Thekla
HOLLIS, Ruby Shaw
HOLLISTER, Leona Stephens
HOLST, Agnes Moller
HOLT, Nora Douglass
HOLTHUSEN, Anita Saunders
HOOD, Helen
HOOVER, Katherine
HOPEKIRK, Helen
HORNBACK, Sister Mary Gisela
HORSLEY, Imogene
HORTON, Marguerite Wagniere
HOSEY, Athena
HOTCHKISS, Evelyn Dissmore
HOUSE, L. Marguerite
HOUSER, Kitty
HOUSMAN, Rosalie
HOVDA, Eleanor
HOWARD, Beatrice Thomas
HOWARD, Helen Willard
HOWE, Mary Alberta Bruce
HOWELL, Alice
HOY, Bonnee L.
HOYLAND, Janet
HOYLE, Aline Isabelle
HOYT, Mary Mack
HRUBY, Dolores Marie
HSU, Wen-Ying
HUDGINS, Mary
HUGHES, Sister Martina
HUGHEY, Evangeline Hart
HUJSAK, Joy Detenbeck
HULL, Anne
HULL, Kathryn B.
HULST, Margaret Gardiner
HUMPHREY, Doris
HUNKINS, Eusebia Simpson
HUNTER, Alberta
HURLBUTT, Patricia

HURLEY, Susan
HURST, Olive
HUTCHINS, Helene Owen
HUTSON, Wihla L.
HYDE, Georgina Colvin
HYNES, Eloise
HYSON, Winifred Prince
HYTREK, Sister Theophane
INGLEFIELD, Ruth Karin
INWOOD, Mary Ruth Brink Berger
IPPOLITO, Carmela
ISLE, Harriet L.
IVEY, Jean Eichelberger
JACKSON, Elizabeth Barnhart
JACKSON, Mary
JACKSON, Marylou L.
JACOBUS, Dale Asher
JAMBOR, Agi
JAMES, Dorothy E.
JANKOWSKI, Loretta Patricia
JAZWINSKI, Barbara
JEBELES, Mrs. Themos
JENKINS, Susan Elaine
JENNEY, Mary Frances
JENNINGS, Carolyn
JENNINGS, Marie Pryor
JESSYE, Eva
JEWELL, Lucina
JOCHSBERGER, Tzipora H.
JOHN, Patricia Spaulding
JOHNSON, Elizabeth
JOHNSON, Eloise Lisle
JOHNSON, Harriet
JOHNSON, J. Rosamond
JOHNSON, Mary Ernestine Clark
JOHNSTON-REID, Sarah Ruth
JOLLEY, Florence Werner
JONES, Catherine
JONES, Dovie Osborn
JONES, Joyce Gilstrap
JONES, Marjorie
JONES, Sister Ida
JORDAN, Alice Yost
JOY, Margaret E.
KABAT, Julie Phyllis
KAHMANN, Chesley
KALLOCH, Doley C.
KAMIEN, Anna
KAMINSKY, Laura
KANACH, Sharon E.
KAPLAN, Lois Jay
KAPP, Corinne
KAVASCH, Deborah Helene
KAYDEN, Mildred
KECK, Pearl
KEIG, Betty
KEISER, Lauren Keith
KELLER, Lue Alice
KELLEY, Dorothea Nolte
KELLEY, Florence Bettray
KELLEY, Patricia Ann
KELLY, Georgia
KELSO, Alice Anne
KEMP, Dorothy Elizabeth Walter
KENDRICK, Virginia Catherine
KENNEDY, Gurney
KER, Ann S.
KESHNER, Joyce Grove
KESSLER, Minuetta Schumiatcher
KETTERER, Ella
KETTERER, Laura
KETTERING, Eunice Lea
KIMPER, Paula M.
KING, Betty Jackson
KING, Mabel Shoup
KING, Patricia
KING, Pearl
KINSCELLA, Hazel Gertrude
KIRBY, Suzanne
KIRKMAN, Merle
KLIMISCH, Sister Mary Jane

KLINGENSMITH, Anne
KLOTZMAN, Dorothy Ann Hill
KNOUSS, Isabelle G.
KNOWLES, Alison
KNOWLTON, Fanny Snow
KOELLING, Eloise
KOHN, Doris
KOLB, Barbara
KORHONEN, S. Gloria
KORN, Clara Anna
KOSSE, Roberta
KRAUS, Rozann Baghdad
KRAUSZ, Susan
KREBS, Suzanne Eigen
KREISS, Hulda E.
KRIMSKY, Katrina
KROFINA, Sharon
KROGMANN, Carrie William
KROSNICK, Mary Louw Wesley
KRUGER, Lilly Canfield
KUESTER, Edith Haines
KUFFLER, Eugenie
KUMMER, Clare
KUNITZ, Sharon Lohse
KUTTEN, Rachel
KUZMYCH, Christina
LA BARBARA, Joan
LA VALLE, Deanna
LACKMAN, Susan C. Cohn
LADEN, Bernice F.
LAITMAN, Lori
LAKE, Bonnie
LAMBERT, Cecily
LAND, Mary
LANDREE, Jaquenote Goldsteen
LANG, Edith
LANG, Margaret Ruthven
LANG, Rosemary Rita
LAPEYRE, Therese
LARSEN, Elizabeth Brown
LARSON, Anna Barbara
LATHAM, Joan Seyler
LATHROP, Gayle Posselt
LATIOLAIS, Desiree Jayne
LAUER, Elizabeth
LAUFER, Beatrice
LAURENT, Ruth Carew
LAURIDSEN, Cora
LAVRANS, Elayne
LAWHON, Gladys Louise
LAYMAN, Pamela
LE SIEGE, Annette
LEACH, Mary Jane
LEAF, Ann
LEAHY, Mary Weldon
LEAVITT, Helen Sewall
LEBARON, Anne
LEBENBOM, Elaine F.
LECLERCQ, Leila Sarah
LEE, Anna Virginia
LEECH, Lida Shivers
LEECH, Renee
LEFEVER, Maxine Lane
LEHMAN, Evangeline Marie
LEIBOW, Ruth Irene
LEON, Tania Justina
LEONARD, Clair
LEONARD, Mamie Grace
LEONE, Mae G.
LEONI, Eva
LEPKE, Charma Davies
LEVEY, Lauren
LEVIN, Erma E.
LEVIN, Rami Yona
LEVINE, Amy Miller
LEVY, Ellen
LEWIS, Carrie Bullard
LEWIS, Margery de
LICHT, Myrtha B.
LIEBLING, Estelle
LIFFER, Binette

LILLENAS, Bertha Mae
LINEBARGER, Iva B.
LINES, Ruth W.
LIPSCOMB, Helen
LITER, Monia
LITTLE, Anita Gray
LIU, Shea-An
LIVINGSTON, Helen
LLOYD, Caroline Parkhurst
LOCKE, Flora Elbertine Huie
LOCKSHIN, Florence Levin
LOCKWOOD, Charlotte Mathewson
LOGAN, Virginia Knight
LOH, Kathy Jean
LOHOEFER, Evelyn
LOMON, Ruth
LORD, Helen Cooper
LORE, Emma Maria Theresa
LORENZ, Ellen Jane
LORING, Nancy
LOVAN, Lydia
LOVE, Loretta
LOVELACE, Carey
LOWELL, Dorothy Dawson
LOWELL, Edith
LUCK, Maude Haben
LUCKE, Katharine E.
LUCKMAN, Phyllis
LUMBY, Betty Louise
LUNDBERG, Harriet
LUNDQUIST, Christie
LUPTON, Belle George
LUSTIG, Leila Sarah
LUTHER, Mary
LUTYENS, Sally
LYNN, Cathy
LYONN LIEBERMAN, Julie
LYONS, Ruth
MAAS, Marguerite Wilson
MACAULAY, Janice Michel
MACKEN, Jane Virginia
MACKIE, Frances C.
MACKIE, Shirley M.
MacARTHUR, Fern
MacARTHUR, Helen
MacDONALD, Catherine
MacENULTY, Rosalind
MacGREGOR, Helen
MacGREGOR, Laurie
MacKOWN, Marjorie T.
MacPHAIL, Frances
McCAIN, Eula Louise
McCARRY, Betty
McCARTHY, Charlotte
McCLEARY, Fiona
McCLEARY, Mary Gilkeson
McCOLLIN, Frances
McDOWELL, Jennifer
McDUFFEE, Mabel Howard
McGOWAN SCOTT, Beatrice
McILWRAITH, Isa Roberta
McKANN-MANCINI, Patricia
McKAY, Frances Thompson
McKEE, Jeanellen
McKINNEY, Mathilde
McLAIN, Margaret Starr
McLAUGHLIN, Erna
McLAUGHLIN, Marian
McLEAN, Priscilla Anne Taylor
McLEMORE, Monita Prine
McLEOD, Evelyn Lundgren
McLIN, Lena
McMILLAN, Ann Endicott
McNAIR, Jacqueline Hanna
McNEIL, Janet L. Pfischner
McPHERSON, Frances Marie
McSWAIN, Augusta Geraldine
McTEE, Cindy Karen
MADISON, Carolyn
MADISON, Clara Duggan
MADSEN, Florence J.

MAGNEY, Ruth Taylor
MAINVILLE, Denise
MAITLAND, Anna Harriet
MAITLAND, S. Marguerite
MAMLOK, Ursula
MANA-ZUCCA
MANGGRUM, Loretta C. Cessor
MANKIN, Linda
MANNING, Kathleen Lockhart
MARCELL, Florence
MARCUS, Ada Belle Gross
MARCUS, Bunita
MARIS, Barbara
MARKS, Jeanne Marie
MARKS, Selma
MARSCHAL-LOEPKE, Grace
MARSH, Gwendolyn
MARSHALL, Jane Manton
MARSHALL, Pamela J.
MARTH, Helen June
MARTIN, Delores J.
MARTIN, Judith Reher
MARTIN, Ravonna G.
MARTINEZ, Odaline de la
MARY BERNICE, Sister
MARY ELAINE, Sister
MASON, Margaret C.
MASON, Marilyn May
MASONER, Elizabeth L.
MAST-BOLDREY, Joyce
MASTERS, Juan
MATHEWS, Blanche Dingley Moore
MATHIS, Judy M.
MATHIS, Kitty
MATRAS, Maude
MATTHEWS, Dorothy White
MATTULLATH, Alice
MAXIM, Florence
MAXWELL, Elsie
MAXWELL, Helen Purcell
MAXWELL, Jacqueline Perkinson
MAY, Laure Castellanes
MAYADAS, Priya
MAYFIELD, Alpha C.
MAYHEW, Grace
MEACHEM, Margaret McKeen
   Ramsey
MEAD, Catherine Pannill
MEADE, Margaret Johnston
MEEK, Ethel Alice
MEEKER, Estelle
MEIGS, Melinda Moore
MEKEEL, Joyce
MELOY, Elizabeth
MELVILLE, Marguerite Liszniewska
MENEELY-KYDER, Sarah Suderley
MERRICK, Marie E.
MERRIMAN, Margarita Leonor
MESNEY, Dorothy Taylor
MEYERS, Lois
MEYSENBURG, Sister Agnes
MIDDLETON, Jean B.
MILAM, Lena Triplett
MILDANTRI, Mary Ann
MILFORD, Mary Jean Ross
MILKULAK, Marcia Lee
MILLER, Alma Grace
MILLER, Jean
MILLER, Joan
MILLER, Lillian Anne
MILLS, Joan Geilfuss
MINEO, Antoinette
MIRANDA, Sharon Moe
MIRELLE, Wilma
MIRON, Tsipora
MISHELL, Kathryn Lee
MITCHELL, Izah Pike
MITCHELL, Janice Misurell
MITCHELL, Norma Jean
MOHNS, Grace Updegraff Bergen
MOLAVA, Pamela May

MONK, Meredith
MONTGOMERY, Merle
MOORE, Anita
MOORE, Dorothy Rudd
MOORE, Luella Lockwood
MOORE, Margaret Crammond
MOORE, Mary Carr
MOORE, Undine Smith
MOORE, Wilda Maurine Ricks
MOOREHEAD, Consuela Lee
MORRIS, Mary S.
MORRIS, Mrs. C.H.
MORRISON, Julia Maria
MORROW, Jean
MORTON, Agnes Louise
MOSCOVITZ, Julianne
MOSSAFER RIND, Bernice
MRACEK, Ann Michelle
MUELLER, Ann
MUG, Sister Mary Theodosia
MUNGER, Millicent Christner
MUNGER, Shirley
MURAD, Elizabeth
MUSTILLO, Lina
MYGATT, Louise
NAKASHIMA, Jeanne Marie
NASH, Grace Helen
NASON, Susanna
NATVIG, Candace
NEAS, Margaret
NEEL, Susan Elizabeth
NEELD, Peggy
NEILY, Anne MacAdams
NELSON, Mary Anne
NEWBARR, Carol
NEWELL, Laura E.
NEWLIN, Dika
NEWMAN-PERPER, Elfie
NEWTON, Rhoda
NICHOLS, Alberta
NICKERSON, Camille Lucie
NIEBEL, Mildred
NIEBERGALL, Julia Lee
NIEMACK, Ilza Louise
NIGHTINGALE, Barbara Diane
NIGHTINGALE, Mae Wheeler
NOBLE, Ann
NOBLITT, Katheryn Marie McCall
NOHE, Beverly
NORDENSTROM, Gladys Mercedes
NORMAN, Ruth
NOWAK, Alison
NOYES, Edith Rowena
NUGENT, Maude Jerome
NUGENT, Trish
NUNLIST, Juli
NYMAN, Amy Utting
NYQUIST, Morine A.
NYSTEL, Louise Gunderson
OBENCHAIN, Virginia
O'BRIEN, Drena
O'BRIEN, Katharine E.
OCHSE, Orpha Caroline
OHLSON, Marion
OLDENBURG, Elizabeth
O'LEARY, Jane Strong
OLIVER, Madra Emogene
OLIVEROS, Pauline
OLIVIER, Blanche
OLSON, Lynn Freeman
OLSON, Mrs. Herbert V.
OMER, Helene
O'NEILL, Denise
O'NEILL, Selena
OPIE, Mary Pickens
ORENSTEIN, Joyce Ellin
OSGOOD, Marion
OSTRANDER, Linda Woodaman
OSTROFF, Esther
OTA, Junka
OTIS, Edna Cogswell

OWEN, Angela Maria
OWEN, Blythe
OWEN, Mollie O.
OWENS, Rochelle
OWENS, Susan Elizabeth
PACK, Beulah Frances
PADGETT, Betty
PAGOTO, Helen
PALMER, Lynne Wainwright
PANETTI, Joan
PARENTE, Sister Elizabeth
PARKER, Alice
PARKER, Muriel
PARR-GERE, Florence
PAUL, Doris A.
PAULL, Barberi
PAYNE, Harriet
PAYNE, Maggi
PEACOCK, Mary O'Kelley
PEARL-MANN, Dora Deborah
PEEK, Betty
PERDEW, Ruth
PERRY, Julia Amanda
PERRY, Kathryn
PERRY, Marilyn Brown
PERRY, Mary Dean
PERRY, Zenobia Powell
PETERSEN, Marian F.
PETERSON, Melody
PFOLH, Bessie Whittington
PHARRIS, Elizabeth
PHILLIPS, Donna
PHILLIPS, Karen Ann
PHILLIPS, Vivian Daphne
PHIPPEN, Laud German
PICKEN, Emele M.
PICKHARDT, Ione
PIERCE, Alexandra
PIERCE, Sarah Anderson
PIETSCH, Edna Frieda
PITCHER, Gladys
PITOT, Genevieve
PITT, Emma
PITTMAN, Evelyn LaRue
PIZER, Elizabeth Faw Hayden
PLANICK, Annette Meyers
PLICQUE, Eveline
PLONSEY, Jennifer
POLIN, Claire
POLK, Grace Porterfield
POLLOCK, Muriel
PONCE, Ethel
POND, Ida L.
POOL, Arlette
POOL, Jeannie Gayle
POOLE, Anna Ware
POOLER, Marie
PORTER, Debra
POST, Jennifer
POWELL, Maud
POWERS, Ada Weigel
POWERS, Jennifer
PRADELL, Leila
PRAY, Ada Jordan
PREOBRAJENSKA, Vera Nicolaevna
PRESTON, Matilee Loeb-Evans
PRICE, Deon Nielsen
PRICE, Florence Beatrice
PRIESING, Dorothy Jean
PRINCE, Mary Lou
PROCTOR, Alice McElroy
PRUNTY, Evelyn Grace Potter
QUEEN, Virginia
QUESADA, Virginia
QUINN-VEES, Deborah
RABINOF, Sylvia
RAIGORODSKY, Leda Natalia
   Heimsath
RALSTON, Frances Marion
RAMSEY, Sister Mary Anastasia
RAPOPORT, Eda

RASKIN, Ruby
RAWLS, Kathryn Hill
RAY, Ruth
REBE, Louise Christine
RED, Virginia Stroh
REED, Ida L.
REED, Marlyce Rae Polk
REED, Mrs. Wallace
REED, Phyllis Luidens
REGAN, Sarah Wren Love
REICH, Amy
REID, Louis C.
REID, Sarah Johnston
REID, Wendy
REISER, Violet
REMER, Jan
REMICK, Bertha
REYNOLDS, Darcy
REYNOLDS, Erma Grey Hogue
REYNOLDS, Laura Lawton
RHEA, Lois
RHOADS, Mary R.
RHODEN, Natalia Naana
RICH, Gladys
RICHARDS, Christine-Louise
RICHARDS, Inez Day
RICHARDS, Laura E.
RICHARDSON, Sharon
RICHMOND, Virginia
RICHTER, Ada
RICHTER, Marga
RICHTER, Marion Morrey
RIDLEY, Ursula
RILEY, Ann Marion
RILEY, Myrtis F.
RINEHART, Marilyn
RISHER, Anna Priscilla
RITTENBAND, Minna Ethel
RITTENHOUSE, Elizabeth Mae
RIVE-KING, Julia
RIVENBURG, Leah Patt
ROBBOY, Rosalie Smotkin
ROBERSON, Ruby Lee Grubbs
ROBERTS, Gertrud Hermine Kuenzel
ROBERTS, Helen
ROBERTS, Jane A.
ROBERTS, Megan L.
ROBERTS, Ruth Olive
ROBERTSON, Donna Lou Nagey
ROBINSON, Berenice
ROBINSON, Frances
ROBINSON, Gertrude Ina
ROBYN, Louise
ROCHEROLLE, Eugenie Katherine
ROCKEFELLER, Helen C.
RODGERS, Mary
ROE, Gloria Ann
ROE, Marion Adelle
ROESSING, Helen
ROGERS, Cornelia P.
ROGERS, Emmy Brady
ROGERS, Ethel Tench
ROGERS, Faith Helen
ROGERS, Patsy
ROGERS, Sharon Elery
ROGERS, Susan Whipple
ROHDE, Q'Adrianne
ROHRER, Gertrude Martin
ROMA, Caro
RONELL, Ann
ROOBENIAN, Amber
ROSCO, B. Jeanie
ROSE OF JESUS, Sister
ROSE, Sister Caroline
ROSS, Gertrude
ROSSER, Annetta Hamilton
ROSSO, Carol L.
ROWAN, Barbara
ROYSE, Mildred Barnes
RUBIN, Anna Ita
RUDOW, Vivian Adelberg

RUSCHE, Marjorie Maxine
RUSH, Ruth
RUSSELL, Anna
RUSSELL, Betsy A.
RUSSELL, Olive Nelson
RYAN, Winifred
RYDER, Theodora Sturkow
SACHS, Carolyn
SADOVNIKOFF, Mary Briggs
SADOWSKY, Reah
SAINT JOHN, Kathleen Louise
SAITO-NODA, Eva
SALTER, Mary Elizabeth
SAM, Carole Nelsom
SAMPSON, Peggy
SAMSON, Valerie Brooks
SAMUEL, Marguerite
SAMUELSON, Laura Byers
SANDERS, Alma M.
SANDIFUR, Ann Elizabeth
SANDRESKY, Margaret Vardell
SANDY, Grace Linn
SANFILIPPO, Margherita Marie
SANFORD, Grace Krick
SANTOS-OCAMPO DE FRANCESCO,
    Amada Amy
SAUNDERS, Carrie Lou
SAWYER, Elizabeth
SCALETTI, Carla
SCHAFMEISTER, Helen
SCHERTZ, Helen Pitkin
SCHIEVE, Catherine
SCHMIDT, Diane Louise
SCHNEIDER, Susan F.
SCHONTHAL, Ruth E.
SCHROEDER, Beatrice
SCHUBERT, Myra Jean
SCHUMAKER, Grace L.
SCHUMANN, Meta
SCHUSTER, Doris Dodd
SCHUYLER, Philippa Duke
SCHWARTZ, Julie
SCHWARTZ, Nan Louise
SCHWERDTFEGER, E. Anne
SCOTT, Molly
SCOTT, Ruth
SCOTT-HUNTER, Hortense
SCOVILLE, Margaret Lee
SEALE, Ruth
SEARCH, Sara Opal
SEARS, Helen
SEARS, Ilene Hanson
SEAVER, Blanche Ebert
SEAY, Virginia
SEIBERT, Irma
SEIDERS, Mary Asenath
SELDON, Margery Stomme
SELMER, Kathryn Lande
SELTZNER, Jennie
SEMEGEN, Daria
SETO, Robin
SEUEL-HOLST, Marie
SEVERY, Violet Cavell
SEWALL, Maud Gilchrist
SHADWELL, Nancy
SHAFFER, Jeanne Ellison
SHARPE, Anna Wright
SHAW, Alice Marion
SHAW, Carrie Burpee
SHEHAN, Helen Falvey
SHELDON, Lillian Tait
SHELLEY, Margaret Vance
SHELTON, Margaret Meier
SHEPARD, Jean Ellen
SHER, Rebecca
SHERMAN, Mary Elizabeth
SHERMAN, Kim Daryl
SHERREY, Mae Ayres
SHEVITZ, Mimi
SHIELDS, Alice Ferree
SHIRAISHI, Iris

SHIRLEY, Constance Jeanette
SHORE, Clare
SHOTWELL, Phyllis
SHREVE, Susan Ellen
SHRUDE, Marilyn
SHURTLEFF, Lynn Richard
SIDDALL, Louise
SIEGFRIED, Lillie Mahon
SILBERTA, Rhea
SILSBEE, Ann L.
SILVER, Sheila Jane
SILVERBURG, Rose
SILVERMAN, Faye-Ellen
SIMONE, Nina
SIMONS, Lorena Cotts
SIMONS, Netty
SIMONS, Virginia Mary
SIMPSON, Mary Jean
SINGER, Jeanne
SIROONI, Alice
SKAGGS, Hazel Ghazarian
SKEENS, Gwendolyn
SKOLFIELD, Alice Jones Tewksbury
SLEETH, Natalie
SLENCZYNSKA, Ruth
SMELTZER, Susan Mary
SMILEY, Pril
SMITH, Anita
SMITH, Edith Gross
SMITH, Eleanor
SMITH, Hilda Josephine
SMITH, Ida Polk
SMITH, Joan Templar
SMITH, Julia Frances
SMITH, LaDonna Carol
SMITH, Linda Catlin
SMITH, Margit
SMITH, Nellie von Gerichten
SMITH, Ruby Mae
SMITH, Selma Moidel
SMITH, Zelma
SNELL, Lillian Lucinda
SNIFFIN, Allison
SNOW, Mary McCarty
SNYDER, Amy
SOLOMON, Elide M.
SOLOMON, Joyce Elaine
SOMMERS, Daria E.
SOUERS, Mildred
SPALDING, G.F.
SPAULDING, Virginia
SPEACH, Sister Bernadette Marie
SPECHT, Anita Socola
SPEKTOR, Mira J.
SPENCER, Williametta
SPIEGEL, Laurie
SPINDLE, Louise Cooper
SPIZIZEN, Louise Myers
SPONGBERG, Viola
SPRAGG, Deborah T.
SPRAGINS, Florence
STAIR, Patty
STAIRS, Lousie E.
STANLEY, Helen Camille
STANLEY, Marion Isabel
STARBUCK, Anna Diller
STEELE, Helen
STEELE, Lynn
STEIN, Gladys Marie
STEINBERG, Carolyn
STEINBOCK, Evalyn
STEINER, Emma Roberto
STEINER, Gitta Hana
STEVENS, Isadore Harmon
STEWART, Hascal Vaughan
STEWART, Ora Pate
STILMAN-LASANSKY, Julia
STINSON, Ethelyn Lenore
STITT, Margaret McClure
STOCKER, Stella
STOEPPELMANN, Janet

STOPHER, Vashti
STORY, Pauline B.
STRATTON, Anne
STREATCH, Alice
STREEB, Barbara Ellen
STRICKLAND, Lily Teresa
STRUTT, Dorothy
STULTZ, Marie Irene
STURE VASA, Mary O'Hara
STURKOW-RYDER, Theodora
STUTSMAN, Grace May
STYLES, Dorothy Geneva
SUCHY, Gregoria Karides
SUESSE, Dana
SUMNER, Sarah
SWADOS, Elizabeth
SWARTZ, Elsa Ellen
SWIFT, Kay
SWISHER, Gloria Agnes Wilson
TALMA, Louise
TANNER, Hilda
TARBOS, Frances
TARLOW, Karen Anne
TARNER, Evelyn Fern
TASHJIAN, B. Charmian
TATTON, Madeleine
TAYLOR, Eleanor
TAYLOR, Mary Virginia
TAYLOR, Maude Cummings
TECK, Katherine
TEMPLAR, Joan
TERHUNE, Anice
TERRY, Frances
THEMMEN, Ivana Marburger
THOMAS, Connie
THOMAS, Gertrude Auld
THOMAS, Helen
THOMAS, Karen P.
THOMAS, Marilyn Taft
THOMAS, Mary Virginia
THOME, Diane
THOMPSON, Ellen
THOMPSON, Leland
THOMPSON, Mary Frances
THREADGILL-MARTIN, Ravonna
TILLETT, Jeanette
TIMOFEYEW, Mrs.
TODD, Alice Weston
TODD, Esther Cox
TODD, M. Flora
TOLLEFSEN, Augusta
TORRANCE, Mrs. Joe Taylor
TOWER, Joan
TOWNSEND, Jill
TRAEGER, Elinor Meissner
TRAUTH, Dorothy Kyle
TREADWAY, Maude Valerie
TRINITAS, Sister M.
TRIPP, Ruth
TROENDLE, Theodora
TUCKER, Mary Jo
TUCKER, Tui St. George
TUNISON, Louise
TURGEON, Frances
TURNELL, Margaret Hoberg
TURNER, Hilda
TURNER, Mildred Cozzens
TURNER, Myra Brooks
TURNER-MALEY, Florence
TURRIETTA, Cheryl Renee
TUTTLE, Thelma Kent
TWOMBLY, Mary Lynn
TWYMAN, Grace
TYEPKEMA, Sandra
TYSON, Mildred Lund
ULEHLA, Ludmila
UNO, Evelyn
UPTON, Anne
URNER, Catherine Murphy
USHER, Ethel Watson
UTTER, Betty

UYEDA, Leslie
VACCARO, Judith Lynne
VAMOS, Grace Becker
VAN APPLEDORN, Mary Jeanne
VAN BUREN, Alicia Keisker
VAN DE VATE, Nancy Hayes
VAN DEN BEEMT, Hedda
VAN ETTEN, Jane
VAN KATWIJK, Viola Edna Beck
VAN OHLEN, Deborah
VAN VLIET, Pearl H.
VANDERVELDE, Jan
VANDEVERE, J. Lilien
VANNAH, Kate
VARLEY, Rene G.
VASHAW, Cecile
VAZQUEZ, Alida
VEHAR, Persis Anne
VERCOE, Elizabeth
VERHAALEN, Sister Marion
VERRILL, Louise Shurtleff Brown
VIERK, Lois
VILLARINI, Awilda
VILLINES, Virginia
VIRGIL, Antha Minerva Patchen
VIRTUE, Constance Cochnower
VITALIS, Sister Mary
VOLKART, Hazel
VON GUNDEN, Heidi
VON PECHY, Valerie
VOSS, Marie Wilson
VREE-BROWN, Marion F.
VRIONIDES, Rosina
VYNER, Mary Bainbridge
WAGNER, Melinda
WALDECKER, Matilde R.
WALDO, Elisabeth
WALDROP, Uda
WALES, Evelyn
WALKER, Ella May
WALKER, Gwyneth van Anden
WALKER, Shirley
WALLACE, Kathryn
WALLACE, Mildred White
WALLACE, Phyllis Joy
WALLACH, Joelle
WALSH, Elizabeth Jameson
WALTERS, Teresa
WALTON, Constance
WANDERMAN, Dorothy
WANG, An-Ming
WARD, Diane
WARD, Louise Taylor
WARD, Nancy
WARD, Sister Mary Louise
WARDE, Ann Maury
WARE, Harriet
WARE, Helen
WARING, Kate
WARNE, Katharine Mulky
WARNER, Sally Slade
WARNER, Sylvia Townsend
WARREN, Betsy
WARREN, Elinor Remick
WARSHAW, Dalit Paz
WARWICK, Mary Carol
WASKO, Christine
WASSALS, Grace
WATERHOUSE, Frances Emery
WATERSTONE, Satella S.
WATSON, Gwendolyn
WEAVER, Carol Ann
WEAVER, Marion
WEAVER, Mary
WEBB, Allienne Brandon
WEBER, Carole
WECKWERTH, Nancy
WEIGL, Vally
WEISS, Helen L.
WENDELBURG, Norma Ruth
WENNERSTROM, Mary Hannah

WESTBROOK, Helen Searles
WESTGATE, Elizabeth
WESTON, Mildred
WEYBRIGHT, June
WHEAT, Margaret Anne
WHITE, Claude Porter
WHITE, Elsie Fellows
WHITE, Grace
WHITE, Ruth Eden
WHITE, Ruth S.
WHITECOTTON, Shirley Ellen
WHITNER, Mary Elizabeth
WICKER, Irene
WICKHAM, Florence Pauline
WICKS, Camilla
WIENER, Eva Hannah
WIGGINS, Mary
WIGHAM, Margaret
WILBER, Clare Marie O'Keefe
WILBRANDT, Susan
WILES, Margaret Jones
WILEY, Dora
WILLIAMS, Carol
WILLIAMS, Frances
WILLIAMS, Jean E.
WILLIAMS, Joan Franks
WILLIAMS, Linda
WILLIAMS, Mary Lou
WILLMAN, Regina Hansen
WILLS, Edwina Florence
WILSON, Elizabeth
WILSON, Gertrude Hoag
WILSON, Jean Dolores
WILSON, Karen
WILSON, Lynn
WINDSOR, Helen J.
WING, Helen
WINTER, Sister Miriam Therese
WIRE, Edith
WISHART, Betty Rose
WITBECK, Ariel Lea
WITKIN, Beatrice
WITNI, Monica
WOLCOTT, Ellen
WOLF, Gwendolyn
WOLF-COHEN, Veronika
WOLLNER, Gertrude Price
WONG, Betty Ann
WONG, Hsiung-Zee
WOOD, Mabel
WOOD, Marilyn
WOOD, Mary Knight
WOOD, Sister Mary Davida
WOODBRIDGE, Charlotte Louise
WOODRUFF, Edith S.
WOODS, Joan Shirley LeSueur
WOODWARD, Martha Clive
WOOLSLEY, Mary Hale
WORRELL, Lola Carrier
WORTH, Amy
WRIGHT, Nannie Louise
WRONIKOWSKI, Florence F.
WUNSCH, Ilse Gerda
WYETH, Ann
WYLIE, Ruth Shaw
YAZBECK, Louise
YDSTIE, Arlene Buckneberg
YOUNG, Donel Marie
YOUNG, Fredricka Agnes
YOUNG, Jane Corner
YOUNG, Rolande Maxwell
YOUSE, Glad Robinson
ZAIMONT, Judith Lang
ZALLMAN, Arlene
ZANARDI, Patricia
ZECKWER, Camille
ZIFFER, Fran
ZIFFRIN, Marilyn Jane
ZIMMER, Nellie
ZIMMERMAN, Phyllis
ZOECKLER, Dorothy Ackerman

ZUZAK, Doris
ZWEIG, Esther
ZWILICH, Ellen Taaffe
Century unknown
AIR, Kathleen
ANDERSON, Joyce
BAKER, Joanne J.
BARTLETT, Gertrude
BLOOMER, Nancy
BONDURANT, Dorothy
BRUNNER, Miriam
BUCKLEY, Caroline Kemper
BUMSTEAD, Gladys
CAWKER, Lenore H.
CHRISTENSEN, Betty
COMBIE, Ida Mae
COOMBS, Mary Woodhull
CORYELL, Marion
COUNTRYMAN, Alice
CROSBY, Marie
DONALDSON, Sadie
ECHOLS, Mrs. James
ERB, Mae Aileen
ERVIN, Emily L.
FERGUS-HOYT, Phyllis
FOSSEY, Elizabeth Jarrell
FRACKER, Cora Robins
FULLAM, Victoria
FUNK, Susan
GRIEVE, Annette
GRISWOLD, Gertrude
HARTLEY, Evaline
HATTON, Anne
HAUSENFLUCK, Frances W.
HEFNER, Leah
HOFFMANN, Mary
KAVELIN, Nellie
KINGSBURY, Lynn C.
KORANDA, Lorraine
KROESEN, Jill
LAVINE, Rhoda J.
LEBARRON, M.H.
LEMERT, Gladys Fulbright
LIVELY, Katherine Allen
McCOY, Nadine
McIVER WOOD, Mrs. Jules
McLARRY, Beverley
MADISON, Ada
MARSHALL, Elisabeth
MARTIN, Elizabeth B.
MENKE, Emma
MIRANDA, Erma Hoag
OLMSTEAD, Bess Heath
ORMAND, Lilla
PENN, Marilyn
PETER, Lily
PEYCKE, Frieda
QUAILLE, Elizabeth
RAPOPORT, Ruth
REED, Edith Lobdell
REYNOLDS, Florence
RICHTER, Rebecca
RICKETTS, Lucy W.
RIND, Bernice M.
RISTAD, Eloise
RITTER, Irene Marschand
RODGERS, Irene
ROGERS, Emmy Brady
ROMA, Elsie P.
ROSSMAN, Floy
RUSSELL, Velma Armistead
RYCOFF, Lalla
SANKS, Mary C.
SANS-SOUCI, Gertrude
SAPAROFF, Andrea
SCHAFER, Ruth
SCHMIDT, Susan
SCHMITT, Alma C.
SEITZ, Inez Rae
SHERWOOD, Josephine
SIEDOFF, Elizabeth

SMITH, Ella May Dunning
SMITH, Mildred Price
SMITH, Virginia B.
SNODGRASS, Louise Harrison
SOMOGI, Judith
STILLING, Kemp
STRONG, May A.
THAIN, Lillian
TISHMAN, Fay
TRAMMER, Gaynor
VELLUCCI, Leonilde
WARD, Beverly A.
WARD, Willa
WATKINS, Mary
WATSON, Mabel Madison
WEAVER, Harriet
WICKDAHL, Lillian S.
WICKHAM, Carol S.
WILSON, Dorothy
WOLLIN, Natalie
WOODSTOCK, Mattie
WOOTTON, Meredith E.
WOZERCRAFT, Marion

URUGUAY
20th Century A.D.
BARRADAS, Carmen
DE PATE, Elisabetta M.S.

U.S.S.R., AFTER 1917
20th Century A.D.
AARNE, Els
ABRAMOVA, Sonia Pinkhasovna
AGABALIAN, Lidia Semyenovna
AKHUNDOVA, Shafiga Gulam kyzy
AKSYANTSEVA, Ninel Moiseyevna
ANDREYEVA, Elena Fedorovna
ANDREYEVA, M.
ANDRIEVSKAYA, Nina
    Konstantinovna
ARAZOVA, Izabella Konstantinovna
ARSEYEVA, Irina Vasilievna
ASTROVA, V.
AUSTER, Lydia Martinovna
AVETISIAN, Aida Konstantinovna
BABAYEVA, Seda Grigorievna
BAIKADAMOVA, Baldyrgan
    Bakhitzhanovna
BAKLANOVA, Natalia
BARAMISHVILI, Olga Ivanovna
BEKMAN-SHCHERBINA, Elena
    Aleksandrovna Kamentseva
BERZON, Asya Yevseyevna
BRYUSSOVA, Nadezhda Yakolevna
CHEBOTARIAN, Gayane
    Movsesovna
CHITCHIAN, Geguni Oganesovna
CHKHEIDZE, Dali Davidovna
CHUDOVA, Tatiana Alekseyevna
DAVIDOVA, V.
DAVITASHVILI, Meri Shalvovna
DIAKVNISHVILI, Mzisavar
    Zakharevna
DROBYAZGINA, Valentina Ivanovna
DYCHKO, Lesya Vasilevna
DZHAFAROVA, Afag Mamed kyzy
EGOROVA, Maria
EKSANISHVILI, Eleonara Grigorevna
ELCHEVA, Irina Mikhailovna
FILZ, Bogdanna
FIRSOVA, Elena
GABASHVILI, Nana
GERCHIK, Vera Petrovna
GOKHMAN, Elena Vladimirovna
GOLOVINA, Olga Akimovna
GONTARENKO, Galina Nikolayevna
GORODOVSKAYA, V.
GUBAIDULINA, Sofia Asgatovna
GUSEINZADE, Sofia Asgatovna
GUTMAN, Natalia Grigorievna
GVAZAVA, Tamara Davidovna

GYANDZHETSIAN, Destrik
    Bogdanovna
IASHVILI, Lili Mikhailovna
IBRAGIMOVA, Ela Imamedinovna
IBRAGIMOVA, Sevda Mirza kyzy
IGENBERGA, Elga Avgustovna
ILLIUTOVICH, Nina Yakovlevna
ISAKOVA, Aida Petrovna
ISMAGILOVA, Leila Zagirovna
KARNITSKAYA, Nina Andreyevna
KATZMAN, Klara Abramovna
KAVARNALIEVA, Konstantina
KAZHAEVA, Tatiana Ibragimovna
KHAIRUTDINOVA, Luisa
KHASANSHINA, D.
KHERESKO, Lidia Petrovna
KHODZHAEVITCH, Asja
KHOLOPOVA, Valentina Nikolayevna
KILICHEVSKAYA, A.
KOLODUB, Zhanna Efimovna
KORNILOVA, Tatiana Dmitrevna
KOVALEVA, Olga Vasilevna
KOZAKIEVICH, Anna Abramovna
KOZHEVNIKOVA, Ekaterina
    Vadimovna
KRASNOGLIADOVA, Vera
    Vladimirovna
KULESHOVA, Galina Grigorevna
KULIEVA, Farida Tairovna
KUSS, Margarita Ivanovna
KUZNETSOVA, Zhanetta
    Alexandrovna
KVERNADZE, Bidzina
LEBEDEVA, A.
LEONCHIK, Svetlana Gavrilovna
LEVI, Natalia Nikolayevna
LEVINA, Zara Alexandrovna
LEVITOVA, Ludmila Vladimirovna
LEVITSKAYA, Viktoria Sergeyevna
LIADOVA, Ludmila Alekseyevna
LICHTENSTEIN, Olga Grigorievna
LITSITE, Paula Yanovna
LVOVA, Julia Fedorovna
LYUBOMIRSKAYA-BOYARSKAYA,
    Revekka Grigorevna
MAILIAN, Elza Antonovna
MAKAROVA, Nina Vladimirovna
MALDYBAYEVA, Zhyldyz
    Abdylasovna
MANUKIAN, Irina Eduardovna
MATEVOSIAN, Araks Surenovna
MATVEYEVA, Novella
METALLIDI, Zhanneta Lazarevna
MIAGI, Ester Kustovna
MIGRANYAN, Emma
MIRSHAKAR, Zarrina Mirsaidovna
MKRTYCHIEVA, Virginia Nikitichna
MSHEVELIDZE, Shalva
MUKHAMEDZHANOVA, Mariam
NAZIROVA, Elmira Mirza Rza kyzy
NIKOLAYEVA, Galina Alexandrovna
NIKOLAYEVA, Tatiana Petrovna
NIKOLSKAYA, Lyubov Borisovna
NIKOLSKAYA, Olga Vasilevna
NISS, Sofia Natanovna
NOVOSELOVA, Ludmila Alexeyevna
OSETROVA-YAKOVLIEVA, Nina
    Alexandrovna
OSHCHERETOVSKAYA, N.
OSTROVSKAYA, T.
PAKHMUTOVA, Alexandra
    Nikolayevna
PETROVA, Olga Andreyevna
PLIEVA, Zhanna Vasilievna
POLIAKOVA, Ludmila Viktorovna
POPATENKO, Tamara Alexandrovna
PRAVOSSUDOVITCH, Natalja
    Michajlovna
RAKHMANKULOVA, Mariam
    Mannanovna
RHEINGOLD, Lauma Yanovna

ROBITASHVILI, Lia Georgievna
ROZHAVSKAYA, Yudif Grigorevna
RUCHEVSKAYA, Ekaterina
  Alexandrovna
RZAYEVA, Agabadzhi Ishmael kykz
SABININA, Marina Dimitrevna
SAFARIAN, Lucia Arisovna
SAIDAMINOVA, Dilorom
SALMANOVA, R.
SALTYKOVA, Tamara Sergeyevna
SAMSUTDINOVA, Magira
SAMVELIAN, Sofia Vardanovna
SCHEIN, Suzanna Fedorovna
SHAGIAKHMETOVA, Svetlana
  Georgievna
SHAIMARDANOVA, Shakhida
SHAVERZASHVILI, Tamara
  Antonovna
SHUKAILO, Ludmila Fedorovna
SHUTENKO, Taisiya Ivanovna
SIDORENKO, Tamara Stepanovna
SIMONIAN, Nadezhda Simonovna
SKREBKOVA, M.
SLENDZINSKA, Julitta
SLIANOVA-MIZANDARI, Dagmara
  Levanovna
SMIRNOVA SOLODCHENKOVA,
  Tatiana Georgievna
SMIRNOVA, Galina Konstantinovna
STANEKAITE-LAUMYANSKENE,
  Elena Ionovna
STEPANIUGINA, E.
STREICHER, Lyubov Lvovna
SUGAREVA, Parashkeva
SULTANOVA, Asya Bakhish kyzy
SVANIDZE, Natela Damianovna
TILICHEYEVA, Elena Nikolayevna
TKACH, Zlata Moiseyevna
TUICHEVA, Zumrad
TUMANIAN, Elizaveta Artashesovna
TUMANISHVILI, Ketevana
  Dmitirevna
TURTYGINA, Pava Grigorevna
TYRMAND, Eta Moiseyevna
USTVOLSKAYA, Galina Ivanovna
UZEINZADZE, Adilea
VAKHVAKHISHVILI, Tamara
  Nikolayevna
VASILIEVA, Tatiana Ivanovna
VETLUGINA, Natalia Alekseyevna
VINOGRADOVA, Vera
VINTULE, Ruta Evaldovna
VORONINA, Tatiana Aleksandrovna
WEISSBERG, Julia Lazerevna
YAGLING, Victoria
YAKHNINA, Yevgenia Yosifovna
YAROSHEVSKAYA, Ludmila
  Anatolievna
YEGEROVA, V.
YUKHNOVSKAYA, Ninel Grigorievna
ZARANEK, Stefania Anatolyevna
ZARIPOVA, Naila Gatinovna
ZAVALISHINA, Maria Semyonovna
ZELIKOVSKAYA, Fania
  Mordukhovna
ZHUBANOVA, Gaziza Akhmetovna
ZHUBINSKAYA, Valentina Yanovna
ZHVANETSKAIA, Inna
  Abramovna
ZIBEROVA, Zinaida Petrovna

VENEZUELA
20th Century A.D.
BEETH, Lola
CARRENO, Teresa
ESCOBAR, Maria Luisa
ESTRELLA, Blanca
LARA, Nelly Mele
OTERO, Mercedes
QUINTANILLA, Alba
RUGELES, Ana Mercedes de

Century unknown
BOR, Modesta

VIETNAM
20th Century A.D.
NGUYEN, Louise

YUGOSLAVIA, AFTER 1918
20th Century A.D.
BEGO-SIMUNIC, Andelka
FRAJT, Ludmila
JANKOVIC, Miroslava
KOZINOVIC, Lujza
LANG-BECK, Ivana
LUDVIG-PECAR, Nada
MARIC, Ljubica
MARINKOVIC, Jelena
MATJAN, Vida
MILENKOVIC, Jelena
MOSUSOVA, Nadezda
NENCIC, Ivanka
PILIS, Heda
PREDIC-SAPER, Branislava
SANCIN, Mirca
SCEK, Breda Friderika
SIMIC, Darinka
SISTEK-DJORDJEVIC, Mirjana
STEFANOVIC, Ivana
ZIVKOVIC, Mirjana
ZRELC, Celeste

NATIONALITY UNKNOWN
12th Century A.D.
CLUZEL, Irene
16th Century A.D.
MOLINARO, Simone
17th Century A.D.
RASSCHENAU, Marianna
VAN SOLDT, Suzanna
18th Century A.D.
ASTORGA, Emmanuelle d'
TABARY, M.A.C. de
TIRINANZI, Nannette
19th Century A.D.
ALBRECHT, Lillie
BARNES, Bertha L.
BOSCH, Elisa
BREITENBACH, Antoinette de
BROWN, Harriet Estelle
BROWNE, Harriet
BRUSCHINI, Ernestina
BUSI, Leonida
CARUTHERS, Julia
CASTELLI, Adele
CONVERT, Josephine
DEPECKER, Rose
DONALDSON, Elizabeth
DORISI, Lina
ELDESE, Renée
FERRARI, Francesca Jessie
GABLER, Jeanette
GOLDSTEIN, M. Anna
HAMAN, Elizabeth
HARVEY, Roberta
HILLEBRAND-LAUSSOT, Jessie
HUNT, Gertrude
JESSUP-MILDRED Marion de
KALB, Janet
KRAINDL, Sophie de
LASCHANZKY, Mme.
LEBER, Antonia
MADURO, Sarah H.L.
MARA, La
MATTFELD, Marie
MELY, Marie, Countess Vanden
  Heuvel
MONTESQUIOU, Odette de
MRASECK, Fraulein
NORRIS, Mary
O'DONNELL, Malvine,
  Countess

OWENS, Priscilla
PERCHERON, Suzanne
PERELLI, Natalie
PICCOLOMINI, Marietta
POLAK, Nina
REED, Florence
ROELOFSON, Emily B.
RUCH-TSCHIEMER, Flora
SCHINDLER, Livia
SPAULDING, Florence Atherton
TRUETTE, Everette
WADIA, Sabra
WALBERG, Emilie
WARDER, Marie
WINTLE, Virginia
YOUNG, Corrine
YOUNG, Matilda
20th Century A.D.
ABOULKER, Isabelle
ADAM, Maria Emma
ALEGRO, Amelia Guilhermina
ANSINK, Caroline
AUBER, Chantal
AVRIL, Mireille
AZARCON, Minda
BADYE, Dyeliba
BAL, Rosita
BALEN, Joan
BALSHONE, Cathy S.
BARATI, Ruth
BARNEKOW, Deborah
BARNETT, Wally
BARNEY, Nancy
BEAMISH, Sally
BELLE, Marie-Paule
BENES, Jara
BERTACCA, Uberta
BIDDER, Helen
BIERMANN, Petra
BILSLAND, Ethel
BIRCH, Ernestine
BIXBY, Allene K.
BORKOWSKI, Marian
BOSHKOFF, Ruth
BOTTELIER, Ina
BOULOGNE, Julia R.C.
BOXALL, Maria
BRANDON, Phyllis
BRENNEN, Sister Rose Immacula
BRICE, Laure
BRODERICK, Deborah Houstle
BUECHNER, Margaret
BURGESS, Brio
BURGESS, Marjorie
BUSCEMI MONTALTO, Margherita
CALANDRA, Matilde T. de
CANAT DE CHIZY, Edith
CANNISTRACI, Helen
CARNECI, Carmen
CARPENTER, Imogen
CARTER, Dorothy
CECILE REGINA, Sister
CHIAPPARIN, Solange
CLAIRE, Paula
COCHEREAU, Nicole
COCHRANE, Peggy
COLLEY, Betty
COLOMER BLAS, Maria
COOLIDGE, Lucy
CORNEILLE
COZETTE, Cynthia
DEDERICH, Hilda
DIESENDRUCK, Tamar
DRIESSLER QUISTORP, Monica
DURAS, Marguerite
EGGELING-SPIES, I.
ERVIN, Karen
EYMAR, Jacqueline
FORSTER, Charlotte
FOWKE, Edith Fulton
FRANCHINO, Raffaela

FRANKLIN-PYKE, Elinor
FRONTIERA, Mary Jo
FROTHINGHAM, Eugenia
GABRIELY, Irith
GABRYS, Ewa Lucja Maria
GALINNE, Rachel
GALLINA, Jill
GARNIER, Ilse
GERENYI, Ilse
GEYRING, E.
GHARACHE-DAGHI, Sheyda
GLENN-COPELANN, Beverly
GLICKMAN, Sylvia
GNEDEL, Mimi
GOLETTI, Nelly
GREENE, Diana
GRERICHS, Doris
GUILBERT, Yvette
HEWITT-JONES, Anita
HILMER, Sally
HINE, Marie M.
HOLMES, Shirlee McGee
HOOVER, Carolyn
HOPKINS, Sarah
HORAK, Hilda
JAMES, Vera
KABOS, Ilona
KARVENO, Wally
KATONOVA, S.
KESSICK, Marlaena
KING, Thea
KIRCH, Irene E.
KNERR, Katrina
KUSUNOKI, Tomoko
LAMBA, Huguette
LASANSKY, Ada Julia
LERCHE, Juliane
LORENZ, Petra
McBURNEY, Mona
MARESCA, Chiara
MARKOV, Katherine Lee
MASSON, Carol Foster
MAYER, Bernadette
MERMAN, Joyce
MESSIAM, Eve
MOLINA, Olivia
MOLINE, Lily Wadham
NEWELL, Eleanor
OCHOA, Elvira
OENNERBERG-MALLING, Berta
O'HEARN, Arletta
ONDISHKO, Denise M.
ORIGO, Iris
ORLANDI, Nora
OSTERTAG, Gertrud
PINE-BLUSTEIN, Cathia
POOLE, Anne
PRITI-PAINTAL
PRUNEDER, Frau
RADEKE, Winifred
RAVISSA
REUCHSEL, Amedée
RICHARDS, Deborah
RICHINSE, Cecile J.
ROEDER, Toni
RZEPECKA, Maria
SAROVA, Dagmar
SASSOLI, Ada
SCHEFFEL, Conny
SCHMIDT, Mia
SCIBOR, Maria
SCOTT, Hazel
SEALY, Helen
SHEPPARD, Suzanne
SMITH, Doreen Wilhelmina
SOEDERG, Gerda
SOHET-BOULNOIS, Suzanne
SOHNIUS, Elfriede
SPECKNER, Anna Barbara
STOCKER, Clara
SUCCARI, Dia

SUGAI, Esther
TANTU, Cornelia
TAYLOR, Iris
TESCHKE, Herma
THOMAS, Janet Owen
THOMSON Geraldine
THOREAU, Rachel
TROTT, Josephine
VAN STEENBERG, Michelim
VANDENBURGH, Mildred
VASCONELLOS, Nana
VELTHUYSEN, Abesritz von
VERNAELDE, Henriette
VIKTOR, Denise
WALSH, Helen Mary
WARSKA, Wanda
WEBER, Bertha
WEISS, Arleta
WELLS, Elsie
WIENER, Elisabeth
WINKLER, Blanka
WRANA, Emilie
YDETTE, Arline
ZEINER, Marliese
ZELINSKA, Lydia
ZIPRICK, Marjorie Jean

Century unknown
ACKERNLEY, Mabel
ALBRECHT, Elise
ALLARD DEMERS, Cecile
ALLEN, Mary
AMARD, Anna
ANDERSON, Edythe
ANDERSON, Elizabeth D.
ANDERSON, Lucy
ARMSTRONG, Susannah
ASHBY, Gertrude
AUSTIN, Roberta Martin
BALL, Rae Eleanor
BARLOW, Sybil
BARRY, Emilie de
BATTY, Florence
BESSON, Maria
BINNS, Jaqueline
BISETTI-BALICE, Rina
BISHOP, Anna
BLAIR-OLIPHANT, Lilian
BRADY, Emma
BRANDES, Renee
BRELING, Jossie
BRENT, Miss
BRESSON, Marie
BRET, Mme. le
BRIL, France-Yvonne
BRUCK, Ester
BRUNET, Jacqueline
BULLIER, Lea
BURNHAM, Mazel
CACCHIATELLI, Adelina
CARBALLO, Celeste
CARLEY, Isabel McNeill
CARTWRIGHT, Patricia
CASPARY, Marie
CASSINIS, Giovannina
CASTELBARCO, Albani Angeline
CHARPENTIER, Louise
CHARPENTREAU, Simone
CHAZOT-LAUCHER, Mme.
CHERBOURG, Mlle.
CHOISY, Laure
CIARLANTINI, Paola
CLEAVER, Esther
COBBE, Linda
COLANGELO, Rita
COLLIER, Elizabeth Mary
COMFORT, Annabel
CORKER, Marjorie
CORNEA, Nely
COURRAS, Jeanne
COWELL, Mrs. Sidney
CRAMM, Helen L.

CRANE, Charlotte M.
CRENDIROPULO, Anna G.
CROFF PORTALUPI, Maddalena
CUNNINGHAME, Agnes Jane
   Winifred
DAHLSTROM, Greta
DARION, Mlle.
DARTY, Paulette
D'AUBISSON, Marguerite
DAUVERGNE DE BEAUVAIS, Mlle.
DAVID, Elizabeth H.
DAVIDSON, Muriel
DE CASTRO, Jessie
DEMAREST, Victoria
DESANGLES, Anny
DINSART, Madeleine
DONATI, Albasini Giuseppina
DONETS-TESSEIR, Marija
DORFNER, Elisabet
DROLENVAUX, Mme.
DUPRE, Mme.
DUROT, Maria
DUSMAN, Linda
EDWARDS, Bella
EICHHORN, Marianne
ELY, Carroll
ENOCH, Yvonne
ESCOMBE, Ester
ESCRIBANO SANCHEZ, Maria
FERRIS, Joan
FORE, Burdette
FORTIER, Julia
FRANK-AUTHENRID, Hedwig
FUNCKE, Kathleen Paula
GABORIT, Marie Josephe
GABRIEL, Alma
GAERTNER, Marie Therese
GALLOS, Mme.
GAMBARO, Alceste
GAMBOGI, Luigia
GATEHOUSE, Lady
GINA, Valentina
GLASS, Jennifer
GORDON, Hope
GORE, Blanche
GORTON, Karen
GOTTSCHALK, Clara
GOULD, Octavia R.
GRACE, Norah
GREEN, Lydia
GREEN, Miss
GRINDELL, Clara Kyle
GUSTAFSON, Vera
HARRINGTON, Mrs. W.C.
HART, Dorothy
HOFFMEYER, Zantha
HOLDBERG, Margaret
HOLZWEISSIG, Erika
HOOVER, Carolyn
HOSCHEK-MUHLHEIM, Klare
IDZIK, Danuta
JACQUET, Marie-Louise
JENNINGS, Marjorie
JENSON, Carol
JOHANSEN, Irene
JOHNDREAU, Audrey
JOHNS, Altona Trent
JOHNSON, Myrna
JOHNSTON-WATSON, Miss
KALLENBACH, Dagmar
KARGER-HOENIG, Friederike
KAUFFMAN, Amanda
KEECH, Diana
KHRISTOVA, Milina
KIEK, Bessie
KLEMM, Roberta
LAIRD, Nancy
LAMB, Myrna
LANGFORD, Olivia
LASON, Olga
LAWSON, May

LE BAS, Gertrude
LEA, Annie
LENKI, Gabriella
LEQUIEN, Colette
LEVAILLANT, Irma
LIECHTI, Grety
LIPSCHUTZ, Lita
LIVINGSTONE, Dorothy
LOEWY, Irma
LOROLLE, Annie
LOTTIN, Phedora
LOVELL, Joan
McDOWALL, Cecilia
MACIEJASZ-KAMINSKA, Anna
MAGARIA, Elvira
MAHLE, Maria Aparecida
MALVEZZI, Peppina
MANACIO-GALDI, Elvira
MANOUKIAS, Virginie
MANTIA, Simone
MARES, Rosita
MARKS, Florence Mary
MARTIN, Gloria
MATTHISON, Adela
MEZZACAPO, Elena
MIGLIARI FERNANDES,
   Marlene
MIKESHINA, Ariadna
MOMONT, Heidi
MOREA, Vincenza della
NERVI, Marta
NICCOLINI, Virginia
NICOLINI, Maria

OREFICE, Olga
ORTWEIN, Gerhild
PADULA, Elvira
PALMER, Peggy Spencer
PARET, Betty
PERERA, Carmen
PEREYERA LIZASO, Nydia
PERRY, Nina
PERUGIA, Noemie
PERWICH, Susanna
PILLING, Dorothy
PLEE, Jo
PORTCH, Margaret
PULER, Clara P.
QUENEDEY, Aglae
RAMOS, Natalia
RAPIN-GERBER, Eleonore
RIEUNIER, Françoise
RILEY, Alice
ROSENWEIG, Florence
ROSS, Clara
ROUCH, Alma
ROWSON, Susannah
RUTTER, Ida
SACHSEN, Caroline von
SAVOY, Anne
SCHIAVO DE GREGORIO,
   Maria
SCHIEMANN, Agnes
SCHLECHTRIEM, Theresia
SHAFFER, Helen Louise
SHINDLER, Mary Dana
SHLEG, Ludmila Karlovna

SOKOLL, Christa
SORELLI, Mariella
SPROED, Anna
STAEHLI, Violette
STANZELEIT, Barbara
STEINBOCK, Evalyn
STERN, Klara
SUTTON, Theodora
TAIROVA, S.
TAVEIRA, Eva
THEMAR, Rosalie
THORBERGS, Ingeborg
TREVALSA, Joan
TRISTAN, Joyeuse
TRUSTEDT, Ulrike
VAUGHAN, Freda
VENTURE, Anna
VERESS, Jolan
VESELA, Alena
VESTERINE, Marja
VON HAGEN, Elizabeth
VOYNICH, Ethel Lillian
WHITE, Evelyn Davidson
WICKOP, Eta
WIEGAND, Elizabeth Grieger
WIESENFELDT, Eva
WILLERT-ORFF, Gertrud
WILLIAMS, Alice Crane
WINOKUR, Roselyn M.
WINTULE, Ruta
WYLIE, Betty Jane
YEARWOOD, Kathleen
ZANETTI, Emilia

APPENDIX 5

List of Pseudonyms

PSEUDONYM	COMPOSER
A.L.	Lehmann, Amelia
AARNE, Els	Paemurru, Elze Janovna
ADRIANETTA, L'	Baroni, Eleanora
ALFRED	McCollin, Frances
ANAIDE, Marulli	Perriere-Pilte, Anais, Countess of
ANOKA, Freddie	Baganier, Janine
AORENA, Mme.	Liliuokalani, Queen of Hawaii
ARRIEU, Claude	Simon, Louise Marie
ASPRI, Orsola	Appignani, Adelhaide
ATTICUS	McCollin, Frances
AWBURY	McCollin, Frances
BASSETT, Beth	Bassett, Henrietta Elizabeth
BEACH, Alden	Beach, Priscilla A.
BERNARDONE, Anka	Sister Mary Ann Joyce
BERNOUX, Leon	Perronnet, Amelie
BEZDEK, Jan	Bezdek, Sister John Joseph
BLANGY, Caroline	Grandval, Marie Felicie
BRAHE, May	Morgan, Mary Hannah
BRISSAC, Jules	MacFarren, Emma Marie
BROWN, Charles	Uyeda, Leslie
CAMPBELL, Aline	Montgomery, Merle
CANNING, Effie I.	Crockett, Effie I.
CANONICUS	McCollin, Frances
CARMEN MARINA	Gioconda, Carmen Manteca
CHALOIX, Erny	Schorlemmer, Erna von
CLARIBEL	Barnard, Charlotte
COMALE	Winkel, Therese Emilie Henriette
CONSEY, Jill	Felix, Margery Edith
CONSTANS, Constantin	Drdova, Marie
COTTON-MARSHALL, Grace	Marschal-Loepke, Grace
CZANYI	Schmitt, Alois
DANIEL	Garcia, Eduarda Mansilla de
DAWE, Margery	Felix, Margery Edith
DE BAUR, Mme.	Bawr, Alexandrine Sophie
DE BOHUN, Lyle	Boone, Clara Lyle
DE LARA, Adelina	Tilbury, Adelina
DE REISET, Maria Felicita	Grandval, Marie Felicie
DE SIVRAI, Jules	Roeckel, Jane
DES ROCHES, Gilbert	Legoux, Julie, Baroness
DEE, Margaret	Diefenthaler, Margaret Kissinger
DELANDE, Jo	Vigneron-Ramakers, Christiane-Josée
DELBOS, Claire	Delbos, Louise Justine
DELYSSE, Jean	Roesgen-Champion, Marguerita Sara
DEWITZ, Hildegard	Kazoreck, Hildegard
DI NOGERO, Francisco	Bauer, Emilie Frances
DINO, Janita	Tajani Mattone, Ida
DOLORES	Dickson, Ellen
D'ORME, Valerie	Atkinson, Dorothy
D'ORSAY, M.L.	Ponsa, Maria Luisa
DOR, Daniela	Kaufman, Barbara
DORIA, Clara	Rogers, Clara Kathleen
DUCELLE, Paul	Krogmann, Carrie William
DURAND, Jean	Rochat, Andree
DUTTON, Theodora	Alden, Blanche Ray
ELIDORA, Donna	Wuiet, Caroline
ELIODD	Oddone Sulli-Rao, Elisabetta
ELL	Loud, Emily L.
ERTIS	Esterhazy, Alexandrine, Countess
ESCARDOT, L.	Karr Y de Alfonsetti, Carmen
ETPA - Ermelinda Talea Pastorella Arcada	Maria Antonia WAlpurgis
FARINETTA, La	Camati, Maria
FARNINGHAM, Marianne	Hearn, Marianne/Mary Ann
FIFE, Duncan	Atkinson, Dorothy
FORREST, Sidney	Stairs, Louise E.
FRANCOIS, M.	Bawr, Alexandrine Sophie
G********	Haxthausen, Aurore M.G. Ch. von
GARRETT	McCollin, Frances
GATELY, Francis Sabine	Rose of Jesus, Sister
GEYRING, E.	* * *

PSEUDONYM	COMPOSER	PSEUDONYM	COMPOSER
GOLDBERG, Sonja	Balenovic, Draga	MORFIDA	Ralph, Kate
GOWER, Beryl	Atkinson, Dorothy	MURDOCK, Jane	Roobenian, Amber
GUSHINGTON, Impulsia	Dufferin, Lady Helen Selina	NOGERO, Francesco	Bauer, Emilie Frances
H.L.L.	Borthwick, Jane Laurie	O'HARA, Mary	Sture Vasa, Mary O'Hara
HADLER, Rosemary	Lorenz, Ellen Jane	PADUCI	Lefebvre, Francoise
HAIGH, Bernard	Edwards, Clara	PALMER, F.H.	Hartmann, Emma Sophie Amalie
HANS, Lio	Scheidl-Hutterstrasser, Lili	PARGETER, Wyatt	Pargeter, Maude
HARA, Kazuko (2)	Yamaguchi, Kazuko	PASTOR	McCollin, Frances
HARDELOT, Guy d'	Rhodes, Helen	PERY, M.	Pferdemenges, Maria Pauline Augusta
HARPER, Mrs. Sydney	WRIGHT, Ellen	PHILHARMONICA, Mrs.	* * *
HEITER, Amalie	Amalie, Marie Friederike Augusta	PILGRIM	McCollin, Frances
HERZ, DR. Albert	Herz, Maria	POLDOWSKI	Wieniawska, Irene Regine
HOPE, Douglas	Wilson, Hilda	RAEDZIELG, Gisella	Delle Grazie, Gisella
HROSTWITHA	Von Rossow, Helene	RAFAELE	Aleotti, Raffaela-Argenta
HUALALAI	Paris, Ella Hudson	RATULD, P.	Zbyszewska-Olechnowska, Maria
HUNTLEY, Helen	Van de Vate, Nancy Hayes	REISET DE TESIER, Maria	Grandval, Marie Felicie
HUNTLEY, William	Van de Vate, Nancy Hayes	RENE, Victor	Hale, Irene
IKA	Peyron, Albertina Fredrika	RHENE-JAQUE	Cartier, Marguerite
JAGIELLA, Jadwiga	Brzowska-Mejean, Jadwiga	RING, Montague	Aldridge, Amanda Ira
JAMES, Allen	Lorenz, Ellen Jane	ROMANINA, La	Archilei, Vittoria
JONES, Hart	Higginbotham, Irene	ROSE	Rosenthal, E.
JORDAN, Mrs.	Bland, Dora/Dorothea	SAINT-AMANS FILS, Leon	La Hye, Louise Genevieve
KAIMEN	Stuart-Bergstrom, Else Marianne	SAINT SIMON, Comtesse de	Bawr, Alexandrine Sophie
KARLTON	McCollin, Frances	SAMAMA, Azuma	Servoz, Harriet
KAWAI, Sawako	Nakamura, Sawako	SAUVAL, Marc	Soulage, Marcelle Fanny Henriette
KENDAL, Sydney	Mason, Gladys Amy	SCAPUS, Mit	Scheepers-van Dommelen, Maria
KERWEY, Julia	Kerr, Julia	SELIN	McCollin, Frances
KING, Gilbert	Harrison, Susan Frances	SERANUS	Harrison, Susan Frances
KING, Wilton	Mullen, Adelaide	SERENA, Amalie	Amalie, Marie Friederike Augusta
KONSTANTIN	Drdova, Marie	SHIBATA, Haruna	Miyake, Haruna
KORD, Mira	Vorlova, Slavka	SILNI, Max	Paigne, Mme.
KUHLMAN, Clara	Haxthausen, Aurore M.G. Ch. von	SKELTON, Violet	Dunlop, Isobel
LAGO	Netzel, Laura	SPENGER, M.T.	Dichler-Sedlacek, Erika
LALAIN, Luc	Daneau, Suzanne	STERLING, Antoinette	MacKinlay, Mrs. J.
LANGHAM, Guy	Atkinson, Dorothy	TEMPLE, Hope	Davies, Dotie
LAREN, Derek	Van Epen-de Groot, Else Antonia	THEODOSIA	Steel, Ann
LEGINSKA, Ethel	Liggins, Ethel	THERESA	Valadon, Giovanna Emma
LIBBEY, Dee	Rohde, Q'Adrianne	THIEME, Karl	Thieme, Kerstin Anja
LIOS	Erdoedy, Luisa, Countess	THORNE, Edgar	Merrick, Marie E.
LOHOEFER, Evelyn	* * *	TRENT, Anthony	Clarke, Rebecca
LOPWEGEN, Benedikt	Jenny, Sister Leonore	VALGRAND, Clemence	Grandval, Marie Felicie
LOVELL, Katharine	Hubicki, Margaret Olive	VAN TWINKLE, Kate	Vannah, Kate
MAERY, H.	Mug, Sister Mary Theodosia	VERNE, Mary J.A.	Wurm, Mary J.A.
MANA-ZUCCA	Zuckermann, Augusta	WALDIN, Hugues	Blanc de Fontbelle, Cecile
MARXHAUSEN, P.F.	Schatzell, Pauline von	WATARI, Koyoko	Natsume, Koyoko
MASTERS, Juan	Eames, Juanita	WEIMAR, Auguste	Goetze, Auguste
MAY, Orchard	Langrishe, May Katherine	WENDEL	McCollin, Frances
MAYFAIR	McCollin, Frances	WHEELWRIGHT	McCollin, Frances
MEDWAY, Carol	Felix, Margery Edith	WURMBACH-STUP-PACH, Ernest	Vrabely-Wurmbach-Stuppachova, Stefania
MEL-BONIS	Domange, Mrs. Albert	ZENTA, Hermann	Holmés, Augusta Mary Anne
MONTGOMERY	Gyllenhaal, Matilda Valeriana		
MONTI, Diana	Kazoreck, Hildegard		
MOORE, Thelma	Miron, Tsipora		
MOREA, Centa Della	Garelli Della Morea, Vincenza		

APPENDIX 6

Operas and Operettas by Women Composers

A GARA COLLE RONDINI
Oddone Sulli-Rao, Elisabetta
A L'HONNEUR DE NANCY (1819)
Amalie, Marie Friederike Augusta
A LA WATTEAU (1906)
Lehman, R.
A NOIVA DO MAR
De Biase Bidart, Lycia
A PROPOS
Sigal, Mme.
ABBOT OF DRIMOCK, THE (1955)
Musgrave, Thea
ABIGAIL, (four acts)
Vito-Delvaux, Berthe di
**ABOU HASSAN, OR THE SLEEPER
AWAKENED, (three acts)**
Gerrish-Jones, Abbie
ABRAHAM LINCOLN THE BOY
Wicker, Irene
ADASHIBA, (one act) (1980)
Szoenyi, Erzsebet
ADEA
Cozette, Cynthia
**ADELHEID, GEMAHLIN OTTOS DES
GROSSEN**
Benfey-Schepe, Anna
ADOLAR UND HILARIA
Anna Amalia, Duchess of
Saxe-Wiemar
ARIADNE AUF NAXOS, (two acts)
Paradis, Maria Theresia von
ADVENTURES OF THUMBELINA, THE
Windsor, Helen J.
A'AGITA
Gideon, Miriam
AGATHA'S DOCTOR
Harraden, R. Ethel
AGNES, (one act) (1763)
Duhamel, Mlle.
AGNETA
Pfeilschifter, Julie von
AIR CASTLES
Galli-Campi
ALADIN
Vieu, Jane
ALCESTE, (three acts) (1882)
Gambaro, Alceste
ALCESTI, (one act)
Respighi, Elsa
ALCESTIAD, THE, (three acts) (1958)
Talma, Louise
ALCHEMIST, THE
Steiner, Emma

ALENKIY TSVETOCHEK (1958)
Nikolskaya, Lyubov Borisovna
ALESHI I CHERNAYA KURITSA (1966)
Vasilieva, Tatiana Ivanovna
ALICE IN WONDERLAND (1957)
Du Page, Florence Elizabeth
**ALICE IN WONDERLAND CONTINUED
(1904)**
Daniels, Mabel Wheeler
ALL ABOUT A BONNET
Harraden, R. Ethel
ALOHA SUGAR MILL
Rich, Gladys
ALPENROSE
Eschborn, Georgine Christine
Maria Anna
ALS ES NOCH KUEHNE RITTER GAB (1907)
Slaughter, Marjorie
ALS HERDERS IN DER NACHT (1959)
Mulder, Johanna Harmina Gerdina
ALTE HAUSMITTEL, (one act) (1901)
Mentzel-Schippel, Elisabeth
**AMANTS DE SESTOS, LES, (three scenes)
(1949)**
Vito-Delvaux, Berthe di
**AMAZON GRACE, OR THE TRUTH ABOUT
THE AMAZONS (1975)**
Buchanan, Dorothy Quita
AME EN PEINE, L', (two acts) (1896)
Ferrari, Gabriella
AMERICANA, L', (1820)
Amalie, Marie Friederike Augusta
AMFIPARNASO, L', (1974)
Evans, Winsome
AMINADE (1863)
Steiner, Emma
AMOUR NON E CIECO, L'
Gasparini, Jola
AMOURS DE MON LORD, LES
Dietrich, Amalia
ANACOANA
Beaton, Isabella
ANACREON
Beaumesnil, Henrietta Adelaide
ANCESTOR MAKER
Wickham, Florence Pauline
ANE QUI JOUAT DE LA LYRE, L', (1975)
Bruzdowicz, Joanna
ANDALUSIANS, THE, (three acts)
Gerrish-Jones, Abbie
ANDREA DEL SARTO (1931)
Rosselli-Nissim, Mary
ANETTE (1945)
Cancino de Cuevas, Sofia

ANGEL ON A HOLIDAY, (three acts) (1954)
Kettering, Eunice Lea
**ANGELA, OU L'ATELIE DE JEAN COUSIN,
(one act)**
Gail, Edmée-Sophie
ANGIOLA DI GHEMME
Crescimano, Fiorita
ANIMAL FARM (1978)
Zaidel-Rudolph, Jeanne
ANNEAUX DE MARINETTE, LES (1895)
Chevalier de Boisval, Mme.
ANNELE (1964)
Igenberga, Elga Avgustovna
ANOEMONE, (two acts)
Urner, Catherine Murphy
ANTINOOS (1908)
Halacsy, Irma von
ANY MAN WILL DO, (three acts) (1954)
Kettering, Eunice Lea
APOCALYPSIS (1977)
Matuszczak, Bernadetta
APRIL FOOL (1898)
Maxim, Florence
APUS DE SOARE
Barberis, Mansi
**ARANYSZARNYU MEHECSKE, AZ, (one
act) (1974)**
Szoeny, Erzsebet
ARETHUSE
Montgomery, Mme. de
ARGENORE
Wilhelmina, Sophie Friederike
ARIADNA (1977)
Sikora, Elzbieta
ARIADNE AND DIONYSUS (1935)
Crews, Lucille
ARIADNE AUF NAXOS
Paradis, Maria Theresia von
ARLETTE
Vieu, Jane
ARTASERSE, (three acts) (1731)
Zamparelli, Dionisia
ARTIST AND THE OTHER, THE (1982)
Swisher, Gloria Agnes Wilson
ARTIST'S PROOF, AN (1882)
Young, Harriet Maitland
AS DIE REENNIMFE VERDWYN
Eagar, Fannie Edith Starke
ASIENS LJUS
Moberg, Ida Georgina
ASPAZJA I PERYKLES, (two acts) (1824)
Milaszewska
ASSANT DE VALETS (1896)
Chevalier de Boisval, Mme.

ASSEPOESTER
Bessem, Saar
ASTARTE
Holmes, Augusta Mary Anne
ASTRID, (three acts)
Labey, Charlotte Sohy
ASTRIFIAMMANTE
Zerr, Anna
ATALA or **I PELLE ROSSE (1894)**
Delle Grazie, Gisella
ATALA
Folville, Eugenie-Emilie Juliette
ATALA (1888)
GRANDVAL, Marie Felicie
ATAMANSHA (1972)
Liadova, Ludmila Alekseyevna
AUCTIONEER, THE (1976)
Jolly, Margaret Anne
AUDIENCE, THE (1981)
Dembo, Royce
AUDITION, THE (1979)
Jebeles, Mrs. Themos
AUTO UND SCHIMMEL
Stein-Schneider, Lena
AUX-AVANT-POSTES (1976)
Michel, Josepha
AVE MARIA, (one act) (1906)
Gubitosi, Emilia
AVENTURE DI UNA GIORNATA, L'
Aspri, Orsola
AZA
Timofeyew, Mrs.
AZTEC PRINCESS, THE
Gerrish-Jones, Abbie
AZURE LILY, THE
Bostelmann, Ida
BABES IN THE WOOD, THE
White, Mary Louisa
BABET ET COLIN
Franchino, Raffaela
BACCANTE (1917)
Testore, Lidia
BACHELETTE, LA (1896)
Dell'acqua, Eva
BAGNO DI VENERE, (three acts) (1915)
Testore, Lidia
BALLAD OF LOLA MONTEZ
Waldo, Elisabeth
BALLET DER ZEIT (1655)
von Braunschweig, Sophie Elisabeth
BALLO DELLE ZINGARE, IL (1614)
Caccini, Francesca
**BALTHAZAR, ou LE MORT VIVANT,
in one act**
Arrieu, Claude
BANCROFT INC.
McLin, Lena
BARBACOLE
Papavoine, Mme.
BASHMAKI BABADZHANY (1968)
Iashvili, Lili Mikhailovna
BATAVI, I, (three acts) (1864)
Tarbe des Sablons, Mme.
BATHILDE ou **LE DUC (1793)**
Candeille, Amelie
BAYOU LEGEND, A
Arvey, Verna
BEAUCOUP DE BRUIT....
Puget, Loise
BEAUTY AND THE BEAST
Ward, Clementine
BEAUTY AND THE BEAST
White, Mary Louisa
BECQUERIANA
Rodrigo, Maria
BELL WITCH OF TENNESSEE (1956)
Simons, Netty
BELLS OF CIRCUMSTANCE, THE (ca. 1928)
Branscombe, Gena
BELLA FANCIULLA DI PERTH, LA
Lucilla D.

BELLA LUCINDA, LA
Farga Pellicer, Onia
BELLE AU BOIS DORMANT, LA
Vieu, Jane
BELLE DU FAR-WEST, LA
RaynaL, Germaine
BELLE MARGUERITE, LA
Steiner, Emma
BEOWULF
Dembo, Royce
BERTA ALLA SIEPE (1908)
Gennai, Emanuela
BERTRAM DE BORN
Tyrell, Agnes
BETWEEN THE SHADOW AND THE DREAM
Gorelli, Olga
BETWEEN TWO STOOLS (ca. 1860)
Gray, Louisa
BEULAH
Stocker, Stella
BEYOND THE BLUE (1947)
Roe, Marion Adelle
BIANCA TORELLA
Fortmagne, Baroness de
BIG BEN
Ellis, Vivian
BIG SISTER'S WEDDING
Elliott, Marjorie Reeve
BILITIS (1930)
Klechniowska, Anna Maria
BILLARNI
Cogan, Morva
BIRDS, THE (1974)
Maconchy, Elizabeth
BIRD'S CHRISTMAS CAROL, THE (1957)
Hagemann, Virginia
BIRTHDAY CAKE, THE
Syner, Sonia
BIRTHMARK, THE (1985)
Ivey, Jean Eichelberger
BLANCA NIEVES, (two acts)
Escobar, Maria Luisa
BLEKITNY KOT
Szajna-Lewandowska, Jadwiga
Helena
BLESS THE BRIDE
Ellis, Vivian
BLESSED EVENT, THE (1958)
Hamill, Roseann
BLUE BELT, THE
Blake, Dorothy Gaynor
BLICK DES BASILISKEN, DER (1846)
Prohaska, Bernhardine
BLIND MEN, THE (1978)
Forman, Joanne
BLIND RAFTERY (1957)
Trimble, Joan
BLUE BEARD
Foster, Fay
BLUE STAR
Dvorkin, Judith
BLUM UND WEISBLUME
Kralik von Mayerswalden, Mathilde
BLUMENZWIST, DER (1906)
Schick, Philippine
BOATSWAIN'S MATE, THE (1916)
Smith, Ethel Mary, Dame
BOBSON ET ABDULLE (1905)
Kroning, Mlle.
BOMBASTES FURIOSO (1938)
Alderman, Pauline
BONNE TERRE, LA
Harvey, Roberta
BOOK OF RUTH
Upton, Anne
BOTTLE, THE, (one act) (1953)
Perry, Julia Amanda
BOUCLIER DE DIAMANT, LE
Grandval, Marie Felicie
BRANNTWEINBRENNER, DER (1894)
Serova, Valentina Semyonovna

BREAK OF TRANSMISSION
Szoenyi, Erzsebet
BRIAN BORU
Gebuhr, Ann K.
BRIDE OF THE CANGO CAVES, THE
Marais, Abelina Jacoba
BRIERY BUSH, THE
Poston, Elizabeth
BRIGANDS (1894)
Steiner, Emma
BRIGANTI, I
Casagemas, Luisa
BRIMSTONE, (three acts) (1953)
Kettering, Eunice Lea
BROUCCI (1938)
Kucerova-Herstova, Marie
**BROWNINGS GO TO ITALY, THE, (one act)
(1936)**
Freer, Eleanor Warner Everest
BURRA PUNDIT
Steiner, Emma
BY DIE WATER VAN LIKWA
Whittington, Joan
**CABARET DU POT-CASSE, LE, (three acts)
(1878)**
Thys, Pauline
CABILDO (1932)
Beach, AMY
CABINE TELEPHONIQUE, LA, (one act)
Arrieu, Claude
CADET-ROUSSEL, (five acts)
Arrieu, Claude
CAEDMON (1933)
Glanville-Hicks, Peggy
**CALL OF JEANNE D'ARC, THE, (one act)
(1923)**
Crews, Lucille
CAMBIO DE CLIMA (1866)
Gonzalez, Dona Paz
CANADA GOOSE, THE
Drynan, Margaret
CANADIER S.V.PL, M. (1875)
Michel, Josepha
CANCION DE AMOR (1925)
Rodrigo, Maria
CANDY FLOSS
Herbert, Muriel
**CAPANNA ARDENTE, LA, (three acts)
(1920)**
Oddone Sulli-Rao, Elisabetta
CAPE COD ANN
Gulesian, Grace Warner
CAPE OF CONFUCIUS, THE (1904)
Allemand, Pauline L'
CAPTAIN KIDD (1959)
Ziffrin, Marilyn Jane
CAPTIF, LE
Ferrari, Gabriella
CARILLON (1952)
Britain, Radie
CARINA
Woolfe, Sophia Julia
CARNEVALE ESIGLIATO, IL
Cazati, Maria
CARNIVAL OF THE FLOWERS
Lewis, Carrie Bullard
CASA BERNARDEI ALBA (1966)
Jerea, Hilda
CASA DISABITATA, LA
Amalie, Marie Friederike Augusta
**CASE BOOK OF SHERLOCK HOLMES, THE,
- THE CONFESSION (1981)**
Hara, Kazuko (1)
**CASE OF THE MISSING PART OF SPEECH,
THE**
Barlow, Betty
CASK OF AMONTILLADO, THE, (one act)
Perry, Julia Amanda
CASTAWAYS, THE
Foster, Fay

CAT AND THE MOON, THE
Clarke, Rosemary

CATHERINE ou LA BELLE FERMIERE (1792)
CandeillE, Amelie

CATS' HOUSE (1959)
Feigin, Sarah

CENA MAGICA, LA
Ziliotto, Elisa

CENDRILLON
Viardot-Garcia, Pauline Michelle
Ferdinande

CENTO DUCATI E BELUCCIA
Recli, Giulia

CEPHALE ET PROCRIS (1694)
La Guerre, Elisabeth-Claude Jacquet
de

CHAMBER DRAMA (1965)
Matuszczak, Bernadetta

CHAMPAGNE, LE (1894)
Chevalier de Boisval, Mme.

CHANSON DE L'AUBEPIN, LA
Perronnet, Amelie

CHANSON DE MIMI PINSON (1952)
Desportes, Yvonne Berthe Melitta

CHANSON DU PRINTEMPS, (one act)
Saint-Croix, Carolina de

CHANTICLEER
Barthelson, Joyce Holloway

CHAPEAU A MUSIQUE, LE, (two acts)
Arrieu, Claude

CHARETTE AUX PAILLACES, LA
Barberis, Mansi

CHARLES, THE CAROUSEL HORSE
Merman, Joyce

CHASI
Streicher, Lyubov Lvovna

CHEVALIERS DE TOLEDE, LES (1872)
Michel, Josepha

CHEST MUNDIRA (1937)
Zaranek, Stefania Anatolyevna

CHICKO-SHO
Hara, Kazuko (1)

CHIEN PERDU, LE
Julien, Jeanne

CHILD OF PROMISE (1964)
Hunkins, Eusebia Simpson

CHILDREN OF THE SUN, (three acts) (1975)
Witni, Monica

CHILKOOT MAIDEN, THE, (one act) (1926)
Freer, Eleanor Warner Everest

CHINESE LEGEND, A (THE IMMORTAL
LOVERS)
Moore, Mary Carr

CHING FOO AND THE EMPEROR
Du Page, Florence Elizabeth

CHITRA (1980)
Phillips, Bryony

CHRISTMAS CAROL, A
Musgrave, Thea

CHRISTMAS CAROL, A
Hagemann, Virginia

CHRISTMAS EVE
Curtis, Elizabeth

CHRISTMAS IN COVENTRY (1953)
Howell, Alice

CHRISTMAS SECRET, THE
Churchill, Beatrice

CHRISTMAS TALE, A, (one act) (1928)
Freer, Eleanor Warner Everest

CHRONPLAN, DER
Kerwey, Julia

CIL
Drdova, Maria

CINDERELLA
Gennai, Emanuela

CINDERELLA
Davis, Katherine Kennicott

CINDERELLA
Seiders, Mary Asenath

CINQUE NANI DELLA MONTAGNA BLU, I
(1932)
Beloch, Dorotea

CIRCUS DEL MONDO, (one act) (1971)
Mulder, Johanna Harmina Gerdina

CIRO IN ARMENIA, in three acts
Agnesi-Pinottini, Maria Teresa d'

CLAIRE (1979)
Sherman, Kim Darryl

CLAIRE DE LUNE (1985)
Larsen, Elizabeth Brown

CLARA D'ARTA
Busky-Benedetti, Albina

CLAVIER POUR UN AUTRE, UN
Arrieu, Claude

CLEOPATRE, REINE D'EGYPTE
Maistre, Baroness of

CLOUDS, THE (1971)
St. John, Kathleen Louise

COBZAR, LE, (one act) (1908)
Ferrari, Gabriella

COCKCROW
Smith, Julia Frances

COLEEN'S EVICTION
Corri, Ghita

COLLEGE DAYS
Dodge, Cynthia

COLUMBINE, (three acts)
Davis, Mary

COLUMBUS
Geiger-Kullman, Rosy Auguste

COLUMBUS, (five acts)
Williams, Margaret

COME ANDO
Gasparini, Jola

COME ON OVER (1941)
Alderman, Pauline

COMMEDIA DI PINOCCHIO, LA, (five acts)
(1927)
Oddone Sulli-Rao, Elisabetta

COMMENT
McLin, Lena

COMPOSER'S DREAM
Stein-Schneider, Lena

COMTESSE EVA, LA, (one act) (1864)
Randval, Marie Felicie

CONCERT, THE (1959)
Crews, Lucille

CONDE DE VIENTO NEGRO, EL (1867)
Preciados Y Manescau, Cecilia

CONGIURA DI CHEVREUSE, LA, (two acts)
(1881)
Thys, Pauline

CONTE DE FEES (1879)
Viardot-Garcia, Pauline Michelle
Ferdinande

CONTE DI BENZEVAL, IL
Lucilla D.

CONTE ROSSO, IL
Lucilla D.

CONTEMPORARY MASS
Du Page, Florence Elizabeth

CONTRABBANDIERE, IL (1842)
Perelli, Natalie

COQUETTE
Rawlinson, Angela

COQUILLE A PLANETES, LA
Arrieu, Claude

CORSARO, IL
Rozwadowski, Contessa Raffaela

CORSARO, IL (1812)
Blewitt, Gionata

CORTE NA ROCO, A
Gonzaga, Chiquinha

COSCRITTO, IL (1900)
Novelli, Mimi

CORSICA (1910)
Berge, Irenee

COSE D'AMERICA
Gasparini, Jola

COSTASO
Arvey, Verna

COUR D'AMOUR, (two acts) (1928)
Thisse-Derouette, Rose

COURT OF HEARTS, THE (1901)
Daniels, Mabel Wheeler

COURTSHIP OF CAMILLA, (one act) (1980)
Schonthal, Ruth E.

COUSIN ESTHER (1954)
Pittman, Evelyn LaRue

COWHERD AND THE WEAVING MAIDEN,
(one act) (1964)
Hsu, Wen-Ying

CRESCENT EYEBROW, THE
Dvorkin, Judith

CRISPINO DE FIUMERI
Procaccini, Teresa

CRISTOFORO COLOMBO
Casella, Felicita

CROW TOO
Oliveros, Pauline

CUENTO DE NAVIDAD, (three acts) (1950)
Blanck, Olga de

CUENTO MUSICAL, (three acts)
Escobar, Maria Luisa

CUPBOARD LOVE
Dring, Madeleine

CUPID AND PSYCHE (1874)
Righton, Mary

CYCLOPE, LE
Charriere, Isabella Agneta
Elisabeth de

CYMBELINE, (two acts)
Arrieu, Claude

CYNTHIA PARKER (1939)
Smith, Julia Frances

CYR A NICE (1904)
Biasini, Marcelle

D'UN OPERA DE POUPEE
Jolas, Betsy

DAISY
Smith, Julia Frances

DAL SONGO ALL'VITA, (three acts)
Mariani-Campolieti, Virginia

DALMA, (three acts) (1952)
Szoenyi, Erzsebet

DAME DE MONTE CARLO, LA
Raynal, Germaine

DANIEL IN DER LOEWENGRUBE
Nikisch, Amelie

DANIEL IN THE LION'S DEN
Walsh, Helen Mary

DAPHNIS ET AMENTHEE (1807)
Guenin, Helene

DARK OF SUMMER, THE, (one act) (1967)
Witni, Monica

DARK PILGRIMAGE (1962)
Tate, Phyllis

DAUGHTER OF MOHAMMED
Cobb, Hazel

DAUGHTER OF SNOW (1901)
Johnston-Watson, Miss

DAVID RIZZIO, (two acts)
Moore, Mary Carr

DAWNPATH (1977)
Lefanu, Nicola Frances

DAY DREAMS (1894)
Steiner, Emma

DAY IN MEXICO (1971)
Walsh, Elizabeth Jameson

DE AMORE
Barkin, Elaine

DEATH OF THE HIRED MAN (1960)
Van de Vate, Nancy

DECISION, THE
Musgrave, Thea

DECK
Fritz, Sherilyn Gail

DEIRDRE OF THE SORROWS
Leclercq, Leila Sarah

DEPART DU ROI, LE
Clerambault, N.

DEPARTURE, THE
Maconchy, Elizabeth

DERNIER AMOUR (1895)
Ferrari, Gabriella

FEU DE PAILLE, LE (1888)
Dell'acqua, Eva

FIAMME, (three acts) (1915)
Rosselli-Nissim, Mary

FIANCAILLES DE PASQUIN, LES (1888)
Dell'acqua, Eva

FIANCEE DE GAEL, LA (1892)
Carissan, Celanie

FIANCEE DU DIABLE, LA (1941)
Karveno, Wally

FIANCEES DE ROSA, LES, (one act) (1863)
Grandval, Marie Felicie

FIGLIA DELLA DORA
White, Maude Valerie

FIGLIO PERDUTO, IL (1931)
Amalie, Marie Friederike Augusta

FILIPPO
CRESCIMANO, Fiorita

FILLA DEL REI BARBUT, LA, (prologue and three acts)
Salvador, Matilde

FIOR DI NEVE, (three acts)
Respighi, Elsa

FIORE INCANTATO, IL (1932)
Beloch, Dorotea

FIRE WORSHIPERS, THE
Ruta, Gilda, Countess

FIRENZE, I (1889)
Munktell, Helena Mathilda

FIRENZEI TRAGEDIA, (one act) (1957)
Szoenyi, Erzsebet

FIRST ATTEMPT, THE (1807)
Morgan, Lady

FIRST LIEUTENANT, THE
Gaynor, Jessie Love

FIRST RAINBOW, THE
Pharris, Elizabeth

FISCHERIN, DIE
Mayer, Emilie

FISHERMAN AND HIS SOUL (1969)
Lomon, Ruth

FISHERMAN AND HIS WIFE, THE
Rappaport, Eda

FLAMING ARROW, THE, (one act)
Moore, Mary Carr

FLEA CIRCUS (1969)
Steele, Lynn

FLEUR D'EPIN, (two acts) (1776)
Louis, Mme.

FLEURETTE
Steiner, Emma

FLIGHT OF TIME, THE
Heckscher, Celeste de Longpre

FLORIAN, (four acts)
Walter, Ida

FLORIS EN BLANCEFLOER
Bessem Sara

FLUTES OF JADE HAPPINESS, (three acts) (1931)
Moore, Mary Carr

FLYNN (1978)
Bingham, Judith

FOLCLORE
Pires de Pires, D. Maria Clementina

FOLIE, OU QUEL CONTE, LA, (two acts) (1789)
Ahlefeldt, Marie Theresia

FOLIES D'AMOUR (1894)
Fortmagne, Baroness de

FOLLIES AND FANCIES (1981)
Allen, Judith Shatin

FOLLIES OF A NIGHT, THE, (two acts) (1860)
Gabriel, Mary Ann Virginia

FOR THE SOUL OF RAFAEL
Manning, Kathleen Lockhart

FOREST, THE (1901)
Smith, Ethel Mary, Dame

FOREST VOICES (1958)
Hunkins, Eusebia Simpson

FORESTER'S WIFE, THE
Donatova, Narcisa

FORGEUR DE MERVEILLES, LE (1965)
Desportes, Yvonne Berthe

FORROBODO, (three) acts (1912)
Gonzaga, Chiquinha

FORTUNATO, (three scenes) (1958)
Gideon, Miriam

FORZA DELL'AMOR, LA
Amalie, Marie Friederike Augusta

FOU SENSE, LA (1971)
TAILLEFERRE, Germaine

FOUR PEEKS ON A BUSHEL OF FUN, or CUPID'S HALLOWEEN (1907)
Cale, Rosalie Balmer Smith

FRANCESCA DA RIMINI
Aspri, Orsola

FRANCINE
Morin-Labrecque, Albertine

FRANCIS
Beath, Betty

FREEDOM'S CHILD
Pittman, Evelyn LaRue

FRIENDSHIP ON PARADE
Niebel, Mildred

FRITHIOF, (two acts) (1929)
Freer, Eleanor Warner Everest

FRITIOFS SAGA
Andree, Elfrida

FROG KING, THE, (two acts)
Wette, Adelheid

FROZEN PRINCESS, THE (1908)
Luttrell, Moira

FRUIT VERT, LE, (three acts)
Thys, Pauline

FUERSTIN VON PAPHOS, DIE
Kinkel, Johanna

G.I. JOE, (one act) (1945)
Rapoport, Eda

GALE (1935)
Leginska, Ethel

GALEOTTO MANFREDI (1839)
Perelli, Natalie

GALLANT TAILOR, THE
Smith, Zelma

GANYMEDE
Stocker, Stella

GARDEN MAGIC
Rich, Gladys

GARDENIA ROSSA, (one act)
Gubitosi, Emilia

GASLIGHT (1982)
Roe, Eileen Betty

GELOEBNIS, DAS, (two acts)
Oosterzee, Cornelia van

GELUKSKINDEREN, (three acts) (1940)
Mulder, Johanna Harmina Gerdina

GENTIL MIGNON
Bensuade, Jane

GEORGE WASHINGTON THE BOY
Wicker, Irene

GET-ACQUAINTED PARTY, A
Blake, Dorothy Gaynor

GHOST OF SUSAN B. ANTHONY, THE (1977)
Shaffer, Jeanne Ellison

GIANT GARDEN, THE
Woolsley, Mary Hale

GIFT OF SONG (1963)
Caldwell, Mary Elizabeth Glockler

GIFT OF THE MAGI, (one act)
Aborn, Lora

GIFT OF THE MAGI, THE
Magney, Ruth Taylor

GIL DRAZE (1844)
Pean de la Roche-Jagu, E. Françoise

GIL GONZALEZ DE AVIL (1937)
Cancino de Cuevas, Sofia

GINGERBREAD MAN
Royse, Mildred Barnes

GIUDITTA, (three acts) (1891)
Thys, Pauline

GIULIANO SALVIATI
Lucilla D.

GLITTERING GATE, THE, (one act)
Glanville-Hicks, Peggy

GLOECKCHEN DES EREMITEN DER LIEBT MICH, DAS
Maillart, Aimée

GOD OF THE SEA
Roma, Caro

GOLDEN BIRD, THE, (six scenes) (1959)
Vorlova, Slavka

GOLDEN KERCHIEF, THE
Kistetenyi, Melinda

GOLUB I KOSUYU LINYEIKU (1974)
Tkach, Zlata Moiseyevna

GONDOLIERO, IL, (three acts)
Correr, Ida, Countess

GOOSEHERD AND THE GOBLIN, THE
Smith, Julia Frances

GOTTIN ZU SAIS, DIE
Bronsart von Schellen dorf, Ingeborg Lena

GOUDHAARTJE EN DE TROUBADOUR
Vladeracken, Geertruida van

GOVERNATORE ED IL CIARLATANO, IL (1897)
Germano, Vittoria

GRAFT
Kalogridou, Maria

GRASS ROOTS
White, Claude Porter

GRASS WIDOWS, THE, (one act) (1873)
GabrieL, Mary Ann Virginia

GREAT CAMPAIGN, THE (1951)
Lee, Bo-Chas

GREAT MOGUL, THE
Owen, Anita

GREEN SYBIL, THE
Genet, Marianne

GREENWICH VILLAGE, 1910
Barthelson, Joyce Holloway

GRETCHEN'S DREAM
Rohde, Q'Adrianne

GROCERIES AND NOTIONS, (three acts) (1931)
Alter, Martha

GROTTO DE MAJO
Perriere-Pilte, Anais

GUIDO FERANTI
Van Etten, Jane

GULNARA (1935)
Weissberg, Julia Lazarevna

GUSI-LEVEDI, (one act) (1937)
Weissberg, Julia Lazarevna

GYPSIES' REWARD, THE (1958)
Norman, Ruth

GYPSY MOON
Elliott, Marjoire Reeve

H.M.S. ALPHABET
Ward, Clementine

HAIL NEW WORLD or TOBACCO BRIDE
Wicker, Irene

HALTE AU MOULIN
Ugalde, Delphine Beauce

HAMLET, THE FLEA
Rabinof, Sylvia

HANEPOORT EN MUSKADEL (1967)
Van der Mark, Maria

HANSEL AND GRETEL
Abeson, Marion

HANUSIA, (one act)
Dorabialska, Julia Helena

HAPPY HEARTS, THE
Woolsley, Mary Hale

HAPPY HYPOCRITE (1965)
Swisher, Gloria Agnes Wilson

HAPPY LAND (1946)
Britain, Radie

HAPPY LAND, OUR AMERICAN HERITAGE IN STORY AND SONG, (one act)
Hunkins, Eusebia Simpson

HAPPY SCARECROW, THE
  Elliott, Marjorie Reeve
HARLEQUIN IN SEARCH OF HIS HEART
  Scott-Hunter, Hortense
HARMONY, (one act)
  Moore, Mary Carr
HASCHISCH (1911)
  Gregory, Else
HAUNTING, THE, (one act)
  Leginska, Ethel
HAWAII
  Townsend, Marie
HAYDEE
  Casella, Felicita
HAZILA
  Thomas, Gertrude Auld
HEDY, FIBICH, ZDENEK (1896)
  Schulzova, Anezka
HEIDI SONGS, THE (1970)
  Dlugoszewski, Lucia
HEILIGE GRAL, DER (1907)
  Kralik von Mayerswalden, Mathilde
HEILIGENSCHEIN DER
  Wolzogen, Else Laura von
HEIMLICHE BUND, DER
  Mizangere, Marquise de la
HEIMLICHE BUND, DER
  Muellner-Gollenhofer, Johanna
HELD MARKO
  Rose
HELIGOLAND
  Vannah, Kate
HELOISES MYSTERIUM, (seven acts) (1975)
  Matuszczak, Bernadetta
HERITER SANS LE SAVOIR, L'
  Thys, Pauline
HERO ET LEANDRE (1874)
  Holmes, Augusta Mary Anne
HERO NERO (1904)
  Terhune, Anice
HERODES UND MARIAMNE (1979)
  Pelegri, Maria Teresa
HEROIQUES, LES (1876)
  Perry-Biagioli, Antoinette
HEUREUSE ERREUR, L'
  Wuiet Caroline
HEUREUSE RENCONTRE, L' (1771)
  Roset, Mme.
HEUREUX STRATAGEME, L' (1786)
  Caroline, Mlle.
HEXENSKAT ODER DER STREIT DER HEXEN
  (1980)
  Koblenz, Babette
HIAWATHA'S CHILDHOOD
  Whitely, Bessie Marshall
HIGH-KING'S DAUGHTER, THE
  Patterson, Annie Wilson
HIREN KARA BUNE (1967)
  Kanai, Kikuko
HIREN TOSEN
  Kanai, Kikuko
HIS LAST CHANCE, (one act) (1891)
  Harraden, R. Ethel
HISTORICAL PAGEANT (1936)
  Reynolds, Laura Lawton
HOELZERNE SCHUH, DER (1906)
  Slaughter, Marjorie
HOLY BRANCH, THE
  Young, Harriet Maitland
HONEYMOON IN 2000, A
  Gulesian, Grace Warner
HONORABLE MME. YEN, THE
  Foster, Fay
HOPITY
  Albright, Lois
HORSE OPERA
  Donaldson, Sadie
HOSANNA, (one act)
  Giuranna, Elena Barbara
HOUSE THAT JACK BUILT, THE
  Gaynor, Jessie Love

HOW CHALEU BECAME CHIEF
  Lavin, Marie Duchnesne
HUMANAE VOCES (1971)
  Matuszczak, Bernadetta
HUMOR AUF REISEN
  Winkler, Blanka
HUMPTY DUMPTY
  McLin, Lena
HUNGER UND DURST
  Dinescu, Violeta
HUT, DER
  Geiger-Kullman, Rosy Auguste
HYPATIA
  Mana-Zucca
HYPOCRYTE SANTIFIE (ca. 1910)
  Polignac, Armande de, Countess
ICARE
  FALCINELLI, Rolande
IDA, L'ORPHELINE DE BERLIN (1807)
  Candeille, Amelie
IDYLLE
  Fortmagne, Baroness de
IF THE SUN WERE NOT TO RETURN (1974)
  Petrova-Krupkova, Elena
IGAZMONDO JUHASZ, AZ (1979)
  Szoenyi, Erzsebet
IGINIA D'ASTI (1942)
  Sanchez de la Madrid, Ventura
IKARUS
  Forman, Joanne
IL ETAIT UN PETIT NAVIRE (1951)
  Tailleferre, Germaine
IL N'Y A PLUS D'ENFANTS (1897)
  Guitty, Madeleine
ILE
  Laufer, Beatrice
ILIA MUROMETZ (1899)
  Serova, Valentina Semyonovna
IMAGE, L' (1864)
  Santa-Colona-Sourget, Eugenie de
IMENINY FIALKI- MALSHKI (1967)
  Robitashvili, Georgievna
IMMER DER ANDERE
  Nikisch, Amelie
IN THE SHADOW OF THE GLEN (1960)
  Van der Vate, Nancy
INCANTESIMO (1915)
  Garelli Della Morea,Vincenza
INCOGNITO, L'
  Charriere, Isabella Agneta Elisabeth
de
INES PEREIRA (1938)
  Policarpo Teixeira, Maria Margarida
INEZ
  Donatova, Narcisa
INFANTA DESDEN, L', (one act)
  Pablos Cerezo, Maria de
INFIDELIO, (seven scenes) (1954)
  Lutyens, Elisabeth
INNER CITY
  Messiam, Eve
INSUBRIA CONSOLATA, L', (two acts)
  Agnesi-Pinottini, Maria Teresa d'
INTERRUPTED SERENADE, AN
  Stair, Patty
INTERVALS AND INTRIGUES (1980)
  Elkoshi, Rivka
INVISIBLE MAIDEN
  Gore, Blanche
IRMA LA DOUCE
  MONNOT, Marguerite Angele
IRMISA (1971)
  Iashvili, Lili Mikhailovna
ISIS AND OSIRIS (1970)
  Lutyens, Elisabeth
ISOLA DEI SANTI (1914)
  Blewitt, Gionata
ISOLA DISABITATA, L'
  Coccia, Maria Rosa
ISOLDA (1881)
  Addi, Renée d'

ISRAELITES POURSUIVIS PAR PHARAON,
LES
  Beaumesnil, Henrietta Adelaide
ISTI AND BEAU VINGT (1945)
  Hardiman, Ellena G.
JACK AND THE BEANSTALK
  McLin, Lena
JALOUX DE SOI, (one act) (1873)
  Perriere-Pilte, Anais
JAMANTO, (three acts) (1914)
  Giurianna, Elena Barbara
JE REVIENS DE COMPIEGNE
  Perronet, Amelie
JEAN DE LA FONTAINE PARMI NOUS (1980)
  Aboulker, Isabelle
JEAN GUETENBERG (1836)
  Pfeiffer, Charlotte Birsch
JERY UND BAETELEY
  Bronsart von Schellendorf, Ingeborg
  Lena
JEU DE L'AMOUR ET DU HASARD, LE
  (1895)
  Chevalier de Boisval, Mme.
JEUNE HOTESSE, LA (1794)
  Candeille, Amelie
JEUNESSE D'HAYDN, LA (1889)
  Carissan, Celanie
JEUNESSE DE LULLY, LA
  Pean de la Roche-Jagu, E. Françoise
JEWELS OF THE DESERT
  Strickland, Lily Teresa
JIG IS UP, THE
  Mainville, Denise
JIGGER O'SCOTCH, A
  Govea Wenonah Milton
JOAN OF ARC
  Leginska, Ethel
JOAN OF ARC, (one act) (1929)
  Freer, Eleanor Warner Everest
JOB (1965)
  Lauridsen, Cora
JOB (1983)
  Allen, Judith Shatin
JOCELYN
  White, Maude Valerie
JOHNNY APPLESEED (1974)
  Lorenz, Ellen Jane
JOLLY BEGGARS, THE
  Wood, Mabel
JOSE, AKING ANAK (1976)
  Kasilag, Lucrecia R.
JOSEPH
  Strickland, Lily Teresa
JOUST, THE, OR THE TOURNAMENT
  Estabrook, G.
JOY (1983)
  Erding, Susanne
JUBELFEST, DAS (1849)
  Wiseneder, Caroline
JUDITH DE BETHULIE (1916)
  Polignac, Armande de, Countess
JULIEN ET JULIETTE
  Charriere, Isabella Agneta
  Elisabeth de
JULIET AND ROMEO, (five scenes) (1967)
  Matuszczak, Bernadetta
JUNIPER TREE (1977)
  Noble, Ann
JUPITER ET LEDA
  Lagier, Suzanne
JURAMENTO DE AMOR (1936)
  Policarpo Teixeira, Maria Margarida
KADZHANA
  Davitashvili, Meri Shalvovna
KAIRE DANCHO (1968)
  Arima, Reiko
KANONENSCHUSS, DER (1828)
  Amalie, Marie Friederike Augusta
KAPITEIN IS JARIG, DE (1966)
  Marez-Oyens, Tera de

KARELSKAYA SKASKA (1940)
Levi, Natalia Nikolayevna
KASA-JIDO (1979)
Kusunoki, Tomoko
KASTAVSKI KAPETAN, (three acts) (1957)
Lang-Beck, Ivana
KAZKA PRO ZAGUBLENII CHAS (1971)
Rozhavskaya, Yudif Grigorevna
KELLERIN, THE
Linwood, Mary
KERA DUDUCA, (three acts)
Barberis, Mansi
KHAI DIEVKA
Serova, Valentina Semyonovna
KHLEB TY MOI (1978)
Kuznetsova, Zhanetta
Aleksandrovna
KIDDY CITY (1961)
Kessler, Minuetta Schumiatcher
KINDER DER PUSZTA
Clement, Mary
KING AND THE GOLDEN RIVER, THE
Maconchy, Elizabeth
KING CHRISTMAS
McCollin, Frances
KING HARALD'S SAGA, (three acts)
Weir, Judith
KING'S BREAKFAST, THE
Barthelson, Joyce Holloway
KLEON
Hansen, Hanna Maria
KOENIG DROSSELBART (1916)
Stein-Schneider, Lena
KOENIG HIERNE
Bronsart von Schellendorf, Ingeborg
Lena
KOL I DRUZIE, (three acts) (1978)
Zavalishina, Maria Semyonovna
KOLTSO SPRAVEDLIVOVOSTI (1970)
Ibragimova, Sevda Mirza kyzy
KOMINEK ZGASL
Garr, Wieslawa
KONINGSKEUZE, DE
Vladeracken, Geertruida van
KOT V SAPOGAKH
Ziberova, Zinaida Petrovna
KOZA S TREMYA KOZLYATAMI (1966)
Tkach, Zlata Moiseyevna
KREPOS U KAMENNOGO BRODA (1940)
Gaigerova, Varvara Andrianovna
KURMANGAZY (1971)
Zhubanova, Gaziza Akhmetovna
KUTHARA (1960)
Britain, Radie
LACUNE, LA (1979)
Aboulker, Isabelle
LADIES' VOICES
Gardner, Kay
LADY OF THE CASTLE
Spektor, Mira J.
LADY IN THE DARK (1962)
Britain, Radie
LADY SAYS YES, THE
Rich, Gladys
LAKE, THE, (one act) (1952)
Pentland, Barbara Lally
LALAPALOO
Norbury, Ethel F.
LAMPS TRIMMED IN BURNING
Cobb, Hazel
LANCELOT DU LAC
Holmes, Augusta Mary Anne
LAND OF CHANCE, THE
Foster, Fay
LAND OF MANANA, THE
Flagge, Mary Houts
LANDPARTIE, DIE
Kinkel, Johanna
LAST SUMMER (1898)
Noyes, Edith Rowena

LAUGHTER
Wieniawska, Irene Regine
LAVINIA E TURNO
Maria Antonia Walpurgis, Princess
of Bavaria
LEALISTA, (two acts) (1985)
Warwick, Mary Carol
LECON IMPREVUE, LA (1903)
Chevalier de Boisval, Mme.
LECON, LA, (one act)
Vito-Delvaux, Berthe di
LEGEND OF HEX MOUNTAIN (1950)
Wickham, Florence Pauline
**LEGEND OF MARIETTA, THE, (one act)
(1909)**
Daniels, Mabel Wheeler
LEGEND OF OKINAWA, A
Kanai, Kikuko
**LEGEND OF RONSARD AND MADELON,
THE**
Belcher, Mary Williams
LEGEND OF SPAIN, THE, (one act) (1931)
Freer, Eleanor Warner Everest
LEGEND OF THE PIPER, THE (1924)
Freer, Eleanor Warner Everest
LEGEND PROVENCALE, (three acts)
Moore, Mary Carr
LEGENDS (1971)
Kavasch, Deborah Helene
LEGISLATRICES, LE
Beaumesnil, Henrietta Adelaide
LENTE CAPRICE (1956)
Van der Vate, Nancy
LEPER, THE, (one act) (1912)
Moore, Mary Carr
LESNIYA CHUDESSA (1967)
Gerchik, Vera Petrovna
LESNOI OPUSHKE
Popatenko, Tamara Alexandrovna
LIANA, (one act) (1925)
Beloch, Dorotea
**LIBERAZIONE DI RUGGIERO DALL'ISOLA
D'ALCINA, LA (1625)**
Caccini, Francesca
LIEBESMAGAZIN (1926)
Frydan, Kamilla
LIEDIE GEZOCHT (1962)
Marez-Oyens, Tera de
LILIPA
Olagnier, Marguerite
LINDORO, (one act) (1879)
Heritte-Viardot, Louise Pauline
LINNET FROM THE LEAF, THE
Lutyens, Elisabeth
LIPANIUSHKA (1976)
Kuznetsova, Zhanetta Alexandrovna
LISA STRATOS
Lackman, Susan C. Cohn
LISIA (1905)
Gasparini, Jola
LIST UN LIST
Schimon, Anna
LITTLE BLACK SAMBO (1983)
DuBois, Shirley Graham
LITTLE DIPPER, THE
Ward, Diane
LITTLE GYPSY BOY
Wales, Evelyn
LITTLE HUSSAR, THE
Steiner, Emma
LITTLE MATCH GIRL, THE
Twombly, Mary Lynn
LITTLE MATCH GIRL, THE (1979)
Charles, S, Robin
LITTLE MERMAID, THE (1976)
Boyd, Anne Elizabeth
LITTLE PRINCE, THE (1972)
Diller, Saralu C.
LITTLE PRINCESS, THE
Bethea, Kay

LITTLE TIN SOLDIER, THE
Forman, Joanne
LITTLE WHITE DOOR, THE
Seiders, Mary Asenath
LODGER, THE (1960)
Tate, Phyllis
LOLITA (1953)
Goodsmith, Ruth B.
LOOK AND LONG
Wicker, Irene
LOOKING UNDER FOOTPRINTS (1983)
Cody, Judith
LOOM, SWORD, RIVER, (three acts)
Allik, Kristi
LOST AND FOUND (1860)
Gabriel, Mary Ann Virginia
LOST CLOWN, THE
Wright, Agnes
LOST HUSBAND, THE (1884)
Harrison, Annie Fortescue
LOUISE DE LA MISERICORDE
Falcinelli, Rolande
LOUP GAROU, LE, (three acts)
Bertin, Louise Angelique
O LOURENÇO DE BRAGA (1934)
Policarpo Teixeira, Maria Margarida
LOVE, POWDER AND PATCHES (1897)
Cale, Rosalie Balmer Smith
LOVE WAGON, THE
Ware, Harriet
LOVE'S A GAMBLE (1961)
Gould, Doris
LUCERO DEL ALBA, EL
Mentes, Maria
LUCETTE ET LUCAS, (one act) (1781)
Dezede, Florine
LUCIEN, (two acts) (1977)
Themmen, Ivana Marburger
LUFTIKUS (1909)
Stein-Schneider, Lena
LUNAR ENCOUNTER
Stanley, Helen Camille
LUSTIGE LIEBE, DIE (1919)
Stein-Schneider, Lena
LYUBAVA (1967)
Katzman, Klara Abramovna
LYUBOV BUVAET RAZNAYA (1957)
Katzman, Klara Abramovna
MACHT DER MUSIK, DIE
Bachmann, Elise
**MADAME DE RABUCOR (RABEUR),
(one act)**
Saint-Croix, Carolina de
**MADAME TALLIEN, (five acts) and
eight scenes**
Vieu, Jane
**MADEMOISELLE DE LAUNAY A LA BAS-
TILLE, (one act) (1813)**
Gail, Edmée-Sophie
MADIA, LA (1936)
Oddone Sulli-Rao, Elisabetta
MADRINI
Morin-Labrecque, Albertine
MAENNERFEINDIN, DIE (1856)
O'Donnell, Malvine, Countess
MAERCHEN DER LIEBE (1924)
Wrana, Emilie
MAERCHEN OPER (1926)
Reiff, Lili
MAGA, LA (1854)
Sanchez de la Madrid, Ventura
**MAGDA, L'ANGE DANS LES TENEBRES,
(four acts) (1961)**
Vito-Delvaux, Berthe di
MAGDALENA
Goetze, Auguste
MAGIC FISH, THE
Neeld, Peggy
MAGIC LAUREL TREES, THE (1974)
Hunkins, Eusebia Simpson

MAGO, IL (1813)
Blewit, Gionata
MAHAILANI
Liliuokalani, Queen of Hawaii
MAID AND THE REAPER, THE, in one act
Young, Eliza
MAISKOYE UTRO, (one act) (1970)
Auster, Lydia Martinovna
MAITRE, LE (1951)
Tailleferre, Germaine
MAITRE CORNELIUS (1940)
Desportes, Yvonne Berthe Melitta
MAITRE PALMA (1830)
Rivay, Mlle.
MAKRANCOS KIRALYLANY, (two acts) (1955)
Szoenyi, Erzsebet
MALCHISH-KIBALCHISH, (three acts) (1969)
Katzman, Klara Abramovna
MALEK-ADEL (1850)
Sanchez de la Madrid, Ventura
MALIBRAN, LA (1946)
Vito-Delvaux, Berthe di
MALZONEK WSZYSTKICH KOBIET, (one act) (1825)
Grodzicka-Rzewuska, Julia
MAN FROM PARIS, THE (1900)
Steiner, Emma
MAN FROM THE MOON, THE
Ace, Joy Milane
MAN IN THE MOON
Newton, Rhoda
MANETTE, (two acts)
Thys, Pauline
MANFRED
Bronsart von Schellendorf, Ingeborg Lena
MANIIAN (1956)
Hunkins, Eusebia Simpson
MARCHESINO, IL (1833)
Amalie, Marie Friederike Augusta
MARCO POLO
Beath, Betty
MARIA (1887)
Morison, Christina W.
MARIA (1933)
Gonzaga, Chiquinha
MARIA D'ORVAL
Serova, Valentina Semyonovna
MARIA MAGDALENA (1921)
Hans, Lio
MARIA REGINA DI SCOZIA (1883)
Skinner, Florence Marian
MARIA TIEPOLO
Crescimano, Fiorita
MARIAGE D'ANTOINE, LE, (one act) (1784)
Gretry, Angelique Dorothée
MARIAGE DE TABARIN, LE (1876)
Thys, Pauline
MARIAGE PAR RUSES, LE
Franchino, Raffaela
MARIAGE PER QUIPROQUO, UN
Sabatier-Blot, Mme.
MARIBEL, (four acts) (1967)
Vito-Delvaux, Berthe di
MARIKO THE MISER
Musgrave, Thea
MARIN DE BOLIVAR, LE (1937)
Tailleferre, Germaine
MARIVAUDAGE (1895)
Chevalier de Boisval, Mme.
MARJOLIJNTJE IN SPROOKJESLAND, (three acts) (1949)
Mulder, Johanna Harmina Gerdina
MARK BEREGOVIK (1955)
Katzman, Klara Abramovna
MARQUISE DE CRECQUI (1891)
Jeske-Choinska-Mikorska, Ludmila
MARTIRIO DI SANT'AGATA, IL (1622)
Caccini, Francesca

MARTYR'S MIRROR, THE
Parker, Alice
MARY, COME RUNNING!
Walker, Gwyneth van Anden
MARY QUEEN OF SCOTS (1977)
Musgrave, Thea
MASK OF ELEANOR, THE
Grigsby, Beverly
MASQUE OF PANDORA, THE, (one act) (1930)
Freer, Eleanor Warner Everest
MASSIMILLIANO/THE COURT JESTER/THE LOVE OF A CALIBAN, (one act)
Freer, Eleanor Warner Everest
MASTER OF SONG (1957)
Roget, Henriette
MATELOTS DE FORMIDABLE, LES
Perry-Biagioli, Antoinette
MATILDE NEL CASTELLO DELLE ALPI
Melia, Gabrielle
MAUVAIS OEIL (1836)
Puget, Loise
MAX, (two acts) (1898)
Rosselli-Nissim, Mary
MAXIMILIAN'S DREAM (1983)
Chlarson, Linda
MAYAKOVSKY AND THE SUN (1972)
Daiken, Melanie
MAYERLING, (three acts) (1961)
Giurianna, Elena Barbara
MAZEPPA
Grandval, Marie Felicie
MEAL, THE
Archer, Violet Balestreri
MEDEE
Gail, Edmée-Sophie
MEDICS AND MERRIMENT
Elliott, Marjorie Reeve
MEINE TANTE, DEINE TANTE
Nikisch, Amelie
MEMORIES (1914)
Moore, Mary Carr
MEMOIRES D'UNE BERGERE (1959)
Tailleferre, Germaine
MENHIRS DE CARNAC, LES
Descat, Henriette
MEPRISE, LA, (one act)
Cecconi-Botella, Monic
MEPRISE, LA, (one act) (1814)
Gail, Edmée-Sophie
MEPRISE VOLONTAIRE, LA
Gretry, Angelique Dorothee
MEPRISE VOLONTAIRE, LA, or LA DOUBLE LECON (1805)
Kercado, Mlle. Le Senechal de
MERCHANT OF PRADO
Origo, Iris
MERLINO
Perriere-Pilte, Anais
MERMAID, THE
More, Margaret Elizabeth
MERRY CHRISTMAS
Richter, Ada
MESSALINA
Giteck, Janice
MESSAOULA
Maurice-Jacquet, H.
METHODICAL MUSIC-MASTER, THE
Lewis, Carrie
MEUNIERE DE SAVENTHEM, LA (1872)
Michel, Josepha
MICE IN COUNCIL, (one act) (1956)
Hunkins, Eusebia Simpson
MICHOACNA (1950)
Cancino de Cuevas, Sofia
MILA AND NELLY (1897)
Lvova, Julia Fedorovna
MILK-MAIDS FAIR, THE, (one act)
Gerrish-Jones, Abbie
MINERVA BANQUETT (1655)
Sophie Elisabeth, von Braunschweig

MIRACLE OF NEMIROV, THE, (one act) (1974)
Silverman, Faye-Ellen
MIRKA
Castegnard, Lola
MIRROR, THE
Davis, Jean Reynolds
MISSION IN BURMA (1970)
Crofts, Inez Altman
MISTER MAN (1963)
Mackie, Shirley M.
MISTER SNOWMAN
Richter, Ada
MITSCHULDIGEN, DIE
Wurm, Mary J.A.
MITTY, (one act)
Aborn, Lora
M'LADY GENIUS (1938)
Kucerova-Herstova, Marie
MOIRA, (three acts) (1930)
Pickhardt, Ione
MOMINETTE (1906)
Guitty, Madeleine
MONEY LENDER, THE
Preobrajenska, Vera Nicolaevna
MONSIEUR GRETRY, (four acts)
Vito-Delvaux, Berthe di
MONTAGNE NOIRE, LA
Holmes, Augusta Mary Anne
MONTONI ou LE CHATEAU D'UDOLPHE (1797)
Gail, Edmée-Sophie
MOON LADY, THE
Foster, Fay
MORGANE, (one act)
Polignac, Armande de, Countess
MOSES
Grigsby, Beverly
MOTA
Arvey, Verna
MOTHER RUN
Lamb, Myrna
MOUETTE BLANCHE, LA (1903)
Kermor, Mireille
MOUSQUETAIRE, LA, or LE JEUNE MILITAIRE, or LA TRAHISON
Pean de la Roche-Jagu, E. Françoise
MR. CUPID, AMERICAN AMBASSADOR
Leoni, Eva
MR. SAMSON OF OMAHA (1880)
Young, Eliza
MR. WU (1926)
Manning, Kathleen Lockhart
MUGNAIO DI MARLINAC, IL (1863)
Grandval, Marie Felicie
MUJERES DE JERUSALEM (1972)
Salvador, Matilde
MURNEIDE TYTAR
Hermann, Miina
MUSIC CLUB, THE (1966)
Blisa, Alice
MUSIC HATER, THE
Newell, Eleanor
MUSIC LAND (1940)
Reynolds, Laura Lawton
MUZHESTVO (1947)
Makarova, Nina Vladimirovna
MY BROTHER'S KEEPER (1968)
Laufer, Beatrice
MYORVAYA TSAREVNA (1937)
Weissberg, Julia Lazarevna
MYSTERIOUS CHARACTERS OF MR. FU, THE
Weber, Bertha
MYSTERIOUS FOREST, THE
Dungan, Olive
NA DEREVHIYU DYEDUVKE (1978)
Chudova, Tatiana Alekseyevna
NA LESNOI OPUSHKE (1961)
Popatenko, Tamara Alexandrovna

NACHOD CASSATION, (six scenes) (1955)
  Vorlova, Slavka
NADA DELWIG, in one act (1910)
  Gubitosi, Emilia
NARCISSA OR THE COST OF EMPIRE, (four acts)
  Moore, Mary Carr
NATIONAL FLOWER, THE
  Adams, Carrie Bell
NATSARKEKIA
  Davitashvili, Meri Shalvovna
NAUGHTY NINKY
  Royse, Mildred Barnes
NAUSICAA, (three acts)
  Glanville-Hicks, Peggy
NEDGEYA, (two acts) (1880)
  Thys, Pauline
NEIGHBORS IN THE HOUSE
  Woolsley, Mary Hale
NELL, OR LE GABIER D'ARTIMON
  Pean de la Roche-Jagu, E. Françoise
NEPHTA, (one act) (1896)
  Rosselli-Nissim, Mary
NEPOFERENNYE (1944)
  Katzman, Klara Abramovna
NEPRIGOSHAYA ILI SOLOMONIDA SABUROVA, (one act) (1873)
  Adajewsky, Ella
NEW DAWN, A (1946)
  House, L. Marguerite
NEW WORLD FOR NELLIE
  Du Page, Florence Elizabeth
NIETZSCHE
  Costre, Adrienne
NIEUWE KLEREN VAN DE KEIZER, DE
  Bessem Saar
NIGHT AT SEA AND DAY IN COURT
  Gyring, Elizabeth
NIGHT OF THE STAR, THE
  Caldwell, Mary Elizabeth Glockler
NIGHTINGALE, THE, (one act)
  Crawford, Dorothy Lamb
NIGHTINGALE AND THE ROSE, THE, (one act) (1973)
  Garwood, Margaret
NIGHTINGALE'S APPRENTICE, THE
  Silsbee, Ann L.
NILTETI
  Cazati, Maria
NINIVE
  Maistre, Baroness of
NITOCRI, (three acts)
  Agnesi-Pinottini, Maria Teresa d'
NOAH, (three acts) (1965)
  Carlos, Wendy
NOE, (three acts)
  Arrieu, Claude
NOTTE A VENEZIA, UNA
  Correr, Ida, Countess
NOUVEL ACTE ABIGAIL (1956)
  Vito-Delvaux, Berthe di
NOZZE DI FIORINA, LE
  Guidi Lionetti, Teresa
NOZZE DI LEPORELLO, LE (1924)
  Garelli Della Morea, Vincenza
NOZZE FUNESTE, LE (1816)
  Amalie, Marie Friederike Augusta
NUIT D'EPREUVE, LA (1867)
  Haenel de Cronenthal, Louise
NUMBERED, THE, (prologue and two acts) (1967)
  Lutyens, Elisabeth
NURSERY RHYMES FOR HOLIDAY TIMES (1979)
  Stultz, Marie Irene
OBIADEK Z MAGDUSIA, (one act)
  Grodzicka-Rzewuska, Julia
OCCURRENCE AT OWL CREEK BRIDGE (1981)
  Musgrave, Thea

ODYSSEY, (one act)
  Shields, Alice Ferree
OEILLET BLANC, L' (1889)
  Dell'acqua, Eva
OGRE, L' (1868)
  Viardot-Garcia, Pauline Michelle Ferdinande
OH! SUSANNA
  Ronell, Ann
OIL FROM THE DEEJAH'S TAIL
  Lowell, Edith
OISEAU BLEU, L'
  Dell'acqua, Eva
OISIN
  Patterson, Annie Wilson
OLD MAN AND THE SEA, THE (1964)
  Carmen Marina
OLD MR. SUNDOWN (1935)
  Solomon, Mirrie Irma
OLHA PAR ISTO
  Travassos Lopes, Maria de Lourdes Alves
OLIMPIADE
  Charriere, Isabella Agneta Elisabeth de
OLINO KOLECHKO (1975)
  Nikolskaya, Lyubov Borisovna
ON THE CLIFFS OF CORNWALL
  Smith, Ethel Mary, Dame
ON THE MERRY NIGHT (1983)
  Hara, Kazuko (1)
ONE AND THE SAME (1973)
  Lutyens, Elisabeth
ONE DAY'S FUN
  Lewis, Carrie
OPERA BUFFET (1982)
  Walker, Gwyneth van Anden
OPERETTA IN MOZARTIAN STYLE
  Manning, Kathleen Lockhart
ORACLE, THE
  Moore, Mary Carr
ORANGE BLOSSOM TIME
  Jenney, Mary Frances
ORLANDO
  Cazati, Maria
ORPHEUS LIVES
  Lebaron, Anne
OSCAR FROM ALVA (1972)
  Ptaszynska, Marta
OSSEOK (1917)
  Noyes, Edith Rowena
OSTI ET NON OSTI (1840)
  Perelli, Natalie
OTTO DER SCHUETZ (1823)
  Schmezer, Elise
OTTO DER SCHUETZ
  Kinkel, Johanna
OUR (THEIR) LAST WAR
  Korn, Clara Anna
OUR NIGHT OUT (1952)
  Briggs, Mary Elizabeth
PABLO Y VIRGINIA, (three acts) (1946)
  Curubeto Godoy, Maria Isabel
PABSTWAHL, DIE (1875)
  Vesvali, Felicita
PAESE EI SUONI, IL (1984)
  Procaccini, Teresa
PAGE DE STELLA, LE (1895)
  Ugalde, Delphine Beauce
PAGEANT OF THE MONTH (1941)
  Reynolds, Laura Lawton
PAISE UNIVERSELLE, LA (1904)
  Chevalier de Boisval, Mme.
PALASTDAME, DIE (1848)
  Wiseneder, Caroline
PALETTE, LA (1964)
  Vito-Delvaux, Berthe di
PAMARO (1907)
  Esterhazy, Alexandrine
PAN
  Urner, Catherine Murphy

PAN! PAN! C'EST L'ESPRIT (1898)
  Chevalier de Boisval, Mme.
PANDORA
  Whitely, Bessie Marshall
PANDORA (1898)
  Moncrieff, Lynedock
PANTAGRUEL
  Tajani Mattone, Ida
PAOLA AND FRANCESCA, (three acts)
  James, Dorothy E.
PARADE CRUELLE (1980)
  Richer, Jeanniné
PARAVENTO E FUOCO, (one act)
  Oddone Sulli-Rao, Elisabetta
PARDONER'S TALE, THE, (one act)
  Nunlist, Juli
PARISIANA (1955)
  Tailleferre, Germaine
PARLOUR, THE (1961)
  Williams, Grace Mary
PARTY, THE
  McLin, Lena
PAS-CHU
  Morin-Labrecque, Albertine
PASKO'I PAG-IBIG (1975)
  Gamilla, Alice Doria
PASSAPORTO DEL DROGHIERE, IL, OR PASSAPORTO
  Delle Grazie, Gisella
PASSEZ MUSCADE (1897)
  Guitty, Madeleine
PASSION, UNE (1888)
  Dell'acqua, Eva
PASTORES, LOS
  Waldo, Elisabeth
PAUL (1974)
  Spicer, Marjorie
PAUL ET JULIE
  Pean de la Roche-Jagu, E. Francoise
PAVEL KORCHAGIN
  Yukhnovskaya, Ninel Grigorievna
PAVILLON AU BORD DE LA RIVIERE, LE, (four acts)
  Jolas, Betsy
PAYS DE COCAGNE, LE, (two acts) (1862)
  Thys, Pauline
PEARL, THE, (three acts) (1972)
  Crawford, Dawn Constance
PIERRE THE DREAMER
  Gaynor, Jessie Love
PELLEAS AND MELISANDE
  Scott-Hunter, Hortense
PENAL COLONY (1968)
  Bruzdowicz, Joanna
PENELOPE (1948)
  Lutyens, Elisabeth
PENITENTE, LA, (one act) (1868)
  Grandval, Marie Felicie
PEPITA L'ANDALOUSE (1896)
  Chevalier de Boisval, Mme.
PEPITO'S GOLDEN FLOWER
  Caldwell, Mary Elizabeth Glockler
PERDON FIO (1895)
  Broca, Carmen L. de
PERLA DEL VILLAGIO (two acts) (1882)
  Gambaro, Alceste
PERLA DELL'ATELIER, LA, (three acts) (1820)
  Testore, Lidia
PERRUQUE DE BAILLI, LA (1860)
  Thys, Pauline
PERSAN, LE, (five acts)
  Olagnier, Marguerite
PET OF THE MET, THE
  Johnson, Harriet
PETITE DACTYL, LE
  Maurice-Jacquet, H.
PETITE SIRENE, LA (1907)
  Polignac, Armande de, Countess
PETITE SIRENE, LA, (three acts) (1958)
  Tailleferre, Germaine

PETKO SAMOKHVALKO (1959)
Klinkova, Zhivka
PETRUCCIO E IL CAVALO CAPPUCCIO
Oddone Sulli-Rao, Elisabetta
PETUKH I LISA (1954)
Nikolskaya, Lyubov Borisovna
PFINGSTKRONE, DIE (1925)
Bock, Bertha
PHENICIENNES, LES
Charriere, Isabella Agneta
Elisabeth de
PIAZZA DELLA MUSICA NO. 1
Procaccini, Teresa
PICCOLINO, (three acts) (1869)
Grandval, Marie Felicie
PIED PIPER, THE (1974)
Blockside, Kathleen Mary
PIEGE D'AMOUR
Vieu, Jane
PIERRE THE DREAMER
Gaynor, Jessie Love
PIERROT PRINCE (1895)
Chevalier de Boisval, Mme.
PIF-PAF
Frondoni Lacombe, Madalena
**PILGRIM'S WAY, THE, OR THE GARDEN
OF LIFE**
Meredith, Margaret
PIONIERSLIED
Whittington, Joan
PIPANDOR
Harrison, Susan Frances
PIRATE'S UMBRELLA, THE
Forman, Addie Walling
PIRATI, I
Aspri, Orsola
PIT, THE (1972)
Lutyens, Elisabeth
PLAIRE, C'EST COMMANDER!
Beaumesnil, Henrietta Adelaide
PLAY OF HEROD (1974)
Evans, Winsome
POD CHORNOI MASKOI (1961)
Liadova, Ludmila Alekseyevna
PODRANILO
Petrova, Mara
POILU, LE
Maurice-Jacquet, H.
POLICEMAN'S SERENADE, THE (1932)
Tate, Phyllis
POLLY BAKER (1977)
Forman, Joanne
POLOVODIE (1962)
Katzman, Klara Abramovna
POMME DE TURQUIE, LA, (one act) (1857)
Thys, Pauline
PONDER HEART, THE
Parker, Alice
POPE, EL, (one act) (1950)
Witni, Monica
POR ELEVAR MISMO NOMBRE
Mena, Carolina
POSLE BALA (1959)
Kuznetsova, Zhanetta Alexandrovna
POUICK!
Raynal, Germaine
**PRAXITELE ou LE CEINTURE,
in one act (1802)**
Devisme, Jeanne-Hippolite
PRAYER, A (1981)
Van Ohlen, Deborah
**PRECIOSA/THE SPANISH STUDENT,
(one act) (1928)**
Freer, Eleanor Warner Everest
PRIDE OF LIONS, A
Tate, Phyllis
PRIGIONIERE, IL (1817)
Amalie, Marie Friederike Augusta
PRIMA NOTTE, LA, (one act)
Procaccini, Teresa

PRINCE AND THE PAUPER, THE (1974)
Skeens, Gwendolyn
PRINCE NOIR, LE (1882)
Dell'acqua, Eva
PRINCE OF ASTURIA, THE
Runcie, Constance Owen Faunt
Le Roy
PRINCE SPRITE (1897)
Marshall, Florence A.
PRINCESA GIRASOL, LA
Escobar, Maria Luisa
PRINCESS AND THE PEA, THE
Selmer, Kathryn Lande
PRINCESS BO-PEEP
Gaynor, Jessie Love
PRINCESS DE BABYLONE, LA, (three acts)
Arrieu, Claude
PRINCESS JU JU
Ward, Clememtine
PRINCESS MARINA
Gulesian, Grace Warner
PRINCESS OF A THOUSAND MOONS
Frank, Jean Forward
PRINCESS OF GEORGIA, THE
Anspach, Elizabeth
PRINCESS WHO COULDN'T LAUGH
Selmer, Kathryn Lande
PRINCIPESSA IRIS, LA (1909)
Meini-Zanotti, Maddalena
PRINCIPINO SMARRITO, IL (1932)
Beloch, Dorotea
**PRINS RUDI EN DE TOVERSTAF,
(three acts) (1938)**
Mulder, Johanna Harmina Gerdina
PRINSES OP DE ERWT, DE
Bessem, Saar
PRINZ HEIDENMUT (1914)
Stein-Schneider, Lena
PRINZESSIN LISA'S FEE (1896)
Wurm, Mary J.A.
PRISCILLA
Ware, Harriet
PRISCILLA, (four acts) (1887)
Gerrish-Jones, Abbie
PROCES VERBAL, LE (1906)
Symiane, Magdaleine
PROFESSOR OWL (1971)
House, L. Marguerite
**PROMESSA D'ARTISTA E PAROLE
DI RE (1952)**
Cancino de Cuevas, Sofia
PROMETHEUS (1981)
Matuszczak, Bernadetta
PROMISE OF PEACE, THE (1969)
Raigorodsky, Leda Natalia Heimsath
PROPOSAL, THE (1985)
Steinbock, Evalyn
PRYANICH NI CHELOVECHEK (1971)
Popatenko, Tamara Alexandrovna
PRZYGODA KROLA ARTURA
Bacewicz, Grazyna
PSYCHE AND THE PSKYSCRAPER
Larsen, Elizabeth Brown
**PUPPENSPIEL VOM ERZZAUBERER
GOETHE, (four acts) (1901)**
Mentzel-Schippel, Elisabeth
PURPLE ON THE MOON
Dunn, Rebecca Welty
PYGMALION, in one act
Saint-Croix, Carolina de
PYGMALION DELIVRE
Falcinelli, Rolande
QUAND DIEU EST DANS LE MENAGE (1860)
Thys, Pauline
QUATTRO RUSTICI, I
Galloni, Adolfa
QUEEN CHRISTINA (1973)
Anderson, Beth
**QUEEN NADA AND THE WOOD NYMPHS
(1912)**
Forster, Charlotte

QUEEN OF THE GARDEN, THE
Lewis, Carrie Bullard
QUEEN'S GARDEN, THE (1938)
Heaton, Eloise Klotz
QUENTIN METZYS (1884)
Dell'acqua, Eva
QUEEN OF HEARTS
Pagoto, Helen
QUEEN OF HEARTS
Stocker, Stella
QUEEN OF HEARTS (1888)
Young, Harriet Maitland
QUEEN OF KI-LU, THE
Mana-Zucca
QUEEN OF THE SAWDUST
Nightingale, Mae Wheeler
QUENILDA
Norbury, Ethel F.
QUESTIONE DI FIDUCIA, (one act)
Procaccini, Teresa
QUONG LUNG'S SHADOW
Bright, Dora Estella
RABBIT WHO WANTED RED WINGS, THE
Barlow, Betty
**RACCAMMONDEMENT DE PIERROT ET DE
NICOLE (1708)**
La Guerre, Elisabeth-Claude
Jacquet de
RAEUBER UND DER SAENGER, DIE (1830)
BlahetkA, Marie Leopoldine
RAGE IN A CAGE, A (1983)
Zaidel-Rudolph, Jeanne
RAINY DAY, A, (one act)
Gabriel, Mary Ann Virginia
RAOUL
Stocker, Stella
RAPPACCINI'S DAUGHTER
Garwood, Margaret
RAPUNZEL
Glanville-Hicks, Peggy
RAY AND THE GOSPEL SINGER
Gould, Elizabeth Davies
REY CUAICAIPURO, EL, (three acts)
Escobar, Marie Luis
REAL MERRY CHRISTMAS, A
Gould, Octavia R.
REINAARD
Bessem, Saar
REINE ARDENTE, LA
Raynal, Germaine
REINE DE L'ONDE, LA
Pean de la Roche-Jagu, E. Françoise
REINE DES REINES, LA (1904)
Biasini, Marcelle
REINE DORT, LA
Delaborde, Elie Mirian
REINEKE FUCHS (1962)
Zechlin, Ruth
**REIS VAN HARLEKINO, DE (three acts)
(1980)**
Mulder, Johanna Harmina Gerdina
RELEASE FROM HELL (1978)
Phillips, Bryony
RELOGHO DE CARDEAL, O
Polonio, Cinira
RELUCTANT HERO (1956)
Hunkins, Eusebia Simpson
RENDEZ-VOUS GALANTS, (one act)
Saint-Croix, Carolina de
RENTING THE HIVE
Rich, Gladys
RESURREZIONE
Arrieu, Claude
RETOUR DE TASSE, LE
Pean de la Roche-Jagu, E. Françoise
RETURN OF THE NATIVE, THE, (three acts)
Coulthard, Jean
REVE DE MAKAR, LE (1964)
Gotkovsky, Ida-Rose Esther
REY CUAICAIPURO, EL, (three acts)
Escobar, Maria Luisa

RIDE 'EM COWBOY
Nightingale, Mae Wheeler
RINALDO INNAMORATO (1616)
Caccini, Francesca
RINALDO UND ALCINA (1797)
Paradis, Maria Theresia von
RITI INDIANI, I
Aspri, Orsola
RITRATTO DI DORIAN GRAY, IL, (one act) (1975)
Ravinale, Irma
RITTER LANCELOT
Geiger-Kullman, Rosy Auguste
ROAM, GYPSIES, ROAM
Pagoto, Helen
ROI BOSSU, LE, (one act)
Barraine, Elsa
ROI JAUNE, LE (1887)
Thys, Pauline
ROMA LIBERATA DALLA SIGNORIA DEI REI, (three acts)
Zamparelli, Dionisia
ROMANCE DE DONA BALADA (1972)
Urreta, Alicia
ROMANITZA
Maurice-Jacquet, H.
ROOFTOPS
Burgess, Brio
ROSA DI PERONA
Guidi Lionetti, Teresa
ROSALYND
Wickham, Florence Pauline
ROSE AND THE RING, THE
Lewis, Carrie Bullard
ROSE AND THE RING, THE (1932)
Leginska, Ethel
ROSE BLANCHE, LA (1925)
Cocq, Rosina Susanna de
ROSE OF DESTINY, (prelude and three acts) (1918)
Heckscher, Celeste de Longpré
ROSE VON LIBANON, DIE
Henn, Angelica
ROSES DU CALIFE, LES (1909)
Polignac, Armande de, Countess
ROTONDE, (one act) (1943)
Bordewijk-Roepman, Johanna
ROUSSALKAS, LES
Maistre, Baroness of
ROZMARYNKA, (four acts) (1955)
Vorlova, Slavka
RUBIOS, LOS, (three acts) (1931)
Moore, Mary Carr
RUEBEZAHL!
Morrison, Julia Maria
RUGGERO (1841)
Sanchez de la Madrid, Ventura
RUMPLESTILTSKIN
McLin, Lena
RUSALOCHKA (1923)
Weissberg, Julia Lazarevna
RUSE DE PIERETTE, UNE (1903)
Dell'acqua, Eva
RUSSKIYE ZHENSHCHINY (1975)
Chudova, Tatiana Alekseyevna
RUTH (1952)
Garland, Kathryn
RUTH (1954)
Kamien, Anna
RUTH AND NAOMI, (one act) (1966)
Harvey, Eva Noel
RYTSARSKAYA BALLADA (1973)
Katzman, Klara Abramovna
SA LAHAT NG ORAS, (two acts) (1974)
GAMILLA, Alice Doria
ST. FRANCOIS
Perronet, Amélie
ST. NIKOLAUS UND SEINE GEHILFEN (1928)
Streit, Else

SAIS
Olagnier, Marguerite
SAKURA-SAN
Gerrish-Jones, Abbie
SALLI VENTADOUR (1875)
Grandval, Marie Felicie
SAM, THE SAD CIRCUS CLOWN
Merman, Joyce
SANCTUARY OF SPIRITS
Bibby, Gillian Margaret
SAMURAI, (three acts)
Respighi, Elsa
SANTA CHIARA (1854)
Pfeiffer, Charlotte Birsch
SAPPHO
Glanville-Hicks, Peggy
SARA, (three acts) (1888)
Marra, Adelina
SARITA
Whitely, Bessie Marshall
SARYA SVOBODY, (four acts) (1873)
Adajewsky, Ella
SAUL (1830)
Uccelli, Carolina
SAUL OF TARSUS (1952)
King, Betty Jackson
SCARECROW (1983)
Tate, Phyllis
SCARECROW, THE
Dunlop, Olive
SCENE FOR ICELANDIC SAGA
Branning, Grace Bell
SCENES FROM LITTLE WOMEN, (two acts)
Freer, Eleanor Warner Everest
SCHAEFERSTUENDCHEN, EIN
Clement, Mary
SCHASTLIVAY MEL
Liadova, Ludmila Alekseyevna
SCHASTLIVUI PUT (1939)
Zaranek, Stefania Anatolyevna
SCHIAVE E REGINA, (three acts) (1881)
Casagemas, Luisa
SCHOOL BOARD, THE
Blisa, Alice
SCHULKANDIDAT, DER (1792)
Paradis, Maria Theresia von
SECRET DE L'ALCADE, LE (1888)
Dell'acqua, Eva
SELEIS
Okey, Maggie
SELFISH GIANT, THE, (three acts)
Perry, Julia Amanda
SEREBRYANOYE KOPITSE (1959)
Nikolskaya, Lyubov Borisovna
SERENADE, LA, (one act) (1818)
Gail, Edmée-Sophie
SERGEANT BRUE (1904)
Lehmann, Liza
SERGENT LAROSSE, LE (1903)
Fortmagne, Baronne Durand de
SEULE
Ugalde, Delphine Beauce
SEVERINA (1939)
Schick, Philippine
SEVILLANE, LA, (one act) (1882)
Chaminade, Cecile Louise Stephanie
SGANARELLE, (one act) (1973)
Archer, Violet Balestreri
SHADOWY WATERS, THE
Swain, Freda Mary
SHAMAN
Shields, Alice Ferree
SHELTER
Ford, Nancy
SHEPHERD OF CORNOUAILLES
Gabriel, Mary Ann Virginia
SHEPHERD, THE
Guerrant, Mary Thorington
SHEPHERD KING, THE, OR THE CONQUEST OF SIDON
Fauche, Marie

SHEPHERDESS AND THE CHIMNEY SWEEP (1966)
Smith, Julia Frances
SHOEMAKER AND THE ELF
Selmer, Kathryn Lande
SHORT OPERA, A (1981)
Gardner, Kay
SIE WAREN SO SCHOEN UND HERRLICH ....
Costre, Adrienna
SIEGESFAHNE, DIE (1834)
Amalie, Marie Friederike Augusta
SILENCIO, DONDE ESTAS TU
Martins, Maria de Lourdes
SILHOUETTE
Dunlop, Olive
SILVER FOX, THE, (one act)
Larsen, Elizabeth Brown
SILVER TANKARD, THE
Anspach, Elizabeth
SIMCHA 73
Friedberg, Patricia Ann
SIMPLE ET COQUETTE
Pean de la Roche-Jagu, E. Françoise
SIMPLE FORMALITE, UNE (1906)
Symiane, Magdaleine
SINDACO DI VILLAGIO
Lucilla D.
SINNER'S SAINT
Ware, Harriet
SIR GAWAIN AND THE GREEN KNIGHT
Aylott, Lydia Georgina Edith
SIRE DE DUCUCU, LE
Matthyssens, Marie
SISTER AIMEE: AN AMERICAN LEGEND (1978)
Martinez, Odaline de la
SISTERS OF FAITH, (one act) (1985)
Warwick, Mary Carol
SIX AND FOUR ARE TEN
Ridley, Ursula
SIX ARIAS FOR L'HUOMO
Wilhelmina, Sophie Friederike
SIX PART CYCLE; ZEME; INDRANI; DRAHO-MIRA; OHEN; VZPOURA, VZLET
Drdova, Marie
SKALA NEVEST (1972)
Akhundova, Shafiga Gulam
SKAZKA O MYORTVOI ISAREVNE I SEMY BOGATERIYACH (1968)
Chudova, Tatiana Alekseyevna
SKAZKA O POTERYANNOM VREMENI (1971)
Rozhavskaya, Yudif Grigorevna
SKOEN KAREN, (one act) (1895)
GriebeL Wandall, Tekla
SKRIKKELJANIE
Rudolf, Anna
SLAUGHTER OF THE INNOCENTS (1974)
Evans, Winsome
SLAVES IN ALGIERS
Rowson, Susannah
SLIDING DOWN A MOONBEAM (1950)
House, L. Marguerite
SMARANDA
White, Maude Valerie
SMILE RIGHT TO THE BONE (1966)
Morrison, Julia Maria
SMOKY MOUNTAIN, (one act) (1954)
Hunkins, Eusebia Simpson
SNEEUWBRUID (1951)
Cocq, Rosina Susanna de
SNEEUWIT EN ROZEROOD
Tenbergen, Maria Elizabeth van Ebbenhorst
SNEEUWMANNETJES, DE
Vladeracken, Geertruida van
SNEZHANKA
Klinkova, Zhivka
SNOW (1966)
Marcus, Ada Belle Gross

SNOW QUEEN, THE
    Gerrish-Jones, Abbie
SNOW QUEEN, THE (1933)
    McPherson, Frances Marie
SNOW QUEEN, THE (1979)
    Alexandra, Liana
SNOW QUEEN, THE, (seven scenes) (1933)
    Maitland, S. Marguerite
SNOW QUEEN, THE, OR THE FROZEN
   HEART
    Carmichael, Mary Grant
SNOW WHITE (1869)
    Mely, Marie, Countess Vanden
      Heuvel
SOFA, THE
    Maconchy, Elizabeth
SOFIA (1896)
    Ferrari, Carlotta
SOFONISBA, (three acts)
    Agnesl-Pinottini, Maria Teresa d'
SOLAR (1983)
    Tate, Phyllis
SOLEIL VANGUER DES NUAGES, LE
    Clerambault, N.
SOLITARIO, IL
    Lucilla D.
SOME PIG (1973)
    Larsen, Elizabeth Brown
SON OF GETRON (1972)
    Evans, Winsome
SONG OF YESTERDAY
    Thomas, Helen
SONGE DE LA RELIGIEUSE, LE
    La Hye, Louise Genevieve
SONGS FROM MOTHER GOOSE'S JUBILEE
  (1900)
    Orth, Lizette Emma
SONHO AO LUAR
    Reis, Manuela Cancio
SORCIER, LE (1886)
    Perriere-Pilte, Anais
SORCIER DE SEVILLE, LE
    Reynac, Mme. de
SORELLE DI MARK, LA (1896)
    Bellincioni, Gemma
SOU DE LISE, (one act) (1859)
    Grandval, Marie Felicie
SOUS LE MASQUE, (one act) (1898)
    Ferrari, Gabriella
SOUTHERN INTERLUDE, A
    Arvey, Verna
SPIDER AND THE BUTTERFLY, THE, (three
  acts) (1953)
    Britain, Radie
SPIRIT OWL, (two acts) (1956)
    Hunkins, Eusebia Simpson
SPONDA MAGICA, LA, (three acts)
    Contini Anselmi, Lucia
SPOTVOGELS, DE (1955)
    Cocq, Rosina Susanna de
SPOUTNIK (1959)
    Vito-Delvaux, Berthe di
STARFLOWER
    Woolsley, Mary Hale
STATUS QUO
    Beyer, Johanna Magdalena
STOCKINGS WERE HUNG, THE (1958)
    House, L. Marguerite
STONE PRINCESS, THE (1974)
    Love, Loretta
STRADELLA
    Schimon, Anna
STRANGE ADVENTURE, A
    Elliott, Marjorie Reeve
STRANGER OF MANZANO (1946)
    Smith, Julia Frances
STRATONICE (1892)
    Fournier, Alice
STREET SINGERS OF MARKET STREET,
  THE (1965)
    Brush, Ruth Damaris

STRIKE, THE
    Aylwin, Josephine Crew
SUDRABOTAIS PUTNS (1938)
    Garuta, Lucia Yanovna
SUEHNE, DIE
    Bronsart von Schellendorf,
      Ingeborg Lena
SUMPAAN NG PUSO, (one act) (1975)
    Gamilla, Alice Doria
SUN PILGRIM, THE
    Urner, Catherine Murphy
SUNNY
    Dunn, Rebecca Welty
SUOCERA (1877)
    Skinner, Florence Marian
SUONATORE DELLE CAMPANE, IL
    Pfeiffer, Charlotte Birsch
SURPRISES DE L'ENFER, LES (1981)
    Aboulker, Isabelle
SUSANNA MONFERT
    Goetze, Auguste
SUSINETTE
    Guidi Lionetti, Teresa
SWING MIKADO, THE
    DuBois, Shirley Graham
SWISS INTERLUDE (1961)
    Allen, Denise
TABOO THE
    Harraden, R. Ethel
TAINA MORYA (1954)
    Zaranek, Stefania Anatolyevna
TALE OF THE TOYS
    Pitcher, Gladys
TALESTRI, REGINA DELLE AMAZONIA
  (1763)
    Maria Antonia Walpurgis, Princess
      of Bavaria
TALISMANN, DER
    Maddison, Adele
TALON D'ACHILLE, LE
    Perriere-Pilte, Anais
TAMARA (1954)
    Abramova, Sonia Pinkhasovna
TAMBOUR BATTANT
    Dell'acqua, Eva
TAMBURLAINE
    Murdoch, Elaine
TAMMANY
    Hatton, Anne
TAMYRIS (1921)
    Polignac, Armande de, Countess
TARASOVA NOCH (1944)
    Levitskaya, Viktoria Sergeyevna
TARTARE, LE, (two acts) (1906)
    Ferrari, Gabriella
TELEMACHUS AND CALYPSO, (four acts)
  (1792)
    Ahlefeldt, Marie Theresia
TENI ILI ZEMLYA DVIZHETSYA (1938)
    Levitskaya, Viktoria Sergeyevna
TEN TEDDY BEARS (1907)
    Maxim, Florence
TERRE BONNE, LA, OR LAND OF THE
  MAPLE LEAF (ca. 1903)
    GEDDES-HARVEY, Roberta
TEUZZONE, IL, (three acts) (1753)
    Zamparelli, Dionisia
THESEE A MARSEILLE
    Demarquez, Suzanne
THIRTEEN CLOCKS
    Johnson, Mary Ernestine Clark
THIRTEEN CLOCKS, THE (1983)
    Zaimont, Judith Lang
THIS IS OUR CAMP (1950)
    Richter, Marion Morrey
THREE LITTLE PIGS
    Ohlson, Marion
THREE STRANGERS, THE
    Maconchy, Elizabeth
TIBULLE ET DELIE, OU LES SATURNALES
    Beaumesnil, Henrietta Adelaide

TIME KILLING, THE
    Cox, Alison Mary
TIME OF OUR LIVES
    Frank, Jean Forward
TIME OFF-NOT A GHOST OF A CHANCE
  (four scenes) (1978)
    Lutyens, Elisabeth
TINY OPERA (1953)
    Dlugoszewski, Lucia
TIZIANELLO (ca. 1860)
    Rose
TLASS ATKA (1922)
    Canal, Marguerite
TO EACH HIS OWN (1964)
    Maitland, Anna Harriet
TO JESSE TREE (1970)
    Maconchy, Elizabeth
TO PLEASE MR. PLUMJOY (1957)
    Hamilton, Marcia
TOINETTE ET LOUIS, (two acts) (1787)
    Gretry, Angelique Dorothée
TOM-TOM (1932)
    DuBois, Shirley Graham
TOM THUMB, (one act)
    Pradell, Leila
TONANTZIN
    Alonso, Julia
TONNELIER DE NUREMBERG, LE
    Mayer, Emilie
TOOVERBAL, DE
    Vladeracken, Geertruida van
TOUGH AT THE TOP
    Ellis, Vivian
TOURISTS, THE
    House, L. Marguerite
TOVERSPIEGEL, DE (three acts) (1958)
    Mulder, Johanna Harmina Gerdina
TOY SHOP, THE
    Gaynor, Jessie Love
TOY-SHOP, THE
    Rich, Gladys
TRANSPOSED HEADS, THE, (six scenes)
  (1950)
    Glanville-Hicks, Peggy
TRAVELLING MUSICIAN
    Holden, Bernice
TRE CINTURE, LE (1817)
    Amalie, Marie Friederike Augusta
TRECCIAIUOLA DI FORENZE, LA
    Delle Grazie, Gisella
TRESOR DE L'EMIR, LE (1884)
    Dell'acqua, Eva
TRETYA LYUBOV (1972)
    Igenberga, Elga Avgustovna
TRI TOVARYSI (1956)
    Kucerova-Herstova, Marie
TRIAL UNIVERSELLE
    Du Page, Florence Elizabeth
TRIBULATIONS D'UN RESERVISTE, LES
  (1901)
    Bellet, Mlle.
TRIONFI DI PARNASSO, I (ca. 1700)
    Sophia, Charlotte
TRIMMING THE CHRISTMAS TREE (1972)
    House, L. Marguerite
TRIOMPHE DU COEUR, LE
    Pierpont, Marie de
TRIONFO DELLA FEDELTA, IL (1754)
    Maria Antonia Walpurgis, Princess
      of Bavaria
TRISTAN AND ISEULT (1975)
    Whitehead, Gillian
TROJAN WOMEN, THE, (one act) (1967)
    Garwood, Margaret
TROP DES FEMMES (1867)
    Viardot-Garcia, Pauline Michelle
TROYENNES, LES (1972)
    Bruzdowich, Joanna
TUMBLEDOWN DICK, (two acts)
    Larsen, Elizabeth Brown

APPENDIX 7

Women Composers influenced by Shakespeare

ADAM, Maria Emma
ANTONIO Y CLEOPATRA — Vocal

ANSPACH, Elizabeth, Margravine of
O MISTRESS MINE, madrigal — Vocal

ARCHER, Violet
SING THE MUSE — Vocal

ARRIEU, Claude
CYMBELINE — Incidental Music
LE MARCHAND DE VENISE — Incidental Music
LA TEMPETE — Incidental Music

AUSTER, Lydia Martinovna
ROMEO, JULIETTA I TMA — Ballet

BARAMISHVILI, Olga Ivanovna
ROMEO AND JULIET — Incidental Music

BARBERIS, Mansi
MERCHANT OF VENICE — Incidental Music

BARKER, Laura Wilson
AS YOU LIKE IT — Incidental Music

BARRAINE, Elsa
KING LEAR — Incidental Music

BAULD, Alison
AS YOU LIKE IT — Incidental Music

BAUMGARTEN, Chris
KOMOEDIE DER IRRUNGEN — Incidental Music

BEACH, Amy Marcy
THREE SHAKESPEARE SONGS, OP. 37 — Vocal

BELLEVILLE-OURY, Emilie
FANTASY ON MERRY WIVES OF WINDSOR — Vocal

BENFEY-SCHUPPE, Anna
ROMEO AND JULIET — Incidental Music

BERK, Adele
SIGH NO MORE LADIES — Vocal

BIANCHINI, Emma
AMLETO — Symphonic Poem

BLIESENER, Ada Elizabeth
FROM A SONNET BY SHAKESPEARE — Vocal

BLISS, Tamara
COME AWAY DEATH (TWELFTH NIGHT) — Vocal

BOBROW, Sanchie
AS YOU LIKE IT — Incidental Music
HENRY V — Incidental Music

BONDS, Margaret
MUSIC FOR SHAKESPEARE IN HARLEM — Incidental Music
ROMIE AND JULIE — Incidental Music

BOONE, Clara Lyle
SONNET — Vocal

BRANDMAN, Margaret Susan
FREEZE FREEZE THOU WINTER WIND — Vocal

BRITAIN, Radie
LADY IN THE DARK (on Shakespearean Sonnets) — Opera

CARTER, Rosetta
MUSIC FOR SHAKESPEARE PLAYS — Incidental Music

CARTWRIGHT, Patricia
THERE IS SWEET MUSIC HERE — Vocal

CHOUQUET, Louise
MACBETH, caprice — Piano

COATES, Gloria Kannenberg
HAMLET — Incidental Music
OPHELIA (lieder) — Vocal

COULTHARD, Jean
THREE SHAKESPEARE SONNETS (1949) — Vocal
THREE SHAKESPEARE SONNETS (1977) — Vocal

DIEMER, Emma Lou
MADRIGALS — Vocal

DONCEANU, Felicia
MEASURE FOR MEASURE — Incidental Music
TWELFTH NIGHT

DRING, Madeleine
THREE SHAKESPEARE SONGS — Vocal

FALTIS, Evelyn
HAMLET — Symphonic Poem

FINE, Vivian
ELIZABETHAN SONGS — Vocal

FALCINELLI, Rolande
OPHELIA — Vocal

FISHER, Jessie
SONNET — Vocal

FISHER, Katherine Danforth	
SONNET	Vocal
FORMAN, Joanne	
TWELFTH NIGHT	Incidental Music
FREER, Eleanor Warner Everest	
SONGS	Vocal
FRITZ, Sherilyn Gail	
KING LEAR	Electronic
A MIDSUMMER NIGHT'S DREAM	Vocal
MUSIC FOR HAMLET	Chamber Music
GERSTMAN, Blanche Wilhelminia	
THREE SONGS FROM SHAKESPEARE	Vocal
GIBB, Prue	
HAMLET ON ICE	Incidental Music
GIDEON, Miriam	
SONNETS FOR SHAKESPEARE	Vocal
GIFFORD, Helen Margaret	
MERCHANT OF VENICE	Incidental Music
OTHELLO	Incidental Music
GILLICK, Emelyn Mildred Samuels	
SOUND ENVIRONMENT FOR MACBETH	Incidental Music
GLATZ, Helen Sinclair	
MERCHANT OF VENICE	Incidental Music
MERRY WIVES OF WINDSOR	Incidental Music
MUCH ADO ABOUT NOTHING	Incidental Music
ROMEO AND JULIET	Incidental Music
GRIEBLING, Karen Jean	
RICHARD III	Incidental Music
GYRING, Elizabeth	
SONG FROM HENRY EIGHTH	Vocal
SONG FROM THE TEMPEST	Vocal
HAENEL DE CRONENTHAL, Louise Augusta Marie Julia	
OPHELIA	vlc and pf.
HALL, Pauline	
AS YOU LIKE IT (LITTLE DANCE SUITE)	Chamber Music
HAMLET	Incidental Music
JULIUS CAESAR, suite	Incidental Music
TAMING OF THE SHREW	Incidental Music
HEINRICH, Adel Verna	
DRAMATIC BANQUET:	
SHAKESPEAREAN MEN	Dance Score
FIVE SHAKESPEAREAN SONNETS	Vocal
ROMEO AND JULIET	Dance Score
SHAKESPEAREAN WOMEN	Dance Score
HERNANDEZ-GONGALO, Gisela	
HAMLET	Incidental Music
HIND O'MALLEY, Pamela	
SHAKESPEAREAN SONGS	Vocal
HOLLAND, Dulcie Sybil	
HE THAT IS THY FRIEND	Vocal
O MISTRESS MINE	Vocal
HOWE, Mary Alberta Bruce	
O MISTRESS MINE	Vocal
HUBICKI, Margaret Olive	
SEVEN SHAKESPEAREAN SKETCHES	Vocal
ISAKOVA, Aida Petrovna	
HAMLET	Ballet
IVEY, Jean Eichelberger	
ABSENT IN THE SPRING	Vocal
JAMES, Dorothy E.	
AS YOU LIKE IT	Incidental Music
JOLAS, Betsy	
LA TEMPETE	Incidental Music

KASILAG, Lucrecia R	
HAMLET	Incidental Music
KATZMAN, Klara Abramovna	
ANTHONY AND CLEOPATRA	Incidental Music
KEMP-POTTER, Joan	
TEMPEST	Incidental Music
KING, Betty Jackson	
A LOVER'S PLEA	Vocal
KISTETENYI, Melinda	
SHAKESPEARE SONNETS	Vocal
KOZAKIEVICH, Anna Abramovna	
OTHELLO	Incidental Music
KRASNOGLIADOVA, Vera Vladimirovna	
THREE SHAKESPEAREAN SONNETS	Vocal
KUZMICH, Natalie	
WHEN ICICLES HANG BY THE WALL	Vocal
LAITMAN, Lori	
THE TAMING OF THE SHREW	Incidental Music
LEONARD, Mamie Grace	
FROM FAIREST CREATURES (sonnet)	Vocal
SO OFT I INVOKED THEE	Vocal
LITTLE, Anita Gray	
THREE SHAKESPEAREAN SONGS	Vocal
LOUDOVA, Ivana	
ROMEO AND JULIET, suite	Chamber Music
LUFF, Enid	
MIDSUMMER NIGHT'S DREAM	fl and pf
THREE SONNETS	Vocal
LUTYENS, Elizabeth	
AS YOU LIKE IT	Incidental Music
JULIUS CAESAR	Incidental Music
LUTYENS, Sally	
MIDSUMMER NIGHT'S DREAM	Vocal
MACDONALD, Catherine	
TWELFTH NIGHT	Incidental Music
MACONCHY, Elizabeth	
OPHELIA'S SONG	Vocal
TAKE O TAKE THOSE LIPS AWAY	Vocal
TWELFTH NIGHT	Chamber
MARCUS, Ada Belle Gross	
A CONSOLATION	Vocal
SEVEN AGES OF MAN	Vocal
A SHAKESPEAREAN DUO	Vocal
MARSHALL, Pamela J.	
AS YOU LIKE IT	Incidental Music
MACBETH	Incidental Music
RICHARD III	Incidental Music
MARTIN, Judith Reher	
MIDSUMMER NIGHT'S DREAM	Incidental Music
MATUSZCZAK, Bernadetta	
JULIET AND ROMEO	Opera
McKENZIE, Sandra	
AS YOU LIKE IT	Incidental Music
MACBETH	Incidental Music
MUCH ADO ABOUT NOTHING	Incidental Music
RICHARD II	Incidental Music
RICHARD III	Incidental Music
ROSENCRANTZ AND GUILDENSTERN ARE DEAD	Incidental Music
TAMING OF THE SHREW	Incidental Music
TWELFTH NIGHT	Incidental Music

McLEOD, Jennifer Helen	
HAMLET	Incidental Music
TROILUS AND CRESSIDA	Incidental Music
TWELFTH NIGHT	Incidental Music
McKEEL, Joyce	
MACBETH	Incidental Music
MERCHANT OF VENICE	Incidental Music
OTHELLO	Incidental Music
RICHARD II	Incidental Music
MOODY, Marie	
HAMLET OVERTURE	Orchestra
KING LEAR OVERTURE	Orchestra
OTHELLO OVERTURE	Orchestra
MUNDELLA, Emma	
YE SPOTTED SNAKES	Vocal
MUSGRAVE, Thea	
THE PHOENIX AND THE TURTLE	Vocal
NOVA-SONDAG, Jacqueline	
JULIUS CAESAR	Incidental Music
MACBETH	Incidental Music
PAYNE, Maggi	
A WINTER'S TALE	Incidental Music
PHILLIPS, Bryoni	
THE MARRIAGE OF TRUE MINDS	Vocal
PIECHOWSKA, Alina	
JULIETTE ET ROMEO	Incidental Music
PIZER, Elizabeth Hayden	
SILENT THOUGHT	Vocal
WHEN TO THE SESSIONS OF SWEET	
PLUMSTEAD, Mary	
TAKE O TAKE THOSE LIPS AWAY	Vocal
SIGH NO MORE LADIES	Vocal
POSTON, Elizabeth	
TWELFTH NIGHT	Incidental Music
POWNALL, Mary Ann	
KISSES SUED FOR	Vocal
RHOADS, Mary R.	
ROMEO AND JULIET	Incidental Music
ROBERTS Jane A.	
TWELFTH NIGHT	Miscellaneous
ROBERTS, Gertrud Hermine Kuenzel	
THE TEMPEST	Incidental Music
RODGERS, MARY	
SELECTIONS FROM SHAKESPEARE	Incidental Music
ROE, Eileen Betty	
FOUR SHAKESPEAREAN SONGS	Vocal
ROECKEL, Jane	
MIRANDA	Piano
ROGERS, Patsy	
THE TEMPEST	Incidental Music
ST. JOHN, Kathleen Louise	
TRESS MINE	Vocal
OPHELIA	Multimedia
SALSBURY, Janet Mary	
FROM SHAKESPEARE'S GARDEN (cycle)	Vocal
SANZ, Rocio	
MACBETH	Incidental Music
TEMPEST	Incidental Music
SCHICK, Philippine	
FIVE SHAKESPEAREAN SONGS	Vocal

SCHLOSS, Myrna Frances	
MUSIC FOR KING LEAR	Electronic Music
SHIELDS, Alice Ferree	
ELECTRONIC MUSIC FOR THE GHOST SCENES IN HAMLET	Incidental Music
WITCHES' SCENES FROM MACBETH	Incidental Music
SMELTZER, Susan Mary	
MIDSUMMER NIGHT'S DREAM	Incidental Music
SMILEY, Pril	
KING LEAR	Incidental Music
MACBETH	Incidental Music
RICHARD III	Incidental Music
SMYTH, Dame Ethel	
ANTHONY AND CLEOPATRA OVERTURE	Orchestra
SPENCER, Marguerita	
FIVE SHAKESPEARE SONGS	Vocal
WHO SEEKETH BEAUTY	Vocal
SPENCER, Williametta	
SONGS FROM THE TEMPEST	Vocal
THREE SONGS FROM WILLIAM SHAKESPEARE	Vocal
SUTHERLAND, Margaret	
MIDSUMMER NIGHT'S DREAM	Incidental Music
O MISTRESS MINE	Vocal
SWAIN, Freda	
SIX SONNETS	Vocal
SWISHER, Gloria	
TWO FACES OF LOVE	Vocal
SZOENY, Erszebet	
PEINE ET PLAISER, ROMANCE DU SAULE	Vocal
TALMA, Louise	
THE TOLLING BELL	Vocal
TATE, Phyllis	
ALL THE WORLD'S A STAGE	Vocal
PHOENIX AND THE TURTLE	Vocal
THOMSEN, Geraldine	
SONNETS	Vocal
MACBETH (ballad)	Vocal
TURNER, Myra Brooks	
MIDSUMMER NIGHT'S DREAM	Incidental Music
ULEHLA, Ludmila	
SONNETS FROM SHAKESPEARE	Vocal
URNER, Catherine	
COME AWAY DEATH	Vocal
USHER, Julia	
TEMPEST	Incidental Music
WASSALS, Grace	
SHAKESPEARIAN SONG CYCLE	Vocal
WEGENER-FRENSEL, Emmy Heil	
SUITE	Orchestra
WEIGL, Vally	
FEAR NO MORE	Vocal
WHITE, Maude Valerie	
OPHELIA'S SONG	Vocal
WICKHAM, Florence Pauline	
ROSALYND (based on As You Like It)	Operetta
WILLIAMS, Grace Mary	
OWEN GLENDOWER (Symphonic Impressions after Henry IV pt 1)	Orchestra
ZALLMAN, Arlene	
TWO SONNETS	Vocal

APPENDIX 8

Women Composers by Instrument and Music Form

ACCORDION
19th Century A.D.
FORTE, Elsa
20th Century A.D.
ALSTED, Birgitte
ARETZ, Isabel
BLOMFIELD-HOLT, Patricia
BRANDMAN, Margaret Susan
BRUGGMANN, Heidi
COQUET, Odile Marie-Lucie
DAVIDSON, Tina
DESPORTES, Yvonne Berthe Melitta
ETHRIDGE, Jean
EUTENEUER-ROHRER, Ursula
Henrietta
KATS-CHERNIN, Elena
LOUIE, Alexina Diane
LUND, Gudrun
McKENZIE, Sandra
NIGHTINGALE, Barbara Diane
OLIVEROS, Pauline
SCHMIDT, Diane Louise

BAGPIPES
20th Century A.D.
FOWLER, Jennifer Joan

BALLET/DANCE MUSIC
17th Century A.D.
SOPHIE ELISABETH von
Braunschweig, Duchess
18th Century A.D.
BARTALOTTI, Signora
DUHAMEL, Mlle.
DUVAL, Louise
LA GUERRE, Elisabeth-Claude
Jacquet de
19th Century A.D.
AUGUSTA MARIA LOUISE, Queen of
Prussia
BALTHASAR, Florence
BOCK, Bertha
CZICZKA, Angela
GALLOIS, Marie
GRANDVAL, Marie Felicie Clemence
de Reiset, Vicomtesse de
PFEILSCHIFTER, Julie von
SALOMONI, Mlle.
WHITE, Maude Valerie
20th Century A.D.
AARON, Yvonne
ABEJO, Sister M. Rosalina
ABORN, Lora
ALCALAY, Luna

ALEXANDER, Leni
ALTER, Martha
ARBUCKLE, Dorothy M.
ARETZ, Isabel
ARRIEU, Claude
ARVEY, Verna
AUSTER, Lydia Martinovna
BACEWICZ, Grażyna
BACH, Maria
BALSHONE, Cathy S.
BARATTA, Maria M. de
BARRAINE, Elsa
BARTHEL, Ursula
BAUER, Marion Eugenie
BECLARD D'HARCOURT,
Marguerite
BEEKHUIS, Hanna
BERTRAND, Ginette
BIASINI, Marcelle
BIBBY, Gillian Margaret
BOND, Victoria Ellen
BONDS, Margaret
BRIGHT, Dora Estella
BRINGUER, Estela
BRITAIN, Radie
BUECHNER, Margaret
CALAME, Genevieve
CALCAGNO, Elsa
CAMPMANY, Montserrat
CARVALHO, Dinora de
CECCONI-BOTELLA, Monic
CHAMINADE, Cécile Louise
Stephanie
CHILDS, Mary Ellen
CHRETIEN-GENARO, Hedwige
CLAMAN, Dolores Olga
CLAYTON, Laura
COCQ, Rosina Susanna de
COGAN, Morva
COHEN, Marcia
COLERIDGE-TAYLOR, Avril
Gwendolen
CONRAD, Laurie M.
CONTINI ANSELMI, Lucia
COOLIDGE, Peggy Stuart
DANIELS, Mabel Wheeler
DANIELSON, Janet Rosalie
DANOWSKI, Helen
DAVIS, Jean Reynolds
DE BIASE BIDART, Lycia
DE CEVEE, Alice
DE FAZIO, Lynette Stevens
DEAN, Laura
DESPORTES, Yvonne Berthe Melitta

DIANDA, Hilda
DINESCU, Violeta
DONATOVA, Narcisa
DRDOVA, Marie
DREYFUS, Francis Kay
DU PAGE, Florence Elizabeth
DUNLOP, Isobel
DYCHKO, Lesya Vasilevna
ECKHARDT-GRAMATTE, Sophie-
Carmen
EISENSTEIN DE VEGA, Silvia
ESCOBAR, Maria Luisa
ESCOT, Pozzi
FALCINELLI, Rolande
FEIGIN, Sarah
FINE, Vivian
FINLEY, Lorraine Noel
FLACH, Elsa
FLEMMING, Elsa
FONTYN, Jacqueline
FORMAN, Ellen
FORMAN, Joanne
FOSTER, Cecily
FRANCE, Jeanne Lelen
FREITAG, Dorothea Hackett
FRIEDBERG, Patricia Ann
FRITTER, Genevieve Davisson
GALAJIKIAN, Florence Grandland
GARCIA MUNOZ, Carmen
GARWOOD, Margaret
GERSTMAN, Blanche Wilhelminia
GILBERT, Pia
GIPPS, Ruth
GIURANNA, Elena Barbara
GLANVILLE-HICKS, Peggy
GLATZ, Helen Sinclair
GOLOVINA, Olga Akimovna
GOTKOVSKY, Ida-Rose Esther
GOULD, Elizabeth Davies
GREENE, Genevieve
GRIEBEL WANDALL, Tekla
GRIEBLING, Karen Jean
GRZADZIELOWNA, Eleonora
GUBAIDULINA, Sofia Asgatovna
GULESIAN, Grace Warner
GYANDZHETSIAN, Destrik
Bogdanovna
HALACSY, Irma von
HALL, Pauline
HARKNESS, Rebekah West
HARVEY, Eva Noel
HAYS, Doris Ernestine
HEIBERG, Ella
HERSCHER-CLEMENT, Jeanne

HIER, Ethel Glen
HOVDA, Eleanor
HOWE, Mary Alberta Bruce
HOWELL, Dorothy
HOY, Bonnee L.
HUBLER, Evelyne
HUMPHREY, Doris
HUNKINS, Eusebia Simpson
HURLEY, Susan
HYDE, Miriam Beatrice
ISAKOVA, Aida Petrovna
JEREA, Hilda
JIRKOVA, Olga
KALOGRIDOU, Maria
KAMINSKY, Laura
KASILAG, Lucrecia R.
KATS-CHERNIN, Elena
KATZMAN, Klara Abramovna
KELLER, Ginette
KERSENBAUM, Sylvia Haydee
KESSLER, Minuetta Schumiatcher
KIRKWOOD, Antoinette
KISTETENYI, Melinda
KLECHNIOWSKA, Anna Maria
KLEES, Gabriele
KLINKOVA, Zhivka
KOLODUB, Zhanna Efimovna
KORHONEN, S. Gloria
KOZAKIEVICH, Anna Abramovna
KUCEROVA-HERSTOVA, Marie
KVERNADZE, Bidzina
LANG-BECK, Ivana
LAPEIRETTA, Ninon de Brouwer
LATZ, Inge
LAUBER, Anne Marianne
LAUER, Elizabeth
LAUFER, Beatrice
LEAHY, Mary Weldon
LEBARON, Anne
LEECH, Renée
LEFANU, Nicola Frances
LELEU, Jeanne
LENNEP, Henrietta van
LEON, Tania Justina
LESICHKOVA, Lili
LOCKSHIN, Florence Levin
LOHOEFER, Evelyn
LOUDOVA, Ivana
LUCAS, Mary Anderson
LUTYENS, Elisabeth
LYONN LIEBERMAN, Julie
MACKIE, Shirley M.
McKELLAN, Irene Mary
McMILLAN, Ann Endicott
MANA-ZUCCA
MAREZ-OYENS, Tera de
MARQUES, Laura Wake
MAURICE, Paule
MAURICE-JACQUET, H.
MAZOUROVA, Jarmila
MEACHEM, Margaret McKeen
    Ramsey
MEISTER, Marianne
METALLIDI, Zhanneta Lazarevna
MIGRANYAN, Emma
MOE, Benna
MORE, Margaret Elizabeth
MORIN-LABRECQUE, Albertine
MORTIFEE, Ann
MUSGRAVE, Thea
NIKOLSKAYA, Lyubov Borisovna
NIKOLSKAYA, Olga Vasilevna
NOVA SONDAG, Jacqueline
NUNLIST, Juli
OFFICER, Bronwyn Lee
OLLER BENLLOCH, Maria Teresa
OSIANDER, Irene
PADE, Else Marie
PEARL-MANN, Dora Deborah
PENGILLY, Sylvia
PENTLAND, Barbara Lally

PERKIN, Helen
PETRA-BASACOPOL, Carmen
PETROVA-KRUPKOVA, Elena
PIECHOWSKA, Alina
PITOT, Genevieve
POLIGNAC, Armande de, Countess
    of Chabannes
POPATENKO, Tamara Alexandrovna
PORTER, Debra
POULET, Defontaine Madeleine
POWERS, Ada Weigel
PREOBRAJENSKA, Vera Nicolaevna
PRIETO, Maria Teresa
PTASZYNSKA, Marta
QUANTIN-SAULNIER, Denise
RAINIER, Priaulx
RAMM, Valentina Iosifovna
RECLI, Giulia
REID, Wendy
RESPIGHI, Elsa
RHEINGOLD, Lauma Yanovna
RICHTER, Marga
ROBERTS, Jane A.
ROFE, Esther
ROGERS, Patsy
ROGET, Henriette
ROHDE, Q'Adrianne
ROMERO BARBOSA, Elena
ROZHAVSKAYA, Yudif Grigorevna
RUBIN, Anna Ita
RUDALL, Eleonor C.
RUEFF, Jeanine
RZAYEVA, Agabadzhi Ishmael kykz
SAIDAMINOVA, Dilorom
SAINT JOHN, Kathleen Louise
SALVADOR, Matilde
SANGUESA, Iris
SANTOS-OCAMPO DE FRANCESCO,
    Amada Amy
SANZ, Rocio
SCHERCHEN, Tona
SCHICK, Philippine
SCHIEVE, Catherine
SCHNEIDER, June
SCHONTHAL, Ruth E.
SCOTT-HUNTER, Hortense
SCRIABINE, Marina
SHAFFER, Jeanne Ellison
SHIDA, Shoko
SIKORA, Elzbieta
SKALSKA-SZEMIOTH, Hanna Wanda
SKOUEN, Synne
SOENSTEVOLD, Maj
SPIEGEL, Laurie
SPIZIZEN, Louise Myers
STANLEY, Helen Camille
STERNICKA-NIEKRASZOWA, Ilza
STREICHER, Lyubov Lvovna
STRICKLAND, Lily Teresa
SUCHY, Gregoria Karides
SUNBLAD-HALME, Heidi Gabriella
    Wilhelmina
SUTHERLAND, Margaret
SWADOS, Elizabeth
SWAIN, Freda Mary
SWIFT, Kay
SZAJNA-LEWANDOWSKA, Jadwiga
    Helena
SZOENYI, Erzsebet
TAILLEFERRE, Germaine
TAL, Ya'ara
TARLOW, Karen Anne
TEMPLE, Hope
TERZIAN, Alicia
THEMMEN, Ivana Marburger
THOME, Diane
THOMPSON, Caroline Lorraine
THOMSEN, Geraldine
TKACH, Zlata Moiseyevna
TOLKOWSKY, Denise
TWOMBLY, Mary Lynn

URRETA, Alicia
VAKHVAKHISHVILI, Tamara
    Nikolayevna
VAN EPEN-DE GROOT, Else Antonia
VAZQUEZ, Alida
VERHAALEN, Sister Marion
VIDAR, Jorunn
VIENNE, Marie-Louise de
VIEU, Jane
VITO-DELVAUX, Berthe di
WARDE, Ann Maury
WARING, Kate
WARWICK, Mary Carol
WATSON, Gwendolyn
WERNER, Tara Louise
WILLMAN, Regina Hansen
WITNI, Monica
WITZIG, Louise
WOOD, Mabel
WYLIE, Ruth Shaw
ZAIDEL-RUDOLPH, Jeanne
ZARANEK, Stefania Anatolyevna
ZHUBANOVA, Gaziza Akhmetovna
ZIBEROVA, Zinaida Petrovna
ZIMMERMANN, Margrit

BAND - JAZZ
20th Century A.D.
AKIYOSHI, Toshiko
BLEY, Carla
FEININGER, Leonore Helene
FULLER-HALL, Sarah Margaret
LYONN LIEBERMAN, Julie
MAIRE, Jacqueline
ROEMER, Hanne
WILLIAMS, Mary Lou

BAND - MILITARY OR BRASS
18th Century A.D.
ANNA AMALIA, Princess of Prussia
19th Century A.D.
ABRECHT, Princess of Prussia
AUGUSTA MARIA LOUISE, Queen of
    Prussia
BROWN, Harriet Estelle
CASTELLI, Adele
CHARLOTTE, Friederike Wilhelmine
Louise, Princess
FRANCOIS, Emmy von
GYLLENHAAL, Matilda Valeriana
    Beatrix, Duchess of Orozco
HORTENSE, Queen of Holland
KOCHANOWSKA, Franciszka
20th Century A.D.
ALVES DE SOUSA, Berta Candida
ANDREE, Elfrida
ARIMA, Reiko
ARQUIT, Nora Harris
BARATI, Ruth
BERK, Adele
BLOCKSIDGE, Kathleen Mary
BRESCHI, Laura
BRUGGMANN, Heidi
BUCHANAN, Dorothy Quita
CAPSIR-TANZI, Mercedes
CHARLES, S. Robin
CHARLOTTE, Princess of Saxe-
    Meiningen
COUTURE, Priscilla
COWLES, Darleen
DIEMER, Emma Lou
DURAND, Nella Wells
FINK, Emma C.
FRASIER, Jane
FREED, Dorothy Whitson
FULLER-HALL, Sarah Margaret
GANNON, Ruth Ellen
GARDNER, Kay
GLATZ, Helen Sinclair
GONZAGA, Chiquinha
HSU, Wen-Ying

JARRATT, Lita
JIRKOVA, Olga
KAPLAN, Lois Jay
KING, Pearl
KLINKOVA, Zhivka
KUZMENKO, Larysa
LANDOWSKA, Wanda
LATHROP, Gayle Posselt
LEAHY, Mary Weldon
LEONE, Mae G.
MACAULAY, Janice Michel
MACKIE, Shirley M.
McLEAN, Priscilla Anne Taylor
McTEE, Cindy Karen
MALHE, Maria Aparecida
MANA-ZUCCA
MARTINS, Maria de Lourdes
MATHIS, Judy M.
MAXWELL, Jacqueline Perkinson
MIRANDA, Sharon Moe
MORIN-LABRECQUE, Albertine
MUNGER, Shirley
MUSGRAVE, Thea
NYQUIST, Morine A.
OWEN, Blythe
PERKIN, Helen
PERRY, Zenobia Powell
PREOBRAJENSKA, Vera Nicolaevna
PRIESING, Dorothy Jean
RHOADS, Mary R.
RICHARDSON, Sharon
RICHTER, Marga
ROCHEROLLE, Eugenie Katherine
ROEMER, Hanne
ROHDE, Q'Adrianne
SCHAFMEISTER, Helen
SHLONSKY, Verdina
SIMONS, Netty
SKARECKY, Jana Milena
SMELTZER, Susan Mary
SMITH, Julia Frances
SMYTH, Ethel Mary, Dame
SPENCER, Williametta
SWISHER, Gloria Agnes Wilson
SZYMANSKA, Iwonka Bogumila
TATE, Phyllis
TEICHMUELLER, Anna
TELFER, Nancy Ellen
TERZIAN, Alicia
TRIMBLE, Joan
TUCKER, Irene
VASHAW, Cécile
VIENNE, Marie-Louise de
WILSON, Marion
Century unknown
ANDERSON, Elizabeth D.

BASSOON
18th Century A.D.
ANNA AMALIA, Duchess of Saxe-
Weimar
ANNA AMALIA, Princess of Prussia
19th Century A.D.
CANDEILLE, Amelie Julie
DESHAYES, Marie
20th Century A.D.
AGUDELO MURGUIA, Graciela
AHRENS, Peg
ALCALAY, Luna
ALEJANDRO-DE LEON, Esther
ALLEN, Judith Shatin
ALTER, Martha
ANDERSON, Olive Jennie Paxton
ANDERSON-WUENSCH, Jean Mary
ARCHER, Violet Balestreri
ARMER, Elinor Florence
ARRIEU, Claude
BACEWICZ, Grażyna
BANCER, Teresa Barbara
BARBILLON, Jeanne
BARON SUPERVIELLE, Susana

BARRELL, Joyce Howard
BARRETT-THOMAS, N.
BAULD, Alison
BECLARD D'HARCOURT,
Marguerite
BERK, Adele
BEYER, Johanna Magdalena
BLOOD, Esta Damesek
BOLZ, Harriet
BOND, Victoria Ellen
BOONE, Clara Lyle
BOUCHARD, Linda L.
BOYD, Anne Elizabeth
BRANDMAN, Margaret Susan
BRINK-POTHUIS, Annie van den
BRITAIN, Radie
BROGUE, Roslyn Clara
BRUSH, Ruth Damaris
BUCHANAN, Dorothy Quita
BUCZEK, Barbara Kazimiera
BUTLER, Patricia Magahay
CABRERA, Silvia Maria Pires
CAMEU, Helza
CECCONI-BATES, Augusta
CHAPIRO, Fania
COATES, Gloria Kannenberg
COHEN, Marcia
COLACO OSORIO-SWAAB, Reine
COQUET, Odile Marie-Lucie
CORY, Eleanor
COULTHARD, Jean
CRAWFORD SEEGER, Ruth
CRAWFORD, Dawn Constance
CRAWFORD, Dorothy Lamb
DANEAU, Suzanne
DANFORTH, Frances A.
DANIELS, Mabel Wheeler
DE FREITAS, Elvira Manuela
Fernandez
DEMBO, Royce
DESPORTES, Yvonne Berthe Melitta
DIANDA, Hilda
DINESCU, Violeta
DITMARS, Elizabeth
DONCEANU, Felicia
DRING, Madeleine
DVORKIN, Judith
ECKHARDT-GRAMATTE, Sophie-
Carmen
ELIAS, Graciela Morales de
FALCINELLI, Rolande
FINE, Vivian
FISHMAN, Marian
FLEITES, Virginia
FONTYN, Jacqueline
FOWLER, Jennifer Joan
FRASIER, Jane
FREED, Dorothy Whitson
GARCIA ROBSON, Magdalena
GARSCIA-GRESSEL, Janina
GARTENLAUB, Odette
GIDEON, Miriam
GIFFORD, Helen Margaret
GIPPS, Ruth
GITECK, Janice
GLANVILLE-HICKS, Peggy
GOOLKASIAN-RAHBEE, Dianne
Zabelle
GOULD, Elizabeth Davies
GRAY, Victoria Winifred
GRIEBLING, Karen Jean
GRIEBLING, Margaret Ann
GRZADZIELOWNA, Eleonora
GUBAIDULINA, Sofia Asgatovna
GURAIEB KURI, Rosa
GYANDZHETSIAN, Destrik
Bogdanovna
GYRING, Elizabeth
HAHN, Sandra Lea
HALL, Pauline
HARRISON, Pamela

HAWLEY, Carolyn Jean
HAYS, Doris Ernestine
HOOVER, Katherine
INWOOD, Mary Ruth Brink Berger
IVEY, Jean Eichelberger
JACOB, Elizabeth Marie
JOHNSTON, Alison Aileen Annie
JONES, Sister Ida
KADIMA, Hagar Yonith
KAHMANN, Chesley
KANACH, Sharon E.
KEEFER, Euphrosyne
KELLER, Ginette
KESHNER, Joyce Grove
KISTETENYI, Melinda
KITAZUME, Yayoi
KNOBLOCHOVA, Antonie
LACHOWSKA, Stefania
LARSEN, Elizabeth Brown
LAUBER, Anne Marianne
LAYMAN, Pamela
LEBARON, Anne
LEE, Hwaeja Yoo
LEE, Young Ja
LOPEZ ROVIROSA, Maria Isabel
LUTYENS, Elisabeth
MACKIE, Shirley M.
MACONCHY, Elizabeth
McKENZIE, Sandra
McLEOD, Jennifer Helen
MEARS, Caroline
MEKEEL, Joyce
MEL-BONIS
MERRIMAN, Margarita Leonor
MUSGRAVE, Thea
NOBLE, Ann
OFFICER, Bronwyn Lee
O'LEARY, Jane Strong
OLIVEROS, Pauline
OSAWA, Kazuko
PELEGRI, Maria Teresa
PENTLAND, Barbara Lally
PERRY, Julia Amanda
PETRA-BASACOPOL, Carmen
PETROVA, Mara
PHILIPPART, Renée
PHILLIPS, Bryony
PIECHOWSKA, Alina
PIRES DOS REIS, Hilda
PIZER, Elizabeth Faw Hayden
POLIN, Claire
PREOBRAJENSKA, Vera Nicolaevna
PROCACCINI, Teresa
PTASZYNSKA, Marta
RAIGORODSKY, Leda Natalia
Heimsath
RAINIER, Priaulx
RENIE, Henriette
REYNOLDS, Erma Grey Hogue
RHEINGOLD, Lauma Yanovna
RODRIGUEZ BELLA, Catalina
ROGER, Denise
RUEFF, Jeanine
RUSCHE, Marjorie Maxine
SAINT JOHN, Kathleen Louise
SAMTER, Alice
SAMUEL, Rhian
SCHORR-WEILER, Eva
SHEPARD, Jean Ellen
SHORE, Clare
SIMONS, Netty
SLIANOVA-MIZANDARI, Dagmara
Levanovna
SNIZKOVA-SKRHOVA, Jitka
STEINER, Gitta Hana
STREATFIELD, Valma June
STRUTT, Dorothy
SUCHY, Gregoria Karides
SZAJNA-LEWANDOWSKA, Jadwiga
Helena
SZOENYI, Erzsebet

TAKAMI, Toyoko
TARLOW, Karen Anne
TATE, Phyllis
THORKELSDOTTIR, Mist Barbara
TOWER, Joan
TUCKER, Tui St. George
VAN DER MARK, Maria
VAN OHLEN, Deborah
VELLERE, Lucie Weiler
VIERK, Lois
VON ZIERITZ, Grete
VORLOVA, Slavka
WALLACH, Joelle
WARNE, Katharine Mulky
WEAVER, Carol Ann
WEGENER-FRENSEL, Emmy Heil
WELANDER, Svea Goeta
WENDELBURG, Norma Ruth
WHITTLE, Chris Mary-Francine
WILDSCHUT, Clara
WOLLNER, Gertrude Price
ZAIDEL-RUDOLPH, Jeanne
ZIELINSKA, Lidia
ZIFFRIN, Marilyn Jane

BASSOON AND ORCHESTRA OR STRINGS
20th Century A.D.
BALLOU, Esther Williamson
ECKHARDT-GRAMATTE, Sophie-
   Carmen
GIPPS, Ruth
GUBAIDULINA, Sofia Asgatovna
LOMON, Ruth
PERISSAS, Madeleine
RHEINGOLD, Lauma Yanovna
VON ZIERITZ, Grete
WILL, Madeleine

BASSOON AND PIANO
20th Century A.D.
ARCHER, Violet Balestreri
BEEKHUIS, Hanna
COULTHARD, Jean
DEMBO, Royce
DUSHKIN, Dorothy Smith
FALCINELLI, Rolande
GARTENLAUB, Odette
GIDEON, Miriam
GIPPS, Ruth
GOULD, Elizabeth Davies
GYANDZHETSIAN, Destrik
   Bogdanovna
HARRISON, Pamela
ISAKOVA, Aida Petrovna
KALTENECKER, Gertraud
KAZHAEVA, Tatiana Ibragimovna
LOMON, Ruth
LORENZ, Ellen Jane
MARI, Pierrette
MARKIEWICZOWNA, Wladyslawa
PIRES DOS REIS, Hilda
PROCACCINI, Teresa
REYNOLDS, Erma Grey Hogue
ROGER, Denise
SEHESTED, Hilda
SIMIC, Darinka
VITO-DELVAUX, Berthe di
VORLOVA, Slavka

BELLS
20th Century A.D.
BEAHM, Jacquelyn Yvette
DANFORTH, Frances A.
DANIELA, Carmen
DESPORTES, Yvonne Berthe Melitta
FIRSOVA, Elena
HAYS, Doris Ernestine
JIRACKOVA, Marta
KIRCH, Irene E.
LORENZ, Ellen Jane
MATUSZCZAK, Bernadetta

MENEELY-KYDER, Sarah Suderley
McLAUGHLIN, Marian
ROGERS, Sharon Elery
SHORE, Clare
STEELE, Lynn
SWAIN, Freda Mary
YOUNG, Gayle

BUGLE
20th Century A.D.
WIGGINS, Mary

CARILLON
20th Century A.D.
BORDEWIJK-ROEPMAN, Johanna
BROCKMAN, Jane E.
BROOK, Gwendolyn Giffen
COOKE, Marjorie Tibbets
DIEMER, Emma Lou
HALSTED, Margo
HINLOPEN, Francina
HOLLAND, Dulcie Sybil
JOHNSTON-REID, Sarah Ruth
LEAHY, Mary Weldon
MILLER, Jean
PIERCE, Alexandra
REED, Marlyce Rae Polk
VAN APPLEDORN, Mary Jeanne
WARNER, Sally Slade
WEEL, Heleen van der
WHITTLE, Chris Mary-Francine

CELESTE
20th Century A.D.
ANDERSON, Julia McKinley
BARKIN, Elaine
BRITAIN, Radie
FALCINELLI, Rolande
FIRSOVA, Elena
GIFFORD, Helen Margaret
GLANVILLE-HICKS, Peggy
HARRIS, Ruth Berman
HSU, Wen-Ying
JAMES, Dorothy E.
MACAULAY, Janice Michel
MOSZUMANSKA-NAZAR, Krystyna
NAITO, Akemi
OLIVEIRA, Jocy de
PELEGRI, Maria Teresa
PIZER, Elizabeth Faw Hayden
ROHDE, Q'Adrianne
TAILLEFERRE, Germaine
TAL, Ya'ara
VON GUNDEN, Heidi

CELLO - see VIOLONCELLO

CIMBALOM
19th Century A.D.
KELEMEN, Mrs. Lajos
20th Century A.D.
ARIMA, Reiko
JIRACKOVA, Marta
MASSUMOTO, Kikuko
MATUSZCZAK, Bernadetta
RUSCHE, Marjorie Maxine
VORLOVA, Slavka

CLARINET
18th Century A.D.
ANNA AMALIA, Duchess of Saxe-
   Weimar
19th Century A.D.
CANDEILLE, Amelie Julie
DESHAYES, Marie
KRAEHMER, Caroline
LEONARDO, Luisa
SMITH, Alice Mary
20th Century A.D.
ABRAMOVA, Sonia Pinkhasovna
AGUDELO MURGUIA, Graciela
AINSCOUGH, Juliana Mary

ALCALAY, Luna
ALEXANDRA, Liana
ALLEN, Judith Shatin
ALLIK, Kristi
ALTER, Martha
ANDERSON, Beth
ANDERSON, Olive Jennie Paxton
ANDERSON, Ruth
ANDERSON-WUENSCH, Jean Mary
ANTHONY, Gina
ARCHER, Violet Balestreri
ARMER, Elinor Florence
ARRIEU, Claude
BACEWICZ, Grazyna
BADIAN, Maya
BAILEY, Judith Margaret
BANCER, Teresa Barbara
BANNISTER, Mary Jeanne Hoggard
BARADAPRANA, Pravrajika
BARBILLON, Jeanne
BARKLUND, Irma L.
BARON SUPERVIELLE, Susana
BARRELL, Joyce Howard
BARRETT-THOMAS, N.
BAUER, Marion Eugenie
BEAT, Janet Eveline
BECKON, Lettie Marie
BECLARD D'HARCOURT,
   Marguerite
BENAVENTE, Regina
BERK, Adele
BEYER, Johanna Magdalena
BIANCHERA, Silvia
BIENVENU, Lily
BINGHAM, Judith
BIRNSTEIN, Renate Maria
BLIESENER, Ada Elizabeth
   Michelman
BOFILL, Anna
BOLZ, Harriet
BOND, Victoria Ellen
BOONE, Clara Lyle
BOYD, Anne Elizabeth
BRANDMAN, Margaret Susan
BRINK-POTHUIS, Annie van den
BRITAIN, Radie
BROCKMAN, Jane E.
BROGUE, Roslyn Clara
BRUSH, Ruth Damaris
BRUZDOWICZ, Joanna
BUCZEK, Barbara Kazimiera
BURKE, Loretto
BURSTON, Maggie
CABRERA, Silvia Maria Pires
CALLAWAY, Ann
CAMPAGNE, Conny
CARLOS, Wendy
CARMEN MARINA
CARTER, Rosetta
CARVALHO, Dinora de
CATUNDA, Eunice do Monte Lima
CECCONI-BATES, Augusta
CHANDLER, Mary
CHAPIRO, Fania
CHARBONNIER, Janine Andree
CHAVES, Mary Elizabeth
CHRETIEN-GENARO, Hedwige
CIOBANU, Maia
CLARKE, Rebecca
CLARKE, Rosemary
COHEN, Marcia
COME, Tilde
CONRAD, Laurie M.
COQUET, Odile Marie-Lucie
CORY, Eleanor
COULOMBE SAINT-MARCOUX,
   Micheline
COULTHARD, Jean
COWLES, Darleen
CRAWFORD SEEGER, Ruth
CRAWFORD, Dawn Constance

DANEAU, Suzanne
DANFORTH, Frances A.
DANIELS, Mabel Wheeler
DE BIASE BIDART, Lycia
DE FREITAS, Elvira Manuela
   Fernandez
DEMBO, Royce
DESPORTES, Yvonne Berthe Melitta
DEYTON, Camilla Hill
DIAMOND, Arline
DIEMER, Emma Lou
DLUGOSZEWSKI, Lucia
DOBSON, Elaine
DONCEANU, Felicia
DRENNAN, Dorothy Carter
DUBANOWICZ, Wanda
DUDLEY, Marjorie Eastwood
DUSHKIN, Dorothy Smith
EAGLES, Moneta M.
ECKHARDT-GRAMATTE, Sophie-
   Carmen
ELIAS, Graciela Morales de
ELWYN-EDWARDS, Dilys
ERDING, Susanne
EVEN-OR, Mary
FAIRLIE, Margaret C.
FEIGIN, Sarah
FINLEY, Lorraine Noel
FINZI, Graciane
FIRSOVA, Elena
FISHMAN, Marian
FONTYN, Jacqueline
FOWLER, Jennifer Joan
FRASIER, Jane
FREED, Dorothy Whitson
FRUMKER, Linda
FULLER-HALL, Sarah Margaret
GABUS, Monique
GARCIA ROBSON, Magdalena
GENTILE, Ada
GEYRING, E.
GIDEON, Miriam
GIFFORD, Helen Margaret
GILBERT, Pia
GIPPS, Ruth
GITECK, Janice
GLATZ, Helen Sinclair
GLAZIER, Beverly
GOEBELS, Gisela
GOOLKASIAN-RAHBEE, Dianne
   Zabelle
GOTKOVSKY, Ida-Rose Esther
GOULD, Elizabeth Davies
GOULD, Janetta
GRAHAM, Janet Christine
GRAY, Victoria Winifred
GREENE, Margo Lynn
GRIEBLING, Karen Jean
GROSSMAN, Deena
GRZADZIELOWNA, Eleonora
GUMMER, Phyllis Mary
GYRING, Elizabeth
HAHN, Sandra Lea
HALL, Pauline
HALPERN, Stella
HARRIS, Ruth Berman
HARRISON, Pamela
HAYS, Doris Ernestine
HENDERSON, Moya
HOLLAND, Dulcie Sybil
HOOVER, Katherine
HOVDA, Eleanor
HSU, Wen-Ying
HUGHES, Sister Martina
HYSON, Winifred Prince
IRMAN-ALLEMANN, Regina
IVEY, Jean Eichelberger
JACOB, Elizabeth Marie
JAMES, Dorothy E.
JIRACKOVA, Marta
JOCHSBERGER, Tzipora H.

JOLLY, Margaret Anne
JONES, Sister Ida
JUENGER, Patricia
KANACH, Sharon E.
KAPRALOVA, Vitezslava
KATS-CHERNIN, Elena
KAVASCH, Deborah Helene
KELLER, Ginette
KING, Thea
KITAZUME, Yayoi
KLEBE, Willemijntje
KLINKOVA, Zhivka
KOBLENZ, Babette
KOELLING, Eloise
KOLB, Barbara
KOSSE, Roberta
KUZMYCH, Christina
LACHARTRE, Nicole Marie
LACHOWSKA, Stefania
LANG, Rosemary Rita
LARSEN, Elizabeth Brown
LATIOLAIS, Desirée Jayne
LAYMAN, Pamela
LEAHY, Mary Weldon
LEBARON, Anne
LEBENBOM, Elaine F.
LEE, Chan-Hae
LEE, Hwaeja Yoo
LEFANU, Nicola Frances
LEJET, Edith
LEVIN, Rami Yona
LIPSCOMB, Helen
LOTTI, Silvana di
LOUIE, Alexina Diane
LOWENSTEIN, Gunilla Marike
LU, Yen
LUCAS, Mary Anderson
LUND, Gudrun
LUNDQUIST, Christie
LUTYENS, Sally
LVOVA, Julia Fedorovna
MACAULAY, Janice Michel
MACKIE, Shirley M.
MACONCHY, Elizabeth
McINTOSH, Diana
McKAY, Frances Thompson
McKENZIE, Sandra
McLAUGHLIN, Marian
McLEOD, Jennifer Helen
MAGEAU, Mary Jane
MALMLOEF-FORSSLING, Carin
MAMLOK, Ursula
MARBE, Myriam
MARCUS, Bunita
MATUSZCZAK, Bernadetta
MAZOUROVA, Jarmila
MEKEEL, Joyce
MEL-BONIS
MERRIMAN, Margarita Leonor
MESRITZ-VAN VELTHUYSEN, Annie
MILENKOVIC, Jelena
MILLER, Elma
MIRON, Tsipora
MOORE, Mary Carr
MORETTO, Nelly
MORRISON, Julia Maria
NIEWIADOMSKA, Barbara
NIKOLSKAYA, Lyubov Borisovna
NOBLE, Ann
NOHE, Beverly
NORRE, Dorcas
OFFICER, Bronwyn Lee
OH, Sook Ja
O'LEARY, Jane Strong
OLIVEROS, Pauline
ORENSTEIN, Joyce Ellin
OSAWA, Kazuko
OWEN, Blythe
PAGH-PAAN, Younghi
PATERSON, Wilma
PATTERSON, Andra

PELEGRI, Maria Teresa
PENTLAND, Barbara Lally
PERETZ-LEVY, Liora
PERKIN, Helen
PETRA-BASACOPOL, Carmen
PETROVA, Mara
PETROVA-KRUPKOVA, Elena
PHILIBA, Nicole
PHILIPPART, Renée
PHILLIPS, Bryony
PHILLIPS, Linda
PIECHOWSKA, Alina
PIERCE, Alexandra
PIERCE, Sarah Anderson
PIRES DOS REIS, Hilda
PIZER, Elizabeth Faw Hayden
PLONSEY, Jennifer
POLIN, Claire
POPOVICI, Elise
POSTON, Elizabeth
PRAVOSSUDOVITCH, Natalja
   Michajlovna
PREOBRAJENSKA, Vera Nicolaevna
PRICE, Beryl
PRICE, Deon Nielsen
PRICE, Florence Beatrice
PROCACCINI, Teresa
PSTROKONSKA-NAVRATIL,
   Grazyna Hanna
PTASZYNSKA, Marta
RAINIER, Priaulx
RAN, Shulamit
RAPOPORT, Eda
RAVINALE, Irma
REID, Sarah Johnston
REYNOLDS, Erma Grey Hogue
RHEINGOLD, Lauma Yanovna
RICHTER, Marga
RILEY, Ann Marion
ROCHAT, Andrée
RODRIGUE, Nicole
RODRIGUEZ BELLA, Catalina
ROE, Eileen Betty
ROGER, Denise
ROGERS, Patsy
ROGERS, Susan Whipple
ROMM, Rosalina Davidovna
ROWAN, Barbara
ROYSE, Mildred Barnes
RUEFF, Jeanine
RUFF-STOEHR, Herta Maria Klara
RUSCHE, Marjorie Maxine
SAINT JOHN, Kathleen Louise
SAMSON, Valerie Brooks
SAMTER, Alice
SCHERCHEN, Tona
SCHIEVE, Catherine
SCHONTHAL, Ruth E.
SCHWARZ, Friederike
SEMEGEN, Daria
SETO, Robin
SHAGIAKHMETOVA, Svetlana
   Georgievna
SHEPARD, Jean Ellen
SHORE, Clare
SILSBEE, Ann L.
SILVERMAN, Faye-Ellen
SISTEK-DJORDJEVIC, Mirjana
SLIANOVA-MIZANDARI, Dagmara
   Levanovna
SMITH, Sharon
SMYTH, Ethel Mary, Dame
SNOW, Mary McCarty
SOUTHAM, Ann
SPENCER PALMER, Florence
   Margaret
SPENCER, Williametta
STEINER, Gitta Hana
STREATFIELD, Valma June
SUCHY, Gregoria Karides
SUH, Kyung-Sun

SUTHERLAND, Margaret
SWAIN, Freda Mary
SWISHER, Gloria Agnes Wilson
SZAJNA-LEWANDOWSKA, Jadwiga
  Helena
SZOENYI, Erzsebet
SZYMANSKA, Iwonka Bogumila
TACK, Annie
TAILLEFERRE, Germaine
TAKAMI, Toyoko
TALMA, Louise
TARIHI, Kamu Yarari Karar
TARLOW, Karen Anne
TATE, Phyllis
THEMMEN, Ivana Marburger
THOME, Diane
THORKELSDOTTIR, Mist Barbara
THREADGILL-MARTIN, Ravonna
TKACH, Zlata Moiseyevna
TOWER, Joan
TRIMBLE, Joan
TUCKER, Tui St. George
USHER, Julia
USTVOLSKAYA, Galina Ivanovna
UYTTENHOVE, Yolande
VAN DE VATE, Nancy Hayes
VAN DER MARK, Maria
VAN DIJCK, Beatrice Madeleine
VAN HAUTE, Anna-Maria
VAN OHLEN, Deborah
VELLERE, Lucie Weiler
VERRALL, Pamela Motley
VIERK, Lois
VIGNERON-RAMAKERS, Christiane-
  Josee
VON GUNDEN, Heidi
VON ZIERITZ, Grete
VORLOVA, Slavka
WALKER, Gwyneth van Anden
WALLACH, Joelle
WANG, An-Ming
WEAVER, Carol Ann
WEGENER-FRENSEL, Emmy Heil
WEIGL, Vally
WELANDER, Svea Goeta
WHITEHEAD, Gillian
WHITLOCK, E. Florence
WHITTLE, Chris Mary-Francine
WIENER, Eva Hannah
WIENIAWSKA, Irene Regine
WILDSCHUT, Clara
WINROW, Barbara
WOLLNER, Gertrude Price
WYLIE, Ruth Shaw
YAROSHEVSKAYA, Ludmila
  Anatolievna
YOUNG, Gayle
ZALLMAN, Arlene
ZIFFRIN, Marilyn Jane

CLARINET (BASS)
19th Century A.D.
CASADESUS, Regina
20th Century A.D.
ALLEN, Judith Shatin
CATUNDA, Eunice do Monte
  Lima
CHARBONNIER, Janine Andrée
CHAVES, Mary Elizabeth
CORY, Eleanor
EVEN-OR, Mary
FREED, Dorothy Whitson
GARDNER, Kay
GIPPS, Ruth
HALPERN, Stella
LANG, Rosemary Rita
LE SIEGE, Annette
LEAHY, Mary Weldon
LVOVA, Julia Fedorovna
MAGEAU, Mary Jane
STRUTT, Dorothy

THEMMEN, Ivana Marburger
WALLACH, Joelle

CLARINET AND ORCHESTRA OR STRINGS
19th Century A.D.
MARSHALL, Florence A.
SMITH, Alice Mary
20th Century A.D.
ABRAMOVA, Sonia Pinkhasovna
ALEXANDRA, Liana
ARCHER, Violet Balestreri
BAILEY, Judith Margaret
BARBERIS, Mansi
CECCONI-BOTELLA, Monic
CONRAD, Laurie M.
DESPORTES, Yvonne Berthe Melitta
FRAJT, Ludmila
GARTENLAUB, Odette
GIPPS, Ruth
GOTKOVSKY, Ida-Rose Esther
GOULD, Elizabeth Davies
LUND, Gudrun
MASON, Marilyn May
MUSGRAVE, Thea
NIKOLSKAYA, Lyubov Borisovna
OSETROVA-YAKOVLIEVA, Nina
  Alexandrovna
PHILIBA, Nicole
RAINIER, Priaulx
RAVINALE, Irma
ROGER, Denise
ROMM, Rosalina Davidovna
RUEFF, Jeanine
SAINT JOHN, Kathleen Louise
SPAIN-DUNK, Susan
SWISHER, Gloria Agnes Wilson
VON ZIERITZ, Grete
VORLOVA, Slavka
WEGENER-FRENSEL, Emmy Heil
WYLIE, Ruth Shaw

CLARINET AND PIANO
19th Century A.D.
ADAJEWSKY, Ella
AMES, Mary Mildred
KRAEHMER, Caroline
MARIE ELIZABETH, Princess of
  Saxe-Meiningen
MUELLER-BENDER, Mme.
20th Century A.D.
AINSCOUGH, Juliana Mary
ALEXANDRA, Liana
ARCHER, Violet Balestreri
ARRIEU, Claude
BACEWICZ, Grażyna
BAILEY, Judith Margaret
BARRATT, Carol Ann
BAUER, Marion Eugenie
BEAT, Janet Eveline
BERK, Adele
BERTRAND, Ginette
BEYER, Johanna Magdalena
BIANCHERA, Silvia
BIENVENU, Lily
BINGHAM, Judith
BOLZ, Harriet
BRANDMAN, Margaret Susan
BROCKMAN, Jane E.
BROGUE, Roslyn Clara
BRUZDOWICZ, Joanna
BURSTON, Maggie
CAMPAGNE, Conny
CHRETIEN-GENARO, Hedwige
CIOBANU, Maia
COLACO OSORIO-SWAAB, Reine
COME, Tilde
COULTHARD, Jean
DEMBO, Royce
DESPORTES, Yvonne Berthe Melitta
DUDLEY, Marjorie Eastwood
EAGLES, Moneta M.

ECKHARDT-GRAMATTE, Sophie-
  Carmen
FEIGIN, Sarah
FINZI, Graciane
FONTYN, Jacqueline
GABUS, Monique
GARTENLAUB, Odette
GARWOOD, Margaret
GEYMULLER, Marguerite Camille-
  Louise de
GIDEON, Miriam
GIPPS, Ruth
GOTKOVSKY, Ida-Rose Esther
GRAHAM, Janet Christine
GRZADZIELOWNA, Eleonora
GYRING, Elizabeth
HARRISON, Pamela
HAYS, Doris Ernestine
HELLER-REICHENBACH, Barbara
HOLLAND, Dulcie Sybil
HYDE, Miriam Beatrice
JANKOVIC, Miroslava
KEEFER, Euphrosyne
KESSLER, Minuetta Schumiatcher
KULIEVA, Farida Tairovna
KUZMENKO, Larysa
LACHOWSKA, Stefania
LAUBER, Anne Marianne
LEE, Young Ja
LIPSCOMB, Helen
LOUDOVA, Ivana
LOVELACE, Carey
LUCAS, Mary Anderson
LUTYENS, Elisabeth
LVOVA, Julia Fedorovna
MACKIE, Shirley M.
MACONCHY, Elizabeth
McLAUGHLIN, Marian
MARBE, Myriam
MAREZ-OYENS, Tera de
MAZOUROVA, Jarmila
MEARS, Caroline
MILLER, Elma
MKRTYCHIEVA, Virginia
  Nikitichna
MOORE, Dorothy Rudd
MOORE, Undine Smith
MOSUSOVA, Nadezda
MOSZUMANSKA-NAZAR, Krystyna
NISS, Sofia Natanovna
NOHE, Beverly
OBROVSKA, Jana
OSETROVA-YAKOVLIEVA, Nina
  Alexandrovna
OSIANDER, Irene
PENTLAND, Barbara Lally
PERRY, Zenobia Powell
PETROVA-KRUPKOVA, Elena
PHILLIPS, Linda
PIERCE, Alexandra
POPOVICI, Elise
RAINIER, Priaulx
REYNOLDS, Erma Grey Hogue
RHENE-JAQUE
RICCIOLI FRAZZI, Eva
RICHTER, Marga
ROBERTS, Jane A.
ROCHAT, Andrée
ROGER, Denise
ROMM, Rosalina Davidovna
ROWAN, Barbara
RUEFF, Jeanine
SAINT JOHN, Kathleen Louise
SAMTER, Alice
SANTOS-OCAMPO DE FRANCESCO,
  Amada Amy
SCHARLI, Ruth
SCHONTHAL, Ruth E.
SEMEGEN, Daria
SETTI, Kilza
SHUTTLEWORTH, Anne-Marie

SIEGRIST, Beatrice
SINGER, Jeanne
SKALSKA-SZEMIOTH, Hanna
   Wanda
SLIANOVA-MIZANDARI, Dagmara
   Levanovna
SNOW, Mary McCarty
SOLOMON, Elide M.
SPENCER, Williametta
STEINER, Gitta Hana
STRUTT, Dorothy
SUTHERLAND, Margaret
SWAIN, Freda Mary
SWISHER, Gloria Agnes
   Wilson
TALMA, Louise
THOMAS, Karen P.
TRIMBLE, Joan
URNER, Catherine Murphy
USHER, Julia
VAN DE VATE, Nancy Hayes
VAZQUEZ, Alida
VEHAR, Persis Anne
VERRALL, Pamela Motley
VIGNERON-RAMAKERS, Christiane-
   Josee
VILLARINI, Awilda
VITO-DELVAUX, Berthe di
VON ZIERITZ, Grete
VORLOVA, Slavka
WARNE, Katharine Mulky
WENDELBURG, Norma Ruth
WYLIE, Ruth Shaw
YAKHNINA, Yevgenia Yosifovna
YAMPOLSCHI, Roseane
YAROSHEVSKAYA, Ludmila
   Anatolievna
YOUNG, Gayle

CLAVICHORD
20th Century A.D.
ARMER, Elinor Florence
BARNETT, Carol Edith
BENNETT, Elsie M.
BIRNSTEIN, Renate Maria
BOLL, Christine E.
BRANDMAN, Margaret Susan
CREES, Kathleen Elsie
JIRACKOVA, Marta
KAESER-BECK, Aida
LEJEUNE-BONNIER, Eliane
OBROVSKA, Jana
OLIVEROS, Pauline
PENTLAND, Barbara Lally
PRICE, Beryl
VON GUNDEN, Heidi

CONCERTO - INSTRUMENTAL see under
INSTRUMENT and ORCHESTRA or
STRINGS

CONCERTO FOR ORCHESTRA
20th Century A.D.
ARAZOVA, Izabella Konstantinovna
BACEWICZ, Grazyna
BUCZEK, Barbara Kazimiera
ECKHARDT-GRAMATTE, Sophie-
   Carmen
GIURANNA, Elena Barbara
GOTKOVSKY, Ida-Rose Esther
HSU, Wen-Ying
MUSGRAVE, Thea
McKAY, Frances Thompson
PAKHMUTOVA, Alexandra
   Nikolayevna
PSTROKONSKA-NAVRATIL,
   Grazyna Hanna
PTASZYNSKA, Marta
SHLONSKY, Verdina
SONNTAG, Brunhilde

CONCERTO GROSSO
20th Century A.D.
BECLARD D'HARCOURT,
   Marguerite
DZHAFAROVA, Afag Mamed kyzy
GEIGER-KULLMANN, Rosy Auguste
KRZANOWSKA, Grażyna
MAGEAU, Mary Jane
MUNGER, Shirley
OSTRANDER, Linda Woodaman
OWEN, Blythe
POSTON, Elizabeth
PRAVOSSUDOVITCH, Natalja
   Michajlovna
PSTROKONSKA-NAVRATIL,
   Grazyna Hanna
PTASZYNSKA, Marta
SAINT JOHN, Kathleen Louise
SUTHERLAND, Margaret
WILKINS, Margaret Lucy
WILL, Madeleine
WYLIE, Ruth Shaw

CONCERTO - OTHER
18th Century A.D.
AGNESI-PINOTTINI, Maria Teresa d'
LACHANTERIE, Elisabeth
20th Century A.D.
ABEJO, Sister M. Rosalina
ACCART, Eveline
ALEXANDRA, Liana
BEECROFT, Norma Marian
BENAVENTE, Regina
CAMPAGNE, Conny
CLARK, Mary Elizabeth
CLARKE, Rosemary
DE LARA, Adelina
DESPORTES, Yvonne Berthe Melitta
DLUGOSZEWSKI, Lucia
FONTYN, Jacqueline
GUBAIDULINA, Sofia Asgatovna
HYTREK, Sister Theophane
JOLAS, Betsy
LAUFER, Beatrice
LEON, Tania Justina
LOUDOVA, Ivana
LUTYENS, Elisabeth
PENTLAND, Barbara Lally
RUSCHE, Marjorie Maxine
SENFTER, Johanna
SUESSE, Dana
SUTHERLAND, Margaret
SWAIN, Freda Mary
SWISHER, Gloria Agnes Wilson
SYNOWIEC, Ewa
VAN EPEN-DE GROOT, Else
   Antonia
WALLACH, Joelle
WILLIAMS, Grace Mary

CONTRABASSOON
20th Century A.D.
ALCALAY, Luna
BADIAN, Maya
BEYER, Johanna Magdalena
BOND, Victoria Ellen
DIANDA, Hilda
ESCOT, Pozzi
KANACH, Sharon E.
KITAZUME, Yayoi
LUND, Gudrun
PROCACCINI, Teresa
SAMTER, Alice
SEMEGEN, Daria
SIMONS, Netty
TASHJIAN, B. Charmian
WILLIAMS, Linda

COR ANGLAIS
19th Century A.D.
WICKINS, Florence

20th Century A.D.
ALLEN, Judith Shatin
ARMER, Elinor Florence
BARBERIS, Mansi
BEAT, Janet Eveline
BEYER, Johanna Magdalena
BLEWITT, Lorna
BOND, Victoria Ellen
CHANDLER, Mary
CHRETIEN-GENARO, Hedwige
CORY, Eleanor
DIAMOND, Arline
DREGE-SCHIELOWA, Lucja
ENDRES, Olive Philomene
FORMAN, Joanne
FROTHINGHAM, Eugenia
GARCIA ROBSON, Magdalena
GARDNER, Kay
GIFFORD, Helen Margaret
GIPPS, Ruth
GRIEBLING, Karen Jean
JOHNSTON-REID, Sarah Ruth
JOLAS, Betsy
LE SIEGE, Annette
LEBENBOM, Elaine F.
LOMON, Ruth
MARKIEWICZOWNA, Wladyslawa
MARTINEZ, Odaline de la
MEKEEL, Joyce
PERKIN, Helen
PERRY, Julia Amanda
PHILLIPS, Bryony
PIZER, Elizabeth Faw
   Hayden
REID, Sarah Johnston
ROWAN, Barbara
RUEFF, Jeanine
RUSCHE, Marjorie Maxine
STRUTT, Dorothy
SUTHERLAND, Margaret
VIGNERON-RAMAKERS, Christiane-
   Josee
WIENIAWSKA, Irene Regine
WITNI, Monica
WOLLNER, Gertrude Price

CORNET
20th Century A.D.
ANDERSON, Julia McKinley
BADIAN, Maya
SEHESTED, Hilda
SMITH, Linda Catlin

DOUBLE BASS
18th Century A.D.
AGNESI-PINOTTINI, Maria Teresa d'
ANNA AMALIA, Duchess of Saxe-
   Weimar
BON, Anna
CHARRIERE, Isabella Agneta
   Elisabeth de
19th Century A.D.
GRANDVAL, Marie Felicie Clemence
   de Reiset, Vicomtesse de
WUIET, Caroline
20th Century A.D.
ABE, Kyoko
AHRENS, Peg
ALCALAY, Luna
ALLIK, Kristi
ANDERSON, Beth
ANDERSON, Olive Jennie Paxton
ARMER, Elinor Florence
AUBERT, Pauline Louise Henriette
AUFDERHEIDE, May
BADIAN, Maya
BARBERIS, Mansi
BARKIN, Elaine
BEECROFT, Norma Marian
BELL, Carla Huston
BERGEN, Sylvia

BLIESENER, Ada Elizabeth Michelman
BOULOGNE, Julia R.C.
BRUGGMANN, Heidi
CALLAWAY, Ann
CARLOS, Wendy
CARROL, Ida Gertrude
CHARBONNIER, Janine Andrée
CHAVES, Mary Elizabeth
CLARKE, Rosemary
COATES, Gloria Kannenberg
DARE, Margaret Marie
DOBSON, Elaine
DUNLOP, Isobel
DUSHKIN, Dorothy Smith
EVEN-OR, Mary
FONTYN, Jacqueline
FORMAN, Joanne
FRITZ, Sherilyn Gail
GAUTHIER, Brigitte
GROSSMAN, Deena
GRZADZIELOWNA, Eleonora
GUBAIDULINA, Sofia Asgatovna
GYRING, Elizabeth
HAYS, Doris Ernestine
HENDERSON, Moya
HOLST, Imogen Clare
HOVDA, Eleanor
IRMAN-ALLEMANN, Regina
JOHNSTON-REID, Sarah Ruth
KATS-CHERNIN, Elena
LANE, Elizabeth
LEAHY, Mary Weldon
LUND, Gudrun
MAIRE, Jacqueline
MAMLOK, Ursula
MARCUS, Bunita
MARIC, Ljubica
MEACHEM, Margaret McKeen Ramsey
MILLER, Elma
MORRISON, Julia Maria
MRACEK, Ann Michelle
MUSGRAVE, Thea
NOWAK, Alison
OLIVEIRA, Jocy de
OLIVEROS, Pauline
PELEGRI, Maria Teresa
PENGILLY, Sylvia
PENTLAND, Barbara Lally
PETRA-BASACOPOL, Carmen
PHILIBA, Nicole
PIECHOWSKA, Alina
POLIN, Claire
PRICE, Florence Beatrice
PTASZYNSKA, Marta
RAPOPORT, Eda
REID, Sarah Johnston
RICHER, Jeannine
RICHTER, Marga
ROBERT, Lucie
RODRIGUE, Nicole
ROE, Eileen Betty
ROE, Helen Mary Gabrielle
RUEFF, Jeanine
SAMTER, Alice
SNIZKOVA-SKRHOVA, Jitka
SOENSTEVOLD, Maj
STRUTT, Dorothy
SZOENYI, Erzsebet
USHER, Julia
USTVOLSKAYA, Galina Ivanovna
VON ZIERITZ, Grete
WALDO, Elisabeth
WHITLOCK, E. Florence
ZAKRZEWSKA-NIKIPORCZYK, Barbara Maria
ZECHLIN, Ruth
ZHVANETSKAIA, Inna Abramovna
Century unknown
MONACHINA

DOUBLE BASS AND ORCHESTRA OR STRINGS
  20th Century A.D.
    AARNE, Els
    BARBERIS, Mansi
    VORLOVA, Slavka
    ZHVANETSKAIA, Inna Abramovna

DOUBLE CONCERTO see TWO INSTRUMENTS and ORCHESTRA

DRUMS
  18th Century A.D.
    MARTINEZ, Marianne
  20th Century A.D.
    ALCALAY, Luna
    BERK, Adele
    BRANDMAN, Margaret Susan
    BREMER, Marrie Petronella
    BURSTON, Maggie
    CABRERA, Silvia Maria Pires
    CRAWFORD SEEGER, Ruth
    GARDNER, Kay
    GIPPS, Ruth
    JUENGER, Patricia
    KABAT, Julie Phyllis
    KEETMAN, Gunild
    LEWIN, Olive
    MacKENNA, Carmela
    McKENZIE, Sandra
    MARCUS, Ada Belle Gross
    MENDOSA, Dot
    NOBLE, Ann
    OWEN, Blythe
    PETROVA, Mara
    PHILLIPS, Bryony
    PRAVOSSUDOVITCH, Natalja Michajlovna
    RUSCHE, Marjorie Maxine
    TAL, Ya'ara
    USTVOLSKAYA, Galina Ivanovna
    UYTTENHOVE, Yolande

DULCIMER
  20th Century A.D.
    OWENS, Rochelle

DUO - OTHER
  18th Century A.D.
    ANNA AMALIA, Princess of Prussia
    BON, Anna
    DE GAMBARINI, Elisabetta
    HOFFMANN, Miss J.
    STECHER, Marianne
  19th Century A.D.
    ADAJEWSKY, Ella
    CRETI, Marianna de Rocchis
    NORRIS, Mary
    RONDONNEAU, Elise
    SZYMANOWSKA, Maria Agata
    WURM, Mary J.A.
  20th Century A.D.
    AARNE, Els
    AAS, Else Berntsen
    ACKLAND, Jeanne Isabel Dorothy
    AINSCOUGH, Juliana Mary
    ALLEN, Judith Shatin
    ALT, Hansi
    ANDERSON, Avril
    ANDERSON, Beth
    ANDERSON-WUENSCH, Jean Mary
    ARIMA, Reiko
    ARMER, Elinor Florence
    BACKES, Lotte
    BADIAN, Maya
    BARAMISHVILI, Olga Ivanovna
    BARKIN, Elaine
    BARKLUND, Irma L.
    BARNETT, Carol Edith
    BARNETT, Wally
    BARRAINE, Elsa

BARRATT, Carol Ann
BARRELL, Joyce Howard
BARRETT-THOMAS, N.
BARTHEL, Ursula
BARTLETT, Ethel Agnes
BAUER, Marion Eugenie
BERK, Adele
BEYER, Johanna Magdalena
BIZONY, Celia
BLOOM, Jane Ira
BOND, Victoria Ellen
BOTTELIER, Ina
BOULANGER, Lili Juliette Marie Olga
BREILH, Fernande
BRIGGS, Dorothy Bell
BRIGHT, Dora Estella
BROCKMAN, Jane E.
BRUSH, Ruth Damaris
BRUZDOWICZ, Joanna
BUCHANAN, Dorothy Quita
BURSTON, Maggie
BUTLER, Patricia Magahay
CALCAGNO, Elsa
CALLAWAY, Ann
CAMPAGNE, Conny
CARMEN MARINA
CARR-BOYD, Ann Kirsten
CHAMINADE, Cecile Louise Stephanie
CHANCE, Nancy Laird
CHANDLER, Mary
CHARBONNIER, Janine Andrée
CHAVES, Mary Elizabeth
CLARKE, Rebecca
CLOSTRE, Adrienne
COLE, Ulric
CONRAD, Laurie M.
COULOMBE SAINT-MARCOUX, Micheline
CRAWFORD, Dawn Constance
CRISWICK, Mary
DANIELSON, Janet Rosalie
DAVIS, Eleanor Maud
DE FREITAS, Elvira Manuela Fernandez
DEMBO, Royce
DESPORTES, Yvonne Berthe Melitta
DIAMOND, Arline
DIANDA, Hilda
DINESCU, Violeta
DLUGOSZEWSKI, Lucia
DOBSON, Elaine
DONCEANU, Felicia
DRING, Madeleine
DUNLOP, Isobel
DUSHKIN, Dorothy Smith
DZIEWULSKA, Maria Amelia
ECKHARDT-GRAMATTE, Sophie-Carmen
EICHENWALD, Sylvia
ERNST, Siegrid
ERVIN, Karen
EVEN-OR, Mary
FALCINELLI, Rolande
FERRAND-TEULET, Denise
FINE, Vivian
FINZI, Graciane
FISCHER, Edith Steinkraus
FISHER, Gladys Washburn
FISHER, Katherine Danforth
FONTYN, Jacqueline
FOWLER, Jennifer Joan
FOX, Erika
FRASER-MILLER, Gloria Jill
FREED, Dorothy Whitson
FRITSCH, Magda von
FULLER-HALL, Sarah Margaret
GABUS, Monique
GALINNE, Rachel
GARR, Wieslawa
GARSCIA-GRESSEL, Janina

GARTENLAUB, Odette
GARUTA, Lucia Yanovna
GENTILE, Ada
GIDEON, Miriam
GILBERT, Pia
GIPPS, Ruth
GITECK, Janice
GLATZ, Helen Sinclair
GOOLKASIAN-RAHBEE, Dianne Zabelle
GOTKOVSKY, Ida-Rose Esther
GOULD, Janetta
GREGER, Luisa
GRIEBLING, Karen Jean
GRILLI GALEFFI, Elvira
GROSSMAN, Deena
GUBAIDULINA, Sofia Asgatovna
GYRING, Elizabeth
HARRIS, Ruth Berman
HARVEY, Eva Noel
HIND O'MALLEY, Pamela
HINLOPEN, Francina
HOENDERDOS, Margriet
HOFFRICHTER, Bertha Chaitkin
HOLLAND, Dulcie Sybil
HOOVER, Katherine
HSU, Wen-Ying
HYSON, Winifred Prince
JENNY, Sister Leonore
JOCHSBERGER, Tzipora H.
JOHNSTON-REID, Sarah Ruth
JOLAS, Betsy
JONES, Catherine
JUENGER, Patricia
KAESER-BECK, Aida
KALTENECKER, Gertraud
KAMINSKY, Laura
KANACH, Sharon E.
KAPP, Corinne
KATS-CHERNIN, Elena
KELLER, Ginette
KING, Rebecca Clift
KINSCELLA, Hazel Gertrude
KISTETENYI, Melinda
KOLB, Barbara
KUBO, Mayako
KURIMOTO, Yoko
KUZMENKO, Larysa
LACHOWSKA, Stefania
LAITMAN, Lori
LAMBERT, Cecily
LAMEGO, Carlinda J.
LARSEN, Elizabeth Brown
LARUELLE, Jeanne-Marie
LAUBER, Anne Marianne
LAYMAN, Pamela
LAZAR, Ella
LEAHY, Mary Weldon
LEE, Hope Anne Keng-Wei
LEE, Hwaeja Yoo
LEFEBVRE, Françoise
LEVIN, Rami Yona
LINNEMANN, Maria Catharina
LITSITE, Paula Yanovna
LOMON, Ruth
LOOTS, Joyce Mary Ann
LOUIE, Alexina Diane
LOWENSTEIN, Gunilla Marike
LUCAS, Mary Anderson
LUNA DE ESPAILLAT, Margarita
LUND, Gudrun
MACONCHY, Elizabeth
McKINNEY, Mathilde
McLAUGHLIN, Marian
McLEAN, Priscilla Anne Taylor
McTEE, Cindy Karen
MAGEAU, Mary Jane
MAMLOK, Ursula
MARCUS, Bunita
MARI, Pierrette
MASSUMOTO, Kikuko

MATTHEISS-BOEGNER, Helga
MEACHEM, Margaret McKeen Ramsey
MEARS, Caroline
MENDELSSOHN, Erna
MERLI-ZWISCHENBRUGGER, Christina
MITCHELL, Janice Misurell
MOON, Chloe Elizabeth
MOORE, Undine Smith
MORRISSEY, Elizabeth
MOSUSOVA, Nadezda
MURAKUMO, Ayako
MURAO, Sachie
MURDOCH, Marjolijn
MUSGRAVE, Thea
MYGATT, Louise
NATVIG, Candace
NAZAROVA, Tatiana Borisovna
NIKOLSKAYA, Lyubov Borisovna
NOBLE, Ann
NOETHLING, Elisabeth
OBROVSKA, Jana
OCHSE, Orpha Caroline
ODAGESCU, Irina
OFFICER, Bronwyn Lee
OH, Sook Ja
O'LEARY, Jane Strong
OLIVE, Vivienne
OLIVEROS, Pauline
OSTROFF, Esther
OWEN, Angela Maria
OWEN, Blythe
PALMER, Lynne Wainwright
PARKER, Alice
PATERSON, Wilma
PATTERSON, Andra
PENNER, Jean Priscilla
PENTLAND, Barbara Lally
PHILIBA, Nicole
PHILIPPART, Renee
PHILLIPS, Bryony
PHILLIPS, Karen Ann
PIECHOWSKA, Alina
PIERCE, Alexandra
PIRES DOS REIS, Hilda
PLONSEY, Jennifer
POLIN, Claire
POSTON, Elizabeth
PRAVOSSUDOVITCH, Natalja Michajlovna
PROCACCINI, Teresa
PSTROKONSKA-NAVRATIL, Grazyna Hanna
PTASZYNSKA, Marta
QUANTIN-SAULNIER, Denise
RAN, Shulamit
REID, Sarah Johnston
REYNOLDS, Erma Grey Hogue
RHEINGOLD, Lauma Yanovna
RICKARD, Sylvia
ROBERT, Lucie
ROE, Eileen Betty
ROGER, Denise
ROGERS, Patsy
ROMM, Rosalina Davidovna
ROSSER, Annetta Hamilton
RUFF-STOEHR, Herta Maria Klara
RUSCHE, Marjorie Maxine
RYDER, Theodora Sturkow
SAITO-NODA, Eva
SALQUIN, Hedy
SAMSON, Valerie Brooks
SAMTER, Alice
SCHERCHEN, Tona
SCHLOSS, Myrna Frances
SCHMIDT-DUISBURG, Margarete Dina Alwina
SCHMITZ-GOHR, Else
SCHONTHAL, Ruth E.
SCHORR-WEILER, Eva

SCHWERDTFEGER, E. Anne
SCOVILLE, Margaret Lee
SEGHIZZI, Cecilia
SHAFFER, Jeanne Ellison
SHELTON, Margaret Meier
SHEPARD, Jean Ellen
SHIRLEY, Constance Jeanette
SILSBEE, Ann L.
SILVERMAN, Faye-Ellen
SIMONS, Netty
SISTEK-DJORDJEVIC, Mirjana
SNIZKOVA-SKRHOVA, Jitka
SOENSTEVOLD, Maj
SOLOMON, Mirrie Irma
SPENCER, Williametta
STEINER, Gitta Hana
STREATFIELD, Valma June
STRUTT, Dorothy
STULTZ, Marie Irene
SUMNER, Clare
SYNOWIEC, Ewa
SZAJNA-LEWANDOWSKA, Jadwiga Helena
SZEKELY, Katalin
SZOENYI, Erzsebet
SZYMANSKA, Iwonka Bogumila
TAILLEFERRE, Germaine
TAL, Marjo
TANN, Hilary
TANNER, Hilda
TARLOW, Karen Anne
TASSO, Joan Maria
TATE, Phyllis
TATTON, Madeleine
TAUTU, Cornelia
TELFER, Nancy Ellen
THEMMEN, Ivana Marburger
THREADGILL-MARTIN, Ravonna
TOWER, Joan
TURRIETTA, Cheryl Renée
USHER, Julia
USTVOLSKAYA, Galina Ivanovna
UYEDA, Leslie
UYTTENHOVE, Yolande
VAN APPLEDORN, Mary Jeanne
VAN DIJCK, Beatrice Madeleine
VOLKART-SCHLAGER, Kaethe
VORLOVA, Slavka
VYNER, Mary Bainbridge
WALDO, Elisabeth
WARNE, Katharine Mulky
WEIGL, Vally
WEISS, Arleta
WILBER, Clare Marie O'Keefe
YAMPOLSCHI, Roseane
ZAIMONT, Judith Lang
ZAKRZEWSKA-NIKIPORCZYK, Barbara Maria
ZAULECK, Gertrud
ZIBEROVA, Zinaida Petrovna
ZIFFRIN, Marilyn Jane
ZIMMERMANN, Margrit
Century unknown
GAMBOGI, Luigia
HOGBEN, Dorothy
ROSS, Clara

DUO - STRINGS
  18th Century A.D.
    COSWAY, Maria Cecilia Louise
    SIRMEN, Maddalena Laura di
  19th Century A.D.
    CRETI, Marianna de Rocchis
    HEIDENREICH, Henrietta
  20th Century A.D.
    ALOTIN, Yardena
    ANDERSON-WUENSCH, Jean Mary
    ARRIEU, Claude
    BACEWICZ, Grazyna
    BACKES, Lotte
    BARRELL, Joyce Howard

BEACH, Amy Marcy
BODENSTEIN-HOYME, Ruth E.
BRINK-POTHUIS, Annie van den
CAMPAGNE, Conny
CAMPMANY, Montserrat
CARMEN MARINA
CLARKE, Rebecca
COLAÇO OSORIO-SWAAB, Reine
CRISWICK, Mary
DALE, Kathleen
DIAMOND, Arline
ECKHARDT-GRAMATTE, Sophie-
    Carmen
FAUTCH, Sister Magdalen
GEORGE, Lila-Gene
GIPPS, Ruth
GLATZ, Helen Sinclair
GREENE, Genevieve
GRIGSBY, Beverly
HAMPE, Charlotte
HARDY, Helen Irene
HARRIS, Ruth Berman
HERBISON, Jeraldine Saunders
HIND O'MALLEY, Pamela
HINLOPEN, Francina
HOLLAND, Dulcie Sybil
IVEY, Jean Eichelberger
KALOGRIDOU, Maria
KERN, Frida
KIM, Kwang-Hee
KLINKOVA, Zhivka
KORNILOVA, Tatiana Dmitrevna
LATHROP, Gayle Posselt
LINDEMAN, Hjelle Signe
LIPSCOMB, Helen
MACONCHY, Elizabeth
MARBE, Myriam
MELOY, Elizabeth
MERLI-ZWISCHENBRUGGER,
    Christina
MOON, Chloe Elizabeth
MOORE, Dorothy Rudd
MUSGRAVE, Thea
McLAUGHLIN, Marian
NOBLE, Ann
NOVI, Anna Beate
OLIVEROS, Pauline
PETERSON, Melody
PROCACCINI, Teresa
RICHER, Jeannine
ROBERTS, Megan L.
ROGER, Denise
SAMVELIAN, Sofia Vardanovna
SEBASTIANI, Pia
SIMONS, Netty
SOULAGE, Marcelle Fanny Henriette
SPECHT, Judy Lavise
STRUTT, Dorothy
SUTHERLAND, Margaret
SWAIN, Freda Mary
TANNER, Hilda
THOME, Diane
TRIMBLE, Joan
TURRIETTA, Cheryl Renée
VAN DER MARK, Maria
VELLERE, Lucie Weiler
VERCOE, Elizabeth
VOLKART-SCHLAGER, Kaethe
VON ZIERITZ, Grete
WALKER, Gwyneth van Anden
WALLACH, Joelle
WARREN, Betsy
WILKINS, Margaret Lucy
YOUNG, Jane Corner

ELECTRONIC INSTRUMENTS -
UNSPECIFIED OR NOT SYNTHESIZED
20th Century A.D.
AESCHLIMANN-ROTH, Esther
ALSTED, Birgitte
AMACHER, Maryanne

BAADER-NOBS, Heidi
BEAT, Janet Eveline
BELLAVANCE, Ginette
BLISS, Marilyn S.
BOESSER, Dagma
BRANDMAN, Margaret Susan
BRIGGS, Nancy Louise
BROUK, Joanna
BRUZDOWICZ, Joanna
BURSTON, Maggie
CALAME, Genevieve
CARL, Tommie Ewert
CIANI, Suzanne Elizabeth
COATES, Gloria Kannenberg
DERBYSHIRE, Delia
DIANDA, Hilda
DIEHL, Paula Jespersen
FAIRLIE, Margaret C.
FRASER-MILLER, Gloria Jill
GRIGSBY, Beverly
HAYS, Doris Ernestine
HEMON, Sedje
HOVDA, Eleanor
HULFORD, Denise Lovona
JOHNSTON-REID, Sarah Ruth
KASILAG, Lucrecia R.
KELLEY, Patricia Ann
KERCHER, Eleanor
LA BARBARA, Joan
LACHARTRE, Nicole Marie
LACKMAN, Susan C. Cohn
LEBARON, Anne
LOCKWOOD, Annea Ferguson
MIZUNO, Shuko
MOLAVA, Pamela May
NORRE, Dorcas
ORE, Cecilie
PHILLIPS, Bryony
PLONSEY, Jennifer
REID, Sarah Johnston
RICHER, Jeannine
RUBIN, Anna Ita
SEMEGEN, Daria
SHIELDS, Alice Ferree
SMITH, Ladonna Carol
SOMMERS, Daria E.
SOUTHAM, Ann
STOEPPELMANN, Janet
TACK, Annie
TASHJIAN, B. Charmian
THOME, Diane
TOYAMA, Michiko Francoise
VAN DE VATE, Nancy Hayes
VAZQUEZ, Alida
VELLERE, Lucie Weiler
WEAVER, Carol Ann

ELECTRONIC MUSIC
20th Century A.D.
ABE, Kyoko
AGUDELO MURGUIA, Graciela
AHRENS, Peg
AIN, Noa
ALCALAY, Luna
ALEXANDRA, Liana
ALLIK, Kristi
ALSTED, Birgitte
AMACHER, Maryanne
ANDERSON, Beth
ANDERSON, Laurie
ANDERSON, Ruth
ARCHER, Violet Balestreri
ARETZ, Isabel
ARRIEU, Claude
AUSTIN, Dorothea
BABITS, Linda
BAILLY, Colette
BANDT, Rosalie Edith
BARBILLON, Jeanne
BARRIERE, Françoise
BAULD, Alison

BEAT, Janet Eveline
BEECROFT, Norma Marian
BELLAVANCE, Ginette
BENAVENTE, Regina
BIBBY, Gillian Margaret
BLEY, Carla
BOFILL, Anna
BOUCHARD, Linda L.
BOYD, Anne Elizabeth
BRENET, Thérèse
BROCKMAN, Jane E.
BRUZDOWICZ, Joanna
CARL, Tommie Ewert
CARLOS, Wendy
CECCONI-BOTELLA, Monic
CHARBONNIER, Janine Andrée
CIANI, Suzanne Elizabeth
CIOBANU, Maia
CLAIRE, Paula
CLARKE, Rosemary
COATES, Gloria Kannenberg
COHEN, Marcia
CORY, Eleanor
COULOMBE SAINT-MARCOUX,
    Micheline
COULTHARD, Jean
COX, Sally
DAIGLE, Sister Anne Cécile
DESPORTES, Yvonne Berthe Melitta
DIANDA, Hilda
DIEMER, Emma Lou
DILLER, Saralu C.
DILLON, Fannie Charles
DU PAGE, Florence Elizabeth
ELLERMAN, Helen
ESCOT, Pozzi
FAIRLIE, Margaret C.
FERREYRA, Beatriz
FINE, Vivian
FOWLER, Jennifer Joan
FRANCO, Clare
FRASER-MILLER, Gloria Jill
FRITZ, Sherilyn Gail
GARDNER, Kay
GARSCIA-GRESSEL, Janina
GILBERT, Janet Monteith
GITECK, Janice
GLATZ, Helen Sinclair
GREENE, Margo Lynn
GREENWALD, Jan Carol
GRIGSBY, Beverly
GRIMAUD, Yvette
GUBAIDULINA, Sofia Asgatovna
HAINES, Julia Howell
HAMMARBERG-AKESSON, Sonja
HAYS, Doris Ernestine
HEDSTROEM, Ase
HEMON, Sedje
HIRSCH, Barbara
HO, Wai On
HOPKINS, Sarah
INJADO
IVEY, Jean Eichelberger
JANKOWSKI, Loretta Patricia
JENKINS, Susan Elaine
JIRACKOVA, Marta
KASILAG, Lucrecia R.
KAVASCH, Deborah Helene
KELLEY, Patricia Ann
KLIMISCH, Sister Mary Jane
KNOWLES, Alison
KORNILOVA, Tatiana Dmitrevna
KROFINA, Sharon
KUBISCH, Christina
KUBO, Mayako
LA BARBARA, Joan
LACHARTRE, Nicole Marie
LEACH, Mary Jane
LEBARON, Anne
LEE, Hope Anne Keng-Wei
LEVEY, Lauren

LOCKWOOD, Annea Ferguson
LOH, Kathy Jean
LORIOD, Yvonne
LOUDOVA, Ivana
LOUIE, Alexina Diane
LUCKMAN, Phyllis
LUTYENS, Elisabeth
LUTYENS, Sally
McKELLAN, Irene Mary
McLEAN, Priscilla Anne Taylor
McLIN, Lena
McMILLAN, Ann Endicott
MALMLOEF-FORSSLING, Carin
MARBE, Myriam
MARCUS, Ada Belle Gross
MAREZ-OYENS, Tera de
MARI, Pierrette
MEACHEM, Margaret McKeen
   Ramsey
MEKEEL, Joyce
MENEELY-KYDER, Sarah Suderley
MILKULAK, Marcia Lee
MONK, Meredith
MORETTO, Nelly
MORRISON, Julia Maria
MOSZUMANSKA-NAZAR, Krystyna
MULDER, Maria Antonia
MUSGRAVE, Thea
NELSON, Mary Anne
NEMTEANU-ROTARU, Doina
NEWLIN, Dika
NIGHTINGALE, Barbara Diane
NOBLE, Ann
NORDENSTROM, Gladys Mercedes
NORRE, Dorcas
NOVA SONDAG, Jacqueline
NOWAK, Alison
OLIVEIRA, Jocy de
OLIVEROS, Pauline
ORAM, Daphne Blake
ORE, Cecilie
PADE, Else Marie
PAULL, Barberi
PAYNE, Maggi
PENGILLY, Sylvia
PHILIBA, Nicole
PHILIPPART, Renee
PIECHOWSKA, Alina
POLIN, Claire
POOL, Jeannie Gayle
POULET DEFONTAINE, Madeleine
PROCACCINI, Teresa
PTASZYNSKA, Marta
QUESADA, Virginia
QUINN-VEES, Deborah
RADERMACHER, Erika
RADIGUE, Eliane
RAN, Shulamit
RANTA-SHIDA, Shoko
REED, Marlyce Rae Polk
REHNQVIST, Karin Birgitta
REID, Sarah Johnston
REID, Wendy
RICHER, Jeannine
ROBERTS, Jane A.
ROBERTS, Megan L.
ROSSO, Carol L.
RUBIN, Anna Ita
RUDOW, Vivian Adelberg
SACHS, Carolyn
SAINT JOHN, Kathleen Louise
SANDIFUR, Ann Elizabeth
SANTOS-OCAMPO DE FRANCESCO,
   Amada Amy
SANZ, Rocio
SCHERCHEN, Tona
SCHIEVE, Catherine
SCHLOSS, Myrna Frances
SCHNEIDER, June
SCRIABINE, Marina
SEMEGEN, Daria

SHEVITZ, Mimi
SHIDA, Shoko
SHIELDS, Alice Ferree
SHIOMI, Mieko
SHUTTLEWORTH, Anne-Marie
SIKORA, Elzbieta
SILSBEE, Ann L.
SILVERMAN, Faye-Ellen
SKARECKY, Jana Milena
SMILEY, Pril
SMITH, Ladonna Carol
SNOW, Mary McCarty
SONNTAG, Brunhilde
SOUTHAM, Ann
SPIEGEL, Laurie
STANLEY, Helen Camille
STOEPPELMANN, Janet
STREATFIELD, Valma June
SUCHY, Gregoria Karides
TANN, Hilary
TARLOW, Karen Anne
TASHJIAN, B. Charmian
THOME, Diane
TOYAMA, Michiko Françoise
ULEHLA, Ludmila
URRETA, Alicia
VAN OHLEN, Deborah
VON GUNDEN, Heidi
WALLACH, Joelle
WHITE, Ruth S.
WILKINS, Margaret Lucy
WILLIAMS, Joan Franks
WITKIN, Beatrice
WOLF-COHEN, Veronika
WONG, Betty Ann
WONG, Hsiung-Zee
ZACCAGNINI, Guiliana
ZANARDI, Patricia

ENSEMBLE CHAMBER
18th Century A.D.
   ETOILE, Mme. de L'
   KOHARY, Marie, Countess of
19th Century A.D.
   BAKA-BAITZ, Irma
   BERTELLI, Clotilde
   BLANC DE FONTBELLE, Cécile
   BRIZZI-GIORGI, Maria
   CHAMBERLAYNE, Edith A.
   DELABORDE, Elie Miriam
   ELDESE, Renee
   FENGER, Johanne
   GABRIEL, Mary Ann Virginia
   GALLONI, Adolfa
   GENGLIS, Stephanie Felicite,
      Countess of Saint-Aubin
   HENN, Angelica
   LAIGHTON, Ruth
   LANZARINI DE ISAJA, Antonietta
   STEIN, Nannette
   VANZO, Vittoria Maria
   ZILIOTTO, Elisa
20th Century A.D.
   ADERHOLDT, Sarah
   ALCALAY, Luna
   ALONSO, Julia
   ALSTED, Birgitte
   ANDERSON, Beth
   ANDERSON, Julia McKinley
   ANTHONY, Gina
   ARIMA, Reiko
   AVETISIAN, Aida Konstantinovna
   BAADER-NOBS, Heidi
   BAKER, Mary Winder
   BARBOUR, Florence Newell
   BARDEL, Germaine
   BARON SUPERVIELLE, Susana
   BARRATT, Carol Ann
   BECKON, Lettie Marie
   BEESON, Elizabeth Ruth
   BENARY, Barbara

BEYER, Johanna Magdalena
BIRNSTEIN, Renate Maria
BIZONY, Celia
BLEY, Carla
BLOCH, Suzanne
BLOOM, Jane Ira
BOND, Victoria Ellen
BOONE, Clara Lyle
BORON, Marion
BRIGHT, Dora Estella
BROCKMAN, Jane E.
BUENAVENTURA, Isabel
CABRERA, Silvia Maria Pires
CALL, Audrey
CAMPAGNE, Conny
CARL, Tommie Ewert
CARR-BOYD, Ann Kirsten
CARROLL, Barbara
CARWITHEN, Doreen
CASAGEMAS, Luisa
CECCONI-BATES, Augusta
CECCONI-BOTELLA, Monic
CHARBONNIER, Janine Andrée
CHUDOVA, Tatiana Alekseyevna
CLAYTON, Susan
COATES, Gloria Kannenberg
COLACO OSORIO-SWAAB, Reine
COLLINS, Janyce
COULOMBE SAINT-MARCOUX,
   Micheline
COX, Alison Mary
DE BIASE BIDART, Lycia
DE MONTEL, Adalgisa
DEMARQUEZ, Suzanne
DESPORTES, Yvonne Berthe Melitta
DLUGOSZEWSKI, Lucia
DRYNAN, Margaret
DUDLEY, Marjorie Eastwood
EIRIKSDOTTIR, Karolina
EKIZIAN, Michelle
ERNEST, Sister M.
FAIRLIE, Margaret C.
FERRER OTERO, Monsita
   Monserrate
FINK, Emma C.
FINLEY, Lorraine Noel
FIUZA, Virginia Salgado
FLORING, Grace Kenny
FONTYN, Jacqueline
FORMAN, Joanne
FREER, Eleanor Warner Everest
FRITTER, Genevieve Davisson
FRYZELL, Regina Holmen
GAMBARINI, Costanza
GARCIA MUNOZ, Carmen
GARDNER, Kay
GASTON, Marjorie Dean
GENTILE, Ada
GERSTMAN, Blanche Wilhelminia
GIFFORD, Helen Margaret
GOMM, Elizabeth
GORELLI, Olga
GRIMES, Doreen
GRZADZIELOWNA, Eleonora
GWILY-BROIDO, Rivka
HANIM, Leyla
HARRIS, Letitia Radcliffe
HARROD, Beth Miller
HAYS, Doris Ernestine
HAZEN, Sara
HEIDRICH, Hermine Margaret
HIGGINBOTHAM, Irene
HINKLE, Daisy Estelle
HIRSCH, Barbara
HOFFMAN, Phyllis Sampson
HORI, Etsuko
HULL, Anne
HURLEY, Susan
IBRAGIMOVA, Sevda Mirza kyzy
JIRACKOVA, Marta
JOLAS, Betsy

KADIMA, Hagar Yonith
KANACH, Sharon E.
KARG, Marga
KAVASCH, Deborah Helene
KLINKOVA, Zhivka
KOLARIKOVA-SEDLACHOVA, Marie
KOLB, Barbara
KOPTAGEL, Yuksel
KOZHEVNIKOVA, Ekaterina
  Vadimovna
KRZANOWSKA, Grażyna
LAITMAN, Lori
LANGE, Anny von
LAPEIRETTA, Ninon de Brouwer
LASRY-HERRBACH, Yvonne
LEECH, Renée
LENNEP, Henrietta van
LEONARD, Mamie Grace
LINNET, Anne
LOMON, Ruth
LORIOD, Yvonne
LUFF, Enid
LUND, Gudrun
MACONCHY, Elizabeth
MARTINEZ, Odaline de la
MASSUMOTO, Kikuko
MILAM, Lena Triplett
MILLER, Elma
MONTIJN, Aleida
MORE, Margaret Elizabeth
MORETTO, Nelly
MOSZUMANSKA-NAZAR, Krystyna
NIEWIADOMSKA, Barbara
NIGHTINGALE, Barbara Diane
NOBLITT, Katheryn Marie McCall
NORMAN, Ruth
NYMAN, Amy Utting
OH, Sook Ja
ORE, Cécilie
OWEN, Blythe
OZAITA, Maria Luisaria Luisa
PADE, Else Marie
PAYNE, Harriet
PETERSEN, Else
PIECHOWSKA, Alina
PLICQUE, Eveline
PRICE, Deon Nielsen
PRITCHARD, Gwyn
PSTROKONSKA-NAVRATIL,
  Grazyna Hanna
PTASZYNSKA, Marta
RAINIER, Priaulx
REMICK, Bertha
RICHARDSON, Sharon
RICHEPIN, Eliane
RICKARD, Sylvia
RITTMAN, Trude
ROCHAT, Andrée
RODRIGUE, Nicole
ROE, Helen Mary Gabrielle
RUBIN, Anna Ita
SADOVNIKOFF, Mary Briggs
SALVADOR, Matilde
SANDERS, Alma M.
SANDIFUR, Ann Elizabeth
SCHIEVE, Catherine
SCHMIDT-DUISBURG, Margarete
  Dina Alwina
SCHUMAKER, Grace L.
SCHWARTZ, Julie
SCRIABINE, Marina
SEAY, Virginia
SELTZNER, Jennie
SETTI, Kilza
SEUEL-HOLST, Marie
SHEPARD, Jean Ellen
SHERMAN, Elna
SHIDA, Shoko
SHLONSKY, Verdina
SMITH, Linda Catlin
SNIZKOVA-SKRHOVA, Jitka

SOMMERS, Daria E.
SOUERS, Mildred
STITT, Margaret McClure
TACK, Annie
TARLOW, Karen Anne
TELFER, Nancy Ellen
THOMAS, Marilyn Taft
TURNER, Sara Scott
USHER, Julia
VAN VLIET, Pearl H.
VYNER, Mary Bainbridge
WALDO, Elisabeth
WALKER, Gwyneth van Anden
WALKER, Nina
WANG, An-Ming
WARD, Nancy
WEIR, Judith
WERTHEIM, Rosy
WILENS, Greta
YOUNG, Gayle
ZAKRZEWSKA-NIKIPORCZYK,
  Barbara Maria
ZIFFRIN, Marilyn Jane
ZWILICH, Ellen Taaffe
Century unknown
CUSENZA, Maria Giacchino
SAPAROFF, Andrea

ENSEMBLE LARGER
  18th Century A.D.
  ANNA AMALIA, Duchess of Saxe-
    Weimar
  MARIA CHARLOTTE AMALIE,
    Princess of Saxe-Meiningen
  TASCA, Mme.
  19th Century A.D.
  BRONSART VON SCHELLENDORF,
    Ingeborg Lena von
  TYRELL, Agnes
  WICKINS, Florence
  20th Century A.D.
  ABEJO, Sister M. Rosalina
  ALEXANDER, Leni
  ANDERSON, Olive Jennie Paxton
  ARMER, Elinor Florence
  BACEWICZ, Grazyna
  BAINBRIDGE, Beryl
  BARKIN, Elaine
  BARRAINE, Elsa
  BARRELL, Joyce Howard
  BARRETT-THOMAS, N.
  BAUER, Marion Eugenie
  BERL WEINFIELD, Christine
  BINET, Jocelyne
  BLAUSTEIN, Susan Morton
  BOSCH Y PAGES, Luisa
  BOUCHARD, Linda L.
  BOYD, Anne Elizabeth
  BRUZDOWICZ, Joanna
  BURCHELL, Henrietta Louise
  COLIN, Jeanne
  CORY, Eleanor
  COULTHARD, Jean
  CRAWFORD SEEGER, Ruth
  DE BIASE BIDART, Lycia
  DEDIEU-PETERS, Madeleine
  DILLON, Fannie Charles
  DLUGOSZEWSKI, Lucia
  DOBIE, Janet
  DUSHKIN, Dorothy Smith
  ERNST, Siegrid
  EUBANKS, Rachel Amelia
  EUTENEUER-ROHRER, Ursula
    Henrietta
  FINZI, Graciane
  FONTYN, Jacqueline
  FRANCO, Clare
  FREED, Dorothy Whitson
  GARDNER, Kay
  GIFFORD, Helen Margaret
  GIPPS, Ruth

GRIEBLING, Karen Jean
GRZADZIELOWNA, Eleonora
GUBAIDULINA, Sofia Asgatovna
GUELL, Elizabeth
HALPERN, Stella
HOENDERDOS, Margriet
HOWE, Mary Alberta Bruce
HULL, Kathryn B.
JANKOWSKI, Loretta Patricia
JOLAS, Betsy
KAMINSKY, Laura
KANACH, Sharon E.
KASILAG, Lucrecia R.
KLINKOVA, Zhivka
LA BARBARA, Joan
LARSEN, Elizabeth Brown
LAUBER, Anne Marianne
LAUER, Elizabeth
LAUFER, Beatrice
LE SIEGE, Annette
LEBARON, Anne
LEE, Hope Anne Keng-Wei
LEGINSKA, Ethel
LEIBOW, Ruth Irene
LEJET, Edith
LELEU, Jeanne
LUCKMAN, Phyllis
LUNA DE ESPAILLAT, Margarita
LUTYENS, Elisabeth
McKAY, Frances Thompson
MARBE, Myriam
MAREZ-OYENS, Tera de
MAZOUROVA, Jarmila
MEACHEM, Margaret McKeen
  Ramsey
MERTENS, Dolores
METALLIDI, Zhanneta Lazarevna
MIAGI, Ester Kustovna
MIRON, Tsipora
MUNGER, Shirley
MUSGRAVE, Thea
NEWLIN, Dika
NIEDERBERGER, Maria A.
OLIVEROS, Pauline
PAGH-PAAN, Younghi
PATTERSON, Andra
PERETZ-LEVY, Liora
PERRY, Julia Amanda
PHILLIPS, Donna
PIERCE, Sarah Anderson
POLIN, Claire
PROCACCINI, Teresa
RAN, Shulamit
ROGERS, Patsy
RUGELES, Ana Mercedes de
RUSCHE, Marjorie Maxine
SANFILIPPO, Margherita Marie
SATOH, Kimi
SCHERCHEN, Tona
SCHIEVE, Catherine
SEMEGEN, Daria
SHAFFER, Jeanne Ellison
SILVER, Sheila Jane
SIMONS, Netty
SNYDER, Amy
SOENSTEVOLD, Maj
SOUTHAM, Ann
STANLEY, Helen Camille
STEINER, Gitta Hana
TAILLEFERRE, Germaine
TAL, Ya'ara
TASHJIAN, B. Charmian
TATE, Phyllis
TAUTU, Cornelia
TERZIAN, Alicia
THOME, Diane
TOWER, Joan
TRIMBLE, Joan
ULEHLA, Ludmila
USHER, Julia
USTVOLSKAYA, Galina Ivanovna

VAN APPLEDORN, Mary Jeanne
VAN DE VATE, Nancy Hayes
VAZQUEZ, Alida
VIERK, Lois
VIGNERON-RAMAKERS, Christiane-
    Josée
VOLKART, Hazel
VON GUNDEN, Heidi
VYNER, Mary Bainbridge
WEAVER, Carol Ann
WENDELBURG, Norma Ruth
WHITLOCK, E. Florence
WIENIAWSKA, Irene Regine
WILL, Madeleine
WITKIN, Beatrice
WYLIE, Ruth Shaw
ZAIDEL-RUDOLPH, Jeanne
ZECHLIN, Ruth
ZIFFRIN, Marilyn Jane

EUPHONIUM
20th Century A.D.
BLISS, Marilyn S.
TASHJIAN, B. Charmian

FLAGEOLET
20th Century A.D.
BRANDMAN, Margaret Susan
TACK, Annie

FLUTE
18th Century A.D.
AHLEFELDT, Marie Theresia,
    Countess
ANNA AMALIA, Duchess of Saxe-
    Weimar
ANNA AMALIA, Princess of Prussia
BARTHELEMON, Cécilia Maria
BON, Anna
VALENTINE, Ann
19th Century A.D.
BAU, Elise
BLANGINI, Mlle.
CHAMBERLAYNE, Edith A.
CRETI, Marianna de Rocchis
CZICZKA, Angela
FARRENC, Louise
GRANDVAL, Marie Felicie Clemence
    de Reiset, Vicomtesse de
LE CLERE, Victoire
LEONARDO, Luisa
POLAK, Nina
RICOTTI, Onestina
SZYMANOWSKA, Maria Agata
VIARDOT-GARCIA, Pauline Michelle
    Ferdinande
WICKINS, Florence
WINTZER, Elisabeth
20th Century A.D.
ABE, Kyoko
ACCART, Eveline
AGABALIAN, Lidia Semyenovna
AGUDELO MURGUIA, Graciela
AHRENS, Peg
AINSCOUGH, Juliana Mary
AKSYANTSEVA, Ninel Moiseyevna
ALCALAY, Luna
ALEXANDRA, Liana
ALLEN, Judith Shatin
ALLIK, Kristi
ALOTIN, Yardena
ALSTED, Birgitte
ALT, Hansi
ALTER, Martha
ANDERSON, Avril
ANDERSON, Beth
ANDERSON, Julia McKinley
ANDERSON, Olive Jennie Paxton
ANDERSON-WUENSCH, Jean Mary
ANDREYEVA, Elena Fedorovna
ANTHONY, Gina

ARCHER, Violet Balestreri
ARMER, Elinor Florence
ARRIEU, Claude
AUSTIN, Dorothea
BAADER-NOBS, Heidi
BACEWICZ, Grazyna
BACKES, Lotte
BADIAN, Maya
BAIL, Grace Shattuck
BAILLY, Colette
BAKKE, Ruth
BANCER, Teresa Barbara
BARADAPRANA, Pravrajika
BARAT, Eliane
BARBOSA, Cacilda Campos Borges
BARKLUND, Irma L.
BARNEY, Nancy
BARON SUPERVIELLE, Susana
BARRETT-THOMAS, N.
BAUER, Marion Eugenie
BAULD, Alison
BEACH, Amy Marcy
BEAT, Janet Eveline
BEATH, Betty
BECLARD D'HARCOURT,
    Marguerite
BEECROFT, Norma Marian
BEEKHUIS, Hanna
BEESON, Elizabeth Ruth
BEHREND, Jeanne
BELL, Lucille Anderson
BENARY, Barbara
BERCKMAN, Evelyn
BERGE, Irenee
BERTRAND, Ginette
BEYER, Johanna Magdalena
BIENVENU, Lily
BINET, Jocelyne
BLISS, Marilyn S.
BLOOD, Esta Damesek
BLOOM, Shirley
BOBROW, Sanchie
BOFILL, Anna
BOLZ, Harriet
BOND, Victoria Ellen
BOONE, Clara Lyle
BORROFF, Edith
BOSMANS, Henriette Hilda
BOTTELIER, Ina
BOUCHARD, Linda L.
BOULANGER, Lili Juliette Marie Olga
BOYD, Anne Elizabeth
BRACQUEMOND, Marthe Henriod
BRANDMAN, Margaret Susan
BRANNING, Grace Bell
BRANSCOMBE, Gena
BREMER, Marrie Petronella
BRENET, Thérèse
BRICE, Jean Anne
BRIGHT, Ann
BRIGHT, Dora Estella
BRINK-POTHUIS, Annie van den
BRITAIN, Radie
BROCKMAN, Jane E.
BROOK, Gwendolyn Giffen
BROUK, Joanna
BROWN, Elizabeth Bouldin
BROWN, Elizabeth van Ness
BRUSH, Ruth Damaris
BRUZDOWICZ, Joanna
BUCZEK, Barbara Kazimiera
BURKE, Loretto
BURSTON, Maggie
BUTLER, Patricia Magahay
CABRERA, Silvia Maria Pires
CALLAWAY, Ann
CARL, Tommie Ewert
CARMEN MARINA
CARVALHO, Dinora de
CECCONI-BATES, Augusta
CHAMPION, Stephanie

CHANCE, Nancy Laird
CHARLES, S. Robin
CHAVES, Mary Elizabeth
CIOBANU, Maia
CLOSTRE, Adrienne
COATES, Gloria Kannenberg
COLACO OSORIO-SWAAB, Reine
COLERIDGE-TAYLOR, Avril
    Gwendolen
COME, Tilde
COONEY, Cheryl Lee
CORNING, Karen Andree
CORY, Eleanor
COULOMBE SAINT-MARCOUX,
    Micheline
COULTHARD, Jean
COWLES, Darleen
COX, Alison Mary
CRAWFORD SEEGER, Ruth
CRAWFORD, Dawn Constance
CRAWFORD, Dorothy Lamb
DANEAU, Suzanne
DANFORTH, Frances A.
DANIELS, Mabel Wheeler
DAVIS, Eleanor Maud
DE BIASE BIDART, Lycia
DE FREITAS, Elvira Manuela
    Fernandez
DEDIEU-PETERS, Madeleine
DELAHAYE, Cecile
DEMARQUEZ, Suzanne
DEMBO, Royce
DESPORTES, Yvonne Berthe Melitta
DIAKVNISHVILI, Mzisavar
    Zakharevna
DIAMOND, Arline
DIANDA, Hilda
DIEMER, Emma Lou
DILLON, Fannie Charles
DINESCU, Violeta
DOBBINS, Lori
DOBSON, Elaine
DONCEANU, Felicia
DOROW, Dorothy
DREYFUS, Francis Kay
DRING, Madeleine
DUDLEY, Marjorie Eastwood
DUSHKIN, Dorothy Smith
DYCHKO, Lesya Vasilevna
ECKHARDT-GRAMATTE, Sophie-
    Carmen
EFREIN, Laurie
EICHENWALD, Sylvia
ELIAS, Graciela Morales de
ERDING, Susanne
ESCOT, Pozzi
EVEN-OR, Mary
EVERETT-SALICCO, Betty Lou
FAIRLIE, Margaret C.
FALCINELLI, Rolande
FAUTCH, Sister Magdalen
FINE, Vivian
FISHER, Katherine Danforth
FISHMAN, Marian
FLEITES, Virginia
FORMAN, Joanne
FOWLER, Jennifer Joan
FRASIER, Jane
FREED, Dorothy Whitson
FRITTER, Genevieve Davisson
FRITZ, Sherilyn Gail
GABRYS, Ewa Lucja Maria
GABUS, Monique
GARDINER, Mary Elizabeth
GARDNER, Kay
GARTENLAUB, Odette
GEBUHR, Ann K.
GEORGE, Lila-Gene
GIDEON, Miriam
GIFFORD, Helen Margaret
GILBERT, Janet Monteith

GITECK, Janice
GLASER, Victoria Merrylees
GLATZ, Helen Sinclair
GLAZIER, Beverly
GOLOVINA, Olga Akimovna
GONTARENKO, Galina Nikolayevna
GOOLKASIAN-RAHBEE, Dianne
  Zabelle
GOULD, Elizabeth Davies
GRAHAM, Janet Christine
GRAY, Victoria Winifred
GREENE, Margo Lynn
GREGORI, Nininha
GRIEBLING, Karen Jean
GRIGSBY, Beverly
GROSSMAN, Deena
GUBITOSI, Emilia
GUMMER, Phyllis Mary
GVAZAVA, Tamara Davidovna
GYRING, Elizabeth
HAHN, Sandra Lea
HALL, Pauline
HARA, Kazuko (1)
HARRIS, Ruth Berman
HAWLEY, Carolyn Jean
HAYAKAWA, Kazuko
HAYS, Doris Ernestine
HECHLER, Ilse
HEINRICH, Adel Verna
HENDERSON, Moya
HERBISON, Jeraldine Saunders
HIER, Ethel Glen
HILDERLEY, Jeriann G.
HINLOPEN, Francina
HOENDERDOS, Margriet
HOOVER, Katherine
HOVDA, Eleanor
HSU, Wen-Ying
HUEGEL, Margrit
HUGHES, Sister Martina
HYDE, Miriam Beatrice
HYSON, Winifred Prince
INWOOD, Mary Ruth Brink Berger
ISZKOWSKA, Zofia
JACOB, Elizabeth Marie
JAMES, Dorothy E.
JANKOWSKI, Loretta Patricia
JIRACKOVA, Marta
JOCHSBERGER, Tzipora H.
JOLAS, Betsy
JONES, Catherine
JONES, Sister Ida
KABAT, Julie Phyllis
KAHMANN, Chesley
KAMINSKY, Laura
KANACH, Sharon E.
KAPP, Corinne
KASILAG, Lucrecia R.
KATS-CHERNIN, Elena
KEEFER, Euphrosyne
KELLER, Ginette
KERN, Frida
KESSICK, Mariaena
KIRKWOOD, Antoinette
KISCH, Eve
KITAZUME, Yayoi
KLINKOVA, Zhivka
KNOBLOCHOVA, Antonie
KOELLING, Eloise
KOLB, Barbara
KOLODUB, Zhanna Efimovna
KONISHI, Nagako
KOSSE, Roberta
KRZANOWSKA, Grazyna
KUBO, Mayako
KUKUCK, Felicitas
KUZMYCH, Christina
LACHARTRE, Nicole Marie
LACHOWSKA, Stefania
LADEN, Bernice F.
LAITMAN, Lori

LANG, Rosemary Rita
LARSEN, Elizabeth Brown
LARUELLE, Jeanne-Marie
LATHROP, Gayle Posselt
LAUBER, Anne Marianne
LAUER, Elizabeth
LAUFER, Beatrice
LAZAR, Ella
LE SIEGE, Annette
LEACH, Mary Jane
LEBARON, Anne
LEBENBOM, Elaine F.
LEE, Hope Anne Keng-Wei
LEE, Hwaeja Yoo
LEECH, Renee
LEJEUNE-BONNIER, Eliane
LEPEUT-LEVINE, Jeannine
LEPLAE, Claire
LEVIN, Rami Yona
LEVITSKAYA, Viktoria Sergeyevna
LIDGI-HERMAN, Sofia
LINNEMANN, Maria Catharina
LOOTS, Joyce Mary Ann
LOPEZ ROVIROSA, Maria Isabel
LORENZ, Ellen Jane
LOUDOVA, Ivana
LOUIE, Alexina Diane
LOWENSTEIN, Gunilla Marike
LU, Yen
LUCAS, Mary Anderson
LUCKMAN, Phyllis
LUFF, Enid
LUND, Gudrun
LUTHER, Mary
LUTYENS, Elisabeth
LUTYENS, Sally
MACAULAY, Janice Michel
MACKIE, Shirley M.
MacKENNA, Carmela
McINTOSH, Diana
McKAY, Frances Thompson
McKENZIE, Sandra
McLAUGHLIN, Marian
McLEOD, Jennifer Helen
McLIN, Lena
McTEE, Cindy Karen
MAGEAU, Mary Jane
MALMLOEF-FORSSLING, Carin
MAMLOK, Ursula
MARBE, Myriam
MARCUS, Bunita
MAREZ-OYENS, Tera de
MARKOV, Katherine Lee
MARTIN, Delores J.
MARTINEZ, Odaline de la
MARTINS, Maria de Lourdes
MATUSZCZAK, Bernadetta
MAXWELL, Jacqueline Perkinson
MAZOUROVA, Jarmila
MEKEEL, Joyce
MINEO, Antoinette
MITCHELL, Janice Misurell
MIYAKE, Haruna
MIZUNO, Shuko
MOON, Chloe Elizabeth
MOORE, Undine Smith
MORETTO, Nelly
MRACEK, Ann Michelle
MURAO, Sachie
MUSGRAVE, Thea
NAITO, Akemi
NAZAROVA, Tatiana Borisovna
NEMTEANU-ROTARU, Doina
NIEWIADOMSKA, Barbara
NIKOLAYEVA, Tatiana Petrovna
NOBLE, Ann
NOHE, Beverly
NORUP, Helle Merete
NOVA SONDAG, Jacqueline
OCHSE, Orpha Caroline
OFFICER, Bronwyn Lee

O'LEARY, Jane Strong
OLIVE, Vivienne
OLIVEROS, Pauline
ORENSTEIN, Joyce Ellin
OWENS, Rochelle
OWENS, Susan Elizabeth
PACK, Beulah Frances
PAGH-PAAN, Younghi
PALMER, Lynne Wainwright
PARKER, Alice
PATERSON, Wilma
PAYNE, Maggi
PENTLAND, Barbara Lally
PERETZ-LEVY, Liora
PERKIN, Helen
PERRY, Zenobia Powell
PHILIBA, Nicole
PHILIPPART, Renée
PHILLIPS, Bryony
PIECHOWSKA, Alina
PIERCE, Sarah Anderson
PIETSCH, Edna Frieda
PIRES DOS REIS, Hilda
PIZER, Elizabeth Faw Hayden
PLONSEY, Jennifer
POLIN, Claire
POOL, Jeannie Gayle
POSTON, Elizabeth
PRADELL, Leila
PRAVOSSUDOVITCH, Natalja
  Michajlovna
PREOBRAJENSKA, Vera Nicolaevna
PRICE, Beryl
PRICE, Florence Beatrice
PROCACCINI, Teresa
PSTROKONSKA-NAVRATIL,
  Grazyna Hanna
PTASZYNSKA, Marta
RADEKE, Winifred
RAIGORODSKY, Leda Natalia
  Heimsath
RAINIER, Priaulx
RAMM, Valentina Iosifovna
RANTA-SHIDA, Shoko
RAPOPORT, Eda
REMER, Jan
RENIE, Henriette
RESPIGHI, Elsa
REYNOLDS, Erma Grey Hogue
RICHARDSON, Enid Dorothy
RICHER, Jeannine
RICHTER, Marga
RICKARD, Sylvia
RILEY, Ann Marion
RILEY, Myrtis F.
ROBERT, Lucie
ROBERTSON, Donna Lou Nagey
ROBLES, Marisa
ROCHAT, Andree
ROCHEROLLE, Eugenie Katherine
RODRIGUE, Nicole
RODRIGUEZ BELLA, Catalina
ROE, Eileen Betty
ROESGEN-CHAMPION, Marguerite
  Sara
ROFE, Esther
ROGER, Denise
ROGERS, Ethel Tench
ROGERS, Sharon Elery
ROHDE, Q'Adrianne
ROSSO, Carol L.
ROWAN, Barbara
RUBIN, Anna Ita
RUEFF, Jeanine
RUFF-STOEHR, Herta Maria Klara
RUSCHE, Marjorie Maxine
SAARIAHO, Kaija
SAINT JOHN, Kathleen Louise
SAITO-NODA, Eva
SALQUIN, Hedy
SAMSON, Valerie Brooks

SAMTER, Alice
SAMUEL, Rhian
SATOH, Kimi
SAUTER, Maya
SCHERCHEN, Tona
SCHIEVE, Catherine
SCHMITZ-GOHR, Else
SCHONTHAL, Ruth E.
SCHORR-WEILER, Eva
SCHWARTZ, Julie
SEARCH, Sara Opal
SEVERY, Violet Cavell
SEWALL, Maud Gilchrist
SHAW, Alice Marion
SHEPARD, Jean Ellen
SHEPPARD, Suzanne
SHERMAN, Kim Daryl
SHREVE, Susan Ellen
SIKORA, Elzbieta
SILSBEE, Ann L.
SILVERMAN, Faye-Ellen
SIMONS, Netty
SIMPSON, Mary Jean
SINGER, Jeanne
SISTEK-DJORDJEVIC, Mirjana
SLIANOVA-MIZANDARI, Dagmara
    Levanovna
SMITH, Julia Frances
SMITH, Margit
SMITH, Sharon
SNIZKOVA-SKRHOVA, Jitka
SOLOMON, Joyce Elaine
SOUBLETTE, Sylvia
SOULAGE, Marcelle Fanny Henriette
SOUTHAM, Ann
SPAIN-DUNK, Susan
SPENCER, Williametta
STEELE, Lynn
STEPHEN, Roberta Mae
STREATFIELD, Valma June
STRUTT, Dorothy
SUCHY, Gregoria Karides
SUGAI, Esther
SUH, Kyung-Sun
SULPIZI, Mira
SUTHERLAND, Margaret
SWAIN, Freda Mary
SWISHER, Gloria Agnes Wilson
SYNOWIEC, Ewa
SZAJNA-LEWANDOWSKA, Jadwiga
    Helena
SZEKELY, Katalin
TACK, Annie
TAILLEFERRE, Germaine
TAKAMI, Toyoko
TALMA, Louise
TANNER, Hilda
TATTON, Madeleine
TAUTU, Cornelia
TELFER, Nancy Ellen
TEMPLAR, Joan
THEMMEN, Ivana Marburger
THOMAS, Karen P.
THOME, Diane
THOMPSON, Caroline Lorraine
THOMSEN, Geraldine
THORKELSDOTTIR, Mist Barbara
TOLKOWSKY, Denise
TOWER, Joan
ULEHLA, Ludmila
USHER, Julia
USTVOLSKAYA, Galina Ivanovna
UYEDA, Leslie
UYTTENHOVE, Yolande
VAN DER MARK, Maria
VAN EPEN-DE GROOT, Else Antonia
VAN OHLEN, Deborah
VELLERE, Lucie Weiler
VERHAALEN, Sister Marion
VIERK, Lois
VISCONTI, Leila

WALKER, Gwyneth van Anden
WALLACH, Joelle
WARDE, Ann Maury
WARING, Kate
WARNE, Katharine Mulky
WEGENER-FRENSEL, Emmy Heil
WEIGL, Vally
WEISSBERG, Julia Lazerevna
WELANDER, Svea Goeta
WENDELBURG, Norma Ruth
WHITEHEAD, Gillian
WHITTLE, Chris Mary-Francine
WIENIAWSKA, Irene Regine
WILBRANDT, Susan
WILDSCHUT, Clara
WOOD, Ruzena Alenka Valda
WYLIE, Ruth Shaw
YOUNG, Gayle
ZAIDEL-RUDOLPH, Jeanne
ZAIMONT, Judith Lang
ZAKRZEWSKA-NIKIPORCZYK,
    Barbara Maria
ZALLMAN, Arlene
ZIELINSKA, Lidia
Century unknown
McDOWALL, Cecilia

FLUTE AND HARPSICHORD
20th Century A.D.
CHRETIEN-GENARO, Hedwige
DIEMER, Emma Lou
HYDE, Miriam Beatrice
INWOOD, Mary Ruth Brink Berger
POST, Jennifer
SAITO-NODA, Eva
SAMTER, Alice
SANZ, Rocio
SCHORR-WEILER, Eva
SCLIAR, Esther
SHLONSKY, Verdina
SNIZKOVA-SKRHOVA, Jitka
UYTTENHOVE, Yolande
VISCONTI, Leila
WALLACH, Joelle
WARING, Kate
ZECHLIN, Ruth

FLUTE AND ORCHESTRA OR STRINGS
18th Century A.D.
WILHELMINA, Sophie Friederike,
    Princess of Prussia
20th Century A.D.
AKSYANTSEVA, Ninel Moiseyevna
ARRIEU, Claude
BARNEKOW, Deborah
BARRATT, Carol Ann
BAUER, Marion Eugenie
BEECROFT, Norma Marian
BOSMANS, Henriette Hilda
BRIGHT, Dora Estella
CHAMINADE, Cécile Louise
    Stephanie
CLARK, Mary Elizabeth
COLIN, Jeanne
DANIELS, Mabel Wheeler
DIEMER, Emma Lou
DOBSON, Elaine
EIRIKSDOTTIR, Karolina
FIRSOVA, Elena
GARTENLAUB, Odette
GLANVILLE-HICKS, Peggy
HOOVER, Katherine
JACKSON, Barbara May
LEJET, Edith
LOUDOVA, Ivana
LUCAS, Mary Anderson
MARI, Pierrette
METALLIDI, Zhanneta Lazarevna
MOON, Chloe Elizabeth
MOSZUMANSKA-NAZAR, Krystyna
McCOLLIN, Frances

OERBECK, Anne-Marie
OLIVE, Vivienne
PLONSEY, Jennifer
POLIN, Claire
RADEKE, Winifred
ROBERT, Lucie
SMITH, Joan Templar
SNIZKOVA-SKRHOVA, Jitka
SWISHER, Gloria Agnes Wilson
SZAJNA-LEWANDOWSKA, Jadwiga
    Helena
TRIPP, Ruth
URNER, Catherine Murphy
VITO-DELVAUX, Berthe di
VON ZIERITZ, Grete
VORLOVA, Slavka
WOODRUFF, Edith S.
ZECHLIN, Ruth

FLUTE AND PIANO
18th Century A.D.
HUNTER, Henrietta Elizabeth
STECHER, Marianne
19th Century A.D.
BLAHETKA, Marie Leopoldina
CZICZKA, Angela
FARRENC, Louise
GRANDVAL, Marie Felicie Clemence
    de Reiset, Vicomtesse de
LASZLO, Anna von
SZYMANOWSKA, Maria Agata
20th Century A.D.
ABORN, Lora
ALLIK, Kristi
ALOTIN, Yardena
ANDERSON, Ruth
ANSINK, Caroline
ARRIEU, Claude
BALLANDS, Etta
BARBILLON, Jeanne
BARKLUND, Irma L.
BARNETT, Carol Edith
BARRELL, Joyce Howard
BATCHELOR, Phyllis
BECLARD D'HARCOURT,
    Marguerite
BEEKHUIS, Hanna
BELL, Lucille Anderson
BIENVENU, Lily
BLIESENER, Ada Elizabeth
    Michelman
BOUCHARD, Linda L.
BOULANGER, Lili Juliette Marie Olga
BOYD, Anne Elizabeth
BRANDMAN, Margaret Susan
BRICE, Jean Anne
BRIGHT, Ann
BRIGHT, Dora Estella
BROGUE, Roslyn Clara
BRUSH, Ruth Damaris
CAMPOS ARAUJO DE, Joaquina
CAPDEVILA I GAYA, Merce
CARVALHO, Dinora de
CHAPIRO, Fania
CHAVES, Mary Elizabeth
CHRETIEN-GENARO, Hedwige
CIOBANU, Maia
COLACO OSORIO-SWAAB, Reine
COLERIDGE-TAYLOR, Avril
    Gwendolen
COME, Tilde
COONEY, Cheryl Lee
COULOMBE SAINT-MARCOUX,
    Micheline
COULTHARD, Jean
DE BIASE BIDART, Lycia
DEMARQUEZ, Suzanne
DEMBO, Royce
DIAKVNISHVILI, Mzisavar
    Zakharevna
DIEMER, Emma Lou

DREYFUS, Francis Kay
DRING, Madeleine
DUSHKIN, Dorothy Smith
ECKHARDT-GRAMATTE, Sophie-
  Carmen
EGGAR, Katharine
ELKOSHI, Rivka
FISHER, Katherine Danforth
FLEITES, Virginia
FONTYN, Jacqueline
FRANCK, Philippine
FRITTER, Genevieve Davisson
GARDNER, Kay
GARDNER, Mildred Alvine
GENTILE, Ada
GEORGE, Lila-Gene
GHANDAR, Ann
GIDEON, Miriam
GIFFORD, Helen Margaret
GILLICK, Emelyn Mildred Samuels
GINDLER, Kathe-Lotte
GIPPS, Ruth
GOERSCH, Ursula Margitta
GOLOVINA, Olga Akimovna
GONTARENKO, Galina Nikolayevna
GONZAGA, Chiquinha
GOULD, Elizabeth Davies
GRIEBLING, Karen Jean
GRZADZIELOWNA, Eleonora
GUBAIDULINA, Sofia Asgatovna
GUMMER, Phyllis Mary
HANIM, Tankuri Faize
HAHN, Sandra Lea
HANNIKAINEN, Ann-Elise
HARRISON, Pamela
HARVEY, Eva Noel
HEDOUX, Yvonne
HELLER-REICHENBACH, Barbara
HOLLAND, Dulcie Sybil
HOOVER, Katherine
HOWE, Mary Alberta Bruce
HSU, Wen-Ying
HUEGEL, Margrit
HYDE, Miriam Beatrice
ISMAGILOVA, Leila Zagirovna
ISZKOWSKA, Zofia
IVEY, Jean Eichelberger
JAMES, Dorothy E.
JOLAS, Betsy
KAZANDJIAN, Sirvart
KELLER, Ginette
KERN, Frida
KESSICK, Marlaena
KESSLER, Minuetta Schumiatcher
KIRKWOOD, Antoinette
KNIGHT, Judyth
KOLB, Barbara
KOLODUB, Zhanna Efimovna
KUBO, Mayako
KUKUCK, Felicitas
KULIEVA, Farida Tairovna
LAGO
LALAUNI, Lila
LARSEN, Elizabeth Brown
LAUBER, Anne Marianne
LAVRANS, Elayne
LEAHY, Mary Weldon
LEIBOW, Ruth Irene
LEONCHIK, Svetlana Gavrilovna
LEVITSKAYA, Viktoria Sergeyevna
LINDEMAN, Anna Severine
LOOTS, Joyce Mary Ann
LUND, Signe
LUTYENS, Elisabeth
LYELL, Margaret
MACKIE, Shirley M.
McINTOSH, Diana
MACONCHY, Elizabeth
MARCUS, Ada Belle Gross
MARI, Pierrette
MARSHALL, Kye

MARTINEZ, Odaline de la
MASSON, Carol Foster
MAZOUROVA, Jarmila
MEL-BONIS
MELL, Gertrud Maria
METALLIDI, Zhanneta Lazarevna
MILENKOVIC, Jelena
MOON, Chloe Elizabeth
MOORE, Mary Carr
MOSUSOVA, Nadezda
MOSZUMANSKA-NAZAR, Krystyna
NAIKHOVICH-LOMAKINA, Fania
  Filippovna
NIEWIADOMSKA, Barbara
NORDENSTROM, Gladys Mercedes
NUNLIST, Juli
ODAGESCU, Irina
OERBECK, Anne-Marie
O'LEARY, Jane Strong
OMER, Helene
OSETROVA-YAKOVLIEVA, Nina
  Alexandrovna
OSIANDER, Irene
PATERSON, Wilma
PAULL, Barberi
PEREIRA DA SILVA, Adelaide
PERISSAS, Madeleine
PETRA-BASACOPOL, Carmen
PEY CASADO, Diana
PHILIBA, Nicole
PIECHOWSKA, Alina
PIERCE, Alexandra
PIETSCH, Edna Frieda
PIRES DE CAMPOS, Lina
POLIN, Claire
PROCACCINI, Teresa
RAIGORODSKY, Leda Natalia
  Heimsath
RHEINGOLD, Lauma Yanovna
RICHARDSON, Enid Dorothy
ROBERT, Lucie
ROBITASHVILI, Lia Georgievna
ROCHAT, Andree
ROE, Eileen Betty
ROESGEN-CHAMPION, Marguerite
  Sara
ROFE, Esther
ROGER, Denise
ROHDE, Q'Adrianne
ROOTH, Anna-Greta
ROSAS FERNANDES, Maria Helena
ROSSER, Annetta Hamilton
RUFF-STOEHR, Herta Maria Klara
RUSCHE, Marjorie Maxine
SAKALLI-LECCA, Alexandra
SALQUIN, Hedy
SAMTER, Alice
SAMUEL, Rhian
SANGUESA, Iris
SCHORR-WEILER, Eva
SEMEGEN, Daria
SETTI, Kilza
SHELTON, Margaret Meier
SHEPARD, Jean Ellen
SHREVE, Susan Ellen
SIEGRIST, Beatrice
SINGER, Jeanne
SMITH, E.M. Monica
SMITH, Julia Frances
SNIZKOVA-SKRHOVA, Jitka
SOMMER, Silvia
SOUBLETTE, Sylvia
SOULAGE, Marcelle Fanny Henriette
SPENCER, Williametta
STEELE, Lynn
STEINER, Gitta Hana
SWAIN, Freda Mary
SZAJNA-LEWANDOWSKA, Jadwiga
  Helena
TAILLEFERRE, Germaine
TAL, Marjo

THEMMEN, Ivana Marburger
THIEME, Kerstin Anja
THOME, Diane
THORKELSDOTTIR, Mist Barbara
TOLKOWSKY, Denise
TOWER, Joan
TRIPP, Ruth
URNER, Catherine Murphy
UYTTENHOVE, Yolande
VAN DE VATE, Nancy Hayes
VAN DIJCK, Beatrice Madeleine
VAN HAUTE, Anna-Maria
VELLERE, Lucie Weiler
VITO-DELVAUX, Berthe di
WALKER, Gwyneth van Anden
WARNE, Katharine Mulky
WASKO, Christine
WOOD, Ruzena Alenka
  Valda
WYLIE, Ruth Shaw
ZAIMONT, Judith Lang
ZARIPOVA, Naila Gatinovna
ZECHLIN, Ruth
ZIMMERMANN, Margrit

FOLK INSTRUMENTS
16th Century A.D.
  MIRA BAI
19th Century A.D.
  HAAPASALO, Kreeta
20th Century A.D.
  ABEJO, Sister M. Rosalina
  AKHUNDOVA, Shafiga Gulam
    kyzy
  ANDREYEVA, Elena Fedorovna
  ANDREYEVA, M.
  ANNAPURNA, Devi
  ARIMA, Reiko
  AUSTER, Lydia Martinovna
  BEATH, Betty
  BENARY, Barbara
  CAREY, Elena
  CHICHERINA, Sofia Nikolayevna
  DARUWALA, Zarine
  GOKHMAN, Elena Vladimirovna
  JASTRZEBSKA, Anna
  JENNY, Sister Leonore
  KASILAG, Lucrecia R.
  KITAZUME, Yayoi
  KLINKOVA, Zhivka
  KONISHI, Nagako
  KOZAKIEVICH, Anna Abramovna
  LAVIN, Marie Duchesne
  MASSUMOTO, Kikuko
  MUKHAMEDZHANOVA, Mariam
  NIKOLSKAYA, Lyubov Borisovna
  NURPEISSOVA, Dina
  OSETROVA-YAKOVLIEVA, Nina
    Alexandrovna
  OSMANOGLU, Gevheri
  PAKHMUTOVA, Alexandra
    Nikolayevna
  ROZHAVSKAYA, Yudif Grigorevna
  RZAYEVA, Agabadzhi Ishmael kykz
  SAMSUTDINOVA, Magira
  SEPULVEDA, Maria Luisa
  SMITH, Margit

GLASS HARMONICA
20th Century A.D.
  KABAT, Julie Phyllis

GLOCKENSPIEL
20th Century A.D.
  COWLES, Darleen
  FIRSOVA, Elena
  MEACHEM, Margaret McKeen
    Ramsey
  MURRAY, Margaret
  SWAIN, Freda Mary
  VAN OHLEN, Deborah

GONG
20th Century A.D.
DLUGOSZEWSKI, Lucia
HOVDA, Eleanor
MATUSZCZAK, Bernadetta
PHILLIPS, Bryony
PTASZYNSKA, Marta

GUITAR
18th Century A.D.
BERTHE, Mme.
CONTAMINE, Mlle. de
19th Century A.D.
BRAASE, Albertine
CONSTANT, Rosalie de
DORIGNY DENOYERS, Mme.
GABRIEL, Mary Ann Virginia
GENTY, Mlle.
GIULIANI-GIULELMI, Emilia
LIND, Jenny
MOUNSEY, Elizabeth
PRATTEN, Mrs. Robert Sidney
PUGET, Loise
REICHARDT, Louise
20th Century A.D.
AGUDELO MURGUIA, Graciela
ALAIN, Marie Claire
ALEJANDRO-DE LEON, Esther
ALLIK, Kristi
ALSTED, Birgitte
ANDERSON, Avril
ANDERSON, Beth
ANDERSON, Olive Jennie
  Paxton
ANDERSON, Ruth
ANIDO, Maria Luisa
ARCHER, Violet Balestreri
BADIAN, Maya
BAILLY, Colette
BARADAPRANA, Pravrajika
BARKLUND, Irma L.
BARNETT, Carol Edith
BARRELL, Joyce Howard
BAULD, Alison
BEAHM, Jacquelyn Yvette
BEECROFT, Norma Marian
BLOOD, Esta Damesek
BOBROW, Sanchie
BOFILL, Anna
BORRAS I FORNELL, Teresa
BOTTELIER, Ina
BOUCHARD, Linda L.
BOYD, Anne Elizabeth
BOYD, Liona Maria
BRAASE, Sophie
BRENET, Thérèse
BRONDI, Rita Maria
CALCAGNO, Elsa
CARMEN MARINA
CARVALHO, Dinora de
CECCONI-BOTELLA, Monic
CIOBANU, Maia
CODY, Judith
COLTRANE, Alice McLeod
CONRAD, Laurie M.
CORY, Eleanor
COULOMBE SAINT-MARCOUX,
  Micheline
COULTHARD, Jean
CRISWICK, Mary
DA SILVA, Adelaide
DE FREITAS, Elvira Manuela
  Fernandez
DIEMER, Emma Lou
DINESCU, Violeta
ERDING, Susanne
ESCOT, Pozzi
EVEN-OR, Mary
FAUTCH, Sister Magdalen
FERRARI, Gabriella
FINZI, Graciane

FLEISCHER-DOLGOPOLSKY,
  Tsipporah
FORMAN, Joanne
FRITZ, Sherilyn Gail
GABUS, Monique
GAMBARINI, Costanza
GARDNER, Kay
GARTENLAUB, Odette
GEYER, Marianne
GIFFORD, Helen Margaret
GILENO, Jean Anthony
GITECK, Janice
GODLA, Mary Ann
GRAHAM, Janet Christine
GRIGSBY, Beverly
GUDAUSKAS, Giedra
GURAIEB KURI, Rosa
HARA, Kazuko (1)
HAWLEY, Carolyn Jean
HO, Wai On
HOOVER, Katherine
HOVDA, Eleanor
IRMAN-ALLEMANN, Regina
JEPPSSON, Kerstin Maria
KANACH, Sharon E.
KAZANDJIAN, Sirvart
KOLB, Barbara
KOPTAGEL, Yuksel
KORNILOVA, Tatiana Dmitrevna
KRZANOWSKA, Grazyna
KUBO, Mayako
KURIMOTO, Yoko
LACHARTRE, Nicole Marie
LAM MAN YEE, Violet
LARSEN, Elizabeth Brown
LATHROP, Gayle Posselt
LAUBER, Anne Marianne
LAVIN, Marie Duchesne
LAYMAN, Pamela
LEJET, Edith
LEJEUNE-BONNIER, Eliane
LEONE, Mae G.
LEVIN, Rami Yona
LEWIN, Olive
LINNEMANN, Maria Catharina
LITER, Monia
LOMON, Ruth
LUTYENS, Elisabeth
McKENZIE, Sandra
MADRIGUERA RODON, Paquita
MARCUS, Bunita
MAREZ-OYENS, Tera de
MARI, Pierrette
MATVEYEVA, Novella
MAZOUROVA, Jarmila
MENEELY-KYDER, Sarah Suderley
MERTENS, Dolores
MIYAKE, Haruna
MORETTO, Nelly
MORRISON, Julia Maria
MOSCOVITZ, Julianne
MURAKUMO, Ayako
MUSGRAVE, Thea
NAITO, Akemi
NAZAROVA, Tatiana Borisovna
NOWAK, Alison
OBROVSKA, Jana
OLIVEIRA, Jocy de
OLIVEROS, Pauline
OSAWA, Kazuko
PARKER, Alice
PATTERSON, Andra
PAULL, Barberi
PEYROT, Fernande
PHILIBA, Nicole
PIECHOWSKA, Alina
PIRES DOS REIS, Hilda
POLIN, Claire
PRADELL, Leila
PREOBRAJENSKA, Vera Nicolaevna
PRESTI, Ida

PRICE, Deon Nielsen
PROCACCINI, Teresa
RAINIER, Priaulx
RAVINALE, Irma
REHNQVIST, Karin Birgitta
RICHER, Jeannine
RICKARD, Sylvia
ROE, Eileen Betty
ROGATIS, Teresa de
RUFF-STOEHR, Herta Maria Klara
RUSCHE, Marjorie Maxine
SAINT JOHN, Kathleen Louise
SAMTER, Alice
SAMUEL, Rhian
SCHONTHAL, Ruth E.
SEPULVEDA, Maria Luisa
SERRANO REDONNET, Ana
SINDE RAMALLAL, Clara
SINGER, Jeanne
STRUTT, Dorothy
SULPIZI, Mira
SWAIN, Freda Mary
SZEKELY, Katalin
SZOENYI, Erzsebet
TACK, Annie
TANN, Hilary
TATE, Phyllis
THOMPSON, Caroline Lorraine
TOWER, Joan
URRETA, Alicia
VAN EPEN-DE GROOT, Else
  Antonia
VAN HAUTE, Anna-Maria
VAN OHLEN, Deborah
VARGAS, Eva
VERHAALEN, Sister Marion
VIERK, Lois
VIGNERON-RAMAKERS, Christiane-
  Josee
VON ZIERITZ, Grete
VORLOVA, Slavka
WALDO, Elisabeth
WALKER, Gwyneth van
  Anden
WALKER, Louise
WARREN, Betsy
WEAVER, Carol Ann
WHITEHEAD, Gillian
WYLIE, Ruth Shaw
YOUNG, Gayle
ZAIDEL-RUDOLPH, Jeanne
ZIFFRIN, Marilyn Jane
ZIMMERMANN, Margrit
Century unknown
FRACKER, Cora Robins

GUITAR AND ORCHESTRA OR STRINGS
20th Century A.D.
ABEJO, Sister M. Rosalina
BALLOU, Esther Williamson
CALANDRA, Matilde T. de
FRENCH, Tania
GODLA, Mary Ann
LE BORDAYS, Christiane
MARI, Pierrette
OBROVSKA, Jana
RAVINALE, Irma
THEMMEN, Ivana Marburger

HANDBELLS
20th Century A.D.
McCLEARY, Mary Gilkeson
PHILLIPS, Vivian Daphne
ROBERTSON, Donna Lou Nagey
SHORE, Clare

HARMONIUM
19th Century A.D.
BLAHETKA, Marie Leopoldina
FARMER, Emily Bardsley
HAASS, Maria Catharina

KERN, Louise
NORRIS, Mary
RONDONNEAU, Elise
20th Century A.D.
BURCHELL, Henrietta Louise
DOANE, Dorothy
DRING, Madeleine
FRANCHI, Dorothea
HELSTED, Bodil
LEPLAE, Claire
MERTENS, Dolores
NOVA SONDAG, Jacqueline
OLIVEIRA, Jocy de
PATERSON, Wilma

HARP
5th Century A.D.
BRIDGET
12th Century A.D.
HILDEGARDE, Saint
16th Century A.D.
MOLZA, Tarquinia
18th Century A.D.
AGNESI-PINOTTINI, Maria Teresa d'
CAMPBELL, Caroline
CROUCH, Anna Maria
DELAVAL, Mme.
DUMUR, Mme.
MIZANGERE, Marquise de la
MUELLNER, Johanna
MUSIGNY, Mme. de
PIO DI SAVOJA, Isabella D.
TRAVENET, Mme. B. de
19th Century A.D.
ABRAMS, Harriet
BEDINI, Guendalina
BELLANI, Caroline
BERTRAND, Aline
BINFIELD, Hanna R.
BISSET, Elizabeth Anne
BLANC DE FONTBELLE, Cécile
BONNAY, Mlle.
BOTTINI, Marianna, Marchioness
BRESSON, Mlle.
CHAMBERLAYNE, Edith A.
CORRI-DUSSEK, Sofia Giustina
CRETI, Marianna de Rocchis
DEMAR, Thérèse
DUFRESNOY, Mme.
DUSSEK, Olivia
ESCHBORN, Georgine Christine
Maria Anna
FARMER, Emily Bardsley
GENGLIS, Stephanie Felicite,
Countess of Saint-Aubin
GRANDVAL, Marie Felicie Clemence
de Reiset, Vicomtesse de
KRUMPHOLTZ PITTAR, Fanny
KRUMPHOLTZ, Anne-Marie
LANNOY, Clementine-Josephine-
Françoise-Thérèse, Countess
LE CLERE, Victoire
MARA, La
MERELLE, Mlle.
MONTESQUIOU, Odette de
MUNDELLA, Emma
POLLET, Marie Nicole Simonin
RENAUD-D'ALLEN, Mme. de
RONSSECY, Mme. de
ROSALES, Cecilia
WINKEL, Thérèse Emilie Henriette
aus dem
20th Century A.D.
ABE, Kyoko
ACCART, Eveline
AGABALIAN, Lidia Semyenovna
ALEXANDRA, Liana
ALLEN, Judith Shatin
ALLEN, Mimi
ALVES DE SOUSA, Berta Candida
ANDERSON, Avril

ANDERSON, Julia McKinley
ANDERSON-WUENSCH, Jean Mary
ANGELI-CATTINI, A. de
ARCHER, Violet Balestreri
ARRIEU, Claude
BAADER-NOBS, Heidi
BACEWICZ, Grażyna
BACKES, Lotte
BAGANIER, Janine
BALLOU, Esther Williamson
BANCER, Teresa Barbara
BARBER, Gail Guseman
BARBERIS, Mansi
BARBILLON, Jeanne
BARRELL, Joyce Howard
BEAT, Janet Eveline
BEATH, Betty
BECLARD D'HARCOURT,
Marguerite
BEECROFT, Norma Marian
BEEKHUIS, Hanna
BELLAMY, Marian Meredith
BERCKMAN, Evelyn
BERGE, Irenee
BIENVENU, Lily
BLOMFIELD-HOLT, Patricia
BLOOD, Esta Damesek
BOLZ, Harriet
BORRAS I FORNELL, Teresa
BOSCH Y PAGES, Luisa
BOUCHARD, Linda L.
BOYD, Anne Elizabeth
BRANSCOMBE, Gena
BRENET, Thérèse
BRITAIN, Radie
BURSTON, Maggie
CALAME, Genevieve
CALCAGNO, Elsa
CALVO-MANZANO, Maria Rosa
CAMPMANY, Montserrat
CANALES PIZARRO, Marta
CARVALHO, Dinora de
CHALLAN, Annie
CHERTOK, Pearl
COATES, Gloria Kannenberg
COLACO OSORIO-SWAAB, Reine
COLERIDGE-TAYLOR, Avril
Gwendolen
COLIN, Jeanne
COLLINS, Janyce
COLTRANE, Alice McLeod
COOLIDGE, Peggy Stuart
COULOMBE SAINT-MARCOUX,
Micheline
COULTHARD, Jean
DAIGLE, Sister Anne Cécile
DAVIS, Eleanor Maud
DEDIEU-PETERS, Madeleine
DEMARQUEZ, Suzanne
DEMBO, Royce
DENBOW, Stefania Bjoerson
DESPORTES, Yvonne Berthe Melitta
DIAMOND, Arline
DILLON, Fannie Charles
DLUGOSZEWSKI, Lucia
DOBBINS, Lori
DONCEANU, Felicia
DUDLEY, Marjorie Eastwood
ELIAS, Graciela Morales de
ERDELI, Xenia Alexandrovna
ERHART, Dorothy
ERVIN, Karen
FALCINELLI, Rolande
FALLADOVA-SKVOROVA, Anezka
FINE, Vivian
FIRSOVA, Elena
FISHER, Katherine Danforth
FITZGERALD, Sister Florence
Therese
FLACH, Elsa
FONTYN, Jacqueline

FORMAN, Joanne
FRAJT, Ludmila
FRANCHI, Dorothea
GABUS, Monique
GARDNER, Kay
GARR, Wieslawa
GARTENLAUB, Odette
GIFFORD, Helen Margaret
GIURANNA, Elena Barbara
GLANVILLE-HICKS, Peggy
GLATZ, Helen Sinclair
GLICK, Nancy Kay
GOODSMITH, Ruth B.
GOOSSENS, Marie Henriette
GOVEA, Wenonah Milton
GRAMEGLIA-GROSSO, Emma
GRIEBLING, Karen Jean
GROSSMAN, Deena
GRZADZIELOWNA, Eleonora
GUBAIDULINA, Sofia Asgatovna
GUBITOSI, Emilia
GUSTAVSON, Nancy Nicholls
GVAZAVA, Tamara Davidovna
HAHN, Sandra Lea
HALL, Pauline
HANSEN, Renée
HARRIS, Ruth Berman
HINLOPEN, Francina
HOLLAND, Dulcie Sybil
HSU, Wen-Ying
HUGH-JONES, Elaine
HUJSAK, Joy Detenbeck
INGEBOS, Louise-Marie
INGLEFIELD, Ruth Karin
IORDAN, Irina Nikolayevna
JAMET, Marie-Claire
JANKOWSKI, Loretta Patricia
JIRACKOVA, Marta
JOEST, Emma
JOHN, Patricia Spaulding
JOLAS, Betsy
KELLER, Ginette
KELLY, Denise Maria Anne
KELLY, Georgia
KERN, Frida
KETTERING, Eunice Lea
KISTETENYI, Melinda
KOLODUB, Zhanna Efimovna
KONISHI, Nagako
KOSTAKOVA-HERODKOVA, Marie
KREISS, Hulda E.
KUZMYCH, Christina
LACHARTRE, Nicole Marie
LAITMAN, Lori
LAJEUNESSE, Emma, Dame
LANG-BECK, Ivana
LAPEYRE, Therese
LARHANTEC, Marie Annick
LARSEN, Elizabeth Brown
LARUELLE, Jeanne-Marie
LAUBER, Anne Marianne
LE DENTU, Odette
LEAHY, Mary Weldon
LEBARON, Anne
LEE, Hope Anne Keng-Wei
LEJET, Edith
LIDGI-HERMAN, Sofia
LITER, Monia
LOMON, Ruth
LOUDOVA, Ivana
LOUIE, Alexina Diane
LUFF, Enid
LUTHER, Mary
LUTYENS, Elisabeth
LYONN LIEBERMAN, Julie
McGILL, Gwendolen Mary Finlayson
McLAUGHLIN, Marian
MAKAROVA, Nina Vladimorovna
MAMLOCK, Ursula
MANZIARLY, Marcelle de
MAREZ-OYENS, Tera de

MARIC, Ljubica
MARKIEWICZOWNA, Wladyslawa
MARSHALL, Pamela J.
MARTINEZ, Odaline de la
MEGEVAND, Denise
MEKEEL, Joyce
MEL-BONIS
MERRIMAN, Margarita Leonor
MIMET, Anne Marie
MORGAN, Maud
MOSSAFER RIND, Bernice
MUSGRAVE, Thea
NAZAROVA, Tatiana Borisovna
NIEWIADOMSKA, Barbara
NOBLE, Ann
NOVI, Anna Beate
OLIVE, Vivienne
OSAWA, Kazuko
PACK, Beulah Frances
PALMER, Lynne Wainwright
PARKER, Alice
PELEGRI, Maria Teresa
PERETZ-LEVY, Liora
PERRY, Julia Amanda
PHARRIS, Elizabeth
PHILIPPART, Renée
PHILLIPS, Bryony
PIERCE, Alexandra
POLIN, Claire
POSTON, Elizabeth
PTASZYNSKA, Marta
RAIGORODSKY, Leda Natalia
    Heimsath
RAPOPORT, Eda
REICH, Amy
REIFF, Lili
REMER, Jan
RENIE, Henriette
RESPIGHI, Elsa
RICHER, Jeannine
ROBERT, Lucie
ROBINSON, Gertrude Ina
ROBLES, Marisa
ROCHAT, Andrée
RODRIGUE, Nicole
ROESGEN-CHAMPION, Marguerite
    Sara
ROGER, Denise
ROHDE, Q'Adrianne
ROMM, Rosalina Davidovna
SAINT JOHN, Kathleen Louise
SANGUESA, Iris
SCHERCHEN, Tona
SCHONTHAL, Ruth E.
SCHROEDER, Beatrice
SEIBERT, Irma
SEPULVEDA, Maria Luisa
SIMONCELLI-PRINCIPE, Giulia
SIMONS, Netty
SINGER, Jeanne
SMITH, Ladonna Carol
SMYTH, Ethel Mary, Dame
SNIZKOVA-SKRHOVA, Jitka
SOENSTEVOLD, Maj
SOUBLETTE, Sylvia
SOULAGE, Marcelle Fanny Henriette
STOEPPELMANN, Janet
STRICKLAND, Lily Teresa
SUESSE, Dana
SUH, Kyung-Sun
SURIANI, Alberta
SZOENYI, Erzsebet
SZYMANSKA, Iwonka Bogumila
TAILLEFERRE, Germaine
TATE, Phyllis
TAUTU, Cornelia
THOMAS, Marilyn Taft
THOME, Diane
THOMSEN, Geraldine
TRIMBLE, Joan
TURNELL, Margaret Hoberg

UYTTENHOVE, Yolande
VIEU, Jane
VORLOVA, Slavka
WARNE, Katharine Mulky
WARREN, Elinor Remick
WHITE, Claude Porter
WILKINSON, Constance Jane
WILLIAMS, Grace Mary
WILLIAMS, Sioned
YOSHIDA, Kazuko
ZAIMONT, Judith Lang
ZIMMER, Nellie
Century unknown
ACHARD, Marguerite
ROSATI, Elvira

HARP AND ORCHESTRA OR STRINGS
20th Century A.D.
BAGANIER, Janine
CALAME, Genevieve
COOLIDGE, Peggy Stuart
FONTYN, Jacqueline
GARTENLAUB, Odette
GLATZ, Helen Sinclair
LANG-BECK, Ivana
PALMER, Lynne Wainwright
POLIN, Claire
PROCACCINI, Teresa
REIFF, Lili
RENIE, Henriette
ROESGEN-CHAMPION, Marguerite
    Sara
SCHONTHAL, Ruth E.
SUESSE, Dana
TAILLEFERRE, Germaine
VON ZIERITZ, Grete
VORLOVA, Slavka

HARP AND OTHER INSTRUMENTS
19th Century A.D.
BRESSON, Mlle.
CORRI-DUSSEK, Sofia Giustina
CRETI, Marianna de Rocchis
DUFRESNOY, Mme.
FARMER, Emily Bardsley
20th Century A.D.
ALLAN, Esther
ANDERSON-WUENSCH, Jean Mary
BAADER-NOBS, Heidi
BACKES, Lotte
BELLAMY, Marian Meredith
BOUCHARD, Linda L.
BRENET, Thérèse
DE BIASE BIDART, Lycia
FALLADOVA-SKVOROVA, Anezka
FLACH, Elsa
HO, Wai On
KAMINSKY, Laura
KERN, Frida
LEBARON, Anne
LEE, Hope Anne Keng-Wei
LITER, Monia
McGILL, Gwendolen Mary Finlayson
McLAUGHLIN, Marian
MARCUS, Bunita
MEGEVAND, Denise
NAZAROVA, Tatiana Borisovna
OBROVSKA, Jana
OH, Sook Ja
PACK, Beulah Frances
PALMER, Lynne Wainwright
PETRA-BASACOPOL, Carmen
PEYROT, Fernande
PIZER, Elizabeth Faw Hayden
POLIN, Claire
PROCACCINI, Teresa
PTASZYNSKA, Marta
RENIE, Henriette
ROCHAT, Andrée
ROESGEN-CHAMPION, Marguerite
    Sara

SIKORA, Elzbieta
TAL, Marjo
TATE, Phyllis
URNER, Catherine Murphy
VELLERE, Lucie Weiler
VYNER, Mary Bainbridge
WASKO, Christine
Century unknown
ACHARD, Marguerite

HARPSICHORD
17th Century A.D.
ASSANDRA, Catterina
BAPTISTA, Gracia
LA PIERRE, Mme.
MENETOU, Françoise-Charlotte de
    Senneterre
18th Century A.D.
AGNESI-PINOTTINI, Maria Teresa d'
ANNA AMALIA, Duchess of Saxe-
    Weimar
ANNA AMALIA, Princess of Prussia
AUENBRUGG, Marianna von
AURENHAMMER, Josefa Barbara
    von
BARTHELEMON, Cecilia Maria
BARTHELEMON, Mary
BENAULT, Mlle.
BON, Anna
BRILLON DE JOUY, Mme.
CAMATI, Maria
CAMPBELL, Caroline
CHARRIERE, Isabella Agneta
    Elisabeth de
CLEREMBAULT, Mme. de
COSWAY, Maria Cécilia Louise
DE GAMBARINI, Elisabetta
HARDING, Elizabeth
HOFFMANN, Miss J.
JACOBSON, Henrietta
LA GUERRE, Elisabeth-Claude
    Jacquet de
LACHANTERIE, Elisabeth
LOUIS, Mme.
MARIA CHARLOTTE AMALIE,
    Princess of Saxe-Meiningen
MIZANGERE, Marquise de la
MONDONVILLE, Mme. de
PARKER, Mrs.
PHILHARMONICA, Mrs.
POUILLAU, Mlle.
SARRET DE COUSSERGUES, Mlle.
SAVAGE, Jane
SCHAUFF, Marie
SIRMEN, Maddalena Laura di
STECHER, Marianne
TIRINANZI, Nannette
TURNER, Eliza
TURNER, Elizabeth
VALENTINE, Ann
19th Century A.D.
BAUER, Katharine
CANDEILLE, Amelie Julie
CONVERT, Josephine
DUCHAMP, Marie Catharine
FORREST, Margret
LANNOY, Clementine-Josephine-
    Françoise-Thérèse, Countess
ROUSSEAU, Louise
WUIET, Caroline
20th Century A.D.
ABE, Kyoko
ALEXANDRA, Liana
ALTER, Martha
ANDERSON, Beth
ARETZ, Isabel
ARHO, Anneli
ARMER, Elinor Florence
ARRIEU, Claude
BAINBRIDGE, Beryl
BARKIN, Elaine

BARRAINE, Elsa
BARTHEL, Ursula
BEATH, Betty
BECLARD D'HARCOURT,
  Marguerite
BILLINGTON, Elizabeth
BINGHAM, Judith
BIZONY, Celia
BOFILL, Anna
BRENET, Thérèse
BROGUE, Roslyn Clara
BRUZDOWICZ, Joanna
CAMPAGNE, Conny
CARR-BOYD, Ann Kirsten
CECCONI-BATES, Augusta
COULOMBE SAINT-MARCOUX,
  Micheline
CRAWFORD, Dorothy Lamb
DANFORTH, Frances A.
DIEMER, Emma Lou
DINESCU, Violeta
DRING, Madeleine
DUSHKIN, Dorothy Smith
ECKHARDT-GRAMATTE, Sophie-
  Carmen
ELLERMAN, Helen
FALCINELLI, Rolande
FINZI, Graciane
FONTYN, Jacqueline
FRESON, Armande
FRITZ, Sherilyn Gail
GARDNER, Kay
GEBUHR, Ann K.
GIFFORD, Helen Margaret
GLASER, Victoria Merrylees
GLATZ, Helen Sinclair
GOULD, Janetta
GRIMES, Doreen
GUBAIDULINA, Sofia Asgatovna
HAHN, Sandra Lea
HARA, Kazuko (1)
HAWLEY, Carolyn Jean
HEATON, Eloise Klotz
HEDOUX, Yvonne
HEINRICH, Adel Verna
HO, Wai On
HOELSZKY, Adriana
JIRACKOVA, Marta
JOLAS, Betsy
KEEFER, Euphrosyne
KOLB, Barbara
LACHARTRE, Nicole Marie
LANDOWSKA, Wanda
LARUELLE, Jeanne-Marie
LEE, Hope Anne Keng-Wei
LOMON, Ruth
LORENZ, Ellen Jane
LOUDOVA, Ivana
LOVAN, Lydia
LUTYENS, Elisabeth
MACONCHY, Elizabeth
McKENZIE, Sandra
McMILLAN, Ann Endicott
McTEE, Cindy Karen
MAGEAU, Mary Jane
MANZIARLY, Marcelle de
MARBE, Myriam
MAREZ-OYENS, Tera de
MARI, Pierrette
MARTINS, Maria de Lourdes
MASSUMOTO, Kikuko
MEGEVAND, Denise
MOLA, Corradina
MURDOCH, Marjolijn
OBROVSKA, Jana
OLIVEIRA, Jocy de
OLIVEROS, Pauline
OMER, Hélène
OWEN, Blythe
OZAITA, Maria Luisaria Luisa
PENTLAND, Barbara Lally

PEYROT, Fernande
PHILLIPS, Bryony
PIECHOWSKA, Alina
PIERCE, Sarah Anderson
POLIN, Claire
POSTON, Elizabeth
PRICE, Deon Nielsen
PTASZYNSKA, Marta
RAINIER, Priaulx
RAN, Shulamit
RAVINALE, Irma
RED, Virginia Stroh
ROBERTS, Gertrud Hermine
  Kuenzel
ROBERTSON, Donna Lou Nagey
ROE, Eileen Betty
ROESGEN-CHAMPION, Marguerite
  Sara
ROGER, Denise
ROGET, Henriette
ROMERO BARBOSA, Elena
RUEFF, Jeanine
SAMTER, Alice
SANDRESKY, Margaret Vardell
SCHMIDT, Mia
SCHONTHAL, Ruth E.
SCHORR-WEILER, Eva
SCHWERDTFEGER, E. Anne
SEVERY, Violet Cavell
SILSBEE, Ann L.
SINGER, Jeanne
SMELTZER, Susan Mary
SOUTHAM, Ann
SUTHERLAND, Margaret
TARLOW, Karen Anne
THEMMEN, Ivana Marburger
VAN DE VATE, Nancy Hayes
VAN OHLEN, Deborah
VIGNERON-RAMAKERS, Christiane-
  Josee
VISCONTI, Leila
VOLKART-SCHLAGER, Kaethe
VON GUNDEN, Heidi
VON PECHY, Valerie
VORLOVA, Slavka
WALLACH, Joelle
WEIR, Judith
WEISSBERG, Julia Lazerevna
WHITEHEAD, Gillian
WHITTLE, Chris Mary-Francine
WIELE, Aimée van der
WILKINS, Margaret Lucy
WILL, Madeleine
WILLIAMS, Grace Mary
WILSON, Jean Dolores
WYLIE, Ruth Shaw
ZECHLIN, Ruth
ZIFFRIN, Marilyn Jane
ZWILICH, Ellen Taaffe
Century unknown
BAZIN, Mlle.
CERUTTI, Paolina
VON HAGEN, Elizabeth

**HARPSICHORD AND ORCHESTRA OR
STRINGS**
18th Century A.D.
GUEST, Jeanne Marie
19th Century A.D.
CANDEILLE, Amelie Julie
PARKE, Maria Hester
20th Century A.D.
BROGUE, Roslyn Clara
DIEMER, Emma Lou
HAYS, Doris Ernestine
ROBERTS, Gertrud Hermine
  Kuenzel
ROESGEN-CHAMPION, Marguerite
  Sara
SCHERCHEN, Tona
ZECHLIN, Ruth

HORN
18th Century A.D.
ANNA AMALIA, Duchess of Saxe-
  Weimar
CECILE, Jeanne
DE GAMBARINI, Elisabetta
19th Century A.D.
CANDEILLE, Amelie Julie
DESHAYES, Marie
DUFRESNOY, Mme.
LA HYE, Louise Genevieve
POLAK, Nina
SZYMANOWSKA, Maria Agata
20th Century A.D.
AARNE, Els
ALCALAY, Luna
ALSTED, Birgitte
ALTER, Martha
ANDERSON, Olive Jennie Paxton
ANDERSON-WUENSCH, Jean Mary
ARCHER, Violet Balestreri
ARHO, Anneli
ARMER, Elinor Florence
ARRIEU, Claude
BACEWICZ, Grazyna
BAILLY, Colette
BALLOU, Esther Williamson
BARRIERE, Françoise
BEAT, Janet Eveline
BEECROFT, Norma Marian
BLOMFIELD-HOLT, Patricia
BOLZ, Harriet
BOND, Victoria Ellen
BORROFF, Edith
BOUCHARD, Linda L.
BOULOGNE, Julia R.C.
BOYD, Anne Elizabeth
BRITAIN, Radie
BROCKMAN, Jane E.
BUCHANAN, Dorothy Quita
BUCZEK, Barbara Kazimiera
BURCHELL, Henrietta Louise
CABRERA, Silvia Maria Pires
CALLAWAY, Ann
CARLOS, Wendy
CECCONI-BATES, Augusta
CHANDLER, Mary
CHAVES, Mary Elizabeth
CHRETIEN-GENARO, Hedwige
CLARKE, Rosemary
COATES, Gloria Kannenberg
COHEN, Marcia
CORY, Eleanor
COULOMBE SAINT-MARCOUX,
  Micheline
COWLES, Darleen
CRAWFORD SEEGER, Ruth
DE BIASE BIDART, Lycia
DEMBO, Royce
DESPORTES, Yvonne Berthe Melitta
DEYTON, Camilla Hill
DIANDA, Hilda
DLUGOSZEWSKI, Lucia
DOBSON, Elaine
DUSHKIN, Dorothy Smith
FREED, Dorothy Whitson
FRITZ, Sherilyn Gail
FULLER-HALL, Sarah Margaret
GARR, Wieslawa
GEORGE, Lila-Gene
GIFFORD, Helen Margaret
GIPPS, Ruth
GLANVILLE-HICKS, Peggy
GLATZ, Helen Sinclair
GYRING, Elizabeth
HALPERN, Stella
HARRISON, Pamela
HINLOPEN, Francina
HOFFMAN, Phyllis Sampson
INWOOD, Mary Ruth Brink Berger
IVEY, Jean Eichelberger

JACOB, Elizabeth Marie
JOHNSTON-REID, Sarah Ruth
KERN, Frida
LAUER, Elizabeth
LAZAR, Ella
LEE, Hwaeja Yoo
LEFANU, Nicola Frances
LEJET, Edith
LEVITSKAYA, Viktoria Sergeyevna
LIDDELL, Claire
LOMON, Ruth
LU, Yen
LUND, Gudrun
LUTHER, Mary
LUTYENS, Elisabeth
MACAULAY, Janice Michel
McKAY, Frances Thompson
McLEOD, Jennifer Helen
MAREZ-OYENS, Tera de
MARSHALL, Pamela J.
MAZOUROVA, Jarmila
MEACHEM, Margaret McKeen
  Ramsey
MEL-BONIS
MERRIMAN, Margarita Leonor
MILLER, Elma
MRACEK, Ann Michelle
NEWLIN, Dika
NOBLE, Ann
NOWAK, Alison
OLIVEROS, Pauline
PATERSON, Wilma
PATTERSON, Andra
PENTLAND, Barbara Lally
PETRA-BASACOPOL, Carmen
PHILIBA, Nicole
PHILLIPS, Bryony
PHILLIPS, Karen Ann
PIRES DOS REIS, Hilda
PIZER, Elizabeth Faw Hayden
POLIN, Claire
POPOVICI, Elise
PRADELL, Leila
PREOBRAJENSKA, Vera Nicolaevna
PROCACCINI, Teresa
PSTROKONSKA-NAVRATIL,
  Grazyna Hanna
RAIGORODSKY, Leda Natalia
  Heimsath
RAINIER, Priaulx
RAVINALE, Irma
REID, Sarah Johnston
ROE, Eileen Betty
ROESGEN-CHAMPION, Marguerite
  Sara
ROGER, Denise
ROGERS, Susan Whipple
ROWAN, Barbara
RUEFF, Jeanine
RUSCHE, Marjorie Maxine
SAARIAHO, Kaija
SACCAGGIO, Adelina Luisa Nicasia
SAMUEL, Rhian
SCHWARTZ, Nan Louise
SHEPARD, Jean Ellen
SHREVE, Susan Ellen
SHRUDE, Marilyn
SILVERMAN, Faye-Ellen
SIMONS, Netty
SINGER, Jeanne
SMEJKALOVA, Vlasta
SMYTH, Ethel Mary, Dame
STANLEY, Helen Camille
STEINER, Gitta Hana
STEPHEN, Roberta Mae
STREATFIELD, Valma June
SUTHERLAND, Margaret
SWAIN, Freda Mary
SZYMANSKA, Iwonka Bogumila
TASHJIAN, B. Charmian
TECK, Katherine

TERZIAN, Alicia
THEMMEN, Ivana Marburger
UYTTENHOVE, Yolande
VAN DE VATE, Nancy Hayes
VAN OHLEN, Deborah
VELLERE, Lucie Weiler
VON ZIERITZ, Grete
WALLACH, Joelle
WARDE, Ann Maury
WARREN, Elinor Remick
WEAVER, Carol Ann
WECKWERTH, Nancy
WEGENER-FRENSEL, Emmy Heil
WEIGL, Vally
WHITLOCK, E. Florence
WHITTLE, Chris Mary-Francine
WIENER, Eva Hannah
WIENIAWSKA, Irene Regine
WILDSCHUT, Clara

HORN AND ORCHESTRA OR STRINGS
20th Century A.D.
AARNE, Els
ANDERSON-WUENSCH, Jean Mary
GIPPS, Ruth
HOFFMAN, Phyllis Sampson
LUTYENS, Elisabeth
MERRIMAN, Margarita Leonor
MUSGRAVE, Thea
SCHONTHAL, Ruth E.
VITO-DELVAUX, Berthe di
WILL, Madeleine

HORN AND PIANO
19th Century A.D.
LA HYE, Louise Genevieve
20th Century A.D.
ALSCHANSKY, Serafine
ARCHER, Violet Balestreri
ARRIEU, Claude
BARNETT, Carol Edith
BARRAINE, Elsa
BORROFF, Edith
BRANSCOMBE, Gena
BUCHANAN, Dorothy Quita
CALLAWAY, Ann
CECCONI-BATES, Augusta
COWLES, Darleen
DEMESSIEUX, Jeanne
DUSHKIN, Dorothy Smith
GARTENLAUB, Odette
GIPPS, Ruth
GOTKOVSKY, Ida-Rose Esther
GOULD, Janetta
HUGHES, Sister Martina
KERN, Frida
LAUBER, Anne Marianne
LEBENBOM, Elaine F.
LEVITSKAYA, Viktoria Sergeyevna
LUTYENS, Elisabeth
McLAUGHLIN, Marian
MIEROWSKA, Jean
MUSGRAVE, Thea
NAIKHOVICH-LOMAKINA, Fania
  Filippovna
NAZAROVA, Tatiana Borisovna
NEEDHAM, Alicia Adelaide
PAKHMUTOVA, Alexandra
  Nikolayevna
PEYROT, Fernande
POPATENKO, Tamara Alexandrovna
PROCACCINI, Teresa
ROE, Eileen Betty
ROGERS, Susan Whipple
RUEFF, Jeanine
SCHONTHAL, Ruth E.
SINGER, Jeanne
STEINER, Gitta Hana
VIGNERY, Jeanne Emilie Virginie
VON ZIERITZ, Grete
ZAVALISHINA, Maria Semyonovna

INCIDENTAL MUSIC - THEATRE, FILM, RADIO ETC.
16th Century A.D.
PIGNETELLI, Mariana
17th Century A.D.
CACCINI, Francesca
COSNARD, Mlle.
SOPHIE ELISABETH von
  Braunschweig, Duchess
18th Century A.D.
AHLEFELDT, Marie Thèrésia,
  Countess
ANNA AMALIA, Duchess of Saxe-
  Weimar
DUVAL, Louise
GRIMANI, Maria Margherita
MATTEI, Beatrice
SCHROETER, Corona Elisabeth
  Wilhelmine
19th Century A.D.
AMERSFOORDT-DYK, Hermina
  Maria
ANSPACH, Elizabeth, Margravine of
ASACHI, Elena
AYLWARD, Florence
BACHMANN, Elise
BARKER, Laura Wilson
BAWR, Alexandrine Sophie
BENFEY-SCHUPPE, Anna
BRUCKEN-FOCK, Emilie von
CARISSAN, Celanie
COLLINS, Laura Sedgwick
CZICZKA, Angela
DELL'ACQUA, Eva
GREATOREX, Martha
GRODZICKA-RZEWUSKA, Julia
GUITTY, Madeleine
HADELN, Nancy von
JAHNOVA, Bozena
KELEMEN, Berta Zathureczky
KINKEL, Johanna
KRALIK VON MAYERSWALDEN,
  Mathilde
NIELSEN, Henriette
PARADIS, Maria Theresia von
PARIS, Salomea
SPAULDING, Florence Atherton
UNTERSTEINER, Antonietta
WARD, Kate Lucy
20th Century A.D.
AARNE, Els
AARON, Yvonne
ACCART, Eveline
ACKLAND, Jeanne Isabel Dorothy
A'DAIR, Jeanne
AHRENS, Peg
AIN, Noa
AKHUNDOVA, Shafiga Gulam
  kyzy
ALBRIGHT, Janet Elaine
ALCALAY, Luna
ALEXANDER, Leni
ALLIK, Kristi
ALLITSEN, Frances
ALSTED, Birgitte
ALTER, Martha
ALVARES-RIOS, Maria
ANDERSON, Beth
ANDERSON, Julia McKinley
ANDERSON, Olive Jennie Paxton
ANDERSON, Ruth
ANDREYEVA, M.
ARCHER, Violet Balestreri
ARMER, Elinor Florence
ARRIEU, Claude
AUZEPY, Michele
AZARCON, Minda
BABAYEVA, Seda Grigorievna
BACEWICZ, Grażyna
BADYE, Dyeliba
BAGANIER, Janine

BAIKADAMOVA, Baldyrgan
   Bakhitzhanovna
BAILEY, Judith Margaret
BAILIN, Harriett
BAILY, Margaret Naismith
   Osborne
BAINBRIDGE, Beryl
BALENOVIC, Draga
BALLASEYUS, Virginia
BALLOU, Esther Williamson
BAMPTON, Ruth
BANDARA, Linda
BARAMISHVILI, Olga Ivanovna
BARBERIS, Mansi
BARKER, Patricia
BARRAINE, Elsa
BARRIERE, Françoise
BARTON, Ann
BASSOT, Anne-Marie
BAUER, Marion Eugenie
BAULD, Alison
BAUMGARTEN, Chris
BEAT, Janet Eveline
BEATH, Betty
BELL, Judith
BELLAVANCE, Ginette
BELLE, Marie-Paule
BELOCH, Dorotea
BENARY, Barbara
BERCKMAN, Evelyn
BERTACCA, Uberta
BILBRO, Anne Mathilde
BIRKETT, Gwenhilda Mary
BJELKE-ANDERSEN, Olga
BLANCK, Olga de
BLOM, Diane
BOBROW, Sanchie
BOND, Victoria Ellen
BONDS, Margaret
BOTTAGISIO, Jacqueline
BOYACK, Jeanette
BOYD, Anne Elizabeth
BOYD, Jeanne Margaret
BRANNING, Grace Bell
BRIGGS, Nancy Louise
BROOKS, Myra Lou
BROWN, Gladys Mungen
BROWN, Norma
BRUZDOWICZ, Joanna
BUCHANAN, Dorothy Quita
CABREIRA, Estefania Loureiro de
   Vasconcelos Leão
CADDEN, Jill
CALCAGNO, Elsa
CALCRAFT, Sharon
CAMPMANY, Montserrat
CARLOS, Wendy
CARPENTER, Imogen
CARTER, Rosetta
CARVALHO, Dinora de
CARWITHEN, Doreen
CECCONI-BOTELLA, Monic
CHARBONNIER, Janine Andree
CHAVES, Laura da Fonseca
CHERTOK, Pearl
CHEVALLIER SUPERVIELLE, Marie
   Louise
CHICHERINA, Sofia Nikolayevna
CHILD, Marjorie
CIANI, Suzanne Elizabeth
CIMAGLIA DE ESPINOSA, Lia
CLAMAN, Dolores Olga
CLARK, Mary Margaret Walker
CLOSTRE, Adrienne
COATES, Gloria Kannenberg
COGAN, Morva
CONTINI ANSELMI, Lucia
COOLIDGE, Lucy
COOLIDGE, Peggy Stuart
COOPER, Rose Marie
COTRON, Fanou

COULOMBE SAINT-MARCOUX, Micheline
COX, Alison Mary
CREES, Kathleen Elsie
CROCHET, Sharon Brandstetter
CULLEN, Trish
CURUBETO GODOY, Maria Isabel
CURZON, Clara-Jean
DAIKEN, Melanie
DAILLY, Claudine
DAMASHEK, Barbara
DANIELA, Carmen
DANIELS, Mabel Wheeler
DAVITASHVILI, Meri Shalvovna
DE CEVEE, Alice
DE FREITAS, Elvira Manuela
   Fernandez
DE JONG, Sarah
DE LYLE, Carlyon
DE PURY, Marianne
DEMARQUEZ, Suzanne
DENEUVILLE, Irene
DERBYSHIRE, Delia
DIMITRIU, Florica
DINESCU, Violeta
DOMINIQUE, Monica
DOMMEL-DIENY, Amy
DONCEANU, Felicia
DOROW, Dorothy
DOYLE, Beth
DREGE-SCHIELOWA, Lucja
DREYFUS, Francis Kay
DRING, Madeleine
DROBYAZGINA, Valentina Ivanovna
DU PAGE, Florence Elizabeth
DUBOIS, Shirley Graham
DUCZMAL-JAROSZEWSKA,
   Agnieszka
DURAS, Marguerite
DZIEWULSKA, Maria Amelia
EAGLES, Moneta M.
EDWARDS, Clara
EGNOS, Bertha
EISENSTEIN DE VEGA, Silvia
EKSANISHVILI, Eleonara Grigorevna
ELKIND, Rachel
ELLIS, Vivian
ESCOT, Pozzi
EVANS, Winsome
FAIRLIE, Margaret C.
FERNANDO, Sarathchandra
   Vichremadithya
FERRE, Susan Ingrid
FERREYRA, Beatriz
FINE, Sylvia
FINE, Vivian
FIRESTONE, Elizabeth
FISHER, Doris
FISHER, Susan
FODY, Ilona
FORD, Nancy
FORMAN, Joanne
FRAJT, Ludmila
FRANGS, Irene
FREED, Dorothy Whitson
FREITAG, Dorothea Hackett
FREIXAS Y CRUELLS, Narcisa
FRIEDBERG, Patricia Ann
FRONTIERA, Mary Jo
FULCHER, Ellen Georgina
GAERTNER, Katarzyna
GALIKIAN, Susanna Avetisovna
GALLINA, Jill
GAMILLA, Alice Doria
GARCIA ROBSON, Magdalena
GARSCIA-GRESSEL, Janina
GARTENLAUB, Odette
GEIGER-KULLMANN, Rosy Auguste
GERSTMAN, Blanche Wilhelminia
GHARACHE-DAGHI, Sheyda
GIBBS, Prue
GIFFORD, Helen Margaret

GILBERT, Pia
GILLICK, Emelyn Mildred Samuels
GLANVILLE-HICKS, Peggy
GLATZ, Helen Sinclair
GLENN-COPELANN, Beverly
GOETSCHIUS, Marjorie
GOKHMAN, Elena Vladimirovna
GOLETTI, Nelly
GONZAGA, Chiquinha
GOOSSENS, Marie Henriette
GORELLI, Olga
GOTKOVSKY, Ida-Rose Esther
GRAHAM, Sybil
GREENE, Genevieve
GREGER, Luisa
GRIEBEL WANDALL, Tekla
GRIEBLING, Karen Jean
GRIGSBY, Beverly
GROSSMAN, Deena
GRUDEFF, Marian
HADDEN, Frances Roots
HAHN, Sandra Lea
HAJDU, Julia
HALACSY, Irma von
HALL, Pauline
HART, Elizabeth Jane Smith
HAYS, Doris Ernestine
HEDOUX, Yvonne
HEILBRON, Valerie
HEINRICH, Adel Verna
HELASVUO, Elsa
HENDERSON, Moya
HERNANDEZ-GONZALO, Gisela
HO, Wai On
HOFER, Maria
HOFFERT, Brenda
HOLBERT, Diana Brown
HOLLAND, Dulcie Sybil
HOOD, Helen
HORROCKS, Amy Elsie
HORST, Carita von
HOSEY, Athena
HULL, Kathryn B.
HUNTER, Alberta
HUTTON, Florence Myra
IASHVILI, Lili Mikhailovna
IBRAGIMOVA, Sevda Mirza kyzy
IGENBERGA, Elga Avgustovna
INWOOD, Mary Ruth Brink Berger
IORDAN, Irina Nikolayevna
ISAKOVA, Aida Petrovna
IVEY, Jean Eichelberger
JAMES, Dorothy E.
JARRATT, Lita
JENNY, Sister Leonore
JESI, Ada
JESSYE, Eva
JIRACKOVA, Marta
JOHNSON, Eloise Lisle
JOHNSTON, Alison Aileen Annie
JOLAS, Betsy
JOLLY, Margaret Anne
JOLY, Suzanne
KABOS, Ilona
KAESER-BECK, Aida
KAHMANN, Chesley
KANACH, Sharon E.
KARNITSKAYA, Nina Andreyevna
KASILAG, Lucrecia R.
KATS-CHERNIN, Elena
KATZMAN, Klara Abramovna
KAYDEN, Mildred
KAZORECK, Hildegard
KEETMAN, Gunild
KETTERING, Eunice Lea
KHANNA, Usha
KICKINGER, Paula
KIELANOWSKI, Alina
KIRKWOOD, Antoinette
KLINKOVA, Zhivka
KOLODUB, Zhanna Efimovna

KOZAKIEVICH, Anna Abramovna
KRALIKOVA, Johana
KRZYZANOWSKA, Halina
KUCEROVA-HERSTOVA, Marie
KUKUCK, Felicitas
KUMMER, Clare
KUSS, Margarita Ivanovna
KVERNADZE, Bidzina
LA BARBARA, Joan
LAITMAN, Lori
LAKE, Bonnie
LAM MAN YEE, Violet
LANG-BECK, Ivana
LARA, Catherine
LARSON, Anna Barbara
LATZ, Inge
LAUBER, Anne Marianne
LAUER, Elizabeth
LEANDRE, Joelle
LEBARON, Anne
LEHMANN, Liza
LEIVISKA, Helvi Lemmiki
LELEU, Jeanne
LENNEP, Henrietta van
LEON, Tania Justina
LEONCHIK, Svetlana Gavrilovna
LESICHKOVA, Lili
LEVI, Natalia Nikolayevna
LEVIN, Erma E.
LEVINA, Zara Alexandrovna
LICHTENSTEIN, Olga Grigorievna
LINDEN VAN SNELREWAARD-
   BOUDEWIJNS, Nelly van der
LINZ VON KRIEGNER, Marta
LISTON, Melba
LOH, Kathy Jean
LUFF, Enid
LUTYENS, Elisabeth
LVOVA, Julia Fedorovna
LYNN, Cathy
LYONN LIEBERMAN, Julie
MacDONALD, Catherine
McFARLANE, Jenny
McINTOSH, Diana
McKENZIE, Sandra
McLEOD, Jennifer Helen
McMILLAN, Ann Endicott
McNEIL, Janet L. Pfischner
MAGEAU, Mary Jane
MAGUY LOVANO, Marguerite
   Schlegel
MAILIAN, Elza Antonovna
MAIRE, Jacqueline
MAKAROVA, Nina Vladimirovna
MALMLOEF-FORSSLING, Carin
MANUKIAN, Irina Eduardovna
MANZONI, Eugenia Tretti
MAREZ-OYENS, Tera de
MARINI, Giovanna
MARKS, Selma
MARTENOT-LAZARD, Ginette-
   Genevieve
MARTIN, Ravonna G.
MARTINEZ DE LA TORRE Y
   SHELTON, Emma
MARTINEZ, Odaline de la
MARTINS, Maria de Lourdes
MATEVOSIAN, Araks Surenovna
MEACHEM, Margaret McKeen
   Ramsey
MEISTER, Marianne
MEKEEL, Joyce
MENDOSA, Dot
MERTENS, Dolores
METALLIDI, Zhanneta Lazarevna
MIAGI, Ester Kustovna
MICHELOW, Sybil
MIGRANYAN, Emma
MIHALITSI, Sophia
MILENKOVIC, Jelena
MILNE, Lorraine

MITCHELL, Janice Misurell
MOELLER, Paulette
MONK, Meredith
MONNOT, Marguerite Angele
MORE, Margaret Elizabeth
MORLEY, Angela
MORRISON, Julia Maria
MORTIFEE, Ann
MOSCOVITZ, Julianne
NARCISSE-MAIR, Denise Lorraine
NARRONE, Claudia
NASON, Susanna
NAZAROVA, Tatiana Borisovna
NAZIROVA, Elmira Mirza Rza kyzy
NEPGEN, Rosa Sophia Cornelia
NICHOLS, Alberta
NIKOLAYEVA, Tatiana Petrovna
NIVELLI SCHWARTZ, Gina
NOVA SONDAG, Jacqueline
NUGENT, Trish
OBAYASHI, Nobichiko
ODDONE SULLI-RAO, Elisabetta
OFFICER, Bronwyn Lee
OLIVEROS, Pauline
OOSTERZEE, Cornelia van
ORAM, Daphne Blake
ORLANDI, Nora
OSETROVA-YAKOVLIEVA, Nina
   Alexandrovna
OWENS, Rochelle
PADE, Else Marie
PAKHMUTOVA, Alexandra Nikolayevna
PALLASTRELLI, Giannina, Countess
PATTERSON, Andra
PAULL, Barberi
PAYNE, Maggi
PENTLAND, Barbara Lally
PERISSAS, Madeleine
PERKIN, Helen
PETROVA-KRUPKOVA, Elena
PEYROT, Fernande
PHILIPPART, Renée
PHILLIPS, Bryony
PHILLIPS, Karen Ann
PIERCE, Alexandra
PIGGOTT, Audrey Margaret
PITTMAN, Evelyn LaRue
POLICARPO TEIXEIRA, Maria
   Margarida Fernandes
POLLOCK, Muriel
POPATENKO, Tamara Alexandrovna
POPOVICI, Elise
POSTON, Elizabeth
PRADELL, Leila
PREDIC-SAPER, Branislava
PRICE, Beryl
PSTROKONSKA-NAVRATIL,
   Grazyna Hanna
PTASZYNSKA, Marta
QUIEL, Hildegard
RADERMACHER, Erika
RADIC, Maureen
RAINIER, Priaulx
RAKHMANKULOVA, Mariam
   Mannanovna
RASKIN, Ruby
RECLI, Giulia
REID, Sarah Johnston
REID, Wendy
RHEINGOLD, Lauma Yanovna
RHOADS, Mary R.
RICHMOND, Virginia
RICKARD, Sylvia
RIVERA, Graciela
ROBERTS, Gertrud Hermine Kuenzel
ROBERTS, Jane A.
ROCHEROLLE, Eugenie Katherine
RODGERS, Mary
ROE, Eileen Betty
ROGERS, Patsy
ROGET, Henriette

ROMITELLI, Sante Maria
ROSALINA, Ana
ROZHAVSKAYA, Yudif Grigorevna
SACHS, Carolyn
SAINT JOHN, Kathleen Louise
SALVADOR, Matilde
SAMIOU, Domna
SAMTER, Alice
SANDERS, Alma M.
SANDIFUR, Ann Elizabeth
SANGUESA, Iris
SANTOJA, Mari Carmen
SANTOS-OCAMPO DE FRANCESCO,
   Amada Amy
SANZ, Rocio
SARASWATIBAI
SATO, Masashiko
SCHERCHEN, Tona
SCHIEVE, Catherine
SCHJELDERUP, Mon Marie Gustava
SCHMITT-LERMANN, Frieda
SCHONTHAL, Ruth E.
SCHORLEMMER, Erna von
SCHULZE-BERGHOF, Luise Doris
   Albertine
SCHUSSLER-BREWAEYS, Marie
   Antoinette
SCIBOR, Maria
SCLIAR, Esther
SCOTT, Molly
SCOTT-HUNTER, Hortense
SERRANO REDONNET, Ana
SHAVERZASHVILI, Tamara Antonovna
SHEMER, Naomi
SHEPARD, Jean Ellen
SHERBOURNE, Janet
SHERMAN, Kim Daryl
SHIELDS, Alice Ferree
SHLONSKY, Verdina
SHOTWELL, Phyllis
SIDORENKO, Tamara Stepanovna
SILSBEE, Ann L.
SIMON, Cécile Paul
SIMONIAN, Nadezhda Simonovna
SKOUEN, Synne
SKOWRONSKA, Janina
SMELTZER, Susan Mary
SMILEY, Pril
SMIRNOVA, Galina Konstantinovna
SNIFFIN, Allison
SNIZKOVA-SKRHOVA, Jitka
SODRE, Joanidia
SOENSTEVOLD, Maj
SOMMER, Silvia
SORALINA, Ana
SOUBLETTE, Sylvia
SOULAGE, Marcelle Fanny Henriette
SPECHT, Judy Lavise
SPEKTOR, Mira J.
SPICER, Marjorie
SPIEGEL, Laurie
SPIZIZEN, Louise Myers
STARBUCK, Anna Diller
STEFANOVIC, Ivana
STRUTT, Dorothy
STULTZ, Marie Irene
SUESSE, Dana
SUTHERLAND, Margaret
SUTZU, Rodica
SWADOS, Elizabeth
SWIFT, Kay
SWISHER, Gloria Agnes Wilson
SZAJNA-LEWANDOWSKA, Jadwiga
   Helena
SZOENYI, Erzsebet
TAILLEFERRE, Germaine
TAL, Ya'ara
TANTU, Cornelia
TATE, Phyllis
TAUTU, Cornelia
TERZIAN, Alicia

TESTORE, Lidia
THISSE-DEROUETTE, Rose
THOMAS, Connie
THOME, Diane
THOMPSON, Caroline Lorraine
THOREAU, Rachel
THREADGILL-MARTIN, Ravonna
TILICHEYEVA, Elena Nikolayevna
TRIMBLE, Joan
TUCKER, Irene
TURNER, Myra Brooks
TURNER, Olive Mary
TUSSENBROEK, Hendrika van
TWOMBLY, Mary Lynn
URRETA, Alicia
USTVOLSKAYA, Galina Ivanovna
UTTER, Betty
UYTTENHOVE, Yolande
VAKHVAKHISHVILI, Tamara
   Nikolayevna
VALDES, Marta
VAN EPEN-DE GROOT, Else Antonia
VASCONELLOS, Nana
VELLERE, Lucie Weiler
VERHAALEN, Sister Marion
VERRALL, Pamela Motley
VIALA, Georgette
VIDAR, Jorunn
VIENNE, Marie-Louise de
VIGNERON-RAMAKERS, Christiane-
   Josée
VILLIN, Marcelle Henriette Marie
VIRTUE, Constance Cochnower
VITO-DELVAUX, Berthe di
VORLOVA, Slavka
VRABELY-WURMBACH-
   STUPPACHOVA, Stefania
WALDO, Elisabeth
WALLACE, Phyllis Joy
WALLNEROVA, Bibiana
WALKER, Shirley
WANG, Qiang
WARSKA, Wanda
WEAVER, Marion
WESTBROOK, Helen Searles
WHITEHEAD, Alison
WHITTAKER, Vivian
WIENECKE, Sigrid Henriette
WIENER, Elisabeth
WILLIAMS, Grace Mary
WILLIAMS, Stella
WILLMAN, Regina Hansen
WITKIN, Beatrice
WITNI, Monica
WOLLNER, Gertrude Price
WONG, Betty Ann
WOOD, Marilyn
ZARANEK, Stefania Anatolyevna
ZAVALISHINA, Maria Semyonovna
ZECHLIN, Ruth
ZHUBANOVA, Gaziza Akhmetovna
ZIBEROVA, Zinaida Petrovna
ZIFFER, Fran
ZIVKOVIC, Mirjana
Century unknown
   SAPAROFF, Andrea
   TAVEIRA, Eva
   TISHMAN, Fay

LUTE
   2nd Century A.D.
      TS'AI, Yen
   9th Century A.D.
      UBAIDA
   11th Century A.D.
      QASMUNA
   16th Century A.D.
      BORGHI, Faustina
      MEDICI ORSINI, Isabella de, Duchess
         of Bracciano
      MILDMAY, Lady

MOLINARO, Simone
MOLZA, Tarquinia
ORSINI, Eleanora, Duchess of Segni
17th Century A.D.
   BOCQUET, Anne
18th Century A.D.
   BERTHE, Mme.
   PINEL, Julie
19th Century A.D.
   WOLZOGEN, Elsa Laura von
20th Century A.D.
   BELOW-BUTTLAR, Gerda von
   BOND, Victoria Ellen
   GARDNER, Kay
   GRAMEGLIA-GROSSO, Emma
   MEGEVAND, Denise
   MENDELSSOHN, Erna
   POSTON, Elizabeth
   WALKER, Gwyneth van Anden

MANDOLIN
   18th Century A.D.
      BERTHE, Mme.
   19th Century A.D.
      BENINGFIELD, Ethel
      PUGET, Loise
   20th Century A.D.
      BARTHEL, Ursula
      BOUCHARD, Linda L.
      CARR-BOYD, Ann Kirsten
      GRILLI GALEFFI, Elvira
      KERN, Frida
      LUTYENS, Elisabeth
      MENDELSSOHN, Erna
      McKENZIE, Sandra
      PREOBRAJENSKA, Vera Nicolaevna
      TEMPLE, Hope
      THOME, Diane
      VIEU, Jane
      WEAVER, Carol Ann
   Century unknown
      GAMBOGI, Luigia
      ROSS, Clara

MARIMBA
   20th Century A.D.
      ABE, Kyoko
      ABEJO, Sister M. Rosalina
      ANDERSON, Julia McKinley
      ARIMA, Reiko
      BARKIN, Elaine
      BARRETT-THOMAS, N.
      BECKON, Lettie Marie
      BORROFF, Edith
      CHENOWETH, Vida
      COWLES, Darleen
      DANFORTH, Frances A.
      DIEMER, Emma Lou
      DUSHKIN, Dorothy Smith
      GIFFORD, Helen Margaret
      GLANVILLE-HICKS, Peggy
      GOULD, Elizabeth Davies
      GREGER, Luisa
      JACOB, Elizabeth Marie
      LEBARON, Anne
      LOWENSTEIN, Gunilla Marike
      McLEOD, Jennifer Helen
      MILLER, Elma
      MORRISON, Julia Maria
      MURAO, Sachie
      NAITO, Akemi
      NOBLE, Ann
      NOWAK, Alison
      OSAWA, Kazuko
      PIERCE, Alexandra
      PTASZYNSKA, Marta
      SAINT JOHN, Kathleen Louise
      SCHERCHEN, Tona
      SHEPPARD, Suzanne
      SZEKELY, Katalin
      TAKAMI, Toyoko

TOWER, Joan
WHITEHEAD, Gillian
WYLIE, Ruth Shaw

MOUTH ORGAN
   20th Century A.D.
      HAMMOND, Fanny Reed
      HOVDA, Eleanor
      McKENZIE, Sandra
      SWAIN, Freda Mary
      VAN EPEN-DE GROOT, Else Antonia

MULTIMEDIA
   20th Century A.D.
      AESCHLIMANN-ROTH, Esther
      AHRENS, Peg
      ALLOUARD CARNY, Odette
      AMACHER, Maryanne
      ANDERSON, Beth
      ANDERSON, Ruth
      ARETZ, Isabel
      BAIRD, Irene
      BARKIN, Elaine
      BOYD, Anne Elizabeth
      BRIGGS, Nancy Louise
      CALAME, Genevieve
      CECCONI-BOTELLA, Monic
      CHANCE, Nancy Laird
      CLARKE, Rosemary
      COHEN, Marcia
      COULOMBE SAINT-MARCOUX,
         Micheline
      CRAWFORD, Dorothy Lamb
      DILLER, Saralu C.
      DIMENTMAN, Esfir Moiseyevna
      DLUGOSZEWSKI, Lucia
      ESCOT, Pozzi
      EVERETT-SALICCO, Betty Lou
      FAIRLIE, Margaret C.
      FELIX, Margery Edith
      FINZI, Graciane
      GILBERT, Janet Monteith
      GITECK, Janice
      GREENWALD, Jan Carol
      HARDY, Helen Irene
      HAYS, Doris Ernestine
      HO, Wai On
      IRMAN-ALLEMANN, Regina
      JIRACKOVA, Marta
      JUENGER, Patricia
      KAHN, Esther
      KASILAG, Lucrecia R.
      KETTERING, Eunice Lea
      KOSSE, Roberta
      LEVIN, Rami Yona
      LUFF, Enid
      McNEIL, Janet L. Pfischner
      MARCUS, Bunita
      MARTIN, Judith Reher
      MEACHEM, Margaret McKeen
         Ramsey
      MEKEEL, Joyce
      MONK, Meredith
      MORETTO, Nelly
      MULDER, Maria Antonia
      OLIVEIRA, Jocy de
      OLIVEROS, Pauline
      OSTRANDER, Linda Woodaman
      PAULL, Barberi
      PAYNE, Maggi
      PENGILLY, Sylvia
      PRADELL, Leila
      PTASZYNSKA, Marta
      QUESADA, Virginia
      RICHER, Jeannine
      RICHTER, Marion Morrey
      ROBERTS, Megan L.
      RODRIGUE, Nicole
      ROSENBACH, Ulrike
      ROSSO, Carol L.
      RUSCHE, Marjorie Maxine

SAINT JOHN, Kathleen Louise
SAMSON, Valerie Brooks
SAMTER, Alice
SANDIFUR, Ann Elizabeth
SANGUESA, Iris
SCHLOSS, Myrna Frances
SHRUDE, Marilyn
SIKORA, Elzbieta
SIMONS, Netty
SMITH, Ladonna Carol
SPIEGEL, Laurie
STANLEY, Helen Camille
STEINER, Emma
STOEPPELMANN, Janet
STRUTT, Dorothy
TARLOW, Karen Anne
THEMMEN, Ivana Marburger
THOME, Diane
WARNE, Katharine Mulky
WHITE, Ruth S.
WHITEHEAD, Gillian
WONG, Betty Ann
WONG, Hsiung-Zee

Century unknown
BRANDES, Renée

MUSIC FOR CHILDREN
19th Century A.D.
BECKER, Ida
BINFIELD, Hanna R.
CHERTKOVA, A.
DUSSEK, Olivia
FELSENTHAL, Amalie
HEITMANN, Matilde
LINDSAY, Miss M.
ORTH, Lizette Emma
THERESA
WARD, Clementine
WICHERN, Caroline
WIGGINS, Kate Douglas

20th Century A.D.
ADAMS, Julia Aurelia
ALOTIN, Yardena
ANDERSEN, Helen Somerville
ANDERSON, Julia McKinley
ANDREYEVA, M.
ARIMA, Reiko
AYLOTT, Lydia Georgina Edith
BADIAN, Maya
BAGANIER, Janine
BALDACCI, Giovanna Bruna
BAMPTON, Ruth
BARBERIS, Mansi
BARBLAN-OPIENSKA, Lydia
BARBOUR, Florence Newell
BARRADAS, Carmen
BARTHEL, Ursula
BARTLETT, Floy Little
BEAT, Janet Eveline
BEKEART, Edna
BEKMAN-SHCHERBINA, Elena
    Aleksandrovna Kamentseva
BELINFANTE-DEKKER, Martha
    Suzanna Betje
BENOIT, Francine Germaine Van
    Gool
BESSEM, Saar
BEZDEK, Sister John Joseph
BLANCK, Olga de
BLIESENER, Ada Elizabeth
    Michelman
BLOCKSIDGE, Kathleen Mary
BOBROW, Sanchie
BORDEWIJK-ROEPMAN, Johanna
BOSHKOFF, Ruth
BOYD, Anne Elizabeth
BRIGGS, Dorothy Bell
BROWN, Elizabeth van Ness
CABREIRA, Estefania Loureiro de
    Vasconcelos Leão
CALAME, Genevieve

CALCAGNO, Elsa
CAMPMANY, Montserrat
CAPERTON, Florence Tait
CAPUIS, Matilde
CARR-BOYD, Ann Kirsten
CHEN, Nira
CHICHERINA, Sofia Nikolayevna
CHITCHIAN, Geguni Oganesovna
CHITTENDEN, Kate Sara
CHKHEIDZE, Dali Davidovna
CHUDOVA, Tatiana Alekseyevna
CITATI-BRACCI, Clelia
CLARK, Mary Margaret Walker
COCQ, Rosina Susanna de
CONSTANTINESCU, Domnica
COOPER, Rose Marie
CURTIS, Natalie
DAILLY, Claudine
DAVITASHVILI, Meri Shalvovna
DE FREITAS, Elvira Manuela Fernandez
DE MOL, Josephine
DELIRE, Alice
DERLIEN, Margarete
DILLER, Saralu C.
DOMMEL-DIENY, Amy
DONATOVA, Narcisa
DREYFUS, Francis Kay
DUNLOP, Isobel
DURAND, Nella Wells
DZIEWULSKA, Maria Amelia
ELKOSHI, Rivka
ESTRELLA, Blanca
FEIGIN, Sarah
FELIX, Margery Edith
FELLOWS, Mrs. Wayne Stanley
FENNER, Beatrice
FERRAND-TEULET, Denise
FISCHER, Edith Steinkraus
FRANCHERE-DESROSIERS, Rose de
    Lima
FREIXAS Y CRUELLS, Narcisa
FRITTER, Genevieve Davisson
FURGERI, Bianca Maria
FURZE, Jessie
GABASHVILI, Nana
GABUS, Monique
GALIKIAN, Susanna Avetisovna
GARSCIA-GRESSEL, Janina
GARUTA, Lucia Yanovna
GARZTECKA-JARZEBSKA, Irena
GAYNOR, Jessie Love
GERCHIK, Vera Petrovna
GERSTMAN, Blanche Wilhelminia
GNESINA, Yelena Fabianovna
GRAUBNER, Hannelore
GUBITOSI, Emilia
HANEFELD, Gertrud
HARA, Kazuko (1)
HARTZER-STIBBE, Marie
HAWLEY, Carolyn Jean
HAYS, Doris Ernestine
HEATON, Eloise Klotz
HEIBERG, Ella
HELBLING, Elsa
HENDERSON, Ruth Watson
HERNANDEZ-GONZALO, Gisela
HESSE, Marjorie Anne
HICKS, Marjorie Kisby
HOFFERT, Brenda
HOLCOMB, Louanah Riggs
HOLLAND, Dulcie Sybil
HUTTON, Florence Myra
IASHVILI, Lili Mikhailovna
IBANEZ, Carmen
JANKOWSKI, Loretta Patricia
JENNINGS, Marie Pryor
JIRACKOVA, Marta
JIRKOVA, Olga
JOCHSBERGER, Tzipora H.
JOEST, Emma
JOHNSON, Eloise Lisle

JOLLY, Margaret Anne
KACZURBINA-ZDZIECHOWSKA,
    Maria
KAHANANUI, Dorothy
KALOGRIDOU, Maria
KANACH, Sharon E.
KARASTOYANOVA, Elena
KAUFMAN, Barbara
KEETMAN, Gunild
KEMP, Dorothy Elizabeth Walter
KENDRICK, Virginia Catherine
KENT, Ada Twohy
KESAREVA, Margarita
    Alexandrovna
KESSLER, Minuetta Schumiatcher
KETTERER, Ella
KIRKBY-MASON, Barbara
KLECHNIOWSKA, Anna Maria
KLINKOVA, Zhivka
KNOWLTON, Fanny Snow
KODOLITSCH, Michaela
KONISHI, Nagako
KOPTAGEL, Yuksel
KORNILOVA, Tatiana Dmitrevna
KRASNOGLIADOVA, Vera
    Vladimirovna
KUCEROVA-HERSTOVA, Marie
LAMBELET, Vivienne Ada Maurice
LAMBRECHTS-VOS, Anna Catharina
LAMEGO, Carlinda J.
LAST, Joan Mary
LATZ, Inge
LAUER, Elizabeth
LAURENT, Ruth Carew
LAVIN, Marie Duchesne
LEBIZAY, Marguerite
LEE, Hope Anne Keng-Wei
LESICHKOVA, Lili
LEVI, Natalia Nikolayevna
LEVINA, Zara Alexandrovna
LEWIS, Carrie Bullard
LIDDELL, Claire
LIDGI-HERMAN, Sofia
LLOYD, Caroline Parkhurst
LOHR, Ina
LORE, Emma Maria Theresa
LORING, Nancy
LOUDOVA, Ivana
LOWELL, Edith
LUDVIG-PECAR, Nada
LUND, Hanna
LUTYENS, Elisabeth
LYUBOMIRSKAYA-BOYARSKAYA,
    Revekka Grigorevna
MACONCHY, Elizabeth
McCOLLIN, Frances
McQUATTIE, Sheila
MALDYBAYEVA, Zhyldyz
    Abdylasovna
MAMLOK, Ursula
MANUKIAN, Irina Eduardovna
MAREZ-OYENS, Tera de
MARIANI-CAMPOLIETI, Virginia
MARTIN, Judith Reher
MATEU, Maria Cateura
MAXIM, Florence
MEL-BONIS
MERMAN, Joyce
METALLIDI, Zhanneta Lazarevna
MICHELI AGOSTINI, Fausta
MIGRANYAN, Emma
MILAM, Lena Triplett
MOBERG, Ida Georgina
MOE, Benna
MONTIJN, Aleida
MOORE, Wilda Maurine Ricks
MOSUSOVA, Nadezda
MULDER, Johanna Harmina Gerdina
NEILY, Anne MacAdams
OLSON, Lynn Freeman
ORAM, Daphne Blake

ORTMANS, Kay Muriel
OSETROVA-YAKOVLIEVA, Nina
    Alexandrovna
PADE, Else Marie
PAGOTO, Helen
PANZERA, Magdeleine
PAUL, Doris A.
PAULL, Barberi
PEGELOW, Hanna G.
PENNER, Jean Priscilla
PENTLAND, Barbara Lally
PETRA-BASACOPOL, Carmen
PILIS, Heda
POPATENKO, Tamara Alexandrovna
PREOBRAJENSKA, Vera Nicolaevna
PTASZYNSKA, Marta
RAVIZE, Angele
RAW, Vera Constance
RENART, Marta Garcia
RENNES, Catharina van
RICHARDS, Laura E.
RICHTER, Ada
ROBYN, Louise
ROGATIS, Térèsa de
ROSAS FERNANDES, Maria Helena
SAFARIAN, Lucia Arisovna
SAMVELIAN, Sofia Vardanovna
SANGUESA, Iris
SANZ, Rocio
SCEK, Breda Friderika
SCHYTTE-JENSEN, Caroline
SEIDERS, Mary Asenath
SELMER, Kathryn Lande
SETO, Robin
SHAFFER, Jeanne Ellison
SHAVERZASHVILI, Tamara
    Antonovna
SHEMER, Naomi
SHEVITZ, Mimi
SHLONSKY, Verdina
SLIANOVA-MIZANDARI, Dagmara
    Levanovna
SMIRNOVA, Galina Konstantinovna
SNIZKOVA-SKRHOVA, Jitka
SOUBLETTE, Sylvia
SPENA, Lita
SPOENDLIN, Elisabeth
STANEKAITE-LAUMYANSKENE,
    Elena Ionovna
STEIN, Gladys Marie
STEPHEN, Roberta Mae
STERNICKA-NIEKRASZOWA, Ilza
STEWART, Katharine
STEWART-NORTH, Isabel
STITT, Margaret McClure
STREICHER, Lyubov Lvovna
STULTZ, Marie Irene
SULTANOVA, Asya Bakhish kyzy
SWAIN, Freda Mary
SZAJNA-LEWANDOWSKA, Jadwiga
    Helena
SZOENYI, Erzsebet
TAL, Ya'ara
TATE, Phyllis
TEGNER, Alice Charlotte
TELFER, Nancy Ellen
TENGBERGEN, Maria Elizabeth van
    Ebbenhorst
TERHUNE, Anice
THOMAS, Muriel Leonora Duncan
THOMPSON, Caroline Lorraine
THOMSEN, Geraldine
TIDEMAN-WIJERS, Bertha
TILICHEYEVA, Elena Nikolayevna
TKACH, Zlata Moiseyevna
TUMANISHVILI, Ketevana
    Dmitirevna
TURNER, Myra Brooks
TURNER-MALEY, Florence
TUSSENBROEK, Hendrika van
USTVOLSKAYA, Galina Ivanovna

UTTER, Betty
VAN EPEN-DE GROOT, Else Antonia
VELLERE, Lucie Weiler
VERRALL, Pamela Motley
VETLUGINA, Natalia Alekseyevna
VITO-DELVAUX, Berthe di
VIVADO ORSINI, Ida
VLADERACKEN, Geertruida van
VOIGT-SCHWEIKERT, Margarete
VOLKART, Hazel
VORLOVA, Slavka
WALLNEROVA, Bibiana
WEIGL, Vally
WEISSBERG, Julia Lazèrevna
WENTZ-JANACEK, Elisabet
ZECHLIN, Ruth
Century unknown
KIEK, Bessie

MUSICAL SAW
20th Century A.D.
KABAT, Julie Phyllis
PROCACCINI, Teresa

NONET
18th Century A.D.
CECILE, Jeanne
19th Century A.D.
FARRENC, Louise
KRALIK VON MAYERSWALDEN,
    Mathilde
20th Century A.D.
AINSCOUGH, Juliana Mary
BARON SUPERVIELLE, Susana
BOFILL, Anna
CLARKE, Rosemary
COATES, Gloria Kannenberg
COLIN, Jeanne
DOBSON, Elaine
ECKHARDT-GRAMATTE, Sophie-
    Carmen
EICHENWALD, Sylvia
FONTYN, Jacqueline
FOWLER, Jennifer Joan
FRANCO, Clare
FURGERI, Bianca Maria
GIURANNA, Elena Barbara
GYRING, Elizabeth
HEMON, Sedje
JOLAS, Betsy
LORENZ, Ellen Jane
LOUIE, Alexina Diane
LUTYENS, Elisabeth
MATUSZCZAK, Bernadetta
MITCHELL, Janice Misurell
MIZUNO, Shuko
MOON, Chloe Elizabeth
MOORE, Dorothy Rudd
MUSGRAVE, Thea
PROCACCINI, Teresa
RODRIGUE, Nicole
SMITH, Linda Catlin
SPOENDLIN, Elisabeth
THOMSEN, Geraldine
VIERK, Lois
WILKINS, Margaret Lucy

OBOE
18th Century A.D.
ANNA AMALIA, Princess of Prussia
CECILE, Jeanne
MARTINEZ, Marianne
19th Century A.D.
DESHAYES, Marie
GRANDVAL, Marie Felicie Clemence
    de Reiset, Vicomtesse de
LASCHANZKY, Mme.
RQSENHOFF, Orla
20th Century A.D.
ALCALAY, Luna
ALLOUARD CARNY, Odette

ALTER, Martha
ANDERSON, Olive Jennie Paxton
ANDERSON-WUENSCH, Jean Mary
ARCHER, Violet Balestreri
ARIMA, Reiko
ARMER, Elinor Florence
ARRIEU, Claude
BACEWICZ, Grażyna
BADIAN, Maya
BAINBRIDGE, Beryl
BARBERIS, Mansi
BARON SUPERVIELLE, Susana
BARRELL, Joyce Howard
BARRETT-THOMAS, N.
BAUER, Marion Eugenie
BAULD, Alison
BEAT, Janet Eveline
BECKON, Lettie Marie
BECLARD D'HARCOURT,
    Marguerite
BEECROFT, Norma Marian
BEYER, Johanna Magdalena
BLIESENER, Ada Elizabeth
    Michelman
BOFILL, Anna
BOLZ, Harriet
BORROFF, Edith
BOUCHARD, Linda L.
BOYD, Anne Elizabeth
BRENET, Thérèse
BRINK-POTHUIS, Annie van den
BRITAIN, Radie
BROGUE, Roslyn Clara
BRUSH, Ruth Damaris
BRUZDOWICZ, Joanna
BURKE, Loretto
BUTLER, Patricia Magahay
CABRERA, Silvia Maria Pires
CAMEU, Helza
CAMPAGNE, Conny
CANAL, Marguerite
CAPUIS, Matilde
CARLOS, Wendy
CARNECI, Carmen
CARVALHO, Dinora de
CECCONI-BATES, Augusta
CHANDLER, Mary
CHAPIRO, Fania
CHAVES, Mary Elizabeth
CLOSTRE, Adrienne
COATES, Gloria Kannenberg
COHEN, Marcia
COLACO OSORIO-SWAAB, Reine
COQUET, Odile Marie-Lucie
CORNING, Karen Andree
CORY, Eleanor
COULOMBE SAINT-MARCOUX,
    Micheline
COULTHARD, Jean
CRAWFORD SEEGER, Ruth
CRAWFORD, Dawn Constance
CRAWFORD, Dorothy Lamb
DANEAU, Suzanne
DANIELS, Mabel Wheeler
DE FREITAS, Elvira Manuela
    Fernandez
DEMBO, Royce
DENBOW, Stefania Bjoerson
DESPORTES, Yvonne Berthe Melitta
DIANDA, Hilda
DIEMER, Emma Lou
DOBBINS, Lori
DONCEANU, Felicia
DRING, Madeleine
DUDLEY, Marjorie Eastwood
DUSHKIN, Dorothy Smith
DVORKIN, Judith
EKIZIAN, Michelle
ERHART, Dorothy
ERVIN, Karen
EVEN-OR, Mary

FINE, Vivian
FINZI, Graciane
FISCHER, Edith Steinkraus
FISHMAN, Marian
FLEITES, Virginia
FONTYN, Jacqueline
FOWLER, Jennifer Joan
FRASIER, Jane
FREED, Dorothy Whitson
FULCHER, Ellen Georgina
GARCIA ROBSON, Magdalena
GARDNER, Kay
GARTENLAUB, Odette
GIFFORD, Helen Margaret
GILBERT, Pia
GIPPS, Ruth
GLANVILLE-HICKS, Peggy
GLATZ, Helen Sinclair
GOOLKASIAN-RAHBEE, Dianne
   Zabelle
GOULD, Elizabeth Davies
GRAHAM, Janet Christine
GRAY, Victoria Winifred
GREENE, Margo Lynn
GRIEBLING, Karen Jean
GRIEBLING, Margaret Ann
GROSSMAN, Deena
GRZADZIELOWNA, Eleonora
GURAIEB KURI, Rosa
GYRING, Elizabeth
HALL, Pauline
HALPERN, Stella
HANEFELD, Gertrud
HEMON, Sedje
HENDERSON, Ruth Watson
HERBISON, Jeraldine Saunders
HIER, Ethel Glen
HIND O'MALLEY, Pamela
HOLLAND, Dulcie Sybil
HOOVER, Katherine
HYDE, Miriam Beatrice
INWOOD, Mary Ruth Brink Berger
IVEY, Jean Eichelberger
JACKSON, Barbara May
JACOB, Elizabeth Marie
JAMES, Dorothy E.
JIRACKOVA, Marta
JOCHSBERGER, Tzipora H.
JOHNSTON-REID, Sarah Ruth
KABAT, Julie Phyllis
KADIMA, Hagar Yonith
KAHMANN, Chesley
KANACH, Sharon E.
KISTETENYI, Melinda
KITAZUME, Yayoi
KOLODUB, Zhanna Efimovna
KUBO, Mayako
KUKUCK, Felicitas
LACHARTRE, Nicole Marie
LARSEN, Elizabeth Brown
LAUBER, Anne Marianne
LAUFER, Beatrice
LEAHY, Mary Weldon
LEBARON, Anne
LEBENBOM, Elaine F.
LEE, Young Ja
LEFANU, Nicola Frances
LEJEUNE-BONNIER, Eliane
LEVIN, Rami Yona
LEVITSKAYA, Viktoria Sergeyevna
LOMON, Ruth
LOPEZ ROVIROSA, Maria Isabel
LOWENSTEIN, Gunilla Marike
LUFF, Enid
LUND, Gudrun
LUTYENS, Elisabeth
MACKIE, Shirley M.
MACONCHY, Elizabeth
McKENZIE, Sandra
McLEOD, Jennifer Helen
MALMLOEF-FORSSLING, Carin

MAZOUROVA, Jarmila
MEACHEM, Margaret McKeen
   Ramsey
MEL-BONIS
MELOY, Elizabeth
MESRITZ-VAN VELTHUYSEN, Annie
MOORE, Dorothy Rudd
MORETTO, Nelly
MURDOCH, Marjolijn
MUSGRAVE, Thea
NAZAROVA, Tatiana Borisovna
NEWLIN, Dika
NIEWIADOMSKA, Barbara
NIKOLSKAYA, Lyubov Borisovna
NOBLE, Ann
OFFICER, Bronwyn Lee
O'LEARY, Jane Strong
ORENSTEIN, Joyce Ellin
OSAWA, Kazuko
OWEN, Blythe
PATTERSON, Andra
PELEGRI, Maria Teresa
PENTLAND, Barbara Lally
PERETZ-LEVY, Liora
PETROVA, Mara
PHILIBA, Nicole
PHILIPPART, Renée
PHILLIPS, Bryony
PHILLIPS, Karen Ann
PHILLIPS, Linda
PIECHOWSKA, Alina
PIERCE, Alexandra
PIRES DOS REIS, Hilda
PIZER, Elizabeth Faw Hayden
POLIN, Claire
PREOBRAJENSKA, Vera Nicolaevna
PROCACCINI, Teresa
PTASZYNSKA, Marta
RADEKE, Winifred
RAINIER, Priaulx
RAVINALE, Irma
REED, Marlyce Rae Polk
REID, Sarah Johnston
RHEINGOLD, Lauma Yanovna
RICKARD, Sylvia
RILEY, Myrtis F.
ROBERT, Lucie
ROBERTSON, Donna Lou Nagey
ROE, Eileen Betty
ROESGEN-CHAMPION, Marguerite Sara
ROGER, Denise
ROSSER, Annetta Hamilton
ROWAN, Barbara
RUSCHE, Marjorie Maxine
SAINT JOHN, Kathleen Louise
SAMTER, Alice
SAMUEL, Rhian
SCHERCHEN, Tona
SCHORR-WEILER, Eva
SCHWARTZ, Julie
SEGHIZZI, Cecilia
SEVERY, Violet Cavell
SEWALL, Maud Gilchrist
SHERMAN, Kim Daryl
SILSBEE, Ann L.
SILVERMAN, Faye-Ellen
SMYTH, Ethel Mary, Dame
SNIZKOVA-SKRHOVA, Jitka
SOLOMON, Joyce Elaine
SPOENDLIN, Elisabeth
STREATFIELD, Valma June
STRUTT, Dorothy
SUTHERLAND, Margaret
SWAIN, Freda Mary
SZAJNA-LEWANDOWSKA, Jadwiga
   Helena
SZOENYI, Erzsebet
TALMA, Louise
TANN, Hilary
TARLOW, Karen Anne
TATE, Phyllis

TAUTU, Cornelia
TELFER, Nancy Ellen
THOMAS, Marilyn Taft
TOWER, Joan
TUCKER, Tui St. George
USHER, Julia
USTVOLSKAYA, Galina Ivanovna
VAN OHLEN, Deborah
VELLERE, Lucie Weiler
VIGNERON-RAMAKERS, Christiane-
   Josée
VOLKART-SCHLAGER, Kaethe
VORLOVA, Slavka
WALLACH, Joelle
WARDE, Ann Maury
WEAVER, Carol Ann
WEGENER-FRENSEL, Emmy Heil
WEIGL, Vally
WELMAN, Sylvia
WENDELBURG, Norma Ruth
WHITTLE, Chris Mary-Francine
WIENIAWSKA, Irene Regine
WILDSCHUT, Clara
WOLLNER, Gertrude Price
WYLIE, Ruth Shaw
YOSHIDA, Kazuko
ZECHLIN, Ruth

Century unknown
   JACQUE, Emilie

OBOE D'AMORE
20th Century A.D.
   CHANDLER, Mary
   LOMON, Ruth
   POSTON, Elizabeth
   SZAJNA-LEWANDOWSKA, Jadwiga
      Helena
   TREMBLOT DE LA CROIX, Francine
   WIENIAWSKA, Irene Regine

OBOE AND ORCHESTRA OR STRINGS
19th Century A.D.
   MACIRONI, Clara Angela
20th Century A.D.
   BALLOU, Esther Williamson
   BARBILLON, Jeanne
   BARTHELSON, Joyce Holloway
   BRITAIN, Radie
   BUTLER, Patricia Magahay
   CAPUIS, Matilde
   CLOSTRE, Adrienne
   GIPPS, Ruth
   GOLUB, Martha Naumovna
   GYRING, Elizabeth
   LOUDOVA, Ivana
   LUND, Gudrun
   MAMLOK, Ursula
   MASON, Gladys Amy
   NOVA SONDAG, Jacqueline
   PERISSAS, Madeleine
   RADEKE, Winifred
   ROBERT, Lucie
   ROE, Evelyn
   ROGER, Denise
   SAINT JOHN, Kathleen Louise
   SCHROEDER, Inge Maria
   SHLONSKY, Verdina
   VIGNERON-RAMAKERS, Christiane-
      Josée
   VORLOVA, Slavka
   WILDSCHUT, Clara
   WILL, Madeleine
   WILLIAMS, Grace Mary
   YAKHNINA, Yevgenia Yosifovna
   ZECHLIN, Ruth

OBOE AND PIANO
19th Century A.D.
   GRANDVAL, Marie Felicie Clemence
      de Reiset, Vicomtesse de
   ROSENHOFF, Orla

20th Century A.D.
ARCHER, Violet Balestreri
ARRIEU, Claude
BACEWICZ, Grazyna
BACKES, Lotte
BAINBRIDGE, Beryl
BARRATT, Carol Ann
BAUER, Marion Eugenie
BELLAMY, Marian Meredith
BEYER, Johanna Magdalena
BLISS, Marilyn S.
BORROFF, Edith
BRIGGS, Nancy Louise
BRITAIN, Radie
CHANDLER, Mary
CHRETIEN-GENARO, Hedwige
COME, Tilde
COOLIDGE, Elizabeth Sprague
COULTHARD, Jean
DE BIASE BIDART, Lycia
DEMBO, Royce
DIMITRIU, Florica
DRING, Madeleine
FINE, Vivian
FINZI, Graciane
FISCHER, Edith Steinkraus
FRASER, Shena Eleanor
GABUS, Monique
GARTENLAUB, Odette
GIPPS, Ruth
HARRISON, Pamela
HARVEY, Eva Noel
HENDERSON, Ruth Watson
HOLLAND, Dulcie Sybil
HYDE, Miriam Beatrice
HYTREK, Sister Theophane
JIRKOVA, Olga
JOLLEY, Florence Werner
KAZANDJIAN, Sirvart
KESSLER, Minuetta Schumiatcher
LE SIEGE, Annette
LEAHY, Mary Weldon
LEBENBOM, Elaine F.
LEJEUNE-BONNIER, Eliane
LEVITSKAYA, Viktoria Sergeyevna
LOUDOVA, Ivana
McALISTER, Mabel
McLAUGHLIN, Marian
MAKAROVA, Nina Vladimirovna
MALDYBAYEVA, Zhyldyz
    Abdylasovna
MAMLOK, Ursula
MANZIARLY, Marcelle de
MAREZ-OYENS, Tera de
MARI, Pierrette
MARKIEWICZOWNA, Wladyslawa
MARKOV, Katherine Lee
MARTINS, Maria de Lourdes
NAIKHOVICH-LOMAKINA, Fania
    Filippovna
PETRA-BASACOPOL, Carmen
PROCACCINI, Teresa
ROBERT, Lucie
ROBERTSON, Donna Lou Nagey
ROGER, Denise
SIMONS, Netty
SNIZKOVA-SKRHOVA, Jitka
SPENCER, Williametta
SUTHERLAND, Margaret
SUTZU, Rodica
SWAIN, Freda Mary
SZAJNA-LEWANDOWSKA, Jadwiga
    Helena
TOWER, Joan
VAN DE VATE, Nancy Hayes
VELLERE, Lucie Weiler
VITO-DELVAUX, Berthe di
VOLKART-SCHLAGER, Kaethe
WEGENER-FRENSEL, Emmy Heil
WELLNER, Elsa
WENDELBURG, Norma Ruth

WILDSCHUT, Clara
WYLIE, Ruth Shaw
ZAVALISHINA, Maria Semyonovna
Century unknown
KEECH, Diana
McDOWALL, Cecilia

OCTET
20th Century A.D.
ABEJO, Sister M. Rosalina
ARCHER, Violet Balestreri
ARIMA, Reiko
ARRIEU, Claude
BAILLY, Colette
BERTRAND, Ginette
BOUCHARD, Linda L.
CHANCE, Nancy Laird
CORY, Eleanor
DUDLEY, Marjorie Eastwood
DUSHKIN, Dorothy Smith
FERRAND-TEULET, Denise
GREENWALD, Jan Carol
GUERRANT, Mary Thorington
HARA, Kazuko (1)
HARRISON, Pamela
INWOOD, Mary Ruth Brink Berger
JOLAS, Betsy
KERN, Frida
LACHOWSKA, Stefania
LUTYENS, Elisabeth
MACAULAY, Janice Michel
MAREZ-OYENS, Tera de
MUSGRAVE, Thea
OLIVE, Vivienne
OLIVEROS, Pauline
OSAWA, Kazuko
PENTLAND, Barbara Lally
PETRA-BASACOPOL, Carmen
PHILLIPS, Bryony
PIZER, Elizabeth Faw Hayden
PREOBRAJENSKA, Vera Nicolaevna
PROCACCINI, Teresa
PTASZYNSKA, Marta
ROGERS, Patsy
SENFTER, Johanna
SMITH, Julia Frances
USTVOLSKAYA, Galina Ivanovna
VIERK, Lois
VIGNERON-RAMAKERS, Christiane-
    Josee
VON ZIERITZ, Grete
WITKIN, Beatrice

ONDES MARTINOT
20th Century A.D.
ARRIEU, Claude
BARRAINE, Elsa
BRENET, Thérèse
CECCONI-BOTELLA, Monic
CHARBONNIER, Janine Andrée
COULOMBE SAINT-MARCOUX,
    Micheline
GRIMAUD, Yvette
HOVDA, Eleanor
LACHARTRE, Nicole Marie
LORIOD, Yvonne
MARI, Pierrette
PHILIBA, Nicole
PHILIPPART, Rénee
PIECHOWSKA, Alina
POULET DEFONTAINE, Madeleine

ORCHESTRA - STRING
19th Century A.D.
MOODY, Marie
SWEPSTONE, Edith
20th Century A.D.
ABEJO, Sister M. Rosalina
ALBRIGHT, Janet Elaine
ANDERSON, Ruth
ANDERSON-WUENSCH, Jean Mary

APPELDOORN, Dina van
ARCHER, Violet Balestreri
ARETZ, Isabel
ARKWRIGHT, Marian Ursula
ARRIEU, Claude
AUSTER, Lydia Martinovna
AUTENRIETH, Helma
BAADER-NOBS, Heidi
BACEWICZ, Grażyna
BACHELLER, Mildred R. Thomas
BAIL, Grace Shattuck
BALLOU, Esther Williamson
BARKLUND, Irma L.
BARRATT, Carol Ann
BARRELL, Joyce Howard
BAUER, Marion Eugenie
BECKON, Lettie Marie
BEECROFT, Norma Marian
BEEKHUIS, Hanna
BENAVENTE, Regina
BERTRAND, Ginette
BIRCHER-REY, Hedy
BLANCK, Olga de
BLOMFIELD-HOLT, Patricia
BODENSTEIN-HOYME, Ruth E.
BOLL, Christine E.
BORDEWIJK-ROEPMAN, Johanna
BOYD, Anne Elizabeth
BRANDMAN, Margaret Susan
BRITAIN, Radie
BRITTON, Dorothy Guyver
BRUNDZAITE, Konstantsiya Kazyo
BUCZEK, Barbara Kazimiera
CADZOW, Dorothy Forrest
CALCAGNO, Elsa
CAMPBELL, Edith Mary
CAPUIS, Matilde
CARVALHO, Dinora de
CARWITHEN, Doreen
CECCONI-BOTELLA, Monic
CHAVES, Mary Elizabeth
CLARK, Florence Durrell
COATES, Gloria Kannenberg
COLE, Ulric
CONTINI ANSELMI, Lucia
CORY, Eleanor
COULTHARD, Jean
DANIELS, Mabel Wheeler
DARE, Margaret Marie
DE BIASE BIDART, Lycia
DE LARA, Adelina
DE PATE, Elisabetta M.S.
DIAKVNISHVILI, Mzisavar
    Zakharevna
DIANDA, Hilda
DIEMER, Emma Lou
DINESCU, Violeta
DU PAGE, Florence Elizabeth
DUSHKIN, Dorothy Smith
ECKHARDT-GRAMATTE, Sophie-
    Carmen
EGGLESTON, Anne E.
EICHENWALD, Sylvia
ENDRES, Olive Philomene
EVEN-OR, Mary
FAUTCH, Sister Magdalen
FERNANDO, Sarathchandra
    Vichremadithya
FINE, Vivian
FISCHER, Edith Steinkraus
FISHER, Katherine Danforth
FONTYN, Jacqueline
FOWLER, Jennifer Joan
FRANK, Jean Forward
FREED, Dorothy Whitson
FRITTER, Genevieve Davisson
GIDEON, Miriam
GIFFORD, Helen Margaret
GIPPS, Ruth
GLATZ, Helen Sinclair
GOTKOVSKY, Ida-Rose Esther

GREY, Edith
GRZADZIELOWNA, Eleonora
GYRING, Elizabeth
HARRISON, Pamela
HELLER-REICHENBACH, Barbara
HERBISON, Jeraldine Saunders
HEWITT-JONES, Anita
HIND O'MALLEY, Pamela
HINLOPEN, Francina
HOLST, Imogen Clare
HOWE, Mary Alberta Bruce
HOWELL, Dorothy
ISAKOVA, Aida Petrovna
JACKSON, Barbara May
JOLAS, Betsy
JUDD, Margaret Evelyn
KAHMANN, Chesley
KALOGRIDOU, Maria
KALTENECKER, Gertraud
KARASTOYANOVA, Elena
KARNITSKAYA, Nina Andreyevna
KERN, Frida
KIRKWOOD, Antoinette
KLINKOVA, Zhivka
KOELLING, Eloise
KOHAN, Celina
LACHOWSKA, Stefania
LANDOWSKA, Wanda
LANE, Elizabeth
LAPEYRE, Therese
LAUBER, Anne Marianne
LEAHY, Mary Weldon
LEBARON, Anne
LEE, Chan-Hae
LEE, Hope Anne Keng-Wei
LEONCHIK, Svetlana Gavrilovna
LEPEUT-LEVINE, Jeannine
LIPSCOMB, Helen
LOOTS, Joyce Mary Ann
LOUDOVA, Ivana
LUCAS, Mary Anderson
LUNA DE ESPAILLAT, Margarita
LUTYENS, Elisabeth
LVOVA, Julia Fedorovna
MACKIE, Shirley M.
MacKENNA, Carmela
McCOLLIN, Frances
McKINNEY, Mathilde
MALDYBAYEVA, Zhyldyz
    Abdylasovna
MALMLOEF-FORSSLING, Carin
MAMLOK, Ursula
MANUKIAN, Irina Eduardovna
MAREZ-OYENS, Tera de
MEYSENBURG, Sister Agnes
MIKUSCH, Margarethe von
MILNE, Helen C.
MIRSHAKAR, Zarrina Mirsaidovna
MKRTYCHIEVA, Virginia Nikitichna
MOBERG, Ida Georgina
MOON, Chloe Elizabeth
MORLEY, Nina Dianne
MOSUSOVA, Nadezda
MOSZUMANSKA-NAZAR, Krystyna
MUSGRAVE, Thea
NAZIROVA, Elmira Mirza Rza kyzy
NORDENSTROM, Gladys Mercedes
NOVA SONDAG, Jacqueline
OBROVSKA, Jana
ODAGESCU, Irina
ORE, Cécilie
OVERMAN, Meta
OWEN, Blythe
PADE, Else Marie
PARKER, Phyllis Norman
PARPAGLIOLO, Iditta
PENTLAND, Barbara Lally
PERISSAS, Madeleine
PETRA-BASACOPOL, Carmen
PETROVA, Mara
PHILIBA, Nicole

PIECHOWSKA, Alina
PIRES DE CAMPOS, Lina
PREOBRAJENSKA, Vera Nicolaevna
RAINIER, Priaulx
RAKHMANKULOVA, Mariam
    Mannanovna
RAPOPORT, Eda
RAVINALE, Irma
RENSHAW, Rosette
REYNOLDS, Erma Grey
    Hogue
RHOADS, Mary R.
RICHTER, Marga
ROESGEN-CHAMPION, Marguerite
    Sara
ROGER, Denise
ROWAN, Barbara
ROYSE, Mildred Barnes
SAINT JOHN, Kathleen Louise
SANTOS-OCAMPO DE FRANCESCO,
    Amada Amy
SCHORR-WEILER, Eva
SCHURZMANN, Katharina
SCHWERDTFEGER, E. Anne
SHAFFER, Jeanne Ellison
SHEPARD, Jean Ellen
SHLONSKY, Verdina
SMYTH, Ethel Mary, Dame
SOLOMON, Joyce Elaine
SOUTHAM, Ann
SPAIN-DUNK, Susan
STEINER, Gitta Hana
STEPHEN, Roberta Mae
STREIT, Else
STRUCK, Ilse
SUNBLAD-HALME, Heidi Gabriella
    Wilhelmina
SUTHERLAND, Margaret
SWAIN, Freda Mary
SZAJNA-LEWANDOWSKA, Jadwiga
    Helena
SZOENYI, Erzsebet
TANN, Hilary
TATE, Phyllis
TELFER, Nancy Ellen
THIEME, Kerstin Anja
TKACH, Zlata Moiseyevna
TOLKOWSKY, Denise
TORRA, Celia
TOWNSEND, Jill
TRIMBLE, Joan
USHER, Julia
VAN DE VATE, Nancy Hayes
VAN DIJCK, Beatrice Madeleine
VAN HAUTE, Anna-Maria
VAZQUEZ, Alida
VEHAR, Persis Anne
VELLERE, Lucie Weiler
WALDO, Elisabeth
WARING, Kate
WARNE, Katharine Mulky
WELANDER, Svea Goeta
WELLNER, Elsa
WHITEHEAD, Gillian
WIERUSZOWSKI, Lili
WILDSCHUT, Clara
WILLIAMS, Grace Mary
Century unknown
BLAIR-OLIPHANT, Lilian
HARVEY, Ella Doreen

ORCHESTRAL - OTHER
16th Century A.D.
VERTOA DA BERGAMO, Sister
    Agostina
18th Century A.D.
BRANDES, Charlotte Wilhelmina
    Franziska
GRIMANI, Maria Margherita
MARIA TERESA BARBARA DE
    BRAGANÇA, Queen of Spain

19th Century A.D.
ALEXANDRA JOSEPHOWNA, Grand
    Duchess
ASPRI, Orsola
BACKER-GROENDAHL, Agathe
    Ursula
BERNOUILLY, Agnes
BERTIN, Louise Angelique
BLAHETKA, Marie Leopoldina
BLEITNER, Rosa
BOSCH, Elisa
BOYCE, Ethel Mary
BRONSART VON SCHELLENDORF,
    Ingeborg Lena von
BRUCKEN-FOCK, Emilie von
CHARLOTTE, Friederike Wilhelmine
    Louise, Princess
COSSOUL, Genoveva Virginia
DAVIES, Llewela
DELL'ACQUA, Eva
ESCHBORN, Georgine Christine
    Maria Anna
GIZYCKA-ZAMOYSKA, Ludmilla,
    Countess
GRANDVAL, Marie Felicie Clemence
    de Reiset, Vicomtesse de
GREENE, Edith
HADELN, Nancy von
HAENEL DE CRONENTHAL, Louise
    Augusta Marie Julia
HOLMES, Augusta Mary Anne
HUNDT, Aline
KARL, Anna
KOWALOWSKA, Wiktoria
LAMBERT, Agnes
LEGOUX, Julie, Baroness
LEONARDO, Luisa
MARCKWALD, Grace
MARIE ELIZABETH, Princess of
    Saxe-Meiningen
MAURY, Renaud
MUNGAY Y PIZARRO, Dona Carolina
OLGA, Grand Duchess
PERRELLI, Giuseppina
PUSICH, D. Antonia Gertrudes
REED, Florence
RIBAS, Medina N.
RODRIGO, Maria
STRANTZ, Louise von
WHITE, Maude Valerie
WURM, Mary J.A.
YEATMAN, Ethel
20th Century A.D.
AARNE, Els
AARON, Marcelle
AARON, Yvonne
ABE, Kyoko
ABEJO, Sister M. Rosalina
ACKLAND, Jeanne Isabel Dorothy
ACOSTA, Josefina, Baroness
ADAM, Maria Emma
ADERHOLDT, Sarah
AHRENS, Peg
AKHUNDOVA, Shafiga Gulam kyzy
AKIYOSHI, Toshiko
ALARCO, Rosa
ALBRIGHT, Janet Elaine
ALCALAY, Luna
ALEXANDER, Leni
ALEXANDRA, Liana
ALLAN, Esther
ALLBRITTON, Florence Ziegler
ALLEN, Judith Shatin
ALLIK, Kristi
ALMESAN, Irma
ALTER, Martha
ALVES DE SOUSA, Berta Candida
ANDERSON, Laurie
APPELDOORN, Dina van
ARAUJO, Gina de
ARBUCKLE, Dorothy M.

ARCHER, Violet Balestreri
ARETZ, Isabel
ARHO, Anneli
ARIMA, Reiko
ARQUIT, Nora Harris
ARRIEU, Claude
AUSTER, Lydia Martinovna
AYARZA DE MORALES, Rosa
  Mercedes
BABITS, Linda
BACH, Maria
BACKES, Lotte
BADIAN, Maya
BAILEY, Judith Margaret
BAILLY, Colette
BAKKE, Ruth
BALLASEYUS, Virginia
BANCER, Teresa Barbara
BANDARA, Linda
BARAMISHVILI, Olga Ivanovna
BARBERIS, Mansi
BARBILLON, Jeanne
BARBOSA, Cacilda Campos Borges
BARCROFT, E. Dorothea
BARKIN, Elaine
BARKLUND, Irma L.
BARNETT, Carol Edith
BARRAINE, Elsa
BARRELL, Joyce Howard
BARRETT-THOMAS, N.
BARTHEL, Ursula
BEACH, Priscilla A.
BEAT, Janet Eveline
BECK, Martha Dillard
BECKMAN, Ellen Josephine
BECKON, Lettie Marie
BEECROFT, Norma Marian
BEEKHUIS, Hanna
BEGO-SIMUNIC, Andelka
BEHREND, Jeanne
BENEDICENTI, Vera
BENNETT, Wilhelmine
BENOIT, Francine Germaine Van
  Gool
BERCKMAN, Evelyn
BERZON, Asya Yevseyevna
BEYER, Johanna Magdalena
BEYERMAN-WALRAVEN, Jeanne
BIBBY, Gillian Margaret
BIENVENU, Lily
BINET, Jocelyne
BIRNSTEIN, Renate Maria
BLAUSTEIN, Susan Morton
BLIESENER, Ada Elizabeth
  Michelman
BLOMFIELD-HOLT, Patricia
BLOOD, Esta Damesek
BODENSTEIN-HOYME, Ruth E.
BOND, Victoria Ellen
BOONE, Clara Lyle
BORRAS I FORNELL, Teresa
BOULANGER, Nadia Juliette
BOYD, Anne Elizabeth
BOYD, Jeanne Margaret
BOYLE, Ina
BRANDMAN, Margaret Susan
BRANSCOMBE, Gena
BRENET, Thérèse
BRIGHT, Dora Estella
BRINGUER, Estela
BRITAIN, Radie
BROWN, Gertrude M.
BRUNDZAITE, Konstantsiya Kazyo
BRUSH, Ruth Damaris
BRUSSELS, Iris
BRUZDOWICZ, Joanna
BUCKLEY, Helen Dallam
BUTLER, Anne Lois
CADZOW, Dorothy Forrest
CALAME, Genevieve
CALCAGNO, Elsa

CALDER, Hattie M.
CALL, Audrey
CAMPMANY, Montserrat
CAPUIS, Matilde
CARR-BOYD, Ann Kirsten
CARREÑO, Teresa
CARTER PAULENA, Elizabeth
CARTER, Buenta MacDaniel
CARTER, Rosetta
CARVALHO, Dinora de
CATUNDA, Eunice do Monte Lima
CECCONI-BATES, Augusta
CECCONI-BOTELLA, Monic
CHACON LASAUCA, Emma
CHAMINADE, Cecile Louise
  Stephanie
CHANCE, Nancy Laird
CHANDLER, Mary
CHARBONNIER, Janine Andrée
CHARLES, S. Robin
CHARLOTTE, Princess of Saxe-
  Meiningen
CHAVES, Mary Elizabeth
CHEBOTARIAN, Gayane Movsesovna
CHICHERINA, Sofia Nikolayevna
CHKHEIDZE, Dali Davidovna
CHRETIEN-GENARO, Hedwige
CIOBANU, Maia
CLAMAN, Dolores Olga
CLAYTON, Susan
CLOSTRE, Adrienne
COATES, Gloria Kannenberg
COCQ, Rosina Susanna de
COHEN, Dulcie M.
COHEN, Marcia
COLE, Ulric
COLERIDGE-TAYLOR, Avril
  Gwendolen
COLIN, Jeanne
CONSTANTINESCU, Domnica
CONTINI ANSELMI, Lucia
COOKE, Edith
COONEY, Cheryl Lee
COOPER, Rose Marie
COQUET, Odile Marie-Lucie
COTRON, Fanou
COULOMBE SAINT-MARCOUX,
  Micheline
COUPER, Mildred
COWLES, Cecil Marion
COX, Alison Mary
CRANE, Helen
CRAWFORD SEEGER, Ruth
CRAWFORD, Dawn Constance
CREWS, Lucille
CROWE, Bonita
DAIGLE, Sister Anne Cécile
DALBERG, Nancy
DANEAU, Suzanne
DANIELS, Mabel Wheeler
DARGEL, Maude
DASCALESCU, Camelia
DAVIS, Hilda Emery
DAVIES, Margaret
DE BIASE BIDART, Lycia
DE CEVEE, Alice
DE FREITAS, Elvira Manuela
  Fernandez
DE LEATH, Vaughn
DE PATE, Elisabetta M.S.
DECARIE, Reine
DEMARQUEZ, Suzanne
DESPORTES, Yvonne Berthe Melitta
DEYTON, Camilla Hill
DIAKVNISHVILI, Mzisavar
  Zakharevna
DIEMER, Emma Lou
DILLON, Fannie Charles
DIMITRIU, Florica
DINESCU, Violeta
DLUGOSZEWSKI, Lucia

DOBSON, Elaine
DONATOVA, Narcisa
DRATTELL, Deborah
DRDOVA, Marie
DRING, Madeleine
DROBYAZGINA, Valentina Ivanovna
DU PAGE, Florence Elizabeth
DUNFORD, Nancy Ridenhour
DUSHKIN, Dorothy Smith
DUVOSEL, Seraphien Lieven
DVORKIN, Judith
DYCHKO, Lesya Vasilevna
DZIEWULSKA, Maria Amelia
EAGLES, Moneta M.
EGGLESTON, Anne E.
EIRIKSDOTTIR, Karolina
EISENSTEIN DE VEGA, Silvia
ERNST, Siegrid
ESCOT, Pozzi
ESTRELLA, Blanca
ETHRIDGE, Jean
EUTENEUER-ROHRER, Ursula
  Henrietta
EVERETT-SALICCO, Betty Lou
FALCINELLI, Rolande
FEININGER, Leonore Helene
FEJARD, Simone
FELDMAN, Joann Esther
FELIX, Margery Edith
FERNANDO, Sarathchandra
  Vichremadithya
FERRARI, Gabriella
FILZ, Bogdanna
FINE, Vivian
FIRSOVA, Elena
FISHER, Susan
FISHMAN, Marian
FLACH, Elsa
FLICK-FLOOD, Dora
FONTYN, Jacqueline
FORMAN, Joanne
FOSTER, Cecily
FOWLER, Jennifer Joan
FOWLER, Marje
FRAJT, Ludmila
FRANCO, Clare
FRASER-MILLER, Gloria Jill
FRASIER, Jane
FROTHINGHAM, Eugenia
GAIGEROVA, Varvara Andrianovna
GALAJIKIAN, Florence Grandland
GALINNE, Rachel
GARCIA ASCOT, Rosa
GARCIA ROBSON, Magdalena
GARDNER, Kay
GARELLI DELLA MOREA, Vincenza
GARTENLAUB, Odette
GARUTA, Lucia Yanovna
GARY, Marianne
GASPARINI, Jola
GAYNOR, Jessie Love
GAZAROSSIAN, Koharik
GEBUHR, Ann Karen
GEIGER-KULLMANN, Rosy Auguste
GERSTMAN, Blanche Wilhelminia
GESSLER, Caroline
GHANDAR, Ann
GHILARDI, Syra
GIDEON, Miriam
GIFFORD, Helen Margaret
GILBERT, Pia
GIURANNA, Elena Barbara
GLANVILLE-HICKS, Peggy
GLASER, Victoria Merrylees
GONTARENKO, Galina Nikolayevna
GONZAGA, Chiquinha
GORELLI, Olga
GOTKOVSKY, Ida-Rose Esther
GOULD, Elizabeth Davies
GRAHAM, Janet Christine
GREENFIELD, Lucille

GREENWALD, Jan Carol
GRIECO, Ida
GRIEF, Marjorie
GRIMES, Doreen
GROOM, Joan Charlene
GRUNBERG, Janeta
GUBITOSI, Emilia
GUNDERSON, Helen Louise
GVAZAVA, Tamara Davidovna
GYANDZHETSIAN, Destrik Bogdanovna
GYRING, Elizabeth
HABAN, Sister Teresine M.
HALACSY, Irma von
HALL, Pauline
HANNIKAINEN, Ann-Elise
HANSEN, Hanna Marie
HARA, Kazuko
HARDIMAN, Ellena G.
HARKNESS, Rebekah West
HARRISON, Pamela
HAYS, Doris Ernestine
HECKSCHER, Céleste de Longpre
HEDOUX, Yvonne
HEDSTROEM, Ase
HEILBRON, Valerie
HEMON, Sedje
HERNANDEZ-GONZALO, Gisela
HERSCHER-CLEMENT, Jeanne
HILSTON, Lucille
HINLOPEN, Francina
HOELSZKY, Adriana
HOFER, Maria
HOKANSON, Margrethe
HOLLAND, Dulcie Sybil
HONEGGER-VAURABOURG, Andree
HONG, Sung-Hee
HOPEKIRK, Helen
HORROCKS, Amy Elsie
HOVDA, Eleanor
HOWE, Mary Alberta Bruce
HOWELL, Dorothy
HSU, Wen-Ying
HUBICKI, Margaret Olive
HUEGEL, Margrit
HUGHES, Sister Martina
HYDE, Miriam Beatrice
HYSON, Winifred Prince
ILLIUTOVICH, Nina Yakovlevna
INWOOD, Mary Ruth Brink Berger
IORDAN, Irina Nikolayevna
ISMAGILOVA, Leila Zagirovna
ISZKOWSKA, Zofia
IVANOVA, Lidia
IVEY, Jean Eichelberger
JAMES, Dorothy E.
JANKOVIC, Miroslava
JANKOWSKI, Loretta Patricia
JANOTHA, Natalia
JAZWINSKI, Barbara
JEPPSSON, Kerstin Maria
JIJON, Ines
JIRACKOVA, Marta
JOHNSTON, Alison Aileen Annie
JOLAS, Betsy
JOLY, Suzanne
JUENGER, Patricia
KABAT, Julie Phyllis
KADIMA, Hagar Yonith
KAHRER, Laura Rappoldy
KANAI, Kikuko
KAPRALOVA, Vitezslava
KASILAG, Lucrecia R.
KAUFMAN, Barbara
KAVARNALIEVA, Konstantina
KAZANDJIAN, Sirvart
KELLER, Ginette
KELLEY, Dorothea Nolte
KEMP, Dorothy Elizabeth Walter
KEMP-POTTER, Joan
KENSWIL, Atma
KERN, Frida

KETTERING, Eunice Lea
KIM, Kwang-Hee
KING, Rebecca Clift
KLEBE, Willemijntje
KLINKOVA, Zhivka
KLOTZMAN, Dorothy Ann Hill
KOLB, Barbara
KOLODUB, Zhanna Efimovna
KORN, Clara Anna
KORNILOVA, Tatiana Dmitrevna
KRASNOGLIADOVA, Vera
  Vladimirovna
KRZANOWSKA, Grażyna
KUCEROVA-HERSTOVA, Marie
KUSS, Margarita Ivanovna
KUYPER, Elizabeth
KUZMENKO, Larysa
KUZMYCH, Christina
KVERNADZE, Bidzina
LACKMAN, Susan C. Cohn
LAITMAN, Lori
LAM MAN YEE, Violet
LAMBELET, Vivienne Ada Maurice
LAMBRECHTS-VOS, Anna Catharina
LARSEN, Elizabeth Brown
LATIOLAIS, Desirée Jayne
LAUER, Elizabeth
LAUFER, Beatrice
LAYMAN, Pamela
LEE, Hope Anne Keng-Wei
LEE, Hwaeja Yoo
LEE, Young Ja
LEFANU, Nicola Frances
LEIBOW, Ruth Irene
LEIVISKA, Helvi Lemmiki
LELEU, Jeanne
LENNEP, Henrietta van
LEON, Tania Justina
LEVEY, Lauren
LEVINA, Zara Alexandrovna
LIADOVA, Ludmila Alekseyevna
LINDEMAN, Hjelle Signe
LITSITE, Paula Yanovna
LLUNELL SANAHUJA, Pepita
LOCKSHIN, Florence Levin
LOPUSKA-WYLEZYNSKA, Helena
LORENZ, Ellen Jane
LORIOD, Yvonne
LOUIE, Alexina Diane
LOVELACE, Carey
LOWENSTEIN, Gunilla Marike
LU, Yen
LUCAS, Mary Anderson
LUCKE, Katharine E.
LUCKMAN, Phyllis
LUFF, Enid
LUNA DE ESPAILLAT, Margarita
LUND, Gudrun
LUND, Signe
LUTHER, Mary
LUTYENS, Elisabeth
LVOVA, Julia Fedorovna
MACAULAY, Janice Michel
MACKIE, Shirley M.
MacKENNA, Carmela
McCOLLIN, Frances
McINTYRE, Margaret
McKAY, Frances Thompson
McLAUGHLIN, Marian
McLEAN, Priscilla Anne Taylor
McLEOD, Jennifer Helen
McLIN, Lena
McTEE, Cindy Karen
MAGEAU, Mary Jane
MAGUY LOVANO, Marguerite Schlegel
MAHLER, Hellgart
MAILIAN, Elza Antonovna
MAIRE, Jacqueline
MALDYBAYEVA, Zhyldyz
  Abdylasovna
MALMLOEF-FORSSLING, Carin

MAMLOK, Ursula
MANA-ZUCCA
MANUKIAN, Irina Eduardovna
MANZIARLY, Marcelle de
MARBE, Myriam
MARCELL, Florence
MARCUS, Ada Belle Gross
MAREZ-OYENS, Tera de
MARI, Pierrette
MARIC, Ljubica
MARSHALL, Pamela J.
MARTINEZ DE LA TORRE Y
  SHELTON, Emma
MARTINS, Maria de Lourdes
MARY BERNICE, Sister
MATUSZCZAK, Bernadetta
MAXWELL, Jacqueline Perkinson
MAYER, Lise Maria
MAZOUROVA, Jarmila
MEEK, Ethel Alice
MEISTER, Marianne
MELL, Gertrud Maria
MERLI-ZWISCHENBRUGGER,
  Christina
MERRIMAN, Margarita Leonor
MERTENS, Dolores
MESRITZ-VAN VELTHUYSEN, Annie
MESTDAGH, Helene
METALLIDI, Zhanneta Lazarevna
MEYSENBURG, Sister Agnes
MIAGI, Ester Kustovna
MIGRANYAN, Emma
MILENKOVIC, Jelena
MILLER, Elma
MINEO, Antoinette
MKRTYCHIEVA, Virginia Nikitichna
MOBERG, Ida Georgina
MOE, Benna
MONTGOMERY, Merle
MOORE, Mary Carr
MORETTO, Nelly
MORIN-LABRECQUE, Albertine
MOSUSOVA, Nadezda
MOSZUMANSKA-NAZAR, Krystyna
MUELLER-HERMANN, Johanna
MURAKUMO, Ayako
MUSGRAVE, Thea
MYSZINSKA-WOJCIECHOWSKA,
  Leokadia
NAZAROVA, Tatiana Borisovna
NIAY, Apolline
NIEMACK, Ilza Louise
NIEWIADOMSKA, Barbara
NOBLE, Ann
NORDENSTROM, Gladys Mercedes
NOVA SONDAG, Jacqueline
NOVI, Anna Beate
NOVOSELOVA, Ludmila Alexeyevna
NOWAK, Alison
NOYES, Edith Rowena
ODAGESCU, Irina
OERBECK, Anne-Marie
OH, Sook Ja
OLLER BENLLOCH, Maria Teresa
O'NEILL, Selena
OOSTERZEE, Cornelia van
OSAWA, Kazuko
OSETROVA-YAKOVLIEVA, Nina
  Alexandrovna
OSIANDER, Irene
OSTRANDER, Linda Woodaman
OTERO, Mercedes
OWEN, Morfydd Llwyn
PADE, Else Marie
PAGH-PAAN, Younghi
PARPAGLIOLO, Iditta
PARR-GERE, Florence
PATERSON, Wilma
PATTERSON, Annie Wilson
PAYNE, Harriet
PELEGRI, Maria Teresa

PENGILLY, Sylvia
PENTLAND, Barbara Lally
PERISSAS, Madeleine
PERRY, Julia Amanda
PERRY, Zenobia Powell
PETRA-BASACOPOL, Carmen
PETROVA-KRUPKOVA, Elena
PEYROT, Fernande
PFEIFFER, Irena
PHILLIPS, Bryony
PHILLIPS, Vivian Daphne
PIECHOWSKA, Alina
PIERCE, Alexandra
PIETSCH, Edna Frieda
PIRES DOS REIS, Hilda
PIZER, Elizabeth Faw Hayden
PLANICK, Annette Meyers
POLIGNAC, Armande de, Countess
  of Chabannes
POLLOCK, Muriel
POSTON, Elizabeth
PRADELL, Leila
PRAVOSSUDOVITCH, Natalja
  Michajlovna
PREDIC-SAPER, Branislava
PREOBRAJENSKA, Vera Nicolaevna
PROCACCINI, Teresa
PSTROKONSKA-NAVRATIL,
  Grazyna Hanna
PTASZYNSKA, Marta
RAINIER, Priaulx
RAMAKERS, Christiane Josée
RAPOPORT, Eda
RAYMOND, Madeleine
RECLI, Giulia
RED, Virginia Stroh
REHNQVIST, Karin Birgitta
REICH, Amy
REIFF, Lili
REISSEROVA, Julie
REMICK, Bertha
RHOADS, Mary R.
RHODEN, Natalia Naana
RICCIOLI FRAZZI, Eva
RICHER, Jeannine
RICHTER, Marga
RILEY, Myrtis F.
ROBERT, Lucie
ROCHEROLLE, Eugenie Katherine
ROE, Marion Adelle
ROFE, Esther
ROGER, Denise
ROMERO BARBOSA, Elena
ROMM, Rosalina Davidovna
ROSE OF JESUS, Sister
ROZHAVSKAYA, Yudif Grigorevna
RUBIN, Anna Ita
RUCHEVSKAYA, Ekaterina
  Alexandrovna
RUEFF, Jeanine
RUSCHE, Marjorie Maxine
RUTA, Gilda, Countess
RZAYEVA, Agabadzhi Ishmael kykz
SADOWSKY, Reah
SALIUTRINSKAYA, Tatiana
SALVADOR, Matilde
SAMSON, Valerie Brooks
SAMVELIAN, Sofia Vardanovna
SANDRESKY, Margaret Vardell
SANGUESA, Iris
SANZ, Rocio
SAROVA, Dagmar
SATOH, Kimi
SAUVREZIS, Alice
SAXTORPH, Gudrun
SCEK, Breda Friderika
SCHAUSS-FLAKE, Magdalene
SCHERCHEN, Tona
SCHMIDT-DUISBURG, Margarete
  Dina Alwina
SCHMITT-LERMANN, Frieda

SCHONTHAL, Ruth E.
SCHORLEMMER, Erna von
SCHORR-WEILER, Eva
SCHUBARTH, Dorothe
SCHUYLER, Philippa Duke
SCHWERDTFEGER, E. Anne
SCLIAR, Esther
SEAVER, Blanche Ebert
SEBASTIANI, Pia
SEHESTED, Hilda
SEMEGEN, Daria
SEPULVEDA, Maria Luisa
SETTI, Kilza
SHAGIAKHMETOVA, Svetlana
  Georgievna
SHAIMARDANOVA, Shakhida
SHAVERZASHVILI, Tamara
  Antonovna
SHELTON, Margaret Meier
SHEPARD, Jean Ellen
SHERMAN, Elna
SHLONSKY, Verdina
SHORE, Clare
SHRUDE, Marilyn
SHUTTLEWORTH, Anne-Marie
SIDORENKO, Tamara Stepanovna
SIKORA, Elzbieta
SILBERTA, Rhea
SILSBEE, Ann L.
SILVER, Sheila Jane
SILVERMAN, Faye-Ellen
SIMON, Cecile Paul
SIMONS, Netty
SKALSKA-SZEMIOTH, Hanna Wanda
SKOUEN, Synne
SLIANOVA-MIZANDARI, Dagmara
  Levanovna
SMEJKALOVA, Vlasta
SMELTZER, Susan Mary
SMITH, Julia Frances
SMITH, Ladonna Carol
SNIZKOVA-SKRHOVA, Jitka
SNYDER, Amy
SOLOMON, Joyce Elaine
SOUBLETTE, Sylvia
SPECHT, Judy Lavise
SPOENDLIN, Elisabeth
STANLEY, Helen Camille
STEELE, Lynn
STEIN, Gladys Marie
STEIN-SCHNEIDER, Lena
STERNICKA-NIEKRASZOWA, Ilza
STREATFIELD, Valma June
STREICHER, Lyubov Lvovna
STREIT, Else
SUCHY, Gregoria Karides
SUTHERLAND, Margaret
SYNOWIEC, Ewa
SZEKELY, Katalin
SZOENYI, Erzsebet
TAILLEFERRE, Germaine
TAKASHIMA, Midori
TAL, Ya'ara
TALMA, Louise
TARLOW, Karen Anne
TATE, Phyllis
TAUTU, Cornelia
TELFER, Nancy Ellen
THIEME, Kerstin Anja
THOMAS, Marilyn Taft
THOME, Diane
TICHARICH, Zdenka
TOWER, Joan
TUICHEVA, Zumrad
UCHENDU, Nellie Uzonna Edith
URNER, Catherine Murphy
USHER, Julia
USTVOLSKAYA, Galina Ivanovna
UYEDA, Leslie
VAN APPLEDORN, Mary Jeanne
VAN DE VATE, Nancy Hayes

VAN DEN BEEMT, Hedda
VAN DEN BOORN-COCLET, Henriette
VAN EPEN-DE GROOT, Else Antonia
VAN OHLEN, Deborah
VANNAH, Kate
VASILIEVA, Tatiana Ivanovna
VAZQUEZ, Alida
VETLUGINA, Natalia Alekseyevna
VIRTUE, Constance Cochnower
VISCONTI, Leila
VITO-DELVAUX, Berthe di
VON ZIERITZ, Grete
VONDRACKOVA, Helena
VORLOVA, Slavka
WALDO, Elisabeth
WALKER, Gwyneth van Anden
WANG, An-Ming
WARREN, Elinor Remick
WARWICK, Mary Carol
WEAVER, Carol Ann
WEBB, Allienne Brandon
WEIR, Judith
WENDELBURG, Norma Ruth
WENNERBERG-REUTER, Sara
  Margareta Eugenia Euphrosyne
WERNER, Tara Louise
WERTHEIM, Rosy
WHITE, Claude Porter
WHITEHEAD, Gillian
WILL, Madeleine
WILLIAMS, Grace Mary
WITKIN, Beatrice
WITNI, Monica
WOLL, Erna
WOLLNER, Gertrude Price
WOOD, Mabel
WYETH, Ann
WYLIE, Ruth Shaw
YAKHNINA, Yevgenia Yosifovna
YAROSHEVSKAYA, Ludmila
  Anatolievna
ZAIDEL-RUDOLPH, Jeanne
ZAKRZEWSKA-NIKIPORCZYK,
  Barbara Maria
ZALLMAN, Arlene
ZARANEK, Stefania Anatolyevna
ZAVALISHINA, Maria Semyonovna
ZECHLIN, Ruth
ZHVANETSKAIA, Inna Abramovna
ZIBEROVA, Zinaida Petrovna
ZIELINSKA, Lidia
ZIFFRIN, Marilyn Jane
ZIMMERMANN, Margrit
ZWILICH, Ellen Taaffe
Century unknown
BOR, Modesta
FERGUS-HOYT, Phyllis
JACQUE, Emilie
PHILIPPINA, Charlotte, Duchess of
  Brunswick
SHLEG, Ludmila Karlovna
SNODGRASS, Louise Harrison

ORCHESTRAL - SUITES, OVERTURES ETC.
18th Century A.D.
  MARIA ANTONIA WALPURGIS,
    Princess of Bavaria
  MARTINEZ, Marianne
19th Century A.D.
  AMERSFOORDT-DYK, Hermina
    Maria
  AUGUSTA MARIA LOUISE, Queen of
    Prussia
  BOTTINI, Marianna, Marchioness
  CALOSSO, Eugenia
  CHAMBERLAYNE, Edith A.
  CIANCHETTINI, Veronica Elisabeth
  DELABORDE, Elie Miriam
  FARRENC, Louise
  HENSEL, Fanny Caecilia
  HOLMES, Augusta Mary Anne

JESKE-CHOINSKA-MIKORSKA,
   Ludmila
KRALIK VON MAYERSWALDEN,
   Mathilde
LODER, Kate Fanny
MANNKOPF, Adolphine
MAYER, Emilie
MOODY, Marie
PRESCOTT, Oliveria Louisa
RAPP, Marguerite
RODRIGO, Maria
SCHAEFFER, Theresa
SMITH, Alice Mary
SWEPSTONE, Edith
TYRELL, Agnes
WAGNER, Virginia De Oliveira
   Bastos
WILLIAMS, Margaret
WOODS, Eliza
WURM, Mary J.A.
ZUMSTEEG, Emilie
20th Century A.D.
AARNE, Els
ABEJO, Sister M. Rosalina
AGABALIAN, Lidia Semyenovna
AKIYOSHI, Toshiko
ALIOTH, Marguerite
ALLITSEN, Frances
ALTER, Martha
ANDERSON-WUENSCH, Jean Mary
ANDREE, Elfrida
ANDREYEVA, Elena Fedorovna
APPELDOORN, Dina van
ARCHER, Violet Balestreri
ARETZ, Isabel
ARKWRIGHT, Marian Ursula
ARRIEU, Claude
AULIN, Laura Valborg
AUSTER, Lydia Martinovna
BABAYEVA, Seda Grigorievna
BACEWICZ, Grażyna
BACH, Maria
BAILEY, Judith Margaret
BANNISTER, Mary Jeanne Hoggard
BARAMISHVILI, Olga Ivanovna
BARNETT, Carol Edith
BARTHEL, Ursula
BARTHELSON, Joyce Holloway
BEATON, Isabella
BEATRICE, Mary Victoria Feodore,
   Princess of Battenberg
BEEKHUIS, Hanna
BEHREND, Jeanne
BELOCH, Dorotea
BERZON, Asya Yevseyevna
BEYERMAN-WALRAVEN, Jeanne
BIELEFELD, Ljuba
BLAKE, Dorothy Gaynor
BORDEWIJK-ROEPMAN, Johanna
BOUCHARD, Linda L.
BOYD, Jeanne Margaret
BRAGGINS, Daphne Elizabeth
BROGUE, Roslyn Clara
BUCKLEY, Helen Dallam
BUECHNER, Margaret
BURKE, Loretto
CALCAGNO, Elsa
CAMEU, Helza
CAPUIS, Matilde
CARMEN MARINA
CARVALHO, Dinora de
CARWITHEN, Doreen
CASTEGNARO, Lola
CHITCHIAN, Geguni Oganesovna
COLACO OSORIO-SWAAB, Reine
CONSTANTINESCU, Domnica
COQUET, Odile Marie-Lucie
COULTHARD, Jean
CRANE, Helen
DANEAU, Suzanne
DAVITASHVILI, Meri Shalvovna

DEMAREST, Anne Shannon
DESPORTES, Yvonne Berthe Melitta
DEYO, Ruth Lynda
DIANDA, Hilda
DIEMER, Emma Lou
DILLON, Fannie Charles
DRDOVA, Marie
DREYFUS, Francis Kay
ELCHEVA, Irina Mikhailovna
ELLICOTT, Rosalind Frances
ERHART, Dorothy
EVERAERTS-ZLICA, Mme.
FINLEY, Lorraine Noel
FOLVILLE, Eugenie-Emilie Juliette
FORMAN, Joanne
FRANCE, Jeanne Lelen
FRUMKER, Linda
GABRYS, Ewa Lucja Maria
GALAJIKIAN, Florence Grandland
GARTENLAUB, Odette
GARUTA, Lucia Yanovna
GARZTECKA-JARZEBSKA, Irena
GIPPS, Ruth
GIURANNA, Elena Barbara
GLICK, Henrietta
GLYN, Margaret Henriette
GOERSCH, Ursula Margitta
GOLOVINA, Olga Akimovna
GRIEBLING, Karen Jean
GUBAIDULINA, Sofia Asgatovna
HIER, Ethel Glen
HOLLAND, Dulcie Sybil
HOLST, Imogen Clare
HOWELL, Dorothy
HSU, Wen-Ying
HYDE, Miriam Beatrice
IASHVILI, Lili Mikhailovna
IORDAN, Irina Nikolayevna
JANKOWSKI, Loretta Patricia
JEREA, Hilda
JESI, Ada
JIRACKOVA, Marta
JOHNSTON-REID, Sarah Ruth
KAHMANN, Chesley
KAPRALOVA, Vitezslava
KASHPEROVA, Leokadia
   Alexandrovna
KERN, Frida
KICKINGER, Paula
KLECHNIOWSKA, Anna Maria
KLINKOVA, Zhivka
KOELLING, Eloise
KRASNOGLIADOVA, Vera
   Vladimirovna
KUSS, Margarita Ivanovna
LACHOWSKA, Stefania
LANG, Margaret Ruthven
LAPEIRETTA, Ninon de Brouwer
LATHAM, Joan Seyler
LAUBER, Anne Marianne
LAUFER, Beatrice
LE BEAU, Louisa Adolpha
LEE, Chan-Hae
LEE, Young Ja
LELEU, Jeanne
LEONCHIK, Svetlana Gavrilovna
LEVITOVA, Ludmila Vladimirovna
LEVITSKAYA, Viktoria Sergeyevna
LICHTENSTEIN, Olga Grigorievna
LOOTS, Joyce Mary Ann
LOPEZ ROVIROSA, Maria Isabel
LORENZ, Ellen Jane
LUCAS, Mary Anderson
LUDVIG-PECAR, Nada
LUND, Gudrun
LUTYENS, Elisabeth
McCLEARY, Fiona
McCOLLIN, Frances
McLAIN, Margaret Starr
McLAUGHLIN, Marian
MAILIAN, Elza Antonovna

MAKAROVA, Nina Vladimirovna
MALDYBAYEVA, Zhyldyz Abdylasovna
MAMLOK, Ursula
MANUKIAN, Irina Eduardovna
MARTINS, Maria de Lourdes
MATEVOSIAN, Araks Surenovna
MEISTER, Marianne
MELOY, Elizabeth
MIGRANYAN, Emma
MKRTYCHIEVA, Virginia Nikitichna
MOBERG, Ida Georgina
MORLEY, Nina Dianne
MOSZUMANSKA-NAZAR, Krystyna
MUELLER-HERMANN, Johanna
MUNKTELL, Helena Mathilda
MUSGRAVE, Thea
NAZAROVA, Tatiana Borisovna
NAZIROVA, Elmira Mirza Rza kyzy
NESTE, Rosane van
NIKOLSKAYA, Lyubov Borisovna
NUNLIST, Juli
OFFICER, Bronwyn Lee
ORTMANS, Kay Muriel
OSETROVA-YAKOVLIEVA, Nina
   Alexandrovna
OSTRANDER, Linda Woodaman
OVERMAN, Meta
OWEN, Blythe
PAKHMUTOVA, Alexandra
   Nikolayevna
PATINO ANDRADE, Graziela
PEJACEVIC, Dora, Countess
PENTLAND, Barbara Lally
PETROVA, Mara
PEYROT, Fernande
PFEIFFER, Irena
PONSA, Maria Luisa
POPATENKO, Tamara Alexandrovna
PRADELL, Leila
PRAVOSSUDOVITCH, Natalja
   Michajlovna
PRICE, Florence Beatrice
RABINOF, Sylvia
RAMM, Valentina Iosifovna
RAPOPORT, Eda
RECLI, Giulia
REID, Sarah Johnston
REISSEROVA, Julie
RENSHAW, Rosette
RESPIGHI, Elsa
REYNOLDS, Erma Grey Hogue
RHEINGOLD, Lauma Yanovna
RHENE-JAQUE
RICHTER, Marion Morrey
ROBINSON, Berenice
ROE, Eileen Betty
ROMERO BARBOSA, Elena
ROMM, Rosalina Davidovna
ROSE OF JESUS, Sister
ROYSE, Mildred Barnes
RYDER, Theodora Sturkow
SALQUIN, Hedy
SAMVELIAN, Sofia Vardanovna
SANTOS-OCAMPO DE FRANCESCO,
   Amada Amy
SAWYER, Elizabeth
SCHICK, Philippine
SCHLEDER, Grizelda Lazzaro
SCHMITZ-GOHR, Else
SIDORENKO, Tamara Stepanovna
SMITH, Julia Frances
SMYTH, Ethel Mary, Dame
SOENSTEVOLD, Maj
SOLOMON, Mirrie Irma
SOULAGE, Marcelle Fanny Henriette
SPAIN-DUNK, Susan
SPENCER, Williametta
SPINDLE, Louise Cooper
STAIR, Patty
STEINER, Gitta Hana
STREATFIELD, Valma June

STRICKLAND, Lily Teresa
STUART-BERGSTROM, Elsa
    Marianne
SUCHY, Gregoria Karides
SUESSE, Dana
SULTANOVA, Asya Bakhish kyzy
SUNBLAD-HALME, Heidi Gabriella
    Wilhelmina
SUSSMAN, Ettel
SUSZCZYNSKA, Anna
SUTHERLAND, Margaret
SVANIDZE, Natela Damianovna
SWADOS, Elizabeth
SWIFT, Kay
SWISHER, Gloria Agnes Wilson
SZOENYI, Erzsebet
SZYMANSKA, Iwonka Bogumila
TAILLEFERRE, Germaine
TAKASHIMA, Midori
TALMA, Louise
TATE, Phyllis
TAUTU, Cornelia
TAYLOR, Eleanor
TERRIER-LAFFAILLE, Anne
THEMMEN, Ivana Marburger
THIEME, Kerstin Anja
THOMSEN, Geraldine
TKACH, Zlata Moiseyevna
TORRA, Celia
TORRENS, Merce
TOYAMA, Michiko Françoise
TUMANIAN, Elizaveta Artashesovna
TUMANISHVILI, Ketevana
    Dmitirevna
TYER, Norma Phyllis
ULEHLA, Ludmila
URNER, Catherine Murphy
URRETA, Alicia
USTVOLSKAYA, Galina Ivanovna
UYTTENHOVE, Yolande
VAKHVAKHISHVILI, Tamara
    Nikolayevna
VAN NESTE, Rosane Micheline Lucie
    Charlotte
VANDENBURGH, Mildred
VELLERE, Lucie Weiler
VILLARINI, Awilda
VITO-DELVAUX, Berthe di
VOLKART, Hazel
VORLOVA, Slavka
VORONINA, Tatiana Aleksandrovna
WARSHAW, Dalit Paz
WARWICK, Mary Carol
WEGENER-FRENSEL, Emmy Heil
WEISSBERG, Julia Lazerevna
WERTHEIM, Rosy
WHITTLE, Chris Mary-Francine
WIENIAWSKA, Irene Regine
WILDSCHUT, Clara
WILLIAMS, Grace Mary
WOOD, Mabel
WYLIE, Ruth Shaw
YAROSHEVSKAYA, Ludmila
    Anatolievna
ZAIDEL-RUDOLPH, Jeanne
ZARIPOVA, Naila Gatinovna
ZECHLIN, Ruth
ZHUBANOVA, Gaziza Akhmetovna
ZHVANETSKAIA, Inna Abramovna

ORCHESTRAL - SYMPHONIC POEMS AND OTHER LARGE WORKS
18th Century A.D.
WILHELMINA, Caroline of
    Anspach
19th Century A.D.
GRANDVAL, Marie Felicie
    Clemènce
    de Reiset, Vicomtesse de
LEGOUX, Julie, Baroness
PURGOLD, Nadezhda Nikolayevna

RAPP, Marguerite
TSCHITSCHERIN, Theodosia de
UNTERSTEINER, Antonietta
20th Century A.D.
AARNE, Els
ABEJO, Sister M. Rosalina
ABORN, Lora
AKHUNDOVA, Shafiga Gulam kyzy
ALVES DE SOUSA, Berta Candida
APPELDOORN, Dina van
ARAUJO, Gina de
ARCHER, Violet Balestreri
ARSEYEVA, Irina Vasilievna
AUSTER, Lydia Martinovna
BACEWICZ, Grażyna
BACKES, Lotte
BARBERIS, Mansi
BARRAINE, Elsa
BAUER, Marion Eugenie
BECLARD D'HARCOURT,
    Marguerite
BELOCH, Dorotea
BIANCHINI, Emma
BIANCHINI, Virginie
BINET, Jocelyne
BLANCK, Olga de
BOULANGER, Lili Juliette Marie Olga
BOYD, Jeanne Margaret
BRANSCOMBE, Gena
BRIGGS, Nancy Louise
BRITAIN, Radie
BRUNDZAITE, Konstantsiya Kazyo
CALCAGNO, Elsa
CAMEU, Helza
CAMPMANY, Montserrat
CANAL, Marguerite
CANCINO DE CUEVAS, Sofia
CARTER, Buenta MacDaniel
CASAGEMAS, Luisa
CLEVE, Cissi
COHEN, Dulcie M.
CONTINI ANSELMI, Lucia
COOLIDGE, Peggy Stuart
COULTHARD, Jean
CRANE, Helen
DANIELS, Mabel Wheeler
DAVIS, Katherine Kennicott
DAVITASHVILI, Meri Shalvovna
DAVY, Ruby Claudia Emily
DE BIASE BIDART, Lycia
DE MONTEL, Adalgisa
DECARIE, Reine
DESPORTES, Yvonne Berthe Melitta
DIAKVNISHVILI, Mzisavar
    Zakharevna
DONATOVA, Narcisa
DONCEANU, Felicia
DUDLEY, Marjorie Eastwood
ERNST, Siegrid
ESTRELLA, Blanca
FALTIS, Evelyn
FLACH, Elsa
FLEISCHER-DOLGOPOLSKY,
    Tsipporah
FLICK-FLOOD, Dora
FOLVILLE, Eugenie-Emilie Juliette
GABUS, Monique
GARCIA ROBSON, Magdalena
GARUTA, Lucia Yanovna
GARZTECKA-JARZEBSKA, Irena
GINDLER, Kathe-Lotte
GIPPS, Ruth
GIURANNA, Elena Barbara
GLYN, Margaret Henriette
GOLOVINA, Olga Akimovna
GOODSMITH, Ruth B.
GRIEBLING, Karen Jean
GRIEBLING, Margaret Ann
GUSEINZADE, Adilia Gadzhi Aga
HANS, Lio
HARDIMAN, Ellena G.

HARDING, Mildred Thompson
HARKNESS, Rebekah West
HEIMERL, Elizabeth
HERTEL, Sister Romana
HOKANSON, Margrethe
HOWE, Mary Alberta Bruce
HOWELL, Dorothy
HUBICKI, Margaret Olive
HYDE, Miriam Beatrice
HYTREK, Sister Theophane
IVANOVA, Lidia
IVEY, Jean Eichelberger
IWAUCHI, Saori
JABOR, Najla
JAELL-TRAUTMANN, Marie
JIRACKOVA, Marta
KARNITSKAYA, Nina Andreyevna
KATZMAN, Klara Abramovna
KORN, Clara Anna
KUSS, Margarita Ivanovna
KVERNADZE, Bidzina
LANDOWSKA, Wanda
LASDAUSKAS, Jacqueline
LAUBER, Anne Marianne
LE BEAU, Louisa Adolpha
LEE, Young Ja
LEGINSKA, Ethel
LEIBOW, Ruth Irene
LEVITSKAYA, Viktoria Sergeyevna
LITSITE, Paula Yanovna
MALLIA-PULVIRENTI, Josie
MANNING, Kathleen Lockhart
MARI, Pierrette
MELL, Gertrud Maria
MOBERG, Ida Georgina
MORE, Margaret Elizabeth
MORIN-LABRECQUE, Albertine
MOSZUMANSKA-NAZAR, Krystyna
MSHEVELIDZE, Shalva
MULDER, Maria Antonia
MUNKTELL, Helena Mathilda
NAIKHOVICH-LOMAKINA, Fania
    Filippovna
NAZAROVA, Tatiana Borisovna
NEPGEN, Rosa Sophia Cornelia
NIKOLAYEVA, Tatiana Petrovna
NIKOLSKAYA, Olga Vasilevna
ODAGESCU, Irina
OOSTERZEE, Cornelia van
ORTMANS, Kay Muriel
OSETROVA-YAKOVLIEVA, Nina
    Alexandrovna
OVERMAN, Meta
PABLOS CEREZO, Maria de
PARPAGLIOLO, Iditta
PATTERSON, Annie Wilson
PAVIA DE MAGALHAES, Isaura
PELEGRI, Maria Teresa
PETROVA, Mara
PEYROT, Fernande
PHILLIPS, Bryony
POPOVICI, Elise
PREOBRAJENSKA, Vera Nicolaevna
PRICE, Florence Beatrice
PRIETO, Maria Teresa
RAN, Shulamit
RAPOPORT, Eda
RECLI, Giulia
RESPIGHI, Elsa
RICHTER, Marion Morrey
ROESGEN-CHAMPION, Marguerite
    Sara
ROHDE, Q'Adrianne
ROSE OF JESUS, Sister
ROZHAVSKAYA, Yudif Grigorevna
SAIDAMINOVA, Dilorom
SANDRESKY, Margaret Vardell
SANTOS-OCAMPO DE FRANCESCO,
    Amada Amy
SAUVREZIS, Alice
SCHEIN, Suzanna Fedorovna

SCHMIDT-DUISBURG, Margarete Dina Alwina
SCHMITT-LERMANN, Frieda
SCHULTE, Eleonore
SCHUYLER, Philippa Duke
SELDEN-GOTH, Gizella
SIMON, Cecile Paul
SLIANOVA-MIZANDARI, Dagmara Levanovna
SPAIN-DUNK, Susan
STRUTT, Dorothy
SUTHERLAND, Margaret
SZYMANSKA, Iwonka Bogumila
TAKAMI, Toyoko
TAUTU, Cornelia
TERRIER-LAFFAILLE, Anne
TERZIAN, Alicia
THIEME, Kerstin Anja
THOMAS, Karen P.
TUMANIAN, Elizaveta Artashesovna
UPTON, Anne
URNER, Catherine Murphy
USTVOLSKAYA, Galina Ivanovna
UZEINZADZE, Adilea
VAN DEN BOORN-COCLET, Henriette
VAN DYCK, Beatrice Madeleine
VEHAR, Persis Anne
VIGNERY, Jeanne Emilie Virginie
VINTULE, Ruta Evaldovna
VOLLENHOVEN, Hanna van
VYNER, Mary Bainbridge
WANG, Jiu-Fang
WARE, Harriet
WEISSBERG, Julia Lazerevna
WIELE, Aimée van der
WILKINS, Margaret Lucy
WILLIAMS, Grace Mary
WILLIAMS, Joan Franks
WILLIAMS, Mary Lou
WILLMAN, Regina Hansen
WOOD, Mabel
YAKHNINA, Yevgenia Yosifovna
ZECHLIN, Ruth
ZHUBANOVA, Gaziza Akhmetovna
ZIBEROVA, Zinaida Petrovna
ZIMMERMANN, Margrit
Century unknown
BOR, Modesta

ORCHESTRAL - SYMPHONIES
18th Century A.D.
ANNA AMALIA, Duchess of Saxe-Weimar
BERTHE, Mme.
MARTINEZ, Marianne
19th Century A.D.
BLANC DE FONTBELLE, Cécile
BOTTINI, Marianna, Marchioness
CALOSSO, Eugenia
CHAMBERLAYNE, Edith A.
FARRENC, Louise
GRANDVAL, Marie Felicie Clemence de Reiset, Vicomtesse de
GREENE, Edith
HAENEL DE CRONENTHAL, Louise Augusta Marie Julia
HOLMES, Augusta Mary Anne
HUND, Alicia
HUNDT, Aline
MAYER, Emilie
PRESCOTT, Oliveria Louisa
RODRIGO, Maria
RUNCIE, Constance Owen Faunt Le Roy
SMITH, Alice Mary
STOLLEWERK, Nina von
SWEPSTONE, Edith
TYRELL, Agnes

20th Century A.D.
AARNE, Els
AARON, Marcelle
AARON, Yvonne
ABEJO, Sister M. Rosalina
ACCART, Eveline
ALEXANDER, Leni
ALEXANDRA, Liana
ALLOUARD CARNY, Odette
ALONSO, Julia
ANDERSON, Ruth
ANDERSON-WUENSCH, Jean Mary
ANDREE, Elfrida
APPELDOORN, Dina van
ARCHER, Violet Balestreri
ARRIEU, Claude
BACEWICZ, Grażyna
BAIKADAMOVA, Baldyrgan Bakhitzhanovna
BAILEY, Judith Margaret
BAILLY, Colette
BANCER, Teresa Barbara
BANDARA, Linda
BARBERIS, Mansi
BARRAINE, Elsa
BARRIENTOS, Maria
BAUER, Marion Eugenie
BEACH, Amy Marcy
BEATON, Isabella
BECLARD D'HARCOURT, Marguerite
BEGO-SIMUNIC, Andelka
BELL, Elizabeth
BENAVENTE, Regina
BENNETT, Wilhelmine
BERZON, Asya Yevseyevna
BEYER, Johanna Magdalena
BIALKIEWICZOWNA-ANDRAULT DE LANGERON, Irena
BIRCHER-REY, Hedy
BLOOD, Esta Damesek
BONDS, Margaret
BORDEWIJK-ROEPMAN, Johanna
BOYLE, Ina
BRATU, Emma
BRENET, Thérèse
BRINGUER, Estela
BRITAIN, Radie
BROCKMAN, Jane E.
BRUSSELS, Iris
BRUZDOWICZ, Joanna
BUENAVENTURA, Isabel
BULTERIJS, Nina
BUTLER, Anne Lois
CALCAGNO, Elsa
CAMEU, Helza
CANCINO DE CUEVAS, Sofia
CAPUIS, Matilde
CARR-BOYD, Ann Kirsten
CARWITHEN, Doreen
CHEBOTARIAN, Gayane Movsesovna
CHICHERINA, Sofia Nikolayevna
CHITCHIAN, Geguni Oganesovna
CHUDOVA, Tatiana Alekseyevna
CLOSTRE, Adrienne
COLERIDGE-TAYLOR, Avril Gwendolen
CONSTANTINESCU, Domnica
COULTHARD, Jean
COWLES, Darleen
DAIKEN, Melanie
DALBERG, Nancy
DAVIS, Jean Reynolds
DESPORTES, Yvonne Bérthe Melitta
DIAMOND, Arline
DIEMER, Emma Lou
DONATOVA, Narcisa
DU PAGE, Florence Elizabeth
DUDLEY, Marjorie Eastwood
DZHAFAROVA, Afag Mamed kyzy

ECKHARDT-GRAMATTE, Sophie-Carmen
ESCOT, Pozzi
FALTIS, Evelyn
FINLEY, Lorraine Noel
FLAGG, Mary Houts
FRAJT, Ludmila
FROMM-MICHAELS, Ilse
FRUMKER, Linda
GAIGEROVA, Varvara Andrianovna
GANNON, Ruth Ellen
GARTENLAUB, Odette
GARZTECKA-JARZEBSKA, Irena
GEIGER-KULLMANN, Rosy Auguste
GERCHIK, Vera Petrovna
GIDEON, Miriam
GIPPS, Ruth
GIURANNA, Elena Barbara
GLANVILLE-HICKS, Peggy
GLYN, Margaret Henriette
GOLDSCHMIDT, Lore
GOLOVINA, Olga Akimovna
GOULD, Elizabeth Davies
GRIECO, Ida
GRZADZIELOWNA, Eleonora
GUBAIDULINA, Sofia Asgatovna
GVAZAVA, Tamara Davidovna
GYRING, Elizabeth
HARDY, Helen Irene
HOFFMAN, Phyllis Sampson
HOLLAND, Dulcie Sybil
INWOOD, Mary Ruth Brink Berger
IORDAN, Irina Nikolayevna
ISZKOWSKA, Zofia
IVEY, Jean Eichelberger
JABOR, Najla
JIRACKOVA, Marta
JOHNSTON-REID, Sarah Ruth
JOLAS, Betsy
KAHMANN, Chesley
KARNITSKAYA, Nina Andreyevna
KASHPEROVA, Leokadia Alexandrovna
KATZMAN, Klara Abramovna
KAVARNALIEVA, Konstantina
KAZHAEVA, Tatiana Ibragimovna
KEAL, Minna
KERN, Frida
KICKINGER, Paula
KIRBY, Suzanne
KIRKWOOD, Antoinette
KLINKOVA, Zhivka
KNOBLOCHOVA, Antonie
KOELLING, Eloise
KOHAN, Celina
KORN, Clara Anna
KOZHEVNIKOVA, Ekaterina Vadimovna
KRZYZANOWSKA, Halina
KUSS, Margarita Ivanovna
KUYPER, Elizabeth
LABEY, Charlotte Sohy
LALAUNI, Lila
LAUFER, Beatrice
LE BEAU, Louisa Adolpha
LEAHY, Mary Weldon
LEAVITT, Helen Sewall
LEE, Chan-Hae
LEIBOW, Ruth Irene
LEIVISKA, Helvi Lemmiki
LEONCHIK, Svetlana Gavrilovna
LEVITSKAYA, Viktoria Sergeyevna
LINNET, Anne
LOTTI, Silvana di
LOUDOVA, Ivana
LUFF, Enid
LUTYENS, Elisabeth
MACKIE, Shirley M.
MACONCHY, Elizabeth
McCLEARY, Fiona
MAKAROVA, Nina Vladimirovna

MAMLOK, Ursula
MARCUS, Ada Belle Gross
MATEVOSIAN, Araks Surenovna
MAURICE, Paule
MAURICE-JACQUET, H.
MAYER, Lise Maria
MEL-BONIS
MELL, Gertrud Maria
MERRIMAN, Margarita Leonor
METALLIDI, Zhanneta Lazarevna
MIAGI, Ester Kustovna
MIDDLETON, Jean B.
MILENKOVIC, Jelena
MINEO, Antoinette
MKRTYCHIEVA, Virginia Nikitichna
MOBERG, Ida Georgina
MONTGOMERY, Merle
MOORE, Dorothy Rudd
MORRISON, Julia Maria
MRACEK, Ann Michelle
MUELLER-HERMANN, Johanna
MUSGRAVE, Thea
NARITA, Kasuko
NIKOLAYEVA, Tatiana Petrovna
NISHIKI, Kayoko
OERBECK, Anne-Marie
OOSTERZEE, Cornelia van
OSAWA, Kazuko
OSIANDER, Irene
OWEN, Blythe
PATINO ANDRADE, Graziela
PEARL-MANN, Dora Deborah
PEJACEVIC, Dora, Countess
PENTLAND, Barbara Lally
PERRY, Julia Amanda
PETRA-BASACOPOL, Carmen
PETROVA-KRUPKOVA, Elena
PHILIBA, Nicole
PHILLIPS, Bryony
PHILLIPS, Karen Ann
PIETSCH, Edna Frieda
POLIGNAC, Armande de, Countess
   of Chabannes
POLIN, Claire
PRAVOSSUDOVITCH, Natalja
   Michajlovna
PRICE, Florence Beatrice
PRIETO, Maria Teresa
RAIGORODSKY, Leda Natalia
   Heimsath
RAINIER, Priaulx
REID, Sarah Johnston
RENSHAW, Rosette
RHENE-JAQUE
ROBERT, Lucie
ROGER, Denise
ROGET, Henriette
ROHDE, Q'Adrianne
RUEFF, Jeanine
SAMUEL, Rhian
SANTOS-OCAMPO DE FRANCESCO,
   Amada Amy
SCHEIN, Suzanna Fedorovna
SCHUYLER, Philippa Duke
SCHWERDTFEGER, E. Anne
SEARCH, Sara Opal
SENFTER, Johanna
SHAIMARDANOVA, Shakhida
SHLONSKY, Verdina
SIDORENKO, Tamara Stepanovna
SIKORA, Elzbieta
SISTEK-DJORDJEVIC, Mirjana
SKOWRONSKA, Janina
SOLOMON, Mirrie Irma
STANLEY, Helen Camille
SUSZCZYNSKA, Anna
SZYMANSKA, Iwonka Bogumila
TERZIAN, Alicia
TILICHEYEVA, Elena Nikolayevna
VAN DIJCK, Beatrice Madeleine
VASILIEVA, Tatiana Ivanovna

VITO-DELVAUX, Berthe di
VORLOVA, Slavka
VYNER, Mary Bainbridge
WALDO, Elisabeth
WALLNEROVA, Bibiana
WARREN, Elinor Remick
WECKWERTH, Nancy
WEISSBERG, Julia Lazerevna
WENDELBURG, Norma Ruth
WILLIAMS, Grace Mary
WILLMAN, Regina Hansen
WITNI, Monica
WYLIE, Ruth Shaw
ZECHLIN, Ruth
ZELINSKA, Lydia
ZHUBANOVA, Gaziza Akhmetovna
ZIMMERMANN, Margrit
ZIVKOVIC, Mirjana
ZUBELDIA, Emiliana de
ZWILICH, Ellen Taaffe

ORGAN
17th Century A.D.
ASSANDRA, Catterina
BACHMANN, Judith
ENTHALLER, Sidonia
18th Century A.D.
BENAULT, Mlle.
GUEST, Jeanne Marie
SANTINI, Maria
STECHER, Marianne
19th Century A.D.
BALTHASAR, Florence
BATTA, Clementine
BINFIELD, Hanna R.
BRESSON, Mlle.
BRZEZINSKA, Filipina
CHAMBERLAYNE, Edith A.
CRUMB, Berenice
FARMER, Emily Bardsley
GYDE, Margaret
HADELN, Nancy von
HENSEL, Fanny Caecilia
HODGES, Faustina Hasse
KERN, Louise
LA HYE, Louise Genevieve
LODER, Kate Fanny
LOUD, Annie Frances
MILANOLLO, Teresa Domenica Maria
MOUNSEY, Elizabeth
MOZART, Maria Anna Walburga
   Ignatia
NORRIS, Mary
PENNA, Catherine
PIERPONT, Marie de
PLATEROWA-BROEL-ZYBERK,
   Maria
REES, Clara H.
RONDONNEAU, Elise
RUNCIE, Constance Owen Faunt Le
   Roy
STIRLING, Elizabeth
TRUETTE, Everette
WAGNER, Virginia De Oliveira
   Bastos
WESTROP, Kate
20th Century A.D.
AAS, Else Berntsen
ABEJO, Sister M. Rosalina
ABORN, Lora
ACKLAND, Jeanne Isabel Dorothy
ADAMS, Elizabeth Kilmer
AHRENS, Sieglinde
AINSCOUGH, Juliana Mary
ALAIN, Marie Claire
ALCALAY, Luna
ALEXANDRA, Liana
ALLEN, Judith Shatin
ALLOUARD CARNY, Odette
ANDERSON, Beth
ANDERSON, Pauline Barbour

ANDREE, Elfrida
ANDRUS, Helen Josephine
ARAUCO, Ingrid Colette
ARCHER, Violet Balestreri
ARMER, Elinor Florence
ASHFORD, Emma Louise
AUBUT-PRATTE, Françoise
AULIN, Laura Valborg
BACEWICZ, Grazyna
BACKES, Lotte
BAGA, Ena Rosina
BAHMANN, Marianne Eloise
BAIL, Grace Shattuck
BAKKE, Ruth
BALLOU, Esther Williamson
BALUTET, Marguerite
BAMPTON, Ruth
BARADAPRANA, Pravrajika
BARBILLON, Jeanne
BARDEL, Germaine
BARRAINE, Elsa
BARTHEL, Ursula
BATE, Jennifer
BAUER, Marion Eugenie
BEACH, Amy Marcy
BEAHM, Jacquelyn Yvette
BEARER, Elaine Louise
BEATON, Isabella
BEEKHUIS, Hanna
BELLMAN, Helene M.
BEYERMAN-WALRAVEN, Jeanne
BIANCHINI, Virginie
BIBBY, Gillian Margaret
BINGHAM, Judith
BISH, Diane
BITGOOD, Roberta
BLACKWELL, Anna Gee
BLOMFIELD-HOLT, Patricia
BOCARD, Sister Cécilia Clair
BOLZ, Harriet
BORKOWSKI, Marian
BORON, Marion
BORROFF, Edith
BOULANGER, Nadia Juliette
BOUTRON, Madeleine
BOYCE, Blanche Ula
BRAGGINS, Daphne Elizabeth
BRANSCOMBE, Gena
BRENNER, Rosamond Drooker
BRICE, Laure
BRIGGS, Cora Skilling
BRINK, Emily R.
BRITAIN, Radie
BROOK, Gwendolyn Giffen
BROWN, Zilda Jennings
BRUECKNER, Monika
BRUSH, Ruth Damaris
BRUSSELS, Iris
BUENAVENTURA, Isabel
BURCHELL, Henrietta Louise
BURROUGHS, Jane Johnson
BYERS, Roxana Weihe
CALE, Rosalie Balmer Smith
CALLAWAY, Ann
CAMPBELL, Edith Mary
CANALES PIZARRO, Marta
CAPUIS, Matilde
CARR-BOYD, Ann Kirsten
CARRINGTON-THOMAS, Virginia
CASAGEMAS, Luisa
CATO, Jane Dickson
CHAMINADE, Cécile Louise
   Stephanie
CHERUBIM, Sister Mary Schaefer
CHESTNUT, Lora Perry
CLARK, Florence Durrell
CLARK, June
CLARKE, Rosemary
CLARKE, Urana
CLOSTRE, Adrienne
COATES, Gloria Kannenberg

COFFMAN, Lillian Craig
COLERIDGE-TAYLOR, Avril Gwendolen
COTE, Helene
COULTHARD, Jean
COWLES, Darleen
CROKER, Catherine Munnell
DAVIS, Eleanor Maud
DE BIASE BIDART, Lycia
DELBOS, Claire
DELORME, Isabelle
DEMESSIEUX, Jeanne
DENBOW, Stefania Bjoerson
DESPORTES, Yvonne Berthe Melitta
DIEMER, Emma Lou
DILLON, Fannie Charles
DINESCU, Violeta
DOBSON, Elaine
DOWNEY, Mary
DRYNAN, Margaret
DU PAGE, Florence Elizabeth
DUNGAN, Olive
DZIEWULSKA, Maria Amelia
EICHHORN, Hermene Warlick
EISENSTEIN, Stella Price
ELST, Nancy van der
EMERY, Dorothy Radde
ENDRES, Olive Philomene
ERNST, Siegrid
ERVIN, Karen
ESCOT, Pozzi
FALCINELLI, Rolande
FALLADOVA-SKVOROVA, Anezka
FALTIS, Evelyn
FARGA PELLICER, Onia
FAUTCH, Sister Magdalen
FAXON, Nancy Plummer
FINK, Emma C.
FINZI, Graciane
FISCHER, Edith Steinkraus
FISHER, Gladys Washburn
FISHER, Katherine Danforth
FLICK-FLOOD, Dora
FOLVILLE, Eugenie-Emilie Juliette
FONDER, Sister Mary Teresine
FORMAN, Joanne
FOSIC, Tarzicija
FOWLER, Jennifer Joan
FOWLER, Marje
FRANCHERE-DESROSIERS, Rose de Lima
FRESON, Armande
FRICKER, Anne
FRITZ, Sherilyn Gail
FULLER-HALL, Sarah Margaret
FURGERI, Bianca Maria
GALAJIKIAN, Florence Grandland
GARSCIA-GRESSEL, Janina
GARUTA, Lucia Yanovna
GASTON, Marjorie Dean
GAUTHIEZ, Cécile
GEORGE, Lila-Gene
GIDEON, Miriam
GILBERT, Pia
GILENO, Jean Anthony
GILLES, Yvette Marie
GIROD-PARROT, Marie-Louise
GLAZIER, Beverly
GLEN, Irma
GLYN, Margaret Henriette
GOOLKASIAN-RAHBEE, Dianne Zabelle
GOULD, Elizabeth Davies
GOULD, Janetta
GRAUBNER, Hannelore
GRIEBLING, Karen Jean
GUBAIDULINA, Sofia Asgatovna
GUBITOSI, Emilia
GUELL, Maria Luisa
GYRING, Elizabeth
HANEFELD, Gertrud

HANSEN, Thyra
HARMS, Signe
HAVEY, Marguerite
HAYS, Doris Ernestine
HEDOUX, Yvonne
HEINRICH, Adel Verna
HEINY, Margaret Harris
HELSTED, Bodil
HEMON, Sedje
HIGGINS, Esther S.
HINLOPEN, Francina
HOFER, Maria
HOFFMAN, Phyllis Sampson
HOFFMANN, Peggy
HOKANSON, Margrethe
HOLLAND, Dulcie Sybil
HOOD, Helen
HORNBACK, Sister Mary Gisela
HOWE, Mary Alberta Bruce
HUBICKI, Margaret Olive
HULST, Margaret Gardiner
HUTSON, Wihla L.
HYTREK, Sister Theophane
JACKSON, Elizabeth Barnhart
JAMES, Dorothy E.
JENNY, Sister Leonore
JEWELL, Lucina
JOHNSTON, Alison Aileen Annie
JOLLY, Margaret Anne
JORDAN, Alice Yost
JOULAIN, Jeanne-Angele-Desirée-Yvonne
JUENGER, Patricia
KAESER-BECK, Aida
KAHMANN, Chesley
KALTENECKER, Gertraud
KANACH, Sharon E.
KASILAG, Lucrecia R.
KER, Ann S.
KETTERING, Eunice Lea
KHOSS VON STERNEGG, Gisela
KING, Betty Jackson
KIRBY, Suzanne
KISTETENYI, Melinda
KLEBE, Willemijntje
KNOBLOCHOVA, Antonie
KOELLING, Eloise
KONISHI, Nagako
KORHONEN, S. Gloria
KOZINOVIC, Lujza
KUNTZE, Olga
LACHARTRE, Nicole Marie
LAGO
LAMBRECHTS-VOS, Anna Catharina
LANDREE, Jaquenote Goldsteen
LANG, Edith
LARSEN, Elizabeth Brown
LAVOIPIERRE, Thérèse
LEAF, Ann
LEAHY, Mary Weldon
LECLERC, Michelle
LEE, Hwaeja Yoo
LEFANU, Nicola Frances
LEFEBVRE, Françoise
LEITE, Clarisse
LEJET, Edith
LEJEUNE-BONNIER, Eliane
LEONE, Mae G.
LEPLAE, Claire
LINDEMAN, Hjelle Signe
LINNET, Anne
LIPSCOMB, Helen
LITSITE, Paula Yanovna
LLUNELL SANAHUJA, Pepita
LOCKWOOD, Charlotte Mathewson
LORENZ, Ellen Jane
LOUDOVA, Ivana
LOVAN, Lydia
LUCKE, Katharine E.
LUMBY, Betty Louise
LUND, Gudrun

MACAULAY, Janice Michel
MACONCHY, Elizabeth
MacPHAIL, Frances
McCOLLIN, Frances
McDUFFEE, Mabel Howard
McILWRAITH, Isa Roberta
McINTOSH, Diana
McKENZIE, Sandra
McKINNEY, Mathilde
McLAUGHLIN, Marian
MAGEAU, Mary Jane
MAGNEY, Ruth Taylor
MALMLOEF-FORSSLING, Carin
MANA-ZUCCA
MARCUS, Ada Belle Gross
MAREZ-OYENS, Tera de
MARI, Pierrette
MARTINEZ, Odaline de la
MASON, Gladys Amy
MASON, Marilyn May
MATTHEISS-BOEGNER, Helga
MATUSZCZAK, Bernadetta
MEEK, Ethel Alice
MEL-BONIS
MELL, Gertrud Maria
MELOY, Elizabeth
MERRIMAN, Margarita Leonor
MIAGI, Ester Kustovna
MILETTE, Juliette
MOBERG, Ida Georgina
MOE, Benna
MOHNS, Grace Updegraff Bergen
MONK, Meredith
MONTGOMERY, Merle
MOORE, Mary Carr
MOORE, Undine Smith
MORIN-LABRECQUE, Albertine
MORLEY, Nina Dianne
MORMONE, Tamara
MUNGER, Millicent Christner
MUNGER, Shirley
MURILLO CABALLERO, Juliana
NEWLIN, Dika
NIELSEN, Olga
NIXON, June
NORDENSTROM, Gladys Mercedes
NOWAK, Alison
OBENCHAIN, Virginia
O'BRIEN, Drena
OCHSE, Orpha Caroline
ODAGESCU, Irina
OLIVEIRA, Sophie Marcondes de Mello
OLIVER, Madra Emogene
OMER, Hélène
O'SHEA, Mary Ellen
OWEN, Angela Maria
OWEN, Blythe
PALMER, Catherine M.
PARKER, Alice
PELEGRI, Maria Teresa
PENTLAND, Barbara Lally
PERONI, Wally
PERRY, Julia Amanda
PETERSON, Melody
PETROVA-KRUPKOVA, Elena
PEYROT, Fernande
PFERDEMENGES, Maria Pauline Augusta
PHILIBA, Nicole
PHILIPPART, Renée
PHILLIPS, Bryony
PHILLIPS, Vivian Daphne
PIERCE, Alexandra
PIERCE, Sarah Anderson
PIERROT, Noëlie Marie Antoinette
PIRES DOS REIS, Hilda
PLE-CAUSSADE, Simone
PLONSEY, Jennifer
POOL, Arlette
POSTON, Elizabeth

PREOBRAJENSKA, Vera Nicolaevna
PRICE, Beryl
PRICE, Deon Nielsen
PRICE, Florence Beatrice
PRIOLLI, Maria Luisa de Matos
PROCACCINI, Teresa
RACOVITZA-FLONDOR, Florica
RAINIER, Priaulx
RALSTON, Frances Marion
RAMSEY, Sister Mary Anastasia
RECLI, Giulia
REES, Winifred Emily
REYNOLDS, Laura Lawton
RHENE-JAQUE
RICHARDSON, Enid Dorothy
RICHTER, Marga
RICHTER, Marion Morrey
RICKARD, Sylvia
RILEY, Ann Marion
ROBERT, Lucie
ROCHEROLLE, Eugenie Katherine
ROE, Eileen Betty
ROESGEN-CHAMPION, Marguerite
  Sara
ROGERS, Ethel Tench
ROGERS, Patsy
ROGERS, Sharon Elery
ROGET, Henriette
ROKSETH, Yvonne
ROSSER, Annetta Hamilton
RUFF-STOEHR, Herta Maria Klara
SAMTER, Alice
SANDRESKY, Margaret Vardell
SCHICK, Philippine
SCHORR-WEILER, Eva
SCHUBARTH, Dorothé
SCHUSSLER-BREWAEYS, Marie
  Antoinette
SCHUSTER, Doris Dodd
SCHWERDTFEGER, E. Anne
SEALE, Ruth
SENFTER, Johanna
SHAFFER, Jeanne Ellison
SHAW, Alice Marion
SHRUDE, Marilyn
SIDDALL, Louise
SIMONS, Lorena Cotts
SMELTZER, Susan Mary
SMITH, Julia Frances
SMITH, Margit
SMITH, Mary Barber
SNIZKOVA-SKRHOVA, Jitka
SONNTAG, Brunhilde
SOUTHGATE, Dorothy
SOUTHGATE, Elsie
SPENCER, Marguerita
STARBUCK, Anna Diller
STREATFIELD, Valma June
STRUCK, Ilse
STRUTT, Dorothy
SULPIZI, Mira
SWAIN, Freda Mary
SZOENYI, Erzsebet
TACK, Annie
TAKAMI, Toyoko
TAL, Marjo
TALMA, Louise
TATE, Phyllis
TAYLOR, Eleanor
TEICHMUELLER, Anna
TELFER, Nancy Ellen
TERZIAN, Alicia
THIEME, Kerstin Anja
THOMAS, Gertrude Evelyn
THOMAS, Mary Virginia
THREADGILL-MARTIN, Ravonna
TISSOT, Mireille
TOBIN, Sister Clare
TORRA, Celia
URNER, Catherine Murphy
VAN APPLEDORN, Mary Jeanne

VAN HAUTE, Anna-Maria
VAN NESTE, Rosane Micheline Lucie
  Charlotte
VERHAALEN, Sister Marion
VIEU, Jane
VIGNERON-RAMAKERS, Christiane-
  Josée
VILLIN, Marcelle Henriette Marie
VOLKART, Hazel
VON GUNDEN, Heidi
VREE-BROWN, Marion F.
WALKER, Gwyneth van Anden
WARNE, Katharine Mulky
WARREN, Elinor Remick
WEAVER, Mary
WENDELBURG, Norma Ruth
WENNERBERG-REUTER, Sara
  Margareta Eugenia Euphrosyne
WENTZ-JANACEK, Elisabet
WESTBROOK, Helen Searles
WIERUSZOWSKI, Lili
WIGGINS, Mary
WILKINS, Margaret Lucy
WILL, Madeleine
WISHART, Betty Rose
WITNI, Monica
WOOD, Mabel
ZAKRZEWSKA-NIKIPORCZYK,
  Barbara Maria
ZECHLIN, Ruth
ZIFFRIN, Marilyn Jane
ZIPRICK, Marjorie Jean
Century unknown
CONSOLINI, Gabriella Elsa
MOLINE, Lily Wadhams
RITTER, Irene Marschand
WARD, Beverly A.
WILLIAMS, Alice Crane

ORGAN AND ORCHESTRA OR STRINGS
18th Century A.D.
DE GAMBARINI, Elisabetta
19th Century A.D.
LA HYE, Louise Genevieve
20th Century A.D.
BORON, Marion
CANALES PIZARRO, Marta
CAPUIS, Matilde
DEMESSIEUX, Jeanne
DIEMER, Emma Lou
FALCINELLI, Rolande
FARGA PELLICER, Onia
GUBITOSI, Emilia
HEINRICH, Adel Verna
JOLAS, Betsy
KISTETENYI, Melinda
LUMBY, Betty Louise
PROCACCINI, Teresa
ROGET, Henriette
SEHESTED, Hilda
SZOENYI, Erzsebet
TREMBLOT DE LA CROIX, Francine
WILL, Madeleine
WITNI, Monica
ZECHLIN, Ruth

PANPIPES
20th Century A.D.
HEMON, Sedje
ROESGEN-CHAMPION, Marguerite
  Sara

PERCUSSION
18th Century A.D.
LACHANTERIE, Elisabeth
20th Century A.D.
ABE, Kyoko
ABEJO, Sister M. Rosalina
ADAIR, Yvonne Madeleine
AKSYANTSEVA, Ninel Moiseyevna
ALCALAY, Luna

ALEXANDRA, Liana
ALLEN, Judith Shatin
ALLIK, Kristi
ALSTED, Birgitte
ALTER, Martha
ANDERSON, Beth
ANDERSON, Julia McKinley
ARETZ, Isabel
ARIMA, Reiko
ARMER, Elinor Florence
AUFDERHEIDE, May
BACEWICZ, Grażyna
BACH, Maria
BACKES, Lotte
BADIAN, Maya
BAILLY, Colette
BAIRD, Irene
BARAT, Eliane
BARBERIS, Mansi
BARBOSA, Cacilda Campos Borges
BARON SUPERVIELLE, Susana
BARRAINE, Elsa
BARRETT-THOMAS, N.
BAULD, Alison
BEAHM, Jacquelyn Yvette
BEAT, Janet Eveline
BEATH, Betty
BECKON, Lettie Marie
BEECROFT, Norma Marian
BELL, Carla Huston
BENAVENTE, Regina
BEYER, Johanna Magdalena
BLAUSTEIN, Susan Morton
BLOCKSIDGE, Kathleen Mary
BLOM, Diane
BLOOD, Esta Damesek
BLOOM, Jane Ira
BOFILL, Anna
BOND, Victoria Ellen
BORROFF, Edith
BOSHKOFF, Ruth
BOUCHARD, Linda L.
BOYD, Anne Elizabeth
BREMER, Marrie Petronella
BRENET, Thérèse
BRITAIN, Radie
BRUZDOWICZ, Joanna
BURSTON, Maggie
CABRERA, Silvia Maria Pires
CALLAWAY, Ann
CARNO, Zita
CARR-BOYD, Ann Kirsten
CARVALHO, Dinora de
CECCONI-BOTELLA, Monic
CHANCE, Nancy Laird
CHANDLER, Mary
CHARBONNIER, Janine Andrée
CHARLES, S. Robin
CHAVES, Mary Elizabeth
CIOBANU, Maia
CLOSTRE, Adrienne
COATES, Gloria Kannenberg
COHEN, Marcia
COLERIDGE-TAYLOR, Avril
  Gwendolen
CORY, Eleanor
COULOMBE SAINT-MARCOUX,
  Micheline
COULTHARD, Jean
CRAWFORD, Dorothy Lamb
DANFORTH, Frances A.
DEDIEU-PETERS, Madeleine
DEMARQUEZ, Suzanne
DESPORTES, Yvonne Berthe Melitta
DIANDA, Hilda
DILLON, Fannie Charles
DINESCU, Violeta
DLUGOSZEWSKI, Lucia
DOBBINS, Lori
DOBSON, Elaine
DRENNAN, Dorothy Carter

DU PAGE, Florence Elizabeth
DUSHKIN, Dorothy Smith
EAKLOR, Vicki
ELIAS, Graciela Morales de
ERVIN, Karen
ESCOT, Pozzi
EUTENEUER-ROHRER, Ursula
   Henrietta
EVEN-OR, Mary
FAIRLIE, Margaret C.
FALCINELLI, Rolande
FAUTCH, Sister Magdalen
FERRAND-TEULET, Denise
FINE, Vivian
FONTYN, Jacqueline
FORMAN, Joanne
FOWLER, Jennifer Joan
FRITZ, Sherilyn Gail
FULLER-HALL, Sarah Margaret
GARDNER, Kay
GARR, Wieslawa
GARSCIA-GRESSEL, Janina
GARTENLAUB, Odette
GIFFORD, Helen Margaret
GILBERT, Pia
GITECK, Janice
GIURANNA, Elena Barbara
GLANVILLE-HICKS, Peggy
GOERSCH, Ursula Margitta
GRAHAM, Janet Christine
GREENFIELD, Marjorie
GREENWALD, Jan Carol
GRIMAUD, Yvette
GUBAIDULINA, Sofia Asgatovna
GUDAUSKAS, Giedra
HAHN, Sandra Lea
HALPERN, Stella
HAWLEY, Carolyn Jean
HILDERLEY, Jeriann G.
HOENDERDOS, Margriet
HOOVER, Katherine
HOVDA, Eleanor
HSU, Wen-Ying
HUMPHREY, Doris
HYDE, Miriam Beatrice
IVEY, Jean Eichelberger
JANKOWSKI, Loretta Patricia
JIRACKOVA, Marta
JOHNSTON-REID, Sarah Ruth
JOLAS, Betsy
JUENGER, Patricia
KABAT, Julie Phyllis
KABE, Mariko
KALOGRIDOU, Maria
KAMINSKY, Laura
KANACH, Sharon E.
KASILAG, Lucrecia R.
KATS-CHERNIN, Elena
KEETMAN, Gunild
KELLER, Ginette
KERN, Frida
KITAZUME, Yayoi
KOBLENZ, Babette
KOLB, Barbara
KROSNICK, Mary Louw Wesley
KUBO, Mayako
KUSUNOKI, Tomoko
LACHARTRE, Nicole Marie
LAM MAN YEE, Violet
LAPEYRE, Thérèse
LARSEN, Elizabeth Brown
LAUBER, Anne Marianne
LAYMAN, Pamela
LE SIEGE, Annette
LEAHY, Mary Weldon
LEBARON, Anne
LEBENBOM, Elaine F.
LEE, Chan-Hae
LEE, Hope Anne Keng-Wei
LEE, Hwaeja Yoo
LEFANU, Nicola Frances

LEFEVER, Maxine Lane
LEJET, Edith
LITER, Monia
LOH, Kathy Jean
LOUDOVA, Ivana
LU, Yen
LUCAS, Mary Anderson
LUNDQUIST, Christie
LUTYENS, Elisabeth
LUTYENS, Sally
MACKIE, Shirley M.
MacGREGOR, Laurie
McKENZIE, Sandra
McLEAN, Priscilla Anne Taylor
McLEOD, Jennifer Helen
McMILLAN, Ann Endicott
McNEIL, Janet L. Pfischner
McTEE, Cindy Karen
MAGEAU, Mary Jane
MAIRE, Jacqueline
MALMLOEF-FORSSLING, Carin
MAMLOK, Ursula
MARBE, Myriam
MARCUS, Bunita
MAREZ-OYENS, Tera de
MARI, Pierrette
MARSHALL, Pamela J.
MARTINS, Maria de Lourdes
MASONER, Elizabeth L.
MATHIS, Judy M.
MATUSZCZAK, Bernadetta
MEACHEM, Margaret McKeen
   Ramsey
MEKEEL, Joyce
MERRIMAN, Margarita Leonor
MILKULAK, Marcia Lee
MILLER, Elma
MINEO, Antoinette
MITCHELL, Janice Misurell
MIZUNO, Shuko
MONK, Meredith
MOORE, Undine Smith
MORRISON, Julia Maria
MOSZUMANSKA-NAZAR, Krystyna
MURAO, Sachie
MURRAY, Margaret
NIEWIADOMSKA, Barbara
NOBLE, Ann
NORUP, Helle Merete
NOVA SONDAG, Jacqueline
NOWAK, Alison
ODAGESCU, Irina
OFFICER, Bronwyn Lee
OH, Sook Ja
OLIVE, Vivienne
OLIVEIRA, Jocy de
OLIVEROS, Pauline
ORENSTEIN, Joyce Ellin
OWEN, Blythe
PADE, Else Marie
PARKER, Alice
PATERSON, Wilma
PAULL, Barberi
PELEGRI, Maria Teresa
PENTLAND, Barbara Lally
PEREIRA DA SILVA, Adelaide
PERETZ-LEVY, Liora
PERRY, Julia Amanda
PHILIBA, Nicole
PHILLIPS, Bryony
PIECHOWSKA, Alina
PIERCE, Sarah Anderson
PRADELL, Leila
PRAVOSSUDOVITCH, Natalja
   Michajlovna
PREOBRAJENSKA, Vera Nicolaevna
PROCACCINI, Teresa
PSTROKONSKA-NAVRATIL,
   Grazyna Hanna
PTASZYNSKA, Marta
RAINIER, Priaulx

RAN, Shulamit
RANTA-SHIDA, Shoko
REID, Sarah Johnston
RICHTER, Marion Morrey
ROBERTS, Megan L.
RODRIGUE, Nicole
ROE, Eileen Betty
ROEDER, Toni
ROGERS, Patsy
ROSAS FERNANDES, Maria Helena
ROYSE, Mildred Barnes
RUBIN, Anna Ita
SAARIAHO, Kaija
SAINT JOHN, Kathleen Louise
SAITO-NODA, Eva
SALQUIN, Hedy
SANGUESA, Iris
SANTOS BARRETO, Adelina
SANTOS-OCAMPO DE FRANCESCO,
   Amada Amy
SCHERCHEN, Tona
SCHORR-WEILER, Eva
SCHWARTZ, Julie
SCOVILLE, Margaret Lee
SHELTON, Margaret Meier
SHORE, Clare
SHRUDE, Marilyn
SIEGRIST, Beatrice
SIKORA, Elzbieta
SILSBEE, Ann L.
SILVER, Sheila Jane
SILVERMAN, Faye-Ellen
SIMONS, Netty
SMITH, Ladonna Carol
SMITH, Margit
SNIZKOVA-SKRHOVA, Jitka
SNYDER, Amy
SOENSTEVOLD, Maj
SOUTHAM, Ann
STANLEY, Helen Camille
STEINER, Gitta Hana
STEPHEN, Roberta Mae
STRUTT, Dorothy
SUH, Kyung-Sun
SULPIZI, Mira
SUTHERLAND, Margaret
SYNOWIEC, Ewa
SZAJNA-LEWANDOWSKA, Jadwiga
   Helena
SZEKELY, Katalin
SZYMANSKA, Iwonka Bogumila
TAILLEFERRE, Germaine
TAKAMI, Toyoko
TASHJIAN, B. Charmian
TAUTU, Cornelia
TELFER, Nancy Ellen
TERZIAN, Alicia
THOME, Diane
THREADGILL-MARTIN, Ravonna
TOLKOWSKY, Denise
TOWER, Joan
USTVOLSKAYA, Galina Ivanovna
VAN DE VATE, Nancy Hayes
VAN HAUTE, Anna-Maria
VAN OHLEN, Deborah
VASILIEVA, Tatiana Ivanovna
VERHAALEN, Sister Marion
VON GUNDEN, Heidi
VON ZIERITZ, Grete
VORLOVA, Slavka
WALDO, Elisabeth
WALKER, Gwyneth van Anden
WALLACH, Joelle
WARNE, Katharine Mulky
WELMAN, Sylvia
WHITEHEAD, Gillian
WIENER, Eva Hannah
WILLIAMS, Linda
WOLLNER, Gertrude Price
WYLIE, Ruth Shaw
ZAIDEL-RUDOLPH, Jeanne

ZAKRZEWSKA-NIKIPORCZYK,
Barbara Maria
ZECHLIN, Ruth
ZIFFRIN, Marilyn Jane

PERCUSSION AND ORCHESTRA OR STRINGS
20th Century A.D.
ARCHER, Violet Balestreri
BALLOU, Esther Williamson
EUTENEUER-ROHRER, Ursula
Henrietta
JEPPSSON, Kerstin Maria
KALOGRIDOU, Maria
LARSEN, Elizabeth Brown
LEBARON, Anne
LOUDOVA, Ivana
MARBE, Myriam
PREDIC-SAPER, Branislava
SHLONSKY, Verdina

PIANO
17th Century A.D.
HOFF, Regina Clara
18th Century A.D.
AGNESI-PINOTTINI, Maria Teresa d'
ANNA AMALIA, Duchess of Saxe-
Weimar
AUENBRUGG, Marianna von
AURENHAMMER, Josefa Barbara
von
BARTHELEMON, Cecilia Maria
BARTHELEMON, Mary
BENAULT, Mlle.
BRANDENSTEIN, Charlotte von
BRANDES, Charlotte Wilhelmina
Franziska
BRILLON DE JOUY, Mme.
BRUCKENTHAL, Bertha von,
Baroness
CAMPET DE SAUJON, Mlle.
CECILE, Jeanne
CHARRIERE, Isabella Agneta
Elisabeth de
CLARKSON, Jane
COURMONT, Countess von
CROUCH, Anna Maria
DANZI, Maria Margarethe
DE GAMBARINI, Elisabetta
DEMILLIERE, Marthèsie
DESFOSSES, Elisabeth Françoise,
Countess
DEZEDE, Florine
DUMUR, Mme.
ESSEX, Margaret
FLEMING, Lady
GUEST, Jeanne Marie
HOFFMANN, Miss J.
HUEBNER, Caroline
KANZLER, Josephine
KAUTH, Maria Magdalena
KOHARY, Marie, Countess of
LEBRUN, Franziska Dorothea
LOUIS, Mme.
MAIER, Catherine
MARTINEZ, Marianne
MEDECK, Mme.
MURRAY, Lady Edith
MacINTOSH, Mary
PARKER, Mrs.
POUILLAU, Mlle.
REICHARDT, Bernhardine Juliane
REYNOLDS, Marie Hester
SAVAGE, Jane
SIRMEN, Maddalena Laura di
STECHER, Marianne
SZCZUKA-JEZIERSKA
TRAVENET, Mme. B. de
VALENTINE, Ann
WOLF, Maria Carolina
ZAMPIERI, Elizabetta

19th Century A.D.
AARUP, Caia
ABRAMS, Harriet
ADAJEWSKY, Ella
ADAMOWITSCH, Elisabeth
ALBRECHT, Lillie
ALESSI, Antonietta
ALEXANDRA JOSEPHOWNA, Grand
Duchess
AMANN, Josephine
AMERSFOORDT-DYK, Hermina
Maria
ANDREWS, Jenny
ANNA, Duchess of Mecklenburg-
Schwerin
APPIANI, Eugenia
ARANCIBIA, Francisca
ATANASIJEVIC, Slavka
AUGUSTENBURG, Caroline
Amelia of
AUSPITZ-KOLAR, Augusta
BACHMANN, Elise
BACKER-GROENDAHL, Agathe
Ursula
BADARZEWSKA-BARANOWSKA,
Tekla
BAJEROWA, Konstancje
BAKA-BAITZ, Irma
BALTHASAR, Florence
BARKER, Laura Wilson
BARNARD, Charlotte
BARNES, Bertha L.
BARNETT, Emma
BARONI-CAVALCABO, Guilia
BARTH, Elise
BARTHOLOMEW, Ann Sheppard
BARTHOLOMEW, Mrs. M.
BATTA, Clementine
BAU, Elise
BAUDISSIN, Sofie, Countess Wolf
BAUER, Charlotte
BAUER, Katharine
BEHR, Louise
BELLANI, Caroline
BELLEVILLE-OURY, Emilie
BENAVIDES, Elena
BERNARD, Eulanie
BERNARD, Vincenzia
BERNOUILLY, Agnes
BERTIN, Louise Angelique
BIEHLER, Ludmilla
BIGOT DE MOROGUES, Marie
BINFIELD, Hanna R.
BISLAND, Margaret Cyrilla
BISSET, Elizabeth Anne
BLAHETKA, Marie Leopoldina
BLAKE, Mary
BLANC DE FONTBELLE, Cécile
BLANGINI, Mlle.
BLOCK, Isabelle McKee
BOCK, Anna
BONNAY, Mlle.
BOPP VON OBERSTADT, Countess
BORGES, Deolinda Eulalia Cordeiro
BORTON, Alice
BOSCH, Elisa
BOTTINI, Marianna, Marchioness
BOYCE, Ethel Mary
BRAGGIOTTI, Augusta
BRANCA-MUSSINI, Adele
BRANCHU, Mme.
BRANDHURST, Elise
BRANDLING, Mary
BRDLIKOVA, Josefina
BREITENBACH, Antoinette de
BRESSON, Mlle.
BRINKMANN, Minna
BRINKMANN, Wilhelmine
BROES, Mlle.
BRONSART VON SCHELLENDORF,
Ingeborg Lena von

BROOMAN, Hanna
BROWN, Harriet Estelle
BROWNE, Augusta
BRUCKEN-FOCK, Emilie von
BRUSCHINI, Ernestina
BRZEZINSKA, Filipina
BUGBEE, L.A.
BUGGE, Magda
BURTIS, Sarah R.
BUSKY-BENEDETTI, Albina
BUTTENSTEIN, Constanze von
CALOSSO, Eugenia
CAMMACK, Amelia
CANDEILLE, Amelie Julie
CANTELLO, Annie
CARISSAN, Celanie
CARMICHAEL, Anne Darling
CASELLA, Felicita
CASTELLI, Adele
CASTRO, Maria Guilhermina de
Noronha E.
CERRINI DE MONTE-VARCHI, Anna
von
CHAMBERLAYNE, Edith A.
CHARLOTTE, Friederike Wilhelmine
Louise, Princess
CHASTENAY, Victorine de
CHEVALIER DE BOISVAL, Mme.
CHEVALIER DE MONTREAL, Julia
CHOUQUET, Louise
CHRZASTOWSKA, Pelagia
CIANCHETTINI, Veronica Elisabeth
CIBBINI, Katherina
CLARKE, Helen Archibald
COATES, Kathleen Kyle
COLLIN, Helene
COLLINS, Laura Sedgwick
CONTIN, Mme.
CONVERT, Josephine
CORRER, Ida, Countess
CORRI-DUSSEK, Sofia Giustina
CRETI, Marianna de Rocchis
CRUMB, Berenice
CUMAN, Harriet Johanna Louise
CZETWERTYNSKA, Marie, Princess
CZETWERTYNSKA-JELOWICKA,
Janina, Princess
CZICZKA, Angela
DABROWSKA, Waleria
DAHL, Emma
DAMCKE, Louise
DANCLA, Alphonsine Genevieve-
Lore
DANZINGER, Laura
DAVIES, Llewela
DAVIS, Marianne
DE CASTRO, Alice
DE LACKNER, Mrs.
DE LISLE, Estelle
DE MICCO, Lora
DEMAR, Thérèse
DEPECKER, Rose
DICK, Edith A.
DIETRICH, Amalia
DONALDS, Belle
DUFRESNOY, Mme.
DUHAN, Mme.
DULCKEN, Louisa
DULCKEN, Sophie
DUPORT, Marie
DUSCHEK, Josefina
DUSSEK, Olivia
DUSSEK, Veronica Rosalie
EATON, Frances
EDELSBERG, Philippine von
EGEBERG, Anna
EGEBERG, Fredrikke Sophie
ELDESE, Renée
ENGER, Nelly
ESCHBORN, Georgine Christine
Maria Anna

EUGENIE, Charlotte Augusta Amalia Albertina, Princess
FABRE, Marie
FARMER, Emily Bardsley
FARRENC, Louise
FARRENC, Victorine Louise
FECHNER, Paulina
FELSENTHAL, Amalie
FERNANDEZ DE LA MORA, Pilar
FERRARI, Carlotta
FERRARI, Francesca Jessie
FILIPOWICZ, Elize-Minelli
FINCH, Miss
FRANCOIS, Emmy von
FRANKEL, Gisela
FRUGONI, Bertha
GABRIEL, Mary Ann Virginia
GALLOIS, Marie
GAMBOGI, Federica Elvira
GARCIA, Eduarda Mansilla de
GARRETT, Mrs. William
GASCHIN-ROSENBERG, Fanny, Countess
GAY, Sophia Maria Francesca
GEIGER, Constanze
GERARD, Miss
GIZYCKA-ZAMOYSKA, Ludmilla, Countess
GLOWACKA, Ludwika
GOLDSTEIN, M. Anna
GORYAINOVNA, A.
GOSSLER, Clara von
GOUBAU D'HAVORST, Leopoldine
GRAB, Isabella von
GRABOWSKA, Clementine, Countess
GRAEVER, Madeleine
GRANDVAL, Marie Felicie Clemence de Reiset, Vicomtesse de
GRAY, Louisa
GRO, Josephine
GROEBENSCHUETZ, Amalie
GUERINI, Rosa
GUIDI LIONETTI, Teresa
GYDE, Margaret
HAASS, Maria Catharina
HADELN, Nancy von
HAENEL DE CRONENTHAL, Louise Augusta Marie Julia
HALE, Irene
HAMBROCK, Mathilde
HAMMER, Marie von
HANIM, Durri Nigar
HARTLAND, Lizzie
HARTMANN, Emma Sophie Amalie
HASWIN, Frances R.
HAXTHAUSEN, Aurore M.G.Ch. von
HAYES, Mrs.
HEINKE, Ottilie
HELLER, Ottilie
HENDRICH-MERTA, Marie
HENSEL, Fanny Caecilia
HERITTE-VIARDOT, Louise Pauline Marie
HERTZ, Hedwig
HERZOGENBERG, Elizabeth von
HEWITT, Estelle
HIBLER, Nellie
HODGES, Faustina Hasse
HOHNSTOCK, Adele
HOLMES, Augusta Mary Anne
HOLMES, Mary
HORTENSE, Queen of Holland
HOVORST, Mme. Gouban d'
HUBER, Nanette
HUENERWADEL, Fanny
HUNDT, Aline
HUTET, Josephine
JAHNOVA, Bozena
JANINA, Olga
JENKS, Maude E.

JESKE-CHOINSKA-MIKORSKA, Ludmila
JONAS, Anna
JOSEPHINE, Queen of Sweden and Norway
KABATH, Augusta de
KALKHOEF, Laura von
KARL, Anna
KAVALIEROVA, Marie
KENDIKOVA, Zdenka
KERN, Louise
KINKEL, Johanna
KIRCHER, Maria Bertha
KNAPP, Phoebe Palmer
KOCHETOVA, Aleksandra, Dorimedontovna
KOENIG, Marie
KOMOROWSKA, Stephanie, Countess
KOSSAKOWSKA, Wanda
KOTSBATREVSKAYA
KRAEHMER, Caroline
KRAINSKA, Justyna
KRALIK VON MAYERSWALDEN, Mathilde
KRYSINSKA, Maria
KURZBOECK, Magdalene von
KYNTZELL-HAGSTROMER, Louise
LA HYE, Louise Genevieve
LAMBERT, Agnes
LANG, Josephine
LANGHANS, Louise
LANGRISHE, May Katherine
LANNOY, Clementine-Josephine-Francoise-Therese, Countess
LARCHER, Maria Amalia
LE CLERE, Victoire
LEAVITT, Josephina
LEFEBURE, Marguerite
LEONARDO, Luisa
LESSEL, Helena
LIEBMANN, Helene
LILIEN, Antoinette von, Baroness
LIND, Jenny
LIPINSKA-PARCZEWSKA, Natalia
LODER, Kate Fanny
LONSDALE, Eva
LORINSER, Gisela von
LOUD, Annie Frances
LOUD, Emily L.
LOWTHIAN, Caroline
LUDWIG, Rosa
LUND, Baroness van der
MACIRONI, Clara Angela
MADDISON, Adele
MALLEVILLE, Charlotte Tardieu de
MARCKWALD, Grace
MARIA PAULOWNA, Grand Duchess of Weimar
MARIE ELIZABETH, Princess of Saxe-Meiningen
MARINELLI, Maria
MARTIN, Giuseppina
MARX, Berthe
MASINI, Giulia
MASSART, Louise Aglae
MATOS, A. de
MATTFELD, Marie
MATTHISON-HANSEN, Nanny Hedwig Christiane
MAYER, Emilie
MENTER, Sophie
METZLER, Bertha
MEYER, Elizabeth
MILANOLLO, Teresa Domenica Maria
MOLINOS-LAFITTE, Mlle. A.
MOLIQUE, Caroline
MOLITOR, Friederike
MOMY, Valerie
MONTGEROULT, Hélène de Nervode

MOODY, Marie
MORANDI, Jennie Jewett
MOSEL, Catherine de
MOUNSEY, Elizabeth
MOZART, Maria Anna Walburga Ignatia
MUNDELLA, Emma
MURIO-CELLI, Adelina
MYERS, Emma F.
MYRBERG, Anne Sophie
NATHAN, Matilde Berendsen
NEGRONE, Luisa
NEUMANN, Elizabeth
NEUVILLE, Mme. Alphonse de
NEWCOMBE, Georgeanne
NEWTON, Adelaide
NICOLAY, Maria Antonia
NIEDERSTETTER, Emilie
NIEWIAROWSKA-BRZOZOWSKA, Julia
NORRIS, Mary
OCKLESTON-LIPPA, Katherine
OLIVEIRA, Alexandrina Maciel de
OLIVER, Mary
OLIVIER, Charlotte
ORGER, Caroline
ORTH, Lizette Emma
OSTIERE, May
OWEN, Anita
PACHLER-KOSCHAK, Marie Leopoldine
PALDI, Mari
PAPARA, Teodozja
PARIS, Salomea
PARK, Jane
PARKE, Maria Hester
PARKYNS, Beatrice
PATTI, Adelina
PERALTA CASTERA, Angela
PERRELLI, Giuseppina
PESADORI, Antoniette de
PESSIAK-SCHMERLING, Anna
PEYRON, Albertina Fredrika
PFEIFFER, Clara-Virginie
PFEILSCHIFTER, Julie von
PIERPONT, Marie de
PIERRET, Phedora
PITTMAN, Alice Locke
PLASENCIA, Ubalda
PLATEROWA-BROEL-ZYBERK, Maria
PLEYEL, Marie Felicity Denise
POLAK, Nina
POLANOWSKA, Teofila
POLKO, Elise Vogel
POSADA Y TORRE, Ana
PRESCOTT, Oliveria Louisa
PUGET, Loise
PURGOLD, Nadezhda Nikolayevna
RABORG, Rosa Ortiz de Zerallos de
RADZIWILL, Princess
RALPH, Kate
RAMANN, Lina
RAMOS, Eudocia
RAYMOND, Emma Marcy
REED, Florence
REES, Clara H.
REICHARDT, Louise
RENAUD-D'ALLEN, Mlle. de
RIBAS, Medina N.
RICHARDSON, Jennie V.
RICHTER, Pauline
RICOTTI, Onestina
RING, Claire
RINGELSBERG, Matilde
ROBINSON, Fanny
RODRIGO, Maria
ROECKEL, Jane
RONDONNEAU, Elise
RONTGEN, Amanda
ROSENHOFF, Orla

ROUSSEAU, Louise
RUCINSKA, Lucja
RUNCIE, Constance Owen Faunt
  Le Roy
SABININ, Martha von
SAFFERY, Eliza
SALIGNY, Clara
SAMUEL, Caroline
SANDELS, Ellen
SANDERS, Alma
SAUGEON, Zelie
SAWATH, Caroline
SCHADEN, Nanette von
SCHAEFFER, Theresa
SCHALE, Mlle.
SCHAUROTH, Delphine von
SCHINDLER, Livia
SCHOLL, Amalie
SCHREINZER, F.M.
SCHUMANN, Clara Josephine
SCHWARZ-SIGMAND,Hermina
SCOTT, Clara H.
SENEKE, Teresa
SEROVA, Valentina Semyonovna
SERVIER, Mme. H.
SICK, Anna
SIEGMUND, Hermine
SIMMONS, Kate
SKELTON, Nellie Bangs
SLOMAN, Jane
SMITH, Alice Mary
SMITH, Hannah
SMITH, Mrs. Gerrit
SOMELLERA DE ESPINOSA,
  Candelaria
SPORLEDER, Charlotte
SQUIRE, Hope
STALEWSKA, Jadwiga
STANG, Erika
STEIN, Nannette
STEMANN, Petronella
STEWART, Elizabeth Kirby
STEWART, F.M.
STIRLING, Elizabeth
STOLLEWERK, Nina von
STRANTZ, Louise von
STUBENBERG, Anna Zichy,
  Countess
SUMOWSKA, Helena
SUTRO, Florence Edith
SWEPSTONE, Edith
SYNGE, Mary Helena
SZARVADY, Wilhelmine Clausz
SZYMANOWSKA, Maria Agata
TAITE, Annie
TARDIEU DE MALLEVILLE, Charlotte
THAMM, Ida
THEGERSTROEM, Hilda Aurora
THERESE, Princess of Saxe-
  Altenburg and of Sweden
THORNE, Beatrice
TONDEUR, Wilhelmine
TONEL, Leonie
TORRY, Jane Sloman
TYRELL, Agnes
UGALDE, Delphine Beauce
VALERO, Matilde
VANZO, Vittoria Maria
VEDRUNA, Dolores
VEGA, Paulina
VEILUVA, Giuseppina Cerruti
VELTHEIM, Charlotte
VENTH, Lydia Kunz
VERGER, Virginie Morel du
VESPERMANN, Marie
VIARDOT-GARCIA, Pauline Michelle
  Ferdinande
VICTORIA MARIA LOUISA, Duchess
  of Kent
VIGNY, Louise von
VILLARD, Nina de

VOLKMANN, Ida
VON HOFF, Elizabeth
VORWERK, Henrietta
WADIA Sabra
WAGNER, Virginia De Oliveira
  Bastos
WALBERG, Emilie
WALDBURG-WURZACH, Julie von,
  Princess
WALDENBURG, Eveline von
WALKER, Ida
WARD, Clementine
WARTEL, Atala Thérèse Annette
WATSON, Regina
WEATHERALL, Nellie G.
WESTENHOLZ, Eleonore Sophie
  Marie
WEYRAUCH, Anna Julie von
WEYRAUCH, Augusta Henrietta von
WEYRAUCH, Sophie Auguste von
WHITE, Emma C.
WHITE, Maude Valerie
WICHERN, Caroline
WICKERHAUSER, Nathalie
WICKINS, Florence
WICKMAN, Fredrika
WIECK, Marie
WIEL, Elise
WILLIAMS, Nora Osborne
WILSON, Addie Anderson
WINTZER, Elisabeth
WOLFF, Luise
WOODS, Eliza
WOOLF, Sophia Julia
WUERTEMBERSKA-
  CZARTORYSKA, Maria, Duchess
WURM, Mary J.A.
YAKUBOVITCH, Elizaveta
YEATMAN, Ethel
YOUNG, Eliza
YOUNG, Matilda
ZAPATER, Rosaria
ZBYSZEWSKA-OLECHNOWSKA,
  Maria
ZEGERS, Isidora
ZENTNER, Clary
ZERNICKOW, Elise
ZIEGLER, Natalie Sophie von
ZIMMERMANN, Agnes Marie
  Jacobina
ZINGLER-SCHREINER, Martha
ZITTELMANN, Helene
ZUMSTEEG, Emilie
20th Century A.D.
AARNE, Els
ABE, Kyoko
ABEJO, Sister M. Rosalina
ABORN, Lora
ABRAMOVA, Sonia Pinkhasovna
ABREU, Julieta Licairac
ACCART, Eveline
ACKLAND, Jeanne Isabel Dorothy
ACKLAND, Jessie Agnes
ACOSTA, Josefina, Baroness
ADAIR, Mildred
ADAM, Margie
ADAM, Maria Emma
ADAMS, Elizabeth Kilmer
ADAMS, Julia Aurelia
AESCHLIMANN-ROTH, Esther
AGABALIAN, Lidia Semyenovna
AGUDELO MURGUIA, Graciela
AINLEY, Julie
AINSCOUGH, Juliana Mary
AKHUNDOVA, Shafiga Gulam kyzy
AKIYOSHI, Toshiko
AKSYANTSEVA, Ninel Moiseyevna
ALCALAY, Luna
ALDEN, Zilpha May
ALEJANDRO-DE LEON, Esther
ALEXANDER, Leni

ALEXANDRA, Liana
ALIOTH, Marguerite
ALLAN, Esther
ALLEN, Judith Shatin
ALLINOWNA, Stefania
ALLOUARD CARNY, Odette
ALMEN, Ruth
ALMESAN, Irma
ALOTIN, Yardena
ALPERT, Pauline Edith
ALSTED, Birgitte
ALT, Hansi
ALTER, Martha
ALVES DE SOUSA, Berta Candida
AMATI, Orlanda
ANACLETO, Aurea
ANDERSEN, Helen Somerville
ANDERSON, Beth
ANDERSON, Julia McKinley
ANDERSON, Olive Jennie Paxton
ANDERSON, Ruth
ANDERSON-WUENSCH, Jean Mary
ANDERSSON, Ellen
ANDREE, Elfrida
ANDREWS, Virginia
ANDREYEVA, Elena Fedorovna
ANDREYEVA, M.
ANDRIESSEN, Caecilia
ANDRUS, Helen Josephine
ANDRZEJOWSKA, Alina
ANTHONY, Gina
APPELDOORN, Dina van
APPLETON, Adeline Carola
ARAUJO, Gina de
ARAZOVA, Izabella Konstantinovna
ARENA, Iris Mae
ARETZ, Isabel
ARIMA, Reiko
ARIZTI SOBRINO, Cécilia
ARLEN, Jeanne Burns
ARMER, Elinor Florence
ARNOLD, Rosanna Luisa Swann
ARRIEU, Claude
ARSEYEVA, Irina Vasilievna
ARTEAGA, Genoveva de
ASHFORD, Emma Louise
ASHMORE, Grace Flournoy
ATKINSON, Dorothy
AUBER, Chantal
AUFDERHEIDE, May
AULIN, Laura Valborg
AUSTER, Lydia Martinovna
AUSTIN, Dorothea
AUTENRIETH, Helma
AVETISIAN, Aida Konstantinovna
AXTENS, Florence
AYLOTT, Lydia Georgina Edith
BAADER-NOBS, Heidi
BABAYEVA, Seda Grigorievna
BACEWICZ, Grażyna
BACH, Maria
BACKES, Lotte
BACON, Viola Ruth Orcutt
BADIAN, Maya
BAGA, Ena Rosina
BAGANIER, Janine
BAIKADAMOVA, Baldyrgan
  Bakhitzhanovna
BAIL, Grace Shattuck
BAILEY, Freda
BAILEY, Judith Margaret
BAILEY-APFELBECK, Marie Louise
BAILLY, Colette
BAINBRIDGE, Beryl
BAIRD, Edith Anna
BAIRD, Lorine Chamberlain
BAKER, Gertrude Tremblay
BAKKE, Ruth
BAL, Rosita
BALDACCI, Giovanna Bruna
BALDWIN, Esther Lillian

BALLANDS, Etta
BALLASEYUS, Virginia
BALLOU, Esther Williamson
BALUTET, Marguerite
BAMBERGER, Regina
BAMPTON, Ruth
BANCER, Teresa Barbara
BANG, Sophy
BANKS, Hilda
BANNISTER, Mary Jeanne Hoggard
BARAMISHVILI, Olga Ivanovna
BARATTA, Maria M. de
BARBERIS, Mansi
BARBI, Alice
BARBILLON, Jeanne
BARBLAN-OPIENSKA, Lydia
BARBOSA, Cacilda Campos Borges
BARBOUR, Florence Newell
BARCROFT, E. Dorothea
BARD, Vivien
BARDEL, Germaine
BARIL, Jeanne
BARKER, Phyllis Elizabeth
BARKIN, Elaine
BARKLUND, Irma L.
BARNS, Ethel
BARON SUPERVIELLE, Susana
BARRADAS, Carmen
BARRAINE, Elsa
BARRATT, Carol Ann
BARRETT-THOMAS, N.
BARRIERE, Françoise
BARTHEL, Ursula
BARTLETT, Ethel Agnes
BARTLETT, Floy Little
BASSETT, Henrietta Elizabeth
BASSOT, Anne-Marie
BATCHELOR, Phyllis
BATES, Anna Craig
BAUER, Marion Eugenie
BAULD, Alison
BAYEVA, Vera
BAYLIS, Lilian Mary
BEACH, Amy Marcy
BEACH, Priscilla A.
BEAHM, Jacquelyn Yvette
BEAN, Mabel
BEARD, Katherine K.
BEAT, Janet Eveline
BEATH, Betty
BEATON, Isabella
BEAUMONT, Vivian
BECK, Martha Dillard
BECKON, Lettie Marie
BECLARD D'HARCOURT,
   Marguerite
BEECROFT, Norma Marian
BEEKHUIS, Hanna
BEESON, Elizabeth Ruth
BEGO-SIMUNIC, Andelka
BEHREND, Jeanne
BEKMAN-SHCHERBINA, Elena
   Aleksandrovna Kamentseva
BELL, Carla Huston
BELL, Elizabeth
BELL, Lucille Anderson
BELLAMY, Marian Meredith
BELLEROSE, Sister Cécilia
BELOCH, Dorotea
BENAVENTE, Regina
BENEDICENTI, Vera
BENOIT, Francine Germaine Van
   Gool
BENTLEY, Berenice Benson
BENZON, Julie
BERAN-STARK, Lola Aloisia Maria
BERG, Lily
BERGE, Irenée
BERGERSEN, Marie Christine
BERK, Adele
BERL WEINFIELD, Christine

BERLINER, Selma
BERNARDONE, Anka
BERNARD, Jeanne
BERRY, Margaret Mary Robinson
BERRYMAN, Alice Davis
BERTRAM, Madge
BERTRAND, Ginette
BERZON, Asya Yevseyevna
BEYER, Johanna Magdalena
BEYERMAN-WALRAVEN, Jeanne
BEZDEK, Sister John Joseph
BIALKIEWICZOWNA-ANDRAULT DE
   LANGERON, Irena
BIANCHERA, Silvia
BIANCHINI, Emma
BIBBY, Gillian Margaret
BIELEFELD, Ljuba
BIELICKA, Eugenia
BIENVENU, Lily
BILBRO, Anne Mathilde
BILLINGTON, Elizabeth
BILSLAND, Ethel
BILTCLIFFE, Florence
BINET, Jocelyne
BINGHAM, Judith
BIRCH, Ernestine
BIRCHER-REY, Hedy
BIRCSAK, Thusnelda
BIRKETT, Gwenhilda Mary
BIRNSTEIN, Renate Maria
BISHOP, Dorothy
BIXBY, Allene K.
BJELKE-ANDERSEN, Olga
BLACKWELL, Anna Gee
BLAIR, Kathleen
BLAKE, Dorothy Gaynor
BLANCK, Olga de
BLASIS, Teresa de
BLAUHUTH, Jenny
BLAUSTEIN, Susan Morton
BLIESENER, Ada Elizabeth
   Michelman
BLISS, Marilyn S.
BLOMFIELD-HOLT, Patricia
BLOOD, Esta Damesek
BLOOMFIELD-ZEISLER, Fannie
BOCARD, Sister Cecilia Clair
BODENSTEIN-HOYME, Ruth E.
BODOM, Erica
BOESGAARDOVA-SCHMIDTOVA,
   Lydie
BOFILL, Anna
BOLL, Christine E.
BOLZ, Harriet
BOND, Carrie Jacobs
BOND, Victoria Ellen
BONDS, Margaret
BOONE, Clara Lyle
BOOSEY, Beatrice Joyce
BORBOM, Maria de Melo Furtado
   Caldeira Giraldes
BORDERS, Barbara Ann
BORDEWIJK-ROEPMAN, Johanna
BORKOWICZ, Maria
BORRAS I FORNELL, Teresa
BORROFF, Edith
BOSMANS, Henriette Hilda
BOSTELMANN, Ida
BOTET, Maria Emma
BOTSFORD, Talitha
BOUCHARD, Linda L.
BOUCHER, Lydia
BOULANGER, Lili Juliette Marie Olga
BOULANGER, Nadia Juliette
BOULOGNE, Julia R.C.
BOUQUET, Marie-Thérèse
BOUTRON, Madeleine
BOYD, Anne Elizabeth
BOYKIN, A. Helen
BRADLEY, Ruth
BRADSHAW, Susan

BRAGGINS, Daphne Elizabeth
BRANDELER, Henriette van den
BRANDMAN, Margaret Susan
BRANDON, Phyllis
BRANDT, Dorothea
BRANNING, Grace Bell
BRANSCOMBE, Gena
BRAUER, Johanna Elisabeth
BREILH, Fernande
BREMER, Marrie Petronella
BRENET, Thérèse
BRENNER, Rosamond Drooker
BRES, Dorothy
BREUIL, Hélène
BRICE, Jean Anne
BRIDGEWATER, Violet Irene
BRIGGS, Dorothy Bell
BRIGGS, Nancy Louise
BRIGHT, Ann
BRIGHT, Dora Estella
BRINK-POTHUIS, Annie van den
BRITAIN, Radie
BROCKMAN, Jane E.
BRODIN, Lena Birgitta Elise
BROGUE, Roslyn Clara
BROOK, Gwendolyn Giffen
BROOKS, Alice M.
BROUK, Joanna
BROWN, Elizabeth Bouldin
BROWN, Elizabeth van Ness
BROWN, Norma
BROWN, Rosemary
BROWN, Veronica
BRUCKSHAW, Kathleen
BRUGGMANN, Heidi
BRUNDZAITE, Konstantsiya Kazyo
BRUNER, Cheryl
BRUSH, Ruth Damaris
BRUSSELS, Iris
BRUZDOWICZ, Joanna
BRYANT, Verna Mae
BRYUSSOVA, Nadezhda
   Yakolevna
BUCHANAN, Dorothy Quita
BUCKLEY, Dorothy Pike
BUCKLEY, Helen Dallam
BULTERIJS, Nina
BURGESS, Brio
BURGESS, Marjorie
BURNETT, Helen Roth
BURROWES, Katherine
BURSTON, Maggie
BURTON, Pixie
BUSCEMI MONTALTO, Margherita
BUSH, Grace E.
BUTCHER, Jane Elizabeth
BUTLER, Anne Lois
BUTLER, Patricia Magahay
BYERS, Roxana Weihe
CABRERA, Ana S. de
CABRERA, Silvia Maria Pires
CADZOW, Dorothy Forrest
CALAME, Genevieve
CALBRAITH, Mary Evelene
CALCAGNO, Elsa
CALE, Rosalie Balmer Smith
CALL, Audrey
CALLAWAY, Ann
CAMEU, Helza
CAMINHA, Alda
CAMPMANY, Montserrat
CAMPOS ARAUJO DE, Joaquina
CANAL, Marguerite
CANALES PIZARRO, Marta
CANCINO DE CUEVAS, Sofia
CAPDEVILA I GAYA, Mercé
CAPERTON, Florence Tait
CAPUIS, Matilde
CARLOS, Wendy
CARMEN MARINA
CARMICHAEL, Mary Grant

CARON-LEGRIS, Albertine
CARR-BOYD, Ann Kirsten
CARRENO, Teresa
CARRIQUE, Ana
CARRIVICK, Olive Amelia
CARSON, Ruby B.
CARSWELL, Francis
CARTER PAULENA, Elizabeth
CARTER, Buenta MacDaniel
CARTER, Rosetta
CARVALHO, Dinora de
CARWITHEN, Doreen
CASAGEMAS, Luisa
CASTAGNETTA, Grace Sharp
CATUNDA, Eunice do Monte Lima
CECCONI-BATES, Augusta
CECCONI-BOTELLA, Monic
CERVANTES, Maria
CHACON LASAUCA, Emma
CHALITA, Laila Maria
CHAMBERS, Wendy
CHAMINADE, Cécile Louise
  Stephanie
CHAMPION, Constance MacLean
CHAMPION, Stephanie
CHANCE, Nancy Laird
CHAPIRO, Fania
CHARBONNIER, Janine Andrée
CHARLES, S. Robin
CHARLOTTE, Princess of Saxe-
  Meiningen
CHASE, Mary Wood
CHAVES, Mary Elizabeth
CHEBOTARIAN, Gayane
  Movsesovna
CHEN, Nira
CHEVALIER, Charlotte Bergersen
CHEVALLIER SUPERVIELLE, Marie
  Louise
CHICHERINA, Sofia Nikolayevna
CHITCHIAN, Geguni Oganesovna
CHITTENDEN, Kate Sara
CHKHEIDZE, Dali Davidovna
CHRETIEN-GENARO, Hedwige
CHRISTENSEN, Anna Mae Parker
CIMAGLIA DE ESPINOSA, Lia
CINTOLESI, Liliana
CIOBANU, Maia
CITATI-BRACCI, Clelia
CLAMAN, Dolores Olga
CLARK, Jane Leland
CLARK, June
CLARKE, Mary Gail
CLARKE, Rebecca
CLARKE, Rosemary
CLARKE, Urana
CLAUDE, Marie
CLEMENT, Mary
CLEMENT, Sheree
CLOSTRE, Adrienne
COATES, Gloria Kannenberg
COBB, Hazel
COCHRANE, Peggy
COCKING, Frances M. Hefford
COCQ, Rosina Susanna de
COELHO, Ernestine Leite
COEN, Augusta
COFFMAN, Lillian Craig
COHEN, Dulcie M.
COHEN, Harriet
COHEN, Marcia
COLACO OSORIO-SWAAB, Reine
COLE, Ulric
COLEMAN, Ellen
COLERIDGE-TAYLOR, Avril
  Gwendolen
COLGAN, Alma Cecilia
COLIN, Jeanne
COLLARD, Marilyn
COLLEY, Betty
COLLVER, Harriet Russell

COLOMER BLAS, Maria
COLTRANE, Alice McLeod
COME, Tilde
CONRAD, Laurie M.
CONSTANTINESCU, Domnica
CONTINI ANSELMI, Lucia
COOKE, Edith
COOLIDGE, Elizabeth Sprague
COOLIDGE, Peggy Stuart
COONEY, Cheryl Lee
COPLAND, Berniece Rose
COPLEY, Maria Kriel
COQUET, Odile Marie-Lucie
CORDULA, Sister M.
CORNEA-IONESCU, Alma
CORNING, Karen Andrée
CORY, Eleanor
COSTA, Maria Helena da
COTRON, Fanou
COULOMBE SAINT-MARCOUX,
  Micheline
COULTHARD, Jean
COUPER, Mildred
COWL, Doreen
COWLES, Cecil Marion
COWLES, Darleen
COX, Alison Mary
CRAIB, Doris
CRANE, Helen
CRAWFORD SEEGER, Ruth
CRAWFORD, Dawn Constance
CRAWFORD, Dorothy Lamb
CRAWFORD, Louise
CREWS, Lucille
CRISP, Barbara
CUNIBERTI, Janet Teresa
CURUBETO GODOY, Maria Isabel
CURZON, Clara-Jean
DAHL, Vivian
DAIGLE, Sister Anne Cécile
DAIKEN, Melanie
DALBERG, Nancy
DALBERT, Anny
DALE, Kathleen
DALE, Phyllis
DANA, Lynn Boardman
DANEAU, Suzanne
DANFORTH, Frances A.
DANIELA, Carmen
DANIELS, Mabel Wheeler
DARE, Margaret Marie
DAVENPORT GOERTZ, Gladys
DAVENPORT, Anne Bridges
DAVIDSON, Tina
DAVIS, Eleanor Maud
DAVIS, Eva May
DAVIS, Genevieve
DAVIS, Katherine Kennicott
DAVIS, Sharon
DAVISON, Martha Taylor
DAVITASHVILI, Meri Shalvovna
DAVY, Ruby Claudia Emily
DE BIASE BIDART, Lycia
DE CEVEE, Alice
DE FREITAS, Elvira Manuela
  Fernandez
DE LARA, Adelina
DE LYLE, Carlyon
DE MOL, Josephine
DE MONTEL, Adalgisa
DE PATE, Elisabetta M.S.
DE VILLIERS, Justina Wilhelmina
  Nancy
DEACON, Mary Connor
DEBRASSINE-PRIJAT, Laure
DECARIE, Reine
DEDERICH, Hilda
DEDIEU-PETERS, Madeleine
DEL CARRETTO, Cristina
DELMOULY, Marie Mathilde
DEMAREST, Anne Shannon

DEMARQUEZ, Suzanne
DEMBO, Royce
DEPPEN, Jessie L.
DESPORTES, Yvonne Berthe Melitta
DEYO, Ruth Lynda
DEYTON, Camilla Hill
DIAKVNISHVILI, Mzisavar
  Zakharevna
DIAMOND, Arline
DIANDA, Hilda
DICHLER-SEDLACEK, Erika
DICK, Ethel A.
DIEFENTHALER, Margaret Kissinger
DIEMER, Emma Lou
DILLER, Angela
DILLER, Saralu C.
DILLON, Fannie Charles
DIMENTMAN, Esfir Moiseyevna
DIMITRIU, Florica
DINESCU, Violeta
DINIZ, Thereza da Fonseca Borges
DITMARS, Elizabeth
DITTENHAVER, Sarah Louise
DLUGOSZEWSKI, Lucia
DOLAN, Hazel
DOLLEY, Betty Grace
DONAHUE, Bertha Terry
DONCEANU, Felicia
DORABIALSKA, Julia Helena
DOROW, Dorothy
DOUGAN, Vera Warnder
DRAKE, Elizabeth Bell
DRDOVA, Marie
DREGE-SCHIELOWA, Lucja
DREYFUS, Francis Kay
DRING, Madeleine
DROBYAZGINA, Valentina Ivanovna
DU PAGE, Florence Elizabeth
DUCOUREAU, Mme. M.
DUDLEY, Marjorie Eastwood
DUFFENHORST, Irma Habeck
DUGAL, Madeleine
DUNGAN, Olive
DUNLOP, Isobel
DURAND, Nella Wells
DUSHKIN, Dorothy Smith
DUTTON, Theodora
DVORKIN, Judith
DYCHKO, Lesya Vasilevna
DZHAFAROVA, Afag Mamed kyzy
DZIELSKA, Jadwiga
DZIEWULSKA, Maria Amelia
EAGLES, Moneta M.
EASTES, Helen Marie
ECKHARDT-GRAMATTE, Sophie-
  Carmen
EDICK, Ethel Vera Ingraham
EGGAR, Katharine
EGGLESTON, Anne E.
EHRMANN, Rosette
EICHHORN, Hermene Warlick
EIRIKSDOTTIR, Karolina
EISENSTEIN DE VEGA, Silvia
EISENSTEIN, Stella Price
EKSANISHVILI, Eleonara Grigorevna
ELIAS, Graciela Morales de
ELKAN, Ida
ELKOSHI, Rivka
ELLEN, Mary
ELLICOTT, Rosalind Frances
ELLIOTT, Janice Overmiller
ELLIOTT, Marjorie Reeve
ELMORE, Cenieth Catherine
ELVYN, Myrtle
ELWYN-EDWARDS, Dilys
EMERY, Dorothy Radde
EMIDIO TAVORA, Florizinha
EMINGEROVA, Katerina
ENDE, Amelia von
ENDRES, Olive Philomene
ERDING, Susanne

ERDMANNSDOERFER, Pauline
ERHART, Dorothy
ERICKSON, Elaine M.
ERNST, Siegrid
ESCOBAR, Maria Luisa
ESCOT, Pozzi
ESTRELLA, Blanca
ETHRIDGE, Jean
EUBANKS, Rachel Amelia
EUTENEUER-ROHRER, Ursula Henrietta
EVANS, Patricia Margaret
EVEN-OR, Mary
EVERETT-SALICCO, Betty Lou
EZELL, Helen Ingle
FAHRBACH, Henrietta
FAHRER, Alison Clark
FAIRLIE, Margaret C.
FAISST, Clara Mathilde
FALCINELLI, Rolande
FALLADOVA-SKVOROVA, Anezka
FALTIS, Evelyn
FARGA PELLICER, Onia
FAULKNER, Elizabeth
FAUTCH, Sister Magdalen
FEIGIN, Sarah
FEININGER, Leonore Helene
FEIST-STEINHAUSEN, Alwine
FELDMAN, Joann Esther
FELIX, Margery Edith
FENNER, Beatrice
FERNANDES, Maria Helena Rosas
FERRAND-TEULET, Denise
FERRARI, Gabriella
FERRER OTERO, Monsita Monserrate
FILIPPONI, Dina
FINE, Vivian
FINK, Emma C.
FINZI, Graciane
FIRNKEES, Gertrud
FIRSOVA, Elena
FISCHER, Edith Steinkraus
FISCHER, Emma Gabriele Marie von, Baroness
FISHER, Charlotte Eleanor
FISHER, Gladys Washburn
FISHER, Katherine Danforth
FITZGERALD, Sister Florence Therese
FIUZA, Virginia Salgado
FLACH, Elsa
FLEITES, Virginia
FLEMMING, Martha
FLICK-FLOOD, Dora
FLORING, Grace Kenny
FLOWER, Amelia Matilda
FOLVILLE, Eugenie-Emilie Juliette
FONTYN, Jacqueline
FOOT, Phyllis Margaret
FORSTER, Dorothy
FOSTER, Cecily
FOSTER, Fay
FOWLER, Jennifer Joan
FRANCHERE-DESROSIERS, Rose de Lima
FRANCO, Clare
FRANK, Jean Forward
FRASER, Shena Eleanor
FRASER-MILLER, Gloria Jill
FRASIER, Jane
FREED, Dorothy Whitson
FREER, Eleanor Warner Everest
FREIXAS Y CRUELLS, Narcisa
FRERICHS, Doris Coulston
FRESON, Armande
FRICKER, Anne
FRITTER, Genevieve Davisson
FRITZ, Sherilyn Gail
FROMM-MICHAELS, Ilse
FRONMUELLER, Frieda

FULLER, Jeanne Weaver
FULLER-HALL, Sarah Margaret
FURGERI, Bianca Maria
FURZE, Jessie
GABRYS, Ewa Lucja Maria
GABUS, Monique
GAIGEROVA, Varvara Andrianovna
GAINSBORG, Lolita Cabrera
GALAJIKIAN, Florence Grandland
GALBRAITH, Nancy Riddle
GAMILLA, Alice Doria
GANNON, Helen Carroll
GARCIA ASCOT, Rosa
GARCIA MUNOZ, Carmen
GARCIA ROBSON, Magdalena
GARDINER, Mary Elizabeth
GARDNER, Kay
GARDNER, Mildred Alvine
GARELLI DELLA MOREA, Vincenza
GARR, Wieslawa
GARSCIA-GRESSEL, Janina
GARTENLAUB, Odette
GARUTA, Lucia Yanovna
GARZTECKA-JARZEBSKA, Irena
GASPARINI, Jola
GAUTHIEZ, Cécile
GAYNOR, Jessie Love
GAZAROSSIAN, Koharik
GEDDES-HARVEY, Roberta
GEIGER-KULLMANN, Rosy Auguste
GENTEMANN, Sister Mary Elaine
GENTIL, Alice
GEORGE, Lila-Gene
GERCHIK, Vera Petrovna
GERRISH-JONES, Abbie
GERSTMAN, Blanche Wilhelminia
GESELSCHAP, Maria
GEST, Elizabeth
GEYMULLER, Marguerite Camille-Louise de
GHANDAR, Ann
GHIGLIERI, Sylvia
GHILARDI, Syra
GIACCHINO CUSENZA, Maria
GIDEON, Miriam
GIFFORD, Helen Margaret
GILBERT, Marie
GILBERT, Pia
GILLES, Yvette Marie
GILLICK, Emelyn Mildred Samuels
GINDLER, Kathe-Lotte
GIPPS, Ruth
GITECK, Janice
GIURANNA, Elena Barbara
GLANVILLE-HICKS, Peggy
GLASER, Victoria Merrylees
GLAZIER, Beverly
GLEN, Irma
GLICKMAN, Sylvia
GNESINA, Yelena Fabianovna
GNUS, Ryta
GODDARD, Arabella
GOEBELS, Gisela
GOETSCHIUS, Marjorie
GOLDSTON, Margaret Nell Stumpf
GOLIA, Maria
GOLOVINA, Olga Akimovna
GOLSON-BATEMAN, Florence
GOMEZ CARRILO, Maria Ines
GONTARENKO, Galina Nikolayevna
GONZAGA, Chiquinha
GOODE, Blanche
GOODSMITH, Ruth B.
GOODWIN, Amina Beatrice
GOOLKASIAN-RAHBEE, Dianne Zabelle
GOTKOVSKY, Ida-Rose Esther
GOULD, Elizabeth Davies
GOULD, Janetta
GRAD-BUCH, Hulda
GRAHAM, Janet Christine

GRAINGER, Ella Viola Strom-Brandelius
GRAUBNER, Hannelore
GRAY, Judith
GRAY, Victoria Winifred
GREENE, Genevieve
GREENE, Margo Lynn
GREGER, Luisa
GRERICHS, Doris
GREVENKOP CASTENKIOLD, Olga
GREVER, Maria
GRIEBEL WANDALL, Tekla
GRIEBLING, Karen Jean
GRIECO, Ida
GRIGSBY, Beverly
GRILLI GALEFFI, Elvira
GRIMAUD, Yvette
GRIMES, Doreen
GROSSMAN, Deena
GRZADZIELOWNA, Eleonora
GUBAIDULINA, Sofia Asgatovna
GUBITOSI, Emilia
GUDAUSKAS, Giedra
GUELL, Maria Luisa
GULESIAN, Grace Warner
GUMMER, Phyllis Mary
GUNDERSON, Helen Louise
GURAIEB KURI, Rosa
GUSEINZADE, Adilia Gadzhi Aga
GVAZAVA, Tamara Davidovna
GWILY-BROIDO, Rivka
GYANDZHETSIAN, Destrik Bogdanovna
GYRING, Elizabeth
HABAN, Sister Teresine M.
HADDEN, Frances Roots
HAENDEL, Ida
HAGAN, Helen Eugenia
HAGER-ZIMMERMANN, Hilde
HAHN, Sandra Lea
HAIMSOHN, Naomi Carrol
HALACSY, Irma von
HALPERN, Stella
HAMER, Janice
HAMILTON, Gertrude Bean
HAMMANN, Rebecca
HANKS, Sybil Ann
HANNIKAINEN, Ann-Elise
HANSEN, Hanna Marie
HANSEN, Joan
HARA, Kazuko (1)
HARDIMAN, Ellena G.
HARDY, Helen Irene
HARLOW, Barbara
HARMS, Signe
HARPER, Marjorie
HARRADEN, R. Ethel
HARRHY, Edith
HARRIS, Dorothy
HARRIS, Ethel Ramos
HARRIS, Letitia Radcliffe
HARRIS, Margaret R.
HARRIS, Ruth Berman
HARRISON, Annie Fortescue
HARRISON, Pamela
HARRISON, Susan Frances
HARROD, Beth Miller
HART, Alice Maud
HART, Elizabeth Jane Smith
HARTER, Louise C.
HARTZER-STIBBE, Marie
HARVEY, Eva Noel
HATCH, Edith
HATCH, Mabel Lee
HAWLEY, Carolyn Jean
HAYS, Doris Ernestine
HAYWARD, Mae Shepard
HAZEN, Sara
HEALE, Helene
HEATON, Eloise Klotz
HEBER, Judith

HECKSCHER, Céleste de Longpre
HEDOUX, Yvonne
HEDSTROEM, Ase
HEIBERG, Ella
HEIMERL, Elizabeth
HEINE, Eleanor
HEINRICH, Adel Verna
HEINRICHS, Agnes
HELLER-REICHENBACH, Barbara
HELSTED, Bodil
HELYER, Marjorie
HEMON, Sedje
HENDERSON, Moya
HENDERSON, Ruth Watson
HERMANSEN, Gudrun
HERNANDEZ-GONZALO, Gisela
HESSE, Marjorie Anne
HEYMAN, Katherine Ruth Willoughby
HEYNSSEN, Adda
HICKS, Marjorie Kisby
HIER, Ethel Glen
HIGGINS, Esther S.
HILDERLEY, Jeriann G.
HILDRETH, Daisy Wood
HILL, May
HILL, Mildred J.
HILLIER-JASPAR, Jeanne
HIND O'MALLEY, Pamela
HINKLE, Daisy Estelle
HIRSCH, Barbara
HO, Wai On
HOENDERDOS, Margriet
HOFF, Vivian Beaumont
HOFFMAN, Phyllis Sampson
HOFFRICHTER, Bertha Chaitkin
HOKANSON, Margrethe
HOLCOMB, Louanah Riggs
HOLLAND, Dulcie Sybil
HOLLAND, Ruby
HOLLWAY, Elizabeth L.
HOLMBERG, Betty
HOLMSEN, Borghild
HOLST, Agnes Moller
HOLST, Imogen Clare
HOLTHUSEN, Anita Saunders
HONEGGER-VAURABOURG, Andrée
HOOD, Helen
HOOVER, Katherine
HOPEKIRK, Helen
HORAK, Hilda
HORROCKS, Amy Elsie
HORSLEY, Imogene
HORTON, Marguerite Wagniere
HOUSMAN, Rosalie
HOVDA, Eleanor
HOWARD, Helen Willard
HOWE, Mary Alberta Bruce
HOWELL, Dorothy
HOY, Bonnee L.
HOYLE, Aline Isabelle
HRUBY, Dolores Marie
HSU, Wen-Ying
HUBICKI, Margaret Olive
HUBLER, Evelyne
HUEBNER, Ilse
HUEGEL, Margrit
HUGHES, Sister Martina
HUGH-JONES, Elaine
HULL, Anne
HULL, Kathryn B.
HULST, Margaret Gardiner
HURLEY, Susan
HYDE, Miriam Beatrice
HYSON, Winifred Prince
HYTREK, Sister Theophane
IBANEZ, Carmen
IBRAGIMOVA, Sevda Mirza kyzy
IGENBERGA, Elga Avgustovna
INWOOD, Mary Ruth Brink Berger
IORDAN, Irina Nikolayevna
IPPOLITO, Carmela

IRGENS-BERGH, Gisela, von
ISAKOVA, Aida Petrovna
ISMAGILOVA, Leila Zagirovna
ISZKOWSKA, Zofia
IVANOVA, Lidia
IVEY, Jean Eichelberger
IWAUCHI, Saori
JABOR, Najla
JACKSON, Barbara May
JACOB, Elizabeth Marie
JACOB-LOEWENSOHN, Alice
JAEGER, Hertha
JAELL-TRAUTMANN, Marie
JAMBOR, Agi
JAMES, Dorothy E.
JAMES, Vera
JANKOVIC, Miroslava
JANKOWSKI, Loretta Patricia
JANOTHA, Natalia
JAQUETTI ISANT, Palmira
JARRATT, Lita
JASTRZEBSKA, Anna
JENKINS, Susan Elaine
JENNINGS, Marie Pryor
JENNY, Sister Leonore
JEPPSSON, Kerstin Maria
JEREA, Hilda
JESI, Ada
JEWELL, Lucina
JIRACKOVA, Marta
JIRKOVA, Olga
JOCHSBERGER, Tzipora H.
JOERGENSEN, Christine
JOEST, Emma
JOHNSON, Mary Ernestine Clark
JOHNSTON, Alison Aileen Annie
JOHNSTON-REID, Sarah Ruth
JOLAS, Betsy
JOLLEY, Florence Werner
JOLLY, Margaret Anne
JOLY, Suzanne
JONES, Dovie Osborn
JUDD, Margaret Evelyn
KABE, Mariko
KADIMA, Hagar Yonith
KAESER-BECK, Aida
KAHMANN, Chesley
KAHN, Esther
KALOGRIDOU, Maria
KALTENECKER, Gertraud
KAMIEN, Anna
KANACH, Sharon E.
KAPP, Corinne
KAPRALOVA, Vitezslava
KARASTOYANOVA, Elena
KARNITSKAYA, Nina Andreyevna
KARVENO, Wally
KASHPEROVA, Leokadia Alexandrovna
KASILAG, Lucrecia R.
KATS-CHERNIN, Elena
KATTS, Letty
KATZMAN, Klara Abramovna
KAUFMAN, Barbara
KAVASCH, Deborah Helene
KAYDEN, Mildred
KAZANDJIAN, Sirvart
KAZHAEVA, Tatiana Ibragimovna
KEEFER, Euphrosyne
KEIG, Betty
KELLER, Ginette
KELLER, Lue Alice
KELLEY, Florence Bettray
KENNEDY-FRASER, Marjory
KENSWIL, Atma
KER, Ann S.
KERN, Frida
KERR, Bessie Maude
KESSICK, Marlaena
KESSLER, Minuetta Schumiatcher
KETTERING, Eunice Lea
KHOSS VON STERNEGG, Gisela

KICKINGER, Paula
KICKTON, Erika
KILBY, Muriel Laura
KIM, Kwang-Hee
KING, Betty Jackson
KING, Patricia
KING, Pearl
KING, Rebecca Clift
KINSCELLA, Hazel Gertrude
KIRBY, Suzanne
KIRCHNER, Elisabeth
KIRKBY-MASON, Barbara
KIRKWOOD, Antoinette
KITAZUME, Yayoi
KJAER, Kirsten
KLEBE, Willemijntje
KLECHNIOWSKA, Anna Maria
KLEES, Gabriele
KLEPPER, Anna Benzia
KLINKOVA, Zhivka
KLOTZMAN, Dorothy Ann Hill
KNIGHT, Judyth
KNOBLOCHOVA, Antonie
KNOUSS, Isabelle G.
KOBLENZ, Babette
KOCHER-KLEIN, Hilda
KODALY, Emma
KODOLITSCH, Michaela
KOEHLER, Estella
KOELLING, Eloise
KOHAN, Celina
KOLB, Barbara
KOLLER-HOPP, Margarete
KOLODUB, Zhanna Efimovna
KOPPEL-HOLBE, Maria
KOPTAGEL, Yuksel
KORN, Clara Anna
KORNILOVA, Tatiana Dmitrevna
KOSTAKOVA-HERODKOVA, Marie
KOZAKIEVICH, Anna Abramovna
KOZANKOVA, Anna
KRALIKOVA, Johana
KRASNOGLIADOVA, Vera
    Vladimirovna
KRAUSZ, Susan
KROGMANN, Carrie William
KROSNICK, Mary Louw Wesley
KRUGER, Lilly Canfield
KRULL, Diana
KRUSE, Lotte
KRZYZANOWSKA, Halina
KUBO, Mayako
KUBOTA, Minako
KUCEROVA-HERSTOVA, Marie
KUESTER, Edith Haines
KUKUCK, Felicitas
KULIEVA, Farida Tairovna
KUNITZ, Sharon Lohse
KUNTZE, Olga
KURIMOTO, Yoko
KUROKAWA, Manae
KUSS, Margarita Ivanovna
KUZMENKO, Larysa
LA BARBARA, Joan
LA VALLE, Deanna
LABEY, Charlotte Sohy
LACHARTRE, Nicole Marie
LACHOWSKA, Stefania
LACKMAN, Susan C. Cohn
LACMANOVA, Anna
LAFLEUR, Lucienne
LAGO
LAJEUNESSE, Emma, Dame
LALAUNI, Lila
LAMBERT, Cecily
LAMEGO, Carlinda J.
LANDOWSKA, Wanda
LANG, Margaret Ruthven
LANG-BECK, Ivana
LANGE, Anny von
LANKMAR, Helen

LAPEIRETTA, Ninon de Brouwer
LAPIN, Lily
LARSEN, Elizabeth Brown
LARSON, Anna Barbara
LARUELLE, Jeanne-Marie
LAST, Joan Mary
LATHAM, Joan Seyler
LATIOLAIS, Desirée Jayne
LATZ, Inge
LAUBER, Anne Marianne
LAUER, Elizabeth
LAUMYANSKENE, Elena Iono
LAVIN, Marie Duchesne
LAVOIPIERRE, Thérèse
LAWRENCE, Emily M.
LAYMAN, Pamela
LAZAR, Ella
LE BEAU, Louisa Adolpha
LE BORDAYS, Christiane
LE SIEGE, Annette
LEAF, Ann
LEAHY, Mary Weldon
LEAVITT, Helen Sewall
LEBARON, Anne
LEBENBOM, Elaine F.
LEBIZAY, Marguerite
LEE, Hope Anne Keng-Wei
LEE, Hwaeja Yoo
LEE, Young Ja
LEFANU, Nicola Frances
LEFEBVRE, Françoise
LEFEVRE, Armande
LEGINSKA, Ethel
LEHMAN, Evangeline Marie
LEHMANN, Liza
LEHOTSKA-KRIZKOVA, Ludmila
LEIBOW, Ruth Irene
LEITE, Clarisse
LEIVISKA, Helvi Lemmiki
LEJEUNE-BONNIER, Eliane
LELEU, Jeanne
LEMAIRE-SINDORFF, Jeanne
LEMCKE, Anna
LEMON, Laura G.
LEON, Tania Justina
LEONARD, Mamie Grace
LEONE, Mae G.
LEPEUT-LEVINE, Jeannine
LEPKE, Charma Davies
LEPLAE, Claire
LESICHKOVA, Lili
LEVIN, Rami Yona
LEVINA, Zara Alexandrovna
LEVITOVA, Ludmila Vladimirovna
LEVITSKAYA, Viktoria Sergeyevna
LEWING, Adele
LIADOVA, Ludmila Alekseyevna
LICHTENSTEIN, Olga Grigorievna
LIDDELL, Claire
LIDGI-HERMAN, Sofia
LIEBLING, Estelle
LIEBMANN, Nanna Magdalene
LIMA CRUZ, Maria Antonietta de
LINDEMAN, Anna Severine
LINDEMAN, Hjelle Signe
LINZ VON KRIEGNER, Marta
LIPSCOMB, Helen
LISSONI, Giulia
LITER, Monia
LITSITE, Paula Yanovna
LLOYD, Caroline Parkhurst
LLUNELL SANAHUJA, Pepita
LOCKSHIN, Florence Levin
LOH, Kathy Jean
LOMON, Ruth
LOOTS, Joyce Mary Ann
LOPEZ ROVIROSA, Maria Isabel
LOPEZ Y PENA, Maria del Carmen
LOPUSKA-WYLEZYNSKA, Helena
LORENZ, Ellen Jane
LORIOD, Yvonne

LOUDOVA, Ivana
LOUIE, Alexina Diane
LOVAN, Lydia
LOWENSTEIN, Gunilla Marike
LU, Yen
LUCKE, Katharine E.
LUDVIG-PECAR, Nada
LUFF, Enid
LUMBY, Betty Louise
LUNA DE ESPAILLAT, Margarita
LUND, Gudrun
LUND, Hanna
LUND, Inger Bang
LUND, Signe
LUO, Jing-Jing
LUTHER, Mary
LUTYENS, Elisabeth
LUTYENS, Sally
LVOVA, Julia Fedorovna
MAAS, Marguerite Wilson
MACIEL, Argentina
MACKIE, Shirley M.
MACONCHY, Elizabeth
MacFARREN, Emma Marie
MacGREGOR, Helen
MacKENNA, Carmela
MacKOWN, Marjorie T.
MacPHAIL, Frances
McALISTER, Mabel
McALLISTER, Rita
McCLEARY, Fiona
McCOLLIN, Frances
McGILL, Gwendolen Mary Finlayson
McGOWAN SCOTT, Beatrice
McINTOSH, Diana
McKAY, Frances Thompson
McKENZIE, Sandra
McKINNEY, Mathilde
McLAUGHLIN, Erna
McLAUGHLIN, Marian
McLEAN, Priscilla Anne Taylor
McLEMORE, Monita Prine
McLEOD, Evelyn Lundgren
McLEOD, Jennifer Helen
McLIN, Lena
McNEIL, Janet L. Pfischner
McPHERSON, Frances Marie
McSWAIN, Augusta Geraldine
McTEE, Cindy Karen
MADISON, Clara Duggan
MAEDLER, Ruth
MAGEAU, Mary Jane
MAGENTA, Maria
MAGNEY, Ruth Taylor
MAIRE, Jacqueline
MAIXANDEAU, Marie-Vera
MAKAROVA, Nina Vladimirovna
MALDYBAYEVA, Zhyldyz Abdylasovna
MALMLOEF-FORSSLING, Carin
MAMLOK, Ursula
MANA-ZUCCA
MANNING, Kathleen Lockhart
MANUKIAN, Irina Eduardovna
MANZIARLY, Marcelle de
MARAIS, Abelina Jacoba
MARBE, Myriam
MARCHI, Giuliana
MARCUS, Ada Belle Gross
MARCUS, Bunita
MARESCA, Chiara
MAREZ-OYENS, Tera de
MARGLES, Pamela
MARI, Pierrette
MARIANI-CAMPOLIETI, Virginia
MARIC, Ljubica
MARINESCU-SCHAPIRA, Ilana
MARKIEWICZOWNA, Wladyslawa
MARKOV, Katherine Lee
MARQUES, Maria Adelaide
MARSCHAL-LOEPKE, Grace
MARSH, Gwendolyn

MARSHALL, Kye
MARTENOT-LAZARD, Ginette-
 Genevieve
MARTIN, Delores J.
MARTIN, Judith Reher
MARTINEZ, Odaline de la
MARY BERNICE, Sister
MARY ELAINE, Sister
MASON, Gladys Amy
MASON, Margaret C.
MASON, Marilyn May
MASONER, Elizabeth L.
MASTERS, Juan
MATEU, Maria Cateura
MATEVOSIAN, Araks Surenovna
MATHEWS, Blanche Dingley Moore
MATJAN, Vida
MATTHEISS-BOEGNER, Helga
MATTHEWS, Dorothy White
MATUSZCZAK, Bernadetta
MAUR, Sophie
MAURICE, Paule
MAXWELL, Jacqueline Perkinson
MAY, Florence
MAYER, Lise Maria
MAZOUROVA, Jarmila
MEACHEM, Margaret McKeen
 Ramsey
MEEK, Ethel Alice
MEISTER, Marianne
MEKEEL, Joyce
MEL-BONIS
MELL, Gertrud Maria
MELOY, Elizabeth
MENDOSA, Dot
MENEELY-KYDER, Sarah Suderley
MERO, Jolanda
MERRICK, Marie E.
MERRIMAN, Margarita Leonor
MERTENS, Dolores
MESRITZ-VAN VELTHUYSEN, Annie
MESTDAGH, Helene
METALLIDI, Zhanneta Lazarevna
MIAGI, Ester Kustovna
MICHELI AGOSTINI, Fausta
MIGRANYAN, Emma
MIKUSCH, Margarethe von
MILA, Leonora
MILKINA, Nina
MILKULAK, Marcia Lee
MILLER, Elma
MILLER, Lillian Anne
MILLS, Joan Geilfuss
MIMET, Anne Marie
MINEO, Antoinette
MIRET, Emilia
MIRON, Tsipora
MIRSHAKAR, Zarrina Mirsaidovna
MITCHELL, Izah Pike
MIYAKE, Haruna
MIZUNO, Shuko
MKRTYCHIEVA, Virginia Nikitichna
MOBERG, Ida Georgina
MOE, Benna
MOELLER, Agnes
MOESTUE, Marie
MOHNS, Grace Updegraff Bergen
MONK, Meredith
MONTGOMERY, Merle
MONTIJN, Aleida
MOON, Chloe Elizabeth
MOORE, Dorothy Rudd
MOORE, Luella Lockwood
MOORE, Mary Carr
MOORE, Undine Smith
MOORE, Wilda Maurine Ricks
MOOREHEAD, Consuela Lee
MORETTO, Nelly
MORHANGE-MOTCHANE, Marthe
MORIN-LABRECQUE, Albertine
MORISON, Christina W.

MORLEY, Nina Dianne
MORRISON, Julia Maria
MORTON, Agnes Louise
MOSHER, Frances Elizabeth
MOSUSOVA, Nadezda
MOSZUMANSKA-NAZAR, Krystyna
MOYSEOWICZ, Gabriela
MRACEK, Ann Michelle
MUKHAMEDZHANOVA, Mariam
MULDER, Johanna Harmina Gerdina
MUNDINGER, Adele Franziska
MUNGER, Millicent Christner
MUNGER, Shirley
MUNKTELL, Helena Mathilda
MUNTHE-MORGENSTIERNE, Anna
MURAO, Sachie
MURRI, Alceste
MUSGRAVE, Thea
MUSTILLO, Lina
MYGATT, Louise
MYSZINSKA-WOJCIECHOWSKA,
   Leokadia
NAESER-OTTO, Martha
NAKAMURA, Sawako
NAKASHIMA, Jeanne Marie
NASH, Grace Helen
NASH, Phyllis V.
NATSUDA, Shoko
NAZAROVA, Tatiana Borisovna
NAZIROVA, Elmira Mirza Rza kyzy
NEAS, Margaret
NEEDHAM, Alicia Adelaide
NEILY, Anne MacAdams
NEMTEANU-ROTARU, Doina
NENCIC, Ivanka
NEPGEN, Rosa Sophia Cornelia
NESTE, Rosane van
NEWLIN, Dika
NEWMAN, Adelaide
NIAY, Apolline
NIEBERGALL, Julia Lee
NIECKS, Christina
NIEWIADOMSKA, Barbara
NIKOLAYEVA, Tatiana Petrovna
NIKOLSKAYA, Lyubov Borisovna
NISS, Sofia Natanovna
NOBLITT, Katheryn Marie McCall
NOHE, Beverly
NORDENFELT, Dagmar
NORDENSON, Ruth
NORDENSTROM, Gladys Mercedes
NORDRAAK-FEYLING, Gudrun
NORLING, Signe
NORMAN, Ruth
NORRE, Dorcas
NOVA SONDAG, Jacqueline
NOVI, Anna Beate
NOVOSELOVA, Ludmila Alexeyevna
NUNLIST, Juli
OBENCHAIN, Virginia
O'BRIEN, Drena
ODAGESCU, Irina
ODDONE SULLI-RAO, Elisabetta
OENNERBERG-MALLING, Berta
OERBECK, Anne-Marie
OFFICER, Bronwyn Lee
OGILVIE, Signe
OH, Sook Ja
OHE, Adele aus der
O'HEARN, Arletta
OHLSON, Marion
OKEY, Maggie
OLDENBURG, Elizabeth
O'LEARY, Jane Strong
OLIVEIRA, Babi de
OLIVEIRA, Jocy de
OLIVEIRA, Sophie Marcondes de
   Mello
OLIVER, Madra Emogene
OLIVEROS, Pauline
OLIVIER, Blanche

OLSON, Lynn Freeman
OLSEN, Sophie
OMER, Helene
OOSTERZEE, Cornelia van
ORAM, Daphne Blake
ORENSTEIN, Joyce Ellin
OSAWA, Kazuko
OSETROVA-YAKOVLIEVA, Nina
   Alexandrovna
OSGOOD, Marion
O'SHEA, Mary Ellen
OSIANDER, Irene
OSTROFF, Esther
OTIS, Edna Cogswell
OWEN, Blythe
OWENS, Susan Elizabeth
PACK, Beulah Frances
PAGOTO, Helen
PAIN, Eva
PAKHMUTOVA, Alexandra
   Nikolayevna
PALMER, Florence Margaret
   Spencer
PALMER, Lynne Wainwright
PANETTI, Joan
PANZERA, Magdeleine
PARENTE, Sister Elizabeth
PARKER, Alice
PARKER, Muriel
PARR, Patricia
PARR-GERE, Florence
PATERSON, Wilma
PATTERSON, Andra
PAULL, Barberi
PEARL-MANN, Dora Deborah
PEJACEVIC, Dora, Countess
PELEGRI, Maria Teresa
PENNER, Jean Priscilla
PEREIRA DA SILVA, Adelaide
PEREIRA, Diana Maria
PERETZ-LEVY, Liora
PERKIN, Helen
PERONI, Wally
PERRY, Julia Amanda
PERRY, Zenobia Powell
PERSCHMANN, Elfriede
PETERSON, Melody
PETRA-BASACOPOL, Carmen
PETROVA, Mara
PETROVA-KRUPKOVA, Elena
PEY CASADO, Diana
PEYROT, Fernande
PFERDEMENGES, Maria Pauline
   Augusta
PHILIBA, Nicole
PHILIPPART, Renée
PHILLIPS, Bryony
PHILLIPS, Karen Ann
PHILLIPS, Linda
PHILLIPS, Lois Elisabeth
PHIPPEN, Laud German
PICKHARDT, Ione
PIECHOWSKA, Alina
PIERCE, Alexandra
PIERROT, Noëlie Marie Antoinette
PIETSCH, Edna Frieda
PIKE, Eleanor B. Franklin
PIRES DE CAMPOS, Lina
PIRES DOS REIS, Hilda
PITCHER, Gladys
PITOT, Genevieve
PITTMAN, Evelyn LaRue
PIZER, Elizabeth Faw Hayden
PLANICK, Annette Meyers
PLE-CAUSSADE, Simone
PLONSEY, Jennifer
POLIGNAC, Armande de, Countess
   of Chabannes
POLIN, Claire
POLLOCK, Muriel
PONCE, Ethel

PONSA, Maria Luisa
POOL, Arlette
POOLE, Anna Ware
POPATENKO, Tamara Alexandrovna
POPOVICI, Elise
POSTON, Elizabeth
POWELL, Maud
POWERS, Ada Weigel
PRADELL, Leila
PRAVOSSUDOVITCH, Natalja
   Michajlovna
PRAY, Ada Jordan
PREDIC-SAPER, Branislava
PREOBRAJENSKA, Vera Nicolaevna
PRESTON, Matilee Loeb-Evans
PRICE, Beryl
PRICE, Deon Nielsen
PRICE, Florence Beatrice
PRIESING, Dorothy Jean
PRIETO, Maria Teresa
PRIOLLI, Maria Luisa de Matos
PRITI-PAINTAL
PROCACCINI, Teresa
PROCTOR, Alice McElroy
PSTROKONSKA-NAVRATIL,
   Grazyna Hanna
PTASZYNSKA, Marta
PUCHE, Sofia
PYKE, Helen
QUANTIN-SAULNIER, Denise
QUEEN, Virginia
QUIEL, Hildegard
QUINLAN, Agnes Clune
QUINTANILLA, Alba
RABER DE REINDERS, Esther
RABINOF, Sylvia
RACOVITZA-FLONDOR, Florica
RADERMACHER, Erika
RAHMN, Elza Loethner
RAIGORODSKY, Leda Natalia
   Heimsath
RAINIER, Priaulx
RAKHMANKULOVA, Mariam
   Mannanovna
RALSTON, Frances Marion
RAMM, Valentina Iosifovna
RAN, Shulamit
RANTA-SHIDA, Shoko
RAPOPORT, Eda
RAVISSA
RAW, Vera Constance
RAYMOND, Madeleine
REBE, Louise Christine
RECLI, Giulia
REID, Louis C.
REID, Sarah Johnston
REIFF, Lili
REISER, Violet
REISSEROVA, Julie
REMICK, Bertha
RENIE, Henriette
RENNES, Catharina van
RENSHAW, Rosette
REUCHSEL, Amedée
REYNOLDS, Erma Grey Hogue
RHEINGOLD, Lauma Yanovna
RHENE-JAQUE
RHOADS, Mary R.
RICHARDS, Christine-Louise
RICHARDSON, Enid Dorothy
RICHEPIN, Eliane
RICHER, Jeannine
RICHTER, Marga
RICHTER, Marion Morrey
RICKARD, Sylvia
RILEY, Ann Marion
RILEY, Myrtis F.
RISHER, Anna Priscilla
RITTENBAND, Minna Ethel
RIVE-KING, Julia
ROBERTS, Gertrud Hermine Kuenzel

ROBERTS, Jane A.
ROBERTS, Megan L.
ROBERTS, Ruth Olive
ROBERTSON, Donna Lou Nagey
ROBINSON, Frances
ROBITASHVILI, Lia Georgievna
ROCHAT, Andrée
ROCHEROLLE, Eugenie Katherine
RODRIGUE, Nicole
RODRIGUEZ, Esther
ROE, Eileen Betty
ROE, Gloria Ann
ROE, Helen Mary Gabrielle
ROE, Marion Adelle
ROESGEN-CHAMPION, Marguerite
    Sara
ROESSING, Helen
ROFE, Esther
ROGATIS, Térèsa de
ROGER, Denise
ROGERS, Clara Kathleen
ROGERS, Ethel Tench
ROGERS, Melicent Joan
ROGERS, Susan Whipple
ROGET, Henriette
ROHDE, Q'Adrianne
ROKSETH, Yvonne
ROLDES FREIXES, Mercedes
ROMERO BARBOSA, Elena
ROMM, Rosalina Davidovna
ROOTH, Anna-Greta
ROSAS FERNANDES, Maria Helena
ROSATO, Clorinda
ROSCO, B. Jeanie
ROWAN, Barbara
ROYSE, Mildred Barnes
ROZET, Sonia
ROZHAVSKAYA, Yudif Grigorevna
RUBIN, Anna Ita
RUEFF, Jeanine
RUFF-STOEHR, Herta Maria Klara
RUGELES, Ana Mercedes de
RUSCHE, Marjorie Maxine
RUTA, Gilda, Countess
RYAN, Winifred
RYBNER, Dagmar de Corval
RYDER, Theodora Sturkow
RYGAARD, Christine
RZAYEVA, Agabadzhi Ishmael kykz
SAARINEN, Gloria Edith
SAFARIAN, Lucia Arisovna
SAINT HELIER, Ivy
SAINT JOHN, Kathleen Louise
SAINT-GEORGES, Didia
SAITO-NODA, Eva
SAIZ-SALAZAR, Marina
SALQUIN, Hedy
SALVADOR, Matilde
SAMSON, Valerie Brooks
SAMTER, Alice
SAMUEL, Marguerite
SAMUEL, Rhian
SAMVELIAN, Sofia Vardanovna
SANCIN, Mirca
SANDELS, Ellen
SANDERS, Alma M.
SANDIFUR, Ann Elizabeth
SANDRESKY; Margaret Vardell
SANDY, Grace Linn
SANFORD, Grace Krick
SANGUESA, Iris
SANTIAGO-FELIPE, Vilma R.
SANTOS-OCAMPO DE FRANCESCO,
    Amada Amy
SANZ, Rocio
SARNECKA, Jadwiga
SASSOLI, Ada
SATOH, Kimi
SAUTER, Maya
SAUVREZIS, Alice
SCEK, Breda Friderika

SCHEIN, Suzanna Fedorovna
SCHELLER ZEMBRANO, Maria
SCHERCHEN, Tona
SCHICK, Philippine
SCHIRMACHER, Dora
SCHLOSS, Myrna Frances
SCHMIDT, Mia
SCHMIDT-DUISBURG, Margarete
    Dina Alwina
SCHMITZ-GOHR, Else
SCHONTHAL, Ruth E.
SCHORR-WEILER, Eva
SCHUBERT, Myra Jean
SCHULZ, Madeleine
SCHULZE-BERGHOF, Luise Doris
    Albertine
SCHULTZOVA, Barbara
SCHURZMANN, Katharina
SCHUSSLER-BREWAEYS, Marie
    Antoinette
SCHUSTER, Doris Dodd
SCHUSTER, Elfriede
SCHUYLER, Philippa Duke
SCHWARZ, Friederike
SCHWARZKOPF-DRESSLER, Maria
SCHWERDTFEGER, E. Anne
SCHYTTE, Anna
SCLIAR, Esther
SCOTT, Georgina Keir
SCOTT, Hazel
SCOVILLE, Margaret Lee
SEALE, Ruth
SEARS, Helen
SEARS, Ilene Hanson
SEAY, Virginia
SEBASTIANI, Pia
SEGHIZZI, Cecilia
SEHESTED, Hilda
SELDEN-GOTH, Gizella
SELTZNER, Jennie
SEMEGEN, Daria
SEPULVEDA, Maria Luisa
SETO, Robin
SETTI, Kilza
SEUEL-HOLST, Marie
SHAFFER, Jeanne Ellison
SHAGIAKHMETOVA, Svetlana
    Georgievna
SHAVERZASHVILI, Tamara Antonovna
SHAW, Alice Marion
SHELTON, Margaret Meier
SHEPARD, Jean Ellen
SHEPPARD, Suzanne
SHERMAN, Kim Daryl
SHIRLEY, Constance Jeanette
SHLONSKY, Verdina
SHORE, Clare
SHRUDE, Marilyn
SHUTTLEWORTH, Anne-Marie
SIDORENKO, Tamara Stepanovna
SIKORA, Elzbieta
SILBERTA, Rhea
SILSBEE, Ann L.
SILVA, Eloisa d'Herbil de
SILVER, Sheila Jane
SILVERMAN, Faye-Ellen
SIMIC, Darinka
SIMON, Cécile Paul
SIMONIAN, Nadezhda Simonovna
SIMONS, Netty
SINGER, Jeanne
SIROONI, Alice
SKAGGS, Hazel Ghazarian
SKALSKA-SZEMIOTH, Hanna Wanda
SKORIK, Irene
SKOUEN, Synne
SKOWRONSKA, Janina
SLENCZYNSKA, Ruth
SLIANOVA-MIZANDARI, Dagmara
    Levanovna
SMEJKALOVA, Vlasta

SMELTZER, Susan Mary
SMITH, Ida Polk
SMITH, Julia Frances
SMITH, Ladonna Carol
SMITH, Linda Catlin
SMITH, Selma Moidel
SMITH, Sharon
SMYTH, Ethel Mary, Dame
SNIZKOVA-SKRHOVA, Jitka
SOEDERG, Gerda
SOENSTEVOLD, Maj
SOHNIUS, Elfriede
SOLLIMA, Donatella
SOLOMON, Elide M.
SOLOMON, Joyce Elaine
SOLOMON, Mirrie Irma
SOMMERS, Daria E.
SONNTAG, Brunhilde
SOUBLETTE, Sylvia
SOUERS, Mildred
SOULAGE, Marcelle Fanny Henriette
SOUTHAM, Ann
SPAGNOLO, Aurelia
SPAIN-DUNK, Susan
SPALDING, Eva Ruth
SPEACH, Sister Bernadette Marie
SPECHT, Anita Socola
SPECHT, Judy Lavise
SPENA, Lita
SPENCER PALMER, Florence
    Margaret
SPENCER, Marguerita
SPENCER, Williametta
SPINDLE, Louise Cooper
SPOENDLIN, Elisabeth
SPOERRI-RENFER, Anna-
    Margaretha
SPONGBERG, Viola
SPOONER, Dorothy Harley
STAIR, Patty
STAIRS, Lousie E.
STANEKAITE-LAUMYANSKENE,
    Elena Ionovna
STANLEY, Helen Camille
STARBUCK, Anna Diller
STEFANOVIC, Ivana
STEIN, Gladys Marie
STEINER, Emma
STEINER, Gitta Hana
STEIN-SCHNEIDER, Lena
STEPHEN, Roberta Mae
STERNICKA-NIEKRASZOWA, Ilza
STEWART, Hascal Vaughan
STEWART, Katharine
STEWART, Ora Pate
STILMAN-LASANSKY, Julia
STINSON, Ethelyn Lenore
STOCKER, Clara
STOCKER, Stella
STORY, Pauline B.
STRAUSS, Elizabeth
STREATFIELD, Valma June
STREET, Arlene Anderson
STREICHER, Lyubov Lvovna
STREIT, Else
STRICKLAND, Lily Teresa
STRUTT, Dorothy
STUART-BERGSTROM, Elsa
    Marianne
STURKOW-RYDER, Theodora
SUCCARI, Dia
SUCHY, Gregoria Karides
SUESSE, Dana
SUH, Kyung-Sun
SULPIZI, Mira
SULTANOVA, Asya Bakhish kyzy
SUMNER, Clare
SUNBLAD-HALME, Heidi Gabriella
    Wilhelmina
SUSSMAN, Ettel
SUSZCZYNSKA, Anna

SUTHERLAND, Margaret
SUTZU, Rodica
SVANIDZE, Natela Damianovna
SWAIN, Freda Mary
SWARTZ, Elsa Ellen
SWIFT, Kay
SWISHER, Gloria Agnes Wilson
SYNER, Sonia
SYNOWIEC, Ewa
SZAJNA-LEWANDOWSKA, Jadwiga
    Helena
SZALITOWNA, Paulina
SZOENYI, Erzsebet
SZYMANSKA, Iwonka Bogumila
TACK, Annie
TAILLEFERRE, Germaine
TAL, Marjo
TAL, Ya'ara
TALMA, Louise
TAMBLYN, Bertha Louise
TANN, Hilary
TANNER, Hilda
TAPPER, Bertha
TARLOW, Karen Anne
TARNOWSKA, Julia
TARTAGLIA, Lidia
TATE, Phyllis
TAUBER, Lotti
TAUTU, Cornelia
TAYLOR, Iris
TEGNER, Alice Charlotte
TEICHMUELLER, Anna
TELFER, Nancy Ellen
TEMPLE, Hope
TENGBERGEN, Maria Elizabeth van
    Ebbenhorst
TERHUNE, Anice
TERRIER-LAFFAILLE, Anne
TERRY, Frances
TERZIAN, Alicia
THEMMEN, Ivana Marburger
THIEME, Kerstin Anja
THOMAS, Helen
THOMAS, Janet Owen
THOMAS, Karen P.
THOMAS, Mary Virginia
THOME, Diane
THOMPSON, Ellen
THOMPSON, Leland
THOMSEN, Geraldine
THORESON, Janice Pearl
THORKELSDOTTIR, Mist Barbara
THREADGILL-MARTIN, Ravonna
TICHARICH, Zdenka
TIDEMAN-WIJERS, Bertha
TILLETT, Jeanette
TOBIN, Sister Clare
TOBLER, Mina
TODD, Esther Cox
TOLKOWSKY, Denise
TORRA, Celia
TORRENS, Merce
TOWER, Joan
TOWERSEY, Phyllis Mary
TREBICKA, Maria
TRIMBLE, Joan
TROENDLE, Theodora
TROUP, Emily Josephine
TRUMAN, Irene
TUCKER, Tui St. George
TUICHEVA, Zumrad
TUMANIAN, Elizaveta Artashesovna
TUMANISHVILI, Ketevana
    Dmitirevna
TURGEON, Frances
TURNER, Myra Brooks
TURNER, Olive Mary
TURNER, Sara Scott
TURNER-MALEY, Florence
TUTTLE, Thelma Kent
TYER, Norma Phyllis

TYRMAND, Eta Moiseyevna
ULEHLA, Ludmila
ULRICHSEN, Ingeborg
UNDERWOOD, Frances Evangeline
UNSCHULD, Marie von
URNER, Catherine Murphy
URRETA, Alicia
USHER, Julia
USTVOLSKAYA, Galina Ivanovna
UYEDA, Leslie
UYTTENHOVE, Yolande
VAN AARDT, Madeiene
VAN APPLEDORN, Mary Jeanne
VAN DE VATE, Nancy Hayes
VAN DEN BOORN-COCLET,
    Henriette
VAN DER MARK, Maria
VAN DIJCK, Beatrice Madeleine
VAN HAUTE, Anna-Maria
VAN KATWIJK, Viola Edna Beck
VAN NESTE, Rosane Micheline Lucie
    Charlotte
VAN OHLEN, Deborah
VANDEVERE, J. Lilien
VANIER, Jeannine
VANNAH, Kate
VASILIEVA, Tatiana Ivanovna
VAUBOURGOIN, Jeanine
VAZQUEZ, Alida
VELLERE, Lucie Weiler
VERCOE, Elizabeth
VERHAALEN, Sister Marion
VERNON, Sylvia
VERRILL, Louise Shurtleff Brown
VIDAR, Jorunn
VIEU, Jane
VIGNERON-RAMAKERS, Christiane-
    Josee
VIKTOR, Denise
VILLA-LOBOS, Arminda Neves de
    Almeida
VILLARINI, Awilda
VILLENEUVE, Marie-Louise Diane
VILLIN, Marcelle Henriette Marie
VINETTE, Alice
VINTULE, Ruta Evaldovna
VIRGIL, Antha Minerva Patchen
VIRTUE, Constance Cochnower
VISCONTI, Leila
VITO-DELVAUX, Berthé di
VIVADO ORSINI, Ida
VLAD, Marina
VLADERACKEN, Geertruida van
VOELLMY-LIECHTI, Grety
VOIGT, Henriette
VOLKART, Hazel
VOLKART-SCHLAGER, Kaethe
VON GUNDEN, Heidi
VON ZIERITZ, Grete
VORLOVA, Slavka
VORONINA, Tatiana Aleksandrovna
VOSS, Marie Wilson
VRABELY-WURMBACH-
    STUPPACHOVA, Stefania
VREE-BROWN, Marion F.
VYNER, Mary Bainbridge
WAGENSONNER, Mimi
WALKER, Ella May
WALKER, Gwyneth van Anden
WALLACE, Kathryn
WALLACH, Joelle
WALTERS, Teresa
WALTON, Constance
WANDERMAN, Dorothy
WANG, An-Ming
WARDE, Ann Maury
WARE, Harriet
WARNE, Katharine Mulky
WARREN, Elinor Remick
WARSHAW, Dalit Paz
WASIAKOWA, M.

WASKO, Christine
WATERHOUSE, Frances Emery
WAUGH, Jane
WEAVER, Carol Ann
WEAVER, Mary
WEBB, Allienne Brandon
WEBB, Mary
WEGENER-FRENSEL, Emmy Heil
WEIGL, Vally
WEISSBERG, Julia Lazerevna
WELANDER, Svea Goeta
WELLNER, Elsa
WELLS, Jane
WENDELBURG, Norma Ruth
WENNERBERG-REUTER, Sara
    Margareta Eugenia Euphrosyne
WENTZEL, Elisabet von
WERFEL-LACHIN, Assia
WERTHEIM, Rosy
WESSELS, Judith Brent
WESTGATE, Elizabeth
WESTON, Mildred
WESTRUP-MILNER, Maria
WEYBRIGHT, June
WHITE, Claude Porter
WHITE, Elsie Fellows
WHITE, Mary Louisa
WHITEHEAD, Gillian
WHITLOCK, E. Florence
WHITTAKER, Vivian
WHITTINGTON, Joan
WHITTLE, Chris Mary-Francine
WIENER, Eva Hannah
WIENIAWSKA, Irene Regine
WIGGINS, Mary
WIGHAM, Margaret
WILBER, Clare Marie O'Keefe
WILDSCHUT, Clara
WILENS, Greta
WILHELM, Grete
WILKINS, Margaret Lucy
WILL, Madeleine
WILLIAMS, Carol
WILLIAMS, Frances
WILLIAMS, Irma
WILLIAMS, Jean E.
WILLIAMS, Joan Franks
WILLIAMS, Kimberley
WILLIAMS, Linda
WILLIAMS, Mary Lou
WILLMAN, Regina Hansen
WILLS, Edwina Florence
WILSON, Gertrude Hoag
WILSON, Jean Dolores
WILSON, Karen
WILSON, Lynn
WIRE, Edith
WISHART, Betty Rose
WITKIN, Beatrice
WITTMAN, Thérèse
WOLF, Winifried
WOLLNER, Gertrude Price
WOOD, Ruzena Alenka Valda
WOODS, Joan Shirley LeSueur
WOOGE, Emma
WORRELL, Lola Carrier
WORTH, Amy
WRIGHT, Nannie Louise
WRONIKOWSKI, Florence F.
WUNSCH, Ilse Gerda
WYETH, Ann
WYLIE, Ruth Shaw
XENOPOL, Margareta
YAKHNINA, Yevgenia Yosifovna
YAMASHITA, Mika
YAMPOLSCHI, Roseane
YAROSHEVSKAYA, Ludmila
    Anatolievna
YAZBECK, Louise
YOGUCHI, Rie
YOUNG, Donel Marie

YOUNG, Jane Corner
YOUNG, Rolande Maxwell
ZAIDEL-RUDOLPH, Jeanne
ZAIMONT, Judith Lang
ZAKRZEWSKA-NIKIPORCZYK,
　Barbara Maria
ZALLMAN, Arlene
ZARANEK, Stefania Anatolyevna
ZARIPOVA, Naila Gatinovna
ZAULECK, Gertrud
ZAVALISHINA, Maria Semyonovna
ZECHLIN, Ruth
ZECKWER, Camille
ZELIKOVSKAYA, Fania
　Mordukhovna
ZHUBANOVA, Gaziza Akhmetovna
ZHUBINSKAYA, Valentina Yanovna
ZHVANETSKAIA, Inna Abramovna
ZIBEROVA, Zinaida Petrovna
ZIFFRIN, Marilyn Jane
ZIMMERMANN, Margrit
ZIPRICK, Marjorie Jean
ZIVKOVIC, Mirjana
ZOECKLER, Dorothy Ackerman
ZUBELDIA, Emiliana de
ZUZAK, Doris

Century not available
ACHARD, Marguerite
ALBRECHT, Elise
BAKER, Joanne J.
BARLOW, Sybil
BARRY, Emilie de
BAZIN, Mlle.
BESSON, Maria
BOR, Modesta
BOTIANO, Helene von
CHOISY, Laure
COMBIE, Ida Mae
CRENDIROPULO, Anna G.
CROFF PORTALUPI, Maddalena
CUBONI, Maria Teresa
DAVIDSON, Muriel
DESCHAMPS, Jacqueline
EDWARDS, Bella
FERGUS-HOYT, Phyllis
FRACKER, Cora Robins
GALEOTTI, Margherita
GAMBOGI, Luigia
GLASS, Jennifer
GORDON, Hope
GOTTSCHALK, Clara
GRAZIANA
HARVEY, Ella Doreen
HOGBEN, Dorothy
JOHNS, Altona Trent
JOUVENEL, Germaine de
KARGER-HOENIG, Friederike
KAUFFMAN, Amanda
KIEK, Bessie
LAWSON, May
LIECHTI, Grety
LOEWY, Irma
LOROLLE, Annie
LOTTIN, Phedora
MANACIO-GALDI, Elvira
MARES, Rosita
MIRANDA, Erma Hoag
MOREA, Vincenza della
OREFICE, Olga
PALMER, Peggy Spencer
PERERA, Carmen
PEYCKE, Frieda
PILLING, Dorothy
PORTCH, Margaret
PROSDOCIMI, Ada
RAPIN-GERBER, Eleonore
RICKETTS, Lucy W.
ROSS, Clara
RYCOFF, Lalla
SMITH, Lilian
SNODGRASS, Louise Harrison

STAEHLI, Violette
TAJANI MATTONE, Ida
THEMAR, Rosalie
THOMSON, Geraldine
VENTURE, Anna
VON HAGEN, Elizabeth
WALTER, Ida
WATSON, Mabel Madison

PIANO AND ORCHESTRA OR STRINGS
18th Century A.D.
GUEST, Jeanne Marie
KAUTH, Maria Magdalena
LA ROCHE, Rosa
MARTINEZ, Marianne
19th Century A.D.
AMERSFOORDT-DYK, Hermina
　Maria
BACKER-GROENDAHL, Agathe
　Ursula
BLAHETKA, Marie Leopoldina
BORTON, Alice
BOTTINI, Marianna, Marchioness
BRONSART VON SCHELLENDORF,
　Ingeborg Lena von
CANDEILLE, Amelie Julie
DUSSEK, Veronica Rosalie
FARRENC, Louise
GRABOWSKA, Clementine,
　Countess
MARKOWSKA-GARLOWSKA, Eliza
MAYER, Emilie
ORGER, Caroline
PARADIS, Maria Theresia von
PARKE, Maria Hester
PRESCOTT, Oliveria Louisa
SCHADEN, Nanette von
SCHUMANN, Clara Josephine
SMITH, Alice Mary
TYRELL, Agnes
WURM, Mary J.A.
20th Century A.D.
AARNE, Els
ABEJO, Sister M. Rosalina
ACCART, Eveline
ACKLAND, Jeanne Isabel Dorothy
ALEXANDRA, Liana
ALLAN, Esther
ALLIK, Kristi
ALMEN, Ruth
ARCHER, Violet Balestreri
ARETZ, Isabel
ARRIEU, Claude
AUSTER, Lydia Martinovna
AVETISIAN, Aida Konstantinovna
BABITS, Linda
BACEWICZ, Grażyna
BACH, Maria
BAGANIER, Janine
BALLOU, Esther Williamson
BARBERIS, Mansi
BARRAINE, Elsa
BARTHELSON, Joyce Holloway
BAUER, Marion Eugenie
BEACH, Amy Marcy
BECKON, Lettie Marie
BERG, Lily
BIALKIEWICZOWNA-ANDRAULT DE
　LANGERON, Irena
BIANCHINI, Emma
BIENVENU, Lily
BONDS, Margaret
BORDEWIJK-ROEPMAN, Johanna
BOSMANS, Henriette Hilda
BOULANGER, Nadia Juliette
BOYKIN, A. Helen
BRANSCOMBE, Gena
BRENET, Thérèse
BRENNER, Rosamond Drooker
BRIGHT, Dora Estella
BRINGUER, Estela

BRITAIN, Radie
BROOK, Gwendolyn Giffen
BRUCKSHAW, Kathleen
BRUZDOWICZ, Joanna
BUCZEK, Barbara Kazimiera
BULTERIJS, Nina
CALCAGNO, Elsa
CAMEU, Helza
CARLOS, Wendy
CARVALHO, Dinora de
CARWITHEN, Doreen
CATUNDA, Eunice do Monte Lima
CECCONI-BOTELLA, Monic
CHAMINADE, Cécile Louise
　Stephanie
CHICHERINA, Sofia Nikolayevna
CHKHEIDZE, Dali Davidovna
CHRETIEN-GENARO, Hedwige
CHUDOVA, Tatiana Alekseyevna
CLARKE, Rosemary
CLAYTON, Laura
COLE, Ulric
COLERIDGE-TAYLOR, Avril
　Gwendolen
CONSTANTINESCU, Domnica
CORY, Eleanor
COTRON, Fanou
COULTHARD, Jean
DAIGLE, Sister Anne Cécile
DALE, Phyllis
DANA, Lynn Boardman
DANEAU, Suzanne
DANIELA, Carmen
DAVIDSON, Tina
DAVITASHVILI, Meri Shalvovna
DAVY, Ruby Claudia Emily
DE BIASE BIDART, Lycia
DE FREITAS, Elvira Manuela
　Fernandez
DE LARA, Adelina
DELMOULY, Marie Mathilde
DELORME, Isabelle
DESPORTES, Yvonne Berthe Melitta
DIEMER, Emma Lou
DILLON, Fannie Charles
DLUGOSZEWSKI, Lucia
DRING, Madeleine
DROBYAZGINA, Valentina Ivanovna
DU PAGE, Florence Elizabeth
DUDLEY, Marjorie Eastwood
DUSHKIN, Dorothy Smith
EAGLES, Moneta M.
ECKHARDT-GRAMATTE, Sophie-
　Carmen
EKSANISHVILI, Eleonara Grigorevna
ELLICOTT, Rosalind Frances
ERHART, Dorothy
ESCOBAR, Maria Luisa
FAIRLIE, Margaret C.
FALCINELLI, Rolande
FALTIS, Evelyn
FENSTOCK, Belle
FERRAND-TEULET, Denise
FINE, Vivian
FIRESTONE, Elizabeth
FISCHER, Emma Gabriele Marie von,
　Baroness
FOLVILLE, Eugenie-Emilie Juliette
FOSTER, Cecily
FRANCE, Jeanne Lelen
FRESON, Armande
FURGERI, Bianca Maria
GAMILLA, Alice Doria
GARCIA ASCOT, Rosa
GARCIA MUNOZ, Carmen
GARDINER, Mary Elizabeth
GARTENLAUB, Odette
GARUTA, Lucia Yanovna
GARY, Marianne
GARZTECKA-JARZEBSKA, Irena
GERSTMAN, Blanche Wilhelminia

GIPPS, Ruth
GLANVILLE-HICKS, Peggy
GOKHMAN, Elena Vladimirovna
GOLUB, Martha Naumovna
GONZAGA, Chiquinha
GOULD, Elizabeth Davies
GRIEBLING, Margaret Ann
GRZADZIELOWNA, Eleonora
GUBAIDULINA, Sofia Asgatovna
GUBITOSI, Emilia
GVAZAVA, Tamara Davidovna
GYANDZHETSIAN, Destrik
   Bogdanovna
HAGAN, Helen Eugenia
HAIK-VANTOURA, Suzanne
HAIMSOHN, Naomi Carrol
HANNIKAINEN, Ann-Elise
HARRIS, Margaret R.
HARRISON, Pamela
HARTZER-STIBBE, Marie
HERZ, Maria
HOPEKIRK, Helen
HORROCKS, Amy Elsie
HOWE, Mary Alberta Bruce
HOWELL, Dorothy
HYDE, Miriam Beatrice
IBRAGIMOVA, Ela Imamedinovna
IBRAGIMOVA, Sevda Mirza kyzy
ISAKOVA, Aida Petrovna
ISMAGILOVA, Leila Zagirovna
ISZKOWSKA, Zofia
JABOR, Najla
JAELL-TRAUTMANN, Marie
JANOTHA, Natalia
JEREA, Hilda
JESI, Ada
JOLAS, Betsy
JOLY, Suzanne
KABE, Mariko
KAHMANN, Chesley
KALOGRIDOU, Maria
KAPRALOVA, Vitezslava
KARNITSKAYA, Nina Andreyevna
KASHPEROVA, Leokadia
   Alexandrovna
KASILAG, Lucrecia R.
KATS-CHERNIN, Elena
KELLER, Ginette
KERN, Frida
KESSLER, Minuetta Schumiatcher
KICKINGER, Paula
KLEES, Gabriele
KOELLING, Eloise
KOLODUB, Zhanna Efimovna
KORN, Clara Anna
KOZAKIEVICH, Anna Abramovna
KRZYZANOWSKA, Halina
KULIEVA, Farida Tairovna
KUROKAWA, Manae
KUSUNOKI, Tomoko
KUZMENKO, Larysa
KUZMYCH, Christina
LACHOWSKA, Stefania
LAGO
LALAUNI, Lila
LANG-BECK, Ivana
LARSON, Anna Barbara
LAUBER, Anne Marianne
LE BEAU, Louisa Adolpha
LEE, Young Ja
LEGINSKA, Ethel
LEIVISKA, Helvi Lemmiki
LELEU, Jeanne
LEMAIRE-SINDORFF, Jeanne
LEON, Tania Justina
LEONCHIK, Svetlana Gavrilovna
LEVINA, Zara Alexandrovna
LIADOVA, Ludmila Alekseyevna
LIMA CRUZ, Maria Antonietta de
LINZ VON KRIEGNER, Marta
LITER, Monia

LOOTS, Joyce Mary Ann
LOPUSKA-WYLEZYNSKA, Helena
LUFF, Enid
LUND, Gudrun
LUO, Jing-Jing
LUTYENS, Elisabeth
MACONCHY, Elizabeth
MacKENNA, Carmela
McBURNEY, Mona
McCOLLIN, Frances
MAILIAN, Elza Antonovna
MANA-ZUCCA
MANNING, Kathleen Lockhart
MANZIARLY, Marcelle de
MARBE, Myriam
MARCUS, Ada Belle Gross
MAREZ-OYENS, Tera de
MARIC, Ljubica
MARINESCU-SCHAPIRA, Ilana
MASON, Gladys Amy
MASTERS, Juan
MATEVOSIAN, Araks Surenovna
MAURICE, Paule
MAZOUROVA, Jarmila
MEL-BONIS
MENEELY-KYDER, Sarah Suderley
MERO, Jolanda
MESRITZ-VAN VELTHUYSEN, Annie
MEYSENBURG, Sister Agnes
MIAGI, Ester Kustovna
MILENKOVIC, Jelena
MINEO, Antoinette
MOORE, Mary Carr
MORIN-LABRECQUE, Albertine
MOSZUMANSKA-NAZAR, Krystyna
MUNGER, Shirley
NAZAROVA, Tatiana Borisovna
NAZIROVA, Elmira Mirza Rza kyzy
NEWLIN, Dika
NGUYEN, Louise
NIEMACK, Ilza Louise
NIKOLAYEVA, Tatiana Petrovna
NIKOLSKAYA, Lyubov Borisovna
NIKOLSKAYA, Olga Vasilevna
NISHIMURA, Yukie
NORDENSTROM, Gladys Mercedes
NORRE, Dorcas
NOVA SONDAG, Jacqueline
NOVOSELOVA, Ludmila Alexeyevna
OBROVSKA, Jana
OERBECK, Anne-Marie
OH, Sook Ja
OHLSON, Marion
OKEY, Maggie
OSETROVA-YAKOVLIEVA, Nina
   Alexandrovna
OWEN, Blythe
PANETTI, Joan
PATINO ANDRADE, Graziela
PEARL-MANN, Dora Deborah
PEJACEVIC, Dora, Countess
PENTLAND, Barbara Lally
PERRY, Julia Amanda
PETRA-BASACOPOL, Carmen
PFERDEMENGES, Maria Pauline
   Augusta
PHILIPPART, Renée
PICKHARDT, Ione
PIETSCH, Edna Frieda
PONCE, Ethel
PRAVOSSUDOVITCH, Natalja
   Michajlovna
PREOBRAJENSKA, Vera Nicolaevna
PRICE, Deon Nielsen
PRICE, Florence Beatrice
PRIETO, Maria Teresa
PRIOLLI, Maria Luisa de Matos
PROCACCINI, Teresa
PSTROKONSKA-NAVRATIL,
   Grazyna Hanna
RALSTON, Frances Marion

RAN, Shulamit
RAPOPORT, Eda
RAYMOND, Madeleine
RICHEPIN, Eliane
RICHTER, Marga
ROBERT, Lucie
ROBITASHVILI, Lia Georgievna
ROESGEN-CHAMPION, Marguerite
   Sara
ROGER, Denise
ROGERS, Patsy
ROGET, Henriette
ROKSETH, Yvonne
ROMERO BARBOSA, Elena
ROMM, Rosalina Davidovna
ROSCO, B. Jeanie
ROZHAVSKAYA, Yudif Grigorevna
RUFF-STOEHR, Herta Maria Klara
RUTA, Gilda, Countess
SAINT JOHN, Kathleen Louise
SALQUIN, Hedy
SAMTER, Alice
SANTOS-OCAMPO DE FRANCESCO,
   Amada Amy
SCHELLER ZEMBRANO, Maria
SCHICK, Philippine
SCHONTHAL, Ruth E.
SCHUSTER, Elfriede
SEBASTIANI, Pia
SEPULVEDA, Maria Luisa
SEUEL-HOLST, Marie
SHLONSKY, Verdina
SHREVE, Susan Ellen
SIMONIAN, Nadezhda Simonovna
SISTEK-DJORDJEVIC, Mirjana
SLIANOVA-MIZANDARI, Dagmara
   Levanovna
SMITH, Julia Frances
SOLOMON, Elide M.
SOLOMON, Joyce Elaine
SOLOMON, Mirrie Irma
SPAIN-DUNK, Susan
SPONGBERG, Viola
STEINER, Emma
STEINER, Gitta Hana
STERNICKA-NIEKRASZOWA, Ilza
SUCHY, Gregoria Karides
SUESSE, Dana
SUSZCZYNSKA, Anna
SUTHERLAND, Margaret
SWAIN, Freda Mary
SZAJNA-LEWANDOWSKA, Jadwiga
   Helena
SZYMANSKA, Iwonka Bogumila
TAILLEFERRE, Germaine
TALMA, Louise
THIEME, Kerstin Anja
THOMAS, Marilyn Taft
THOMSEN, Geraldine
TOLKOWSKY, Denise
TUMANISHVILI, Ketevana
   Dmitirevna
TWOMBLY, Mary Lynn
TYRMAND, Eta Moiseyevna
URRETA, Alicia
USTVOLSKAYA, Galina Ivanovna
UYEDA, Leslie
VAMOS, Grace Becker
VAN APPLEDORN, Mary Jeanne
VAN DE VATE, Nancy Hayes
VAN NESTE, Rosane Micheline Lucie
   Charlotte
VASILIEVA, Tatiana Ivanovna
VIDAR, Jorunn
VIEU, Jane
VINOGRADOVA, Vera
VINTULE, Ruta Evaldovna
VISCONTI, Leila
VITO-DELVAUX, Berthe di
VON ZIERITZ, Grete
VORONINA, Tatiana Aleksandrovna

VYNER, Mary Bainbridge
WARD, Louise Taylor
WARD, Nancy
WARE, Harriet
WEGENER-FRENSEL, Emmy Heil
WERTHEIM, Rosy
WIENIAWSKA, Irene Regine
WIGHAM, Margaret
WILL, Madeleine
WILLIAMS, Grace Mary
WILLIAMS, Jean E.
WITNI, Monica
WRIGHT, Nannie Louise
YAKHNINA, Yevgenia Yosifovna
ZAIMONT, Judith Lang
ZAKRZEWSKA-NIKIPORCZYK,
  Barbara Maria
ZARANEK, Stefania Anatolyevna
ZECHLIN, Ruth
ZHUBINSKAYA, Valentina Yanovna
ZIVKOVIC, Mirjana
Century unknown
VENTURE, Anna

PIANO QUARTET
18th Century A.D.
KANZLER, Josephine
19th Century A.D.
HENSEL, Fanny Caecilia
HERITTE-VIARDOT, Louise Pauline
  Marie
LIEBMANN, Helene
MAYER, Emilie
ORGER, Caroline
PRESCOTT, Oliveria Louisa
SANDERS, Alma
SMITH, Alice Mary
20th Century A.D.
ANDREE, Elfrida
BACH, Maria
BARBILLON, Jeanne
BOLZ, Harriet
BROCKMAN, Jane E.
BROGUE, Roslyn Clara
BUCKLEY, Helen Dallam
COULTHARD, Jean
DIEMER, Emma Lou
EGGLESTON, Anne E.
ESTRELLA, Blanca
FOLVILLE, Eugenie-Emilie
  Juliette
GHANDAR, Ann
GIPPS, Ruth
GOKHMAN, Elena Vladimirovna
GYANDZHETSIAN, Destrik
  Bogdanovna
HALACSY, Irma von
HARA, Kazuko
HIER, Ethel Glen
HOFFMAN, Phyllis Sampson
HORROCKS, Amy Elsie
HUGHES, Sister Martina
KAPP, Corinne
LACHOWSKA, Stefania
LATIOLAIS, Desirée Jayne
LE BEAU, Louisa Adolpha
LEIVISKA, Helvi Lemmiki
LELEU, Jeanne
MEL-BONIS
MITCHELL, Janice Misurell
MOSUSOVA, Nadezda
ODDONE SULLI-RAO, Elisabetta
OWEN, Blythe
PEJACEVIC, Dora, Countess
PENTLAND, Barbara Lally
POPOVICI, Elise
RAPOPORT, Eda
RHENE-JAQUE
RILEY, Myrtis F.
SEHESTED, Hilda
SOMMER, Silvia

SOULAGE, Marcelle Fanny
  Henriette
VIEU, Jane
WANG, An-Ming
WEIR, Judith

PIANO QUINTET
19th Century A.D.
FARRENC, Louise
HOLMES, Augusta Mary Anne
LA HYE, Louise Genevieve
SWEPSTONE, Edith
20th Century A.D.
ABEJO, Sister M. Rosalina
AGABALIAN, Lidia Semyenovna
ANDREE, Elfrida
BACEWICZ, Grażyna
BACH, Maria
BANNISTER, Mary Jeanne
  Hoggard
BEACH, Amy Marcy
BECK, Martha Dillard
BIRNSTEIN, Renate Maria
BLIESENER, Ada Elizabeth,
  Michelman
BRUCKSHAW, Kathleen
CALCAGNO, Elsa
CIOBANU, Maia
CONSTANTINESCU, Domnica
COULTHARD, Jean
COUPER, Mildred
CRAWFORD SEEGER, Ruth
DEDIEU-PETERS, Madeleine
DESPORTES, Yvonne Berthe Melitta
EGGAR, Katharine
EKSANISHVILI, Eleonara Grigorevna
EMERY, Dorothy Radde
FRESON, Armande
GONTARENKO, Galina Nikolayevna
GRIEBLING, Karen Jean
GUBAIDULINA, Sofia Asgatovna
GYANDZHETSIAN, Destrik
  Bogdanovna
HOWE, Mary Alberta Bruce
HOY, Bonnee L.
HSU, Wen-Ying
IORDAN, Irina Nikolayevna
JESI, Ada
KAMIEN, Anna
KASILAG, Lucrecia R.
KICKINGER, Paula
LANG, Margaret Ruthven
LEIBOW, Ruth Irene
LITSITE, Paula Yanovna
MacKOWN, Marjorie T.
McCOLLIN, Frances
MARCUS, Ada Belle Gross
MELVILLE, Marguerite Liszniewska
METALLIDI, Zhanneta Lazarevna
MOORE, Mary Carr
MUELLER-HERMANN, Johanna
NAIKHOVICH-LOMAKINA, Fania
  Filippovna
NIKOLAYEVA, Tatiana Petrovna
OWEN, Blythe
PEJACEVIC, Dora, Countess
PHILIBA, Nicole
PIETSCH, Edna Frieda
PRICE, Florence Beatrice
ROWAN, Barbara
RUEFF, Jeanine
RUFF-STOEHR, Herta Maria Klara
SAINT JOHN, Kathleen Louise
SAMUEL, Rhian
SANFORD, Grace Krick
SOULAGE, Marcelle Fanny Henriette
SWAIN, Freda Mary
SZAJNA-LEWANDOWSKA, Jadwiga
  Helena
TOWER, Joan
VAN DE VATE, Nancy Hayes

PIANO TRIO
19th Century A.D.
BERTIN, Louise Angelique
CANDEILLE, Amelie Julie
FARMER, Emily Bardsley
FARRENC, Louise
FILIPOWICZ, Elize-Minelli
HENDRICH-MERTA, Marie
HENSEL, Fanny Caecilia
KOTSBATREVSKAYA
KRALIK VON MAYERSWALDEN,
  Mathilde
LIEBMANN, Helene
LODER, Kate Fanny
MAYER, Emilie
NAVA D'ADDA, Francesca,
  Countess
ORGER, Caroline
PARADIS, Maria Theresia von
SANDERS, Alma
SCHUMANN, Clara Josephine
SMITH, Alice Mary
TAITE, Annie
ZIMMERMANN, Agnes Marie
  Jacobina
20th Century A.D.
ABORN, Lora
AKHUNDOVA, Shafiga Gulam kyzy
ALCALAY, Luna
ALLIK, Kristi
ALOTIN, Yardena
ALTER, Martha
ALVES DE SOUSA, Berta Candida
ANDREE, Elfrida
ARCHER, Violet Balestreri
ARETZ, Isabe!
ARIZTI SOBRINO, Cecilia
ARRIEU, Claude
AYLOTT, Lydia Georgina Edith
BAGANIER, Janine
BALLOU, Esther Williamson
BARBILLON, Jeanne
BARKLUND, Irma L.
BARNS, Ethel
BEACH, Amy Marcy
BECLARD D'HARCOURT,
  Marguerite
BERGERSEN, Marie Christine
BINET, Jocelyne
BLISS, Marilyn S.
BOND, Victoria Ellen
BOULANGER, Lili Juliette Marie Olga
BOUTRON, Madeleine
BRESCHI, Laura
BRITAIN, Radie
BUCHANAN, Dorothy Quita
BUCKLEY, Helen Dallam
BULTERIJS, Nina
BUTLER, Patricia Magahay
CAMPMANY, Montserrat
CARR-BOYD, Ann Kirsten
CLARKE, Rebecca
CLARKE, Rosemary
COCQ, Rosina Susanna de
COLE, Ulric
CORY, Eleanor
COULTHARD, Jean
CRANE, Helen
DAVIS, Eleanor Maud
DAVITASHVILI, Meri Shalvovna
DAVY, Ruby Claudia Emily
DE BIASE BIDART, Lycia
DEMBO, Royce
DENBOW, Stefania Bjoerson
DILLON, Fannie Charles
DREGE-SCHIELOWA, Lucja
DUCOUREAU, Mme. M.
ECKHARDT-GRAMATTE, Sophie-
  Carmen
ELLICOTT, Rosalind Frances
ENDRES, Olive Philomene

ERHART, Dorothy
EZELL, Helen Ingle
FALTIS, Evelyn
FERRAND-TEULET, Denise
FINZI, Graciane
FONTYN, Jacqueline
FRANCK, Philippine
GARCIA ROBSON, Magdalena
GARUTA, Lucia Yanovna
GOEBELS, Gisela
GOKHMAN, Elena Vladimirovna
GOULD, Elizabeth Davies
GRIEBEL WANDALL, Tekla
GUELL, Elizabeth
GUMMER, Phyllis Mary
GYANDZHETSIAN, Destrik Bogdanovna
HAHN, Sandra Lea
HALACSY, Irma von
HARRADEN, R. Ethel
HARTZER-STIBBE, Marie
HAYWARD, Mae Shepard
HEDOUX, Yvonne
HENDERSON, Moya
HERNANDEZ-GONZALO, Gisela
HOFFRICHTER, Bertha Chaitkin
HOLLAND, Dulcie Sybil
HOOD, Helen
HOOVER, Katherine
HOWE, Mary Alberta Bruce
HOY, Bonnee L.
HSU, Wen-Ying
HUBICKI, Margaret Olive
IBRAGIMOVA, Ela Imamedinovna
IBRAGIMOVA, Sevda Mirza kyzy
JAMES, Dorothy E.
JIRACKOVA, Marta
JOHNSTON, Alison Aileen Annie
JOLLY, Margaret Anne
KADIMA, Hagar Yonith
KALOGRIDOU, Maria
KANACH, Sharon E.
KASILAG, Lucrecia R.
KAZANDJIAN, Sirvart
KERN, Frida
KESSLER, Minuetta Schumiatcher
KOSTAKOVA-HERODKOVA, Marie
KUYPER, Elizabeth
LABEY, Charlotte Sohy
LAGO
LAPIN, Lily
LEAHY, Mary Weldon
LEHMAN, Evangeline Marie
LEONCHIK, Svetlana Gavrilovna
LITSITE, Paula Yanovna
LUCKE, Katharine E.
LUND, Gudrun
McCOLLIN, Frances
McKINNEY, Mathilde
MAGEAU, Mary Jane
MAILIAN, Elza Antonovna
MAMLOK, Ursula
MANA-ZUCCA
MANZIARLY, Marcelle de
MAREZ-OYENS, Tera de
MARI, Pierrette
MARTINS, Maria de Lourdes
MATEU, Maria Cateura
MATEVOSIAN, Araks Surenovna
MAYER, Lise Maria
MEL-BONIS
MELOY, Elizabeth
MESRITZ-VAN VELTHUYSEN, Annie
MIAGI, Ester Kustovna
MIKUSCH, Margarethe von
MOORE, Dorothy Rudd
MOORE, Mary Carr
MORE, Margaret Elizabeth
MOSUSOVA, Nadezda
MUNKTELL, Helena Mathilda
MYSZINSKA-WOJCIECHOWSKA,
  Leokadia

NAKAMURA, Sawako
NEPGEN, Rosa Sophia Cornelia
NEWLIN, Dika
NIECKS, Christina
NIKOLSKAYA, Lyubov Borisovna
NIKOLSKAYA, Olga Vasilevna
NOBLITT, Katheryn Marie McCall
NOETHLING, Elisabeth
NOYES, Edith Rowena
OMER, Helene
OOSTERZEE, Cornelia van
OSTRANDER, Linda Woodaman
OWEN, Blythe
PEJACEVIC, Dora, Countess
PETRA-BASACOPOL, Carmen
PEY CASADO, Diana
PHILIBA, Nicole
PHILLIPS, Linda
PIETSCH, Edna Frieda
PIKE, Eleanor B. Franklin
PIRES DOS RIES, Hilda
PLIEVA, Zhanna Vasilievna
POLIN, Claire
POPOVICI, Elise
PRIOLLI, Maria Luisa de Matos
PROCACCINI, Teresa
QUIEL, Hildegard
RADERMACHER, Erika
RAINIER, Priaulx
RAPOPORT, Eda
RECLI, Giulia
RHENE-JAQUE
RICHER, Jeannine
RICHTER, Marga
RICHTER, Marion Morrey
ROGERS, Melicent Joan
ROSATO, Clorinda
RUSCHE, Marjorie Maxine
SAMTER, Alice
SANDRESKY, Margaret Vardell
SANFORD, Grace Krick
SCHICK, Philippine
SCHMITZ-GOHR, Else
SCHUSTER, Elfriede
SELTZNER, Jennie
SIDORENKO, Tamara Stepanovna
SIMON, Cecile Paul
SISTEK-DJORDJEVIC, Mirjana
SKAGGS, Hazel Ghazarian
SMYTH, Ethel Mary, Dame
SOLOMON, Mirrie Irma
SOULAGE, Marcelle Fanny
  Henriette
SPAIN-DUNK, Susan
SPENCER, Marguerita
SZOENYI, Erzsebet
TAILLEFERRE, Germaine
TAL, Ya'ara
TRIMBLE, Joan
TURGEON, Frances
URNER, Catherine Murphy
USTVOLSKAYA, Galina Ivanovna
VELLERE, Lucie Weiler
VELTHUYSEN, Abesritz von
VERNE-BREDT, Alice
VIRTUE, Constance Cochnower
VITO-DELVAUX, Berthe di
WELANDER, Svea Goeta
WHITEHEAD, Gillian
WHITTLE, Chris Mary-Francine
ZELIKOVSKAYA, Fania
  Mordukhovna
ZIFFRIN, Marilyn Jane
Century unknown
  GALEOTTI, Margherita
  SNODGRASS, Louise Harrison

PICCOLO
20th Century A.D.
  ARMER, Elinor Florence
  BAULD, Alison

BOUCHARD, Linda L.
BOYD, Anne Elizabeth
CHARLES, S. Robin
CORY, Eleanor
COULOMBE SAINT-MARCOUX,
  Micheline
DUNLOP, Isobel
GABUS, Monique
GARDNER, Kay
GIFFORD, Helen Margaret
GRIGSBY, Beverly
HOOVER, Katherine
INWOOD, Mary Ruth Brink Berger
JOLAS, Betsy
KEEFER, Euphrosyne
LE SIEGE, Annette
LOUIE, Alexina Diane
LUFF, Enid
MEACHEM, Margaret McKeen
  Ramsey
MEKEEL, Joyce
MIYAKE, Haruna
MIZUNO, Shuko
MUSGRAVE, Thea
OLIVEROS, Pauline
RODRIGUE, Nicole
RUSCHE, Marjorie Maxine
SIMONS, Netty
TOWER, Joan
USHER, Julia
USTVOLSKAYA, Galina Ivanovna
VON ZIERITZ, Grete
WARNE, Katharine Mulky

PSALTERY
20th Century A.D.
  BAADER-NOBS, Heidi
  LU, Yen
  LUND, Gudrun
  POSTON, Elizabeth
  ZIFFRIN, Marilyn Jane

QUARTET-OTHER
17th Century A.D.
  PRIOLI MORISINA, Marietta
18th Century A.D.
  ANNA AMALIA, Duchess of Saxe-
    Weimar
  CHARRIERE, Isabella Agneta
    Elisabeth de
  LA GUERRE, Elisabeth-Claude
    Jacquet de
  PHILHARMONICA, Mrs.
19th Century A.D.
  BALTHASAR, Florence
  BAU, Elise
  BLANGINI, Mlle.
  CANDEILLE, Amelie Julie
  FARMER, Emily Bardsley
  JOSEPHINE, Queen of Sweden and
    Norway
20th Century A.D.
  ABE, Kyoko
  ACCART, Eveline
  AGUDELO MURGUIA, Graciela
  ALLEN, Judith Shatin
  ALLIK, Kristi
  ANDERSON, Olive Jennie Paxton
  ANDERSON-WUENSCH, Jean Mary
  ARIMA, Reiko
  BACEWICZ, Grażyna
  BAILEY, Judith Margaret
  BARKIN, Elaine
  BARRAINE, Elsa
  BARRETT-THOMAS, N.
  BERGEN, Sylvia
  BERK, Adele
  BINGHAM, Judith
  BLOOM, Jane Ira
  BOFILL, Anna
  BOND, Victoria Ellen

BOUCHARD, Linda L.
BRANDMAN, Margaret Susan
BRENET, Therese
BRIGGS, Nancy Louise
BRITAIN, Radie
BRUGGMANN, Heidi
BRUSH, Ruth Damaris
BRUZDOWICZ, Joanna
CAMPAGNE, Conny
CAMPMANY, Montserrat
CAPDEVILA I GAYA, Merce
CATUNDA, Eunice do Monte Lima
CECCONI-BATES, Augusta
CHAMPION, Stephanie
CHANCE, Nancy Laird
CLOSTRE, Adrienne
COATES, Gloria Kannenberg
COLAÇO OSORIO-SWAAB, Reine
CORY, Eleanor
COWLES, Darleen
CULP, Paula Newell
DANEAU, Suzanne
DARE, Margaret Marie
DE BIASE BIDART, Lycia
DEMBO, Royce
DIAMOND, Arline
DIEMER, Emma Lou
DILLER, Saralu C.
DU PAGE, Florence Elizabeth
DUSHKIN, Dorothy Smith
ENDRES, Olive Philomene
ERDING, Susanne
EUTENEUER-ROHRER, Ursula
  Henrietta
EVEN-OR, Mary
FINE, Vivian
FINZI, Graciane
FISHER, Gladys Washburn
FISHMAN, Marian
FONTYN, Jacqueline
FORMAN, Joanne
FRASIER, Jane
FRUMKER, Linda
FULLER-HALL, Sarah Margaret
GARR, Wieslawa
GLATZ, Helen Sinclair
GOTKOVSKY, Ida-Rose Esther
GOULD, Elizabeth Davies
GOULD, Janetta
GRAHAM, Janet Christine
GRESHAM, Ann
GROSSMAN, Deena
GRZADZIELOWNA, Eleonora
GUBAIDULINA, Sofia Asgatovna
HAHN, Sandra Lea
HARRIS, Ruth Berman
HARRISON, Pamela
HAZEN, Sara
HEDSTROEM, Ase
HOELSZKY, Adriana
HOOVER, Katherine
HOVDA, Eleanor
IRMAN-ALLEMANN, Regina
JANACEKOVA, Viera
JOLLY, Margaret Anne
JOLY, Suzanne
KAMINSKY, Laura
KELLER, Ginette
KEMP, Dorothy Elizabeth Walter
KITAZUME, Yayoi
KOLB, Barbara
KONISHI, Nagako
KRULL, Diana
LANG, Rosemary Rita
LARSEN, Elizabeth Brown
LEAHY, Mary Weldon
LEBARON, Anne
LEE, Hwaeja Yoo
LEECH, Renée
LEFANU, Nicola Frances
LEJET, Edith

LEJEUNE-BONNIER, Eliane
LIFFER, Binette
LINNEMANN, Maria Catharina
LITER, Monia
LOMON, Ruth
LU, Yen
LUCAS, Mary Anderson
LUNA DE ESPAILLAT, Margarita
LUND, Gudrun
MACKIE, Shirley M.
MACONCHY, Elizabeth
McINTOSH, Diana
MAGEAU, Mary Jane
MAIRE, Jacqueline
MAMLOK, Ursula
MARI, Pierrette
MARKIEWICZOWNA, Wladyslawa
MARTINS, Maria de Lourdes
MENEELY-KYDER, Sarah Suderley
MERRIMAN, Margarita Leonor
MESNEY, Dorothy Taylor
MIAGI, Ester Kustovna
MOORE, Anita
MORETTO, Nelly
MUNGER, Shirley
MURAKUMO, Ayako
MURAO, Sachie
NAZAROVA, Tatiana Borisovna
NEMTEANU-ROTARU, Doina
NIEDERBERGER, Maria A.
NIEMACK, Ilza Louise
NOBLE, Ann
NOWAK, Alison
OH, Sook Ja
O'LEARY, Jane Strong
OWEN, Angela Maria
OWEN, Blythe
PAGH-PAAN, Younghi
PELEGRI, Maria Teresa
PENGILLY, Sylvia
PETROVA, Mara
PHILIBA, Nicole
PHILLIPS, Linda
PIRES DOS REIS, Hilda
PIZER, Elizabeth Faw Hayden
POSTON, Elizabeth
POULET DEFONTAINE, Madeleine
PRAVOSSUDOVITCH, Natalja
  Michajlovna
PRICE, Deon Nielsen
PROCACCINI, Teresa
PSTROKONSKA-NAVRATIL,
  Grazyna Hanna
PTASZYNSKA, Marta
RAINIER, Priaulx
RAMAKERS, Christiane Josée
RAPOPORT, Eda
REED, Marlyce Rae Polk
RHOADS, Mary R.
RICHER, Jeannine
RILEY, Myrtis F.
ROBERTSON, Donna Lou Nagey
RODRIGUE, Nicole
ROE, Eileen Betty
ROEDER, Toni
ROSCO, B. Jeanie
RUEFF, Jeanine
SAMSON, Valerie Brooks
SAMTER, Alice
SAMUEL, Rhian
SANGUESA, Iris
SCHONTHAL, Ruth E.
SCHORR-WEILER, Eva
SEGHIZZI, Cécilia
SEMEGEN, Daria
SHRUDE, Marilyn
SIEBER, Susanne
SIEGRIST, Beatrice
SILSBEE, Ann L.
SIMONS, Netty
SINGER, Jeanne

SLIANOVA-MIZANDARI, Dagmara
  Levanovna
SMELTZER, Susan Mary
SMYTH, Ethel Mary, Dame
SODRE, Joanidia
SOENSTEVOLD, Maj
SOLOMON, Elide M.
SOUTHAM, Ann
STANLEY, Helen Camille
STEINER, Gitta Hana
STILMAN-LASANSKY, Julia
STREATFIELD, Valma June
STRUTT, Dorothy
SUTHERLAND, Margaret
SWAIN, Freda Mary
SYNOWIEC, Ewa
TATE, Phyllis
THEMMEN, Ivana Marburger
THOME, Diane
TOLKOWSKY, Denise
TOWER, Joan
TUMANISHVILI, Ketevana
  Dmitirevna
TURRIETTA, Cheryl Renée
URNER, Catherine Murphy
USTVOLSKAYA, Galina Ivanovna
UYTTENHOVE, Yolande
VAN DE VATE, Nancy Hayes
VAN DIJCK, Beatrice Madeleine
VAN HAUTE, Anna-Maria
VEHAR, Persis Anne
VIGNERON-RAMAKERS, Christiane-
  Josée
VITO-DELVAUX, Berthe di
VORLOVA, Slavka
WALLACH, Joelle
WARREN, Betsy
WECKWERTH, Nancy
WEIGL, Vally
WILLIAMS, Mary Lou
WITNI, Monica
WOLLNER, Gertrude Price
WYLIE, Ruth Shaw
ZAIDEL-RUDOLPH, Jeanne
ZAULECK, Gertrud
ZIMMERMANN, Margrit
ZWILICH, Ellen Taaffe

QUARTET - PIANO see PIANO QUARTET

QUARTET - STRING see STRING QUARTET

QUARTET - UNSPECIFIED
19th Century A.D.
AMERSFOORDT-DYK, Hermina
  Maria
20th Century A.D.
ABEJO, Sister M. Rosalina
ALONSO, Julia
ANDREYEVA, Elena Fedorovna
BOLZ, Harriet
CAPUIS, Matilde
CECCONI-BATES, Augusta
CECCONI-BOTELLA, Monic
CHRETIEN-GENARO, Hedwige
DIANDA, Hilda
DRDOVA, Marie
ELLICOTT, Rosalind Frances
FIUZA, Virginia Salgado
FLEITES, Virginia
GLATZ, Helen Sinclair
GREENWALD, Jan Carol
GUBAIDULINA, Sofia Asgatovna
HERBISON, Jeraldine Saunders
KAESER-BECK, Aida
KOZAKIEVICH, Anna Abramovna
MESNEY, Dorothy Taylor
PENTLAND, Barbara Lally
POPATENKO, Tamara Alexandrovna
PTASZYNSKA, Marta
ROYSE, Mildred Barnes

SACCAGGIO, Adelina Luisa Nicasia
SCHEIN, Suzanna Fedorovna
SOLOMON, Joyce Elaine
STREICHER, Lyubov Lvovna
TERRIER-LAFFAILLE, Anne
WELLNER, Elsa
WOLF, Ilda von
Century unknown
PARGETER, Maude

QUARTET - WIND see WIND QUARTET

QUINTET - OTHER
18th Century A.D.
ANNA AMALIA, Duchess of Saxe-
Weimar
19th Century A.D.
CASELLA, Felicita
DESHAYES, Marie
LASCHANZKY, Mme.
20th Century A.D.
ABORN, Lora
AINSCOUGH, Juliana Mary
ALCALAY, Luna
ALEXANDRA, Liana
ALLEN, Judith Shatin
ALLIK, Kristi
ANDERSON-WUENSCH, Jean Mary
ANDREYEVA, Elena Fedorovna
ANTHONY, Gina
BAINBRIDGE, Beryl
BALLOU, Esther Williamson
BARBILLON, Jeanne
BARKLUND, Irma L.
BARRELL, Joyce Howard
BARRETT-THOMAS, N.
BEACH, Amy Marcy
BECLARD D'HARCOURT,
Marguerite
BELLAMY, Marian Meredith
BIRNSTEIN, Renate Maria
BLOOD, Esta Damesek
BLOOM, Shirley
BODENSTEIN-HOYME, Ruth E.
BORDERS, Barbara Ann
BOULOGNE, Julia R.C.
BRITAIN, Radie
BROOK, Gwendolyn Giffen
BUCZEK, Barbara Kazimiera
CAPDEVILA I GAYA, Merce
CAPUIS, Matilde
CARTER, Rosetta
CARWITHEN, Doreen
CATUNDA, Eunice do Monte Lima
CHANCE, Nancy Laird
CHAVES, Mary Elizabeth
CORY, Eleanor
COWLES, Darleen
CRAWFORD, Dawn Constance
DANFORTH, Frances A.
DEYTON, Camilla Hill
DIANDA, Hilda
DINESCU, Violeta
DLUGOSZEWSKI, Lucia
DU PAGE, Florence Elizabeth
DUDLEY, Marjorie Eastwood
DUSHKIN, Dorothy Smith
ELIAS, Graciela Morales de
ERHART, Dorothy
EVEN-OR, Mary
FONTYN, Jacqueline
FULCHER, Ellen Georgina
GARDNER, Kay
GEYRING, E.
GIPPS, Ruth
GODLA, Mary Ann
GOLOVINA, Olga Akimovna
GREENE, Margo Lynn
GRIEBLING, Karen Jean
GVAZAVA, Tamara Davidovna
GYRING, Elizabeth

HALL, Pauline
HALPERN, Stella
HARRISON, Pamela
HAYS, Doris Ernestine
HIND O'MALLEY, Pamela
HOOVER, Katherine
INWOOD, Mary Ruth Brink Berger
IVEY, Jean Eichelberger
JAMES, Dorothy E.
JOLY, Suzanne
KAMINSKY, Laura
KERN, Frida
KITAZUME, Yayoi
KOZAKIEVICH, Anna Abramovna
KUZMENKO, Larysa
LACHARTRE, Nicole Marie
LACKMAN, Susan C. Cohn
LATHROP, Gayle Posselt
LAUBER, Anne Marianne
LAZAR, Ella
LEBARON, Anne
LEE, Young Ja
LEFANU, Nicola Frances
LEJET, Edith
LORENZ, Ellen Jane
LOUDOVA, Ivana
LUNA DE ESPAILLAT, Margarita
LUND, Gudrun
LUSTIG, Leila Sarah
MACAULAY, Janice Michel
MACKIE, Shirley M.
MACONCHY, Elizabeth
MAGEAU, Mary Jane
MANUKIAN, Irina Eduardovna
MANZIARLY, Marcelle de
MARBE, Myriam
MARCUS, Bunita
MAREZ-OYENS, Tera de
MARSHALL, Pamela J.
MARTIN, Delores J.
MAYER, Lise Maria
MAZOUROVA, Jarmila
MEKEEL, Joyce
MERRIMAN, Margarita Leonor
MOORE, Mary Carr
MUNGER, Shirley
MUSGRAVE, Thea
NAITO, Akemi
NEMTEANU-ROTARU, Doina
NOWAK, Alison
OLIVEROS, Pauline
OSTRANDER, Linda Woodaman
PENTLAND, Barbara Lally
PERRY, Julia Amanda
PHILIPPART, Renee
PHILLIPS, Bryony
PIRES DOS REIS, Hilda
PIZER, Elizabeth Faw Hayden
POLIN, Claire
PREOBRAJENSKA, Vera Nicolaevna
PROCACCINI, Teresa
PTASZYNSKA, Marta
QUINTANILLA, Alba
RAVINALE, Irma
REID, Sarah Johnston
RICHER, Jeannine
ROBERT, Lucie
ROBERTSON, Donna Lou Nagey
ROESGEN-CHAMPION, Marguerite
Sara
ROGER, Denise
ROGERS, Patsy
RUBIN, Anna Ita
RUFF-STOEHR, Herta Maria
Klara
RUSCHE, Marjorie Maxine
SCHERCHEN, Tona
SCHWARTZ, Nan Louise
SCHWARZ, Friederike
SIKORA, Elzbieta
SILVERMAN, Faye-Ellen

SLIANOVA-MIZANDARI, Dagmara
Levanovna
SMYTH, Ethel Mary, Dame
SNYDER, Amy
SOENSTEVOLD, Maj
SOLOMON, Joyce Elaine
STEINER, Gitta Hana
STREATFIELD, Valma June
SWAIN, Freda Mary
SZAJNA-LEWANDOWSKA, Jadwiga
Helena
TAKAMI, Toyoko
TALMA, Louise
TELFER, Nancy Ellen
THEMMEN, Ivana Marburger
TKACH, Zlata Moiseyevna
USHER, Julia
VAN DE VATE, Nancy Hayes
VASILIEVA, Tatiana Ivanovna
VITO-DELVAUX, Berthe di
VON ZIERITZ, Grete
VORLOVA, Slavka
WARREN, Elinor Remick
WECKWERTH, Nancy
WEIGL, Vally
WHITLOCK, E. Florence
WHITTLE, Chris Mary-Francine
WILDSCHUT, Clara
WISHART, Betty Rose
WITKIN, Beatrice
ZAIDEL-RUDOLPH, Jeanne
ZAKRZEWSKA-NIKIPORCZYK,
Barbara Maria
ZECHLIN, Ruth
ZIFFRIN, Marilyn Jane
ZIMMERMANN, Margrit
ZIVKOVIC, Mirjana
Century unknown
JACQUE, Emilie

QUINTET - PIANO see PIANO QUINTET

QUINTET - STRING see STRING QUINTET

QUINTET - UNSPECIFIED
19th Century A.D.
DESHAYES, Marie
MAYER, Emilie
20th Century A.D.
BECLARD D'HARCOURT,
Marguerite
BOYD, Anne Elizabeth
BUCKLEY, Helen Dallam
CALCAGNO, Elsa
CAPUIS, Matilde
CECCONI-BOTELLA, Monic
CHRETIEN-GENARO, Hedwige
COLE, Ulric
DEMARQUEZ, Suzanne
EZELL, Helen Ingle
GAZAROSSIAN, Koharik
GLATZ, Helen Sinclair
HERBISON, Jeraldine Saunders
HOY, Bonnee L.
MATUSZCZAK, Bernadetta
MOORE, Mary Carr
POLIGNAC, Armande de, Countess
of Chabannes
SAINT JOHN, Kathleen Louise
SHLONSKY, Verdina
VON ZIERITZ, Grete
Century unknown
BOR, Modesta

QUINTET - WIND see WIND QUINTET

RECORDER
20th Century A.D.
ABE, Kyoko
AHRENS, Peg
ALCALAY, Luna

ALSTED, Birgitte
ANDERSON, Olive Jennie Paxton
ARCHER, Violet Balestreri
BAINBRIDGE, Beryl
BANDT, Rosalie Edith
BARNETT, Carol Edith
BARRELL, Joyce Howard
BEATH, Betty
BELL, Carla Huston
BOEHN, Liselotte
BOESSER, Dagma
BOYD, Anne Elizabeth
BRODIN, Lena Birgitta Elise
BROGUE, Roslyn Clara
CAMPAGNE, Conny
CHAMPION, Stephanie
COLACO OSORIO-SWAAB, Reine
COONEY, Cheryl Lee
CRAWFORD, Dorothy Lamb
DEMBO, Royce
DINESCU, Violeta
DINN, Freda
DOBSON, Elaine
DUSHKIN, Dorothy Smith
EGGLESTON, Anne E.
EHRHARDT, Else
ETHRIDGE, Jean
EVEN-OR, Mary
FREED, Dorothy Whitson
FRITSCH, Magda von
GAMBARINI, Costanza
GARDNER, Kay
GARTENLAUB, Odette
GLANVILLE-HICKS, Peggy
GLATZ, Helen Sinclair
GRAUBNER, Hannelore
HAZELRIG, Sylvia Jean Earnhart
HEINRICH, Adel Verna
HELBLING, Elsa
HELLER-REICHENBACH, Barbara
HOLLAND, Dulcie Sybil
HOVDA, Eleanor
HUNTER, Hilda
JANACEKOVA, Viera
JOCHSBERGER, Tzipora H.
JOHNSTON, Alison Aileen Annie
KEETMAN, Gunild
KING, Rebecca Clift
KUKUCK, Felicitas
KURIMOTO, Yoko
LARUELLE, Jeanne-Marie
LEAHY, Mary Weldon
LEECH, Renée
LUND, Gudrun
McINTOSH, Diana
McKENZIE, Sandra
McKINNEY, Mathilde
MAGEAU, Mary Jane
MALMLOEF-FORSSLING, Carin
MAREZ-OYENS, Tera de
MASSUMOTO, Kikuko
MURRAY, Margaret
OWEN, Angela Maria
PHILLIPS, Bryony
PIERCE, Alexandra
POSTON, Elizabeth
PTASZYNSKA, Marta
QUANTIN-SAULNIER, Denise
RAVIZE, Angele
REYNOLDS, Erma Grey Hogue
ROE, Eileen Betty
ROWE, Victoria
SAMSON, Valerie Brooks
SAMTER, Alice
SANDRESKY, Margaret Vardell
SANTOS-OCAMPO DE FRANCESCO,
    Amada Amy
SANZ, Rocio
SCHORR-WEILER, Eva
SILVER, Sheila Jane
STEELE, Lynn

STRUTT, Dorothy
SWAIN, Freda Mary
SZOENYI, Erzsebet
TACK, Annie
TAL, Marjo
TELFER, Nancy Ellen
TUCKER, Tui St. George
UIES, Margret
USHER, Julia
VANIER, Jeannine
VERRALL, Pamela Motley
VORLOVA, Slavka
WARNE, Katharine Mulky
WEISS, Arleta
ZIFFRIN, Marilyn Jane
Century unknown
SOKOLL, Christa

SAXOPHONE
19th Century A.D.
PICCOLOMINI, Marietta
20th Century A.D.
ALCALAY, Luna
ANDERSON, Beth
BAILEY, Judith Margaret
BANCER, Teresa Barbara
BIENVENU, Lily
BLOOM, Jane Ira
BORROFF, Edith
BOUCHARD, Linda L.
BRANDMAN, Margaret Susan
BREILH, Fernande
BRENET, Thérèse
BRITAIN, Radie
BROCKMAN, Jane E.
BROGUE, Roslyn Clara
BRUGGMANN, Heidi
BRUNER, Cheryl
BUCZEK, Barbara Kazimiera
CATUNDA, Eunice do Monte Lima
CECCONI-BOTELLA, Monic
CHANCE, Nancy Laird
CHRETIEN-GENARO, Hedwige
CLARKE, Rosemary
CLAYTON, Laura
CLOSTRE, Adrienne
COLIN, Jeanne
COME, Tilde
COWLES, Darleen
CRAWFORD, Dorothy Lamb
DESPORTES, Yvonne Berthe Melitta
ESCOT, Pozzi
FERRAND-TEULET, Denise
FINZI, Graciane
FONTYN, Jacqueline
GABRYS, Ewa Lucja Maria
GABUS, Monique
GILBERT, Janet Monteith
GILBERT, Pia
GONZAGA, Chiquinha
GOTKOVSKY, Ida-Rose Esther
GRESHAM, Ann
GROSSMAN, Deena
HAIK-VANTOURA, Suzanne
HANKS, Sybil Ann
HAZEN, Sara
HO, Wai On
HOLLAND, Dulcie Sybil
HOOVER, Katherine
HURLEY, Susan
JOLAS, Betsy
KLINKOVA, Zhivka
KOBLENZ, Babette
KOLB, Barbara
KUZMYCH, Christina
LAUBER, Anne Marianne
LEJET, Edith
LELEU, Jeanne
LOUVIER, Nicole
LUTYENS, Elisabeth
McMILLAN, Ann Endicott

MAURICE, Paule
MAYER, Lise Maria
MITCHELL, Janice Misurell
MORRISON, Julia Maria
NOBLE, Ann
OSAWA, Kazuko
OSTRANDER, Linda Woodaman
PERRY, Julia Amanda
PHILIBA, Nicole
POLIN, Claire
POULET DEFONTAINE, Madeleine
PREOBRAJENSKA, Vera Nicolaevna
REED, Marlyce Rae Polk
RICHER, Jeannine
ROBERT, Lucie
ROESGEN-CHAMPION, Marguerite
    Sara
ROGER, Denise
RUEFF, Jeanine
SHREVE, Susan Ellen
SHRUDE, Marilyn
SILVERMAN, Faye-Ellen
STILMAN-LASANSKY, Julia
STREATFIELD, Valma June
SWAIN, Freda Mary
SWISHER, Gloria Agnes Wilson
TAILLEFERRE, Germaine
TAKAMI, Toyoko
TATE, Phyllis
THEMMEN, Ivana Marburger
VAN APPLEDORN, Mary Jeanne
VAN DE VATE, Nancy Hayes
VAN HAUTE, Anna-Maria
VEHAR, Persis Anne
VIGNERON-RAMAKERS, Christiane-
    Josee
WALLACH, Joelle
WARING, Kate
WARREN, Betsy
WELANDER, Svea Goeta
WIENER, Eva Hannah
ZAKRZEWSKA-NIKIPORCZYK,
    Barbara Maria

SAXOPHONE AND ORCHESTRA OR STRINGS
20th Century A.D.
BIENVENU, Lily
GOTKOVSKY, Ida-Rose Esther
HAIK-VANTOURA, Suzanne
HANKS, Sybil Ann
KLOTZMAN, Dorothy Ann Hill
MAURICE, Paule
PHILIBA, Nicole
REED, Marlyce Rae Polk
RUEFF, Jeanine
THIEME, Kerstin Anja
VEHAR, Persis Anne
WARING, Kate

SAXOPHONE AND PIANO
20th Century A.D.
ARCHER, Violet Balestreri
BARRAINE, Elsa
BRANDMAN, Margaret Susan
BREILH, Fernande
BRUNER, Cheryl
CECCONI-BOTELLA, Monic
CLARKE, Rosemary
CLOSTRE, Adrienne
COME, Tilde
FERRAND-TEULET, Denise
FINZI, Graciane
FONTYN, Jacqueline
GOTKOVSKY, Ida-Rose Esther
HOLLAND, Dulcie Sybil
LE SIEGE, Annette
LELEU, Jeanne
LEONARD, Clair
MARI, Pierrette
MIMET, Anne Marie

OWEN, Blythe
PHILIBA, Nicole
PRICE, Deon Nielsen
RICCIOLI FRAZZI, Eva
ROBERT, Lucie
RUEFF, Jeanine
SHRUDE, Marilyn
SOLOMON, Elide M.
SWAIN, Freda Mary
SWISHER, Gloria Agnes Wilson
TATE, Phyllis
VAN DIJCK, Beatrice Madeleine
VEHAR, Persis Anne
WARWICK, Mary Carol
WEAVER, Carol Ann
YOUNG, Gayle

SEPTET
20th Century A.D.
ALCALAY, Luna
BAILEY, Judith Margaret
BODENSTEIN-HOYME, Ruth E.
BOFILL, Anna
BOLZ, Harriet
CHARBONNIER, Janine Andrée
CLARKE, Rosemary
CORY, Eleanor
CRAWFORD, Dorothy Lamb
DEDIEU-PETERS, Madeleine
DEMBO, Royce
DINESCU, Violeta
DUSHKIN, Dorothy Smith
DZIEWULSKA, Maria Amelia
ERNST, Siegrid
FALCINELLI, Rolande
FRONMUELLER, Frieda
FULLER-HALL, Sarah Margaret
GIFFORD, Helen Margaret
GITECK, Janice
GLATZ, Helen Sinclair
GRAHAM, Janet Christine
HSU, Wen-Ying
IVEY, Jean Eichelberger
KNOBLOCHOVA, Antonie
KUBO, Mayako
LEJET, Edith
LOPEZ ROVIROSA, Maria Isabel
LU, Yen
LUND, Gudrun
MACKIE, Shirley M.
McCOLLIN, Frances
McLEOD, Jennifer Helen
MAMLOK, Ursula
MAREZ-OYENS, Tera de
MARIC, Ljubica
MEKEEL, Joyce
MEL-BONIS
NOWAK, Alison
OLIVE, Vivienne
PENTLAND, Barbara Lally
PERRY, Julia Amanda
RICHTER, Marga
SILSBEE, Ann L.
STRUTT, Dorothy
SWAIN, Freda Mary
WHITLOCK, E. Florence
WISHART, Betty Rose
ZIELINSKA, Lidia

SEXTET
18th Century A.D.
ANNA AMALIA, Princess of Prussia
19th Century A.D.
FARRENC, Louise
ROSENHOFF, Orla
20th Century A.D.
ALCALAY, Luna
ALTER, Martha
ARIMA, Reiko
BACKES, Lotte
BALLOU, Esther Williamson

BARKIN, Elaine
BAUER, Marion Eugenie
BEECROFT, Norma Marian
BENAVENTE, Regina
BERGE, Irenee
BIRNSTEIN, Renate Maria
BOLZ, Harriet
BOUCHARD, Linda L.
BRUSH, Ruth Damaris
BUCZEK, Barbara Kazimiera
CAMPAGNE, Conny
CANAL, Marguerite
CARLOS, Wendy
CARNO, Zita
CHANDLER, Mary
CHRETIEN-GENARO, Hedwige
CORY, Eleanor
COULTHARD, Jean
COWLES, Darleen
CRAWFORD SEEGER, Ruth
DE BIASE BIDART, Lycia
DESPORTES, Yvonne Berthe Melitta
DIEMER, Emma Lou
DUSHKIN, Dorothy Smith
FALCINELLI, Rolande
FINE, Vivian
FINZI, Graciane
FISHER, Gladys Washburn
GARCIA ROBSON, Magdalena
GARTENLAUB, Odette
GITECK, Janice
GYRING, Elizabeth
HANNIKAINEN, Ann-Elise
HARA, Kazuko
HARRISON, Pamela
HIER, Ethel Glen
INWOOD, Mary Ruth Brink Berger
JANKOWSKI, Loretta Patricia
JAZWINSKI, Barbara
JIRACKOVA, Marta
JUENGER, Patricia
KATS-CHERNIN, Elena
KEMP, Dorothy Elizabeth Walter
KESSLER, Minuetta Schumiatcher
LEBARON, Anne
LEE, Hope Anne Keng-Wei
LEPEUT-LEVINE, Jeannine
LESICHKOVA, Lili
LOUDOVA, Ivana
LOWENSTEIN, Gunilla Marike
LUND, Gudrun
McCOLLIN, Frances
MAMLOK, Ursula
MARCUS, Bunita
MAREZ-OYENS, Tera de
MEKEEL, Joyce
MEL-BONIS
MESRITZ-VAN VELTHUYSEN, Annie
MUSGRAVE, Thea
NISHIKI, Kayoko
NOBLE, Ann
NORDENSTROM, Gladys Mercedes
NOWAK, Alison
OBROVSKA, Jana
OH, Sook Ja
OLIVE, Vivienne
OLIVEROS, Pauline
OSTRANDER, Linda Woodaman
PELEGRI, Maria Teresa
PHILLIPS, Bryony
PTASZYNSKA, Marta
RENIE, Henriette
SCHERCHEN, Tona
SEVERY, Violet Cavell
SMITH, Linda Catlin
SNYDER, Amy
SOLOMON, Elide M.
SPOENDLIN, Elisabeth
TAKAMI, Toyoko
TASHJIAN, B. Charmian
THEMMEN, Ivana Marburger

URNER, Catherine Murphy
USTVOLSKAYA, Galina Ivanovna
VAN HAUTE, Anna-Maria
WALDO, Elisabeth
WEAVER, Carol Ann
WEGENER-FRENSEL, Emmy Heil
WEIR, Judith
WYLIE, Ruth Shaw
Century unknown
JACQUE, Emilie

SPINET
17th Century A.D.
PRIOLI MORISINA, Marietta
SUARDA, Maria Virginia
20th Century A.D.
LOUIE, Alexina Diane

STRING QUARTET
18th Century A.D.
MIZANGERE, Marquise de la
MUELLNER, Johanna
SIRMEN, Maddalena Laura di
19th Century A.D.
BARKER, Laura Wilson
BERTIN, Louise Angelique
BLAHETKA, Marie Leopoldina
DAVIES, Llewela
HAENEL DE CRONENTHAL, Louise
  Augusta Marie Julia
HENSEL, Fanny Caecilia
HERITTE-VIARDOT, Louise Pauline
  Marie
KRALIK VON MAYERSWALDEN,
  Mathilde
LANGHANS, Louise
LODER, Kate Fanny
MAYER, Emilie
MOODY, Marie
POTT, Aloyse
PRESCOTT, Oliveria Louisa
RODRIGO, Maria
RONTGEN, Amanda
SMITH, Alice Mary
SWEPSTONE, Edith
WURM, Mary J.A.
20th Century A.D.
ABEJO, Sister M. Rosalina
ACCART, Eveline
ADERHOLDT, Sarah
AGABALIAN, Lidia Semyenovna
AHRENS, Peg
AINSCOUGH, Juliana Mary
ALCALAY, Luna
ALEXANDER, Leni
ALLIK, Kristi
ALMEN, Ruth
ALOTIN, Yardena
ALSTED, Birgitte
ANDERSON, Beth
ANDERSON, Ruth
ANDERSON-WUENSCH, Jean Mary
ANDREE, Elfrida
ARCHER, Violet Balestreri
ARIMA, Reiko
ARSEYEVA, Irina Vasilievna
AULIN, Laura Valborg
AUSTER, Lydia Martinovna
BACEWICZ, Grażyna
BACH, Maria
BACKES, Lotte
BALLOU, Esther Williamson
BANNISTER, Mary Jeanne Hoggard
BARBERIS, Mansi
BARBILLON, Jeanne
BARKIN, Elaine
BARON SUPERVIELLE, Susana
BARRELL, Joyce Howard
BARTHEL, Ursula
BAUER, Marion Eugenie
BAYEVA, Vera

KUZMYCH, Christina
LABEY, Charlotte Sohy
LACHARTRE, Nicole Marie
LACHOWSKA, Stefania
LACKMAN, Susan C. Cohn
LAMBERT, Cecily
LAMBRECHTS-VOS, Anna Catharina
LANG, Margaret Ruthven
LATHAM, Joan Seyler
LAUBER, Anne Marianne
LE BEAU, Louisa Adolpha
LEAHY, Mary Weldon
LEE, Chan-Hae
LEE, Hope Anne Keng-Wei
LEE, Hwaeja Yoo
LEE, Young Ja
LEECH, Renée
LEFANU, Nicola Frances
LEGINSKA, Ethel
LEIBOW, Ruth Irene
LEJEUNE-BONNIER, Eliane
LEVIN, Rami Yona
LEVITOVA, Ludmila Vladimirovna
LEVITSKAYA, Viktoria Sergeyevna
LIMA CRUZ, Maria Antonietta de
LINDEMAN, Anna Severine
LINNET, Anne
LLOYD, Caroline Parkhurst
LLUNELL SANAHUJA, Pepita
LOH, Kathy Jean
LOMON, Ruth
LONGWORTH, Helen
LOPUSKA-WYLEZYNSKA, Helena
LORENZ, Ellen Jane
LOUDOVA, Ivana
LOUIE, Alexina Diane
LUDVIG-PECAR, Nada
LUFF, Enid
LUND, Gudrun
LUSTIG, Leila Sarah
LUTHER, Mary
LUTYENS, Elisabeth
LVOVA, Julia Fedorovna
MACAULAY, Janice Michel
MACONCHY, Elizabeth
MacARTHUR, Fern
MacKENNA, Carmela
McALLISTER, Rita
McCLEARY, Fiona
McCOLLIN, Frances
McINTOSH, Diana
McKANN-MANCINI, Patricia
McKINNEY, Mathilde
McLAIN, Margaret Starr
McLAUGHLIN, Marian
McSWAIN, Augusta Geraldine
McTEE, Cindy Karen
MAGEAU, Mary Jane
MAILIAN, Elza Antonovna
MALDYBAYEVA, Zhyldyz
   Abdylasovna
MAMLOK, Ursula
MANNING, Kathleen Lockhart
MANUKIAN, Irina Eduardovna
MANZIARLY, Marcelle de
MARCUS, Ada Belle Gross
MAREZ-OYENS, Tera de
MARIC, Ljubica
MARKOV, Katherine Lee
MARSHALL, Kye
MARSHALL, M.E.
MARTIN, Delores J.
MARTINS, Maria de Lourdes
MARY BERNICE, Sister
MASON, Marilyn May
MATEVOSIAN, Araks Surenovna
MAUR, Sophie
MAYADAS, Priya
MAYER, Lise Maria
MEKEEL, Joyce
MELL, Gertrud Maria

MELOY, Elizabeth
MESRITZ-VAN VELTHUYSEN, Annie
MIAGI, Ester Kustovna
MIGRANYAN, Emma
MIKUSCH, Margarethe von
MILENKOVIC, Jelena
MILNE, Helen C.
MIRSHAKAR, Zarrina Mirsaidovna
MITCHELL, Janice Misurell
MKRTYCHIEVA, Virginia Nikitichna
MOE, Benna
MOON, Chloe Elizabeth
MOORE, Dorothy Rudd
MOORE, Mary Carr
MOORE, Wilda Maurine Ricks
MORETTO, Nelly
MORI, Junko
MOSUSOVA, Nadezda
MOSZUMANSKA-NAZAR, Krystyna
MRACEK, Ann Michelle
MUNKTELL, Helena Mathilda
MUSGRAVE, Thea
NAIKHOVICH-LOMAKINA, Fania
   Filippovna
NAZAROVA, Tatiana Borisovna
NAZIROVA, Elmira Mirza Rza kyzy
NELSON, Mary Anne
NEMTEANU-ROTARU, Doina
NEWMAN, Adelaide
NIEMACK, Ilza Louise
NIGHTINGALE, Barbara Diane
NIKOLSKAYA, Olga Vasilevna
NOETHLING, Elisabeth
NORUP, Helle Merete
NUNLIST, Juli
OBROVSKA, Jana
ODAGESCU, Irina
ODDONE SULLI-RAO, Elisabetta
OH, Sook Ja
O'LEARY, Jane Strong
OLIVEIRA, Sophie Marcondes de
   Mello
OLIVEROS, Pauline
OOSTERZEE, Cornelia van
ORENSTEIN, Joyce Ellin
OSETROVA-YAKOVLIEVA, Nina
   Alexandrovna
OSIANDER, Irene
OSTRANDER, Linda Woodaman
OTA, Junka
OWEN, Angela Maria
OWEN, Blythe
PABLOS CEREZO, Maria de
PALMER, Jane Hetherington
PARKER, Alice
PATINO ANDRADE, Graziela
PATTERSON, Andra
PAULL, Barberi
PEJACEVIC, Dora, Countess
PELEGRI, Maria Teresa
PENGILLY, Sylvia
PENTLAND, Barbara Lally
PEREIRA, Diana Maria
PERKIN, Helen
PERONI, Wally
PERRY, Julia Amanda
PERRY, Zenobia Powell
PETROVA-KRUPKOVA, Elena
PEYROT, Fernande
PFEIFFER, Irena
PHILLIPS, Karen Ann
PIECHOWSKA, Alina
PIETSCH, Edna Frieda
PIRES DOS REIS, Hilda
POINTON, Barbara
POLIGNAC, Armande de, Countess
   of Chabannes
POLIN, Claire
POULET DEFONTAINE, Madeleine
PRAVOSSUDOVITCH, Natalja
   Michajlovna

PREDIC-SAPER, Branislava
PREOBRAJENSKA, Vera Nicolaevna
PRICE, Florence Beatrice
PRIETO, Maria Teresa
PRIOLLI, Maria Luisa de Matos
PROCACCINI, Teresa
PSTROKONSKA-NAVRATIL,
   Grazyna Hanna
RADERMACHER, Erika
RAINIER, Priaulx
RAMM, Valentina Iosifovna
RAPOPORT, Eda
RECLI, Giulia
REED, Marlyce Rae Polk
RICHTER, Marga
RICKARD, Sylvia
ROBERT, Lucie
ROBERTSON, Donna Lou Nagey
RODRIGUEZ, Esther
ROE, Helen Mary Gabrielle
ROESGEN-CHAMPION, Marguerite
   Sara
ROGER, Denise
ROGERS, Clara Kathleen
ROGERS, Melicent Joan
ROMERO BARBOSA, Elena
ROMM, Rosalina Davidovna
ROOBENIAN, Amber
ROSAS FERNANDES, Maria Helena
ROSATO, Clorinda
ROSE OF JESUS, Sister
RUDALL, Eleonor C.
RUEFF, Jeanine
RUFF-STOEHR, Herta Maria Klara
RUSCHE, Marjorie Maxine
RUSSELL, Betsy A.
SAINT JOHN, Kathleen Louise
SAMUEL, Rhian
SAMVELIAN, Sofia Vardanovna
SANFORD, Grace Krick
SANTOS-OCAMPO DE FRANCESCO,
   Amada Amy
SANZ, Rocio
SCHELLER ZEMBRANO, Maria
SCHICK, Philippine
SCHONTHAL, Ruth E.
SCHORR-WEILER, Eva
SCHUBARTH, Dorothe
SCHWARTZ, Julie
SCLIAR, Esther
SCOVILLE, Margaret Lee
SEHESTED, Hilda
SELDEN-GOTH, Gizella
SELDON, Margery Stomme
SEMEGEN, Daria
SETTI, Kilza
SEWALL, Maud Gilchrist
SHAFFER, Jeanne Ellison
SHAVERZASHVILI, Tamara
   Antonovna
SHEPARD, Jean Ellen
SHEVITZ, Mimi
SHLONSKY, Verdina
SHORE, Clare
SIDORENKO, Tamara Stepanovna
SIKORA, Elzbieta
SILSBEE, Ann L.
SILVER, Sheila Jane
SILVERMAN, Faye-Ellen
SIMONS, Netty
SISTEK-DJORDJEVIC, Mirjana
SKALSKA-SZEMIOTH, Hanna Wanda
SKOWRONSKA, Janina
SMITH, Julia Frances
SMITH, Linda Catlin
SMYTH, Ethel Mary, Dame
SNIZKOVA-SKRHOVA, Jitka
SOLOMON, Joyce Elaine
SOLOMON, Mirrie Irma
SOMMERS, Daria E.
SOULAGE, Marcelle Fanny Henriette

SPAIN-DUNK, Susan
SPALDING, Eva Ruth
SPECHT, Judy Lavise
SPENCER, Marguerita
SPENCER, Williametta
SPOERRI-RENFER, Anna-
    Margaretha
SPONGBERG, Viola
STANLEY, Helen Camille
STEFANOVIC, Ivana
STEINER, Gitta Hana
STERNICKA-NIEKRASZOWA, Ilza
STILMAN-LASANSKY, Julia
STREICHER, Lyubov Lvovna
STRUTT, Dorothy
SUCHY, Gregoria Karides
SUTHERLAND, Margaret
SUZUE, Mariko
SWAIN, Freda Mary
SZEKELY, Katalin
SZYMANSKA, Iwonka Bogumila
TAILLEFERRE, Germaine
TAL, Marjo
TALMA, Louise
TATE, Phyllis
TAUTU, Cornelia
TELFER, Nancy Ellen
TERRY, Frances
TERZIAN, Alicia
THIEME, Kerstin Anja
THOMAS, Karen P.
THOMAS, Marilyn Taft
THOME, Diane
THOMSEN, Geraldine
THORKELSDOTTIR, Mist Barbara
TILICHEYEVA, Elena Nikolayevna
TUCKER, Tui St. George
TUCZEK, Felicia
TUICHEVA, Zumrad
TUMANIAN, Elizaveta Artashesovna
TURNER, Sara Scott
TURRIETTA, Cheryl Renée
TYER, Norma Phyllis
ULEHLA, Ludmila
UNDERWOOD, Frances Evangeline
URNER, Catherine Murphy
URRETA, Alicia
USTVOLSKAYA, Galina Ivanovna
UYEDA, Leslie
VAN BUREN, Alicia Keisker
VAN DE VATE, Nancy Hayes
VAN DIJCK, Beatrice Madeleine
VAN HAUTE, Anna-Maria
VASILIEVA, Tatiana Ivanovna
VAZQUEZ, Alida
VELLERE, Lucie Weiler
VINOGRADOVA, Vera
VINTULE, Ruta Evaldovna
VIRTUE, Constance Cochnower
VITO-DELVAUX, Berthe di
VLAD, Marina
VOLLENHOVEN, Hanna van
VON ZIERITZ, Grete
VORLOVA, Slavka
VORONINA, Tatiana Aleksandrovna
WALLACH, Joelle
WARNE, Katharine Mulky
WARNER, Sylvia Townsend
WEGENER-FRENSEL, Emmy Heil
WEIGL, Vally
WEISSBERG, Julia Lazerevna
WELANDER, Svea Goeta
WENDELBURG, Norma Ruth
WERTHEIM, Rosy
WHITEHEAD, Gillian
WHITLOCK, E. Florence
WILDSCHUT, Clara
WILES, Margaret Jones
WILLIAMS, Joan Franks
WILLS, Edwina Florence
WINROW, Barbara

WITBECK, Ariel Lea
WITNI, Monica
WOOD, Mabel
WYLIE, Ruth Shaw
YAKHNINA, Yevgenia Yosifovna
YAMPOLSCHI, Roseane
ZAKRZEWSKA-NIKIPORCZYK,
    Barbara Maria
ZARIPOVA, Naila Gatinovna
ZECHLIN, Ruth
ZHUBANOVA, Gaziza Akhmetovna
ZHVANETSKAIA, Inna Abramovna
ZIELINSKA, Lidia
ZIFFRIN, Marilyn Jane
ZIMMERMANN, Margrit
ZUBELDIA, Emiliana de
ZWILICH, Ellen Taaffe
Century unknown
SNODGRASS, Louise Harrison
WATKINS, Mary

STRING QUINTET
19th Century A.D.
ROSENHOFF, Orla
20th Century A.D.
BEACH, Amy Marcy
BIELEFELD, Ljuba
COX, Alison Mary
DANIELS, Nellie
DARE, Margaret Marie
DEDIEU-PETERS, Madeleine
DENBOW, Stefania Bjoerson
ERHART, Dorothy
FOWLER, Jennifer Joan
GOEBELS, Gisela
HOLST, Imogen Clare
KASILAG, Lucrecia R.
KERN, Frida
KICKINGER, Paula
LE BEAU, Louisa Adolpha
LVOVA, Julia Fedorovna
McLAUGHLIN, Marian
MESRITZ-VAN VELTHUYSEN, Annie
MUELLER-HERMANN, Johanna
NISS, Sofia Natanovna
ORENSTEIN, Joyce Ellin
PEYROT, Fernande
PHILLIPS, Vivian Daphne
PLONSEY, Jennifer
POPOVICI, Elise
PREOBRAJENSKA, Vera Nicolaevna
ROGERS, Patsy
ROKSETH, Yvonne
SAINT JOHN, Kathleen Louise
SZEKELY, Katalin
VON ZIERITZ, Grete
WHITLOCK, E. Florence
ZIFFRIN, Marilyn Jane

STRING TRIO
18th Century A.D.
SIRMEN, Maddalena Laura di
19th Century A.D.
BLANGINI, Mlle.
20th Century A.D.
ALOTIN, Yardena
ANDERSON, Olive Jennie Paxton
ANDERSON-WUENSCH, Jean Mary
ARCHER, Violet Balestreri
BADIAN, Maya
BAIL, Grace Shattuck
BALLOU, Esther Williamson
BARKIN, Elaine
BARREL, Joyce Howard
BECKON, Lettie Marie
BECLARD D'HARCOURT,
    Marguerite
BERG, Lily
BLOOD, Esta Damesek
BOBROW, Sanchie
BORROFF, Edith

BOUCHARD, Linda L.
BRINK-POTHUIS, Annie van den
BROCKMAN, Jane E.
BRUSH, Ruth Damaris
BURSTON, Maggie
CAMEU, Helza
CLARK, Florence Durrell
COX, Alison Mary
CRANE, Helen
DANEAU, Suzanne
DANIELS, Nellie
DAVIDSON, Tina
DIAMOND, Arline
DONAHUE, Bertha Terry
ECKHARDT-GRAMATTE, Sophie-
    Carmen
FINE, Vivian
GENTILE, Ada
GERSTMAN, Blanche Wilhelminia
GHANDAR, Ann
GRIEBLING, Karen Jean
GRZADZIELOWNA, Eleonora
GYRING, Elizabeth
HARRISON, Pamela
HAWLEY, Carolyn Jean
JENNINGS, Marie Pryor
JOHNSTON, Alison Aileen Annie
JOLLY, Margaret Anne
KANACH, Sharon E.
KICKINGER, Paula
KUZMYCH, Christina
LACKMAN, Susan C. Cohn
LAUBER, Anne Marianne
LAUFER, Beatrice
LEIBOW, Ruth Irene
LUND, Gudrun
LUTYENS, Elisabeth
MACONCHY, Elizabeth
McINTOSH, Diana
McLEOD, Jennifer Helen
MARTINEZ, Odaline de la
MIKUSCH, Margarethe von
MOON, Chloe Elizabeth
MOORE, Mary Carr
MOORE, Undine Smith
MOSZUMANSKA-NAZAR, Krystyna
NOWAK, Alison
OSTRANDER, Linda Woodaman
PAGH-PAAN, Younghi
PENTLAND, Barbara Lally
PERONI, Wally
PHILLIPS, Karen Ann
PRICE, Beryl
PROCACCINI, Teresa
RAINIER, Priaulx
RAPOPORT, Eda
ROGER, Denise
ROHNSTOCK, Sofie
RUFF-STOEHR, Herta Maria Klara
SAINT JOHN, Kathleen Louise
SAMUEL, Rhian
SHELTON, Margaret Meier
SMYTH, Ethel Mary, Dame
SOLOMON, Mirrie Irma
SPOENDLIN, Elisabeth
SPONGBERG, Viola
STEINER, Gitta Hana
STREATFIELD, Valma June
STRUTT, Dorothy
SUTHERLAND, Margaret
TAL, Marjo
TATE, Phyllis
TELFER, Nancy Ellen
THOME, Diane
TURRIETTA, Cheryl Rénée
URNER, Catherine Murphy
VAN DE VATE, Nancy Hayes
VELLERE, Lucie Weiler
WEGENER-FRENSEL, Emmy Heil
WILKINS, Margaret Lucy
ZWILICH, Ellen Taaffe

SYNTHESIZER
20th Century A.D.
ANDERSON, Julia McKinley
BANDT, Rosalie Edith
BROUK, Joanna
COULOMBE SAINT-MARCOUX,
  Micheline
GREENWALD, Jan Carol
KABAT, Julie Phyllis
MARTIN, Judith Reher
McLEAN, Priscilla Anne Taylor
OFFICER, Bronwyn Lee
PIZER, Elizabeth Faw Hayden
RADIGUE, Eliane
ROBERTS, Megan L.
ROSSO, Carol L.
SHEVITZ, Mimi
YOUNG, Gayle

TAPE RECORDER
20th Century A.D.
ABE, Kyoko
AHRENS, Peg
ALEXANDRA, Liana
ALLIK, Kristi
ANDERSON, Beth
ANDERSON, Ruth
ARCHER, Violet Balestreri
ARETZ, Isabel
AUSTIN, Dorothea
BABITS, Linda
BAILLY, Colette
BAIRD, Irene
BANDT, Rosalie Edith
BARKIN, Elaine
BARRIERE, Françoise
BAULD, Alison
BEECROFT, Norma Marian
BELLAVANCE, Ginette
BENAVENTE, Regina
BERTRAND, Ginette
BIBBY, Gillian Margaret
BLEY, Carla
BOFILL, Anna
BOUCHARD, Linda L.
BOYD, Anne Elizabeth
BRIGGS, Nancy Louise
CIOBANU, Maia
CLARKE, Rosemary
CLAYTON, Laura
COATES, Gloria Kannenberg
COHEN, Marcia
COULOMBE SAINT-MARCOUX,
  Micheline
COULTHARD, Jean
COWLES, Darleen
COX, Sally
DAIGLE, Sister Anne Cécile
DANFORTH, Frances A.
DAVIDSON, Tina
DIANDA, Hilda
DIEMER, Emma Lou
DITMARS, Elizabeth
DOBSON, Elaine
ELLERMAN, Helen
ESCOT, Pozzi
EVERETT-SALICCO, Betty Lou
FERREYRA, Beatriz
FRAJT, Ludmila
FRANCO, Clare
FRASER-MILLER, Gloria Jill
FRITZ, Sherilyn Gail
GABURO, Elizabeth
GALLINA, Jill
GARDNER, Kay
GARSCIA-GRESSEL, Janina
GILBERT, Janet Monteith
GILLICK, Emelyn Mildred Samuels
GITECK, Janice
GREENE, Margo Lynn
GREENWALD, Jan Carol

GRIGSBY, Beverly
GUBAIDULINA, Sofia Asgatovna
HAINES, Julia Howell
HAYS, Doris Ernestine
HOENDERDOS, Margriet
HOPKINS, Sarah
HOVDA, Eleanor
INJADO
IVEY, Jean Eichelberger
JANKOWSKI, Loretta Patricia
JENKINS, Susan Elaine
JUENGER, Patricia
KANACH, Sharon E.
KAVASCH, Deborah Helene
KELLEY, Patricia Ann
KOLB, Barbara
KUBO, Mayako
LA BARBARA, Joan
LACHARTRE, Nicole Marie
LARSON, Anna Barbara
LEACH, Mary Jane
LEBARON, Anne
LEE, Hope Anne Keng-Wei
LOCKWOOD, Annea Ferguson
LOH, Kathy Jean
LOUDOVA, Ivana
LOUIE, Alexina Diane
LUTYENS, Sally
McINTOSH, Diana
McKENZIE, Sandra
McLEAN, Priscilla Anne Taylor
McMILLAN, Ann Endicott
MAGEAU, Mary Jane
MAMLOK, Ursula
MARCUS, Ada Belle Gross
MARCUS, Bunita
MAREZ-OYENS, Tera de
MARTINEZ, Odaline de la
MATUSZCZAK, Bernadetta
MEACHEM, Margaret McKeen
  Ramsey
MEIGS, Melinda Moore
MEKEEL, Joyce
MENEELY-KYDER, Sarah Suderley
MILKULAK, Marcia Lee
MILLER, Elma
MORETTO, Nelly
MOSZUMANSKA-NAZAR, Krystyna
MUSGRAVE, Thea
NATVIG, Candace
NEMTEANU-ROTARU, Doina
NEWLIN, Dika
NOBLE, Ann
NORDENSTROM, Gladys Mercedes
NORRE, Dorcas
NOVA SONDAG, Jacqueline
OFFICER, Bronwyn Lee
OLIVEIRA, Jocy de
OLIVEROS, Pauline
ORAM, Daphne Blake
OSTRANDER, Linda Woodaman
PADE, Else Marie
PAULL, Barberi
PAYNE, Maggi
PENGILLY, Sylvia
PENTLAND, Barbara Lally
PIECHOWSKA, Alina
PIERCE, Alexandra
PIZER, Elizabeth Faw Hayden
POLIN, Claire
POOL, Jeannie Gayle
PRADELL, Leila
PSTROKONSKA-NAVRATIL,
  Grażyna Hanna
PTASZYNSKA, Marta
QUESADA, Virginia
RAN, Shulamit
RANTA-SHIDA, Shoko
REED, Marlyce Rae Polk
REID, Wendy
ROBERTS, Megan L.

SANGUESA, Iris
SCOVILLE, Margaret Lee
SEMEGEN, Daria
SHELTON, Margaret Meier
SHIELDS, Alice Ferree
SHORE, Clare
SIKORA, Elzbieta
SMITH, Ladonna Carol
SPIEGEL, Laurie
STANLEY, Helen Camille
TANN, Hilary
THOME, Diane
TURRIETTA, Cheryl Renée
ULEHLA, Ludmila
VAN DE VATE, Nancy Hayes
VAZQUEZ, Alida
VON GUNDEN, Heidi
WALLACH, Joelle
YOUNG, Gayle

TAPE AND INSTRUMENTS
20th Century A.D.
ALEJANDRO-DE LEON, Esther
ANDERSON, Beth
ANDERSON, Julia McKinley
BACKES, Lotte
BEAT, Janet Eveline
BEECROFT, Norma Marian
BELLAVANCE, Ginette
BENAVENTE, Regina
BERTRAND, Ginette
BLEY, Carla
BLISS, Marilyn S.
BOFILL, Anna
BOUCHARD, Linda L.
BOYD, Anne Elizabeth
BRUZDOWICZ, Joanna
CALAME, Genevieve
CAPDEVILA I GAYA, Merce
CLARKE, Rosemary
CLAYTON, Laura
COATES, Gloria Kannenberg
COHEN, Marcia
CORY, Eleanor
COULTHARD, Jean
DANFORTH, Frances A.
DIANDA, Hilda
DIEMER, Emma Lou
DITMARS, Elizabeth
DOBSON, Elaine
ESCOT, Pozzi
EVERETT-SALICCO, Betty Lou
FERREYRA, Beatriz
FRAJT, Ludmila
FRASER-MILLER, Gloria Jill
FRITZ, Sherilyn Gail
GRIGSBY, Beverly
HAYS, Doris Ernestine
HO, Wai On
INJADO
IVEY, Jean Eichelberger
JOLLEY, Florence Werner
JUENGER, Patricia
KELLEY, Patricia Ann
KOLB, Barbara
LA BARBARA, Joan
LACKMAN, Susan C. Cohn
LEE, Michelle
LEVEY, Lauren
LOCKWOOD, Annea Ferguson
LOUDOVA, Ivana
LOUIE, Alexina Diane
McINTOSH, Diana
McLEAN, Priscilla Anne Taylor
McMILLAN, Ann Endicott
MAGEAU, Mary Jane
MAREZ-OYENS, Tera de
MARTIN, Judith Reher
MEACHEM, Margaret McKeen
  Ramsey
MOLAVA, Pamela May

MONK, Meredith
OLIVEROS, Pauline
ORAM, Daphne Blake
PADE, Else Marie
PAULL, Barberi
PAYNE, Maggi
PENGILLY, Sylvia
PENTLAND, Barbara Lally
POOL, Jeannie Gayle
PSTROKONSKA-NAVRATIL,
  Grażyna Hanna
RANTA-SHIDA, Shoko
REID, Wendy
SAINT JOHN, Kathleen Louise
SANDIFUR, Ann Elizabeth
SCOVILLE, Margaret Lee
SETO, Robin
SIKORA, Elzbieta
SILSBEE, Ann L.
SILVERMAN, Faye-Ellen
SNOW, Mary McCarty
SOUTHAM, Ann
STANLEY, Helen Camille
THOMAS, Karen P.
THOMAS, Marilyn Taft
THOME, Diane
TOYAMA, Mihoko
TURRIETTA, Cheryl Renée
VERHAALEN, Sister Marion
VIERK, Lois
VON GUNDEN, Heidi
WASKO, Christine
WHITE, Ruth S.

THEORBO
18th Century A.D.
BERTHE, Mme.
LOUVENCOURT, Mlle. de
20th Century A.D.
BERZON, Asya Yevseyevna
DELAHAYE, Cécile
MATUSZCZAK, Bernadetta

THREE INSTRUMENTS AND ORCHESTRA OR STRINGS
20th Century A.D.
ACCART, Eveline
ARRIEU, Claude
BALLOU, Esther Williamson
CALCAGNO, Elsa
ECKHARDT-GRAMATTE, Sophie-
  Carmen
ELIAS, Graciela Morales de
FINE, Vivian
MATUSZCZAK, Bernadetta
NEWLIN, Dika
PLE-CAUSSADE, Simone
PROCACCINI, Teresa
RAVINALE, Irma
ROESGEN-CHAMPION, Marguerite
  Sara
VON ZIERITZ, Grete

TIMPANI
18th Century A.D.
DE GAMBARINI, Elisabetta
20th Century A.D.
ANDERSON, Olive Jennie Paxton
ARCHER, Violet Balestreri
BARRETT-THOMAS, N.
BEECROFT, Norma Marian
BLOM, Diane
BRITAIN, Radie
BROCKMAN, Jane E.
CHANCE, Nancy Laird
COATES, Gloria Kannenberg
COLERIDGE-TAYLOR, Avril
  Gwendolen
COULTHARD, Jean
CULP, Paula Newell
DANFORTH, Frances A.

DEDIEU-PETERS, Madeleine
DILLON, Fannie Charles
ECKHARDT-GRAMATTE, Sophie-
  Carmen
ERNST, Siegrid
FULLER-HALL, Sarah Margaret
GLANVILLE-HICKS, Peggy
GLATZ, Helen Sinclair
GRIMAUD, Yvette
GYRING, Elizabeth
HARRIS, Ruth Berman
HO, Wai On
HOVDA, Eleanor
HYDE, Miriam Beatrice
KAHMANN, Chesley
KERN, Frida
KUZMYCH, Christina
LA BARBARA, Joan
LAPEYRE, Therese
LEON, Tania Justina
LITTLEJOHN, Joan Anne
LUTYENS, Elisabeth
MIRANDA, Sharon Moe
MORRISON, Julia Maria
NOBLE, Ann
PARKER, Alice
PETROVA, Mara
PHILLIPS, Bryony
POLIN, Claire
PREDIC-SAPER, Branislava
PREOBRAJENSKA, Vera Nicolaevna
RAVINALE, Irma
ROGERS, Sharon Elery
RUSCHE, Marjorie Maxine
SALQUIN, Hedy
STANLEY, Helen Camille
VIGNERON-RAMAKERS, Christiane-
  Josee
WANG, An-Ming
WEIGL, Vally
WENDELBURG, Norma Ruth
ZAKRZEWSKA-NIKIPORCZYK,
  Barbara Maria

TRIO-OTHER
17th Century A.D.
SUARDA, Maria Virginia
18th Century A.D.
ANNA AMALIA, Princess of Prussia
BARTHELEMON, Cecilia Maria
BON, Anna
LOUIS, Mme.
PHILHARMONICA, Mrs.
POUILLAU, Mlle.
19th Century A.D.
CANDEILLE, Amelie Julie
CIBBINI, Katherina
CORMONTAN, Theodora
CRETI, Marianna de Rocchis
GRANDVAL, Marie Felicie Clemence
  de Reiset, Vicomtesse de
KERN, Louise
KRAEHMER, Caroline
LEONARDO, Luisa
LIND, Jenny
NORRIS, Mary
POLAK, Nina
20th Century A.D.
AARNE, Els
AGABALIAN, Lidia Semyenovna
AGUDELO MURGUIA, Graciela
AHRENS, Peg
AINSCOUGH, Juliana Mary
ALCALAY, Luna
ALEXANDRA, Liana
ALLEN, Judith Shatin
ALLIK, Kristi
ALTER, Martha
ALVES DE SOUSA, Berta Candida
ANDERSON, Ruth
AUFDERHEIDE, May

AUTENRIETH, Helma
BAADER-NOBS, Heidi
BACEWICZ, Grazyna
BACKES, Lotte
BADIAN, Maya
BAILEY, Judith Margaret
BAILLY, Colette
BALLOU, Esther Williamson
BANNISTER, Mary Jeanne Hoggard
BARADAPRANA, Pravrajika
BARKLUND, Irma L.
BARNS, Ethel
BARRELL, Joyce Howard
BARTHEL, Ursula
BARTLETT, Floy Little
BAUER, Marion Eugenie
BEAT, Janet Eveline
BEATH, Betty
BEATON, Isabella
BECLARD D'HARCOURT, Marguerite
BIENVENU, Lily
BINGHAM, Judith
BIRNSTEIN, Renate Maria
BLISS, Marilyn S.
BLOOD, Esta Damesek
BLOOM, Jane Ira
BOFILL, Anna
BOLZ, Harriet
BOND, Victoria Ellen
BOONE, Clara Lyle
BORRAS I FORNELL, Teresa
BOYD, Anne Elizabeth
BRANSCOMBE, Gena
BRENET, Therese
BRIGGS, Nancy Louise
BRINK-POTHUIS, Annie van den
BRITAIN, Radie
BROCKMAN, Jane E.
BROGUE, Roslyn Clara
BRUSH, Ruth Damaris
BRUZDOWICZ, Joanna
BUCZEK, Barbara Kazimiera
BURKE, Loretto
BURSTON, Maggie
CALLAWAY, Ann
CAMPAGNE, Conny
CAPDEVILA I GAYA, Merce
CARMEN MARINA
CECCONI-BATES, Augusta
CECCONI-BOTELLA, Monic
CHAMPION, Stephanie
CHANDLER, Mary
CHAPIRO, Fania
CHARBONNIER, Janine Andrée
CHAVES, Mary Elizabeth
CIOBANU, Maia
CLARKE, Rosemary
COATES, Gloria Kannenberg
COHEN, Marcia
COLAÇO OSORIO-SWAAB, Reine
COLTRANE, Alice McLeod
CONRAD, Laurie M.
CORY, Eleanor
COULTHARD, Jean
COWLES, Darleen
DANFORTH, Frances A.
DANIELA, Carmen
DANIELS, Mabel Wheeler
DAVIES, Margaret
DAVIS, Eleanor Maud
DE BIASE BIDART, Lycia
DEMBO, Royce
DIAMOND, Arline
DIEMER, Emma Lou
DLUGOSZEWSKI, Lucia
DOBSON, Elaine
DONAHUE, Bertha Terry
DORABIALSKA, Julia Helena
DRING, Madeleine
DUBANOWICZ, Wanda
DUDLEY, Marjorie Eastwood

DUSHKIN, Dorothy Smith
DVORKIN, Judith
EAKLOR, Vicki
EASTES, Helen Marie
EIRIKSDOTTIR, Karolina
ERDING, Susanne
EUBANKS, Rachel Amelia
EUTENEUER-ROHRER, Ursula
  Henrietta
EVEN-OR, Mary
FAIRLIE, Margaret C.
FINE, Vivian
FISHER, Gladys Washburn
FLEITES, Virginia
FONTYN, Jacqueline
FORMAN, Joanne
FRASER-MILLER, Gloria Jill
FRASIER, Jane
FULLER-HALL, Sarah Margaret
GARCIA ROBSON, Magdalena
GARDNER, Kay
GARSCIA-GRESSEL, Janina
GARTENLAUB, Odette
GEBUHR, Ann Karen
GEORGE, Lila-Gene
GIDEON, Miriam
GIFFORD, Helen Margaret
GILBERT, Pia
GIPPS, Ruth
GLANVILLE-HICKS, Peggy
GLATZ, Helen Sinclair
GLAZIER, Beverly
GOEBELS, Gisela
GOULD, Elizabeth Davies
GREGORI, Nininha
GRIEBLING, Karen Jean
GROSSMAN, Deena
GUMMER, Phyllis Mary
GURAIEB KURI, Rosa
GYRING, Elizabeth
HAHN, Sandra Lea
HALL, Pauline
HARA, Kazuko (1)
HARRIS, Ruth Berman
HART, Elizabeth Jane Smith
HAYS, Doris Ernestine
HAZELRIG, Sylvia Jean Earnhart
HEALE, Helene
HERBISON, Jeraldine Saunders
HIER, Ethel Glen
HIND O'MALLEY, Pamela
HOOVER, Katherine
HORNBACK, Sister Mary Gisela
HUGHES, Sister Martina
HUGH-JONES, Elaine
HYDE, Miriam Beatrice
HYSON, Winifred Prince
INGLEFIELD, Ruth Karin
IRMAN-ALLEMANN, Regina
ISSLE, Christa
ISZKOWSKA, Zofia
JACKSON, Barbara May
JAMES, Dorothy E.
JEPPSSON, Kerstin Maria
JOHNSTON, Alison Aileen Annie
JOLAS, Betsy
JOLLY, Margaret Anne
JONES, Sister Ida
KAHMANN, Chesley
KAMINSKY, Laura
KANACH, Sharon E.
KARNITSKAYA, Nina Andreyevna
KATS-CHERNIN, Elena
KEEFER, Euphrosyne
KELLER, Ginette
KERN, Frida
KETTERING, Eunice Lea
KITAZUME, Yayoi
KLEBE, Willemijntje
KNOBLOCHOVA, Antonie
KOBLENZ, Babette

KOELLING, Eloise
KOSSE, Roberta
KUKUCK, Felicitas
LACHOWSKA, Stefania
LACKMAN, Susan C. Cohn
LAGO
LAITMAN, Lori
LARSEN, Elizabeth Brown
LATHROP, Gayle Posselt
LAUBER, Anne Marianne
LEBARON, Anne
LEE, Hope Anne Keng-Wei
LEE, Hwaeja Yoo
LEE, Young Ja
LEFANU, Nicola Frances
LEJEUNE-BONNIER, Eliane
LIPSCOMB, Helen
LOMON, Ruth
LOWENSTEIN, Gunilla Marike
LUNA DE ESPAILLAT, Margarita
LUND, Gudrun
LUTYENS, Elisabeth
LUTYENS, Sally
MACKIE, Shirley M.
MacKENNA, Carmela
McINTOSH, Diana
McLAUGHLIN, Marian
McLEAN, Priscilla Anne Taylor
MAGEAU, Mary Jane
MAGENTA, Maria
MANZIARLY, Marcelle de
MARBE, Myriam
MARCUS, Ada Belle Gross
MARIC, Ljubica
MARKIEWICZOWNA, Wladyslawa
MASONER, Elizabeth L.
MASSUMOTO, Kikuko
MAXWELL, Jacqueline Perkinson
MAZOUROVA, Jarmila
MEGEVAND, Denise
MEL-BONIS
MELOY, Elizabeth
MILENKOVIC, Jelena
MIYAKE, Haruna
MOON, Chloe Elizabeth
MOORE, Undine Smith
MORRISON, Julia Maria
MOSZUMANSKA-NAZAR, Krystyna
MURAKUMO, Ayako
MURAO, Sachie
MUSGRAVE, Thea
NIEWIADOMSKA, Barbara
NIKOLAYEVA, Tatiana Petrovna
NIKOLSKAYA, Lyubov Borisovna
NOBLE, Ann
NOHE, Beverly
NOVA SONDAG, Jacqueline
NOVI, Anna Beate
NOWAK, Alison
OBROVSKA, Jana
O'LEARY, Jane Strong
OLIVE, Vivienne
OLIVEROS, Pauline
ORENSTEIN, Joyce Ellin
OSAWA, Kazuko
OWEN, Angela Maria
OWEN, Blythe
PACK, Beulah Frances
PALMER, Lynne Wainwright
PATERSON, Wilma
PATTERSON, Andra
PELEGRI, Maria Teresa
PENGILLY, Sylvia
PENTLAND, Barbara Lally
PERRY, Zenobia Powell
PEYROT, Fernande
PHILIBA, Nicole
PHILLIPS, Karen Ann
PIECHOWSKA, Alina
PIERCE, Alexandra
PIERCE, Sarah Anderson

PIRES DOS REIS, Hilda
PLONSEY, Jennifer
POLIN, Claire
POPOVICI, Elise
POSTON, Elizabeth
PRAVOSSUDOVITCH, Natalja
  Michajlovna
PREOBRAJENSKA, Vera Nicolaevna
PRICE, Deon Nielsen
PRICE, Florence Beatrice
RAN, Shulamit
RAPOPORT, Eda
RAVINALE, Irma
REID, Sarah Johnston
RENIE, Henriette
RESPIGHI, Elsa
REYNOLDS, Erma Grey Hogue
ROBERT, Lucie
ROBERTSON, Donna Lou Nagey
ROBLES, Marisa
ROCHAT, Andrée
ROCHEROLLE, Eugenie Katherine
RODRIGUEZ BELLA, Catalina
ROESGEN-CHAMPION, Marguerite
  Sara
ROGER, Denise
ROGERS, Susan Whipple
ROWE, Victoria
ROYSE, Mildred Barnes
RUFF-STOEHR, Herta Maria Klara
SAITO-NODA, Eva
SALQUIN, Hedy
SAMSON, Valerie Brooks
SAMSUTDINOVA, Magira
SAMTER, Alice
SANDRESKY, Margaret Vardell
SCHLOSS, Myrna Frances
SCHORR-WEILER, Eva
SCHUBARTH, Dorothe
SHEPARD, Jean Ellen
SHLONSKY, Verdina
SHUTTLEWORTH, Anne-Marie
SILSBEE, Ann L.
SILVER, Sheila Jane
SILVERMAN, Faye-Ellen
SIMONS, Netty
SINGER, Jeanne
SMYTH, Ethel Mary, Dame
SNIZKOVA-SKRHOVA, Jitka
SODRE, Joanidia
SOLOMON, Joyce Elaine
STANLEY, Helen Camille
STEELE, Lynn
STEFANOVIC, Ivana
STEINER, Gitta Hana
STERNICKA-NIEKRASZOWA, Ilza
STREATFIELD, Valma June
STRUCK, Ilse
STRUTT, Dorothy
SUCHY, Gregoria Karides
SWISHER, Gloria Agnes Wilson
SYNOWIEC, Ewa
SZOENYI, Erzsebet
SZYMANSKA, Iwonka Bogumila
TAKAMI, Toyoko
TAL, Marjo
TARLOW, Karen Anne
TATE, Phyllis
TATTON, Madeleine
TAUTU, Cornelia
TELFER, Nancy Ellen
TERZIAN, Alicia
THEMMEN, Ivana Marburger
THOME, Diane
THORKELSDOTTIR, Mist Barbara
TOWER, Joan
TUCKER, Tui St. George
URNER, Catherine Murphy
USTVOLSKAYA, Galina Ivanovna
UYTTENHOVE, Yolande
VAN DE VATE, Nancy Hayes

VAN DYCK, Beatrice Madeleine
VAN EPEN-DE GROOT, Else
　Antonia
VANIER, Jeannine
VELLERE, Lucie Weiler
VON GUNDEN, Heidi
VON ZIERITZ, Grete
VORLOVA, Slavka
WALLACH, Joelle
WALTERS, Teresa
WANG, An-Ming
WANG, Qiang
WARING, Kate
WARNE, Katharine Mulky
WARREN, Betsy
WEIGL, Vally
WELANDER, Svea Goeta
WHITTLE, Chris Mary-Francine
WOLLNER, Gertrude Price
WOOD, Mary Knight
ZAIMONT, Judith Lang
ZALLMAN, Arlene
ZECHLIN, Ruth
Century unknown
　RAPIN-GERBER, Eleonore

TRIO - PIANO see PIANO TRIO

TRIO - STRING - see STRING TRIO

TRIO - WIND see WIND TRIO

TRIO - UNSPECIFIED
18th-century
　BERTHE, Mme.
　SIRMEN, Maddalena Laura di
19th Century A.D.
　GRANDVAL, Marie Felicie Clemence
　　de Reiset, Vicomtesse de
　HAASS, Maria Catharina
　LAMBERT, Agnes
20th Century A.D.
　AARNE, Els
　ARQUIT, Nora Harris
　BAILLY, Colette
　BECLARD D'HARCOURT,
　　Marguerite
　BOSMANS, Henriette Hilda
　CARTER, Buenta MacDaniel
　CHACON LASAUCA, Emma
　CHAMINADE, Cecile Louise
　　Stephanie
　CHANCE, Nancy Laird
　CHEBOTARIAN, Gayane
　　Movsesovna
　COLTRANE, Alice McLeod
　CRISP, Barbara
　EMERY, Dorothy Radde
　FINE, Vivian
　GARUTA, Lucia Yanovna
　GREENWALD, Jan Carol
　HAIK-VANTOURA, Suzanne
　HEDSTROEM, Ase
　HERBISON, Jeraldine Saunders
　HOWE, Mary Alberta Bruce
　KOZAKIEVICH, Anna Abramovna
　KRZANOWSKA, Grażyna
　LARKIN, Deirdre
　LE BEAU, Louisa Adolpha
　MARSHALL, M.E.
　MESNEY, Dorothy Taylor
　RISHER, Anna Priscilla
　RUFF-STOEHR, Herta Maria
　　Klara
　SCHEIN, Suzanna Fedorovna
　SOLOMON, Joyce Elaine
　TERRIER-LAFFAILLE, Anne
　WILLIAMS, Joan Franks

**TRIPLE CONCERTO see THREE
　INSTRUMENTS and ORCHESTRA**

TROMBONE
20th Century A.D.
　AGUDELO MURGUIA, Graciela
　ALCALAY, Luna
　ALEXANDRA, Liana
　ALLEN, Judith Shatin
　ANTHONY, Gina
　ARCHER, Violet Balestreri
　ARMER, Elinor Florence
　BADIAN, Maya
　BARRAINE, Elsa
　BARRATT, Carol Ann
　BIRNSTEIN, Renate Maria
　BLISS, Marilyn S.
　BOND, Victoria Ellen
　BRANDMAN, Margaret Susan
　BREUIL, Helene
　BRITAIN, Radie
　BUMP, Mary Crane
　CABRERA, Silvia Maria Pires
　CALAME, Genevieve
　CALLAWAY, Ann
　CECCONI-BOTELLA, Monic
　CHARBONNIER, Janine Andrée
　CHRETIEN-GENARO, Hedwige
　CIOBANU, Maia
　CLARKE, Rosemary
　COATES, Gloria Kannenberg
　COME, Tilde
　CORY, Eleanor
　COULTHARD, Jean
　CRAWFORD, Dorothy Lamb
　DESPORTES, Yvonne Berthe Melitta
　DIANDA, Hilda
　DLUGOSZEWSKI, Lucia
　DRENNAN, Dorothy Carter
　DU PAGE, Florence Elizabeth
　EASTES, Helen Marie
　ENDRES, Olive Philomene
　FORMAN, Joanne
　FRITZ, Sherilyn Gail
　FRONMUELLER, Frieda
　GARTENLAUB, Odette
　GIFFORD, Helen Margaret
　GITECK, Janice
　GLATZ, Helen Sinclair
　GLAZIER, Beverly
　GONTARENKO, Galina Nikolayevna
　GUBAIDULINA, Sofia Asgatovna
　HOOVER, Katherine
　IVEY, Jean Eichelberger
　JACOB, Elizabeth Marie
　KADIMA, Hagar Yonith
　KATS-CHERNIN, Elena
　KORNILOVA, Tatiana Dmitrevna
　KUBO, Mayako
　LARSEN, Elizabeth Brown
　LEBARON, Anne
　LEJET, Edith
　LOMON, Ruth
　LOUDOVA, Ivana
　LU, Yen
　LUND, Gudrun
　MACAULAY, Janice Michel
　McLEAN, Priscilla Anne Taylor
　MAREZ-OYENS, Tera de
　MARIC, Ljubica
　MAZOUROVA, Jarmila
　MILLER, Elma
　MORRISON, Julia Maria
　NATVIG, Candace
　NIKOLSKAYA, Lyubov Borisovna
　PATTERSON, Andra
　PENTLAND, Barbara Lally
　PEYROT, Fernande
　PHILIBA, Nicole
　PHILLIPS, Bryony
　PIRES DOS REIS, Hilda
　POLIN, Claire
　POPOVICI, Elise
　PTASZYNSKA, Marta

RICHER, Jeannine
RICHTER, Marga
ROBERTSON, Donna Lou Nagey
RUEFF, Jeanine
RUSCHE, Marjorie Maxine
SCHERCHEN, Tona
SEMEGEN, Daria
SIEGRIST, Beatrice
SNYDER, Amy
SPENCER, Williametta
STANLEY, Helen Camille
STEINER, Gitta Hana
THEMMEN, Ivana Marburger
VAN DE VATE, Nancy Hayes
VELLERE, Lucie Weiler
VIERK, Lois
VON GUNDEN, Heidi
VON ZIERITZ, Grete
WEIGL, Vally
WHITEHEAD, Gillian
WIENER, Eva Hannah
ZECHLIN, Ruth

**TROMBONE AND ORCHESTRA OR
STRINGS**
20th Century A.D.
　BALENOVIC, Draga
　DESPORTES, Yvonne Berthe Melitta
　GOTKOVSKY, Ida-Rose Esther
　ISAKOVA, Aida Petrovna
　LUND, Gudrun
　MARSHALL, Kye
　MORLEY, Nina Dianne
　SCHERCHEN, Tona
　THEMMEN, Ivana Marburger
　UYTTENHOVE, Yolande

TROMBONE AND PIANO
20th Century A.D.
　ARRIEU, Claude
　BARTHEL, Ursula
　BREUIL, Helene
　CHUDOVA, Tatiana Alekseyevna
　COME, Tilde
　DESPORTES, Yvonne Berthe Melitta
　DU PAGE, Florence Elizabeth
　GARTENLAUB, Odette
　GONTARENKO, Galina Nikolayevna
　GOTKOVSKY, Ida-Rose Esther
　KATS-CHERNIN, Elena
　LOUDOVA, Ivana
　METALLIDI, Zhanneta Lazarevna
　ROBERTSON, Donna Lou Nagey
　SIEGRIST, Beatrice
　SPENCER, Williametta
　STEINER, Gitta Hana
　VITO-DELVAUX, Berthe di
　WENDELBURG, Norma Ruth

TRUMPET
18th Century A.D.
　ANNA AMALIA, Princess of Prussia
　MARTINEZ, Marianne
19th Century A.D.
　SZYMANOWSKA, Maria Agata
20th Century A.D.
　ABE, Kyoko
　ABRAMOVA, Sonia Pinkhasovna
　ACCART, Eveline
　ALCALAY, Luna
　ALEXANDRA, Liana
　ALLEN, Judith Shatin
　ALTER, Martha
　ANDERSON, Olive Jennie Paxton
　ANDERSON-WUENSCH, Jean Mary
　ANTHONY, Gina
　ARCHER, Violet Balestreri
　ARMER, Elinor Florence
　BACEWICZ, Grażyna
　BACKES, Lotte
　BADIAN, Maya

BAIKADAMOVA, Baldyrgan
   Bakhitzhanovna
BAIL, Grace Shattuck
BAILLY, Colette
BALLOU, Esther Williamson
BARON SUPERVIELLE, Susana
BARRATT, Carol Ann
BARRELL, Joyce Howard
BLOOM, Jane Ira
BOND, Victoria Ellen
BOULOGNE, Julia R.C.
BRANDMAN, Margaret Susan
BRENET, Therese
BRUSH, Ruth Damaris
BUCHANAN, Dorothy Quita
CABRERA, Silvia Maria Pires
CALAME, Genevieve
CALLAWAY, Ann
CECCONI-BATES, Augusta
CHANDLER, Mary
CHARBONNIER, Janine Andrée
CHRETIEN-GENARO, Hedwige
CLARKE, Rosemary
CLOSTRE, Adrienne
COME, Tilde
CORY, Eleanor
COULTHARD, Jean
COWLES, Darleen
CRAWFORD, Dawn Constance
CRAWFORD, Dorothy Lamb
DEDIEU-PETERS, Madeleine
DESPORTES, Yvonne Berthe Melitta
DIAMOND, Arline
DIANDA, Hilda
DLUGOSZEWSKI, Lucia
DOBBINS, Lori
ECKHARDT-GRAMATTE, Sophie-
   Carmen
ENDRES, Olive Philomene
EVEN-OR, Mary
FAUTCH, Sister Magdalen
FINE, Vivian
FORMAN, Joanne
FRASER-MILLER, Gloria Jill
FRITZ, Sherilyn Gail
FRONMUELLER, Frieda
FULLER-HALL, Sarah Margaret
GIFFORD, Helen Margaret
GRZADZIELOWNA, Eleonora
GUBAIDULINA, Sofia Asgatovna
HALL, Pauline
HARRIS, Ruth Berman
HAYS, Doris Ernestine
HOOVER, Katherine
IVEY, Jean Eichelberger
JACOB, Elizabeth Marie
JANKOWSKI, Loretta Patricia
KADIMA, Hagar Yonith
KAHMANN, Chesley
KALOGRIDOU, Maria
KAVASCH, Deborah Helene
KELLER, Ginette
KITAZUME, Yayoi
KLINKOVA, Zhivka
KOBLENZ, Babette
LAUFER, Beatrice
LAYMAN, Pamela
LEJET, Edith
LOMON, Ruth
LU, Yen
LUND, Gudrun
MACAULAY, Janice Michel
McKENZIE, Sandra
McLIN, Lena
MAMLOK, Ursula
MAREZ-OYENS, Tera de
MATUSZCZAK, Bernadetta
MAZOUROVA, Jarmila
MEACHEM, Margaret McKeen
   Ramsey
MIRON, Tsipora

MORETTO, Nelly
MORRISON, Julia Maria
NOBLE, Ann
NOWAK, Alison
OH, Sook Ja
OLIVEROS, Pauline
OWEN, Blythe
PATTERSON, Andra
PAULL, Barberi
PENTLAND, Barbara Lally
PERRY, Julia Amanda
PEYROT, Fernande
PHILIBA, Nicole
PHILLIPS, Bryony
PIRES DOS REIS, Hilda
PLE-CAUSSADE, Simone
PLONSEY, Jennifer
POLIN, Claire
POPOVICI, Elise
PROCACCINI, Teresa
PSTROKONSKA-NAVRATIL,
   Grażyna Hanna
PTASZYNSKA, Marta
ROBERTSON, Donna Lou Nagey
ROCHAT, Andrée
ROE, Eileen Betty
ROGER, Denise
ROGERS, Sharon Elery
RUEFF, Jeanine
RUSCHE, Marjorie Maxine
SAINT JOHN, Kathleen Louise
SCHERCHEN, Tona
SHADWELL, Nancy
STILMAN-LASANSKY, Julia
STREATFIELD, Valma June
SWAIN, Freda Mary
SWISHER, Gloria Agnes Wilson
SYNOWIEC, Ewa
TELFER, Nancy Ellen
THEMMEN, Ivana Marburger
URNER, Catherine Murphy
UYTTENHOVE, Yolande
VAN APPLEDORN, Mary Jeanne
VAN DE VATE, Nancy Hayes
VAN OHLEN, Deborah
VELLERE, Lucie Weiler
VIERK, Lois
VON ZIERITZ, Grete
WALDO, Elisabeth
WALLACH, Joelle
WARNE, Katharine Mulky
WECKWERTH, Nancy
WELMAN, Sylvia
WENDELBURG, Norma Ruth
WHITEHEAD, Gillian
WIENER, Eva Hannah
WILL, Madeleine
ZAIDEL-RUDOLPH, Jeanne
ZAIMONT, Judith Lang

TRUMPET AND ORCHESTRA OR STRINGS
20th Century A.D.
ARRIEU, Claude
BAIKADAMOVA, Baldyrgan
   Bakhitzhanovna
BUCHANAN, Dorothy Quita
CLOSTRE, Adrienne
DAIGLE, Sister Anne Cécile
FERRAND-TEULET, Denise
FULLER-HALL, Sarah Margaret
GOTKOVSKY, Ida-Rose Esther
GOULD, Elizabeth Davies
KALOGRIDOU, Maria
LARSEN, Elizabeth Brown
LEONCHIK, Svetlana Gavrilovna
LUND, Gudrun
PADE, Else Marie
PAKHMUTOVA, Alexandra
   Nikolayevna
PHILIBA, Nicole
ROE, Eileen Betty

VAN APPLEDORN, Mary Jeanne
VORLOVA, Slavka
WILL, Madeleine
WILLIAMS, Grace Mary

TRUMPET AND PIANO
20th Century A.D.
ABRAMOVA, Sonia Pinkhasovna
ARCHER, Violet Balestreri
ARRIEU, Claude
BARRAINE, Elsa
BOLZ, Harriet
BRENET, Thérèse
COME, Tilde
COULTHARD, Jean
DE BIASE BIDART, Lycia
EVEN-OR, Mary
FERRAND-TEULET, Denise
FONTYN, Jacqueline
FULLER-HALL, Sarah Margaret
GABRYS, Ewa Lucja Maria
GARTENLAUB, Odette
GOTKOVSKY, Ida-Rose Esther
GOULD, Elizabeth Davies
HABAN, Sister Teresine M.
JANKOWSKI, Loretta Patricia
JIRKOVA, Olga
KASILAG, Lucrecia R.
KELLER, Ginette
KERN, Frida
KOLODUB, Zhanna Efimovna
McLAUGHLIN, Marian
MARI, Pierrette
MARKIEWICZOWNA, Wladyslawa
MIAGI, Ester Kustovna
MISHELL, Kathryn Lee
OSETROVA-YAKOVLIEVA, Nina
   Alexandrovna
OSTROVSKAYA, T.
PAKHMUTOVA, Alexandra
   Nikolayevna
PHILIBA, Nicole
PIRES DOS REIS, Hilda
ROGER, Denise
RUEFF, Jeanine
SMIRNOVA SOLODCHENKOVA,
   Tatiana Georgievna
USHER, Julia
VEHAR, Persis Anne
VITO-DELVAUX, Berthe di
WECKWERTH, Nancy
ZAIMONT, Judith Lang
ZHUBANOVA, Gaziza Akhmetovna

TUBA
20th Century A.D.
ALEXANDRA, Liana
ANDERSON, Beth
ANDERSON, Olive Jennie Paxton
ANTHONY, Gina
ARCHER, Violet Balestreri
BARRAINE, Elsa
BARRATT, Carol Ann
BRITAIN, Radie
BUCZEK, Barbara Kazimiera
CABRERA, Silvia Maria Pires
CECCONI-BOTELLA, Monic
DESPORTES, Yvonne Berthé Melitta
DEYTON, Camilla Hill
DIAMOND, Arline
DU PAGE, Florence Elizabeth
FRITZ, Sherilyn Gail
FULLER-HALL, Sarah Margaret
GOTKOVSKY, Ida-Rose Esther
GRIEBLING, Karen Jean
HART, Elizabeth Jane Smith
HYDE, Miriam Beatrice
LAUBER, Anne Marianne
LEAHY, Mary Weldon
LU, Yen
MACAULAY, Janice Michel

McLEAN, Priscilla Anne Taylor
POLIN, Claire
PREOBRAJENSKA, Vera Nicolaevna
PTASZYNSKA, Marta
REED, Marlyce Rae Polk
RICHARDSON, Sharon
ROBERT, Lucie
ROBERTSON, Donna Lou Nagey
RUEFF, Jeanine
RUSCHE, Marjorie Maxine
SCHWERDTFEGER, E. Anne
SIKORA, Elzbieta
SILVERMAN, Faye-Ellen
SOLOMON, Joyce Elaine
STEINER, Gitta Hana
USHER, Julia
USTVOLSKAYA, Galina Ivanovna
WARING, Kate
WITKIN, Beatrice
ZIFFRIN, Marilyn Jane
Century unknown
GLASS, Jennifer

TWO INSTRUMENTS AND ORCHESTRA OR STRINGS
18th Century A.D.
WILHELMINA, Sophie Friederike,
Princess of Prussia
20th Century A.D.
ALEXANDRA, Liana
ARRIEU, Claude
BACEWICZ, Grazyna
CHANDLER, Mary
CHRETIEN-GENARO, Hedwige
CLOSTRE, Adrienne
COLE, Ulric
DANEAU, Suzanne
ECKHARDT-GRAMATTE, Sophie-
Carmen
FISHER, Katherine Danforth
FONTYN, Jacqueline
FRANCHI, Dorothea
FRANCO, Clare
GIFFORD, Helen Margaret
GIPPS, Ruth
GOTKOVSKY, Ida-Rose Esther
GRZADZIELOWNA, Eleonora
HARA, Kazuko (1)
KALTENECKER, Gertraud
KLINKOVA, Zhivka
LOWENSTEIN, Gunilla Marike
LUND, Gudrun
MACONCHY, Elizabeth
MARCUS, Ada Belle Gross
MIAGI, Ester Kustovna
OBROVSKA, Jana
PALMER, Lynne Wainwright
PROCACCINI, Teresa
RAPOPORT, Eda
RAVINALE, Irma
ROBERT, Lucie
ROBERTS, Gertrud Hermine
Kuenzel
SALQUIN, Hedy
SHUKAILO, Ludmila Fedorovna
SPONGBERG, Viola
TKACH, Zlata Moiseyevna
VON ZIERITZ, Grete

TWO STRINGED INSTRUMENTS
see DUO - STRINGS

UGUBO BOW
20th Century A.D.
MAGOGO KA DINIZULU, Constance,
Princess

UKELELE
20th Century A.D.
ABEJO, Sister M. Rosalina
ANDERSON, Julia McKinley

ARMER, Elinor Florence
COLERIDGE-TAYLOR, Avril
Gwendolen
JIRACKOVA, Marta

VIBRAPHONE
20th Century A.D.
AGUDELO MURGUIA, Graciela
ALLIK, Kristi
ALSTED, Birgitte
ANDERSON, Beth
ARMER, Elinor Florence
BAILLY, Colette
BARBOSA, Cacilda Campos Borges
BARKIN, Elaine
BARNETT, Carol Edith
BARRELL, Joyce Howard
BAULD, Alison
BEECROFT, Norma Marian
BLOOM, Jane Ira
BOND, Victoria Ellen
BROCKMAN, Jane E.
BRUZDOWICZ, Joanna
BUCZEK, Barbara Kazimiera
CHANCE, Nancy Laird
CLARKE, Rosemary
CORY, Eleanor
CRAWFORD, Dorothy Lamb
DANFORTH, Frances A.
DANIELA, Carmen
DESPORTES, Yvonne Berthé
Melitta
DIEMER, Emma Lou
DILLON, Fannie Charles
DU PAGE, Florence Elizabeth
FRASIER, Jane
GIFFORD, Helen Margaret
GROSSMAN, Deena
GRZADZIELOWNA, Eleonora
HSU, Wen-Ying
ISZKOWSKA, Zofia
JANKOWSKI, Loretta Patricia
KOLB, Barbara
LE SIEGE, Annette
LOUIE, Alexina Diane
LUFF, Enid
MATUSZCZAK, Bernadetta
MEACHEM, Margaret McKeen
Ramsey
MORRISON, Julia Maria
McLEOD, Jennifer Helen
NAITO, Akemi
NOWAK, Alison
OLIVE, Vivienne
PERETZ-LEVY, Liora
PIERCE, Alexandra
PROCACCINI, Teresa
PTASZYNSKA, Marta
RODRIGUE, Nicole
SCHERCHEN, Tona
SILVERMAN, Faye-Ellen
STEINER, Gitta Hana
STREATFIELD, Valma June
SYNOWIEC, Ewa
TAKAMI, Toyoko
TAL, Ya'ara
TOWER, Joan
VERCOE, Elizabeth
WALLACH, Joelle
ZAIDEL-RUDOLPH, Jeanne
ZAKRZEWSKA-NIKIPORCZYK,
Barbara Maria

VIOLA
18th Century A.D.
ANNA AMALIA, Duchess of Saxe-
Weimar
CHARRIERE, Isabella Agneta
Elisabeth de
KANZLER, Josephine
LEVI, Mme.

19th Century A.D.
BLAHETKA, Marie Leopoldina
HEIDENREICH, Henrietta
LASCHANZKY, Mme.
LIEBMANN, Helene
MONTGEROULT, Helene de Nervode
WICKINS, Florence
20th Century A.D.
AGABALIAN, Lidia Semyenovna
ALCALAY, Luna
ALEXANDRA, Liana
ALLEN, Judith Shatin
ANDERSON, Beth
ANDERSON, Olive Jennie Paxton
ANDERSON, Ruth
ANDERSON-WUENSCH, Jean Mary
ANDREYEVA, Elena Fedorovna
ARHO, Anneli
BACEWICZ, Grażyna
BAILEY, Judith Margaret
BANCER, Teresa Barbara
BARBERIS, Mansi
BARRETT-THOMAS, N.
BEAT, Janet Eveline
BECLARD D'HARCOURT,
Marguerite
BEECROFT, Norma Marian
BEHREND, Jeanne
BELL, Carla Huston
BENAVENTE, Regina
BERGE, Irenée
BERGEN, Sylvia
BERK, Adele
BEYER, Johanna Magdalena
BEYERMAN-WALRAVEN, Jeanne
BIENVENU, Lily
BLOMFIELD-HOLT, Patricia
BLOOD, Esta Damesek
BOBROW, Sanchie
BODENSTEIN-HOYME, Ruth E.
BOFILL, Anna
BOLZ, Harriet
BOND, Victoria Ellen
BORROFF, Edith
BOUCHARD, Linda L.
BRINK-POTHUIS, Annie van den
BRUZDOWICZ, Joanna
CAMPAGNE, Conny
CARMEN MARINA
CATUNDA, Eunice do Monte Lima
CECCONI-BATES, Augusta
CHARBONNIER, Janine Andrée
CHAVES, Mary Elizabeth
CHEVALLIER SUPERVIELLE, Marie
Louise
CIOBANU, Maia
CLARKE, Rebecca
CLARKE, Rosemary
COATES, Gloria Kannenberg
COLACO OSORIO-SWAAB, Reine
COLIN, Jeanne
CONRAD, Laurie M.
CORY, Eleanor
COULTHARD, Jean
COX, Alison Mary
CRANE, Helen
CRAWFORD, Dawn Constance
CREWS, Lucille
CRISP, Barbara
DARE, Margaret Marie
DAVIS, Eleanor Maud
DE BIASE BIDART, Lycia
DEDIEU-PETERS, Madeleine
DELORME, Isabelle
DIAMOND, Arline
DIEMER, Emma Lou
DINN, Freda
DOBBINS, Lori
DUDLEY, Marjorie Eastwood
DUNLOP, Isobel
DUSHKIN, Dorothy Smith

DZHAFAROVA, Afag Mamed kyzy
ECKHARDT-GRAMATTE, Sophie-
  Carmen
ELLICOTT, Rosalind Frances
ERDING, Susanne
ERHART, Dorothy
FALCINELLI, Rolande
FELDMAN, Joann Esther
FINE, Vivian
FISCHER, Edith Steinkraus
FOSTER, Cecily
FOX, Kalitha Dorothy
FREED, Dorothy Whitson
FRITZ, Sherilyn Gail
FUCHS, Lillian
FULCHER, Ellen Georgina
GARDNER, Kay
GARR, Wieslawa
GIFFORD, Helen Margaret
GIPPS, Ruth
GITECK, Janice
GIURANNA, Elena Barbara
GLATZ, Helen Sinclair
GODLA, Mary Ann
GOEBELS, Gisela
GOKHMAN, Elena Vladimirovna
GOLOVINA, Olga Akimovna
GONTARENKO, Galina Nikolayevna
GOULD, Janetta
GRAHAM, Janet Christine
GREGORI, Nininha
GRIEBLING, Karen Jean
GRZADZIELOWNA, Eleonora
GUMMER, Phyllis Mary
GYANDZHETSIAN, Destrik
  Bogdanovna
GYRING, Elizabeth
HAMPE, Charlotte
HARA, Kazuko (1)
HARRISON, Pamela
HAWLEY, Carolyn Jean
HAYS, Doris Ernestine
HIER, Ethel Glen
HIND O'MALLEY, Pamela
HOOVER, Katherine
JACKSON, Barbara May
JAMES, Dorothy E.
JIRACKOVA, Marta
JOHNSON, Elizabeth
JOHNSTON, Alison Aileen Annie
JOLAS, Betsy
JOLLY, Margaret Anne
KANACH, Sharon E.
KEEFER, Euphrosyne
KERN, Frida
KICKINGER, Paula
KITAZUME, Yayoi
KLINKOVA, Zhivka
KNOBLOCHOVA, Antonie
KOBLENZ, Babette
KOELLING, Eloise
KONISHI, Nagako
KUBO, Mayako
KUKUCK, Felicitas
LACHOWSKA, Stefania
LAUBER, Anne Marianne
LAZAR, Ella
LE BEAU, Louisa Adolpha
LEAHY, Mary Weldon
LEJET, Edith
LEJEUNE-BONNIER, Eliane
LEPEUT-LEVINE, Jeannine
LOH, Kathy Jean
LOPEZ ROVIROSA, Maria Isabel
LORENZ, Ellen Jane
LOUDOVA, Ivana
LUCAS, Mary Anderson
LUND, Gudrun
LUTYENS, Elisabeth
LVOVA, Julia Fedorovna
MACONCHY, Elizabeth

MacKENNA, Carmela
McLEOD, Jennifer Helen
McMILLAN, Ann Endicott
MAGEAU, Mary Jane
MAMLOK, Ursula
MARSHALL, Pamela J.
MAYADAS, Priya
MAYER, Lise Maria
MAZOUROVA, Jarmila
MILNE, Helen C.
MOON, Chloe Elizabeth
MYGATT, Louise
NIKOLAYEVA, Tatiana Petrovna
OBROVSKA, Jana
ODAGESCU, Irina
O'LEARY, Jane Strong
ORENSTEIN, Joyce Ellin
PAULL, Barberi
PELEGRI, Maria Teresa
PENGILLY, Sylvia
PENNER, Jean Priscilla
PENTLAND, Barbara Lally
PEREIRA DA SILVA, Adelaide
PERRY, Julia Amanda
PHILIPPART, Renée
PHILLIPS, Bryony
PHILLIPS, Karen Ann
PHILLIPS, Lois Elisabeth
PIETSCH, Edna Frieda
POLIN, Claire
POPATENKO, Tamara Alexandrovna
POPOVICI, Elise
POSTON, Elizabeth
PRADELL, Leila
PRAVOSSUDOVITCH, Natalja
  Michajlovna
PREOBRAJENSKA, Vera Nicolaevna
PRICE, Beryl
PRICE, Deon Nielsen
PRICE, Florence Beatrice
PRIETO, Maria Teresa
PROCACCINI, Teresa
PTASZYNSKA, Marta
RADMALL, Peggy
RAINIER, Priaulx
RAMM, Valentina Iosifovna
RAPOPORT, Eda
RAVINALE, Irma
REID, Wendy
RESPIGHI, Elsa
RHENE-JAQUE
RICHARDSON, Enid Dorothy
RICHARDSON, Sharon
RICHTER, Marga
RILEY, Ann Marion
RILEY, Myrtis F.
ROGER, Denise
ROYSE, Mildred Barnes
SAINT JOHN, Kathleen Louise
SAMSON, Valerie Brooks
SANDRESKY, Margaret Vardell
SCHERCHEN, Tona
SCHONTHAL, Ruth E.
SCHORR-WEILER, Eva
SCHUBARTH, Dorothé
SHERMAN, Kim Daryl
SIDORENKO, Tamara Stepanovna
SILVERMAN, Faye-Ellen
SIMONS, Netty
SMITH, Julia Frances
SMITH, Linda Catlin
SMYTH, Ethel Mary, Dame
SNIFFIN, Allison
SNIZKOVA-SKRHOVA, Jitka
SOULAGE, Marcelle Fanny
  Henriette
SOUTHAM, Ann
STREATFIELD, Valma June
STRUTT, Dorothy
SUCHY, Gregoria Karides
SUTHERLAND, Margaret

SUZUE, Mariko
SWAIN, Freda Mary
SYNOWIEC, Ewa
TALMA, Louise
TANN, Hilary
TARLOW, Karen Anne
TASHJIAN, B. Charmian
TATE, Phyllis
TATTON, Madeleine
TERZIAN, Alicia
THEMMEN, Ivana Marburger
THOME, Diane
THOMSEN, Geraldine
THORKELSDOTTIR, Mist
  Barbara
TOWER, Joan
TUICHEVA, Zumrad
TUMANIAN, Elizaveta Artashesovna
TUMANISHVILI, Ketevana
  Dmitirevna
TURNER, Sara Scott
VAN DE VATE, Nancy Hayes
VAN EPEN-DE GROOT, Else
  Antonia
VASILIEVA, Tatiana Ivanovna
VELLERE, Lucie Weiler
VOLKART-SCHLAGER, Kaethe
VON ZIERITZ, Grete
VORLOVA, Slavka
WALLACH, Joelle
WANG, An-Ming
WARING, Kate
WEIGL, Vally
WHITLOCK, E. Florence
WILL, Madeleine
WISHART, Betty Rose
WITBECK, Ariel Lea
WITNI, Monica
WOLLNER, Gertrude Price
WYLIE, Ruth Shaw
ZAIDEL-RUDOLPH, Jeanne
ZAIMONT, Judith Lang
ZECHLIN, Ruth
ZIELINSKA, Lidia
ZIFFRIN, Marilyn Jane
Century unknown
  MONACHINA
  SNODGRASS, Louise Harrison

VIOLA AND ORCHESTRA OR STRINGS
20th Century A.D.
  ALLEN, Judith Shatin
  BACEWICZ, Grazyna
  BALLOU, Esther Williamson
  BIENVENU, Lily
  COLIN, Jeanne
  COULTHARD, Jean
  ELLIOTT, Janice Overmiller
  GIPPS, Ruth
  GLANVILLE-HICKS, Peggy
  HOFFMAN, Phyllis Sampson
  HOLST, Imogen Clare
  JEPPSSON, Kerstin Maria
  LAUFER, Beatrice
  LUTYENS, Elisabeth
  MACONCHY, Elizabeth
  MARBE, Myriam
  MERLI-ZWISCHENBRUGGER,
    Christina
  MESRITZ-VAN VELTHUYSEN,
    Annie
  MUSGRAVE, Thea
  PAYNE, Harriet
  PIETSCH, Edna Frieda
  RICHARDSON, Sharon
  RICHTER, Marga
  ROGERS, Patsy
  SOLOMON, Mirrie Irma
  VELLERE, Lucie Weiler
  VORLOVA, Slavka
  WITNI, Monica

VIOLA AND PIANO

19th Century A.D.
HUNDT, Aline
PARADIS, Maria Theresia von
WIECK, Marie

20th Century A.D.
ACCART, Eveline
AHRENS, Peg
ALLEN, Judith Shatin
ANDERSON-WUENSCH, Jean Mary
BAKLANOVA, Natalia
BARBERIS, Mansi
BARNETT, Carol Edith
BARRETT-THOMAS, N.
BAUER, Marion Eugenie
BEAT, Janet Eveline
BEHREND, Jeanne
BEYERMAN-WALRAVEN, Jeanne
BIENVENU, Lily
BORROFF, Edith
BRUZDOWICZ, Joanna
CLARKE, Rebecca
COLACO OSORIO-SWAAB, Reine
COULTHARD, Jean
CREWS, Lucille
CRISP, Barbara
DARE, Margaret Marie
DE BIASE BIDART, Lycia
ECKHARDT-GRAMATTE, Sophie-
Carmen
ELLICOTT, Rosalind Frances
FELDMAN, Joann Esther
FINZI, Graciane
FORMAN, Joanne
GAIGEROVA, Varvara Andrianovna
GIDEON, Miriam
GIPPS, Ruth
GOKHMAN, Elena Vladimirovna
GOLUB, Martha Naumovna
GOTKOVSKY, Ida-Rose Esther
GOULD, Elizabeth Davies
GRIEBLING, Karen Jean
GRZADZIELOWNA, Eleonora
HARMS, Signe
HARRISON, Pamela
HO, Wai On
HOLST, Imogen Clare
HOWE, Mary Alberta Bruce
HYDE, Miriam Beatrice
IORDAN, Irina Nikolayevna
IRMAN-ALLEMANN, Regina
ISZKOWSKA, Zofia
IVEY, Jean Eichelberger
KERN, Frida
KONISHI, Nagako
KUKUCK, Felicitas
LAUBER, Anne Marianne
LE BEAU, Louisa Adolpha
LEJEUNE-BONNIER, Eliane
LEVINA, Zara Alexandrovna
LOUDOVA, Ivana
LUTYENS, Elisabeth
LVOVA, Julia Fedorovna
McLAUGHLIN, Marian
MANA-ZUCCA
MARBE, Myriam
MAREZ-OYENS, Tera de
MARI, Pierrette
MAXWELL, Elsie
MOODY, Pamela
NIEMACK, Ilza Louise
NORRE, Dorcas
NOVI, Anna Beate
NUNLIST, Juli
PAYNE, Harriet
PENNER, Jean Priscilla
PENTLAND, Barbara Lally
PETROVA-KRUPKOVA, Elena
PHILLIPS, Karen Ann
POPATENKO, Tamara Alexandrovna
POPOVICI, Elise

PRICE, Beryl
PROCACCINI, Teresa
RADMALL, Peggy
RAINIER, Priaulx
RAPOPORT, Eda
RILEY, Ann Marion
ROGER, Denise
SCHONTHAL, Ruth E.
SENFTER, Johanna
SHUKAILO, Ludmila Fedorovna
SIMONS, Netty
SMITH, Julia Frances
SNIZKOVA-SKRHOVA, Jitka
SOLOMON, Joyce Elaine
SOULAGE, Marcelle Fanny Henriette
SUTHERLAND, Margaret
SWAIN, Freda Mary
SZOENYI, Erzsebet
THOMSEN, Geraldine
TKACH, Zlata Moiseyevna
TUMANIAN, Elizaveta Artashesovna
TUMANISHVILI, Ketevana
Dmitirevna
URNER, Catherine Murphy
VAN DE VATE, Nancy Hayes
VON ZIERITZ, Grete
WALKER, Gwyneth van Anden
WELANDER, Svea Goeta
WHITEHEAD, Gillian
WILDSCHUT, Clara
WYLIE, Ruth Shaw
ZUBELDIA, Emiliana de

Century unknown
BOR, Modesta
LOVELL, Joan

VIOLIN

16th Century A.D.
BOLEYN, Anne, Queen of England

17th Century A.D.
PRIOLI MORISINA, Marietta
SUARDA, Maria Virginia

18th Century A.D.
AGNESI-PINOTTINI, Maria Teresa d'
ANNA AMALIA, Duchess of Saxe-
Weimar
ANNA AMALIA, Princess of Prussia
BARTHELEMON, Mary
BERTHE, Mme.
BRUCKENTHAL, Bertha von,
Baroness
CECILE, Jeanne
CHARRIERE, Isabella Agneta
Elisabeth de
COSWAY, Maria Cécilia Louise
DANZI, Maria Margarethe
DE GAMBARINI, Elisabetta
DESFOSSES, Elisabeth Françoise,
Countess
KANZLER, Josephine
LA GUERRE , Elisabeth-Claude
Jacquet de
LEBRUN, Franziska Dorothea
LOUIS, Mme.
MARTINEZ, Marianne
PHILHARMONICA, Mrs.
POUILLAU, Mlle.
REYNOLDS, Marie Hester
SIRMEN, Maddalena Laura di
VALENTINE, Ann

19th Century A.D.
AMALIE, Marie Friederike Augusta,
Princess of Saxony
BAU, Elise
BERTIN, Louise Angelique
BLAHETKA, Marie Leopoldina
BLANC DE FONTBELLE, Cécile
BLANGINI, Mlle.
BRESSON, Mlle.
BRONSART VON SCHELLENDORF,
Ingeborg Lena von

CALOSSO, Eugenia
CANDEILLE, Amelie Julie
CARISSAN, Celanie
COLLINS, Laura Sedgwick
CORRER, Ida, Countess
CRUMB, Berenice
DAVIES, Llewela
ELDESE, Renee
FARMER, Emily Bardsley
FARRENC, Louise
FILIPOWICZ, Elize-Minelli
GRANDVAL, Marie Felicie Clemence
de Reiset, Vicomtesse de
HEIDENREICH, Henrietta
KENDIKOVA, Zdenka
KERN, Louise
KRAEHMER, Caroline
KRALIK VON MAYERSWALDEN,
Mathilde
LANNOY, Clementine-Josephine-
Françoise-Thérèse, Countess
LASCHANZKY, Mme.
LEONARDO, Luisa
LIEBMANN, Helene
LIND, Jenny
LODER, Kate Fanny
LONSDALE, Eva
MARX, Berthe
MATTFELD, Marie
MILANOLLO, Teresa Domenica
Maria
MOLIQUE, Caroline
PARKE, Maria Hester
PEYRON, Albertina Fredrika
PFEIFFER, Clara-Virginie
PITTMAN, Alice Locke
POLAK, Nina
RALPH, Kate
REED, Florence
RIBAS, Medina N.
RICOTTI, Onestina
RODRIGO, Maria
RONTGEN, Amanda
ROSALES, Cecilia
SMITH, Alice Mary
SMITH, Rosalie Balmer
SWEPSTONE, Edith
TOWNSEND, Pearl Dea Etta
TSCHETSCHULIN, Agnes
TURNEY, Ruthyn
VANZO, Vittoria Maria
VIARDOT-GARCIA, Pauline Michelle
Ferdinande
WHITE, Maude Valerie
WICKINS, Florence
WINKEL, Thérèse Emilie Henriette
aus dem
WINTZER, Elisabeth
WUIET, Caroline

20th Century A.D.
ABE, Kyoko
ABEJO, Sister M. Rosalina
ABRAMOVA, Sonia Pinkhasovna
ACKLAND, Jessie Agnes
AKSYANTSEVA, Ninel Moiseyevna
ALCALAY, Luna
ALEXANDRA, Liana
ALLIK, Kristi
ALLOUARD CARNY, Odette
ALMEN, Ruth
ALMESAN, Irma
ALOTIN, Yardena
ALSTED, Birgitte
ALT, Hansi
ALTER, Martha
ANDERSON, Beth
ANDERSON, Olive Jennie Paxton
ANDERSON, Ruth
ANDERSON-WUENSCH, Jean Mary
ARAUCO, Ingrid Colette
ARBEL, Re Chaya

ARCHER, Violet Balestreri
ARHO, Anneli
BAADER-NOBS, Heidi
BABAYEVA, Seda Grigorievna
BACEWICZ, Grazyna
BADIAN, Maya
BAIKADAMOVA, Baldyrgan Bakhitzhanovna
BAIL, Grace Shattuck
BAILLY, Colette
BAINBRIDGE, Beryl
BAKKE, Ruth
BANCER, Teresa Barbara
BARADAPRANA, Pravrajika
BARKIN, Elaine
BARKLUND, Irma L.
BARNS, Ethel
BARRETT-THOMAS, N.
BARRIERE, Françoise
BARTLETT, Floy Little
BAUER, Marion Eugenie
BAULD, Alison
BEACH, Amy Marcy
BEAT, Janet Eveline
BEATON, Isabella
BECK, Martha Dillard
BECKON, Lettie Marie
BECLARD D'HARCOURT, Marguerite
BEECROFT, Norma Marian
BEEKHUIS, Hanna
BEESON, Elizabeth Ruth
BELL, Carla Huston
BELL, Elizabeth
BELOCH, Dorotea
BENAVENTE, Regina
BENOIT, Francine Germaine Van Gool
BERAN-STARK, Lola Aloisia Maria
BERBERIAN, Cathy
BERGE, Irenee
BERGEN, Sylvia
BERK, Adele
BEYER, Johanna Magdalena
BIALKIEWICZOWNA-ANDRAULT DE LANGERON, Irena
BIENVENU, Lily
BILLINGTON, Elizabeth
BILTCLIFFE, Florence
BINET, Jocelyne
BIRCHER-REY, Hedy
BIZONY, Celia
BLAKE, Dorothy Gaynor
BLOMFIELD-HOLT, Patricia
BLOOD, Esta Damesek
BLOOM, Jane Ira
BOBROW, Sanchie
BODENSTEIN-HOYME, Ruth E.
BOFILL, Anna
BOLZ, Harriet
BOND, Victoria Ellen
BORDEWIJK-ROEPMAN, Johanna
BORGE, Michele
BORKOWICZ, Maria
BOSMANS, Henriette Hilda
BOSTELMANN, Ida
BOUCHARD, Linda L.
BOULANGER, Lili Juliette Marie Olga
BOULOGNE, Julia R.C.
BOUTRON, Madeleine
BOYD, Anne Elizabeth
BRANNING, Grace Bell
BRANSCOMBE, Gena
BRAUER, Johanna Elisabeth
BRENET, Thérèse
BRESCHI, Laura
BRIGHT, Dora Estella
BRINK-POTHUIS, Annie van den
BRITAIN, Radie
BRODIN, Lena Birgitta Elise
BROOK, Gwendolyn Giffen

BROWN, Elizabeth van Ness
BRUCKSHAW, Kathleen
BRUSH, Ruth Damaris
BRUSSELS, Iris
BRUZDOWICZ, Joanna
BUCHANAN, Dorothy Quita
BUCKLEY, Helen Dallam
BUCZEK, Barbara Kazimiera
BULTERIJS, Nina
BURROUGHS, Jane Johnson
BURSTON, Maggie
BUTLER, Anne Lois
BUTLER, Patricia Magahay
CALCAGNO, Elsa
CALL, Audrey
CALLAWAY, Ann
CAMEU, Helza
CAMINHA, Alda
CAMPAGNE, Conny
CAMPMANY, Montserrat
CANAL, Marguerite
CANALES PIZARRO, Marta
CANAT DE CHIZY, Edith
CAPERTON, Florence Tait
CAPUIS, Matilde
CARLOS, Wendy
CARMEN MARINA
CARR-BOYD, Ann Kirsten
CARRIVICK, Olive Amelia
CARTER, Rosetta
CARVALHO, Dinora de
CARWITHEN, Doreen
CATUNDA, Eunice do Monte Lima
CECCONI-BATES, Augusta
CHAMINADE, Cecile Louise Stephanie
CHAMPION, Stephanie
CHANCE, Nancy Laird
CHARBONNIER, Janine Andree
CHARLOTTE, Princess of Saxe-Meiningen
CHAVES, Mary Elizabeth
CHEVALLIER SUPERVIELLE, Marie Louise
CHICHERINA, Sofia Nikolayevna
CHITCHIAN, Geguni Oganesovna
CHKHEIDZE, Dali Davidovna
CHRETIEN-GENARO, Hedwige
CHUDOVA, Tatiana Alekseyevna
CIMAGLIA DE ESPINOSA, Lia
CIOBANU, Maia
CLARKE, Rebecca
CLOSTRE, Adrienne
COATES, Gloria Kannenberg
COCQ, Rosina Susanna de
COHEN, Marcia
COLACO OSORIO-SWAAB, Reine
COLE, Ulric
COLIN, Jeanne
COLLVER, Harriet Russell
CONRAD, Laurie M.
CONTINI ANSELMI, Lucia
COQUET, Odile Marie-Lucie
CORNING, Karen Andree
CORY, Eleanor
COTRON, Fanou
COULOMBE SAINT-MARCOUX, Micheline
COULTHARD, Jean
CRANE, Helen
CRAWFORD SEEGER, Ruth
CRAWFORD, Dawn Constance
CRAWFORD, Dorothy Lamb
CRAWFORD, Louise
CROKER, Catherine Munnell
DAIGLE, Sister Anne Cecile
DALE, Kathleen
DANEAU, Suzanne
DANIELA, Carmen
DANIELS, Mabel Wheeler
DARE, Margaret Marie

DAVENPORT GOERTZ, Gladys
DAVIDSON, Tina
DAVIS, Eleanor Maud
DAVITASHVILI, Meri Shalvovna
DAVY, Ruby Claudia Emily
DE BIASE BIDART, Lycia
DE LYLE, Carlyon
DEBRASSINE-PRIJAT, Laure
DEDIEU-PETERS, Madeleine
DELAHAYE, Cécile
DELMOULY, Marie Mathilde
DELORME, Isabelle
DEMARQUEZ, Suzanne
DEMBO, Royce
DENBOW, Stefania Bjoerson
DESPORTES, Yvonne Berthe Melitta
DIAKVNISHVILI, Mzisavar Zakharevna
DIAMOND, Arline
DIEMER, Emma Lou
DILLON, Fannie Charles
DIMITRIU, Florica
DINESCU, Violeta
DINN, Freda
DLUGOSZEWSKI, Lucia
DOBBINS, Lori
DOBSON, Elaine
DRAKE, Elizabeth Bell
DREGE-SCHIELOWA, Lucja
DRENNAN, Dorothy Carter
DROBYAZGINA, Valentina Ivanovna
DU PAGE, Florence Elizabeth
DUCOUREAU, Mme. M.
DUDLEY, Marjorie Eastwood
DUGGAN, Beatrice Abbott
DUSHKIN, Dorothy Smith
DUTTON, Theodora
DYCHKO, Lesya Vasilevna
DZHAFAROVA, Afag Mamed kyzy
ECKHARDT-GRAMATTE, Sophie-Carmen
EHRMANN, Rosette
EIRIKSDOTTIR, Karolina
EISENSTEIN, Stella Price
EMINGEROVA, Katerina
ENDRES, Olive Philomene
ERHART, Dorothy
ESCOT, Pozzi
ETHRIDGE, Jean
EUTENEUER-ROHRER, Ursula Henrietta
EVEN-OR, Mary
EZELL, Helen Ingle
FAIRLIE, Margaret C.
FALCINELLI, Rolande
FALTIS, Evelyn
FARGA PELLICER, Onia
FAUTCH, Sister Magdalen
FEIGIN, Sarah
FELDMAN, Joann Esther
FERRAND-TEULET, Denise
FINE, Vivian
FINLEY, Lorraine Noel
FIRSOVA, Elena
FISCHER, Edith Steinkraus
FISHER, Katherine Danforth
FLACH, Elsa
FLEITES, Virginia
FLICK-FLOOD, Dora
FOLVILLE, Eugenie-Emilie Juliette
FOSTER, Fay
FOWLER, Jennifer Joan
FRANCHI, Dorothea
FRASER-MILLER, Gloria Jill
FREED, Dorothy Whitson
FRITTER, Genevieve Davisson
FRONMUELLER, Frieda
FUCHS, Lillian
FULCHER, Ellen Georgina
FULLER-HALL, Sarah Margaret
FURGERI, Bianca Maria

GALAJIKIAN, Florence Grandland
GARCIA ROBSON, Magdalena
GARDNER, Kay
GARR, Wieslawa
GARUTA, Lucia Yanovna
GEIGER-KULLMANN, Rosy Auguste
GEORGE, Lila-Gene
GERSTMAN, Blanche Wilhelminia
GEYER, Stefi
GHERTOVICI, Aida
GIFFORD, Helen Margaret
GINDLER, Kathe-Lotte
GIPPS, Ruth
GITECK, Janice
GLATZ, Helen Sinclair
GODLA, Mary Ann
GODWIN-FOSTER, Dorothy
GOEBELS, Gisela
GOETSCHIUS, Marjorie
GOKHMAN, Elena Vladimirovna
GOLOVINA, Olga Akimovna
GOMM, Elizabeth
GONTARENKO, Galina Nikolayevna
GOTKOVSKY, Ida-Rose Esther
GRAHAM, Janet Christine
GREENE, Genevieve
GREENE, Margo Lynn
GREGORI, Nininha
GRIEBLING, Karen Jean
GRIGSBY, Beverly
GROSSMAN, Deena
GUBAIDULINA, Sofia Asgatovna
GUBITOSI, Emilia
GUELL, Maria Luisa
GVAZAVA, Tamara Davidovna
GYANDZHETSIAN, Destrik Bogdanovna
GYRING, Elizabeth
HALACSY, Irma von
HALPERN, Stella
HAMPE, Charlotte
HANEFELD, Gertrud
HARA, Kazuko
HARDY, Helen Irene
HARRISON, Pamela
HART, Elizabeth Jane Smith
HARWOOD, Sylvia Rowell
HASKELL, Doris Burd
HAWLEY, Carolyn Jean
HAYS, Doris Ernestine
HEALE, Helene
HEGELER, Anna
HEGNER, Anna
HEIBERG, Ella
HEMON, Sedje
HERBISON, Jeraldine Saunders
HIER, Ethel Glen
HIND O'MALLEY, Pamela
HOELSZKY, Adriana
HOFFRICHTER, Bertha Chaitkin
HOLLAND, Dulcie Sybil
HOLMBERG, Betty
HOLMSEN, Borghild
HOOD, Helen
HOOVER, Katherine
HORTON, Marguerite Wagniere
HOY, Bonnee L.
HSU, Wen-Ying
HULST, Margaret Gardiner
HUNKINS, Eusebia Simpson
HURLEY, Susan
HYDE, Miriam Beatrice
HYTREK, Sister Theophane
IRMAN-ALLEMANN, Regina
IVEY, Jean Eichelberger
IWAUCHI, Saori
JACOB, Elizabeth Marie
JAMES, Dorothy E.
JENNINGS, Marie Pryor
JENNY, Sister Leonore
JIRACKOVA, Marta
JOCHSBERGER, Tzipora H.

JOHNSON, Elizabeth
JUENGER, Patricia
KABAT, Julie Phyllis
KADIMA, Hagar Yonith
KAHMANN, Chesley
KAHN, Esther
KALOGRIDOU, Maria
KAMIEN, Anna
KANACH, Sharon E.
KAPRALOVA, Vitezslava
KARNITSKAYA, Nina Andreyevna
KAUFMAN, Barbara
KEEFER, Euphrosyne
KELLER, Ginette
KERN, Frida
KESSLER, Minuetta Schumiatcher
KIM, Kwang-Hee
KIRKMAN, Merle
KISTETENYI, Melinda
KITAZUME, Yayoi
KLECHNIOWSKA, Anna Maria
KLINKOVA, Zhivka
KNOBLOCHOVA, Antonie
KNOUSS, Isabelle G.
KOBLENZ, Babette
KOELLING, Eloise
KOHAN, Celina
KOLB, Barbara
KONISHI, Nagako
KORN, Clara Anna
KOZANKOVA, Anna
KRASNOGLIADOVA, Vera
    Vladimirovna
KROSNICK, Mary Louw Wesley
KRULL, Diana
KRUSE, Lotte
KRZANOWSKA, Grażyna
KRZYZANOWSKA, Halina
KUBO, Mayako
KUKUCK, Felicitas
KURIMOTO, Yoko
KUSS, Margarita Ivanovna
KUZMYCH, Christina
LABEY, Charlotte Sohy
LACHOWSKA, Stefania
LAGO
LAMBERT, Cecily
LANG-BECK, Ivana
LATHAM, Joan Seyler
LAUBER, Anne Marianne
LAUFER, Beatrice
LAYMAN, Pamela
LAZAR, Ella
LE BEAU, Louisa Adolpha
LEAHY, Mary Weldon
LEBARON, Anne
LEBIZAY, Marguerite
LEE, Chan-Hae
LEE, Hwaeja Yoo
LEE, Young Ja
LEFANU, Nicola Frances
LEHMANN, Liza
LEIVISKA, Helvi Lemmiki
LEJET, Edith
LEONARD, Mamie Grace
LEPEUT-LEVINE, Jeannine
LEVIN, Rami Yona
LEWING, Adele
LIDGI-HERMAN, Sofia
LIEDBERGIUS, Camilla
LIMA CRUZ, Maria Antonietta de
LINDEMAN, Hjelle Signe
LINZ VON KRIEGNER, Marta
LIPSCOMB, Helen
LOH, Kathy Jean
LOMON, Ruth
LONGWORTH, Helen
LOPEZ ROVIROSA, Maria Isabel
LOPUSKA-WYLEZYNSKA, Helena
LOUDOVA, Ivana
LU, Yen

LUDVIG-PECAR, Nada
LUND, Gudrun
LUTYENS, Elisabeth
LVOVA, Julia Fedorovna
LYONN LIEBERMAN, Julie
MacKENNA, Carmela
McCOLLIN, Frances
McINTOSH, Diana
McKENZIE, Sandra
McLEOD, Evelyn Lundgren
McLEOD, Jennifer Helen
McPHERSON, Frances Marie
MAGENTA, Maria
MAKAROVA, Nina Vladimirovna
MAMLOK, Ursula
MARBE, Myriam
MARINKOVIC, Jelena
MARSHALL, Pamela J.
MARTINEZ, Odaline de la
MATEVOSIAN, Araks Surenovna
MAYADAS, Priya
MAYER, Lise Maria
MEKEEL, Joyce
MIAGI, Ester Kustovna
MIKUSCH, Margarethe von
MIZUNO, Shuko
MOESTUE, Marie
MONK, Meredith
MOON, Chloe Elizabeth
MORRISON, Julia Maria
MOSELEY, Caroline Carr
MYGATT, Louise
NATVIG, Candace
NEMTEANU-ROTARU, Doina
NESTE, Rosane van
NEUWIRTH, Goesta
NOBLE, Ann
NOHE, Beverly
NORDENSON, Ruth
NORUP, Helle Merete
NOVA SONDAG, Jacqueline
NOVI, Anna Beate
OFFICER, Bronwyn Lee
OH, Sook Ja
O'LEARY, Jane Strong
OLIVE, Vivienne
OSAWA, Kazuko
PACK, Beulah Frances
PADE, Else Marie
PAGH-PAAN, Younghi
PALMER, Lynne Wainwright
PAULL, Barberi
PELEGRI, Maria Teresa
PENGILLY, Sylvia
PENNER, Jean Priscilla
PENTLAND, Barbara Lally
PERKIN, Helen
PERRY, Julia Amanda
PERSCHMANN, Elfriede
PETERSON, Melody
PEYROT, Fernande
PHILIBA, Nicole
PHILIPPART, Renée
PHILLIPS, Bryony
PHILLIPS, Karen Ann
PHILLIPS, Linda
PHILLIPS, Lois Elisabeth
PIECHOWSKA, Alina
PIKE, Eleanor B. Franklin
PLONSEY, Jennifer
POLIGNAC, Armande de, Countess
    of Chabannes
POLIN, Claire
POPATENKO, Tamara Alexandrovna
POPOVICI, Elise
POWELL, Maud
POWERS, Ada Weigel
PRADELL, Leila
PRAVOSSUDOVITCH, Natalja
    Michajlovna
PREDIC-SAPER, Branislava

PREOBRAJENSKA, Vera Nicolaevna
PRICE, Beryl
PRICE, Florence Beatrice
PRIESING, Dorothy Jean
PRIETO, Maria Teresa
PRIOLLI, Maria Luisa de Matos
PROCACCINI, Teresa
PSTROKONSKA-NAVRATIL,
  Grazyna Hanna
PTASZYNSKA, Marta
QUANTIN-SAULNIER, Denise
QUIEL, Hildegard
RADMALL, Peggy
RAINIER, Priaulx
RALSTON, Frances Marion
RAMM, Valentina Iosifovna
RAN, Shulamit
RANTA-SHIDA, Shoko
RAPOPORT, Eda
RAVINALE, Irma
RECLI, Giulia
REIFF, Lili
RENIE, Henriette
REYNOLDS, Erma Grey Hogue
RHENE-JAQUE
RICHARDSON, Enid Dorothy
RICHTER, Marga
RICHTER, Marion Morrey
RILEY, Myrtis F.
ROBERTS, Megan L.
ROBERTSON, Donna Lou Nagey
ROCHAT, Andrée
ROCHEROLLE, Eugenie Katherine
ROE, Eileen Betty
ROE, Helen Mary Gabrielle
ROESGEN-CHAMPION, Marguerite
  Sara
ROGER, Denise
ROGERS, Clara Kathleen
ROGERS, Ethel Tench
ROGERS, Patsy
ROKSETH, Yvonne
ROMERO BARBOSA, Elena
ROMM, Rosalina Davidovna
ROSATO, Clorinda
ROYSE, Mildred Barnes
ROZHAVSKAYA, Yudif Grigorevna
RUEGGER, Charlotte
RUFF-STOEHR, Herta Maria Klara
RUSCHE, Marjorie Maxine
RUTA, Gilda, Countess
RYBNER, Dagmar de Corval
SAINT JOHN, Kathleen Louise
SAMTER, Alice
SAMVELIAN, Sofia Vardanovna
SAXTORPH, Gudrun
SCHJELDERUP, Mon Marie Gustava
SCHLOSS, Myrna Frances
SCHONTHAL, Ruth E.
SCHUMAKER, Grace L.
SEBASTIANI, Pia
SEGHIZZI, Cecilia
SEMEGEN, Daria
SENFTER, Johanna
SHAW, Alice Marion
SIKORA, Elzbieta
SILSBEE, Ann L.
SIMONS, Netty
SINGER, Jeanne
SLIANOVA-MIZANDARI, Dagmara
  Levanovna
SMITH, Anita
SMITH, Julia Frances
SMITH, Linda Catlin
SMYTH, Ethel Mary, Dame
SNIZKOVA-SKRHOVA, Jitka
SOLOMON, Mirrie Irma
SOUBLETTE, Sylvia
SOULAGE, Marcelle Fanny Henriette
SOUTHAM, Ann
SOUTHGATE, Dorothy

SOUTHGATE, Elsie
SPAIN-DUNK, Susan
SPALDING, Eva Ruth
SPENCER, Marguerita
SPOENDLIN, Elisabeth
SPONGBERG, Viola
STAIR, Patty
STEINER, Gitta Hana
STREICHER, Lyubov Lvovna
STREIT, Else
STRUTT, Dorothy
STUDENY, Herma
STULTZ, Marie Irene
STURKOW-RYDER, Theodora
SUCHY, Gregoria Karides
SUH, Kyung-Sun
SULTANOVA, Asya Bakhish kyzy
SUTHERLAND, Margaret
SUZUE, Mariko
SWAIN, Freda Mary
SYNOWIEC, Ewa
SZEKELY, Katalin
SZOENYI, Erzsebet
TAILLEFERRE, Germaine
TAL, Ya'ara
TALMA, Louise
TATE, Phyllis
TATTON, Madeleine
TEMPLE, Hope
TERZIAN, Alicia
THEMMEN, Ivana Marburger
THOME, Diane
THOMSEN, Geraldine
TILICHEYEVA, Elena Nikolayevna
TODD, Esther Cox
TOLKOWSKY, Denise
TOWER, Joan
TROTT, Josephine
TUCKER, Tui St. George
TUICHEVA, Zumrad
TUMANIAN, Elizaveta Artashesovna
TUMANISHVILI, Ketevana
  Dmitirevna
UNDERWOOD, Frances Evangeline
USTVOLSKAYA, Galina Ivanovna
VAN DE VATE, Nancy Hayes
VAN DEN BOORN-COCLET,
  Henriette
VAN DER MARK, Maria
VASILIEVA, Tatiana Ivanovna
VELLERE, Lucie Weiler
VERCOE, Elizabeth
VIERK, Lois
VIRTUE, Constance Cochnower
VISCONTI, Leila
VITO-DELVAUX, Berthé di
VLADERACKEN, Geertruida van
VOIGT-SCHWEIKERT, Margarete
VOLKART, Hazel
VON ZIERITZ, Grete
VRABELY-WURMBACH-
  STUPPACHOVA, Stefania
VYNER, Mary Bainbridge
WALLACE, Phyllis Joy
WALLACH, Joelle
WANG, An-Ming
WARNE, Katharine Mulky
WEGENER-FRENSEL, Emmy Heil
WEIGL, Vally
WELANDER, Svea Goeta
WELMAN, Sylvia
WENDELBURG, Norma Ruth
WENNERBERG-REUTER, Sara
  Margareta Eugenia Euphrosyne
WERTHEIM, Rosy
WEYBRIGHT, June
WHITEHEAD, Gillian
WHITLOCK, E. Florence
WIENER, Eva Hannah
WIGGINS, Mary
WILLIAMS, Joan Franks

WISHART, Betty Rose
WITBECK, Ariel Lea
WOLLNER, Gertrude Price
WORRELL, Lola Carrier
YAROSHEVSKAYA, Ludmila
  Anatolievna
ZAKRZEWSKA-NIKIPORCZYK,
  Barbara Maria
ZIELINSKA, Lidia
ZIMMERMANN, Margrit
ZIVKOVIC, Mirjana

Century unknown
ACHARD, Marguerite
COMBIE, Ida Mae
CONSOLINI, Gabriella Elsa
FERGUS-HOYT, Phyllis
GALEOTTI, Margherita
GAMBOGI, Luigia
JACQUE, Emilie
MONACHINA
RAPIN-GERBER, Eleonore
ROSS, Clara
SNODGRASS, Louise Harrison

VIOLIN AND ORCHESTRA OR STRINGS
18th Century A.D.
KOHARY, Marie, Countess of
SIRMEN, Maddalena Laura di
19th Century A.D.
BALTHASAR, Florence
FILIPOWICZ, Elize-Minelli
FORTMAGNE, Baroness de
RUNCIE, Constance Owen Faunt Le
  Roy
SALOMONI, Mlle.
TURNEY, Ruthyn
20th Century A.D.
ABEJO, Sister M. Rosalina
ARCHER, Violet Balestreri
ARRIEU, Claude
AUSTER, Lydia Martinovna
AVETISIAN, Aida Konstantinovna
BAADER-NOBS, Heidi
BACEWICZ, Grazyna
BARBERIS, Mansi
BARNS, Ethel
BECKON, Lettie Marie
BENAVENTE, Regina
BIALKIEWICZOWNA-ANDRAULT DE
  LANGERON, Irena
BOLL, Christine E.
BRODIN, Lena Birgitta Elise
BUCKLEY, Helen Dallam
BUCZEK, Barbara Kazimiera
BULTERIJS, Nina
CALL, Audrey
CIOBANU, Maia
COLIN, Jeanne
COQUET, Odile Marie-Lucie
COULTHARD, Jean
DAIGLE, Sister Anne Cécile
DESPORTES, Yvonne Berthe Melitta
ECKHARDT-GRAMATTE, Sophie-
  Carmen
FIRSOVA, Elena
FOLVILLE, Eugenie-Emilie Juliette
FONTYN, Jacqueline
FRANCHI, Dorothea
FULCHER, Ellen Georgina
GARR, Wieslawa
GARZTECKA-JARZEBSKA, Irena
GIPPS, Ruth
GRAUBNER, Hannelore
GUBAIDULINA, Sofia Asgatovna
GUBITOSI, Emilia
GYRING, Elizabeth
HALACSY, Irma von
HEMON, Sedje
HOY, Bonnee L.
IORDAN, Irina Nikolayevna
JIRKOVA, Olga

KARNITSKAYA, Nina Andreyevna
KERN, Frida
KLINKOVA, Zhivka
KOELLING, Eloise
KOHAN, Celina
KORN, Clara Anna
KULIEVA, Farida Tairovna
KUYPER, Elizabeth
KVERNADZE, Bidzina
LARSEN, Elizabeth Brown
LAUFER, Beatrice
LEE, Young Ja
LEJET, Edith
LEONCHIK, Svetlana Gavrilovna
LINZ VON KRIEGNER, Marta
LOCKWOOD, Annea Ferguson
LOUDOVA, Ivana
LUTYENS, Elisabeth
MAILIAN, Elza Antonovna
MANA-ZUCCA
MARCUS, Ada Belle Gross
MATRAS, Maude
MEREDITH, Margaret
MIAGI, Ester Kustovna
NIEDERBERGER, Maria A.
NIEMACK, Ilza Louise
NIKOLSKAYA, Olga Vasilevna
NOVOSELOVA, Ludmila
    Alexeyevna
OH, Sook Ja
PANETTI, Joan
PAYNE, Harriet
PERRY, Julia Amanda
PETRA-BASACOPOL, Carmen
PRICE, Florence Beatrice
PRIETO, Maria Teresa
RAINIER, Priaulx
RAPOPORT, Eda
RAVINALE, Irma
ROESGEN-CHAMPION, Marguerite
    Sara
ROGERS, Patsy
RUEGGER, Charlotte
SCHEIN, Suzanna Fedorovna
SCHORR-WEILER, Eva
SENFTER, Johanna
SHAIMARDANOVA, Shakhida
SHLONSKY, Verdina
SOLOMON, Mirrie Irma
STEINER, Gitta Hana
SUTHERLAND, Margaret
SWAIN, Freda Mary
SZYMANSKA, Iwonka Bogumila
TAILLEFERRE, Germaine
TERZIAN, Alicia
THIEME, Kerstin Anja
TIDEMAN-WIJERS, Bertha
TKACH, Zlata Moiseyevna
TUMANISHVILI, Ketevana
    Dmitirevna
UYEDA, Leslie
UYTTENHOVE, Yolande
VAKHVAKHISHVILI, Tamara
    Nikolayevna
VAN DE VATE, Nancy Hayes
VELLERE, Lucie Weiler
VERCOE, Elizabeth
VISCONTI, Leila
VITO-DELVAUX, Berthe di
VON ZIERITZ, Grete
VORLOVA, Slavka
WALDO, Elisabeth
WALLACE, Phyllis Joy
WHITE, Grace
WHITLOCK, E. Florence
WILLIAMS, Grace Mary
YAROSHEVSKAYA, Ludmila
    Anatolievna
ZAKRZEWSKA-NIKIPORCZYK,
    Barbara Maria
ZECHLIN, Ruth

ZHUBANOVA, Gaziza Akhmetovna
ZIELINSKA, Lidia
ZWILICH, Ellen Taaffe
Century unknown
JACQUE, Emilie

VIOLIN AND ORGAN
18th Century A.D.
BERTHE, Mme.
19th Century A.D.
AYLWARD, Florence
DELL'ACQUA, Eva
HAASS, Maria Catharina
WICHERN, Caroline
WICKINS, Florence
ZIMMERMANN, Agnes Marie
    Jacobina
20th Century A.D.
AHRENS, Sieglinde
BACKES, Lotte
BAKKE, Ruth
BOUTRON, Madeleine
FALCINELLI, Rolande
FRENCH, Tania
GUMMER, Phyllis Mary
KAHN, Esther
KALTENECKER, Gertraud
KARVENO, Wally
LEFANU, Nicola Frances
LEIVISKA, Helvi Lemmiki
POOL, Arlette
POPATENKO, Tamara Alexandrovna
POPOVICI, Elise
RHOADS, Mary R.
SIMPSON, Mary Jean
SOLOMON, Mirrie Irma
SOUTHGATE, Dorothy
SOUTHGATE, Elsie
SULTANOVA, Asya Bakhish kyzy
THOMSEN, Geraldine
TILICHEYEVA, Elena Nikolayevna
TUMANISHVILI, Ketevana
    Dmitirevna
VILLIN, Marcelle Henriette Marie
WARE, Helen
WHITE, Elsie Fellows
WICKS, Camilla
ZHVANETSKAIA, Inna Abramovna

VIOLIN AND PIANO
18th Century A.D.
AURENHAMMER, Josefa Barbara
    von
BARTHELEMON, Cécilia Maria
BARTHELEMON, Mary
BRANDENSTEIN, Charlotte von
BRUCKENTHAL, Bertha von,
    Baroness
DANZI, Maria Margarethe
DESFOSSES, Elisabeth Françoise,
    Countess
ESSEX, Margaret
LEBRUN, Franziska Dorothea
MOREL, Virginie
MURRAY, Lady Edith
REYNOLDS, Marie Hester
19th Century A.D.
AMALIE, Marie Friederike Augusta,
    Princess of Saxony
AMES, Mary Mildred
BALTHASAR, Florence
BARKER, Laura Wilson
BOYCE, Ethel Mary
BRESSON, Mlle.
BRONSART VON SCHELLENDORF,
    Ingeborg Lena von
CALOSSO, Eugenia
CANDEILLE, Amelie Julie
CARISSAN, Celanie
COLLINS, Laura Sedgwick
CORRER, Ida, Countess

CRUMB, Berenice
DAVIES, Llewela
DELL'ACQUA, Eva
EGEBERG, Anna
EUAN-SMITH, Lady
FARMER, Emily Bardsley
FARRENC, Louise
FILIPOWICZ, Elize-Minelli
GRANDVAL, Marie Felicie Clemence
    de Reiset, Vicomtesse de
GREENE, Edith
GUERINI, Rosa
GYDE, Margaret
HAMBROCK, Mathilde
HENSEL, Fanny Caecilia
HUNDT, Aline
KALKHOEF, Laura von
KENDIKOVA, Zdenka
KLETZINSKY, Adele
KRALIK VON MAYERSWALDEN,
    Mathilde
LANGHANS, Louise
LANGRISHE, May Katherine
LASZLO, Anna von
LIEBMANN, Helene
LODER, Kate Fanny
LONSDALE, Eva
MALLARD, Clarisse
MARIE ELIZABETH, Princess of
    Saxe-Meiningen
MASSART, Louise Aglae
MAYER, Emilie
MEYER, Elizabeth
MILANOLLO, Teresa Domenica
    Maria
MOLIQUE, Caroline
MUNDELLA, Emma
NAVA D'ADDA, Francesca,
    Countess
NEUVILLE, Mme. Alphonse de
OLIVER, Mary
PARADIS, Maria Theresia von
PARKE, Maria Hester
PARKYNS, Beatrice
PFEIFFER, Clara-Virginie
PITTMAN, Alice Locke
RALPH, Kate
RIBAS, Medina N.
RODRIGO, Maria
RONTGEN, Amanda
RUNCIE, Constance Owen Faunt Le
    Roy
SANDERS, Alma
SCHUMANN, Clara Josephine
SPORLEDER, Charlotte
SZYMANOWSKA, Maria Agata
TOWNSEND, Pearl Dea Etta
TREW, Susan
TSCHETSCHULIN, Agnes
VERGER, Virginie Morel du
VIARDOT-GARCIA, Pauline Michelle
    Ferdinande
WILHELMJ, Maria
WITKOWSKA-JABLONSKA, Maria
WURM, Mary J.A.
ZIEGLER, Natalie Sophie von
20th Century A.D.
AARNE, Els
ABEJO, Sister M. Rosalina
ABORN, Lora
ABRAMOVA, Sonia Pinkhasovna
ACCART, Eveline
ACOCK, Gwendolyn
AGABALIAN, Lidia Semyenovna
AGUDELO MURGUIA, Graciela
AKSYANTSEVA, Ninel Moiseyevna
ALMEN, Ruth
ALMESAN, Irma
ALOTIN, Yardena
ALVES DE SOUSA, Berta Candida
ANDREE, Elfrida

ANDREYEVA, Elena Fedorovna
ANTHONY, Evangeline
ARCHER, Violet Balestreri
ARIMA, Reiko
ARIZTI SOBRINO, Cecilia
ARRIEU, Claude
AUSTER, Lydia Martinovna
AVETISIAN, Aida Konstantinovna
AXTENS, Florence
BABAYEVA, Seda Grigorievna
BACEWICZ, Grażyna
BADIAN, Maya
BAGANIER, Janine
BAIKADAMOVA, Baldyrgan
    Bakhitzhanovna
BAIL, Grace Shattuck
BAILEY, Judith Margaret
BAINBRIDGE, Beryl
BAKLANOVA, Natalia
BALLANDS, Etta
BALLOU, Esther Williamson
BALUTET, Marguerite
BANNISTER, Mary Jeanne Hoggard
BARBERIS, Mansi
BARBILLON, Jeanne
BARKER, Phyllis Elizabeth
BARNS, Ethel
BARRADAS, Carmen
BARRAINE, Elsa
BARRELL, Joyce Howard
BARTHEL, Ursula
BATCHELOR, Phyllis
BAUER, Marion Eugenie
BAYEVA, Vera
BEACH, Amy Marcy
BEAT, Janet Eveline
BECK, Martha Dillard
BEESON, Elizabeth Ruth
BEHREND, Emilie
BELOCH, Dorotea
BENOIT, Francine Germaine Van
    Gool
BERAN-STARK, Lola Aloisia Maria
BERK, Adele
BEYER, Johanna Magdalena
BIALKIEWICZOWNA-ANDRAULT DE
    LANGERON, Irena
BILLINGTON, Elizabeth
BILTCLIFFE, Florence
BINET, Jocelyne
BLOMFIELD-HOLT, Patricia
BLOOD, Esta Damesek
BORDEWIJK-ROEPMAN, Johanna
BORKOWICZ, Maria
BORROFF, Edith
BOULANGER, Lili Juliette Marie Olga
BOUTRON, Madeleine
BRANSCOMBE, Gena
BRAUER, Johanna Elisabeth
BRESCHI, Laura
BRIGHT, Dora Estella
BRINK-POTHUIS, Annie van den
BROOK, Gwendolyn Giffen
BROWN, Norma
BRUCKSHAW, Kathleen
BRUSH, Ruth Damaris
BRUZDOWICZ, Joanna
BUCHANAN, Dorothy Quita
BULTERIJS, Nina
BUTLER, Anne Lois
CALCAGNO, Elsa
CALL, Audrey
CAMEU, Helza
CAMINHA, Alda
CANAL, Marguerite
CANALES PIZARRO, Marta
CAPERTON, Florence Tait
CAPUIS, Matilde
CARMEN MARINA
CARR-BOYD, Ann Kirsten
CARRIVICK, Olive Amelia

CARTER, Rosetta
CARWITHEN, Doreen
CATUNDA, Eunice do Monte Lima
CECCONI-BATES, Augusta
CHACON LASAUCA, Emma
CHAMINADE, Cécile Louise
    Stephanie
CHAMPION, Stephanie
CHARLOTTE, Princess of Saxe-
    Meiningen
CHICHERINA, Sofia Nikolayevna
CHITCHIAN, Geguni Oganesovna
CHKHEIDZE, Dali Davidovna
CHRETIEN-GENARO, Hedwige
CIMAGLIA DE ESPINOSA, Lia
CIOBANU, Maia
CLARK, Jane Leland
CLARKE, Emily
CLARKE, Rebecca
CLEMENT, Mary
COCQ, Rosina Susanna de
COHEN, Marcia
COLACO OSORIO-SWAAB, Reine
COLE, Ulric
COLERIDGE-TAYLOR, Avril
    Gwendolen
COLIN, Jeanne
CONTINI ANSELMI, Lucia
COQUET, Odile Marie-Lucie
CORNING, Karen Andrée
COTRON, Fanou
COULTHARD, Jean
CRAWFORD SEEGER, Ruth
DAIGLE, Sister Anne Cécile
DALE, Kathleen
DANEAU, Suzanne
DANIELS, Mabel Wheeler
DARE, Margaret Marie
DAVENPORT GOERTZ, Gladys
DAVITASHVILI, Meri Shalvovna
DAVY, Ruby Claudia Emily
DE BIASE BIDART, Lycia
DE LYLE, Carlyon
DEBRASSINE-PRIJAT, Laure
DELMOULY, Marie Mathilde
DEMARQUEZ, Suzanne
DESPORTES, Yvonne Berthe Melitta
DIAKVNISHVILI, Mzisavar
    Zakharevna
DIAMOND, Arline
DIEMER, Emma Lou
DIMITRIU, Florica
DINESCU, Violeta
DONIACH, Shula
DORABIALSKA, Julia Helena
DRAKE, Elizabeth Bell
DREGE-SCHIELOWA, Lucja
DROBYAZGINA, Valentina Ivanovna
DU PAGE, Florence Elizabeth
DUCOUREAU, Mme. M.
DUDLEY, Marjorie Eastwood
DYER, Susan
DZIEWULSKA, Maria Amelia
ECKHARDT-GRAMATTE, Sophie-
    Carmen
EGGELING-SPIES, I.
EHRMANN, Rosette
EISENSTEIN, Stella Price
EMINGEROVA, Katerina
ENDRES, Olive Philomene
ERDMANNSDOERFER, Pauline
ESCOBAR, Maria Luisa
ESCOT, Pozzi
ETHRIDGE, Jean
EUTENEUER-ROHRER, Ursula
    Henrietta
FAISST, Clara Mathilde
FALCINELLI, Rolande
FALTIS, Evelyn
FARGA PELLICER, Onia
FAUTCH, Sister Magdalen

FEIGIN, Sarah
FELDMAN, Joann Esther
FERRAND-TEULET, Denise
FINE, Vivian
FINZI, Graciane
FISCHER, Emma Gabriele Marie von,
    Baroness
FISHER, Katherine Danforth
FLACH, Elsa
FLICK-FLOOD, Dora
FOLVILLE, Eugenie-Emilie Juliette
FONTYN, Jacqueline
FORSTER, Dorothy
FREED, Dorothy Whitson
FRESON, Armande
FROMM-MICHAELS, Ilse
FULCHER, Ellen Georgina
FULLER-HALL, Sarah Margaret
FURGERI, Bianca Maria
GABUS, Monique
GALAJIKIAN, Florence Grandland
GARTENLAUB, Odette
GARUTA, Lucia Yanovna
GARZTECKA-JARZEBSKA, Irena
GEORGE, Lila-Gene
GERCHIK, Vera Petrovna
GERSTMAN, Blanche Wilhelminia
GEST, Elizabeth
GIDEON, Miriam
GINDLER, Kathe-Lotte
GIPPS, Ruth
GOETSCHIUS, Marjorie
GOKHMAN, Elena Vladimirovna
GOLOVINA, Olga Akimovna
GOLSON-BATEMAN, Florence
GOLUB, Martha Naumovna
GONTARENKO, Galina Nikolayevna
GONZAGA, Chiquinha
GOTKOVSKY, Ida-Rose Esther
GOULD, Elizabeth Davies
GRAHAM, Janet Christine
GRAUBNER, Hannelore
GRAY, Victoria Winifred
GREVENKOP CASTENKIOLD, Olga
GRIECO, Ida
GRZADZIELOWNA, Eleonora
GUBITOSI, Emilia
GURAIEB KURI, Rosa
GYANDZHETSIAN, Destrik
    Bogdanovna
HAENDEL, Ida
HAGER-ZIMMERMANN, Hilde
HALACSY, Irma von
HALL, Beatrice Mary
HANSEN, Hanna Marie
HARA, Kazuko (1)
HARDING, Mildred Thompson
HARRADEN, R. Ethel
HART, Elizabeth Jane Smith
HARVEY, Eva Noel
HAYS, Doris Ernestine
HEALE, Helene
HEBER, Judith
HECKSCHER, Céleste de Longpre
HEDOUX, Yvonne
HEDSTROEM, Ase
HEILBRON, Valerie
HEINRICHS, Agnes
HERNANDEZ-GONZALO, Gisela
HESSE, Marjorie Anne
HIER, Ethel Glen
HOEK, Agnes
HOLLINS, Dorothea
HOLMBERG, Betty
HONEGGER-VAURABOURG, Andrée
HOOD, Helen
HOPEKIRK, Helen
HORROCKS, Amy Elsie
HOUSMAN, Rosalie
HOWE, Mary Alberta Bruce
HOWELL, Dorothy

HSU, Wen-Ying
HUBICKI, Margaret Olive
HUEGEL, Margrit
HYDE, Cicely
HYTREK, Sister Theophane
IASHVILI, Lili Mikhailovna
IBRAGIMOVA, Sevda Mirza kyzy
IORDAN, Irina Nikolayevna
IPPOLITO, Carmela
IRMINGER, Caroline
ISMAGILOVA, Leila Zagirovna
ISZKOWSKA, Zofia
IVEY, Jean Eichelberger
JAELL-TRAUTMANN, Marie
JAMES, Dorothy E.
JANKOVIC, Miroslava
JEREA, Hilda
JOEST, Emma
JOLLY, Margaret Anne
KAHMANN, Chesley
KAHN, Esther
KAMIEN, Anna
KAPP, Corinne
KAPRALOVA, Vitezslava
KARASTOYANOVA, Elena
KARHILO, Liisa
KARNITSKAYA, Nina Andreyevna
KASILAG, Lucrecia R.
KATS-CHERNIN, Elena
KAUFMAN, Barbara
KAZANDJIAN, Sirvart
KEAL, Minna
KENNEDY-FRASER, Marjory
KERN, Frida
KESSLER, Minuetta Schumiatcher
KILBY, Muriel Laura
KLECHNIOWSKA, Anna Maria
KOELLING, Eloise
KOZANKOVA, Anna
KRASNOGLIADOVA, Vera
  Vladimirovna
KRZANOWSKA, Grazyna
KUKUCK, Felicitas
KUSS, Margarita Ivanovna
KUYPER, Elizabeth
KUZNETSOVA, Zhanetta
  Alexandrovna
LABEY, Charlotte Sohy
LAGO
LAMBERT, Cecily
LAMBRECHTS-VOS, Anna Catharina
LAMEGO, Carlinda J.
LANG-BECK, Ivana
LARA, Nelly Mele
LATHAM, Joan Seyler
LATIOLAIS, Desirée Jayne
LAUBER, Anne Marianne
LAWRENCE, Emily M.
LE BEAU, Louisa Adolpha
LEAHY, Mary Weldon
LEBARON, Anne
LEFANU, Nicola Frances
LEFEVRE, Jeanne
LEHMAN, Evangeline Marie
LEHMANN, Liza
LEHOTSKA-KRIZKOVA, Ludmila
LEIBOW, Ruth Irene
LEMON, Laura G.
LEONARD, Mamie Grace
LEONCHIK, Svetlana Gavrilovna
LEPLAE, Claire
LESUR, Mme. A.R.
LEVINA, Zara Alexandrovna
LIMA CRUZ, Maria Antonietta de
LINDEMAN, Anna Severine
LINZ VON KRIEGNER, Marta
LOUDOVA, Ivana
LUCAS, Blanche
LUDVIG-PECAR, Nada
LUNA DE ESPAILLAT, Margarita
LUND, Hanna

LUND, Inger Bang
LUND, Signe
LUTYENS, Elisabeth
LVOVA, Julia Fedorovna
MacKENNA, Carmela
McCLEARY, Fiona
McINTOSH, Diana
McKINNEY, Mathilde
McLAIN, Margaret Starr
McLAUGHLIN, Marian
McLEOD, Jennifer Helen
McPHERSON, Frances Marie
MAGEAU, Mary Jane
MAILIAN, Elza Antonovna
MAKAROVA, Nina Vladimirovna
MALDYBAYEVA, Zhyldyz
  Abdylasovna
MANA-ZUCCA
MARCUS, Ada Belle Gross
MARCUS, Bunita
MAREZ-OYENS, Tera de
MARI, Pierrette
MARIC, Ljubica
MARSHALL, M.E.
MARTINEZ DE LA TORRE Y
  SHELTON, Emma
MARTINS, Maria de Lourdes
MARY BERNICE, Sister
MATEVOSIAN, Araks Surenovna
MAZOUROVA, Jarmila
MEL-BONIS
MELL, Gertrud Maria
MELVILLE, Marguerite Liszniewska
MESRITZ-VAN VELTHUYSEN, Annie
METALLIDI, Zhanneta Lazarevna
MIAGI, Ester Kustovna
MIGRANYAN, Emma
MIKUSCH, Margarethe von
MIRSHAKAR, Zarrina Mirsaidovna
MKRTYCHIEVA, Virginia Nikitichna
MOORE, Dorothy Rudd
MOORE, Mary Carr
MORE, Margaret Elizabeth
MORIN-LABRECQUE, Albertine
MORLEY, Nina Dianne
MUELLER-HERMANN, Johanna
MUKHAMEDZHANOVA, Mariam
MUNGER, Shirley
MUNKTELL, Helena Mathilda
MUSGRAVE, Thea
MYSZINSKA-WOJCIECHOWSKA,
  Leokadia
NAZAROVA, Tatiana Borisovna
NAZIROVA, Elmira Mirza Rza kyzy
NEPGEN, Rosa Sophia Cornelia
NESTE, Rosane van
NEWLIN, Dika
NIEMACK, Ilza Louise
NIKOLAYEVA, Tatiana Petrovna
NIKOLSKAYA, Olga Vasilevna
NISS, Sofia Natanovna
NORRE, Dorcas
NOVI, Anna Beate
NOWAK, Alison
NOYES, Edith Rowena
OBROVSKA, Jana
ODAGESCU, Irina
OERBECK, Anne-Marie
OHE, Adele aus der
OKEY, Maggie
OSETROVA-YAKOVLIEVA, Nina
  Alexandrovna
OSGOOD, Marion
OSIANDER, Irene
OSTRANDER, Linda Woodaman
OSTROFF, Esther
OWEN, Blythe
PARPAGLIOLO, Iditta
PATERSON, Wilma
PATINO ANDRADE, Graziela
PATTERSON, Andra

PAYNE, Harriet
PEJACEVIC, Dora, Countess
PENTLAND, Barbara Lally
PEREIRA DA SILVA, Adelaide
PERONI, Wally
PERRY, Julia Amanda
PETRA-BASACOPOL, Carmen
PETROVA, Mara
PETROVA-KRUPKOVA, Elena
PEYROT, Fernande
PHILIPPART, Renée
PHILLIPS, Karen Ann
PHILLIPS, Linda
PIECHOWSKA, Alina
PIKE, Eleanor B. Franklin
PIRES DOS REIS, Hilda
PIZER, Elizabeth Faw Hayden
POLIGNAC, Armande de, Countess
  of Chabannes
POLIN, Claire
POPATENKO, Tamara Alexandrovna
POWELL, Maud
PRAVOSSUDOVITCH, Natalja
  Michajlovna
PREDIC-SAPER, Branislava
PREOBRAJENSKA, Vera Nicolaevna
PRICE, Florence Beatrice
PRIESING, Dorothy Jean
PRITI-PAINTAL
PROCACCINI, Teresa
QUANTIN-SAULNIER, Denise
QUIEL, Hildegard
RADERMACHER, Erika
RAINIER, Priaulx
RALSTON, Frances Marion
RAMM, Valentina Iosifovna
RAPOPORT, Eda
RAY, Ruth
RECLI, Giulia
REID, Wendy
REYNOLDS, Erma Grey Hogue
RHENE-JAQUE
RICHINSE, Cecile J.
RICHTER, Marga
RICKARD, Sylvia
RILEY, Myrtis F.
ROCHAT, Andrée
ROCHEROLLE, Eugenie Katherine
ROGER, Denise
ROGERS, Clara Kathleen
ROKSETH, Yvonne
ROSAS FERNANDES, Maria Helena
ROYSE, Mildred Barnes
ROZHAVSKAYA, Yudif Grigorevna
RUDALL, Eleonor C.
RUEGGER, Charlotte
RUFF-STOEHR, Herta Maria Klara
RUTA, Gilda, Countess
RYBNER, Dagmar de Corval
RYDER, Theodora Sturkow
SAKALLI-LECCA, Alexandra
SAMSON, Valerie Brooks
SAMTER, Alice
SANFORD, Grace Krick
SANTOS-OCAMPO DE FRANCESCO,
  Amada Amy
SAUVREZIS, Alice
SCHARWENKA-STRESOW,
  Marianne
SCHELLER ZEMBRANO, Maria
SCHICK, Philippine
SCHMITZ-GOHR, Else
SCHONTHAL, Ruth E.
SCHORR-WEILER, Eva
SEALY, Helen
SEHESTED, Hilda
SELTZNER, Jennie
SENFTER, Johanna
SEPULVEDA, Maria Luisa
SERVOZ, Harriet
SETO, Robin

SHARPE, Anna Wright
SHLONSKY, Verdina
SIMIC, Darinka
SIMON, Cécile Paul
SIMONIAN, Nadezhda Simonovna
SINGER, Jeanne
SISTEK-DJORDJEVIC, Mirjana
SOLOMON, Joyce Elaine
SOLOMON, Mirrie Irma
SOULAGE, Marcelle Fanny Henriette
SPAIN-DUNK, Susan
SPALDING, Eva Ruth
STAIR, Patty
STANEKAITE-LAUMYANSKENE,
Elena Ionovna
STEWART-BAXTER, Maud
STREICHER, Lyubov Lvovna
STREIT, Else
STRUTT, Dorothy
STURKOW-RYDER, Theodora
SUTHERLAND, Margaret
SVANIDZE, Natela Damianovna
SWAIN, Freda Mary
SZOENYI, Erzsebet
TAILLEFERRE, Germaine
TAKASHIMA, Midori
TAL, Marjo
TALMA, Louise
TARLOW, Karen Anne
TATE, Phyllis
TEICHMUELLER, Anna
TELFER, Nancy Ellen
TENGBERGEN, Maria Elizabeth van
Ebbenhorst
TERRY, Frances
THOME, Diane
TKACH, Zlata Moiseyevna
TOLKOWSKY, Denise
TORRA, Celia
TOWERSEY, Phyllis Mary
TROMBONE, Giuseppina
TROOSTWYCK, Hendrika
TROUP, Emily Josephine
TUMANIAN, Elizaveta Artashesovna
TYRMAND, Eta Moiseyevna
URNER, Catherine Murphy
USTVOLSKAYA, Galina Ivanovna
VAN DEN BOORN-COCLET,
Henriette
VAN NESTE, Rosane Micheline Lucie
Charlotte
VAZQUEZ, Alida
VELLERE, Lucie Weiler
VERCOE, Elizabeth
VIDAR, Jorunn
VIEU, Jane
VIGNERY, Jeanne Emilie Virginie
VILLIN, Marcelle Henriette Marie
VINOGRADOVA, Vera
VISCONTI, Leila
VITO-DELVAUX, Berthe di
VOLKART-SCHLAGER, Kaethe
VON ZIERITZ, Grete
VORONINA, Tatiana Aleksandrovna
VRABELY-WURMBACH-
STUPPACHOVA, Stefania
VYNER, Mary Bainbridge
WALLACH, Joelle
WARNE, Katharine Mulky
WARSHAW, Dalit Paz
WEAVER, Carol Ann
WEGENER-FRENSEL, Emmy Heil
WEIR, Judith
WEISSBERG, Julia Lazerevna
WENDELBURG, Norma Ruth
WENNERBERG-REUTER, Sara
Margareta Eugenia Euphrosyne
WHITE, Elsie Fellows
WHITLOCK, E. Florence
WHITTLE, Chris Mary-Francine
WIENIAWSKA, Irene Regine

WILKINS, Margaret Lucy
WILLIAMS, Joan Franks
WITKIN, Beatrice
WOODRUFF, Edith S.
WYLIE, Ruth Shaw
YAKHNINA, Yevgenia Yosifovna
YAROSHEVSKAYA, Ludmila
Anatolievna
YOUNG, Donel Marie
ZARIPOVA, Naila Gatinovna
ZAVALISHINA, Maria Semyonovna
ZECHLIN, Ruth
ZHUBANOVA, Gaziza Akhmetovna
ZHUBINSKAYA, Valentina Yanovna
ZIMMERMANN, Margrit
ZIVKOVIC, Mirjana
ZWILICH, Ellen Taaffe
Century unknown
BALL, Rae Eleanor
BOR, Modesta
COMBIE, Ida Mae
RAPIN-GERBER, Eleonore

VIOLONCELLO
17th Century A.D.
PRIOLI MORISINA, Marietta
SUARDA, Maria Virginia
18th Century A.D.
ANNA AMALIA, Duchess of Saxe-
Weimar
BON, Anna
BRUCKENTHAL, Bertha von,
Baroness
CECILE, Jeanne
DESFOSSES, Elisabeth Françoise,
Countess
KANZLER, Josephine
LOUIS, Mme.
POUILLAU, Mlle.
19th Century A.D.
BATTA, Clementine
BAUDISSIN, Sofie, Countess Wolf
BERTIN, Louise Angelique
BLAHETKA, Marie Leopoldina
BLANGINI, Mlle.
BRONSART VON SCHELLENDORF,
Ingeborg Lena von
CIBBINI, Katherina
CRETI, Marianna de Rocchis
DAHL, Emma
FARRENC, Louise
FILIPOWICZ, Elize-Minelli
GRANDVAL, Marie Felicie Clemence
de Reiset, Vicomtesse de
HAMMER, Marie von
KRAEHMER, Caroline
KRALIK VON MAYERSWALDEN,
Mathilde
LANG, Josephine
LANNOY, Clementine-Josephine-
Françoise-Thérèse, Countess
LIEBMANN, Helene
LODER, Kate Fanny
NORRIS, Mary
PUGET, Loise
SMITH, Alice Mary
VANZO, Vittoria Maria
VIARDOT-GARCIA, Pauline Michelle
Ferdinande
WAGNER, Virginia De Oliveira
Bastos
WHITE, Maude Valerie
WICKINS, Florence
20th Century A.D.
ABE, Kyoko
ACKLAND, Jessie Agnes
AKSYANTSEVA, Ninel Moiseyevna
ALEXANDRA, Liana
ALLEN, Judith Shatin
ALLIK, Kristi
ALLOUARD CARNY, Odette

ALOTIN, Yardena
ALTER, Martha
ANDERSON, Beth
ANDERSON, Julia McKinley
ANDERSON, Olive Jennie Paxton
ANDERSON, Ruth
ANDERSON-WUENSCH, Jean Mary
ANDREYEVA, Elena Fedorovna
ARAZOVA, Izabella Konstantinovna
ARCHER, Violet Balestreri
ARHO, Anneli
ARMER, Elinor Florence
ARSEYEVA, Irina Vasilievna
AUTENRIETH, Helma
BABAYEVA, Seda Grigorievna
BACEWICZ, Grażyna
BACH, Maria
BACKES, Lotte
BADIAN, Maya
BAIKADAMOVA, Baldyrgan
Bakhitzhanovna
BANCER, Teresa Barbara
BARADAPRANA, Pravrajika
BARBOSA, Cacilda Campos Borges
BARKLUND, Irma L.
BARRETT-THOMAS, N.
BARTLETT, Ethel Agnes
BAULD, Alison
BEACH, Amy Marcy
BEAT, Janet Eveline
BEATH, Betty
BECLARD D'HARCOURT,
Marguerite
BEECROFT, Norma Marian
BELL, Carla Huston
BELL, Elizabeth
BELLAMY, Marian Meredith
BENAVENTE, Regina
BENEDICENTI, Vera
BERCKMAN, Evelyn
BERGE, Irenee
BERGEN, Sylvia
BERNARD, Jeanne
BEYER, Johanna Magdalena
BIELEFELD, Ljuba
BIENVENU, Lily
BINET, Jocelyne
BIRCHER-REY, Hedy
BIRCSAK, Thusnelda
BIRKETT, Gwenhilda Mary
BIRNSTEIN, Renate Maria
BLAUSTEIN, Susan Morton
BLIESENER, Ada Elizabeth
Michelman
BLOMFIELD-HOLT, Patricia
BLOOD, Esta Damesek
BOBROW, Sanchie
BODENSTEIN-HOYME, Ruth E.
BOFILL, Anna
BOLZ, Harriet
BOND, Victoria Ellen
BORGE, Michele
BORRAS I FORNELL, Teresa
BOSMANS, Henriette Hilda
BOUCHARD, Linda L.
BOULANGER, Lili Juliette Marie Olga
BOUTRON, Madeleine
BOYD, Anne Elizabeth
BRANDMAN, Margaret Susan
BRESCHI, Laura
BRINK-POTHUIS, Annie van den
BRITAIN, Radie
BRODIN, Lena Birgitta Elise
BROOK, Gwendolyn Giffen
BRUZDOWICZ, Joanna
BUCHANAN, Dorothy Quita
BUCZEK, Barbara Kazimiera
BULTERIJS, Nina
BURSTON, Maggie
BUTLER, Patricia Magahay
CALCAGNO, Elsa

CALLAWAY, Ann
CAMPAGNE, Conny
CAMPMANY, Montserrat
CANAL, Marguerite
CAPUIS, Matilde
CARLOS, Wendy
CARMEN MARINA
CARNECI, Carmen
CARR-BOYD, Ann Kirsten
CARVALHO, Dinora de
CATUNDA, Eunice do Monte Lima
CECCONI-BATES, Augusta
CHANCE, Nancy Laird
CHARBONNIER, Janine Andrée
CHAVES, Mary Elizabeth
CHITCHIAN, Geguni Oganesovna
CHRETIEN-GENARO, Hedwige
CIMAGLIA DE ESPINOSA, Lia
CIOBANU, Maia
CLARKE, Rebecca
CLARKE, Rosemary
COATES, Gloria Kannenberg
COCQ, Rosina Susanna de
COLACO OSORIO-SWAAB, Reine
COLE, Ulric
CONRAD, Laurie M.
COONEY, Cheryl Lee
CORY, Eleanor
COULOMBE SAINT-MARCOUX,
 Micheline
COULTHARD, Jean
COWLES, Darleen
CRAIB, Doris
CRANE, Helen
CRAWFORD, Dawn Constance
CRAWFORD, Dorothy Lamb
CRAWFORD SEEGER, Ruth
DAHL, Vivian
DARE, Margaret Marie
DAVIDSON, Tina
DAVIS, Eleanor Maud
DAVITASHVILI, Meri Shalvovna
DEBRASSINE-PRIJAT, Laure
DEDIEU-PETERS, Madeleine
DELORME, Isabelle
DEMARQUEZ, Suzanne
DEMBO, Royce
DENBOW, Stefania Bjoerson
DIAMOND, Arline
DIANDA, Hilda
DIEMER, Emma Lou
DILLON, Fannie Charles
DINESCU, Violeta
DINN, Freda
DOBBINS, Lori
DOLMETSCH, Hélène
DREGE-SCHIELOWA, Lucja
DUCOUREAU, Mme. M.
DUDLEY, Marjorie Eastwood
DUSHKIN, Dorothy Smith
DZHAFAROVA, Afag Mamed kyzy
EARLEY, Judith
ECKHARDT-GRAMATTE, Sophie-
 Carmen
EGGAR, Katharine
ELLICOTT, Rosalind Frances
ERDOEDY, Luisa, Countess
ERHART, Dorothy
EVEN-OR, Mary
FALCINELLI, Rolande
FAUTCH, Sister Magdalen
FINE, Vivian
FINZI, Graciane
FIRSOVA, Elena
FISHER, Gladys Washburn
FLEISCHER-DOLGOPOLSKY,
 Tsipporah
FLEITES, Virginia
FLICK-FLOOD, Dora
FOLVILLE, Eugenie-Emilie Juliette
FORMAN, Joanne

FRANCO, Clare
FRASIER, Jane
FREED, Dorothy Whitson
FROMM-MICHAELS, Ilse
GARCIA ROBSON, Magdalena
GARDNER, Kay
GARR, Wieslawa
GARSCIA-GRESSEL, Janina
GARUTA, Lucia Yanovna
GEIGER-KULLMANN, Rosy Auguste
GENTILE, Ada
GEORGE, Lila-Gene
GIDEON, Miriam
GIFFORD, Helen Margaret
GIPPS, Ruth
GITECK, Janice
GLATZ, Helen Sinclair
GLAZIER, Beverly
GODLA, Mary Ann
GOEBELS, Gisela
GOKHMAN, Elena Vladimirovna
GOLOVINA, Olga Akimovna
GONTARENKO, Galina Nikolayevna
GOODSMITH, Ruth B.
GOTKOVSKY, Ida-Rose Esther
GRAHAM, Janet Christine
GREENE, Margo Lynn
GRIGSBY, Beverly
GRONOWETTER, Freda
GROSSMAN, Deena
GUBAIDULINA, Sofia Asgatovna
GUBITOSI, Emilia
GUDAUSKAS, Giedra
GVAZAVA, Tamara Davidovna
GYANDZHETSIAN, Destrik
 Bogdanovna
GYRING, Elizabeth
HAHN, Sandra Lea
HALPERN, Stella
HARA, Kazuko (1)
HARDY, Helen Irene
HARRIS, Ruth Berman
HARRISON, Pameia
HAWLEY, Carolyn Jean
HECKSCHER, Celeste de Longpre
HERBISON, Jeraldine Saunders
HIER, Ethel Glen
HILDERLEY, Jeriann G.
HIND O'MALLEY, Pamela
HO, Wai On
HOLLAND, Dulcie Sybil
HOLST, Imogen Clare
HOOVER, Katherine
HOPKINS, Sarah
HSU, Wen-Ying
HUEGEL, Margrit
HYSON, Winifred Prince
ISZKOWSKA, Zofia
JAMES, Dorothy E.
JANKOWSKI, Loretta Patricia
JENNY, Sister Leonore
JIRACKOVA, Marta
JOHNSON, Elizabeth
JOLAS, Betsy
KADIMA, Hagar Yonith
KAHMANN, Chesley
KALOGRIDOU, Maria
KANACH, Sharon E.
KAPRALOVA, Vitezslava
KATS-CHERNIN, Elena
KATZMAN, Klara Abramovna
KAVASCH, Deborah Helene
KELLER, Ginette
KERN, Frida
KESSLER, Minuetta Schumiatcher
KICKINGER, Paula
KING, Patricia
KIRKWOOD, Antoinette
KISTETENYI, Melinda
KITAZUME, Yayoi
KLECHNIOWSKA, Anna Maria

KNOBLOCHOVA, Antonie
KOELLING, Eloise
KOLB, Barbara
KONISHI, Nagako
KOPPEL-HOLBE, Maria
KOSSE, Roberta
KREISS, Hulda E.
KRZANOWSKA, Grażyna
KUBO, Mayako
KURIMOTO, Yoko
KUSUNOKI, Tomoko
KUZMYCH, Christina
LABEY, Charlotte Sohy
LACHOWSKA, Stefania
LAGO
LAITMAN, Lori
LANG-BECK, Ivana
LATHROP, Gayle Posselt
LATZ, Inge
LAUBER, Anne Marianne
LAVOIPIERRE, Thérèse
LAZAR, Ella
LE BEAU, Louisa Adolpha
LE SIEGE, Annette
LEAHY, Mary Weldon
LEBENBOM, Elaine F.
LEBIZAY, Marguerite
LEE, Chan-Hae
LEE, Hope Anne Keng-Wei
LEE, Hwaeja Yoo
LEE, Young Ja
LEFANU, Nicola Frances
LEIVISKA, Helvi Lemmiki
LEJET, Edith
LEJEUNE-BONNIER, Eliane
LELEU, Jeanne
LEON, Tania Justina
LEPEUT-LEVINE, Jeannine
LEVIN, Rami Yona
LEVITOVA, Ludmila Vladimirovna
LIMA CRUZ, Maria Antonietta de
LINDEMAN, Hjelle Signe
LINZ VON KRIEGNER, Marta
LIPSCOMB, Helen
LITSITE, Paula Yanovna
LLOYD, Caroline Parkhurst
LOH, Kathy Jean
LOMON, Ruth
LOPEZ ROVIROSA, Maria Isabel
LOWENSTEIN, Gunilla Marike
LUCAS, Mary Anderson
LUCKMAN, Phyllis
LUDVIG-PECAR, Nada
LUFF, Enid
LUND, Gudrun
LUTYENS, Elisabeth
LUTYENS, Sally
MACKIE, Shirley M.
MACONCHY, Elizabeth
MacKOWN, Marjorie T.
McCLEARY, Fiona
McCOLLIN, Frances
McGILL, Gwendolen Mary Finlayson
McINTOSH, Diana
McKENZIE, Sandra
McLEOD, Evelyn Lundgren
McLEOD, Jennifer Helen
MAGEAU, Mary Jane
MALMLOEF-FORSSLING, Carin
MAMLOK, Ursula
MAREZ-OYENS, Tera de
MARKOV, Katherine Lee
MARSHALL, Kye
MARTIN, Delores J.
MARTINEZ, Odaline de la
MAYADAS, Priya
MAYER, Lise Maria
MERRIMAN, Margarita Leonor
MOON, Chloe Elizabeth
MOORE, Dorothy Rudd
MOSELEY, Caroline Carr

MUNGER, Shirley
NEMTEANU-ROTARU, Doina
NIEDERBERGER, Maria A.
NOHE, Beverly
NOVOSELOVA, Ludmila Alexeyevna
NOWAK, Alison
ODAGESCU, Irina
OH, Sook Ja
O'LEARY, Jane Strong
ORENSTEIN, Joyce Ellin
PALMER, Lynne Wainwright
PARKER, Alice
PATTERSON, Andra
PAULL, Barberi
PELEGRI, Maria Teresa
PENGILLY, Sylvia
PERETZ-LEVY, Liora
PERRY, Julia Amanda
PETERSON, Melody
PHILIBA, Nicole
PHILIPPART, Renée
PHILLIPS, Bryony
PHILLIPS, Karen Ann
PHILLIPS, Linda
PIECHOWSKA, Alina
PIGGOTT, Audrey Margaret
PIKE, Eleanor B. Franklin
PLE-CAUSSADE, Simone
POLIN, Claire
POPOVICI, Elise
PRADELL, Leila
PRAVOSSUDOVITCH, Natalja
   Michajlovna
PREOBRAJENSKA, Vera Nicolaevna
PRICE, Beryl
PRICE, Deon Nielsen
PRICE, Florence Beatrice
PRIETO, Maria Teresa
PROCACCINI, Teresa
PSTROKONSKA-NAVRATIL,
   Grazyna Hanna
PTASZYNSKA, Marta
QUIEL, Hildegard
RAINIER, Priaulx
RAMM, Valentina Iosifovna
RAN, Shulamit
RAPOPORT, Eda
RAVINALE, Irma
REID, Wendy
REIFF, Lili
RENIE, Henriette
RHEINGOLD, Lauma Yanovna
RHENE-JAQUE
RICHTER, Marga
RICHTER, Marion Morrey
RICKARD, Sylvia
RILEY, Myrtis F.
RISHER, Anna Priscilla
ROBERTS, Megan L.
ROCHEROLLE, Eugenie Katherine
RODRIGUE, Nicole
RODRIGUEZ, Esther
ROE, Eileen Betty
ROESGEN-CHAMPION, Marguerite
   Sara
ROGER, Denise
ROGERS, Clara Kathleen
ROGERS, Melicent Joan
ROGERS, Patsy
ROGET, Henriette
ROSATO, Clorinda
RUBIN, Anna Ita
RUEFF, Jeanine
RUSCHE, Marjorie Maxine
RUTA, Gilda, Countess
SAITO-NODA, Eva
SAMSON, Valerie Brooks
SAMTER, Alice
SAMVELIAN, Sofia Vardanovna
SANGUESA, Iris
SCHERCHEN, Tona

SCHONTHAL, Ruth E.
SEARS, Ilene Hanson
SEMEGEN, Daria
SHAW, Alice Marion
SHEPARD, Jean Ellen
SHERMAN, Kim Daryl
SILSBEE, Ann L.
SILVERMAN, Faye-Ellen
SIMONS, Netty
SLIANOVA-MIZANDARI, Dagmara
   Levanovna
SMITH, Julia Frances
SMITH, Linda Catlin
SMYTH, Ethel Mary, Dame
SNIZKOVA-SKRHOVA, Jitka
SOLOMON, Joyce Elaine
SOULAGE, Marcelle Fanny Henriette
SOUTHAM, Ann
SPAIN-DUNK, Susan
SPENCER PALMER, Florence
   Margaret
SPENCER, Marguerita
STEINER, Gitta Hana
STREATFIELD, Valma June
STREICHER, Lyubov Lvovna
STREIT, Else
STRUTT, Dorothy
STURKOW-RYDER, Theodora
SUCHY, Gregoria Karides
SUH, Kyung-Sun
SUTHERLAND, Margaret
SUZUE, Mariko
SWAIN, Freda Mary
SYNOWIEC, Ewa
SZEKELY, Katalin
SZOENYI, Erzsebet
TAL, Ya'ara
TALMA, Louise
TATE, Phyllis
TELFER, Nancy Ellen
THEMMEN, Ivana Marburger
THOME, Diane
THOMSEN, Geraldine
TOWER, Joan
TUICHEVA, Zumrad
TUMANISHVILI, Ketevana
   Dmitirevna
USTVOLSKAYA, Galina Ivanovna
UYEDA, Leslie
VAN DE VATE, Nancy Hayes
VAN DEN BOORN-COCLET,
   Henriette
VAN OHLEN, Deborah
VASILIEVA, Tatiana Ivanovna
VERCOE, Elizabeth
VIERK, Lois
VIRTUE, Constance Cochnower
VOLKART, Hazel
VOLKART-SCHLAGER, Kaethe
WALKER, Gwyneth van Anden
WALLACH, Joelle
WANG, An-Ming
WANG, Qiang
WARDE, Ann Maury
WARING, Kate
WEGENER-FRENSEL, Emmy Heil
WEIGL, Vally
WELANDER, Svea Goeta
WEYBRIGHT, June
WHITEHEAD, Gillian
WHITLOCK, E. Florence
WHITTLE, Chris Mary-Francine
WISHART, Betty Rose
WITBECK, Ariel Lea
WOLLNER, Gertrude Price
WYLIE, Ruth Shaw
XENOPOL, Margareta
YAGLING, Victoria
YAROSHEVSKAYA, Ludmila
   Anatolievna
ZAIDEL-RUDOLPH, Jeanne

ZALLMAN, Arlene
ZECHLIN, Ruth
ZIBEROVA, Zinaida Petrovna
ZIELINSKA, Lidia
Century unknown
GALEOTTI, Margherita
MOREA, Vincenza della
RAPIN-GERBER, Eleonore
SNODGRASS, Louise Harrison

**VIOLONCELLO AND ORCHESTRA OR
STRINGS**
  19th Century A.D.
    HADELN, Nancy von
  20th Century A.D.
    BERGMAN, Ellen
    BOSMANS, Henriette Hilda
    BRODIN, Lena Birgitta Elise
    CALCAGNO, Elsa
    CAPUIS, Matilde
    COULTHARD, Jean
    DIANDA, Hilda
    ECKHARDT-GRAMATTE, Sophie-
     Carmen
    FIRSOVA, Elena
    GARY, Marianne
    GOODSMITH, Ruth B.
    GOTKOVSKY, Ida-Rose Esther
    GRONOWETTER, Freda
    HSU, Wen-Ying
    IORDAN, Irina Nikolayevna
    KALOGRIDOU, Maria
    KELLER, Ginette
    KORNILOVA, Tatiana Dmitrevna
    LEJET, Edith
    LUNA DE ESPAILLAT, Margarita
    MACONCHY, Elizabeth
    MacKOWN, Marjorie T.
    MORLEY, Angela
    NIKOLAYEVA, Tatiana Petrovna
    PENTLAND, Barbara Lally
    PETRA-BASACOPOL, Carmen
    PHILLIPS, Karen Ann
    PRICE, Beryl
    PRICE, Deon Nielsen
    PRIETO, Maria Teresa
    RAINIER, Priaulx
    RAPOPORT, Eda
    ROGET, Henriette
    RUEFF, Jeanine
    SHLONSKY, Verdina
    THOMSEN, Geraldine
    TOWER, Joan
    WILL, Madeleine
    YAGLING, Victoria
    YAROSHEVSKAYA, Ludmila
     Anatolievna

VIOLONCELLO AND PIANO
  18th Century A.D.
    BRUCKENTHAL, Bertha von,
     Baroness
  19th Century A.D.
    BLAHETKA, Marie Leopoldina
    BOPP VON OBERSTADT,
     Countess
    BRONSART VON SCHELLENDORF,
     Ingeborg Lena von
    DANZINGER, Laura
    FARRENC, Louise
    GRANDVAL, Marie Felicie Clemence
     de Reiset, Vicomtesse de
    HAENEL DE CRONENTHAL, Louise
     Augusta Marie Julia
    HAMMER, Marie von
    HEINKE, Ottilie
    HENSEL, Fanny Caecilia
    HERITTE-VIARDOT, Louise Pauline
     Marie
    LANG, Josephine
    LASZLO, Anna von

LIEBMANN, Helene
MAYER, Emilie
MOLIQUE, Caroline
NAVA D'ADDA, Francesca, Countess
ORGER, Caroline
PARADIS, Maria Theresia von
PESADORI, Antoinette de
SEIPT, Sophie
SWEPSTONE, Edith
SZYMANOWSKA, Maria Agata
VILLARD, Nina de
WHITE, Maude Valerie
WICHERN, Caroline
WIECK, Marie
WITKOWSKA-JABLONSKA, Maria
WURM, Mary J.A.
ZIMMERMANN, Agnes Marie Jacobina

20th Century A.D.

AARNE, Els
ACCART, Eveline
AKSYANTSEVA, Ninel Moiseyevna
ALLEN, Judith Shatin
ALVES DE SOUSA, Berta Candida
ARCHER, Violet Balestreri
ARMER, Elinor Florence
ARRIEU, Claude
ARSEYEVA, Irina Vasilievna
AVETISIAN, Aida Konstantinovna
BABAYEVA, Seda Grigorievna
BACEWICZ, Grażyna
BACH, Maria
BACKES, Lotte
BAIKADAMOVA, Baldyrgan Bakhitzhanovna
BAILEY, Judith Margaret
BAKLANOVA, Natalia
BALLANDS, Etta
BALLOU, Esther Williamson
BALUTET, Marguerite
BARBILLON, Jeanne
BARTLETT, Ethel Agnes
BELL, Elizabeth
BERNARD, Jeanne
BIENVENU, Lily
BLIESENER, Ada Elizabeth Michelman
BLOMFIELD-HOLT, Patricia
BOLZ, Harriet
BOND, Victoria Ellen
BORROFF, Edith
BOSMANS, Henriette Hilda
BOULANGER, Lili Juliette Marie Olga
BOULANGER, Nadia Juliette
BOUTRON, Madeleine
BRIGHT, Dora Estella
BRITAIN, Radie
BROGUE, Roslyn Clara
BUCHANAN, Dorothy Quita
CAPUIS, Matilde
CARLOS, Wendy
CECCONI-BATES, Augusta
CHITCHIAN, Geguni Oganesovna
CHRETIEN-GENARO, Hedwige
CIMAGLIA DE ESPINOSA, Lia
COCQ, Rosina Susanna de
COLEMAN, Ellen
COULTHARD, Jean
COWLES, Darleen
CRAIB, Doris
CRANE, Helen
CRAWFORD, Dorothy Lamb
CRAWFORD, Louise
DAHL, Vivian
DARE, Margaret Marie
DAVIDSON, Tina
DE BIASE BIDART, Lycia
DE FREITAS, Elvira Manuela Fernandez
DEBRASSINE-PRIJAT, Laure

DEL RIEGO, Thérèsa
DEMARQUEZ, Suzanne
DIAMOND, Arline
DUNLOP, Isobel
ECKHARDT-GRAMATTE, Sophie-Carmen
ELLICOTT, Rosalind Frances
ERDING, Susanne
FALCINELLI, Rolande
FAUTCH, Sister Magdalen
FINE, Vivian
FINZI, Graciane
FLEITES, Virginia
FOLVILLE, Eugenie-Emilie Juliette
FONTYN, Jacqueline
FRESON, Armande
GALAJIKIAN, Florence Grandland
GARSCIA-GRESSEL, Janina
GARTENLAUB, Odette
GIDEON, Miriam
GOEBELS, Gisela
GONZAGA, Chiquinha
GOULD, Elizabeth Davies
GOULD, Janetta
GRAHAM, Janet Christine
GRIECO, Ida
GRIMAUD, Yvette
GUBITOSI, Emilia
GUMMER, Phyllis Mary
GUSEINZADE, Adilia Gadzhi Aga
GVAZAVA, Tamara Davidovna
GYANDZHETSIAN, Destrik Bogdanovna
HAGER-ZIMMERMANN, Hilde
HARRADEN, R. Ethel
HARRISON, Pamela
HECKSCHER, Céleste de Longpre
HEDOUX, Yvonne
HERBISON, Jeraldine Saunders
HOPEKIRK, Helen
HORROCKS, Amy Elsie
HOWE, Mary Alberta Bruce
HSU, Wen-Ying
HUBICKI, Margaret Olive
HUEGEL, Margrit
HUGH-JONES, Elaine
IORDAN, Irina Nikolayevna
IVEY, Jean Eichelberger
JACKSON, Barbara May
JAELL-TRAUTMANN, Marie
JOLAS, Betsy
KAHMANN, Chesley
KALTENECKER, Gertraud
KANACH, Sharon E.
KAPRALOVA, Vitezslava
KARHILO, Liisa
KASHPEROVA, Leokadia Alexandrovna
KATZMAN, Klara Abramovna
KAVASCH, Deborah Helene
KERN, Frida
KESSLER, Minuetta Schumiatcher
KIRKWOOD, Antoinette
KLECHNIOWSKA, Anna Maria
KOELLING, Eloise
KOPPEL-HOLBE, Maria
KOPTAGEL, Yuksel
KORNILOVA, Tatiana Dmitrevna
KUYPER, Elizabeth
LAGO
LANG-BECK, Ivana
LATIOLAIS, Desirée Jayne
LAYMAN, Pamela
LE BEAU, Louisa Adolpha
LEAHY, Mary Weldon
LEE, Young Ja
LEHMAN, Evangeline Marie
LEIBOW, Ruth Irene
LEIVISKA, Helvi Lemmiki
LEONCHIK, Svetlana Gavrilovna
LEVINA, Zara Alexandrovna

LEVITOVA, Ludmila Vladimirovna
LIMA CRUZ, Maria Antonietta de
LINDEMAN, Anna Severine
LINZ VON KRIEGNER, Marta
LITSITE, Paula Yanovna
LOMON, Ruth
LUCKMAN, Phyllis
LUFF, Enid
LUTYENS, Elisabeth
MACONCHY, Elizabeth
McGILL, Gwendolen Mary Finlayson
MAKAROVA, Nina Vladimirovna
MALDYBAYEVA, Zhyldyz Abdylasovna
MANA-ZUCCA
MANZIARLY, Marcelle de
MAREZ-OYENS, Tera de
MARSHALL, Kye
MARTINS, Maria de Lourdes
MAZOUROVA, Jarmila
MEACHEM, Margaret McKeen Ramsey
MEL-BONIS
MERRIMAN, Margarita Leonor
MESRITZ-VAN VELTHUYSEN, Annie
MIAGI, Ester Kustovna
MOORE, Dorothy Rudd
MUELLER-HERMANN, Johanna
MUKHAMEDZHANOVA, Mariam
MUKLE, May Henrietta
MYSZINSKA-WOJCIECHOWSKA, Leokadia
NAZAROVA, Tatiana Borisovna
NAZIROVA, Elmira Mirza Rza kyzy
NIKOLSKAYA, Lyubov Borisovna
NORRE, Dorcas
NOVA SONDAG, Jacqueline
NOVI, Anna Beate
OSETROVA-YAKOVLIEVA, Nina Alexandrovna
OWEN, Blythe
PATERSON, Wilma
PEJACEVIC, Dora, Countess
PENTLAND, Barbara Lally
PERKIN, Helen
PERONI, Wally
PETRA-BASACOPOL, Carmen
PEYROT, Fernande
PIRES DOS REIS, Hilda
POPATENKO, Tamara Alexandrovna
POPOVICI, Elise
POSTON, Elizabeth
PRAVOSSUDOVITCH, Natalja Michajlovna
PRICE, Deon Nielsen
PROCACCINI, Teresa
PSTROKONSKA-NAVRATIL, Grazyna Hanna
RADERMACHER, Erika
RAN, Shulamit
RAPOPORT, Eda
RHEINGOLD, Lauma Yanovna
RHOADS, Mary R.
RISHER, Anna Priscilla
ROBERT, Lucie
ROCHAT, Andrée
RODRIGUEZ, Esther
ROESGEN-CHAMPION, Marguerite Sara
ROGERS, Clara Kathleen
ROGET, Henriette
RUEFF, Jeanine
RUFF-STOEHR, Herta Maria Klara
RUTA, Gilda, Countess
SAMTER, Alice
SANFORD, Grace Krick
SANZ, Rocio
SCHICK, Philippine
SEHESTED, Hilda
SENFTER, Johanna

SHAVERZASHVILI, Tamara
Antonovna
SHLONSKY, Verdina
SIDORENKO, Tamara Stepanovna
SMITH, Ethel
SMYTH, Ethel Mary, Dame
SNIZKOVA-SKRHOVA, Jitka
SOLOMON, Joyce Elaine
SOLOMON, Mirrie Irma
SOULAGE, Marcelle Fanny Henriette
SPENCER PALMER, Florence
Margaret
SPOERRI-RENFER, Anna-
Margaretha
STANEKAITE-LAUMYANSKENE,
Elena Ionovna
STEIN-SCHNEIDER, Lena
STREICHER, Lyubov Lvovna
STRUTT, Dorothy
SUTZU, Rodica
SWAIN, Freda Mary
SWIFT, Kay
SZOENYI, Erzsebet
TAL, Marjo
TATE, Phyllis
THEMMEN, Ivana Marburger
THOME, Diane
TORRENS, Merce
TRICHT, Nora von
TUMANISHVILI, Ketevana
Dmitirevna
URNER, Catherine Murphy
USTVOLSKAYA, Galina Ivanovna
VAN DE VATE, Nancy Hayes
VAN DEN BOORN-COCLET,
Henriette
VAN NESTE, Rosane Micheline Lucie
Charlotte
VELLERE, Lucie Weiler
VIDAR, Jorunn
VIEU, Jane
VITO-DELVAUX, Berthe di
VOLKART-SCHLAGER, Kaethe
VORLOVA, Slavka
WALKER, Gwyneth van Anden
WEGENER-FRENSEL, Emmy Heil
WELANDER, Svea Goeta
WHITTINGTON, Joan
WILLIAMS, Kimberley
WILLS, Edwina Florence
WILSON, Lynn
WITKIN, Beatrice
XENOPOL, Margareta
YAGLING, Victoria
YAROSHEVSKAYA, Ludmila
Anatolievna
ZAIDEL-RUDOLPH, Jeanne
ZAVALISHINA, Maria Semyonovna
ZELIKOVSKAYA, Fania
Mordukhovna
ZHUBANOVA, Gaziza Akhmetovna
ZIBEROVA, Zinaida Petrovna
ZIFFRIN, Marilyn Jane
ZIMMERMANN, Margrit
Century unknown
BOR, Modesta
CORKER, Marjorie
GORE, Blanche

**VIOLS INCLUDING VIOLA D'AMORE AND
VIOLA DA GAMBA**
16th Century A.D.
MOLZA, Tarquinia
18th Century A.D.
LA GUERRE, Elisabeth-Claude
Jacquet de
PHILHARMONICA, Mrs.
THICKNESSE, Miss
20th Century A.D.
ALSTED, Birgitte
AUSTIN, Dorothea

BARRELL, Joyce Howard
BARRIERE, Françoise
BARTHEL, Ursula
BEHREND, Jeanne
BLOOM, Jane Ira
DEMBO, Royce
ECKHARDT-GRAMATTE, Sophie-
Carmen
FREER, Eleanor Warner Everest
FRITZ, Sherilyn Gail
GARDNER, Kay
KUKUCK, Felicitas
MANZIARLY, Marcelle de
MASSUMOTO, Kikuko
NEWLIN, Dika
OLIVEROS, Pauline
PETROVA-KRUPKOVA, Elena
POSTON, Elizabeth
SAMPSON, Peggy
SCHORR-WEILER, Eva
USHER, Julia

VIRGINAL
17th Century A.D.
VAN SOLDT, Suzanna
20th Century A.D.
ARMER, Elinor Florence
PRICE, Beryl

**WIND ENSEMBLE AND ORCHESTRA OR
STRINGS**
18th Century A.D.
BRANDES, Charlotte Wilhelmina
Franziska
20th Century A.D.
ARRIEU, Claude
CALCAGNO, Elsa
CHANDLER, Mary
GRZADZIELOWNA, Eleonora
HYTREK, Sister Theophane
LAUER, Elizabeth
LEHMAN, Evangeline Marie
LOUDOVA, Ivana
LOUIE, Alexina Diane
RAINIER, Priaulx
RAMM, Valentina Iosifovna
RAVINALE, Irma
SCHWARTZ, Julie
SHLONSKY, Verdina
THIEME, Kerstin Anja
WALLACH, Joelle

WIND QUARTET
20th Century A.D.
AKHUNDOVA, Shafiga Gulam kyzy
ALEXANDRA, Liana
ANDERSON, Beth
ARCHER, Violet Balestreri
ARRIEU, Claude
AUSTER, Lydia Martinovna
AUSTIN, Dorothea
BAILEY, Judith Margaret
BARKIN, Elaine
BEEKHUIS, Hanna
BOLZ, Harriet
BOUCHARD, Linda L.
BOYD, Anne Elizabeth
CECCONI-BATES, Augusta
CECCONI-BOTELLA, Monic
CHANDLER, Mary
COATES, Gloria Kannenberg
DIEMER, Emma Lou
FREED, Dorothy Whitson
FRUMKER, Linda
GABRYS, Ewa Lucja Maria
GARDNER, Mildred Alvine
GIDEON, Miriam
GOERSCH, Ursula Margitta
GOOLKASIAN-RAHBEE, Dianne
Zabelle
HARRISON, Pamela

HIRSCHFELDT, Ingrid
KANACH, Sharon E.
KICKINGER, Paula
KOBLENZ, Babette
LACHARTRE, Nicole Marie
LOH, Kathy Jean
LOWENSTEIN, Gunilla Marike
LUNA DE ESPAILLAT, Margarita
LUTHER, Mary
McINTOSH, Diana
MARKIEWICZOWNA, Wladyslawa
MASON, Gladys Amy
MRACEK, Ann Michelle
NIKOLSKAYA, Lyubov Borisovna
OFFICER, Bronwyn Lee
PEYROT, Fernande
PIZER, Elizabeth Faw Hayden
PRICE, Beryl
RAMM, Valentina Iosifovna
RILEY, Ann Marion
ROGER, Denise
SAINT JOHN, Kathleen Louise
SANGUESA, Iris
SCHWARTZ, Nan Louise
THOMSEN, Geraldine
VAN DE VATE, Nancy Hayes
VELLERE, Lucie Weiler
VOLKART, Hazel
WALLACH, Joelle
WARING, Kate
WASKO, Christine
WENDELBURG, Norma Ruth
YOUNG, Gayle
ZAIMONT, Judith Lang

WIND QUINTET
19th Century A.D.
RODRIGO, Maria
20th Century A.D.
AARNE, Els
ALEXANDRA, Liana
ALLEN, Judith Shatin
ALVES DE SOUSA, Berta Candida
ANDERSON, Ruth
ARHO, Anneli
ARMER, Elinor Florence
ARRIEU, Claude
BACEWICZ, Grażyna
BADIAN, Maya
BAILEY, Judith Margaret
BARKLUND, Irma L.
BARRAINE, Elsa
BAUER, Marion Eugenie
BEACH, Amy Marcy
BEECROFT, Norma Marian
BEEKHUIS, Hanna
BENNETT, Wilhelmine
BEYER, Johanna Magdalena
BOLZ, Harriet
BORRAS I FORNELL, Teresa
BOYD, Anne Elizabeth
BRITAIN, Radie
BROCKMAN, Jane E.
BROGUE, Roslyn Clara
BUCZEK, Barbara Kazimiera
BUTLER, Patricia Magahay
CARR-BOYD, Ann Kirsten
CHANDLER, Mary
COULOMBE SAINT-MARCOUX,
Micheline
CRAWFORD SEEGER, Ruth
CRAWFORD, Dawn Constance
DANIELSON, Janet Rosalie
DAVIS, Jean Reynolds
DEMBO, Royce
DIANDA, Hilda
DIEMER, Emma Lou
DINESCU, Violeta
DOBIE, Janet
ECKHARDT-GRAMATTE, Sophie-
Carmen

ERVIN, Karen
EVERETT-SALICCO, Betty Lou
FAIRLIE, Margaret C.
FINZI, Graciane
FONTYN, Jacqueline
FRASIER, Jane
FREED, Dorothy Whitson
FRITTER, Genevieve Davisson
FROMM-MICHAELS, Ilse
GALBRAITH, Nancy Riddle
GARTENLAUB, Odette
GOULD, Elizabeth Davies
GRAY, Victoria Winifred
HARDY, Helen Irene
HARRIS, Ruth Berman
HAWLEY, Carolyn Jean
HEILBRON, Valerie
HOOVER, Katherine
HOWE, Mary Alberta Bruce
HUNKINS, Eusebia Simpson
IVEY, Jean Eichelberger
JACOB, Elizabeth Marie
JIRKOVA, Olga
JOLAS, Betsy
KANACH, Sharon E.
KEAL, Minna
KERN, Frida
KETTERING, Eunice Lea
KLEBE, Willemijntje
KOELLING, Eloise
KOLB, Barbara
LACHARTRE, Nicole Marie
LACKMAN, Susan C. Cohn
LANG, Rosemary Rita
LEAHY, Mary Weldon
LEBENBOM, Elaine F.
LEE, Hwaeja Yoo
LEVY, Ellen
LIPSCOMB, Helen
LOMON, Ruth
LUFF, Enid
LUNA DE ESPAILLAT, Margarita
LUND, Gudrun
LUTHER, Mary
LUTYENS, Elisabeth
MACKIE, Shirley M.
MACONCHY, Elizabeth
McCOLLIN, Frances
McINTOSH, Diana
McLAUGHLIN, Marian
McNEIL, Janet L. Pfischner
MAMLOK, Ursula
MAREZ-OYENS, Tera de
MARI, Pierrette
MARIC, Ljubica
MARKOV, Katherine Lee
MARSHALL, Pamela J.
MARTINS, Maria de Lourdes
MEARS, Caroline
METALLIDI, Zhanneta Lazarevna
MIAGI, Ester Kustovna
NAKAMURA, Sawako
NEMTEANU-ROTARU, Doina
NORDENSTROM, Gladys Mercedes
OBROVSKA, Jana
ORE, Cecilie
OSETROVA-YAKOVLIEVA, Nina
    Alexandrovna
PATERSON, Wilma
PATTERSON, Andra
PERISSAS, Madeleine
PERRY, Julia Amanda
PETROVA-KRUPKOVA, Elena
PHILIPPART, Renee
PIZER, Elizabeth Faw Hayden
PLONSEY, Jennifer
POLIN, Claire
POPOVICI, Elise
PROCACCINI, Teresa
RAIGORODSKY, Leda Natalia
    Heimsath

RAINIER, Priaulx
RAPOPORT, Eda
REED, Marlyce Rae Polk
REYNOLDS, Erma Grey Hogue
ROE, Eileen Betty
ROOTH, Anna-Greta
ROWAN, Barbara
RUSCHE, Marjorie Maxine
SAINT JOHN, Kathleen Louise
SANDRESKY, Margaret Vardell
SANTOS-OCAMPO DE FRANCESCO,
    Amada Amy
SANZ, Rocio
SCHERCHEN, Tona
SCHORR-WEILER, Eva
SCHUBARTH, Dorothe
SEVERY, Violet Cavell
SHLONSKY, Verdina
SHORE, Clare
SHREVE, Susan Ellen
SILVERMAN, Faye-Ellen
SKARECKY, Jana Milena
STANLEY, Helen Camille
STEELE, Lynn
STILMAN-LASANSKY, Julia
STRUTT, Dorothy
TAKAMI, Toyoko
TARLOW, Karen Anne
TELFER, Nancy Ellen
THOMAS, Marilyn Taft
VAN DE VATE, Nancy Hayes
VAN EPEN-DE GROOT, Else Antonia
VAN HAUTE, Anna-Maria
VITO-DELVAUX, Berthe di
VORLOVA, Slavka
WALDO, Elisabeth
WEAVER, Carol Ann
WECKWERTH, Nancy
WEIR, Judith
YAMPOLSCHI, Roseane
ZECHLIN, Ruth
ZHVANETSKAIA, Inna Abramovna
ZIVKOVIC, Mirjana

Century unknown
GORTON, Karen

WIND TRIO
19th Century A.D.
SANTA-COLONA-SOURGET,
    Eugenie
20th Century A.D.
AINSCOUGH, Juliana Mary
ALEXANDER, Leni
ARCHER, Violet Balestreri
ARRIEU, Claude
BACEWICZ, Grażyna
BEYER, Johanna Magdalena
BOLZ, Harriet
BORDERS, Barbara Ann
BRANDMAN, Margaret Susan
BRUNER, Cheryl
CRAWFORD, Dorothy Lamb
DANFORTH, Frances A.
DEMBO, Royce
ECKHARDT-GRAMATTE, Sophie-
    Carmen
EVERETT-SALICCO, Betty Lou
FRASER-MILLER, Gloria Jill
FRASIER, Jane
FREED, Dorothy Whitson
FRENCH, Tania
FRITTER, Genevieve Davisson
GOTKOVSKY, Ida-Rose Esther
GRAUBNER, Hannelore
HAYS, Doris Ernestine
HSU, Wen-Ying
INWOOD, Mary Ruth Brink Berger
JACOB, Elizabeth Marie
JOCHSBERGER, Tzipora H.
KANACH, Sharon E.
KAYDEN, Mildred

KETTERING, Eunice Lea
KLINKOVA, Zhivka
KUZMYCH, Christina
LAUER, Elizabeth
LE SIEGE, Annette
McLAUGHLIN, Marian
MARCUS, Bunita
MAREZ-OYENS, Tera de
MARINESCU-SCHAPIRA, Ilana
MEACHEM, Margaret McKeen
    Ramsey
MOON, Chloe Elizabeth
MUSGRAVE, Thea
NOWAK, Alison
OLIVEROS, Pauline
OWEN, Blythe
PERKIN, Helen
PETROVA, Mara
PIETSCH, Edna Frieda
POULET DEFONTAINE, Madeleine
ROGER, Denise
RUEFF, Jeanine
SAINT JOHN, Kathleen Louise
SAMTER, Alice
SHEVITZ, Mimi
SIEGRIST, Beatrice
SUTHERLAND, Margaret
TESCHKE, Herma
VAN DER MARK, Maria
VEHAR, Persis Anne
VELLERE, Lucie Weiler
VERNAELDE, Henriette
VIERK, Lois
WELANDER, Svea Goeta
WENDELBURG, Norma Ruth
YAMPOLSCHI, Roseane

WOODWIND ENSEMBLE
20th Century A.D.
ABEJO, Sister M. Rosalina
ARKWRIGHT, Marian Ursula
BALLOU, Esther Williamson
BARTHEL, Ursula
BAUER, Marion Eugenie
BEAT, Janet Eveline
BENNETT, Wilhelmine
BLISS, Marilyn S.
BOND, Victoria Ellen
BORROFF, Edith
BROCKMAN, Jane E.
CAMPMANY, Montserrat
CECCONI-BATES, Augusta
CORY, Eleanor
CREWS, Lucille
DIAMOND, Arline
DRING, Madeleine
DUSHKIN, Dorothy Smith
DZHAFAROVA, Afag Mamed kyzy
FLEMMING, Martha
FULLER, Jeanne Weaver
FULLER-HALL, Sarah Margaret
GIDEON, Miriam
GRIEBLING, Karen Jean
GYRING, Elizabeth
HANNIKAINEN, Ann-Elise
HENDERSON, Moya
HURLEY, Susan
INWOOD, Mary Ruth Brink Berger
KITAZUME, Yayoi
KLECHNIOWSKA, Anna Maria
KOELLING, Eloise
KORNILOVA, Tatiana Dmitrevna
LAPEIRETTA, Ninon de Brouwer
LE SIEGE, Annette
LESICHKOVA, Lili
LEVIN, Rami Yona
LIFFER, Binette
LOTTI, Silvana di
LUND, Gudrun
MARSHALL, Pamela J.
MITCHELL, Janice Misurell

MOORE, Dorothy Rudd
NIKOLSKAYA, Olga Vasilevna
OSETROVA-YAKOVLIEVA, Nina
   Alexandrovna
PENGILLY, Sylvia
PRICE, Deon Nielsen
SCHWARTZ, Nan Louise
SHAVERZASHVILI, Tamara
   Antonovna
SHEPARD, Jean Ellen
SIEGRIST, Beatrice
SMITH, Julia Frances
STRUTT, Dorothy
UYTTENHOVE, Yolande
VEHAR, Persis Anne
VERRALL, Pamela Motley
Century unknown
   BINNS, Jaqueline

XYLOPHONE
20th Century A.D.
   BARKIN, Elaine
   BARRETT-THOMAS, N.
   DESPORTES, Yvonne Berthe Melitta
   DIEMER, Emma Lou
   DU PAGE, Florence Elizabeth
   GUDAUSKAS, Giedra
   IVEY, Jean Eichelberger
   LOUDOVA, Ivana
   MARSHALL, Pamela J.
   MAZOUROVA, Jarmila
   MEACHEM, Margaret McKeen
      Ramsey
   MORRISON, Julia Maria
   MURRAY, Margaret
   ODAGESCU, Irina
   OSAWA, Kazuko
   PETRA-BASACOPOL, Carmen
   PHILLIPS, Bryony
   PTASZYNSKA, Marta
   STREATFIELD, Valma June
   ZIBEROVA, Zinaida Petrovna
   ZIFFRIN, Marilyn Jane

ZITHER
12th Century A.D.
   HILDEGARDE, Saint
19th Century A.D.
   ADELUNG, Olga
   CHRIST, Fanny
   KAVALIEROVA, Marie
   SIEGMUND, Hermine
   STUBENBERG, Anna Zichy,
      Countess
   WIMMER, Marianne
   ZAUBITZER, Ida
20th Century A.D.
   PADE, Else Marie
   PIECHOWSKA, Alina

VOCAL MUSIC- SECULAR

CANTATAS
17th Century A.D.
   STROZZI, Barbara
18th Century A.D.
   AGNESI-PINOTTINI, Maria Teresa d'
   DELAVAL, Mme.
   GRIMANI, Maria Margherita
   GUEST, Jeanne Marie
   GUIDICCIONI, Laura
   LA GUERRE, Elisabeth-Claude
      Jacquet de
   LOUVENCOURT, Mlle. de
   MARTINEZ, Marianne
   SAVAGE, Jane
19th Century A.D.
   ASACHI, Elena
   ASPRI, Orsola
   BARKER, Laura Wilson
   BOYCE, Ethel Mary

BRIZZI-GIORGI, Maria
DEMAR, Thérèse
EATON, Frances
FERRARI, Carlotta
GABRIEL, Mary Ann Virginia
HARTLAND, Lizzie
HERITTE-VIARDOT, Louise Pauline
   Marie
HOLLAND, Caroline
HOLMES, Augusta Mary Anne
KINKEL, Johanna
KNAPP, Phoebe Palmer
MARSHALL, Florence A.
MELY, Marie, Countess Vanden
   Heuvel
MEYER, Elizabeth
PARADIS, Maria Theresia von
PLITT, Agathe
PRESCOTT, Oliveria Louisa
RAMSAY, Lady Katherine
RUDERSDORF, Erminie
RUNCIE, Constance Owen Faunt Le
   Roy
SAINT-DIDIER, Countess
SAINTON-DOLBY, Charlotte Helen
SMITH, Alice Mary
SONTAG, Henriette
SWEPSTONE, Edith
WARD, Clementine
20th Century A.D.
AARNE, Els
ABEJO, Sister M. Rosalina
ADAMS, Julia Aurelia
ALCALAY, Luna
ALEXANDER, Leni
ALEXANDRA, Liana
ALLITSEN, Frances
ALOTIN, Yardena
ANDREE, Elfrida
ANDREYEVA, M.
ARETZ, Isabel
ARRIEU, Claude
AUSTER, Lydia Martinovna
BACEWICZ, Grażyna
BACH, Maria
BALLANDS, Etta
BARAMISHVILI, Olga Ivanovna
BARBERIS, Mansi
BARBLAN-OPIENSKA, Lydia
BARRAINE, Elsa
BARRELL, Joyce Howard
BEACH, Amy Marcy
BECK, Martha Dillard
BELLEROSE, Sister Cécilia
BIENVENU, Lily
BJELKE-ANDERSEN, Olga
BODENSTEIN-HOYME, Ruth E.
BOND, Victoria Ellen
BOULANGER, Lili Juliette
   Marie Olga
BOULANGER, Nadia Juliette
BOYD, Jeanne Margaret
BRANSCOMBE, Gena
BRENNER, Rosamond Drooker
BRIGGS, Dorothy Bell
BROGUE, Roslyn Clara
BUENAVENTURA, Isabel
BULTERIJS, Nina
BURKE, Loretto
CATUNDA, Eunice do Monte Lima
CECCONI-BATES, Augusta
CECCONI-BOTELLA, Monic
CHEBOTARIAN, Gayane
   Movsesovna
CHUDOVA, Tatiana Alekseyevna
COATES, Gloria Kannenberg
COHEN, Dulcie M.
COONEY, Cheryl Lee
COTRON, Fanou
CREWS, Lucille
DAVY, Ruby Claudia Emily

DE FREITAS, Elvira Manuela
   Fernandez
DERLIEN, Margarete
DILLON, Fannie Charles
DIMITRIU, Florica
DINESCU, Violeta
DONATOVA, Narcisa
DUSHKIN, Dorothy Smith
ELKOSHI, Rivka
ELLICOTT, Rosalind Frances
ELLIOTT, Janice Overmiller
ELMORE, Cenieth Catherine
ELST, Nancy van der
ERNST, Siegrid
FILZ, Bogdanna
FINE, Vivian
FINLEY, Lorraine Noel
FISHER, Katherine Danforth
FOLVILLE, Eugenie-Emilie Juliette
FORMAN, Addie Walling
FRAJT, Ludmila
FRASER, Shena Eleanor
FURGERI, Bianca Maria
GAIGEROVA, Varvara Andrianovna
GARUTA, Lucia Yanovna
GARY, Marianne
GARZTECKA-JARZEBSKA, Irena
GITECK, Janice
GOERSCH, Ursula Margitta
GOLSON-BATEMAN, Florence
GONTARENKO, Galina Nikolayevna
GRIEBEL WANDALL, Tekla
GRZADZIELOWNA, Eleonora
GUBAIDULINA, Sofia Asgatovna
GUSEINZADE, Adilia Gadzhi Aga
GYRING, Elizabeth
HARRADEN, R. Ethel
HARRISON, Annie Fortescue
HEDOUX, Yvonne
HENDERSON, Ruth Watson
HIER, Ethel Glen
HOLLAND, Dulcie Sybil
HOLST, Imogen Clare
HORROCKS, Amy Elsie
INWOOD, Mary Ruth Brink Berger
IORDAN, Irina Nikolayevna
ISAKOVA, Aida Petrovna
JAMES, Dorothy E.
JOLAS, Betsy
KASHPEROVA, Leokadia
   Alexandrovna
KATZMAN, Klara Abramovna
KAZHAEVA, Tatiana Ibragimovna
KELLER, Ginette
KESSLER, Minuetta Schumiatcher
KETTERING, Eunice Lea
KLECHNIOWSKA, Anna Maria
KLINKOVA, Zhivka
KLOTZMAN, Dorothy Ann Hill
KOLODUB, Zhanna Efimovna
KOVALEVA, Olga Vasilevna
KRASNOGLIADOVA, Vera
   Vladimirovna
KUKUCK, Felicitas
KUSUNOKI, Tomoko
KUYPER, Elizabeth
LAMBRECHTS-VOS, Anna Catharina
LANG, Margaret Ruthven
LASANSKY, Ada Julia
LAWRENCE, Emily M.
LE BEAU, Louisa Adolpha
LEE, Chan-Hae
LEHMAN, Evangeline Marie
LEIVISKA, Helvi Lemmiki
LELEU, Jeanne
LENNEP, Henrietta van
LESICHKOVA, Lili
LEVITOVA, Ludmila Vladimirovna
LEVITSKAYA, Viktoria Sergeyevna
LEWIS, Carrie Buliard
LIADOVA, Ludmila Alekseyevna

LITTLEJOHN, Joan Anne
LOCKWOOD, Annea Ferguson
LOPUSKA-WYLEZYNSKA, Helena
LORENZ, Ellen Jane
LOUDOVA, Ivana
LUND, Signe
LUTYENS, Elisabeth
MACONCHY, Elizabeth
McALLISTER, Rita
McCOLLIN, Frances
McINTOSH, Diana
McLIN, Lena
MAKAROVA, Nina Vladimirovna
MARBE, Myriam
MARIANI-CAMPOLIETI, Virginia
MARIC, Ljubica
MASON, Gladys Amy
MAURICE, Paule
MEACHEM, Margaret McKeen
  Ramsey
MIAGI, Ester Kustovna
MILLER, Joan
MIRSHAKAR, Zarrina Mirsaidovna
MONK, Meredith
MOORE, Mary Carr
MORLEY, Nina Dianne
MOTTA, Giovanna
MUELLER-HERMANN, Johanna
MUSGRAVE, Thea
NAZAROVA, Tatiana Borisovna
NEPGEN, Rosa Sophia Cornelia
NIKOLAYEVA, Tatiana Petrovna
NIKOLSKAYA, Lyubov Borisovna
NIKOLSKAYA, Olga Vasilevna
NUNLIST, Juli
ODAGESCU, Irina
OOSTERZEE, Cornelia van
OSETROVA-YAKOVLIEVA, Nina
  Alexandrovna
PAKHMUTOVA, Alexandra
  Nikolayevna
PARKER, Alice
PATTERSON, Annie Wilson
PERETZ-LEVY, Liora
PERKIN, Helen
PERRY, Julia Amanda
PETERSEN, Marian F.
PETRA-BASACOPOL, Carmen
PETROVA-KRUPKOVA, Elena
PETYREK, Felika
PEYROT, Fernande
PFEIFFER, Irena
PHILLIPS, Bryony
POPATENKO, Tamara Alexandrovna
PREOBRAJENSKA, Vera Nicolaevna
QUINTANILLA, Alba
RAMM, Valentina Iosifovna
RAPOPORT, Eda
RECLI, Giulia
RENNES, Catharina van
REYNOLDS, Erma Grey Hogue
RHEINGOLD, Lauma Yanovna
RICHEPIN, Eliane
ROBERT, Lucie
ROE, Eileen Betty
ROESGEN-CHAMPION, Marguerite
  Sara
ROWAN, Barbara
ROZHAVSKAYA, Yudif Grigorevna
SANDRESKY, Margaret Vardell
SANZ, Rocio
SCHICK, Philippine
SCHUBARTH, Dorothe
SEHESTED, Hilda
SETTI, Kilza
SHELTON, Margaret Meier
SHIELDS, Alice Ferree
SHLONSKY, Verdina
SIDORENKO, Tamara Stepanovna
SKARECKY, Jana Milena
SMITH, Eleanor

SMYTH, Ethel Mary, Dame
SNIZKOVA-SKRHOVA, Jitka
SOUBLETTE, Sylvia
STAIRS, Lousie E.
STILMAN-LASANSKY, Julia
STOLL, Helene Marianne
STRUTT, Dorothy
SULTANOVA, Asya Bakhish kyzy
SUSSMAN, Ettel
SWAIN, Freda Mary
SZOENYI, Erzsebet
SZPINTER-KINIECKA, Maria
TAILLEFERRE, Germaine
TARNER, Evelyn Fern
TEGNER, Alice Charlotte
TERZIAN, Alicia
THOME, Diane
TILICHEYEVA, Elena Nikolayevna
TKACH, Zlata Moiseyevna
TUCKER, Tui St. George
TUMANISHVILI, Ketevana
  Dmitirevna
TYRMAND, Eta Moiseyevna
URNER, Catherine Murphy
VAKHVAKHISHVILI, Tamara
  Nikolayevna
VAN APPLEDORN, Mary Jeanne
VASILIEVA, Tatiana Ivanovna
VENDELHAVEN, Harriet
VITO-DELVAUX, Berthe di
VLADERACKEN, Geertruida van
VORLOVA, Slavka
VORONINA, Tatiana Aleksandrovna
WALKER, Gwyneth van Anden
WARE, Harriet
WARREN, Elinor Remick
WEGENER-KOOPMAN, Bertha
  Frensel
WEIGL, Vally
WEISSBERG, Julia Lazerevna
WELLNER, Elsa
WOLL, Erna
YAKHNINA, Yevgenia Yosifovna
ZECHLIN, Ruth
ZHUBANOVA, Gaziza Akhmetovna
ZIVKOVIC, Mirjana
ZWEIG, Esther

Century unknown
CONSOLINI, Gabriella Elsa
SNODGRASS, Louise Harrison
SOKOLL, Christa
TRANETTINA
VOYNICH, Ethel Lillian

CHORUS AND ORCHESTRA
18th Century A.D.
  ANNA AMALIA, Princess of Prussia
19th Century A.D.
  BARKER, Laura Wilson
  HOLLAND, Caroline
  HOLMES, Augusta Mary Anne
  MATTFELD, Marie
  RODRIGO, Maria
  SMITH, Alice Mary
  THOMPSON, Alexandra
20th Century A.D.
  AARNE, Els
  ABEJO, Sister M. Rosalina
  ABRAMOVA, Sonia Pinkhasovna
  AINSCOUGH, Juliana Mary
  AKSYANTSEVA, Ninel Moiseyevna
  ALEJANDRO-DE LEON, Esther
  ALVES DE SOUSA, Berta Candida
  ARAZOVA, Izabella Konstantinovna
  ARCHER, Violet Balestreri
  ARRIEU, Claude
  AULIN, Laura Valborg
  AUSTER, Lydia Martinovna
  AVETISIAN, Aida Konstantinovna
  BACH, Maria
  BALLOU, Esther Williamson

BANCER, Teresa Barbara
BARBERIS, Mansi
BARRAINE, Elsa
BARTHELSON, Joyce Holloway
BAUER, Marion Eugenie
BAULD, Alison
BERCKMAN, Evelyn
BERTRAND, Ginette
BLOM, Diane
BRANSCOMBE, Gena
BRUGGMANN, Heidi
BRUNDZAITE, Konstantsiya Kazyo
CALCAGNO, Elsa
CHAMINADE, Cécile Louise
  Stephanie
CHARLES, S. Robin
CIOBANU, Maia
COATES, Gloria Kannenberg
CONRAD, Laurie M.
COULTHARD, Jean
COWLES, Darleen
DANIELS, Mabel Wheeler
DANOWSKI, Helen
DE BIASE BIDART, Lycia
DE FREITAS, Elvira Manuela
  Fernandez
DEL RIEGO, Theresa
DEMESSIEUX, Jeanne
DINESCU, Violeta
DROSTE, Doreen
DUSHKIN, Dorothy Smith
DYCHKO, Lesya Vasilevna
DZIEWULSKA, Maria Amelia
FALCINELLI, Rolande
FOSTER, Cecily
FRENCH, Tania
GABUS, Monique
GHIGLIERI, Sylvia
GIURANNA, Elena Barbara
GLANVILLE-HICKS, Peggy
GOODSMITH, Ruth B.
GOULD, Elizabeth Davies
GRZADZIELOWNA, Eleonora
GUBITOSI, Emilia
GYANDZHETSIAN, Destrik
  Bogdanovna
HERNANDEZ-GONZALO, Gisela
KALTENECKER, Gertraud
KATZMAN, Klara Abramovna
KENSWIL, Atma
KUBO, Mayako
LEE, Hope Anne Keng-Wei
LEITE, Clarisse
LEIVISKA, Helvi Lemmiki
LEVI, Natalia Nikolayevna
LIMA CRUZ, Maria Antonietta de
LINZ VON KRIEGNER, Marta
LOCKSHIN, Florence Levin
LUNA DE ESPAILLAT, Margarita
MACKIE, Shirley M.
MacKENNA, Carmela
McCOLLIN, Frances
McINTYRE, Margaret
McLAUGHLIN, Marian
MAGUY LOVANO, Marguerite
  Schlegel
MANUKIAN, Irina Eduardovna
MAREZ-OYENS, Tera de
MARIC, Ljubica
MARTINS, Maria de Lourdes
MAYER, Lise Maria
MEKEEL, Joyce
MIGRANYAN, Emma
MIRSHAKAR, Zarrina Mirsaidovna
MOBERG, Ida Georgina
MONTGOMERY, Merle
MORLEY, Angela
MOSZUMANSKA-NAZAR, Krystyna
MUELLER-HERMANN, Johanna
MUNGER, Millicent Christner
MUSGRAVE, Thea

NORDENSTROM, Gladys Mercedes
NOVA SONDAG, Jacqueline
OLIVIERI SAN GIACOMO, Elsa
OSETROVA-YAKOVLIEVA, Nina
  Alexandrovna
PABLOS CEREZO, Maria de
PARKER, Alice
PETRA-BASACOPOL, Carmen
PEYROT, Fernande
PHILIPPART, Renee
PHILLIPS, Bryony
PIERCE, Sarah Anderson
PRAVOSSUDOVITCH, Natalja
  Michajlovna
PRICE, Florence Beatrice
PRIETO, Maria Teresa
PTASZYNSKA, Marta
QUINTANILLA, Alba
RABINOF, Sylvia
RAINIER, Priaulx
RAMAKERS, Christiane Josée
RAVINALE, Irma
RECLI, Giulia
REED, Marlyce Rae Polk
REISSEROVA, Julie
RENNES, Catharina van
REYNOLDS, Erma Grey Hogue
ROBERT, Lucie
ROCHEROLLE, Eugenie Katherine
ROMM, Rosalina Davidovna
ROSSELLI-NISSIM, Mary
SAINT JOHN, Kathleen Louise
SAMUEL, Rhian
SAMUELSON, Laura Byers
SCHICK, Philippine
SHORE, Clare
SIDORENKO, Tamara Stepanovna
SISTEK-DJORDJEVIC, Mirjana
SMYTH, Ethel Mary, Dame
SODRE, Joanidia
SOLOMON, Joyce Elaine
SOUBLETTE, Sylvia
SPICER, Marjorie
STANLEY, Helen Camille
STILMAN-LASANSKY, Julia
STULTZ, Marie Irene
SZYMANSKA, Iwonka Bogumila
TAILLEFERRE, Germaine
TATE, Phyllis
TELFER, Nancy Ellen
THIEME, Kerstin Anja
TUCKER, Irene
TUMANISHVILI, Ketevana
  Dmitirevna
TWOMBLY, Mary Lynn
URNER, Catherine Murphy
USHER, Julia
USTVOLSKAYA, Galina Ivanovna
VAN DE VATE, Nancy Hayes
VAN HAUTE, Anna-Maria
VASHAW, Cecile
VASILIEVA, Tatiana Ivanovna
VIDAR, Jorunn
VON ZIERITZ, Grete
VORLOVA, Slavka
WALDO, Elisabeth
WALKER, Gwyneth van Anden
WELANDER, Svea Goeta
WENDELBURG, Norma Ruth
WENNERBERG-REUTER, Sara
  Margareta Eugenia Euphrosyne
WHITLOCK, E. Florence
WILLIAMS, Grace Mary
WOODWARD, Martha Clive
YOUNG, Donel Marie
ZAIMONT, Judith Lang
ZAKRZEWSKA-NIKIPORCZYK,
  Barbara Maria
ZHVANETSKAIA, Inna Abramovna
ZIVKOVIC, Mirjana

CHORAL WORKS
7th Century B.C.
  MEGALOSTRATA OF SPARTA
6th Century B.C.
  TELESILLA OF ARGOS
6th Century A.D.
  CORINNA
16th Century A.D.
  BOURGES, Clementine de
18th Century A.D.
  AGNESI-PINOTTINI, Maria Teresa d'
  CAMBIASI BRANCA, Cirilla
  MUELLER, Elise
19th Century A.D.
  ASACHI, Elena
  AYLWARD, Florence
  BARKER, Laura Wilson
  BARTHOLOMEW, Mrs. M.
  BEHR, Louise
  BERTIN, Louise Angelique
  CALOSSO, Eugenia
  CARISSAN, Celanie
  COLLETT, Sophia Dobson
  DULCKEN, Louisa
  EATON, Frances
  FRANKEL, Gisela
  GEIGER, Constanze
  HARTLAND, Lizzie
  HERTZ, Hedwig
  HOLMES, Augusta Mary Anne
  HUNDT, Aline
  KINKEL, Johanna
  KRAEHMER, Caroline
  LANGHANS, Louise
  MALLARD, Clarisse
  NORRIS, Mary
  ORSINI, Teresa
  PARKHURST, Susan
  PESSIAK-SCHMERLING, Anna
  PLITT, Agathe
  PUGET, Loise
  REES, Cathrine Felicie van
  RICOTTI, Onestina
  ROECKEL, Jane
  RUCH-TSCHIEMER, Flora
  RUNCIE, Constance Owen Faunt Le
    Roy
  TOWNSEND, Marie
  VESPERMANN, Marie
  VORWERK, Henrietta
  WAKEFIELD, Augusta Mary
  WURM, Mary J.A.
  YOUNG, Harriet Maitland
  ZIMMERMANN, Agnes Marie
    Jacobina
  ZUMSTEEG,Emilie
20th Century A.D.
  AARNE, Els
  AAS, Else Berntsen
  ABE, Kyoko
  ABRAMOVA, Sonia Pinkhasovna
  ACOSTA, Josefina, Baroness
  ADAMS, Carrie Bell
  AESCHLIMANN-ROTH, Esther
  AKHUNDOVA, Shafiga Gulam kyzy
  ALCALAY, Luna
  ALEJANDRO-DE LEON, Esther
  ALLEN, Denise
  ALLIK, Kristi
  ALOTIN, Yardena
  ALTER, Martha
  ALTMAN, Adella C.
  ALVES DE SOUSA, Berta
    Candida
  ANDERSEN, Helen Somerville
  ANDERSON, Beth
  ANDERSON, Julia McKinley
  ANDERSON-WUENSCH, Jean Mary
  ANDREE, Elfrida
  ANDREYEVA, Elena Fedorovna
  ANDRIESSEN, Caecilia

ANDRIEVSKAYA, Nina
  Konstantinovna
ANTHONY, Gina
ARAZOVA, Izabella Konstantinovna
ARIMA, Reiko
ARKWRIGHT, Marian Ursula
ARMER, Elinor Florence
ARSEYEVA, Irina Vasilievna
ARVEY, Verna
ASHFORD, Emma Louise
AUSTIN, Grace Leadenham
AYLOTT, Lydia Georgina Edith
BAADER-NOBS, Heidi
BACEWICZ, Grazyna
BACHELLER, Mildred R. Thomas
BACKES, Lotte
BAIL, Grace Shattuck
BAILLY, Colette
BAINBRIDGE, Beryl
BAKER, Gertrude Tremblay
BAKKE, Ruth
BALCKE, Frida Dorothea
BALDACCI, Giovanna Bruna
BALLOU, Esther Williamson
BAMPTON, Ruth
BANDARA, Linda
BARAT, Eliane
BARBERIS, Mansi
BARBILLON, Jeanne
BARBOSA, Cacilda Campos Borges
BARBOUR, Florence Newell
BARIL, Jeanne
BARKIN, Elaine
BARKLUND, Irma L.
BARNETT, Carol Edith
BARON SUPERVIELLE, Susana
BARRELL, Joyce Howard
BARRETT-THOMAS, N.
BARTHEL, Ursula
BARTHELSON, Joyce Holloway
BARTON, Ann
BASSETT, Karolyn Wells
BASSOT, Anne-Marie
BAUER, Marion Eugenie
BAULD, Alison
BAUMGARTEN, Chris
BAYEVA, Vera
BEAHM, Jacquelyn Yvette
BEAMISH, Sally
BEAT, Janet Eveline
BEATH, Betty
BEEKHUIS, Hanna
BEESON, Elizabeth Ruth
BEHREND, Jeanne
BELL, Carla Huston
BELOCH, Dorotea
BERK, Adele
BERNARDONE, Anka
BERRY, Margaret Mary Robinson
BEZDEK, Sister John Joseph
BIBBY, Gillian Margaret
BILLSON, Ada
BILTCLIFFE, Florence
BINET, Jocelyne
BIRCSAK, Thusnelda
BITGOOD, Roberta
BIXBY, Allene K.
BLAKE, Dorothy Gaynor
BLANCK, Olga de
BLAUSTEIN, Susan Morton
BOBROW, Sanchie
BOCARD, Sister Cécilia Clair
BOLZ, Harriet
BORDEWIJK-ROEPMAN, Johanna
BORRAS I FORNELL, Teresa
BOUCHARD, Linda L.
BOULANGER, Lili Juliette Marie Olga
BRANDMAN, Margaret Susan
BRANSCOMBE, Gena
BRITAIN, Radie
BROCKMAN, Jane E.

BROOKS, Alice M.
BROWN, Mary Helen
BRUNDZAITE, Konstantsiya Kazyo
BUCHANAN, Annabel Morris
BURSTON, Maggie
BUTTERFIELD, Hattie May
CABRERA, Silvia Maria Pires
CAESAR, Shirley
CALCAGNO, Elsa
CALE, Rosalie Balmer Smith
CAMPAGNE, Conny
CAMPMANY, Montserrat
CANALES PIZARRO, Marta
CARR-BOYD, Ann Kirsten
CARTER, Buenta MacDaniel
CATUNDA, Eunice do Monte Lima
CHAMINADE, Cécile Louise
    Stephanie
CHAMPION, Constance MacLean
CHEATHAM, Kitty
CHERUBIM, Sister Mary Schaefer
CHESTNUT, Lora Perry
CIOBANU, Maia
CLARK, June
CLARK, Ruth Scott
CLINGAN, Judith Ann
COLERIDGE-TAYLOR, Avril Gwen-
dolen
CONSTANTINESCU, Domnica
CONWAY, Olive
COONEY, Cheryl Lee
COOPER, Esther Sayward
COULTHARD, Jean
COUTURE, Priscilla
COVERT, Mary Ann Hunter
COWLES, Darleen
CRAWFORD, Dawn Constance
CRAWFORD, Dorothy Lamb
CROFTS, Inez Altman
CROWE, Bonita
CURRAN, Pearl Gildersleeve
CURTWRIGHT, Carolee
CUTLER, Mary J.
DALBERT, Anny
DANIELA, Carmen
DANIELS, Mabel Wheeler
DAVIS, Margaret Munger
DAVISON, Martha Taylor
DAVITASHVILI, Meri Shalvovna
DAVY, Ruby Claudia Emily
DE BIASE BIDART, Lycia
DE FREITAS, Elvira Manuela
    Fernandez
DEMBO, Royce
DENBOW, Stefania Bjoerson
DESPORTES, Yvonne Berthe Melitta
DIEMER, Emma Lou
DINESCU, Violeta
DIXON, Esther
DOBIE, Janet
DOBSON, Elaine
DOLLEY, Betty Grace
DONCEANU, Felicia
DRDOVA, Marie
DROBYAZGINA, Valentina Ivanovna
DROSTE, Doreen
DRYE, Sarah Lynn
DRYNAN, Margaret
DUNGAN, Olive
DUNLOP, Isobel
DUNN, Rebecca Welty
DZIEWULSKA, Maria Amelia
EAGAR, Fannie Edith Starke
EASTES, Helen Marie
EDWARDS, Clara
EDWARDS, Jessie B.
EGGLESTON, Anne E.
EICHENWALD, Sylvia
EILERS, Joyce Elaine
EIRIKSDOTTIR, Karolina
EISENSTEIN DE VEGA, Silvia

ELLICOTT, Rosalind Frances
ELLIOTT, Marjorie Reeve
ELLIS, Cecil Osik
ELWYN-EDWARDS, Dilys
EMERY, Dorothy Radde
EMINGEROVA, Katerina
ENDRES, Olive Philomene
ERHART, Dorothy
ERNST, Siegrid
ESCOT, Pozzi
EVEN-OR, Mary
FAHRER, Alison Clark
FAISST, Clara Mathilde
FELDMAN, Joann Esther
FERNANDEZ, Helen Lorenzo
FERRIS, Isabel D.
FINE, Vivian
FISHER, Katherine Danforth
FITZGERALD, Sister Florence
    Thérèse
FLACH, Elsa
FLEISCHER-DOLGOPOLSKY,
    Tsipporah
FLICK-FLOOD, Dora
FOSTER, Cecily
FOSTER, Fay
FRANCO, Clare
FRASIER, Jane
FREEHOFF, Ruth Williams
FREER, Eleanor Warner Everest
FRITZ, Sherilyn Gail
FULLER-HALL, Sarah Margaret
GALINNE, Rachel
GANNON, Ruth Ellen
GARDINER, Mary Elizabeth
GARDNER, Kay
GARTENLAUB, Odette
GAUTHIEZ, Cécile
GERCHIK, Vera Petrovna
GESSLER, Caroline
GHIKA-COMANESTI, Ioana
GIDEON, Miriam
GILBERT, Janet Monteith
GILENO, Jean Anthony
GIPPS, Ruth
GIURANNA, Elena Barbara
GLANVILLE-HICKS, Peggy
GLATZ, Helen Sinclair
GLAZIER, Beverly
GLICKMAN, Sylvia
GOKHMAN, Elena Vladimirovna
GOLUB, Martha Naumovna
GOMM, Elizabeth
GONTARENKO, Galina Nikolayevna
GORELLI, Olga
GOULD, Elizabeth Davies
GOVEA, Wenonah Milton
GRAHAM, Janet Christine
GRAY, Dorothy
GUILBERT, Christiane
GULESIAN, Grace Warner
GUMMER, Phyllis Mary
HANKS, Sybil Ann
HARLEY, Frances Marjorie
HARPER, Marjorie
HARROD, Beth Miller
HARTER, Louise C.
HASHIMOTO, Kunihiko
HAWLEY, Carolyn Jean
HEALE, Helene
HEGGE, Mrs. M.H.
HEIDRICH, Hermine Margaret
HELLER, Ruth
HENDERSON, Elizabeth
HENDERSON, Ruth Watson
HERBERT, Dorothy
HERBISON, Jeraldine Saunders
HERMANN, Miina
HICKS, Marjorie Kisby
HIER, Ethel Glen
HIGGINS, Esther S.

HIRSCH, Barbara
HO, Wai On
HOFFRICHTER, Bertha Chaitkin
HOLLIS, Ruby Shaw
HOLST, Imogen Clare
HOLTHUSEN, Anita Saunders
HOYLAND, Janet
HSU, Wen-Ying
HUGHEY, Evangeline Hart
HURLEY, Susan
HUTSON, Wihla L.
IVANOVA, Lidia
JACKSON, Mary
JACOB, Elizabeth Marie
JACOBUS, Dale Asher
JAMES, Dorothy E.
JANKOWSKI, Loretta Patricia
JENNY, Sister Leonore
JEREA, Hilda
JIRACKOVA, Marta
JOCHSBERGER, Tzipora H.
JOHNSON, Eloise Lisle
JOLAS, Betsy
JOLLEY, Florence Werner
JOLLY, Margaret Anne
JUENGER, Patricia
KABE, Mariko
KAESER-BECK, Aida
KALTENECKER, Gertraud
KAMINSKY, Laura
KANACH, Sharon E.
KANAKA'OLE, Edith Ke-Kuhikuhi-I-
    Pu'u-one-o-Na-Ali'i-O-Kohala
KAPRALOVA, Vitezslava
KARASTOYANOVA, Elena
KARG, Marga
KARVENO, Wally
KASILAG, Lucrecia R.
KAYDEN, Mildred
KAZHAEVA, Tatiana Ibragimovna
KECK, Pearl
KELLY, Denise Maria Anne
KERN, Frida
KESAREVA, Margarita Alexandrovna
KESSLER, Minuetta Schumiatcher
KETTERER, Laura
KETTERING, Eunice Lea
KLECHNIOWSKA, Anna Maria
KLEPPER, Anna Benzia
KLINKOVA, Zhivka
KNOBLOCHOVA, Antonie
KNOUSS, Isabelle G.
KNOWLTON, Fanny Snow
KOELLING, Eloise
KOHAN, Celina
KONISHI, Nagako
KOPPEL-HOLBE, Maria
KOSSE, Roberta
KRASNOGLIADOVA, Vera
    Vladimirovna
KRUSE, Lotte
KUBO, Mayako
KUNTZE, Olga
KURIMOTO, Yoko
KUSS, Margarita Ivanovna
KUYPER, Elizabeth
KUZMENKO, Larysa
KUZMICH, Natalie
KUZMYCH, Christina
LACHARTRE, Nicole Marie
LACMANOVA, Anna
LAITMAN, Lori
LAMEGO, Carlinda J.
LANDOWSKA, Wanda
LARSEN, Elizabeth Brown
LARSON, Anna Barbara
LATIOLAIS, Desirée Jayne
LATZ, Inge
LAUBER, Anne Marianne
LAUER, Elizabeth
LAUFER, Beatrice

LAURENT, Ruth Carew
LAVIN, Marie Duchesne
LAZAR, Ella
LE BEAU, Louisa Adolpha
LEAHY, Mary Weldon
LEBARON, Anne
LEBEDEVA, A.
LEE, Chan-Hae
LEECH, Renee
LEFANU, Nicola Frances
LEHMAN, Evangeline Marie
LEIBOW, Ruth Irene
LEJET, Edith
LEJEUNE-BONNIER, Eliane
LEPEUT-LEVINE, Jeannine
LEVITSKAYA, Viktoria Sergeyevna
LEWIN, Olive
LIDDELL, Claire
LIPSCOMB, Helen
LITSITE, Paula Yanovna
LITTLE, Anita Gray
LIU, Tyan-Khua
LLOYD, Caroline Parkhurst
LOCKSHIN, Florence Levin
LOMON, Ruth
LOPEZ ROVIROSA, Maria Isabel
LOPUSKA-WYLEZYNSKA, Helena
LORD, Helen Cooper
LORE, Emma Maria Theresa
LOUDOVA, Ivana
LUCK, Maude Haben
LUCKE, Katharine E.
LUFF, Enid
LUNA DE ESPAILLAT, Margarita
LUTYENS, Elisabeth
LVOVA, Julia Fedorovna
MACAULAY, Janice Michel
MACKIE, Shirley M.
MACONCHY, Elizabeth
MacDONALD, Catherine
McALISTER, Mabel
McCARTHY, Charlotte
McCOLLIN, Frances
McINTOSH, Diana
McLAIN, Margaret Starr
McLAUGHLIN, Marian
McLEAN, Priscilla Anne Taylor
McLEOD, Jennifer Helen
McLIN, Lena
McPHERSON, Frances Marie
McSWAIN, Augusta Geraldine
MADISON, Carolyn
MADSEN, Florence J.
MALDYBAYEVA, Zhyldyz
  Abdylasovna
MALHE, Maria Aparecida
MALMLOEF-FORSSLING, Carin
MAMLOK, Ursula
MANA-ZUCCA
MARAIS, Abelina Jacoba
MARBE, Myriam
MARCUS, Ada Belle Gross
MAREZ-OYENS, Tera de
MARGLES, Pamela
MARIC, Ljubica
MARINESCU-SCHAPIRA, Ilana
MARKOV, Katherine Lee
MARSCHAL-LOEPKE, Grace
MARTIN, Judith Reher
MARTINEZ, Odaline de la
MARTINS, Maria de Lourdes
MASON, Gladys Amy
MATEVOSIAN, Araks Surenovna
MAY, Florence
MAYFIELD, Alpha C.
MAZOUROVA, Jarmila
MEACHEM, Margaret McKeen
  Ramsey
MEARS, Caroline
MEKEEL, Joyce
MEL-BONIS

MELOY, Elizabeth
MENEELY-KYDER, Sarah Suderley
MEREDITH, Margaret
MERLI-ZWISCHENBRUGGER,
  Christina
MERRICK, Marie E.
MERTENS, Dolores
MIAGI, Ester Kustovna
MILENKOVIC, Jelena
MILFORD, Mary Jean Ross
MITCHELL, Janice Misurell
MOBERG, Ida Georgina
MODRAKOWSKA, M.
MOE, Benna
MOESTUE, Marie
MOHNS, Grace Updegraff Bergen
MONK, Meredith
MONTGOMERY, Merle
MOON, Chloe Elizabeth
MOORE, Dorothy Rudd
MOORE, Undine Smith
MORIN-LABRECQUE, Albertine
MORLEY, Nina Dianne
MRACEK, Ann Michelle
MULDER, Johanna Harmina Gerdina
MUNGER, Shirley
MUSGRAVE, Thea
MYSZINSKA-WOJCIECHOWSKA,
  Leokadia
NARCISSE-MAIR, Denise Lorraine
NASH, Grace Helen
NAZAROVA, Tatiana Borisovna
NEPGEN, Rosa Sophia Cornelia
NICKERSON, Camille Lucie
NIGHTINGALE, Mae Wheeler
NIKOLSKAYA, Lyubov Borisovna
NIKOLSKAYA, Olga Vasilevna
NISS, Sofia Natanovna
NOETHLING, Elisabeth
NORBURY, Ethel F.
NORDRAAK-FEYLING, Gudrun
NORMAN, Ruth
NOVA SONDAG, Jacqueline
NOVI, Anna Beate
NOVOSELOVA, Ludmila Alexeyevna
NOZAWA, Kazuyo
NUNLIST, Juli
NYQUIST, Morine A.
O'BRIEN, Katharine E.
ODAGESCU, Irina
OERBECK, Anne-Marie
OIKONOMOPOULOS, Eleni N.
OLDENBURG, Elizabeth
O'LEARY, Jane Strong
OLIVE, Vivienne
OLIVEIRA, Alda de Jesus
OLIVEIRA, Sophie Marcondes de
  Mello
OLIVEROS, Pauline
OLLER BENLLOCH, Maria Teresa
OOSTERZEE, Cornelia van
ORE, Cecilie
OSAWA, Kazuko
OSETROVA-YAKOVLIEVA, Nina
  Alexandrovna
OTIS, Edna Cogswell
OWEN, Blythe
PAGH-PAAN, Younghi
PAKHMUTOVA, Alexandra
  Nikolayevna
PARASKEVAIDIS, Graciela
PARKER, Alice
PATTERSON, Andra
PATTERSON, Annie Wilson
PAULL, Barberi
PELEGRI, Maria Teresa
PENGILLY, Sylvia
PENNER, Jean Priscilla
PENTLAND, Barbara Lally
PEREIRA DA SILVA, Adelaide
PERONI, Wally

PERSCHMANN, Elfriede
PETROVA, Mara
PETROVA, Olga Andreyevna
PETROVA-KRUPKOVA, Elena
PEYROT, Fernande
PFEIFFER, Irena
PFERDEMENGES, Maria Pauline
  Augusta
PFOLH, Bessie Whittington
PHILIBA, Nicole
PHILLIPS, Bryony
PICHE, Eudore
PIERCE, Alexandra
PIRES DE CAMPOS, Lina
PITCHER, Gladys
PITTMAN, Evelyn LaRue
PIZER, Elizabeth Faw Hayden
PLE-CAUSSADE, Simone
PLUMSTEAD, Mary
POLIN, Claire
POOL, Arlette
POPATENKO, Tamara Alexandrovna
POPOVICI, Elise
POULET, Defontaine Madeleine
PRAVOSSUDOVITCH, Natalja
  Michajlovna
PREDIC-SAPER, Branislava
PRICE, Florence Beatrice
PRIESING, Dorothy Jean
PROCACCINI, Teresa
PROCTOR, Alice McElroy
PSTROKONSKA-NAVRATIL,
  Grazyna Hanna
PTASZYNSKA, Marta
QUIEL, Hildegard
QUINTANILLA, Alba
RALSTON, Frances Marion
RAPOPORT, Eda
RAVINALE, Irma
RAVIZE, Angele
RAW, Vera Constance
RECLI, Giulia
RED, Virginia Stroh
REED, Ida L.
REES, Winifred Emily
REHNQVIST, Karin Birgitta
REID, Louis C.
RENART, Marta Garcia
RHEA, Lois
RHOADS, Mary R.
RICHARDSON, Enid Dorothy
RICHER, Jeannine
RICHTER, Ada
RICHTER, Marion Morrey
RILEY, Ann Marion
ROBERTSON, Donna Lou Nagey
ROBITASHVILI, Lia Georgievna
ROCHEROLLE, Eugenie Katherine
RODRIGUEZ BELLA, Catalina
RODRIGUEZ, Esther
ROE, Gloria Ann
ROGER, Denise
ROGET, Henriette
ROHDE, Q'Adrianne
ROHRER, Gertrude Martin
ROMM, Rosalina Davidovna
ROSAS FERNANDES, Maria Helena
ROSATO, Clorinda
ROSSO, Carol L.
ROWAN, Barbara
ROYSE, Mildred Barnes
ROZHAVSKAYA, Yudif Grigorevna
RUBIN, Anna Ita
RUEGGER, Charlotte
RUFF-STOEHR, Herta Maria Klara
RUSCHE, Marjorie Maxine
RUSSELL, Olive Nelson
RZAYEVA, Agabadzhi Ishmael kykz
SAARIAHO, Kaija
SADOVNIKOFF, Mary Briggs
SAINT JOHN, Kathleen Louise

SALQUIN, Hedy
SAMTER, Alice
SAMUEL, Rhian
SANZ, Rocio
SCHLOSS, Myrna Frances
SCHMIDT, Margot Alice
SCHMIDT-DUISBURG, Margarete
  Dina Alwina
SCHUBERT, Myra Jean
SCHUSSLER-BREWAEYS, Marie
  Antoinette
SEAY, Virginia
SEPULVEDA, Maria Luisa
SEUEL-HOLST, Marie
SEWALL, Maud Gilchrist
SHAFFER, Jeanne Ellison
SHELDON, Lillian Tait
SHELLEY, Margaret Vance
SHELTON, Margaret Meier
SHERMAN, Kim Daryl
SIDDALL, Louise
SINGER, Jeanne
SISTEK-DJORDJEVIC, Mirjana
SKARECKY, Jana Milena
SKOWRONSKA, Janina
SLEETH, Natalie
SMEJKALOVA, Vlasta
SMITH, Julia Frances
SMYTH, Ethel Mary, Dame
SNIZKOVA-SKRHOVA, Jitka
SNYDER, Amy
SOLOMON, Elide M.
SPENCER, Williametta
SPIZIZEN, Louise Myers
SPRAGINS, Florence
STANEKAITE-LAUMYANSKENE,
  Elena Ionovna
STEINER, Gitta Hana
STEWART, Ora Pate
STITT, Margaret McClure
STREATCH, Alice
STREATFIELD, Valma June
STRUCK, Ilse
STRUTT, Dorothy
STUART-BERGSTROM, Elsa
  Marianne
STULTZ, Marie Irene
SUTZU, Rodica
SVANIDZE, Natela Damianovna
SWIFT, Kay
SZOENYI, Erzsebet
SZYMANSKA, Iwonka Bogumila
TAKASHIMA, Midori
TALMA, Louise
TAMBLYN, Bertha Louise
TARLOW, Karen Anne
TASHJIAN, B. Charmian
TATE, Phyllis
TAUTU, Cornelia
TELFER, Nancy Ellen
TERZIAN, Alicia
THIEME, Kerstin Anja
THISSE-DEROUETTE, Rose
THOMSEN, Geraldine
THORKELSDOTTIR, Mist Barbara
THREADGILL-MARTIN, Ravonna
TIDEMAN-WIJERS, Bertha
TILICHEYEVA, Elena Nikolayevna
TILLETT, Jeanette
TODD, M. Flora
TORRA, Celia
TOWERSEY, Phyllis Mary
TRINITAS, Sister M.
TRIPP, Ruth
TUCKER, Mary Jo
TUMANIAN, Elizaveta Artashesovna
TURGEON, Frances
TURNER, Myra Brooks
TURNER-MALEY, Florence
TURRIETTA, Cheryl Renée
TUSSENBROEK, Hendrika van

TYER, Norma Phyllis
TYRMAND, Eta Moiseyevna
TYSON, Mildred Lund
USHER, Julia
VACCARO, Judith Lynne
VAN APPLEDORN, Mary Jeanne
VAN DER MARK, Maria
VASHAW, Cecile
VASILIEVA, Tatiana Ivanovna
VELLERE, Lucie Weiler
VERHAALEN, Sister Marion
VIEU, Jane
VIGNERON-RAMAKERS, Christiane-
  Josée
VINTULE, Ruta Evaldovna
VISCONTI, Leila
VITO-DELVAUX, Berthe di
VON ZIERITZ, Grete
VORLOVA, Slavka
VREE-BROWN, Marion F.
VRIONIDES, Rosina
WAALER, Fredrikke Holtemann
WAINWRIGHT, Harriet
WALKER, Ella May
WANG, An-Ming
WANG, Qiang
WARE, Harriet
WARREN, Elinor Remick
WASKO, Christine
WEAVER, Mary
WEBB, Allienne Brandon
WEISSBERG, Julia Lazerevna
WELANDER, Svea Goeta
WELLNER, Elsa
WENDELBURG, Norma Ruth
WENTZ-JANACEK, Elisabet
WERTHEIM, Rosy
WHITE, Claude Porter
WHITEHEAD, Gillian
WHITNER, Mary Elizabeth
WHITTAKER, Vivian
WHITTINGTON, Joan
WHITTLE, Chris Mary-Francine
WICKHAM, Florence Pauline
WIGGINS, Mary
WILDSCHUT, Clara
WILHELM, Grete
WILKINS, Margaret Lucy
WILLIAMS, Frances
WILLIAMS, Grace Mary
WILLIAMS, Jean E.
WILLMAN, Regina Hansen
WOLCOTT, Ellen
WOLF, Ilda von
WOLL, Erna
WOODRUFF, Edith S.
YAKHNINA, Yevgenia Yosifovna
YAMPOLSCHI, Roseane
YDSTIE, Arlene Buckneberg
YOUNG, Fredricka Agnes
YOUNG, Gayle
YOUSE, Glad Robinson
ZAIDEL-RUDOLPH, Jeanne
ZAIMONT, Judith Lang
ZAKRZEWSKA-NIKIPORCZYK,
  Barbara Maria
ZALLMAN, Arlene
ZAULECK, Gertrud
ZAVALISHINA, Maria Semyonovna
ZEINER, Marliese
ZHUBANOVA, Gaziza Akhmetovna
ZHUBINSKAYA, Valentina Yanovna
ZIBEROVA, Zinaida Petrovna
ZIELINSKA, Lidia

Century unknown
ACHARD, Marguerite
BOR, Modesta
FERGUS-HOYT, Phyllis
MIRANDA, Erma Hoag
PFUND, Jeanne
SCHLECHTRIEM, Thérèsia

MADRIGALS
  16th Century A.D.
    ALEOTTI, Raffaela-Argenta
    ALEOTTI, Vittoria
    ANIMUCIA, Giovanna
    ARCHINTA, Marguerite
    BAGLIONCELLA, Francesca
    BOLEYN, Anne, Queen of
      England
    BOVIA, Laura
    CAPPELLO, Laura Beatrice
    CARAFA, Livia
    CASULANA, Maddalena
    COTTA, Anastasia
    LA MAINA
    LA PEREGO
    MASSARENGHI, Paola
    RICCI, Cesarina di Tingoli
    VARISI, Giulia
  17th Century A.D.
    BERTOLAJO-CAVALETTI, Orsola
    CACCINI, Francesca
    CACCINI-GHIVIZZANI, Settimia
    CALEGARI, Cornelia
    CAMPANA, Francesca
    NASCIMBENI, Maria Francesca
    QUINCIANI, Lucia
    STROZZI, Barbara
    TARRONI, Antonia
    VIZANA, Lucretia Orsina
  19th Century A.D.
    BARKER, Laura Wilson
    CALOSSO, Eugenia
    THOMPSON, Alexandra
  20th Century A.D.
    BALDACCI, Giovanna Bruna
    BOLZ, Harriet
    CHAMINADE, Cécile Louise
      Stephanie
    CLARKE, Rosemary
    COSTA, Maria Helena da
    FLEISCHER-DOLGOPOLSKY,
      Tsipporah
    FONTYN, Jacqueline
    FREEHOFF, Ruth Williams
    FURZE, Jessie
    GEORGE, Lila-Gene
    GIDEON, Miriam
    GOULD, Elizabeth Davies
    JEREA, Hilda
    JOLAS, Betsy
    KOBLENZ, Babette
    MacDONALD, Catherine
    MARTINEZ, Odaline de la
    MONTGOMERY, Merle
    ROSSELLI-NISSIM, Mary
    SINGER, Jeanne
    SPENCER, Williametta
    SZEKELY, Katalin
    THIEME, Kerstin Anja
    WALKER, Gwyneth van Anden
    WALLACH, Joelle
    WHITE, Elsie Fellows
    WORTH, Amy
    ZIMMERMAN, Phyllis

OPERAS
  16th Century A.D.
    CATERINA
    MANCINI, Eleonora
  17th Century A.D.
    BEMBO, Antonia
    CACCINI, Francesca
    DOROTHEA SOPHIA, Duchess
    FRANCESCHINI, Petronia
  18th Century A.D.
    AGNESI-PINOTTINI, Maria Teresa d'
    AHLEFELDT, Marie Theresia,
      Countess
    ANNA AMALIA, Duchess of Saxe-
      Weimar

BEAUMESNIL, Henrietta Adelaide
  Villard de
BOYD, Elisabeth
CAROLINE, Mlle.
CAZATI, Maria
CHARRIERE, Isabella Agneta
  Elisabeth de
CLERAMBAULT, N.
DEZEDE, Florine
GRETRY, Angelique Dorothée Lucie
LA GUERRE, Elisabeth-Claude
  Jacquet de
MARIA ANTONIA WALPURGIS,
  Princess of Bavaria
MIZANGERE, Marquise de la
MUELLNER, Johanna
PAPAVOINE, Mme.
ROSET, Mme.
SOPHIA CHARLOTTE
WILHELMINA, Sophie Friederike,
  Princess of Prussia
ZAMPARELLI, Dionisia

19th Century A.D.
ADAJEWSKY, Ella
ADDI, Renée d'
AMALIE, Marie Friederike Augusta,
  Princess of Saxony
ANSPACH, Elizabeth, Margravine of
ASPRI, Orsola
BELLINCIONI, Gemma
BENFEY-SCHUPPE, Anna
BERTIN, Louise Angelique
BLAHETKA, Marie Leopoldina
BLEWIT, Gionata
BOCK, Bertha
BRONSART VON SCHELLENDORF,
  Ingeborg Lena von
BUSKY-BENEDETTI, Albina
CALOSSO, Eugenia
CANDEILLE, Amelie Julie
CASADESUS, Regina
CASELLA, Felicita
CHAMBERLAYNE, Edith A.
CHEVALIER DE BOISVAL, Mme.
COCCIA, Maria Rosa
COLLINET, Clara
CORRER, Ida, Countess
CRESCIMANO, Fiorita
DELABORDE, Elie Miriam
DELLE GRAZIE, Gisella
DEVISME, Jeanne-Hippolite
  Moyroud
FARMER, Emily Bardsley
FAUCHE, Marie
FERRARI, Carlotta
FORTMAGNE, Baroness de
FOURNIER, Alice
GAIL, Edmée-Sophie
GALLONI, Adolfa
GAMBARO, Alceste
GIGNOUX, Jeanne
GOETZE, Auguste
GRANDVAL, Marie Felicie Clemence
  de Reiset, Vicomtesse de
GRODZICKA-RZEWUSKA, Julia
GUENIN, Helene
GUIDI LIONETTI, Teresa
HAENEL DE CRONENTHAL, Louise
  Augusta Marie Julia
HARVEY, Roberta
HENN, Angelica
HOLMES, Augusta Mary Anne
JESKE-CHOINSKA-MIKORSKA,
  Ludmila
JESSUP-MILDRED Marion de
JULIEN, Jeanne
KERMOR, Mireille
KINKEL, Johanna
KRALIK VON MAYERSWALDEN,
  Mathilde
LA HYE, Louise Genevieve

LAGIER, Suzanne
LINWOOD, Mary
LODER, Kate Fanny
LUCILLA D.
MADDISON, Adele
MAILLART, Aimee
MAISTRE, Baroness of
MARRA, Adelina
MATTHYSSENS, Marie
MELIA, Gabrielle
MENK-MAYER, Florence
MENTZEL-SCHIPPEL, Elisabeth
MICHEL, Josepha
MILASZEWSKA
MONCRIEFF, Lynedock
MONTGOMERY, Mme. de
MORPURGO, Irene
OLAGNIER, Marguerite
OWEN, Anita
PAIGNE, Mme.
PARADIS, Maria Theresia von
PEAN DE LA ROCHE-JAGU, E.
  Françoise
PERELLI, Natalie
PERRIERE-PILTE, Anais, Countess of
PERRONNET, Amelie
PERRY-BIAGIOLI, Antoinette
PFEIFFER, Charlotte Birsch
PFEILSCHIFTER, Julie von
PIERPONT, Marie de
PROHASKA, Bernhardine
PUGET, Loise
RAPP, Marguerite
RAYMOND, Emma Marcy
REYNAC, Mme. de
RIGHTON, Mary
RIVAY, Mlle.
RODRIGO, Maria
ROSE
ROZWADOWSKI, Contessa Raffaela
RUNCIE, Constance Owen Faunt Le
  Roy
SABATIER-BLOT, Mme.
SANCHEZ DE LA MADRID, Ventura
SANTA-COLONA-SOURGET,
  Eugenie
SCHIMON, Anna
SCHMEZER, Elise
SCHULZOVA, Anezka
SENEKE, Térèsa
SEROVA, Valentina Semyonovna
SIGAL, Mme.
SKINNER, Florence Marian
THYS, Pauline
TOWNSEND, Marie
TYRELL, Agnes
UCCELLI, Carolina
UGALDE, Delphine Beauce
VESVALI, Felicita
VIARDOT-GARCIA, Pauline Michelle
  Ferdinande
WARD, Clementine
WHITE, Maude Valerie
WHITELY, Bessie Marshall
WILLIAMS, Margaret
WISENEDER, Caroline
WOLZOGEN, Elsa Laura von
WOOLF, Sophia Julia
WRIGHT, Agnes
WUIET, Caroline
WURM, Mary J.A.
YOUNG, Eliza
ZERR, Anna
ZILIOTTO, Elisa

20th Century A.D.
ABORN, Lora
ABRAMOVA, Sonia Pinkhasovna
ADAM, Maria Emma
ADAMS, Carrie Bell
AKHUNDOVA, Shafiga Gulam kyzy
ALBRIGHT, Lois

ALDERMAN, Pauline
ALEXANDRA, Liana
ALLEN, Judith Shatin
ALLIK, Kristi
ALLITSEN, Frances
ALONSO, Julia
ANDERSON, Beth
ANDREE, Elfrida
APPLETON, Adeline Carola
ARCHER, Violet Balestreri
ARRIEU, Claude
ARSEYEVA, Irina Vasilievna
ARVEY, Verna
AUSTER, Lydia Martinovna
AYLOTT, Lydia Georgina Edith
AYLWIN, Josephine Crew
BABAYEVA, Seda Grigorievna
BACEWICZ, Grazyna
BACH, Maria
BALSHONE, Cathy S.
BARBERIS, Mansi
BARKIN, Elaine
BARLOW, Betty
BARRAINE, Elsa
BARTHELSON, Joyce Holloway
BEACH, Amy Marcy
BEATH, Betty
BEATON, Isabella
BECLARD D'HARCOURT,
  Marguerite
BELCHER, Mary Williams
BELOCH, Dorotea
BENARY, Barbara
BENES, Jara
BENSUADE, Jane
BERGE, Irenee
BESSEM, Saar
BETHEA, Kay
BEUSCHER, Elisabeth
BEYER, Johanna Magdalena
BIBBY, Gillian Margaret
BINGHAM, Judith
BLISA, Alice
BLISS, Pearl
BLOM, Diane
BOESING, Martha
BONHOMME, Marie Thérèse
BORDEWIJK-ROEPMAN, Johanna
BORROFF, Edith
BORRONI, Virginia
BOULANGER, Nadia Juliette
BOYD, Anne Elizabeth
BRADLEY, Ruth
BRANSCOMBE, Gena
BRATU, Emma
BRIGGS, Mary Elizabeth
BRIGHT, Dora Estella
BRITAIN, Radie
BRUSH, Ruth Damaris
BRUZDOWICZ, Joanna
BUCHANAN, Dorothy Quita
BURDICK, Elizabeth Tucker
BURGESS, Brio
CADZOW, Dorothy Forrest
CALDWELL, Mary Elizabeth Glockler
CANCINO DE CUEVAS, Sofia
CARLOS, Wendy
CARMEN MARINA
CARMON, Helen Bidwell
CASAGEMAS, Luisa
CECCONI-BOTELLA, Monic
CHAMINADE, Cécile Louise
  Stephanie
CHARLES, S. Robin
CHLARSON, Linda
CHUDOBA, Blanka
CHUDOVA, Tatiana Alekseyevna
CHURCHILL, Beatrice
CLARKE, Rosemary
CLAYTON, Laura
CLOSTRE, Adrienne

COCQ, Rosina Susanna de
COLEMAN, Ellen
COULTHARD, Jean
COX, Alison Mary
CRAWFORD, Dawn Constance
CRAWFORD, Dorothy Lamb
CREWS, Lucille
CROFTS, Inez Altman
CURTIS, Elizabeth
CURUBETO GODOY, Maria Isabel
DAVIS, Jean Reynolds
DAVIS, Katherine Kennicott
DAVIS, Mary
DAVITASHVILI, Meri Shalvovna
DE BIASE BIDART, Lycia
DE LA MARTINEZ, Odaline
DEMBO, Royce
DESCAT, Henriette
DESPORTES, Yvonne Berthe Melitta
DEYO, Ruth Lynda
DIEMER, Emma Lou
DILLER, Saralu C.
DODGE, Cynthia
DODGE, May Hewes
DONATOVA, Narcisa
DONCEANU, Felicia
DORABIALSKA, Julia Helena
DRDOVA, Marie
DRING, Madeleine
DROBYAZGINA, Valentina Ivanovna
DU PAGE, Florence Elizabeth
DUBOIS, Shirley Graham
DUNLOP, Isobel
DVORKIN, Judith
EGGELING-SPIES, I.
EGGLESTON, Anne E.
ELKAN, Ida
ELKOSHI, Rivka
ELLIOTT, Marjorie Reeve
ERDING, Susanne
ESCOBAR, Maria Luisa
ESTERHAZY, Alexandrine, Countess
EVANS, Winsome
FAHRBACH, Henrietta
FALCINELLI, Rolande
FARGA PELLICER, Onia
FARR, Hilda Butler
FEIGIN, Sarah
FERRARI, Gabriella
FINE, Vivian
FIRSOVA, Elena
FOLVILLE, Eugenie-Emilie Juliette
FORD, Mrs. Raymond C.
FORD, Nancy
FORMAN, Joanne
FOSTER, Fay
FRANCHINO, Raffaela
FRANK, Jean Forward
FREER, Eleanor Warner Everest
FRIEDBERG, Patricia Ann
GAIGEROVA, Varvara Andrianovna
GALLI-CAMPI
GANNON, Ruth Ellen
GARDNER, Kay
GARLAND, Kathryn
GARR, Wieslawa
GARUTA, Lucia Yanovna
GARWOOD, Margaret
GASPARINI, Jola
GEDDES-HARVEY, Roberta
GEIGER-KULLMANN, Rosy Auguste
GENNAI, Emanuela
GERRISH-JONES, Abbie
GIDEON, Miriam
GIFFORD, Helen Margaret
GITECK, Janice
GIURANNA, Elena Barbara
GLANVILLE-HICKS, Peggy
GOLOVINA, Olga Akimovna
GOODSMITH, Ruth B.
GORELLI, Olga

GOTKOVSKY, Ida-Rose Esther
GOULD, Doris
GOULD, Elizabeth Davies
GREGORY, Else
GRIEBEL WANDALL, Tekla
GRIGSBY, Beverly
GRIMES, Doreen
GUBITOSI, Emilia
GUERRANT, Mary Thorington
GYRING, Elizabeth
HAGEMANN, Virginia
HALACSY, Irma von
HAMILL, Roseann
HAMILTON, Marcia
HANCHETT, Sybil Croly
HANS, Lio
HANSEN, Hanna Marie
HARA, Kazuko (1)
HARDIMAN, Ellena G.
HARRADEN, R. Ethel
HARRISON, Annie Fortescue
HARRISON, Susan Frances
HARVEY, Eva Noel
HECKSCHER, Céleste de Longpre
HEIDRICH, Hermine Margaret
HEIMLICH, Florentine
HEMENWAY, Edith
HERBERT, Dorothy
HERBERT, Muriel
HILLIER-JASPAR, Jeanne
HOLDEN, Bernice
HOTCHKISS, Evelyn Dissmore
HOUSE, L. Marguerite
HOWELL, Alice
HUNKINS, Eusebia Simpson
IBRAGIMOVA, Sevda Mirza kyzy
JACOBUS, Dale Asher
JAMES, Dorothy E.
JEBELES, Mrs. Themos
JEREA, Hilda
JOHNSON, Harriet
JOHNSON, Mary Ernestine Clark
JOLAS, Betsy
JOY, Margaret E.
KALOGRIDOU, Maria
KAMIEN, Anna
KANAI, Kikuko
KARVENO, Wally
KATZMAN, Klara Abramovna
KAVASCH, Deborah Helene
KERWEY, Julia
KING, Betty Jackson
KISTETENYI, Melinda
KLINKOVA, Zhivka
KOBLENZ, Babette
KODOLITSCH, Michaela
KOMPANUETS, Lidia
KORN, Clara Anna
KRONING, Mlle.
KUCEROVA-HERSTOVA, Marie
KULESHOVA, Galina Grigorevna
KUZNETSOVA, Zhanetta
  Alexandrovna
LABEY, Charlotte Sohy
LACKMAN, Susan C. Cohn
LANG-BECK, Ivana
LARSEN, Elizabeth Brown
LAUER, Elizabeth
LAUFER, Beatrice
LAURIDSEN, Cora
LE BEAU, Louisa Adolpha
LEBARON, Anne
LECLERCQ, Leila Sarah
LEE, Bo-Chas
LEFANU, Nicola Frances
LEGINSKA, Ethel
LEHMAN, R.
LEHMANN, Liza
LEONI, Eva
LEVI, Natalia Nikolayevna
LEVITSKAYA, Viktoria Sergeyevna

LEWIS, Carrie Bullard
LIDGI-HERMAN, Sofia
LINZ VON KRIEGNER, Marta
LLOYD, Caroline Parkhurst
LOMON, Ruth
LOPEZ Y PENA, Maria del Carmen
LOVE, Loretta
LUTYENS, Elisabeth
LVOVA, Julia Fedorovna
MACKIE, Shirley M.
McCOLLIN, Frances
McINTOSH, Diana
McKEE, Jeanellen
McLEOD, Jennifer Helen
McLIN, Lena
McPHERSON, Frances Marie
MAGNEY, Ruth Taylor
MAINVILLE, Denise
MAITLAND, Anna Harriet
MAITLAND, S. Marguerite
MAJLATH, Julia
MAKAROVA, Nina Vladimirovna
MANA-ZUCCA
MANNiNG, Kathleen Lockhart
MARAIS, Abelina Jacoba
MARCUS, Ada Belle Gross
MAREZ-OYENS, Tera de
MARIANI-CAMPOLIETI, Virginia
MARTINS, Maria de Lourdes
MATUSZCZAK, Bernadetta
MAURICE-JACQUET, H.
MAXWELL, Elsie
MAYER, Lise Maria
MEREDITH, Margaret
MESSIAM, Eve
MILLER, Alma Grace
MIREILLE, Saint Plante
MOBERG, Ida Georgina
MONK, Meredith
MOORE, Mary Carr
MORE, Margaret Elizabeth
MORIN-LABRECQUE, Albertine
MORISON, Christina W.
MORRISON, Julia Maria
MUNKTELL, Helena Mathilda
MURDOCH, Elaine
MUSGRAVE, Thea
NEELD, Peggy
NEWELL, Eleanor
NEWLIN, Dika
NICHOLS, Alberta
NIEBEL, Mildred
NIKOLSKAYA, Lyubov Borisovna
NOBLE, Ann
NORBURY, Ethel F.
NORMAN, Ruth
NOWAK, Alison
NOYES, Edith Rowena
NUNLIST, Juli
ODDONE SULLI-RAO, Elisabetta
OH, Sook Ja
OKEY, Maggie
OLIVEROS, Pauline
ORIGO, Iris
PABLOS CEREZO, Maria de
PADE, Else Marie
PARKER, Alice
PATTERSON, Annie Wilson
PELEGRI, Maria Teresa
PENTLAND, Barbara Lally
PERRY, Julia Amanda
PETROVA-KRUPKOVA, Elena
PHILLIPS, Bryony
PICKHARDT, Ione
PIRES DE PIRES, D. Maria
Clementina
PITTMAN, Evelyn LaRue
POLIGNAC, Armande de, Countess
  of Chabannes
POSTON, Elizabeth
PREOBRAJENSKA, Vera Nicolaevna

PROCACCINI, Teresa
PTASZYNSKA, Marta
RAIGORODSKY, Leda Natalia
  Heimsath
RAPOPORT, Eda
RAVINALE, Irma
RECLI, Giulia
REIFF, Lili
RESPIGHI, Elsa
RHEINGOLD, Lauma Yanovna
RICHER, Jeannine
RICHTER, Marion Morrey
RIDLEY, Ursula
ROBERT, Lucie
ROBITASHVILI, Lia Georgievna
ROE, Eileen Betty
ROGERS, Patsy
ROGET, Henriette
ROHRER, Gertrude Martin
ROMA, Caro
ROSSELLI-NISSIM, Mary
ROZHAVSKAYA, Yudif Grigorevna
RUDALL, Eleonor C.
RUEFF, Jeanine
RUTA, Gilda, Countess
SALVADOR, Matilde
SAMTER, Alice
SCHICK, Philippine
SCHONTHAL, Ruth E.
SCOTT-HUNTER, Hortense
SEHESTED, Hilda
SELMER, Kathryn Lande
SHAFFER, Jeanne Ellison
SHERMAN, Kim Daryl
SHIELDS, Alice Ferree
SIKORA, Elzbieta
SILSBEE, Ann L.
SILVERMAN, Faye-Ellen
SKEENS, Gwendolyn
SKOUEN, Synne
SMILEY, Pril
SMITH, Julia Frances
SMITH, Nellie von Gerichten
SMITH, Zelma
SMYTH, Ethel Mary, Dame
SODRE, Joanidia
SPEKTOR, Mira J.
STAIR, Patty
STEELE, Lynn
STEINER, Emma
STITT, Margaret McClure
STOCKER, Stella
STREICHER, Lyubov Lvovna
STREIT, Else
STRICKLAND, Lily Teresa
SUTHERLAND, Margaret
SWAIN, Freda Mary
SWISHER, Gloria Agnes Wilson
SZOENYI, Erzsebet
TAILLEFERRE, Germaine
TALMA, Louise
TARBOS, Frances
TATE, Phyllis
TEICHMUELLER, Anna
TERHUNE, Anice
THEMMEN, Ivana Marburger
THOMAS, Gertrude Auld
TIMOFEYEW, Mrs.
TKACH, Zlata Moiseyevna
TRIMBLE, Joan
TRIPP, Ruth
TUSSENBROEK, Hendrika van
TWOMBLY, Mary Lynn
UPTON, Anne
URRETA, Alicia
UZEINZADZE, Adilea
VAN DE VATE, Nancy Hayes
VAN DER MARK, Maria
VAN ETTEN, Jane
VANNAH, Kate
VASILIEVA, Tatiana Ivanovna

VIEU, Jane
VITO-DELVAUX, Berthe di
VORLOVA, Slavka
WALES, Evelyn
WALSH, Helen Mary
WARD, Diane
WARE, Harriet
WARWICK, Mary Carol
WEBER, Bertha
WEIR, Judith
WEISSBERG, Julia Lazerevna
WELMAN, Sylvia
WHITE, Claude Porter
WHITEHEAD, Gillian
WICKER, Irene
WILLAERT, Caterina
WILLIAMS, Grace Mary
WINDSOR, Helen J.
WINKLER, Blanka
WITNI, Monica
WOOD, Mabel
WRANA, Emilie
YUKHNOVSKAYA, Ninel Grigorievna
ZAIDEL-RUDOLPH, Jeanne
ZAIMONT, Judith Lang
ZAVALISHINA, Maria Semyonovna
ZECHLIN, Ruth
ZHUBANOVA, Gaziza Akhmetovna

Century unknown
BRADY, Emma
DANZIGER, Rosa
FERGUS-HOYT, Phyllis
GOULD, Octavia R.
GREEN, Lydia
GRINDELL, Clara Kyle
HATTON, Anne
JOHNSTON-WATSON, Miss
LAMB, Myrna
MIRANDA, Erma Hoag
PULER, Clara P.
ROWSON, Susannah
STEINBOCK, Evalyn
TARBE DES SABLONS, Mme.
WALTER, Ida

OPERETTAS
18th Century A.D.
DUBOIS, Dorothea
LOUIS, Mme.
19th Century A.D.
AMALIE, Marie Friederike Augusta,
  Princess of Saxony
BARTLETT, Agnes
BELLET, Mlle.
BOTTINI, Marianna, Marchioness
CARISSAN, Celanie
CHEVALIER DE BOISVAL, Mme.
DEJAZET, Hermine
DELL'ACQUA, Eva
DIETRICH, Amalia
DORISI, Lina
ESCHBORN, Georgine Christine
  Maria Anna
ESTABROOK, G.
GABRIEL, Mary Ann Virginia
GERMANO, Vittoria
GRANDVAL, Marie Felicie Clemence
  de Reiset, Vicomtesse de
GRAY, Louisa
GUITTY, Madeleine
HERITTE-VIARDOT, Louise Pauline
  Marie
JACQUES, Charlotte
KERCADO, Mlle. le Senechal de
KINKEL, Johanna
LANGHANS, Louise
LILIUOKALANI, Queen of Hawaii
LUCILLA D.
MARSHALL, Florence A.
MATHIEU, Emilie
MAYER, Emilie

MELY, Marie, Countess Vanden
  Heuvel
MICHEL, Josepha
MORGAN, Lady
O'DONNELL, Malvine, Countess
OLAGNIER, Marguerite
ORTH, Lizette Emma
PARADIS, Maria Theresia von
PERRIERE-PILTE, Anais, Countess of
PERRONNET, Amelie
PUGET, Loise
RAWLINSON, Angela
RICHINGS, Caroline
SAINT-CROIX, Caroline de
SPAULDING, Florence Atherton
SYMIANE, Magdaleine
THYS, Pauline
UGALDE, Delphine Beauce
VIARDOT-GARCIA, Pauline Michelle
  Ferdinande
WARD, Clementine
WETTE, Adelheid
WINTLE, Virginia
WURM, Mary J.A.
YOUNG, Harriet Maitland
20th Century A.D.
AARON, Yvonne
ABOULKER, Isabelle
ACE, Joy Milane
ACKLAND, Jeanne Isabel Dorothy
AKHUNDOVA, Shafiga Gulam kyzy
ALDERMAN, Pauline
ALLEMAND, Pauline L'
ALLEN, Denise
ALTER, Martha
ALTMAN, Adella C.
ARIMA, Reiko
ARKWRIGHT, Marian Ursula
BARKLUND, Irma L.
BESSEM, Saar
BIASINI, Marcelle
BILBRO, Anne Mathilde
BLAKE, Dorothy Gaynor
BLANCK, Olga de
BOSTELMANN, Ida
BROWN, Mary Helen
CALE, Rosalie Balmer Smith
CARMICHAEL, Mary Grant
CASTEGNARO, Lola
CLARK, Mary Margaret Walker
CLEMENT, Mary
COBB, Hazel
COGAN, Morva
CORRI, Ghita
DANIELS, Mabel Wheeler
DARGEL, Maude
DOBSON, Elaine
DODD, Dorothy
DONAHUE, Bertha Terry
DRYNAN, Margaret
DUNGAN, Olive
DUNN, Rebecca Welty
EAGAR, Fannie Edith Starke
ELLIOTT, Marjorie Reeve
ELLIS, Vivian
ESCOBAR, Maria Luisa
FAHRBACH, Henrietta
FLAGG, Mary Houts
FORMAN, Addie Walling
FORSTER, Charlotte
FOSTER, Fay
FRANK, Jean Forward
FRONDONI LACOMBE, Madalena
FRYDAN, Kamilla
GAMILLA, Alice Doria
GARELLI DELLA MOREA, Vincenza
GASPARINI, Jola
GAYNOR, Jessie Love
GENET, Marianne
GINDLER, Kathe-Lotte
GONZAGA, Chiquinha

GOVEA, Wenonah Milton
GULESIAN, Grace Warner
HAJDU, Julia
HARDELOT, Guy d'
HARRADEN, R. Ethel
HEATON, Eloise Klotz
HORST, Carita von
HOUSE, L. Marguerite
HUME, Phyllis
IASHVILI, Lili Mikhailovna
IGENBERGA, Elga Avgustovna
JENNEY, Mary Frances
JOLLY, Margaret Anne
KASILAG, Lucrecia R.
KATZMAN, Klara Abramovna
KEMP-POTTER, Joan
KESSLER, Minuetta Schumiatcher
KETTERING, Eunice Lea
KLINKOVA, Zhivka
KRALIKOVA, Johana
KUSUNOKI, Tomoko
LARKIN, Deirdre
LAVIN, Marie Duchesne
LEHMANN, Liza
LEWIS, Carrie Bullard
LIADOVA, Ludmila Alekseyevna
LORENZ, Ellen Jane
LOWELL, Edith
LUTTRELL, Moira
MACONCHY, Elizabeth
McCOLLIN, Frances
MAITLAND, Anna Harriet
MANNING, Kathleen Lockhart
MARCUS, Bunita
MAURICE-JACQUET, H.
MAXIM, Florence
MEINI-ZANOTTI, Maddalena
MERMAN, Joyce
MONNOT, Marguerite Angele
MOORE, Mary Carr
MUELLER, Charlotte
MULDER, Johanna Harmina Gerdina
NEWTON, Rhoda
NIGHTINGALE, Mae Wheeler
NIKISCH, Amelie
NORBURY, Ethel F.
NOVELLI, Mimi
NOYES, Edith Rowena
OBENCHAIN, Virginia
ODDONE SULLI-RAO, Elisabetta
OHLSON, Marion
PAGOTO, Helen
PETERSEN, Marian F.
PETROVA, Mara
PHARRIS, Elizabeth
PHILLIPS, Bryony
PITCHER, Gladys
POLICARPO TEIXEIRA, Maria
    Margarida Fernandes
POLK, Grace Porterfield
POLONIO, Cinira
POPATENKO, Tamara Alexandrovna
RABINOF, Sylvia
RAYNAL, Germaine
REIS, Manuela Cancio
REYNOLDS, Laura Lawton
RICH, Gladys
RICHTER, Ada
RICHTER, Marion Morrey
ROE, Marion Adelle
ROHDE, Q'Adrianne
ROYSE, Mildred Barnes
RUDOLPH, Anna
SCHICK, Philippine
SCHLEDER, Grizelda Lazzaro
SEIDERS, Mary Asenath
SHERREY, Mae Ayres
SIEGFRIED, Lillie Mahon
SLAUGHTER, Marjorie
STAIR, Patty
STANLEY, Helen Camille

STEELE, Lynn
STEINER, Emma
STEIN-SCHNEIDER, Lena
STULTZ, Marie Irene
SYNER, Sonia
SZAJNA-LEWANDOWSKA, Jadwiga
    Helena
TAILLEFERRE, Germaine
TATE, Phyllis
TEMPLE, Hope
TENGBERGEN, Maria Elizabeth van
    Ebbenhorst
TERHUNE, Anice
TESTORE, Lidia
THOMAS, Helen
TKACH, Zlata Moiseyevna
TRAVASSOS LOPES, Maria de
    Lourdes Alves
TRIPP, Ruth
TWOMBLEY, Mary Lynn
URNER, Catherine Murphy
VAN DER MARK, Maria
VIALA, Georgette
VLADERACKEN, Geertruida van
VOIGT, Henriette
VOIGT-SCHWEIKERT, Margarete
VORLOVA, Slavka
WALSH, Elizabeth Jameson
WARD, Diane
WARE, Harriet
WHITE, Mary Louisa
WHITTINGTON, Joan
WICKHAM, Florence Pauline
WOOLSLEY, Mary Hale
XENOPOL, Margareta
ZARANEK, Stefania Anatolyevna
ZIBEROVA, Zinaida Petrovna
Century unknown
DONALDSON, Sadie
GORE, Blanche
HARVEY, Ella Doreen
MacDONNELL, Lilly
TAJANI MATTONE, Ida

SONGS
30th Century B.C.
    INANNA
25th Century B.C.
    ITI
12th Century B.C.
    DEBORAH
10th Century B.C.
    HENUTTAUI
    MUTYUNET
9th Century B.C.
    TENTIOH
7th Century B.C.
    DAMOPHILA
    ERINNA
6th Century B.C.
    DE-ESIHEBSED
    SAPPHO
    TELESILLA OF ARGOS
5th Century B.C.
    PRAXILLA
1st Century A.D.
    CALPURNIA
    THYMELE
2nd Century A.D.
    TS'AI, Yen
3rd Century A.D.
    SIRIN
6th Century A.D.
    CORINNA
    GUINEVERE, Queen
    HIND BINT'UTBA
    HURAIRA
    KHULAIDA II
7th Century A.D.
    AZZA AL-MAILA
    QU'AD
    SALLAMA AL-ZARQA

8th Century A.D.
    ALYA
    BASBAS
    HABBABA
    INAN
    JAMILA
    MUTAYYAM AL-HASHIMIYYA
    SALLAMA AL-QASS
    ULAYYA
9th Century A.D.
    BADHL
    BANAN
    BID'A
    DANANIR AL BARMAKIYYA
    FADL(1)
    FARIDA
    HSUEH, T'ao
    IRFAN
    MAHBUBA
    NASIB AL-MUTAWAKKILIYA
    ORAIB
    QALAM
    QALAM AL-SALAHIYYA
    QAMAR
    RAIQ
    THEODOSIA
11th Century A.D.
    AZALAIS D'ALTIER
    MARGARET, Queen of Scotland
    QASMUNA
    UMM AL-HIRAM
12th Century A.D.
    ALAIS
    ALAMANDA
    ALMUCS DE CASTELNAU
    AZALAIS DE PORCAIRAGUES
    CHARTRES, La Vidame de
    CHIEVRE DE REINS, La
    ELEANOR OF AQUITAINE
    FAYEL, La Dame du
    GARSENDA, Countess of Provence
    ISABELLA
    ISELDA
    ISEUT DE CAPIO, Dame
    MARIA de VENTADORN
    MARIE DE FRANCE
    TIBORS
13th Century A.D.
    BEATRICE DE DIA, Contessa
    BIEIRIS DE ROMANS
    BLANCHE DE CASTILLE
    CARENZA
    CASTELLOZA, Dame
    CAUDAIRENCA
    DOETE
    DOMNA H.
    D'ANDUZA, Clara
    GUILLELMA DE ROSERS
    HADEWIJCH OF BRABANT
    KUNEGUNDE, Queen
    NATIBORS
    SAINT GILLES, La Chatelaine De
14th Century A.D.
    AGNES DE NAVARRE-CHAMPAGNE,
        Comtesse de Foix
    FLASSAN, Flandrine de
    LORRAINE, La Duchesse de
    RUPAMATI, Rani
15th Century A.D.
    BOURGOGNE, Marie de
    CHRISTINE DE PISAN
    HATZLERIN, Sister Clara
    HOYA, Katherina von
    PEPARARA, Laura
    PINAR, Florencia del
16th Century A.D.

    ARCHILEI, Vittoria
    ARCHINTA, Marguerite
    BAGLIONCELLA, Francesca
    BERNARDI-BELLATI, Eleonora

BOLEYN, Anne, Queen of England
BOLOGNESE, Isabella
BRAUNSCHWEIG, Anna Maria,
  Duchess
ELIZABETH I, Queen of England
GINES, Teodora
MARGARET OF AUSTRIA
MARY STUART, Queen of Scots
MEDICI ORSINI, Isabella de, Duchess
  of Bracciano
MILDMAY, Lady
MOLZA, Tarquinia
MRIGANAYANA, Queen
ORSINI, Eleanora, Duchess of Segni
RUFFIN, Fraulein
SESSA, Claudia
TERESA

17th Century A.D.
AMALIE JULIANE, Countess of
  Schwarzenberg
ANGELINI, Maria Vittoria
BARONI, Eleanora
BASSANO, Mlle.
BIBER, Maria Anna Magdalena von
BIRNIE, Patie
CACCINI, Francesca
CACCINI-GHIVIZZANI, Settimia
CAMPANA, Francesca
CERVONI, Isabella di Colle
CHURAI, Marusya
DERING, Lady Mary
DILCARO, Mrs.
DOROTHEA SOPHIA, Duchess
ESCAMILLA, Manuela de
FEDELE, Diacinta
FRANCK, Elsbeth
HUME, Agnes
LACERDA, Bernarda Ferreira de
MacLEOD, Mary
MENETOU, Françoise-Charlotte de
  Senneterre
PATTARINA, Maria
SIEFERT, Justina
SOPHIE ELISABETH von
  Braunschweig, Duchess
STROZZI, Barbara

18th Century A.D.
AHLEFELDT, Marie Theresia,
  Countess
ALESSANDRA, Caterina
ANNA AMALIA, Duchess of Saxe-
  Weimar
ANNA AMALIA, Princess of Prussia
ASTORGA, Emmanuelle d'
AUBIGNY VON ENGELBRUNNER,
  Nina d'
AURELIA, Sister
AURENHAMMER, Josefa Barbara
  von
BACH, Maria Barbara
BACHMANN, Charlotte Caroline
  Wilhelmine
BARTHELEMON, Cecilia Maria
BARTHELEMON, Mary
BONITA, Domina S. Delia
BOUVARDINSKA, Mlle.
BRANDES, Charlotte Wilhelmina
  Franziska
BRUCKENTHAL, Bertha von,
  Baroness
BUTTIER, Mlle.
CAMATI, Maria
CAMPBELL, Caroline
CANTELO, Anne
CARVER, Miss
CASSON, Margaret
CATLEY, Anne
CAVENDISH, Georgiana
CERINI, Geronda
CHARRIERE, Isabella Agneta
  Elisabeth de

CONTAMINE, Mlle. de
COSWAY, Maria Cecilia Louise
COURMONT, Countess von
CROUCH, Anna Maria
CUMBERLAND, Mrs. William
CZARTORYSKA, Izabela de,
  Princess
DALL, Miss
DASHKOVA, Ekaterina Romanovna,
  Princess
DAWSON, Nancy
DE GAMBARINI, Elisabetta
DOLORES, Maria Francisca de los
DONI, Antonia
EICHNER, Adelheid Marie
ESSEX, Margaret
FERRIERES, Mme. de
FIELD, Miss A.
GUIDICCIONI, Laura
HARDING, Elizabeth
HARLOW, Clarissa
HODGES, Ann Mary
HOFFMANN, Miss J.
KALFA, Dilhayat
KANZLER, Josephine
KAUTH, Maria Magdalena
KNIGHT, Julia Baylis
LA GUERRE, Elisabeth-Claude
  Jacquet de
LANTI, Teresa
LESZCZYNSKA, Marie, Queen
LOUIS, Mme.
MARIA CHARLOTTE AMALIE,
  Princess of Saxe-Meiningen
MARIE ANTOINETTE, Archduchess
  of Austria, Queen of France
MARIE THERESE LOUISE OF
  SAVOY-CARIGNANO, Princess of
  Lamballe
MARTINEZ, Marianne
MELLISH, Miss
MORE, Isabella Theaker
MUELLER, Elise
MUELLNER, Johanna
MUSIGNY, Mme. de
MacINTOSH, Mary
OLIN, Elizabeth
PAPAVOINE, Mme.
PINEL, Julie
PIO DI SAVOJA, Isabella D.
POOLE, Caroline
POOLE, Maria
POWNALL, Mary Ann
REICHARDT, Bernhardine Juliane
RICHMOND, Heiress
SAVAGE, Jane
SCHAUFF, Marie
SCHROETER, Corona Elisabeth
  Wilhelmine
SOPHIA, Charlotte
STIRLING, Magdalene
SUBLIGNY, Mme.
TRAVENET, Mme. B. de
TURNER, Elizabeth
VENIER DE PETRIS, Teresa
VIDAMPIERRE, Countess of
WOLDERSLEBEN, Juliane
  Charlotte
WORGAN, Mary
ZAMOYSKA, Zofia, Princess

19th Century A.D.
AARUP, Caia
ABBOTT, Jane
ABLAMOWICZ, Anna
ABRAMS, Harriet
ABRANTES, Duchess of
ACQUAVIVA-D'ARAGONA, Sofia
ADAJEWSKY, Ella
ALBRECHT, Lillie
ALEXANDROVA, A.
ALLEN, Mary Wood

ALSOP, Frances
AMERSFOORDT-DYK, Hermina
  Maria
AMES, Mrs. Henry
ANDREWS, Jenny
ANDREWS, Mrs. George H.
ANLEY, Charlotte
APPIANI, Eugenia
ARAGO, Victoria
ARKWRIGHT, Mrs. Robert
ARMSTRONG, Annie
ARNIM, Bettina von
ASACHI, Elena
ASTLE-ALLAM, Agnes Mary
ATHERTON, Grace
AUSPITZ-KOLAR, Augusta
AYLWARD, Florence
BABNIGG, Emma
BACHE, Constance
BACHMANN, Elise
BACKER-GROENDAHL, Agathe
  Ursula
BAER, Louisa
BAILY, Mrs. James S.
BAKA-BAITZ, Irma
BAKER, Maude
BALLIO, Hilda
BARNARD, Charlotte
BARNETT, Emma
BARONI-CAVALCABO, Guilia
BARONI-PASOLINI, Silvia
BARTHOLOMEW, Ann Sheppard
BARTHOLOMEW, Mrs. M.
BAUDISSIN, Sofie, Countess Wolf
BAUER, Charlotte
BAUM, Katherine
BAWR, Alexandrine Sophie
BEARDSMORE, Mrs.
BECKER, Ida
BEHR, Louise
BELLANI, Caroline
BELLCHAMBERS, Julliet
BELLINCIONI, Gemma
BENINGFIELD, Ethel
BENNETT, Mimi
BERTIN, Louise Angelique
BERTINOTTI, Teresa
BEYDALE, Cecile
BLACK, Jennie Price
BLAHETKA, Marie Leopoldina
BLANC DE FONTBELLE, Cecile
BLAND, Maria Theresa
BLANGINI, Mlle.
BLEITNER, Rosa
BOCHKOLTZ-FALCONI, Anna
BOCK, Bertha
BONNAY, Mlle.
BOPP VON OBERSTADT, Countess
BORTON, Alice
BOSCH, Elisa
BOTTINI, Marianna, Marchioness
BOULEAU-NELDY, Mlle. A.
BOVET, Hermine
BOYCE, Ethel Mary
BRAGGIOTTI, Augusta
BRAMBILLA, Marietta
BRANCHU, Mme.
BRANCOVAN, Princess of
BRANDHURST, Elise
BRAY, Anna Eliza
BRDLIKOVA, Josefina
BREITENBACH, Antoinette de
BREMONT, Countess de
BRIGHAM, Helena
BRINE, Mary D.
BRONIKOWSKA, Charlotte von
BRONSART VON SCHELLENDORF,
  Ingeborg Lena von
BROOMAN, Hanna
BROWN, Caroline Curtis
BROWN, Clemmon May

BROWNE, Augusta
BROWNE, Harriet
BRYAN, Mrs. M.A.
BRZEZINSKA, Filipina
BUCHLEITNER, Therese
BUELOW, Charlotte von
BUERDE, Jeanette Antonie
BUGGE, Magda
BUTTENSTEIN, Constanze von
CALOSSO, Eugenia
CAMMACK, Amelia
CAMPBELL, Mary Maxwell
CANDEILLE, Amelie Julie
CAPUCCI, Lida
CAREW, Lady Henry
CARTER, Christine Nordstrom
CARTWRIGHT, Mrs. Robert
CARUTHERS, Julia
CASADESUS, Regina
CASELLA, Felicita
CASPERS, Agnes B.
CASSEL, Flora Hamilton
CASTRO GUIMARAES, Floripes de
CATALANI, Angelica
CHAMBERLAYNE, Edith A.
CHARLOTTE, Friederike Wilhelmine
    Louise, Princess
CHERTKOVA, A.
CHEVALIER DE MONTREAL, Julia
CHICKERING, Mrs. Charles F.
CHODKIEWICZ, Comtesse
CHRIST, Fanny
CLARKE, Helen Archibald
CLARKE, Jessie Murray
CLAY, Melesina
COCCIA, Maria Rosa
COEN, Anna
COLE, Charlotte
COLLETT, Sophia Dobson
COLLINET, Clara
COLLINS, Laura Sedgwick
COLTELLANI, Celeste
CONFORTINI-ZAMBUSI, Lucietta
CONSTANT, Rosalie de
CONTIN, Mme.
COOK, Eliza
CORMONTAN, Theodora
CORRER, Ida, Countess
CRAMENT, J. Maude
CROWNINGSHIELD, Mary Bradford
CRUMB, Berenice
CRUVELLI, Sofia
CZETWERTYNSKA-JELOWICKA,
    Janina, Princess
DABROWSKA, Konstancja
DAHL, Emma
DALY, Julia
DAMON, Frances Brackett
DAMOREAU-CINTI, Laure
DANCLA, Alphonsine Genevieve-
    Lore
DANILEVSKAYA, V.
DAVIES, Llewela
DAVIS, Marianne
DAVIS, Miss
DE MICCO, Lora
DE SOUSA HOLSTEIN, Donna
    Teresa
DECKER, Pauline
DEDEKAM, Sophie
DEICHMANN, Julie
DELABORDE, Elie Miriam
DELL'ACQUA, Eva
DEMAR, Therese
DEMING, Mrs. L.L.
DESHAYES, Marie
DIBDIN, Isabelle Perkins
DICK, Edith A.
DICKSON, Ellen
DIETRICH, Amalia
DOLE, Caroline

DONALDS, Belle
DONALDSON, Elizabeth
DRAPER, Mrs. J.T.
DREIFUSS, Henrietta
DRIEBURG, Louise von
DROSTE-HUELSHOFF, Annette Elise
    von, Baroness
DUCHAMBGE, Pauline
DUCHAMP, Marie Catharine
DUFFERIN, Lady Helen Selina
DUSCHEK, Josefina
DUSSEK, Olivia
EATON, Frances
EBERLIN, Anna Margrethe
EDELSBERG, Philippine von
EGEBERG, Anna
EGEBERG, Fredrikke Sophie
ELSCHNIG, Marietta
ELSSLER, Fanny
ERARD, Mlle.
ESCHBORN, Georgine Christine
    Maria Anna
ESTABROOK, G.
EUAN-SMITH, Lady
EUGENIE, Charlotte Augusta Amalia
    Albertina, Princess
EVERETT, Alice
EVERSOLE, Rose M.
FARE, Florence
FARLEY, Marion
FARMER, Emily Bardsley
FARRENC, Louise
FECHNER, Paulina
FENGER, Johanne
FERRARI, Francesca Jessie
FISCHEL, Marguerite
FITZGERALD, Lady Edward
FLOTOW, Marthe von
FLOWER, Eliza
FONSECA, Ida Henriette da
FORTEY, Mary Comber
FOWLES, Margaret F.
FRUGONI, Bertha
GABLER, Jeanette
GABRIEL, Mary Ann Virginia
GADE, Margaret
GAIL, Edmée-Sophie
GALLOIS, Marie
GALLONI, Adolfa
GAMBOGI, Federica Elvira
GARCIA, Eduarda Mansilla de
GATES, Alice Avery
GAY, Sophia Maria Francesca
GEIGER, Constanze
GENTY, Mlle.
GERING, Karoline
GERZSO, Angela
GIACOMELLI, Genevieve-Sophie
    Bille
GIBSON, Isabella Mary
GIBSON, Louisa
GILBERT, Florence
GIZYCKA-ZAMOYSKA, Ludmilla,
    Countess
GOETZE, Auguste
GOODEVE, Mrs. Arthur
GORE, Katharina
GORONCY, Emilie
GOSSLER, Clara von
GRANDVAL, Marie Felicie Clemence
    de Reiset, Vicomtesse de
GRAY, Louisa
GRISI, Mme.
GRO, Josephine
GRODZICKA-RZEWUSKA, Julia
GROOM, Mrs.
GROTTGEROWA, Krystyna
GRUNBAUM, Theresa
GUERINI, Rosa
GUIDI LIONETTI, Teresa
GYDE, Margaret

GYLLENHAAL, Matilda Valeriana
    Beatrix, Duchess of Orozco
HAAPASALO, Kreeta
HAASS, Maria Catharina
HABICHT, Mrs. C.E.
HACKETT, Marie
HADELN, Nancy von
HAENEL DE CRONENTHAL, Louise
    Augusta Marie Julia
HAGUE, Harriet
HAHR, Emma
HALE, Irene
HAMAN, Elizabeth
HAMBROCK, Mathilde
HAMMER, Marie von
HAMPDEN, Elizabeth
HARDY, Mrs. Charles S.
HART, Imogine
HARTMANN, Emma Sophie Amalie
HASWIN, Frances R.
HAWES, Charlotte W.
HAWES, Maria
HAXTHAUSEN, Aurore M.G.Ch. von
HEIBERG, Johanne Louise
HEINEMANN, Jenny
HEITMANN, Matilde
HELLER, Ottilie
HENDRICH-MERTA, Marie
HENN, Angelica
HENSEL, Fanny Caecilia
HERRESHOFF, Constance
HERTZ, Hedwig
HERZOGENBERG, Elizabeth von
HEUBERGER, Jenny
HIBLER, Nellie
HINRICHS, Marie
HJORT, Thecla
HODGES, Faustina Hasse
HOEGSBRO-CHRISTENSEN, Inge
HOLLAND, Caroline
HOLMBERG, Emelie Augusta
    Kristina
HOLMES, Augusta Mary Anne
HUENERWADEL, Fanny
HUNDT, Aline
HUNEEUS, Isidora Zegers de
HUNT, Gertrude
HUNTER, Anne
INVERARITY, Eliza
JAHNOVA, Bozena
JENKS, Maude E.
JESKE-CHOINSKA-MIKORSKA,
    Ludmila
JEWELL, Althea Grant
JOACHIM, Amalie
JOYCE, Florence Buckingham
KABATH, Augusta de
KALB, Janet
KARL, Anna
KAVALIEROVA, Marie
KELEMEN, Berta Zathureczky
KELEMEN, Mrs. Lajos
KEMBLE, Adelaide
KERBY, Caroline
KERR, Louisa
KING, Frances Isabella
KINGSTON, Marie Antoinette
KINKEL, Johanna
KLAGE, Marie
KLENZE, Irene von
KLETZINSKY, Adele
KNAPP, Phoebe Palmer
KNUDSEN, Lynne
KOCHETOVA, Aleksandra
    Dorimedontovna
KOENIG, Marie
KOMOROWSKA, Stephanie,
    Countess
KOTSBATREVSKAYA
KRALIK VON MAYERSWALDEN,
    Mathilde

KRAUSE, Anna
KRAUSE, Ida
KREBS, Mrs.
KRYSINSKA, Maria
KURZBOECK, Magdalene von
KYNTZELL-HAGSTROMER, Louise
LA HYE, Louise Genevieve
LAMSON, Georgie
LANGHANS, Louise
LANGRISHE, May Katherine
LANNOY, Clementine-Josephine-
    Françoise-Thérèse, Countess
LANUZA Y VAZQUEZ, Agustina
LATY, Mme.
LE CLERE, Victoire
LE ROUX, Nanine
LEAVITT, Josephina
LEHMANN, Amelia
LEMMEL, Helen Howarth
LEONARD, Antonia Sitcher de Mendi
LEONARDO, Luisa
LIEBMANN, Helene
LIGHTFOOT, Mils
LIKELIKE, Miriam Cleghorn, Princess
LILIUOKALANI, Queen of Hawaii
LIND, Jenny
LINDSAY, Miss M.
LINEVA, Yevgeniya Eduardovna
LINWOOD, Mary
LLANOVER, Lady
LODER, Kate Fanny
LOEWE, Auguste
LONSDALE, Eva
LORINSER, Gisela von
LOUD, Annie Frances
LOWTHIAN, Caroline
LUNDBERG, Ada
MacKINLEY, Mrs. J.
McKINNEY, Ida Scott Taylor
MACIRONI, Clara Angela
MACKENZIE, Grace
MADDISON, Adele
MADURO, Sarah H.L.
MAILLART, Aimée
MALIBRAN, Maria Felicitas
MALLARD, Clarisse
MANNKOPF, Adolphine
MARA, La
MARCHESI, Mathilde de Castrone
MARCHISIO, Barbara
MARCKWALD, Grace
MARRA, Adelina
MARSHALL, Florence A.
MARSHALL, Mrs. William
MARTIN, Angelica
MASSON, Elizabeth
MATTHISON-HANSEN, Nanny
    Hedwig Christiane
MAYER, Emilie
MAZEL, Helen Roberts
MEADER, Emily Peace
MELY, Marie, Countess Vanden
    Heuvel
MENESSIER-NODIER, Marie
    Antoinette Elisabeth
MERSANNE, Maddalena
METZGER-VESPERMANN, Clara
METZLER, Bertha
MEYER, Elizabeth
MIER, Countess Anna von
MILLAR, Marian
MILLARD, Mrs. Philip
MITFORD, Eliza
MOLINOS-LAFITTE, Mlle. A.
MOLIQUE, Caroline
MOLITOR, Friederike
MONCRIEFF, Lynedock
MONGRUEL, Georgiana Catherine
    Eugenia Leonard
MONTGEROULT, Helene de Nervode
MORGAN, Lady

MOULTON, Mrs. Charles
MULLEN, Adelaide
MUNCH, Natalie
MUNDELLA, Emma
MURIO-CELLI, Adelina
NAIRNE, Carolina, Baroness
NARBUTOWNA, Constance
NATHUSIUS, Marie
NEGRONE, Luisa
NEWCOMBE, Georgeanne
NEWTON, Adelaide
NIEMIERZYC, Antonia
NIEWIAROWSKA-BRZOZOWSKA,
    Julia
NIKOLSKY, Mlle.
NORRIS, Mary
NORTON, Caroline Elizabeth Sarah
NORTON, The Hon. Mrs.
NOVELLO, Mary Sabilla
NUNN, Elizabeth Annie
NYSTROEM, Elisabeth
OCKLESTON-LIPPA, Katherine
OLAGNIER, Marguerite
OLCOTT, Grace
OLDHAM, Emily
O'LEARY, Rosetta
OLIVER, Mary
ORGER, Caroline
ORSINI, Teresa
ORTH, Lizette Emma
OSTIERE, May
OWEN, Anita
PAPOT, Marie Anne
PAPPENHEIM, Marie, Countess
PARADIS, Maria Theresia von
PARCELLO, Marie
PARK, Edna Rosalind
PARKE, Maria Hester
PARKHURST, Susan
PARKYNS, Beatrice
PATTI, Adelina
PEASE, Jessie L.
PELLEGRINI CELONI, Anna
PENNA, Catherine
PERCHERON, Suzanne
PERRONNET, Amelie
PESCHKA, Minna
PESSIAK-SCHMERLING, Anna
PEYRON, Albertina Fredrika
PFEILSCHIFTER, Julie von
PHILP, Elizabeth
PIERPONT, Marie de
PIERRET, Phedora
PITTMAN, Alice Locke
PLATEROWA-BROEL-ZYBERK, Maria
PLITT, Agathe
POLKO, Elise Vogel
POSADA Y TORRE, Ana
POTOCKA-PILAVA, Laura
POTT, Aloyse
POWELL, Mrs. Watkins
PRESCOTT, Oliveria Louisa
PRICE, Sara A.
PUCIC-SORKOCEVIC, Yelena
PUGET, Loise
PURGOLD, Nadezhda Nikolayevna
POZZONE, Maria
PUZZI, Fanny
REED Mrs Wallace
RADECKI, Olga von
RADNOR, Helen, Countess of
RALPH, Kate
RAMSAY, Lady Katherine
RAWLINSON, Angela
RAYMOND, Emma Marcy
READ, Sarah Ferriss
REBAUDI, Virginia
RECKE, Caroline
REES, Clara H.
REICHARDT, Louise
RENAUD-D'ALLEN, Mlle. de

REVIAL, Marie Pauline
RICHINGS, Caroline
RICHTER, Pauline
RICOTTI, Onestina
RIDDERSTOLPE, Caroline Johanna
    Lovisa
RING, Claire
RITTER, Fanny Malone Raymond
ROBERT-MAZEL, Helene
ROBERTS, Nellie Wilkinson
ROBINSON, Fanny
RODRIGO, Maria
ROECKEL, Jane
ROELOFSON, Emily B.
RON, Helene de
RONALDS, Belle
ROOT, Grace W.
ROSENHOFF, Orla
ROSENTHAL, Pauline
ROTHSCHILD, Matilde, Baroness
    Willy de
RUCH-TSCHIEMER, Flora
RUDERSDORF, Erminie
RUNCIE, Constance Owen Faunt Le
    Roy
RUTTENSTEIN, Baroness Constance
SABININ, Martha von
SAFFERY, Eliza
SAHLBERG, Alma
SAINT JOHN, Georgie Boyden
SAINTON-DOLBY, Charlotte Helen
SALM-DYCK, Constance-Marie de
    Theis, Princess
SAMUEL, Caroline
SANCHEZ, Manuela Cornejo de
SANDFORD, Lucy A.
SANTA-COLONA-SOURGET,
    Eugenie
SARGENT, Cora Decker
SAUGEON, Zelie
SAWYER, Harriet P.
SCHAEFFER, Theresa
SCHATZELL, Pauline von
SCHIMON, Anna
SCHLICK, Elise, Countess of
SCHMEZER, Elise
SCHMITT, Alois
SCHNORR VON CAROLSFELD,
    Malvina
SCHOLL, Amalie
SCHREINZER, F.M.
SCHUBERT, Georgine
SCHULZOVA, Anezka
SCHUMANN, Clara Josephine
SCHUYLER, Georgina
SCHWERTZELL, Wilhelmine von
SCOTT, Clara H.
SCOTT, Lady John Douglas
SCOTT, M.B.
SENEKE, Teresa
SEROVA, Valentina Semyonovna
SESSI, Marianne
SHASHINA, Elizaveta Sergeyevna
SHELLEY, Mary Wollstonecraft
SHERRINGTON, Grace
SHERRINGTON, Helena Lemmens
SICK, Anna
SKELTON, Nellie Bangs
SKINNER, Fannie Lovering
SLAVYANSKAYA, Olga
    Khristoforovna Agreneva
SLEIGH, Mrs.
SLOMAN, Jane
SMART, Harriet Anne
SMITH, Alice Mary
SMITH, Eleanor Louise
SMITH, Gertrude
SMITH, Laura Alexandrine
SMITH, May Florence
SMITH, Mrs. Gerrit
SMITH, Nettie Pierson

SNEED, Anna
SOMELLERA, Josefa
SPENCER, Fannie Morris
SPORLEDER, Charlotte
STANG, Erika
STEIN, Nannette
STENHAMMAR, Fredrika
STEPHENSON, Maria Theresa
STEWART, Annie M.
STEWART, Elizabeth Kirby
STEWART, F.M.
STIRLING, Elizabeth
STITH, Mrs. Townsend
STOLBERG, Louise von
STOLLEWERK, Nina von
STOLTZ, Rosina
STRANTZ, Louise von
STUBENBERG, Anna Zichy,
　　Countess
SULLIVAN, Marian Dix
SUTRO, Florence Edith
SWEPSTONE, Edith
SWIFT, Gertrude H.
SYNGE, Mary Helena
SZUMINSKA, Flora
SZYMANOWSKA, Maria Agata
TAITE, Annie
TAMMELIN, Bertha
TAYLOR, Mrs. A.H.
TENNYSON, Emily Sarah, Lady
THAMM, Ida
THEGERSTROEM, Hilda Aurora
THERESA
THERESE, Princess of Saxe-
　　Altenburg and of Sweden
THOMPSON, Alexandra
THURBER, Nettie C.
THYS, Pauline
TONDEUR, Wilhelmine
TORRENS, Grace
TORRY, Jane Sloman
TOWNSEND, Marie
TOWNSEND, Pearl Dea Etta
TRAIN, Adelaine
TRETBAR, Helen
TROSCHKE UND ROSENWEHRT,
　　Wilhelmine von, Baroness
TROWBRIDGE, Leslie Eliot
TSCHETSCHULIN, Agnes
TSCHIERSCHKY, Wilhelmine von
TURNER, Harriet
TYRELL, Agnes
UGALDE, Delphine Beaucé
UNGHER-SABATIER, Caroline
UNTERSTEINER, Antonietta
VANDERPOEL, Kate
VANE, Florence
VELTHEIM, Charlotte
VESPERMANN, Marie
VIARDOT-GARCIA, Pauline Michelle
　　Ferdinande
VICTORIA MARIA LOUISA, Duchess
　　of Kent
VIGNY, Louise von
VOLKONSKAYA, Zinanda
　　Alexandrovna, Princess
VORONTSOVA, M.
WAGNER, Virginia De Oliveira
　　Bastos
WAKEFIELD, Augusta Mary
WALDBURG-WURZACH, Julie von,
　　Princess
WALKER, Ida
WARD, Clementine
WARD, Kate Lucy
WARDER, Marie
WATSON, Regina
WEATHERALL, Nellie G.
WEBENAU, Julie
WEIR, Mary Brinckley
WENSLEY, Frances Foster

WEST, Lottie
WESTROP, Kate
WEYRAUCH, Augusta Henrietta von
WHITE, Emma C.
WHITE, Maude Valerie
WHITELY, Bessie Marshall
WICHERN, Caroline
WICKERHAUSER, Nathalie
WICKINS, Florence
WICKMAN, Fredrika
WIECK, Marie
WIEL, Elise
WIGGINS, Kate Douglas
WILLS, Harriet Burdett
WILSON, Addie Anderson
WILSON, Hilda
WILSON, Mrs. Cornwall Baron
WISENEDER, Caroline
WOLFF-FRITZ, Sophie
WOLZOGEN, Elsa Laura von
WOOD, Mrs. George
WOODFORDE-FINDEN, Amy
WOODHULL, Mary G.A.
WOODS, Eliza
WOOLF, Sophia Julia
WORALECK, Josephine
WORTH, Adelaide
WRIGHT, Agnes
WRIGHT, Ellen
WUERTEMBERSKA-
　　CZARTORYSKA, Maria, Duchess
WUIET, Caroline
WURM, Mary J.A.
WURZER, Gabriella
YAKUBOVITCH, Elizaveta
YOUNG, Corrine
YOUNG, Eliza
YOUNG, Harriet Maitland
YOUNG, Matilda
ZAFFAUK, Theresa
ZAMOYSKA, Maria
ZANTEN, Cornelia van
ZEGERS, Isidora
ZIEGLER, Natalie Sophie von
ZIMMERMANN, Agnes Marie
　　Jacobina
ZITTELMANN, Helene
ZUMSTEEG, Emilie
ZYBINE, Mme. S.

20th Century A.D.
AARNE, Els
AARON, Yvonne
ABEJO, Sister M. Rosalina
ABESON, Marion
ABORN, Lora
ABRAMOVA, Sonia Pinkhasovna
ACE, Joy Milane
ACKLAND, Jeanne Isabel Dorothy
ACKLAND, Jessie Agnes
A'DAIR, Jeanne
ADAM, Maria Emma
ADAMS, Carrie Bell
ADAMS, Elizabeth Kilmer
ADAMS, Julia Aurelia
ADERHOLDT, Sarah
AGUDELO MURGUIA, Graciela
AGUIRRE, Diana V.
AHRENS, Peg
AHRENS, Sieglinde
AINSCOUGH, Juliana Mary
AKHUNDOVA, Shafiga Gulam kyzy
AKIYOSHI, Toshiko
AKSYANTSEVA, Ninel Moiseyevna
ALAIN, Marie Claire
ALDERMAN, Pauline
ALDRIDGE, Amanda Ira
ALEJANDRO-DE LEON, Esther
ALEXANDER, Leni
ALIOTH, Marguerite
ALLAIN, Edmee J.
ALLEN, Denise

ALLEN, Judith Shatin
ALLIK, Kristi
ALLITSEN, Frances
ALLOUARD CARNY, Odette
ALMEN, Ruth
ALMESAN, Irma
ALOTIN, Yardena
ALT, Hansi
ALTER, Martha
ALVARES-RIOS, Maria
ALVES DE SOUSA, Berta Candida
ANDERSON, Avril
ANDERSON, Beth
ANDERSON, Jay
ANDERSON, Laurie
ANDERSON, Ruth
ANDERSON-WUENSCH, Jean Mary
ANDREE, Elfrida
ANDREYEVA, Elena Fedorovna
ANDREYEVA, M.
ANDRIEVSKAYA, Nina
　　Konstantinovna
APPELDOORN, Dina van
APPLETON, Adeline Carola
ARAUCO, Ingrid Colette
ARAUJO, Gina de
ARAZOVA, Izabella Konstantinovna
ARBUCKLE, Dorothy M.
ARCHER, Violet Balestreri
ARETZ, Isabel
ARIMA, Reiko
ARIZTI SOBRINO, Cecilia
ARKWRIGHT, Marian Ursula
ARLEN, Jeanne Burns
ARMER, Elinor Florence
ARRIEU, Claude
ARSEYEVA, Irina Vasilievna
ARTEAGA, Genoveva de
ARVEY, Verna
ASHFORD, Emma Louise
ASHMORE, Grace Flournoy
ASTROVA, V.
ATKINSON, Dorothy
ATRE, Prabha
AULIN, Laura Valborg
AUSTER, Lydia Martinovna
AUSTIN, Grace Leadenham
AUZEPY, Michele
AXTENS, Florence
AYARZA DE MORALES, Rosa
　　Mercedes
AYLOTT, Lydia Georgina Edith
BABAYEVA, Seda Grigorievna
BACEWICZ, Grazyna
BACH, Maria
BAGANIER, Janine
BAIKADAMOVA, Baldyrgan
　　Bakhitzhanovna
BAIL, Grace Shattuck
BAILY, Margaret Naismith Osborne
BAINBRIDGE, Beryl
BAINBRIDGE, Katharine
BAIRD, Lorine Chamberlain
BAKER, Gertrude Tremblay
BAKKE, Ruth
BALCKE, Frida Dorothea
BALL, Ida W.
BALLANDS, Etta
BALLASEYUS, Virginia
BALLOU, Esther Williamson
BALSHONE, Cathy S.
BAMPTON, Ruth
BANDARA, Linda
BANG, Sophy
BANKOVA-MARINOVA, Angelina
BARAMISHVILI, Olga Ivanovna
BARATTA, Maria M. de
BARBERIS, Mansi
BARBI, Alice
BARBILLON, Jeanne
BARBLAN-OPIENSKA, Lydia

BARBOUR, Florence Newell
BARCROFT, E. Dorothea
BARDEL, Germaine
BARKER, Phyllis Elizabeth
BARKLUND, Irma L.
BARNETT, Alice
BARNS, Ethel
BARON SUPERVIELLE, Susana
BARRADAS, Carmen
BARRAINE, Elsa
BARRELL, Joyce Howard
BARRETT-THOMAS, N.
BARTLETT, Floy Little
BASSETT, Karolyn Wells
BATCHELOR, Phyllis
BATES, Anna Craig
BAUER, Emilie Frances
BAUER, Marion Eugenie
BAULD, Alison
BAUMGARTEN, Chris
BAYEVA, Vera
BAYLIS, Lilian Mary
BEACH, Amy Marcy
BEAHM, Jacquelyn Yvette
BEAMER, Helen Desha
BEARER, Elaine Louise
BEAT, Janet Eveline
BEATH, Betty
BEATON, Isabella
BEATRICE, Mary Victoria Feodore,
    Princess of Battenberg
BEAUMONT, Vivian
BECK, Martha Dillard
BECLARD D'HARCOURT,
    Marguerite
BEECROFT, Norma Marian
BEEKHUIS, Hanna
BEESON, Elizabeth Ruth
BEGO-SIMUNIC, Andelka
BEHREND, Jeanne
BEKEART, Edna
BEKMAN-SHCHERBINA, Elena
    Aleksandrovna Kamentseva
BELINFANTE-DEKKER, Martha
    Suzanna Betje
BELL, Carla Huston
BELL, Elizabeth
BELL, Lucille Anderson
BELLEROSE, Sister Cecilia
BELOCH, Dorotea
BELOW-BUTTLAR, Gerda von
BENEDICENTI, Vera
BENNETT, Elsie M.
BENNETT, Wilhelmine
BENOIT, Francine Germaine Van
    Gool
BENSUADE, Jane
BENTLEY, Berenice Benson
BENTZON, Karen Johanne
BENZON, Julie
BERAN-STARK, Lola Aloisia Maria
BERBERIAN, Cathy
BERCKMAN, Evelyn
BERG, Lily
BERGE, Irenée
BERGMAN, Ellen
BERGSTROM, Anna
BERK, Adele
BERLINER, Selma
BERRY, Margaret Mary Robinson
BERTRAM, Madge
BERZON, Asya Yevseyevna
BEUSCHER, Elisabeth
BEYER, Johanna Magdalena
BEYERMAN-WALRAVEN, Jeanne
BEZDEK, Sister John Joseph
BIALKIEWICZOWNA-ANDRAULT DE
    LANGERON, Irena
BIANCHINI, Emma
BIANCHINI, Virginie
BIBBY, Gillian Margaret

BIENVENU, Lily
BILBRO, Anne Mathilde
BILTCLIFFE, Florence
BINET, Jocelyne
BINGHAM, Judith
BIRCHER-REY, Hedy
BIRCSAK, Thusnelda
BISHOP, Dorothy
BIXBY, Allene K.
BIZONY, Celia
BJELKE-ANDERSEN, Olga
BLAIR, Kathleen
BLAKE, Dorothy Gaynor
BLANCK, Olga de
BLEY, Carla
BLIESENER, Ada Elizabeth
    Michelman
BLISS, Marilyn S.
BLISS, Tamara
BLOCKSIDGE, Kathleen Mary
BLOMFIELD-HOLT, Patricia
BLOOD, Esta Damesek
BLOOMFIELD-ZEISLER, Fannie
BODENSTEIN-HOYME, Ruth E.
BOESE, Helen
BOETZELAER, Josina Anna
    Petronella
BOFILL, Anna
BOISEN, Elisabeth
BOLZ, Harriet
BOND, Carrie Jacobs
BOND, Victoria Ellen
BONDS, Margaret
BONINCONTRO, Gabrielle
BOONE, Clara Lyle
BOOSEY, Beatrice Joyce
BORDERS, Barbara Ann
BORDEWIJK-ROEPMAN, Johanna
BORRAS I FORNELL, Teresa
BORROFF, Edith
BORRONI, Virginia
BOSCH Y PAGES, Luisa
BOSMANS, Henriette Hilda
BOSTELMANN, Ida
BOTET, Maria Emma
BOUCHARD, Linda L.
BOUCHER, Lydia
BOULANGER, Lili Juliette Marie Olga
BOULANGER, Nadia Juliette
BOUTRON, Madeleine
BOYACK, Jeanette
BOYCE, Blanche Ula
BOYD, Anne Elizabeth
BOYD, Jeanne Margaret
BRADLEY, Ruth
BRAGA, Henriqueta Rosa Fernandes
BRAGGINS, Daphne Elizabeth
BRANDELER, Henriette van den
BRANDMAN, Margaret Susan
BRANNING, Grace Bell
BRANSCOMBE, Gena
BRATU, Emma
BRAUER, Johanna Elisabeth
BREEN, May Singhi
BRENET, Thérèse
BRENNER, Rosamond Drooker
BRESCHI, Laura
BRICE, Laure
BRIDGEWATER, Violet Irene
BRIGGS, Cora Skilling
BRIGGS, Dorothy Bell
BRIGGS, Nancy Louise
BRIGHT, Ann
BRIGHT, Dora Estella
BRINK-POTHUIS, Annie van den
BRITAIN, Radie
BROADWOOD, Lucy E.
BRODERICK, Deborah Houstle
BROGUE, Roslyn Clara
BROOK, Gwendolyn Giffen
BROWN, Mary Helen

BROWN, Norma
BROWN, Rosemary
BROWN, Veronica
BROWNING, Bertha Hecker
BRUNDZAITE, Konstantsiya Kazyo
BRUNNER, Maria
BRUSH, Ruth Damaris
BRUZDOWICZ, Joanna
BRYANT, Verna Mae
BRYUSSOVA, Nadezhda Yakolevna
BUCHANAN, Annabel Morris
BUCHANAN, Dorothy Quita
BUCK, Era Marguerite
BUCKLEY, Beatrice Barron
BUCKLEY, Dorothy Pike
BUCKLEY, Helen Dallam
BUENAVENTURA, Isabel
BULTERIJS, Nina
BURDICK, Elizabeth Tucker
BURNETT, Helen Roth
BURROUGHS, Jane Johnson
BURSTON, Maggie
BURT, Virginia M.
BURTON, Pixie
BURZYNSKA, Jadwiga
BUSH, Gladys B.
BUSH, Grace E.
BUTLER, Anne Lois
BUTT, Thelma
BYERS, Roxana Weihe
CABREIRA, Estefania Loureiro de
    Vasconcelos Leao
CABRERA, Ana S. de
CABRERA, Silvia Maria Pires
CADZOW, Dorothy Forrest
CALBRAITH, Mary Evelene
CALCAGNO, Elsa
CALE, Rosalie Balmer Smith
CALL, Audrey
CALLAWAY, Ann
CALVIN, Susan Heath
CAMEU, Helza
CAMPAGNE, Conny
CAMPMANY, Montserrat
CAMPOS ARAUJO DE, Joaquina
CANAL, Marguerite
CANALES PIZARRO, Marta
CANCINO DE CUEVAS, Sofia
CANNING, Effie I.
CAPUIS, Matilde
CAPURSO, Elisabetta
CARMEN MARINA
CARMICHAEL, Mary Grant
CARON-LEGRIS, Albertine
CARRENO, Teresa
CARRILLO, Isolina
CARRIQUE, Ana
CARROLL, Barbara
CARSON, Zeula Miller
CARSWELL, Francis
CARTER, Buenta MacDaniel
CARVALHO, Dinora de
CASAGEMAS, Luisa
CASTAGNETTA, Grace Sharp
CASTEGNARO, Lola
CASTELLANOS, Tania
CATUNDA, Eunice do Monte Lima
CECCONI-BATES, Augusta
CECCONI-BOTELLA, Monic
CECILE REGINA, Sister
CERVANTES, Maria
CHAMINADE, Cécile Louise
    Stephanie
CHAMPION, Constance MacLean
CHANCE, Nancy Laird
CHANDLER, Mary
CHARBONNIER, Janine Andrée
CHARLES, S. Robin
CHARTRES, Vivien
CHASE, Mary Wood
CHAVES, Mary Elizabeth

FERRAND-TEULET, Denise
FERRARI, Gabriella
FERRER OTERO, Monsita
  Monserrate
FILZ, Bogdanna
FINE, Sylvia
FINE, Vivian
FINLEY, Lorraine Noel
FINZI, Graciane
FIRESTONE, Idabelle
FIRNKEES, Gertrud
FIRSOVA, Elena
FISCHER, Edith Steinkraus
FISCHER, Emma Gabriele Marie von,
  Baroness
FISHER, Charlotte Eleanor
FISHER, Doris
FISHER, Gladys Washburn
FISHER, Jessie
FISHER, Katherine Danforth
FIUZA, Virginia Salgado
FLACH, Elsa
FLAGG, Mary Houts
FLEISCHER-DOLGOPOLSKY,
  Tsipporah
FLEITES, Virginia
FLICK-FLOOD, Dora
FLORING, Grace Kenny
FODY, Ilona
FOLVILLE, Eugenie-Emilie Juliette
FONTYN, Jacqueline
FORD, Mrs. Raymond C.
FORD, Olive Elizabeth
FORMAN, Addie Walling
FORMAN, Joanne
FORSTER, Dorothy
FORSYTH, Josephine
FOSTER, Cecily
FOSTER, Dorothy Godwin
FOSTER, Fay
FOWLER, Jennifer Joan
FOWLER, Marje
FOX, Erika
FRAJT, Ludmila
FRANCHERE-DESROSIERS, Rose de
  Lima
FRANGS, Irene
FRANK, Jean Forward
FRASER, Shena Eleanor
FRASIER, Jane
FRAZER, Mrs. Allan H.
FREED, Dorothy Whitson
FREEHOFF, Ruth Williams
FREER, Eleanor Warner Everest
FREGA, Ana Lucia
FREIXAS Y CRUELLS, Narcisa
FRESON, Armande
FRICKER, Anne
FRITTER, Genevieve Davisson
FRITZ, Sherilyn Gail
FROMM-MICHAELS, Ilse
FRONMUELLER, Frieda
FRUMKER, Linda
FULCHER, Ellen Georgina
FULLER, Jeanne Weaver
FURGERI, Bianca Maria
FURZE, Jessie
GABASHVILI, Nana
GABURO, Elizabeth
GABUS, Monique
GAERTNER, Katarzyna
GAIGEROVA, Varvara Andrianovna
GAINSBORG, Lolita Cabrera
GALAJIKIAN, Florence Grandland
GALIKIAN, Susanna Avetisovna
GAMILLA, Alice Doria
GANNON, Helen Carroll
GANNON, Ruth Ellen
GARCIA MUNOZ, Carmen
GARCIA ROBSON, Magdalena
GARDINER, Mary Elizabeth

GARDNER, Kay
GARDNER, Mildred Alvine
GARELLI DELLA MOREA, Vincenza
GARNETT, Luisa Aires
GARSCIA-GRESSEL, Janina
GARTENLAUB, Odette
GARWOOD, Margaret
GASPARINI, Jola
GASTON, Marjorie Dean
GAUTHIEZ, Cecile
GAYNOR, Jessie Love
GAZAROSSIAN, Koharik
GEBUHR, Ann Karen
GEDDES-HARVEY, Roberta
GEIGER-KULLMANN, Rosy Auguste
GENET, Marianne
GENTEMANN, Sister Mary Elaine
GERCHIK, Vera Petrovna
GERRISH-JONES, Abbie
GERSTMAN, Blanche Wilhelminia
GESELSCHAP, Maria
GEST, Elizabeth
GEYER, Marianne
GEYMULLER, Marguerite Camille-
  Louise de
GHANDAR, Ann
GHIKA-COMANESTI, Ioana
GIDEON, Miriam
GIFFORD, Helen Margaret
GILBERT, Janet Monteith
GILBERT, Marie
GILLES, Yvette Marie
GINDLER, Kathe-Lotte
GIPPS, Ruth
GITECK, Janice
GIURANNA, Elena Barbara
GLANVILLE-HICKS, Peggy
GLASER, Victoria Merrylees
GLATZ, Helen Sinclair
GLYN, Margaret Henriette
GNUS, Ryta
GOEBELS, Gisela
GOETSCHIUS, Marjorie
GOKHMAN, Elena Vladimirovna
GOLLAHON, Gladys
GOLSON-BATEMAN, Florence
GOLUB, Martha Naumovna
GOMEZ CARRILO, Maria Ines
GOMM, Elizabeth
GONTARENKO, Galina Nikolayevna
GONZAGA, Chiquinha
GOODE, Blanche
GOODMAN, Lillian Rosedale
GORELLI, Olga
GOTKOVSKY, Ida-Rose Esther
GOULD, Elizabeth Davies
GOULD, Janetta
GRAHAM, Janet Christine
GRAINGER, Ella Viola Strom-
  Brandelius
GRANT, Louise
GRAUBNER, Hannelore
GRAY, Dorothy
GREEN, Mary Thompson
GREENE, Pauline
GREENFIELD, Lucille
GREENFIELD, Marjorie
GREENWALD, Jan Carol
GREGER, Luisa
GREGORI, Nininha
GREGORY, Else
GREVENKOP CASTENKIOLD, Olga
GRIEBLING, Karen Jean
GRIEF, Marjorie
GRIFFINS, Vashti Rogers
GRIGSBY, Beverly
GRILLI GALEFFI, Elvira
GRIMES, Doreen
GROOM, Joan Charlene
GRUNBERG, Janeta
GRZADZIELOWNA, Eleonora

GUBAIDULINA, Sofia Asgatovna
GUBITOSI, Emilia
GUDAUSKAS, Giedra
GUILBERT, Yvette
GULESIAN, Grace Warner
GUMMER, Phyllis Mary
GURAIEB KURI, Rosa
GUSEINZADE, Adilia Gadzhi Aga
GVAZAVA, Tamara Davidovna
GWILY-BROIDO, Rivka
GYANDZHETSIAN, Destrik
  Bogdanovna
GYLDENKRONE, Clara
GYRING, Elizabeth
HACKLEY, Emma Azalia Smith
HADDEN, Frances Roots
HAENDEL, Ida
HAGER-ZIMMERMANN, Hilde
HAIMSOHN, Naomi Carrol
HAINES, Julia Howell
HAJDU, Julia
HALL, Frances
HALL, Pauline
HALPERN, Stella
HAMILTON, Gertrude Bean
HAMMANN, Rebecca
HAMMOND, Fanny Reed
HAMPE, Charlotte
HANIM, Leyla
HANKS, Sybil Ann
HANSEN, Hanna Marie
HARA, Kazuko (1)
HARA, Kazuko (2)
HARDELOT, Guy d'
HARDIMAN, Ellena G.
HARDY, Helen Irene
HARKNESS, Rebekah West
HARMS, Signe
HARPER, Marjorie
HARRADEN, R. Ethel
HARRHY, Edith
HARRIS, Dorothy
HARRIS, Ethel Ramos
HARRIS, Letitia Radcliffe
HARRISON, Annie Fortescue
HARRISON, Pamela
HARRISON, Susan Frances
HART, Elizabeth Jane Smith
HARTER, Louise C.
HARTZER-STIBBE, Marie
HARVEY, Eva Noel
HARVEY, Vivien
HARWOOD, Sylvia Rowell
HAUSMAN, Ruth Langley
HAWLEY, Carolyn Jean
HAYS, Doris Ernestine
HAYWARD, Mae Shepard
HEALE, Helene
HEATON, Eloise Klotz
HEBER, Judith
HECKSCHER, Celeste de Longpre
HEDOUX, Yvonne
HEGELER, Anna
HEGNER, Anna
HEIBERG, Ella
HEIDRICH, Hermine Margaret
HEIMERL, Elizabeth
HEIMLICH, Florentine
HEINRICH, Adel Verna
HEINSIUS, Clara
HELBLING, Elsa
HELLER-REICHENBACH, Barbara
HELLMERS, Ellen
HELSINGIUS, Barbara
HELSTED, Bodil
HEMMENT, Marguerite E.
HENDERSON, Elizabeth
HENDERSON, Moya
HENDERSON, Ruth Watson
HERBERT, Dorothy
HERICARD, Jeanne

HERMANN, Miina
HERMANSEN, Gudrun
HERNANDEZ-GONZALO, Gisela
HERSCHER-CLEMENT, Jeanne
HERZ, Maria
HESSE, Marjorie Anne
HEYMAN, Katherine Ruth Willoughby
HICKS, Marjorie Kisby
HIER, Ethel Glen
HIGGINBOTHAM, Irene
HIGGINS, Esther S.
HILDERLEY, Jeriann G.
HILDRETH, Daisy Wood
HILL, May
HILL, Mildred J.
HIND O'MALLEY, Pamela
HINLOPEN, Francina
HO, Wai On
HOENDERDOS, Margriet
HOFER-SCHNEEBERGER, Emma
HOFFERT, Brenda
HOFFRICHTER, Bertha Chaitkin
HOKANSON, Margrethe
HOLLAND, Dulcie Sybil
HOLLINS, Dorothea
HOLLISTER, Leona Stephens
HOLLWAY, Elizabeth L.
HOLMES, Shirlee McGee
HOLMSEN, Borghild
HONEGGER-VAURABOURG, Andree
HONG, Sung-Hee
HOOD, Helen
HOOVER, Katherine
HOPPE, Clara
HORROCKS, Amy Elsie
HORTON, Marguerite Wagniere
HOTCHKISS, Evelyn Dissmore
HOUSE, L. Marguerite
HOUSMAN, Rosalie
HOVDA, Eleanor
HOWARD, Beatrice Thomas
HOWE, Mary Alberta Bruce
HOWELL, Dorothy
HOY, Bonnee L.
HOYT, Mary Mack
HRUBY, Dolores Marie
HSU, Wen-Ying
HUEGEL, Margrit
HUGHES, Sister Martina
HUGHEY, Evangeline Hart
HUGH-JONES, Elaine
HULL, Kathryn B.
HULST, Margaret Gardiner
HUNKINS, Eusebia Simpson
HUTTON, Florence Myra
HYDE, Miriam Beatrice
HYLIN, Birgitta Charlotta Kristina
HYSON, Winifred Prince
IASHVILI, Lili Mikhailovna
IBRAGIMOVA, Ela Imamedinovna
IBRAGIMOVA, Sevda Mirza kyzy
IGENBERGA, Elga Avgustovna
ILLIUTOVICH, Nina Yakovlevna
INGBER, Anita Rahel
INGLEFIELD, Ruth Karin
INWOOD, Mary Ruth Brink Berger
IORDAN, Irina Nikolayevna
IRMINGER, Caroline
ISAKOVA, Aida Petrovna
ISMAGILOVA, Leila Zagirovna
ISZKOWSKA, Zofia
IVANOVA, Lidia
IVEY, Jean Eichelberger
JABOR, Najla
JACKSON, Elizabeth Barnhart
JACKSON, Mary
JACOB, Elizabeth Marie
JACOBUS, Dale Asher
JAEGER, Hertha
JAELL-TRAUTMANN, Marie
JAMA, Agnes

JAMES, Dorothy E.
JANKOVIC, Miroslava
JANKOWSKI, Loretta Patricia
JANOTHA, Natalia
JAQUETTI ISANT, Palmira
JARRATT, Lita
JASTRZEBSKA, Anna
JENNINGS, Carolyn
JENNINGS, Marie Pryor
JENSEN, Helga
JEPPSSON, Kerstin Maria
JEREA, Hilda
JESI, Ada
JESSYE, Eva
JEWELL, Lucina
JIRACKOVA, Marta
JIRKOVA, Olga
JOERGENSEN, Christine
JOEST, Emma
JOHNSON, Eloise Lisle
JOHNSON, Harriet
JOHNSON, J. Rosamond
JOHNSTON, Alison Aileen Annie
JOLAS, Betsy
JOLLEY, Florence Werner
JOLLY, Margaret Anne
JOLY, Suzanne
JONES, Dovie Osborn
JONES, Marjorie
JONES-DAVIES, Maude
JOSEPH, Rosa
JOY, Margaret E.
JUDD, Margaret Evelyn
JUENGER, Patricia
KABAT, Julie Phyllis
KACZURBINA-ZDZIECHOWSKA, Maria
KAESER-BECK, Aida
KAHANANUI, Dorothy
KAHMANN, Chesley
KAHN, Esther
KALLOCH, Doley C.
KALOGRIDOU, Maria
KAMIEN, Anna
KAMINSKY, Laura
KANAI, Kikuko
KANAKA'OLE, Edith Ke-Kuhikuhi-I-Pu'u-one-o-Na-Ali'i-O-Kohala
KAPLAN, Lois Jay
KAPP, Corinne
KAPRALOVA, Vitezslava
KARASTOYANOVA, Elena
KARG, Marga
KARNITSKAYA, Nina Andreyevna
KARR Y DE ALFONSETTI, Carmen
KARVENO, Wally
KASHPEROVA, Leokadia Alexandrovna
KASILAG, Lucrecia R.
KATTS, Letty
KATZMAN, Klara Abramovna
KAUFMAN, Barbara
KAVASCH, Deborah Helene
KAYDEN, Mildred
KAZANDJIAN, Sirvart
KAZORECK, Hildegard
KEEFER, Euphrosyne
KEIG, Betty
KELLER, Lue Alice
KELLY, Denise Maria Anne
KEMP, Dorothy Elizabeth Walter
KEMP-POTTER, Joan
KENDRICK, Virginia Catherine
KENNEDY-FRASER, Marjory
KENSWIL, Atma
KENT, Ada Twohy
KER, Ann S.
KERN, Frida
KERR, Bessie Maude
KERSENBAUM, Sylvia Haydee
KERWEY, Julia

KESAREVA, Margarita Alexandrovna
KESSLER, Minuetta Schumiatcher
KETTERER, Laura
KETTERING, Eunice Lea
KHASANSHINA, D.
KHOSS VON STERNEGG, Gisela
KICKINGER, Paula
KICKTON, Erika
KILBY, Muriel Laura
KING, Betty Jackson
KING, Mabel Shoup
KING, Patricia
KING, Rebecca Clift
KINSCELLA, Hazel Gertrude
KIRBY, Suzanne
KIRCHNER, Elisabeth
KIRKMAN, Merle
KIRKWOOD, Antoinette
KISCH, Eve
KISTETENYI, Melinda
KLEBE, Willemijntje
KLEIN, Ivy Frances
KLEPPER, Anna Benzia
KLINKOVA, Zhivka
KLOTZMAN, Dorothy Ann Hill
KNIGHT, Judyth
KNOBLOCHOVA, Antonie
KNOUSS, Isabelle G.
KNOWLTON, Fanny Snow
KOBLENZ, Babette
KODOLITSCH, Michaela
KOELLING, Eloise
KOHAN, Celina
KOLARIKOVA-SEDLACHOVA, Marie
KOLB, Barbara
KOLLER-HOPP, Margarete
KOLODUB, Zhanna Efimovna
KOMPANUETS, Lidia
KONISHI, Nagako
KOPPEL-HOLBE, Maria
KOPTAGEL, Yuksel
KOSHETZ, Nina
KOSSE, Roberta
KOVALEVA, Olga Vasilevna
KOZAKIEVICH, Anna Abramovna
KOZHEVNIKOVA, Ekaterina Vadimovna
KOZINOVIC, Lujza
KRALIKOVA, Johana
KRASNOGLIADOVA, Vera Vladimirovna
KREBS, Suzanne Eigen
KREISS, Hulda E.
KROGMANN, Carrie William
KRUSE, Lotte
KRZANOWSKA, Grazyna
KRZYZANOWSKA, Halina
KUBISCH, Christina
KUESTER, Edith Haines
KUKUCK, Felicitas
KULESHOVA, Galina Grigorevna
KULIEVA, Farida Tairovna
KUMMER, Clare
KUNITZ, Sharon Lohse
KURIMOTO, Yoko
KUSS, Margarita Ivanovna
KUZMENKO, Larysa
KUZMYCH, Christina
KUZNETSOVA, Zhanetta Alexandrovna
LA BARBARA, Joan
LABEY, Charlotte Sohy
LACHOWSKA, Stefania
LACKMAN, Susan C. Cohn
LACMANOVA, Anna
LADEN, Bernice F.
LAFLEUR, Lucienne
LAGO
LAITMAN, Lori
LALAUNI, Lila

LAMBELET, Vivienne Ada Maurice
LAMBERT, Cecily
LAMBRECHTS-VOS, Anna Catharina
LAMEGO, Carlinda J.
LANDOWSKA, Wanda
LANDREE, Jaquenote Goldsteen
LANE, Elizabeth
LANG, Edith
LANG, Margaret Ruthven
LANG-BECK, Ivana
LANGE, Anny von
LANKMAR, Helen
LAPEIRETTA, Ninon de Brouwer
LAPIN, Lily
LARKIN, Deirdre
LARSEN, Elizabeth Brown
LARSON, Anna Barbara
LATIOLAIS, Desirée Jayne
LATZ, Inge
LAUER, Elizabeth
LAUFER, Beatrice
LAUMYANSKENE, Elena Iono
LAURENT, Ruth Carew
LAVIN, Marie Duchesne
LAVOIPIERRE, Therese
LAWRENCE, Emily M.
LAYMAN, Pamela
LE BEAU, Louisa Adolpha
LEAF, Ann
LEAHY, Mary Weldon
LEBARON, Anne
LEBEDEVA, A.
LEBENBOM, Elaine F.
LEBIZAY, Marguerite
LEE, Young Ja
LEFANU, Nicola Frances
LEGINSKA, Ethel
LEHMAN, Evangeline Marie
LEHMANN, Liza
LEHOTSKA-KRIZKOVA, Ludmila
LEIBOW, Ruth Irene
LEITE, Clarisse
LEIVISKA, Helvi Lemmiki
LELEU, Jeanne
LEMCKE, Anna
LEMON, Laura G.
LENNEP, Henrietta van
LEON, Tania Justina
LEONARD, Mamie Grace
LEONCHIK, Svetlana Gavrilovna
LEONE, Mae G.
LEPEUT-LEVINE, Jeannine
LEPKE, Charma Davies
LESICHKOVA, Lili
LEVEY, Lauren
LEVI, Natalia Nikolayevna
LEVIN, Rami Yona
LEVINA, Zara Alexandrovna
LEVITE, Miriam
LEVITOVA, Ludmila Vladimirovna
LEVITSKAYA, Viktoria Sergeyevna
LEWING, Adele
LIADOVA, Ludmila Alekseyevna
LICHT, Myrtha B.
LICHTENSTEIN, Olga Grigorievna
LIDDELL, Claire
LIDGI-HERMAN, Sofia
LIEBLING, Estelle
LIEBMANN, Nanna Magdalene
LIEDBERGIUS, Camilla
LIMA CRUZ, Maria Antonietta de
LINNET, Anne
LINZ VON KRIEGNER, Marta
LIPSCOMB, Helen
LITSITE, Paula Yanovna
LITTLE, Anita Gray
LITTLEJOHN, Joan Anne
LIU, Tyan-Khua
LLOYD, Caroline Parkhurst
LLUNELL SANAHUJA, Pepita
LOCKWOOD, Annea Ferguson

LOH, Kathy Jean
LOHR, Ina
LOMON, Ruth
LOOTS, Joyce Mary Ann
LOPEZ ROVIROSA, Maria Isabel
LORD, Helen Cooper
LORE, Emma Maria Theresa
LORENZ, Ellen Jane
LORENZ, Petra
LORIOD, Yvonne
LOUDOVA, Ivana
LOUIE, Alexina Diane
LOUVIER, Nicole
LOWELL, Edith
LOWENSTEIN, Gunilla Marike
LU, Yen
LUCAS, Mary Anderson
LUCK, Maude Haben
LUCKE, Katharine E.
LUDVIG-PECAR, Nada
LUMBY, Betty Louise
LUND, Inger Bang
LUND, Signe
LUPTON, Belle George
LUTHER, Mary
LUTYENS, Elisabeth
LVOVA, Julia Fedorovna
LYELL, Margaret
LYONN LIEBERMAN, Julie
LYONS, Ruth
LYUBOMIRSKAYA-BOYARSKAYA,
  Revekka Grigorevna
MAAS, Marguerite Wilson
MACHADO, Lena
MACKEN, Jane Virginia
MACKIE, Shirley M.
MACONCHY, Elizabeth
MacARTHUR, Helen
McALISTER, Mabel
McALLISTER, Rita
McCARTHY, Charlotte
McCOLLIN, Frances
McDUFFEE, Mabel Howard
McGOWAN SCOTT, Beatrice
McILWRAITH, Isa Roberta
McINTYRE, Margaret
McKELLAN, Irene Mary
McKENZIE, Sandra
McLAIN, Margaret Starr
McLAUGHLIN, Marian
McLEMORE, Monita Prine
McLIN, Lena
McNEIL, Janet L. Pfischner
McPHERSON, Frances Marie
McSWAIN, Augusta Geraldine
McTEE, Cindy Karen
MADISON, Clara Duggan
MADRIGUERA RODON, Paquita
MADSEN, Florence J.
MAEDLER, Ruth
MAGENTA, Maria
MAGOGO KA DINIZULU, Constance,
  Princess
MAGUY LOVANO, Marguerite
  Schlegel
MAHLER, Alma Maria
MAJLATH, Julia
MAKAROVA, Nina Vladimirovna
MALDYBAYEVA, Zhyldyz
  Abdylasovna
MALHE, Maria Aparecida
MALMLOEF-FORSSLING, Carin
MAMLOK, Ursula
MANA-ZUCCA
MANGGRUM, Loretta C. Cessor
MANNING, Kathleen Lockhart
MANUKIAN, Irina Eduardovna
MANZIARLY, Marcelle de
MARAIS, Abelina Jacoba
MARBE, Myriam
MARCUS, Ada Belle Gross

MAREZ-OYENS, Tera de
MARIANI-CAMPOLIETI, Virginia
MARIC, Ljubica
MARINESCU-SCHAPIRA, Ilana
MARKIEWICZOWNA, Wladyslawa
MARKOV, Katherine Lee
MARKS, Jeanne Marie
MARQUES, Fernandina Lagos
MARQUES, Laura Wake
MARSCHAL-LOEPKE, Grace
MARSH, Gwendolyn
MARSHALL, Jane Manton
MARSHALL, Kye
MARTENOT-LAZARD, Ginette-
  Genevieve
MARTIN, Judith Reher
MARTIN, Ravonna G.
MARTINEZ DE LA TORRE Y
  SHELTON, Emma
MARTINEZ, Odaline de la
MASON, Gladys Amy
MASSUMOTO, Kikuko
MASTERS, Juan
MATEU, Maria Cateura
MATEVOSIAN, Araks Surenovna
MATHEWS, Blanche Dingley Moore
MATHIESON, Ann Emily
MATJAN, Vida
MATTHEISS-BOEGNER, Helga
MATTHEWS, Dorothy White
MATTULLATH, Alice
MATVEYEVA, Novella
MATZEN, Margarete
MAUR, Sophie
MAXWELL, Elsie
MAXWELL, Helen Purcell
MAXWELL, Jacqueline Perkinson
MAY, Florence
MAYER, Lise Maria
MAYHEW, Grace
MEAD, Catherine Pannill
MEADE, Margaret Johnston
MEARS, Caroline
MEISTER, Marianne
MEKEEL, Joyce
MEL-BONIS
MELL, Gertrud Maria
MELOY, Elizabeth
MELVILLE, Marguerite Liszniewska
MENDELSSOHN, Erna
MENEELY-KYDER, Sarah Suderley
MEREDITH, Margaret
MERO, Jolanda
MERRICK, Marie E.
MERRIMAN, Margarita Leonor
MERTENS, Dolores
MESNEY, Dorothy Taylor
MESRITZ-VAN VELTHUYSEN, Annie
METALLIDI, Zhanneta Lazarevna
MIAGI, Ester Kustovna
MIGRANYAN, Emma
MIKUSCH, Margarethe von
MILA, Leonora
MILAM, Lena Triplett
MILENKOVIC, Jelena
MILLER, Elma
MILLER, Lillian Anne
MINEO, Antoinette
MIREILLE, Saint Plante
MITCHELL, Izah Pike
MITCHELL, Norma Jean
MIYAKE, Haruna
MKRTYCHIEVA, Virginia Nikitichna
MOE, Benna
MOELLER, Paulette
MOESTUE, Marie
MONK, Meredith
MONNOT, Marguerite Angele
MONTGOMERY, Merle
MONTIJN, Aleida
MOORE, Dorothy Rudd

MOORE, Luella Lockwood
MOORE, Mary Carr
MOORE, Undine Smith
MOOREHEAD, Consuela Lee
MORGAN, Mary Hannah
MORISON, Christina W.
MORITZEN, Gunda
MORLEY, Nina Dianne
MORRIS, Mrs. C.H.
MORRISON, Julia Maria
MORRISSEY, Elizabeth
MORROW, Jean
MORTIFEE, Ann
MORTON, Agnes Louise
MOSCOVITZ, Julianne
MOSELEY, Caroline Carr
MOSHER, Frances Elizabeth
MOSS, Katie
MOSSMAN, Bina
MOSUSOVA, Nadezda
MOTTA, Giovanna
MRACEK, Ann Michelle
MUELLER-HERMANN, Johanna
MUELLER-WELTI, Hedwig
MUENTZING, Paula
MUKHAMEDZHANOVA, Mariam
MUKLE, May Henrietta
MUNDINGER, Adele Franziska
MUNGER, Millicent Christner
MUNKTELL, Helena Mathilda
MUNTHE-MORGENSTIERNE, Anna
MURDOCH, Heather
MURRI, Alceste
MUSGRAVE, Thea
MUSTILLO, Lina
MYSZINSKA-WOJCIECHOWSKA,
  Leokadia
NAESER-OTTO, Martha
NAIKHOVICH-LOMAKINA, Fania
  Filippovna
NAKAMURA, Sawako
NAKASHIMA, Jeanne Marie
NAMAKELUA, Alice K.
NASH, Phyllis V.
NATVIG, Candace
NAUMANN, Ida
NEEDHAM, Alicia Adelaide
NEPGEN, Rosa Sophia Cornelia
NEWELL, Laura E.
NEWLIN, Dika
NEWMAN, Adelaide
NEWMAN-PERPER, Elfie
NICKERSON, Camille Lucie
NIEBEL, Mildred
NIEDERBERGER, Maria A.
NIEMACK, Ilza Louise
NIEWIADOMSKA, Barbara
NIGHTINGALE, Mae Wheeler
NIKOLAYEVA, Tatiana Petrovna
NIKOLSKAYA, Lyubov Borisovna
NILSSON, Christine
NISHUDA, Yamiko
NOBLE, Ann
NOBLITT, Katheryn Marie McCall
NOETHLING, Elisabeth
NORBURY, Ethel F.
NORDENFELT, Dagmar
NORDENSTROM, Gladys Mercedes
NORDRAAK-FEYLING, Gudrun
NORRE, Dorcas
NORUP, Helle Merete
NOVA SONDAG, Jacqueline
NOVELLO-DAVIES, Clara
NOVI, Anna Beate
NOVOSELOVA, Ludmila Alexeyevna
NOYES, Edith Rowena
NUGENT, Maude Jerome
OBENCHAIN, Virginia
O'BRIEN, Drena
OBROVSKA, Jana
ODAGESCU, Irina

ODDONE SULLI-RAO, Elisabetta
OENNERBERG-MALLING, Berta
OERBECK, Anne-Marie
OGILVIE, Signe
OH, Sook Ja
OIKONOMOPOULOS, Eleni N.
OLDENBURG, Elizabeth
O'LEARY, Jane Strong
OLIVE, Vivienne
OLIVEIRA, Babi de
OLIVER, Madra Emogene
OLLER BENLLOCH, Maria Teresa
OLSON, Lynn Freeman
OMER, Helene
ORE, Cecilie
ORENSTEIN, Joyce Ellin
OSAWA, Kazuko
OSETROVA-YAKOVLIEVA, Nina
  Alexandrovna
OSGOOD, Marion
OSIANDER, Irene
OSMANOGLU, Gevheri
OSTROFF, Esther
OWEN, Angela Maria
OWEN, Blythe
OWEN, Morfydd Llwyn
OWENS, Susan Elizabeth
OZDENSES, Semahat
PACK, Beulah Frances
PADE, Else Marie
PAGOTO, Helen
PAKHMUTOVA, Alexandra
  Nikolayevna
PALMER, Florence Margaret Spencer
PANETTI, Joan
PARKE, Dorothy
PARKER, Alice
PARPAGLIOLO, Iditta
PARR-GERE, Florence
PARS, Melahat
PATINO ANDRADE, Graziela
PATTERSON, Andra
PATTERSON, Annie Wilson
PAUL, Doris A.
PAULL, Barberi
PAVIA DE MAGALHAES, Isaura
PEACOCK, Mary O'Kelley
PEGELOW, Hanna G.
PEJACEVIC, Dora, Countess
PENGILLY, Sylvia
PENNER, Jean Priscilla
PENTLAND, Barbara Lally
PEREIRA DA SILVA, Adelaide
PERISSAS, Madeleine
PERKIN, Helen
PERRY, Zenobia Powell
PERSCHMANN, Elfriede
PETERSEN, Else
PETERSON, Melody
PETRA-BASACOPOL, Carmen
PETROVA, Mara
PETROVA-KRUPKOVA, Elena
PEYROT, Fernande
PFERDEMENGES, Maria Pauline
  Augusta
PFOLH, Bessie Whittington
PFUND, Leonore
PHARRIS, Elizabeth
PHILIBA, Nicole
PHILIPPART, Renée
PHILLIPS, Bryony
PHILLIPS, Donna
PHILLIPS, Karen Ann
PHILLIPS, Linda
PHILLIPS, Lois Elisabeth
PHILLIPS, Vivian Daphne
PICCONI, Maria Antonietta
PIECHOWSKA, Alina
PIERROT, Noelie Marie Antoinette
PIETSCH, Edna Frieda
PIGGOTT, Audrey Margaret

PILIS, Heda
PIRES DE CAMPOS, Lina
PIRES DOS REIS, Hilda
PITCHER, Gladys
PITOT, Genevieve
PITT, Emma
PIZER, Elizabeth Faw Hayden
PLANICK, Annette Meyers
PLE-CAUSSADE, Simone
PLUMSTEAD, Mary
POINTON, Barbara
POLIGNAC, Armande de, Countess
  of Chabannes
POLIN, Claire
POLK, Grace Porterfield
POLLOCK, Muriel
PONSA, Maria Luisa
POOLE, Anna Ware
POOLE, Anne
POOLER, Marie
POPATENKO, Tamara Alexandrovna
POPOVICI, Elise
PORTER, Debra
POSTON, Elizabeth
POWERS, Ada Weigel
PRADELL, Leila
PRAVOSSUDOVITCH, Natalja
  Michajlovna
PRAY, Ada Jordan
PREDIC-SAPER, Branislava
PREOBRAJENSKA, Vera Nicolaevna
PRESTON, Matilee Loeb-Evans
PRICE, Beryl
PRICE, Deon Nielsen
PRICE, Florence Beatrice
PRIESING, Dorothy Jean
PRIETO, Maria Teresa
PRIOLLI, Maria Luisa de Matos
PROCACCINI, Teresa
PROCTOR, Alice McElroy
PSTROKONSKA-NAVRATIL,
  Grazyna Hanna
PUCHE, Sofia
PUKUI, Mary Abigail
QUANTIN-SAULNIER, Denise
QUIEL, Hildegard
QUINLAN, Agnes Clune
QUINTANILLA, Alba
RABEN-LEVETZAU, Nina
RAHMN, Elza Loethner
RAINIER, Priaulx
RAKHMANKULOVA, Mariam
  Mannanovna
RALSTON, Frances Marion
RAN, Shulamit
RAVIZE, Angele
RAW, Vera Constance
REBULL, Teresa
RECLI, Giulia
REED, Marlyce Rae Polk
REID, Sarah Johnston
REID, Wendy
REID, Mrs. Wallace
REIFF, Lili
REIS, Hilda Pires dos
REISER, Violet
REMICK, Bertha
RENIE, Henriette
RENNES, Catharina van
RENSHAW, Rosette
RESPIGHI, Elsa
RHEINGOLD, Lauma Yanovna
RHENE-JAQUE
RICH, Gladys
RICHARDS, Inez Day
RICHARDS, Laura E.
RICHARDSON, Cornelia Heintzman
RICHARDSON, Enid Dorothy
RICHMOND, Virginia
RICHNER-HEIM, Erika
RICHTER, Ada

RICHTER, Marga
RICHTER, Marion Morrey
RILEY, Ann Marion
RILEY, Myrtis F.
RITTENBAND, Minna Ethel
ROBERT, Lucie
ROBERTS, Gertrud Hermine Kuenzel
ROBERTS, Jane A.
ROBERTS, Ruth Olive
ROBERTSON, Donna Lou Nagey
ROBINSON, Frances
ROCHAT, Andrée
ROCHEROLLE, Eugenie Katherine
RODGERS, Mary
RODRIGUEZ, Esther
ROE, Marion Adelle
ROES, Carol
ROESGEN-CHAMPION, Marguerite
  Sara
ROFE, Esther
ROGATIS, Teresa de
ROGER, Denise
ROGERS, Clara Kathleen
ROGERS, Faith Helen
ROGERS, Melicent Joan
ROGERS, Patsy
ROGET, Henriette
ROHDE, Q'Adrianne
ROHRER, Gertrude Martin
ROMA, Caro
ROMM, Rosalina Davidovna
ROOBENIAN, Amber
ROOTH, Anna-Greta
ROSATO, Clorinda
ROSE, Sister Caroline
ROSS, Gertrude
ROSSELLI-NISSIM, Mary
ROSSER, Annetta Hamilton
ROWAN, Barbara
ROYSE, Mildred Barnes
ROZHAVSKAYA, Yudif Grigorevna
RUDOLPH, Anna
RUEGGER, Charlotte
RUFF-STOEHR, Herta Maria Klara
RUGELES, Ana Mercedes de
RUSCHE, Marjorie Maxine
RUSSELL, Anna
RUTA, Gilda, Countess
RYAN, Winifred
RYBNER, Dagmar de Corval
RYDER, Theodora Sturkow
RYLEK-STANKOVA, Blazena
RZAYEVA, Agabadzhi Ishmael kykz
SAARIAHO, Kaija
SACCAGGIO, Adelina Luisa Nicasia
SADERO GENI, Maria Scarpa
SADOVNIKOFF, Mary Briggs
SAFARIAN, Lucia Arisovna
SAINT JOHN, Kathleen Louise
SAINT-GEORGES, Didia
SAKALLI-LECCA, Alexandra
SALMANOVA, R.
SALSBURY, Janet Mary
SALTER, Mary Elizabeth
SALVADOR, Matilde
SAMTER, Alice
SAMUELSON, Laura Byers
SAMVELIAN, Sofia Vardanovna
SANCIN, Mirca
SANDERS, Alma M.
SANDIFUR, Ann Elizabeth
SANDRESKY, Margaret Vardell
SANDY, Grace Linn
SANFILIPPO, Margherita Marie
SANFORD, Grace Krick
SANNA CAMPAGNA, Myriam
SANZ, Rocio
SARNECKA, Jadwiga
SAUNDERS, Carrie Lou
SAUVREZIS, Alice
SAXTORPH, Gudrun

SCEK, Breda Friderika
SCHAFMEISTER, Helen
SCHAUSS-FLAKE, Magdalene
SCHEEPERS-VAN DOMMELEN, Maria
SCHEIN, Suzanna Fedorovna
SCHERCHEN, Tona
SCHICK, Philippine
SCHIRMACHER, Dora
SCHJELDERUP, Mon Marie Gustava
SCHMIDT, Margot Alice
SCHMIDT-DUISBURG, Margarete
  Dina Alwina
SCHMITT-LERMANN, Frieda
SCHONTHAL, Ruth E.
SCHORLEMMER, Erna von
SCHORR-WEILER, Eva
SCHUBARTH, Dorothe
SCHULTE, Eleonore
SCHULZ, Madeleine
SCHULZE-BERGHOF, Luise Doris
  Albertine
SCHUMAKER, Grace L.
SCHUMANN, Meta
SCHURZMANN, Katharina
SCHUSSLER-BREWAEYS, Marie
  Antoinette
SCHUSTER, Elfriede
SCHUYLER, Philippa Duke
SCHWARTZ, Julie
SCHWARTZ, Nan Louise
SCHWARZ, Friederike
SCHWARZKOPF-DRESSLER, Maria
SCHWEIZER, Gertrude
SCHWERDTFEGER, E. Anne
SCHYTTE-JENSEN, Caroline
SCLIAR, Esther
SCOTT, Georgina Keir
SCOTT, Molly
SCOTT-HUNTER, Hortense
SCOVILLE, Margaret Lee
SEALE, Ruth
SEARS, Helen
SEAVER, Blanche Ebert
SEAY, Virginia
SEBASTIANI, Pia
SEGHIZZI, Cecilia
SEHESTED, Hilda
SELDEN-GOTH, Gizella
SELMER, Kathryn Lande
SEMEGEN, Daria
SENFTER, Johanna
SEPULVEDA, Maria Luisa
SERRANO REDONNET, Ana
SETO, Robin
SETTI, Kilza
SEUEL-HOLST, Marie
SEVERY, Violet Cavell
SEWALL, Maud Gilchrist
SHAFFER, Jeanne Ellison
SHAIMARDANOVA, Shakhida
SHARPE, Emma
SHATAL, Miriam
SHAVERZASHVILI, Tamara
  Antonovna
SHAW, Alice Marion
SHAW, Carrie Burpee
SHELDON, Lillian Tait
SHELTON, Margaret Meier
SHEMER, Naomi
SHER, Rebecca
SHERMAN, Ingrid
SHEVITZ, Mimi
SHIDA, Shoko
SHIELDS, Alice Ferree
SHLONSKY, Verdina
SIDORENKO, Tamara Stepanovna
SIEGFRIED, Lillie Mahon
SIEGRIST, Beatrice
SILBERTA, Rhea
SILSBEE, Ann L.
SILVA, Eloisa d'Herbil de

SILVER, Sheila Jane
SILVERBURG, Rose
SILVERMAN, Faye-Ellen
SIMIC, Darinka
SIMON, Cecile Paul
SIMONE, Nina
SIMONIAN, Nadezhda Simonovna
SIMONS, Lorena Cotts
SIMONS, Netty
SINGER, Jeanne
SKAGGS, Hazel Ghazarian
SKALSKA-SZEMIOTH, Hanna Wanda
SKOWRONSKA, Janina
SLEETH, Natalie
SLIANOVA-MIZANDARI, Dagmara
  Levanovna
SMEJKALOVA, Vlasta
SMELTZER, Susan Mary
SMILEY, Pril
SMIRNOVA SOLODCHENKOVA,
  Tatiana Georgievna
SMIRNOVA, Galina Konstantinovna
SMITH, Anita
SMITH, Eleanor
SMITH, Hilda Josephine
SMITH, Julia Frances
SMITH, Mary Barber
SMITH, Ruby Mae
SMYTH, Ethel Mary, Dame
SNELL, Lillian Lucinda
SNIFFIN, Allison
SNIZKOVA-SKRHOVA, Jitka
SODRE, Joanidia
SOENSTEVOLD, Maj
SOLOMON, Joyce Elaine
SOLOMON, Mirrie Irma
SOMMER, Silvia
SONNTAG, Brunhilde
SOUBLETTE, Sylvia
SOUERS, Mildred
SOULAGE, Marcelle Fanny Henriette
SPALDING, Eva Ruth
SPAULDING, Virginia
SPEACH, Sister Bernadette Marie
SPECHT, Judy Lavise
SPEKTOR, Mira J.
SPENA, Lita
SPENCER PALMER, Florence
  Margaret
SPENCER, Marguerita
SPENCER, Williametta
SPINDLE, Louise Cooper
SPIZIZEN, Louise Myers
SPOENDLIN, Elisabeth
SPOERRI-RENFER, Anna-
  Margaretha
SPONGBERG, Viola
STAIR, Patty
STANEKAITE-LAUMYANSKENE,
  Elena Ionovna
STANLEY, Helen Camille
STANLEY, Marion Isabel
STARBUCK, Anna Diller
STEELE, Helen
STEFANOVIC, Ivana
STEIN, Gladys Marie
STEINER, Emma
STEINER, Gitta Hana
STEIN-SCHNEIDER, Lena
STEPANIUGINA, E.
STEPHEN, Roberta Mae
STERNICKA-NIEKRASZOWA, Ilza
STEVENS, Isadore Harmon
STEVENS, Joan Frances
STEWART, Hascal Vaughan
STEWART, Katharine
STEWART, Ora Pate
STEWART-BAXTER, Maud
STEWART-NORTH, Isabel
STITT, Margaret McClure
STOBEAUS, Kristina

STOCKER, Stella
STOEPPELMANN, Janet
STRATTON, Anne
STRAUSS, Elizabeth
STREATCH, Alice
STREATFIELD, Valma June
STREICHER, Lyubov Lvovna
STREIT, Else
STRICKLAND, Lily Teresa
STRUCK, Ilse
STRUTT, Dorothy
STUART-BERGSTROM, Elsa
   Marianne
STUDENY, Herma
STURKOW-RYDER, Theodora
STYLES, Dorothy Geneva
SUBBALAKSHMI, M.S.
SUCHY, Gregoria Karides
SUESSE, Dana
SUH, Kyung-Sun
SULPIZI, Mira
SULTAN, Aishe
SULTAN, Fatma
SULTAN, Hatidje
SULTANOVA, Asya Bakhish kyzy
SUMNER, Clare
SUMNER, Sarah
SUNBLAD-HALME, Heidi Gabriella
   Wilhelmina
SUSSMAN, Ettel
SUTHERLAND, Margaret
SUTZU, Rodica
SVANIDZE, Natela Damianovna
SWADOS, Elizabeth
SWAIN, Freda Mary
SWISHER, Gloria Agnes Wilson
SZAJNA-LEWANDOWSKA, Jadwiga
   Helena
SZOENYI, Erzsebet
SZPINTER-KINIECKA, Maria
TAKAMI, Toyoko
TAL, Marjo
TAL, Ya'ara
TALMA, Louise
TAMBLYN, Bertha Louise
TANNER, Hilda
TAPPER, Bertha
TARBOS, Frances
TARLOW, Karen Anne
TASHJIAN, B. Charmian
TAUTU, Cornelia
TAYLOR, Eleanor
TAYLOR, Mary Virginia
TAYLOR, Maude Cummings
TE RANGI-PAI, Princess
TEGNER, Alice Charlotte
TELFER, Nancy Ellen
TEMPLE, Hope
TENGBERGEN, Maria Elizabeth van
   Ebbenhorst
TERHUNE, Anice
TERRIER-LAFFAILLE, Anne
TERZIAN, Alicia
THISSE-DEROUETTE, Rose
THOMAS, Helen
THOMAS, Karen P.
THOMAS, Marilyn Taft
THOMAS, Mary Virginia
THOMAS, Muriel Leonora Duncan
THOME, Diane
THOMPSON, Caroline Lorraine
THOMPSON, Leland
THOMSEN, Geraldine
TICHARICH, Zdenka
TIDEMAN-WIJERS, Bertha
TIMMERMANN, Leni
TKACH, Zlata Moiseyevna
TOBIN, Sister Clare
TODD, Alice Weston
TODD, Esther Cox
TOLER, Anne

TOLKOWSKY, Denise
TOLLEFSEN, Augusta
TORRA, Celia
TORRANCE, Mrs. Joe Taylor
TORRENS, Merce
TOWERSEY, Phyllis Mary
TOYAMA, Michiko Françoise
TRAEGER, Elinor Meissner
TRAVASSOS LOPES, Maria de
   Lourdes Alves
TREADWAY, Maude Valerie
TRIMBLE, Joan
TRINITAS, Sister M.
TRIPP, Ruth
TROUP, Emily Josephine
TRUMAN, Irene
TUCKER, Irene
TUICHEVA, Zumrad
TUMANIAN, Elizaveta Artashesovna
TUMANISHVILI, Ketevana
   Dmitirevna
TUNISON, Louise
TURGEON, Frances
TURNELL, Margaret Hoberg
TURNER, Mildred Cozzens
TURNER, Myra Brooks
TURNER, Olive Mary
TURNER, Sara Scott
TURNER-MALEY, Florence
TURRIETTA, Cheryl Renée
TURTYGINA, Pava Grigorevna
TUSSENBROEK, Hendrika van
TUXEN, Elisabeth
TWOMBLY, Mary Lynn
TWOREK, Wandy
TWYMAN, Grace
TYER, Norma Phyllis
TYSON, Mildred Lund
ULEHLA, Ludmila
UNDERWOOD, Frances Evangeline
UPTON, Anne
URNER, Catherine Murphy
USHER, Ethel Watson
USHER, Julia
UYTTENHOVE, Yolande
VALDES, Marta
VAN AARDT, Madelene
VAN APPLEDORN, Mary Jeanne
VAN BUREN, Alicia Keisker
VAN DE VATE, Nancy Hayes
VAN DEN BOORN-COCLET,
   Henriette
VAN DER MARK, Maria
VAN EPEN-DE GROOT, Else Antonia
VAN ETTEN, Jane
VAN HAUTE, Anna-Maria
VAN KATWIJK, Viola Edna Beck
VAN NESTE, Rosane Micheline Lucie
   Charlotte
VAN OHLEN, Deborah
VAN VLIET, Pearl H.
VARGAS, Eva
VASILIEVA, Tatiana Ivanovna
VAZQUEZ, Alida
VEHAR, Persis Anne
VEIGA OLIVEIRA, Sofia Helena da
VENDELHAVEN, Harriet
VERCOE, Elizabeth
VERHAALEN, Sister Marion
VERNE, Adela
VERRALL, Pamela Motley
VERRILL, Louise Shurtleff Brown
VIALA, Georgette
VIDAR, Jorunn
VIEU, Jane
VIGGO, Eleanor Margaret Green,
   Princess
VIGNERON-RAMAKERS, Christiane-
   Josee
VIGNERY, Jeanne Emilie Virginie
VILLARINI, Awilda

VILLENEUVE, Marie-Louise Diane
VILLIN, Marcelle Henriette Marie
VILLINES, Virginia
VINTULE, Ruta Evaldovna
VIRTUE, Constance Cochnower
VITALI-AUGUSTI, Giuseppina
VITO-DELVAUX, Berthe di
VIVADO ORSINI, Ida
VLADERACKEN, Geertruida van
VOELLMY-LIECHTI, Grety
VOIGT, Henriette
VOIGT-SCHWEIKERT, Margarete
VOLKART, Hazel
VOLKART-SCHLAGER, Kaethe
VOLKSTEIN, Pauline
VOLLENHOVEN, Hanna van
VON ZIERITZ, Grete
VORLOVA, Slavka
VORONINA, Tatiana Aleksandrovna
VOSS, Marie Wilson
VREE-BROWN, Marion F.
WAALER, Fredrikke Holtemann
WAGENSONNER, Mimi
WAINWRIGHT, Harriet
WALDO, Elisabeth
WALDROP, Uda
WALKER, Gwyneth van Anden
WALLACE, Mildred White
WALLACE, Phyllis Joy
WALLACH, Joelle
WALLNEROVA, Bibiana
WALSH, Elizabeth Jameson
WANG, An-Ming
WARD, Diane
WARE, Harriet
WARE, Helen
WARNE, Katharine Mulky
WARNER, Sylvia Townsend
WASKO, Christine
WASSALS, Grace
WATERHOUSE, Frances Emery
WATERSTONE, Satella S.
WEAVER, Carol Ann
WEAVER, Marion
WEAVER, Mary
WEBB, Allienne Brandon
WEGENER-KOOPMAN, Bertha
   Frensel
WEIGL, Vally
WEIR, Judith
WEISSBERG, Julia Lazerevna
WEISS-MANN, Edith
WELANDER, Svea Goeta
WELDON, Georgina
WELLNER, Elsa
WENDELBURG, Norma Ruth
WENNERBERG-REUTER, Sara
   Margareta Eugenia Euphrosyne
WENTZEL, Elisabet von
WENTZ-JANACEK, Elisabet
WERFEL-LACHIN, Assia
WERTHEIM, Rosy
WESSELS, Judith Brent
WESSELS, Marlene
WESTBROOK, Helen Searles
WESTGATE, Elizabeth
WEYBRIGHT, June
WHITE, Claude Porter
WHITE, Elizabeth Estelle
WHITE, Elsie Fellows
WHITE, Mary Louisa
WHITECOTTON, Shirley Ellen
WHITEHEAD, Gillian
WHITLOCK, E. Florence
WHITTINGTON, Joan
WHITTLE, Chris Mary-Francine
WICKHAM, Florence Pauline
WIENECKE, Sigrid Henriette
WIENIAWSKA, Irene Regine
WIERUSZOWSKI, Lili
WIGGINS, Mary

WILDSCHUT, Clara
WILEY, Dora
WILKINSON, Constance Jane
WILLIAMS, Grace Mary
WILLIAMS, Irma
WILLMAN, Regina Hansen
WILSON, Elizabeth
WILSON, Gertrude Hoag
WILSON, Jean Dolores
WILSON, Marion
WINROW, Barbara
WINTER, Sister Miriam Therese
WISHART, Betty Rose
WITTICH, Martha von
WITTMAN, Therese
WOLF, Ilda von
WOLL, Erna
WOLLNER, Gertrude Price
WONG, Hsiung-Zee
WOOD, Mabel
WOOD, Mary Knight
WOOD, Sister Mary Davida
WOODRUFF, Edith S.
WOODWARD, Martha Clive
WOOGE, Emma
WOOLSLEY, Mary Hale
WORRELL, Lola Carrier
WORTH, Amy
WRONIKOWSKI, Florence F.
WYETH, Ann
WYLIE, Ruth Shaw
XENOPOL, Margareta
YAGLING, Victoria
YAKHNINA, Yevgenia Yosifovna
YAROSHEVSKAYA, Ludmila
    Anatolievna
YAZBECK, Louise
YDSTIE, Arlene Buckneberg
YI, Heung-Yull
YOUNG, Gayle
YOUNG, Jane Corner
YOUNG, Rolande Maxwell
YOUSE, Glad Robinson
ZAIDEL-RUDOLPH, Jeanne
ZAIMONT, Judith Lang
ZARANEK, Stefania Anatolyevna
ZARIPOVA, Naila Gatinovna
ZAULECK, Gertrud
ZAVALISHINA, Maria Semyonovna
ZECHLIN, Ruth
ZELIKOVSKAYA, Fania
    Mordukhovna
ZHUBANOVA, Gaziza Akhmetovna
ZHUBINSKAYA, Valentina Yanovna
ZHVANETSKAIA, Inna Abramovna
ZIBEROVA, Zinaida Petrovna
ZIFFRIN, Marilyn Jane
ZIMMERMANN, Margrit
ZIPRICK, Marjorie Jean
ZIVKOVIC, Mirjana
ZOECKLER, Dorothy Ackerman
ZUZAK, Doris
ZWEIG, Esther
ZWILICH, Ellen Taaffe
Century not available
  ALBRECHT, Elise
  BAZIN, Mlle.
  CACCHIATELLI, Adelina
  CAI, Wen Ji, Princess
  CARAFA D'ANDRIA, Anna
  CARTWRIGHT, Patricia
  CIARLANTINI, Paola
  COBBE, Linda
  COOMBS, Mary Woodhull
  CORYELL, Marion
  CUSENZA, Maria Giacchino
  DONALDSON, Sadie
  ELENA
  FERGUS-HOYT, Phyllis
  FERRIS, Joan
  GALEOTTI, Margherita

GALLI, Signora
GAMBOGI, Luigia
GOTTSCHALK, Clara
GREEN, Miss
GRISWOLD, Gertrude
GUEDON DE PRESLES, Mlle.
HART, Dorothy
HARVEY, Ella Doreen
JACQUE, Emilie
KAUFFMAN, Amanda
LANGFORD, Olivia
LE BAS, Gertrude
LOTTIN, Phedora
MINGHELLA, Aida
MIRANDA, Erma Hoag
MOREA, Vincenza della
MUDDUPALANI
NERVI, Marta
NICCOLINI, Virginia
PENN, Marilyn
PERERA, Carmen
PEYCKE, Frieda
PROSDOCIMI, Ada
RICHTER, Rebecca
RICKETTS, Lucy W.
RIVET, Jeanne
ROSENWEIG, Florence
ROST, Emilie
ROUCH, Alma
RYCOFF, Lalla
SANI, Maria Teresa
SNODGRASS, Louise Harrison
STILLING, Kemp
TAJANI MATTONE, Ida
TEDESCHI, Angela
THAIN, Lillian
TREVALSA, Joan
TRISTAN, Joyeuse
VAUGHAN, Freda
WALTER, Ida
WEAVER, Harriet
WERBER, Elise
WONG, Zhao, Princess
WOODSTOCK, Mattie

VOCAL ENSEMBLE
  18th Century A.D.
    CUZZONI, Francesca
    MARTINEZ, Marianne
    MUELLER, Elise
  19th Century A.D.
    BARNARD, Charlotte
    BARTHOLOMEW, Mrs. M.
    BATTAGINI, Giuseppina
    BENNETT, Mimi
    BLAKE, Mary
    DAVIS, Miss
    DE SOUSA HOLSTEIN, Donna Teresa
    ESCHBORN, Georgine Christine
        Maria Anna
    MUNDELLA, Emma
    PEYRON, Albertina Fredrika
    POLKO, Elise Vogel
    RITTER, Fanny Malone Raymond
    WERNER, Hildegard
  20th Century A.D.
    ALVES DE SOUSA, Berta Candida
    ANDRIEVSKAYA, Nina
        Konstantinovna
    BAINBRIDGE, Beryl
    BAKKE, Ruth
    BARBERIS, Mansi
    BARRADAS, Carmen
    BARTHEL, Ursula
    BAUER, Marion Eugenie
    BERGE, Irenee
    BIRNSTEIN, Renate Maria
    BODENSTEIN-HOYME, Ruth E.
    BOUCHARD, Linda L.
    CALLINAN, Maureen
    CECCONI-BATES, Augusta

CHARLES, S. Robin
CORNING, Karen Andree
COULTHARD, Jean
DALBERG, Nancy
DROBYAZGINA, Valentina
    Ivanovna
DUNLOP, Isobel
FLACH, Elsa
GEBUHR, Ann Karen
GOEBELS, Gisela
GRAINGER, Ella Viola Strom-
    Brandelius
HARDING, Mildred Thompson
HAYS, Doris Ernestine
HEILBRON, Valerie
HURLEY, Susan
JENNINGS, Carolyn
JIRACKOVA, Marta
KANACH, Sharon E.
KIP, Yuksel
LATZ, Inge
LEBARON, Anne
LEE, Hope Anne Keng-Wei
LEJET, Edith
LITTLE, Anita Gray
LOH, Kathy Jean
MANZIARLY, Marcelle de
MARCUS, Ada Belle Gross
MARTINS, Maria de Lourdes
MOE, Benna
MUNKTELL, Helena Mathilda
OLIVEROS, Pauline
PATERSON, Wilma
PEREIRA DA SILVA, Adelaide
PEYROT, Fernande
PFERDEMENGES, Maria Pauline
    Augusta
PHILIPPART, Renee
PHILLIPS, Bryony
PRICE, Deon Nielsen
RAINIER, Priaulx
RENNES, Catharina van
RHEINGOLD, Lauma Yanovna
SAMTER, Alice
SHIOMI, Mieko
SHURTLEFF, Lynn Richard
TACK, Annie
TELFER, Nancy Ellen
THOMAS, Karen P.
VETLUGINA, Natalia Alekseyevna
VIERK, Lois
VON ZIERITZ, Grete
WALDO, Elisabeth
WALLACH, Joelle
WARNE, Katharine Mulky
WEGENER-FRENSEL, Emmy Heil
WILKINSON, Constance Jane
WOOD, Mabel
Century unknown
  RYCOFF, Lalla

VOICE (SOLO) AND ENSEMBLE
  17th Century A.D.
    CACCINI-GHIVIZZANI, Settimia
    CAMPANA, Francesca
  18th Century A.D.
    AHLEFELDT, Marie Theresia,
        Countess
    MARIA ANTONIA WALPURGIS,
        Princess of Bavaria
    MARTINEZ, Marianne
  19th Century A.D.
    PUGET, Loise
    RICOTTI, Onestina
    ROECKEL, Jane
    ZYBINE, Mme. S.
  20th Century A.D.
    AARNE, Els
    ABE, Kyoko
    ABORN, Lora
    ADAIR, Yvonne Madeleine

AINSCOUGH, Juliana Mary
ALCALAY, Luna
ALEXANDER, Leni
ALEXANDRA, Liana
ALLEN, Judith Shatin
ALTER, Martha
ANDERSON, Beth
ANDERSON, Ruth
ANDERSON-WUENSCH, Jean Mary
AOKE, Haruna
ARCHER, Violet Balestreri
ARHO, Anneli
ARMER, Elinor Florence
BAADER-NOBS, Heidi
BAHMANN, Marianne Eloise
BALLOU, Esther Williamson
BANCER, Teresa Barbara
BARBERIS, Mansi
BARBILLON, Jeanne
BARON SUPERVIELLE, Susana
BARRETT-THOMAS, N.
BAULD, Alison
BEAHM, Jacquelyn Yvette
BEATH, Betty
BEEKHUIS, Hanna
BIRNSTEIN, Renate Maria
BLAUSTEIN, Susan Morton
BLISS, Marilyn S.
BLOMFIELD-HOLT, Patricia
BLOOD, Esta Damesek
BLOOM, Jane Ira
BOLZ, Harriet
BOND, Victoria Ellen
BOUCHARD, Linda L.
BRENET, Therese
BROCKMAN, Jane E.
BUCZEK, Barbara Kazimiera
BURSTON, Maggie
CALCAGNO, Elsa
CALLAWAY, Ann
CAMPAGNE, Conny
CAPUIS, Matilde
CARMEN MARINA
CECCONI-BATES, Augusta
CHAVES, Mary Elizabeth
CLARKE, Rebecca
COATES, Gloria Kannenberg
CONRAD, Laurie M.
CORY, Eleanor
COWLES, Darleen
COX, Alison Mary
CRAWFORD, Dorothy Lamb
DAVIDSON, Tina
DE BIASE BIDART, Lycia
DE FREITAS, Elvira Manuela
    Fernandez
DEMBO, Royce
DOBBINS, Lori
DOBSON, Elaine
DONAHUE, Bertha Terry
DRATTELL, Deborah
EICHENWALD, Sylvia
EKIZIAN, Michelle
ESCOT, Pozzi
EVEN-OR, Mary
FALCINELLI, Rolande
FISHER, Katherine Danforth
FONTYN, Jacqueline
FORMAN, Joanne
FOWLER, Jennifer Joan
FRASER, Shena Eleanor
GARDINER, Mary Elizabeth
GARDNER, Kay
GARR, Wieslawa
GARZTECKA-JARZEBSKA, Irena
GIDEON, Miriam
GIFFORD, Helen Margaret
GOLOVINA, Olga Akimovna
GOTKOVSKY, Ida-Rose Esther
GRAHAM, Janet Christine
GRAINGER, Ella Viola Strom-Brandelius

GROSSMAN, Deena
HARRIS, Ruth Berman
HOLMES, Shirlee McGee
IRMAN-ALLEMANN, Regina
JAZWINSKI, Barbara
JENKINS, Susan Elaine
JIRACKOVA, Marta
JOLY, Suzanne
JUENGER, Patricia
KADIMA, Hagar Yonith
KAMINSKY, Laura
KARVENO, Wally
KASILAG, Lucrecia R.
KATTS, Letty
KURIMOTO, Yoko
KUZMYCH, Christina
LARSEN, Elizabeth Brown
LATIOLAIS, Desirée Jayne
LAYMAN, Pamela
LAZAR, Ella
LE BEAU, Louisa Adolpha
LEBARON, Anne
LEE, Hope Anne Keng-Wei
LICHTENSTEIN, Olga Grigorievna
LIDDELL, Claire
LINDEMAN, Hjelle Signe
LU, Yen
LUSTIG, Leila Sarah
LUTYENS, Elisabeth
MACONCHY, Elizabeth
McINTOSH, Diana
McKAY, Frances Thompson
McLAUGHLIN, Marian
McNEIL, Janet L. Pfischner
MAGEAU, Mary Jane
MANZIARLY, Marcelle de
MARBE, Myriam
MARESCA, Chiara
MAREZ-OYENS, Tera de
MARGLES, Pamela
MARKIEWICZOWNA, Wladyslawa
MARSHALL, Pamela J.
MARTIN, Ravonna G.
MARTINS, Maria de Lourdes
MATUSZCZAK, Bernadetta
MEACHEM, Margaret McKeen
    Ramsey
MEADE, Margaret Johnston
MEEK, Ethel Alice
MEKEEL, Joyce
MENEELY-KYDER, Sarah Suderley
MERRIMAN, Margarita Leonor
MESRITZ-VAN VELTHUYSEN, Annie
MIGRANYAN, Emma
MITCHELL, Janice Misurell
MOORE, Mary Carr
MOSZUMANSKA-NAZAR, Krystyna
MRACEK, Ann Michelle
MURAKUMO, Ayako
McTEE, Cindy Karen
NIEDERBERGER, Maria A.
NIEWIADOMSKA, Barbara
NIKOLSKAYA, Lyubov Borisovna
NOBLE, Ann
NOBLITT, Katheryn Marie McCall
NORUP, Helle Merete
NUNLIST, Juli
OH, Sook Ja
O'LEARY, Jane Strong
OLIVE, Vivienne
OLIVEROS, Pauline
ORE, Cecilie
ORENSTEIN, Joyce Ellin
PAGH-PAAN, Younghi
PARKER, Alice
PATERSON, Wilma
PATTERSON, Andra
PAULL, Barberi
PENTLAND, Barbara Lally
PERETZ-LEVY, Liora
PEYROT, Fernande

PHILLIPS, Bryony
PIECHOWSKA, Alina
PIGGOTT, Audrey Margaret
PIZER, Elizabeth Faw Hayden
POLIN, Claire
POSTON, Elizabeth
PRADELL, Leila
PREOBRAJENSKA, Vera Nicolaevna
PROCACCINI, Teresa
PTASZYNSKA, Marta
QUINN-VEES, Deborah
RADERMACHER, Erika
RAINIER, Priaulx
RAMM, Valentina Iosifovna
RAN, Shulamit
RAPOPORT, Eda
RAVINALE, Irma
REHNQVIST, Karin Birgitta
REID, Sarah Johnston
RHOADS, Mary R.
RICKARD, Sylvia
ROBITASHVILI, Lia Georgievna
ROBLES, Marisa
ROCHAT, Andrée
ROE, Eileen Betty
ROE, Helen Mary Gabrielle
ROESGEN-CHAMPION, Marguerite
    Sara
ROGER, Denise
ROGERS, Patsy
ROOBENIAN, Amber
ROSAS FERNANDES, Maria Helena
ROWAN, Barbara
RUBIN, Anna Ita
RUSCHE, Marjorie Maxine
RZAYEVA, Agabadzhi Ishmael kykz
SAMTER, Alice
SAMUEL, Rhian
SANDRESKY, Margaret Vardell
SCEK, Breda Friderika
SCHERCHEN, Tona
SCHIEVE, Catherine
SCHLOSS, Myrna Frances
SCHONTHAL, Ruth E.
SCHUBARTH, Dorothé
SHRUDE, Marilyn
SHURTLEFF, Lynn Richard
SHUTTLEWORTH, Anne-Marie
SIEBER, Susanne
SIKORA, Elzbieta
SILSBEE, Ann L.
SKOUEN, Synne
SMILEY, Pril
SMITH, Ladonna Carol
SNIFFIN, Allison
SNYDER, Amy
SOENSTEVOLD, Maj
SOUBLETTE, Sylvia
SPECHT, Judy Lavise
SPEKTOR, Mira J.
STANLEY, Helen Camille
STEELE, Lynn
STREATFIELD, Valma June
STULTZ, Marie Irene
SULPIZI, Mira
SUTHERLAND, Margaret
SZEKELY, Katalin
TACK, Annie
TASHJIAN, B. Charmian
TATE, Phyllis
TELFER, Nancy Ellen
THIEME, Kerstin Anja
THOMAS, Karen P.
THOME, Diane
THOMPSON, Caroline Lorraine
TOYAMA, Michiko Françoise
TUCKER, Irene
URNER, Catherine Murphy
USHER, Julia
VEHAR, Persis Anne
VIERK, Lois

VITO-DELVAUX, Berthe di
VIVADO ORSINI, Ida
VON ZIERITZ, Grete
VORONINA, Tatiana Aleksandrovna
WALKER, Gwyneth van Anden
WALLACH, Joelle
WARING, Kate
WEAVER, Carol Ann
WEISSBERG, Julia Lazerevna
WELANDER, Svea Goeta
WELMAN, Sylvia
WHITEHEAD, Gillian
WILKINS, Margaret Lucy
WILLIAMS, Grace Mary
WILLIAMS, Joan Franks
WITKIN, Beatrice
WOOD, Mabel
YOUNG, Jane Corner
ZAIMONT, Judith Lang
ZECHLIN, Ruth
ZHUBANOVA, Gaziza Akhmetovna
ZIBEROVA, Zinaida Petrovna
ZIMMERMANN, Margrit
ZIVKOVIC, Mirjana
Century unknown
ESCRIBANO SANCHEZ, Maria
MONACHINA
VISCONTI, Caterina
VOYNICH, Ethel Lillian

VOICE AND ORCHESTRA
8th Century A.D.
HABBABA
18th Century A.D.
ANNA AMALIA, Duchess of Saxe-
Weimar
MARTINEZ, Marianne
TABARY, M.A.C. de
19th Century A.D.
CALOSSO, Eugenia
CARISSAN, Célanie
POTT, Aloyse
PRESCOTT, Oliveria Louisa
WESTENHOLZ, Eleonore Sophie
Marie
WURM, Mary J.A.
YOUNG, Eliza
ZIMMERMANN, Agnes Marie
Jacobina
20th Century A.D.
AARNE, Els
ABEJO, Sister M. Rosalina
AKHUNDOVA, Shafiga Gulam kyzy
ALEXANDRA, Liana
ALOTIN, Yardena
ALTER, Martha
ALVES DE SOUSA, Berta Candida
ANCONA, Solange
ANDERSON, Beth
ARETZ, Isabel
AUTENRIETH, Helma
BACEWICZ, Grażyna
BACH, Maria
BADIAN, Maya
BAINBRIDGE, Beryl
BALEN, Joan
BANCER, Teresa Barbara
BARAMISHVILI, Olga Ivanovna
BARBERIS, Mansi
BARBILLON, Jeanne
BARBLAN-OPIENSKA, Lydia
BARKLUND, Irma L.
BARRAINE, Elsa
BATES, Katherine Lee
BAUER, Marion Eugenie
BEACH, Amy Marcy
BEAN, Mabel
BEATH, Betty
BEEKHUIS, Hanna
BELOCH, Dorotea
BENNETT, Claudia

BERCKMAN, Evelyn
BEYERMAN-WALRAVEN, Jeanne
BORDEWIJK-ROEPMAN, Johanna
BORROFF, Edith
BOSMANS, Henriette Hilda
BRANDELER, Henriette van den
BRANSCOMBE, Gena
BURSTON, Maggie
CALAME, Genevieve
CALCAGNO, Elsa
CAMEU, Helza
CANAT DE CHIZY, Edith
CAPSIR-TANŻI, Mercedes
CECCONI-BOTELLA, Monic
CHUDOVA, Tatiana Alekseyevna
CLARKE, Rosemary
COATES, Gloria Kannenberg
CONRAD, Laurie M.
CONSTANTINESCU, Domnica
CONTINI ANSELMI, Lucia
COULTHARD, Jean
DANIELS, Mabel Wheeler
DANOWSKI, Helen
DAVIDSON, Tina
DE BIASE BIDART, Lycia
DEL RIEGO, Thérèsa
DIAKVNISHVILI, Mzisavar
Zakharevna
DIMITRIU, Florica
DONCEANU, Felicia
DVORKIN, Judith
EGGLESTON, Anne E.
ERDING, Susanne
EUBANKS, Rachel Amelia
FALCINELLI, Rolande
FAUTCH, Sister Magdalen
FEIGIN, Sarah
FIRESTONE, Idabelle
GABUS, Monique
GARTENLAUB, Odette
GARUTA, Lucia Yanovna
GARY, Marianne
GEBUHR, Ann Karen
GEIGER-KULLMANN, Rosy Auguste
GERSTMAN, Blanche Wilhelminia
GIURANNA, Elena Barbara
GOERSCH, Ursula Margitta
GOLOVINA, Olga Akimovna
GREENE, Pauline
GREVER, Maria
GRZADZIELOWNA, Eleonora
GUBAIDULINA, Sofia Asgatovna
HALL, Pauline
HANS, Lio
HARA, Kazuko (1)
HARVEY, Eva Noel
HEILBRON, Valerie
HO, Wai On
HOLLAND, Dulcie Sybil
HOOVER, Katherine
HOWE, Mary Alberta Bruce
HULFORD, Denise Lovona
IVANOVA, Lidia
JOCHSBERGER, Tzipora H.
JOLAS, Betsy
KASILAG, Lucrecia R.
KELLER, Ginette
KESSLER, Minuetta Schumiatcher
KORN, Clara Anna
KRASNOGLIADOVA, Vera
Vladimirovna
LACHOWSKA, Stefania
LANG-BECK, Ivana
LARSEN, Elizabeth Brown
LEBARON, Anne
LEBIZAY, Marguerite
LEHMAN, Evangeline Marie
LEHMANN, Liza
LEON, Tania Justina
LEVINA, Zara Alexandrovna
LEVITE, Miriam

LINDEMAN, Hjelle Signe
LITTLEJOHN, Joan Anne
LOPEZ Y PENA, Maria del Carmen
LUO, Jing-Jing
LUTYENS, Elisabeth
LVOVA, Julia Fedorovna
McALLISTER, Rita
McINTOSH, Diana
McKAY, Frances Thompson
MAILIAN, Elza Antonovna
MANNING, Kathleen Lockhart
MAREZ-OYENS, Tera de
MARIC, Ljubica
MATUSZCZAK, Bernadetta
MEACHEM, Margaret McKeen
Ramsey
MEISTER, Marianne
MENDOSA, Dot
MERLI-ZWISCHENBRUGGER,
Christina
MESRITZ-VAN VELTHUYSEN, Annie
MKRTYCHIEVA, Virginia Nikitichna
MOE, Benna
MORLEY, Nina Dianne
MUNKTELL, Helena Mathilda
MUSGRAVE, Thea
NAZIROVA, Elmira Mirza Rza kyzy
NEWLIN, Dika
NIKOLAYEVA, Tatiana Petrovna
NIKOLSKAYA, Lyubov Borisovna
NIKOLSKAYA, Olga Vasilevna
NUNLIST, Juli
OERBECK, Anne-Marie
OSETROVA-YAKOVLIEVA, Nina
Alexandrovna
PALMER, Jane Hetherington
PARKER, Alice
PEARL-MANN, Dora Deborah
PELEGRI, Maria Teresa
PENTLAND, Barbara Lally
PERONI, Wally
PETRA-BASACOPOL, Carmen
PHILIBA, Nicole
PHILIPPART, Renée
PHILLIPS, Bryony
PIECHOWSKA, Alina
PILIS, Heda
POPOVICI, Elise
POSTON, Elizabeth
PRICE, Florence Beatrice
PRIETO, Maria Teresa
PROCACCINI, Teresa
PTASZYNSKA, Marta
QUINTANILLA, Alba
RAKHMANKULOVA, Mariam
Mannanovna
RAMM, Valentina Iosifovna
REISSEROVA, Julie
RHEINGOLD, Lauma Yanovna
ROESGEN-CHAMPION, Marguerite
Sara
ROGATIS, Teresa de
ROZHAVSKAYA, Yudif Grigorevna
SAINT JOHN, Kathleen Louise
SAMUEL, Rhian
SANTOS-OCAMPO DE FRANCESCO,
Amada Amy
SAUVREZIS, Alice
SCHERCHEN, Tona
SCHICK, Philippine
SCHMIDT-DUISBURG, Margaret
Dina Alwina
SILBERTA, Rhea
SLIANOVA-MIZANDARI, Dagmara
Levanovna
SMYTH, Ethel Mary, Dame
SOENSTEVOLD, Maj
SOMMER, Silvia
STEINER, Emma
STREICHER, Lyubov Lvovna
SUESSE, Dana

SULTANOVA, Asya Bakhish kyzy
SUNBLAD-HALME, Heidi Gabriella Wilhelmina
SUTHERLAND, Margaret
SUTZU, Rodica
SWIFT, Kay
SZAJNA-LEWANDOWSKA, Jadwiga Helena
SZEKELY, Katalin
TAILLEFERRE, Germaine
TAL, Ya'ara
TALMA, Louise
TELFER, Nancy Ellen
TERZIAN, Alicia
THEMMEN, Ivana Marburger
THIEME, Kerstin Anja
THORKELSDOTTIR, Mist Barbara
TILICHEYEVA, Elena Nikolayevna
TUCKER, Irene
USHER, Julia
USTVOLSKAYA, Galina Ivanovna
UZEINZADZE, Adilea
VAKHVAKHISHVILI, Tamara Nikolayevna
VAN APPLEDORN, Mary Jeanne
VANIER, Jeannine
VEHAR, Persis Anne·
VIGNERON-RAMAKERS, Christiane-Josee
VIGNERY, Jeanne Emilie Virginie
VITO-DELVAUX, Berthe di
VORLOVA, Slavka
VYNER, Mary Bainbridge
WHITTLE, Chris Mary-Francine
WILLIAMS, Grace Mary
WYLIE, Ruth Shaw
ZAIMONT, Judith Lang
ZAKRZEWSKA-NIKIPORCZYK, Barbara Maria
ZECHLIN, Ruth
ZHUBANOVA, Gaziza Akhmetovna
Century unknown
WYLIE, Betty Jane

VOICE AND PIANO
18th Century A.D.
MUELLER, Elise
MUELLNER, Johanna
MUSIGNY, Mme. de
19th Century A.D.
BERTIN, Louise Angelique
CORMONTAN, Theodora
HJORT, Thecla
HUENERWADEL, Fanny
LIEBMANN, Helene
MATTFELD, Marie
MELY, Marie, Countess Vanden Heuvel
MERSANNE, Maddalena
MONGRUEL, Georgiana Catherine Eugenia Leonard
MUNCH, Natalie
NYSTROEM, Elisabeth
OLAGNIER, Marguerite
ORSINI, Teresa
PARADIS, Maria Theresia von
PARKHURST, Susan
PATTI, Adelina
PUGET, Loise
VANE, Florence
20th Century A.D.
ABOULKER, Isabelle
AINSCOUGH, Juliana Mary
BELL, Elizabeth
BOFILL, Anna
BOSMANS, Henriette Hilda
BRODERICK, Deborah Houstle
CAMPOS ARAUJO DE, Joaquina
CHUDOVA, Tatiana Alekseyevna
COOLIDGE, Lucy
CORNEILLE

DALBERT, Anny
DAVIES, Margaret
DAVIS, Sharon
DE BIASE BIDART, Lycia
DE FREITAS, Elvira Manuela Fernandez
DEBRASSINE-PRIJAT, Laure
ELCHEVA, Irina Mikhailovna
EUTENEUER-ROHRER, Ursula Henrietta
GOVEA, Wenonah Milton
GRAINGER, Ella Viola Strom-Brandelius
GURAIEB KURI, Rosa
GWILY-BROIDO, Rivka
HALL, Pauline
HENDERSON, Ruth Watson
HULL, Kathryn B.
HUTTON, Florence Myra
INGBER, Anita Rahel
JEPPSSON, Kerstin Maria
KALTENECKER, Gertraud
KAMINSKY, Laura
KARVENO, Wally
KING, Patricia
KUZMENKO, Larysa
LAGO
LAMEGO, Carlinda J.
LAPIN, Lily
LARSON, Anna Barbara
LATIMER, Ella May Elizabeth
LAUBER, Anne Marianne
LAUMYANSKENE, Elena Iono
LAVOIPIERRE, Thérèse
LEECH, Renee
LEHMAN, Evangeline Marie
LEIBOW, Ruth Irene
LEVITE, Miriam
LEVITSKAYA, Viktoria Sergeyevna
LICHTENSTEIN, Olga Grigorievna
LIMA CRUZ, Maria Antonietta de
LITTLEJOHN, Joan Anne
LLUNELL SANAHUJA, Pepita
LOOTS, Joyce Mary Ann
LUFF, Enid
LUND, Gudrun
LUND, Signe
MACAULAY, Janice Michel
MACKIE, Shirley M.
MACONCHY, Elizabeth
MacKENNA, Carmela
MacPHAIL, Frances
McALISTER, Mabel
McDUFFEE, Mabel Howard
McILWRAITH, Isa Roberta
McINTOSH, Diana
McLAUGHLIN, Marian
MAHLER, Alma Maria
MAKAROVA, Nina Vladimirovna
MALDYBAYEVA, Zhyldyz Abdylasovna
MALMLOEF-FORSSLING, Carin
MAMLOK, Ursula
MANNING, Kathleen Lockhart
MARAIS, Abelina Jacoba
MARBE, Myriam
MARCUS, Ada Belle Gross
MARCUS, Bunita
MAREZ-OYENS, Tera de
MARIC, Ljubica
MARKIEWICZOWNA, Wladyslawa
MARKOV, Katherine Lee
MARTIN, Ravonna G.
MARTINEZ, Odaline de la
MASSUMOTO, Kikuko
MATEU, Maria Cateura
MATEVOSIAN, Araks Surenovna
MATTULLATH, Alice
MAXWELL, Helen Purcell
MAZOUROVA, Jarmila
MEADE, Margaret Johnston

MELL, Gertrud Maria
MENEELY-KYDER, Sarah Suderley
MERALI-ZWISCHENBRUGGER, Christina
MERRIMAN, Margarita Leonor
MESRITZ-VAN VELTHUYSEN, Annie
MIAGI, Ester Kustovna
MIGRANYAN, Emma
MILENKOVIC, Jelena
MILLER, Elma
MIRET, Emilia
MIRSHAKAR, Zarrina Mirsaidovna
MITCHELL, Norma Jean
MIYAKE, Haruna
MKRTYCHIEVA, Virginia Nikitichna
MODRAKOWSKA, M.
MOE, Benna
MOELLER, Paulette
MONK, Meredith
MOON, Chloe Elizabeth
MOORE, Mary Carr
MOORE, Undine Smith
MORGAN, Mary Hannah
MORITZEN, Gunda
MORLEY, Nina Dianne
MORRISON, Julia Maria
MORRISSEY, Elizabeth
MOSHER, Frances Elizabeth
MOSZUMANSKA-NAZAR, Krystyna
MRACEK, Ann Michelle
MUKLE, May Henrietta
MUNDINGER, Adele Franziska
MURDOCH, Heather
MURRI, Alceste
NAIKHOVICH-LOMAKINA, Fania Filippovna
NAZAROVA, Tatiana Borisovna
NAZIROVA, Elmira Mirza Rza kyzy
NEPGEN, Rosa Sophia Cornelia
NEWLIN, Dika
NIEBEL, Mildred
NIKOLSKAYA, Lyubov Borisovna
NIKOLSKAYA, Olga Vasilevna
NILSSON, Christine
NISHUDA, Yamiko
NISS, Sofia Natanovna
NORRE, Dorcas
NOVI, Anna Beate
OERBECK, Anne-Marie
OFFICER, Bronwyn Lee
OGILVIE, Signe
OIKONOMOPOULOS, Eleni N.
OLDENBURG, Elizabeth
OLIVE, Vivienne
OLIVEIRA, Babi de
OLIVEIRA, Sophie Marcondes de Mello
OLIVEROS, Pauline
OMER, Helene
OSAWA, Kazuko
OSETROVA-YAKOVLIEVA, Nina Alexandrovna
OSIANDER, Irene
OWEN, Blythe
OWEN, Morfydd Llwyn
PADE, Else Marie
PAGOTO, Helen
PARKE, Dorothy
PARKER, Alice
PATERSON, Wilma
PATTERSON, Andra
PAULL, Barberi
PAVIA DE MAGALHAES, Isaura
PELEGRI, Maria Teresa
PENGILLY, Sylvia
PENNER, Jean Priscilla
PEREIRA DA SILVA, Adelaide
PERKIN, Helen
PERRY, Julia Amanda
PERRY, Zenobia Powell
PETRA-BASACOPOL, Carmen
PETROVA, Mara

PETROVA-KRUPKOVA, Elena
PEYROT, Fernande
PHILIBA, Nicole
PHILIPPART, Renee
PHILLIPS, Linda
PIERCE, Sarah Anderson
PIERROT, Noelie Marie
    Antoinette
PILIS, Heda
PIRES DE CAMPOS, Lina
PIRES DOS REIS, Hilda
PIZER, Elizabeth Faw Hayden
PLUMSTEAD, Mary
PRAVOSSUDOVITCH, Natalja
    Michajlovna
PREOBRAJENSKA, Vera
    Nicolaevna
PRICE, Beryl
PRICE, Florence Beatrice
PRIETO, Maria Teresa
PRIOLLI, Maria Luisa
    de Matos
PROCACCINI, Teresa
PSTROKONSKA-NAVRATIL,
    Grażyna Hanna
QUANTIN-SAULNIER, Denise
QUINTANILLA, Alba
REID, Sarah Johnston
REID, Wendy
RICCIOLI FRAZZI, Eva
ROBERT, Lucie
ROCHAT, Andrée
SAKALLI-LECCA, Alexandra
SALQUIN, Hedy
SAMUEL, Rhian
SCHMIDT-DUISBURG, Margarete
    Dina Alwina
SCHORR-WEILER, Eva
SHAVERZASHVILI, Tamara
    Antonovna
SHIMIZU, Chisako
SHUTTLEWORTH, Anne-Marie
SIDORENKO, Tamara Stepanovna
STEELE, Lynn
SULTANOVA, Asya Bakhish kyzy
TAL, Marjo
TAL, Ya'ara
TANN, Hilary
TARLOW, Karen Anne
TASHJIAN, B. Charmian
THOMAS, Muriel Leonora Duncan
THREADGILL-MARTIN, Ravonna
TYSON, Mildred Lund
VAN DE VATE, Nancy Hayes
VAN NESTE, Rosane Micheline Lucie
    Charlotte
VAZQUEZ, Alida
VEHAR, Persis Anne
VEIGA OLIVEIRA, Sofia
    Helena da
VENDELHAVEN, Harriet
VIGNERON-RAMAKERS, Christiane-
    Josee
VILLARINI, Awilda
WALKER, Gwyneth van Anden
WARDE, Ann Maury
WARSHAW, Dalit Paz
WEAVER, Carol Ann
WIENER, Eva Hannah
WIKSTROM, Inger
YAGLING, Victoria
YAMASHITA, Toyoko
YAMPOLSCHI, Roseane
ZIMMERMANN, Margrit
ZWILICH, Ellen Taaffe

Century unknown
NICCOLINI, Virginia
PENN, Marilyn
PFUND, Jeanne
PROSDOCIMI, Ada
STAEHLI, Violette

ZARZUELAS
  19th Century A.D.
    GONZALEZ, Dona Paz
    MENA, Carolina
    MENTES, Maria
    PRECIADOS Y MANESCAU, Cecilia
    RODRIGO, Maria
  20th Century A.D.
    BROCA, Carmen L. de
    GAMILLA, Alice Doria
    SELDEN-GOTH, Gizella

VOCAL MUSIC - SACRED

ANTHEMS AND HYMNS
  25th Century B.C.
    APALA
  24th Century B.C.
    ENHEDUANNA
  13th Century B.C.
    VISVAVARA
  7th Century B.C.
    DAMOPHILA
  4th Century B.C.
    MOERO
  5th Century A.D.
    ELPIS DE BOECE, Dame
  9th Century A.D.
    KASIA
    THEKLA
  12th Century A.D.
    HILDEGARDE, Saint
    SPONHEIM, Sister Jutta von
  14th Century A.D.
    JANABAI
  16th Century A.D.
    CIERA, Hippolita
  17th Century A.D.
    BAPTISTA, Gracia
    CALEGARI, Cornelia
    CLARISSE DE ROME, Sister
    CONSTANCE OF AUSTRIA, Queen of
      Poland
    HUDSON, Mary
  18th Century A.D.
    BARTHELEMON, Mary
    CLARKE, Jane
    GRAEFIN, Sophia Regina
    GRAZIANINI, Caterina Benedicta
    HUDSON, Mary
    SANTINI, Maria
    STEEL, Ann
    WILBRAHAM, Mrs.
    WILHELMINA, Caroline of Anspach
  19th Century A.D.
    ADAMS, Sarah
    ALEXANDER, Mrs. Cecil Frances
    AUSTEN, Augusta Amherst
    BARTHOLOMEW, Ann Sheppard
    BLAHETKA, Marie Leopoldina
    BLANGINI, Mlle.
    BOERNER-SANDRINI, Marie
    BORTHWICK, Jane Laurie
    BOTTINI, Marianna, Marchioness
    BRADSHAW, Nellie Shorthill
    BRONTE, Anne
    BUTLER, Mary
    BUTTENSTEIN, Constanze von
    CAETANI-RZEWUSKA, Calista,
      Princess
    COCCIA, Maria Rosa
    COLLINET, Clara
    DRAPER, Mrs. J.T.
    ELLIOTT, Charlotte
    EUAN-SMITH, Lady
    FARNINGHAM, Marianne
    FERRARI, Carlotta
    FLOWER, Eliza
    FOWLES, Margaret F.
    HAVERGAL, Frances Ridley
    HENSEL, Fanny Caecilia

IRVINE, Jessie Seymour
JENTSCH, May
KAINERSTORFER, Clotilde
KALLEY, Sara Poulton
KERR, Louisa
KINKEL, Johanna
KNAPP, Phoebe Palmer
KRALIK VON MAYERSWALDEN,
    Mathilde
LANNOY, Clementine-Josephine-
    Françoise-Thérèse, Countess
LAWRENCE, Elizabeth S.
LOUD, Annie Frances
MACIRONI, Clara Angela
MOODY, Marie
MOUNSEY, Elizabeth
MUNDELLA, Emma
OCKLESTON-LIPPA, Katherine
OWENS, Priscilla
PRESCOTT, Oliveria Louisa
RADNOR, Helen, Countess of
REES, Cathrine Felicie van
RUNCIE, Constance Owen Faunt Le
    Roy
SALE, Sophia
SMART, Harriet Anne
SPENCER, Fannie Morris
STOWE, Harriet Beecher
UGALDE, Delphine Beauce
VIARDOT-GARCIA, Pauline Michelle
    Ferdinande
WHITE, Maude Valerie
ZIMMERMANN, Agnes Marie
    Jacobina
20th Century A.D.
    ABEJO, Sister M. Rosalina
    ADAMS, Carrie Bell
    ALLEN, Mimi
    ALMESAN, Irma
    ANDERSON-WUENSCH, Jean Mary
    ANDRUS, Helen Josephine
    ASHFORD, Emma Louise
    BAIL, Grace Shattuck
    BAILEY, Judith Margaret
    BAMPTON, Ruth
    BARBOUR, Florence Newell
    BARKER, Phyllis Elizabeth
    BARRELL, Joyce Howard
    BARROWS, Margaret Bentley
      Hamilton
    BARTHEL, Ursula
    BARTHELSON, Joyce Holloway
    BAUER, Marion Eugenie
    BEACH, Amy Marcy
    BEATON, Isabella
    BEATRICE, Mary Victoria Feodore,
      Princess of Battenberg
    BEHREND, Jeanne
    BEZDEK, Sister John Joseph
    BIRCSAK, Thusnelda
    BIRD, Sister Mary Rafael
    BOLZ, Harriet
    BONDS, Margaret
    BOYD, Anne Elizabeth
    BRANDT, Dorothea
    BRESCHI, Laura
    BRIGGS, Cora Skilling
    BRINK, Emily R.
    BROWN, Elizabeth Bouldin
    BROWN, Elizabeth van Ness
    BROWN, Gladys Mungen
    BROWN, Zilda Jennings
    BRUGGMANN, Heidi
    CANALES PIZARRO, Marta
    CARMON, Helen Bidwell
    CHANDLER, Mary
    CHARLES, S. Robin
    CHEATHAM, Kitty
    CHESTER, Isabel
    CHITTENDEN, Kate Sara
    CLARK, Florence Durrell

CLARK, June
CLINGAN, Judith Ann
COCKING, Frances M. Hefford
COLERIDGE-TAYLOR, Avril
  Gwendolen
COLLVER, Harriet Russell
COOPER, Rose Marie
CROSBY, Fannie
CURRIE, Edna R.
DALE, Phyllis
DAVIES, Margaret
DAVIS, Eleanor Maud
DAVIS, Fay Simmons
DAVIS, Hazel E.
DEMBO, Royce
DEMESSIEUX, Jeanne
DIEMER, Emma Lou
DITTENHAVER, Sarah Louise
DORTCH, Eileen Wier
DROSTE, Doreen
DUNGAN, Olive
EAGER, Mary Ann
EAKIN, Vera O.
EGGAR, Katharine
EISENSTEIN, Stella Price
ELLIOTT, Marjorie Reeve
EMERY, Dorothy Radde
EVANTI, Lillian
FISCHER, Edith Steinkraus
FISHER, Katherine Danforth
FONDER, Sister Mary Teresine
FOWLER, Jennifer Joan
FRANCHERE-DESROSIERS, Rose de
  Lima
FREEHOFF, Ruth Williams
FRITTER, Genevieve Davisson
FROHBEITER, Ann W.
GABUS, Monique
GAMILLA, Alice Doria
GANNON, Ruth Ellen
GEDDES-HARVEY, Roberta
GENET, Marianne
GENTEMANN, Sister Mary Elaine
GHILARDI, Syra
GILLES, Yvette Marie
GIROD-PARROT, Marie-Louise
GIURANNA, Elena Barbara
GLEN, Irma
GOULD, Elizabeth Davies
GRAU, Irene Rosenberg
GRIEBLING, Karen Jean
GUELL, Elizabeth
HABAN, Sister Teresine M.
HALACSY, Irma von
HEATON, Eloise Klotz
HEDOUX, Yvonne
HIND O'MALLEY, Pamela
HINEBAUGH, Bessie
HOFFMANN, Peggy
HOLST, Agnes Moller
HOOD, Helen
HORNBACK, Sister Mary Gisela
HOWELL, Dorothy
HSU, Wen-Ying
HUTSON, Wihla L.
HYSON, Winifred Prince
IVEY, Jean Eichelberger
JACKSON, Barbara May
JACKSON, Elizabeth Barnhart
JACKSON, Marylou I.
JENNINGS, Marie Pryor
JENNY, Sister Leonore
JONES-DAVIES, Maude
JORDAN, Alice Yost
KAHMANN, Chesley
KENDRICK, Virginia Catherine
KENT, Ada Twohy
KERN, Frida
KERR, Bessie Maude
KIRCH, Irene E.
KLIMISCH, Sister Mary Jane

KOELLING, Eloise
KOZANKOVA, Anna
LAFLEUR, Lucienne
LAVIN, Marie Duchesne
LAWRENCE, Emily M.
LEONARD, Mamie Grace
LEVITE, Miriam
LIPSCOMB, Helen
LOCKWOOD, Charlotte Mathewson
LUCAS, Blanche
McALISTER, Mabel
McCOLLIN, Frances
McDUFFEE, Mabel Howard
McNAIR, Jacqueline Hanna
McQUATTIE, Sheila
MACKEN, Jane Virginia
MADISON, Clara Duggan
MAGOGO KA DINIZULU, Constance,
  Princess
MANKIN, Linda
MAQUISO, Elena G.
MAREZ-OYENS, Tera de
MARQUES, Fernandina Lagos
MARQUES, Laura Wake
MARSH, Gwendolyn
MARSHALL, Jane Manton
MARTH, Helen June
MARY ELAINE, Sister
MELOY, Elizabeth
MESNEY, Dorothy Taylor
MORGAN, Hilda
MORRIS, Mrs. C.H.
MUNGER, Millicent Christner
NIKOLSKAYA, Olga Vasilevna
NIXON, June
NOBLITT, Katheryn Marie McCall
NOYES, Edith Rowena
OHLSON, Marion
OPIE, Mary Pickens
O'SHEA, Mary Ellen
OWEN, Angela Maria
OWEN, Blythe
PALMER, Catherine M.
PALMER, Florence Margaret
  Spencer
PALMER, Jane Hetherington
PALMER, Lynne Wainwright
PARIS, Ella Hudson
PARKER, Alice
PATTERSON, Annie Wilson
PEEK, Betty
PFOLH, Bessie Whittington
PIERCE, Alexandra
POINTON, Barbara
PONSA, Maria Luisa
POOLER, Marie
POSTON, Elizabeth
PRICE, Deon Nielsen
RALSTON, Frances Marion
RAMSEY, Sister Mary Anastasia
REEKS, Kathleen Doris
REES, Winifred Emily
RICHTER, Marion Morrey
RIVERA, Graciela
ROBERSON, Ruby Lee Grubbs
ROCKEFELLER, Helen C.
ROE, Eileen Betty
ROGERS, Ethel Tench
ROGERS, Patsy
ROYSE, Mildred Barnes
RUGELES, Ana Mercedes de
SANDRESKY, Margaret Vardell
SANGUESA, Iris
SCHUBERT, Myra Jean
SCHWEIZER, Gertrude
SCHWERDTFEGER, E. Anne
SHAFFER, Jeanne Ellison
SHAW, Alice Marion
SHEPARD, Jean Ellen
SHERMAN, Elna
SILSBEE, Ann L.

SKOLFIELD, Alice Jones Tewksbury
SMITH, Eleanor
SMITH, Hilda Josephine
SMITH, Ida Polk
SPONGBERG, Viola
STREATFIELD, Valma June
STRUTT, Dorothy
STULTZ, Marie Irene
STUTSMAN, Grace May
STYLES, Dorothy Geneva
SWAIN, Freda Mary
TAMBLYN, Bertha Louise
TARTAGLIA, Lidia
TAYLOR, Mary Virginia
TAYLOR, Maude Cummings
TELFER, Nancy Ellen
TERZIAN, Alicia
THIEME, Kerstin Anja
THOMAS, Gertrude Evelyn
TOBIN, Sister Clare
TUCKER, Tui St. George
TURGEON, Frances
URBAYI-KRASNODEBSKA, Zofia
  Jadwiga
VAN DE VATE, Nancy Hayes
VERHAALEN, Sister Marion
VERRALL, Pamela Motley
VIENNE, Marie-Louise de
VILLIN, Marcelle Henriette
  Marie
VIRTUE, Constance Cochnower
WALKER, Gwyneth van Anden
WALLACH, Joelle
WANG, An-Ming
WEAVER, Marion
WEBB, Allienne Brandon
WEIGL, Vally
WELANDER, Svea Goeta
WENNERBERG-REUTER, Sara
  Margareta Eugenia Euphrosyne
WILLIAMS, Mary Lou
YDSTIE, Arlene Buckneberg
ZIMMERMAN, Phyllis
ZIPRICK, Marjorie Jean
Century unknown
DEMAREST, Victoria
GHOSHA
LOPAMUDRA
MORRIGU, Queen

CANTATAS
15th Century A.D.
HOYA, Katherina von
17th Century A.D.
BADALLA, Rosa Giacinta
18th Century A.D.
ANNA AMALIA, Princess of Prussia
ASTORGA, Emmanuelle d'
BONITA, Domina S. Delia
CARVER, Miss
GUIDICCIONI, Laura
LA GUERRE, Elisabeth-Claude
  Jacquet de
RODRIGUES, Maria Joachina
ROSSI, Camilla de
19th Century A.D.
AMERSFOORDT-DYK, Hermina
  Maria
BARTHOLOMEW, Ann Sheppard
BECKER, Ida
BOTTINI, Marianna, Marchioness
BOULEAU-NELDY, Mlle. A.
BOYCE, Ethel Mary
COCCIA, Maria Rosa
DANILEVSKAYA, V.
FERRARI, Carlotta
HORTENSE, Queen of Holland
KRALIK VON MAYERSWALDEN,
  Mathilde
ROBERT-MAZEL, Helene
ROBINSON, Fanny

RUNCIE, Constance Owen Faunt Le
  Roy
VOLKONSKAYA, Zinanda
  Alexandrovna, Princess
20th Century A.D.
ABEJO, Sister M. Rosalina
ALOTIN, Yardena
ALTER, Martha
ANDERSON, Pauline Barbour
ANDRUS, Helen Josephine
ARCHER, Violet Balestreri
ASHFORD, Emma Louise
AYLOTT, Lydia Georgina Edith
BACEWICZ, Grazyna
BAIL, Grace Shattuck
BALCKE, Frida Dorothea
BALLANDS, Etta
BASSETT, Henrietta Elizabeth
BEEKHUIS, Hanna
BENOIT, Francine Germaine Van
  Gool
BITGOOD, Roberta
BOLZ, Harriet
BONDS, Margaret
BROWNING, Bertha Hecker
CADORET, Charlotte
CALDWELL, Mary Elizabeth Glockler
CAPUIS, Matilde
CECILE REGINA, Sister
CHANDLER, Mary
CHESTNUT, Lora Perry
CLARK, June
CLOSTRE, Adrienne
COULTHARD, Jean
CRAWFORD, Dorothy Lamb
DANIELS, Mabel Wheeler
DAVIS, Katherine Kennicott
DECARIE, Reine
DESPORTES, Yvonne Berthé
  Melitta
DIEMER, Emma Lou
DONAHUE, Bertha Terry
DRENNAN, Dorothy Carter
DUNLOP, Isobel
EICHHORN, Hermene Warlick
EISENSTEIN, Judith Kaplan
EMIG, Lois Irene
FAIRCHILD, Helen
FERRARI, Gabriella
FISHMAN, Marian
FLAGG, Mary Houts
FORD, Olive Elizabeth
FRASER, Shena Eleanor
FRESON, Armande
FRONMUELLER, Frieda
GARNETT, Luisa Aires
GEIGER-KULLMANN, Rosy Auguste
GERSTMAN, Blanche Wilhelminia
GIDEON, Miriam
GRIGSBY, Beverly
GUBAIDULINA, Sofia Asgatovna
GUBITOSI, Emilia
HANEFELD, Gertrud
HARVEY, Eva Noel
HEATON, Eloise Klotz
HEINRICH, Adel Verna
HOFFMANN, Peggy
HULFORD, Denise Lovona
HYSON, Winifred Prince
JONES, Joyce Gilstrap
JONES, Marjorie
KALTENECKER, Gertraud
KARG, Marga
KERN, Frida
KESSLER, Minuetta Schumiatcher
KETTERING, Eunice Lea
KING, Betty Jackson
KINSCELLA, Hazel Gertrude
KLOTZMAN, Dorothy Ann Hill
KOVALEVA, Olga Vasilevna
KUKUCK, Felicitas

KULIEVA, Farida Tairovna
LAFLEUR, Lucienne
LAMBRECHTS-VOS, Anna Catharina
LEFEBVRE, Françoise
LEHMAN, Evangeline Marie
LEONCHIK, Svetlana Gavrilovna
LORENZ, Ellen Jane
LUCAS, Blanche
LUNA DE ESPAILLAT, Margarita
McCOLLIN, Frances
McINTOSH, Diana
McKINNEY, Mathilde
McLIN, Lena
McNAIR, Jacqueline Hanna
McPHERSON, Frances Marie
McQUATTIE, Sheila
MAIXANDEAU, Marie-Vera
MALMLOEF-FORSSLING, Carin
MANGGRUM, Loretta C. Cessor
MAREZ-OYENS, Tera de
MARTH, Helen June
MARTINS, Maria de Lourdes
MILETTE, Juliette
MOORE, Undine Smith
NEPGEN, Rosa Sophia Cornelia
PALMER, Jane Hetherington
PERONI, Wally
PEY CASADO, Diana
PEYROT, Fernande
PHILLIPS, Lois Elisabeth
PREOBRAJENSKA, Vera Nicolaevna
PRICE, Beryl
PROCACCINI, Teresa
PSTROKONSKA-NAVRATIL,
  Grazyna Hanna
RABINOF, Sylvia
RAMM, Valentina Iosifovna
RECLI, Giulia
RESPIGHI, Elsa
RICH, Gladys
ROCHAT, Andrée
ROE, Eileen Betty
ROE, Gloria Ann
ROGER, Denise
ROGERS, Ethel Tench
ROGERS, Sharon Elery
ROSE, Sister Caroline
SCHICK, Philippine
SCOTT-HUNTER, Hortense
SHAFFER, Jeanne Ellison
SKARECKY, Jana Milena
SPEKTOR, Mira J.
SPENCER, Williametta
SPINDLE, Louise Cooper
STRICKLAND, Lily Teresa
TACK, Annie
TALMA, Louise
TEICHMUELLER, Anna
TELFER, Nancy Ellen
THIEME, Kerstin Anja
THOMPSON, Mary Frances
UPTON, Anne
VAN DER MARK, Maria
VILLIN, Marcelle Henriette
  Marie
VITO-DELVAUX, Berthe di
VOELLMY-LIECHTI, Grety
WALTERS, Teresa
WARREN, Betsy
WEISS, Helen L.
WELANDER, Svea Goeta
WENNERBERG-REUTER, Sara
  Margareta Eugenia Euphrosyne
WHITECOTTON, Shirley Ellen
WILLIAMS, Frances
WOLL, Erna
WOOD, Sister Mary Davida
WORTH, Amy
YDSTIE, Arlene Buckneberg
Century unknown
WARD, Beverly A.

CHORAL WORKS
9th Century A.D.
KASIA
MARTHA
THEKLA
12th Century A.D.
SEIDENWEBERIN, Metzi
15th Century A.D.
HOYA, Katherina von
PALAEOLOGINA
17th Century A.D.
ASSANDRA, Catterina
LEONARDA, Sister Isabella
TIRS, Katharina
18th Century A.D.
ANNA AMALIA, Duchess of Saxe-
  Weimar
ANNA AMALIA, Princess of Prussia
HUDSON, Mary
LA GUERRE, Elisabeth-Claude
  Jacquet de
TURNER, Elizabeth
19th Century A.D.
ADAJEWSKY, Ella
BALTHASAR, Florence
BARTHOLOMEW, Mrs. M.
BROWNE, Augusta
FLOWER, Eliza
KAINERSTORFER, Clotilde
KINKEL, Johanna
LOUD, Annie Frances
MAISTRE, Baroness of
MANNKOPF, Adolphine
MATTFELD, Marie
MILANOLLO, Teresa Domenica
  Maria
MILLAR, Marian
MOMY, Valerie
MUNDELLA, Emma
PARKHURST, Susan
RADNOR, Helen, Countess of
RUNCIE, Constance Owen Faunt Le
  Roy
THOMAS, Adelaide Louise
WAGNER, Virginia De Oliveira
  Bastos
ZIMMERMANN, Agnes Marie
  Jacobina
20th Century A.D.
ABEJO, Sister M. Rosalina
ABORN, Lora
ADAIR, Dorothy
AINSCOUGH, Juliana Mary
ALEJANDRO-DE LEON, Esther
ALLEN, Judith Shatin
ALLOUARD CARNY, Odette
ALVES DE SOUSA, Berta Candida
ANDERSON, Ruth
ASHFORD, Emma Louise
AULIN, Laura Valborg
BACKES, Lotte
BAHMANN, Marianne Eloise
BALCKE, Frida Dorothea
BALDACCI, Giovanna Bruna
BALLOU, Esther Williamson
BARADAPRANA, Pravrajika
BARDEL, Germaine
BARKER, Phyllis Elizabeth
BARNETT, Carol Edith
BASSETT, Henrietta Elizabeth
BATCHELOR, Phyllis
BAUER, Marion Eugenie
BEACH, Amy Marcy
BEAHM, Jacquelyn Yvette
BEECROFT, Norma Marian
BEEKHUIS, Hanna
BERK, Adele
BEZDEK, Sister John Joseph
BIRD, Sister Mary Rafael
BITGOOD, Roberta
BOBROW, Sanchie

BOLZ, Harriet
BOOZER, Patricia P.
BORBOM, Maria de Melo Furtado
  Caldeira Giraldes
BOULANGER, Lili Juliette Marie Olga
BRITAIN, Radie
BRUGGMANN, Heidi
BRUSH, Ruth Damaris
BUCHANAN, Dorothy Quita
CALCAGNO, Elsa
CALDWELL, Mary Elizabeth Glockler
CALVIN, Susan Heath
CARR, Bess Berry
CHERUBIM, Sister Mary Schaefer
COATES, Gloria Kannenberg
CORY, Eleanor
COWLES, Darleen
DANIELS, Mabel Wheeler
DAVIES, Eiluned
DAVIES, Margaret
DE BIASE BIDART, Lycia
DE FREITAS, Elvira Manuela
  Fernandez
DE MONTEL, Adalgisa
DEACON, Mary Connor
DELORME, Isabelle
DEMBO, Royce
DENBOW, Stefania Bjoerson
DIEMER, Emma Lou
DOUROUX, Margaret Pleasant
DROSTE, Doreen
EAGAR, Fannie Edith Starke
EISENSTEIN, Stella Price
ELLIOTT, Marjorie Reeve
EMIG, Lois Irene
ESCOT, Pozzi
EUBANKS, Rachel Amelia
EVEN-OR, Mary
FAUTCH, Sister Magdalen
FELLOWS, Mrs. Wayne Stanley
FISHER, Katherine Danforth
FITZGERALD, Sister Florence
  Thérèse
FLACH, Elsa
FLEMING, Shari Beatrice
FRASIER, Jane
FREER, Eleanor Warner Everest
FRONMUELLER, Frieda
FRYZELL, Regina Holmen
GARDINER, Mary Elizabeth
GAYNOR, Jessie Love
GENTEMANN, Sister Mary Elaine
GERSTMAN, Blanche Wilhelminia
GESSLER, Caroline
GHILARDI, Syra
GRIMES, Doreen
GUBAIDULINA, Sofia Asgatovna
HAIRSTON, Jacqueline Butler
HANEFELD, Gertrud
HEINRICHS, Agnes
HELLER, Ruth
HENDERSON, Rosamon
HENDERSON, Ruth Watson
HICKS, Marjorie Kisby
HOFFMANN, Peggy
HOUSMAN, Rosalie
HOY, Bonnee L.
HRUBY, Dolores Marie
HULFORD, Denise Lovona
HUTSON, Wihla L.
JENNY, Sister Leonore
JOCHSBERGER, Tzipora H.
JONES, Sister Ida
JORDAN, Alice Yost
KALTENECKER, Gertraud
KASILAG, Lucrecia R.
KAVASCH, Deborah Helene
KELLY, Denise Maria Anne
KER, Ann S.
KESSLER, Minuetta Schumiatcher
KETTERING, Eunice Lea

KOELLING, Eloise
KRZYZANOWSKA, Halina
LAGO
LAJEUNESSE, Emma, Dame
LANG, Margaret Ruthven
LARSEN, Elizabeth Brown
LATIMER, Ella May Elizabeth
LAUFER, Beatrice
LAVOIPIERRE, Thérèse
LEAHY, Mary Weldon
LEE, Chan-Hae
LEFANU, Nicola Frances
LEFEBVRE, Francoise
LEIBOW, Ruth Irene
LIDDELL, Claire
LINES, Ruth W.
LORE, Emma Maria Thérèsa
LORENZ, Ellen Jane
LORING, Nancy
LOUDOVA, Ivana
LOWELL, Dorothy Dawson
LUFF, Enid
LUNA DE ESPAILLAT, Margarita
MACAULAY, Janice Michel
MACKIE, Frances C.
MACKIE, Shirley M.
MacKENNA, Carmela
McCOLLIN, Frances
McDUFFEE, Mabel Howard
McILWRAITH, Isa Roberta
McKINNEY, Mathilde
McLAIN, Margaret Starr
McLAUGHLIN, Marian
McLIN, Lena
McTEE, Cindy Karen
MAGEAU, Mary Jane
MAGNEY, Ruth Taylor
MALMLOEF-FORSSLING, Carin
MARAIS, Abelina Jacoba
MARCUS, Ada Belle Gross
MARKOV, Katherine Lee
MARSHALL, Jane Manton
MARSHALL, Pamela J.
MARTIN, Ravonna G.
MARY ELAINE, Sister
MATUSZCZAK, Bernadetta
MAXWELL, Jacqueline Perkinson
MEACHEM, Margaret McKeen
  Ramsey
MEEKER, Estelle
MEL-BONIS
MELL, Gertrud Maria
MERRIMAN, Margarita Leonor
MILDANTRI, Mary Ann
MILLER, Alma Grace
MIRELLE, Wilma
MOHNS, Grace Updegraff Bergen
MOORE, Undine Smith
MORIN-LABRECQUE, Albertine
MORMONE, Tamara
MORRISON, Julia Maria
MOYSEOWICZ, Gabriela
MURRAY, Margaret
NEEL, Susan Elizabeth
NEPGEN, Rosa Sophia Cornelia
NEWLIN, Dika
NIXON, June
NOHE, Beverly
NOYES, Edith Rowena
O'BRIEN, Katharine E.
OLIVEIRA, Sophie Marcondes de
  Mello
OLIVIERI SAN GIACOMO, Elsa
OPIE, Mary Pickens
OWEN, Blythe
PALMER, Lynne Wainwright
PARKER, Alice
PAUL, Doris A.
PERRY, Julia Amanda
PEYROT, Fernande
PFEIFFER, Irena

PHILLIPS, Bryony
PHILLIPS, Lois Elisabeth
PHILLIPS, Vivian Daphne
PIERCE, Sarah Anderson
PIZER, Elizabeth Faw Hayden
POLIN, Claire
POOLER, Marie
POSTON, Elizabeth
PRAVOSSUDOVITCH, Natalja
  Michajlovna
PRICE, Beryl
PRICE, Florence Beatrice
QUEEN, Virginia
RAW, Vera Constance
RECLI, Giulia
RED, Virginia Stroh
RESPIGHI, Elsa
REYNOLDS, Erma Grey Hogue
REYNOLDS, Laura Lawton
RICHARDSON, Enid Dorothy
RINEHART, Marilyn
ROBERTSON, Donna Lou Nagey
ROCHEROLLE, Eugenie Katherine
ROGERS, Ethel Tench
ROGERS, Patsy
ROGERS, Sharon Elery
ROKSETH, Yvonne
ROSATO, Clorinda
ROSE OF JESUS, Sister
RUFF-STOEHR, Herta Maria Klara
RUSCHE, Marjorie Maxine
SAKALLI-LECCA, Alexandra
SANFORD, Grace Krick
SCHICK, Philippine
SCHMITT-LERMANN, Frieda
SCHUBARTH, Dorothe
SCHYTTE-JENSEN, Caroline
SHAW, Carrie Burpee
SHELTON, Margaret Meier
SLEETH, Natalie
SPENCER, Williametta
SPIZIZEN, Louise Myers
STERNICKA-NIEKRASZOWA, Ilza
STEVENS, Isadore Harmon
STRUCK, Ilse
STULTZ, Marie Irene
SUCHY, Gregoria Karides
SWAIN, Freda Mary
SZEKELY, Katalin
TACK, Annie
TALMA, Louise
TERZIAN, Alicia
THEMMEN, Ivana Marburger
THOMA, Annette
THOMAS, Gertrude Evelyn
THOMAS, Karen P.
THOMPSON, Mary Frances
THREADGILL-MARTIN, Ravonna
TYER, Norma Phyllis
URBAYI-KRASNODEBSKA, Zofia
  Jadwiga
VACCARO, Judith Lynne
VAN DER MARK, Maria
VANIER, Jeannine
VEHAR, Persis Anne
VERRALL, Pamela Motley
VIERK, Lois
VILLIN, Marcelle Henriette Marie
VITO-DELVAUX, Berthe di
VREE-BROWN, Marion F.
WALKER, Gwyneth van Anden
WALLACH, Joelle
WARNE, Katharine Mulky
WARREN, Elinor Remick
WEAVER, Carol Ann
WEAVER, Mary
WEBB, Allienne Brandon
WEGENER-KOOPMAN, Bertha
  Frensel
WEIGL, Vally
WEINREICH, Waltraub

WENDELBURG, Norma Ruth
WENTZ-JANACEK, Elisabet
WHITE, Ruth Eden
WHITEHEAD, Gillian
WHITTINGTON, Joan
WHITTLE, Chris Mary-Francine
WILCOCK, Anthea
WILKINS, Margaret Lucy
WILLIAMS, Frances
WILLIAMS, Grace Mary
WISHART, Betty Rose
WOLL, Erna
WOOD, Mary Knight
WORTH, Amy
XENOPOL, Margareta
YOUNG, Fredricka Agnes
ZIPRICK, Marjorie Jean
Century unknown
BOR, Modesta
ISIS
KINGSBURY, Lynn C.

MASSES AND REQUIEMS
12th Century A.D.
HILDEGARDE, Saint
13th Century A.D.
MECHTHILD
ROTTERIN ALHEIT
16th Century A.D.
ANIMUCIA, Giovanna
ECHENFELD, Katharina
17th Century A.D.
CALEGARI, Leonarda
LEONARDA, Sister Isabella
18th Century A.D.
ASTORGA, Emmanuelle d'
BONITA, Domina S. Delia
MARTINEZ, Marianne
SANTINI, Maria
19th Century A.D.
BALTHASAR, Florence
BOTTINI, Marianna, Marchioness
BOULEAU-NELDY, Mlle. A.
CORRER, Ida, Countess
FERRARI, Carlotta
GRANDVAL, Marie Felicie Clemence
   de Reiset, Vicomtesse de
HENN, Angelica
KRALIK VON MAYERSWALDEN,
   Mathilde
LA HYE, Louise Genevieve
LANNOY, Clementine-Josephine-
   Françoise-Thérèse, Countess
MATTFELD, Marie
NEUVILLE, Mme. Alphonse de
NUNN, Elizabeth Annie
PESSIAK-SCHMERLING, Anna
POTT, Aloyse
RUNCIE, Constance Owen Faunt Le
   Roy
STOLLEWERK, Nina von
TROWBRIDGE, Leslie Eliot
WHITE, Maude Valerie
20th Century A.D.
ABEJO, Sister M. Rosalina
ADAMS, Julia Aurelia
ANDREE, Elfrida
ARAUJO, Gina de
ARKWRIGHT, Marian Ursula
ARTEAGA, Genoveva de
AUBUT-PRATTE, Françoise
AVRIL, Mireille
AYLOTT, Lydia Georgina Edith
BACKES, Lotte
BARBOSA, Cacilda Campos Borges
BARNETT, Carol Edith
BEACH, Amy Marcy
BEZDEK, Sister John Joseph
BIRD, Sister Mary Rafael
BOHMANN, Hedwig
BONDS, Margaret

BORROFF, Edith
BOUTRON, Madeleine
BRANDELER, Henriette van den
BROGUE, Roslyn Clara
BUCHANAN, Dorothy Quita
CADORET, Charlotte
CANAL, Marguerite
CANALES PIZARRO, Marta
CARL, Tommie Ewert
CARMICHAEL, Mary Grant
CARVALHO, Dinora de
CECCONI-BATES, Augusta
CLARK, June
COATES, Gloria Kannenberg
COLEMAN, Ellen
COWLES, Cecil Marion
DE BIASE BIDART, Lycia
DE FREITAS, Elvira Manuela
   Fernandez
DE MONTEL, Adalgisa
DECARIE, Reine
DEL CARRETTO, Cristina
DERHEIMER, Cecile
DORABIALSKA, Julia Helena
DOWNEY, Mary
DREYFUS, Francis Kay
DRYNAN, Margaret
DU PAGE, Florence Elizabeth
DZIEWULSKA, Maria Amelia
ESCOT, Pozzi
ETHRIDGE, Jean
EUBANKS, Rachel Amelia
FALCINELLI, Rolande
FALTIS, Evelyn
FARGA PELLICER, Onia
FAUTCH, Sister Magdalen
FINE, Vivian
FONDER, Sister Mary Teresine
FOSIC, Tarzicija
FOSTER, Dorothy Godwin
FRASIER, Jane
FRITZ, Sherilyn Gail
FURGERI, Bianca Maria
GAERTNER, Katarzyna
GARR, Wieslawa
GAUTHIEZ, Cècile
GENTEMANN, Sister Mary Elaine
GORELLI, Olga
GRIMES, Doreen
GYRING, Elizabeth
HABAN, Sister Teresine M.
HARLOW, Barbara
HARRHY, Edith
HAWLEY, Carolyn Jean
HEINRICHS, Agnes
HERSCHER-CLEMENT, Jeanne
HICKS, Marjorie Kisby
HILL, Sister M. Mildred
HINLOPEN, Francina
HOFER, Maria
HOOVER, Katherine
HOWELL, Dorothy
HRUBY, Dolores Marie
HUGHES, Sister Martina
HUNKINS, Eusebia Simpson
HYTREK, Sister Theophane
IBANEZ, Carmen
JENNY, Sister Leonore
KAHMANN, Chesley
KALTENECKER, Gertraud
KARG, Marga
KASILAG, Lucrecia R.
KING, Betty Jackson
KISTETENYI, Melinda
KLIMISCH, Sister Mary Jane
KNOBLOCHOVA, Antonie
KORHONEN, S. Gloria
KOZINOVIC, Lujza
KUKUCK, Felicitas
LABEY, Charlotte Sohy
LAVIN, Marie Duchesne

LEAHY, Mary Weldon
LEONE, Mae G.
LOMON, Ruth
LORE, Emma Maria Theresa
LUCAS, Blanche
LUNA DE ESPAILLAT, Margarita
LUND, Gudrun
LUND, Hanna
LUTYENS, Elisabeth
MacKENNA, Carmela
McCOLLIN, Frances
McLIN, Lena
MAGEAU, Mary Jane
MAREZ-OYENS, Tera de
MARY BERNICE, Sister
MARY ELAINE, Sister
MEYSENBURG, Sister Agnes
MILLER, Alma Grace
MINEO, Antoinette
MORONEY, Sister Mary Emmeline
NYSTEL, Louise Gunderson
OIKONOMOPOULOS, Eleni N.
O'SHEA, Mary Ellen
PARENTE, Sister Elizabeth
PARKER, Alice
PELEGRI, Maria Teresa
PERONI, Wally
PERRY, Julia Amanda
PERRY, Mary Dean
PERRY, Zenobia Powell
PETROVA, Mara
PEYROT, Fernande
PFEIFFER, Irena
PFERDEMENGES, Maria Pauline
   Augusta
PHILIPPART, Renee
PHILLIPS, Bryony
POLIN, Claire
PREOBRAJENSKA, Vera
   Nicolaevna
PRUNEDER, Frau
RAIGORODSKY, Leda Natalia
   Heimsath
RAINIER, Priaulx
RECLI, Giulia
ROE, Eileen Betty
ROGER, Denise
ROGERS, Sharon Elery
ROSCO, B. Jeanie
ROSE OF JESUS, Sister
ROSE, Sister Caroline
SCHMITT-LERMANN, Frieda
SCHORR-WEILER, Eva
SCHWERDTFEGER, E. Anne
SEAVER, Blanche Ebert
SENIOR, Kay
SHORE, Clare
SKARECKY, Jana Milena
SKOLFIELD, Alice Jones
   Tewksbury
SMYTH, Ethel Mary, Dame
SNIZKOVA-SKRHOVA, Jitka
SNYDER, Amy
STRUTT, Dorothy
SULPIZI, Mira
TAL, Marjo
TEICHMUELLER, Anna
THEMMEN, Ivana Marburger
THOMA, Annette
THOMAS, Karen P.
TOBIN, Sister Clare
VINETTE, Alice
VON GUNDEN, Heidi
WALDO, Elisabeth
WALKER, Gwyneth van Anden
WALLACH, Joelle
WARD, Sister Mary Louise
WARREN, Elinor Remick
WEIGL, Vally
WHITTLE, Chris Mary-Francine
WILL, Madeleine

CARVALHO, Dinora de
CHARLES, S. Robin
CLARKE, Rebecca
COOPER, Rose Marie
COTRON, Fanou
DANIELS, Mabel Wheeler
DE FREITAS, Elvira Manuela
   Fernandez
DECARIE, Reine
FALCINELLI, Rolande
FAUTCH, Sister Magdalen
FELLOWS, Mrs. Wayne
   Stanley
FINE, Vivian
FISHER, Gladys Washburn
FISHER, Katherine Danforth
FONTYN, Jacqueline
FOSTER, Cecily
FRENCH, Tania
FRONMUELLER, Frieda
FULLER, Jeanne Weaver
GARTENLAUB, Odette
GEBUHR, Ann K.
GHIGLIERI, Sylvia
GILBERT, Janet Monteith
GIROD-PARROT, Marie-Louise
GLATZ, Helen Sinclair
GRIEBLING, Karen Jean
HALACSY, Irma von
HARTZER-STIBBE, Marie
HEATON, Eloise Klotz
HERSCHER-CLEMENT, Jeanne
HICKS, Marjorie Kisby
HILL, Sister M. Mildred
HIND O'MALLEY, Pamela
HINLOPEN, Francina
HOFFRICHTER, Bertha Chaitkin
HUGHES, Sister Martina
HULFORD, Denise Lovona
HUTTON, Florence Myra
HYTREK, Sister Theophane
JACKSON, Elizabeth Barnhart
JAELL-TRAUTMANN, Marie
JAMBOR, Agi
JOCHSBERGER, Tzipora H.
JONES, Joyce Gilstrap
JORDAN, Alice Yost
KAZANDJIAN, Sirvart
KINSCELLA, Hazel Gertrude
KISTETENYI, Melinda
KRUGER, Lilly Canfield
LAGO
LANE, Elizabeth
LEIVISKA, Helvi Lemmik
LEONARD, Mamie Grace
LEONE, Mae G.
LOHR, Ina
McCOLLIN, Frances
McLIN, Lena
McPHERSON, Frances Marie
McTEE, Cindy Karen
MAMLOK, Ursula
MANKIN, Linda
MAREZ-OYENS, Tera de
MARTIN, Ravonna G.
MARTINEZ, Odaline de la
MASON, Gladys Amy
MATUSZCZAK, Bernadetta
MAXWELL, Jacqueline
   Perkinson
MORLEY, Nina Dianne
MORRISON, Julia Maria
NEPGEN, Rosa Sophia Cornelia
NEWLIN, Dika
NIECKS, Christina
NOVA SONDAG, Jacqueline
OERBECK, Anne-Marie
PATTERSON, Annie Wilson
PERETZ-LEVY, Liora
PEYROT, Fernande
PFEIFFER, Irena

PFERDEMENGES, Maria Pauline
   Augusta
PHILIPPART, Rénee
PHILLIPS, Bryony
PLE-CAUSSADE, Simone
RAIGORODSKY, Leda Natalia
   Heimsath
RICHTER, Marga
ROBERTSON, Donna Lou Nagey
ROE, Eileen Betty
ROE, Marion Adelle
ROESGEN-CHAMPION, Marguerite
   Sara
ROGER, Denise
SACCAGGIO, Adelina Luisa
   Nicasia
SANDRESKY, Margaret Vardell
SCHICK, Philippine
SCHORR-WEILER, Eva
SEMEGEN, Daria
SEVERY, Violet Cavell
SKARECKY, Jana Milena
SMELTZER, Susan Mary
SPOERRI-RENFER, Anna-
   Margaretha
STREIT, Else
STULTZ, Marie Irene
SWAIN, Freda Mary
TELFER, Nancy Ellen
THIEME, Kerstin Anja
THOME, Diane
UYTTENHOVE, Yolande
VAN DE VATE, Nancy Hayes
VON ZIERITZ, Grete
WALLACH, Joelle
WARNE, Katharine Mulky
WENDELBURG, Norma Ruth
WHITTINGTON, Joan
WIENECKE, Sigrid Henriette
WOLL, Erna

SONGS
30th Century B.C.
INANNA
13th Century B.C.
· TUY
8th Century B.C.
MERESAMENT
TENTNAU
7th Century B.C.
'ANKH-AMENARDAIS
'ANKH-SHEPENWEPT
6th Century B.C.
NEIT
4th Century A.D.
MACRINA, Saint
9th Century A.D.
KODHAI
THEODOSIA
10th Century A.D.
ASSUNCÃO, Sister Arcangela Maria
   de
11th Century A.D.
HROSTWITHA
12th Century A.D.
HILDEGARDE, Saint
SEIDENWEBERIN, Metzi
13th Century A.D.
HEDWIG, Sister
MECHTHILD
14th Century A.D.
JANABAI
15th Century A.D.
BUNGE, Jungfer Gertrud
HATZLERIN, Sister Clara
HOYA, Katherina von
TUORNABUONI, Lucrezia
16th Century A.D.
AGOSTINO, Corona
ALEOTTI, Raffaela-Argenta
BERNARDI-BELLATI, Eleonora

COLONNA, Vittoria, Duchess of
   Amalfi and Marchioness of
   Pescara
MARGARET OF AUSTRIA
MIRA BAI
17th Century A.D.
BAHINABAI
BEMBO, Antonia
CACCINI, Francesca
COZZOLANI, Chiara Margarita
ERPACH, Amalia Katharina, von,
   Countess
GRECA, Antonia La
HOIJER, Anna Ovena
LEONARDA, Sister Isabella
MARGARITA da Monaco
MURATORI SCANNABECCHI,
   Angiola Teresa
RUSCA, Claudia Francesca
SOPHIE ELISABETH von
   Braunschweig, Duchess
TIRS, Katharina
18th Century A.D.
ASTORGA, Emmanuelle d'
CAZATI, Maria
DECAIX, Marianne Ursula
EBERLIN, Maria Barbara Caecilia
ENGELBRETSDATTER, Dorthe
ETOILE, Mme. de L'
JORDAN, Mrs.
STEEL, Ann
TURNER, Elizabeth
VIELANDA, Mengia
WILKINS, Elizabeth
19th Century A.D.
ADAJEWSKY, Ella
ARKWRIGHT, Mrs. Robert
BALLIO, Hilda
BARTHOLOMEW, Ann Sheppard
BATTA, Clementine
BECKER, Ida
BOERNER-SANDRINI, Marie
BORTON, Alice
BOUNDY, Kate
BRANDLING, Mary
BRANHAM, Norma Wood
BRZEZINSKA, Filipina
BURNHAM, Georgiana
CAPPIANI, Luisa
CARISSAN, Celanie
COLE, Elizabeth Shirk
COLLETT, Sophia Dobson
CORMONTAN, Theodora
CROWNINGSHIELD, Mary Bradford
CRUMB, Berenice
CZETWERTYNSKA-JELOWICKA,
   Janina, Princess
DANA, Mary S.B.
DAVIS, Miss
DRAPER, Mrs. J.T.
DUSSEK, Olivia
EGEBERG, Anna
EGEBERG, Fredrikke Sophie
ELLIOTT, Charlotte
ESCHBORN, Georgine Christine
   Maria Anna
EUGENIE, Charlotte Augusta Amalia
   Albertina, Princess
FARRENC, Victorine Louise
GABRIEL, Mary Ann Virginia
GEIGER, Constanze
GRANDVAL, Marie Felicie Clemence
   de Reiset, Vicomtesse de
HACKETT, Marie
HARTLAND, Lizzie
HODGES, Faustina Hasse
HORTENSE, Queen of Holland
JENKS, Maude E.
KNYVETT, Mrs. Edmund
LANG, Josephine
LASZLO, Anna von

LAVATER, Magdalena Elisabeth
LOUD, Annie Frances
MACIRONI, Clara Angela
MALIBRAN, Maria Felicitas
MANNKOPF, Adolphine
MATTFELD, Marie
MILANOLLO, Teresa Domenica
    Maria
MILLAR, Marian
MOMY, Valerie
MURIO-CELLI, Adelina
NATHUSIUS, Marie
NEUVILLE, Mme. Alphonse de
O'LEARY, Rosetta
PARKHURST, Susan
PERRELLI, Giuseppina
PUGET, Loise
RAYMOND, Emma Marcy
REICHARDT, Louise
RICHINGS, Caroline
ROSALES, Cecilia
RUNCIE, Constance Owen Faunt Le
    Roy
RUTTENSTEIN, Baroness Constance
SALE, Sophia
SANCHEZ, Manuela Cornejo de
SAWYER, Harriet P.
SCOTT, Clara H.
SMITH, May Florence
STANG, Erika
STEWART, Elizabeth Kirby
TRUETTE, Everette
VELA DE ARNAO, Sofia
VESPERMANN, Marie
WALKER, Ida
WHITE, Maude Valerie
WICHERN, Caroline
WICKINS, Florence
WICKMAN, Fredrika
WIECK, Marie
WIENECKE, Henriette Stadfeldt
YOUNG, Eliza
ZAMOYSKA, Maria

20th Century A.D.
ABEJO, Sister M. Rosalina
ABORN, Lora
ACKERMANN, Dorothy
ADAMS, Elizabeth Kilmer
AKERS, Doris Mae
ALLITSEN, Frances
ALVARES-RIOS, Maria
ANDERSON, Pauline Barbour
ANDERSON, Ruth
ARAUJO, Gina de
ARBEL, Re Chaya
ARBUCKLE, Dorothy M.
ARCHER, Violet Balestreri
ARETZ, Isabel
BAIL, Grace Shattuck
BAINBRIDGE, Beryl
BAINBRIDGE, Katharine
BAMPTON, Ruth
BARADAPRANA, Pravrajika
BARBLAN-OPIENSKA, Lydia
BARKER, Phyllis Elizabeth
BARTHEL, Ursula
BEACH, Amy Marcy
BEAHM, Jacquelyn Yvette
BEAN, Mabel
BEEKHUIS, Hanna
BERK, Adele
BERROA, Catalina
BIANCHINI, Virginie
BILTCLIFFE, Florence
BITGOOD, Roberta
BLAIR, Kathleen
BLIESENER, Ada Elizabeth
    Michelman
BOISEN, Elisabeth
BOLZ, Harriet
BOND, Carrie Jacobs

BONDS, Margaret
BORBOM, Maria de Melo Furtado
    Caldeira Giraldes
BOSMANS, Henriette Hilda
BOUTRON, Madeleine
BRACQUEMOND, Marthe Henriod
BRANDELER, Henriette van den
BRANSCOMBE, Gena
BRAUER, Johanna Elisabeth
BRECK, Carrie Ellis
BRIGGS, Cora Skilling
BRINK, Emily R.
BROCK, Blanche Kerr
BROWN, Gladys Mungen
BRUSH, Ruth Damaris
BUTLER, Anne Lois
BYLES, Blanche D.
CADORET, Charlotte
CALDWELL, Mary Elizabeth Glockler
CALVIN, Susan Heath
CAMPBELL, Edith Mary
CANALES PIZARRO, Marta
CANNISTRACI, Helen
CAPERTON, Florence Tait
CAPUIS, Matilde
CARON-LEGRIS, Albertine
CARR, Wynona
CAWTHORN, Janie M.
CHACON LASAUCA, Emma
CHARLES, S. Robin
CHERUBIM, Sister Mary Schaefer
CLARK, Florence Durrell
CLARK, Mary Margaret Walker
CLINGAN, Judith Ann
COFFMAN, Lillian Craig
COLAÇO OSORIO-SWAAB, Reine
COLLVER, Harriet Russell
COOPER, Esther Sayward
COOPER, Rose Marie
COTE, Helene
COULTHARD, Jean
COWLES, Darleen
CROKER, Catherine Munnell
CURRAN, Pearl Gildersleeve
CURRIE, Edna R.
DANIELS, Mabel Wheeler
DANOWSKI, Helen
DAVIES, Eiluned
DAVIS, Katherine Kennicott
DAVIS, Margaret Munger
DE BIASE BIDART, Lycia
DE PATE, Elisabetta M.S.
DEACON, Mary Connor
DECARIE, Reine
DELORME, Isabelle
DEMAREST, Alison
DENBOW, Stefania Bjoerson
DERHEIMER, Cécile
DIEMER, Emma Lou
DITTENHAVER, Sarah Louise
DONAHUE, Bertha Terry
DOUROUX, Margaret Pleasant
DRETKE, Leora N.
DREYFUS, Francis Kay
DRYNAN, Margaret
DU PAGE, Florence Elizabeth
DUCOUREAU, Mme. M.
DUNGAN, Olive
DUNLOP, Isobel
DUNN, Rebecca Welty
EASTES, Helen Marie
EDWARDS, Clara
EGGLESTON, Anne E.
EILERS, Joyce Elaine
ELLIOTT, Marjorie Reeve
ELST, Nancy van der
ELWYN-EDWARDS, Dilys
EMERY, Dorothy Radde
ENDRES, Olive Philomene
ERICKSON, Elaine M.
EVANTI, Lillian

EZELL, Helen Ingle
FALTIS, Evelyn
FAY, Amy
FEDERHOF-MOLLER, Betty
FELLOWS, Mrs. Wayne Stanley
FENNER, Beatrice
FERRARI, Gabriella
FERRER OTERO, Monsita
    Monserrate
FISCHER, Edith Steinkraus
FISHER, Gladys Washburn
FISHER, Katherine Danforth
FITZGERALD, Sister Florence
    Thérèse
FLACH, Elsa
FOLVILLE, Eugenie-Emilie Juliette
FORD, Olive Elizabeth
FORMAN, Joanne
FORSYTH, Josephine
FOWLER, Marje
FRANK, Jean Forward
FRASER, Shena Eleanor
FREEHOFF, Ruth Williams
FREER, Eleanor Warner Everest
FRESON, Armande
FRONMUELLER, Frieda
FRYZELL, Regina Holmen
GARDNER, Mildred Alvine
GARELLI DELLA MOREA, Vincenza
GASPARINI, Jola
GAYNOR, Jessie Love
GEBUHR, Ann K.
GEDDES-HARVEY, Roberta
GERRISH-JONES, Abbie
GERSTMAN, Blanche Wilhelminia
GESSLER, Caroline
GHIKA-COMANESTI, Ioana
GIDEON, Miriam
GIFFORD, Helen Margaret
GIPPS, Ruth
GLATZ, Helen Sinclair
GLAZIER, Beverly
GLEN, Irma
GOERSCH, Ursula Margitta
GOLLAHON, Gladys
GONZAGA, Chiquinha
GOODMAN, Lillian Rosedale
GOULD, Elizabeth Davies
GOVEA, Wenonah Milton
GRAINGER, Ella Viola Strom-
    Brandelius
GRAU, Irene Rosenberg
GUBITOSI, Emilia
HAIMSOHN, Naomi Carrol
HAMBLEN, Suzy
HANEFELD, Gertrud
HARPER, Marjorie
HARRIS, Ruth Berman
HART, Elizabeth Jane Smith
HARVEY, Eva Noel
HAUSMAN, Ruth Langley
HAVEY, Marguerite
HAZEN, Sara
HEATON, Eloise Klotz
HEIMERL, Elizabeth
HEINRICH, Adel Verna
HEINRICHS, Agnes
HEINY, Margaret Harris
HENDERSON, Rosamon
HENDERSON, Ruth Watson
HERNANDEZ-GONZALO, Gisela
HETRICK, Patricia Anne
HIER, Ethel Glen
HINLOPEN, Francina
HOFF, Vivian Beaumont
HOKANSON, Margrethe
HOLCOMB, Louanah Riggs
HOLST, Imogen Clare
HOOVER, Katherine
HOPEKIRK, Helen
HOPPE, Clara

HOUSE, L. Marguerite
HOWE, Mary Alberta Bruce
HRUBY, Dolores Marie
HSU, Wen-Ying
HUGHES, Sister Martina
HUGH-JONES, Elaine
HUNKINS, Eusebia Simpson
HYDE, Miriam Beatrice
INGBER, Anita Rahel
INWOOD, Mary Ruth Brink Berger
IVEY, Jean Eichelberger
JACKSON, Elizabeth Barnhart
JACKSON, Marylou I.
JAMES, Dorothy E.
JANOTHA, Natalia
JENNINGS, Marie Pryor
JESSYE, Eva
JOCHSBERGER, Tzipora H.
JOLLEY, Florence Werner
JOLLY, Margaret Anne
JONES, Sister Ida
JORDAN, Alice Yost
JUDD, Margaret Evelyn
KALLOCH, Doley C.
KASILAG, Lucrecia R.
KAZORECK, Hildegard
KEMP, Dorothy Elizabeth Walter
KENDRICK, Virginia Catherine
KESSLER, Minuetta Schumiatcher
KETTERING, Eunice Lea
KING, Mabel Shoup
KING, Patricia
KINSCELLA, Hazel Gertrude
KIRCHGASSNER, Elisabeth
KLEIN, Ivy Frances
KLIMISCH, Sister Mary Jane
KLOTZMAN, Dorothy Ann Hill
KOELLING, Eloise
KORHONEN, S. Gloria
KRUGER, Lilly Canfield
KUKUCK, Felicitas
KUNITZ, Sharon Lohse
LACKMAN, Susan C. Cohn
LAFLEUR, Lucienne
LAJEUNESSE, Emma, Dame
LANE, Elizabeth
LANG, Margaret Ruthven
LAURENT, Ruth Carew
LAVOIPIERRE, Thérèse
LEAHY, Mary Weldon
LEECH, Lida Shivers
LEHMAN, Evangeline Marie
LEIBOW, Ruth Irene
LEONE, Mae G.
LEWIS, Carrie Bullard
LIDDELL, Claire
LILLENAS, Bertha Mae
LITTLE, Anita Gray
LIVINGSTON, Helen
LLUNELL SANAHUJA, Pepita
LOHR, Ina
LOOTS, Joyce Mary Ann
LORENZ, Ellen Jane
LOWELL, Dorothy Dawson
LOWENSTEIN, Gunilla Marike
LUTYENS, Elisabeth
MACEDA, Corazon S.
MacPHAIL, Frances
McCOLLIN, Frances
McDUFFEE, Mabel Howard
McLIN, Lena
MADISON, Clara Duggan
MAEDLER, Ruth
MANA-ZUCCA
MARAIS, Abelina Jacoba
MAREZ-OYENS, Tera de
MARIANI-CAMPOLIETI, Virginia
MARKS, Jeanne Marie
MARQUES, Fernandina Lagos
MARSHALL, Jane Manton
MARTIN, Ravonna G.

MATHIESON, Ann Emily
MAYHEW, Grace
MEADE, Margaret Johnston
MEL-BONIS
MENDELSSOHN, Luise
MEREDITH, Margaret
MESNEY, Dorothy Taylor
MEYER, Ilse
MEYERS, Lois
MILA, Leonora
MILETTE, Juliette
MILLER, Lillian Anne
MORGAN, Hilda
MORTIFEE, Ann
MORTON, Agnes Louise
NEEDHAM, Alicia Adelaide
NEPGEN, Rosa Sophia Cornelia
NEWTON, Rhoda
NOBLITT, Katheryn Marie McCall
NOETHLING, Elisabeth
NOVI, Anna Beate
OHLSON, Marion
OIKONOMOPOULOS, Eleni N.
O'SHEA, Mary Ellen
OWEN, Blythe
PALMER, Jane Hetherington
PARENTE, Sister Elizabeth
PELEGRI, Maria Teresa
PERONI, Wally
PERRY, Julia Amanda
PFERDEMENGES, Maria Pauline
    Augusta
PHILIPPART, Rénee
PIRES DOS REIS, Hilda
PLUMSTEAD, Mary
POLIN, Claire
PRICE, Florence Beatrice
PRIETO, Maria Teresa
PRIOLLI, Maria Luisa de Matos
PUKUI, Mary Abigail
RAIGORODSKY, Leda Natalia
    Heimsath
RAINIER, Priaulx
RAW, Vera Constance
RHENE-JAQUE
RICH, Gladys
RICHTER, Marga
RITTENHOUSE, Elizabeth Mae
ROBERSON, Ruby Lee Grubbs
ROCHAT, Andree
ROE, Eileen Betty
ROGATIS, Térèsa de
ROHDE, Q'Adrianne
ROKSETH, Yvonne
ROSSER, Annetta Hamilton
SALSBURY, Janet Mary
SALTER, Mary Elizabeth
SANDRESKY, Margaret Vardell
SAUNDERS, Carrie Lou
SCEK, Breda Friderika
SCHAFMEISTER, Helen Louise
SCHAUSS-FLAKE, Magdalene
SCHMIDT, Carola
SCHMITT-LERMANN, Frieda
SCHONE, Elna
SCHUSSLER-BREWAEYS, Marie
    Antoinette
SCHWERDTFEGER, E. Anne
SCHYTTE-JENSEN, Caroline
SCOTT, Molly
SEALE, Ruth
SEARS, Ilene Hanson
SEAVER, Blanche Ebert
SEPULVEDA, Maria Luisa
SHATAL, Miriam
SHERMAN, Ingrid
SHIELDS, Alice Ferree
SILVERBURG, Rose
SIMONS, Lorena Cotts
SIMONS, Netty
SINGER, Jeanne

SKARECKY, Jana Milena
SKOVGAARD, Irene
SLEETH, Natalie
SMITH, Eleanor
SMITH, Julia Frances
SMITH, Ruby Mae
SOUBLETTE, Sylvia
SOUERS, Mildred
SPEACH, Sister Bernadette Marie
SPECHT, Judy Lavise
SPEKTOR, Mira J.
SPENCER, Williametta
SPINDLE, Louise Cooper
SPOERRI-RENFER, Anna-
    Margaretha
SPONGBERG, Viola
STAIR, Patty
STAIRS, Lousie E.
STANLEY, Marion Isabel
STEVENS, Isadore Harmon
STEWART, Hascal Vaughan
STREATFIELD, Valma June
STREIT, Else
STRICKLAND, Lily Teresa
STRUCK, Ilse
STURE VASA, Mary O'Hara
SUBBALAKSHMI, M.S.
SWISHER, Gloria Agnes Wilson
TAMBLYN, Bertha Louise
TARNER, Evelyn Fern
TATE, Phyllis
TAYLOR, Maude Cummings
TEICHMUELLER, Anna
TELFER, Nancy Ellen
TERHUNE, Anice
THOMAS, Helen
THOMAS, Marilyn Taft
TIMMERMANN, Leni
TOBIN, Sister Clare
TORRANCE, Mrs. Joe Taylor
TUCKER, Irene
TWOMBLY, Mary Lynn
TWYMAN, Grace
USHER, Ethel Watson
UYTTENHOVE, Yolande
VANNAH, Kate
VIEU, Jane
VILLENEUVE, Marie-Louise Diane
VILLINES, Virginia
VITALIS, Sister Mary
VON ZIERITZ, Grete
VOSS, Marie Wilson
WALLACE, Kathryn
WALLACE, Mildred White
WALLACH, Joelle
WANG, An-Ming
WARE, Harriet
WARREN, Elinor Remick
WEAVER, Carol Ann
WEAVER, Mary
WEIGL, Vally
WENDELBURG, Norma Ruth
WESTBROOK, Helen Searles
WESTGATE, Elizabeth
WESTRUP-MILNER, Maria
WHITE, Elizabeth Estelle
WHITECOTTON, Shirley Ellen
WHITEHEAD, Gillian
WIENECKE, Sigrid Henriette
WIERUSZOWSKI, Lili
WILKINS, Margaret Lucy
WILLIAMS, Frances
WILLIAMS, Grace Mary
WILLIAMS, Joan
WILLIAMS, Mary Lou
WILLMAN, Regina Hansen
WILSON, Elizabeth
WINTER, Sister Miriam Thérèse
WOOD, Mary Knight
WOOD, Ruzena Alenka Valda
WOOGE, Emma

WORTH, Amy
WUNSCH, Ilse Gerda
WYLIE, Ruth Shaw
YDSTIE, Arlene Buckneberg
YOUSE, Glad Robinson
ZAKRZEWSKA-NIKIPORCZYK,
   Barbara Maria
ZIFFRIN, Marilyn Jane
ZIMMERMAN, Phyllis
ZOECKLER, Dorothy
   Ackerman
Century unknown
COLLIER, Elizabeth Mary
DONALDSON, Sadie
FUNK, Susan
PROSDOCIMI, Ada
RENNUTET
ROSS, Clara
VAUGHAN, Freda
WIEGAND, Elizabeth Grieger

VOICE AND ORGAN
17th Century A.D.
ENTHALLER, Sidonia
19th Century A.D.
BALTHASAR, Florence
BLAHETKA, Marie
   Leopoldina
KAINERSTORFER, Clotilde
MASINI, Giulia
PLATEROWA-BROEL-ZYBERK,
   Maria
SZTARAY, Margit
VESPERMANN, Marie
WICKINS, Florence

20th Century A.D.
AINSCOUGH, Juliana Mary
ANDERSON, Pauline Barbour
BARADAPRANA, Pravrajika
BISH, Diane
BITGOOD, Roberta
BUSH, Gladys B.
DIMENTMAN, Esfir Moiseyevna
DONCEANU, Felicia
ELST, Nancy van der
FALCINELLI, Rolande
FAUTCH, Sister Magdalen
FISHER, Katherine Danforth
FRANCK, Philippine
GLAZIER, Beverly
GNUS, Ryta
GUBITOSI, Emilia
HANEFELD, Gertrud
HEDOUX, Yvonne
HRUBY, Dolores Marie
JENNY, Sister Leonore
JORDAN, Alice Yost
KALTENECKER, Gertraud
KAYDEN, Mildred
LAGO
LANG-BECK, Ivana
LAWRENCE, Emily M.
LEIBOW, Ruth Irene
LEJEUNE-BONNIER, Eliane
LELEU, Jeanne
LEPEUT-LEVINE, Jeannine
MACKIE, Frances C.
McALISTER, Mabel
McCOLLIN, Frances
MAGEAU, Mary Jane

MARCUS, Ada Belle Gross
MILETTE, Juliette
MOE, Benna
MONK, Meredith
MORLEY, Nina Dianne
OWEN, Blythe
PALMER, Catherine M.
PALMER, Jane Hetherington
PFEIFFER, Irena
PHILIPPART, Renée
PHILLIPS, Vivian Daphne
PIZER, Elizabeth Faw Hayden
ROBERT, Lucie
ROE, Eileen Betty
SANDRESKY, Margaret
   Vardell
SCHUBARTH, Dorothé
SPEACH, Sister Bernadette
   Marie
STRUTT, Dorothy
TORRA, Celia
VAN APPLEDORN, Mary Jeanne
VAN NESTE, Rosane Micheline Lucie
   Charlotte
VANIER, Jeannine
VILLIN, Marcelle Henriette Marie
VLADERACKEN, Geertruida van
WALKER, Gwyneth van Anden
WARREN, Elinor Remick
WEAVER, Mary
WELANDER, Svea Goeta
WENDELBURG, Norma Ruth
WENNERBERG-REUTER, Sara
   Margareta Eugenia Euphrosyne
WHITLOCK, E. Florence

APPENDIX 9

Women composers by occupation, calling or profession

ACTRESS
1st Century A.D.
THYMELE
17th Century A.D.
ESCAMILLA, Manuela de
18th Century A.D.
JORDAN, Mrs.
POWNALL, Mary Ann
SCHROETER, Corona Elisabeth
Wilhelmine
19th Century A.D.
ARKWRIGHT, Mrs. Robert
CANDEILLE, Amelie Julie
COLLINS, Laura Sedgwick
HEIBERG, Johanne Louise
LEONARDO, Luisa
20th Century A.D.
BELL, Carla Huston
BERBERIAN, Cathy
BROWN, Gladys Mungen
CANNING, Effie I.
COATES, Gloria Kannenberg
DILLER, Angela
DRING, Madeleine
FENSTOCK, Belle
GLEN, Irma
KALTENECKER, Gertraud
LEANDRE, Joelle
LEVI, Natalia Nikolayevna
MONK, Meredith
NUGENT, Maude Jerome
POLONIO, Cinira
THOMPSON, Caroline Lorraine
YOUNG, Rolande Maxwell

ARISTOCRACY
12th Century A.D.
GARSENDA, Countess of Provence
HILDEGARDE, Saint
13th Century A.D.
CASTELLOZA, Dame
LORRAINE, La Duchesse de
14th Century A.D.
RUPAMATI, Rani
15th Century A.D.
HOYA, Katherina von
16th Century A.D.
ARCHINTA, Marguerite
BRAUNSCHWEIG, Anna Maria,
Duchess
COLONNA, Vittoria, Duchess of
Amalfi and Marchioness of
Pescara
DE CASTRO, Maria

17th Century A.D.
AMALIE JULIANE, Countess of
Schwarzenberg
DOROTHEA SOPHIA, Duchess
ERPACH, Amalia Katharina, von,
Countess
LACERDA, Bernarda Ferreira de
SOPHIE ELISABETH von
Braunschweig, Duchess
STROZZI, Barbara
18th Century A.D.
AGNESI-PINOTTINI, Maria Teresa d'
ANNA AMALIA, Duchess of Saxe-
Weimar
BRUCKENTHAL, Bertha von,
Baroness
CAVENDISH, Georgiana
CHARRIERE, Isabella Agneta
Elisabeth de
COURMONT, Countess von
DESFOSSES, Elisabeth Francoise,
Countess
FLEMING, Lady
KOHARY, Marie, Countess of
LESZCZYNSKA, Marie, Queen
PIO DI SAVOJA, Isabella D.
VENIER DE PETRIS, Teresa
VIDAMPIERRE, Countess of
19th Century A.D.
ABRANTES, Duchess of
ABRECHT, Princess of Prussia
AMALIE, Marie Friederike Augusta,
Princess of Saxony
ANNA, Duchess of Mecklenburg-
Schwerin
ANSPACH, Elizabeth, Margravine of
BAWR, Alexandrine Sophie
BOTTINI, Marianna, Marchioness
CAETANI-RZEWUSKA, Calista,
Princess
CHODKIEWICZ, Comtesse
CORRER, Ida, Countess
DAHL, Emma
DE SOUSA HOLSTEIN, Donna Teresa
DUCHAMBGE, Pauline
DUFFERIN, Lady Helen Selina
EUAN-SMITH, Lady
FORTMAGNE, Baroness de
GASCHIN-ROSENBERG, Fanny,
Countess
GIZYCKA-ZAMOYSKA, Ludmilla,
Countess
GRABOWSKA, Clementine,
Countess

GRANDVAL, Marie Felicie Clemence
de Reiset, Vicomtesse de
GYLLENHAAL, Matilda Valeriana
Beatrix, Duchess of Orozco
HAENEL DE CRONENTHAL, Louise
Augusta Marie Julia
KINGSTON, Marie Antoinette
KOMOROWSKA, Stephanie,
Countess
LANNOY, Clementine-Josephine-
Francoise-Therese, Countess
LEGOUX, Julie, Baroness
LILIEN, Antoinette von,
Baroness
LLANOVER, Lady
LODER, Kate Fanny
LUND, Baroness van der
MARIA PAULOWNA, Grand Duchess
of Weimar
MIER, Countess Anna von
NAIRNE, Carolina, Baroness
O'DONNELL, Malvine, Countess
PERRIERE-PILTE, Anais,
Countess of
RADNOR, Helen, Countess of
RAMSAY, Lady Katherine
RENAUD-D'ALLEN, Mlle. de
RIDDERSTOLPE, Caroline Johanna
Lovisa
RUTTENSTEIN, Baroness Constance
SAINT-DIDIER, Countess
SCHLICK, Elise, Countess of
SONTAG, Henriette
SPORLEDER, Charlotte
STOLBERG, Louise von
STUBENBERG, Anna Zichy,
Countess
SZTARAY, Margit
TENNYSON, Emily Sarah, Lady
UCCELLI, Carolina
20th Century A.D.
BOETZELAER, Josina Anna
Petronella
BORBOM, Maria de Melo Furtado
Caldeira Giraldes
ERDOEDY, Luisa, Countess
ESTERHAZY, Alexandrine, Countess
FISCHER, Emma Gabriele Marie von,
Baroness
HARRISON, Annie Fortescue
PEJACEVIC, Dora, Countess
RUTA, Gilda, Countess
SILVA, Eloisa d'Herbil de
TE RANGI-PAI, Princess

Century unknown
PHILIPPINA, Charlotte, Duchess of
Brunswick

ARRANGER
17th Century A.D.
MENETOU, Francoise-Charlotte de
Senneterre
18th Century A.D.
VALENTINE, Ann
19th Century A.D.
BORTON, Alice
CORRI-DUSSEK, Sofia Giustina
HAENEL DE CRONENTHAL, Louise
Augusta Marie Julia
MATOS, A. de
PERRELLI, Giuseppina
RAMANN, Lina
SANDELS, Ellen
SZARVADY, Wilhelmine Clausz
VIARDOT-GARCIA, Pauline Michelle
Ferdinande
20th Century A.D.
ANDERSON, Ruth
AYARZA DE MORALES, Rosa
Mercedes
BARTLETT, Floy Little
BIRCSAK, Thusnelda
BONDS, Margaret
CADZOW, Dorothy Forrest
CARLOS, Wendy
CASTAGNETTA, Grace Sharp
CLARK, Mary Margaret Walker
CLAUDE, Marie
CLEMENS, Margaret
DE FAZIO, Lynette Stevens
DRETKE, Leora N.
ELKIND, Rachel
EMINGEROVA, Katerina
ESCOBAR, Maria Luisa
GAIGEROVA, Varvara Andrianovna
GEST, Elizabeth
GILLICK, Emelyn Mildred Samuels
GIURANNA, Elena Barbara
GODLA, Mary Ann
GUBITOSI, Emilia
HAIRSTON, Jacqueline Butler
HARKNESS, Rebekah West
HARRADEN, R. Ethel
HAUSMAN, Ruth Langley
HECHLER, Ilse
HELLER, Ruth
HIGGINS, Esther S.
HOKANSON, Margrethe
HOUSE, L. Marguerite
JAQUETTI ISANT, Palmira
KASILAG, Lucrecia R.
KEMP, Dorothy Elizabeth Walter
KETTERING, Eunice Lea
LINNET, Anne
LOUVIER, Nicole
LVOVA, Julia Fedorovna
McGILL, Gwendolen Mary Finlayson
McLEMORE, Monita Prine
MASON, Margaret C.
MASTERS, Juan
MATHIS, Judy M.
MAXWELL, Jacqueline Perkinson
MITCHELL, Norma Jean
MOORE, Undine Smith
MOOREHEAD, Consuela Lee
NICKERSON, Camille Lucie
NIGHTINGALE, Mae Wheeler
O'BRIEN, Katharine E.
PAGOTO, Helen
PARKER, Alice
PFOLH, Bessie Whittington
PITOT, Genevieve
PREOBRAJENSKA, Vera Nicolaevna
PRICE, Florence Beatrice
RAMSEY, Sister Mary Anastasia

REISER, Violet
SAKALLI-LECCA, Alexandra
SAMVELIAN, Sofia Vardanovna
SANDELS, Ellen
SCHIEVE, Catherine
SCHUYLER, Philippa Duke
SCHWARTZ, Nan Louise
SELVA, Blanche
SIDORENKO, Tamara Stepanovna
SIEGRIST, Beatrice
SINDE RAMALLAL, Clara
SINGER, Jeanne
STEELE, Lynn
STEINER, Emma
SUESSE, Dana
SURIANI, Alberta
VERNE, Adela
VIRTUE, Constance Cochnower
WALKER, Shirley
WARWICK, Mary Carol
WILLIAMS, Mary Lou
YOUNG, Fredricka Agnes
Century unknown
SANI, Maria Teresa
SNODGRASS, Louise Harrison

ARTIST
18th Century A.D.
MARIA ANTONIA WALPURGIS,
Princess of Bavaria
MONDONVILLE, Mme. de
SCHROETER, Corona Elisabeth
Wilhelmine
19th Century A.D.
CAETANI-RZEWUSKA, Calista, Princess
20th Century A.D.
BACH, Maria
BOND, Carrie Jacobs
BRESCHI, Laura
BRYUSSOVA, Nadezhda Yakolevna
BUENAVENTURA, Isabel
GLASER, Victoria Merrylees
GRAINGER, Ella Viola Strom-
Brandelius
GRIFFINS, Vashti Rogers
HYLIN, Birgitta Charlotta Kristina
JANOTHA, Natalia
KNOWLES, Alison
KRALIKOVA, Johana
MAGUY LOVANO, Marguerite
Schlegel
MOSHER, Frances Elizabeth
McDUFFEE, Mabel Howard
PERRY, Marilyn Brown
ROSSELLI-NISSIM, Mary
SCHIEVE, Catherine
SMITH, Ruby Mae
SOUERS, Mildred
THEMMEN, Ivana Marburger
WEAVER, Marion
WEBER, Carole
WHITTINGTON, Joan
WONG, Hsiung-Zee
WYETH, Ann

BUSINESS WOMAN
20th Century A.D.
BOONE, Clara Lyle
BRYAN, Betty Sue
CROCHET, Sharon Brandstetter
HIRSCH, Barbara
SANDIFUR, Ann Elizabeth

CHOREOGRAPHER
20th Century A.D.
DE FAZIO, Lynette Stevens
DEAN, Laura
FORMAN, Ellen
HUMPHREY, Doris
KANAKA'OLE, Edith Ke-Kuhikuhi-I-
Pu'u-one-o-Na-Ali'i-O-Kohala

KRAUS, Rozann Baghdad
MONK, Meredith
TYRMAND, Eta Moiseyevna

CONCERT MISTRESS
20th Century A.D.
CABRERA, Silvia Maria Pires
CAPERTON, Florence Tait
DAVITASHVILI, Meri Shalvovna
DIMENTMAN, Esfir Moiseyevna
DZHAFAROVA, Afag Mamed kyzy
FRITTER, Genevieve Davisson
GAIGEROVA, Varvara Andrianovna
GREENE, Genevieve
GVAZAVA, Tamara Davidovna
IBRAGIMOVA, Ela Imamedinovna
IGENBERGA, Elga Avgustovna
KULIEVA, Farida Tairovna
KUYPER, Elizabeth
LEVITOVA, Ludmila Vladimirovna
LICHTENSTEIN, Olga Grigorievna
NAZAROVA, Tatiana Borisovna
OSETROVA-YAKOVLIEVA, Nina
Alexandrovna
TYRMAND, Eta Moiseyevna
VINTULE, Ruta Evaldovna
WILES, Margaret Jones

CONDUCTOR (CHORAL)
8th Century A.D.
JAMILA
17th Century A.D.
TIRS, Katharina
19th Century A.D.
BLANGINI, Mlle.
FOWLES, Margaret F.
HOLLAND, Caroline
KALLEY, Sara Poulton
KINKEL, Johanna
O'LEARY, Rosetta
ROSENTHAL, Pauline
WICHERN, Caroline
20th Century A.D.
ADAMS, Carrie Bell
ADAMS, Elizabeth Kilmer
AKERS, Doris Mae
ALDEN, Zilpha May
ANDRIESSEN, Caecilia
AVETISIAN, Aida Konstantinovna
BALCKE, Frida Dorothea
BAMPTON, Ruth
BARBOSA, Cacilda Campos Borges
BARNES-WOOD, Zilpha
BARTHEL, Ursula
BARTHELSON, Joyce Holloway
BAUMGARTEN, Chris
BAYEVA, Vera
BECKMAN, Ellen Josephine
BENOIT, Francine Germaine Van
Cool
BERROA, Catalina
BERRY, Margaret Mary Robinson
BITGOOD, Roberta
BOLZ, Harriet
BRANSCOMBE, Gena
BRENNER, Rosamond Drooker
BRINGUER, Estela
BROWN, Elizabeth van Ness
BROWN, Norma
BUCHANAN, Annabel Morris
BURCHELL, Henrietta Louise
BURT, Virginia M.
BUTLER, Anne Lois
CALDWELL, Mary Elizabeth Glockler
CAMPBELL, Edith Mary
CARRILLO, Isolina
CARTER, Rosetta
CECCONI-BATES, Augusta
CHERUBIM, Sister Mary Schaefer
CLINGAN, Judith Ann
DAHL, Vivian

DALBERT, Anny
DIMENTMAN, Esfir Moiseyevna
DIMITRIU, Florica
DOUROUX, Margaret Pleasant
DRYNAN, Margaret
DU PAGE, Florence Elizabeth
EICHHORN, Hermene Warlick
ELLIOTT, Marjorie Reeve
ELST, Nancy van der
ERDELI, Xenia Alexandrovna
FAHRBACH, Henrietta
FEHRS, Anna Elisbeth
FELLOWS, Mrs. Wayne Stanley
FISHER, Katherine Danforth
FLACH, Elsa
FOSTER, Dorothy Godwin
FOWLER, Marje
FRASIER, Jane
GARDINER, Mary Elizabeth
GHILARDI, Syra
GLASER, Victoria Merrylees
GOLDSTON, Margaret Nell Stumpf
HARLOW, Barbara
HAVEY, Marguerite
HAWLEY, Carolyn Jean
HENDERSON, Ruth Watson
HERMANN, Miina
HERNANDEZ-GONZALO, Gisela
HOFF, Vivian Beaumont
HORNBACK, Sister Mary Gisela
HRUBY, Dolores Marie
IGENBERGA, Elga Avgustovna
JENNEY, Mary Frances
JENNY, Sister Leonore
JESSYE, Eva
JIRKOVA, Olga
JOLLEY, Florence Werner
KACZURBINA-ZDZIECHOWSKA,
    Maria
KAMIEN, Anna
KER, Ann S.
KIP, Yuksel
KLINKOVA, Zhivka
KORHONEN, S. Gloria
KOZINOVIC, Lujza
KUCEROVA-HERSTOVA, Marie
LAWRENCE, Emily M.
LEE, Anna Virginia
LIDGI-HERMAN, Sofia
LOHR, Ina
LORENZ, Ellen Jane
LORING, Nancy
MACAULAY, Janice Michel
MacDONALD, Catherine
McCLEARY, Mary Gilkeson
McCOLLIN, Frances
McDUFFEE, Mabel Howard
McILWRAITH, Isa Roberta
McLEMORE, Monita Prine
McLIN, Lena
McNAIR, Jacqueline Hanna
MAITLAND, Anna Harriet
MARCUS, Bunita
MAREZ-OYENS, Tera de
MARTH, Helen June
MELL, Gertrud Maria
MILDANTRI, Mary Ann
MILFORD, Mary Jean Ross
MILLER, Alma Grace
MINEO, Antoinette
MOHNS, Grace Updegraff Bergen
MOORE, Undine Smith
MOOREHEAD, Consuela Lee
MOSSMAN, Bina
MULDER, Johanna Harmina Gerdina
MUNGER, Millicent Christner
MUSGRAVE, Thea
MUSTILLO, Lina
NARCISSE-MAIR, Denise Lorraine
NEILY, Anne MacAdams
NIXON, June

NOHE, Beverly
NOVELLO-DAVIES, Clara
OLLER BENLLOCH, Maria Teresa
OTERO, Mercedes
PAGOTO, Helen
PARENTE, Sister Elizabeth
PENNER, Jean Priscilla
PERRY, Mary Dean
PERSCHMANN, Elfriede
PFEIFFER, Irena
PICHE, Eudore
PIERCE, Sarah Anderson
PIKE, Eleanor B. Franklin
PITTMAN, Evelyn LaRue
RABINOF, Sylvia
RAMSEY, Sister Mary Anastasia
RAW, Vera Constance
REED, Phyllis Luidens
REIS, Manuela Cancio
RENART, Marta Garcia
RENNES, Catharina van
RICHARDSON, Enid Dorothy
ROBBOY, Rosalie Smotkin
ROE, Eileen Betty
ROGERS, Faith Helen
ROGERS, Sharon Elery
ROSAS FERNANDES, Maria Helena
RYAN, Winifred
RYDER, Theodora Sturkow
SCEK, Breda Friderika
SCHLEDER, Grizelda Lazzaro
SCHUBARTH, Dorothe
SCHUSTER, Doris Dodd
SHORE, Clare
SHREVE, Susan Ellen
SIMONS, Netty
SKOLFIELD, Alice Jones
    Tewksbury
SMEJKALOVA, Vlasta
SOERLIE, Caroline Volla
SOUBLETTE, Sylvia
SPONGBERG, Viola
SPOONER, Dorothy Harley
STAIR, Patty
STEELE, Helen
STULTZ, Marie Irene
STYLES, Dorothy Geneva
SUCHY, Gregoria Karides
SZOENYI, Erzsebet
TACK, Annie
TELFER, Nancy Ellen
THOMPSON, Ellen
TORRA, Celia
TURNER, Myra Brooks
TYSON, Mildred Lund
URBAYI-KRASNODEBSKA, Zofia
    Jadwiga
VAZQUEZ, Alida
VIERK, Lois
VILLENEUVE, Marie-Louise
    Diane
VITALIS, Sister Mary
VOIGT, Henriette
VORLOVA, Slavka
WAALER, Fredrikke Holtemann
WARNER, Sally Slade
WARREN, Elinor Remick
WEBB, Allienne Brandon
WELDON, Georgina
WENTZ-JANACEK, Elisabet
WERTHEIM, Rosy
WHITE, Ruth S.
WIERUSZOWSKI, Lili
WILLS, Edwina Florence
WOLF, Ilda von
WORTH, Amy
WUNSCH, Ilse Gerda
YDSTIE, Arlene Buckneberg
YOUNG, Fredricka Agnes
ZOECKLER, Dorothy Ackerman
ZWEIG, Esther

CONDUCTOR (ORCHESTRA)
8th Century A.D.
JAMILA
16th Century A.D.
COTTA, Anastasia
MOLZA, Tarquinia
18th Century A.D.
DE GAMBARINI, Elisabetta
19th Century A.D.
AMANN, Josephine
BLANC DE FONTBELLE, Cecile
CALOSSO, Eugenia
HARTLAND, Lizzie
HOLMES, Augusta Mary Anne
HUND, Alicia
HUNDT, Aline
KINKEL, Johanna
KRAEHMER, Caroline
MARSHALL, Florence A.
RADNOR, Helen, Countess of
RIDDERSTOLPE, Caroline Johanna
    Lovisa
RODRIGO, Maria
VANZO, Vittoria Maria
WURM, Mary J.A.
20th Century A.D.
ABEJO, Sister M. Rosalina
ALMESAN, Irma
ALVES DE SOUSA, Berta Candida
ARQUIT, Nora Harris
ARTEAGA, Genoveva de
BAILEY, Judith Margaret
BARBOSA, Cacilda Campos Borges
BARRIENTOS, Maria
BARTHELSON, Joyce Holloway
BEARER, Elaine Louise
BOND, Victoria Ellen
BONHOMME, Marie Therese
BOUCHARD, Linda L.
BOULANGER, Nadia Juliette
BRAGA, Henriqueta Rosa Fernandes
BUTLER, Anne Lois
CARRENO, Teresa
CARVALHO, Dinora de
CASTEGNARO, Lola
CATUNDA, Eunice do Monte Lima
CECCONI-BATES, Augusta
CHAMINADE, Cecile Louise
    Stephanie
COLERIDGE-TAYLOR, Avril Gwendolen
COOLIDGE, Peggy Stuart
COONEY, Cheryl Lee
CRANE, Helen
DAIKEN, Melanie
DANIELS, Mabel Wheeler
DASCALESCU, Camelia
DAVY, Ruby Claudia Emily
DE BIASE BIDART, Lycia
DE FREITAS, Elvira Manuela
    Fernandez
DE LA MARTINEZ, Odaline
DE PATE, Elisabetta M.S.
DEBRASSINE-PRIJAT, Laure
DIANDA, Hilda
DIMITRIU, Florica
DRETKE, Leora N.
DUCZMAL-JAROSZEWSKA,
    Agnieszka
DZIEWULSKA, Maria Amelia
EICHENWALD, Sylvia
EISENSTEIN DE VEGA, Silvia
ENGBERG, M. Davenport
ERHART, Dorothy
FARGA PELLICER, Onia
FERNANDO, Sarathchandra
    Vichremadithya
FOLVILLE, Eugenie-Emilie Juliette
FRONMUELLER, Frieda
GILLUM, Ruth Helen
GIPPS, Ruth
GUNDERSON, Helen Louise

GWILY-BROIDO, Rivka
HARRIS, Margaret R.
HAWLEY, Carolyn Jean
HERBISON, Jeraldine Saunders
HOKANSON, Margrethe
HOLST, Imogen Clare
JABOR, Najla
JESI, Ada
KAPLAN, Lois Jay
KAPRALOVA, Vitezslava
KAZURO-TROMBINI, Margerita
KEMP, Dorothy Elizabeth Walter
KEMP-POTTER, Joan
KESHNER, Joyce Grove
KIRKWOOD, Antoinette
KLOTZMAN, Dorothy Ann Hill
KOSSE, Roberta
KUYPER, Elizabeth
LARSON, Anna Barbara
LAUBER, Anne Marianne
LEFANU, Nicola Frances
LEFEVER, Maxine Lane
LEGINSKA, Ethel
LEON, Tania Justina
LEONE, Mae G.
LIDGI-HERMAN, Sofia
LINZ VON KRIEGNER, Marta
MACAULAY, Janice Michel
MACKIE, Shirley M.
McINTYRE, Margaret
McKANN-MANCINI, Patricia
McKELLAN, Irene Mary
MAILIAN, Elza Antonovna
MANZIARLY, Marcelle de
MARCUS, Bunita
MAREZ-OYENS, Tera de
MARIANI-CAMPOLIETI, Virginia
MARIC, Ljubica
MAURICE-JACQUET, H.
MAYER, Lise Maria
MEISTER, Marianne
MILDREN, Margaret Joyce
MOBERG, Ida Georgina
MOORE, Mary Carr
MORLEY, Angela
MRACEK, Ann Michelle
MUSGRAVE, Thea
NELSON, Mary Anne
OH, Sook Ja
OHLSON, Marion
OLIVEROS, Pauline
OWEN, Angela Maria
OZAITA, Maria Luisaria Luisa
PARKER, Alice
PARS, Melahat
PAUL, Doris A.
PEARL-MANN, Dora Deborah
PERRY, Julia Amanda
PETROVA, Mara
PIECHOWSKA, Alina
PIRES DOS REIS, Hilda
POLIGNAC, Armande de, Countess
    of Chabannes
PRICE, Beryl
QUINTANILLA, Alba
RAMAKERS, Christiane Josee
RAMSEY, Sister Mary Anastasia
RASKIN, Ruby
REED, Marlyce Rae Polk
RISHER, Anna Priscilla
ROMERO BARBOSA, Elena
SALQUIN, Hedy
SANGUESA, Iris
SCHERCHEN, Tona
SCLIAR, Esther
SEGHIZZI, Cecilia
SERRANO REDONNET, Ana
SHURTLEFF, Lynn Richard
SMYTH, Ethel Mary, Dame
SNYDER, Amy
SODRE, Joanidia

SPAIN-DUNK, Susan
STEINER, Emma
STREICHER, Lyubov Lvovna
SUNBLAD-HALME, Heidi Gabriella
    Wilhelmina
TERZIAN, Alicia
THOMAS, Karen P.
TORRA, Celia
TOYAMA, Michiko Francoise
TUCKER, Tui St. George
TURNER, Mildred Cozzens
TWOMBLY, Mary Lynn
URBAYI-KRASNODEBSKA, Zofia
    Jadwiga
URRETA, Alicia
VAN EPEN-DE GROOT, Else Antonia
VAN HAUTE, Anna-Maria
VIGNERON-RAMAKERS, Christiane-
    Josee
WAALER, Fredrikke Holtemann
WALKER, Shirley
WHITLOCK, E. Florence
WILES, Margaret Jones
WILKINS, Margaret Lucy
WILLIAMS, Frances
WILLIAMS, Mary Lou
WOODS, Joan Shirley LeSueur
ZAIDEL-RUDOLPH, Jeanne
ZECHLIN, Ruth
ZIBEROVA, Zinaida Petrovna
ZIMMERMANN, Margrit

CRITIC

19th Century A.D.
GARCIA, Eduarda Mansilla de
SEROVA, Valentina Semyonovna
20th Century A.D.
ADAMS, Julia Aurelia
ALVES DE SOUSA, Berta Candida
BAUER, Emilie Frances
BAUER, Marion Eugenie
BEAT, Janet Eveline
BENOIT, Francine Germaine Van Gool
BOULANGER, Nadia Juliette
BRUZDOWICZ, Joanna
CALCAGNO, Elsa
DEMARQUEZ, Suzanne
ELST, Nancy van der
FULCHER, Ellen Georgina
GERRISH-JONES, Abbie
GLANVILLE-HICKS, Peggy
GODDARD, Arabella
HALL, Pauline
HERRERA Y OGAZON, Alba
HOLCK, Sine
HOLMSEN, Borghild
IASHVILI, Lili Mikhailovna
KAPLAN, Lois Jay
KISCH, Eve
LAUER, Elizabeth
LEIVISKA, Helvi Lemmiki
LIMA CRUZ, Maria Antonietta de
McNAIR, Jacqueline Hanna
MARI, Pierrette
MATTHEWS, Dorothy White
MEAD, Catherine Pannill
MORRISON, Julia Maria
PHILLIPS, Linda
PICKHARDT, Ione
POOL, Jeannie Gayle
RAIGORODSKY, Leda Natalia
    Heimsath
ROGERS, Emmy Brady
SALQUIN, Hedy
SANTIAGO-FELIPE, Vilma R.
SERRANO REDONNET, Ana
SKOUEN, Synne
SOULAGE, Marcelle Fanny Henriette
TURNER-MALEY, Florence
WENNERSTROM, Mary Hannah

ECCLESIASTIC

30th Century B.C.
INANNA
24th Century B.C.
ENHEDUANNA
13th Century B.C.
VISVAVARA
4th Century A.D.
MACRINA, Saint
5th Century A.D.
BRIDGET
9th Century A.D.
KASIA
MARTHA
THEKLA
THEODOSIA
10th Century A.D.
ASSUNCAO, Sister Arcangela Maria
    de
11th Century A.D.
HROSTWITHA
12th Century A.D.
HILDEGARDE, Saint
ISELDA
SEIDENWEBERIN, Metzi
SPONHEIM, Sister Jutta von
13th Century A.D.
GERTRUDE OF HELFTA, Saint
HADEWIJCH OF BRABANT
MECHTHILD
ROTTERIN ALHEIT
15th Century A.D.
HATZLERIN, Sister Clara
HOYA, Katherina von
PALAEOLOGINA
16th Century A.D.
ALEOTTI, Raffaela-Argenta
ALEOTTI, Vittoria
CAMALDULI, Sorella
CASULANA, Maddalena
ECHENFELD, Katharina
MIRA BAI
SESSA, Claudia
VERTOA DA BERGAMO, Sister
    Agostina
17th Century A.D.
ASSANDRA, Catterina
BADALLA, Rosa Giacinta
CALEGARI, Cornelia
CALEGARI, Leonarda
CEPPARELLI, Soura Costanza
CLARISSE DE ROME, Sister
COZZOLANI, Chiara Margarita
ENTHALLER, Sidonia
LEONARDA, Sister Isabella
MEDA, Sister Bianca Maria
MURATORI SCANNABECCHI,
    Angiola Teresa
PERUCONA, Sister Maria Saveria
QUINZANA, Sister Rosalba
RASSCHENAU, Marianna
RUSCA, Claudia Francesca
SERA, Beatrice del
SUARDA, Maria Virginia
TIRS, Katharina
VIZANA, Lucretia Orsina
18th Century A.D.
ARCANGELA-MARIA, Sister
AURELIA, Sister
KIERNICKA, Anna
WOHL, Maria Viktoria
19th Century A.D.
BOPP VON OBERSTADT, Countess
CHASTENAY, Victorine de
KALLEY, Sara Poulton
MASINI, Giulia
RAPP, Marguerite
20th Century A.D.
ANCELE, Sister Mary
BARADAPRANA, Pravrajika
BARIL, Jeanne

BEAUCHEMIN, Marie
BELLEROSE, Sister Cecilia
BERNARDONE, Anka
BEZDEK, Sister John Joseph
BIRD, Sister Mary Rafael
BOCARD, Sister Cecilia Clair
BOUCHER, Lydia
CADORET, Charlotte
CECILE REGINA, Sister
CHERUBIM, Sister Mary Schaefer
CORDULA, Sister M.
COTE, Helene
DAHL, Vivian
DAIGLE, Sister Anne Cecile
DECARIE, Reine
ERNEST, Sister M.
FAUTCH, Sister Magdalen
FITZGERALD, Sister Florence Therese
FONDER, Sister Mary Teresine
GENTEMANN, Sister Mary Elaine
HABAN, Sister Teresine M.
HERTEL, Sister Romana
HILL, Sister M. Mildred
HORNBACK, Sister Mary Gisela
HUGHES, Sister Martina
HYTREK, Sister Theophane
JENNY, Sister Leonore
JONES, Sister Ida
KER, Ann S.
KLIMISCH, Sister Mary Jane
KORHONEN, S. Gloria
LAFLEUR, Lucienne
LEFEBVRE, Francoise
LILLENAS, Bertha Mae
MARY BERNICE, Sister
MARY ELAINE, Sister
MEYSENBURG, Sister Agnes
MILETTE, Juliette
MORONEY, Sister Mary Emmeline
MUG, Sister Mary Theodosia
O'SHEA, Mary Ellen
PAQUIN, Louisa
PARENTE, Sister Elizabeth
RAMSEY, Sister Mary Anastasia
RHENE-JAQUE
RITTENHOUSE, Elizabeth Mae
ROMITELLI, Sante Maria
ROSE OF JESUS, Sister
ROSE, Sister Caroline
SCHWERDTFEGER, E. Anne
SPEACH, Sister Bernadette Marie
TOBIN, Sister Clare
TRINITAS, Sister M.
VERHAALEN, Sister Marion
VILLENEUVE, Marie-Louise Diane
VINETTE, Alice
VITALIS, Sister Mary
WARD, Sister Mary Louise
WILSON, Elizabeth
WINTER, Sister Miriam Therese
WOOD, Sister Mary Davida
Century unknown
CESIS, Sister Sulpizia
GHOSHA

FOLKLORIST
20th Century A.D.
ARETZ, Isabel
AYARZA DE MORALES, Rosa
Mercedes
BARATTA, Maria M. de
BEATH, Betty
BECLARD D'HARCOURT, Marguerite
BROADWOOD, Lucy E.
BUCHANAN, Annabel Morris
CABRERA, Ana S. de
CALCAGNO, Elsa
CARRIQUE, Ana
CHICHERINA, Sofia Nikolayevna
CONSTANTINESCU, Domnica
CRAWFORD SEEGER, Ruth

CURTIS, Natalie
DE PATE, Elisabetta M.S.
DELIZ, Monserrate
DIMENTMAN, Esfir Moiseyevna
DONCEANU, Felicia
DURAND, Nella Wells
ESCOBAR, Maria Luisa
FERRER OTERO, Monsita Monserrate
FIUZA, Virginia Salgado
FREIXAS Y CRUELLS, Narcisa
GAIGEROVA, Varvara Andrianovna
GUSEINZADE, Adilia Gadzhi Aga
HARRISON, Susan Frances
HOLST, Imogen Clare
HUNKINS, Eusebia Simpson
JAQUETTI ISANT, Palmira
KAZANDJIAN, Sirvart
KENNEDY-FRASER, Marjory
KESAREVA, Margarita Alexandrovna
KOZINOVIC, Lujza
LANG-BECK, Ivana
LEVI, Natalia Nikolayevna
LORENZ, Ellen Jane
LVOVA, Julia Fedorovna
MEKEEL, Joyce
PATTERSON, Annie Wilson
PUKUI, Mary Abigail
REIS, Manuela Cancio
RENSHAW, Rosette
SADERO GENI, Maria Scarpa
SAMVELIAN, Sofia Vardanovna
SEPULVEDA, Maria Luisa
SERRANO REDONNET, Ana
SETTI, Kilza
SIDORENKO, Tamara Stepanovna
STREICHER, Lyubov Lvovna
TAUTU, Cornelia
THOMA, Annette
THOMSEN, Geraldine
VORLOVA, Slavka
WALDO, Elisabeth

LECTURER
19th Century A.D.
CAPPIANI, Luisa
CLARKE, Helen Archibald
HAWES, Charlotte W.
HOEGSBRO-CHRISTENSEN, Inge
LA HYE, Louise Genevieve
PESSIAK-SCHMERLING, Anna
PLEYEL, Marie Felicity Denise
PRESCOTT, Oliveria Louisa
ROSALES, Cecilia
SCHNORR VON CAROLSFELD,
Malvina
WAKEFIELD, Augusta Mary
ZANTEN, Cornelia van
ZIEGLER, Natalie Sophie von
20th Century A.D.
AARNE, Els
ABEJO, Sister M. Rosalina
ABRAMOVA, Sonia Pinkhasovna
ADAMS, Julia Aurelia
AKSYANTSEVA, Ninel Moiseyevna
ALEXANDRA, Liana
AMATI, Orlanda
ANDREYEVA, Elena Fedorovna
ARAUCO, Ingrid Colette
ARAZOVA, Izabella Konstantinovna
ARHO, Anneli
ARMER, Elinor Florence
BABAYEVA, Seda Grigorievna
BACEWICZ, Grazyna
BAILEY, Judith Margaret
BANDT, Rosalie Edith
BARKIN, Elaine
BARTHELSON, Joyce Holloway
BAUER, Marion Eugenie
BAULD, Alison
BEAT, Janet Eveline
BECK, Martha Dillard

BEHREND, Jeanne
BENNETT, Wilhelmine
BERBERIAN, Cathy
BERK, Adele
BERL WEINFIELD, Christine
BESSEM, Saar
BEZDEK, Sister John Joseph
BILBRO, Anne Mathilde
BIZONY, Celia
BLAUSTEIN, Susan Morton
BOLZ, Harriet
BONDS, Margaret
BOSCH Y PAGES, Luisa
BOULANGER, Nadia Juliette
BOYCE, Blanche Ula
BOYD, Anne Elizabeth
BREMER, Marrie Petronella
BRIGHT, Ann
BRINK, Emily R.
BROGUE, Roslyn Clara
BRUSSELS, Iris
BRUZDOWICZ, Joanna
BRYUSSOVA, Nadezhda Yakolevna
BUCHANAN, Annabel Morris
BUCK, Era Marguerite
BUSH, Grace E.
CARR-BOYD, Ann Kirsten
CHANDLER, Mary
CHEATHAM, Kitty
CHEBOTARIAN, Gayane
Movsesovna
CHEVALIER, Charlotte Bergersen
CHITCHIAN, Geguni Oganesovna
CHITTENDEN, Kate Sara
CHKHEIDZE, Dali Davidovna
CHUDOVA, Tatiana Alekseyevna
CLAYTON, Susan
CLEMENS, Margaret
COATES, Gloria Kannenberg
CONSTANTINESCU, Domnica
CORNEA-IONESCU, Alma
CORY, Eleanor
CREES, Kathleen Elsie
DAIGLE, Sister Anne Cecile
DANEAU, Suzanne
DAVIS, Sharon
DAVY, Ruby Claudia Emily
DEMESSIEUX, Jeanne
DESPORTES, Yvonne Berthe Melitta
DOBSON, Elaine
DONCEANU, Felicia
DROBYAZGINA, Valentina Ivanovna
DUBOIS, Shirley Graham
DZHAFAROVA, Afag Mamed kyzy
EICHENWALD, Sylvia
EKSANISHVILI, Eleonara Grigorevna
ELMORE, Cenieth Catherine
ELST, Nancy van der
ELWYN-EDWARDS, Dilys
ERNST, Siegrid
ESCOT, Pozzi
EUBANKS, Rachel Amelia
EVANS, Patricia Margaret
FERNANDEZ, Helen Lorenzo
FINE, Vivian
FISHER, Katherine Danforth
FLEISCHER-DOLGOPOLSKY,
Tsipporah
FRASER, Shena Eleanor
FRERICHS, Doris Coulston
FRUMKER, Linda
GABUS, Monique
GALIKIAN, Susanna Avetisovna
GANNON, Helen Carroll
GARCIA MUNOZ, Carmen
GARDNER, Mildred Alvine
GARSCIA-GRESSEL, Janina
GARUTA, Lucia Yanovna
GARWOOD, Margaret
GAUTHIEZ, Cecile
GENTILE, Ada

GERSTMAN, Blanche Wilhelminia
GHANDAR, Ann
GIACCHINO CUSENZA, Maria
GITECK, Janice
GOKHMAN, Elena Vladimirovna
GOLSON-BATEMAN, Florence
GONTARENKO, Galina Nikolayevna
GOODE, Blanche
GOOLKASIAN-RAHBEE, Dianne
    Zabelle
GOULD, Janetta
GUSEINZADE, Adilia Gadzhi Aga
GUSTAVSON, Nancy Nicholls
GVAZAVA, Tamara Davidovna
GYANDZHETSIAN, Destrik
    Bogdanovna
HARRIS, Ethel Ramos
HATCH, Edith
HAYS, Doris Ernestine
HERNANDEZ-GONZALO, Gisela
HERTEL, Sister Romana
HESSE, Marjorie Anne
HILL, Sister M. Mildred
HO, Wai On
HOLCOMB, Louanah Riggs
HOLLAND, Dulcie Sybil
HOPEKIRK, Helen
HORNBACK, Sister Mary Gisela
HOUSMAN, Rosalie
HSU, Wen-Ying
HUJSAK, Joy Detenbeck
HUNTER, Hilda
HYDE, Miriam Beatrice
IASHVILI, Lili Mikhailovna
IBRAGIMOVA, Sevda Mirza kyzy
ISAKOVA, Aida Petrovna
ISMAGILOVA, Leila Zagirovna
JAZWINSKI, Barbara
JOCHSBERGER, Tzipora H.
JOHNSTON-REID, Sarah Ruth
JOLLEY, Florence Werner
JOLY, Suzanne
JONES, Sister Ida
KACZURBINA-ZDZIECHOWSKA,
    Maria
KARASTOYANOVA, Elena
KAVASCH, Deborah Helene
KEMP-POTTER, Joan
KER, Ann S.
KERN, Frida
KIM, Kwang-Hee
KIRKBY-MASON, Barbara
KISCH, Eve
KNIGHT, Judyth
KOPPEL-HOLBE, Maria
KOSSE, Roberta
KRAUS, Rozann Baghdad
KRAUSZ, Susan
KRUSE, Lotte
KULIEVA, Farida Tairovna
KUYPER, Elizabeth
KUZMENKO, Larysa
LARSEN, Elizabeth Brown
LARSON, Anna Barbara
LATIOLAIS, Desiree Jayne
LAUBER, Anne Marianne
LAUER, Elizabeth
LAWHON, Gladys Louise
LAYMAN, Pamela
LEBARON, Anne
LEFANU, Nicola Frances
LEFEVER, Maxine Lane
LELEU, Jeanne
LEONCHIK, Svetlana Gavrilovna
LEPKE, Charma Davies
LESICHKOVA, Lili
LEVEY, Lauren
LICHTENSTEIN, Olga Grigorievna
LIPSCOMB, Helen
LORD, Helen Cooper
LORENZ, Ellen Jane

LORIOD, Yvonne
LOTTI, Silvana di
LOUIE, Alexina Diane
LUCAS, Blanche
LUCKE, Katherine E.
LUTYENS, Sally
LYUBOMIRSKAYA-BOYARSKAYA,
    Revekka Grigorevna
MAAS, Marguerite Wilson
MACAULAY, Janice Michel
MACEDA, Corazon S.
MACKIE, Shirley M.
McCOLLIN, Frances
McINTOSH, Diana
McKAY, Frances Thompson
McLAUGHLIN, Marian
McLEMORE, Monita Prine
McMILLAN, Ann Endicott
McQUATTIE, Sheila
MAGEAU, Mary Jane
MAILIAN, Elza Antonovna
MALDYBAYEVA, Zhyldyz Abdylasovna
MANKIN, Linda
MANZIARLY, Marcelle de
MAREZ-OYENS, Tera de
MARSHALL, Pamela J.
MARTIN, Ravonna G.
MARTINEZ DE LA TORRE Y
    SHELTON, Emma
MARTINEZ, Odaline de la
MARY BERNICE, Sister
MARY ELAINE, Sister
MASON, Margaret C.
MASONER, Elizabeth L.
MASSUMOTO, Kikuko
MASTERS, Juan
MATEVOSIAN, Araks Surenovna
MAURICE, Paule
MAZOUROVA, Jarmila
MEARS, Caroline
MESNEY, Dorothy Taylor
METALLIDI, Zhanneta Lazarevna
MIAGI, Ester Kustovna
MICHELOW, Sybil
MIGRANYAN, Emma
MILAM, Lena Triplett
MILETTE, Juliette
MILLER, Elma
MIRON, Tsipora
MIRSHAKAR, Zarrina Mirsaidovna
MISHELL, Kathryn Lee
MITCHELL, Janice Misurell
MKRTYCHIEVA, Virginia Nikitichna
MOHNS, Grace Updegraff Bergen
MOLAVA, Pamela May
MONK, Meredith
MONTGOMERY, Merle
MOON, Chloe Elizabeth
MOORE, Mary Carr
MUELLER-HERMANN, Johanna
NARCISSE-MAIR, Denise Lorraine
NASH, Grace Helen
NEPGEN, Rosa Sophia Cornelia
NEUWIRTH, Goesta
NIAY, Apolline
NIGHTINGALE, Mae Wheeler
NIKOLAYEVA, Tatiana Petrovna
NIKOLSKAYA, Lyubov Borisovna
NIKOLSKAYA, Olga Vasilevna
NISHIKI, Kayoko
NIXON, June
NORBURY, Ethel F.
NOVOSELOVA, Ludmila Alexeyevna
ODAGESCU, Irina
O'LEARY, Jane Strong
OLIVEROS, Pauline
OLLER BENLLOCH, Maria Teresa
OLSON, Lynn Freeman
ORAM, Daphne Blake
OSTRANDER, Linda Woodaman
PABLOS CEREZO, Maria de

PALMER, Lynne Wainwright
PARKER, Alice
PARKER, Muriel
PATTERSON, Annie Wilson
PAUL, Doris A.
PAYNE, Harriet
PAYNE, Maggi
PENGILLY, Sylvia
PENTLAND, Barbara Lally
PEREIRA DA SILVA, Adelaide
PERRY, Julia Amanda
PERRY, Mary Dean
PERRY, Zenobia Powell
PETERSEN, Marian F.
PETERSON, Melody
PETRA-BASACOPOL, Carmen
PETROVA-KRUPKOVA, Elena
PEYROT, Fernande
PHILLIPS, Lois Elisabeth
PIERCE, Alexandra
PIETSCH, Edna Frieda
PIRES DOS REIS, Hilda
PLE-CAUSSADE, Simone
POINTON, Barbara
POLK, Grace Porterfield
POOL, Jeannie Gayle
POPOVICI, Elise
PRICE, Deon Nielsen
PRIESING, Dorothy Jean
PROCTOR, Alice McElroy
PTASZYNSKA, Marta
PUKUI, Mary Abigail
QUINTANILLA, Alba
RAIGORODSKY, Leda Natalia
    Heimsath
RALSTON, Frances Marion
RAMSEY, Sister Mary Anastasia
RICHER, Jeannine
RICHTER, Ada
RICHTER, Marion Morrey
RILEY, Myrtis F.
ROBITASHVILI, Lia Georgievna
RODRIGUEZ BELLA, Catalina
ROGATIS, Teresa de
ROGERS, Sarah Wren Love
RUDALL, Eleonor C.
RYBNER, Dagmar de Corval
RZAYEVA, Agabadzhi Ishmael kykz
SACCAGGIO, Adelina Luisa Nicasia
SAINT JOHN, Kathleen Louise
SALTER, Mary Elizabeth
SALVADOR, Matilde
SAMSON, Valerie Brooks
SAMUEL, Rhian
SAMVELIAN, Sofia Vardanovna
SANTOS-OCAMPO DE FRANCESCO,
    Amada Amy
SASSOLI, Ada
SAXTORPH, Gudrun
SCEK, Breda Friderika
SCHEIN, Suzanna Fedorovna
SCHERCHEN, Tona
SCHICK, Philippine
SCHLOSS, Myrna Frances
SCHMIDT-DUISBURG, Margarete
    Dina Alwina
SCHNEIDER, June
SCHWERDTFEGER, E. Anne
SCOTT, Molly
SEARS, Ilene Hanson
SEMEGEN, Daria
SHAVERZASHVILI, Tamara
    Antonovna
SHERMAN, Ingrid
SHIELDS, Alice Ferree
SIEGRIST, Beatrice
SILSBEE, Ann L.
SINGER, Jeanne
SMITH, Eleanor
SMITH, Joan Templar
SMITH, Ladonna Carol

SOENSTEVOLD, Maj
SOLOMON, Mirrie Irma
SOUBLETTE, Sylvia
SOULAGE, Marcelle Fanny Henriette
SOUTHAM, Ann
SPALDING, Eva Ruth
SPINDLE, Louise Cooper
SPIZIZEN, Louise Myers
STAIR, Patty
STANLEY, Helen Camille
STEVENS, Joan Frances
STEWART, Hascal Vaughan
STINSON, Ethelyn Lenore
STOCKER, Stella
STREICHER, Lyubov Lvovna
STREIT, Else
STRUTT, Dorothy
SUCHY, Gregoria Karides
SUH, Kyung-Sun
SUNBLAD-HALME, Heidi Gabriella
  Wilhelmina
SUSSMAN, Ettel
SUTHERLAND, Margaret
SUTZU, Rodica
SVANIDZE, Natela Damianovna
SWISHER, Gloria Agnes Wilson
SZOENYI, Erzsebet
TACK, Annie
TASHJIAN, B. Charmian
THOME, Diane
TICHARICH, Zdenka
TILICHEYEVA, Elena Nikolayevna
TOBIN, Candida
TOYAMA, Michiko Francoise
TUMANISHVILI, Ketevana Dmitirevna
TURNER, Myra Brooks
TURNER, Sara Scott
TURRIETTA, Cheryl Renee
TUTTLE, Thelma Kent
TYRMAND, Eta Moiseyevna
TYSON, Mildred Lund
URBAYI-KRASNODEBSKA, Zofia
  Jadwiga
URNER, Catherine Murphy
URRETA, Alicia
USHER, Julia
UYTTENHOVE, Yolande
VACCARO, Judith Lynne
VAKHVAKHISHVILI, Tamara
  Nikolayevna
VAN APPLEDORN, Mary Jeanne
VAN DE VATE, Nancy Hayes
VAN HAUTE, Anna-Maria
VAN KATWIJK, Viola Edna Beck
VANIER, Jeannine
VASILIEVA, Tatiana Ivanovna
VAZQUEZ, Alida
VEHAR, Persis Anne
VERHAALEN, Sister Marion
VILLARINI, Awilda
VIRTUE, Constance Cochnower
VITALIS, Sister Mary
VITO-DELVAUX, Berthe di
VIVADO ORSINI, Ida
VON GUNDEN, Heidi
VORLOVA, Slavka
VYNER, Mary Bainbridge
WAGENSONNER, Mimi
WALDO, Elisabeth
WEAVER, Carol Ann
WEAVER, Mary
WEIGL, Vally
WEIR, Judith
WELANDER, Svea Goeta
WENNERSTROM, Mary Hannah
WERNER, Tara Louise
WERTHEIM, Rosy
WEYBRIGHT, June
WHITE, Grace
WHITE, Ruth S.
WHITEHEAD, Gillian

WILBER, Clare Marie O'Keefe
WILES, Margaret Jones
WILKINS, Margaret Lucy
WILL, Madeleine
WILLIAMS, Irma
WILSON, Karen
WOLLNER, Gertrude Price
WOODS, Joan Shirley LeSueur
WYLIE, Ruth Shaw
YOUNG, Jane Corner
ZAIDEL-RUDOLPH, Jeanne
ZAIMONT, Judith Lang
ZARANEK, Stefania Anatolyevna
ZAVALISHINA, Maria Semyonovna
ZECHLIN, Ruth
ZHUBINSKAYA, Valentina Yanovna
ZHVANETSKAIA, Inna Abramovna
ZIELINSKA, Lidia
ZIMMERMAN, Agnes Marie Jacobina
ZIPRICK, Marjorie Jean
ZWILICH, Ellen Taaffe
Century unknown
BAKER, Joanne J.
PEYCKE, Frieda
SNODGRASS, Louise Harrison

MUSIC LIBRARIAN/ARCHIVIST
20th Century A.D.
ANDERSON, Pauline Barbour
DIMITRIU, Florica
FRASIER, Jane
FREED, Dorothy Whitson
HAGAN, Helen Eugenia
HIRSCH, Barbara
KAVASCH, Deborah Helene
LEE, Hope Anne Keng-Wei
LEIVISKA, Helvi Lemmiki
LYONS, Ruth
MILLER, Elma
ROKSETH, Yvonne
SHORE, Clare
ZAKRZEWSKA-NIKIPORCZYK,
  Barbara Maria

MUSIC THERAPIST
20th Century A.D.
BELINFANTE-DEKKER, Martha
  Suzanna Betje
BYERS, Roxana Weihe
FERREYRA, Beatriz
HUEBNER, Ilse
KABAT, Julie Phyllis
LATZ, Inge
LVOVA, Julia Fedorovna
PAULL, Barberi
SCHARLI, Ruth
SCHNEIDER, June
SKAGGS, Hazel Ghazarian
STINSON, Ethelyn Lenore
WEIGL, Vally
YOUNG, Jane Corner

MUSICOLOGIST
16th Century A.D.
DE CASTRO, Maria
19th Century A.D.
ADAJEWSKY, Ella
HILLEBRAND-LAUSSOT, Jessie
20th Century A.D.
ANDREYEVA, Elena Fedorovna
ANDRIEVSKAYA, Nina Konstantinovna
ARETZ, Isabel
BAIL, Grace Shattuck
BEARER, Elaine Louise
BECLARD D'HARCOURT, Marguerite
BENARY, Barbara
BORROFF, Edith
BOUQUET, Marie-Therese
BRAGA, Henriqueta Rosa Fernandes
BRENET, Therese
BRENNER, Rosamond Drooker

BROWN, Norma
BRYUSSOVA, Nadezhda Yakolevna
CAMEU, Helza
CECCONI-BATES, Augusta
CHEBOTARIAN, Gayane
  Movsesovna
DALE, Kathleen
DIANDA, Hilda
DOMMEL-DIENY, Amy
DORABIALSKA, Julia Helena
DUGGAN, Beatrice Abbott
EISENSTEIN DE VEGA, Silvia
ELST, Nancy van der
FRANGS, Irene
GARCIA MUNOZ, Carmen
GIDEON, Miriam
GLYN, Margaret Henriette
GRIMAUD, Yvette
HAIK-VANTOURA, Suzanne
HERNANDEZ-GONZALO, Gisela
HORSLEY, Imogene
HOUSMAN, Rosalie
HSU, Wen-Ying
INGLEFIELD, Ruth Karin
JACOB-LOEWENSOHN, Alice
KESHNER, Joyce Grove
KINSCELLA, Hazel Gertrude
KISCH, Eve
KLIMISCH, Sister Mary Jane
KUBO, Mayako
LACHARTRE, Nicole Marie
LANDOWSKA, Wanda
LE BORDAYS, Christiane
LIMA CRUZ, Maria Antonietta de
LITTLEJOHN, Joan Anne
LOVELACE, Carey
LUND, Gudrun
McALLISTER, Rita
MARI, Pierrette
MARY ELAINE, Sister
MOSUSOVA, Nadezda
NEWLIN, Dika
NOVOSELOVA, Ludmila Alexeyevna
OLIVEIRA, Sophie Marcondes de
  Mello
OWEN, Angela Maria
PIZER, Elizabeth Faw Hayden
POLIN, Claire
POOL, Jeannie Gayle
PSTROKONSKA-NAVRATIL,
  Grazyna Hanna
PUKUI, Mary Abigail
REIS, Manuela Cancio
ROKSETH, Yvonne
SAINT JOHN, Kathleen Louise
SCRIABINE, Marina
SEAY, Virginia
SELDEN-GOTH, Gizella
SNIZKOVA-SKRHOVA, Jitka
SOMMERS, Daria E.
SPENCER, Williametta
TERZIAN, Alicia
WALDO, Elisabeth
WOOD, Ruzena Alenka Valda
ZIFFRIN, Marilyn Jane

PLAYWRIGHT
19th Century A.D.
PUSICH, D. Antonia Gertrudes
20th Century A.D.
BURSTON, Maggie
CHAVES, Laura da Fonseca
FORMAN, Joanne
HUTTON, Florence Myra
KUMMER, Clare
MAXIM, Florence
OWENS, Rochelle
PEACOCK, Mary O'Kelley
STURE VASA, Mary O'Hara
TURNER, Myra Brooks
TWOMBLY, Mary Lynn

CHRETIEN-GENARO, Hedwige
CIOBANU, Maia
CLARKE, Rosemary
COHEN, Harriet
CRAIB, Doris
DAIGLE, Sister Anne Cecile
DE FREITAS, Elvira Manuela
    Fernandez
DEBRASSINE-PRIJAT, Laure
DIANDA, Hilda
DIEMER, Emma Lou
DIMITRIU, Florica
DIRKS, Jewel Dawn
DOMMEL-DIENY, Amy
DORABIALSKA, Julia Helena
DROBYAZGINA, Valentina Ivanovna
DUDLEY, Marjorie Eastwood
DZIEWULSKA, Maria Amelia
ECKHARDT-GRAMATTE, Sophie-
    Carmen
ELMORE, Cenieth Catherine
ELST, Nancy van der
EMINGEROVA, Katerina
ESCOT, Pozzi
EVERETT-SALICCO, Betty Lou
FALLADOVA-SKVOROVA, Anezka
FELDMAN, Joann Esther
FISCHER, Edith Steinkraus
FISHER, Gladys Washburn
FITZGERALD, Sister Florence
    Therese
FOLVILLE, Eugenie-Emilie Juliette
FONDER, Sister Mary Teresine
FONTYN, Jacqueline
FRANCK, Philippine
FROMM-MICHAELS, Ilse
FUCHS, Lillian
GARTENLAUB, Odette
GEBUHR, Ann K.
GENTEMANN, Sister Mary Elaine
GHIGLIERI, Sylvia
GIDEON, Miriam
GILBERT, Janet Monteith
GILBERT, Pia
GNESINA, Yelena Fabianovna
GOODSMITH, Ruth B.
GRAU, Irene Rosenberg
GRIGSBY, Beverly
GUERRANT, Mary Thorington
GUNDERSON, Helen Louise
GURAIEB KURI, Rosa
HABAN, Sister Teresine M.
HAMPE, Charlotte
HARA, Kazuko
HEINRICH, Adel Verna
HEMON, Sedje
HERRERA Y OGAZON, Alba
HERTEL, Sister Romana
HOKANSON, Margrethe
HONG, Sung-Hee
HOWELL, Dorothy
HSU, Wen-Ying
HYTREK, Sister Theophane
INGLEFIELD, Ruth Karin
JAMBOR, Agi
JAMES, Dorothy E.
JOCHSBERGER, Tzipora H.
JOULAIN, Jeanne-Angele-Desiree-
    Yvonne
KEETMAN, Gunild
KERN, Frida
KETTERING, Eunice Lea
KINSCELLA, Hazel Gertrude
KLECHNIOWSKA, Anna Maria
KLIMISCH, Sister Mary Jane
KLOTZMAN, Dorothy Ann Hill
KOELLING, Eloise
KOLB, Barbara
KRAUSZ, Susan
LANG-BECK, Ivana
LAST, Joan Mary

LAUMYANSKENE, Elena Iono
LEBIZAY, Marguerite
LEE, Chan-Hae
LEITE, Clarisse
LEJET, Edith
LEJEUNE-BONNIER, Eliane
LUDVIG-PECAR, Nada
LUMBY, Betty Louise
LUNA DE ESPAILLAT, Margarita
McILWRAITH, Isa Roberta
McKINNEY, Mathilde
McLAIN, Margaret Starr
McLEOD, Jennifer Helen
McNEIL, Janet L. Pfischner
McPHERSON, Frances Marie
McSWAIN, Augusta Geraldine
MAITLAND, Anna Harriet
MAMLOK, Ursula
MARBE, Myriam
MARCUS, Bunita
MARIC, Ljubica
MARKIEWICZOWNA, Wladyslawa
MARSHALL, Jane Manton
MARTINS, Maria de Lourdes
MAYER, Lise Maria
MEACHEM, Margaret McKeen
    Ramsey
MEKEEL, Joyce
MELOY, Elizabeth
MERRIMAN, Margarita Leonor
MOORE, Undine Smith
MOOREHEAD, Consuela Lee
MOSUSOVA, Nadezda
MOSZUMANSKA-NAZAR, Krystyna
MUNGER, Shirley
MUSGRAVE, Thea
NARCISSE-MAIR, Denise Lorraine
NAZIROVA, Elmira Mirza Rza kyzy
NEWLIN, Dika
NICKERSON, Camille Lucie
NIEMACK, Ilza Louise
NIKOLAYEVA, Tatiana Petrovna
OCHSE, Orpha Caroline
OLIVEIRA, Jocy de
OLIVEIRA, Sophie Marcondes de
    Mello
OLIVEROS, Pauline
OSTRANDER, Linda Woodaman
OTTAWOWA, Helena
OWEN, Blythe
PANETTI, Joan
PARR, Patricia
PATTERSON, Annie Wilson
PAVIA DE MAGALHAES, Isaura
PERRY, Mary Dean
PETERSEN, Marian F.
PHILIBA, Nicole
PHILLIPS, Lois Elisabeth
PIERCE, Alexandra
PIERROT, Noelie Marie Antoinette
PIKE, Eleanor B. Franklin
PIRES DOS REIS, Hilda
PRESTI, Ida
PRIESING, Dorothy Jean
QUEEN, Virginia
RADERMACHER, Erika
RAINIER, Priaulx
RAN, Shulamit
RANTA-SHIDA, Shoko
REID, Sarah Johnston
RILEY, Ann Marion
RIVERA, Graciela
ROBERTSON, Donna Lou Nagey
ROBLES, Marisa
ROGET, Henriette
SAARINEN, Gloria Edith
SALSBURY, Janet Mary
SANCIN, Mirca
SANDRESKY, Margaret Vardell
SANTIAGO-FELIPE, Vilma R.
SCHLEDER, Grizelda Lazzaro

SCHMITZ-GOHR, Else
SCHUSTER, Doris Dodd
SELVA, Blanche
SEMEGEN, Daria
SEVERY, Violet Cavell
SHAFFER, Jeanne Ellison
SIDORENKO, Tamara Stepanovna
SILVERMAN, Faye-Ellen
SIMPSON, Mary Jean
SISTEK-DJORDJEVIC, Mirjana
SLENCZYNSKA, Ruth
SNIZKOVA-SKRHOVA, Jitka
SNOW, Mary McCarty
SODRE, Joanidia
SOLOMON, Mirrie Irma
SONNTAG, Brunhilde
SPENCER, Williametta
STANEKAITE-LAUMYANSKENE,
    Elena Ionovna
STEINER, Gitta Hana
SUCHY, Gregoria Karides
SUTZU, Rodica
SWAIN, Freda Mary
TAILLEFERRE, Germaine
TALMA, Louise
TANN, Hilary
THOMAS, Marilyn Taft
THOME, Diane
THOMPSON, Ellen
TRIMBLE, Joan
ULEHLA, Ludmila
VAN APPLEDORN, Mary Jeanne
VAN DE VATE, Nancy Hayes
VAN DEN BOORN-COCLET,
    Henriette
VERHAALEN, Sister Marion
VIGNERON-RAMAKERS, Christiane-
    Josee
VILLA-LOBOS, Arminda Neves de
    Almeida
VON ZIERITZ, Grete
WALKER, Gwyneth van Anden
WARNE, Katharine Mulky
WARWICK, Mary Carol
WENNERSTROM, Mary Hannah
WICKS, Camilla
WILKINSON, Constance Jane
WILLIAMS, Sioned
WINTER, Sister Miriam Therese
WOLL, Erna
WOODRUFF, Edith S.
WUNSCH, Ilse Gerda
WYLIE, Ruth Shaw
YI, Heung-Yull
YOUNG, Fredricka Agnes
ZAIMONT, Judith Lang
ZALLMAN, Arlene
ZECHLIN, Ruth
ZIFFRIN, Marilyn Jane
ZIVKOVIC, Mirjana

PUBLISHER/EDITOR
19th Century A.D.
    CLARKE, Helen Archibald
    CORMONTAN, Theodora
    HAASS, Maria Catharina
    HAWES, Charlotte W.
    PUSICH, D. Antonia Gertrudes
    RADNOR, Helen, Countess of
20th Century A.D.
    ANDREYEVA, Elena Fedorovna
    ANDRIEVSKAYA, Nina
        Konstantinovna
    AUSTER, Lydia Martinovna
    BARBER, Gail Guseman
    BARKIN, Elaine
    BAUER, Emilie Frances
    BAUER, Marion Eugenie
    BLISS, Marilyn S.
    BOONE, Clara Lyle
    BOYD, Anne Elizabeth

BRITAIN, Radie
BROADWOOD, Lucy E.
BRYUSSOVA, Nadezhda Yakolevna
BUTT, Thelma
CHAVES, Laura da Fonseca
CLARKE, Urana
COLE, Ulric
CORY, Eleanor
DANEAU, Suzanne
DASCALESCU, Camelia
DAVIS, Hazel E.
DOANE, Dorothy
DRYNAN, Margaret
DZHAFAROVA, Afag Mamed kyzy
FAHRER, Alison Clark
FAUTCH, Sister Magdalen
FISHER, Charlotte Eleanor
HELSINGIUS, Barbara
HILL, May
IBRAGIMOVA, Ela Imamedinovna
JOHN, Patricia Spaulding
JOLAS, Betsy
KOBLENZ, Babette
KORNILOVA, Tatiana Dmitrevna
LACHOWSKA, Stefania
LEVITOVA, Ludmila Vladimirovna
LEVITSKAYA, Viktoria Sergeyevna
LITTLEJOHN, Joan Anne
LORENZ, Ellen Jane
LU, Yen
LUTYENS, Elisabeth
MANUKIAN, Irina Eduardovna
MARBE, Myriam
MAXWELL, Helen Purcell
MINEO, Antoinette
NAKASHIMA, Jeanne Marie
OBROVSKA, Jana
ODAGESCU, Irina
ORE, Cecilie
PILIS, Heda
PITCHER, Gladys
PREDIC-SAPER, Branislava
PREOBRAJENSKA, Vera Nicolaevna
RAMM, Valentina Iosifovna
RICHARDS, Christine-Louise
RICHMOND, Virginia
ROBERTSON, Donna Lou Nagey
ROKSETH, Yvonne
SACHS, Carolyn
SANDELS, Ellen
SANDIFUR, Ann Elizabeth
SCHUSSLER-BREWAEYS, Marie
  Antoinette
SILVERMAN, Faye-Ellen
SKALSKA-SZEMIOTH, Hanna Wanda
SKOUEN, Synne
SMITH, Ruby Mae
SOLOMON, Elide M.
TANN, Hilary
TAPPER, Bertha
VERHAALEN, Sister Marion
VIRTUE, Constance Cochnower
WALLACE, Mildred White
WALLNEROVA, Bibiana
WEISSBERG, Julia Lazerevna
WILLIAMS, Frances
WOOLSLEY, Mary Hale
ZIMMER, Nellie

RADIO/TV
20th Century A.D.
AUSTER, Lydia Martinovna
BABAYEVA, Seda Grigorievna
BARCROFT, E. Dorothea
BARRAINE, Elsa
BAYEVA, Vera
BEECROFT, Norma Marian
BROUK, Joanna
CABREIRA, Estefania Loureiro de
  Vasconcelos Leao
CASTELLANOS, Tania

DANIELSON, Janet Rosalie
FRAJT, Ludmila
FRANGS, Irene
GIURANNA, Elena Barbara
GOETSCHIUS, Marjorie
HERNANDEZ-GONZALO, Gisela
IBRAGIMOVA, Ela Imamedinovna
JIRACKOVA, Marta
KRASNOGLIADOVA, Vera
  Vladimirovna
LEON, Tania Justina
LUSTIG, Leila Sarah
LYONS, Ruth
MATTHEWS, Dorothy White
MORETTO, Nelly
ORTMANS, Kay Muriel
PADE, Else Marie
PATERSON, Wilma
POOL, Jeannie Gayle
PSTROKONSKA-NAVRATIL,
  Grazyna Hanna
RAIGORODSKY, Leda Natalia
  Heimsath
RITTENHOUSE, Elizabeth Mae
SANDIFUR, Ann Elizabeth
SANZ, Rocio
SCHIEVE, Catherine
SCHWARTZ, Nan Louise
SERRANO REDONNET, Ana
SIMIC, Darinka
SIMONS, Netty
UPTON, Anne
VERCOE, Elizabeth
WALLNEROVA, Bibiana
WARD, Diane

ROYALTY
16th Century B.C.
HATSHEPSUT, Queen
15th Century B.C.
AHMES-NEFRETERE, Queen
6th Century A.D.
GUINEVERE, Queen
11th Century A.D.
MARGARET, Queen of Scotland
12th Century A.D.
ELEANOR OF AQUITAINE
13th Century A.D.
KUNEGUNDE, Queen
16th Century A.D.
BOLEYN, Anne, Queen of England
ELIZABETH I, Queen of England
MARGARET OF AUSTRIA
MARY STUART, Queen of Scots
MIRA BAI
MRIGANAYANA, Queen
17th Century A.D.
CONSTANCE OF AUSTRIA, Queen of
  Poland
18th Century A.D.
ANNA AMALIA, Princess of Prussia
CZARTORYSKA, Izabela de,
  Princess
DASHKOVA, Ekaterina Romanovna,
  Princess
MARIA ANTONIA WALPURGIS,
  Princess of Bavaria
MARIA CHARLOTTE AMALIE,
  Princess of Saxe-Meiningen
MARIA TERESA BARBARA DE
  BRAGANCA, Queen of Spain
MARIE ANTOINETTE, Archduchess
  of Austria, Queen of France
MARIE THERESE LOUISE OF
  SAVOY-CARIGNANO, Princess of
  Lamballe
ZAMOYSKA, Zofia, Princess
19th Century A.D.
AUGUSTA MARIA LOUISE, Queen of
  Prussia
AUGUSTENBURG, Caroline Amelia of

BRANCOVAN, Princess of
CAETANI-RZEWUSKA, Calista,
  Princess
CHARLOTTE, Friederike Wilhelmine
  Louise, Princess
CZETWERTYNSKA, Marie, Princess
CZETWERTYNSKA-JELOWICKA,
  Janina, Princess
EUGENIE, Charlotte Augusta Amalia
  Albertina, Princess
HORTENSE, Queen of Holland
JOSEPHINE, Queen of Sweden and
  Norway
LIKELIKE, Miriam Cleghorn,
  Princess
LILIUOKALANI, Queen of Hawaii
MARIE ELIZABETH, Princess of
  Saxe-Meiningen
SALM-DYCK, Constance-Marie de
  Theis, Princess
THERESE, Princess of Saxe-
  Altenburg and of Sweden
VICTORIA MARIA LOUISA, Duchess
  of Kent
VOLKONSKAYA, Zinanda
  Alexandrovna, Princess
WALDBURG-WURZACH, Julie von,
  Princess
WUERTEMBERSKA-
  CZARTORYSKA, Maria, Duchess
20th Century A.D.
BEATRICE, Mary Victoria Feodore,
  Princess of Battenberg
CHARLOTTE, Princess of Saxe-
  Meiningen
MAGOGO KA DINIZULU, Constance,
  Princess
VIGGO, Eleanor Margaret Green,
  Princess
Century unknown
CAI, Wen Ji, Princess
DE, Li, Princess
WONG, Zhao, Princess

SINGER
2nd Century A.D.
TS'AI, YEN
12th Century A.D.
TIBORS
13th Century A.D.
BIEIRIS DE ROMANS
BLANCHE DE CASTILLE
MECHTHILD
PEREZ, Maria
14th Century A.D.
BIENVEIGNANT, Liegart
15th Century A.D.
PEPARARA, Laura
16th Century A.D.
ARCHILEI, Vittoria
BELLINA, Madonna
BOLEYN, Anne, Queen of England
CASULANA, Maddalena
GINES, Teodora
MOLZA, Tarquinia
SESSA, Claudia
17th Century A.D.
BEMBO, Antonia
CACCINI, Francesca
CACCINI-GHIVIZZANI, Settimia
CALEGARI, Cornelia
CHURAI, Marusya
COZZOLANI, Chiara Margarita
ESCAMILLA, Manuela de
QUINZANA, Sister Rosalba
STROZZI, Barbara
TIRS, Katharina
VIZANA, Lucretia Orsina
18th Century A.D.
AUBIGNY VON ENGELBRUNNER,
  Nina d'

AUENBRUGG, Marianna von
BACHMANN, Charlotte Caroline
   Wilhelmine
BARTHELEMON, Cecilia Maria
BARTHELEMON, Mary
BEAUMESNIL, Henrietta Adelaide
   Villard de
BRANDES, Charlotte Wilhelmina
   Franziska
CAMATI, Maria
CANTELO, Anne
CASSON, Margaret
COURMONT, Countess von
CROUCH, Anna Maria
CUZZONI, Francesca
DALL, Miss
DANZI, Maria Margarethe
DE GAMBARINI, Elisabetta
DUVAL, Louise
EICHNER, Adelheid Marie
JORDAN, Mrs.
KALFA, Dilhayat
LEBRUN, Franziska Dorothea
LOUIS, Mme.
MARIA ANTONIA WALPURGIS,
   Princess of Bavaria
MARTINEZ, Marianne
MUELLNER, Johanna
OLIN, Elizabeth
POOLE, Maria
POWNALL, Mary Ann
QUINAULT, Marie Anne
REICHARDT, Bernhardine Juliane
SCHROETER, Corona Elisabeth
   Wilhelmine
SIRMEN, Maddalena Laura di
TIBALDI, Rosa
ZAMOYSKA, Zofia, Princess

19th Century A.D.
ABRAMS, Harriet
ALEXANDROVA, A.
AMALIE, Marie Friederike Augusta,
   Princess of Saxony
ARNIM, Bettina von
ASPRI, Orsola
AUENHEIM, Marianna
BAWR, Alexandrine Sophie
BERTIN, Louise Angelique
BERTINOTTI, Teresa
BLAND, Maria Theresa
BOCHKOLTZ-FALCONI, Anna
BOCK, Bertha
BOERNER-SANDRINI, Marie
BRADSHAW, Nellie Shorthill
BRAMBILLA, Marietta
BRANCHU, Mme.
BRDLIKOVA, Josefina
BUERDE, Jeanette Antonie
CANDEILLE, Amelie Julie
CAPPIANI, Luisa
CASELLA, Felicita
CATALANI, Angelica
COLE, Charlotte
COLLINS, Laura Sedgwick
COLTELLANI, Celeste
CORRI-DUSSEK, Sofia Giustina
CZETWERTYNSKA-JELOWICKA,
   Janina, Princess
DAHL, Emma
DAMOREAU-CINTI, Laure
DE SOUSA HOLSTEIN, Donna Teresa
DECKER, Pauline
DESHAYES, Marie
DEVISME, Jeanne-Hippolite Moyroud
DIBDIN, Isabelle Perkins
DRIEBURG, Louise von
DUCHAMP, Marie Catharine
DUSCHEK, Josefina
EDELSBERG, Philippine von
ESCHBORN, Georgine Christine
   Maria Anna

FERRARI, Carlotta
FLOWER, Eliza
FOWLES, Margaret F.
GAIL, Edmee-Sophie
GARCIA, Eduarda Mansilla de
GIACOMELLI, Genevieve-Sophie Bille
GIBSON, Isabella Mary
GOETZE, Auguste
GORONCY, Emilie
GRODZICKA-RZEWUSKA, Julia
GROOM, Mrs.
GYLLENHAAL, Matilda Valeriana
   Beatrix, Duchess of Orozco
HAAPASALO, Kreeta
HAWES, Maria
HEINEMANN, Jenny
HERITTE-VIARDOT, Louise Pauline
   Marie
HEUBERGER, Jenny
HOLMBERG, Emelie Augusta Kristina
HUENERWADEL, Fanny
INVERARITY, Eliza
JESKE-CHOINSKA-MIKORSKA,
   Ludmila
JOACHIM, Amalie
KEMBLE, Adelaide
KENDIKOVA, Zdenka
KLAGE, Marie
KOCHANOWSKA, Franciszka
KOCHETOVA, Aleksandra
   Dorimedontovna
LA HYE, Louise Genevieve
LANG, Josephine
LANUZA Y VAZQUEZ, Agustina
LEHMANN, Amelia
LEONARD, Antonia Sitcher de Mendi
LIND, Jenny
LOEWE, Auguste
MacKINLEY, Mrs. J.
MALIBRAN, Maria Felicitas
MANNKOPF, Adolphine
MARCHESI, Mathilde de Castrone
MARCHISIO, Barbara
MARRA, Adelina
MASSON, Elizabeth
MATTHYSSENS, Marie
METZGER-VESPERMANN, Clara
MULLEN, Adelaide
NEWCOMBE, Georgeanne
NEWTON, Adelaide
NORTON, Caroline Elizabeth Sarah
O'LEARY, Rosetta
PARADIS, Maria Theresia von
PARIS, Salomea
PARKE, Maria Hester
PATON, Mary Anne
PATTI, Adelina
PELLEGRINI CELONI, Anna
PENNA, Catherine
PERALTA CASTERA, Angela
PESCHKA, Minna
PHILP, Elizabeth
POLKO, Elise Vogel
POSADA Y TORRE, Ana
PUGET, Loise
RADNOR, Helen, Countess of
REICHARDT, Louise
RICHINGS, Caroline
SAINTON-DOLBY, Charlotte Helen
SANTA-COLONA-SOURGET, Eugenie
SCHATZELL, Pauline von
SCHIMON, Anna
SCHNORR VON CAROLSFELD, Malvina
SCHUBERT, Georgine
SESSI, Marianne
SHERRINGTON, Grace
SHERRINGTON, Helena Lemmens
SKINNER, Fannie Lovering
SMITH, Mrs. Gerrit
STENHAMMAR, Fredrika
STOLTZ, Rosina

STRANTZ, Louise von
SYNGE, Mary Helena
THERESA
TROWBRIDGE, Leslie Eliot
UGALDE, Delphine Beauce
UNGHER-SABATIER, Caroline
VELA DE ARNAO, Sofia
VELTHEIM, Charlotte
VIARDOT-GARCIA, Pauline Michelle
   Ferdinande
VOLKONSKAYA, Zinanda
   Alexandrovna
WAKEFIELD, Augusta Mary
WARD, Clementine
WEST, Lottie
WESTENHOLZ, Eleonore Sophie
   Marie
WICHERN, Caroline
WILSON, Hilda
WOLFF-FRITZ, Sophie
ZAMOYSKA, Maria
ZANTEN, Cornelia van
ZAPATER, Rosaria
ZEGERS, Isidora
ZUMSTEEG, Emilie

20th Century A.D.
A'DAIR, Jeanne
AGUIRRE, Diana V.
AKERS, Doris Mae
ALLEN, Denise
ALLITSEN, Frances
ALVARES-RIOS, Maria
ANNAPURNA, Devi
AOKE, Haruna
ARAUJO, Gina de
ASHFORD, Emma Louise
ASHMORE, Grace Flournoy
ATRE, Prabha
BABITS, Linda
BAHMANN, Marianne Eloise
BAILY, Margaret Naismith Osborne
BALENOVIC, Draga
BANKOVA-MARINOVA, Angelina
BARBI, Alice
BARBLAN-OPIENSKA, Lydia
BARDEL, Germaine
BARRIENTOS, Maria
BASSETT, Karolyn Wells
BELINFANTE-DEKKER, Martha
   Suzanna Betje
BELL, Carla Huston
BENARY, Barbara
BERAN-STARK, Lola Aloisia Maria
BERBERIAN, Cathy
BESSEM, Saar
BIALKIEWICZOWNA-ANDRAULT DE
   LANGERON, Irena
BILLINGTON, Elizabeth
BIZONY, Celia
BLISS, Marilyn S.
BLOCH, Suzanne
BOEHN, Liselotte
BOESGAARDOVA-SCHMIDTOVA,
   Lydie
BOND, Carrie Jacobs
BROADWOOD, Lucy E.
BROCK, Blanche Kerr
BUCKLEY, Beatrice Barron
BUCKLEY, Helen Dallam
BUMP, Mary Crane
CAPSIR-TANZI, Mercedes
CAREY, Elena
CARMEN MARINA
CARRENO, Teresa
CARSON, Zeula Miller
CASAGEMAS, Luisa
CHEATHAM, Kitty
CHUDOBA, Blanka
CLEVE, Cissi
CLINGAN, Judith Ann
COATES, Gloria Kannenberg

COLBRAN, Isabella Angela
CORRI, Ghita
COWL, Doreen
CRAWFORD, Dorothy Lamb
CREWS, Lucille
CRISWICK, Mary
CROFTS, Inez Altman
DAILLY, Claudine
DALBERT, Anny
DANIELS, Mabel Wheeler
DASCALESCU, Camelia
DAVIS, Eva May
DAVIS, Genevieve
DE LEATH, Vaughn
DE VILLIERS, Justina Wilhelmina
    Nancy
DEL RIEGO, Theresa
DERHEIMER, Cecile
DOROW, Dorothy
DRETKE, Leora N.
DRING, Madeleine
DRYNAN, Margaret
EDGERLY, Cora Emily
EDWARDS, Clara
EVANTI, Lillian
FELLOWS, Mrs. Wayne Stanley
FERNANDEZ, Terresita
FINLEY, Lorraine Noel
FISCHER, Edith Steinkraus
FISHER, Charlotte Eleanor
FISHER, Doris
FLACH, Elsa
FORD, Olive Elizabeth
FORSYTH, Josephine
FOSIC, Tarzicija
FOSTER, Dorothy Godwin
FRANCHERE-DESROSIERS, Rose de
    Lima
FRANGS, Irene
FREEHOFF, Ruth Williams
FREER, Eleanor Warner Everest
GALLI-CAMPI
GERRISH-JONES, Abbie
GLASER, Victoria Merrylees
GOETSCHIUS, Marjorie
GOLSON-BATEMAN, Florence
GOODMAN, Lillian Rosedale
GREEN, Mary Thompson
GRIEBLING, Karen Jean
GUDAUSKAS, Giedra
HACKLEY, Emma Azalia Smith
HARA, Kazuko (1)
HARLEY, Frances Marjorie
HARRIS, Ethel Ramos
HARVEY, Eva Noel
HAYS, Doris Ernestine
HEIBERG, Ella
HELLER, Ruth
HELSINGIUS, Barbara
HERMANN, Miina
HEYNSSEN, Adda
HILL, May
HOLCK, Sine
HOPPE, Clara
HOUSE, L. Marguerite
HULFORD, Denise Lovona
HUTTON, Florence Myra
HYLIN, Birgitta Charlotta Kristina
INJADO
JESI, Ada
JOLAS, Betsy
JONES, Marjorie
KABAT, Julie Phyllis
KAHMANN, Chesley
KALLOCH, Doley C.
KALTENECKER, Gertraud
KANAKA'OLE, Edith Ke-Kuhikuhi-I-
    Pu'u-one-o-Na-Ali'i-O-Kohala
KAVASCH, Deborah Helene
KAZANDJIAN, Sirvart
KEEFER, Euphrosyne

KELLY, Denise Maria Anne
KENNEDY-FRASER, Marjory
KIP, Yuksel
KLEIN, Ivy Frances
KOPPEL-HOLBE, Maria
KOSHETZ, Nina
KOSTAKOVA-HERODKOVA, Marie
KOVALEVA, Olga Vasilevna
KRALIKOVA, Johana
KUFFLER, Eugenie
LA BARBARA, Joan
LAGO
LAJEUNESSE, Emma, Dame
LAMBELET, Vivienne Ada Maurice
LAZAR, Ella
LE BEAU, Louisa Adolpha
LEANDRE, Joelle
LEHMAN, Evangeline Marie
LEHMANN, Liza
LIDGI-HERMAN, Sofia
LIEBLING, Estelle
LIEBMANN, Nanna Magdalene
LINNET, Anne
LITSITE, Paula Yanovna
LLUNELL SANAHUJA, Pepita
LOPEZ Y PENA, Maria del Carmen
LORE, Emma Maria Theresa
LORING, Nancy
LOUVIER, Nicole
LUPTON, Belle George
LYONN LIEBERMAN, Julie
McLAUGHLIN, Marian
McQUATTIE, Sheila
MACHADO, Lena
MAGOGO KA DINIZULU, Constance,
    Princess
MANA-ZUCCA
MANNING, Kathleen Lockhart
MARQUES, Fernandina Lagos
MARQUES, Laura Wake
MATVEYEVA, Novella
MEAD, Catherine Pannill
MEIGS, Melinda Moore
MENDELSSOHN, Erna
MENDELSSOHN, Luise
MESNEY, Dorothy Taylor
MICHELOW, Sybil
MOE, Benna
MONK, Meredith
MOORE, Dorothy Rudd
MOORE, Mary Carr
MORTIFEE, Ann
MRACEK, Ann Michelle
MUG, Sister Mary Theodosia
MUNDINGER, Adele Franziska
NAKASHIMA, Jeanne Marie
NAMAKELUA, Alice K.
NATVIG, Candace
NAUMANN, Ida
NEILY, Anne MacAdams
NICKERSON, Camille Lucie
NILSSON, Christine
NOETHLING, Elisabeth
NORDRAAK-FEYLING, Gudrun
NOVELLO-DAVIES, Clara
ODDONE SULLI-RAO, Elisabetta
OLIVER, Madra Emogene
OWEN, Morfydd Llwyn
OWENS, Susan Elizabeth
ODENSES, Semahat
PAGOTO, Helen
PARS, Melahat
PENNER, Jean Priscilla
PHARRIS, Elizabeth
PHILLIPS, Bryony
PHILLIPS, Donna
PILIS, Heda
POLK, Grace Porterfield
POLONIO, Cinira
PONCE, Ethel
POOLE, Anna Ware

PUKUI, Mary Abigail
RADERMACHER, Erika
RAKHMANKULOVA, Mariam
    Mannanovna
RAMM, Valentina Iosifovna
REED, Phyllis Luidens
RENNES, Catharina van
RESPIGHI, Elsa
RIVERA, Graciela
ROBBOY, Rosalie Smotkin
ROE, Eileen Betty
ROE, Marion Adelle
ROGERS, Clara Kathleen
ROMA, Caro
RUDOLPH, Anna
RUSSELL, Anna
SADERO GENI, Maria Scarpa
SAKALLI-LECCA, Alexandra
SALTER, Mary Elizabeth
SAMSUTDINOVA, Magira
SANDERS, Alma M.
SAUNDERS, Carrie Lou
SAXTORPH, Gudrun
SCEK, Breda Friderika
SCHEEPERS-VAN DOMMELEN,
    Maria
SCHUMANN, Meta
SCHUSSLER-BREWAEYS, Marie
    Antoinette
SCHWARTZ, Nan Louise
SCOTT, Molly
SELMER, Kathryn Lande
SHAFFER, Jeanne Ellison
SHIELDS, Alice Ferree
SHORE, Clare
SILBERTA, Rhea
SINDE RAMALLAL, Clara
SMITH, Eleanor
SNYDER, Amy
SOUBLETTE, Sylvia
SPECHT, Anita Socola
SPEKTOR, Mira J.
SPIZIZEN, Louise Myers
SPOERRI-RENFER, Anna-
    Margaretha
SPONGBERG, Viola
STANLEY, Marion Isabel
STEPHEN, Roberta Mae
STOBEAUS, Kristina xxx
STRICKLAND, Lily Teresa
SUBBALAKSHMI, M.S.
SWADOS, Elizabeth
TACK, Annie
TELFER, Nancy Ellen
THOMAS, Helen
THOMAS, Muriel Leonora Duncan
TODD, Alice Weston
TREADWAY, Maude Valerie
TURNER, Mildred Cozzens
TURNER, Olive Mary
TURNER-MALEY, Florence
UCHENDU, Nellie Uzonna Edith
URNER, Catherine Murphy
VAN ETTEN, Jane
VIENNE, Marie-Louise de
VITALI-AUGUSTI, Giuseppina
VITALIS, Sister Mary
VLADERACKEN, Geertruida van
VOIGT, Henriette
VORLOVA, Slavka
WALLACE, Mildred White
WALLACE, Phyllis Joy
WALLACH, Joelle
WALSH, Elizabeth Jameson
WARD, Diane
WARREN, Betsy
WEBB, Allienne Brandon
WELDON, Georgina
WICKHAM, Florence Pauline
WILEY, Dora
YAMPOLSCHI, Roseane

Century unknown
ELENA
GALLI, Signora
RENNUTET
TAJANI MATTONE, Ida

SONGSTRESS (before 10th-century A.D.)
25th Century B.C.
ITI
16th Century B.C.
BAKIT
HATSHEPSUT, Queen
15th Century B.C.
AHMES-NEFRETERE, Queen
MERIT
13th Century B.C.
MIRIAM
TUY
12th Century B.C.
DEBORAH
10th Century B.C.
HENUTTAUI
MUTYUNET
9th Century B.C.
MILH AL-ATTARA
TENTIOH
8th Century B.C.
MERESAMENT
TENTNAU
7th Century B.C.
'ANKH-AMENARDAIS
'ANKH-SHEPENWEPT
MEGALOSTRATA OF SPARTA
RAYYA AL-ZARQA
6th Century B.C.
DE-ESIHEBSED
NEIT
SAPPHO
TELESILLA OF ARGOS
3rd Century A.D.
AFARIN
SIRIN
4th Century A.D.
MACRINA, Saint
5th Century A.D.
AZADE
6th Century A.D.
HIND BINT'UTBA
HURAIRA
KHULAIDA II
7th Century A.D.
AZZA AL-MAILA
MAYSUNAH
QU'AD
SALLAMA AL-ZARQA
THAMAD
8th Century A.D.
ALYA
BASBAS
HABBABA
INAN
JAMILA
KHULAIDA I
MAKNUNA
MUTAYYAM AL-HASHIMIYYA
SALLAMA AL-QASS
SHARIYYA
ULAYYA
9th Century A.D.
BADHL
BANAN
BID'A
DANANIR AL BARMAKIYYA
FADL(1)
FADL(2)
FARIDA
HSUEH, T'ao
IRFAN
MAHBUBA
NASIB AL-MUTAWAKKILIYA
ORAIB

QALAM
QALAM AL-SALAHIYYA
QAMAR
RAIQ
UBAIDA
Century unknown
TAUHERT

TEACHER
6th Century B.C.
SAPPHO
4th Century A.D.
MACRINA, Saint
8th Century A.D.
JAMILA
12th Century A.D.
SPONHEIM, Sister Jutta von
17th Century A.D.
BARONI BASILE, Adriana
18th Century A.D.
BERTHE, Mme.
GUEST, Jeanne Marie
LOUIS, Mme.
MARTINEZ, Marianne
MUELLNER, Johanna
SCHROETER, Corona Elisabeth
Wilhelmine
ZAMPIERI, Elizabetta
19th Century A.D.
ANDREWS, Jenny
ASACHI, Elena
ASTLE-ALLAM, Agnes Mary
AUENHEIM, Marianna
BACKER-GROENDAHL, Agathe
Ursula
BAJEROWA, Konstancje
BARTH, Elise
BARTHOLOMEW, Ann Sheppard
BIGOT DE MOROGUES, Marie
BINFIELD, Hanna R.
BLAHETKA, Marie Leopoldina
BLEITNER, Rosa
BOCHKOLTZ-FALCONI, Anna
BOVET, Hermine
BRADSHAW, Nellie Shorthill
BRAMBILLA, Marietta
BROOMAN, Hanna
BUERDE, Jeanette Antonie
CAPPIANI, Luisa
CLARKE, Jessie Murray
COLE, Charlotte
CORMONTAN, Theodora
CZICZKA, Angela
DAMOREAU-CINTI, Laure
DANCLA, Alphonsine Genevieve-
Lore
DELABORDE, Elie Miriam
DUCHAMP, Marie Catharine
DULCKEN, Louisa
DUSSEK, Veronica Rosalie
ENGER, Nelly
FARNINGHAM, Marianne
FARRENC, Louise
FERNANDEZ DE LA MORA,
Pilar
GOETZE, Auguste
GRAEVER, Madeleine
GROEBENSCHUETZ, Amalie
HAHR, Emma
HARTLAND, Lizzie
HAWES, Charlotte W.
HERITTE-VIARDOT, Louise Pauline
Marie
HEUBERGER, Jenny
JACQUES, Charlotte
JAHNOVA, Bozena
JANINA, Olga
JENTSCH, May
KALLEY, Sara Poulton
KINKEL, Johanna
KIRCHER, Maria Bertha

KOCHETOVA, Aleksandra
Dorimedontovna
KRAEHMER, Caroline
KUCZOR, Hilda
LANNOY, Clementine-Josephine-
Francoise-Therese, Countess
LAVATER, Magdalena Elisabeth
LEFEBURE, Marguerite
LEONARD, Antonia Sitcher de Mendi
LEONARDO, Luisa
LOUD, Annie Frances
MACIRONI, Clara Angela
MARA, La
MARCHESI, Mathilde de Castrone
MARCHISIO, Barbara
MARTIN, Angelica
MASINI, Giulia
MASSART, Louise Aglae
MASSON, Elizabeth
MILANOLLO, Teresa Domenica
Maria
MONGRUEL, Georgiana Catherine
Eugenia Leonard
MONTGEROULT, Helene de Nervode
MOZART, Maria Anna Walburga
Ignatia
MUNDELLA, Emma
MURIO-CELLI, Adelina
NICOLAY, Maria Antonia
O'LEARY, Rosetta
PARADIS, Maria Theresia von
PEASE, Jessie L.
PELLEGRINI CELONI, Anna
PFEIFFER, Clara-Virginie
PHILP, Elizabeth
PIERRET, Phedora
PLITT, Agathe
POLLET, Marie Nicole Simonin
PRESCOTT, Oliveria Louisa
RAMANN, Lina
RENAUD-D'ALLEN, Mlle. de
REVIAL, Marie Pauline
RICHINGS, Caroline
RICOTTI, Onestina
ROBERT-MAZEL, Helene
ROBINSON, Fanny
RODRIGO, Maria
ROECKEL, Jane
ROSENHOFF, Orla
ROSENTHAL, Pauline
SAINTON-DOLBY, Charlotte Helen
SALE, Sophia
SANCHEZ, Manuela Cornejo de
SANCHEZ DE LA MADRID, Ventura
SAUGEON, Zelie
SCHIMON, Anna
SCHREINZER, F.M.
SCHUMANN, Clara Josephine
SERVIER, Mme. H.
SHERRINGTON, Helena Lemmens
SKINNER, Fannie Lovering
SUTRO, Florence Edith
SWEPSTONE, Edith
SZYMANOWSKA, Maria Agata
THEGERSTROEM, Hilda Aurora
TURNEY, Ruthyn
UGALDE, Delphine Beauce
VANZO, Vittoria Maria
VERGER, Virginie Morel du
VIARDOT-GARCIA, Pauline Michelle
Ferdinande
VOJACKOVA-WETCHE, Ludmila
VOLKMANN, Ida
VON HOFF, Elizabeth
WALKER, Caroline Holme
WERNER, Hildegard
WHITELY, Bessie Marshall
WICHERN, Caroline
WICKMAN, Fredrika
WIECK, Marie
WILSON, Hilda

WINKEL, Therese Emilie Henriette
    aus dem
WISENEDER, Caroline
WOLFF-FRITZ, Sophie
WUIET, Caroline
ZAPATER, Rosaria
ZINGLER-SCHREINER, Martha
ZUMSTEEG, Emilie

20th Century A.D.

ABORN, Lora
ABRAMOVA, Sonia Pinkhasovna
ACKLAND, Jessie Agnes
ADAIR, Mildred
ADAIR, Yvonne Madeleine
ADAMS, Carrie Bell
AESCHLIMANN-ROTH, Esther
AGUDELO MURGUIA, Graciela
AINSCOUGH, Juliana Mary
AKIYOSHI, Toshiko
ALAIN, Marie Claire
ALARCO, Rosa
ALBRIGHT, Janet Elaine
ALCALAY, Luna
ALDRIDGE, Amanda Ira
ALEXANDER, Leni
ALLEN, Judith Shatin
ALLEN, Mimi
ALLITSEN, Frances
ALMEN, Ruth
ALONSO, Julia
ALOTIN, Yardena
ALT, Hansi
ALVARES-RIOS, Maria
ALVES DE SOUSA, Berta Candida
AMACHER, Maryanne
ANCELE, Sister Mary
ANDERSON, Beth
ANDERSON, Jay
ANDERSON, Julia McKinley
ANDERSON, Pauline Barbour
ANDERSON-WUENSCH, Jean Mary
ANDREE, Elfrida
ANDRIESSEN, Caecilia
APPELDOORN, Dina van
ARENA, Iris Mae
ARIZTI SOBRINO, Cecilia
ARTEAGA, Genoveva de
ASHFORD, Emma Louise
ASHMORE, Grace Flournoy
AUBUT-PRATTE, Francoise
AULIN, Laura Valborg
AUTENRIETH, Helma
AVETISIAN, Aida Konstantinovna
AYLOTT, Lydia Georgina Edith
BABITS, Linda
BACHELLER, Mildred R. Thomas
BACON, Viola Ruth Orcutt
BAHMANN, Marianne Eloise
BAIKADAMOVA, Baldyrgan
    Bakhitzhanovna
BAIL, Grace Shattuck
BAKLANOVA, Natalia
BALCKE, Frida Dorothea
BALDACCI, Giovanna Bruna
BALDWIN, Esther Lillian
BALL, Frances de Villa
BALLANDS, Etta
BALSHONE, Cathy S.
BANNISTER, Mary Jeanne Hoggard
BARATTA, Maria M. de
BARBERIS, Mansi
BARBLAN-OPIENSKA, Lydia
BARBOSA, Cacilda Campos Borges
BARIL, Jeanne
BARKER, Phyllis Elizabeth
BARKIN, Elaine
BARKLUND, Irma L.
BARNES-WOOD, Zilpha
BARNETT, Alice
BARRADAS, Carmen
BARRELL, Joyce Howard

BARTHEL, Ursula
BASSETT, Henrietta Elizabeth
BAUER, Emilie Frances
BEAHM, Jacquelyn Yvette
BEARER, Elaine Louise
BECKMAN, Ellen Josephine
BEKEART, Edna
BEKMAN-SHCHERBINA, Elena
    Aleksandrovna Kamentseva
BELINFANTE-DEKKER, Martha
    Suzanna Betje
BENARY, Barbara
BENOIT, Francine Germaine Van
    Gool
BERAN-STARK, Lola Aloisia Maria
BERGMAN, Ellen
BERGSTROM, Anna
BERROA, Catalina
BERRYMAN, Alice Davis
BEZDEK, Sister John Joseph
BIALKIEWICZOWNA-ANDRAULT DE
    LANGERON, Irena
BIANCHINI, Emma
BIENVENU, Lily
BILBRO, Anne Mathilde
BILTCLIFFE, Florence
BINET, Jocelyne
BIRCSAK, Thusnelda
BIRD, Sister Mary Rafael
BIRKETT, Gwenhilda Mary
BIXBY, Allene K.
BIZONY, Celia
BLACKWELL, Anna Gee
BLAKE, Dorothy Gaynor
BLANCK, Olga de
BLASIS, Teresa de
BLAUHUTH, Jenny
BLAUVELT, Bula Caswell
BLIESENER, Ada Elizabeth
    Michelman
BLOCH, Suzanne
BLOCKSIDGE, Kathleen Mary
BLOMFIELD-HOLT, Patricia
BLOOD, Esta Damesek
BODENSTEIN-HOYME, Ruth E.
BODOM, Erica
BOESSER, Dagma
BOLL, Christine E.
BOLZ, Harriet
BONDS, Margaret
BOONE, Clara Lyle
BOOZER, Patricia P.
BORDERS, Barbara Ann
BOTET, Maria Emma
BOUCHARD, Linda L.
BOUCHER, Lydia
BOUTRON, Madeleine
BOYD, Jeanne Margaret
BOYKIN, A. Helen
BRAGGINS, Daphne Elizabeth
BRANDMAN, Margaret Susan
BRANDT, Dorothea
BRANNING, Grace Bell
BRATU, Emma
BRAUER, Johanna Elisabeth
BREEN, May Singhi
BRENNER, Rosamond Drooker
BRICE, Jean Anne
BRIDGEWATER, Violet Irene
BRINK, Emily R.
BRINK-POTHUIS, Annie van den
BRITAIN, Radie
BROCKMAN, Jane E.
BRODIN, Lena Birgitta Elise
BROUWER, Margaret Lee
BROWN, Norma
BROWN, Veronica
BROWN, Zilda Jennings
BRUNNER, Maria
BRUSSELS, Iris
BRUZDOWICZ, Joanna

BRYANT, Verna Mae
BUCHANAN, Annabel Morris
BUCHANAN, Dorothy Quita
BUCK, Era Marguerite
BUCKLEY, Dorothy Pike
BUCKLEY, Helen Dallam
BUCZEK, Barbara Kazimiera
BUENAVENTURA, Isabel
BULTERIJS, Nina
BURCHELL, Henrietta Louise
BURGER, Hester Aletta Sophie
BURKE, Loretto
BURROUGHS, Jane Johnson
BURSTON, Maggie
BURT, Virginia M.
BUTCHER, Jane Elizabeth
BUTLER, Anne Lois
BYERS, Roxana Weihe
CADORET, Charlotte
CADY, Harriette
CADZOW, Dorothy Forrest
CALE, Rosalie Balmer Smith
CAMEU, Helza
CAMPAGNE, Conny
CAMPMANY, Montserrat
CAMPOS ARAUJO DE, Joaquina
CAPSIR-TANZI, Mercedes
CAPUIS, Matilde
CARMEN MARINA
CARRENO, Teresa
CARRINGTON-THOMAS, Virginia
CARRIVICK, Olive Amelia
CARTER, Buenta MacDaniel
CARTER, Rosetta
CASTAGNETTA, Grace Sharp
CECCONI-BATES, Augusta
CHANCE, Nancy Laird
CHAVES, Mary Elizabeth
CHEN, Nira
CHERTOK, Pearl
CHESTNUT, Lora Perry
CHEVALLIER SUPERVIELLE, Marie
    Louise
CHRISTENSEN, Anna Mae Parker
CLARK, June
CLARK, Mary Margaret Walker
CLARKE, Mary Gail
CLARKE, Phyllis Chapman
CLAUDE, Marie
CLINGAN, Judith Ann
COBB, Hazel
CONRAD, Laurie M.
COOKE, Marjorie Tibbets
COOLIDGE, Peggy Stuart
COONEY, Cheryl Lee
COPLAND, Berniece Rose
CORDULA, Sister M.
CORNEA-IONESCU, Alma
COTE, Helene
COULOMBE SAINT-MARCOUX,
    Micheline
COUPER, Mildred
COWLES, Darleen
CRAIB, Doris
CRAWFORD SEEGER, Ruth
CRAWFORD, Dawn Constance
CRAWFORD, Dorothy Lamb
CREWS, Lucille
CRISWICK, Mary
CROFTS, Inez Altman
CROSBY, Fannie
CURRIE, Edna R.
CURUBETO GODOY, Maria Isabel
CURZON, Clara-Jean
DALE, Kathleen
DALE, Phyllis
DAMASHEK, Barbara
DANFORTH, Frances A.
DANIELA, Carmen
DANIELS, Nellie
DAVIDSON, Tina

DAVIES, Eiluned
DAVIS, Eleanor Maud
DAVIS, Eva May
DAVIS, Fay Simmons
DAVIS, Jean Reynolds
DAVIS, Katherine Kennicott
DAVIS, Margaret Munger
DE CEVEE, Alice
DE LARA, Adelina
DE MOL, Josephine
DE VILLIERS, Justina Wilhelmina Nancy
DEACON, Mary Connor
DECARIE, Reine
DELIRE, Alice
DELIZ, Monserrate
DELORME, Isabelle
DEMAREST, Anne Shannon
DEMBO, Royce
DESPORTES, Yvonne Berthe Melitta
DIAMOND, Arline
DIEFENTHALER, Margaret Kissinger
DIEMER, Emma Lou
DILLER, Angela
DILLON, Fannie Charles
DIMITRIU, Florica
DINESCU, Violeta
DITTENHAVER, Sarah Louise
DLUGOSZEWSKI, Lucia
DOBIE, Janet
DODGE, May Hewes
DOMINIQUE, Monica
DORABIALSKA, Julia Helena
DOROW, Dorothy
DOUROUX, Margaret Pleasant
DRENNAN, Dorothy Carter
DRETKE, Leora N.
DREYFUS, Francis Kay
DRYNAN, Margaret
DUGGAN, Beatrice Abbott
DUNGAN, Olive
DURAND, Nella Wells
DZIEWULSKA, Maria Amelia
EAGAR, Fannie Edith Starke
EDICK, Ethel Vera Ingraham
EGGLESTON, Anne E.
EILERS, Joyce Elaine
EIRIKSDOTTIR, Karolina
EISENSTEIN, Stella Price
EISENSTEIN DE VEGA, Silvia
ELIAS, Graciela Morales de
ELKAN, Ida
ELKOSHI, Rivka
ELLIOTT, Marjorie Reeve
EMIG, Lois Irene
EMINGEROVA, Katerina
ENDE, Amelia von
ENGBERG, M. Davenport
ERDELI, Xenia Alexandrovna
ESCOT, Pozzi
ESTRELLA, Blanca
ETHRIDGE, Jean
EUTENEUER-ROHRER, Ursula Henrietta
EVERETT-SALICCO, Betty Lou
EZELL, Helen Ingle
FAHRBACH, Henrietta
FALCINELLI, Rolande
FAUTCH, Sister Magdalen
FEHRS, Anna Elisbeth
FEIGIN, Sarah
FELIX, Margery Edith
FELLOWS, Mrs. Wayne Stanley
FERNANDEZ, Helen Lorenzo
FINE, Vivian
FINZI, Graciane
FIRNKEES, Gertrud
FISCHER, Emma Gabriele Marie von, Baroness
FISHER, Gladys Washburn
FISHER, Renee Breger

FISHMAN, Marian
FITZGERALD, Sister Florence Therese
FIUZA, Virginia Salgado
FLAGG, Mary Houts
FLEITES, Virginia
FLICK-FLOOD, Dora
FLORING, Grace Kenny
FLOWER, Amelia Matilda
FODY, Ilona
FOLVILLE, Eugenie-Emilie Juliette
FONDER, Sister Mary Teresine
FOOT, Phyllis Margaret
FORD, Olive Elizabeth
FORMAN, Jeanne
FOSIC, Tarzicija
FOSTER, Cecily
FOSTER, Fay
FOWLER, Jennifer Joan
FOWLER, Marje
FRANCHERE-DESROSIERS, Rose de Lima
FRANGS, Irene
FRASER-MILLER, Gloria Jill
FRASIER, Jane
FREEHOFF, Ruth Williams
FREER, Eleanor Warner Everest
FREGA, Ana Lucia
FREITAG, Dorothea Hackett
FREIXAS Y CRUELLS, Narcisa
FRITZ, Sherilyn Gail
FRONMUELLER, Frieda
FRYZELL, Regina Holmen
FUCHS, Lillian
FULCHER, Ellen Georgina
FULLER, Jeanne Weaver
FURGERI, Bianca Maria
FURZE, Jessie
GAMILLA, Alice Doria
GANNON, Ruth Ellen
GARCIA ROBSON, Magdalena
GARDINER, Mary Elizabeth
GARDNER, Kay
GARSCIA-GRESSEL, Janina
GARTENLAUB, Odette
GARUTA, Lucia Yanovna
GAYNOR, Jessie Love
GENET, Marianne
GEORGE, Lila-Gene
GESELSCHAP, Maria
GESSLER, Caroline
GEST, Elizabeth
GHERTOVICI, Aida
GIDEON, Miriam
GILBERT, Marie
GILLUM, Ruth Helen
GINDLER, Kathe-Lotte
GITECK, Janice
GIURANNA, Elena Barbara
GLASER, Victoria Merrylees
GLAZIER, Beverly
GLICK, Nancy Kay
GNUS, Ryta
GODDARD, Arabella
GOERSCH, Ursula Margitta
GOLDSTON, Margaret Nell Stumpf
GOLOVINA, Olga Akimovna
GOODMAN, Lillian Rosedale
GOOLKASIAN-RAHBEE, Dianne Zabelle
GORELLI, Olga
GOULD, Janetta
GOVEA, Wenonah Milton
GRAD-BUCH, Hulda
GRAHAM, Janet Christine
GRANJE, Rosa
GREENE, Margo Lynn
GREENFIELD, Lucille
GRIMES, Doreen
GRONOWETTER, Freda
GROSSMAN, Deena

GRUDEFF, Marian
GRZADZIELOWNA, Eleonora
GUBITOSI, Emilia
GULESIAN, Grace Warner
GWILY-BROIDO, Rivka
HAGAN, Helen Eugenia
HAHN, Sandra Lea
HAIK-VANTOURA, Suzanne
HAIRSTON, Jacqueline Butler
HALPERN, Stella
HALSTED, Margo
HAMMOND, Fanny Reed
HANEFELD, Gertrud
HANSEN, Hanna Marie
HARDING, Mildred Thompson
HARLEY, Frances Marjorie
HART, Alice Maud
HARTZER-STIBBE, Marie
HASKELL, Doris Burd
HAWLEY, Carolyn Jean
HEATON, Eloise Klotz
HEDOUX, Yvonne
HEGNER, Anna
HEINRICH, Adel Verna
HEINRICHS, Agnes
HEINY, Margaret Harris
HELBLING, Elsa
HELLER-REICHENBACH, Barbara
HELSINGIUS, Barbara
HELYER, Marjorie
HENDERSON, Ruth Watson
HERBISON, Jeraldine Saunders
HERMANN, Miina
HETRICK, Patricia Anne
HICKS, Marjorie Kisby
HIER, Ethel Glen
HIGGINS, Esther S.
HILL, May
HILL, Sister M. Mildred
HIND O'MALLEY, Pamela
HIRSCH, Barbara
HOFF, Vivian Beaumont
HOLCK, Sine
HOLMSEN, Borghild
HOLTHUSEN, Anita Saunders
HOOD, Helen
HOPPE, Clara
HORROCKS, Amy Elsie
HOUSE, L. Marguerite
HOVDA, Eleanor
HOWARD, Beatrice Thomas
HOWELL, Dorothy
HOY, Bonnee L.
HRUBY, Dolores Marie
HUBICKI, Margaret Olive
HUEBNER, Ilse
HUGHES, Sister Martina
HUGH-JONES, Elaine
HUJSAK, Joy Detenbeck
HULFORD, Denise Lovona
HULL, Kathryn B.
HUNKINS, Eusebia Simpson
HUTTON, Florence Myra
HYDE, Miriam Beatrice
HYSON, Winifred Prince
IASHVILI, Lili Mikhailovna
IBANEZ, Carmen
IBRAGIMOVA, Sevda Mirza kyzy
INWOOD, Mary Ruth Brink Berger
IRMAN-ALLEMANN, Regina
ISZKOWSKA, Zofia
IVEY, Jean Eichelberger
JACKSON, Elizabeth Barnhart
JAMES, Dorothy E.
JANKOVIC, Miroslava
JENNEY, Mary Frances
JENNINGS, Marie Pryor
JENNY, Sister Leonore
JEREA, Hilda
JESI, Ada
JEWELL, Lucina

JOHN, Patricia Spaulding
JOHNSON, Mary Ernestine Clark
JOHNSTON, Alison Aileen Annie
JOLLEY, Florence Werner
JONES, Marjorie
JONES-DAVIES, Maude
JUDD, Margaret Evelyn
KABAT, Julie Phyllis
KAESER-BECK, Aida
KAHMANN, Chesley
KAMIEN, Anna
KANACH, Sharon E.
KANAKA'OLE, Edith Ke-Kuhikuhi-I-Pu'u-one-o-Na-Ali'i-O-Kohala
KAPLAN, Lois Jay
KARNITSKAYA, Nina Andreyevna
KASHPEROVA, Leokadia Alexandrovna
KASILAG, Lucrecia R.
KATS-CHERNIN, Elena
KAVASCH, Deborah Helene
KAYDEN, Mildred
KEEFER, Euphrosyne
KEETMAN, Gunild
KELLEY, Florence Bettray
KELLEY, Patricia Ann
KELLY, Denise Maria Anne
KENT, Ada Twohy
KERR, Bessie Maude
KESHNER, Joyce Grove
KESSLER, Minuetta Schumiatcher
KETTERING, Eunice Lea
KHOSS VON STERNEGG, Gisela
KICKTON, Erika
KINSCELLA, Hazel Gertrude
KLECHNIOWSKA, Anna Maria
KLEIN, Ivy Frances
KLEPPER, Anna Benzia
KLOTZMAN, Dorothy Ann Hill
KNOBLOCHOVA, Antonie
KNOUSS, Isabelle G.
KOMIAZYK, Magdalena
KORN, Clara Anna
KOSHETZ, Nina
KOZINOVIC, Lujza
KRALIKOVA, Johana
KRAUSZ, Susan
KREISS, Hulda E.
KRIMSKY, Katrina
KRUGER, Catharina Maria
KRUGER, Lilly Canfield
KRULL, Diana
KRZYZANOWSKA, Halina
KUCEROVA-HERSTOVA, Marie
KUESTER, Edith Haines
KUNITZ, Sharon Lohse
KUZMYCH, Christina
LACHOWSKA, Stefania
LACKMAN, Susan C. Cohn
LACMANOVA, Anna
LAFLEUR, Lucienne
LAITMAN, Lori
LAJEUNESSE, Emma, Dame
LAMEGO, Carlinda J.
LANDOWSKA, Wanda
LANG, Edith
LANG, Rosemary Rita
LANG-BECK, Ivana
LAPIN, Lily
LARKIN, Deirdre
LARSON, Anna Barbara
LATHROP, Gayle Posselt
LATZ, Inge
LEAVITT, Helen Sewall
LEBENBOM, Elaine F.
LEE, Anna Virginia
LEE, Hope Anne Keng-Wei
LEECH, Lida Shivers
LEECH, Renee
LEFEBVRE, Francoise
LEGINSKA, Ethel

LEHMAN, Evangeline Marie
LEHMANN, Liza
LEITE, Clarisse
LEIVISKA, Helvi Lemmiki
LEMAIRE-SINDORFF, Jeanne
LEON, Tania Justina
LEONARD, Mamie Grace
LEPEUT-LEVINE, Jeannine
LESICHKOVA, Lili
LEVIN, Rami Yona
LEVINA, Zara Alexandrovna
LEVITSKAYA, Viktoria Sergeyevna
LEWING, Adele
LIEBLING, Estelle
LIEBMANN, Nanna Magdalene
LINDEMAN, Anna Severine
LINDEMAN, Hjelle Signe
LINNEMANN, Maria Catharina
LITTLEJOHN, Joan Anne
LLOYD, Caroline Parkhurst
LLUNELL SANAHUJA, Pepita
LOCKE, Flora Elbertine Huie
LOCKSHIN, Florence Levin
LOCKWOOD, Annea Ferguson
LOHOEFER, Evelyn
LOHR, Ina
LOMON, Ruth
LOPUSKA-WYLEZYNSKA, Helena
LORE, Emma Maria Theresa
LOWENSTEIN, Gunilla Marike
LUCKMAN, Phyllis
LUMBY, Betty Louise
LUNA DE ESPAILLAT, Margarita
LUND, Gudrun
LUND, Hanna
LUPTON, Belle George
LVOVA, Julia Fedorovna
LYONN LIEBERMAN, Julie
MACHADO, Lena
MACKIE, Shirley M.
MacARTHUR, Helen
MacDONALD, Catherine
MacGREGOR, Laurie
McGILL, Gwendolen Mary Finlayson
McINTYRE, Margaret
McKANN-MANCINI, Patricia
McKELLAN, Irene Mary
McLEAN, Priscilla Anne Taylor
McLEOD, Evelyn Lundgren
McLIN, Lena
McNAIR, Jacqueline Hanna
MADISON, Clara Duggan
MAILIAN, Elza Antonovna
MAITLAND, Anna Harriet
MALMLOEF-FORSSLING, Carin
MANGGRUM, Loretta C. Cessor
MARCUS, Ada Belle Gross
MARKOV, Katherine Lee
MARTENOT-LAZARD, Ginette-Genevieve
MARY ELAINE, Sister
MASON, Gladys Amy
MASON, Marilyn May
MASTERS, Juan
MATEU, Maria Cateura
MATHEWS, Blanche Dingley Moore
MATJAN, Vida
MATTHEWS, Dorothy White
MAUR, Sophie
MAURICE-JACQUET, H.
MAXWELL, Jacqueline Perkinson
MEEK, Ethel Alice
MEIGS, Melinda Moore
MEKEEL, Joyce
MELL, Gertrud Maria
MELOY, Elizabeth
MERLI-ZWISCHENBRUGGER, Christina
MERRIMAN, Margarita Leonor

MESNEY, Dorothy Taylor
MESRITZ-VAN VELTHUYSEN, Annie
MEYSENBURG, Sister Agnes
MIEROWSKA, Jean
MILAM, Lena Triplett
MILDANTRI, Mary Ann
MILDREN, Margaret Joyce
MILFORD, Mary Jean Ross
MILLER, Lillian Anne
MILNE, Helen C.
MIRET, Emilia
MIRON, Tsipora
MISHELL, Kathryn Lee
MITCHELL, Norma Jean
MOBERG, Ida Georgina
MOE, Benna
MOELLER, Agnes
MOESTUE, Marie
MOHNS, Grace Updegraff Bergen
MONTGOMERY, Merle
MOORE, Luella Lockwood
MOORE, Wilda Maurine Ricks
MORGAN, Maud
MORIN-LABRECQUE, Albertine
MORONEY, Sister Mary Emmeline
MRACEK, Ann Michelle
MUKHAMEDZHANOVA, Mariam
MUNDINGER, Adele Franziska
MUNGER, Millicent Christner
MUSTILLO, Lina
MYSZINSKA-WOJCIECHOWSKA, Leokadia
NAIKHOVICH-LOMAKINA, Fania Filippovna
NAMAKELUA, Alice K.
NASH, Grace Helen
NAZAROVA, Tatiana Borisovna
NAZIROVA, Elmira Mirza Rza kyzy
NEAS, Margaret
NEEL, Susan Elizabeth
NEILY, Anne MacAdams
NEUWIRTH, Goesta
NEWPORT, Doreen
NICKERSON, Camille Lucie
NIEDERBERGER, Maria A.
NIEMACK, Ilza Louise
NIGHTINGALE, Mae Wheeler
NIKISCH, Amelie
NOBLITT, Katheryn Marie McCall
NOETHLING, Elisabeth
NOHE, Beverly
NORDENFELT, Dagmar
NORRE, Dorcas
NOVELLO-DAVIES, Clara
NOYES, Edith Rowena
NUNLIST, Juli
OBENCHAIN, Virginia
O'BRIEN, Drena
O'BRIEN, Katharine E.
OLIVEIRA, Jocy de
OLIVER, Madra Emogene
OLIVEROS, Pauline
OLLER BENLLOCH, Maria Teresa
OLSON, Lynn Freeman
O'NEILL, Selena
ORE, Cecilie
ORTMANS, Kay Muriel
OSETROVA-YAKOVLIEVA, Nina Alexandrovna
OSGOOD, Marion
O'SHEA, Mary Ellen
OSTROFF, Esther
OTIS, Edna Cogswell
OTTAWOWA, Helena
OWEN, Angela Maria
OWEN, Blythe
OZDENSES, Semahat
PACK, Beulah Frances
PAGOTO, Helen

PALMER, Florence Margaret Spencer
PAQUIN, Anna
PAQUIN, Louisa
PARENTE, Sister Elizabeth
PARKER, Alice
PARS, Melahat
PATINO ANDRADE, Graziela
PAUL, Doris A.
PAULL, Barberi
PEGELOW, Hanna G.
PENNER, Jean Priscilla
PEREIRA, Diana Maria
PERONI, Wally
PERRY, Mary Dean
PEY CASADO, Diana
PFEIFFER, Irena
PFOLH, Bessie Whittington
PHILLIPS, Donna
PHILLIPS, Karen Ann
PHIPPEN, Laud German
PICCONI, Maria Antonietta
PIECHOWSKA, Alina
PIERCE, Sarah Anderson
PIERROT, Noelie Marie Antoinette
PIETSCH, Edna Frieda
PIRES DE CAMPOS, Lina
PITCHER, Gladys
PITTMAN, Evelyn LaRue
POLICARPO TEIXEIRA, Maria
    Margarida Fernandes
PONCE, Ethel
POOL, Arlette
POOLE, Anna Ware
POOLER, Marie
POPOVICI, Elise
PRAY, Ada Jordan
PREOBRAJENSKA, Vera Nicolaevna
PRESTI, Ida
PRICE, Florence Beatrice
PRIESING, Dorothy Jean
PRIOLLI, Maria Luisa de Matos
PROCACCINI, Teresa
PRUNTY, Evelyn Grace Potter
PTASZYNSKA, Marta
PUCHE, Sofia
PUKUI, Mary Abigail
QUIEL, Hildegard
QUINLAN, Agnes Clune
RABER DE REINDERS, Esther
RAINIER, Priaulx
RAMAKERS, Christiane Josee
RAMM, Valentina Iosifovna
RAVINALE, Irma
RAVIZE, Angele
RAW, Vera Constance
RAY, Ruth
REBE, Louise Christine
REEKS, Kathleen Doris
REES, Winifred Emily
REHNQVIST, Karin Birgitta
REID, Wendy
REIS, Hilda Pires dos
REISER, Violet
RENIE, Henriette
RENNES, Catharina van
REYNOLDS, Erma Grey Hogue
REYNOLDS, Laura Lawton
RHEINGOLD, Lauma Yanovna
RHENE-JAQUE
RHOADS, Mary R.
RICH, Gladys
RICHARDSON, Enid Dorothy
RICHNER-HEIM, Erika
RICHTER, Ada
RICHTER, Marga
RICKARD, Sylvia
RITTENBAND, Minna Ethel
RIVE-KING, Julia
ROBBOY, Rosalie Smotkin
ROBERSON, Ruby Lee Grubbs
ROBERT, Lucie

ROBERTS, Gertrud Hermine Kuenzel
ROBERTS, Jane A.
ROBERTS, Megan L.
ROBERTS, Ruth Olive
ROBERTSON, Donna Lou Nagey
ROBLES, Marisa
ROBYN, Louise
RODRIGUE, Nicole
ROE, Eileen Betty
ROE, Marion Adelle
ROEMER, Hanne
ROESGEN-CHAMPION, Marguerite
    Sara
ROGERS, Clara Kathleen
ROGERS, Ethel Tench
ROGERS, Melicent Joan
ROGERS, Patsy
ROGERS, Sharon Elery
ROGERS, Susan Whipple
ROGET, Henriette
ROKSETH, Yvonne
ROLDES FREIXES, Mercedes
ROMM, Rosalina Davidovna
ROSAS FERNANDES, Maria Helena
ROSATO, Clorinda
ROSCO, B. Jeanie
ROSE OF JESUS, Sister
ROSSO, Carol L.
ROYSE, Mildred Barnes
ROZET, Sonia
RUBIN, Anna Ita
RUDALL, Eleonor C.
RUDOLPH, Anna
RUDOW, Vivian Adelberg
RUEFF, Jeanine
RUEGGER, Charlotte
RUFF-STOEHR, Herta Maria Klara
RUGELES, Ana Mercedes de
RUTA, Gilda, Countess
RYDER, Theodora Sturkow
RYLEK-STANKOVA, Blazena
SAFARIAN, Lucia Arisovna
SAITO-NODA, Eva
SAMTER, Alice
SAMUEL, Marguerite
SANDERS, Alma M.
SANDY, Grace Linn
SANFILIPPO, Margherita Marie
SANFORD, Grace Krick
SANZ, Rocio
SARNECKA, Jadwiga
SCHAFMEISTER, Helen
SCHARLI, Ruth
SCHMIDT-DUISBURG, Margarete
    Dina Alwina
SCHMITZ-GOHR, Else
SCHONTHAL, Ruth E.
SCHUBARTH, Dorothe
SCHUBERT, Myra Jean
SCHULZE-BERGHOF, Luise Doris
    Albertine
SCHUMAKER, Grace L.
SCHURZMANN, Katharina
SCHUSTER, Doris Dodd
SCHUSTER, Elfriede
SCHWARTZ, Julie
SCHWEIZER, Gertrude
SCLIAR, Esther
SCOTT, Georgina Keir
SEAVER, Blanche Ebert
SEGHIZZI, Cecilia
SELTZNER, Jennie
SEPULVEDA, Maria Luisa
SETO, Robin
SETTI, Kilza
SEUEL-HOLST, Marie
SHARPE, Emma
SHAW, Alice Marion
SHAW, Carrie Burpee
SHERMAN, Ingrid
SHIRLEY, Constance Jeanette

SHLONSKY, Verdina
SHORE, Clare
SHREVE, Susan Ellen
SHRUDE, Marilyn
SIDDALL, Louise
SIDORENKO, Tamara Stepanovna
SIEBER, Susanne
SILBERTA, Rhea
SILSBEE, Ann L.
SILVERMAN, Faye-Ellen
SIMIC, Darinka
SIMONE, Nina
SIMONS, Lorena Cotts
SIMONS, Netty
SIMPSON, Mary Jean
SINDE RAMALLAL, Clara
SINGER, Jeanne
SIROONI, Alice
SISTEK-DJORDJEVIC, Mirjana
SKAGGS, Hazel Ghazarian
SKALSKA-SZEMIOTH, Hanna
    Wanda
SKARECKY, Jana Milena
SLENDZINSKA, Julitta
SLIANOVA-MIZANDARI, Dagmara
    Levanovna
SMEJKALOVA, Vlasta
SMELTZER, Susan Mary
SMILEY, Pril
SMITH, Edith Gross
SMITH, Eleanor
SMITH, Hilda Josephine
SMITH, Ruby Mae
SMITH, Selma Moidel
SNOW, Mary McCarty
SOLOMON, Elide M.
SOUERS, Mildred
SPAIN-DUNK, Susan
SPEACH, Sister Bernadette Marie
SPECHT, Judy Lavise
SPENCER PALMER, Florence
    Margaret
SPENCER, Marguerite
SPIEGEL, Laurie
SPIZIZEN, Louise Myers
SPOONER, Dorothy Harley
STAINKAMPH, Eileen Freda
STAIRS, Lousie E.
STANEKAITE-LAUMYANSKENE,
    Elena Ionovna
STANLEY, Marion Isabel
STEELE, Helen
STEELE, Lynn
STEIN, Gladys Marie
STEPHEN, Roberta Mae
STEWART, Katharine
STRAUSS, Elizabeth
STREATFIELD, Valma June
STRICKLAND, Lily Teresa
STULTZ, Marie Irene
STURKOW-RYDER, Theodora
STYLES, Dorothy Geneva
SUMNER, Clare
SURIANI, Alberta
SUSZCZYNSKA, Anna
SWARTZ, Elsa Ellen
SYNER, Sonia
SZOENYI, Erzsebet
TACK, Annie
TAKAMI, Toyoko
TAL, Marjo
TALMA, Louise
TANN, Hilary
TAPPER, Bertha
TARLOW, Karen Anne
TAUBER, Lotti
TAYLOR, Mary Virginia
TAYLOR, Maude Cummings
TEGNER, Alice Charlotte
TEICHMUELLER, Anna
TELFER, Nancy Ellen

TENGBERGEN, Maria Elizabeth van
    Ebbenhorst
TERRY, Frances
TERZIAN, Alicia
THEMMEN, Ivana Marburger
THIEME, Kerstin Anja
THOMAS, Elizabeth
THOMAS, Mary Virginia
THOMAS, Muriel Leonora Duncan
THOMPSON, Caroline Lorraine
THOMPSON, Ellen
THORESON, Janice Pearl
THORKELSDOTTIR, Mist Barbara
TIMMERMANN, Leni
TKACH, Zlata Moiseyevna
TOBLER, Mina
TORRA, Celia
TOWER, Joan
TOWERSEY, Phyllis Mary
TRAEGER, Elinor Meissner
TRINITAS, Sister M.
TROTT, Josephine
TURNER, Mildred Cozzens
TURNER-MALEY, Florence
TUSSENBROEK, Hendrika van
ULEHLA, Ludmila
UNDERWOOD, Frances Evangeline
USHER, Julia
USTVOLSKAYA, Galina Ivanovna
VACCARO, Judith Lynne
VAN AARDT, Madelene
VAN DE VATE, Nancy Hayes
VAN DEN BOORN-COCLET,
    Henriette
VAN DIJCK, Beatrice Madeleine
VAN EPEN-DE GROOT, Else Antonia
VAN NESTE, Rosane Micheline Lucie
    Charlotte
VANDEVERE, J. Lilien
VERCOE, Elizabeth
VERHAALEN, Sister Marion
VERRALL, Pamela Motley
VIDAR, Jorunn
VIENNE, Marie-Louise de
VIGNERON-RAMAKERS, Christiane-
    Josee
VILLENEUVE, Marie-Louise Diane
VINETTE, Alice
VIRGIL, Antha Minerva Patchen
VISCONTI, Leila
VOELLMY-LIECHTI, Grety
VOIGT, Henriette
VOLKART, Hazel
VOLKART-SCHLAGER, Kaethe
VON PECHY, Valerie
VON ZIERITZ, Grete
VORONINA, Tatiana Aleksandrovna
VREE-BROWN, Marion F.
WAALER, Fredrikke Holtemann
WALKER, Louise
WALLACH, Joelle
WALSH, Elizabeth Jameson
WANG, Qiang
WARD, Diane
WARD, Sister Mary Louise
WARING, Kate
WARNE, Katharine Mulky
WARNER, Sally Slade
WARREN, Betsy
WATERSTONE, Satella S.
WEBER, Carole
WECKWERTH, Nancy
WEISSBERG, Julia Lazerevna
WEISS-MANN, Edith
WESTGATE, Elizabeth
WESTON, Mildred
WEYBRIGHT, June
WHITE, Mary Louisa
WHITECOTTON, Shirley Ellen
WHITEHEAD, Gillian
WHITLOCK, E. Florence

WIGGINS, Mary
WILKINSON, Constance Jane
WILLIAMS, Grace Mary
WILLS, Edwina Florence
WILSON, Jean Dolores
WINTER, Sister Miriam Therese
WISHART, Betty Rose
WITZIG, Louise
WOLF-COHEN, Veronika
WOLCOTT, Ellen
WOLL, Erna
WOLLNER, Gertrude Price
WONG, Betty Ann
WOOD, Mabel
WOODRUFF, Edith S.
WOODWARD, Martha Clive
WORTH, Amy
WRIGHT, Nannie Louise
WUNSCH, Ilse Gerda
WYLIE, Ruth Shaw
YAKHNINA, Yevgenia Yosifovna
YAZBECK, Louise
YDSTIE, Arlene Buckneberg
ZECHLIN, Ruth
ZIFFRIN, Marilyn Jane
ZIMMERMANN, Margrit
ZUBELDIA, Emiliana de
ZWEIG, Esther
Century unknown
BOR, Modesta
FRACKER, Cora Robins
HARVEY, Ella Doreen
MIRANDA, Erma Hoag
TAJANI MATTONE, Ida

TROUBADOUR
11th Century A.D.
AZALAIS D'ALTIER
12th Century A.D.
ALAIS
ALAMANDA
ALMUCS DE CASTELNAU
AZALAIS DE PORCAIRAGUES
CHARTRES, La Vidame de
CHIEVRE DE REINS, La
ELEANOR OF AQUITAINE
FAYEL, La Dame du
GARSENDA, Countess of Provence
ISABELLA
ISELDA
ISEUT DE CAPIO, Dame
LOMBARDA
MARIA de VENTADORN
TIBORS
13th Century A.D.
BEATRICE DE DIA, Contessa
BIEIRIS DE ROMANS
BLANCHE DE CASTILLE
CARENZA
CASTELLOZA, Dame
CAUDAIRENCA
DOETE
DOMNA H.
D'ANDUZA, Clara
GUILLELMA DE ROSERS
GUILLELMA of MONJA
NATIBORS
SAINT GILLES, La Chatelaine De
14th Century A.D.
ADELINE L'ANGLOIS
BIENVEIGNANT, Liegart
CHARTAINE, Marcella La
FLASSAN, Flandrine de
GUERIN, Alipson
ISABEL LA LORRAINE
ISABELET LA ROUSSELLE
JEHANE LA FERPIERE
LORRAINE, La Duchesse de
MARGUERITE AU MOINE
15th Century A.D.
ALEGRE, Gracieuse

WRITER
9th Century A.D.
DANANIR AL BARMAKIYYA
11th Century A.D.
HROSTWITHA
12th Century A.D.
HILDEGARDE, Saint
13th Century A.D.
GERTRUDE OF HELFTA, Saint
MECHTHILD
15th Century A.D.
BUNGE, Jungfer Gertrud
CHRISTINE DE PISAN
PINAR, Florencia del
17th Century A.D.
CALEGARI, Cornelia
LACERDA, Bernarda Ferreira de
LEONARDA, Sister Isabella
MacLEOD, Mary
18th Century A.D.
AUBIGNY VON ENGELBRUNNER,
    Nina d'
CHARRIERE, Isabella Agneta
    Elisabeth de
DUBOIS, Dorothea
DUVAL, Louise
GOUGELET, Mme.
KANZLER, Josephine
LA GUERRE, Elisabeth-Claude
    Jacquet de
LOUIS, Mme.
19th Century A.D.
AMALIE, Marie Friederike Augusta,
    Princess of Saxony
ANSPACH, Elizabeth, Margravine of
ARNIM, Bettina von
AYLWARD, Florence
BAWR, Alexandrine Sophie
BERNARD, Vincenzia
BERTIN, Louise Angelique
BOVET, Hermine
BRONTE, Anne
CANDEILLE, Amelie Julie
CASTRO GUIMARAES, Floripes de
CHEVALIER DE MONTREAL,
    Julia
CLARKE, Helen Archibald
CLARKE, Jessie Murray
COOK, Eliza
CROWNINGSHIELD, Mary Bradford
DUHAN, Mme.
DUSSEK, Olivia
FARNINGHAM, Marianne
FARRENC, Louise
FECHNER, Paulina
FERRARI, Carlotta
FORTEY, Mary Comber
GAY, Sophia Maria Francesca
GENGLIS, Stephanie Felicite,
    Countess of Saint-Aubin
GIBSON, Louisa
GOETZE, Auguste
GORE, Katharina
HAASS, Maria Catharina
HACKETT, Marie
HAXTHAUSEN, Aurore M.G.Ch. von
HEIBERG, Johanne Louise
HERITTE-VIARDOT, Louise Pauline
    Marie
HILLEBRAND-LAUSSOT, Jessie
HODGES, Faustina Hasse
HOEGSBRO-CHRISTENSEN, Inge
HUBER, Nanette
JANINA, Olga
JESKE-CHOINSKA-MIKORSKA,
    Ludmila
KALLEY, Sara Poulton
KINKEL, Johanna
LEONARDO, Luisa
LILIUOKALANI, Queen of Hawaii
MARSHALL, Florence A.

MILLAR, Marian
MONGRUEL, Georgiana Catherine Eugenia Leonard
MORGAN, Lady
McKINNEY, Ida Scott Taylor
NATHUSIUS, Marie
NEWCOMBE, Georgeanne
NIELSEN, Henriette
NORTON, Caroline Elizabeth Sarah
NOVELLO, Mary Sabilla
OWENS, Priscilla
PERRONNET, Amelie
POLKO, Elise Vogel
PURGOLD, Nadezhda Nikolayevna
PUSICH, D. Antonia Gertrudes
RAMANN, Lina
RICOTTI, Onestina
RITTER, Fanny Malone Raymond
ROSALES, Cecilia
RUDERSDORF, Erminie
RUNCIE, Constance Owen Faunt Le Roy
SAINTON-DOLBY, Charlotte Helen
SALM-DYCK, Constance-Marie de Theis, Princess
SCHUMANN, Clara Josephine
SEROVA, Valentina Semyonovna
SERVIER, Mme. H.
SMITH, Hannah
SMITH, Laura Alexandrine
SMITH, May Florence
STOWE, Harriet Beecher
SUTRO, Florence Edith
THOMAS, Adelaide Louise
THYS, Pauline
TRETBAR, Helen
VIARDOT-GARCIA, Pauline Michelle Ferdinande
VOLKONSKAYA, Zinanda Alexandrovna, Princess
WAKEFIELD, Augusta Mary
WOLFF, Luise
WOLFF-FRITZ, Sophie
WUERTEMBERSKA-CZARTORYSKA, Maria, Duchess
WUIET, Caroline
ZANTEN, Cornelia van
ZBYSZEWSKA-OLECHNOWSKA, Maria

20th Century A.D.
ACE, Joy Milane
ADAMS, Julia Aurelia
ANDERSON, Ruth
ARHO, Anneli
ARLEN, Jeanne Burns
ARMER, Elinor Florence
ARTEAGA, Genoveva de
ARVEY, Verna
ATKINSON, Dorothy
BACEWICZ, Grazyna
BADIAN, Maya
BAGANIER, Janine
BAILIN, Harriett
BAINBRIDGE, Katharine
BARDEL, Germaine
BAUER, Marion Eugenie
BAULD, Alison
BEACH, Amy Marcy
BEAT, Janet Eveline
BEATH, Betty
BECLARD D'HARCOURT, Marguerite
BEECROFT, Norma Marian
BEHREND, Jeanne
BELINFANTE-DEKKER, Martha Suzanna Betje
BENEDICENTI, Vera
BENNETT, Elsie M.
BENOIT, Francine Germaine Van Gool
BERCKMAN, Evelyn

BEZDEK, Sister John Joseph
BILBRO, Anne Mathilde
BILLINGTON, Elizabeth
BLAKE, Dorothy Gaynor
BLANCK, Olga de
BOLZ, Harriet
BOND, Carrie Jacobs
BOND, Victoria Ellen
BONDS, Margaret
BORBOM, Maria de Melo Furtado Caldeira Giraldes
BORON, Marion
BORROFF, Edith
BOSCH Y PAGES, Luisa
BOULANGER, Nadia Juliette
BOUQUET, Marie-Therese
BRAGA, Henriqueta Rosa Fernandes
BRANDMAN, Margaret Susan
BREEN, May Singhi
BRESCHI, Laura
BRIGGS, Nancy Louise
BRITAIN, Radie
BROADWOOD, Lucy E.
BROWN, Gladys Mungen
BRYUSSOVA, Nadezhda Yakolevna
BUCHANAN, Annabel Morris
BUENAVENTURA, Isabel
BURGER, Hester Aletta Sophie
BUTT, Thelma
CABREIRA, Estefania Loureiro de Vasconcelos Leao
CARMEN MARINA
CARMICHAEL, Mary Grant
CARRENO, Teresa
CASTAGNETTA, Grace Sharp
CATUNDA, Eunice do Monte Lima
CAWTHORN, Janie M.
CECCONI-BATES, Augusta
CHALITA, Laila Maria
CHANDLER, Mary
CHARLES, S. Robin
CHAVES, Laura da Fonseca
CHEATHAM, Kitty
CHITTENDEN, Kate Sara
CHUDOBA, Blanka
CLARKE, Rebecca
CLARKE, Urana
CONSTANTINESCU, Domnica
CORDULA, Sister M.
CORNEA-IONESCU, Alma
CORY, Eleanor
COTE, Helene
COULOMBE SAINT-MARCOUX, Micheline
CRAWFORD, Dawn Constance
CRAWFORD SEEGER, Ruth
CURRAN, Pearl Gildersleeve
CURTIS, Natalie
DALE, Kathleen
DAVIS, Jean Reynolds
DE PATE, Elisabetta M.S.
DEACON, Mary Connor
DELIZ, Monserrate
DEMARQUEZ, Suzanne
DESPORTES, Yvonne Berthe Melitta
DIANDA, Hilda
DILLER, Angela
DINN, Freda
DITTENHAVER, Sarah Louise
DLUGOSZEWSKI, Lucia
DOANE, Dorothy
DOMMEL-DIENY, Amy
DONCEANU, Felicia
DORABIALSKA, Julia Helena
DREYFUS, Francis Kay
DRYNAN, Margaret
DUBOIS, Shirley Graham
DUGGAN, Beatrice Abbott
DUNN, Rebecca Welty
DZIEWULSKA, Maria Amelia
EICHHORN, Hermene Warlick

ELKAN, Ida
ELLIOTT, Marjorie Reeve
ELLIOTT, Mary Sims
ELLIS, Vivian
ELMORE, Cenieth Catherine
ELST, Nancy van der
EMINGEROVA, Katerina
ENDE, Amelia von
ERHART, Dorothy
ESCOBAR, Maria Luisa
ESCOT, Pozzi
EZELL, Helen Ingle
FAHRER, Alison Clark
FAIRLIE, Margaret C.
FALCINELLI, Rolande
FELIX, Margery Edith
FENNER, Beatrice
FERREYRA, Beatriz
FINE, Sylvia
FINE, Vivian
FINLEY, Lorraine Noel
FISHER, Doris
FISHER, Renee Breger
FIUZA, Virginia Salgado
FLICK-FLOOD, Dora
FONDER, Sister Mary Teresine
FORD, Olive Elizabeth
FORMAN, Joanne
FRASER, Shena Eleanor
FRASIER, Jane
FREED, Dorothy Whitson
FREER, Eleanor Warner Everest
FREGA, Ana Lucia
FRIEDBERG, Patricia Ann
FRONDONI LACOMBE, Madalena
FURGERI, Bianca Maria
GARCIA MUNOZ, Carmen
GARNETT, Luisa Aires
GARTENLAUB, Odette
GAUTHIEZ, Cecile
GAYNOR, Jessie Love
GERRISH-JONES, Abbie
GEST, Elizabeth
GIDEON, Miriam
GITECK, Janice
GLANVILLE-HICKS, Peggy
GLEN, Irma
GLYN, Margaret Henriette
GNUS, Ryta
GODLA, Mary Ann
GOETSCHIUS, Marjorie
GONZAGA, Chiquinha
GOODMAN, Lillian Rosedale
GOODSMITH, Ruth B.
GOODWIN, Amina Beatrice
GOTKOVSKY, Ida-Rose Esther
GRAINGER, Ella Viola Strom-Brandelius
GRAU, Irene Rosenberg
GREENE, Margo Lynn
GRIEBEL WANDALL, Tekla
GUBITOSI, Emilia
GULESIAN, Grace Warner
HACKLEY, Emma Azalia Smith
HAIK-VANTOURA, Suzanne
HAJDU, Julia
HALL, Pauline
HAMILTON, Gertrude Bean
HANIM, Leyla
HANSEN, Joan
HARRIS, Ethel Ramos
HAUSMAN, Ruth Langley
HAYS, Doris Ernestine
HEALE, Helene
HEINRICH, Adel Verna
HELLER, Ruth
HEMMENT, Marguerite E.
HERNANDEZ-GONZALO, Gisela
HEYMAN, Katherine Ruth Willoughby
HIGGINS, Esther S.

HILDERLEY, Jeriann G.
HILL, May
HILL, Mildred J.
HINLOPEN, Francina
HOFF, Vivian Beaumont
HOLCOMB, Louanah Riggs
HOLLAND, Dulcie Sybil
HOLST, Imogen Clare
HORSLEY, Imogene
HOUSE, L. Marguerite
HOWARD, Beatrice Thomas
HOWARD, Helen Willard
HOYT, Mary Mack
HSU, Wen-Ying
HUEBNER, Ilse
HUNKINS, Eusebia Simpson
HYDE, Miriam Beatrice
HYTREK, Sister Theophane
IBANEZ, Carmen
IVEY, Jean Eichelberger
JAELL-TRAUTMANN, Marie
JANOTHA, Natalia
JENNEY, Mary Frances
JOHNSON, Mary Ernestine Clark
JOHNSTON, Alison Aileen Annie
JOLAS, Betsy
JOLLEY, Florence Werner
JORDAN, Alice Yost
KACZURBINA-ZDZIECHOWSKA,
    Maria
KAHMANN, Chesley
KALOGRIDOU, Maria
KANACH, Sharon E.
KAPLAN, Lois Jay
KARR Y DE ALFONSETTI, Carmen
KASILAG, Lucrecia R.
KAVASCH, Deborah Helene
KAYDEN, Mildred
KEETMAN, Gunild
KETTERER, Ella
KICKTON, Erika
KINSCELLA, Hazel Gertrude
KISCH, Eve
KISTETENYI, Melinda
KNIGHT, Judyth
KNOWLES, Alison
KOBLENZ, Babette
KORN, Clara Anna
KOVALEVA, Olga Vasilevna
KOZINOVIC, Lujza
KREISS, Hulda E.
KRUGER, Lilly Canfield
KUMMER, Clare
LA BARBARA, Joan
LACHARTRE, Nicole Marie
LAJEUNESSE, Emma, Dame
LANDOWSKA, Wanda
LAST, Joan Mary
LE BEAU, Louisa Adolpha
LE SIEGE, Annette
LEECH, Lida Shivers
LEHMAN, Evangeline Marie
LEONE, Mae G.
LEVI, Natalia Nikolayevna
LEVINA, Zara Alexandrovna
LIDDELL, Claire
LIEBLING, Estelle
LILLENAS, Bertha Mae
LIMA CRUZ, Maria Antonietta de
LITTLEJOHN, Joan Anne
LOCKE, Flora Elbertine Huie
LOCKWOOD, Annea Ferguson
LOGAN, Virginia Knight
LOHOEFER, Evelyn
LOHR, Ina
LORENZ, Ellen Jane
LORING, Nancy
LOVELACE, Carey
LUNA DE ESPAILLAT, Margarita
LUND, Signe
LUTYENS, Elisabeth

LYONN LIEBERMAN, Julie
LYONS, Ruth
MACKEN, Jane Virginia
MacFARREN, Emma Marie
McILWRAITH, Isa Roberta
McLEAN, Priscilla Anne Taylor
McLEMORE, Monita Prine
McLEOD, Evelyn Lundgren
McMILLAN, Ann Endicott
McNAIR, Jacqueline Hanna
MAHLER, Alma Maria
MARKS, Jeanne Marie
MARQUES, Laura Wake
MARSHALL, Jane Manton
MARTH, Helen June
MILAM, Lena Triplett
MILLER, Lillian Anne
MILNE, Helen C.
MIRON, Tsipora
MONTGOMERY, Merle
MOSHER, Frances Elizabeth
NAKASHIMA, Jeanne Marie
NEWTON, Rhoda
NIGHTINGALE, Mae Wheeler
NIKOLSKAYA, Lyubov Borisovna
NIVELLI SCHWARTZ, Gina
NOBLITT, Katheryn Marie McCall
NUGENT, Maude Jerome
OBENCHAIN, Virginia
O'BRIEN, Katharine E.
OCHSE, Orpha Caroline
ODAGESCU, Irina
OHLSON, Marion
OLIVER, Madra Emogene
OLSON, Lynn Freeman
OSTERZEE, Cornelia van
ORE, Cecilie
OWENS, Rochelle
PATERSON, Wilma
PATTERSON, Annie Wilson
PAUL, Doris A.
PAULL, Barberi
PEACOCK, Mary O'Kelley
PERRY, Marilyn Brown
PETERSON, Melody
PETRA-BASACOPOL, Carmen
PHILLIPS, Bryony
PIECHOWSKA, Alina
PITT, Emma
PITTMAN, Evelyn LaRue
POOL, Jeannie Gayle
POSTON, Elizabeth
PREOBRAJENSKA, Vera
    Nicolaevna
PRICE, Florence Beatrice
PRIESING, Dorothy Jean
PUKUI, Mary Abigail
QUINLAN, Agnes Clune
RABER DE REINDERS, Esther
RABINOF, Sylvia
RAKHMANKULOVA, Mariam
    Mannanovna
RALSTON, Frances Marion
RAMM, Valentina Iosifovna
RAW, Vera Constance
REIS, Hilda Pires dos
RESPIGHI, Elsa
RICHMOND, Virginia
RITTENHOUSE, Elizabeth Mae
ROGERS, Clara Kathleen
ROKSETH, Yvonne
ROMA, Caro
ROSE OF JESUS, Sister
RUBIN, Anna Ita
RUSSELL, Anna
SACHS, Carolyn
SALQUIN, Hedy
SALSBURY, Janet Mary
SANDRESKY, Margaret Vardell
SANFILIPPO, Margherita Marie
SANTIAGO-FELIPE, Vilma R.

SANZ, Rocio
SCHICK, Philippine
SCHLEDER, Grizelda Lazzaro
SCHMITZ-GOHR, Else
SCHURZMANN, Katharina
SCHUSSLER-BREWAEYS, Marie
    Antoinette
SCHUYLER, Philippa Duke
SCRIABINE, Marina
SEARCH, Sara Opal
SEAVER, Blanche Ebert
SELDEN-GOTH, Gizella
SEMEGEN, Daria
SERRANO REDONNET, Ana
SHAFFER, Jeanne Ellison
SHERMAN, Ingrid
SILVERMAN, Faye-Ellen
SIMONS, Netty
SKAGGS, Hazel Ghazarian
SLENCZYNSKA, Ruth
SMITH, Julia Frances
SMITH, Ruby Mae
SMITH, Selma Moidel
SMYTH, Ethel Mary, Dame
SNIZKOVA-SKRHOVA, Jitka
SODRE, Joanidia
SOLOMON, Mirrie Irma
SOMMERS, Daria E.
SPENCER PALMER, Florence
    Margaret
SPIZIZEN, Louise Myers
SPONGBERG, Viola
STAINKAMPH, Eileen Freda
STEELE, Helen
STEIN, Gladys Marie
STEIN-SCHNEIDER, Lena
STRICKLAND, Lily Teresa
STUDENY, Herma
STURE VASA, Mary O'Hara
STUTSMAN, Grace May
STYLES, Dorothy Geneva
SUESSE, Dana
SUTHERLAND, Margaret
SWADOS, Elizabeth
TATE, Phyllis
TAYLOR, Mary Virginia
TECK, Katherine
TERHUNE, Anice
TERZIAN, Alicia
THIEME, Kerstin Anja
THOMA, Annette
THOMAS, Helen
THOMAS, Mary Virginia
THOMPSON, Ellen
TIDEMAN-WIJERS, Bertha
TILICHEYEVA, Elena Nikolayevna
TOBIN, Candida
TODD, Alice Weston
TRAEGER, Elinor Meissner
TURGEON, Frances
TURNER, Mildred Cozzens
TURNER, Myra Brooks
ULEHLA, Ludmila
UPTON, Anne
VAN APPLEDORN, Mary Jeanne
VAN DE VATE, Nancy Hayes
VAN DER MARK, Maria
VANNAH, Kate
VASHAW, Cecile
VERHAALEN, Sister Marion
VIGNERON-RAMAKERS, Christiane-
    Josee
VIRGIL, Antha Minerva Patchen
VLADERACKEN, Geertruida van
VOIGT-SCHWEIKERT, Margarete
WAINWRIGHT, Harriet
WALDO, Elisabeth
WALLACE, Mildred White
WALLNEROVA, Bibiana
WANG, An-Ming
WARD, Diane

WATERHOUSE, Frances Emery
WEAVER, Mary
WEISSBERG, Julia Lazerevna
WESTGATE, Elizabeth
WHITE, Elsie Fellows

WHITTINGTON, Joan
WINTER, Sister Miriam
   Therese
WOLLNER, Gertrude Price
WOOD, Ruzena Alenka Valda

WOODRUFF, Edith S.
WOODS, Joan Shirley LeSueur
WOOLSLEY, Mary Hale
YI, Heung-Yull
YOUNG, Rolande Maxwell

APPENDIX 10

Women composers by the instruments they play

ACCORDION
20th Century A.D.
BENNETT, Elsie M.
BOLL, Christine E.
BRANDMAN, Margaret Susan
BRUGGMANN, Heidi
FISHER, Renee Breger
GRIMES, Doreen
HETRICK, Patricia Anne
HOLMES, Shirlee McGee
KEMP, Dorothy Elizabeth Walter
NIGHTINGALE, Barbara Diane
SAMSUTDINOVA, Magira
SCHIEVE, Catherine
SCHMIDT, Diane Louise
SPECHT, Judy Lavise

BASSOON
20th Century A.D.
GRIEBLING, Karen Jean
JARRATT, Lita
MILDREN, Margaret Joyce
VAZQUEZ, Lilia

CARILLON
19th Century A.D.
WILSON, Addie Anderson
20th Century A.D.
COOKE, Marjorie Tibbets
HALSTED, Margo
WARNER, Sally Slade
WEEL, Heleen van der

CIMBALOM
20th Century A.D.
GHILARDI, Syra
HOUSE, L. Marguerite
KJAER, Kirsten
MAZOUROVA, Jarmila

CLARINET
19th Century A.D.
KRAEHMER, Caroline
20th Century A.D.
ARQUIT, Nora Harris
BRANDMAN, Margaret Susan
GRIMES, Doreen
HOY, Bonnee L.
KJAER, Kirsten
KOLB, Barbara
LANG, Rosemary Rita
MACKIE, Shirley M.
MARCUS, Bunita
MILLER, Elma

McLAUGHLIN, Marian
REED, Marlyce Rae Polk
SMELTZER, Susan Mary

COR ANGLAIS
20th Century A.D.
LANG, Rosemary Rita
REID, Sarah Johnston

CORNET
16th Century A.D.
BORGHI, Faustina

DOMRA
20th Century A.D.
GORODOVSKAYA, V.
NURPEISSOVA, Dina
SAMSUTDINOVA, Magira

DOUBLE BASS
20th Century A.D.
AESCHLIMANN-ROTH, Esther
FISHER, Renée Breger
GERSTMAN, Blanche Wilhelminia
LEANDRE, Joelle
WITNI, Monica

ELECTRONIC INSTRUMENTS
20th Century A.D.
AMACHER, Maryanne
BEECROFT, Norma Marian
BIBBY, Gillian Margaret
BROUK, Joanna
BRUZDOWICZ, Joanna
CARLOS, Wendy
CIANI, Suzanne Elizabeth
DIANDA, Hilda
FERREYRA, Beatriz
FOWLER, Jennifer Joan
FRASER-MILLER, Gloria Jill
HAYS, Doris Ernestine
IVEY, Jean Eichelberger
JOHNSTON-REID, Sarah Ruth
KANACH, Sharon E.
KELLEY, Patricia Ann
LA BARBARA, Joan
LACHARTRE, Nicole Marie
LEBARON, Anne
LEE, Hope Anne Keng-Wei
LOCKWOOD, Annea Ferguson
LORIOD, Yvonne
LOUIE, Alexina Diane
McLEAN, Priscilla Anne Taylor
MARTIN, Judith Reher

MILLER, Elma
MOLAVA, Pamela May
MONK, Meredith
MULDER, Maria Antonia
ORAM, Daphne Blake
POOL, Jeannie Gayle
RANTA-SHIDA, Shoko
SAINT JOHN, Kathleen Louise
SANDIFUR, Ann Elizabeth
SCRIABINE, Marina
SEARCH, Sara Opal
SEMEGEN, Daria
SHIELDS, Alice Ferree
SHIOMI, Mieko
SMILEY, Pril
SOUTHAM, Ann
SPIEGEL, Laurie
STOEPPELMANN, Janet
THOME, Diane
TOYAMA, Michiko Françoise
TWOMBLY, Mary Lynn
URRETA, Alicia
VAZQUEZ, Alida
WALLACH, Joelle
WOLF-COHEN, Veronika

FLUTE
20th Century A.D.
ANDERSON, Ruth
BEECROFT, Norma Marian
BLISS, Marilyn S.
BOUCHARD, Linda L.
BOYD, Anne Elizabeth
BRICE, Jean Anne
CROCHET, Sharon Brandstetter
DUCZMAL-JAROSZEWSKA,
    Agnieszka
EICHENWALD, Sylvia
FISHER, Susan
GARDNER, Kay
GEBUHR, Ann Karen
GROSSMAN, Deena
HOOVER, Katherine
HOY, Bonnee L.
KUFFLER, Eugenie
KUKUCK, Felicitas
LAITMAN, Lori
LATHROP, Gayle Posselt
LEE, Hope Anne Keng-Wei
LEE, Michelle
MEACHEM, Margaret McKeen
    Ramsey
MILDREN, Margaret Joyce
MITCHELL, Janice Misurell

OMER, Hélène
PAYNE, Maggi
PERISSAS, Madeleine
POLIN, Claire
SANFILIPPO, Margherita Marie
SCHARLI, Ruth
SCHIEVE, Catherine
SIMPSON, Mary Jean
SMITH, Joan Templar
SWAIN, Freda Mary
TURRIETTA, Cheryl Renée
USHER, Julia
UYEDA, Leslie
WARING, Kate
WEBER, Carole
WOODWARD, Martha Clive
WYLIE, Ruth Shaw
Century unknown
CAI, Wen Ji, Princess
DE, Li, Princess

FRENCH HORN
20th Century A.D.
FRUMKER, Linda
HOFFMAN, Phyllis Sampson
KEMP, Dorothy Elizabeth Walter
LANG, Rosemary Rita
MARSHALL, Pamela J.
ROGERS, Susan Whipple
SKARECKY, Jana Milena
TECK, Katherine
TELFER, Nancy Ellen
WECKWERTH, Nancy

GUITAR
17th Century A.D.
BARONI BASILE, Adriana
CACCINI, Francesca
18th Century A.D.
BERTHE, Mme.
KALFA, Dilhayat
19th Century A.D.
CONSTANT, Rosalie de
LIKELIKE, Miriam Cleghorn,
    Princess
MARCHISIO, Barbara
MOUNSEY, Elizabeth
PRATTEN, Mrs. Robert Sidney
20th Century A.D.
ABEJO, Sister M. Rosalina
ANIDO, Maria Luisa
ASHFORD, Emma Louise
BARTHEL, Ursula
BECKON, Lettie Marie
BELL, Carla Huston
BERROA, Catalina
BOYD, Liona Maria
BRONDI, Rita Maria
CARMEN MARINA
CRISWICK, Mary
DAILLY, Claudine
FERNANDEZ, Terresita
GODLA, Mary Ann
GRIMES, Doreen
HYLIN, Birgitta Charlotta Kristina
IRMAN-ALLEMANN, Regina
KANAKA'OLE, Edith Ke-Kuhikuhi-I-
    Pu'u-one-o-Na-Ali'i-O-Kohala
KOKDES, Veveser
LATHROP, Gayle Posselt
LE BORDAYS, Christiane
LINNEMANN, Maria Catharina
MACHADO, Lena
MERTENS, Dolores
NAMAKELUA, Alice K.
NICKERSON, Camille Lucie
OSMANOGLU, Gevheri
OTERO, Mercedes
PRESTI, Ida
ROEMER, Hanne
ROGATIS, Teresa de

SERRANO REDONNET, Ana
SINDE RAMALLAL, Clara
SPEACH, Sister Bernadette Marie
SPIEGEL, Laurie
VALDES, Marta
VAZQUEZ, Alida
WALKER, Louise
Century unknown
FRACKER, Cora Robins

HANDBELL RINGER
20th Century A.D.
LORENZ, Ellen Jane

HARP
25th Century B.C.
HEKENU
16th Century B.C.
BAKIT
5th Century A.D.
AZADE
BRIDGET
15th Century A.D.
PEPARARA, Laura
17th Century A.D.
BARONI BASILE, Adriana
18th Century A.D.
BARTHELEMON, Cecilia Maria
DELAVAL, Mme.
DUMUR, Mme.
MARIE ANTOINETTE, Archduchess
    of Austria, Queen of France
MUELLNER, Johanna
MUSIGNY, Mme. de
19th Century A.D.
BERTRAND, Aline
BINFIELD, Hanna R.
BISSET, Elizabeth Anne
BOTTINI, Marianna, Marchioness
CANDEILLE, Amelie Julie
CRETI, Marianna de Rocchis
DEMAR, Thrèse
DUSSEK, Olivia
ESCHBORN, Georgine Christine
    Maria Anna
GENGLIS, Stephanie Felicite,
    Countess of Saint-Aubin
GIBSON, Isabella Mary
KRUMPHOLTZ PITTAR, Fanny
KRUMPHOLTZ, Anne-Marie
MORGAN, Lady
O'LEARY, Rosetta
PARIS, Salomea
PATON, Mary Anne
POLLET, Marie Nicole Simonin
RONSSECY, Mme. de
WINKEL, Thérèse Emilie Henriette
    aus dem
20th Century A.D.
ALLEN, Mimi
BARBER, Gail Guseman
BERROA, Catalina
BOSCH Y PAGES, Luisa
BOULANGER, Lili Juliette Marie Olga
BRANDMAN, Margaret Susan
CHALLAN, Annie
CHERTOK, Pearl
COLTRANE, Alice McLeod
ERDELI, Xenia Alexandrovna
FALLADOVA-SKVOROVA, Anezka
FITZGERALD, Sister Florence
    Therese
GIURANNA, Elena Barbara
GLICK, Nancy Kay
GOOSSENS, Marie Henriette
GOVEA, Wenonah Milton
GRAMEGLIA-GROSSO, Emma
GUSTAVSON, Nancy Nicholls
HANSEN, Renee
HARRIS, Ruth Berman
HINLOPEN, Francina

HORNBACK, Sister Mary Gisela
HUJSAK, Joy Detenbeck
INGLEFIELD, Ruth Karin
JAMET, Marie-Claire
JOHN, Patricia Spaulding
JONES, Sister Ida
KELLY, Denise Maria Anne
KJAER, Kirsten
KOSTAKOVA-HERODKOVA, Marie
KREISS, Hulda E.
LANDREE, Jaquenote Goldsteen
LEBARON, Anne
LORE, Emma Maria Theresa
McGILL, Gwendolen Mary Finlayson
MARIANI-CAMPOLIETI, Virginia
MEGEVAND, Denise
MERTENS, Dolores
MORGAN, Maud
MOSSAFER RIND, Bernice
PALMER, Lynne Wainwright
PHARRIS, Elizabeth
QUINTANILLA, Alba
RENIE, Henriette
ROBBOY, Rosalie Smotkin
ROBINSON, Gertrude Ina
ROBLES, Marisa
SASSOLI, Ada
SCALETTI, Carla
SCHROEDER, Beatrice
SEIBERT, Irma
SHARPE, Emma
SMITH, Edith Gross
SURIANI, Alberta
VON PECHY, Valerie
WILKINS, Margaret Lucy
WILLIAMS, Sioned
WILSON, Jean Dolores
Century unknown
ACHARD, Marguerite
ROSATI, Elvira

HARPSICHORD
16th Century A.D.
ALEOTTI, Vittoria
17th Century A.D.
CACCINI, Francesca
MENETOU, Françoise-Charlotte de
    Senneterre
18th Century A.D.
AGNESI-PINOTTINI, Maria Teresa d'
ANNA AMALIA, Princess of Prussia
AUENBRUGG, Marianna von
BACHMANN, Charlotte Caroline
    Wilhelmine
BARTHELEMON, Cecilia Maria
BRILLON DE JOUY, Mme.
CAMATI, Maria
CASSON, Margaret
GUEST, Jeanne Marie
LA GUERRE, Elisabeth-Claude
    Jacquet de
LA ROCHE, Rosa
LACHANTERIE, Elisabeth
LOUIS, Mme.
MARIA ANTONIA WALPURGIS,
    Princess of Bavaria
MARIA CHARLOTTE AMALIE,
    Princess of Saxe-Meiningen
MARIA TERESA BARBARA DE
    BRAGANÇA, Queen of Spain
MARTINEZ, Marianne
POUILLAU, Mlle.
SAVAGE, Jane
SIRMEN, Maddalena Laura di
19th Century A.D.
AMALIE, Marie Friederike Augusta,
    Princess of Saxony
BAUER, Katharine
CASADESUS, Regina
CHODKIEWICZ, Comtesse
CORRI-DUSSEK, Sofia Giustina

MOZART, Maria Anna Walburga
Ignatia
WESTENHOLZ, Eleonore Sophie
Marie
20th Century A.D.
ABE, Kyoko
ALBRIGHT, Janet Elaine
AUBERT, Pauline Louise
Henriette
BARTLETT, Ethel Agnes
BILLINGTON, Elizabeth
BIZONY, Celia
BREMER, Marrie Petronella
BROGUE, Roslyn Clara
CLAYTON, Susan
COVERT, Mary Ann Hunter
CREES, Kathleen Elsie
DIEMER, Emma Lou
ERHART, Dorothy
GABRYS, Ewa Lucja Maria
GHIGLIERI, Sylvia
GOULD, Janetta
HEINRICH, Adel Verna
KELLY, Denise Maria Anne
KRIMSKY, Katrina
LANDOWSKA, Wanda
LEE, Hwaeja Yoo
LUMBY, Betty Louise
MACAULAY, Janice Michel
MAGEAU, Mary Jane
MAREZ-OYENS, Tera de
MARTINS, Maria de Lourdes
MASON, Margaret C.
MEIGS, Melinda Moore
MEKEEL, Joyce
NARCISSE-MAIR, Denise Lorraine
OLIVE, Vivienne
OZAITA, Maria Luisaria Luisa
PRICE, Deon Nielsen
QUINTANILLA, Alba
RICHARDSON, Enid Dorothy
ROBERTS, Gertrud Hermine Kuenzel
ROBERTSON, Donna Lou Nagey
ROESGEN-CHAMPION, Marguerite
Sara
SLENDZINSKA, Julitta
SMELTZER, Susan Mary
SMITH, Linda Catlin
SPIZIZEN, Louise Myers
STOEPPELMANN, Janet
VEHAR, Persis Anne
VISCONTI, Leila
WHITTLE, Chris Mary-Francine
WIELE, Aimée van der
ZECHLIN, Ruth

LUTE
7th Century A.D.
AZZA AL-MAILA
8th Century A.D.
JAMILA
KHULAIDA I
9th Century A.D.
BADHL
FADL(1)
FARIDA
MAHBUBA
ORAIB
16th Century A.D.
ARCHILEI, Vittoria
BOLEYN, Anne, Queen of England
BOLOGNESE, Isabella
CASULANA, Maddalena
FERRA, Susana
17th Century A.D.
BOCQUET, Anne
CACCINI, Francesca
18th Century A.D.
BERTHE, Mme.
19th Century A.D.
WOLZOGEN, Elsa Laura von

20th Century A.D.
BLOCH, Suzanne
GREGORY, Else
MENDELSSOHN, Erna
OSMANOGLU, Gevheri
SPIEGEL, Laurie
Century unknown
CESIS, Sister Sulpizia

LYRE
6th Century B.C.
SAPPHO
17th Century A.D.
BARONI BASILE, Adriana
20th Century A.D.
OZDENSES, Semahat
OSMANOGLU, Gevheri
PARS, Melahat
Century unknown
DILAL

MANDOLIN
18th Century A.D.
BERTHÉ, Mme.
19th Century A.D.
SONTAG, Henriette

MARIMBA
20th Century A.D.
ABEJO, Sister M. Rosalina
BECKON, Lettie Marie
BUMP, Mary Crane
CHENOWETH, Vida
KILBY, Muriel Laura

MUSICAL BOW
20th Century A.D.
MAGOGO KA DINIZULU, Constance,
Princess

OBOE
19th Century A.D.
HAGUE, Harriet
20th Century A.D.
CHANDLER, Mary
FERNANDO, Sarathchandra
Vichremadithya
GIPPS, Ruth
GRIEBLING, Margaret Ann
HUNTER, Hilda
LANG, Rosemary Rita
LEVIN, Rami Yona
PHILLIPS, Bryony
RAMAKERS, Christiane Josee
REID, Sarah Johnston
SANFILIPPO, Margherita Marie
SHORE, Clare

ORGAN
16th Century A.D.
ALEOTTI, Raffaela-Argenta
BORGHI, Faustina
17th Century A.D.
CALEGARI, Cornelia
ENTHALLER, Sidonia
18th Century A.D.
CLARKE, Jane
DE GAMBARINI, Elisabetta
HUDSON, Mary
LA GUERRE, Elisabeth-Claude
Jacquet de
LACHANTERIE, Elisabeth
STECHER, Marianne
VALENTINE, Ann
WORGAN, Mary
19th Century A.D.
ARENS-ROGER, Adelia
ASTLE-ALLAM, Agnes Mary
AUSTEN, Augusta Amherst
AYLWARD, Florence
BARTHOLOMEW, Ann Sheppard

BERNARD, Vincenzia
BINFIELD, Hanna R.
BRADSHAW, Nellie Shorthill
BRIZZI-GIORGI, Maria
DUSSEK, Olivia
FOWLES, Margaret F.
HODGES, Faustina Hasse
HOLMBERG, Emelie Augusta
Kristina
HUENERWADEL, Fanny
LA HYE, Louise Genevieve
LAWRENCE, Elizabeth S.
LOUD, Annie Frances
MOSEL, Catherine de
MOUNSEY, Elizabeth
NEWCOMBE, Georgeanne
PARADIS, Maria Theresia von
PIERPONT, Marie de
PYNE, Louisa Aubert
REES, Clara H.
SALE, Sophia
SMITH, Eleanor Louise
STIRLING, Elizabeth
TRUETTE, Everette
VON HOFF, Elizabeth
WARD, Clementine
WESTROP, Kate
WILSON, Addie Anderson
20th Century A.D.
ABORN, Lora
ACKLAND, Jeanne Isabel Dorothy
ADAMS, Carrie Bell
ADAMS, Elizabeth Kilmer
ADAMS, Julia Aurelia
AHRENS, Sieglinde
AINSCOUGH, Juliana Mary
ALAIN, Marie Claire
ALDEN, Zilpha May
ALLBRITTON, Florence Ziegler
ALLOUARD CARNY, Odette
ALONSO, Julia
ANDREE, Elfrida
ANDRUS, Helen Josephine
ARENA, Iris Mae
ARTEAGA, Genovéva de
ASHFORD, Emma Louise
AUBUT-PRATTE, Françoise
BACKES, Lotte
BAGA, Ena Rosina
BAKKE, Ruth
BAMPTON, Ruth
BARKER, Phyllis Elizabeth
BARTHEL, Ursula
BASSETT, Henrietta Elizabeth
BATE, Jennifer
BECKON, Lettie Marie
BEESON, Elizabeth Ruth
BERGSTROM, Anna
BERROA, Catalina
BITGOOD, Roberta
BIXBY, Allene K.
BLACKWELL, Anna Gee
BLAUVELT, Bula Caswell
BOESSER, Dagma
BORDERS, Barbara Ann
BORON, Marion
BOULANGER, Nadia Juliette
BOYCE, Blanche Ula
BRACQUEMOND, Marthe Henriod
BRAGA, Henriqueta Rosa Fernandes
BRAGGINS, Daphne Elizabeth
BRANDMAN, Margaret Susan
BRANNING, Grace Bell
BREMER, Marrie Petronella
BRENNER, Rosamond Drooker
BRIGGS, Cora Skilling
BRIGHT, Dora Estella
BRITAIN, Radie
BROGUE, Roslyn Clara
BROWN, Elizabeth van Ness
BROWN, Zilda Jennings

BRUSH, Ruth Damaris
BRYAN, Betty Sue
BUCHANAN, Annabel Morris
BUCK, Era Marguerite
BURCHELL, Henrietta Louise
BURT, Virginia M.
BUTLER, Anne Lois
CALDWELL, Mary Elizabeth Glockler
CAMPBELL, Edith Mary
CARL, Tommie Ewert
CARRINGTON-THOMAS, Virginia
CARRIVICK, Olive Amelia
CARSON, Zeula Miller
CARTER, Buenta MacDaniel
CECCONI-BATES, Augusta
CHERUBIM, Sister Mary Schaefer
CHESTNUT, Lora Perry
CHITTENDEN, Kate Sara
CLARK, Florence Durrell
CLARKE, Phyllis Chapman
COFFMAN, Lillian Craig
COLGAN, Alma Cecilia
COLTRANE, Alice McLeod
CROFTS, Inez Altman
CROKER, Catherine Munnell
CROWE, Bonita
CURRIE, Edna R.
DAVIS, Eleanor Maud
DAVIS, Margaret Munger
DE VILLIERS, Justina Wilhelmina
   Nancy
DEACON, Mary Connor
DEMESSIEUX, Jeanne
DENBOW, Stefania Bjoerson
DIEMER, Emma Lou
DOWNEY, Mary
DRYNAN, Margaret
DU PAGE, Florence Elizabeth
DURAND, Nella Wells
EAGLES, Moneta M.
EAKIN, Vera O.
EDGERLY, Cora Emily
EICHHORN, Hermene Warlick
EMIG, Lois Irene
ENDRES, Olive Philomene
FALCINELLI, Rolande
FAUTCH, Sister Magdalen
FISHER, Renée Breger
FONDER, Sister Mary Teresine
FORMAN, Addie Walling
FOSIC, Tarzicija
FOSTER, Fay
FRANCHERE-DESROSIERS, Rose de
   Lima
FROHBEITER, Ann W.
FRONMUELLER, Frieda
FRYZELL, Regina Holmen
FURGERI, Bianca Maria
GEDDES-HARVEY, Roberta
GENET, Marianne
GERRISH-JONES, Abbie
GIACCHINO CUSENZA, Maria
GIROD-PARROT, Marie-Louise
GLEN, Irma
GOVEA, Wenonah Milton
GRIMES, Doreen
HAGAN, Helen Eugenia
HAIK-VANTOURA, Suzanne
HALSTED, Margo
HATCH, Edith
HAVEY, Marguerite
HEIMERL, Elizabeth
HEINRICH, Adel Verna
HEINY, Margaret Harris
HENDERSON, Ruth Watson
HERMANN, Miina
HICKS, Marjorie Kisby
HIGGINS, Esther S.
HILL, May
HILL, Mildred J.
HOFER, Maria

HOFFMANN, Peggy
HOKANSON, Margrethe
HORNBACK, Sister Mary Gisela
HOY, Bonnee L.
HUJSAK, Joy Detenbeck
HUTTON, Florence Myra
HYTREK, Sister Theophane
IVANOVA, Lidia
JACKSON, Elizabeth Barnhart
JENNEY, Mary Frances
JEWELL, Lucina
JOHNSTON, Alison Aileen Annie
JOLAS, Betsy
JOLLEY, Florence Werner
JOLLY, Margaret Anne
JONES, Sister Ida
JORDAN, Alice Yost
JOULAIN, Jeanne-Angele-Desirée-
   Yvonne
JUENGER, Patricia
KALTENECKER, Gertraud
KENDRICK, Virginia Catherine
KENT, Ada Twohy
KER, Ann S.
KISTETENYI, Melinda
KNOBLOCHOVA, Antonie
KOZINOVIC, Lujza
KUESTER, Edith Haines
KUNTZE, Olga
LAFLEUR, Lucienne
LAMBRECHTS-VOS, Anna Catharina
LANDREE, Jaquenote Goldsteen
LANG, Edith
LARUELLE, Jeanne-Marie
LAWRENCE, Emily M.
LEAF, Ann
LEAVITT, Helen Sewall
LECLERC, Michelle
LEE, Anna Virginia
LEE, Hope Anne Keng-Wei
LEE, Hwaeja Yoo
LEECH, Lida Shivers
LEECH, Renée
LEHOTSKA-KRIZKOVA, Ludmila
LEJEUNE-BONNIER, Eliane
LEONE, Mae G.
LEPKE, Charma Davies
LOCKWOOD, Charlotte Mathewson
LORENZ, Ellen Jane
LUMBY, Betty Louise
LYONS, Ruth
MACAULAY, Janice Michel
McCLEARY, Mary Gilkeson
McCOLLIN, Frances
McDUFFEE, Mabel Howard
McILWRAITH, Isa Roberta
MANGGRUM, Loretta C. Cessor
MARCELL, Florence
MARTH, Helen June
MARTIN, Judith Reher
MARY BERNICE, Sister
MASON, Marilyn May
MEADE, Margaret Johnston
MEEK, Ethel Alice
MELL, Gertrud Maria
MELOY, Elizabeth
MILDREN, Margaret Joyce
MILETTE, Juliette
MILLER, Alma Grace
MIRON, Tsipora
MITCHELL, Norma Jean
MOE, Benna
MOHNS, Grace Updegraff Bergen
MORONEY, Sister Mary Emmeline
MORTON, Agnes Louise
MUG, Sister Mary Theodosia
MUNGER, Millicent Christner
MUSTILLO, Lina
NEEL, Susan Elizabeth
NEILY, Anne MacAdams
NEPGEN, Rosa Sophia Cornelia

NEWTON, Rhoda
NIXON, June
NOHE, Beverly
OCHSE, Orpha Caroline
ODDONE SULLI-RAO, Elisabetta
OHLSON, Marion
OLIVE, Vivienne
OLIVER, Madra Emogene
PAQUIN, Anna
PARENTE, Sister Elizabeth
PATTERSON, Annie Wilson
PEGELOW, Hanna G.
PERRY, Mary Dean
PFERDEMENGES, Maria Pauline
   Augusta
PFOLH, Bessie Whittington
PHILLIPS, Vivian Daphne
PICHE, Eudore
PIERCE, Sarah Anderson
PIERROT, Noelie Marie Antoinette
POLLOCK, Muriel
POSTON, Elizabeth
PRICE, Florence Beatrice
PROCACCINI, Teresa
RAHMN, Elza Loethner
RAMSEY, Sister Mary Anastasia
REED, Phyllis Luidens
REES, Winifred Emily
REISER, Violet
RENSHAW, Rosette
REYNOLDS, Laura Lawton
RISHER, Anna Priscilla
RITTENBAND, Minna Ethel
ROBBOY, Rosalie Smotkin
ROBERSON, Ruby Lee Grubbs
ROBERT, Lucie
ROBERTS, Ruth Olive
ROBERTSON, Donna Lou Nagey
ROE, Eileen Betty
ROE, Marion Adelle
ROGERS, Ethel Tench
ROGERS, Faith Helen
ROGERS, Sharon Elery
ROGET, Henriette
ROKSETH, Yvonne
ROOBENIAN, Amber
ROSE OF JESUS, Sister
RYAN, Winifred
SALSBURY, Janet Mary
SANDRESKY, Margaret Vardell
SANDY, Grace Linn
SCHORR-WEILER, Eva
SCHUSTER, Doris Dodd
SCOTT, Georgina Keir
SCRIABINE, Marina
SEUEL-HOLST, Marie
SEWALL, Maud Gilchrist
SHAW, Carrie Burpee
SHELDON, Lillian Tait
SIEGRIST, Beatrice
SILVERBURG, Rose
SIMONE, Nina
SKARECKY, Jana Milena
SKOLFIELD, Alice Jones Tewksbury
SLEETH, Natalie
SMELTZER, Susan Mary
SMITH, Hilda Josephine
SPEACH, Sister Bernadette Marie
SPECHT, Judy Lavise
SPENCER, Marguerita
SPENCER, Williametta
SPONGBERG, Viola
STAIR, Patty
STAIRS, Lousie E.
STARBUCK, Anna Diller
STEVENS, Isadore Harmon
STRICKLAND, Lily Teresa
STRUCK, Ilse
STYLES, Dorothy Geneva
SUESSE, Dana
SUMNER, Clare

TACK, Annie
TAYLOR, Maude Cummings
TERHUNE, Anice
THIEME, Kerstin Anja
THOMAS, Gertrude Evelyn
THOMAS, Marilyn Taft
THOMAS, Mary Virginia
TISSOT, Mireille
TODD, Alice Weston
TURNELL, Margaret Hoberg
TYSON, Mildred Lund
USHER, Ethel Watson
VANIER, Jeannine
VANNAH, Kate
VIGNERON-RAMAKERS, Christiane-
    Josee
VILLENEUVE, Marie-Louise Diane
VILLIN, Marcelle Henriette Marie
VINETTE, Alice
VIRTUE, Constance Cochnower
VOELLMY-LIECHTI, Grety
VOLKART, Hazel
VRIONIDES, Rosina
WALKER, Ella May
WARD, Sister Mary Louise
WARNER, Sally Slade
WELANDER, Svea Goeta
WENNERBERG-REUTER, Sara
    Margareta Eugenia Euphrosyne
WENTZ-JANACEK, Elisabet
WESTBROOK, Helen Searles
WESTGATE, Elizabeth
WHITE, Ruth Eden
WIERUSZOWSKI, Lili
WIGGINS, Mary
WITNI, Monica
WORTH, Amy
WUNSCH, Ilse Gerda
YDSTIE, Arlene Buckneberg
ZECHLIN, Ruth
ZIPRICK, Marjorie Jean
ZOECKLER, Dorothy Ackerman
Century unknown
DONALDSON, Sadie
RITTER, Irene Marschand

PANDORA
20th Century A.D.
BIANCHINI, Virginie
HOKANSON, Margrethe
VIRGIL, Antha Minerva Patchen
WARREN, Elinor Remick

PERCUSSION
20th Century A.D.
BREMER, Marrie Petronella
CULP, Paula Newell
DRYNAN, Margaret
FEDERHOF-MOLLER, Betty
IRMAN-ALLEMANN, Regina
MACHADO, Lena
MASONER, E.L.
MATHIS, Judy M.
PORTER, Debra
PTASZYNSKA, Marta
SANGUESA, Iris

PIANO
18th Century A.D.
AHLEFELDT, Marie Theresia,
    Countess
ANNA AMALIA, Princess of Prussia
AURENHAMMER, Josefa Barbara von
BENAULT, Mlle.
BRANDES, Charlotte Wilhelmina
    Franziska
BRILLON DE JOUY, Mme.
CLARKSON, Jane
DUMUR, Mme.
EICHNER, Adelheid Marie
GUEST, Jeanne Marie

KANZLER, Josephine
KOHARY, Marie, Countess of
LA ROCHE, Rosa
LEBRUN, Franziska Dorothea
MAIER, Catherine
MARIA ANTONIA WALPURGIS,
    Princess of Bavaria
MARTINEZ, Marianne
MEDECK, Mme.
MOREL, Virginie
MUELLER, Elise
POUILLAU, Mlle.
REICHARDT, Bernhardine Juliane
ZAMPIERI, Elizabetta
19th Century A.D.
ADAJEWSKY, Ella
ALEXANDROVA, A.
AMANN, Josephine
AMERSFOORDT-DYK, Hermina
    Maria
ARANCIBIA, Francisca
ARENS-ROGER, Adelia
ASPRI, Orsola
ASTLE-ALLAM, Agnes Mary
ATANASIJEVIC, Slavka
AUSPITZ-KOLAR, Augusta
AYLWARD, Florence
BACHMANN, Elise
BACKER-GROENDAHL, Agathe
    Ursula
BADARZEWSKA-BARANOWSKA,
    Tekla
BAJEROWA, Konstancje
BARONI-CAVALCABO, Guilia
BARTH, Elise
BARTHOLOMEW, Ann Sheppard
BAUER, Katharine
BAWR, Alexandrine Sophie
BELLEVILLE-OURY, Emilie
BERNARD, Vincenzia
BERTIN, Louise Angelique
BIGOT DE MOROGUES, Marie
BISLAND, Margaret Cyrilla
BLAHETKA, Marie Leopoldina
BLEITNER, Rosa
BLOCK, Isabelle McKee
BOCK, Bertha
BOERNER-SANDRINI, Marie
BORTON, Alice
BOVET, Hermine
BOYCE, Ethel Mary
BRANCA-MUSSINI, Adele
BRANCHU, Mme.
BRESSON, Mlle.
BRINKMANN, Minna
BRIZZI-GIORGI, Maria
BROES, Mlle.
BRONSART VON SCHELLENDORF,
    Ingeborg Lena von
BRZEZINSKA, Filipina
BUERDE, Jeanette Antonie
BUGGE, Magda
BUIXO, Paulina
CAETANI-RZEWUSKA, Calista,
    Princess
CANTELLO, Annie
CAPUCCI, Lida
CARMICHAEL, Anne Darling
CHARLOTTE, Friederike Wilhelmine
    Louise, Princess
CHASTENAY, Victorine de
CHEVALIER DE BOISVAL, Mme.
CHOUQUET, Louise
CHRZASTOWSKA, Pelagia
CIBBINI, Katherina
COATES, Kathleen Kyle
COLLIN, Helene
COLLINS, Laura Sedgwick
CONTIN, Mme.
CORRER, Ida, Countess
CORRI-DUSSEK, Sofia Giustina

CRUMB, Berenice
CUMAN, Harriet Johanna Louise
CZETWERTYNSKA, Marie, Princess
CZICZKA, Angela
DAMCKE, Louise
DAMOREAU-CINTI, Laure
DAVIES, Llewela
DE CASTRO, Alice
DELABORDE, Elie Miriam
DEVISME, Jeanne-Hippolite
    Moyroud
DIETRICH, Amalia
DULCKEN, Louisa
DULCKEN, Sophie
DUSCHEK, Josefina
DUSSEK, Olivia
DUSSEK, Veronica Rosalie
EDELSBERG, Philippine von
ENGER, Nelly
FARRENC, Louise
FARRENC, Victorine Louise
FECHNER, Paulina
FERNANDEZ DE LA MORA, Pilar
FERRARI, Carlotta
FORTEY, Mary Comber
FOWLES, Margaret F.
GABRIEL, Mary Ann Virginia
GASCHIN-ROSENBERG, Fanny,
    Countess
GAY, Sophia Maria Francesca
GEIGER, Constanze
GIZYCKA-ZAMOYSKA, Ludmilla,
    Countess
GRABOWSKA, Clementine,
    Countess
GRAEVER, Madeleine
GROEBENSCHUETZ, Amalie
GYDE, Margaret
HAHR, Emma
HALE, Irene
HARTLAND, Lizzie
HASWIN, Frances R.
HAWES, Charlotte W.
HELLER, Ottilie
HENSEL, Fanny Caecilia
HERZOGENBERG, Elizabeth von
HOLMBERG, Emelie Augusta
    Kristina
HOLMES, Augusta Mary Anne
HUENERWADEL, Fanny
HUNDT, Aline
JACQUES, Charlotte
JAHNOVA, Bozena
JANINA, Olga
JENTSCH, May
JOSEPHINE, Queen of Sweden and
    Norway
KAVALIEROVA, Marie
KENDIKOVA, Zdenka
KINKEL, Johanna
KIRCHER, Maria Bertha
KOMOROWSKA, Stephanie,
    Countess
KRAINDL, Sophie de
KUCZOR, Hilda
LA HYE, Louise Genevieve
LANG, Josephine
LANGHANS, Louise
LANGRISHE, May Katherine
LANNOY, Clementine-Josephine-
    Françoise-Therese, Countess
LAVATER, Magdalena Elisabeth
LEONARDO, Luisa
LIEBMANN, Hélène
LIKELIKE, Miriam Cleghorn,
    Princess
LILIEN, Antoinette von, Baroness
LIPINSKA-PARCZEWSKA, Natalia
LODER, Kate Fanny
LORINSER, Gisela von
MACIRONI, Clara Angela

MALIBRAN, Maria Felicitas
MALLEVILLE, Charlotte Tardieu de
MARIA PAULOWNA, Grand Duchess
    of Weimar
MARINELLI, Maria
MARTIN, Giuseppina
MARX, Berthe
MASSART, Louise Aglae
MATOS, A. de
MATTHISON-HANSEN, Nanny
    Hedwig Christiane
MATTHYSSENS, Marie
MAYER, Emilie
MEADER, Emily Peace
MENTER, Sophie
MILLAR, Marian
MOLINOS-LAFITTE, Mlle. A.
MONTGEROULT, Helene de Nervode
MORANDI, Jennie Jewett
MOSEL, Catherine de
MOUNSEY, Elizabeth
MOZART, Maria Anna Walburga
    Ignatia
MUELLER-BENDER, Mme.
MUNDELLA, Emma
NATHAN, Matilde Berendsen
NIEWIAROWSKA-BRZOZOWSKA,
    Julia
O'LEARY, Rosetta
OLIVEIRA, Alexandrina Maciel de
ORGER, Caroline
PACHLER-KOSCHAK, Marie
    Leopoldine
PARADIS, Maria Theresia von
PARIS, Salomea
PARKE, Maria Hester
PEASE, Jessie L.
PELLEGRINI CELONI, Anna
PERALTA CASTERA, Angela
PESADORI, Antoniette de
PEYRON, Albertina Fredrika
PFEIFFER, Clara-Virginie
PFEILSCHIFTER, Julie von
PIERRET, Phedora
PLASENCIA, Ubalda
PLEYEL, Marie Felicity Denise
PLITT, Agathe
POLANOWSKA, Teofila
POSADA Y TORRE, Ana
POTT, Aloyse
PURGOLD, Nadezhda Nikolayevna
PUSICH, D. Antonia Gertrudes
RABORG, Rosa Ortiz de Zerallos de
RALPH, Kate
RAMOS, Eudocia
RAPP, Marguerite
RICHINGS, Caroline
RICOTTI, Onestina
ROBERT-MAZEL, Helene
ROBINSON, Fanny
RODRIGO, Maria
ROECKEL, Jane
RUNCIE, Constance Owen Faunt Le
    Roy
SAINTON-DOLBY, Charlotte Helen
SAMUEL, Caroline
SANDERS, Alma
SANTA-COLONA-SOURGET,
    Eugenie
SCHADEN, Nanette von
SCHAUROTH, Delphine von
SCHINDLER, Livia
SCHREINZER, F.M.
SCHUMANN, Clara Josephine
SCHWARZ-SIGMAND, Hermina
SEROVA, Valentina Semyonovna
SERVIER, Mme. H.
SICK, Anna
SKELTON, Nellie Bangs
SMITH, Eleanor Louise
SMITH, Hannah

SOMELLERA, Josefa
STEIN, Nannette
STENHAMMAR, Fredrika
STIRLING, Elizabeth
STRANTZ, Louise von
SUTRO, Florence Edith
SYNGE, Mary Helena
SZARVADY, Wilhelmine Clausz
SZYMANOWSKA, Maria Agata
TAITE, Annie
TARDIEU DE MALLEVILLE, Charlotte
THAMM, Ida
THEGERSTROEM, Hilda Aurora
THOMAS, Adelaide Louise
THORNE, Beatrice
TONDEUR, Wilhelmine
TORRENS, Grace
TREW, Susan
TYRELL, Agnes
UGALDE, Delphine Beauce
UNTERSTEINER, Antonietta
VALERO, Matilde
VEDRUNA, Dolores
VEGA, Paulina
VELTHEIM, Charlotte
VENTH, Lydia Kunz
VERGER, Virginie Morel du
VESPERMANN, Marie
VIARDOT-GARCIA, Pauline Michelle
    Ferdinande
VOJACKOVA-WETCHE, Ludmila
VOLKMANN, Ida
VON HOFF, Elizabeth
WAKEFIELD, Augusta Mary
WALKER, Caroline Holme
WARTEL, Atala Therese Annette
WENSLEY, Frances Foster
WERNER, Hildegard
WEST, Lottie
WESTROP, Kate
WHITELY, Bessie Marshall
WIECK, Marie
WIGGINS, Kate Douglas
WOOLF, Sophia Julia
WUIET, Caroline
WURM, Mary J.A.
ZAPATER, Rosaria
ZIEGLER, Natalie Sophie von
ZIMMERMANN, Agnes Marie
    Jacobina
ZUMSTEEG, Emilie

20th Century A.D.
AARNE, Els
ABE, Kyoko
ABEJO, Sister M. Rosalina
ABORN, Lora
ABRAMOVA, Sonia Pinkhasovna
ACCART, Eveline
ACKLAND, Jeanne Isabel Dorothy
ACKLAND, Jessie Agnes
ACOSTA, Josefina, Baroness
A'DAIR, Jeanne
ADAIR, Mildred
ADAM, Margie
ADAMS, Julia Aurelia
AESCHLIMANN-ROTH, Esther
AINSCOUGH, Juliana Mary
AKIYOSHI, Toshiko
ALBRIGHT, Janet Elaine
ALCALAY, Luna
ALDEN, Zilpha May
ALDERMAN, Pauline
ALDRIDGE, Amanda Ira
ALIOTH, Marguerite
ALLAN, Esther
ALLBRITTON, Florence Ziegler
ALLINOWNA, Stefania
ALLOUARD CARNY, Odette
ALMEN, Ruth
ALMESAN, Irma
ALOTIN, Yardena

ALPERT, Pauline Edith
ALT, Hansi
ALTER, Martha
ALVARES-RIOS, Maria
ALVES DE SOUSA, Berta Candida
AMATI, Orlanda
ANCELE, Sister Mary
ANDERSEN, Helen Somerville
ANDERSON, Beth
ANDERSSON, Ellen
ANDRIESSEN, Caecilia
AOKE, Haruna
APPELDOORN, Dina van
ARBEL, Re Chaya
ARCHER, Violet Balestreri
ARENA, Iris Mae
ARIZTI SOBRINO, Cecilia
ARMER, Elinor Florence
ARNOLD, Rosanna Luisa Swann
ARTEAGA, Genoveva de
ARVEY, Verna
AUBER, Chantal
AUBUT-PRATTE, Françoise
AYARZA DE MORALES, Rosa
    Mercedes
BABITS, Linda
BACKES, Lotte
BACON, Viola Ruth Orcutt
BAGA, Ena Rosina
BAGANIER, Janine
BAHMANN, Marianne Eloise
BAIL, Grace Shattuck
BAILEY-APFELBECK, Marie Louise
BALDACCI, Giovanna Bruna
BALDWIN, Esther Lillian
BALL, Frances de Villa
BALL, Ida W.
BALLANDS, Etta
BALLOU, Esther Williamson
BALSHONE, Cathy S.
BANKS, Hilda
BANNISTER, Mary Jeanne Hoggard
BARATTA, Maria M. de
BARBILLON, Jeanne
BARBOSA, Cacilda Campos Borges
BARBOUR, Florence Newell
BARRADAS, Carmen
BARRIENTOS, Maria
BARTHEL, Ursula
BARTHELSON, Joyce Holloway
BARTLETT, Ethel Agnes
BASSETT, Henrietta Elizabeth
BASSETT, Karolyn Wells
BATCHELOR, Phyllis
BAUER, Emilie Frances
BEACH, Amy Marcy
BEAHM, Jacquelyn Yvette
BEATON, Isabella
BECKON, Lettie Marie
BEECROFT, Norma Marian
BEEKHUIS, Hanna
BEESON, Elizabeth Ruth
BEHREND, Jeanne
BEKMAN-SHCHERBINA, Elena
    Aleksandrovna Kamentseva
BELL, Carla Huston
BELL, Lucille Anderson
BELLAMY, Marian Meredith
BELOW-BUTTLAR, Gerda von
BENAVENTE, Regina
BENEDICENTI, Vera
BENOIT, Francine Germaine Van
    Gool
BERAN-STARK, Lola Aloisia Maria
BERCKMAN, Evelyn
BERG, Lily
BERGERSEN, Marie Christine
BERL WEINFIELD, Christine
BERLINER, Selma
BERNARDONE, Anka
BERROA, Catalina

BERRY, Margaret Mary Robinson
BERRYMAN, Alice Davis
BERTRAM, Madge
BERTRAND, Ginette
BEYERMAN-WALRAVEN, Jeanne
BEZDEK, Sister John Joseph
BIANCHINI, Emma
BIANCHINI, Virginie
BIBBY, Gillian Margaret
BIENVENU, Lily
BILBRO, Anne Mathilde
BILTCLIFFE, Florence
BINET, Jocelyne
BJELKE-ANDERSEN, Olga
BLACKWELL, Anna Gee
BLAKE, Dorothy Gaynor
BLASIS, Teresa de
BLAUHUTH, Jenny
BLAUSTEIN, Susan Morton
BLEY, Carla
BLOMFIELD-HOLT, Patricia
BLOOD, Esta Damesek
BLOOMFIELD-ZEISLER, Fannie
BODENSTEIN-HOYME, Ruth E.
BODOM, Erica
BOEHN, Liselotte
BOESE, Helen
BOESGAARDOVA-SCHMIDTOVA,
    Lydie
BOESSER, Dagma
BOLZ, Harriet
BOND, Victoria Ellen
BONDS, Margaret
BORDERS, Barbara Ann
BORKOWICZ, Maria
BORROFF, Edith
BOSMANS, Henriette Hilda
BOTET, Maria Emma
BOTSFORD, Talitha
BOULANGER, Lili Juliette Marie
    Olga
BOUTRON, Madeleine
BOYCE, Blanche Ula
BOYD, Anne Elizabeth
BOYD, Jeanne Margaret
BOYKIN, A. Helen
BRAGA, Henriqueta Rosa Fernandes
BRANDELER, Henriette van den
BRANDMAN, Margaret Susan
BRANDT, Dorothea
BRANNING, Grace Bell
BRANSCOMBE, Gena
BRATU, Emma
BRAUER, Johanna Elisabeth
BRENET, Thérèse
BRIGGS, Dorothy Bell
BRIGGS, Nancy Louise
BRIGHT, Ann
BRIGHT, Dora Estella
BRITAIN, Radie
BROCK, Blanche Kerr
BROGUE, Roslyn Clara
BROOK, Gwendolyn Giffen
BROOKS, Myra Lou
BROWN, Norma
BROWN, Rosemary
BROWN, Veronica
BROWN, Zilda Jennings
BRUCKSHAW, Kathleen
BRUGGMANN, Heidi
BRUSH, Ruth Damaris
BRUSSELS, Iris
BRUZDOWICZ, Joanna
BRYAN, Betty Sue
BRYANT, Verna Mae
BRYUSSOVA, Nadezhda Yakolevna
BUCHANAN, Annabel Morris
BUCK, Era Marguerite
BUCKLEY, Beatrice Barron
BUCKLEY, Dorothy Pike
BUCZEK, Barbara Kazimiera

BUENAVENTURA, Isabel
BULTERIJS, Nina
BUMP, Mary Crane
BURGER, Hester Aletta Sophie
BURNETT, Helen Roth
BURSTON, Maggie
BURTON, Pixie
BUSH, Grace E.
BUTCHER, Jane Elizabeth
BYERS, Roxana Weihe
CADORET, Charlotte
CADY, Harriette
CALAME, Genevieve
CALBRAITH, Mary Evelene
CALCAGNO, Elsa
CALDWELL, Mary Elizabeth Glockler
CALE, Rosalie Balmer Smith
CAMEU, Helza
CAMPOS ARAUJO DE, Joaquina
CANCINO DE CUEVAS, Sofia
CANNING, Effie I.
CAPSIR-TANZI, Mercedes
CAPUIS, Matilde
CAREY, Elena
CARMICHAEL, Mary Grant
CARON-LEGRIS, Albertine
CARRENO, Térèsa
CARRIVICK, Olive Amelia
CARROLL, Barbara
CARSON, Ruby B.
CARTER PAULENA, Elizabeth
CARTER, Buenta MacDaniel
CARVALHO, Dinora de
CASAGEMAS, Luisa
CASTAGNETTA, Grace Sharp
CATUNDA, Eunice do Monte Lima
CECCONI-BOTELLA, Monic
CERVANTES, Maria
CHACON LASAUCA, Emma
CHALITA, Laila Maria
CHAMINADE, Cecile Louise
    Stephanie
CHANCE, Nancy Laird
CHAPIRO, Fania
CHAVES, Mary Elizabeth
CHEBOTARIAN, Gayane
    Movsesovna
CHEN, Nira
CHENOWETH, Vida
CHEVALIER, Charlotte Bergersen
CHEVALLIER SUPERVIELLE, Marie
    Louise
CHICHERINA, Sofia Nikolayevna
CHITCHIAN, Geguni Oganesovna
CHITTENDEN, Kate Sara
CHKHEIDZE, Dali Davidovna
CHRISTENSEN, Anna Mae Parker
CHUDOBA, Blanka
CIMAGLIA DE ESPINOSA, Lia
CIOBANU, Maia
CLAMAN, Dolores Olga
CLARK, Florence Durrell
CLARK, June
CLARKE, Mary Gail
CLARKE, Phyllis Chapman
CLAUDE, Marie
CLAYTON, Laura
CLAYTON, Susan
CLEMENS, Margaret
CLEMENT, Mary
CLOSTRE, Adrienne
COATES, Gloria Kannenberg
COBB, Hazel
COCKING, Frances M. Hefford
COCQ, Rosina Susanna de
COELHO, Ernestine Leite
COEN, Augusta
COFFMAN, Lillian Craig
COHEN, Dulcie M.
COHEN, Harriet
COLE, Ulric

COLERIDGE-TAYLOR, Avril
    Gwendolen
COLGAN, Alma Cecilia
COLLARD, Marilyn
COLLVER, Harriet Russell
COLTRANE, Alice McLeod
CONRAD, Laurie M.
CONSTANTINESCU, Domnica
COOLIDGE, Elizabeth Sprague
COOLIDGE, Peggy Stuart
COOPER, Esther Sayward
COPLAND, Berniece Rose
COPLEY, Maria Kriel
CORDULA, Sister M.
CORNEA-IONESCU, Alma
COTE, Helene
COTRON, Fanou
COULTHARD, Jean
COUPER, Mildred
COVERT, Mary Ann Hunter
COWL, Doreen
COWLES, Cecil Marion
CRANE, Helen
CRAWFORD SEEGER, Ruth
CREES, Kathleen Elsie
CREWS, Lucille
CROKER, Catherine Munnell
CROWE, Bonita
CUNIBERTI, Janet Teresa
CURRIE, Edna R.
CURTIS, Natalie
CURUBETO GODOY, Maria Isabel
CURZON, Clara-Jean
DAHL, Vivian
DAHMEN, Mona Scholte
DAIGLE, Sister Anne Cecile
DALBERT, Anny
DALE, Kathleen
DALE, Phyllis
DANA, Lynn Boardman
DANEAU, Suzanne
DANFORTH, Frances A.
DANIELA, Carmen
DANIELS, Mabel Wheeler
DANIELS, Nellie
DASCALESCU, Camelia
DAVENPORT, Anne Bridges
DAVIDSON, Tina
DAVIES, Eiluned
DAVIS, Eleanor Maud
DAVIS, Eva May
DAVIS, Fay Simmons
DAVIS, Genevieve
DAVIS, Jean Reynolds
DAVIS, Katherine Kennicott
DAVIS, Sharon
DAVITASHVILI, Meri Shalvovna
DAVY, Ruby Claudia Emily
DE BIASE BIDART, Lycia
DE FREITAS, Elvira Manuela
    Fernandez
DE LARA, Adelina
DE LEATH, Vaughn
DE MONTEL, Adalgisa
DE PATE, Elisabetta M.S.
DE VILLIERS, Justina Wilhelmina
    Nancy
DEACON, Mary Connor
DECARIE, Reine
DEL RIEGO, Theresa
DELIZ, Monserrate
DELMOULY, Marie Mathilde
DEMAREST, Anne Shannon
DEPPEN, Jessie L.
DESPORTES, Yvonne Berthe Melitta
DEYO, Ruth Lynda
DICHLER-SEDLACEK, Erika
DIEFENTHALER, Margaret Kissinger
DIEMER, Emma Lou
DILLER, Angela
DILLON, Fannie Charles

DIMENTMAN, Esfir Moiseyevna
DIMITRIU, Florica
DITTENHAVER, Sarah Louise
DLUGOSZEWSKI, Lucia
DOANE, Dorothy
DOBSON, Elaine
DODGE, May Hewes
DOMINIQUE, Monica
DONIACH, Shula
DORABIALSKA, Julia Helena
DOWNEY, Mary
DREYFUS, Francis Kay
DRING, Madeleine
DRYNAN, Margaret
DU PAGE, Florence Elizabeth
DUCZMAL-JAROSZEWSKA,
   Agnieszka
DUGAL, Madeleine
DUGGAN, Beatrice Abbott
DUNGAN, Olive
DUNN, Rebecca Welty
DURAND, Nella Wells
DUTTON, Theodora
EAGAR, Fannie Edith Starke
EAGLES, Moneta M.
EAKIN, Vera O.
ECKHARDT-GRAMATTE, Sophie-
   Carmen
EDICK, Ethel Vera Ingraham
EDWARDS, Clara
EGGAR, Katharine
EGGLESTON, Anne E.
EICHENWALD, Sylvia
EISENSTEIN DE VEGA, Silvia
EISENSTEIN, Stella Price
EKSANISHVILI, Eleonara
   Grigorevna
ELKOSHI, Rivka
ELLEN, Mary
ELLICOTT, Rosalind Frances
ELLIOTT, Marjorie Reeve
ELVYN, Myrtle
EMERY, Dorothy Radde
EMIG, Lois Irene
EMINGEROVA, Katerina
ENDE, Amelia von
ENDRES, Olive Philomene
ERDELI, Xenia Alexandrovna
ERDMANNSDOERFER, Pauline
ERDOEDY, Luisa, Countess
ERNST, Siegrid
ESCOBAR, Maria Luisa
ESTRELLA, Blanca
ETHRIDGE, Jean
EUBANKS, Rachel Amelia
EUTENEUER-ROHRER, Ursula
   Henrietta
EVANS, Patricia Margaret
EVERETT-SALICCO, Betty Lou
EZELL, Helen Ingle
FAHRER, Alison Clark
FAIRLIE, Margaret C.
FAISST, Clara Mathilde
FALCINELLI, Rolande
FARGA PELLICER, Onia
FAUTCH, Sister Magdalen
FEDERHOF-MOLLER, Betty
FEHRS, Anna Elisbeth
FEIGIN, Sarah
FEININGER, Leonore Helene
FEIST-STEINHAUSEN, Alwine
FENSTOCK, Belle
FERRAND-TEULET, Denise
FERRARI, Gabriella
FERRER OTERO, Monsita
   Monserrate
FERREYRA, Beatriz
FILIPPONI, Dina
FINE, Vivian
FINLEY, Lorraine Noel
FIRNKEES, Gertrud

FISCHER, Emma Gabriele Marie von,
   Baroness
FISHER, Charlotte Eleanor
FISHER, Renée Breger
FITZGERALD, Sister Florence
   Therese
FLACH, Elsa
FLEMMING, Martha
FLEURY, Helene
FLICK-FLOOD, Dora
FLORING, Grace Kenny
FOLVILLE, Eugenie-Emilie Juliette
FONTYN, Jacqueline
FOOT, Phyllis Margaret
FORMAN, Addie Walling
FORSTER, Dorothy
FOSTER, Cecily
FOSTER, Fay
FRANCHERE-DESROSIERS, Rose de
   Lima
FRANCO, Clare
FRANGS, Irene
FRASER, Shena Eleanor
FREEHOFF, Ruth Williams
FRESON, Armande
FROMM-MICHAELS, Ilse
FRUMKER, Linda
FRYZELL, Regina Holmen
FURGERI, Bianca Maria
FURZE, Jessie
GABUS, Monique
GAIGEROVA, Varvara Andrianovna
GAINSBORG, Lolita Cabrera
GALAJIKIAN, Florence Grandland
GALIKIAN, Susanna Avetisovna
GALINNE, Rachel
GAMILLA, Alice Doria
GANNON, Helen Carroll
GARCIA ASCOT, Rosa
GARCIA MUNOZ, Carmen
GARCIA ROBSON, Magdalena
GARDNER, Mildred Alvine
GARELLI DELLA MOREA, Vincenza
GARSCIA-GRESSEL, Janina
GARTENLAUB, Odette
GARUTA, Lucia Yanovna
GARWOOD, Margaret
GARZTECKA-JARZEBSKA, Irena
GASPARINI, Jola
GAYNOR, Jessie Love
GAZAROSSIAN, Koharik
GEIGER-KULLMANN, Rosy Auguste
GENTEMANN, Sister Mary Elaine
GENTILE, Ada
GEORGE, Lila-Gene
GERRISH-JONES, Abbie
GERSTMAN, Bianche Wilhelminia
GESELSCHAP, Maria
GEYMULLER, Marguerite Camille-
   Louise de
GHIGLIERI, Sylvia
GHILARDI, Syra
GIACCHINO CUSENZA, Maria
GIDEON, Miriam
GIFFORD, Helen Margaret
GILBERT, Marie
GILLES, Yvette Marie
GILLUM, Ruth Helen
GINDLER, Kathe-Lotte
GIPPS, Ruth
GITECK, Janice
GIURANNA, Elena Barbara
GLASER, Victoria Merrylees
GLEN, Irma
GLICK, Nancy Kay
GNESINA, Yelena Fabianovna
GNUS, Ryta
GODDARD, Arabella
GOEBELS, Gisela
GOETSCHIUS, Marjorie
GOLDSCHMIDT, Lore

GOMEZ CARRILO, Maria Ines
GOMM, Elizabeth
GONZAGA, Chiquinha
GOODE, Blanche
GOODMAN, Lillian Rosedale
GOODSMITH, Ruth B.
GOODWIN, Amina Beatrice
GOOLKASIAN-RAHBEE, Dianne
   Zabelle
GOTKOVSKY, Ida-Rose Esther
GOULD, Elizabeth Davies
GOULD, Janetta
GRAD-BUCH, Hulda
GRAHAM, Janet Christine
GRAU, Irene Rosenberg
GREENE, Genevieve
GREENE, Margo Lynn
GREVER, Maria
GRIEBEL WANDALL, Tekla
GRIEBLING, Karen Jean
GRIECO, Ida
GRIMAUD, Yvette
GRIMES, Doreen
GRUDEFF, Marian
GRZADZIELOWNA, Eleonora
GUBAIDULINA, Sofia Asgatovna
GUBITOSI, Emilia
GUDAUSKAS, Giedra
GULESIAN, Grace Warner
GUNDERSON, Helen Louise
GURAIEB KURI, Rosa
GUSTAVSON, Nancy Nicholls
GYANDZHETSIAN, Destrik
   Bogdanovna
HADDEN, Frances Roots
HAGAN, Helen Eugenia
HAHN, Sandra Lea
HAIMSOHN, Naomi Carrol
HAINES, Julia Howell
HAJDU, Julia
HALL, Pauline
HALPERN, Stella
HAMMOND, Fanny Reed
HANIM, Leyla
HANNIKAINEN, Ann-Elise
HANSEN, Hanna Marie
HANSEN, Joan
HARDIMAN, Ellena G.
HARDING, Mildred Thompson
HARDY, Helen Irene
HARLEY, Frances Marjorie
HARPER, Marjorie
HARRIS, Ethel Ramos
HARRIS, Letitia Radcliffe
HARRIS, Margaret R.
HARRISON, Pamela
HARRISON, Susan Frances
HARTZER-STIBBE, Marie
HARVEY, Eva Noel
HATCH, Edith
HAUSMAN, Ruth Langley
HAWLEY, Carolyn Jean
HAYS, Doris Ernestine
HAZEN, Sara
HEALE, Helene
HEATON, Eloise Klotz
HEBER, Judith
HECKSCHER, Celeste de Longpre
HEDOUX, Yvonne
HEILBRON, Valerie
HEIMERL, Elizabeth
HEINRICHS, Agnes
HEINY, Margaret Harris
HELBLING, Elsa
HELLER, Ruth
HELLER-REICHENBACH, Barbara
HELYER, Marjorie
HENDERSON, Ruth Watson
HERNANDEZ-GONZALO, Gisela
HERRERA Y OGAZON, Alba
HERZ, Maria

HESSE, Marjorie Anne
HETRICK, Patricia Anne
HEYMAN, Katherine Ruth Willoughby
HEYNSSEN, Adda
HICKS, Marjorie Kisby
HIER, Ethel Glen
HIGGINBOTHAM, Irene
HILL, Mildred J.
HILL, Sister M. Mildred
HIND O'MALLEY, Pamela
HO, Wai On
HOFER, Maria
HOFF, Vivian Beaumont
HOFFMANN-BEHRENDT, Lydia
HOLCK, Sine
HOLCOMB, Louanah Riggs
HOLLAND, Dulcie Sybil
HOLLAND, Ruby
HOLMSEN, Borghild
HOLST, Imogen Clare
HONEGGER-VAURABOURG, Andree
HOOD, Helen
HOPEKIRK, Helen
HORNBACK, Sister Mary Gisela
HORROCKS, Amy Elsie
HORSLEY, Imogene
HORTON, Marguerite Wagniere
HOUSMAN, Rosalie
HOWARD, Helen Willard
HOWE, Mary Alberta Bruce
HOWELL, Dorothy
HOY, Bonnee L.
HOYLE, Aline Isabelle
HOYT, Mary Mack
HRUBY, Dolores Marie
HSU, Wen-Ying
HUBICKI, Margaret Olive
HUEBNER, Ilse
HUEGEL, Margrit
HUGHES, Sister Martina
HUGH-JONES, Elaine
HUJSAK, Joy Detenbeck
HULFORD, Denise Lovona
HULL, Kathryn B.
HUNKINS, Eusebia Simpson
HUNTER, Hilda
HUTTON, Florence Myra
HYDE, Miriam Beatrice
HYLIN, Birgitta Charlotta Kristina
HYSON, Winifred Prince
IBRAGIMOVA, Sevda Mirza kyzy
IGENBERGA, Elga Avgustovna
ILLIUTOVICH, Nina Yakovlevna
INWOOD, Mary Ruth Brink Berger
IRMAN-ALLEMANN, Regina
ISAKOVA, Aida Petrovna
ISMAGILOVA, Leila Zagirovna
ISZKOWSKA, Zofia
IVANOVA, Lidia
IVEY, Jean Eichelberger
IWAUCHI, Saori
JACKSON, Barbara May
JACOBINA, Agnes Marie
JAEGER, Hertha
JAELL-TRAUTMANN, Marie
JAMBOR, Agi
JANKOWSKI, Loretta Patricia
JANOTHA, Natalia
JAQUETTI ISANT, Palmira
JENNEY, Mary Frances
JEREA, Hilda
JESI, Ada
JEWELL, Lucina
JIRKOVA, Olga
JOCHSBERGER, Tzipora H.
JOHNSON, Mary Ernestine Clark
JOHNSTON, Alison Aileen Annie
JOLAS, Betsy
JOLLEY, Florence Werner
JOLY, Suzanne
JONES, Catherine

JONES, Sister Ida
JONES-DAVIES, Maude
JUENGER, Patricia
KACZURBINA-ZDZIECHOWSKA,
   Maria
KALOGRIDOU, Maria
KALTENECKER, Gertraud
KAMIEN, Anna
KARNITSKAYA, Nina Andreyevna
KASHPEROVA, Leokadia Alexandrovna
KASILAG, Lucrecia R.
KATS-CHERNIN, Elena
KAZANDJIAN, Sirvart
KELLY, Denise Maria Anne
KEMP, Dorothy Elizabeth Walter
KENDRICK, Virginia Catherine
KENNEDY-FRASER, Marjory
KENSWIL, Atma
KENT, Ada Twohy
KERR, Bessie Maude
KERSENBAUM, Sylvia Haydee
KESHNER, Joyce Grove
KESSLER, Minuetta Schumiatcher
KHOSS VON STERNEGG, Gisela
KICKINGER, Paula
KICKTON, Erika
KILBY, Muriel Laura
KINSCELLA, Hazel Gertrude
KIRCHNER, Elisabeth
KIRKBY-MASON, Barbara
KISTETENYI, Melinda
KJAER, Kirsten
KLECHNIOWSKA, Anna Maria
KLEES, Gabriele
KLEIN, Ivy Frances
KLINKOVA, Zhivka
KNIGHT, Judyth
KNOUSS, Isabelle G.
KOEHLER, Estella
KOHAN, Celina
KOKDES, Veveser
KOLODUB, Zhanna Efimovna
KOMIAZYK, Magdalena
KOPPEL-HOLBE, Maria
KOPTAGEL, Yuksel
KORN, Clara Anna
KOSTAKOVA-HERODKOVA, Marie
KOZAKIEVICH, Anna Abramovna
KRALIKOVA, Johana
KRASNOGLIADOVA, Vera
   Vladimirovna
KRAUSZ, Susan
KRIMSKY, Katrina
KROSNICK, Mary Louw Wesley
KRUSE, Lotte
KRZYZANOWSKA, Halina
KUBO, Mayako
KUBOTA, Minako
KUCEROVA-HERSTOVA, Marie
KUESTER, Edith Haines
KUKUCK, Felicitas
KULIEVA, Farida Tairovna
KUNTZE, Olga
KUROKAWA, Manae
KUZMENKO, Larysa
LACHOWSKA, Stefania
LACKMAN, Susan C. Cohn
LACMANOVA, Anna
LAFLEUR, Lucienne
LAGO
LAJEUNESSE, Emma, Dame
LALAUNI, Lila
LAMEGO, Carlinda J.
LANDOWSKA, Wanda
LANDREE, Jaquenote Goldsteen
LANG, Margaret Ruthven
LANG-BECK, Ivana
LANKMAR, Helen
LAOUREUX DE GUCHTENAERE,
   Marguerite
LAPEIRETTA, Ninon de Brouwer

LAPIN, Lily
LARKIN, Deirdre
LARSON, Anna Barbara
LAST, Joan Mary
LATIOLAIS, Desirée Jayne
LATZ, Inge
LAUBER, Anne Marianne
LAUER, Elizabeth
LAUMYANSKENE, Elena Iono
LAWHON, Gladys Louise
LAWRENCE, Emily M.
LAYMAN, Pamela
LAZAR, Ella
LE BEAU, Louisa Adolpha
LE BORDAYS, Christiane
LEAF, Ann
LEAHY, Mary Weldon
LEAVITT, Helen Sewall
LEBENBOM, Elaine F.
LEBIZAY, Marguerite
LEE, Hope Anne Keng-Wei
LEECH, Lida Shivers
LEECH, Renée
LEGINSKA, Ethel
LEHMAN, Evangeline Marie
LEHMANN, Liza
LEHOTSKA-KRIZKOVA, Ludmila
LEIBOW, Ruth Irene
LEITE, Clarisse
LEIVISKA, Helvi Lemmiki
LELEU, Jeanne
LEMAIRE-SINDORFF, Jeanne
LEON, Tania Justina
LEONARD, Mamie Grace
LEONE, Mae G.
LEPKE, Charma Davies
LESICHKOVA, Lili
LEVIN, Rami Yona
LEVINA, Zara Alexandrovna
LEVITE, Miriam
LEWING, Adele
LIADOVA, Ludmila Alekseyevna
LICHTENSTEIN, Olga Grigorievna
LIDDELL, Claire
LIDGI-HERMAN, Sofia
LIEBMANN, Nanna Magdalene
LIEDBERGIUS, Camilla
LIMA CRUZ, Maria Antonietta de
LINDEMAN, Anna Severine
LINDEMAN, Hjelle Signe
LINNEMANN, Maria Catharina
LINNET, Anne
LIPSCOMB, Helen
LISSONI, Giulia
LITTLE, Anita Gray
LITTLEJOHN, Joan Anne
LLUNELL SANAHUJA, Pepita
LOCKE, Flora Elbertine Huie
LOCKSHIN, Florence Levin
LOH, Kathy Jean
LOHOEFER, Evelyn
LOMON, Ruth
LOOTS, Joyce Mary Ann
LOPUSKA-WYLEZYNSKA, Helena
LORENZ, Ellen Jane
LORIOD, Yvonne
LOTTI, Silvana di
LOUDOVA, Ivana
LOUIE, Alexina Diane
LOWELL, Edith
LOWENSTEIN, Gunilla Marike
LUCAS, Mary Anderson
LUDVIG-PECAR, Nada
LUFF, Enid
LUNA DE ESPAILLAT, Margarita
LUND, Gudrun
LUND, Hanna
LUND, Signe
LUO, Jing-Jing
LUTHER, Mary
LVOVA, Julia Fedorovna

LYONS, Ruth
LYUBOMIRSKAYA-BOYARSKAYA,
　Revekka Grigorevna
MAAS, Marguerite Wilson
MacARTHUR, Helen
MacFARREN, Emma Marie
MacKENNA, Carmela
McCLEARY, Fiona
McCLEARY, Mary Gilkeson
McCOLLIN, Frances
McGILL, Gwendolen Mary Finlayson
McINTOSH, Diana
McKANN-MANCINI, Patricia
McKAY, Frances Thompson
McKELLAN, Irene Mary
McKINNEY, Mathilde
McLEAN, Priscilla Anne Taylor
McLEMORE, Monita Prine
McLEOD, Evelyn Lundgren
McLEOD, Jennifer Helen
McLIN, Lena
McNAIR, Jacqueline Hanna
McPHERSON, Frances Marie
McQUATTIE, Sheila
McSWAIN, Augusta Geraldine
MACHADO, Lena
MADISON, Clara Duggan
MADRIGUERA RODON, Paquita
MAHLER, Alma Maria
MAILIAN, Elza Antonovna
MAITLAND, Anna Harriet
MALMLOEF-FORSSLING, Carin
MAMLOK, Ursula
MANA-ZUCCA
MANGGRUM, Loretta C. Cessor
MANKIN, Linda
MANNING, Kathleen Lockhart
MANZIARLY, Marcelle de
MARAIS, Abelina Jacoba
MARBE, Myriam
MARCUS, Ada Belle Gross
MARCUS, Bunita
MAREZ-OYENS, Tera de
MARI, Pierrette
MARIANI-CAMPOLIETI, Virginia
MARKIEWICZOWNA, Wladyslawa
MARQUES, Fernandina Lagos
MARQUES, Laura Wake
MARSCHAL-LOEPKE, Grace
MARSHALL, Kye
MARTENOT-LAZARD, Ginette-
　Genevieve
MARTIN, Delores J.
MARTIN, Judith Reher
MARTIN, Ravonna G.
MARTINEZ DE LA TORRE Y
　SHELTON, Emma
MARTINEZ, Odaline de la
MARTINS, Maria de Lourdes
MARY BERNICE, Sister
MARY ELAINE, Sister
MASON, Margaret C.
MASSUMOTO, Kikuko
MASTERS, Juan
MATEU, Maria Cateura
MATEVOSIAN, Araks Surenovna
MATJAN, Vida
MATTHEWS, Dorothy White
MAUR, Sophie
MAURICE-JACQUET, H.
MAXIM, Florence
MAXWELL, Jacqueline Perkinson
MAY, Florence
MAYER, Lise Maria
MAZOUROVA, Jarmila
MEACHEM, Margaret McKeen
　Ramsey
MEADE, Margaret Johnston
MEEK, Ethel Alice
MEISTER, Marianne
MEKEEL, Joyce

MELL, Gertrud Maria
MELVILLE, Marguerite Liszniewska
MENEELY-KYDER, Sarah Suderley
MERLI-ZWISCHENBRUGGER,
　Christina
MERO, Jolanda
MERTENS, Dolores
MESNEY, Dorothy Taylor
MESRITZ-VAN VELTHUYSEN, Annie
MESTDAGH, Helene
MICHELOW, Sybil
MIEROWSKA, Jean
MIGRANYAN, Emma
MIKUSCH, Margarethe von
MILA, Leonora
MILDANTRI, Mary Ann
MILDREN, Margaret Joyce
MILENKOVIC, Jelena
MILETTE, Juliette
MILKINA, Nina
MILKULAK, Marcia Lee
MILLER, Elma
MILLER, Lillian Anne
MINEO, Antoinette
MIRET, Emilia
MIRON, Tsipora
MISHELL, Kathryn Lee
MITCHELL, Izah Pike
MITCHELL, Norma Jean
MIYAKE, Haruna
MOBERG, Ida Georgina
MOE, Benna
MOELLER, Agnes
MOHNS, Grace Updegraff Bergen
MOLAVA, Pamela May
MONK, Meredith
MONNOT, Marguerite Angele
MOORE, Luella Lockwood
MOORE, Undine Smith
MOORE, Wilda Maurine Ricks
MOOREHEAD, Consuela Lee
MORETTO, Nelly
MORIN-LABRECQUE, Albertine
MORLEY, Nina Dianne
MORONEY, Sister Mary Emmeline
MOSZUMANSKA-NAZAR, Krystyna
MUELLER-WELTI, Hedwig
MULDER, Johanna Harmina Gerdina
MUNDINGER, Adele Franziska
MUNGER, Millicent Christner
MUNKTELL, Helena Mathilda
MYSZINSKA-WOJCIECHOWSKA,
　Leokadia
NAIKHOVICH-LOMAKINA, Fania
　Filippovna
NAKASHIMA, Jeanne Marie
NARCISSE-MAIR, Denise Lorraine
NAZAROVA, Tatiana Borisovna
NEAS, Margaret
NEEL, Susan Elizabeth
NEILY, Anne MacAdams
NEPGEN, Rosa Sophia Cornelia
NESTE, Rosane van
NEWLIN, Dika
NEWMAN, Adelaide
NEWPORT, Doreen
NIAY, Apolline
NICKERSON, Camille Lucie
NIGHTINGALE, Mae Wheeler
NIKOLAYEVA, Tatiana Petrovna
NISHIMURA, Yukie
NIXON, June
NOBLITT, Katheryn Marie McCall
NORDENFELT, Dagmar
NORDRAAK-FEYLING, Gudrun
NORMAN, Ruth
NORRE, Dorcas
NOVELLO-DAVIES, Clara
NOVI, Anna Beate
NOYES, Edith Rowena
OBROVSKA, Jana

ODAGESCU, Irina
OERBECK, Anne-Marie
OHE, Adele aus der
OHLSON, Marion
OIKONOMOPOULOS, Eleni N.
OKEY, Maggie
O'LEARY, Jane Strong
OLIVEIRA, Babi de
OLIVEIRA, Jocy de
OLIVEIRA, Sophie Marcondes de
　Mello
OLLER BENLLOCH, Maria Teresa
OLSEN, Lynn Freeman
OMER, Helene
ORE, Cecilie
OSIANDER, Irene
OTTAWOWA, Helena
OWEN, Blythe
OWEN, Morfydd Llwyn
OZAITA, Maria Luisaria Luisa
PACK, Beulah Frances
PAGOTO, Helen
PALMER, Florence Margaret
　Spencer
PANETTI, Joan
PARENTE, Sister Elizabeth
PARKER, Muriel
PARPAGLIOLO, Iditta
PARR, Patricia
PARR-GERE, Florence
PAULL, Barberi
PEACOCK, Mary O'Kelley
PEARL-MANN, Dora Deborah
PENNER, Jean Priscilla
PENTLAND, Barbara Lally
PEREIRA DA SILVA, Adelaide
PEREIRA, Diana Maria
PERETZ-LEVY, Liora
PERKIN, Helen
PERONI, Wally
PERRY, Julia Amanda
PERRY, Marilyn Brown
PERRY, Mary Dean
PERRY, Zenobia Powell
PETERSEN, Else
PETROVA-KRUPKOVA, Elena
PFERDEMENGES, Maria Pauline
　Augusta
PHILIBA, Nicole
PHILLIPS, Donna
PHILLIPS, Karen Ann
PHILLIPS, Linda
PHILLIPS, Lois Elisabeth
PHILLIPS, Vivian Daphne
PHIPPEN, Laud German
PICCONI, Maria Antonietta
PICKHARDT, Ione
PIECHOWSKA, Alina
PIERCE, Alexandra
PIETSCH, Edna Frieda
PIGGOTT, Audrey Margaret
PIKE, Eleanor B. Franklin
PIRES DE CAMPOS, Lina
PIRES DOS REIS, Hilda
PITOT, Genevieve
PIZER, Elizabeth Faw Hayden
PLE-CAUSSADE, Simone
POLICARPO TEIXEIRA, Maria
　Margarida Fernandes
POLLOCK, Muriel
PONCE, Ethel
PONSA, Maria Luisa
POOL, Arlette
POOLE, Anna Ware
POPOVICI, Elise
PORTER, Debra
POSTON, Elizabeth
POWERS, Ada Weigel
PRADELL, Leila
PRAVOSSUDOVITCH, Natalja
　Michajlovna

PRAY, Ada Jordan
PREOBRAJENSKA, Vera Nicolaevna
PRESTON, Matilee Loeb-Evans
PRICE, Beryl
PRICE, Deon Nielsen
PRICE, Florence Beatrice
PRIETO, Maria Teresa
PRIOLLI, Maria Luisa de Matos
PROCACCINI, Teresa
PROCTOR, Alice McElroy
PRUNTY, Evelyn Grace Potter
PTASZYNSKA, Marta
PUCHE, Sofia
PYKE, Helen
QUANTIN-SAULNIER, Denise
QUINLAN, Agnes Ciune
QUINTANILLA, Alba
RABINOF, Sylvia
RADERMACHER, Erika
RAHMN, Elza Loethner
RALSTON, Frances Marion
RAMAKERS, Christiane Josee
RAN, Shulamit
RANTA-SHIDA, Shoko
RAYMOND, Madeleine
REBE, Louise Christine
REES, Winifred Emily
REGAN, Sarah Wren Love
REHNQVIST, Karin Birgitta
REIFF, Lili
REISER, Violet
RENART, Marta Garcia
RENNES, Catharina van
RENSHAW, Rosette
REYNOLDS, Laura Lawton
RHEINGOLD, Lauma Yanovna
RHOADS, Mary R.
RICHARDS, Christine-Louise
RICHARDSON, Cornelia Heintzman
RICHARDSON, Enid Dorothy
RICHEPIN, Eliane
RICHTER, Marga
RICHTER, Marion Morrey
RISHER, Anna Priscilla
RITTENBAND, Minna Ethel
RITTMAN, Trude
RIVE-KING, Julia
ROBBOY, Rosalie Smotkin
ROBERT, Lucie
ROBERTS, Jane A.
RODRIGUEZ BELLA, Catalina
ROE, Gloria Ann
ROESGEN-CHAMPION, Marguerite
  Sara
ROGER, Denise
ROGERS, Ethel Tench
ROGERS, Faith Helen
ROGET, Henriette
ROLDES FREIXES, Mercedes
ROMERO BARBOSA, Elena
ROOBENIAN, Amber
ROOTH, Anna-Greta
ROSATO, Clorinda
ROSCO, B. Jeanie
ROSE OF JESUS, Sister
ROSS, Gertrude
ROZET, Sonia
ROZMAN, Sarah
RUBIN, Anna Ita
RUDOW, Vivian Adelberg
RUSH, Ruth
RUTA, Gilda, Countess
RYBNER, Dagmar de Corval
RYDER, Theodora Sturkow
SAARINEN, Gloria Edith
SADOWSKY, Reah
SAINT JOHN, Kathleen Louise
SAINT-GEORGES, Didia
SAITO-NODA, Eva
SAKALLI-LECCA, Alexandra
SALQUIN, Hedy

SALVADOR, Matilde
SAMTER, Alice
SAMUEL, Marguerite
SANCIN, Mirca
SANDERS, Alma M.
SANFILIPPO, Margherita Marie
SANGUESA, Iris
SANTIAGO-FELIPE, Vilma R.
SANTOS-OCAMPO DE FRANCESCO,
  Amada Amy
SARNECKA, Jadwiga
SASSOLI, Ada
SAUTER, Maya
SAXTORPH, Gudrun
SCHAFMEISTER, Helen
SCHARLI, Ruth
SCHARWENKA-STRESOW,
  Marianne
SCHICK, Philippine
SCHIRMACHER, Dora
SCHJELDERUP, Mon Marie Gustava
SCHLEDER, Grizelda Lazzaro
SCHLOSS, Myrna Frances
SCHMIDT-DUISBURG, Margarete
  Dina Alwina
SCHMITT-LERMANN, Frieda
SCHMITZ-GOHR, Else
SCHNEIDER, June
SCHONTHAL, Ruth E.
SCHORR-WEILER, Eva
SCHUBERT, Myra Jean
SCHULZE-BERGHOF, Luise Doris
  Albertine
SCHUSSLER-BREWAEYS, Marie
  Antoinette
SCHUSTER, Doris Dodd
SCHUSTER, Elfriede
SCHUYLER, Philippa Duke
SCHWARTZ, Julie
SCHWARTZ, Nan Louise
SCHWEIZER, Gertrude
SCHYTTE, Anna
SCLIAR, Esther
SCOTT, Georgina Keir
SEARS, Ilene Hanson
SEBASTIANI, Pia
SEHESTED, Hilda
SEIDERS, Mary Asenath
SELDEN-GOTH, Gizella
SELTZNER, Jennie
SELVA, Blanche
SEMEGEN, Daria
SENFTER, Johanna
SEPULVEDA, Maria Luisa
SETO, Robin
SEUEL-HOLST, Marie
SHARPE, Emma
SHAVERZASHVILI, Tamara Antonovna
SHAW, Carrie Burpee
SHELTON, Margaret Meier
SHEPARD, Jean Ellen
SHER, Rebecca
SHERMAN, Kim Daryl
SHERREY, Mae Ayres
SHIRLEY, Constance Jeanette
SHLONSKY, Verdina
SIDORENKO, Tamara Stepanovna
SILBERTA, Rhea
SILVA, Eloisa d'Herbil de
SILVERMAN, Faye-Ellen
SIMIC, Darinka
SIMONE, Nina
SIMONIAN, Nadezhda Simonovna
SIMONS, Netty
SINGER, Jeanne
SIROONI, Alice
SKAGGS, Hazel Ghazarian
SKARECKY, Jana Milena
SKOLFIELD, Alice Jones Tewksbury
SLENCZYNSKA, Ruth
SLENDZINSKA, Julitta

SLIANOVA-MIZANDARI, Dagmara
  Levanovna
SMEJKALOVA, Vlasta
SMELTZER, Susan Mary
SMITH, Edith Gross
SMITH, Hilda Josephine
SMITH, Julia Frances
SMYTH, Ethel Mary, Dame
SNELL, Lillian Lucinda
SNIFFIN, Allison
SNIZKOVA-SKRHOVA, Jitka
SODRE, Joanidia
SOENSTEVOLD, Maj
SOLOMON, Elide M.
SOLOMON, Mirrie Irma
SOMMER, Silvia
SOUERS, Mildred
SOULAGE, Marcelle Fanny Henriette
SOUTHAM, Ann
SPALDING, Eva Ruth
SPAULDING, Virginia
SPEACH, Sister Bernadette Marie
SPECHT, Anita Socola
SPECHT, Judy Lavise
SPENCER PALMER, Florence
  Margaret
SPENCER, Marguerita
SPIZIZEN, Louise Myers
SPOENDLIN, Elisabeth
SPOERRI-RENFER, Anna-
  Margaretha
SPOONER, Dorothy Harley
STAIR, Patty
STAIRS, Lousie E.
STANEKAITE-LAUMYANSKENE,
  Elena Ionovna
STANLEY, Helen Camille
STARBUCK, Anna Diller
STEELE, Helen
STEELE, Lynn
STEIN, Gladys Marie
STEINER, Gitta Hana
STEPHEN, Roberta Mae
STERNICKA-NIEKRASZOWA, Ilza
STEVENS, Joan Frances
STILMAN-LASANSKY, Julia
STINSON, Ethelyn Lenore
STOCKER, Clara
STOCKER, Stella
STORY, Pauline B.
STREATFIELD, Valma June
STREIT, Else
STRICKLAND, Lily Teresa
STRUTT, Dorothy
STUART-BERGSTROM, Elsa
  Marianne
STURKOW-RYDER, Theodora
STUTSMAN, Grace May
STYLES, Dorothy Geneva
SUCHY, Gregoria Karides
SUESSE, Dana
SUH, Kyung-Sun
SUMNER, Clare
SUNBLAD-HALME, Heidi Gabriella
  Wilhelmina
SUSZCZYNSKA, Anna
SUTHERLAND, Margaret
SUTZU, Rodica
SWAIN, Freda Mary
SWIFT, Kay
SWISHER, Gloria Agnes Wilson
SZAJNA-LEWANDOWSKA, Jadwiga
  Helena
SZALITOWNA, Paulina
SZOENYI, Erzsebet
SZYMANSKA, Iwonka Bogumila
TAKAMI, Toyoko
TAL, Marjo
TAL, Ya'ara
TAMBLYN, Bertha Louise
TAPPER, Bertha

TARBOS, Frances
TARTAGLIA, Lidia
TATE, Phyllis
TAUBER, Lotti
TEGNER, Alice Charlotte
TELFER, Nancy Ellen
TEMPLE, Hope
TERHUNE, Anice
TERRY, Frances
TERZIAN, Alicia
THEMMEN, Ivana Marburger
THIEME, Kerstin Anja
THOMAS, Karen P.
THOMAS, Marilyn Taft
THOMAS, Mary Virginia
THOMAS, Muriel Leonora Duncan
THOME, Diane
THOMPSON, Caroline Lorraine
THORESON, Janice Pearl
THORKELSDOTTIR, Mist Barbara
TICHARICH, Zdenka
TIDEMAN-WIJERS, Bertha
TIMMERMANN, Leni
TOBIN, Candida
TODD, Alice Weston
TOLKOWSKY, Denise
TOWER, Joan
TOYAMA, Michiko Françoise
TRIMBLE, Joan
TRUMAN, Irene
TUMANISHVILI, Ketevana
    Dmitirevna
TURNELL, Margaret Hoberg
TURNER, Mildred Cozzens
TURNER-MALEY, Florence
TURRiETTA, Cheryl Renée
TURTYGINA, Pava Grigorevna
TUTTLE, Thelma Kent
TWOMBLY, Mary Lynn
TYRMAND, Eta Moiseyevna
TYSON, Mildred Lund
UNDERWOOD, Frances Evangeline
UNSCHULD, Marie von
URBAYI-KRASNODEBSKA, Zofia
    Jadwiga
URRETA, Alicia
USHER, Ethel Watson
USHER, Julia
UYEDA, Leslie
UYTTENHOVE, Yolande
VAKHVAKHISHVILI, Tamara
    Nikolayevna
VAN APPLEDORN, Mary Jeanne
VAN DE VATE, Nancy Hayes
VAN EPEN-DE GROOT, Else Antonia
VAN HAUTE, Anna-Maria
VAN KATWIJK, Viola Edna Beck
VAN NESTE, Rosane Micheline Lucie
    Charlotte
VAN VLIET, Pearl H.
VANNAH, Kate
VASCONCELOS, Maria Regina
    Quintanilha de
VAZQUEZ, Alida
VAZQUEZ, Lilia
VEHAR, Persis Anne
VERNE, Adela
VERNE-BREDT, Alice
VERRILL, Louise Shurtleff Brown
VIDAR, Jorunn
VIERK, Lois
VIGNERON-RAMAKERS, Christiane-
    Josee
VILLARINI, Awilda
VILLENEUVE, Marie-Louise Diane
VILLIN, Marcelle Henriette Marie
VINETTE, Alice
VINOGRADOVA, Vera
VIRGIL, Antha Minerva Patchen
VIRTUE, Constance Cochnower
VISCONTI, Leila

VITALIS, Sister Mary
VITO-DELVAUX, Berthe di
VIVADO ORSINI, Ida
VOELLMY-LIECHTI, Grety
VOIGT-SCHWEIKERT, Margarete
VOLKART, Hazel
VOLKART-SCHLAGER, Kaethe
VOLLENHOVEN, Hanna van
VON ZIERITZ, Grete
VORLOVA, Slavka
VORONINA, Tatiana Aleksandrovna
VRABELY-WURMBACH-
    STUPPACHOVA, Stefania
WALLACH, Joelle
WALSH, Elizabeth Jameson
WALTERS, Teresa
WANG, An-Ming
WARE, Harriet
WARREN, Elinor Remick
WARSHAW, Dalit Paz
WARWICK, Mary Carol
WATERHOUSE, Frances Emery
WATERSTONE, Satella S.
WEAVER, Carol Ann
WEAVER, Marion
WEAVER, Mary
WEGENER-FRENSEL, Emmy Heil
WEGENER-KOOPMAN, Bertha
    Frensel
WEIGL, Vally
WENNERSTROM, Mary Hannah
WENTZEL, Elisabet von
WESTGATE, Elizabeth
WEYBRIGHT, June
WHITE, Ruth S.
WHITTLE, Chris Mary-Francine
WIKSTROM, Inger
WILLIAMS, Linda
WILLIAMS, Stella
WILSON, Gertrude Hoag
WILSON, Lynn
WINDSOR, Helen J.
WING, Helen
WISHART, Betty Rose
WITNI, Monica
WONG, Betty Ann
WCODS, Joan Shirley
    LeSueur
WRIGHT, Nannie Louise
WYETH, Ann
WYLIE, Ruth Shaw
YAMASHITA, Mika
YAMPOLSCHI, Roseane
YOGUCHI, Rie
YOUNG, Fredricka Agnes
YOUNG, Jane Corner
YOUNG, Rolande Maxwell
ZAIDEL-RUDOLPH, Jeanne
ZAIMONT, Judith Lang
ZARANEK, Stefania Anatolyevna
ZELIKOVSKAYA, Fania
    Mordukhovna
ZHUBINSKAYA, Valentina
    Yanovna
ZIBEROVA, Zinaida Petrovna
ZIMMERMANN, Margrit
ZIPRICK, Marjorie Jean
ZIVKOVIC, Mirjana
Century unknown
BAKER, Joanne J.
CUBONI, Maria Teresa
FERGUS-HOYT, Phyllis
GALEOTTI, Margherita
GRAZIANA
RYCOFF, Lalla
SNODGRASS, Louise Harrison
TAJANI MATTONE, Ida

PSALTERY
7th Century A.D.
    AZZA AL-MAILA

RECORDER
20th Century A.D.
    BARTHEL, Ursula
    BLOCH, Suzanne
    BOESSER, Dagma
    BOYD, Anne Elizabeth
    BREMER, Marrie Petronella
    HAZELRIG, Sylvia Jean Earnhart
    HELBLING, Elsa
    HUNTER, Hilda
    KRAUS, Rozann Baghdad
    LEE, Michelle
    LEVIN, Rami Yona
    MAZOUROVA, Jarmila
    OWEN, Angela Maria
    SIEBER, Susanne
    STREATFIELD, Valma June
    TUCKER, Tui St. George

SAXOPHONE
18th Century A.D.
    DANZI, Maria Margarethe
20th Century A.D.
    BLOOM, Jane Ira
    LANG, Rosemary Rita
    LINNET, Anne
    ROEMER, Hanne
    SANFILIPPO, Margherita Marie
    SHORE, Clare
    SNELL, Lillian Lucinda

THEORBO
18th Century A.D.
    BERTHÉ, Mme.
    LOUVENCOURT, Mlle. de
20th Century A.D.
    NAZIROVA, Elmira Mirza Rza kyzy

TROMBONE
20th Century A.D.
    BERGMAN, Ellen
    BUMP, Mary Crane
    KAPLAN, Lois Jay
    LEE, Hope Anne Keng-Wei
    LISTON, Melba
    SNELL, Lillian Lucinda

TRUMPET
20th Century A.D.
    ORTMANS, Kay Muriel

TUBA
20th Century A.D.
    SANFILIPPO, Margherita Marie
    WECKWERTH, Nancy

UKELELE
19th Century A.D.
    LIKELIKE, Miriam Cleghorn,
        Princess
20th Century A.D.
    BREEN, May Singhi
    KANAKA'OLE, Edith Ke-Kuhikuhi-I-
        Pu'u-one-o-Na-Ali'i-O-Kohala
    MACHADO, Lena
    SHARPE, Emma

VIOLA
18th Century A.D.
    LEVI, Mme.
20th Century A.D.
    ALBRIGHT, Janet Elaine
    BITGOOD, Roberta
    BROGUE, Roslyn Clara
    CLARK, Florence Durrell
    CLARKE, Rebecca
    FUCHS, Lillian
    FULCHER, Ellen Georgina
    GOEBELS, Gisela
    GOMM, Elizabeth
    GRAHAM, Janet Christine

GRIEBLING, Karen Jean
HAMPE, Charlotte
HEGELER, Anna
HUBICKI, Margaret Olive
JARRATT, Lita
KELLEY, Dorothea Nolte
KISCH, Eve
LUTYENS, Elisabeth
MILAM, Lena Triplett
MILNE, Helen C.
PAYNE, Harriet
PHILLIPS, Karen Ann
RADMALL, Peggy
ROZMAN, Sarah
SANFILIPPO, Margherita Marie
SEPULVEDA, Maria Luisa
SMELTZER, Susan Mary
SPAIN-DUNK, Susan
SPOENDLIN, Elisabeth
STANLEY, Helen Camille
THOMAS, Mary Virginia

VIOLA DA GAMBA
18th Century A.D.
THICKNESSE, Miss
20th Century A.D.
DOLMETSCH, Helene
HSU, Wen-Ying
LINDEMAN, Hjelle Signe
POLICARPO TEIXEIRA, Maria
    Margarida Fernandes
WILLIAMS, Mary Lou

VIOLIN
17th Century A.D.
BIRNIE, Patie
18th Century A.D.
BAYER, Karoline
SIRMEN, Maddalena Laura di
TASCA, Mme.
19th Century A.D.
AMANN, Josephine
BARKER, Laura Wilson
BLANGINI, Mlle.
BRESSON, Mlle.
FILIPOWICZ, Elize-Minelli
GYDE, Margaret
KRAEHMER, Caroline
KRAINSKA, Justyna
MILANOLLO, Teresa Domenica
    Maria
PATON, Mary Anne
RONTGEN, Amanda
SALOMONI, Mlle.
SCHUMANN, Clara Josephine
TURNEY, Ruthyn
WESTENHOLZ, Eleonore Sophie
    Marie
20th Century A.D.
ABE, Kyoko
ABEJO, Sister M. Rosalina
ACKLAND, Jeanne Isabel Dorothy
ALSTED, Birgitte
ANTHONY, Evangeline
ARAUCO, Ingrid Colette
ARBEL, Re Chaya
BAADER-NOBS, Heidi
BACEWICZ, Grażyna
BAGANIER, Janine
BAIL, Grace Shattuck
BARBERIS, Mansi
BARBI, Alice
BARBILLON, Jeanne
BARNS, Ethel
BARRIENTOS, Maria
BARTHEL, Ursula
BARTLETT, Floy Little
BAYLIS, Lilian Mary
BEATON, Isabella
BECKON, Lettie Marie
BELL, Carla Huston

BELOW-BUTTLAR, Gerda von
BERROA, Catalina
BINET, Jocelyne
BOBROW, Sanchie
BOTSFORD, Talitha
BOULANGER, Lili Juliette Marie Olga
BRINK-POTHUIS, Annie van den
BROGUE, Roslyn Clara
BROUWER, Margaret Lee
BROWN, Elizabeth van Ness
BRYAN, Betty Sue
BUCHANAN, Dorothy Quita
BUTLER, Anne Lois
CALL, Audrey
CANALES PIZARRO, Marta
CAPERTON, Florence Tait
CHAMINADE, Cecile Louise
    Stephanie
CHARTRES, Vivien
CLARK, Florence Durrell
CLARKE, Rebecca
DAHL, Vivian
DAVENPORT GOERTZ, Gladys
DAVIS, Sharon
DE BIASE BIDART, Lycia
DELBOS, Claire
DELORME, Isabelle
DILLER, Saralu C.
DODGE, May Hewes
DUNLOP, Isobel
ECKHARDT-GRAMATTE, Sophie-
    Carmen
EISENSTEIN, Stella Price
ELIAS, Graciela Morales de
ENGBERG, M. Davenport
FARGA PELLICER, Onia
FAUTCH, Sister Magdalen
FELLOWS, Mrs. Wayne Stanley
FERREYRA, Beatriz
FINLEY, Lorraine Noel
FISCHER, Edith Steinkraus
FISHER, Charlotte Eleanor
FITZGERALD, Sister Florence
    Therese
FOLVILLE, Eugenie-Emilie Juliette
FOWLER, Marje
FRASER, Shena Eleanor
FRITTER, Genevieve Davisson
FULCHER, Ellen Georgina
GEYER, Stefi
GOMM, Elizabeth
GREENE, Genevieve
HAENDEL, Ida
HALACSY, Irma von
HAMPE, Charlotte
HANEFELD, Gertrud
HARDING, Mildred Thompson
HARVEY, Eva Noel
HARWOOD, Sylvia Rowell
HASKELL, Doris Burd
HEGNER, Anna
HEMON, Sedje
HERBISON, Jeraldine Saunders
HERTEL, Sister Romana
HILL, Sister M. Mildred
HOFFMAN, Phyllis Sampson
HOLMBERG, Betty
HUTTON, Florence Myra
IPPOLITO, Carmela
JACKSON, Barbara May
JENNINGS, Marie Pryor
JENNY, Sister Leonore
KAUFMAN, Barbara
KAVASCH, Deborah Helene
KAZURO-TROMBINI, Margerita
KIRKMAN, Merle
KOLODUB, Zhanna Efimovna
KRUSE, Lotte
LANG, Margaret Ruthven
LAUBER, Anne Marianne
LE BEAU, Louisa Adolpha

LEBENBOM, Elaine F.
LINNEMANN, Maria Catharina
LINZ VON KRIEGNER, Marta
LOH, Kathy Jean
LOHR, Ina
LUND, Gudrun
LYONN LIEBERMAN, Julie
McINTYRE, Margaret
McLIN, Lena
MAREZ-OYENS, Tera de
MARY BERNICE, Sister
MATTHEWS, Dorothy White
MILAM, Lena Triplett
MILNE, Helen C.
MOLAVA, Pamela May
MOON, Chloe Elizabeth
NATVIG, Candace
NIEDERBERGER, Maria A.
NIEMACK, Ilza Louise
NIGHTINGALE, Mae Wheeler
NOVI, Anna Beate
OSGOOD, Marion
PAYNE, Harriet
PEJACEVIC, Dora, Countess
PENNER, Jean Priscilla
PHILLIPS, Vivian Daphne
PIETSCH, Edna Frieda
POWELL, Maud
RADMALL, Peggy
RAINIER, Priaulx
RAY, Ruth
REGAN, Sarah Wren Love
ROZMAN, Sarah
RUEGGER, Charlotte
SANFILIPPO, Margherita
    Marie
SCHARWENKA-STRESOW,
    Marianne
SCOTT, Georgina Keir
SEGHIZZI, Cecilia
SENFTER, Johanna
SEPULVEDA, Maria Luisa
SEWALL, Maud Gilchrist
SMELTZER, Susan Mary
SPAIN-DUNK, Susan
SPENCER, Marguerita
SPOENDLIN, Elisabeth
SPONGBERG, Viola
STANLEY, Helen Camille
STEFANOVIC, Ivana
STEPHEN, Roberta Mae
STEWART-BAXTER, Maud
STINSON, Ethelyn Lenore
STREATFIELD, Valma June
STREICHER, Lyubov Lvovna
STREIT, Else
STUDENY, Herma
SUMNER, Sarah
SWAIN, Freda Mary
TORRA, Celia
TROENDLE, Theodora
TROTT, Josephine
TWOREK, Wandy
UNSCHULD, Marie von
VAN NESTE, Rosane Micheline Lucie
    Charlotte
VIGNERY, Jeanne Emilie Virginie
VRIONIDES, Rosina
VYNER, Mary Bainbridge
WAALER, Fredrikke Holtemann
WALDO, Elisabeth
WARE, Helen
WEGENER-FRENSEL, Emmy Heil
WHITE, Elsie Fellows
WHITE, Grace
WHITLOCK, E. Florence
WICKS, Camilla
WILES, Margaret Jones
WING, Helen
ZIELINSKA, Lidia
ZWILICH, Ellen Taaffe

VIOLONCELLO
  19th Century A.D.
    POTT, Aloyse
  20th Century A.D.
    ADERHOLDT, Sarah
    BLIESENER, Ada Elizabeth
      Michelman
    BOULANGER, Lili Juliette
      Marie Olga
    CRAIB, Doris
    CROKER, Catherine Munnell
    DARE, Margaret Marie
    DOLMETSCH, Hélène
    GOEBELS, Gisela
    GOETSCHIUS, Marjorie
    GRONOWETTER, Freda
    HILL, Sister M. Mildred
    HIND O'MALLEY, Pamela
    HOLLAND, Dulcie Sybil
    HOUSE, L. Marguerite

HOY, Bonnee L.
HSU, Wen-Ying
IORDAN, Irina Nikolayevna
LAPIN, Lily
LEE, Hope Anne Keng-Wei
LOWELL, Edith
LUCKMAN, Phyllis
McGILL, Gwendolen Mary Finlayson
MARSHALL, Kye
MUKLE, May Henrietta
OWEN, Blythe
PAVIA DE MAGALHAES, Isaura
PIGGOTT, Audrey Margaret
RISHER, Anna Priscilla
SANFILIPPO, Margherita Marie
SCOTT, Georgina Keir
SPENCER, Marguerita
STRUTT, Dorothy
TODD, Alice Weston
WATSON, Gwendolyn

WILLS, Edwina Florence
YAGLING, Victoria

VIOLS (OTHER)
  20th Century A.D.
    PELEGRI, Maria Teresa

XYLOPHONE
  20th Century A.D.
    BECKON, Lettie Marie

ZITHER
  19th Century A.D.
    ADELUNG, Olga
    CHRIST, Fanny
    KAVALIEROVA, Marie
    ZAUBITZER, Ida
  20th Century A.D.
    LEBARON, Anne
    WOOD, Ruzena Alenka Valda

APPENDIX 11

International Council of Women and Affiliates

13 Rue Caumartin, 75009 Paris, FRANCE

This is a non-governmental organization comprising the National Councils of Women of nearly every country in the world. It is a federation of women of all nations, races, creeds and cultural traditions. Founded in Washington in 1888, its aim is to help women to be aware of their rights and their civic, social and political responsibilities to society. It has first category consultative status with the Economic and Social Councils of the United Nations (ECOSOC) and the ICW representatives at the United Nations keep the Councils' conveners in touch with inter-governmental work in their respective fields.

The international standing committees conduct studies in depth and each has a specific term of reference in the following categories:

Arts, letters and music; Child and family; Economics; Education; Environment and habitat; Home economics; International relations and peace; Law and the status of women; Mass media; Migration; Social welfare; Women and employment.

The National Councils in each country are made up of affiliated organizations and individual members. These councils carry on their own activities under similar categories and benefit from the inspiration and new ideas through contact and discussion with women of other groups in their own countries and in other countries. The National Councils are frequently consulted by their respective governments when new laws are being drafted and often succeed in having existing laws changed and made more favourable to women.

For administrative purposes there are two regional councils:

CANADA
American Regional Council
8020 Arthur Drive RR No 1
SAARNICHTON BC V05 1M0

NETHERLANDS:
European Centre of the International Council of Women
Stadionkade 13
AMSTERDAM 1077 VJ

The postal addresses of the affiliated National Councils are listed below:

ARGENTINA
Consejo de Mujeres de la Republica
  Argentina
Casilla de Correo 116
Sucursal 48
1060
BUENOS AIRES

AUSTRALIA
National Council of Women of Australia
P.O. Box 161
STEPNEY SA 5069

AUSTRIA
Bund Oesterreichischer Frauenvereine
Wilhelm Exnergasse 34-36
A-1090 VIENNA 9

BAHAMAS
The Council of Women in the Bahamas
P.O. Box 1145
NASSAU

BARBADOS
Barbados Council of Women
Lyrias
CHRISTCHURCH

BELGIUM
Conseil National des Femmes Belges/
  Nationale Vrouwenraad
Louisalaan 183
1050 BRUSSELS

BOLIVIA
Consejo Nacional de Mujeres de Bolivia
Castilla 2573
LE PAZ

BOTSWANA
Botswana Council of Women
P.O. Box 339
GABORONE

BRAZIL
Conselho Nacional de Mulheres do Brazil
Rue Baratra
Ribeiro 539, Apt. 201
Copacabana
RIO DE JANEIRO

BURMA
Council of Women's Associations
280a U Wishara Rd.
RANGOON

CAMEROON
Organisation des Femmes du
Rassemblement Democratique
du Peuple Camerounais
Comite Central
B.P. 867
YAOUNDE

CANADA
National Council of Women of Canada
270 MacLaren St., Suite 20
OTTAWA 4
K2P OM3 ONTARIO

CHILE
Secretaria Nacional de la Mujer
Villavicencio 341 OF 21
SANTIAGO

COLUMBIA
Consejo Nacional de Mujeres de Colombia
Calle 82 14A-17, Oficinas 308/309
BOGOTA

CONGO
Union révolutionnaire des Femmes du
Congo
B.P. 309
BRAZZAVILLE

DENMARK
Danske Kvinders Nationalraad
Niels Hemmingsensgade 8 (2nd Floor)
1153 COPENHAGEN K

DOMINICAN REPUBLIC
Consejo Nacional de Mujeres Inc.
de la Republica Dominicana
El Conde St. 23A
SANTO DOMINGO

ECQUADOR
Union Nacional de Mujeres del Ecuador
Avenida America No. 5573
y San Francisco
QUITO

EGYPT
National Women's Organization
Arab Socialist Union (Women's Section)
Cornish El Nil
CAIRO

FIJI
The Fiji National Council of Women
P.O. Box 840
SUVA

FINLAND
The National Council of Women of Finland
Rauhankatu 7
00170 HELSINKI

FRANCE
Conseil National des Femmes Françaises
11 Rue de Viarmes
B.P. 115-01
75022 PARIS
CEDEX 01

GAMBIA
Gambia Women's Federation
P.O. Box 83
BANJUL

GERMAN FEDERAL REPUBLIC
Deutscher Frauenring E.V.
Wall 42
2300 KIEL 1

GHANA
Ghana Assembly of Women
P.O. Box 459
ACCRA

GREECE
Conseil National des Femmes Hellenes
38 Rue Voulis
ATHENS 10557

GUATEMALA
Consejo Nacional de Mujeres de Guatemala
13 Calle 3-15
Zona 10
GUATEMALA CITY

HAITI
Conseil National des Femmes d'Haiti
B.P. 1082
PORT-AU-PRINCE

HONG KONG
Hong Kong Council of Women
P.O. Box 819
HONG KONG

INDIA
National Council of Women in India
14 Sonmarg
Nepean Sea Rd.
BOMBAY 400 006

INDONESIA
Kongres Wanita Indonesia (Kowani)
Jl. Imam Bonjol No. 58
JAKARTA PUSAT 10310

ISRAEL
Council of Women's Organizations in Israel
Wizo Club
1 Mapu St.
JERUSALEM

ITALY
Consiglio Nazionale delle Donne Italiane
Piazza dei Quiriti 3
00192 ROME

IVORY COAST
Association des Femmes Ivoiriennes
B.P. 2005
ABIDJAN

KENYA
National Council of Women of Kenya
Moi Ave.
P.O. Box 43741
NAIROBI

KOREA
Korean National Council of Women
40-427, 428 3rd St.
Han River
Yongsan-ku
SEOUL 140

LEBANON
Conseil des Femmes Libanaises
B.P. 16.5640
BEIRUT

LESOTHO
Lesotho National Council of Women
P.O. Box MS. 1340
MASERU

LIBERIA
National Federation of Liberian Women
P.O. Box 2703
MONROVIA

LUXEMBOURG
Fédération Nationale des Femmes
Luxembourgeoises
B.P. 172
LUXEMBOURG VILLE

MADAGASCAR
Conseil National des Associations de
Femmes de Madagascar
90 bis. Avenue Marechal Foch
ANTANANARIVO 101

MALAYSIA
National Council of Women's Organizations Malaysia
157 Jalan tun
Razak
50400 KUALA LUMPUR

MALTA
The Council of Women
23 St. Andrew St.
VALLETTA

MEXICO
Consejo Nacional de Mujeres de Mexico
Cuvier 45
MEXICO CITY 5 D.F.

MOROCCO
Union Nationale des Femmes Marocaines
3 Rue El Afghani
B.P. 30
RABAT

NEPAL
Nepal Women's Organization
Central Committee
Pulchok
Lalitpur
KATMUNDU

NETHERLANDS
Netherlands Council of Women
Laan van Meerdervoort 30
2517 AL DEN HAAG

NEW ZEALAND
National Council of Women of New Zealand
P.O. Box 12-117
WELLINGTON NORTH

NIGER
Association des Femmes du Niger
B.P. 28-18
NIAMEY

NIGERIA
National Council of Women's Societies,
Nigeria
P.O. Box 3063
Tafawa Balewa Square Complex
LAGOS

NORWAY
Norske Kvinners Nasjonalrad
Fr. Nansens Plass 6
OSLO 1

PAKISTAN
All Pakistan Women's Association
67/B Garden Rd.
KARACHI 3

PAPUA NEW GUINEA
National Council of Women of Papua New
Guinea
P.O. Box 154 UPNG
PORT MORESBY

PERU
Consejo Nacional de Mujeres del Peru
Francia 706
Miraflores
LIMA 18

PHILIPPINES
Civic Assembly of Women of the Philippines
c/o Philippines Women's University
1743 Taft Ave.
MANILA

SAUDI ARABIA
Saudi Arabia Women's Association
B.P. 6, RIYADH

SIERRA LEONE
Sierra Leone Federation of Women's
Organisations
P.O. Box 811
FREETOWN

SINGAPORE
National Council of Women, Singapore
9 Balmoral Rd.
SINGAPORE 1025

SOUTH AFRICA
National Council of Women of South Africa
161 Pietermaritz St.
PIETERMARITZBURG 3201

SPAIN
Consell de Dones
Diputacio, 306
Pral
BARCELONA 08009

SURINAM
National Council of Women of Surinam
Rust en Vredestraat 64B
P.O. Box 1574
PARAMARIBO

SWITZERLAND
Alliance de Sociétés Feminines Suisses
P.O. Box 185
8033 ZURICH

SYRIA
Union Générale des Femmes Arabes
Syriennes
Rue Mahdi Ben Barakeh
Abou Roumane
DAMASCUS

TANZANIA
Umoja wa Wananaka wa Tanzania
P.O. Box 1473
DAR-ES-SALAAM

THAILAND
National Council of Women of Thailand
Manangkasilla Mansion
Larnluang Rd.
BANGKOK

TRINIDAD AND TOBAGO
National Council of Women of Trinidad and
Tobago
118 Saddle Rd., Cor. Lynch Dr.
MARAVAL

TUNISIA
Union Nationale des Femmes de Tunisie
56 Boulevard Bab Benat
TUNIS

TURKEY
National Council of Turkish Women
Posta Kutusu 44
Yenisehir
ANKARA

UGANDA
The National Council of Women of Uganda
P.O. Box 1663
KAMPALA

UNITED KINGDOM
National Council of Women of Great Britain
34 Lower Sloane St.
LONDON SW1 8BP

UNITED STATES OF AMERICA
National Council of Women of U.S.A., Inc.
777 United Nations Plaza
NEW YORK NY 10017

URUGUAY
Consejo Nacional de Mujeres del Uruguay
Rambla Republica de Peru 815
Apt. 1101
MONTEVIDEO

WESTERN SAMOA
National Council of Women of Western
  Samoa
P.O. Box 1162
APIA

ZAIRE
Union Révolutionnaire des Femmes
  du Zaire
B.P. 309
KINSHASA

ZIMBABWE
National Council of Women of Zimbabwe
P.O. Box MR 37
Marlborough
HARARE

APPENDIX 12

International Music Societies and Institutions

This selection of some of the important music institutions and information centers excludes the music faculties and music departments of the universities and university colleges in each of the countries listed.

Whilst this listing is by no means all-inclusive, it would be appreciated if pertinent societes and associations would submit their names and addresses for inclusion in the next edition or supplement. Please write to the Director, International Institute for the Study Women in Music, California State University Northridge CA 91330 U.S.A.

ALGERIA
Conservatoire de Musique
2 Blvd. Che Guevara
ALGIERS

Conservatoire Municipal de Musique
5 Rue d'Igli
ORAN

ARGENTINA
Conservatorio Nacionale de Musica
Callao 1521
1024 BUENOS AIRES

Conservatorio de Musica
Sarmiento 1551
1042 BUENOS AIRES

AUSTRALIA
Australian Council for the Arts
P.O. Box 302
NORTH SYDNEY
NSW 2060

Australian Music Centre Ltd
P.O. Box N9
Grosvenor Street
SYDNEY
NSW 2000

Canberra School of Music
P.O. Box 804
CANBERRA CITY
ACT 2601

Fellowship of Australian Composers
Box 522
STRATHFIELD
NSW

AUSTRIA
Gesellschaft der Musikfreunde in Wien
Bösendorferstrasse 12
A 1010 VIENNA

International Music Centre
Lothringerstr 20
1030 VIENNA

Konservatorium der Stadt Wien
Johannesgasse 4A
A 1010 VIENNA

Oesterreichische Gesellschaft für Musik
Hanuschgasse 3
A 1010 VIENNA

Oesterreichischer Komponistenbund
Baumannstraase 8-10
A 1030 VIENNA

BELGIUM
Belgian Centre for Music Documentation (CEBEDEM)
Rue d'Arolon 75-77
B. 1040 BRUSSELS

Conservatoire Royale de Musique de Bruxelles
30 Rue de la Regence
1000 BRUSSELS

Fédération Internationale de Jeunesses Musicales
4 Palais de Beaux-Arts
10 Rue Royale
1000 BRUSSELS

Koninklyk Vlaams Conservatorium van Antwerpen
Des guinlei 25
2018 ANTWERP

Société Belge de Musicologie
30 Rue de la Regence
1000 BRUSSELS

BOLIVIA
Conservatorio Nacional de Musica
Avenida 6 de Agosto 2092
LA PAZ

BRAZIL
Conservatorio Brasiliero de Musica
Avenida Graca Aranha 57-12
RIO DE JANEIRO

BULGARIA
Bulgarian State Conservatoire
K. Gotwald 11
1505 SOFIA

Union of Bulgarian Composers
Vasov 2
1000 SOFIA IV

BURMA
Department of Fine Arts
1 Narawat Yeiktha Rd.
Dagon P.O.
RANGOON

State School of Music and Drama
Jubilee Hall
Shwedagon Pagoda Rd.
RANGOON

CANADA
Canadian Music Center
Chalmers House
20 St. Joseph Street
TORONTO
M4Y IJ9

Conservatoire de Musique de Montréal
100 Est Rue Notre-Dame
MONTREAL
H2Y 1C1

CHINA (TAIWAN)
National Taiwan Academy of Arts
Pan-chiao Park
TAIPEI

CHINESE PEOPLE'S REPUBLIC
Research Institute of Music
Dong Zhi Men Wai
BEJING (PEKING)

COLOMBIA
Centro de Documentacion Nacional
Carrera 5 # 10-09
BOGOTA D.E.

CUBA
Conservatorio de Musica Amadeo Roldan
Rastro y Lealtad
HAVANA

CZECHOSLOVAKIA
Academy of Music and Dramatic Art
Jiraskova 3
813 01 BRATISLAVA

Brno Conservatory
Trida kpt Jarose 43
600 00 BRNO

Czech Music Society
Valdstejnoke nam 1
110 00 PRAGUE

Czech Society for Chamber Music
Barrandov 327
152 00 PRAGUE

Music Information Centre of the Czech Music Fund
Besedni 3
118 00 PRAGUE 1

Music Information Centre of the Slovak Music Fund
Fucikova
801 00 BRATISLAVA

Prague Conservatory
Na rejdisti 1
110 00 PRAGUE

Union of Czech Composers
Skroupova nam 9
130 00 PRAGUE 3

Union of Slovak Composers
Sladkovicova 11
BRATISLAVA

DENMARK
Dansk Komponist Forening
Valkindorfsgade 3
DK 1151 COPENHAGEN

Dansk Tonkunstler Forening
Radhusstraede 1
1000 COPENHAGEN K

Musikinformations-Centret
Skoubogade 2
COPENHAGEN 1158 KBH K

Royal Danish Academy of Music
Niels Brocksgade 1
1574 COPENHAGEN V

ECUADOR
Conservatorio Nacional de Musica
Carrion 14 y Reina Victoria
QUITO

EGYPT
Higher Institute of Music
CAIRO

FINLAND
Finnish Music Information Centre
Runeberginkatu 15 A1
SF 00100 HELSINKI

Sibelius Academy
Toolonkatu 28
00260 HELSINKI 26

Society of Finnish Composers
Runeberginkatu 15A 11
00100 HELSINKI 17

FRANCE
Centre de Documentation de la Musique Contemporaine
225 Avenue Charles de Gaulle
F 92521 Neuilly-sur-Seine

Conservatoire National Supérieur de Musique
14 Rue de Madrid
75008 PARIS

International Music Council
UNESCO
1 Rue Miollis
Cedex 15
75732 PARIS

International Musicological Society
UNESCO
1 Rue Miollis
Cedex 15
75732 PARIS

Scola Cantorum de Musique
269 Rue St. Jacques
75008 PARIS

GERMAN DEMOCRATIC REPUBLIC
Hochschule für Musik 'Franz Liszt'
Platz der Demokratie
5300 WEIMAR

GERMAN FEDERAL REPUBIC
Deutsche Komponisten Verband
Bergengruen Str 28
1000 BERLIN 38

Frau und Musik - Internationaler Arbeitskreis
c/o Antje Olivier
Frobenstrasse 6
D4000 DUESSELDORF 30

Gesellschaft für Neue Musik
c/o Musik Heckel N7 i3
6800 MANNHEIM

International Institute for Comparative
 Music Studies and Documentation
Winklerstr 20
1000 BERLIN 33

Internationales Musikinstitut Darmstadt
Nieder-Ramstadter Strasse 190
D-6100 DARMSTADT

GREECE
Pan-Hellenic Musical Association
C/o Agios Constantinou 51
ATHENS

State Conservatory of Music
Odos Olympion Diamanti 7
THESSALONIKI

GUATEMALA
Conservatorio Nacional de Musica
GUATEMALA CITY

HUNGARY
Association of Hungarian Musicians
Vorosmarty ter 1
1051 BUDAPEST

Music Information Centre
P.O.B. 47
H-1364 BUDAPEST

Ferenc Liszt Academy of Music
P.O.B. 206
1391 BUDAPEST

ICELAND
Iceland Music Information Centre
Laufaswegi 40
REYKJAVIK

Reykjavik College of Music
Skipholti 33
105 REYKJAVIK

INDIA
Music Academy
306 T.T.K. Rd.
Royapittah
MADRAS 600014

Sangeet Natak Akademi
Rabindra Bhavan
Feroze Shah Rd.
NEW DELHI 110001

IRELAND
Music Association of Ireland
11 Suffolk St.
DUBLIN 2

Royal Irish Academy of Music
36 Westland Row
DUBLIN 2

ISRAEL
Israel Music Institute
6 Chen Blvd.
P.O Box 11253
TEL AVIV

Jerusalem Rubin Academy of Music
7 Smolenski St.
JERUSALEM

ITALY
Conservatorio di Musica 'Gioacchino Rossini'
Piazza Olivieri 5
6110 PESARO

Conservatorio di Musica Niccolo Piccinni
Via Brigata Bari 26
70124 BARI

Conservatorio di Musica Santa Cecilia
Via del Greci 18
ROME

Conservatorio Statale di Musica "Giuseppi Verdi"
Via Mazzini 11
TURIN

Conservatorio Statale di Musica "G B Martini"
Piazza Rossini 2
BOLOGNA

Conservatorio Statale di Musica "C. Monteverdi"
Piazza Domenicane 19
39100 BOLZANO

Sindicato Nationale dei Musicisti
Via Vicenza 52
ROME

Unione Donne Italiani
Via Della Colonna Antonini 41
00186 ROME

JAPAN
Japan Federation of Composers
Ogawa Building
3-7-15 Akasaka, Minato-Ku
TOKYO

Japanese Musicological Society
Ueno Park, Taito-ku
TOKYO

Kunitachi College of Music
5-5-1 Kasheiva-cho
Tachikawa-shi
190 TOKYO

Tokyo College of Music
3-4-5 Minami
Ikebukuro, Toshimaku
TOKYO

KOREA
Music Association of Korea
303 Faco Building
86-6 Sechon-Ro
Chongro ku
SEOUL

MEXICO
Conservatorio Nacional de Musica
Avenida Presidente Masaryk 582
MEXICO 5 DF

MOROCCO
Association des Amateurs de la Musique Andalouse
c/o 133 Ave. Ziraoui
CASABLANCA

Conservatoire National de Musique
RABAT

NETHERLANDS
Donemus Foundation
Paulus Potterstraat 14
NL 1071 CZ AMSTERDAM

Royal Conservatory of Music and Dance
Juliana van Stolberglaan 1
THE HAGUE

Royal Netherland Association of Musicians
Van Miereveldstraat 13
1071 Dw AMSTERDAM

Werkgroep Vrouw en Muziek
Swammersdamstraat 38
1091 Rv AMSTERDAM

NEW ZEALAND
Composers' Association of New Zealand
P.O. Box 4065
WELLINGTON

International Society for Music Education
School of Music
University of Canterbury
CHRISTCHURCH 1

NORWAY
Norsk Komponist Forening
Postboks 1666 Vika
OSLO 1

Norwegian State Academy of Music
Nordahl Brusgt 8
OSLO 1

Norwegian Music Information Centre
Tordenskioldsgt 6B
OSLO 1

PAKISTAN
Music Foundation of Pakistan
Buch Terrace
Preedy St.
KARACHI 3

PERU
Conservatorio Nacional de Musica
Emancipacion 180 Apdo 2957
LIMA

POLAND
Academy of Music
Ul Powstancow Slaskich 204
53-140 WROCLAW

Academy of Music
Ul Zacisze 3
40-025 KATOWICE

Polish Music Centre
Rynek Starego Miasta 27
PL 00 272 WARSAW

PORTUGAL
Calouste Gulbenkian Foundation
Avenidea de Berna 45
LISBON

Conservatorio Nacional
Rua dos Caetanos 29
LISBON

PUERTO RICO
Conservatory of Music of Puerto Rico
Box 41227
Minillas Station
SANTURCE 00940

Instituto de Cultura Puertorriquena
Apartado 4184
SAN JUAN DE PUERTO RICO 00905

RUMANIA
Conservatorul 'George Enescu'
Str. Closca 9
IASI

Conservatorul de Musica 'Ciprian Porumbescu'
Str. Stirbei Voda Nr 33
BUCHAREST

SOUTH AFRICA
Johannesburg Musical Society
P.O. Box 5747
JOHANNESBURG
2000

Human Sciences Research Council
Private Bag X41
PRETORIA
0001

SPAIN
Conservatorio Superior de Musica de Barcelona
Alle Bruch 112
BARCELONA

Real Conservatorio Superior de Musica de Madrid
Plaza de Isabel 11
MADRID

SWEDEN
Musikhogskolan i Stockholm
Valhallavagen 103-109
115 31 STOCKHOLM

Royal Academy of Music
Blasieholmstorg 8
111 48 STOCKHOLM

Swedish Music Information Centre
Box 27327
S 10251 STOCKHOLM

SWITZERLAND
Association des Musiques Suisses
Ave du Graumont 11 bis
1000 LAUSANNE

Conservatoire de Musique
Place Neuve
GENEVA

European Associations of Music Festivals
Centre Européen de la Culture
122 Rue de Lausanne
GENEVA

Federation of International Music Competitions
12 Rue de l'Hôtel de ville
1204 GENEVA

Frauenmusik Forum
Wiesenstr 14
5000 AARAU

International Federation of Musicians
Hofackerst 7
8032 ZURICH

International Society for Contemporary Music
c/o Studio de Musique Contemporaine
7 Blvd. Jacques-Dalcroze
CH 1204 GENEVA

Swiss Music Archives
Bellariastraase 82
CH 8038 ZURICH

TAIWAN see **CHINA**

UNITED KINGDOM
British Music Information Centre
10 Stratford Place
LONDON
W1N 9AE

Composers Guild of Great Britain
c/o British Music Information Centre
10 Stratford Place
LONDON
W1N 9AE

Royal Academy of Music
Marylebone Rd.
LONDON
NW1

Royal College of Music
Prince Consort Road
South Kensington
LONDON
SW7

Society for the Promotion of New Music
c/o British Music Information Centre
10 Stratford Place
LONDON
W1N 9AE

Trinity College of Music
Mandeville Place
LONDON
W1M 6AQ

UNITED STATES OF AMERICA

American Composers Alliance
170 West 74th Street
NEW YORK
NY 10023

American Music Center
250 West 57th Street
NEW YORK
NY 10019

American Women Composers Inc.
6192 Oxon Hill RD.
Suite 406
WASHINGTON
DC 20021

Anchorage Community College
Music Department
2533 Providence Ave.
ANCHORAGE 99504

International Institute for the Study of Women in Music
California State University
NORTHRIDGE
CA 91330

International Council for Traditional Music
Department of Music
Columbia University
NEW YORK
NY 10027

International League of Women Composers
P.O. Box 42
THREE MILE BAY
NY 13693

Juilliard School of Music
Lincoln Center
NEW YORK
NY 10023

MacDowell Colony Inc.
(National Affiliate Organization)
100 High Street
PETERBOROUGH
NH 03458

UNION SOVIET SOCIALIST REPUBLICS

Azerbaijan State Conservatory
Ul Dimitrova 98
370014 BAKU

Leningrad State Conservatory
Teatralnaya pl 3
192041 LENINGRAD

Moscow State Conservatory
Ul Gerzena 13
MOSCOW K9

YUGOSLAVIA

Academy of Music
Gunduliceva 6
41001 ZAGREB

Association of Composers of Bosnia and Herzegovina
Radiceva 15
71000 SARAJEVO

Society of Slovene Composers
Françoske revolucize 6
LJUBLJANA

Union of Yugoslav Composers
Borte Postale 213
11000 BEOGRAD

APPENDIX 13

The International Music and Performing Rights Societies

A few generations ago the enjoyment of music was, by and large, confined to the privileged upper strata of the community. But the development of 20th-century technology has changed all that. Today the radio, the gramophone and the tape recorder bring music into every home, into offices, shops and restaurants, into trains, ships and aircraft, into factories and hospitals, on to playgrounds and sporting fields and beaches. Music is now available to everyone, everywhere and at all times. The composers who create all this music, bring not only enjoyment to millions of people all over the world, but also rich profits to the many who exploit their works - singers, pianists, orchestras, impresarios, theatre owners, film producers, broadcasters, industrialists and many others. Moreover, this enjoyment and these profits continue long after the death of the composer - often for centuries. It is therefore, only fair that, just as any other laborers are worthy of their hire, the composers should be entitled to claim a just reward for the use of their works by others.

For a long time musical works had no legal protection and their creators suffered great hardship. Many a composer lived and died in shocking penury while many people were making fortunes out of the use of the composer's works. The tragic injustice of those cases led to a world-wide movement to protect the composer against such ruthless exploitation. In 1884 an international conference to discuss this problem was held in Berne, Switzerland, and that conference led to the formation in 1886, of an "International Union for the Protection of Literary and Artistic Works", known as the "Berne Union" for short. All member countries of the Union signed the "Berne Convention", thereby undertaking to give a certain minimum copyright protection to each other's literary, dramatic and artistic works.

Whilst the United States does not belong to the Berne Convention, it is however, party to the Universal Copyright Convention of 1952, which came into force in 1955 and to which some 60 or 70 countries are members. Practically, their purpose is to minimise the formalities to securing copyright amongst them. Similarly there are the Pan-American Conventions as well as some bi-lateral conventions among countries in regard to any special conditions relative to the copyright arrangements between them.

However, what did confirm the necessity for copyright and accelerated the improvement of its legislation was the sudden realization of the astounding economic importance of copyright. Surveys undertaken in the United States, Canada, England and other European countries revealed that the ramifications of the copyright industry was of vast importance, being responsible for more than two and a half percent of the Gross National Product of the countries. In fact, it rated a higher percentage than that of the automobile industry or of the food packaging and even many other industries. What was previously a matter of sectional concern had now blossomed into a major economic force.

Notwithstanding the adoption of copyright legislation in many countries, the pirating of musical works was still rife and it became clear that the composers needed some means of enforcing their legal rights. For that purpose a world-wide network of music rights organizations was created and these organizations are all members of the Confédération Internationale des Sociétés d'Auteurs et Compositeurs (CISAC), one of whose objects is to promote uniformity of copyright protection and copyright administration throughout the world. These organizations have a dual task - on the one hand to protect the interests of the composers, and on the other hand to assist the users of music and facilitate matters for them. For this purpose all the organizations in that world-wide network are bound by a system of reciprocal agreements to protect and administer each other's work in their respective countries. The copyright legislation in each of the countries concerned affirms that music is the property of the person who created it and that the composer alone is entitled to exercise certain rights in that property in order to earn a living. One of these is the right to perform the music in public and that includes any kind of performance, whether 'live' - ie. given by an orchestra, a pianist, an organist, a singer, etc. - or by mechanical means such as a record player, a juke box, a tape machine, a cassette player, or a radio or television receiving set. This means that no one may publicly perform music in any of these ways without first obtaining the permission of all the composers of the works to be performed. To do so would amount to an infringement of the copyrights of those composers. Furthermore the purchase of a piece of music in printed or recorded form does not authorize the purchaser to perform in public the work embodied in that printed copy or recording. It only entitles performance in the purchaser's domestic circle. The question of an admission charge to a public performance does not affect the copyright position, for it is immaterial whether the performance is given for commercial or for charitable purposes.

The music or performing rights organizations are thus absolutely indispensible to the composer. Collectively they search out wherever music is performed or used. They assess and collect the royalties due and eventually remit to the composer, her share of the royalties earned. It becomes a vital necessity therefore, for each composer to become a member of such an organization in her country.

Listed on the following pages are the names and addresses of every one of these organizations throughout the world. In addition for convenience, those organizations relating to literary works, recordings and mechanical reproductions have been included.

ALGERIA
Office National du Droit d'Auteur (ONDA)
88 rue Mourad-Didouche
ALGER

ARGENTINA
Sociedad Argentina de Autores y Compositores de Musica
(SADAIC)
Lavalle 1547
Apartado Especial No. 11
Suc 44
BUENOS AIRES, 1444

Sociedad Argentina de Escritores (SADE)
Uruguay 1371
BUENOS AIRES

Sociedad General de Autores de la Argentina (ARGENTORES)
Pacheo de Melo 1820
BUENOS AIRES, 1444

AUSTRALIA
Australasian Performing Right Association (APRA)
P.O. Box 567
CROWS NEST
NSW 2065

Australasian Mechanical Copyright Owners Society Ltd (AMCOS)
P.O. Box Q 291
Queen Victoria Bldgs
SYDNEY
2000

Australian Music Publishers Association Ltd. (AMPAL)
P.O.Box Q291
Queen Victoria Blds.
SYDNEY
2000

Copyright Agency Ltd.
Suite 301, Glen St.
MILSONS POINT
2061

AUSTRIA
Staatlich Genehmigte Gesellschaft der Autoren, Komponisten und
Musikverieger (AKM)
Baumannstrasse 8
1031 VIENNA 3

Gesellschaft zur Verwaltung und Auswertung mechanisch-
musikalischer Urheberrechte (AUSTRO-MECHANA)
Baumannstrasse 10
1031 VIENNA 3

Staatlich Genehmigte Literarische Verwertungsgesellschaft
(LVG)
Linke Wienzelle 18
A-1060 VIENNA 6

Verwertungsgesellschaft bildender Künstler (VBK)
Maria Theresienstrasse 11
3 Stock A
1090 VIENNA

Wahrnehmungsgellschaft für Urheberrechte
(LITERAR-MECHANA)
Linke Wienzelle 18
A-1060 VIENNA 6

BELGIUM
Société Belges des Auteurs, Compositeurs et Editeurs (SABAM)
75-77 rue d'Arlon
1040 BRUSSELS 4

Association Belge des Auteurs de Films
8, rue Eugene Hubert
B-1090 BRUSSELS

Société des Auteurs - Photographes (SOFAM)
1 blvd. Charlemagne
BOLTE 54
1041 BRUSSELS

BRAZIL
Sociedade Independente de Compositores e Autores Musicals
(SICAM)
Largo Paissandu 51
11 Andar
SAO PAULO

Sociedade Brasileira de Autores Teatrais (SBAT)
Caixa Postal 1503
RIO de JANEIRO

União Brasileira de Compositores (UBC)
rua Visconde de Inhauma 104
20091 RIO de JANEIRO RJ

BULGARIA
Agence pour la Protection des Droits d'Auteur (JUSTAUTOR)
Pl. Slaveikov 11
SOFIA

Federation Internationale des Traducteurs (FIT)
rue Sveta Gora 17
SOFIA

CAMEROON
Société Camerounaise de Droit d'Auteur (SOCADRA)
BP 5515
DOUALA

CANADA
Performing Rights' Organization of Canada Ltd. (PROCAN)
41 Valleybrook Drive
Don Mills
ONTARIO M3B 2S6

Société Canadienne-Française de Protection du Droit
d'Auteur (SCFPDA)
1151 rue Alexandre Desève
MONTREAL H2L 2T7

Composers', Authors' and Publishers' Association
of Canada Ltd. (CAPAC)
1240 Bay St.
Toronto
ONTARIO M5R 2C2

Société des Auteurs, Recherchistes, Documentalistes (SARDeC)
1229 rue Panet
MONTREAL H2L 2Y6

CHILE
Sociedad Administrativa de Autores y
Compositores (SAIC-CHILE)
Manuel de Salas No. 335
SANTIAGO

Sociedad de Autores Teatrales de Chile (SATCH)
San Diego 246
SANTIAGO

Universidad de Chile, Departamento del Pequeño
Derecho do Autor (DAIC)
San Antonio 427
SANTIAGO

COLOMBIA
Sociedad de Autores y Compositores de Colombia (SAYCO)
Carrera 19
No. 40-42 Apartado Areo 6482
BOGOTA

CZECHOSLOVAKIA
Divadelni a Literarni Agentura (DILIA)
Vyserhradska 28
PRAGUE 2

Ochranny Svaz Autorsky (OSA)
Tr. Cs. Armady 20
160 56 PRAGUE - BUBENEC.

Slovenska Literarna Agentura (LITA)
Ulica Cs. Armady 37/111
894 20 BRATISLAVA

Slovensky Ochranny Sväz Autorsky (SOZA)
Zivnostenska 1
BRATISLAVA

DENMARK
Nordisk Copyright Bureau (N.C.B.)
Frederiksgade 17
DK - 1265
COPENHAGEN

Selskabet til Forvaltning af Internationale
Komponistrettighede i Danmark (KODA)
Rosenvaengets Hovedvej 14
2100 COPENHAGEN 0

EGYPT
Société des Auteurs, Compositeurs et Editeurs de la Republique
Arabe d'Egypte (SACERAU)
10 rue Elfi Bey
CAIRO

EQUADOR
Sociedad de Autores y Compositores Ecuatorianos (SAYCE)
Avenida 10 de Agosto, No. 6877 y Rio Coca
QUITO

FINLAND
Säveltäjäin Tekijänolkeustoimisto (TEOSTO)
Lauttasaarentie 1
00200 HELSINKI 20

Suomen Näytelmäkirjallijallitto (SUNKLO)
Vironkatu 12 B
13 Estnasgatan
00170 HELSINKI 17

FRANCE
Société des Auteurs, Compositeurs et
Editeurs de Musique (SACEM)
225 Ave. Charles de Gaulle
92521 NEUILLY-SUR-SEINE CEDEX

Société des Auteurs et Compositeurs Dramatiques (SACD)
9-11 rue Ballu
75442 PARIS CEDEX 09

Société de la Propriété Artistique et
des Dessins et Modeles (SPADEM)
12 rue Henner
75009 PARIS

Société des Gens de Lettres de France (SGDL)
Hôtel de Massa
38 rue du Faubourg Saint-Jacques
75014 PARIS

Société pour l'Administration du Droit de Réproduction
Mechanique des Auteurs, Compositeurs et Editeurs (SDRM)
225 Ave. Charles de Gaulle
92521 NEUILLY-SUR-SEINE CEDEX

Syndicat National des Auteurs et Compositeurs de Musique
(SNAC)
80 rue Taitbout
75442 PARIS CEDEX 09

GERMAN DEMOCRATIC REPUBLIC
Anstalt zur Wahrung des Aufführungsrechte auf dem Gebiete der
Musik (AWA)
Storkower-St. 134
1055 BERLIN

Büro für Urheberrechte
Clara-Zetkin-Strasse 105
108 BERLIN

GERMAN FEDERAL REPUBLIC
Gesellschaft für musikalishe Aufführungs-und-mechanische
Vervielfältigungsrechte (GEMA)
Bayreuther St. 37/38
1 Berlin 30
Herzog-Wilhelm St. 28
8 MÜNICH 2

Bild-Kunst
Poppelsdorfer Allee 43
53 BONN 1

Bild-Kunst
Stollbergstrasse 1
8000 MUNICH 22

Dramatiker-Union E.V.
Bismarckstr. 17
1000 BERLIN 12

Verwertungsgesellschaft WORT
Goethestrasse 49,
8000 MUNICH 2

GREECE
Société Anonyme Hellénique pour la Protection Intellectuelle
(AEPI)
14 rue Delighianni
ATHENS (148)

Société des Auteurs Dramatiques Hellènes (SADH)
33 rue Asclipiou
ATHENS (144)

Société de Protection du Droit d'Auteur (SOPE)
14, rue Delighianni
ATHENS (148)

HONG KONG
Composers' and Authors' Society of Hong Kong Ltd. (CASH)
South-Seas Center Tower 1, 3/F
75 Mody Rd
Tsinshatsuí
EAST KOWLOON

HUNGARY
Bureau Hongrois pour la Protection des Droits (ARTISJUS)
Vörösmarty Ter 1
1051 BP 67 H 1364
BUDAPEST V

ICELAND
Samband Tonskaida og Elgenda Flutnigsrettar (STEF)
Laufasvegi 40
REYKJAVIK

INDIA
The Indian Performing Right Society Ltd (IPRS)
717 Dalamal Towers
Nariman Point
BOMBAY 400 021

ISRAEL
Société des Auteurs, Compositeurs et Editeurs de
Musique en Israël (ACUM)
ACUM-House
Bvld. Rothschild 118-120
P.O. Box 14220
TEL AVIV 61440

ITALY
Società Italiana degli Autori ed Editori (SIAE)
Viale della Letteratura 30
ROME (E.U.R.)

IVORY COAST
Bureau Ivoirien du Droit d'Auteur (BURIDA)
B.P. v. 258
ABIDJAN

JAPAN
Japanese Society of Rights of Authors, Composers
and Publishers (JASRAC)
JASRAC-House
7-13 1-chome Nishishimbashi
MINATO-KU
TOKYO 105

KENYA
The Musicians' Performing Right Society of Kenya (MPRSK)
P.O. Box 28777
NAIROBI

MALTA
Guild of Maltese Composers and Authors (UKAM)
3 Church Ave.
PAOLA

MAURITIUS
Société Mauricienne des Auteurs et Compositeurs (SMAC)
8, rue Gustave Collin
BEAU-BASSIN

MEXICO
Sociedad de Autores y Compositores de Musica, S. de A. (SACM)
San Felipe 143
Col. General Anaya
MEXICO 13 D.F.

Sociedad Generale de Escritores de Mexico (SOGEM)
J.M. Velasco 59
MEXICO 19 D.F.

Sociedad Mexicana de Directores-Realizadores de Cine, Radio y
Television, S de. A. de I.P. (DIRECTORES)
Felix Parra 130
San José Insurgentes
MEXICO 19 D.F.

MOROCCO
Bureau Marocain du Droit d'Auteur (BMDA)
B.P. 35
6 Zankat Laghouat
RABAT

NETHERLANDS
Het Bureau voor Muziek-Auteursrecht (BUMA)
Buma/Stemra-huis
Postbus 725
1180 AS AMSTELVEEN

Beeldrecht
Nieuwe Keizersgracht 58
1018 DT AMSTERDAM

Stichting tot Ultoefening en handhaving van mechansiche
Reproduktierechten des Auteurs (STEMRA)
Buma/Stemra-huis
POSTBUS 725
1180 AS AMSTELVEEN

Vereniging van Letterkundigen
Het Schrijvershuis
Huddelstraat 7
1018 HB AMSTERDAM

NEW GUINEA
Bureau Guinéen de Droit d'Auteur (BGDA)
c/o Ministère de l'Enseignement Supérior et de la
Recherche Scientifique
CONAKRY

NEW ZEALAND See AUSTRALIA

NORWAY
Norsk Komponistforenings Internasjonale Musikkbyra (TONO)
Klingenberg Gt. 5
Postboks 1666 - Vika
OSLO 1

PARAGUAY
Autores Paraguayos Asociados (APA)
Ave. Chile 1850
ASUNCION

PERU
Asociación Peruana de Autores y Compositores (APDAYC)
Jr. Ica 559
LIMA

POLAND
Stowarzyszenie Autorow ''ZAIKS''
Ul. Hipoteczna 2-Boite Postale P-16
00-092 WARSAW 1.

PORTUGAL
Sociedade Portuguesa de Autores (SPA)
Av. Duque de Louié 31,
1098 LISBONNE CEDEX

PUERTO RICO
Associacion Puertorriquena de Compositores y Autores (APCA)
Colorado 1709
RIO PIEDRAS
PR 00926

RUMANIA
Fondul Literar al Schriltorilor din RSR
Ralonul 30 Decembrie, Sos
Kisseleff 10
BUCHAREST

SENEGAL
Bureau Sénégalais du Droit d'Auteur (BSDA)
B.P. 126
DAKAR

SOUTH AFRICA
Southern African Music Rights Organisation (SAMRO)
P.O. Box 9292
JOHANNESBURG
2000

Dramatic, Artistic and Literary Rights Organisation (DALRO)
P.O. Box 9292
JOHANNESBURG
2000

South African Recording Rights Association Limited (SARRAL)
1017/19 Bosman Bldg.
99 Eloff St.
JOHANNESBURG
2001

SPAIN
Sociedad General de Autores de Espana (SGAE)
Fernando V1
4 MADRID

SWEDEN
Svenska Tonsattares Internationella Musikbyra (STIM)
Box 1539
S-111 85 STOCKHOLM

Kónstnårernas Riksorganisation (KRO)
Sandbacksgatan 5
116 21 STOCKHOLM

Sveriges författarförbund
Linnegatan 12-14
Box 5252
102 45 STOCKHOLM 5

SWITZERLAND
Société Suisse pour les Droits des Auteurs d'OEuvres Musicales
(SUISA)
Bellariastrasse 82
8038 ZURICH

TAHITI
Société Polynesienne des Auteurs, Compositeurs et
Editeurs de Musique (SPACEM)
Bld d'Alsace
B.P. 324
PAPEETE

TUNISIA
Société des Auteurs et Compositeurs de Tunisie (SODACT)
11 rue Al-Djazira
TUNIS

UNITED KINGDOM
The Performing Right Society Ltd (PRS)
Copyright House
22/33 Berners St.
LONDON W1P 4AA

The Authors' Lending and Copyright Society Ltd. (ALCS)
430 Edgware Rd.
LONDON W2 1EH

Mechanical Copyright Protection Society Ltd (MCPS)
Elgar House
41 Streatham High Road
LONDON SW16 1ER

Mechanical Rights Society (MRS)
Elgar House
41 Streatham High Rd.
LONDON SW16 1ER

Music Copyright (Overseas) Services Ltd (MCOS)
26 Berners St.
LONDON SW10 9SD

The Society of Authors
84 Drayton Gdns.
LONDON W2 1EH

The Writers' Guild of Great Britain
430 Edgware Rd.
LONDON W2 1EH

UNITED STATES OF AMERICA
American Society of Composers, Authors and Publishers (ASCAP)
One Lincoln Plaza
NEW YORK NY 10023

Broadcast Music Inc. (BMI)
320 West 57th St.
NEW YORK NY 10019

American Mechanical Rights' Assocation (AMRA)
250 West 57th St.
NEW YORK NY 10107

National Music Publishers' Association Inc. (NMPA)
110 East 59 St.
NEW YORK NY 10022

Screen Composers of America (SCA)
2451 Nichols Canyon
LOS ANGELES CA

SESAC Inc.
10 Columbia Circle
NEW YORK NY 10091

Visual Artists and Galleries Association, Inc. (VAGA)
One World Trade Center
Suite 1535
NEW YORK NY 10048

UNION OF SOVIET SOCIALIST REPUBLICS
Vseojuznoje Agentstvo po Avtorskim Pravam (VAAP)
Bolchaia Bronnaia 6-a
MOSCOW 103670 GJP

URAGUAY
Asociación General de Autores del Uruguay (AGADU)
Calle Canelones 1130
MONTEVIDEO

VENEZUELA
Sociedad de Autores y Compositores de Venezuela (SACVEN)
Ave. Andrés Bello, Edf. VAM
Torre Oeste Piso 9
CARACAS

YUGOSLAVIA
Jugoslovenska Autorska Agencija (JAA)
Majke Jevrosime 38
11001 BELGRADE

Savez Organizacija Kompozitora Jugoslavije (SOKOJ)
Misarska 12-14
B.P. 213
1100 BELGRADE

ZAIRE
Société Nationale des Editeurs, Compositeurs et Auteurs (SONECA)
Boite Postale 460
KINSHASA

APPENDIX 14

The National Federation of Music Clubs

1336 North Delaware St. Indianapolis IN 46202 U.S.A.

This organization, although confined to the United States is without doubt the largest of its kind in the world. Its congregation of some 4 000 music clubs, musical groups etc., representing a membership of over 600 000, probably exerts the greatest concerted influence in the study and dissemination of music, the vocal arts and the dance in the United States.

Its beginnings date back to the 1860s just after the American Civil War, when women began to promote a greater interest and participation in music through the formation of music clubs in the towns and cities, spurred on, it must be confessed, by the prevailing centuries-old prejudice against the participation by women in certain aspects of music.

In 1893, the first national assembly of women's amateur musical clubs met at the invitation of Mrs. Theodore Thomas to plan for a four day festival at the World's Columbian Exposition in June 1897 in Chicago. Mrs. Thomas was the wife of Theodore Thomas, the celebrated conductor who founded his symphony orchestra in 1891, which later became the Chicago Symphony Orchestra. An ad-hoc committee was formed and at the time of the meeting of the Music Teachers' National Association (founded by Theodore Presser in 1876) invitations were issued to all members of music clubs and friends interested in organizing a National Federation of Music Clubs. A nominated committee was then instructed to draw up a constitution at a meeting to be held at the Congress Hotel, Chicago under the temporary presidency of Mrs. Florence Sutro.

On January 26 1898, Mrs. Edwin T. Uhl of Grand Rapids, MI, was elected the first president and 19 members constituted the board of directors. An application for Charter to the State of Illinois was made and granted along with the Certificate of Incorporation. The aims of the new federation related to its dedication to music education and its promotion of the creative and performing arts in America and there were no restrictions as to gender in membership.

But it was not until the administration of Mrs. Maurice (Hinda) Honigman (1967 to 1971), the 21st president of the Federation that positive steps were taken to improve the recognition and opportunities for performances of music composed by women. With the appointment of Marion Morrey Richter as chairlady of American music and of Julia Smith as first chairlady of women composers, three awards of $1 000 each were made. These were won by Miriam Gideon (symphony/chamber music); Emma Lou Diemer (choral and educational works) and Hansi Alt (piano teaching pieces).

This encouragement of the recognition of women composers has been carried on by subsequent administrations, notwithstanding the striving for the improvement of the music of both men and women in general. The steadily growing membership of the Federation necessitated a much wider administration and the 50 states were separated into 14 districts, administered by a national council of district co-ordinators and state presidents.

Some of the achievements of the National Federation of Music Clubs are as follows:

PERFORMING ARTS

1. Young artist auditions – for young performers ready for concert careers. Cash and supplemental awards.
2. Artist presentation awards – presenting national winners in concert.
3. Student auditions - providing cash awards and scholarships for students aged 16-25.
4. Parade of American music - stimulates performance of American composers in and out of America.
5. National music week - sponsored annually to focus attention on music as an integral part in the life of America.
6. Awards providing for the concert appearance, debut recitals and one opera contract for individually selected NFMC artist winners.
7. Opera promotion and performance.
8. Opera for youth.
9. Radio and television programs presenting young talent in local, national and international broadcasts.
10. Choral music – concerts and festivals for choruses and choirs.
11. Folk music – solo and group performances at local, state and national levels.

CREATIVE ARTS

1. Young composers' contest – cash awards and public performance, ages 18-25.
2. Junior composers' contest – cash awards and public performance, ages under 19.
3. Adult composers' contest – cash awards and public performance.
4. Dance choreography.
5. Essay contest – National Music Week.

The listing on the following pages of the names and addresses of the music clubs is not complete, but is made up from all of those which have been received prior to going to press. Will those clubs not listed please communicate with the Director, International Institute for the Study Women in Music California State University, Northridge. CA. 91330. U.S.A.

ALABAMA

Leeds Music Study
460 Katherine St. SW
LEEDS
AL 35094

Birmingham Shades Mountain Music Club
1509 Primrose Pl.
BIRMINGHAM
AL 35209

Melodia Music Club
2333 Hawksbury Ln.
BIRMINGHAM
AL 35226

Etude Music Club
270 East Main Street
CENTER
AL 35960

Wedowee Music Club
Box 321
WEDOWEE
AL 36278

Enterprise State Junior College
Box 1300
ENTERPRISE
AL 36331

Union Harmony Club
Box 489
FAUNSDALE
AL 36738

Birmingham Woodlawn Music Study Club
1121 Del Ray Dr.
BIRMINGHAM
AL 35213

Enterprise Music Club
308 Lakeshore Rd.
ENTERPRISE
AL 35330

Scottsboro Music Study Club
403 Lora St.
SCOTTSBORO
AL 35768

North East Alabama State Junior College
Box 159
RAINSVILLE
AL 35986

Montgomery Music Study Club
1241 Kirkwood Dr.
MONTGOMERY
AL 36117

Dothan Harmony Club
Box 27
DOTHAN
AL 36302

Evergreen Orpheus Club
101 Belleville St.
EVERGREEN
AL 36401

Greensboro Music Study Club
1205 Tuscaloosa St.
GREENSBORO
AL 36744

Talladega Music Club
1013 Southwood Ave.
TALLADEGA
AL 35160

Bush Hills' Music Club
2861 Thornhill Rd.
BIRMINGHAM
AL 35213

Allegro Music Club
837 Jeffrey Ln.
BIRMINGHAM
AL 35235

Stillman College
3600 15th St.
TUSCALOOSA
AL 35401

Decatur Music Study Club
1708 Devonshire Dr. SE
DECATUR
AL 35601

Huntsville Music Study Club
1708 Laverne Dr. NW
HUNTSVILLE
AL 35805

Tallassee Music Club
Box 515
TALLASSEE
AL 36078

Birmingham Shades Valley Music Club
3804 Briar Oak Dr.
BIRMINGHAM
AL 36243

George C. Wallace State Commercial College
St. #6
DOTHAN
AL 36303

Schuman Club of Mobile
36 Ridgeview Dr.
CHICKASAW
AL 36611

Music Appreciation Club of Clanton
305 Second Ave. S.
CLANTON
AL 35045

Shepherd Center Singers
118 84th Street N.
BIRMINGHAM
AL 35206

Birmingham Music Teachers
2713 Vestavia Forest Pl.
BIRMINGHAM
AL 35216

Tuscaloosa Music Club
51 Cherokee Hills
TUSCALOOSA
AL 35404

Florence Music Study Club
506 Pamplin Ave.
FLORENCE
AL 35630

Gadsden Music Club
2416 Scenic Dr.
GADSDEN
AL 35901

Troy Music Club
926 University Ave.
TROY
AL 36081

Roanoke Music Study Club
Box 894
ROANOKE
AL 36274

Valley Music Study Club
Box 164
LANETT
AL 36863

ALASKA

Anchorage Community College Music Dept.
2533 Providence Ave.
ANCHORAGE
AK 99504

ARIZONA

La Fuerza Club
4033 W. Rovey Ave.
PHOENIX
AZ 85019

Douglas Music Club
1320 Eleventh St.
DOUGLAS
AZ 85607

White Mountain Musical Arts Club
Box 964
SHOW LOW
AZ 85901

Tucson Musical Arts Club
781 W. Kovaya Dr.
TUCSON
AZ 85704

Desert Music Club
920 Briggs
AJO
AZ 85321

Philharmonia Orchestra of Tucson
2301 E. Drachman
TUCSON
AZ 85719

Musical Arts Club
Box 2373
GLOBE
AZ 85501

ARKANSAS

Southern Arizona University
Box 1277 SAU
MAGNOLIA
AR 71753

Philharmonic Club
1016 Clinton
ARKADELPHIA
AR 71923

Brinkley Mc Dowell Club
Rt. 1
BRINKLEY
AR 72021

Hendrix College Music Dept.
CONWAY
AR 72032

Little Rock Musical Coterie
1516 Garland
NORTH LITTLE ROCK
AR 72116

Little Rock Arkansas Opera Theatre
908 Rock St.
LITTLE ROCK
AR 72202

Blytheville Orpheus Club
1504 Normandy Ln.
BLYTHEVILLE
AR 72315

Monticello Music Club
382 Willis
MONTICELLO
AR 71655

Hope Friday Music club
Rt. 2, Box 355A
HOPE
AR 71801

Musical Coterie of Brinkley
108 E. Cloverdale
BRINKLEY
AR 72021

Cotton Plant Crescendo Club
P.O. Box 246
COTTON PLANT
AR 72036

Earle Music Coterie
910 Ruth St.
EARLE
AR 72331

Jenson Musical Coterie
1015 W. 11th Ave.
PINE BLUFF
AR 71601

Thursday Musicale
Rt. 1, Box 851
CAMDEN
AR 71701

Foreman Thursday Music Club
Rt. 1, Box 255
FOREMAN
AR 71836

Conway Orpheus Club
359 Watkins St.
CONWAY
AR 72032

Musical Arts Club
1229 Dyer St.
MALVERN
AR 72104

Searcy Beethoven Club
14 Jamestown Dr.
SEARCY
AR 72143

Little Rock Chorale of Woman's City Club
1324 Fair Park Blvd.
LITTLE ROCK
AR 72204

Pine Bluff Musical Coterie
1219 W. 19th
PINE BLUFF
AR 71603

Magnolia Music Club
503 Smith St.
MAGNOLIA
AR 71753

Hot Springs' Music Club
4 Edgewood
HOT SPRINGS NATIONAL PARK
AR 71901

Mac Dowell Music Club
1801 Hidden Valley Dr.
BENTON
AR 72015

University of Central Arkansas Music Dept.
CONWAY
AR 72032

Newport MacDowell Music Club
1501 Fairway St.
NEWPORT
AR 72112

Stuttgart Fine Arts Club
Box 391
STUTTGART
AR 72160

Little Rock Ballet of Arkansas
P.O. Box 7574
LITTLE ROCK
AR 72217

Treble Clef
1117 Kennesaw
JONESBORO
AR 72401

Musical Arts Club
1690 College St.
BATESVILLE
AR 72501

Russellville Music Club
408 Honeysuckle Ln.
RUSSELLVILLE
AR 72801

Fort Smith Music Coterie
3203 Hendricks Blvd.
FORT SMITH
AR 72903

Jonesboro Nocturne
3000 Hillridge Cove
JONESBORO
AR 72401

Clef-Hangers Music Society
Star Rt.
EVENING SHADE
AR 72532

Arkansas Technical University Music Dept.
RUSSELLVILLE
AR 72801

Schubert Music Club of Walnut Ridge
415 Eastwood Circle
WALNUT RIDGE
AR 72476

Andante Club
113 Mayfair Dr.
BELLA VISTA
AR 72714

Danville Music Club
Box 566
DANVILLE
AR 72833

Wednesday Music Club
10 Cambridge
TEXARKANA
AR 75502

CALIFORNIA
Spinet Club
1685 Country Club Dr.
REDLANDS
CA 92373

Music Academy of the West
1070 Fairway Rd.
SANTA BARBARA
CA 93108

Grand Staff Seniors Club
2637 N. 1st St.
FRESNO
CA 93703

Fresno Musical Club
1132 E. Santa Ana
FRESNO
CA 93704

Burlingame Music Club
1425 Bellevue Ave. #5
BURLINGAME
CA 94010

San Francisco Musical Club
280 San Fernando Way
DALY CITY
CA 94015

Matinee Musical Club-LA
1835 Outpost Dr.
HOLLYWOOD
CA 90068

Saint Cecilia Club
920 Singingwood Dr.
ARCADIA
CA 91006

Opera Reading Club
1952 Carmen Ave.
HOLLYWOOD
CA 90068

Manuscript Club of Los Angeles
639 Orange Grove Ave.
SOUTH PASADENA
CA 91030

Santa Barbara Music Club
161 Rametto Rd.
SANTA BARBARA
CA 93108

Fresno Opera League
2741 N. Channing Way
FRESNO
CA 93705

Pacific Musical Society
3634 Jackson St.
SAN FRANCISCO
CA 94115

Namn Georgia Laster Br.
2455 S. St. Andrews Pl. #730
LOS ANGELES
CA 90018

Four Arts Club of Los Angeles
1278 Monte Ceilo Dr.
BEVERLY HILLS
CA 90210

Phi Beta Fraternity, Pi Iota Chapter
23942 Via Flamenco
VALENCIA
CA 91355

American Guild of Organists
San Joaquin Valley Chapter
2504 Sixteenth Ave.
KINGSBURG
CA 93631

Music Teachers' Assoc.
Fresno County Branch
150 N. Duke
FRESNO
CA 93727

San Francisco Conservatory of Music
1201 Ortega St.
SAN FRANCISCO
CA 94122

COLORADO
Lamar Music Club
P.O. Box 392
LAMAR
CO 81052

Mesa College
P.O. Box 2647
GRAND JUNCTION
CO 81501

Boulder Federation Music Club
2155 Topaz
BOULDER
CO 80302

Wednesday Music Club
168 Rainbow Dr.
GRAND JUNCTION
CO 81503

Fort Collins Senior Music Club
1420 Hillside Dr.
FORT COLLINS
CO 80524

Instru-Voca
1205 Walz Ave.
GLENWOOD SPRINGS
CO 81601

Denver Musicians' Society
1433 Williams St. # 801
DENVER
CO 90218

CONNECTICUT
Hartt College of Music
200 Bloomfield Ave.
WEST HARTFORD
CT 06117

Wednesday Afternoon Musical Club
P.O. Box 243
STRATFORD
CT 06497

Musical Arts Society of Branford
32 Meadow Wood Rd.
BRANFORD
CT 06405

Neighborhood Music School
100 Aubodon St.
NEW HAVEN
CT 06511

Darien Music Club
7 Highland Ave.
DARIEN
CT 06820

John P. Testa Music Club
457 Oak View Dr.
ORANGE
CT 03477

Connecticut Experimental Theatre
1730 State St. Unit 311
HAMDEN
CT 06511

Beethoven Club
496 Trinity Pass
NEW CANAAN
CT 06840

Connecticut Institute of Vocal Arts
141 Tainter Dr.
SOUTHPORT
CT 06490

St. Ambrose Music Club
11 Belden Rd.
HAMDEN
CT 06514

Schubert Club of Fairfield County
73 Tall Oaks Ct.
STAMFORD
CT 06903

DISTRICT OF COLUMBIA
New York Avenue Presbyterian Club
1313 New York Ave. NW
WASHINGTON
DC 20005

Callahan Student Club
3803 Ingomar St. NW
WASHINGTON
DC 20015

Chanticleers' Club
3113 Tennyson St. NW
WASHINGTON
DC 20015

Dmitrieff Club
1313 Potomac St. NW
WASHINGTON
DC 20007

Pianoforte 88ers
3308 Runnymeade Pl.
WASHINGTON
DC 20015

Beethoven Society
5000 Klingle St. NW
WASHINGTON
DC 20016

FLORIDA
St. Cecilia Music Club
5 Dogwood Circle
LAKE CITY
FL 32055

Stephen Foster Music Club
P.O. Box 26
WHITE SPRINGS
FL 32096

Wednesday Musicals
704 E. Palmetto St.
WAUCHULA
FL 33873

Winter Haven Music Club
156 Audobon Ct.
WINTER HAVEN
FL 33880

Haines City Music Club
P.O. Box 1253
HAINES CITY
FL 33844

Lake Wales Music Club
826 Lorraine Circle
LAKE WALES
FL 33853

Calusa Musicale
3413 SE 18th Ave.
CAPE CORAL
FL 33904

Harmony Music Club
3308 Sunnybrook Ave.
JACKSONVILLE
FL 32205

Capital City Music Club
101 Westwood Dr. N.
TALLAHASSE
FL 32302

Reaves Family String Quartet
1930 NW 8th Ave.
GAINESVILLE
FL 32603

Suncoast Music Club
11584 W. Kingfisher Ct.
CRYSTAL RIVER
FL 32629

Orlando Music Club
P.O. Box 240
GOTHA
FL 32734

Dryan Memorial Methodist
3713 Main Highway
CORAL GABLES
FL 33133

Miami Music Club
8310 SW 81st Terrace
MIAMI
FL 33134

South Miami Music Club
11780 SW 81st Rd.
MIAMI
FL 33156

Morning Musicale of Fort Lauderdale
4224 NW 2nd St.
PLANTATION
FL 33317

Beethoven Music Club
2802 14th St. W.
BRADENTON
FL 33505

Sarasota Music Club
1645 Hawthorne
SARASOTA
FL 33579

Friday Morning Musicale
4717 Bullock Ct.
TAMPA
FL 33624

Perry Music Club
706 E. Marguerite St.
PERRY
FL 32347

Gainesville Music Club
5702 SW 35th Way
GAINESVILLE
FL 32608

Keystone Heights Community Church
Palmetto Ave.
KEYSTONE HEIGHTS
FL 32656

East Coast Music Club
28 Magruder Ave.
ROCKLEDGE
FL 32955

St. Stephens' Episcopal
2750 Mc Farlane Rd.
MIAMI
FL 33133

Dale Willoughby
Granada Presbyterian Church
950 University Dr.
CORAL GABLES
FL 33134

Margaret Mill's Music Club
22990 SW 179 Ave.
MIAMI
FL 33170

West Palm Beach Club
1408 Beta Circle
Lake Clarke Shores
WEST PALM BEACH
FL 33406

Brooksville Music Club
23390 Eppley Dr.
BROOKSVILLE
FL 33512

Nina Kor Voice Studio
1645 Hawthorne
SARASOTA
FL 33579

Panama City Music Club
7618 Old Bicycle Rd.
PANAMA CITY
FL 32404

Ocala Music Club
10 Emerald Ct.
OCALA
FL 32672

Wednesday Music Club
Orlando & Winter Park
1804 Meritt Park Dr.
ORLANDO
FL 32803

Tuesday Morning Music
5790 Stirling Rd. Apt 311
HOLLYWOOD
FL 33021

Choir-Presbyterian Church
121 Alhambra Plaza
CORAL GABLES
FL 33131

University Baptist Church
624 Anastasia Ave.
CORAL GABLES
FL 33134

Caribbean Music Club of Miami
9830 Santos Dr.
MIAMI
FL 33189

Boca Raton Musical Club
301 SW 1st St. Apt D-304
BOCA RATON
FL 33432

Springhill Music Club
7413 Acorn Circle
SPRINGHILL
FL 33526

Sarasota Opera Assoc.
4205 Higel Ave.
SARASOTA
FL 33581

Lakeland Tuesday Music Club
502 Cassandra Ln.
Lakeland Hills Estate
LAKELAND
FL 33805

Choctaw Bay Music Club
206 Vicki Leigh Dr.
FORT WALTON BEACH
FL 32548

Riverland Music Club
Rt. 1, Box 364
BROOKER
FL 32622

Central Florida Music Club
3283 El Primo Way
ORLANDO
FL 32808

First United Methodist
536 Coral Way
CORAL GABLES
FL 33134

Coral Gables Music Club
5110 San Amaro Dr.
CORAL GABLES
FL 33146

Cecilian Music Society
2260 Lakewood Ln.
NOKOMIS
FL 33555

Sarasota Evening Musicale
3020 Cambridge Dr.
SARASOTA
FL 33582

St. Davids Singles of Lakeland
145 Edgewood Dr.
LAKELAND
FL 33805

GEORGIA
Camerata Club
Shorter College
ROME
GA 30161

Gainesville Music Club
2360 Thompson Bridge Rd.
GAINESVILLE
GA 30501

Sandersville Music Club
403 Ridgeland Dr.
SANDERSVILLE
GA 31082

Rome Music Lovers' Club
9 Wilson Dr.
ROME
GA 30161

Georgia Academy of Music
P.O. Box 19877
Station N.
ATLANTA
GA 30325

Macon Federated Music Club
247 Riley Ave.
MACON
GA 31204

Floyd Fine Arts' Club
126 Wildwood Way
ROME
GA 30161

College Park Music Club
2002 Rugby Ave.
COLLEGE PARK
GA 30337

Cordele Symphony Club
Rt. 1, Box 284
CORDELE
GA 31015

Montezuma Music Lovers' Club
Rt. 1, Box 36
Engville Highway
ANDERSONVILLE
GA 31711

Berry College Music Dept.
Student Music Club
MOUNT BERRY
GA 30149

Pike Music Club
Rt. 1, Box 43
MOLENA
GA 30258

Cordele Fine Arts
Rt. 1, Rebecca Rd.
CORDELE
GA 31015

Orpheus Club
5801 Windsor Dr.
COLUMBUS
GA 31909

IDAHO
Pocatello Music Club
723 Hubbard Ave.
POCATELLO
ID 83201

Burley Music Club
Rt. 2, Box 154
RUPERT
ID 83350

Nampa Musicale
417 Meadow Dr.
NAMPA
ID 83651

Boise Tuesday Musicale
165 Horizon Dr.
BOISE
ID 83702

Idaho Falls Music Club
Rt. 3, Box 48A
IDAHO FALLS
ID 83401

Scenic Valleys Music Club
Box 774
CASCADE
ID 83611

Parma Musicale
Rt. 1, A-M Ct. #32
PARMA
ID 83660

Boise Choristers
618 W. Highland View Dr.
BOISE
ID 83702

Twin Falls Music Club
1242 Lawndale Dr.
TWIN FALLS
ID 83301

Margaret Goering Mussettes
297 Davis Ave.
NAMPA
ID 83651

Payette Friday Musicale
411 S. 12th St.
PAYETTE
ID 83661

Boise Valley Dance Teachers' Assoc.
2813 Malibu St.
BOISE
ID 83705

Boise Master Chorale
College of Southern Idaho
TWIN FALLS
ID 83301

Caldwell Thursday Musicale
3511 S. Ohio
CALDWELL
ID 83605

Boise Philharmonic
205 N. 10th St.
BOISE
ID 83702

Bosie Civic Opera
6000 Elkhorn Ave.
BOISE
ID 83709

ILLINOIS
Chicago Chapter
National Harp Society
401 E. 32nd St.
CHICAGO
IL 60616

Ottawa Amateur Musical Club
15 Oaklane Dr.
OTTAWA
IL 61350

Lincoln Musical Arts Club
703 N. Union St.
LINCOLN
IL 62656

Musicians' Club of Women
2438 Pomona
WILMETTE
IL 60091

Lincoln Park Music Center
3652 N. Janssen
CHICAGO
IL 60618

Fine Arts Music Club of Morton
2615 N. Morton Ave.
MORTON
IL 61550

Chicago Symphony Orchestra
220 S. Michigan
CHICAGO
IL 60604

Chicago Musical Society Arts Club
4912 W. Berenice St.
CHICAGO
IL 60641

Orpheus Club
204 N. Cornell Dr.
NORMAL
IL 61761

Lake View Musical Society
2456 N. Surrey Ct.
CHICAGO
IL 60614

Chicago Club of Women Organists
5618 N. Talman
CHICAGO
IL 60659

INDIANA
Anderson Evening Musical
2560 W. 12th St.
ANDERSON
IN 46011

Indianapolis Piano Teachers' Assoc.
57 Turner Ct.
MORRESVILLE
IN 46158

Joyful Sounds Choir
4506 Avon Dr.
ANDERSON
IN 46014

Phi Beta Fraternity
1801 W. 51st St.
INDIANAPOLIS
IN 46208

Mu Phi Epsilon Patron Club
248 N. Yandes St.
FRANKLIN
IN 46131

La Porte Symphony
1108 Jefferson
LA PORTE
IN 46350

M C Community Chorus
2408 Oak St.
MICHIGAN CITY
IN 46360

Dist. 5 Federated Music Club
1511 North St.
LOGANSPORT
IN 46947

Folklore Weavers
3800 N. Vernon Dr.
MUNCIE
IN 47304

Bloomington Friday Musicale
9380 E. Conrad Dr.
BLOOMINGTON
IN 47401

Hillsboro Harmony Club
HILLSBORO
IN 47949

Michigan City Community Strings
9781 W. County Rd. 300 N.
MICHIGAN CITY
IN 46360

Friends of Music
P.O. Box 5
SAINT PAUL
IN 47272

Lee Meyer Singers & Repertoire Music Club
1412 York St.
MICHIGAN CITY
IN 46360

Morning Musicale Fort Wayne
5302 Brookview Dr.
FORT WAYNE
IN 46815

Muncie Chamber Players
3900 Burlington
MUNCIE
IN 47302

Muncie Matinee Musicale
704 E. Washington St.
MUNCIE
IN 47305

Oakland City Philharmonic
RR 1, Box 99
OAKLAND CITY
IN 47660

Michigan City Monday Musical
3955 Woznak Rd.
MICHIGAN CITY
IN 46360

Kokomo Morning Musicale
830 East Hall
GREENTOWN
IN 46936

Muncie Matinee Musical
406 N. Chinquapin Way
MUNCIE
IN 47304

Delaware County Music Teachers' Assoc.
1516 N. Colton Drive
MUNCIE
IN 47804

IOWA
Shenandoah Korner Keynotes
507 East Temple
LENOX
IA 50851

Paullina Federated Music Club
418 South Maple
PAULLINA
IA 51046

Spencer Clef Club
1523 1st Ave. W.
SPENCER
IA 51301

Tri-County Music Teachers' Assoc.
RR 1
IRWIN
IA 51446

Atlantic Nishna
Valley Musicales
RR 1
MARNE
IA 51552

Glenwood Mills County Music Teachers' Assoc.
Box 372
PACIFIC JUNCTION
IA 51561

Iowa City Piano Teachers' Assoc.
1033 Sandusky Dr.
IOWA CITY
IA 52240

Junior Counselors Club
92 16th Ave. SW
CEDAR RAPIDS
IA 52404

Centerville Ensemble Music Club
708 North 18th St.
CENTERVILLE
IA 52544

Davenport Music Students
330 Grant
BETTENDORF
IA 52722

Davenport Come and Sing
2530 Bayberry Ct.
BETTENDORF
IA 52722

Waterloo B Natural Club
1434 Lyon
WATERLOO
IA 50702

Triangle Club
P.O. Box 94
DIAGONAL
IA 50845

Siouxland Music Teachers' Assoc.
1371 Vandenberg Circle
SERGEANT BLUFF
IA 51054

Le Mars Soo-Mar Music Teachers' Assoc.
317 6th St. SE
SIOUX CENTER
IA 51250

Council Bluffs Music Teachers' Assoc.
RR 4, Box 266
COUNCIL BLUFFS
IA 51501

District 7 Teachers' Assoc.
P.O. Box 2
DUNLAP
IA 51529

Luther College Music Dept.
DECORAH
IA 52101

Benton County Music Teachers' Assoc.
107 Prospect St. NW
BLAIRSTOWN
IA 52209

Cedar Rapids Women's Club, Fine Arts Dept.
658-26th St. SE
CEDAR RAPIDS
IA 52403

Fairfield Women's Club and Chorus
1234 Glenview Circle
FAIRFIELD
IA 52556

Federated Teachers and Counsellors
330 Grant St.
BETTENDORF
IA 52722

Etude Club
COLUMBUS JUNCTION
IA 52738

Davenport Etude Club
2510 Scott St.
DAVENPORT
IA 52803

Indianola Federated Music Club
Rt. 2
INDIANOLA
IA 50125

Marshalltown-Bach to Bop
2011 Skyline Dr.
MARSHALLTOWN
IA 50158

Des Moines Music and Drama
3833 Greenwood Dr.
DES MOINES
IA 50312

Mason City Matinee Musicale
671 East State St.
MASON CITY
IA 50401

Storm Lake Melody Club
1021 North Walnut
STORM LAKE
IA 50588

Hampton Treble Clef Club
Rt. 2, Box 266
HAMPTON
IA 50441

Madrigal Music Club
3009 Meadow Ln.
DES MOINES
IA 50265

Grandview College Music Dept.
DES MOINES
IA 50316

Philharmonic Club of Sheffield
Box 612
LATIMER
IA 50452

Independence Ladies' Musical Society
1119 4th St. NE
INDEPENDENCE
IA 50644

Winterset Music Club
100 - 8th Ave.
WINTERSET
IA 50273

Junior Counsellors
7025 Sheridan Circle
DES MOINES
IA 50322

Osage Musicale
RR #5, Box 159A
OSAGE
IA 50461

Wartburg College Music Dept.
WAVERLY
IA 50677

KANSAS
Lawrence Music Club
1701 St. Andrews Dr.
LAWRENCE
KS 66044

Kansas City Music Club
Student Division
8117 High Dr.
LEAWOOD
KS 66206

Merriam Music & Study Club
4102 W. 94th Terrace
PRAIRIE VILLAGE
KS 66207

Music Study Club of Topeka
1289 Pembroke Ln.
TOPEKA
KS 66604

Girard Music Club
501 N. Summit
GIRARD
KS 66743

Treble Clef Club of Pittsburg
RR 4, Box 234B
PITTSBURG
KS 66762

Arkansas City Music & Dramatics' Club
606 North Third
ARKANSAS CITY
KS 67005

Newton Treble Clef Club
4 Ambleside
NEWTON
KS 67114

Treble Clef Club
1106 N. Washington
WELLINGTON
KS 67152

Encore Club
1508 W. 19th
WICHITA
KS 67203

Crescendo Music Club
RR 2
CHERRYVALE
KS 67335

Matinee Musicale
106 Wilshire
COFFEYVILLE
KS 67337

Treble Clef Club
521 E. Wayne
SALINA
KS 67401

Allegro Music Club
RR 4
BELOIT
KS 67420

Polyphonic Music Club
2219 Dover Dr.
HUTCHINSON
KS 67502

Larned Music Club
548 W. 4th
LARNED
KS 67550

Atwood Music Club
707 Blaine
ATWOOD
KS 67730

Goodland Federated Music Club
Midwest Village #F-10
GOODLAND
KS 67735

Sharon Springs Music Club
P.O. Box 28
SHARON SPRINGS
KS 67758

Scott City Federated Music Club
711 East 7th
SCOTT CITY
KS 67871

Concordia Music Club
RR 3
CONCORDIA
KS 66901

Kensington Music Club
P.O. Box 325
KENSINGTON
KS 66951

Pratt Music Club
714 Ridgeway
PRATT
KS 67124

Zenda Music Club
RAGO
KS 67128

Wichita Musical Club
1643 Harlan
WICHITA
KS 67212

Monday Music Club
2713 Country Club Circle
INDEPENDENCE
KS 67301

Salina Staccato Notes
326 South 9th
SALINA
KS 67401

Beloit Music Club
723 North Hersey
BELOIT
KS 67420

Hutchinson Music Club
3314 Clove Circle
HUTCHINSON
KS 67501

Russell Federated Music Club
P.O. Box 37
BUNKER HILL
KS 67626

WA Keeney Harmony Club
408 N. Fourth
WA KEENEY
KS 67672

Goodland Allegro Music Club
1528 Wyoming
GOODLAND
KS 67735

St. Francis Music Club
P.O. Box 119
SAINT FRANCIS
KS 67756

Mozart Music Club
6100 Leavenworth
Road No. 1010
KANSAS CITY
KS 66104

Borger Music Club
612 S. 10th
KANSAS CITY
KS 66105

Manhattan Music Repertoire
1926 Montgomery
MANHATTAN
KS 66502

Civic Music Club
2308 Seaton
MANHATTAN
KS 66702

Civic Music Club of Topeka
100 E. 9th, Apt. 906
TOPEKA
KS 66612

KENTUCKY
Stephen Foster Music Club
Apt. B-1
418 W. Breckenridge St.
LOUISVILLE
KY 40203

Saturday Matinee Musicale
103 Moberly Ave.
RICHMOND
KY 40475

Middlesboro Music Club
125 Alpine Rd.
MIDDLESBORO
KY 40965

Glasgow Musicale
511 N. Race St.
GLASGOW
KY 42141

Henderson Music Club
440 Crestview Dr.
HENDERSON
KY 42420

Mac Dowell Music Club
4734 Southern Parkway
LOUISVILLE
KY 40214

Middlesboro Music Club
A-353 Sherwood Rd.
MIDDLESBORO
KY 40965

Saturday Musicale
1330 St. Ann St.
OWENSBORO
KY 42301

Winchester Music Club
240 Boone Ave.
WINCHESTER
KY 40391

Richmond Cecilian Club
222 S. 3rd St.
RICHMOND
KY 40475

Mount Auburn Music Club
3 Trinity Pl.
FORT THOMAS
KY 41075

Aeolian Club
516 Broadway
CENTRAL CITY
KY 42330

Daniel Boone Music Club
417 Estes Dr.
WINCHESTER
KY 40391

Lexington Federated Music Club
273-B Fontaine Circle
LEXINGTON
KY 40502

Matinee Music Club
2226 Madison
PADUCAH
KY 42001

Madisonville Music Society
RR 1, Box 249
DAWSON SPRINGS
KY 42408

LOUISIANA
Greater New Orleans Music Club
6079 General Haig St.
NEW ORLEANS
LA 70124

Metairie Music Club
4116 Rye St.
Apt. #B
METAIRIE
LA 70002

Thiboudaux Music Club
304 Levert Dr.
THIBOUDAUX
LA 70301

L'Heure de Musique
129 Teche Dr.
LAFAYETTE
LA 70503

West Tech Junior Counsellors' Club
P.O. Box 334
JENNINGS
LA 70546

Aurora Music Club
1537 Calhoun St.
NEW ORLEANS
LA 70118

Music Guild of Monroe
15 Camelia Dr.
MONROE
LA 70122

Donaldsville Music Club
P.O. Box 487
DONALDSVILLE
LA 70346

Bogalusa Philharmonic Music Club
1004 N. Border Dr.
BOGALUSA
LA 70427

Baton Rouge Music Club Chorus
P.O. Box 335
GONZALES
LA 70737

Counsellors' Club of Baton Rouge
147 Clara Dr.
BATON ROUGE
LA 70808

Lyric Opera Theatre
1214 Ross Ave.
BATON ROGE
LA 70808

Music Club of Baton Rouge
2843 Valcour Amie Dr.
BATON ROUGE
LA 70808

Mildren Bevill Music Club
Homer Rd.
Rt. 3, Box 234
HAYNESVILLE
LA 71038

Musicians' Club
3820 Fairfield #91
SHREVEPORT
LA 71104

Music Guild
3018 River Oaks Dr.
MONROE
LA 71201

Musical Coterie of Monroe
113 Louisiana Ave.
WEST MONROE
LA 71291

Alexandria Matinee Musical Club
213 Susan Gay
PINEVILLE
LA 71360

Baton Rouge Philharmonic Club
3328 Broussard St.
BATON ROUGE
LA 70808

Baton Rouge Music Club Auxilliary
12333 Brookshire
BATON ROUGE
LA 70815

Music Forum
6658 Gilbert Pl.
SHREVEPORT
LA 71106

Shreveport District Junior Counselors' Club
2502 Conrad
BOSSIER CITY
LA 71111

Monroe District Music Teachers' Assoc.
504 Bayou Shores Dr.
MONROE
LA 71203

Louis Gottschalk Music Club
408 Forest Circle
RUSTON
LA 71270

Natchez Musical Arts League
Box 186
VIDALIA
LA 71373

Cane River Music Club
213 College Ave.
NATCHITOCHES
LA 71457

MAINE
Annie Louise Carey Club
36 Narraganseit St.
GORHAM
ME 04038

Louise Armstrong Club
9 Lawn Ave.
GORHAM
ME 04038

Mac Dowell Club of Portland
104 West St.
PORTLAND
ME 04102

Marston-Kotzschmar Club
696 Allen Ave.
PORTLAND
ME 04103

Philharmonic Club of Auburn & Lewiston
P.O. Box 7
TURNER
ME 04282

Cecilia Club of Augusta
163 West Hill Rd.
GARDINER
ME 04345

Westbrook Chopin Club
46 Waltham St.
WESTBROOK
ME 04092

Portland Symphony Orchestra
30 Myrtle St.
PORTLAND
ME 04101

Portland Community Chorus
17 Karynel Dr.
Dow's Woods
SOUTH PORTLAND
ME 04106

Portland Rossini Club
Algonquin Rd.
CAPE ELIZABETH
ME 04107

MARYLAND
Friday Morning Music Club
9212 Villa Dr.
BETHESDA
MD 20817

Sligo Federated Music Club
1008 Venice Dr.
SILVER SPRINGS
MD 20904

Baltimore Music Teachers' Assoc.
101 Garrison Forest Rd.
OWINGS MILLS
MD 21117

Baltimore Opera Co.
524 N. Charles St.
BALTIMORE
MD 21201

Allegany County Chorus
Box 42
FLINTSTONE
MD 21503

Friday Morning Music Club
9212 Villa Dr.
BETHESDA
MD 20817

Helmut Braunlich Club
5901 Sonoma Rd.
BETHESDA
MD 20817

Women's Club of Towson
2800 Merrmans Mill Rd.
PHOENIX
MD 21131

Baltimore Music Club
19 East Mt. Vernon Pl.
BALTIMORE
MD 21202

Music & Arts Club of Cumberland
511 Baltimore Ave.
CUMBERLAND
MD 21502

Julio Esteban Music Club
1111 Park Ave.
Sutton Pl.
BALTIMORE
MD 21201

MASSACHUSETTS
Kneisel Hall of Blue hill
24 Quincy Rd.
CHESTNUT HILL
MA 02147

MICHIGAN
Fenton Music Study Club
614 S. East St.
FENTON
MI 48430

Port Huron Musicale
8536 Lakeview Ave.
LEXINGTON
MI 48450

Flint Institute of Music
1025 E. Kearsley
FLINT
MI 48503

Lansing Senior Music Club
DIMONDALE
MI 48821

Matinee Musicale of Lansing
4100 Dobie Rd.
OKEMOS
MI 48864

Owosso Musicale
513 Dean Dr.
OWOSSO
MI 48867

Battle Creek Morning Musical Club
272 Capital Ave. NE #1
BATTLE CREEK
MI 49017

Fortnightly Music Club
137 Harrison St.
COLDWATER
MI 49036

Niles Music Club
1650 Mayflower Rd.
NILES
MI 49120

Tecumseh Music Club
316 W. Michigan Ave.
P.O. Box 557
CLINTON
MI 49236

Muskegon Cecilian Civic Music Club
1092 W. Larch Ave.
MUSKEGON
MI 49441

St. Cecilia Music Society of Grand Rapids
1424 Sherwood SE
EAST GRAND RAPIDS
MI 49506

Grand Rapids Baptist College
1001 E. Beltine NE
GRAND RAPIDS
MI 49506

Hope College School of Music
HOLLAND
MI 49653

Traverse City Musicale
726 Kingston Ct. #B-3
TRAVERSE CITY
MI 49684

Flint St. Cecilia Society
3505 Yale St.
FLINT
MI 48503

Flint Council Choir
1637 Pontiac St.
FLINT
MI 48503

Michigan State University
103 Music Bld.
EAST LANSING
MI 48824

Ionia Music Assoc.
775 Prairie Creek Rd.
IONIA
MI 48846

St. Johns' Morning Musicale
2883 Loomis Rd.
ST JOHNS
MI 48879

Olivet College Music Dept.
OLIVET
MI 49076

Benton Harbour & St. Joseph Monday Musical Club
319 Dunham Ave.
SAINT JOSEPH
MI 49085

Jackson Tuesday Musicale
3825 Kirkwood
JACKSON
MI 49203

Albion College Music Depart.
ALBION
MI 49224

Celebration Club
1705 Bonneville Dr.
MUSKEGON
MI 49441

Rubenstein Club
556 Main
SAUGATUCK
MI 49453

Cadillac Philharmonic Club
617 E. Division St.
CADILLAC
MI 49601

National Music Camp
World Youth Symphony Orchestra
INTERLOCHEN
MI 49643

Crystal Falls Musicale
714 Forest Parkway
CRYSTAL FALLS
MI 49920

Student League of Tuesday Musical
858 Woodland
BIRMICHIGAN
MI 48009

Sigma Alpha Iota
Alumnae Chapter Detroit
447 Wilshire Dr.
BLOOMFIELD HILLS
MI 48013

Farmington Musicale
5403 Picadilly Circle, S.
WEST BLOOMFIELD
MI 48033

Lake Orion Choral Creations
770 Lakeville Rd.
LAKEVILLE
MI 48036

Oxford Music Club
2020 Noble Rd.
OXFORD
MI 48051

Pontiac Tuesday Musicale
3365 Watkins Lake Rd. Apt. B-3
PONTIAC
MI 48054

St. Clair Music Study Club
4626 Yankee Rd.
SAINT CLAIR
MI 48079

Warren Vivace Music Club
11464 Briarcliff
WARREN
MI 48093

Camerata
18430 Golfview
LIVONIA
MI 48154

Sister Edith Maria Madonna College
36600 Schoolcraft
LIVONIA
MI 48159

Music Study Club
8586 N. River Rd.
ALGONAC
MI 48001

Camerata Music Society
16773 Spenger
EAST DETROIT
MI 48021

Tuesday Musicale of Detroit
23907 Wesley Dr.
FARMINGTON
MI 48024

Milford Musicale
5600 Ford Rd.
Box 386
MILFORD
MI 48042

Mount Clemens Monday Musical
5 Westerndorf Court
MOUNT CLEMENS
MI 48043

Michigan Christian College
800 W. Avon Rd.
ROCHESTER
MI 48063

Rochester Tuesday Musicale
125 Briggs Dr.
ROCHESTER
MI 48063

Amity Music Club
3804 Hillside Dr.
ROYAL OAK
MI 48072

Royal Oak Musicale
2709 Vinsetta
ROYAL OAK
MI 48073

Birmingham Musicale
4158 Walnut Hill Dr.
TROY
MI 48098

Milan Music Study Club
320 East Arkona Rd.
MILAN
MI 48160

Music Study Club of Metropolitan Detroit
8544 Huntington Rd.
HUNTINGTON WOODS
MI 48070

MINNESOTA
North Central Bible College
910 Elliot Ave.
MINNEAPOLIS
MN 55404

Mesabi Musicale
Box 958
GILBERT
MN 55741

Hibbling Musicale
1109 Wisconsin
HIBBING
MN 55746

Barnum Music Study Club
1000 Almac Dr.
DULUTH
MN 55810

Mankato Music Club
Rt. 1, Box 34
MADISON LAKE
MN 56063

West Central Keyboard Club
Rt. 2, Box 1788
SPICER
MN 56288

Euterpean Music Club
Rt. 1, Box 264
ALEXANDRIA
MN 56308

MPLS Alumnae Chapter
Mu Phi Epsilon
6626 Rainbow Dr.
Eden Prairie
MN 55344

Andahazy Ballet Company
3208 Zenwood Ave. S.
ST LOUIS PARK
MN 55416

Richfield Chapter, Mu Phi Epsilon
5137 Know Ave. S.
MINNEAPOLIS
MN 55419

Symphonions
RR 3, Box 765
GRAND MARAIS
MN 55604

Duluth Music Teachers' Assoc.
156 Wildwood Dr.
ESKO
MN 55733

Duluth Cecilian Society
334 Kenilworth Ave.
DULUTH
MN 55804

Duluth Matinee Musicale
216 North 33rd Ave. W
DULUH
MN 55805

Willmar Musicale
1712 Hanson Dr. S.W.
WILLMAR MN 56201

Olivia County Music Teachers' Assoc.
801 S. Pine
OLIVIA
MN 56277

MISSISSIPPI
Oxford Music Club
1601 Buchanan
OXFORD
MS 38655

Fortnightly Musicale
14 Quail Creek
TUPELO
MS 38801

Beethoven Club
2206 Hickory Rd.
CORINTH
MS 38834

Pontotoc Music Club
136 N. Brooks St.
PONTOTOC
MS 38863

Belzoni Music Lovers' Club
Rt. 2
Four Mile Rd.
BELZONI
MS 39038

Canton Music Study Club
Rt. 4, Box 167
CANTON
MS 39046

Mount Olive Music Lovers' Club
P.O. Box 123
MOUNT OLIVE
MS 39119

Taylorsville Music Club
TAYLORSVILLE
MS 39168

Mac Dowell Music Club
834 Newland St.
JACKSON
MS 39211

Philharmonic Club of Meridian
Rt. 9, Box 316
MERIDIAN
MS 39304

Lydian Music Club
804 Azalea Dr.
PHILADELPHIA
MS 39350

Hattiesburg Music Club
1003 Stratford
HATTIESBURG
MS 39401

Columbus Music Study Club
3109 Apple Valley Rd.
COLUMBUS
MS 39701

Nocturne Music Club
2501 Plum Rd.
STARKVILLE
MS 39759

Opera Study House
715 Maple Ave.
CLARKSDALE
MS 38614

Amory Wednesday Musicale
505 8th Ave. N.
AMORY
MS 38821

Corinth Music Club
1412 Pine Rd.
CORINTH
MS 38834

Matinee Musicale
Gilliam Place
GREENWOOD
MS 38930

Sumner Music Club
P.O. Box 369
SUMNER
MS 38957

Crystal Springs Mac Dowell Club
Box 305
GALLMAN
MS 39077

Simpson County Sinfonia Music
Box 518
MENDENHALL
MS 39114

Vicksburg Matinee Musical
617 Holly Ridge
VICKSBURG
MS 39180

Mozart Music Club
P.O. Box 780
YAZOO CITY
MS 39194

Matinee Musical Club
2113 – 41st Ave.
MERIDIAN
MS 39305

Newton Music Lovers
300 New Ireland
NEWTON
MS 39345

Biloxi Music Club
Oakwood Apt. # 28
2870 West Beach
BILOXI
MS 39531

Wiggins Music Club
P.O. Box 729
WIGGINS
MS 39577

MISSOURI
Musical Research Club
3869A Connecticut St.
ST. LOUIS
MO 63116

Morning Etude
3851 Keats Dr.
ST. LOUIS
MO 63134

Music Study Club
143 Royal Manor Ct.
CREVE COEUR
MO 63141

Bach Music Club
622 W. Martin
CAMPBELL
MO 63833

Etude Music Club of Hornersville
HORNERSVILLE
MO 63855

M.E. Pierce Music Club
4022 S. Fuller
INDEPENDENCE
MO 64052

Carthage Musical Devotees' Club
1433 S. Maple
CARTHAGE
MO 64836

Morning Music Club
144 Boonville
JEFFERSON CITY
MO 65101

Mount Vernon Music Club
520 Oak Ln.
MOUNT VERNON
MO 65712

Springfield Music Club
931 W. State
SPRINGFIELD
MO 65806

Woerner Music Club
4528 Tomahawk
ST. LOUIS
MO 63123

Rubenstein Music Club
10374 Badgley
ST. LOUIS
MO 63126

Hannibal Evening Etude
1215 Bird St.
HANNIBAL
MO 63401

Perry Musique Club
Rt. 1, Box 116A
PERRY
MO 63462

Wednesday Morning Music Club
1009 David Dr.
KENNETT
MO 63857

Adene Keller Music Club
909 Towery
MALDEN
MO 63863

Kansas City Musical Club
2453 Lister
KANSAS CITY
MO 64127

Butler Music Club
311 N. Fulton
BUTLER
MO 64730

Moberly Music Club
320 S. 4th St.
MOBERLY
MO 65270

Thursday Musicale of Bolivar
330 W. Gordon
BOLIVAR
MO 65613

MONTANA
Tuesday Music Club
426 4th Ave. N.
GREAT FALLS
MT 59401

Rainbow Hill Dance Studios
600 1st Ave. SW
GREAT FALLS
MT 59404

Great Falls Music Teachers' Assoc.
504 23rd Ave. NE
GREAT FALLS
MT 59404

High Line Federation
954 Westwood Ave.
SHELBY
MT 59474

Kalispell Music Club
813 2nd Ave. E.
KALISPELL
MT 59901

Havre Area Music Teachers' Club
P.O. Box 1179
CHINOOK
MT 59523

Canzone Music Club
70 Town Pump East
Highway 10A East
MT 59711

NEBRASKA
Blair-Tekamah Group
2007 Scott Ave.
TEKAMAH
NE 68061

Crescendo
7332 Washington
OMAHA
NE 68127

Bellevue Federated
14310 S. 63rd St.
PAPILLION
NE 68133

Arpeggios
8781 Templeton Dr.
OMAHA
NE 68134

Omaha Suzuki Piano Assoc.
5620 Howard St.
OMAHA
NE 68132

Tenutos
6023 Lafayette Ct.
OMAHA
NE 68132

Rocky Ridge Music Center
3600 Sumner St.
LINCOLN
NE 68506

NEW MEXICO
Sigmas Alpha Iota Patronesses
5404 Montgomery NE. #412A
ALBUQUERQUE
NM 87108

Albuquerque Light Opera Assoc.
4201 Ellison NE
ALBUQUERQUE
NM 87109

New Mexico Symphony Orchestra
P.O. Box 769
ALBUQUERQUE
NM 87103

Sai Alumnae Choir
Star Rt. Box 260
CORRALES
NM 87048

New Mexico Women's Composers Guild
8304 Della Rd. N. E.
ALBUQUERQUE
NM 87109

Albuquerque Music Club
4601 San Andres NE
ALBUQUERQUE
NM 87110

Alpha Sigma Choir SAI
7210 Settlement Way NW
ALBUQUERQUE
NM 87120

Santa Fe Opera
P.O. Box 2408
SANTE FE
NM 87501

Friends of Music
9700 Pebble Beach Dr. NE
ALBUQUERQUE
NM 87111

Junior Counselors' Senior Club
5401 Tioga NE
ALBUQUERQUE
NM 87120

Terpsica Dance Theatre
P.O. Box 25567
ALBUQUERQUE
NM 87125

Taos School of Music
P.O. Box 1879
TAOS
NM 87571

NEW YORK
Meadowmont School for Strings
170 W. 73rd St. Apt 10A
NEW YORK
NY 10023

Juilliard School of Music
Lincoln Center Plaza
NEW YORK
NY 10023

Hoff Barthelson Music School
25 School Ln.
SCARSDALE
NY 10583

Westchester Conservatory of Music
20 Southern Ave.
WHITE PLAINS
NY 10605

Watertown Morning Musicales
232 Elm St.
WATERTOWN
NY 13601

Music Forum Club of Piano Teachers
249 Wellingwood Dr.
EAST AMHERST
NY 14051

Amherst Symphony Orchestra
90 Harrogate Square
WILLIAMSVILLE
NY 14221

Nazareth College Music Dept.
4245 East Ave.
ROCHESTER
NY 14610

D. Hachstein Memorial Music School
50 N. Plymouth Ave.
ROCHESTER
NY 14614

Ithaca Music Club
386 The Parkway
ITHACA
NY 14850

Tompkins Country Junior Counselors' Club
1109 East State St.
ITHACA
NY 14850

Fransohnian Musical Society
141 Moore St.
WAVERLY
NY 14892

New York Philomusica Chamber Ensemble
105 W. 73rd St. Apt 4G
NEW YORK
NY 10023

Aspen Music School
1860 Broadway
NEW YORK
NY 10023

Manhattan School of Music
120 Claremont Ave.
NEW YORK
NY 10027

CUNY Music Dept.
Davis Center
138 St. & Convent Ave.
NEW YORK
NY 10031

Port Washington Music Study Club
464 Main St.
PORT WASHINGTON
NY 11050

Vassar College Music Dept.
Box 18
POUGHKEEPSIE
NY 12601

Crane Music School
State University Potsdam
POTSDAM
NY 13676

Morning Evening Musical Club
72 Pleasant St.
NORWICH
NY 13815

Villa Maria Institute of Music
240 Pine Ridge Rd.
CHEEKTOWAGA
NY 14225

Sunny Buffalo
Amherst Campus Music Dept.
222 Baird Hall
BUFFALO
NY 14260

Chautauqua Institute of Music
CHAUTAUQUA
NY 14722

Euterpean Club
174 Broad St.
SALAMANCA
NY 14779

NORTH CAROLINA
North Carolina School of The Arts
P.O. Box 12189
WINSTON SALEM
NC 27107

Troy Music Club
P.O. Box 848
BISCOE
NC 27209

Musical Art Club of High Point
911 N. Hamilton St.
HIGH POINT
NC 27262

Musical Art Club of High Point
c/o Schubert
1020 Wellington Ct.
HIGH POINT
NC 27262

Euterpean Club of Greensboro
605 Kemp Rd. W.
GREENSBORO
NC 27410

Gastonia Music Club
304 N. Ransom St.
GASTONIA
NC 28052

Gastonia Sharps & Flats Music Club
Rt. 1, Box 182
KINGS MOUNTAIN
NC 28085

Cecilia Music Club
810 Brittain Dr.
SHELBY
NC 28150

Queen City Music Club
2341 Richardson Dr.
CHARLOTTE
NC 28211

Thursday Morning Music Club of Wilmington
3949 Halifax Rd.
WILMINGTON
NC 28403

East Carolina Music Club
P.O. Box 1147
NEW BERN
NC 28560

Schubert Music Club of Morgantown
P.O. Box 35
DREXEL
NC 28619

Weaverville Music Study Club
P. O. Box 152
WEAVERVILLE
NC 28787

Asheville Music Club
c/o Sams
54 W. Oakvie Rd.
ASHVILLE
NC 28806

Holly Hill Music Club
Rt. 2, Box 1107
HOLLY HILL
SC 29059

Winston-Salem Thursday Morning Music Club
2461 Ardmore Manor
WINSTON SALEM
NC 27103

Burlington Music Club
904 Kimberly Rd.
BURLINGTON
NC 27215

Gibonsville Music Club
Box 3307
Kivette House Rd.
GIBONSVILLE
NC 27249

Lexington Music Study Club
321 W. 2nd St.
LEXINGTON
NC 27292

Euterpean Music Club of Lexington
500 Country Club Dr.
LEXINGTON
NC 27292

Robertsonville Mac Dowell Music Club
EVERETTS
NC 27825

Lucille Wall Music Club
207 Hall St.
FOREST CITY
NC 28043

Lamar Stringfield Club
204 South Ridgecrest St.
RUTHERFORDTON
NC 28139

Salisbury Music Club
Rt. 1, Box 273
SALISBURY
NC 28144

Charlotte Music Club
10028 Santa Fe Lane
CHARLOTTE
NC 28212

Chaminade Music Club of Fayetteville
215 Valley Rd.
FAYETTEVILLE
NC 28305

La Musique Club of Cartaret County
Rt. 3, Box 99B
NEWPORT
NC 28570

Hickory Music Club
Rt. 10, Box 70A
HICKORY
NC 28601

Mac Dowell Music Club of Statesville
440 Oakhurst Rd.
STATESVILLE
NC 28677

Brevard Music Lovers' Club
37 Dogwood Lane.
BREVARD
NC 28712

Valdese Music Club
P.O. Box 145
HILDEBRAN
NC 28637

NORTH DAKOTA

Devils Lake Music Club
112 - 19th St.
DEVILS LAKE
ND 58301

Bismarck-Mandan Thursday Music
818 C. West
BISMARCK
ND 58501

Fargo-Moorhead Area Music Club
2814 7th St. N.
FARGO
ND 58102

Thursday Music Club
506 28th Ave. S.
GRAND FORKS
ND 58201

St. Cecilia Club
1087 17th Ave. W.
DICKINSON
ND 58601

Thursday Musical
Rt. 3, Box 30
WILLISTON
ND 58801

OHIO

Delaware Music Club
128 N. Washington St. Apt. #4
DELAWARE
OH 43015

Westerville Women's Music Club
4638 N. Shore Dr.
WESTERVILLE
OH 43081

Cecilian Music Club
325 E. Temple St.
WASHINGTON COURT HOUSE
OH 4316

Columbus Women's Music Club
5657 Godown Rd.
COLUMBUS
OH 43220

Saturday Music Club
2044 Quail Ridge Dr.
COLUMBUS
OH 43229

Lecture Recital Club
16042 Co. Rd. 115, Rt. 5
UPPER SANDUSKY
OH 43351

Music Club of Newcomerstown
125 Chapman Ave.
NEWCOMERSTOWN
OH 43832

Cleveland Institutems
11021 E. Boulevard
CLEVELAND
OH 44106

Fortnighly Musical Club of Cleveland
1874 Bromton Dr.
LYNDHURST
OH 44124

Coyahoga Falls Music Club
261 Washburn Rd.
TALLMADGE
OH 44278

Tuesday Musical Club
1240 Ashford Lane #1-A
AKRON
OH 44313

Columbiana Music Study Club
47 South Cross St.
COLUMBIANA
OH 44408

1st United Methodist Church
Joy Ringer's Bell Choir
206 Manor Dr.
COLUMBIANA
OH 44408

Monday Musical Club
2242 5th Ave.
YOUNGSTOWN
OH 44504

Alliance Music Study Club
1058 Vincent Blvd.
ALLIANCE
OH 44601

Mac Dowell Music Study Club
Dover - N. Phil.
508 Evergreen Dr.
DOVER
OH 44622

Fortnightly Music Club of New Philadelphia
Rt. 2, Box 12
DOVER
OH 44622

Ashland Musical Club
1531 Edgewood Dr.
ASHLAND
OH 44805

Ashland College Music Dept.
ASHLAND
OH 44805

Mansfield Music Study Club
535 Eby Rd. Box 230
SHILOH
OH 44878

Middleton Music Club
3794 Julia Dr.
FRANKLIN
OH 45005

Oxford Women's Music Club
720 Erin Dr.
OXFORD
OH 45056

Wilmington Music Club
1104 Berlin Rd.
WILMINGTON
OH 45177

Cincinnati Symphony Club
3640 Brotherton Rd.
CINCINNATI
OH 45209

Norther Hills Piano Teachers' Forum
411 Flembrook Ct.
CINCINNATI
OH 45231

Greenville Music Club
126 Winchester Rd.
GREENVILLE
OH 45331

Melodieres
3684 Harry Truman Dr.
DAYTON
OH 45432

Irontown Women's Music Club
2543 South Seventh St.
IRONTON
OH 45638

Athens Women's Music Club
Strouds Run Rd.
ATHENS
OH 45701

Music Club Upper Sandusky
9530 TR 32
ARLINGTON
OH 45814

Keyboard Club
1616 Grant Blvd.
FINDLAY
OH 45840

Beethoven Club
601 E. Gambier St.
MOUNT VERNON
OH 43050

Newark Music and Study Club
977 Grafton Rd. Apt #6
NEWARK
OH 43055

Worthington Music Club
6653 Merwin Rd.
WORTHINGTON
OH 43085

Euterpean Club
56 Orchard St.
LOGAN
OH 43138

Jefferson Academy of Music
66 Jefferson Ave.
COLUMBUS
OH 43215

Hanby Music Club
3245 Minerva Lake
COLUMBUS
OH 43229

Kenton Music Club
16092 Tr 39
BELLE CENTER
OH 43310

New Lexington Musical Study Club
3740 Rt. 1 NE
NEW LEXINGTON
OH 43764

Oberlin College Conservatory of Music
OBERLIN
OH 44074

Cleveland Music School Settlement
11125 Magnolis Dr.
CLEVELAND
OH 44106

Musical Arts Club
Medina County
921 Clovedale Ave.
MEDINA
OH 44256

Salem Music Study Club
206 Manor Dr.
COLUMBIANA
OH 44408

Lisbon Music Study Club
43623 Sr 154
LISBON
OH 44432

Warren Music Club
197 Adelaide SE
WARREN
OH 44483

Mount Junior College Music Dept.
ALLIANCE
OH 44601

Carrollton Music Study Club
211 Gallo Rd. NW
CARROLLTON
OH 44613

Mac Dowell Club
5110 Millersburg Rd.
WOOSTER
OH 44691

Bellville Butler Music
98 Ogle St.
BELLVILLE
OH 44813

Western Reserve Piano Teachers' Guild
1001 Beachside Ln.
HURON
OH 44839

Musical Arts Club of Hamilton
704 Shultz Dr.
HAMILTON
OH 45013

Warren Country Music Club
405 Clippinger
LEBANON
OH 45036

Greenfield Music and Drama Club
230 South Street
GREENFIELD
OH 45123

West Hills Music Club
3679 Crestnoll Ln.
CINCINNATI
OH 45211

Fortnightly Musical Club
170 Weinland
NEW CARLISLE
OH 45344

Xenia Woman's Music Club
303 Orton Rd.
YELLOW SPRINGS
OH 45387

Dayton Music Club
6515 Willow Hill Ct.
DAYTON
OH 45459

OKLAHOMA
Chickasha Mac Dowell Music Club
916 Shepard
CHICKASHA
OK 73018

Atlas Mac Dowell Club of Allied Arts
2049 Willard Dr.
ALTUS
OK 73521

Duncan Music Club
423 N. 20th
DUNCAN
OK 73533

Stillwater St. Cecilia Music Club
2826 North Keller Dr.
STILLWATER
OK 74075

Hyechka Club of Tulsa
4321 E. 35th
TULSA
OK 74135

Mc Alester Fortnightly Music Club
313 Bluebird Ln.
MC ALESTER
OK 74501

Coalgate Music Club
Box 36
ALLEN
OK 74825

Norman Music Club
23100 Ravenwood
NORMAN
OK 73069

Schubert Federated Music Club
2014 Lakeview Dr.
SULPHUR
OK 73086

Erick MacDowell Music Club
ERICK
OK 73645

Bartlesville Musical Research Society
2901 Oakdale Pl.
BARTLESVILLE
OK 74006

Musical Arts Society
Box 427
WARNER
OK 74469

Poteau Musical Arts Society
Rt. 3, Box 98M
POTEAU
OK 74953

OREGON

Federated Junior Music Leaders
4030 SW Fairhaven Dr.
CORVALLIS
OR 97333

Mothers' Music Club of Oregon
16933 S. Bradley Rd.
OREGON CITY
OR 97045

Melody Moms
3811 SE 40th Ave.
PORTLAND
OR 97202

Portland Monday Musical Club
6214 SW 41st Ave.
PORTLAND
OR 97221

Progressive Music Teachers' Assoc.
7675 SW 136th Ave.
BEAVERTON
OR 97005

Federation of Music Teachers
1306 E. 5th St.
MCMINNVILLE
OR 97128

Allied Arts Club
2525 NE 20th Ave.
PORTLAND
OR 97212

Salem Federated Music Club
3645 12th Ct. SE
SALEM
OR 97302

Portland Junior Leaders
19515 SW Butternut St.
ALOHA
OR 97007

Tillamook Monday Musical Club
840 Sollie Smith Rd. N.
TILLAMOOK
OR 97141

Sing and Strum
1732 NE Schuyler St.
PORTLAND
OR 97212

Society of Oregon Composers
2615 SW Orchard Hill Ln.
LAKE OSWEGO
OR 97034

Pro Musica Club of Oregon
2806 SE 19th
PORTLAND
OR 97202

Opus 14 Recital Club
4107 Vermont St.
PORTLAND
OR 97219

PENNSYLVANIA

North Hills Music Club
1391 Parkview Dr.
ALLISON PARK
PA 15101

Tuesday Musical Club of Butler
211 Belmont Rd.
BUTLER
PA 16001

Grove City Music Club
109 Mc Chesney Dr.
GROVE CITY
PA 16127

St. John's Recorder Consort
174 Forker Blvd.
SHARON
PA 16146

Elizabethtown College Music Dept.
Rider Hall
ELIZABETHTOWN
PA 17022

Williamsport Music Club
Rt. 1, Box 591
COGAN STATION
PA 17728

Slatington Music Club
212 Lincoln Dr.
WALNUTPORT
PA 18088

Wyalusing Musical Society
Rd. 1
SUGAR RUN
PA 18846

Matinee Musical Club
609 Hathaway House
515 W. Chelten Ave.
PHILADELPHIA
PA 19144

MC Keesport Music Club
1404 California Ave.
MC KEESPORT
PA 15131

Uniontown Music Club
Box 87
HOPWOOD
PA 15445

North Butler County Music Club
Box 95
CHICORA
PA 16025

Sandy Lake & Stoneboro Monday Music Club
Rd. 1
JACKSON CENTER
PA 16133

Schubert Musical & Literary Club
1121 W. First St.
OIL CITY
PA 16301

Harmonica Club
400 S. Lincoln Ave.
LEBANON
PA 17042

Lock Haven Music Club
124 N. Hillview St.
LOCK HAVEN
PA 17745

Allentown Music Club
1455 Grace St.
ALLENTOWN
PA 18103

Towanda Musical Society
28 Main St.
TOWANDA
PA 18848

Pittsburgh Piano Teachers' Assoc.
1397 Navahoe Dr.
PITTSBURGH
PA 15228

Indiana Monday Musical Club
128 N. Coulter Ave.
INDIANA
PA 15701

Treble Clef Music Club
P.O. Box 26
KARNS CITY
PA 16041

Mercer Music Club
200 S. Erie St.
MERCER
PA 16187

Musical Art Society
2141 Kentwood Dr.
LANCASTER
PA 17601

Cecilian Club
601 Dewart
SHAMOKIN
PA 17892

Music Study Club of Stroudsburg
2206 N. 5th St.
STROUDSBURG
PA 18360

New School of Music
301 S. 21st St.
PHILADELPHIA
PA 19103

Octave Club
66 N. Whitehall Rd.
NORRISTOWN
PA 19403

Pittsburgh Tuesday Musical Club
145 Calmont Dr.
PITTSBURGH
PA 15235

Johnstown Senior Music League
137 Daisy St.
JOHNSTOWN
PA 15902

Sharon Music Club
411 Tamplin St.
SHARON
PA 16146

Troy Music Club
460 Elmira St.
TROY
PA 16947

Canton Music Club
123 N. Minnequa
CANTON
PA 17724

Tri-County Music Club
1625 Cloverleaf
BETHLEHEM
PA 18017

Mozart Club
Rt. 1, Box 130
PITTSTON
PA 18640

Curtis Institute of Music
1726 Locust St.
PHILADELPHIA
PA 19103

RHODE ISLAND
Chopin Club
175 Lloyd Ave.
PROVIDENCE
RI 02906

Chaminade Club
241 Narragansett Parkway
WARWICK
RI 02888

Mac Dowell Club
14 Kearsarge Dr.
CRANSTON
RI 02920

Schubert Club
350 Olney St.
PROVIDENCE
RI 02906

Chopin Student Musicians
49 Edgehill Rd.
PROVIDENCE
RI 02906

SOUTH CAROLINA
Union Music Club
713 E. Main St.
UNION
SC 29379

Chopin Music Club
1454 Jebaily Dr.
FLORENCE
SC 29501

Marion Music Club
505 Lipscombe St.
MARION
SC 29571

Belton Music Club
Rt. 1, Box 16
BELTON
SC 29627

Music Lovers' Club of Ninety Six
405 N. Church St.
NINETY SIX
SC 29666

Travelers Rest Club
P.O. Box 144
TRAVELERS REST
SC 29690

Clinton Music Club
304 Hickory St.
CLINTON
SC 29325

Charleston Music Study Club
1239 Harrow St.
CHARLESTON
SC 29407

Mac Dowell Evening Music Club
514 Iris Dr.
FLORENCE
SC 29501

Crescent Music Club
52 Fernwood Ln.
GREENVILLE
SC 29607

Easley Piano Teachers' Guild Assoc.
408 S. 54th St.
EASLEY
SC 29640

Pickens Music Club
Star Rt.
PICKENS
SC 29671

Allegro Music Club
224 Bailey Ave.
ROCK HILL
SC 29730

Afternoon Music Club
57 Olde Springs Rd.
COLUMBIA
SC 29223

Women's Music Club of Spartanburg
181 Fairview Ave.
SPARTANBURG
SC 29302

Mc Dowell Music Club
505 Welch St.
KERSHAW
SC 29067

Women's Afternon Music Club
126 Nash St.
SUMTER
SC 29150

Converse College
Dept. Pre College Club
SPARTANBURG
SC 29301

Apollo Music Club
320 N. Carlisle St.
BAMBERG
SC 29003

Lancaster Music Study Club
Rt. 3, Box 192
KERSHAW
SC 29067

Quida Eich Music Club
613 Hatrick Rd.
COLUMBIA
SC 29209

Spartanburg Music Teachers' Club
501 Camelot Dr.
FOXFIRE
SC 29301

Bishopville Music Club
Rt. 3, Box 272
BISHOPVILLE
SC 29010

Newberry Music Club
1720 College St.
NEWBERRY
SC 29018

Eau Claire Music Club
7821 St. Margaret St.
COLUMBIA
SC 29209

Converse College of Music
580 E. Main St.
SPARTANBURG
SC 29301

Cora Cox Lucas Music Club
523 Chestnut St.
LAURENS
SC 29360

Musical Arts Club
203 Sycamore Dr.
FLORENCE
SC 29501

Greer Music Club
108 Wilson Dr. Box 141
GREER
SC 29651

Tri-City Music Educators
P.O. Box 143
SENECA
SC 29679

Rock Hill Music Club
231 Bailey Ave.
ROCK HILL
SC 29730

Spartanburg Philharmonic Music Club
P.O. Box 132
PAULINE
SC 29374

Summerville Music Club
106 Race Club Rd.
SUMMERVILLE
SC 29483

Hartsville Music Study Club
112 Pine Lake Dr.
HARTSVILLE
SC 29550

Music Club of Greenville
102 Merrifield Ct.
GREENVILLE
SC 29615

Anderson Music Club
P.O. Box 558
IVA
SC 29655

Fountain Inn Music Club
Rt. 4, Box 233
SIMPSONVILLE
SC 29681

Orangeburg Music Club
106 Dragon Fly Ct.
ORANGEBURG
SC 29115

SOUTH DAKOTA
Vermillion Music Club
RR 2, Box 74
ELK POINT
SD 57025

Huron Senior Choraleers
438 8th St. SW
HURON
SD 57350

Huron Thursday Musicale
Box 376
DOLAND
SD 57436

Beresford Musical Arts Club
RR 1
BERESFORD
SD 57004

Aberdeen Monday Musicale
1312 3rd Ave. SE
ABERDEEN
SD 57401

Pierre Monday Musicale
117 Lakeview Dr.
PIERRE
SD 57501

Augustana College
2101 S. Summit Ave.
SIOUX FALLS
SD 57197

Aeolian Music Club
RR 4, Box 114
BROOKINGS
SD 57006

Musical Medley Club
400 9th St. NE
WATERTOWN
SD 57201

Lyre Music Club
220 7th Ave. SE
ABERDEEN
SD 57401

TENNESSEE
Frances Bohannon Music Club
1123 Wiseman Pl.
MURFREESBORO
TN 37130

Tullahoma Music Club
306 Oak Park Ln.
TULLAHOMA
TN 37388

Newport Music Club
Terrace Apts. #31, Rt. 6
NEWPORT
TN 37821

Thursday Evening Musicale
115 Thompson Dr.
RIPLEY
TN 38063

Stephen Foster Music Club
Horner Dr.
SELMER
TN 38375

Springfield Music Study Club
Black Patch Dr.
SPRINGFIELD
TN 37172

Bristol Music Club
2115 Edgemont Ave.
BRISTOL
TN 37620

Tuesday Evening Music Club
609 Creek View
SEVIERVILLE
TN 37862

Martin Philharmonic Music Guild
205 University
MARTIN
TN 38237

Monday Evening Music Club
2575 Memorial Dr. Ext.
CLARKSVILLE
TN 3043

Athens Music Club
111 Highland Ave.
ATHENS
TN 37303

Tuesday Morning Musicale
3308 Timberlake Dr.
KNOXVILE
TN 37920

Matinee Music Club
506 E. Jackson St.
UNION CITY
TN 38261

Thursday Music Study Club
R.F.D. # 2
ENGLEWOOD
TN 37329

Maryville Music Club
504 Belle Meade Dr.
MARYVILLE
TN 27801

Brownsville Wednesday Morning Musicale
625 West College St.
BROWNSVILLE
TN 38012

Dyer Senior Music Lovers' Club
Rt. 1, Box 30
DYER
TN 38330

TEXAS
Athens Music Study Club
Rt. 5, Box 96
ATHENS
TX 75751

Tarrant County Junior College
Northeast Campus
828 Harwood Rd.
HURST
TX 76053

League of Composers
5120 Malinda Ln. S.
FORT WORTH
TX 76112

Vernon Musicians' Club
Rt. 3
VERNON
TX 76384

Rockdale Matinee Music Club
903 Cady Rd.
ROCKDALE
TX 76567

McLennan Community College Music Dept.
WACO
TX 76708

Philharmonic Society
2215 Delker Dr.
SAN ANGELO
TX 76904

Port Arthur Symphony
3016 Grand Ave.
PORT ARTHUR
TX 77642

New Braunfels Music Study Club
105 Briarwood
NEW BRAUNFELS
TX 78130

Bishop Music Study Club
703 Henderson
BISHOP
TX 78343

Stephen Foster Music Club
1015 Jones St.
FUFKIN
TX 75901

Mozart Music Club
2816 Montgomery Circle
VERNON
TX 76384

Taylor Wednesday Music Club
509 W. 11th
TAYLOR
TX 76574

Musical Notes Club
725 Kipling Dr.
WACO
TX 76710

Galveston Musical Club
4415 S. 1/2
GALVESTON
TX 77550

Music Study Club
840 Central
BEAUMONT
TX 77706

San Antonio Etude Music Club
210 Lovera
SAN ANTONIO
TX 78216

Music Club of Kingsville
425 E. Kennedy
KINGSVILLE
TX 78363

Marshall Music Club
413 Lynoak
MARSHALL
TX 75670

Center Music Study
Rt. 3, Box 1445
CENTER
TX 75935

Euterpean Club
4336 Lovell
FORT WORTH
TX 76107

SW Baptist Theological Seminary
P.O. Box 22000
FORT WORTH
TX 76122

Cisco Music Study Club
Rt. 3
CISCO
TX 76437

Schubert Club
Box 96
BROWNWOOD
TX 76804

Pasadena Federated Music Club
222 Viceroy
HOUSTON
TX 77034

Port Arthur Choral Club
4148 Willow Oak
GROVES
TX 77619

Navasota Music Study Club
509 Senior Circle
NAVASOTA
TX 77868

Tyler Music Coterie
1221 Old Hickory Rd.
TYLER
TX 75703

Arlington Music Club
1020 Anita
ARLINGTON
TX 76013

Harmony Club
2628 Stadium
FORT WORTH
TX 76109

Wichita Falls Musicians' Club
1205 Grace
WICHITA FALLS
TX 76308

Eastland Music Study Club
Rt. 2, Box 185A
EASTLAND
TX 76448

Euterpean Music Club
603 N 33rd St.
WACO
TX 76707

Damrosch Music Club
507 W. 13th St.
BRADY
TX 76825

Gulf Coast Music Assoc.
15814 Crestbrook
HOUSTON
TX 77059

Orange Chamber Musicians
708 West Cherry
ORANGE
TX 77630

Victoria Music Club
2307 Terrace
VICTORIA
TX 77901

Alice Music Study Club
2619 N Texas Blvd. #116
ALICE
TX 78332

Musical Culture Club
Rt. 1, Box 689
ALAMO
TX 78516

Mc Allen Music Club
Rt. 4, Box 225
MISSION
TX 78572

Del Rio Music Club
300 Westward Way
DEL RIO
TX 78840

Levelland Music Club
102 Ave. U
LEVELLAND
TX 79336

Lufkin Music Study
135 East Denman
LUFKIN
TX 79501

Abilene Harmony Club
542 Highland
ABILENE
TX 79605

Del Mar College
548 Naples
CORPUS CHRISTI
TX 78404

Bastrop Harmony Club
Rt. 2, Box 188
Steiner Ranch
BASTROP
TX 78602

Dawn Music Club
Box 87
DAWN
TX 79025

Stratford Federated Music Club
Box 122
STRATFORD
TX 79084

Euterpean Club
Box 728
PADUCAH
TX 79248

Plains Fine Arts Club
Box 423
PLAINS
TX 79355

Snyder Music Coterie
3300 48th St.
SNYDER
TX 79549

Thursday Music club
518 Miramar
CORPUS CHRISTI
TX 78411

Music lovers' Club
2813 Blake Ave.
HARLINGEN
TX 78550

Music Study Club
213 St. Andrew
GONZALES
TX 78629

Wednesday Morning Music
3303 Hyclimb Circle
AUSTIN
TX 78723

Gruver Music Club
Box 29
GRUVER
TX 79040

Mac Dowell Music Club
7210 Calumet
AMARILLO
TX 79106

Harmony Music Club
433 South Ivy
CROSBYTON
TX 7932

Seminole Music Club
805 SW Highway
SEMINOLE
TX 79359

Lubbock Music Club
2322 61st St.
LUBBOCK
TX 79413

Stamford Music Club
1306 Portland
STAMFORD
TX 79553

Musicians' Club
2604 Bluebird Lane
MIDLAND
TX 79705

Stanton Music Club
Box 1128
STANTON
TX 79782

Corpus Christi Harmony Club
4600 Ocean Dr. #606
CORPUS CHRISTI
TX 78412

Mercedes Music Club
P.O. Box 171
MERCEDES
TX 78370

San Marcos Crescendo Club
17 Northcrest
SAN MARCOS
TX 78666

Odessa Tuesday Morning Music and Arts Club
1509 Parker
ODESSA
TX 78761

Music Study Club
102 North Texas
HEREFORD
TX 79045

Philharmonic Music Club
4127 Van Buren
AMARILLO
TX 79110

South Plains College
LEVELLAND
TX 79336

Seagraves Music Club
Box 144
SEAGRAVES
TX 79359

Allegro Music Club
4602 10th St.
LUBBOCK
TX 79416

Abilene Christian University
P.O. Box 8274
ABILENE
TX 79601

Big Spring Music Study Club
3609 Wasson # 36
BIG SPRING
TX 79720

Dallas Federation of Music Club
708 Rollingwood
RICHARDSON
TX 75080

Music and Drama Club
4414 Colgate
DALLAS
TX 75225

Carthage Music Club
Rt. 3, Box 21V
CARTHAGE
TX 75633

Nevin Club
644 West 5th
CORSICANA
TX 75110

Mountain View College
4849 W. Illinois Ave.
DALLAS
TX 75211

Melodie Club
3619 Townsend
DALLAS
TX 75229

Gladewater Music Club
Rt. 2, Box 195-B
GLADEWATER
TX 75647

Garland Music Club
502 Reinosa
GARLAND
TX 75043

Cecilian Club
515 Feather Crest Dr.
MESQUITE
TX 75150

Christine Palmer Club
6232 Pemberton Dr.
DALLAS
TX 75230

Longview Music Club
311 South Highe
LONGVIEW
TX 75601

Plano Federated Music Club
1505 Scotsdale
PLANO
TX 75075

Fine Arts Dept.
Dallas Public Library
1515 Young
DALLAS
TX 75201

Wednesday Morning Choral Club
6746 Lupton
DALLAS
TX 75225

Beckville Music club
RR 1, Box 225
BECKVILLE
TX 75631

Mac Dowell Club
Rt. 2, Box 58
CELINA
TX 75009

Odesa Music Study Club
2109 Verde
ODESSA
TX 79761

Lubbock Christian College
LUBBOCK
TX 79407

VIRGINIA
Fairfax Music Guild
9600 Bel Glade
FAIRFAX
VA 22031

Rappahannock Music Society
15 Mount Vernon Ave.
FREDERICKSBURG
VA 22405

Matthews Music Study Club
MATTHEWS
VA 23109

Norfolk Keynote Music Club
5409 Count Turf Rd.
VIRGINIA BEACH
VA 23462

Tidewater Community College Music Dept.
Fred Campus St. Rd. 135
PORTSMOUTH
VA 23703

Virtuoso Club
2517 Maycrest St. NE
ROANOKE
VA 24012

Galax Music Club
Rt. 1
ELK CREEK
VA 24326

Clifton Forge Civic Music Club
Rt. 1, Box 215
MILLBORO
VA 24460

Les Cantatrices
1704 Warner Ave.
MC LEAN
VA 22101

Caroline Music Club
Box 423
BOWLING GREEN
VA 22427

Scherzo Music Club
6425 Drew Dr.
VIRGINIA BEACH
VA 23464

Portsmouth Music Study Club
5009 Garner Ave.
PORTSMOUTH
VA 23703

Thursday Morning Music Club
2644 Willowlawn St.
ROANOKE
VA 24018

Oak Hill Academy Music Dept.
MOUTH OF WILSON
VA 24363

Piedmont Music Club
8301 Claremont St.
MANASSAS
VA 22110

Rappahannock Music Study Club
Box 372
WHITE STONE
VA 22578

Richmond Music Study Club
9 South Dooley Ave.
RICHMOND
VA 23221

Governor's Magnet School for the Arts
P.O. Box 1357
NORFOLK
VA 23501

Franklin Music Study Club
405 West Second Ave.
FRANKLIN
VA 23851

Big Stone Gap Music Study Club
213 East 1st St.
BIG STONE GAP
VA 24219

Mac Dowell Music Club
Rt. 1, Box 4
RURAL RETREAT
VA 24368

Tazewell Music Club
Box 838
TAZEWELL
VA 24651

Northern Virginia Music Teachers' Assoc.
13720 Penwith Ct.
CHANTILLY
VA 22021

Springfield Music Club
700 N. Naylor St.
ALEXANDRIA
VA 22304

Front Royal Music Study Club
10 S. Charles St.
FRONT ROYAL
VA 22630

Thoroughgood Music Club
4816 Haygood Point Rd.
VIRGINIA BEACH
VA 23455

Cradock Music Club
Box 2118
PORTSMOUTH
VA 23702

South Hill Music Club
611 Raleigh Ave.
SOUTH HILL
VA 23970

Pulaski Music Club
Rt. 1, Box 184 G-7
DRAPER
VA 24324

Annabell Morris Buchanan Music Club of Smyth Co.
Rt. 1, Box 156A
SUGAR GROVE
VA 24375

Lynchburg Music Teachers' Assoc.
156 Norfolk Ave.
LYNCHBURG
VA 24503

WASHINGTON
Seattle Musical Arts Society
5543 37th Ave. NE
SEATTLE
WA 98105

Bremerton-Kitsap Youth Symphony
1113 6th St.
BREMERTON
WA 98310

Shelton Music Club
P.O. Box 66
SHELTON
WA 98584

Seattle Youth Symphony Orchestra
11065 Fifth NE, Suite #E
SEATTLE
WA 98125

Bowling Piano Studio
7216 Chico Way NW
BREMERTON
WA 98312

Ellensburg Music Study Club
Rt. 6, Box 145
ELLENSBURG
WA 98926

Music Study Club of Seattle
1403 NW 195th
SEATTLE
WA 98177

Bremerton Ladies' Chorale
15481 Clear Creek Rd. NE
POULSBO
WA 98370

Edmonds Music and Art Club
19518 94th Pl. W.
EDMONDS
WA 98020

Bellingham Women's Music Club
1612 Lakeway Dr.
BELLINGHAM
WA 98225

Capital Music Club
1331 E. 4th Ave.
OLYMPIA
WA 98501

WEST VIRGINIA
Chaminade Music Club
525 Lilly Dr.
BECKLEY
WV 25801

Crescendo Music Club
242 South Heber St.
BECKLEY
WV 25801

Monday Music Club
104 Phill Ave.
BECKLEY
WV 25801

Flippin School of Dance
P.O. Box 8024
HUNTINGTON
WV 25705

WISCONSIN

Oconomowoc Music Club
422 E. Greenland Ave.
OCONOMOWOC
WI 53066

Delta Omicron
1075 Wilson Dr.
BROOKFIELD
WI 53005

Kenosha Schubert Club
8051 25th Ave.
KENOSHA
WI 53140

Janesville McDowell Music Club
232 S. Pontiac Dr.
JANESVILLE
WI 53545

Galesville Music Study Club
Rt. 2, Box 389
GALESVILLE
WI 54630

Harmony Club
1432 N. 120th St.
WAUWATOSA
WI 53224

Milwaukee Music Teachers' Assoc.
N. 90 W. 16819 Roosevelt Dr.
MENOMONEE FALLS
WI 53051

Carthage College Music Dept.
KENOSHA
WI 53141

Civic Music Assoc.
1630 E. Royall Pl.
MILWAUKEE
WI 53202

Madison Federated Music Club
702 Anthony Ln.
MADISON
WI 53711

Monomonie Music Study Club
RR 2, Box 108
ELMWOOD
WI 54740

Wauwatosa Music Club
2550 N. 67th
WAUWATOSA
WI 53213

Treble Clef
1918 Prairie Ave.
BELOIT
WI 53511

Baraboo Federated Music Club
Rt. 4, Box 278B
BARABOO
WI 53913

Sheboygan Music Club
2743 N. 12th St.
SHEBOYGAN
WI 53081

Mac Fadyen Music Club
3715 N. 50th
MILWAUKEE
WI 53216

Fine Arts Club
326 S. Wisconsin
JANESVILLE
WI 53545

Peninsula Arts Festival
10990 S. Sand Bay Ln.
SISTER BAY
WI 54234

Cumberland Federated Music Club
Box 838
CUMBERLAND
WI 54829

Ashland Wednesday Music Club
1423 9th Ave. N.
ASHLAND
WI 54806

Barron Federated Music Club
RFD #1
BARRON
WI 54812

WYOMING

Octavo Music Club
Box 35
CHUGWATER
WY 82210

Friends of Music
Rt. 1, Box 390
TORRINGTON
WY 82240

Cheyenne Music Study Club
1844 Milton Dr.
CHEYENNE
WY 82001

Thermopolis Music Study Club
105 Cedar Ridge
THERMOPOLIS
WY 82443

Cheyenne Staff and Clef
7014 Bomar Dr.
CHEYENNE
WY 82009

Buffalo Music Study Club
Box 86
BUFFALO
WY 82834

Discography of the Women Composers

Preface

In this day and age it would appear that a composer may be said to have "arrived" if his or her compositions have been commercially recorded on discs and a claim to fame would seem to be proportionate to the number of their recorded compositions. Judging from the names of the composers and the quantity of records listed under them in the standard catalogues, this would seem in some way to be true, but in the realm of concert or art music, the odds are always greater against the recording of women's compositions.

Contrary to general masculine thought, there is a wealth of very good material available for recording, and it is the author's belief that there are a large number of women's works available that are as good as any and better than many of the men's compositions of the last twenty years. This may seem to be a sweeping statement, but when one considers the outpourings of tens of thousands of men composers it is surprising that so few, comparatively, find their way to the turntable, other than the standard composers and their standard compositions.

The total number of women composers listed in the discography is five hundred and seventy seven. There are still a number about whose recordings no information was available at the time of going to press. A few composers appear in the discography who are not mentioned in the general biographies. This is due to the fact that their information was received after the first half of this book had gone to press. These new composers are designated by a triple x (xxx) following their name.

Almost all of the records listed (nearly 2800 titles) are available commercially, and the coverage is of LP and EP records only. As far as 78's or acoustic records are concerned, there was no point in listing them at all. Not only were most of them unobtainable, but those that were available were re-recorded under LP labels. Any listing therefore would be purely academic and of no practical value in a work that sets itself out to make the music of women more accessible. Open reels and cassettes have also been excluded.

It will be noted that in some instances the titles of the works differ slightly from those appearing in the relative biographies. This is probably due to the musician's license exhibited by the performers or producers, and it is rarely that they give the musical key signatures or opus numbers. Most of these records are not listed in the standard catalogues like Schwann, The Gramophone, Diapason, or Bielefelder, since it is rare that the output of the small companies merits even a mention in the standard catalogues. Nevertheless it is gratifying to note that more and more record companies are beginning to record the works of women composers, and certain musicians, especially pianists, are devoting whole albums to the works of these composers.

All record labels have been coded and these acronyms have been alphabetically tabulated with the names of the record companies and their addresses. Since a number of these addresses were not available at the time of going to press, the receipt of any information to complete the list would be much appreciated. Sometimes, however, the names of distributing companies have been given. A number of recordings have not been listed owing to the paucity of information supplied by composers themselves and other sources. However, the records have been listed as long as the titles and the record labels are known. It is hoped that the missing information will be supplied by the record companies or by interested persons and readers to be included in a later edition.

Due to space limitations, re-issues of the same recording have generally been omitted, except where the same recording has been issued under different labels and numbers, subsequent to their release in different countries. Some women have composed and recorded both classical and 'pop' music, but only the recordings of the classical/art music have been listed.

It frequently happens that recordings of the better known composers are published by different companies under their own particular labels. These are all separately listed. But sometimes a record company will change the label of an existing recording with no change in the numbering. Confusion also arises when an album consists of several records of which the woman composer is featured on only one of them. The listing is of the record number and not of the album number. Re-issues are sometimes given different numbers, but the listing is only of the original number. A source of great irritation occurs when an advance notice is given of a new recording. The work etc. is specified, likewise the number of the recording. But when the record is finally issued some months later, it has been found that the record number is quite different. This has occurred several times especially among the smaller companies.

It is the editor's sincere hope that this discography will not only add to the repertoire of the performing musicians, but will also encourage the record companies, the musicians, and the program directors and conductors to be a little more adventurous than they have been up to now.

Recordings

AARNE, Els (1917-   )

ARRIVAL OF SPRING
  E. Maazik (S.)
  **MELOD
  D 00017865/6**

GUESS WHO WE ARE
  G. Ots (Bar.), E. Aarne (pf.)
  **MELOD
  D 3956/7**

ABEJO, Sister M. Rosalina S.F.C.C. (1922-   )

FILIPINA 'IMELDA', LA (MARIMBA AND ORCHESTRA)
  Petra Molas (mar.) with Philippine Symphony
    Orchestra
  (cond.) Sister M. Rosalina Abejo
  SRA 001

GUERILLA SYMPHONY, THE
  Philippine Symphony Orchestra
  (cond.) Sister M. Rosalina Abejo
  SRA 001

HATING GABING TAHIMIK
  Sisters' Concert Chorus
  SRA 005

LARAWAN (SONG-CYCLE)
  Fides Santos Cuyugan Asensio (vce.) with
  Philippine Symphony Orchestra
  (cond.) Sister M. Rosalina Abejo
  SRA 003

LEYTE CHIMES
  Bill Guerrerro (gtr.) with Philippine Symphony
    Orchestra
  (cond.) Sister M. Rosalina Abejo
  SRA 003

MALACANANG GARDENS
  Bill Guerrerro (gtr.) with Philippine Symphony
    Orchestra
  (cond.) Sister M. Rosalina Abejo
  SRA 003

MANILA MEMORIES
  Bill Guerrerro (gtr.) with Philippine Symphony
    Orchestra
  (cond.) Sister M. Rosalina Abejo
  SRA 003

ODE TO A STATESMAN
  Philippine Symphony Orchestra
  (cond.) Sister M. Rosalina Abejo
  SRA 002

ORATORIO PAGTUTUBOS
  Soloists and combined choruses with Philippine
    Symphony Orchestra
  (cond.) Sister M. Rosalina Abejo
  SRA 004

OVERTURE 1081
  Philippine Symphony Orchestra
  (cond.) Sister M. Rosalina Abejo
  SRA 002

TIME UNYIELDING
  Roda Pepito (vce.) with Philippine
  Symphony Orchestra
  (cond.) Sister M. Rosalina Abejo
  SRA 003

VILLANCICO FILIPINO
  Sisters' Concert Chorus
  SRA 005

ADAM, Margie (-   )

NAKED KEYS
  * * * * * *
  PLEID - - -

ADERHOLDT, Sarah (1955-   )

STRING QUARTET
  Crescent Quartet: Alicia Edelberg, Nancy
  Diggs, Jill Jaffe, Maxine Neumann
  LEONA LPI 111

AIN, Noa (1941-   )

USED TO CALL ME SADNESS
  (A PORTRAIT OF YOKO MATSUA)
  Yoko Matsua (vln.)
  **FOLKW
  FTS 33904**

AKHUNDOVA, Shafiga Gulam kyzy (1924-   )

SKALA NEVEST (OPERA HIGHLIGHTS)
  Soloists with Choir and Azerbaijanian
  State Theatre Opera Orchestra
  (cond.) Rauf Abdullayev
  **MELOD
  C 10 14999**

ALCALAY, Luna (1928-   )

PLATITUDES EN OCCASION FOR VOCALISTS,
  STRING QUINTET AND PERCUSSION
  Pro-Arte-Ensemble, Graz
  (cond.) Karl Ernst Hoffmann
  ORF 0120064

ALEXANDRA, Liana (1947-   )

COLAJE PENTRU CVINTET DE ALAMURI
  Armonia Quintet
  **ELECT
  ST ECE 01545**

INCANTATIONS II
  Gaudeamus String Quartet
  **ELECT
  ST ECE 01694**

SINFONIA NO. 1 (RITMI CONTEMPORANE) (1985)
Banatul din Timisoara Symphony Orchestra
(cond.) Remus Georgescu — **ELECT STCS 0194**

SONATA PENTRU FLAUT SOLO
Voicu Vasinca (fl.) — **ELECT ST ECE 01459**

SYMPHONY NO. 2 (ANTHEMS)
Rumanian RTV Symphony Orchestra
(cond.) Iosif Conta — **ELECT ST ECE 02183**

SYMPHONY NO. 3 (DIACRONICS)
Rumanian RTV Symphony Orchestra
(cond.) Liviu Ionescu — **ELECT ST ECE 02183**

ALLAN, Esther (1914-)

AUTUMN NOCTURNE
Esther Allan (pf.), Elyze Yockey Ilku (hp.) — **NORET 09100**

BETHIE'S THEME
Esther Allan (pf.) with Detroit Sinfonietta
(cond.) Felix Resnick — **NORET 30221**

ENCHANTMENT
Esther Allan (pf.) with Detroit Sinfonietta
(cond.) Felix Resnick — **NORET 30221**

FREDDIE'S RUNNING
Esther Allan (pf.) with Detroit Sinfonietta
(cond.) Felix Resnick — **NORET 30221**

INTERLUDE
Esther Allan (pf.) with Detroit Sinfonietta
(cond.) Felix Resnick — **NORET 30221**

KAREN'S BUTTERFLIES
Esther Allan (pf.) — **NORET 09100**

MEDITATION
Esther Allan (pf.) with Detroit Sinfonietta
(cond.) Felix Resnick — **NORET 09100**

NANCY'S WALTZ
Esther Allan (pf.) — **NORET 09100**

NORMAN CONCERTO
Esther Allan (pf.) with Detroit Sinfonietta
(cond.) Felix Resnick — **NORET 09100**

OCEAN RHAPSODY
Esther Allan (pf.) with Detroit Sinfonietta
(cond.) Felix Resnick — **NORET 09100**

ROMANTIC CONCERTO
Esther Allan (pf.) with Detroit Sinfonietta
(cond.) Felix Resnick — **NORET 09100**

SUMMER WALTZ
Esther Allan (pf.) with Detroit Sinfonietta
(cond.) Felix Resnick — **NORET 30221**

TRAILING
Esther Allan (pf.) with Detroit Sinfonietta
(cond.) Felix Resnick — **NORET 30221**

ALLEN, Judith Shatin (1949-)

WIND SONGS FOR WIND QUINTET (1980)
Clarion Wind Quintet — **OPONE 87**

ANDERSON, Beth (1950-)

I CAN'T STAND IT
Beth Anderson (S.), Warton Tiers (perc.) — **BETHA 45**

I CAN'T STAND IT
Beth Anderson (S.) — **WIDEM 8619**

IF I WERE A POET
Beth Anderson (S.) — **WIDEM 8619**

OCEAN MOTION MILDEW MIND
Beth Anderson (S.), Warton Tiers (perc.) — **BETHA 45**

ODE, AN AMERICAN SONG
Beth Anderson (S.) — **WIDEM 8619**

PEOPLE RUMBLE LOUDER THAN
THE POET SPEAKER, THE
Beth Anderson (S.) — **WIDEM 8619**

PREPARATION FOR THE DOMINANT
Beth Anderson (S.) — **WIDEM 8619**

SHAKUHACHI RUN
* * * * * * — **WIDEM 8619**

TORERO PIECE (1973)
Beth Anderson, Marjorie Celeste Anderson — **ARCH 1752**

YES SIR REE
Beth Anderson (S.) — **WIDEM 8619**

ANDERSON, Laurie (1947-)

BLUE LAGOON (7'03)
Laurie Anderson with Ensemble — **WARNE 25077**

BORN, NEVER ASKED (FROM
UNITED STATES PART I) (4'30)
Farisa, handclaps, violin, marimba — **GIORN GPS 020/1**

CLOSED CIRCUITS (FROM
UNITED STATES PART I) (7'26)
For microphone turned through
harmonizer and woodblock — **GIORN GPS 020/1**

DR. MILLER (WITH PERRY HOBERMAN)
Laurie Anderson (syn. and perc.),
Perry Hoberman (sax.) — **GIORN GPS 020/1**

DRUMS (FROM UNITED STATES PART II) (0'30)
Wharton Tiers (dr.) — **GIORN GPS 020/1**

EXCELLENT BIRDS (3'12)
Laurie Anderson with Ensemble — **WARNE 25077**

FOR ELECTRONIC DOGS
(FROM UNITED STATES PART II)
Laurie Anderson (vln. and elects.),
Wharton Tiers (dr.) — **GIORN GPS 020/1**

GRAVITY'S ANGEL (6'02)
Laurie Anderson with Ensemble — **WARNE 25077**

HOME OF THE BRAVE (FILM)
* * * * * * — **WARNE 25400 1**

IT WAS UP IN THE MOUNTAINS (2'49)
Narrator — **GIORN GPS 020/1**

KOKOKU (7'03)
Laurie Anderson with Ensemble — **WARNE 25077**

LANGUE D'AMOUR (6'12)
Laurie Anderson with Ensemble — **WARNE 25077**

MISTER HEARTBREAK
Laurie Anderson with Ensemble — **WARNE 25077**

NEW YORK SOCIAL LIFE (1977)
Laurie Anderson (vce. and telephone),
Scott Johnson (tamboura) — **ARCH S 1765**

SHARKEY'S DAY (7'41)
Laurie Anderson with Ensemble — **WARNE 25077**

SHARKEY'S NIGHT (2'29)
Laurie Anderson with Ensemble — **WARNE 25077**

STRUCTURALIST FILM-MAKING (FROM
DARK DOGS, AMERICAN DREAMS)
Giorno Poetry Systems Institute — **GIORN GPS 020/1**

TIME TO GO (FOR DIEGO, 1977)
Laurie Anderson (vce. and vln.),
Scott Johnson (gtr. and org.) — **ARCH S 1765**

ANDERSON, Ruth (1928-   )

DUMP (1970)
Electronically Derived Tape Collage   **OPONE 70**

I COME OUT OF YOUR SLEEP (1979)
Electronically Derived Sounds   **OPONE 63**

POINTS (1973-74)
Hunter College Electronic Music Studio   **ARCH S 1765**

SUM (STATE OF THE UNION MESSAGE) (1975)
Electronically Derived Tape Collage   **OPONE 70**

ANDREE, Elfrida (1841-1929)

I TEMPLET
Ola Waessman (S.)   **HR 4002**

ORGAN SYMPHONY IN B-MINOR (17'5)
Gotthard Arner (org.)   **PROPR 7848**

QUINTET IN E-MINOR (not E-major as shown on label)
(ALLEGRO MOLTO VIVACE)   **GEMIN**
Michael May (pf.) with Vieuxtemps Quartet   **RAP 1010**

SYMPHONY NO. 2
Olle Johansson (T.) with Musikhoegskolans
Brass Ensemble
(cond.) John Eriksson   **URIEL LP 7**

ANIDO, Maria Luisa (1909-   )

ARGENTINE MELODY   **MELOD**
V. Shirokov (gtr.)   **SM 03737/8**

DANCE OF THE NORTH ARGENTINE INDIANS   **MELOD**
V. Shirokov (gtr.)   **SM 03737/8**

SONGS OF YUCATAN   **MELOD**
V. Shirokov (gtr.)   **C 20 07889/90**

ANNA AMALIA, Duchess of Saxe-Weimar (1739-1807)

AUF DEM LAND UND IN DER STADT (1'54)
Dietrich Fischer-Dieskau (Bar.),   **ARCIV**
Jorg Demus (pf.)   **DGG 2533 149**

CONCERTO FOR TWELVE INSTRUMENTS AND
CEMBALO OBBLIGATO
Vienna Chamber Orchestra
(cond.) K. Rapf   **TURNA 34754**

DIVERTIMENTO FOR PIANO AND STRINGS
Rosario Marciano (pf.) with Vienna
Chamber Orchestra
(cond.) K. Rapf   **TURNA 34754**

ERWIN UND ELMIRE (SELECTION)
Berenice Bramson (S.) with Instrumental
Accompaniment   **GEMIN RAP 1010**

SIE SCHEINEN ZU SPIELEN
Dietrich Fischer-Dieskau (Bar.),
Jorg Demus (pf.)   **ARCIV DGG 2533 149**

ANNA AMALIA, Princess of Prussia (1723-1787)

MARCH FOR THE REGIMENT OF GENERAL
VON BUELOW
Thomas Theis (d-b.) with Vieuxtemps
Quartet   **GEMIN RAP 1010**

MARCH FOR THE REGIMENT OF
GENERAL VON SALDERN
Thomas Theis (d-b.) with Vieuxtemps
Quartet   **GEMIN RAP 1010**

MARCH FOR THE REGIMENT,
GRAF LOTTUM
Thomas Theis (d-b.) with Vieuxtemps
Quartet   **GEMIN RAP 1010**

REGIMENTAL MARCH: GENERAL
VON BUELOW
Austrian Tonkünstler Orchestra
(cond.) Dietfried Bernet   **MUHER MHS 660**

REGIMENTAL MARCH: GENERAL
VON MOLLENDORF
Austrian Tonkünstler Orchestra
(cond.) Dietfried Bernet   **MUHER MHS 660**

REGIMENTAL MARCH: GENERAL
VON SALDERN
Austrian Tonkünstler Orchestra
(cond.) Dietfried Bernet   **MUHER MHS 660**

REGIMENTAL MARCH: GRAF LOTTUM
Austrian Tonkünstler Orchestra
(cond.) Dietfried Bernet   **MUHER MHS 660**

ARBUCKLE, Dorothy M. (1910-   )

TALL CATHEDRAL WINDOWS, THE,
FOR WOMEN'S CHORUS
* * * * * *   **TROPI 202**

ARCHER, Violet Balestreri (1913-   )

APRIL WEATHER, FOR MEZZO AND PIANO
* * * * * *   **CBC RCI 108**

BELL, THE (MIXED CHORUS AND ORCHESTRA)
Montreal Bach Choir
(cond.) George Little   **CBC RCI 130**

CALEIDOSCOPIO (9'13)
Roxolana Roslak (S.), William Aide (pf.)   **CENTR CMC 1183**

CHORALE IMPROVISATION ON
"O WORSHIP THE KING"
Hugh Bancroft (org.)   **ASCED ST 56722/23**

CHRISTMAS
Ruth Henderson (pf.), Ann-Elise Keefer (fl.)
with Toronto Children's Chorus
(cond.) Jean Ashworth Bartle   **TCC D 003**

CRADLE SONG (MEZZO-SOPRANO
AND PIANOFORTE)
* * * * * *   **CBC RCI 108**

DIVERTIMENTO, FOR OBOE,
CLARINET AND BASSOON
* * * * * *   **CBC RCI 192**

ELEVEN SHORT PIANO PIECES
(NOS. 3, 4, 5, 6, 7 AND 9 ONLY)
* * * * * *   **CCM 1**

EPISODES
Bick (elec.)   **MELBO SMLP 4024**

FANFARE AND PASSACAGLIA,
FOR ORCHESTRA
* * * * * *   **CBC RCI 130**

IMPROVISATIONS FOR PIANO
Antonin Kubalek (pf.)   **MELBO SMLP 4031**

LANDSCAPES
* * * * * *   **CBC RCI 70**

LANDSCAPES (MIXED CHOIR)
* * * * * *   **CBC RCI 10**

LANDSCAPES (MIXED CHOIR)
Festival Singers of Canada
(cond.) E. Iseler   **CBC SM 274**

NORTHERN LANDSCAPES
Phyllis Mailing (m-S.), William Aide (pf.)　　　**CMC 1083**

O SING UNTO THE LORD
Gilbert Patenaude (org.), Didier Seutin (trp.)
with Les Petits Chanteurs de Mont
Royal Choir　　　**✱ ✱ ✱ SNE 528**

PRELUDE AND ALLERGO, FOR
VIOLIN AND PIANO
Arthur Leblanc (vln.), Herbert Ruff (pf.)　　　**CBC RCI 136**

PROUD HORSES (MIXED CHOIR)
✱ ✱ ✱ ✱ ✱ ✱　　　**CBC RCI 189**

SINFONIETTA
CBC Vancouver Chamber Orchestra
(cond.) John Avison　　　**CBC SM 226**

SONATA FOR ALTO SAXOPHONE AND PIANO
Paul Brodie (sax.), George Brough (pf.)　　　**CBC RCI 412**

SONATA FOR CELLO AND PIANO
Walter Joachim (vlc.), John Newmark (pf.)　　　**CBC RCI 139**

SONATA FOR CLARINET AND PIANO
James Campbell (cl.), Gloria Saarinen (pf.)　　　**CBC RCI 412**

SONATA FOR HORN AND PIANO
Pierre Del Vescovo (hn.), Armas Maiste (pf.)　　　**CBC RCI 412**

SONATA NO. 1, FOR VIOLIN AND PIANO
Charles Joseph (vln.), Digby Bell (pf.)　　　**CBC RCI 196**

SONATINA NO. 2
✱ ✱ ✱ ✱ ✱ ✱　　　**CBC RCI 132**

TEN FOLK SONGS (4 HANDS)
✱ ✱ ✱ ✱ ✱ ✱　　　**CBC RCI 113**

THEME AND VARIATIONS ON LA-HAUT　　　**CENTR**
Charles Foreman (pf.)　　　**CMC 1684**

THREE FRENCH CANADIAN FOLK SONGS　　　**TURNA**
✱ ✱ ✱ ✱ ✱ ✱　　　**CTC 32003**

THREE FRENCH CANADIAN FOLK SONGS
Montreal Bach Choir
(cond.) George Little　　　**VOX PL 11 860**

THREE MINIATURES FOR PIANO
✱ ✱ ✱ ✱ ✱ ✱　　　**CCM 1**

THREE SKETCHES FOR ORCHESTRA
Winnipeg Orchestra　　　**CBC**
(cond.) Eric Wild　　　**BR SM 119**

TRIO NO. 1, FOR VIOLIN, CELLO AND PIANO
Hyman Bress (vln.), Walter Joachim (vlc.),
John Newmark (pf.)　　　**CBC RCI 112**

TRIO NO. 2
Halifax Trio　　　**CBC RCI 241**

TRIO NO. 2, FOR PIANO, VIOLIN AND CELLO
Walter Balsam (pf.), Marc Gottlieb (vln.),
Irving Klein (vlc.)　　　**CBC BR SM 5**

TRIO NO. 2, FOR PIANO, VIOLIN AND CELLO
Walter Balsam (pf.), Marc Gottlieb (vln.),
Irving Klein (vlc.)　　　**CBC RCI 196**

TWENTY-THIRD PSALM, THE
(MEZZOSOPRANO AND PIANO)
✱ ✱ ✱ ✱ ✱ ✱　　　**CBC RCI 108**

UNDER THE SUN (SOPRANO AND PIANO)
✱ ✱ ✱ ✱ ✱ ✱　　　**CBC RCI 108**

ARCHILEI, Vittoria (1550-　　)

DALLE PIU ALTE SFERE
Linde Choeur de Chambre de Stockholm,　　　**EMI**
Linde Consort　　　**CO 63 30114/5**

ARETZ, Isabel (1909-　　)

MOVIMENTOS DE PERCUSION
(BALLET FOR 11 PERFORMERS AND
40 PERCUSSION INSTRUMENTS)
✱ ✱ ✱ ✱ ✱ ✱　　　**MTV LP 001**

POEMA ARAUCANO (SOPRANO AND
SMALL ORCHESTRA)
(cond.) L.F. Ramon Y Rivera　　　**RCAV P 1507**

ARIMA, Reiko (1933-　　)

AS BAROQUE FOSTER
✱ ✱ ✱ ✱ ✱ ✱　　　**COLUJ OS 10131 N**

CHILDREN'S YARD: BALLET OF THE SYLPHS
Kazuko Ina (pf.)　　　**VICTO SJV 1167**

CHILDREN'S YARD: PYGMY'S MARCH
Kazuko Ina (pf.)　　　**VICTO SJV 1167**

CHILDREN'S YARD: WHISTLING LEAVES
Kazuko Ina (pf.)　　　**VICTO SJV 1167**

FAIRY TALES, FOR PIANO DUET
✱ ✱ ✱ ✱ ✱ ✱　　　**COLUJ GS 7059**

FOUR SEASONS OF JAPAN
✱ ✱ ✱ ✱ ✱ ✱　　　**COLUJ OS 10101 N**

ARNIM, Bettina von (1785-1859)

O SCHAUDRE NICHT　　　**ARCIV**
D. Fischer-Dieskau (Bar.) Jorg Demus (pf.)　　　**DGG 2533 149**

ARRIEU, Claude (1903-　　)

BRAVE HOMME
Pierre Laurent　　　**CHDUM LD A 6006**

CHANSON DE LA COTE 1
Fabien Lorris　　　**CHDUM LD A 6006**

CHANSON DE LA PATIENCE
Jacques Douai　　　**BAM 20328**

CHANSON DE MAURICE
Jacques Douai　　　**BAM LD 370**

CHANSON DE PERLIMPIN
Claire Leclerc　　　**CHDUM 4031**

CHANSON DE PERLIMPIN
Catherine Sauvage　　　**PHILI B 77376 L**

CINQ MOUVEMENTS POUR
QUATOUR DE CLARINETTES (1969)
Quatuor de Clarinettes de Paris: G. Dort,
P. Dovillez, R. Bianciotto, M. Gizard　　　**CALLI CAL 1849**

COMPLAINTE DES GUEUX AUX PARADIS　　　**ADES**
Marc and Andre　　　**TS 30 LA 503**

DEPECHE-TOI DE RIRE
Jacques Douai　　　**BAM LD 354**

ESPECE DE COMPTINE
Aime Doniat　　　**VEGA L 30 PO 389**

FIACRE, UN
✱ ✱ ✱ ✱ ✱ ✱　　　**BAM LD 312**

FIVE MOVEMENTS FOR FOUR CLARINETS
Lutece Clarinet Quartet　　　**CYBEL 656**

MICHKA
✱ ✱ ✱ ✱ ✱ ✱　　　**DUCRE 460 V 426**

NATHALIE
Jacques Douai　　　**BAM LD 312**

ORGUE, L' (L'ALLEGRO HUIT)
* * * * * *
CHDUM LD A 6006

PAUVRE JEAN
* * * * * *
BAM LD 370

QU'AVEZ-VOUS VU, BERGERS?
(CHORUS A CAPELLA)
Chorale de Saulsure sur Liselotte
ODEON FOC 1022

QU'AVEZ-VOUS VU, BERGERS?
(CHORUS A CAPELLA)
Chorale de Provence
DISQU SM 3310

QUINTETTE IN C-MAJOR FOR FLUTE, OBOE,
CLARINET, BASSOON AND HORN
Soni Ventorum Wind Quintet
CRYST S 253

QUINTETTE IN C-MAJOR FOR FLUTE, OBOE,
CLARINET, BASSOON AND HORN
Quintette a Vent des Flandres
**EMI
C 065 12 116**

QUINTETTE IN C-MAJOR FOR FLUTE, OBOE,
CLARINET, BASSOON AND HORN
Quintette à Vent Français
OISEU 01 50122

ROI QUI NE POUVER PAS ETERNUER, LE
* * * * * *
DUCRE 460 V 427

TRIO FOR OBOE, CLARINET AND BASSOON
Soni Ventorum
CRYST S 254

TRIO POUR PIPEAUX
A. Berge, M. Ene, J. Burel
ERATO LDE 1076

TROIS CHANSONS DE CHARLES CROS
* * * * * *
CHDUM LD A 6006

AUFDERHEIDE, May (-   )

PELHAM WALTZES (ARR. MORATH)
Morath (pf.)
VANGR VSD 79429

AURENHAMMER, Josefa Barbara von (1758-1820)
SONATE A-DUR FUER KLAVIER
EMI

Werner Genuit (pf.)
IC 187 28 836/39

AUSTER, Lydia Martinovna (1912-   )

AUTUMN IN TALLIN
V. Gurev (T.)
MELOD D 0009553/4

CONCERTO IN G, FOR PIANO AND ORCHESTRA
K. Sepp (pf.) with Estonian State
Symphony Orchestra
(cond.) Neeme Jarvi
**MELOD
D 0205 77/8**

CONCERTO IN G, FOR PIANO AND ORCHESTRA
Arbo Valdma (pf.) with Estonian State
Symphony Orchestra
(cond.) Neeme Jarvi
**MELOD
C 10 08797/8**

LENTO
A. Klas, B. Lukk (pf. duet)
MELOD D 5480/1

NORTHERN DREAM, A (SERVERNI SON)
EXCERPTS FROM THE BALLET
Estonian State Symphony Orchestra
(cond.) Neeme Jarvi
**MELOD
D 9555/6**

ROMEO, JULIET AND DARKNESS, EXCERPTS
FROM THE BALLET
Estonian State Symphony Orchestra
(cond.) Neeme Jarvi
**MELOD
C 10 08797/8**

TIINA, EXCERPTS FROM THE BALLET
Estonian State Symphony Orchestra
(cond.) Neeme Jarvi
**MELOD
C 10 08797 8**

TIINA, EXCERPTS FROM THE BALLET
Estonian State Symphony Orchestra
(cond.) Raudsepp
**MELOD
D 3926/27**

TIINA, MONOLOGUE
Estonian State Symphony Orchestra
(cond.) Raudsepp
**MELOD
D 15719 20**

TIINA, THREE DANCES FROM THE BALLET
* * * * * *
RIGA 28 4888/9

TIINA, TWO PIECES FROM THE BALLET
Livontas (vln.)
**MELOD
D 23563/4**

AUTENRIETH, Helma (1896-   )

JUBILEUM VARIATIONS ON AN
ORIGINAL THEME, FOR TWO PIANOS
Richard Laugs (pf.), Katya Laugs (pf.)
DACAM SM 93127

PIANO SONATA (1967)
Richard Laugs (pf.)
DACAM SM 93127

SONATA FOR TWO CELLOS AND PIANO
Hans Adomeit (vlc.),
Margaret Gutbrod (vlc.),
Richard Laugs (pf.)
DACAM SM 93127

SUITE FOR PIANO
Richard Laugs (pf.)
DACAM SM 93127

AZALAIS DE PORCAIRAGUES (-1140)

AR EM AL FREG TEMPS VENTENT FOR
SOPRANO, NARRATOR, VIELE,
DULCIMER, REBEC AND DRUM
Clemencic Consort
HARMU HM 397

BACEWICZ, Grazyna (1909-1969)

CAPRICES, NO. 2 (1968)
Jenny Abel (vln.)
CONAS CON POD 3

CONCERTO FOR ORCHESTRA
Warsaw National Philharmonic
Symphony Orchestra
(cond.) Witold Rowicki
MUZA SX 0274

CONCERTO FOR STRING ORCHESTRA
Polish Radio Chamber Orchestra
(cond.) Jerzy Maksymiuk
MUZA SXL 1256

CONCERTO FOR STRING ORCHESTRA
Polish Radio Chamber Orchestra
(cond.) Jan Krenz
MUZA SXL 0274

CONCERTO FOR STRING ORCHESTRA
Polish Radio Chamber Orchestra
(cond.) Jan Krenz
MUZA L 0010

CONCERTO FOR TWO PIANOS
AND ORCHESTRA
Jerzy Maksymiuk (pf.), Jerzy Witkowski (pf.)
with Warsaw National Philharmonic
Symphony Orchestra
(cond.) Stanislaw Wislocki
MUZA SXL 0875

CONCERTO FOR VIOLA AND ORCHESTRA
Stefan Kamasa (vla.) with
Warsaw National Philharmonic
Symphony Orchestra
(cond.) Stanislaw Wislocki
MUZA SXL 0875

CONCERTO NO. 2, FOR CELLO
AND ORCHESTRA
Gaspar Cassado (vlc.) with Warsaw
National Philharmonic Orchestra
(cond.) W. Krzemienski
MUZA W 877/8

CONCERTO NO. 7, FOR VIOLIN
AND ORCHESTRA
Piotr Janowski (vln.) with Warsaw
National Philharmonic Orchestra
(cond.) Andrzej Markowski **MUZA M 3XW 1183**

CONTRADIZIONE FOR CHAMBER
ORCHESTRA
Warsaw National Philharmonic
Symphony Orchestra
(cond.) Witold Rowicki **MUZA M 3XW 890/1**

DIVERTIMENTO, FOR STRINGS
Warsaw Philharmonic Chamber
Orchestra (cond.) K. Teutsch **MUZA SXL 0586**

ESQUISSE FOR ORGAN
Jean Guillou (org.) **PHILI S 6504 039**

IN UNA PARTE FOR ORCHESTRA
Warsaw National Philharmonic
Symphony Orchestra
(cond.) Stanislaw Wislocki **MUZA SXL 0875**

KLEINES TRIPTYCHON
Rosario Marciano (pf.) **FONO FSM 53 0 36**

MUSIC FOR STRINGS, TRUMPETS
AND PERCUSSION
USSR String Orchestra
(cond.) Anosov **MELOD D 013193/6**

MUSIC FOR STRINGS, TRUMPETS
AND PERCUSSION
Polish Radio Orchestra
(cond.) Jan Krenz **MUZA XW 567**

MUSIC FOR STRINGS, TRUMPETS
AND PERCUSSION
Polish Radio Orchestra
(cond.) Jan Krenz **MUZA W 614**

MUSIC FOR STRINGS, TRUMPETS
AND PERCUSSION
Warsaw National Philharmonic
Symphony Orchestra
(cond.) Witold Rowicki **PHILI 839 260**

MUSIC FOR STRINGS, TRUMPETS
AND PERCUSSION
Warsaw National Philharmonic
Symphony Orchestra
(cond.) Witold Rowicki **MUZA SXL 0171**

MUSICA SINFONICA IN TRE MOVIMENTI
Warsaw National Philharmonic
Symphony Orchestra
(cond.) Witold Rowicki **MUZA SX 0274**

NO. 2 AND NO. 8, FROM TEN
CONCERT STUDIES
Virginia Eskin (pf.) **MUHER MHS 4236**

OBEREK, FOR VIOLIN AND PIANO
Kaja Danczowska (vln.), Janusz
Olejniczak (pf.) **VIFON LP 055 PRITV**

OVERTURE
Warsaw National Philharmonic
Symphony Orchestra
(cond.) Witold Rowicki **MUZA SX 0274**

PENSIERI NOTTURNI FOR CHAMBER
ORCHESTRA
Warsaw National Philharmonic
Symphony Orchestra
(cond.) Witold Rowicki **MUZA SX 0274**

PETIT TRIPTYQUE FOR PIANO
Rosario Marciano (pf.) **TURNA TV 34685**

PETIT TRIPTYQUE FOR PIANO
Regina Smendzianka (pf.) **MUZA SXL 0977**

PIANO QUINTET, NO. 1
Warsaw Piano Quintet **MUZA SXL 0608**

PIANO QUINTET, NO. 2
Warsaw Piano Quintet **MUZA SXL 0608**

PIANO SONATA, NO. 2
K. Zimmerman (pf.) **MUZA SX 1510**

PIANO SONATA, NO. 2
Nancy Fierro (pf.) **AVANT AV 1012**

PIANO SONATA, NO. 2
Regina Smendzianka (pf.) **MUZA SXL 0977**

POLISH CAPRICE (1950)
Jenny Abel (vln.) **CONAS CON POD 3**

QUARTET NO. 3, FOR STRINGS
Wilanow String Quartet **MUZA SX 1597**

QUARTET NO. 4, FOR STRINGS
Parrenin Quartet **MUZA W 180**

QUARTET NO. 4, FOR STRINGS
Grazyna Bacewicz with
Warsaw String Quartet **MUZA SX 1598**

QUARTET NO. 5, FOR STRINGS
Wilanow String Quartet **MUZA SX 1597**

QUARTET NO. 6, FOR STRINGS
Parrenin Quartet **MUZA W 679**

QUARTET NO. 7, FOR STRINGS
Grazyna Bacewicz with
Warsaw String Quartet **MUZA SX 1598**

QUARTET NO. 7, FOR STRINGS
Bulgarian Quartet **MUHER MHS 1889**

QUARTET NO. 7, FOR STRINGS
Dimov Quartet **MUZA XW 716**

QUARTET NO. 7, FOR STRINGS
Bulgarian Quartet **HARMU HMO 34708**

QUARTET, FOR FOUR CELLI
A. Ciechanski (vlc.), J. Weslawski (vlc.),
R. Suchecki (vlc.), M. Raczak (vlc.) **MUZA W 969**

SELECTION OF SHORT VIOLIN PIECES
* * * * * * **MUZA 82870/1**

SELECTION OF SHORT VIOLIN PIECES
* * * * * * **MUZA ZND 2892/3**

SONATA FOR VIOLIN SOLO (1958)
Jenny Abel (vln.) **CONAS CON POD 3**

SONATA NO. 4, FOR VIOLIN AND PIANO
Edward Statkiewicz (vln.),
Aleksandra Utrecht (pf.) **MUZA SXL 0505**

SONATA NO. 4, FOR VIOLIN AND PIANO
Grazyna Bacewicz (vln.),
Kieistut Bacewicz (pf.) **MUZA XL 0033**

TEN CONCERT STUDIES
Regina Smendzianka (pf.) **MUZA SXL 0977**

TRIPTYCH, FOR PIANO
Virginia Eskin (pf.) **MUHER MHS 4236**

BACKER-GROENDAHL, Agathe Ursula (1847-1907)

BALLADE B-MOLL, OP. 36, NO. 5 (1895)
(B-FLAT MAJOR)
Liv Glaser (pf.) **NCC NKF 30 008**

EIN VOGEL SCHRIE, OP. 31
(VILHELM KRAG) (1'47)
Tuula Nienstedt (Cont.), Uwe Wegner (pf.) **MUSVI MV 30 1104**

ETUDE DE CONCERT,
A-MINOR, OP. 11, NO. 6
Doris Pines (pf.) **GENES GS 1024**

ETUDE DE CONCERT,
D-FLAT MAJOR, OP. 11, NO. 2
Doris Pines (pf.) **GENES GS 1024**

FANTASY PIECES, OP. 36
    (AFTONVIND: ALVALEK)
    Stig Ribbing (pf.)   ★ ★ ★ **7 C 137 35736 9**

FANTASY PIECES, OP. 45 (SOMMARISA)
    Stig Ribbing (pf.)   ★ ★ ★ **7 C 137 35736 9**

FOUR SKIZZER, OP. 19
    Doris Pines (pf.)   **GENES GS 1024**

FUENF LIEDER NACH GEDICHTEN
    VON VILHELM KRAG, OP. 31
    Tuula Nienstedt (Cont.),
    Uwe Wegner (pf.)   **MUSVI MV 30 1104**

HUMORESKE, G MINOR, OP. 15, NO. 3
    Doris Pines (pf.)   **GENES GS 1024**

I BLAFJELLET, EVENTYRSUITE I
    6 KLAVERSTYKKER, OP. 44 (1894)
    Liv Glaser (pf.)   **NCC NKF 30 008**

KONSERTETYDE A-MOLL, OP. 57,
    NO. 1 (1903)
    Doris Pines (pf.)   **GENES GS 1024**

KONSERTETYDE A-MOLL, OP. 57,
    NO. 1 (1903)
    Liv Glaser (pf.)   **NCC NKF 30 008**

KONSERTETYDE B-MOLL, OP. 11,
    NO. 1 (1881)
    Doris Pines (pf.)   **GENES GS 1024**

KONSERTETYDE B-MOLL, OP. 11,
    NO. 1 (1881)
    Liv Glaser (pf.)   **NCC NKF 30 008**

KONSERTETYDE G-MOLL, OP. 11,
    NO. 3 (1881)
    Liv Glaser (pf.)   **NCC NKF 30 008**

KONSERTETYDE G-MOLL, OP. 58,
    NO. 2 (1903)
    Liv Glaser (pf.)   **NCC NKF 30 008**

MEERESNACHT, OP. 31,
    (VILHELM KRAG) (2'05)
    Tuula Nienstedt (Cont.),
    Uwe Wegner (pf.)   **MUSVI MV 30 1104**

PAA BALLET, D-FLAT MAJOR,
    OP. 15, NO. 2
    Doris Pines (pf.)   **GENES GS 1024**

ROSERNES SANG, OP. 39, NO. 4 (1896)
    Liv Glaser (pf.)   **NCC NKF 30 008**

SCHWANE DER MADONNA, DIE,
    OP. 1, (VILHELM KRAG) (3'48)
    Tuula Nienstedt (Cont.),
    Uwe Wegner (pf.)   **MUSVI MV 30 1104**

SERENADE, F-MAJOR, OP. 15, NO. 1 (1882)
    Doris Pines (pf.)   **GENES GS 1024**

SERENADE, F-MAJOR, OP. 15, NO. 1 (1882)
    Liv Glaser (pf.)   **NCC NKF 30 008**

SEVENTEEN SONGS
    Kari Frisell (S.), Liv Glaser (pf.)   **NCC NKF 30 007**

SOMMERVISE, OP. 45, NO. 3 (1897)
    Liv Glaser (pf.)   **NCC NKF 30 008**

SONGS
    Kirsten Flagstad (S.)   **HARVS 1305 H 1004**

SONGS
    Norwegian Students' Choir   **NCC NKF 30022**

STURM, OP. 31 (VILHELM KRAG) (1'00)
    Tuula Nienstedt (Cont.),
    Uwe Wegner (pf.)   **MUSVI MV 30 1104**

THREE ETUDES, OP. 11
    (FROM SIX ETUDES DE CONCERT)
    Judith Alstadter (pf.)   **EDUCO 3146**

UNGDOMSSANG, OP. 36, NO. 6
    Rosario Marciano (pf.)   **TURNA TV 34685**

UNGDOMSSANG, OP. 36, NO. 6
    Rosario Marciano (pf.)   **FONO FSM 53 0 36**

VISNET, OP. 39, NO. 9
    Rosario Marciano (pf.)   **TURNA TV 34685**

VISNET, OP. 39, NO. 9
    Rosario Marciano (pf.)   **FONO FSM 53 0 36**

WALPURGISNACHT AUF DEM MEER,
    OP. 31 (VILHELM KRAG) (2'29)
    Tuula Nienstedt (Cont.),
    Uwe Wegner (pf.)   **MUSVI MV 30 1104**

BACKES, Lotte (1901-   )

CAPRICCIO
    Helmut Plattner (org.)   **MIXTR BSW 30576**

CHROMATISCHE FANTASIE (1959)
    Heinz Lohmann (org.)   **MIXTR BSW 30576**

CONCERTO PER VIOLINO E ORGANO
    Rudolf Schulz (vln.), Rudolf
    Heinemann (org.)   **MIXTR BSW 35 676**

DE INVOCATIONE SPIRITUS SANCTI (LITANEI)
    Eberhard Grunz (org.)   **MIXTR BSW 30 176**

ET REPLETI SUNT OMNES SPIRITU SANCTO
    Eberhard Grunz (org.)   **MIXTR BSW 30 176**

ET REPLETI SUNT OMNES SPIRITU SANCTO
    Feliks Raczowski (org.)   **MIXTR BSW 30576**

ET SPIRITUS DEI FEREBATUR SUPER AQUAS
    Eberhard Grunz (org.)   **MIXTR BSW 30 176**

IMPRESSIONI DIVERTIMENTI,
    FUR ORGEL (1980) (5'55)
    Eberhard Kraus (org.)   **MIXTR MXT 35881**

IMPROVISATION UEBER EIN
    ORIGINAL-THEMA (B-A-C-C-E-S-)
    Helmut Plattner (org.)   **MIXTR BSW 30576**

IMPROVISATION UEBER EIN
    ORIGINAL-THEMA
    Eberhard Grunz (org.)   **MIXTR BSW 30 176**

IN SACRATISSIMA NOCTE (HEILIGE NACHT)
    Eberhard Grunz (org.)   **MIXTR BSW 30 176**

IN SACRATISSIMA NOCTE (HEILIGE NACHT) (8'50)
    Eberhard Kraus (org.)   **MIXTR MXT 35881**

INTRODUKTION UND PASSACAGLIA
    Helmut Plattner (org.)   **MIXTR BSW 30576**

MYSTERIUM DEI (1974)
    Helmut Plattner (org.)   **MIXTR BSW 30576**

PARTITA, DEIN LOB, HER ....
    Helmut Plattner (org.)   **MIXTR BSW 30576**

PARTITA, ERSCHIENEN IST
    DER HERRLICHE TAG, FUR ORGEL
    ★ ★ ★ ★ ★ ★   **KASKA BLN 6001**

PARTITA-WIE MEIN GOTT WILL (9'45)
    Gerhardt Blum (org.) with Hugo-Distler
    Choir, Berlin
    (cond.) Klaus Fischer-Dieskau   **MIXTR MXT 35881**

PSALM 24, FOR MIXED CHOIR,
    BARITONE SOLO AND ORGAN
    Martin Lucker (org.), Heiner Eckels (Bar.)
    with Bachchor Gutersloh
    (cond.) H. Krentz   **MIXTR BSW 35 676**

PSALM 47 (1963)
    Gerhard Blum (org.) with Hugo-Distler
    Choir, Berlin
    (cond.) Klaus Fischer-Dieskau   **MIXTR MXT 35881**

TE DEUM (16'20)
Helmut Kuehn (org.) with Hugo-Distler
Choir, Berlin
(cond.) Klaus Fischer-Dieskau   **MIXTR MXT 35881**

BADARZEWSKA-BARANOWSKA, Tekla (1834-1861)

LA PRIERE D'UNE VIERGE
* * * * * *   **ARIOL 51095 K**

MAIDEN'S PRAYER
Allan Etherden (pf.)   **GAMUT HMP 0284**

PRIERE D'UNE VIERGE, LA
Hans Kann (pf.)   **MUHER MHS 1139**

BADIAN, Maya (1945-   )

MOVIMENTO
Musica Rediviva Orchestra
(cond.) Ludovic Baci   **ELECT ST ECE 02331**

SIMFONIETTA
Sibiu Philharmonic Orchestra
(cond.) Petre Sbarcea   **ELECT ST ECE 02331**

BAHMANN, Marianne Eloise (1933-   )

ELECTRO-VOICE SERIES D ORGAN
SPEAKS WITH AUTHORITY, THE
Jon Spong (org.)   **ELECT E V 1092**

BAIL, Grace Shattuck (1898-   )

AUTUMN LOVE
* * * * * *   **MSR 3091 H**

HUSHABY
* * * * * *   **MSR 3091 H**

BALLOU, Esther Williamson (1915-1973)

PRELUDE AND ALLEGRO, FOR
PIANO AND STRING ORCHESTRA
Vienna Orchestra
(cond.) F. Charles Adler   **CRI 115**

SONATA FOR TWO PIANOS (1949)
Toni Grunschlag (pf.), Rosi Grunschlag (pf.)   **CRI 472**

BAPTISTA, Gracia (-   )

CONDITOR ALME (HYMNUS)
Pablo Cano (hpcd.)   **HARMU F 1001**

BARADAPRANA, Pravrajika (1923-   )

EAST INDIAN CHANTS
Gita Scott (org.) with Sarada Math Choir
(cond.) Pravrajika Baradaprana   **SHEFF M 5 S 5**

BARBERIS, Mansi (1899-   )

CVARTETTINO PENTRU COARDE
IN STIL NEO-CLASSIC   **ELECT**
Philharmonia Quartet   **ST ECE 01545**

BARBOSA, Cacilda Campos Borges (1914-   )

PROCISSAO DA CHUVA
Corais Escolares Do Rio De Janeiro   **CASAB LPC 3000**

QUATRO ESTUDOS BRASILEIROS
Alberto Boavista (pf.)   **LONDO LLB 1095**

BARKIN, Elaine (1932-   )

PLEIN CHANT
Harvey Sollberger (a-fl.)   **CRI SD 513**

STRING QUARTET (1969)
American Quartet   **CRI SD 338**

TWO EMILY DICKINSON CHORUSES
New England Conservatory Chorus
(cond.) Lorna Cooke de Varon   **CRI SD 482**

BARRADAS, Carmen (1888-1963)

FABRICACION
Neffer Kroger (pf.)   **ORFEO 90598**

BARRIERE, Françoise (1944-   )

CORDES-CI, CORDES CA   **PATHE**
Groupe Musicale Experimentale Bourges   **C 053 12 112**

BARTHEL, Ursula (1913-   )

CHRISTKIND KOMMT, DAS
* * * * * *   **DGG DG 6331100**

FROEHLICHE MUSIKANTEN (COLLECTION)   **TONST**
* * * * * *   **72601 73786 29**

HEUT'WANDERN WIR INS BLAU
* * * * * *   **ARIOL 74 79 ZU**

MINDENER SONNTAGSKONZERT,
DAS (COLLECTION)
* * * * * *   **DGG DG 666064**

MUSIKALISCHER KALENDAR
(AFTER JAMES KRUSS)
* * * * * *   **DGG DG 633 143**

NEUE KINDERLIEDER (AFTER JAMES KRUSS)
* * * * * *   **DGG DG 633 113**

STILLE NACHT, HEILIGE NACHT
* * * * * *   **METRO HLP 10 060**

BATE, Jennifer (1944-   )

INTRODUCTION AND VARIATIONS ON AN
OLD FRENCH CHRISTMAS SONG (9'40)
Jennifer Bate (org.)   **HYPER A 66083**

TOCCATA ON A THEME BY MARTIN SHAW
Jennifer Bate (org.)   **UNICO DKP 9007**

TOCCATA, FOR ORGAN
Jennifer Bate (org.)   **UNICO DKP 9007**

BAUER, Marion Eugenie (1887-1955)

FOUR PIANO PIECES (CHROMATICON,
OSTINATO, TOCCATA, SYNCOPE)   **MUHER**
Virginia Eskin (pf.)   **MHS 4236**

FROM NEW HAMPSHIRE WOODS,
OP. 12, NOS. 1-3 (1921)
Virginia Eskin (pf.)   **NORTH NR 204**

PRELUDE AND FUGUE,
FOR FLUTE AND STRINGS
Vienna Orchestra
(cond.) F. Charles Adler   **CRI 101**

SONATA FOR VIOLA AND PIANO, OP. 22
Arnold Steinhardt (vla.),
Virginia Eskin (pf.)   **NORTH NR 222**

SONATA FOR VIOLIN AND PIANO
Arnold Steinhardt (vln.),
Virginia Eskin (pf.)   **NORTH NR 222**

SUITE FOR STRING ORCHESTRA
Vienna Orchestra
(cond.) F. Charles Adler   **CRI 101**

TURBULENCE, OP. 17, NO.2 (1942)
Virginia Eskin (pf.)   **NORTH NR 204**

BEACH, Amy Marcy (1867-1944)

AH LOVE BUT A DAY
Jussi Bjorling (T.), Ivor Newton (pf.)   **EMI IC 147 0335455 M**

BALKAN VARIATIONS
Virginia Eskin (pf.)   **NORTH NR 223**

BALLAD OP. 6 (1894)
Virginia Eskin (pf.)   **GENES GS 1054**

BY THE STILL WATERS, OP. 114 (1925)
Virginia Eskin (pf.)   **NORTH NR 204**

CONCERTO IN C-SHARP MINOR, FOR
PIANOFORTE AND ORCHESTRA, OP. 45
Mary Louise Boehm (pf.) with
Westphalian Symphony Orchestra
(cond.) Siegfried Landau   **TURNA QTV S 34665**

FIVE IMPROVISATIONS
Virginia Eskin (pf.)   **GENES GS 1054**

FIVE IMPROVISATIONS FOR PIANO, OP. 148
Herbert Rogers (pf.)   **DORIN 1006**

FOUR PIECES FOR PIANO, OP. 15 (1892)
Virginia Eskin (pf.)   **GENES GS 1054**

FRENCH SUITE
Virginia Eskin (pf.)   **NORTH NR 223**

FROM GRANDMOTHER'S GARDEN,
OP. 97, NOS. 1-5
Virginia Eskin (pf.)   **NORTH NR 204**

GAELIC SYMPHONY IN E-MINOR, OP. 32
Royal Philharmonic Orchestra, London
(cond.) Karl Krueger   **MUSAM MIA 139**

HERMIT THRUSH AT EVE,
OP. 92, NO. 1 (1922)
Virginia Eskin (pf.)   **GENES GS 1054**

HERMIT THRUSH AT MORN,
OP. 92, NO. 2 (1922)
Virginia Eskin (pf.)   **GENES GS 1054**

HUMMING BIRD, A (1937)
Virginia Eskin (pf.)   **NORTH NR 204**

IMPROVISATION, FROM OP. 118, NO. 1
Rosario Marciano (pf.)   **TURNA TV 34685**

INVOCATION, OP. 55
Arnold Steinhardt (vln.),
Virginia Eskin (pf.)   **NORTH NR 222**

MAID SINGS LIGHT, A, OP. 56, NO. 3
Virginia Eskin (pf.)   **NEWOR NWD 247**

NOCTURNE, OP. 107 (1924)
Virginia Eskin (pf.)   **GENES G5 1054**

PRELUDE AND FUGUE, OP. 81 (1914)
Virginia Eskin (pf.)   **GENES GS 1054**

QUINTET IN F-SHARP MINOR, FOR PIANO
AND STRINGS, OP. 67
Mary Louise Boehm (pf.) with Kooper
Quartet:
Kees Kooper (vln.), Alvin Rogers
(vln.),
Richard Maximoff (vla.), Fred
Sherry (vlc.)   **TURNA TV S 34556**

SCHERZINO
Stanley Waldoff (pf.)   **MUHER MHS 3808**

SONATA IN A, FOR VIOLIN
AND PIANO, OP. 34
Joseph Silverstein (vln.),
Gilbert Kalish (pf.)   **NEWOR NW 268**

SONGS AND VIOLIN PIECES
D'Anna Fortunato (m-S.),
Joseph Silverstein (vln.),
Virginia Eskin (pf.)   **NORTH NR 202**

STRING QUARTET, OP. 89 (1929)
Crescent Quartet: Alicia Edelberg,
Nancy Diggs, Jill Jaffe, Maxine Neuman   **LEONA LP1 111**

THEME AND VARIATIONS, OP. 80
Diane Gold (fl.) with Alard Quartet   **LEONA LP1 105**

THREE BROWNING SONGS,
OP. 44 (1899) (7'44)
Carolyn Heafner (S.), Dixie Ross Neill (pf.)   **CRI SD 462**

THREE BROWNING SONGS, OP. 44, NO. 1
(THE YEAR'S AT THE SPRING)
* * * * * *   **VICTO 87026**

THREE BROWNING SONGS, OP. 44, NO. 1
(THE YEAR'S AT THE SPRING)
Ina Souez (S.), Loyd Simpson (pf.)   **NEWSO 5001**

THREE BROWNING SONGS, OP. 44, NO. 1
(THE YEAR'S AT THE SPRING)
Johanna Gadski (S.)   **NEWOR NW 247**

THREE BROWNING SONGS, OP. 44, NO. 1
(THE YEAR'S AT THE SPRING)
Michael Aspinall (S.)   **DECCA SDD 507**

THREE BROWNING SONGS, OP. 44, NO. 1
(THE YEAR'S AT THE SPRING)
* * * * * *   **VICTO 88008**

THREE MORCEAUX CARACTERISTIQUES,
OP. 28 (1894)
Virginia Eskin (pf.)   **GENES GS 1054**

TRIO FOR PIANO, VIOLIN AND CELLO, OP. 150
Macalester Trio   **VOX SVBX 5112**

TRIO FOR PIANO, VIOLIN AND CELLO, OP. 150
Clio Trio   **DORIN 1007**

VALSE CAPRICE, OP. 4 (1889)
Virginia Eskin (pf.)   **GENES GS 1054**

VARIATIONS ON BALKAN THEMES, OP. 60
Virginia Eskin (pf.)   **MUHER MHS 4236**

WOODWIND QUINTET: PASTORALE
E. Lawrence (fl.), W. Arrowsmith (ob.),
I. Neidich (cl.), R. Vrotney (bsn.),
B. Tillotson (hn.)   **MUHER MHS 3578**

BEAT, Janet Eveline (1937-   )

DANCING ON MOONBEAMS
Peter Mountain (vla.), A. Dale (pf.)   **SCOTS SSC 001**

BEATRICE DE DIA, Contessa (1160-1212)

A CHANTER M'ER DE SO QU'EU NO VOLRIA
Montserrat Figuera (S.)
EMI IC 065 30 941

A CHANTER M'ER DE SO QU'EU NO VOLRIA
Martin Best Mediaeval Ensemble
NIMBU 45023

A CHANTER M'ER DE SO QU'EU
NO VOLRIA (11'45)
Rogers and Studio der frühen Musik
TELEF 6 41 126 AS

A CHANTER M'ER DE SO QU'EU
NO VOLRIA (11'45)
Studio der frühen Musik
TELDE SAW T 9567

A CHANTER M'ER DE SO QU'EU
NO VOLRIA (14'47)
Clemencic Consort
HARMU HM F 397

PLANG (1'58)
Musiciens de Provence
ARION ARN 34260

BECLARD D'HARCOURT, Marguerite (1884-1964)

MARIPOSACA, NINACA
Baily van Walleghem (S.)
PAVAN ADW 7 036

BEECROFT, Norma Marian (1934-   )

11 AND 7 FOR 5+, FOR BRASS QUINTET
AND 2-CHANNEL TAPE
Canadian Brass Quintet
CBC SM 320

ELEGY AND TWO WENT TO SLEEP, FOR
SOPRANO, FLUTE, PERCUSSION AND TAPE
Lyric Arts Trio
CBC RCI 404

FROM DREAMS OF BRASS, FOR NARRATOR,
MIXED CHORUS, ORCHESTRA AND TAPE
* * * * * *
RCAY CC CCS 1008

FROM DREAMS OF BRASS, FOR NARRATOR,
MIXED CHORUS, ORCHESTRA AND TAPE
Barry Morse (narr.), Mary Morrison (S.) with
Toronto Chorus and Symphony Orchestra
(cond.) John Avison
CBC RCI 214

IMPROVVISAZIONI CONCERTANTI NO. 1,
FOR FLUTE AND MEDIUM ORCHESTRA
Karl Kraber (fl.) with Santa Cecilia
Orchestra

(cond.) Daniele Paris
AUDAT 477 4001

IMPROVVISAZIONI CONCERTANTI NO. 2
National Arts Center Orchestra
(cond.) Mario Bernardi
CBC RCI 382

IMPROVVISAZIONI CONCERTANTI NO. 2
National Arts Center Orchestra
(cond.) Mario Bernardi
RCA KRL 1 0007

LIVING FLAME OF LOVE, THE
Festival Singers of Canada
POLYD 2917 009

RASAS I FOR FLUTE, HARP, VIOLIN, VIOLA,
CELLO, PERCUSSION AND PIANO
Ensemble de la Societe de Musique
Contemporaine du Quebec
CBC RCI 301

TRE PEZZI BREVI, FOR FLUTE AND HARP
(OR GUITAR AND PIANO)
Gazzeloni (fl.), Campary (gtr.)
DOMIN S 69006

TRE PEZZI BREVI, FOR FLUTE AND HARP
(OR GUITAR AND PIANO)
Aitken (fl.), Ross (pf.)
DOMIN S 69006

**BEKMAN-SHCHERBINA, Elena Aleksandrovna Kamentseva
(1882-1951)**

PIANO MUSIC
Elena Bekman-Shcherbina (pf.)
MELOD 028617 8

BENARY, Barbara (1946-   )

BRAID, SLEEPING BRAID
Gamelan Son of Lion
FOLKW FS 31313

IN SCROLLS OF LEAVES
Gamelan Son of Lion
FOLKW FS 31312

PIECES FOR GAMELAN SON OF LION
Gamelan Son of Lion
NEWIL 8542

PIECES FOR GAMELAN SON OF LION
Gamelan Son of Lion
NEWIL 8442

BENEDICENTI, Vera (1913-   )

NINNA NANNA
* * * * * *
BIEM DPR 107

OTTO BOZZETTI MUSICALI
* * * * * *
STUDA VBG 19

PER SOPRAVVIVERE (FANTASY) FOR ORCHESTRA
* * * * * *
STUDA VBG 19

PICCOLA SUITE
* * * * * *
STUDA VBG 19

QUINDICI CANONI A DUE PARTI
* * * * * *
STUDA VBG 19

SERENATA SUI TETTI
* * * * * *
STUDA VBG 19

TU ERI IL MIO UNICO FIORE
* * * * * *
BIEM DPR 107

BERBERIAN, Cathy (1925-1983)

STRIPSODY FOR VOICE AND VIOLIN
Cathy Berberian (m-S.), Canino (vln.) **WERGO WER 60 054**

BERTIN, Louise Angelique (1805-1877)

NINNA NANNA (LULLABY) FOR VOICE AND PIANO
* * * * * *
PHILI A 00427 L

BEYER, Johanna Magdalena (1888-1944)

MUSIC OF THE SPHERES
Electric Weasel Ensemble
ARCH S 1765

BISH, Diane (-   )

PASSION SYMPHONY
Kennedy (narr.), Diane Bish (org.)
SNCM SCJP 792

BITGOOD, Roberta (1908-   )

CHORAL PRELUDE ON SILOAM
C. Warren Becker (org.)
CHAPL LP 5 134 ST 134

OFFERTORIES FROM AFAR: CHILDREN'S
PRAYER FROM SWEDEN (CHILDREN OF THE
HEAVENLY FATHER)
C. Warren Becker (org.)
CHAPL LP 5 134 ST 134

BLACKWELL, Anna Gee (1928-   )

THERE'S A NEW WORLD COMING
* * * * * *
QCA RJ 3115

BLANCHE DE CASTILLE (1188-1252)

AMOURS, OU TROP TARD ME SUIS PRIS
Julian Skowron (rebec),
Guy Robert (gtr. maresque)
Jean Belliard (counter-T.),
Elizabeth Robert (medieval lutes)   **CEZAM CEZ 1055**

AMOURS, OU TROP TARD ME SUIS PRIS
Julian Skowron (rebec),
Guy Robert (gtr. maresque),
Jean Belliard (counter-T.),
Elizabeth Robert (medieval lutes)   **ALVAR C 485**

BLEY, Carla (1938-   )

DINNER MUSIC
Carla Bley Band   **WATT 6**

ESCALATOR OVER THE HILL
Carla Bley Band   **JCOA EOTH - - -**

HEAVY HEART
Steve Slagle (Bar.), Carla Bley (vce., org.
and pf.) with Ensemble   **ECM 14**

JESUS MARIA AND OTHER SPANISH STRAINS
Carla Bley Band   **WATT 9**

LIVE!
Carla Bley (vce., org. and pf.) with
Wind Ensemble   **WATT 12**

LIVE!
Carla Bley Band   **WATT 11**

MUSIQUE MECANIQUE I
Carla Bley Band   **WATT 9**

MUSIQUE MECANIQUE II (AT MIDNIGHT)
Carla Bley Band   **WATT 9**

MUSIQUE MECANIQUE III
Carla Bley Band   **WATT 9**

SOCIAL STUDIES
Carla Bley Band   **WATT 12**

TROPIC APPETITES
Carla Bley (vce., org. and pf.) with Wind
Ensemble and Percussion   **WATT 1**

BLOOM, Jane Ira (1955-   )

ALL OUT #8
* * * * * *   **ANIMA 1 J 35**

MIGHTY LIGHTS #8, 9, 10, 11
* * * * * *   **ENJA 4044**

OF THE WIND'S EYE, #12
* * * * * *   **ENJA 3089**

SECOND WIND, #5, 6 AND 7
* * * * * *   **OUTLI 138**

WE ARE - OUTLINE, #1, #2, #3, #4
* * * * * *   **OUTLI 137**

BOLEYN, Anne, Queen of England (1507-1536)

O DEATH ROCK ME A-SLEEP (ATTRIB.)
* * * * * *   **PYE CCL 30121**

O DEATH ROCK ME A-SLEEP (ATTRIB.)
Paris Polyphonic Ensemble of the ORTF
(cond.) Charles Ravier   **MUHER MHS 905**

THREE MADRIGALS WITH FIDDLE ACCOMP:
SWEET AMARILLIS STAY, ALAS WHAT A
WRETCHED LIFE, O FAIREST MAID
* * * * * *   **PYE CCL 30121**

BOND, Carrie Jacobs (1862-1946)

PERFECT DAY, A
Palmer (S.), Constable (pf.)   **ARGO ZK 97**

PERFECT DAY, A,
Burrows (T.), Constable (pf.)   **OISEU 324**

BOND, Victoria Ellen (1949-   )

MONOLOGUE (PART OF TRIO FOR
VIOLIN, CELLO AND PIANO)
Ronald Leonard (vlc.)   **PROTO PR 150**

PETER QUINCE AT THE CLAVIER
(MONODRAMA)
Penny Orloff (S. and perc.), Zita Carno (pf.)   **PROTO PR 150**

SONATA FOR CELLO AND PIANO
Munguia (vlc.), V. Bond (pf.)   **LAUPR LP 13**

BONDS, Margaret (1913-1972)

SONG
* * * * * *   **MICHI SM 0015**

TROUBLED WATERS (1967)
Ruth Norman (pf.)   **OPONE 39**

BOSMANS, Henriette Hilda (1895-1952)

ANNEAU, L' (1'28)
Noemie Perugia (S.), Hans Henkemans (pf.)   **BABEL 8314 4**

AURORE (1'32)
Noemie Perugia (S.), Henriette Bosmans (pf.)   **BABEL 8314 4**

AVE MARIA (2'11)
Noemie Perugia (S.), Hans Henkemans (pf.)   **BABEL 8314 4**

CHANSON (1'59)
Noemie Perugia (S.), Hans Henkemans (pf.)   **BABEL 8314 4**

CHANSON (2'43)
Noemie Perugia (S.), Henriette Bosmans (pf.)   **BABEL 8314 4**

CHANSON DES MARINS HALES, LA (3'21)
Noemie Perugia (S.), Henriette Bosmans (pf.)   **BABEL 8314 4**

CHANSON DU CHIFFONIER, LA (3'52)
Noemie Perugia (S.), Henriette Bosmans (pf.)   **BABEL 8314 4**

CHANSON FATALE, LA (2'47)
Noemie Perugia (S.), Henriette Bosmans (pf.)   **BABEL 8314 4**

CHANSONS DES ESCARGOTS QUI VONT A
L'ENTERREMENT (1950)
Max van Egmond (Bar.), Thom Bollen (pf.)   **CBS LSP 14514**

COMPLAINTE DU PETIT CHEVAL BLANC
Cora Canne Meijer (m-S.), Thom Bollen (pf.)   **CBS LSP 14514**

COMPLAINTE DU PETIT CHEVAL BLANC (2'09)
Noemie Perugia (S.), Henriette Bosmans (pf.)   **BABEL 8314 4**

CONCERT PIECE, FOR VIOLIN AND
ORCHESTRA (1934) (20'00)
Vera Beths (vln.) with Radio Philharmonic
Orchestra
(cond.) Lucas Vis   **BABEL 8314 4**

CONCERTINO, FOR PIANO AND
ORCHESTRA (1928) (15'24)
Jacob Bogaart (pf.) with Radio Philharmonic
Orchestra
(cond.) Jan Stulen   **BABEL 8314 4**

JE NE SUIS PAS SEUL (1'23)
Noemie Perugia (S.), Henriette Bosmans (pf.)   **BABEL 8314 4**

LIED VOOR SPANJE, EEN
Anne Haenen (S.), Ton Hartsuiker (pf.)   **CBS LSP 14514**

MEDISANTS, LES
Cora Canne Meijer (m-S.), Thom Bollen (pf.) **CBS LSP 14514**

MEDISANTS, LES (0'53)
Noemie Perugia (S.), Hans Henkemans (pf.) **BABEL 8314 4**

NAUFRAGE, LE (2'24)
Noemie Perugia (S.), Hans Henkemans (pf.) **BABEL 8314 4**

ON FRAPPE (1'45)
Noemie Perugia (S.), Henriette Bosmans (pf.) **BABEL 8314 4**

POUR TOI MON AMOUR (1'28)
Noemie Perugia (S.), Henriette Bosmans (pf.) **BABEL 8314 4**

REGARD ETERNAL, LE (3'12)
Noemie Perugia (S.), Henriette Bosmans (pf.) **BABEL 8314 4**

RONDEL (2'01)
Noemie Perugia (S.), Hans Henkemans (pf.) **BABEL 8314 4**

THREE SONGS ON GERMAN TEXTS
Norah Raphael-Tours (S.), Anja Gosman (pf.) **BABEL 8104**

BOULANGER, Lili Juliette Marie Olga (1893-1918)

ATTENTE (19'00)
Sharon Mabry (S.), Rosemary Platt (pf.) **CORON LPS 3127**

CLARIERES DANS LE CIEL (1914) (33'35)
Kristine Ciesinski (S) Ted Taylor (pf.) **LEONA LPI 118**

CLARIERES DANS LE CIEL (SELECTIONS)
FOR SOPRANO/TENOR AND PIANO
Berenice Bramson (S.), Roger Rundle (pf.) **GEMIN RAP 1010**

CLARIERES DANS LE CIEL (SELECTIONS)
FOR SOPRANO/TENOR AND PIANO
Stark (S.), Garvey (pf.) **SPECT SR 126**

CLARIERES DANS LE CIEL (SELECTIONS)
FOR SOPRANO/TENOR AND PIANO
Tappy (T.), Francaix (pf.) **HMV CVC 2077**

CORTEGE
Arnold Steinhardt (vln.), Virginia Eskin (pf.) **NORTH NR 222**

CORTEGE
* * * * * * **RCA ARM 4 0942/7**

CORTEGE
Joseph Roche (vln.), Paul Freed (pf.) **VOX SVBX 5112**

CORTEGE
Nancy Fierro (pf.) **AVANT AV 1012**

CORTEGE
Barry Griffiths (vln.), Eric Parkin (pf.) **UNICO DKP 9021**

D'UN JARDIN CLAIR
Eric Parkin (pf.) **UNICO DKP 9021**

D'UN MATIN DE PRINTEMPS
Laurence (fl.) **MUHER MHS 4339**

D'UN MATIN DE PRINTEMPS
Barry Griffiths (vln.), Keith Harvey (vlc.),
Eric Parkin (pf.) **UNICO DKP 9021**

D'UN MATIN DE PRINTEMPS
Katharine Hoover (fl.), Virginia Eskin (pf.) **LEONA LP1 104**

D'UN SOIR TRISTE
Barry Griffiths (vln.), Keith Harvey (vlc.)
Eric Parkin (pf.) **UNICO DKP 9021**

D'UN VIEUX JARDIN
Eric Parkin (pf.) **UNICO DKP 9021**

D'UN VIEUX JARDIN
Nancy Fierro (pf.) **AVANT AV 1012**

DU FOND DE L'ABIME (PSALM), CONTRALTO,
TENORS, CHORUS AND ORCHESTRA
Oralia Dominguez (Cont.) with Elizabeth
Brasseur Chorale and Orchestre
Lamoureux (cond.) Igor Markevitch **HMV CO 65 95520**

DU FOND DE L'ABIME, FOR CONTRALTO,
TENORS, CHORUS AND ORCHESTRA (PSALM 130)
Oralia Dominguez (Cont.) with Elizabeth
Brasseur Chorale and Orchestre Lamoureux
(cond.) Igor Markevitch **EVERS SDBR 3059**

FAUST ET HELENE, FOR SOLOIST,
CHORUS AND ORCHESTRA
Lyne Dourian (m-S.), Andre Malla-
brera (T.), Michael Carey (Bar.)
with Monte Carlo National Opera
Orchestra and Chorus
(cond.) Igor Markevitch **VARES VC 81095**

HARMONIES DU SOIR
Barry Griffiths (vln.), Keith Harvey (vlc.),
Eric Parkin (pf.) **UNICO DKP 9021**

NOCTURNE
Arnold Steinhardt (vln.), Virginia Eskin (pf.) **NORTH NR 222**

NOCTURNE
Barry Griffiths (vln.), Eric Parkin (pf.) **UNICO DKP 9021**

NOCTURNE
* * * * * * **RCA ARM 4 0942/7**

NOCTURNE
Katharine Hoover (fl.), Virginia Eskin (pf.) **LEONA LPI 104**

NOCTURNE
Joseph Roche (vln.), Paul Freed (pf.) **VOX SVBX 5112**

NOCTURNE
Pasquier (vln.), Heisser (pf.) **FONO FSM 53 3 31**

NOCTURNE
Pasquier (vln.), Heisser (pf.) **HARMU HMU 387**

NOCTURNE
Masaka Yanagita (vln.), Michael May (pf.) **GEMIN RAP 1010**

PIE JESUS
Gisele Peyron (vce.) with Instrumental
Ensemble **TURNA TV 4183**

PIE JESUS
Oralia Dominguez (Cont.) with Elizabeth
Brasseur Chorale and Orchestre
Lamoureux (cond.) Igor Markevitch **HMV CO 65 95520**

PIE JESUS
Oralia Dominguez (Cont.) with Elizabeth
Brasseur Chorale and Orchestre
Lamoureux (cond.) Igor Markevitch **EVERS SDBR 3059**

POUR LES FUNERAILLES D'UN SOLDAT
Carey (Bar.) with Monte Carlo National
Opera Orchestra
(cond.) Igor Markevitch **VARES VC 81095**

PSALMS 24 AND 129
Oralia Dominguez (Cont.) with
Elizabeth Brasseur Chorale
(cond.) Igor Markevitch **HMV CO 65 95520**

PSALMS 24 AND 129, FOR SOLOISTS,
CHORUS AND ORCHESTRA
Oralia Dominguez (Cont.) with Elizabeth
Brasseur Chorale and Orchestre
Lamoureux (cond.) Igor Markevitch **EVERS SDBR 3059**

REFLETS
Sharon Mabry (S.), Rosemary Platt (pf.) **CORON LPS 3127**

RETOUR, LE
Sharon Mabry (S.), Rosemary Platt (pf.) **CORON LPS 3127**

THREE PIECES FOR VIOLIN AND PIANO
Y. Menuhin (vln.), C. Curzon (pf.) **HMV CVC 2077**

VIELLE PRIERE BOUDDHIQUE FOR
VOICE, CHORUS AND ORCHESTRA
Oralia Dominguez (Cont.) with Elizabeth
Brasseur Chorale and Orchestre
Lamoureux (cond.) Igor Markevitch **EVERS SDBR 3059**

BOULANGER, Nadia Juliette (1887-1979)

IMPROMPTU, FOR CELLO AND PIANO
J. Gavrish (vln.), T. Sadovskaya (pf.)　　**MELOD SM 02109/10**

BOURGOGNE, Marie de (1450-　　)

BASSE-DANSE: BEAULTE
Studio fuer Alte Musik, Duesseldorf　　**MUHER MHS 1442**

BASSE-DANSE: BEAULTE
Studio fuer Alte Musik, Duesseldorf　　**DACAM SM 91702**

BASSE-DANSE: LA FRANCHOISE NOUVELLE
Studio fuer Alte Musik, Duesseldorf　　**MUHER MHS 1442**

BASSE-DANSE: LA FRANCHOISE NOUVELLE
Studio fuer Alte Musik, Duesseldorf　　**DACAM SM 91702**

BOYD, Liona Maria (1950-　　)

CANTARELL, FOR GUiTAR
Liona Boyd (gtr.)　　**LONDO CS 7068**

PERSONA
Liona Maria Boyd (gtr.)　　**CBS FM 42120**

SUN CHILD
Liona Marie Boyd (gtr.)　　**CBS 42120**

BRANDENSTEIN, Charlotte von (1754-1813)

SONATA IN D-MAJOR, FOR VIOLIN AND PIANO
Mannheim Chamber Duo: Hanno Haag (vln.),
Anneliese Schlicker (pf.)　　**FONO FSM 43 7 51**

SONATA IN D-MAJOR, FOR VIOLIN AND PIANO
Mannheim Chamber Duo: Hanno Haag (vln.),
Anneliese Schlicker (pf.)　　**NOCTR SM 1051**

BREMER, Marrie Petronella (1933-　　)

CHROAI (WITH MARGIT SMITH)
Marrie Bremer, Margit Smith (chin,
hpcd., pf. and kayagum)　　**MUSMU MC 18038**

ELEVENSEVENSEVEN (WITH MARGIT SMITH)
Marrie Bremer, Margit Smith (kayagum and
renaissance b-fl.)　　**MUSMU MC 18038**

MAQAM (WITH MARGIT SMITH)
Marrie Bremer (org.), Margit Smith (org.)　　**MUSMU MC 18038**

MOBILE (WITH MARGIT SMITH)
Marrie Bremer (org.), Margit Smith (org.)　　**MUSMU MC 18038**

OMBRE (WITH MARGIT SMITH)
Marrie Bremer (org.), Margit Smith (org.)　　**MUSMU MC 18038**

TRAJECT 1 (WITH MARGIT SMITH)
Marrie Bremer, Margit Smith (org, baroque
vce-fl. and Peruvian fl.)　　**MUSMU MC 18038**

TRAJECT 2 (WITH MARGIT SMITH)
Marrie Bremer, Margit Smith (org., 2
African fl, gemshorn, b-fl., shakuhachi,
Nepalese and Thai fl.)　　**MUSMU MC 18038**

BRITTON, Dorothy Guyver (1922-　　)

TOKYO IMPRESSION (1967)
Orchestra　　**CAPIT T 10123**

YEDO FANTASY (1956)
Orchestra　　**CAPIT T 10123**

BROCKMAN, Jane E. (1949-　　)

TELL-TALE FANTASY (1978)
Rosemary Platt (pf.)　　**CORON LP 53105**

BRONSART VON SCHELLENDORF, Ingeborg Lena von (1840-1913)

DUET FROM THE OPERA JERY UND BAETELY
Berenice Bramson (S.),
Mertine Johns (m-S.) with
Instrumental Accompaniment　　**GEMIN RAP 1010**

LIED FROM THE OPERA, JERY UND BAETELY
Berenice Bramson (S.) with Instrumental
Accompaniment　　**GEMIN RAP 1010**

VALSE CAPRICE
Rosario Marciano (pf.)　　**FONO FSM 53 0 36**

VALSE CAPRICE
Rosario Marciano (pf.)　　**TURNA TV 34685**

BROWN, Gladys Mungen (1926-　　)

BLACK TEA
Gladys Mungen Brown (narr.)　　**OPONE 53**

BROWN, Rosemary (　　-　　)

KOMPOSITIONEN AUS DEM JENSEITS,
UEBERMITTELT VON BRAHMS, BEETHOVEN,
CHOPIN, DEBUSSY, LISZT, SCHUBERT,
RACHMANINOFF
Howard Shelley (pf.)　　**AVES INT 160 819**

ROSEMARY BROWN'S MUSIC (INSPIRED
BY BEETHOVEN, BRAHMS, CHOPIN,
DEBUSSY, LISZT, SCHUBERT, RACHMANINOFF)
Rosemary Brown (pf.), Peter Katin (pf.)　　**PHILI 6500 059**

BRUECKNER, Monika (1957-　　)

IM SOMMER
Christian Ridel with Augsburger Vokalensemble **MDG G 1082**

RICERCARE BY 3＋1 TONE SERIES (1978)
J. Dorfmuller (org.)　　**SCHW O 609**

BRUNDZAITE, Konstantsiya Kazyo (1942-1971)

DIALOGUES, FOR ORGAN AND ORCHESTRA
B. Vasilyauskas (org.) with Lithuanian
Chamber Orchestra
(cond.) Sondetskis　　**MELOD SM 03435/6**

SEVEN ENIGMAS FROM LITHUANIAN FOLKLORE
Kaunas State Choir
(cond.) Bingyalis　　**MELOD SM 03435/6**

TWO SONGS
N. Ambrazaitite (m-S.)　　**MELOD SM 03435/6**

BRUZDOWICZ, Joanna (1943-　　)

DUM SPIRO SPERO, FOR FLUTE AND TAPE
March Grauwels (fl.) with Studio IPEM Gand　　**PAVAN ADW 7064**

EROTIQUES
Delle Vigne-Fabbri (pf.)　　**PAVAN ADW 7052 53**

HOMO FABER (TRILOGIE ELECTRONIQUE)
Studio IPEM Gand　　**PAVAN ADW 7064**

MARLOS GROSSO BRASILEIRAS,
CHANT D'AMITIE POUR FLUTE, VIOLON,
CLAVECIN ET BANDE MAGNETIQUE
Trio Baroque: Maria Piech (hpcd.),
Jan Poda (vln.), March Grauwels (fl.)　　**PAVAN ADW 7035**

OCTOBER SONATA
Aquilles Delle Vigne (pf.)　　**PAVAN ADW 7054**

PIANO PIECE
Nelson Delle Vigne **PAVAN ADW 7052/3**

SONATE D'OCTOBRE, FOR PIANO
Delle Vigne-Fabbri (pf.) **PAVAN ADW 7064**

STRING QUARTET NO. 1 (LA VITA) (18'32)
Varsovia String Quartet **PAVAN ADW 7149**

TRIO DEI DUO MONDI (1980) (16'50)
Kinnstedt, Groger, Foster **MARUS 30 8329 Z**

WORKS FOR FLUTE AND MAGNETIC TAPE
Marc Grauwels (fl.) **PAVAN ADW 7064**

BULTERIJS, Nina (1929-   )

SYMPHONY FOR LARGE ORCHESTRA
Belgian National Orchestra
(cond.) Daniel Sternefeld **CULTU 5071 1**

TRIO FOR PIANO, VIOLIN AND CELLO
Bel Arte Trio **ALPHA DBM V 187**

CACCINI, Francesca (1587-1640)

CHE DESIA DI SAPER', CHE COS
E AMORE (1'55)
Carol Plantamura (S.) with Ensemble **LEONA LPI 123**

JESU CORONA VIRGINUM
Anfosa (S.), Bedois (org.) **ARION ARN 38532**

LIBERAZIONE DI RUGGIERO DALL'ISOLA
D'ALCINA, LA (SELECTIONS)
(BALLET OPERA)
Mertine Johns (m-S.), Michael May (hpcd.),
Yvonne Cable (vlc.) **GEMIN RAP 1010**

O CHE NUOVO STUPOR
Max van Egmond (Bar.) with Leonhardt
Consort **SELEC 641088**

O CHE NUOVO STUPOR
D. Munrow Recorder Consort with **EMI**
Early Music Consort, London **ICI 87 05 865/6**

O CHE NUOVO STUPOR (ARIA FOR VOICE,
RECORDER AND BASSO CONTINUO) **TELDE**
Max van Egmond (Bar.) **SAWT 9525**

PASTORELLA MIA TRI I FIORI, LA (3'24)
Carol Plantamura (S.) with Ensemble **LEONA LPI 123**

CACCINI-GHIVIZZANI, Settimia (1590-1640)

GIA SPERAI, NON SPERO HOR' PIU (1'53)
Carol Plantamura (S.) with Ensemble **LEONA LPI 123**

CALLAWAY, Ann (1949-   )

THEME AND SEVEN VARIATIONS
Rosemary Platt (pf.) **CORON LPS 3105**

CAMEU, Helza (1903-   )

ACALANTO
Sarita Gloria (S), Anthony Chanaka (pf.) **WASHI WR 408**

CIDADE NOVA FOR OBOE AND BASSOON
Bras Limonges (ob.), Noel Devos (bsn.) **ANGEL 3 CBX 442**

CAMINHA, Alda (-   )

PRELUDIO, OP. 16
Henryk Szeryng (vln.), Claude Maillols (pf.) **PHILI 6500 016**

CAMPANA, Francesca (-   )

PARGOLETTA, VEZZOSETTA
Carol Plantamura (S.) with Ensemble **LEONA LPI 123**

CAPUIS, Matilde (1913-   )

FIABA ARMONIOSA FOR PIANO
* * * * * * **KULKO SCHOE 4**

PUPPENMÄRCHEN (FÜR CLAVIER)
Schoell (pf.) **MARHE MA 25035**

SONATA IN C-MINOR,
FOR CELLO AND PIANO
* * * * * * **CETRA LPU 0057**

SONATA IN F-SHARP MINOR,
FOR CELLO AND PIANO
* * * * * * **KULKO SCHOE 5**

TEME VARIATO, FOR CELLO AND PIANO
* * * * * * **KULKO SCHOE 4**

THREE LIRICHE FOR VOICE,
CELLO AND PIANO
* * * * * * **KULKO SCHOE 5**

CAREY, Elena (1939-   )

D.N.A.
Gamelan Son of Lion **FOLKW FTS 31313**

CARLOS, Wendy (1939-   )

BACH-BRANDENBURG CONCERTOS
(SYNTHESIZER)
* * * * * * **COLUM M 2 X 35895**

BY REQUEST
* * * * * * **COLUM M 1 32088**

CLOCKWORK ORANGE (SCORE)
Wendy Carlos (elec.) **COLUM KC 31480**

COSMOLOGICAL IMPRESSIONS
Wendy Carlos (syn.) **CBS IM 39340**

DIALOGUES FOR PIANO AND
TWO LOUDSPEAKERS
Phillip Ramsey (pf.) **COLUM XM 32088**

DIALOGUES FOR PIANO AND
TWO LOUDSPEAKERS
Phillip Ramsey (pf.) **VOX TV 34004**

EPISODES FOR PIANO AND
ELECTRIC SOUND
Phillip Ramsey (pf.) **COLUM XM 32088**

GEODESIC DANCE
* * * * * * **COLUM XM 32088**

MOONSCAPES
Wendy Carlos (syn.) **CBS IM 39340**

POMPOUS CIRCUMSTANCES
* * * * * * **COLUM XM 32088**

ROCKY MOUNTAINS (WITH RACHEL ELKIND)
(FROM THE SHINING, FILM)
* * * * * * **WARNE HS 3449**

SHINING, THE (WITH RACHEL ELKIND)
(FROM FILM SOUND TRACK)
* * * * * * **WARNE HS 3449**

SONIC SEASONINGS
Wendy Carlos (elec.) **COLUM PG 31234**

SWITCHED-ON BACH
Wendy Carlos with Moog Synthesizer **COLUM MS 7194**

TIMESTEPS FOR SYNTHESIZER
* * * * * * **COLUM KC 31480**

VARIATIONS, FOR FLUTE AND
ELECTRONIC SOUND
John Heiss (fl.)   **VOX TV 34004**

WELL TEMPERED SYNTHESIZER
* * * * * *   **COLUM MS 7286**

CARNO, Zita (-)

SEXTET FOR PERCUSSION
University of Michigan
Percussion Ensemble   **MICHI SM 0016**

CARRENO, Teresa (1853-1917)

BARCAROLE, OP. 33 (FROM
2 ESQUISSES ITALIENNES)
Judith Alstadter (pf.)   **EDUCO 3146**

FANTAISIE, OP. 27 (REVUE A PRAGUE)
Judith Alstadter (pf.)   **EDUCO 3146**

INTERMEZZO SCHERZOSO, OP. 34
Rosario Marciano (pf.)   **TURNA TV 34685**

INTERMEZZO SCHERZOSO, OP. 34
Judith Alstadter (pf.)   **EDUCO 3146**

MIA TERESITA
Monique Duphil (pf.)   **CONAV LPE 1018431**

REVERIE-BARCAROLLE, VENISE, FROM
OP. 33 (DEUX ESQUISSES ITALIENNES)
Rosario Marciano (pf.)   **TURNA TV 34685**

REVERIE-BARCAROLLE, VENISE, FROM
OP. 33 (DEUX ESQUISSES ITALIENNES)
Rosario Marciano (pf.)   **FSM 53036**

STRING QUARTET, IN B-MINOR
Joseph Roche (vln.), Robert Zelnick (vln.),   **VOX**
Tamas Strasser (vla.), Camilla Heller (vlc.)   **SVBX 5112**

VALSE, OP. 25 (LE PRINTEMPS)
Judith Alstadter (pf.)   **EDUCO 3146**

VALSE, OP. 9 (LA CORBEILLE DE FLEURS)
Judith Alstadter (pf.)   **EDUCO 3146**

CARVALHO, Dinorah de (1905-)

ACALANTO
Madalena Lebeis (S.), Fritz Jank (pf.)   **RGE NAC 1076**

COQUEIRO
Lenice Prioli (S.), Selma Asprino (pf.)   **ASC 103**

POBRE CEGA
Maria Livia Sao Marcos (vla.)   **EVERS SDBR 3248**

SONATA NO. 1, FOR PIANO
Isis Moreira (pf.)   **FERMA 308 0026**

CASTEGNARO, Lola (1905-)

LASCIATE AMARE
Monserrat Caballe   **VRG 775**

CECCONI-BOTELLA, Monic (1936-)

SILENCES
Quatuor D'Anches Francais:
J. Vandeville (ob.),
J. Brion (cl.), P. Pareille (sax.),
D. Neuranter (bsn.)   **EDFRA EFM 011**

CHALLAN, Annie (1940-)

BALLADE
Annie Challan (hp.)   **HMV CO 3 12135**

MAGIQUE BOITE A MUSIQUE
Annie Challan (hp.)   **HMV CO 53 12135**

CHAMINADE, Cecile Louise Stephanie (1857-1944)

ARABESQUE, G-MINOR, OP. 61
Laval (pf.)   **EMI 2 C 069 16410**

AUTOMNE, OP. 35 (KONZERTSTUCK)
Albert Ferber (pf.)   **MERID E 77018**

AUTOMNE, OP. 35 (KONZERTSTUCK)
John Ogdon (pf.)   **HMV HQS 1287**

AUTREFOIS IN A-MINOR, OP. 87
S. Cherkassky (pf.)   **OISEU DSL 07**

BERCEUSE
Joan Sutherland (S.), Richard Bosynge (pf.)   **DECCA 12503**

CALLIRHOE
* * * * * *   **TURNA TV 34685**

CAPRICE ESPAGNOLE, OP. 67, FOR PIANO
Michael May (pf.)   **GEMIN RAP 1010**

CHANSON (SERENADE) ESPAGNOL
Ferras (vln.), Ambrosini (pf.)   **DGG DG 2538 016**

CHANSON (SERENADE) ESPAGNOL
Bisztriczky (vln.), Shroeder (pf.)   **DGG DG 133008**

CHANSON (SERENADE) ESPAGNOL
Bisztriczky (vln.), Shroeder (pf.)   **DGG DG LPM 17161**

CHANSON (SERENADE) ESPAGNOL
Ferras (vln.), Ambrosini (pf.)   **DGG DG 135133**

CHANSON (SERENADE) ESPAGNOL
Auclair (vln.), Schulhof (pf.)   **REMIN 199 128**

CHANSON (SERENADE) ESPAGNOL
Perlman (vln.), Sanders (pf.)   **EMI 065 03449**

CHANSON (SERENADE) ESPAGNOL
Soloviev (vln.), Ebert (pf.)   **CUPOL 6038**

CHANSON (SERENADE) ESPAGNOL
Renardy (vln.), Lush (pf.)   **LONDO R 10137**

CHANSON (SERENADE) ESPAGNOL
Morini (vln.), Dommers (pf.)   **WESTM XWN 18087**

CHANSON (SERENADE) ESPAGNOL
Ferras (vln.), Ambrosini (pf.)   **DGG DG 2535 612**

CHANSON SLAVE
Gerville-Riche (m-S.)   **DIPHL KIS KGG 3**

CONCERTINO FOR FLUTE AND
ORCHESTRA, OP. 107
James Galway (fl.), with Royal
Philharmonic Orchestra
(cond.) C. Dutoit   **RCA ARL 1 3777**

CONCERTINO FOR FLUTE AND ORCHESTRA, OP. 107
James Galway (fl.) with Royal
Philharmonic Orchestra
(cond.) C. Dutoit   **RCA RL 25109**

CONCERTINO FOR FLUTE AND
ORCHESTRA, OP. 107
Pellerite (fl.) with Indiana University
Wind Ensemble   **CORON S 1724**

CONCERTINO FOR FLUTE AND
ORCHESTRA, OP. 107
Hoberman (fl.), Stannard (pf.)   **AVANT 1015**

CONCERTINO FOR FLUTE
AND ORCHESTRA, OP. 107
A. Armonas (fl.), M. Dvarionaite (pf.)   **MELOD D 23577 8**

CONCERTINO FOR FLUTE AND
ORCHESTRA, OP. 107
Karl Bernhard Sebon (fl.) with Radio
Symphony Orchestra, Berlin **SCHW VMS 1608**

CONCERTINO FOR FLUTE AND
ORCHESTRA, OP. 107
Karl Bernhard Sebon (fl.) with Radio
Symphony Orchestra, Berlin
(cond.) Uros Lajovic **MUSMU VMS 1608 F**

CONCERTINO FOR FLUTE AND
ORCHESTRA, OP. 107
James Galway (fl.) with Royal Philharmonic
Orchestra
(cond.) C. Dutoit *** * * GL 85448**

CONCERTINO FOR FLUTE
AND PIANO, OP. 107
Karlheinz Zoller (fl.), Bruno Canino (pf.) **EMI C 187 30681/2**

CONCERTINO, FOR FLUTE (1902)
Graf (fl.), Kobayashi (pf.) **CLAVE 0 704**

CONCERTSTUCK, FOR PIANO
AND ORCHESTRA
Johnson (pf.) with Royal Philharmonic
Orchestra
(cond.) Freeman **ORION 78296**

CONCERTSTUCK, FOR PIANO
AND ORCHESTRA
Marciano (pf.), with Radio Luxembourg
Orchestra
(cond.) Froment **TURNA TV 34754**

GAVOTTE IN A-MINOR, OP. 9, NO. 2
D. Pines (pf) **GENES GS 1024**

INTERMEDE, OP. 36, NO. 1
I. Beyer, H. Dagul (pf. duo) *** * * FHM 842**

LISONJERA, LA, IN G-FLAT MAJOR, OP. 50
Rosario Marciano (pf.) **FONO 53 0 36**

LISONJERA, LA, IN G-FLAT MAJOR, OP. 50
Rosario Marciano (pf.) **TURNA TV 34685**

LISONJERA, LA, IN G-FLAT MAJOR, OP. 50
D. Pines (pf.) **GENES GS 1024**

LISONJERA, LA, IN G-FLAT MAJOR, OP. 50
Hans Kann (pf.) **MUHER MHS 1139**

LITTLE SILVER RING
Michel Dens (Bar.) **EMI CO 53 12540**

LITTLE SILVER RING
Dame Clara Butt (Cont.) **OLYMP ORL 222**

LITTLE SILVER RING
John McCormack (T.) *** * * EX 2900073**

PAS DES ECHARPES, OP. 37
Rosario Marciano (pf.) **FONO 53 0 36**

PAS DES ECHARPES, OP. 37
Rosario Marciano (pf.) **TURNA TV 34685**

PIECE IN OLD STYLE, E-MINOR, OP. 74
Laval (pf.) **EMI 2 C 069 16410**

PIERRETTE
Arnold Steinhardt (vln.), Virginia
Eskin (pf.) **NORTH NR 222**

PIERRETTE (AIR DE BALLET) IN E-FLAT
MAJOR, OP. 41
D. Pines (pf.) **GENES GS 1024**

ROMANZA APPASSIONATA
Arnold Steinhardt (vln.), Virginia
Eskin (pf.) **NORTH NR 222**

SCARF DANCE
Virginia Eskin (pf.) **CONOS CSQ 2065**

SERENADE ESPAGNOLE
Itzak Perlman (vln.), Sanders (pf.) **ANGEL SZ 37630 SD**

SERENADE ESPAGNOLE
Arnold Steinhardt (vln.), Virginia
Eskin (pf.) **NORTH NR 222**

SERENADE ESPAGNOLE (ARR. F. KREISLER)
G. Barinova (vln.) **MELOD D 1185 6**

SERENADE ESPAGNOLE (ARR. F. KREISLER)
Nishizaki (vln.) **CAMER CMTX 1504**

SERENADE ESPAGNOLE, OP. 24
(ARR. F. KREISLER)
Yo Yo Ma (vlc.), Zander (pf.) **CBS IM 37280**

SPANISH SERENADE see below

SERENADE IN D-MAJOR, OP. 29
D. Pines (pf.) **GENES GS 1024**

SIX CONCERT STUDIES, OP. 35
(NOS. 1, 2, 3, 5 AND 6)
Laval (pf.) **EMI 2 C 069 16410**

SONATA IN C-MINOR, OP. 21
Laval (pf.) **EMI 2 C 069 16410**

SONATA IN C-MINOR, OP. 21
Nancy Fierro (pf.) **PELIC LP 2017**

SONATA IN C-MINOR, OP. 21
D. Pines (pf.) **GENES GS 1024**

SONATA IN C-MINOR, OP. 21
Judith Alstadter (pf.) **EDUCO 3146**

SONGS WITHOUT WORDS,
OP. 76, NOS. 3 AND 5
Laval (pf.) **EMI 2 C 069 16410**

SPANISH SERENADE, OP. 24 (ARR. F. KREISLER)
Peter Csaba (vln.), Kocsis (pf.) **HUNGA SLPX 12437**

SERENADE ESPAGNOLE see above

TRIO FOR PIANO, VIOLIN AND CELLO, OP. 11,
NO. 1, IN G-MINOR
Macalester Trio **VOX SVBX 5112**

VALSE CAPRICE, IN D-FLAT MAJOR, OP. 33
D. Pines (pf.) **GENES GS 1024**

CHANCE, Nancy Laird (1931-)

DAYSONGS, FOR FLUTE AND PERCUSSION (1974)
* * * * * * **OPONE 72**

DUOS III
Joel Lester (vln.), Andre Ameliahoff (vlc.) **OPONE 85**

EXULTATION AND LAMENT, FOR ALTO
SAXOPHONE AND TIMPANI (1980)
Kenneth Hitchcock (sax.), William Trigg (tim.) **OPONE 79**

RITUAL SOUNDS FOR BRASS AND PERCUSSION
Weisberg with Apple Brass Quintet: J. Kraus
G. Schall, G. Yelez (perc.) **OPONE 69**

SONGS
Wills and Mutter **IND MA 377**

CHARRIERE, Isabella Agneta Elisabeth de (1740-1805)

SONATE NO. 3, POUR CLAVECIN
Germaine Vaucher-Clerc (hpcd.) **SWISS CT 64 4**

CHERTOK, Pearl (1919-1981)

AROUND THE CLOCK
Pearl Chertok (hp.) **ORION ORS 76231**

DRIFTWOOD
Pearl Chertok (hp.)   **ORION ORS 76231**

SEAFOAM
Pearl Chertok (hp.)   **ORION ORS 76231**

CIANI, Suzanne Elizabeth (1946-   )

SEVEN WAVES
Suzanne Ciani (syn.)   **FINNA 90175 1**

CIBBINI, Katherina (1790-1858)

SIX VALSES, OP. 6
Rosario Marciano (pf.)   **FONO FSM 53 0 36**

SIX VALSES, OP. 6
Rosario Marciano (pf.)   **TURNA TV 34685**

CIOBANU, Maia (1952-   )

DA SUONARE, FOR PIANO
Razvan Cernat (pf.)   **ELECT ST ECE 02591**

DECOR, FOR CLARINET AND PIANO
Rezvan Cernat (pf.)   **ELECT ST ECE 02591**

EARTH MUST LIVE, THE
Razvan Cernat (pf.)   **ELECT ST ECE 02591**

CLARKE, Rebecca (1886-1979)

COLOR OF LIFE (1'43)
John Ostendorf (B-Bar.), Shirley Seguin (pf.) **LEONA LPI 120**

DONKEY, THE (2'07)
John Ostendorf (B-Bar.), Shirley Seguin (pf.) **LEONA LPI 120**

DOWN BY THE SALLEY GARDENS (1'33)
John Ostendorf (B-Bar.), Shirley Seguin (pf.) **LEONA LPI 120**

DREAM, A (2'17)
John Ostendorf (B-Bar.), Shirley Seguin (pf.),
Kristine Ciesinski (S.)   **LEONA LPI 120**

DUO FOR VIOLA AND CLARINET
Patricia McCarty (vla.), Peter Hadcock (cl.) **NORTH NR 212**

GOD MADE A TREE (2'03)
John Ostendorf (B-Bar.), Shirley Seguin (pf.) **LEONA LPI 120**

JUNE TWILIGHT (2'36)
Kristine Ciesinski (S.), John Ostendorf (B-Bar.)
Shirley Sequin (pf.)   **LEONA LPI 120**

PASSACAGLIA FOR VIOLA AND PIANO
Patricia McCarty (vla.), Virginia Eskin (pf.) **NORTH NR 212**

SEAL MAN, THE (5'47)
Kristine Ciesinski (S.), Shirley Seguin (pf.),
John Ostendorf (B-Bar.)   **LEONA LPI 120**

SONATA FOR VIOLA AND PIANO   **SUPRA**
Josef Kodousek (vla.), Kveta Novotna (pf.)   **1111 2694 G**

SONATA FOR VIOLA AND PIANO (1919)
Michael Ponder (vla.), John Alley (pf.)   **ENSEM ENS 123**

SONATA FOR VIOLIN AND PIANO
Patricia McCarty (vln.), Virginia Eskin (pf.) **NORTH NR 212**

TRIO FOR VIOLIN, CELLO AND PIANO
Clementi Trio   **LARGO 5003**

TRIO FOR VIOLIN, CELLO AND PIANO (1921)
Suzanne Ornstein (vln.), James Kreger (vlc.),
Virginia Eskin (pf.)   **LEONA LPI 103**

TWO PIECES FOR VIOLA AND CELLO
Patricia McCarty (vla.), Martha Babcock (vlc.) **NORTH NR 212**

CLAYTON, Laura (-   )

CREE SONGS TO THE NEWBORN, FOR
SOPRANO AND CHAMBER ENSEMBLE (1978)
Bryn-Johnson (S.) with Weisberg
Contemporary Chamber Ensemble   **CRI SD 498**

CLOSTRE, Adrienne (1921-   )

BROTHER BLUE, SUITE FOR CELTIC HARP
Megevand (hp.)   **SFP 1054**

COATES, Gloria Kannenberg (1938-   )

MUSIC ON OPEN STRINGS (16'41)
Bavarian Radio Symphony Orchestra
(cond.) Elgar Howarth   **PROVI ISVP 128**

STRING QUARTET NO. 1
(ANDANTE AGITATO) (4'30)
Kronos Quartet   **PROVI ISPV 128**

STRING QUARTET NO. 2 (GRAVE) (5'40)
Kronos Quartet   **PROVI ISVP 128**

STRING QUARTET NO. 4 (11'15)
Kronos Quartet   **PROVI ISVP 128**

COLTRANE, Alice McLeod (1937-   )

BLISS, THE ETERNAL NOW
Alice Coltrane (acoustic pf. and hp.),
Carlos Santana (gtr.)   **COLUM PCQ 32900**

JOURNEY IN SATCHIDNANDA
* * * * * *   **IMPUL AS 9 203**

MONASTIC TRIO, A
* * * * * *   **ABC AS 9156**

UNIVERSAL CONSCIOUSNESS
* * * * * *   **IMPUL AS 9 210**

COOLIDGE, Peggy Stuart (1913-1981)

NEW ENGLAND AUTUMN (11'42)
Westphalian Symphony Orchestra
(cond.) Siegfried Landau   **MUHER MHS 4387**

NEW ENGLAND AUTUMN (SUITE) FOR
CHAMBER ORCHESTRA
Aristid von Wurtzler (hp.) with
Westphalian Symphony Orchestra
(cond.) Siegfried Landau   **TURNA QTV S 34635**

PIONEER DANCES
Aristid von Wurtzler (hp.) with
Westphalian Symphony Orchestra
(cond.) Siegfried Landau   **TURNA QTV S 34635**

PIONEER DANCES (12'34)

Aristid von Wurtzler (hp.) with
Westphalian Symphony Orchestra
(cond.) Siegfried Landau   **MUHER MHS 4387**

RHAPSODY FOR HARP AND ORCHESTRA
Aristid von Wurtzler (hp.) with
Westphalian Symphony Orchestra
(cond.) Siegfried Landau   **TURNA QTV S 34635**

RHAPSODY FOR HARP AND ORCHESTRA (13'06)
Aristid von Wurtzler (hp.) with
Westphalian Symphony Orchestra
(cond.) Siegfried Landau   **MUHER MHS 4387**

SPIRITUALS IN SUNSHINE AND SHADOW
New York Harp Ensemble
(cond.) Aristid von Wurtzler   **MUHER MHS 3307**

SPIRITUALS IN SUNSHINE AND SHADOW
Aristid von Wurtzler (hp.) with
Westphalian Symphony Orchestra
(cond.) Siegfried Landau   **TURNA QTV S 34635**

SPIRITUALS IN SUNSHINE AND SHADOW (11'30)
Aristid von Wurtzler (hp.) with
Westphalian Symphony Orchestra   **MUHER**
(cond.) Siegfried Landau   **MHS 4387**

COOPER, Rose Marie (1937-   )

LORD MOST HOLY (SACRED CANTATA) FOR
WOMEN'S CHORUS, ORGAN OR PIANO
* * * * * *   **BROAD 452 062**

TELL THE BLESSED TIDINGS (SACRED CHORUS)
FOR UNISON CHORUS, ORGAN OR PIANO
* * * * * *   **BROAD 452 062**

CORMONTAN, Theodora (1840-1920)

AFTENDAEMRING (ANDERSON) (3'11)
Niels Eje (ob.), Inge Muldrad (vlc.),
Lillian Torquist (hp.)   **OLUFS DOC 5004**

CORY, Eleanor (1943-   )

DESIGNS (11'15)
Arioso Trio   **CRI SD 459**

OCTAGONS (1976)
Blumenthal with
Composers Chamber Ensemble   **OPONE 69**

COSTA, Maria Helena da (-   )

ATENCAO
Madrigal Renascentista de Belo Horizonte   **PROME**
(cond.) Afranio Lacerda   **MMB 79 014**

COULOMBE SAINT-MARCOUX, Micheline (1938-1985)

ASSEMBLAGES
Christina Petrowska (pf.)   **CBC RCI 396**

BROUILLARD EPIAS, RAYON DE CLARTE,
FROM DOREANES
* * * * * *   **DOMIN S 69001**

GENESIS
Quintette a Vent du Quebec   **SNE 501**

ISHUMA
Marthe Forget (S.) with Ensemble
de la Société de Musique
(cond.) S. Garant   **CBC RCI 422**

MANDALA I
Days, Months and Years to Come   **CBC RCI 525**

MOMENTS
* * * * * *   **CBC RCI 525**

QUATUOR A CORDES
Classical Quartet of Montreal   **CBC RCI 363**

REGARDS
Ensemble de la Societe de Musique

Contemporaine du Quebec
(cond.) S. Garant   **CBC RCI 525**

SEQUENCES
2 Ondes Martenot and Percussion   **CBC RCI 492**

TRAKADIE   **CBC RCI**
Guy Lachapelle (perc.)   **CAPAC RM 222**

ZONES
* * * * * *   **CBC RCI 373**

COULTHARD, Jean (1908-   )

AEGEAN SKETCHES
Antonin Kubalek (pf.)   **MELBO SMLP 4031**

BALLADE
* * * * * *   **CBC PR 1082**

BELL SONG
Patrick Wedd (org.) with Vancouver
Bach Choir and Vancouver Symphony
Orchestra (brass)
(cond.) Bruce Pullan   * * * **VBC 001 L**

CRADLE SONG
* * * * * *   **WESTM WGS 8124**

CRADLE SONG
Maureen Forrester (A.)   **CBC WST 17137**

CYCLE OF THREE LOVE SONGS
* * * * * *   **CBC RCI 109**

ECSTASY FROM SPRING RHAPSODY

David Mills (B.), Marjorie Mutter (pf.)   **MASTE MA 377**

FIVE MEDIEVAL LOVE SONGS
Jon Vickers (T.), Richard Woitach (pf.)   **CBC SM 180**

FIVE PART SONGS
Rogers (pf.) with CBC Vancouver Chorus
(cond.) Hugh McLean   **CBC RCI 226**

FIVE PART SONGS
Rogers (pf.) with CBC Vancouver Chorus   **RCA**
(cond.) Hugh McLean   **CC CCS 1020**

FOUR ETUDES, NO. 4
* * * * * *   **CBC RCI 134**

FOUR ETUDES, NOS. 1 AND 4
Mario Varro (pf.)   **BAROQ BC 2837**

FOUR PROPHETIC SONGS
Roxolana Roslak (S.),
Coenraad Bloemendal (vlc.),
William Aide (pf.)   **CENTR 1183**

IMAGE ASTRALE
Charles Foreman (pf.)   **CENTR CMC 1684**

LEAN OUT OF THE WINDOW, GOLDEN HAIR
David Mills (Bar.), Marjorie Mutter (pf.)   **MASTE MA 377**

LEAN OUT OF THE WINDOW, GOLDEN HAIR
* * * * * *   **CBC RCI 109**

LYRIC SONATINA
Christopher Weait (bsn.), Monica
Gaylord (pf.)   **MELBO SMLP 4032**

MORE LOVELY GROWS THE EARTH
FOR MIXED CHORUS
* * * * * *   **CBC RCI 35**

NOON SIESTA FOR PIANO
* * * * * *   **CCM 1**

QUEBEC MAY, FOR MIXED CHORUS
* * * * * *   **CBC RCI 35**

QUIET SONG
* * * * * *   **CBC RCI 93**

SIX IRISH SONGS FOR MAUREEN,
FOR ALTO AND PIANO
Maureen Forrester (A.)   **CBC WST 17137**

SIX MEDIEVAL LOVE SONGS
Jon Vickers (T.), Richard Woitach (pf.)   **CMC 2185**

SKETCHES FROM THE WESTERN WOODS
Bruce (pf.) — **CCM BVC 357**

SONATA FOR CELLO AND PIANO
Roland Leduc (vlc.), John Newmark (pf.) — **COLUM ML 5942**

SONATA FOR CELLO AND PIANO
Vladimir Orloff (vlc.), Marietta Orloff (pf.) — **CBC SM 305**

SONATA FOR CELLO AND PIANO
Ernst Friedlander (vlc.),
Marc Friedlander (pf.) — **ODYSS 32 16 0415**

SONATA FOR CELLO AND PIANO
Ernst Friedlander (vlc.),
Marc Friedlander (pf.) — **COLUM ML 5942**

SONATA FOR OBOE AND PIANO
Claude Perrier (ob.), John Newmark (pf.) — **CBC RCI 4**

SONATA FOR PIANO
John Ogdon (pf.) — **CBC RCI 289**

SONG TO THE SEA
Atlantic Symphony
(cond.) Kenneth Elloway — **CBC SM 215**

SPRING RHAPSODY
* * * * * * — **CBC RCI 203**

STRING QUARTET, NO. 2 (THRENODY)
University of Alberta String Quartet — **CBC RCI 386**

THREE SONGS FOR MEDIUM VOICE (MEZZO-SOPRANO AND PIANO)
* * * * * * — **CBC RCI 20**

TWELVE ESSAYS ON A CANTABILE THEME (STRING OCTET)
* * * * * * — **CBC RCI 495**

VARIATIONS ON B.A.C.H.
John Ogdon (pf.) — **CBC RCI 289**

COWLES, Darleen (1942-   )

TRANSLUCENT UNREALITY (6'58)
Mary Stolper (fl.), Melody Lord (pf.) — **CAPIO CR 1001**

CRAWFORD SEEGER, Ruth (1901-1953)

CHANT
* * * * * * — **VOX SVBX 5353**

CLASSIC SONATAS FOR VIOLIN AND PIANO
Ida Karafian (vln.), Vivian Fine (pf.) — **CRI SD 508**

DIAPHONIC SUITE NO. 1 (1930)
James Ostryniec (ob.) — **CRI SD 423**

DIAPHONIC SUITE NO. 2, FOR BASSOON AND CELLO (1931)
Eifert (bsn.), Christensen (vlc.) — **GASPA 108 CX**

NINE PRELUDES FOR PIANO
Bloch (pf.) — **CRI SD 247**

NINE PRELUDES FOR PIANO, NOS. 6 TO 9
Alan Mandel (pf.) — **DESTO DC 6445 7**

PIANO STUDY IN MIXED ACCENTS
Rosemary Platt (pf.) — **CORON LPS 3121**

PRELUDES (1924-1928)
Rosemary Platt (pf.) — **CORON LPS 3121**

PRELUDES, NOS. 6-9 (1927-1928)
Virginia Eskin (pf.) — **NORTH NR 204**

SONATA FOR VIOLIN AND PIANO (15'28)
Ida Kavafian (vln.), Vivian Fine (pf.) — **CRI SD 508**

STRING QUARTET
Amati Quartet — **COLUM AMS 6142**

STRING QUARTET
Composers Quartet — **NONSU 471280**

STRING QUARTET (1931)
Fine Arts Quartet — **GASPA GS 205**

STUDY IN MIXED ACCENTS, FOR PIANO (1930)
Virginia Eskin (pf.) — **NORTH NR 204**

STUDY IN MIXED ACCENTS, FOR PIANO (1930)
Bloch (pf.) — **CRI SD 247**

SUITE FOR WIND QUINTET
Lark Quintet — **CRI SD 249**

SUITE NO. 2, FOR FOUR STRINGS AND PIANO
New Music Consort — **NEWOR NW 319**

THREE SONGS
B. Morgan (m-S.) with New Jersey
Percussion Ensemble — **NEWOR NWD 285**

THREE SONGS
Berlin (m-S.), Maxmilian (pf.) — **CR1 SD 501**

TWO MOVEMENTS FOR CHAMBER ORCHESTRA
Boston Musica Viva
(cond.) Pittman — **DELOS 25405**

CURRAN, Pearl Gildersleeve (1875-1941)

LIFE
Beniamino Gigli (T.), Dino Fedri (pf.) — **RCA LM 1972**

DANIELS, Mabel Wheeler (1878-1971)

DEEP FOREST, OP. 34, NO.1
Tokyo Imperial Philharmonic Orchestra
(cond.) William Strickland — **CRI 145**

THREE OBSERVATIONS FOR THREE WOODWINDS, OP. 41
R. Roseman (ob.), J. Rabbay (cl.),
McCord (bsn.) — **DESTO DC 7117**

DANZI, Maria Margarethe (1768-1800)

SONATA FOR PIANO AND VIOLIN, IN E-FLAT MAJOR, OP. 1, NO. 1
Monica von Saalfeld (pf.),
Werner Grobholz (vln.) — **MUBAV MB 70 902**

DAVIS, Katherine Kennicott (1892-1981)

CAROL OF THE DRUM
Augustana Choir
(cond.) Henry Veld — **RCA LBC 1075**

RAISING OF LAZARUS, THE
Frederick Jagel (T.),
Ruth Barrett Phelps (org.) — * * * - - -

DAVIS, Sharon (-   )

COCKTAIL ETUDES: 4 CONCERT ETUDES FOR PIANO Sharon Davis (pf.) — **WIM WIMR 16**

SIX SONGS ON POEMS BY WILLIAM PILLIN, FOR SOPRANO, CLARINET AND PIANO
Delcina Stevenson (S.), Sharon Davis (pf.),
David Atkins (cl.) — **WIM WIMR 23**

THOUGH MEN CALL US FREE (10'10)
Delcina Stevenson (S.), David Atkins (cl.),
Sharon Davis (pf.)
(cond.) Robert Henderson — **WIM WIMR 13**

THOUGH MEN CALL US FREE, FOR SOPRANO, CLARINET AND PIANO
Delcina Stevenson (S.), David Atkins (cl.),
Sharon Davis (pf.) — **WIM WIMR 23**

THREE MOODS OF EMILY DICKINSON,
FOR SOPRANO, VIOLIN,
VIOLONCELLO AND PIANO
Delcina Stevenson (S.), Haslop (vln.),
D. Davis (vlc.), Sharon Davis (pf.) **WIM WIMR 23**

THREE POEMS OF WILLIAM BLAKE
Delcina Stevenson (S.), Spear (cl.) **WIM WIMR 10**

DELL'ACQUA, Eva (1856-1930)

HIRONDELLE, L'
G. Gasparian (S.) **MELOD D 1901 2**

HIRONDELLE, L'
A. Nezhdanova (S.) **MELOD D 028361 2**

HIRONDELLE, L'
Bogna Sokorska (S.) with Polish Radio
Orchestra
(cond.) Stefan Rachon **MUZA SX 0228**

VILLANELLE
Beverly Sills (S.) with Columbia Symphony
Orchestra
(cond.) Andre Kostelanetz **CBS 76502**

VILLANELLE
Lily Pons (S.), Frances Blaisdell (fl.) with
Orchestra
(cond.) Andre Kostelanetz **CAMDE 1011**

VILLANELLE
Edita Gruberova (S.) with R.S.O. Stuttgartt **ORFEO S 072831**

VILLANELLE (3'10)
Miliza Korjus (S.) **EMI IC 147 30 819/20 M**

VILLANELLE (3'10)
Miliza Korjus (S.) **VENUS LP 963 M**

VILLANELLE (4'19)
Dorothy Dorow (S.), Gunilla von Bahr (fl.),
Lucia Negro (pf.) **BIS LP 45**

DEMAR, Therese (1801-   )

CAVATINE VARIÉE DI TANTI PALPITI,
AFTER TANCREDE, BY ROSSINI
Laskine (hp.), Nordmann (hp.) **ERATO STU 70721**

DEMARQUEZ, Suzanne (1899-1965)

SONATINE, FOR FLUTE AND PIANO
* * * * * * **PACIF LDPE 5102**

DEMESSIEUX, Jeanne (1921-1968)

ETUDES FOR ORGAN, NOS. 1-6
Pierre Labric (org.) **MUHER MHS 3044**

MEDITATIONS, NOS. 1-7
Pierre Labric (org.) **MUHER MHS 3042/4**

PRELUDE AND FUGUE IN C-MAJOR
Graham Barber (org.) **MIXTR VPS 1025**

PRELUDE AND FUGUE, OP. 13
Pierre Labric (org.) **MUHER 3043**

REPONS POUR LE TEMPS DE PAQUES
Nicholas Kynaston (org.) **OISEU SOL 326**

REPONSE FOR EASTER
Pierre Labric (org.) **MUHER MHS 3044**

TE DEUM
Pierre Labric (org.) **MUHER MHS 3044**

TE DEUM, OP. 11
Zimmerman (org.) **SCHW 2614**

TE DEUM, OP. 11
Graham Barber (org.) **MIXTR VPA 1032**

TRYPTIQUE
Pierre Labric (org.) **MUHER MHS 3043**

TRYPTIQUE, OP. 11
Graham Barber (org.) **MIXTR VPS 1032**

TWELVE CHORALE PRELUDES
Pierre Labric (org.) **MUHER MHS 3043**

DIAMOND, Arline (1928-   )

CLARINET COMPOSITION
Phillip Rehfeldt (cl.) **ADVAN FGR 4**

DIANDA, Hilda (1925-   )

A-7, FOR CELLO AND MAGNETIC TAPE
* * * * * * **MCBA 0010**

AFTER THE SILENCE (FOR AMPLIFIED FLUTE)
Choir of the Catholic University of Chile **TACU TE 12**

DOS ESTUDIOS EN OPOSICION
* * * * * * **MCBA 0010**

DIEMER, Emma Lou (1927-   )

CHORAL MUSIC
University Chorale of West Texas
State University **GOLDE GC 5063**

DECLARATIONS FOR ORGAN (6'18)
Emma Lou Diemer (org.) **CAPIO CR 1001**

QUARTET FOR PIANO, VIOLIN, VIOLA
AND CELLO (1954)
Obercracker, Copes, Ohyama, Rutkowski **ORION OC 693**

SEXTET FOR PIANO AND WOODWIND QUINTET
Emma Lou Diemer (pf.)
with Woodwind Quintet **ORION OC 693**

SONATA FOR FLUTE AND PIANO (1958)
Mark Thomas (fl.), Christine Croshaw (pf.) **GOLDE GC 7074**

SUMMER OF '82, FOR CELLO
AND PIANO (1982)
Rutkowski (vlc.), Nelson (pf.) **ORION OC 693**

TOCCATA AND FUGUE FOR ORGAN (5'37)
Emma Lou Diemer (org.) **CAPIO CR 1001**

TOCCATA FOR FLUTE CHORUS
Armstrong Flute Ensemble **GOLDE S 4088**

TOCCATA FOR PIANO (1979)
Rosemary Platt (pf.) **CORON LPS 3105**

TRIO FOR FLUTE, OBOE,
HARPSICHORD AND TAPE (1973)
Emma Lou Diemer (pf.), Atkinson, Wilson **ORION OC 693**

YOUTH OVERTURE
D.C. Youth Orchestra
(cond.) Lyn McLain **INTAM OAS 007**

DILLON, Fannie Charles (1881-1947)

FROM THE CHINESE, OP. 93
* * * * * * **DORIN 1014**

WOODLAND FLUTE CALL
(ARR. ALEXANDER SCHREINER)
Alexander Schreiner (org.) **COLUM
ML 5425 MS 6101**

DLUGOSZEWSKI, Lucia (1925-)

ANGELS OF THE INMOST HEAVEN (7'27)
Schwarz Instrumental Ensemble: Mark Gould (trp.),
Louis Ranger (trp.), Per Brevig (trb.),
David Taylor (trb.), Martin Smith (hn.)
(cond.) Gerard Schwarz — **FOLKW FTS 33902**

FIRE FRAGILE FLIGHT (1976) (8'30)
Johanna Albrecht (m-S.) with Orchestra
Of Our Time
(cond.) Joel Thome — **CANDI CE 31113**

SPACE IS A DIAMOND (SOLO TRUMPET) (10'29)
Gerard Schwarz (trp.) — **NONSU H 71275**

TENDER THEATRE FLIGHT NAGEIRE,
FOR BRASS AND PERCUSSION (18'00)
Schwarz Instrumental Ensemble: Schwarz (trp.),
Carroll (trp.), Smith (trp.), Taylor (b-trb.),
Langlitz (t-trb.), Dlugoszewski (perc.)
(cond.) Gerard Schwarz — **CRI SD 388**

DOBIE, Janet (1936-)

DIMENSIONS FOR STRINGS
West Australian Symphony Orchestra
(cond.) Patrick Thomas — **FESTI L 4 2040**

DIMENSIONS FOR STRINGS (10'00)
South Australian Symphony Orchestra (strs.)
(cond.) Patrick Thomas — **FESTI FC 80027**

DONCEANU, Felicia (1931-)

PONTI EUXINI, CLEPSIDRA, SKETCH
FOR OBOE, CLARINET, SOPRANO,
HARP AND PERCUSSION (20'00)
Contemporan Quartet: Manu (S.),
Chisu (ob.), Blaga (cl.),
Nemteanu (hp.), Badea (perc.) — **ELECT ST ECE 01406**

DOROW, Dorothy (-)

DREAM (5'32)
Dorothy Dorow (vce.) — **BIS LP 45**

PASTOURELLES, PASTOUREAUX (1'26)
Dorothy Dorow (vce.) — **BIS LP 45**

DRING, Madeleine (1923-1977)

AMERICAN DANCE (2'10)
Leigh Kaplan (pf.) — **CAMBR C 1014**

CARIBBEAN DANCE (2'10)
Leigh Kaplan (pf.), Susan Pitts (pf.) — **CAMBR C 1014**

COLOUR SUITE (12'45)
Leigh Kaplan (pf.) — **CAMBR C 1014**

DANZA GAYA (2'40)
Leigh Kaplan (pf.), Susan Pitts (pf.) — **CAMBR C 1014**

DEDICATIONS (HERRICK)
Robert Tear (T.), P. Ledger (pf.) — **CBS E 77050**

FIVE BETJEMAN SONGS
Robert Tear (T.), P. Ledger (pf.) — **CBS E 77050**

FIVE BETJEMAN SONGS
Margery Mackay (m-S.),
Leigh Kaplan (pf.) — **CAMBR CT 1020**

FOUR NIGHT SONGS
Robert Tear (T.), P. Ledger (pf.) — **CBS E 77050**

ITALIAN DANCE
Robin Paterson (duo pf.) — **CAMBR C 1015**

ITALIAN DANCE (2'09)
Tommy Reilly (har.), Skaila Kanga (hp).,
James Moody (pf.) — **ARGO ZK 55**

JIG
Leigh Kaplan (pf.) — **CAMBR C 1015**

MARCH FOR THE NEW YEAR
Leigh Kaplan (pf.) — **CAMBR C 1015**

MELISANDE, THE FAR AWAY
PRINCESS (AITKEN)
Robert Tear (T.), P. Ledger (pf.) — **CBS E 77050**

MOTO PERPETUO
Leigh Kaplan (pf.) — **CAMBR C 1016**

PASTEL PANACHE
Instrumental Ensemble — **CAMBR C 1016**

SHADES OF DRING
Instrumental Ensemble — **CAMBR C 1016**

TARANTELLE
Robin Paterson (pf.) — **CAMBR C 1015**

THREE DANCES
Leigh Kaplan (pf.) — **CAMBR C 1015**

THREE PIECES FOR FLUTE AND PIANO
Louise di Tullio (fl.), Leigh Kaplan (pf.) — **CAMBR C 1015**

THREE SHAKESPEARE SONGS
Robert Tear (T.), P. Ledger (pf.) — **CBS E 77050**

VALSE FRANCAISE
Leigh Kaplan (pf.) — **CAMBR C 1015**

VALSE FRANCAISE (3'45)
Leigh Kaplan (pf.), Susan Pitts (pf.) — **CAMBR C 1015**

VALSE FRANCAISE (3'56)
Natalie Field (pf.), Leigh Kaplan (pf.) — **CAMBR C 1023**

WALTZ FINALE
Leigh Kaplan (pf.) — **CAMBR C 1015**

WEST INDIAN DANCE
Robin Paterson (pf.) — **CAMBR C 1015**

DROSTE-HUELSHOFF, Annette Elise von, Baroness (1797-1848)

ES STEHET EIN FISCHLEIN IN EINEM
TIEFEN SEE
Chorus of Birnauer Kantorei
(cond.) K. Reiners — **HGBS - - -**

FOUR SONGS FOR BARITONE AND PIANO
Wolfgang Schone (Bar.),
Rudolf Reuter (pf.) — **FONO FSM 123003/4**

LIEDER IM CHORSATZ VON KLAUS REINERS
Chorus of Birnauer Kantorei
(cond.) K. Reiners — **HGBS - - -**

DVORKIN, Judith (1930-)

MAURICE, A SHAGGY TALE
Randolph Singers
(cond.) David Randolph — **CRI 102**

DYER, Susan (-1923)

OUTLANDISH SUITE, AN: FLORIDA NIGHT
SONG (CHUCK WILL'S WIDOW)
Jascha Heifetz (vln.), Emanuel Bay (pf.) — **DECCA DL 9760**

ECKHARDT-GRAMATTE, Sophie-Carmen (1902-1974)

BRASS CHAMBER MUSIC
Composers Brass Group — **MGE 34**

CONCERTO FOR UNACCOMPANIED
VIOLIN (A-MINOR)
Sophie-Carmen Eckhardt-Gramatte (vln.) **MASTE MB 1031**

CONCERTO IN A, FOR VIOLIN SOLO
* * * * * * **ODEON 0 6973 6**

DUO CONCERTANTE FOR CELLO AND PIANO
* * * * * * **CBC RCI 224**

DUO CONCERTANTE FOR CELLO
AND PIANO (15'40)
Peggie Samson (vlc.), Diedre Irons (pf.) **RCA CC/CCS 1018**

SUITE NO. 6 (THREE PIANO PIECES)
Diedre Irons (pf.) **RCA CC/CCS 1018**

SUITE NO. 6 (THREE PIANO PIECES) (14'40)
Sophie-Carmen Eckhardt-Gramatte (pf.) **CBC RCI 224**

SYMPHONY-CONCERTO FOR PIANO
AND ORCHESTRA
* * * * * * **CBC SM 107**

SYMPHONY-CONCERTO FOR PIANO
AND ORCHESTRA
Anton Kueriti (pf.) **RCA LSC 3175**

TEN CAPRICES, FOR VIOLIN SOLO
Chaplin (vln.) **MASTE MB 2018**

TRIPLE CONCERTO FOR TRUMPET,
CLARINET AND BASSOON
Collins (trp.), Morton (cl.), Corey (bsn.) with
National Arts Center Orchestra
(cond.) Marco Bernardi **CBS SM 272**

EDWARDS, Clara (1887-1974)

BY THE BEND IN THE RIVER
Robert White (T.), Samuel Sanders (pf.) **RCA ARL 1 1698**

INTO THE NIGHT
Ezio Pinza (B.), Gibner King (pf.) **COLUM ML 2142**

EGGLESTON, Anne (1934-   )

PIANO QUARTET
* * * * * * **CBC RCI 472**

ELKIND, Rachel (1937-   )

ROCKY MOUNTAINS (WITH WENDY
CARLOS) (FROM THE SHINING, FILM)
* * * * * * **WARNE HS 3449**

SHINING, THE (WITH WENDY CARLOS)
(EXCERPT FROM FILM SOUND TRACK)
* * * * * * **WARNE HS 3449**

ELWYN-EDWARDS, Dilys (-   )

CANEUON Y TRI ADERYN
Kenneth Bowen (T.), Anthony Saunders (pf.),
Elinor Bennett (hp.) **ARGO ZRG 769**

EMIDIO TAVORA, Florizinha (-   )

SAUDOSINHO AO VIOLAO
Arnaldo Rebello (pf.) **CORCO CDEM 9**

ESCOBAR, Maria Luisa (1908-   )

CANTO CARIBE
* * * * * * **ARCO 002**

CONCIERTO SENTIMENTALE FOR
PIANO AND ORCHESTRA
Rose Marie Sader (pf.) with Orchestra
(cond.) P.A. Rios Reyna **PREST 7138**

COSTA MONTANA Y LLANO
* * * * * * **ARCO 001**

ESCOT, Pozzi (1933-   )

EURE PAX FOR SOLO VIOLIN
* * * * * * **SPECT SR 136**

FERGUS ARE
Martha Folts (org.) **DELOS 25448**

NEYRAC LUX (FOR 1 PERFORMER, 3 GUITARS)
Harry Chalmiers (12 str, classical and
elec. gtr.) **SPECT SR 128**

EUGENIE, Charlotte Augusta Amalia Albertina, Princess (1830-1889)

DROTTNING JOSEPHINAS POLONAISE (2'16)
Arnold Ostman (pf.) **SWEDI SLT 33243**

HJERTATS HEM (1'36)
Elisabeth Soderstrom (S.),
Kerstin Meyer (m-S.),
Arnold Ostman (pf.) **SWEDI SLT 33243**

NOVEMBERKVAELLEN
Nicolai Gedda (Bar.) **POLAR POLS 410**

NOVEMBERKVAELLEN (BOETTIGER) (1'43)
Carl-Axel Hallgren (Bar.),
Arnold Ostman (pf.) **SWEDI SLT 33243**

SOMMERDAG, EN (1'21)
Elisabeth Soderstrom (S.),
Kerstin Meyer (m-S.),
Arnold Ostman (pf.) **SWEDI SLT 33243**

TILL VAAGEN (2'13)
Erik Saeden (Bar.),
Elisabeth Soderstrom (S.),
Arnold Ostman (pf.) **SWEDI SLT 33243**

EUTENEUER-ROHRER, Ursula Henrietta (1953-   )

... FUER AKKORDEON (1981) (4'00)
Teodoro Anzellotti (acdn.) **TTR TTR 001**

PERCUSSION QUARTET (5'09)
Percussion Ensemble of Badisches
Konservatorium: Leader M. Rohrer (perc.)
T. Anzellotti (acdn.), U. Euteneuer-Rohrer (pf.) **SOUND SST 0164**

TRIO NO. 1, FOR ACCORDION, PIANO AND
PERCUSSION (1980) (7'52)
Percussion Ensemble of Badisches
Konservatorium: Leader M. Rohrer (perc.),
T. Anzellotti (acdn.), U. Euteneuer-Rohrer (pf.) **TTR TTR 002**

TRIO NO. 2, FOR ACCORDION, PIANO AND
PERCUSSION (1980) (4'48)
Percussion Ensemble of Badisches
Konservatorium: Leader M. Rohrer (perc.),
T. Anzellotti (acdn.) U. Euteneuer-Rohrer (pf.) **TTR TTR 002**

TRIO NO. 4, FOR ACCORDION, PIANO AND
PERCUSSION (2'20)
Percussion Ensemble of Badisches
Konservatorium: Leader M. Rohrer (perc.),
T. Anzellotti (acdn.), U. Euteneuer-
Rohrer (pf.) **SOUND SST 0164**

TRIO NO. 5, FOR ACCORDION, PIANO AND
PERCUSSION (4'04)
Percussion Ensemble of Badisches
Konservatorium: Leader M. Rohrer (perc.),
T. Anzellotti (acdn.), U. Euteneuer-
Rohrer (pf.) **SOUND SST 0164**

FALCINELLI, Rolande (1920-   )

OEUVRES POUR ORGUE, VIOLIN ET ORGUE,
FLUTE ET ORGUE
Rolande Falcinelli (org.)   **REMST 10897**

SERMON SUR LA MONTAGNE, OP. 46
Rolande Falcinelli (org.)   **REMST 10882**

TRIPTIQUE, OP. 11
Rolande Falcinelli (org.)   **REMST 10882**

VARIATIONS SUR UNE BERCEUSE, OP. 48
Rolande Falcinelli (org.)   **REMST 10882**

FARRENC, Louise (1804-1875)

AIR RUSSE VARIE, OP. 17 (8'36)
Gena Raps (pf.)   **MUHER MHS 3766**

ETUDES FOR PIANO, OP. 26 (12'08)
Gena Raps (pf.)   **MUHER MHS 3766**

NONETTO, OP. 38
Bronx Arts Ensemble   **LEONA LPI 110**

SCHERZO FROM THE QUINTET, OP. 31
M. Hall (vln.), M. Middleton (vla.),
E. Steinbeck (vlc.), T. Theis (d-b.)
M. May (pf.)   **GEMIN RAP 1010**

TRIO IN E-MINOR, OP. 45 (22'49)
Katherine Hoover (fl.), Carter Brey (vlc.),
Barbara Weintraub (pf.)   **LEONA LPI 104**

TRIO NO. 2, IN D-MINOR, OP. 34 (21'10)
New York Lyric Arts Trio: Mary Freeman
Blankstein (vln.), Marion Feldman (vlc.),   **MUHER**
Gena Raps (pf.)   **MHS 3766**

FAXON, Nancy Plummer (1914-   )

ADAGIO ESPRESSIVO
Ruth Barrett Phelps (org.)   **WASHI WAS 13**

FEININGER, Leonore Helene (1901-   )

HOCHZEITSGLOCKEN, FOR PIANO
* * * * * *   **ROYAL 3989**

STERNEN BLUES, FOR PIANO
* * * * * *   **ROYAL 4062**

VALSE MUSETTE, FOR PIANO
* * * * * *   **ROYAL 4062**

FERNANDES, Maria Helena Rosas (-   )

CYCLE
Ruth Serrao   **FUNAR MMB 8403**

FERREYRA, Beatriz (1937-   )

MEDISANCES
* * * * * *   **PHILI 6 521 006**

SOLFEGE DE L'OBJET SONORE
* * * * * *   **ORTF SR 2**

FINE, Vivian (1913-   )

ALCESTIS
Imperial Philharmonic Orchestra of Tokyo
(cond.) William Strickland   **CRI SD 145**

CONCERTANTE FOR PIANO
AND ORCHESTRA (1944) (17'29)
Reiko Honsho (pf.) with Japan Philharmonic
(cond.) Akeo Watanabe   **CRI SD 135**

MISSA BREVIS (1976) FOR FOUR CELLOS AND
MEZZO SOPRANO (20'15)
DeGaetani (m-S.), Bartlett (vlc.), Finckel (vlc.),
Finckel (vlc.), Neuman (vlc.)   **CRI SD 434**

MOMENTI (1978) (8'50)
Lionel Nowark (pf.)   **CRI SD 434**

PAEAN (11'35)
F. Baker with Narrator, Eastman Brass
Ensemble and Bennington Choral Ensemble
(cond.) Vivian Fine   **CRI SD 260**

QUARTET FOR BRASS (1978) (11'20)
Anderson (trp), Dean (trp.), Jolly (hn.),
Benz (b-trb.)   **CRI SD 434**

SINFONIA AND FUGATO FOR PIANO
* * * * * *   **RCA LSC 7042**

SINFONIA AND FUGATO FOR PIANO (5'40)
Robert Helps (pf.)   **CRI SD 288**

FINZI, Graciane (1945-   )

PROFIL SONORE (5'10)
Elizabeth Chojnacka (hpcd.)   **PHILI 6526 009**

FIRESTONE, Idabelle (1874-1954)

BLUEBIRDS
Rise Stevens (m-S.) with Orchestra
(cond.) Howard Barlow   **VICTO ERA 149**

IF I COULD TELL YOU
Rise Stevens (m-S.) with Orchestra
(cond.) Howard Barlow   **VICTO ERA 149**

IN MY GARDEN
Rise Stevens (m-S.) with Orchestra
(cond.) Howard Barlow   **VICTO ERA 149**

YOU ARE THE SONG IN MY HEART
Rise Stevens (m-S.) with Orchestra
(cond.) Howard Barlow   **VICTO ERA 149**

FIRSOVA, Elena (1950-   )

CHAMBER CONCERTO FOR
FLUTE AND STRINGS
Alexander Korniev (fl.) with Members of   **MELOD**
Soviet State Orchestra   **C 10 18255 6**

FISHER, Katherine Danforth (1913-   )

MUSIC FOR FRIENDS
* * * * * *   **CENTU 36095**

SONG OF SUMMER (CANTATA) FOR
WOMEN'S CHORUS AND PIANO   **KENDA**
* * * * * *   **KRC 60 LP 398**

FLICK-FLOOD, Dora (1895-   )

HUAJILLA
Dora Flick-Flood (pf.)   **STAND 406**

THEME AND VARIATIONS
Dora Flick-Flood (pf.)   **STAND 406**

WATERFALL
Dora Flick-Flood (pf.)   **STAND 406**

FONTYN, Jacqueline (1930-   )

DIALOGUES FOR SAXOPHONE AND PIANO
F. Daneels (a-sax.), P. Mercks (pf.) (13'17)   **ALPHA DBM F 214**

FILIGRANE, FOR FLUTE AND HARP
Dieks Viller (fl.), Erika Waardenburg (hp.)   **TERPS 1982 024**

FOUGERES, FOR VIOLA AND HARP
Pieter Hans König (vla.), Erika
Waardenburg (hp.)   **TERPS 1982 024**

FRISES, FOR ORCHESTRA
Great Symphonic Band of the Belgium
Guides
(cond.) Norbert Nozy   **TERPS - - -**

HALO, FOR HARP AND CHAMBER ORCHESTRA
Yoko Nagae-Ceschina (hp.) with London
Sinfonietta
(cond.) Ronald Zollman   **TERPS 1982 024**

HET WAS EEN MAGHET UITVERCOREN
Ensemble Vocal de Bruxelles
(cond.) Fritz Hoyois   **ALPHA 5067 8**

HET WAS EEN MAGHET UITVERCOREN (2'23)
Ensemble Vocale de Bruxelles
(cond.) Fritz Hoyois   **CULTU 5067 8**

INTERMEZZO
Yoko Nagae-Ceschina   **TERPS 1982 024**

MIME 1, FOR FLUTE AND HARP
Dieks Visser (fl.),
Erika Waardenburg (hp.)   **TERPS 1982 024**

MOSAIQUES FOR CLARINET AND PIANO
* * * * * *   **BUFCM BCB 103**

MOUVEMENTS CONCERTANTS,
FOR TWO PIANOS AND STRINGS
* * * * * *   **ALPHA DBM 141 C**

PIEDIGROTTA
* * * * * *   **DECCA 173 476**

PSALMUS TERTIUS FOR BARITONE,
MIXED CHORUS AND ORCHESTRA (17'15)
Albrecht Klora (Bar.) with B.R.T.
Omroepkoor de Philharmonie van
Antwerpen (cond.) Leonce Gras   **CULTU 5071 1**

SIX EBAUCHES (10'03)
National Orkest van Belgie
(cond.) Daniel Sternefeld   **CULTU 5067 2**

SPIRALS FOR TWO PIANOS (15'43)
Raya Birguer (pf.), Pauline Marcelle (pf.)   **ALPHA DBM F 259**

TRIO FOR PIANO, VIOLIN AND CELLO
* * * * * *   **ALPHA DB 93**

FORMAN, Joanne (1934-   )

I THANK YOU GOD FOR MOST THIS AMAZING
DAY (E.E. CUMMINGS) (2'36)
Kristen Woolf (S.), Carla Scaletti (hp.),
Geoffrey Butcher (org.)   **OPONE 34**

IN TIME OF DAFFODILS/WHO KNOW
(E.E. CUMMINGS) (2'22)
Kristen Woolf (S.), Carla Scaletti (hp.),
Geoffrey Butcher (org.)   **OPONE 34**

MAGGIE AND MILLY AND MOLLY AND MAY
(E.E. CUMMINGS) (1'26)
Kristen Woolf (S.), Carla Scaletti (hp.),
Geoffrey Butcher (org.)   **OPONE 34**

NOCHE (LORCA) (1'22)

Kristen Woolf (S.), Carla Scaletti (hp.),
Geoffrey Butcher (org.)   **OPONE 34**

THREE LORCA SONGS (ARBOLE,
ES VERDAD, LA LUNA ASMA)
Sally Bissell (S.), Glenn McFarland (gtr.)   **OPONE 44**

FOWLER, Jennifer Joan (1939-   )

CHIMES, FRACTURED, FOR TWO FLUTES,
TWO CLARINETS, TWO BASSOONS,
ORGAN, BAGPIPES AND PERCUSSION
Sydney Symphony Orchestra
(cond.) John Hopkins   **FESTI L 42020**

CHIMES, FRACTURED, FOR TWO FLUTES,
TWO CLARINETS, TWO BASSOONS, ORGAN,
BAGPIPES AND PERCUSSION (7'39)
Sydney Symphony Orchestra
(cond.) John Hopkins   **FESTI FC 800 27**

FRAJT, Ludmila (1919-   )

DVANAEST MESECI, SONG CYCLE FOR
WOMEN'S CHORUS AND ORCHESTRA
* * * * * *   **RTB EP 61048**

NEOBICNI SVIRACI,
SYMPHONY STORY FOR CHILDREN
* * * * * *   **RTB EP 61026**

NOKTURNO (9'00)
Radio Belgrade Electronic Studio   **RTB EP 3130037**

PESMA SUNCU U MAJU
* * * * * *   **RTB EP 61033**

PESME NOCI, CANTATA FOR WOMEN'S CHORUS,
STRING ORCHESTRA, PIANO AND HARP
RTB Women's Chorus with String Orchestra
(cond.) Simic   **RTB LP 2509**

PESME RASTANKA, SONG CYCLE FOR MIXED
CHOIR A CAPPELLA
* * * * * *   **RTB JSM 1**

TUZBALICA (LAMENT) FOR WOMEN'S CHORUS
RTB Women's Chorus
(cond.) Simic   **RTB LP 2509**

FREED, Dorothy Whitson (1919-   )

WHENCE COMES THIS RUSH OF WINGS (CAROL)
(ARR WOMEN'S CHORUS A-CAPELLA)
Choir of St. Mary's Cathedral, Auckland
(cond.) Peter Godfrey   **KIWI EC 28**

FRITZ, Sherilyn Gail (1957-   )

MASS OF THE MORNING SUN
* * * * * *   **DULCI DR 1002**

FRONMUELLER, Frieda (1901-   )

BUSSTAGSKANTATE, FOR TENOR, BASS,
HORUS AND ORCHESTRA (1947)
Lange (T.), Hartmann (B.), Lehrergesang-
verein,Furth; Chor des Heinrich-
Schliemann-Gymnasiums, Furth;
Erlanger Kammerorchester
(cond.) Otmar Ruhland   **ABANO ABL 827**

BUSSTAGSKANTATE, FOR TENOR, BASS,
CHORUS AND ORCHESTRA (1947)
Lange (T.), Hartmann (B.), Lehrergesang-
verein, Furth; Chor des Heinrich-
Schliemann-Gymnasiums, Furth;
Erlanger Kammerorchester
(cond.) Otmar Ruhland   **MIXTR MXT 0 827**

CHRIST IST ERSTANDEN (CHORALINTRADE)
FOR WIND CHORUS
Posaunenchor Rosstal
(cond.) Martin Vogelhuber   **MIXTR MXT 0 827**

CHRIST IST ERSTANDEN (CHORALINTRADE)
FOR WIND CHORUS
Posaunenchor, Rosstal
(cond.) Martin Vogelhuber   **ABANO ABL 827**

FESTLICHE MUSIK NO. 11, FOR THREE
TRUMPETS AND FOUR TROMBONES
Collegium Aulos   **UNISO 22497**

HERR, WIE SIND DEINE WERKE SO GROSS
UND VIEL (PSALM-MOTETTE)
Der Junge Chor Furth
(cond.) Hildegard Appel   **ABANO ABL 827**

HERR, WIE SIND DEINE WERKE SO GROSS
UND VIEL (PSALM-MOTETTE)
Der Junge Chor Furth
(cond.) Hildegard Appel   **MIXTR MXT 0 827**

IN WALD UND FLUR (KINDERKANTATE) (GOTZ)
Knolle/Kinderchor U. Instr'Kreis
St. Petri Hamburg
(cond.) Harden   **MUSIC MV 20 1072**

JERUSALEM DU HOCHGEBAUTE STADT
(CHORALKANTATE) (FOR CHORUS,
BRASS CHOIR AND SOLO TRUMPET)
Karl Pfann (trp.), Lehrergesangverein
Furth, Chor des Heinrich Schliemann-
ymnasiums, Furth; Posaunenchor
Schniegling (cond.) Otmar Ruhland   **ABANO ABL 827**

JERUSALEM, DU HOCHGEBAUTE STADT
(CHORALKANTATE) (FOR CHORUS,
BRASS CHOIR AND SOLO TRUMPET)
Karl Pfann (trp.), Lehrergesangverein,
Furth, Chor des Heinrich-Schliemann-
Gymnasiums, Furth; Posaunenchor
Schniegling (cond.) Otmar Ruhland   **MIXTR MXT 0 827**

RUF INTRADE
Posaunenchor Baden   **JSV 657 614**

RUF INTRADE
Posaunenchor Rosstal
(cond.) Frieda Fronmueller   **MIXTR MXT 0 827**

RUF INTRADE
Posaunenchor, Rosstal
(cond.) Frieda Fronmueller   **ABANO ABL 827**

FRYZELL, Regina Holmen (1899-   )

CHRISTMAS WISH (1957)
Augustana Choir
(cond.) Henry Veld   **WORD 4012**

FUCHS, Lillian (1910-   )

JOTA, FOR VIOLIN AND PIANO
Bezrodny (vln.), Makarova (pf.)   **MONIT MC 2028**

JOTA, FOR VIOLIN AND PIANO
* * * * * *   **VOX D VCL 9057**

GAIGEROVA, Varvara Andrianovna (1903-1944)

FORTRESS AT STONE FORD, OPERA
ARIA OF PECHORIN
I. Kozlovsky (T.)   **MELOD D 028059 62**

GAINSBORG, Lolita Cabrera (1896-1981)

LULLABY (2'23)
Fierro (pf.) (2'23)   **PELIC LP 2017**

GAMILLA, Alice Doria (1931-   )

ALIW NG TUGTUGAN (BALITAW)
* * * * * *   **VILLA MLS 5174**

ANG PASKO'I PAG-IBIG
* * * * * *   **VILLA 4 1880**

I GIVE YOU MY HEART AT CHRISTMAS
* * * * * *   **VILLA 4 2238**

I PRAY SO HARD
* * * * * *   **ZODIA ZS 1 040**

MAGPAHANGGANG LANGIT (DANZA)
* * * * * *   **DYNA DNS 1065**

MILLION THANKS TO YOU, A
* * * * * *   **VILLA MLS 5185**

MILLION THANKS TO YOU, A
* * * * * *   **VILLA MLPO 5089 S**

MILLION THANKS TO YOU, A
* * * * * *   **CORAL CRL 757472**

MILLION THANKS TO YOU, A
* * * * * *   **VILLA MLP 5050**

MY CHRISTMAS LOVE AFFAIR
* * * * * *   **VILLA 4 2238**

MY WONDERFUL WORLD IS YOU (BALLAD)
* * * * * *   **JONAL JLP 506**

SA LAHAT NG ORAS (DANZA)
* * * * * *   **VICER TSP 5047**

GARCIA MUNOZ, Carmen (1929-   )

UNA MONTANA PASANDO
* * * * * *   **PHILI 6747 004**

GARDINER, Mary Elizabeth (1932-   )

MOSAIC
Mary Elizabeth Gardiner (pf.)   * * * **EK 1**

MOSAIC (TORONTO, 1984)
Elaine Keillor (pf.)   **KEILL WRCI 3315**

GARUTA, Lucia Yanovna (1902-   )

CONCERTO FOR PIANO AND ORCHESTRA
H. Braun (pf.) with Latvian Radio
Orchestra
(cond.) Tons   **MELOD D 010989 90**

LIVING FLAME (ORATORIO)
Daine (m-S.), Zabers (Bar.) with Kalnyny
Choir and Latvian Radio Orchestra   **MELOD D 028415 6**

MEDITATION
P. Sipolniek (org.)   **MELOD SM 03523 4**

SEVEN LATVIAN FOLK SONGS FOR PIANO
H. Braun (pf.)   **MELOD D 029273 4**

THREE PRELUDES IN E-MAJOR, D-FLAT MAJOR AND
C-SHARP MAJOR
H. Braun (pf.)   **MELOD D 010989 90**

GIDEON, Miriam (1906-   )

ADORABLE MOUSE, THE, FOR VOICE
AND STRING QUARTET
Reardon (vce.) with Ariel Quartet   **SEREN SRS 12050**

CONDEMNED PLAYGROUND, THE (1963) (15'45)
Bryn-Julson (S.), Cassolas (T.), Galimir (vln.),
Toromeo (vla.), Arico (vlc.), Dunkel (fl.)
Shapiro (vln.), Heller (bsn.)
(cond.) Fritz Jahoda   **CRI SD 343**

FANTASY ON A JAVANESE MOTIVE (1948)
Seymour Barab (vlc.), William Masselos (pf.)
PARAD PL 10001

HOUND OF HEAVEN (1945)
Metcalf (Bar.), Roseman (ob.), Cohen (vln.),
Phillips (vla.), Sherry (vlc.)
(cond.) Fritz Jahoda
CRI SD 286

HOW GOODLY ARE THY TENTS (1947)
* * * * * *
WESTM XWN 18857

HOW GOODLY ARE THY TENTS (1947)
Chizuk Amuno Congregation
Choral Society (cond.) Hugo Weisgall
WESTM W 9634

LYRIC PIECE (1941)
Imperial Philharmonic Orchestra, Tokyo
(cond.) William Strickland
CRI 170

NOCTURNES (7'52)
J. Raskin (S.) with Da Capo Chamber Players
and Guest Artists
(cond.) John Demain
CRI SD 401

PIANO SUITE, NO. 3
* * * * * *
VICTO LSC 7042

PIANO SUITE, NO. 3 (3'48)
Robert Helps (pf.)
CRI SD 288

QUESTIONS ON NATURE (1965) (9'35)
Jan deGaetani (m-S.), Philip West (ob.),
S. Lipman (pf.), B. Jekofsky (perc.)
CRI SD 343

RESOUNDING LYRE, THE
Constantine Cassolas (T.), Robert Black (lyre)
with Constantine Speculum Musical
CRI SD 493

RHYMES FROM THE HILL (1968) (7'35)
Gaetani (m-S.), Bloom (cl.), Sherry (vlc.),
Raymond Des Roches (mar.)
(cond.) David Gilbert
CRI SD 286

SEASONS OF TIME, THE: TANKA POETRY OF
ANCIENT JAPAN (1969)
Paul Sperry (T.), M. Lobel, G. Schwarz
SEREN 12078

SEASONS OF TIME, THE: TANKA POETRY OF
ANCIENT JAPAN (1969)
Mandac (S.), Kraber (fl.),
Arico (vlc.), Jahoda (pf.)
DESTO DC 7117

SLOW, SLOW FRESH FOUNT (1941)
Bushnell Choir
(cond.) Alexander Dashnaw
GOLDE CRS 4172

SONATA FOR PIANO
Robert Black (pf.)
CRI SD 481

SONGS OF YOUTH AND MADNESS (1977) (14'36)
J. Raskin (vce.) with American Composers
Orchestra (cond.) James Dixon
CRI SD 401

SONNETS FROM SHAKESPEARE, FOR BARITONE
AND ORCHESTRA
William Sharp (Bar.) with Prism Orchestra
(cond.) Robert Black
CRI SD 527

SPIRIT ABOVE THE DUST
Elaine Bonazzi (m-S.) with Contemporary
Chamber Ensemble
(cond.) Arthur Weisberg
CRI SD 493

SYMPHONIA BREVIS
Radio Orchestra, Zurich
(cond.) Jacques Monod
CRI SD 128

WING'D HOUR, FOR TENOR AND ORCHESTRA
Constantine Cassolas (T.) with Prism
Orchestra
(cond.) Robert Black
CRI SD 527

GIFFORD, Helen Margaret (1935-   )

CANZONE
Tasmanian Orchestra
(cond.) Patrick Thomas
ABC RRCS 72

CHIMAERA
South Australian Symphony Orchestra
(cond.) Patrick Thomas
ABC RRCS 386

IMPERIUM
Melbourne Symphony Orchestra
(cond.) Keith Humble
ABC RRCS 387

PHANTASMA FOR STRINGS
Strings of West Australian Symphony
Orchestra
(cond.) Patrick Thomas
ABC RRCS 124

GILBERT, Pia (1921-   )

INTERRUPTED SUITE
Gary Gray (cl.), Dolores Stevens (pf.),
Richard Grayson (pf.),
Susan Savage (prep. pf.)
PROTO PR 150

TRANSMUTATIONS
Thomas Harmon (org.), Scott Shepherd (perc.) **PROTO PR 150**

GIROD-PARROT, Marie Louise (1915-   )

INTERLUDE SUR LE PSAUME 47
Marie Louise Girod-Parrot (org.)
VOGUE CV 25001

GLANVILLE-HICKS, Peggy (1912-   )

CONCERTINO DA CAMERA
Carlo Bussoti (pf.) with New York
Woodwind Ensemble
COLUM ML 4990

CONCERTINO ROMANTICO FOR
VIOLA AND ORCHESTRA
Walter Trampler (vla.) with MGM Orchestra
(cond.) Carlos Surinach
MGM 3559

ETRUSCAN CONCERTO FOR
PIANO AND ORCHESTRA
Carlo Bussoti (pf.) with MGM Orchestra
(cond.) Carlos Surinach
MGM 3557

GYMNOPEDICS 1-3
Radio Symphony Orchestra of Berlin
(cond.) Jonel Perlea
COLOS COL V 81046

LETTERS FROM MOROCCO
Loren Driscoll (T.) with MGM Orchestra
(cond.) Carlos Surinach
MGM E 3549

NAUSICAA
Soloists with Athens Symphony Orchestra
and Chorus
(cond.) Carlos Surinach
CRI 175

PRELUDE FOR A PENSIVE PUPIL (2'22)
Robert Helps (pf.)
CRI SD 288

SINFONIA DA PACIFICA
MGM Orchestra
(cond.) C. Surinach
MGM E 3336

SONATA
N. Zabaleta (hp.)
CLASS 920 111

SONATA FOR HARP (PASTORALE)
N. Zabaleta (hp.)
ESOTE ES 523

SONATA FOR HARP (PASTORALE) (2'21)
John Marson (hp.)
DISCO ABK 15

SONATA FOR PIANO AND PERCUSSION
Carlo Bussoti (pf.) with New York
Percussion Group
COLUM ML 4990

THREE GYMNOPEDIES
Berlin Radio Symphony Orchestra
(cond.) Jonel Perea
VARES VC 81046

THREE GYMNOPEDIES (1934)
MGM Chamber Orchestra
(cond.) Carlos Surinach   **MGM E 3336**

TRANSPOSED HEADS, THE
* * * * * *   **LOUIS 545 6**

GLEN, Irma (1902-   )

BRIDGE TO HIGHER CONSCIOUSNESS, A
* * * * * *   **NUMIN LB 2897**

CHRISTMAS MIRACLES NOW!
* * * * * *   **NUMIN PC 136**

CHURCH OF RELIGIOUS SCIENCE AND ITS
MUSIC, THE
* * * * * *   **TEMPO RSC 1**

DON BLANDING'S VAGABOND'S HOUSE
* * * * * *   **TEMPO TR 460**

DON BLANDING'S VAGABOND'S HOUSE
* * * * * *   **TEMPO TR 458**

DON BLANDING'S VAGABOND'S HOUSE
* * * * * *   **TEMPO TR 456**

DON BLANDING'S VAGABOND'S HOUSE
* * * * * *   **TEMPO
UR 14146**

MUSIC, ECOLOGY AND YOU
* * * * * *   **NUMIN CFS 2155**

PRAYER THERAPY
* * * * * *   **NUMIN 2899/2900**

PROMISES OF CHRIST JESUS, THE
* * * * * *   **NUMIN CFS 2156**

STORY BOOK LADY
* * * * * *   **MEMO 9201/2/3**

GONZAGA, Chiquinha (1847-1935)

A MORENA (3'25)
Vania Carvalho (S.) with Chamber
Ensemble   **ESTEL 13 79 0333**

A NOITE
Arnaldo Rebello (pf.)   **CORCO CDEM 9**

ATRAENTE (1'58)
Leci Brandao (S.) with Chamber Ensemble **ESTEL 13 79 0333**

BIONNE (3'25)
Chamber Ensemble   **ESTEL 13 79 0333**

EM GUARDA (2'13)
Chamber Ensemble   **ESTEL 13 79 0333**

LUA BRANCA (2'32)
Vania Carvalho (S.) with Chamber
Ensemble   **ESTEL 13 79 0333**

MACHUCA (2'50)
Leci Brandao (S.) with Chamber Ensemble **ESTEL 13 79 0333**

MANHA DE AMOR (3'15)
Manha De Amor   **ESTEL 13 79 0333**

MUSICIANA (2'42)
Chamber Ensemble   **ESTEL 13 79 0333**

OS NAMORADOS DA LUA (4'28)
Vania Carvalho (S.) with Strings   **ESTEL 13 79 0333**

PLANGENTE (5'35)
Chamber Ensemble   **ESTEL 13 79 0333**

TIM TIM (2'13)
Chamber Ensemble   **ESTEL 13 79 0333**

GOOLKASIAN-RAHBEE, Dianne Zabelle (1938-   )

PHANTASIE VARIATIONS FOR PIANO, OP. 12
Lehrer (pf.)   **EDUCO 3130**

GOTKOVSKY, Ida-Rose Esther (1933-   )

BRILLIANCE, FOR SAXOPHONE AND PIANO
Jackson (sax.), Mainous (pf.)   **MUHER
MHS 3623**

BRILLIANCE, FOR SAXOPHONE AND PIANO
Daneels (sax.), Gotkovsky (pf.)   **DECCA 153 006**

GRAD-BUCH, Hulda (1912-   )

CONCERTS
* * * * * *   **KOL - - -**

OTHER COMPOSITIONS
* * * * * *   **KOL - - -**

SWEET FOR YOUTH, A (PIANO, 4 HANDS)
* * * * * *   **KOL - - -**

GRAINGER, Ella Viola Strom-Brandelius (1889-   )

FAREWELL TO AN ATOLL
* * * * * *   **EMI OASD 7606**

GREENWALD, Jan Carol (1952-   )

DURATION 2 (12'50)
Electronic Music Studio, California
Institute of the Arts   **CRI SD 443**

GREVER, Maria (1885-1951)

JURAME
Careras (T.) with English Chamber
Orchestra   **PHILI 9500 894**

TE QUIERO, DIJISTE
J. Carreras (T.)   **PHILI 411 422 1 PH**

GRIMANI, Maria Margherita (-   )

SINFONIE (1713)
New England Women's Symphony
(cond.) Jean Lamon   **GALAX GAL 004**

GUBAIDULINA, Sofia Asgatovna (1931-   )

CHACONNE FOR PIANO, IN B-MINOR
A. Cherkasov (pf.)   **MELOD D 02155 6**

CONCERTO FOR BASSOON AND
STRING ORCHESTRA
Valeri Popov (bsn.) with State
Symphony Orchestra
(cond.) L. Mestaninov   **MELOD
C 10 12749 50**

CONCORDANZA FOR CHAMBER ENSEMBLE
Prague Musica Viva
(cond.) Z. Vostrak   **PANTN 11 0342 3**

DE PROFUNDIS (FROM SOWJETISCHE
MEISTER DER BALLADENKUNST)
* * * * * *   **MELOD
C 20 16633 4**

DETTO II, FOR CELLO AND CHAMBER
ENSEMBLE (15'00)
Ivan Monigetti (vlc.) with Soloists from
Academic Symphony Orchestra
of Moscow (cond.) Dmitri Kitayenko   **MELOD
C 10 10167 63**

IN CROCE, FOR VIOLONCELLO AND ORGAN
Jozef Podhoransky (vlc.), Vladimir Ruso (org.) **OPUS 9111 1277**

NOCH V MEMFIS, CANTATA
* * * * * * **MELOD C 10 15059 60**

RUBAYAT, CANTATA FOR BARITONE AND
CHAMBER ENSEMBLE
Sergei Vakovenko (Bar.) with
Chamber Orchestra
(cond.) Gennadi Rozhdestvensky **MELOD C 10 15059 60**

GYRING, Elizabeth (1906-1970)

PIANO SONATA, NO. 2 (1957)
Mitchell Andrews **CRI SD 252**

HAGER-ZIMMERMANN, Hilde (1907-)

FRUHLINGSGESCHENK
* * * * * * **LORBY BI 668**

MEDITATION
* * * * * * **LORBY BI 624**

HAIK-VANTOURA, Suzanne (1912-)

BURNING BUSH, THE (EXODUS, CH. 3, V. 1)
Emile Kasmann (B.) with Choir **HARMU HMU 989**

ELEGY OF DAVID (II SAMUEL, CH. 1, V. 19)
Adolphe Attia (T.) **HARMU HMU 989**

ESTHER (CH. 5, V. 1)
Adolphe Attia (T.) **HARMU HMU 989**

HEAR, O HEAR (DEUTERONOMY, CH. 6, V. 4)
Michel Scherb (Bar.) **HARMU HMU 989**

LAMENTATIONS (CH. 1, V. 1)
Emile Kasmann (B.) **HARMU HMU 989**

PSALM 3
Xavier Tamalet (B.), Michele
Gonzales (celtic hp.) **ERATO STU 71269**

PSALM 6
Adolphe Attia (T.) **HARMU HMU 989**

PSALM 8
Adolphe Attia (T.), Michele
Gonzales (celtic hp.) **ERATO STU 71269**

PSALM 19
Adolphe Attia (T.) with Choir and
Instrumental Ensemble
(cond.) Stephane Caillat **ERATO STU 71269**

PSALM 23
Michel Scherb (Bar.) **HARMU HMU 989**

PSALM 24
Adolphe Attia (T.) **HARMU HMU 989**

PSALM 122
Michel Scherb (Bar.) **HARMU HMU 989**

PSALM 123
Choral Ensemble **HARMU HMU 989**

PSALM 130
Bernard Fabre-Garrus (Bar.), Michele
Gonzales (celtic hp.) with Petit
Choeur Final **ERATO STU 71269**

PSALM 133
Adolphe Attia (T.) **HARMU HMU 989**

PSALM 150
Choral Ensemble **HARMU HMU 989**

PSAUME 27
Bernard Fabre-Garus (Bar.), Michele
Gonzales (celtic hp.) with Petit
Choeur Final **ERATO STU 71269**

PSAUME 29
Choir with Instrumental Ensemble
(cond.) Stephane Caillat **ERATO STU 71269**

PSAUME 93
Choir with Instrumental Ensemble
(cond.) Stephane Caillat **ERATO STU 71269**

PSAUME 96
Choir with Instrumental Ensemble
(cond.) Stephane Caillat **ERATO STU 71269**

PSAUME 131
Adolphe Attia (T.), Michele Gonzales
(celtic hp.) with Petit Choeur Final **ERATO STU 71269**

PSAUME 137
Xavier Tamalet (B.), Michele
Gonzales (celtic hp.) **ERATO STU 71269**

SACERDOTAL BENEDICTION
(NUMBERS, CH. 6, V. 22)
Michel Scherb (Bar.) **HARMU HMU 989**

SONG OF SONGS, THE (CH. 1, V. 1)
Adolphe Attia (T.) **HARMU HMU 989**

TEN COMMANDMENTS, THE
(EXODUS, CH. 20, V. 1-17)
Bernard Fabre-Garrus (Bar.) **ERATO STU 71269**

VISION D'ISAIE (ISAIAH, CH. 11, V. 1-9)
Xavier Tamalet (B.) **ERATO STU 71269**

HALL, Pauline (1890-1969)

BLACKBIRDS, THE (VERLAINE)
Bergen Symphony Orchestra
(cond.) K. Andersen **PHILI 6507 038**

CIRCUS PICTURES
Norwegian Broadcasting Orchestra
(cond.) Bergh **PHILI 839 239 AY**

ORNELAND
Knut Skram (B.), Robert Levin (pf.) **PHILI 6507 001**

SUITE FOR WIND QUINTET
Norwegian Wind Quintet **PHILI 839 256 AY**

HARDELOT, Guy d' (1858-1936)

BECAUSE, SONG (1902)
Jose Carreras (T.) **PHILI 411422 IPH**

BIG LADY MOON
* * * * * * **ARGO ZK 97**

I KNOW A LOVELY GARDEN
Felicity Palmer (S.), John Constable (pf.) **ARGO ZE 97 PSI**

THREE GREEN BONNETS
Felicity Palmer (S.), John Christopher (pf.) **ARGO ZK 45**

HARKNESS, Rebekah West (1915-)

BARCELONA SUITE
Symphony Orchestra
(cond.) Sylvan Levin **VANGR VRS 1058**

GIFT OF THE MAGI
Symphony Orchestra
(cond.) Sylvan Levin **VANGR VRS 1058**

JOURNEY TO LOVE (1958)
* * * * * * **WESTM YWM 18745**

SAFAFRI (1955)
* * * * * * **CAVAL DC 1000**

HAYAKAWA, Kazuko (1944-   )

INSISTENCE II, FOR FLUTE SOLO
Masahiro Itoi (fl.)   **JAPAN JFC 8302**

HAYS, Doris Ernestine (1941-   )

ARABELLA AND 21 OTHER RAGS
* * * * * *   **SOUTH MQLP 38**

BLUES FRAGMENTS FROM SOUTHERN
VOICES, FOR ORCHESTRA
* * * * * *   **FOLKW FTS 37476**

CELEBRATION OF NO
* * * * * *   **FOLKW FTS 37476**

EXPLOITATION
* * * * * *   **FOLKW FTS 37476**

FOLLOW THE LEADER, FOR MIXED CHORUS
AND INSTRUMENTAL ENSEMBLE
* * * * * *   **SILVE 74 185 10**

JUNCTURE DANCE II, FOR MIXED CHORUS
AND INSTRUMENTAL ENSEMBLE
* * * * * *   **SILVE 74 185 10**

LOOK OUT, FOR MIXED CHORUS
* * * * * *   **SILVE 74 185 02**

MAKE A MELODY, MAKE A SONG,
FOR SOPRANO
* * * * * *   **SILVE 74 185 11**

OL'CLO'
Clifford Synder (Bar.), Doris Hays (pf.) **SILVE 74 183 08**

ON THE WAY TO ...., FOR MIXED CHORUS
AND INSTRUMENTAL ENSEMBLE
* * * * * *   **SILVE 74 186 10**

SOUND PIECE ONE, FOR CHAMBER GROUP
* * * * * *   **SILVE 74 184 01**

SOUND PIECE TWO
* * * * * *   **SILVE 74 183 04**

SOUTHERN VOICES FOR TAPE
Daisy Newman (S.), Phil Thomas (pf.)   **FOLKW FTS 37476**

SPECTRUM, FOR FOUR, AND
OTHER COMPOSITIONS
* * * * * *   **SILVE 74 183/4/5/6**

SUNDAY NIGHTS
Doris Hays (pf.)   **FINNA SR 9025**

TRR, CLICK, POP, POP, FOR MIXED CHORUS
* * * * * *   **SILVE 74 184 03**

WALKIN' TALKIN' BLUES
Doris Hays (vce.), Georges Deviviers (d-b.) **SILVE 74 184 05**

HELSINGIUS, Barbara (-   )

BARBARA'S BLANDADE
Barbara Helsingius (vce.)   **RCA PL 40207**

DET VAR EN GAENG (1977)
Barbara Helsingius (vce.)   **RCA PL 40042**

FRA BARBARA MED KJAERLIGHET
Barbara Helsingius (vce.)   **RCA PLY 40274**

KAHLAAJATYTTOE (POEMS BY AALE
TYNNI AND AILA MERILUOTO) (1984)
Barbara Helsingius (vce.)   **KERBE KEL 634**

OLIPA KERRAN (1978)
Barbara Helsingius (vce.)   **RCA PL 40093**

RAKKAUDELLA
Barbara Helsingius (vce.)   **PLAY LP 6024**

REFLECTION (1984)
Barbara Helsingius (vce.)   **KERBE KEL 633**

SPEGLING
Barbara Helsingius (vce.)   **RCA PL 71006**

SPEILING (1982)
Barbara Helsingius (vce.)   **RCA PLY 40273**

HENDERSON, Ruth Watson (1932-   )

FOUR MUSICAL ANIMAL TALES
Toronto Children's Choir   **WRCI 1456**

HENSEL, Fanny Caecilia (1805-1847)

A CAPELLA (PART SONGS)
Lieder Krief Ensemble   **NORTH NR 213**

ABENDBILD, OP. 10, NO. 3 (1'48)
Brigitte Lafon (m-S.), Françoise
Tillard (pf.)   **CALLI CAL 121314**

BERGESLUST
Berenice Bramson (S.), Roger Rundle (pf.) **GEMIN RAP 1010**

BERGESLUST, OP. 10, NO. 5 (1'23)
Aline Dumas (S.), Françoise Tillard (pf.) **CALLI CAL 121314**

ERSEHNTE, DIE, OP. 9, NO. 1 (2'30)
Aline Dumas (S.), Françoise Tillard (pf.) **CALLI CAL 121314**

FERNE, OP. 9, NO. 2 (2'33)
Brigitte Lafon (m-S.), Françoise
Tillard (pf.)   **CALLI CAL 121314**

FOUR LIEDER (DIE NONNE, IM HERBSTE,
DU BIST DIE RUH, VORWORT)
John Ostendorf (B-Bar.), Katherine
Ciesinski (m-S.), Rudolph Palmer (pf.) **LEONA LPI 107**

FOUR LIEDER FOR PIANO, OP. 2 (10'15)
Virginia Eskin (pf.)   **NORTH NR 215**

FOUR LIEDER FOR PIANO, OP. 8 (11'10)
Virginia Eskin (pf.)   **NORTH NR 215**

FÜNF LIEDER, OP. 10, NO. 5 (BERGESLUST)
(1847) (1'20)
Susan Larson (S.)   **NORTH NR 215**

GARTENLIEDER, OP. 3
Susan Larson (S.) with Liederkreis
Ensemble   **NORTH NR 213**

GARTENLIEDER, OP. 3, NO. 1, HÖRST DU NICHT
DIE BAEUME RAUSCHEN (1846) (2'15)
Liederkreis Ensemble   **NORTH NR 215**

GARTENLIEDER, OP. 3, NO. 3, IM
HERBSTE (1846) (2'20)
Liederkreis Ensemble   **NORTH NR 215**

GARTENLIEDER, OP. 3, NO. 4,
MORGENGRUSS (1846) (1'55)
Liederkreis Ensemble   **NORTH NR 215**

GONDELLIED, OP. 1, NO. 6 (3'26)
Aline Dumas (S.), Françoise
Tillard (pf.)   **CALLI CAL 121314**

GONDOLLIED, OP. 1, NO. 6 (4'09)
Grayson Hirst (T.), Michel Yuspeh (pf.) **LEONA LPI 112**

HEIMWEH, DAS (ROBERT) (1'48)
Tuula Nienstedt (Cont.), Uwe Wegner (pf.) **MUSVI MV 30 1104**

HEIMWEH, DAS, OP. 8, NO. 2 (1'50)
Brigitte Lafon (m-S.), Françoise Tillard (pf.) **CALLI CAL 121314**

IM HERBSTE, OP. 10, NO. 4 (2'37)
Aline Dumas (S.), Françoise Tillard (pf.) **CALLI CAL 121314**

ITALIEN (GRILLPARZER) (1'37)
Tuula Nienstedt (Cont.), Uwe Wegner (pf.) **MUSVI MV 30 1104**

ITALIEN, OP. 8, NO. 3
Berenice Bramson (S.), Roger Rundle (pf.) **GEMIN RAP 1010**

ITALIEN, OP. 8, NO. 3 (1'30)
Brigitte Lafon (m-S.), Françoise Tillard (pf.) **CALLI CAL 121314**

MAIABEND, DER, OP. 9, NO. 5 (1'10)
Aline Dumas (S.), Françoise Tillard (pf.) **CALLI CAL 121314**

MAINACHT, DIE, OP. 9, NO. 6 (2'20)
Brigitte Lafon (m-S), Françoise Tillard (pf.) **CALLI CAL 121314**

MAINACHT, DIE, OP. 9, NO. 6 (HOELTY) (2'25) **MUSVI**
Tuula Nienstedt (Cont.), Uwe Wegner (pf.) **MV 30 1104**

MAYENLIED, OP. 1, NO. 4 (1'21)
Grayson Hirst (T.), Michel Yuspeh (pf.) **LEONA LPI 112**

MAYENLIED, OP. 1, NO. 4 (1'30)
Aline Dumas (S.), Françoise Tillard (pf.) **CALLI CAL 121314**

MELODIES FOR PIANO, OP. 4, NOS. 4-6
AND OP. 5, NOS. 2 AND 4
Judith Alstadter (pf.) **MUHER MHS 4163**

MORGENSTÄNDCHEN, OP. 1, NO. 5 (1'31)
Grayson Hirst (T.), Michel Yuspeh (pf.) **LEONA LPI 112**

MORGENSTÄNDCHEN, OP. 1, NO. 5 (2'04)
Aline Dumas (S.), Françoise Tillard (pf.) **CALLI CAL 121314**

ORATORIO BASED ON STORIES FROM THE BIBLE
Soloists with choir and Orchestra der
Kölner Kurrende **TELDE**
(cond.) Elke Mascha Blanckenburg **BEST 999009**

PIANO PIECES, OP. 2
Virginia Eskin (pf.) **NORTH NR 213**

PIANO PIECES, OP. 7
Virginia Eskin **NORTH NR 213**

PRAELUDIUM FOR ORGAN (1829) (4'20)
Victoria Sirota (org.) **NORTH NR 215**

PRELUDE IN E-MINOR
Rosario Marciano (pf.) **FONO FSM 53 0 36**

PRELUDE IN E-MINOR (2'13)
Rosario Marciano (pf.) **TURNA TV 34685**

PRELUDE IN F-MAJOR
Victoria Sirota (org.) **NORTH NR 213**

ROMANCE WITHOUT WORDS, FOR PIANO,
OP. 2, NO. 4, IN A-MAJOR (2'55)
Françoise Tillard (pf.) **CALLI CAL 121314**

ROMANCE WITHOUT WORDS, FOR PIANO,
OP. 4, NO. 2, IN C-SHARP MINOR (1'34)
Françoise Tillard (pf.) **CALLI CAL 121314**

ROMANCE WITHOUT WORDS, FOR PIANO,
OP. 4, NO. 3, IN E-MAJOR (3'37)
Françoise Tillard (pf.) **CALLI CAL 121314**

ROMANCE WITHOUT WORDS, FOR PIANO,
OP. 5, NO. 3 IN E-FLAT MAJOR (4'30)
Françoise Tillard (pf.) **CALLI CAL 121314**

ROMANCE WITHOUT WORDS, FOR PIANO,
OP. 8, NO. 1, IN B-MINOR (4'10)
Françoise Tillard (pf.) **CALLI CAL 121314**

ROMANCE WITHOUT WORDS, FOR PIANO,
OP. 8, NO. 2, IN A-MAJOR (2'45)
Françoise Tillard (pf.) **CALLI CAL 121314**

ROMANCE WITHOUT WORDS, FOR PIANO,
OP. 8, NO. 3, IN D-FLAT MAJOR (2'30)
Françoise Tillard (pf.) **CALLI CAL 121314**

ROSENKRANZ, DER, OP. 9, NO. 3 (2'05)
Aline Dumas (S.), Françoise Tillard (pf.) **CALLI CAL 121314**

SCHWANENLIED, OP. 1, NO. 1 (2'45)
Brigitte Lafon (m-S.), Françoise Tillard (pf.) **CALLI CAL 121314**

SCHWANENLIED, OP. 1, NO. 1 (3'51)
Grayson Hirst (T.), Michel Yuspeh (pf.) **LEONA LPI 112**

SECHS LIEDER, OP. 7, NO. 3,
FRÜHLING (1846) (1'30)
Susan Larson (S.) **NORTH NR 215**

SECHS LIEDER, OP. 7, NO. 5, BITTE (1846) (1'10)
Susan Larson (S.) **NORTH NR 215**

SECHS LIEDER, OP. 7, NO. 6, DEIN IS MEIN
HERZ (1846) (2'20)
Susan Larson (S.) **NORTH NR 215**

SECHS LIEDER, OP. 9, NO. 2, FERNE (1823) (2'05)
Susan Larson (S.) **NORTH NR 215**

SECHS LIEDER, OP. 9, NO. 4, DIE FRÜHEN
GRÄBER (1828) (4'10)
Susan Larson (S.) **NORTH NR 215**

SECHS LIEDER, OP. 9, NO. 4, DIE FRÜHEN
GRÄBER (3'09)
Brigitte Lafon (m-S.), Françoise
Tillard (pf.) **CALLI CAL 121314**

SECHS LIEDER, OP. 9, NO. 4, DIE FRÜHEN
GRÄBER (KLOPSTOCK)
Tuula Nienstedt (Cont.), Uwe Wegner (pf.) **MUSVI MV 30 1104**

SECHS LIEDER, OP. 9, NO. 6, DIE
MAINACHT (1838) (1'50)
Susan Larson (S.) **NORTH NR 215**

SEHNSUCHT (DROYSEN) (2'00)
Tuula Nienstedt (Cont.), Uwe Wegner (pf.) **MUSVI MV 30 1104**

SEHNSUCHT, OP. 9, NO. 7 (OF FELIX
MENDELSSOHN) (2'17)
Aline Dumas (S.), Françoise Tillard (pf.) **CALLI CAL 121314**

SENNIN, DIE (2'06)
Aline Dumas (S.), Françoise Tillard (pf.) **CALLI CAL 121314**

SIX SONGS, OP. 1
Grayson Hirst (T.), Michel Yuspeh (pf.) **LEONA LPI 112**

SOLO SONGS FOR SOPRANO AND PIANO
Susan Larson (S.), Virginia Eskin (pf.) **NORTH NR 213**

SONGS FROM OP. 7, 9 AND 10
Susan Larson (S.) **NORTH NR 213**

SONGS WITHOUT WORDS, OP. 2 AND 8
Virginia Eskin (pf.) **NORTH NR 213**

SULEIKA AND HATEM, OP. 8, NO. 12
(OF FELIX MENDELSSOHN)
* * * * * * **ANGEL ANG 36712**

SULEIKA AND HATEM, OP. 8, NO. 12
(OF FELIX MENDELSSOHN) (2'37)
Aline Dumas (S.), Françoise Tillard (pf.) **CALLI CAL 121314**

TRIO FOR VIOLIN, CELLO AND PIANO,
IN D-MINOR Clementi Trio **LARGO 5003**

TRIO FOR VIOLIN, CELLO AND PIANO,
IN D-MINOR, OP. 11 (11'18)

Trio Fidelio **CALLI CAL 121314**

TRIO FOR VIOLIN, CELLO AND PIANO,
IN D-MINOR,
OP. 11 (24'10)
Camerata Canada: Victor Martin (vln.)
Coenraad Bloemendal (vlc.), Elyakim
Taussig (pf.) **CRYST S 642**

TRIO FOR VIOLIN, CELLO AND PIANO,
IN D-MINOR,
OP. 11 (25'21)
Macalester Trio **VOX SVBX 5112**

TWO LIEDER (NACHTWANDERER,
ROSENKRANZ)
John Ostendorf (B-Bar.), Rudolph Palmer (pf.) **LEONA LPI 107**

VERLUST, OP. 9, NO. 10 (OF FELIX
MENDELSSOHN) (1'38)
Aline Dumas (S.), Françoise Tillard (pf.) **CALLI CAL 121314**

VORWURF, OP. 10, N0. 2 (2'33)
Brigitte Lafon (m-S.), Françoise Tillard (pf.) **CALLI CAL 121314**

WANDERLIED, OP. 1, NO. 2 (1'29)
Grayson Hirst (T.), Michel Yuspeh (pf.) **LEONA LPI 112**

WANDERLIED, OP. 1, NO. 2 (1'34)
Brigitte Lafon (m-S.), Françoise Tillard (pf.) **CALLI CAL 121314**

WARUM SIND DENN DIE ROSEN SO BLASS,
OP. 1, NO. 3 (2'30)
Brigitte Lafon (m-S.), Françoise Tillard (pf.) **CALLI CAL 121314**

WARUM SIND DENN DIE ROSEN SO BLASS,
OP. 1, NO. 3 (2'59)
Grayson Hirst (T.), Michel Yuspeh (pf.) **LEONA LPI 112**

HERITTE-VIARDOT, Louise Pauline Marie (1841-1918)

SERENADE FROM QUARTET, OP. 11
M. Yanagita (vln.), Middleton (vla.),
Steinbock (vlc.), M. May (pf.) **GEMIN RAP 1010**

HERMANN, Miina (1864-1941)

CHILDHOOD SONG
Estonian Radio Choir **MELOD D 00018133/4**

FORMERLY AND NOW
Estonian Men's Choir **MELOD D 00018133/4**
FORMERLY AND NOW
Estonian Men's Choir **MELOD D 014871/2**

HOW BEAUTIFUL WAS MY FLOWER
K. Ots (T.) **MELOD D 31225/6**

I MUST NOT KEEP SILENT
Female Choir and Estonian Men's Choir **MELOD D 024549/50**

KALEV AND LINDA (CANTATA),
FINAL CHORUS
Estonian Radio Choir **MELOD D 00018133/4**

SONG OF THE MEN
Estonian Men's Choir **MELOD D 00018133/4**

TULYAK
Estonian Men's Choir **MELOD D 024563/4**

WHEN YOU COME, BRING SOME FLOWERS
R. Iyks **MELOD D 17649 56**

WHEN YOU COME, BRING SOME FLOWERS
J. Siymon (m-S.) **MELOD D 27181 92**

HERNANDEZ-GONZALO, Gisela (1910-1971)

LIEDER CUBANOS
Yolanda Hernandez (S.),
Emma Norka Ruiz (pf.) **ARIET LDA 3386**

PALMAS REALES
* * * * * * **PUCHI SP 112**

PIANO WORKS
* * * * * * **WESTM XWN 18430**

PIANO WORKS
* * * * * * **ETERN 5 20 463**

SON DE NAVIDAD
* * * * * * **PUCHI SP 112**

HESSE, Marjorie Anne (1911-   )

CURIOUS PIANO
Cooke (pf.) **W & G B S 5589**

HICKS, Marjorie Kisbey (1905-   )

TWO INDISPOSITIONS (NO. 1 ONLY)
* * * * * * **CCM 2**

HILDEGARDE, Saint (1098-1179)

AVE, GENEROSA
Gothic Voices
(cond.) Christopher Page **HYPER A 66039**

COLUMBA ASPEXIT
Gothic Voices
(cond.) Christopher Page **HYPER A 66039**

FOUR INSTRUMENTAL PIECES **HARMU**
Sequentia Medieval Music Ensemble **IC 069 19971**

GESÄNGE VON HILDEGARD VON BINGEN,
Schola der Benediktinerinnenabtei.
Rudesheim-Eibingen/Rheingau **PSALL**
(cond.) Im. Ritscher **242 04079 PET**

GLOCKEN DER ABTEIKIRCHE, DIE
Schola der Benediktinerinnenabtei.
St. Hildegard, Rudesheim- **PSALL**
Eibingen/Rheingau **PEX 138 250 973**

KYRIE
Schola der Benediktinerinnenabtei.
St. Hildegard Rudesheim- **PSALL**
Eibingen/Rheingau **PEX 138 250 973**

KYRIE
Schola Cantorum, University of Arkansas
(cond.) Jack Groh **LEONA LPI 115**

LIEDER AND ANTIPHONIES
Almut-Teichart, Hailperin (S.) **CHRIS SCGLV 66 22387**

O CLARISSIMA MATER
Sequentia Medieval Music Ensemble **HARMU IC 069 19971**

O ECCLESIA
Gothic Voices
(cond.) Christopher Page **HYPER A 66039**

O EUCHARI
Gothic Voices
(cond.) Christopher Page **HYPER A 66039**

O IERUSALEM
Gothic Voices
(cond.) Christophe Page **HYPER A 66039**

O IGNIS SPIRITUS
Gothic Voices
(cond.) Christopher Page **HYPER A 66039**

O LUCIDISSIMA APOSTOLORUM TURBA
Sequentia Medieval Music Ensemble **HARMU IC 069 19971**

O PRESUL VERE CIVITATIS
Gothic Voices
(cond.) Christopher Page **HYPER A 66039**

O PULCHRAE FACIES
Sequentia Medieval Music Ensemble **HARMU IC 069 19971**

O QUAM MIRABILIS EST
Sequentia Medieval Music Ensemble **HARMU IC 069 19971**

O SUCCESSORES FORTISSIMA LEONIS
Sequentia Medieval Music Ensemble **HARMU IC 069 19971**

O VIRGA AC DIADEMA
Sequentia Medieval Music Ensemble **HARMU IC 069 19971**

O VIRIDISSIMA VIRGA
Gothic Voices
(cond.) Christopher Page **HYPER A 66039**

O VIRTUS FLORUM ROSARUM
Sequentia Medieval Music Ensemble **HARMU IC 069 19971**

O VIRTUS SAPIENTIAE
Sequentia Medieval Music Ensemble **HARMU IC 069 19971**

O VOS FELICES RADICES
Sequentia Medieval Music Ensemble **HARMU IC 069 19971**

ORDO VIRTUTUM (DRAMA MUSICALE
DU MOYEN-AGE)
Sequentia Medieval Music Ensemble **HARMU HM 20395 6**

SEQUENZ AN MARIA
Schola Der Benediktinerinnenabtei.
St. Hildegard Rudesheim-
Eibingen/Rheigau **PSALL PEX 138 250 973**

SEVEN ANTIPHONS AND OTHER CHANTS
Helga Weber Group **IHW 66 2237**

SPIRITU SANCTO HONOR SIT
Sequentia Medieval Music Ensemble **HARMU IC 069 19971**

VOS FLORUM ROSARUM
Sequentia Medieval Music Ensemble **HARMU IC 069 19971**

HILDERLEY, Jeriann G. (1937-   )

HOUSE OF MANY COLOURS
* * * * * * **SWAVE 17 180**

I POKE A SEED
* * * * * * **SWAVE 17 180**

SEA WAVE
* * * * * * **SWAVE 17 180**

THRU YOUR BLUE VEIL
* * * * * * **SWAVE 17 180**

HIRSCHFELDT, Ingrid (-   )

WIR ALLE ESSEN VON EINEM
BROT (ZENETTI)
Heidelberger Kantorei &
Jugend Kantorei (cond.) E. Hubner **LAUDA HV 91516**

HOLLAND, Dulcie Sybil (1913-   )

AT THE EDGE OF THE SEA (MEZZO-SOPRANO,
SOPRANO AND PIANO)
* * * * * * **ABC O N 40525**

BALLADE, FOR CLARINET AND PIANO
Clive Amadio (cl.), Olga Krasnik (pf.) **COLUM 330 S 7560**

BERYL TREE, THE (VOICE AND PIANO)
* * * * * * **COLUM DO 3766**

CHRISTMAS GREETING (PIANO)
* * * * * * **ABC PRX 5616**

END OF SUMMER, THE (PIANO)
* * * * * * **ABC PRX 5616**

FLAGS IN THE BREEZE (PIANO)
Cooke (pf.) **W & G B S 5589**

LAKE, THE (PIANO)
* * * * * * **ABC PRX 5616**

SCATTERING OF THE LEAVES, THE
* * * * * * **ABC PRX 5616**

THIS LAND IS MINE, FOR
BASS AND ORCHESTRA
* * * * * * **ABC PRX 4558**

HOLMES, Augusta Mary Anne (1847-1903)

NOEL (TROIS ANGES SONT
VENUS CE SOIR) (2'50)
Michel Dens (Bar.) with Choeurs
Rene Duclos, Orchestre de
L'Association de Concerts Colonne
(cond.) R. Challan **HMV C 053 10932**

TROIS PETITES PIECES
Hoberman (fl.), Stannard (pf.) **ORION ORS 76257**

HOOVER, Katherine (1937-   )

DIVERTIMENTO FOR FLUTE, VIOLIN,
VIOLA AND CELLO
Diane Gold (fl.), Joanne Zagst (vln.),
Raymond Page (vla.), Leonard Feldman (vlc.) **LEONA LPI 105**

MEDIEVAL SUITE, THE (19'18)
Katherine Hoover (fl.), Mary Ann Brown (pf.) **LEONA LPI 121**

ON THE BETROTHAL OF PRINCESS
ISABELLA OF FRANCE, AGED SIX (3'04)
Katherine Hoover (fl.), Virginia Eskin (pf.) **LEONA LPI 104**

REFLECTIONS (6'46)
Katherine Hoover (fl.) **LEONA LPI 121**

SINFONIA (10'54)
New York Bassoon Quartet **LEONA LPI 102**

TRIO FOR VIOLIN, CELLO
AND PIANO (1978) (18'04)
Rogeri Trio: Karen Clarke (vln.),
Carter Brey (vlc.), Barbara Wentraub (pf.) **LEONA LPI 103**

HORTENSE, Queen of Holland (1783-1837)

ROMANCES
Margreet van Gunsteren (m-S.),
Christian Lambour (pf.) **DURAP HD 261**

SIX ROMANCES
Margreet van Gunsteren (m-S.),
Christian Lambour (pf.) **SOUND HD 261**

HOWE, Mary Alberta Bruce (1882-1964)

CASTELLANA, FOR TWO PIANOS AND ORCHESTRA
Cellus Dougherty (pf.), Vincent Ruzicka (pf.)
with Vienna Orchestra
(cond.) C.W. Strickland **CRI 124**

CAVALIERS
Howard University Choir
(cond.) Warner Lawson **WCFM 13**

CHAIN GANG SONG (1925)
Howard University Choir
(cond.) Warner Lawson **WCFM 13**

FRAGMENT
Katharine Hansel (S.), Theodore Schaefer (pf.) **WCFM 13**

GOETHE LIEDER (11'29)
Sharon Mabry (S.), Rosemary Platt (pf.) **CORON LPS 3127**

HORSEMAN, THE
Howard University Choir
(cond.) Warner Lawson **WCFM 13**

INNISFREE
Harold Ronk (T.), Theodore Schaefer (pf.) **WCFM 13**

INTERLUDE BETWEEN 2 PIECES
Chamber Arts Society of Catholic University
of America
(cond.) Emerson Meyers **WCFM 9**

LULLABY FOR A FORESTER'S CHILD
Harold Ronk (T.), Theodore Schaefer (pf) **WCFM 13**

MA DOULEUR
Katharine Hansel (S.), Theodore Schaefer (pf.)　**WCFM 13**

MEIN HERZ
Katharine Hansel (S.), Theodore Schaefer (pf.)　**WCFM 13**

MUSIC WHEN SOFT VOICES DIE
Howard University Choir
(cond.) Warner Lawson　**WCFM 13**

O PROSERPINA
Katharine Hansel (S.), Theodore Schaefer (pf.)　**WCFM 13**

RAG PICKER, THE
Harold Ronk (T.), Theodore Schaefer (pf.)　**WCFM 13**

SAND (1938)
Vienna Orchestra
(cond.) William Strickland　**CRI 103**

SAND (1938)
Vienna Orchestra
(cond.) William Strickland　**CRI 124**

SONG OF RUTH
Howard University Choir
(cond.) Warner Lawson　**WCFM 13**

SPRING PASTORAL
Imperial Philharmonic Orchestra Tokyo
(cond.) William Strickland　**CRI 145**

STARS (1937)
Vienna Orchestra
(cond.) William Strickland　**CRI 103**

STARS (1937)
Vienna Orchestra
(cond.) William Strickland　**CRI 124**

STARS (1937)
Maganini Chamber Symphony
(cond.) Quinto Maganini　**NEWMU 1514**

SUITE, PIANO AND STRING QUARTET (1923)
Chamber Arts Society of Catholic University
of America
(cond.) Emerson Meyers　**WCFM 9**

THREE PIECES AFTER EMILY DICKINSON
Chamber Arts Society of Catholic University
of America
(cond.) Emerson Meyers　**WCFM 9**

TO THE UNKNOWN SOLDIER
Harold Ronk (T.), Theodore Schaefer (pf.)　**WCFM 13**

WHEN I DIED IN BERNERS STREET
Katharine Hansel (S.), Theodore Schaefer (pf.)　**WCFM 13**

WILLIAMSBURG SUNDAY
Howard University Choir
(cond.) Warner Lawson　**WCFM 13**

HOY, Bonnee L. (1936-　)

DE MAZIA QUINTET, THE
Bonnee Hoy (pf.) with Amado String Quartet　**ENCOR EN 3003**

EIGHT PRELUDES (PIANO) (1969)
* * * * * *　**ENCOR 1001**

FREEMAN CELEBRATION, THE (1971)
Kathryn Bouleyn (S.), David Barg (fl.),
Peter Wiley (vlc.), Bonnee Hoy (pf.)　**ENCOR EN 2002**

LAMENT
Carol Stein (vln.)　**ENCOR EN 3003**

PIANO SONATA, NO. 2 (1971)
* * * * * *　**ENCOR 1001**

VERLAINE SONGS, THE
Baillis Webb (Bar.), Bonnee Hoy (pf.)　**ENCOR EN 2002**

WINTER CYCLE, THE
Kathryn Bouleyn (S.), Bonnee Hoy (pf.)　**ENCOR EN 2002**

HYDE, Miriam Beatrice (1913-　)

FOUNTAIN, THE , OP. 8, NO. 2
* * * * * *　**BROLG CTX 1122**

FOUR SONGS, OP. 43 (VOICE AND PIANO)
(A BRIDAL SONG, LAUGHTER, THE
WIND IN THE HEDGES, UNKNOWN)
* * * * * *　**ABC 0 N 40525**

LENTO IN E-MINOR (ORCHESTRA)
* * * * * *　**ABC RRCS 377**

SONATA IN G-MINOR, OP. 121
* * * * * *　**ABC PRX 5334**

STUDY IN A-MINOR, FOR PIANO
Cooke (pf.)　**WANDG BS 55899**

STUDY IN E-MINOR, FOR PIANO
Cooke (pf.)　**WANDG BS 55899**

INGBER, Anita Rahel (1917-　)

HORAT HANOAR (YOUTH HORA)
* * * * * *

ISMAGILOVA, Leila Zagirovna (1946-　)

OCTET
Melodiya Octet　**MELOD C 10 21907 004**

PIANO SONATA
Leila Ismagilova (pf.)　**MELOD C 10 21907 004**

IVEY, Jean Eichelberger (1923-　)

ALDEBARAN, FOR VIOLA AND TAPE (10'00)
Jacob Glick (vla.)　**FOLKW FTS 33439**

CORTEGE FOR CHARLES KENT (ELECTRONIC
PIECE) (5'20)
Peabody Conservatory Electronic
Music Studio　**FOLKW FTS 33439**

HERA, HUNG FROM THE SKY, OP. 9 (1974) (12'50)
Elaine Bonazzi (m-S.) with Tape and
Underground Group
(cond.) Andrew Thomas　**CRI SD 325**

PINBALL
Jean Ivey (modified, re-assembled
pinball machines)　**FOLKW FM 3436**

PINBALL (EXCERPT)
* * * * * *　**COLSP P 11597**

TERMINUS (10'00)
Elaine Bonazzi (m-S.)　**FOLKW FTS 33439**

THREE SONGS OF NIGHT (1971) (14'43)
Catherine Rowe (S.) with Peabody
Contemporary Music Ensemble
and Tape (cond.) Leonard Pearlman　**FOLKW FTS 33439**

IWAUCHI, Saori (1970-　)

HUNTERS, THE (5'03)
Saori Iwauchi (pf.)　**RJOCR YL 8102 3 19 282**

MILKYWAY TRAIN, THE (8'12)
Saori Iwauchi (pf.)　**RJOCR YL 8102 3 19 282**

JEPPSSON, Kerstin Maria (1948-　)

OCTOBER 1974
Elisabeth Klein (pf.)　**DANIC DLP 8017**

JEREA, Hilda (1916-   )

CINTEC DE INTRECERE, FOR MIXED CHORUS
Alexandru Tassian (vce.)　　　　　**ELECT EXE 046**

CINTEC HAIDUCESC (3'20)
Gheza Duma (pf.), Valentin　　　　**ELECT**
Teodorian (T.)　　　　　　　　**ST ECE 01406**

CINTECE DE LUPTA
Alexandru Tassian (vce.)　　　　　**ELECT EXE 046**

MELANCOLIE (4'08)
Steliana Calos (S.), Adrian Tomescu (pf.),　**ELECT**
Voicu Vasinca (fl.)　　　　　　**ST ECE 01406**

PIERDA-VARA (3'15)　　　　　　　**ELECT**
Dan Zancu (T.), Gheza Duma (pf.)　**ST ECE 01406**

RAMEAUX FLEURIS (SUITE) FOR CHILDREN'S CHORUS
AND PIANO
* * * * * *　　　　　　　　　　**ELECT EXE 147**

SUS LA MURFATLAR IN VIE, FOR FOLK CHORUS
AND ORCHESTRA
Folk Chorus and Orchestra of Rumanian
Radio Television
(cond.) Victor Predescu　　　　　**ELECT EXA 3125**

ULCIORUL (4'54)
Steliana Calos (S.), Adrian Tomescu (pf.),　**ELECT**
Voicu Vasinca (fl.)　　　　　　**ST ECE 01406**

UNDE UN CINTEC ESTE (4'53)
Steliana Calos (S.), Adrian Tomescu (pf.),　**ELECT**
Voicu Vasinca (fl.)　　　　　　**ST ECE 01406**

VESELIE (2'00)
Valentine Teodorian (T.), Ghezaws**ELECT**
Duma (pf.)　　　　　　　　　**ST ECE 01406**

JOCHSBERGER, Tzipora H. (1920-   )

EIN KAMOKHA
* * * * * *　　　　　　　　　　**MEDIA EMB 1500**

YIZKOR
* * * * * *　　　　　　　　　　**MEDIA EMB 1500**

JOHNSON, Elizabeth (1913-   )

STRING QUARTET (1938) (21'12)
R. Kimstedt (vln.), I. Schliephake (vln.),　**MARUS**
C. Lelong (vla.), W. Groeger (vlc.)　**MRS 308329**

JOHNSON, J. Rosamond (1873-1954)

LIT'L GAL (1917)
Paul Robenson (Bar.), Lawrence Brown (pf.) **NEWOR NW 247**

AUTOUR
Elizabeth Chojnacka (hpcd.)　　**ERATO STU 71010**

D'UN OPERA DE VOYAGE
* * * * * *　　　　　　　　　**ADES ADE 1 7001**

D'UN OPERA DE VOYAGE
* * * * * *　　　　　　　　　**ADES ADE 1 2001**

D'UN OPERA DE VOYAGE
Orchestre du Domaine Musical
(cond.) Gilbert Amy　　　　　　**ADES ADE 1 6012**

FUSAIN, POUR UN FLAUTISTE
Artaud (fl.)　　　　　　　　**CHDUM LDX 78 700**

J.D.E. (FOR 14 INSTRUMENTS)
Ensemble Ars Nova
(cond.) M. Constant　　　　　　**ADES 1 4013**

MON AMI
Michele Boegner (pf.)　　　　　**ADES 2001**

POINTS D'AUBE, FOR ALTO AND 13 WIND
INSTRUMENTS (1969)
Collot (A.) with Ensemble Ars Nova
(cond.) Marius Constant　　　　　**ADES 1 4013**

QUATOUR II, FOR SOPRANO
AND STRING TRIO
* * * * * *　　　　　　　　　　**EMI CVB 2190**

QUATOUR II, FOR SOPRANO
AND STRING TRIO (15'16)
M. Mesple (S.) with French String Trio　**ANGEL S 36655**

QUATOUR III (9 ETUDES) FOR
STRING QUARTET (17'15)
Concord String Quartet: M. Sokoi (vln.),
A. Jenning (vln.), J. Kochanowski (vla.),
N. Fischer (vla.)　　　　　　　**CRI SD 332**

SONATE A DOUZE, FOR MIXED CHOIR
AND TWELVE SOLOISTS
Soloistes des Choeurs de L'ORTF
(cond.) Marcel Courand　　　　　**ORTF 99503**

STANCES, FOR PIANO AND ORCHESTRA (1978)
Helffer (pf.) with New Philharmonic
Orchestra of Radio France
(cond.) M. Constant　　　　　　**ADES 1 4013**

TRANCHE
Jamet (hp.)　　　　　　　　**ERATO STU 71 160**

TRANCHE, FOR HARP
Marcelle Decray (hp.)　　　　**CORON 850 C 2508**

JORDAN, Alice Yost (1916-   )

FIFTH PSALM
Sherill Milnes (Bar.), Jon Sprong (org.)　**VICTO ARL 1 1403**

JOSEPHINE, Queen of Sweden and Norway (1807-1876)

ROMANCE ISLANDAISE (2'01)
Elizabeth Soderstrom　　　　**SWEDI SWS SLT 33243**

KABAT, Julie Phyllis (1947-   )

A MI HIJA (4'04)
Julie Kabat (vce. and saw)　　　**LEONA LPI 119**

FIVE POEMS BY H.D. (13'04)
Julie Kabat (vce., glass har. and saw),
Ben Hudson (vln.)　　　　　　**LEONA LPI 119**

INVOCATION IN CENTRIFUGAL FORM (9'54)
Julie Kabat (vce. and glass har.)　**LEONA LPI 119**

KALIMBA ALIGHT (2'17)
Julie Kabat (vce. and kalimba)　　**LEONA LPI 119**

ON EDGE (13'00)
Julie Kabat (vce. and African drs.),
Marilyn Crispell (pf.),
Abraham Adzenyah
(African drs. and congas)　　　　**LEONA LPI 119**

KALOGRIDOU, Maria (1922-   )

FOUR SONGS
* * * * * *　　　　　　　　**RENAT 35828 7231 73**

TWENTY CHILDREN'S SONGS
* * * * * *　　　　　　　　　**RENAT 103**

KAPRALOVA, Vitezslava (1915-   )

APRIL ......
* * * * * *　　　　　　　　**SUPRA 1 19 1748 G**

MILITARY SINFONIETTA, FOR
    LARGE ORCHESTRA, OP. 11
    Brno State Philharmonic Orchestra
    (cond.) B. Bakala   **SUPRA DM 5649**

PARTITA, FOR PIANO AND
    STRING ORCHESTRA, OP. 20
    Duras (pf.) with Brno State
    Symphony Orchestra
    (cond.) Josef Blacky   **SUPRA 1 19 1748 G**

PARTITA, FOR PIANO AND
    STRING ORCHESTRA, OP. 20
    Milan Masa (pf.) with Pilsen Radio
    Symphony Orchestra
    (cond.) O. Trhlik   **SUPRA DV 5961**

PRELUDE FOR PIANO, OP. 13
    Pidermannova (pf.)   **SUPRA 1 19 1748 G**

RUSTIC SUITE, OP. 19
    Brno State Philharmonic Orchestra
    (cond.) J. Pinkas   **SUPRA 1 19 1748 G**

WAVING FAREWELL, FOR SOPRANO
    AND ORCHESTRA, OP. 14
    Kareninova (S.) with Brno State
    Philharmonic Orchestra
    (cond.) J. Pinkas   **SUPRA 1 19 1748 G**

KARNITSKAYA, Nina Andreyevna (1906-   )
CONCERTO NO. 1, FOR PIANO AND
    ORCHESTRA, IN D-MINOR
    B. Friedman (pf.) with North-Ossetian
    Symphonic Orchestra
    (cond.) P. Yadykh   **MELOD D 6971 2**

IN THE MOUNTAINS, IN THE FIELD
    North-Ossetian Symphonic Orchestra
    (cond.) P. Yadykh   **MELOD
C 10 08319 20**

PICTURES OF AN OSSETIAN
    COLLECTIVE FARM
    North-Ossetian Symphonic Orchestra
    (cond.) P. Yadykh   **MELOD D 7535 6**

KASILAG, Lucrecia R. (1918-   )

CONCERTO FOR VIOLIN AND ORCHESTRA
    Carmencita Lozada (vln.) with Philippine
    Philharmonic Orchestra
    (cond.) Francisco Feliciano **MARCO 6 220419**

DIVERSIONS
    * * * * * *   **KUBIN C 1979**

DIVERTISSEMENT
    * * * * * *   **KUBIN C 1979**

DULARAWAN
    * * * * * *   **KUBIN C 1979**

PHILIPPINE SCENES
    * * * * * *   **DISCR DLP 10027**

SISA
    * * * * * *   **KUBIN C 1979**

TOCCATA
    * * * * * *   **KUBIN C 1979**

KAZHAEVA, Tatiana Ibragimova (1950-   )

PRELUDE AND INVENTION
    Terence Judd (pf.)   **MELOD C 10 14493 4**

PRELUDE AND INVENTION
    Terence Judd (pf.)   **CHAND ABR 1090**

KELLY, Georgia (-)

SEAPEACE (1978)
    * * * * * *   **HERU - - -**

KELSO, Alice Anne (-)

MOURNFUL SOUNDS IN MEMORY
    OF ABRAHAM LINCOLN
    * * * * * *   **PARNO LPS 3101**

KENNEDY-FRASER, Marjory (1857-1930)

ERISKAY LOVE-LILT, AN (FROM
    SONGS OF THE HEBRIDES)
    Isobel Baillie (S.), Gerald Moore (pf.) **HMV HQM 1118**

ISLAND SHEILING SONG, AN
    * * * * * *   **MARQ MAR 102**

KESSLER, Minuetta Schumiatcher (1914-   )

BALLET SONATINA (1946)
    Minuetta Kessler (pf.)   **AFKA SK 288**

CHILDHOOD CAMEOS
    Jennifer Paterson (S.), John Oliver (Bar.),
    Minuetta Kessler (pf.)   **AFKA S 4663**

FANTASY FOR OBOE AND PIANO
    Patricia Moorhead (ob.), Minuetta Kessler (pf.) **AFKA SK 288**

SONATE CONCERTANTE, FOR
    VIOLIN AND PIANO (1957)
    Marylou Speaker (vln.), Minuetta Kessler (pf.) **AFKA SK 288**

SONATE FOR CLARINET AND PIANO
    William Wrzesian (cl.), Minuetta Kessler (pf.) **AFKA SK 288**

KETTERING, Eunice Lea (1906-   )

JOHN JAMES AUDUBON, CANTATA FOR
    MIXED CHORUS SOPRANO AND TENOR
    SOLOISTS, NARRATOR AND ORCHESTRA
    Dayton Philharmonic Orchestra,
    American Psalm Choir   **CORON**
    (cond.) Dr. Paul E. Katz   **U 4 RS 9860**

LAMB, THE, FOR MIXED CHORUS A CAPPELLA
    Chapel Choir of Capital University
    Columbus, Ohio
    (cond.) Dr. Ellis Snyder   **CORON TV 27028**

KINKEL, Johanna (1810-1858)

AN DEN MOND, OP. 7, NO. 5 (GOETHE) (3'13) **MUSVI**
    Tuula Nienstedt (Cont.), Uwe Wegner (pf.) **MV 30 1104**

GEISTER HABEN'S VERNOMMEN, DIE,
    OP. NO. 6.3 (HEINE) (3'56)   **MUSVI**
    Tuula Nienstedt (Cont.), Uwe Wegner (pf.) **MV 30 1104**

LORELEI, DIE, OP. 7. NO. 4 (HEINE) (3'37) **MUSVI**
    Tuula Nienstedt (Cont.), Uwe Wegner (pf.) **MV 30 1104**

ZIGEUNER, DIE, OP. 7, NOS. 7 AND 9
    (GIEBEL) (1'53)   **MUSVI**
    Tuula Nienstedt (Cont.), Uwe Wegner (pf.) **MV 30 1104**

KIRCHGASSNER, Elisabeth (1864-1941)

MANNHEIMER KINDERMESSE
    Kinderchöre Christ Koenig und Heilig
    Geist Mannheim with Instrumental
    Ensemble   **STUDU 17 363**

KITAZUME, Yayoi (1945-)

INNER SPACE, FOR TWO PIANOS
* * * * * *   **JAPAN JFC 7909**

KOLB, Barbara (1939-)

CHANSONS BAS (1966)
V. Lamoree (S.) with Chamber Group
(cond.) C. Kolb   **DESTO DC 7143**

CROSSWINDS (1974)
New England Women's Symphony
(cond.) Kay Gardner   **GALAX GAL 004**

FIGMENTS (1967)
Herlinger (fl.), Selzer (pf.)   **DESTO DC 7143**

HOMAGE TO KEITH JARRETT
AND GARY BURTON (8'48)
Katherine Hoover (fl.),
William Noersch (vibes.)   **LEONA LPI 121**

HOMAGE TO KEITH JARRETT
AND GARY BURTON, FOR FLUTE
AND VIBRAPHONE
Tambous Duo   **CRS 8425**

LOOKING FOR CLAUDIO (1975)
D. Starobin (gtr. and man.), G. Gottlieb (perc.),
A. Ivanoff (S.), P. Mason (Bar.)   **CRI SD 361**

REBUTTAL (1964)
G. McGee (cl.), G. Hirner (cl.)   **OPONE 14**

SENTENCES, THE (PINSKY) FOR VOICE
AND GUITAR (1976)
R. Rees (S.), David Starobin (gtr.)   **TURNA TV 34727**

SOLITAIRE (PIANO AND
VIBRAPHONE) (1971) (13'32)
C. Selzer (pf.), R. Fitz (vibes)   **TURNA TV 34487**

SONGS BEFORE AN ADIEU
Rosalind Rees (S.), David Starobin (gtr.),
Susan Palma (fl.)   **BRIDG BDG 2004**

SPRING, RIVER, FLOWERS, MOON, NIGHT (1976) (19'00)
R. Phillips (pf.), F. Renzulli (pf.) with
Brooklyn College Percussion Ensemble   **CRI SD 361**

THREE LULLABIES (1980)
D. Starobin (gtr.)   **BRIDG BDG 2001**

THREE PLACE SETTINGS
Eastman (narr.), Williams, Haupt,
Yadzinsky, C. Michii
(cond.) C. Kolb   **DESTO DC 7143**

TROBAR CLUS (1970)
Chicago University Contemporary
Chamber Players
(cond.) C. Kolb   **TURNA TV 34487**

KOLODUB, Zhanna Efimovna (1930-)

POEM: NOCTURNE
O. Kudkyashov (fl.), Z. Kolodub (pf.)   **MELOD D 00029805 6**

TWO UKRAINIAN SONGS
A. Ponomarenko (vce.), Z. Kolodub (pf.) **MELOD D 00029805 6**

KONISHI, Nagako (1945-)

GRAVE POST
* * * * * *   **JAPAN JFC 8011**

KOSHETZ, Nina (1894-1965)

TO THE SUN
Nina Koshetz (S.)   **CLUB CL 99 36**

KOSSE, Roberta (1947-)

RETURN OF THE GREAT MOTHER (ORATORIO)
Item for Chorus and Instrumental Ensemble
(cond.) Roberta Kosse   **ARSPR ST APF 77**

KOTSBATREVSKAYA (-)

FORGET ALL BYGONE LOVES AND PASSIONS
Alexandrovich (T.) with Andreas Trio: **MUHER**
Drucker (vln.), Catell (vlc.), Kaye (pf.)   **MHS 3809 SD**

GROVE WAS STILL, THE
Alexandrovich (T) with Andreas Trio:
Drucker (vln.), Catell (vlc.),   **MUHER**
Kaye (pf.)   **MHS 3809 SD**

KOZHEVNIKOVA, Ekaterina Vadimovna (1954-)

ELEGIE (KRZHIZHANOVSKY)
I. Kozlovsky (T.), S. Aidenko (org.)
with Bolshoi Theatre Orchestra and Chorus   **MELOD**
(cond.) Gusman   **D 028059/62**

VOCAL TRIPTYCH   **MELOD**
Alexei Martinov (T.)   **C 10 13247/8**

KRIMSKY, Katrina (1938-)

EPILOGUE (WITH WOODY SHAW) (1'51)
Katrina Krimsky (pf.)   **SONIC - - -**

SPECS (WITH WOODY SHAW) (6'04)
Katrina Krimsky (pf.)   **SONIC - - -**

KUBISCH, Christina (1948-)

DIVERSO NO. 10, TEMPO LIQUIDO
Christina Kubisch, Fabrizio
Plessi (tape and insts)   **CRAMP 5206210**

KUBOTA, Minako (1972-)

CHEERFUL DUMBO   **RJOCR**
Minako Kubota (pf.)   **C 25 R 8001 19 298**

KUKUCK, Felicitas (1914-)

BRUECKE SUITE, THE, WITH SONGS FOR
SOPRANO, RECORDER AND LUTE
Faringer, Pehrsson, Rorby, Pehrsson   **DISCB 0 002**

ES BEGAB SICH ABER
* * * * * *   **FIDUL 3018**

HEILIGEN DREI KOENIGE, DIE
* * * * * *   **FIDUL 1114**

HERBEI, IHR GROSS UND KLEIN
Gerhard Trubel Dortmunder Kantorei   **ELREC EL E 3237**

MARIAE VERKUENDIGUNG (MOTET)   **MOSEL**
* * * * * *   **CMS 17035 EP**

MUSIK VON FELICITAS KUKUCK IN
COMPONISTINNEN UNSERER ZEIT

ilfred Jochims (T.) with Chamber Choir of
the Volkshochschule, Duelken   **CAMER**
(cond.) H.J. Roth   **CMS 17121 EP**

SOMMERCANTATA
* * * * * *   **FIDUL 1123**

WEIHNACHTSMESSE
* * * * * *   **FIDUL 1123**

KURIMOTO, Yoko (1951-   )

JUNE END SONGS (1982)
* * * * * *   JAPAN JFC 8403

KUROKAWA, Manae (1966-   )

PIANO CONCERTO IN G-MAJOR (14'18)
Manae Kurokawa (pf.) with National
Symphony Orchestra   **RJOCR**
(cond.) Mstislav Rostropovich   YL 8102 3 19 282

RAINBOW FANTASY (9'33) **RJOCR**
Manae Kurokawa (pf.)   YL 8102 3 19 282

KUSS, Margarita Ivanovna (1921-   )

AH, THOU MY NIGHT
N. Isakova (m-S.) with Orchestra of Folk   **MELOD**
Instruments   SM 03587/8

HEADACHE FOR THE YOUNG LADS AND GIRLS, A
N. Isakova (m-S.) with Orchestra of Folk   **MELOD**
Instruments   SM 03587/8

I WALKED IN THE GARDEN
N. Isakova (m-S.) with Orchestra   **MELOD**
of Folk Instruments   SM 03687/8

LYRICAL SONGS OF THE FOOTHILLS
S. Danilyan (domra) with Moscow Youth
Orchestra of Russian Folk Instruments   **MELOD**
(cond.) N. Kalinin   33 C 20 06429/30

SONATA FOR VIOLIN AND PIANO, IN E-MINOR   **MELOD**
N. Shkolnikova (vln.), L. Yedlina (pf.)   D 17085/6

SONATA IN C
N. Shkolnikova (vln.), L. Yedlina (pf.)   **MEZHD D 11064**

KUSUNOKI, Tomoko (1949-   )

LAKE, THE (VIOLONCELLO AND
PERCUSSION) (1981)
* * * * * *   JAPAN JFC 8216

KVERNADZE, Bidzina (1929-   )

BERIKOABA (MUSIC FROM THE BALLET)
Georgian Symphony Orchestra
(cond.) Kakhidze   **MELOD 510 05979/80**

CHOREOGRAPHIC POEM
Georgian Symphony Orchestra
(cond.) Kakhidze   **MELOD D 015721/2**

CONCERTO FOR VIOLIN AND ORCHESTRA
A. Markov (vln.) with Radio Orchestra
(cond.) Khurodze   **MELOD D 4826/7**

DANCE FANTASIA
Georgian Symphony Orchestra
(cond.) Khurodze   **MELOD D 7579/80**

INCIDENT AT THE WEIR
Georgian Symphony Orchestra
(cond.) Khurodze   **MELOD D 00010883/4**

KYROU, Mireille (-   )

ETUDE 1
* * * * * *   **PHILI 835487 AY**

LA BARBARA, Joan (1947-   )

AS LIGHTNING COMES, IN FLASHES
* * * * * *   **WIZAR RVW 2283**

AUTUMN SIGNAL (13'16)
Joan La Barbara (vce.) with
Quadraphonic Sounds   **WIZAR RVW 2279**

CATHING (1977) (8'02)
Joan La Barbara (vce.)   **CHIAR CR 196**

CIRCULAR SONG (7'41)
* * * * * *   **WIZAR RVW 2266**

ERIN
* * * * * *   **WIZAR RVW 2283**

KLEE ALEE (16'00)
Joan La Barbara (vce.) with multi-
layered tape   **WIZAR RVW 2279**

OCTOBER MUSIC
Joan La Barbara (vce.) with Ensemble   **NONSU 78029**

Q-UATRE PETITES BETES (7'21)
Joan La Barbara with quadraphonic sounds **WIZAR RVW 2279**

SHADOWSONG (5'03)
Joan La Barbara with multi-layered tape **WIZAR RVW 2279**

SOLAR WIND, THE (1983)
Joan La Barbara (vce.) with Ensemble   **NONSU 78029**

STAR SHOWERS AND EXTRA
TERRESTRIALS (1980)
Joan La Barbara (vce.) with Ensemble   **NONSU 78029**

THUNDER (SIX TIMPANI,
SOLO VOICE AND
ELECTRONICS (1976) (22'59)
La Barbara (vce. and tape), Smith (perc.)
Ditmas (perc.)   **CHIAR CR 196**

TWELVESONG
* * * * * *   **WIZAR RVW 2293**

VISSINGEN HARBOUR (1982)
Joan La Barbara (vce.) with Ensemble   **NONSU 78029**

VOCAL EXTENSIONS (18'17)   **WIZAR**
Joan La Barbara (vce.) with Electronic Music **RVW 2266**

VOICE PIECE: ONE-NOTE INTERNAL
RESONANCE INVESTIGATION (15'41)   **WIZAR**
Joan La Barbara (vce.)   **RVW 2266**

LA GUERRE, Elisabeth-Claude Jacquet de (1664-1729)

AIR AND RECITATIVE, FROM THE
CANTATA SUZANNE
Mertine Johns (m-S.), M. May (hpcd.),
Y. Cable (vlc.)   **GEMIN RAP 1010**

AIR FROM THE CANTATA
JACOB AND RACHEL
Mertine Johns (m-S.), M. May (hpcd.),
Y. Cable (vlc.)   **GEMIN RAP 1010**

RONDEAU IN G-MINOR (1'57)
Rosario Marciano (pf.)   **TURNA TV 34685**

SAMSON
John Ostendorf (B-Bar.) with Bronx
Arts Ensemble Chamber Orchestra
(cond.) Johannes Somary   **LEONA LP1 109**

SARABANDE IN G-MAJOR, FOR
HARPSICHORD
L. Boulay (hpcd.)   **MUHER MHS 930**

SARABANDE IN G-MAJOR, FOR
HARPSICHORD
Van de Wiele (hpcd.)   **MUSID RC 896**

SECOND GIGUE IN D-MINOR, FOR
HARPSICHORD (1'68)
L. Boulay (hpcd.)   **MUHER MHS 930**

SOMMEIL D'ULISSEZ, LE
John Ostendorf (B-Bar.) with Bronx Arts
Ensemble Chamber Orchestra
(cond.) Johannes Somary   **LEONA LP1 109**

SONATA IN D-MINOR (EXTRACTS) FOR VIOLIN,
BASS VIOL AND HARPSICHORD
F. Jaros (vln.), J. Lamy (b-viol.)
A. Geoffrey Dechaume (hpcd.)   **ORTF 995039**

SUITE IN A-MINOR
Emer Buckley (hpcd.)   **HARMU 1098**

SUITE IN D-MINOR
Emer Buckley (hpcd.)   **HARMU 1098**

SUITE IN D-MINOR
Kenneth Gilbert (hpcd.)   **ARGO ZK 64**

SUITE IN D-MINOR (9'04)
Nancy Fierro (pf.)   **AVANT AV 1012**

SUITE IN F-MAJOR
Emer Buckley (hpcd.)   **HARMU 1098**

SUITE IN G-MINOR
Emer Buckley (hpcd.)   **HARMU 1098**

LA VALLE, Deanna (-)

PIECE FOR PIANO (1971)
Rebecca La Brecque (pf.)   **OPONE 76**

LAMEGO, Carlinda J. (1910-)

A SAUDADE DE VOCE
Belchior dos Santos (Bar.)   **ACADS ASC 10**

LANDOWSKA, Wanda (1879-1959)

BOUREE D'AUVERGNE
Wanda Landowska (hpcd.)   **RCA LM 2830**

HOP, THE (WEDDING SONG) (3'27)
Wanda Landowska (hpcd.)   **RCA LM 2830**

LANG, Josephine (1815-1880)

LOVE SONGS:
WIE GLANZT SO HELL DEIN AUGE;
O, SEHNTEST DU DICH SO NACH MIR
John Ostendorf (B-Bar.), Katherine
Ciesinski (m-S.), Rudolph Palmer (pf.)   **LEONA LPI 107**

NINE SONGS FOR SOPRANO AND PIANO
Christel Kromer (S.) Jutta Vornehm (pf.)   **MUBAV MB 902**

SIE LIEBT MICH
Berenice Bramson (S.) Roger Rundle (pf.)   **GEMIN RAP 1010**

SONGS OF THE SEASONS
John Ostendorf (B-Bar.), Katherine
Ciesinski (m-S.), Rudolph Palmer (pf.)   **LEONA LPI 107**

LANG, Margaret Ruthven (1867-1972)

IRISH LOVE SONG, OP. 22
* * * * * *   **VICTR 87022**

IRISH LOVE SONG, OP. 22
Ernestine Schumann-Heink (A.)   **PELIC LP 2008**

LARSEN, Elizabeth Brown (1950-)

AUBADE
Eugenia Zukerman (fl.), Lisa
Emenheiser (pf.)   **PROAT PRO 1086**

IN A WINTER GARDEN (43'32)
Janis Hardy (m-S.), Dan Dressen (T.) with
Plymouth Festival Chorus and Orchestra
(cond.) Philip Brunelle   **PROAT PAD 151**

ULLOA'S RING
Eugenia Zukerman (fl.), Lisa Emenheiser
(pf.)   **PROAT PRO 1086**

LAUBER, Anne Marianne (1943-)

AFFAIRE COFFIN, L'
Piano and Youth Orchestra   **SNE 503**

PETIT PRINCE, LE
(narr. and pf.)   **SNE 503**

LAYMAN, Pamela (1949-)

GRAVITATION I (1974)
Oliveira (vln.)   **GRENA 1032**

LEANDRE, Joelle (-)

DOUZE SONS, LES
Joelle Leandre (d-b.) with others   **NATO 82**

SINCERELY
Joelle Leandre   **PLANI SA 1267 15**

LEBARON, Anne (1953-)

BUTTERFLY COLLECTION
Anne Lebaron, LaDonna Smith,
Davey Williams (chamber improvisations)   **TRANS - - -**

CONCERTO FOR ACTIVE FROGS
Ron Pate's Debonairs   **SAYDA 1**

DOGGONE CATACT
Anne Lebaron (hp.)   **OPONE - - -**

DRUNK UNDERWATER KOTO
Anne Lebaron, LaDonna Smith,
Davey Williams
(chamber improvisations)   **TRANS - - -**

EUPHORBIA (WITH JON ENGLISH
AND CANDACE NATVIG)
Anne Lebaron (hp.), Candace Natvig (vce.
and vln.), Jon English (trb.)   **OPONE OP 58**

JEWELS
Anne Lebaron, LaDonna Smith,
Davey Williams (chamber improvisations)   **TRANS - - -**

LITTLE LEFT OF CENTER, A (WITH
JON ENGLISH AND CANDACE NATVIG)
Anne Lebaron (hp.), Candace Natvig (vce.
and vln.), Jon English (trb.)   **OPONE OP 58**

RARE SEAL WOLVES
Anne Lebaron, LaDonna Smith,
Davey Williams (chamber improvisations)   **TRANS - - -**

SIESTA
Anne Lebaron, LaDonna Smith,
Davey Williams (chamber improvisations)   **TRANS - - -**

SUDDEN NOTICING OF TREES
Anne Lebaron, LaDonna Smith,
Davey Williams (chamber improvisations)   **TRANS - - -**

TRANSPARENT ZEBRA
Anne Lebaron, LaDonna Smith,
Davey Williams (chamber improvisations)   **TRANS - - -**

UKRANIAN ICE EGGS
Anne Lebaron, LaDonna Smith,
Davey Williams (chamber improvisations)   **TRANS - - -**

LEBRUN, Franziska Dorothea (1756-1791)

RONDO ALLEGRETTO, FROM THE
SONATA FOR PIANO AND VIOLIN
IN F-MAJOR, OP. 1, NO. 3
Monica von Saalfeld (pf.),
Werner Grobholz (vln.)　　　　　　**MUVAV MB 902**

LECLERC, Michelle (1939-　　)

IMPROVISATIONS FOR ORGAN
Michelle Leclerc (org.)　　　　　　**MXT BMG 267**

TOCCATA (1961)
Michelle Leclerc (org.)　　　　　　**MXT F 082**

LEE, Young Ja (1931-　　)

PIANO SONATINE
* * * * * *　　　　　　**JIGU 7703 4868**

LEFANU, Nicola Frances (1947-　　)

BUT STARS REMAINING,
FOR SOPRANO (1970)
J Manning (S.)　　　　　　**CHAND ABR 1017**

DEVA, FOR SOLO CELLO AND
SEVEN PLAYERS (1979)
C. Van Kampen (vlc.)
with Nash Ensemble　　　　　　**CHAND ABR 1017**

SAME DAY DAWNS, THE (FRAGMENTS FROM
A BOOK OF SONGS) (1974)
J. Manning (S.) with Gemini Ensemble:
Lukas (fl.), Mitchell (cl.), Levine (vln),
Smith (vlc.), Wood (perc.)
(cond.) Nicola Lefanu　　　　　　**CHAND ABR 1017**

LEGINSKA, Ethel (1890-1970)

THREE VICTORIAN PORTRAITS,
FOR PIANO (9'52)
Jeaneane Dowis (pf.)　　　　　　**ORION ORS 75188**

LEHMANN, Liza (1862-1918)

AT LOVE'S BEGINNING (CAMPBELL) (2'45)
Carole Rosen (Cont.), David Wilson-
Johnson (Bar.), A. Saunders (pf.)　　　　　　**HYPER A 66063**

CUCKOO, THE
Michael Aspinall (S.)　　　　　　**ACEDI SDD 507**

FOUR CAUTIONARY TALES AND
A MORAL (1909)
Robert Tear (T.), Gareth Morell (pf.)　　　　　　**ABAL CDN 5004**

IN A PERSIAN GARDEN
Elizabeth Harwood (S.), Bernadette
Greevy (Cont.), Philip Langridge (T.),
Forbes Robinson (B.), John Constable (pf.)　　　　　　**ARGO ZK 87**

THERE ARE FAIRIES AT THE BOTTOM
OF OUR GARDEN
Cathy Berberian (S.) Bruno Canino (pf.)　　　　　　**RCA LRL 1 5007**

THERE ARE FAIRIES AT THE BOTTOM
OF OUR GARDEN (3'00)
Carole Rosen (Cont.)　　　　　　**HYPER A 66063**

LEIVISKA, Helvi Lemmiki (1902-1982)

NOUSE, OLE KIRKAS
Maiju Kuusoja (S.), Taneli Kuusisto (pf.)　　　　　　**FENIC ST 19**

LEON, Tania Justina (1944-　　)

FOUR PIECES FOR CELLO
Michale Rudiakov (vlc.)　　　　　　**OPONE 101**

HAIKU
Narrator with Ensemble
(cond.) Tania Leon　　　　　　**OPONE 101**

I GOT OVAH
Johana (S.), Yolanda Liepa (pf.),
Tom Goldstein (perc.)　　　　　　**OPONE 101**

VOICES AND PICCOLO FLUTE
Tania Leon (elec. tape)　　　　　　**OPONE 101**

LEONARD, Clair (1901-　　)

RECITATIVO AND ABRACADABRA
Sigurd Rascher (sax.), David Tudor (pf.)　　**CONHA CHS 1156**

LEONARDA, Sister Isabella (1620-1704)

PRIMA MESSA, OP. 18
Schola Cantorum, University of Arkansas
(cond.) Jack Groh　　　　　　**LEONA LP1 115**

LEONCHIK, Svetlana Gavrilovna (1939-　　)

CONCERTO FOR TRUMPET AND ORCHESTRA
A. Maksimenko (trp.) with Bolshoi Theatre
Orchestra　　　　　　**MELOD**
(cond.) B. Khaikin　　　　　　**D 015505 6**

LEPLAE, Claire (1912-　　)

DANSES IMAGINAIRES
Frederick Gevers (pf.)　　　　　　**MUSAG MAG 70001**

SUITE CLASSIQUE
Robert Leuridon (pf.)　　　　　　**MUSAG MAG 70001**

SUITE IMPRESSIONISTE
Robert Leuridon (pf.)　　　　　　**MUSAG MAG 70001**

TABLEAU D'EXTREME ORIENT
Frederick Gevers (pf.)　　　　　　**MUSAG MAG 70001**

LEVI, Natalia Nikolayevna (1901-1972)

I STROLL ALONG THE FOREST PATH
B. Kazantsev (B.)　　　　　　**MELOD D 0008565/6**

LEVINA, Zara Alexandrovna (1907-1976)

CONCERTO FOR PIANO AND ORCHESTRA
Leonid Brumberg (pf.) with Bolshoi
Symphony Orchestra　　　　　　**MELOD**
(cond.) V. Kin　　　　　　**M 10 3809/12**

DANCE, IN A-FLAT MAJOR　　　　　　**MELOD**
Leonid Brumberg (pf.)　　　　　　**M 10 3809/12**

EIGHT ROMANCES FROM POEMS BY ESENIN　　**MELOD**
* * * * * *　　　　　　**M 10 3809/12**

FOUR SONGS　　　　　　**MELOD**
* * * * * *　　　　　　**M 10 3809/12**

FOURTEEN SONGS
Ivanova (S.), Milashkina (S.),
Kibkalo (B.), Isakova (m-S.),　　　　　　**MELOD**
Zara Levina (pf.)　　　　　　**D 20709/10**

FROM UNDER A MYSTERIOUS COLD HALF MASK
AND ALBUM IN VERSE (LERMONTOV)
N. Shpiller (S.) — **MELOD D 14301/2**

ODE TO A SOLDIER (VOCAL SYMPHONY)
Postavnicheva (m-S.), Selivanov (Bar.),
Muntyan (pf.), Dizhur (org.) with Radio
Chorus and Orchestra
(cond.) Aranovich — **MELOD D 16559/60**

SONATA FOR VIOLIN AND PIANO
D. Oistrakh (vln.), Zara Levina (pf.) — **MELOD M 10 3809/12**

THREE SONGS
Myasnikova (m-S.) — **MELOD D 29275/6**

THREE SONGS
N. Isakova (m-S.), Zara Levina (pf.) — **MELOD SM 03587/8**

TOCCATA, IN E-MINOR
* * * * * *
(cond.) Leonid Brumberg — **MELOD M 10 3809/12**

LIDDELL, Claire (-   )

KINDLING FIRE, THE
Claire Liddell, John Laurie, Patti Duncan,
James Boyd — **EMWAV SZLP 2141**

LINDEMAN, Anna Severine (1859-1938)

STRING QUARTET IN G-MINOR
Copenhagen String Quartet — **SIMAX PN 2010**

LIU, Tyan-Khua (1895-1932)
CHINESE FOLK DANCE
Central House Vocal Ensemble — **MELOD D 016831 2**

LLOYD, Caroline Parkhurst (1924-   )

DONA BARBARA (OPERA)
R Castillo (S.), M. Munoz (m-S.),
W. Rodriguez, D. Ramirez,
J. Castro (T.), R. Iriate (Bar.)
with Corey Orquestra Sinfonia,
Venezuela (cond.) Carlos Mendoza — **CYMBL 5054/5**

LLUNELL SANAHUJA, Pepita (1926-   )

PEL MATEIX CAMI (SARDANA)
* * * * * * — **DISCP STER 145**

TARRAGONA CARA AL MAR (SARDANA)
* * * * * * — **PICAP DL B 38 222 25**

LOCKWOOD, Annea Ferguson (1939-   )

AND SOUND FLEW LIKE A BIRD (1973)
Annea Lockwood (tape) — **NEWIL 7704**

CLOUD MUSIC (1974)
Annea Lockwood (tape) — **NEWIL 7704**

END
Annea Lockwood (tape) — **SVR RELP 1102**

GLASS WORLD OF ANNA LOCKWOOD, THE
Annea Lockwood — **TANGE TGS 104**

GLIDE (1977)
Wine Glass Quartet: Annea Lockwood
Emily Derr, Julie Winter, Ruth Anderson — **NEWIL 7704**

MALAMAN
Annea Lockwood, Julie Weber (vces. a-cap.) — **NEWIL 7704**

MALAMAN (1974)
Annea Lockwood, Julie Weber (vces. a-cap.) — **BRETH - - -**

MALOLO (1984)
Three Female Voices (a-cap.) — **FINNA 90226 1**

SOUND MAP OF THE HUDSON RIVER -
ENGLEWOOD FALLS (1982)
Annea Lockwood (tape) — **AUDIO VOL 6**

TIGER BALM
Annea Lockwood (tape) — **SORCE 9**

TIGER BALM (1971)
Annea Lockwood (tape) — **OPONE 70**

TIGER BALM (1971)
Annea Lockwood (tape) — **NEWIL 7704**

WOMAN MURDER (1978)
Annea Lockwood (tape) — **NEWIL 7704**

WORLD RHYTHMS (1975)
Hunter College Electronic Music Studio — **ARCH S 1765**

WORLD RHYTHMS (1975)
Annea Lockwood (10 channel tape) — **NEWIL 7704**

LOMON, Ruth (1930-   )

DUST DEVILS
Susan Allen (hp.) — **ARCH S 1787**

FIVE CEREMONIAL MASKS (1980)
Rosemary Platt (pf.) — **CORON LPS 3121**

SOUNDINGS (6'33)
Ruth Lomon (pf.), Iris Graffman Wenglin (pf.) — **CAPIO CR 2**

TRIPTYCH (6'15)
Ruth Lomon (pf.), Iris Graffman Wenglin (pf.) — **CAPIO CR 2**

LOUDOVA, Ivana (1941-   )

AIR (DUO) FOR BASS CLARINET
AND PIANO (5'18)
Emma Kovarnova (pf.), Josef Horak (b-cl.) — **PANTN P 11 0369**

CHORALE FOR ORCHESTRA
Vladimir Vlasak (perc.), Jan Klouda (perc.)
with Prague Symphony Orchestra
(cond.) L. Slovak — **PANTN 11 0490**

CHORALE FOR WIND ORCHESTRA,
PERCUSSION AND ORGAN
Koon, Boudreau with American Wind Symphony — **AWS 102**

CONCERTO FOR PERCUSSION, ORGAN
AND WIND SYMPHONY ORCHESTRA
American Wind Symphony — **AWS 103**

FORTUNE - LITTLE CANTATA FOR MALE,
FEMALE AND CHILDREN'S CHOIRS
A CAPPELLA (1984)
Bambini di Praga with Kuehn Mixed
Choir (cond.) Pavel Kuehn and
Bohumil Kulinsky — **PANTN 8112 0403**

KUROSHYO (DRAMATIC FRESCOES)
(SOPRANO SOLO AND MIXED CHOIR)
J. Jonasova (S.) with Czechoslovak
Radio Choir — **PANTN 11 0358**

MEETING WITH LOVE, FOR MEN'S CHOIR,
FLUTE AND PIANO
Prague Men's Choir
(cond.) M. Kosler — **SUPRA SP 20424**

MUSICA FESTIVA, FOR THREE TRUMPETS
AND THREE TROMBONES
Prague Brass Soloists — **PANTN 8111 0282**

RHAPSODY IN BLACK (BALLET)
Jiri Kaniak (ob.), Vladimir Vlasak (perc.),
Oldrich Satava (perc.) with Musici Di Praga
(cond.) Mario Klemens **PANTN 8110 0001 2**

SPLEEN, HOMMAGE A CHARLES BAUDELAIRE
Vadimir Vlasak (perc.), Jan Klouda (perc.)
with Prague Symphony Orchestra
(cond.) L. Slovak **PANTN 11 0490**

STRING QUARTET NO. 2 (DEM ANDENKEN AN
SMETANA) (1976)
Kocian Quartet **PANTN 81 110 030**

STRING QUARTET NO. 2 (DEM ANDENKEN AN
SMETANA) (1976)
Kocian Quartet **PANTN 81 110 738**

LOWENSTEIN, Gunilla Marike (1928-1981)

TELLUS MATER, FOR FLUTE, MARIMBA
AND STRING ORCHESTRA (1980) (17'58)
Barbro Lindvall (fl.), Bengt Stark (mar.)
with Royal Swedish Chamber Orchestra
(cond.) Mats Wiljefors **CAPRI CAP 1266**

LUO, Jing-Jing (1953-   )

PIANO CONCERTO (19'40)
Wu Ying (pf.) with Orchestra of the
Central Opera, Beijing
(cond.) Zheng Xiao-ying **HONGK HK 6 340161**

PIANO SOLO PIECES, BASED ON THREE
DUNHUANG POEMS: ACAOPUO,
TIANXIANZI, ZHETAZHI (13'00)
Cheui Shi-Guang (pf.) **HONGK HK 6 340161**

TWO MOVEMENTS FOR PIANO, MEZZOSOPRANO AND
ORCHESTRA (13'05)
Luo Tian-xian (m-S.), Chuei Shi-Guang (pf.)
with Central Philharmonic
Orchestra, Beijing (cond.) Li De-lun **HONGK HK 6 340161**

LUTYENS, Elisabeth (1906-1983)

AND SUDDENLY IT'S EVENING, OP. 66
(TENOR AND ELEVEN INSTRUMENTS)
H. Handt (T.) with Members of BBC
Symphony Orchestra **ARGO ZRG 638**

FIVE BAGATELLES
Richard Deering (pf.) **PEARL SHE 537**

FIVE BAGATELLES
Katharine Wolpe (pf.) **ARGO ZRG 5425**

FIVE INTERMEZZI FOR PIANO
Richard Deering (pf.) **PEARL SHE 537**

MOTET, OP. 27
John Alldis Choir
(cond.) John Alldis **ARGO ZRG 5426**

O SAISONS, O CHATEAUX, OP. 13 (CANTATA)
FOR SOPRANO AND ORCHESTRA
Marilyn Tyler (S.) with Royal Philharmonic
Orchestra
(cond.) Del Mar **ARGO ZRG 754**

O SAISONS, O CHATEAUX, OP. 13 (CANTATA)
FOR SOPRANO AND ORCHESTRA
Marilyn Tyler (S.) with Royal Philharmonic
Orchestra
(cond.) Del Mar **EMI ASD 612**

O SAISONS, O CHATEAUX, OP. 13 (CANTATA)
FOR SOPRANO AND ORCHESTRA
Marilyn Tyler (S.) with Royal Philharmonic
Orchestra
(cond.) Del Mar **EMI FALP 870**

O SAISONS, O CHATEAUX, OP. 13 (CANTATA)
FOR SOPRANO AND ORCHESTRA
Marilyn Tyler (S.) with Royal Philharmonic
Orchestra
(cond.) Del Mar **EMI ALP 2064**

PIANO E FORTE, OP. 43
Richard Deering (pf.) **PEARL SHE 537**

PLENUM 1, OP. 87
Richard Deering (pf.) **PEARL SHE 537**

PLENUM 4, OP. 100 (WHAT IS THE WIND)
Cleobury (org.), Cleobury (org.) **MIXTR YPS 1039**

QUINCUNX, OP. 44, FOR SOPRANO AND
BARITONE SOLOISTS AND ORCHESTRA
Josephine Nendick (S.), John Shirley-
Quirk (Bar.) with BBC Symphony
Orchestra (cond.) Del Mar **ARGO ZRG 622**

RING OF BONE (1976)
Peter Lawson (pf.) **NORWA ECR 001**

STEVIE SMITH SONGS
Meriel Dickinson (m-S.), Peter Dickinson (pf.) **UNICO UNS 268**

STRING QUARTET NO. 6, OP. 25
Dartington String Quartet **ARGO ZRG 5425**

THIS GREEN TIDE, FOR CLARINET/
BASSET HORN AND PIANO, OP. 103
Georgina Dobrey (cl.), Morris Pert (pf.) **CHANT CHT 005**

VALEDICTION, FOR CLARINET AND
PIANO, OP. 28
Georgina Dobrey (cl.), Morris Pert (pf.) **CHANT CHT 005**

WIND QUINTET, OP. 45
Leonardo Ensemble **ARGO ZRG 5425**

LYONN LIEBERMAN, Julie (1954-   )

ARTUCUS
Deborah Rothrock, Stephen Browman,
Omar Mesa, Marty Quinn, Tim Rusco,
Perkin Barnes (vln. and band) **THIRD TE 1501**

EMPHATIC CONNECTIONS
Laraaji Venus, Sri Vina (vce. and vln.) **HUIKS 01**

MACGREGOR, Laurie (1951-   )

INTRUSION OF THE HUNTER, FOR
PERCUSSION (1973-1974)
New Jersey Percussion Ensemble
(cond.) Raymond des Roches **CRI SD 444**

MACONCHY, Elizabeth (1907-   )

ARIADNE (DRAMATIC MONOLOGUE)
FOR SOPRANO AND ORCHESTRA
Heather Harper (S.) with Chamber
Orchestra (cond.) R. Leppard **OISEU SOL 331**

CAROL NOWELL
King's College Choir, Cambridge **EMI ALP 2290**

PROUD THAMES: OVERTURE
London Philharmonic Orchestra **LYRIT SRCS 57**

SERENATA CONCERTANTE, FOR
VIOLIN AND ORCHESTRA (21'33)
Manoug Parikian (vln.) with London
Symphony Orchestra
(cond.) V. Handley **LYRIT SRCS 116**

STRING QUARTET, NO. 5 (1948)
Allegri String Quartet **ARGO ZRG 5329**

STRING QUARTET, NO. 9
Allegri String Quartet **ARGO ZRG 672**

STRING QUARTET, NO. 10 (21'50)
University of Alberta String Quartet **CBC RCI 386**

SYMPHONY FOR DOUBLE STRING
ORCHESTRA (1953) (21'50)
London Symphony Orchestra
(cond.) V. Handley **LYRIT SRCS 116**

TAKE, O TAKE THOSE LIPS AWAY
(SHAKESPEARE) (1965)
S. Eaves (S.), C. Kerney (pf.) **CAMEO GOCLP 9020**

THREE BAGATELLES
E. Barbirolli (ob.), V. Aveling (hpcd.),
D. Nesbitt (vln.) **HMV HQS 1298**

TWELFTH NIGHT SONG
Scottish Festival Chorus **EMI CLP 3598**

MADISON, Carolyn (1907-   )

TWO PIECES (BITTE, N. LENAU;
WELTLAUF, HEINE) (2'27)
Gregg Smith Singers
(cond.) Gregg Smith **VOX SVBX 5354**

MADRIGUERA RODON, Paquita (1900-   )

HUMORADA, FOR GUITAR
* * * * * * **LYRIC LLST 7299**

HUMORADA, FOR GUITAR
* * * * * * **TELDE 648 029 DX**

HUMORADA, FOR GUITAR
John Williams (gtr) **DECCA SDD R 329**

MAGEAU, Mary Jane (1934-   )

CONTRASTS
Gary Williams (vlc.) **GREVL GRV 1070**

NEW LACRIMAE, A
Duluth Madgrigal Singers **SOND S 80 1995**

SCARBOROUGH FAIR VARIATIONS
Brisbane Baroque Trio **GREVL GRV 1081**

SONATE CONCERTATE
Brisbane Baroque Trio **GREVL GRV 1080**

MAGOGO KA DINIZULU, Constance, Princess (1900-1984)

BAMBULAL'UJESU YAMAJUDA (2'09)
Princess Constance Magogo Ka Dinizulu (vce.) **GALLO**
Mangosuthu Buthelezi (ugubu bow) **SGALP 1678**

MAHLER, Alma Maria (1879-1964)
FÜNF LIEDER – EKSTASE
Mary Sindoni (S.) **AFKA S 4686**

FÜNF LIEDER – ERKENNENDE
Mary Sindoni (S.) **AFKA S 4686**

FÜNF LIEDER – HYMNE
Mary Sindoni (S.) **AFKA S 4686**

FÜNF LIEDER – HYMNE AN DIE NACHT
Mary Sindoni (S.) **AFKA S 4686**

FÜNF LIEDER – LOBGESANG
Mary Sindoni (S.) **AFKA S 4686**

ICH WANDLE UNTER BLUMEN
Christopher Norton-Welsh (Bar.),
Charles Spencer (pf.) **PREIS 120653**

LAUE SOMMERNACHT
Christopher Norton-Welsh (Bar.),
Charles Spencer (pf.) **PREIS 120653**

STILLE STADT, DIE (DEHMEL)
Christopher Norton-Welsh (Bar.),
Charles Spencer (pf.) **PREIS 120653**

VIER LIEDER (14'26)
Katherine Ciesinski (m-S.), Ted Taylor (pf.) **LEONA LPI 118**

MAKAROVA, Nina Vladimirovna (1908-1976)

DREAMS
N. Postavnicheva (m-S.) **MELOD M 10 42077**

FIVE PIANO ETUDES
Nina Makarova (pf.) **MELOD M 10 42077**

MARIANNA PINEDA, FRAGMENTS
M. Postavnicheva (m-S.) **MELOD M 10 42077**

MELODY AND SCHERZO,
OP. 18, NOS. 1 AND 2
V. Pikaizen (vln), Nina Makarova (pf.) **MELOD D 21195/6**

MELODY, OP. 18, NO. 1
USSR Bolshoi Theatre Violinist Ensemble
(cond.) B. Khaikin **MELOD C 10 07029/30**

MY NIGHTINGALE (PUSHKIN)
V. Gomova (S.), N. Diominov (T.),
B. Dobrin (Bar.) **MELOD M 10 42077**

PATH, THE (PRISHELITZ)
V. Gomova (S.), N. Diominov (T.),
B. Dobrin (Bar.) **MELOD M 10 42077**

SONG OF THE POPLAR (FROM,
HOW STEEL IS HARDENED)
V. Gomova (S.), N. Diominov (T.),
B. Dobrin (Bar.) **MELOD M 10 42077**

SYMPHONY IN D-MINOR (1938)
USSR State Symphony Orchestra
(cond.) O. Koch **MELOD D 020989/90**

SYMPHONY IN D-MINOR (1938)
USSR State Symphony Orchestra
(cond.) O. Koch **MELOD SO 1585/6**

TO A FRIEND (KETLINSKAYA)
V. Gomova (S.), N. Diominov (T.),
B. Dobrin (Bar.) **MELOD M 10 42077**

TWO PIECES FOR CELLO AND PIANO
K. Georgian (vlc.), Nina Makarova (pf.) **MELOD M 10 42077**

TWO PIECES FOR HARP
Natalia Shameyeva (hp.) **MELOD M 10 42077**

TWO PIECES FOR VIOLIN AND PIANO
Pikaizen (vln.), Nina Makarova (pf.) **MELOD M 10 42077**

TWO ROMANCES (PUSHKIN)
V. Gomova (S.), N. Diominov (T.),
B. Dobrin (Bar.) **MELOD M 10 42077**

VOCALISE, AND, A MEMORY
E. Altman (vlc.), Nina Makarova (pf.) **MELOD D 21195 6**

ZOYA, HIGHLIGHT FROM THE OPERA
N. Postavnicheva (m-S.), V. Gomova (S.),
N. Diominov (T.), B. Dobrin (Bar.)
Nina Makarova (pf.) **MELOD M 10 42077**

ZOYA, THE DREAM (EXCERT
FROM THE OPERA) (ARR. PIANO)
Nina Makarova (pf.) **MELOD M 10 42077**

MALIBRAN, Maria Felicitas (1808-1836)

REVEIL D'UN BEAU JOUR, LE
Berenice Bramson (S.), Roger Rundle (pf.) **GEMIN RAP 1010**

MALMLOEF-FORSSLING, Carin (1916-   )

LALENDO, FOR SOLO CELLO (1970) (8'07)
Elmer Lavotha (vlc.)   **BLUEB BELL 179**

LITANIA, THREE SONGS (WERNER
ASPENSTROM) (1966) (4'10)
Margareta Jonth (S.)   **BLUEB BELL 179**

ORIZZONTE (1981) (8'45)
Margareta Jonth (S.)   **BLUEB BELL 179**

RELEASE, FOR STRING ORCHESTRA (4'05)
String Orchestra of the Landsting
Higher Music School   **WISLP 510**

SONATA SVICKEL, FOR SOLO
FLUTE (1964) (7'29)
Georgia Mohammar (fl.)   **BLUEB BELL 179**

THREE EXPERIENCES (1976) (4'38)
Margareta Jonth (S.)   **BLUEB BELL 179**

VOLLMOND – THREE JAPANESE HAIKU (3'23)
Margareta Jonth (S.)   **BLUEB BELL 179**

MAMLOK, Ursula (1928-   )

HAIKU SETTINGS, FOR SOPRANO
AND FLUTE (1967)
Shelton, Kahn   **GRENA 1015**

PANTA RHEI
Ben Hudson (vln.), Chris Finckel (vlc.),
Aleck Karis (pf.)   **CRI SD 518**

PANTA RHEI
Makara, Smith, Smith   *** * * S 101**

SEXTET (12'50)
Parnassus: Leader Anthony Korf   **CRI SD 480**

STRAY BIRDS (1963) (14'20)
P. Bryn-Julson (S.), S. Sollberger (fl.),
F. Sherry (vlc.)   **CRI 301**

VARIATIONS, FOR SOLO FLUTE (1961)
Samuel Brown (fl.)   **CRI 212**

VARIATIONS, FOR SOLO FLUTE (1961)
Hoover (fl.)   **OPONE 72**

WHEN SUMMER SANG (1980) (8'16)
Da Capo Chamber Players   **CRI SD 480**

MANA-ZUCCA (1894-   )

I LOVE LIFE, OP. 83
* * * * * *   **VICTO 1986**

PIANO CONCERTO IN E-FLAT MAJOR
Mana-Zucca (pf.) with Pasdeloup
Symphony Orchestra
(cond.) Jean Allain   **COMPT LP 1601**

RACHEM, OP. 60, NO. 1
* * * * * *   **VICTO 1986**

SEVENTEEN SONGS, FOR
BARITONE AND PIANO
James Farrar (Bar.), Mana-Zucca (pf.)   **COMPT LP 1006**

VIOLIN CONCERTO, OP. 224
Eddy Brown (vln.) with Pasdeloup
Symphony Orchestra
(cond.) Jean Allain   **COMPT LP 1501**

MANNING, Kathleen Lockhart (1890-1951)

SHOES
Nancy Tatum (S.), Geoffrey Parson (pf.) **LONDO OS 26053**

MANZIARLY, Marcelle de (1899-   )

DIALOGUE FOR CELLO AND PIANO
G. Munguia (vlc.), T. Hrunkiv (pf.)   **LAUPR LP 13**

OISEAU BLESSE, L' (LA FONTAINE)
Marie-Therese Holley with Instrumental
Ensemble   **TURNA TV 4183**

TRILOGUE FOR VIOLIN,
CELLO AND PIANO (9'16)
The Western Arts Trio: Brian Hanly (vln.),
David Tomatz (vlc.), Werner Rose (pf.) **LAURE LR 109**

TROIS FABLES DE LA FONTAINE (1935) (5'05)
H. Cuenod (T.), G. Parsons (pf.)   **NIMBU 2118**

MARBE, Myriam (1931-   )

CONCERTO FOR HARPSICHORD AND EIGHT
INSTRUMENTALISTS
Adrian Tomescu (hpcd.) with   **ELECT**
Instrumental Assemble
(cond.) Anatol Vieru   **ST ECE 01862**

CYCLE FOR FLUTE, GUITAR AND PERCUSSION   **ELECT**
Voicu Vasinca (fl. and perc.)   **ST ECE 01459**

INCANTATION (SONATA) FOR CLARINET SOLO   **ELECT**
Aurelian-Octav Popa (cl.)   **ECE 0389**

JOC SECUND   **ELECT**
Musica Nova Chamber Ensemble   **ECE 01237**

PIECE FOR PIANO AND HARPSICHORD   **ELECT**
Adrian Tomescu (pf. and hpcd.)   **ST ECE 02040**

RITUAL FOR THE THIRST OF THE EARTH
Madrigal Chamber Group   **ELECT**
(cond.) Constantin   **ST ECE 0416**

SERENATA
Formatia Consortium Violae   **ELECT**
(cond.) Anatol Vieru   **ST ECE 01862**

SERENATA (EINE KLEINE SONNENMUSIK)
G. Dima of Brasov Symphonic Orchestra   **ELECT**
(cond.) I. Ionesu-Galati   **ST ECE 01862**

TIME FOUND AGAIN
Emilia Petrescu (S.), with Consortium Violae **ELECT**
(cond.) Anatol Vieru   **ST ECE 01862**

MAREZ-OYENS, Tera de (1932-   )

AMBIVERSION, FOR BASS
CLARINET AND TAPE (15'08)
Harry Spaarmaay (b-cl.)   **BVHAS 054**

BALLERINA ON A CLIFF (1980) (7'08)
Tera de Marez-Oyens (pf.)   **BVHAS 054**

CHARON'S GIFT, FOR PIANO AND TAPE (13'50)
Tera de Marez-Oyens (pf.)   **BVHAS 054**

DEATH TO BIRTH (1974) (18'40)
Netherlands Vocal Ensemble   **BVHAS 054**

ELECTRONIC MUSIC (1954-1968)
* * * * * *   **COMPO CV 7803**

ELECTRONIC MUSIC (1967-1976)
* * * * * *   **COMPO CV 7903**

SOLANG AS MENSCHEN GIBT
Heinrich Schultz Kantorei, Freiburg
(cond.) Schneider   **LAUDA HV 91516**

VIOLIN CONCERTO (STRUCTURES
AND DANCE)
Robert Szreder (vln) and Dutch
Radio S.O. (cond.) Kenneth Montgomeryr   **SONOTONE - - -**

MARGARET OF AUSTRIA (1480-1530)

LIVRES DE BASSES DANCES (SELECTIONS)
Clemencic Consort
HARMU HMU 939

LIVRES DE BASSES DANCES (SELECTIONS) (4'59)
Clemencic Consort
HARMU HMU 990

LIVRES DE BASSES DANSES (SELECTIONS)
Clemencic Consort
HARMU HMU 2 472

MARI, Pierrette (1929-   )

ESPAGNOLETTE
Sandanowsky (gtr.)
VERSE M 10 034

MARIC, Ljubica (1909-   )

PESME PROSTORA (SONGS OF SPACE)
Radio Televizija Beograd Chorus
and Symphony Orchestra
(cond.) Jagust
RTB LP 2502

WIND QUINTET (12'00)
Belgrade Wind Quintet
RTB LP 2602

MARTINEZ, Marianne (1744-1812)

CONCIERTO (FOR HARPSICHORD),
IN A-MAJOR
Maria Teresa Chenlo (hpcd.) with Orquesta
Da Camara Espanola
(cond.) Victor Martin
ETNOS 02 A X 1

SINFONIA IN C-MAJOR
Orquesta Da Camara Espanola
(cond.) Victor Martin
ETNOS 02 A X 1

SONATA IN A-MAJOR (7'27)
Nancy Fierro (pf.)
PELIC LP 2017

MARTINS, Maria de Lourdes (1926-   )

DIVERTIMENTO FOR WIND QUINTET
Clarion Wind Quintet
EDUCO 4101

MASSUMOTO, Kikuko (1937-   )

THREE SONGS FROM MEDIEVAL JAPAN:
AWARE, HAYASHI, SHI-TE-TEN
Hiroko Asaoka (S.)
JAPAN JFC 8108

MATUSZCZAK, Bernadetta (1937-   )

CHAMBER DRAMA FOR BARITONE,
SPOKEN VOICE AND INSTRUMENTAL
ENSEMBLE, A
* * * * * *
MUZA M 3 XW 890

SALMI (PER UN GRUPPO DI CINQUE)
* * * * * *
MUZA S 3 XW 1883

MATVEYEVA, Novella (1934-   )

SONGS
Novelle Matveyeva (S. and gtr.)
MELOD C 40 07679/80

MAURICE, Paule (1910-1967)

TABLEAUX DE PROVENCE, FOR
SAXOPHONE AND PIANO
Pittel (sax.), Grierson (pf.)
CRYST S 105

MAZOUROVA, Jarmila (1941-   )

INVENTION FOR FLUTE, VIOLIN
AND CIMBALOM
Julius Kessner (fl.), Bohumil Smijdal (vln.),
Helena Cervenkova (cimbalom)
PANTN 8110 0001/2

MCLEAN, Priscilla Anne Taylor (1942-   )

BENEATH THE HORIZON III
Melvyn Poore (tba.) with Tape
OPUS 96

DANCE OF DAWN (22'05)
Indiana University South Bend Electronic
Music Studio
CRI SD 335

INNER UNIVERSE – SALT CANYONS
Priscilla McLean (pf.) with Tape
OPONE 96

INTERPLANES, FOR TWO PIANOS (12'33)
Robert Hamilton (pf.), Christine
Douberteen (pf.)
ADVAN FGR 195

INVISIBLE CHARIOTS
Priscilla McLean (elec.)
FOLKW FIS 33450

INVISIBLE CHARIOTS (MOVEMENT ONE –
VOICES OF THE INVISIBLE)
Priscilla McLean (elec.)
FOLKW FPX 6050

NIGHT IMAGES
Priscilla McLean (elec.)
FOLKW FPX 6050

VARIATIONS AND MOZAICS ON A THEME OF
STRAVINSKY (17'46)
Louisville Orchestra
(cond.) Juan Matteucci
LOUIS LS 762

MCLEOD, Jennifer Helen (1941-   )

CAMBRIDGE SUITE FOR ORCHESTRA (5'54)
Youth Orchestra
(cond.) Juan Matteucci
KIWI SLC 72

PIANO PIECE (1965)
Tessa Birnie (pf.)
KIWI SLD 19

UNDER THE SUN
Narrators, Choirs and Orchestras
(cond.) Peter Tulloch
PHILI 6641 009

McLIN, Lena (1929-   )

GLORY, GLORY, HALLELUJAH
Virginia Union University Choir
(cond.) Odell Hobbs
RISST RSSWO 626

SANCTUS
Virginia Union University Choir
(cond.) Odell Hobbs
GELER MC 8806

McMILLAN, Ann Endicott (1923-   )

AMBER, '75
Ann McMillan (elec.)
FOLKW FTS 33451

CARREFOURS (1971) (6'12)
Ann McMillan (elec.)
FOLKW FTS 33904

EPISODE
Ann McMillan (elec.)
FOLKW FTS 33451

GATEWAY SUMMER SOUND
Abstracted Animal and Other Sounds
FOLKW 33451

GONG SONG (1969)
Ann McMillan (elec.)
FOLKW 33451

LITTLE COSMIC DUST, A, FOR PIANO
AND TAPE (1981-1982)
Lifchitz, Chance
OPONE 79

SYRINX
Ann McMillan (elec.) **FOLKW FTS 33451**

WHALE 1 (5'02)
Ann McMillan (elec.) **FOLKW FTS 33904**

MEGEVAND, Denise (-   )

HARPE CELTIQUE DES ILES
HEBRIDES, LA (ARR. MEGEVAND)
Denise Megevand (celtic hp.) with
Instrumental Accompaniment **ARION ARN 33 351**

MEKEEL, Joyce (1931-   )

ALARUMS AND EXCURSIONS (7'26)
K. Lenel (m-S.) with Boston Musica Viva

(cond.) R. Pittman **NORTH NR 203**

CORRIDORS OF DREAM, FOR MEZZO-SOPRANO
AND CHAMBER ORCHESTRA (11'30)
Curtis (m-S.) with Boston Musica Viva
(cond.) R. Pittman **DELOS 25405**

PLANH, FOR SOLO VIOLIN (1975) (13'02)
Nancy Cirilloa (vln.) **DELOS 25405**

RUNE (1977) (6'28)
J. Fenwick Smith (fl.), D. Anderson (perc.) **NORTH NR 203**

VIGIL, FOR ORCHESTRA
* * * * * *
(cond.) Mester **LOUIS 768**

MELL, Gertrud Maria (1947-   )

FANTAISIE IN A-MINOR, OP. 1, FOR PIANO
Gertrud Mell (pf.) **MELL 1**

IMPROVISATION IN C-MINOR
Gertrud Mell (pf.) **MELL 1**

STRING QUARTET, NO. 1, IN C-MINOR
(E-FLAT MAJOR)
Medlemmar ur Kungl. Hof Kapelle **MELL 1**

MEYERS, Lois (1925-   )

CARRY CANDLES TO THE MANGER
Da Camera Singers, Edmonton **CMB SM 256**

MIAGI, Ester Kustovna (1922-   )

KALEVIPOEG'S JOURNEY INTO
FINLAND (CANTATA)
Estonian Men's Chorus and Estonian
Radio Orchestra **MELOD D 10089/90**

OSTINATA
Estonian Radio Wind Quintet **MELOD D 29547/8**

PIANO TRIO (1950)
Juri Gerrets (vln.), Toomas Velmet (vlc.),
Valdur Roots (pf.) **MELOD C 10 05333/4**

SERENADE FOR VIOLIN AND
SYMPHONY ORCHESTRA (13'25)
E. Lippus (vln.), with Estonian Radio
Symphony Orchestra
(cond.) R. Maisov **MELOD 33 D 05906/7**

SYMPHONY NO. 1 (1968)
Estonian Radio Television Orchestra
(cond.) Neeme Jarvi **MELOD C 10 05333/4**

THREE PIECES FOR TWO PIANOS
A. Klas (pf.), B. Lukk (pf.) **MELOD D 3900/1**

VARIATIONS, FOR PIANO, CLARINET
AND STRING ORCHESTRA
Valdur Roots (pf.), Rein Karin (cl.) with
Tallin Chamber Orchestra
(cond.) Neeme Jarvi **MELOD C 10 05333/4**

MIGRANYAN, Emma (1940-   )

SONATINA
Emma Migranyan (pf.) **MELOD C 10 07763/4**

MIRA BAI (1498-1547)

BHAJANS
M.S. Subbalakshmi (vce.),
V.V. Subramaniam (vln.),
T.K. Murthy (dr.) **EMI EALP 1297**

MIRSHAKAR, Zarrina Mirsaidovna (1947-   )

THREE PAMIR FRESCOS,
FOR VIOLIN AND PIANO
Alexander Vinnitski (vln.),
Valerie Petash (pf.) **MELOD C 10 14821/22**

MIYAKE, Haruna Shibata (1942-   )

FLOWER FANTASY FOR SOPRANO,
PIANO AND TRUMPET
Mari Kitahara (S.), Haruna Miyake (pf.),
Toshio Itakura (trp.) **VICTJ SJX 9522**

WHY NOT, MY BABY? FOR SOPRANO,
PIANO AND TRUMPET
Mari Kitahara (S.), Haruna Miyake (pf.),
Toshio Itakura (trp.) **VICTJ SJX 9522**

MIZUNO, Shuko (1934-   )

TONE, FOR PIANO
Aki Takahashi (pf.) **CP 2 3 5**

MOLINARO, Simone (1565-1615)

FANTASIA NOVA, FOR LUTE
Yasunori Imamura (lute) **CLAVS D 8206**

MONK, Meredith (1943-   )

DOLMEN MUSIC
Meredith Monk (vce.) with Chorus **MUZA ECM 1 1197**

ENGINE STEPS
Meredith Monk (vce.) with Ensemble **ECM ECM 23792**

ESTER'S SONG
Meredith Monk (vce.) with Ensemble **ECM ECM 23792**

KEY (EIGHT COMPOSITIONS FOR
VOICE AND ORGAN)
* * * * * * **INCRE 1001**

OUR LADY OF LATE (SIXTEEN COMPOSITIONS
FOR VOICE AND GLASS HARMONICA)
Meredith Monk (vce.), Collin Walcott (glass har.) **MINON 1001**

SONGS FROM THE HILL (1976)
Meredith Monk (vce. and pf.), Andrea
Goodman (vce., pf. and rec.), Susan
Kempe (vce. and pf.), Monica Solem (vce.) **WERGO SM 1022**

TABLET (1977)
Meredith Monk (vce. and pf.), Andrea
Goodman (vce., pf. and rec.), Susan
Kempe (vce and pf.), Monica Solem (vce.)
**WERGO
SM 1022**

TURTLE DREAMS
Meredith Monk (vce.) with Ensemble
ECM ECM 23792

TURTLE DREAMS
Meredith Monk (vce. and org.) with Ensemble
**ECM
ECM 1240**

VIEW 1
Meredith Monk (vce.) with Ensemble
ECM ECM 23792

VIEW 2
Meredith Monk (vce.) with Ensemble
ECM ECM 23792

MONNOT, Marguerite Angele (1903-1961)

IRMA LA DOUCE (OPERETTA)
Juhnke (vce.), Ferrari (vce.)
PHONO 9072 226

IRMA LA DOUCE (OPERETTA)
Elizabeth Seal, Keith Mitchell with
Chorus
CBS AOS 2029

MOON, Chloe (1952-   )

SHADOWS, SEVEN PIECES FOR STRING ORCHESTRA (10'33)
Schola Musica
(cond.) Ashley Musica
KIWI SLD 71

MOORE, Dorothy Rudd (1940-   )

DIRGE AND DELIVERANCE
K. Moore (vlc.), Johnson (pf.)
PERF CR 7001

FROM THE DARK TOWER
Harris (m-S.)
PERF CR 7003

MOORE, Mary Carr (1873-1957)

SIXTEEN ART SONGS
Evelyn de la Rosa (S.), David Rudat (T.),
Andre Lenz (pf.)
CAMBR C 1022

MOORE, Undine Smith (1905-   )

AFRO-AMERICAN SUITE (FLUTE/ALTO FLUTE,
AND PIANO)
Trio Pro-Viva
EASTE ERS 513

LAMB, THE, TWO PART CANON,
FOR TREBLE VOICES
St. Stephen's Church Choir
(cond.) Clarence Whiteman
EASTE ERS 542

LAMB, THE, TWO PART CANON,
FOR TREBLE VOICES
Virginia State College Choir
(cond.) Carl Harris
RICHS 4112 N 10

LET US MAKE MAN IN OUR IMAGE
(FOR MIXED CHORUS A CAPPELLA)
Virginia State College Choir
(cond.) Carl Harris
RICHS 4112 N 10

LORD, WE GIVE THANKS TO THEE
(FOR MIXED CHORUS A CAPPELLA)
Virginia State College Choir
(cond.) Carl Harris
RICHS 4112 N 10

LORD, WE GIVE THANKS TO THEE
(FOR MIXED CHORUS A CAPPELLA)
Virginia Union University Choir
(cond.) Odell Hobbs
EASTE ERS 549

LORD, WE GIVE THANKS TO THEE
(FOR MIXED CHORUS A CAPPELLA)
Massanetta Chorus
(cond.) John Motley
MARK MC 8568

LOVE LET THE WINDS CRY
HOW I ADORE THEE
* * * * * *
MICHI SM 0015

MOTHER TO SON, FOR DOUBLE
MIXED CHORUS A CAPPELLA
Virginia Union University Choir
(cond.) Odell Hobbs
EASTE ERS 549

STRIVING AFTER GOD, FOR MIXED
CHORUS A CAPELLA
Virginia District Five All Regional Chorus
(cond.) John Motley
MARK MC 8458

STRIVING AFTER GOD, FOR MIXED
CHORUS A CAPPELLA
Virginia State College Choir
(cond.) Carl Harris
RICHS 4112 N 10

MORETTO, Nelly (1925-   )

COMPOSICION NO. 9B, SOMBRE POEMAS DE
GUSTAVO MORETTO
* * * * * *
MCBA 0010

MORGAN, Mary Hannah (1885-1956)

BLESS THIS HOUSE
John McCormack (T.)
* * * EX 2900073

BLESS THIS HOUSE (BALLAD)
Janet Baker (S.), P. Ledger (pf.)
EMI ASD 3981

BLESS THIS HOUSE (BALLAD)
Felicity Palmer (S.), John Constable (pf.)
ARGO ZK 97

TWO LITTLE WORDS (BALLAD)
Felicity Palmer (S.); John Constable (pf.)
ARGO ZK 45

MORLEY, Angela (1924-   )

WATERSHIP DOWN - KEHAAR'S THEME
City of Birmingham Symphony Orchestra
(cond.) Marcus Dods
HMV ASD 3797

MORTIFEE, Ann (1947-   )

BAPTISM
Ann Mortifee
* * * CAP ST 6437

ECSTASY OF RITA JOE, THE
Ann Mortifee
**KERYG
KRS 1005 UA LA 126 F**

MOSS, Katie (1881-   )

FLORAL DANCE, THE
Robert Easton (B.)
SUNOP SYO 12

MOSZUMANSKA-NAZAR, Krystyna (1924-   )

INTERPRETATIONS FOR FLUTE, PERCUSSION
AND MAGNETIC TAPE
B. Swiatek (fl.), J. Stefanski (perc.)
**MUZA
M 3 XW 1034**

KONSTELLATIONEN (1972)
Alex Blin (pf.)
RBM 3022

THREE MINIATURES FOR CLARINET
AND PIANO
B. Listokin (cl.), A. Listokin (pf.)
GOLDE RE 7052

VARIAZIONI CONCERTANTE FOR FLUTE
AND CHAMBER ORCHESTRA
E. Dastych-Szwarc (fl.) with Silesian
Philharmonic Orchestra — **MUZA ARCH 246**

MURAKUMO, Ayako (1949-   )

PROJECTION, FOR MEZZOSOPRANO,
VIOLONCELLO AND PIANO
* * * * * * — **JAPAN JFC 8508**

MURAO, Sachie (1945-   )

7290 (KLEINES STÜCK FÜR KLAVIER, NR. 6)
* * * * * * — **JAPAN 7910**

MURDOCH, Marjolijn (1943-   )

FANTASIE IN D-MINOR, FOR OBOE
AND HARPSICHORD
* * * * * * — **EMI HQS 1298**

MUSGRAVE, Thea (1928-   )

CHAMBER CONCERTO NO. 2 (15'56)
Boston Musica Viva
(cond.) R. Pittman — **DELOS 25405**

CHRISTMAS CAROL (COMPLETE OPERA)
Virginia Opera Association
(cond.) Peter Mark — **MOSSM MMG 302**

COLLOQUY FOR VIOLIN AND PIANO
Parikian (vln.), Crowson (pf.) — **ARGO ZRG 5328**

CONCERTO FOR CLARINET AND ORCHESTRA
De Peyer (cl.) with London Symphony
Orchestra (cond.) Del Mar — **ARGO ZRG 726**

CONCERTO FOR HORN AND ORCHESTRA
* * * * * * — **DECCA ZAL 13447**

CONCERTO FOR HORN AND ORCHESTRA
Tuckwell (hn.) with Scottish National
Orchestra (cond.) Thea Musgrave — **DECCA HEAD 8**

CONCERTO FOR ORCHESTRA
* * * * * * — **DECCA ZAL 13447**

CONCERTO FOR ORCHESTRA
Keith Pearson (cl.) with Scottish National
Orchestra
(cond.) A. Gibson — **DECCA HEAD 8**

EXCURSIONS
Thea Musgrave (pf.) — **ARGO ZRG 704**

FOUR MADRIGALS (SIR THOMAS WYATT)
(FOR MIXED CHORUS) (1953)
Leonine Consort — **ARIKA AR 002**

MARY, QUEEN OF SCOTS
Virginia Opera Chorus and Orchestra
(cond.) Peter Mark — **FONO FSM MO 301**

MARY, QUEEN OF SCOTS (COMPLETE OPERA)
Virginia Opera Chorus and Orchestra
(cond.) Peter Mark — **MOSSM MMG 301**

MONOLOGUES FOR PIANO
Thea Musgrave (pf.) — **ARGO ZRG 704**

MUSIC FOR HORN AND PIANO (10'40)
Charles Kavalovski (hn.), E.
Zuckermann (pf.) — **MUHER MHS 3547**

NIGHT MUSIC, FOR TWO HORNS
AND ORCHESTRA
Tuckwell (hn.), Chidell (hn.) with
London Sinfonietta
(cond.) Prausnitz — **ARGO ZRG 702**

PRIMAVERA
Dorothy Dorow (S.) — **CAPRI RIKS LP 59**

RORATE COELI
BBC Northern Singers
(cond.) Wilkinson — **ABBEY LPB 798**

SOLILOQUY I, FOR GUITAR AND
PRE-RECORDED TAPE
Siegfried Behrend (gtr.) with Tape — **DGG DG 2530 079**

TRIO FOR FLUTE, OBOE AND PIANO
Mabillon Trio — **DELTA SDEL 18005**

TRIPTYCH, FOR TENOR AND ORCHESTRA
Duncan Robertson (T.) with Scottish
National Orchestra
(cond.) Gibson — **HMV ASD 2279**

NAITO, Akemi (1956-   )

MAYA, FOR SOLO VIOLIN (1983)
* * * * * * — **JAPAN JFC 8409**

NATSUDA, Shoko (-   )

PREMIERE PIECE (2'20)
Nelson Delle-Vigne Fabbri (pf.) — **PAVAN ADW 7053**

NATVIG, Candace (1947-   )

EUPHORBIA (WITH JON ENGLISH
AND ANNE LEBARON)
Candace Natvig (vln. and vce.), Jon
English (hp.), Anne Lebaron (hp.) — **OPONE OP 58**

IDYLLE UND KATASTROPHEN (WITH ALEX
SCHLIPPENBACH, SVEN A. JOHANSSON ET. AL.)
* * * * * * — **TORCH - - -**

IOWA EAR MUSIC
* * * * * * — **CORNP - - -**

LITTLE LEFT OF CENTER, A (WITH
JON ENGLISH AND ANNE LEBARON)
Anne Lebaron (hp.), Candace Natvig (vce.
and vln.), Jon English (trb.) — **OPONE OP 58**

ONE, NOT TWO
Candace Natvig (S. and vln.) — **ARCH S 1797**

TRAVELS OF DOG AND CAT
Candace Natvig, Anne Lebaron, Jon English — **ARCH - - -**

NAZIROVA, Elmira Mirza Rza Kyzy (1928-   )

CONCERTO FOR PIANO AND ORCHESTRA (ON
ARABIAN MOTIFS)
Elmira Nazirova with Radio Orchestra
(cond.) Svetlanov — **MELOD D 4216/7**

NEWLIN, Dika (1923-   )

MACHINE SHOP
Gamelan Son of Lion — **FOLKW FTS 31313**

PIANO TRIO, OP. 2 (1948)
London Czech Trio: Liza Marketta (pf.),
Jack Rothstein (vln.), Karel Horitz (vlc.) — **CRI 170**

NIKOLAYEVA, Tatiana Petrovna (1924-   )

CONCERTO FOR PIANO AND ORCHESTRA,
IN B-MAJOR
Tatiana Nikolayeva (pf.) with USSR
String Orchestra
(cond.) Kondrashin — **MELOD D 0263/4**

ETUDE IN E-FLAT MAJOR
Tatiana Nikolayeva (pf.)   **MELOD D 6125/6**

NISHIMURA, Yukie (1968-   )

PIANO CONCERTO NO. 3, IN D-MAJOR
Yukie Nishimura (pf.) with NHK
Symphony Orchestra   **RJOCR**
(cond.) Mstislav Rostropovich   **C 25 R 8001 19 298**

NORDENSTROM, Gladys Mercedes (1924-   )

ZEIT XXIV (RENATA PANDULA) (1976)
Neva Pilgrim (S.), Dennis Helmrich (pf.)   **ORION ORS 79348**

NORMAN, Ruth (1927-   )

MOLTO ALLEGRO, FROM FOUR
PIANO PIECES (1970)
Ruth Norman (pf.)   **OPONE 35**

PRELUDE IV FOR PIANO, FROM
FOUR PIANO PIECES (1970)
Ruth Norman (pf.)   **OPONE 35**

NUNLIST, Juli (1916-1964)

RILKE LIEDER – DU GEHST MIT
Mary Sindoni (S.)   **AFKA S 4686**

RILKE LIEDER – LIEBESLIED
Mary Sindoni (S.)   **AFKA S 4686**

RILKE LIEDER – LIED VOM MEER
Mary Sindoni (S.)   **AFKA S 4686**

RILKE LIEDER – LÖSCH MIR DIE AUGEN AUS
Mary Sindoni (S.)   **AFKA S 4686**

RILKE LIEDER – MIR WAR SO WEH
Mary Sindoni (S.)   **AFKA S 4686**

RILKE LIEDER – PFAUENFEDER
Mary Sindoni (S.)   **AFKA S 4686**

RILKE LIEDER – SCHLAFLIED
Mary Sindoni (S.)   **AFKA S 4686**

SPELLS (1963)
Philharmonic Chorale   **ADVEN USR 5005**

TWO PIANO PIECES (1961)
Arthur Loesser (pf.)   **CRI 183**

ZWEI NACHTSTÜCKE – GNOMENREIGEN
Mary Sindoni (S.)   **AFKA S 4685**

ZWEI NACHTSTÜCKE – MONDSÜCHTIG
Mary Sindoni (S.)   **AFKA S 4686**

OBROVSKA, Jana (1930-   )

CONCERTO FOR TWO GUITARS AND
ORCHESTRA
Milan Zelenka (gtr.), Lubomir
Brabec (gtr.) with Plzen Radio Symphony
Orchestra (cond.) Rostislav Haliska   **PANTO 8110 0185**

CONCERTO FOR TWO GUITARS AND
ORCHESTRA (18'00)
Milan Zelenka (gtr.), Lubomir
Brabec (gtr.) with State Symphony
Orchestra (cond.) Rostislav Haliska   **PANTN 11 0742**

DUE MUSICI (4'49)
Milan Zelenka (gtr.), Lubomir Brabec (gtr.)   **PANTN 8110 0185**

PRELUDES FOR GUITAR
Milan Zelenka (gtr.)   **SUPRA 1 110969**

STRING QUARTET
Talichovo Quartet   **PANTN 11 0631 G**

ODAGESCU, Irina (1937-   )

BATALIA CU FACLE, OP. 31
(CHOREOGRAPHIC POEM)
Rumanian RTV Symphony Orchestra   **ELECT**
(cond.) Emanuel Elenescu   **ST ECE 01866**

CINTEC INALT, OP. 51
Orchestra Simfonic din Radio Clevizuri   **ELECT**
(cond.) Paul Popescu   **ST ECE 02589**

CINTIND PLAIUL MIORITEI
(FOR WOMEN'S CHOIR)
* * * * * *   **ELECT ST EXE 01822**

HIGH SONG
Rumanian Radio TV Symphony Orchestra   **ELECT**
(cond.) Paul Popescu   **ST ECE 02589**

IMPROVISATU DRAMATICE, OP. 22
Orchestra Simfonic din Radio Clevizuri   **ELECT**
(cond.) Cristian Brancuzi   **ST ECE 02589**

MOMENTE, OP. 25
Filarmonica din Arad   **ELECT**
(cond.) Nicolae Boboc   **ST ECE 02589**

OGLINDIRE, CHORAL POEM   **ELECT**
* * * * * *   **STM ECE 01127**

PE NIMB DE VULTURI, CHORAL POEM   **ELECT**
* * * * * *   **ST EXE 01973**

PISCURI, OP. 15 (SYMPHONIC POEM)
Rumanian RTV Symphony Orchestra   **ELECT**
(cond.) Emanuel Elenescu   **ST ECE 01866**

SONATA PENTRU VIOARA SI PIAN (12'46)
Victoria Basta (vln.), Crimhilda   **ELECT**
Cristescu (pf.)   **ST ECE 01545**

OERBECK, Anne-Marie (1911-   )

MARCIA INDOMABILE (2'07)
Eva Knardahl (pf.)   **PHILI 6507 051**

PASTORALE AND ALLEGRO FOR FLUTE AND
STRINGS (1959) (9'54)
Per Oien (fl.) with Norwegian
Chamber Orchestra   **BIS LP 103**

SEVEN POEMS BY HANS HENRIK HOLM (13'17)
Froydis Klausberger (S.), Einar
Steen-Nokleberg (pf.)   **PHILI 6507 051**

SONATINA FOR PIANO (8'59)
Eva Knardahl (pf.)   **PHILI 6507 051**

VALSE PICCANTE (1'01)
Eva Knardahl (pf.)   **PHILI 6507 051**

OH, Sook Ja (1941-   )

CONTEMPORARY MUSIC SOCIETY IN SEOUL   **SUNG**
* * * * * *   **SEL 100135**

CONTEMPORARY MUSIC SOCIETY IN SEOUL   **SUNG**
* * * * * *   **SEL 100071**

OH SOOK JA'S ART SONGS   **SUNG**
* * * * * *   **SEL RS 001**

OIKONOMOPOULOS, Eleni N. (1912-   )

CHRISTMAS SONGS (SELECTIONS)
* * * * * *   **COLUM 33 G 62**

EASTER (PASCHALIA) SELECTIONS
* * * * * *   **COLUM AZS 5**

JOYOUS VOICES (HAROPES FONES)
(SELECTIONS)
* * * * * *   **COLUM 33 XAZ 1251**

JOYOUS VOICES (HAROPES FONES)
(SELECTIONS)
* * * * * *   **COLUM AZE 202**

KITTEN, THE (TO GATAKI) (SELECTIONS)
* * * * * *   **COLUM AZS 3**

MY COUNTRY (PATRIDA MOU)
(SELECTIONS)
* * * * * *   **COLUM 33 XAZ 1251**

MY COUNTRY (PATRIDA MOU)
(SELECTIONS)
* * * * * *   **COLUM AZE 201**

O KOINONIKOS (COMMUNION SONG)
(ORATORIO)
* * * * * *   **COLUM 33 AZ 1107/8**

ONE HEART (MIA KARDIA) (SELECTIONS)
* * * * * *   **COLUM AZS 2**

PINDOS (SELECTIONS)
* * * * * *   **COLUM AZS 12**

TA THEOPHANIA (ORATORIO)
* * * * * *   **COLUM 33 YAZ 1256/7**

TODAY (HIMERA) (SELECTIONS)
* * * * * *   **COLUM AZS 1**

TOWARDS THE LIGHT (PROS TO FOS)
(SELECTIONS)
* * * * * *   **COLUM 33 XAZ 1251**

TOWARDS THE LIGHT (PROS TO FOS)
(SELECTIONS)
* * * * * *   **COLUM AZE 203**

OLAGNIER, Marguerite (1844-1906)

SAIS
* * * * * *   **PACIF PIZ 1539**

OLIVEIRA, Babi de (-   )

CABOCLO AMAZONESE
Arnaldo Rebello (pf.)   **CORCO CDEM 9**

SONGS
Lauricy Avila Prochet (S.), Vitor Prochet (T.),
Babi de Oliviera (pf.)   **ASC 49**

SONGS – A ESTRELA DO CELI
Luzia Marques Mathias (vce.), Murillo
Loures (vln.), Babi de Oliveira (pf.)   **ASC 11**

OLIVEIRA, Jocy de (1936-   )

ESTORIA II (FOR VOICE, TAPE
AND PERCUSSION)
* * * * * *   **NEMUC - - -**

OLIVEROS, Pauline (1932-   )

1 OF IV (1967)
* * * * * *   **ODYSS 32 16 0160**

BYE BYE BUTTERFLY, FOR OSCILLATORS,
AMPLIFIERS AND ASSORTED TAPE (1965)
Pauline Oliveros   **ARCH S 1765**

GENTLE, THE (1985)
Pauline Oliveros (vce.) with Ensemble   **HATAR 2020**

GENTLE, THE (1985)
Pauline Oliveros (acc.)   **EIGEL ES 2025/6**

HORSE SINGS FROM CLOUD (1977)
Pauline Oliveros (vce. and acc.)   **LOVE VR 1901**

HORSE SINGS FROM CLOUD (HARMONIUM,
ACCORDION, CONCERTINA AND
BANDONEON) (1975)
Gold (har.), Haines (acc.), Montano
(concertina), Pauline Oliveros (bandoneon)   **LOVE VR 1902**

JAR PIECE (1968)
* * * * * *   **MARAT MS 2111**

LOVE SONG, A
Pauline Oliveros (vce.)   **EIGEL ES 2025/6**

LULLABY FOR DAISY PAULINE (1985)
Queens College Choral Society   **FINNA 90266 1**

OUTLINE, FOR FLUTE, PERCUSSION
AND STRING BASS (14'19)
N. Turetzky (fl.), R. Georgo (perc.),
B. Turetzky (d-b.)   **NONSU H 71237**

PREPONDERANCE OF THE GREAT
Pauline Oliveros (vce.) with the Ensemble
for Contemporary Music   **HATAR 2020**

RATTLESNAKE MOUNTAIN (1982)
Pauline Oliveros (acc.)   **LOVE VR 1901**

RECEPTIVE, THE
Guy Klucevsek (acc.)   **ZOAR ZCS 8**

RECEPTIVE, THE (1985)
Guy Klucevsek (acc.)   **HATAR 2020**

SOUND PATTERNS FOR CHORUS AND
SYNTHESIZER (1969) (4'00)
New Music Choral Ensemble
(cond.) Kenneth Gaburo   **ARSNO AN 1005**

SOUND PATTERNS, FOR CHORUS AND
SYNTHESIZER (1967) (4'00)
Brandeis University Chamber Choir
(cond.) Alvin Lucier   **ODYSS 32 16 0156**

THREE MEDITATIONS: THE WELL;
PREPONDERANCE OF THE
GREAT; THE GENTLE (1985)
* * * * * *   **HATAR 2020**

TRIO FOR FLUTE, PIANO AND
PAGE TURNER (1973)
* * * * * *   **ADVAN FGR 9 S**

WANDERER, THE, FOR SOLO ACCORDION
AND ACCORDION ORCHESTRA (1984)
Pauline Oliveros (acdn.) with Springfield
Accordion Orchestra
(cond.) Falcetti   **LOVE VR 1902**

WELL, THE
Pauline Oliveros with Ensemble for
Contemporary Music   **HATAR 2020**

ORAM, Daphne Blake (1925-   )

ELECTRONIC SOUND PATTERNS
Daphne Oram   **HMV 7 EG 8762**

ELECTRONIC SOUND PATTERNS
Daphne Oram   **HMV CLP 3762**

OSAWA, Kazuko (1926-   )

WORDS FROM ROSE
All Japan Chorus   **COLUM GZ 7043**

OWEN, Blythe (1898-   )

HOW LOVELY ARE THY DWELLINGS
(NINE PIECES FOR DUO-PIANO)
* * * * * *   CHAPL S 4028

OWEN, Morfydd Llwyn (1891-1918)

TWO MADONNA SONGS
Janet Price (S.), Anthony Saunders (pf.)   ARGO ZRG 769

PACK, Beulah Frances (1896-1971)

SING ROBIN SING AND OTHER SONGS
* * * * * *   CUSTO CF 1457

PAIN, Eva (-   )

DUNMOW FLITCH
* * * * * *   ERATO LDEV 492

PAKHMUTOVA, Alexandra Nikolayevna (1929-   )

CONCERTO IN E-FLAT MINOR, FOR TRUMPET
AND ORCHESTRA (13'45)
Sergei Popov (trp.) with State
Radio Orchestra
(cond.) Y. Svetlanov   MONIT MC 2030

CONCERTO IN E-FLAT MINOR, FOR TRUMPET
AND ORCHESTRA
T. Dokshitser (trp.) with Bolshoi Theatre   MELOD
Orchestra   C 10 11990

DO YOU KNOW THE KIND OF LAD HE WAS?   MELOD
A. Zykina   C 60 08037 8

GOODBYE MOSCOW
L. Leshchenko, T. Antsiferova with
Orchestra of the U.S.S.R.
Cinematography Committee   MELOD
(cond.) O. Dimitriadi   33 C 60 14423/4

LENIN IN OUR HEARTS (CANTATA)
FOR CHILDREN'S CHORUS AND
NARRATORS
Children's Chorus with Orchestra
(cond.) A. Birchansky   MELOD M 50 39443/4

MOSCOW GIVES THE START
L. Leshchenko, V. Tolkunova with U.S.S.R.
Symphony Orchestra   MELOD
(cond.) Y. Svetlanov   33 C 60 14423/4

ODE ON THE LIGHTING OF THE
OLYMPIC FLAME
Moscow Chamber Chorus with U.S.S.R.
Academic Symphony Orchestra   MELOD
(cond.) Y. Svetlanov   33 C 60 14423/4

RUSSIAN FESTIVAL OVERTURE
Moscow Youth Orchestra
(cond.) C.N. Kalinin   MELOD C 20 06429/30

RUSSIAN SUITE
Radio Orchestra
(cond.) Belousov   MELOD D 3188/9

STREET OF PEACE, A
Children's Chorus   MELOD C 50 07877/8

WHO'LL ANSWER
Pyalnitzky Folk Chorus   MELOD C 20 07241/2

YOUTH OVERTURE
U.S.S.R. State Radio Orchestra
(cond.) Belousov   MONIT 2038

PALMER, Jane Hetherington (1952-   )

PRAISE OUR LORD (EIGHT JUNIOR HYMNS)
* * * * * *   JOSEP CLM 226

PARADIS, Maria Theresia von (1759-1824)

SICILIANA
J. Thibaud (vln.)   MELOD D 23271/2

SICILIANA (ARR. G. ZABOROV)
Violin Ensemble of the Bolshoi
Theatre Orchestra   MELOD SMO 3281/2

SICILIANA (ARR. VIOLIN)
G. Baranova (vln.)   MELOD D 1185/6

SICILIANA (ARR. VIOLONCELLO)
S. Koussevitsky (vlc.)   MELOD D 028137/8

SICILIANA (ARR. VIOLONCELLO)
D. Shafran (vlc.)   MELOD D 9157/8

SICILIENNE
S. Accardo (vln.)   EMI EL 270 186/1

SICILIENNE
Jacqueline du Pre (vlc.)   ANGEL S 37900

SICILIENNE
Bemant (vln.)   DESTO DC 7191

SICILIENNE
* * * * * *   HARMU MHY 386

SICILIENNE
Perlman (vln.), Sanders (pf)   ANGEL SZ 37560

SICILIENNE
Bobesco (vln.), Bemant (pf.)   MIXTR MXT 153 009

SICILIENNE
Thibaud (vln.)   TRIAN C 045 00887

SICILIENNE
Solisti di Zagreb   VANGR VSL 11065

SICILIENNE
Nora Grumlikova (vln.)   SUPRA 50708

SICILIENNE
Evalyn Steinbock (vlc.), Michael May (pf.) GEMIN RAP 1010

SICILIENNE
Bobesco (vln.), Guttman (pf.)   MIXTR MXT 20

SICILIENNE
Pasquier (vln.), Heisser (pf.)   FONO FSM 53 3 28

SICILIENNE
Perlman (vln.), Sanders (pf.)   EMI ASD 3810

SICILIENNE
Chapman, J. Pawlyk with City of London
Junior Chamber Orchestra
(cond.) C. Henderson   * * * MS 1000

SICILIENNE
Ginette Niveu (vln.)   * * * RLS 739

SICILIENNE
Jacqueline du Pre (vlc.), G. Moore (pf.) HMV HQS 1437

SICILIENNE
Elmar Oliveira (vln.), McDonald (pf.) VOX D VCL 9057

SICILIENNE (1'56)
Rosario Marciano (pf.)   TURNA TV 34685

TOCCATA IN A, FOR PIANO
* * * * * *   EMBER GVC 28

PARASKEVAIDIS, Graciela (1940-   )

E DESIDERO SOLO COLORI, FOR CHORUS
Rio de Janeiro Contemporary
Arts Ensemble   TACU TE 11

PARKER, Alice (1925-   )

ECHOES FROM THE HILLS (SIX POEMS BY
EMILY DICKINSON)
Shelton (S.) with Manhattan Quartet   **MUHER**
and others   **MHS 827161**

GAUDETE (SIX LATIN CHRISTMAS HYMNS)   **TURNA**
* * * * * *   **QTV 34647/8**

SONGS FOR EVE (TWENTY-EIGHT
SHORT STORIES BY ARCHIBALD MCLEISH)   **MUHER**
Shelton (S.) with Manhattan Quartet and others **MHS 827161**

PATERSON, Wilma (1944-   )

CASIDA DEL LLANTO
Peter Mountain (vln.), A. Dale (pf.)   **SCOTS SSC 001**

PATTI, Adelina (1843-1919)

BACIO D'ADDIO, IL (BYRON) (3'40)
Patricia Adkins Chiti (m-S.),   **EDMUS**
Gian Paolo Chiti (pf.)   **PAN NRC 5016**

PAYNE, Maggi (1945-   )

CRYSTAL
* * * * * *   **LOVE VR 2061**

LUNAR DUSK
* * * * * *   **LOVE VR 101 06**

LUNAR EARTHRISE
* * * * * *   **LOVE VR 101 06**

SCIROCCO
* * * * * *   **LOVE VR 2061**

SOLAR WIND
* * * * * *   **LOVE VR 2061**

WHITE NIGHT
* * * * * *   **LOVE VR 2061**

PEJACEVIC, Dora, Countess (1885-1923)

CAPRICCIO, OP. 47
Ksenija Kos (pf.)   **JUGOT LSY 66154**

CAPRICIOUS MOOD, OP. 54B
Ksenija Kos (pf.)   **JUGOT LSY 66154**

HUMORESQUE, OP. 54A
Ksenija Kos (pf.)   **JUGOT LSY 66154**

IMPROMPTU, OP. 32B
Ksenija Kos (pf.)   **JUGOT LSY 66154**

NIGHTFALL, OP. 32A
Ksenija Kos (pf.)   **JUGOT LSY 66154**

NOCTURNE, OP. 50, NO. 1
Ksenija Kos (pf.)   **JUGOT LSY 66154**

NOCTURNE, OP. 50, NO. 2
Ksenija Kos (pf.)   **JUGOT LSY 66154**

PIANO QUINTET IN B-MINOR
Ranko Filjak (pf.) with Klima Quartet   **JUGOT LSY 66154**

PELEGRI, Maria Teresa (1907-   )

TRES PECES PER A PIANO
Antoni Besses (pf.)   **ENSAY ENY A 1001**

PENTLAND, Barbara Lally (1912-   )

CONCERTO FOR PIANO AND
STRING ORCHESTRA
Mario Bernardi (pf.) with Radio-Canada
Symphony Orchestra
(cond.) V. Feldbrill   **CBC RCI 184**

DUO FOR VIOLA AND PIANO
* * * * * *   **CBC RCI 223**

DUO FOR VIOLA AND PIANO   **RCA**
Harry Adaskin (vla.), Frances Marr (pf.) **CC CC 5 1017**

ECHOES ONE AND TWO
* * * * * *   **CCM 2**

EPHEMERA
Robert G. Rogers (pf.)   **CENTR CMC 1985**

FANTASY
Leonard Stein (pf.)   **CBC RCI 242**

HANDS ACROSS THE C
* * * * * *   **CCM 2**

INTERPLAY FOR FREE BASS ACCORDION
AND STRING QUARTET   **MELBO**
Macarello (acc.) with Purcell String Quartet **SMLP 4034**

PIANO WORKS   **MELBO**
Antonin Kubalek (pf.)   **SMLP 4031**

SHADOWS – OMBRES
* * * * * *   **CBC RCI 242**

SONG CYCLE FOR SOPRANO AND PIANO
Frances James (S.), Barbara Pentland (pf.) **CBC RCI 20**

SONGS
Mary Morrison (S.), Joseph Macarello (acc.) **MELBO**
with Purcell String Quartet   **SMLP 4034**

SPACE STUDIES
* * * * * *   **CCM 2**

STRING QUARTET, NO. 1
* * * * * *   **CBC RCI 141**

STRING QUARTET, NO. 1
Canadian String Quartet   **COLUM MS 6364**

STRING QUARTET, NO. 1
Canadian String Quartet   **COLUM ML 5764**

STRING QUARTET, NO. 3
Purcell String Quartet   **CBC RCI 353**

STRING QUARTET, NO. 4
Purcell String Quartet   **CMC 0782**

STRING QUARTET, NO. 4 (15'12)
Purcell String Quartet   **CENTR WRC 1 2429**

STUDIES IN LINE
* * * * * *   **CCM 2**

STUDIES IN LINE
* * * * * *   **CBC RCI 134**

STUDIES IN LINE
* * * * * *   **CBC RCI 496**

SUITE BOREALIS
Antonin Kubalek (pf.)   **MELBO SMLP 4031**

SUITE BOREALIS
Robert G. Rogers (pf.)   **CENTR CMC 1985**

SUITE BOREALIS (1966)
Robert G. Rogers (pf.)   **CENTR CMC 1985**

SYMPHONY FOR TEN PARTS
* * * * * *   **CBC RCI 215**

SYMPHONY FOR TEN PARTS
* * * * * *   **RCA CC CCS 1009**

THREE DUETS, AFTER PICTURES
BY PAUL KLEE
Barbara Pentland (pf.), Robert Rogers (pf.) **CBC RCI 242**

THREE PAIRS, FOR PIANO
* * * * * * **CCM 2**

TOCCATA
* * * * * * **CBC RCI 242**

TOCCATA
Buczynski (pf.) **CBC BR 162**

TRIO FOR VIOLIN, CELLO AND PIANO
Halifax Trio **CBC RCI 242**

TWO SUNG SONGS
Phyllis Mailing (m-S.) **CENTR CMC 1083**

VINCULA (1983)
Robert G. Rogers (pf.) **CENTR CMC 1985**

VITA BREVIS
Robert G. Rogers (pf.) **CENTR CMC 1985**

PEREIRA, Diana Maria (1932-   )

SONATA NO. 2, OP. 3, FOR PIANO
Elisabeth Klein (pf.) **DANIC DLP 8017**

SONATA NO. 3, FOR PIANO
Elisabeth Klein (pf.) **DANIC DLP 8017**

PERISSAS, Madeleine (1906-   )

CAROL OF THE VILLAGE
Andre Marchal (org.), Ghislaine
Lardennois (org.) with
Reims Cathedral Choir
(cond.) A. Muzerelle **MUHER MHS 818**

PERKIN, Helen (1909-   )

BURLESQUE
Newsome, Howard with Sun Life
Stanshaw Band **CHAND BBR 1005**

PERRY, Julia (1924-1979)

HOMUNCULUS, C.F. FOR
TEN PERCUSSIONISTS
Manhattan Percussion Ensemble
(cond.) P. Price **CRI SD 252**

SHORT PIECE FOR ORCHESTRA, A
Tokyo Imperial Philharmonic Orchestra
(cond.) William Strickland **CRI SD 145**

STABAT MATER
Makiko Asakura (m-S.) with Japan
Philharmonic Orchestra
(cond.) W. Strickland **CRI SD 133**

PETRA-BASACOPOL, Carmen (1926-   )

CONCERTINO FOR HARP, STRING ORCHESTRA
AND TIMPANI, OP. 40 (13'32)
Elena Gantolea (hp.) with Rumanian
Radio Symphony Orchestra **ELECT**
(cond.) Josif Conta **ST ECE 01862**

CONCERTINO FOR VIOLIN AND ORCHESTRA
George Hamza (vln.) with
Rumanian Radio Symphony Orchestra
(cond.) Ludovic Baci **ELECT ECE 0404**

CONCERTO NO. 2, OP. 25
(VIOLIN AND ORCHESTRA) **ELECT**
* * * * * * **ECE 0607**

MIORITZA, CHOREOGRAPHIC POEM (1980)
Rumanian RTV Symphony Orchestra **ELECT**
(cond.) Iosif Conta **ST ECE 02329**

SONATA PENTRU FLAUT SI
HARPA, OP. 16, NO. 2 **ELECT**
Voicu Vasinca (fl.), Liana Pasquali (hp.) **ST ECE 01545**

SUITE FOR HARP, OP. 10
* * * * * * **ELECT ST ECE 01927**

PETROVA-KRUPKOVA, Elena (1929-   )

INVOCATION
Harak (b-cl.), Kovarnova (pf.) **PANTN 11 064**

SUNFLOWER BALLET SUITE
Prague National Theatre Orchestra
(cond.) J. Chaloupka **PANTN 8110 0001/2**

VZYVANI (CYCLE) FOR MEN'S
CHAMBER CHOIR
Men's Chamber Choir Concentus
(cond.) Hanus Krupka **SUPRA 119 2406 G**

PEYROT, Fernande (1888-1978)

DEUX CHANSONS
Fernande Peyrot **AMADO AVRS 6062**

DIMANCHE DES RAMEAUX
Frances James (S.) **AMADO AVRS 6062**

PETITE SUITE POUR GUITARE (1954)
(5'00) Herman Leeb (gtr.) **SWISS CT 64 24**

PHILIPPART, Renee (1905-   )

BUCHE DE NOEL, LA
Christiane Chantal (vce.) with Jacques
Lacome Orchestra **DURAN 275**

NOEL CANADIEN
Christiane Chantal (vce.) with Jacques
Lacome Orchestra **DURAN 276**

NOEL DES NEIGES
Christiane Chantal (vce.) with Jacques
Lacome Orchestra **DURAN 276**

NOEL DU ZOO
Christiane Chantal (vce.) with Jacques
Lacome Orchestra **DURAN 275**

PHILIPPINA, Charlotte (Duchess of Brunswick) (-   )

MARCH, FOR WIND ORCHESTRA
* * * * * * **TELEF SLT 43104**

PHILLIPS, Linda (-   )

ASH TREES (2'12)
Muriel Luyk (m-Cont.) **WANDG WG B S 5537**

BRACKEN BROWN (2'49)
Muriel Luyk (m-Cont.) **WANDG WG B S 5537**

BUSH EVENING (VIOLIN SOLO) (5'31)
Leonard Dommett (vln.) **WANDG WG B S 5537**

CRADLE SONG (3'02)
Muriel Luyk (m-Cont.) **WANDG WG B S 5537**

DAYDREAMS (TRIO FOR VOICE, VIOLIN
AND PIANO) (2'36)
Muriel Luyk (m-Cont.), Leonard
Dommett (vln.), Linda Phillips (pf.) **WANDG WG B S 5537**

EVENING CANTICLE – TRIO FOR VOICE
CLARINET AND PIANO (4'25)
Muriel Luyk (m-Cont.), Eugene
Danilov (cl.), Linda Phillips (pf.)   **WANDG WG B S 5537**

IRIS MARSHES (3'02)
Muriel Luyk (m-Cont.)   **WANDG WG B S 5537**

SERENADE (VIOLIN SOLO) (3'11)
Leonard Dommett (vln.)   **WANDG WG B S 5537**

SHADOW DANCE (VIOLIN SOLO) (5'30)
Leonard Dommett (vln.)   **WANDG WG B S 5537**

TWO MOODS FOR CLARINET
(GRAVE: GIOCOSO) (7'16)
Eugene Danilov (cl.)   **WANDG WG B S 5537**

WHEN THE TWILIGHT TURNS
TO AMETHYST (2'09)
Muriel Luyk (m-Cont.)   **WANDG WG B S 5537**

PIERCE, Alexandra (1934-   )

JOB 22:28 (CLARINET DUO)
* * * * * *   **ZANJA ZR 2**

VARIATIONS 7 (7'27)
Alexandra Pierce (pf.)   **CAPIO CR 2**

PILIS, Heda (1925-   )

I'LL MARRY YOU
* * * * * *   **JUGOT LPY S 61135**

MARY
* * * * * *   **JUGOT LPY V S 60902**

MERRY VOCALS
* * * * * *   **JUGOT EPY 4369**

MY GRANNY
* * * * * *   **JUGOT LPY V S 60979**

OUR PUSSY-CAT
* * * * * *   **JUGOT EPY 4369**

PIRES DE CAMPOS, Lina (1918-   )

PONTEIO E TOCATINA
Sergio Assad (vla.)   **PROME MMB 81 002**

PLUMSTEAD, Mary (1905-1980)

CLOSE THINE EYES (QUARLES)
Janet Baker (S.), P. Ledger (pf.)   **HMV ASD 3981**

GRATEFUL HEART (HERBERT)
Janet Baker (S.), P. Ledger (pf.)   **HMV ASD 3981**

SIGH NO MORE LADIES (SHAKESPEARE)
Graham Trew (Bar.), R. Vignoles (pf.)   **HYPER A 66026**

TAKE, O TAKE THOSE LIPS AWAY
(SHAKESPEARE)
Graham Trew (Bar.), R. Vignoles (pf.)   **HYPER A 66026**

POLIN, Claire (1926-   )

CADER IDRIS (1970)
Apple Brass Quintet   **OPONE 61**

KUEQUENAKU-CAMBRIOLA
* * * * * *   **OPONE - - -**

MARGOA, FOR SOLO FLUTE
Loren N. Lind (fl.)   **ORION ORS 79330**

O, ADERYN PUR (1972)
M. Taylor (a-sax.), Claire Polin (fl.)
with Bird Tape   **OPONE 62**

SUMMER SETTINGS, SUITE (1965)
Claire Polin (fl.), Phyllis Schlomovitz (hp.)   **EDUCO 4031**

SUMMER SETTINGS, SUITE (1965)
Claire Polin (fl.), Phyllis Schlomovitz (hp.)   **ARSNO AN 1004**

SYNAULIA II
John Russo (cl. and b-cl.),
Loren N. Lind (fl. and a-fl.),
Lydia Walton Ignacio (pf.)   **ORION ORS 79330**

POSTON, Elizabeth (1905-   )

JESUS CHRIST THE APPLE TREE
Kensington Gore Singers   **WEALD WS 156**

JESUS CHRIST THE APPLE TREE
David Slater (org.) with Felstead Junior
School Choir   **ABBEY PHB 755**

JESUS CHRIST THE APPLE TREE
King's College Choir, Cambridge
(cond.) David Willcocks   **EMI SEOM 5**

JESUS CHRIST THE APPLE TREE
King's College Choir, Cambridge
(cond.) David Willcocks   **HMV ASD 2290**

JESUS CHRIST THE APPLE TREE
Choir of the Liverpool Metropolitan
Cathedral of Christ the King
(cond.) Phillip Duffy   **ABBEY LPB 816**

JESUS CHRIST THE APPLE TREE
St. George's Chapel Choir   **ABBEY MVP 827**

JESUS CHRIST THE APPLE TREE
Westminster Abbey Choir   **DGG
DG 410590 1 GH**

TRIO FOR VIOLA, FLUTE AND HARP (12'29)
Nederburg Harp Trio: Walter Mony (vla.),
Lucien Grujon (fl.), Kathleen Alister (hp.)   **RPMR
RPM 1093**

PRAVOSSUDOVITCH, Natalija Michajlovna (1899-   )

OEVRES POUR PIANO (1979)
Georges Bernand (pf.)   **BVM ST 2281**

OEVRES POUR PIANO (1979)
Georges Bernand (pf.)   **BVM ST 2267**

PREOBRAJENSKA, Vera Nicolaevna (1926-   )

FOUND (AMERICAN FOLK SONG)
Darrell Walker (vce.)   **INTRA ISR 19**

THINGS THAT MAKE ME CARE, THE
Jimmy Edwards (vce.) with Western
All Star Orchestra   **INTRA ISR 26**

PRESTI, Ida (1924-1967)

DANSE D'AVILA (3'48)
Ito (gtr.), Dorigny (gtr.)   **DELOS FY 008**

ETUDE DU MATIN
Mc. Cutcheon (gtr.)   **ADES 14 047**

ETUDE FANTASQUE
* * * * * *   **PHILI 6730 009**

ETUDE FANTASQUE
  Ida Presti (gtr.), Alexander Lagoya (gtr.)   **PHILI 6747 353**

ETUDE FANTASQUE
  Ida Presti (gtr.), Alexander Lagoya (gtr.)   **PHILI 6504 049**

ETUDE NO. 2
  McCutcheon (gtr.)   **ADES 14 047**

PRICE, Florence Beatrice (1888-1953)

WERE YOU THERE?
  Salli Terri (S.) with Roger Wagner Chorale
  (cond.) Roger Wagner   **CAPIT P 8365**

PRIESING, Dorothy Jean (1910-   )

NOW IS THE CAROLLING SEASON
  * * * * * *   **CAPIT T 896**

PROCACCINI, Teresa (1934-   )

ANDANTE E RONDO, OP. 50
  Trio d'archi di Roma   **PAN PRC S 20 11**

BAMBINO DI PLASTICA, IL, OP. 81   **EDMUS**
  * * * * * *   **EDI PAN MB 703**

CAVALLINO AVVENTUROSO, UN, OP. 22   **EDMUS**
  * * * * * *   **EDI PAN MB 703**

DIALOGO PER VIOLA E PIANOFORTE,
  OP. 34 (6'05)
  Paolo Centurioni (vla.), Teresa
  Procaccini (pf.)   **PAN PRC S 20 10**

DUO PER VIOLINI E VIOLA (4'17)
  Antonio Salvatore (vln.), Paolo
  Centurioni (vla.)   **PAN PRC S 20 10**

FANTASIA, OP. 10 (9'45)
  Antonio Salvatore (vln.), Teresa
  Procaccini (pf.)   **PAN PRC S 20 10**

IMPROVVISAZONI FOR STRING TRIO,
  OP. 37 (9'28)
  Antonio Salvatore (vln.), Paolo
  Centurioni (vla.) Mario Centurioni (vlc.)   **PAN PRC S 20 10**

INTRODUZIONE E ALLEGRO, OP. 39
  Trio d'Archi di Roma   **PAN PRC S 20 11**

MARIONETTE FOR PIANOFORTE, TEN
  INSTRUMENTS AND MIME   **EDMUS**
  Dauni Soloists   **EDI PAN MB 701**

NOVE PRELUDI, OP. 29
  Teresa Procaccini (pf.) with Trio
  d'Archi di Roma   **PAN PRC S 20 11**

PESTE DI ATENE, LA: CANTATA FOR CORO
  ET ORCHESTRA
  Banatul din Timisoara Symphony Orchestra   **ELECT**
  (cond.) Remus Georgescu   **STCS 0194**

PIAZZA DELLA MUSICA NO. 1 (FOR TWENTY
  INSTRUMENTS AND RECITATIVE)
  R. Antini (reciter) with Ensemble   **EDMUS**
  (cond.) D. Losavio   **EDI PAN MB 701**

PICCOLI PEZZI PER PIANOFORTE, OP. 91   **EDMUS**
  * * * * * *   **EDI PAN MB 703**

QUARTETTO PER ARCHI, OP. 42
  Teresa Procaccini (pf.) with Trio
  D'Archi di Roma   **PAN PRC S 20 11**

SENSAZIONE SONORE – 4 PEZZI PAR
  ORCHESTRA, OP. 41 (1969)
  Banatul din Timisoara Symphony Orchestra   **ELECT**
  (cond.) Remus Georgescu   **STCS 0194**

SONATINA NO. 2, OP. 43
  Trio d'Archi di Roma   **PAN PRC S 20 11**

SONATINA PER VIOLONCELLO. OP. 28 (6'94)
  Mario Centurioni (vlc.)   **PAN PRC S 20 10**

PTASZYNSKA, Marta (1943-   )

DREAM LANDS, MAGIC SPACES
  * * * * * *   **ARCH 1983**

GRAND SOMMEIL NOIR, UN
  * * * * * *   **POLSK SZ 18479**

MOBILE
  * * * * * *   **ARCH 1979**

RAINIER, Priaulx (1903-1986)

CYCLE FOR DECLAMATION
  P. Pears (T.), B. Britten (pf.)   **ARGO ZK 28 9**

QUANTA
  London Oboe Quartet   **ARGO ZRG 660**

STRING QUARTET (1939) (17'57)
  Alard Quartet   **LEONA LPI 117**

STRING TRIO
  Members of London Oboe Quartet   **ARGO ZRG 660**

RAN, Shulamit (1949-   )

APPREHENSIONS
  Judith Nicosia (S.), Laura Flax (cl.),
  Alan Feinberg (pf.)   **CRI SD 509**

HATZVI ISRAEL EULOGY, FOR VOICE AND
  ENSEMBLE
  Reid-Parsons (m-S.) with Dal Segno
  Ensemble   **CRITI CC 1703**

O, THE CHIMNEYS (18'18)
  Gloria Davy (S.), Shulamit Ran (pf.) with
  Philomusica Chamber Ensemble   **TURNA**
  (cond.) A. Robert Johnson   **TV S 34492**

PRIVATE GAME (3'58)
  Laura Flax (cl.), Andre Emelianoff (vlc.)   **CRI SD 441**

REBULL, Teresa (-   )

CHANTS CATALANS (J. SALVAT PAPPASEIT)
  Teresa Rebull (vce.) with Instrumental   **SPALA**
  Ensemble   **SPX 6807**

REICHARDT, Louise (1779-1826)

NINE SONGS
  Grayson Hirst (T.), Michel Yuspeh (pf.)   **LEONA LPI 112**

REISER, Violet (1905-   )

IN GAY MADRID
  Eliot Lawrence Septet   **SESAC 1107/8**

MORNING IN MANHATTEN
  Eddie Safranski's Rhythm and Romance
  Orchestra   **SESAC 909/10**

PLANTATION PICNIC
  Savoy Orchestra   **SESAC N 4801/2**

SMITTEN KITTENS
  Buddy Weeds Quartet   **SESAC PA 209/10**

RENIE, Henriette (1875-1956)

CONCERTO
Wurtzler (hp.) with New York Harp
Ensemble   **MUHER MHS 3611**

CONTEMPLATION
Susann McDonald (hp.)   **KLAVI KS 543**

DANSE DES LUTINS
Chantal Mathieu (hp.)   **ARIOL AR 202 181 366**

DANSE DES LUTINS
N. Shameyeva (hp.)   **MELOD C 10 07879/80**

DANSE DES LUTINS (3'10)
Susan McDonald (hp.)   **KLAVI KS 525**

LEGENDE
Susan McDonald (hp.)   **KLAVI KS 543**

PIECE SYMPHONIQUE
Susan McDonald (hp.)   **KLAVI KS 543**

ROSSIGNOL, LE
Chantal Mathieu (hp.)   **ARIOL AR 202 181 366**

RESPIGHI, Elsa (1894-   )

MAMMA POVERA, LA (COMPOSER)
Alba Anzellotti (S.), Giorgio Favaretto (pf.)   **ADRIA E 5**

RHENE-JAQUE (1918-   )

DEUXIEME SUITE POUR PIANO
Antonin Kubalek (pf.)   **MELBO SMLP 4031**

RIBONI, Liliane (-   )

JEANNE D'ARC
Liliane Riboni with Company   **BOURG BG 6002 3**

RICHTER, Marga (1926-   )

ARIA AND TOCCATA FOR VIOLA AND STRINGS
Walter Trampler (vla.) with MGM Chamber
Orchestra
(cond.) Carlos Surinach   **MGM 3559**

CONCERTO FOR PIANO AND VIOLAS,
CELLOS AND BASSES (1955)
William Masselos (pf.) with MGM String
Orchestra
(cond.) Carlos Surinach   **MGM E 3547**

FISHING PICTURE
Dorothy Renzi (S.), Maro Ajemian (pf.)   **MGM E 3546**

HERMIT, THE
Dorothy Renzi (S.), Maro Ajemian (pf.)   **MGM E 3546**

LAMENT, FOR STRING ORCHESTRA
MGM String Orchestra
(cond.) Izler Solomon   **MGM E 3422**

LANDSCAPES OF THE MIND II (17'15)
Daniel Heifetz (vln.), Michael Skelly (pf.)   **LEONA LPI 122**

SONATA, FOR PIANO
Peter Basquin (pf.) with Long Island
Chamber Ensemble, New York   **GRENA GS 1010**

SONATA, FOR PIANO
Menachem Pressler (pf.)   **MGM E 3244**

SONGS
Dorothy Renzi (S.), Maro Ajemian (pf.)   **MGM E 3546**

SONORA: FOR TWO CLARINETS AND TWO
PIANOS (10'19)
Drucker Trio (2 cl. and pf.)   **LEONA LPI 122**

TRANSMUTATION, EIGHT SONGS
TO CHINESE TEXTS
Dorothy Renzi (S.), Maro Ajemian (pf.)   **MGM E 3546**

TWO SHORT SUITES FOR YOUNG PIANISTS
Marga Richter (pf.)   **MGM E 3147**

ROBERT, Lucie (1936-   )

CADENZA (10'23)
Jean-Marie Londeix (a-sax.), Anne-Marie
Schielin (pf.)   **GOLDE RE 7066**

SONATA, FOR ALTO SAXOPHONE AND PIANO
Trent Kynaston (sax.), T. Turner-Jones (pf.)   **CORON 3044**

SUPPLICATIONS
Trio Evolution: Serge Bichon (a-sax.),
Christian Ognibene (ob.), Patrick
Gabard (vlc.)   **REM 10 875 X**

TOURBILLONS STROPHES
Jean-Marie Londeix (sax.),
Lucie Robert (pf.)   **GOLDE RE 7098**

VARIATIONS
Iwan Roth (sax.), Gerard Wyss (pf.)   **BASIL ST 7801**

ROBERTS, Gertrud Hermine Kuenzel (1906-   )

WORKS FOR PIANO AND HARPSICHORD
* * * * * *   **HOOKA 781219**

ROBERTS, Megan L. (1952-   )

I COULD SIT HERE ALL DAY (6'22)
Phil Loarie (vce.), William Novak (vce.),
Danny Sofer (dr.), Megan Roberts
(Moog syn.)   **ARCH S 1765**

ROBLES, Marisa (1937-   )

HORSE AND HIS BOY, THE (C.S. LEWIS)
M. Hordern (narr.), Marisa Robles (hp.)
C. Hyde Smith (fl.)   **ASV SWD 353**

LAST BATTLE, THE (C.S. LEWIS)
M. Hordern (narr.), Marisa Robles (hp.),
C. Hyde Smith (fl.)   **ASV SWD 357**

LION, THE WITCH AND THE WARDROBE, THE
(C.S. LEWIS)
M. Hordern (narr.), Marisa Robles (hp.),
C. Hyde Smith (fl.)   **ASV SWD 352**

MAGICIAN'S NEPHEW, THE (C.S. LEWIS)
M. Hordern (narr.), Marisa Robles (hp.),
C. Hyde Smith (fl.)   **ASV SWD 351**

NARNIA SUITE, THE
Marisa Robles (hp.), Rachel Masters (hp.),
Gillian Tingay (hp.), Ruth Faber (hp.)
C. Hyde Smith (fl. and picc.)   **ASV DCA 513**

PRINCE CASPIAN (C.S. LEWIS)
M. Hordern (narr.), Marisa
Robles (hp.), C. Hyde Smith (f.)   **ASV SWD 354**

SILVER CHAIR, THE (C.S. LEWIS)
M. Hordern (narr.), M. Robles (hp.),
C. Hyde Smith (fl.)   **ASV SWD 356**

VOYAGE OF THE DAWN TREADER, THE
M. Hordern (narr.), Marisa Robles (hp.),
C. Hyde Smith (fl.)   **ASV SWD 355**

1124

ROCHEROLLE, Eugenie Katherine (1936-   )

BABY BOY
King's Heralds — **CHAPL S 5242**

RODRIGUE, Nicole (1943-   )

FISSION, FOR TWO PERCUSSIONS
* * * * * * — **CAPAC QC 1274**

LAUDES (REQUIEM) FOR CHORUS AND
CHAMBER ORCHESTRA
* * * * * * — **CAPAC QC 1274**

MODULES, FOR HARP, DOUBLE-BASS
AND SEVEN TAMTAMS
* * * * * * — **CAPAC QC 1274**

NASCA, FOR CLARINET, ALTO, PIANO
AND VIBRAPHONE
* * * * * * — **CAPAC QC 1274**

SOUFRIERE, FOR TWO FLUTES AND
TWO PICCOLOS
* * * * * * — **CAPAC QC 1274**

TOI, FOR HARP
* * * * * * — **CAPAC QC 1274**

TWO ATMOSPHERES
* * * * * * — **CAPAC QC 1274**

ROE, Eileen Betty (1930-   )

A.D. ONE, MASQUE FOR CHRISTMAS
Three's Company Plus — **PEARL SHE 542**

PREFABULOUS ANIMILES
Robert Stanton (narr.), Betty Roe (pf.)
with Colet Court Boys' Choir
(cond.) Ian T. Hunter — **PEARL SHE 542**

THREE ECCENTRICS
Betty Roe (pf.) with Colet Court Boys' Choir
(cond.) Ian T. Hunter — **PEARL SHE 542**

ROESGEN-CHAMPION, Marguerite Sara (1894-1976)

COMPLAINTE AND RONDEAU, FOR FLUTE
AND HARP (SUITE FRANCAISE)
* * * * * * — **PHILI N 00695 R**

ROGER, Denise (1924-   )

THREE MOVEMENTS FOR CLARINET QUARTET
Quatuor de Clarinettes de Geneve — **GALLO 30 391**

ROGET, Henriette (1910-   )

CORTEGE FUNEBRE
Robert Owen (org.) — **WESTM XWN 18363**

RUEFF, Jeanine (1922-   )

SONATE (3'42)
Daniel Deffayet (a-sax.) — **GOLDE RE 7051**

RUSSELL, Anna (1911-   )

ANNA RUSSEL SINGS?
Anna Russell (S.), Harry Dvorkin (pf.) — **PHILI B 07031 L**

ANNA RUSSELL IN DARKEST AFRICA
Anna Russell (S.) — **CBS BLD 7084**

ANNA RUSSELL SINGS AGAIN?
Anna Russell (S.), John Coveast (pf.) — **CBS BLD 7046**

DECLINE AND FALL OF THE POPULAR SONG
Anna Russell (S.) with Jenny Carrol
and Ensemble — **COLUM ML 5036**

GUIDE TO CONCERT AUDIENCES
Anna Russell (S.), Eugene Rankin (pf.) — **COLUM ML 4928**

SURVEY OF SINGING FROM MADRIGALS
TO MODERN OPERA
Anna Russell (S.), Eugene Rankin (pf.),
Arthur Hoberman (fl.) — **COLUM ML 5036**

RUTA, Gilda Countess (1853-1932)

ADDIO, MELODIA ROMANTICA (3'52)
Patricia Adkins Chiti (m-S.),
Gian Paolo Chiti (pf.) — **EDMUS PAN NRC 5016**

MESTA SERENATA (3'25)
Gian Paolo Chiti (pf.) — **EDMUS PAN NRC 5016**

POVERO AMORE (2'48)
Patricia Adkins Chiti (m-S.),
Gian Paolo Chiti (pf.) — **EDMUS PAN NRC 5016**

SAIDAMINOVA, Dilorom (1943-   )

SUITE FROM THE BALLET FIERY STONE
Uzbek SSR Symphony Orchestra
(cond.) Z. Khaknazarov — **MELOD C 10 06949/50**

SYMPHONIC POEM
Uzbek SSR Symphony Orchestra
(cond.) Z. Khaknazarov — **MELOD C 10 06949/50**

SALQUIN, Hedy (1928-   )

'NOEL' EIN WEIHNACHTSSTÜCK
Hedy Salquin (pf.) — **SORIS - - -**

NOVEMBER AM THURNERSEE
Hedy Salquin (pf.) — **SORIS - - -**

THEME AND VARIATIONS
Hedy Salquin (pf.) — **SORIS - - -**

TOCCATA IN ES
Hedy Salquin (pf.) — **SORIS - - -**

ZWEI KLAVIERSTÜCKE AUS SEVENTEEN
Hedy Salquin (pf.) — **SORIS - - -**

SAMPSON, Peggy (-   )

IMPROVISATION
Peggy Sampson — **MUSIC MGE 7**

SAMTER, Alice (1908-   )

DIALOG FOR VIOLIN AND PIANO
Marianne Boettcher (vln.), Phillip Moll (pf.) — **MIXTR 1002**

ESKAPADEN
Irma Hofmeister (pf.) — **MIXTR 1002**

EXTREMES SE TOUCENT, LES (1974) (8'09)
Schubert-Weber Trio — **MARS 308328**

KONTRAPOST (1974) (9'46)
Kassner (fl.), Chemin-Petit (rec.),
Irma Hofmeister (pf.) — **MARS 308328**

KONTRAPOST TRIO FOR FLUTE,
RECORDER AND PIANO
Kassner (fl.), Chemin-Petit (rec.),
Irma Hofmeister (pf.) **MARS 207741**

LIEDER, NOS. 1-4 (8'12)
Christa-Sylvia Gröschke (S.),
Siegfried Schubert-Weber (pf.) **MARS 308328**

MATCH FOR PIANO (4'02)
Siegfried Schubert-Weber (pf.) **MARS 308328**

MOSAIK (1978) (6'09)
Wolfgang Guttler (d-b.), Manfred Theilen (pf.) **MARS 308328**

RIVALITES (1974) (8'42)
Senn (fl.), Hartmann (cl.), Forest (vlc.),
Goebel (pf.) **MARS 308328**

SKETCH FOR THREE WOODWINDS (1970) (5'53)
Berlin Wind Trio **MARS 308328**

TANZERINNEN (3 SONGS) (1975) (7'38)
Christa-Sylvia Gröschke (S.) **MARS 308328**

SAMUEL, Rhian (1944-   )

SONGS OF EARTH AND AIR: THE KINGFISHER,
APRIL RISE (1983) (15'38) **CORON**
Sharon Mabry (S.), Rosemary Platt (pf.) **LPS 3127**

SAMUELSON, Laura Byers (-   )

SHADES: A NEW MUSICAL FOR THE
BICENTENNIAL (COMPOSER)
Octaves of Washington **MARK MC 8634**

SATOH, Kimi (1949-   )

LE BLEU DU CIEL
* * * * * * **JAPAN JFC 8009**

SCALETTI, Carla (1956-   )

MOTET FOR NARRATOR, MEZZO,
BASS CLARINET AND HARP (1977)
Irwin Hoffman (narr.), Kathy
Ives-Clawson (m-S.), Floyd Williams (b-cl),
Carla Scaletti (hp.) **OPONE 42**

SCHARLI, Ruth (1929-   )

PARTHENON FOR BASS CLARINET
AND PIANO
Josef Horak (b-cl.), Emma Kovarnova (pf.) **FONO FSM 53 1 114**

PARTHENON FOR BASS CLARINET
AND PIANO (5'50)
Josef Horak (b-cl.), Emma **CORON**
Kovarnova (pf.) **GEMA SM 30071**

SCHAUSS-FLAKE, Magdalene (1921-   )

MORGENSTERN IST AUFGEDRUNGEN, DER,
FOR FOUR TO SIX WIND INSTRUMENTS,
SOPRANO AND VOCAL CHORUS (2'24)
Stuttgarter Bläserkantorei **CARUS**
(cond.) C.B. Kohler **FSM 43 1 27**

OHREN GABST DU MIR (RUPPEL)
Motetten Chor, Jugend Kantorei
Bläserensemble und Mitglieder des
Bachorchesters Pforzheim
(cond.) R. Schweizer **LAUDA HV 91 516**

SUITE IN G, FUR BLASER (8'15)
Blech und Holzblaser Ensemble
(cond.) Wilhelm Ehmann **CANTA GEMA 658 224**

SUITE IN G, FÜR BLÄSER (8'15)
Collegium Aulos **UNISO UNS 22 497**

SCHERCHEN, Tona (1938-   )

SHEN (10'50)
Percussion de Strasbourg **PHILI 6521 030**

YI POUR MARIMBAPHONE (10'48)
Kieffer (mar.), Askill (mar.) **APOST AS 37334**

SCHIEVE, Catherine (1956-   )

MABLICK
* * * * * * **FOLKW FTS 33875**

SERPENTINE
* * * * * * **FOLKW FTS 33875**

SCHMITZ-GOHR, Else (1901-   )

KOMPOSITIONEN FUER VIOLINE
UND KLAVIER
* * * * * * **KASKA 1 BLN 30**

SCHONTHAL, Ruth E. (1924-   )

FANTASY FOR VIOLIN AND PIANO, OP. 47 (1949)
Gross (vla.), Grayson (pf.) **ORION ORS 74147**

FOUR EPIPHANIES (1976)
Paul Doktor (vla.) **ORION ORS 83444**

FRAGMENTS FROM A WOMAN'S DIARY (1982)
Gary Steigerwalt (pf.) **ORION ORS 85490**

IN HOMAGE OF ....
Gary Steigerwalt (pf.) **ORION ORS 85490**

LOVE LETTERS, FOR CLARINET
AND CELLO (11'25)
Esther Lamnech (cl.), Michale Rudlakov (vlc.) **CAPIO CR 1001**

MUSIC FOR HORN AND
CHAMBER ORCHESTRA
Meir Rimon (hn.) with members of Israel
Philharmonic Orchestra
(cond.) Shalom Ronly-Riklis **CRYST S 673**

QUARTET 1, FOR STRINGS (1962)
Crescent Quartet **LEONA LPI 111**

REVERBERATIONS
Gary Steigerwalt (pf.) **ORION ORS 81413**

SONATA BREVE
Gary Steigerwalt (pf.) **ORION ORS 81413**

SONATA CONCERTANTE
Maxine Neuman (vlc.), Joan Stein (pf.) **ORION ORS 83444**

SONATENSATZ
Gary Steigerwalt (pf.) **ORION ORS 81413**

TOTENGESÄNGE (1963)
Berenice Branson (S.), Ruth Schonthal (pf.) **LEONA LPI 106**

VARIATIONS IN SEARCH OF A THEME
Gary Steigerwalt (pf.) **ORION ORS 81413**

SCHUMANN, Clara Josephine (1819-1896)

AM STRAND (BURNS)
Udo Reinemann (Bar.), Christian
Ivaldi (pf.) **ARION ARN 38575**

AM STRAND (BURNS) (2'47)
Patricia Adkins Chiti (m-S.), Gian
Paolo Chiti (pf.)
EDMUS PAN NRC 5016

AN EINEM LICHTEN MORGEN, OP. 23, NO. 2
(HERMAN ROLLET)
Udo Reinemann (Bar.), Christian
Ivaldi (pf.)
ARION ARN 38575

ANDANTE ESPRESSIVO (D-MAJOR)
Christian Ivaldi (pf.)
ARION ARN 38575

AUF EINEM GRÜNEN HÜGEL, OP. 23, NO. 4
(HERMANN ROLLET)
Udo Reinemann (Bar.), Christian
Ivaldi (pf.)
ARION ARN 38575

CONCERTO FOR PIANO AND ORCHESTRA,
IN A-MINOR, OP. 7
* * * * * *
FONO FSM 31 038

CONCERTO FOR PIANO AND ORCHESTRA,
IN A-MINOR, OP. 7
M. Ponti (pf.) with Berlin
Symphony Orchestra
(cond.) V. Schmidt-Gertenbach
VOX STGBY 649

DAS IST EIN TAG, DER KLINGEN MAG
Katherine Ciesinski (m-S.), Rudolph
Palmer (pf.)
LEONA LPI 107

DAS IST EIN TAG, DER KLINGEN MAG
Berenice Bramson (S.), Roger
Rundle (pf.)
GEMIN RAP 1010

DAS IST EIN TAG, DER KLINGEN MAG
Tuula Nienstedt (Cont.), Uwe
Wegner (pf.)
MUSVI MV 301104

DAS IST EIN TAG, DER KLINGEN MAG,
OP. 23, N0. 5 (HERMANN ROLLET)
Udo Reinemann (Bar.), Christian Ivaldi (pf.) **ARION ARN 38575**

ER IST GEKOMMEN IN STURM UND
REGEN OP. 12,
NO. 2 (F. RUCKERT)
Katherine Ciesinski (m-S.),
Rudolph Palmer (pf.)
LEONA LPI 107

ER IST GEKOMMEN IN STURM UND
REGEN, OP. 12, NO. 2 (F. RUCKERT)
Udo Reinemann (Bar.), Christian Ivaldi (pf.) **ARION ARN 38575**

ER IST GEKOMMEN IN STURM UND
REGEN, OP. 12 (F. RUCKERT) (2'37)
Tuula Nienstedt (Cont.), Uwe Wegner (pf.) **MUSVI MV 301104**

GEHEIMES FLÜSTERN HIER UND DORT,
OP. 23, NO. 3 (HERMANN ROLLET)
Udo Reinemann (Bar.),
Christian Ivaldi (pf.)
ARION ARN 38575

ICH HAB'IN DEINEM AUGE, OP. 13,
NO. 5 (F. RUCKERT)
Udo Reinemann (Bar.),
Christian Ivaldi (pf.)
ARION ARN 38575

SCHUMANN, Clara Josephine (1819-1896)

ICH STAND IN DUNKLEN TRAUMEN OP. 13,
NO. 1 (HEINE)
Udo Reinemann (Bar.),
Christian Ivaldi (pf.)
ARION ARN 38575

ICH STAND IN DUNKLEN TRAUMEN, OP. 13,
NO. 1 (HEINE)
Katherine Ciesinski (m-S),
Rudolph Palmer (pf.)
LEONA LPI 107

IMPROMPTU
Michael May (pf.)
GEMIN RAP 1010

IMPROMPTU (2'39)
Nancy Fierro (pf.)
PELIC LP 2017

IMPROMPTU, OP. 9
Altstandter (pf.)
MUHER MHS 4163

LIEBESZAUBER, OP. 13, NO. 3 (GEIBEL)
Udo Reinemann (Bar.),
Christian Ivaldi (pf.)
ARION ARN 38575

LIEBST DU UM SCHOENHEIT, OP. 12, NO. 4
Mertine Johns (m-S.),
Roger Rundle (pf.)
GEMIN RAP 1010

LIEBST DU UM SCHOENHEIT, OP. 12
(F. RUCKERT) (2'27)
Tuula Nienstedt, (Cont.),
Uwe Wegner (pf.)
MUSVI MV 301104

LIEBST DU UM SCHONHEIT OP. 12,
NO. 4 (F. RUCKERT)
Katherine Ciesinski (m-S.),
Rudolph Palmer (pf.)
LEONA LPI 107

LIEBST DU UM SCHONHEIT, OP. 12,
NO. 4 (F. RUCKERT)
Udo Reinemann (Bar.),
Christian Ivaldi (pf.)
ARION ARN 38575

LIEBST DU UM SCHONHEIT, OP. 12,
NO. 4 (F. RUCKERT) (2'11)
Patricia Adkins Chiti (m-S.),
Gian Paolo Chiti (pf.)
EDMUS PAN NRC 5016

MAZURKA IN G, OP. 6
Sykes
ORION 75182

MOND KOMMT STILL GEGANGEN,
DER, OP. 13, NO. 4 (GIEBEL)
Udo Reinemann (Bar.),
Christian Ivaldi (pf.)
ARION ARN 38575

O LUST, O LUST, OP. 23,
NO. 6 (HERMANN ROLLET)
Udo Reinemann (Bar.),
Christian Ivaldi (pf.)
ARION ARN 38575

PIECES FOR PIANO
Helene Boschi (pf.)
CALLI 1211

PRAELUDIUM AND FUGUE
IN G-MINOR, OP. 16
Monica von Saalfeld (pf.)
MUHER MHS 1339

PRELUDE AND FUGUE, OP. 16
Monica von Saalfeld (pf.)
DACAM SM 93116

PRELUDE AND FUGUE, OP. 16
Monica von Saalfeld (pf.)
ORYX 1819

PRELUDE AND FUGUE, OP. 16, NO. 2
Nancy Fierro (pf.)
PELIC LP 2017

QUATRE PIECES FUGITIVES, OP. 15
M. Ponti (pf.)
FONO FSM 31 038

QUATRE PIECES FUGITIVES, OP. 15
M. Ponti (pf.)
VOX STGBY 649

QUATRE PIECES FUGITIVES, OP. 15
(NO. 1 ONLY) (2'28)
Nancy Fierro (pf.)
PELIC LP 2017

QUATRE PIECES FUGITIVES, OP. 15
(NO. 3 ONLY) (5'45)
Helene Boschi (pf.)
CALLI CAL 121112

ROMANCE IN B-MAJOR, OP. 5, NO. 3
Demus (pf.)
INTCO 180 812

ROMANCE IN B-MAJOR, OP. 5, NO. 3
Demus (pf.)
EMI 151 99773/4

ROMANCE IN B-MAJOR, OP. 5, NO. 3
Demus (pf.)
HARMU HM 828

ROMANCE IN B-MAJOR, OP. 5, NO. 3
Demus (pf.)
HARMU HM 2920327 1

ROMANCE VARIEE, OP. 3, FOR PIANO
Goebels (pf.)
BAREN BM 1916

ROMANCE, IN B-MINOR (5'25)
Helene Boschi (pf.)
CALLI CAL 121112

ROMANCE, OP. 11, NO. 3, IN A-FLAT MAJOR
Christian Ivaldi (pf.) **ARION ARN 38575**

ROMANCES FOR VIOLIN AND PIANO, OP. 22
H. Boschi (pf.), A. Jodry (vln.) **CALLI 1212**

ROMANCES FOR VIOLIN AND PIANO, OP. 22
Luca (vln.), Epperson (pf.) **NONSU 79007**

ROMANCES, OP. 22, NOS. 1-3
Marianne Boettcher (vln.), Ursula
Frede-Boettcher (pf.) **MARUS MRS 308226**

ROMANCES, OP. 22, NOS. 1-3
Sergio Luca (vln.), Anne Epperson (pf.) **TELDE TIS 79007**

RUCKERT SONGS (ER IST GEKOMMEN IN
STURM UND REGEN, LIEBST DU UM
SCHONHEIT, WARUM WILLST DU
AND'RE FRAGEN)
Katherine Ciesinski (m-S.),
Rudolph Palmer (pf.) **LEONA LPI 107**

SCHERZO IN C-MINOR, OP. 14
Christian Ivaldi (pf.) **ARION ARN 38575**

SCHERZO IN C-MINOR, OP. 14 (3'18)
Nancy Fierro (pf.) **PELIC LP 2017**

SCHERZO IN G-MAJOR, OP. 15, NO. 4
Christian Ivaldi (pf.) **ARION ARN 38575**

SCHERZO NO. 1 IN D-MINOR, OP. 10
Michael Ponti (pf.) **FONO FSM 31 038**

SCHERZO NO. 1 IN D-MINOR, OP. 10
Michael Ponti (pf.) **VOX STGBY 649**

SCHERZO NO. 2 IN C-MINOR, OP. 14
Michael Ponti (pf.) **VOX STGBY 649**

SCHERZO NO. 2 IN C-MINOR, OP. 14
Michael Ponti (pf.) **FONO FSM 31 038**

SCHERZO NO. 2 IN C-MINOR, OP. 14
Altstadter (pf.) **MUHER MHS 4163**

SIE LIEBTEN SICH BEIDE, OP. 13,
NO. 2 (HEINE) 0
Udo Reinemann (Bar.), Christian Ivaldi (pf.) **ARION ARN 38575**

SIE LIEBTEN SICH BEIDE, OP. 13,
NO. 2 (HEINE) (2'03)
Tuula Nienstedt (Cont.), Uwe Wegner (pf.) **MUSVI MV 30 1104**

SOUVENIR DE VIENNE, IMPROMPTU, OP. 9
Monica von Saalfeld (pf.) **DACAM SM 93116**

SOUVENIR DE VIENNE, IMPROMPTU, OP. 9
Monica von Saalfeld (pf.) **MUHER MHS 1339**

SOUVENIR DE VIENNE, IMPROMPTU, OP. 9
Monica von Saalfeld (pf.) **ORYX 1819**

STILLE LOTUSBLUME, DIE, OP. 13,
NO. 6 (GEIBEL)
Udo Reinemann (Bar.), Christian Ivaldi (pf.) **ARION ARN 38575**

STILLE LOTUSBLUME, DIE, OP. 13,
NO. 6 (GEIBEL)
Katherine Ciesinski (m-S.), Rudolph
Palmer (pf.) **LEONA LPI 107**

THREE PRELUDES AND FUGUES, OP. 16
(1845) (14'39)
Helene Boschi (pf.) **CALLI CAL 121112**

THREE ROMANCES FOR PIANO, OP. 11 (12'30)
Helene Boschi (pf.) **CALLI CAL 121112**

THREE ROMANCES FOR VIOLIN AND PIANO
Sergio Luca (vln.), Anne Epperson (pf.) **NONSU D 79007**

THREE ROMANCES FOR VIOLIN AND
PIANO, OP. 22 (10'00)
Helene Boschi (pf.), Annie Jodry (vln.) **CALLI CAL 121112**

THREE ROMANCES, OP. 21 (1853) (10'30)
Helene Boschi (pf.) **CALLI CAL 121112**

TRIO FOR PIANO, VIOLIN AND CELLO, IN
G-MINOR, OP. 17
Beaux Arts Trio **PHILI 6700 051**

TRIO FOR PIANO, VIOLIN AND CELLO, IN
G-MINOR, OP. 17
Beaux Arts Trio **PHILI 6500 296**

TRIO FOR PIANO, VIOLIN AND CELLO, IN
G-MINOR, OP. 17
Wieck Trio **ORYX 1819**

TRIO FOR PIANO, VIOLIN AND CELLO, IN
G-MINOR, OP. 17
Macalester Trio **VOX SVBX 5112**

TRIO FOR PIANO, VIOLIN AND CELLO, IN
G-MINOR, OP. 17
Monica von Saalfeld (pf.),
F. Koscielny (vln.), Gisela Reith (vlc.) **MUHER MHS 1339**

TRIO FOR PIANO, VIOLIN AND CELLO, IN
G-MINOR, OP. 17
Monica von Saalfeld (pf.), F. Koscielny (vln.),
Gisela Reith (vlc.) **DACAM SM 93116**

TRIO FOR PIANO, VIOLIN AND CELLO, IN
G-MINOR, OP. 17
Helene Boschi (pf.), Annie Jodry (vln.),
Etienne Peclard (vlc.) **CALLI CAL 121112**

TWO ROMANCES, OP. 21
Sykes (pf.) **ORION 75182**

VARIATIONS ON A THEME
BY ROBERT SCHUMANN, OP. 20
Monica von Saalfeld (pf.) **DACAM SM 93116**

VARIATIONS ON A THEME
BY ROBERT SCHUMANN, OP. 20
Goebels (pf.) **BAREN BM 1916**

VARIATIONS ON A THEME
BY ROBERT SCHUMANN, OP. 20
M. Ponti (pf.) **VOX STGBY 649**

VARIATIONS ON A THEME
BY ROBERT SCHUMANN, OP. 20
Monica von Saalfeld (pf.) **ORYX 1819**

VARIATIONS ON A THEME
BY ROBERT SCHUMANN, OP. 20
Sykes (pf.) **ORION 75182**

VARIATIONS ON A THEME
BY ROBERT SCHUMANN, OP. 20
Monica von Saalfeld (pf.) **MUHER MHS 1339**

VARIATIONS ON A THEME
BY ROBERT SCHUMANN, OP. 20
Rosario Marciano (pf.) **TURNA TV 34685**

VARIATIONS ON A THEME
BY ROBERT SCHUMANN, OP. 20
Judith Alstadter (pf.) **MUHER MHS 4163**

VARIATIONS ON A THEME
BY ROBERT SCHUMANN, OP. 20
M. Ponti (pf.) **FONO FSM 31 038**

VARIATIONS ON A THEME
BY ROBERT SCHUMANN, OP. 20
Rosario Marciano (pf.) **FONO FSM 53 0 36**

VARIATIONS ON A THEME
BY ROBERT SCHUMANN, OP. 20
Evelinde Trenkner (pf.) **PAIR AG - - -**

VARIATIONS ON A THEME BY ROBERT
SCHUMANN, OP. 20 (10'25)
Helene Boschi (pf.) **CALLI CAL 121112**

WARUM WILLST DU AND'RE FRAGEN,
OP. 12, NO. 11 (F. RUCKERT)
Udo Reinemann (Bar.), Christian Ivaldi (pf.) **ARION ARN 38575**

WARUM WILLST DU AND'RE FRAGEN, OP. 12,
NO. 11 (F. RUCKERT)
Katherine Ciesinski (m-S.),
Rudolph Palmer (pf.) **LEONA LPI 107**

WAS WEINST DU BLUEMLEIN, OP. 23, NO. 1
(HERMANN ROLLET) (12'00)
Tuula Nienstedt (Cont.), Uwe Wegner (pf.) **MUSVI MV 301104**

WAS WEINST DU BLUEMLEIN, OP. 23,
NO. 1 (HERMANN ROLLET)
Udo Reinemann (Bar.), Christian Ivaldi (pf.) **ARION ARN 38575**

WAS WEINST DU BLUEMLEIN, OP. 23,
NO. 1 (HERMANN ROLLET)
Katherine Ciesinski (m-S), Rudolph
Palmer (pf.) **LEONA LPI 107**

SCHUYLER, Philippa Duke (1932-1967)

INTERNATIONAL FAVORITES
Philippa Duke Schuyler (pf.) **MIDLE - - -**

SCLIAR, Esther (1926-)

ETUDE NO. 1, FOR GUITAR
* * * * * * **FUNAR MMB 84 037**

IMBRICATA FOR FLUTE,
OBOE AND PIANO
* * * * * * **FUNAR MMB 84 037**

SIX CHORAL SONGS
* * * * * * **FUNAR MMB 84 037**

SONATA FOR PIANO
* * * * * * **FUNAR MMB 84 037**

SCOTT, Lady John Douglas (1810-1900)

ANNIE LAURIE
* * * * * * **ORION ORS 77271**

ANNIE LAURIE
* * * * * * **PELIC LP 2005**

THINK ON ME
Isobel Baillie (S.), Gerald Moore (pf.) **EMI HQM 1118**

SCOVILLE, Margaret Lee (1944-)

OSTINATO, FANTASY AND FUGUE
George Skipworth (pf.) **EDUCO 3097**

PENTACYCLE
George Skipworth (pf.) **EDUCO 3097**

SEAVER, Blanche Ebert (1891-)

JUST FOR TODAY
Igor Gorin (Bar.) with Orchestra
(cond.) Donald Voorhees **ALIDE 2000**

JUST FOR TODAY
John McCormack (T.) with Orchestra **CAMDE CAL 635**

SEMEGEN, Daria (1946-)

ARC: MUSIC FOR DANCERS (1977))
Electronic Music Studios, State
University of New York **FINNA SR 9020**

ELECTRONIC COMPOSITION NO. 1
Columbia-Princetown Electronic
Music Center **OFYSS Y 34139**

JEUX DES QUATRES FOR CELLO, PIANO,
CLARINET AND TROMBONE
Stony Brook Players: Calhoun, Fisher,
Hill, Schecher **OPONE 59**

MUSIC FOR VIOLIN SOLO (1973)
Carol Sadowski (vln.) **OPONE 59**

SPECTRA: ELECTRONIC COMPOSITION NO. 2
Electronic Music Studio of State
University of New York **CRI SD 443**

SHADWELL, Nancy (-)

THEME AND VARIATIONS FOR TRUMPET
Endsley (trp.) **CLARI SLP 1006**

SHAIMARDANOVA, Shakhida (1938-)

SYMPHONY IN C-MAJOR
Symphony Orchestra of the State
Philharmonia of the Uzbek SSR
(cond.) Z. Khaknazarov **MELOD D 026785 6**

SHASHINA, Elizaveta Sergeyevna (-)

I GO ALONE ALONG THE ROAD
D. Golovin (Bar.) **MELOD D 032713 4**

I GO ALONE ALONG THE ROAD
Boys' Chorus of Lenin State Acedemy **MELOD D 18411 2**

I GO ALONE ALONG THE ROAD
I. Kozlovsky (T.) **MELOD D 028059 62**

I GO ALONE ALONG THE ROAD
B. Shtokolov (B.) **MELOD S 01 277 8**

I GO ALONE ALONG THE ROAD
N. Obukhova (m-S.) **MELOD D 021667 8**

VYKHOZHU ODIN YA NA DOROGU
Louis Danto (T.), Hans Dieter Wagner (pf.) **MUHER MHS 1185**

VYKHOZHU ODIN YA NA DOROGU (3'32)
Louis Danto (T.), Hans Dieter Wagner (pf.) **DACAM SM 90012**

SHIELDS, Alice Ferree (1943-)

COYOTE
Alice Shields (tape) **CRI SD 495**

EL'S ARIA (FROM OPERA SHAMAN)
Carrie Rockwood (S.), David McBride (pf.),
Tamsin Fitzgerald (fl.), Tom Goldstein (perc.) **OPONE 90**

FAREWELL TO A HILL
* * * * * * **FINNA QD 9010**

NERUDA SONGS
Johana Arnold (S.),
Andre Emelianoff (vlc.) **OPONE 83**

O GRACIOUS LIGHT
* * * * * * **OPONE - - -**

RHAPSODY FOR PIANO AND TAPE
(HOMAGE TO BRAHMS) (1983)
Yolande Liepa (pf.) with tape **OPONE 94**

TRANSFORMATION OF ANI, THE, FOR TAPE (1970)
* * * * * * **CR SD 268**

WILDCAT SONGS
Turash (S.), Dunkle (picc.) **OPONE 13**

SHIOMI, Mieko (1938-)

IF I WERE A PENTAGONAL MEMORY DEVICE
* * * * * * **JAPAN JFC 7907**

SPRING
* * * * * * **JAPAN JFC ---**

SIKORA, Elzbieta (1943-   )

ARIADNA (OPERA) (1977)
Eva Ignatowicz (S.), Lidia Juranek (m-S.)
with Warsaw Chamber Orchestra
(cond.) Jacek Kasprzyk   **MUZA SX 1778**

IL VIAGGIO I
Zdzislaw Piernik (tba.),
Maciej Paderewski (pf.)   **NTP DAU ISPV 102**

SILSBEE, Ann L. (1930-   )

SPIRALS, FOR ORCHESTRA
* * * * * *   **TURNA TV 34704**

SPIRALS, FOR STRING QUARTET AND
PIANO (19'30) Nancy Cirillo (vln.), Valerie Kuchment
(vln.), Katherine Murdock (vla.), Joel
Moerschel (vlc.), Randall Hodgkinson
(pf.) (cond.) Richard Pittman   **NORTH NR 221**

SILVER, Sheila Jane (1946-   )

STRING QUARTET (1975)
Atlantic String Quartet   **CRI CRI 520**

SILVERMAN, Faye-Ellen (1947-   )

OBOE-STHENICS FOR OBOE SOLO (1980)
Ostryniec (ob.)   **FINNA SR 90008 1**

SIMONS, Netty (1913-   )

DESIGN GROUPS NO. 1
Ron George (perc.)   **DESTO DC 7128**

DESIGN GROUPS NO. 2
Nancy Turetzky (fl.), Bertram Turetzky (d-b.) **DESTO DC 7128**

PIED PIPER OF HAMELIN, THE
(ROBERT BROWNING)
Lou Gilbert (narr.), Paul Dunkel (fl.),
Netty Simons (pf.) with Violin Orchestra
(cond.) Richard Dufallo   **CRI SD 309**

PUDDINTAME
Barbara Britton (limericist),
Lou Gilbert (Limericist)
Jean-Charles Francois (perc.),
Ron George (perc.)   **CRI SD 309**

SET OF POEMS FOR CHILDREN (ROSETTI,
SANDBERG, STEPHENS AND STEVENSON)
Barbara Britten (narr.) with String
and Wind Octet
(cond.) Edwin London   **CRI SD 309**

SILVER THAW
Bertram Turezky (d-b.)   **DESTO DC 7128**

SKOUEN, Synne (1950-   )

HAIL DOMITILA!
Elisabeth Klein (pf.)   **DANIC 8017**

SMILEY, Pril (1943-   )

ECLIPSE
* * * * * *   **FINNA 9010**

ECLIPSE
* * * * * *   **TURNA TV 34301**

KOLYOSA
* * * * * *   **CRI SD 268**

**SMIRNOVA SOLODCHENKOVA, Tatiana
Georgievna (1940-   )**

SONATA BALLAD, FOR TRUMPET AND PIANO   **MELOD**
Yuri Usov (trp.), Tatiana Smirnova (pf.)   **M 10 39303/4**

SMITH, Alice Mary (1839-1884)

O, THAT WE TWO WERE MAYING
Molyneux (m-S.), Van Asch (B.),
Miall (pf.)   **DESTO DC 6449**

SMITH, Julia Frances (1911-   )

DAISY (OPERA HIGHLIGHTS)
Chorus and Orchestra of Charlotte
Opera Association
(cond.) C. Rosekrans   **ORION ORS 76248**

QUARTET FOR STRINGS
Kohon Quartet   **DESTO DC 7117**

SMITH, Ladonna Carol (1951-   )

AMERIGREEN FOR ENSEMBLE, IMPROVISATION
AND FOUR LAWNMOWERS
* * * * * *   **TRANS 2002**

ARMED FORCES DAY
Blue Denim Deals   **SAYDA 2**

PRELUDE, DAY MUSIC
* * * * * *   **TRANS 2005**

RAUDELUNAS, PATAPHYSICAL REVUE
* * * * * *   **SAYDA 1**

SCHOOL
Eugene Chadbourne, John Zorn   **PARAC 004 006**

SOLO, FOR AMATEUR ORCHESTRA
* * * * * *   **TRANS 2001**

USA CONCERTS
Andre Centazzo   **ICTUS 0018**

SMITH, Margit (-   )

CHROAI (WITH MARRIE BREMER)
Marrie Bremer, Margit Smith (chin,
hpcd., pf. and kayagum)   **MUSMU MC 18038**

ELEVENSEVENSEVEN
(WITH MARRIE BREMER)
Marrie Bremer, Margit Smith
(kayagum and renaissance b-fl.)   **MUSMU MC 18038**

MAQAM (WITH MARRIE BREMER)
Marrie Bremer (org.), Margit Smith (org.) **MUSMU MC 18038**

MOBILE (WITH MARRIE BREMER)
Marrie Bremer (org.), Margit Smith (org.) **MUSMU MC 18038**

OMBRE (WITH MARRIE BREMER)
Marrie Bremer (org.), Margit Smith (org.) **MUSMU MC 18038**

TRAJECT 1 (WITH MARRIE BREMER)
Marrie Bremer, Margit Smith (org,
Baroque vce-fl. and Peruvian fl.)   **MUSMU MC 18038**

TRAJECT 2 (WITH MARRIE BREMER)
Marrie Bremer, Margit Smith (org., 2
African fl., gemshorn, b-fl.,
shakuhachi, Nepalese and Thai fl.   **MUSMU MC 18038**

SMYTH, Ethel Mary, Dame (1858-1944)

BOATSWAIN'S MATE, THE: SUPPOSE YOU
MEAN TO DO A GIVEN THING AND ARIA:
WHAT IF I WERE YOUNG AGAIN (8'22)
Tommy Crowell Anderson (S.)   **OPERV OV 101/2**

WRECKERS, THE (COMPLETE OPERA)
Bradford Opera Group
(cond.) David Dawson   **RARER SRRE 193 4**

WRECKERS, THE, OVERTURE
Scottish National Orchestra
(cond.) Gibson   **HMV ASD 2400**

SNYDER, Amy (1949-   )

OZARK BRUSH MEETING (1983) (14'40)
Aemstel Quartet and Ensemble   **BVHAS 052**

SOENSTEVOLD, Maj (1917-   )

ELEVEN POLYTONAL BLUES
Elisabeth Klein (pf.)   **DANIC DLP 8017**

MEGET LITE STYKKE FOR HARPE
Elisabeth Soenstevold (hp.)   **PHILI 6754 002**

NINE HAIKU FOR ALTO, FLUTE AND HARP
Else Nedburg (A.), Per Oeien (fl.),
Elisabeth Soenstevold (hp.)   **PHILI 6507 018**

PECULIAR DREAM OF AN OLD MAJOR
Norwegian Broadcasting Orchestra
(cond.) O. Bergh   **PHILI 6830 027**

PIANO SONATA
Anne Eline Riisnes (pf.)   **PHILI 6754 002**

SNOW WHITE AND THE SEVEN DWARFS
* * * * * *   **RCA REP 337**

SORLANDSOMMER
* * * * * *   **PHILI 839 239**

STILLNESS, FOR EIGHT VOICES, FLUTE,
CLARINET, PIANO, PERCUSSION, VIOLA
AND VIOLONCELLO
Chamber Choir with New Music
Ensemble (cond.) Ole Viggo Bang   **PHILI 6754 002**

SUITE FOR PIANO
Anne Eline Riisnes (pf.)   **PHILI 6754 002**

THORN ROSE
* * * * * *   **RCA REP 345**

SOLOMON, Mirrie Irma (1892-   )

ABORIGINAL THEMES
Adelaide Symphony Orchestra
(cond.) Krips   **WRC R 03154**

AND EVERYONE WILL LOVE ME
* * * * * *   **M7 MLX 147**

AVINU MOLKEINU
Adelaide Symphony Orchestra
(cond.) Krips   **WRC R 03154**

SOUTHAM, Ann (1937-   )

BOAT, RIVER, MOON
Brick (elec. insts)   **MELBO SMLP 4024**

EMERGING GROUND (1983)
Ann Southam   **HATHO HS 290147**

FOUR BAGATELLES, FOR PIANO
* * * * * *   **MELBO SMLP 4031**

QUODLIBET, FOR PIANO
* * * * * *   **CCM 2**

REPRIEVE (1975)
Ann Southam   **HATHO 290147**

RHAPSODIC INTERLUDE, FOR VIOLIN
David Zaffer (vln.)   **MELBO SMLP 4021**

RIVERS (SECOND SET)
Ann Southam (pf.)   **★ ★ ★ EK 1**

RIVERS (SECOND SET) NO. 7
Elaine Keillor (pf.)   **KEILL WRCI 3315**

SKY-SAILS
David Zaffer (vln.)   **MHIC MH 93**

THREE IN BLUE FOR PIANO
* * * * * *   **CCM 2**

SPEKTOR, Mira J. (-   )

HOUSEWIVES' CANTATA, THE
* * * * * *   **ORICA OC 8133**

SPENCER, Williametta (1932-   )

DEATH BE NOT PROUD
* * * * * *   **OMNIS N 1009**

SPIEGEL, Laurie (1945-   )

APPALACHIAN GROVE 1 (1974)
* * * * * *   **1750A S 1765**

DRUMS (7'06)
Laurie Spiegel (elect.)   **CAPIO CR 2**

EXPANDING UNIVERSE, THE
* * * * * *   **PHILO PH 9003**

OLD WAVE
* * * * * *   **PHILO PH 9003**

PATCHWORK
* * * * * *   **PHILO PH 9003**

PENTACHROME
* * * * * *   **PHILO PH 9003**

VOICES WITHIN (14'36)
Laurie Spiegel (syn.)   **CAPIO CR 2**

SPINAROVA, Vera (-   )

ANDROMEDA
Ivo Pavlik Group   **PANTN 11 0327**

SQUIRE, Hope (1878-1936)

VARIATIONS ON BLACK EYED SUSAN
Frank Merrick (pf.)   **RARER SRRE 118**

STANEKAITE-LAUMYANSKENE, Elena Ionovna (1880-   )

REMEMBRANCE, TARANTELL, MAZURKA   **MELOD**
E. Kalinauskaite   **D 009587/8**

STEWART, Ora Pate (-   )

CROSSING THE BAR, FOR WOMEN'S
CHORUS AND OPTIONAL ORGAN
* * * * * *   **PREVI 1**

GOLDEN PROMISE
* * * * * *   **PREVI 2**

JAMIE'S CHRISTMAS, FOR WOMEN'S
CHORUS AND PIANO
* * * * * *   **MEDAL KM 1421**

LIKEWISE
* * * * * *   **PREVI 17**

MOTHER-SONG, FOR WOMEN'S
CHORUS AND PIANO
* * * * * *   **PREVI 3**

PEBBLE BEACH, FOR WOMEN'S
CHORUS AND PIANO
* * * * * *   **PREVI 6**

SONG OF LOVE, FOR SOLO SOPRANO
AND PIANO
* * * * * *   **MEDAL 1418**

TO A CHILD, FOR WOMEN'S CHORUS, PIANO,
OPTIONAL VIOLIN AND VIOLA
* * * * * *   **KENNA 23041**

TREE STOOD TALL, FOR WOMEN'S
CHORUS AND PIANO
* * * * * *   **PREVI 2**

STOBEAUS, Kristina xxx (1942-   )

GAMLA FAAGELN, DEN
Kristina Stobeaus (S.)   **BLUEB BELL 193**

STREET, Arlene Anderson (1933-   )

DROWSY DILEMMA, FOR PIANO
* * * * * *   **CCM 1**

STRICKLAND, Lily Teresa (1887-1958)

MAH LINDY LOU
Paul Robeson (B-Bar.) with Columbia
Concert Orchestra
(cond.) Emanuel Balaban   **COLUM ML 4105**

MAH LINDY LOU
William Warfield (Bar.) with Columbia
Symphony Orchestra
(cond.) Lehman Engel   **COLUM AAL 32**

STROZZI, Barbara (1620-1664)

ASTRATO: LUCIBELLE, OP. 8
Judith Nelson (S.) with Clavichord,
Violoncello and Harp   **HARMU 1114**

CHE SI PUO FARE? (11'37)
Carol Plantamura (S.) with Ensemble   **LEONA LPI 123**

LAMENTO: APPRESSO A I MOLLI ARGENTI, OP. 7
Judith Nelson (S.) with Clavichord,
Violoncello, and Harp   **HARMU 1114**

LAMENTO: SU'L RODANO SEVERO, OP. 3
Montserrat Figueras (S.), Judith Nelson (S.),
With Clavichord, Violoncello and Harp   **HARMU 1114**

LUCI BELLE, OP. 8
Judith Nelson (S.) with Clavichord,
Violoncello, and Harp   **HARMU 1114**

MORALITA AMOROSA
Judith Nelson (S.) with Clavichord,
Violoncello and Harp   **HARMU 1114**

NON PAVENTO CO DI TE, OP. 6
Judith Nelson (S.) with Clavichord,
Violoncello and Harp   **HARMU 1114**

NON PAVENTO IO NON DI TE (4'10)
Carol Plantamura (S.) with Ensemble   **LEONA LPI 123**

NON TI DOLER MIO COR (2'53)
Teresa Berganza (m-S.)   **CLAVS D 8206**

RISSOLVETEVI PENSIERI (3'27)
Teresa Berganza (m-S.)   **CLAVS D 8206**

S'UL RODANO SEVERO (IL LAMENTO) (15'05)
Montserrat Figueras (S.) with Ensemble
Hesperion   **ARCIV 2533468**

SU'L RODANO SEVERO, OP. 3
Savall with Ensemble Hesperion   **DG 2533468**

TRADIMENTO! (2'40)
Carol Plantamura (S.) with Ensemble   **LEONA LPI 123**

STULTZ, Marie Irene (1945-   )

HORSESHOE NAIL (FROM FIRESIDE
AMUSEMENTS) (1982)
Treble Voices   **VOGT - - -**

SONG OF JUBILATION, OP. 2
Treble or Soprano Voices,
Mixed Choir and Organ   **GOLDE - - -**

SUESSE, Dana (1911-   )

BLUE MOONLIGHT
Paul Whiteman and his Concert Orchestra   **JJA 19751**

SULPIZI, Mira (1923-   )

ANTICHI CANTO SPAGNOLI
* * * * * *   **FONIT VP 10019**

MESSA MELODICA
* * * * * *   **CARAR 42 3045**

OTTO CANTI MEDIOEVALI
* * * * * *   **OMNIA OLC 19008**

SUTHERLAND, Margaret (1897-   )

DITHYRAMB
Australian Youth Orchestra
(cond.) Sir Bernard Heinze   **PHILI S 10839 L**

DIVERTIMENTO, FOR STRING TRIO
* * * * * *   **CHERR CPF 1030**

HAUNTED HILLS, THE
Melbourne Symphony Orchestra
(cond.) John Hopkins   **FESTI L 42013**

HAUNTED HILLS, THE
Melbourne Symphony Orchestra
(cond.) John Hopkins   **FESTI SFC 800 20**

NOCTURNE IN A-FLAT
Rosario Marciano   **TURNA TV 34685**

NOCTURNE IN B-FLAT
* * * * * *   **TURNA TV 34685**

SONATA FOR CLARINET AND PIANO
* * * * * *   **FESTI L 42018**

SONATA FOR CLARINET AND PIANO
Jack Harrison (cl.), Stephen Dornan (pf.)   **FESTI SFC 800 25**

SONATINA FOR PIANO
Penelope Thwaites — **DSCOU ABM 30**

TRIO
Jiri Tancibudek (ob.), Sybil
Copeland (vln.), John Glickman (vla.) — **BROLG BXM 02**

YOUNG KABBARLI, THE
New Opera of South Australia
(cond.) Patrick Thomas — **EMI 040 ASD 7569**

SZOENYI, Erzsebet (1924-)

CONCERTO FOR ORGAN AND ORCHESTRA
Gabor Lehotka (org.) with Hungarian
State Orchestra
(cond.) Gyula Nemeth — **HUNGA SLPX 11 808**

FIVE PRELUDES FOR PIANO (7'00)
Laszlo Almasy (pf.) — **HUNGA SLPX 12623**

PICCOLA OUVERTURA
Orchestra of Budapest Municipal
Music School
(cond.) Margit Kutassy — **QUALI LPX 1188**

RADNOTI CANTATA, ON POEMS BY MIKLOS
RADNOTI (24'40)
M. Laszlo (S.), J. Horvath (T.),
G. Melis (Bar.) with Radnoti Children's
and Budapest Choruses and
Budapest MAV Symphony Orchestra
(cond.) Sandor Margittay — **HUNGA SLPX 12623**

SIX PIECES FOR ORGAN
* * * * * * — **QUALI LPX 1222**

SIX PIECES FOR ORGAN
Sebestyen Pecsi (org.) — **DACAM SM 93 267**

THREE IDEAS IN FOUR MOVEMENTS, FOR
PIANO AND CHAMBER ENSEMBLE (8'35)
Laszlo Almasy (pf.) with Corelli
Chamber Ensemble
(cond.) Istvan Ella — **HUNGA SLPX 12623**

TRIO SONATA, FOR VIOLIN,
CELLO AND PIANO (9'12)
Laszlo Koete (vln.), Laszlo Mezoe (vlc.),
Laszlo Almasy (pf.) — **HUNGA SLPX 12623**

SZYMANOWSKA, Maria Agata (1789-1831)

BALLADE (MADAME
SAINTE-ONGE) (1822) (2'13)
Patricia Adkins Chiti (m-S.),
Gian Paola Chiti (pf.) — **EDMUS PAN NRC 5016**

DANSE POLONAISE
P. Bowyer (pf.) — **ARION ARN 336 029**

EARLY POLISH PIANO MUSIC
Lidia Kozubek (pf.) — **MUZA XL 0559**

ETUDE IN C-MAJOR
Nancy Fierro (pf.) — **AVANT AV 1012**

ETUDE IN C-MAJOR
Georges Alexandrovitch (pf.) — **MUSID RC 782**

ETUDE IN D-MINOR
Georges Alexandrovitch (pf.) — **MUSID RC 782**

ETUDE IN E-FLAT MAJOR
Georges Alexandrovitch (pf.) — **MUSID RC 782**

ETUDE IN E-MAJOR
Nancy Fierro (pf.) — **AVANT AV 1012**

ETUDE IN E-MAJOR
Georges Alexandrovitch (pf.) — **MUSID RC 782**

ETUDE IN F-MAJOR
Nancy Fierro (pf.) — **AVANT AV 1012**

ETUDE IN F-MAJOR
Georges Alexandrovitch (pf.) — **MUSID RC 782**

MENUET
Georges Alexandrovitch (pf.) — **MUSID RC 782**

NOCTURNE IN A-FLAT MAJOR (LE MURMURE)
Rosario Marciano (pf.) — **FONO FSM 530 36**

NOCTURNE IN A-FLAT MAJOR (LE MURMURE)
Rosario Marciano (pf.) — **TURNA TV 34685**

NOCTURNE IN A-FLAT MAJOR (LE MURMURE)
Georges Alexandrovitch (pf.) — **MUSID RC 782**

NOCTURNE IN B FLAT MAJOR
M. Federova (pf.) — **MELOD D 004998/9**

NOCTURNE IN B-FLAT MAJOR
Rosario Marciano (pf.) — **FONO FSM 53 0 36**

NOCTURNE IN B-FLAT MAJOR
Rosario Marciano (pf.) — **TURNA TV 34685**

NOCTURNE IN B-FLAT MAJOR
Nancy Fierro (pf.) — **AVANT AV 1012**

PEINE ET PLAISIR (SERGE PUSHKIN) (2'25)
Patricia Adkins Chiti (m-S),
Gian Paolo Chiti (pf.) — **EDMUS PAN NRC 5016**

POLISH PRE-ROMANTIC PIANO MUSIC
Regina Smendzianka (pf.) — **MUZA XL 0355**

POLONAISE IN F-MINOR
Georges Alexandrovitch (pf.) — **MUSID RC 782**

TAILLEFERRE, Germaine (1892-1983)

BALLADE FOR PIANO AND ORCHESTRA
Rosario Marciano (pf.) with Orchestra
of Radio Luxembourg
(cond.) Louis de Froment — **FONO FSM 53 0 42**

BALLADE FOR PIANO AND ORCHESTRA
Rosario Marciano (pf.) with Orchestra
of Radio Luxembourg
(cond.) Louis de Froment — **TURNA TV 34754**

CONCERTINO FOR HARP AND ORCHESTRA
Susan Allen (hp.) with New England
Women's Symphony
(cond.) Antonia Brico — **GALAX GAL 004**

CONCERTINO FOR HARP AND ORCHESTRA
Zabaleta (hp.), Robert White (reed drones)
with ORTF Orchestra Muskett
(cond.) Jean Martinon — **DGG DG 2530 008**

CONCERTINO FOR HARP AND ORCHESTRA
Zabaleta (hp.) with ORTF Orchestra
(cond.) Jean Martinon — **DGG DG 2543 806**

DEUX VALSES
Corre-Exejean Piano Duo — **PIEVE PV 786091**

FLEURS DE FRANCE
Leigh Kaplan (pf.) — **CAMBR C 1014**

JEUX DE PLEIN AIR, FOR TWO PIANOS
Leigh Kaplan (pf.), Susan Pitts (pf.) — **CAMBR C 1014**

JEUX DE PLEIN AIR:
CACHE-CACHE MITOULA (2'47)
Genevieve Picavet (pf.),
Bernard Picavet (pf.) — **AUVID AV 4828**

JEUX DE PLEIN AIR: LA
TIRELITENTAINE (1'45)
Genevieve Picavet (pf.), Bernard Picavet (pf.) — **AUVID AV 4828**

MARIES DE LA TOUR EIFFEL, LES:
VALSE DES DEPECHES; QUADRILLE
* * * * * * — **ADES 15501**

PARTITA: PERPETUUM MOBILE
Virginia Eskin (pf.) — **MUHER MHS 4236**

PASTORALE
Boyd (fl.), Schmidt (pf.) — **STOLA SZM 0119**

PASTORALE
Hoover (fl.), Eskin (pf.) — **LEONA LPI 104**

PASTORALE
Pratz (vln.) with Orchestra — **ACEDI SDL 2118**

PASTORALE IN D
Leigh Kaplan (pf.) — **CAMBR C 1014**

PREMIERES PROUESSES
Corre-Exejean Piano Duo — **PIEVE PV 786091**

QUADRILLE (FROM BALLET LES MARIES
DE LA TOUR EIFFEL) (3'00)
Philharmonic Orchestra
(cond.) Geoffrey Simon — **CHAND ABRD 1119**

QUARTET FOR STRINGS
Vieuxtemps Quartet — **GEMIN RAP 1010**

QUARTET FOR STRINGS
Quatuor De Provence — **CALLI CAL 1803**

SICILIENNE
Leigh Kaplan (pf.) — **CAMBR C 1014**

SICILIENNE
Rosario Marciano (pf.) — **TURNA TV 34685**

SIX CHANSONS FRANCAISES
Carol Bogard (S.), John Moriarty (pf.) — **CAMBR 2777**

SONATA FOR HARP
V. Dulova (hp.) — **MELOD D 19485 6**

SONATA FOR HARP
* * * * * * — **CLASS 0920 111**

SONATA FOR HARP
Zabaleta (hp.) — **DGG DG 2531 051**

SONATA FOR HARP
Geliot (hp.) — **HMV CO 65 12 115**

SONATA FOR VIOLIN AND PIANO,
IN C-SHARP MINOR
Joseph Roche (vln.), Paul Freed (pf.) — **VOX SVBX 55112**

SONATA NO. 1
Arnold Steinhardt (vln.), Virginia Eskin (pf.) — **NORTH NR 222**

SOUVENT UN AIR DE VERITE
* * * * * * — **CHDUM LDX 78 410**

SUITE BURLESQUE
Corre-Exejean Piano Duo — **PIEVE PV 786091**

TOMBEAU DE COUPERIN
Rosario Marciano (pf.) — **FONO FSM 53036**

VALSE DES DEPECHES (FROM BALLET LES
MARIES DE LA TOUR EIFFEL) (2'29)
Philharmonic Orchestra
(cond.) Geoffrey Simon — **CHAND ABRD 1119**

VALSE LENTE FOR DUO PIANO
Leigh Kaplan (pf.), Susan Pitts (pf.) — **CAMBR C 1014**

TAKASHIMA, Midori (1954-   )

STATUE, FOR VIOLIN AND PIANO
* * * * * * — **JAPAN JFC 8510**

TAL, Marjo (1915-   )

CHANSONS DES AMOURS DECHIRANTES **PHILI**
Catherine Sauvage (m-S.) — **SB 77 892 L**

CHANSONS DES AMOURS ET DE TENDRESSE **PHILI**
Catherine Sauvage (m-S.) — **SB 77 892 L**

COPLA DE ANDALUCIA (ANON)
Meinard Kraak (Bar.), Marjo Tal (pf.) — **CBS LSP 14514**

EL VIAJE DEL ALMA, FROM SIETE CANCIONES
ESPANOLAS (LOPE DE VEGA) (1973)
Meinard Kraak (Bar.), Marjo Tal (pf.) — **CBS LSP 14514**

HET ONBEREIKBARE, FROM ACHT
ENGELMAN LIEDEREN
Meinard Kraak (Bar.), Marjo Tal (pf.) — **CBS LSP 14514**

REED PIPE, THE (ALEXANDER BLOK) (1975)
Meinard Kraak (Bar.), Marjo Tal (pf.) — **CBS LSP 14514**

WOLKEN FROM ACHT ENGELMAN LIEDEREN
Meinard Kraak (Bar.), Marjo Tal (pf.) — **CBS LSP 14514**

TALMA, Louise (1906-   )

ALLELUIA IN FORM OF TOCCATA
Nancy Fierro (pf.) — **AVANT AV 1012**

CORONA, LA (SEVEN SONNETS BY JOHN DONNE)
FOR MIXED CHORUS A CAPPELLA
Dorian Chorale
(cond.) Harold Aks — **CRI SD 187**

DIADEM
Paul Sperry (T.) with Da Capo Chamber
Players — **NEWOR 317**

LET'S TOUCH THE SKY
* * * * * * — **TURNA SVBX 5363**

PIANO SONATA, NO. 1
Virginia Eskin (pf.) — **MUHER MHS 4236**

PIANO SONATA, NO. 2
Herbert Rogers (pf.) — **CRI SD 281**

SIX ETUDES FOR PIANO
Webster (pf.) — **DESTO DC 7117**

THREE DUOLOGUES, FOR CLARINET AND PIANO
Michael Webster (cl.), B. Webster (pf.) — **CRI SD 374**

TOCCATA, FOR ORCHESTRA
Tokyo Imperial Philharmonic Orchestra
(cond.) William Strickland — **CRI 145**

TASHJIAN, Charmian B. (1950-   )

RESAN (13'48)
Jeffrey Bradelich (d-b.), Nancy Brown (vla.),
S. Caplan (hn.), Don Horisberger (hpcd.)
with Seven Percussionists
(cond.) James MacDonald — **CAPIO CR 1001**

TATE, Phyllis (1911-   )

APPARITIONS FOR TENOR, HARMONICA,
STRING QUARTET AND PIANO
English, Lockhart with
Cardiff Festival Players — **ARGO ZRG 691**

LONG AGO IN BETHLEHEM
(MORAVIAN CAROL)
Devon Fellowship of Music — **EXONA EAS 13**

SONATA FOR CLARINET AND CELLO
Georgina Dobree (cl.), Jack Kirsten (vlc.) — **CHANT CHT 004**

SONATA FOR CLARINET AND CELLO
G. de Peyer (cl.), W. Pleeth (vlc.) — **ARGO ZRG 5475**

THREE GAELIC BALLADS
M. Price (S.), J. Lockhart (pf.) — **ARGO ZRG 691**

VIRGIN AND CHILD (CAROL)
Elizabethan Singers — **ARGO ZRG 5499**

TAUBER, Lotti (1944-   )

AUFGEHOBEN (1981)
* * * * * * — **★ ★ ★ LT 30 747**

BESTIMMUNG (1982)
* * * * * *   * * * LT 30 778

COURAGE (1982)
* * * * * *   * * * LT 30 768

I GING (1984)
* * * * * *   * * * LT 307

PLANETEN (1983)
* * * * * *   * * * LT 30 842

ROUNDABOUT WAYS (1981)
* * * * * *   * * * LT 30 720

VON ZEIT ZU ZEIT (1982)
* * * * * *   * * * LT 30 801

TE RANGI-PAI (-)

HINE E HINE (FROM A MAORI SUITE) (HEENAN)
Combined Youth Orchestras of New Zealand
(cond.) C.J. Matteuci   **KIWI SLC 72**

TEGNER, Alice Charlotte (1864-1943)

BETLEHEMS STJAERNA
Iwa Soerenson (S.)   **LKK 1**

BETLEHEMS STJAERNA
* * * * * *   **PROPR 7861**

HERDARNA
Eva Bohlin (S.)   **LKK 1**

JULDAGSMORGEN
Eva Bohlin (S.)   **LKK 1**

TELFER, Nancy Ellen (1950-)

SAILING DAY, THE (1979)
Mixed Choir with Woodwind Quintet   **WORLD WRCI 1141**

TERZIAN, Alicia (1938-)

JUEGOS PARA DIANA
Nelson Delle-Vigne Fabbri (pf.)   **PAVAN ADW 7032/3**

THREE MADRIGALS FOR WOMEN'S CHORUS
Female Chorus of San Justo
(cond.) Roberte Saccente   **QUALI 1025**

THREE PIECES ON ARMENIAN FOLK
MATERIAL, FOR STRING QUARTET, OP. 5
Quarteto Contemporaneo   **EMBA 0004**

TOCCATA
Sahan Arzruni (pf.)   **MUHER MHS 1843**

VIOLIN CONCERTO
Katanian (vln.) with Armenian
State Orchestra   **ILP 3001**

THEMMEN, Ivana Marburger (1935-)

ODE TO AKHMATOVA
Jean Kraft (m-S.), Linda Jones (pf.)   **OPONE 54**

SHELTER THIS CANDLE FROM THE WIND
Paula Seibel (S.) with Louisville Orchestra
(cond.) Jorge Mester   **LOUIS LS 767**

THERESA (1837-1913)

JOY IS LIKE THE RAIN
Mennonite Children's Choir   **CBC SM 203**

THERESE, Princess of Saxe-Altenburg and of Sweden (1836-1914)

GONDOLIERA
Carl-Axel Hallgren (Bar.),
Arnold Ostman (pf.)   **SWEDI SLT 33243**

THOMA, Annette (1886-1974)

KLEINE MESSE, DIE
Ebersberger Volksmusik   **TELEF 6 22 149 AG**

KLEINE MESSE, DIE
Roaner Saengerinnen   **EMI EMI 066 32 042**

KLEINE MESSE, DIE
Kerber Musikanten   **DAU PLPS 30 159**

KLEINE MESSE, DIE
Waakirchner Saenger
(cond.) Schmid   **AVES INT 160 807**

THOME, Diane (1942-)

ANAIS, FOR PIANO, CELLO AND TAPE (8'53)
Diane Thome (pf.), Finckel (vlc.)   **CRI SD 437**

NOMBRES, LOS, FOR PIANO,
PERCUSSION AND COMPUTER
* * * * * *   **TULST - - -**

YEW TREE, THE (9'31)
Montserrat Alavedra (S.) with Contemporary
Group of University of Washington
(cond.) Michel Singher   **CRYST S 257**

TIMMERMANN, Leni (1901-)

BUNTE BAELLCHEN, DAS
* * * * * *   **KOLIB 33083**

CHRISTIAN BRÜCKNER LIEST
WEIHNACHTSGESCHICHTEN
Christian Brueckner (narr.)   **FSM 43518**

GEHST DU DER SONNE ENTGEGEN
* * * * * *   **OCEAN 33066**

LIEDER AUS DEM SAÜRLAND
* * * * * *   **SUN SR 1001**

MIRACLE IN BETHLEHEM
John Scott (org.) with
Louis Halsey Singers   **PEARL SHE 581**

WEIHNACHTSERWARTUNG
* * * * * *   **OCEAN 133 068**

TISSOT, Mireille (-)

MEDITATION FUER ORGEL
Mireille Tissot (org.)   **PSALL PET 176 060 875**

TORRENS, Grace (-)

HOW PANSIES GROW
Michael Aspinall (S.)   **ACEDI SDD 507**

TOWER, Joan (1938-)

AMAZON (1977)
Da Capo Chamber Players   **CRI SD 517**

BREAKFAST RHYTHMS ONE AND TWO, FOR
CLARINET AND FIVE INSTRUMENTS (1975)
Da Capo Chamber Players   **CRI S 354**

HEXACHORDS FOR FLUTE
Da Capo Chamber Players — **CRI S 354**

MOVEMENTS
Spencer (fl.), Joan Tower (pf.) — **ADVAN FGR 245**

NOON DANCE (1982)
Da Capo Chamber Players — **CRI SD 517**

PETROUSHSKATES (5'32)
Da Capo Chamber Players — **CRI SD 441**

PLATINUM SPIRALS, FOR SOLO VIOLIN (1976)
Joe Smirnoff (vln.) — **CRI SD 517**

PRELUDE FOR FIVE PLAYERS (1970)
Da Capo Chamber Players: J. Tower (pf.),
P. Spencer (fl.), J. Lester (vln.),
A. Blustine (cl.), H. Harbison (vlc.) — **CRI SD 302**

SEQUOIA FOR ORCHESTRA
St. Louis Symphony Orchestra
(cond.) Leonard Slatkin — **NONSU 9 79118 1 F**

WINGS, FOR SOLO CLARINET (1981)
Laura Flaz (cl.) — **CRI SD 517**

TOYAMA, Michiko Francoise (1913-)

AOI NO UE (PRINCESS HOLLYHOCK)
(FOR TAPE AND NARRATION)
Beate Gordon (narr.) with Tape — **FOLKW FW 8881**

JAPANESE SUITE
Juilliard Student Orchestra
(cond.) Michiko Toyama — **FOLKW FW 8881**

TAKAI YAMA KARA (FROM
THE HIGH MOUNTAINS)
Hana Ito (S.) — **FOLKW FW 8881**

TORIANSE (LET US PASS)
Hana Ito (S.) — **FOLKW FW 8881**

VOICE OF YAMATO, FOR SOPRANO
AND ORCHESTRA
Rassmussen (S.) with Juilliard Student
Orchestra — **FOLKW FW 8881**

WAKA, FOR TAPE AND NARRATION
Beate Gordon (narr.) with tape — **FOLKW FW 8881**

TREADWAY, Maude Valerie (-)

FIVE POEMS (JUDITH HELEN BROWN)
Maude Valerie Treadway (m-S.) — **ORION ORS 84476**

TREVALSA, Joan (-)

MY TREASURE
Michael Aspinall (S.) — **ACEDI SDD 507**

TURNER, Mildred Cozzens (1897-)

HAWAII CALLS AT TWILIGHT
* * * * * * — **CAPIT T 1152**

I WISH THEY DIDN'T MEAN GOODBYE
* * * * * * — **DECCA 9 31057**

TYRMAND, Eta Moiseyevna (1917-)

POEM FOR VIOLIN AND PIANO
R. Nodel (vln.), N. Temkina (pf.) — **MELOD D 31427 8**

TYSON, Mildred Lund (-)

SEA MOODS, FOR MIXED
CHORUS AND PIANO
* * * * * * — **RCAV LM 1870**

UCHENDU, Nellie Uzonna Edith (1953-)

AKA BU EZE
* * * * * * — **HOMZY HCE 012**

EZIGBO DIM
* * * * * * — **DECCA DWAPS 2168**

LOVE NWANTINTI
* * * * * * — **HOMZY HCE 013**

MAMA-AUSA
* * * * * * — **DECCA DWAPS 2066**

YEGHEYEGHE
* * * * * * — **DECCA DWAPS 2168**

ULEHLA, Ludmila (1923-)

ELEGY FOR A WHALE
Hoover, (fl.), Brey (vlc.), Weintraub (pf.)
with Whales from Pacific and
Atlantic Oceans — **LEONA LPI 104**

USTVOLSKAYA, Galina Ivanovna (1919-)

CHILDREN'S SUITE
Leningrad State Philharmonic
Society Orchestra
(cond.) E. Mravinsky — **MELOD 04430/31**

CONCERTO FOR PIANO AND ORCHESTRA,
IN G-MINOR
P. Serebryakov (pf.) with Leningrad
Philharmonic Chamber Orchestra — **MELOD SM 02439/40**

LIGHTS IN THE STEPPE
Symphony Orchestra of Leningrad
Philharmonic Society
(cond.) Yansons — **MELOD 010305/06**

OCTET FOR TWO OBOES, FOUR
VIOLINS, TIMBALES AND PIANO
Kosoyan (ob.), Chinakov (ob.),
Stangh (vln.), Liskovich (vln.),
Dukor (vln.), Saakov (vln.),
Znamensky (timbales), Karandashova
(pf.) — **MELOD C 10 07151/2**

SONATA NO. 3, FOR PIANO
O. Malov (pf.) — **MELOD C 10 07151/2**

UYTTENHOVE, Yolande (1925-)

CENDRILLON FOR PIANO, FOUR HANDS
Renaud De Macq (pf.),
Yolande Uyttenhove (pf.) — **FLY F 40 714**

SONATA FOR VIOLIN AND PIANO, OP. 95 (1980)
Fernand Leonard (vln.),
Yolande Uyttenhove (pf.) — **EMS SB 001**

VAN APPLEDORN, Mary Jeanne (1927-)

BONNIE BARNETT'S TUNNEL HUM (1984)
* * * * * * — **OPONE 110**

COMMUNIQUE
Judith Klinger (S.) M.J. Van Appledorn (pf.) — **OPONE 52**

CONCERTO FOR TRUMPET AND CONCERT BAND
Birch (trp.) with Texas Technical
University Symphonic Band
(cond.) Sudduth   **OPONE 110**

PASSACAGLIA AND CHORALE
Texas Technical University Symphonic Band
(cond.) Sudduth   **OPONE 110**

SET OF FIVE
Virginia Eskin (pf.)   **NORTH NR 204**

SET OF FIVE
Mary Jeanne van Appledorn (pf.)   **OPONE 52**

SONNET FOR ORGAN
Maynard (org.)   **OPONE 43**

VAN DE VATE, Nancy Hayes (1930-   )

CONCERT PIECE FOR VIOLONCELLO
AND SMALL ORCHESTRA
Elizabeth Goy (vlc.) with New England
Women's Symphony
(cond.) Miriam Barnot-Webb   **GALAX GAL 004**

MUSIC FOR VIOLA, PERCUSSION AND PIANO
Johnson (vla.), Wiley (perc.),
Zuckerman (pf.)   **ORION ORS 80386**

NINE PRELUDES
Max Lifchitz (pf.)   **OPONE 118**

NINE PRELUDES FOR PIANO
Max Lifchitz (pf.)   **OPONE - - -**

SECOND SONATA FOR PIANO
Paula Ennis-Dwyer (pf.)   **CORON - - -**

SONATA (1978)
Rosemary Platt (pf.)   **CORON LPS 3105**

SONATA FOR VIOLA AND PIANO
Johnson (vla.), Unger (pf.)   **ORION ORS 83444**

STRING QUARTET, NO. 1
Ridge String Quartet   **ORION ORS 83444**

VAN EPEN-DE GROOT, Else Antonia (1919-   )

EPISODES FROM THE BIBLE, VOL. 1
International Studio Orchestra
(cond.) Hugh Granville   **DW LP 3051**

EPISODES FROM THE BIBLE, VOL. 2
Dutch Chamber Orchestra
(cond.) Else van Epen-De Groot   **DW LP 3241**

JACQUELINE WALTZ
Orchestra
(cond.) Jos Cleber   **PHILI PF 318650**

KLOP OP DE DEUR, DE
Orchestra
(cond.) Hugo de Groot   **CNR 141106**

MUSIC FOR A HISTORICAL ERA
(AS DEREK LAREN)
Symphonic Ensemble
(cond.) Hugo de Groot   **DW LP 2852**

WALTZ THEME FROM FILM HET HUIS
Orchestra
(cond.) Hugo de Groot   **CNR 141106**

VAN SOLDT, Suzanna (-   )

ALMANDE
Garnier (vir.)   **ARION ARN 36572**

ALMANDE BRUN SMEEDELIN
Garnier (vir.)   **ARION ARN 36572**

ALMANDE D'AMOUR
Garnier (vir.)   **ARION ARN 36572**

ALMANDE DE LA NONNETTE
Garnier (vir.)   **ARION ARN 36572**

ALMANDE PRYNCE
Garnier (vir.)   **ARION ARN 36572**

DE FRANCE GALLIARD
Garnier (vir.)   **ARION ARN 36572**

VANIER, Jeannine (1929-   )

CINQ PIECES ENFANTINES
* * * * * *   **BMI - - -**

FANTASIE (2'02)
Mario Duschenes Recorder Trio   **BAROQ BC 1857**

SALVE REGINA
Montreal Bach Choir   **RCI 206**

VARGAS, Eva (-   )

VON ZEIT ZU ZEIT FOR VOICE AND GUITAR
Eva Vargas (vce. and gtr.)   **CANTA 656014**

WENN GOTT ES WILL FOR VOICE AND GUITAR
Eva Vargas (vce. and gtr.)   **CANTA 656014**

VEIGA OLIVEIRA, Sofia Helena da (-   )

MURMURIOS DE UM REGATO (GUIMARAES)
L. Prioli (m-S.), S. Asprino (pf.)   **ASC 103**

VELLERE, Lucie (1896-1966)

CHANSONNETTES FOR CHILDREN'S
CHOIR AND PIANO
Pavane D'Argenteuil Chorale   **DISPT PT 119**

QUARTET FOR FOUR CLARINETS
Ancion, Segers, Gerard, Zinque (cl qrt.)   **MIXTR
MXT DB 276**

STRING QUARTET, NO. 3
Crescent Quartet: Alicia Edelberg, Nancy
Diggs, Jill Jaffe, Maxine Neuman   **LEONA LPI 111**

VERCOE, Elizabeth (1941-   )

FANTASY (1975)
Rosemary Platt (pf.)   **CORON LPS 3105**

HERSTORY II (13 JAPANESE LYRICS
FOR SOPRANO, PIANO AND
PERCUSSION) (17'45)
Elsa Charlston (S.), Randal Hodgkin
son (pf.), Dean Anderson (perc.)
(cond.) Richard Pittman   **NORTH NR 221**

IRREVERIES FROM SAPPHO (1981) (6'12)
Sharon Mabry (S.), Rosemary Platt (pf.)   **CORON LPS 3127**

SYNAPSE FOR VIOLA AND COMPUTER
Thompson   **CRI S 393**

SYNTHESISM
Princeton University Computer Center   **NONSU 71245**

VIARDOT-GARCIA, Pauline Michelle Ferdinande (1821-1910)

CENDRILLON
Price, Eaves, Harlte, Busch, Adams,
Fieldsend, Lawlor, Leggo (pf.)   **UNOPR UORC 136**

DITES QUE FAUT-IL FAIRE
Mertine Johns (m-S.), Roger Rundle (pf.)   **GEMIN RAP 1010**

FLÜSTERN, ATHEMSCHEUS, LAÜSCHEN
Mertine Johns (m-S.), Roger Rundle (pf.)   **GEMIN RAP 1010**

PUSHKIN SONGS: DES NACHTS; DAS
VOEGLEIN; DIE BESCHWOERUNG
John Ostendorf (B-Bar.),
Rudolph Palmer (pf.)   **LEONA LPI 107**

STERNE, DIE: ICH STARRTE UND
STAND UNBEWEGLICH
Mertine Johns (m-S.), Y. Cable (vlc.),
M. May (pf.)   **GEMIN RAP 1010**

VITO-DELVAUX, Berthe di (1915-   )

CHAMELLE A MARIER, LA, FOR VOICE
AND WIND QUINTET
* * * * * *   **BUFCM BCB 101**

SUITE FOR STRING QUARTET
* * * * * *   **ALPHA LC 2007**

VIVADO ORSINI, Ida (1916-   )

ESTUDIOS (FIFTEEN STUDIES FOR PIANO)
Elvira Savi (pf.)   **INSTI - - -**

VLAD, Marina (-   )

PIANO SONATA
Serban Soreanu (pf.)   **ELECT ST ECE 02442**

STRING QUARTET NO. 2
George Enescu String Quartet   **ELECT ST ECE 02442**

VON ZIERITZ, Greta (1899-   )

SUITE FOR VIOLA (1976) (12'32)
Claude Lelong (vla.)   **MARUS 308 329**

VONDRACKOVA, Helena (-   )

FILM MELODIES
* * * * * *   **SUPRA 1 13 1805**

ISLE OF HELENA
Prague Radio Dance Orchestra
(cond.) Vobruba   **SUPRA 1 13 0857**

VORLOVA, Slavka (1894-1973)

EMERGENCE, OP. 93, FOR
VIOLIN AND ORCHESTRA
Bruno Belcik (vln.) with Moravia
Philharmonic Orchestra
(cond.) Jaromir Nohejl   **SUPRA 1 19 1575 G**

IMMANENCE, OP. 87, FOR FLUTE, BASS
CLARINET, PIANO AND PERCUSSION
Munclinger (fl.), J. Horak (b-cl.),
Kovarnova (pf.), Satava (perc.) and
Kiesliech (perc.)   **SUPRA 1 19 1235 G**

WALDO, Elisabeth (1923-   )

DE ANZA MARCH, THE
Elisabeth Waldo Orchestra   **SOUTH PSO 002**

ENTRANCE OF THE PIZZARO, FOR ORCHESTRA
Elisabeth Waldo Orchestra   **GNPCR 603**

REALM OF THE INCAS
Elisabeth Waldo Orchestra   **GNPCR 603**

RITES OF THE PAGAN
Elisabeth Waldo Orchestra   **GNPCR 601**

SERPENT AND THE EAGLE, THE
Elisabeth Waldo Orchestra   **GNPCR 601**

VIVA CALIFORNIA
St. Charles Choir and Elisabeth Waldo
Folklorico Orchestra   **SOUTH PSO 002**

WALKER, Louise (-   )

SMALL VARIATIONS ON A
CATALONIAN FOLK SONG
Louise Walker (gtr.)   **SUPRA 1 11 1230**

WANG, Jiu-Fang (1937-   )

RED LADY (WITH JU WEI) (12'33)
Shanghai Philharmonic Orchestra
(cond.) Huang Yi-jun   **HONGK HK 6 340163**

WANG, Qiang (1935-   )

FOLK DANCE-JIU-JIE-BIAN (NINE-JOIN-WHIP)
* * * * * *   **CHINA DL - - -**

GA DA MEI LIN, CELLO CONCERTO
Gao Long (vlc.) with Shanghai
Symphony Orchestra
(cond.) Cao Peng   **CHINA DL 0019**

RIVERS OF HAPPINESS, CANTATA
* * * * * *   **CHINA DL 0108**

TRUMPET AND DRUM
Shanghai Philharmonic Orchestra
(cond.) Cao Peng   **HONGK 6 340163**

WARREN, Elinor Remick (1906-   )

ABRAM IN EGYPT, FOR CHORUS
AND ORCHESTRA
Ronald Lewis (Bar.) with Roger Wagner
Chorale and London Philharmonic Orchestra
(cond.) Roger Wagner   **CRI 172**

SUITE FOR ORCHESTRA
Oslo Philharmonic Orchestra
(cond.) William Strickland   **CRI 172**

WEIGL, Vally (1889-1982)

BRIEF ENCOUNTERS, FOR WIND QUARTET
City Winds   **ORION 80393**

DEAR EARTH (1956) (QUINTET)
R. Shiesley (Bar.), M. Dubow (vln.),
D. Moore (vlc.), P. Gordon (hn.),
I. Sass (pf.)   **ORION 80393**

ECHOES FROM POEMS, FOR CLARINET,
VIOLIN, HORN AND PIANO
J. Bunke (cl.), M. Dubow (vln.),
P. Gordon (hn.), I. Sass (pf.)   **MUHER MHS 3880**

LYRICAL SUITE, FOR MEZZO SOPRANO,
CLARINET, CELLO AND PIANO
L. Muller (m-S.), J. Bunke (cl.),
K. Moore (vlc.), I. Sass (pf.)   **MUHER MHS 3880**

NATURE MOODS, FOR TENOR,
CLARINET AND VIOLIN
George Shirley (T.), Stanley Drucker (cl.),
Kenneth Gordon (vln.)　　　　　**CRI SD 326**

NEW ENGLAND SUITE, FOR CLARINET,
PIANO AND CELLO
Stanley Drucker (cl.), Ilse Sass (pf.),
Kermit Moore (vlc.)　　　　　**CRI SD 326**

SONGS OF LOVE AND LEAVING
S. Love (m-S.), D. Holloway (Bar.),
R. Woitach (pf.), L. Sobol (cl.)　　　　　**ORION 80393**

SONGS, FROM DO NOT AWAKE ME, FOR
BARITONE, CLARINET AND PIANO
D. Holloway (Bar.), J. Bunke (cl.),
Vally Weigl (pf.)　　　　　**MUHER MHS 3880**

SONGS, FROM NO BOUNDARY, FOR
MEZZO SOPRANO, VIOLA AND PIANO
L. Miller (m-S.), K. Phillips (vla.),
Vally Weigl (pf.)　　　　　**MUHER MHS 3880**

WEISS, Helen L. (1920-1948)

I AM THE PEOPLE, CANTATA
* * * * * *　　　　　**FELLO FM 1 FS 1**

WHITE, Maude Valerie (1855-1937)

CHANTEZ, CHANTEZ, JEUNE INSPIREE
Felicity Lott (S.)　　　　　**HARMU HMC 1138**

SO WE'LL GO NO MORE A ROVING
Gervase Elwes (T.)　　　　　**OPAL 806**

WHITE, Ruth S. (1925-)

FLOWERS OF EVIL
* * * * * *　　　　　**LIMET LS 86058**

PINIONS
* * * * * *　　　　　**LIMET LS 86058**

SEVEN TRUMPS FOR TAROT CARDS
* * * * * *　　　　　**LIMET LS 86058**

SHORT CIRCUITS
Ruth White　　　　　**ANGEL S 36042**

WHITEHEAD, Gillian (1941-)

CADENZA SIA CORTA, LA
Bruce Field (pf.)　　　　　**KIWI SLD 50**

FANTASIA ON THREE NOTES
Tessa Birnie (pf.)　　　　　**KIWI SLD 19**

MISSA BREVIS (SANCTUS,
BENEDICTUS, AGNUS DEI)
Auckland Dorian Choir
(cond.) Peter Godfrey　　　　　**KIWI SLD 56**

QUI NATUS EST (ANON)
Cathy MacDonald (S.), Elizabeth Dickson (S.)
with University of Auckland Festival Choir
(cond.) Peter Godfrey　　　　　**KIWI SLD 31**

WIENIAWSKA, Irene Regine (1880-1932)

IMPRESSION FAUSSE
Mertine Johns (m-S.), Roger Rundle (pf.)　**GEMIN RAP 1010**

TANGO
* * * * * *　　　　　**RCA ARM 4 0942 7**

WIKSTROM, Inger (-)

AN DIE MUSIK, OP. 12, NO. 2 (2'45)
Chesne Ryman (S.), Inger Wikstrom (pf.)　**BLUE BELL 144**

DU BIST DIE ZUKUNFT, GROSSES
MORGENROT, OP. NO. 3 (3'16)
Kerstin Meyer (m-S.), Inger Wikstrom (pf.)　**BLUE BELL 144**

LIEBESLIED, OP. 12, NO. 1 (2'25)
Chesne Ryman (S.), Inger Wikstrom (pf.)　**BLUE BELL 144**

ORFEUS EURYDIKE HERMES, OP. 11 (16'10)
Kerstin Meyer (m-S.), Inger Wikstrom (pf.)　**BLUE BELL 144**

SECHS LIEDER, OP. 10 (11'36)
Chesne Ryman (S.), Inger Wikstrom (pf.)　**BLUE BELL 144**

WILCOCK, Anthea (-)

CHRISTUS NATUS EST
Exeter Musical Society　　　　　**EXONA EAS 13**

WILHELMINA, Sophie Friederike, Princess of Prussia (1709-1758)

CONCERTO FOR HARPSICHORD AND
ORCHESTRA, IN G-MINOR
J.B. Hoffman (hpcd.) with Chamber
Orchestra of Venice
(cond.) Franco Piva　　　　　**MONDI MON 11002**

CONCERTO FOR HARPSICHORD AND
ORCHESTRA, IN G-MINOR
Hilda Langfort (hpcd.) with Austrian
Tonkuenstler Orchestra, Vienna
(cond.) Dietfried Bernet　　　　　**MUHER MHS 660**

WILKINSON, Constance Jane (1944-)

PHOENIX 1, FOR HARP
Elizabeth Blakeslee (hp.)　　　　　**OPONE 117**

WILLIAMS, Grace Mary (1906-1977)

AVE MARIS STELLA
Richard Hickox Singers with City of
London Sinfonia
(cond.) Richard Hickox　　　　　**CHAND ABRD 1116**

BALLADS
BBC Orchestra
(cond.) Vernon Handley　　　　　**BBC REG L 381**

CARILLONS FOR OBOE AND ORCHESTRA
Camden (ob.) with London Symphony
Orchestra (cond.) Sir Charles Groves　**ORIEL ORM 1005**

CARILLONS, FOR OBOE AND ORCHESTRA
Camden (ob.) with London Symphony
Orchestra (cond.) Sir Charles Groves　**EMI ASD 3006**

CHORAL SUITE – THE DANCERS
Eiddwen Harrhy (S.), Caryl Thomas (hp.),
Richard Hickox Singers with City of
London Sinfonia
(cond.) Richard Hickox　　　　　**CHAND ABRD 1116**

CONCERTO FOR TRUMPET AND ORCHESTRA
Snell (trp.) with London Symphony
Orchestra
(cond.) Sir Charles Groves　　　　　**EMI ASD 3006**

CONCERTO FOR TRUMPET AND ORCHESTRA
Snell (trp.) with London Symphony
Orchestra
(cond.) Sir Charles Groves　　　　　**ORIEL ORM 1005**

FAIREST OF STARS, FOR SOPRANO
AND ORCHESTRA
J. Price (S.) with London Symphony
Orchestra (cond.) Sir Charles Groves **EMI ASD 3006**

FAIREST OF STARS, FOR SOPRANO
AND ORCHESTRA
J. Price (S.) with London Symphony
Orchestra
(cond.) Sir Charles Groves **ORIEL ORM 1005**

FANTASIA ON WELSH NURSERY TUNES
London Symphony Orchestra
(cond.) Sir Charles Groves **EMI ASD 3006**

FANTASIA ON WELSH NURSERY TUNES
London Symphony Orchestra
(cond.) Sir Charles Groves **ORIEL ORM 1005**

HARP SONG OF THE DANE WOMEN
(KIPLING) (1975)
Caryl Thomas (hp.), Frank LLoyd
(hn.), Christopher Larkin (hn.),
Richard Hickox Singers with
City of London Sinfonia
(cond.) Richard Hickox **CHAND ABRD 1116**

MARINERS' SONG (BEDDOES)
Caryl Thomas (hp.) with Richard Hickox
Singers and City of London Sinfonia
(cond.) Richard Hickox **CHAND ABRD 1116**

PENILLION (1955)
Royal Philharmonic Orchestra
(cond.) Sir Charles Groves **EMI ASD 2739**

PENILLION (1955)
Royal Philharmonic Orchestra
(cond.) Sir Charles Groves **ORIEL ORM 1001**

SEA SKETCHES
English Chamber Orchestra
(cond.) Atherton **DECCA SXL 6468**

SIX POEMS BY GERALD MANLEY HOPKINS
Helen Watts (Cont.) with City of London
Sinfonia Sextet **CHAND ABRD 1116**

SYMPHONY NO. 2
BBC Orchestra
(cond.) Vernon Handley **BBC REG L 381**

WELSH SONGS (TRADITIONAL,
ARR. WILLIAMS)
Margaret Price (S.), James Lockhart (pf.) **OISEU SOL 345**

WILLIAMS, Mary Lou (1910-1981)

ANIMA CHRISTI
Mitchell (vce.), Johnson (b-cl.),
Gales (d-b), Green (gtr). with George
Gordon Singers **FOLKW FJ 2843**

BLACK CHRIST OF THE ANDES
(ST. MARTIN DE PORRES)
Mary Lou Williams (pf.) with Howard
Robert's Chorus **FOLKW FJ 2843**

DEVIL, THE (CHORALE VOCAL)
Howard Robert's Chorus **FOLKW FJ 2843**

DIRGE BLUES
Mary Lou Williams (pf.) **FOLKW FJ 2843**

FUNGUS AMUNGUS, A
Mary Lou Williams (pf.) **FOLKW FJ 2843**

GLORIA
Milton Suggs (B.), Mary Lou Williams (pf.),
Tony Waters (conga) **FOLKW FTS 33901**

GRAND NITE FOR SWINGING, A
Percy Heath (B.), Mary Lou Williams (pf.) **FOLKW FJ 2843**

IT AIN'T NECESSARILY SO
Mary Lou Williams (pf.) **FOLKW FJ 2843**

KANSAS CITY JAZZ
* * * * * * **DECCA DL 8044**

KEYBOARD HISTORY, A
* * * * * * **JAZZT 1206**

MARY LOU WILLIAMS LIVE AT THE COOKERY
* * * * * * **CHIAR CR 146**

MISS D.D.
Mary Lou Williams (pf.) **FOLKW FJ 2843**

MY BLUE HEAVEN
Percy Heath (B.), Mary Lou Williams (pf.),
Tim Kennedy (perc.) **FOLKW FJ 2843**

PRAISE THE LORD
J. Mitchell (vce.), B. Johnson (vce.),
G. Green (gtr.), P. Brice (perc.) **FOLKW FJ 2843**

ZONING FUNGUS II
Mary Lou Williams (pf.), Zita Carno (pf.),
Bob Cranshaw (B.), Mickey Roker (dr.) **FOLKW FTS 33901**

WINTER, Sister Miriam Therese (1938-   )

GOLD, INCENSE AND MYRRH (CONTEMPORARY
CHRISTMAS CAROLS)
Medical Mission Sisters and Friends **AVANT AVS 136**

I KNOW THE SECRET
* * * * * * **AVANT AVS 105**

JOY IS LIKE THE RAIN
* * * * * * **AVANT AVS 101**

KNOCK, KNOCK
* * * * * * **AVANT AVS 109**

SEASONS
* * * * * * **AVANT AVS 126**

WITKIN, Beatrice (1916-   )

BREATH AND SOUNDS, FOR TUBA AND TWO
TRACK ELECTRONIC TAPE
Hanks (tba.) with Tape **OPONE 12**

CHIAROSCURO, FOR CELLO AND PIANO
Robert Sylvester (vlc.), Zita Carno (pf.) **OPONE 10**

CONTOUR, FOR PIANO
Zita Carno (pf.) **OPONE 10**

DUO, FOR VIOLIN AND PIANO
Louis Simon (vln.), Zita Carno (pf.) **OPONE 10**

INTERLUDES, FOR FLUTE
Paul Klinkel (fl.) **OPONE 12**

PARAMETERS, FOR EIGHT INSTRUMENTS
* * * * * * **OPONE 12**

PROSE POEM, FOR SOPRANO, NARRATOR,
HORN, CELLO AND PERCUSSION
J. Kraft (m-S.), J. Silver (narr.),
B. Tillotson (hn.), R. Sylverster (vlc.)
R. des Roches (perc.)
(cond.) A. Brehm **OPONE 10**

TRIADS AND THINGS, FOR BRASS QUINTET
* * * * * * **OPONE 12**

WITNI, Monica (-   )

SUMMER HOLIDAY
* * * * * * **AGON 102**

SWEET ONE
* * * * * *　　　　　　　　　　**AGON 102**

TWILIGHT SERENADE
* * * * * *　　　　　　　　**PLANC OOX 12**

WOLF-COHEN, Veronika (1944-)

BAT-DAVID
Robin Heifetz　　　　　　**FOLKW FS 533878**

WOLL, Erna (1917-)

ALLE ZEIT IST GOTTES ZEIT
Church Singers
(cond.) Karl Berg　　　　　**FIDUL FF 1135**

DU HAST UNS GERUFEN (CHILDREN'S MASS)　　**CHRIS**
* * * * * *　　　　　　　　　**SEV 75144**

ES BEGAB SICH ABER
Wilhelm Precker (org.) with Chamber Chorus
of Pedagogic College,
Rheinland/Cologne　　　　　　**LAUMA**
(cond.) G. Speer　　　　　**LAU 280970**

FEIER DER WEIHNACHT
Church Singers
(cond.) Karl Berg　　　　　**FIDUL FF 3020**

FEIER DES ADVENT
Church Singers
(cond.) Karl Berg　　　　　**FIDUL FF 3010**

FORT-MOTETTEN, LE
Lower Rhineland Chamber Choir of
Viersen-Dulken
(cond.) H.J. Roth　　　　　**EMI F 665705**

GOTT, WIR SUCHEN DICH　　　　　**LAUMA**
Church Singers
(cond.) Karl Berg　　　　**LAU 3 007 111271**

LIEDER VON NEUEN LEBEN
* * * * * *　　　　　　　　**FIDUL FF 1201**

MESSE FÜR KINDER
* * * * * *　　　　　　　　**FIDUL FF 1149**

MESSE FÜR KINDER UND IHRE ELTERN　　**LAUMA**
* * * * * *　　　　　　　　**LAU 230370**

NEUE LIEDER ZUR FEIER　　　　　**LAUMA**
* * * * * *　　　　　　　**LAU W 76 210675**

NEUE LIEDER ZUR VERLOBUNG UND
HOCHZEIT: DASEIN FÜREINANDER
Church Singers
(cond.) Karl Berg　　　　　**FIDUL FF 1202**

STERN, GOLDNER STERN
* * * * * *　　　　　　　　**FIDUL FF 1240**

SUESSES SAITENSPIEL
Wilfred Jochims (T.) with Chamber
Choir of the Duelken High School　　**CAMER**
(cond.) H.J. Roth　　　　　**EMS 17121 EP**

WIR GLAUBEN (MASS)
* * * * * *　　　　　　　　**FIDUL FF 1148**

WIR LOBEN DICH
* * * * * *　　　　　　**CHRIS SELP 75527**

WOODFORDE-FINDEN, Amy (-1919)

ALLAH BE WITH US (TOWNE)
Carole Rosen (Cont.), David Wilson-
Johnson (Bar.), A. Saunders (pf.)　**HYPER A 66063**

KASHMIRI SONG (PALE HANDS I LOVED)
Molyneux (m-S), Van Asch (B.),
Miall (pf.)　　　　　　**DESTO DC 6449**

KASHMIRI SONG (PALE HANDS I LOVED)
Benjamin Luxon (Bar.),　　　　**DECCA**
S. Burrows (T.)　　　　　**DEC 411 642 1**

WYLIE, Betty Jane (-)

BEOWULF (WITH VICTOR DAVIES)
Vocal Soloists with Holiday Festival Singers
with Winipeg Symphony Orchestra　**IND LFR 1 83**

WYLIE, Ruth Shaw (1916-)

PSYCHOGRAM, OP. 25, FOR PIANO
Rosemary Catanese (pf.)　　　　**CRI SD 353**

XENOPOL, Margareta (1928-1979)

ALLONS MARIN
Valentin Teodorian Male Choir　　**ELECT EPC 5087**

CHANT D'AUTOMNE
Valentin Teodorian (T.)　　　**ELECT EPE 01490**

FOUR ROMANCES
Angela Moldovan (S.)　　　　**ELECT 1012**

FUMEE BLEUE DE CIGARETTE
C. Dumitrescu (S.)　　　　**ELECT EPE 10461**

J'AI VOULU TE FUIR
Sonia Cruceru (S.)　　　　**ELECT 789**

J'AI VOULU TE FUIR
Sonia Cruceru (S.)　　　　**ELECT EDC 683**

J'AI VOULU TE FUIR
Lizeta Chirculescu (S.)　　　**ELECT EPE 02419**

J'AIME COMME JE N'AI JAMAIS AIME
Angela Moldovan (S.)　　　　**ELECT EPC 588**

JE REST A TE REGARDER
C. Dumitrescu (S.)　　　　**ELECT EPC 10461**

JOURS PASSENT, MAIS L'AMOUR
DEMEURRE, LES
Pusa Neicu (T.)　　　　**ELECT EPE 01490**

NOCTURNE
Angela Moldovan (S.)　　　　**ELECT EPC 10129**

POURQUOI JE ME LIE D'UN REVE
Lizeta Chirculescu (S.)　　　**ELECT EPE 01446**

QUE TU OUBLIE LA ROMANCE
Angela Moldovan (S.)　　　　**ELECT EPC 10129**

RETOUR
Lizeta Chirculescu (S.)　　　**ELECT EPC 10461**

ROMANCE DE L'AUTOMNE, LA
Elena Cernei (S.)　　　　**ELECT EPE 0936**

ROMANCE DE L'AUTOMNE, LA
Angela Moldovan (S.)　　　　**ELECT EPC 10129**

ROMANCE DE L'AUTOMNE, LA
Dorel Livianu (S.)　　　　**ELECT EPE 01534**

ROMANCE DU COEUR, LA
Elena Cernei (S.)　　　　**ELECT EPE 0936**

ROMANCE DU COUR, LA
Angela Moldovan (S.)　　　　**ELECT EPC 10129**

ROMANCES SANS MUSIQUE
Lizeta Chirculescu (S.)　　　**ELECT EPD 1240**

SI TU VEUX QUI JE MEURE
Elena Cernei (S.)　　　　**ELECT EPE 0936**

THREE ROMANCES
Elena Cernei (S.)　　　　**ELECT EPE 0936**

TOUJOURS LA MER
Lizeta Chirculescu (S.)　　　**ELECT EPC 10461**

YAGLING, Victoria (1946-   )

SUITE FOR VIOLONCELLO AND
STRING ORCHESTRA
Victoria Yagling (vlc.) with
Roskontserta
Chamber Orchestra
(cond.) Georgi Vetwitski   **MELOD**
                                            C 10 19803 002

YAMASHITA, Mika (1968-   )

DANCE OF A COMIC DOLL (6'03)   **RJOCR**
Mika Yamashita (pf.)   **YL 8102 3 19 282**

YOGUCHI, Rie (1971-   )

FANTASY OF CHATEAU AND
THE SILHOUETTE (5'48)   **RJOCR**
Rie Yoguchi (pf.)   **YL 8102 3 19 282**

YOUNG, Jane Corner (1915-   )

DRAMATIC SOLILOQUY FOR PIANO (1961)
Arthur Loesser (pf.)   **CRI 183**

WE PEOPLE (1967)
Phyllis Brown (S.), Warren Downs (vlc.)
Jane Young (pf.)   **ADVEN USR 5005**

YOUSE, Glad Robinson (1898-   )

APRIL IS FOREVER, FOR WOMEN'S
CHORUS AND PIANO
* * * * * *   **GOLDE CRS 4138**

MY DREAM OF SPRINGTIME, FOR
SOLO SOPRANO AND PIANO
* * * * * *   **GOLDE CRS 4138**

SALUTE TO AMERICA, A, FOR MIXED
CHORUS AND PIANO
* * * * * *   **DDREC 1075**

SOME LOVELY THING, FOR SOLO
SOPRANO AND PIANO
* * * * * *   **GOLDE CRS 4138**

THIS NATION UNDER GOD, FOR MIXED
CHORUS AND PIANO
* * * * * *   **DDREC 1075**

THOU WILT LIGHT MY CANDLE, FOR SOLO
SOPRANO AND PIANO
* * * * * *   **GOLDE CRS 4138**

ZAIMONT, Judith Lang (1945-   )

CALENDAR SET, A (TWELVE PRELUDES
FOR SOLO PIANO)
Gary Steigerwalt (pf.)   **LEONA LPI 101**

CHANSONS NOBLES ET SENTIMENTALES,
FOR HIGH VOICE AND PIANO
Charles Bressler (T.), Judith Zaimont (pf.) **LEONA LPI 101**

GREYED SONNETS
E. Olbrycht (S.), Judith Zaimont (pf.)   **GOLDE ATH 5051**

MAGIC WORLD, THE (RITUAL MUSIC FOR
THREE) (1979) (23'00)
David Evitts (Bar.), Alan
Feinberg (pf.), Richard Fitz (perc.)   **LEONA LPI 116**

NOCTURNE: LA FIN DE SIECLE
Judith Zaimont (pf.)   **LEONA LPI 101**

SONGS OF INNOCENCE, FOR SOPRANO,
TENOR, FLUTE, CELLO AND HARP
E. Olbrycht (S.), P. Browne (T.),
P. Spencer (fl.), B. Bogatin (vlc.),
N. Allen (hp.)
(cond.) R. Nierenberg   **GOLDE ATH 5051**

SUNNY AIRS AND SOBER (A BOOK
OF MADRIGALS)
Gregg Smith Singers: R. Rees (S.),
P. Magdamo (A.)
(cond.) Gregg Smith   **GOLDE ATH 5051**

THREE AYRES
Gregg Smith Singers
(cond.) Gregg Smith   **GOLDE ATH 5051**

TWO SONGS, FOR SOPRANO AND HARP
B. Bramson (S.), S. Cutler (hp.)   **LEONA LPI 106**

ZAVALISHINA, Maria Semyonovna (1903-   )

TOYS (CHILDREN'S SUITE)
Ukrainian Radio Symphony Orchestra   **MELOD**
(cond.) I. Ostrovsky   **33 D 11713/14**

ZECHLIN, Ruth (1926-   )

CHAMBER SYMPHONY
Berlin Chamber Orchestra
(cond.) Helmut Koch   **ETERN 885026**

FOUR STRING QUARTETS
* * * * * *   **NOVA 885033**

LIDICE (CANTATA)
* * * * * *   **ETERN 720080**

MUSIK FUER ORCHESTER
Berlin Symphony Orchestra
(cond.) Guenther Herbig   **VEB - - -**

REFLEXIONEN FUER 14 STREICHER
Dresden Chamber Orchestra
(cond.) Manfred Scherzer   **VEB - - -**

SITUATIONEN FUER ORCHESTER
Orchestra of the Comic Opera, Berlin
(cond.) Joachim Willert   **VEB - - -**

SONATA, FOR FLUTE AND PIANO
* * * * * *   **MELOD D 21399**

TRIO FOR OBOE, VIOLA AND CELLO
Hans Werner Watzig (ob.),
Hugo Fricke (vla.), Werner Haupt (vlc.) **ETERN 520205**

ZHUBANOVA, Gaziza Akhmetovna (1928-   )

ARIAS FROM KURMANGAZY
Kazakh Opera Orchestra
(cond.) T. Osmanov   **MELOD C 10 07619/20**

ARIAS FROM YENLIK AND KEBEK
Kazakh Opera Orchestra
(cond.) T. Osmanov   **MELOD C 10 07619/20**

ARIAS FROM YENLIK AND KEBEK
B. Tulugenova, Y. Serbebaev,
M. Musabaev, K. Baktaev,
S. Umbetaliev   **MELOD C 10 12905**

DAYBREAK OVER THE STEPPES (ORATORIO)
Derbina (m-S), Kuznetsov (B.),
Dobrin (B.) with Radio Chorus and
Orchestra (cond.) Mansurov   **MELOD D 33401/2**

FESTIVE OVERTURE
Kazakh State Symphony Orchestra
(cond.) T. Mynbayev   **MELOD C 10 07619/20**

ZHIGER SYMPHONY
Kazakh State Symphony Orchestra
(cond.) T. Mynbayev   **MELOD C 10 07619/20**

ZIFFRIN, Marilyn Jane (1926-   )

FOUR PIECES FOR TUBA
Barton Cummings (tba.)   **CRYST S 391**

TRIO FOR XYLOPHONE,
SOPRANO AND TUBA
Dean Anderson (xy.), Neva Pilgrim (S.),
Barton Cummings (tba.)   **CAPRA CRS 1210**

ZUBELDIA, Emiliana de (1948-   )

CONCIERTO INOLVIDABLE
Coro de la Universidad de Sonora   **UNSON MC 0090**

ZWILICH, Ellen Taaffe (1939-   )

CELEBRATION
Indianapolis Symphony Orchestra   **NEWOR NW 336**

ELISABETH
John Ostendorf (B-Bar.),
Shirley Seguin (pf.)   **LEONA LPI 120**

MÜCKENSCHWARM
John Ostendorf (B-Bar.),
Shirley Seguin (pf.)   **LEONA LPI 120**

PASSAGES (22'25)
Janice Felty (m-S.) with
Boston Musica Viva   **NORTH NR 218**

PROLOGUE AND VARIATIONS
Indianapolis Symphonic Orchestra
(cond.) John Nelson   **NEWOR NW 336**

SCHICKSAL
John Ostendorf (B-Bar.),
Shirley Seguin (pf.)   **LEONA LPI 120**

STRING TRIO (1981) (14'09)
Nancy Cirillo (vln.),
Katherine Murdock (vla.),
Ronald Thomas (vlc.)   **NORTH NR 218**

SYMPHONY NO. 1
Indianapolis Symphony Orchestra
(cond.) John Nelson   **NEWOR NW 336**

ÜBER DIE FELDER
John Ostendorf (B-Bar.),
Shirley Seguin (pf.)   **LEONA LPI 120**

WIE SIND DIE TAGE SCHWER
John Ostendorf (B-Bar.),
Shirley Seguin (pf.)   **LEONA LPI 120**

WOHL LIEB ICH DIE FINSTRE NACHT
John Ostendorf (B-Bar.),
Shirley Seguin (pf.)   **LEONA LPI 120**

Record Companies

CODE	LABEL	ADDRESS
ABANO	Abanori	Verein zur Kirchenmusikpflege in Furth, 851 Furth/Bay, Amalienstrasse 70, Germany.
ABBEY	Abbey	Abbey Recording Co., Abbey St., Eynsham, Oxford, England.
ABC	ABC Records	Australian Broadcasting Corp., P.O. Box 487 GPO, Sydney, NSW 2001, Australia.
ACANT	Acanta	19-21 Nile St., London N1 7LR, England.
ACADS	Academia Santa	See ASC.
ACEDI	Ace of Diamonds	Decca Record Co., Decca House, 9 Albert Embankment, London SEI 7SW, England.
ADES	Ades	Disques Ades, 54 Rue Saint-Lazare, 75009 Paris, France.
ADRIA	Adriano	Adriano Records, P.O. Box CH-8022, Zurich, Switzerland.
ADVAN	Advance	New Music Distribution Service, 500 Broadway, New York, NY 10012. **Composers, 170 W 74 St., New York, NY 10023, U.S.A.
ADVEN	Advent	Advent Productions, P.O. Box 772, El Cerrito, CA 94530, U.S.A.
AFKA	Afka	B.K.M. Associates, P.O. Box 22, Wilmington, MA 01887, U.S.A.
AGON	Agon	Dragon Records, 872 Morris Park Ave., Bronx, NY 10462, U.S.A.
ALIDE	Allied	* * * * * *
ALPHA	Alpha	Alpha, 47-51 Chalton St., London NWI IHY, England. Leman & Gorle Sprl., 52 Avenue Nôtre Dame de Lourdes, B-1009 Bruxelles, Belgium.
ALVAR	Alvares	Disc. Az, Rue François 1, Paris VIII, France.
AMADO	Amadeo	Apon Records Co. Inc., P.O. Box 3087, Long Island City, NY 11030, U.S.A.
AMS	AMS Studio	Studio for New Church Music.
ANGEL	Angel	Capitol Records Inc., 1750 North Vine St., Hollywood, CA 90028, U.S.A.
ANIMA	Anima Records	* * * * * *
APOST	Apostrophe	Prodisc, 19 Rue de Rhinau, 67100 Strasbourg, France.
ARABE	Arabesque	Caedmon/Arabesque, 1995 Broadway, New York, NY 10023, U.S.A.
ARC	Arc	Arc Publications, P.O. Box 3044, Vancouver, BC, Canada.
ARCH	Arch	1750 Arch Records, 1750 Arch St., Berkeley CA 94709, U.S.A.
ARCIV	Archiv	Polygram Classics, 13-14 St. George St., London W1R 9DE, England.
ARCO	Arcophon	* * * * * * Italy.
AREIT	Areito	* * * * * *
ARGO	Argo	Decca Record Co., Ltd., Argo Division, 115 Fulham Road, London SW3 6RR, England. **810 7th Ave., New York, NY 10019, U.S.A.
ARIKA	Arika	Fifth Continent Music Corp. 1200 Newell Hill Place, Suite 302, Walnut Creek, CA 94596, U.S.A.
ARIOL	Ariola	Ariola Eurodisc Benelux BV., P.O. Box 6033, Haarlem, Holland. RCA, 1133 Ave. of the Americas New York, NY 10036, U.S.A.
ARION	Arion	Disques Arion, 36 Ave., Hoche, 75008 Paris, France.
ARSNO	Ars Nova	Ars Antiqua Recordings, P.O. Box 7048, S.E., Washington DC 20032, U.S.A.
ARSPR	Ars Pro Femina	Ars Pro Femina, Inc., 129 Berkeley Place, Brooklyn, NY 11217, U.S.A.
ARTIUM	Artium	See BBC.
ASC	ASC	Academia Santa Cecilia de Discos Ltd., Rua des Lavanjeiras 519, Rio de Janeiro, Brazil.
ASCED	Asced	All Saints Cathedral, Edmonton, Canada.
ASUC	Asuc	European America Retail Music Inc., P.O. Box 850, Valley Forge, PA 19482, U.S.A.
ASV	ASV	Academy Sound and Vision Ltd. 115 Fulham Rd., London SW3 6RL, England.
AUDAT	Audat	World Records, P.O. Box 2000, Bowmanville, Ontario, LIC 3Z3, Canada.

CODE	LABEL	ADDRESS
AUDIO	Audio Arts	6 Briarwood Rd., London SW4 9PX, England.
AUVID	Auvidis	See Harmonia Mundi.
AVANT	Avant	Avant Records, 6331 Quebec Dr., Hollywood CA 90068, U.S.A. Crystal Records, 2235 Willida Lane, Sedro Woolley, WA 98284, U.S.A.
AVES	Aves	Intercord Tongesellschaft GmbH., Box 750270, Stuttgart, West Germany.
AWS	AWS	American Wind Symphony, New York, U.S.A.
BABEL	Attacca Babel	BV Haast Records, 99 Prinseneiland, 1013 LN Amsterdam, Netherlands.
BAM	Boite a Musique	Disc AZ, 32 Rue François 1, Paris VIII, France.
BAREN	Barenreiter	Barenreiter Tonkunstverlag, Barenreiterweg 6-8, (35) Kassel, West Germany.
BAROQ	Baroque	Everest Records, 2020 Ave. of the Stars, Century City, CA 90067, U.S.A.
BASIL	Basilisk	* * * * * *
BBC	BBC Artium	BBC Records & Tapes, The Langham, Portland Place, London W1A 1AA, England.
BETHA	Beth Anderson	New Music Distribution Service, 500 Broadway, New York, NY 10012, U.S.A.
BIEM	Biem	Verlag Der Elektroniker, Aarau, Stuttgart, West Germany.
BIS	Bis	Grammafonfirma BIS, Robert von Bahr, Bragevagen 2, S-182 64 Djursholm, Sweden. **Qualiton, 39-28 Crescent St., Long Island City, NY 11101, U.S.A.
BLUEB	Bluebell of Sweden	Polygram Special Imports, 810 Seventh Ave., New York, NY 10019, USA Conifer Records, Horton Rd., West Drayton, Middlesex, UB7 SNP, England. * * * * * *
BMI	BMI Canada	
BOOSH	Boosh	Boosey & Hawkes, 24 West 57th St., New York, NY 10019, U.S.A.
BOURG	Bourg	Qualiton Import Ltd., 39-38 Crescent St., Long Island, NY 11101, U.S.A
BRETH	Breathing Space	P.O. Box 4174, Washington, DC 20015, U.S.A.
BRIDG	Bridge	Bridge Record Productions,. P.O. Box 1864, New York, NY 10023, U.S.A.
BROAD	Broadman	Broadman Records, P.O. Box 12157 Southern Baptist Convention, Fort Worth, TX 76116, U.S.A. * * * * * *
BROLG	Brolga	
BUFCM	Buffet-Crampon	Classijazz, Rue du Midi 149, B 1000, Brussels, Belgium.
BVHAS	BVHaast	99 Prinsen Eiland, 1013 LN Amsterdam, Netherlands. * * * * * *
BVM	BVM Geneva	
CABAL	Cabaletta	Fowlmere House, Fowlmere, Royston, Herts SG8 75U, England.
CALLI	Calliope	Calliope Records, 19-21 Nile St., London, N1 7LR, England. **Qualiton, 39-28 Crescent St., Long Island City, NY 11101, U.S.A.
CAMBR	Cambria	Cambria Records, P.O. Box 2163, Palos Verdes, CA 90274, U.S.A.
CAMDE	Camden	1133 Ave. of the Americas, New York, NY 10036, U.S.A.

CODE	LABEL	ADDRESS
CAMEO	Cameo Classics	7 Gartside St., Manchester, M3 3EL, England.
CAMER	Camerata	Camerata Schallplatten, Moseler Verlag, Hoffmann-von-Fallersleben Strasse 8, (334) Wolfenbuttel, West Germany.
CAMGE	Cambridge	Cambridge Records, 125 Irving St., Framingham, MA 01701, U.S.A.
CANDI	Candide	Moss Music Group Inc., 211 East 43rd St., New York, NY 10017, U.S.A. **48 West 38 St., New York, NY 10018 U.S.A.
CANTA	Cantata	Barenreiter Tonkunstverlag, Barenreiter Weg 6-8, (35) Kassel, West Germany.
CAPAC	Capac	* * * * * *
CAPIO	Capriccio	Capriccio Records, 7315 Hooking Rd., McLean, VA 22101, U.S.A.
CAPIT	Capitol	Capitol Records Inc., 1750 N. Vine St., Hollywood, CA 90028, U.S.A.
CAPRA	Capra	Capra Records, 1908 Perry Ave., Redondo Beach, CA 90278, U.S.A. **317 Nobel Dr., Santa Cruz, CA 95060, U.S.A.
CAPRI	Caprice	Rikskonserter, P.O. Box 1225, S-11182 Stockholm, Sweden. **40-11 24 St., Long Island City, NY 11101, U.S.A.
CARAR	Carrere	Carrere Records (U.K.) Ltd., 22 Queen Street, London W1X 7PJ, England. **51 W 52 St., New York, NY 10019, U.S.A.
CARUS	Carus	Carus Verlag, Wannenstr. 45, 7000 Stuttgart 1, West Germany.
CASAB	Casablanca	PYE Records Ltd., ATV House, Great Cumberland Pl., London W1A 1AG, England. Polygram Records, Inc., 810 Seventh Ave., New York, NY 10019, U.S.A.
CAVAL	Cavalcade	American Entertainment Industries Inc., P.O. Box 3324, Hollywood, CA 90028, U.S.A.
CBC	CBC	CBS Merchandising, P.O. Box 500, Station A, Toronto, M5W 1E6, Canada.
CBS	CBS	Columbia Records/CBS Inc., 51 West 52nd St., New York, NY 10019, U.S.A.
CCM	Contemporary	Canadian Music Center, 1263 Bay St., Canadian Music Toronto, M5R 261, Ontario, Canada.
CENTR	Centredisc	See CMC.
CENTU	Century	Century Records, 6550 Sunset Blvd., Los Angeles, CA 90028, U.S.A.
CETRA	Cetra	Fonit-Cetra Sp.A., Via Bertola 34, 1-10122, Torino, Italy.
CEZ	Cezame	RCA Immeuble, Martignon-Mermoz, 9 Ave., Martignon, 7008 Paris. France
CHAND	Chandos	Sinequa Non, 1 Charles St., Providence, RI 02904. Chandos Records Ltd., 93 Sheppenden Rd., London N1 3DF, England P.O. Box 64503, Los Angeles, CA 90064, U.S.A.

CODE	LABEL	ADDRESS
CHANT	Chantry	Chimes Music Shop, 65 Marylebone High St., London W1M 3AH, England. ******
CHAPL	Chapel	
CHDUM	Chant du Monde	Disques Chant du Monde, 24-32 Rue des Amandiero, 75020 Paris, France.
CHERR	Cherry Pie	Cherry Pie Records, P.O. Box 225, 34 Warne St., Pennant Hills, NSW 2120, Australia.
CHIAR	Chiaroscura	Chiaroscura Records, Audiofidelity Enterprise, Inc., 221 West 57th St., New York, NY 10019, U.S.A.
CHINA	China Record	Company Peking, China.
CHRIS	Christophorus	Christophorus Verlag Herder GmbH., Hermann-Herder-Strasse 4, 7800 Freiburg, West Germany. ******
CLARI	Clarino	
CLASS	Classic	Howard International, 43-57 Union St., Flushing, NY 11355, U.S.A.
CLAVE	Clave	New Music Distribution Service, 500 Broadway, New York, NY 10012, U.S.A.
CLAVS	Claves	Editions de Disque Claves, Treulweg 14, 3600 Thun, Switzerland. **Qualiton, 39-28 Crescent St., Long Island City, NY 11101, U.S.A.
CLUB	Club 99	Club 99, 42-39 81st St., Elmhurst, NY 11373, U.S.A. ******
CMB	CMB	
CMC	CMC	Centerdiscs Collection, Canadian Music Center, 1263 Bay St., Toronto, Ontario, M5R 2C1, Canada.
CNR	CNR	Netherlands.
COLOS	Colosseum	Varese-Sarabande, 13006 Saticoy St., North Hollywood, CA 91605, U.S.A.
COLSP	Columbia Special	See CBS. Products
COLUJ	Columbia Japan	Nippon Columbia Co., Ltd., AK 4 14 4, U.S.A. Minato-k, Tokyo 107, Japan.
COLUM	Columbia	CBS Records, 51 West 52nd St., New York, NY 10019, U.S.A.
COMPO	Composers Voice	Donemus, Paulus Potterstraat 14, 1071 CZ, Amsterdam, Holland.
COMPT	Compatible	******
CONAS	Connaisseur Music	Postfach 1807, Karlsruhe, West Germany. ******
CONAV	Conciertos	Avila
CONHA	Concert Hall	Concert Hall Record Club, 18-20 St. Ann's Cres., London, SW18 2DU, England.
CONOS	Connoiseur	Connoiseur Society, 300 West End Ave., New York, NY 10024, U.S.A.
CORAL	Coral	MCA Records, Inc., 70 Universal City Plaza, Universal City, CA 91608, U.S.A. ****** Brazil.
CORCO	Corcovado	
CORNP	Corn Pride Records	******
CORO	Corona	Carus-Verlag GmbH., Gebelsbergstr. 34B, D7000 Stuttgart, West Germany.
CORON	Coronet	Coronet Recording Co., 4971 North High St., Columbus, OH 43214, U.S.A.
CP 2	CP2	Musical Observations Inc. 45 West Co St., New York, NY 10023, U.S.A. *******
CRAMP	Cramp	

CODE	LABEL	ADDRESS
CRI	CRI	Composers Recordings Inc. 170 West 74th St., New York, NY 10023, U.S.A.
CRITI	Critics Choice	Critics Choice Artist Management, 2067 Broadway, New York, NY 10023, U.S.A.
CRYST	Crystal	Crystal Records, 2235, Willida Lane, Sedro Woolley, WA 98284, U.S.A.
CULTU	Cultura	Alpha Records, 47-51 Chalton Street, London NW1 IHY, England. Leman & Gorle Sprl., 52 Ave Nôtre Dame de Lourdes, B 1009 Bruxelles, Belgium.
CUPOL	Cupolo	Swedish Information Center, Box 27327, 102 54 Stockholm, Sweden. ******
CUSTO	Custom Fidelity Records	
CYBEL	Cybelia	Disco Shop, 22 Rue de la Republic, 94160 Sainte Mande, Paris, France. Qualiton Imports, 39-28 Crescent St. Long Island City, NY 11101, U.S.A. ******
CYMBL	Cymbal	
DACAM	Da Camera Magna	Da Camera, Lameystrasse 10-12, Mannheim, West Germany. ******
DANIC	Danica	
DAU	Dau	Deutsche Austrophon GmbH., Auf dem Esch 8, D 2840, Diepholz, West Germany. ******
DDREC	DD Records	
DECCA	Decca	Decca Record Co., Decca House, 9 Albert Embankment, London SE1 7SW, England. MCA Records Inc., 100 Universal City Plaza, Universal City, CA 91608, U.S.A. **810 7th Ave., New York, NY 10019, U.S.A.
DELOS	Delos	Delos Records, Inc., 855 Via de la Paz, Pacific Palisades, CA 90272, U.S.A. **2210 Wilshire Blvd, Santa Monica, CA 90403, U.S.A.
DELTA	Delta	Europese Fonoclub, 262 Singel, Amsterdam, Holland.
DESTO	Desto	Desto Records, Inc. 1860 Broadway, New York, NY 10023, U.S.A. **226 Washington St., Mt. Vernon, NY 10553, U.S.A.
DG	DG	See DGG.
DGG	Deutsche	Deutsche Grammophon Gesellschaft, Grammophon Polydor Inc., 1700 Broadway, New York, NY 10019, U.S.A. **810 7th Ave., New York, NY 10019, U.S.A
DIPHL	Discophil	STIM. P.O. Box 1539, S 11185 Stockholm, Sweden.
DISCB	Disco Center	Disco Center Vereinigte Schallplatten Vertriebsgesellschaft Postfach 10 1029, 3500 Kassel, Germany.
DISCO	Disco	Jecklin Disco-Center, Ramistrasse 42, Zurich 1, Switzerland.
DISCP	Discophon	******
DISCR	Discorporation	******
DISPT	Dispt	Disques Paul Tassier, Cebedem, Rue de l'Hopital 31, Brussels 1, Belgium.
DISQU	Disques SM	Studio SM, 3 Rue Nicolas Chuquet, 75017, Paris, France.

CODE	LABEL	ADDRESS
DOMIN	Dominion	* * * * * *
DORIN	Dorian	R. Brown Co., 1709 N. Kenmore Ave., Hollywood, CA 90027, U.S.A.
DSCOU	Discourses	Discourses Ltd., 30 Crescent Rd., Tunbridge Wells TN1 1XF, Kent, England.
DUCRE	Ducretet-Thomson	Pathe-Marconi, 19 Rue Lord Byron, Paris VIII, France.
DULCI	Dulcian Recordings	* * * * * *
DURAN	Durand	* * * * * *
DURAP	Duraphon	Sound-Star-Tonproduction, Heideweg 20, D 3074 Steyerberg, West Germany.
DW	De Wolfe	80-88 Wardour St. London, England.
DYNA	Dyna	Gillette-Madison, Box 134, Gillette, NJ 07933, U.S.A.
EASTE	Eastern	* * * * * *
ECM	ECM Records	Gleichmannstrasse 10, 8000 Muenchen 60, West Germany.
EDFRA	Editions	Editions Françaises de Musique-Francais Technisonor, 12 Rue Magellan, 75008 Paris, France.
EDMUS	Edizioni Musicali	Edizioni Musicali Edi Pan, Viale Mazzini 6, 00195 Roma, Italy.
EDUCO	Educo	Educo Records, P.O. Box 3006, Ventura, CA 93003, U.S.A.
EIGEL	Eigelstein	* * * * * *
ELECT	Electrecord	Electrecord Recording 60, Str. Luigi Cazzavillan 14-16. Bucharest. Rumania.
ELEMI	Electrola	EMI - Electrola GmbH., Postfach, 450363, Koln, West Germany.
ELREC	Engelsmann	Engelsmann Life Records GmbH., Burghardt, West Germany.
EMBA	Embassy	CBS Records, 17-19 Soho Square, London W1V 6HE, England.
EMBER	Ember	Ember Records, Suite 4, Carlton Tower Place, Sloane St., London, SW1X 9PZ, England.
EMI	EMI	EMI Records Ltd., 20 Manchester Square, London, W1A 1ES, England.
EMS	Studio EMS	Waterloo, Belgium.
EMWAV	EMI Waverley	EMI Records Ltd., 20 Manchester Sq., London W1A 1ES, England.
ENCOR	Encore	EMI Records Ltd., 20 Manchester Sq., London W1A 1ES, England.
ENJA	Enja Records	* * * * * *
ENSAY	Ensayo	Qualiton Imports, 39-28 Crescent St., Long Island City, NY 11101, U.S.A.
ENSEM	Ensemble	See Electrola.
ERATO	Erato	Conifer Records, Horton Rd., West Drayton, Middelsex UB7 8NP, England. Erato Disques, 60 Rue de la Chaussée d'Anlin, Paris VIII, France. **1133 Ave. of the Americas, New York, NY 10036, U.S.A.
ESOTE	Esoteric	Everest Record Group, 2020 Ave. of the Stars, Century City, CA 90067, U.S.A.
ESTEL	Estudio Eldorado	Estudio Eldorado, Rua Major Quedinho 90, Sao Paolo, Brazil.
ETERN	Eterna	Eterna Schallplatten, Leipziger St. 26, Berlin 102, East Germany.
ETNOS	Etnos	Gabriel Moralejo, P.O.Box 53 046, Madrid, Spain.
EVERS	Everest	Everest Records, 2020 Ave. of the Stars, Century City, CA. 90067, U.S.A.

CODE	LABEL	ADDRESS
EXONA	Exon Audio	* * * * * *
FELLO	Fellowship	* * * * * *
FENIC	Fennica	Society of Finnish Composers, Runeberginkatu 15A 11, SF 00100, Helsinki, Finland.
FERMA	Fermata	Discos RGE - Fermata Ltd., Rua de Triumfo 117, São Paulo, Brazil.
FESTI	Festival	Musidisque (Festival), 99 Rue de la République, F 92 Puteaux, France. Label also used by: Festival Records (Pty.) Ltd., Australian Broadcasting Commission, P.O. Box 487 GPO, Sydney, NSW 2001, Australia.
FIDEL	Fidulafon	* * * * * *
FINNA	Finnadar	Finnadar Records, 75 Rockefeller Plaza, New York, NY 10019, U.S.A.
FLY	Fly	Sprl Fly Music, Chaussée de Nivelles 133-6521 Arquennes. France
FOLKW	Folkways	712 Broadway, 5th floor, New York, NY 10003, U.S.A. **632 Broadway, New York, NY 10012, U.S.A.
FONIT	Fonit	Fonit-Cetra Sp A., Via Bertola 34, 1-10122 Torino, Italy. **810 7th Ave., New York, NY 10019, U.S.A.
FONO	Fono	Fono Schallplatten GmbH., P.O. Box 2780, Muenster, West Germany.
FSM	FSM	Fono Schallplatten GmbH., P.O. Box 2780, Muenster, West Germany.
FUNAR	Funarte	* * * * * *
GALAX	Galaxia	Galaxia Records, P.O. Box 212, Woburn, MA 01801, U.S.A.
GALLO	Gallo	Gallo (Africa) Ltd., P.O. Box 6216, Johannesburg 2000, South Africa. **Qualiton, 39-28 Crescent St., Long Island City, NY 11101, U.S.A.
GASPA	Gasparo	Gasparo Co., P.O. Box 90574, Nashville, TN 37209, U.S.A. P.O. Box. 120069, Nashville, TN 37212, U.S.A.
GELER	Gerald Lewis Recording	* * * * * *
GEMIN	Gemini Hall	Gemini Records, 808 West End Ave., New York, NY 10025, U.S.A.
GENES	Genesis	Wayne Stahnke Assoc., 8244 Tuscany Ave., Playa Del Rey, CA 90291, U.S.A. **Grush, Box 773512, Steamboat Springs, CO 80477, U.S.A.
GIORN	Giorno	Giorno Poetry Systems Records, 222 Bowery, New York, NY 10012, U.S.A.
GM	GM	GM Recordings, 167 Dudley Road, Newton Center, MA 02159, U.S.A.
GNPCR	GNP-Crescendo	GNP-Crescendo Records Inc., 8560 Sunset Boulevard, Suite 603, Los Angeles, CA 90069, U.S.A.
GOLDE	Golden Crest	Golden Crest Records, 220 Broadway, Huntington Station, New York, NY 11746, U.S.A.
GRENA	Grenadilla	New Music Distribution Service, 500 Broadway, New York, NY 10012, U.S.A. **R. Gilbert, 142-25 Pershing, Kew Gardens, NY 11435, U.S.A.
GREVL	Grevillea	1200 Newell Hill Place, Walnut Creek, CA 94596, U.S.A.
GAMUT	Harvest Moon/Gamut	1 All Saints Passage, Cambridge CB2 3LT, England.

CODE	LABEL	ADDRESS
HATAR	Hat Art	New Music Distribution, 500 Broadway, New York, NY 10012, U.S.A.
HARMU	Harmonia Mundi	Harmonia Mundi Inc., 2351 Westwood Blvd., Los Angeles, CA 90064, U.S.A. Harmonia Mundi (U.K.) Ltd., 19-21 Nile St., London N1 7LR, England. **Box 64503, Los Angeles, CA 90064, U.S.A.
HATHO	Hathor Sound	60A Oriole Rd., Toronto, M4W 261, Canada.
HARVS	Harvest	EMI Records Ltd., 20 Manchester Sq., London W1A 1ES, England. **Hollywood and Vine, Hollywood, CA 90028, U.S.A.
HERU	Heru Records	* * * * * *
HGBS	HGBS Studio and Music Productions	* * * * * *
HM	HM	See Harmonia Mundi.
HMV	His Masters Voice	EMI Records Ltd., 20 Manchester Sq., London W1A 1ES, England.
HOMZY	Homzy Records	* * * * * *
HONGK	Hong Kong Records	China Records Inc., Beijing, Peking, China.
HOOKA	Ho'Okani	* * * * * *
HR	HR	Haninge Records, Box 4001, S 136 04 Handen.
HRE	HRE	Historical Recordings Inc., P.O. Box 12, Kew Gardens, New York, NY 11415, U.S.A.
HUIKS	Huiksu Music	P.O. Box 511, Hastings, NY 10706, U.S.A.
HUNGA	Hungaroton	Parnote Distribution Ltd., 47-51 Chalton St., London NW1 1HY, England. Qualiton Records Ltd., 39-28 Crescent St., Long Island City, NY 11101, U.S.A.
HYPER	Hyperion	Hyperion Records Ltd., P.O. Box 25, Eltham, London SE9 1AX, England. **Box 64503, Los Angeles, CA 90064, U.S.A.
ICTUS	Ictus	See CLAVE.
IHW	IHW Plattenversand	P.O. Box 800506, D 2050 Hamburg, West Germany.
ILP	ILP	* * * * * *
IMPUL	Impulse	EMI Records Ltd., 20 Manchester Square, London W1A 1ES, England. MCA Records Inc., 70 Universal City Plaza, University City, CA 91608, U.S.A.
INCRE	Increase	* * * * * *
IND	Independent	Independent Recordings, Canadian Music Center, 1263 Bay St., Toronto, Ontario, M5R 2C1, Canada.
INSTI	Institute	Institute de Extension University of Chile, Ave Bernado O'Higgins 1058, Casilla 10 D, Santiago, Chile.
INTAM	Inter American	Technical Unit on Music, Organization of American States, Washington, DC 20006, U.S.A.
INTCO	Intercord	Intercord Tongesellschaft GmbH., Postfach 750270, 7000 Stuttgart 75, West Germany.
INTPV	Intersound	Intersound GmbH., Schleibinger Str. 10, 8000 Muenchen 80, West Germany.
INTRA	Intrastate	* * * * * *
JAPAN	Japan Federation of Composers	Japan Federation of Composers, Shinanomachi Bldg., 602 33 Shinanomachi, Shinjuku-ku, Tokyo, Japan.

CODE	LABEL	ADDRESS
JAZZ	Jazztone	* * * * * *
JCOA	JCOA	See CLAVE.
JIGU	Jigu Records Corp.	* * * * * *
JJA	JA	Box Office Records (private recording).
JONAL	Jonal	* * * * * *
JOSEP	Joseph Weinberger Ltd.	Joseph Weinberger Ltd., 10-16 Rathbone St., London W1P 2BJ, England.
JSV	JSV	Joh. Stauda Verlag, Kassel, West Germany.
JUGOT	Jugoton	Jugoton Poduzece za Izradu Gramofonskin, Trnjanska BB., YV 41000 Zagreb-Dubrnva, Yugoslavia.
KASKA	Kaskade	* * * * * *
KEILL	Keillor	102 Rykert Cres., Toronto, M4G 259, Canada.
KENDA	Kendall	* * * * * *
KENNA	Kennard	* * * * * *
KERBE	Kerberos	* * * * * *
KIWI	Kiwi	Kiwi/Pacific Records Ltd., 182 Wakefield St., Wellington, New Zealand.
KLAVI	Klavier	Klavier Records, 5652 Willowcrest Ave., North Hollywood, CA 91601, U.S.A. **10520 Burbank Blvd, New Hollywood, CA 90601, U.S.A.
KOL	Kol Israel	* * * * * *
KOLIB	Kolibri	* * * * * *
KRS	Keryga	* * * * * *
KUBIN	Kubing Records	* * * * * *
KULKO	Kulko	* * * * * *
LARGO	Largo	International Book and Record Distributors, 40-11 24th St., Long Island City, NY 11101, U.S.A.
LAUDA	Laudate	Hanssler-Verlag, Postfach 1220, D 7303 Neuhausen-Stuttgart, West Germany.
LAUMA	Laumann	* * * * * *
LAUPR	Laurel-Protone	Laurel-Protone Records, 2451 Nichols Canyon, Los Angeles, CA 90046, U.S.A.
LAURE	Laurel	**Consortium, 2451 Nichols Canyon, Los Angeles, CA 90046, U.S.A.
LEONA	Leonarda	Leonarda Productions, P.O. Box 124, Radio City Station, New York, NY 10101, U.S.A.
LIMET	Limelight	Mercury Recording Corp., 35 East Wacker Drive, Chicago, IL 60601, U.S.A. **810 Seventh Ave., New York, NY 10019, U.S.A.
LKK	LKK	Lunds Kommunala Musikskola, Laurentugaten 1, S 122 21 Lund. Sweden
LONDO	London	London Records Co., 539 West 25th St., New York, NY 10001, U.S.A. **810 Seventh Ave., New York, NY 10019, U.S.A.
LORBY	Lorby	* * * * * *
LOUIS	Louisville	Louisville Orchestra, 333 West Broadway, Louisville, KY 40202, U.S.A. **Composers, 170 West 74th St., New York, NY 10023, U.S.A.
LOVE	Lovely Music	Lovely Music Ltd., 325 Spring St., New York, NY 10013, U.S.A.
LYRIC	Lyrichord	Lyrichord Records, 141 Perry St., New York, NY 10014, U.S.A.
LYRIT	Lyrita	Phonographic Performances Ltd., Ganton House, 14-22 Ganton St., London W1V 11B, England.

CODE	LABEL	ADDRESS	CODE	LABEL	ADDRESS
M7	M7 Records	* * * * * *	MOVE	Move	Move Records, P.O. Box 266, Carlton South 3053, Australia.
MAKOL	Makolit	Makolit Ltd., 15 Hamanor St., Tel-Aviv, Israel.			
MARAT	Marathon	* * * * * *	MSR	MSR Records	Venice Boulevard, Los Angeles, CA 90034, U.S.A.
MARCO	Marco Polo	Records International, Box 1140, Goleta, CA 93116, U.S.A.	MTV	MTV	Ministerio de Trabejo de Venezuela, Caracas, Venezuela.
MARHE	Marhel	Konzertdirection H. Schoell, Postfach 301, 7300 Esslingen, West Germany.	MUBAV	Music Bavaria	Musica Bavarica, Thalkirchner Strasse 11, 8 Munchen 2, West Germany.
MARK	Mark	Mark Records, 10815 Bodine Rd., Clarence, NY 14031, U.S.A.	MUHER	Musical Heritage	Musical Heritage Society, Inc., 14 Park Rd., Tinton Falls, NJ 07724, U.S.A.
MARQ	Marquis	Qualiton Imports, 39-28 Crescent St., Long Island City, NY 11101, U.S.A.			
MARS	Mars	* * * * * *	MUS	Musica Magna	* * * * * *
			MUSAG	Musica Magna	* * * * * *
MARUS	Marus	Marus Schallplatten, Joachim-Friedrich-Str. 55, 1000 Berlin 3l, West Germany.	MUSAM	Music in America	The Society for the Preservation of the American Musical Heritage, Inc., P.O. Box 4244, Grand Central Station, New York, NY 10017, U.S.A.
MARY	Mary	Folkways Records, 43 West 61st St., New York, NY 10023, U.S.A. **Box 32, Hamilton Grange, New York, NY 10031, U.S.A.	MUSIC	Musicus	* * * * * *
			MUSID	Musidisc	Disques Musidisc Europe, 13-15 Rue Pages, Suresnes, France.
MASTE	Masters of the Bow	Le Connoiseur Schallplatten, Postfach 4807, 7500 Karlsruhe 1, West Germany.	MUSMU	Musica Mundi	Musica Mundi, P.O. Box 8226, Washington, DC 20024, U.S.A.
MCBA	Municipalidad de la Ciudad de Buenos Aires	Secretaria de Cultura, LS1 Radio Municipal de la Cuidad de Buenos Aires, Buenos Aires, Argentina.	MUSVI	Musica Viva	German News Co., Inc., 218 E. 86th St., New York, NY 10028, U.S.A.
MDG	MDG	Musikprodukt Dabinhaus, u Grimm Detmold, See ELEMI.	MUZA	Muza	Ars Polonia, P.O. Box 1001, Warszawa, Poland.
MEDAL	Medallion	* * * * * *	NATO	Nato Records	3 Rue de Duras, 5008 Paris, France.
MEDIA	Media Judaiea	* * * * * *	NCC	Norwegian Cultural Council	Norwegian Music Information Center, Tordenskioldsgt 6B, Oslo 1, Norway.
MELBO	Melbourne	London Records of Canada Ltd., P.O. Box 651, Peterborough, Ontario, Canada.	NEMUC	New Music Circle	New Music Circle, 6912 Wise Ave., St. Louis, MO 63139, U.S.A.
MELL	Mell	G.M. Mell, Stromstadsvagen 30, 66800 ED, Sweden.	NEWMU	New Music Quarterly	See New Music Distribution.
MELOD	Melodiya	Collets Holdings Ltd., Denington Estate, Wellingborough, Northants, NN8 2QR, England. Four Continent Book Corp., 149 Fifth Avenue, New York, NY 10010, U.S.A.	NEWIL	New Wilderness Audiographics	35 Spring St., Room 208, New York, NY 10013, U.S.A.
			NEWOR	New World	Recorded Anthology of American Music, 231 E. 51 St., New York, NY 10022, U.S.A.
MEMO	Memo	* * * * * *	NEWSO	New Sound	* * * * * *
MERID	Meridian	Reference Monitor Inc., 6074 Corte del Cedro, Carlsbad, CA 92008, U.S.A.	NIMBU	Nimbus	Nimbus Records Ltd., Waystone Leys, Monmouth, Wales U.K.
METRO	Metronome	Metronome Musik GmbH., Postfach 601740, 2000 Hamburg, Germany. **810 7th Ave., New York, NY 10019, U.S.A.	NOCTR	Nocturne	Schallplattenfabrik Pallas GmbH., Diepholz, West Germany.
			NONSU	Nonesuch	Electra/Asylum/Nonesuch Records, 665 Fifth Ave., New York, NY 10022, U.S.A.
MEZHD	Mezhdunarodnaya Kniga	See MELOD.	NORET	Noret	Nor-Est Recordings Inc., 17540 Wyoming Ave., Detroit, MI 48221, U.S.A.
MGE	MGE	Music Gallery Editions Recordings, Canadian Music Centre 1263 Bay St., Toronto, Ontario, M5R 2C1, Canada.	NORTH	North	North Eastern Records, P.O. Box 116, Boston, MA 02117, U.S.A.
MGM	MGM	MGM Records, 7165 Sunset Blvd, Hollywood, CA 90046, U.S.A.	NORWE	Northwest Arts	* * * * * *
MHIC	Mhic	Mhic Company, 359 Howland Ave., Toronto, Canada.	NOVA	Nova	Nova Sound Recording Studios, 27-31 Bryanston St., London W1H 7AB, England.
MICHI	Michi	University of Michigan, School of Music, Ann Arbor, M1 48109, U.S.A.	NUMIN	Numinus	* * * * * *
			OCEAN	Ocean	* * * * * *
MIDLE	Middle Tone Records	* * * * * *	ODEON	Odeon	Pathe-Marconi, 19 Rue Lord Byron, Paris VIII, France.
MINON	Minon	* * * * * *	ODYSS	Odyssey	CBS Records, 51 West, 52nd St., New York, NY 10019, U.S.A.
MIXTR	Mixtur	Mixtur Schallplatten GmbH., Rosenheimer Strasse 35, 1000 Berlin 30, West Germany.	OISEU	Oiseau-Lyre	Decca House, 9 Albert Embankment, London SE1 7SW, England. **810 7th Ave., New York, NY 10019, U.S.A.
MONDI	Mondiodis	Mondiodis, 8 Place Violet, 75015 Paris, France.			
MONIT	Monitor	Monitor, 156 Fifth Ave., New York, NY 10010, U.S.A.	OLUFS	Olufsen	Hallingsgade 30, 2100 Copenhagen, Denmark.
MOSEL	Moseler Camerata	See CAMER.	OLYMP	Olympic	University of Washington, Seattle, WA 98195, U.S.A.
MOSSM	Moss Music Group	Moss Music Group Inc., 211 East 43rd St., New York, NY 10017, U.S.A.	OMEGA	Omega	Fonior Brussels, I.P.G.

CODE	LABEL	ADDRESS
OMNIA	Omnia	Omnia Music Co., France.
OMNIS	Omnisound	Omnisound, Inc., Delaware Water Gap, PA 18327, U.S.A.
ONETE	One Ten	New Music Distribution Service, 500 Broadway, New York, NY 10012, U.S.A.
OPAL	Pearl/Opal	See Qualiton.
OPONE	Opus One	Opus One, P.O. Box 604, Greenville, ME 04441, U.S.A.
ORF	Orf	Orf-Studios, Oesterreich Rund Funk, Graz, Austria.
ORFEO	Orpheo	Orfeo Classic Schallplatten und Musikfilm GmbH., Heilmannstrasse 17, D 8000 Munich. West Germany **Box 64503, Los Angeles, CA 90064, U.S.A.
ORICA	Original Cast	Broadway/Hollywood Recordings, P.O. Box 496, Georgetown, CT 06829, U.S.A.
ORIEL	Oriel	EMI Records, 20 Manchester Sq., London, W1A 1ES, England.
ORION	Orion	Orion Master Recordings, 3802 Castlerock Rd., Malibu, CA 90265, U.S.A. **5840 Bush Drive, Malibu, CA 90265, U.S.A.
ORTF	Ortf-Inedits	Radiodiffusion-Television Français, Centre Bourdan, 5 Ave. du Recteur Poincare, F 75 Paris 16, France.
ORYX	Oryx	Oryx Recordings Ltd., 28 Snowdon Quay, Porthmadog Gwynedd, Wales.
OUTLI	Outline Records	* * * * * *
PACIF	Pacific	
PAIR	Pair Music Schoenwalde	Pair Records, 84-184 Dayton Ave., Bldg. 5D, Passaic, NJ 07055, U.S.A.
PAN	Edi-Pan	Editioni Musicali Edi-Pan, Viale Mazzini 6, 00195, Roma, Italy.
PANTN	Panton	Panton, Vydavetelstvi, Ceskeno Hudebnijo Fondu, Ricni 12, 118, 39 Praha 1, Czechoslovakia. **Jungmannova 30, Prague, Czechoslovakia.
PARAC	Parachute	New Music Distribution Service 500 Broadway, New York, NY 10012, U.S.A.
PARAD	Paradox	* * * * * *
PARNO	Parnote	Parnote Records, 47-51 Chalton St., London NW1 1HY, England.
PATHE	Pathe-Marconi	Pathé-Marconi, 19 Rue Lord Byron, Paris 8, France.
PAVAN	Pavane	Harmonia Mundi (Uis) Ltd., 19-21 Nile St., London N1 7LR, England.
PEARL	Pearl	Pavilion Records Ltd., 48 High St., Pembury, Kent, TN2 4NU, England. **4243 North Lincoln, Chicago, IL 60618, U.S.A.
PELIC	Pelican	Pelican Records, P.O. Box 34732, Los Angeles, CA 90034, U.S.A.
PERF	Performance	See CLAVE.
PHILI	Philips	Phonographic Performances Ltd., Ganton House, 14-22 Ganton St., London W1V 1LB, England. **810 7th Ave., New York, NY 10019, U.S.A.
PHILO	Philharmonic	* * * * * * U.S.A.
PHONO	Phonogram	Mercury Recording Corp. (Philips), 35 East Wacker Dr., Chicago, IL 60601, U.S.A.
PICAP	Picap Productions	* * * * * *
PIEVE	Pierre Verany	Records International, Box 1140, Goleta, 93116, U.S.A.
PLANC	Planchette	* * * * * *
PLANI	Plainisphere	* * * * * *
PLAY	Play	* * * * * *

CODE	LABEL	ADDRESS
PLEID	Pleiades	Southern Illinois University Press, Carbondale, IL 62901, U.S.A.
POLAR	Polar	* * * * * *
POLSK	Polskie Nagranie	See Melodia.
POLYD	Polydor	Polygram Classics, 13-14 St. George St., London, W1R 9DE, England. **810 Seventh Ave., New York, NY 10019, U.S.A.
PREIS	Preiser	See Harmonia Mundi.
PREST	Polydor-Prestigo	Polygram Classics, 13-14 St. George St., London, W1R 9DE, England. * * * * * *
PREVI	Pre-view	
PROAT	Pro-Arte	Intersound Inc. 14025, 23rd Ave., N. Minneapolis, MN 55441, U.S.A.
PRODI	Prodisc	Prodisc, 19 Rue de Rhinau, 67100 Strassbourg, West Germany.
PROME	Promenus	Ministerio da Educatão e Cultura, Rio de Janeiro, Brazil.
PROPR	Proprius	Audio Source, 1185 Chess Dr., Foster City, CA 94404, U.S.A. Proprius Bocker e Musik, Vartavagen 35 nb, S 115, 29 Stockholm, Sweden.
PROTO	Protone	Laurel-Protone Records, 2451 Nichols Canyon, Los Angeles, CA 90046, U.S.A.
PROVI	Pro Viva	Deutsche Austrophon GmbH., 2480 Diepholz, Germany.
PSALL	Psallite	Nordd.Tonstudio füer Kirchenmusik, 3079 Warmsen 1, Bohnhorst 145, Germany.
PSO	PSO	Peer Southern Organization, 1740 Broadway, New York, NY 10019, U.S.A.
PUCHI	Puchito	* * * * * *
PYE	Pye	Pye Records Ltd., 17 St. Cumberland Place, London W1H 1AG, England.
QCA	QCA/rejoice	Cincinnati, OH 45255, U.S.A.
QUALI	Qualiton	Qualiton Records Ltd., 39-28 Crescent St., Long Island City, NY 11101, U.S.A.
RARER	Rare Recorded Editions	Rare Recorded Editions, 14A Seymour St., London W1, England.
RBM	RBM	RBM Musikproduktion GmbH., Seckenheimer Str. 4-6, 6800 Mannheim, West Germany.
RCA	RCA	RCA Ltd., (Record Division), 1 Bedford Ave., London WC1, England.
RCAJ	RCA Japan	RVC Corp., 1-7-8- Shibuya, Shibuya-ku, Tokyo 150, Japan.
RCAV	RCA Victor	RCA Records, 1133 Ave. of the Americas, New York, NY 10036, U.S.A.
RCI	RCI	Radio Canada International, National Arts Center, Ottawa, Canada.
REFEX	Reflexe	See: ELEMI.
REM	REM	* * * * * *
REMIN	Remington	American Tape Corp., 1116 Edgewater Ave., Ridgefield, NJ 07657, U.S.A.
REMST	Rem Studio	* * * * * *
RENAT	Serenata	* * * * * *
REPRI	Reprise	Warner Bros. Records Inc., 4000 Warner Blvd., Burbank, CA 91505, U.S.A.
RGE		See FERMA.
RICHS	Richsound	* * * * * *
RIGA	Riga	* * * * * *
RISST	Richmond Sound Stages	See POLYD.
RJOCR	RJOCRN	Yamaha Music Foundation, Tokyo, Japan.
ROYAL	Royale	* * * * * *

CODE	LABEL	ADDRESS
RPMR	RPM	RPM Record Co., P.O. Box 2807, Johannesburg 2000, South Africa.
RTB	RTB	Radio Television Belgrade, Hilendarska 2, YU-1000, Beograd, Yugoslavia. ******
RYPRO	Rhythm Productions	
SAYDA	Say Day-Bew	University of Alabama-Tuskelora, Birmingham, AL 35294, U.S.A.
SCOTS	Scottish Society of Composers	C/o Scottish Music Archiv, 7 Lilybank Gdns., Glasgow, G12 8RZ, Scotland.
SELEC	Selecta-Telefunken	Teldec Telefunken-Decca Schallplatten GmbH., Heussweg 25, 2000 Hamburg 19, Germany. Selecta (London), 125-7 Lee High Rd., London SE13 5 NX, England.
SEREN	Serenus	Serenus Corporation, 145 Palisade St., Dobbs Ferry, NY 10522, U.S.A. Serenus Records, 30 Atney Rd., Putney, London SW15 2PS, England.
SESAC	Sesac	******
SFP	SFP	******
SHEFF	Sheffield	Sheffield Records, P.O. Box 5332, Santa Barbara, CA 93108, U.S.A.
SILVE	Silver Burdett	Silver Burdett Co., 250 James St., Morristown, NJ 07960, U.S.A.
SIMAX	Simax	Pro-Musica A/5, Wergelandsveien 5 N 1010 Oslo 1, Norway.
SIRIS	Sirius	STIM. P.O. Box 1539, S 11185 Stockholm, Sweden.
SNE	SNE	Société Nouvelle D'enregistrement Recordings, Canadian Music Center, 1263 Bay St., Toronto, Ontario, M5R 2C1, Canada.
SNCM	Suncoast Management	Ars Antiqua, 1707 E. Second St., Bloomington, IN 47401, U.S.A.
SOND	Sound 80	Sound 80, 2709 E. 25th St., Minneapolis, MN 55406, U.S.A.
SONIC	Transonic	P.O. Box 40553, San Franscisco, CA 94190, U.S.A.
SONOT	Sonoton	Sonoton Munich. W. Germany
SORCE	Source (Music of the Avant Garde)	Out of print: copies of issue #9 from Larry Austin, Music Dept. North Texas State University, Denton, TX 67203, U.S.A.
SORIS	Sorriso	Sorriso Editions, CH 6010 Kriens, Lucerne, Switzerland.
SOUND	Sound-Star-Ton	Sound-Star-Ton Productions, Heideway 20, D 3074, Steyerberg, West Germany.
SOUTH	Southern Library	Peer-Southern Org., 1740 Broadway, New York, NY 10019, U.S.A.
SPALA	Spalax	******
SPECT	Spectrum	Uni-Pro Records Inc. (Spectrum Division), Harriman, New York, NY 10926, U.S.A.
SRA	SRA	Sister Rosalina Abejo SFCC. 37950, No. 62 Fremont Bldg., Fremont, CA 94536, U.S.A.
STAND	Standard	******
STOLA	Stolat	******
STORY	Storyville	Moss Music Group, Inc., 48 W. 38th St., New York, NY 10018, U.S.A.
STUDA	Studio Angelicum	Sciascia Sas, Via Brodolini, 20089. Rozzano, Milan, Italy.
STUDU	Studu	Studio Union im Lahn Verlag, Limburg, Netherlands.

CODE	LABEL	ADDRESS
SUN	Sun	Selby Shingle Enterprises, 3106 Belmont Blvd., Nashville, IN 37212, U.S.A.
SUNGE	Sung Eum Company	******
SUNOP	Sunday Opera	109 Cromwell Rd., St. Andrews, Bristol, BS6 5EX, England.
SUPRA	Supraphon	Qualiton Records Ltd., 39-28 Crescent St., Long Island City, NY 11101, U.S.A. Bond St. Music, 100 New Bond St., London W1Y 9GL, England. **Na Ujezdi 15, Prague, Czechoslovakia.
SVR	Sveriges Radio	Sveriges Radio, P.O. Box 955, S 10510 Stockholm, Sweden.
SWAVE	Seewave	Seewave Records, P.O. Box 4407, Madison Square Station, New York, NY 10010, U.S.A.
SWEDI	Swedish Society Discofil	STIM. P.O. Box 1539, Stockholm, Sweden.
SWISS	Anthology of Swiss Music	Communaute de Travail, 11 bis, Ave. de Grammont, 1007 Lausanne, Switzerland.
TACU	Tacuabe	******
TAKTJ	Taktj	****** Japan.
TANGE	Tangent	Tangent, Suite 11, 52 Shaftsbury Ave., London W1V 7DE, England.
TCC	***	******
TELDE	Teldec	Teldec Schallplatten GmbH., Huessweg 25, Hamburg 19, West Germany. Decca (U.K.) Ltd., 50 New Bond St., London W1Y 9HA, England.
TELEF	Telefunken	See: DECCA **810 7th Ave., New York, NY 10019, U.S.A.
TEMPO	Tempo	Multiple Sound Distributors, 79 Blyth Rd., London W14 OHP, England.
TERPS	Terpsichore	N.V. Phonic, S.A. Belgium.
THIRD	Third Ear Music	******
TONST		See ELREC.
TORCH	P O Torch Records	******
TRANS	Transmuseq	6 Glen Iris Park Birmingham, AL 35205, U.S.A.
TRIAN	Trianon	Sonopresse, 26 Rue de Berri, 75008 Paris, France.
TROPI	Tropic	Tropic Records, 1650 Broadway, New York, NY 10019, U.S.A.
TTR	Tom-Tom	Tonstudio Bauer GmbH., & Co. 7140 Ludwigsburg, West Germany.
TULST	Tulstar	******
TURNA	Turnabout	The Moss Music Group, 48 West 38th St., New York, NY 10018, U.S.A. Parnote Distribution Ltd., 47-51 Chalton St., London NW1 1HY, England.
UNICO	Unicorn	Euroclass Record Distributors Ltd., 155 Ave. of the Americas, New York, NY 10013, U.S.A. Unicorn-Kanchana Ltd., 12 Hillgate Place, London W8, England.
UNISO	Unisono	Unisono Tontechnik Pfeifer-Koch, Theodor-Heuss-Strasse 90, 6712 Bobenheim-Roscheim 2, West Germany.
UNOPR	Unique Opera Records	******
UNSON	UNSON	Universidad de Sonora, APDO Postal 336 Y 106, Hermosillo, Sonora, Mexico.
URIEL	Uriel	******

CODE	LABEL	ADDRESS
VANGR	Vanguard	Vanguard Recording Society, 154 West 14th St., New York, U.S.A. **71 W 23 St., New York, NY 10010, U.S.A.
VARES	Varese	Varese Saraband Records Inc., 6404 Wilshire Blvd., Suite 1127, Los Angeles, CA 90048, U.S.A **13006 Saticoy St, North Hollywood, CA 91603, U.S.A.
VEGA	Vega	Société Française du Son, 30 Rue Beaujon, F 75008 Paris, France.
VENUS	Venus	Venus Recording Co., P.O. Box 1451, Beverley Hills, CA 90213, U.S.A.
VERSE	Verseau	Disco Shop, 22 Rue de la Republic, 94160 Sainte Mande, Paris, France.
VERVE	Verve	MGM Records, 7165 Sunset Blvd., Hollywood, CA 90046, U.S.A. **810 Seventh Ave., New York, NY 10019, U.S.A. * * * * * *
VICER	Viceroy	
VICTJ	Victor Japan	Victor Musical Instruments, 26-18 Jingu-Mae 4-Chome, Shibuya-Ku, Tokyo 150, Japan.
VICTO	Victor	RCA Records, 1133 Ave. of the Americas, New York, NY 10036, U.S.A. * * * * * *
VICTR	Victoria	* * * * * *
VIFON	Vifon	* * * * * *
VILLA	Villar	* * * * * *
VOGT	Vogt Quality	* * * * * *
VOGUE	Vogue	Vogue, 82 Rue Maurice-Grancoing, 93430, Villetaneuse, France.
VOX	Vox	Vox Records, Decca House, 9 Albert Embankment, London SE1 7SW, England. Moss Music Group Inc., 211 East 43rd St., New York, NY 10017, U.S.A. * * * * * *
VRG	VRG	

CODE	LABEL	ADDRESS
WANDG	WANDG	White & Gillespie Record Processing Co., Melbourne, Australia.
WARNE	Warner	Warner Bros Inc., 3300 Warner Blvd., Burbank, CA 91510, U.S.A.
WASHI	Washington	Dept. of Music, University of St. Louis, 221 North Grand Blvd., St. Louis, MO 63130, U.S.A.
WATT	Watt	Import Music Services, 54, Maddox St., London W1, England. **New Music, 6 West 95 St., New York, NY 10025, U.S.A. * * * * * *
WCFM	WCFM	
WEALD	Wealden Studios	Old Forge Meadow, Platts Heath, Lenham, Kent ME17 2NX, England.
WERGO	Wergo	Wergo Schallplatten GmbH., Postfach 3640 (Weihergarten) D 6500 Mainz, West Germany.
WESTM	Westminster	Westminster Recording Sale Corp., 257 Seventh Ave., New York, U.S.A. * * * * * *
WIDEM	Widemouth	
WIM	WIM	Western International Music Inc., 2859 Holt Ave., Los Angeles, CA 90034, U.S.A. Crystal Records, P.O. Box 65661, Los Angeles, CA 90065, U.S.A.
WISLP	Wisa	Wisa Grammafon AB, Angsvagen 3, 77700 Smedjebacken, Sweden.
WIZAR	Wizard	New Music Distribution Service, 500 Broadway, New York, NY 10012, U.S.A.
WORD	Word	Word (UK) Ltd., Park Lane, Hemel Hempstead, Herts HP2 4TD, England. **4800 W. Waco Dr., Waco, TX 76710, U.S.A.
WRC	WRC	World Record Club, England. * * * * * *
WRCI	World Record Co.	* * * * * *
ZANJA	Zanja	* * * * * *
ZOAH	Zoah	
ZODIA	Zodiac	Zodiac Records, 7447 N. Linden Ave., Skokie, IL 60076, U.S.A.